The Norton Anthology of Poetry

DISCARD

FOURTH EDITION

Editors Emeriti

Alexander Allison
LATE OF THE UNIVERSITY OF MICHIGAN

Herbert Barrows
PROFESSOR EMERITUS, UNIVERSITY OF MICHIGAN

Caesar R. Blake
UNIVERSITY OF TORONTO

Arthur J. Carr
LATE OF WILLIAMS COLLEGE

Arthur M. Eastman
PROFESSOR EMERITUS, VIRGINIA POLYTECHNIC INSTITUTE AND STATE UNIVERSITY

Hubert M. English, Jr.
UNIVERSITY OF MICHIGAN

The Norton Anthology of Poetry

FOURTH EDITION

◆◆◆

Margaret Ferguson
COLUMBIA UNIVERSITY

Mary Jo Salter
MOUNT HOLYOKE COLLEGE

Jon Stallworthy
OXFORD UNIVERSITY

W. W. NORTON & COMPANY · *New York* · *London*

The text of this book is composed in Electra
with the display set in Bernhard Modern
Composition by Maple-Vail Composition Services
Cover illustration: *Beatrice Addressing Dante From the Car (Purgatorio, Canto XXIX)*, by
William Blake. The Tate Gallery, London

Library of Congress Cataloging-in-Publication Data

The Norton anthology of poetry / [edited by] Margaret Ferguson,
Mary Jo Salter, Jon Stallworthy.—4th ed.
p.   cm.
Includes bibliographical references and index.
1. English poetry.   2. American poetry.   I. Ferguson, Margaret W.,
1948–   .   II. Salter, Mary Jo.   III. Stallworthy, Jon.
PR1174.N6   1996
821.009–dc20   96-8035

ISBN 0-393-96820-0 (pbk.)

W. W. Norton & Company, Inc. 500 Fifth Avenue, New York, N.Y. 10110
http://web.wwnorton.com
W. W. Norton & Company Ltd., 10 Coptic Street, London WC1A 1PU

2 3 4 5 6 7 8 9 0

Contents

Preface to the Fourth Edition

A poem is a record of remarkable language, written or spoken; in the case of a good poem, a record undamaged by the centuries and continents it may have crossed since poet or scribe put pen to paper. This dramatically expanded Fourth Edition of *The Norton Anthology of Poetry* brings together more than sixteen hundred such records from "the round earth's imagined corners." We have set out to provide readers with a wide and deep sampling of the best poetry written in the English language. That previous editions have succeeded in this endeavor, within the limits of the pages available in a single volume, seems manifest in the acceptance of those editions by teachers and students alike. But, as our friend and advisor M. H. Abrams has said in another context, "a vital literary culture is always on the move," both in the appearance of new works and in the altering response to existing texts: hence, a Fourth Edition, which broadens and refines that cultural tradition. Our efforts have been crucially helped by the practical criticism and informed suggestions provided to us by the many teachers who have used the anthology in their classes. In the best sense, then, the vitality of our literary culture has been demonstrated by this collaboration.

In assembling the new edition we, like our predecessors, have worked toward a balance between the older and the newer. Thus, while more than one hundred twentieth-century voices are heard here for the first time, forty earlier poets are also new to the book. This signal increase in poets and poems reflects the book's strengthened geographic and ethnic diversity: the many traditions of American poetry are more fully represented by better than double the number of African-American, Hispanic, Native American, and Asian-American poets (fifteen newly included). In addition to thirty-seven new English poets, the anthology includes fifty-four poets from Australia, Canada, New Zealand, Ireland, Scotland, Wales, the Caribbean, South Africa, and India. The work of women poets, with special attention to the early periods, is dramatically expanded with fifty-five new voices, seventy-nine in all. Even so, we would have wished to include many more voices in every category, had space permitted, and regretted having to exclude poets born after 1960.

The broadened representation of poets in the Fourth Edition speaks as well to greater historical and formal range and expanded pedagogical possibilities. The beginnings of poetry in English are now richly represented by Old English selections, including Cædmon's *Hymn*, selections from *Beowulf*, *The Seafarer*, *The Wife's Lament*, and popular riddles; and the Middle English selections newly include selections from the great long poems *Pearl* and *Piers Plowman*. These additions enable the study of the history of the English language and English poetic meters from Anglo-Saxon times to the present day.

The vernacular tradition, in which the poet "Anon" has spoken eloquently over the centuries, is now brought forward from medieval lyrics and Elizabethan and Jacobean poems to African-American spirituals and popular ballads of the twentieth century, two new clusters of poems. Teachers can trace the history of the epic by comparing openings and selections from *Beowulf, The Faerie Queene* (which we now represent with the complete first canto of book 1), *Paradise Lost*, Anne Killigrew's unfinished *Alexandreis*, Pope's (mock-epic) *The Rape of the Lock*, and Wordsworth's *Prelude*. Light verse, too, can now be taught more nimbly, with new selections by Wendy Cope, James Fenton, and John Updike to add to those by Lewis Carroll, W. S. Gilbert, Edward Lear, Ogden Nash, and Dorothy Parker.

In addition, the Fourth Edition opens up intertextual "dialogues" among poets in their time, such as Alexander Pope, Matthew Green, and Anne Finch on "the spleen"; within a traditional form, as in the way Jean Elliot's eighteenth-century ballad "The Flowers of the Forest" resonates in C. Day Lewis' song "I've heard them lilting at loom and belting" and Pete Seeger's ballad "Where Have All the Flowers Gone?"; across centuries and cultures, as, for example, William Wordsworth's "Nuns Fret Not at Their Convent's Narrow Room" and Gwendolyn Brooks' "birth in a narrow room" meditate on the limits and possibilities of the sonnet form; or in response to a common text, as in the four versions of Psalm 58 (Mary Sidney's, that of *The Massachusetts Bay Psalm Book*, Isaac Watts', and Christopher Smart's). To bring these potential dialogues to readers' attention, we have added a number of cross-referencing annotations.

The Fourth Edition includes many longer poems, since these belong in a collection representative not merely of the lyric and epigrammatic, but of the entire range of poetic genres in English. Among the longer poems new to this edition are Aemilia Lanyer's "The Description of Cooke-ham" and Richard Howard's "Nikolaus Mardruz to His Master Ferdinand, Count of Tyrol, 1565," as well as teachable excerpts from John Skelton's "Phillip Sparow" and "Colin Clout," Charlotte Smith's "Beachy Head," Elizabeth Barrett Browning's *Aurora Leigh*, William Carlos Williams' "Asphodel, That Greeny Flower," and James Merrill's *The Changing Light at Sandover*. Although it is impossible to include all of *The Faerie Queene, Paradise Lost, The Prelude, Song of Myself*, or *The Dream Songs*, students will find representative and self-sufficient selections from each of these works.

In addition to expanding representation, we have made a special effort to reconsider, and in some instances reselect, the work of poets retained from earlier editions. Almost all poets who have produced important works since our last edition have been updated; among them are Seamus Heaney, Margaret Atwood, and Derek Walcott. But Chaucer has been reexamined, too; so also, to name a few of the many other poets of the past, have Spenser, Shakespeare, Bradstreet, Tennyson, Dickinson, and Moore.

Editorial Procedures

The order is chronological, poets appearing according to their dates of birth and their poems according to dates of publication (estimated dates of composition in the case of Old and Middle English poets) in volume form. These dates are printed at the end of the poem, and to the right; when two dates are printed at the end of the poem, they indicate published versions that differ in an important way. Dates on the left, when given, are those of composition.

We have in several areas reconsidered texts with an eye to restoring spellings and punctuation that are subtly integral to metrical and visual character of the poem. In editing the Middle English poems, we have retained as many old spellings as possible to give the modern reader a sense of the period's difference from our own in matters orthographical. The forms "thorn" (used for the "th" sound) and "yogh" (used for "g," "gh," and "y" or "z" depending on the context) have been replaced by their appropriate modern equivalents. The letters "u/v" and "i/j" and "i/y," which are often used interchangeably in manuscripts, have been regularized according to modern usage. Because there was no standard English spelling, it varies from manuscript to manuscript and is affected by the marked variations in dialects spoken in different parts of Britain. For the early modern texts, we have modernized spellings and punctuation except where there is a clear semantic dimension to the original spelling and/or punctuation practices, as in Wyatt's poems (many of which appear in his own handwriting in manuscript form) or Spenser's (which are replete with graphic puns). Beginning with Emerson for American poets and Hardy for British poets, we have started the ongoing project of restoring original spelling and punctuation, in the belief that the poets' choices, when they pose no difficulties for student readers, should be respected.

Annotation in the Fourth Edition has been thoroughly revised. In keeping with recent developments in editing, we have introduced notes that mention significant textual variants. These are intended to spark classroom discussion about poems whose multiple versions challenge and problematize the idea of textual "authority." We have added many new notes that provide contextual information and clarify archaisms and allusions; however, as in previous editions, we make a special effort to minimize commentary that is interpretive rather than, in a limited sense, explanatory. Marginal glosses for archaic, dialect, or unfamiliar words have been reconsidered and, for many poems, increased in number. For the convenience of the student, we have used square brackets to indicate titles supplied by the editors and have, whenever a portion of a text has been omitted, indicated that omission with three asterisks.

Two other features within the anthology facilitate its usefulness in the classroom. Jon Stallworthy's Essay on Versification has been selectively expanded and moved to the beginning of the volume, where it can give students a valuable grounding in rhythm, meter, rhyme, and poetic forms as a prelude to their reading. Versification terms, indicated in boldfaced type within the essay, are now integrated within the primary index at the back of the book. A new appendix of biographical sketches situates the poets' lives and works in brief compass.

The Course Guide to accompany *The Norton Anthology of Poetry*, by Mark Jeffreys and Debra Fried, makes available to instructors varied reading lists that help shape a course or courses along a number of lines—according to form, figurative language, traditions and counter-traditions, and topics—and to establish relationships among poets and poems of different genres, periods, and concerns. A new electronic ancillary, *The Norton Poetry Workshop CD-ROM*, edited by James F. Knapp, contains texts and recordings of thirty of the most-taught poems from the anthology, supported by a rich array of multimedia, exercises, and study aids. Information for ordering these materials may be obtained from the publisher.

We are indebted to our predecessors, the editors emeriti of *The Norton Anthology of Poetry*, whose presence on the title page signals their ongoing contribution, and to M. H. Abrams, advisor to the Norton English list, for his wise and ready counsel. We also thank the staff at Norton who helped this book come into being: Julia Reidhead used her remarkable resources of energy, intelligence, and good humor to keep the book on course; Marian Johnson gave us important editorial advice early in our labors; Diane O'Connor guided the book through production; Tara Parmiter gracefully facilitated

communications and meetings; Fred Courtright handled the massive task of
securing permissions; and Anna Karvellas made the dream of a CD-ROM
accompaniment come true. Finally, our project editor, Kurt Wildermuth,
paid attention to (and in many cases perfected) the book's "minute particulars"
in ways that William Blake would have admired; Kurt also kept a steady eye
on the book's larger shape and primary goal: to bring English-language poems
originating in different times and places to modern readers—who will, we
hope, find pleasure within these covers.

Acknowledgments

Among our many critics, advisors, and friends, the following were of especial help in the preparation of the Fourth Edition. For assisting us in researching and preparing texts and other materials, thanks to John Barrell, Mike Bell, Reed Bye, Alfred E. David, Ed Doughtie, Harriet Guest, Skip Hamilton (reference librarian and bibliographer at the University of Colorado at Boulder), David Scott Kastan, Cathy Preston, Mike Preston, Julie Radliff, Jeffrey Robinson, Beth Robertson, James Shapiro, John Stevenson, Dana Symons, James Winn. For preparing the biographical sketches, thanks to Sherri Vanden Akker. Special thanks for their invaluable help goes to Andrea Bundy, Sandie Byrne, Tony Edwards, Charles Middleton (dean of arts and sciences at the University of Colorado at Boulder), Donna Mlinek, David Simpson, and Laura Wilson.

We take pleasure in thanking those teachers who provided critiques and questionnaire responses: Sally B. Allen (North Georgia College), Peter Balakian (Colgate University), Sharon Bartling (Eastern Illinois University), Judith Baumel (Adelphi University), Thomas L. Blanton (Central Washington University), Florence S. Boos (University of Iowa), Paul R. Brandt (Kent State University), Alison Byerly (Middlebury College), Thomas Carper (University of Southern Maine), William C. Cavanaugh (De Pauw University), Jonathan F. Chancey (Chemeketa Community College), Robert Cram (University of Florida), Steven S. Curry (University of Hawaii at Manoa), M. Godman (University of Kansas), Eli Goldblatt (Villanova University), R. I. C. Graziami (University College, University of Toronto), Anthony Grooms (University of Georgia), Thomas Grundy (University of Oregon), Laura Haigwood (Saint Mary's College), W. Harmon (University of North Carolina, Chapel Hill), Dayton Haskin (Boston College), Terry Heller (Coe College), Richard Hoffpauir (University of Alberta), Nicholas Jones (Oberlin College), Bruce Kawin (University of Colorado, Boulder), Robert Kern (Boston College), P. B. Labadie (University of Dayton), Barbara Leavy (Queens College), Tim Logue (University of North Carolina, Chapel Hill), Carol S. Long (Willamette University), M. K. Louis (University of Victoria), Paul Loukides (Albion College), Martin Maner (Wright State University), S. Mayne (University of Ottawa), Kerry McSweeney (McGill University), Lewis H. Miller, Jr. (Indiana University), Malcolm Nelson (State University of New York, Fredonia), Shirley Neuman (University of Alberta, Edmonton), Kevin O'Derman (West Virginia University), Linda Pratt (University of Nebraska), Bin Ramke (University of Denver), Victor J. Ramraj (University of Calgary), Magdalene Redekop (Victoria College, University of Toronto), Christine Rose (Portland State University), Ron Shreiber (University of Massachusetts, Boston), Lloyd Schwartz (University of Massachusetts, Boston), Barbara Sebek (University of Illinois), W. David Shaw (Victoria College, University of Toronto), John Shoptaw (Princeton University), Kathleen Skubikowski (Middlebury College), Thomas Small (Western Michigan University), Edith Suyama (University of Hawaii at Manoa), Avril Torrence (Mount Royal College), Paul S. Upton (University of Lethbridge), Helen Vendler (Harvard University), Sidney Wade (University of Florida), David Walton (University of Pittsburgh), Clifford Warier (Mount Royal College).

Versification

A poem is a composition written for performance by the human voice. What your eye sees on the page is the composer's verbal score, waiting for your voice to bring it alive as you read it aloud or hear it in your mind's ear. Unlike our reading of a newspaper, the best reading—that is to say, the most satisfying reading—of a poem involves a simultaneous engagement of eye and ear: the eye attentive not only to the meaning of words, but to their grouping and spacing as lines on a page; the ear attuned to the grouping and spacing of sounds. The more one understands of musical notation and the principles of musical composition, the more one will understand and appreciate a composer's score. Similarly, the more one understands of versification (the principles and practice of writing verse), the more one is likely to understand and appreciate poetry and, in particular, the intimate relationship between its form and its content. What a poem says or means is the result of how it is said, a fact that poets are often at pains to emphasize. "All my life," said W. H. Auden, "I have been more interested in technique than anything else." And T. S. Eliot claimed that "the conscious problems with which one is concerned in the actual writing are more those of a quasi-musical nature, in the arrangement of metric and pattern, than of a conscious exposition of ideas." Fortunately, the principles of versification are easier to explain than those of musical composition.

The oldest classification of poetry into three broad categories still holds:

1. **Epic:** a long narrative poem, frequently extending to several "books" (sections of several hundred lines), on a great and serious subject. See, for example, Spenser's *The Faerie Queene* (p. 152), Milton's *Paradise Lost* (p. 380), Wordsworth's *The Prelude* (p. 714), and Barrett Browning's *Aurora Leigh* (p. 857). With one notable exception, James Merrill's *The Changing Light at Sandover* (p. 1615), the few poems of comparable length to have been written in the twentieth century—for example, Williams' *Paterson* and Pound's *Cantos*—have a freer, less formal structure.

2. **Dramatic:** poetry, monologue or dialogue, written in the voice of a character assumed by the poet. Space does not permit the inclusion in this anthology of speeches from the many great verse dramas of English literature, but see such dramatic monologues as Tennyson's "Ulysses" (p. 896), Browning's "My Last Duchess" (p. 911), and Richard Howard's response to that poem, "Nikolaus Mardruz to his Master Ferdinand, Count of Tyrol, 1565" (p. 1666).

3. **Lyric:** originally, a song performed in ancient Greece to the accompaniment of a small harplike instrument called a lyre. The term is now used for any fairly short poem in the voice of a single speaker, although that speaker may sometimes quote others. The reader should be wary of identifying the lyric speaker with the poet, since the "I" of a poem will frequently be that of a fictional character invented by the poet. The majority of poems in this book

are lyrics, and the principal types of lyric will be found set out under "Forms" (p. lxxi).

Rhythm

Poetry is the most compressed form of language, and rhythm is an essential component of language. When we speak, we hear a sequence of **syllables**. These, the basic units of pronunciation, can consist of a vowel sound alone or a vowel with attendant consonants: *oh; syl-la-ble*. Sometimes *m*, *n*, and *l* are counted as vowel sounds, as in *riddle (rid-dl)* and *prism (pri-zm)*. In words of two or more syllables, one is almost always given more emphasis or, as we say, is more heavily stressed than the others, so that what we hear in ordinary speech is a sequence of such units, variously stressed and unstressed as, for example:

A poem is a composition written for performance by the human voice.

We call such an analysis of stressed and unstressed syllables **scansion** (the action or art of **scanning** a line to determine its division into metrical feet); and a simple system of signs has been evolved to denote stressed and unstressed syllables and any significant pause between them. Adding such scansion marks will produce the following:

A poĕm ĭs ă compŏsĭtiŏn ‖ wrĭttĕn fŏr pĕrfórmănce bȳ thĕ húmăn voíce.

The double bar, known as a **caesura** (from the Latin word for "cut"), indicates a natural pause in the speaking voice, which may be short (as here) or long (as between sentences); the ✗ sign indicates an unstressed syllable, and the ´ sign indicates one that is stressed.

The pattern of emphasis, stress, or accent can vary from speaker to speaker and situation to situation. If someone were to contradict my definition of a poem, I might reply:

A poĕm ís ă compŏsĭtiŏn . . .

with a heavier stress on **is** than on any other syllable in the sentence. The signs ✗ and ´ make no distinction between varying levels of stress and unstress—it being left to the reader to supply such variations—but some analysts use a third sign ˋ to indicate a stress falling between heavy and light.

Most people pay little or no attention to the sequence of stressed and unstressed syllables in their speaking and writing, but to a poet there is no more important element of a poem.

Meter

If a poem's rhythm is structured into a recurrence of regular—that is, approximately equal—units, we call it meter (from the Greek word for "measure"). There are four metrical systems in English poetry: the accentual, the accentual-syllabic, the syllabic, and the quantitative. Of these, the second accounts for more poems in the English language—and in this anthology—than do the other three together.

Accentual meter, sometimes called "strong-stress meter," is the oldest. The earliest recorded poem in the language—that is, the oldest of Old English or

Anglo-Saxon poems, Caedmon's seventh-century "Hymn" (p. 1)—employs a line divided in two by a heavy caesura, each half dominated by the two strongly stressed syllables:

> Hé aérĕst sčĕŏp ‖ aéldă béarnŭm
> [He first created for men's sons]
> héofŏn tŏ hrofĕ ‖ háliğ Sćyppĕnd
> [heaven as a roof holy creator]

Here, as in most Old English poetry, each line is organized by stress and by **alliteration** (the repetition of speech sounds—vowels or, more usually, consonants—in a sequence of nearby words). One and generally both of the stressed syllables in the first half-line alliterate with the first stressed syllable in the second half-line.

Accentual meter continued to be used into the late fourteenth century, as in Langland's *Piers Plowman*, which begins:

> Iñ ă sómĕr sésŏn, ‖ whăn sóft wăs thĕ sónnĕ,
> [In a summer season when mild was the sun,]
> Ĭ shópe mĕ iñ shróuds, ‖ ăs Í ă shépe wĕre . . .
> [I clad myself in clothes as if I'd become a sheep . . .]

However, following the Saxons' conquest by the Normans in 1066, Saxon native meter was increasingly supplanted by the metrical patterns of Old French poetry brought to England in the wake of William the Conqueror, although the nonalliterative four-stress line would have a long and lively continuing life—structuring, for example, section 2 of Eliot's "The Dry Salvages" (p. 1250). The Old English metrical system has been occasionally revived in more recent times, as for Heaney's translation of "The Seafarer" (p. 1794), Morgan's translation of *Beowulf* (p. 2), or the four-stress lines of Coleridge's "Christabel" and Wilbur's "Junk" (p. 1532); and many English poets from Spenser onward have used alliteration in ways that recall the character of Old and Middle English verse.

Accentual-syllabic meter provided the metrical structure of the new poetry to emerge in the fourteenth century, and its basic unit was the **foot**, a combination of two or three stressed and/or unstressed syllables. The four most common metrical feet in English poetry are:

1. **Iambic** (the noun is "iamb"): an unstressed followed by a stressed syllable, as in "New **York**." Between the Renaissance and the rise of free verse (p. lxxviii) in this century, iambic meter was the dominant rhythm of English poetry, considered by many English as well as classical Latin writers the meter closest to that of ordinary speech. For this reason, iambic meter is also to be found occasionally in the work of prose writers. Dickens' novel *A Tale of Two Cities*, for example, begins:

> Ĭt wàs | thĕ bést | ŏf tiḿes, ‖ ĭt wàs | thĕ wórst | ŏf tiḿes . . .

2. **Trochaic** (the noun is "trochee"): a stressed followed by an unstressed syllable, as in the word "**Lon**don" or the line from the nursery rhyme,

> Lóndŏn | brídge iš | fálliñg | dówn . . .

This is not to say that "London" can appear only in a trochaic line. Provided its natural stress is preserved, it can take its place comfortably in an iambic line, like that from Eliot's *The Waste Land*:

Ă crówd | flow̌ed óv | ĕr Lón | dŏn brídge . . .

Whereas iambic meter has a certain gravity, making it a natural choice for poems on solemn subjects, the trochaic foot has a lighter, quicker, more buoyant movement. Hence, for example, its use in Milton's "L'Allegro" (lines 25–29, for example, on p. 366) and Blake's "Introduction" to *Songs of Innocence* (p. 671).

3. **Anapestic** (the noun is "anapest"): two unstressed syllables followed by a stressed syllable, as in "Tennessee" or the opening of Byron's "The Destruction of Sennacherib" (p. 766).

Thĕ Ăssýr | iăn căme dówn | likĕ thĕ wólf | ŏn thĕ fóld . . .

The last three letters of the word "Assyrian" should be heard as one syllable, a form of contraction known as **elision.**

4. **Dactylic** (the noun is "dactyl"): a stressed syllable followed by two unstressed syllables, as in "**Len**ingrad." This, like the previous "triple" (three-syllable) foot, the anapest, has a naturally energetic movement, making it suitable for poems with vigorous subjects, though not these only. See Hardy's "The Voice" (p. 1056), which begins:

Wómăn mŭch | mised, hŏw yŏu | cáll tŏ mĕ, | cáll tŏ mĕ . . .

Iambs and anapests, which have a strong stress on the last syllable, are said to constitute a **rising meter**, whereas trochees and dactyls, ending with an unstressed syllable, constitute a **falling meter.** In addition to these four standard metrical units, there are two other (two-syllable) feet that occur only as occasional variants of the others:

5. **Spondaic** (the noun is "spondee"): two successive syllables with approximately equal strong stresses, as on the words "draw back" in the second of these lines from Arnold's "Dover Beach":

Lístĕn! | yŏu héar | thĕ grát | iňg róar
Ŏf péb | blĕs whĭch | thĕ wáves | dráw báck, | ăňd flíng . . .

6. **Pyrrhic** (the noun is also "pyrrhic"): two successive unstressed or lightly stressed syllables, as in the second foot of the second line above, where the succession of light syllables seems to mimic the rattle of light pebbles that the heavy wave slowly draws back.

Poets, who consciously or instinctively will select a meter to suit their subject, have also a variety of line lengths from which to choose:

1. **Monometer** (one foot): see the fifth and sixth lines of each stanza of Herbert's "Easter Wings" (p. 330), which reflect, in turn, the poverty and thinness of the speaker. Herrick's "Upon His Departure Hence" is a rare example of a complete poem in iambic monometer. The fact that each line is a solitary foot (× ´) suggests to the eye the narrow inscription of a gravestone, and to the ear the brevity and loneliness of life.

Thus I
Pass by
And die,
As one,

Unknown,
And gone:
I'm made
A shade,
And laid
I'th grave,
There have
My cave.
Where tell
I dwell,
Farewell.

2. **Dimeter** (two feet): iambic dimeter alternates with iambic pentameter in Donne's "A Valediction of Weeping" (p. 270); and dactylic dimeter (´ × × | ´ × ×) gives Tennyson's "The Charge of the Light Brigade" (p. 907) its galloping momentum:

Cannon to right of them,
Cannon to left of them,
Cannon in front of them
 Volleyed and thundered;
Stormed at with shot and shell,
Boldly they rode and well,
Into the jaws of Death,
Into the mouth of hell
 Rode the six hundred.

Lines 4 and 9 each lack a final unstressed syllable—in technical terms such lines are **catalectic.** This shortening, which gives prominence to the stressed syllable necessary for rhyme (p. lxix), is a common feature of rhyming lines in trochaic and dactylic poems.

3. **Trimeter** (three feet): Ralegh's "The Lie" (p. 142) and Roethke's "My Papa's Waltz" (p. 1386) are written in iambic trimeter; and all but the last line of each stanza of Shelley's "To a Skylark" (p. 805) in trochaic trimeter.

4. **Tetrameter** (four feet): Marvell's "To His Coy Mistress" (p. 435) is written in iambic tetrameter; and Shakespeare's "Fear No More the Heat o' the Sun" (p. 247) in trochaic tetrameter.

5. **Pentameter** (five feet): the most popular metrical line in English poetry, the iambic pentameter provides the basic rhythmical framework, or **base rhythm,** of countless poems from the fourteenth century to the twentieth, from Chaucer's "General Prologue" to *The Canterbury Tales* (p. 17) and Shakespeare's sonnets (p. 234) to Hill's "Lachrimae" (p. 1724) and Dunn's "In the Grounds" (p. 1808). It even contributes to the stately prose of the Declaration of Independence:

We hóld | thése trúths | tŏ be | sélf-év | ĭdeńt . . .

Anapestic pentameter is to be found in Browning's "Saul":

Ăs thў lóve | ĭs dĭscóv | erĕd ălmíght | ў, ălmíght | ў, bĕ próved
Thў power, | thăt ĕxísts | wĭth ańd fór | ĭt, ŏf be | ĭńg bĕlovéd!

A missing syllable in the first foot of the second line gives emphasis to the important word "power."

6. **Hexameter** (six feet): The opening sonnet of Sidney's "Astrophil and Stella" (p. 192) and Dowson's "Non sum qualis eram bonae sub regno Cynarae" (p. 1106) are written in iambic hexameter, a line sometimes known as an **alexandrine** (probably after a twelfth-century French poem, the *Roman d'Alexandre*). A single alexandrine is often used to provide a resonant termination to a stanza of shorter lines, as, for example, the Spenserian stanza (p. lxxiii) or Hardy's "The Convergence of the Twain" (p. 1053), in which the shape of the stanza suggests the iceberg that is the poem's subject. Swinburne's "The Last Oracle" is written in trochaic hexameter:

Dáy bў̆ | dáy thў̆ | shădŏw | shínes iñ | heáven bĕ | hóldĕn . . .

7. **Heptameter** (seven feet): Kipling's "Tommy" (p. 1076) is written in iambic heptameter (or **fourteeners**, as they are often called, from the number of their syllables), with an added initial syllable in three of the four lines that make up the second half of each stanza.

8. **Octameter** (eight feet): Browning's "A Toccata of Galuppi's" (p. 926) is the most famous example of the rare trochaic octameter.

Poets who write in strict conformity to a single metrical pattern will achieve the music of a metronome and soon drive their listeners away. Variation, surprise, is the very essence of every artist's trade; and one of the most important sources of metrical power and pleasure is the perpetual tension between the regular and the irregular, between the expected and the unexpected, the base rhythm and the variation.

John Hollander has spoken of the "metrical contract" that poets enter into with their readers from the first few words of a poem. When Frost begins "The Gift Outright" —

Thĕ lánd | wăs oúrs | bĕfóre | ẃe wĕre | thĕ lánd's

—we expect what follows to have an iambic base rhythm, but the irregularity or variation in the fourth foot tells us that we are hearing not robot speech but human speech. The stress on "we" makes it, appropriately, one of the two most important words in the line, "we" being the most important presence in the "land."

Frost's poem will serve as an example of ways in which skillful poets will vary their base rhythm:

1. Thĕ lánd | wăs oúrs | bĕfóre | ẃe wĕre | thĕ lánd's.
2. Shé wăs | oúr lánd || móre thăn | ă hún | drĕd yéars
3. Bĕfóre | ẃe wĕre | hér péo | plĕ. || Shé|wăs oúrs
4. Iñ Máss | ăchú | seĭ̆ts, || iñ | Vĭ̆rgín | ĭ̆ă,
5. Bŭt ẃe | wĕre Éng | lăñd's, || still | cŏlón | ĭ̆als,
6. Pŏsséss | iñg whát | wĕ stíll | wĕre ún | pŏssessed | bў̆.
7. Pŏssessed | bў̆ whát | w̆e nów | ˌno móre | pŏssessed.
8. Sómethĭ̆ng | wĕ wĕre | wĭ̆thhold | iñg máde | ŭs wéak
9. Uñtíl | wĕ foúnd | oút thăt | it wăs | oŭrselves
10. Wé wĕre | wĭ̆thhóld | iñg frŏm | oŭr lánd | ŏf lív | iñg,
11. Ăñd fórth | wĭ̆th foúnd | săĺva | tĭ̆oñ iñ | sŭrrén | dĕr.
12. Súch ăs | wĕ wére | wĕ gáve | oŭrselves | oŭtríght
13. (Thĕ déed | ŏf gíft | wăs mán | ў̆ deéds | ŏf wár)

14. Tŏ thĕ lánd | vaguelў̆ | reăl | ĭžĭng | wéstwárd,
15. Bŭt still | uñstór | iĕd, || art | lĕss, || ún | ĕnhánced,
16. Súch ăs | shé wás, || súch ăs | shé woŭld | bĕcóme.

The iambic pentameter gives the poem a stately movement appropriate to the unfolding history of the United States. In the trochaic "reversed feet" at the start of lines 2, 10, 12, and 16, the stress is advanced to lend emphasis to a key word or, in the case of line 8, an important syllable. Spondees in lines 2 ("our land") and 3 ("her people") bring into equal balance the two partners whose union is the theme of the poem. Such additional heavy stresses are counterbalanced by the light pyrrhic feet at the end of lines 4 and 5, in the middle of line 10, or toward the end of line 14. The multiple irregularities of that line give a wonderful impression of the land stretching westward into space, just as the variations of line 16 give a sense of the nation surging toward its destiny in time. It must be added, however, that scansion is to some extent a matter of interpretation, in which the rhetorical emphasis a particular reader prefers alters the stress pattern. Another reader might—no less correctly—prefer to begin line 9, for example:

Uñtil | we foŭnd . . .

An important factor in varying the pattern of a poem is the placing of its pauses or caesurae. One falling in the middle of a line—as in line 4 above—is known as a medial caesura; one falling near the start of a line, an initial caesura; and one falling near or at the end of a line, a terminal caesura. When a caesura occurs as in lines 13 and 14 above, those lines are said to be **endstopped**. Lines 3 and 9, however, are called **run-on lines** (or, to use a French term, they exhibit **enjambment**—"a striding over"), because the thrust of the incompleted sentence carries on over the end of the verse line. Such transitions tend to increase the pace of the poem, as the end-stopping of lines 10 through 16 slows it down.

A strikingly original and influential blending of the Old English accentual and more modern accentual-syllabic metrical systems was **sprung rhythm**, conceived and pioneered by Gerard Manley Hopkins.

Finding the cadences of his Victorian contemporaries—what he called their "common rhythm"—too measured and mellifluous for his liking, he sought for a stronger, more muscular verse movement. Strength he equated with stress, arguing that "even one stressed syllable may make a foot, and consequently two or more stresses may come running [one after the other], which in common rhythm can, regularly speaking, never happen." In his system of sprung rhythm, each foot began with a stress and could consist of a single stressed syllable (´), a trochee (´ x), a dactyl (´ x x), or what he called a **first paeon** (´ x x x). His lines will, on occasion, admit other unstressed syllables, as in the sonnet "Felix Randal" (p. 1063):

Félĭx | Rándăl, || thĕ | fárriĕr, || Ŏ ĭš hĕ | deád thĕn? || mы̆ | dútў̆ ăll | éndĕd,
Who hăve | watched hĭs | móuld ŏf măn, || bĭg- | bóned ănd | hárdў̆-| hándsŏme
Pínĭng, || pínĭng, || tĭll | tíme whĕn | réasŏn | rámblĕd ĭñ ĭt | ańd sŏme
Fátăl | fóur dĭs | órdĕrs, || fléshed thĕre, || áll cŏn | téndĕd?

A poetry structured on the principle that strength is stress is particularly well suited to stressful subjects, and the sprung rhythm of what Hopkins called his "terrible sonnets" (p. 1064/67), for example, gives them a dramatic urgency, a sense of anguished struggle that few poets have equalled in accentual-syllabic meter.

A number of other poets have experimented with two other metrical systems. **Syllabic meter** measures only the number of syllables in a line, without regard to their stress. Being an inescapable feature of the English language, stress will of course appear in lines composed on syllabic principles, but will fall variously, and usually for rhetorical emphasis, rather than in any formal metrical pattern. When Marianne Moore wished to attack the pretentiousness of much formal "Poetry" (p. 1218), she shrewdly chose to do so in **syllabics,** as lines in syllabic meter are called. The effect is carefully informal and prosaic, and few unalerted readers will notice that there are 19 syllables in the first line of each stanza; 22 in the second; 11 in the third (except for the third line of the third stanza, which has 7); 5 in the fourth; 8 in the fifth; and 13 in the sixth. That the poem succeeds in deflating Poetry (with a capital P) while at once celebrating poetry and creating it is not to be explained by Moore's talent for arithmetic so much as by her unobtrusive skill in modulating the stresses and pauses of colloquial speech. The result is a music like that of good free verse (p. lxxviii).

Because stress plays a less important role in such Romance languages as French and Italian and in Japanese, their poetry tends to be syllabic in construction, and Pound brilliantly adapts the form of three-line, seventeen-syllable Japanese **haiku** in a poem whose title is an integral part of the whole:

In a Station of the Metro

The apparition of these faces in the crowd;
Petals on a wet, black bough.

The syllable count (8, 12, 7) bears only a token relation to that of the strict Japanese pattern (5, 7, 5), but the poem succeeds largely because its internal rhymes (p. lxix)—*Station* / appa*rition; Met*ro / *pet*als / *wet; crowd* / *bough*— point up a series of distinct stressed syllables that suggest, in an impressionist fashion, a series of distinct white faces.

A number of other modern poets—among them Auden, Dylan Thomas, and Gunn—have written notable poems in syllabics; their efforts to capture the spirit—if not the letter—of a foreign linguistic and poetic tradition may be compared with those of many poets since the Renaissance who have attempted to render Greek and Latin meters into English verse, using the fourth metrical system to be considered here.

Quantitative meter, which structures most Greek, Sanskrit, and later Roman poetry, is based on notions of a syllable's duration in time or its *length.* This is determined by various conventions of spelling as well as by the type of vowel sound it contains. Complexities arise because Latin has more word-stress than does ancient Greek, and hence there is often an alignment of stress and quantity in foot-patterns of later Roman verse. This is ironic in light of the efforts, on the part of some Renaissance English poets, to "ennoble" the vernacular tradition by following classical metrical models. Although poets like Spenser and Sidney devised elaborate rules for determining the "length" of English syllables according to ancient rules, the theoretical prescriptions often generated poems in which "long" syllables are in fact stressed syllables. Indeed, one defender of quantitative meter in English, Thomas Campion, explicitly recommended a metrical system aligning stress with quantity; he illustrated his theory with some highly successful poems such as "Rose-cheeked Laura" (p. 251). Although some Renaissance experiments in quantitative meter produced poems distinctly less pleasing to the ear than to the (highly educated) eye, others such as those in Sidney's *Arcadia*, work well and can be compared to the elegant and beautiful **alcaics** that Tennyson addressed to Milton. (An alcaic is a four-line stanza of considerable metrical complexity, named after the ancient Greek poet Alcaeus.) In that poem, Tennyson reminds us that experiments in cultural translation—some more successful than others—have been an enduring part of the English poetic tradition from the Anglo-Saxon era to the present.

Rhyme

Ever since the poetry of Chaucer sprang from the fortunate marriage of Old French and Old English, rhyme (the concurrence, in two or more lines, of the last stressed vowel and of all speech sounds following that vowel) has been closely associated with rhythm in English poetry. It is to be found in the early poems and songs of many languages. Most English speakers meet it first in nursery rhymes, many of which involve numbers ("One, two, / Buckle my shoe"), a fact supporting the theory that rhyme may have had its origin in primitive religious rites and magical spells. From such beginnings, poetry has been inextricably linked with music—Caedmon's "Hymn" (p. 1) and the earliest popular ballads (p. 81) were all composed to be sung—and rhyme has been a crucial element in the music of poetry. More than any other factor it has been responsible for making poetry memorable. Its function is a good deal more complicated than may at first appear, in that by associating one rhyme-word with another, poets may introduce a remote constellation of associations that may confirm, question, or on occasion deny the literal meaning of their words. Consider, for example, the opening eight lines, or "octet" (p. lxxv) of Hopkins' sonnet "God's Grandeur" (p. 1062):

1. The world is charged with the grandeur of God.
2. It will flame out, like shining from shook foil;
3. It gathers to a greatness, like the ooze of oil
4. Crushed. Why do men then now not reck his rod?
5. Generations have trod, have trod, have trod;
6. And all is seared with trade; bleared, smeared with toil;
7. And wears man's smudge and shares man's smell: the soil
8. Is bare now, nor can foot feel, being shod.

The grand statement of the first line is illustrated, not by the grand examples that the opening of lines 2 and 3 seem to promise, but by the surprising similes of shaken tin foil and olive oil oozing from its press. The down-to-earthiness that these objects have in common is stressed by the *foil / oil* rhyme that will be confirmed by the *toil / soil* of lines 6 and 7. At the other end of the cosmic scale, "The grandeur of *God*" no less appropriately rhymes with "his *rod*." But what of the implicit coupling of grand God and industrial man in the ensuing *trod / shod* rhymes of lines 5 and 8? These rhymes remind Hopkins' reader that Christ, too, was a worker, a walker of hard roads, and that "the grandeur of God" is manifest in the world through which the weary generations tread.

Rhymes appearing like these at the end of a line are known as **end rhymes,** but poets frequently make use of such **internal rhyme** as the *then / men* of Hopkins' line 4, the *seared / bleared / smeared* of line 6, or the *wears / shares* of line 7. **Assonance** (the repetition of identical or similar vowel sounds) is present in the *not / rod* of line 4. This sonnet also contains two examples of a related sound effect, **onomatopoeia**, sometimes called "echoism," a combination of words whose sound seems to resemble the sound it denotes. So, in lines 3 and 4, the long, slow, alliterative vowels—"ooze of oil"—seem squeezed out by the crushing pressure of the heavily stressed verb that follows. So, too, the triple repetition of "have trod" in line 5 seems to echo the thudding boots of the laboring generations.

All the rhymes so far discussed have been what is known as **masculine rhymes** in that they consist of a single stressed syllable. Rhyme words in which a stressed syllable is followed by an unstressed syllable—*chiming / rhyming*—are known as **feminine rhymes.** Single (one-syllable) and double (two-syllable) rhymes are the most common, but triple and even quadruple rhymes are also to be found, usually in a comic context like that of Gilbert's "I Am the Very Model of a Modern Major-General" (p. 1041) or Byron's *Don Juan:*

> But—Oh! ye lords of ladies intell*ectual,*
> Inform us truly, have they not hen-*pecked you all?*

If the correspondence of rhyming sounds is exact, it is called **perfect rhyme** or else "full" or "true rhyme." For many centuries almost all English writers of serious poems confined themselves to rhymes of this sort, except for an occasional **poetic license** (or violation of the rules of versification) such as **eye rhymes,** words whose endings are spelled alike, and in most instances were pronounced alike, but have in the course of time acquired a different pronunciation: *prove / love, daughter / laughter.* Since the nineteenth century, however, an increasing number of poets have felt the confident chimes of perfect rhymes inappropriate for poems of doubt, frustration, and grief, and have used various forms of **imperfect rhyme:**

Off-rhyme (also known as half rhyme, near rhyme, or slant rhyme) differs from perfect rhyme in changing the vowel sound and / or the concluding consonants expected of perfect rhyme. See Byron's *gone / alone* rhyme in the second stanza of "On This Day I Complete My Thirty-sixth Year" (p. 792), or Dickinson's rhyming of *Room / Storm, firm / Room,* and *be / Fly* in "I heard a Fly buzz—when I died—" (p. 1016).

Vowel rhyme goes beyond off-rhyme to the point at which rhyme words have only their vowel sound in common. See for example, the muted but musically effective rhymes of Dylan Thomas' "Fern Hill" (p. 1464): *boughs / towns, green / leaves, starry / barley, climb / eyes / light.*

Pararhyme, in which the stressed vowel sounds differ but are flanked by identical or similar consonants, is a term coined by Edmund Blunden to describe Owen's pioneering use of such rhymes. Although they had occurred on occasion before—see *trod / trade* in lines 5 and 6 of "God's Grandeur"— Owen was the first to employ pararhyme consistently. In such a poem as "Strange Meeting" (p. 1279) the second rhyme is usually lower in pitch (has a deeper vowel sound) than the first, producing effects of dissonance, failure, and unfulfillment that subtly reinforce Owen's theme. The last stanza of his "Miners" shows a further refinement:

> The centuries will burn rich loads
> With which we groaned,
> Whose warmth shall lull their dreaming lids,
> While songs are crooned.
> But they will not dream of us poor lads,
> Left in the ground.

Here, the pitch of the pararhyme rises to reflect the dream of a happier future—*loads / lids*—before plunging to the desolate reality of *lads*, a rise and fall repeated in *groaned / crooned / ground*.

The effect of rhyming—whether the chime is loud or muted—is to a large extent dictated by one rhyme's distance from another, a factor frequently dictated by the rhyme scheme of the poet's chosen stanza form. At one extreme stands Dylan Thomas' "Author's Prologue," a poem of 102 lines, in which line 1 rhymes with line 102, line 2 with 101, and so on down to the central couplet of lines 51–52. Rhyme schemes, however, are seldom so taxing for poets (or their readers) and, as with their choice of meter, are likely to be determined consciously or subconsciously by their knowledge of earlier poems written in this or that form.

Forms

BASIC FORMS

Having looked at—and listened to—the ways in which metrical feet combine in a poetic line, one can move on to see—and hear—how such lines combine in the larger patterns of the dance, what are known as the forms of poetry.

1. **Blank verse,** at one end of the scale, consists of unrhymed (hence "blank") iambic pentameters. Introduced to England by Surrey in his translations from the *Aeneid* (1554), it soon became the standard meter for Elizabethan poetic drama. No verse form is closer to the natural rhythms of spoken English or more adaptive to different levels of speech. Following the example of Shakespeare, whose kings, clowns, and countryfolk have each their own voice when speaking blank verse, it has been used by dramatists from Marlowe to Eliot. Milton chose it for his religious epic *Paradise Lost* (p. 380), Wordsworth for his autobiographical epic *The Prelude* (p. 714), and Coleridge for his meditative lyric "Frost at Midnight" (p. 742). During the nineteenth century it became a favorite form of such **dramatic monologues** as Tennyson's "Ulysses" (p. 896) and Browning's "Fra Lippo Lippi" (p. 918), in which a single speaker (who is not the poet himself) addresses a dramatically defined listener in a specific situation and at a critical moment. All of these poems are divided into **verse paragraphs** of varying length, as distinct from the **stanzas** of equal length that make up Tennyson's "Tears, Idle Tears" (p. 898) or Stevens' "Sunday Morning" (p. 1151).

2. The **couplet,** two lines of verse, usually coupled by rhyme, has been a principal unit of English poetry since rhyme entered the language. The first of the anonymous thirteenth- and fourteenth-century lyrics in this anthology (p. 13) is in couplets, but the first poet to use the form consistently was Chaucer, whose "General Prologue" to *The Canterbury Tales* (p. 17) exhibits great flexibility. His narrative momentum tends to overrun line endings, and his pentameter couplets are seldom the self-contained syntactic units one finds in Jonson's "On My First Son" (p. 291). The sustained use of such **closed couplets** attained its ultimate sophistication in what came to be known as **heroic couplets** ("heroic" because of their use in epic poems or plays), pioneered by Denham in the seventeenth century and perfected by Dryden and Pope in the eighteenth. The Chaucerian energies of the iambic pentameter were

reined in, and each couplet made a balanced whole within the greater balanced whole of its poem, "Mac Flecknoe" (p. 473), for example, or "The Rape of the Lock" (p. 574). As if in reaction against the elevated ("heroic" or "mock heroic") diction and syntactic formality of the heroic couplet, more-recent users of the couplet have tended to veer toward the other extreme of informality. Colloquialisms, frequent enjambment, and variable placing of the caesura mask the formal rhyming of Browning's "My Last Duchess" (p. 911), as the speaker of that dramatic monologue seeks to mask its diabolical organization. Owen, with the pararhymes of "Strange Meeting" (p. 1279), and Yeats, with the off-rhymed tetrameters of "Under Ben Bulben" (p. 1103), achieve similarly informal effects.

3. The **tercet** is a stanza of three lines usually linked with a single rhyme, although Williams' "Poem" (p. 1167) is unrhymed. It may also be a three-line section of a larger poetic structure, as, for example, the sestet of a sonnet (p. lxxv). Tercets can be composed of lines of equal length—iambic tetrameter in Herrick's "Upon Julia's Clothes" (p. 323), trochaic octameter in Browning's "A Toccata of Galuppi's" (p. 926)—or of different length, as in Hardy's "The Convergence of the Twain" (p. 1053). An important variant of this form is the linked tercet, or **terza rima**, in which the second line of each stanza rhymes with the first and third lines of the next. A group of such stanzas is commonly concluded with a final line supplying the missing rhyme, as in Wilbur's "First Snow in Alsace" (p. 1526), although Shelley expanded the conclusion to a couplet in his "Ode to the West Wind" (p. 801). No verse form in English poetry is more closely identified with its inventor than is terza rima with Dante, who used it for his *Divine Comedy*. Shelley invokes the inspiration of his great predecessor in choosing the form for his "Ode" written on the outskirts of Dante's Florence, and T. S. Eliot similarly calls the *Divine Comedy* to mind with the tercets—unrhymed, but aligned on the page like Dante's— of a passage in part 2 of "Little Gidding" that ends:

> "From wrong to wrong the exasperated spirit
> Proceeds, unless restored by that refining fire
> Where you must move in measure, like a dancer."
> The day was breaking. In the disfigured street
> He left me, with a kind of valediction,
> And faded on the blowing of the horn.

4. The **quatrain**, a stanza of four lines, rhymed or unrhymed, is the most common of all English stanzaic forms. And the most common type of quatrain is the **ballad stanza**, in which lines of iambic tetrameter alternate with iambic trimeter, rhyming *abcb* (lines 1 and 3 being unrhymed) or, less commonly, *abab*. This, the stanza of such popular ballads as "Sir Patrick Spens" (p. 87), Coleridge's literary ballad "The Rime of the Ancient Mariner" (p. 744), and Dickinson's "I felt a Funeral, in my Brain" (p. 1013), also occurs in many hymns and is there called **common meter**. The expansion of lines 2 and 4 to tetrameters produces a quatrain known (particularly in hymnbooks) as **long meter**, the form of Hardy's "Channel Firing" (p. 1054). When, on the other hand, the first line is shortened to a trimeter, matching lines 2 and 4, the stanza is called **short meter**. Gascoigne uses it for "And If I Did What Then?" (p. 132) and Hardy uses it for "I Look into My Glass"(p. 1050). Stanzas of iambic pentameter rhyming *abab*, as in Gray's "Elegy Written in a Country Churchyard" (p. 609), are known as **heroic quatrains**. The pentameter stanzas of FitzGerald's "Rubáiyát of Omar Khayyám of Naishápúr" (p. 866) are

rhymed *aaba*, a rhyme scheme that Frost elaborates in "Stopping by Woods on a Snowy Evening" (p. 1131), where the third line (unrhymed in the "Rubáiyát") rhymes with lines 1, 2, and 4 of the following stanza, producing an effect like that of terza rima. Quatrains can also be in **monorhyme**, as in Rossetti's "The Woodspurge" (p. 1004); composed of two couplets, as in "Now Go'th Sun Under Wood" (p. 13); or rhymed *abba*, as in Tennyson's "In Memoriam A. H. H." (p. 899).

5. **Rhyme royal,** a seven-line iambic-pentameter stanza rhyming *ababbcc*, was introduced by Chaucer in *Troilus and Criseide* (p. 52), but its name is thought to come from its later use by King James I of Scotland in "The Kingis Quair." Later examples include Wyatt's "They Flee from Me" (p. 115) and those somber stanzas in Auden's "The Shield of Achilles" (p. 1372) that describe the present century, as a contrast to the eight-line stanzas with a ballad rhythm that describe a mythic past.

6. **Ottava rima** is an eight-line stanza, as its Italian name indicates, and it rhymes *abababcc*. Like terza rima and the sonnet (below), it was introduced to English literature by Sir Thomas Wyatt. Byron put it to brilliant use in *Don Juan* (p. 769), frequently undercutting with a comic couplet the seeming seriousness of the six preceding lines. Yeats used ottava rima more gravely in "Sailing to Byzantium" (p. 1094) and "Among School Children" (p. 1096).

7. The **Spenserian stanza** has nine lines, the first eight being iambic pentameter and the last an iambic hexameter (an **alexandrine**), rhyming *ababbcbcc*. Chaucer had used two such quatrains, linked by three rhymes, as the stanza form of "The Monk's Tale," but Spenser's addition of a concluding alexandrine gave the stanza he devised for *The Faerie Queene* (p. 152) an inequality in its final couplet, a variation reducing the risk of monotony that can overtake a long series of iambic pentameters. Keats and Hopkins wrote their earliest known poems in this form, and Keats went on to achieve perhaps the fullest expression of its intricate harmonies in "The Eve of St. Agnes" (p. 833). Partly, no doubt, in tribute to that poem, Shelley used the Spenserian stanza in his great elegy on Keats, *Adonais* (p. 807); later, the form was a natural choice for the narcotic narrative of Tennyson's "The Lotos-Eaters"(p. 892).

Ottava rima and the Spenserian stanza each open with a quatrain and close with a couplet. These and other of the shorter stanzaic units similarly recur as component parts of certain lyrics with a fixed form.

8. The **sonnet,** traditionally a poem of fourteen iambic pentameters linked by an intricate rhyme scheme, is one of the oldest verse forms in English. Used by almost every notable poet in the language, it is the best example of how rhyme and meter can provide the imagination not with a prison but with a theater. The sonnet originated in Italy and, since being introduced to England by Sir Thomas Wyatt (see his "Whoso List to Hunt," p. 113) in the early sixteenth century, has been the stage for the soliloquies of countless lovers and for dramatic action ranging from a dinner party (p. 1007) to the rape of Leda and the fall of Troy (p. 1095). There are two basic types of sonnet—the Italian or Petrarchan (named after the fourteenth-century Italian poet Petrarch) and the English or Shakespearean—and a number of variant types, of which the most important is the Spenserian. They differ in their rhyme schemes, and consequently their structure, as follows:

The Spenserian Sonnet

First quatrain
a
b
a
b

Second quatrain
b
c
b
c

Third quatrain
c
d
c
d

Couplet
e
e

couplet link

couplet link

The English Sonnet

First quatrain
a
b
a
b

Second quatrain
c
d
c
d

Third quatrain
e
f
e
f

Couplet
g
g

Turn

The Italian Sonnet

First quatrain
a
b
b
a

Second quatrain
a
b
b
a

Octave

First tercet
c
d
e

Second tercet
c
d
e

Sestet

Turn

The Italian sonnet, with its distinctive division into **octave** (an eight-line unit) and **sestet** (a six-line unit), is structurally suited to a statement followed by a counterstatement, as in Milton's "When I Consider How My Light Is Spent" (p. 378). The blind poet's questioning of divine justice is checked by the voice of Patience, whose haste "to prevent That murmur" is conveyed by the accelerated **turn** (change in direction of argument or narrative) on the word "but" in the last line of the octave, rather than the first of the sestet. Shelley's "Ozymandias" (p. 799) follows the same pattern of statement and counterstatement, except that its turn comes in the traditional position. Another pattern common to the Italian sonnet—observation (octave) and amplifying conclusion (sestet)—underlies Keats' "On First Looking into Chapman's Homer" (p. 831) and Hill's "The Laurel Axe" (p. 1725). Of these, only Milton's has a sestet conforming to the conventional rhyme scheme: others, such as Donne's "Holy Sonnets" (p. 287), end with a couplet, sometimes causing them to be mistaken for sonnets of the other type.

The English sonnet falls into three quatrains, with a turn at the end of line 12 and a concluding couplet often of a summary or epigrammatic character. M. H. Abrams has well described the unfolding of Drayton's "Since there's no help, come let us kiss and part" (p. 215): "The lover brusquely declares in the first two quatrains that he is glad the affair is cleanly broken off, pauses in the third quatrain as though at the threshold, and in the last two rhymed lines suddenly drops his swagger to make one last plea." Spenser, in the variant form that bears his name, reintroduced to the English sonnet the couplets characteristic of the Italian sonnet. This interweaving of the quatrains, as in sonnet 75 of his "Amoretti" (p. 169), makes possible a more musical and closely developed argument, and tends to reduce the sometimes excessive assertiveness of the final couplet. That last feature of the English sonnet is satirized by Brooke in his "Sonnet Reversed," which turns romantic convention upside down by *beginning* with the couplet:

> Hand trembling towards hand; the amazing lights
> Of heart and eye. They stood on supreme heights.

The three quatrains that follow record the ensuing anticlimax of suburban married life. Meredith in "Modern Love" (p. 1007) stretched the sonnet to sixteen lines; Hopkins cut it short in what he termed his **curtal** (a curtailed form of "curtailed") **sonnet** "Pied Beauty" (p. 1063); while Shakespeare concealed a sonnet in *Romeo and Juliet* (1.5.95 ff.). Shakespeare's 154 better-known sonnets form a carefully organized progression or **sonnet sequence**, following the precedent of such earlier sonneteers as Sidney with his "Astrophil and Stella" (p. 192) and Spenser with his "Amoretti" (p. 165). In the nineteenth century, Elizabeth Barrett Browning's "Sonnets from the Portuguese" (p. 856) continued a tradition in which the author of "Berryman's Sonnets" has since, with that title, audaciously challenged the author of Shakespeare's sonnets.

9. The **villanelle**, a French verse form derived from an earlier Italian folk song, retains the circular pattern of a peasant dance. It consists of five tercets rhyming *aba* followed by a quatrain rhyming *abaa*, with the first line of the initial tercet recurring as the last line of the second and fourth tercets and the third line of the initial tercet recurring as the last line of the third and fifth tercets, these two **refrains** (lines of regular recurrence) being again repeated as the last two lines of the poem. If A^1 and A^2 may be said to represent the first

and third lines of the initial tercet the rhyme scheme of the villanelle will look like this:

$$\text{tercet 1: } A^1 \; B \; A^2$$
$$2: A \; B \; A^1$$
$$3: A \; B \; A^2$$
$$4: A \; B \; A^1$$
$$5: A \; B \; A^2$$
$$\text{quatrain: } A \; B \; A^1 \; A^2$$

The art of writing complicated forms like the villanelle and sestina (see below) is to give them the graceful momentum of good dancing, and the vitality of the dance informs such triumphant examples as Roethke's "The Waking" (p. 1391), Bishop's "One Art" (p. 1419), and Thomas' "Do Not Go Gentle into That Good Night" (p. 1465).

10. The **sestina,** the most complicated of the verse forms initiated by the twelfth-century wandering singers known as troubadours, is composed of six stanzas of six lines each, followed by an **envoy,** or concluding stanza, that incorporates lines or words used before: in this case the *words* (instead of *rhymes*) end each line in the following pattern:

$$\text{stanza 1: } A \; B \; C \; D \; E \; F$$
$$2: F \; A \; E \; B \; D \; C$$
$$3: C \; F \; D \; A \; B \; E$$
$$4: E \; C \; B \; F \; A \; D$$
$$5: D \; E \; A \; C \; F \; B$$
$$6: B \; D \; F \; E \; C \; A$$

envoy: E C A or A C E [these lines should contain the remaining three end words]

The earliest example in this anthology is, in fact a *double* sestina: Sidney's "Ye Goatherd Gods" (p. 188). Perhaps daunted by the intricate brilliance of this, few poets attempted the form for the next three centuries. It was reintroduced by Swinburne and Pound, who prepared the way for such notable contemporary examples as Bishop's "Sestina" (p. 1412), Hecht's "The Book of Yolek" (p. 1566), and Ashbery's "The Painter" (p. 1626).

11. The **limerick** (to end this section on a lighter note) is a five-line stanza thought to take its name from an old custom at convivial parties whereby each person was required to sing an extemporized "nonsense verse," which was followed by a chorus containing the words "Will you come up to Limerick?" The acknowledged Old Master of the limerick is Edward Lear (p. 942), who required that the first and fifth lines end with the same word (usually a place name), a restriction abandoned by many Modern Masters, though triumphantly retained by the anonymous author of this:

> There once was a man from Nantucket
> Who kept all his cash in a bucket;
> But his daughter named Nan
> Ran away with a man,
> And as for the bucket, Nantucket.

COMPOSITE FORMS

Just as good poets have always varied their base rhythm, there have always been those ready to bend, stretch, or in some way modify a fixed form to suit the demands of a particular subject. The earliest systematic and successful pioneer of such variation was John Skelton, who gave his name to what has come to be called **Skeltonic verse.** His poems typically—and see, for example, the extract from "Colin Clout" (p. 76)—have short lines of anything from three to seven syllables containing two or three stresses (though more of both are not uncommon), and exploit a single rhyme until inspiration and the resources of the language run out. The breathless urgency of this form has intrigued and influenced such modern poets as Graves and Auden.

Another early composite form employed longer lines: iambic hexameter (twelve syllables) alternating with iambic heptameter (fourteen syllables). This form, known as "poulter's measure"—from the poultryman's practice of giving twelve eggs for the first dozen and fourteen for the second—was used by such sixteenth-century poets as Wyatt (p. 113), Queen Elizabeth (p. 130), and Sidney (p. 188), but has not proved popular since.

The element of the unexpected often accounts for much of the success of poems in such a composite form as Donne's "The Sun Rising" (p. 265). His stanza might be described as a combination of two quatrains (the first rhyming *abba*, the second *cdcd*), and a couplet (*ee*). That description would be accurate but inadequate in that it takes no account of the variation in line length, which is a crucial feature of the poem's structure. It opens explosively with the outrage of the interrupted lover:

> Busy old fool, unruly sun,
> Why dost thou thus
> Through windows and through curtains call on us?

Short lines, tetrameter followed by dimeter, suggest the speaker's initial shock and give place, as he begins to recover his composure, to the steadier pentameters that complete the first quatrain. Continuing irritation propels the brisk tetrameters that form the first half of the second quatrain. This, again, is completed by calmer pentameters, and the stanza rounded off like an English sonnet, with a summary pentameter couplet:

> Love, all alike, no season knows nor clime
> Nor hours, days, months, which are the rags of time.

This variation in line length achieves a different effect in the third stanza, where the brief trimeter suggests an absence contrasting with the royal presences in the preceding tetrameter:

> She's all states, and all princes, I,
> Nothing else is.

And these lines prepare, both rhetorically and visually, for the contraction and expansion so brilliantly developed in the poem's triumphant close. Similar structural considerations account for the composite stanza forms of Arnold's "The Scholar-Gypsy" (p. 988) and Lowell's "Skunk Hour" (p. 1493), though variations of line length and rhyme scheme between the six-line stanzas of Lowell's poem bring it close to the line that divides composite form from the next category.

IRREGULAR FORMS

A poet writing in irregular form will use rhyme and meter but follow no fixed pattern. A classic example is Milton's "Lycidas" (p. 354), which is written in iambic pentameters interspersed with an occasional trimeter, probably modeled on the occasional half-lines that intersperse the hexameters of Virgil's

Aeneid. Milton's rhyming in this **elegy** (a formal lament for a dead person) is similarly varied, and a few lines are unrhymed. The most extensive use of irregular form is to be found in one of the three types of **ode.** Long lyric poems of elevated style and elaborate stanzaic structure, the original odes of the Greek poet Pindar were modeled on songs sung by the chorus in Greek drama. The three-part structure of the regular **Pindaric ode** has been attempted once or twice in English, but more common and more successful has been the irregular Pindaric ode, which has no three-part structure but sections of varying length, varying line length, and varying rhyme scheme. Each of Pindar's odes was written to celebrate someone, and celebration has been the theme of many English Pindaric odes, among them Dryden's "A Song for St. Cecilia's Day" (p. 480), Tate's "Ode to the Confederate Dead" (p. 1309), and Lowell's "The Quaker Graveyard in Nantucket" (p. 1485). The desire to celebrate someone or something has also prompted most English odes of the third type, those modeled on the subject matter, tone, and form of the Roman poet Horace. More meditative and restrained than the boldly irregular Pindaric ode, the **Horatian ode** is usually written in a repeated stanza form—Marvell's "An Horatian Ode upon Cromwell's Return from Ireland" (p. 444) in quatrains, for example, and Keats' "To Autumn" (p. 849) in a composite eleven-line stanza.

OPEN FORMS OR FREE VERSE

At the opposite end of the formal scale from the fixed forms (or, as they are sometimes called, **closed forms**) of sonnet, villanelle, and sestina, we come to what was long known as free verse, poetry that makes little or no use of traditional rhyme and meter. The term is misleading, however, suggesting to some less thoughtful champions of open forms (as free-verse structures are now increasingly called) a false analogy with political freedom as opposed to slavery, and suggesting to traditionalist opponents the disorder or anarchy implied by Frost's in/famous remark that "writing free verse is like playing tennis with the net down." There has been much unprofitable debate in this century over the relative merits and "relevance" of closed and open forms, unprofitable because, as will be clear to any reader of this anthology, good poems continue to be written in both. It would be foolish to wish that Larkin wrote like Whitman, or Atwood like Dickinson. Poets must find forms and rhythms appropriate to their voices. When, around 1760, Smart chose an open form for "Jubilate Agno" (p. 625), that incantatory catalogue of the attributes of his cat Jeoffry proclaimed its descent from the King James translation of the Old Testament and, specifically, such parallel cadences as those of Psalm 150:

> Praise ye the Lord. Praise God in his sanctuary:
> praise him in the firmament of his power.
> Praise him for his mighty acts: praise him
> according to his excellent greatness.
> Praise him with the sound of the trumpet: praise
> him with the psaltery and harp.

These rhythms and rhetorical repetitions, audible also in Blake's Prophetic Books, resurfaced in the work of the nineteenth-century founder of American poetry, as we know it today. Whitman's elegy for an unknown soldier, "Vigil Strange I Kept on the Field One Night" (p. 970), may end with a traditional image of the rising sun, like Milton's "Lycidas" (p. 354), but its cadences are those of the Old Testament he read as a boy:

And there and then and bathed by the rising sun, my son in his grave, in
     his rude-dug grave I deposited,
Ending my vigil strange with that, vigil of night and battle-field dim,
Vigil for boy of responding kisses, (never again on earth responding,)
Vigil for comrade swiftly slain, vigil I never forget, how as day brighten'd.
I rose from the chill ground and folded my soldier well in his blanket,
And buried him where he fell.

Whitman's breakaway from the prevailing poetic forms of his time was truly
revolutionary, but certain traditional techniques he would use for special
effect: the concealed *well / fell* rhyme that gives his elegy its closing chord, for
example, or the bounding anapests of an earlier line:

> One look | I but gave | which your dear | eyes return'd |
> with a look | I shall nev | er forget . . .

The poetic revolution that Whitman initiated was continued by Pound, who
wrote of his predecessor:

> It was you that broke the new wood,
> Now is a time for carving.

Pound, the carver, unlike Whitman, the pioneer, came to open forms by way
of closed forms, a progression reflected in the first four sections of Pound's
partly autobiographical portrait of the artist, "Hugh Selwyn Mauberley"
(p. 1191). Each section is less "literary," less formal than the last, quatrains
with two rhymes yielding to quatrains with one rhyme and, in section IV, to
Whitmanian free verse. A similar progression from the mastery of closed forms
to the mastery of open forms can be seen in the development of such other
poets as Lawrence, Eliot, Lowell, and Rich (pp. 1176–86, 1230–55, 1485–98,
1679–88, respectively).

Pound may have called himself a carver, but he, too, proved a pioneer,
opening up terrain that has been more profitably mined by his successors than
the highlands, the rolling cadences explored by Smart, Blake, and Whitman.
Pound recovered for poets territory then inhabited only by novelists, the low
ground of everyday speech, a private rather than a public language. He was
aided by Williams, who, in such a poem as "The Red Wheelbarrow," used
the simplest cadences of common speech to reveal the extraordinary nature of
"ordinary" things:

> so much depends
> upon
>
> a red wheel
> barrow
>
> glazed with rain
> water
>
> beside the white
> chickens.

Each line depends upon the next to complete it, indicating the interdepen-
dence of things in the poem and, by extension, in the world. "The Red Wheel-
barrow" bears out the truth of Auden's statement that in free verse "you need
an infallible ear to determine where the lines should end."

Some poets have ventured even further into the no man's land between prose and poetry with **prose poems**. Hill's "Mercian Hymns" may look like prose, but the poet insists that his lines are to be printed exactly as they appear on pages 1722–24; and the reader's ear will detect musical cadences no less linked and flowing than in good free verse. Eye and ear together—to return to the opening of this essay—are never more dramatically engaged than in the reading of such **shaped poems** as Herbert's "Easter Wings" (p. 331) and Hollander's "Swan and Shadow" (p. 1664).

Further Reading

Poets have been making poems for as long as composers have been making music or carpenters furniture, and, just as it would be unreasonable to expect to find the lore and language of music or carpentry distilled into one short essay, so there is more to be said about the making and appreciating of poems than is said here. The fullest treatment of the subject is to be found in *A History of English Prosody from the Twelfth Century to the Present Day* by George Saintsbury (3 vols., New York, 1906–1910) and the *Princeton Encyclopedia of Poetry and Poetics*, edited by Alex Preminger, Frank J. Warnke, and O. B. Hardison, Jr. (Princeton, 1965; enl. ed., 1974). More suitable for students are *Poetic Meter and Poetic Form* by Paul Fussell (New York, 1965; rev. ed. 1979), *The Structure of Verse*, edited by Harvey Gross (New York, 1966; rev. ed. 1979), *Rhyme's Reason: A Guide to English Verse* by John Hollander (New Haven, 1981; enl. ed., 1989), and the appropriate entries in *A Glossary of Literary Terms* by M. H. Abrams (New York, 1957; 6th ed., 1990). Each of these has its own more detailed suggestions for further reading.

JON STALLWORTHY

CÆDMON'S HYMN[1]

Nu sculon *h*erigean	*h*eofonrices Weard
Now we must praise	heaven-kingdom's Guardian,
*M*eotodes *m*eahte	and his *m*odgeþanc
the Measurer's might	and his mind-plans,
*w*eorc Wuldor-Fæder	swa he *w*undra gehwæs
the work of the Glory-Father,	when he of wonders of every one,
ece Drihten	or onstealde
eternal Lord,	the beginning established.[2]
5 He *ærest* sceop	*i*elda[3] bearnum
He first created	for men's sons
*h*eofon to *h*rofe	*h*alig Scyppend
heaven as a roof,	holy Creator;
ða *m*iddangeard	*m*oncynnes Weard
then middle-earth	mankind's Guardian,
ece Drihten	*æ*fter teode
eternal Lord,	afterwards made —
*f*irum *f*oldan	*F*rea ælmihtig
for men earth,	Master almighty.

1. Cædmon's "Hymn" is probably the earliest extant Old English poem (composed sometime between 658 and 680). Old English texts have been preserved in copies of the Latin *Ecclesiastical History of the English People*, written by the great scholar Bede (ca. 673–735). Bede tells how Cædmon, an illiterate herdsman employed by the monastery of Whitby, miraculously received the gift of religious song, was received by the monks as a lay brother, and became the founder of a school of Christian poetry. At feasts where the farmhands were accustomed to take turns performing songs to the accompaniment of a harp, Cædmon would withdraw to his bed in the stable whenever the harp was being passed his way. One night a man appeared to him in a dream and commanded, "Cædmon, sing me something." When Cædmon protested that he didn't know how to sing, the man insisted, and told him to sing about the Creation. "At this, Cædmon immediately began to sing verses in praise of God the Creator, which he had never heard before." (After transcribing the hymn, Bede remarks that "this is the general sense but not the exact order of the words that he [Cædmon] sang in his sleep; for it is impossible to make a literal translation, no matter how well written, of poetry into another language without losing some of the beauty and dignity." Bede refers here to his translation of the poem from Old English to Latin, but the poem also changes significantly from an oral to a written medium.) After Cædmon told the story to his foreman, the monks tested him to establish that the gift was from God, and he composed other religious poems based on biblical stories they told him. The Germanic tribes had oral poets (the *Beowulf* poet portrays such a bard, or "scop," performing in the mead hall), and we may suspect that Cædmon had been trained as such a singer, who concealed his knowledge of pagan poetry—what Bede calls "vain and idle songs." The "Hymn" is typical of Germanic verse: two half-lines, each containing two stressed and two or more unstressed syllables, linked by alliteration; interweaving of syntactically parallel formulaic expressions. For example, eight of the poem's half-lines consist of varying epithets for God: He is *Weard* ("Guardian"), *Meotod* ("Measurer"), *Wuldor-Fæderu* ("Glory-Father"), *Drihten* ("Lord"), *Scyppend* ("Creator"), and *Frea* ("Master"). The poem is given here in a West Saxon form with a literal interlinear translation. In Old English spelling, æ (as in Cædmon's name and line 3) is a vowel symbol that has not survived; it represented the vowel of Modern English "cat"; þ (line 2) and ð (line 7) both represented the sound *th*. The large space in the middle of the line indicates the caesura. The alliterating sounds that connect the half-lines have been italicized.

2. I.e., when he established the beginning of every wonder.

3. Later manuscript copies have *eorþan* ("earth") in place of *ælda* (West Saxon *ielda*; "men's").

1

FROM BEOWULF[1]

[Introductory: history and praise of the Danes,
and account of Grendel's attacks on Heorot]

How that glory remains in remembrance,
Of the Danes and their kings in days gone,
The acts and valor of princes of their blood!
Scyld Scefing:[2] how often he thrust from their feast-halls
5 The troops of his enemies, tribe after tribe,
Terrifying their warriors: he who had been found
Long since as a waif and awaited his desert
While he grew up and throve in honor among men
Till all the nations neighboring about him
10 Sent as his subjects over the whale-fields
Their gifts of tribute: king worth the name!
Then there was born a son to succeed him,
A boy for that house, given by God
As a comfort to the folk for all the wretchedness
15 He saw they had lived in, from year to year
Lacking an overlord; and the overlord of Life,
Of Glory, gave the man worldly excelling,
Till his fame spread far, the fame of Beowulf
The son of Scyld, on Scandinavian soil.
20 So should magnanimity be the young man's care,
Rich gifts and royal in his father's household,
That when he is old his ready companions
Will remain with him still, his people stand by him
When war returns; a man shall flourish
25 By acts of merit in every land.
    Then Scyld departed in the ripeness of time,
Old in deeds, to the Lord's keeping.
They carried him down to the restless sea,[3]
His beloved retainers, as he himself had asked
30 While words served him, the lord of the Scyldings
And their dear king who had ruled them long.
There at the harbor stood the ring-prowed boat,
The prince's vessel, ice-cased, sea-keen;
Deep in the ship they laid him down,
35 Their beloved lord, the giver of rings,
The hero by the mast. Great treasures there,

1. This epic poem was written in an Old English dialect sometime between the first part of the eighth century and the tenth century A.D. Preserved in a late-tenth-century manuscript, it was probably composed by a literate poet following the versification and style of Germanic oral poetry; the translation here is by Edwin Morgan. The poem deals with the Germanic forebears of the English people, specifically the Danes, who inhabited the Danish island of Zealand, and the Geats of southern Sweden. In recounting the heroic feats of Beowulf of the Geats, the poem mixes elements of the Christian tradition (the Germanic settlers in England had been converted to Christianity by the time the poem was written) with the heroic ideals of a non-Christian, warrior society. Cf. Seamus Heaney, "A Ship of Death," which translates lines 26–52 (p. 1794).
2. A mythical king of the Scyldings (Danes), of divine origin and associated with agricultural fertility. Scyld is father of Beowulf the Dane, not Beowulf of the Geats.
3. Sea burials for chieftains, such as this one for Scyld Scefing, were probably more mythical than historical.

Far-gathered trappings were taken and set:
No ship in fame more fittingly furnished
With weapons of war and battle-armor;
40 With mail-coat and sword; there lay to his hand
Precious things innumerable that would go at his side
Voyaging to the distant holds of the flood.
By no means poorer were their rich offerings,
The treasures they gave him, than those given
45 By the men who cast him at his life's beginning
A child out over the waves alone.[4]
Lastly they put up high above his head
A gold-woven banner, and let the sea bear him,
Gave him to the main;° their hearts grieved,   *sea*
50 Mourning was in their minds. And whose were the shores—
Who can say with truth, whether counsellor in hall
Or warrior on earth—where this freight was washed?
    That country then saw Beowulf of the Scyldings
Renowned among the peoples, a beloved king
55 Ruling many years—his father and lord
Having gone from the world—until there was born to him
Noble Healfdene; war-grim, aged,
Lifelong guardian of the illustrious Scyldings.
By him four children reckoned in all
60 Were born into this world, princes of men,
Heorogar and Hrothgar and the good Halga
And she [. . . . . .],[5] who was Onela's queen,
The dear consort of the warlike Swede.
To Hrothgar in time came triumph in battle,
65 The glory of the sword, and his friendly kinsmen
Flocked to serve him till the band of them was great,
A host of eager retainers. And his mind
Stirred him to command a hall to be built,
A huger mead-house to be made and raised
70 Than any ever known to the children of men,
Where he under its roof to young and old
Would distribute such gifts as God gave him,
Everything but the lands and lives of his people.
Not few, we are told, were the tribes who then
75 Were summoned to the work far throughout this world,
To adorn that dwelling-place. And so in due time,
Quickly as men labored, it was all prepared,
Most massive of halls; and he called it Heorot
Whose word was authority far and wide.
80 And his promise he performed, he presented rings,[6]
Treasure at banqueting. The hall towered up
Clifflike, broad-gabled: (it awaited flame-battling,
Fire's hostility; and not far off
Lay that sword-hatred ready to be roused

4. Scyld appeared from the sea as a child, apparently on a divinely ordained mission.
5. The text here is faulty, so the name of Healfdene's daughter is unknown; her husband, Onela, was a Swedish king.

6. Early Germanic tribal kings, such as Hrothgar here, traditionally presented their retainers with rings or other treasures to seal a mutual bond of loyalty between them.

85 In the deadly feud of father and son-in-law).[7]
But the outcast spirit[8] haunting darkness
Began to suffer bitter sorrow
When day after day he heard the happiness
Of the hall resounding: the harp ringing,
90 Sweet minstrelsinging—as the tongue skilled
In the distant conception and creation of men
Sang how the Almighty made the earth-fields
Brilliant in beauty, bound by the sea,
Set exulting sun and moon
95 As lamps for the light of living men,
And loaded the acres of the world with jewelwork
Of branch and leaf, bringing then to life
Each kind of creature that moves and breathes.
—So those retainers lived on in joy
100 Happy all, till this one spirit,
Hell in his mind, his malice began.
Grendel the fiend's name: grim, infamous,
Wasteland-stalker, master of the moors
And the fen-fortress; the world of demonkind
105 Was for long the home of the unhappy creature
After his Creator had cast him out
With the kin of Cain,[9] the everlasting Lord
Destining for the death of Abel killed;
A joyless feud, for he banished him far,
110 His Maker for his crime, far from mankind.
Progenitor he was of the miscreations,
Kobolds and gogmagogs, lemurs and zombies[1]
And the brood of titans that battled with God
Ages long; for which he° rewarded them.°   God / the titans
115 He went then to visit at the fall of night
That lofty hall, to see how the Danes
Fared as they lay at the end of their carousing.
Within it he found the band of warriors
Sleeping after the feast; they were far from sorrow
120 And the misery of men. The creature was like pestilence
Raging and ravenous, quick at his task,
Savage and unsparing, seizing thirty
Soldiers from their beds; then off again
Glutlusty with booty making for his home,
125 Seeking his dwelling laden with the slain.
When the dawn broke and day began
And Grendel's battle-strength filled men's eyes,
Then weeping arose where feasting had been,
Loud morning crying. The illustrious king,
130 The man old in worth sat unrejoicing,
Bearing, enduring grief, strong

---

7. An allusion to the future destruction of Heorot in a family feud. The father is Hrothgar; the son-in-law, Ingeld, is the chief of the Heathobards.
8. First reference to Grendel, an evil being who haunts the moors and is angered by the singing and merrymaking coming from the great hall, Heorot.
9. Grendel's descent is traced back to the biblical Cain, son of Adam and Eve. For the crime of killing his brother Abel, Cain was marked by God and sentenced to roam the Earth as an outcast (Genesis 4).
1. I.e., all monstrous creatures, such as giants, ogres, ghouls, and goblins.

Sorrow for his soldiers, when they saw the footprint
Of the hated, of the accursed spirit; that strife
Was too strong, too long, and too malignant!
135 And after no longer than a single night
He went further in murder and mourned none for it,
In hatred, in violence—in these ways too set.
Then it wasn't rare for a man elsewhere
At a greater distance to look for his rest,
140 For a bed in the outbuildings, when once he knew,
Truly told by a sure token,
The hall-haunter's hate; to escape the fiend
Was to keep himself thereafter farther off and safer.
So he held sway and struggled against the right,
145 Solitary against all, till empty and unvisited
Stood the best of halls. Long was the time,
Twelve years passing, that the lord of the Scyldings[2]
Spent to learn pain, each grief there was,
Each bursting sorrow; and so it became known,
150 Became open to men, grievously recounted
To the children of men, how Grendel fought
That time with Hrothgar, waging his enmity,
His sin-forced feud for many seasons,
His seasonless strife; what peace would he have
155 With any man of the host of Denmark?
His deadliness was unshakeable: no settling with money:
Nor did any counsellor have cause to expect
Glorious reparation from the killer's hands;[3]
But that was a monster remorseless to persecute,
160 Dark with death's shadow, both veteran and untried;
He lay hid and plotted, he held the moors,
Mist, endless night; and what man's knowledge
Can map the gliding-ground of demon and damned?
   So mankind's enemy, the terrible solitary
165 Went on accomplishing outrage on outrage,
Heavy humiliations. Heorot was his house,
That treasure-strewn hall through the hours of blackness.
(—No coming openly to the throne or its gifts
Or feeling its favor, forbidden by God.)[4]
170 It was sharp distress to the lord of the Scyldings,
Heartbreak it was; often his chief men
Gathered in council to debate the means
That might seem best to the brave in mind
For combating the panic terror of the raids.
175 At times in their temples they made pagans' vows,
Sacrifices to their idols, in their speeches beseeching
The destroyer of souls to help the people
In their common affliction. Such was their custom,
The hope of the heathen,[5] it was hell that came

---

2. I.e., Hrothgar.
3. A Germanic law, called *wergild*, required compensatory payment by a criminal to the victim of a crime, or to his or her kin.
4. These lines imply that Grendel, who entered the hall at will, was unable ("forbidden by God")
to approach Hrothgar's throne.
5. Here we see that the Christian elements of the poem are not part of the culture presented in the story, though they play a significant role in its telling.

180 Called back to their minds, of the Creator they knew nothing,
The Judge of all acts, the Lord God was strange to them,
And indeed they were ignorant of the praise of heaven's King,
The Ruler of Glory, O unhappy man
Who will thrust his soul through terrible perversity
185 Into Fire's embrace, eschewing solace
All unregenerate! O happy the man
To be drawn to the Lord when his death-day falls,
In his Father's embrace to implore his peace!
— So the son of Healfdene's[6] heart was surging
190 With the cares of that time, nor could the wise man
Turn aside his trouble; the strife too severe,
Too long, too malignant, that settled on that people,
Fierce-forcing persecution, night-frightfulness unequalled.

*   *   *

[The Last Survivor's Speech]

* * * and one man remained[7]
From the host of the people, the last wanderer there,
A watchman grieving over friends, to augur°   *foretell*
2240 For his own life the same: brief use, brief love
Of long-prized wealth. The barrow of the dead
Stood ready on the plain near the breaking sea,
New-made on the headland, built hard of access;
Into its interior the jewel-guardian took
2245 That cherishable mass of the treasures of men,
Of the beaten gold, and uttered these words:
"Now earth hold fast, since heroes have failed to,
The riches of the race! Was it not from you
That good men once won it? Battle-death, evil
2250 Mortal and terrible has taken every man
Of this folk of mine that has left life and time,
That has gazed its last on feast and gladness.
No one I have to be sword-bearer or burnisher
Of the beaten-gold goblet, the dearly-loved drinking-cup:
2255 That chivalry has slipped away. Hard helmet must shed
Its flashing furnishing, its plating of gold;
Burnishers sleep who should sheen° the battle-mask;   *polish*
So too the mail-coat that has met the biting
Of iron war-blades above clashed shields
2260 Crumbles after its wearer; nor can this chain-armor
Follow the fight's commander into far-off regions
At the heroes' side. There is no harp-pleasure
And no happy minstrelsy, there is no good hawk
To swoop through the hall, there is no swift horse
2265 With hoofbeats in the courtyard. Hatred and death

6. I.e., Hrothgar's.
7. This passage comes near the end of the poem. Beowulf, now an old king who has ruled the Geats for fifty years, must fight a fierce flying dragon that guards a treasure hoard and terrorizes the region. These lines tell the history of the treasure: it is the accumulated wealth of a tribe of warriors, now perished. The "wanderer" is the last survivor of the tribe. He carries the treasure to the barrow where his people are buried and speaks these words on the transience of earthly things.

Have driven out on their voyage the hosts of the living!"
So one sad-minded spoke out the misery
He felt for all, moving unconsoled
Restless day and night, till the tidewater of death
2270 Rose touching his heart.

[*The Last Survivor's Speech in Old English*]

"Heald þu nu, hruse,   nu hæleð ne mostan,
eorla æhte!   Hwæt, hyt ær on ðe
gode begeaton.   Guþ-deað fornam,
2250 feorh-bealo frecne   fyra gehwylcne
leoda minra,   þara ðe þis lif ofgeaf,
gesawon sele-dreamas.   Nah hwa sweord wege
oððe feormie   fæted wæge,
drync-fæt deore;   duguð ellor scoc.
2255 Sceal se hearda helm   hyrsted golde
fætum befeallen;   feormynd swefað,
þa ðe beado-griman   bywan sceoldon;
ge swylce seo here-pad,   sio æt hilde gebad
ofer borda gebræc   bite irena,
2260 brosnað æfter beorne;   ne mæg byrnan hring
æfter wig-fruman   wide feran
hæleðum be healfe.   Næs hearpan wyn
gomen gleo-beames,   ne god hafoc
geond sæl swingeð,   ne se swifta mearh
2265 burh-stede beateð.   Bealo-cwealm hafað
fela feorh-cynna   forð onsended!"

RIDDLES[1]

1

I am a lonely being, scarred by swords,
Wounded by iron, sated with battle-deeds,
Wearied by blades. Often I witness war,
Perilous fight, nor hope for consolation,
5 That any help may rescue me from strife
Before I perish among fighting men;
But hammered swords, hard edged and grimly sharp,
Batter me, and the handwork of the smith
Bites in the castles; I must ever wait
10 A contest yet more cruel. I could never
In any habitation find the sort
Of doctor who could heal my wounds with herbs;

1. The Old English riddles, like their counterparts in Latin poetic tradition (from which many of them are derived), are poems in which beings or objects from ordinary life are presented disguised in metaphoric terms. The riddles below are among those found in the Exeter Book, a tenth-century manuscript collection of Old English poetry. The "answers" appear in note 3, below.

But cuts from swords ever increase on me
Through deadly contest, both by day and night.

2

My dress is silent when I tread the ground
Or stay at home or stir upon the waters.
Sometimes my trappings and the lofty air
Raise me above the dwelling-place of men,
5   And then the power of clouds carries me far
Above the people; and my ornaments
Loudly resound, send forth a melody
And clearly sing, when I am not in touch
With earth or water, but a flying spirit.

3

A moth ate words; a marvellous event
I thought it when I heard about that wonder,
A worm had swallowed some man's lay,[2] a thief
In darkness had consumed the mighty saying
5   With its foundation firm. The thief was not
One whit the wiser when he ate those words.[3]

[Riddle 3 in Old English]

Moððe word fræt.   Me þæt þuhte
wrætlicu wyrd,   þa ic þæt wundor gefrægn,
þæt se wyrm forswealg   wera gied sumes,
þeof in þystro   þrymfæstne cwide
5   and þæs strangan staþol.   Stælgiest ne wæs
wihte þy gleawra,   þe he þam wordum swealg.

THE WIFE'S LAMENT[1]

I sing this song about myself, full sad,
My own distress, and tell what hardships I
Have had to suffer since I first grew up,

2. A short poem intended to be sung.
3. The solutions to these riddles are "shield," "swan," and "bookworm," respectively.
1. This poem appears in the Exeter Book, a tenth-century manuscript collection of Old English poetry, immediately following a series of riddles. Different translations offer somewhat different interpretations of the poem; the one below suggests that the poem is a dramatic monologue spoken by a wife separated from her husband. Some critics have suggested that the poem may be an allegory in which the speaker represents either the soul or the children of Israel during the Babylonian captivity.

Present and past, but never more than now;
5 I ever suffered grief through banishment.
For since my lord departed from this people
Over the sea, each dawn have I had care
Wondering where my lord may be on land.
When I set off to join and serve my lord,
10 A friendless exile in my sorry plight,
My husband's kinsmen plotted secretly
How they might separate us from each other
That we might live in wretchedness apart
Most widely in the world: and my heart longed.
15 In the first place my lord had ordered me
To take up my abode here, though I had
Among these people few dear loyal friends;[2]
Therefore my heart is sad. Then had I found
A fitting man, but one ill-starred, distressed,
20 Whose hiding heart was contemplating crime,[3]
Though cheerful his demeanor. We had vowed
Full many a time that nought should come between us
But death alone, and nothing else at all.
All that has changed, and it is now as though
25 Our marriage and our love had never been,
And far or near forever I must suffer
The feud of my beloved husband dear.
So in this forest grove they made me dwell,
Under the oak-tree, in this earthy barrow.
30 Old is this earth-cave, all I do is yearn.
The dales are dark with high hills up above,
Sharp hedge surrounds it, overgrown with briars,
And joyless is the place. Full often here
The absence of my lord comes sharply to me.
35 Dear lovers in this world lie in their beds,
While I alone at crack of dawn must walk
Under the oak-tree round this earthy cave,
Where I must stay the length of summer days,
Where I may weep my banishment and all
40 My many hardships, for I never can
Contrive to set at rest my careworn heart,
Nor all the longing that this life has brought me.
A young man always must be serious,
And tough his character; likewise he should
45 Seem cheerful, even though his heart is sad
With multitude of cares. All earthly joy
Must come from his own self. Since my dear lord
Is outcast, far off in a distant land,
Frozen by storms beneath a stormy cliff
50 And dwelling in some desolate abode
Beside the sea, my weary-hearted lord
Must suffer pitiless anxiety.

---

2. The speaker seems to have come from a faraway
place to her husband's home.
3. The speaker's husband seems to have been
exiled overseas for a crime he committed. His kin,
meanwhile, have sent his wife to the "earth-cave"
where she dwells.

And all too often he will call to mind
A happier dwelling. Grief must always be
55 For him who yearning longs for his beloved.

THE SEAFARER[1]

I sing my own true story, tell my travels,
How I have often suffered times of hardship
In days of toil, and have experienced
Bitter anxiety, my troubled home
5 On many a ship has been the heaving waves,
Where grim night-watch has often been my lot
At the ship's prow as it beat past the cliffs.
Oppressed by cold my feet were bound by frost
In icy bonds, while worries simmered hot
10 About my heart, and hunger from within
Tore the sea-weary spirit. He knows not,
Who lives most easily on land, how I
Have spent my winter on the ice-cold sea,
Wretched and anxious, in the paths of exile,
15 Lacking dear friends, hung round by icicles,
While hail flew past in showers. There heard I nothing
But the resounding sea, the ice-cold waves.
Sometimes I made the song of the wild swan
My pleasure, or the gannet's° call, the cries   *fish-eating seabird's*
20 Of curlews for the missing mirth of men,
The singing gull instead of mead in hall.
Storms beat the rocky cliffs, and icy-winged
The tern replied, the horn-beaked eagle shrieked.
No patron had I there who might have soothed
25 My desolate spirit. He can little know
Who, proud and flushed with wine, has spent his time
With all the joys of life among the cities,
Safe from such fearful venturings, how I
Have often suffered weary on the seas.
30 Night shadows darkened, snow came from the north,
Frost bound the earth and hail fell on the ground,
Coldest of corns.[2] And yet the heart's desires
Incite me now that I myself should go
On towering seas, among the salt waves' play;
35 And constantly the heartfelt wishes urge
The spirit to venture, that I should go forth
To see the lands of strangers far away.
Yet no man in the world's so proud of heart,

1. This poem appears in the Exeter Book, a tenth-century manuscript collection of Old English poetry. Although the poem realistically describes the hardships of a seafaring life, the shift to Christian homily at line 64 has led some critics to sug-gest that it is an allegory in which life is represented as a difficult journey over rough seas toward the harbor of heaven.
2. Small hard particles or grains.

So generous of gifts, so bold in youth,
40　In deeds so brave, or with so loyal lord,
That he can ever venture on the sea
Without great fears of what the Lord may bring.
His mind dwells not on the harmonious harp,
On ring-receiving,[3] or the joy of woman,
45　Or wordly hopes, or anything at all
But the relentless rolling of the waves;
But he who goes to sea must ever yearn.
The groves bear blossom, cities grow more bright,
The fields adorn themselves, the world speeds up;
50　Yet all this urges forth the eager spirit
Of him who then desires to travel far
On the sea-paths. Likewise the cuckoo calls
With boding voice, the harbinger of summer
Offers but bitter sorrow in the breast.
55　The man who's blest with comfort does not know
What some then suffer who most widely travel
The paths of exile. Even now my heart
Journeys beyond its confines, and my thoughts
Over the sea, across the whale's domain,
60　Travel afar the regions of the earth,
And then come back to me with greed and longing.
The cuckoo cries, incites the eager breast
On to the whale's roads irresistibly,
Over the wide expanses of the sea,
65　Because the joys of God mean more to me
Than this dead transitory life on land.
That earthly wealth lasts to eternity
I don't believe. Always one of three things
Keeps all in doubt until one's destined hour.
70　Sickness, old age, the sword, each one of these
May end the lives of doomed and transient men.
Therefore for every warrior the best
Memorial is the praise of living men
After his death, that ere he must depart
75　He shall have done good deeds on earth against
The malice of his foes, and noble works
Against the devil, that the sons of men
May after praise him, and his glory live
For ever with the angels in the splendor
80　Of lasting life, in bliss among those hosts.
The great old days have gone, and all the grandeur
Of earth; there are not Caesars now or kings
Or patrons such as once there used to be,
Amongst whom were performed most glorious deeds,
85　Who lived in lordliest renown. Gone now
Is all that host, the splendors have departed.
Weaker men live and occupy the world,

---

3. Rings or gold or other valuable objects were customarily given by Anglo-Saxon kings to their retainers to affirm a mutual bond of loyalty and protection.

Enjoy it but with care. Fame is brought low,
Earthly nobility grows old, decays,
90 As now throughout this world does every man.
Age comes on him, his countenance grows pale,
Gray-haired he mourns, and knows his former lords,
The sons of princes, given to the earth.
Nor when his life slips from him may his body
95 Taste sweetness or feel pain or stir his hand
Or use his mind to think. And though a brother
May strew with gold his brother's grave, and bury
His corpse among the dead with heaps of treasure,
Wishing them to go with him, yet can gold
100 Bring no help to the soul that's full of sins,
Against God's wrath, although he hide it here
Ready before his death while yet he lives.
Great is the might of God, by which earth moves;
For He established its foundations firm,
105 The land's expanses, and the sky above.
Foolish is he who does not fear his Lord,
For death will come upon him unprepared.
Blessed is he who humble lives; for grace
Shall come to him from heaven. The Creator
110 Shall make his spirit steadfast, for his faith
Is in God's might. Man must control himself
With strength of mind, and firmly hold to that,
True to his pledges, pure in all his ways.
With moderation should each man behave
115 In all his dealings with both friend and foe.
No man will wish the friend he's made to burn
In fires of hell, or on an earthly pyre,
Yet fate is mightier, the Lord's ordaining
More powerful than any man can know.
120 Let us think where we have our real home,
And then consider how we may come thither;
And let us labor also, so that we
May pass into eternal blessedness,
Where life belongs amid the love of God,
125 Hope in the heavens. The Holy One be thanked
That He has raised us up, the Prince of Glory,
Lord without end, to all eternity.
                                        Amen.

[*The First Lines of "The Seafarer" in Old English*]

Mæg ic be me sylfum   soðgied wrecan,
siþas secgan,   hu ic geswincdagum
earfoðhwile   oft þrowade,
bitre breostceare   gebiden hæbbe,
5 gecunnad in ceole   cearselda fela,
atol yþa gewealc,   þær mec oft bigeat
nearo nihtwaco   æt nacan stefnan
þonne he be clifum cnossað. . .

ANONYMOUS LYRICS OF THE THIRTEENTH AND FOURTEENTH CENTURIES

Now Go'th Sun Under Wood[1]

Nou goth sonne under wode—
Me reweth, Marie,[2] thi faire rode.°   *face*
Nou goth sonne under tre—
Me reweth, Marie, thi sone and the.°   *thee*

The Cuckoo Song[3]

Sing, cuccu, nu.° Sing, cuccu.   *now*
Sing, cuccu. Sing, cuccu, nu.

Sumer is i-cumen in—
    Lhude° sing, cuccu!   *loudly*
5 Groweth sed and bloweth° med°   *blooms / field*
    And springth° the wude° nu.   *buds / wood*
    Sing, cuccu!

Awe° bleteth after lomb,   *ewe*
    Lhouth° after calve cu,°   *lows / cow*
10 Bulluc sterteth,° bucke verteth[4]—   *leaps*
    Murie° sing, cuccu!   *merrily*
    Cuccu, cuccu.
Wel singes thu,° cuccu.   *thou*
Ne swik thu naver nu![5]

Ubi Sunt Qui Ante Nos Fuerunt?[6]

Were beth they biforen us weren,
    Houndes ladden° and haukes beren°   *led / hawks carried*
    And hadden° feld and wode?°   *owned / wood*
    The riche levedies° in hoere bour,°   *ladies / their bower*
5   That wereden gold in hoere tressour,°   *headdress*
    With hoere brightte rode,°   *face*

1. This is one of the earliest Middle English lyrics presenting the Passion of Christ (his Crucifixion at Calvary). The subject occurs frequently in Middle English lyrics. This poem, which was perhaps originally part of a longer one on the Passion, is notable for its wordplay, e.g., "sonne" means both "sun" and "son"; and the "wode" of line 1 refers both to the woods behind which the sun is setting and to Christ's wooden cross; "rode" (line 2) also plays on "cross" (the Old English "rood"), as does "tre" (line 3).
2. Christ's mother, the Virgin Mary, who, according to John 19.25, witnessed the Crucifixion; "me reweth": I pity.
3. This song about summer or spring "coming in" is one of the earliest surviving Middle English lyrics. It is written, with music, in a manuscript that was owned by a religious house.
4. Farts; thought to derive from the Old English *feortan*, although some commentators suggest a derivation from the Latin *vertere*, "to turn" or "to cavort."
5. Cease ("swik") thou never now, i.e., don't ever stop.
6. The first line translates the Latin title: "Where are now those who lived before us?" It is part of an extensive medieval tradition of *ubi sunt* poems lamenting the mutability of human life and institutions; for an Old English example, see "The Seafarer" (p. 10).

Eten and drounken and maden hem° glad;   *them*
Hoere lif was al with gamen° i-lad;°   *pleasure / led*
Men keneleden° hem biforen;   *knelt*
10   They beren hem wel swithe heye°—   *very haughtily*
And in a twincling of an eye
Hoere soules weren forloren.°   *completely lost*

Were is that lawing° and that song,   *laughing*
That trayling and that proude yong,[7]
15   Tho hauekes and tho houndes?
Al that joye is went away;
That wele° is comen to welaway,°   *happiness / sadness*
To manie harde stoundes.°   *times*

Hoere paradis hy nomen° here,   *they took*
20   And nou they lien in helle i-fere°—   *together*
The fuir° hit brennes° hevere.°   *fire / burns / ever*
Long is ay° and long is ho,°   *ah / oh*
Long is wy° and long is wo°—   *alas / woe*
Thennes° ne cometh they nevere.   *thence*

25   Dreghy° here, man, thenne if thou wilt,   *suffer*
A luitel pine,° that me the bit.[8]   *pain*
Withdrau thine eyses ofte.
They° thi pine be ounrede,°   *though / severe*
And° thou thenke on thi mede,°   *if / reward*
30   Hit sal the thinken softe.[9]

If that fend,[1] that foule thing,
Thorou wikke roun,° thorou fals egging,°   *temptation / urging*
Nethere° the haveth i-cast,   *down*
Oup,° and be god chaunpioun!   *up*
35   Stond, ne fal° namore adoun   *fall*
For a luytel blast.°   *puff of wind*

Thou tak the rode[2] to° thi staf   *to be*
And thenk on him that thereonne yaf°   *gave*
His lif that wes so lef.°   *dear*
40   He hit yaf for the; thou yelde° hit him.   *yield*
Ayein° his fo that staf thou nim,°   *against / take*
And wrek him of that thef.[3]

Of rightte bileve[4] thou nim that sheld
The wiles° that thou best° in that feld.   *while / are*
45   Thin° hond to strenkthen fonde[5]   *then*

---

7. I.e., that trailing (of garments) and that proud gait.
8. That you are asked to bear. Literally, one ("me") that bids thee.
9. It shall seem soft to thee.
1. Fiend, or enemy (German *Feind*); that is, Satan, whose name means "adversary" in Hebrew; cf. "fo" (line 41): foe.

2. "Rod," but here also referring to Christ's cross ("rood").
3. I.e., he gave it [his life] for thee; thou repay him for it. Against his foe take thou that staff [the Cross] and revenge him upon that thief [the devil].
4. I.e., right belief, or true faith.
5. I.e., try to strengthen your hand; an allusion to the "shield of faith" (Ephesians 6.16).

And kep thy fo with staves ord[6]
And do that traytre seien that word.[7]
Biget° that murie londe   *gain*

Thereinne is day withouten night,
50 Withouten ende strenkthe and might,
And wreche of° everich fo,   *vengeance on*
Mid° god himselwen eche° lif   *with / eternal*
And pes and rest withoute strif,
Wele° withouten wo.   *happiness*

55 Mayden moder, hevene quene,
Thou might and const° and owest° to bene°   *can / ought / be*
Oure sheld ayein° the fende.   *against*
Help ous sunne for to flen[8]
That we moten° thi sone i-seen   *might*
60 In joye withouten hende.°   *end*

Amen.

Alison[9]

Bytwene Mersh° and Averil,   *March*
When spray° biginneth to springe,°   *twigs / open, leaf out*
The lutel° foul° hath hire° wyl   *little / bird / its*
On hyre lud° to synge.   *birdsong*
5 Ich° libbe° in love-longinge   *I / live*
For semlokest° of alle thinge—   *seemliest*
He° may me blisse bringe;   *she*
Ich am in hire baundoun°   *power*
An hendy hap ichabbe yhent[1]—
10 *Ichot° from hevene it is me sent:*   *I know*
From alle wymmen mi love is lent°   *turned*
And lyht° on Alysoun.   *fallen*

On heu° hire her° is fayr ynoh,°   *in color / hair / enough*
Hire browe broune, hire eye blake—
15 With lossum chere he on me loh[2]—
With middel° smal and wel ymake.°   *waist / made*
Bote° he° me wolle to hire take,   *unless / she*
Forte buen hire owen make,[3]
Longe to lyven ichulle° forsake   *I will*
20 And feye° fallen adoun   *dead, lifeless*
An hendy hap ichabbe yhent—. . .

---

6. I.e., the point of your staff.
7. I.e., make the traitor say the word (of surrender). Some editors place a comma after "word" and a period after "londe" in the next line. Our editorial decision about punctuating these difficult lines—a decision that breaks the pattern of syntactically self-contained stanzas—requires "thereinne" of line 49 to be interpreted as "wherein."
8. I.e., help us to flee from sin—with a play on "sunne" (line 58) and "sone" (line 59).

9. This lyric (like most Middle English poems, originally untitled) occurs in a famous anthology containing the so-called Harley Lyrics, written in the west of England in the early fourteenth century; the manuscript is now in the British Library (Ms. Harley 2253).
1. I.e., a happy chance I have received.
2. I.e., with lovely face she laughed at ("loh" "on") me.
3. I.e., for to be her own mate.

Nightes when I wende° and wake—   *turn*
Forthi° myn wonges° waxeth won°—   *therefore / cheeks / wan, pale*
Levedi,° al for thine sake   *lady*
25   Longinge is ylent me on.[4]
In world nis non so wyter mon[5]
That al hire bounte° telle con.   *excellence*
Hire swyre° is whittore then the swon,°   *neck / swan*
And feyrest may° in toune.   *maid*
30   An hendy hap ichabbe yhent—...

Icham for wowyng al forwake,[6]
Wery so° water in wore,[7]   *as*
Lest eny° reve me my make[8]   *anyone*
Ichabbe y-yerned yore.[9]
35   Betere is tholien° whyle sore[1]   *suffer*
Then mournen evermore.
Geynest under gore,[2]
Herkne° to my roun.°   *listen / song*
An hendy hap ichabbe yhent—...

Fowls in the Frith[3]

Fowles° in the frith,°   *birds / woods*
The fisshes in the flood,
And I mon waxe wood:[4]
Much sorwe° I walke with   *sorrow*
5   For beste[5] of boon° and blood.   *bone*

I Am of Ireland[6]

Ich° am of Irlonde,   *I*
And of the holy londe
Of Irlonde.

Goode sire, praye ich thee,
5   For of° sainte° charitee,   *sake of / holy*
Com and dance with me
In Irlonde.

4. I.e., come upon me.
5. I.e., in the world there is no man so wise.
6. I.e., I am entirely worn out from wooing.
7. Weir, a pool made by damming up water.
8. I.e., deprive me of my mate, "reve" being a form of the old verb "reave," to rob.
9. I.e., [the mate] I have desired a long time.
1. I.e., sorely for a while.
2. I.e., kindest of ladies (persons "under gown").
3. This poem, with a musical accompaniment designed for two voices, appears on one side of a page in a manuscript comprised mainly of legal texts (it contains no other poems).
4. Must go mad.
5. Either "the best" or "beast." The ambiguity allows for both a religious and an erotic interpretation.
6. This poem may be a fragment or an extract from a longer poem; it is written in prose in the manuscript. The first three lines are the burden, or refrain.

GEOFFREY CHAUCER

ca. 1343–1400

From The Canterbury Tales

The General Prologue

Whan that April with his° showres soote°	*its / fresh*
The droughte of March hath perced to the roote,	
And bathed every veine[1] in swich° licour,°	*such / liquid*
Of which vertu[2] engendred is the flowr;	
5 Whan Zephyrus eek° with his sweete breeth	*also*
Inspired[3] hath in every holt° and heeth°	*grove / field*
The tendre croppes,° and the yonge sonne[4]	*shoots*
Hath in the Ram his halve cours yronne,	
And smale fowles° maken melodye	*birds*
10 That sleepen al the night with open yë°—	*eye*
So priketh hem° Nature in hir corages[5]—	*them*
Thanne longen folk to goon° on pilgrimages,	*go*
And palmeres for to seeken straunge strondes	
To ferne halwes,[6] couthe° in sondry° londes;	*known / various*
15 And specially from every shires ende	
Of Engelond to Canterbury they wende,	
The holy blisful martyr[7] for to seeke	
That hem hath hŏlpen° whan that they were seke.°	*helped / sick*
Bifel° that in that seson on a day,	*It happened*
20 In Southwerk[8] at the Tabard as I lay,	
Redy to wenden on my pilgrimage	
To Canterbury with ful° devout corage,	*very*
At night was come into that hostelrye	
Wel nine and twenty in a compaignye	
25 Of sondry folk, by aventure° yfalle	*chance*
In felaweshipe, and pilgrimes were they alle	
That toward Canterbury wolden° ride.	*would*
The chambres and the stables weren wide,	
And wel we weren esed° at the beste.[9]	*accommodated*
30 And shortly, whan the sonne was to reste,[1]	
So hadde I spoken with hem everichoon°	*every one*
That I was of hir felaweshipe anoon,°	*at once*
And made forward[2] erly for to rise,	
To take oure way ther as[3] I you devise.°	*describe*
35 But nathelees,° whil I have time and space,[4]	*nevertheless*

1. I.e., in plants.
2. By the power of which.
3. Breathed into. "Zephyrus": the west wind.
4. The sun is young because it has run only half-way through its course in Aries, the Ram—the first sign of the zodiac in the solar year.
5. Their hearts.
6. Far-off shrines. "Palmeres": palmers, wide-ranging pilgrims—especially those who sought out the "straunge strondes" (foreign shores) of the Holy Land.

7. St. Thomas à Becket, murdered in Canterbury Cathedral in 1170; his shrine was associated with healing.
8. Southwark, site of the Tabard Inn, was then a suburb of London, south of the Thames River.
9. In the best possible way.
1. Had set.
2. I.e., (we) made an agreement.
3. Where.
4. I.e., opportunity.

Er° that I ferther in this tale pace,°   *before / proceed*
Me thinketh it accordant to resoun[5]
To telle you al the condicioun
Of eech of hem, so as it seemed me,
40 And whiche they were, and of what degree,°   *social rank*
And eek in what array that they were inne:
And at a knight thanne° wol I first biginne.   *then*
   A Knight ther was, and that a worthy man,
That fro the time that he first bigan
45 To riden out, he loved chivalrye,
Trouthe and honour, freedom and curteisye.[6]
Ful worthy was he in his lordes werre,°   *war*
And therto hadde he riden, no man ferre,°   *further*
As wel in Cristendom as hethenesse,°   *heathen lands*
50 And[7] evere honoured for his worthinesse.
At Alisandre[8] he was whan it was wonne;
Ful ofte time he hadde the boord bigonne[9]
Aboven alle nacions in Pruce;
In Lettou had he reised,° and in Ruce,   *campaigned*
55 No Cristen man so ofte of his degree;
In Gernade° at the sege eek hadde he be   *Granada*
Of Algezir, and riden in Belmarye;
At Lyeis was he, and at Satalye,
Whan they were wonne; and in the Grete See[1]
60 At many a noble arivee° hadde he be.   *military landing*
   At mortal batailes[2] hadde he been fifteene,
And foughten for oure faith at Tramissene
In listes[3] thries,° and ay° slain his fo.   *thrice / always*
   This ilke° worthy Knight hadde been also   *same*
65 Somtime with the lord of Palatye[4]
Again° another hethen in Turkye;   *against*
And everemore he hadde a soverein pris.°   *reputation*
And though that he were worthy, he was wis,[5]
And of his port° as meeke as is a maide.   *demeanor*
70 He nevere yit no vilainye° ne saide   *rudeness*
In al his lif unto no manere wight:[6]
He was a verray,° parfit,° gentil° knight.   *true / perfect / noble*
But for to tellen you of his array,
His hors° were goode, but he was nat gay.   *horses*
75 Of fustian° he wered° a gipoun[7]   *thick cloth / wore*
Al bismotered with his haubergeoun,[8]
For he was late° come from his viage,°   *lately / expedition*

---

5. It seems to me according to reason.
6. Courtesy; "trouthe": integrity; "freedom": generosity of spirit.
7. I.e., and he was.
8. The Knight has taken part in campaigns fought against three groups who threatened Christian Europe during the fourteenth century: the Moslems in the Near East, from whom Alexandria was seized after a famous siege; the northern barbarians in Prussia, Lithuania, and Russia; and the Moors in North Africa. The place names in the following lines refer to battlegrounds in these continuing wars.
9. Sat in the seat of honor at military feasts.

1. The Mediterranean.
2. Tournaments fought to the death.
3. Lists, tournament grounds.
4. "The lord of Palatye" was a Moslem: alliances of convenience were often made during the Crusades between Christians and Moslems.
5. I.e., he was wise as well as bold.
6. Any sort of person. In Middle English, negatives are multiplied for emphasis, as in these two lines: "nevere," "no," "ne," "no."
7. Tunic worn underneath the coat of mail. "Gay": i.e., gaily dressed.
8. All rust-stained from his hauberk (coat of mail).

And wente for to doon his pilgrimage.
　　With him ther was his sone, a yong Squier,[9]
80　A lovere and a lusty bacheler,
　　With lokkes crulle° as° they were laid in presse.　　　　*curly / as if*
　　Of twenty yeer of age he was, I gesse.
　　Of his stature he was of evene° lengthe,　　　　*moderate*
　　And wonderly delivere,° and of greet° strengthe.　　*agile / great*
85　And he hadde been som time in chivachye[1]
　　In Flandres, in Artois, and Picardye,
　　And born him wel as of so litel space,[2]
　　In hope to stonden in his lady° grace.　　　　*lady's*
　　Embrouded° was he as it were a mede,[3]　　　　*embroidered*
90　Al ful of fresshe flowres, white and rede;°　　　　*red*
　　Singing he was, or floiting,° al the day:　　　　*whistling*
　　He was as fressh as is the month of May.
　　Short was his gowne, with sleeves longe and wide.
　　Wel coude he sitte on hors, and faire ride;
95　He coude songes make, and wel endite,°　　　　*compose verse*
　　Juste[4] and eek° daunce, and wel portraye° and write.　*also / sketch*
　　So hote° he loved that by nightertale[5]　　　　*hotly*
　　He slepte namore than dooth a nightingale.
　　Curteis he was, lowely,° and servisable,　　　　*humble*
100　And carf biforn his fader at the table.[6]
　　　A Yeman hadde he[7] and servants namo°　　　　*no more*
　　At that time, for him liste[8] ride so;
　　And he[9] was clad in cote and hood of greene.
　　A sheef of pecok arwes,° bright and keene,　　　　*arrows*
105　Under his belt he bar° ful thriftily;°　　　　*bore / properly*
　　Wel coude he dresse° his takel° yemanly:[1]　　*tend to / gear*
　　His arwes drouped nought with fetheres lowe.
　　And in his hand he bar a mighty bowe.
　　A not-heed° hadde he with a brown visage.　　　　*close-cut head*
110　Of wodecraft wel coude° he al the usage.　　　　*knew*
　　Upon his arm he bar a gay bracer,[2]
　　And by his side a swerd° and a bokeler,[3]　　　　*sword*
　　And on that other side a gay daggere,
　　Harneised° wel and sharp as point of spere;　　　　*mounted*
115　A Cristophre[4] on his brest of silver sheene;°　　　*bright*
　　An horn he bar, the baudrik[5] was of greene.
　　A forster° was he soothly,° as I gesse.　　　　*forester / truly*
　　　Ther was also a Nonne, a Prioresse,[6]
　　That of hir smiling was ful simple° and coy.°　　*sincere / mild*

---

9. The vague term "Squier" (Squire) here seems to be the equivalent of "bacheler," a young knight still in the service of an older one.
1. On cavalry expeditions. The places in the next line are sites of skirmishes in the constant warfare between the English and the French.
2. I.e., considering the little time he had been in service.
3. Mead, meadow.
4. Joust, fight in a tournament.
5. At night.
6. It was a squire's duty to carve his lord's meat.

7. The Knight. "Yeman" (Yeoman) is an independent commoner who acts as the Knight's military servant.
8. It pleased him to.
9. I.e., the Yeoman.
1. In a workmanlike way.
2. Wristguard for archers.
3. Buckler (a small shield).
4. St. Christopher medal.
5. Baldric (a supporting strap).
6. The Prioress is the mother superior of her nunnery.

120	Hir gretteste ooth was but by sainte Loy![7]	
	And she was cleped° Madame Eglantine.	*named*
	Ful wel she soong° the service divine,	*sang*
	Entuned° in hir nose ful semely;[8]	*chanted*
	And Frenssh she spak ful faire and fetisly,°	*elegantly*
125	After the scole° of Stratford at the Bowe[9]—	*school*
	For Frenssh of Paris was to hire unknowe.	
	At mete° wel ytaught was she withalle:°	*meals / besides*
	She leet° no morsel from hir lippes falle,	*let*
	Ne wette hir fingres in hir sauce deepe;	
130	Wel coude she carve a morsel, and wel keepe°	*take care*
	That no drope ne fille° upon hir brest.	*should fall*
	In curteisye was set ful muchel hir lest.[1]	
	Hir over-lippe wiped she so clene	
	That in hir coppe° ther was no ferthing° seene	*cup / bit*
135	Of grece,° whan she dronken hadde hir draughte;	*grease*
	Ful semely after hir mete she raughte.°	*reached*
	And sikerly° she was of greet disport,[2]	*certainly*
	And ful plesant, and amiable of port,°	*mien*
	And pained hire to countrefete cheere[3]	
140	Of court, and to been statlich° of manere,	*dignified*
	And to been holden digne[4] of reverence.	
	But, for to speken of hir conscience,	
	She was so charitable and so pitous°	*merciful*
	She wolde weepe if that she saw a mous	
145	Caught in a trappe, if it were deed° or bledde.	*dead*
	Of[5] smale houndes hadde she that she fedde	
	With rosted flessh, or milk and wastelbreed;°	*fine white bread*
	But sore wepte she if oon of hem were deed,	
	Or if men smoot it with a yerde smerte;[6]	
150	And al was conscience and tendre herte.	
	Ful semely hir wimpel° pinched° was,	*headdress / pleated*
	Hir nose tretis,° hir yën° greye[7] as glas,	*well-formed / eyes*
	Hir mouth ful smal, and therto° softe and reed,°	*moreover / red*
	But sikerly° she hadde a fair forheed:	*certainly*
155	It was almost a spanne brood,[8] I trowe,°	*believe*
	For hardily,° she was nat undergrowe.	*assuredly*
	Ful fetis° was hir cloke, as I was war;°	*becoming / aware*
	Of smal° coral aboute hir arm she bar	*dainty*
	A paire of bedes, gauded al with greene,[9]	
160	And theron heeng° a brooch of gold ful sheene,°	*hung / bright*
	On which ther was first writen a crowned A,[1]	
	And after, *Amor vincit omnia.*[2]	
	Another Nonne with hire hadde she	

7. Eloi, or Eligius, a saint associated with journeys and craftsmanship, was also famous for his personal beauty, courtesy, and refusal to swear.
8. In a seemly manner.
9. The French learned in a convent school in Stratford-at-the-Bow, a suburb of London, was evidently not up to the Parisian standard.
1. I.e., her chief delight lay in good manners.
2. Of great good cheer.
3. And took pains to imitate the behavior.
4. And to be considered worthy.

5. I.e., some.
6. If someone struck it with a rod sharply.
7. Gray was a conventional color for the eyes of heroines in romances.
8. A handsbreadth wide.
9. Provided with green beads to mark certain prayers; "paire": string (i.e., a rosary).
1. An A with an ornamental crown on it.
2. A Latin motto meaning "Love conquers all."

That was hir chapelaine,° and preestes three.[3]   *secretary*
165   A Monk ther was, a fair for the maistrye,[4]
    An outridere[5] that loved venerye,°   *hunting*
    A manly man, to been an abbot able.°   *worthy*
    Ful many a daintee° hors hadde he in stable,   *fine*
    And whan he rood,° men mighte his bridel heere   *rode*
170   Ginglen° in a whistling wind as clere   *jingle*
    And eek as loude as dooth the chapel belle
    Ther as this lord was kepere of the celle.[6]
    The rule of Saint Maure or of Saint Beneit,
    By cause that it was old and somdeel strait[7] —
175   This ilke° Monk leet olde thinges pace,°   *same / pass away*
    And heeld° after the newe world the space.[8]   *held*
    He yaf nought of that text a pulled hen[9]
    That saith that hunteres been° nought holy men,   *are*
    Ne that a monk, whan he is recchelees,[1]
180   Is likned til° a fissh that is waterlees —   *to*
    This is to sayn, a monk out of his cloistre;
    But thilke° text heeld he nat worth an oystre.   *that same*
    And I saide his opinion was good:
    What° sholde he studye and make himselven wood°   *why / crazy*
185   Upon a book in cloistre alway to poure,°   *pour, read intently*
    Or swinke° with his handes and laboure,   *work*
    As Austin bit?[2] How shal the world be served?
    Lat Austin have his swink to him reserved!
    Therfore he was a prikasour° aright.   *hard rider*
190   Grehoundes he hadde as swift as fowl in flight.
    Of priking° and of hunting for the hare   *riding*
    Was al his lust,° for no cost wolde he spare.   *pleasure*
    I sawgh his sleeves purfiled° at the hand   *fur-lined*
    With gris,° and that the fineste of a land;   *gray fur*
195   And for to festne his hood under his chin
    He hadde of gold wrought a ful curious[3] pin:
    A love-knotte in the grettere° ende ther was.   *greater*
    His heed was balled,° that shoon as any glas,   *bald*
    And eek his face, as he hadde been anoint:
200   He was a lord ful fat and in good point;[4]
    His yën steepe,° and rolling in his heed,   *protruding*
    That stemed as a furnais of a leed,[5]
    His bootes souple,° his hors in greet estat° —   *supple / condition*
    Now certainly he was a fair prelat.[6]
205   He was nat pale as a forpined° gost: *wasted away*
    A fat swan loved he best of any rost.
    His palfrey° was as brown as is a berye.   *saddle horse*

---

3. Later there is only one priest, who tells "The Nun's Priest's Tale."
4. I.e., a superlatively fine one.
5. A monk charged with supervising property distant from the monastery.
6. Prior of an outlying cell (branch) of the monastery.
7. Somewhat straight. "Saint Maure" and "Saint Beneit": St. Maurus and St. Benedict, authors of monastic rules.

8. The course, or direction. I.e., he followed the new direction of things.
9. He didn't give a plucked hen for that text.
1. Reckless, careless of rule.
2. I.e., as St. Augustine bids. St. Augustine had written that monks should perform manual labor.
3. Of careful workmanship.
4. In good shape, plump.
5. That glowed like a furnace with a pot in it.
6. Prelate (an important churchman).

A Frere[7] ther was, a wantoune° and a merye,   *jovial*
A limitour, a ful solempne° man.   *ceremonious*
210   In alle the ordres foure is noon that can°   *knows*
So muche of daliaunce° and fair langage: *sociability*
He hadde maad ful many a mariage
Of yonge wommen at his owene cost;
Unto his ordre he was a noble post.[8]
215   Ful wel biloved and familier was he
With frankelains over al[9] in his contree,
And with worthy wommen of the town—
For he hadde power of confessioun,
As saide himself, more than a curat,°   *parish priest*
220   For of° his ordre he was licenciat.[1]   *by*
Ful swetely herde he confessioun,
And plesant was his absolucioun.
He was an esy man to yive penaunce
Ther as he wiste to have[2] a good pitaunce;°   *donation*
225   For unto a poore ordre for to yive
Is signe that a man is wel yshrive;[3]
For if he yaf, he dorste make avaunt°   *boast*
He wiste° that a man was repentaunt;   *knew*
For many a man so hard is of his herte
230   He may nat weepe though him sore smerte:[4]
Therfore, in stede of weeping and prayeres,
Men mote° yive silver to the poore freres.[5]   *may*
    His tipet° was ay farsed° ful of knives   *scarf / packed*
And pinnes, for to yiven faire wives;
235   And certainly he hadde a merye note;
Wel coude he singe and playen on a rote;°   *fiddle*
Of yeddinges he bar outrely the pris.[6]
His nekke whit was as the flowr-de-lis;°   *lily*
Therto he strong was as a champioun.
240   He knew the tavernes wel in every town,
And every hostiler° and tappestere,°   *innkeeper / barmaid*
Bet° than a lazar or a beggestere.[7]   *better*
For unto swich a worthy man as he
Accorded nat, as by his facultee,[8]
245   To have with sike° lazars aquaintaunce: *sick*
It is nat honeste,° it may nought avaunce,°   *dignified / profit*
For to delen with no swich poraile,[9]
But al with riche, and selleres of vitaile;°   *foodstuffs*
And over al ther as profit sholde arise,
250   Curteis he was, and lowely of servise.

---

7. The "Frere" (Friar) is a member of one of the
four religious orders whose members live by beg-
ging; as a "limitour" (line 209) he has been
granted exclusive begging rights within a certain
limited area.
8. I.e., pillar, a staunch supporter.
9. I.e., with franklins everywhere. Franklins were
well-to-do country men.
1. I.e., licensed to hear confessions.
2. Where he knew he would have.
3. Shriven, absolved.
4. Though he is sorely grieved.
5. Before granting absolution, the confessor must

be sure the sinner is contrite; moreover, the abso-
lution is contingent upon the sinner's performance
of an act of satisfaction. In the case of Chaucer's
Friar, a liberal contribution served both as proof of
contrition and as satisfaction.
6. He absolutely took the prize for ballads.
7. Female beggar; "lazar": leper.
8. It was not suitable because of his position.
9. I.e., poor people. The oldest order of friars had
been founded by St. Francis to administer to the
spiritual needs of precisely those classes the Friar
avoids.

Ther was no man nowher so vertuous:°   *effective*
He was the beste beggere in his hous.°   *friary*
And yaf a certain ferme for the graunt:[1]
Noon of his bretheren cam ther in his haunt.°   *assigned territory*
255 For though a widwe° hadde nought a sho,°   *widow / shoe*
So plesant was his *In principio*[2]
Yit wolde he have a ferthing° er he wente;   *small coin*
His purchas was wel bettre than his rente.[3]
And rage he coude as it were right a whelpe,[4]
260 In love-dayes[5] ther coude he muchel° helpe,   *much*
For ther he was nat lik a cloisterer,
With a thredbare cope, as is a poore scoler,
But he was lik a maister[6] or a pope.
Of double worstede was his semicope,°   *short robe*
265 And rounded as a belle out of the presse.°   *bell mold*
Somwhat he lipsed° for his wantounesse°   *lisped / affectation*
To make his Englissh sweete upon his tonge;
And in his harping, whan he hadde songe,°   *sung*
His yën twinkled in his heed aright
270 As doon the sterres° in the frosty night.   *stars*
This worthy limitour was cleped Huberd.
    A Marchant was ther with a forked beerd,
In motelee,[7] and hye on hors he sat,
Upon his heed a Flandrissh° bevere hat,   *Flemish*
275 His bootes clasped faire and fetisly.°   *elegantly*
His resons° he spak ful solempnely,   *opinions*
Souning° alway th'encrees° of his winning.   *sounding / increase*
He wolde the see were kept for any thing[8]
Bitwixen Middelburgh and Orewelle.
280 Wel coude he in eschaunge sheeldes[9] selle.
This worthy man ful wel his wit bisette:°   *employed*
Ther wiste° no wight° that he was in dette,   *knew / person*
So statly° was he of his governaunce,[1]   *dignified*
With his bargaines,° and with his chevissaunce.°   *bargainings / borrowing*
285 Forsoothe he was a worthy man withalle;
But, sooth to sayn, I noot° how men him calle.   *don't know*
    A Clerk[2] ther was of Oxenforde also
That unto logik hadde longe ygo.[3]
As lene was his hors as is a rake,
290 And he was nought right fat, I undertake,
But looked holwe,° and therto sobrely.   *hollow*
Ful thredbare was his overeste courtepy,

1. And he paid a certain rent for the privilege of begging.
2. A friar's usual salutation: "In the beginning [was the Word]" (John 1.1).
3. I.e., the money he got through such activity was more than his regular income.
4. And he could flirt wantonly, as if he were a puppy.
5. Days appointed for the settlement of lawsuits out of court.
6. A man of recognized learning.
7. Motley, a cloth of mixed color.
8. I.e., he wished the sea to be guarded at all costs. The sea route between Middleburgh (in the Neth-

erlands) and Orwell (in Suffolk) was vital to the Merchant's export and import of wool—the basis of England's chief trade at the time.
9. Shields, *écus* (French coins), were units of transfer in international credit, which he exchanged at a profit.
1. The management of his affairs.
2. The Clerk is a student at Oxford; in order to become a student, he would have had to signify his intention of becoming a cleric, but he was not bound to proceed to a position of responsibility in the church.
3. Who had long since matriculated in philosophy.

For he hadde geten him yit no benefice,[4]
Ne was so worldly for to have office.°   *secular employment*
295 For him was levere[5] have at his beddes heed
Twenty bookes, clad in blak or reed,
Of Aristotle and his philosophye,
Than robes riche, or fithele,° or gay sautrye.[6]   *fiddle*
But al be that he was a philosophre[7]
300 Yit hadde he but litel gold in cofre;°   *coffer*
But al that he mighte of his freendes hente,°   *take*
On bookes and on lerning he it spente,
And bisily gan for the soules praye
Of hem that yaf him wherwith to scoleye.°   *study*
305 Of studye took he most cure° and most heede.   *care*
Nought oo° word spak he more than was neede,   *one*
And that was said in forme[8] and reverence,
And short and quik,° and ful of heigh sentence:[9]   *lively*
Souning° in moral vertu was his speeche,   *resounding*
310 And gladly wolde he lerne, and gladly teche.
    A Sergeant of the Lawe, war and wis,[1]
That often hadde been at the Parvis[2]
Ther was also, ful riche of excellence.
Discreet he was, and of greet reverence—
315 He seemed swich, his wordes weren so wise.
Justice he was ful often in assise°   *circuit courts*
By patente° and by plein° commissioun.   *royal warrant / full*
For his science° and for his heigh renown   *knowledge*
Of fees and robes hadde he many oon.
320 So greet a purchasour° was nowher noon;   *speculator in land*
Al was fee simple[3] to him in effect—
His purchasing mighte nat been infect.[4]
Nowher so bisy a man as he ther nas;°   *was not*
And yit he seemed bisier than he was.
325 In termes hadde he caas and doomes[5] alle
That from the time of King William[6] were falle.
Therto he coude endite and make a thing,[7]
Ther coude no wight pinchen° at his writing;   *cavil*
And every statut coude° he plein° by rote.[8]   *knew / entire*
330 He rood but hoomly° in a medlee cote,[9]   *unpretentiously*
Girt with a ceint° of silk, with barres° smale.   *belt / transverse stripes*
Of his array telle I no lenger tale.
    A Frankelain[1] was in his compaignye:
Whit was his beerd as is the dayesye;°   *daisy*

4. Ecclesiastical living, such as the income a parish priest receives. "Overeste courtepy": outer cloak.
5. He would rather.
6. Psaltery (a kind of harp).
7. The word may also mean "alchemist," someone who tries to turn base metals into gold. The Clerk's "philosophy" does not pay either way.
8. With decorum.
9. Elevated thought.
1. Wary and wise; the Sergeant is not only a practicing lawyer, but one of the high justices of the nation.
2. The "Paradise," the porch of St. Paul's Cathedral, a meeting place for lawyers and their clients.
3. Owned outright without legal impediments.
4. Invalidated on a legal technicality.
5. Lawcases and decisions; "in termes": yearbooks of laws arranged by legal phrases referred to as "terms."
6. I.e., the Conqueror (reigned 1066–87).
7. Compose and draw up a deed.
8. By heart.
9. A coat of mixed color.
1. The "Frankelain" (Franklin) is a prosperous country man, whose lower-class ancestry is no impediment to the importance he has attained in his county.

335 Of his complexion he was sanguin.[2]
Wel loved he by the morwe a sop in win.[3]
To liven in delit° was evere his wone,°   *sensual delight / wont*
For he was Epicurus[4] owene sone,
That heeld opinion that plein° delit   *full*
340 Was verray felicitee parfit.
An housholdere and that a greet was he:
Saint Julian[5] he was in his contree.
His breed, his ale, was always after oon;[6]
A bettre envined° man was nevere noon.   *wine-stocked*
345 Withouten bake mete was nevere his hous,
Of fissh and flessh, and that so plentevous°   *plenteous*
It snewed° in his hous of mete° and drinke, *snowed / food*
Of alle daintees that men coude thinke.
After° the sondry sesons of the yeer   *according to*
350 So chaunged he his mete° and his soper.° *dinner / supper*
Ful many a fat partrich hadde he in mewe,°   *cage*
And many a breem,° and many a luce° in stewe.° *carp / pike / fishpond*
Wo was his cook but if his sauce were
Poinant° and sharp, and redy all his gere.   *pungent*
355 His table dormant in his halle alway
Stood redy covered all the longe day.[7]
At sessions ther was he lord and sire.
Ful ofte time he was Knight of the Shire.[8]
An anlaas° and a gipser° al of silk   *dagger / purse*
360 Heeng at his girdel,[9] whit as morne° milk.   *morning*
A shirreve° hadde he been, and countour.[1]   *sheriff*
Was nowher swich a worthy vavasour.[2]
  An Haberdasshere and a Carpenter,
A Webbe,° a Dyere, and a Tapicer°— *weaver / tapestry maker*
365 And they were clothed alle in oo liveree[3]
Of a solempne and greet fraternitee.
Ful fresshe and newe hir gere apiked° was;   *trimmed*
Hir knives were chaped° nought with bras,   *mounted*
But al with silver; wrought ful clene and weel
370 Hir girdles and hir pouches everydeel.°   *altogether*
Wel seemed eech of hem a fair burgeis°   *burgher*
To sitten in a yeldehalle° on a dais.   *guildhall*
Everich, for the wisdom that he can,[4]
Was shaply° for to been an alderman.   *suitable*
375 For catel° hadde they ynough and rente,° *property / income*
And eek hir wives wolde it wel assente—
And elles certain were they to blame:
It is ful fair to been ycleped° "Madame,"   *called*

2. A reference to the fact that the Franklin's temperament is dominated by blood as well as to his red face (see note to line 431).
3. I.e., in the morning he was very fond of a piece of bread soaked in wine.
4. The Greek philosopher whose teaching is popularly believed to make pleasure the chief goal of life.
5. The patron saint of hospitality.
6. Always of the same high quality.
7. Tables were usually dismounted when not in use, but the Franklin kept his mounted and set

("covered"), hence "dormant."
8. County representative in Parliament. "Sessions": i.e., sessions of the justices of the peace.
9. Hung at his belt.
1. Auditor of county finances.
2. Feudal landholder of lowest rank; a provincial gentleman.
3. In one livery, i.e., the uniform of their "fraternitee," or guild, a partly religious, partly social organization.
4. Was capable of.

And goon to vigilies all bifore,[5]
380 And have a mantel royalliche ybore.[6]
  A Cook they hadde with hem for the nones,[7]
To boile the chiknes with the marybones,°   marrowbones
And powdre-marchant tart and galingale.[8]
Wel coude he knowe° a draughte of London ale.   recognize
385 He coude roste, and seethe,° and broile, and frye,   boil
Maken mortreux,° and wel bake a pie.   stews
But greet harm was it thoughte° me,   seemed to
That on his shine a mormal° hadde he.   ulcer
For blankmanger,[9] that made he with the beste.
390   A Shipman was ther, woning° fer by weste—   dwelling
For ought I woot,° he was of Dertemouthe.[1]   know
He rood upon a rouncy° as he couthe,[2]   large nag
In a gowne of falding° to the knee.   heavy wool
A daggere hanging on a laas° hadde he   strap
395 Aboute his nekke, under his arm adown.
The hote somer hadde maad his hewe° al brown;   color
And certainly he was a good felawe.
Ful many a draughte of win hadde he drawe[3]
Fro Burdeuxward, whil that the chapman sleep:[4]
400 Of nice° conscience took he no keep;°   fastidious / heed
If that he faught and hadde the hyer hand,
By water he sente hem hoom to every land.[5]
But of his craft, to rekene wel his tides,
His stremes° and his daungers° him bisides,[6]   currents / hazards
405 His herberwe° and his moone, his lodemenage,°   anchorage / pilotage
There was noon swich from Hulle to Cartage.[7]
Hardy he was and wis to undertake;
With many a tempest hadde his beerd been shake;
He knew alle the havenes° as they were   harbors
410 Fro Gotlond to the Cape of Finistere,[8]
And every crike° in Britaine° and in Spaine.   inlet / Brittany
His barge ycleped was the Maudelaine.°   Magdalene
  With us ther was a Doctour of Physik:°   medicine
In al this world ne was ther noon him lik
415 To speken of physik and of surgerye.
For° he was grounded in astronomye,°   because / astrology
He kepte° his pacient a ful greet deel[9]   tended to
In houres by his magik naturel.[1]
Wel coude he fortunen the ascendent

5. I.e., at the head of the procession; "vigilies": feasts held on the eve of saints' days.
6. "Mantel": a covering or cloak with a train, royally carried.
7. For the occasion.
8. "Powdre-marchant" and "galingale" are flavoring materials.
9. A white stew or mousse, from the French blanc ("white") + manger ("to eat").
1. Dartmouth, a port in the southwest of England.
2. As best he could.
3. Drawn, i.e., stolen.
4. Merchant slept; "Fro Burdeuxward": from Bor-

deaux; i.e., while carrying wine from Bordeaux (the wine center of France).
5. I.e., he drowned his prisoners.
6. Around him.
7. From Hull (in northern England) to Cartagena (in Spain).
8. From Gotland (an island in the Baltic) to Finisterre (the westernmost point in Spain).
9. Closely.
1. Natural—as opposed to black—magic; "in houres": i.e., the astrologically important hours (when conjunctions of the planets might help his recovery).

420   Of his images[2] for his pacient.
      He knew the cause of every maladye,
      Were it of hoot or cold or moiste or drye,
      And where engendred and of what humour:[3]
      He was a verray parfit praktisour.[4]

425   The cause yknowe,° and of his° harm the roote,   *known / its*
      Anoon he yaf the sike man his boote.°   *remedy*
        Ful redy hadde he his apothecaries
      To senden him drogges° and his letuaries,°   *drugs / medicines*
      For eech of hem made other for to winne:
430   Hir frendshipe was nought newe to biginne.
      Wel knew he the olde Esculapius,[5]
      And Deiscorides and eek Rufus,
      Olde Ipocras, Hali, and Galien,
      Serapion, Razis, and Avicen,
435   Averrois, Damascien, and Constantin,
      Bernard, and Gatesden, and Gilbertin.
      Of his diete mesurable° was he,   *moderate*
      For it was of no superfluitee,
      But of greet norissing° and digestible.   *nourishment*
440   His studye was but litel on the Bible.
      In sanguin° and in pers° he clad was al,   *blood red / blue*
      Lined with taffata and with sendal;°   *silk*
      And yit he was but esy of dispence;°   *expenditure*
      He kepte that he wan in pestilence.[6]
445   For° gold in physik is a cordial,[7]   *because*
      Therfore he loved gold in special.
        A good Wif was ther of biside Bathe,
      But she was somdeel deef, and that was scathe.°   *a pity*
      Of cloth-making she hadde swich an haunt,°   *practice*
450   She passed° hem of Ypres and of Gaunt.[8]   *surpassed*
      In al the parissh wif ne was ther noon
      That to the offring[9] bifore hire sholde goon,
      And if ther dide, certain so wroth° was she   *angry*
      That she was out of alle charitee.
455   Hir coverchiefs ful fine were of ground° —   *texture*
      I dorste° swere they weyeden° ten pound   *dare / weighed*
      That on a Sonday weren° upon hir heed.   *were*
      Hir hosen weren of fin scarlet reed,°   *red*

2. Assign the propitious time, according to the position of stars, for using talismanic images. Such images, representing either the patient himself or points in the zodiac, were thought to influence the course of the disease.
3. Diseases were thought to be caused by a disturbance of one or another of the four bodily "humors," each of which, like the four elements, was a compound of two of the elementary qualities mentioned in line 422: the melancholy humor, seated in the black bile, was cold and dry (like earth); the sanguine, seated in the blood, hot and moist (like air); the choleric, seated in the yellow bile, hot and dry (like fire); the phlegmatic, seated in the phlegm, cold and moist (like water).
4. True perfect practitioner.
5. The Doctor is familiar with the treatises that the Middle Ages attributed to the "great names" of medical history, whom Chaucer names in lines 431–36: the purely legendary Greek demigod Aesculapius; the Greeks Dioscorides, Rufus, Hippocrates, Galen, and Serapion; the Persians Hali and Rhazes; the Arabians Avicenna and Averroës; the early Christians John (?) of Damascus and Constantine Afer; the Scotsman Bernard Gordon; the Englishmen John of Gatesden and Gilbert, the former an early contemporary of Chaucer.
6. He saved the money he made during the plague time.
7. A stimulant. Gold was thought to have some medicinal properties.
8. Ypres and Ghent ("Gaunt") were Flemish cloth-making centers.
9. The offering in church, when the congregation brought its gifts forward.

Ful straite yteyd,[1] and shoes ful moiste° and newe.   *supple*
460 Bold was hir face and fair and reed of hewe.
She was a worthy womman al hir live:
Housbondes at chirche dore[2] she hadde five,
Withouten° other compaigny in youthe—   *not counting*
But therof needeth nought to speke as nouthe.°   *now*
465 And thries hadde she been at Jerusalem;
She hadde passed many a straunge° streem;   *foreign*
At Rome she hadde been, and at Boloigne,
In Galice at Saint Jame, and at Coloigne:[3]
She coude° muchel of wandring by the waye.   *knew*
470 Gat-toothed[4] was she, soothly for to saye.
Upon an amblere[5] esily she sat,
Ywimpled° wel, and on hir heed an hat   *veiled*
As brood as is a bokeler or a targe,[6]
A foot-mantel° aboute hir hipes large,   *riding skirt*
475 And on hir feet a paire of spores° sharpe.   *spurs*
In felaweshipe wel coude she laughe and carpe:°   *talk*
Of remedies of love she knew parchaunce,°   *as it happened*
For she coude of that art the olde daunce.[7]
A good man was ther of religioun,
480 And was a poore Person° of a town,   *parson*
But riche he was of holy thought and werk.
He was also a lerned man, a clerk,
That Cristes gospel trewely° wolde preche;   *faithfully*
His parisshens° devoutly wolde he teche.   *parishioners*
485 Benigne he was, and wonder° diligent,   *wonderfully*
And in adversitee ful pacient,
And swich he was preved° ofte sithes.°   *proved / times*
Ful loth were him to cursen for his tithes,[8]
But rather wolde he yiven, out of doute,[9]
490 Unto his poore parisshens aboute
Of his offring[1] and eek of his substaunce:°   *property*
He coude in litel thing have suffisaunce.°   *sufficiency*
Wid was his parissh, and houses fer asonder,
But he ne lafte° nought for rain ne thonder,   *neglected*
495 In siknesse nor in meschief,° to visite   *misfortune*
The ferreste° in his parissh, muche and lite,[2]   *farthest*
Upon his feet, and in his hand a staf.
This noble ensample° to his sheep he yaf   *example*
That first he wroughte,[3] and afterward he taughte.
500 Out of the Gospel he tho° wordes caughte,°   *those / took*
And this figure° he added eek therto: *metaphor*
That if gold ruste, what shal iren do?
For if a preest be foul, on whom we truste,

---

1. Tightly laced.
2. In medieval times, weddings were performed at the church door.
3. Rome, Boulogne (in France), St. James (of Compostella) in Galicia (Spain), Cologne (in Germany) were all sites of shrines much visited by pilgrims.
4. Gap-toothed; in medieval physiognomy such teeth indicated an irreverent, luxurious, sexualized nature.
5. Horse with an easy gait.
6. "Bokeler" and "targe": small shields.
7. I.e., she knew all the tricks of that trade.
8. He would be most reluctant to invoke excommunication in order to collect his tithes.
9. Without doubt.
1. The offering made by the congregation of his church was at the Parson's disposal.
2. I.e., great and small.
3. I.e., he practiced what he preached.

No wonder is a lewed° man to ruste. *uneducated*
505 And shame it is, if a preest take keep,° *heed*
A shiten° shepherde and a clene sheep. *befouled*
Wel oughte a preest ensample for to yive
By his clennesse how that his sheep sholde live.
He sette nought his benefice[4] to hire
510 And leet his sheep encombred in the mire
And ran to London, unto Sainte Poules,[5]
To seeken him a chaunterye[6] for soules,
Or with a bretherhede to been withholde,[7]
But dwelte at hoom and kepte wel his folde,
515 So that the wolf ne made it nought miscarye:
He was a shepherde and nought a mercenarye.
And though he holy were and vertuous,
He was to sinful men nought despitous,° *scornful*
Ne of his speeche daungerous° ne digne,° *disdainful / haughty*
520 But in his teching discreet and benigne,
To drawen folk to hevene by fairnesse
By good ensample—this was his bisinesse.
But it° were any persone obstinat, *if there*
What so he were, of heigh or lowe estat,
525 Him wolde he snibben° sharply for the nones:[8] *scold*
A bettre preest I trowe° ther nowher noon is. *believe*
He waited after[9] no pompe and reverence,
Ne maked him a spiced conscience,[1]
But Cristes lore° and his Apostles twelve *teaching*
530 He taughte, but first he folwed it himselve.
  With him ther was a Plowman, was his brother,
That hadde ylad° of dong° ful many a fother.° *carried / dung / load*
A trewe swinkere° and a good was he, *worker*
Living in pees° and parfit charitee. *peace*
535 God loved he best with al his hoole° herte *whole*
At alle times, though him gamed or smerte,[2]
And thanne his neighebor right as himselve.
He wolde thresshe, and therto dike° and delve,° *work hard / dig*
For Cristes sake, for every poore wight,
540 Withouten hire, if it laye in his might.
His tithes payed he ful faire and wel,
Bothe of his propre swink[3] and his catel.° *property*
In a tabard° he rood upon a mere.° *workman's smock / mare*
  Ther was also a Reeve° and a Millere, *estate manager*
545 A Somnour, and a Pardoner[4] also,
A Manciple,° and myself—ther were namo. *steward*
  The Millere was a stout carl° for the nones. *fellow*

---

4. I.e., his parish. A priest might rent his parish to
another and take a more profitable position.
"Leet": i.e., he did not leave.
5. St. Paul's Cathedral.
6. Chantry, i.e., a foundation that employed
priests for the sole duty of saying masses for the
souls of certain persons. St. Paul's had many of
them.
7. Or to be employed by a brotherhood; i.e., to
take a lucrative and fairly easy position as chaplain
with a parish guild.

8. On any occasion.
9. I.e., expected.
1. Nor did he assume an overfastidious con-
science.
2. Whether he was pleased or grieved.
3. His own work.
4. "Somnour" (Summoner): server of summonses
to the ecclesiastical court; "Pardoner": dispenser of
papal pardons. See lines 625 and 671, and notes,
below.

Ful big he was of brawn° and eek of bones—   *muscle*
That preved[5] wel, for overal ther he cam
550 At wrastling he wolde have alway the ram.[6]
He was short-shuldred, brood,° a thikke° knarre.°   *broad / stout / fellow*
Ther was no dore that he nolde heve of harre,[7]
Or breke it at a renning° with his heed.°   *running / head*
His beerd as any sowe or fox was reed,°   *red*
555 And therto brood, as though it were a spade;
Upon the cop° right of his nose he hade   *tip*
A werte,° and theron stood a tuft of heres,   *wart*
Rede as the bristles of a sowes eres;°   *ears*
His nosethirles° blake were and wide.   *nostrils*
560 A swerd and a bokeler° bar° he by his side.   *shield / bore*
His mouth as greet was as a greet furnais.°   *furnace*
He was a janglere° and a Goliardais,[8]   *chatterer*
And that was most of sinne and harlotries.°   *obscenities*
Wel coude he stelen corn and tollen thries[9]—
565 And yit he hadde a thombe[1] of gold, pardee.°   *by heaven*
A whit cote and a blew hood wered° he.   *wore*
A baggepipe wel coude he blowe and soune,°   *sound*
And therwithal° he broughte us out of towne.   *therewith*
A gentil Manciple[2] was ther of a temple,
570 Of which achatours° mighte take exemple   *buyers of food*
For to been wise in bying of vitaile;°   *victuals*
For wheither that he paide or took by taile,[3]
Algate he waited so in his achat[4]
That he was ay biforn and in good stat.[5]
575 Now is nat that of God a ful fair grace
That swich a lewed° mannes wit shal pace°   *uneducated / surpass*
The wisdom of an heep of lerned men?
Of maistres° hadde he mo than thries ten   *masters*
That weren of lawe expert and curious,°   *cunning*
580 Of whiche ther were a dozeine in that hous
Worthy to been stiwardes of rente° and lond   *income*
Of any lord that is in Engelond,
To make him live by his propre good[6]
In honour dettelees but if[7] he were wood,°   *insane*
585 Or live as scarsly° as him list° desire,   *economically / it pleases*
And able for to helpen al a shire
In any caas° that mighte falle° or happe,   *event / befall*
And yit this Manciple sette hir aller cappe![8]
The Reeve was a sclendre° colerik[9] man;   *slender*
590 His beerd was shave as neigh° as evere he can;   *close*

---

5. Proved, i.e., was evident.
6. A ram was frequently offered as the prize in wrestling.
7. He would not heave off (its) hinge.
8. Goliard, teller of ribald stories.
9. Take toll thrice—i.e., deduct from the grain far more than the lawful percentage.
1. Possibly an ironic reference to the proverb "an honest miller hath a golden thumb," which apparently means "there are no honest millers."
2. The Manciple is the steward of a community of lawyers in London (a "temple").

3. By talley, i.e., on credit.
4. Always he was on the watch in his purchasing.
5. Financial condition; "ay biforn": i.e., ahead of the game.
6. His own money.
7. Out of debt unless.
8. This Manciple made fools of them all.
9. "Colerik" (choleric) describes a person whose dominant humor is yellow bile (choler)—i.e., a hot-tempered person. The Reeve is the superintendent of a large farming estate.

His heer was by his eres ful round yshorn;
His top was dokked[1] lik a preest biforn;
Ful longe were his legges and ful lene,
Ylik a staf, ther was no calf yseene.°   *visible*
595 Wel coude he keepe° a gerner° and a binne—   *guard / granary*
Ther was noon auditour coude on him winne.[2]
Wel wiste° he by the droughte and by the rain   *knew*
The yeelding of his seed and of his grain.
His lordes sheep, his neet,° his dayerye,°   *cattle / dairy herd*
600 His swin, his hors, his stoor,° and his pultrye   *stock*
Was hoolly° in this Reeves governinge,   *wholly*
And by his covenant yaf[3] the rekeninge,
Sin° that his lord was twenty-yeer of age.   *since*
There coude no man bringe him in arrerage.[4]
605 Ther nas baillif, hierde, nor other hine,
That he ne knew his sleighte and his covine[5]—
They were adrad° of him as of the deeth.°   *afraid / plague*
His woning° was ful faire upon an heeth;°   *dwelling / meadow*
With greene trees shadwed was his place.
610 He coude bettre than his lord purchace.°   *acquire goods*
Ful riche he was astored° prively.°   *stocked / secretly*
His lord wel coude he plesen subtilly,
To yive and lene° him of his owene good,°   *lend / property*
And have a thank, and yit a cote and hood.
615 In youthe he hadde lerned a good mister:°   *occupation*
He was a wel good wrighte, a carpenter.
This Reeve sat upon a ful good stot°   *stallion*
That was a pomely° grey and highte° Scot.   *dapple / was named*
A long surcote° of pers° upon he hade,[6]   *overcoat / blue*
620 And by his side he bar° a rusty blade.   *bore*
Of Northfolk was this Reeve of which I telle,
Biside a town men clepen Baldeswelle.°   *Bawdswell*
Tukked[7] he was as is a frere aboute,
And evere he rood the hindreste of oure route.[8]
625   A Somnour[9] was ther with us in that place
That hadde a fir-reed° cherubinnes[1] face,   *fire-red*
For saucefleem° he was, with yën narwe,   *pimply*
And hoot° he was, and lecherous as a sparwe,[2]   *hot*
With scaled° browes blake and piled[3] beerd: *scabby*
630 Of his visage children were aferd.°   *afraid*
Ther nas quiksilver, litarge, ne brimstoon,
Boras, ceruce, ne oile of tartre noon,[4]

---

1. Cut short; the clergy wore the head partially
shaved.
2. I.e., find him in default.
3. And according to his contract he gave.
4. Convict him of being in arrears financially.
5. There was no bailiff (i.e., foreman), shepherd,
nor other farm laborer whose craftiness and plots
he didn't know.
6. He had on.
7. With clothing tucked up.
8. Hindmost of our group.
9. The "Somnour" (Summoner) is an employee
of the ecclesiastical court, whose defined duty is to

bring to court persons whom the archdeacon—the
justice of the court—suspects of offenses against
canon law. By this time, however, summoners had
generally transformed themselves into corrupt
detectives who spied out offenders and black-
mailed them by threats of summonses.
1. Cherub's, often depicted in art with a red face.
2. The sparrow was traditionally associated with
lechery.
3. Uneven, partly hairless.
4. These are all ointments for diseases affecting
the skin, probably diseases of venereal origin.

Ne oinement that wolde clense and bite,
That him mighte helpen of his whelkes° white,   *pimples*
635 Nor of the knobbes° sitting on his cheekes.   *lumps*
Wel loved he garlek, oinons, and eek leekes,
And for to drinke strong win reed as blood.
Thanne wolde he speke and crye as he were wood;°   *mad*
And whan that he wel dronken hadde the win,
640 Thanne wolde he speke no word but Latin:
A fewe termes hadde he, two or three,
That he hadde lerned out of som decree;
No wonder is—he herde it al the day,
And eek ye knowe wel how that a jay°   *parrot*
645 Can clepen "Watte"[5] as wel as can the Pope—
But whoso coude in other thing him grope,°   *examine*
Thanne hadde he spent all his philosophye;[6]
Ay *Questio quid juris*[7] wolde he crye.
He was a gentil harlot° and a kinde;   *rascal*
650 A bettre felawe sholde men nought finde:
He wolde suffre,° for a quart of win,   *permit*
A good felawe to have his concubin
A twelfmonth, and excusen him at the fulle;[8]
Ful prively° a finch eek coude he pulle.[9]   *secretly*
655 And if he foond° owher° a good felawe   *found / anywhere*
He wolde techen him to have noon awe
In swich caas of the Ercedekenes curs,[1]
But if[2] a mannes soule were in his purs,
For in his purs he sholde ypunisshed be.
660 "Purs is the Ercedekenes helle," saide he.
    But wel I woot he lied right in deede:
Of cursing° oughte eech gilty man drede,   *excommunication*
For curs wol slee° right as assoiling° savith—   *slay / absolution*
And also war him of a *significavit*.[3]
665 In daunger[4] hadde he at his owene gise°   *disposal*
The yonge girles of the diocise,
And knew hir conseil,° and was al hir reed.[5]   *secrets*
A gerland hadde he set upon his heed
As greet as it were for an ale-stake;[6]
670 A bokeler hadde he maad him of a cake.
    With him ther rood a gentil Pardoner[7]
Of Rouncival, his freend and his compeer,°   *comrade*

5. Call out "Walter"—like modern parrots' "Polly."
6. I.e., learning.
7. "What point of law does this investigation involve?": a phrase frequently used in ecclesiastical courts.
8. Fully. Ecclesiastical courts had jurisdiction over many offenses that today would come under civil law, including sexual offenses.
9. I.e., "to pluck a finch": to swindle someone; also, an expression for sexual intercourse.
1. Archdeacon's sentence of excommunication.
2. Unless.
3. And also one should be careful of a *significavit*

(the writ that transferred the guilty offender from the ecclesiastical to the civil arm for punishment).
4. Under his domination.
5. Was their chief source of advice.
6. A tavern was signalized by a pole ("alestake"), rather like a modern flagpole, projecting from its front wall; on this hung a garland, or "bush."
7. A Pardoner dispensed papal pardon for sins to those who contributed to the charitable institution that he was licensed to represent; this Pardoner purported to be collecting for the hospital of Roncesvalles ("Rouncival") in Spain, which had a London branch.

That straight was comen fro the Court of Rome.
Ful loude he soong,° "Com hider, love, to me."   *sang*
675   This Somnour bar to him a stif burdoun:[8]
Was nevere trompe° of half so greet a soun.   *trumpet*
    This Pardoner hadde heer as yelow as wex,
But smoothe it heeng° as dooth a strike° of flex;°   *hung / hank / flax*
By ounces[9] heenge his lokkes that he hadde,
680   And therwith he his shuldres overspradde,°   *overspread*
But thinne it lay, by colpons,° oon by oon;   *strands*
But hood for jolitee° wered° he noon,   *nonchalance / wore*
For it was trussed up in his walet:°   *pack*
Him thoughte he rood al of the newe jet.°   *fashion*
685   Dischevelee° save his cappe he rood al bare.   *with hair down*
Swiche glaring yën hadde he as an hare.
A vernicle[1] hadde he sowed upon his cappe,
His walet biforn him in his lappe,
Bretful° of pardon, comen from Rome al hoot.°   *brimful / hot*
690   A vois he hadde as smal° as hath a goot;°   *fine / goat*
No beerd hadde he, ne nevere sholde have;
As smoothe it was as it were late yshave:
I trowe° he were a gelding or a mare.[2]   *believe*
But of his craft, fro Berwik into Ware,[3]
695   Ne was ther swich another pardoner;
For in his male° he hadde a pilwe-beer°   *bag / pillowcase*
Which that he saide was Oure Lady veil;
He saide he hadde a gobet° of the sail   *piece*
That Sainte Peter hadde whan that he wente
700   Upon the see, til Jesu Crist him hente.°   *seized*
He hadde a crois° of laton,° ful of stones,   *cross / brassy metal*
And in a glas he hadde pigges bones,
But with thise relikes[4] whan that he foond°   *found*
A poore person° dwelling upon lond,[5]   *parson*
705   Upon° a day he gat° him more moneye   *in / got*
Than that the person gat in monthes twaye;
And thus with feined° flaterye and japes°   *false / tricks*
He made the person and the peple his apes.°   *dupes*
But trewely to tellen at the laste,
710   He was in chirche a noble ecclesiaste;
Wel coude he rede a lesson and a storye,°   *liturgical narrative*
But alderbest° he soong an offertorye,[6]   *best of all*
For wel he wiste° whan that song was songe,   *knew*
He moste° preche and wel affile° his tonge   *must / sharpen*
715   To winne silver, as he ful wel coude—
Therfore he soong the merierly° and loude.   *more merrily*
    Now have I told you soothly in a clause[7]

---

8. I.e., provided him with a strong bass accompa-
niment.
9. I.e., thin strands.
1. Portrait of Christ's face as it was said to have
been impressed on St. Veronica's handkerchief,
i.e., a souvenir reproduction of a famous relic in
Rome.
2. A female horse; "gelding": a castrated male

horse.
3. I.e., from one end of England to another.
4. Relics—i.e., the pigs' bones that the Pardoner
represented as saints' bones.
5. Upcountry.
6. Part of the mass sung before the offering of
alms.
7. I.e., in a short space.

Th'estaat, th'array, the nombre, and eek the cause
Why that assembled was this compaignye
720 In Southwerk at this gentil hostelrye
That highte the Tabard, faste° by the Belle;[8]   *close*
But now is time to you for to telle
How that we baren us[9] that ilke° night   *same*
Whan we were in that hostelrye alight;
725 And after wol I telle of oure viage,°   *trip*
And al the remenant of oure pilgrimage.
But first I praye you of youre curteisye
That ye n'arette it nought my vilainye[1]
Though that I plainly speke in this matere
730 To telle you hir wordes and hir cheere,°   *behavior*
Ne though I speke hir wordes proprely;°   *accurately*
For this ye knowen also wel as I:
Who so shal telle a tale after a man
He moot° reherce,° as neigh as evere he can,   *must / repeat*
735 Everich a word, if it be in his charge,°   *responsibility*
Al speke he[2] nevere so rudeliche and large,°   *broadly*
Or elles he moot telle his tale untrewe,
Or feine° thing, or finde° wordes newe;   *falsify / devise*
He may nought spare[3] although he were his brother:
740 He moot as wel saye oo word as another.
Crist spake himself ful brode° in Holy Writ,   *broadly*
And wel ye woot no vilainye° is it;   *rudeness*
Eek Plato saith, who so can him rede,
The wordes mote be cosin to the deede.
745   Also I praye you to foryive it me
Al° have I nat set folk in hir degree   *although*
Here in this tale as that they sholde stonde:
My wit is short, ye may wel understonde.
   Greet cheere made oure Host[4] us everichoon,
750 And to the soper sette he us anoon.°   *at once*
He served us with vitaile° at the beste.   *food*
Strong was the win, and wel to drinke us leste.°   *it pleased*
A semely man oure Hoste was withalle
For to been a marchal[5] in an halle;
755 A large man he was, with yën steepe,°   *prominent*
A fairer burgeis° was ther noon in Chepe[6]—   *burgher*
Bold of his speeche, and wis, and wel ytaught,
And of manhood him lakkede right naught.
Eek therto he was right a merye man,
760 And after soper playen he bigan,
And spak of mirthe amonges othere thinges—
Whan that we hadde maad oure rekeninges[7]—
And saide thus, "Now, lordinges, trewely,
Ye been to me right welcome, hertely.°   *heartily*

---

8. Another tavern in Southwark, possibly a brothel.
9. Bore ourselves.
1. That you do not charge it to my boorishness.
2. Although he speak.
3. I.e., spare anyone.

4. The Host is the landlord of the Tabard Inn.
5. Marshal, one who was in charge of feasts.
6. Cheapside, business center of London.
7. Had paid our bills.

765 For by my trouthe, if that I shal nat lie,
    I sawgh nat this yeer so merye a compaignye
    At ones in this herberwe° as is now.   *inn*
    Fain° wolde I doon you mirthe, wiste I[8] how.   *gladly*
    And of a mirthe I am right now bithought,
770 To doon you ese, and it shal coste nought.
       "Ye goon to Canterbury—God you speede;
    The blisful martyr quite you youre meede.[9]
    And wel I woot as ye goon by the waye
    Ye shapen you[1] to talen° and to playe,   *converse*
775 For trewely, confort ne mirthe is noon
    To ride by the waye domb as stoon;°   *stone*
    And therfore wol I maken you disport
    As I saide erst,° and doon you som confort;   *before*
    And if you liketh alle, by oon assent,
780 For to stonden at[2] my juggement,
    And for to werken as I shal you saye,
    Tomorwe whan ye riden by the waye—
    Now by my fader° soule that is deed,   *father's*
    But° ye be merye I wol yive you myn heed!°   *unless / head*
785 Holde up youre handes withouten more speeche."
       Oure counseil was nat longe for to seeche;°   *seek*
    Us thoughte it was nat worth to make it wis,[3]
    And graunted him withouten more avis,°   *deliberation*
    And bade him saye his voirdit° as him leste.[4]   *verdict*
790   "Lordinges," quod he, "now herkneth for the beste;
    But taketh it nought, I praye you, in desdain.
    This is the point, to speken short and plain,
    That eech of you, to shorte° with oure waye   *shorten*
    In this viage, shal tellen tales twaye°—   *two*
795 To Canterburyward, I mene it so,
    And hoomward he shal tellen othere two,
    Of aventures that whilom° have bifalle;   *once upon a time*
    And which of you that bereth him best of alle—
    That is to sayn, that telleth in this cas
800 Tales of best sentence° and most solas°—   *meaning / delight*
    Shal have a soper at oure aller cost,[5]
    Here in this place, sitting by this post,
    Whan that we come again fro Canterbury.
    And for to make you the more mury°   *merry*
805 I wol myself goodly° with you ride—   *kindly*
    Right at myn owene cost—and be youre gide.
    And who so wol my juggement withsaye°   *contradict*
    Shal paye al that we spende by the waye.
    And if ye vouche sauf that it be so,
810 Telle me anoon, withouten wordes mo,°   *more*
    And I wol erly shape me[6] therfore."

8. If I knew.
9. Pay you your reward.
1. Intend.
2. Abide by.
3. We didn't think it worthwhile to make an issue

of it.
4. It pleased.
5. At the cost of us all.
6. Prepare myself.

This thing was graunted and oure othes swore
With ful glad herte, and prayden⁷ him also
That he wolde vouche sauf for to do so,
815 And that he wolde been oure governour,
And of oure tales juge and reportour,°   *accountant*
And sette a soper at a certain pris,°   *price*
And we wol ruled been at his devis,°   *disposal*
In heigh and lowe; and thus by oon assent
820 We been accorded to his juggement.
And therupon the win was fet° anoon;   *fetched*
We dronken and to reste wente eechoon
Withouten any lenger° taryinge.   *longer*
Amorwe° whan that day bigan to springe   *in the morning*
825 Up roos oure Host and was oure aller cok,⁸
And gadred us togidres in a flok,
And forth we riden, a litel more than pas,°   *walking pace*
Unto the watering of Saint Thomas;⁹
And ther oure Host bigan his hors arreste,°   *halt*
830 And saide, "Lordes, herkneth if you leste:°   *it please*
Ye woot youre forward° and it you recorde:¹   *agreement*
If evensong and morwesong° accorde,°   *morningsong / agree*
Lat see now who shal telle the firste tale.
As evere mote° I drinken win or ale,   *may*
835 Who so be rebel to my juggement
Shal paye for al that by the way is spent.
Now draweth cut er that we ferre twinne:²
He which that hath the shorteste shal biginne.
"Sire Knight," quod he, "my maister and my lord,
840 Now draweth cut, for that is myn accord.°   *will*
Cometh neer," quod he, "my lady Prioresse,
And ye, sire Clerk, lat be youre shamefastnesse°—   *modesty*
Ne studieth nought. Lay hand to, every man!"
Anoon to drawen every wight bigan,
845 And shortly for to tellen as it was,
Were it by aventure, or sort, or cas,³
The soothe° is this, the cut fil° to the Knight;   *truth / fell*
Of which ful blithe and glad was every wight,
And telle he moste° his tale, as was resoun,   *must*
850 By forward and by composicioun,⁴
As ye han herd. What needeth wordes mo?
And whan this goode man sawgh that it was so,
As he that wis was and obedient
To keepe his forward by his free assent,
855 He saide, "Sin I shal biginne the game,
What, welcome be the cut, in Goddes name!
Now lat us ride, and herkneth what I saye."
And with that word we riden forth oure waye,
And he bigan with right a merye cheere°   *countenance*
860 His tale anoon, and saide as ye may heere.

7. I.e., we prayed.
8. Was rooster for us all.
9. A watering place near Southwark.
1. You recall it.

2. Go farther; "draweth cut": i.e., draw straws.
3. Whether it was luck, fate, or chance.
4. By agreement and compact.

The Pardoner's Prologue and Tale[1]

The Introduction: The Wordes of the Host to the Phisicien and the Pardoner

Oure Hoste gan to swere as he were wood;°   *insane*
"Harrow,"° quod he, "by nailes and by blood,[2]   *help*
This was a fals cherl and a fals justice.[3]
As shameful deeth as herte may devise
5 Come to thise juges and hir advocats.
Algate° this sely° maide is slain, allas! *at any rate / innocent*
Allas, too dere° boughte she beautee!   *dear*
Wherfore I saye alday° that men may see   *always*
The yiftes of Fortune and of Nature
10 Been cause of deeth to many a creature.
As bothe yiftes that I speke of now,
Men han ful ofte more for harm than prow.°   *benefit*
 "But trewely, myn owene maister dere,
This is a pitous tale for to heere.
15 But nathelees, passe over, is no fors:[4]
I praye to God so save thy gentil cors,°   *body*
And eek thine urinals and thy jurdones,[5]
Thyn ipocras and eek thy galiones,[6]
And every boiste° ful of thy letuarye°— *box / medicine*
20 God blesse hem, and oure lady Sainte Marye.
So mote I theen,[7] thou art a propre man,
And lik a prelat, by Saint Ronian![8]
Saide I nat wel? I can nat speke in terme.[9]
But wel I woot,° thou doost° myn herte to erme° *know / make / grieve*

---

1. The medieval pardoner's function was to collect money for charitable enterprises supported by branches of the church and to act as the pope's agent in rewarding donors with some temporal remission of their sins. According to theological doctrine, St. Peter—and through him his papal successors—received from Christ the power to make a gift of mercy from God's infinite treasury to those of the faithful who had earned special favor, such as contributors to charity. The charitable enterprises themselves—generally hospitals—hired pardoners to raise money, but the pardoners had also to be licensed by the pope to pass on to contributors the papal indulgence. By canon law a pardoner was permitted to work only in a prescribed area; within that area he might visit churches during Sunday service, briefly explain his mission, receive contributions, and in the pope's name, issue indulgence, which was considered not a sale but a free gift made in return for a free gift. In actual fact pardoners seem seldom to have behaved as the law required them. Because a parish priest was forbidden to exclude properly licensed pardoners, a pardoner often made his way into a church at will and, once there, did not confine himself to a mere statement of his business but rather, to encourage the congregation to give freely, preached a highly emotive sermon and boasted of the extraordinarily efficacy of his own particular pardon, claiming for it powers that not even the pope could have invested it with. An honest pardoner, if such existed, was entitled to a percentage of his collections; dishonest pardoners took more than their share, and some took everything; indeed, some were complete frauds, bearing forged credentials that, in an age when even clerical illiteracy was common, were no less impressive than if they had been real.
 "The Pardoner's Prologue and Tale" follow "The Physician's Tale."
2. I.e., Christ's (God's) nails and blood.
3. The Host refers to the Physician's tragic tale of the Roman maiden Virginia, whose great beauty caused a judge to try to gain possession of her person through a trumped-up lawsuit in which he connived with a "churl," who claimed her as his slave. In order to preserve Virginia's chastity, her father killed her.
4. I.e., never mind.
5. Jordans (chamber pots): the Host is somewhat confused in his use of technical medical terms; "urinals": vessels for examining urine.
6. A medicine, probably fabricated on the spot by the Host, named after the ancient Greek physician and writer Galen; "ipocras": a medicinal drink named after the ancient Greek physician Hippocrates.
7. So might I prosper.
8. St. Ronan or St. Ninian, with a possible pun on "runnion" (sexual organ).
9. Speak in technical language.

25   That I almost have caught a cardinacle.[1]
      By corpus bones,[2] but if° I have triacle.°   unless / medicine
      Or elles a draughte of moiste° and corny° ale,   fresh / malty
      Or but I here anoon° a merye tale,   at once
      Myn herte is lost for pitee of this maide.
30   "Thou bel ami,[3] thou Pardoner," he saide,
      "Tel us som mirthe or japes° right anoon."   joke
      "It shal be doon," quod he, "by Saint Ronion.
      But first," quod he, "here at this ale-stake[4]
      I wol bothe drinke and eten of a cake."
35   And right anoon thise gentils gan to crye,
      "Nay, lat him telle us of no ribaudye.°   ribaldry
      Tel us som moral thing that we may lere,°   learn
      Som wit,[5] and thanne wol we gladly heere."
      "I graunte, ywis,"° quod he, "but I moot° thinke   certainly / must
40   Upon som honeste° thing whil that I drinke.   decent

The Prologue

      Lordinges—quod he—in chirches whan I preche,
      I paine me[6] to han° an hautein° speeche,   have / loud
      And ringe it out as round as gooth a belle,
      For I can al by rote[7] that I telle.
45   My theme is alway oon,[8] and evere was:
      Radix malorum est cupiditas.[9]
      First I pronounce whennes° that I come,   whence
      And thanne my bulles shewe I alle and some:[1]
      Oure lige lordes seel on my patente,[2]
50   That shewe I first, my body to warente,°   keep safe
      That no man be so bold, ne preest ne clerk,
      Me to destourbe of Cristes holy werk.
      And after that thanne telle I forth my tales[3]—
      Bulles of popes and of cardinales,
55   Of patriarkes and bisshopes I shewe,
      And in Latin I speke a wordes fewe,
      To saffron with[4] my predicacioun,°   preaching
      And for to stire hem to devocioun.
      Thanne shewe I forth my longe crystal stones,°   jars
60   Ycrammed ful of cloutes° and of bones—   rags
      Relikes been they, as weenen° they eechoon.°   suppose / every one
      Thanne have I in laton° a shulder-boon   brass
      Which that was of an holy Jewes sheep.
      "Goode men," I saye, "take of my wordes keep:°   notice
65   If that this boon be wasshe in any welle,
      If cow, or calf, or sheep, or oxe swelle,

1. Apparently a cardiac condition, which the Host confuses with a cardinal.
2. An illiterate oath, mixing the Latin *corpus dei* ("Christ's body") with "God's bones."
3. "Fair friend" (French), perhaps used derisively.
4. Sign of a tavern.
5. I.e., something with significance.
6. Take pains.
7. I know all by heart.

8. I.e., the same. "Theme": biblical text on which the sermon is based.
9. "Avarice is the root of evil "(1 Timothy 6.10).
1. Each and every one; "bulles": papal bulls, official documents.
2. I.e., the Pope's seal on my papal license.
3. I continue with my yarn.
4. To add spice to.

That any worm hath ete or worm ystonge,[5]
Take water of that welle and wassh his tonge,
And it is hool° anoon. And ferthermoor,   *sound*
70 Of pokkes° and of scabbe and every soor°   *pox / sore*
Shal every sheep be hool that of this welle
Drinketh a draughte. Take keep eek° that I telle: *also*
If that the goode man that the beestes oweth°   *owns*
Wol every wike,° er° that the cok him croweth,   *week / before*
75 Fasting drinken of this welle a draughte—
As thilke° holy Jew oure eldres taughte—   *that same*
His beestes and his stoor° shal multiplye.   *stock*
    "And sire, also it heleth jalousye:
For though a man be falle in jalous rage,
80 Lat maken with this water his potage,°   *soup*
And nevere shal he more his wif mistriste,°   *mistrust*
Though he the soothe of hir defaute wiste,[6]
Al hadde she[7] taken preestes two or three.
    "Here is a mitein° eek that ye may see: *mitten*
85 He that his hand wol putte in this mitein
He shal have multiplying of his grain,
Whan he hath sowen, be it whete or otes—
So that he offre pens or elles grotes.[8]
    "Goode men and wommen, oo thing warne I you:
90 If any wight be in this chirche now
That hath doon sinne horrible, that he
Dar nat for shame of it yshriven° be,   *absolved*
Or any womman, be she yong or old,
That hath ymaked hir housbonde cokewold,°   *cuckold*
95 Swich folk shal have no power ne no grace
To offren to[9] my relikes in this place;
And whoso findeth him out of swich blame,
He wol come up and offre in Goddes name,
And I assoile° him by the auctoritee   *absolve*
100 Which that by bulle ygraunted was to me."
    By this gaude° have I wonne, yeer by yeer,   *trick*
An hundred mark[1] sith° I was pardoner.   *since*
I stonde lik a clerk in my pulpet,
And whan the lewed° peple is down yset,   *ignorant*
105 I preche so as ye han herd bifore,
And telle an hundred false° japes° more.   *deceitful / tales*
Thanne paine I me[2] to strecche forth the nekke,
And eest and west upon the peple I bekke°   *nod*
As dooth a douve,° sitting on a berne;°   *dove / barn*
110 Mine handes and my tonge goon so yerne°   *fast*
That it is joye to see my bisinesse.
Of avarice and of swich cursednesse°   *sin*
Is al my preching, for to make hem free°   *generous*
To yiven hir° pens, and namely° unto me,   *their / especially*
115 For myn entente is nat but for to winne,[3]

5. That has eaten any worm or been bitten by any
snake.
6. Knew the truth of her infidelity.
7. Even if she had.
8. Pennies, or else groats (silver coins).

9. To make offerings in reverence of.
1. Marks (pecuniary units).
2. I take pains.
3. My intent is only to make money.

And no thing for correccion of sinne:
I rekke° nevere whan that they been beried°   care / buried
Though that hir soules goon a-blakeberied.[4]
For certes, many a predicacioun°   sermon
120   Comth ofte time of yvel entencioun:
Som for plesance of folk and flaterye,
To been avaunced° by ypocrisye,   promoted
And som for vaine glorye, and som for hate;
For whan I dar noon otherways debate,°   fight
125   Thanne wol I stinge him with my tonge smerte
In preching, so that he shal nat asterte°   escape
To been defamed falsly, if that he
Hath trespassed to my bretheren[5] or to me.
For though I telle nought his propre name,
130   Men shal wel knowe that it is the same
By signes and by othere circumstaunces.
Thus quite° I folk that doon us displesaunces;[6]   pay back
Thus spete° I out my venim under hewe°   spit / false colors
Of holinesse, to seeme holy and trewe.
135   But shortly myn entente I wol devise:°   describe
I preche of no thing but for coveitise;°   greed
Therfore my theme is yit and evere was
Radix malorum est cupiditas.
Thus can I preche again° that same vice   against
140   Which that I use, and that is avarice.
But though myself be gilty in that sinne,
Yit can I make other folk to twinne°   separate
From avarice, and sore to repente—
But that is nat my principal entente:
145   I preche no thing but for coveitise.
Of this matere it oughte ynough suffise.
Thanne telle I hem ensamples[7] many oon
Of olde stories longe time agoon,
For lewed° peple loven tales olde—   ignorant
150   Swiche° thinges can they wel reporte and holde.[8]   such
What, trowe° ye that whiles I may preche,   believe
And winne gold and silver for° I teche,   because
That I wol live in poverte wilfully?°   voluntarily
Nay, nay, I thoughte° it nevere, trewely,   intended
155   For I wol preche and begge in sondry landes;
I wol nat do no labour with mine handes,
Ne make baskettes and live therby,
By cause I wol nat beggen idelly.[9]
I wol none of the Apostles countrefete:°   imitate
160   I wol have moneye, wolle,° cheese, and whete,   wool
Al were it[1] yiven of the pooreste page,
Or of the pooreste widwe in a village—
Al sholde hir children sterve[2] for famine.
Nay, I wol drinke licour of the vine

---

4. Go blackberrying, i.e., go to hell.
5. Injured by fellow pardoners.
6. Make trouble for us.
7. Exempla (stories illustrating moral principles).

8. Repeat and remember.
9. I.e., without profit.
1. Even though it were.
2. Even though her children should die.

pleasure

165 And have a joly wenche in every town.
But herkneth, lordinges, in conclusioun,
Youre liking° is that I shal telle a tale: *pleasure*
Now have I dronke a draughte of corny ale,
By God, I hope I shal you telle a thing
170 That shal by reson been at youre liking;
For though myself be a ful vicious man,
A moral tale yit I you telle can,
Which I am wont° to preche for to winne.   *accustomed*
Now holde youre pees, my tale I wol biginne.

The Tale

175   In Flandres whilom° was a compaignye   *once*
Of yonge folk that haunteden° folye—   *practiced*
As riot, hasard, stewes,[3] and tavernes,
Wher as with harpes, lutes, and giternes°   *guitars*
They daunce and playen at dees° bothe day and night,   *dice*
180 And ete also and drinke over hir might,[4]
Thurgh which they doon the devel sacrifise
Within that develes temple in cursed wise
By superfluitee° abhominable.   *overindulgence*
Hir othes been so grete and so dampnable
185 That it is grisly for to heere hem swere:
Oure blessed Lordes body they totere[5]—   *tore*
Hem thoughte that Jewes rente° him nought ynough.   *tore*
And eech of hem at otheres sinne lough.°   *laughed*
And right anoon thanne comen tombesteres,°   *dancing girls*
190 Fetis° and smale,° and yonge frutesteres,[6]   *shapely / slim*
Singeres with harpes, bawdes,° wafereres[7]—   *pimps*
Whiche been the verray develes officeres,
To kindle and blowe the fir of lecherye
That is annexed unto glotonye:[8]
195 The Holy Writ take I to my witnesse
That luxure° is in win and dronkenesse.   *lechery*
Lo, how that dronken Lot[9] unkindely°   *unnaturally*
Lay by his doughtres two unwitingly:
So dronke he was he niste° what he wroughte.   *didn't know*
200 Herodes, who so wel the stories soughte,[1]
Whan he of win was repleet° at his feeste,   *filled*
Right at his owene table he yaf° his heeste°   *gave / command*
To sleen° the Baptist John, ful giltelees.   *slay*
   Senek[2] saith a good word doutelees:
205 He saith he can no difference finde
Bitwixe a man that is out of his minde
And a man which that is dronkelewe,°   *drunken*

---

3. Wild parties, gambling, brothels.
4. Beyond their capacity.
5. Tear apart (a reference to oaths that name parts of Christ's body, such as "God's bones!" or "God's teeth!").
6. Fruit-selling girls.
7. Cake-selling girls.

8. I.e., closely related to gluttony.
9. See Genesis 19.30–36.
1. For the story of Herod and St. John the Baptist, see Mark 6.17–29. "Who so . . . sought": i.e., whoever looked it up in the Gospel would find.
2. Seneca (first century A.D.), Roman Stoic philosopher.

But that woodnesse, yfallen in a shrewe,[3]
Persevereth lenger than dooth dronkenesse.
210 O glotonye, ful of cursednesse!°   *wickedness*
O cause first of oure confusioun!°   *downfall*
O original of oure dampnacioun,°   *damnation*
Til Crist hadde bought° us with his blood again!   *redeemed*
Lo, how dere, shortly for to sayn,
215 Abought° was thilke° cursed vilainye;   *paid for / that same*
Corrupt was al this world for glotonye:
Adam oure fader and his wif also
Fro Paradis to labour and to wo
Were driven for that vice, it is no drede.°   *doubt*
220 For whil that Adam fasted, as I rede,
He was in Paradis; and whan that he
Eet° of the fruit defended° on a tree,   *ate / forbidden*
Anoon he was out cast to wo and paine.
O glotonye, on thee wel oughte us plaine!°   *complain*
225   O, wiste a man[4] how manye maladies
Folwen of excesse and of glotonies,
He wolde been the more mesurable°   *moderate*
Of his diete, sitting at his table.
Allas, the shorte throte, the tendre mouth,
230 Maketh that eest and west and north and south,
In erthe, in air, in water, men to swinke,°   *work*
To gete a gloton daintee mete and drinke.
Of this matere, O Paul, wel canstou trete:
"Mete unto wombe,° and wombe eek unto mete,   *belly*
235 Shal God destroyen bothe," as Paulus saith.[5]
Allas, a foul thing is it, by my faith,
To saye this word, and fouler is the deede
Whan man so drinketh of the white and rede[6]
That of his throte he maketh his privee°   *privy*
240 Thurgh thilke cursed superfluitee.°   *overindulgence*
    The Apostle[7] weeping saith ful pitously,
"Ther walken manye of which you told have I—
I saye it now weeping with pitous vois—
They been enemies of Cristes crois,°   *cross*
245 Of whiche the ende is deeth—wombe is hir god!"[8]
O wombe, O bely, O stinking cod,°   *bag*
Fulfilled° of dong° and of corrupcioun!   *filled full / dung*
At either ende of thee foul is the soun.°   *sound*
How greet labour and cost is thee to finde!°   *provide for*
250 Thise cookes, how they stampe° and straine and grinde,   *pound*
And turnen substance into accident[9]
To fulfillen al thy likerous° talent!°   *dainty / appetite*
Out of the harde bones knokke they

---

3. Except that madness, occurring in a wicked man.
4. If a man knew.
5. See 1 Corinthians 6.13: "Meats for the belly and the belly for meats; but God shall destroy both it and them."
6. I.e., white and red wines.
7. I.e., St. Paul.

8. See Philippians 3.18–19: "For many walk, of whom I have told you often . . . whose God is their belly, and whose glory is in their shame, who mind earthly things."
9. A philosophic joke, depending on the distinction between inner reality (substance) and outward appearance (accident).

The mary,° for they caste nought away   *marrow*
255   That may go thurgh the golet¹ softe and soote.°   *sweetly*
Of spicerye° of leef and bark and roote   *spices*
Shal been his sauce ymaked by delit,
To make him yit a newer appetit.
But certes, he that haunteth swiche delices°   *pleasures*
260   Is deed° whil that he liveth in tho° vices.   *dead / those*
     A lecherous thing is win, and dronkenesse
Is ful of striving° and of wrecchednesse.   *quarreling*
O dronke man, disfigured is thy face!
Sour is thy breeth, foul artou to embrace!
265   And thurgh thy dronke nose seemeth the soun
As though thou saidest ay,° "Sampsoun, Sampsoun."   *always*
And yit, God woot,° Sampson drank nevere win.²   *knows*
Thou fallest as it were a stiked swin;³
Thy tonge is lost, and al thyn honeste cure,⁴
270   For dronkenesse is verray sepulture°   *burial*
Of mannes wit° and his discrecioun.   *intelligence*
In whom that drinke hath dominacioun
He can no conseil° keepe, it is no drede.°   *secrets / doubt*
Now keepe you fro the white and fro the rede—
275   And namely° fro the white win of Lepe⁵   *particularly*
That is to selle in Fisshstreete or in Chepe:⁶
The win of Spaine creepeth subtilly
In othere wines growing faste° by,   *close*
Of which ther riseth swich fumositee°   *heady fumes*
280   That whan a man hath dronken draughtes three
And weeneth° that he be at hoom in Chepe,   *supposes*
He is in Spaine, right at the town of Lepe,
Nat at The Rochele ne at Burdeux town;⁷
And thanne wol he sayn, "Sampsoun, Sampsoun."
285   But herkneth, lordinges, oo° word I you praye,   *one*
That alle the soverein actes,⁸ dar I saye,
Of victories in the Olde Testament,
Thurgh verray God that is omnipotent,
Were doon in abstinence and in prayere:
290   Looketh° the Bible and ther ye may it lere.°   *behold / learn*
     Looke Attila, the grete conquerour,⁹
Deide° in his sleep with shame and dishonour,   *died*
Bleeding at his nose in dronkenesse:
A capitain sholde live in sobrenesse.
295   And overal this, aviseth° you right wel   *consider*
What was comanded unto Lamuel¹—
Nat Samuel, but Lamuel, saye I—
Redeth the Bible and finde it expresly,

---

1. Through the gullet.
2. Before Samson's birth an angel told his mother that he would be a Nazarite throughout his life; members of this sect took no strong drink.
3. Stuck pig.
4. Care for self-respect.
5. A town in Spain.
6. Fishstreet and Cheapside in the London market district.

7. The Pardoner is joking about the illegal custom of adulterating fine wines of Bordeaux and La Rochelle with strong Spanish wine.
8. Distinguished deeds.
9. I.e., look at Attila, leader of the Huns who captured Rome in the fifth century; he died of a nosebleed resulting from excessive drinking.
1. Lemuel's mother told him that kings should not drink (Proverbs 31.4–5).

Of win-yiving° to hem that han[2] justise: *wine-serving*
300   Namore of this, for it may wel suffise.
     And now that I have spoken of glotonye,
  Now wol I you defende° hasardrye:°   *prohibit / gambling*
  Hasard is verray moder° of lesinges,°   *mother / lies*
  And of deceite and cursed forsweringes,°   *perjuries*
305   Blaspheme of Crist, manslaughtre, and wast° also   *waste*
  Of catel° and of time; and ferthermo,   *property*
  It is repreve° and contrarye of honour   *disgrace*
  For to been holden a commune hasardour,°   *gambler*
  And evere the hyer he is of estat
310   The more is he holden desolat.[3]
  If that a prince useth hasardrye,
  In alle governance and policye
  He is, as by commune opinioun,
  Yholde the lasse° in reputacioun.   *less*
315   Stilbon, that was a wis embassadour,[4]
  Was sent to Corinthe in ful greet honour
  Fro Lacedomye° to make hir alliaunce,   *Sparta*
  And whan he cam him happede° parchaunce   *it happened*
  That alle the gretteste° that were of that lond   *greatest*
320   Playing at the hasard he hem foond,°   *found*
  For which as soone as it mighte be
  He stal him[5] hoom again to his contree,
  And saide, "Ther wol I nat lese° my name,   *lose*
  N'I wol nat take on me so greet defame°   *dishonor*
325   You to allye unto none hasardours:
  Sendeth othere wise embassadours,
  For by my trouthe, me were levere[6] die
  Than I you sholde to hasardours allye.
  For ye that been so glorious in honours
330   Shal nat allye you with hasardours
  As by my wil, ne as by my tretee."°   *treaty*
  This wise philosophre, thus saide he.
    Looke eek that to the king Demetrius
  The King of Parthes, as the book[7] saith us,
335   Sente him a paire of dees° of gold in scorn,   *dice*
  For he hadde used hasard therbiforn,
  For which he heeld his glorye or his renown
  At no value or reputacioun.
  Lordes may finden other manere play
340   Honeste° ynough to drive the day away.   *honorable*
    Now wol I speke of othes false and grete
  A word or two, as olde bookes trete:
    Greet swering is a thing abhominable,
  And fals swering is yit more reprevable.°   *reprehensible*
345   The hye God forbad swering at al—

---

2. I.e., administer.
3. I.e., dissolute.
4. Perhaps the ancient Greek philosopher Stilbo, but the story is from John of Salisbury's *Policraticus* (twelfth century), in which the ambassador's name is Chilon; he is sent to Corinth, a city famous for luxury.
5. Stole away.
6. I had rather.
7. The story is also from John of Salisbury's *Policraticus*; "Parthes": Parthia, northern Persia.

Witnesse on Mathew.[8] But in special
Of swering saith the holy Jeremie,[9]
"Thou shalt swere sooth° thine othes and nat lie,   *true*
And swere in doom° and eek in rightwisnesse,°   *equity / righteousness*
350   But idel swering is a cursedness."°   *wickedness*
     Biholde and see that in the firste Table[1]
Of hye Goddes heestes° honorable   *commandments*
How that the seconde heeste of him is this:
"Take nat my name in idel or amis."
355   Lo, rather° he forbedeth swich swering   *earlier*
Than homicide, or many a cursed thing.
I saye that as by ordre thus it stondeth—
This knoweth that[2] his heestes understondeth
How that the seconde heeste of God is that.
360   And fertherover,° I wol thee telle al plat°   *furthermore / flat*
That vengeance shal nat parten° from his hous   *depart*
That of his othes is too outrageous.
"By Goddes precious herte!" and "By his nailes!"°   *fingernails*
And "By the blood of Crist that is in Hailes,[3]
365   Sevene is my chaunce, and thyn is cink and traye!"[4]
"By Goddes armes, if thou falsly playe
This daggere shal thurghout thyn herte go!"
This fruit cometh of the bicche bones[5] two—
Forswering, ire, falsnesse, homicide.
370   Now for the love of Crist that for us dyde,°   *died*
Lete° youre othes bothe grete and smale.   *leave*
But sires, now wol I telle forth my tale.
     Thise riotoures° three of whiche I telle,   *revelers*
Longe erst er prime[6] ronge of any belle,
375   Were set hem in a taverne to drinke,
And as they sat they herde a belle clinke
Biforn a cors° was caried to his grave.   *corpse*
That oon of hem gan callen to his knave:°   *servant*
"Go bet,"[7] quod he, "and axe° redily°   *ask / promptly*
380   What cors is this that passeth heer forby,
And looke° that thou reporte his name weel."° *be sure / well*
     "Sire," quod this boy, "it needeth neveradeel:[8]
It was me told er ye cam heer two houres.
He was, pardee,° an old felawe of youres,   *by God*
385   And sodeinly he was yslain tonight,°   *last night*
Fordronke° as he sat on his bench upright;   *very drunk*
Ther cam a privee° thief men clepeth° Deeth, *stealthy / call*
That in this contree al the peple sleeth,°   *slays*
And with his spere he smoot his herte atwo,
390   And he wente his way withouten wordes mo.
He hath a thousand slain this° pestilence.   *during this*

---

8. "But I say unto you, Swear not at all" (Matthew 5.34).
9. "And thou shalt swear, the Lord liveth, in truth, in judgment, and in righteousness" (Jeremiah 4.2).
1. I.e., the first three of the Ten Commandments.
2. I.e., he who.
3. An abbey in Gloucestershire supposed to possess some of Christ's blood.

4. Five and three; "Sevene": winning number; the Pardoner is imitating a player in a game of dice.
5. I.e., damned dice.
6. According to Catholic ritual, this is the first hour of the day, rung between 6 and 9 A.M.
7. Better, i.e., quick.
8. It isn't a bit necessary.

And maister, er ye come in his presence,
Me thinketh that it were necessarye
For to be war of swich an adversarye;
395 Beeth redy for to meete him everemore:
Thus taughte me my dame.° I saye namore."   *mother*
    "By Sainte Marye," saide this taverner,
"The child saith sooth, for he hath slain this yeer,
Henne° over a mile, within a greet village,   *hence*
400 Bothe man and womman, child and hine° and page.   *farm laborer*
I trowe° his habitacion be there.   *believe*
To been avised° greet wisdom it were   *forewarned*
Er that he dide a man a dishonour."
    "Ye, Goddes armes," quod this riotour,
405 "Is it swich peril with him for to meete?
I shal him seeke by way and eek by streete,⁹
I make avow to Goddes digne° bones.   *worthy*
Herkneth, felawes, we three been alle ones:°   *of one mind*
Lat eech of us holde up his hand to other
410 And eech of us bicome otheres brother,
And we wol sleen this false traitour Deeth.
He shal be slain, he that so manye sleeth,
By Goddes dignitee, er it be night."
    Togidres han thise three hir trouthes plight¹
415 To live and dien eech of hem with other,
As though he were his owene ybore° brother.   *born*
And up they sterte,° al dronken in this rage,   *started*
And forth they goon towardes that village
Of which the taverner hadde spoke biforn,
420 And many a grisly ooth thanne han they sworn,
And Cristes blessed body they torente:°   *tore apart*
Deeth shal be deed° if that they may him hente.°   *dead / catch*
    Whan they han goon nat fully half a mile,
Right as they wolde han treden° over a stile,   *stepped*
425 An old man and a poore with hem mette;
This olde man ful mekely hem grette,°   *greeted*
And saide thus, "Now lordes, God you see."²
    The pruddeste° of thise riotoures three   *proudest*
Answerde again, "What, carl° with sory grace,   *churl*
430 Why artou al forwrapped° save thy face?   *muffled up*
Why livestou so longe in so greet age?"
    This olde man gan looke in his visage,
And saide thus, "For° I ne can nat finde   *because*
A man, though that I walked into Inde,°   *India*
435 Neither in citee ne in no village,
That wolde chaunge his youthe for myn age;
And therfore moot° I han myn age stille,   *must*
As longe time as it is Goddes wille.
    "Ne Deeth, allas, ne wol nat have my lif.
440 Thus walke I lik a resteless caitif,°   *captive, wrench*
And on the ground which is my modres° gate   *mother's*

9. By highway and byway.   2. May God protect you.
1. Pledged their words of honor.

I knokke with my staf both erly and late,
And saye, 'Leve° moder, leet me in: *dear*
Lo, how I vanisshe, flessh and blood and skin.
445 Allas, whan shal my bones been at reste?
Moder, with you wolde I chaunge° my cheste[3]   *exchange*
That in my chambre longe time hath be,
Ye, for an haire-clout[4] to wrappe me.'
But yit to me she wol nat do that grace,
450 For which ful pale and welked° is my face.   *withered*
But sires, to you it is no curteisye
To speken to an old man vilainye,°   *rudeness*
But° he trespasse° in word or elles in deede.   *unless / offend*
In Holy Writ ye may yourself wel rede,
455 'Agains[5] an old man, hoor° upon his heed,   *hoar, white*
Ye shal arise.'[6] Wherfore I yive you reed,°   *advice*
Ne dooth unto an old man noon harm now,
Namore than that ye wolde men dide to you
In age, if that ye so longe abide.[7]
460 And God be with you wher ye go° or ride: *walk*
I moot° go thider as I have to go."   *must*
    "Nay, olde cherl, by God thou shalt nat so,"
Saide this other hasardour anoon.
"Thou partest nat so lightly,° by Saint John!   *easily*
465 Thou speke° right now of thilke traitour Deeth,   *spoke*
That in this contree alle oure freendes sleeth:
Have here my trouthe, as thou art his espye,°   *spy*
Tel wher he is, or thou shalt it abye,°   *pay for*
By God and by the holy sacrament!
470 For soothly thou art oon of his assent[8]
To sleen us yonge folk, thou false thief."
    "Now sires," quod he, "if that ye be so lief°   *anxious*
To finde Deeth, turne up this crooked way,
For in that grove I lafte° him, by my fay,°   *left / faith*
475 Under a tree, and ther he wol abide:
Nat for youre boost° he wol him no thing hide.   *boast*
See ye that ook?° Right ther ye shal him finde.   *oak*
God save you, that boughte again[9] mankinde,
And you amende." Thus saide this olde man.
480   And everich of thise riotoures ran
Til he cam to that tree, and ther they founde
Of florins° fine of gold ycoined rounde   *coins*
Wel neigh an eighte busshels as hem thoughte—
Ne lenger thanne after Deeth they soughte,
485 But eech of hem so glad was of the sighte,
For that the florins been so faire and brighte,
That down they sette hem by this precious hoord.
The worste of hem he spak the firste word:
    "Bretheren," quod he, "take keep° what that I saye: *heed*

---

3. Chest for one's belongings, used here as the symbol for life—or perhaps a coffin.
4. Haircloth, for a winding sheet.
5. In the presence of.
6. Cf. Leviticus 19.32: "You shall rise up before the hoary head, and honor the face of an old man, and you shall fear your God: I am the Lord."
7. I.e., if you live so long.
8. I.e., one of his party.
9. Redeemed.

490 My wit is greet though that I bourde° and playe.   *joke*
This tresor hath Fortune unto us yiven
In mirthe and jolitee oure lif to liven,
And lightly° as it cometh so wol we spende.   *easily*
Ey, Goddes precious dignitee, who wende[1]
495 Today that we sholde han so fair a grace?
But mighte this gold be caried fro this place
Hoom to myn hous—or elles unto youres—
For wel ye woot that al this gold is oures—
Thanne were we in heigh felicitee.
500 But trewely, by daye it mighte nat be:
Men wolde sayn that we were theves stronge,°   *flagrant*
And for oure owene tresor doon us honge.[2]
This tresor moste ycaried be by nighte,
As wisely and as slyly as it mighte.
505 Therfore I rede° that cut° amonges us alle   *advise / straws*
Be drawe, and lat see wher the cut wol falle;
And he that hath the cut with herte blithe
Shal renne° to the town, and that ful swithe,°   *run / quickly*
And bringe us breed and win ful prively;°   *in secret*
510 And two of us shal keepen° subtilly   *guard*
This tresor wel, and if he wol nat tarye,
Whan it is night we wol this tresor carye
By oon assent wher as us thinketh best."
That oon of hem the cut broughte in his fest°   *fist*
515 And bad hem drawe and looke wher it wol falle;
And it fil° on the yongeste of hem alle,   *fell*
And forth toward the town he wente anoon.
And also° soone as that he was agoon,°   *as / gone away*
That oon of hem spak thus unto that other:
520 "Thou knowest wel thou art my sworen brother;
Thy profit wol I telle thee anoon:
Thou woost wel that oure felawe is agoon,
And here is gold, and that ful greet plentee,
That shal departed° been among us three.   *divided*
525 But nathelees, if I can shape° it so   *arrange*
That it departed were among us two,
Hadde I nat doon a freendes turn to thee?"
That other answerde, "I noot° how that may be: *don't know*
He woot that the gold is with us twaye.
530 What shal we doon? What shal we to him saye?"
"Shal it be conseil?"[3] saide the firste shrewe.°   *villain*
"And I shal telle in a wordes fewe
What we shul doon, and bringe it wel aboute."
"I graunte," quod that other, "out of doute,
535 That by my trouthe I wol thee nat biwraye."°   *expose*
"Now," quod the firste, "thou woost wel we be twaye,
And two of us shal strenger° be than oon: *stronger*
Looke whan that he is set that right anoon
Aris as though thou woldest with him playe,

1. Who would have supposed.   3. A secret.
2. Have us hanged.

540 And I shal rive° him thurgh the sides twaye,   *pierce*
Whil that thou strugelest with him as in game,
And with thy daggere looke thou do the same;
And thanne shal al this gold departed be,
My dere freend, bitwixe thee and me.
545 Thanne we may bothe oure lustes° al fulfille,   *desires*
And playe at dees° right at oure owene wille."   *dice*
And thus accorded been thise shrewes twaye
To sleen the thridde, as ye han herd me saye.
    This yongeste, which that wente to the town,
550 Ful ofte in herte he rolleth up and down
The beautee of thise florins newe and brighte.
"O Lord," quod he, "if so were that I mighte
Have al this tresor to myself allone,
Ther is no man that liveth under the trone°   *throne*
555 Of God that sholde live so merye as I."
And at the laste the feend oure enemy°   *Satan*
Putte in his thought that he sholde poison beye,°   *buy*
With which he mighte sleen his felawes twaye—
Forwhy° the feend° foond him in swich livinge   *because / devil*
560 That he hadde leve° him to sorwe bringe:[4]   *permission*
For this was outrely° his fulle entente,   *plainly*
To sleen hem bothe, and nevere to repente.
    And forth he gooth—no lenger wolde he tarye—
Into the town unto a pothecarye,°   *apothecary*
565 And prayed him that he him wolde selle
Som poison that he mighte his rattes quelle,°   *kill*
And eek ther was a polcat[5] in his hawe°   *yard*
That, as he saide, his capons hadde yslawe,°   *slain*
And fain he wolde wreke him[6] if he mighte
570 On vermin that destroyed him[7] by nighte.
    The pothecarye answerde, "And thou shalt have
A thing that, also° God my soule save,   *as*
In al this world there is no creature
That ete or dronke hath of this confiture°—   *mixture*
575 Nat but the mountance° of a corn° of whete—   *amount / kernel*
That he ne shal his lif anoon forlete.°   *lose*
Ye, sterve° he shal, and that in lasse° while   *die / less*
Than thou wolt goon a paas[8] nat but a mile,
The poison is so strong and violent."
580 This cursed man hath in his hand yhent°   *taken*
This poison in a box and sith° he ran   *then*
Into the nexte streete unto a man
And borwed of him large botels three,
And in the two his poison poured he—
585 The thridde he kepte clene for his drinke,
For al the night he shoop him[9] for to swinke°   *work*
In carying of the gold out of that place.

4. Christian doctrine teaches that the devil may not tempt people except with God's permission.
5. A weasel-like animal.
6. He would gladly avenge himself.
7. I.e., were ruining his farming.
8. Take a walk.
9. He was preparing.

And whan this riotour with sory grace
Hadde filled with win his grete botels three,
590   To his felawes again repaireth he.
     What needeth it to sermone of it more?
For right as they had cast° his deeth bifore,   *plotted*
Right so they han him slain, and that anoon.
And whan that this was doon, thus spak that oon:
595   "Now lat us sitte and drinke and make us merye,
And afterward we wol his body berye."°   *bury*
And with that word it happed him par cas[1]
To take the botel ther the poison was,
And drank, and yaf his felawe drinke also,
600   For which anoon they storven° bothe two.   *died*
     But certes I suppose that Avicen
Wroot nevere in no canon ne in no *fen*[2]
Mo wonder signes[3] of empoisoning
Than hadde thise wrecches two er hir ending:
605   Thus ended been thise homicides two,
And eek the false empoisonere also.
     O cursed sinne of alle cursednesse!
O traitours homicide, O wikkednesse!
O glotonye, luxure,° and hasardrye!   *lechery*
610   Thou blasphemour of Crist with vilainye
And othes grete of usage° and of pride!   *habit*
Allas, mankinde, how may it bitide
That to thy Creatour which that thee wroughte,
And with his precious herte blood thee boughte,°   *redeemed*
615   Thou art so fals and so unkinde,° allas?   *unnatural*
     Now goode men, God foryive you youre trespas,
And ware° you fro the sinne of avarice: *guard*
Myn holy pardon may you alle warice°—   *save*
So that ye offre nobles or sterlinges,[4]
620   Or elles silver brooches, spoones, ringes.
Boweth your heed under this holy bulle!
Cometh up, ye wives, offreth of youre wolle!°   *wool*
Youre name I entre here in my rolle: anoon
Into the blisse of hevene shul ye goon.
625   I you assoile° by myn heigh power—   *absolve*
Ye that wol offre—as clene and eek as cleer
As ye were born.—And lo, sires, thus I preche.
And Jesu Crist that is oure soules leeche°   *physician*
So graunte you his pardon to receive,
630   For that is best—I wol you nat deceive.

The Epilogue

"But sires, oo word forgat I in my tale:
I have relikes and pardon in my male°   *bag*

---

1. By chance.
2. The *Canon of Medicine*, by Avicenna, an eleventh-century Arabic philosopher, was divided into sections called "fens."
3. More wonderful symptoms.
4. "Nobles" and "sterlinges" were valuable coins.

As faire as any man in Engelond,
Whiche were me yiven by the Popes hond.
635 If any of you wol of devocioun
Offren and han myn absolucioun,
Come forth anoon, and kneeleth here adown,
And mekely receiveth my pardoun,
Or elles taketh pardon as ye wende,°   *ride along*
640 Al newe and fressh at every miles ende—
So that ye offre alway newe and newe[5]
Nobles or pens whiche that be goode and trewe.
It is an honour to everich° that is heer   *everyone*
That ye have a suffisant° pardoner   *competent*
645 T'assoile you in contrees as ye ride,
For aventures whiche that may bitide:
Paraventure° ther may falle oon or two   *by chance*
Down of his hors and breke his nekke atwo;
Looke which a suretee° is it to you alle   *safeguard*
650 That I am in youre felaweshipe yfalle
That may assoile you, bothe more and lasse,[6]
Whan that the soule shal fro the body passe.
I rede° that oure Hoste shal biginne,   *advise*
For he is most envoluped° in sinne.   *involved*
655 Com forth, sire Host, and offre first anoon,
And thou shalt kisse the relikes everichoon,°   *each one*
Ye, for a grote: unbokele° anoon thy purs."   *unbuckle*
"Nay, nay," quod he, "thanne have I Cristes curs!
Lat be," quod he, "it shal nat be, so theech!°   *may I prosper*
660 Thou woldest make me kisse thyn olde breech°   *breeches*
And swere it were a relik of a saint,
Though it were with thy fundament° depeint.°   *anus / stained*
But, by the crois which that Sainte Elaine foond,[7]
I wolde I hadde thy coilons° in myn hond,   *testicles*
665 In stede of relikes or of saintuarye.°   *relic-box*
Lat cutte hem of: I wol thee helpe hem carye.
They shal be shrined in an hogges tord."°   *turd*
This Pardoner answerde nat a word:
So wroth he was no word ne wolde he saye.
670 "Now," quod oure Host, "I wol no lenger playe
With thee, ne with noon other angry man."
But right anoon the worthy Knight bigan,
Whan that he sawgh that al the peple lough,°   *laughed*
"Namore of this, for it is right ynough.
675 Sire Pardoner, be glad and merye of cheere,
And ye, sire Host that been to me so dere,
I praye you that ye kisse the Pardoner,
And Pardoner, I praye thee, draw thee neer,
And as we diden lat us laughe and playe."
680 Anoon they kiste and riden forth hir waye.

---

5. Over and over.
6. Both high and low (i.e., everybody).
7. I.e., by the cross that St. Helena found. Helena,   mother of the Roman emperor Constantine the Great, was reputed to have found the True Cross.

From Troilus and Criseide[1]

Cantus Troili[2]

400　"If no love is, O God, what feele I so?
　　And if love is, what thing and which is he?
　　If love be good, from whennes cometh my wo?
　　If it be wikke, a wonder thinketh me,
　　Whan every torment and adversitee
405　That cometh of him may to me savory° thinke,°　　　*pleasant / seem*
　　For ay thurste I, the more that ich° it drinke.　　　　*I*

　　And if that at myn owene lust I brenne,°　　　　　　　　*burn*
　　From whennes cometh my wailing and my plainte?°　　*lament*
　　If harm agree me, wherto plaine I thenne?[3]—
410　I noot, ne why unwery that I fainte.[4]
　　O quikke° deeth, O sweete harm so quainte,°　　　*living / strange*
　　How may° of thee in me swich quantitee,　　　　*can there be*
　　But if° that I consente that it be?　　　　　　　　　*except*

　　And if that I consente, I wrongfully
415　Complaine: ywis,° thus possed° to and fro,　　　*indeed / tossed*
　　Al stereless° within a boot am I　　　　　　　　*rudderless*
　　Amidde the see, bitwixen windes two,
　　That in contrarye° stonden everemo.　　　　　　*opposition*
　　Allas, what is this wonder maladye?
420　For hoot° of cold, for cold of hoot I die."[5]　　　*heat*

LYRICS AND OCCASIONAL VERSE

To Rosamond

　　Madame, ye been of alle beautee shrine
　　As fer as cercled is the mapemounde:[6]
　　For as the crystal glorious ye shine,
　　And like ruby been° youre cheekes rounde.　　　*are*
5　　Therwith ye been so merye and so jocounde
　　That at a revel whan that I see you daunce
　　It is an oinement unto my wounde,
　　Though ye to me ne do no daliaunce.[7]

---

1. In this long poem Chaucer tells the tragic story of the love between Troilus, the son of King Priam of Troy, and Criseide, the daughter of Calkas (a Trojan priest who defects to the Greek side during the Trojan War).
2. "The Song of Troilus" (Latin); Troilus sings this song just after he has fallen in love with Criseide in book 1. Prior to falling in love, Troilus had spurned love and mocked other lovers. These stanzas were taken by Chaucer from the eighty-eighth sonnet of the Italian poet Petrarch (1304–1374).
3. I.e., if suffering is agreeable to me, why, then, do I lament?
4. I.e., I know not, nor why I faint even though I am not weary.
5. Such oxymorons were a convention of Petrarchan love poetry.
6. I.e., to the shrine of all beauty, to the farthest circumference of the map of the world.
7. I.e., show me no encouragement.

For though I weepe of teres ful a tine,°   *tub*
10 Yit may that wo myn herte nat confounde;
    Youre semy° vois, that ye so smale outtwine,[8]   *small*
    Maketh my thought in joye and blis haboundе:°   *abound*
    So curteisly I go with love bounde
    That to myself I saye in my penaunce,[9]
15 "Suffiseth me to love you, Rosemounde,
    Though ye to me ne do no daliaunce."

    Was nevere pik walwed in galauntine[1]
    As I in love am walwed and ywounde,
    For which ful ofte I of myself divine
20 That I am trewe Tristam[2] the secounde;
    My love may not refreide nor affounde;[3]
    I brenne° ay in amorous plesaunce: *burn*
    Do what you list, I wol youre thral° be founde,   *slave*
    Though ye to me ne do no daliaunce.

Truth

    Flee fro the prees and dwelle with soothfastnesse;[4]
    Suffise unto thy thing,[5] though it be smal;
    For hoord hath[6] hate, and climbing tikelnesse;°   *insecurity*
    Prees hath envye, and wele° blent° overal.   *prosperity / blinds*
5 Savoure° no more than three bihoove shal;   *relish*
    Rule wel thyself that other folk canst rede:°   *advise*
    And Trouthe shal delivere,[7] it is no drede.°   *doubt*

    Tempest thee nought al crooked to redresse[8]
    In trust of hire that turneth as a bal;[9]
10 Muche wele stant in litel bisinesse;[1]
    Be war therfore to spurne ayains an al.[2]
    Strive nat as dooth the crokke° with the wal.[3]   *pot*
    Daunte° thyself that dauntest otheres deede: *master*
    And Trouthe shal delivere, it is no drede.

15 That thee is sent, receive in buxomnesse;°   *obedience*
    The wrastling for the world axeth° a fal;   *asks for*
    Here is noon hoom, here nis but wildernesse:[4]
    Forth, pilgrim, forth! Forth, beest, out of thy stal!
    Know thy countree, looke up, thank God of al.

8. That you so delicately spin out.
9. I.e., pangs of unrequited love.
1. Pike rolled in galantine sauce.
2. The famous lover of Isolt (Iseult, Isolde) in medieval legend, renowned for his constancy.
3. Cool nor chill.
4. Truthfulness; "prees": crowd; also, ambition. In some early manuscripts and printed editions, this poem is subtitled "Balade de Bon Conseyl" ("Ballad of Good Counsel").
5. Be content with your possessions.
6. Hoarding causes.
7. I.e., truth shall make you free; cf. John 8.32.

8. Do not struggle to correct all that's crooked.
9. I.e., trust in Fortune, who turns like a ball in that she is always presenting a different aspect to people.
1. I.e., much happiness will be found in little activity.
2. I.e., be careful therefore not to kick against an awl (a small, sharply pointed tool).
3. I.e., do not strive against impossible odds (as when a clay pot fights with a wall).
4. Here is no home, here is nothing but wilderness.

20 Hold the heigh way and lat thy gost° thee lede: *spirit*
    And Trouthe shal delivere, it is no drede.

Envoy

Therfore, thou Vache,[5] leve thyn olde wrecchednesse
Unto the world; leve[6] now to be thral.
Crye him mercy that of his heigh goodnesse
25 Made thee of nought, and in especial
Draw unto him, and pray in general,
For thee and eek for othere, hevenelich meede:°   *reward*
And Trouthe shal delivere, it is no drede.

Complaint to His Purse

To you, my purs, and to noon other wight,°   *person*
Complaine I, for ye be my lady dere.
I am so sory, now that ye be light,
For certes, but if° ye make me hevy cheere,   *unless*
5   Me were as lief[7] be laid upon my beere;°   *bier*
For which unto youre mercy thus I crye:
Beeth hevy again, or elles moot° I die.   *must*

Now voucheth sauf[8] this day er° it be night   *before*
That I of you the blisful soun may heere,
10 Or see youre colour, lik the sonne bright,
That of yelownesse hadde nevere peere.
Ye be my life, ye be myn hertes steere,°   *rudder, guide*
Queene of confort and of good compaignye:
Beeth hevy again, or elles moot I die.

15 Ye purs, that been to me my lives light
And saviour, as in this world down here,
Out of this towne[9] helpe me thurgh your might,
Sith that ye wol nat be my tresorere;°   *treasurer*
For I am shave as neigh as any frere.[1]
20 But yit I praye unto youre curteisye:
Beeth hevy again, or elles moot I die.

Envoy to Henry IV

O conquerour of Brutus Albioun,[2]
Which that by line and free eleccioun
Been verray king, this song to you I sende:
25 And ye, that mowen° alle oure harmes amende,   *may*
Have minde upon my supplicacioun.

---

5. Probably Sir Philip de la Vache, with a pun on
the French for "cow."
6. I.e., cease.
7. I'd just as soon.
8. Grant.
9. Probably Westminster, where Chaucer had
rented a house.
1. Shaved as close as any (tonsured) friar, an
expression for being broke.
2. Britain (Albion) was said to have been founded
by Brutus, the grandson of Aeneas, the founder of
Rome.

To His Scribe[3] Adam

Adam scrivain,° if evere it thee bifalle   *scribe*
Boece or *Troilus*[4] for to writen newe,
Under thy longe lokkes thou moste have the scalle,[5]
But after my making thou write more trewe,
So ofte a day I moot° thy werk renewe,   *must*
It to correcte, and eek° to rubbe and scrape:[6]   *also*
And al is thurgh thy necligence and rape.°   *haste*

From PEARL[1]

1375–1400

I

1

Perle plesaunte to prynces paye	Pearl,[2] the precious prize of a king,

Perle plesaunte to prynces paye | Pearl,[2] the precious prize of a king,
To clanly clos in golde so clere | Chastely set in cherished gold,
Oute of Oryent I hardyly saye | In all the East none equalling,
Ne proued I neuer her precios pere | No peer to her could I behold.
So rounde so reken in vche araye | So round, so rare, a radiant thing,
So smal so smoþe her sydeʒ were | So smooth she was, so small of mold,
Quere so euer I jugged gemmeʒ gaye | Wherever I judged gems glimmering
I sette hyr sengely in synglure | I set her apart, her price untold.
Allas I leste hyr in on erbere | Alas, I lost her in earth's green fold;
Þurʒ gresse to grounde hit fro me yot | Through grass to the ground, I searched in vain.
I dewyne fordolked of luf daungere | I languish alone; my heart grows cold

3. Copyist, responsible for making copies of the poet's work.
4. Chaucer's long poem "Troilus and Criseide" (see p. 52); "Boece": Chaucer's translation of the *Consolation of Philosophy* by Boethius (ca. A.D. 480–524).
5. I.e., may you have scurf, a scaly or scabby disease of the scalp.
6. Corrections on parchment were made by scraping off the ink and rubbing the surface smooth again.
1. *Pearl* was written in the latter half of the fourteenth century by an unknown author who probably lived in the northwest midlands of England. The one manuscript of the poem still extant also contains the poems *Sir Gawain and the Green Knight, Purity,* and *Patience,* all generally thought to be by the same author. *Pearl,* in the form of a dream vision, a popular convention of the time, is an elegy on the death of a child, perhaps the poet's daughter. Many scholars, however, read the poem as an allegory. In the poem's 101 stanzas, the dreamer carries on a dialogue with the Pearl maiden, who instructs him in Christian doctrine. The intricate pattern of the poem involves rhyme and repeated words and phrases that link the stanzas, forming, finally, a circular structure. The translation used here was done by Sara deFord and a group of her students at Goucher College. The translators chose to print their translation side by side with the original in Middle English (they modernized only the capitalization). They have attempted to remain true to the original form, retaining, where possible, the four-beat alliterative line, rhyme pattern, and repetition of words and phrases of the original. The first five stanzas of the poem, reproduced here, recount the narrator's grief at the loss of his Pearl, and the beginning of the "slumber" that will produce his dream vision of the maid. (The roman numeral reprinted below marks the first five-stanza section of the original text.)
2. In medieval tradition, the pearl is a symbol of the pure and precious.

Of þat pryuy perle wythouten
    spot

For my precious pearl without a
    stain.[3]

2

Syþen in þat spote hit fro me
    sprange
Ofte haf I wayted wyschande þat
    wele
15 Þat wont watȝ whyle deuoyde my
    wrange
& heuen my happe & al my
    hele
Þat dotȝ bot þrych my hert þrange
My breste in bale bot bolne &
    bele
Ȝet þoȝt me neuer so swete a sange
20 As stylle stounde let to me stele
For soþe þer fleten to me
    fele
To þenke hir color so clad in
    clot
O moul þou marreȝ a myry
    iuele
My priuy perle wythouten spotte

Since in that spot it slipped from
    me,
I lingered, longing for that
    delight
That from my sins once set me
    free
And my happiness raised to the
    highest height.
Her going wounds me grievously;
It burns my breast both day and
    night.
Yet I never imagined a melody
So sweet as she, so brief, and slight.
But memory flowed through my
    mind's sight:
I thought how her color in clods[4]
    had lain
O dust that dims what once was
    bright,
My precious pearl without a stain.

3

25 Þat spot of spyseȝ [mo] t nedeȝ
    sprede
Þer such rycheȝ to rot is runne
Blomeȝ blayke & blwe & rede
Þer schyneȝ ful schyr agayn þe
    sunne
Flor & fryte may not be fede
30 Þer hit doun drof in moldeȝ
    dunne
For vch gresse mot grow of grayneȝ
    dede
No whete were elleȝ to woneȝ
    wonne
Of goud vche goude is ay bygonne
So semly a sede moȝt fayly
    not
35 Þat spryg ande spyceȝ vp ne
    sponne
Of þat precios perle wythouten
    spotte

Rare spices on that spot must
    spread:
Such riches there to rot have run,
Blooms of yellow and blue and red,
Their sheen a shimmer against the
    sun.
Flower and fruit nor faded nor dead,
Where the pearl dropped down in
    mouldering dun;[5]
Each grass from a lifeless grain is
    bred,
Else to harvest no wheat were
    won:[6]
Always from good is good begun.
So seemly[7] a seed could not die in
    vain,
That sprig nor spice there would be
    none
Of that precious pearl without a
    stain.

---

3. The translators note that the word "spot" is used in the first five stanzas, but because of the limited rhyme possibilities, they have substituted "stain" in the terminal position.
4. I.e., clods of earth.
5. The original "moldeȝ dunne" may be translated "dark clods of earth."

6. Christ uses this metaphor in reference to his own crucifixion: "Verily, verily, I say unto you, Except a corn of wheat fall into the ground and die, it abideth alone; but if it die, it bringeth forth much fruit" (John 12.24).
7. Beautiful.

4

To þat spot þat I in speche
    expoun
I entred in þat erber grene
In Augoste in a hyȝ seysoun
40 Quen corne is coruen wyth crokeȝ
    kene
On huyle þer perle hit trendeled
    doun
Schadowed þis worteȝ ful schyre &
    schene
Gilofre gyngure & gromylyoun
& pyonys powdered ay
    bytwene
45 ȝif hit watȝ semly on to sene
A fayr reflayr ȝet fro hit
    flot
Þer wonys þat worþyly I wot &
    wene
My precious perle wythouten spot

To the spot which I in speech
    portray,
I entered in that arbor green,
In August on a holy day,
When the corn is cut with sickles
    keen.
On the little rise where my pearl
    rolled away,
The fairest flowers formed a screen:
Gillyflower, ginger, gromwell spray,
With peonies[8] powdered in
    between.
If they were seemly to be seen,
Far sweeter the scents from that
    domain,
More worthy her dwelling, well I
    ween,[9]
My precious pearl without a stain.

5

Bifore þat spot my honde I
    spenn[e]d
50 For care ful colde þat to me
    caȝt
A deuely dele in my hert denned
Þaȝ resoun sette myseluen
    saȝt
I playned my perle þat þer watȝ
    spenned
Wyth fyrte skylleȝ þat faste
    faȝt
55 Þaȝ kynde of Kryst me comfort
    kenned
My wreched wylle in wo ay
    wraȝte
I felle vpon þat floury flaȝt
Suche odour to my herneȝ schot
I slode vpon a slepyng-slaȝte
60 On þat prec[i]os perle wythouten
    spot

I mourned, hands clenched, before
    that mound,
For the piercing cold of grief had
    caught
Me in the doleful dread and bound
My heart, though reason solace
    sought.
I longed for my pearl, locked in the
    ground,
While fierce contentions in me
    fought.
In Christ, though comfort could be
    found,
My wretched will was still dis-
    traught.
I fell upon that flowery plot.
Such odors eddied in my brain,
To sudden slumber I was brought
By that precious pearl without a
    stain.

8. All these plants are types of spices; spices were
precious plants valued for their rich scent.

9. Know.

WILLIAM LANGLAND

fl. 1375

Piers Plowman[1]

In a somer seson, whan softe was the sonne,°   *sun*
I shoop me into shroudes as I a sheep were,[2]
In habite as an heremite unholy of werkes,[3]
Wente wide in this world wondres to here.°   *hear*
5   Ac° on a May morwenynge[4] on Malverne Hilles   *but, and*
Me bifel a ferly, of Fairye me thoghte.[5]
I was wery [of]wandred and wente me to reste
Under a brood bank by a bournes° syde;   *stream's*
And as I lay and lenede and loked on the watres,
10   I slombred into a slepyng, it sweyed so murye.°   *merry*
    Thanne gan [me] to meten° a merveillous swevene°—   *dream / dream*
That I was in a wildernesse, wiste° I nevere where.   *knew*
As I biheeld into the eest an heigh to the sonne,[6]
I seigh a tour° on a toft° trieliche ymaked,[7]   *tower / knoll*
15   A deep dale° bynethe, a dongeon° therinne,   *valley / dungeon*
With depe diches and derke and dredfulle of sighte.
A fair feeld ful of folk[8] fond° I ther bitwene—   *found*
Of alle manere° of men, the meene° and the riche,   *kinds / lowly*
Werchynge° and wandrynge as the world asketh.°   *working / requires*
20   Somme putten hem° to the plough, pleiden° ful   *themselves / playing*
    selde,°   *seldom*
In settynge° and sowynge swonken° ful harde,   *planting / toiled*
And wonnen that thise wastours with glotonye destroyeth[9]

1. Probably composed between 1360 and 1387, *The Vision of Piers Plowman* is a long religious, social, and political allegory. It is written in alliterative verse in a west-midlands dialect, which differs in many ways from that used by Chaucer in the nearly contemporaneous *Canterbury Tales. Piers* survives in several distinct versions that scholars refer to as the A-, B-, C-, and Z-texts. The A-text (about twenty-four hundred lines long) breaks off inconclusively; the B-text, which we follow here, is about four thousand lines longer. The C-text is poetically and doctrinally more conservative. Recently, scholars have started to focus on the Z-text as possibly being an earlier text than the other three. The large number of manuscripts (and two sixteenth-century printed editions) that survive suggest that the poem was quite popular during the early modern period. While scholars generally attribute authorship to William Langland, little is known about the author other than what has been inferred from the poem itself, and it is possible that the figure of William Langland is a fiction of the poem. Generally, his name has been derived from the speaker's claim that "I have lived in land . . . my name is Long Will" (line 152, Passus 15; the sections of the poem are called "Passus," Latin for "step"). The poem takes the form of a dream vision, a popular genre during the Middle Ages in which the author presents a story as the dream of the main character. The selection here from the poem's prologue introduces the dreamer's vision of the Field of Folk, which represents fourteenth-century English society and its failures to live in accordance with Christian principles.
2. I.e., I dressed in garments as if I were either a sheep or a shepherd.
3. Perhaps meaning one without holy works to his credit, but not necessarily one of sinful works; "in habite as an heremite": thus, the simple clothes resemble those of a hermit.
4. Traveling forth on a May morning often initiated a dream vision in medieval poetry. As the setting of the vision, the "Malverne hills" in the west midlands are generally thought to have been the site of Langland's early home (if such a person existed).
5. I.e., a marvel ("ferly") that seemed to be from fairyland.
6. I.e., looked toward the east on high, toward the sun. Both the east and the sun are symbols of Christ.
7. This has several possible meanings, including well or wonderfully made; and made like a tree, i.e., like the Cross.
8. The fair field of folk is commonly interpreted as a representation of the world, situated between heaven (the tower) and hell (the dungeon in the valley).
9. I.e., and won that which wasters destroyed with gluttony. An opposition between winners and wasters was a common idea during the period.

And somme putten hem° to pride, apparailed hem therafter,   *themselves*
In contenaunce of clothynge comen disgised.[1]

25 In preieres° and penaunce putten hem manye,   *prayers*
Al for love of Oure Lord lyveden° ful streyte°   *living / strictly*
In hope to have heveneriche° blisse—   *heavenly*
As ancres and heremites that holden hem in hire selles,
Coveiten noght in contree to cairen aboute
30 For no likerous liflode hire likame to plese.[2]
    And somme chosen chaffare;° they cheveden° the   *trade / succeeded*
        bettre—
As it semeth to oure sight that swiche men thryveth;
And somme murthes° to make as mynstralles   *entertainments*
        konne,°   *know how*
And geten gold with hire glee°—synnelees,° I   *singing / guiltless*
        leeve.°   *believe*
35 Ac japeres° and jangeleres, Judas children,[3]   *jesters*
Feynen hem fantasies, and fooles hem maketh,
And han wit at wille to werken if they sholde.[4]
That Poul[5] precheth of hem I wol nat preve° it here: *prove*
Qui loquitur turpiloquium is Luciferes hyne.[6]
40   Bidderes° and beggeres faste aboute yede°   *beggars / went*
[Til] hire bely and hire bagge [were] bredful ycrammed;[7]
Faiteden° for hire foode, foughten at the ale.°   *begged falsely / alehouse*
In glotonye, God woot,° go thei to bedde,   *knows*
And risen with ribaudie,° tho Roberdes knaves;[8]   *obscenities*
45 Sleep and sory° sleuthe° seweth hem evere.°   *wretched / sloth / follow*
    Pilgrymes and palmeres plighten hem togidere
To seken Seint Jame and seintes in Rome;[9]
Wenten forth in hire wey° with many wise tales,°   *way / speeches*
And hadden leve° to lyen° al hire lif after.   *leave / tell lies*
50 I seigh° somme that seiden° thei hadde ysought seintes: *saw / said*
To ech a tale that thei tolde hire tonge was tempred° to lye   *tuned*
Moore than to seye sooth,° it semed bi hire speche.   *truth*
    Heremytes on an heep° with hoked° staves   *crowd / crooked*
Wenten to Walsyngham[1]—and hire wenches after:

1. I.e., and dressed themselves accordingly, disguised in an outward show of finery.
2. I.e., like anchorites and hermits who keep to their cells, instead of coveting to wander ("cairen") about the land ("contree") in order to indulge their bodies ("likame") with a luxurious way of life ("likerous liflode"). An anchorite (male) or anchoress (female) vowed to live a reclusive, religious life in a cell.
3. A proverbial term for sinners.
4. I.e., they devise fantasies and make fools of themselves even though they possess intelligence if they should choose to work.
5. Perhaps an allusion to St. Paul's words in 2 Thessalonians 3.10: "For even when we were with you, this we commanded you, that if any would not work, neither should he eat."
6. "He who utters foul speech" (Latin) is the devil's servant; the quotation is not from St. Paul (nor does Langland say that it is), but it does bear some resemblance to his words in Ephesians 5.4 and Colossians 3.8.
7. I.e., until their bellies and their bags were

crammed to the brimful; a bag was carried by beggars for receiving the food bestowed on them as alms.
8. A term for robbers; "roberdes" men were lawless vagabonds, notorious for their crimes during the period when *Piers Plowman* was written. A statute by King Richard II ordained that the statute of King Edward concerning "Roberdesmen, wastours and drawlacches" must be strictly observed.
9. I.e., pilgrims and palmers pledged themselves to visit famous shrines of the day. Palmers were pilgrims who had gone to the Holy Land, and carried a palm leaf or a badge in token of their journey. The shrine of St. James, or Santiago, was a famous place of pilgrimage in Spain, and one of the four pilgrimages assigned as penance for particularly grave sins. Rome was known for its many shrines.
1. The Walsingham shrine was the most famous shrine in England dedicated to the Virgin Mary. Cf. "A Lament for Our Lady's Shrine at Walsingham" (p. 104).

55 Grete lobies and longe that lothe were to swynke
    Clothed hem in copes to ben knowen from othere,
    And shopen hem heremytes hire ese to have.[2]
        I fond there freres, alle the foure ordres,[3]
    Prechynge the peple for profit of [the] womb[e]:°   belly
60 Glosed the gospel as hem good liked;[4]
    For coveitise of copes construwed it as thei wolde.
    Manye of this maistres freres mowe clothen hem at likyng[5]
    For hire moneie° and marchaundise marchen togideres.   money
    For sith charite hath ben chapman and chief to shryve lordes[6]
65 Manye ferlies° han fallen in a fewe yeres.   wondrous events
    But Holy Chirche and hii holde bettre togidres
    The mooste meschief on molde is mountynge up faste.[7]
        Ther preched a pardoner as he a preest were:[8]
    Broughte forth a bulle with bisshopes seles,
70 And seide that hymself myghte assoillen° hem alle   absolve
    Of falshede° of fastynge, of avowes° ybroken.   deceit / vows
    Lewed° men leved hym wel and liked hise wordes,   unlearned
    Comen up knelynge to kissen hise bulles.
    He bonched hem with his brevet and blered hire eighen,
75 And raughte with his rageman rynges and broches.[9]
    Thus [ye] gyven [youre] gold glotons to helpe,
    And leneth it losels that leccherie haunten![1]
    Were the bisshop yblessed and worth bothe his eris,
    His seel[2] sholde noght be sent to deceyve the peple.
80 Ac it is noght by the bisshop that the boy° precheth[3] —   rogue
    For the parisshe preest and the pardoner parten° the silver   divide
    That the povere° [peple] of the parissche sholde have if they   poor
        ne were.
        Persons° and parisshe preestes pleyned° hem to   rectors / complained
        the bisshop
    That hire parisshes weren povere sith the pestilence tyme,°   plague
85 To have a licence and leve° at London to dwelle,   permission

---

2. Lubbers ("lobies") or tall ("longe") idle louts, who are loath to work ("swynke"), disguised themselves as hermits in order to have their comfort. "Copes": the special dress of a friar or monk.
3. The four orders of friars: the Carmelites, Augustinians, Dominicans or Jacobins, and Franciscans.
4. Complaints were frequently made in medieval literature that friars interpreted ("glosed") the Scriptures to serve their own purposes.
5. I.e., many of these masters can ("mowe") dress themselves as they like.
6. I.e., since Charity (or those who claim to work for it) has become a merchant and first ("chief") to hear the confessions ("shryve") of noblemen; alluding to money received by friars for hearing confessions.
7. I.e., unless Holy Church and they ("hii": i.e., the friars) hold together better, then great misfortune ("meschief") on earth ("molde") is coming.
8. I.e., as if he were a priest. A pardoner was empowered by the Pope to supply an indulgence for a sin, in return for some payment toward the Church. An indulgence granted remission of pun-

ishment by the Church for the sin, but not forgiveness from the guilt of the sin. While the payment was supposed to be a voluntary contribution to the works of the Church, the system was open to the kind of abuse shown in this pardoner. A papal bull was a formal statement of "indulgence," and the seals of bishops in whose diocese the pardoner was (ostensibly) licensed to preach were affixed to it.
9. I.e., he struck ("bonched") them with his document ("brevet"), and bleared their eyes, and thus got ("raughte") rings and brooches with his bull ("rageman": a long parchment with ragged edges), in payment for pardon.
1. I.e., thus you give your gold to help gluttons, and hand it ("leneth") to wretches ("losels") who indulge in lechery.
2. Seal of authorization. "Worth bothe his eris": i.e., worthy to have his ears, being alert and vigilant.
3. I.e., it is not with the bishop's permission; thus, the pardoner has illicitly obtained the bishop's seal; moreover, he has bribed the parish priest and divides the money with him.

And syngen ther for symonie[4] for silver is swete.
Bisshopes and bachelers, bothe maistres and doctours—
That han cure under Crist, and crownynge in tokene
And signe that thei sholden shryven hire parisshens,
90 Prechen and praye for hem, and the povere fede—
Liggen in Londoun in Lenten and ellis.[5]
Somme serven the King and his silver tellen,°   keep account of
In the Cheker and in the Chauncelrie chalangen hise dettes
Of wardes and of wardemotes, weyves and streyves.[6]
95 And somme serven as servaunts lordes and ladies,
And in stede° of stywardes sitten and demen.°   position / judge
Hire messe° and hire matyns° and many of   masses / morning prayers
    hire houres°   divine offices
Arn doone undevoutliche;° drede is at the laste   undevoutly
Lest Crist in his Consistorie[7] acorse° ful manye!   condemn
100 I parcevved° of the power that Peter hadde to kepe—   comprehended
To bynden and to unbynden, as the Book telleth[8]—
How he it lefte with love as Oure Lorde highte°   commanded
Amonges foure vertues,[9] most vertuous of alle vertues,
That cardinals ben called and closynge yates[1]
105 There Crist is in kyngdom, to close and to shette,°   shut
And to opene it to hem and hevene blisse shewe.
Ac of the Cardinals at court that kaughte of that name
And power presumed in hem a Pope to make
To han the power that Peter hadde, impugnen I nelle[2]—
110 For in love and lettrure° the eleccion[3] bilongeth;   learning
Forthi° I kan and kan naught of court speke moore.   therefore

4. I.e., and sing masses for payment ("simony": the practice of buying or selling ecclesiastical preferment); after the plague caused depopulation and a loss of tithes and income, many priests went to London to make money by saying masses for the souls of rich dead persons.
5. I.e., those who have responsibility under Christ, and clerical tonsure (or "crownynge": the part of a monk's or priest's head that has been shaved) as a symbol of their responsibility to hear the confessions of their parishioners, instead reside ("Liggen") in London in Lent (the busiest time of the Christian year) and at other times ("ellis").
6. In the courts, those serving the king claim dues arising to him from guardianship cases ("wardes"), meetings held in each ward ("wardemotes"), lost property ("weyves") and stray animals ("streyves"). The Exchequer ("Cheker") was the commission to receive revenue and the audit of accounts; the Chancery ("Chauncelrie") heard petitions addressed to the king.
7. A consistory court was held by a bishop or his official to consider any case in which an ecclesias

tic was involved.
8. In Matthew 16.15, Christ tells Peter: "And I will give unto thee the keys of the kingdom of heaven: and whatsoever thou shalt bind on earth shall be bound in heaven: and whatsoever thou shalt loose on earth shall be loosed in heaven."
9. The four cardinal virtues: prudence, temperance, fortitude, and justice.
1. Closing gates. A rough translation of Latin cardinalis, which is derived from cardo, or "hinge"; thus the power of the four cardinal virtues is made into the power of the hinges on the gates to heaven, where Christ rules. The word "cardinals" also plays on a double meaning, referring to the cardinals of the papal consistory.
2. I.e., but of the cardinals (or church officials) who grabbed ("kaughte") that name, and presumed to claim they have the power St. Peter had to name a pope, I will not find fault with them. Perhaps an allusion to the French cardinals who elected an antipope in 1378 (Clement VII, a Frenchman), thus resulting in the Great Schism.
3. Election of popes; also a reference to salvation.

CHARLES D'ORLÉANS[1]

1391–1465

The Smiling Mouth

The smiling mouth and laughing eyen° gray,	*eyes*
The breastes round and long small° armes twain,°	*slender / two*
The handes smooth, the sides straight and plain,	
Your feetes lit°—what should I further say?	*little*
5 It is my craft° when ye are far away	*practice*
To muse thereon in stinting° of my pain—	*soothing*
The smiling mouth and laughing eyen gray,	
The breastes round and long small armes twain.	
So would I pray you, if I durst or may,	
10 The sight to see as I have seen,	
Forwhy° that craft me is most fain,°	*because / pleasing*
And will be to the hour in which I day°—	*die*
The smiling mouth and laughing eyen gray,	
The breastes round and long small armes twain.	

Oft in My Thought

Oft in my thought full busily have I sought,	
Against the beginning of this fresh new year,	
What pretty thing that I best given ought	
To her that was mine hearte's lady dear;[2]	
5 But all that thought bitane° is fro° me clear	*taken / from*
Since death, alas, hath closed her under clay	
And hath this world fornaked° with her here—	*stripped bare*
God have her soul, I can no better say.	
But for to keep in custom, lo, my thought,	
10 And of my seely° service the manere,	*simple*
In showing als° that I forget her not	*also*
Unto each wight,[3] I shall to my powere	
This dead her serve with masses and prayere;[4]	
For all too foul a shame were me, mafay,°	*by my faith*
15 Her to forget this time that nigheth° near—	*draws*
God have her soul, I can no better say.	
To her profit now nis° there to be bought	*is not*
None other thing all° will I buy it dear;[5]	*although*
Wherefore, thou Lord that lordest° all aloft,	*rules*

1. Imprisoned in England for nearly twenty-five years at the end of the Hundred Years War, d'Orléans wrote many poems in English as well as in his native French. This lyric is a *rondel*, with a refrain in lines 1 and 2, 7 and 8, and 13 and 14.
2. The occasion of the poem is the approaching New Year; New Year's Day was the day for gift-giving during the Middle Ages. The speaker asks what gift he can give his love, who is dead. He can endow masses, but the poem itself, a *ballade*, is a symbolic gift in memory of the lady.
3. Person; the speaker wants to show everyone that he does not forget his lady.
4. I.e., I will serve this dead woman ("her") to the best of my power with masses and prayer.
5. I.e., if anything else could help her, I would pay any cost.

20 My deedes take, such as goodness steer,
    And crown her, Lord, within thine heavenly sphere
        As for most truest lady, may I say,
    Most good, most fair, and most benign of cheer° —   *countenance*
    God have her soul, I can no better say.

25 When I her praise, or praising of her hear,
    Although it whilom° were to me pleasere,   *formerly*
        It fill enough it doth mine heart today,
    And doth° me wish I clothed had my bier[6] —   *makes*
    God have her soul, I can no better say.

ANONYMOUS LYRICS OF THE FIFTEENTH CENTURY[1]

Adam Lay I-bounden[2]

Adam lay i-bounden,° bounden in a bond;   *bound*
Foure thousand winter[3] thought he not too long.
And all was for an apple, an apple that he took,
As clerkes finden written in theire book.

5   Ne hadde the apple taken been,[4] the apple taken been,
    Ne hadde never our Lady aye been Heaven's queen.[5]
    Blessed be the time that apple taken was,
    Therefore we may singen, "*Deo gracias!*"[6]

I Sing of a Maiden[7]

I sing of a maiden
    That is makeles:[8]
King of alle kinges
    To° her sone she chees.°   *for / chose*

6. A movable stand on which a corpse is placed before burial; i.e., I wish that I had died.
1. The poems in this section do not appear in chronological order, since they cannot be dated with any certainty. Like the "Anonymous Lyrics of the Thirteenth and Fourteenth Centuries," these works often blend religious and secular themes; the line between sacred love and erotic love is particularly ambiguous in poems such as "I Have a Young Sister" and "The Corpus Christi Carol."
   English poems explicitly titled "carols" first appear in fifteenth-century manuscripts. In earlier centuries, the term usually denoted a ring-dance accompanied by singing that originated in France (the French *carole*) and was fashionable during Chaucer's lifetime. In the fifteenth and sixteenth centuries, carols were poems with uniform stanzas often rhyming *aaab* and linked by the last rhyme to a "burden" or refrain. The burden typically appears at the beginning of the carol and after each stanza. Carols initially treated many subjects, even celebrations of battle-victories as in the "Carol of Agincourt" below. Gradually, however, they became associated, as they are today, with the feast of Christmas.
2. This poem survives only in a fifteenth-century manuscript collection of carols. It explores the theological idea of the *felix culpa* ("happy fault" [Latin]). The poet, in a kind of humorous, courtly gesture, identifies the happy event not as humankind's redemption but as the elevation of the Virgin Mary as queen of heaven.
3. One tradition placed the Creation at about 4000 B.C.
4. I.e., if the apple had not been taken.
5. I.e., Christ's mother, Mary.
6. "Thanks be to God" (Latin).
7. This poem celebrating the "immaculate conception" of Christ appears in a manuscript containing a variety of English ballads and carols as well as several songs in Latin.
8. A triple pun: mateless, matchless, and spotless.

5   He cam also° stille°   *as / silently*
      Ther° his moder° was   *where / mother*
      As dewe in Aprille
      That falleth on the gras.

      He cam also stille
10   To his modres bowr[9]
      As dewe in Aprille
      That falleth on the flowr.

      He cam also stille
      Ther his moder lay
15   As dewe in Aprille
      That falleth on the spray.°   *budding twig*

      Moder and maiden°   *virgin*
      Was nevere noon but she:
      Well may swich° a lady   *such*
20   Godes moder be.

Out of Your Sleep Arise and Wake

Noel, noel, noel,[1]
Noel, noel, noel!

Out of your sleep[2] arise and wake,
For God mankind° now hath i-take,°   *human nature / taken*
5   All of° a maid without any make:°   *from / match, mate*
      Of all women she beareth the bell.[3]

    Noel, noel, noel . . .

And through a maide fair and wise
Now man is made of full great price;°   *worth*
10   Now angels kneel to man's servise,
      And at this time all this befell.

    Noel, noel, noel . . .

Now man is brighter than the sun;
Now man in heaven on high shall wone;°   *dwell*
15   Blessed be God this game[4] is begun,
      And his mother empress of hell.[5]

    Noel, noel, noel . . .

9. A covert made of leafy branches; also, a bed-chamber.
1. A word sung as an expression of joy, originally to commemorate Christ's birth; in this carol, included with music in two fifteenth-century manuscripts, the refrain celebrates both Christ and his virgin mother.
2. Figuratively, the repose of death; also, inactivity or sluggishness.
3. I.e., takes the prize; also, takes the foremost position; also, with a pun on bearing a child.
4. I.e., joy, delight.
5. According to medieval Catholic doctrine, Mary, as queen of heaven, had the power to intercede for those sent to hell.

That° ever was thrall,° now is he free;   *who / captive*
That ever was small, now great is she;
20   Now shall God deem° both thee and me   *judge*
      Unto his bliss if we do well.

      Noel, noel, noel . . .

      Now man may to heaven wend;°   *go*
      Now heaven and earth to him they bend;
25   He that was foe now is our friend.
      This is no nay that I you tell.[6]

      Noel, noel, noel . . .

      Now, blessèd brother, grant us grace
      At doomesday[7] to see thy face
30   And in thy court to have a place,
      That we may there sing noel.

      Noel, noel, noel . . .

I Have a Young Sister

      I have a yong sister
          Fer° beyond the sea;   *far*
      Manye be the druries°   *love tokens*
          That she sente me.

5   She sente me the cherry
          Withouten any stone,
      And so she did the dove
          Withouten any bone.

      She sente me the brere°   *briar*
10   Withouten any rinde;°   *bark*
      She bade me love my lemman°   *sweetheart*
          Without longing.

      How should any cherry
          Be withoute stone?
15   And how should any dove
          Be withoute bone?

      How should any brere
          Be withoute rind?
      How should I love my lemman
20   Without longing?

      When the cherry was a flowr,
          Then hadde it no stone.

6. I.e., what I tell you cannot be denied.   7. Day of God's final judgment.

When the dove was an ey,°   *egg*
Then hadde it no bone.

25   When the briar was unbred,[8]
Then hadde it no rinde.
When the maiden hath that she loveth,
She is without longinge.

I Have a Gentle Cock

I have a gentle° cock,   *noble*
Croweth me day;
He doth me risen[9] early
My matins° for to say.   *morning prayers*

5   I have a gentle cock,
Comen he is of great;°   *lofty lineage*
His comb is of red coral,
His tail is of jet.°   *black*

I have a gentle cock,
10   Comen he is of kind;°   *good stock*
His comb is of red coral,
His tail is of inde.°   *indigo*

His legges be of azure,
So gentle and so small;°   *slender*
15   His spurres are of silver white
Into the wortewale.[1]

His eyen° are of crystal,   *eyes*
Locked° all in amber;   *set*
And every night he percheth him
20   In my lady's chamber.

Timor Mortis[2]

In what estate[3] so ever I be
Timor mortis conturbat me.

As I went on a merry morning,
I heard a bird both weep and sing.
5   This was the tenor° of her talking: *meaning*
"*Timor mortis conturbat me.*"

8. Ungrown, i.e., still in the seed.
9. Makes me rise. "Croweth me day": crows at daybreak.
1. I.e., down to the base or imbedded portion of the spurs. "Spurres": back claws.
2. The title and refrain of this poem come from a prayer recited (in Latin) during the Catholic religious rite known as the Office of the Dead. "Since I have been sinning daily and repenting not," the prayer says, "the fear of death dismays me" (*timor mortis conturbat me*). A number of other medieval

lyrics use the same line as their refrain, as does the later poem by William Dunbar (see p. 71). This poem is unusual in combining the carol form with a narrative convention—that of the "unexpected encounter"—typical of the *chanson d'aventure* ("adventure song" [French]).
3. Condition; also, more specifically, an allusion to the medieval view of society as divided into three great "estates," the nobility, the clergy, and the workers.

I asked that bird what she meant.
"I am a musket[4] both fair and gent;°   *gentle, noble*
For dread of death I am all shent:°   *ruined*
10   *Timor mortis conturbat me.*

"When I shall die, I know no day;
What country or place I cannot say;
Wherefore this song sing I may:
Timor mortis conturbat me.

15   "Jesu Christ, when he should die,
To his Father he gan° say,   *began [to]*
'Father,' he said, 'in Trinity,[5]
Timor mortis conturbat me.'

"All Christian people, behold and see:
20   This world is but a vanity
And replete with necessity.
Timor mortis conturbat me.

"Wake I or sleep, eate or drink,
When I on my last end° do think,   *death*
25   For greate fear my soul do shrink:
Timor mortis conturbat me.

"God grant us grace him for to serve,
And be at our end when we sterve,°   *die*
And from the fiend° he us preserve.   *devil*
30   *Timor mortis conturbat me.*"

The Corpus Christi Carol[6]

Lully, lullay, lully, lullay,[7]
The falcon hath born my make° away.   *mate*

He bore him up, he bore him down,
He bore him into an orchard brown.

5   *Lully, lullay, lully, lullay, . . .*

In that orchard there was a hall
That was hanged with purple and pall.°   *black velvet*

---

4. Male sparrowhawk.
5. The Christian doctrine that God the Father, God the Son, and God the Holy Ghost form one true eternal God.
6. The title of this carol, Latin for "body of Christ," alludes both to the sacrament of the Holy Communion and to a feast of the Church in celebration of that sacrament. The appearance of the words on a stone in the poem's final line has led some critics to interpret the wounded knight as the crucified Christ and/or as the "Fisher King," a Christianized version of a hero in an ancient fertility myth.
The version of the carol printed here first appears in a sixteenth-century manuscript anthology, and some scholars believe that the poem itself dates from that century rather than from the fifteenth. The late dating has given rise to a historical-allegorical interpretation that takes the knight as a figure for King Henry VIII (1492–1547). He divorced his first wife, Katherine of Aragon, in order to marry Anne Boleyn, whose heraldic badge was a falcon.
7. This lullabylike refrain appears only in the version of the carol printed here, although several other versions have been recorded by folk-song collectors.

Lully, lullay, lully, lullay, . . .

And in that hall there was a bed,
10   It was hanged with gold so red.

Lully, lullay, lully, lullay, . . .

And in that bed there lieth a knight,
His woundes bleeding day and night.

Lully, lullay, lully, lullay, . . .

15   By that bed's side there kneeleth a may°   maiden
And she weepeth both night and day.

Lully, lullay, lully, lullay, . . .

And by that bed's side there standeth a stone,
Corpus Christi written thereon.

20   *Lully, lullay, lully, lullay, . . .*

Western Wind[8]

Western wind, when will thou blow,
The small rain down can rain?
Christ, if my love were in my arms
And I in my bed again!

A Lyke-Wake Dirge[9]

This ae° night, this ae night,   one
   Every night and all,
Fire and sleet[1] and candle-light,
   And Christ receive thy saul.°   soul

5   When thou from hence away are past,
      Every night and all,
   To Whinny-muir thou comest at last:
      And Christ receive thy saul.

   If ever thou gavest hosen and shoon,°   stockings and shoes
10   *Every night and all,*
   Sit thee down and put them on:
      And Christ receive thy saul.

8. This lyric survives, with music, in an early-sixteenth-century manuscript. Although it seems to be a secular love song, several Tudor composers used it in settings of the Mass.
9. A dirge is a lament for the dead and is linked here to the traditional watch ("wake") over the corpse ("lyke"). The poem dramatizes the soul's progress after death: to "Whinny-muir" (line 6), or "prickly moor," *whin* being a name for various prickly shrubs; to "Brig" (bridge) of Dread (line 21); and to purgatory (line 23). These places represent different stages of possible punishment in the afterlife. The opening refrain, or burden, is repeated in its entirety at the end; intervening stanzas repeat only its second and fourth lines.
1. Salt, sometimes placed with earth on the breast of the dead as emblematic of soul and body.

If hosen and shoon thou ne'er gavest nane,°   *none*
   Every night and all,
15   The whins shall prick thee to the bare bane:°   *bone*
   And Christ receive thy saul.

From Whinny-muir when thou mayst pass,
   Every night and all,
To Brig o' Dread thou comest at last:
20   *And Christ receive thy saul.*

From Brig o' Dread when thou mayst pass,
   Every night and all,
To purgatory fire thou comest at last:
   And Christ receive thy saul.

25   If ever thou gavest meat or drink,
   Every night and all,
The fire shall never make thee shrink:
   And Christ receive thy saul.

If meat or drink thou ne'er gavest nane,
30   *Every night and all,*
The fire will burn thee to the bare bane:
   And Christ receive thy saul.

This ae night, this ae night,
   Every night and all,
35   *Fire and sleet and candle-light:*
   And Christ receive thy saul.

A carol of Agincourt[2]

Deo gracias, Anglia,
Redde pro victoria.[3]

Oure kinge went forth to Normandy
With grace and might of chivalry.°   *men at arms*
5   Ther God for him wrought mervelusly:
Wherefore Englonde may calle and cry.

Deo gracias . . .

He sette a sege, the sothe° for to say,   *truth*
To Harflu towne with ryal array:[4]
10   That towne he wan and made affray°   *terror*
That Fraunce shall riwe° till Domesday.°   *rue / Last Judgment*

2. This is one of several poems in carol form celebrating the English victory over the French at Agincourt in 1415. This version is accompanied by music for solo voices and chorus. Contemporary accounts record a number of celebratory processions on Henry V's triumphant return to London at which such songs were sung. "Carol" is used here in the sense of a poem in short stanzas with a burden or refrain ("Deo gracias . . .") that is repeated after each stanza.
3. "Return thanks to God, England, for victory" (Latin).
4. Display of his military forces; Henry laid siege to and captured the French port of Harfleur shortly before the victory at Agincourt.

Deo gracias . . .

	Than went oure kinge with alle his hoste°	*army*
	Thorwe Fraunce, for alle the Frenshe boste:[5]	
15	He spared, no drede, of lest ne moste,[6]	
	Till he come to Agincourt coste.°	*district*

Deo gracias . . .

	Than, forsoth,° that knight comely°	*truly / handsome*
	In Agincourt feld° he faught manly.	*field*
20	Thorw grace of God most mighty	
	He had bothe the felde and the victory.	

Deo gracias . . .

	There dukis and erlis, lorde and barone,	
	Where take° and slaine, and that well sone,°	*captured / quickly*
25	And summe were ladde° into Lundone°	*led / London*
	With joye and merthe and grete renone.°	*pomp*

Deo gracias . . .

	Now gracious God he save oure kinge,[7]	
	His peple and alle his well-willinge:°	*friends*
30	Yef° him gode life and gode ending,	*give*
	That we with merthe mowe° safely singe,	*may*

Deo gracias . . .

The Sacrament of the Altar[8]

	It semes white and is red;	
	It is quike° and semes dede;°	*living / dead*
	It is fleshe and semes bred;	
	It is on and semes too;[9]	
5	It is God body and no mo.°	*more*

See! here, my heart[1]

	O! Mankinde,	
	Have in thy minde	
	My Passion smert,°	*painful*
	And thou shall finde	
5	Me full kinde—	
	Lo! here my hert.	

---

5. I.e., in spite of French boasts or threats.
6. I.e., he spared, no doubt, neither the great nor the humble; some editors print this line without punctuation, in which case it may be read: he avoided no dangers, great or small.
7. I.e., may he save our king.
8. This poem, which dates from about 1450, examines the paradox of the sacrament of the bread used in the Communion service; according to the doctrine of transubstantiation, the bread becomes the living body of Christ.
9. Two, probably a reference to the bread and wine of the Eucharist; "on": one.
1. This poem is an early type of "emblem poem," a verse that interprets a symbolic picture. In a manuscript from the early 1500s, the poem appears to the right of the face of a naked and wounded Christ who is offering a kneeling suppliant a large and bleeding heart with a wound in its center.

WILLIAM DUNBAR

ca. 1460–ca. 1525

Lament for the Makaris[1]

I that in heill° was and gladness,	*health*
Am troublit now with great seikness,°	*sickness*
And feeblit with infirmity:	
Timor Mortis conturbat me.[2]	

5	Our plesance here is all vain-glory	
	This false warld is bot transitory,	
	The flesh is brukill,° the Fiend is sle;°	*frail / sly*
	Timor Mortis conturbat me.	

	The state of man dois change and vary,	
10	Now sound, now seik, now blyth,° now sary,°	*happy / sorry*
	Now dansand merry, now like to die;[3]	
	Timor Mortis conturbat me.	

	No state in erd° here standis siccar;°	*earth / securely*
	As with the wind wavis° the wicker,°	*waves / willow*
15	Wavis this warldis vanitie;	
	Timor Mortis conturbat me.	

	Unto the deid gois all Estatis,[4]	
	Princes, Prelatis,° and Potestatis,°	*prelates / potentates*
	Baith rich and puir° of all degree;	*poor*
20	*Timor Mortis conturbat me.*	

	He takis the knichtis into the field,	
	Enarmit under helm and shield;	
	Victor he is at all mêlée;°	*battles*
	Timor Mortis conturbat me.	

25	That strang° unmerciful tyrand	*strong*
	Takis on the moderis breist soukand°	*sucking*
	The babe, full of benignite;°	*gentleness*
	Timor Mortis conturbat me.	

	He takis the champion in the stour,°	*battle*
30	The capitane closit in the tour,°	*tower*
	The lady in bour° full of beautie;	*bedroom*
	Timor Mortis conturbat me.	

	He sparis no lord for his puissance,	
	Na clerk° for his intelligence;	*scholar*

---

1. Poets.
2. "The fear of death dismays me" (Latin); a line from the Office of the Dead. Cf. the anonymous fifteenth-century poem with the same refrain (p. 66).
3. I.e., now dance and be merry, now likely to die.
4. Estates; society was said to be divided into three estates, or groups: those who ruled, those who prayed, and those who labored.

35 His awful straik° may no man flee;   stroke
   Timor Mortis conturbat me.

   Art magicianis,[5] and astrologis,°   astrologers
   Rethoris,° logicianis, and theologis,   rhetoricians
   Them helpis no conclusionis sle;°   sly, clever
40 *Timor Mortis conturbat me.*

   In medicine the most° practicianis,   greatest
   Leechis,° surigianis, and phisicianis,   doctors
   Them-self fra deid° may not supple;°   death / help
   Timor Mortis conturbat me.

45 I see that makaris amang the lave°   remainder
   Playis here their pageant, syne° gois to grave;   then
   Sparit° is nocht° their facultie;   spared / not
   Timor Mortis conturbat me.

   He has done piteously devour
50 The noble Chaucer, of makaris flour,°   flower
   The Monk of Bery, and Gower,[6] all three;
   Timor Mortis conturbat me.

   The gude Sir Hew of Eglintoun,[7]
   And eik° Heriot, and Wintoun,   also
55 He has ta'en out of this countrie;
   Timor Mortis conturbat me.

   That scorpion fell has done infec'°   infected
   Maister John Clerk and James Affleck,
   Fra ballad-making and tragedie;
60 *Timor Mortis conturbat me.*

   Holland and Barbour he has bereavit;
   Alas! that he nought with us leavit
   Sir Mungo Lockhart of the Lea;
   Timor Mortis conturbat me.

65 Clerk of Tranent eke he has ta'en,
   That made the Aunteris° of Gawain;[8]   adventures
   Sir Gilbert Hay endit has he;
   Timor Mortis conturbat me.

   He has Blind Harry, and Sandy Traill
70 Slain with his shour° of mortal hail,   shower
   Whilk° Patrick Johnstoun micht nocht flee;   which
   Timor Mortis conturbat me.

5. Those practicing the art of magic.
6. Three English poets. "The Monk of Bery":
John Lydgate (1370?–1451?) wrote a great variety
of verse; he was considered second only to Chau-
cer during the sixteenth century. "Gower": John
Gower (1325?–1408), whose main poem is the
Confessio Amantis.

7. The first in a list of Scots poets, some well-
known (e.g., Dunbar's contemporary Robert Hen-
ryson, line 82), some obscure. Dunbar presented
Walter Kennedy (line 89) as his adversary in the
poem *Flyting of Dunbar and Kennedie.*
8. A hero of Arthurian romance.

He has reft Merser endite,[9]
That did in luve so lively write,
75 So short, so quick, of sentence hie;°   *lively*
    Timor Mortis conturbat me.

He has ta'en Roull of Aberdeen,
And gentle Roull of Corstorphin;
Two better fellowis did no man see;
80   *Timor Mortis conturbat me.*

In Dunfermline he has done roune°   *made a circuit*
With Maister Robert Henryson;
Sir John the Ross embraced has he;
    Timor Mortis conturbat me.

85 And he has now ta'en, last of a',
Gude gentle Stobo and Quintin Shaw,
Of wham all wichtis° has pitie: *creatures*
    Timor Mortis conturbat me.

Gude Maister Walter Kennedy
90 In point of deid lies verily,
Great ruth° it were that so suld be;   *pity*
    Timor Mortis conturbat me.

Sen he has all my brether° ta'en,   *brothers*
He will nocht lat me live alane,
95 On force I maun° his next prey be;   *must*
    Timor Mortis conturbat me.

Sen for the deid remead° is none,   *remedy*
Best is that we for deid dispone,°   *prepare*
Eftir our deid that live may we;
100   *Timor Mortis conturbat me.*

             1508

In Prais of Wemen[1]

Now of wemen this I say for me,
Of erthly thingis nane° may bettir be;   *none*
Thay should haif wirschep° and grit° honoring   *worship / great*
Of men, aboif all othir erthly thing;
5 Rycht° grit dishonour upoun him self he takkis   *right*
In word or deid quha° evir wemen lakkis;°   *who / faults*
Sen that of wemen cumin all are we,
Wemen are wemen and sa° will end and de.°   *so / die*
Wo wirth the fruct wald put the tre to nocht,[2]
10 And wo wirth him rycht so that sayis ocht°   *anything*
Of womanheid that may be ony lak°   *any lack, default*

9. I.e., Death has taken the practice of poetry from Mercer.
1. This poem first appears in the manuscript written for George Bannatyne in 1568, and may have been written for James IV's queen, Margaret, to whom Dunbar addressed several poems.
2. I.e., woe come to the son who would denigrate the mother.

Or sic grit shame upone him for to tak.
Thay us consaif° with pane, and by thame fed   *conceived*
Within thair breistis thair we be boun to bed;
15 Grit pane and wo, and murnyng° mervellus,   *mourning*
Into thair birth thay suffir sair° for us;   *sore*
Than meit and drynk to feid us get we nane,
Bot that we sowk° out of thair breistis bane.°   *suck / harm*
Thay are the confort that we all haif heir,
20 Thair may no man be till us half so deir;
Thay are our verry nest of nurissing;
In lak of thame quha can say ony thing,
That fowll his nest he fylis,° and for thy°   *flees / that*
Exylit° he should be of all gud cumpany;   *exiled*
25 Thair should na wyis° man gif audience,   *wise*
To sic ane without intelligence.
Christ to his fader he had nocht ane man;
Se quhat° wirschep wemen should haif than.   *what*
That Sone is Lord, that Sone is King of kingis,
30 In heaven and earth his majestie ay ringis.
Sen scho[3] hes borne him in hir halines,
And he is well and grund° of all gudnes,   *ground*
All wemen of us should haif honoring,
Service and luve, aboif all othir thing.

1500–10?

JOHN SKELTON

1460–1529

Mannerly Margery Milk and Ale[1]

Ay, beshrew° you! by my fay,°   *curse / faith*
These wanton clerks be nice[2] alway!
Avaunt,° avaunt, my popinjay![3]   *get out*
What, will ye do nothing but play?
5 Tilly vally, straw,[4] let be I say!
    Gup, Christian Clout, gup, Jack of the Vale![5]
    With Mannerly Margery Milk and Ale.

---

3. Since she, i.e., the Virgin Mary.
1. Two copies of this poem survive, with considerable variation between them. Critics disagree about which lines belong to which speaker and about what "happens" between the third and fourth stanzas. The refrain could be divided between Margery and James, or it could be spoken by a third party, as is suggested by an early musical setting that makes the poem a song for three voices.
  "Margery Milk and Ale": an epithet for a servant girl. "Mannerly": well-mannered, with a possible ironic reflection on a serving girl's aspirations.
2. Variously meant foolish, finicky, or lascivious.

The term "clerk" was originally used to describe a member of the clergy (from Latin, *clericus*), although it became a general name for a scholar or student.
3. Parrot; a symbol of vanity.
4. Expressions of contemptuous rejection: fiddlesticks, poppycock, nonsense.
5. A contemptuous name. "Gup": contracted (?) from "go up"; sometimes an exclamation of derision, remonstrance, or surprise, sometimes a command: get along, get out; get up; also, a command to a horse, giddy up. "Christian Clout": an epithet for a rural fellow.

By God, ye be a pretty pode,°   toad
And I love you an whole cart-load.[6]
10 Straw, James Foder,[7] ye play the fode,°   deceiver
I am no hackney[8] for your rod:°   riding
Go watch a bull, your back is broad![9]
    Gup, Christian Clout, gup, Jack of the Vale!
    With Mannerly Margery Milk and Ale.

15 Ywis° ye deal uncourteously;   for certain
What, would ye frumple[1] me? now fy!
What, and ye shall be my pigesnye?[2]
By Christ, ye shall not, no hardely:°   indeed
I will not be japèd[3] bodily!
20   Gup, Christian Clout, gup, Jack of the Vale!
    With Mannerly Margery Milk and Ale.

Walk forth your way, ye cost me nought;
Now have I found that I have sought:
The best cheap flesh that ever I bought.
25 Yet, for his love that all hath wrought,
Wed me, or else I die for thought.
    Gup, Christian Clout, your breath is stale!
    Go, Mannerly Margery Milk and Ale!
    Gup, Christian Clout, gup, Jack of the Vale!
30 With Mannerly Margery Milk and Ale.

ca. 1495   1523

To Mistress Margaret Hussey[4]

Merry Margaret,[5]
    As midsummer flower,
Gentle as falcon
Or hawk of the tower:[6]
5 With solace and gladness,
Much mirth and no madness,
All good and no badness;
    So joyously,
    So maidenly,
10 So womanly
    Her demeaning°   demeanour
In every thing,
Far, far passing
That I can indite,°   compose

6. I.e., a large amount.
7. Jamesweed, ragwort, useless stuff; "straw": expression of contempt.
8. I.e., an ordinary riding horse (as distinct from a warhorse or a plowhorse); a prostitute.
9. I.e., go look after farm animals.
1. Wrinkle, muss up.
2. Pet; also, a common flower.
3. Tricked, with a reference to sexual intercourse.
4. This poem is one of ten lyrics included in Skelton's *The Garland of Laurel*, in which the poet is crowned with a laurel wreath (the symbol of poetic

achievement) by the countess of Surrey and her ladies; in return, he writes a poem in praise of each of them. "Margaret Hussey," while not identified with any certainty, was perhaps the daughter of Simon Blount of Mangotsfield and married to John Hussey; she died in August 1492. "Mistress": title for an upper-class married woman; a courteous form.
5. "Margaret": meaning daisy, a midsummer flower.
6. A hawk bred and trained to fly high.

15   Or suffice to write
        Of Merry Margaret
            As midsummer flower,
        Gentle as falcon
        Or hawk of the tower.
20   As patient and still
        And as full of good will
        As fair Isaphill,⁷
        Coriander,⁸
        Sweet pomander,⁹
25   Good Cassander,¹
        Steadfast of thought,
        Well made, well wrought,
        Far may be sought
        Ere that ye can find
30   So courteous, so kind
        As Merry Margaret,
            This midsummer flower,
        Gentle as falcon
        Or hawk of the tower.

1495, 1522   1523

From Colin Clout²

HEREAFTER FOLLOWETH A LITTLE BOOK CALLED COLIN CLOUT,
COMPILED BY MASTER SKELTON, POET LAUREATE.

*Quis consurget mecum adversus malignantes? aut quis stabit mecum adversus
operantes iniquitatem? Nemo, Domine!*³

        What can it avail⁴
        To drive forth a snail,
        Or to make a sail
        Of an herring's tail;
5   To rhyme or to rail,
        To write or to indict,
        Either for delight

---

7. Hypsipyle, mythological daughter of Thaos, king of Lemnos, was noted for her endurance. She saved her father when the women of Lemnos killed the men of the island, bore twin sons to Jason, and was then deserted by him. She endured slavery while searching for her father and her sons.
8. An aromatic herb, believed to soothe pain.
9. A mixture of perfumed or aromatic substances made into a ball.
1. Cassandra, mythological daughter of Priam, king of Troy; another figure of steadfastness. After she refused him as a lover, Apollo made her a prophet whom listeners would always disbelieve, as they did when she foretold the fall of Troy.
2. Colin, from the Latin *colonus* ("farmer"), was a stock name for a person of humble birth in the late-medieval and Renaissance periods; "clout" has multiple meanings relevant to the poetic persona that Skelton creates and that Spenser significantly imitates in his *Shepheardes Calender* (see his "January Eclogue," p. 147). Skelton plays on meanings not only of humble birth but also of satirical force:

"clout" (variously spelled in this era) can signify a patch of cloth such as those worn by vagrant clerks, a clot or clod of earth (recalling Langland's persona Piers Plowman; see p. 58), a type of rough shoe, and also a blow with the hand. In this poem of more than twelve hundred lines, Skelton uses his verse as a satirical weapon against bishops and archbishops of the English Church who placed worldly ambitions above their ecclesiastical duties. Skelton's prime opponent is Cardinal Thomas Wolsey (ca. 1475–1530), who rose to and fell from great power during Henry VIII's reign (1509–47), and who began the dissolution of monasteries—a process of alleged "reform" that Skelton abhorred.
3. From Psalm 94.14: "Who will rise up for me against the evil-doers? or who will stand up for me against the workers of iniquity?" (Latin). From John 8.11: "No one, lord."
4. I.e., what good can it do; the first four lines and many others in the poem are based on well-known proverbs.

Or else for despight;
Or books to compile
10 Of divers manner of style,
Vice to revile
And sin to exile;
To teach or to preach,
As reason will reach?
15 Say this, and say that,
His⁵ head is so fat,
He wotteth° never what   *knows*
Nor whereof he speaketh;
He crieth and he creaketh,
20 He prieth and he peeketh,⁶
He chides and he chatters,
He prates and he patters,
He clitters° and he clatters,   *chatters*
He meddles and he smatters,
25 He gloses° and he flatters;   *interprets*
Or if he speak plain,
Then he lacketh brain,
He is but a fool;
Let him go to school,
30 On a three footed stool
That he may down sit,
For he lacketh wit;
And if that he hit
The nail on the head,
35 It standeth in no stead;
The devil, they say, is dead,
The devil is dead.⁷
    It may well so be,
Or else they would see
40 Otherwise, and flee
From worldly vanity,
And foul covetousness,
And other wretchedness,
Fickle falseness,
45 Variableness,
With unstableness.
    And if ye stand in doubt
Who brought this rhyme about,
My name is Colin Clout.
50 I purpose° to shake out   *aim*
All my connying bag,
Like a clerkly hag;⁸
For though my rhyme be ragged,

5. Apparently refers to the poet as seen by his detractors, who scorn him whether he writes and prophesies through allegory or speaks "plainly" (line 26).
6. I.e., he pries into things and goads us (or, possibly, he pries and peeks into things).
7. Based on a proverbial saying, these lines evidently express the reaction of an imaginary audience that doesn't want to be bothered by Skelton's critique of evil.
8. Wandering clerks typically carried pouches; although "hag" usually referred to an old woman, it was sometimes used as a general term of abuse. The image of the clerk's "connying" bag, to which the poet compares his own bag of poetic tricks, plays on the meanings of "cunning" both as "knowledge" and as "cheating," duping through cleverness.

Tattered and jagged,
55   Rudely rain beaten,
Rusty and moth eaten,
If ye take well therewith,
It hath in it some pith.°   *meaning*

ca. 1521–22   ca. 1531

Phillip Sparow

HEREAFTER FOLLOWETH [*SELECTIONS FROM*] THE BOOK OF
PHILLIP SPAROW, COMPILED BY MASTER SKELTON, POET LAUREATE.[9]

Pla ce bo,[1]
Who is there, who?
Di le xi,[2]
Dame Margery;
5   Fa, re, my, my,[3]
Wherefore and why, why?
For the soul of Phillip Sparow,
That was late slain at Carow,[4]
Among the Nuns Black,
10   For that sweet soul's sake,
And for all sparrows' souls,
Set in our bead-rolls,[5]
Pater noster qui,
With an *Ave Mari,*[6]
15   And with the corner of a creed,[7]
The more shall be your meed,°   *reward*
Whan I remember again
How my Phillip was slain,
Never half the pain
20   Was between you twain,
Pyramus and Thisbe,[8]

9. In 1488, Skelton received the honorable title of
"laureate" from Oxford University. His *Phillip
Sparow*, a poem of approximately 1380 lines,
begins with a long elegy (lines 1–884) for the pet
sparrow of a gentlewoman named Jane Scrope.
(The second part eulogizes Jane herself, and in the
third part Skelton defends himself against a
detractor.) Imitating classical elegies for dead birds
by Catullus and Ovid and perhaps also the descrip-
tion of how a fox killed Chantekler's daughter in
William Caxton's early printed translation of the
Dutch *Reynard the Fox* (1481), Skelton's poem
makes Jane the first-person comic narrator of the
first part, interweaving her lamenting verse (in the
runnning-rhyme form known as "Skeltonic"; see
"Essay on Versification," p. lxxvii) with Latin
phrases from the solemn Catholic funeral service
called the Office of the Dead.
1. "I shall please [the Lord]," from Psalm 114.9.
The Psalms are cited according to their numbering
in the Catholic Bible known as the "Vulgate."
"Placebo," like all other citations of the Psalms in
this poem, is a phrase used in the "Vespers," or
evening service of the Office of the Dead. The
spacing of the Latin syllables suggests the
plainsong music of the Mass.

2. "I love [the Lord, because he hath heard my
voice]," Psalm 114.1.
3. Musical notes used at the close of the Office of
the Dead.
4. Carrow Abbey, where Jane Scrope went to live
after her mother was widowed for the second time
in 1502. A senior nun named Margery is men-
tioned in the records of this abbey, which was
founded by the Benedictines. "Nuns Black" refers
to the black robes worn by members of the Bene-
dictine order.
5. List of people for whom the nuns prayed with
the "beads" of their rosaries.
6. "Hail Mary"; the previous Latin phrase opens
the Lord's Prayer ("Our Father which . . .").
7. A prayer about Christian beliefs (from *credere*,
Latin for "to believe") that was typically printed,
along with the "Hail Mary" and "Our Father," on
the first page of elementary reading books (prim-
ers). Skelton probably refers to the "corner" of the
"creed" because only part of that prayer usually fit
on the first page of the primer.
8. Lovers tragically separated in a story told by
Ovid (*Metamorphoses*) and Chaucer (*Legend of
Good Women*), among others.

As then befell° to me: *happened*
I wept and I wailèd,
The tears down hailèd;
25 But nothing it availèd[9]
To call Phillip again,
Whom Gib our cat hath slain.
   Gib, I say, our cat
Worrowed[1] her on that
30 Which I loved best:
It can not be expressed
My sorowful heaviness,
But all without redress;
For within that stound,°   *moment*
35 Half slumb'ring, in a sound°   *faint*
I fell down to the ground.
   Unneth° I cast mine eyes   *scarcely*
Toward the cloudy skies:
But when I did behold
40 My sparow dead and cold,
No creature but that would
Have rewed° upon me,   *had pity*
To behold and see
What heaviness did me pang;°   *affect with pain*
45 Wherewith my hands I wrang,
That my sinews cracked,
As though I had been racked,°   *tortured*
So painèd and so strainèd
That no life wellnigh remainèd.
50   I sighed and I sobbed,
For that I was robbed
Of my sparow's life.
O maiden, widow, and wife,
Of what estate ye be,
55 Of high or low degree,
Great sorow then° ye might see,   *then*
And learn to weep at° me!   *from*
Such pains did me fret,
That mine heart did beat,
60 My visage pale and dead,
Wan, and blue as lead;
The pangs of hateful death
Wellnigh had stopped my breath.

                 *   *   *

   Though I have enrolled°   *inscribed*
750 A thousand new and old
Of these historious° tales,   *historical*
To fill bougets° and males°   *bags / pouches*
With books that I have read,
Yet I am nothing sped . . .[2]

9. I.e., it did no good.
1. Worried, i.e., bit. "Gib," short for Gilbert, was a standard name for a cat, as Phillip was for a pet
sparow.
2. I.e., I've gotten nowhere.

* * *

For, as I tofore° have said,   *before*
770 I am but a young maid,
And cannot in effect
My style as yet direct
With English words elect:[3]
Our natural tongue is rude,[4]
775 And hard to be ennewed°   *revived*
With polished terms lusty;
Our language is so rusty,
So cankered,° and so full   *infected*
Of frowards,° and so dull,   *badly formed words*
780 That if I would apply°   *try*
To write ornately,[5]
I wot° not where to find   *know*
Terms to serve my mind.

* * *

Wherefore hold me excused
If I have not well perused°   *studied carefully*
815 Mine English half abused;
Though it be refused,
In worth I shall it take,[6]
And fewer words make.
But, for my sparow's sake,
820 Yet as a woman may,
My wit I shall assay
An epitaph to write
In Latin plain and light,
Whereof the elegy
825 Followeth by and by:
Flos volucrum formose, vale![7]
Philippe, sub isto
Marmore jam recubas,
Qui mihi carus eras.
830 *Semper erunt nitido*
Radiantia sidera cælo;
Impressusque meo
Pectore semper eris.
Per me laurigerum
835 *Britonum Skeltonida vatem*

---

3. Well-chosen; one early edition substitutes "clere" (clear) for "elect."
4. Uneducated, lacking in polish.
5. With rhetorical embellishment of the kind taught in the grammar schools, which focused during Skelton's era on Latin rather than English composition and which were generally closed to girls.
6. I.e., I'll take it in good part.
7. Although Jane claims to write the following lines, Skelton implicitly (and perhaps ironically) undermines her claim by switching to Latin; he explicitly asserts his own authorship of the entire first part of the poem in lines 827–44. Translated, the final lines of the first part of the poem go as follows: "Farewell, flower of birds, beautiful one! Phillip, you lie now beneath this marble, you who were dear to me. So long as the stars shine in the sky, you will always be engraved in my heart. By me, Skelton, the laureate poet of Britain, these things could be sung under a feigned likeness. She whose bird you were is a maiden of surpassing beauty. Nias [presumably one of the classical water nymphs known as 'naiads'] was fair, but Jane is lovelier; Corinna was learned, but Jane is wiser." Corinna is the name of the woman who laments her dead parrot in Ovid's *Amores*.

> *Hæc cecinisse licet*
> *Ficta sub imagine texta.*
> *Cujus eras volucris,*
> *Præstanti corpore virgo:*
> 840 *Candida Nais erat,*
> *Formosior ista Joanna est;*
> *Docta Corinna fuit,*
> *Sed magis ista sapit.*
> *Bien men souient.*[8]

ca. 1505–07   ca. 1545

EARLY MODERN BALLADS[1]

The Douglas Tragedy[2]

1
"Rise up, rise up, now, Lord Douglas," she says,
  "And put on your armor so bright;
Let it never be said that a daughter of thine
  Was married to a lord under night.

2
5 "Rise up, rise up, my seven bold sons,
  And put on your armor so bright,
And take better care of your youngest sister,
  For your eldest's awa'° the last night."   away

3
He's mounted her on a milk-white steed,
10 And himself on a dapple gray,
With a bugelet° horn hung down by his side,   small bugle
  And lightly they rode away.

4
Lord William looked o'er his left shoulder,
  To see what he could see,
15 And there he spied her seven brethren bold,
  Come riding over the lea.°   meadow

---

8. "I remember it well"; translates a French phrase Skelton also uses elsewhere in his poetry.
1. The following ballads exist in numerous versions, many of which are printed in the great collection of F. J. Child, *English and Scottish Popular Ballads* (five volumes, 1882–98). Child's different versions, designated by alphabetical letters here and in his edition, reveal different political and ethical interpretations of a given story; see, for example, the two versions of "Mary Hamilton" included below. Ballads often contain topical allusions, and most popular ballads from the fourteenth through the seventeenth centuries, in contrast to later literary instances of the genre, were sung to well-known tunes. While some ballads originated as folk-songs and were written down (and/or printed) much later (sometimes centuries later), other ballads were initially made to be read—and sold—as printed objects. Even manuscript or printed versions of ballads, among the latter being the "broadsides" printed cheaply on a single sheet and sold at fairs and by peddlers along the road, might subsequently be orally transmitted, since they could be heard and memorized by the non- or partially literate person.
2. From Child, No. 7.B.

5

"Light down, light down, Lady Margret," he said,
  "And hold my steed in your hand,
Until that against your seven brethren bold,
20   And your father, I mak a stand."

6

She held his steed in her milk-white hand,
  And never shed one tear,
Until that she saw her seven brethren fa',°   *fall*
  And her father hard fighting, who loved her so dear.

7

25 "O hold your hand, Lord William!" she said,
  "For your strokes they are wondrous sair;°   *sore*
True lovers I can get many a ane,°   *one*
  But a father I can never get mair."°   *more*

8

O she's ta'en out her handkerchief,
30   It was o' the holland° sae° fine,   *linen / so*
And aye she dighted° her father's bloody wounds, *dressed*
  That were redder than the wine.

9

"O choose, O choose, Lady Margret," he said,
  "O whether will ye gang° or bide?"   *go*
35 "I'll gang, I'll gang, Lord William," she said,
  "For ye have left me no other guide."

10

He's lifted her on a milk-white steed,
  And himself on a dapple gray,
With a bugelet horn hung down by his side,
40   And slowly they baith rade away.

11

O they rade on, and on they rade,
  And a' by the light of the moon,
Until they came to yon wan° water,   *pale*
  And there they lighted down.

12

45 They lighted down to tak a drink
  Of the spring that ran sae clear,
And down the stream ran his good heart's blood,
  And sair she 'gan to fear.

13

"Hold up, hold up, Lord William," she says,
50   "For I fear that you are slain."
" 'Tis naething but the shadow of my scarlet cloak,
  That shines in the water sae plain."

14

O they rade on, and on they rade,
  And a' by the light of the moon,

55 Until they cam to his mother's ha'° door,   *hall*
    And there they lighted down.

15

"Get up, get up, lady mother," he says,
    "Get up, and let me in!
Get up, get up, lady mother," he says,
60   "For this night my fair lady I've win.

16

"O mak my bed, lady mother," he says,
    "O mak it braid° and deep,   *broad*
And lay Lady Margret close at my back,
    And the sounder I will sleep."

17

65 Lord William was dead lang° ere midnight,   *long*
    Lady Margret lang ere day,
And all true lovers that go thegither,°   *together*
    May they have mair luck than they!

18

Lord William was buried in St. Mary's kirk,
70   Lady Margret in Mary's choir;
Out o' the lady's grave grew a bonny red rose,
    And out o' the knight's a briar.

19

And they twa met, and they twa plat,°   *plaited*
    And fain they wad° be near;   *would*
75 And a' the warld might ken° right weel   *know*
    They were twa lovers dear.

20

But by and rade the Black Douglas,
    And wow but he was rough!
For he pulled up the bonny briar,
80   And flang 't in St. Mary's Loch.°   *lake*

Lord Randal[3]

1

"O where ha' you been, Lord Randal, my son?
And where ha' you been, my handsome young man?"
"I ha' been at the greenwood; mother, mak my bed soon,
For I'm wearied wi' huntin', and fain wad° lie down."   *would*

2

5 "And wha° met ye there, Lord Randal, my son?   *who*
And wha met you there, my handsome young man?"
"O I met wi' my true-love; mother, mak my bed soon,
For I'm wearied wi' huntin', and fain wad lie down."

3. Child, No. 12.A.

3

"And what did she give you, Lord Randal, my son?
10 And what did she give you, my handsome young man?"
"Eels fried in a pan; mother, mak my bed soon,
For I'm wearied wi' huntin', and fain wad lie down."

4

"And wha gat your leavin's, Lord Randal, my son?
And wha gat your leavin's, my handsome young man?"
15 "My hawks and my hounds; mother, mak my bed soon,
For I'm wearied wi' huntin', and fain wad lie down."

5

"And what becam of them, Lord Randal, my son?
And what becam of them, my handsome young man?"
"They stretched their legs out and died; mother, mak my bed soon,
20 For I'm wearied wi' huntin', and fain wad lie down."

6

"O I fear you are poisoned, Lord Randal, my son!
I fear you are poisoned, my handsome young man!"
"O yes, I am poisoned; mother, mak my bed soon,
For I'm sick at the heart, and I fain wad lie down."

7

25 "What d' ye leave to your mother, Lord Randal, my son?
What d'ye leave to your mother, my handsome young man?"
"Four and twenty milk kye°; mother, mak my bed soon,   *kine, cattle*
For I'm sick at the heart, and I fain wad lie down."

8

"What d' ye leave to your sister, Lord Randal, my son?
30 What d' ye leave to your sister, my handsome young man?"
"My gold and my silver; mother, mak my bed soon,
For I'm sick at the heart, and I fain wad lie down."

9

"What d' ye leave to your brother, Lord Randal, my son?
What d' ye leave to your brother, my handsome young man?"
35 "My houses and my lands; mother, mak my bed soon,
For I'm sick at the heart, and I fain wad lie down."

10

"What d' ye leave to your true-love, Lord Randal, my son?
What d' ye leave to your true-love, my handsome young man?"
"I leave her hell and fire; mother, mak my bed soon,
40 For I'm sick at the heart, and I fain wad lie down."

Edward[4]

1

"Why does your brand° sae° drap wi' bluid,   *sword / so*
Edward, Edward,
Why does your brand sae drap wi' bluid,
And why sae sad gang° ye, O?"   *go*

4. Child, No. 13.B.

5 "O I ha'e killed my hawk sae guid,°   *good*
  Mither, mither,
O I ha'e killed my hawk sae guid,
  And I had nae mair but he, O."

2

"Your hawke's bluid was never sae reid,°   *red*
10   Edward, Edward,
Your hawke's bluid was never sae reid,
  My dear son I tell thee, O."
"O I ha'e killed my reid-roan steed,
  Mither, mither,
15 O I ha'e killed my reid-roan steed,
  That erst was sae fair and free, O."

3

"Your steed was auld, and ye ha'e gat mair,°   *more*
  Edward, Edward,
Your steed was auld, and ye ha'e gat mair,
20   Some other dule° ye drie,° O."   *grief / suffer*
"O I ha'e killed my fader dear,
  Mither, mither,
O I ha'e killed my fader dear,
  Alas, and wae° is me, O!"   *woe*

4

25 "And whatten° penance wul ye drie for that,   *what sort of*
  Edward, Edward?
And whatten penance wul ye dree for that,
  My dear son, now tell me O?"
"I'll set my feet in yonder boat,
30   Mither, mither,
I'll set my feet in yonder boat,
  And I'll fare over the sea, O."

5

"And what wul ye do wi' your towers and your ha',
  Edward, Edward?
35 And what wul ye do wi' your towers and your ha',
  That were sae fair to see, O?"
"I'll let them stand tul they down fa',
  Mither, mither,
I'll let them stand tul they down fa',
40   For here never mair maun° I be, O."   *must*

6

"And what wul ye leave to your bairns° and your wife,   *children*
  Edward, Edward?
And what wul ye leave to your bairns and your wife,
  Whan ye gang over the sea, O?"
45 "The warlde's room,[5] let them beg thrae° life,   *through*
  Mither, mither,
The warlde's room, let them beg thrae life,
  For them never mair wul I see, O."

---

5. I.e., the wide world.

7

"And what wul ye leave to your ain mither dear,
50   Edward, Edward?
And what wul ye leave to your ain mither dear,
    My dear son, now tell me, O?"
"The curse of hell frae° me sall° ye bear,   *from / shall*
    Mither, mither,
55 The curse of hell frae me sall ye bear,
    Sic° counsels ye gave to me, O."   *such*

The Three Ravens[6]

1

There were three ravens sat on a tree,
    Down a down, hay down, hay down.
There were three ravens sat on a tree,
    With a down,
5 There were three ravens sat on a tree,
They were as black as they might be.
    With a down derry, derry, derry, down, down.

2

The one of them said to his mate,
"Where shall we our breakfast take?"

3

10 "Down in yonder greene field,
There lies a knight slain under his shield.

4

"His hounds they lie down at his feet,
So well they can their master keep.

5

"His hawks they fly so eagerly,°   *fiercely*
15 There's no fowl dare him come nigh."

6

Down there comes a fallow[7] doe,
As great with young as she might go.

7

She lift up his bloody head
And kissed his wounds that were so red.

8

20 She got him up upon her back
And carried him to earthen lake.°   *ditch*

9

She buried him before the prime;[8]
She was dead herself ere even-song time.

---

6. Child, No. 26; first printed in a songbook in 1611. All stanzas follow the pattern of the first, with the refrain in lines 2, 4, and 7, and the first line repeated in line 5.
7. A species of deer distinguished by color ("fal-low": pale brownish or reddish yellow) from the red deer.
8. According to Catholic Church ritual, the first hour of the day, between 6 and 9 A.M.

10

God send every gentleman
25   Such hawks, such hounds, and such a leman.°   *lover, sweetheart*

Sir Patrick Spens⁹

1

The king sits in Dumferling town,
    Drinking the blude-reid° wine: *blood-red*
"O whar will I get guid sailor,
    To sail this ship of mine?"

2

5   Up and spak° an eldern knicht,   *spoke*
    Sat at the king's richt knee:
"Sir Patrick Spens is the best sailor
    That sails upon the sea."

3

The king has written a braid¹ letter
10   And signed it wi' his hand,
And sent it to Sir Patrick Spens,
    Was walking on the sand.

4

The first line that Sir Patrick read,
    A loud lauch° lauched he;   *laugh*
15   The next line that Sir Patrick read,
    The tear blinded his ee.°   *eye*

5

"O wha is this has done this deed,
    This ill deed done to me,
To send me out this time o' the year,
20   To sail upon the sea?

6

"Mak haste, mak haste, my mirry men all,
    Our guid ship sails the morn."
"O say na sae,° my master dear,   *so*
    For I fear a deadly storm.

7

25   "Late, late yestre'en I saw the new moon
    Wi' the auld moon in hir arm,
And I fear, I fear, my dear master,
    That we will come to harm."

---

9. Child, No. 58.A. "Sir Patrick Spens," first printed in 1765, tells a story that may be based on two voyages of thirteenth-century Scots noblemen to conduct princesses to royal marriages. Margaret, daughter of Alexander III, was married in 1281 to Eric of Norway, and many members of her escort were drowned on the voyage home. Her daughter, also named Margaret, was drowned with her escort on the way to a marriage in Scotland in 1290. In Child version H, Patrick is sent to Norway to bring the king's daughter home. In all versions, Patrick is sent to sea against his will.
1. Broad, i.e., long.

8

O our Scots nobles were richt laith°   *loath*
30   To weet° their cork-heeled shoon,°   *wet / shoes*
But lang or° a' the play were played   *before*
    Their hats they swam aboon.[2]

9

O lang,° lang may their ladies sit,   *long*
    Wi' their fans into their hand,
35   Or ere they see Sir Patrick Spens
    Come sailing to the land.

10

O lang, lang may the ladies stand
    Wi' their gold kems° in their hair,   *combs*
Waiting for their ain dear lords,
40   For they'll see them na mair.

11

Half o'er, half o'er to Aberdour
    It's fifty fadom deep,
And there lies guid Sir Patrick Spens
    Wi' the Scots lords at his feet.

The Unquiet Grave[3]

1

"The wind doth blow today, my love,
    And a few small drops of rain;
I never had but one true-love,
    In cold grave she was lain.

2

5   "I'll do as much for my true-love
    As any young man may;
I'll sit and mourn all at her grave
    For a twelvemonth and a day."

3

The twelvemonth and a day being up,
10   The dead began to speak:
"Oh who sits weeping on my grave,
    And will not let me sleep?"

4

" 'T is I, my love, sits on your grave,
    And will not let you sleep;
15   For I crave one kiss of your clay-cold lips,
    And that is all I seek."

5

"You crave one kiss of my clay-cold lips,
    But my breath smells earthy strong;

---

2. I.e., their hats swam above (them).
3. Child, No. 78.A, from a nineteenth-century ver-   sion collected in the journal *Folk Lore Record*.

If you have one kiss of my clay-cold lips,
20   Your time will not be long.

6

" 'T is down in yonder garden green,
    Love, where we used to walk,
The finest flower that e'er was seen
    Is withered to a stalk.

7

25 "The stalk is withered dry, my love,
    So will our hearts decay;
So make yourself content, my love,
    Till God calls you away."

The Wife of Usher's Well[4]

1

There lived a wife at Usher's Well,
    And a wealthy wife was she;
She had three stout and stalwart sons,
    And sent them o'er the sea.

2

5 They hadna been a week from her,
    A week but barely ane,°   *one*
Whan word came to the carlin° wife   *old*
    That her three sons were gane.

3

They hadna been a week from her,
10   A week but barely three,
Whan word came to the carlin wife
    That her sons she'd never see.

4

"I wish the wind may never cease,
    Nor fashes° in the flood,   *troubles*
15 Till my three sons come hame to me,
    In earthly flesh and blood."

5

It fell about the Martinmass,[5]
    When nights are lang and mirk,°   *murky*
The carlin wife's three sons came hame,
20   And their hats were o' the birk.°   *birch*

6

It neither grew in syke° nor ditch,   *trench*
    Nor yet in any sheugh;°   *furrow*
But at the gates o' Paradise,
    That birk grew fair eneugh.

---

4. Child, No. 79.A, from Sir Walter Scott's *Minstrelsy of the Scottish Border* (1802–03).

5. The feast of St. Martin (the martyred Pope Martin I, died A.D. 655), November 11.

7

25   "Blow up the fire, my maidens,
          Bring water from the well;
      For a' my house shall feast this night,
          Since my three sons are well."

8

      And she has made to them a bed,
30   She's made it large and wide,
      And she's ta'en her mantle° her about,   *cloak*
          Sat down at the bed-side.

9

      Up then crew the red, red cock,
          And up and crew the gray;
35   The eldest to the youngest said,
          " 'T is time we were away."

10

      The cock he hadna crawed but once,
          And clapped his wings at a',
      When the youngest to the eldest said,
40   "Brother, we must awa'.

11

      "The cock doth craw, the day doth daw,
          The channerin'° worm doth chide;   *fretting*
      Gin° we be missed out o' our place,   *if*
          A sair° pain we maun° bide.   *sore / must*

12

45   "Fare ye weel, my mother dear!
          Fareweel to barn and byre!°   *cowhouse*
      And fare ye weel, the bonny lass,
          That kindles my mother's fire!"

Bonny Barbara Allan[6]

1

      It was in and about the Martinmas[7] time,
          When the green leaves were a falling,
      That Sir John Græme, in the West Country,
          Fell in love with Barbara Allan.

2

5   He sent his man down through the town,
          To the place where she was dwelling:
      "O haste and come to my master dear,
          Gin° ye be Barbara Allan."   *if*

3

      O hooly,° hooly rose she up,   *slowly, gently*
10   To the place where he was lying,

---

6. Child, No. 84.A, from the *Tea Table Miscellany*   7. See n. 5, p. 89.
(1763).

And when she drew the curtain by:
  "Young man, I think you're dying."

4

"O it's I'm sick, and very, very sick,
  And 'tis a' for Barbara Allan."
15 "O the better for me ye s'° never be,   *ye shall*
  Though your heart's blood were a-spilling.

5

"O dinna° ye mind, young man," said she,   *don't*
  "When ye was in the tavern a drinking,
That ye made the healths gae° round and round,   *go*
20   And slighted Barbara Allan?"

6

He turned his face unto the wall,
  And death was with him dealing:
"Adieu, adieu, my dear friends all,
  And be kind to Barbara Allan."

7

25 And slowly, slowly raise she up,
  And slowly, slowly left him,
And sighing said, she could not stay,
  Since death of life had reft him.

8

She had not gane a mile but twa,
30   When she heard the dead-bell ringing,
And every jow° that the dead-bell geid,°   *stroke / gave*
  It cried, "Woe to Barbara Allan!"

9

"O mother, mother, make my bed!
  O make it saft and narrow!
35 Since my love died for me to-day,
  I'll die for him to-morrow."

Mary Hamilton[8]

Version A

1

Word's gane to the kitchen,
  And word's gane to the ha',°   *hall*

8. Child, No. 173.A. "Mary Hamilton," first cited in 1790 and first printed in the early nineteenth century, is probably set at the court of Mary Stuart (1542–1587). According to the Calendar of State Papers, Mary, queen of Scotland, had four maids-in-waiting who bore her first name. The Protestant writer John Knox, hostile both to female rulers and to Catholics like Mary Stuart, denounced one of the maids-in-waiting for murdering a child she had conceived illicitly with the court apothecary (*History of the Reformation*). Most versions of the story in ballad form identify the baby's father as the king, probably alluding to Lord Darnley, Mary Stuart's frequently unfaithful second husband. To illustrate how different versions of the ballad disagree on the question of Mary Hamilton's degree of guilt for the child's death, we print Child 173.A and 173.B. Child believes that this ballad alludes to events that occurred in the Russian court of Peter the Great (1672–1725) rather than in that of Mary Stuart.

That Marie Hamilton gangs° wi' bairn°   *goes / child*
    To the hichest° Stewart of a'.   *highest*

2

5 He's courted her in the kitchen,
    He's courted her in the ha',
    He's courted her in the laigh cellar,[9]
    And that was warst of a'.

3

She's tied it in her apron
10   And she's thrown it in the sea;
    Says, "Sink ye, swim ye, bonny wee babe!
    You'll ne'er get mair o' me."

4

Down then cam the auld queen,
    Goud° tassels tying her hair: *gold*
15 "O Marie, where's the bonny wee babe
    That I heard greet sae sair?"[1]

5

"There was never a babe intill° my room,   *in*
    As little designs to be;
    It was but a touch o' my sair° side,   *sore*
20   Come o'er my fair body."

6

"O Marie, put on your robes o' black,
    Or else your robes o' brown,
    For ye maun° gang wi' me the night,   *must*
    To see fair Edinbro' town."

7

25 "I winna° put on my robes o' black,   *won't*
    Nor yet my robes o' brown;
    But I'll put on my robes o' white,
    To shine through Edinbro' town."

8

When she gaed° up the Cannogate,[2]   *went*
30   She laughed loud laughters three;
    But when she cam down the Cannogate
    The tear blinded her ee.°   *eye*

9

When she gaed up the Parliament stair,
    The heel cam aff her shee;
35 And lang or° she cam down again   *before*
    She was condemned to dee.

---

9. Low cellar, basement.
1. "Greet sae sair": cry so sorely.
2. The Canongate is the Edinburgh street leading
uphill from Holyrood House (where the queen

and the "four Maries" of line 69 lived) to the Tol-
booth, which was both jail and judicial chamber
and, on occasion, the place where Parliament (line
33) sat.

10

When she cam down the Cannogate,
    The Cannogate sae free,
Many a lady looked o'er her window,
    Weeping for this lady.

11

"Ye need nae weep for me," she says,
    "Ye need nae weep for me;
For had I not slain mine own sweet babe,
    This death I wadna dee.

12

"Bring me a bottle of wine," she says,
    "The best that e'er ye ha'e,
That I may drink to my weil-wishers,
    And they may drink to me.

13

"Here's a health to the jolly sailors,
    That sail upon the main;
Let them never let on to my father and mother
    But what I'm coming hame.

14

"Here's a health to the jolly sailors,
    That sail upon the sea;
Let them never let on to my father and mother
    That I cam here to dee.

15

"Oh little did my mother think,
    The day she cradled me,
What lands I was to travel through,
    What death I was to dee.

16

"Oh little did my father think,
    The day he held up me,
What lands I was to travel through,
    What death I was to dee.

17

"Last night I washed the queen's feet,
    And gently laid her down;
And a' the thanks I've gotten the night[3]
    To be hanged in Edinbro' town!

18

"Last night there was four Maries,
    The night there'll be but three;
There was Marie Seton, and Marie Beton,
    And Marie Carmichael, and me."

3. I.e., tonight.

Mary Hamilton

Version B

1

There were ladies, they lived in a bower,°   *chamber*
   And oh but they were fair!
The youngest o them is to the king's court,
   To learn some unco lair.[4]

2

5   She hadna been in the king's court
   A twelve month and a day,
Till of her they could get na wark,
   For wantonness and play.

3

Word is to the kitchen gane,
10   And word is to the ha,°   *hall*
And word is up to Madame the Queen,
   And that is warst of a',
That Mary Hamilton has born a bairn,°   *child*
   To the hichest Stewart of a'.

4

15   "O rise, O rise, Mary Hamilton,
   O rise, and tell to me
What thou did with thy sweet babe
   We sair° heard weep by thee."   *sorely*

5

"Hold your tongue, madame," she said,
20   "And let your folly be;
It was a shouir° o sad sickness   *paroxysm*
   Made me weep sae° bitterlie."   *so*

6

"O rise, O rise, Mary Hamilton,
   O rise, and tell to me
25   What thou did with thy sweet babe
   We sair heard weep by thee."

7

"I put it in a piner-pig,[5]
   And set it on the sea;
I bade it sink, or it might swim,
30   It should neer come hame to me."

8

"O rise, O rise, Mary Hamilton,
   Arise, and go with me;
There is a wedding in Glasgow town
   This day we'll go and see."

4. I.e., unusual lore or knowledge.
5. An earthen vessel in which money was usually kept.

9

35 She put not on her black clothing,
    She put not on her brown,
But she put on the glistering gold,
    To shine thro Edinburgh town.

10

As they came into Edinburgh town,
40   The city for to see,
The bailie's wife and the provost's wife[6]
    Said, Och an alace° for thee!   *alas*

11

"Gie° never alace for me," she said,   *give*
    "Gie never alace for me;
45 It's all for the sake of my poor babe,
    This death that I maun die."

12

As they gaed up the Tolbuith[7] stair,
    The stair it was sae hie,
The bailie's son and the provost's son
50   Said, Och an alace for thee!

13

"Gie never alace for me," she said,
    "Gie never alace for me!
It's all for the sake of my puir babe,
    This death that I maun° die.   *must*

14

55 "But bring to me a cup," she says,
    "A cup bot and a can,[8]
And I will drink to all my friends,
    And they'll drink to me again.

15

"Here's to you all, travellers,
60   Who travels by land or sea;
Let na wit to my father nor mother
    The death that I must die.

16

"Here's to you all, travellers,
    That travels on dry land;
65 Let na wit to my father nor mother
    But I am coming hame.

17

"Little did my mother think,
    First time she cradled me,
What land I was to travel on,
70   Or what death I would die.

---

6. I.e., the wives of two types of municipal offi-
cials, the bailiff being an alderman or steward, the
provost being in this context a chief magistrate or
perhaps a policeman.

7. For Edinburgh's Tolbooth, see n. 2, p. 92.
8. I.e., a cup and also ("bot") a larger container
("can").

18

"Little did my mother think,
    First time she tied my head,
What land I was to tread upon,
    Or whare I would win my bread.

19

75   "Yestreen Queen Mary had four Maries,
    This night she'll hae but three;
She had Mary Seaton, and Mary Beaton,
    And Mary Carmichael, and me.

20

"Yestreen I wush Queen Mary's feet,
80   And bore her till° her bed;   *to*
This day she's given me my reward,
    This gallows-tree to tread.

21

"Cast off, cast off my goun," she said,
    "But let my petticoat be,
85 And tye a napkin on my face,
    For that gallows I downa see."

22

By and cum the king himsell,
    Lookd up with a pitiful ee:°   *eye*
"Come down, come down, Mary Hamilton,
90   This day thou wilt dine with me."

23

"Hold your tongue, my sovereign leige,
    And let your folly be;
An ye had a mind to save my life,
    Ye should na shamed me here."

Get Up and Bar the Door[9]

1

It fell about the Martinmas[1] time,
    And a gay time it was then,
When our goodwife got puddings to make,
    And she's boiled them in the pan.

2

5 The wind sae° cauld blew south and north,   *so*
    And blew into the floor;
Quoth our goodman to our goodwife,
    "Gae° out and bar the door."   *go*

---

9. Child, No. 275.A, from David Herd, *The Ancient and Modern Scots Songs* (1769).   1. See n. 5, p. 89.

3

"My hand is in my hussyfskap.°   *housewife's work*
10   Goodman, as ye may see;
An° it should nae be barred this hundred year,   *if*
It s'° no be barred for me."   *shall*

4

They made a paction° 'tween them twa,   *pact*
They made it firm and sure,
15   That the first word whae'er should speak,
Should rise and bar the door.

5

Then by there came two gentlemen,
At twelve o'clock at night,
And they could neither see house nor hall,
20   Nor coal nor candle-light.

6

"Now whether is this a rich man's house,
Or whether is it a poor?"
But ne'er a word wad° ane o' them speak,   *would*
For barring of the door.

7

25   And first they ate the white puddings,
And then they ate the black;
Though muckle° thought the goodwife to hersel,   *much, a lot*
Yet ne'er a word she spak.

8

Then said the one unto the other,
30   "Here, man, tak ye my knife;
Do ye tak aff° the auld man's beard,   *off*
And I'll kiss the goodwife."

9

"But there's nae water in the house,
And what shall we do then?"
35   "What ails ye at² the pudding-broo,°   *-broth*
That boils into the pan?"

10

O up then started our goodman,
An angry man was he:
"Will ye kiss my wife before my een,°   *eyes*
40   And scad° me wi' pudding-bree?"°   *scald / -broth*

11

Then up and started our goodwife,
Gied° three skips on the floor: *gave*
"Goodman, you've spoken the foremost word,
Get up and bar the door."

---

2. I.e., what's the matter with.

The Bitter Withy[3]

1

As it fell out on a holy day,
  The drops of rain did fall, did fall,
Our Saviour asked leave of his mother Mary
  If he might go play at ball.

2

5 "To play at ball, my own dear son,
  It's time you was going or gone,
But be sure let me hear no complain of you,
  At night when you do come home."

3

It was upling scorn and downling scorn,[4]
10   Oh, there he met three jolly jerdins;°   *fellows*
Oh, there he asked the jolly jerdins
  If they would go play at ball.

4

"Oh, we are lords' and ladies' sons,
  Born in bower° or in hall,   *private bedroom*
15 And you are some poor maid's child
  Borned in an ox's stall."

5

"If you are lords' and ladies' sons,
  Borned in bower or in hall,
Then at last I'll make it appear
20   That I am above you all."

6

Our Saviour built a bridge with the beams of the sun,[5]
  And over it he gone, he gone he.
And after followed the three jolly jerdins,
  And drownded they were all three.

7

25 It was upling scorn and downling scorn,
  The mothers of them did whoop and call,
Crying out, "Mary mild, call home your child,
  For ours are drownded all."

8

Mary mild, Mary mild, called home her child,
30   And laid our Saviour across her knee,
And with a whole handful of bitter withy
  She gave him slashes three.

---

3. This ballad was first published in full in 1905, but is believed to be of much earlier origin. It describes an event found not in canonical Christian writings but rather in pseudo-evangelical chronicles of Christ's childhood. "Withy": willow.

4. I.e., there was scorn everywhere ("upling," "downling").
5. The miracle of the bridge of sunbeams derives from a legend about Christ frequently found in medieval lives of the saints.

9

Then he says to his mother, "Oh! the withy, oh! the withy,
  The bitter withy that causes me to smart, to smart,
35 Oh! the withy, it shall be the very first tree
  That perishes at the heart."

The Knight and Shepherd's Daughter[6]

1

There was a shepherd's dochter
  Kept sheep on yonder hill;
Bye cam a knicht frae° the High College,[7]   *from*
  And he wad° hae° his will.   *would / have*

2

5 Whan he had got his wills o her,
  His will as he has taen:°   *taken*
"Wad ye be sae° gude° and kind   *so / good*
  As tell to me your name?"[8]

3

"Some ca's me Jock, some ca's me John,
10 Some disna ken my name,
But whan I 'm into the king's court,
  Mitchcock[9] is my name."

4

"Mitchcock! hey!" the lady did say,
  And spelt it oure° again;   *over*
15 "If that 's your name in the Latin tongue,
  Earl Richard is your name!"

5

O jumpt he upon his horse,
  And said he wad go ride;
Kilted° she her green claithing,   *tucked up*
20 And said she wad na° bide.°   *not / stay*

6

The knicht rade on, the lady ran,
  A live-lang simmer's° day,   *summer's*
Till they cam to a wan° water   *black*
  Was calld the river Tay.[1]

7

25 "Jump on behind, ye weill-faurd° may,°   *well-favored / maid*
  Or do ye chuse to ride?"

---

6. This Scottish ballad has several variants in which the identities of the knight and the shepherd's daughter vary but the events and outcome are similar. The version printed here, the C variant of Child Ballad No. 110, is from Kinloch's *Ancient Scottish Ballads*.

7. King's court.
8. The shepherd's daughter asks this question.
9. The knight gives the shepherd's daughter a false name (though she is not fooled); "disna ken": do not know.
1. The longest river in Scotland.

"No, thank ye, sir," the lady said,
　"I rather chuse to wade";
And afore that he was mid-water,
30　She was at the ither side.

8

"Turn back, turn back, ye weill-faurd may,
　My heart will brak in three:"
"And sae did mine in yon bonny hill-side,
　Whan ye was [na] lat me be."

9

35　"Whare gat ye that gay° claithing　　　　　　　　　　*fine*
　This day I see on thee?"
"My mither was a gude milk-nurse,
　And a gude nourice° was she;　　　　　　　　　　　*nurse*
She nursd the Earl of Stockford's daughter,
40　And gat aw this to me."

10

Whan she cam to the king's court,
　She rappit wi a ring;[2]
Sae ready as the king himsel
　Was to let the lady in!

11

45　"There is a knicht into your court
　This day has robbed me:"
"O has he taen your gowd,"° he says,　　　　　　　　*gold*
　"Or has he taen your fee?"°　　　　　　*wealth, possessions*

12

"He has na taen my gowd," she says,
50　"Nor yet has he my fee;
But he has taen my maiden-head,
　The flowr o° my fair bodie."　　　　　　　　　　　*of*

13

Then out bespak° the queen hersel,　　　　　　　　*spoke*
　Wha sat by the king's knee:
55　There 's na a knicht in aw° our court　　　　　　　　*all*
　Wad hae dune that to thee,
Unless it war my brither, Earl Richard,
　And forbid it it war he!

14

Wad ye ken° your love,　　　　　　　　　　　　*know*
60　Amang a hunder° men?　　　　　　　　　　　*hundred*
"I wad," said the bonnie ladie,
　"Amang five hunder and ten."

15

The king made aw his merry men pass,
　By ane,° by twa, and three;　　　　　　　　　　　*one*

2. I.e., rapped with the door knocker.

65 Earl Richard us'd to be the first man,
　　But he was hinmost man that day.

16

He cam hauping° on ane foot,　　　　　　　　*hopping*
　　And winking with ae° ee;°　　　　　　　　*one / eye*
But "Ha! ha!" said the bonnie ladie,
70　　"That same young man are ye."

17

He 's taen° her up to a hie towr-head　　　　*taken*
　　And offerd her hunder punds in a glove:[3]
"Gin° ye be a courteous maid,　　　　　　　　*if*
　　Ye 'll choice° anither love."　　　　　　*choose*

18

75 "What care I for your hunder pund?
　　Na mair° than ye wad for mine;　　　　　　*more*
What 's a hunder pund to me,
　　To a marriage wi a king!"

19

Whan the marriage it was oure,
80　　And ilk° ane took them horse,　　　　　　*each*
"It never set a beggar's brat
　　At nae knicht's back to be."[4]

20

The ladie met wi a beggar-wife,
　　And gied her half o crown:
85 "Tell aw your neebours, whan ye gang hame,
　　That Earl Richard's your gude-son."°　　　*son-in-law*

21

"O hold your tongue, ye beggar's brat,
　　My heart will brak in three";
"And sae did mine on yon bonny hill-side,
90　　Whan ye wad na let me be."

22

Whan she cam to yon nettle-dyke,°　　　*nettle-covered ditch*
　. . . . .
　　　　　　　　　　5
"An my auld° mither she was here,　　　　　　*old*
　　Sae weill as she wad pu.[6]

23

95 "She wad boil ye weill and butter ye weill,
　　And sup till she war fu,[7]
And lay her hed upon her dish-doup,[8]
　　And sleep like onie° sow."　　　　　　　　*any*

---

3. I.e., a hundred pounds tied up in a glove (which he offers in exchange for having to marry her).
4. I.e., it never suited a beggar's child to ride behind a lord.
5. Line 92 is missing; this folk ballad, like most, was transcribed from sung versions. Other printed versions suggest, however, that the line describes how the nettles were spread on the ground.
6. I.e., you would have to pull ("pu") the plough as well as she does.
7. I.e., and eat till she was full.
8. The bottom of her bowl.

24

Whan she cam to Earl Richard's house,
100   The sheets war holland fine:⁹
"O haud° awa thae linen sheets,   *hold*
And bring to me the linsey clouts¹
    I hae been best used° in.°"   *accustomed / to*

25

["Awa, awa wi your siller° spoons,   *silver*
105   Haud them awa frae me;
It would set° me better to feed my flocks   *suit*
    Wi the brose-cap° on me knee: *oatmeal sack*
Sae bring to me the gude ram's horn,
    The spoons I've been used wi."]²

26

110 "Hold your tongue, ye beggar's brat,
    My heart will brak in three";
"And sae did mine on yon bonnie hillside,
    Whan ye wadna lat me be."

27

"I wish I had drank the well-water
115   Whan first I drank the wine!
Never a shepherd's dochter
    Wad hae been a love o mine."

28

"O I wish I'd drank the well-water
    Whan first I drank the beer,
120 That ever a shepherd's dochter
    Shoud hae been my only dear!"

     *   *   *   *   *   *   *   *   *³

29

"Ye 'll turn about, Earl Richard,
    And mak some mair° o me;   *more*
An ye mak me lady o ae puir plow,⁴
125   I can mak ye laird° o three."   *lord*

30

"If ye be the Earl of Stockford's dochter,
    As I 've taen some thouchts ye be,
Aft° hae I waited at your father's yett,°   *oft / gate*
    But your face I coud never see."⁵

---

9. A linen fabric made in Holland.
1. Woven patches of coarse wool and flax.
2. Stanza 25 is in brackets because it was an insertion in Kinloch's own copy of *Ancient Scottish Ballads*.
3. The asterisks signal an apparent gap in the narrative.
4. I.e., if you make me the lady of one poor plow

(the area of land one plow will till in a year).
5. With the suggestion that she can make the knight lord of three plows, the narrative begins its revelation that the shepherd's daughter is in truth high-born. In some versions, however, her social status is mysterious at the end; and in one text, the knight is revealed to be a blacksmith's son whereas the lady is a king's daughter.

ANONYMOUS ELIZABETHAN AND JACOBEAN POEMS

Love Me Little, Love Me Long[1]

Love me little, love me long,
Is the burden° of my song.　　　　　　　　　*refrain*
Love that is too hot and strong
　　Burneth soon to waste.
5　Still, I would not have thee cold,
Not too backward, nor too bold;
Love that lasteth till 'tis old
　　Fadeth not in haste.
　　　　Love me little, love me long,
10　　　*Is the burden of my song.*

If thou lovest me too much,
It will not prove as true as touch;[2]
Love me little, more than such,
　　For I fear the end.
15　I am with little well content,
And a little from thee sent
Is enough, with true intent
　　To be steadfast friend.
　　　　Love me little, love me long,
20　　　*Is the burden of my song.*

Say thou lov'st me while thou live;
I to thee my love will give,
Never dreaming to deceive
　　Whiles that life endures.
25　Nay, and after death, in sooth,
I to thee will keep my truth,
As now, when in my May of youth;
　　This my love assures.
　　　　Love me little, love me long,
30　　　*Is the burden of my song.*

Constant love is moderate ever,
And it will through life persever;
Give me that, with true endeavor
　　I will it restore.
35　A suit of durance° let it be,　　　　　*durability*
For all weathers that for me,
For the land or for the sea,
　　Lasting evermore.

1. This song was registered in 1569–70 with the Stationers' Company, which authorized all printed texts from 1557 onward. Our source is the *Extracts from the Stationers' Company* (1848).

2. Touchstone or basanite; gold or silver rubbed on touchstone produces a streak, the appearance of which was formerly used as a test for the purity of the metal.

> *Love me little, love me long,*
> 40   *Is the burden of my song.*

Winter's cold, or summer's heat,
Autumn's tempests on it beat,
It can never know defeat,
    Never can rebel.
45 Such the love that I would gain,
Such the love, I tell thee plain,
Thou must give, or woo in vain;
    So to thee, farewell!
        Love me little, love me long,
50   *Is the burden of my song.*

ca. 1570

A Lament for Our Lady's Shrine at Walsingham[3]

In the wracks° of Walsingham   *ruins*
  Whom should I choose,
But the Queen of Walsingham[4]
  To be guide to my muse.
5 Then thou Prince of Walsingham,[5]
  Grant me to frame
Bitter plaints° to rue thy wrong,   *complaints*
  Bitter woe for thy name.
Bitter was it so to see
10   The seely[6] sheepe
Murd'red by the ravening° wolves   *plundering*
  While the shepherds did sleep;
Bitter was it oh, to view
  The sacred vine,
15 Whiles the gardeners played all close,[7]
  Rooted up by the swine;
Bitter, bitter, oh to behold,
  The grass to grow
Where the walls of Walsingham
20   So stately did show;
Such were the works of Walsingham,
  While she did stand;
Such are the wracks as now do show
  Of that holy land.
25 Level, level with the ground,

---

3. Walsingham, a small town in Norfolk, was the site of a famous shrine of the Virgin Mary and one of the most popular places of pilgrimage in medieval England. A relic of the Virgin's milk brought by Crusaders from Palestine was believed to be enclosed in a jeweled crucifix there. In 1538 the shrine was desecrated and despoiled of its icons and wealth in Henry VIII's programmatic dissolution of the Catholic monasteries. This poem is from a manuscript containing several Catholic works. The manuscript, in Oxford's Bodleian Library, probably dates from around 1600.
4. The Virgin Mary.
5. Probably King Henry VIII.
6. The word has a range of apt meanings: innocent, holy, pitiable.
7. Amused themselves nearby.

The towers do lie,
Which with their golden glittering tops
Pierced once to the sky;
Where were gates no gates are now,
30   The ways unknown
Where the press° of peers° did pass   *throng / nobles*
While her fame far was blown.
Owls do scrike° where the sweetest hymns   *screech*
Lately were sung;
35 Toads, and serpents hold their dens,
Where the Palmers° did throng.   *pilgrims*
Weep, weep, o Walsingham,
Whose days are nights,
Blessings turned to blasphemies,
40   Holy deeds to despites!°   *outrages*
Sin is where our Lady sat,
Heaven turned is to Hell;
Satan sits where our Lord did sway:°   *rule*
Walsingham, oh farewell!

ca. 1600?

Fine Knacks for Ladies[8]

Fine knacks for ladies, cheap, choice, brave and new!
Good pennyworths—but money cannot move:
I keep a fair but for the fair to view;
A beggar may be liberal of love.
5 Though all my wares be trash, the heart is true,
        The heart is true.

Great gifts are guiles° and look for gifts again;   *deceits*
My trifles come as treasures from my mind.
It is a precious jewel to be plain;
10 Sometimes in shell the orient'st° pearls we find.   *most lustrous*
Of others take a sheaf, of me a grain!
        Of me a grain!

Within this pack pins, points,[9] laces, and gloves,
And divers toys fitting a country fair;
15 But in my heart, where duty serves and loves,
Turtles and twins,[1] court's brood, a heavenly pair.
Happy the heart that thinks of no removes!
        Of no removes!

1600

---

8. This anonymous peddler's song was set for lute accompaniment by John Dowland, a well-known Elizabethan composer, and included in his *Second book of songs or ayres* (1600).
9. A lace (such as a shoelace) with the ends tagged or pointed for convenience in lacing.
1. Turtledoves ("turtles") and the "heavenly pair" of twins, Castor and Pollux of the constellation Gemini, were symbols of true love and constancy.

To His Love[2]

Come away! come, sweet love!
The golden morning breaks;
All the earth, all the air,
Of love and pleasure speaks.

5 Teach thine arms then to embrace,
And sweet rosy lips to kiss,
And mix our souls in mutual bliss.
Eyes were made for beauty's grace,
Viewing, rueing, love's long pain,
10 Procured by beauty's rude disdain.

Come away! come, sweet love!
The golden morning wastes,
While the sun from his sphere
His fiery arrows casts,
15 Making all the shadows fly,
Playing, staying in the grove,
To entertain the stealth of love.
Thither, sweet love, let us hie°   go
Flying, dying, in desire,
20 Wing'd with sweet hopes and heavenly fire.

Come away! come, sweet love!
Do not in vain adorn
Beauty's grace that should rise
Like to the naked morn.
25 Lilies on the river's side,
And fair Cyprian[3] flowers new-blown,
Desire no beauties but their own;
Ornament is nurse of pride.
Pleasure, measure love's delight.
30 Haste then, sweet love, our wishèd flight!

1600

Weep You No More, Sad Fountains[4]

Weep you no more, sad fountains;
What need you flow so fast?
Look how the snowy mountains
Heaven's sun doth gently waste.
5 But my sun's heavenly eyes
View not your weeping,

---

2. Included in *England's Helicon* (1600), an influential anthology of verse.
3. An allusion to Venus, the goddess of love; the center of her cult was the island of Cyprus.
4. From John Dowland's *Songs or Airs*, Book 3 (1603).

That now lie sleeping
Softly, now softly lies
Sleeping.

10   Sleep is a reconciling,
     A rest that peace begets.
   Doth not the sun rise smiling
      When fair at even° he sets?   *evening*
     Rest you then, rest, sad eyes,
15   Melt not in weeping
      While she lies sleeping
     Softly, now softly lies
      Sleeping.

                                  1603

There Is a Lady Sweet and Kind[5]

There is a lady sweet and kind,
Was never face so pleased my mind;
I did but see her passing by,
And yet I love her till I die.

5   Her gesture, motion and her smiles,
   Her wit, her voice, my heart beguiles,
   Beguiles my heart, I know not why,
   And yet I love her till I die.

   Her free behavior, winning looks,
10 Will make a lawyer burn his books.
   I touched her not, alas, not I,
   And yet I love her till I die.

   Had I her fast betwixt mine arms,
   Judge you that think such sports were harms,
15 Were't any harm? No, no, fie, fie!
   For I will love her till I die.

   Should I remain confinèd there,
   So long as Phoebus[6] in his sphere,
   I to request, she to deny,
20 Yet would I love her till I die.

   Cupid is wingèd and doth range;
   Her country so my love doth change,
   But change she earth, or change she sky,
   Yet will I love her till I die.

                                    1607

5. From Thomas Ford's *Music of Sundry Kinds*   6. Apollo, god of the sun.
(1607).

The Silver Swan[7]

The silver swan, who living had no note,
When death approached, unlocked her silent throat;
Leaning her breast against the reedy shore,
Thus sung her first and last, and sung no more:
5 "Farewell, all joys; Oh death, come close mine eyes;
More geese than swans now live, more fools than wise."

1612

Yet If His Majesty, Our Sovereign Lord[8]

Yet if his majesty, our sovereign lord,
Should of his own accord
Friendly himself invite,
And say, "I'll be your guest tomorrow night,"
5 How should we stir ourselves, call and command
All hands to work! "Let no man idle stand.
Set me fine Spanish tables in the hall,
See they be fitted all;
Let there be room to eat,
10 And order taken that there want no meat.
See every sconce[9] and candlestick made bright,
That without tapers they may give a light.
Look to the presence:[1] are the carpets spread,
The dais° o'er the head,   canopy
15 The cushions in the chair,
And all the candles lighted on the stair?
Perfume the chambers, and in any case
Let each man give attendance in his place."
Thus if the king were coming would we do,
20 And 'twere good reason too;
For 'tis a duteous thing
To show all honor to an earthly king,
And, after all our travail° and our cost,   labor, pain
So he be pleased, to think no labor lost.
25 But at the coming of the King of Heaven
All's set at six and seven:[2]
We wallow in our sin;
Christ cannot find a chamber in the inn.
We entertain him always like a stranger,
30 And, as at first, still lodge him in the manger.

1625

---

7. From Orlando Gibbons' *First Set of Madrigals and Motets* (1612). Gibbons, one of the last madrigalists, may be implying an analogy between himself and the swan.
8. Preserved in manuscripts now in Christ Church, Oxford (MSS 736–38), this poem was set to music by a court musician, Thomas Ford, some- time after 1620.
9. An ornamented bracket for holding candles, often backed by a mirror; also, a screen on a candlestick made to protect the light from wind.
1. The area around the place where the king will sit.
2. In disorder.

A Song Bewailing the Time of Christmas, So Much Decayed in England[3]

Christmas is my name, far have I gone, have I gone, have I gone,
     have I gone without regard,
     Whereas great men, by flocks they be flown, they be flown,
     they be flown, they be flown to London ward,
5   Where they in pomp and pleasure do waste
     that which Christmas had wont to feast;
          Wellay day.
     Houses where music was wonted° to ring,   *used*
          Nothing but bats, and owls now do sing
10   Wellay day, wallay day, wallay day, where should I stay.

     Christmas bread and beef is turned into stones, into stones, into stones,
     Into stones and silken rags.
     And lady money[4] it doth sleep, it doth sleep, it doth sleep,
     It doth sleep in misers' bags.
15   Where many gallants once abound,
     Nought but a dog and a shepherd is found,
          Wellay day.
     Places where Christmas revels did keep,
          Are now become habitations for sheep.
20   Wallay day, wallay day, wellay day, where should I stay.

     Pan, the shepherd's god, doth deface, doth deface, doth deface,
     doth deface, Lady Ceres' crown,[5]
     And tilliges° doth decay, doth decay, doth decay,   *plowed land*
     doth decay in every town.[6]
25   Landlords their rents so highly enhance,
     That Peares the plowman[7] barefoot doth dance,
          Wellay day.

     Farmers that Christmas would entertain,
          hath scarsely withal them selves to maintain,
30   Wellay day, wellay day, wellay day, where should I stay.

     Go to the Protestant, he'll protest, he'll protest, he'll protest,
     he will protest and boldly boast,

---

3. This lament for Christmas festivities banned by Protestants after the Reformation (and for other social changes the speaker deplores) comes from a manuscript in the British Library (MS Additional 38599); a longer version of the poem was printed around 1635.
4. Probably a reference to the money traditionally given out for charity on "Lady-Days," dates in the Roman Catholic calendar devoted to celebrating events in the life of the Virgin Mary. One such celebration occurred (before the Reformation) on December 8, when the Virgin's immaculate conception was honored.
5. Ceres was the goddess of grain and hence of the harvest; Pan, god of shepherds and huntsmen,

here symbolizes Protestants who "defaced" Catholic rituals and works of art, especially statues of religious figures; Protestant "iconoclasts" frequently beheaded or otherwise mutilated such statues in Catholic churches.
6. Probably a reference to the practice of "enclosure," whereby peasant farmers who were tenants of a manor lost their traditional access to "common" lands; during the sixteenth century many wealthy landowners enclosed "tilled" land for the sake of the sheep being raised for England's expanding wool trade.
7. "Peares" is a traditional name for a plowman; compare Langland's *Piers Plowman* (p. 58).

And to the Puritan, he is so hot, he is so hot, he is so hot,
he is so hot he will burn the roast,
35   The Catholic good deeds will not scorn,
nor will not see poor Christmas forlorn,
        Wellay day.
Since Holiness no good deeds will do,
    Protestants had best turn Papists too,
40 Wellay day, wellay day, wellay day, where should I stay.

Pride and Luxury doth devour, doth devour, doth devour,
doth devour house keeping quite,°   *completely*
    And beggary doth beget, doth beget, doth beget,
doth beget in many a knight.
45   Madam for° sooth° in coach she must reel   *in / truth*
Although she wear her hose out at heel,
        Wellay day.
And on her back were that for her weed,
    that would both me, and many other feed,
50 Wellay day, wellay day, wellay day, where should I stay.

Briefly for to end, here I find, here I find,
here I find such great vacation°   *emptying*
    That some great houses do seem to have, seem to have,
        seem to have,
for to have some great purgation,
55   With purging pills, such effects they have showed,
that out of doors, their owners they have spewed.[8]
        Wellay day.
And when Christmas goes by and calls,
    Nothing but solitude, and naked walls,
60 Wellay day, wellay day, wellay day, where should I stay.

Philomel's cottages are turned into gold, into gold,
Into gold for harboring Jove.[9]
    And great mens' houses up for to hold, up for to hold,
up for to hold, make great men moan,
65   But in the city they say they do live,
Where gold by handfuls away they do give,
        Wellay day.
And therefor thither I purpose to pass,
    hoping at London to find the golden ass,
70 I'll away, I'll away, I'll away, I'll no longer stay.

ca. 1624   1635

8. Probably a reference to the widespread "dissolution" of ecclesiastical manors that began during the reign of Henry VIII; the king (and his successors) raised money by dispossessing monasteries of their lands and houses.

9. An allusion to the myth of Philemon, a poor man who was visited by Jove and Mercury in disguise. For entertaining the gods well, Philemon and his wife, Baucis, were rewarded by having their cottage transformed into a luxurious temple.

Tom o' Bedlam's Song[1]

From the hagg° and hungry goblin   *haggard*
That into rags would rend ye,
And the spirit that stands by the naked man
In the Book of Moons[2] defend ye!
5 That of your five sound senses
You never be forsaken,
Nor wander from your selves with Tom
Abroad to beg your bacon.

While I do sing "any food, any feeding,
10 *Feeding, drink or clothing,"*
Come dame or maid, be not afraid,
Poor Tom will injure nothing.

Of thirty bare years have I
Twice twenty been enragèd,°   *mad*
15 And of forty been three times fifteen
In durance° soundly cagèd.   *confinement, prison*
On the lordly lofts of Bedlam,
With stubble soft and dainty,
Brave bracelets strong, sweet whips ding-dong,
20 With wholesome hunger plenty.

And now I sing "any food, any feeding, . . .

With a thought I took for Maudline[3]
And a cruse° of cockle pottage,°   *pitcher / shellfish soup*
With a thing thus tall, sky bless you all,
25 I befell into this dotage.
I slept not since the Conquest,[4]
Till then I never wakèd,
Till the roguish boy° of love where I lay   *Cupid*
Me found and stripped me naked.

30 *And now I sing "any food, any feeding, . . .*

When I short have shorn my sour face
And swigged my horny barrel,
In an oaken inn I pound my skin
As a suit of gilt apparel.
35 The moon's my constant Mistress,

---

1. This poem, like a number of other anonymous lyrics, purports to be sung by a madman, Tom, from "Bedlam," that is, the Hospital of St. Mary of Bethlehem, an asylum in London that housed the mentally ill from the fifteenth century on. The earliest known version of this poem is in a manuscript of songs and verses in the British Museum. Edgar in Shakespeare's *King Lear* assumes the persona of "Poor Tom," and this poem has been echoed by writers from Ben Jonson through Sir Walter Scott to Rudyard Kipling.
2. Probably an astrological book.
3. Tom's "lady" is frequently named Maudline (short for Magdalene and probably an allusion to the New Testament character Mary Magdalene).
4. William of Normandy's conquest of England in 1066.

And the lowly owl my morrow,
The flaming Drake° and the Nightcrow make   *male duck*
Me music to my sorrow.

While I do sing "any food, any feeding, . . .

40 The palsy plagues my pulses
When I prigg° your pigs or pullen,°   *steal / chicken*
Your culvers° take, or matchless make   *wood pigeons*
Your Chanticleare,[5] or sullen.
When I want provant,° with Humfry   *food*
45 I sup,[6] and when benighted,
I repose in Paul's with waking souls
Yet never am affrighted.

But I do sing "any food, any feeding, . . .

I know more than Apollo,[7]
50 For oft, when hee lies sleeping,
I see the stars at bloody wars
In the wounded welkin° weeping;   *sky*
The moon embrace her shepherd,
And the queen of Love her warrior,
55 While the first doth horn the star of morn,
And the next the heavenly Farrier.[8]

While I do sing "any food, any feeding, . . .

The Gipsy Snap and Pedro[9]
Are none of Tom's comrados.
60 The punk I scorn and the cut purse sworn
And the roaring boys bravado.
The meek, the white, the gentle,
Me handle touch and spare not,
But those that cross Tom Rynosseros
65 Do what the panther dare not.

Although I sing "any food, any feeding, . . .

With an host of furious fancies,
Whereof I am commander,
With a burning spear, and a horse of air,
70 To the wilderness I wander.
By a knight of ghosts and shadows
I summoned am to tourney°   *take part in a tournament*

5. I.e., take away your rooster's mate.
6. Refers to the legendary "Duke Humphrey's Walk," in front of St. Paul's Cathedral in London ("Paul's," line 46), where the poor congregated.
7. Greek god of poetry and the sun.
8. In Greek myth the Moon loved the shepherd Endymion, and Venus, the goddess of love, preferred Mars (god of war) to her husband, Hephaestos, god of metalworking and hence a "heavenly Farrier," or horseshoer. The verb "horn," printed as "born" in some texts of the poem, suggests an image of the new moon "embracing" the morning star; in the second clause governed by this verb, there is a play on horn's figurative meaning as cuckold.
9. I.e., a gypsy rogue (with "Snap" probably connoting thievery) and a Spaniard.

Ten leagues beyond the wide world's end.
Me think it is no journey.

75   *Yet will I sing "any food, any feeding, . . .*

Before 1615   1656

THOMAS WYATT*

1503–1542

The Long Love, That in My Thought Doth Harbor[1]

The long° love, that in my thought doth harbor,°   *enduring / lodge*
And in mine heart doth keep his residence,
Into my face presseth with bold pretense,
And therein campeth, spreading his banner.[2]
5 She that me learneth° to love and suffer,   *teaches*
And wills that my trust and lust's negligence
Be reined[3] by reason, shame and reverence,
With his hardiness° taketh displeasure.   *boldness*
Wherewithal, unto the heart's[4] forest he fleeth,
10 Leaving his enterprise with pain and cry;
And there him hideth, and not appeareth.
What may I do when my master feareth
But in the field with him to live and die?
For good is the life, ending faithfully.

E. MS.

Whoso List to Hunt[5]

Whoso list to hunt, I know where is an hind,°   *female deer*
But as for me, alas, I may no more:

---

*Though Wyatt apparently meant to publish a collection of his poems, only a few of the poems were printed before his death (several appeared in a collection published between 1536 and 1540 entitled *The Court of Venus*). Most of his works circulated in manuscript among aristocratic readers. After his death, however, the printer Richard Tottel published ninety-seven poems attributed to Wyatt—along with forty attributed to Surrey (see pp. 123–26) and Grimald (see pp. 127–28) respectively, and some by "Uncertain Authors"—in a book entitled *Songs and Sonnets* (1557). Usually known as *Tottel's Miscellany*, this anthology is considered by literary historians one of the epochal books of English literature.

Wyatt's translations of Petrarch's Italian sonnets were particularly important to Tottel's stated project of showing that the English "tongue" is capable of producing poems written no less "praisworthily" than those in Latin and Italian ("The Printer to the Reader"). While praising the "weightiness of the deepwitted Sir Thomas Wyatt," Tottel quietly "emended" Wyatt's lines to make them more metrically regular. Sometimes Tottel's versions differ strikingly, in diction as well as rhythm, from those found in manuscript. To illustrate such differences, we print "They Flee from Me" both in Tottel's version and in that of the Egerton manuscript.

That manuscript (E. MS.) contains a number of poems in Wyatt's own hand as well as his corrections of poems in other scribes' hands. Whenever possible, we have used this manuscript's versions of Wyatt's poems. We also print poems from the Devonshire manuscript (D. MS.) and several others in which some of Wyatt's texts are preserved. To maintain the integrity of the manuscript versions, we have not modernized punctuation, although for the sake of accessibility we have modernized some spellings.
1. Translated from Petrarch, *Rime* 140. Compare the translation by Henry Howard, earl of Surrey, "Love, That Doth Reign and Live Within My Thought" (p. 123–24).
2. Raising the flag, i.e., taking up a position for battle and, figuratively, blushing.
3. Checked; with a probable pun on "reigned."
4. With a pun on "heart" and "hart" (as deer).
5. "Whoso list": whoever likes.

The vain travail hath wearied me so sore.
I am of them that farthest cometh behind;
5   Yet may I by no means my wearied mind
Draw from the deer: but as she fleeth afore,
Fainting I follow. I leave off therefore,
Since in a net I seek to hold the wind.
Who list her hunt, I put him out of doubt,
10   As well as I may spend his time in vain:
And, graven with diamonds, in letters plain
There is written her fair neck round about:
Noli me tangere,[6] for Caesar's I am;
And wild for to hold, though I seem tame.

E. MS.

My Galley[7]

My galley charged° with forgetfulness   *laden*
Thorough° sharp seas in winter nights doth pass   *through*
'Tween rock and rock; and eke° mine enemy,[8] alas,   *also*
That is my lord, steereth with cruelness;
5   And every oar a thought in readiness,
As though that death were light in such a case.
An endless wind doth tear the sail apace
Of forced sighs and trusty fearfulness.
A rain of tears, a cloud of dark disdain,
10   Hath done the wearied cords[9] great hinderance;
Wreathed with error and eke with ignorance.
The stars be hid[1] that led me to this pain;
Drowned is reason that should me consort,°   *accompany*
And I remain despairing of the port.

E. MS.

Madam, Withouten Many Words

Madam, withouten many words
Once I am sure ye will or no;
And if ye will, then leave your bords,°   *jests*
And use your wit and show it so.

5   And with a beck[2] ye shall me call,
And if of one that burneth alway

---

6. "Touch me not" (Latin). The phrase (in Italian in Petrarch) has roots both in Petrarch's sonnet *Rime* 190—Wyatt's main source—and in the Bible (see especially the Catholic Bible, the Vulgate: John 20.17 and Matthew 22.21). Renaissance commentators on Petrarch maintained that the deer in Caesar's royal forest wore collars bearing a similar inscription, to prevent anyone from hunting the animals. The allusion raises questions about Wyatt's relation to King Henry VIII ("Caesar," line 14). Wyatt was accused during his lifetime of having been the lover of Anne Boleyn, who became Henry VIII's second wife and a major cause of his break with the Roman Catholic church.

7. It is difficult to say with certainty when Wyatt intended an -*ed* ending to be pronounced as a second syllable and when not. Hence no attempt has been made to mark syllabic endings with an accent in any of Wyatt's poems (although in this particular poem such endings may occur in lines 1, 8, 11, and 13). Wyatt's poem is based on Petrarch's *Rime* 189.
8. I.e., love.
9. The worn lines of the sail, with a possible pun on the Latin for heart (*cor, cordis*).
1. I.e., the lady's eyes.
2. A gesture, such as a nod of the head or a motion of the forefinger.

Ye have any pity at all,
  Answer him fair with yea or nay.

If it be yea I shall be fain;°   *well-pleased*
10   If it be nay, friends as before;
Ye shall another man obtain,
  And I mine own and yours no more.

                                         E. MS.

They Flee from Me

They flee from me that sometime did me seek
  With naked foot stalking in my chamber.
I have seen them gentle tame and meek
  That now are wild and do not remember
5   That sometime they put themselves in danger
To take bread at my hand; and now they range
Busily seeking with a continual change.

Thanked be fortune, it hath been otherwise
  Twenty times better;[3] but once in special,
10 In thin array after a pleasant guise,[4]
  When her loose gown from her shoulders did fall,
  And she me caught in her arms long and small;°   *slender*
And therewithal sweetly did me kiss,
And softly said, *Dear heart,*[5] *how like you this?*

15 It was no dream, I lay broad waking.[6]
  But all is turned thorough° my gentleness   *through*
Into a strange fashion of forsaking;
  And I have leave to go of her goodness[7]
  And she also to use newfangleness.
20 But since that I so kindely[8] am served,
I would fain know what she hath deserved.

                                       E. MS.

The Lover Showeth How He Is Forsaken
of Such as He Sometime Enjoyed

[*They Flee from Me*]

They flee from me, that sometime did me seek
With naked foot stalking within my chamber.
Once have I seen them gentle, tame, and meek
That now are wild, and do not once remember
5   That sometime they have put themselves in danger

---

3. I.e., more than twenty times.
4. In a thin gown, made in a pleasing fashion.
5. With a pun on "heart" and "hart" (as deer).
6. I.e., wide awake.
7. Because of her goodness (ironic).

8. I.e., in the way typical of female nature, or "kind"; with kindness (ironic). "Newfangleness": a new fashion; novelty or inconstancy in her erotic relationships with men.

To take bread at my hand, and now they range,
Busily seeking in continual change.

Thanked be fortune, it hath been otherwise,
Twenty times better; but once especial,
10 In thin array, after a pleasant guise,
When her loose gown did from her shoulders fall,
And she me caught in her arms long and small,
And therewithal, so sweetly did me kiss
And softly said, "Dear heart, how like you this?"

15 It was no dream, for I lay broad awaking.
But all is turned now, through my gentleness,
Into a bitter fashion of forsaking.
And I have leave to go, of her goodness,
And she also to use newfangleness.
20 But since that I unkindly so am served,
How like you this, what hath she now deserved?

Tottel, 1557

Patience, Though I Have Not

Patience, though I have not
     The thing that I require,
I must of force, God wot,°   knows
     Forbear my most desire;[9]
5   For no ways can I find
     To sail against the wind.

Patience, do what they will
     To work me woe or spite,
I shall content me still
10   To think both day and night,
To think and hold my peace,
     Since there is no redress.

Patience, withouten blame[1]
     For I offended nought;
15 I know they know the same,
     Though they have changed their thought.
Was ever thought so moved
     To hate that it hath loved?

Patience of all my harm,[2]
20   For fortune is my foe;
Patience must be the charm
     To heal me of my woe:
Patience without offence
     Is a painful patience.

E. MS.

9. I.e., restrain or endure my strongest desire.   2. I.e., in all the harm I suffer.
1. I.e., when one is without blame.

My Lute Awake!

My lute awake! Perform the last
Labor that thou and I shall waste,
   And end that I have now begun;
For when this song is sung and past,
5   My lute be still, for I have done.

As to be heard where ear is none,
As lead to grave° in marble stone,[3]   *engrave*
   My song may pierce her heart as soon;
Should we then sigh, or sing, or moan?
10   No, no, my lute, for I have done.

The rocks do not so cruelly
Repulse the waves continually
   As she my suit and affection.
So that I am past remedy:
15   Whereby my lute and I have done.

Proud of the spoil that thou hast got
Of simple hearts thorough° love's shot,[4]   *through*
   By whom, unkind, thou hast them won,
Think not he hath his bow forgot,
20   Although my lute and I have done.

Vengeance shall fall on thy disdain,
That makest but game[5] on earnest pain;
   Think not alone under the sun
Unquit° to cause thy lovers plain,°   *unrequited / lamentation*
25   Although my lute and I have done.

Perchance thee lie withered and old,
The winter nights that are so cold,
   Plaining in vain unto the moon;
Thy wishes then dare not be told;
30   Care then who list,° for I have done.   *likes*

And then may chance thee to repent
The time that thou hast lost and spent
   To cause thy lovers sigh and swoon;
Then shalt thou know beauty but lent,
35   And wish and want as I have done.

Now cease, my lute, this is the last
Labor that thou and I shall waste,
   And ended is that we begun;
Now is this song both sung and past:
40   My lute be still, for I have done.

E. MS.

---

3. I.e., it is as likely that sound will be heard with no ear to hear it, or soft lead will be able to engrave hard marble, as it is that my song will move her.

4. Cupid's arrow. The referent for "thou" is unclear.

5. Makes fun of or plays games with one in pain.

Is It Possible

Is it possible
That so high debate,
So sharp, so sore, and of such rate,°   pace
Should end so soon and was begun so late?
5   Is it possible?

Is it possible
So cruel intent,
So hasty heat and so soon spent,
From love to hate, and thence for to relent?
10   Is it possible?

Is it possible
That any may find
Within one heart so diverse mind,
To change or turn as weather and wind?
15   Is it possible?

Is it possible
To spy it in an eye[6]
That turns as oft as chance on die?[7]
The troth° whereof can any try?   truth, faith
20   Is it possible?

It is possible
For to turn so oft,
To bring that lowest that was most aloft,
And to fall highest[8] yet to light soft?
25   It is possible.

All is possible,
Whoso list° believe;   cares to
Trust therefore first, and after preve:[9]
As men wed ladies by license and leave,
30   All is possible.

                                                  D. MS.

Forget Not Yet

Forget not yet the tried intent
Of such a truth as I have meant,
My great travail so gladly spent
Forget not yet.

---

6. I.e., to spy love; the eyes were often said to be where a person's true feelings could be seen.
7. I.e, as often as fortune changes in tosses of the dice.
8. From the highest place. The imagery here plays on the Renaissance figure of the wheel of life, the frequent turning of which causes people's fortunes to rise and fall unpredictably.
9. I.e., learn by experience.

5 Forget not yet when first began
The weary life ye know since whan,°   *when*
The suit, the service none tell¹ can.
        Forget not yet.

Forget not yet the great assays,°   *trials*
10 The cruel wrong, the scornful ways,
The painful patience in denays,°   *denials*
        Forget not yet.

Forget not yet, forget not this,
How long ago hath been and is
15 The mind that never meant amiss,
        Forget not yet.

Forget not then thine own approved,²
The which so long hath thee so loved,
Whose steadfast faith yet never moved,
20   Forget not this.

                                        D. MS.

What Should I Say

What should I say
        Since faith is dead,
And truth away
        From you is fled?
5   Should I be led
With doubleness?
Nay, nay, Mistress!³

I promised you
        And you promised me,
10 To be as true
        As I would be;
        But since I see
Your double heart,
Farewell my part!⁴

15 Though for to take
        It is not my mind
But to forsake —
        I am not blind —
        And as I find
20 So will I trust.
Farewell, unjust!

Can ye say nay?
        But you said

---

1. Give an account of, estimate. In courtly rhetoric, "service" often meant the actions of a male lover.
2. I.e., the one of whom you approved.

3. Title for an upper-class married woman; a courteous form.
4. Share in the relationship; possible pun on the French word for loss *(perte)*.

That I alway°   *always*
25   Should be obeyed;[5]
And thus betrayed
Or° that I wist°—   *before / knew*
Farewell, unkist!°   *unkissed*

D. MS.

Of Such as Had Forsaken Him

Lux,[6] my fair falcon, and thy fellows all:
How well pleasant it were your liberty:
Ye not forsake me, that fair might you fall.[7]
But they that sometime° liked my company: *formerly*
5   Like lice away from dead bodies they crawl.
Lo, what a proof in light adversity?
But ye my birds, I swear by all your bells,[8]
Ye be my friends, and very few else.

Tottel, 1557

Stand Whoso List[9]

Stand whoso list° upon the slipper° top   *likes / slippery*
Of court's estates, and let me here rejoice;
And use me quiet without let or stop,°   *hindrance*
Unknown in court, that hath such brackish[1] joys:
5   In hidden place, so let my days forth pass,
That when my years be done, withouten noise,
I may die aged after the common trace.°   *way*
For him death gripeth right hard by the crope°   *throat*
That is much known of other; and of himself, alas,
10   Doth die unknown, dazed with dreadful[2] face.

Arundel Castle MS.

Mine Own John Poins[3]

Mine own John Poins, since ye delight to know
The cause why that homeward I me draw,
And flee the press of courts whereso they go,[4]

---

5. Some contemporary marriage services included a vow by the woman to obey the man; the point raises the possibility that the poem is addressed to the speaker's wife.
6. This poem appears in all editions of *Tottel's Miscellany* and in one manuscript (Additional MS 36529) in the British Museum. Scholars speculate that the poem was written shortly before Wyatt was imprisoned in 1541. The title was added by Tottel.
7. The original punctuation has been retained for these difficult lines, which initiate a contrast between the falcons who do not forsake their master and humans who do. In the manuscript version, the words "might ye befall" appear where Tottel prints "mought [might] you fall."
8. A bell was attached by a leather strap to each leg of a falcon.
9. This poem, a translation of Seneca's play *Thy-*

estes, lines 391–404, was printed in a quite different version by Tottel under the title "Of the meane and sure estate." The same passage from Seneca was later translated into English verse by Andrew Marvell (1621–1678) and by Abraham Cowley (1618–1667).
1. Spoiled, like water that has gone bad.
2. Has a variety of possible meanings, including awful, terrified, and frightening.
3. Wyatt's friend; a member of Henry VIII's court. This verse epistle of informal satire is based on the tenth satire of the Italian Luigi Alamanni, but Wyatt Anglicizes it and adds personal details. It apparently was written during Wyatt's banishment from court in 1536.
4. The royal court frequently moved residence in Renaissance England, sometimes through highly elaborate "progresses" or processions.

Rather than to live thrall, under the awe
5 Of lordly looks, wrapped within my cloak,
  To will and lust° learning to set a law;[5]   *pleasure*
It is not for because I scorn and mock
  The power of them, to whom fortune hath lent
  Charge over us, of right, to strike the stroke:[6]
10 But true it is that I have always meant
  Less to esteem them than the common sort,[7]
  Of outward things that judge in their intent,
Without regard what doth inward resort.
  I grant sometime that of glory the fire
15 Doth touch my heart: me list not[8] to report
Blame by honor and honor to desire.[9]
  But how may I this honor now attain
  That cannot dye the color black a liar?[1]
My Poins, I cannot frame me tune to feign,[2]
20 To cloak the truth, for praise without desert,° *undeservedly*
  Of them that list all vice for to retain.[3]
I cannot honor them that sets their part
  With Venus and Bacchus[4] all their life long;
  Nor hold my peace of them although I smart.
25 I cannot crouch nor kneel to do so great a wrong,
  To worship them, like God on earth alone,
  That are as wolves these sely° lambs among.   *innocent*
I cannot with my words complain and moan,
  And suffer naught; nor smart without complaint,
30 Nor turn the word that from my mouth is gone.
I cannot speak and look like a saint,
  Use wiles° for wit or make deceit a pleasure,   *cunning*
  And call craft° counsel, for profit still to paint;° *scheming / flatter*
I cannot wrest the law to fill the coffer
35 With innocent blood to feed myself fat,
  And do most hurt where most help I offer.
I am not he that can allow° the state   *accept*
  Of high Caesar and damn Cato to die,
  That with his death did 'scape out of the gate
40 From Caesar's hands (if Livy do not lie)[5]
  And would not live where liberty was lost:
  So did his heart the common weal apply.[6]
I am not he such eloquence to boast,
  To make the crow singing as the swan,[7]
45 Nor call the lion of coward beasts the most[8]
That cannot take a mouse as the cat can:

5. I.e., learning to set a law to (or keep in check) my passions.
6. I.e., rightfully empowered to command and to punish us.
7. I.e., to have less esteem for them than do the common people (line 11), who base their judgment on what appears outwardly (lines 12–13).
8. "Me list not": I care not.
9. I.e., I have no wish to represent faults as virtues or pleasure as honor.
1. A common proverb held that "black will take no other hue."

2. I.e., shape my style falsely.
3. I.e., desire to keep vice in their service.
4. Venus was the Roman goddess of love; Bacchus, the Roman god of wine.
5. The Roman historian Livy recounts the death of Cato the Younger, who committed suicide rather than submit to Caesar's tyranny.
6. I.e., so did his heart practice the common good.
7. Swans supposedly sang beautifully just before dying.
8. Nor call a lion (a symbol of bravery) a coward.

And he that dieth for hunger of the gold
Call him Alexander;[9] and say that Pan
Passeth Apollo in music manifold;[1]
50   Praise Sir Thopas for a noble tale,
And scorn the story that the Knight told.[2]
Praise him for counsel that is drunk of ale;
Grin when he laugheth that beareth all the sway,
Frown when he frowneth and groan when he is pale;
55 On others' lust to hang both night and day:
None of these points would ever frame in me;[3]
My wit is naught—I cannot learn the way.
And much the less of things that greater be,
That asken help of colors of device[4]
60   To join the mean° with each extremity,   *middle*
With the nearest virtue to cloak° alway the vice: *soften, cover*
And as to purpose likewise it shall fall,
To press° the virtue that it may not rise;[5]   *to press down*
As drunkenness good fellowship to call;
65   The friendly foe with his double face
Say he is gentle and courteous therewithal;
And say that favel° hath a goodly grace   *flattery*
In eloquence; and cruelty to name
Zeal of justice and change in time and place;
70 And he that suff'reth offense without blame
Call him pitiful; and him true and plain
That raileth reckless[6] to every man's shame.
Say he is rude that cannot lie and feign;
The lecher a lover; and tyranny
75   To be the right of a prince's reign.
I cannot, I. No, no, it will not be.
This is the cause° that I could never yet   *reason*
Hang on their sleeves that weigh as thou mayst see
A chip[7] of chance more than a pound of wit.
80   This maketh me at home to hunt and hawk
And in foul weather at my book to sit.
In frost and snow then with my bow to stalk,
No man doth mark whereso I ride or go;
In lusty leas° at liberty I walk,   *pleasant meadows*
85 And of these news I feel nor weal° nor woe,   *happiness*
Save that a clog doth hang yet at my heel:[8]
No force° for that for it is ordered so,   *no matter*
That I may leap both hedge and dike[9] full well.
I am not now in France to judge the wine,

9. Say that he is Alexander the Great (356–323 B.C.), who was said to prefer glory and action to riches; i.e., he cannot say that one who is greedy for gold instead prefers glory.
1. The god Pan played simple ditties on his pipe; Apollo played divine melodies on his lyre.
2. Chaucer's tale of Sir Thopas (in *The Canterbury Tales*) is a deliberately dull parody that is cut off after a few stanzas by the Host. "The Knight's Tale," according to other pilgrims, is "a noble storie."
3. I.e., suit my character.
4. Artful language that "colors" or falsifies.
5. I.e., and intention will be subsumed by the deceit.
6. Rants abusively.
7. A small amount.
8. A clog was a heavy object tied to a prisoner's foot to impede motion.
9. Ditch, used as a boundary.

90   With sav'ry sauce those delicates to feel;[1]
Nor yet in Spain where one must him incline
    Rather than to be, outwardly to seem.
    I meddle not with wits that be so fine,
Nor Flanders' cheer letteth° not my sight to deem   *hinders*
95   Of black and white,[2] nor taketh my wit away
    With beastliness, they beasts do so esteem;
Nor am I not where Christ is given in prey
    For money, poison, and treason at Rome,[3]
    A common practice used night and day:
100   But here I am in Kent and Christendom
    Among the Muses where I read and rhyme;
    Where if thou list, my Poins, for to come,
Thou shalt be judge how I do spend my time.

                   E. MS.

HENRY HOWARD, EARL OF SURREY

ca. 1517–1547

The Soote Season[1]

The soote° season, that bud and bloom forth brings,   *sweet*
With green hath clad the hill and eke° the vale;   *also*
The nightingale with feathers new she sings;
The turtle° to her make° hath told her tale.   *turtledove / mate*
5 Summer is come, for every spray now springs;
The hart hath hung his old head on the pale;[2]
The buck in brake° his winter coat he flings,   *the bushes*
The fishes float with new repairèd scale;
The adder all her slough away she slings,
10 The swift swallow pursueth the flies small;
The busy bee her honey now she mings.°   *discharges*
Winter is worn, that was the flowers' bale.°   *harm*
    And thus I see among these pleasant things,
    Each care decays, and yet my sorrow springs.

                 1557

Love, That Doth Reign and Live Within My Thought[3]

Love, that doth reign and live within my thought,
And built his seat within my captive breast,
Clad in the arms° wherein with me he fought,   *heraldic insignia*

---

1. To savor exquisite food.
2. I.e., to be able to tell the difference between black and white. "Flanders' cheer": in the sixteenth century the Flemings were notorious for drinking.
3. In *Tottel's Miscellany*, published in 1557, during the reign of the Catholic Queen Mary, these lines read: "where truth is given prey / For money, poison and treason; of some."
1. An adaptation of Petrarch's *Rime* 310; first pub-

lished, along with poems by Wyatt and others, in Tottel's *Songs and Sonnets*, commonly known as Tottel's *Miscellany* (1557), an important early anthology.
2. I.e., has hung his antlers on the fence, or paling.
3. Translated from Petrarch, *Rime* 140. Compare the translation by Sir Thomas Wyatt, "The Long Love, That in My Thought Doth Harbor" (p. 113).

Oft in my face he doth his banner rest.
5　But she that taught me love and suffer pain,
　　My doubtful hope and eke° my hot desire　　　　　　　　　*also*
　　With shamefast° look to shadow and refrain,　　　　　　*shamefaced*
　　Her smiling grace converteth straight to ire.
　　And coward Love, then, to the heart apace°　　　　　　*quickly*
10　Taketh his flight, where he doth lurk and plain,°　　　*complain*
　　His purpose lost, and dare not show his face.
　　For my lord's guilt thus faultless bide° I pain,　　　*endure*
　　Yet from my lord shall not my foot remove:[4]
　　Sweet is the death that taketh end by love.

1557

Wyatt Resteth Here[5]

　　Wyatt resteth here, that quick° could never rest;　　*living*
　　Whose heavenly gifts increasèd by disdain,[6]
　　And virtue sank the deeper in his breast;
　　Such profit he of envy could obtain.
5　A head where wisdom mysteries[7] did frame,
　　Whose hammers beat still in that lively brain
　　As on a stithy,° where some work of fame　　　　　　*anvil*
　　Was daily wrought, to turn to Britain's gain.
　　A visage stern and mild, where both did grow,
10　Vice to contemn, in virtues to rejoice,
　　Amid great storms, whom grace assurèd so,
　　To live upright, and smile at fortune's choice.
　　A hand that taught what might be said in rhyme;
　　That reft° Chaucer the glory of his wit;　　　　　　*bereft*
15　A mark, the which—unperfited,° for time—　　　　*uncompleted*
　　Some may approach, but never none shall hit.
　　A tongue that served in foreign realms his king;
　　Whose courteous talk to virtue did enflame
　　Each noble heart; a worthy guide to bring
20　Our English youth, by travail, unto fame.
　　An eye whose judgment no affect° could blind,　　*passion*
　　Friends to allure, and foes to reconcile;
　　Whose piercing look did represent a mind
　　With virtue fraught, reposèd, void of guile.
25　A heart where dread yet never so impressed
　　To hide the thought that might the truth advance;
　　In neither fortune lost, nor so repressed,
　　To swell in wealth, nor yield unto mischance.
　　A valiant corps,° where force and beauty met,　　*body*
30　Happy, alas! too happy, but for foes,
　　Livèd, and ran the race that nature set;
　　Of manhood's shape, where she the mold did lose.
　　But to the heavens that simple soul is fled,
　　Which left with such as covet Christ to know[8]

---

4. I.e., I will not leave his side.
5. Surrey's epitaph on Thomas Wyatt (1503–1542), published in 1542, soon after Wyatt's death.
6. I.e., by others' disdain (as in line 4, of others'
"envy").
7. Hidden or subtle meanings.
8. I.e., Christians.

35 Witness of faith that never shall be dead,
Sent for our health, but not receivèd so.
Thus, for our guilt, this jewel have we lost;
The earth his bones, the heavens possess his ghost.

1557

So Cruel Prison[9]

So cruel prison how could betide,° alas,   *befall*
As proud Windsor?[1] Where I in lust° and joy   *pleasure*
With a king's son my childish° years did pass   *youthful*
In greater feast than Priam's sons of Troy;[2]
5 Where each sweet place returns a taste full sour:
The large green courts where we were wont to hove°   *linger*
With eyes cast up unto the maidens' tower,
And easy sighs, such as folk draw in love;
The stately sales,° the ladies bright of hue,   *halls*
10 The dances short, long tales of great delight;
With words and looks that tigers could but rue,[3]
Where each of us did plead the other's right;
The palm play,° where, despoilèd° for the game,   *handball / disrobed*
With dazèd eyes oft we by gleams of love
15 Have missed the ball and got sight of our dame,
To bait[4] her eyes, which kept the leads above;
The graveled ground, with sleeves tied on the helm,[5]
On foaming horse, with swords and friendly hearts,
With cheer, as though the one should overwhelm;
20 Where we have fought, and chasèd oft with darts,
With silver drops the meads° yet spread for ruth,°   *meadows / pity*
In active games of nimbleness and strength,
Where we did strain, trailed by swarms of youth,
Our tender limbs that yet shot up in length;
25 The secret groves which oft we made resound
Of pleasant plaint and of our ladies' praise,
Recording soft what grace each one had found,
What hope of speed, what dread of long delays;
The wild forest, the clothèd holt° with green,   *small wood*
30 With reins avaled,° and swift ybreathèd° horse,   *slackened / exercised*
With cry of hounds and merry blasts between,
Where we did chase the fearful hart aforce;°   *strenuously*
The void walls eke° that harbored us each night,   *also*
Wherewith, alas, revive within my breast
35 The sweet accord; such sleeps as yet delight,
The pleasant dreams, the quiet bed of rest;
The secret thoughts imparted with such trust,

9. As a boy and young man, Surrey had enjoyed the life at Windsor Palace as the close friend of Henry Fitzroy, an illegitimate son of Henry VIII. In 1537, a year after the death of his friend, Surrey was imprisoned temporarily at Windsor for striking another courtier.
1. I.e., how could proud Windsor (Castle) have become such a cruel prison?
2. Priam, king of Troy.

3. The tiger conventionally symbolized unfeeling savagery.
4. To feed, as a fire with fuel. The "leads" from which the lady watches may be either a leaded window or a flat, leaded roof.
5. A knight would customarily tie a favor received from a lady to his sleeve or helmet and wear it into a joust or a battle. "Graveled ground": tiltyard; space strewn with gravel for jousting.

The wanton talk, the divers change of play,
The friendship sworn, each promise kept so just,
40 Wherewith we passed the winter nights away.
And with this thought the blood forsakes my face,
The tears berain° my cheeks of deadly hue,   *wet*
The which as soon as sobbing sighs, alas,
Upsuppèd° have, thus I my plaint renew: *absorbed*
45 O place of bliss, renewer of my woes,
Give me accompt⁶—where is my noble fere?°   *companion*
Whom in thy walls thou didst each night enclose,
To other lief,° but unto me most dear!   *beloved*
Echo, alas, that doth my sorrow rue,
50 Returns thereto a hollow sound of plaint.
Thus I, alone, where all my freedom grew,
In prison pine with bondage and restraint;
And with remembrance of the greater grief
To banish the less, I find my chief relief.

1557

Norfolk Sprung Thee, Lambeth Holds Thee Dead⁷

Norfolk sprung° thee, Lambeth holds thee dead;   *gave birth to*
Clere, of the Count of Cleremont,⁸ thou hight!°   *are called*
Within the womb of Ormond's race thou bred,
And saw'st thy cousin crowned in thy sight.⁹
5 Shelton for love, Surrey for lord thou chase;¹
(Aye, me! whilst life did last that league° was tender)   *bond*
Tracing whose steps thou sawest Kelsal blaze,²
Landrecy burnt, and battered Boulogne render.³
At Montreuil gates, hopeless of all recure,⁴
10 Thine Earl, half dead, gave in thy hand his will;
Which cause did thee this pining death procure,
Ere summers four times seven thou couldst fulfill.
Ah! Clere! if love had booted° care or cost,   *valued*
Heaven had not won, nor earth so timely° lost.   *early*

ca. 1545   1605

---

6. I.e., tell me.
7. This epitaph is for Thomas Clere, Surrey's squire who died in 1545 from a wound he received while saving Surrey's life. It was first published in William Camden, *Remaines of a greater worke concerning Britaine.*
8. Clere was the youngest son of Sir Robert Clere, of Ormesby in Norfolk, a descendant of Clere, of Cleremont in Normandy; Clere was buried in Lambeth churchyard.
9. Clere was first cousin to Anne Boleyn, Henry VIII's second wife, who was crowned in 1533 and executed in 1536. Clere was the great-grandson of Thomas Boteler, earl of Ormond.
1. Chose; Clere married Mary Shelton.

2. Surrey and Clere were with the British forces that burned Kelsal, a Scottish town, in 1542.
3. Surrender. Surrey took part in a siege of the French city of Landrecy by allied English and Spanish forces in 1543; although the city was not taken, it was set on fire by a battery of mortars. Surrey was the marshall of the field when the French city of Boulogne surrendered to the British in 1544.
4. Rescue. In 1544, Surrey lead an attack against the besieged French city of Montreuil. Due to a lack of adequate reinforcements, the attack failed and the wounded Surrey was rescued by Clere; during this rescue Clere received the wound from which he died in April 1545.

NICHOLAS GRIMALD

1519?–1562?

From A Funeral Song, Upon the Decease of Annes His Mother[1]

Yea, and a good cause why thus should I plain.
For what is he, can quietly sustain
So great a grief, with mouth as still as stone?
My love, my life, of joy my jewel is gone.
5   This hearty zeal if any wight° disprove,   *creature*
As woman's work, whom feeble mind doth move:
He neither knows the mighty nature's laws,
Nor touching elders' deeds hath seen old saws.
Martius, to vanquish Rome, was set on fire:
10   But vanquisht fell, at mother's boon,° his ire.[2]   *request*

*   *   *

And should not I express my inward woe,
When you, most loving dam, so soon hence go?
I, in your fruitful womb conceived, born was,
30   While wandering moon ten months did overpass.
Me, brought to light, your tender arms sustained:
And, with my lips, your milky paps I strained.°   *squeezed*
You me embraced, in bosom soft you me
Cherished, as I your only childe had be.°   *been*
35   Of yssue° fair with numbers were you blest: *children*
Yet I, the best-beloved of all the rest.
Good luck, certain fore-reading° mothers have,   *able to foresee the future*
And you of me a special judgement gave.
Then, when firm pase° I fixèd on the ground,   *foot, pace*
40   When tongue gan° cease to break the lisping sound: *began*
You me straightway did to the Muses send,
Ne° suffered long a loitering life to spend   *nor*
What gain the wool, what gain the web has brought;[3]
It was his meed,° that me there daily taught.   *reward*
45   When with Minerve I had acquaintance won:
And Pheobus[4] seemed to love me, as his son:
Brownshold[5] I bad, at parents' hest,° farewell: *behest*
And gladly there in schools I gan to dwell:
Where Granta° gives the ladies nine° such place,   *Cambridge / the Muses*
50   That they rejoice to see their blisful case.
With joys at heart, in this Pernasse[6] I bode,

---

1. Grimald's mother, Agnes (of which name "Annes" is a common variation), died sometime after her son left Oxford in January 1552; the poem was first published in Richard Tottel's *Songs and Sonnets* (1557).
2. Gaius Martius Coriolanus, insulted by the Romans, led an enemy force against Rome; he spared the city because his mother begged him to do so.
3. "What gain the wool . . . the web": the products of both nature and cultivation. "Muses": nine sister goddesses thought to be the sources of inspiration for the arts.
4. God of poetry. Minerva, goddess of wisdom.
5. "Brownshold": Grimald was born in Leighton-Bromswold in Huntingdonshire.
6. Parnassus, home of the Muses.

While, through his signs, five times great Titan glode:°   *glided*
And twice as long, by that fair ford,° whereas   *Oxford*
Swanfeeder Temms° no furder course can pass.   *Thames River*
55 O, what desire had you, therewhile, of me?
Mid doubtful dreads, what joys were wont to be?
Now linen clothes, wrought with those fingers fine,
Now other things of yours did you make mine:
Till your last threads gan Clotho[7] to untwine,
60 And of your days the date extreme assign.
Hearing the chance, your neighbors made much moan:
A dearworth dame, they thought their comfort gone.
Kinswomen wept: your charge, the maidens wept:
Your daughters wept, whom you so well had kept.
65 But my good sire° gave, with soft words, relief: *father*
And cloaks, with outward cheer, his inward grief:
Lest, by his care, your sickness should augment,
And on his case your thoughtful heart be bent.
You, not forgetting yet a mother's mood,
70 When at the door dart-hurling death there stood,
Did say: Adieu, dear spouse, my race is run;
Where so he be, I have left you a son,
And Nicolas you named, and named again:
With other speech, aspiring° heavenly reign: *aspiring to*
75 When into air your sprite departed fled,
And left the corpse a cold in lukewarm bed.
Ah, could you thus, dear mother, leave us all?
Now, should you live: that yet, before your fall,
My songs you might have sung, have heard my voice,
80 And in commodities of your own rejoyce.

✧   ✧   ✧

1557

ANNE ASKEW

1521–1546

The Ballad Which Anne Askewe Made and Sang When She Was in Newgate[1]

Like as the armèd knight
Appointed to the field,
With this world will I fight

---

7. One of the three Fates (from Greek *Klothes*, "spinners").
1. Askew was arrested and examined for heresy in June 1545. She was released, but was arrested again in June 1546, subjected to torture, and burned at the stake in July 1546. This ballad was included in the Protestant Bishop John Bale's two accounts of her examination and death, printed in 1546 and 1547, respectively. "Newgate": a London prison.

And faith shall be my shield.[2]
5   Faith is that weapon strong
Which will not fail at need;
My foes therefore among
Therewith will I proceed.
  As it is had in strength
10 And force of Christ's way,
It will prevail at length
Though all the devils say nay.
  Faith in the father's old
Obtainèd rightwiseness°   *righteousness*
15 Which make me very bold
To fear no world's distress.
  I now rejoice in heart
And hope bid me do so,
For Christ will take my part
20 And ease me of my woe.
  Thou sayst lord, who so kneck,[3]
To them wilt thou attend;
Undo therefore the lock
And thy strong power send.
25   More enemies now I have
Than hairs upon my head
Let them not me deprave,°   *villify*
But fight thou in my stead.
  On thee my care I cast
30 For all their cruel spite
I set not by their haste,[4]
For thou art my delight.
  I am not she that list°   *chooses*
My anchor to let fall
35 For every drizzling mist
My ship substantial.
  Not oft use I to write
In prose nor yet in rhyme,
Yet will I show one sight
40 That I saw in my time.
  I saw a royal throne
Where Justice should have sit,
But in her stead was one
Of modie° cruel wit.   *wrathful*
45   Absorbed° was rightwiseness   *swallowed up*
As of the raging flood;
Satan in his excess
Sucked up the guiltless blood.
  Then thought I, Jesus lord,

---

2. Ephesians 6.13–17 exhorts the Christian to put on "the whole armor of God," including "the shield of faith, with which ye shall be able to quench all the fiery darts of the wicked."

3. Knocks. Matthew 7.7: "Ask, and it shall be given you; seek, and ye shall find; knock, and it shall be opened unto you."

4. I have no regard for their haste or rashness.

50 When thou shalt judge us all,
Hard is it to record
On these men what will fall.
  Yet lord I thee desire
For that° they do to me,   *what*
55 Let them not taste the hire°   *reward*
Of their iniquity.[5]

1546

QUEEN ELIZABETH I

1533–1603

When I Was Fair and Young[1]

When I was fair and young, then favor graced me.
Of many was I sought their mistress° for to be,   *sweetheart*
But I did scorn them all and answered them therefore:
Go, go, go, seek some other where, importune me no more.

5 How many weeping eyes I made to pine in woe,
How many sighing hearts I have not skill to show,
But I the prouder grew and still this spake therefore:
Go, go, go, seek some other where, importune me no more.

Then spake fair Venus' son,° that proud victorious boy,   *Cupid*
10 Saying: You dainty dame, for that you be so coy,
I will so pluck your plumes[2] as you shall say no more:
Go, go, go, seek some other where, importune me no more.

As soon as he had said, such change[3] grew in my breast
That neither night nor day I could take any rest.
15 Wherefore I did repent that I had said before:
Go, go, go, seek some other where, importune me no more.

ca. 1585?   1964

---

5. Christ on the cross also asks mercy for his persecutors: "Father, forgive them; for they know not what they do" (Luke 23.34).

1. This poem is found with many variations in five manuscripts. We follow Leicester Bradner, *The Poems of Queen Elizabeth,* in using the British Museum's Harleian 7392 as the basis for our text. The Bodleian Library's Rawlinson manuscript, written between 1590 and 1600, also contains a version of the poem and states, furthermore, that it was written when Elizabeth "was suposed to be in love with mounsyre," that is, her French suitor, the duke of Alençon. Some modern scholars doubt that Elizabeth wrote the poem, but all accept it as an important cultural document about her.

2. I.e., remove your pride; a reference to the brightly colored plumes of the peacock, a traditional symbol of pride.

3. One manuscript, in the Folger Library, substitutes "care" for "change"; in the Bodleian's copy, the phrase "When he had spake these words" appears in lieu of "As soon as he had said."

[The doubt of future foes exiles my present joy][4]

The doubt of future foes exiles my present joy,
And wit me warns to shun such snares as threaten mine annoy;[5]
For falsehood now doth flow, and subjects' faith doth ebb,
Which should not be if reason ruled or wisdom weaved the web.
5 But clouds of joys untried do cloak aspiring minds,
Which turn to rain of late repent by changed course of winds.
The top of hope supposed the root upreared° shall be,[6]   *exalted*
And fruitless all their grafted guile,[7] as shortly ye shall see.
The dazzled eyes with pride, which great ambition blinds,
10 Shall be unsealed[8] by worthy wights° whose foresight falsehood   *people*
    finds.
The daughter of debate that discord aye doth sow
Shall reap no gain where former rule still peace hath taught to know.
No foreign banished wight[9] shall anchor in this port;
Our realm brooks° not seditious sects, let them elsewhere resort.   *tolerates*
15 My rusty sword through rest shall first his edge employ
To poll their tops[1] that seek such change or gape° for future joy.   *long*
ca. 1570   1589

[Ah silly pugg wert thou so sore afraid][2]

Ah silly pugg wert thou so sore afraid,
mourn not (my Wat[3]) nor be thou so dismayed,
it passeth fickle fortune's power and skill,
to force my heart to think thee any ill.
5 No fortune base thou saiest shall alter thee,
and may so blind a Witch[4] so conquer me?
no no my pugg, though fortune were not blind,
assure thy self she could not rule my mind.
fortune I know sometimes doth conquer kings
10 and rules & reigns on earth & earthly things
But never think fortune can bear the sway,
if virtue watch & will not her obey

---

4. This poem is written in poulter's measure—alternating lines of six and seven beats (see "Essay on Versification" [p. lxxvii])—a popular form at this time (see Philip Sidney, "What Length of Verse?" [pp. 190–91]). It appears to answer a sonnet written by Elizabeth's Catholic cousin Mary Stuart, queen of Scotland, in which Mary, who had fled to England from imprisonment in Scotland in 1568, asks to see Elizabeth. Until her execution in 1587, Mary was a constant threat, the impetus of many plots to depose Elizabeth and seat herself on the English throne. "The daughter of debate" in line 11 and the "foreign banished wight" in line 13 apparently both refer to Mary.
    Versions of this poem appear in six manuscripts and two early printed texts, including George Puttenham's *Arte of English Poesie* (1589). Our text follows that of Bodleian Ms. Rawlinson, thought to have been compiled around 1570.
    "Doubt": danger or thing to be dreaded.
5. I.e., cause me discomfort or trouble.

6. Variants on this line include: "The top of hope suppressed the root upreared shall be" and "The top of hope supposed the root of ruth will be."
7. The image of grafting, or inserting a shoot into the root stock of another tree or plant, suggests that conspirators have attempted to plant their own seditious thoughts in the minds of others.
8. Unsewn or unopened, as the eyes of a hawk in the sport of hawking.
9. I.e., no person exiled to a foreign land.
1. I.e., cut off their heads.
2. This poem was written in answer to a poem by Sir Walter Ralegh, probably "Fortune hath taken thee away, my love" (p. 146). "Silly": deserving of pity or compassion; also foolish, lacking in judgment, helpless, defenseless, insignificant, or lowly; "pugg": a term of endearment.
3. A diminutive of Walter.
4. Fortune was often personified as a fickle woman and was sometimes depicted as blind or blind-folded.

ne° chose I thee by fickle fortune's rede,°   *neither / advice*
ne° she shall force me alter° with such speed   *nor / to change*
15 But if to try this mistress jest with thee,
. 5

Pull up thy heart suppress thy brackish° tears,   *salty*
torment thee not, but put away thy fears;
Dead to all joys & living unto woe,
Slain quite by her that nere gave wiseman blow
20 Revive again & live without all dread,
the less afraid the better thou shalt speed.°   *succeed, prosper*

ca. 1578–88   1992

GEORGE GASCOIGNE

ca. 1535–1577

And If I Did What Then?

"And if I did what then?
Are you aggrieved therefore?
The sea hath fish for every man,
And what would you have more?"

5 Thus did my mistress once
Amaze my mind with doubt,
And popped a question for the nonce[1]
To beat my brains about.

Whereto I thus replied:
10 "Each fisherman can wish
That all the sea at every tide
Were his alone to fish.

And so did I, in vain;
But since it may not be,
15 Let such fish there as find the gain,
And leave the loss for me.

And with such luck and loss
I will content myself,
Till tides of turning time may toss
20 Such fishers on the shelf.

And when they stick on sands,
That every man may see,
Then will I laugh and clap my hands,
As they do now at me."

---

5. A portion of the poem appears to be missing at   1. Expressly for the purpose of.
this point.

For That He Looked Not upon Her

You must not wonder, though you think it strange,
To see me hold my louring° head so low,   *sullen*
And that mine eyes take no delight to range
About the gleams which on your face do grow.
5   The mouse which once hath broken out of trap
Is seldom 'ticèd° with the trustless bait,   *enticed*
But lies aloof for fear of more mishap,
And feedeth still in doubt° of deep deceit.   *suspicion*
The scorchèd fly, which once hath 'scaped the flame,
10 Will hardly come to play again with fire,
Whereby I learn that grievous is the game
Which follows fancy dazzled by desire:
    So that I wink[2] or else hold down my head,
    Because your blazing eyes my bale° have bred.   *anguish*

Gascoigne's Lullaby

Sing lullaby, as women do,
Wherewith they bring their babes to rest,
And lullaby can I sing too,
As womanly as can the best.
5   With lullaby they still the child,
And if I be not much beguiled,
Full many wanton babes have I,
Which must be stilled with lullaby.

First, lullaby, my youthful years,
10 It is now time to go to bed,
For crooked age and hoary hairs
Have won the haven within my head.
With lullaby then, youth, be still,
With lullaby content they will,
15 Since courage quails° and comes behind,   *shrinks*
Go sleep, and so beguile thy mind.

Next, lullaby, my gazing eyes,
Which wonted were[3] to glance apace.°   *directly*
For every glass may now suffice
20 To show the furrows in my face.
With lullaby then wink[4] awhile,
With lullaby your looks beguile.
Let no fair face nor beauty bright
Entice you eft° with vain delight.   *after*

25 And lullaby, my wanton will,
Let reason's rule now rein thy thought,
Since all too late I find by skill°   *experience*

---

2. Close my eyes; also, blink.   4. I.e., shut your eyes.
3. Which were accustomed.

How dear I have thy fancies bought.
With lullaby now take thine ease,
30   With lullaby thy doubts appease.
For trust to this, if thou be still,
My body shall obey thy will.

Eke° lullaby, my loving boy,   *also*
My little Robin,[5] take thy rest.
35   Since age is cold and nothing coy,°   *lascivious*
Keep close thy coin, for so is best.
With lullaby be thou content,
With lullaby thy lusts relent.
Let others pay which° hath mo° pence;   *who / more*
40   Thou art too poor for such expense.

Thus, lullaby, my youth, mine eyes,
My will, my ware, and all that was.
I can no mo delays devise,
But welcome pain, let pleasure pass.
45   With lullaby now take your leave,
With lullaby your dreams deceive,
And when you rise with waking eye,
Remember Gascoigne's lullaby.

                                        1573

ISABELLA WHITNEY

fl. 1567–1573

FROM A SWEET NOSEGAY

A Communication Which the Author Had to London, Before She Made Her Will[1]

The time is come, I must depart
   from thee, ah famous city;
I never yet to rue my smart,
   did find that thou had'st pity.
5   Wherefore small cause there is, that I
   should grieve from thee to go;
But many women foolishly,
   like me, and other moe,°   *more*

---

5. I.e., a nickname for his penis.
1. This poem and the poetic testament that follows it conclude Whitney's volume *A Sweet Nosegay* (1573), a collection of poems that begins with 110 verse couplets of advice explicitly borrowed from Hugh Plat's *Flowers of Philosophy* (1572). While Plat's classicizing verses were aimed at an audience of university men and lawyers, Whitney's book seems designed for less privileged readers of both sexes. Her "will," occasioned not by impending death but rather by the poverty that compels her to leave London, plays on the fantasy that all of the city's riches are the author's to bequeath as she likes.

Do such a fixèd fancy set,
10   on those which least deserve,
That long it is ere wit we get
    away from them to swerve.
But time with pity oft will tell
    to those that will her try,
15 Whether it best be more to mell,°   *mix with*
    or utterly defy.
And now hath time me put in mind
    of thy great cruelness,
That never once a help would find,
20   to ease me in distress.
Thou never yet would'st credit give
    to board me for a year;
Nor with apparel me relieve,
    except thou payèd were.
25 No, no, thou never did'st me good,
    nor ever wilt, I know.
Yet am I in no angry mood,
    but will, or ere² I go,
In perfect love and charity,
30   my testament here write,
And leave to thee such treasury,
    as I in it recite.
Now stand aside and give me leave
    to write my latest will;
35 And see that none you do deceive
    of that I leave them till.°   *in the coffer*

From The Manner of Her Will, & What She Left to London, and to All Those in It, at Her Departing

I whole in body, and in mind,
    but very weak in purse,
Do make, and write my testament
    for fear it will be worse.
5 And first I wholly do commend
    my soul and body eke,°   *also*
To God the Father and the Son,
    so long as I can speak.
And after speech, my soul to him,
10   and body to the grave,
Till time that all shall rise again,
    their Judgement for to have.
And then I hope they both shall meet,
    to dwell for aye° in joy;   *ever*
15 Whereas° I trust to see my friends   *when*
    released from all annoy.
Thus have you heard touching my soul,
    and body what I mean:
I trust you all will witness bear,

---

2. In early modern English "or" was often used with "ere" to mean "before."

20   I have a steadfast brain.
O God, now let me dispose such things,
    as I shall leave behind,
That those which shall receive the same,
    may know my willing mind.
25   I first of all to London leave,
    because I there was bred,
Brave buildings rare, of churches store,
    and Paul's to the head.[3]
Between the same, fair treats there be,
30   and people goodly store;
Because their keeping craveth cost,
    I yet will leave him° more.   *them*
First for their food, I butchers leave,
    that every day shall kill;
35   In Thames you shall have brewers' store,
    and bakers at your will.
And such as orders do observe,
    and eat fish thrice a week,[4]
I leave two streets, full fraught therewith,[5]
40   they need not far to seek.
Watling Street, and Canwick Street,
    I full of wollen° leave;   *woolen goods*
And linen store in Friday Street,
    if they me not deceive.
45   And those which are of calling such,
    that costlier they require,
I mercers° leave, with silk so rich,   *textile merchants*
    as any would desire.[6]
In Cheap of them, they store shall find,
50   and likewise in that street,
I goldsmiths leave, with jewels such,[7]
    as are for ladies meet.

        ✧   ✧   ✧

Now when the folk are fed and clad
90   with such as I have named,
For dainty mouths, and stomachs weak
    some junckets° must be framed.   *sweet cakes*
Wherefore I potecaries leave,
    with banquets in their shop;[8]
95   Physicians also for the sick,

---

3. The greatest of the "store" (repository) of London's sixteenth-century churches was St. Paul's Cathedral.

4. Evidently playing on religious and secular meanings of "order," i.e., the clergy (those "in orders") and also anyone who obeyed the Act of 1563, which sought to stimulate the fishing trade by decreeing that fish was to be eaten three days a week rather than the two days stipulated in an Act of 1548.

5. Possibly "Old Fish Street," London's original fish market, and "New Fish Street," in a different part of the city. There were, however, other streets in which fish was sold.

6. Possibly an ironic allusion to the Sumptuary Laws that prevented persons below certain social ranks (or "callings," a Protestant term for vocation) from wearing luxurious fabrics.

7. I.e., she bequeathes to goldsmiths their own street, "Goldsmith's Row," which was on the south side of Cheapside Market ("Cheap"); there, those who "require costlier" things may find many (a "store") of them.

8. Apothecaries carried not only drugs but also spices; hence one could supply "banquets" in their shops.

Diseases for to stop.
Some roysters° still must bide in thee,   *revellers*
    and such as cut it out;°   *show off*
That with the guiltless quarrel will,
100   to let their blood about.
For them I cunning surgeons[9] leave,
    some plasters to apply,
That ruffians may not still be hanged,
    nor quiet persons die.

✻   ✻   ✻

To all the bookbinders by Paul's,
    because I like their art,
195 They every week shall money have,
    when they from books depart.
Among them all, my printer must
    have somewhat to his share;
I will my friends these books to buy
200   of him, with other ware.
For maidens poor, I widowers rich
    do leave, that oft shall dote:
And by that means shall marry them,
    to set the girls afloat.
205 And wealthy widows will I leave
    to help young gentlemen;
Which when you have, in any case,
    be courteous to them then:
And see their plate° and jewels eke°   *silverware / also*
210   may not be marred with rust;
Nor let their bags too long be full,
    for fear that they do burst.

✻   ✻   ✻

225 And Bedlam[1] must not be forgot,
    for that was oft my walk:
I people there too many leave,
    that out of tune do talk.

✻   ✻   ✻

235 At th' Inns of Court, I lawyers leave
    to take their case in hand.
And also leave I at each Inn
    of Court, or Chancery,[2]
Of gentlemen, a youthful roote,°   *rout, throng*
240   full of activity,
For whom I store of books have left,
    at each bookbinder's stall:

---

9. Surgeons generally practiced "manual" arts of healing and operating in the early modern era and hence were often regarded as distinct from (and inferior to) physicians (see line 95).
1. The Hospital of St. Mary of Bethlehem, for the mentally ill; compare "Tom o' Bedlam's Song" (p. 111).
2. The court of the lord chancellor of England, in which a number of young men lived and trained as clerks; the Inns of Court housed and trained students in the Common Law.

And part of all that London hath,
    to furnish them withal.
245 And when they are with study cloyed,°   *overfed*
    to recreate their mind,
Of tennis courts, of dancing schools,
    and fence° they store shall find.   *fencing*
And every Sunday at the least,
250   I leave to make them sport,
In divers places players, that
    of wonders shall report.
Now, London, have I (for thy sake)
    within thee, and without,[3]
255 As comes into my memory,
    dispersèd 'round about
Such needful things as they should have,
    here left now unto thee;
When I am gone, with conscience,
260   let them dispersèd be.
And though I nothing namèd have,
    to bury me withal,
Consider that above the ground,
    annoyance be I shall.
265 And let me have a shrouding sheet
    to cover me from shame,
And in oblivion bury me,
    and never more me name.
Ringings nor other ceremonies
270   use you not for cost,
Nor at my burial, make no feast,
    your money were but lost.

*   *   *

This xx of October, I,
    in ANNO DOMINI,°   *year of our Lord*
A thousand, v. hundred seventy-three,
315   as almanacs descry,°   *show*
Did write this will with mine own hand,
    and it to London gave;
In witness of the standers-by,
    whose names, if you will have,
320 paper, pen and standish° were,   *writing stand*
    at that same present by,°   *nearby*
With Time, who promised to reveal
    so fast as she could buy
The same, lest of my nearer kin
325   for any thing should vary;[4]
So finally I make an end
    no longer can I tarry.

1573

---

3. A number of the places and institutions described, including the theaters, were outside the city proper, in suburbs called the "liberties."

4. I.e., lest anything should change for my close relatives, Time promised to reveal my bequests as fast as she could buy them.

CHIDIOCK TICHBORNE

d. 1586

Tichborne's Elegy

Written with his own hand in the Tower before his execution[1]

My prime of youth is but a frost of cares,
My feast of joy is but a dish of pain,
My crop of corn is but a field of tares,°   *weeds*
And all my good is but vain hope of gain;
5   The day is past, and yet I saw no sun,
And now I live, and now my life is done.

My tale was heard and yet it was not told,
My fruit is fallen and yet my leaves are green,
My youth is spent and yet I am not old,
10 I saw the world and yet I was not seen;
My thread is cut and yet it is not spun,[2]
And now I live, and now my life is done.

I sought my death and found it in my womb,
I looked for life and saw it was a shade,
15 I trod the earth and knew it was my tomb,
And now I die, and now I was but made;
My glass° is full, and now my glass is run,   *hourglass*
And now I live, and now my life is done.

1586

SIR WALTER RALEGH

ca. 1552–1618

A Vision upon the Fairy Queen[1]

Methought I saw the grave where Laura[2] lay,
Within that temple where the vestal flame[3]
Was wont° to burn; and, passing by that way,   *accustomed*
To see that buried dust of living fame,

---

1. Tichborne was imprisoned in the Tower of London and executed after being implicated in a Catholic plot against Queen Elizabeth. Only three poems by Tichborne were preserved in manuscripts.
2. An allusion to the three Fates, who spun the thread that determined the length of a person's life and cut it when he or she was destined to die.
1. This poem appeared in both the 1590 and the

1596 editions of Edmund Spenser's epic poem *The Faerie Queene* (pp. 152–65).
2. The woman to whom the Italian poet Petrarch (1304–1374) addressed his sonnet sequence; with a pun on "laurel," a symbol of poetic achievement.
3. The sacred fire, guarded by virgin priestesses, in the temple of Vesta, Roman goddess of the hearth; thus an allusion to Laura's chastity and purity.

5   Whose tomb fair Love, and fairer Virtue kept:
    All suddenly I saw the Fairy Queen;
    At whose approach the soul of Petrarch wept,
    And, from thenceforth, those Graces[4] were not seen:
  For they this queen attended; in whose stead
10   Oblivion laid him down on Laura's hearse:°   *tomb*
    Hereat the hardest stones were seen to bleed,
  And groans of buried ghosts the heavens did pierce:
    Where Homer's spright[5] did tremble all for grief,
    And cursed the access of that celestial thief!

1590

The Nymph's Reply to the Shepherd[6]

If all the world and love were young,
And truth in every shepherd's tongue,
These pretty pleasures might me move
To live with thee and be thy love.

5   Time drives the flocks from field to fold
When rivers rage and rocks grow cold,
And Philomel[7] becometh dumb;
The rest complains of cares to come.

The flowers do fade, and wanton fields[8]
10 To wayward winter reckoning yields;
A honey tongue, a heart of gall,°   *bitterness*
Is fancy's spring, but sorrow's fall.

Thy gowns, thy shoes, thy beds of roses,
Thy cap, thy kirtle,[9] and thy posies
15 Soon break, soon wither, soon forgotten—
In folly ripe, in reason rotten.

Thy belt of straw and ivy buds,
Thy coral clasps and amber studs,°   *buttons*
All these in me no means can move
20 To come to thee and be thy love.

But could youth last and love still breed,
Had joys no date[1] nor age no need,

---

4. I.e., Love and Virtue.
5. Ghost of the Greek poet (eighth century B.C.) credited with composing the epic poems the *Iliad* and the *Odyssey*.
6. Written in reply to Christopher Marlowe's "The Passionate Shepherd to His Love" (p. 233).
7. Philomel, the nightingale, who sings a mournful song in the springtime: according to myth, Philomela was raped by her brother-in-law, Tereus, who then tore out her tongue so that she could not

speak. She wove the story in a tapestry and sent it to her sister, who rescued her. She was later changed into a nightingale while in flight from Tereus.
8. I.e, carelessly cultivated fields; also, fields with luxuriant summer growth.
9. A long dress, often worn under an outer garment.
1. I.e., terminal date.

Then these delights my mind might move
To live with thee and be thy love.

1600

The Passionate Man's Pilgrimage

Give me my scallop-shell[2] of quiet,
My staff of faith to walk upon,
My scrip[3] of joy, immortal diet,
My bottle of salvation,
5 My gown of glory, hope's true gage,°   *pledge*
And thus I'll take my pilgrimage.

Blood must be my body's balmer,°   *embalmer*
No other balm[4] will there be given,
Whilst my soul like a white palmer[5]
10 Travels to the land of heaven,
Over the silver mountains,
Where spring the nectar fountains;
And there I'll kiss
The bowl of bliss,
15 And drink my eternal fill
On every milken hill.
My soul will be a-dry° before,   *dried out, thirsty*
But after it will ne'er thirst more;[6]
And by the happy blissful way
20 More peaceful pilgrims I shall see
That have shook off their gowns of clay[7]
And go appareled fresh like me.
I'll bring them first
To slake° their thirst,   *quench*
25 And then to taste those nectar suckets,°   *confections*
At the clear wells
Where sweetness dwells,
Drawn up by saints in crystal buckets.

And when our bottles and all we
30 Are filled with immortality,
Then the holy paths we'll travel,
Strewed with rubies thick as gravel,
Ceilings of diamonds, sapphire floors,
High walls of coral, and pearl bowers,
35 From thence to heaven's bribeless hall
Where no corrupted voices brawl,

2. A scallop shell or something resembling it was worn as the sign of a pilgrim.
3. Pilgrim's knapsack or bag.
4. An aromatic preparation for embalming the dead.
5. A person wearing a palm leaf as a sign that he had made a pilgrimage to the Holy Land.

6. Alludes to John 4.14: "But whosoever drinketh of the water that I shall give him shall never thirst. . . ." In line 16, "milken hill" alludes to the Promised Land as a land flowing in milk and honey (Joshua 5.6).
7. Earth, i.e., earthly bodies.

No conscience molten into gold,
Nor forged accusers bought and sold,
No cause deferred, nor vain-spent journey,
40 For there Christ is the king's attorney,
Who pleads for all, without degrees,
And he hath angels,[8] but no fees.
When the grand twelve million jury
Of our sins and sinful fury,
45 'Gainst our souls black verdicts give,
Christ pleads his death, and then we live.
Be thou my speaker, taintless pleader,
Unblotted lawyer, true proceeder;
Thou movest salvation even for alms,°   *charitable deeds*
50 Not with a bribed lawyer's palms.
And this is my eternal plea
To him that made heaven, earth, and sea,
Seeing my flesh must die so soon,
And want° a head to dine next noon,   *need, lack*
55 Just at the stroke when my veins start and spread,
Set on my soul an everlasting head.
Then am I ready, like a palmer fit,[9]
To tread those blest paths which before I writ.

1604

The Lie

Go, soul, the body's guest,
Upon a thankless errand;
Fear not to touch the best;
The truth shall be thy warrant.°   *guarantee, proof*
5 Go, since I needs must die,
And give the world the lie.[1]

Say to the court, it glows
And shines like rotten wood;
Say to the church, it shows
10 What's good, and doth no good.
If church and court reply,
Then give them both the lie.

Tell potentates,° they live   *rulers*
Acting by others' action;
15 Not loved unless they give,
Not strong but by a faction.
If potentates reply,
Give potentates the lie.

8. A punning reference to the gold coin of that name, ten shillings in value. "Without degrees": without respect to rank.
9 Outfitted (refers back to the first stanza); Ralegh is imagining his death by beheading, which occurred in 1618. When he wrote this poem he was in prison, charged with treason.
1. To "give the lie" means to contradict, or to prove the falsity of something.

Tell men of high condition,
20 That manage the estate,[2]
Their purpose is ambition,
Their practice only hate.
And if they once reply,
Then give them all the lie.

25 Tell them that brave it most,[3]
They beg for more by spending,
Who, in their greatest cost,
Seek nothing but commending.
And if they make reply,
30 Then give them all the lie.

Tell zeal it wants devotion;
Tell love it is but lust;
Tell time it is but motion;
Tell flesh it is but dust.
35 And wish them not reply,
For thou must give the lie.

Tell age it daily wasteth;
Tell honor how it alters;
Tell beauty how she blasteth;°   withers
40 Tell favor how it falters.
And as they shall reply,
Give every one the lie.

Tell wit how much it wrangles
In tickle° points of niceness;   delicate, unreliable
45 Tell wisdom she entangles
Herself in overwiseness.
And when they do reply,
Straight give them both the lie.

Tell physic° of her boldness;   medicine
50 Tell skill it is pretension;
Tell charity of coldness;
Tell law it is contention.
And as they do reply,
So give them still the lie.

55 Tell fortune of her blindness;
Tell nature of decay;
Tell friendship of unkindness;
Tell justice of delay.
And if they will reply,
60 Then give them all the lie.

---

2. Condition of human beings with respect to worldly prosperity; also, an implied analogy between England and a nobleman's estate or land.

3. I.e., show off the most; also, to dress extravagantly.

Tell arts they have no soundness,
But vary by esteeming;
Tell schools they want profoundness,
And stand too much on seeming.
65   If arts and schools reply,
  Give arts and schools the lie.

Tell faith it's fled the city;
Tell how the country erreth;
Tell° manhood shakes off pity;   *say how*
70   Tell virtue least preferreth.[4]
  And if they do reply,
  Spare not to give the lie.

So when thou hast, as I
Commanded thee, done blabbing°—   *revealing secrets*
75   Although to give the lie
  Deserves no less than stabbing—
  Stab at thee he that will,
  No stab the soul can kill.

                                   1608

Nature, That Washed Her Hands in Milk

Nature, that washed her hands in milk,
And had forgot to dry them,
Instead of earth took snow and silk,
At love's request to try them,
5   If she a mistress could compose
  To please love's fancy out of those.

Her eyes he would should be of light,
A violet breath, and lips of jelly;
Her hair not black, nor overbright,
10   And of the softest down her belly;
  As for her inside he'd have it
  Only of wantonness and wit.

At love's entreaty such a one
Nature made, but with her beauty
15   She hath framed a heart of stone;
  So as love, by ill destiny,
  Must die for her whom nature gave him,
  Because her darling would not save him.

But time (which nature doth despise,
20   And rudely gives her love the lie,
  Makes hope a fool, and sorrow wise)
  His hands do neither wash nor dry;

---

4. I.e., tell virtue that it is least preferred or esteemed (?).

But being made of steel and rust,
Turns snow and silk and milk to dust.

25 The light, the belly, lips, and breath,
He dims, discolors, and destroys;
With those he feeds but fills not death,
Which sometimes° were the food of joys.   *formerly*
Yea, time doth dull each lively wit,
30 And dries all wantonness with it.

Oh, cruel time! which takes in trust
Our youth, our joys, and all we have,
And pays us but with age and dust;
Who in the dark and silent grave
35 When we have wandered all our ways
Shuts up the story of our days.[5]

ca. 1610

Three Things There Be

Three things there be that prosper up apace°   *quickly*
And flourish, whilst they grow asunder far,
But on a day, they meet all in one place,
And when they meet, they one another mar;
5 And they be these: the wood, the weed, the wag.°   *mischievous youth*
The wood is that which makes the gallow tree,
The weed is that which strings the hangman's bag,
The wag, my pretty knave, betokeneth thee.
Mark well, dear boy, whilst these assemble not,
10 Green springs the tree, hemp grows, the wag is wild;
But when they meet, it makes the timber rot,
It frets° the halter, and it chokes the child.[6]   *frays*
    Then bless thee, and beware, and let us pray
    We part not with thee at this meeting day.

ca. 1610

If Cynthia Be a Queen, a Princess, and Supreme[7]

If Cynthia be a queen, a princess, and supreme,
Keep these among the rest,[8] or say it was a dream,

---

5. Another version of this stanza, traditionally supposed to have been written by Ralegh on the night before his execution, was published in 1628. In it the first three words are changed to "Even such is time," and the following couplet is added at the end: "And from which earth, and grave, and dust / The Lord shall raise me up, I trust." The poem as a whole existed only in manuscript form until 1902.
6. I.e., the youth being hanged.
7. This enigmatic poem probably was written at a time when Ralegh had fallen out of the queen's favor. It appears in a manuscript before a fragment of the longer poem "The Ocean to Cynthia." The

"thou" of the poem may be the queen, Ralegh himself, or a third party. "Cynthia": also known as Diana; the virgin goddess of the moon, chastity, the hunt, and childbirth. The figure of Cynthia was often used for Queen Elizabeth I and was one that she approved of. By referring to himself as the "Ocean," Ralegh suggests that the queen rules him as the Moon rules the tides.
8. If Ralegh is addressing himself, "keep" may mean "don't send to her"; if the poet addresses the queen, he is telling her to keep his verses with the rest of the many poems of courtly love and praise she has received from him and other court poets.

For those that like, expound, and those that loathe express
Meanings according as their minds are moved more or less;
5   For writing what thou art, or showing what thou were,
Adds to the one disdain, to the other but despair,
      Thy mind of neither needs, in both seeing it exceeds.

1589?   1870

[Fortune hath taken thee away, my love][9]

Fortune hath taken thee away, my love,
My life's soul and my soul's heaven above;
Fortune hath taken thee away, my princess;
My only light and my true fancy's mistress.

5   Fortune hath taken all away from me,
Fortune hath taken all by taking thee.
Dead to all joy, I only live to woe,
So fortune now becomes my mortal foe.

In vain you eyes, you eyes do waste your tears,
10   In vain you sighs do smoke forth my despairs,
In vain you search the earth and heaven above,
In vain you search, for fortune rules in love.

Thus now I leave my love in fortune's hands,
Thus now I leave my love in fortune's bands,
15   And only love the sorrows due to me;
Sorrow henceforth it shall my princess be.

I joy in this, that fortune conquers kings;
Fortune that rules on earth and earthly things
Hath taken my love in spite of Cupid's[1] might;
20   So blind a dame[2] did never Cupid right.

With wisdom's eyes had but blind Cupid seen,
Then had my love my love for ever been;
But love farewell; though fortune conquer thee,
No fortune base shall ever alter me.

Before 1589   1992

---

9. This poem appears to have been written to
Queen Elizabeth I, who replied to it with her
poem "Ah silly pugg wert thou so sore afraid" (p.
131). Both poems are included in a manuscript of
the 1620s in the Wiltshire record office, and both
were written before 1589; George Puttenham
quotes from both poems in his *Arte of English Poe-*

sie, published in that year.
1. Cupid, the god of love, is often depicted as a
blind and winged boy.
2. Fortune was often personified as a fickle
woman and was sometimes depicted as blind or
blindfolded. "Fortune My Foe" was a popular
tune.

EDMUND SPENSER*

ca. 1552–1599

From The Shepheardes Calender

Januarye[1]

Aegloga prima[2]

ARGUMENT[3]

In this fyrst Aeglogue *Colin cloute*[4] a shepheardes boy complaineth him of his
unfortunate love, being but newly (as semeth) enamoured of a countrie lasse

*Because Spenser adopted many archaisms in
order to lend the appearance of antiquity to his
poetry, Ben Jonson said that Spenser "writ no lan-
guage." For example, he imitated the archaic form
of the participle common in Chaucer in which *y*
represents a reduced form of the Old English pre-
fix *ge*. Spenser was innovative as well as archaizing
in his language: he coined many new words and
played—often fancifully—with the native and for-
eign etymologies of English words. He thus partici-
pated in a project dear to the hearts of many
educated Elizabethan writers—a project of
"enriching" the vernacular with borrowings from
classical and modern languages and dialects in
order to create a "kingdom of our own language,"
as Spenser called it in a letter to his friend Gabriel
Harvey (for Harvey's possible participation in the
learned annotation of Spenser's *Shepheardes Cal-
ender*, see below, p. 150). In recognition of the fact
that Spenser's verbal wit depends in part on show-
ing words' multiple meanings and various "roots,"
historical and imaginary, we have chosen not to
modernize Spenser's texts except in minor ways.
We do regularize "i's," "j's," "u's," and "v's"
according to modern conventions, we replace dip-
thongs with separate characters, and we occasion-
ally repunctuate lines when they seem particularly

difficult for modern readers. We also print in
roman type words italicized in the editions printed
during Spenser's lifetime. (In general, we follow
the first editions of his texts except in the case of
the *Faerie Queene*, where we rely on the 1596 edi-
tion rather than the one of 1590.) Finally, to aid
the reader in pronouncing and scanning Spenser's
poetry, which often plays on correspondences and
differences between the way words might sound
and the ways in which they may appear on the
page, we add some metrical accents.
1. "The Shepheardes Calender" is a series of
twelve eclogues, or pastoral poems. For each
poem, a woodcut depicts the month's zodiacal sign
and the poem's scenario, although the picture may
add features not in the poem. "Januarye" is a
rejected lover's "complaint"—a lyric poem that
expresses the speaker's misery over an unrespon-
sive mistress.
2. "First eclogue" (Latin).
3. The argument gives a short synopsis of the
action of the poem.
4. A conventional name in pastoral poetry and one
that Spenser uses for himself in his poem "Colin
Clouts Come Home Againe" (1595). See also n. 8,
p. 150.

called *Rosalinde:* with which strong affection being very sore traveled, he compareth his carefull case[5] to the sadde season of the yeare, to the frostie ground, to the frosen trees, and to his owne winterbeaten flocke. And lastlye, fynding himselfe robbed of all former pleasaunce and delights, hee breaketh his Pipe[6] in peeces, and casteth him selfe to the ground.

COLIN CLOUTE

A Shepeheards boye (no better doe him call)
When Winters wastful spight was almost spent,
All in a sunneshine day, as did befall,
Led forth his flock, that had bene long ypent.°   penned up
5 So faynt they woxe,° and feeble in the folde,   grew
That now unnethes° their feete could them uphold.   scarcely

All as the Sheepe, such was the shepeheards looke,
For pale and wanne he was, (alas the while,)
May seeme he lovd, or els some care he tooke:[7]
10 Well couth° he tune his pipe, and frame his stile.[8]   could
Tho to a hill his faynting flocke he ledde,
And thus him playnd,° the while his shepe there fedde.   lamented

Ye Gods of love, that pitie lovers payne,
(If any gods the paine of lovers pitie:)
15 Looke from above, where you in joyes remaine,
And bowe your eares unto my dolefull dittie.°   song
And Pan thou shepheards God,[9] that once didst love,
Pitie the paines, that thou thy selfe didst prove.°   experience

Thou barrein ground, whome winters wrath hath wasted,
20 Art made a myrrhour, to behold my plight:
Whilome° thy fresh spring flowrd, and after hasted   formerly
Thy sommer prowde with Daffadillies dight.°   clothed
And now is come thy wynters stormy state,
Thy mantle mard, wherein thou maskedst[1] late.

25 Such rage as winters, reigneth in my heart,
My life bloud friesing with unkindly° cold: unnatural
Such stormy stoures° do breede my balefull smart,   tumults
As if my yeare were wast,° and woxen° old.   wasted / grew
And yet alas, but now my spring begonne,
30 And yet alas, yt is already donne.

---

5. Sorrowful plight. "Sore traveled": troubled, burdened.
6. The shepherd's reed pipe, a rudimentary flute, was a symbol of poetic composition.
7. I.e., or else he was afflicted by some troubles.
8. I.e., compose a poem or song.
9. Pan, the Greek god of shepherds, had the torso and arms of a man but the legs, ears, and horns of a goat; the nymph Syrinx, fleeing his advances, begged her sisters to change her shape so she could escape his assault. She was transformed into a reed.
1. Took part in a masque, a form of court entertainment that included dancing, song, drama, and spectacle; thus the earth is compared to a reveler whose costume is marred ("mard") by the winter's storms.

You naked trees, whose shady leaves are lost,
Wherein the byrds were wont° to build their bowre: *accustomed*
And now are clothd with mosse and hoary° frost, *grayish white*
Instede of bloosmes, wherwith your buds did flowre:
35 I see your teares, that from your boughes doe raine,
Whose drops in drery ysicles remaine.

All so my lustfull° leafe is drye and sere,° *vigorous / withered*
My timely° buds with wayling all are wasted: *seasonable*
The blossome, which my braunch of youth did beare,
40 With breathed sighes is blowne away, and blasted,
And from mine eyes the drizling teares descend,
As on your boughes the ysicles depend.° *hang*

Thou feeble flocke, whose fleece is rough and rent,° *torn*
Whose knees are weake through fast and evill fare:
45 Mayst witnesse well by thy ill governement,[2]
Thy maysters mind is overcome with care.
Thou weake, I wanne: thou leane, I quite forlorne:
With mourning pyne I, you with pyning mourne.

A thousand sithes° I curse that carefull hower, *times*
50 Wherein I longd the neighbour towne to see:
And eke tenne thousand sithes I blesse the stoure,° *time of turmoil*
Wherein I sawe so fayre a sight, as shee.
Yet all for naught: such sight hath bred my bane.° *ruin*
Ah God, that love should breede both joy and payne.

55 It is not Hobbinol,[3] wherefore I plaine,
Albee° my love he seeke with dayly suit: *although*
His clownish° gifts and curtsies° I disdaine, *rustic / courtesies*
His kiddes, his cracknelles,° and his early fruit. *biscuits*
Ah foolish Hobbinol, thy gyfts bene vayne:
60 Colin them gives to Rosalind againe.

I love thilke° lasse, (alas why doe I love?) *this*
And am forlorne, (alas why am I lorne?°) *wretched*
Shee deignes° not my good will, but doth reprove, *accepts*
And of my rurall musick holdeth scorne.
65 Shepheards devise° she hateth as the snake, *song, speech*
And laughes the songes, that Colin Clout doth make.

Wherefore my pype, albee rude Pan thou please,
Yet for thou pleasest not, where most I would:
And thou unlucky Muse, that wontst° to ease *was accustomed*
70 My musing mynd, yet canst not, when thou should:

---

2. Poor care.
3. A conventional name in pastoral poetry; the original notes to the September eclogue (see note 7, below) identify Hobbinol as Spenser's Cambridge associate Gabriel Harvey.

Both pype and Muse, shall sore the while abye.[4]
So broke his oaten pype, and downe dyd lye.

By that, the welked Phoebus gan availe
His weary waine,[5] and nowe the frosty Night
75 Her mantle black through heaven gan overhaile.°   *draw over*
Which seene, the pensife boy halfe in despight
Arose, and homeward droue his sonned° sheepe,   *sunned*
Whose hanging heads did seeme his carefull case to weepe.

Colins Embleme.

Anchôra Speme.[6]

GLOSSE[7]

1 COLIN Cloute) is a name not greatly used, and yet have I sene a Poesie of M. Skeltons[8] under that title. But indeede the word Colin is Frenche, and used of the French Poete Marot (if he be worthy of the name of a Poete) in a certein Aeglogue.[9] Under which name this Poete secretly shadoweth himself, as sometime did Virgil under the name of Tityrus, thinking it much fitter, then such Latine names, for the great unlikelyhoode of the language.[1]
6 unnethes) scarcely.
10 couthe) commeth of the verbe Conne, that is, to know or to have skill. As well interpreteth the same the worthy Sir Tho. Smith in his booke of goverment: wherof I have a perfect copie in wryting,[2] lent me by his kinseman, and my verye singular good freend, M. Gabriel Harvey: as also of some other his most grave and excellent wrytings.
37 Sere) withered.   *49* Sythe) time.
50 Neighbour towne) the next towne: expressing the Latine Vicina.
51 Stoure) a fitt.   *57* His clownish gyfts) imitateth Virgils verse,
Rusticus es Corydon, nec munera curat Alexis.[3]
59 Hobbinol) is a fained country name, whereby, it being so commune and usuall, seemeth to be hidden the person of some his very speciall and most familiar freend, whom he entirely and extraordinarily beloved, as peradventure shall be more largely declared hereafter. In thys place seemeth to be some savour of disor-

---

4. I.e., shall pay dearly for that time (of failure); or, perhaps, shall pay dearly for a while.
5. Phoebus, the Greek god of the sun, was imagined as driving his chariot (here a more humble "waine," or wagon) across the sky each day. "Welked": faded; "gan availe": began to lower.
6. "Still (there is) hope" (Italian), with a pun on anchor, a conventional symbol of hope.
7. Explanatory notes that appeared at the end of each eclogue in the original version of the poem, provided by someone identified only as "E. K." Speculations concerning the identity of E. K. include Spenser himself and Spenser's Cambridge associate Gabriel Harvey; the notes may represent a combined effort by both men. The glosses are sometimes useful, sometimes misleading or irrelevant, and frequently humorously pedantic.

8. John Skelton's poem "Colin Clout" (1529; pp. 76–78) lampooned Thomas Woolsey (ca. 1475–1530), English cardinal and statesman.
9. "Eclogue de Mme Louise de Savoye" by Clément Marot (1496?–1544), one of the greatest poets of the French Renaissance.
1. I.e., Latin pastoral names would have been incongruent with the English setting of the poem; the Roman poet Virgil (70–19 B.C.), author of the *Aeneid*, also wrote a series of pastoral eclogues.
2. *De Republica Anglorum* (1556) by Sir Thomas Smith was not published until 1581, two years after E. K. wrote this gloss; thus "I have a perfect copie in wryting" means he had it in manuscript form.
3. "You, Corydon, are a yokel, and Alexis doesn't care for gifts" (Latin).

derly love, which the learned call paederastice:[4] but it is gathered beside his meaning. For who that hath red Plato his dialogue called Alcybiades, Xenophon and Maximus Tyrius of Socrates opinions,[5] may easily perceive, that such love is muche to be alowed and liked of, specially so meant, as Socrates used it: who sayth, that in deede he loved Alcybiades extremely, yet not Alcybiades person, but hys soule, which is Alcybiades owne selfe. And so is paederastice much to be praeferred before gynerastice,[6] that is the love whiche enflameth men with lust toward woman kind. But yet let no man thinke, that herein I stand with Lucian or hys develish disciple Unico Aretino,[7] in defence of execrable and horrible sinnes of forbidden and unlawful fleshlinesse. Whose abominable errour is fully confuted of Perionius,[8] and others.

60 Rosalinde) is also a feigned name, which being wel ordered, wil bewray[9] the very name of hys love and mistresse, whom by that name he coloureth. So as Ovide shadoweth hys love under the name of Corynna, which of some is supposed to be Julia, th' emperor Augustus his daughter, and wyfe to Agryppa. So doth Aruntius Stella every where call his Lady Asteris and Ianthis, albe it is wel knowen that her right name was Violantilla: as witnesseth Statius in his Epithalamium. And so the famous Paragone of Italy, Madonna Coelia in her letters envelopeth her selfe under the name of Zima: and Petrona[1] under the name of Bellochia. And this generally hath bene a common custome of counterfeicting the names of secret Personages.

61 I love) a prety Epanorthosis in these two verses, and withall a Paronomasia[2] or playing with the word, where he sayth (I love thilke lasse (alas &c.

73 Avail) bring downe.   75 Overhaile) drawe over.

Embleme.

His Embleme or Poesye[3] is here under added in Italian, Anchóra speme: the meaning wherof is, that notwithstande his extreme passion and lucklesse love, yet leaning on hope, he is some what recomforted.

1579

4. Love of boys; sodomy.
5. See Plato's *Symposium* 1.31; Xenophon (ca. 431–ca. 352 B.C.) was a Greek general, philosopher, and historian, and a student of Socrates; "Maximus Tyrius": Cassius Maximus Tyrius (fl. second century A.D.), Greek rhetorician and philosopher, some of whose forty-one essays, or "discourses," especially those concerning Plato's views on God, were copied by Renaissance humanist scholars.
6. This word appears to be a coinage by Spenser (it does not appear in the Oxford English Dictionary).
7. Pietro Aretino (1492–1556), author of pornographic comedies and satires, was, according to Gabriel Harvey, very popular at Cambridge; Lucian (ca. 120–180) was a Greek author of satirical but not particularly licentious dialogues, although he was notorious for his impiety.
8. Joachim Perion (1499–1559), a Benedictine

humanist, attacked Aretino in his *In Petrum Aretinum Oratio*.
9. Reveal; "wel ordered": carefully arranged.
1. Unidentified. Ovid addressed his *Amores* to a woman named Corinna, believed by some to be a reference to the daughter of Augustus (63 B.C.–A.D. 14), first Roman emperor. Statius (ca. A.D. 45–96), Roman epic poet and imitator of Virgil; these characters are found in his *Silvae*, a book of occasional verses. "Epithalamium": a kind of poem written to celebrate a marriage; Madonna Coelia was the author of *Lettere Amorose* (Venice, 1562).
2. A play on words that sound alike; a pun (Greek); "Epanorthosis": a rhetorical figure in which a word is recalled in order to substitute a more correct or stronger term (Greek, "a setting straight"); the Oxford English Dictionary cites this passage as the first usage of these two words in an English text.
3. A motto or short inscription.

From The Faerie Queene

The First Booke

Contayning
The Legende of the
Knight of the Red Crosse,
or
Of Holinesse[4]

1

Lo I the man, whose Muse[5] whilome° did maske,   *formerly*
  As time her taught, in lowly Shepheards weeds,[6]
  Am now enforst a far unfitter taske,
  For trumpets sterne to chaunge mine Oaten reeds,[7]
5 And sing of Knights and Ladies gentle° deeds;   *noble*
  Whose prayses having slept in silence long,
  Me, all too meane, the sacred Muse areeds[8]
  To blazon[9] broad emongst her learned throng:
Fierce warres and faithfull loves shall moralize my song.

2

10 Helpe then, O holy Virgin chiefe of nine,
  Thy weaker° Novice to performe thy will,   *too weak*
  Lay forth out of thine everlasting scryne[1]
  The antique rolles, which there lye hidden still,
  Of Faerie knights and fairest Tanaquill,[2]
15 Whom that most noble Briton Prince[3] so long
  Sought through the world, and suffered so much ill,

4. In a letter to the English poet Sir Walter Ralegh (see pp. 139–46) published with the first edition, Spenser declares that his principal intention in writing the poem is "to fashion a gentleman or noble person in virtuous and gentle discipline." Thus he sets forth a plan to write twelve books, each one having a hero distinguished for one of the private virtues; twelve books on the public virtues will follow. The six books that Spenser actually completed (the first three published in 1590, and the remaining three published in 1596) present the virtues of Holiness, Temperance, Chastity, Friendship, Justice, and Courtesy. In addition, two cantos on Mutability (the principle of constant change in nature) were published in 1609 after Spenser's death, although no known authority exists for their division and numbering, or for the running title, "The Seventh Booke." The title of the poem contains a dual reference to its character, Gloriana, the Fairy Queen who bids the poem's heroes to set out on particular adventures, and to Queen Elizabeth I (see pp. 130–32), England's ruler from 1558 until 1603, or for almost all of Spenser's life; as an "Allegory, or darke conceit" (again, a claim that Spenser makes in the letter to Ralegh), the poem mirrors Queen Elizabeth not only in the figure of Gloriana, but also in several other characters. In addition to various modes of allegory, the poem draws on many Renaissance genres, some of the most important being the cour-

tesy book, the romance, and the epic.
5. One of nine Greek goddesses believed to be sources of inspiration for the arts.
6. Garments; i.e., the poet who before wrote humble pastoral poetry. Lines 1–4 imitate verses prefixed to Renaissance editions of Virgil's epic poem the *Aeneid* and signal Spenser's imitation of Virgil, who began his poetic career with pastoral poetry and moved on to the epic, a move that Spenser copied (with the 1579 publication of *The Shepheardes Calender*, followed by the 1590 publication of *The Faerie Queene*). Spenser's organization of each book into twelve cantos also imitates the twelve books of Virgil's *Aeneid*.
7. Or pipes, a symbol of pastoral poetry; "trumpets": a symbol of epic poetry.
8. Commands and instructs. "Sacred Muse": perhaps Clio, the Muse of history, often said to be the eldest of the nine Muses; or perhaps Calliope, the Muse of epic poetry; the "holy Virgin chiefe of nine" (line 10) also seems to refer to one of these two Muses.
9. To proclaim (from "blaze," to announce by blowing a trumpet).
1. A coffer, or a shrine.
2. The wife of Tarquin, the first Etruscan king of Rome; noted for her chastity; i.e., a reference to Gloriana.
3. I.e., Arthur, first named in canto 9.

That I must rue his undeservèd wrong:
O helpe thou my weake wit, and sharpen my dull tong.

3

And thou most dreaded impe[4] of highest Jove,
20   Faire Venus sonne, that with thy cruell dart
At that good knight so cunningly didst rove,°   *shoot*
That glorious fire it kindled in his hart,
Lay now thy deadly Heben° bow apart,   *ebony*
And with thy mother milde come to mine ayde:
25   Come both, and with you bring triumphant Mart,[5]
In loves and gentle jollities arrayd,
After his murdrous spoiles and bloudy rage allayd.

4

And with them eke,° O Goddesse heavenly bright,   *also*
Mirrour of grace and Majestie divine,
30   Great Lady of the greatest Isle, whose light
Like Phoebus lampe[6] throughout the world doth shine,
Shed thy faire beames into my feeble eyne,
And raise my thoughts too humble and too vile,
To thinke of that true glorious type of thine,
35   The argument° of mine afflicted stile:[7]   *subject*
The which to heare, vouchsafe, O dearest dred[8] a-while.

Canto 1

The Patron of true Holinesse,
Foule Errour doth defeate:
Hypocrisie him to entrappe,
Doth to his home entreate.

1

A Gentle Knight was pricking° on the plaine,   *riding briskly*
Ycladd in mightie armes and silver shielde,
Wherein old dints of deepe wounds did remaine,
The cruell markes of many a bloudy fielde;
5   Yet armes till that time did he never wield:
His angry steede did chide his foming bitt,
As much disdayning to the curbe to yield:
Full jolly[9] knight he seemd, and faire did sitt,
As one for knightly giusts° and fierce encounters fitt.   *jousts*

2

10   But on his brest a bloudie Crosse he bore,
The deare remembrance of his dying Lord,
For whose sweete sake that glorious badge he wore,
And dead as living ever him ador'd:

---

4. Offspring, i.e., Cupid (Eros), the god of love whose arrows ("cruell dart") caused their victims to fall in love; he was the son of Venus, goddess of love and beauty. Ares or Hermes was often said to be Cupid's father, but Spenser stresses the line of descent from Jove, Venus' father and ruler of the gods.
5. Mars, god of war and lover of Venus.

6. The sun; Phoebus Apollo was god of the sun.
7. Humble pen; also, "stile" may refer to the poem itself.
8. Object of awe and fear; "vouchsafe": bestow (i.e., confer your ear upon my poem).
9. The range of meanings includes gallant, handsome, amorous, brave.

Upon his shield the like was also scor'd,
For soveraine hope, which in his helpe he had:
Right faithfull true[1] he was in deede and word,
But of his cheere did seeme too solemne sad;°   *grave*
Yet nothing did he dread, but ever was ydrad.°   *dreaded*

3

Upon a great adventure he was bond,[2]
That greatest Gloriana to him gave,
That greatest Glorious Queene of Faerie lond,
To winne him worship,° and her grace to have,   *honor*
Which of all earthly things he most did crave;
And ever as he rode, his hart did earne°   *yearn*
To prove his puissance° in battell brave   *strength*
Upon his foe, and his new force to learne;
Upon his foe, a Dragon horrible and stearne.

4

A lovely Ladie rode him faire beside,
Upon a lowly Asse more white then snow,
Yet she much whiter, but the same did hide
Under a vele, that wimpled° was full low,   *lying in folds*
And over all a blacke stole she did throw,
As one that inly° mourned: so was she sad,   *inwardly*
And heavie sat upon her palfrey slow:
Seemèd in heart some hidden care she had,
And by her in a line a milke white lambe she lad.

5

So pure an innocent, as that same lambe,
She was in life and every vertuous lore,[3]
And by descent from Royall lynage came
Of ancient Kings and Queenes, that had of yore
Their scepters stretcht from East to Westerne shore,
And all the world in their subjection held;
Till that infernall feend with foule uprore°   *revolt*
Forwasted° all their land, and them expeld: *laid waste*
Whom to avenge, she had this Knight from far compeld.°   *summoned*

6

Behind her farre away a Dwarfe did lag,
That lasie seemd in being ever last,
Or wearied with bearing of her bag
Of needments at his backe. Thus as they past,
The day with cloudes was suddeine overcast,
And angry Jove an hideous storme of raine
Did poure into his Lemans[4] lap so fast,
That every wight° to shrowd° it did constrain,   *creature / take cover*
And this faire couple eke to shroud themselves were fain.°   *obliged*

1. Echoes Revelation 19.11: "And I saw heaven opened; and behold a white horse; and he that sat upon him was called Faithfull and True . . ."
2. Going; also, bound by a vow.
3. Moral doctrine.
4. His lover, i.e., the Earth; Jove was the ruler of the classical gods.

7

55 Enforst to seeke some covert nigh at hand,
   A shadie grove not far away they spide,
   That promist ayde the tempest to withstand:
   Whose loftie trees yclad with sommers pride,
   Did spred so broad, that heavens light did hide,
60 Not perceable° with power of any starre: *penetrable*
   And all within were pathes and alleies wide,
   With footing worne, and leading inward farre:
Faire harbour that them seemes; so in they entred arre.

8

   And foorth they passe, with pleasure forward led,
65 Joying to heare the birdes sweete harmony,
   Which therein shrouded from the tempest dred,°   *fearful*
   Seemd in their song to scorne the cruell sky.
   Much can° they prayse the trees so straight and hy,   *did*
   The sayling Pine,⁵ the Cedar proud and tall,
70 The vine-prop Elme, the Poplar never dry,
   The builder Oake, sole king of forrests all,
The Aspine good for staves, the Cypresse funerall.

9

   The Laurell, meed° of mightie Conquerours   *reward*
   And Poets sage, the Firre that weepeth still,
75 The Willow worne of forlorne Paramours,
   The Eugh obedient to the benders will,
   The Birch for shaftes, the Sallow for the mill,
   The Mirrhe sweete bleeding in the bitter wound,
   The warlike Beech, the Ash for nothing ill,
80 The fruitful Olive, and the Platane round,
The carver Holme, the Maple seeldom inward sound.

10

   Led with delight, they thus beguile the way,
   Untill the blustring storme is overblowne;
   When weening° to returne, whence they did stray,   *intending*
85 They cannot finde that path, which first was showne,
   But wander too and fro in wayes unknowne,
   Furthest from end then, when they neerest weene.⁶
   That makes them doubt, their wits be not their owne:
   So many pathes, so many turnings seene,
90 That which of them to take, in diverse doubt they been.

---

5. Spenser's catalog of trees imitates similar catalogs in Chaucer's *Parliament of Fowls*, Virgil's *Aeneid*, and Ovid's *Metamorphoses*. Ships or masts were made of "Sayling" pine; the "Poplar" grew by water; the "Oake" was used in building; the "Cypresse" was used to decorate graves. Garlands made from the "Laurell" were a sign of military or poetic achievement; the "Firre" continually exudes resin; the "Eugh" (yew) was traditionally used for bows; the "Sallow" (willow) was associated with stagnant water like that found at a millpond; the "Mirrhe" (myrrh), used as incense because of its sweet smell, was one of the gifts presented by the Wise Men to the infant Christ; the "Beech" was used to make the axle of the war chariot, according to Homer's *Iliad*; the "Platane" is perhaps listed as a classical contrast (as Socrates and his friends sat by a plane tree, *Phaedrus* 230b) to the olive tree, with its Christian associations; the "Holme" (Holly) was suitable for carving.
6. I.e., think to be nearest to it.

11

At last resolving forward still to fare,
   Till that some end they finde or in or out,
   That path they take, that beaten seemd most bare,
   And like to lead the labyrinth about;°   *out of*
95   Which when by tract° they hunted had throughout,   *track*
   At length it brought them to a hollow cave,
   Amid the thickest woods. The Champion stout°   *brave*
   Eftsoones° dismounted from his courser brave,   *forthwith*
And to the Dwarfe a while his needlesse spere[7] he gave.

12

100 Be well aware, quoth then that Ladie milde,
   Least suddaine mischiefe° ye too rash provoke: *misfortune*
   The danger hid, the place unknowne and wilde,
   Breedes dreadfull doubts: Oft fire is without smoke,
   And perill without show: therefore your stroke
105   Sir knight with-hold, till further triall made.
   Ah Ladie (said he) shame were to revoke°   *draw back*
   The forward footing for an hidden shade:
Vertue gives her selfe light, through darkenesse for to wade.

13

Yea but (quoth she) the perill of this place
110   I better wot then[8] you, though now too late
   To wish you backe returne with foule disgrace,
   Yet wisedome warnes, whilest foot is in the gate,
   To stay the steppe, ere forcèd to retrate.°   *retreat*
   This is the wandring wood, this Errours den,
115   A monster vile, whom God and man does hate:
   Therefore I read° beware. Fly fly (quoth then   *advise*
The fearefull Dwarfe:) this is no place for living men.

14

But full of fire and greedy hardiment,°   *boldness*
   The youthfull knight could not for ought° be staide,   *anything*
120   But forth unto the darksome hole he went,
   And lookèd in: his glistring° armor made   *shining*
   A litle glooming light, much like a shade,
   By which he saw the ugly monster plaine,
   Halfe like a serpent horribly displaide,
125   But th' other halfe did womans shape retaine,
Most lothsom, filthie, foule, and full of vile disdaine.°   *loathsomeness*

15

And as she lay upon the durtie ground,
   Her huge long taile her den all overspred,
   Yet was in knots and many boughtes° upwound,   *coils*
130   Pointed with mortall sting. Of her there bred
   A thousand yong ones, which she dayly fed,
   Sucking upon her poisonous dugs, eachone
   Of sundry shapes, yet all ill favorèd:

---

7. "Needlesse" because the spear is generally used   8. Know than.
only on horseback.

Soone as that uncouth° light upon them shone,   *unfamiliar*
135 Into her mouth they crept, and suddain all were gone.

16

Their dam upstart, out of her den effraide,°   *alarmed*
 And rushèd forth, hurling her hideous taile
 About her cursèd head, whose folds displaid° *extended*
 Were stretcht now forth at length without entraile.° *winding*
140 She lookt about, and seeing one in mayle
 Armèd to point,⁹ sought backe to turne againe;
 For light she hated as the deadly bale,°   *evil*
 Ay wont° in desert darknesse to remaine, *accustomed*
Where plaine none might her see, nor she see any plaine.

17

145 Which when the valiant Elfe¹ perceiv'd, he lept
 As Lyon fierce upon the flying pray,
 And with his trenchand° blade her boldly kept *sharp*
 From turning backe, and forcèd her to stay:
 Therewith enrag'd she loudly gan to bray,
150 And turning fierce, her speckled taile advaunst,
 Threatning her angry sting, him to dismay:° *defeat*
 Who nough° aghast, his mightie hand enhaunst:° *now / raised up*
The stroke down from her head unto her shoulder glaunst.

18

Much daunted with that dint,° her sence was dazd, *blow*
155 Yet kindling rage, her selfe she gathered round,° *coiled*
 And all attonce her beastly body raizd
 With doubled forces high above the ground:
 Tho° wrapping up her wrethèd sterne arownd, *then*
 Lept fierce upon his shield, and her huge traine° *tail*
160 All suddenly about his body wound,
 That hand or foot to stirre he strove in vaine:
God helpe the man so wrapt in Errours endlesse traine.

19

His Lady sad to see his sore constraint,°   *fettered state*
 Cride out, Now now Sir knight, shew what ye bee,
165 Add faith unto your force, and be not faint:
 Strangle her, else she sure will strangle thee.
 That when he heard, in great perplexitie,
 His gall² did grate for griefe° and high disdaine, *anger*
 And knitting all his force got one hand free,
170 Wherewith he grypt her gorge° with so great paine, *throat*
That soone to loose her wicked bands did her constraine.

20

Therewith she spewd out of her filthy maw
 A floud of poyson horrible and blacke,
 Full of great lumpes of flesh and gobbets raw,³

---

9. Fully armed.   2. The seat of anger.
1. I.e., a knight from fairyland as distinct from a 3. Chunks of undigested food.
Briton knight.

175 Which stunck so vildly, that it forst him slacke
   His grasping hold, and from her turne him backe:
   Her vomit full of bookes and papers was,[4]
   With loathly frogs and toades, which eyes did lacke,
   And creeping sought way in the weedy gras:
180 Her filthy parbreake° all the place defilèd has.   *vomit*

21

As when old father Nilus[5] gins to swell
   With timely° pride above the Aegyptian vale,   *in season*
   His fattie° waves do fertile slime outwell,   *rich*
   And overflow each plaine and lowly dale:
185 But when his later spring gins to avale,°   *subside*
   Huge heapes of mudd he leaves, wherein there breed
   Ten thousand kindes of creatures, partly male
   And partly female of his fruitfull seed;
Such ugly monstrous shapes elswhere may no man reed.°   *see*

22

190 The same so sore annoyèd has the knight,
   That welnigh chokèd with the deadly stinke,
   His forces faile, ne can no longer fight.
   Whose corage when the feend perceived to shrinke,
   She pourèd forth out of her hellish sinke[6]
195 Her fruitfull cursèd spawne of serpents small,
   Deformèd monsters, fowle, and blacke as inke,
   Which swarming all about his legs did crall,
And him encombred sore, but could not hurt at all.

23

As gentle Shepheard in sweete even-tide,
200 When ruddy Phoebus gins to welke° in west,   *sink*
   High on an hill, his flocke to vewen wide,
   Markes° which do byte their hasty supper best;   *observes*
   A cloud of combrous° gnattes do him molest,   *encumbering*
   All striving to infixe their feeble stings,
205 That from their noyance he no where can rest,
   But with his clownish° hands their tender wings   *rustic*
He brusheth oft, and oft doth mar their murmurings.

24

Thus ill bestedd,° and fearfull more of shame,   *situated*
   Then of the certaine perill he stood in,
210 Halfe furious unto his foe he came,
   Resolv'd in minde all suddenly to win,
   Or soone to lose, before he once would lin;°   *cease*
   And strooke at her with more then manly force,
   That from her body full of filthie sin
215 He raft° her hatefull head without remorse;   *struck off*
A streame of cole black bloud forth gushèd from her corse.°   *corpse*

---

4. Among other meanings, the "bookes and papers" may include a reference to Catholic books and pamphlets that attacked the Protestant Queen Elizabeth, in which case Error may be, among other things, an allegorical representation of the Catholic Church.
5. The Nile River was commonly said to breed strange monsters.
6. I.e., her mouth.

25

Her scattred brood, soone as their Parent deare
   They saw so rudely° falling to the ground,   *violently*
   Groning full deadly, all with troublous feare,
220   Gathred themselves about her body round,
   Weening° their wonted entrance to have found   *thinking*
   At her wide mouth: but being there withstood
   They flockèd all about her bleeding wound,
   And suckèd up their dying mothers blood,
225 Making her death their life, and eke her hurt their good.

26

That detestable sight him much amazde,
   To see th' unkindly Impes[7] of heaven accurst,
   Devoure their dam; on whom while so he gazd,
   Having all satisfide their bloudy thurst,
230   Their bellies swolne he saw with fulnesse burst,
   And bowels gushing forth: well worthy end
   Of such as drunke her life, the which them nurst;
   Now needeth him no lenger labour spend,
His foes have slaine themselves, with whom he should contend.

27

235 His Ladie seeing all, that chaunst, from farre
   Approcht in hast to greet° his victorie,   *congratulate*
   And said, Faire knight, borne under happy° starre,   *auspicious*
   Who see your vanquisht foes before you lye:
   Well worthy be you of that Armorie,°   *armor*
240   Wherein ye have great glory wonne this day,
   And proov'd your strength on a strong enimie,
   Your first adventure: many such I pray,
And henceforth ever wish, that like succeed it may.

28

Then mounted he upon his Steede againe,
245   And with the Lady backward sought to wend;°   *go*
   That path he kept, which beaten was most plaine,
   Ne ever would to any by-way bend,
   But still did follow one unto the end,
   The which at last out of the wood them brought.
250   So forward on his way (with God to frend)[8]
   He passèd forth, and new adventure sought;
Long way he travellèd, before he heard of ought.

29

At length they chaunst to meet upon the way
   An aged Sire, in long blacke weedes yclad,[9]
255   His feete all bare, his beard all hoarie° gray,   *ancient*
   And by his belt his booke he hanging had;
   Sober he seemde, and very sagely sad,°   *pensive*
   And to the ground his eyes were lowly bent,
   Simple in shew, and voyde of malice bad,

---

7. Unnatural offspring.   9. Dressed in long black garments.
8. As a friend.

260 And all the way he prayèd, as he went,
And often knockt his brest, as one that did repent.

30

He faire the knight saluted, louting° low,   *bowing*
 Who faire him quited,° as that courteous was: *answered*
 And after askèd him, if he did know
265 Of straunge adventures, which abroad did pas.
 Ah my deare Sonne (quoth he) how should, alas,
 Silly° old man, that lives in hidden cell,   *simple*
 Bidding his beades[1] all day for his trespas,
 Tydings of warre and worldly trouble tell?
270 With holy father sits not with such things to mell.°   *meddle*

31

But if of daunger which hereby doth dwell,
 And homebred evill ye desire to heare,
 Of a straunge man I can you tidings tell,
 That wasteth all this countrey farre and neare.
275 Of such (said he) I chiefly do inquere,
 And shall you well reward to shew the place,
 In which that wicked wight his dayes doth weare:°   *spend*
 For to all knighthood it is foule disgrace,
 That such a cursed creature lives so long a space.

32

280 Far hence (quoth he) in wastfull° wildernesse   *desolate*
 His dwelling is, by which no living wight
 May ever passe, but thorough great distresse.
 Now (sayd the Lady) draweth toward night,
 And well I wote, that of your later° fight   *recent*
285 Ye all forwearied be: for what so strong,
 But wanting rest will also want of might?
 The Sunne that measures heaven all day long,
At night doth baite° his steedes the Ocean waves emong.   *feed*

33

Then with the Sunne take Sir, your timely rest,
290 And with new day new worke at once begin:
 Untroubled night they say gives counsell best.
 Right well Sir knight ye have advisèd bin,
 (Quoth then that aged man;) the way to win
 Is wisely to advise:° now day is spent;   *take thought*
295 Therefore with me ye may take up your In°   *lodging*
 For this same night. The knight was well content:
So with that godly father to his home they went.

34

A little lowly Hermitage it was,
 Downe in a dale, hard by a forests side,
300 Far from resort of people, that did pas
 In travell to and froe: a little wyde°   *apart*

---

1. Saying his prayers, i.e., counting rosary beads.

There was an holy Chappell edifyde,°   *built*
    Wherein the Hermite dewly wont to say
    His holy things° each morne and eventyde: *prayers*
305   Thereby a Christall streame did gently play,
    Which from a sacred fountaine wellèd forth alway.

35

    Arrivèd there, the little house they fill,
    Ne looke for entertainement, where none was:
    Rest is their feast, and all things at their will;
310   The noblest mind the best contentment has.
    With faire discourse the evening so they pas:
    For that old man of pleasing wordes had store,
    And well could file° his tongue as smooth as glas;   *polish*
    He told of Saintes and Popes, and evermore
315 He strowd an Ave-Mary[2] after and before.

36

    The drouping Night thus creepeth on them fast,
    And the sad humour[3] loading their eye liddes,
    As messenger of Morpheus[4] on them cast
    Sweet slombring deaw, the which to sleepe them biddes.
320   Unto their lodgings then his guestes he riddes:°   *dispatches*
    Where when all drownd in deadly sleepe[5] he findes,
    He to his study goes, and there amiddes
    His Magick bookes and artes of sundry kindes,
    He seekes out mighty charmes, to trouble sleepy mindes.

37

325 Then choosing out few wordes most horrible,
    (Let none them read) thereof did verses frame,
    With which and other spelles like terrible,
    He bade awake blacke Plutoes griesly Dame,[6]
    And cursèd heaven, and spake reprochfull shame
330 Of highest God, the Lord of life and light;
    A bold bad man, that dared to call by name
    Great Gorgon,[7] Prince of darknesse and dead night,
    At which Cocytus quakes, and Styx is put to flight.

38

    And forth he cald out of deepe darknesse dred
335   Legions of Sprights, the which like little flyes[8]
    Fluttring about his ever damnèd hed,
    A-waite whereto their service he applyes,
    To aide his friends, or fray° his enimies: *frighten*
    Of those he chose out two, the falsest twoo,
340 And fittest for to forge true-seeming lyes;
    The one of them he gave a message too,
    The other by him selfe staide other worke to doo.

---

2. "Hail Mary" (Latin); a Catholic prayer.
3. Heavy moisture, the "deaw" (line 319) of sleep.
4. God of dreams.
5. Sleep like death.
6. Proserpina, goddess of the underworld; patron of witches.

7. Demogorgon, whose power is so great that the mention of his name causes hell's rivers (Cocytus and Styx) to quake.
8. The simile connects him to Beelzebub, lord of the flies.

39

He making speedy way through spersèd° ayre,   *dispersed*
  And through the world of waters wide and deepe,
345 To Morpheus house doth hastily repaire.
  Amid the bowels of the earth full steepe,
  And low, where dawning day doth never peepe,
  His dwelling is; there Tethys[9] his wet bed
  Doth ever wash, and Cynthia[1] still° doth steepe   *continually*
350 In silver deaw his ever-drouping hed,
Whiles sad° Night over him her mantle black doth spred.   *sober*

40

Whose double gates he findeth lockèd fast,
  The one faire fram'd of burnisht Yvory,
  The other all with silver overcast;
355 And wakefull dogges before them farre do lye,
  Watching to banish Care their enimy,
  Who oft is wont° to trouble gentle Sleepe.   *accustomed*
  By them the Sprite doth passe in quietly,
  And unto Morpheus comes, whom drownèd deepe
360 In drowsie fit he findes: of nothing he takes keepe.°   *notice*

41

And more, to lulle him in his slumber soft,
  A trickling streame from high rocke tumbling downe
  And ever-drizling raine upon the loft,
  Mixt with a murmuring winde, much like the sowne°   *sound*
365 Of swarming Bees, did cast him in a swowne:°   *faint*
  No other noyse, nor peoples troublous cryes,
  As still° are wont t'annoy the wallèd towne,   *always*
  Might there be heard: but carelesse° Quiet lyes,   *free from care*
Wrapt in eternall silence farre from enemyes.

42

370 The messenger approching to him spake,
  But his wast° wordes returnd to him in vaine: *wasted*
  So sound he slept, that nought mought° him awake.   *might*
  Then rudely he him thrust, and pusht with paine,°   *effort*
  Whereat he gan to stretch: but he againe
375 Shooke him so hard, that forced him to speake.
  As one then in a dreame, whose dryer braine[2]
  Is tost with troubled sights and fancies° weake,   *fantasies*
He mumbled soft, but would not all° his silence breake.   *altogether*

43

The Sprite then gan more boldly him to wake,
380 And threatned unto him the dreaded name
  Of Hecate:[3] whereat he gan to quake,
  And lifting up his lumpish head, with blame
  Halfe angry askèd him, for what he came.

---

9. Goddess of the sea, wife of Neptune.
1. Goddess of the moon.
2. Renaissance ideas of physiology held that being too "dry," or lacking a proper balance of bodily moisture, resulted in troubled dreams.
3. A goddess of Hades; associated with witches, magic, and dreams.

Hither (quoth he) me Archimago[4] sent,
385 He that the stubborne Sprites can wisely tame,
He bids thee to him send for his intent
A fit false dreame, that can delude the sleepers sent.°   *senses*

44

The God obayde, and calling forth straight way
A diverse° dreame out of his prison darke,   *misleading*
390 Delivered it to him, and downe did lay
His heavie head, devoide of carefull carke,[5]
Whose sences all were straight benumbd and starke.°   *paralyzed*
He backe returning by the Yvorie dore,[6]
Remounted up as light as chearefull Larke,
395 And on his litle winges the dreame he bore
In hast unto his Lord, where he him left afore.

45

Who all this while with charmes and hidden artes,
Had made a Lady of that other Spright,
And fram'd of liquid ayre her tender partes
400 So lively,° and so like in all mens sight,   *lifelike*
That weaker sence it could have ravisht quight:
The maker selfe for all his wondrous witt,
Was nigh beguilèd with so goodly sight:
Her all in white he clad, and over it
405 Cast a blacke stole, most like to seeme for Una[7] fit.

46

Now when that ydle dreame was to him brought,
Unto that Elfin knight he bad him fly,
Where he slept soundly void of evill thought,
And with false shewes abuse his fantasy,°   *imagination*
410 In sort as[8] he him schoolèd privily:
And that new creature borne without her dew,[9]
Full of the makers guile, with usage sly
He taught to imitate that Lady trew,
Whose semblance she did carrie under feignèd hew.°   *form*

47

415 Thus well instructed, to their worke they hast
And comming where the knight in slomber lay
The one upon his hardy head him plast,°   *placed*
And made him dreame of loves and lustfull play,
That nigh his manly hart did melt away,
420 Bathèd in wanton blis and wicked joy:
Then seemèd him his Lady by him lay,
And to him playnd,° how that false wingèd boy,[1]   *complained*
Her chast hart had subdewd, to learne Dame pleasures[2] toy.

---

4. Archmagician or chief deceiver, from the Latin *archi* ("first") + *magus* ("magician"); also, the arch-imago, or chief image-maker.
5. Anxious concerns.
6. According to Homer (*Odyssey*) and Virgil (*Aeneid*), false dreams came through the ivory door.

7. "One," or "unity" (Latin). Many Elizabethan readers would have known the Latin phrase *Una Vera Fides* ("one true faith").
8. In the way that.
9. Unnaturally.
1. Cupid.
2. Venus; "toy": lustful play.

48

And she her selfe of beautie soveraigne Queene
425   Faire Venus seemde unto his bed to bring
    Her, whom he waking evermore did weene°   *think*
    To be the chastest flowre, that ay° did spring   *ever*
    On earthly braunch, the daughter of a king,
    Now a loose Leman° to vile service bound: *lover*
430   And eke the Graces seemèd all to sing,
    Hymen iô Hymen, dauncing all around,
Whilst freshest Flora[3] her with Yvie girlond crownd.

49

In this great passion of unwonted° lust,   *unaccustomed*
    Or wonted feare of doing ought amis,
435   He started up, as seeming to mistrust°   *suspect*
    Some secret ill, or hidden foe of his:
    Lo there before his face his Lady is,
    Under blake stole hyding her bayted hooke,
    And as halfe blushing offred him to kis,
440   With gentle blandishment° and lovely° looke,   *flattering speech / loving*
Most like that virgin true, which for her knight him took.

50

All cleane dismayd to see so uncouth° sight,   *strange*
    And halfe enragèd at her shamelesse guise,
    He thought have slaine her in his fierce despight:°   *indignation*
445   But hasty heat tempring with sufferance wise,
    He stayde his hand, and gan himselfe advise
    To prove his sense, and tempt° her faignèd truth.   *test*
    Wringing her hands in wemens pitteous wise,
    Tho can[4] she weepe, to stirre up gentle ruth,°   *pity*
450 Both for her noble bloud, and for her tender youth.

51

And said, Ah Sir, my liege Lord and my love,
    Shall I accuse the hidden cruell fate,
    And mightie causes wrought in heaven above,
    Or the blind God, that doth me thus amate,°   *dismay*
455   For° hopèd love to winne me certaine hate?   *instead of*
    Yet thus perforce° he bids me do, or die.   *forcibly*
    Die is my dew:[5] yet rew° my wretched state   *feel sorry for*
    You, whom my hard avenging destinie
Hath made judge of my life or death indifferently.

52

460 Your owne deare sake forst me at first to leave
    My Fathers kingdome, There she stopt with teares;
    Her swollen hart her speach seemd to bereave,
    And then againe begun, My weaker yeares
    Captiv'd to fortune and frayle worldly feares,

---

3. Flower goddess; sometimes referred to as sexu-
ally unchaste. "Graces": handmaids of Venus;
here, they sing in praise of the marriage bed.

"Hymen": god of marriage.
4. Then did.
5. I.e., I deserve to die.

465 Fly to your faith for succour and sure ayde:
Let me not dye in languor° and long teares.   *sorrow*
Why Dame (quoth he) what hath ye thus dismayd?
What frayes° ye, that were wont to comfort me affrayd?   *frightens*

53

Love of your selfe, she said, and deare° constraint   *dire*
470 Lets me not sleepe, but wast the wearie night
In secret anguish and unpittied plaint,
Whiles you in carelesse sleepe are drownèd quight.
Her doubtfull words made that redoubted⁶ knight
Suspect her truth: yet since no untruth he knew,
475 Her fawning love with foule disdainefull spight°   *contempt*
He would not shend,° but said, Deare dame I rew,°   *reject / pity*
That for my sake unknowne such griefe unto you grew.

54

Assure your selfe, it fell not all to ground;
For all so deare as life is to my hart,
480 I deeme your love, and hold me to you bound;
Ne let vaine feares procure° your needlesse smart,   *cause*
Where cause is none, but to your rest depart.
Not all content, yet seemd she to appease°   *cease*
Her mournefull plaintes, beguilèd° of her art,   *deprived*
485 And fed with words, that could not chuse but please,
So slyding softly forth, she turnd° as to her ease.   *returned*

55

Long after lay he musing at her mood,
Much griev'd to thinke that gentle Dame so light,⁷
For whose defence he was to shed his blood.
490 At last dull wearinesse of former fight
Having yrockt a sleepe his irkesome spright,⁸
That troublous dreame gan freshly tosse his braine,
With bowres, and beds, and Ladies deare delight:
But when he saw his labour all was vaine,
495 With that misformèd spright he backe returnd againe.

From Amoretti⁹

Sonnet 1

Happy ye leaves¹ when as those lilly hands,
Which hold my life in their dead doing might²

---

6. Dreaded, also doubting again; "doubtfull": fearful, also questionable.
7. I.e., so unchaste.
8. Spirit, in various senses.
9. "Little loves" (Italian). This sequence of eighty-nine sonnets was published in 1595, together with *Epithalamion* (p. 171), a kind of poem written to celebrate a marriage. It is generally believed that these poems were written to Spenser's bride-to-be, Elizabeth Boyle. The Petrarchan sonnet cycle was popular at this time, but Spenser's sequence is unusual because the desire expressed is directed not at an unattainable mistress but toward the woman who became the poet's second wife. The rhyme scheme is *abab bcbc cdcd ee*, a difficult pattern in English because of the frequency of the repeating rhymes.
1. Pages; in this sonnet the poet addresses his poems as "leaves," "lines," and "rhymes."
2. Death-dealing power.

Shall handle you and hold in loves soft bands,
Lyke captives trembling at the victors sight.
5   And happy lines, on which with starry light,
Those lamping° eyes will deigne sometimes to look   *shining*
And reade the sorrowes of my dying spright,°   *spirit*
Written with teares in harts close° bleeding book.   *secret*
And happy rymes bath'd in the sacred brooke,
10   Of Helicon³ whence she derived is,
When ye behold that Angels blessed looke,
My soules long lacked foode, my heavens blis.
Leaves, lines, and rymes, seeke her to please alone,
Whom if ye please, I care for other none.

Sonnet 8

More then° most faire, full of the living fire,   *than*
Kindled above unto the maker neere:
No eies⁴ but joyes, in which al powers conspire,
That to the world naught else be counted deare.
5   Thrugh your bright beames doth not the blinded guest⁵
Shoot out his darts to base affections wound?
But Angels come to lead fraile mindes to rest
In chast desires on heavenly beauty bound.
You frame my thoughts and fashion me within,
10   You stop my toung, and teach my hart to speake,
You calme the storme that passion did begin,
Strong thrugh your cause, but by your vertue weak.
Dark is the world, where your light shined never;
Well is he borne, that may behold you ever.

Sonnet 10

Unrighteous Lord of love what law is this,
That me thou makest thus tormented be?
The whiles she lordeth in licentious blisse
Of her freewill, scorning both thee and me.
5   See how the Tyrannesse doth joy to see
The huge massàcres which her eyes do make:
And humbled harts brings captives unto thee,
That thou of them mayst mightie vengeance take.
But her proud hart doe thou a little shake
10   And that high look, with which she doth comptroll°   *control*
All this worlds pride bow to a baser make,⁶
And al her faults in thy black booke enroll.
That I may laugh at her in equall sort,
As she doth laugh at me and makes my pain her sport.

---

3. The Hippocrene Spring on Mt. Helicon was the haunt of the Muses, the nine Greek goddesses believed to be the source of inspiration for the arts.
4. The lover's eyes are imagined as the source of love, both erotic and spiritual (Platonic).
5. I.e., Cupid.
6. The poet asks the Lord of love ("thou") to lower ("bow") the lady's look to a "baser" mate ("make"), i.e., the poet himself.

Sonnet 15[7]

Ye tradefull[8] Merchants that with weary toyle,
Do seeke most pretious things to make your gain:
And both the Indias[9] of their treasures spoile,°   *despoil*
What needeth you to seeke so farre in vaine?
5 For loe my love doth in her selfe containe
All this worlds riches that may farre be found,
If Saphyres, loe her eies be Saphyres plaine,°   *perfect*
If Rubies, loe hir lips be Rubies sound:° *free from defect*
If Pearles, hir teeth be pearles both pure and round;
10 If Yvorie, her forhead yvory weene;[1]
If Gold, her locks are finest gold on ground;°   *Earth*
If silver, her faire hands are silver sheene;°   *bright*
But that which fairest is, but few behold,
Her mind adornd with vertues manifold.

Sonnet 23

Penelope for her Ulisses sake,
Deviz'd a Web her wooers to deceave:
In which the worke that she all day did make
The same at night she did again unreave:[2]
5 Such subtile° craft my Damzell doth conceave,° *fine, clever / devise*
Th' importune° suit of my desire to shonne: *importunate*
For all that I in many dayes doo weave,
In one short houre I find by her undonne.
So when I thinke to end that° I begonne,   *that which*
10 I must begin and never bring to end:
For with one looke she spils° that long I sponne,   *destroys*
And with one word my whole years work doth rend.
Such labour like the Spyders web I fynd,
Whose fruitlesse worke is broken with least wynd.

Sonnet 37

What guyle° is this, that those her golden tresses,   *deceit*
She doth attyre under a net of gold:
And with sly skill so cunningly them dresses,
That which is gold or heare,° may scarse be told?   *hair*
5 Is it that mens frayle eyes, which gaze too bold,
She may entangle in that golden snare:
And being caught may craftily enfold
Theyr weaker harts, which are not wel aware?
Take heed therefore, myne eyes, how ye doe stare
10 Henceforth too rashly on that guilefull° net,   *deceitful*

---

7. This sonnet is a "blazon," a series of comparisons or depictions cataloging the lady's parts.
8. Fully occupied with trading (this is the Oxford English Dictionary's first recorded usage of the word).
9. The East and West Indies.
1. Beautiful; or, possibly, may be read as an imperative, i.e., "think her forehead ivory."
2. During the long absence of her husband, Odysseus, Penelope warded off the proposals of her suitors by telling them she would choose one of them as soon as she finished weaving a shroud. Each night for three years she undid her day's work (Homer, *Odyssey* 2).

In which if ever ye entrapped are,
Out of her bands ye by no meanes shall get.
Fondnesse° it were for any being free,   *folly*
To covet fetters, though they golden bee.

Sonnet 54

Of this worlds Theatre in which we stay,
My love lyke the Spectàtor ydly sits
Beholding me that all the pageants° play,   *roles*
Disguysing diversly my troubled wits.
5 Sometimes I joy when glad occasion fits,
And mask³ in myrth lyke to a Comedy:
Soone after when my joy to sorrow flits,
I waile and make my woes a Tragedy.
Yet she beholding me with constant eye,
10 Delights not in my merth nor rues° my smart: *pities*
But when I laugh she mocks, and when I cry
She laughes, and hardens evermore her hart.
What then can move her? if nor merth nor mone,
She is no woman, but a sencelesse stone.

Sonnet 67⁴

Lyke as a huntsman after weary chace,
Seeing the game from him escapt away,
Sits downe to rest him in some shady place,
With panting hounds beguilèd of their pray:
5 So after long pursuit and vaine assay,
When I all weary had the chace forsooke,
The gentle deare⁵ returnd the selfe-same way,
Thinking to quench her thirst at the next brooke.
There she beholding me with mylder looke,
10 Sought not to fly, but fearelesse still did bide:
Till I in hand her yet halfe trembling tooke,
And with her owne goodwill hir fyrmely tyde.
Strange thing me seemd⁶ to see a beast so wyld,
So goodly wonne with her owne will beguyld.

Sonnet 68

Most glorious Lord of lyfe that on this day,⁷
Didst make thy triumph over death and sin:
And having harrowd hell⁸ didst bring away
Captivity thence captive us to win:⁹
5 This joyous day, deare Lord, with joy begin,
And grant that we for whom thou diddest dye
Being with thy deare blood clene washt from sin,
May live for ever in felicity.

---

3. To cover (or mask) his emotions.
4. An imitation of Petrarch's *Rime* 190, although with a dissimilar ending. Cf. Wyatt, "Whoso List to Hunt" (p. 113).
5. With a pun on "deer" and "dear" (beloved).
6. I.e., it seemed to me.

7. Easter.
8. A reference to the apocryphal account of Christ's descent into hell, after his crucifixion, in order to rescue the captive souls of the just.
9. "When he ascended up on high, he led captivity captive" (Ephesians 4.8).

And that thy love we weighing[1] worthily,
10   May likewise love thee for the same againe:[2]
And for thy sake that all lyke deare[3] didst buy,
With love may one another entertayne.
So let us love, deare love, lyke as we ought,
Love is the lesson which the Lord us taught.[4]

Sonnet 70

Fresh spring the herald of loves mighty king,
In whose cote armour° richly are displayd   *coat of arms*
All sorts of flowers the which on earth do spring
In goodly colours gloriously arrayd:
5   Goe to my love, where she is carelesse layd,
Yet in her winters bowre not well awake:
Tell her the joyous time wil not be staid°   *detained*
Unless she doe him by the forelock take.[5]
Bid her therefore her selfe soone ready make,
10   To wayt on love amongst his lovely crew:
Where every one that misseth then her make,°   *mate*
Shall be by him amearst° with penance dew.   *punished*
Make hast therefore sweet love,[6] whilest it is prime,°   *spring*
For none can call againe the passèd time.

Sonnet 71

I joy to see how in your drawen work,[7]
Your selfe unto the Bee ye doe compare;
And me unto the Spyder that doth lurke,
In close° awayt° to catch her unaware.   *secret / ambush*
5   Right so your selfe were caught in cunning snare
Of a deare foe, and thralled° to his love: *enslaved*
In whose streight° bands ye now captived are   *tight*
So firmely, that ye never may remove.
But as your worke is woven all about,
10   With woodbynd flowers and fragrant Eglantine:[8]
So sweet your prison you in time shall prove,°   *find*
With many deare delights bedecked fyne.
And all thensforth eternall peace shall see
Betweene the Spyder and the gentle Bee.

Sonnet 75

One day I wrote her name upon the strand,°   *shore*
But came the waves and washèd it away:
Agayne I wrote it with a second hand,°   *time*
But came the tyde, and made my paynes his pray.°   *prey*

1. I.e., grant also that we, weighing thy love rightly, might love thee in the same way.
2. I.e., for thy love.
3. I.e., at the same cost.
4. "This is my commandment, That ye love one another, as I have loved you" (John 15.12).
5. "To take time by the forelock" is to act promptly.
6. The addressee of the poem changes here from Spring, as the herald of love, to the loved one herself.
7. Ornamental work done in textile fabrics by drawing out some of the threads so as to form patterns.
8. Sweetbrier or wild rose; "woodbynd": honeysuckle.

5   Vayne man, sayd she, that doest in vaine assay,°   *attempt*
A mortall thing so to immortalize,
For I my selve shall lyke to this decay,
And eek° my name bee wypèd out lykewize.   *also*
Not so, (quod° I) let baser things devize°   *quoth / plan*
10   To dy in dust, but you shall live by fame:
My verse your vertues rare shall eternize,
And in the hevens wryte your glorious name.
Where whenas death shall all the world subdew,
Our love shall live, and later life renew.

Sonnet 79

Men call you fayre, and you doe credit° it,   *believe*
For that your selfe ye dayly such doe see:
But the trew fayre,° that is the gentle wit,   *beauty*
And vertuous mind, is much more praysd of me.
5   For all the rest, how ever fayre it be,
Shall turne to nought and loose that glorious hew:°   *form*
But onely that is permanent and free
From frayle corruption, that doth flesh ensew.[9]
That is true beautie: that doth argue you
10   To be divine and borne of heavenly seed:
Deriv'd from that fayre Spirit, from whom al true
And perfect beauty did at first proceed.
He[1] onely fayre, and what he fayre hath made,
All other fayre lyke flowres untymely fade.

Sonnet 81

Fayre is my love, when her fayre golden heares,°   *hairs*
With the loose wynd ye waving chance to marke:°   *notice*
Fayre when the rose in her red cheekes appeares,
Or in her eyes the fyre of love does sparke.
5   Fayre when her brest lyke a rich laden barke,
With pretious merchandize she forth doth lay:
Fayre when that cloud of pryde, which oft doth dark
Her goodly light with smiles she drives away.
But fayrest she, when so she doth display
10   The gate with pearles and rubyes richly dight:°   *adorned*
Throgh which her words so wise do make their way
To beare the message of her gentle spright.°   *spirit*
The rest be works of natures wonderment,
But this the worke of harts astonishment.

Sonnet 89

Lyke as the Culver[2] on the barèd bough,
Sits mourning for the absence of her mate:
And in her songs sends many a wishfull vow,
For his returne that seemes to linger late.

---

9. I.e., corruption that overtakes all flesh; "ensew":
follow.
1. I.e., God, the "fayre Spirit" (line 11).

2. Dove; a bird associated with fidelity, peace, and
the Holy Spirit.

5   So I alone now left disconsolate,
     Mourne to my selfe the absence of my love:
     And wandring here and there all desolate,
     Seek with my playnts° to match that mournful   *lamentations, complaints*
          dove:
     Ne joy of ought that under heaven doth hove,°   *abide*
10   Can comfort me, but her owne joyous sight:
     Whose sweet aspèct both God and man can move,
     In her unspotted pleasauns³ to delight.
     Dark is my day, whyles her fayre light I mis,
     And dead my life that wants such lively blis.

                                                                          1595

Epithalamion⁴

     Ye learned sisters⁵ which have oftentimes
     Beene to me ayding, others to adorne:
     Whom ye thought worthy of your gracefull⁶ rymes,
     That even the greatest did not greatly scorne
5   To heare theyr names sung in your simple layes,°   *songs*
     But joyèd in theyr prayse.
     And when ye list° your owne mishaps to mourne,   *desire*
     Which death, or love, or fortunes wreck did rayse,
     Your string could soone to sadder tenor° turne,   *strain*
10   And teach the woods and waters to lament
     Your dolefull dreriment.°   *sadness*
     Now lay those sorrowfull complaints aside,
     And having all your heads with girland crownd,
     Helpe me mine owne loves prayses to resound,
15   Ne let the same of any be envìde:
     So Orpheus⁷ did for his owne bride,
     So I unto my selfe alone will sing,
     The woods shall to me answer and my Eccho ring.

     Early before the worlds light giving lampe,⁸
20   His golden beame upon the hils doth spred,

---

3. Charm or pleasing manners; also, a garden's pleasure area; compare Song of Solomon 4.12, in which the bride is compared to an enclosed garden.

4. A wedding song or poem; its Greek name conveys that it was sung on the threshold of the bridal chamber. The genre, practiced by the Latin poets, characteristically includes the invocation to the Muses, the bringing home of the bride, the singing and dancing at the wedding party, and the preparations for the wedding night. Published in 1595 with the *Amoretti*, Spenser's *Epithalamion* has a uniquely complex structure. The central section on the church ceremony (lines 185–222) is flanked by two symmetrical ten-stanza sections, each of which is divided into units of three-four-three. Furthermore, the poem's structure reinforces the theme of time, with exactly 365 long lines, matching the number of days in the year,

and twenty-four stanzas (including the envoy), matching the number of hours in one day. The first sixteen stanzas describe the day, making "night . . . come" (line 300) after sixteen and one-quarter stanzas: contemporary almanacs indicate sixteen and one-quarter hours of daylight in southern Ireland on June 11, 1594, the day Spenser was married.

5. The nine Muses, Greek goddesses believed to be sources of inspiration for the arts.

6. Graceful; also, conferring grace.

7. Orpheus, the son of Calliope, one of the Muses; his music was said to charm wild animals and to make stones and trees move. According to one tradition, he won his wife, Euridyce, with music. However, he failed to free her from the underworld after her death because he looked back at her on the journey out.

8. I.e., the sun.

Having disperst the nights unchearefull dampe,
Doe ye awake, and with fresh lusty hed,°   *cheerfulness*
Go to the bowre° of my belovèd love,   *bedchamber*
My truest turtle dove,
25   Bid her awake; for Hymen[9] is awake,
And long since ready forth his maske to move,
With his bright Tead that flames with many a flake,°   *spark*
And many a bachelor to waite on him,
In theyr fresh garments trim.
30   Bid her awake therefore and soone her dight,°   *dress*
For lo the wishèd day is come at last,
That shall for al the paynes and sorrowes past,
Pay to her usury° of long delight: *interest*
And whylest she doth her dight,
35   Doe ye to her of joy and solace° sing,   *pleasure*
That all the woods may answer and your eccho ring.

Bring with you all the Nymphes that you can heare[1]
Both of the rivers and the forrests greene:
And of the sea that neighbours to her neare,
40   Al with gay girlands goodly wel beseene.[2]
And let them also with them bring in hand
Another gay girland
For my fayre love of lillyes and of roses,
Bound truelove wize[3] with a blew silke riband.
45   And let them make great store of bridale poses,°   *posies*
And let them eeke° bring store of other flowers   *also*
To deck the bridale bowers.
And let the ground whereas° her foot shall tread,   *whereon*
For feare the stones her tender foot should wrong
50   Be strewed with fragrant flowers all along,
And diapred lyke the discolored mead.[4]
Which done, doe at her chamber dore awayt,
For she will waken strayt,°   *straightway*
The whiles doe ye this song unto her sing,
55   The woods shall to you answer and your Eccho ring.

Ye Nymphes of Mulla[5] which with carefull heed,
The silver scaly trouts doe tend full well,
And greedy pikes which use therein to feed,
(Those trouts and pikes all others doo excell)
60   And ye likewise which keepe the rushy lake,
Where none doo fishes take,
Bynd up the locks[6] the which hang scatterd light,
And in his waters which your mirror make,
Behold your faces as the christall bright,
65   That when you come whereas my love doth lie,

---

9. The Greek god of the wedding feast, repre-
sented as a young man bearing a torch ("Tead")
and leading a "maske" or procession.
1. I.e., that can hear you. "Nymphes": nymphs;
mythological female spirits inhabiting a particular
place, object, or natural phenomenon.

2. I.e., beautiful.
3. I.e., in the manner of true love.
4. And variegated like the many-colored meadow.
5. The vale of Mulla, near Spenser's home in Ire-
land.
6. I.e., the rushes.

No blemish she may spie.
And eke ye lightfoot mayds which keepe the deere,
That on the hoary mountayne use to towre,[7]
And the wylde wolves which seeke them to devoure,
70 With your steele darts doo chace from comming neer,
Be also present heere,
To helpe to decke her and to help to sing,
That all the woods may answer and your eccho ring.

Wake, now my love, awake; for it is time,
75 The Rosy Morne long since left Tithones bed,[8]
All ready to her silver coche° to clyme,   *coach*
And Phoebus[9] gins to shew his glorious hed.
Hark how the cheerefull birds do chaunt theyr laies°   *songs*
And carroll of loves praise.
80 The merry Larke hir mattins° sings aloft,[1]   *morning prayers*
The thrush replyes, the Mavis descant° playes,   *melodic counterpart*
The Ouzell shrills, the Ruddock warbles soft,
So goodly all agree with sweet consent,
To this dayes merriment.
85 Ah my deere love why doe ye sleepe thus long,
When meeter° were that ye should now awake,   *more appropriate*
T' awayt the comming of your joyous make,°   *mate*
And hearken to the birds lovelearnèd song,
The deawy leaves among.
90 For they of joy and pleasance to you sing,
That all the woods them answer and theyr eccho ring.

My love is now awake out of her dreames,
And her fayre eyes like stars that dimmèd were
With darksome cloud, now shew theyr goodly beams
95 More bright then Hesperus[2] his head doth rere.
Come now ye damzels, daughters of delight,
Helpe quickly her to dight,
But first come ye fayre houres[3] which were begot
In Joves sweet paradice, of Day and Night,
100 Which doe the seasons of the yeare allot,
And al that ever in this world is fayre
Doe make and still° repayre.   *continually*
And ye three handmayds of the Cyprian Queene,[4]
The which doe still adorne her beauties pride,
105 Helpe to addorne my beautifullest bride:
And as ye her array, still throw betweene°   *at intervals*
Some graces to be seene,

---

7. A hawking term meaning "to climb high."
"Lightfoot mayds": i.e., the nymphs.
8. The dawn, personified in mythology as the goddess Eos, or Aurora, was married to Tithonus, a mortal Trojan prince who aged while his wife stayed young.
9. Phoebus Apollo, the sun god.
1. The lark (a songbird) was associated with dawn. The mavis (song thrush), the ouzell (European blackbird), and the ruddock (robin) are all varieties of thrush. The birds' concert is a convention of love poetry.
2. The evening star, sacred to Venus.
3. The Horae, or Hours, were three daughters of Jove, commonly associated with the seasons and the principle of order.
4. Venus, whose handmaids were the three Graces: Aglaia, Thalia, and Euphrosyne. Their names mean "the brilliant one," "she who brings flowers," and "she who rejoices the heart."

And as ye use to Venus, to her sing,
The whiles the woods shal answer and your eccho ring.

110 Now is my love all ready forth to come,
Let all the virgins therefore well awayt,
And ye fresh boyes that tend upon her groome[5]
Prepare your selves; for he is comming strayt.
Set all your things in seemely good aray
115 Fit for so joyfull day,
The joyfulst day that ever sunne did see.
Faire Sun, shew forth thy favourable ray,
And let thy lifull° heat not fervent be   *lifegiving*
For feare of burning her sunshyny face,
120 Her beauty to disgrace.°   *spoil*
O fayrest Phoebus, father of the Muse,[6]
If ever I did honour thee aright,
Or sing the thing, that mote° thy mind delight,   *might*
Doe not thy servants simple boone° refuse,   *request*
125 But let this day let this one day be myne,
Let all the rest be thine.
Then I thy soverayne prayses loud wil sing,
That all the woods shal answer and theyr eccho ring.

Harke how the Minstrels gin to shrill aloud
130 Their merry Musick that resounds from far,
The pipe, the tabor,° and the trembling Croud,[7]   *drum*
That well agree withouten breach or jar.°   *discord*
But most of all the Damzels doe delite,
When they their tymbrels° smyte,   *tambourines*
135 And thereunto doe daunce and carrol sweet,
That all the sences they doe ravish quite,
The whyles the boyes run up and downe the street,
Crying aloud with strong confusèd noyce,
As if it were one voyce.
140 Hymen iô[8] Hymen, Hymen they do shout,
That even to the heavens theyr shouting shrill
Doth reach, and all the firmament doth fill,
To which the people standing all about,
As in approvance doe thereto applaud
145 And loud advaunce her laud,°   *praise*
And evermore they Hymen Hymen sing,
That al the woods them answer and theyr eccho ring.

Loe where she comes along with portly° pace,   *stately*
Lyke Phoebe[9] from her chamber of the East,
150 Arysing forth to run her mighty race,
Clad all in white, that seemes° a virgin best.   *befits*

5. Her bridegroom, i.e., the speaker of the poem himself.
6. Usually, Zeus was considered father of the Muses; in contrast, Spenser names Phoebus as their father.
7. Primitive fiddle.
8. A shout of joy or triumph (Greek). "Hymen":

god of marriage.
9. Another name for the moon goddess, Diana, commonly associated with chastity. This stanza and the two following praise her chaste beauty, which, by association, is identified with that of the speaker's betrothed.

So well it her beseemes that ye would weene
Some angell she had beene.
Her long loose yellow locks lyke golden wyre,
155 Sprinckled with perle, and perling° flowres a tweene,   *intermingling*
Doe lyke a golden mantle her attyre,
And being crownèd with a girland greene,
Seeme lyke some mayden Queene.
Her modest eyes abashèd to behold
160 So many gazers, as on her do stare,
Upon the lowly ground affixèd are.
Ne dare lift up her countenance too bold,
But blush to heare her prayses sung so loud,
So farre from being proud.
165 Nathlesse° doe ye still loud her prayses sing,   *nevertheless*
That all the woods may answer and your eccho ring.

Tell me ye merchants daughters did ye see
So fayre a creature in your towne before?
So sweet, so lovely, and so mild as she,
170 Adornd with beautyes grace and vertues store,°   *wealth*
Her goodly eyes lyke Saphyres shining bright,
Her forehead yvory white,
Her cheekes lyke apples which the sun hath rudded,
Her lips lyke cherryes charming men to byte,
175 Her brest like to a bowle of creame uncrudded,[1]
Her paps lyke lyllies budded,
Her snowie necke lyke to a marble towre,
And all her body lyke a pallace fayre,
Ascending uppe with many a stately stayre,
180 To honors seat and chastities sweet bowre.
Why stand ye still ye virgins in amaze,
Upon her so to gaze,
Whiles ye forget your former lay to sing,
To which the woods did answer and your eccho ring?

185 But if ye saw that which no eyes can see,
The inward beauty of her lively spright,°   *spirit*
Garnisht with heavenly guifts of high degree,
Much more then would ye wonder at that sight,
And stand astonisht lyke to those which red°   *saw*
190 Medusaes mazeful hed.[2]
There dwels sweet love and constant chastity,
Unspotted fayth and comely womanhed,
Regard of honour and mild modesty,
There Vertue raynes as Queene in royal throne,
195 And giveth lawes alone.
The which the base affections° doe obay,   *lowly emotions*
And yeeld theyr services unto her will,
Ne thought of thing uncomely ever may
Thereto approch to tempt her mind to ill.
200 Had ye once seene these her celestial threasures,

---

1. Uncurdled, or fresh.
2. The Gorgon Medusa had serpents for hair; whoever looked upon her was turned to stone. She was sometimes associated with chastity.

And unrevealèd pleasures,
Then would ye wonder and her prayses sing,
That al the woods should answer and your echo ring.

Open the temple gates unto my love,
205 Open them wide that she may enter in,
And all the postes adorne as doth behove,[3]
And all the pillours deck with girlands trim,
For to recyve this Saynt with honour dew,
That commeth in to you.
210 With trembling steps and humble reverence,
She commeth in, before th' almighties vew:
Of her ye virgins learne obedience,
When so ye come into those holy places,
To humble your proud faces;
215 Bring her up to th' high altar that she may,
The sacred ceremonies there partake,
The which do endlesse matrimony make,
And let the roring Organs loudly play
The praises of the Lord in lively notes,
220 The whiles with hollow throates
The Choristers the joyous Antheme sing,
That al the woods may answere and their eccho ring.

Behold whiles she before the altar stands
Hearing the holy priest that to her speakes
225 And blesseth her with his two happy hands,
How the red roses flush up in her cheekes,
And the pure snow with goodly vermill° stayne,   scarlet
Like crimsin dyde in grayne,[4]
That even th' Angels which continually,
230 About the sacred Altare doe remaine,
Forget their service and about her fly,
Ofte peeping in her face that seemes more fayre,
The more they on it stare.
But her sad° eyes still fastened on the ground,   sober
235 Are governèd with goodly modesty,
That suffers not one looke to glaunce awry,
Which may let in a little thought unsownd.°   unsound
Why blush ye love to give to me your hand,
The pledge of all our band?°   bond
240 Sing ye sweet Angels, Alleluya sing,
That all the woods may answere and your eccho ring.

Now al is done; bring home the bride againe,
Bring home the triumph of our victory,
Bring home with you the glory of her gaine,[5]
245 With joyance bring her and with jollity.
Never had man more joyfull day then this,
Whom heaven would heape with blis.

---

3. I.e., as is fitting.   5. I.e., of gaining her.
4. I.e., dyed with colorfast dye.

Make feast therefore now all this live long day,
This day for ever to me holy is,
250 Poure out the wine without restraint or stay,
Poure not by cups, but by the belly full,
Poure out to all that wull,°   *will*
And sprinkle all the postes and wals with wine,
That they may sweat, and drunken be withall.
255 Crowne ye God Bacchus[6] with a coronall,°   *garland*
And Hymen also crowne with wreathes of vine,
And let the Graces daunce unto the rest;
For they can doo it best:
The whiles the maydens doe theyr carroll sing,
260 To which the woods shal answer and theyr eccho ring.

Ring ye the bels, ye yong men of the towne,
And leave your wonted labors for this day:
This day is holy; doe ye write it downe,
That ye for ever it remember may.
265 This day the sunne is in his chiefest hight,
With Barnaby the bright,[7]
From whence declining daily by degrees,
He somewhat loseth of his heat and light,
When once the Crab[8] behind his back he sees.
270 But for this time it ill ordainèd was,
To chose the longest day in all the yeare,
And shortest night, when longest fitter weare:
Yet never day so long, but late° would passe.   *finally*
Ring ye the bels, to make it weare away,
275 And bonefiers° make all day,   *bonfires*
And daunce about them, and about them sing:
That all the woods may answer, and your eccho ring.

Ah when will this long weary day have end,
And lende me leave to come unto my love?
280 How slowly do the houres theyr numbers spend?
How slowly does sad Time his feathers move?
Hast° thee O fayrest Planet to thy home[9]   *haste*
Within the Westerne fome:
Thy tyred steedes long since have need of rest.
285 Long though it be, at last I see it gloome,
And the bright evening star with golden creast
Appeare out of the East.
Fayre childe of beauty, glorious lampe of love
That all the host of heaven in rankes doost lead,
290 And guydest lovers through the nights dread,
How chearefully thou lookest from above,
And seemst to laugh atweene thy twinkling light
As joying in the sight

---

6. Bacchus, god of wine and ecstasy.
7. St. Barnabas's Day (June 11) was also the day of the summer solstice (the longest day of the year) in the calendar used during Spenser's time.
8. Cancer the Crab, the fourth constellation in the zodiac, through which the sun passes in July.
9. The sun, drawn in its chariot (by "tyred steedes"); in Ptolemaic astronomy, still often accepted in Spenser's time, the sun was one of the planets, which revolved about the Earth.

Of these glad many which for joy doe sing,
295   That all the woods them answer and their echo ring.

Now ceasse ye damsels[1] your delights forepast;
Enough is it, that all the day was youres:
Now day is doen, and night is nighing fast:
Now bring the Bryde into the brydall boures.[2]
300   Now night is come,[3] now soone her disaray,°   undress
And in her bed her lay;
Lay her in lillies and in violets,
And silken courteins° over her display,   curtains
And odourd sheetes, and Arras[4] coverlets.
305   Behold how goodly my faire love does ly
In proud humility;
Like unto Maia,[5] when as Jove her tooke,
In Tempe, lying on the flowry gras,
Twixt sleepe and wake, after she weary was,
310   With bathing in the Acidalian brooke.
Now it is night, ye damsels may be gon,
And leave my love alone,
And leave likewise your former lay to sing:
The woods no more shal answere, nor your echo ring.

315   Now welcome night, thou night so long expected,°   awaited
That long daies labour doest at last defray,°   requite
And all my cares, which cruell love collected,
Hast sumd in one, and cancellèd for aye:
Spread thy broad wing over my love and me,
320   That no man may us see,
And in thy sable mantle us enwrap,
From feare of perrill and foule horror free.
Let no false treason seeke us to entrap,
Nor any dread disquiet once annoy
325   The safety of our joy:
But let the night be calme and quietsome,
Without tempestuous storms or sad afray:°   dark terror
Lyke as when Jove with fayre Alcmena[6] lay,
When he begot the great Tirynthian groome:
330   Or lyke as when he with thy selfe did lie,
And begot Majesty.
And let the mayds and yongmen cease to sing:
Ne let the woods them answer, nor theyr eccho ring.

Let no lamenting cryes, nor dolefull teares,
335   Be heard all night within nor yet without:
Ne let false whispers breeding hidden feares,

1. I.e., all the aforementioned nymphs and spirits.
2. Bowers, or private bedrooms.
3. On the placement of this phrase, see the end of note 4, p. 171.
4. A northeastern French city famous for its tapestries.
5. Said to be the most beautiful of the Pleiades, the seven daughters of Atlas and the Oceanid Plei-
one; Maia was the mother of the god Hermes (and Jove was his father). The "Acidalian brooke" (line 310) is associated with Venus.
6. According to several versions of the story, Jove ordered the sun not to shine in order to make the night longer; the "Tirynthian groome" conceived by Alcmena was Heracles.

Breake gentle sleepe with misconceivèd dout.°   *fear*
Let no deluding dreames, nor dreadful sights
Make sudden sad affrights;
340 Ne let housefyres, nor lightnings helpelesse harmes,
Ne let the Pouke,[7] nor other evill sprights,
Ne let mischìvous witches with theyr charmes,
Ne let hob Goblins, names whose sence we see not,
Fray us with things that be not.
345 Let not the shriech Oule, nor the Storke be heard:
Nor the night Raven[8] that still° deadly yels,   *continually*
Nor damnèd ghosts cald up with mighty spels,
Nor griesly vultures make us once affeard:
Ne let th' unpleasant Quyre of Frogs still croking
350 Make us to wish theyr choking.
Let none of these theyr drery accents sing;
Ne let the woods them answer, nor theyr eccho ring.

But let stil Silence trew night watches keepe,
That sacred peace may in assurance rayne,
355 And tymely sleep, when it is tyme to sleepe,
May poure his limbs forth on your pleasant playne,°   *plain*
The whiles an hundred little wingèd loves,°   *cupids*
Like divers fethered doves,
Shall fly and flutter round about your bed,
360 And in the secret darke, that none reproves,
Their prety stealthes shal worke, and snares shal spread
To filch away sweet snatches of delight,
Conceald through covert night.
Ye sonnes of Venus, play your sports at will,
365 For greedy pleasure, carelesse of your toyes,°   *amorous sports*
Thinks more upon her paradise of joyes,
Then what ye do, albe it good or ill.
All night therefore attend your merry play,
For it will soone be day:
370 Now none doth hinder you, that say or sing,
Ne will the woods now answer, nor your Eccho ring.

Who is the same, which at my window peepes?
Or whose is that faire face, that shines so bright,
Is it not Cinthia,[9] she that never sleepes,
375 But walkes about high heaven al the night?
O fayrest goddesse, do thou not envỳ
My love with me to spy:
For thou likewise didst love, though now unthought,[1]
And for a fleece of woll,° which privily,   *wool*
380 The Latmian shephard once unto thee brought,

---

7. Puck, also called Hobgoblin; a small supernatural creature popular in English folklore and a character in Shakespeare's *A Midsummer Night's Dream*.
8. The night raven and the owl were birds of ill omen; the stork was sometimes figured as an avenger of adultery.
9. Another name for Diana, the moon goddess; in addition to chastity, she was associated with childbirth.
1. According to some versions of the story, Cynthia and Endymion, the "Latmian shephard," made love on Mount Latmos, after he brought her a fleece. In revenge, Zeus made Endymion sleep eternally.

His pleasures with thee wrought.
Therefore to us be favorable now;
And sith of wemens labours thou hast charge,
And generation goodly dost enlarge,
385   Encline thy will t' effect our wishfull vow,
And the chast wombe informe with timely seed,
That may our comfort breed:
Till which we cease our hopefull hap to sing,
Ne let the woods us answere, nor our Eccho ring.

390   And thou great Juno,[2] which with awful° might   *awe-inspiring*
The lawes of wedlock still dost patronize,
And the religion° of the faith first plight   *sanctity*
With sacred rites hast taught to solemnize:[3]
And eeke for comfort often callèd art
395   Of women in their smart,°   *pains of childbirth*
Eternally bind thou this lovely band,
And all thy blessings unto us impart.
And thou glad Genius,[4] in whose gentle hand,
The bridale bowre and geniall° bed remaine,   *marriage*
400   Without blemish or staine,
And the sweet pleasures of theyr loves delight
With secret ayde doest succour and supply,
Till they bring forth the fruitfull progeny,
Send us the timely fruit of this same night.
405   And thou fayre Hebe,[5] and thou Hymen free,
Grant that it may so be.
Til which we cease your further prayse to sing,
Ne any woods shal answer, nor your Eccho ring.

And ye high heavens, the temple of the gods,
410   In which a thousand torches flaming bright
Doe burne, that to us wretched earthly clods,
In dreadful darknesse lend desirèd light;
And all ye powers which in the same remayne,
More then we men can fayne,°   *imagine*
415   Poure out your blessing on us plentiously,
And happy influence upon us raine,
That we may raise a large posterity,
Which from the earth, which they may long possesse,
With lasting happinesse,
420   Up to your haughty pallaces may mount,
And for the guerdon° of theyr glorious merit   *reward*
May heavenly tabernacles there inherit,
Of blessed Saints for to increase the count.
So let us rest, sweet love, in hope of this,
425   And cease till then our tymely joyes to sing,
The woods no more us answer, nor our eccho ring.

---

2. Goddess of marriage and childbirth.
3. I.e., the marriage vows.
4. A spirit presiding over generation. By invoking both Juno and a Genius as patrons of the marriage bed, Spenser draws also on the belief that each individual is watched over from birth by a tutelary spirit called a "Juno" (for girls) or a "Genius" (for boys).
5. Daughter of Juno and goddess of youth.

Song made in lieu of many ornaments,
With which my love should duly have bene dect,°   *adorned*
Which cutting off[6] through hasty° accidents,   *sudden*
430   Ye would not stay your dew time to expect,°   *await*
But promist both to recompens,
Be unto her a goodly ornament,
And for short time an endlesse moniment.

1595

Prothalamion[7]

Calme was the day, and through the trembling ayre,
Sweete breathing Zephyrus[8] did softly play
A gentle spirit, that lightly did delay
Hot Titans[9] beames, which then did glyster° fayre: *shine*
5   When I whom sullein care,
Through discontent of my long fruitlesse stay
In Princes Court, and expectation vayne
Of idle hopes, which still doe fly away,
Like empty shaddowes, did aflict my brayne,
10   Walkt forth to ease my payne
Along the shoare of silver streaming Themmes,°   *Thames River*
Whose rutty° Bancke, the which his River hemmes,°   *rooty / hems in*
Was paynted all with variable flowers,
And all the meades adornd with daintie gemmes,
15   Fit to decke maydens bowres,
And crowne their Paramours,°   *loves*
Against the Brydale day, which is not long:
    Sweete Themmes runne softly, till I end my Song.

There, in a Meadow, by the Rivers side,
20   A flocke of Nymphes[1] I chauncèd to espy,
All lovely Daughters of the Flood° thereby,   *river*
With goodly greenish locks all loose untyde,
As each had bene a Bryde,
And each one had a little wicker basket,
25   Made of fine twigs entraylèd° curiously,   *entwined*
In which they gathered flowers to fill their flasket:[2]
And with fine Fingers, cropt full feateously°   *dexterously*
The tender stalkes on hye.[3]
Of every sort, which in that Meadow grew,
30   They gathered some; the Violet pallid blew,°   *blue*
The little Dazie, that at evening closes,
The virgin Lillie, and the Primrose trew,
With store of vermeil° Roses,   *scarlet*

6. Preventing; also, running away.
7. Literally, "before the bridal chamber" (Greek). A nuptial song celebrating the double betrothal of Elizabeth and Katherine Somerset, daughters of the earl of Worcester. These sisters are figured as the two swans in the poem.
8. The west wind, often associated with morning and spring.
9. The sun's.
1. Mythological female spirits inhabiting a particular place, object, or natural phenomenon.
2. A long, shallow basket.
3. Hurriedly.

To decke their Bridegromes posies,
35 Against the Brydale day, which was not long:
　Sweete Themmes runne softly, till I end my Song.

With that I saw two Swannes of goodly hewe,
Come softly swimming downe along the Lee;[4]
Two fairer Birds I yet did never see:
40 The snow which doth the top of Pindus[5] strew,
Did never whiter shew,
Nor Jove himselfe when he a Swan would be
For love of Leda,[6] whiter did appeare:
Yet Leda was they say as white as he,
45 Yet not so white as these, nor nothing neare;
So purely white they were,
That even the gentle streame, the which them bare,
Seem'd foule to° them, and bad his billowes spare　　　*compared to*
To wet their silken feathers, least° they might　　　　　*lest*
50 Soyle their fayre plumes with water not so fayre,
And marre their beauties bright,
That shone as heavens light,
Against their Brydale day, which was not long:
　Sweete Themmes runne softly, till I end my Song.

55 Eftsoones° the Nymphes, which now had Flowers their fill,　*forthwith*
Ran all in haste, to see that silver brood,
As they came floating on the Christal Flood,
Whom when they sawe, they stood amazèd still,
Their wondring eyes to fill.
60 Them seem'd they never saw a sight so fayre,
Of Fowles so lovely, that they sure did deeme
Them heavenly borne, or to be that same payre
Which through the Skie draw Venus silver Teeme,[7]
For sure they did not seeme
65 To be begot of any earthly Seede,
But rather Angels or of Angels breede:
Yet were they bred of Somers-heat[8] they say,
In sweetest Season, when each Flower and weede
The earth did fresh aray,
70 So fresh they seem'd as day,
Even as their Brydale day, which was not long:
　Sweete Themmes runne softly, till I end my Song.

Then forth they all out of their baskets drew
Great store of Flowers, the honour of the field,
75 That to the sense did fragrant odours yield,
All which upon those goodly Birds they threw,
And all the Waves did strew,

4. Then a tributary of the Thames.
5. A mountain range in central Greece, the highest peak of which is Parnassus.
6. Jove took the shape of a swan and raped the maiden Leda; according to some traditions of the story, she gave birth as a result to two pairs of twins: Castor and Pollux, and Helen and Clytemnestra.

In line 173, the two knights, or bridegrooms, are compared to the "twins of Jove."
7. Contemporary pictures often showed Venus' chariot drawn by two swans.
8. A play on "summer's heat" and their family name, Somerset.

That like old Peneus[9] Waters they did seeme,
When downe along by pleasant Tempes shore
80 Scattred with Flowres, through Thessaly they streeme,
That they appeare through Lillies plenteous store,
Like a Brydes Chamber flore:°   *floor*
Two of those Nymphes, meane while, two Garlands bound,
Of freshest Flowres which in that Mead° they found,   *meadow*
85 The which presenting all in trim° Array,   *perfect*
Their snowie Foreheads therewithall they crownd,
Whil'st one did sing this Lay,
Prepar'd against that Day,
Against their Brydale day, which was not long:
90   Sweete Themmes runne softly, till I end my Song.

Ye gentle Birdes, the worlds faire ornament,
And heavens glorie, whom this happie hower°   *hour*
Doth leade unto your lovers blisfull bower,
Joy may you have and gentle hearts content
95 Of your loves couplement:°   *union*
And let faire Venus, that is Queene of love,
With her heart-quelling Sonne[1] upon you smile,
Whose smile they say, hath vertue° to remove   *power*
All Loves dislike, and friendships faultie guile
100 For ever to assoile.°   *absolve*
Let endlesse Peace your steadfast hearts accord,
And blessed Plentie wait upon your bord,°   *table*
And let your bed with pleasures chast abound,
That fruitfull issue may to you afford,°   *produce*
105 Which may your foes confound,
And make your joyes redound,°   *overflow*
Upon your Brydale day, which is not long:
  Sweete Themmes run softlie, till I end my Song.

So ended she; and all the rest around
110 To her redoubled that her undersong,[2]
Which said, their bridale daye should not be long.
And gentle Eccho from the neighbour ground,
Their accents did resound.
So forth those joyous Birdes did passe along,
115 Adowne the Lee,° that to them murmurde low,   *meadow*
As he would speake, but that he lackt a tong,°   *tongue*
Yet did by signes his glad affection show,
Making his streame run slow.
And all the foule which in his flood did dwell
120 Gan° flock about these twaine, that did excell   *did*
The rest, so far, as Cynthia doth shend[3]
The lesser starres. So they enrangèd° well,   *arranged*
Did on those two attend,
And their best service lend,

---

9. A river in Thessaly, Greece, that flows through the Tempe valley, the beauty of which was praised by several poets.

1. I.e., Cupid.
2. Repeated her refrain.
3. I.e., as the moon doth surpass.

125   Against their wedding day, which was not long:
       Sweete Themmes run softly, till I end my Song.

    At length they all to mery London came,
    To mery London, my most kyndly Nurse,
    That to me gave this Lifes first native sourse:°   *source*
130   Though from another place I take my name,
    An house of auncient fame.[4]
    There when they came, whereas those bricky towres,[5]
    The which on Themmes brode agèd backe doe ryde,
    Where now the studious Lawyers have their bowers,
135   There whylome° wont the Templer Knights to byde,   *formerly*
    Till they decayd through pride:
    Next whereunto there standes a stately place,[6]
    Where oft I gaynèd giftes and goodly grace
    Of that great Lord, which therein wont to dwell,
140   Whose want too well, now feeles my freendles case:
    But Ah here fits not well
    Olde woes but joyes to tell
    Against the bridale daye, which is not long:
       Sweete Themmes runne softly, till I end my Song.

145   Yet therein now doth lodge a noble Peer,[7]
    Great Englands glory and the Worlds wide wonder,
    Whose dreadfull name, late through all Spaine did thunder,[8]
    And Hercules two pillors standing neere,[9]
    Did make to quake and feare:
150   Faire branch of Honor, flower of Chevalrie,
    That fillest England with thy triumphes fame,
    Joy have thou of thy noble victorie,
    And endlesse happinesse of thine owne name
    That promiseth the same:[1]
155   That through thy prowesse and victorious armes,
    Thy country may be freed from forraine harmes:
    And great Elìsaes° glorious name may ring   *Elizabeth's*
    Through al the world, fil'd with thy wide Alarmes,[2]
    Which some brave muse may sing
160   To ages following,
    Upon the Brydale day, which is not long:
       Sweete Themmes runne softly, till I end my Song.

    From those high Towers, this noble Lord issuing,[3]
    Like Radiant Hesper° when his golden hayre   *evening star*
165   In th'Ocean billowes he hath Bathèd fayre,

4. Spenser is making a claim, debated by modern scholars, that he is related to the Spencers of Althorpe, Northampton.
5. The Temple, residence of law students in London, formerly occupied by the Knights Templars, whose military and religious order was dissolved on suspicion of heretical practices.
6. Leicester House, palace of Spenser's patron, the earl of Leicester; called Essex House after its occupation by the earl of Essex in 1596.
7. I.e., Robert Devereux, earl of Essex (1566?–1601).
8. The earl of Essex had sacked the city of Cádiz in Spain during August 1596.
9. According to legend, the two cliffs on both sides of the Straits of Gibraltar were erected by Hercules.
1. A pun on his name, Devereux: *dev(enir) (h)eureux,* "to become happy" (French).
2. Calls to arms (military campaigns).
3. I.e., coming out of the Towers.

Descended to the Rivers open viewing,
With a great traine ensuing.
Above the rest were goodly to bee seene
Two gentle Knights of lovely face and feature
170   Beseeming well the bower of anie Queene,
With gifts of wit and ornaments of nature,
Fit for so goodly stature:
That like the twins of Jove[4] they seem'd in sight,
Which decke the Bauldricke[5] of the Heavens bright.
175   They two forth pacing to the Rivers side,
Received those two faire Brides, their Loves delight,
Which at th'appointed tyde,
Each one did make his Bryde,
Against their Brydale day, which is not long:
180   Sweete Themmes runne softly, till I end my Song.

                                      1596

FULKE GREVILLE, LORD BROOKE

1554–1628

From Mustapha

Chorus Sacerdotum[1]

O wearisome condition of humanity!
Born under one law, to another bound;
Vainly begot and yet forbidden vanity;
Created sick,[2] commanded to be sound.
5   What meaneth nature by these diverse laws?
Passion and reason, self-division cause.
Is it the mark or majesty of power
To make offenses that it may forgive?
Nature herself doth her own self deflower
10   To hate those errors she herself doth give.
For how should man think that he may not do,
If nature did not fail and punish, too?
Tyrant to others, to herself unjust,
Only commands things difficult and hard,
15   Forbids us all things which it knows is lust,°   *pleasure, desire*
Makes easy pains, unpossible reward.
If nature did not take delight in blood,
She would have made more easy ways to good.
We that are bound by vows and by promotion,[3]
20   With pomp of holy sacrifice and rites,

4. Castor and Pollux, who as the Gemini form the third constellation in the "Bauldricke of the Heavens," the zodiac.
5. Baldric: a belt or girdle worn over one shoulder and across the chest to support a sword, bugle, etc.
1. I.e., chorus of priests; the final chorus of Greville's closet tragedy *Mustapha,* in which the hero, son of the Turkish emperor, is falsely accused by his stepmother of desiring to kill his father. Mustapha's execution despite his virtuous innocence prompts the chorus to meditate on the meaning of human life.
2. A reference to the Christian doctrine of original sin.
3. I.e., stirring of the mind.

To teach belief in good and still° devotion,   *instill*
To preach of heaven's wonders and delights;
Yet when each of us in his own heart looks
He finds the God there, far unlike his books.

1609

From Caelica[4]

4

You little stars that live in skies
And glory in Apollo's[5] glory,
In whose aspècts conjoinèd lies
The heaven's will and nature's story,[6]
5   Joy to be likened to those eyes,[7]
Which eyes make all eyes glad or sorry;
     For when you force thoughts from above,
     These overrule your force by love.

And thou, O Love, which in these eyes
10   Hast married Reason with Affection,
And made them saints of Beauty's skies,
Where joys are shadows of perfection,
Lend me thy wings that I may rise
Up, not by worth, but thy election;[8]
15   For I have vowed in strangest fashion
     To love and never seek compassion.

ca. 1580   1633

39

The *nurse-life°* wheat within his green husk growing,   *life-fostering*
Flatters our hope, and tickles our desire,
Nature's true riches in sweet beauties showing,
Which set all hearts, with labor's love, on fire.

5   No less fair is the wheat when golden ear
Shows unto hope the joys of near enjoying;
Fair and sweet is the bud, more sweet and fair
The rose, which proves that time is not destroying.

Caelica, your youth, the morning of delight,
10   Enamel'd o'er with beauties white and red,
All sense and thoughts did to belief invite,
That love and glory there are brought to bed;

4. *Caelica* (Latin for "heavenly"), the title of Gre-
ville's poetic sequence, refers to one of three ladies
he addresses in the poems; the others are Cynthia
and Myra. Heavily influenced by Sidney's
Astrophil and Stella, the 110 poems in the first edi-
tion of *Caelica* treat religious and political themes
as well as erotic ones.
5. Apollo was god of the sun; here, the sun itself.
6. As in astrology. The "aspect" of a star or planet
was its position in the sky from an observation
point on earth. When two heavenly bodies occu-
pied approximately the same position, their aspects
were said to be "conjoined" or "in conjunction," a
circumstance thought to exert a powerful influ-
ence ("the heaven's will") on mundane affairs
("nature's story").
7. I.e., the stars.
8. Calvinist theology held that salvation depended
not on human merit but on "election" by God.

And your ripe year's love-noon; he goes no higher,[9]
Turns all the spirits of man into desire.

ca. 1580–1600   1633

JOHN LYLY

1554–1606

Cupid and My Campaspe[1]

Cupid and my Campaspe played
At cards for kisses; Cupid paid.
He stakes his quiver, bow, and arrows,
His mother's[2] doves and team of sparrows,
5   Loses them too; then down he throws
The coral of his lip, the rose
Growing on 's cheek (but none knows how),
With these the crystal of his brow,
And then the dimple of his chin:
10   All these did my Campaspe win.
At last he set her both his eyes;
She won, and Cupid blind did rise.
        Oh Love! has she done this to thee?
        What shall (alas) become of me?

1632

Oh, For a Bowl of Fat Canary[3]

Oh, for a bowl of fat Canary,
Rich Palermo, sparkling Sherry,
Some nectar else, from Juno's dairy;[4]
Oh, these draughts would make us merry!

5   Oh, for a wench (I deal in faces,
And in other daintier things);
Tickled am I with her embraces,
Fine dancing in such fairy rings.[5]

Oh, for a plump fat leg of mutton,
10   Veal, lamb, capon, pig, and coney;[6]
None is happy but a glutton,
None an ass but who wants money.

9. I.e., your year or present age is love's noon; he (the morning sun) goes no higher.
1. This song appears in Act 3, Scene 5 of Lyly's play *Campaspe* (published in 1584), which tells the story of Alexander the Great's love for his Theban captive, Campaspe. Sung by Apelles, the painter who falls in love with Campaspe while painting her portrait, the song expresses his erotic frustration.
2. I.e., Venus'.
3. Also from *Campaspe* (see note 1, above). Three servant boys (Granichus, Psyllus, and Manes) sing this song as they prepare to feast at someone else's expense (1.2). Each boy sings one stanza, and all three sing the final verse.
4. "Nectar": the drink of the gods, hence coming from the "dairy" of Juno, the queen of the gods. "Canary": a light sweet wine; "fat": meaning well-bodied. "Palermo": a wine from Palermo in Sicily.
5. Circles of grass, differing in color from the surrounding grass; a phenomenon commonly supposed to be caused by dancing fairies.
6. Rabbit; "capon": a castrated rooster, especially one fattened for eating.

Wines indeed and girls are good,
But brave victuals° feast the blood;   *provisions, food*
15 For wenches, wine, and lusty cheer,
Jove[7] would leap down to surfeit here.

1640

SIR PHILIP SIDNEY

1554–1586

Ye Goatherd Gods[1]

STREPHON.[2] Ye goatherd gods, that love the grassy mountains,
Ye nymphs which haunt the springs in pleasant valleys,
Ye satyrs[3] joyed with free and quiet forests,
Vouchsafe your silent ears to plaining music,
5   Which to my woes gives still an early morning,
And draws the dolor on till weary evening.

KLAIUS. O Mercury,[4] foregoer to the evening,
O heavenly huntress of the savage mountains,
O lovely star, entitled of the morning,
10   While that my voice doth fill these woeful valleys,
Vouchsafe your silent ears to plaining music,
Which oft hath Echo tired in secret forests.

STREPHON. I, that was once free burgess° of the forests,   *citizen*
Where shade from sun, and sport I sought in evening,
15 I, that was once esteemed for pleasant music,
Am banished now among the monstrous mountains
Of huge despair, and foul affliction's valleys,
Am grown a screech owl[5] to myself each morning.

KLAIUS. I, that was once delighted every morning,
20   Hunting the wild inhabiters of forests,
I, that was once the music of these valleys,
So darkened am that all my day is evening,
Heartbroken so, that molehills seem high mountains
And fill the vales with cries instead of music.

---

7. Chief of the gods (also known as Zeus).
1. The poem is in the form of a double sestina, two sets of six six-line stanzas, with a triplet concluding the whole. The same six key words end the lines of each stanza; their order is always a permutation of the order in the stanza just preceding: the pattern is 6 1 5 2 4 3, i.e., the last word of line 1 of any stanza is always the same as the last word of line 6 in the preceding stanza. Line 2's end is like line 1 of the preceding stanza; line 3 like line 5; line 4 like line 2; line 5 like line 4; and line 6 like line 3. All six key words appear in the triplet in the same order as that of the first and seventh stanzas.
2. Strephon and Klaius are shepherds, both in love with the absent Urania, in Sidney's heroic romance *Arcadia*, in which this poem appears.
3. Woodland deities, usually having the head and torso of a man, and the lower body of a goat; commonly associated with merriment and lust.
4. The evening star. The "heavenly huntress" is the goddess Diana, the moon.
5. Named for the sound of its voice, and considered to be a bird of ill omen.

25 STREPHON. Long since, alas, my deadly swannish[6] music
Hath made itself a crier of the morning,
And hath with wailing strength climbed highest moun-
tains;
Long since my thoughts more desert be than forests,
Long since I see my joys come to their evening,
30 And state° thrown down to overtrodden   *high position*
valleys.

KLAIUS. Long since the happy dwellers of these valleys
Have prayed me leave my strange exclaiming music,
Which troubles their day's work and joys of evening;
Long since I hate the night, more hate the morning;
35 Long since my thoughts chase me like beasts in forests,
And make me wish myself laid under mountains.

STREPHON. Meseems° I see the high and stately   *it seems to me*
mountains
Transform themselves to low dejected valleys;
Meseems I hear in these ill-changèd forests
40 The nightingales do learn of owls their music;
Meseems I feel the comfort of the morning
Turned to the mortal serene[7] of an evening.

KLAIUS. Meseems I see a filthy cloudy evening
As soon as sun begins to climb the mountains;
45 Meseems I feel a noisome° scent, the morning   *offensive*
When I do smell the flowers of these valleys;
Meseems I hear, when I do hear sweet music,
The dreadful cries of murdered men in forests.

STREPHON. I wish to fire the trees of all these forests;
50 I give the sun a last farewell each evening;
I curse the fiddling finders-out of music;
With envy I do hate the lofty mountains,
And with despite despise the humble valleys;
I do detest night, evening, day, and morning.

55 KLAIUS. Curse to myself my prayer is, the morning;
My fire is more than can be made with forests,
My state more base than are the basest valleys.
I wish no evenings more to see, each evening;
Shamèd, I hate myself in sight of mountains
60 And stop mine ears, lest I grow mad with music.

STREPHON. For she whose parts maintained a perfect music,
Whose beauties shined more than the blushing morning,
Who much did pass[8] in state the stately mountains,
In straightness passed the cedars of the forests,

---

6. The swan was supposed to sing only just before it died.
7. Damp evening air, thought to produce sickness

("mortal": deadly). The stress is on the first syllable.
8. Surpass.

65   Hath cast me, wretch, into eternal evening
                     By taking her two suns[9] from these dark valleys.

KLAIUS.   For she, with whom compared, the Alps are valleys,
                     She, whose least word brings from the spheres their
                            music,[1]
                     At whose approach the sun rose in the evening,
70   Who where she went bare° in her forehead   *bore*
                          morning,
                     Is gone, is gone, from these our spoilèd forests,
                     Turning to deserts our best pastured mountains.

STREPHON.   These mountains witness shall, so shall these valleys,

KLAIUS.   These forests eke,° made wretched by our music,   *also*
75   Our morning hymn this is, and song at evening.
1577–83   1593

What Length of Verse?[2]

What length of verse can serve brave° Mopsa's good to show,   *splendid*
Whose virtues strange, and beauties such, as no man them may
    know?
Thus shrewdly° burden, then, how can my Muse escape?   *severally*
The gods must help, and precious things must serve to show her
    shape.

5   Like great god Saturn, fair, and like fair Venus, chaste;[3]
    As smooth as Pan, as Juno mild, like goddess Iris fast.[4]
    With Cupid she foresees, and goes° god Vulcan's pace;   *walks with*
    And for a taste of all these gifts, she borrows Momus' grace.

    Her forehead jacinth-like, her cheeks of opal[5] hue,
10   Her twinkling eyes bedecked with pearl, her lips of sapphire blue,

---

9. I.e., her eyes.
1. Music of the spheres: a popular theory during the period, based on the Pythagorean idea that the movement of the celestial bodies produced a musical harmony, inaudible to human ears.
2. This fourteen-line poem parodies the sonnet form and a number of conventions of pastoral love poetry. Written in "poulter's measure"—alternating lines of six and seven iambic feet—the poem occurs early in the first version of Sidney's pastoral romance, a version known now as the *Old Arcadia*. The poem is attributed to Alethes, whose name plays on a Greek word meaning "truth" or "sincerity"; in his verses Alethes ironically praises "Mistress Mopsa," ugly daughter of boorish rural parents. Mopsa's qualities are associated with those of the verse itself. Although popular for much of the sixteenth century, poulter's measure is here defined as antiquated and "vulgar." For a different perspective on the meter, see Queen Elizabeth I, "The doubt of future foes exiles my present joy"

(p. 131).
3. This line initiates an inversion of classical gods' and goddesses' qualities: Saturn is ugly; Venus, unchaste; Cupid, blind; Vulcan, lame; and Momus, god of laughter and rebuke, censorious.
4. Iris is goddess of the rainbow, the ephemeral quality of which leads us to interpret the adjective spelled "faste" in several manuscripts as "fast"—meaning "steadfast"—rather than as "faced." William Ringler and several other modern editors choose "faced," and Ringler attempts to make this choice work by emending "Iris" (the reading of all manuscripts) to "Isis," an Egyptian goddess sometimes depicted as "cow-faced." But Ringler's reason for rejecting "Iris"—that she was "fast" in the sense of speedy, and hence the line so read would lose its irony—disappears if one reads "fast" as "steadfast."
5. Many-colored; "jacinth-like": yellow, reddish-orange, or blue.

Her hair pure crapall stone,[6] her mouth, O heavenly wide,
Her skin like burnished gold, her hands like silver ore untried.

As for those parts unknown, which hidden sure are best,
Happy be they which will believe, and never seek the rest.

ca. 1580   1593

The Nightingale[7]

The nightingale, as soon as April bringeth
Unto her rested sense a perfect waking,
While late° bare earth, proud of new clothing, springeth,   *recently*
Sings out her woes, a thorn her song-book making,
5   And mournfully bewailing,
Her throat in tunes expresseth
What grief her breast oppresseth
For Tereus' force on her chaste will prevailing.
Oh Philomela fair, Oh take some gladness,
10   That here is juster cause of plaintful sadness:
Thine earth now springs, mine fadeth;
Thy thorn without, my thorn my heart invadeth.

Alas, she hath no other cause of anguish
But Tereus' love, on her by strong hand wroken,[8]
15   Wherein she suffering, all her spirits languish;
Full womanlike complains her will was broken.
But I, who daily craving,
Cannot have to content me,
Have more cause to lament me,
20   Since wanting is more woe than too much having.
O Philomela fair, O take some gladness,
That here is juster cause of plaintful sadness:
Thine earth now springs, mine fadeth;
Thy thorn without, my thorn my heart invadeth.

1581   1598

Ring Out Your Bells

Ring out your bells, let mourning shows be spread,
For Love is dead.
All Love is dead, infected
With plague of deep disdain;
5   Worth as naught worth rejected,

---

6. With a pun on "crap," the line refers to "chelo-
nitis"—according to bestiaries, a stone in the head
of a frog. The stone was described as green or tor-
toise-shell colored.
7. Philomela, the nightingale, who sings a mourn-
ful song in the springtime: according to myth, Phil-
omela was raped by her brother-in-law, Tereus,
who then tore out her tongue so that she could not
reveal his crime. She wove the story in a tapestry

and sent it to her sister, who rescued her. She was
later changed into a nightingale while in flight
from Tereus. This and the following poem are
from the *Certain Sonnets*, a collection of poems in
various forms and meters that Sidney wrote before
1581; they were first published in 1593, after his
death.
8. Old past participle of *wreak*, "to urge or force
upon."

And Faith fair scorn doth gain.[9]
From so ungrateful fancy,
From such a female franzy,°   frenzy
From them that use men thus,
10   *Good Lord, deliver us!*

Weep, neighbors, weep; do you not hear it said
That Love is dead?
His deathbed peacock's folly,[1]
His winding sheet° is shame,   shroud
15   His will false-seeming holy,
His sole exec'tor blame.
From so ungrateful fancy, . . .

Let dirge be sung and trentals[2] rightly read,
For Love is dead.
20   Sir Wrong his tomb ordaineth
My mistress, marble heart,
Which epitaph containeth,
"Her eyes were once his dart."
From so ungrateful fancy, . . .

25   Alas, I lie, rage hath this error bred;
Love is not dead.
Love is not dead, but sleepeth
In her unmatchèd mind,
Where she his counsel keepeth,
30   Till due desert she find.
Therefore from so vile fancy,
To call such wit a franzy,
Who Love can temper thus,
Good Lord, deliver us!

1581   1598

From Astrophil and Stella[3]

1

Loving in truth, and fain° in verse my love to show,   eager
That she dear she might take some pleasure of my pain,
Pleasure might cause her read, reading might make her know,
Knowledge might pity win, and pity grace obtain,
5   I sought fit words to paint the blackest face of woe:

9. I.e., scorn from a fair lady.
1. I.e., ostentatious pride, as peacocks were a symbol of pride.
2. A series of thirty masses for the dead, designed to mitigate the pains of purgatory; in Sidney's day, no longer accepted as a service by the Church of England.
3. Sidney's *Astrophil and Stella* ("Starlover and Star") is the first of the great Elizabethan sonnet cycles that relied heavily on the conventions developed by Petrarch. It has 108 sonnets and eleven songs. The sequence alludes to Sidney's ambiguous relationship with Penelope Devereux, who married Lord Robert Rich in 1581. Thought to have been composed around 1582, the sequence was circulated in manuscript form during Sidney's lifetime.

Studying inventions[4] fine, her wits to entertain,
Oft turning others' leaves, to see if thence would flow
Some fresh and fruitful showers upon my sunburned brain.
But words came halting forth, wanting Invention's stay;°   *support*
10   Invention, Nature's child, fled stepdame Study's blows;
And others' feet[5] still seemed but strangers in my way.
Thus, great with child to speak, and helpless in my throes,[6]
Biting my truant pen, beating myself for spite:
"Fool," said my Muse to me, "look in thy heart, and write."

14

Alas, have I not pain enough, my friend,
Upon whose breast a fiercer gripe° doth tire°   *vulture / tear*
Than did on him who first stale° down the fire,[7]   *stole*
While Love° on me doth all his quiver spend,   *Cupid*
5   But with your rhubarb° words you must contend   *cynical*
To grieve me worse, in saying that Desire
Doth plunge my well-formed soul even in the mire
Of sinful thoughts, which do in ruin end?
If that be sin which doth the manners° frame,[8]   *morals*
10   Well stayed° with truth in word and faith of deed,   *supported*
Ready of wit, and fearing naught but shame;
If that be sin which in fixed hearts doth breed
A loathing of all loose unchastity,
Then love is sin, and let me sinful be.

21[9]

Your words my friend (right healthful caustics[1]) blame
My young mind marred, whom Love doth windlass° so,   *ensnare*
That mine own writings like bad servants show
My wits, quick in vain thoughts, in virtue lame,
5   That Plato I read for nought, but if he tame
Such coltish gyres,[2] that to my birth I owe
Nobler desires, least else that friendly foe,
Great expectation,[3] wear a train of shame.
For since mad March great promise made of me,
10   If now the May of my years much decline,
What can be hoped my harvest time will be?
Sure you say well, your wisdom's golden mine
Dig deep with learning's spade, now tell me this,
Hath this world ought° so fair as Stella is?   *anything*

---

4. In art and literary composition, the devising of a subject or idea by the exercise of the intellect or imagination.
5. With a pun on the units of poetic measure (called feet).
6. I.e., birth-throes.
7. Prometheus, for having stolen fire for man's benefit, was chained to a rock and preyed upon daily by a vulture that tore at his vitals.
8. "Doth the manners frame": builds character.
9. One of several sonnets addressed to a friend—

perhaps the English poet Fulke Greville (see pp. 185–87)—who takes a skeptical view of the poet's love.
1. Medicines used for burning away diseased tissue.
2. Young gyrations. "But if he": i.e., if he did not.
3. Hope of prestigious public employment and / or recognition. "Birth": position in society; Sidney was the eldest son in a rich and powerful aristocratic family.

25

The wisest scholar of the wight° most wise   *creature*
By Phoebus' doom,[4] with sugared sentence says
That Virtue, if it once met with our eyes,
Strange flames of love it in our souls would raise;
5   But, for that° man with pain this truth descries,[5]   *because*
While he each thing in sense's balance weighs,
And so nor will nor can behold those skies
Which inward sun to heroic mind displays,
Virtue of late, with virtuous care to stir
10 Love of herself, takes Stella's shape, that she[6]
To mortal eyes might sweetly shine in her.[7]
It is most true, for since I her did see,
Virtue's great beauty in that face I prove,°   *experience*
And find th'effect, for I do burn in love.

31

With how sad steps, Oh Moon, thou climb'st the skies,
How silently, and with how wan° a face!   *pale*
What, may it be that even in heav'nly place
That busy archer[8] his sharp arrows tries?
5   Sure, if that long-with-love-acquainted eyes
Can judge of love, thou feel'st a lover's case;
I read it in thy looks: thy languished grace,
To me that feel the like, thy state descries.°   *reveals*
Then even of fellowship, Oh Moon, tell me,
10 Is constant love deemed there but want of wit?
Are beauties there as proud as here they be?
Do they above love to be loved, and yet
Those lovers scorn whom that love doth possess?
Do they call virtue there ungratefulness?[9]

39

Come sleep, Oh sleep, the certain knot of peace,
The baiting place[1] of wit, the balm of woe,
The poor man's wealth, the prisoner's release,
Th'indifferent° judge between the high and low;   *impartial*
5   With shield of proof[2] shield me from out the prease° *press, multitude*
Of those fierce darts Despair at me doth throw;
Oh make in me[3] those civil wars to cease;
I will good tribute pay, if thou do so.
Take thou of me smooth pillows, sweetest bed,
10 A chamber deaf to noise and blind to light,
A rosy garland and a weary head;

---

4. Judgment. The "wight most wise" was Socrates, so called by the oracle of Apollo (Phoebus) at Delphi. His "wisest scholar," or pupil, was Plato, who (in *Phaedrus* 250D) provides the basis for lines 3–8.
5. Discovers or perceives.
6. I.e., Virtue.
7. I.e., Stella.

8. I.e., Cupid.
9. I.e., do they give the name of virtue to ungratefulness?
1. Resting; a place where a traveler might stop for rest and refreshment.
2. Of proven strength.
3. The speaker is offering these things to Sleep as a tribute.

And if these things, as being thine by right,
Move not thy heavy grace, thou shalt in me,
Livelier° than elsewhere, Stella's image see.   *more lifelike*

47

What, have I thus betrayed my liberty?
Can those black beams such burning marks[4] engrave
In my free side? or am I born a slave,
    Whose neck becomes° such yoke of tyranny?   *befits*
5 Or want I sense to feel my misery?
Or sprite,° disdain of such disdain to have?   *spirit*
Who for long faith, though daily help I crave,
May get no alms but scorn of beggary.
Virtue, awake! Beauty but beauty is;
10 I may, I must, I can, I will, I do
Leave following that which it is gain to miss.
Let her go. Soft, but here she comes. Go to,
Unkind, I love you not! O me, that eye
Doth make my heart give to my tongue the lie!

48

Soul's joy, bend not those morning stars from me,
Where virtue is made strong by beauty's might,
Where love is chasteness, pain doth learn delight,
And humbleness grows one with majesty.
5 Whatever may ensue, O let me be
Co-partner of the riches of that sight;
Let not mine eyes be hell-driv'n[5] from that light;
O look, O shine, O let me die and see.
For though I oft my self of them bemoan,
10 That through my heart their beamy darts be gone,
Whose cureless wounds even now most freshly bleed,
Yet since my death wound is already got,
Dear killer,[6] spare not thy sweet cruel shot;
A kind of grace it is to slay with speed.

49

I on my horse, and Love on me, doth try
Our horsemanships, while by strange work I prove
A horseman to my horse, a horse to Love,
And now man's wrongs in me, poor beast, descry.°   *discern*
5 The reins wherewith my rider doth me tie
Are humbled thoughts, which bit of reverence move,
Curbed[7] in with fear, but with gilt boss above
Of hope, which makes it seem fair to the eye.
The wand[8] is will; thou, fancy, saddle art,
10 Girt fast by memory; and while I spur

---

4. Brands; i.e., disdainful looks from his lover.
5. I.e., driven to hell.
6. With a pun on "dear" and "deer."
7. The curb is a short chain or strap connecting

the upper branches of the bit and ornamented, in
this case, with a metal "boss" or decorative stud.
8. A stick or switch for urging on a horse.

My horse, he spurs with sharp desire my heart;
He sits me fast, however I do stir;
And now hath made me to his hand so right
That in the manage⁹ myself takes delight.

52

A strife is grown between Virtue and Love,
While each pretends that Stella must be his:
Her eyes, her lips, her all, saith Love, do this,
Since they do wear his badge, most firmly prove.
5   But Virtue thus that title doth disprove,
That Stella (O dear name) that Stella is
That virtuous soul, sure heir of heav'nly bliss;
Not this fair outside, which our hearts doth move.
And therefore, though her beauty and her grace
10 Be Love's indeed, in Stella's self he may
By no pretense claim any manner place.¹
Well, Love, since this demur² our suit doth stay,°   detain
Let Virtue have that Stella's self; yet thus,
That Virtue but that body grant to us.

63

O Grammer rules, ô now your virtues show;
So children still read you with awful° eyes,   awed
As my young Dove may in your precepts wise
Her grant to me, by her own virtue know.
5   For late with heart most high, with eyes most low,
I crav'd the thing which ever she denies:
She lightning Love, displaying Venus' skies,³
Least once should not be heard, twice said, No, No.
Sing then my Muse, now Io Pean⁴ sing,
10 Heav'ns envy not at my high triumphing:
But Grammer's force with sweet success confirme,
For Grammer sayes (ô this deare Stella weigh,)
For Grammer sayes (to Grammer who says nay)
That in one speech two Negatives affirm.⁵

71

Who will in fairest book of Nature know
How virtue may best lodged in beauty be,
Let him but learn of love to read in thee,
Stella, those fair lines which true goodness show.
5   There shall he find all vices' overthrow,

9. The schooling or handling of a horse.
1. I.e., any kind of place.
2. Demurrer; one who demurs, or delays.
3. Venus is the goddess of love and beauty; some editors modernize "lightning" as "lightening," a present participle parallel to "displaying," but one can also read the word as a noun comparing Stella to lightning that "displays" the night sky.
4. A hymn of thanksgiving for victory. Ovid uses this phrase in the opening of the second book of

the Ars Amatoria to celebrate success with a long-pursued love. "Muse": one of the nine Greek goddesses believed to be sources of inspiration for the arts.
5. In several of the preceding sonnets, Stella has engaged in scholastic disputation; the poet's reasoning here is sophistic, since the lady's double "no" is emphatic rather than a grammatical double negative signifying "yes"—as it did in Latin, but not in Elizabethan English.

Not by rude force, but sweetest sovereignty
Of reason, from whose light those night birds fly,
That inward sun in thine eyes shineth so.
And, not content to be perfection's heir
10   Thyself, dost strive all minds that way to move,
Who mark in thee what is in thee most fair.
So while thy beauty draws the heart to love,
As fast thy virtue bends that love to good.
"But ah," Desire still cries, "give me some food."

Fourth Song

Only joy, now here you are,
Fit to hear and ease my care;
Let my whispering voice obtain,
Sweet reward for sharpest pain;
5   Take me to thee, and thee to me.
No, no, no, no, my dear, let be.[6]

Night hath closed all in her cloak,
Twinkling stars love-thoughts provoke:
Danger hence good care doth keep,
10   Jealousy itself doth sleep;
Take me to thee, and thee to me.
No, no, no, no, my dear, let be.

Better place no wit can find,
Cupid's yoke to loose or bind:
15   These sweet flowers on fine bed too,
Us in their best language woo;
Take me to thee, and thee to me.
No, no, no, no, my dear, let be.

This small light the moon bestows,
20   Serves thy beams but to disclose,
So to raise my hap° more high;   chances
Fear not else, none can us spy:
Take me to thee, and thee to me.
No, no, no, no, my dear, let be.

25   That° you heard was but a mouse,   what
Dumb sleep holdeth all the house;
Yet asleep, methinks they say,
Young folks, take time while you may:[7]
Take me to thee, and thee to me.
30   *No, no, no, no, my dear, let be.*

Niggard° Time threats, if we miss   miserly
This large offer of our bliss,

---

6. Stella's "reply" to Astrophil occurs after each
stanza and becomes the refrain. This poem was set
to music by Henry Youll in 1608.

7. An allusion to the traditional *carpe diem* (Latin,
"seize the day") motif of seduction lyrics.

Long stay ere he grant the same;
Sweet then, while each thing doth frame,
35 Take me to thee, and thee to me.
No, no, no, no, my dear, let be.

Your fair mother is abed,
Candles out, and curtains spread:
She thinks you do letters write.
40 Write, but first let me indite:°   *dictate*
Take me to thee and thee to me.
No, no, no, no, my dear, let be.

Sweet, alas, why strive you thus?
Concord better fitteth us:
45 Leave to Mars[8] the force of hands,
Your power in your beauty stands;
Take me to thee, and thee to me.
No, no, no, no, my dear, let be.

Woe to me, and do you swear
50 Me to hate, but I forbear,
Cursèd be my destines all
That brought me so high to fall:
Soon with my death I will please thee.
No, no, no, no, my dear, let be.

Seventh Song

Whose senses in so evil consort,[9] their stepdame Nature lays,
That ravishing delight in them most sweet tunes do not raise;
Or if they do delight therein, yet are so cloyed° with wit,   *sated, burdened*
As with sententious° lips to set a title vain on it: *aphoristic*
5 O let them hear these sacred tunes, and learn in wonder's schools,
To be (in things past bounds of wit) fools, if they be not fools.[1]

Who have so leaden eyes, as not to see sweet beauty's show,
Or seeing, have so wooden° wits, as not that worth to know;   *dull*
Or knowing, have so muddy minds, as not to be in love;
10 Or loving, have so frothy° thoughts, as eas'ly thence to   *shallow, trifling*
move:
Or let them see these heavenly beams, and in fair letters read
A lesson fit, both sight and skill, love and firm love to breed.

Hear then, but then with wonder hear; see but adoring see,
No mortal gifts, no earthly fruits, now here descended be;
15 See, do you see this face? a face? nay, image of the skies,
Of which the two life-giving lights[2] are figured in her eyes:
Hear you this soul-invading voice, and count it but a voice?
The very essence of their tunes, when Angels do rejoice.

8. The classical god of war.
9. Company; accord or agreement.
1. I.e., the music will teach them (if they are not
fools) that, in things that are beyond the limitations
of reason and intellect ("wit"), they are deficient in
understanding ("fools").
2. I.e., the sun and the moon.

90

Stella, think not that I by verse seek fame,
Who seek, who hope, who love, who live but thee;
Thine eyes my pride, thy lips my history;
If thou praise not, all other praise is shame.
5 Nor so ambitious am I, as to frame
A nest for my young praise in laurel tree:[3]
In truth I sweare, I wish not there should be
Graved in mine epitaph a Poet's name:
Nay if I would, could I just title make,
10 That any laud° to me thereof should grow,   *praise*
Without my plumes from others' wings I take.
For nothing from my wit or will doth flow,
Since all my words thy beauty doth endite,[4]
And love doth hold my hand, and makes me write.

107

Stella, since thou so right a princess art
Of all the powers which life bestows on me,
That ere by them aught undertaken be
They first resort unto that sovereign part;
5 Sweet, for a while give respite to my heart,
Which pants as though it still should leap to thee,
And on my thoughts give thy lieutenancy
To this great cause, which needs both use° and art,   *experience*
And as a queen, who from her presence sends
10 Whom she employs, dismiss from thee my wit,
Till it have wrought what thy own will attends.[5]
On servants' shame oft master's blame doth sit.
Oh let not fools in me thy works reprove,
And scorning say, "See what it is to love."

1582   1591

MARY SIDNEY

1568–1621

Psalm 58: *Si Vere Utique*[1]

And call ye this to utter what is just,
  You that of justice hold the sov'reign throne?

3. The laurel was a symbol of poetic achievement.
4. A variation of both "indict" (to proclaim) and "indite" (to inscribe or give literary form to).
5. Is concerned about.
1. "If, indeed, it is true" (Latin). Frequently the Latin titles for Psalms were taken from the Psalm's first line in the Vulgate version of the Bible. However, in this case the first line in the Vulgate is *Numquid vere* ("Is it true?"). Mary Sidney probably derived her title from one of her source Psalters, the most important of which was the *CL Pseaumes de David* (1562) containing metrical versions by Clément Marot and Théodore de Bèze. Sidney also used (and changed) the version of the Psalms done in fourteener couplets by Thomas Sternhold and John Hopkins in 1562. This version, set to music, was often printed after the prose Psalter in the Book of Common Prayer.

And call ye this to yield, O sons of dust,
    To wronged brethren ev'ry man his own?
5 O no: it is your long malicious will
    Now to the world to make by practice known,
With whose oppression you the balance fill,
    Just to your selves, indiff'rent° else to none.[2]   *impartial*

But what could they, who even in birth declined,[3]
10   From truth and right to lies and injuries?
To show the venom of their cankred° mind   *corrupt, malignant*
    The adder's image scarcely can suffice;
Nay scarce the aspic° may with them contend,   *asp*
    On whom the charmer all in vain applies
15 His skillfull'st spells: ay° missing of his end,   *always*
    While she self-deaf, and unaffected lies.[4]

Lord crack their teeth, Lord crush these lion's jaws,
    So let them sink as water in the sand:
When deadly bow their aiming fury draws,
20   Shiver° the shaft ere° past the shooter's hand.   *shatter / before*
So make them melt as the dishoused snail
    Or as the embryo, whose vital band
Breaks ere it holds,[5] and formless eyes do fail
    To see the sun, though brought to lightful land.

25 O let their brood, a brood of springing thorns,
    Be by untimely rooting overthrown[6]
Ere bushes waxt,° they push with pricking horns,   *grew*
    As fruits yet green are oft by tempest blown.[7]
The good with gladness this revenge shall see,
30   And bathe his feet in blood of wicked one
While all shall say: the just rewarded be,
    There is a God that carves to each his own.[8]

1599   1823

2. I.e., now to make known to the world, through continual repetition, with whose oppression you fill the balance, being just to yourselves, but impartial to no one else.

3. I.e., but what else could they do, those who from birth turned aside?

4. The snake is "unaffected" by the snake charmer's music because she is "self-deaf," i.e., she stops her ears.

5. A reference to premature birth.

6. The Hebrew original here is problematic and hinges on the translation of an ambiguous word, *sir*, which can be variously translated as "pot" or "thorns." The verse has thus been rendered in a variety of ways, including: "Sooner than your poets can feel the heat of thorns, whether green or ablaze, may he sweep them away" (RSV); "Before your thorns have ripened on the thornbush, a wrath will tear them out while they are still green" (Luther). Luther interpreted the "thorns" as the Jews.

7. I.e., before the bushes have fully grown, they [already] begin to grow thorns, and, as still unripe fruits, are often blown by the tempest. A further elaboration of the images of the thorns in the lines above.

8. I.e., the good person is glad to see the wicked overthrown in this manner, and bathes his feet in the blood of the wicked one, who has been destroyed before he has come to fruition. Seeing this, everyone will recognize that the just are rewarded and that God gives each person what he deserves.

To the Thrice-Sacred Queen Elizabeth[9]

1

Even now that care,° which on thy crown attends   *burden*
And with thy happy° greatness daily grows,   *fortunate*
Tells me, thrice-sacred Queen, my muse[1] offends,
And of respect to thee the line out goes.[2]
5   One instant will or willing can she lose[3]
I say not reading, but receiving rhymes,
On whom in chief dependeth to dispose°   *settle*
What Europe acts in these most active times?

2

Yet dare I so, as humbleness may dare,
10   Cherish some hope they° shall acceptance find;   *the poems*
Not weighing less thy state, lighter thy care,
But knowing more thy grace, abler thy mind.[4]
What heavenly powers thee highest throne assigned,
Assigned thee goodness suiting that degree,°   *position or rank*
15   And by thy strength thy burthen so defined,
To others toil, is exercise to thee.[5]

3

Cares, though still° great, cannot be greatest still,   *always*
Business must ebb, though leisure never flow;
Then these the posts[6] of duty and goodwill
20   Shall press° to offer what their senders owe,   *hurry*
Which once in two, now in one subject go,[7]
The poorer left, the richer reft° away,   *stolen*
Who better might (O might, ah word of woe)
Have given for me what I for him defray.°   *pay*

4

25   How can I name whom sighing signs extend,[8]
And not unstop my tears' eternal spring?
But he did warp, I weaved this web to end;[9]

---

9. This is a dedicatory poem originally prefixed to a translation of the Psalms of David, begun by Mary Sidney's brother Sir Philip Sidney and completed by Mary Sidney after Philip's death. The poem, preserved in a unique manuscript copy, was probably prepared for a presentation volume to be given to the queen when she visited the Sidney home in 1599. The expected visit did not occur. Sir Philip Sidney had been exiled from court after incurring Elizabeth's disfavor by counseling against a marriage with the duke of Anjou; furthermore, the Sidneys, devoted to the cause of Protestantism, felt that the queen should adopt a more aggressive policy in support of Protestant factions on the continent (especially the Netherlands). "Thrice": to a high degree.
1. The Muses were nine Greek goddesses believed to be the daughters of memory and the source of inspiration for the arts.
2. I.e., the meter fails.
3. I.e., will she, or can she willingly, lose one instant?

4. I.e., not because I judge your status or responsibilities to be less than they are, but because I know how great is your grace and how able your mind.
5. I.e., your "burthen" is defined according to your strength, such that what would be burdensome labor to others is mere "exercise," i.e., customary practice, to you.
6. Postmen or letter carriers, here referring to the poems that convey the poet's "duty" and "goodwill" to the queen.
7. Sir Philip Sidney wrote the first forty-three translations (of 150 Psalms); the rest are Mary's. Philip died in 1586 fighting for the Protestant cause in the Netherlands.
8. I.e., how can I name him (Philip Sidney) whose memory is extended by "sighing signs" (i.e., the signs of grief)?
9. To completion; in cloth making, the warp threads on a loom run lengthwise and are set first; the woof threads are then woven crosswise through them.

The stuff[1] not ours, our work no curious° thing,　　　*novel or ingenious*
Wherein yet well we thought the Psalmist King[2]
30　Now English denizened, though Hebrew born,[3]
Would to thy music undispleasèd sing,
Oft having worse, without repining,° worn;[4]　　　*complaining*

5

And I the cloth in both our names present,
A livery robe[5] to be bestowed by thee;
35　Small parcel of that undischargèd° rent,　　　*unpaid*
From which nor° pains nor payments can us free.　　　*neither*
And yet enough to cause our neighbors see
We will[6] our best, though scanted° in our will;　　　*limited or restricted*
And those nigh° fields where sown thy favors be　　　*nearby*
40　Unwealthy do, not else unworthy, till.[7]

6

For in our work what bring we but thine own?
What English is, by many names is thine,
There humble laurels[8] in thy shadows grown
To garland others would themselves repine.[9]
45　Thy breast the cabinet,° thy seat[1] the shrine,　　　*small room*
Where muses hang their vowèd° memories;　　　*consecrated*
Where wit,° where art, where all that is divine　　　*intelligence*
Conceivèd best, and best defended lies.

7

Which if men did not (as they do) confess,[2]
50　And wronging worlds would otherwise consent,
Yet here who minds so meet° a patroness[3]　　　*suitable or proper*
For authors' state° or writings' argument?°　　　*financial condition / subject*
A King should only to a Queen be sent;
God's lovèd choice unto his chosen love;
55　Devotion to devotion's president;[4]
What all applaud, to her whom none reprove.

8

And who sees ought, but sees how justly square°　　　*fit or correspond*
His haughty ditties° to thy glorious days?[5]　　　*songs*

---

1. Raw material (i.e., the Hebrew Scriptures).
2. King David, the second king of Israel, believed to have written many of the Psalms of the Bible.
3. I.e., admitted to English citizenship, though born a Hebrew.
4. I.e., often having worn worse (than "thy music," i.e., the English language) without complaining; "worse" probably refers to translations of the Psalms in other languages; these two lines might also refer to David's service, as a youth, to the tyrant Saul, whom David often soothed with his singing.
5. A suit of clothes bestowed by a noble upon his male retainers by which they may be recognized as his servants. "Cloth": the poems. Sidney seems to be saying that she presents the poems to Elizabeth, who will then give them a "livery robe" as a sign that they are her servants.
6. Want to do.
7. I.e., we till those nearby fields where your favors are sown without a show of wealth, but not other-

wise unworthily.
8. Leaves used to crown the heads of great poets; hence, the symbol of poetic achievement.
9. I.e., the laurels grown in your shadow would complain at being worn by others besides you.
1. Place of abode as well as Elizabeth's throne.
2. I.e., if people did not (as they do) agree that Elizabeth is the source of all English works.
3. I.e., who in England can remember so suitable a supporter (as Elizabeth)?
4. One who presides over, perhaps referring to the fact that as queen, Elizabeth was head of the Church of England. The first element in each of lines 53 through 56 refers to King David, the second to Queen Elizabeth. King David was God's choice to be king of Israel; he wrote Psalms of devotion to God that were generally acclaimed and often translated.
5. I.e., who sees anything without seeing how well his lofty songs correspond to your glorious days?

How well beseeming° thee his triumphs[6] are?   *resembling or matching*
60 His hope, his zeal, his prayer, plaint,° and praise,   *lamentation*
Needless thy person to their height to raise;
Less need to bend them down to thy degree;
These holy garments[7] each good soul assays,°   *tries on*
Some sorting all, all sort to none but thee.[8]

9

65 For even thy rule is painted° in his reign;[9]   *represented*
Both clear in right; both nigh by wrong oppressed;[1]
And each at length (man crossing God in vain)
Possessed of place, and each in peace possessed.
Proud Philistines did interrupt his rest,
70 The foes of heaven no less have been thy foes;[2]
He with great conquest, thou with greater blessed;
Thou sure to win, and he secure to lose.[3]

10

Thus hand in hand with him thy glories walk;
But who can trace them[4] where alone they go?
75 Of thee two hemispheres on honor talk,[5]
And lands and seas thy trophies jointly show.
The very winds did on thy party blow,
And rocks in arms thy foemen eft[6] defy.
But soft, my muse, thy pitch[7] is earthly low;
80 Forbear° this heaven where only eagles fly.   *avoid*

11

Kings on a Queen enforced their states to lay;[8]
Mainlands for empire waiting on an isle;[9]
Men drawn by worth a woman to obey;
One moving all, herself unmoved[1] the while;
85 Truth's restitution, vanity exile,[2]
Wealth sprung of want, war held without annoy,°   *vexation*

6. Both victories and triumphal songs.
7. I.e., the Psalms.
8. I.e., some fitting everyone, but all fitting no one but you.
9. I.e., David's reign.
1. Defeated (rather than its modern meaning); "nigh": almost. David's succession to the throne of Israel was opposed by Saul, the first king of Israel, who tried to kill David. Elizabeth's succession to the crown of England was disputed (especially by Catholics who championed her cousin, Mary, queen of Scots) because of the questionable legality of Henry VIII's second marriage to Anne Boleyn, Elizabeth's mother. Despite opposition, both David and Elizabeth came to possess their respective thrones, although "each in peace possessed" is a questionable claim. David continued to put down rebellions, including one by his own son, until late in his life. In 1587 Elizabeth had her cousin, Mary, beheaded, ending that particular claim to her throne.
2. Elizabeth and David both reigned in times of war; their enemies, the Spanish (who were Catholic) and the Philistines respectively, were perceived as enemies of the true religion.
3. Enigmatic phrasing; probably secure (sure) against losing, so as not to contradict line 79.

4. I.e., thy glories. "Trace": follow or put down in writing.
5. I.e., about you, the whole world talks on the topic of honor.
6. Afterwards. The British defeated the Spanish Armada in 1588, aided by favorable winds; the remnant of the defeated Spanish fleet lost more ships when storms drove them onto the western coast of Ireland.
7. The height to which a falcon or other bird of prey soars before swooping down on its prey, but also height in a figurative sense: degree, rank, status.
8. I.e., kings compelled to humble their greatness, splendor, power (all meanings of "state") to Elizabeth.
9. Continental countries, because of the greatness of Elizabeth's empire, serving England.
1. Perhaps a reference to Aristotle's idea of God as an "Unmoved Mover" (in *Nichomachean Ethics* 10 and *Metaphysics* 12).
2. Perhaps a reference to Elizabeth's restoration of the Protestant faith ("truth") in England after the reign of her half-sister, the Catholic Mary Tudor. The banishment of "vanity" would then refer to the banishment of the ornate rituals of the Catholic religion.

Let subject be of some inspired style,
Till then the object of her subjects' joy.

12

Thy utmost can but offer to her sight
90   Her handmaids' task, which most her will endears,[3]
And pray unto thy pains life from that light
Which lively lightsome,° court and kingdom cheers,[4]   *luminous or bright*
What° wish she may (far past her living peers   *who*
And rival still to Judah's faithful king)[5]
95   In more than he and more triumphant years,
Sing what God doth, and do what men may sing.[6]

1599   1962

GEORGE PEELE

1557–1596

His Golden Locks Time Hath to Silver Turned[1]

His golden locks time hath to silver turned;
    Oh, time too swift, oh, swiftness never ceasing!
His youth 'gainst time and age hath ever spurned.°   *kicked*
    But spurned in vain; youth waneth by increasing.
5   Beauty, strength, youth, are flowers but fading seen;
    Duty, faith, love, are roots, and ever green.

His helmet now shall make a hive for bees,
    And lover's sonnets turned to holy psalms,
A man-at-arms must now serve on his knees,
10   And feed on prayers, which are age his[2] alms;
But though from court to cottage he depart,
    His saint[3] is sure of his unspotted heart.

And when he saddest sits in homely cell,
    He'll teach his swains this carol for a song:
15   Blest be the hearts that wish my sovereign well,
    Cursed be the souls that think her any wrong!
Goddess, allow this aged man his right,
    To be your beadsman[4] now, that was your knight.

1590

3. I.e., the most you can do is offer her the work of a handmaid, which most endears itself to her will. "Thy" seems to refer to Sidney's muse.
4. I.e., and pray to get, for your pains, life from that light, whose lively brightness the court and kingdom cheer (or alternatively, that light, whose lively brightness brings cheer to the court and kingdom).
5. I.e., far more so than other kings and queens, and still as rival to King David (king of the tribe of Judah before he became king of all Israel).
6. I.e., having more reasons and more triumphant

years than David, sing what God sings and do whatever is worthy to have men sing of.
1. This poem refers to Sir Henry Lee, for years Queen Elizabeth's champion in courtly jousts or contests of arms. At the age of sixty, too old to take part in the queen's birthday tournament of 1590, he retired in favor of a younger man.
2. "Age his": age's.
3. Seems to refer to Queen Elizabeth, as does "Goddess" in line 17.
4. One who offers prayers for the soul of another.

When As the Rye Reach to the Chin

When as the rye reach to the chin,
And chopcherry,[5] chopcherry ripe within,
Strawberries swimming in the cream,
And schoolboys playing in the stream;
5   Then O, then O, then O my truelove said,
Till that time come again
She could not live a maid.[6]

1595

Hot Sun, Cool Fire

Hot sun, cool fire, tempered with sweet air,
Black shade, fair nurse, shadow my white hair.
Shine, sun; burn, fire; breathe, air, and ease me;
Black shade, fair nurse, shroud me and please me.
5   Shadow, my sweet nurse, keep me from burning;
Make not my glad cause cause of mourning.
     Let not my beauty's fire
     Inflame unstaid desire,
     Nor pierce any bright eye
10   That wandereth lightly.

1599

THOMAS LODGE

1558–1625

Rosalind's Madrigal[1]

Love in my bosom like a bee
     Doth suck his sweet;
Now with his wings he plays with me,
     Now with his feet.
5   Within mine eyes he makes his nest,
His bed amidst my tender breast;
My kisses are his daily feast,
And yet he robs me of my rest.
     Ah, wanton, will ye?

10   And if I sleep, then percheth he
     With pretty flight,
And makes his pillow of my knee
     The livelong night.
Strike I my lute, he tunes the string;
15   He music plays if so I sing;
He lends me every lovely thing;

5. A game in which one tries to catch a suspended
cherry with one's teeth.
6. An unmarried woman; a virgin.

1. "Madrigal": a short lyrical poem, usually about
love, suitable for a musical setting; a song.

Yet cruel he my heart doth sting.
　　Whist,° wanton, still ye!　　　　　　　　　　　　*be silent*

Else I with roses every day
20　　Will whip you hence,
And bind you, when you long to play,
　　For your offense.
I'll shut mine eyes to keep you in,
I'll make you fast it for your sin,
25　I'll count your power not worth a pin.
Alas! what hereby shall I win
　　If he gainsay me?

What if I beat the wanton boy
　　With many a rod?
30　He will repay me with annoy,
　　Because a god.
Then sit thou safely on my knee,
And let thy bower my bosom be;
Lurk in mine eyes, I like of thee.
35　O Cupid, so thou pity me,[2]
　　Spare not, but play thee!

　　　　　　　　　　　　　　　　　　　　　　1590

ROBERT SOUTHWELL

ca. 1561–1595

The Burning Babe

As I in hoary winter's night stood shivering in the snow,
Surprised I was with sudden heat which made my heart to glow;
And lifting up a fearful eye to view what fire was near,
A pretty babe all burning bright did in the air appear;
5　Who, scorchèd with excessive heat, such floods of tears did shed
As though his floods should quench his flames which with his tears
　　were fed.
"Alas," quoth he, "but newly born in fiery heats I fry,
Yet none approach to warm their hearts or feel my fire but I!
My faultless breast the furnace is, the fuel wounding thorns,
10　Love is the fire, and sighs the smoke, the ashes shame and scorns;
The fuel justice layeth on, and mercy blows the coals,
The metal in this furnace wrought are men's defilèd souls,
For which, as now on fire I am to work them to their good,
So will I melt into a bath to wash them in my blood."
15　With this he vanished out of sight and swiftly shrunk away,
And straight I callèd unto mind that it was Christmas day.

---

2. I.e., as long as you show me some pity.

New Heaven, New War

Come to your heaven, you heavenly choirs,
Earth hath the heaven of your desires.
Remove your dwelling to your God;
A stall is now his best abode.
5   Sith° men their homage do deny,   *since*
Come, angels, all their fault supply.

His chilling cold doth heat require;
Come, seraphins,[1] in lieu of fire.
This little ark no cover hath;
10 Let cherubs' wings his body swathe.°   *enwrap*
Come, Raphael,[2] this babe must eat;
Provide our little Toby meat.

Let Gabriel be now his groom,
That first took up his earthly room.
15 Let Michael stand in his defense,
Whom love hath linked to feeble sense.
Let graces rock when he doth cry,
And angels sing his lullaby.

The same you saw in heavenly seat
20 Is he that now sucks Mary's teat;
Agnize° your king a mortal wight,°   *acknowledge / person*
His borrowed weed° lets° not your sight.   *clothing / hinders*
Come, kiss the manger where he lies,
That is your bliss above the skies.

25 This little babe, so few days old,
Is come to rifle Satan's fold;
All hell doth at his presence quake,
Though he himself for cold do shake,
For in this weak unarmèd wise°   *manner*
30 The gates of hell he will surprise.

With tears he fights and wins the field;
His naked breast stands for a shield;
His battering shot are babish cries,
His arrows looks of weeping eyes,
35 His martial ensigns cold and need,
And feeble flesh his warrior's steed.

His camp is pitchèd in a stall,
His bulwark but a broken wall,
The crib his trench, hay stalks his stakes,
40 Of shepherds he his muster[3] makes;

---

1. Seraphim and cherubs (line 10) were generally understood to be orders among the angels, derived in Christian theology from Hebrew Old Testament terms.
2. One of the seven archangels, the companion and protector of Tobias in the book of Tobit (one of the apocryphal books of the Old Testament). Gabriel (line 13) and Michael (line 15) are also archangels.
3. An assembly of troops for inspection.

And thus, as sure his foe to wound,
The angels' trumps° alarum sound.   *trumpets*

My soul, with Christ join thou in fight;
Stick to the tents that he hath pight;°   *pitched*
45   Within his crib is surest ward,°   *protection*
This little babe will be thy guard.
If thou wilt foil thy foes with joy,
Then flit not from this heavenly boy.

1602

SAMUEL DANIEL
ca. 1562–1619

From Delia[1]

1

Unto the boundless Ocean of thy beauty
Runs this poor river, charged with streams of zeal:
Returning thee the tribute of my duty,
Which here my love, my youth, my plaints reveal.
5   Here I unclasp the book of my charged soul,
Where I have cast th'accounts of all my care:
Here have I summed my sighs, here I enroll°   *register*
How they were spent for thee; look what they are.
Look on the dear expenses of my youth,
10 And see how just I reckon with thine eyes:
Examine well thy beauty with my truth,
And cross my cares ere greater sum arise.
Read it sweet maid, though it be done but slightly;
Who can show all his love, doth love but lightly.

2

Go wailing verse, the infants of my love,
Minerva-[2]like, brought forth without a Mother:
Present the image of the cares I prove,
Witness your Father's grief exceeds all other.
5   Sigh out a story of her cruel deeds,
With interrupted accents of despair:
A monument that whosoever reads,
May justly praise, and blame my loveless Fair.
Say her disdain hath dried up my blood,
10 And starved you, in succours° still denying: *aid*

1. A sequence of fifty sonnets. The title, which
recalls Maurice Scève's poetic collection *Délie*
(1544), plays on the lady's status as the poet's
"Ideal." A dedicatory sonnet addressed to Mary
Sidney, countess of Pembroke, appears in early
editions of the sequence. The numbering of the
sonnets varies by edition; we have followed the
numbering and the text of the first authorized edi-
tion (1592).
2. Minerva, the mythological goddess of war, wis-
dom, arts, and justice, sprang fully formed from
the head of her father, Jove.

Press to her eyes, importune me some good;
Waken her sleeping pity with your crying.
Knock at that hard heart, beg till you have moved her;
And tell th'unkind, how dearly I have loved her.

6

Fair is my love, and cruel as she's fair:
Her brow shades frowns, although her eyes are sunny,
Her smiles are lightning, though her pride despair,
And her disdains are gall,° her favors honey.   *bitterness*
5   A modest maid, decked with a blush of honor,
Whose feet do tread green paths of youth and love;
The wonder of all eyes that look upon her,
Sacred on earth, designed a Saint above.
Chastity and Beauty, which were deadly foes,
10 Live reconcilèd friends within her brow;
And had she pity to conjoin with those,
Then who had heard the plaints I utter now?
Oh had she not been fair and thus unkind,
My Muse had slept, and none had known my mind.

31

Look, Delia, how we 'steem° the half-blown rose,   *esteem*
The image of thy blush and Summer's honor,
Whilst in her tender green she doth inclose
That pure sweet beauty Time bestows upon her.
5   No sooner spreads her glory in the air
But straight her full-blown pride is in declining.
She then is scorned that late adorned the fair;
So clouds thy beauty after fairest shining.
No April can revive thy withered flowers,
10 Whose blooming grace adorns thy glory now;
Swift speedy Time, feathered with flying hours,
Dissolves the beauty of the fairest brow.
Oh let not then such riches waste in vain,
But love whilst that thou mayst be loved again.

32

But love whilst that thou mayst be loved again,
Now whilst thy May hath filled thy lap with flowers,
Now whilst thy beauty bears without a stain,
Now use the summer smiles, ere winter lowers.
5   And whilst thou spread'st unto the rising sun
The fairest flower that ever saw the light,
Now joy thy time before thy sweet be done,
And, Delia, think thy morning must have night,
And that thy brightness sets at length to west,
10 When thou wilt close up that which now thou shew'st;
And think the same becomes thy fading best
Which then shall most inveil and shadow most.
Men do not weigh the stalk for what it was,
When once they find her flower, her glory, pass.

33

When men shall find thy flower, thy glory pass,
And thou, with careful° brow sitting alone,   *sorrowful*
Receivèd hast this message from thy glass,
That tells thee truth, and says that all is gone,
5 Fresh shalt thou see in me the wounds thou madest,
Though spent thy flame, in me the heat remaining,
I that have loved thee thus before thou fadest,
My faith shall wax, when thou art in thy waning.
The world shall find this miracle in me,
10 That fire can burn when all the matter's spent;
Then what my faith hath been thyself shall see,
And that thou wast unkind thou mayst repent.
Thou mayst repent that thou hast scorned my tears,
When Winter snows upon thy golden hairs.

49

Care-charmer Sleep, son of the sable° Night,   *black*
Brother to Death, in silent darkness born.
Relieve my languish and restore the light;
With dark forgetting of my cares, return.
5 And let the day be time enough to mourn
The shipwreck of my ill-adventured youth;
Let waking eyes suffice to wail their scorn
Without the torment of the night's untruth.
Cease, dreams, th' imagery of our day desires,
10 To model forth[3] the passions of the morrow;
Never let rising sun approve° you liars,   *prove*
To add more grief to aggravate my sorrow.
Still let me sleep, embracing clouds in vain,
And never wake to feel the day's disdain.

50

Let others sing of knights and paladins°   *chivalric heroes*
In agèd accents, and untimely° words;   *outdated*
Paint shadows in imaginary lines
Which well the reach of their high wits records;
5 But I must sing of thee, and those fair eyes
Authentic° shall my verse in time to come,   *authenticate*
When yet th' unborn shall say, "Lo where she lies,
Whose beauty made him speak that else was dumb."
These are the arks, the trophies I erect,
10 That fortify thy name against old age;
And these thy sacred virtues must protect
Against the dark and time's consuming rage.
Though th' error of my youth they shall discover,
Suffice, they show I lived and was thy lover.

1592

3. "Model forth": portray.

Ulysses and the Siren[4]

SIREN. Come, worthy Greek, Ulysses, come,
Possess these shores with me;
The winds and seas are troublesome,
And here we may be free.
5   Here may we sit and view their toil
That travail in the deep,
And joy the day in mirth the while,
And spend the night in sleep.

ULYSSES. Fair nymph, if fame or honor were
10 To be attained with ease,
Then would I come and rest me there,
And leave such toils as these.
But here it dwells, and here must I
With danger seek it forth;
15 To spend the time luxuriously
Becomes not men of worth.

SIREN. Ulysses, Oh be not deceived
With that unreal name;
This honor is a thing conceived,
20 And rests on others' fame.
Begotten only to molest
Our peace, and to beguile
The best thing of our life, our rest,
And give us up to toil.

25 ULYSSES. Delicious nymph, suppose there were
Nor honor nor report,
Yet manliness would scorn to wear
The time in idle sport.
For toil doth give a better touch,
30 To make us feel our joy;
And ease finds tediousness, as much
As labor yields annoy.

SIREN. Then pleasure likewise seems the shore
Whereto tends all your toil,
35 Which you forgo to make it more,
And perish oft the while.
Who may disport them diversly,
Find never tedious day,
And ease may have variety
40 As well as action may.

ULYSSES. But natures of the noblest frame
These toils and dangers please,

---

4. In Greek mythology, the Sirens were beautiful but only partly human creatures who sang so sweetly that passing sailors would forget their work and homes and be lured to their destruction. When Ulysses, the hero of Homer's *Odyssey*, passed by, he had his sailors' ears filled with beeswax and himself tied to the ship's mast so that he could listen without succumbing to their song.

And they take comfort in the same
As much as you in ease,
45 And with the thoughts of actions past
Are recreated still;
When pleasure leaves a touch at last
To show that it was ill.

SIREN. That doth opinion only cause
50 That's out of custom bred,
Which makes us many other laws
Than ever nature did.
No widows wail for our delights,
Our sports are without blood;
55 The world, we see, by warlike wights°   persons
Receives more hurt than good.

ULYSSES. But yet the state of things require
These motions of unrest,
And these great spirits of high desire
60 Seem born to turn them best,
To purge the mischiefs that increase
And all good order mar;
For oft we see a wicked peace
To be well changed for war.

65 SIREN. Well, well, Ulysses, then I see
I shall not have thee here,
And therefore I will come to thee,
And take my fortunes there.
I must be won that cannot win,
70 Yet lost were I not won;
For beauty hath created been
T' undo, or be undone.

1605

Are They Shadows

Are they shadows that we see?
And can shadows pleasure give?
Pleasures only shadows be
Cast by bodies we conceive
5 And are made the things we deem
In those figures which they seem.

But these pleasures vanish fast
Which by shadows are expressed;
Pleasures are not, if they last;
10 In their passing is their best.
Glory is most bright and gay
In a flash, and so away.

Feed apace° then, greedy eyes,   quickly
On the wonder you behold;

15

Take it sudden as it flies,
Though you take it not to hold.
When your eyes have done their part,
Thought must length° it in the heart.   *lengthen*
                                                          1610

MICHAEL DRAYTON

1563–1631

A Roundelay Between Two Shepherds[1]

1 Shep. Tell me, thou gentle shepherd swain,°   *lover, rustic*
          Who's yonder in the vale is set?
2 Shep. Oh, it is she, whose sweets do stain
          The lily, rose, the violet!

5

1 Shep. Why doth the sun against his kind,°   *nature*
          Fix his bright chariot in the skies?[2]
2 Shep. Because the sun is stricken blind
          With looking on her heavenly eyes.

1 Shep. Why do thy flocks forbear their food,
10   Which sometime° were thy chief delight?   *formerly*
2 Shep. Because they need no other good
          That live in presence of her sight.

1 Shep. Why look these flowers so pale and ill,
          That once attired this goodly heath?
15 *2 Shep.* She hath robb'd Nature of her skill,
          And sweetens all things with her breath.

1 Shep. Why slide these brooks so slow away,
          Whose bubbling murmur pleased thine ear?
2 Shep. Oh, marvel not although they stay,°   *stand still*
20   When they her heavenly voice do hear!

1 Shep. From whence come all these shepherd swains,
          And lovely nymphs attired in green?
2 Shep. From gathering garlands on the plains,
          To crown our fair the shepherds' queen.

25 *Both.*   The sun that lights this world below,
          Flocks, flowers, and brooks will witness bear:

1. This roundelay, or simple song, was included in the anthology called *England's Helicon* (1600); it also appeared (in a slightly different form) in the Ninth Eclogue of Drayton's "Pastorals," published in his collected *Poems* (1619). Pastoral poems, or eclogues, a classical form practiced by Virgil and others, are populated by shepherds and nymphs, and usually portray a simple, happy life of singing and dancing, rather than a life of farm labor. The Ninth Eclogue describes a "Shepherd's Board," or feast, and contains several songs by shepherds, or "swains," in praise of their lovers.

2. According to myth, the sun was a chariot driven daily across the sky by Apollo; "fix": make motionless.

These nymphs and shepherds all do know,
That it is she is only fair.

1600

From Idea[3]

To the Reader of these Sonnets

Into these loves who but for passion looks,
At this first sight here let him lay them by
And seek elsewhere, in turning other books,
Which better may his labor satisfy.
5 No far-fetched sigh shall ever wound my breast,
Love from mine eye a tear shall never wring,
Nor in *Ah me*'s my whining sonnets dressed,
A libertine,[4] fantastically° I sing.   *capriciously*
My verse is the true image of my mind,
10 Ever in motion, still desiring change;
And as thus to variety inclined,
So in all humors sportively I range:
   My muse is rightly of the English strain,
   That cannot long one fashion entertain.

6

How many paltry, foolish, painted things,
That now in coaches trouble every street,
Shall be forgotten, whom no poet sings,
Ere they be well wrapped in their winding-sheet?°   *shroud*
5 Where I to thee eternity shall give,
When nothing else remaineth of these days,
And queens hereafter shall be glad to live
Upon the alms of thy superfluous praise.
Virgins and matrons reading these my rhymes
10 Shall be so much delighted with thy story
That they shall grieve they lived not in these times,
To have seen thee, their sex's only glory.
   So shalt thou fly above the vulgar throng,
   Still to survive in my immortal song.

14

If he from heaven that filched that living fire[5]
Condemned by Jove to endless torment be,
I greatly marvel how you still go free,

---

3. Drayton's fifty-nine sonnets addressed to "Idea" are concerned with the embodiment of the Platonic ideas of virtue and beauty: the sequence represents his lifelong devotion (in the manner of a courtly lover) to Anne Goodyere, Lady Rainsford. His sequence first appeared as *Idea's Mirror* in 1594, and after revisions as *Idea* in 1619.

4. One not bound by conventional morality.
5. Prometheus, a Greek hero who stole fire from heaven and gave it to humans. He was chained by Jove (Zeus) to a rock and preyed upon daily by a vulture that tore at his vitals. In some versions of the myth, Prometheus created humankind out of clay.

That far beyond Prometheus did aspire.
5   The fire he stole, although of heavenly kind,
Which from above he craftily did take,
Of liveless clods,[6] us living men to make,
He did bestow in temper of the mind.
But you broke into heaven's immortal store,
10   Where virtue, honor, wit, and beauty lay;
Which taking thence you have escaped away,
Yet stand as free as ere you did before;
    Yet old Prometheus punished for his rape.[7]
    Thus poor thieves suffer when the greater 'scape.°   *escape*

61

Since there's no help, come let us kiss and part;
Nay, I have done, you get no more of me,
And I am glad, yea glad with all my heart
That thus so cleanly I myself can free;
5   Shake hands forever, cancel all our vows,
And when we meet at any time again,
Be it not seen in either of our brows
That we one jot of former love retain.
Now at the last gasp of love's latest breath,
10   When, his pulse failing, Passion speechless lies,
When Faith is kneeling by his bed of death,
And Innocence is closing up his eyes,
    Now if thou wouldst, when all have given him over,
    From death to life thou mightst him yet recover.

63

Truce, gentle love, a parley° now I crave,   *conference*
Methinks 'tis long since first these wars begun;
Nor thou nor I the better yet can have;
Bad is the match where neither party won.
5   I offer free conditions of fair peace,
My heart for hostage that it shall remain;
Discharge our forces, here let malice cease,
So for my pledge thou give me pledge again.
Or if no thing but death will serve thy turn,
10   Still thirsting for subversion of my state,
Do what thou canst, raze, massacre, and burn,
Let the world see the utmost of thy hate;
    I send defiance, since if overthrown,
    Thou vanquishing, the conquest is mine own.

1619

---

6. Lumps of earth or clay.
7. "Rape" referred not only to sexual assault but to other acts of forceful appropriation such as Prometheus' theft of heavenly fire.

CHRISTOPHER MARLOWE

1564–1593

Hero and Leander

First Sestiad[1]

On Hellespont,[2] guilty of true love's blood,
In view and opposite, two cities stood,
Sea-borderers, disjoined by Neptune's[3] might;
The one Abydos, the other Sestos hight.°   *called*
5 At Sestos Hero dwelt; Hero the fair,
Whom young Apollo courted for her hair,
And offered as a dower his burning throne,
Where she should sit for men to gaze upon.[4]
The outside of her garments were of lawn,[5]
10 The lining purple silk, with gilt stars drawn;
Her wide sleeves green, and bordered with a grove
Where Venus in her naked glory strove
To please the careless and disdainful eyes
Of proud Adonis,[6] that before her lies;
15 Her kirtle° blue, whereon was many a stain,   *gown*
Made with the blood of wretched lovers slain.
Upon her head she ware a myrtle wreath,
From whence her veil reached to the ground beneath.
Her veil was artificial flowers and leaves,
20 Whose workmanship both man and beast deceives;
Many would praise the sweet smell as she passed,
When 'twas the odor which her breath forth cast;
And there for honey, bees have sought in vain,
And, beat from thence, have lighted there again.
25 About her neck hung chains of pebble-stone,
Which, lightened° by her neck, like diamonds shone.   *illuminated*
She ware no gloves, for neither sun nor wind
Would burn or parch her hands, but to her mind[7]
Or warm or cool them, for they took delight
30 To play upon those hands, they were so white.
Buskins[8] of shells all silvered, usèd she,
And branched with blushing coral to the knee,
Where sparrows perched, of hollow pearl and gold,
Such as the world would wonder to behold;
35 Those with sweet water oft her handmaid fills,
Which, as she went, would chirrup through the bills.

---

1. A term for a book or canto (from Hero's city, Sestos). George Chapman, who wrote a four-part continuation of this poem, divided it into sestiads. The poem belongs to the genre of the minor epic, or *epyllion*, which flourished in the 1590s and showed the strong influence of Ovid. Ovid told the story of Hero and Leander in two of his *Heroides* (fictional love letters) and in one of the *Elegies* Marlowe had translated.
2. The modern Dardanelles, a strait between the Aegean Sea and the Sea of Marmora, one mile wide at its narrowest point.
3. Neptune was the god of the sea.
4. Apollo was the god of the sun.
5. A sheer cotton or linen fabric.
6. Venus passionately loved the young hunter Adonis, who was killed by a boar; in lines 91–93, Marlowe claims that the men of Sestos hold a festival in honor of Adonis every year.
7. As she wished.
8. Laced foot coverings reaching halfway or more to the knees.

Some say, for her the fairest Cupid pined,
And looking in her face, was strooken blind.
But this is true: so like was one the other,
40 As he imagined Hero was his mother;[9]
And oftentimes into her bosom flew,
About her naked neck his bare arms threw,
And laid his childish head upon her breast,
And with still panting rocked, there took his rest.
45 So lovely fair was Hero, Venus' nun,
As Nature wept, thinking she was undone,
Because she took more from her than she left
And of such wondrous beauty her bereft;
Therefore, in sign her treasure suffered wrack,[1]
50 Since Hero's time hath half the world been black.
Amorous Leander, beautiful and young,
(Whose tragedy divine Musaeus[2] sung)
Dwelt at Abydos; since him dwelt there none
For whom succeeding times make greater moan.
55 His dangling tresses that were never shorn,
Had they been cut and unto Colchos[3] borne,
Would have allured the vent'rous youth of Greece
To hazard more than for the Golden Fleece.
Fair Cynthia[4] wished his arms might be her sphere;°   *orbit*
60 Grief makes her pale, because she moves not there.
His body was as straight as Circe's wand;[5]
Jove might have sipped out nectar from his hand.[6]
Even as delicious meat is to the taste,
So was his neck in touching, and surpassed
65 The white of Pelops' shoulder.[7] I could tell ye
How smooth his breast was, and how white his belly,
And whose immortal fingers did imprint
That heavenly path, with many a curious° dint,   *exquisite*
That runs along his back; but my rude pen
70 Can hardly blazon forth the loves of men,
Much less of powerful gods; let it suffice
That my slack° muse sings of Leander's eyes,   *feeble*
Those orient[8] cheeks and lips, exceeding his
That leapt into the water for a kiss
75 Of his own shadow,[9] and despising many,
Died ere he could enjoy the love of any.
Had wild Hippolytus[1] Leander seen,
Enamored of his beauty had he been;
His presence made the rudest peasant melt,

---

9. I.e., Venus.
1. I.e., therefore, as a sign that her (Nature's) wealth had suffered a shipwreck (i.e., been harmed by Hero's beauty), Nature made half the world dark-haired or -complexioned.
2. A fifth-century Alexandrian whose poem on Hero and Leander served Marlowe as a source. Marlowe's term "divine" suggests that he may have identified him with an earlier, legendary Musaeus.
3. The country in Asia where Jason and his Argonauts found the Golden Fleece.
4. The moon. Leander is being compared to the moon's lover, Endymion.

5. The enchantress Circe, in the *Odyssey*, possessed a magical wand capable of turning men into beasts.
6. Leander is being compared to Jove's beloved Ganymede.
7. Pelops' father, Tantalus, killed, cut up, cooked, and served his son at a dinner of the gods. The goddess Demeter ate his shoulder. Hermes later reconstituted Pelops, giving him a shoulder of ivory.
8. Glowing, like eastern skies or gems.
9. I.e., Narcissus.
1. A great hunter, contemptuous of love.

80   That in the vast uplandish° country dwelt;   *wild*
     The barbarous Thracian soldier, moved with naught,
     Was moved with him, and for his favor sought.
     Some swore he was a maid in man's attire,
     For in his looks were all that men desire:
85   A pleasant smiling cheek, a speaking° eye,   *expressive*
     A brow for love to banquet royally;
     And such as knew he was a man, would say,
     "Leander, thou art made for amorous play;
     Why art thou not in love, and loved of all?
90   Though thou be fair, yet be not thine own thrall."°   *captive*
        The men of wealthy Sestos every year,
     For his sake whom their goddess held so dear,
     Rose-cheeked Adonis, kept a solemn feast.
     Thither resorted many a wandering guest
95   To meet their loves; such as had none at all
     Came lovers home from this great festival;
     For every street, like to a firmament,
     Glistered with breathing stars, who, where they went,
     Frighted the melancholy earth, which deemed
100 Eternal heaven to burn, for so it seemed
     As if another Phaeton[2] had got
     The guidance of the sun's rich chariot.
     But, far above the loveliest, Hero shined,
     And stole away the enchanted gazer's mind;
105 For like sea nymphs' inveigling° harmony,   *beguiling*
     So was her beauty to the standers by.
     Nor that night-wandering pale and watery star[3]
     (When yawning dragons draw her thirling[4] car
     From Latmus' mount up to the gloomy sky,
110 Where, crowned with blazing light and majesty,
     She proudly sits) more over-rules° the flood,   *rules over*
     Than she the hearts of those that near her stood.
     Even as when gaudy nymphs pursue the chase,
     Wretched Ixion's shaggy-footed race,[5]
115 Incensed with savage heat, gallop amain
     From steep pine-bearing mountains to the plain,
     So ran the people forth to gaze upon her,
     And all that viewed her were enamored on her.
     And as in fury of a dreadful fight,
120 Their fellows being slain or put to flight,
     Poor soldiers stand with fear of death dead-strooken,
     So at her presence all, surprised and tooken,
     Await the sentence of her scornful eyes;
     He whom she favors lives, the other dies.
125 There might you see one sigh, another rage,
     And some, their violent passions to assuage,°   *ease*

2. Son of Apollo, the sun god, who reluctantly
allowed him to drive the chariot of the sun across
the sky for one day. When the plunging horses
drew the sun below its normal path, the Earth was
set on fire and Phaeton was destroyed.
3. The moon.

4. Piercing, like a flying arrow; also, whirling. Lat-
mus was the home of the shepherd Endymion,
loved by Diana, the moon goddess.
5. The centaurs, offspring of Ixion and a cloud.
For loving Juno, Ixion was made "wretched" by
being chained to a ceaselessly rolling wheel.

Compile sharp satires; but alas, too late,
For faithful love will never turn to hate.
And many, seeing great princes were denied,
130 Pined as they went, and thinking on her, died.
On this feast day, oh, cursed day and hour!
Went Hero thorough° Sestos, from her tower   *through*
To Venus' temple, where unhappily,
As after chanced, they did each other spy.
135 So fair a church as this had Venus none;
The walls were of discolored° jasper stone,   *varicolored*
Wherein was Proteus carvèd, and o'erhead
A lively° vine of green sea-agate spread,   *lifelike*
Where, by one hand, light-headed Bacchus° hung,   *god of wine*
140 And with the other, wine from grapes out-wrung.
Of crystal shining fair the pavement was;
The town of Sestos called it Venus' glass;
There might you see the gods in sundry shapes,
Committing heady° riots, incest, rapes;   *violent, impetuous*
145 For know that underneath this radiant floor
Was Danae's statue in a brazen tower;[6]
Jove slyly stealing from his sister's bed
To dally with Idalian Ganymed,
And for his love Europa bellowing loud,
150 And tumbling with the rainbow in a cloud;
Blood-quaffing Mars heaving the iron net[7]
Which limping Vulcan and his Cyclops set;
Love kindling fire to burn such towns as Troy;
Silvanus weeping for the lovely boy
155 That now is turned into a cypress tree,[8]
Under whose shade the wood gods love to be.
And in the midst a silver altar stood;
There Hero sacrificing turtles'° blood,   *turtledoves'*
Veiled to the ground, veiling her eyelids close,
160 And modestly they opened as she rose;
Thence flew love's arrow with the golden head,[9]
And thus Leander was enamorèd.
Stone still he stood, and evermore he gazed,
Till with the fire that from his countenance blazed,
165 Relenting Hero's gentle heart was strook;
Such force and virtue hath an amorous look.
    It lies not in our power to love or hate,
For will in us is over-ruled by fate.

6. In the next lines, specific examples of the "riots, incest, rapes" are given. Jove frequently left Juno, his sister and wife, to pursue other women; whether his actions constituted seduction or rape often depends upon the particular account of a given myth, as well as on interpretation. Danae was the daughter of the king of Argos, who imprisoned her because of a prophecy that a son born to her would kill him; Jove came to her in the form of a shower of gold, and as a result she became the mother of Perseus. Jove took the form of an eagle to abduct Ganymede, a beautiful young Trojan boy, to serve as his cup-bearer; the sexual nature of their relationship was a topic of great interest during the Renaissance. Jove took the form of a bull in order to rape Europa. The goddess of the rainbow (line 150) was Iris, a messenger of the gods.
7. Vulcan and his helpers, the Cyclopes (correct plural form), trapped his wife, Venus, in bed with Mars and exposed them to the laughter of the other gods.
8. Cyparissus, changed by Apollo into a cypress tree, was mourned by the forest god, Sylvanus.
9. According to Ovid, Cupid's arrows were tipped with gold or lead, the one producing love and the other loathing.

When two are stripped,[1] long ere the course begin
170   We wish that one should lose, the other win;
And one especially do we affect°   *prefer*
Of two gold ingots, like in each respect.
The reason no man knows, let it suffice,
What we behold is censured by our eyes.
175   Where both deliberate, the love is slight;
Who ever loved, that loved not at first sight?
      He kneeled, but unto her devoutly prayed;
Chaste Hero to herself thus softly said:
"Were I the saint he worships, I would hear him";
180   And as she spake these words, came somewhat near him.
He started up; she blushed as one ashamed;
Wherewith Leander much more was inflamed.
He touched her hand; in touching it she trembled;
Love deeply grounded hardly is dissembled.
185   These lovers parled° by the touch of hands;   *spoke*
True love is mute, and oft amazed stands.
Thus while dumb signs their yielding hearts entangled,
The air with sparks of living fire was spangled,°   *speckled*
And night, deep drenched in misty Acheron,[2]
190   Heaved up her head, and half the world upon
Breathed darkness forth (dark night is Cupid's day).
And now begins Leander to display
Love's holy fire with words, with sighs, and tears,
Which like sweet music entered Hero's ears;
195   And yet at every word she turned aside,
And always cut him off as he replied.
At last, like to a bold sharp sophister,[3]
With cheerful hope thus he accosted her:
      "Fair creature, let me speak without offense;
200   I would my rude words had the influence
To lead thy thoughts as thy fair looks do mine!
Then shouldst thou be his prisoner who is thine.
Be not unkind and fair; misshapen stuff°   *persons*
Are of behavior boisterous and rough.
205   Oh, shun me not, but hear me ere you go,
God knows I cannot force love, as you do.
My words shall be as spotless as my youth,
Full of simplicity and naked truth.
This sacrifice, whose sweet perfume descending
210   From Venus' altar to your footsteps bending,
Doth testify that you exceed her far,
To whom you offer, and whose nun you are.
Why should you worship her? her you surpass
As much as sparkling diamonds flaring glass.
215   A diamond set in lead his worth retains;
A heavenly nymph, beloved of human swains,°   *rustics*
Receives no blemish, but ofttimes more grace;
Which makes me hope, although I am but base,

1. I.e., for a race.
2. The river of woe in the underworld.
3. One who reasons adroitly rather than soundly;

also, a university student in his junior or senior
year.

Base in respect of thee, divine and pure,
220 Dutiful service may thy love procure,
And I in duty will excel all other,
As thou in beauty dost exceed Love's mother.[4]
Nor heaven, nor thou, were made to gaze upon;
As heaven preserves all things, so save thou one.
225 A stately builded ship, well rigged and tall,
The ocean maketh more majestical;
Why vowest thou then to live in Sestos here,
Who on love's seas more glorious wouldst appear?
Like untuned golden strings all women are,
230 Which long time lie untouched,[5] will harshly jar.
Vessels of brass, oft handled, brightly shine;
What difference betwixt the richest mine°   ore
And basest mold,° but use? for both, not used,   earth
Are of like worth. Then treasure is abused,
235 When misers keep it; being put to loan,
In time it will return us two for one.
Rich robes themselves and others do adorn;
Neither themselves nor others, if not worn.
Who builds a palace, and rams up the gate,
240 Shall see it ruinous and desolate.
Ah, simple Hero, learn thyself to cherish!
Lone women, like to empty houses, perish.
Less sins the poor rich man that starves himself
In heaping up a mass of drossy pelf,°   base riches
245 Than such as you; his golden earth remains,
Which, after his decease, some other gains;
But this fair gem, sweet in the loss alone,
When you fleet hence, can be bequeathed to none.
Or if it could, down from th' enameled sky
250 All heaven would come to claim this legacy,
And with intestine° broils the world destroy,   civil
And quite confound nature's sweet harmony.
Well therefore by the gods decreed it is
We human creatures should enjoy that bliss.
255 One is no number;[6] maids are nothing, then,
Without the sweet society of men.
Wilt thou live single still? one shalt thou be
Though never-singling Hymen[7] couple thee.
Wild savages, that drink of running springs,
260 Think water far excels all earthly things,
But they that daily taste neat wine, despise it;
Virginity, albeit some highly prize it,
Compared with marriage, had you tried them both,
Differs as much as wine and water doth.
265 Base bullion for the stamp's[8] sake we allow;
Even so for men's impression do we you,

4. I.e., Venus, mother of Cupid.
5. I.e., which, if they lie untouched for a long time.
6. The theory that one is not a number appears in Aristotle's *Metaphysics* and was often discussed by later, Neoplatonic philosophers.
7. The god of marriage.
8. I.e., the impression that turns a mere piece of metal into a coin.

By which alone, our reverend fathers say,
Women receive perfection every way.
This idol which you term virginity
270 Is neither essence⁹ subject to the eye,
No, nor to any one exterior sense,
Nor hath it any place of residence,
Nor is 't of earth or mold celestial,
Or capable of any form at all.
275 Of that which hath no being, do not boast;
Things that are not at all, are never lost.
Men foolishly do call it virtuous;
What virtue is it, that is born with us?
Much less can honor be ascribed thereto;
280 Honor is purchased by the deeds we do.
Believe me, Hero, honor is not won
Until some honorable deed be done.
Seek you, for chastity, immortal fame,
And know that some have wronged Diana's¹ name?
285 Whose name is it, if she be false or not,
So she be fair, but some vile tongues will blot?
But you are fair, ay me, so wondrous fair,
So young, so gentle, and so debonair,
As Greece will think, if thus you live alone,
290 Some one or other keeps you as his own.
Then, Hero, hate me not, nor from me fly
To follow swiftly blasting infamy.
Perhaps thy sacred priesthood makes thee loath;
Tell me, to whom mad'st thou that heedless oath?"
295   "To Venus," answered she, and as she spake,
Forth from those two tralucent° cisterns brake   translucent
A stream of liquid pearl, which down her face
Made milk-white paths, whereon the gods might trace°   go
To Jove's high court. He thus replied: "The rites
300 In which love's beauteous empress most delights
Are banquets, Doric music,² midnight revel,
Plays, masques, and all that stern age counteth evil.
Thee as a holy idiot° doth she scorn,   untutored person
For thou, in vowing chastity, hast sworn
305 To rob her name and honor, and thereby
Commit'st a sin far worse than perjury,
Even sacrilege against her deity,
Through regular and formal purity.
To expiate which sin, kiss and shake hands;
310 Such sacrifice as this Venus demands."
        Thereat she smiled, and did deny him so
As, put° thereby, yet might he hope for mo.°   put off / more
Which makes him quickly reinforce his speech,
And her in humble manner thus beseech:
315   "Though neither gods nor men may thee deserve,
Yet for her sake whom you have vowed to serve,

---

9. An existing thing.
1. Diana was the goddess of chastity. Nevertheless, some stories attribute amorous relationships to her.

2. Leander apparently confuses Doric music, which was stirring and martial, with Lydian music, which was soft and voluptuous.

Abandon fruitless cold virginity,
The gentle queen of love's sole enemy.
Then shall you most resemble Venus' nun,
320 When Venus' sweet rites are performed and done.
Flint-breasted Pallas[3] joys in single life,
But Pallas and your mistress are at strife.
Love, Hero, then, and be not tyrannous,
But heal the heart that thou hast wounded thus;
325 Nor stain thy youthful years with avarice;
Fair fools delight to be accounted nice.°   *reticent*
The richest corn dies if it be not reaped;
Beauty alone is lost, too warily kept."
      These arguments he used, and many more,
330 Wherewith she yielded, that was won before.
Hero's looks yielded, but her words made war;
Women are won when they begin to jar.°   *argue*
Thus having swallowed Cupid's golden hook,
The more she strived, the deeper was she strook;°   *love-struck*
335 Yet, evilly feigning anger, strove she still,
And would be thought to grant against her will.
So having paused awhile, at last she said:
"Who taught thee rhetoric to deceive a maid?
Ay me! such words as these should I abhor,
340 And yet I like them for the orator."
      With that Leander stooped to have embraced her,
But from his spreading arms away she cast her,
And thus bespake him: "Gentle youth, forbear
To touch the sacred garments which I wear.
345 Upon a rock, and underneath a hill,
Far from the town, where all is whist° and still   *silent*
Save that the sea playing on yellow sand
Sends forth a rattling murmur to the land,
Whose sound allures the golden Morpheus°   *god of sleep*
350 In silence of the night to visit us,
My turret stands; and there, God knows, I play
With Venus' swans and sparrows all the day.
A dwarfish beldame° bears me company,   *old woman*
That hops about the chamber where I lie,
355 And spends the night, that might be better spent,
In vain discourse and apish° merriment.   *silly*
Come thither." As she spake this, her tongue tripped,
For unawares, "Come thither," from her slipped;
And suddenly her former color changed,
360 And here and there her eyes, through anger, ranged.
And like a planet moving several ways
At one self instant, she, poor soul, assays,
Loving, not to love at all, and every part
Strove to resist the motions of her heart;
365 And hands so pure, so innocent, nay such
As might have made heaven stoop to have a touch,
Did she uphold to Venus, and again

---

3. Pallas Athena, the virgin goddess of wisdom.

Vowed spotless chastity, but all in vain.
Cupid beats down her prayers with his wings;
370   Her vows above the empty air he flings;
All deep enraged, his sinewy bow he bent,
And shot a shaft that burning from him went;
Wherewith she, strooken, looked so dolefully,
As made Love sigh to see his tyranny.
375   And as she wept, her tears to pearl he turned,
And wound them on his arm, and for her mourned.
Then towards the palace of the Destinies,
Laden with languishment and grief, he flies,
And to those stern nymphs humbly made request,
380   Both might enjoy each other, and be blest.
But with a ghastly dreadful countenance,
Threatening a thousand deaths at every glance,
They answered Love, nor would vouchsafe so much
As one poor word, their hate to him was such.
385   Hearken awhile, and I will tell you why:
Heaven's winged herald, Jove-born Mercury,
The selfsame day that he asleep had laid
Enchanted Argus,[4] spied a country maid,
Whose careless hair, instead of pearl t' adorn it,
390   Glistered with dew, as one that seemed to scorn it;
Her breath as fragrant as the morning rose,
Her mind pure, and her tongue untaught to gloze;°   *flatter*
Yet proud she was, for lofty pride that dwells
In towered courts is oft in shepherds' cells,
395   And too too well the fair vermilion° knew,   *scarlet*
And silver tincture of her cheeks, that drew
The love of every swain. On her this god
Enamored was, and with his snaky rod[5]
Did charm her nimble feet, and made her stay,
400   The while upon a hillock down he lay,
And sweetly on his pipe began to play,
And with smooth speech her fancy to assay;°   *try*
Till in his twining arms he locked her fast,
And then he wooed with kisses, and at last,
405   As shepherds do, her on the ground he laid,
And tumbling in the grass, he often strayed
Beyond the bounds of shame, in being bold
To eye those parts which no eye should behold.
And like an insolent commanding lover,
410   Boasting his parentage, would needs discover
The way to new Elysium;[6] but she,
Whose only dower was her chastity,
Having striv'n in vain, was now about to cry,
And crave the help of shepherds that were nigh.
415   Herewith he stayed his fury, and began
To give her leave to rise; away she ran;

---

4. The watchman with a hundred eyes set by Juno to guard Io, beloved of Jupiter. Mercury lulled Argus asleep with his music, then killed him, at Jove's command.

5. The caduceus, Mercury's magic staff.
6. In Greek mythology, a place of ideal happiness inhabited by the blessed dead.

After went Mercury, who used such cunning,
As she, to hear his tale, left off her running;
Maids are not won by brutish force and might,
420 But speeches full of pleasure and delight;
And knowing Hermes[7] courted her, was glad
That she such loveliness and beauty had
As could provoke his liking, yet was mute,
And neither would deny nor grant his suit.
425 Still vowed he love, she wanting no excuse
To feed him with delays, as women use,
Or thirsting after immortality—
All women are ambitious naturally—
Imposed upon her lover such a task
430 As he ought not perform, nor yet she ask.
A draught of flowing nectar she requested,
Wherewith the king of gods and men is feasted.
He, ready to accomplish what she willed,
Stole some from Hebe[8] (Hebe Jove's cup filled)
435 And gave it to his simple rustic love;
Which being known (as° what is hid from Jove?)   *for*
He inly° stormed, and waxed more furious   *inwardly*
Than for the fire filched by Prometheus,[9]
And thrusts him down from heaven; he wandering here
440 In mournful terms,° with sad and heavy cheer,   *state*
Complained to Cupid. Cupid, for his sake,
To be revenged on Jove did undertake;
And those on whom heaven, earth, and hell relies,
I mean the adamantine Destinies,
445 He wounds with love, and forced them equally
To dote upon deceitful Mercury.
They offered him the deadly fatal knife
That shears the slender threads of human life;
At his fair-feathered feet the engines laid
450 Which th' earth from ugly Chaos' den upweighed;[1]
These he regarded not, but did entreat
That Jove, usurper of his[2] father's seat,
Might presently be banished into hell,
And aged Saturn in Olympus dwell.
455 They granted what he craved, and once again
Saturn and Ops began their golden reign.
Murder, rape, war, lust, and treachery
Were with Jove closed in Stygian[3] empery.
But long this blessed time continued not;
460 As soon as he his wishèd purpose got,
He, reckless of his promise, did despise
The love of th' everlasting Destinies.
They seeing it, both Love and him abhorred,

---

7. Another name for Mercury.
8. Jove's cup-bearer before Jove ravished Ganymede (see n. 6, p. 219).
9. Prometheus angered Jove by stealing fire from the gods for the benefit of humans.
1. The Fates also controlled the "beams" that "upweighed," or supported, the Earth, since it was formed out of Chaos, the undifferentiated mass

from which all things came.
2. I.e., Jove's father, Saturn, whose peaceful reign in Italy, after Jove had dethroned him, was known as the Golden Age; Ops was the Roman name for Saturn's wife.
3. Pertaining to the river Styx in Hades; "empery": dominion.

And Jupiter unto his place restored.
465 And but that Learning,[4] in despite of Fate,
Will mount aloft, and enter heaven gate,
And to the seat of Jove itself advance,
Hermes had slept in hell with Ignorance;
Yet as a punishment they added this,
470 That he and Poverty should always kiss.
And to this day is every scholar poor;
Gross gold from them runs headlong to the boor.[5]
Likewise, the angry sisters thus deluded,
To venge themselves on Hermes, have concluded
475 That Midas'[6] brood shall sit in Honor's chair,
To which the Muses' sons are only heir;
And fruitful wits that inaspiring are
Shall, discontent, run into regions far;
And few great lords in virtuous deeds shall joy,
480 But be surprised with every garish toy;[7]
And still enrich the lofty servile clown,
Who with encroaching guile keeps learning down.
Then muse not Cupid's suit no better sped,
Seeing in their loves the Fates were injurèd.

Second Sestiad

By° this, sad Hero, with love unacquainted,   *at*
Viewing Leander's face, fell down and fainted.
He kissed her and breathed life into her lips,
Wherewith, as one displeased, away she trips.
5 Yet as she went, full often looked behind,
And many poor excuses did she find
To linger by the way, and once she stayed
And would have turned again, but was afraid,
In offering parley, to be counted light.°   *wanton*
10 So on she goes, and in her idle flight,
Her painted fan of curlèd plumes let fall,
Thinking to train° Leander therewithal.   *draw along*
He, being a novice, knew not what she meant,
But stayed, and after her a letter sent,
15 Which joyful Hero answered in such sort
As he had hoped to scale the beauteous fort
Wherein the liberal graces locked their wealth,
And therefore to her tower he got by stealth.
Wide open stood the door, he need not climb;
20 And she herself, before the 'pointed time,
Had spread the board, with roses strewed the room,
And oft looked out, and mused he did not come.
At last he came; Oh, who can tell the greeting
These greedy lovers had at their first meeting?
25 He asked, she gave, and nothing was denied;
Both to each other quickly were affied.°   *affianced*

4. Mercury, the god of learning; i.e., Learning, because it is so divine, always rises, despite the downward pull of fate.
5. I.e., large amounts (a "gross") of gold go swiftly to the "boor," one who lacks refinement, rather than to the "scholar."
6. The king whose touch turned objects to gold.
7. I.e., be delighted with trivial things.

Look how their hands, so were their hearts united,
And what he did she willingly requited.
(Sweet are the kisses, the embracements sweet,
30   When like desires and affections meet;
For from the earth to heaven is Cupid raised,
Where fancy is in equal balance peised.°)   *weighed*
Yet she this rashness suddenly repented,
And turned aside, and to herself lamented,
35   As if her name and honor had been wronged
By being possessed of him for whom she longed;
Aye, and she wished, albeit not from her heart,
That he would leave her turret and depart.
The mirthful god of amorous pleasure smiled
40   To see how he this captive nymph beguiled;
For hitherto he did but fan the fire,
And kept it down that it might mount the higher.
Now waxed she jealous lest his love abated,
Fearing her own thoughts made her to be hated.
45   Therefore unto him hastily she goes,
And like light Salmacis,[8] her body throws
Upon his bosom, where with yielding eyes
She offers up herself, a sacrifice
To slake his anger if he were displeased.
50   Oh, what god would not therewith be appeased?
Like Aesop's cock,[9] this jewel he enjoyed,
And as a brother with his sister toyed,
Supposing nothing else was to be done,
Now he her favor and good will had won.
55   But know you not that creatures wanting sense[1]
By nature have a mutual appetence,°   *affinity*
And wanting organs to advance a step,
Moved by love's force, unto each other leap?
Much more in subjects having intellect,
60   Some hidden influence breeds like effect.
Albeit Leander, rude° in love and raw,   *untutored*
Long dallying with Hero, nothing saw
That might delight him more, yet he suspected
Some amorous rites or other were neglected.
65   Therefore unto his body hers he clung;
She, fearing on the rushes to be flung,
Strived with redoubled strength; the more she strived,
The more a gentle pleasing heat revived,
Which taught him all that elder lovers know;
70   And now the same gan so to scorch and glow,
As in plain terms, yet cunningly, he craved it;
Love always makes those eloquent that have it.
She, with a kind of granting, put him by it,[2]
And ever as he thought himself most nigh it,

8. A nymph who became enamored of Hermaphroditus when she saw him bathing in her lake. Throwing herself upon him in spite of his resistance, she called upon the gods to keep them forever together. In answer to her prayer their two bodies united and became one, both male and female.
9. Finding a jewel in a dung heap, the cock had no notion of its value and was willing to trade it for a grain of corn.
1. Inanimate objects.
2. Deflected him.

75   Like to the tree of Tantalus[3] she fled,
And, seeming lavish, saved her maidenhead.
Ne'er king more sought to keep his diadem,
Than Hero this inestimable gem.
Above our life we love a steadfast friend,
80   Yet when a token of great worth we send,
We often kiss it, often look thereon,
And stay the messenger that would be gone;
No marvel then though Hero would not yield
So soon to part from that she dearly held;
85   Jewels being lost are found again, this never;
'Tis lost but once, and once lost, lost forever.
    Now had the morn espied her lover's steeds,[4]
Whereat she starts, puts on her purple weeds,
And, red for anger that he stayed so long,
90   All headlong throws herself the clouds among.
And now Leander, fearing to be missed,
Embraced her suddenly, took leave, and kissed.
Long was he taking leave, and loath to go,
And kissed again, as lovers use to do.
95   Sad Hero wrung him by the hand and wept,
Saying, "Let your vows and promises be kept."
Then, standing at the door, she turned about,
As loath to see Leander going out.
And now the sun that through th' horizon peeps,
100   As pitying these lovers, downward creeps,
So that in silence of the cloudy night,
Though it was morning, did he take his flight.
But what the secret trusty night concealed,
Leander's amorous habit° soon revealed;   *clothing*
105   With Cupid's myrtle was his bonnet crowned,
About his arms the purple riband° wound   *ribbon*
Wherewith she wreathed her largely spreading hair;
Nor could the youth abstain, but he must wear
The sacred ring wherewith she was endowed,
110   When first religious chastity she vowed;
Which made his love through Sestos to be known,
And thence unto Abydos sooner blown
Than he could sail; for incorporeal Fame,
Whose weight consists in nothing but her name,
115   Is swifter than the wind, whose tardy plumes
Are reeking[5] water and dull earthly fumes.
Home, when he came, he seemed not to be there,
But like exilèd air thrust from his sphere,
Set in a foreign place;[6] and straight from thence,
120   Alcides° like, by mighty violence   *Hercules*
He would have chased away the swelling main°   *ocean*
That him from her unjustly did detain.

3. For stealing nectar from the gods to give to humans, Jove punished Tantalus by placing him in a pool in Hades. Whenever Tantalus bent to drink, the water receded from his lips; when he reached for the fruit that dangled above his head, it rose up out of his grasp.
4. The horses that pull the sun's chariot.
5. Producing fog and mist.
6. I.e., air rushes to fill a vacuum.

Like as the sun in a diameter[7]
Fires and inflames objects removèd far,
125 And heateth kindly, shining laterally,
So beauty sweetly quickens when 'tis nigh,
But being separated and removed,
Burns where it cherished, murders where it loved.
Therefore even as an index to a book,
130 So to his mind was young Leander's look.
Oh, none but gods have power their love to hide;
Affection by the countenance is descried.°   made known
The light of hidden fire itself discovers,
And love that is concealed betrays poor lovers.
135 His secret flame apparently[8] was seen;
Leander's father knew where he had been,
And for the same mildly rebuked his son,
Thinking to quench the sparkles new begun.
But love, resisted once, grows passionate,
140 And nothing more than counsel lovers hate;
For as a hot proud horse highly disdains
To have his head controlled, but breaks the reins,
Spits forth the ringled° bit, and with his hooves   ringed
Checks° the submissive ground, so he that loves,   stamps
145 The more he is restrained, the worse he fares.
What is it now but mad Leander dares?
"Oh Hero, Hero!" thus he cried full oft,
And then he got him to a rock aloft,
Where having spied her tower, long stared he on 't,
150 And prayed the narrow toiling Hellespont
To part in twain, that he might come and go;
But still the rising billows answered "No."
With that he stripped him to the ivory skin,
And crying, "Love, I come!" leaped lively in.
155 Whereat the sapphire-visaged god[9] grew proud,
And made his capering Triton sound aloud,
Imagining that Ganymede,[1] displeased,
Had left the heavens; therefore on him he seized.
Leander strived; the waves about him wound,
160 And pulled him to the bottom, where the ground
Was strewed with pearl, and in low coral groves
Sweet singing mermaids sported with their loves
On heaps of heavy gold, and took great pleasure
To spurn in careless sort the shipwreck treasure.
165 For here the stately azure palace stood,
Where kingly Neptune and his train abode.
The lusty god embraced him, called him love,
And swore he never should return to Jove.
But when he knew it was not Ganymede,
170 For under water he was almost dead,

---

7. Directly overhead, where it appears to be farther off than when low in the sky.
8. I.e., it was apparent.
9. Neptune, god of the sea. "Triton": his son and trumpeter.

1. A beautiful young Trojan boy abducted by Jove to serve as his cup-bearer; the sexual nature of their relationship was a topic of great interest during the Renaissance.

He heaved him up, and looking on his face,
Beat down the bold waves with his triple mace,[2]
Which mounted up, intending to have kissed him,
And fell in drops like tears, because they missed him.
175   Leander, being up, began to swim,
And looking back, saw Neptune follow him;
Whereat aghast, the poor soul gan to cry:
"Oh, let me visit Hero ere I die!"
The god put Helle's[3] bracelet on his arm,
180   And swore the sea should never do him harm.
He clapped his plump cheeks, with his tresses played,
And smiling wantonly, his love bewrayed.°   *revealed*
He watched his arms, and as they opened wide,
At every stroke betwixt them would he slide,
185   And steal a kiss, and then run out and dance,
And as he turned, cast many a lustful glance,
And threw him gaudy toys to please his eye,
And dive into the water, and there pry
Upon his breast, his thighs, and every limb,
190   And up again, and close beside him swim,
And talk of love. Leander made reply:
"You are deceived, I am no woman, I."
Thereat smiled Neptune, and then told a tale
How that a shepherd, sitting in a vale,
195   Played with a boy so lovely, fair, and kind,
As for his love both earth and heaven pined;
That of the cooling river durst not drink
Lest water nymphs should pull him from the brink;
And when he sported in the fragrant lawns,
200   Goat-footed satyrs and up-staring fauns
Would steal him thence. Ere half this tale was done,
"Ay me," Leander cried, "th' enamored sun,
That now should shine on Thetis' glassy bower,[4]
Descends upon my radiant Hero's tower.
205   Oh, that these tardy arms of mine were wings!"
And as he spake, upon the waves he springs.
Neptune was angry that he gave no ear,
And in his heart revenging malice bare;
He flung at him his mace, but as it went
210   He called it in, for love made him repent.
The mace returning back, his own hand hit,
As meaning to be venged for darting it.
When this fresh bleeding wound Leander viewed,
His color went and came, as if he rued
215   The grief which Neptune felt. In gentle breasts
Relenting thoughts, remorse, and pity rests;
And who have hard hearts and obdurate minds
But vicious, harebrained, and illiterate hinds?°   *rustics*

---

2. The three-pronged fork carried by Neptune.
3. Fleeing from her stepmother with her brother Phrixus on the back of a wonderful golden ram that bore them through the air, Helle fell into the strait that separates Europe and Asia, whence the name Hellespont. Marlowe seems to have invented the detail of the bracelet.
4. I.e., the sea. Thetis was a daughter of the sea god Nereus.

The god, seeing him with pity to be moved,
220 Thereon concluded that he was beloved.
(Love is too full of faith, too credulous,
With folly and false hope deluding us.)
Wherefore, Leander's fancy to surprise,
To the rich ocean for gifts he flies.
225 'Tis wisdom to give much; a gift prevails
When deep persuading oratory fails.
    By this, Leander, being near the land,
Cast down his weary feet and felt the sand.
Breathless albeit he were, he rested not
230 Till to the solitary tower he got,
And knocked and called, at which celestial noise
The longing heart of Hero much more joys
Than nymphs or shepherds when the timbrel° rings,   *tambourine*
Or crooked° dolphin when the sailor sings;   *curving*
235 She stayed not for her robes, but straight arose,
And drunk with gladness, to the door she goes;
Where seeing a naked man, she screeched for fear,
(Such sights as this to tender maids are rare)
And ran into the dark herself to hide.
240 Rich jewels in the dark are soonest spied;
Unto her was he led, or rather drawn,
By those white limbs which sparkled through the lawn.
The nearer that he came, the more she fled,
And seeking refuge, slipped into her bed.
245 Whereon Leander sitting, thus began,
Through numbing cold all feeble, faint, and wan:°   *pale*
    "If not for love, yet, love, for pity sake,
Me in thy bed and maiden bosom take;
At least vouchsafe these arms some little room,
250 Who, hoping to embrace thee, cheerly° swum;   *gladly*
This head was beat with many a churlish billow,
And therefore let it rest upon thy pillow."
Herewith affrighted Hero shrunk away,
And in her lukewarm place Leander lay,
255 Whose lively heat like fire from heaven fet,°   *fetched*
Would animate gross clay, and higher set
The drooping thoughts of base declining souls,
Than dreary° Mars carousing nectar bowls.   *cruel, bloody*
His hands he cast upon her like a snare;
260 She, overcome with shame and sallow° fear,   *pale, yellowish*
Like chaste Diana, when Actaeon spied her,[5]
Being suddenly betrayed, dived down to hide her;
And as her silver body downward went,
With both her hands she made the bed a tent,
265 And in her own mind thought herself secure,
O'ercast with dim and darksome coverture.
And now she lets him whisper in her ear,
Flatter, entreat, promise, protest, and swear;
Yet ever as he greedily assayed

---

5. Actaeon, a hunter who saw the naked Diana about to bathe in her favorite pool; as punishment, he was turned into a stag and killed by hounds.

270 To touch those dainties, she the harpy[6] played,
And every limb did, as a soldier stout,
Defend the fort and keep the foeman out;
For though the rising ivory mount he scaled,
Which is with azure circling lines empaled,
275 Much like a globe (a globe may I term this,
By which love sails to regions full of bliss)
Yet there with Sisyphus[7] he toiled in vain,
Till gentle parley did the truce obtain.
Wherein Leander on her quivering breast,
280 Breathless spoke something, and sighed out the rest;
Which so prevailed, as he with small ado
Enclosed her in his arms and kissed her too.
And every kiss to her was as a charm,
And to Leander as a fresh alarm,°   summons to action
285 So that the truce was broke, and she, alas,
Poor silly maiden, at his mercy was.
Love is not full of pity, as men say,
But deaf and cruel where he means to prey.
Even as a bird, which in our hands we wring,
290 Forth plungeth and oft flutters with her wing,
She trembling strove; this strife of hers, like that
Which made the world, another world begat
Of unknown joy. Treason was in her thought,
And cunningly to yield herself she sought.
295 Seeming not won, yet won she was at length;
In such wars women use but half their strength.
Leander now, like Theban Hercules,
Entered the orchard of th' Hesperides,[8]
Whose fruit none rightly can describe but he
300 That pulls or shakes it from the golden tree.
And now she wished this night were never done,
And sighed to think upon th' approaching sun;
For much it grieved her that the bright daylight
Should know the pleasure of this blessed night,
305 And them like Mars and Erycine[9] display,
Both in each other's arms chained as they lay.
Again she knew not how to frame her look,
Or speak to him who in a moment took
That which so long, so charily she kept;
310 And fain by stealth away she would have crept,
And to some corner secretly have gone,
Leaving Leander in the bed alone.
But as her naked feet were whipping out,
He on the sudden clinged her so about,
315 That mermaid-like unto the floor she slid,
One half appeared, the other half was hid.

---

6. Harpies were often pictured as hideous crea-
tures, half woman and half bird; several harpies
seized the meal of an old prophet in Virgil's
Aeneid.
7. Sisyphus was condemned to Hades and made

to roll a stone uphill forever.
8. Daughters of Atlas and custodians of a wonder-
ful tree that bore golden apples.
9. Venus; see note to First Sestiad, line 151.

Thus near the bed she blushing stood upright,
And from her countenance behold ye might
A kind of twilight break, which through the hair,
320 As from an orient cloud, glimpse here and there;
And round about the chamber this false morn
Brought forth the day before the day was born.
So Hero's ruddy cheek Hero betrayed,
And her all naked to his sight displayed;
325 Whence his admiring eyes more pleasure took
Than Dis[1] on heaps of gold fixing his look.
By this, Apollo's golden harp began
To sound forth music to the ocean;[2]
Which watchful Hesperus no sooner heard,
330 But he the day-bright-bearing car prepared,
And ran before, as harbinger of light,
And with his flaring beams mocked ugly night
Till she, o'ercome with anguish, shame, and rage,
Danged° down to hell her loathsome carriage.   *drove violently*
                                                    1598

The Passionate Shepherd to His Love[3]

Come live with me and be my love,
And we will all the pleasures prove°   *try*
That valleys, groves, hills, and fields,
Woods, or steepy mountain yields.

5   And we will sit upon the rocks,
Seeing the shepherds feed their flocks,
By shallow rivers to whose falls
Melodious birds sing madrigals.

And I will make thee beds of roses
10   And a thousand fragrant posies,
A cap of flowers, and a kirtle°   *gown*
Embroidered all with leaves of myrtle;

A gown made of the finest wool
Which from our pretty lambs we pull;
15   Fair lined slippers for the cold,
With buckles of the purest gold;

A belt of straw and ivy buds,
With coral clasps and amber studs:°   *buttons*
And if these pleasures may thee move,
20   Come live with me, and be my love.

---

1. Pluto, god of the underworld and god of wealth.
2. Presaging the rising of the sun. Hesperus is normally the evening star; Marlowe here applies the name to the morning star, usually called Phosphorus.
3. See the response by Sir Walter Ralegh, "The Nymph's Reply to the Shepherd" (p. 140); also see C. Day Lewis' version of this poem (pp. 1341–42).

The shepherds' swains shall dance and sing
For thy delight each May morning:
If these delights thy mind may move,
Then live with me and be my love.

1599, 1600

WILLIAM SHAKESPEARE
1564–1616

From Sonnets

To the Only Begetter of
These Ensuing Sonnets
MR. W. H. All Happiness
and That Eternity
Promised
By
Our Ever-Living Poet
Wisheth
the Well-Wishing
Adventurer in
Setting Forth
T.T.[1]

1

From fairest creatures we desire increase,
That thereby beauty's rose might never die,
But as the riper should by time decease,
His tender° heir might bear his memory;   young
5   But thou, contracted[2] to thine own bright eyes,
Feed'st thy light's flame with self-substantial[3] fuel,
Making a famine where abundance lies,
Thyself thy foe, to thy sweet self too cruel.
Thou that art now the world's fresh ornament
10   And only° herald to the gaudy spring,   principal, solitary
Within thine own bud buriest thy content,[4]
And, tender churl, mak'st waste in niggarding.[5]
    Pity the world, or else this glutton be,
    To eat the world's due, by the grave and thee.

1. There is much critical debate about this dedication and its first set of initials (the second set refers to the publisher, Thomas Thorpe). "Mr. W. H." has been identified with William Herbert, earl of Pembroke, and also with Henry Wriothesley, earl of Southampton; the former is a dedicatee of the volume of Shakespeare's plays known as the First Folio, while the latter is the dedicatee of Shakespeare's narrative poems *Venus and Adonis* and *Lucrece*. Patrons were often flatteringly depicted as "begetters" of poems, and it is therefore tempting to see an association between "Mr. W. H." and the beloved young man addressed in many of Shakespeare's sonnets, especially because the opening poems in the sequence (1–17) stress the young man's need to marry and beget heirs. There is, however, no clear evidence identifying a specific historical person either with the young man addressed in the sonnets or with the "Dark Lady" evoked as the third member of the erotic triangle Shakespeare dramatizes in these poems. The sonnets evidently circulated in manuscript for some years before they were first published as a group in 1609 (a few appeared separately in anthologies). There is no evidence that the ordering of the 153 poems in the 1609 Quarto reflects authorial design.
2. Betrothed; also implying "withdrawn into," shrunken (not increased).
3. Of your own (unique) substance.
4. What contents you and also what you contain (generative potential).
5. Hoarding; "tender churl": gentle boor.

3

Look in thy glass° and tell the face thou viewest,   *mirror*
Now is the time that face should form another,
Whose fresh repair[6] if now thou not renewest,
Thou dost beguile the world, unbless some mother.
5   For where is she so fair whose uneared[7] womb
Disdains the tillage of thy husbandry?
Or who is he so fond° will be the tomb   *foolish*
Of his self-love, to stop posterity?
Thou art thy mother's glass, and she in thee
10 Calls back the lovely April of her prime;
So thou through windows of thine age shalt see,
Despite of wrinkles, this thy golden time.
    But if thou live rememb'red not to be,
    Die single, and thine image dies with thee.

12

When I do count the clock that tells the time,
And see the brave° day sunk in hideous night;   *resplendent*
When I behold the violet past prime,
And sable curls all silvered o'er with white;
5   When lofty trees I see barren of leaves,
Which erst° from heat did canopy the herd,   *formerly*
And summer's green all girded up in sheaves,
Borne on the bier[8] with white and bristly beard,
Then of thy beauty do I question make,
10 That thou among the wastes of time must go,
Since sweets and beauties do themselves forsake
And die as fast as they see others grow;
    And nothing 'gainst Time's scythe can make defense
    Save breed,° to brave° him when he takes thee hence.   *progeny / defy*

18

Shall I compare thee to a summer's day?
Thou art more lovely and more temperate:
Rough winds do shake the darling buds of May,
And summer's lease° hath all too short a date;   *alloted time*
5   Sometimes too hot the eye of heaven shines,
And often is his gold complexion dimmed;
And every fair from fair sometimes declines,
By chance or nature's changing course untrimmed;[9]
But thy eternal summer shall not fade,
10 Nor lose possession of that fair thou ow'st;[1]
Nor shall death brag thou wand'rest in his shade,
When in eternal lines to Time thou grow'st:[2]
    So long as men can breathe, or eyes can see,
    So long lives this, and this gives life to thee.

---

6. "Fresh repair": unfaded condition.
7. Immature; also, unplowed.
8. A frame for carrying harvested grain; also, a stand on which a corpse is carried to the grave.

9. Divested of its beauty.
1. Beauty you own, with a play on "owe."
2. I.e., when you are grafted to Time in this immortal poetry.

20

A woman's face, with nature's own hand painted,[3]
Hast thou, the master mistress of my passion—
A woman's gentle heart, but not acquainted
With shifting change, as is false women's fashion;
5 An eye more bright than theirs, less false in rolling,°   *roving*
Gilding the object whereupon it gazeth;
A man in hue all hues in his controlling,
Which steals men's eyes and women's souls amazeth.
And for a woman wert thou first created,
10 Till nature as she wrought thee fell a-doting,
And by addition me of thee defeated,
By adding one thing to my purpose nothing.
    But since she pricked thee out for women's pleasure,
    Mine be thy love and thy love's use their treasure.[4]

29

When, in disgrace[5] with fortune and men's eyes,
I all alone beweep my outcast state,
And trouble deaf heaven with my bootless° cries,   *futile*
And look upon myself, and curse my fate,
5 Wishing me like to one more rich in hope,
Featured° like him, like him with friends possessed,   *formed, handsome*
Desiring this man's art° and that man's scope,[6]   *skill*
With what I most enjoy contented least;
Yet in these thoughts myself almost despising,
10 Haply I think on thee—and then my state,
Like to the lark at break of day arising
From sullen earth, sings hymns at heaven's gate;
    For thy sweet love rememb'red such wealth brings
    That then I scorn to change my state with kings.

30

When to the sessions of sweet silent thought
I summon up[7] remembrance of things past,
I sigh the lack of many a thing I sought,
And with old woes new wail my dear time's waste:
5 Then can I drown an eye, unused to flow,
For precious friends hid in death's dateless° night,   *endless*
And weep afresh love's long since canceled woe,
And moan the expense° of many a vanished sight: *loss*
Then can I grieve at grievances foregone,°   *past*
10 And heavily from woe to woe tell° o'er   *count*
The sad account[8] of fore-bemoanèd moan,
Which I new pay as if not paid before.

---

3. I.e., not made up with cosmetics.
4. Modern editors usually punctuate this line with a comma after "love," but some recent critics argue instead for a comma after "use"; we follow the 1609 Quarto in not punctuating the line internally, thereby allowing for more than one interpre-

tation of the final couplet.
5. "In disgrace": out of favor.
6. Freedom, range of ability.
7. One may be "summoned" to the "sessions" (sittings) of a court.
8. Report; financial record.

But if the while I think on thee, dear friend,
All losses are restored and sorrows end.

33

Full many a glorious morning have I seen
Flatter the mountain-tops with sovereign eye,
Kissing with golden face the meadows green,
Gilding pale streams with heavenly alchemy;
5 Anon° permit the basest clouds to ride   *soon*
With ugly rack⁹ on his celestial face,
And from the forlorn world his visage hide,
Stealing unseen to west with this disgrace:
Even so my sun one early morn did shine
10 With all-triumphant splendor on my brow;
But, out, alack! he was but one hour mine,
The region cloud¹ hath masked him from me now.
    Yet him for this my love no whit disdaineth;
    Suns of the world may stain² when heaven's sun staineth.

55

Not marble, nor the gilded monuments
Of princes, shall outlive this powerful rhyme;
But you shall shine more bright in these contènts
Than unswept stone, besmeared with sluttish time.
5 When wasteful war shall statues overturn,
And broils root out the work of masonry,³
Nor Mars his⁴ sword nor war's quick fire shall burn
The living record of your memory.
'Gainst death and all-oblivious enmity⁵
10 Shall you pace forth; your praise shall still find room
Even in the eyes of all posterity
That wear this world out to the ending doom.°   *Judgment Day*
    So, till the judgment that yourself arise,⁶
    You live in this, and dwell in lovers' eyes.

65

Since brass, nor⁷ stone, nor earth, nor boundless sea
But sad mortality o'er-sways their power,
How with this rage shall beauty hold a plea,
Whose action is no stronger than a flower?
5 O, how shall summer's honey breath hold out
Against the wrackful° siege of batt'ring days,   *destructive*
When rocks impregnable are not so stout,
Nor gates of steel so strong, but time decays?
O fearful meditation! where, alack,
10 Shall time's best jewel from time's chest lie hid?

---

9. A wind-driven mass of high, broken clouds.
1. I.e., the clouds in the vicinity.
2. I.e., be stained.
3. Products of the stonemason's work; made of stone. "Broils": disturbances.

4. I.e., Mars'.
5. The enmity of being forgotten.
6. I.e., until the Judgment Day when ("that") you rise from the dead.
7. I.e., since there is neither brass nor.

Or what strong hand can hold his swift foot back?
Or who his spoil of beauty[8] can forbid?
   O, none, unless this miracle have might,
   That in black ink my love may still shine bright.

71

No longer mourn for me when I am dead
Than you shall hear the surly sullen bell[9]
Give warning to the world that I am fled
From this vile world, with vilest worms to dwell:
5 Nay, if you read this line, remember not
The hand that writ it; for I love you so,
That I in your sweet thoughts would be forgot,
If thinking on me then should make you woe.
Oh, if, I say, you look upon this verse
10 When I (perhaps) compounded am with clay,
Do not so much as my poor name rehearse,
But let your love even with my life decay;
   Lest the wise world should look into your moan,
   And mock you with me after I am gone.

73

That time of year thou mayst in me behold
When yellow leaves, or none, or few, do hang
Upon those boughs which shake against the cold,
Bare ruined choirs, where late the sweet birds sang.
5 In me thou see'st the twilight of such day
As after sunset fadeth in the west;
Which by and by black night doth take away,
Death's second self, that seals up all in rest.
In me thou see'st the glowing of such fire,
10 That on the ashes of his youth doth lie,
As the deathbed whereon it must expire,
Consumed with that which it was nourished by.
   This thou perceiv'st, which makes thy love more strong,
   To love that well which thou must leave ere long.

94

They that have power to hurt and will do none,
That do not do the thing they most do show,[1]
Who, moving others, are themselves as stone,
Unmovèd, cold, and to temptation slow;
5 They rightly do inherit heaven's graces
And husband nature's riches from expense;[2]
They are the lords and owners of their faces,
Others but stewards° of their excellence.   *hired managers*
The summer's flower is to the summer sweet,

---

8. Ravaging of beauty; the Quarto has "or" for "of," and some modern editors follow that reading.
9. The bell rang to announce the death of a member of the parish, one stroke for each year he or she had lived.
1. I.e., what their appearance indicates they will do.
2. I.e., guard against squandering nature's riches.

10 Though to itself it only live and die,
But if that flower with base infection meet,
The basest weed outbraves° his dignity: *surpasses*
    For sweetest things turn sourest by their deeds;
    Lilies that fester smell far worse than weeds.

106

When in the chronicle of wasted° time   *past, destroyed*
I see descriptions of the fairest wights,°   *persons*
And beauty making beautiful old rhyme
In praise of ladies dead and lovely knights,
5 Then, in the blazon³ of sweet beauty's best,
Of hand, of foot, of lip, of eye, of brow,
I see their antique pen would have expressed
Even such a beauty as you master now.
So all their praises are but prophecies
10 Of this our time, all you prefiguring;
And, for° they looked but with divining eyes,   *because*
They had not skill enough your worth to sing:
    For we, which now behold these present days,
    Have eyes to wonder, but lack tongues to praise.

107

Not mine own fears, nor the prophetic soul
Of the wide world dreaming on things to come,
Can yet the lease of my true love control,
Supposed as forfeit to a cònfined doom.⁴
5 The mortal moon⁵ hath her eclipse endured,
And the sad augurs mock their own presage;°   *prediction*
Incertainties now crown themselves assured,
And peace proclaims olives of endless age.
Now with the drops of this most balmy time
10 My love looks fresh, and death to me subscribes,°   *submits*
Since, spite of him, I'll live in this poor rhyme,
While he insults o'er dull and speechless tribes:
    And thou in this shalt find thy monument,
    When tyrants' crests and tombs of brass are spent.°   *destroyed*

116

Let me not to the marriage of true minds
Admit impediments. Love is not love
Which alters when it alteration finds,
Or bends with the remover to remove:
5 Oh, no! it is an ever-fixèd mark,
That looks on tempests and is never shaken;
It is the star to every wandering bark,

3. A catalog of attributes; a literary form character-ized by a standardized description of the woman's body parts.
4. Playing on metaphors of real estate, the lines suggest that despite his fears, the poet's love has not yet suffered the fate of being limited ("con-fined") by death.
5. Queen Elizabeth, whose sixty-third year had been erroneously anticipated by astrologers ("augurs") as a time of disaster.

Whose worth's unknown, although his height be taken.[6]
Love's not Time's fool, though rosy lips and cheeks
Within his bending sickle's compass come;
Love alters not with his brief hours and weeks,
But bears it out even to the edge of doom.[7]
    If this be error and upon me proved,
    I never writ, nor no man ever loved.

129

Th' expense of spirit in a waste of shame
Is lust in action; and till action, lust
Is perjured, murderous, bloody, full of blame,
Savage, extreme, rude, cruel, not to trust;
Enjoyed no sooner but despisèd straight:
Past reason hunted; and no sooner had,
Past reason hated, as a swallowed bait,
On purpose laid to make the taker mad:
Mad in pursuit, and in possession so;
Had, having, and in quest to have, extreme;
A bliss in proof,[8] and proved, a very woe;
Before, a joy proposed; behind, a dream.
    All this the world well knows; yet none knows well
    To shun the heaven that leads men to this hell.

130

My mistress' eyes are nothing like the sun;
Coral is far more red than her lips' red;
If snow be white, why then her breasts are dun;°   *dull grayish brown*
If hairs be wires, black wires grow on her head.
I have seen roses damasked,° red and white,   *variegated*
But no such roses see I in her cheeks;
And in some perfumes is there more delight
Than in the breath that from my mistress reeks.
I love to hear her speak, yet well I know
That music hath a far more pleasing sound;
I grant I never saw a goddess go;°   *walk*
My mistress, when she walks, treads on the ground.
    And yet, by heaven, I think my love as rare
    As any she° belied with false compare.   *woman*

138

When my love swears that she is made of truth,
I do believe her, though I know she lies,[9]
That° she might think me some untutored youth,   *so that*
Unlearnèd in the world's false subtleties.
Thus vainly thinking that she thinks me young,
Although she knows my days are past the best,[1]

---

6. I.e., although its elevation may be measured.
7. Judgment Day, the end of the world.
8. I.e., in the experience.
9. Does not tell the truth, with a pun on "lies"

with men.
1. This sonnet was first published in 1599, in the anthology called *The Passionate Pilgrim*; Shakespeare was then thirty-five.

Simply I credit her false-speaking tongue:
On both sides thus is simple truth suppressed.
But wherefore says she not she is unjust?[2]
10 And wherefore say not I that I am old?
Oh, love's best habit is in seeming trust,
And age in love loves not to have years told.
    Therefore I lie with her and she with me,
    And in our faults by lies we flattered be.

146

Poor soul, the center of my sinful earth,
Lord of[3] these rebel powers that thee array,°   *dress, deck out*
Why dost thou pine within and suffer dearth,
Painting thy outward walls so costly gay?
5 Why so large cost, having so short a lease,
Dost thou upon thy fading mansion[4] spend?
Shall worms, inheritors of this excess,
Eat up thy charge? Is this thy body's end?
Then, soul, live thou upon thy servant's loss,
10 And let that pine to[5] aggravate° thy store;   *increase*
Buy terms divine in selling hours of dross;[6]
Within be fed, without be rich no more.
    So shalt thou feed on death, that feeds on men,
    And death once dead, there's no more dying then.

                                            1609

The Phoenix and the Turtle[7]

Let the bird[8] of loudest lay,°   *song*
On the sole° Arabian tree,   *unique*
Herald sad° and trumpet be,   *solemn*
To whose sound chaste wings obey.

5 But thou shrieking harbinger,[9]
Foul precurrer° of the fiend,[1]   *forerunner*
Augur of the fever's end,[2]
To this troop come thou not near!

From this session interdict°   *forbid*
10 Every fowl of tyrant wing,[3]

---

2. I.e., why does she not say that she is unjust?
3. The 1609 Quarto repeats "My sinful earth," apparently a mistake, in place of "Lord of" (an editorial conjecture) at the beginning of this line. Other possibilities have been suggested, e.g., "Rebuke," "Thrall to," "Pressed by."
4. Dwelling place, or house.
5. "Pine to": suffer in order to; "that": i.e., the body.
6. I.e., purchase ages of immortality through selling hours of mortal time; "dross": rubbish.
7. Turtledove, famous for steadfastness in love.

The phoenix is a legendary bird, the only one of its kind. It is represented as living five hundred years in the Arabian desert before setting itself on fire, then rising anew from its own ashes.
8. This bird's identity has been much debated; most critics agree that it is not the phoenix, which left "no posterity" (line 59).
9. I.e., the screech owl, harbinger of death.
1. I.e., Satan.
2. I.e., presager of death.
3. I.e., every predator.

Save the eagle, feathered king:
Keep the obsequy° so strict.　　　　　　　　　　*funeral rites*

Let the priest in surplice° white,　　　　　　　*vestment*
That defunctive° music can,°　　　　　　　*funereal / knows*
15　Be the death-divining swan,[4]
Lest the requiem lack his right.[5]

And thou treble-dated crow,[6]
That thy sable° gender mak'st　　　　　　　　　*black*
With the breath thou giv'st and tak'st,
20　'Mongst our mourners shalt thou go.

Here the anthem doth commence:
Love and constancy is dead,
Phoenix and the turtle fled
In a mutual flame from hence.

25　So they loved as love in twain
Had the essence but in one;
Two distincts, division none:
Number there in love was slain.[7]

Hearts remote, yet not asunder;
30　Distance, and no space was seen
'Twixt this turtle and his queen;
But in them it were a wonder.[8]

So between them love did shine
That the turtle saw his right
35　Flaming in the phoenix' sight:°　　　　　　　*eyes*
Either was the other's mine.[9]

Property was thus appalled,
That the self[1] was not the same;
Single nature's double name
40　Neither two nor one was called.

Reason, in itself confounded,
Saw division grow together,
To themselves yet either neither,
Simple were so well compounded;

45　That it cried, "How true a twain
Seemeth this concordant one!

---

4. Since the swan was said to sing only as its death
drew near, it "divined" (knew) the time of its
death.
5. Its due ceremony.
6. The crow was supposed to live three times
longer than humans and to conceive its young
("sable gender") through its beak.
7. Refers to the Aristotelian theory that "one is no

number," as Marlowe puts it in *Hero and Leander*
(l. 255, p. 221).
8. I.e., in anyone except ("but") them, it would
have been a wonder.
9. I.e., self; with a pun on source of (mineral)
wealth.
1. Single nature. "Property": essential quality.

Love hath reason, reason none,
If what parts can so remain."[2]

Whereupon it made this threne[3]
50 To the phoenix and the dove,
Co-supremes and stars of love,
As chorus to their tragic scene.

Threnos

Beauty, truth, and rarity,
Grace in all simplicity,
55 Here enclosed in cinders lie.

Death is now the phoenix' nest;
And the turtle's loyal breast
To eternity doth rest,

Leaving no posterity:
60 'Twas not their infirmity,
It was married chastity.

Truth may seem, but cannot be;
Beauty brag, but 'tis not she:
Truth and Beauty buried be.

65 To this urn let those repair
That are either true or fair;
For these dead birds sigh a prayer.

1601

Songs from the Plays

When Daisies Pied[4]

Spring

When daisies pied° and violets blue   *variegated*
  And lady-smocks all silver-white
And cuckoo-buds of yellow hue[5]
  Do paint the meadows with delight,
5 The cuckoo then, on every tree,
Mocks married men;[6] for thus sings he,
       Cuckoo;
Cuckoo, cuckoo: Oh word of fear,
Unpleasing to a married ear!

2. I.e., if what is separate can remain joined, then reason yields to love as more reasonable.
3. Threnos or threnody (Greek), a lyrical lament over the dead.
4. This song concludes *Love's Labour's Lost*. Announced as a "Dialogue . . . in praise of the Owl and the Cuckoo," it provides a lyric commentary on the bittersweet mood that pervades the play's final scene.
5. Modern commentators differ in identifying these flowers.
6. The cuckoo's song was often translated as "cuckold," a word for a husband whose wife is unfaithful.

10   When shepherds pipe on oaten straws,[7]
            And merry larks[8] are plowmen's clocks,
        When turtles tread, and rooks, and daws,[9]
            And maidens bleach their summer smocks,
        The cuckoo then, on every tree,
15   Mocks married men; for thus sings he,
                        Cuckoo;
        Cuckoo, cuckoo: Oh word of fear,
        Unpleasing to a married ear!

                    Winter

        When icicles hang by the wall
20   And Dick the shepherd blows his nail[1]
        And Tom bears logs into the hall,
            And milk comes frozen home in pail.
        When blood is nipped and ways be foul,
        Then nightly sings the staring owl,
25   Tu-who;
        Tu-whit, tu-who: a merry note,
        While greasy Joan doth keel[2] the pot.

        When all aloud the wind doth blow,
            And coughing drowns the parson's saw,°   *wise saying*
30   And birds sit brooding in the snow,
            And Marian's nose looks red and raw,
        When roasted crabs° hiss in the bowl,   *crab apples*
        Then nightly sings the staring owl,
                        Tu-who;
35   Tu-whit, tu-who: a merry note
        While greasy Joan doth keel the pot.

1595?   1598

Under the Greenwood Tree[3]

        Under the greenwood tree
        Who loves to lie with me,
            And turn° his merry note   *attune*
            Unto the sweet bird's throat,
5   Come hither, come hither, come hither:
                Here shall he see
                No enemy
        But winter and rough weather.

        Who doth ambition shun
10   And loves to live i' the sun,
            Seeking the food he eats,
            And pleased with what he gets,

---

7. Reed pipes.
8. "Larks" sing at sunrise.
9. Two kinds of crows; "when turtles tread": i.e., when turtledoves mate.
1. I.e., breathes on his fingers to warm them; also, waits patiently while he has nothing to do.

2. Keep from boiling over by stirring.
3. From *As You Like It* (2.5). Sung by Amiens, a lord attending the banished duke in the Forest of Arden, the song addresses the play's concern with the traditional opposition between pastoral and courtly modes of life.

Come hither, come hither, come hither:
   Here shall he see
15   No enemy
   But winter and rough weather.

1599?   1623

Blow, Blow, Thou Winter Wind[4]

Blow, blow, thou winter wind,
  Thou art not so unkind
    As man's ingratitude;
  Thy tooth is not so keen,
5 Because thou art not seen,
    Although thy breath be rude.
Heigh-ho! sing, heigh-ho! unto the green holly:[5]
Most friendship is feigning, most loving mere folly:
Then, heigh-ho, the holly!
10   *This life is most jolly.*

Freeze, freeze, thou bitter sky,
  That dost not bite so nigh
    As benefits forgot:
  Though thou the waters warp,[6]
15   Thy sting is not so sharp
    As friend remembered not.
Heigh-ho! sing, heigh-ho! unto the green holly . . .

1599?   1623

It Was a Lover and His Lass[7]

It was a lover and his lass,
  With a hey, and a ho, and a hey nonino,
That o'er the green corn field[8] did pass
  In springtime, the only pretty ring time,[9]
5 *When birds do sing, hey ding a ding, ding:*
  Sweet lovers love the spring.

Between the acres of the rye,[1]
  With a hey, and a ho, and a hey nonino,
These pretty country folks would lie,
10   *In springtime, the only pretty ring time . . .*

This carol° they began that hour,   song
  With a hey, and a ho, and a hey nonino,
How that a life was but a flower
  In springtime, the only pretty ring time . . .

4. From *As You Like It* (2.7). Sung by Amiens, a lord attending the banished duke in the Forest of Arden, this lyric elaborates on the play's thematic contrast between nature and human behavior.
5. An emblem of mirth.
6. I.e., freeze.
7. From *As You Like It* (5.3). Sung by two pages to the clown, Touchstone, and the "country wench," Audrey; in the next (and final) scene, this couple (and two other couples) will marry.
8. Wheat field.
9. Marriage season.
1. On unplowed ground between the planted fields.

15 And therefore take the present time,
      With a hey, and a ho, and a hey nonino;
    For love is crownèd with the prime°   springtime
      In springtime, the only pretty ring time . . .

1599?   1623

Oh Mistress Mine²

Oh mistress mine! where are you roaming?
Oh! stay and hear; your true love's coming,
    That can sing both high and low.
Trip no further, pretty sweeting;
5 Journeys end in lovers meeting,
    Every wise man's son doth know.

What is love? 'tis not hereafter;
Present mirth hath present laughter;
    What's to come is still unsure:
10 In delay there lies no plenty;
    Then come kiss me, sweet and twenty,
    Youth's a stuff will not endure.

1602   1623

Come Away, Come Away, Death³

Come away, come away, death,
    And in sad cypress⁴ let me be laid.
Fly away, fly away, breath;
    I am slain by a fair cruel maid.
5 My shroud of white, stuck all with yew,⁵
        O, prepare it!
My part of death, no one so true
        Did share it.

Not a flower, not a flower sweet,
10   On my black coffin let there be strown.
Not a friend, not a friend greet
    My poor corpse, where my bones shall be thrown.
A thousand thousand sighs to save,
        Lay me, O, where
15 Sad true lover never find my grave,
        To weep there!

1602   1623

2. From *Twelfth Night* (2.3). Sung by the clown, Feste, in response to a request by Sir Toby and Sir Andrew for a "love-song."
3. From *Twelfth Night* (2.4). Sung by the clown, Feste, in response to the lovesick duke's melan-choly request for a song.
4. Often used to decorate graves.
5. A tree symbolizing sadness, often planted in churchyards.

When That I Was and a Little Tiny Boy[6]

When that I was and a little tiny boy,
  With hey, ho, the wind and the rain,
A foolish thing was but a toy,[7]
  For the rain it raineth every day.

5 But when I came to man's estate,°   state, condition
  With hey, ho, the wind and the rain,
'Gainst knaves and thieves men shut their gate,
  For the rain it raineth every day.

But when I came, alas! to wive,
10 With hey, ho, the wind and the rain,
By swaggering° could I never thrive,   blustering
  For the rain it raineth every day.

But when I came unto my beds,
  With hey, ho, the wind and the rain,
15 With toss-pots° still had drunken heads,   drunkards
  For the rain it raineth every day.

A great while ago the world begun,
  With hey, ho, the wind and the rain,
But that's all one, our play is done,
20 And we'll strive to please you every day.

1602   1623

Fear No More the Heat o' the Sun[8]

Fear no more the heat o' the sun,
  Nor the furious winter's rages;
Thou thy worldly task hast done,
  Home art gone, and ta'en thy wages:
5 Golden lads and girls all must,
  As chimney-sweepers, come to dust.

Fear no more the frown o' the great;
  Thou art past the tyrant's stroke;
Care no more to clothe and eat;
10 To thee the reed is as the oak:[9]
The scepter, learning, physic,[1] must
  All follow this, and come to dust.

---

6. Sung by the clown Feste to conclude *Twelfth Night*.
7. I.e., my mischief was not taken seriously; "toy": trifle.
8. From *Cymbeline* (4.2). A lament sung by two singers for the young boy named Fidele, who is actually Imogen in disguise; the singers mistakenly believe that "he" is dead.
9. I.e., to you, what is fragile ("the reed") is the same as what is enduring ("the oak").
1. Medicine; "scepter": ruling power.

Fear no more the lightning flash,
  Nor the all-dreaded thunder stone;[2]
15 Fear not slander, censure rash;
  Thou hast finished joy and moan:
All lovers young, all lovers must
Consign to thee, and come to dust.[3]

No exorciser harm thee!
20 Nor no witchcraft charm thee!
Ghost unlaid forbear thee!
Nothing ill come near thee!
Quiet consummation have;
And renownèd be thy grave!

1610?   1623

When Daffodils Begin to Peer[4]

When daffodils begin to peer,
  With heigh! the doxy[5] over the dale,
Why, then comes in the sweet o' the year;
  For the red blood reigns in the winter's pale.[6]

5 The white sheet bleaching on the hedge,
  With heigh! the sweet birds, Oh, how they sing!
Doth set my pugging° tooth on edge;   *thieving*
  For a quart of ale is a dish for a king.

The lark, that tirra-lirra chants,
10 With heigh! with heigh! the thrush and the jay,
Are summer songs for me and my aunts,[7]
  While we lie tumbling in the hay.

1611   1623

Full Fathom Five[8]

Full fathom five thy father lies;
  Of his bones are coral made;
Those are pearls that were his eyes:
  Nothing of him that doth fade,
5 But doth suffer a sea change
Into something rich and strange.
Sea nymphs hourly ring his knell:
  Ding-dong.
Hark! now I hear them—Ding-dong, bell.

1611   1623

2. Thunder was thought to be caused by meteorites falling from the sky.
3. I.e., accept the same terms that have governed you.
4. From *The Winter's Tale* (4.3). Sung by the rogue Autolycus, to himself.
5. Beggar's lover; a prostitute.
6. Territory, as well as lack of color.
7. Sweethearts; prostitutes.
8. From *The Tempest* (1.2). Ariel, the airy spirit of the enchanted isle, sings this song to lead the shipwrecked Ferdinand, prince of Naples, to Prospero.

Where the Bee Sucks, There Suck I[9]

Where the bee sucks, there suck I:
In a cowslip's bell I lie;
There I couch when owls do cry.
On the bat's back I do fly
5   After summer merrily.
Merrily, merrily shall I live now
Under the blossom that hangs on the bough.

1611   1623

THOMAS CAMPION

1567–1620

My Sweetest Lesbia[1]

My sweetest Lesbia, let us live and love,
And though the sager sort our deeds reprove,
Let us not weigh° them. Heaven's great lamps do dive   *heed*
Into their west, and straight again revive,
5 But soon as once set is our little light,
Then must we sleep one ever-during night.

If all would lead their lives in love like me,
Then bloody swords and armor should not be;
No drum nor trumpet peaceful sleeps should move,
10 Unless alarm came from the camp of love.
But fools do live, and waste their little light,
And seek with pain their ever-during night.

When timely death my life and fortune ends,
Let not my hearse be vexed with mourning friends,
15 But let all lovers, rich in triumph, come
And with sweet pastimes grace my happy tomb;
And Lesbia, close up thou my little light,
And crown with love my ever-during night.

1601

I Care Not for These Ladies

I care not for these ladies,
That must be wooed and prayed:
Give me kind Amaryllis,
The wanton country maid.
5 Nature art disdaineth,
Her beauty is her own.

---

9. From *The Tempest* (1.2). Ariel, the airy spirit of the enchanted isle, sings this song in anticipation of his approaching freedom from servitude.

1. The Roman poet Catullus (87?–54 B.C.) sang the praises of his beloved Lesbia in a poem here imitated and partly translated by Campion.

Her when we court and kiss,
She cries, "Forsooth, let go!"
But when we come where comfort is,
10 She never will say no.

If I love Amaryllis,
She gives me fruit and flowers:
But if we love these ladies,
We must give golden showers.[2]
15 Give them gold, that sell love,
Give me the nut-brown lass,
    Who, when we court and kiss,
    She cries, "Forsooth, let go!"
But when we come where comfort is,
20 She never will say no.

These ladies must have pillows,
And beds by strangers wrought;
Give me a bower° of willows,   bedchamber
Of moss and leaves unbought,
25 And fresh Amaryllis,
With milk and honey fed;
    Who, when we court and kiss,
    She cries, "Forsooth, let go!"
But when we come where comfort is,
30 She never will say no.

                                                1601

Follow Thy Fair Sun

Follow thy fair sun, unhappy shadow;
Though thou be black as night,
And she made all of light,
Yet follow thy fair sun, unhappy shadow.

5 Follow her whose light thy light depriveth;
Though here thou liv'st disgraced,
And she in heaven is placed,
Yet follow her whose light the world reviveth!

Follow those pure beams whose beauty burneth,
10 That so have scorchèd thee,
As thou still black must be,[3]
Till her kind beams thy black to brightness turneth.

Follow her while yet her glory shineth;
There comes a luckless night,
15 That will dim all her light;
And this the black unhappy shade divineth.

2. An allusion to the Greek myth in which Jove
takes the form of a shower of gold to ravish Danae.

3. In Renaissance England, dark skins were often
held to be caused by the sun's burning.

Follow still since so thy fates ordained;
The sun must have his shade,
Till both at once do fade;
20 The sun still proved,° the shadow still disdained.   *approved*
                                                            1601

When to Her Lute Corinna Sings

When to her lute Corinna sings,
Her voice revives the leaden strings,
And doth in highest notes appear
As any challenged echo clear;
5 But when she doth of mourning speak,
Ev'n with her sighs the strings do break.

And as her lute doth live or die,
Led by her passion, so must I:
For when of pleasure she doth sing,
10 My thoughts enjoy a sudden spring,
But if she doth of sorrow speak,
Ev'n from my heart the strings do break.

                                                            1601

When Thou Must Home

When thou must home to shades of underground,
And there arrived, a new admirèd guest,
The beauteous spirits do engirt° thee round,   *encircle*
White Iope, blithe° Helen,[4] and the rest,   *happy*
5 To hear the stories of thy finished love
From that smooth tongue whose music hell can move,[5]

Then wilt thou speak of banqueting delights,
Of masques[6] and revels which sweet youth did make,
Of tourneys and great challenges of knights,
10 And all these triumphs for thy beauty's sake;
When thou hast told these honors done to thee,
Then tell, Oh tell, how thou didst murther° me.   *murder*
                                                            1601

Rose-cheeked Laura[7]

Rose-cheeked Laura, come,
Sing thou smoothly with thy beauty's
Silent music, either other
Sweetly gracing.

4. Iope, or Cassiopeia, and Helen of Troy, the first renowned for beauty and vanity, the second for beauty and fickleness.
5. I.e., whose music can move hell.
6. Elaborate court entertainments in which aristo-crats performed a dignified play, usually allegorical and mythological, that ended in a formal dance.
7. This poem exemplifies Campion's interest in quantitative verse (see "Essay on Versification," pp. lxviii–lxix).

5   Lovely forms do flow
      From concent° divinely framed;   *sounds in harmony*
      Heav'n is music, and thy beauty's
          Birth is heavenly.

      These dull notes we sing
10   Discords need for helps to grace them;
      Only beauty purely loving
          Knows no discord,

      But still moves delight,
      Like clear springs renewed by flowing,
15   Ever perfect, ever in them-
          Selves eternal.

                                        1602

Now Winter Nights Enlarge

      Now winter nights enlarge
          The number of their hours;
      And clouds their storms discharge
          Upon the airy towers.
5   Let now the chimneys blaze
          And cups o'erflow with wine,
      Let well-tuned words amaze
          With harmony divine.
      Now yellow waxen lights
10   Shall wait on honey love
      While youthful revels, masques,[8] and courtly sights
          Sleep's leaden spells remove.

      This time doth well dispense
          With[9] lovers' long discourse;
15   Much speech hath some defense,
          Though beauty no remorse.
      All do not all things well;
          Some measures comely tread,[1]
      Some knotted riddles tell,
20   Some poems smoothly read.
      The summer hath his joys,
          And winter his delights;
      Though love and all his pleasures are but toys,
          They shorten tedious nights.

                                        1617

8. Elaborate court entertainments in which aristo-
crats performed a dignified play, usually allegorical
and mythological, that ended in a formal dance.
9. I.e., this time deals indulgently with lovers' long

discourse.
1. I.e., some dance (tread measures) in a beautiful
way.

There Is a Garden in Her Face

There is a garden in her face,
Where roses and white lilies grow,
A heavenly paradise is that place,
Wherein all pleasant fruits do flow.
5   There cherries grow, which none may buy
Till "Cherry ripe!"[2] themselves do cry.

Those cherries fairly do enclose
Of orient pearl a double row,
Which when her lovely laughter shows,
10   They look like rosebuds filled with snow.
Yet them nor peer nor prince can buy,
Till "Cherry ripe!" themselves do cry.

Her eyes like angels watch them still;
Her brows like bended bows do stand,
15   Threatening with piercing frowns to kill
All that attempt with eye or hand
Those sacred cherries to come nigh,
Till "Cherry ripe!" themselves do cry.

1617

THOMAS NASHE

1567–1601

From Summer's Last Will

Spring, the Sweet Spring[1]

Spring, the sweet spring, is the year's pleasant king,
Then blooms each thing, then maids dance in a ring,
Cold doth not sting, the pretty birds do sing:
   Cuckoo, jug-jug, pu-we, to-witta-woo![2]

5   The palm and may[3] make country houses gay,
Lambs frisk and play, the shepherds pipe all day,
And we hear aye birds tune this merry lay:°   *song*
   Cuckoo, jug-jug, pu-we, to-witta-woo!

The fields breathe sweet, the daisies kiss our feet,
10   Young lovers meet, old wives a-sunning sit,
In every street these tunes our ears do greet:
   Cuckoo, jug-jug, pu-we, to-witta-woo!
   Spring, the sweet spring!

---

2. A London street vendor's cry.
1. This song is sung by Ver ("spring" in Latin) in Nashe's allegorical drama *Summer's Last Will and Testament*, performed in 1592 in the palace of the archbishop of Canterbury and first published in 1600.

2. Bird songs of the cuckoo, nightingale, lapwing, owl.
3. Hawthorn blossoms; "palm": perhaps palms left over from the religious celebration known as Palm Sunday, which occurs a week before Easter and commemorates Christ's entry into Jerusalem.

"Adieu, farewell, earth's bliss"[4]

Adieu, farewell, earth's bliss;
This world uncertain is;
Fond° are life's lustful joys;   *foolish*
Death proves them all but toys;°   *trifles*
5 None from his darts can fly;
I am sick, I must die.
    Lord, have mercy on us![5]

Rich men, trust not in wealth,
Gold cannot buy you health;
10 Physic himself must fade.
All things to end are made,
The plague full swift goes by;
I am sick, I must die.
    Lord, have mercy on us!

15 Beauty is but a flower
Which wrinkles will devour;
Brightness falls from the air;
Queens have died young and fair;
Dust hath closed Helen's[6] eye.
20 I am sick, I must die.
    Lord, have mercy on us!

Strength stoops unto the grave,
Worms feed on Hector[7] brave;
Swords may not fight with fate,
25 Earth still holds ope her gate.
"Come, come!" the bells do cry.
I am sick, I must die.
    Lord, have mercy on us.

Wit with his wantonness
30 Tasteth death's bitterness;
Hell's executioner
Hath no ears for to hear
What vain art can reply.
I am sick, I must die.
35   Lord, have mercy on us.

4. Often entitled by editors "A Litany in Time of Plague," this lyric comes from Nashe's allegorical drama *Summer's Last Will and Testament.* Performed during the summer of 1592 before the archbishop of Canterbury, the play repeatedly alludes to the epidemic of plague that had driven the archbishop and his aristocratic guests from London. Summer, who according to the jester-character Will Summers enters the play already sick, requests a "doleful ditty to the lute" that will lament his "near-approaching death."
5. These recurring words come from the Litany, a standard prayer in Church of England services; these words were also inscribed in red letters on plague-stricken houses.
6. Helen was renowned for her beauty, which was said to be the cause of the war between the Trojans and the Greeks; married to Menelaus, she was abducted and/or seduced by Paris, thus initiating the war.
7. Renowned for his bravery, he was the son of Priam and leader of the Trojans against the Greeks.

Haste, therefore, each degree,[8]
To welcome destiny;
Heaven is our heritage,
Earth but a player's stage;
40   Mount we unto the sky.
I am sick, I must die.
    Lord, have mercy on us.

1592   1600

AEMILIA LANYER

1569–1645

From Salve Deus Rex Judaeorum[1]

Sith° *Cynthia*[2] is ascended to that rest   *since*
Of endless joy and true eternity,
That glorious place that cannot be expressed
By any wight° clad in mortality,   *person*
5 In her almighty love so highly blessed,
And crowned with everlasting sov'reignty;
    Where saints and angels do attend her throne,
    And she gives glory unto God alone.

To thee great Countess[3] now I will apply
10 My pen, to write thy never dying fame;
That when to heaven thy blessed soul shall fly,
These lines on earth record thy reverend name:
And to this task I mean my Muse to tie,
Though wanting skill I shall but purchase blame:
15   Pardon (dear Lady) want of woman's wit
    To pen thy praise, when few can equal it.

                *   *   *

745 Now *Pontius Pilate* is to judge the cause[4]
Of faultless *Jesus*, who before him stands;
Who neither hath offended prince, nor laws,
Although he now be brought in woeful bands:

8. Rank; social station.
1. "Hail God, King of the Jews" (Latin); a variant of the inscription on Christ's cross. Lanyer claimed that the title came to her in a dream. This long text is prefaced by a prose address ("To the virtuous Reader") and by a series of dedicatory poems to women patrons including Queen Anne of Denmark (wife of James I), Princess Elizabeth (daughter of Ann and James), and Mary Sidney, countess of Pembroke (see pp. 199–204). To the latter, Lanyer recounts (in four-line stanzas) a dream she had about an idyllic community of virgins. She concludes the dream narrative with praises of the countess's poetry. The main part of Lanyer's poem begins and ends with praise of Margaret Clifford, countess of Cumberland, Lanyer's friend and primary patron. The poem itself is divided into four parts: "The Passion of Christ," "Eve's Apology," "The Tears of the Daughters of Jerusalem," and "The Salutation and Sorrow of the Virgin Mary." The stanzas reprinted here are from the opening of the poem and its second section respectively.
2. A mythological name for the virgin goddess of the moon, frequently applied to Queen Elizabeth I (1533–1603; see pp. 130–32). As a powerful and much-revered queen, she is an appropriate "first muse" for Lanyer to invoke.
3. Margaret Clifford, countess of Cumberland (see note 1, above).
4. Case; Pontius Pilate was the Roman governor of Jerusalem from A.D. 26 to 36. For his condemnation of Christ, see Matthew 27.11–24.

O noble governor, make thou yet a pause,
750   Do not in innocent blood imbrue thy hands;
      But hear the words of thy most worthy wife,
      Who sends to thee, to beg her Savior's life.[5]

      Let barb'rous cruelty far depart from thee,
      And in true justice take affliction's part;
755   Open thine eyes, that thou the truth may'st see,
      Do not the thing that goes against thy heart,
      Condemn not him that must thy Savior be;
      But view his holy life, his good desert.
         Let not us women glory in men's fall,
760   Who had power given to over-rule us all.[6]

Eve's Apology

      Till now[7] your indiscretion sets us free,
      And makes our former fault much less appear;
      Our Mother *Eve*, who tasted of the Tree,
      Giving to *Adam* what she held most dear,
765   Was simply good, and had no power to see,
      The after-coming harm did not appear;
      The subtle° serpent that our sex betrayed,   *crafty*
      Before our fall so sure a plot had laid.

      That undiscerning Ignorance[8] perceived
770   No guile, or craft that was by him° intended: *the serpent*
      For, had she known of what we were bereaved,[9]
      To his request she had not condescended.
      But she (poor soul) by cunning was deceived[1]
      No hurt therein her harmless heart intended:
775   For she alleged God's word, which he denies,
      That they should die, but even as gods, be wise.[2]

      But surely *Adam* cannot be excused,
      Her fault, though great, yet he was most to blame;
      What weakness offered, strength might have refused,[3]
780   Being lord of all, the greater was his shame:

5. In Matthew 27.19, Pontius Pilate's wife sends a message saying "Have thou nothing to do with that just man: for I have suffered many things this day in a dream because of him." Lanyer gives this minor biblical character a major narrative role, making her the dramatic advocate both of Christ and of Eve and hence a fulcrum linking the first and second parts of the poem; Eve's "Apology" flows directly from Pontius Pilate's (unwise) refusal to heed his wife's words about her prophetic dream.
6. According to Genesis 3.16, Eve was punished for the Fall by being made subject to her husband.
7. I.e., men "over-ruled" women until this (imagined) moment of Christ's judgment, when your error in condemning Christ (Pilate's error and by extension that of men in general) frees women by making Eve's sin seem much less by comparison.

8. I.e., Eve.
9. I.e., of eternal life. In Genesis 3, Eve is enticed by the serpent to eat the forbidden fruit, and Adam then eats when she offers it to him. God expels them from Eden, condemning Adam to hard work, Eve to pain in childbirth, and both to suffering and death.
1. Compare 1 Timothy 2.14: "And Adam was not deceived but the woman being deceived was in the transgression."
2. In condensed syntactic form the couplet mimics Eve's argument with the serpent. She put forward God's "word" (that humans would die if they disobeyed), and the serpent denied that idea, arguing instead that humans would become "wise" as gods.
3. I.e., what Eve offered, Adam might have refused.

Although the serpent's craft had her abused,
God's holy word ought all his actions frame:
For he was lord and king of all the earth,
Before poor *Eve* had either life or breath.

785 Who being framed by God's eternal hand,
The perfect'st man that ever breathed on earth,
And from God's mouth received that strait° command,   *strict, narrow*
The breach whereof he knew was present death:
Yea having power to rule both sea and land,
790 Yet with one apple won to lose that breath,
Which God hath breathèd in his beauteous face,
Bringing us all in danger and disgrace.

And then to lay the fault on Patience back,[4]
That we (poor women) must endure it all;
795 We know right well he did discretion lack,
Being not persuaded thereunto at all;
If Eve did err, it was for knowledge sake,
The fruit being fair persuaded him° to fall: *Adam*
No subtle serpent's falsehood did betray him,
800 If he would eat it, who had power to stay him?

Not *Eve*, whose fault was only too much love,
Which made her give this present to her dear,
That what she tasted, he likewise might prove,°   *experience*
Whereby his knowledge might become more clear;
805 He never sought her weakness to reprove,
With those sharp words, which he of God did hear;
Yet men will boast of knowledge, which he took
From *Eve's* fair hand, as from a learnèd book.

If any evil did in her remain,
810 Being made of him, he was the ground of all;[5]
If one of many worlds[6] could lay a stain
Upon our sex, and work so great a fall
To wretched man, by Satan's subtle train;°   *trickery*
What will so foul a fault amongst you all?
815 Her weakness did the serpent's words obey,
But you in malice God's dear Son betray.[7]

Whom, if unjustly you condemn to die,
Her° sin was small, to what you do commit;   *Eve's*
All mortal sins that do for vengeance cry,
820 Are not to be comparèd unto it:
If many worlds would altogether try,

---

4. Eve is allegorized as Patience, with a glance at the literary tradition of the wronged but patient wife (for example, the "patient Griselda" in Chaucer's "Clerk's Tale").
5. With a pun on Adam's name (*hā'ādam*) and on the word for ground (*hā'ādamâ*); Eve was created from Adam's rib: "And the rib, which the Lord God had taken from man, made he a woman, and brought her unto the man" (Genesis 2.22).

6. An allusion to the popular seventeenth-century belief in a plurality of inhabited globes in the universe, or at least in the solar system. Cf. Milton, *Paradise Lost* 3.565 ff. "One": Satan.
7. Here and in the preceding question, Pontius Pilate's wife addresses both men in general ("you all") and her husband, recalling the specific dramatic situation of Christ's trial.

By all their sins the wrath of God to get;
This sin of yours, surmounts them all as far
As doth the sun, another little star.

825 Then let us have our liberty again,
And challenge° to your selves no Sov'reignty;   *claim*
You came not in the world without our pain,
Make that a bar against[8] your cruelty;
Your fault being greater, why should you disdain
830 Our being your equals, free from tyranny?
If one weak woman simply did offend,
This sin of yours[9] hath no excuse, nor end.

To which (poor souls) we never gave consent,
Witness thy wife (O *Pilate*) speaks for all;
835 Who did but dream, and yet a message sent,
That thou should'st have nothing to do at all
With that just man; which, if thy heart relent,
Why wilt thou be a reprobate with *Saul?*[1]
To seek the death of him that is so good,
840 For thy soul's health to shed his dearest blood.

The Description of Cooke-ham[2]

Farewell (sweet *Cooke-ham*) where I first obtained
Grace[3] from that grace where perfect grace remained;
And where the muses[4] gave their full consent,
I should have power the virtuous to content;
5 Where princely palace willed me to indite,[5]
The sacred story[6] of the soul's delight.
Farewell (sweet place) where virtue then did rest,
And all delights did harbor in her breast;
Never shall my sad eyes again behold
10 Those pleasures which my thoughts did then unfold.
Yet you (great Lady) Mistress of that place,
From whose desires did spring this work of grace;

8. I.e., let that prevent. "Pain": of childbirth.
9. I.e., again a reference to Pilate's (and men's) sin of condemning Christ.
1. I.e., morally unprincipled like Saul, a reference to the first king of Israel, who was rejected by God for disobedience, and who plotted to kill David, his successor (1 Samuel 22–23). (Or perhaps another Saul, who was an early persecutor of the first Christians, and who later converted to Christianity himself, changing his name to Paul [Acts 9.1–31]).
2. This poem followed the title poem in the first edition of Lanyer's *Salve Deus Rex Judaeorum* (1611). Cooke-ham was the crown manor leased to William Russell; his sister, Margaret Clifford, the countess of Cumberland, resided there periodically until 1605. The countess was Lanyer's friend and her primary patron. The unhappiness alluded to in this poem refers to the countess's alienation from her husband, George Clifford, third earl of Cumberland, and her legal battles with his rela-

tives after his death in 1605. The countess fought for the claims of her daughter, Cumberland's only heir, Anne Clifford, to his estates. King James and the court bureaucracy offered only a cash settlement—far less than the value of Cumberland's lands and titles—which the countess and her daughter refused to accept. This poem, which probably dates from 1609–10, is an early example of what would become the popular genre of the "country house poem"; see Ben Jonson's "To Penshurst" (pp. 296–98).
3. Respectively (line 2), favor, noble person (i.e., Margaret Clifford, countess of Cumberland, God-given virtues.
4. The nine Greek goddesses believed to be sources of inspiration for the arts.
5. Compose or write.
6. Perhaps a reference to the story of Christ's passion in the "Salve Deus Rex Judaeorum," or to the story of this poem.

Vouchsafe to think upon those pleasures past,
As fleeting worldly joys that could not last,
15   Or, as dim shadows[7] of celestial° pleasures,   *heavenly*
Which are desired above all earthly treasures.
Oh how (methought) against you thither came,[8]
Each part did seem some new delight to frame!
The house received all ornaments to grace it,
20   And would endure no foulness to deface it.
And walks put on their summer liveries,°   *uniforms*
And all things else did hold like similes.[9]
The trees with leaves, with fruits, with flowers clad,
Embraced each other, seeming to be glad,
25   Turning themselves to beauteous Canopies,
To shade the bright sun from your brighter eyes;
The crystal streams with silver spangles graced,
While by the glorious sun they were embraced;
The little birds in chirping notes did sing,
30   To entertain both you and that sweet spring.
And *Philomela*[1] with her sundry lays,
Both you and that delightful place did praise.
Oh how me thought each plant, each flower, each tree
Set forth their beauties then to welcome thee!
35   The very hills right humbly did descend,
When you to tread on them did intend.
And as you set your feet, they still did rise,
Glad that they could receive so rich a prize.
The gentle winds did take delight to be
40   Among those woods that were so graced by thee,
And in sad° murmur uttered pleasing sound,   *constant*
That pleasure in that place might more abound.
The swelling banks delivered all their pride
When such a *Phoenix*[2] once they had espied.
45   Each arbor, bank, each seat, each stately tree,
Thought themselves honored in supporting thee.
The pretty birds would oft come to attend thee,
Yet fly away for fear they should offend thee;
The little creatures in the burrough° by   *burrow*
50   Would come abroad to sport them in your eye,
Yet fearful of the bow in your fair hand.[3]
Would run away when you did make a stand.
Now let me come unto that stately tree,
Wherein such goodly prospects you did see;
55   That oak that did in height his fellows pass,
As much as lofty trees, low growing grass,
Much like a comely cedar straight and tall,

7. Reflections or images.
8. I.e., when you went there.
9. I.e., did the same; "similies": similarities.
1. The nightingale, whose various songs ("sundry lays") were said to express lovesickness and/or mourning. According to a classical myth that was widely known during the Renaissance, Philomela was raped by her brother-in-law, Tereus, who then tore out her tongue so that she could not speak. She wove the story in a tapestry and sent it to her sister, who rescued her. She was later changed into a nightingale while in flight from Tereus.
2. A legendary bird, the only one of its kind, represented as living five hundred years in the Arabian desert before setting itself on fire, then rising anew from its own ashes; here, also a reference to the countess.
3. I.e., the countess is figured as Diana, the classical goddess of hunting, the moon, and chastity.

Whose beauteous stature far exceeded all.
How often did you visit this fair tree,
60   Which seeming joyful in receiving thee,
Would like a palm tree spread his arms abroad,
Desirous that you there should make abode;
Whose fair green leaves much like a comely° veil,   *attractive*
Defended *Phoebus*[4] when he would assail;
65   Whose pleasing boughs did yield a cool fresh air,
Joying his happiness when you were there.
Where being seated, you might plainly see
Hills, vales, and woods, as if on bended knee
They had appeared, your honor to salute,
70   Or to prefer° some strange unlooked-for suit;°   *offer / request*
All interlaced with brooks and crystal springs,
A prospect fit to please the eyes of kings.
And° thirteen shires appeared all in your sight,   *if*
Europe could not afford much more delight.
75   What was there then but gave you all content,
While you the time in meditation spent
Of their Creator's power, which there you saw,
In all his creatures held a perfect law;°   *order*
And in their beauties did you plain descry
80   His beauty, wisdom, grace, love, majesty.
In these sweet woods how often did you walk,
With Christ and his Apostles there to talk;
Placing his holy Writ in some fair tree
To meditate what you therein did see.
85   With *Moses*[5] you did mount his holy hill
To know his pleasure, and perform his will.
With lowly *David*[6] you did often sing
His holy hymns to Heaven's eternal King.
And in sweet music did your soul delight
90   To sound his praises, morning, noon, and night.
With blessed *Joseph*[7] you did often feed
Your pined brethren, when they stood in need.
And that sweet Lady sprung from *Clifford's* race,[8]
Of noble *Bedford's* blood, fair stem of grace,
95   To honorable *Dorset* now espoused,
In whose fair breast true virtue then was housed,
Oh what delight did my weak spirits find
In those pure parts of her well framèd mind.
And yet it grieves me that I cannot be
100   Near unto her, whose virtues did agree
With those fair ornaments of outward beauty,
Which did enforce from all both love and duty.
Unconstant Fortune, thou art most to blame,

4. I.e., protected you from the sun; Phoebus Apollo was the mythological god of the sun.
5. Moses spoke with God on a mountaintop (Exodus 24.13–18).
6. The psalmist of the Bible; the second king of Judah and Israel.
7. Joseph was sold by his brothers into Egypt; after

he became powerful, they had to petition him for food during the great famine (Genesis 37.42–45).
8. Anne Clifford, countess of Dorset, the countess of Cumberland's daughter. Her father came from the Cliffords, earls of Cumberland; her mother came from the Russells, earls of Bedford. She married into the Sackville family, earls of Dorset.

Who casts us down into so low a frame
105 Where our great friends we cannot daily see,
So great a difference is there in degree.
Many are placed in those orbs of state,[9]
Parters in honor,[1] so ordained by Fate,
Nearer in show, yet farther off in love,
110 In which, the lowest always are above.[2]
But whither am I carried in conceit,
My wit too weak to conster° of the great.   *consider, understand*
Why not? although we are but born of earth.
We may behold the heavens, despising death;
115 And loving heaven that is so far above,
May in the end vouchsafe us entire love.[3]
Therefore sweet memory do thou retain
Those pleasures past, which will not turn again:
Remember beauteous *Dorset's* former sports,
120 So far from being touched by ill reports,
Wherein myself did always bear a part,
While reverend love presented my true heart.
Those recreations let me bear in mind,
Which her sweet youth and noble thoughts did find,
125 Whereof deprived, I evermore must grieve,
Hating blind Fortune, careless to relieve.
And you sweet Cooke-ham, whom these ladies leave,
I now must tell the grief you did conceive
At their departure, when they went away,
130 How everything retained a sad dismay.
Nay long before, when once an inkling came,
Methought each thing did unto sorrow frame:
The trees that were so glorious in our view,
Forsook both flowers and fruit, when once they knew
135 Of your depart, their very leaves did wither,
Changing their colors as they grew together.
But when they saw this had no power to stay you,
They often wept, though, speechless, could not pray you,[4]
Letting their tears in your fair bosoms fall,
140 As if they said, Why will ye leave us all?
This being vain, they cast their leaves away
Hoping that pity would have made you stay:
Their frozen tops, like age's hoary° hairs,   *grayish white*
Shows their disasters, languishing in fears.
145 A swarthy riveled rind[5] all over spread,
Their dying bodies half alive, half dead.
But your occasions called you so away
That nothing there had power to make you stay.
Yet did I see a noble grateful mind
150 Requiting° each according to their kind,   *rewarding*

9. I.e., the political realm.
1. Separated in rank.
2. I.e., while circumstance may place the high and the low near to each other, the lower-born are more devoted to the higher-born. In *Nichomachean Ethics,* the Greek philosopher Aristotle (384–322 B.C.) says that in friendship between

unequals, "the better and more useful partner should receive more affection than he gives" (7.1158).
3. I.e., may bestow all love on us.
4. I.e., beg you (to stay).
5. A dark rough covering.

Forgetting not to turn and take your leave
Of these sad creatures, powerless to receive
Your favor, when with grief you did depart,
Placing their former pleasures in your heart,
155 Giving great charge to noble memory
There to preserve their love continually.
But specially the love of that fair tree,
That first and last you did vouchsafe to see,
In which it pleased you oft to take the air
160 With noble *Dorset*, then a virgin fair,[6]
Where many a learned book was read and scanned,
To this fair tree, taking me by the hand,
You did repeat the pleasures which had passed,
Seeming to grieve they could no longer last.
165 And with a chaste, yet loving kiss took leave,
Of which sweet kiss I did it soon bereave,[7]
Scorning a senseless creature should possess
So rare a favor, so great happiness.
No other kiss it could receive from me,
170 For fear to give back what it took of thee,
So I ungrateful creature did deceive° it   *deprive*
Of that which you in love vouchsafed° to leave it.   *bestowed*
And though it oft had given me much content,
Yet this great wrong I never could repent;
175 But of the happiest made it most forlorn,
To show that nothing's free from Fortune's scorne,
While all the rest with this most beauteous tree
Made their sad consort[8] sorrow's harmony.
The flowers that on the banks and walks did grow,
180 Crept in the ground, the grass did weep for woe.
The winds and waters seemed to chide together
Because you went away they knew not whither;
And those sweet brooks that ran so fair and clear,
With grief and trouble wrinkled did appear.
185 Those pretty birds that wonted° were to sing,   *accustomed*
Now neither sing, nor chirp, nor use their wing,
But with their tender feet on some bare spray,
Warble forth sorrow, and their own dismay.
Fair *Philomela* leaves her mournful ditty,°   *song*
190 Drowned in deep sleep, yet can procure no pity.
Each arbor, bank, each seat, each stately tree
Looks bare and desolate now for want° of thee,   *lack*
Turning green tresses[9] into frosty gray,
While in cold grief they wither all away.
195 The sun grew weak, his beams no comfort gave,
While all green things did make the earth their grave.
Each brier, each bramble, when you went away
Caught fast your clothes, thinking to make you stay;
Delightful Echo[1] wonted to reply

---

6. I.e., before marriage.
7. I.e., Lanyer claims to have kissed the tree after
the countess did, and so deprived the tree of the
countess's kiss.

8. Company, with a pun on "consort" as a musical
group.
9. I.e., leaves.
1. A personification of the sound effect.

200   To our last words, did now for sorrow die;
        The house cast off each garment that might grace it,
        Putting on dust and cobwebs to deface it.
        All desolation then there did appear,
        When you were going whom they held so dear.
205   This last farewell to *Cooke-ham* here I give,
        When I am dead thy name in this may live,
        Wherein I have performed her noble hest°   bidding
        Whose virtues lodge in my unworthy breast,
        And ever shall, so long as life remains,
210   Tying my life to her by those rich chains.

                                                          1611

JOHN DONNE

1572–1631

The Good-Morrow[1]

        I wonder, by my troth, what thou and I
        Did, till we loved? were we not weaned till then?
        But sucked on country[2] pleasures, childishly?
        Or snorted° we in the Seven Sleepers' den?[3]   snored
5   'Twas so; but° this, all pleasures fancies be.   except for
        If ever any beauty I did see,
        Which I desired, and got, 'twas but a dream of thee.

        And now good-morrow to our waking souls,
        Which watch not one another out of fear;
10   For love, all love of other sights controls,
        And makes one little room an everywhere.[4]
        Let sea-discoverers to new worlds have gone,
        Let maps[5] to others, worlds on worlds have shown,
        Let us possess one[6] world, each hath one, and is one.

---

1. This poem and the others in this anthology up to "The Relic" are usually printed under the rubric *Songs and Sonnets*, a title given to a grouping of Donne's love poems in the second edition of his *Poems* (1635). There is no authorial warrant for that title, however, since even the first edition of Donne's *Poems* (1633) appeared after his death, and no copies of his poems in his own handwriting survive. Instead, the poems exist in posthumous printed editions as well as in a large number of manuscript copies, many of which circulated during Donne's lifetime; some manuscripts include musical settings for the poems. We cannot date most of Donne's love poems with any certainty, and the multiple copies, printed and in manuscript, show many variations in stanza forms, punctuation, spelling, and even diction and grammar. Like most modern editors, we base our texts on the 1633 *Poems*; significant variations are mentioned in the notes.
    Donne's poems frequently have an apostrophe between words to indicate that the neighboring syllables are fused in pronunciation and counted as one metrically. Such contractions occur only under certain phonetic conditions (e.g., when one word ends, and the next begins, with a vowel). They continue to be common in modern speech, although in writing we now limit use of the apostrophe to those contractions that omit letters from the usual spelling of the words, as in "you're" and "don't."
2. Also with a sexual connotation.
3. Seven Christian youths, under the persecutions of the Roman Emperor Decius (who ruled A.D. 249–51), were said to have been sealed in a cave, where they slept for nearly two centuries. On awakening, they found Christianity established as a world religion.
4. The common Renaissance trope of the individual as a microcosm of the universe.
5. Terrestrial maps or sky charts.
6. In some manuscripts, "our."

15   My face in thine eye, thine in mine appears,
And true plain hearts do in the faces rest;
Where can we find two better hemispheres,
Without sharp North, without declining West?
Whatever dies was not mixed equally;[7]
20   If our two loves be one, or, thou and I
Love so alike that none do slacken, none can die.

1633

Song

Go and catch a falling star,
  Get with child a mandrake root,[8]
Tell me where all past years are,
  Or who cleft the Devil's foot,
5   Teach me to hear mermaids[9] singing,
  Or to keep off envy's stinging,
       And find
       What wind
Serves to advance an honest mind.

10   If thou beest born to strange sights,[1]
  Things invisible to see,
Ride ten thousand days and nights,
  Till age snow white hairs on thee,
Thou, when thou return'st, wilt tell me
15   All strange wonders that befell thee,
       And swear
       Nowhere
Lives a woman true, and fair.

If thou find'st one, let me know,
20   Such a pilgrimage were sweet;
Yet do not, I would not go,
  Though at next door we might meet;
Though she were true when you met her,
And last till you write your letter,
25   Yet she
       Will be
False, ere I come, to two, or three.

1633

---

7. In medieval and Renaissance medical theory, death was often considered the result of an imbalance in the body's elements. When elements were "not mixed equally," matter was mutable and mortal, but when they were mixed perfectly, it was changing and immortal.
8. The large, forked root of the mandrake roughly resembles a human body and was thought to be an aphrodisiac.

9. Identified with the Sirens (in Homer's *Odyssey*), whose seductive song only the cunning Odysseus successfully resisted.
1. I.e., if your nature inclines you to seek strange sights; alternatively, if you are carried ("borne," as the word is spelled in the 1633 text and most manuscript versions) to strange sights (cf. "return'st," line 14).

Woman's Constancy

Now thou hast loved me one whole day,
Tomorrow when thou leav'st, what wilt thou say?
Wilt thou then antedate² some new-made vow?
    Or say that now
5 We are not just those persons which we were?
Or, that oaths made in reverential fear
Of Love, and his wrath, any may forswear?
Or, as true° deaths, true marriages untie,   *real*
So lovers' contracts, images of those,³
10 Bind but till sleep, death's image, them unloose?
    Or, your own end to justify,
For having purposed change, and falsehood, you
Can have no way but falsehood to be true?
Vain lunatic,⁴ against these 'scapes° I could   *escapes, deceptions*
15   Dispute, and conquer, if I would,
    Which I abstain to do,
For by tomorrow, I may think so too.

            1633

The Sun Rising

    Busy old fool, unruly sun,
      Why dost thou thus,
Through windows, and through curtains call on us?
Must to thy motions lovers' seasons run?
5   Saucy pedantic wretch, go chide
    Late school boys and sour prentices,°   *apprentices*
Go tell court huntsmen⁵ that the king will ride,
Call country ants to harvest offices;⁶
Love, all alike,⁷ no season knows nor clime,
10 Nor hours, days, months, which are the rags° of time. *fragments*

    Thy beams, so reverend and strong
      Why shouldst thou think?⁸
I could eclipse and cloud them with a wink,
But that I would not lose her sight so long;
15   If her eyes have not blinded thine,
    Look, and tomorrow late, tell me,
Whether both th' Indias⁹ of spice and mine
Be where thou leftst them, or lie here with me.
Ask for those kings whom thou saw'st yesterday,
20 And thou shalt hear, All here in one bed lay.

2. Affix an earlier date than the true date. I.e., will you pretend that a new vow of love is older than that you have made to me?
3. I.e., of true marriages.
4. The word has for Donne the additional meaning of "inconstant" or "fickle," since lunacy (from *luna*, "moon") was supposed to be affected by the changing phases of the moon.
5. I.e., courtiers who hunt office by emulating King James' passion for hunting.
6. "Harvest" may be read both as part of a noun phrase ("duties of the harvest," in which case "country ants" would refer to farm workers) and as a verb, in which case the "ants" would be provincial courtiers seeking to collect ("harvest") paid positions.
7. The same at all times.
8. I.e., what makes you think your light is so awesome?
9. India and the West Indies, whence came spices and gold (from mines) respectively.

She's all states, and all princes, I,[1]
Nothing else is.
Princes do but play us; compared to this,
All honor's mimic, all wealth alchemy.[2]
25   Thou, sun, art half as happy as we,[3]
In that the world's contracted thus.
Thine age asks ease, and since thy duties be
To warm the world, that's done in warming us.
Shine here to us, and thou art everywhere;
30   This bed thy center is, these walls, thy sphere.[4]

1633

The Canonization[5]

For God's sake hold your tongue, and let me love,
Or chide my palsy, or my gout,
My five gray hairs, or ruined fortune, flout,
With wealth your state, your mind with arts improve,
5   Take you a course, get you a place,[6]
Observe his honor, or his grace,
Or the King's real, or his stampéd face[7]
Contémplate; what you will, approve,°   try
So you will let me love.

10   Alas, alas, who's injured by my love?
What merchant's ships have my sighs drowned?
Who says my tears have overflowed his ground?
When did my colds a forward° spring remove?[8]   early
When did the heats which my veins fill
15   Add one more to the plaguy bill?[9]
Soldiers find wars, and lawyers find out still
Litigious° men, which quarrels move,   contentious
Though she and I do love.

Call us what you will, we're made such by love;
20   Call her one, me another fly,[1]
We're tapers too, and at our own cost die,

1. One manuscript has "She is all princes, and all states, I, . . ."
2. A metallic composition imitating gold; i.e., a fraud.
3. The sun, being one thing, is half as happy as two lovers.
4. I.e., the bedroom and the lovers are a microcosm of the solar system, with the bed itself as the point around which the sun revolves.
5. The title refers to admission into the canon of Church saints, often attested by martyrdom. As part of the canonization process, a "devil's advocate" sought to ensure that the whole truth, including faults, emerged about a candidate.
6. An appointment, at court or elsewhere; "take you a course": begin a career.

7. I.e., on coins. The contrast is complicated by the fact that "real," spelled "royall" in several manuscripts, is also a term for a Spanish coin.
8. A common poetic conceit figured lovers as frozen by their mistresses' neglect; i.e., the speaker protests that his "colds" have not removed the warmth of an early spring.
9. Weekly list of plague victims; many manuscripts have "man" instead of "more."
1. I.e., we're both "fly" (a moth or any winged insect) and "tapers," the self-consuming candles that attract winged insects. "Dying" was a popular metaphor for sexual climax in seventeenth-century English. "At our own cost" reflects the common superstition that each orgasm shortened the man's life by a day.

And we in us find th' eagle and the dove.[2]
  The phoenix riddle hath more wit°   *sense*
  By us: we two being one, are it.
25 So, to one neutral thing both sexes fit.
  We die and rise the same,[3] and prove
    Mysterious by this love.

We can die by it, if not live by love,
  And if unfit for tombs and hearse
30 Our legend be, it will be fit for verse;
  And if no piece of chronicle° we prove,[4]   *history*
  We'll build in sonnets pretty rooms;[5]
  As well a well-wrought urn becomes°   *befits*
The greatest ashes, as half-acre tombs;
35 And by these hymns,[6] all shall approve
    Us canonized for love.

And thus invoke us: You whom reverend love
  Made one another's hermitage;
You, to whom love was peace, that now is rage,° *lust*
40 Who did the whole world's soul contract, and drove[7]
    Into the glasses of your eyes
    So made such mirrors, and such spies,
That they did all to you epitomize,[8]
  Countries, towns, courts: Beg from above
45 A pattern of your love![9]

        1633

Song

Sweetest love, I do not go
  For weariness of thee,
Nor in hope the world can show
  A fitter love for me;
5   But since that I
Must die at last, 'tis best
To use myself in jest,
  Thus by feigned deaths to die.[1]

2. A common symbol of peace and meekness; the "eagle" signifies strength. "Eagle" and "dove" are also alchemical terms for processes leading to the rise of "phoenix," a stage in the transmutation of metals. The phoenix is a legendary bird; it was thought to be the only one of its kind, to contain both sexes, and to live five hundred years in the Arabian desert before setting itself on fire. Because a new phoenix supposedly arose from fire's ashes, the bird was often a symbol of the resurrected Christ.
3. A reference to the phoenix and to orgasm.
4. One manuscript has "Chronicles." The biblical book of 1 Chronicles (1–9) lists the genealogies of the tribes of Israel. The speaker may be implying that if the "timeless" lovers leave no "progeny," they will leave poetry.
5. The "rooms" (punning on the Italian word for

room, *stanza*) will hold the ashes, i.e., record their deeds.
6. I.e., the lover's poems.
7. Some manuscripts have "extract" for "contract" and "draw" for "drove."
8. I.e., you in whose eyes the essence of the world has been distilled so they now mirror and reveal all human relations.
9. Interpretations of this syntactically complex stanza turn, in part, on where one thinks that the direct address ends. Some editors put quotation markes before "You" (line 37) and after "love," and some manuscripts have "our" for "your."
1. Partings, and perhaps orgasms, as rehearsals for the final death of life. "Dying" was a popular metaphor for sexual climax in seventeenth-century English.

Yesternight the sun went hence,
10   And yet is here today;
He hath no desire nor sense,
    Nor half so short a way:
      Then fear not me,
But believe that I shall make
15 Speedier journeys, since I take
    More wings and spurs than he.

O how feeble is man's power,
    That if good fortune fall,
Cannot add another hour,
20   Nor a lost hour recall!
      But come bad chance,
And we join to'it our strength,
And we teach it art and length,
    Itself o'er us to'advance.

25 When thou sigh'st, thou sigh'st not wind,
    But sigh'st my soul away;
When thou weep'st, unkindly kind,
    My life's blood doth decay.
      It cannot be
30 That thou lov'st me, as thou say'st,
If in thine my life thou waste;
    Thou art the best of me.

Let not thy divining° heart   *foreseeing*
    Forethink me any ill;
35 Destiny may take thy part,
    And may thy fears fulfill;
      But think that we
Are but turned aside to sleep;
They who one another keep
40   Alive, ne'er parted be.

          1633

The Anniversary

All kings, and all their favorites,
All glory'of honors, beauties, wits,
The sun itself, which makes times, as they pass,
Is elder by a year, now, than it was
5 When thou and I first one another saw:
All other things to their destruction draw,
    Only our love hath no decay;
This, no tomorrow hath, nor yesterday;
Running it never runs from us away,
10 But truly keeps his first, last, everlasting day.

Two graves must hide thine and my corse;°   *corpse*
    If one might, death were no divorce.
Alas, as well as other princes, we

(Who prince enough in one another be)
15 Must leave at last in death, these eyes, and ears,
Oft fed with true oaths, and with sweet salt tears;
    But souls where nothing dwells but love
(All other thoughts being inmates°) then shall   *lodgers*
    prove°   *experience*
This, or a love increasèd there above,
20 When bodies to their graves, souls from their graves remove.

    And then we shall be throughly° blest,   *thoroughly*
    But we no more than all the rest;[2]
Here upon earth, we're kings, and none but we
Can be such kings, nor of such subjects be;[3]
25 Who is so safe as we, where none can do
Treason to us, except one of us two?
    True and false fears let us refrain,
Let us love nobly,'and live, and add again
Years and years unto years, till we attain
30 To write threescore, this is the second of our reign.

                                                         1633

Love's Growth[4]

I scarce believe my love to be so pure
    As I had thought it was,
    Because it doth endure
Vicissitude,° and season, as the grass;   *change*
5   Methinks I lied all winter, when I swore
My love was infinite, if spring make'it more.

But if this medicine, love, which cures all sorrow
With more, not only be no quìntessence,[5]
But mixed of all stuffs paining soul or sense,
10 And of the sun his working vigor borrow,
Love's not so pure, and abstract, as they use
To say, which have no mistress but their muse,
But as all else, being elemented[6] too,
Love sometimes would contémplate, sometimes do.

15 And yet no greater, but more eminent,°   *conspicuous, evident*
    Love by the spring is grown;
    As, in the firmament,
Stars by the sun are not enlarged, but shown,
Gentle love deeds, as blossoms on a bough,
From love's awakened root do bud out now.

2. Scholastic philosophers maintained that all souls are equally content in heaven but not equally blessed.
3. The conceit is that each lover is the other's king, and therefore each is also the other's only subject.
4. In some manuscripts the poem is titled "Spring." If "love's growth" refers to the swelling of pregnancy, then the irregular "growing" shape of the stanzas in the early editions and some manuscripts may be an instance of imitative form. The

stanzas play on (by inverting) the Italian sonnet pattern of an octave followed by a sestet.
5. According to many ancient and medieval philosophers, there was a fifth or "quintessential" element more pure than the four elements of ordinary life (earth, air, fire, and water); the quintessence was thought to be a cure for all diseases. "This medicine": in the early seventeenth century, cures were often sought according to a principle of likeness between medicine and illness.
6. Made up of a mixture of elements.

20

If, as in water stirred more circles be
Produced by one, love such additions take,
Those, like so many spheres, but one heaven make,
For they are all concentric unto thee;[7]
25 And though each spring do add to love new heat,
As princes do in times of action get
New taxes, and remit them not in peace,
No winter shall abate the spring's increase.

1633

A Valediction[8] of Weeping

Let me pour forth
My tears before thy face whilst I stay here,
For thy face coins them, and thy stamp they bear,[9]
And by this mintage they are something worth,
5   For thus they be
       Pregnant of thee;
Fruits of much grief they are, emblems of more;
When a tear falls, that Thou falls which it bore,[1]
So thou and I are nothing then, when on a diverse shore.

10   On a round ball
A workman that hath copies by, can lay
An Europe, Afric, and an Asïa,
And quickly make that, which was nothing, all,[2]
       So doth each tear
15   Which thee doth wear,[3]
A globe, yea world, by that impression grow,
Till thy tears mixed with mine do overflow
This world; by waters sent from thee, my heaven dissolvèd so.

       O more than moon,
20 Draw not up seas[4] to drown me in thy sphere;
Weep me not dead,[5] in thine arms, but forbear
To teach the sea what it may do too soon.
       Let not the wind
       Example find
25 To do me more harm than it purposeth;
Since thou and I sigh one another's breath,
Whoe'er sighs most is cruelest, and hastes the other's death.

1633

7. Astronomers up to Donne's time conceived of nine concentric spheres, each of transparent crystal, turning around the Earth. The various heavenly bodies were thought to be fixed in the surfaces of these spheres.
8. A departure speech or discourse; a bidding of farewell. Several manuscripts place a colon after "Valediction," but many, along with the 1633 edition, do not.
9. I.e., they reflect her face (among other meanings).
1. With a play on the image of pregnancy in the preceding lines. "That" is a demonstrative adjective modifying "Thou"; the tear of the speaker bears the impression of the lover.
2. I.e., an artist can paste maps of the continents on a blank globe. The "o" of the globe's shape is echoed in the word "nothing."
3. Can be read as either "which bears your impression" (i.e., the speaker's tears), or "which you weep" (i.e., bearing the speaker's impression).
4. I.e., by heavy sighing.
5. I.e., do not weep me to death.

A Valediction[6] of the Book

I'll tell thee now (dear Love) what thou shalt do
To anger destiny, as she doth us,
How I shall stay, though she esloygne° me thus   *remove far off*
And how posterity shall know it too;
5   How thine may out-endure
Sybil's[7] glory, and obscure
Her[8] who from Pindar could allure,
And her,[9] through whose help Lucan is not lame,
And her, whose book (they say) Homer did find, and name.[1]

10   Study our manuscripts, those myriads
Of letters, which have past twixt thee and me,
Thence write our annals, and in them will be
To all whom love's subliming fire invades,
Rule and example found;
15   There, the faith of any ground[2]
No schismatic[3] will dare to wound,
That sees, how Love this grace to us affords,
To make, to keep, to use, to be these his records.

This book, as long-lived as the elements,
20   Or as the world's form, this all-graved tome
In cipher writ, or new made idiom;[4]
We for love's clergy only'are instruments,[5]
When this book is made thus,
Should again the ravenous
25   Vandals and the Goths[6] invade us,
Learning were safe; in this our universe
Schools might learn sciences, spheres music, angels verse.[7]

---

6. A departure speech or discourse; a bidding of farewell. Several manuscripts place a colon after "Valediction," but many, along with the 1633 edition, do not.

7. The best-known "sibyl," or prophetess, was Virgil's Cumaean Sibyl, who lived for a thousand years. In a trancelike frenzy she wrote inspired prophecies on leaves, which were scattered abroad by the wind. Her prophecies concerning the destiny of the Roman state were gathered into the Sibylline Books, which were preserved in the Roman temple of Capitoline Jupiter. These books were consulted during national emergencies and required interpretation by male priests.

8. According to tradition, Corinna the Boeotian (fl. ca. 500 B.C.?) taught writing to and competed successfully with the Greek lyric poet Pindar (ca. 522–ca. 438 B.C.). His poems are extant; Corinna's are not, except in fragments.

9. Polla Argentaria, the wife of Lucan (A.D. 39–65), a Roman poet, who helped him write his historical epic *Pharsalia*.

1. One tradition holds that Homer, the supposed author of the *Iliad* (and the *Odyssey*), took the subject of the siege of Troy from an epic poem on that event by Phantasia of Memphis. In another version of Donne's poem, the last three lines of this stanza read: "Her who from old allure, / And, through whose help Lucan is not lame, / And her, whose (they say) Homer did find, and name." Note that this variant substitutes "look" for "book" and omits Corinna and Phantasia. The "her" of this last line refers to Helen of Troy, wife of the Greek King Menelaus, whose abduction (or seduction) by Paris, son of the king of Troy, began the Trojan War.

2. I.e., the trustworthiness of any fundamental doctrine.

3. One who promotes schism, or breach of unity in the Church; in this stanza and the next, the poet speaks of love as a sort of religion.

4. Language or dialect. "All-graved": indelibly written. "Tome": a heavy book; one manuscript has "tomb" and another has "to me."

5. I.e., we are, in these letters, documents for love's initiates only; one variant has "are only" for "only'are."

6. Vandals and Goths were Germanic tribes that invaded Western Europe during the third, fourth, and fifth centuries; the words are used to refer to those who willfully and ignorantly destroy anything beautiful or worthy of preservation.

7. I.e., angelic hymns; "schools": scholastic philosophers; "spheres music": according to Pythagorean tradition, the motion of the planetary spheres created a music inaudible to human ears.

Here Love's divines° (since all divinity   *prophets, priests*
    Is love or wonder) may find all they seek,
30   Whether abstract spiritual love they like,
Their souls exhaled with[8] what they do not see,
        Or loth so to amuse
        Faith's[9] infirmity, they choose
        Something which they may see and use;
35   For, though mind be the heaven, where love doth sit,
Beauty'a convenient type[1] may be to figure° it.   *represent*

Here more than in their books may lawyers find,
    Both by what titles[2] mistresses are ours,
    And how prerogative these states[3] devours,
40   Transferred from Love himself, to womankind.[4]
        Who though from heart, and eyes,
        They exact great subsidies,
        Forsake him who on them relies
    And for the cause, honor, or conscience give,
45   Chimeras, vain as they, or their prerogative.[5]

Here statesmen (or of them, they which can read)
    May of their occupation find the grounds,°   *basic principles*
    Love and their art alike it deadly wounds,
If to consider what'tis, one proceed,[6]
50   In both they do excel
        Who the present govern well,[7]
        Whose weakness[8] none doth, or dares tell;
In this thy book, such will there nothing see,
As in the Bible some can find out alchemy.[9]

55   Thus vent thy thoughts; abroad[1] I'll study thee,
    As he removes far off, that° great heights[2] takes;°   *who / measures*
    How great love is, presence best trial makes,
But absence tries° how long this love will be;

---

8. Drawn out by.
9. One variant has "doth" for "loth" and "faithless" for "Faith's."
1. A symbol or earthly reflection of the celestial original.
2. I.e., legal rights to the possession of property.
3. I.e., estates, presumably the "titles" mentioned in the above line; "prerogative": official right or privilege; Donne alludes here to the feudal practice by which a lord could demand from his vassals dues over and above those that were customary; also, at issue in the Parliament of 1601 was the prerogative of the monarch to levy special grants against noblemen's estates at time of need.
4. The "ours" of line 38 seems to refer to men. Thus the first four lines of this stanza might be paraphrased "Here, more than in their books, lawyers may discover both by what titles (legal rights to property, with, perhaps, a pun on 'names') mistresses belong to us (men), and how women's usurpation of the prerogative (privileges attendant on those legal rights), which rightfully belongs to

Love, eats away at those rights ('states')."
5. I.e., and for their reason they please conscience or honor, both illusions as empty as themselves or their prerogative.
6. I.e., neither love nor politics can bear close scrutiny.
7. The suggestion of these lines seems to be that opportunists do well in both love and politics.
8. I.e., the weakness of lovers and politicians, about which "none doth, or dares tell" because they have been either deceived or intimidated.
9. The science applied to the pursuit of transmutation of baser metals into gold and also to the search for a panacea or universal remedy. "Such": such people. "Nothing": worthlessness; one variant (printed in the 1633 edition) has "something" in place of "nothing." "Find out": show the falsity of, or possibly, find support for (the Bible could be used to show the falsity of alchemy, but alchemists found support for their theories there).
1. I.e., while I'm away; "vent": give expression to.
2. One variant has "shadows" for "great heights."

To take a latitude
60 Sun, or stars, are fitliest viewed
    At their brightest, but to conclude,
Of longitudes, what other way have we,
But to mark when, and where the dark eclipses be?[3]

                                                    1633

Love's Alchemy

Some that have deeper digged love's mine than I,
Say where his centric° happiness doth lie;   *central, essential*
    I've loved, and got, and told,[4]
But should I love, get, tell, till I were old,
5   I should not find that hidden mystery;
    O, 'tis imposture all:
And as no chemic° yet th' elixir[5] got,   *alchemist*
    But glorifies his pregnant pot,
    If by the way to him befall
10 Some odoriferous thing, or mèdicinal;
    So lovers dream a rich and long delight,
    But get a winter-seeming summer's night.

Our ease, our thrift, our honor, and our day,
Shall we for this vain bubble's shadow pay?
15   Ends love in this, that my man°   *servant*
Can be as happy'as I can if he can
Endure the short scorn of a bridegroom's play?
    That loving wretch that swears,
'Tis not the bodies marry, but the minds,
20   Which he in her angelic finds,
    Would swear as justly that he hears,
In that day's rude hoarse minstrelsy, the spheres.[6]
    Hope not for mind in women; at their best
    Sweetness and wit they're but mummy[7] possessed.

                                                    1633

---

3. The latitude of a place may be measured by calculating its distance from the zenith of a star whose altitude (its distance from the equator) is known; longitude can be measured by noting the time at which an eclipse occurs at different points on the Earth's surface. Donne here puns on the word "longitude," as it suggests (but does not mean) length or duration.
4. Tallied (counted) or estimated the quality of.
5. A hypothetical substance, the goal of the alchemists' endeavors, supposedly capable of transmuting base metals into gold, curing all illnesses, and prolonging life indefinitely.
6. I.e., the music of the spheres, or concentric transparent shells containing the heavenly bodies in Ptolemaic astronomy; they were thought to pro-

duce angelic music as they turned. Here, they are contrasted with the "charivari," a raucous serenade using pots, pans, and trumpets, traditionally performed on the wedding night.
7. Lifeless flesh; also, a medication prepared from mummified remains. The poem is entitled "Mummy" in some manuscripts.
    The syntax of the last two lines is obscure; the last line may be read with a comma after "wit," after "are," after "but," and / or after "mummy." The final word may modify "mummy," to signify "mummy with a demon in it," or "they," to signify "women, once possessed by men" (i.e., married) or "women, after men possess them" (i.e., after marriage). Some manuscripts have a comma after "best."

A Nocturnal upon St. Lucy's Day,
Being the Shortest Day[8]

'Tis the year's midnight, and it is the day's,
Lucy's,[9] who scarce seven hours herself unmasks;
The sun is spent, and now his flasks[1]
Send forth light squibs, no constant rays;
5   The world's whole sap is sunk:[2]
The general balm th' hydroptic[3] earth hath drunk,
Whither, as to the bed's-feet, life is shrunk,
Dead and interred; yet all these seem to laugh,
Compared with me, who am their epitaph.[4]

10 Study me then, you who shall lovers be
At the next world, that is, at the next spring:
For I am every dead thing,
In whom love wrought new alchemy.
For his art did express°   *squeeze out*
15 A quintessence[5] even from nothingness,
From dull privations, and lean emptiness:
He ruined me, and I am re-begot
Of absence, darkness, death; things which are not.

All others, from all things, draw all that's good,
20 Life, soul, form, spirit, whence they being have;
I, by love's limbeck,[6] am the grave
Of all that's nothing. Oft a flood
Have we two wept, and so
Drowned the whole world, us two; oft did we grow
25 To be two chaoses,[7] when we did show
Care to aught else;[8] and often absences
Withdrew our souls, and made us carcasses.

But I am by her death (which word wrongs her)
Of the first nothing, the elixir grown;[9]
30   Were I a man, that I were one
I needs must know; I should prefer,

---

8. The "nocturns" of the Roman Catholic Church were night offices or prayers; the title may also allude to an astronomical instrument used for telling time at night. According to the calendar in use during Donne's time, the winter solstice or shortest day of the year fell on December 12, the eve of St. Lucy's Day. St. Lucy was patron saint of the blind. Her festival is celebrated with lights and candles, and her name itself recalls the Latin word for light (*lux, lucis*). Lucy was the name of Donne's patron, the countess of Bedford, and some commentators have suggested that the poem was written on her death in 1627. Other believe that the "she" of the poem is Donne's wife, Anne, who died in 1617. Donne's daughter, named Lucy after the countess of Bedford, also died in 1627.
9. In Latin, *lux, lucis* also means "day"; "Lucy's" here is an appositive to "day's."
1. Powder flasks. I.e., the sun is compared to a gun shooting powder from powder flasks, but in "squibs" like small fireworks that spurt and fizzle as they burn.
2. Like that of trees and vegetation in winter.
3. Implies both saturation and insatiable thirst; i.e., insatiably thirsty. "General balm": probably refers to the sap of line 5. In the winter a plant's sap recedes into the roots (to be stored).
4. Inscription on a tombstone.
5. A highly concentrated essence or extract, often identified with the "fifth essence" of ancient and medieval philosophy (see note 5, p. 269, and n. 5, p. 273).
6. An alembic, an apparatus often used by alchemists (see line 13).
7. Includes a reference to the primordial emptiness out of which all form arises.
8. I.e., when we turned our attention from each other.
9. He is now "grown" (become) the "elixir of the first nothing," i.e., the quintessence of the nothing that preceded creation of the world.

If I were any beast,
Some ends, some means; yea plants, yea stones detest,
And love;[1] all, all some properties invest;°   *put on*
35   If I an ordinary nothing were,
As shadow, 'a light and body must be here.

But I am none; nor will my sun[2] renew.
You lovers, for whose sake the lesser sun
    At this time to the Goat is run
40   To fetch new lust, and give it you,
          Enjoy your summer all;
Since she enjoys her long night's festival,
Let me prepare towards her, and let me call
This hour her vigil,[3] and her eve, since this
45   Both the year's, and the day's deep midnight is.

                                      1633

A Valediction Forbidding Mourning[4]

As virtuous men pass mildly' away,
    And whisper to their souls to go,
Whilst some of their sad friends do say
    The breath goes now, and some say, no;

5   So let us melt, and make no noise,
    No tear-floods, nor sigh-tempests move,
        'Twere profanation of our joys
        To tell the laity[5] our love.

Moving of th' earth brings harms and fears,
10   Men reckon what it did and meant;
But trepidation of the spheres,[6]
        Though greater far, is innocent.

Dull sublunary[7] lovers' love
    (Whose soul is sense) cannot admit
15   Absence, because it doth remove
        Those things which elemented° it.   *composed*

But we by'a love so much refined
    That our selves know not what it is,
    Inter-assurèd of the mind,
20   Care less,[8] eyes, lips, and hands to miss.

1. I.e., even plants and stones (like lodestones) have attractions and antipathies; even "beasts" have intentions.
2. I.e., the dead woman. The "lesser sun" is the real sun, which is in the constellation of Capricorn ("the Goat") during the month of December. Goats were proverbial for their lustfulness.
3. The watch kept on the eve of a feast, with prayer.
4. One of Donne's friends, Izaak Walton, reported that this poem was written to Donne's wife when Donne went to the Continent in 1611. "Valedic-tion": a departure speech or discourse; a bidding of farewell.
5. I.e., those who do not understand such love.
6. A trembling of the celestial spheres, hypothesized by Ptolemaic astronomers to account for unpredicted variations in the paths of the heavenly bodies.
7. Beneath the moon; earthly, hence, changeable.
8. At least one manuscript and many editions from 1639 to 1654 give "carelesse" for "care lesse"; we choose the latter form because it allows for two grammatical interpretations.

Our two souls therefore, which are one,
　　Though I must go, endure not yet
A breach, but an expansion,
　　Like gold to airy thinness beat.

25　If they be two, they are two so
　　As stiff twin compasses[9] are two;
Thy soul, the fixed foot, makes no show
　　To move, but doth, if th' other do.

And though it in the center sit,
30　　Yet when the other far doth roam,
It leans and hearkens after it,
　　And grows erect, as that comes home.

Such wilt thou be to me, who must
　　Like th' other foot, obliquely° run.　　　　*diagonally, aslant*
35　Thy firmness makes my circle[1] just,
　　And makes me end where I begun.

　　　　　　　　　　　　　　　　　　1633

The Ecstasy[2]

Where, like a pillow on a bed,
　　A pregnant bank swelled up to rest
The violet's[3] reclining head,
　　Sat we two, one another's best.
5　Our hands were firmly cèmented
　　With a fast balm,[4] which thence did spring.
Our eye-beams twisted, and did thread
　　Our eyes upon one double string;
So to'intergraft our hands, as yet
10　Was all the means to make us one,[5]
　　And pictures° in our eyes to get°　　　　*reflections / beget*
Was all our propagation.
　　As 'twixt two equal armies, Fate
Suspends uncertain victory,
15　Our souls (which to advance their state,
　　Were gone out) hung 'twixt her and me.
And whilst our souls negotiate there,
　　We like sepulchral statues lay;
All day the same our postures were,
20　　And we said nothing all the day.
If any, so by love refined

9. I.e., compasses used in drawing circles.
1. The circle was a symbol of perfection; with a dot in the middle, it was also the alchemist's symbol for gold.
2. Literally, "a standing out"; a term used by religious mystics to describe the experience in which the soul seemed to leave the body and rise superior to it in a state of heightened awareness.

3. An emblem of faithful love and truth.
4. I.e., perspiration; also, a moisture that preserves them steadfast.
5. The lovers are joined "as yet" only by hands and eyes; "eye-beams" are invisible shafts of light, thought of as going out of the eyes and so enabling one to see.

That he soul's language understood,
And by good love were grown all mind,
    Within convenient distance stood,
25 He (though he knew not which soul spake,
    Because both meant, both spake the same)
Might thence a new concoction[6] take,
    And part far purer than he came.
This ecstasy doth unperplex,
30   We said, and tell us what we love;
We see by this it was not sex;
    We see we saw not what did move;[7]
But as all several° souls contain   *separate*
    Mixture of things, they know not what,
35 Love these mixed souls doth mix again,
    And makes both one, each this and that.
A single violet transplant,
    The strength, the color, and the size
(All which before was poor, and scant)
40   Redoubles still, and multiplies.
When love, with one another so
    Interinanimates two souls,
That abler soul, which thence doth flow,[8]
    Defects of loneliness controls.
45 We then, who are this new soul, know,
    Of what we are composed, and made,
For, th' atomies° of which we grow,   *atoms, components*
    Are souls, whom no change can invade.
But O alas, so long, so far
50   Our bodies why do we forbear?
They're ours, though they're not we; we are
    Th' intelligences, they the spheres.[9]
We owe them thanks because they thus
    Did us to us at first convey,
55 Yielded their forces, sense, to us,
    Nor are dross to us, but allay.[1]
On man heaven's influence works not so,
    But that it first imprints the air,[2]
So soul into the soul may flow,
60   Though it to body first repair.
As our blood labors to beget
    Spirits[3] like souls as it can,
Because such fingers need to knit
    That subtle knot which makes us man:

6. Mixture of diverse elements refined (literally, cooked together) by heat (an alchemical term).
7. I.e., we see that we did not understand before what "did move" (motivated) us.
8. The "abler soul" derives from the union of the two lesser ones. "Interanimates": i.e., mutually breathes life into and mutually removes the consciousness of.
9. The nine orders of angels ("intelligences") were believed to govern the nine spheres of Ptolemaic astronomy.
1. Alloy, an impurity that strengthens metal; "dross": an impurity that weakens metal.
2. Astrological influences were conceived of as being transmitted through the medium of the air; also, angels were thought to assume bodies of air in their dealings with humans.
3. Vapors believed to permeate the blood and to mediate between the body and the soul.

65 So must pure lovers' souls descend
      To'affections,° and to faculties,[4]   *feelings*
   Which sense may reach and apprehend;
      Else a great Prince in prison lies.
   To'our bodies turn we then, that so
70   Weak men on love revealed may look;
   Love's mysteries in souls do grow,
      But yet the body is his book.
   And if some lover, such as we,
      Have heard this dialogue of one,
75 Let him still mark us; he shall see
      Small change when we're to bodies gone.

                                                          1633

The Funeral

Whoever comes to shroud me, do not harm
      Nor question much
That subtle wreath of hair which crowns my arm;
The mystery, the sign you must not touch,
5   For 'tis my outward soul,
Viceroy to that, which then to heaven being gone,
      Will leave this to control,
And keep these limbs, her[5] provinces, from dissolution.

For if the sinewy thread[6] my brain lets fall
10   Through every part
Can tie those parts and make me one of all;
These hairs, which upward grew, and strength and art
      Have from a better brain,
Can better do'it; except° she meant that I   *unless*
15   By this should know my pain,
As prisoners then are manacled, when they're condemned to die.

Whate'er she meant by 'it, bury it with me,
      For since I am
Love's martyr, it might breed idolatry,[7]
20 If into other's hands these relics came;
      As 'twas humility
To'afford to it all that a soul can do,
      So 'tis some bravery,
That since you would save none of me, I bury some of you.

                                                          1633

4. Dispositions, powers of the body.
5. The soul's, but also the mistress's (cf. "she," line 14). "Victory": one who acts in the name and by the authority of the supreme ruler.
6. One theory during the period maintained that the body is held in organic order by sinews or

nerves emanating from the brain to every part.
7. A reference to the Roman Catholic practice of idolizing martyrs as saints and venerating objects (relics) associated with them, such as bones or clothing.

The Flea[8]

Mark but this flea, and mark in this,
How little that which thou deniest me is;
It sucked me first, and now sucks thee,
And in this flea, our two bloods mingled be;
5 Thou know'st that this cannot be said
A sin, nor shame nor loss of maidenhead,[9]
    Yet this enjoys before it woo,[1]
    And pampered swells with one blood made of two,[2]
    And this, alas, is more then we would do.

10 Oh stay,[3] three lives in one flea spare,
Where we almost, yea more than married are.
This flea is you and I, and this
Our marriage bed, and marriage temple is;
Though parents grudge, and you, w'are met,
15 And cloisered in these living walls of jet.[4]
    Though use° make you apt to kill me,   *custom*
    Let not to that, self murder added be,
    And sacrilege,[5] three sins in killing three.

Cruel and sudden, hast thou since
20 Purpled thy nail, in blood of innocence?
Wherein could this flea guilty be,
Except in that drop which it sucked from thee?
Yet thou triumph'st, and say'st that thou
Find'st not thy self, nor me the weaker now;[6]
25 'Tis true, then learn how false, fears be;
    Just so much honor, when thou yield'st to me,
    Will waste, as this flea's death took life from thee.[7]

1633

The Relic[8]

When my grave is broke up again
Some second guest to entertain[9]
(For graves have learned that woman-head°   *womanhood*
To be to more than one a bed),
5   And he that digs it, spies

---

8. The flea was a popular subject of Renaissance erotic poems in which, frequently, the narrator envies the flea for the liberties it takes with his lady and for its death at her hands (both "die" and "kill" were Renaissance slang terms for orgasm; the act of sexual intercourse was believed to reduce the man's life span). The narrator here addresses a woman who has scorned his advances.
9. I.e., loss of virginity; the maidenhead is the hymen.
1. I.e., the flea enjoys this liberty without the effort of wooing the lady.
2. Renaissance medical theory held that blood was mingled during sexual intercourse, leading to conception; thus, the image of swelling suggests pregnancy.
3. I.e., refrain from killing the flea.
4. Black marble; the "living walls of jet" here refer to the body of the flea.
5. Since the flea is a "marriage temple," killing it would be sacrilege.
6. I.e., now that she has killed the flea.
7. I.e., when she yields to the narrator, the lady's honor will be diminished by the same amount as her life was diminished by the death of the flea.
8. See note 7, p. 278.
9. Reuse of a grave after an interval of several years was a common seventeenth-century practice (the bones of previous occupants were deposited in charnel houses).

A bracelet of bright hair about the bone,[1]
   Will he not let'us alone,
And think that there a loving couple lies,
Who thought that this device might be some way
10 To make their souls, at the last busy day,[2]
Meet at this grave, and make a little stay?

     If this fall° in a time, or land,   *happen*
     Where mis-devotion[3] doth command,
     Then he that digs us up, will bring
15   Us to the Bishop and the King,
       To make us relics; then
Thou shalt be'a Mary Magdalen,[4] and I
     A something else thereby;
All women shall adore us, and some men;
20 And since at such time, miracles are sought,
I would have that age by this paper taught
What miracles we harmless lovers wrought.

     First, we loved well and faithfully,
     Yet knew not what we loved, nor why,
25   Difference of sex no more we knew,
     Than our guardian angels do;
       Coming and going, we
Perchance might kiss, but not between those meals;[5]
     Our hands ne'er touched the seals,
30 Which nature, injured by late law,[6] sets free:
These miracles we did; but now, alas,
All measure and all language I should pass,
Should I tell what a miracle she was.

                                   1633

Elegy VII[7]

Nature's lay idiot,[8] I taught thee to love,
And in that sophistry, oh, thou dost prove
Too subtle: Fool, thou didst not understand
The mystic language of the eye nor hand:

---

1. I.e., a lock of hair that he had tied about his arm.
2. Judgment Day, when all parts of the body would be reassembled and reunited with the soul in resurrection.
3. False devotion; seems to be a reference to Catholicism.
4. The woman out of whom Christ had cast seven devils (Luke 8.2), traditionally identified with the repentant prostitute of Luke 7.37–50. Renaissance painters often depicted her with long golden hair.
5. I.e., customary kisses of greeting and parting; "meals": kisses were thought to be food for the soul.
6. I.e., human law puts prohibitions ("seals," which may also here signify sexual organs) on that which nature originally set free.
7. Donne's "Elegies," heavily influenced by Ovid's *Amores*, are written in heroic couplets

(rhyming iambic pentameter lines) that provide an apt English equivalent for the Latin elegiac meter of alternating dactyllic pentameter and hexameter lines. In Donne's time, elegies were reflective poems treating various topics including love and (increasingly often) death. Donne's elegies are thought to be early poems, mostly written in the 1590s. Five of the thirteen elegies designed for printing in the 1633 edition of the *Poems* were refused a licence by the official censors; the second edition of 1635 printed seventeen elegies, and others were added to later editions, such as the 1669. There is still no scholarly consensus on the canon of Donne's elegies, and the Roman numerals in the titles first appeared in twentieth-century editions.
8. I.e., one who is ignorant of the workings of nature.

expresses

5 Nor couldst thou judge the difference of the air
   Of sighs, and say, this lies, this sounds° despair:
   Nor by the'eye's water call a malady
   Desperately hot, or changing feverously.
   I had not taught thee then, the alphabet
10 Of flowers, how they devicefully° being set   *ingeniously*
   And bound up, might with speechless secrecy
   Deliver errands mutely, and mutually.
   Remember since° all thy words used to be   *when*
   To every suitor, "I,[9] 'if my friends agree";
15 Since, household charms,[1] thy husband's name to teach,
   Were all the love-tricks, that thy wit could reach;
   And since, an hour's discourse could scarce have made
   One answer in thee,[2] and that ill arrayed
   In broken proverbs, and torn sentences.
20 Thou art not by so many duties his,
   That from the'world's common having severed thee,
   Inlaid thee,[3] neither to be seen, nor see,
   As mine: who have with amorous delicacies
   Refined thee'into a blissful paradise.
25 Thy graces and good words my creatures be;
   I planted knowledge and life's tree[4] in thee,
   Which oh, shall strangers taste? Must I alas
   Frame and enamel plate, and drink in glass?[5]
   Chafe° wax for others' seals? break a colt's force   *heat*
30 And leave him then, being made a ready horse?

1633

Elegy XIX. To His Mistress Going to Bed[6]

   Come, madam, come, all rest my powers defy,
   Until I labor, I in labor[7] lie.
   The foe oft-times having the foe in sight,
   Is tired with standing though he never fight.
5 Off with that girdle, like heaven's zone[8] glistering,
   But a far fairer world encompassing.
   Unpin that spangled breastplate which you wear,
   That th' eyes of busy fools may be stopped there.
   Unlace yourself, for that harmonious chime[9]
10 Tells me from you that now it is bed time.
   Off with that happy busk,° which I envy,   *corset*
   That still can be, and still can stand so nigh.

---

9. Some modern editions change "I"—the reading of all early editions and manuscripts—to "Ay."
1. Magic used to learn her future "husband's name."
2. I.e., could hardly have elicited a response from you.
3. I.e., "laid thee in," set thee aside for his own use, with an allusion to the contested Renaissance practice of "enclosing" common agricultural lands for private uses.
4. The first paradise, Eden, included the Tree of Knowledge and the Tree of Life (Genesis 2.9).
5. I.e., must I fashion and decorate a silver cup but drink from a glass one?
6. This poem was one of the five refused license for the 1633 edition (see note 7, above).
7. Meaning "get to work" in the first instance and "distress" (as of a woman in childbirth) in the second.
8. The belt of Orion.
9. The noise made in removing her "breastplate," or bodice.

Your gown going off, such beauteous state reveals,
As when from flowry meads° th'hill's shadow steals. *meadows*
15 Off with that wiry coronet° and show *headpiece*
The hairy diadem which on you doth grow:
Now off with those shoes, and then safely[1] tread
In this love's hallowed temple, this soft bed.
In such white robes, heaven's angels used to be
20 Received by men; thou, Angel, bring'st with thee
A heaven like Mahomet's Paradise;[2] and though
Ill spirits walk in white, we easily know
By this these angels from an evil sprite:
Those set our hairs, but these our flesh upright.
25 License my roving hands, and let them go
Before, behind, between, above, below.
O my America! my new-found-land,
My kingdom, safeliest when with one man manned,
My mine of precious stones, my empery,° *empire*
30 How blest am I in this discovering thee!
To enter in these bonds is to be free;
Then where my hand is set, my seal shall be.
Full nakedness! All joys are due to thee,
As souls unbodied, bodies unclothed must be,
35 To taste whole joys. Gems which you women use
Are like Atlanta's balls,[3] cast in men's views,
That when a fool's eye lighteth on a gem,
His earthly soul may covet theirs, not them:
Like pictures, or like books' gay coverings made
40 For lay-men, are all women thus arrayed.
Themselves are mystic books,[4] which only we
(Whom their imputed grace will dignify)
Must see revealed. Then, since that I may know,
As liberally as to a midwife, show
45 Thyself: cast all, yea, this white linen hence,
There is no penance due to innocence:[5]
To teach thee, I am naked first; why than,° *then*
What needst thou have more covering than a man?

1669

1. Here and elsewhere in this poem we substitute some manuscript variants for phrases in the 1669 edition, which has "softly" for "safely," "revealed to" (for "received by") in line 20, and "court" (for "covet") in line 38.
2. A heaven of sensual pleasures.
3. According to Greek mythology, Atalanta agreed to marry Hippomenes if he could defeat her in a foot race. As she was about to overtake him, he cast in her path three golden apples (or "balls") given to him by Venus. Distracted by their beauty, Atalanta stopped to retrieve them, and Hippomenes won the race.
4. A manuscript variant for "books" is "bodies."
5. Some manuscripts have "here is no penance much less innocence." White clothing was often considered penitential vestment; the speaker seems to be arguing that the women should cast off such clothing since innocence does not require penance.

Satire III[6]

Kind pity chokes my spleen;[7] brave scorn forbids
Those tears to issue which swell my eyelids;
I must not laugh,° nor weep° sins, and be wise,   *mock / lament*
Can railing then cure these worn maladies?
5 Is not our mistress fair Religion,
As worthy' of all our souls' devotion,
As virtue was to the first blinded age?[8]
Are not heaven's joys as valiant to assuage
Lusts, as earth's honor was to them?[9] Alas,
10 As we do them in means, shall they surpass
Us in the end, and shall thy father's spirit
Meet blind philosophers in heaven, whose merit
Of strict life may be' imputed faith, and hear
Thee, whom he taught so easy ways and near
15 To follow, damned? O, if thou dar'st, fear this;
This fear great courage and high valor is.
Dar'st thou aid mutinous Dutch,[1] and dar'st thou lay
Thee in ships, wooden sepulchers, a prey
To leaders' rage, to storms, to shot, to dearth?
20 Dar'st thou dive seas and dungeons of the earth?
Hast thou courageous fire to thaw the ice
Of frozen North discoveries? and thrice
Colder than salamanders, like divine
Children in the oven,[2] fires of Spain, and the line,°   *equator*
25 Whose countries limbecks to our bodies be,
Canst thou for gain bear?[3] And must every he
Which cries not, "Goddess!" to thy mistress, draw,[4]
Or eat thy poisonous words? Courage of straw!
O desperate coward, wilt thou seem bold, and
30 To thy foes and his (who made thee to stand
Sentinel in his world's garrison) thus yield,

6. In this poem Donne adapts techniques of classical Roman satirists (e.g., Horace, Juvenal, and Persius) to a contemporary problem: the proliferating divisions of belief among Christians in the period after the Protestant break with the Roman Catholic Church. Donne himself was raised in an old Catholic household and seems to have retained considerable sympathy for Catholic beliefs even after he abandoned them in the 1590s; still dubious about the "official" Church of England's doctrines, he refused to take Anglican orders in 1607 despite King James' wish that Donne pursue a career in the Church. Later, he did become an Anglican minister and in 1621 was appointed dean of St. Paul's Cathedral. When Satire III was written, however—probably in the 1590s—Donne like many other English people was in a state of doubt about religious "truth."
    Donne's five satires are among the first formal experiments in the genre in English; they were initially refused a publication license, but the ban was later removed.
7. The seat of bile, and thus of scorn and ridicule (according to Renaissance physiology).
8. I.e., the age of paganism, "blinded" to Chris-

tianity, but capable of a natural devotion to "virtue."
9. I.e., hope of heaven's "joys" should be as capable of calming our "lusts" as earthly "honor" was able to appease the lusts of the pagans.
1. In the last twenty years of the sixteenth century, the English aided the Protestant Dutch in their revolt against Spanish (and Catholic) rule. Donne himself had sailed in two raiding expeditions against the Spanish.
2. After alluding to expeditions to discover the Northwest Passage, Donne invokes the "divine children" Shadrach, Meshach, and Abednego, who are described in the Book of Daniel (3.20–30) as surviving a fiery furnace unharmed after refusing to worship a golden idol. "Salamanders" were thought to be so cold-blooded that they could endure fire.
3. The object of "bear" is "fires of Spain, and the line." "Fires of Spain" refers to the Inquisition, in which heretics were burned at the stake. Inquisitorial and equatorial heats burn people as chemists heat materials in "limbecks," apparatuses used for distilling liquids.
4. I.e., fight a duel.

And for forbidden wars, leave th'appointed field?
Know thy foes: The foul Devil he is, whom thou
Strivest to please: for hate, not love, would allow
35 Thee fain his whole realm to be quit;[5] and as
The world's all parts wither away and pass,
So the world's self, thy other loved foe, is
In her decrepit wane, and thou, loving this,
Dost love a withered and worn strumpet; last,
40 Flesh (itself's death) and joys which flesh can taste,
Thou lovest; and thy fair goodly soul, which doth
Give this flesh power to taste joy, thou dost loathe;
Seek true religion. O, where? Mirreus,[6]
Thinking her unhoused here, and fled from us,
45 Seeks her at Rome; there, because he doth know
That she was there a thousand years ago.
He loves her rags so, as we here obey
The statecloth[7] where the Prince sat yesterday.
Crantz to such brave loves will not be enthralled,
50 But loves her only, who at Geneva[8] is called
Religion—plain, simple, sullen, young,
Contemptuous, yet unhandsome; as among
Lecherous humors,° there is one that judges   *dispositions*
No wenches wholesome but coarse country drudges.
55 Graius[9] stays still at home here, and because
Some preachers, vile ambitious bawds, and laws
Still new, like fashions, bid him think that she
Which dwells with us, is only perfect, he
Embraceth her whom his Godfathers will
60 Tender to him, being tender, as wards still
Take such wives as their guardians offer, or
Pay values. Careless Phrygius[1] doth abhor
All, because all cannot be good, as one
Knowing some women whores, dares marry none.
65 Graccus[2] loves all as one, and thinks that so
As women do in divers countries go
In divers habits, yet are still one kind,
So doth, so is religion; and this blind-
ness too much light breeds;[3] but unmovèd thou
70 Of force must one, and forced but one allow;
And the right; ask thy father which is she,
Let him ask his; though truth and falsehood be
Near twins, yet truth a little elder is;

5. I.e., the devil would willingly ("fain")—but for hate, not love—give you his whole realm of hell to be free ("quit") of it.
6. The fictional characters that follow represent different creeds. "Mirreus," from myrrh, which gives incense its smell, is a Roman Catholic.
7. The royal canopy; a symbol of royal power.
8. The center of Calvinism; "Crantz" is a Geneva Presbyterian.
9. "Graius" is probably an Erastian, i.e., one who believes that religious belief should be determined by the state; he could also be an Anglican, a follower of England's state religion after the Reformation.

1. "Phrygius" seems to represent a skeptic or one who rejects all creeds. "Values," or fines, had to be paid by young men (of "tender" years) who rejected the marriages arranged by their guardians; Catholics also had to pay fines if they refused to attend Anglican services.
2. "Graccus" represents a Universalist, or one who considers all creeds basically alike.
3. I.e., "too much light" grows for anyone to see the truth. Unlike Graccus, who finds the "light of truth" in every creed, the reader is advised to find the one "right" religion without being moved by other forces.

Be busy to seek her, believe me this,
75　He's not of none, nor worst, that seeks the best.[4]
To'adore, or scorn an image, or protest,[5]
May all be bad; doubt wisely; in strange way
To stand inquiring right, is not to stray;
To sleep, or run wrong, is. On a huge hill,
80　Craggèd and steep, Truth stands, and he that will
Reach her, about° must, and about must go,　　　　　　　　*around*
And what th'hill's suddenness° resists, win so;　*unexpected abruptness*
Yet strive so, that before age, death's twilight,
Thy soul rest, for none can work in that night.[6]
85　To will[7] implies delay, therefore now do.
Hard deeds, the body's pains; hard knowledge too
The mind's endeavors reach,[8] and mysteries
Are like the sun, dazzling, yet plain to'all eyes.
Keep the'truth which thou hast found; men do not stand
90　In so ill case that God hath with his hand
Signed kings' blank charters to kill whom they hate,
Nor are they vicars, but hangmen to fate.[9]
Fool and wretch, wilt thou let thy Soul be tied
To man's laws, by which she shall not be tried
95　At the last day? O, will it then boot° thee　　　　　　　*profit*
To say a Philip, or a Gregory,
A Harry, or a Martin[1] taught thee this?
Is not this excuse for mere° contraries　　　　*absolute, complete*
Equally strong? Cannot both sides say so?
100　That thou mayest rightly'obey power, her° bounds know;　*power's*
Those passed, her nature'and name is changed; to be
Then humble to her is idolatry.
As streams are, power is; those blest flowers that dwell
At the rough stream's calm head, thrive and do well,
105　But having left their roots, and themselves given
To the stream's tyrannous rage, alas, are driven
Through mills, and rocks, and woods, and at last, almost
Consumed in going, in the sea are lost:
So perish souls, which more choose men's unjust
110　Power from God claimed, than God himself to trust.

1633

4. I.e., the person who seeks the true church is not an unbeliever ("of none") nor the "worst" sort of believer.
5. "To'adore" alludes to Catholic worship, whereas to "scorn an image" and to "protest" are typical Protestant gestures.
6. See John 9.4: "I must work the work of him that sent me, while it is day. The night cometh, when no man can work."
7. To intend a future action.
8. I.e., just as the body's pains achieve ("reach") hard deeds, the mind's endeavors reach hard knowledge.
9. The lines are syntactically and conceptually difficult, appropriately, perhaps, since they concern a politically sensitive issue. They seem to say that God has not given earthly rulers unconditional authority ("blank charters") to kill whomever they choose; when they do kill, they are serving not as God's "vicars" but rather as hangmen to "fate."
1. Martin Luther (1483–1546), German Reformation leader. "Philip": Philip II of Spain; "Gregory": any one of several Pope Gregorys (VII, XIII, XIV); "Harry": Henry VIII of England.

Good Friday,[2] 1613. Riding Westward

Let man's soul be a sphere, and then, in this,
The'intelligence that moves,[3] devotion is,
And as the other spheres, by being grown
Subject to foreign motions, lose their own,
And being by others hurried every day,   5
Scarce in a year their natural form obey;
Pleasure or business, so, our souls admit
For their first mover, and are whirled by it.[4]
Hence is 't, that I am carried towards the West
This day, when my soul's form bends towards the East.   10
There I should see a Sun,[5] by rising, set,
And by that setting endless day beget;
But that Christ on this cross did rise and fall,
Sin had eternally benighted all.
Yet dare I'almost be glad I do not see   15
That spectacle, of too much weight for me.
Who sees God's face, that is self-life, must die;[6]
What a death were it then to see God die?
It made his own lieutenant, Nature, shrink;
It made his footstool crack, and the sun wink.[7]   20
Could I behold those hands which span the poles,
And tune[8] all spheres at once, pierced with those holes?
Could I behold that endless height which is
Zenith to us, and to'our antipodes,[9]
Humbled below us? Or that blood which is   25
The seat of all our souls, if not of His,
Make dirt of dust, or that flesh which was worn
By God, for his apparel, ragg'd and torn?
If on these things I durst not look, durst I
Upon his miserable mother cast mine eye,   30
Who was God's partner here, and furnished thus
Half of that sacrifice which ransomed us?
Though these things, as I ride, be from mine eye,
They're present yet unto my memory,
For that looks towards them; and thou look'st towards me,   35
O Saviour, as thou hang'st upon the tree.
I turn my back to thee but to receive
Corrections, till thy mercies bid thee leave.°   *desist*
O think me worth thine anger; punish me;

2. The Friday before Easter, observed as the anniversary of Christ's death.
3. I.e., just as an angel was believed to govern the movements of each of the nine concentric celestial spheres, so "devotion" is or should be the guiding principle for the movements of humans.
4. I.e., just as spheres are deflected from their true orbits by outside influences, so our souls are diverted by "Pleasure or business." According to the Ptolemaic astronomy, each sphere, in addition to its own motion, was influenced by the motions of those outside it ("foreign motions," line 4), the outermost being known as the *primum mobile* or "first mover" (line 8).

5. With a pun on "Son."
6. God told Moses: "Thou canst not see my face: for there shall no man see me and live" (Exodus 33.20).
7. An earthquake and an eclipse accompanied the Crucifixion (Matthew 27.45, 51).
8. The motion of the celestial spheres was believed to produce music; some manuscripts have "turn," which accords with the notion that God was the *primum mobile*, or "first mover."
9. The zenith is that part of the heavens directly above any point on earth; the antipodes are that part of earth diametrically opposite such a point.

40　Burn off my rusts and my deformity;
　　Restore thine image so much, by thy grace,
　　That thou may'st know me, and I'll turn my face.

1633

From Holy Sonnets[1]

1

　　Thou hast made me, and shall thy work decay?
　　Repair me now, for now mine end doth haste;
　　I run to death, and death meets me as fast,
　　And all my pleasures are like yesterday.
5　I dare not move my dim eyes any way,
　　Despair behind, and death before doth cast
　　Such terror, and my feeble flesh doth waste
　　By sin in it, which it towards hell doth weigh.
　　Only thou art above, and when towards thee
10　By thy leave I can look, I rise again;
　　But our old subtle foe° so tempteth me　　　　　　*Satan*
　　That not one hour myself I can sustain.
　　Thy grace may wing me[2] to prevent° his art,　　*forestall*
　　And thou like adamant[3] draw mine iron° heart.　*obdurate*

1635

5

　　I am a little world[4] made cunningly
　　Of elements,° and an angelike sprite;°　　　　*matter / spirit*
　　But black sin hath betrayed to endless night
　　My world's both parts, and O, both parts must die.
5　You which beyond that heaven which was most high
　　Have found new spheres, and of new lands can write,[5]
　　Pour new seas in mine eyes, that so I might
　　Drown my world with my weeping earnestly,
　　Or wash it if it must be drowned no more.[6]
10　But O, it must be burnt![7] Alas, the fire
　　Of lust and envy'have burnt it heretofore,
　　And made it fouler; let their flames retire,
　　And burn me, O Lord, with a fiery zeal
　　Of thee'and thy house, which doth in eating heal.[8]

1635

1. Donne's religious poetry is collectively known as the *Divine Poems*, of which the nineteen *Holy Sonnets* form the largest group. Although Donne probably began writing them around 1609, at least a decade after leaving the Catholic Church, the sonnets display an interest in the formal meditative exercise of the Jesuits. Our selections are numbered according to Sir Herbert Grierson's influential edition of 1912, but there is no reason to believe that Donne intended this ordering.
2. Give wings to.
3. Lodestone, a magnetic stone; or adamantine rock, a proverbially hard stone.
4. The individual as microcosm of the world was a common Renaissance notion.

5. Copernican astronomy (which placed the sun at the center of our system, unlike Ptolemaic astronomy, which placed the Earth at the center) had changed peoples' ideas about the universe just as recent terrestrial exploration had changed peoples' ideas about the world.
6. God promised Noah that he would never again cover the Earth with a flood (Genesis 9.11).
7. The Bible predicts that the world will be destroyed by fire (2 Peter 3.10).
8. "The zeal of thine house hath eaten me up" (Psalms 59.9); probably also a reference to the Christian rite of Communion in which Christ's blood and body (his "house") are eaten.

7

At the round earth's imagined corners, blow
Your trumpets, angels;[9] and arise, arise
From death, you numberless infinities
Of souls, and to your scattered bodies go;
5   All whom the flood did, and fire shall,[1] o'erthrow,
All whom war, dearth, age, agues, tyrannies,
Despair, law, chance, hath slain, and you whose eyes
Shall behold God, and never taste death's woe.[2]
But let them sleep, Lord, and me mourn a space;
10 For, if above all these, my sins abound,
'Tis late to ask abundance of thy grace
When we are there. Here on this lowly ground,
Teach me how to repent; for that's as good
As if thou'hadst sealed my pardon with thy blood.

1633

9

If poisonous minerals, and if that tree
Whose fruit threw death on else° immortal us,   *otherwise*
If lecherous goats, if serpents envious
Cannot be damned,[3] alas, why should I be?
5   Why should intent or reason, born in me,
Make sins, else equal, in me more heinous?
And mercy being easy and glorious
To God, in his stern wrath why threatens he?
But who am I, that dare dispute with thee,
10 O God? Oh! of thine only worthy blood,
And my tears, make a heavenly Lethean[4] flood,
And drown in it my sins' black memory.
That thou remember them, some claim as debt;[5]
I think it mercy if thou wilt forget.

1633

10

Death, be not proud, though some have called thee
Mighty and dreadful, for thou are not so;
For those whom thou think'st thou dost overthrow
Die not, poor Death, nor yet canst thou kill me.
5   From rest and sleep, which but thy pictures be,
Much pleasure; then from thee much more must flow,

---

9. The first eight lines of the poem recount the events of the end of the world and the second coming of Christ; Donne alludes specifically to Revelation 7.1: "I saw four angels standing on the four corners of the earth, holding the four winds of the earth."

1. At the end of the world, "the elements shall melt with fervent heat, the earth also and the works that are therein shall be burned up" (2 Peter 3.10).

2. "But I tell you of a truth, there be some standing here, which shall not taste of death, till they see the kingdom of God" (Christ's words to his disciples, Luke 9.27). According to 1 Thessalonians

4.17, believers who are alive at the time of Christ's second coming will not die but will be taken directly to heaven.

3. I.e., only creatures with the ability to reason can be damned. The tree refers to the Tree of Knowledge of Good and Evil, the fruit of which Adam and Eve were forbidden to eat or touch.

4. Lethe was a river in the classical underworld; drinking its waters caused one to forget the past.

5. Perhaps a reference to those who falsely profess on Judgment Day to be God's servants and who call on him to remember their "wonderful works" (Matthew 7.21–22).

And soonest our best men with thee do go,
Rest of° their bones, and soul's delivery.   *for*
Thou'art slave to fate, chance, kings, and desperate men,
10 And dost with poison, war, and sickness dwell,
And poppy'or° charms can make us sleep as well   *opium or*
And better than thy stroke; why swell'st thou then?[6]
One short sleep past, we wake eternally,
And death shall be no more; Death, thou shalt die.

1633

14

Batter my heart, three-personed God;[7] for You
As yet but knock, breathe, shine, and seek to mend;
That I may rise and stand, o'erthrow me,'and bend
Your force to break, blow, burn, and make me new.
5 I, like an usurped town, to'another due,
Labor to'admit You, but O, to no end;
Reason, Your viceroy[8] in me, me should defend,
But is captived, and proves weak or untrue.
Yet dearly'I love you,'and would be loved fain,°   *with pleasure*
10 But am betrothed unto your enemy.
Divorce me,'untie or break that knot again;
Take me to you, imprison me, for I,
Except you'enthrall[9] me, never shall be free,
Nor ever chaste, except you ravish me.

1633

18

Show me, dear Christ, thy spouse[1] so bright and clear.
What! is it she which on the other shore
Goes richly painted? or which, robbed and tore,
Laments and mourns in Germany and here?
5 Sleeps she a thousand, then peeps up one year?
Is she self-truth, and errs? now new, now'outwore?
Doth she,'and did she, and shall she evermore
On one, on seven, or on no hill[2] appear?
Dwells she with us, or like adventuring knights
10 First travel[3] we to seek, and then make love?
Betray,° kind husband, thy spouse to our sights,   *reveal*
And let mine amorous soul court thy mild dove,[4]
Who is most true and pleasing to thee then
When she's embraced and open to most men.[5]

after 1615

6. I.e., puffed up with pride.
7. The Trinity: Father, Son, and Holy Spirit.
8. One who acts in the name and by the authority of the supreme ruler.
9. Make a prisoner of.
1. The true church, "the bride of Christ" (compare Matthew 25.1–13). Lines 2–4 ask whether God's spouse is the Roman Catholic Church (in power in Continental countries such as France, Spain, and Italy, i.e., lands on the "other shore") or the Protestant church "here," i.e., in England.
2. The church on "no hill" could be either the Presbyterian church of Geneva or the Episcopal Church of England, based in Canterbury. The church of "one" hill is an unclear reference, but perhaps it is Mt. Moriah (site of Solomon's temple). The church of "seven" hills is that of Rome.
3. Formerly, "labor" as well as "journey."
4. The dove was a symbol of the Holy Spirit.
5. Universal, without division. An echo of the Song of Solomon (5.2), which was frequently interpreted as the song of love between Christ and the church.

Hymn to God My God, in My Sickness

Since I am coming to that holy room
   Where, with thy choir of saints for evermore,
I shall be made thy music; as I come
   I tune the instrument here at the door,
5   And what I must do then, think here before.

Whilst my physicians by their love are grown
   Cosmographers,[6] and I their map, who lie
Flat on this bed, that by them may be shown
   That this is my southwest discovery
10   *Per fretum febris,*[7] by these straits to die,

I joy, that in these straits, I see my West;[8]
   For, though their currents yield return to none,
What shall my West hurt me? As West and East
   In all flat maps (and I am one) are one,[9]
15   So death doth touch the resurrection.

Is the Pacific Sea my home? Or are
   The Eastern riches? Is Jerusalem?
Anyan,° and Màgellan, and Gìbraltar,[1]   *Bering Straits*
   All straits, and none but straits, are ways to them,
20   Whether where Japhet dwelt, or Cham, or Shem.[2]

We think that Paradise and Calvary,
   Christ's cross, and Adam's tree, stood in one place;
Look, Lord, and find both Adams[3] met in me;
   As the first Adam's sweat surrounds my face,
25   May the last Adam's blood my soul embrace.

So, in his purple[4] wrapped, receive me, Lord;
   By these his thorns give me his other crown;
And, as to others' souls I preached Thy word,
   Be this my text, my sermon to mine own:
30   Therefore that he may raise the Lord throws down.[5]

1635

---

6. Ones who map the general features of the celestial and terrestrial worlds.
7. "Through the straits of fever" (Latin). Donne puns on the word "strait" as both a passageway between two bodies of water and a situation of distress. Compare Christ's words in Matthew 7.4: "Because strait is the gate and narrow is the way, which leadeth unto life, and few there be that find it." Magellan had discovered the straits that bear his name in 1520. They lie at the southern tip of South America and are hence southwest from England.
8. Where the sun sets; hence, where life ends.
9. In one of his sermons (no. 55 in the collection *LXXX Sermons*), Donne noted that when a flat map is "pasted" upon a round body, "then West and East are all one."
1. Behind these locations lie many ancient speculations about the location of paradise, which is analogous to heaven, as the various straits are to death.
2. The three sons of Noah, who settled in Europe, Africa, and Asia respectively after the Flood.
3. I.e., Adam and Christ. "Adam's tree": the Tree of Knowledge of Good and Evil in the Garden of Eden; "in one place": in the same region.
4. I.e., in the purple of Christ's blood or his purple robe (Mark 15.17).
5. Adapted from Psalms 146.8: "the Lord raiseth them that are bowed down."

BEN JONSON

1572–1637

To the Reader[1]

Pray thee, take care, that tak'st my book in hand,
To read it well: that is, to understand.

1616

To Doctor Empirick[2]

When men a dangerous disease did 'scape
Of old, they gave a cock to Aesculape;[3]
Let me give two, that doubly am got free
From my disease's danger, and from thee.

1616

On My First Daughter

Here lies, to each her parents' ruth,°   sorrow
Mary, the daughter of their youth;
Yet all heaven's gifts being heaven's due,
It makes the father less to rue.
5   At six months' end she parted hence
With safety of her innocence;
Whose soul heaven's queen, whose name she bears,
In comfort of her mother's tears,
Hath placed amongst her virgin-train:[4]
10 Where, while that severed doth remain,[5]
This grave partakes the fleshly birth;
Which cover lightly, gentle earth!

1616

On My First Son

Farewell, thou child of my right hand,[6] and joy;
My sin was too much hope of thee, loved boy:
Seven years thou'wert lent to me, and I thee pay,

---

1. From the book of epigrams that Jonson published along with a collection of poems called *The Forrest* in his *First Folio* of 1616. He seems initially to have planned another book of epigrams, but he published later examples of the genre in his supplemental collection of poems, *The Underwood.* That book, with a preface and (partial) arrangement by Jonson, was not published until after his death, in the *Second Folio* of 1640. Jonson's teacher, the historian William Camden, described "Epigrammes" as "short and sweet poems, framed to praise or dispraise." Modeled on poems by the Latin poet Martial (ca. A.D. 40–ca. 103), an "epigram" (originally an inscription, then extended to include any short poem) was a terse and pointed verse, usually ending with a witty turn of thought.
2. An empiric was an untrained physician; the name comes from an ancient sect of physicians called Empirici, who relied on experience rather than on philosophical theory.
3. Aesculapius, the Roman god of medicine and healing.
4. I.e., among those in attendance on the Virgin Mary.
5. I.e., while her soul remains separate from her body (the soul and body will reunite at Resurrection).
6. A literal translation of the Hebrew *Benjamin,* the boy's name.

Exacted by thy fate, on the just day.[7]
5   O could I lose all father now![8] for why
Will man lament the state he should envỳ,
To have so soon 'scaped world's and flesh's rage,
And, if no other misery, yet age?
Rest in soft peace, and asked, say, "Here doth lie
10   Ben Jonson his best piece of poetry."
For whose sake henceforth all his[9] vows be such
As what he loves may never like too much.

1616

On Spies

Spies, you are lights in state,[1] but of base stuff,
Who, when you've burnt yourselves down to the snuff,°   *candle end*
Stink and are thrown away. End fair enough.

1616

To Fool or Knave

Thy praise or dispraise is to me alike:
One doth not stroke me, nor the other strike.

1616

To Fine Lady Would-Be

Fine Madam[2] Would-Be, wherefore° should you fear,   *why*
That love to make so well, a child to bear?
The world reputes you barren; but I know
Your 'pothecary,[3] and his drug says no.
5   Is it the pain affrights? That's soon forgot.
Or your complexion's loss? You have a pot[4]
That can restore that. Will it hurt your feature?°   *good form*
To make amends, you're thought a wholesome° creature.   *healthy*
What should the cause be?[5] Oh, you live at court,
10   And there's both loss of time and loss of sport
In a great belly. Write, then, on thy womb,
Of the not born, yet buried, here's the tomb.

1616

To Sir Henry Cary[6]

That neither fame nor love might wanting be
To greatness, Cary, I sing that and thee;

---

7. Jonson's son died on his seventh birthday in 1603.
8. I.e., let go all fatherly thoughts and sorrow.
9. I.e., Ben Jonson the father's.
1. Condition or form; with a likely pun on "state" as government.
2. "Madame" and "Lady" were courteous designa-

tions for a woman of high social rank.
3. An apothecary prepared and sold drugs for medicinal purposes.
4. I.e., a makeup pot.
5. I.e., that you do not have children.
6. Henry Cary became Viscount Falkland in 1620 and was the father of Jonson's friend Lucius Cary.

Whose house,[7] if it no other honor had,
In only thee might be both great and glad;
5   Who, to upbraid° the sloth of this our time,   *chastise*
Durst valor make almost, but not, a crime;[8]
Which deed I know not, whether were more high,
Or thou more happy, it to justify
Against thy fortune: when no foe, that day,
10   Could conquer thee but chance, who did betray.
Love thy great loss, which a renown hath won,
To live when Broick not stands, nor Ruhr doth run.[9]
Love honors, which of best example be
When they cost dearest and are done most free;
15   Though every fortitude deserves applause,
It may be much or little in the cause.
He's valiant'st that dares fight, and not for pay;
That virtuous is, when the reward's away.

                                                                    1616

On Playwright

Playwright, convict° of public wrongs to men,   *convicted*
Takes private beatings and begins again.
Two kinds of valor he doth show at once:
Active in 's° brain, and passive in his bones.   *his*
                                                                    1616

To Elizabeth, Countess of Rutland[1]

That poets are far rarer births than kings
Your noblest father proved; like whom before,
Or then, or since, about our Muses' springs,
Came not that soul exhausted so their store.[2]
5   Hence was it that the destinies decreed
(Save that most masculine issue of his brain)[3]
No male unto him; who could so exceed
Nature, they thought, in all that he would fain.°   *make*
At which she, happily[4] displeased, made you,
10   On whom, if he were living now to look,
He should those rare and absolute numbers[5] view,
As he would burn or better far his book.
                                                                    1616

---

7. Family (lineage). Cary's wife, Elizabeth, also perhaps honored the "house"; her play *The Tragedy of Mariam* was published in 1613.
8. In October 1605, Cary was with a group of English and Dutch soldiers who fled from a smaller Italian force—hence Cary, who tried to stop the rout and was captured, almost made "valor" a crime in English eyes.
9. "The castle and river near where he was taken" [Jonson's note]. Cary was captured near the confluence of the Rhur and the Rhine rivers.

1. (1584–1612); daughter of the poet Sir Philip Sidney (1554–1586), she married Roger Manners, fifth earl of Rutland.
2. I.e., no one before or since Sidney has so well used up the sources of poetic inspiration, or springs of the Muses (goddesses of poetry in Greek myth).
3. I.e., his books.
4. I.e., by good fortune.
5. Metrical feet, hence lines or verses; perhaps also, "proportions."

On English Monsieur

Would you believe, when you this monsieur[6] see,
That his whole body should speak French, not he?
That so much scarf of France, and hat, and feather,
And shoe, and tie, and garter should come hether,°   *hither*
5   And land on one whose face durst never be
Toward the sea farther than Half-Way Tree?[7]
That he, untraveled, should be French so much
As Frenchmen in his company should seem Dutch?
Or had his father, when he did him get,
10   The French disease,[8] with which he labors yet?
Or hung some monsieur's picture on the wall,
By which his dam conceived him, clothes and all?
Or is it some French statue? No: 'T° doth move,   *it*
And stoop, and cringe. O then, it needs must prove
15   The new French tailor's motion,° monthly made,   *puppet*
Daily to turn in Paul's,[9] and help the trade.

1616

To John Donne

Who shall doubt, Donne, where° I a poet be,   *whether*
When I dare send my epigrams[1] to thee?
That so alone canst judge, so'alone dost make;
And, in thy censures, evenly dost take
5   As free simplicity to disavow
As thou hast best authority t' allow.
Read all I send, and if I find but one
Marked by thy hand, and with the better stone,[2]
My title's sealed.[3] Those that for claps° do write,   *applause*
10   Let pui'nies', porters', players'[4] praise delight,
And, till they burst, their backs like asses load:[5]
A man should seek great glory, and not broad.° *widespread, unrefined*

1616

Inviting a Friend to Supper[6]

Tonight, grave sir, both my poor house, and I
Do equally desire your company;

6. Stress on first syllable; often spelled *monser* in Jonson's time, suggesting an Anglicized pronunciation.
7. Perhaps a landmark between London and Dover, where a traveler would embark for France.
8. I.e., syphilis.
9. St. Paul's Cathedral in London. In the seventeenth century St. Paul's was a popular gathering place; merchants hired men to walk up and down in the yard advertising their wares.
1. On epigrams, see note 1, p. 291.
2. The allusion may be to the Thracian custom of recording the good or evil fortunes of each day by placing a stone counter of corresponding color in

an urn. Jonson refers elsewhere to Pliny's description of this custom in his *Natural History* 7.40.
3. I.e., as a poet.
4. Actors; "pui'nies' ": puisnies (pronounced like punies), insignificant persons.
5. The obscure grammar seems to mean: let the praises made by insignificant persons ("pui'nies', porters', players' ") load the backs of those who write for applause ("claps") until their backs break ("burst"). "Asses": beasts of burden, with a probable pun on "ass" as an ignorant person.
6. The versified invitation to share a meal was a popular type of classical and Renaissance verse epistle.

Not that we think us worthy such a guest,
But that your worth will dignify our feast
5   With those that come, whose grace may make that seem
Something, which else could hope for no esteem.
It is the fair acceptance, sir, creates
The entertainment perfect, not the cates.°   *food*
Yet shall you have, to rectify your palate,
10   An olive, capers,[7] or some better salad
Ushering the mutton; with a short-legged hen,
If we can get her, full of eggs, and then
Lemons, and wine for sauce; to these a cony°   *rabbit*
Is not to be despaired of, for our money;
15   And, though fowl now be scarce, yet there are clerks,
The sky not falling, think we may have larks.[8]
I'll tell you of more, and lie, so you will come:
Of partridge, pheasant, woodcock, of which some
May yet be there, and godwit,[9] if we can;
20   Knot, rail, and ruff too. Howsoe'er, my man
Shall read a piece of Virgil, Tacitus,
Livy,[1] or of some better book to us,
Of which we'll speak our minds, amidst our meat;
And I'll profess[2] no verses to repeat.
25   To this, if aught appear which I not know of,
That will the pastry, not my paper, show of.[3]
Digestive[4] cheese and fruit there sure will be;
But that which most doth take my Muse and me,
Is a pure cup of rich Canary wine,
30   Which is the Mermaid's[5] now, but shall be mine;
Of which had Horace, or Anacreon[6] tasted,
Their lives, as do their lines, till now had lasted.
Tobacco, nectar, or the Thespian spring,[7]
Are all but Luther's beer[8] to this I sing.
35   Of this we will sup free, but moderately,
And we will have no Pooley, or Parrot[9] by,
Nor shall our cups make any guilty men;
But, at our parting we will be as when
We innocently met. No simple word
40   That shall be uttered at our mirthful board,
Shall make us sad next morning or affright
The liberty that we'll enjoy tonight.

1616

---

7. Pickled flower-buds of the caper shrub.
8. According to an old proverb, "When the sky falls we shall have larks." "Clerks": i.e., scholars (pronounced "clarks").
9. The godwit, knot, rail, and ruff are all wading birds related to the curlew or sandpiper. They were formerly regarded as delicacies.
1. (59 B.C.–A.D. 17); Roman historian. Virgil (70–19 B.C.), Roman poet, author of the *Aeneid*; Tacitus (ca. A.D. 56–ca. 120), Roman historian.
2. I.e., promise.
3. I.e., if papers appear, they will be only under pies ("pastry"; to keep them from sticking to the pan). "To this": add to this.
4. Promoting or aiding digestion.

5. The Mermaid tavern in London, a favorite haunt of Jonson's. Canary is a light sweet wine.
6. Anacreon of Teos (ca. 582–ca. 485 B.C.), a Greek poet, and Horace (65–68 B.C.), a Roman poet, both wrote many poems praising wine.
7. Associated with the nine Muses, Greek goddesses believed to be sources of inspiration for the arts; smoking was often called "drinking tobacco"; "nectar": the drink of the classical gods.
8. German beer, considered inferior.
9. Robert Pooly and (probably) Henry Parrot were government spies; Pooly was present when the poet Christopher Marlowe was killed in a tavern brawl in 1593. With a pun on the chattering of parrots ("Polly," a name for a parrot).

On Gut

Gut eats all day and lechers all the night;
So all his meat he tasteth[1] over twice;
And, striving so to double his delight,
He makes himself a thoroughfare of vice.
5   Thus in his belly can he change a sin:
Lust it comes out, that gluttony went in.

               1616

Epitaph on Elizabeth, L. H.[2]

Wouldst thou hear what man can say
In a little? Reader, stay.
Underneath this stone doth lie
As much beauty as could die;
5   Which in life did harbor give
To more virtue than doth live.
If at all she had a fault,
Leave it buried in this vault.
One name was Elizabeth;
10   Th' other, let it sleep with death:
Fitter, where it died, to tell,
Than that it lived at all. Farewell.

               1616

To Penshurst[3]

Thou art not, Penshurst, built to envious show,
Of touch[4] or marble; nor canst boast a row
Of polished pillars, or a roof of gold;
Thou hast no lantern,[5] whereof tales are told,
5   Or stair, or courts; but stand'st an ancient pile,
And, these grudged at, art reverenced the while.[6]
Thou joy'st in better marks, of soil, of air,
Of wood, of water; therein thou art fair.
Thou hast thy walks for health, as well as sport;
10   Thy mount,[7] to which the dryads° do resort,   *wood nymphs*
Where Pan and Bacchus[8] their high feasts have made,
Beneath the broad beech and the chestnut shade;
That taller tree, which of a nut was set

---

1. Also meaning to know carnally.
2. The subject of this epitaph (a poem written as if it were inscribed on a tombstone) has not been identified, although it is likely that the "L" stood for "Lady."
3. The country estate of the Sidney family, in Kent. An important early example of the "country house" poem in English, this poem was imitated by Jonson's contemporaries.
4. Touchstone, a fine black (costly) variety of basalt.

5. A glassed or open structure raised above the roof of a house.
6. I.e., while other buildings are envied, Penshurst is admired.
7. Some high ground on the estate.
8. Classical god of wine and revelry. "Pan": classical god of shepherds and hunters; half goat, half man, he was raised by Bacchus, and was associated with lust and music.

At his great birth where all the Muses[9] met.
15 There in the writhèd bark are cut the names
Of many a sylvan, taken with his flames;[1]
And thence the ruddy satyrs oft provoke
The lighter fauns to reach thy Lady's Oak.
Thy copse too, named of Gamage,[2] thou hast there,
20 That never fails to serve thee seasoned deer
When thou wouldst feast or exercise thy friends.
The lower land, that to the river bends,
Thy sheep, thy bullocks, kine,° and calves do feed;   *cows*
The middle grounds thy mares and horses breed.
25 Each bank doth yield thee conies;° and the tops,   *rabbits*
Fertile of wood, Ashore and Sidney's copse,[3]
To crown thy open table, doth provide
The purpled pheasant with the speckled side;
The painted partridge lies in every field,
30 And for thy mess° is willing to be killed.   *meal*
And if the high-swollen Medway[4] fail thy dish,
Thou hast thy ponds, that pay thee tribute fish,
Fat aged carps that run into thy net,
And pikes, now weary their own kind to eat,
35 As loath the second draught[5] or cast to stay,°   *await*
Officiously° at first themselves betray;   *dutifully*
Bright eels that emulate them, and leap on land
Before the fisher, or into his hand.
Then hath thy orchard fruit, thy garden flowers,
40 Fresh as the air, and new as are the hours.
The early cherry, with the later plum,
Fig, grape, and quince, each in his time doth come;
The blushing apricot and woolly peach
Hang on thy walls, that every child may reach.
45 And though thy walls be of the country stone,
They're reared with no man's ruin, no man's groan;
There's none that dwell about them wish them down;
But all come in, the farmer and the clown,°   *countryman*
And no one empty-handed, to salute
50 Thy lord and lady, though they have no suit.
Some bring a capon,[6] some a rural cake,
Some nuts, some apples; some that think they make
The better cheeses bring them, or else send
By their ripe daughters, whom they would commend
55 This way to husbands, and whose baskets bear

---

9. The nine Greek goddesses believed to be sources of inspiration for the arts; "at his great birth": i.e., Sir Philip Sidney's birth (on November 30, 1554), when an oak was planted to commemorate the day.
1. I.e., the fires of love; perhaps the woodsman ("sylvan") is in love because of reading Sidney's poems. The "ruddy satyrs" (woodland gods associated with lust and drinking) challenge the "lighter fauns" (woodland gods described as less wild than the satyrs) to race to the tree named after a Lady

Leicester, who is said to have entered into labor under its branches.
2. Barbara Gamage, wife of Sir Robert Sidney (Philip's younger brother and the current owner of Penshurst).
3. Two groves on the estate.
4. The local river.
5. The drawing in of a net.
6. A castrated rooster, especially one fattened for eating.

An emblem of themselves in plum or pear.
But what can this (more than express their love)
Add to thy free provisions, far above
The need of such? whose liberal board° doth flow   *table*
60   With all that hospitality doth know;
Where comes no guest but is allowed to eat,
Without his fear, and of thy lord's own meat;
Where the same beer and bread, and selfsame wine,
That is his lordship's shall be also mine,
65   And I not fain° to sit (as some this day   *obliged*
At great men's tables), and yet dine away.[7]
Here no man tells° my cups; nor, standing by,   *counts*
A waiter doth my gluttony envy,
But gives me what I call, and lets me eat;
70   He knows below he shall find plenty of meat.
Thy tables hoard not up for the next day;
Nor, when I take my lodging, need I pray
For fire, or lights, or livery;° all is there,   *provisions*
As if thou then wert mine, or I reigned here:
75   There's nothing I can wish, for which I stay.°   *wait*
That found King James when, hunting late this way
With his brave son, the prince, they saw thy fires
Shine bright on every hearth, as the desires
Of thy Penates[8] had been set on flame
80   To entertain them; or the country came
With all their zeal to warm their welcome here.
What (great I will not say, but) sudden cheer
Didst thou then make 'em! and what praise was heaped
On thy good lady then, who therein reaped
85   The just reward of her high housewifery;
To have her linen, plate, and all things nigh,
When she was far; and not a room but dressed
As if it had expected such a guest!
These, Penshurst, are thy praise, and yet not all.
90   Thy lady's noble, fruitful, chaste withal.
His children thy great lord may call his own,
A fortune in this age but rarely known.
They are, and have been, taught religion; thence
Their gentler spirits have sucked innocence.
95   Each morn and even they are taught to pray,
With the whole household, and may, every day,
Read in their virtuous parents' noble parts
The mysteries of manners, arms, and arts.
Now, Penshurst, they that will proportion° thee   *compare*
100   With other edifices, when they see
Those proud, ambitious heaps, and nothing else,
May say their lords have built, but thy lord dwells.

1616

---

7. I.e., to be insufficiently fed at "great men's   8. Roman household gods.
tables," and so to dine elsewhere to finish.

Song: To Celia (I)⁹

Come, my Celia, let us prove,°   *experience*
While we can, the sports of love;
Time will not be ours forever;
He at length our good will sever.
5   Spend not then his gifts in vain.
Suns that set may rise again;
But if once we lose this light,
'Tis with us perpetual night.
Why should we defer our joys?
10 Fame and rumor are but toys.
Cannot we delude the eyes
Of a few poor household spies,
Or his easier ears beguile,
So removèd by our wile?
15 'Tis no sin love's fruit to steal;
But the sweet thefts to reveal,
To be taken, to be seen,
These have crimes accounted been.

1606   1616

Song: To Celia (II)¹

Drink to me only with thine eyes,
And I will pledge² with mine;
Or leave a kiss but in the cup,
And I'll not look for wine.
5   The thirst that from the soul doth rise,
Doth ask a drink divine:
But might I of Jove's nectar³ sup,°   *taste*
I would not change for thine.⁴
I sent thee late a rosy wreath,
10 Not so much honoring thee,
As giving it a hope, that there
It could not withered be.
But thou thereon did'st only breathe,
And sent'st it back to me;
15 Since when it grows and smells, I swear,
Not of itself, but thee.

1616

9. From Jonson's play *Volpone* (1606). The lecherous Volpone is attempting to seduce Celia, the virtuous wife of Corvino, whom Volpone has gotten out of the way by a stratagem (line 14). The poem draws on Catullus 5, a poem translated by a number of English poets in this period. Cf. Thomas Campion, "My Sweetest Lesbia" (p. 249).
1. Based on five separate passages in the *Epistles* of the Greek rhetorician Philostratus (ca. A.D. 170–ca. 245).
2. Vow, with the added meaning "drink a toast."
3. The drink of the gods of classical mythology, hence belonging to Jove, the king of the gods.
4. Although the lines are ambiguous, the speaker seems to be saying that "even if I might taste (sup) Jove's nectar, I would not take it in exchange for thine."

A Fit of Rhyme Against Rhyme[5]

Rhyme, the rack° of finest wits,   *instrument of torture*
 That expresseth but by fits
   True conceit,
 Spoiling senses of their treasure,
5 Cozening judgment with a measure,
   But false weight;[6]
 Wresting words from their true calling;
 Propping verse for fear of falling
   To the ground;
10 Jointing syllabes,[7] drowning letters,
 Fastening vowels, as with fetters
   They were bound!
 Soon as lazy thou wert known,
 All good poetry hence was flown,
15   And art banished:
 For a thousand years together,[8]
 All Parnassus'[9] green did wither,
   And wit vanish'd!
 Pegasus[1] did fly away,
20 At the wells no Muse did stay,
   But bewailed,
 So to see the fountain dry,
 And Apollo's music die,
   All light failed!
25 Starveling rhymes did fill the stage,
 Not a poet in an age
   Worthy crowning.
 Not a work deserving bays,[2]
 Nor a line deserving praise,
30   Pallas[3] frowning:
 Greek was free from rhyme's infection,
 Happy Greek, by this protection,
   Was not spoiled.
 Whilst the Latin, queen of tongues,
35 Is not yet free from rhyme's wrongs,

---

5. The issue of rhyme was hotly debated by many sixteenth and seventeenth century poets including John Milton and John Dryden; some who denigrated rhyme in theory used it effectively in their poetic practice. In 1587 Christopher Marlowe attacked the "jigging veins of rhyming motherwits" in the prologue to *Tamburlaine the Great*, part 1, and in 1602 Thomas Campion published a treatise arguing for the superiority of classical "quantitative meters" to English rhyming verse. In 1603, Samuel Daniel published his *Defense of Rhyme*; Jonson entered the fray with a witty poem he described to a friend as written "both against Campion and Daniel." A "fit" is an old term for a part of a poem, a canto; Jonson also plays (e.g., in line 2) on the term's meaning of "convulsion."
6. Punning on "measure" as a unit of poetical or musical rhythm and as a standard amount of a commodity, the line suggests that the rhyming poet cheats the buyer-reader by failing to "weigh" sounds properly, i.e., according to the system used

in Latin prosody.
7. I.e., making a rhyme by breaking a word on a syllabic unit (as Jonson himself does in some poems).
8. Classical Latin poetry did not use rhyme, but beginning in the third and fourth centuries A.D., Christian poets rhymed in Latin. Jonson's view that true poetry's "banishment" lasted a thousand years implies that the Italian humanists of the fourteenth century rescued poetry from the "wrongs" (line 35) of rhyme.
9. Mount Parnassus, in central Greece, was considered sacred to the Muses, goddesses of the arts and sciences, and to Phoebus (Apollo), god of sunlight, prophecy, music, and poetry.
1. The winged horse Pegasus made the Hippocrene spring ("wells") for the Muses by striking his hoof on the ground.
2. I.e., the evergreen garland symbolizing a poet's superiority.
3. Pallas Athena, goddess of wisdom.

But rests foiled.
Scarce the hill again doth flourish,
Scarce the world a wit doth nourish,
  To restore
40 Phoebus to his crown again;
And the Muses to their brain;
  As before.
Vulgar[4] languages that want
Words, and sweetness, and be scant
45 Of true measure,
Tyrant rhyme hath so abused,
That they long since have refused,
  Other cesure.°   *caesura*
He that first invented thee,
50 May his joints tormented be,
  Cramp'd for ever;
Still may syllabes° jar with time,   *syllables*
Still may reason war with rhyme,
  Resting never!
55 May his sense when it would meet
The cold tumor in his feet,
  Grow unsounder;
And his title be long fool,[5]
That in rearing such a school
60 Was the founder!

1616?   1640–41

A Hymn to God the Father

Hear me, O God!
A broken heart,
Is my best part;
Use still thy rod,[6]
5 That I may prove°   *experience*
Therein thy love.

If thou hadst not
Been stern to me,
But left me free,
10 I had forgot
Myself and thee.

For sin's so sweet,
As° minds ill bent   *that*
Rarely repent,
15 Until they meet
Their punishment.

Who more can crave
Than thou hast done,

---

4. Vernacular, as opposed to Latin.   ("art is long, life short").
5. A play on the Latin saying *ars longa, vita brevis* 6. I.e., punishment.

> That gav'st a Son,[7]
> 20   To free a slave?
> First made of naught,
> With all since bought.[8]
>
> Sin, Death, and Hell,
> His glorious Name
> 25   Quite overcame,
> Yet I rebel,
> And slight the same.
>
> But I'll come in
> Before my loss
> 30   Me farther toss,
> As sure to win
> Under his Cross.

1640–41

Her Triumph[9]

See the chariot at hand here of Love,
    Wherein my lady rideth!
Each that draws is a swan or a dove,[1]
    And well the care Love guideth.
5   As she goes, all hearts do duty
        Unto her beauty;
And, enamored, do wish, so they might
        But enjoy such a sight,
That they still° were to run by her side,   always
10   Through[2] swords, through seas, whither° she would ride.   wherever

Do but look on her eyes; they do light
    All that Love's world compriseth!
Do but look on her hair; it is bright
    As Love's star[3] when it riseth!
15   Do but mark, her forehead's smoother
        Than words that soothe her!
And from her arched brows, such a grace
        Sheds itself through the face,
As alone there triumphs to the life
20   All the gain, all the good, of the elements' strife.[4]

---

7. I.e., who could crave more than what God ("Thou") has already done, in giving his "Son" (Christ).
8. I.e., redeemed by Christ.
9. Published after Jonson's death, this poem was included in "A Celebration of Charis in Ten Lyric Pieces"; although Jonson may have arranged these lyrics as they stand, they were (probably) not composed as a unit. The Greek word *charis* means "grace" or "loveliness"; the three Graces are *Charites*. "Charis" is also related to the Latin term for love, *caritas*. "Triumph": following Petrarch, many Renaissance poets used the image of the triumphal procession to celebrate a person or concept (such as chastity, time, etc.). "Charis" is also an obsolete form of "cherish."
1. Venus ("Love") was said to drive a chariot drawn by swans or doves.
2. Here pronounced as two syllables (often spelled "thorough").
3. I.e., Venus.
4. The four elements (earth, water, air, and fire) were thought to be constantly at war; according to Platonic theory, heavenly harmony reconciles the skirmishing elements.

Have you seen but a bright lily grow,
  Before rude hands have touched it?
Ha' you marked but the fall o' the snow
  Before the soil hath smutched° it?   smudged
25 Ha' you felt the wool o' the beaver?
      Or swan's down⁵ ever?
Or have smelt o' the bud o' the brier?
      Or the nard in the fire?
Or have tasted the bag⁶ o' the bee?
30 O so white, O so soft, O so sweet is she!

                                                      1640–41

An Elegy⁷

Though beauty be the mark of praise,
  And yours of whom I sing be such
  As not the world can praise too much,
Yet is 't your virtue now I raise.

5   A virtue, like allay,° so gone   alloy
      Throughout your form as, though that⁸ move
      And draw and conquer all men's love,
This⁹ subjects you to love of one.

Wherein you triumph yet; because
10   'Tis of yourself, and that you use
      The noblest freedom, not to choose
Against or faith or honor's laws.

But who should less expect from you,
  In whom alone Love¹ lives again?
15   By whom he is restored to men,
And kept, and bred,² and brought up true.

His falling temples you have reared,
  The withered garlands ta'en away;
  His altars kept from the decay
20 That envy wished, and nature feared;

And on them burn so chaste a flame,
  With so much loyalties' expense,
  As Love, t' acquit³ such excellence,
Is gone himself into your name.⁴

25 And you are he; the deity
      To whom all lovers are designed

---

5. I.e., the softness of the beaver's fur and the swan's down.
6. Sack of honey. "Nard": spikenard, an aromatic plant used in preparing incense (as here) and perfumes.
7. Originally a poem written in elegiac meter; in English tradition an elegy dealt either with love or (increasingly from the seventeenth century on) with grief for a dead person.

8. I.e., your beauty.
9. I.e., your virtue.
1. I.e., Cupid.
2. Educated, or properly trained.
3. I.e., to reward.
4. I.e., the lady's name includes the letters of "love." Based on this hint, some scholars have suggested Lady Covell as the person addressed.

That would their better objects find;
Among which faithful troop am I.

Who, as an offspring[5] at your shrine,
30   Have sung this hymn, and here entreat
One spark of your diviner heat
To light upon a love of mine.

Which, if it kindle not, but scant
Appear, and that to shortest view,
35   Yet give me leave t' adore in you
What I in her am grieved to want.

1640–41

An Ode to Himself[6]

Where dost thou careless lie
    Buried in ease and sloth?
Knowledge that sleeps doth die;
    And this security,°   *overconfidence*
5   It is the common moth
That eats on wits and arts, and oft destroys them both.

Are all th' Aonian springs
    Dried up?[7] Lies Thespia waste?
Doth Clarius' harp[8] want strings,
10   That not a nymph now sings;
        Or droop they as disgraced,
To see their seats and bowers by chattering pies[9] defaced?

If hence thy silence be,
    As 'tis too just a cause,
15   Let this thought quicken thee:
    Minds that are great and free
        Should not on fortune pause;
'Tis crown enough to virtue still, her own applause.

What though the greedy fry[1]
20   Be taken with false baits
Of worded balladry,
    And think it poesy?°   *poetry*
        They die with their conceits,
And only piteous scorn upon their folly waits.

25   Then take in hand thy lyre,
    Strike in thy proper strain,

---

5. Possibly a misprint for "offering."
6. A Horatian ode (see "Essay on Versification," p. lxxviii).
7. Aonia was the region in Greece near Mount Helicon, home of the nine Muses, Greek goddesses believed to be sources of inspiration for the arts. "Thespia": a town near Helicon, center of the cult of the Muses.
8. The lyre of Apollo, god of music and poetry (from his temple at Clarus, on the Ionian coast.)
9. The Muses changed the nine daughters of King Pierus into magpies ("pies") for challenging their supremacy in poetry.
1. Youth, with a pun on "fry" (young fishes).

With Japhet's line,[2] aspire°   *aspire to*
   Sol's chariot for new fire
      To give the world again;
30 Who aided him will thee, the issue of Jove's brain.[3]

And since our dainty age
   Cannot endure reproof,
   Make not thyself a page
To that strumpet the stage,
35   But sing high and aloof,
Safe from the wolve's black jaw, and the dull ass's hoof.

                                  1640

To the Immortal Memory and Friendship of That Noble Pair, Sir Lucius Cary and Sir Henry Morison[4]

The Turn[5]

Brave infant of Saguntum,[6] clear°   *explain or describe*
Thy coming forth in that great year,
When the prodigious Hannibal did crown
His rage with razing your immortal town.
5 Thou, looking then about,
   Ere thou wert half got out,
Wise child, didst hastily return,
And mad'st thy mother's womb thine urn.[7]
How summed a circle didst thou leave mankind
10 Of deepest lore, could we the center find!

The Counterturn

Did wiser Nature draw thee back
From out the horror of that sack,
Where shame, faith, honor, and regard of right
Lay trampled on; the deeds of death and night
15 Urged, hurried forth, and hurled
   Upon th' affrighted world;
Sword, fire, and famine, with fell fury met,
And all on utmost ruin set,
As, could they but life's miseries foresee,
20 No doubt all infants would return like thee?

2. Prometheus, the son of Iapetus, stole fire from the gods for the benefit of mankind.
3. Minerva or Pallas Athena, who was said to have sprung fully grown from the head of her father, Jove.
4. Sir Henry Morison (ca. 1608–1629) was knighted in 1627. His good friend Sir Lucius Cary (ca. 1610–1643), who married Morison's sister in 1630, was killed at the battle of Newbury in September 1643, fighting for the Royalist cause.
5. Unlike other "odes" by Jonson modeled on Horace's *Odes* (see, e.g., "An Ode to Himself," pp. 304–05), this one is modeled on a poetic structure used by the Greek poet Pindar (ca. 522–ca. 438 B.C.). Pindar's odes are typically arranged in groups of three stanzas (strophe, antistrophe, and epode)

designed to be sung by a chorus; the chorus moved in one direction while chanting the strophe, reversed direction for the antistrophe, and stood still for the epode. Jonson's "turn," "counterturn," and "stand," (more or less translated from the Greek terms) imitate Pindar's pattern. As in Pindar, the metrical pattern of the turn is repeated in the counterturn, then varied in the stand. The pattern of these first three stanzas is then repeated exactly in the remaining sets of stanzas.
6. A town sacked by Hannibal in 219 B.C. The Roman naturalist Pliny the Elder (A.D. 23–79) records the story of a "brave infant," who returned to his mother's womb upon witnessing the city's destruction.
7. I.e., tomb.

The Stand

For what is life, if measured by the space,[8]
Not by the act?
Or maskèd man, if valued by his face
Above his fact?
25 Here's one outlived his peers
And told forth fourscore years;
He vexèd time and busied the whole state,
Troubled both foes and friends;
But ever to no ends:
30 What did this stirrer but die late?
How well at twenty had he fall'n or stood!
For three of his fourscore he did no good.

The Turn

He[9] entered well, by virtuous parts,
Got up and thrived with honest arts;
35 He purchased friends, and fame, and honors then,
And had his noble name advanced with men;
But weary of that flight
He stooped in all men's sight
To sordid flatteries, acts of strife,
40 And sunk in that dead sea of life
So deep, as he did then death's waters sup,°   *taste*
But that the cork of title buoyed him up.

The Counterturn

Alas, but Morison fell young;
He never fell, thou fall'st,[1] my tongue.
45 He stood, a soldier to the last right end,
A perfect patriot, and a noble friend,
But most a virtuous son.
All offices° were done   *duties in life*
By him so ample, full, and round,
50 In weight, in measure, number, sound,
As, though his age imperfect° might appear,   *incomplete*
His life was of humanity the sphere.[2]

The Stand

Go now, and tell out[3] days summed up with fears,
And make them years;
55 Produce thy mass of miseries on the stage
To swell thine age;
Repeat of things a throng,
To show thou hast been long,
Not lived; for life doth her great actions spell
60 By what was done and wrought

8. I.e., by the length of time.
9. I.e., another man, a separate example.
1. Slip, with a possible pun on the Latin *fallere* (to

make a mistake).
2. I.e., the perfect model.
3. Count, number.

In season, and so brought
To light: her measures are, how well
Each syllabe° answered, and was formed how fair;   *syllable*
These make the lines of life, and that's her air.[4]

The Turn

65 It is not growing like a tree
In bulk doth make man better be;
Or standing long an oak, three hundred year,
To fall a log at last, dry, bald, and sere:°   *withered*
A lily of a day
70 Is fairer far in May;
Although it fall and die that night,
It was the plant and flower of light.
In small proportions we just beauties see,
And in short measures life may perfect be.

The Counterturn

75 Call, noble Lucius, then for wine,
And let thy looks with gladness shine;
Accept this garland, plant it on thy head,
And think, nay know, thy Morison's not dead.
He leaped the present age,
80 Possessed with holy rage
To see that bright eternal day;
Of which we priests and poets say
Such truths as we expect for happy men,
And there he lives with memory, and Ben

The Stand

85 Jonson! who sung this of him, ere he went
Himself to rest,
Or taste a part of that full joy he meant
To have expressed
In this bright asterism;°   *constellation*
90 Where it were friendship's schism
(Were not his Lucius long with us to tarry)
To separate these twi-
Lights, the Dioscuri,[5]
And keep the one half from his Harry.
95 But fate doth so altérnate the design,
Whilst that in heaven, this light on earth must shine.

The Turn

And shine as you exalted are,
Two names of friendship, but one star:
Of hearts the union. And those not by chance

---

4. I.e., life's "measures" are its metrical patterns, and the standards by which it is judged; "air": melody, song.
5. Castor and Pollux, twin sons of Zeus, famous for brotherly devotion. When Castor was killed,

Zeus granted Pollux' prayer that he be allowed to share his life with his brother; henceforward each lived half the time on earth and half in heaven. Their constellation is Gemini, the Twins.

100   Made, or indenture,° or leased out t'advance   *contracted for*
The profits for a time.
No pleasures vain did chime
Of rimes, or riots, at your feasts,
Orgies of drink, or feigned protests,°   *protestations*
105   But simple love of greatness and of good;
That knits brave minds and manners more than blood.

The Counterturn

This made you first to know the why
You liked, then after to apply
That liking, and approach so one the tother,°   *other*
110   Till either grew a portion of the other:
Each styled by his end
The copy of his friend.
You lived to be the great surnames
And titles by which all made claims
115   Unto the virtue. Nothing perfect done,
But as a Cary, or a Morison.

The Stand

And such a force the fair example had,
As they that saw
The good, and durst not practice it, were glad
120   That such a law
Was left yet to mankind;
Where they might read and find
Friendship, indeed, was written, not in words;
And with the heart, not pen,
125   Of two so early men,
Whose lines her rolls were, and recòrds,
Who, ere the first down bloomèd on the chin,[6]
Had sowed these fruits, and got the harvest in.

1640

Still to Be Neat[7]

Still to be neat, still to be dressed,
As you were going to a feast;
Still to be powdered, still perfumed;
Lady, it is to be presumed,
5   Though art's hid causes are not found,
All is not sweet, all is not sound.

Give me a look, give me a face
That makes simplicity a grace;
Robes loosely flowing, hair as free;
10   Such sweet neglect more taketh me

---

6. I.e., before they had grown beards.
7. From Jonson's play *Epicoene, the Silent Woman* (1609). Sung by a servant upon Clerimont's request (1.1); Clerimont is irritated with the Lady Haughty, who, he says, overdoes the art of makeup. The lyric perhaps derives from an anonymous Latin poem in the *Anthologia latina* (sixteenth century).

Then all th' adulteries of art.
They strike mine eyes, but not my heart.

1609   1640–41

Though I Am Young and Cannot Tell[8]

Though I am young, and cannot tell
    Either what Death or Love is well,
Yet I have heard they both bear darts,
    And both do aim at human hearts.
5 And then again, I have been told
    Love wounds with heat, as Death with cold;
So that I fear they do but bring
    Extremes to touch, and mean one thing.

As in a ruin we it call
10 One thing to be blown up, or fall;
Or to our end like way may have
    By a flash of lightning, or a wave;
So Love's inflaméd shaft or brand
    May kill as soon as Death's cold hand;
15 Except Love's fires the virtue have
    To fright the frost out of the grave.

1640–41

To the Memory of My Beloved, the Author Mr. William Shakespeare

And What He Hath Left Us[9]

To draw no envy, Shakespeare, on thy name,
Am I thus ample[1] to thy book and fame,
While I confess thy writings to be such
As neither man nor Muse can praise too much.
5 'Tis true, and all men's suffrage.° But these ways   *consent*
Were not the paths I meant unto thy praise:
For silliest ignorance on these may light,
Which, when it sounds at best, but echoes right;
Or blind affection,° which doth ne'er advance   *feeling*
10 The truth, but gropes, and urgeth all by chance;
Or crafty malice might pretend this praise,
And think to ruin where it seemed to raise.
These are as some infamous bawd or whore
Should praise a matron.[2] What could hurt her more?
15 But thou art proof against them, and, indeed,
Above th' ill fortune of them, or the need.
I therefore will begin. Soul of the age!
The applause! delight! the wonder of our stage!

---

8. From Jonson's play *The Sad Shepherd* (1640). The monosyllables of the poem (1.5) echo the pastoral simplicity of the character Karalin, who sings it.
9. Prefixed to the first collected edition—the first folio edition—of Shakespeare's works, 1623.
1. Copious, i.e., in this relatively lengthy poem.
2. A married woman with moral and social dignity. "As": i.e., as if.

My Shakespeare, rise; I will not lodge thee by
20 Chaucer or Spenser, or bid Beaumont lie[3]
    A little further to make thee a room:
    Thou art a monument without a tomb,
    And art alive still while thy book doth live,
    And we have wits to read and praise to give.
25 That I not mix thee so, my brain excuses,
    I mean with great, but disproportioned Muses;[4]
    For, if I thought my judgment were of years,[5]
    I should commit° thee surely with thy peers,   unite, connect
    And tell how far thou didst our Lyly outshine,
30 Or sporting Kyd, or Marlowe's mighty line.[6]
    And though thou hadst small Latin and less Greek,[7]
    From thence to honor thee I would not seek
    For names, but call forth thund'ring Aeschylus,
    Euripides, and Sophocles to us,
35 Pacuvius, Accius, him of Cordova dead,[8]
    To life again, to hear thy buskin[9] tread
    And shake a stage; or, when thy socks were on,
    Leave thee alone for the comparison
    Of all that insolent Greece or haughty Rome
40 Sent forth, or since did from their ashes come.
    Triumph, my Britain; thou hast one to show
    To whom all scenes° of Europe homage owe.   stages
    He was not of an age, but for all time!
    And all the Muses still were in their prime
45 When like Apollo he came forth to warm
    Our ears, or like a Mercury[1] to charm.
    Nature herself was proud of his designs,
    And joyed to wear the dressing of his lines,
    Which were so richly spun, and woven so fit,
50 As, since, she will vouchsafe no other wit:
    The merry Greek, tart Aristophanes,
    Neat Terence, witty Plautus[2] now not please,
    But antiquated and deserted lie,
    As they were not of Nature's family.
55 Yet must I not give Nature all; thy Art,
    My gentle Shakespeare, must enjoy a part.
    For though the poet's matter Nature be,

3. All three authors—Geoffrey Chaucer (ca. 1340–1400), Edmund Spenser (ca. 1552–1599), Francis Beaumont (1584–1616)—are buried in Westminster Abbey, London. Shakespeare is buried in the Holy Trinity Church, Stratford-on-Avon (see "Avon," line 71).
4. I.e., that I do not place you with the other authors, whose poetry is "great" but still not comparable ("disproportioned") with your poetry; "muses": the nine Greek goddesses believed to be sources of inspiration for the arts.
5. I.e., over the course of extended periods of time.
6. John Lyly (1554–1606), Thomas Kyd (1558–1594), and Christopher Marlowe (1564–1593), all Elizabethan dramatists; with "sporting" as a pun on Kyd ("kid," meaning little goat).
7. By modern standards, Shakespeare had an ade-

quate command of Latin (as well as French and Italian); but he lacked Jonson's knowledge of classical literature.
8. I.e., the Roman tragedian Seneca, of the first century A.D.; Marcus Pacuvius and Lucius Accius were Roman tragedians of the second century B.C. Aeschylus (525–456 B.C.), Euripides (ca. 484–406 B.C.), and Sophocles (496–406 B.C.) were all Greek dramatists.
9. The high-heeled boot worn by Greek tragic actors; the "sock" or light shoe was worn in comedies.
1. Associated with good luck and enchantment, "Apollo": the classical god of music.
2. Aristophanes (Greek) and Terence and Plautus (Roman) were comic writers of the fourth to second centuries B.C.

His Art doth give the fashion;° and that he　　　　　*form, style*
Who casts° to write a living line must sweat　　　　*undertakes*
60　(Such as thine are) and strike the second heat
Upon the muses' anvil; turn the same,
And himself with it, that he thinks to frame,
Or for the laurel he may gain a scorn;
For a good poet's made as well as born.
65　And such wert thou! Look how the father's face
Lives in his issue, even so the race
Of Shakespeare's mind and manners brightly shines
In his well-turnèd and true-filèd° lines,　　　　　　*well-polished*
In each of which he seems to shake a lance,³
70　As brandished at the eyes of ignorance.
Sweet swan of Avon, what a sight it were
To see thee in our waters yet appear,
And make those flights upon the banks of Thames
That so did take Eliza and our James!⁴
75　But stay; I see thee in the hemisphere
Advanced and made a constellation there!
Shine forth, thou star of poets, and with rage
Or influence⁵ chide or cheer the drooping stage,
Which, since thy flight from hence, hath mourned like night,
80　And despairs day, but for thy volume's light.
1623　　　　　　　　　　　　　　　　　　　　　　　1640–41

A Sonnet to the Noble Lady, the Lady Mary Wroth⁶

I that have been a lover, and could show it,
　　Though not in these,⁷ in rithmes not wholly dumb,
　　Since I exscribe° your sonnets, am become　　　　*copy out*
A better lover, and much better poet.
5　Nor is my Muse⁸ or I ashamed to owe it
　　To those true numerous graces, whereof some
　　But charm the senses, others overcome
Both brains and hearts; and mine now best do know it:
For in your verse all cupid's armory,
10　His flames, his shafts, his quiver, and his bow,
　　His very eyes are yours to overthrow.
But then his mother's sweets you so apply,
　　Her joys, her smiles, her loves, as readers take
For Venus' ceston° every line you make.　　　　　　*girdle*
　　　　　　　　　　　　　　　　　　　　　　　1640–41

---

3. With a pun on "Shake-speare" (also see line 37).
4. I.e., to travel on the river banks as did Queen Elizabeth and King James.
5. "Rage" and "influence" describe a supposed emanation of power from the stars, affecting the Earth's events. "Rage" also implies poetic inspira-tion.
6. For samples of Wroth's own sonnets, see pp. 314–15. Jonson dedicated his play *The Alchemist* (1610) to Wroth.
7. I.e., the sonnet form, typically used for love poetry but not by Jonson.
8. Source of poetic inspiration.

Slow, Slow, Fresh Fount[9]

Slow, slow, fresh fount, keep time with my salt tears;
Yet slower, yet, O faintly, gentle springs!
List to the heavy part the music bears,
Woe weeps out her division,[1] when she sings.
5   Droop herbs and flowers;
      Fall grief in showers;
Our beauties are not ours. O, I could still,
Like melting snow upon some craggy hill,
      Drop, drop, drop, drop,
10 Since nature's pride is now a withered daffodil.

1600

Queen and Huntress[2]

Queen and huntress, chaste and fair,
Now the sun is laid to sleep,
Seated in thy silver chair,
State in wonted manner keep;
5 Hesperus entreats thy light,
Goddess excellently bright.

Earth, let not thy envious shade
Dare itself to interpose;
Cynthia's shining orb was made
10 Heaven to clear, when day did close.
Bless us then with wishéd sight,
Goddess excellently bright.

Lay thy bow of pearl apart,
And thy crystal-shining quiver;
15 Give unto the flying hart[3]
Space to breathe, how short soever.
Thou that mak'st a day of night,
Goddess excellently bright.

1600

9. From Jonson's play *Cynthia's Revels* (1600), which deals satirically with the sin of self-love, this song is sung by Echo for Narcissus, who fell in love with his own reflection and was changed into the flower that bears his name (1.2). The daffodil (line 11) is a species of narcissus. "Fount": spring.
1. Part in a song, as well as grief at parting.

2. From *Cynthia's Revels* (1600), like the previous poem, this lyric is sung by Hesperus, the evening star, to Cynthia (also known as Diana), goddess of the moon and of the hunt (5.6). Cynthia was often identified with Queen Elizabeth by poets of this period.
3. With a pun on "heart" and "hart" (as deer).

JOHN FLETCHER

1579–1625

Take, Oh, Take Those Lips Away[1]

Take, oh, take those lips away
That so sweetly were forsworn
And those eyes, like break of day,
Lights that do mislead the morn;
5   But my kisses bring again,
Seals of love, though sealed in vain.

Hide, oh, hide those hills of snow,
Which thy frozen bosom bears,
On whose tops the pinks that grow
10 Are of those that April wears;
But first set my poor heart free,
Bound in those icy chains by thee.

1639

MARY WROTH

1587?–1651?

From Pamphilia to Amphilanthus[1]

37

Night, welcome art thou to my mind destrest,°   *distressed*
Dark, heavy, sad, yet not more sad than I;
Never could'st thou find fitter company
For thine own humor than I thus oprest.

5   If thou beest dark, my wrongs still unredrest°   *unremedied*
Saw never light, nor smallest bliss can spy;
If heavy, joy from me too fast doth hy°   *hurry away*
And care outgoes my hope of quiet rest,

---

1. The first stanza of this song appears as a complete poem in Shakespeare's play *Measure for Measure* (1604–05). It is likely that Fletcher simply appropriated it.
1. Mary Wroth wrote the first work of prose fiction by an Englishwoman, her long but unfinished *The Countess of Montgomery's Urania.* Including a number of poems and modeled on her uncle Sir Philip Sidney's romance, *The Arcadia,* Wroth's text covertly alludes to various personages and scandals of the Jacobean court, and was met with a storm of criticism when published in 1621. Appended to *Urania* is *Pamphilia to Amphilanthus,* a sonnet sequence (the only one by an Englishwoman of her time) consisting of eighty-three sonnets and twenty songs. Pamphilia ("All-loving") is the protagonist of *Urania;* Amphilanthus ("Lover of Two") is her unfaithful beloved. Their names reflect the main theme of both the romance and the appended sonnet sequence—constancy in the face of unfaithfulness. *Pamphilia to Amphilanthus* is divided into several separately numbered series (the first of which includes forty-eight sonnets, with songs inserted after every sixth sonnet). Of the selections below, "Night, welcome art thou" comes in the first section (as sonnet #37, according to the original edition), and the Song ("Love a child") comes unnumbered in the second section of the sequence.

Then now in friendship join with hapless me,
10   Who am as sad, and dark as thou canst be
Hating all pleasure, or delight of life;

Silence, and grief, with thee I best do love
And from you three, I know I can not move,
Then let us live companions without strife.

Song

Love a child[2] is ever crying,
    Please him, and he straight is flying,
    Give him he the more is craving[3]
    Never satisfied with having;

5 His desires have no measure,
    Endless folly is his treasure,
    What he promiseth he breaketh
    Trust not one word that he speaketh;

He vows nothing but false matter,
10   And to cousen you he'll flatter,[4]
    Let him gain the hand[5] he'll leave you,
    And still glory to deceive you;

He will triumph in your wailing,
    And yet cause be of your failing,
15   These his virtues are, and slighter
    Are his gifts, his favors lighter,

Feathers are as firm in staying
    Wolves no fiercer in their praying.
    As a child then leave him crying
20   Nor seek him[6] so given to flying.

From A *Crown of Sonnets Dedicated to Love*[7]

In this strange labyrinth how shall I turn,
Ways[8] are on all sides, while the way I miss:
If to the right hand, there in love I burn,
Let me[9] go forward, therein danger is.

2. Depicting love as Cupid, the mythological young son of Venus, the goddess of love, was a Renaissance commonplace, although a "crying" Cupid is unusual; in this section of her sonnet sequence, Wroth uses the image to explore Pamphilia's frustration in love.
3. I.e., the more he is given, the more he craves.
4. I.e., to deceive or cheat ("cousen") you, he'll flatter you.
5. I.e., the upper hand.
6. I.e., he who is so given to leaving ("flying").
7. The "crown" is a complex poetic form, in which the last line of each poem serves as the first line of the next poem, until a circle is completed by the last line of the final poem, which is the same as the first line of the sequence. Originally an Italian form that could be used to praise or condemn (and often known by its Italian name,

corona); various kinds of poems could be used for the sequence, with the number of poems ranging from seven to fourteen (as in Wroth's crown of fourteen sonnets). Sir Philip Sidney, Wroth's uncle, included one of the first examples of the corona in English in the first version of his prose romance, the *Old Arcadia*; her father, Sir Robert Sidney, wrote an incomplete crown thought to be in praise of a specific lady. Wroth, however, dedicates her crown more generally to "Love"; as a temporary recantation of the harsh judgement of love depicted in the preceding part of the *Pamphilia to Amphilanthus* sequence (of which Wroth's crown is one part), Love is here portrayed as a monarch whose true service ennobles lovers.
8. I.e., paths.
9. I.e., if I.

5   If to the left, suspicion hinders bliss:
    Let me turn back, shame cries I ought return:
    Nor faint,[1] though crosses° with my fortunes kiss.   *troubles, adversity*
    Stand still is harder, although sure to mourn.
    Thus let me take the right, or left hand way,
10   Go forward, or stand still, or back retire:
    I must these doubts endure without allay°   *alleviation*
    Or help, but travail[2] find for my best hire.
    Yet that which most my troubled sense doth move,
    Is to leave all and take the thread of Love.[3]

2

15   Is to leave all and take the thread of Love,
    Which line straight leads unto the soul's content,
    Where choice delights with pleasure's wings do move,
    And idle fant'sy never room had lent.[4]
    When chaste thoughts guide us, then our minds are bent
20   To take that good which ills from us remove:
    Light of true love brings fruit which none repent;
    But constant lovers seek and wish to prove.°   *try*
    Love is the shining star of blessings light,
    The fervent fire of zeal, the root of peace,
25   The lasting lamp, fed with the oil of right,
    Image of faith, and womb for joys increase.°   *children*
    Love is true virtue, and his ends delight,
    His flames are joys, his bands true lovers might.[5]

6

    He[6] may our prophet, and our tutor prove,
    In whom alone we do this power find,
    To join two hearts as in one frame to move;
    Two bodies, but one soul to rule the mind.[7]
75   Eyes which must care to one dear object bind,
    Ears to each others' speech as if above
    All else, they sweet, and learned were; this kind
    Content of lovers witnesseth true love.
    It doth enrich the wits, and make you see
80   That in your self which you knew not before,
    Forcing you to admire such gifts should be
    Hid from your knowledge, yet in you the store.
    Millions of these adorn the throne of Love,
    How blest are they then, who his favors prove.°   *experience*

---

1. Lose heart; Wroth occasionally used "nor" without including other negatives.
2. I.e., I find hard labor (or suffering) to be the reward for my best efforts. Instead of "traveile" (Folger Library manuscript), the 1621 edition prints "travell."
3. An allusion to the thread that Ariadne, in defiance of her father, gave Theseus to unwind behind him in the labyrinth at Crete. After killing the Minotaur, he was able to find his way out by following the thread; shortly thereafter he abandoned Ariadne.
4. I.e., where room or space had never been loaned to idle fantasy.
5. I.e., Love's bands are the strength of true lovers, and not their shackles.
6. I.e., love personified.
7. Two hearts joined in one body, or two bodies joined in one soul; common Renaissance metaphors for true love.

From Urania

Song[8]

Love what art thou? A vain thought
  In our minds by phant'sie° wrought,   *fancy*
  Idle smiles did thee beget
  While fond wishes made the net
5 Which so many fools have caught;

Love what art thou? light, and fair,
  Fresh as morning, clear as th'air,
  But too soon thy evening change
  Makes thy worth with coldness range;
10 Still thy joy is mixed with care.

Love what art thou? A sweet flow'r
  Once full blown, dead in an hour,
  Dust in wind as staid° remains   *steadfast*
  As thy pleasure, or our gains
15 If thy humor change to lour.°   *gloomy*

Love what art thou? childish, vain,
  Firm as bubbles made by rain;
  Wantonness thy greatest pride,
  These foul faults thy virtues hide,
20 But babes can no staidness gain.

Love what art thou? causeless curse,
  Yet alas these not the worst,
  Much more of thee may be said
  But thy law I once obeyed
25 Therefore say no more at first.

1621

WILLIAM BROWNE
1591?–1643?

On the Countess Dowager of Pembroke[1]

Underneath this sable hearse[2]
Lies the subject of all verse:
Sidney's sister, Pembroke's mother.
Death, ere thou hast slain[3] another
5 Fair and learn'd and good as she,
Time shall throw a dart at thee.

8. Sung at the end of book 1 by a "delicate Mayd" with a sweet voice who seemed to have "falne out with Love"; on Wroth's long prose romance, see 2nd n. 1, p. 313.
1. Mary (Sidney) Herbert (see pp. 199–204), poet, patron, sister of Sir Philip Sidney (see pp. 188–99), and mother of William Herbert, third earl of Pem-broke. Philip Sidney wrote the first version of his *Arcadia* for her, and they coauthored a translation of the Psalms. She died in 1621.
2. Tomb; some manuscripts have "marble" instead of "sable" (black).
3. Some manuscripts have "kill'd."

Marble piles let no man raise
To her name, for after-days
Some kind woman, born as she,
10   Reading this, like Niobe[4]
Shall turn marble, and become
Both her mourner and her tomb.

1623

ROBERT HERRICK

1591–1674

The Argument of His Book[1]

I sing of brooks, of blossoms, birds, and bowers,
Of April, May, of June, and July flowers.
I sing of Maypoles, hock carts, wassails, wakes,[2]
Of bridegrooms, brides, and of their bridal cakes.
5   I write of youth, of love, and have access
By these to sing of cleanly wantonness.
I sing of dews, of rains, and, piece by piece,
Of balm, of oil, of spice, and ambergris.[3]
I sing of times trans-shifting, and I write
10   How roses first came red and lilies white.
I write of groves, of twilights, and I sing
The court of Mab[4] and of the fairy king.
I write of hell; I sing (and ever shall)
Of heaven, and hope to have it after all.

The Vine

I dreamed this mortal part of mine
Was metamorphosed to a vine,
Which crawling one and every way
Enthralled° my dainty Lucia.   *imprisoned*
5   Methought her long small° legs and thighs   *slender*
I with my tendrils did surprise;
Her belly, buttocks, and her waist
By my soft nervelets° were embraced.   *tendrils*
About her head I writhing hung,
10   And with rich clusters (hid among
The leaves) her temples I behung,
So that my Lucia seemed to me

4. Niobe, queen of Thebes, mourning the deaths of her seven sons and seven daughters at the hands of the gods Apollo and Diana, continued to weep even after she had been turned to stone.
1. "Argument": subject matter. The "book" is a thick volume containing all of Herrick's poems— over fourteen hundred of them—divided into a religious set entitled *Noble Numbers* and a secular set entitled *Hesperides*. The latter title alludes to the mythical daughters of Atlas and Hesperis (or, in another tradition, of Night) who guarded a tree

of golden apples in a far-western garden that Herrick often likens to his home in the western county of Devon.
Since all of Herrick's poems were published in 1648, we do not repeat the date for each poem.
2. Parish festivals as well as watches over the dead; "hock carts" brought in the last load of the harvest; "wassails": drinking to the health of others.
3. A waxlike substance used in making perfumes, i.e., something rare.
4. Queen of the fairies.

Young Bacchus ravished by his tree.[5]
My curls about her neck did crawl,
15 And arms and hands they did enthrall,
So that she could not freely stir
(All parts there made one prisoner).
But when I crept with leaves to hide
Those parts which maids keep unespied,
20 Such fleeting pleasures there I took
That with the fancy I awoke;
And found (ah me!) this flesh of mine
More like a stock[6] than like a vine.

To the Sour Reader

If thou dislik'st the piece thou light'st on first,
Think that of all that I have writ the worst;
But if thou read'st my book unto the end,
And still dost this and that verse reprehend,
5 O perverse man! If all disgustful be,
The extreme scab[7] take thee and thine, for me.

Delight in Disorder

A sweet disorder in the dress
Kindles in clothes a wantonness.
A lawn[8] about the shoulders thrown
Into a fine distraction;
5 An erring lace, which here and there
Enthralls the crimson stomacher;[9]
A cuff neglectful, and thereby
Ribbons to flow confusedly;
A winning wave, deserving note,
10 In the tempestuous petticoat;
A careless shoestring, in whose tie
I see a wild civility;
Do more bewitch me than when art
Is too precise in every part.

Corinna's Going A-Maying

Get up! get up for shame! the blooming morn
Upon her wings presents the god unshorn.[1]

5. Bacchus was the classical god of wine and revelry; his "tree" is the grapevine.
6. The hardened stem of a plant.
7. The mange. "The extreme scab" is a borrowing from Horace's Art of Poetry (lines 416–18), in which an unpracticed dabbler in poetry is represented as saying, "Ego mira poemata pango: / Occupet extremum scabies, mihi turpe relinqui / Et quod non didici sane nescire fateri." In the translation of Herrick's admired master, Ben Jonson, these lines are: "I make / An admirable verse: the great scab take / Him that is last, I scorn to come behind / Or, of the things that ne'er came in my mind, / Once say I'm ignorant. . . ."
8. A very fine transparent linen.
9. An ornamental piece worn under the open (and often laced) front of a bodice; the "erring" ("wandering," with an overtone of moral straying) lace thus "enthralls" (literally, makes a slave of) the stomacher.
1. Apollo, the sun god, whose hair (the rays of the sun) is never cut.

See how Aurora[2] throws her fair
Fresh-quilted colors through the air:
5   Get up, sweet slug-a-bed, and see
The dew bespangling herb and tree.
Each flower has wept and bowèd toward the east
Above an hour since, yet you not dressed;
Nay, not so much as out of bed?
10 When all the birds have matins° said,   *morning prayers*
And sung their thankful hymns, 'tis sin,
Nay, profanation to keep in,
Whenas a thousand virgins on this day
Spring, sooner than the lark, to fetch in May.[3]

15 Rise, and put on your foliage, and be seen
To come forth, like the springtime, fresh and green,
And sweet as Flora.[4] Take no care
For jewels for your gown or hair;
Fear not; the leaves will strew
20 Gems in abundance upon you;
Besides, the childhood of the day has kept,
Against you come, some orient pearls[5] unwept;
Come and receive them while the light
Hangs on the dew-locks of the night,
25 And Titan[6] on the eastern hill
Retires himself, or else stands still
Till you come forth. Wash, dress, be brief in praying:
Few beads[7] are best when once we go a-Maying.

Come, my Corinna, come; and, coming mark
30 How each field turns a street,[8] each street a park
Made green and trimmed with trees; see how
Devotion gives each house a bough
Or branch: each porch, each door ere this,
An ark, a tabernacle is,[9]
35 Made up of whitethorn neatly interwove,
As if here were those cooler shades of love.
Can such delights be in the street
And open fields, and we not see 't?
Come, we'll abroad; and let's obey
40 The proclamation made for May,
And sin no more, as we have done, by staying;
But, my Corinna, come, let's go a-Maying.

There's not a budding boy or girl this day
But is got up and gone to bring in May;
45 A deal of youth, ere this, is come

2. The goddess of the dawn, tossing her blankets aside and spreading over the Earth a newly made coverlet of light.
3. Boughs of white hawthorn, traditionally gathered to decorate streets and houses on May Day; "larks" sing at sunrise.
4. Goddess of flowers.
5. "Orient": lustrous and glowing; also, "Eastern," as pearls come from the "Orient"; i.e., in readiness for the time when.
6. The sun.
7. I.e., prayers (with overtones of the rosary of Catholicism).
8. Turns into a street.
9. I.e., the doorways are like the Hebrew "ark" of the Covenant, or the sanctuary ("tabernacle") that housed it; i.e., May sprigs are the central mystery of the religion of nature.

Back, and with whitethorn laden home.
Some have dispatched their cakes and cream
Before that we have left to dream;
And some have wept, and wooed, and plighted troth,
50 And chose their priest, ere we can cast off sloth.
     Many a green-gown has been given,[1]
     Many a kiss, both odd and even,[2]
     Many a glance, too, has been sent
     From out the eye, love's firmament;°   sky
55 Many a jest told of the keys betraying
     This night, and locks picked; yet we're not a-Maying.

Come, let us go while we are in our prime,
And take the harmless folly of the time.
     We shall grow old apace,° and die   quickly
60 Before we know our liberty.
     Our life is short, and our days run
     As fast away as does the sun;
And, as a vapor or a drop of rain
Once lost, can ne'er be found again;
65 So when or you or I are made
     A fable, song, or fleeting shade,
     All love, all liking, all delight
     Lies drowned with us in endless night.
Then while time serves, and we are but decaying,
70 Come, my Corinna, come, let's go a-Maying.

To the Virgins, to Make Much of Time

Gather ye rosebuds while ye may,
     Old time is still a-flying;
And this same flower that smiles today
     Tomorrow will be dying.

5   The glorious lamp of heaven, the sun,
     The higher he's a-getting,
The sooner will his race be run,
     And nearer he's to setting.

That age is best which is the first,
10   When youth and blood are warmer;
But being spent, the worse, and worst
     Times still succeed the former.

Then be not coy, but use your time,
     And, while ye may, go marry;
15   For, having lost but once your prime,
     You may forever tarry.

---

1. I.e., by rolling in the grass.   2. Kisses are odd and even in kissing games.

Upon Julia's Breasts

Display thy breasts, my Julia, there let me
Behold that circummortal³ purity;
Between whose glories, there my lips I'll lay,
Ravished in that fair *Via Lactea.*⁴

Upon a Child That Died

Here she lies, a pretty bud,
Lately made of flesh and blood,
Who as soon fell fast asleep
As her little eyes did peep.°   open
5   Give her strewings,⁵ but not stir
The earth that lightly covers her.

To Daffodils

Fair daffodils, we weep to see
    You haste away so soon:
As yet the early-rising sun
    Has not attained his noon.
5   Stay, stay,
    Until the hasting day
        Has run
    But to the evensong;
And, having prayed together, we
10   Will go with you along.

We have short time to stay as you;
    We have as short a spring;
As quick a growth to meet decay,
    As you or anything.
15   We die,
    As your hours do, and dry
        Away
    Like to the summer's rain;
Or as the pearls of morning's dew,
20   Ne'er to be found again.

His Prayer to Ben Jonson

When I a verse shall make,
Know I have prayed thee,

---

3. A coinage by Herrick, literally "around or encompassing what is mortal"; therefore, perhaps, beyond or more than mortal.
4. "Milky Way" (Latin); with reference to the color white, and the constellation; also, figuratively, a way brilliant in appearance and leading to heaven.
5. Flowers scattered on a grave.

For old religion's sake,[6]
   Saint Ben, to aid me.

5 Make the way smooth for me,
   When I, thy Herrick,
   Honoring thee, on my knee
   Offer my lyric.

Candles I'll give to thee,
10 And a new altar;
   And thou, Saint Ben, shalt be
   Writ in my psalter.[7]

The Night Piece, to Julia

Her eyes the glowworm[8] lend thee;
The shooting stars attend thee;
   And the elves also,
   Whose little eyes glow
5 Like the sparks of fire, befriend thee.

No will-o'-the-wisp[9] mislight thee;
Nor snake or slowworm° bite thee;   *adder*
   But on, on thy way,
   Not making a stay,
10 Since ghost there's none to affright thee.

Let not the dark thee cumber;°   *trouble*
What though the moon does slumber?
   The stars of the night
   Will lend thee their light,
15 Like tapers clear without number.

Then, Julia, let me woo thee,
Thus, thus to come unto me;
   And when I shall meet
   Thy silvery feet,
20 My soul I'll pour into thee.

---

6. Herrick, who had been ordained in the Church of England, plays on the fact that Jonson was for a while a Catholic (of the "old religion"), as well as a saint in the mock religion of poetry. The Puritans (who came to power in the civil war, which began in 1642) were hostile to the invocation of saints and, especially, of secular "saints" such as Ben Jonson; Herrick was dispossessed by the Puritans in 1647, shortly before his poems were published. "Religion" may also mean the sacredness of an oath, i.e., the vows of friendship.

7. A collection of sacred poems called Psalms; also, the Book of Psalms, one of the books of the Old Testament, composed of such poems.
8. An insect, the female of which emits a shining green light from the abdomen. I.e., may the glowworm lend her eyes to thee.
9. The will-o'-the-wisp was said to draw travelers astray by holding a false light before them; the phenomenon of nocturnal light is caused by the combustion of marsh gas.

Upon Julia's Clothes

Whenas in silks my Julia goes,
Then, then, methinks, how sweetly flows
That liquefaction[1] of her clothes.

Next, when I cast mine eyes, and see
5   That brave[2] vibration, each way free,
O, how that glittering taketh me!

Upon Prue, His Maid

In this little urn is laid
Prudence Baldwin, once my maid,
From whose happy spark here let
Spring the purple violet.

Upon Ben Jonson

Here lies Jonson with the rest
Of the poets; but the best.
Reader, would'st thou more have known?
Ask his story, not this stone.
5   That will speak what this can't tell
Of his glory. So farewell.

An Ode for Him

Ah, Ben!
Say how or when
Shall we, thy guests,
Meet at those lyric feasts
5   Made at the Sun,
The Dog, the Triple Tun,[3]
Where we such clusters° had   wine
As made us nobly wild, not mad;
And yet each verse of thine
10   Outdid the meat, outdid the frolic wine.

My Ben!
Or come again,
Or send to us
Thy wit's great overplus;
15   But teach us yet
Wisely to husband[4] it,
Lest we that talent spend,

1. Process of liquefying.
2. Glorious, splendid.
3. The names of taverns.
4. Manage with thrift and prudence.

And having once brought to an end
That precious stock, the store
20   Of such a wit the world should have no more.

The Pillar of Fame[5]

Fame's pillar here at last we set,[6]
Out-during° marble, brass or jet;   *outlasting*
Charmed and enchanted so
As to withstand the blow
5   Of   o v e r t h r o w ;
Nor   shall   the   seas,
Or   o u t r a g e s
Of storms, o'erbear
What   we   uprear;
10   Tho'   kingdoms   fall,
This   pillar   never   shall
Decline   or   waste   at   all;
But   stand   for   ever   by   his   own
Firm and well-fixed foundation.

Neutrality Loathsome[7]

God will have all or none; serve Him, or fall
Down before Baal, Bel, or Belial.[8]
Either be hot or cold: God doth despise,
Abhor, and spew out all neutralities.[9]

To His Conscience

Can I not sin, but thou wilt be
My private protonotary?[1]
Can I not woo thee to pass by
A short and sweet iniquity?
5   I'll cast a mist and cloud upon
My delicate transgression,
So utter dark, as that no eye
Shall see the hugged° impiety.   *cherished*
Gifts blind the wise,[2] and bribes do please,
10   And wind° all other witnesses;   *pervert*
And wilt not thou, with gold, be tied
To lay thy pen and ink aside?
That in the murk° and tongueless night,   *murky*
Wanton I may, and thou not write?

---

5. This poem is "shaped" to resemble a pillar; on the significance of shaped poems, see Herbert, n. 2 (p. 329).
6. Black marble or a hard form of lignite.
7. This and the following poems are from *His Noble Numbers*, the collection of religious poems in Herrick's 1648 volume.
8. Baal (or Bel) and Belial were pagan divinities; hence, false gods in general.
9. See Revelation 3.16: ". . . because thou art luke-warm, and neither cold nor hot, I will spew thee out of my mouth."
1. Chief recorder in a law court.
2. Deuteronomy 16.19: ". . . a gift doth blind the eyes of the wise, and pervert the words of the righteous."

15 It will not be; and therefore now,
For times to come, I'll make this vow:
From aberrations to live free;
So I'll not fear the judge³ or thee.

To Find God⁴

Weigh me the fire; or canst thou find
A way to measure out the wind?
Distinguish° all those floods that are   separate
Mixed in that wat'ry theater,⁵
5   And taste thou them as saltless there,
As in their channel first they were.
Tell° me the people that do keep   count
Within the kingdoms of the deep;
Or fetch me back that cloud again,
10   Beshivered° into seeds of rain.   shattered
Tell me the motes, dust, sands, and spears
Of corn, when summer shakes his ears;
Show me that world of stars, and whence
They noiseless spill their influence.
15   This if thou canst;⁶ then show me Him
That rides the glorious cherubim.⁷

The White Island, or Place of the Blest

In this world, the isle of dreams,
While we sit by sorrow's streams,
Tears and terrors are our themes
Reciting:

5   But when once from hence we fly,
More and more approaching nigh
Unto young eternity,
Uniting:

In that whiter island, where
10   Things are evermore sincere;
Candor° here and luster there   whiteness, truthfulness
Delighting:

---

3. I.e., God on the final judgment day (continuing the poem's metaphor of a law court).
4. The "impossibility" theme was much used by seventeenth century poets such as Donne ("Go and catch a falling star," p. 264) and Marvell ("To His Coy Mistress," pp. 435–36); here it emphasizes the challenge issued by the concluding line: if you can do these things, then show me the supreme sight, a vision of God. The poem alludes to an Apocryphal book of the Bible, 2 Esdras: "Weigh me the weight of fire, or measure me the day that is past. . . . How many dwellings are there in the heart of the sea, or how many streams at the source of the deep, or how many ways above the firmament . . ." (4.5–7).
5. I.e., the ocean.
6. Perhaps an echo of Ecclesiasticus 1.2–3: "The sand of the deep, and the drops of rain, and the days of eternity—who can count them? The height of the heavens, and the breadth of the earth, and the deep, and wisdom—who can track them out?"
7. One of the nine orders of angels; cf. Psalms 18.10: "he [the Lord] rode upon a cherub."

There no monstrous fancies shall
Out of hell an horror call,
15   To create, or cause at all,
                Affrighting.

There, in calm and cooling sleep
We our eyes shall never steep,
But eternal watch shall keep,
20   Attending

Pleasures, such as shall pursue
Me immortalized, and you;
And fresh joys, as never too
                Have ending.

                                                                        1648

HENRY KING
1592–1669

An Exequy to His Matchless, Never-to-Be-Forgotten Friend[1]

Accept, thou shrine of my dead saint,
Instead of dirges, this complaint;[2]
And for sweet flowers to crown thy hearse,
Receive a strew° of weeping verse   *scattering*
5   From thy grieved friend, whom thou might'st see
Quite melted into tears for thee,

Dear loss! since thy untimely fate
My task hath been to meditate
On thee, on thee; thou art the book,
10   The library whereon I look,
Though almost blind. For thee, loved clay,
I languish out, not live, the day,
Using no other exercise
But what I practice with mine eyes;
15   By which wet glasses I find out
How lazily time creeps about
To one that mourns: this, only this,
My exercise and business is.
So I compute the weary hours
20   With sighs dissolvèd into showers.

Nor wonder if my time go thus
Backward and most preposterous;
Thou hast benighted me, thy set[3]

---

1. Written for his wife, Anne King, who died in 1623 (after eight years of marriage); "exequy": a funeral ceremony.
2. A plaintive poem; "dirges": mourning songs.

3. Setting, death. "Preposterous": in reverse order (from the Latin, literally, "hind side first"). "Benighted me": i.e., placed me in darkness.

This eve of blackness did beget,
25 Who wast my day, though overcast
Before thou hadst thy noontide passed;
And I remember must in tears,
Thou scarce hadst seen so many years
As day tells° hours. By thy clear sun   *counts*
30 My love and fortune first did run;
But thou wilt never more appear
Folded within my hemisphere,
Since both thy light and motiòn
Like a fled star is fallen and gone;
35 And 'twixt me and my soul's dear wish
An earth now interposèd is,
Which such a strange eclipse doth make
As ne'er was read in almanac.

I could allow thee for a time
40 To darken me and my sad clime;[4]
Were it a month, a year, or ten,
I would thy exile live till then,
And all that space my mirth adjourn,
So thou wouldst promise to return;
45 And putting off thy ashy shroud,
At length disperse this sorrow's cloud.

But woe is me! the longest° date   *most distant*
Too narrow is to calculate
These empty hopes; never shall I
50 Be so much blest as to descry°   *discern*
A glimpse of thee, till that day come
Which shall the earth to cinders doom,
And a fierce fever must calcine[5]
The body of this world—like thine,
55 My little world! That fit of fire
Once off, our bodies shall aspire
To our souls' bliss; then we shall rise
And view ourselves with clearer eyes
In that calm region where no night
60 Can hide us from each other's sight.

Meantime, thou hast her, earth: much good
May my harm[6] do thee. Since it stood°   *agreed*
With heaven's will I might not call
Her longer mine, I give thee all
65 My short-lived right and interest
In her whom living I loved best;
With a most free and bounteous grief
I give thee what I could not keep.
Be kind to her, and prithee look
70 Thou write into thy doomsday[7] book

4. Climate, part of the earth.
5. Reduce to dust by heat.

6. I.e., her death that harms me so much.
7. Day of God's final judgment.

Each parcel of this rarity
Which in thy casket shrined doth lie.
See that thou make thy reckoning straight,
And yield her back again by weight;
75 For thou must audit on thy trust
Each grain and atom of this dust,
As thou wilt answer him that lent,
Not gave thee, my dear monument.

So close the ground, and 'bout her shade
80 Black curtains draw; my bride is laid.

Sleep on, my love, in thy cold bed,
Never to be disquieted!
My last good-night! Thou wilt not wake
Till I thy fate shall overtake;
85 Till age, or grief, or sickness must
Marry my body to that dust
It so much loves; and fill the room
My heart keeps empty in thy tomb.
Stay for me there; I will not fail
90 To meet thee in that hollow vale.
And think not much of my delay;
I am already on the way,
And follow thee with all the speed
Desire can make, or sorrows breed.
95 Each minute is a short degree,
And every hour a step towards thee.
At night when I betake to rest,
Next morn I rise nearer my west
Of life, almost by eight hours' sail,
100 Than when sleep breathed his drowsy gale.

Thus from the sun my bottom° steers,   *vessel*
And my day's compass downward bears;
Nor labor I to stem the tide
Through which to thee I swiftly glide.

105 'Tis true, with shame and grief I yield,
Thou like the van° first took'st the field,   *vanguard*
And gotten hast the victory
In thus adventuring to die
Before me, whose more years might crave
110 A just precèdence in the grave.
But hark! my pulse like a soft drum
Beats my approach, tells thee I come;
And slow howe'er my marches be,
I shall at last sit down by thee.

115 The thought of this bids me go on,
And wait my dissolutìon.
With hope and comfort. Dear (forgive

The crime), I am content to live
Divided, with but half a heart,
120 Till we shall meet, and never part.

1657

GEORGE HERBERT

1593–1633

FROM THE TEMPLE: SACRED POEMS AND PRIVATE EJACULATIONS[1]

The Altar[2]

A broken A L T A R , Lord, thy servant rears,
Made of a heart, and cemented with tears:
    Whose parts are as thy hand did frame;
    No workman's tool hath touched the same.[3]
5   A H E A R T alone
           Is such a stone,
           As nothing but
           Thy power doth cut.
           Wherefore each part
10   Of my hard heart
           Meets in this frame,
           To praise thy Name:
    That, if I chance to hold my peace,
    These stones to praise thee may not cease.[4]
15 Oh let thy blessed S A C R I F I C E be mine,
And sanctify this A L T A R to be thine.

Redemption[5]

Having been tenant long to a rich lord,
  Not thriving, I resolvèd to be bold,

---

1. Posthumously published in 1633, *The Temple* includes 160 poems, which Herbert carefully arranged to dramatize the central Christian concept of the believer's body as the "temple of the Holy Ghost" (Paul's first letter to the Corinthians, 6.19). Designed to illustrate the myriad links between the human "temple" and the Church of England that Herbert served—its doctrines, its rituals, even the physical construction of its churches—Herbert's book begins with a poem entitled "The Church Porch" and proceeds to a long section called "The Church," from which the following poems are taken.
    Since all of Herbert's poems were published in 1633, we do not print the date for each one.
2. The first poem in the section of *The Temple* called "The Church," this poem, like "Easter Wings" below, is shaped to resemble the object evoked by its title. Its placement suggests that all of the following poems are offered as "sacrifices" on the symbolic altar constituted here.
3. A reference to the altar of uncut stone described in Exodus 20.25 and in Deuteronomy 27.5–8.
4. I.e., whether the poem is read or spoken, and whether its author is living or dead, he wants the words to praise God. Here, as so often in Herbert's poems, the "praise" involves echoing words of the scriptures; see Luke 19.40: "I tell you that, if these should hold their peace, the stones would immediately cry out."
5. Redemption means, literally, buying back; in Christian doctrine, Christ's death redeemed human beings from the consequences of their sin.

And make a suit unto him, to afford°   grant
A new small-rented lease, and cancel th' old.[6]

5   In heaven at his manor I him sought;
          They told me there that he was lately gone
          About some land, which he had dearly bought
Long since on earth, to take possessiòn.

I straight returned, and knowing his great birth,
10   Sought him accordingly in great resorts;°   gatherings, crowds
          In cities, theaters, gardens, parks, and courts;
At length I heard a ragged noise and mirth

Of thieves and murderers; there I him espied,
Who straight, *Your suit is granted*, said, and died.

Easter Wings[7]

Lord, who createdst man in wealth and store,°   abundance
Though foolishly he lost the same,[8]
Decaying more and more
Till   he   became
5   Most poor:
With   thee
O   let   me   rise
As   larks,[9]   harmoniously,
And sing this day thy victories:
10 Then shall the fall further the flight in me.[1]

My   tender   age   in   sorrow   did   begin;
And still with sicknesses and shame
Thou didst so punish sin,
That   I   became
15   Most thin.
With   thee
Let me combine,
And feel this day[2] thy victory;
For, if I imp[3] my wing on thine,
20 Affliction shall advance the flight in me.

6. I.e., to ask for a new lease, with a smaller rent, and to cancel the old lease.
7. As a "pattern poem," the typographical shape of these lines represents some part of their subject. Below this version we reproduce the poem as it was first published. The stanzas were printed on two pages and arranged to suggest two birds flying upward, wings outspread.
8. I.e., in the Fall from Eden.
9. Larks sing at sunrise.
1. I.e., paradoxically, the joy of Easter and

redemption from sin (the "flight" to heaven) is greater because the Fall from Eden occurred.
2. The words "this day," which are superfluous in the metrical scheme of the poem, were perhaps included in the early editions to emphasize the occasion, Easter. They are omitted, however, in the only surviving manuscript book of Herbert's poems.
3. A term from falconry: additional feathers were "imped" or grafted onto the wing of a hawk to improve its power of flight.

Easter Wings

Lord, who createdst man in wealth and store,
Though foolishly he lost the same,
Decaying more and more,
Till he became
Most poore:
With thee
O let me rise
As larks, harmoniously,
And sing this day thy victories:
Then shall the fall further the flight in me.

My tender age in sorrow did beginne
And still with sicknesses and shame
Thou didst so punish sinne,
That I became
Most thinne.
With thee
Let me combine,
And feel this day thy victorie:
For, if I imp my wing on thine,
Affliction shall advance the flight in me.

Sin (I)[4]

    Lord, with what care hast thou begirt° us round!　　　　*girdled*
      Parents first season us: then schoolmasters
      Deliver us to laws; they send us bound
    To rules of reason, holy messengers,
5 Pulpits and Sundays, sorrow dogging sin,
      Afflictions sorted, anguish of all sizes,
      Fine nets and stratagems to catch us in,
    Bibles laid open, millions of surprises,
    Blessings beforehand, ties of gratefulness,
10   The sound of glory ringing in our ears:
      Without, our shame; within, our consciences;
    Angels and grace, eternal hopes and fears.
      Yet all these fences and their whole array
      One cunning bosom-sin blows quite away.[5]

Affliction (I)

    When first thou didst entice to thee my heart,
      I thought the service brave°:　　　　*splendid*
    So many joys I writ down for my part,
      Besides what I might have
5 Out of my stock of natural delights,
    Augmented with thy gracious benefits.

---

4. Herbert frequently used the same title for several different poems; editors differentiate between them by adding numbers.
5. I.e., a sin within the heart.

I lookèd on thy furniture so fine,
        And made it fine to me;
Thy glorious household stuff did me entwine,
10   And 'tice me unto thee.
Such stars I counted mine: both heaven and earth
Paid me my wages in a world of mirth.

What pleasures could I want, whose king I served,
        Where joys my fellows were?
15 Thus argued into hopes, my thoughts reserved
        No place for grief or fear;
Therefore my sudden soul caught at the place,
And made her youth and fierceness seek thy face:

At first thou gav'st me milk and sweetnesses;
20   I had my wish and way:
My days were strawed° with flowers and happiness;   strewed
        There was no month but May.
But with my years sorrow did twist and grow.
And made a party unawares for woe.

25 My flesh began unto my soul in pain,
        "Sicknesses cleave my bones;
Consuming agues° dwell in every vein,   fevers
        And tune my breath to groans."
Sorrow was all my soul; I scarce believed,
30 Till grief did tell me roundly,° that I lived.   bluntly

When I got health, thou took'st away my life,
        And more; for my friends die:
My mirth and edge was lost: a blunted knife
        Was of more use than I.
35 Thus thin and lean without a fence or friend,
I was blown through with ev'ry storm and wind.

Whereas my birth and spirit rather took
        The way that takes the town,[6]
Thou didst betray me to a lingering book,
40   And wrap me in a gown.
I was entangled in the world of strife,
Before I had the power to change my life.

Yet, for I threatened oft the siege to raise,
        Not simpering all mine age,
45 Thou often didst with academic praise
        Melt and dissolve my rage.

6. An allusion to the career at court that Herbert had sought until 1625; his hopes for advancement disappointed, he "betook himself to a Retreat from London" and resolved to "enter into Sacred Orders." Many poems of The Temple were composed after Herbert was ordained a deacon in 1626—a period during which he suffered from ill-health.

I took thy sweetened pill, till I came where
I could not go away, nor persevere.

Yet lest perchance I should too happy be
50   In my unhappiness,
Turning my purge to food, thou throwest me
          Into more sicknesses.
Thus doth thy power cross-bias[7] me, not making
Thine own gift good, yet me from my ways taking.

55 Now I am here, what thou wilt do with me
          None of my books will show:
I read, and sigh, and wish I were a tree,
          For sure then I should grow
To fruit or shade; at least, some bird would trust
60 Her household to me, and I should be just.

Yet, though thou troublest me, I must be meek;
          In weakness must be stout:[8]
Well, I will change the service, and go seek
          Some other master out.
65 Ah, my dear God! though I am clean forgot,
Let me not love thee, if I love thee not.

Prayer (I)

Prayer, the church's banquet, angels' age,[9]
    God's breath in man returning to his birth,
    The soul in paraphrase, heart in pilgrimage,
The Christian plummet[1] sounding heav'n and earth;

5 Engine against th' Almighty, sinner's tower,
    Reversèd thunder, Christ-side-piercing spear,
    The six-days' world[2] transposing in an hour,
A kind of tune, which all things hear and fear;

Softness, and peace, and joy, and love, and bliss,
10   Exalted manna,[3] gladness of the best,
    Heaven in ordinary,[4] man well dressed,
The Milky Way, the bird of Paradise,[5]

---

7. A term from the game of bowls: to cause the natural path of the ball to be altered. I.e., thy power frustrates me.
8. Cf. Malachi 3.13: "Your words have been stout against me, saith the Lord."
9. Prayer acquaints humans with the timeless existence of the "angels' age" (in contrast to finite human life).
1. A plummet is a piece of metal attached to a line, used for sounding or measuring a vertical distance. "Paraphrase": usually a fuller, simpler version of a text.
2. God created the world in six days (Genesis 1).

Also, of course, the six weekdays might be thought of as a "world" distinct from that of the Sabbath.
3. Spiritual nourishment, or food divinely supplied. Manna was the substance miraculously supplied as food to the Israelites during their time in the wilderness (Exodus 16).
4. In the everyday course of things. More specifically, "ordinary" also meant a daily allowance of food or an established order or form, as of the divine service.
5. Perhaps chosen for its name, or for its brilliant coloring.

Church bells beyond the stars heard, the soul's blood,
The land of spices; something understood.

The Temper (I)

How should I praise thee, Lord! how should my rhymes
    Gladly engrave thy love in steel,
    If what my soul doth feel sometimes,
        My soul might ever feel!

5   Although there were some forty heavens, or more,
    Sometimes I peer above them all;
    Sometimes I hardly reach a score;
        Sometimes to hell I fall.

O rack me not to such a vast extent;
10   Those distances belong to thee:
    The world's too little for thy tent,
        A grave too big for me.

Wilt thou meet arms with man, that thou dost stretch
    A crumb of dust from heaven to hell?
15   Will great God measure with a wretch?
        Shall he thy stature spell?

O let me, when thy roof my soul hath hid,
    O let me roost and nestle there;
    Then of a sinner thou art rid,
20   And I of hope and fear.

Yet take thy way; for, sure, thy way is best:
    Stretch or contract me, thy poor debtor:
    This is but tuning of my breast,
        To make the music better.

25   Whether I fly with angels, fall with dust,
    Thy hands made both, and I am there.
    Thy power and love, my love and trust,
        Make one place everywhere.

1633

Jordan (I)[6]

Who says that fictions only and false hair
    Become a verse? Is there in truth no beauty?
    Is all good structure in a winding stair?
    May no lines pass, except they do their duty
5   Not to a true, but painted chair?[7]

---

6. The only river of ancient Palestine; the Israelites crossed it to enter the Promised Land, and Christ was baptized in it. The title may also allude to the many windings of the Jordan.

7. It was customary to bow or "do one's duty" to the king's chair of state even when unoccupied; also alludes to the false imitation critiqued by Plato in *The Republic* 10.

Is it no verse, except enchanted groves
And sudden arbors shadow coarse-spun lines?[8]
Must purling streams refresh a lover's loves?
Must all be veiled while he that reads, divines,
10   Catching the sense at two removes?

Shepherds are honest people; let them sing:
Riddle who list,° for me, and pull for prime:[9]   *likes*
I envy no man's nightingale or spring;
Nor let them punish me with loss of rhyme,
15   Who plainly say, *My God, My King.*

The Windows

Lord, how can man preach thy eternal word?
    He is a brittle crazy° glass;   *flawed, distorting*
Yet in thy temple thou dost him afford
    This glorious and transcendent place,
5   To be a window, through thy grace.

But when thou dost anneal[1] in glass thy story,
    Making thy life to shine within
The holy preachers, then the light and glory
    More reverend grows, and more doth win;
10   Which else shows waterish, bleak, and thin.

Doctrine and life, colors and light, in one
    When they combine and mingle, bring
A strong regard and awe; but speech alone
    Doth vanish like a flaring thing,
15   And in the ear, not conscience, ring.[2]

Denial

When my devotions could not pierce
        Thy silent ears,
Then was my heart broken, as was my verse;
    My breast was full of fears
5   And disorder.

My bent thoughts, like a brittle bow,
        Did fly asunder:
Each took his way; some would to pleasures go,
    Some to the wars and thunder
10   Of alarms.

8. I.e., is it not true poetry unless enchanted groves and suddenly appearing trees (effects sought by landscape architects) shade (but also overshadow) humble lines?
9. To draw a lucky card in the game of primero. Lines 11–12 have been variously interpreted; their ambiguity and syntactical density work to complicate the contrast Herbert seems to be drawing between a "plain" style (exemplified by the shepherds) and the artificial, worldly style described in line 12. "For me": as far as I'm concerned.
1. Fix the colors, after painting, by heating the glass.
2. The last stanza seems to challenge directly the Puritan belief in the efficacy of the spoken word alone.

"As good go anywhere," they say,
        "As to benumb
Both knees and heart, in crying night and day,
        Come, come, my God, O come!
15   But no hearing."

O that thou shouldst give dust a tongue
        To cry to thee,
And then not hear it crying! All day long
        My heart was in my knee,³
20   But no hearing.

Therefore my soul lay out of sight,
        Untuned, unstrung:
My feeble spirit, unable to look right,
        Like a nipped blossom, hung
25   Discontented.

O cheer and tune my heartless breast,
        Defer no time;
That so thy favors granting my request,
        They and my mind may chime,⁴
30   And mend my rhyme.

Vanity (I)

The fleet astronomer can bore°   pierce
And thread the spheres⁵ with his quick-piercing mind:
He views their stations, walks from door to door,
        Surveys, as if he had designed
5   To make a purchase there; he sees their dances,
        And knoweth long before
Both their full-eyed aspècts,⁶ and secret glances.

        The nimble diver with his side⁷
Cuts through the working waves, that he may fetch
10 His dearly-earnèd pearl, which God did hide
        On purpose from the venturous wretch;
That he might save his life, and also hers
        Who with excessive pride
Her own destruction and his danger wears.

15   The subtle chymic° can divest   chemist
And strip the creature naked, till he find
The callow° principles within their nest: bald, immature

3. I.e., my heart was bowed and bent in reverence, like my knee.
4. I.e., agree.
5. Concentric transparent shells containing the heavenly bodies, according to Ptolemaic astronomy; they were thought to produce angelic music as they turned.
6. The relative positions of the heavenly bodies as they appear to an observer on the Earth at a given time, and their supposed influence on Earthly matters.
7. I.e., swimming on his side.

There he imparts to them his mind,
Admitted to their bed-chamber,[8] before
20   They appear trim and dressed
To ordinary suitors at the door.

What hath not man sought out and found,
But his dear God? who yet his glorious law
Embosoms in us, mellowing the ground
25   With showers and frosts, with love and awe,
So that we need not say, "Where's this command?"
             Poor man, thou searchest round
To find out death, but missest life at hand.

Virtue

Sweet day, so cool, so calm, so bright,
    The bridal of the earth and sky:
The dew shall weep thy fall tonight;
    For thou must die.

5 Sweet rose, whose hue, angry and brave,[9]
    Bids the rash gazer wipe his eye:
Thy root is ever in its grave,
    And thou must die.

Sweet spring, full of sweet days and roses,
10   A box where sweets° compacted lie;   *perfumes*
My music shows ye have your closes,[1]
    And all must die.

Only a sweet and virtuous soul,
    Like seasoned timber, never gives;
15 But though the whole world turn to coal,[2]
    Then chiefly lives.

Man

My God, I heard this day
That none doth build a stately habitation,
But he that means to dwell therein.
What house more stately hath there been,
5 Or can be, than is Man? to[3] whose creation
    All things are in decay.

---

8. Herbert implies that the chemist examining creatures' inner natures in an overly intimate way is forming them according to his own intellect ("imparts to them his mind") rather than discovering their God-given reality.
9. Splendid; "angry": i.e., red, the color of anger.

1. A close is a cadence, the conclusion of a musical strain.
2. An allusion to Judgment Day, when the world will end in a great fire (2 Peter 3.10).
3. I.e., compared to.

For Man is every thing,
And more: he is a tree, yet bears more fruit;[4]
A beast, yet is or should be more:
10   Reason and speech we only bring.
Parrots may thank us, if they are not mute,
They go upon the score.[5]

Man is all symmetry,
Full of proportions, one limb to another,
15   And all to all the world besides:[6]
Each part may call the furthest, brother;
For head with foot hath private amity,°   friendship
And both with moons and tides.[7]

Nothing hath got so far,
20   But man hath caught and kept it, as his prey.
His eyes dismount the highest star:
He is in little all the sphere.
Herbs gladly cure our flesh, because that they
Find their acquaintance there.

25   For us the winds do blow,
The earth doth rest, heaven move, and fountains flow.
Nothing we see but means our good,
As our delight or as our treasure:
The whole is either our cupboard of food,
30   Or cabinet of pleasure.

The stars have us to bed;
Night draws the curtain, which the sun withdraws;
Music and light attend our head.
All things unto our flesh are kind°   kin
35   In their descent and being; to our mind
In their ascent and cause.

Each thing is full of duty:[8]
Waters united are our navigation;
Distinguishèd, our habitation;
40   Below, our drink; above, our meat;
Both are our cleanliness. Hath one such beauty?
Then how are all things neat?[9]

---

4. This line presents a serious textual problem, since all early printed versions of the poem have "no" instead of "more" "fruit." We follow the reading of the one surviving manuscript, which Herbert saw, but the alternate reading has strong claims. See, for instance, "Affliction (I)," lines 57–60 (p. 333), where Herbert contrasts the uncertainty of human "fruitfulness"—dependant partly on God's hidden will—with the tree's natural cycle of growth.
5. "Man" is the only creature with "[r]eason and speech": the parrot may seem to be an exception, but it talks on credit ("upon the score"), i.e., because humans taught it how.

6. I.e., man is also symmetrical to—a microcosm of—the world.
7. Refers to the notion that parts of the body are affected by the motions of the moon and stars.
8. I.e., all the elements serve humans. Oceans ("waters united") are valuable for navigation; the dividing of the waters ("distinguished") during the Creation allowed humans to live on the Earth (Genesis 1.6). Water on Earth provides drink, while water from "above" (i.e., manna or dew) is food.
9. I.e., if one element can serve so abundantly, how wonderful ("neat") is the sum of all things.

More servants wait on Man
Than he'll take notice of: in every path
45   He treads down that which doth befriend him[1]
When sickness makes him pale and wan.
O mighty love! Man is one world, and hath
Another to attend him.

Since then, my God, thou hast
50   So brave a palace built, O dwell in it,
That it may dwell with thee at last!
Till then, afford us so much wit,
That, as the world serves us, we may serve thee,
And both thy servants be.

Life

I made a posy, while the day ran by:
"Here will I smell my remnant° out, and tie   *remaining time*
My life within this band."
But Time did beckon to the flowers, and they
5   By noon most cunningly did steal away,
And withered in my hand.

My hand was next to them, and then my heart;
I took, without more thinking, in good part
Time's gentle admonition;
10   Who did so sweetly death's sad taste convey,
Making my mind to smell my fatal day,
Yet sug'ring the suspicion.

Farewell dear flowers, sweetly your time ye spent,
Fit, while ye lived, for smell or ornament,
15   And after death for cures.[2]
I follow straight without complaints or grief,
Since, if my scent be good, I care not if
It be as short as yours.

Artillery

As I one evening sat before my cell,
Methought[3] a star did shoot into my lap.
I rose and shook my clothes, as knowing well
That from small fires comes oft no small mishap;
5   When suddenly I heard one say,
"Do as thou usest, disobey,
Expel good motions from thy breast,
Which have the face of fire, but end in rest."[4]

---

1. I.e., he treads down the herb that cures ill-
nesses.
2. Roses were sometimes used as an ingredient in
medicines.

3. It seemed to me.
4. I.e., divine impulses, like falling stars, may have
the appearance of dangerous fires, but ultimately
end quietly.

I, who had heard of music in the spheres,[5]
10 But not of speech in stars, began to muse;
But turning to my God, whose ministers
The stars and all things are: "If I refuse,
    Dread Lord," said I, "so oft my good,
    Then I refuse not ev'n with blood
15   To wash away my stubborn thought;
For I will do or suffer what I ought.

"But I have also stars and shooters too,
Born where thy servants both artilleries use.
My tears and prayers night and day do woo
20 And work up to thee; yet thou dost refuse.
    Not but I am (I must say still)
    Much more obliged to do thy will
Than thou to grant mine; but because
Thy promise now hath ev'n set thee thy laws.

25 "Then we are shooters both, and thou dost deign°   *condescend*
To enter combat with us, and contest
With thine own clay. But I would parley fain:[6]
Shun not my arrows, and behold my breast.
    Yet if thou shunnest, I am thine:
30   I must be so, if I am mine.
    There is no articling° with thee: *negotiating*
I am but finite, yet thine infinitely."

The Collar[7]

I struck the board° and cried, "No more;   *table*
    I will abroad!
What? shall I ever sigh and pine?
My lines and life are free, free as the road,
5   Loose as the wind, as large as store.°   *abundance*
      Shall I be still in suit?[8]
Have I no harvest but a thorn
To let me blood, and not restore
What I have lost with cordial° fruit?   *life-giving*
10   Sure there was wine
Before my sighs did dry it; there was corn
Before my tears did drown it.
Is the year only lost to me?
Have I no bays[9] to crown it,
15 No flowers, no garlands gay? All blasted?
      All wasted?
Not so, my heart; but there is fruit,
    And thou hast hands.

---

5. The spheres of Ptolemaic astronomy, concentric transparent shells containing the heavenly bodies, were thought to produce angelic music as they turned.
6. "Parley fain": speak gladly.
7. A band of metal fixed round a prisoner's neck; also, something worn about the neck as a badge of servitude.
8. I.e., in attendance upon someone for a favor.
9. A laurel garland symbolizing poetic fame.

Recover all thy sigh-blown age
20 On double pleasures: leave thy cold dispute
Of what is fit and not. Forsake thy cage,
     Thy rope of sands,[1]
Which petty thoughts have made, and made to thee
Good cable, to enforce and draw,
25   And be thy law,
While thou didst wink[2] and wouldst not see.
     Away! take heed;
     I will abroad.
Call in thy death's-head[3] there; tie up thy fears.
30   He that forbears
     To suit and serve his need,
     Deserves his load."
But as I raved and grew more fierce and wild
     At every word,
35 Methought I heard one calling, *Child!*
     And I replied, *My Lord.*

The Pulley[4]

When God at first made man,
Having a glass of blessings standing by,
     "Let us," said he, "pour on him all we can.
Let the world's riches, which dispersèd lie,
5   Contract into a span."[5]

So strength first made a way;
Then beauty flowed, then wisdom, honor, pleasure.
     When almost all was out, God made a stay,
Perceiving that, alone of all his treasure,
10   Rest[6] in the bottom lay.

     "For if I should," said he,
"Bestow this jewel also on my creature,
     He would adore my gifts instead of me,
And rest in Nature, not the God of Nature;
15   So both should losers be.

     "Yet let him keep the rest,
But keep them with repining restlessness.
     Let him be rich and weary, that at least,
If goodness lead him not, yet weariness
20   May toss him to my breast."

---

1. I.e., the restrictions on behavior, which the "petty thoughts" have made into "good" (or strong) cable.
2. Shut your eyes.
3. A representation of a human skull intended to serve as a reminder that all men and women must die (*memento mori*).
4. A simple mechanical device, made of a rope, a wheel, and sometimes a block, used for changing the direction of a pulling force in order to lift weights.
5. A small space; the distance from the end of the thumb to the end of the little finger of a spread hand.
6. Meaning both "remainder" and "repose."

The Flower

How fresh, oh Lord, how sweet and clean
Are thy returns! even as the flowers in spring;
    To which, besides their own demean,[7]
The late-past frosts tributes of pleasure bring.
5   Grief melts away
               Like snow in May,
         As if there were no such cold thing.

         Who would have thought my shriveled heart
Could have recovered greenness? It was gone
10   Quite underground; as flowers depart   bloomed
To see their mother-root, when they have blown,°
               Where they together
               All the hard weather,
         Dead to the world, keep house unknown.

15   These are thy wonders, Lord of power,
Killing and quickening°, bringing down to hell   reviving
    And up to heaven in an hour;
Making a chiming of a passing-bell.[8]
               We say amiss
20   This or that is:
         Thy word is all, if we could spell.

         Oh that I once past changing were,
Fast in thy Paradise, where no flower can wither!
    Many a spring I shoot up fair,
25 Offering° at heaven, growing and groaning thither;   aiming
               Nor doth my flower
               Want a spring shower,[9]
         My sins and I joining together.

         But while I grow in a straight line,
30 Still upwards bent, as if heaven were mine own,
    Thy anger comes, and I decline:
What frost to that? what pole is not the zone
               Where all things burn,
               When thou dost turn,
35   And the least frown of thine is shown?[1]

         And now in age I bud again,
After so many deaths I live and write;
    I once more smell the dew and rain,
And relish versing. Oh, my only light,
40   It cannot be

---

7. Demeanor or bearing (spelled "demean" in the first edition); also *demesne*, "estate," i.e., the estate of one's own beauty or pleasure.
8. A monotone bell tolled to announce a death; a chiming offers a pleasing variety.

9. I.e., the tears of contrition caused by the "joining" together of the poet's sins and his conscience.
1. I.e., what cold compares to God's anger? What chill would not seem like the heat of the equator, compared to God's wrath?

      That I am he
On whom thy tempests fell all night.

      These are thy wonders, Lord of love,
To make us see we are but flowers that glide;[2]
45   Which when we once can find and prove,°   *experience*
Thou hast a garden for us where to bide;
      Who would be more,
      Swelling through store,°   *possessions*
Forfeit their Paradise by their pride.

Bitter-Sweet

Ah, my dear angry Lord,
Since thou dost love, yet strike;
Cast down, yet help afford;
Sure I will do the like.

5   I will complain, yet praise;
I will bewail, approve;
And all my sour-sweet days
I will lament and love.

The Forerunners

The harbingers[3] are come. See, see their mark:
White is their color, and behold my head.[4]
But must they have my brain? Must they dispark[5]
Those sparkling notions, which therein were bred?
5   Must dullness turn me to a clod?
Yet have they left me, *Thou art still my God.*

Good men ye be, to leave me my best room,
Ev'n all my heart, and what is lodgèd there:
I pass not,[6] I, what of the rest become,
10 So *Thou art still my God* be out of fear.
     He will be pleasèd with that ditty;
And if I please him, I write fine and witty.

Farewell sweet phrases, lovely metaphors.
But will ye leave me thus? When ye before
15 Of stews and brothels only knew the doors,
     Then did I wash you with my tears, and more,

2. Pass silently away.
3. The advance agents of the king and his party on a royal progress or tour. They marked with chalk the doors of those dwellings where the court would be accommodated.
4. I.e., the poet has been marked by the appearance of white hairs, a sign that all of his "sparkling notions" must be dispossessed, to make room for his coming Lord.

5. I.e., *dis-park*, to turn out, as of a park; there may also be a play on *dis-spark* (from "sparkling notions" in the next line).
6. I care not. I.e., all the other thoughts in the house (my mind, my soul) can be turned out of doors, as long as you leave my heart ("my best room") and its one inhabitant, the thought "Thou art still my God."

Brought you to church well dressed and clad:
My God must have my best, ev'n all I had.

Lovely enchanting language, sugar-cane,
20 Honey of roses, wither wilt thou fly?
Hath some fond lover 'ticed thee to thy bane?° *destruction*
And wilt thou leave the church and love a sty?[7]
    Fie, thou wilt soil thy broidered coat,
And hurt thyself, and him that sings the note.

25 Let foolish lovers, if they will love dung,
With canvas, not with arras,[8] clothe their shame:
Let folly speak in her own native tongue.
True beauty dwells on high: ours is a flame
    But borrowed thence to light us thither.
30 Beauty and beauteous words should go together.

Yet if you go, I pass not; take your way:
For *Thou art still my God* is all that ye
Perhaps with more embellishment can say.
Go, birds of spring: let winter have his fee;
35   Let a bleak paleness chalk the door,
So all within be livelier than before.

Discipline

Throw away thy rod,[9]
Throw away thy wrath:
    O my God,
Take the gentle path.

5 For my heart's desire
Unto thine is bent:
    I aspire
To a full consent.

Not a word or look
10 I affect to own,
    But by book,
And thy book alone.[1]

Though I fail, I weep:
Though I halt in pace,
15   Yet I creep
To the throne of grace.

Then let wrath remove;
Love will do the deed:
    For with love
20 Stony hearts will bleed.

---

7. Pigsty; also, a place of moral contamination.   9. Instrument of punishment.
8. I.e., with coarse cloth, not with tapestry.   1. I.e., the Bible.

Love is swift of foot;
Love's a man of war,[2]
      And can shoot,
And can hit from far.

25   Who can 'scape his bow?
That which wrought on thee,
      Brought thee low,
Needs must work on me.

Throw away thy rod;
30   Though man frailties hath,
      Thou art God:
Throw away thy wrath.

The Elixir[3]

Teach me, my God and King,
  In all things thee to see,
And what I do in anything,
  To do it as for thee.

5   Not rudely, as a beast,
  To run into an action;
But still to make thee prepossest,[4]
  And give it his° perfection.   *its*

A man that looks on glass,
10   On it may stay his eye,
Or, if he pleaseth, through it pass,
  And then the heaven espy.

All may of thee partake:
  Nothing can be so mean
15   Which with his tincture *(for thy sake)*[5]
  Will not grow bright and clean.

A servant with this clause
  Makes drudgery divine:
Who sweeps a room as for thy laws,
20   Makes that and th' action fine.

This is the famous stone
  That turneth all to gold;
For that which God doth touch[6] and own
  Cannot for less be told.

2. A song by Moses in Exodus 15 calls the Lord a "man of war"; also, a possible reference to the classical image of Cupid and his arrow.
3. An elixir is a drug or essence supposed to have the property of indefinitely prolonging life; here, it is identified with the "famous stone" (line 21), believed by the alchemists to have the property of turning other metals to gold. Figuratively, the quintessence or soul of a thing.
4. I.e., always to give thee a prior claim.
5. I.e., nothing is so insignificant ("mean") that it can't grow bright and clean for thy sake by means of its tincture (an immaterial principle that transformed substances, according to alchemical theory).
6. To test (gold) for purity by rubbing it with a touchstone.

Death

Death, thou wast once an uncouth hideous thing,
        Nothing but bones,
      The sad effect of sadder groans:
Thy mouth was open, but thou couldst not sing.

5   For we considered thee as at some six
        Or ten years hence,
      After the loss of life and sense,
Flesh being turned to dust, and bones to sticks.

We looked on this side of thee, shooting short;
10   Where we did find
      The shells of fledge souls left behind,
Dry dust, which sheds no tears, but may extort.[7]

But since our Savior's death did put some blood
        Into thy face,
15   Thou art grown fair and full of grace,
Much in request, much sought for as a good.

For we do now behold thee gay and glad,
        As at Doomsday;[8]
      When souls shall wear their new array,
20 And all thy bones with beauty shall be clad.

Therefore we can go die as sleep, and trust
        Half that we have
      Unto an honest faithful grave;
Making our pillows either down, or dust.

Love (III)[9]

Love bade me welcome: yet my soul drew back,
        Guilty of dust and sin.
But quick-eyed Love, observing me grow slack[1]
        From my first entrance in,
5   Drew nearer to me, sweetly questioning
        If I lacked any thing.

"A guest," I answered, "worthy to be here":
        Love said, "You shall be he."
"I, the unkind, ungrateful? Ah, my dear,
10   I cannot look on thee."
Love took my hand, and smiling did reply,
        "Who made the eyes but I?"

7. "Fledge souls" that have left the body and gone to heaven are like fledgling chicks that have left the shell behind. The shell (i.e., the corpse) can draw ("extort") tears from survivors, although it cannot shed them itself.
8. Day of God's final judgment.

9. This is the last lyric in "The Church" both in the early Williams manuscript and in the 1633 edition of *The Temple*; some critics have therefore interpreted the poem as describing the soul's reception into heaven.
1. I.e., become hesitant because of misgivings.

"Truth, Lord; but I have marred them; let my shame
Go where it doth deserve."
15 "And know you not," says Love, "who bore the blame?"[2]
"My dear, then I will serve."
"You must sit down," says Love, "and taste my meat."[3]
So I did sit and eat.

JAMES SHIRLEY

1596–1666

FROM AJAX

Dirge[1]

The glories of our blood and state
Are shadows, not substantial things;
There is no armor against fate;
Death lays his icy hand on kings.
5   Scepter and crown
      Must tumble down
And in the dust be equal made
With the poor crooked scythe and spade.

Some men with swords may reap the field
10   And plant fresh laurels[2] where they kill,
But their strong nerves at last must yield;
They tame but one another still.
      Early or late
      They stoop to fate
15   And must give up their murmuring breath,
When they, pale captives, creep to death.

The garlands wither on your brow,
Then boast no more your mighty deeds;
Upon death's purple altar now
20   See where the victor-victim bleeds.
      Your heads must come
      To the cold tomb;
Only the actions of the just
Smell sweet and blossom in their dust.

1659

2. I.e., Christ, who took on the "blame" for human beings' original sin.
3. A reference to the sacrament of Communion; according to Anglicans, the ritual taking of bread and wine in remembrance of Christ's body; also a reference to the final Communion in heaven, when God "shall gird himself, and make them to sit down to meat, and will come forth and serve them" (Luke 12.37).

1. This poem concludes Shirley's play The Contention of Ajax and Ulysses for the Armor of Achilles, which retells a story from Ovid's Metamorphoses.
2. The laurel was an emblem of victory, as well as a symbol of distinction in poetry.

THOMAS CAREW
1598?–1639?

A Song

Ask me no more where Jove[1] bestows,
When June is past, the fading rose;
For in your beauty's orient deep,
These flowers, as in their causes,[2] sleep.

5 Ask me no more whither doth stray
The golden atoms of the day;
For in pure love heaven did prepare
Those powders to enrich your hair.

Ask me no more whither doth haste
10 The nightingale when May is past;
For in your sweet dividing[3] throat
She winters, and keeps warm her note.

Ask me no more where those stars light,
That downwards fall in dead of night;
15 For in your eyes they sit, and there
Fixèd become, as in their sphere.

Ask me no more if east or west
The phoenix[4] builds her spicy nest;
For unto you at last she flies,
20 And in your fragrant bosom dies.

1640

The Spring

Now that the winter's gone, the earth hath lost
Her snow-white robes, and now no more the frost
Candies° the grass, or casts an icy cream   ices
Upon the silver lake or crystal stream;
5 But the warm sun thaws the benumbèd earth
And makes it tender, gives a sacred[5] birth
To the dead swallow, wakes in hollow tree
The drowsy cuckoo and the humble bee.
Now do a choir of chirping minstrels bring
10 In triumph to the world the youthful spring.
The valleys, hills, and woods in rich array
Welcome the coming of the longed-for May.
Now all things smile: only my love doth lour,°   frown
Nor hath the scalding noonday sun the power

---

1. The ruling god of classical mythology.
2. Aristotelian philosophy regarded that from which a thing is made or comes into being as the "material cause" of the thing.
3. Executing a "division," an embellished musical phrase.

4. A legendary bird, the only one of its kind, represented as living five hundred years in the Arabian desert, being consumed in fire, then rising anew from its own ashes.
5. Swallows were sacred to the Roman household gods.

15   To melt that marble ice which still doth hold
      Her heart congealed, and makes her pity cold.
      The ox, which lately did for shelter fly
      Into the stall, doth now securely lie
      In open fields; and love no more is made
20   By the fireside, but in the cooler shade:
      Amyntas now doth with his Chloris[6] sleep
      Under a sycamore, and all things keep
      Time with the season. Only she doth carry
      June in her eyes, in her heart January.

1640

Mediocrity[7] in Love Rejected

    Give me more love, or more disdain;
      The torrid or the frozen zone
    Bring equal ease unto my pain;
      The temperate affords me none:
5   Either extreme, of love or hate,
    Is sweeter than a calm estate.°   *condition*

    Give me a storm; if it be love,
      Like Danae in that golden shower,[8]
    I swim in pleasure; if it prove
10   Disdain, that torrent will devour
    My vulture hopes; and he's possessed
    Of heaven that's but from hell released.
      Then crown my joys, or cure my pain;
      Give me more love, or more disdain.

1640

Song. To My Inconstant Mistress

    When thou, poor excommunicate
      From all the joys of love, shalt see
    The full reward and glorious fate
      Which my strong faith shall purchase me,
5   Then curse thine own inconstancy.

    A fairer hand than thine shall cure
      That heart which thy false oaths did wound,
    And to my soul a soul more pure
      Than thine shall by Love's hand be bound,
10   And both with equal glory crowned.

6. Conventional names for a shepherd and shepherdess.
7. Temperance, moderation.
8. Jove, the ruling god in classical mythology, frequently left Juno, his sister and wife, to pursue other women; whether his actions constituted seduction or rape often depends upon the particular account of a common myth, as well as on interpretation. Danae was the daughter of the king of Argos, who imprisoned her because of a prophecy that a son born to her would kill him; Jove came to her in the form of a shower of gold, and as a result she became the mother of Perseus.

Then shalt thou weep, entreat, complain
To Love, as I did once to thee;
When all thy tears shall be as vain
As mine were then, for thou shalt be
15   Damned for thy false apostasy.[9]

1640

An Elegy upon the Death of the Dean of Paul's, Dr. John Donne

Can we not force from widowed poetry,
Now thou art dead, great Donne, one elegy
To crown thy hearse? Why yet did we not trust,
Though with unkneaded dough-baked[1] prose, thy dust,
5   Such as the unscissored[2] lect'rer from the flower
Of fading rhetoric, short-lived as his hour,
Dry as the sand that measures it,[3] should lay
Upon the ashes on the funeral day?
Have we nor tune, nor voice? Didst thou dispense[4]
10   Through all our language both the words and sense?
'Tis a sad truth. The pulpit may her plain
And sober Christian precepts still retain;
Doctrines it may, and wholesome uses, frame,
Grave homilies° and lectures; but the flame   *sermons*
15   Of thy brave soul, that shot such heat and light
As burnt our earth and made our darkness bright,
Committed holy rapes[5] upon our will,
Did through the eye the melting heart distill,
And the deep knowledge of dark truths so teach
20   As sense might judge what fancy could not reach,[6]
Must be desired forever. So the fire
That fills with spirit and heat the Delphic choir,[7]
Which, kindled first by thy Promethean[8] breath,
Glowed here a while, lies quenched now in thy death.
25   The Muses' garden, with pedantic weeds
O'erspread, was purged by thee; the lazy seeds
Of servile imitation thrown away,
And fresh invention planted; thou didst pay
The debts of our penurious° bankrupt age;   *poverty-stricken*
30   Licentious thefts, that make poetic rage

9. Abandonment of one's allegiance, often to a religious faith or god.
1. I.e., badly finished, flat.
2. I.e., with uncut hair; in the first edition, Carew wrote "church-man" instead of "lecturer," and thus signalled an aim to distinguish this figure from Roman Catholic priests, whose hair was cut (tonsured) when they entered the Church. The line seems to have been altered to soften the critique of Protestant clergymen implicit in the evocation of a "dry," inadequate elegy on the occasion of Donne's official funeral. Donne himself was born a Catholic; although he later became a famous Anglican preacher, he expressed doubts about vari-

ous religious claims to truth in "Satire III" (pp. 283–85) and other writings.
3. I.e., the sand in an hourglass.
4. Use up or lay out.
5. Forcible seizures. For Donne's use of the metaphor of a religious "rape," see Holy Sonnet 14 (p. 289).
6. I.e., so that things too intangible and elevated even to be imagined might be made plain to sense.
7. I.e., the choir of poets. Delphi was the site of an oracle of Apollo, the god of poetry.
8. Prometheus stole fire from the gods for the benefit of mortals.

A mimic fury, when our souls must be
Possessed, or with Anacreon's ecstasy,
Or Pindar's,[9] not their own; the subtle cheat
Of sly exchanges, and the juggling feat
35 Of two-edged words, or whatsoever wrong
By ours was done the Greek or Latin tongue,
Thou hast redeemed, and opened us a mine
Of rich and pregnant fancy, drawn a line
Of masculine expression, which had good
40 Old Orpheus[1] seen, or all the ancient brood
Our superstitious fools admire, and hold
Their lead more precious than thy burnished gold,
Thou hadst been their exchequer,° and no more   *treasury*
They in each other's dung had searched for ore.
45 Thou shalt yield no precèdence, but of time
And the blind fate of language, whose tuned chime
More charms the outward sense; yet thou mayest claim
From so great disadvantage greater fame,
Since to the awe of thy imperious wit
50 Our troublesome language bends, made only fit
With her tough thick-ribbed hoops, to gird about
Thy giant fancy, which had proved too stout
For their soft melting phrases.[2] As in time
They had the start, so did they cull the prime
55 Buds of invention many a hundred year,
And left the rifled fields, besides the fear
To touch their harvest; yet from those bare lands
Of what is only thine, thy only hands
(And that their smallest work) have gleanèd more
60 Than all those times and tongues could reap before.
    But thou art gone, and thy strict laws will be
Too hard for libertines in poetry.
They will recall the goodly exiled train
Of gods and goddesses, which in thy just reign
65 Were banished° nobler poems; now with these   *banished from*
The silenced tales i' th' *Metamorphoses*[3]
Shall stuff their lines and swell the windy page,
Till verse, refined by thee in this last age,
Turn ballad-rhyme, or those old idols be
70 Adored again with new apostasy.[4]
    O pardon me, that break with untuned verse
The reverend silence that attends thy hearse,
Whose solemn awful° murmurs were to thee,   *awestruck*
More than these faint lines, a loud elegy,
75 That did proclaim in a dumb eloquence
The death of all the arts, whose influence,
Grown feeble, in these panting numbers lies
Gasping short-winded accents, and so dies:

9. Anacreon (sixth–fifth c. B.C.) and Pindar (fifth c. B.C.) were famous Greek poets.
1. In Greek mythology, the son of one of the Muses and the greatest of poets and musicians.
2. I.e., a metaphor describing Donne's wit as a barrel-maker bending hoops of metal around the "wine" of his genius.
3. Earlier poets had drawn heavily on the stories in Ovid's *Metamorphoses* for the materials of their poetry.
4. Abandonment of one's allegiance, especially to a religious faith or a god.

So doth the swiftly turning wheel not stand
80   In th' instant we withdraw the moving hand,
But some small time retain a faint weak course
By virtue of the first impulsive force;
And so whilst I cast on thy funeral pile
Thy crown of bays,⁵ oh, let it crack awhile
85   And spit disdain, till the devouring flashes
Suck all the moisture up; then turn to ashes.
    I will not draw thee envy to engross⁶
All thy perfections, or weep all the loss;
Those are too numerous for one elegy,
90   And this too great to be expressed by me.
Let others carve the rest; it shall suffice
I on thy grave this epitaph incise:

        Here lies a king, that ruled as he thought fit
        The universal monarchy of wit;
95   *Here lie two flamens,° and both those the best:*   *priests*
        Apollo's⁷ first, at last the true God's priest.

        1633, 1640

EDMUND WALLER

1607–1687

On a Girdle¹

    That which her slender waist confined,
Shall now my joyful temples bind;
No monarch but would give his crown,
His arms might do what this has done.

5   It was my heaven's extremest sphere,²
The pale° which held that lovely dear;   *enclosure*
My joy, my grief, my hope, my love
Did all within this circle move!

    A narrow compass! and yet there
10   Dwelt all that's good, and all that's fair;
Give me but what this ribbon bound,
Take all the rest the sun goes round!

        1645

Song

Go, lovely rose!
Tell her that wastes her time and me

---

5. A crown of bays or laurel was the traditional reward of the victor in a poetic competition.
6. Write, copy out, with a pun on the word's economic meanings: to buy up, monopolize.

7. I.e., the god of poetry.
1. A belt or sash worn around the waist.
2. The outermost sphere of the Ptolemaic universe; a supposed source of cosmic harmonies.

That now she knows,
When I resemble° her to thee,   *liken*
5 How sweet and fair she seems to be.

Tell her that's young,
And shuns to have her graces spied,
  That hadst thou sprung
In deserts, where no men abide,
10 Thou must have uncommended died.

Small is the worth
Of beauty from the light retired;
  Bid her come forth,
Suffer herself to be desired,
15 And not blush so to be admired.

Then die! that she
The common fate of all things rare
  May read in thee;
How small a part of time they share
20 That are so wondrous sweet and fair!

                                                      1645

Of the Last Verses in the Book[3]

When we for age could neither read nor write,
The subject made us able to indite;°   *utter, dictate*
The soul, with nobler resolutions decked,
The body stooping, does herself erect.
5 No mortal parts are requisite to raise
Her that, unbodied, can her Maker praise.
  The seas are quiet when the winds give o'er;
So calm are we when passions are no more!
For then we know how vain it was to boast
10 Of fleeting things, so certain to be lost.
Clouds of affection° from our younger eyes   *emotion*
Conceal that emptiness which age descries.°   *discerns*
  The soul's dark cottage, battered and decayed,
Lets in new light through chinks that time has made;
15 Stronger by weakness, wiser men become,
As they draw near to their eternal home.
Leaving the old, both worlds at once they view,
That stand upon the threshold of the new.
                          —*Miratur Limen Olympi*
                                   Vergil[4]

                                                      1686

---

3. I.e., his book *Divine Poems*, first published in 1685.
4. From a sentence in Virgil's Fifth Eclogue that reads, in translation, "Arrayed in dazzling white, he stands *enraptured at heaven's unfamiliar threshold.*" Through this Latin quotation, Waller gives the last words in his poem about his "divine poems" to a pagan author. Many Christian writers, most notably Dante, viewed Virgil as a precursor of Christianity, one who stood on its threshold without being able to enter.

JOHN MILTON
1608–1674

Lycidas

*In This Monody the Author Bewails a Learned Friend,[1] Unfortunately
Drowned in His Passage from Chester on the Irish Seas, 1637. And by
Occasion Foretells the Ruin of Our Corrupted Clergy, Then in Their
Height.*

Yet once more, O ye laurels[2] and once more
Ye myrtles brown,° with ivy never sere,°   *dark / withered*
I come to pluck your berries harsh and crude,°   *unripe*
And with forced fingers rude,
5 Shatter your leaves before the mellowing year.
Bitter constraint, and sad occasion dear,°   *severe*
Compels me to disturb your season due;
For Lycidas is dead, dead ere his prime,
Young Lycidas, and hath not left his peer.
10 Who would not sing for Lycidas? He knew
Himself to sing, and build the lofty rhyme.
He must not float upon his watery bier[3]
Unwept, and welter° to the parching wind,   *roll about*
Without the meed° of some melodious tear.   *tribute*
15   Begin then, sisters of the sacred well
That from beneath the seat of Jove doth spring,
Begin, and somewhat loudly sweep the string.[4]
Hence with denial vain, and coy excuse;
So may some gentle Muse
20 With lucky words favor my destined urn,[5]
And as he passes turn,
And bid fair peace be to my sable° shroud.   *black*
For we were nursed upon the selfsame hill,
Fed the same flock, by fountain, shade, and rill.°   *brook*
25   Together both, ere the high lawns° appeared   *pastures*
Under the opening eyelids of the morn,
We drove afield, and both together heard
What time the grayfly winds her sultry horn,[6]
Battening° our flocks with the fresh dews of night,   *fattening*
30 Oft till the star that rose at evening bright[7]
Toward Heaven's descent had sloped his westering wheel.
Meanwhile the rural ditties were not mute,
Tempered to th' oaten flute,

---

1. Edward King, a young scholar, poet, and clergy-
man at Cambridge with Milton. This poem, which
draws heavily upon pastoral traditions, was first
published with some elegies by King's friends at
Cambridge in 1638 after King's ship mysteriously
foundered on a clear day in August 1637. Milton
added this headnote when he published the elegy
in his 1645 *Poems*. "Monody": an elegy or dirge
sung by a single voice.
2. Laurel, myrtle, and ivy were all traditional
materials for poetic garlands.
3. A stand on which a corpse is carried to the

grave.
4. I.e., play your music. "Sisters of the sacred
well": The Muses, nine Greek goddesses believed
to be sources of inspiration for the arts and god-
desses of song; the well sacred to them was Aga-
nippe, at the foot of Mt. Helicon, where they
danced about the altar of Jove.
5. I.e., place of burial.
6. I.e., the insect hum of midday, as the grayfly
blows ("winds") her horn in the ("sultry") heat of
day.
7. I.e., Hesperus, the evening star.

Rough satyrs danced, and fauns with cloven heel[8]
35 From the glad sound would not be absent long,
And old Damoetas[9] loved to hear our song.
    But O the heavy change, now thou art gone,
Now thou art gone, and never must return!
Thee, shepherd,[1] thee the woods and desert caves,
40 With wild thyme and the gadding° vine o'ergrown,   *wandering*
And all their echoes mourn.
The willows and the hazel copses[2] green
Shall now no more be seen,
Fanning their joyous leaves to thy soft lays.
45 As killing as the canker° to the rose,   *cankerworm*
Or taint-worm to the weanling herds that graze,
Or frost to flowers that their gay wardrobe wear,
When first the white thorn blows;°   *blooms*
Such, Lycidas, thy loss to shepherd's ear.
50   Where were ye, nymphs,[3] when the remorseless deep
Closed o'er the head of your loved Lycidas?
For neither were ye playing on the steep,
Where your old Bards, the famous Druids lie,
Nor on the shaggy top of Mona high,
55 Nor yet where Deva spreads her wizard stream:[4]
Ay me! I fondly° dream—   *foolishly*
Had ye been there—for what could that have done?
What could the Muse[5] herself that Orpheus bore,
The Muse herself, for her inchanting son
60 Whom universal Nature did lament,
When by the rout that made the hideous roar,
His gory visage° down the stream was sent,   *face*
Down the swift Hebrus to the Lesbian shore?
    Alas! What boots° it with uncessant care   *profits*
65 To tend the homely slighted shepherd's trade,
And strictly meditate[6] the thankless Muse?
Were it not better done as others use,
To sport with Amaryllis[7] in the shade,
Or with the tangles of Neaera's hair?
70 Fame is the spur that the clear spirit doth raise
(That last infirmity of noble mind)
To scorn delights, and live laborious days;[8]
But the fair guerdon° when we hope to find,   *reward*
And think to burst out into sudden blaze,

---

8. The half-goat, half-man woodland gods associated with lust and drinking (although the fauns were sometimes described as less wild than the satyrs).
9. A conventional pastoral name, here perhaps referring to one of the tutors at Cambridge.
1. I.e., Lycidas.
2. Small thickets of trees.
3. Mythological female spirits inhabiting a particular place, object, or natural phenomenon.
4. The "steep" is probably the mountain Kerig-y-Druidion in northern Wales, a Druid burial ground. Mona is the Isle of Anglesey, Deva the river Dee, called "wizard" because its changes of course were supposed to foretell the country's fortune. All three places are just south of that part of the Irish Sea where King was drowned.
5. Calliope, the Muse of epic poetry. Her son, Orpheus, the greatest of all poets and musicians, was torn limb from limb by a band of Thracian Maenads, who flung his head into the river Hebrus, whence it drifted across the Aegean to the island of Lesbos.
6. I.e., do a poet's work.
7. A conventional pastoral name for a woman, like Neaera in the next line.
8. I.e., fame is an incentive to virtue and hard work.

75   Comes the blind Fury[9] with th' abhorrèd shears,
    And slits the thin spun life. "But not the praise,"
    Phoebus[1] replied, and touched my trembling ears;
    "Fame is no plant that grows on mortal soil,
    Nor in the glistering foil[2]
80   Set off to th' world, nor in broad rumor lies,
    But lives and spreads aloft by those pure eyes,
    And perfect witness of all-judging Jove;[3]
    As he pronounces lastly on each deed,
    Of so much fame in Heaven expect thy meed."°   *reward*
85   O fountain Arethuse,[4] and thou honored flood,
    Smooth-sliding Mincius, crowned with vocal reeds,
    That strain I heard was of a higher mood.
    But now my oat[5] proceeds,
    And listens to the herald of the sea[6]
90   That came in Neptune's plea.
    He asked the waves, and asked the felon winds,
    "What hard mishap hath doomed this gentle swain?"°   *rustic fellow*
    And questioned every gust of rugged wings
    That blows from off each beakèd promontory;
95   They knew not of his story,
    And sage Hippotades[7] their answer brings,
    That not a blast was from his dungeon strayed,
    The air was calm, and on the level brine,[8]
    Sleek Panope[9] with all her sisters played.
100   It was that fatal and perfidious bark[1]
    Built in th' eclipse, and rigged with curses dark,
    That sunk so low that sacred head of thine.
      Next Camus,[2] reverend sire, went footing slow,
    His mantle hairy, and his bonnet sedge,
105   Inwrought with figures dim, and on the edge
    Like to that sanguine flower inscribed with woe.
    "Ah! who hath reft," quoth he, "my dearest pledge?"°   *child*
    Last came and last did go
    The pilot of the Galilean lake,[3]
110   Two massy keys he bore of metals twain°   *two*
    (The golden opes,° the iron shuts amain).°   *opens / vehemently*
    He shook his mitered locks, and stern bespake:

9. Atropos, the third of the three Fates, who cut the thread of a person's life after it had been spun and measured by her sisters.
1. Phoebus Apollo, god of poetic inspiration, who plucked Virgil's ears as a warning against impatient ambition (see Virgil's *Eclogues* 6.3–4).
2. The setting for a gem, especially one that enhances the appearance of an inferior or false stone.
3. The most powerful of the classical gods.
4. A fountain in Sicily, associated with the pastoral poems of Theocritus, a Greek poet of the third century B.C. The "Mincius" is a river in Italy described in one of Virgil's pastorals.
5. Oaten pipe, song.
6. The merman Triton, who came to plead his master Neptune's innocence of Lycidas' death.
7. Aeolus, son of Hippotas and god of the winds.

8. I.e., the surface; "brine": saltwater.
9. One of the Nereids, daughters of Nereus, the Old Man of the Sea.
1. I.e., the ship.
2. The god of the river Cam, representing Cambridge University, personified as wearing an academic robe ("mantle" and "bonnet") with colors like the dark reeds ("sedge") on its banks, but relieved by the crimson hyacinth ("sanguine flower"). Certain markings on the hyacinth—created by Apollo from the blood of the youth Hyacinthus, whom he had killed by accident with a discus—are supposed to be the letters AIAI ("Alas, alas!"), inscribed by Apollo.
3. St. Peter, the Galilean fisherman, to whom Christ promised the keys of the kingdom of heaven (Matthew 16.19). He wears the bishop's miter (line 112) as the first head of Christ's Church.

"How[4] well could I have spared for thee, young swain,
Enow° of such as for their bellies' sake,   *enough*
115 Creep and intrude, and climb into the fold!
Of other care they little reckoning make,
Than how to scramble at the shearers' feast,
And shove away the worthy bidden guest.
Blind mouths! That scarce themselves know how to hold
120 A sheep-hook, or have learned aught else the least
That to the faithful herdsman's art belongs!
What recks it them?[5] What need they? They are sped;[6]
And when they list, their lean and flashy° songs *insipid*
Grate on their scrannel° pipes of wretched straw. *meager*
125 The hungry sheep look up, and are not fed,
But swoln with wind, and the rank mist they draw,
Rot inwardly, and foul contagion spread,
Besides what the grim wolf with privy paw[7]
Daily devours apace,° and nothing said.   *quickly*
130 But that two-handed engine at the door
Stands ready to smite once, and smite no more."[8]
  Return, Alpheus,[9] the dread voice is past,
That shrunk thy streams; return, Sicilian muse,
And call the vales, and bid them hither cast
135 Their bells and flowerets of a thousand hues.
Ye valleys low where the mild whispers use,° *frequent*
Of shades° and wanton winds, and gushing brooks, *shadows*
On whose fresh lap the swart star[1] sparely looks,
Throw hither all your quaint enameled eyes,
140 That on the green turf suck the honeyed showers,
And purple all the ground with vernal° flowers.[2] *springtime*
Bring the rathe° primrose that forsaken dies, *early*
The tufted crow-toe, and pale jessamine,
The white pink, and the pansy freaked° with jet, *mottled*
145 The glowing violet,
The musk-rose, and the well attired woodbine.
With cowslips wan° that hang the pensive head, *pale*
And every flower that sad embroidery wears:
Bid amaranthus[3] all his beauty shed,
150 And daffadillies fill their cups with tears,
To strew the laureate hearse° where Lycid lies. *bier*
For so to interpose a little ease,

4. Here begins the speech condemning the "corrupted clergy" and foretellling their "ruin" as described in the argument. Camus uses the common metaphor of the shepherd as the pastor (from *pastor*, the Latin for shepherd) and the sheep as the congregation.
5. I.e., what does it matter to them?
6. I.e., they have prospered.
7. I.e., anti-Protestant forces, either Roman Catholic or Anglican; "privy": furtive, sly.
8. A satisfactory explanation of these two lines has yet to be made, although many have been attempted. Most have taken the "two-handed engine" as an instrument of retribution against those clergy who neglect their responsibilities (such as the ax of reformation, the two-handed

sword of the archangel Michael, the two houses of Parliament, or death and damnation).
9. A river god who fell in love with the nymph Arethusa. When she fled to Sicily he pursued her by diving under the sea and emerging on the island. There she was turned into a fountain (see line 85), and their waters mingled.
1. Sirius, the Dog Star, thought to have a swart or malignant influence; perhaps because this star is in the zenith in late summer, when vegetation often withers.
2. Here begins a catalog of flowers, a traditional element of pastoral elegy. "Crow-toe": a name for various plants, either wild hyacinth or buttercups; "jessamine": jasmine, fragrant white flowers.
3. A legendary flower, supposed never to fade.

Let our frail thoughts dally with false surmise.°   *conjecture*
Ay me! Whilst thee the shores and sounding seas
155   Wash far away, where'er thy bones are hurled,
Whether beyond the stormy Hebrides,[4]
Where thou perhaps under the whelming tide
Visit'st the bottom of the monstrous world;
Or whether thou, to our moist vows[5] denied,
160   Sleep'st by the fable of Bellerus old,[6]
Where the great vision of the guarded mount
Looks toward Namancos and Bayona's hold;
Look homeward angel now, and melt with ruth:°   *pity*
And, O ye dolphins, waft° the hapless youth.[7]   *transport*
165   Weep no more, woeful shepherds, weep no more,
For Lycidas your sorrow is not dead,
Sunk though he be beneath the watery floor,
So sinks the day-star° in the ocean bed,   *sun*
And yet anon° repairs his drooping head,   *soon*
170   And tricks° his beams, and with new-spangled ore,°   *dresses / gold*
Flames in the forehead of the morning sky:
So Lycidas sunk low, but mounted high,
Through the dear might of him that walked the waves,[8]
Where other groves, and other streams along,
175   With nectar pure his oozy locks he laves,°   *bathes*
And hears the unexpressive° nuptial song,[9]   *inexpressible*
In the blest kingdoms meek of joy and love.
There entertain him all the saints above,
In solemn troops and sweet societies
180   That sing, and singing in their glory move,
And wipe the tears forever from his eyes.
Now, Lycidas, the shepherds weep no more;
Henceforth thou art the genius of the shore,[1]
In thy large recompense, and shalt be good
185   To all that wander in that perilous flood.
Thus sang the uncouth° swain to th' oaks and rills,   *unlettered*
While the still morn went out with sandals gray;
He touched the tender stops of various quills,[2]
With eager thought warbling his Doric[3] lay:
190   And now the sun had stretched out all the hills,
And now was dropped into the western bay;
At last he rose, and twitched his mantle° blue: *cloak*
Tomorrow to fresh woods, and pastures new.

1637   1645

---

4. The islands that lie west of Scotland's coast.
5. I.e., tearful prayers.
6. A legendary figure supposedly buried at Land's End in Cornwall. The "mount" of the next line is St. Michael's Mount at the tip of Land's End, "guarded" by the archangel Michael, who gazes southward toward Namancos and the stronghold of Bayona in northwestern Spain.
7. Perhaps a reference to the pagan myth of Palaemon, who became known as a protector of sailors after he drowned near Corinth and a temple was built on the spot where his body was supposed to

have been brought ashore by a dolphin.
8. I.e., Christ (Matthew 14.26).
9. Perhaps a reference to the "marriage supper of the lamb" (i.e., Christ), as described by St. John in the Apocalypse (Revelations 19.9).
1. The local divinity who protects navigators on the Irish Sea ("flood").
2. The individual reeds in a set of panpipes.
3. Pastoral, because Doric was the dialect of the ancient Greek pastoral writers Theocritus, Bion, and Moschus.

On the Morning of Christ's Nativity[4]

1

This is the month, and this the happy morn,
Wherein the Son of Heaven's Eternal King,
Of wedded maid and virgin mother born,
Our great redemption from above did bring;
5　For so the holy sages[5] once did sing,
　　That he our deadly forfeit[6] should release,
And with his Father work us a perpetual peace.

2

That glorious form, that light unsufferable,
And that far-beaming blaze of majesty,
10　Wherewith he wont° at Heaven's high council-table　　　*was accustomed*
To sit the midst of Trinal° Unity,　　　　　　　　　　　　*three-fold*
He laid aside, and, here with us to be,
　　Forsook the courts of everlasting day,
And chose with us a darksome house of mortal clay.[7]

3

15　Say, Heavenly Muse,[8] shall not thy sacred vein
Afford a present to the Infant God?
Hast thou no verse, no hymn, or solemn strain,
To welcome him to this his new abode,
Now while the heaven, by the Sun's team untrod,[9]
20　　Hath took no print of the approaching light,
And all the spangled host[1] keep watch in squadrons bright?

4

See how from far upon the eastern road
The star-led wizards[2] haste with odors sweet!
Oh run, prevent° them with thy humble ode,[3]　　　　　　　*go before*
25　And lay it lowly at his blessèd feet;
　　Have thou the honor first thy Lord to greet,
　　And join thy voice unto the angel choir
From out his secret altar touched with hallowed fire.[4]

The Hymn

1

　　It was the winter wild,
30　　While the heaven-born child

---

4. Milton's poem portrays the triumphs of the infant Christ over pagan gods, a theme of interest to both Catholics and Protestants of the early seventeenth century. This is the first poem in Milton's first published volume of poetry (1645); we follow his corrected text of 1673.
5. I.e., the Hebrew prophets.
6. The penalty of death, occasioned by the sin of Adam.
7. I.e., a human body.
8. Perhaps a reference to Urania, the Muse of astronomy, later identified in Milton's epic poem *Paradise Lost* with divine wisdom and treated by Milton as the source of creative inspiration. The Muses were nine Greek goddesses believed to be sources of inspiration for the arts.
9. A reference to Apollo, the pagan god of the sun, who drove the chariot of the sun behind mighty steeds (the "Sun's team").
1. An armed multitude (i.e., the angels).
2. The "wise men from the east" (Matthew 2.1), who brought gifts of gold, myrrh, and frankincense ("odors sweet").
3. A rhymed lyric, generally dignified or lofty in subject and style.
4. Cf. Isaiah 16.6, in which a seraph touches a prophet's lips with a burning coal from the altar.

All meanly wrapt in the rude manger lies;
   Nature, in awe to him,
   Had doffed° her gaudy trim,   *taken off*
With her great Master so to sympathize:
35   It was no season then for her
To wanton with the Sun, her lusty paramour.°   *beloved, lover*

2

   Only with speeches fair
   She woos the gentle air
To hide her guilty front with innocent snow,
40   And on her naked shame,
    Pollute with sinful blame,
The saintly veil of maiden white to throw;
Confounded, that her Maker's eyes
Should look so near upon her foul deformities.

3

45   But he, her fears to cease,
   Sent down the meek-eyed Peace:
She, crowned with olive green, came softly sliding
   Down through the turning sphere,[5]
   His ready harbinger,[6]
50   With turtle° wing the amorous clouds dividing;   *dove*
And, waving wide her myrtle wand,
She strikes a universal peace through sea and land.

4

   No war, or battle's sound,
   Was heard the world around;
55   The idle spear and shield were high uphung;
   The hookèd chariot[7] stood,
   Unstained with hostile blood;
The trumpet spake not to the armèd throng;
And kings sat still with awful eye,[8]
60   As if they surely knew their sovran Lord was by.

5

   But peaceful was the night
   Wherein the Prince of Light
His reign of peace upon the earth began.
   The winds, with wonder whist,°   *hushed*
65   Smoothly the waters kissed,
Whispering new joys to the mild Ocean,
Who now hath quite forgot to rave,
While birds of calm[9] sit brooding on the charmèd wave.

---

5. The heavens as a whole, which "turn" once daily about the Earth because of the Earth's rotation.
6. One who prepares the way, or makes an announcement.
7. War chariots were sometimes armed with sicklelike hooks projecting from the hubs of the wheels.
8. I.e., with a look full of awe and reverence.
9. Halcyons, or kingfishers, which in ancient times were believed to build floating nests at sea about the time of the winter solstice, and to calm the waves during the incubation of their young.

6

70

The stars, with deep amaze,°   *amazement*
Stand fixed in steadfast gaze,
Bending one way their precious influence,[1]
And will not take their flight,
For all the morning light,
Or Lucifer[2] that often warned them thence;

75

But in their glimmering orbs[3] did glow,
Until their Lord himself bespake, and bid them go.

7

And, though the shady gloom
Had given day her room,
The Sun himself withheld his wonted° speed,   *usual*

80

And hid his head for shame,
As his inferior flame
The new-enlightened world no more should need:
He saw a greater Sun appear
Than his bright throne or burning axletree[4] could bear.

8

85

The shepherds on the lawn,°   *meadow*
Or ere the point of dawn,
Sat simply chatting in a rustic row;
Full little thought they than°   *then*
That the mighty Pan[5]

90

Was kindly come to live with them below:
Perhaps their loves, or else their sheep,
Was all that did their silly° thoughts so busy keep.   *simple*

9

When such music sweet
Their hearts and ears did greet

95

As never was by mortal finger strook,°   *struck*
Divinely-warbled voice
Answering the stringéd noise,
As all their souls in blissful rapture took:
The air, such pleasure loth to lose,

100

With thousand echoes still prolongs each heavenly close.° *cadence*

10

Nature, that heard such sound
Beneath the hollow round
Of Cynthia's seat[6] the airy region thrilling,
Now was almost won

105

To think her part was done,
And that her reign had here its last fulfilling:

---

1. Medieval astrologers believed that stars emitted an ethereal liquid ("influence") that had the power to nourish or otherwise affect all things on Earth.
2. Here, the morning star, although Milton sometimes uses this word for Satan.
3. The concentric crystalline spheres of Ptolemaic astronomy; each sphere was supposed to contain one or more of the heavenly bodies in its surface and to revolve about the Earth, creating beautiful music.
4. I.e., the sun's chariot.
5. The Greek god of shepherds, whose name means "all," was often associated with Christ in Renaissance poetry.
6. I.e., beneath the sphere of the moon.

She knew such harmony alone
Could hold all Heaven and Earth in happier uniòn.

11

At last surrounds their sight
110   A globe of circular light,
That with long beams the shamefaced Night arrayed;
The helmèd cherubim
And sworded seraphim[7]
Are seen in glittering ranks with wings displayed,
115 Harping loud and solemn quire,°   *choir*
With unexpressive° notes, to Heaven's new-born Heir. *inexpressible*

12

Such music (as 'tis said)
Before was never made,
But when of old the sons of morning sung,[8]
120   While the Creator great
His constellations set,
And the well-balanced world on hinges hung,
And cast the dark foundations deep,
And bid the weltering waves their oozy channel keep.

13

125 Ring out, ye crystal spheres,[9]
Once bless our human ears,
If ye have power to touch our senses so;
And let your silver chime
Move in melodious time;
130 And let the bass of heaven's deep organ blow;
And with your ninefold harmony
Make up full consort° to th' angelic symphony.   *harmony*

14

For, if such holy song
Enwrap our fancy long,
135 Time will run back and fetch the age of gold;[1]
And speckled vanity
Will sicken soon and die;
And leprous sin will melt from earthly mold;[2]
And Hell itself will pass away,
140 And leave her dolorous mansions to the peering day.

15

Yea, Truth and Justice then
Will down return to men,
Orbed in a rainbow; and, like° glories wearing,   *similar*
Mercy will sit between,
145   Throned in celestial sheen,

7. Seraphim and cherubim (both are plural forms) are the two highest of the nine orders of angels in the medieval classification.
8. Job speaks of the creation of the universe as the time "when the morning stars sang together, and all the sons of God shouted for joy" (Job 38.7).
9. A reference to the Pythagorean idea that the music of the spheres would be audible only to sin-less humans (see note 3, above).
1. According to a Roman belief, Saturn, after his dethronement by Jupiter, fled to Italy and there brought in the Golden Age, a time of perfect peace and happiness.
2. I.e., the Earth; also, mortal humans; "leprous sin": i.e., sin that is like the loathsome disease leprosy.

With radiant feet the tissued clouds down steering;
And Heaven, as at some festival,
Will open wide the gates of her high palace-hall.

16

But wisest Fate says no,
150   This must not yet be so;
The Babe lies yet in smiling infancy
   That on the bitter cross
   Must redeem our loss,
So both himself and us to glorify:
155 Yet first, to those ychained in sleep,[3]
The wakeful° trump of doom must thunder through   *awakening*
   the deep,

17

With such a horrid clang
   As on Mount Sinai rang,[4]
While the red fire and smoldering clouds outbrake:
160   The aged Earth, aghast,
   With terror of that blast,
Shall from the surface to the center shake,
When, at the world's last sessiòn,
The dreadful Judge in middle air shall spread his throne.

18

165   And then at last our bliss
   Full and perfect is,
But now begins; for from this happy day
   Th' old Dragon° under ground,   *Satan*
   In straiter limits bound,
170 Not half so far casts his usurpèd sway,
And, wroth to see his kingdom fail,
Swinges° the scaly horror of his folded tail.   *lashes*

19

The Oracles[5] are dumb;
   No voice or hideous hum
175 Runs through the archéd roof in words deceiving.
   Apollo from his shrine
   Can no more divine,
With hollow shriek the steep of Delphos leaving.
No nightly trance, or breathéd spell,
180 Inspires the pale-eyed priest from the prophetic cell.

20

The lonely mountains o'er,
   And the resounding shore,
A voice of weeping heard and loud lament;

---

3. I.e., death; "ychained": Milton uses the archaic form of the participle, common in Chaucer and imitated by Spenser, in which y- represents a reduced form of the Old English prefix *ge-*. Lines 155–64 allude to the Apocalypse as described in Revelation.
4. Moses received the Ten Commandments on Mount Sinai: "there were thunders and lightnings . . . and the voice of the trumpet exceeding loud" (Exodus 19.16).
5. Prophecies revealed at shrines consecrated to the worship and consultation of classical gods. Apollo's shrine at Delphi ("Delphos") lay on the upper slopes ("steep") of Mount Parnassus.

From haunted spring, and dale
185   Edged with poplar pale,
The parting genius° is with sighing sent;   *local spirit*
With flower-inwoven tresses torn
The Nymphs[6] in twilight shade of tangled thickets mourn.

21

In consecrated earth,
190   And on the holy hearth,
The Lars and Lemures[7] moan with midnight plaint;
In urns and altars round,
A drear and dying sound
Affrights the flamens° at their service quaint;°   *priests / elaborate*
195 And the chill marble seems to sweat,
While each peculiar power forgoes his wonted seat.

22

Peor[8] and Baalim
Forsake their temples dim,
With that twice-battered God of Palestine;[9]
200   And moonèd Ashtaroth,[1]
Heaven's queen and mother both,
Now sits not girt° with tapers'° holy shine: *encircled / candles'*
The Libyc Hammon[2] shrinks his horn;
In vain the Tyrian maids their wounded Thammuz mourn.[3]

23

205   And sullen Moloch,[4] fled,
Hath left in shadows dread
His burning idol all of blackest hue;
In vain with cymbals' ring
They call the grisly king,
210   In dismal dance about the furnace blue;
The brutish gods of Nile as fast,
Isis, and Orus, and the dog Anubis,[5] haste.

24

Nor is Osiris seen
In Memphian grove or green,
215   Trampling the unshowered[6] grass with lowings loud;
Nor can he be at rest
Within his sacred chest;
Nought but profoundest Hell can be his shroud;

6. Mythological female spirits inhabiting a particular place, object, or natural phenomenon.
7. Hostile spirits of the unburied dead; "Lars": tutelary gods or spirits of the ancient Romans associated with particular places.
8. Baal, or Baal-Peor, the highest Canaanite god, whose shrine was at Mount Peor. Baalim (the plural form) were lesser gods related to him.
9. Dagon, god of the Philistines, whose statue twice fell to the ground before the ark of the Lord (1 Samuel 5.1–4).
1. Astarte, a Phoenician goddess identified with the moon.
2. The Egyptian god Ammon, represented as a horned ram. He had a famous temple and oracle at an oasis in the Libyan desert.
3. The death of the god Thammuz, Ashtaroth's lover, symbolized the coming of winter. The Tyrian (Phoenician) women mourned for him in an annual ceremony.
4. A pagan god to whom children were sacrificed. Their cries were drowned out by the clang of cymbals.
5. The Egyptian goddess Isis was represented as a cow, the gods Orus and Anubis as a hawk and a dog (hence "brutish"). Osiris (line 213) the creator, who had a shrine at Memphis, was represented as a bull.
6. I.e., the rainless Egyptian landscape.

In vain, with timbreled° anthems dark,   *with tambourines*
220   The sable-stolèd sorcerers bear his worshipped ark.

25

He feels from Juda's land
The dreaded Infant's hand;[7]
The rays of Bethlehem blind his dusky eyn;°   *eyes*
Nor all the gods beside
225   Longer dare abide,
Not Typhon[8] huge ending in snaky twine:
Our Babe, to show his Godhead true,
Can in his swaddling° bands control the damnèd crew.   *binding*

26

So, when the sun in bed,
230   Curtained with cloudy red,
Pillows his chin upon an orient° wave,   *eastern*
The flocking shadows pale
Troop to th' infernal[9] jail;
Each fettered ghost slips to his several° grave,   *separate*
235   And the yellow-skirted fays°   *fairies*
Fly after the night-steeds, leaving their moon-loved maze.[1]

27

But see! the Virgin blest
Hath laid her Babe to rest.
Time is our tedious song should here have ending:
240   Heaven's youngest-teemèd star[2]
Hath fixed her polished car,
Her sleeping Lord with handmaid lamp attending;
And all about the courtly stable
Bright-harnessed[3] angels sit in order serviceable.

1629   1645

L'Allegro[4]

Hence[5] loathèd Melancholy
Of Cerberus[6] and blackest midnight born,
In Stygian[7] cave forlorn
'Mongst horrid shapes, and shrieks, and sights unholy,
5   Find out some uncouth[8] cell,
Where brooding Darkness spreads his jealous wings,
And the night-raven sings;

7. I.e., the hand of Christ, who was descended from the tribe of Judah. Perhaps an allusion to Matthew 2.6, referring to Micah 5.2, on the power resident in Bethlehem in the land of Judah.
8. A hundred-headed monster destroyed by Zeus.
9. Of the realm of the dead; i.e., hell(ish).
1. I.e., the woods.
2. I.e., newest-born star, the star that guided the wise men, now imagined as having halted its "car" or chariot over the manger.
3. I.e., clad in bright armor. "Courtly": i.e., because it houses Christ, the king.

4. "L'Allegro" ("the happy man" [Italian]) is a companion poem to "Il Penseroso" ("the pensive man" [Italian]). Probably written late in Milton's years at Cambridge, the poems influenced many later poets and were illustrated by William Blake.
5. A command to depart.
6. The three-headed dog that guarded the gates of hell.
7. Pertaining to the Styx, one of the rivers of the classical underworld.
8. Unknown and dreadful.

There under ebon° shades, and low-browed rocks,   *black*
As ragged as thy locks,
10   In dark Cimmerian[9] desert ever dwell.
But come thou goddess fair and free,
In Heaven yclept° Euphrosyne,[1]   *called*
And by men, heart-easing Mirth,
Whom lovely Venus at a birth
15   With two sister Graces more
To ivy-crownèd Bacchus[2] bore;
Or whether (as some sager sing)[3]
The frolic wind that breathes the spring,
Zephyr with Aurora playing,
20   As he met her once a-Maying,
There on beds of violets blue,
And fresh-blown° roses washed in dew,   *newly bloomed*
Filled her with thee a daughter fair,
So buxom,° blithe, and debonair.°   *merry / pleasant*
25   Haste thee nymph, and bring with thee
Jest and youthful Jollity,
Quips and Cranks,° and wanton Wiles,   *jests*
Nods, and Becks,° and wreathèd Smiles,   *curtseys*
Such as hang on Hebe's[4] cheek,
30   And love to live in dimple sleek;
Sport that wrinkled Care derides,
And Laughter, holding both his sides.
Come, and trip it as ye go
On the light fantastic toe,
35   And in thy right hand lead with thee,
The mountain nymph, sweet Liberty;
And if I give thee honor due,
Mirth, admit me of thy crew
To live with her and live with thee,
40   In unreprovèd° pleasures free;   *unreprovable*
To hear the lark[5] begin his flight,
And, singing, startle the dull night,
From his watch-tower in the skies,
Till the dappled dawn doth rise;
45   Then to come in spite° of sorrow,   *contempt*
And at my window bid good morrow,
Through the sweetbriar, or the vine,
Or the twisted eglantine.[6]
While the cock with lively din,
50   Scatters the rear of darkness thin,
And to the stack, or the barn door,
Stoutly struts his dames before;
Oft listening how the hounds and horn

9. In classical mythology the Cimmerians lived in a mysterious land somewhere across the ocean, where the sun never shone.
1. One of the three Graces, who were believed to bring joy to humans. Her name means "mirth."
2. The god of wine. "Two sister Graces": Aglaia and Thalia.
3. It is generally believed that the following mythi-cal account of the birth of Euphrosyne is Milton's own invention. Zephyr is the west wind; Aurora, the dawn.
4. The cupbearer of Zeus, a goddess who personi-fied youth.
5. Larks sing at sunrise.
6. The sweetbriar, possibly used here to mean the honeysuckle.

Cheerly rouse the slumbering morn,
55 From the side of some hoar[7] hill,
Through the high wood echoing shrill.
Sometime walking not unseen
By hedgerow elms, on hillocks green,
Right against the eastern gate,
60 Where the great sun begins his state,°   *progress*
Robed in flames, and amber light,
The clouds in thousand liveries dight;°   *dressed*
While the plowman near at hand,
Whistles o'er the furrowed land,
65 And the milkmaid singeth blithe,
And the mower whets his scythe,
And every shepherd tells his tale,
Under the hawthorn in the dale.
Straight mine eye hath caught new pleasures
70 Whilst the landscape round it measures,
Russet° lawns and fallows° gray,   *reddish brown / plowed land*
Where the nibbling flocks do stray,
Mountains on whose barren breast
The laboring clouds do often rest;
75 Meadows trim with daisies pied,°   *variegated*
Shallow brooks, and rivers wide.
Towers and battlements it sees
Bosomed high in tufted trees,
Where perhaps some beauty lies,
80 The cynosure[8] of neighboring eyes.
Hard by, a cottage chimney smokes,
From betwixt two aged oaks,
Where Corydon and Thyrsis[9] met,
Are at their savory dinner set
85 Of herbs, and other country messes,°   *dishes*
Which the neat-handed Phyllis dresses;°   *prepares*
And then in haste her bower she leaves,
With Thestylis to bind the sheaves;
Or if the earlier season lead
90 To the tanned haycock[1] in the mead.
Sometimes with secure° delight   *carefree*
The upland hamlets will invite,
When the merry bells ring round
And the jocund° rebecks[2] sound   *merry*
95 To many a youth and many a maid,
Dancing in the checkered shade;
And young and old come forth to play
On a sunshine holiday,
Till the livelong daylight fail;
100 Then to the spicy nut-brown ale,
With stories told of many a feat,

---

7. Grayish white, perhaps because of a morning frost.
8. The North Star, or anything that attracts attention.
9. Conventional male names in pastoral poetry,
like Thestylis (line 88); Phyllis (line 86) is a conventional female pastoral name.
1. A conical heap of hay in the field ("mead").
2. A rebeck is a kind of three-stringed fiddle.

How fairy Mab the junkets eat;[3]
She was pinched and pulled, she said,
And he, by Friar's lantern[4] led,
105 Tells how the drudging goblin[5] sweat
To earn his cream-bowl, duly set,
When in one night, ere glimpse of morn,
His shadowy flail hath threshed the corn
That ten day-laborers could not end;
110 Then lies him down the lubber° fiend,   *loutish*
And, stretched out all the chimney's° length,   *fireplace's*
Basks at the fire his hairy strength;
And crop-full out of doors he flings
Ere the first cock his matin° rings.   *morning*
115 Thus done the tales, to bed they creep,
By whispering winds soon lulled asleep.
Towered cities please us then,
And the busy hum of men,
Where throngs of knights and barons bold,
120 In weeds° of peace high triumphs hold,   *garments*
With store of ladies, whose bright eyes
Rain influence,[6] and judge the prize
Of wit, or arms, while both contend
To win her grace, whom all commend.
125 There let Hymen[7] oft appear
In saffron° robe, with taper clear,   *orange-yellow*
And pomp, and feast, and revelry,
With masque,[8] and antique pageantry;
Such sights as youthful poets dream
130 On summer eves by haunted stream.
Then to the well-trod stage anon,
If Jonson's learnèd sock[9] be on,
Or sweetest Shakespeare, fancy's child,
Warble his native wood-notes wild.
135 And ever against eating cares
Lap me in soft Lydian airs[1]
Married to immortal verse
Such as the meeting soul may pierce
In notes, with many a winding bout°   *turn*
140 Of linkèd sweetness long drawn out,
With wanton heed, and giddy cunning,
The melting voice through mazes running;
Untwisting all the chains that tie

---

3. I.e., Mab, queen of the fairies, ate the delicacies ("junkets"). The behavior attributed to fairies here and in the following lines reflects traditional rustic lore.
4. The will-o'-the-wisp, which was said to draw travelers astray by holding a false light before them; the phenomenon of nocturnal light is caused by the combustion of marsh gas.
5. A hobgoblin, also known as Robin Goodfellow or Puck, was a small supernatural creature popular in northern European folk traditions. He is an important character in Shakespeare's *A Midsummer Night's Dream*, a play that "L'Allegro" frequently echoes.

6. The ladies' eyes are compared to stars, alluding to the idea held by medieval astrologers that the stars emitted an ethereal liquid ("influence") that could powerfully affect human lives.
7. God of marriage.
8. An elaborate form of court entertainment, in which aristocrats performed a dignified play, usually allegorical and mythological, that ended in a formal dance.
9. The light shoe worn by Greek comic actors, here standing for the comedies of Ben Jonson.
1. Lydian music was noted for its voluptuous sweetness.

The hidden soul of harmony;
145 That Orpheus' self[2] may heave his head
From golden slumber on a bed
Of heaped Elysian° flowers, and hear   *glorious*
Such strains as would have won the ear
Of Pluto, to have quite set free
150 His half-regained Eurydice.
These delights if thou canst give,
Mirth, with thee I mean to live.

ca. 1631   1645

Il Penseroso[3]

Hence[4] vain deluding Joys,
   The brood of Folly without father bred.
How little you bestead,°   *profit*
   Or fill the fixèd mind with all your toys;°   *trifles*
5 Dwell in some idle brain,
   And fancies fond° with gaudy shapes possess,   *foolish*
As thick and numberless
   As the gay motes° that people the sunbeams,   *specks*
Or likest hovering dreams,
10   The fickle pensioners° of Morpheus'[5] train.   *attendants*
But hail thou Goddess, sage and holy,
Hail, divinest Melancholy,
Whose saintly visage is too bright
To hit° the sense of human sight;   *affect*
15 And therefore to our weaker view,
O'erlaid with black, staid Wisdom's hue.
Black, but such as in esteem,
Prince Memnon's sister[6] might beseem,
Or that starred Ethiope queen[7] that strove
20 To set her beauty's praise above
The sea nymphs, and their powers offended.
Yet thou art higher far descended;
Thee bright-haired Vesta long of yore
To solitary Saturn bore;[8]
25 His daughter she (in Saturn's reign
Such mixture was not held a stain).
Oft in glimmering bowers and glades
He met her, and in secret shades
Of woody Ida's inmost grove,

2. The great poet and musician of classical mythology, whose wife, Eurydice, died on their wedding day. He won permission from Pluto, god of the underworld, to lead her back to the land of the living, but only on the condition that he not look to see if she was following him. Unable to resist a backward glance, he lost her forever.
3. See "L'Allegro," n. 4 (p. 365).
4. A command to depart.
5. God of sleep.
6. Memnon, an Ethiopian prince, was called the handsomest of men. His sister was Hemera, whose name means "day."
7. Cassiopeia, who boasted that her beauty (or her daughter's, in some accounts) surpassed that of the daughters of the sea god Nereus. "Starred" refers to the fact that a constellation bears her name.
8. The parentage here attributed to Melancholy is Milton's invention. Saturn, who ruled on Mt. Ida before being overthrown by his son Jove, was associated with melancholy because of the supposedly "saturnine" influence of the planet that bears his name. His daughter Vesta was the goddess of purity.

30   While yet there was no fear of Jove.[9]
     Come pensive nun, devout and pure,
     Sober, steadfast, and demure,
     All in a robe of darkest grain,°   color
     Flowing with majestic train,
35   And sable° stole of cypress lawn[1]   black
     Over thy decent shoulders drawn.
     Come, but keep thy wonted state,
     With even step and musing gait,
     And looks commercing with the skies,
40   Thy rapt soul sitting in thine eyes:
     There held in holy passion still,
     Forget thyself to marble, till
     With a sad° leaden downward cast,   serious
     Thou fix them on the earth as fast.
45   And join with thee calm Peace and Quiet,
     Spare Fast, that oft with gods doth diet,
     And hears the Muses[2] in a ring
     Aye round about Jove's altar sing.
     And add to these retired Leisure,
50   That in trim gardens takes his pleasure;
     But first, and chiefest, with thee bring,
     Him that yon soars on golden wing,
     Guiding the fiery-wheelèd throne,
     The cherub Contemplation;[3]
55   And the mute Silence hist° along   beckon
     'Less Philomel[4] will deign a song,
     In her sweetest, saddest plight,
     Smoothing the rugged brow of night,
     While Cynthia[5] checks her dragon yoke
60   Gently o'er th' accustomed oak;
     Sweet bird that shunn'st the noise of folly,
     Most musical, most melancholy!
     Thee chantress oft the woods among,
     I woo to hear thy evensong;
65   And missing thee, I walk unseen
     On the dry smooth-shaven green,
     To behold the wandering moon,
     Riding near her highest noon,
     Like one that had been led astray
70   Through the Heaven's wide pathless way;
     And oft as if her head she bowed,
     Stooping through a fleecy cloud.
     Oft on a plat° of rising ground,   plot

9. The most powerful god of classical mythology.
1. A gauzy, crepelike material, usually dyed black and used for mourning garments; "cypress": Cyprus, where the material was originally made.
2. The nine Greek goddesses believed to be sources of inspiration for the arts; at the foot of Mt. Helicon, they danced about the altar of Jove.
3. A reference to the vision of the four cherubim (a high order of angels) stationed beside four wheels of fire under the throne of the Lord (Ezekiel 1 and 10).

4. I.e., or else Philomel will condescend to sing a song. Philomel, the nightingale, who sings a mournful song in the springtime: according to Ovid's version of this popular myth, Philomela was raped by her brother-in-law, Tereus, who then tore out her tongue so that she could not speak. She wove the story in a tapestry and sent it to her sister, who rescued her. She was later changed into a nightingale while in flight from Tereus.
5. Goddess of the moon, sometimes represented as driving a team of dragons.

I hear the far-off curfew sound,[6]
75 Over some wide-watered shore,
Swinging slow with sullen roar;
Or if the air will not permit,
Some still removèd place will fit,
Where glowing embers through the room
80 Teach light to counterfeit a gloom
Far from all resort of mirth,
Save the cricket on the hearth,
Or the bellman's° drowsy charm,   night-watchman's
To bless the doors from nightly harm;
85 Or let my lamp at midnight hour
Be seen in some high lonely tower,
Where I may oft outwatch the Bear,[7]
With thrice great Hermes, or unsphere[8]
The spirit of Plato to unfold
90 What worlds, or what vast regions hold
The immortal mind that hath forsook
Her mansion in this fleshly nook;
And of those demons[9] that are found
In fire, air, flood, or underground,
95 Whose power hath a true consent°   correspondence
With planet, or with element.
Some time let gorgeous Tragedy
In sceptered pall° come sweeping by,   robe
Presenting Thebes, or Pelops' line,
100 Or the tale of Troy divine.[1]
Or what (though rare) of later age
Ennobled hath the buskined[2] stage.
But, O sad virgin, that thy power
Might raise Musaeus[3] from his bower,
105 Or bid the soul of Orpheus sing
Such notes as, warbled to the string,
Drew iron tears down Pluto's cheek,
And made Hell grant what Love did seek.
Or call up him[4] that left half told
110 The story of Cambuscan bold,
Of Camball, and of Algarsife,
And who had Canacee to wife,
That owned the virtuous° ring and glass,   potent
And of the wondrous horse of brass,
115 On which the Tartar king did ride;

6. The customary ringing of a bell at a fixed hour in the evening.
7. The Great Bear, or Big Dipper, which in northern latitudes never sets.
8. Call back from his present sphere; Hermes Trismegistus ("thrice-great"), a name given by Neoplatonists to the Egyptian god Thoth, who was sometimes identified with the Greek Hermes. He was thought to be the actual author of some forty books embodying mystical, theosophical, astrological, and alchemical doctrines.
9. Supernatural beings inhabiting each of the four "elements": fire, air, water, and earth.
1. The city of Thebes, the descendants of Pelops, and the Trojan War afforded the subjects of most Greek tragedies.
2. The buskin was the high boot worn by Greek tragic actors.
3. A legendary Greek poet, contemporary of Orpheus (line 105); for the story of Orpheus see "L'Allegro," n. 2 (p. 369).
4. Chaucer, whose "Squire's Tale" leaves unfinished the story of the Tartar King Cambuscan, his two sons, Camball and Algarsife, and his daughter, Canacee. At a banquet celebrating Cambuscan's reign, a mysterious guest offered several magical gifts to the king, including a brass horse, a mirror ("glass"), and a ring.

And if aught else great bards beside
In sage and solemn tunes have sung,
Of tourneys and of trophies hung,
Of forests and enchantments drear,
120   Where more is meant than meets the ear.
Thus, Night, oft see me in thy pale career,
Till civil-suited morn[5] appear,
Not tricked and frounced° as she was wont,   *curled*
With the Attic boy to hunt,
125   But kerchiefed in a comely cloud,
While rocking winds are piping loud,
Or ushered with a shower still,
When the gust hath blown his fill,
Ending on the rustling leaves,
130   With minute-drops from off the eaves.
And when the sun begins to fling
His flaring beams, me, Goddess, bring
To archèd walks of twilight groves,
And shadows brown that Sylvan[6] loves
135   Of pine or monumental oak,
Where the rude ax with heavèd stroke,
Was never heard the nymphs[7] to daunt,
Or fright them from their hallowed haunt.
There in close covert by some brook,
140   Where no profaner eye may look,
Hide me from day's garish eye,
While the bee with honeyed thigh,
That at her flowery work doth sing,
And the waters murmuring
145   With such consort° as they keep,   *harmony*
Entice the dewy-feathered sleep;
And let some strange mysterious dream,
Wave at his wings in airy stream,
Of lively portraiture displayed,
150   Softly on my eyelids laid.
And as I wake, sweet music breathe
Above, about, or underneath,
Sent by some spirit to mortals good,
Or th' unseen genius° of the wood.   *indwelling spirit*
155   But let my due feet never fail
To walk the studious cloister's pale,°   *enclosure*
And love the high embowèd roof,
With antic° pillars massy proof,   *fancifully decorated*
And storied windows[8] richly dight,°   *dressed*
160   Casting a dim religious light.
There let the pealing organ blow,
To the full-voiced choir below,
In service high, and anthems clear,
As may with sweetness, through mine ear,

5. Aurora, goddess of the dawn, soberly dressed
("civil-suited"); she loved Cephalus ("the Attic
boy," line 124).
6. Sylvanus, god of forests.

7. Mythological female spirits inhabiting a
particular place, object, or natural phenomenon.
8. Windows with representations of biblical stories
in stained glass. "Massy proof": massive solidity.

165 Dissolve me into ectasies,
    And bring all heaven before mine eyes.
    And may at last my weary age
    Find out the peaceful hermitage,
    The hairy gown and mossy cell,
170 Where I may sit and rightly spell°   *speculate*
    Of every star that Heaven doth show,
    And every herb that sips the dew
    Till old experience do attain
    To something like prophetic strain.
175 These pleasures, Melancholy, give,
    And I with thee will choose to live.

ca. 1631   1645

On Shakespeare[9]

What needs my Shakespeare for his honored bones
    The labor of an age in pilèd stones?
    Or that his hallowed reliques should be hid
    Under a star-ypointing[1] pyramid?
5 Dear son of Memory,[2] great heir of Fame,
    What need'st thou such weak witness of thy name?
    Thou in our wonder and astonishment
    Hast built thyself a livelong monument.
    For whilst, to th' shame of slow-endeavoring art,
10 Thy easy numbers° flow, and that each heart   *verses*
    Hath from the leaves of thy unvalued° book   *invaluable*
    Those Delphic[3] lines with deep impression took,
    Then thou, our fancy of itself bereaving,
    Dost make us marble with too much conceiving,
15 And so sepùlchred in such pomp dost lie
    That kings for such a tomb would wish to die.

1630   1645

How Soon Hath Time[4]

How soon hath Time, the subtle thief of youth,
    Stoln on his wing my three and twentieth year!
    My hasting days fly on with full career,
    But my late spring no bud or blossom shew'th.°   *showeth*
5 Perhaps my semblance° might deceive the truth,   *outward appearance*
    That I to manhood am arrived so near,
    And inward ripeness doth much less appear,
    That some more timely-happy spirits endu'th.°   *endoweth*

---

9. Milton's poem was printed in the Second Folio of Shakespeare's plays (1632), under the title "An Epitaph on the Admirable Dramatic Poet W. Shakespear."
1. Milton uses the archaic form of the past participle, common in Chaucer and imitated by Spenser, in which *y-* represents a reduced form of the Old English prefix *ge-*.
2. Memory (Mnemosyne) was the mother of the

Muses, the nine Greek goddesses believed to be sources of inspiration for the arts.
3. Pertaining to Apollo, god of poetry, who had an oracle at Delphi.
4. Milton's twenty-third birthday was on December 9, 1631. He enclosed a copy of this poem in a letter to a friend who, according to Milton, had accused him of dreaming away his "years in the arms of a studious retirement."

Yet be it less or more, or soon or slow,
10   It shall be still in strictest measure even°   *equal*
To that same lot, however mean or high,
Toward which Time leads me, and the will of Heaven;
All is, if I have grace to use it so,
As ever in my great Taskmaster's eye.

1631   1645

From Comus[5]

Song[6]

Sweet Echo, sweetest nymph, that liv'st unseen
    Within thy airy shell,[7]
By slow Meander's margent green,[8]
And in the violet-embroider'd vale,
5   Where the love-lorn nightingale[9]
Nightly to thee her sad song mourneth well;

Canst thou not tell me of a gentle pair
    That likest thy Narcissus are?
      O, if thou have
10   Hid them in some flowery cave,
      Tell me but where,
Sweet queen of parley, daughter of the sphere![1]
So mayst thou be translated to the skies,
And give resounding grace to all heav'n's harmonies.[2]

---

5. Titled by Milton simply "A Mask Presented at Ludlow Castle," and produced in collaboration with the English composer Henry Lawes (1569–1662), who wrote music for these songs. Masques, popular in the seventeenth century, were court entertainments that included dance, song, drama, and spectacle; they usually celebrated an occasion—in this case, the earl of Bridgewater's assuming the presidency of Wales and the Marches. In the action of this masque the Lady (played by the earl's daughter, Alice) is separated from her two younger brothers in a wood and accosted by Comus (a classical god of feast and revelry) and his band of revelers. Comus attempts to persuade the chaste and virtuous Lady to join their revelry, but she resists and is rescued by her brothers with help from the river nymph, Sabrina.
6. Lost in the forest, the Lady calls upon the nymph Echo for assistance.
7. The sphere of air around the earth; Echo, in love with the handsome youth Narcissus, who spurned her love, pined away until only her voice remained (see Ovid, *Metamorphosis* 3.359–401).
8. Meander is a river in Phrygia with a very winding (thus "slow") course; "margent": margin, i.e., bank.
9. The nightingale is known for its sweet nocturnal song; there are many classical myths about this bird. The Ovidian story of Philomela seems a likely subtext for the Lady's song because Philomela, like Echo, loses her full powers of speech. Philomela, however, was "love-lorn" only in the ironic sense of being victimized by another's passion; she was raped by her brother-in-law, Tereus, who then tore out her tongue so that she could not speak. She wove the story into a tapestry and sent it to her sister, who rescued her. She was later changed into a nightingale while in flight from Tereus.
1. Echo was, according to some accounts, the daughter of Air and Earth; "parley": speech. Before her encounter with Narcissus, Echo was a talkative nymph, whose chatter distracted Hera, the queen of the gods, while her husband, Zeus, consorted with other nymphs and mortal women. Hera punished Echo by depriving her of the ability to speak, except to repeat the words of others.
2. In myth, a traditional method of bestowing immortality is transformation into a star or constellation; thus "translated to the skies," Echo will provide, with her echoes, a resonance to "heav'n's harmonies," perhaps the songs of the angels or the music of the spheres—a music, according to Pythagorean tradition, caused by the motion of the planetary spheres.

Song[3]

Sabrina fair,
    Listen where thou art sitting
Under the glassy, cool, translucent wave,
    In twisted braids of lilies knitting
5   The loose train of thy amber-dropping hair;[4]
    Listen for dear honor's sake,
    Goddess of the silver lake,
        Listen and save.

Sabrina rises, attended by water-nymphs, and sings.

By the rushy-fringèd bank,
10 Where grows the willow and the osier[5] dank,
    My sliding chariot stays,°   *halts*
Thick set with agate, and the azure sheen
Of turkis[6] blue, and emerald green,
    That in the channel strays;
15 Whilst from off the waters fleet,
    Thus I set my printless feet
O'er the cowslip's velvet head,
    That bends not as I tread;
Gentle Swain,[7] at thy request
20   I am here.

1634   1645

To Mr. H. Lawes, On His Airs[8]

Harry, whose tuneful and well-measured song
    First taught our English music how to span°   *measure*
Words with just note and accent, not to scan
With Midas' ears,[9] committing° short and long,   *misjoining*
5 Thy worth and skill exempts thee from the throng,
    With praise enough for Envy to look wan;°   *pale*
To after-age thou shalt be writ the man
That with smooth air couldst humor best our tongue.
Thou honor'st Verse, and Verse must lend her wing
10   To honor thee, the priest of Phœbus' choir,[1]

---

3. The attendant Spirit, who has helped the brothers in their search for the Lady, calls upon Sabrina to assist in her rescue. Sabrina was the goddess of the Severn; according to a story retold by Spenser, among others, she was a mortal girl thrown into the river by her vengeful stepmother, who was angry at the illicit liaison that resulted in Sabrina's birth. Milton adds to the legend Sabrina's magical powers and her special concern for virgins. In the text of the masque that Milton published in 1645, the Spirit speaks twenty-one lines of poetry between the first and second segments of this song. 4. Amber may refer to the color of her hair, i.e., blonde, through which water drips; or perhaps her hair is wet with amber-colored water; or amber is a perfume (from ambergris, a product of the whale), and thus her hair is shedding perfume. 5. A species of willow. 6. Turquoise; "agate": a precious stone; "azure sheen": deep blue luster. 7. Shepherd; the attendant Spirit is dressed as a shepherd. 8. Melodies; the composer Henry Lawes (see note 5, p. 374) had written the music for Milton's masque *Comus* (and printed the masque without Milton's name in 1637). 9. Midas was given ass's ears for having preferred Pan's music to Apollo's. 1. Phoebus Apollo was god of music and poetry.

That tun'st their happiest lines in hymn or story.[2]
Dante shall give Fame leave to set thee higher
Than his Casella,[3] whom he wooed to sing,
Met in the milder shades of Purgatory.

1645   1648

From Samson Agonistes[4]

60 But peace, I must not quarrel with the will
     Of highest dispensation,[5] which herein
     Haply° had ends above my reach to know: *perhaps*
     Suffices that to me strength is my bane,[6]
     And proves the source of all my miseries,
65 So many, and so huge, that each apart,
     Would ask° a life to wail; but chief of all,   *need*
     O loss of sight, of thee I most complain!
     Blind among enemies, O worse than chains,
     Dungeon, or beggary, or decrepit age!
70 Light the prime work of God to me is extinct,
     And all her various objects of delight
     Annull'd, which might in part my grief have eased,
     Inferior to the vilest now become
     Of man or worm; the vilest here excel me,
75 They creep, yet see; I dark in light exposed
     To daily fraud, contempt, abuse, and wrong.
     Within doors, or without, still° as a fool   *always*
     In power of others, never in my own;
     Scarce half I seem to live, dead more than half.
80 O dark, dark, dark, amid the blaze of noon,
     Irrecoverably dark, total eclipse
     Without all hope of day!
     O first created beam, and thou great word,
     Let there be light, and light was over all;[7]
85 Why am I thus bereaved° thy prime decree?   *robbed of*
     The sun to me is dark
     And silent as the moon,
     When she deserts the night

---

2. Perhaps a reference to "The Story," a poem by William Cartwright (1611–1643) that Lawes set to music.
3. In the *Divine Comedy* Dante represents himself, on the threshold of Purgatory, as meeting the shade of his musician friend Casella, who sings a ballad to him.
4. Milton's dramatic poem *Samson Agonistes* tells the story of the biblical Samson (Judges 13–16) from the time of his captivity to his death. Samson was given great strength by God to deliver his people from their longtime enemies, the Philistines. The source of his strength was his long hair. His Philistine wife, Dalila, badgered him into revealing the secret of his strength, then cut his hair and betrayed him to the Philistines, who blinded him and set him to work as a slave. In these lines Samson laments his fate. T. S. Eliot echoed this speech in his *Four Quartets.*
5. I.e., God; dispensation refers to the ordering of events by divine providence.
6. I.e., It is sufficient that (I know?) my strength is the cause of my downfall.
7. Genesis 1.3: "And God said, Let there be light: and there was light"; this is God's "prime work" (line 70) and his "prime decree" (line 85) because it was his first (and perhaps most important) creation.

Hid in her vacant interlunar cave.[8]
90 Since light so necessary is to life,
And almost life itself, if it be true
That light is in the soul,
She[9] all in every part; why was the sight
To such a tender ball as th' eye confined,
95 So obvious° and so easy to be quench'd,   *exposed*
And not, as feeling, through all parts diffused,
That she might look at will through every pore?
Then had I not been thus exiled from light,
As in the land of darkness yet in light,
100 To live a life half dead, a living death,
And buried; but O yet more miserable!
Myself my sepulchre, a moving grave,
Buried, yet not exempt
By privilege of death and burial
105 From worst of other evils, pains, and wrongs,
But made hereby obnoxious° more   *exposed*
To all the miseries of life,
Life in captivity
Among inhuman foes.

1647–70?   1671

I Did But Prompt the Age

I did but prompt the age to quit their clogs[1]
    By the known rules of ancient liberty,
    When straight a barbarous noise environs me
Of owls and cuckoos, asses, apes, and dogs;[2]
5 As when those hinds that were transformed to frogs
    Railed at Latona's twin-born progeny,[3]
    Which after held the sun and moon in fee.°   *possession*
But this is got by casting pearl to hogs,[4]
That bawl for freedom in their senseless mood,
10   And still revolt when truth would set them free.[5]
    License they mean when they cry liberty;
For who loves that must first be wise and good:
    But from that mark how far they rove we see,
    For all this waste of wealth and loss of blood.

1645   1673

8. The Romans called the moon, when it was in conjunction with the sun, *silentiis lunae*; thus, "silent" means "not shining." This phase of the moon was called the interlunar time (*interlunii*); during this time, according to myth, the moon retired to a cave somewhere beneath the earth; "vacant," from the Latin *vacare*, to be at leisure, i.e., resting.
9. I.e., the soul; according to Augustine (*De Trinitate* 5.6) the soul is whole in every part of the body.
1. Heavy objects tied to prisoners' feet to impede motion.
2. Milton had been attacked for advocating liberalized divorce laws. "Ancient liberty" (line 2) refers to the law of divorce set forth in Deuteronomy

24.1.
3. Apollo and Diana, afterwards deities of the sun and moon respectively. Their mother, Latona, was refused a drink by Lycian peasants ("hinds"), who were thereupon transformed into frogs by the twins' father, Jove.
4. I.e., I receive this response because I gave something valuable to those who could not appreciate its value. Compare Matthew 7.6: "Give not that which is holy unto the dogs, neither cast your pearls before swine, lest they trample them under their feet, and turn again and rend you."
5. Compare John 8.32: "And ye shall know the truth and the truth shall make you free."

When I Consider How My Light Is Spent[6]

When I consider how my light is spent
   Ere half my days, in this dark world and wide,
   And that one talent which is death to hide[7]
   Lodged with me useless, though my soul more bent
5 To serve therewith my Maker, and present
   My true account, lest he returning chide;
   "Doth God exact day-labor, light denied?"
   I fondly° ask; but Patience to prevent   *foolishly*
That murmur, soon replies, "God doth not need
10 Either man's work or his own gifts; who best
   Bear his mild yoke, they serve him best. His state
Is kingly. Thousands at his bidding speed
And post o'er land and ocean without rest:
They also serve who only stand and wait."

ca. 1652   1673

On the Late Massacre in Piedmont[8]

Avenge, O Lord, thy slaughtered saints, whose bones
   Lie scattered on the Alpine mountains cold,
   Even them who kept thy truth so pure of old
   When all our fathers worshiped stocks° and stones,[9]   *idols*
5 Forget not: in thy book record their groans
   Who were thy sheep and in their ancient fold
   Slain by the bloody Piedmontese that rolled
   Mother with infant down the rocks. Their moans
The vales redoubled to the hills, and they
10 To Heaven. Their martyred blood and ashes sow
   O'er all th' Italian fields where still doth sway
The triple tyrant:[1] that from these may grow
A hundredfold, who having learnt thy way
Early may fly the Babylonian woe.[2]

1655   1673

---

6. Milton had become totally blind in 1651.
7. An allusion to the parable of the talents, in which the servant who buried the single talent his lord had given him, instead of investing it, was deprived of all he had and cast "into outer darkness" at the lord's return (Matthew 25.14–30).
8. Some seventeen hundred members of the Protestant Waldensian sect in the Piedmont in northwestern Italy died as a result of a treacherous attack by the duke of Savoy's forces on Easter Day, 1655.

9. The Waldenses had existed as a sect, first within the Catholic Church and then as heretics, since the twelfth century. They were particularly critical of materialistic tendencies in the Church.
1. The pope, whose tiara has three crowns.
2. Babylon, as a city of luxury and vice, was often linked with the Papal Court by Protestants, who took the destruction of the city described in Revelation 18 as an allegory of the fate in store for the Roman Church.

Cyriack,[3] Whose Grandsire

Cyriack, whose grandsire on the royal bench
    Of British Themis,[4] with no mean applause,
    Pronounced, and in his volumes taught, our laws,
    Which others at their bar so often wrench,
5 Today deep thoughts resolve with me to drench
    In mirth that after no repenting draws;
    Let Euclid rest, and Archimedes pause,[5]
    And what the Swede intend, and what the French.[6]
To measure life learn thou betimes,° and know   *early*
10   Toward solid good what leads the nearest way;
    For other things mild Heaven a time ordains,
And disapproves that care, though wise in show,
    That with superfluous burden loads the day,
    And, when God sends a cheerful hour, refrains.

ca. 1655   1673

Methought I Saw

Methought I saw my late espousèd saint[7]
    Brought to me like Alcestis[8] from the grave,
    Whom Jove's great son to her glad husband gave,
    Rescued from Death by force, though pale and faint.
5 Mine, as whom washed from spot of child-bed taint
    Purification in the Old Law did save,[9]
    And such, as yet once more I trust to have
    Full sight of her in heaven without restraint,
Came vested all in white, pure as her mind.
10   Her face was veiled; yet to my fancied sight
    Love, sweetness, goodness, in her person shined
So clear as in no face with more delight.
    But O, as to embrace me she inclined,
    I waked, she fled, and day brought back my night.

ca. 1658   1673

3. Cyriack Skinner, a pupil of Milton's and grandson of Sir Edward Coke, the great jurist who had been chief justice of the King's Bench under James I.
4. The Greek goddess of justice.
5. Euclid and Archimedes (third century B.C.), Greek mathematicians; Skinner's interest in Greek mathematics may have begun when he was a pupil in Milton's school on Aldersgate Street.
6. In 1655, Charles X of Sweden was leading military campaigns against the Poles; Cardinal Mazarin was leading French policy.
7. The "saint," or soul in heaven, is probably Milton's second wife, Katherine Woodcock, to whom

he had been married less than two years (hence "late espousèd") when she died in 1658; since Milton had become blind in 1651, he almost certainly had never seen his wife. However, critics do not agree on the identity of the "saint." It is possibly a reference to Mary Powell, Milton's first wife, who died in childbirth in 1652.
8. The wife brought back from the dead to her husband, Admetus, by Hercules ("Jove's great son") in Euripides' *Alcestis*.
9. Hebrew law (Leviticus 12) prescribed certain sacrificial rituals for the purification of women after childbirth.

FROM PARADISE LOST[1]

The Verse[2]

The measure is English heroic verse[3] without rhyme, as that of Homer in Greek, and of Virgil in Latin;[4] rhyme being no necessary adjunct or true ornament of poem or good verse, in longer works especially, but the invention of a barbarous age, to set off wretched matter and lame meter; graced indeed since by the use of some famous modern poets, carried away by custom, but much to their own vexation, hindrance, and constraint, to express many things otherwise, and for the most part worse, than else they would have expressed them. Not without cause, therefore, some both Italian and Spanish poets of prime note, have rejected rhyme both in longer and shorter works, as have also, long since, our best English tragedies, as a thing of itself, to all judicious ears, trivial and of no true musical delight; which consists only in apt numbers, fit quantity of syllables, and the sense variously drawn out from one verse into another, not in the jingling sound of like endings, a fault avoided by the learned ancients both in poetry and all good oratory. This neglect then of rhyme, so little is to be taken for a defect, though it may seem so perhaps to vulgar readers, that it rather is to be esteemed an example set, the first in

1. John Milton wrote his epic poem *Paradise Lost* in order to "justify the ways of God to men," as he asserts in the invocation to Book 1. Although he eschews the traditional subject matter of epic poetry—"fabled knights / In battles feigned" (9.30–31)—he nevertheless follows many conventions of the epic form, including the beginning *in medias res* ("in the middle of things"), the invocation of a muse (a request for divine aid in the writing of the poem), the division of the poem into twelve books, the use of epic similes (extended and elaborately detailed comparisons that temporarily draw the reader's attention from the subject at hand), and the epic catalog (as of ships in Homer's *Iliad* and fallen angels in *Paradise Lost*). While Milton clearly establishes that his poem is part of an epic tradition that includes Homer's *Iliad* and Virgil's *Aeneid*, he simultaneously questions some of the assumptions of that tradition (he introduces, for example, a different concept of heroism) and introduces other generic elements such as pastoral and drama into his poem.

The poem begins in hell, where Satan and his fallen angels plot their revenge against God through the destruction of his newest creation, the human race (Books 1 and 2). In Book 3, the scene shifts to heaven, where God predicts the disobedience of Adam and Eve, and Christ volunteers to undertake their redemption. In Book 4, Satan enters Eden and appears to Eve in a dream. God sends the angel Raphael to warn Adam and Eve of Satan's intentions. In Books 5 and 6, Raphael narrates to Adam the story of the war in heaven between Satan and his followers, and God, Christ, and the angels loyal to God. Raphael goes on to relate the creation of the world and its inhabitants by God (Book 7). Adam, in Book 8, tells Raphael what he remembers of his own creation and of Eve's. Book 9, reprinted here, chronicles the temptation and fall of Adam and Eve. Christ descends from heaven to the garden to pronounce punishment upon the humans, and Sin and Death create a broad highway between hell and earth (Book 10).

Finally God sends the angel Michael to expel Adam and Eve from the garden, but first Michael shows Adam the history of the world up through the coming of Christ, relating God's promise to redeem the human race through the sacrifice of his Son (Books 11 and 12). Adam and Eve, heartened by this promise, depart the garden "hand in hand with wand'ring steps and slow") (12.648). Although Milton draws on biblical accounts of the events he narrates, he both embellishes these accounts and adds entire events of his own devising (such as the war in heaven, modeled on classical stories of battles among gods).

While there are many ways of approaching this poem, any approach will benefit from a careful consideration of Milton's language and the formal features of his poetry. Milton is a master of prosody, and he frequently varies the meter of his blank verse in ways that enhance or complicate the meaning of the words. His wordplay and the ambiguous syntax of his long, complexly subordinated sentences allow the reader the experience, in small, of the freedom to choose within a predetermined structure, an experience not unlike that of the characters in his poem.

2. This note first appeared in a 1668 reissue of the first edition of *Paradise Lost*, following a note in which the printer, S. Simmons, claimed that he had "procured" the note to satisfy many readers curious about why "the poem rhymes not." Milton's decision to add the note may have been influenced by a debate between John Dryden and Sir Robert Howard. Dryden's *Essay on Dramatic Verse* (1668) records the controversy, in which Dryden argues the merits of rhyme and Howard champions blank verse.

3. English heroic verse was the iambic line of five feet, or ten syllables.

4. Homer (ninth–eighth century B.C.) is the supposed author of the epic poems the *Iliad* and the *Odyssey*; Virgil (70–19 B.C.) is the author of the *Aeneid*; heroic verse in Greek and Latin poetry was the hexameter.

English, of ancient liberty recovered to heroic poem from the troublesome and modern bondage of rhyming.

Book 1

[The Invocation][5]

Of man's first disobedience, and the fruit
Of that forbidden tree whose mortal taste
Brought death into the world, and all our woe,
With loss of Eden, till one greater Man[6]
5   Restore us, and regain the blissful seat,
Sing, Heavenly Muse,[7] that, on the secret top
Of Oreb, or of Sinai, didst inspire
That shepherd who first taught the chosen seed
In the beginning how the Heavens and Earth
10   Rose out of Chaos: or, if Sion hill
Delight thee more, and Siloa's brook that flowed
Fast by the oracle of God, I thence
Invoke thy aid to my adventurous song,
That with no middle flight intends to soar
15   Above th' Aonian mount, while it pursues
Things unattempted yet in prose or rhyme.
And chiefly thou, O Spirit, that dost prefer
Before all temples th' upright heart and pure,
Instruct me, for thou know'st; thou from the first
20   Wast present, and, with mighty wings outspread,
Dovelike sat'st brooding on the vast abyss,
And mad'st it pregnant: what in me is dark
Illumine; what is low, raise and support;
That, to the height of this great argument,°   *theme*
25   I may assert Eternal Providence,
And justify the ways of God to men.

Book 9

The Argument[8]

Satan, having compassed the Earth, with meditated guile returns as a mist by night into Paradise; enters into the Serpent sleeping. Adam and Eve in the

---

5. In these opening lines Milton follows long-established epic tradition by stating his subject and invoking divine aid in the treatment of it.

6. Christ, the second Adam.

7. The invocation of the muse is an epic convention. In the invocation to Book 7, Milton specifically calls upon Urania, the patroness of astronomy and one of the nine Muses of Greek tradition, to assist him in telling the story of Creation. But he insists that it is the "meaning, not the Name I call" (7.5), suggesting that the non-Christian name is inadequate to his true intentions.

Here, the muse seems to represent the Spirit of God, the same Spirit that spoke to Moses ("That shepherd") out of the burning bush on Mount Horeb (also called Sinai) and called upon him to lead Israel ("the chosen seed") out of Egypt. God's

Spirit might also be found at Jerusalem in the Temple of Mount Sion ("the oracle of God") overlooking the stream Siloam, here contrasted with such haunts of the pagan Muses as "th' Aonian mount" (Helicon, in Greece). Milton asks this Spirit not only for inspiration but for instruction, since God alone was present "from the first" and knows the whole truth of the events Milton is about to relate.

8. The Argument is a prose summary of the action of the book. *Paradise Lost* was originally published without these summaries, but because many readers found the poem difficult the printer asked Milton to provide these short prose explanations at the beginning of each book. They first appeared, with the note on the verse, in a 1668 reissue of the first edition.

morning go forth to their labors, which Eve proposes to divide in several places, each laboring apart: Adam consents not, alleging the danger lest that enemy of whom they were forewarned should attempt her found alone. Eve, loth to be thought not circumspect or firm enough, urges her going apart, the rather desirous to make trial of her strength; Adam at last yields. The Serpent finds her alone: his subtle approach, first gazing, then speaking, with much flattery extolling Eve above all other creatures. Eve, wondering to hear the Serpent speak, asks how he attained to human speech and such understanding not till now; the Serpent answers that by tasting of a certain tree in the Garden he attained both to speech and reason, till then void of both. Eve requires him to bring her to that tree, and finds it to be the Tree of Knowledge forbidden; the Serpent, now grown bolder, with many wiles and arguments induces her at length to eat. She, pleased with the taste, deliberates a while whether to impart thereof to Adam or not; at last brings him of the fruit; relates what persuaded her to eat thereof. Adam, at first amazed, but perceiving her lost, resolves, through vehemence of love, to perish with her, and, extenuating the trespass, eats also of the fruit. The effects thereof in them both; they seek to cover their nakedness; then fall to variance and accusation of one another.

No more of talk where God or angel guest[9]
With man, as with his friend, familiar used
To sit indulgent, and with him partake
Rural repast, permitting him the while
5   Venial° discourse unblamed. I now must change   *allowable*
Those notes to tragic—foul distrust, and breach
Disloyal, on the part of man, revolt
And disobedience; on the part of Heaven,
Now alienated, distance and distaste,
10   Anger and just rebuke, and judgment given,
That brought into this world a world of woe,
Sin and her shadow Death, and Misery,
Death's harbinger. Sad task, yet argument
Not less but more heroic than the wrath
15   Of stern Achilles on his foe pursued
Thrice fugitive about Troy wall; or rage
Of Turnus for Lavinia disespoused;
Or Neptune's ire, or Juno's, that so long
Perplexed the Greek, and Cytherea's son:[1]
20   If answerable° style I can obtain   *suitable, fitting*
Of my celestial Patroness,[2] who deigns°   *condescends to grant*
Her nightly visitation unimplored,
And dictates to me slumbering, or inspires
Easy my unpremeditated verse,
25   Since first this subject for heroic song
Pleased me, long choosing and beginning late,
Not sedulous° by nature to indite°   *diligent / write about*
Wars, hitherto the only argument

9. Adam has just concluded a conversation with the angel Raphael at the end of Book 8.
1. Important moments in important epics. Achilles, whose "wrath" is the epic subject announced in the first line of the *Iliad*, pursued Hector three times around the walls of Troy before slaying him. Turnus (in the *Aeneid*) fought with Aeneas for the hand of Lavinia. Neptune hindered Odysseus ("the Greek") in his attempts to return home after the Trojan War, and Juno, hostile to Venus ("Cytherea"), made difficulties for Venus' son Aeneas.
2. Urania, the "Heavenly Muse" whose aid Milton had invoked at the beginning of Book 1.

Heroic deemed, chief mastery to dissect
30   With long and tedious havoc fabled knights
In battles feigned (the better fortitude
Of patience and heroic martyrdom
Unsung), or to describe races and games,
Or tilting furniture,³ emblazoned shields,
35   Impresses quaint, caparisons and steeds,
Bases and tinsel trappings, gorgeous knights
At joust and tournament; then marshaled feast
Served up in hall with sewers and seneschals:⁴
The skill of artifice or office mean;
40   Not that which justly gives heroic name
To person or to poem. Me, of these
Nor skilled nor studious, higher argument
Remains,⁵ sufficient of itself to raise
That name,⁶ unless an age too late, or cold
45   Climate, or years, damp my intended wing
Depressed; and much they may if all be mine,
Not hers who brings it nightly to my ear.⁷
        The sun was sunk, and after him the star
Of Hesperus, whose office is to bring
50   Twilight upon the Earth, short arbiter
'Twixt day and night, and now from end to end
Night's hemisphere had veiled the horizon round,
When Satan, who late fled before the threats
Of Gabriel out of Eden, now improved
55   In meditated fraud and malice, bent
On man's destruction, maugre° what might hap   *despite*
Of heavier on himself, fearless returned.
By night he fled, and at midnight returned
From compassing the Earth—cautious of day
60   Since Uriel, regent of the sun,⁸ descried
His entrance, and forewarned the Cherubim
That kept their watch. Thence, full of anguish, driven,
The space of seven continued nights he rode
With darkness; thrice the equinoctial line
65   He circled, four times crossed the car of Night
From pole to pole, traversing each colure;⁹
On the eighth returned, and on the coast averse°   *side opposite*
From entrance or cherubic watch by stealth

---

3. The equipment used in a "tilt" or tournament, examples of which follow. "Impresses": heraldic emblems displayed on shields. "Caparisons": ornamented coverings spread over the saddle or harness of a horse. "Bases": skirtlike coverings, sometimes of mail, intended to decorate and protect warhorses.
4. High-ranking household servants.
5. I.e., to me, not skilled or learned in these things, remains a more important subject.
6. I.e., "heroic name" (from line 40).
7. I.e., these things, "an age too late" (the age of the world), "cold Climate," or "years" (the poet's age), might indeed "damp" or benumb his intent if the effort of writing the poem were all his instead of "hers," i.e., that of his "celestial Patroness."

8. In medieval astronomy, each of the concentric crystalline spheres containing one of the heavenly bodies was supposed to be inhabited by an angel, its "intelligence," who governed its motion; Uriel is one of the four great archangels of the Jewish tradition, along with Raphael, Gabriel and Michael.
9. The "equinoctial line" is the equator. The colures (line 66) are two of the great circles that pass through the celestial poles, one intersecting the ecliptic at the equinoxes, the other at the solstices. Satan circles the earth for the space of seven days, first along the equator and then over the poles, always timing his flight so as to remain hidden on the dark side.

Found unsuspected way. There was a place
70   (Now not, though Sin, not Time, first wrought the change)
Where Tigris, at the foot of Paradise,
Into a gulf shot under ground, till part
Rose up a fountain by the Tree of Life.
In with the river sunk and with it rose
75   Satan, involved in rising mist; then sought
Where to lie hid. Sea he had searched and land,
From Eden over Pontus,[1] and the pool
Maeotis, up beyond the river Ob;
Downward as far antarctic; and, in length,
80   West from Orontes to the ocean barred
At Darien, thence to the land where flows
Ganges and Indus. Thus the orb he roamed
With narrow search, and with inspection deep
Considered every creature, which of all
85   Most opportune might serve his wiles, and found
The serpent subtlest beast of all the field.[2]
Him, after long debate, irresolute
Of thoughts revolved, his final sentence chose
Fit vessel, fittest imp° of fraud, in whom   *graft*
90   To enter, and his dark suggestions hide
From sharpest sight; for in the wily snake
Whatever sleights° none would suspicious mark,   *cunning, dexterity*
As from his wit and native subtlety
Proceeding, which, in other beasts observed,
95   Doubt° might beget of diabolic power   *suspicion*
Active within beyond the sense of brute.
Thus he resolved, but first from inward grief
His bursting passion into plaints thus poured:
   "O Earth, how like to Heaven, if not preferred
100   More justly, seat worthier of Gods, as built
With second thoughts, reforming what was old!
For what God, after better, worse would build?
Terrestrial Heaven, danced round by other Heavens,
That shine, yet bear their bright officious° lamps,   *obliging*
105   Light above light, for thee alone, as seems,
In thee concentring all their precious beams
Of sacred influence![3] As God in Heaven
Is center, yet extends to all, so thou
Centring receiv'st from all those orbs; in thee,
110   Not in themselves, all their known virtue appears,
Productive in herb, plant, and nobler birth
Of creatures animate with gradual life
Of growth, sense, reason, all summed up in man.[4]
With what delight could I have walked thee round,

1. Satan's search had extended from the Black Sea (Pontus) to the connecting Sea of Azov (the pool Maeotis) and northward beyond the river Ob in Siberia: southward to the antarctic; and westward from the Orontes River in Syria to the isthmus of Panama (Darien) and on around the world to India.
2. Milton here follows Genesis 3.1: "Now the serpent was more subtle than any beast of the field which the Lord God had made."
3. Satan seems to describe here a Ptolemaic system of the universe in which the Earth is the center around which many heavenly bodies turn.
4. The Earth is populated with forms of life on a graduated scale ranging from plants, which merely grow; to animals, which both grow and feel; to humans, who grow, feel, and think.

115   If I could joy in aught; sweet interchange
Of hill and valley, rivers, woods, and plains,
Now land, now sea, and shores with forest crowned,
Rocks, dens, and caves! But I in none of these
Find place or refuge; and, the more I see
120   Pleasures about me, so much more I feel
Torment within me, as from the hateful siege
Of contraries; all good to me becomes
Bane,° and in Heaven much worse would be my state.   *poison, evil*
But neither here seek I, no, nor in Heaven,
125   To dwell, unless by mastering Heaven's Supreme;
Nor hope to be myself less miserable
By what I seek, but others to make such
As I, though thereby worse to me redound.°   *return*
For only in destroying I find ease
130   To my relentless thoughts; and him destroyed,
Or won to what may work his utter loss,
For whom all this was made, all this will soon
Follow, as to him linked in weal° or woe: *happiness*
In woe then, that destruction wide may range!
135   To me shall be the glory sole among
The infernal Powers, in one day to have marred
What he, Almighty styled, six nights and days
Continued making, and who knows how long
Before had been contriving; though perhaps
140   Not longer than since I in one night freed
From servitude inglorious well nigh half
The angelic name,[5] and thinner left the throng
Of his adorers. He, to be avenged,
And to repair his numbers thus impaired—
145   Whether such virtue,° spent of old, now failed   *power, energy*
More angels to create (if they at least
Are his created),[6] or to spite us more—
Determined to advance into our room
A creature formed of earth,[7] and him endow,
150   Exalted from so base original,
With Heavenly spoils, our spoils. What he decreed
He effected; Man he made, and for him built
Magnificent this World, and Earth his seat,
Him Lord pronounced, and, O indignity!
155   Subjected to his service angel-wings
And flaming ministers, to watch and tend
Their earthy charge. Of these the vigilance
I dread, and to elude, thus wrapped in mist
Of midnight vapor, glide obscure, and pry
160   In every bush and brake, where hap° may find   *luck*
The serpent sleeping, in whose mazy folds

5. I.e., half the angels. Satan alludes to the revolt he led against God, the consequence of which was that he and his supporters (whose number he exaggerates here) were cast out of heaven into hell.
6. Only once (at the beginning of Book 4, line 43) does Satan speak of the angels as created by God, instead of self-created (as he implies here).

7. Milton explains in Book 7 (lines 524–26) that Adam is made from earth: "he form'd thee, Adam, thee O man / Dust of the ground, and in thy nostrils breath'd / The breath of Life," following Genesis 2:7: "And the Lord God formed man of the dust of the ground, and breathed into his nostrils the breath of life."

To hide me, and the dark intent I bring.
O foul descent! that I, who erst contended
With Gods to sit the highest, am now constrained
165 Into a beast, and, mixed with bestial slime,
This essence to incarnate and imbrute,[8]
That to the height of deity aspired!
But what will not ambition and revenge
Descend to? Who aspires must down as low
170 As high he soared, obnoxious,° first or last,   *subject*
To basest things. Revenge, at first though sweet,
Bitter ere long back on itself recoils.
Let it; I reck° not, so it light well aimed,   *care*
Since higher I fall short, on him who next
175 Provokes my envy, this new favorite
Of Heaven, this man of clay, son of despite,°   *spite, scorn*
Whom, us the more to spite, his Maker raised
From dust: spite then with spite is best repaid."
      So saying, through each thicket, dank or dry,
180 Like a black mist low-creeping, he held on
His midnight search, where soonest he might find
The serpent. Him fast sleeping soon he found,
In labyrinth of many a round self-rolled,
His head the midst, well stored with subtle wiles:
185 Not yet in horrid shade or dismal den,
Nor nocent° yet, but on the grassy herb,   *harmful*
Fearless, unfeared, he slept. In at his mouth
The Devil entered, and his brutal sense,
In heart or head, possessing soon inspired
190 With act intelligential; but his sleep
Disturbed not, waiting close° the approach of morn.   *hidden*
      Now, whenas sacred light began to dawn
In Eden on the humid flowers, that breathed
Their morning incense, when all things that breathe
195 From th' Earth's great altar send up silent praise
To the Creator, and his nostrils fill
With grateful smell, forth came the human pair,
And joined their vocal worship to the choir
Of creatures wanting° voice; that done, partake   *lacking*
200 The season, prime° for sweetest scents and airs;   *best*
Then cómmune how that day they best may ply
Their growing work; for much their work outgrew
The hands' dispatch of two gardening so wide:
And Eve first to her husband thus began:
205   "Adam, well may we labor still° to dress   *constantly*
This garden, still to tend plant, herb, and flower,
Our pleasant task enjoined; but, till more hands
Aid us, the work under our labor grows,
Luxurious° by restraint: what we by day   *luxuriant*
210 Lop overgrown, or prune, or prop, or bind,
One night or two with wanton growth derides,
Tending to wild. Thou, therefore, now advise,

---

8. Satan's incarnation in the body of the serpent is a grotesque parody of Christ's incarnation in human form.

Or hear what to my mind first thoughts present.
Let us divide our labors; thou where choice
215   Leads thee, or where most needs, whether to wind
The woodbine round this arbor, or direct
The clasping ivy where to climb; while I
In yonder spring° of roses intermixed   *growth*
With myrtle⁹ find what to redress till noon.
220   For, while so near each other thus all day
Our task we choose, what wonder if so near
Looks intervene and smiles, or object new
Casual discourse draw on, which intermits
Our day's work, brought to little, though begun
225   Early, and the hour of supper comes unearned!"
      To whom mild answer Adam thus returned:
"Sole Eve, associate sole, to me beyond
Compare above all living creatures dear!
Well hast thou motioned,° well thy thoughts employed   *suggested*
230   How we might best fulfil the work which here
God hath assigned us, nor of me shalt pass
Unpraised; for nothing lovelier can be found
In woman than to study household good,
And good works in her husband to promote.
235   Yet not so strictly hath our Lord imposed
Labor as to debar us when we need
Refreshment, whether food, or talk between,
Food of the mind, or this sweet intercourse
Of looks and smiles; for smiles from reason flow,
240   To brute denied, and are of love the food;
Love, not the lowest end of human life.
For not to irksome toil, but to delight,
He made us, and delight to reason joined.
These paths and bowers doubt not but our joint hands
245   Will keep from wilderness with ease, as wide
As we need walk, till younger hands ere long
Assist us. But, if much converse perhaps
Thee satiate, to short absence I could yield;
For solitude sometimes is best society,
250   And short retirement urges sweet return.
But other doubt possesses me, lest harm
Befall thee, severed from me; for thou know'st
What hath been warned us—what malicious foe,
Envying our happiness, and of his own
255   Despairing, seeks to work us woe and shame
By sly assault, and somewhere nigh at hand
Watches, no doubt, with greedy hope to find
His wish and best advantage, us asunder,
Hopeless to circumvent° us joined, where each   *outwit*
260   To other speedy aid might lend at need.
Whether his first design be to withdraw
Our fealty from God, or to disturb
Conjugal love—than which perhaps no bliss

---

9. The myrtle tree, having shiny green leaves and white flowers; associated with Venus, and an emblem of love. "Woodbine": a name for various climbing plants.

Enjoyed by us excites his envy more—
265 Or this, or worse, leave not the faithful side
That gave thee being,[1] still shades thee and protects.
The wife, where danger or dishonor lurks,
Safest and seemliest by her husband stays,
Who guards her, or with her the worst endures."
270   To whom the virgin° majesty of Eve,   *innocent*
As one who loves, and some unkindness meets,
With sweet austere composure thus replied:
   "Offspring of Heaven and Earth, and all Earth's lord!
That such an enemy we have, who seeks
275 Our ruin, both by thee informed I learn,
And from the parting angel overheard,
As in a shady nook I stood behind,
Just then returned at shut of evening flowers.
But that thou shouldst my firmness therefore doubt
280 To God or thee, because we have a foe
May tempt it, I expected not to hear.
His violence thou fear'st not, being such
As we, not capable of death or pain,
Can either not receive, or can repel.
285 His fraud is, then, thy fear; which plain infers
Thy equal fear that my firm faith and love
Can by his fraud be shaken or seduced:
Thoughts, which how found they harbor in thy breast,
Adam, misthought of her to thee so dear?"
290   To whom, with healing words, Adam replied:
"Daughter of God and Man, immortal Eve!
For such thou art, from sin and blame entire°   *wholly free*
Not diffident° of thee do I dissuade   *mistrustful*
Thy absence from my sight, but to avoid
295 Th' attempt itself, intended by our foe.
For he who tempts, though in vain, at least asperses[2]
The tempted with dishonor foul, supposed
Not incorruptible of faith, not proof
Against temptation. Thou thyself with scorn
300 And anger wouldst resent the offered wrong,
Though ineffectual found; misdeem not, then,
If such affront I labor to avert
From thee alone, which on us both at once
The enemy, though bold, will hardly dare;
305 Or, daring, first on me th' assault shall light.
Nor thou his malice and false guile contemn°—   *regard scornfully*
Subtle he needs must be who could seduce
Angels—nor think superfluous others' aid.
I from the influence of thy looks receive
310 Access° in every virtue—in thy sight   *increase*
More wise, more watchful, stronger, if need were
Of outward strength; while shame, thou looking on,
Shame to be overcome or overreached,

---

1. In Book 8 (lines 465–71) Adam describes God's creation of Eve out of a rib taken from his side, following Genesis 2:22: "And the rib, which the Lord God had taken from man, made he a woman, and brought her unto the man."
2. Maligns (literally, "sprinkles").

Would utmost vigor raise, and raised unite.
315 Why shouldst not thou like sense within thee feel
When I am present, and thy trial choose
With me, best witness of thy virtue tried?"
    So spake domestic Adam in his care
And matrimonial love; but Eve, who thought
320 Less àttributed to her faith sincere,
Thus her reply with accent sweet renewed:
    "If this be our condition, thus to dwell
In narrow circuit straitened° by a foe,   *constrained, limited*
Subtle or violent, we not endued°   *endowed*
325 Single with like defense wherever met,
How are we happy, still in fear of harm?
But harm precedes not sin: only our foe
Tempting affronts us with his foul esteem
Of our integrity: his foul esteem
330 Sticks no dishonor on our front,° but turns   *brow*
Foul on himself; then wherefore shunned or feared
By us, who rather double honor gain
From his surmise proved false, find peace within,
Favor from Heaven, our witness, from the event?
335 And what is faith, love, virtue, unassayed°   *untested*
Alone, without exterior help sustained?
Let us not then suspect our happy state
Left so imperfect by the Maker wise
As not secure to single or combined.
340 Frail is our happiness, if this be so;
And Eden were no Eden, thus exposed."
    To whom thus Adam fervently replied:
"O woman, best are all things as the will
Of God ordained them; his creating hand
345 Nothing imperfect or deficient left
Of all that he created, much less man,
Or aught that might his happy state secure,
Secure from outward force. Within himself
The danger lies, yet lies within his power;
350 Against his will he can receive no harm.
But God left free the will; for what obeys
Reason is free; and reason he made right,
But bid her[3] well beware, and still erect,°   *alert*
Lest, by some fair appearing good surprised,
355 She dictate false, and misinform the will
To do what God expressly hath forbid.
Not then mistrust, but tender love, enjoins
That I should mind° thee oft; and mind thou me.   *remind*
Firm we subsist, yet possible to swerve,
360 Since reason not impossibly may meet
Some specious° object by the foe suborned,[4]   *fair-appearing*
And fall into deception unaware,
Not keeping strictest watch, as she was warned.
Seek not temptation, then, which to avoid

3. I.e., Reason.
4. Procured by corrupt means and with a sinister motive.

365 Were better, and most likely if from me
Thou sever not: trial will come unsought.
Wouldst thou approve° thy constancy, approve   *prove*
First thy obedience; the other who can know,
Not seeing thee attempted, who attest?
370 But, if thou think trial unsought may find
Us both securer[5] than thus warned thou seem'st,
Go; for thy stay, not free, absents thee more.
Go in thy native innocence; rely
On what thou hast of virtue; summon all;
375 For God towards thee hath done his part: do thine."
    So spake the patriarch of mankind; but Eve
Persisted; yet submiss,° though last, replied: *submissive*
    "With thy permission, then, and thus forewarned,
Chiefly by what thy own last reasoning words
380 Touched only, that our trial, when least sought,
May find us both perhaps far less prepared,
The willinger I go, nor much expect
A foe so proud will first the weaker seek;
So bent, the more shall shame him his repulse."
385 Thus saying, from her husband's hand her hand
Soft she withdrew, and like a wood nymph light,
Oread or dryad,[6] or of Delia's train,
Betook her to the groves, but Delia's self
In gait surpassed and goddesslike deport,
390 Though not as she with bow and quiver armed,
But with such gardening tools as art yet rude,
Guiltless of fire had formed,[7] or angels brought.
To Pales, or Pomona, thus adorned,
Likest she seemed, Pomona when she fled
395 Vertumnus, or to Ceres in her prime,
Yet virgin of Proserpina from Jove.[8]
Her long with ardent look his eye pursued
Delighted, but desiring more her stay.
Oft he to her his charge of quick return
400 Repeated; she to him as oft engaged
To be returned by noon amid the bower,
And all things in best order to invite
Noontide repast, or afternoon's repose.
O much deceived, much failing, hapless Eve,
405 Of thy presumed return! Event perverse!
Thou never from that hour in Paradise
Found'st either sweet repast, or sound repose;
Such ambush hid among sweet flowers and shades
Waited with hellish rancor imminent
410 To intercept thy way, or send thee back

---

5. Milton may be playing on both senses of the Latin word *securus*, which means both "safe" or "free from care" and "careless" or "negligent."
6. Mountain or wood nymph. Delia is Diana (born at Delos), goddess of the hunt, who was accompanied by a band of nymphs when she hunted.
7. There was no need of fire in Eden; the associa-

tion of guilt with fire suggests the myth of Prometheus, who stole fire from the gods to give to humans.
8. Roman goddesses, the first of flocks, the second of fruits. Pomona's suitor, Vertumnus, won her only after long wooing. Ceres, the supreme agricultural goddess, bore Proserpina to Jove.

Despoiled of innocence, of faith, of bliss.
For now, and since first break of dawn, the fiend,
Mere serpent in appearance, forth was come,
And on his quest, where likeliest he might find
415 The only two of mankind, but in them
The whole included race, his purposed prey.
In bower and field he sought, where any tuft
Of grove or garden-plot more pleasant lay,
Their tendance° or plantation for delight;   *object of care*
420 By fountain or by shady rivulet
He sought them both, but wished his hap might find
Eve separate; he wished, but not with hope
Of what so seldom chanced; when to his wish,
Beyond his hope, Eve separate he spies,
425 Veiled in a cloud of fragrance, where she stood,
Half spied, so thick the roses bushing round
About her glowed, oft stooping to support
Each flower of slender stalk, whose head though gay
Carnation, purple, azure, or specked with gold,
430 Hung drooping unsustained, them she upstays
Gently with myrtle band, mindless the while
Herself, though fairest unsupported flower,
From her best prop so far, and storm so nigh.
Nearer he drew, and many a walk traversed
435 Of stateliest covert, cedar, pine, or palm;
Then voluble° and bold, now hid, now seen   *twining*
Among thick-woven arborets° and flowers   *shrubs*
Embordered on each bank, the hand° of Eve: *handiwork*
Spot more delicious than those gardens feigned[9]
440 Or of revived Adonis, or renowned
Alcinous, host of old Laertes' son,
Or that, not mystic, where the sapient king
Held dalliance with his fair Egyptian spouse.
Much he° the place admired, the person more.   *Satan*
445 As one who long in populous city pent,
Where houses thick and sewers annoy° the air,   *pollute*
Forth issuing on a summer's morn to breathe
Among the pleasant villages and farms
Adjoined, from each thing met conceives delight,
450 The smell of grain, or tedded[1] grass, or kine,°   *cattle*
Or dairy, each rural sight, each rural sound:
If chance with nymphlike step fair virgin pass,
What pleasing seemed, for her now pleases more,
She most, and in her look sums all delight.
455 Such pleasure took the serpent to behold
This flowery plat,° the sweet recess of Eve   *plot*
Thus early, thus alone; her heavenly form
Angelic, but more soft, and feminine,

---

9. Mythical or legendary gardens. In the first, Adonis was nursed by Venus after having been wounded by a boar; the second was visited by Odysseus ("Laertes' son"), who found spring time and harvest time both continuous there. The third garden mentioned—the garden of Solomon ("the sapient king") and his bride, the pharaoh's daughter—Milton regards as historical, not "mystic" or mythical.
1. Spread out to dry to make hay.

Her graceful innocence, her every air°   *manner*
460 Of gesture or least action overawed
His malice, and with rapine° sweet bereaved   *robbery*
His fierceness of the fierce intent it brought:
That space the evil one abstracted stood
From his own evil, and for the time remained
465 Stupidly good, of enmity disarmed,
Of guile, of hate, of envy, of revenge.[2]
But the hot Hell that always in him burns,
Though in mid Heaven, soon ended his delight,
And tortures him now more, the more he sees
470 Of pleasure not for him ordained: then soon
Fierce hate he recollects, and all his thoughts
Of mischief, gratulating,° thus excites: *exulting*
         "Thoughts, whither have ye led me? with what sweet
Compulsion thus transported to forget
475 What hither brought us? hate, not love, nor hope
Of Paradise for Hell, hope here to taste
Of pleasure, but all pleasure to destroy,
Save what is in destroying; other joy
To me is lost. Then let me not let pass
480 Occasion which now smiles; behold alone
The woman, opportune° to all attempts,   *open to*
Her husband, for I view far round, not nigh,
Whose higher intellectual° more I shun,   *intellect*
And strength, of courage haughty, and of limb
485 Heroic built, though of terrestrial mold;[3]
Foe not informidable, exempt from wound,
I not; so much hath Hell debased, and pain
Enfeebled me, to what I was in Heaven.
She fair, divinely fair, fit love for gods,
490 Not terrible,° though terror be in love   *exciting fear*
And beauty, not° approached by stronger hate,   *unless*
Hate stronger, under show of love well feigned,
The way which to her ruin now I tend."
         So spake the enemy of mankind, enclosed
495 In serpent, inmate bad, and toward Eve
Addressed his way, not with indented wave,
Prone on the ground, as since, but on his rear,
Circular base of rising folds, that towered
Fold above fold a surging maze; his head
500 Crested aloft, and carbuncle° his eyes;   *ruby-colored*
With burnished neck of verdant gold, erect
Amidst his circling spires,° that on the grass   *coils*
Floated redundant.° Pleasing was his shape,   *waving, excessive*
And lovely; never since of serpent kind
505 Lovelier, not those that in Illyria changed
Hermione and Cadmus, or the god
In Epidaurus; nor to which transformed
Ammonian Jove, or Capitoline was seen,

---

2. Amazed by Eve's beauty, Satan is momentarily   tated, is insensibly good.
stunned into inaction and, while thus incapaci-   3. Made of earth.

He with Olympias, this with her who bore
510 Scipio, the height of Rome.[4] With tract oblique
At first, as one who sought access, but feared
To interrupt, sidelong he works his way.
As when a ship by skillful steersman wrought
Nigh river's mouth or foreland, where the wind
515 Veers oft, as oft so steers, and shifts her sail:
So varied he, and of his tortuous train
Curled many a wanton wreath in sight of Eve,
To lure her eye: she busied heard the sound
Of rustling leaves, but minded not, as used
520 To such disport before her through the field,
From every beast, more duteous at her call,
Than at Circean call the herd disguised.[5]
He bolder now, uncalled before her stood:
But as in gaze admiring; oft he bowed
525 His turret crest, and sleek enameled neck,
Fawning, and licked the ground whereon she trod.
His gentle dumb expression turned at length
The eye of Eve to mark his play: he, glad
Of her attention gained, with serpent tongue
530 Organic, or impulse of vocal air,[6]
His fraudulent temptation thus began.
    "Wonder not, sovereign mistress, if perhaps
Thou canst, who art sole wonder; much less arm
Thy looks, the heaven of mildness, with disdain,
535 Displeased that I approach thee thus, and gaze
Insatiate, I thus single, nor have feared
Thy awful° brow, more awful thus retired.   *awe-inspiring*
Fairest resemblance of thy Maker fair,
Thee all things living gaze on, all things thine
540 By gift, and thy celestial beauty adore
With ravishment° beheld, there best beheld   *rapture, ecstasy*
Where universally admired: but here
In this enclosure wild, these beasts among,
Beholders rude, and shallow to discern
545 Half what in thee is fair, one man except,
Who sees thee? (and what is one?) who shouldst be seen
A goddess among gods, adored and served
By angels numberless, thy daily train."
    So glozed° the tempter, and his proem tuned;   *flattered*
550 Into the heart of Eve his words made way,
Though at the voice much marveling: at length,
Not unamazed, she thus in answer spake.
    "What may this mean? Language of man pronounced

---

4. Cadmus, king of Thebes, and his wife, Harmonia ("Hermione"), were transformed into serpents after their retirement to Illyria. The "god in Epidaurus" is Aesculapius, god of healing, whose art included the use of serpents and who sometimes appeared in the form of a serpent at his temple in Epidaurus. Jove (here called Ammonian and Capitoline after temples associated with him) was said to have coupled with Olympias and Sempronia in the form of a serpent. Alexander the Great was born of the first union, and the Roman leader Scipio Africanus was born of the second.
5. In the *Odyssey* (Book 10) the enchantress Circe changed men into swine, who then dutifully followed her about.
6. I.e., Satan speaks through the serpent either using the serpent's own tongue or by directly impelling the air to make it seem voicelike.

By tongue of brute, and human sense expressed?
555 The first at least of these I thought denied
To beasts, whom God on their creation-day
Created mute to all articulate sound;
The latter I demur,° for in their looks   *hesitate about*
Much reason, and in their actions oft appears.
560 Thee, serpent, subtlest beast of all the field
I knew, but not with human voice endued:°   *endowed*
Redouble then this miracle, and say,
How cam'st thou speakable of mute, and how
To me so friendly grown above the rest
565 Of brutal kind, that daily are in sight?
Say, for such wonder claims attention due."
    To whom the guileful tempter thus replied:
"Empress of this fair world, resplendent Eve!
Easy to me it is to tell thee all
570 What thou command'st and right thou shouldst be obeyed:
I was at first as other beasts that graze
The trodden herb, of abject thoughts and low,
As was my food, nor aught but food discerned
Or sex, and apprehended nothing high:
575 Till on a day, roving the field, I chanced
A goodly tree far distant to behold
Loaden with fruit of fairest colors mixed,
Ruddy and gold; I nearer drew to gaze;
When from the boughs a savory odor blown,
580 Grateful to appetite, more pleased my sense
Than smell of sweetest fennel,[7] or the teats
Of ewe or goat dropping with milk at even,
Unsucked of lamb or kid, that tend their play.
To satisfy the sharp desire I had
585 Of tasting those fair apples, I resolved
Not to defer: hunger and thirst at once,
Powerful persuaders, quickened at the scent
Of that alluring fruit, urged me so keen.
About the mossy trunk I wound me soon,
590 For, high from ground, the branches would require
Thy utmost reach, or Adam's: round the tree
All other beasts that saw, with like desire
Longing and envying stood, but could not reach.
Amid the tree now got, where plenty hung
595 Tempting so nigh, to pluck and eat my fill
I spared not; for such pleasure till that hour
At feed or fountain never had I found.
Sated at length, ere long I might perceive
Strange alteration in me, to degree
600 Of reason in my inward powers, and speech
Wanted not long, though to this shape retained.
Thenceforth to speculations high or deep
I turned my thoughts, and with capacious° mind   *wide, spacious*
Considered all things visible in Heaven,

---

7. It was popularly believed that snakes were especially fond of fennel (an herb) and that they stole milk
from sheep and goats.

605 Or Earth, or middle,° all things fair and good: *regions between*
But all that fair and good in thy divine
Semblance, and in thy beauty's heavenly ray
United I beheld: no fair° to° thine   *beauty / compared to*
Equivalent or second, which compelled
610 Me thus, though importune° perhaps, to come   *inopportunely*
And gaze, and worship thee of right declared
Sovereign of creatures, universal dame."
    So talked the spirited° sly snake: and Eve   *spirit-possessed*
Yet more amazed, unwary thus replied:
615 "Serpent, thy overpraising leaves in doubt
The virtue of that fruit, in thee first proved.
But say, where grows the tree, from hence how far?
For many are the trees of God that grow
In Paradise, and various, yet unknown
620 To us; in such abundance lies our choice,
As leaves a greater store of fruit untouched,
Still hanging incorruptible, till men
Grow up to their provision, and more hands
Help to disburden Nature of her birth."[8]
625   To whom the wily adder, blithe and glad:
"Empress, the way is ready, and not long,
Beyond a row of myrtles, on a flat,
Fast by a fountain, one small thicket past
Of blowing° myrrh and balm: if thou accept   *blooming*
630 My conduct, I can bring thee thither soon."
    "Lead then," said Eve. He leading swiftly rolled
In tangles, and made intricate seem straight,
To mischief swift. Hope elevates, and joy
Brightens his crest; as when a wandering fire
635 Compact° of unctuous vapor,[9] which the night   *composed*
Condenses, and the cold environs round,
Kindled through agitation to a flame
(Which oft, they say, some evil spirit attends),
Hovering and blazing with delusive light,
640 Misleads th' amazed night-wanderer from his way
To bogs and mires, and oft through pond or pool,
There swallowed up and lost, from succor° far: *help*
So glistered the dire snake, and into fraud
Led Eve our credulous mother, to the tree
645 Of prohibition,[1] root of all our woe:
Which when she saw, thus to her guide she spake:
    "Serpent, we might have spared our coming hither,
Fruitless to me, though fruit be here to excess,
The credit of whose virtue rest with thee;[2]
650 Wondrous indeed, if cause of such effects!
But of this tree we may not taste nor touch:
God so commanded, and left that command
Sole daughter of his voice; the rest,[3] we live

8. I.e., what Nature bears.
9. Made of oily vapor. The allusion is to the will-o'-the-wisp *(ignis fatuus)*, which was said to draw travelers astray by holding a false light before them; the phenomenon of nocturnal light is caused by the combustion of marsh gas.
1. I.e., the prohibited tree.
2. I.e., my belief in the effects of the fruit must continue to depend solely on your testimony.
3. I.e., in everything else.

Law to ourselves; our reason is our law."
655   To whom the Tempter guilefully replied:
"Indeed? Hath God then said that of the fruit
Of all these garden trees ye shall not eat,
Yet lords declared of all in Earth or air?"
      To whom thus Eve, yet sinless: "Of the fruit
660   Of each tree in the garden we may eat,
But of the fruit of this fair tree amidst
The garden, God hath said, 'Ye shall not eat
Thereof, nor shall ye touch it, lest ye die.' "
      She scarce had said, though brief, when now more bold,
665   The tempter, but with show of zeal and love
To man, and indignation at his wrong,
New part puts on, and as° to passion moved,   *as if*
Fluctuates disturbed, yet comely,° and in act°   *attractive / bearing*
Raised, as of some great matter to begin.
670   As when of old some orator renowned
In Athens or free Rome, where eloquence
Flourished, since mute, to some great cause addressed,
Stood in himself collected, while each part,
Motion, each act, won audience ere the tongue,
675   Sometimes in height began, as no delay
Of preface brooking, through his zeal of right.[4]
So standing, moving, or to height upgrown
The tempter all impassioned thus began:
      "O sacred, wise, and wisdom-giving plant,
680   Mother of science!° now I feel thy power   *knowledge*
Within me clear, not only to discern
Things in their causes, but to trace the ways
Of highest agents, deemed however wise.
Queen of this universe! do not believe
685   Those rigid threats of death. Ye shall not die;
How should ye? By the fruit? it gives you life
To° knowledge; by the Threatener? look on me,   *in addition to*
Me who have touched and tasted, yet both live,
And life more perfect have attained than Fate
690   Meant me, by venturing higher than my lot.
Shall that be shut to man, which to the beast
Is open? Or will God incense his ire
For such a petty trespass, and not praise
Rather your dauntless virtue, whom the pain
695   Of death denounced, whatever thing death be,
Deterred not from achieving what might lead
To happier life, knowledge of good and evil?
Of good, how just! Of evil, if what is evil
Be real, why not known, since easier shunned?
700   God therefore cannot hurt ye, and be just;
Not just, not God; not feared then, nor obeyed:
Your fear itself of death removes the fear.
Why then was this forbid? Why but to awe,
Why but to keep ye low and ignorant,

---

4. I.e., the orator, convinced of the rightness of his cause, bursts directly into his argument, impatient of the "delay" of an introduction.

705 His worshippers? He knows that in the day
Ye eat thereof, your eyes that seem so clear,
Yet are but dim, shall perfectly be then
Opened and cleared, and ye shall be as gods,
Knowing both good and evil, as they know.
710 That ye should be as gods, since I as man,
Internal man,[5] is but proportion meet,
I, of brute, human; ye, of human, gods.
So ye shall die perhaps, by putting off
Human, to put on gods: death to be wished,
715 Though threatened, which no worse than this can bring.
And what are gods that man may not become
As they, participating° godlike food?   *sharing*
The gods are first, and that advantage use
On our belief, that all from them proceeds.
720 I question it; for this fair Earth I see,
Warmed by the sun, producing every kind,
Them nothing: If they all things,[6] who enclosed
Knowledge of good and evil in this tree,
That whoso eats thereof forthwith attains
725 Wisdom without their leave? And wherein lies
Th' offense, that man should thus attain to know?
What can your knowledge hurt him, or this tree
Impart against his will if all be his?
Or is it envy, and can envy dwell
730 In heavenly breasts? These, these, and many more
Causes import° your need of this fair fruit.   *imply, indicate*
Goddess humane,[7] reach then, and freely taste!"
    He ended, and his words, replete with guile,
Into her heart too easy entrance won:
735 Fixed on the fruit she gazed, which to behold
Might tempt alone, and in her ears the sound
Yet rung of his persuasive words, impregned°   *impregnated*
With reason, to her seeming, and with truth;
Meanwhile the hour of noon drew on, and waked
740 An eager appetite, raised by the smell
So savory of that fruit, which with desire,
Inclinable now grown to touch or taste,
Solicited her longing eye;[8] yet first
Pausing a while, thus to herself she mused:
745   "Great are thy virtues, doubtless, best of fruits,
Though kept from man, and worthy to be admired,
Whose taste, too long forborn, at first essay°   *testing*
Gave elocution to the mute, and taught
The tongue not made for speech to speak thy praise:
750 Thy praise he also who forbids thy use,
Conceals not from us, naming thee the Tree
Of Knowledge, knowledge both of good and evil;
Forbids us then to taste; but his forbidding

5. I.e., internally man.
6. A verb here, probably "producing" from line 721, is understood.
7. "Humane" probably means "kindly" or "gracious," but also suggests the oxymoron "human

Goddess," expressing Satan's prediction of what Eve will become if she eats the fruit.
8. All five of Eve's senses—sight, hearing, smell, taste, and touch—are involved in her temptation.

Commends thee more, while it infers the good
755 By thee communicated, and our want:
For good unknown, sure is not had, or had
And yet unknown, is as not had at all.
In plain[9] then, what forbids he but to know?
Forbids us good, forbids us to be wise!
760 Such prohibitions bind not. But if Death
Bind us with after-bands, what profits then
Our inward freedom? In the day we eat
Of this fair fruit, our doom is, we shall die.
How dies the serpent? He hath eaten and lives,
765 And knows, and speaks, and reasons, and discerns,
Irrational till then. For us alone
Was death invented? Or to us denied
This intellectual food, for beasts reserved?
For beasts it seems: yet that one beast which first
770 Hath tasted, envies not, but brings with joy
The good befallen him, author unsuspect,[1]
Friendly to man, far from deceit or guile.
What fear I then, rather what know to fear
Under this ignorance of good and evil,
775 Of God or death, of law or penalty?
Here grows the cure of all, this fruit divine,
Fair to the eye, inviting to the taste,
Of virtue° to make wise: what hinders then   *power*
To reach, and feed at once both body and mind?"
780   So saying, her rash hand in evil hour,
Forth reaching to the fruit, she plucked, she eat.°   *ate*
Earth felt the wound, and Nature from her seat
Sighing through all her works gave signs of woe,
That all was lost. Back to the thicket slunk
785 The guilty serpent, and well might, for Eve
Intent now wholly on her taste, naught else
Regarded; such delight till then, as seemed,
In fruit she never tasted, whether true
Or fancied so, through expectation high
790 Of knowledge; nor was godhead from her thought.[2]
Greedily she engorged without restraint,
And knew not eating death:[3] satiate at length,
And heightened as with wine, jocund and boon,°   *jovial*
Thus to herself she pleasingly began:
795   "O sovereign, virtuous, precious of all trees
In Paradise! of operation blest
To sapience,[4] hitherto obscured, infamed,°   *defamed*
And thy fair fruit let hang, as to no end
Created; but henceforth my early care,
800 Not without song each morning, and due praise
Shall tend thee, and the fertile burden ease
Of thy full branches offered free to all;

---

9. In plain language.
1. I.e., authority whose testimony does not arouse
suspicion.
2. I.e., she also expected to achieve godhead.
3. I.e., she was eating death and did not know it;

also, she was unaware while she ate death.
4. Wisdom, for the wise and those good of taste,
from the Latin *sapere*, "to be wise," which has its
roots in the verb "to taste."

Till dieted by thee I grow mature
In knowledge, as the gods who all things know;
805 Though others[5] envy what they cannot give:
For had the gift been theirs, it had not here
Thus grown. Experience, next to thee I owe,
Best guide; not following thee I had remained
In ignorance; thou open'st Wisdom's way,
810 And giv'st access, though secret she retire.
And I perhaps am secret;° Heaven is high,   unseen
High and remote to see from thence distinct
Each thing on Earth; and other care perhaps
May have diverted from continual watch
815 Our great Forbidder, safe with all his spies
About him. But to Adam in what sort°   guise
Shall I appear? Shall I to him make known
As yet my change, and give him to partake
Full happiness with me, or rather not,
820 But keep the odds of knowledge in my power
Without copartner? so to add what wants
In female sex, the more to draw his love,
And render me more equal, and perhaps,
A thing not undesirable, sometime
825 Superior: for, inferior, who is free?
This may be well: but what if God have seen
And death ensue? Then I shall be no more,
And Adam, wedded to another Eve,
Shall live with her enjoying, I extinct;
830 A death to think. Confirmed then I resolve,
Adam shall share with me in bliss or woe:
So dear I love him, that with him all deaths
I could endure, without him live no life."
        So saying, from the tree her step she turned,
835 But first low reverence done, as to the power
That dwelt within, whose presence had infused
Into the plant sciental° sap, derived   knowledge-giving
From nectar, drink of gods. Adam the while
Waiting desirous her return, had wove
840 Of choicest flowers a garland to adorn
Her tresses, and her rural labors crown,
As reapers oft are wont their harvest queen.
Great joy he promised to his thoughts, and new
Solace in her return, so long delayed:
845 Yet oft his heart, divine° of something ill,   apprehensive
Misgave him; he the faltering measure[6] felt;
And forth to meet her went, the way she took
That morn when first they parted. By the Tree
Of Knowledge he must pass; there he her met,
850 Scarce from the tree returning; in her hand
A bough of fairest fruit that downy smiled,
New gathered, and ambrosial smell diffused.
To him she hastened, in her face excuse

5. I.e., the other gods; Eve here echoes the lesson   6. I.e., the irregular beat (of his heart).
taught her by the serpent.

Came prologue, and apology to prompt,[7]
855 Which with bland words at will she thus addressed:
  "Hast thou not wondered, Adam, at my stay?
  Thee I have missed, and thought it long, deprived
  Thy presence, agony of love till now
  Not felt, nor shall be twice; for never more
860 Mean I to try, what rash untried I sought,
  The pain of absence from thy sight. But strange
  Hath been the cause, and wonderful to hear:
  This tree is not as we are told, a tree
  Of danger tasted, nor to evil unknown
865 Opening the way, but of divine effect
  To open eyes, and make them gods who taste;
  And hath been tasted such. The serpent wise,
  Or not restrained as we, or not obeying,
  Hath eaten of the fruit, and is become,
870 Not dead, as we are threatened, but thenceforth
  Endued with human voice and human sense,
  Reasoning to admiration,[8] and with me
  Persuasively hath so prevailed, that I
  Have also tasted, and have also found
875 Th' effects to correspond—opener mine eyes
  Dim erst,° dilated spirits, ampler heart, *previously*
  And growing up to godhead; which for thee
  Chiefly I sought, without thee can despise.
  For bliss, as thou hast part, to me is bliss,
880 Tedious, unshared with thee, and odious soon.
  Thou therefore also taste, that equal lot
  May join us, equal joy, as equal love;
  Lest, thou not tasting, different degree[9]
  Disjoin us, and I then too late renounce
885 Deity for thee, when Fate will not permit."
    Thus Eve with countenance blithe her story told;
  But in her cheek distemper flushing glowed.
  On th' other side, Adam, soon as he heard
  The fatal trespass done by Eve, amazed,
890 Astonied[1] stood and blank, while horror chill
  Ran through his veins, and all his joints relaxed;
  From his slack hand the garland wreathed for Eve
  Down dropped, and all the faded roses shed.
  Speechless he stood and pale, till thus at length
895 First to himself he inward silence broke:
    "O fairest of creation, last and best
  Of all God's works, creature in whom excelled
  Whatever can to sight or thought be formed,
  Holy, divine, good, amiable, or sweet!
900 How art thou lost, how on a sudden lost,
  Defaced, deflowered, and now to death devote?° *doomed*
  Rather how hast thou yielded to transgress

---

7. Her excuse, apparent in her expression, is a pro-
logue to her "apology" or formal defense of her
actions.
8. So as to produce admiration.

9. I.e., different rank, since she, as she believes,
has grown "up to godhead" while he has not.
1. Stunned, with a likely pun on "turned to
stone."

The strict forbiddance, how to violate
The sacred fruit forbidden! Some cursèd fraud
905 Of enemy hath beguiled thee, yet unknown,
And me with thee hath ruined, for with thee
Certain my resolution is to die.
How can I live without thee, how forgo
Thy sweet converse and love so dearly joined,
910 To live again in these wild woods forlorn?
Should God create another Eve, and I
Another rib afford, yet loss of thee
Would never from my heart; no, no! I feel
The link of nature draw me: flesh of flesh,
915 Bone of my bone thou art, and from thy state
Mine never shall be parted, bliss or woe."
    So having said, as one from sad dismay
Recomforted, and after thoughts disturbed
Submitting to what seemed remediless,
920 Thus in calm mood his words to Eve he turned:
    "Bold deed thou hast presumed, adventurous Eve
And peril great provoked, who thus hast dared
Had it been only coveting to eye
That sacred fruit, sacred° to abstinence,   *dedicated*
925 Much more to taste it, under ban to touch.
But past who can recall, or done undo?
Not God omnipotent, nor Fate! Yet so
Perhaps thou shalt not die, perhaps the fact°   *deed*
Is not so heinous now, foretasted fruit,
930 Profaned first by the serpent, by him first
Made common and unhallowed ere our taste,
Nor yet on him found deadly; he yet lives,
Lives, as thou saidst, and gains to live as man
Higher degree of life: inducement strong
935 To us, as likely, tasting, to attain
Proportional ascent, which cannot be
But to be gods, or angels, demigods.
Nor can I think that God, Creator wise,
Though threatening, will in earnest so destroy
940 Us his prime creatures, dignified so high,
Set over all his works, which in our fall,
For us created, needs with us must fail,
Dependent made; so God shall uncreate,
Be frustrate, do, undo, and labor lose;
945 Not well conceived of God, who, though his power
Creation could repeat, yet would be loath
Us to abolish, lest the adversary
Triumph and say: 'Fickle their state whom God
Most favors; who can please him long? Me first
950 He ruined, now mankind; whom will he next?'
Matter of scorn, not to be given the foe.
However, I with thee have fixed my lot,
Certain° to undergo like doom: if death   *resolved*
Consort° with thee, death is to me as life;   *keep company*
955 So forcible within my heart I feel

The bond of nature draw me to my own,
My own in thee, for what thou art is mine;
Our state cannot be severed; we are one,
One flesh; to lose thee were to lose myself."
960 So Adam, and thus Eve to him replied:
"O glorious trial of exceeding love,
Illustrious evidence, example high!
Engaging me to emulate; but short
Of thy perfection, how shall I attain,
965 Adam? from whose dear side I boast me sprung,
And gladly of our union hear thee speak,
One heart, one soul in both; whereof good proof
This day affords, declaring thee resolved,
Rather than death or aught than death more dread
970 Shall separate us, linked in love so dear,
To undergo with me one guilt, one crime,
If any be, of tasting this fair fruit;
Whose virtue (for of good still good proceeds,
Direct, or by occasion°) hath presented   indirect
975 This happy trial of thy love, which else
So eminently never had been known.
Were it I thought death menaced would ensue
This my attempt, I would sustain alone
The worst, and not persuade thee, rather die
980 Deserted, than oblige° thee with a fact   involve in guilt
Pernicious to thy peace, chiefly assured
Remarkably so late of thy so true,
So faithful love unequaled; but I feel
Far otherwise th' event°—not death, but life   outcome
985 Augmented, opened eyes, new hopes, new joys,
Taste so divine, that what of sweet before
Hath touched my sense, flat seems to this, and harsh.
On my experience, Adam, freely taste,
And fear of death deliver to the winds."
990 So saying, she embraced him, and for joy
Tenderly wept, much won that he his love
Had so ennobled, as of choice to incur
Divine displeasure for her sake, or death.
In recompense (for such compliance bad
995 Such recompense best merits), from the bough
She gave him of that fair enticing fruit
With liberal hand; he scrupled not to eat,
Against his better knowledge, not deceived,[2]
But fondly° overcome with female charm.   foolishly
1000 Earth trembled from her entrails, as again
In pangs, and Nature gave a second groan,
Sky lowered, and muttering thunder, some sad drops
Wept at completing of the mortal sin
Original; while Adam took no thought,
1005 Eating his fill, nor Eve to iterate
Her former trespass feared, the more to soothe

2. Here Milton follows 1 Timothy 2.14: "And Adam was not deceived, but the woman being deceived was in the transgression."

Him with her loved society; that now
As with new wine intoxicated both,
They swim in mirth, and fancy that they feel
1010 Divinity within them breeding wings
Wherewith to scorn the Earth. But that false fruit
Far other operation first displayed,
Carnal desire inflaming; he on Eve
Began to cast lascivious eyes, she him
1015 As wantonly repaid; in lust they burn,
Till Adam thus 'gan Eve to dalliance move:
    "Eve, now I see thou art exact° of taste,   *discriminating*
And elegant, of sapience no small part,
Since to each meaning savor we apply,
1020 And palate call judicious. I the praise
Yield thee, so well this day thou hast purveyed.°   *provisioned us*
Much pleasure we have lost, while we abstained
From this delightful fruit, nor known till now
True relish, tasting; if such pleasure be
1025 In things to us forbidden, it might be wished,
For this one tree had been forbidden ten.
But come; so well refreshed, now let us play,
As meet is, after such delicious fare;
For never did thy beauty, since the day
1030 I saw thee first and wedded thee, adorned
With all perfections, so enflame my sense
With ardor to enjoy thee, fairer now
Than ever, bounty of this virtuous tree."
    So said he, and forbore not glance or toy°   *caress*
1035 Of amorous intent, well understood
Of° Eve, whose eye darted contagious fire.   *by*
Her hand he seized, and to a shady bank,
Thick overhead with verdant roof embowered
He led her, nothing loath; flowers were the couch,
1040 Pansies, and violets, and asphodel,[3]
And hyacinth—Earth's freshest, softest lap.
There they their fill of love and love's disport
Took largely, of their mutual guilt the seal,
The solace of their sin, till dewy sleep
1045 Oppressed them, wearied with their amorous play.
    Soon as the force of that fallacious fruit,
That with exhilarating vapor bland
About their spirits had played, and inmost powers
Made err, was now exhaled, and grosser sleep
1050 Bred of unkindly° fumes, with conscious dreams   *unnatural*
Encumbered, now had left them, up they rose
As from unrest, and each the other viewing,
Soon found their eyes how opened, and their minds
How darkened. Innocence, that as a veil
1055 Had shadowed them from knowing ill, was gone;
Just confidence, and native righteousness,
And honor from about them, naked left

---

3. A flower conventionally held to be immortal and said to cover the Elysian meadows.

To guilty Shame; he[4] covered, but his robe
Uncovered more. So rose the Danite strong,
1060 Herculean Samson, from the harlot-lap
Of Philistean Dalilah, and waked
Shorn of his strength;[5] they destitute and bare
Of all their virtue. Silent, and in face
Confounded, long they sat, as strucken mute;
1065 Till Adam, though not less than Eve abashed,
At length gave utterance to these words constrained:
"O Eve, in evil hour thou didst give ear
To that false worm,° of whomsoever taught   serpent
To counterfeit man's voice, true in our fall,
1070 False in our promised rising; since our eyes
Opened we find indeed, and find we know
Both good and evil, good lost, and evil got:
Bad fruit of knowledge, if this be to know,
Which leaves us naked thus, of honor void,
1075 Of innocence, of faith, of purity,
Our wonted° ornaments now soiled and stained,   customary
And in our faces evident the signs
Of foul concupiscence;° whence evil store,   lust
Even shame, the last of evils; of the first
1080 Be sure then. How shall I behold the face
Henceforth of God or angel, erst with joy
And rapture so oft beheld? Those heavenly shapes
Will dazzle now this earthly with their blaze
Insufferably bright. O might I here
1085 In solitude live savage, in some glade
Obscured, where highest woods, impenetrable
To star or sunlight, spread their umbrage° broad,   shade
And brown as evening! Cover me, ye pines,
Ye cedars, with innumerable boughs
1090 Hide me, where I may never see them more!
But let us now, as in bad plight, devise
What best may for the present serve to hide
The parts of each from other, that seem most
To shame obnoxious,° and unseemliest seen;   liable
1095 Some tree whose broad smooth leaves together sewed,
And girded on our loins, may cover round
Those middle parts, that this newcomer, Shame,
There sit not, and reproach us as unclean."
So counseled he, and both together went
1100 Into the thickest wood; there soon they chose
The figtree, not that kind for fruit renowned,
But such as at this day, to Indians known,
In Malabar or Deccan[6] spreads her arms
Branching so broad and long, that in the ground
1105 The bended twigs take root, and daughters grow
About the mother tree, a pillared shade

---

4. I.e., Shame.
5. The Philistine Dalilah betrayed her husband, Samson (of the tribe of Dan), by cutting off his hair, the source of his strength, while he slept.

Their story is told in Judges 16. Cf. Milton's "Samson Agonistes," n. 4 (p. 376).
6. Sections of southern India.

High overarched, and echoing walks between;
There oft the Indian herdsman, shunning heat,
Shelters in cool, and tends his pasturing herds
1110   At loopholes cut through thickest shade. Those leaves
They gathered, broad as Amazonian targe,[7]
And with what skill they had, together sewed,
To gird their waist; vain covering, if to hide
Their guilt and dreaded shame! O how unlike
1115   To that first naked glory! Such of late
Columbus found th' American, so girt
With feathered cincture,° naked else and wild   *belt*
Among the trees on isles and woody shores.
Thus fenced, and, as they thought, their shame in part
1120   Covered, but not at rest or ease of mind,
They sat them down to weep; nor only tears
Rained at their eyes, but high winds worse within
Began to rise, high passions, anger, hate,
Mistrust, suspicion, discord, and shook sore
1125   Their inward state of mind, calm region once
And full of peace, now tossed and turbulent:
For Understanding ruled not, and the Will
Heard not her lore, both in subjection now
To sensual Appetite, who, from beneath
1130   Usurping over sovereign Reason, claimed
Superior sway.[8] From thus distempered breast,
Adam, estranged in look and altered style,
Speech intermitted thus to Eve renewed:
    "Would thou hadst hearkened to my words, and stayed
1135   With me, as I besought thee, when that strange
Desire of wandering, this unhappy morn,
I know not whence possessed thee! we had then
Remained still happy, not as now, despoiled
Of all our good, shamed, naked, miserable.
1140   Let none henceforth seek needless cause to approve°   *prove*
The faith they owe;° when earnestly they seek   *own*
Such proof, conclude, they then begin to fail."
    To whom, soon moved with touch of blame, thus Eve:
"What words have passed thy lips, Adam severe?
1145   Imput'st thou that to my default, or will
Of wandering, as thou call'st it, which who knows
But might as ill have happened, thou being by,
Or to thyself perhaps? Hadst thou been there,
Or here th' attempt, thou couldst not have discerned
1150   Fraud in the serpent, speaking as he spake;
No ground of enmity between us known,
Why he should mean me ill, or seek to harm?
Was I to have never parted from thy side?
As good have grown there still a lifeless rib.
1155   Being as I am, why didst not thou, the head,[9]

---

7. The Amazons, mythical female warriors, carried large, crescent-shaped shields called "targes."
8. As a result of the Fall, the higher faculties, Reason and Understanding, are subjected to Appetite and the physical senses.
9. Cf. Corinthians 11.3: "the head of the woman is the man."

Command me absolutely not to go,
Going into such danger, as thou saidst?
Too facile° then, thou didst not much gainsay,   *easy*
Nay, didst permit, approve, and fair dismiss.
1160   Hadst thou been firm and fixed in thy dissent,
Neither had I transgressed, nor thou with me."
        To whom, then first incensed, Adam replied:
"Is this the love, is this the recompense°   *repayment*
Of mine to thee, ingrateful Eve, expressed°   *revealed*
1165   Immutable° when thou were lost, not I,   *constant*
Who might have lived and joyed immortal bliss,
Yet willingly chose rather death with thee?
And am I now upbraided as the cause
Of thy transgressing? not enough severe,
1170   It seems, in thy restraint! What could I more?
I warned thee, I admonished thee, foretold
The danger, and the lurking enemy
That lay in wait: beyond this had been force,
And force upon free will hath here no place.
1175   But confidence then bore thee on, secure
Either to meet no danger, or to find
Matter of glorious trial; and perhaps
I also erred in overmuch admiring
What seemed in thee so perfect, that I thought
1180   No evil durst attempt thee! but I rue
That error now, which is become my crime,
And thou th' accuser. Thus it shall befall
Him who, to worth in women overtrusting,
Lets her will rule; restraint she will not brook,°   *tolerate*
1185   And, left to herself, if evil thence ensue,
She first his weak indulgence will accuse."
        Thus they in mutual accusation spent
The fruitless hours, but neither self-condemning;
And of their vain contèst appeared no end.
1660–65   1667, 1674

To the Lord General Cromwell[1]

Cromwell, our chief of men, who through a cloud,
        Not of war only, but detractions rude,
        Guided by faith and matchless fortitude,
        To peace and truth thy glorious way hast ploughed,[2]
5   And on the neck[3] of crownèd Fortune proud
        Hast reared God's trophies, and His work pursued,
        While Darwen stream, with blood of Scots imbrued,
        And Dunbar field, resounds thy praises loud,
And Worcester's laureate wreath: yet much remains
10   To conquer still; peace hath her victories

---

1. Oliver Cromwell, successor to Sir Thomas Fairfax as commander in chief of the Parliamentary armies.
2. In 1651, Parliament issued a coin bearing the words "Truth and Peace," to express confidence in the results of Cromwell's victories over the Scots at Preston on the banks of the "Darwen" (line 7) and at "Dunbar" (line 8) and "Worcester" (line 9).
3. Charles I was beheaded in 1649.

No less renowned than war: new foes arise,
  Threatening to bind our souls with secular chains.[4]
  Help us to save free conscience from the paw
  Of hireling wolves, whose gospel is their maw.[5]

1652   1694

SIR JOHN SUCKLING
1609–1642

Song[1]

Why so pale and wan, fond° lover?   *foolish*
  Prithee,° why so pale?   *pray thee*
Will, when looking well can't move her,
  Looking ill prevail?
5   Prithee, why so pale?

Why so dull and mute, young sinner?
  Prithee, why so mute?
Will, when speaking well can't win her,
  Saying nothing do 't?
10   Prithee, why so mute?

Quit, quit, for shame; this will not move,
  This cannot take her.
If of herself she will not love,
  Nothing can make her:
15   The devil take her!

                                                                       1638

Sonnet II[2]

Of thee, kind boy, I ask no red and white,[3]
  To make up my delight;
  No odd becoming graces,
Black eyes, or little know-not-whats in faces;
5 Make me but mad enough, give me good store
Of love for her I count;
  I ask no more,
'Tis love in love that makes the sport.

---

4. A possible reference to the clergy who in 1652 asked Parliament to establish the English Church on broad Protestant principles but with a State-salaried and State-controlled ministry.
5. Indicating a voracious appetite; see Christ's warning to "[b]eware of false prophets, which come to you in sheep's clothing, but inwardly they are ravening wolves" (Matthew 7.15).
1. First printed in Suckling's play *Aglaura* (1638). Orsames, a friend to the prince (Thersames), sings it upon request, and then claims it is "a little fool-ish counsell (Madam) I gave a friend of mine foure or five yeares agoe" (4.2). It was evidently popular, occurring in at least five musical settings, with the first probably written by Henry Lawes for the first performance of the play in 1637.
2. The term "sonnet" was formerly applied to any short love lyric.
3. The colors conventionally used to depict female beauty in love poetry (in the Petrarchan tradition); "kind boy": Cupid, as god of love.

There's no such thing as that we beauty call,
10   It is mere cozenage° all;   *fraud*
    For though some, long ago,
Liked certain colors mingled so and so,[4]
That doth not tie me now from choosing new;
If I a fancy take
15   To black and blue,
That fancy doth it beauty make.

'Tis not the meat, but 'tis the appetite
    Makes eating a delight;
    And if I like one dish
20   More than another, that a pheasant is;
What in our watches, that in us is found:
So to the height and nick°   *critical point*
    We up be wound,
No matter by what hand or trick.

                              1646

Upon My Lady Carlisle's Walking in Hampton Court Garden

Dialogue[5]

T.C.   J.S.

Thom.

Didst thou not find the place inspired,
And flowers, as if they had desired
No other sun, start from their beds,
And for a sight steal out their heads?
5   Heardst thou not music when she talked?
And didst not find that as she walked
She threw rare perfumes all about,
Such as bean-blossoms newly out,
Or chafed spices give?—

J.S.

10   I must confess those perfumes, Tom,
I did not smell; nor found that from
Her passing by ought sprung up new.
The flowers had all their birth from you;
For I passed o'er the self-same walk
15   And did not find one single stalk
Of anything that was to bring
This unknown after-after-spring.

---

4. I.e., the "red and white" of line 1.
5. Lucy Hay, countess of Carlisle (1599–1660), was a patron of many poets. The "T.C." or "Thom" of this dialogue is the poet Thomas Carew (1598?–1639?; see pp. 348–52), who wrote two poems to Hay; "J.S." is a figure for John Suckling himself.

Thom.

Dull and insensible, couldst see
A thing so near a deity
20 Move up and down, and feel no change?

J.S.

None, and so great, were alike strange;
I had my thoughts, but not your way.
All are not born, sir, to the bay.[6]
Alas! Tom, I am flesh and blood,
25 And was consulting how I could
In spite of masks and hoods descry°   *reveal*
The parts denied unto the eye.
I was undoing all she wore,
And had she walked but one turn more,
30 Eve in her first state had not been
More naked or more plainly seen.

Thom.

'Twas well for thee she left the place;
There is great danger in that face.
But hadst thou viewed her leg and thigh,
35 And upon that discovery
Searched after parts that are more dear
(As fancy seldom stops so near),
No time or age had ever seen
So lost a thing as thou hadst been.

1646

A Ballad upon a Wedding[7]

I tell thee, Dick,[8] where I have been,
Where I the rarest things have seen,
   Oh, things without compare!
Such sights again cannot be found
5 In any place on English ground,
   Be it at wake° or fair.   *festival*

At Charing Cross,[9] hard by the way
Where we (thou know'st) do sell our hay,

---

6. A crown of bay (or laurel) leaves was the traditional recognition of poetic achievement.
7. This poem parodies the "epithalamion," a poem written to celebrate a marriage, the Greek name of which conveys that it was sung on the threshold of the bridal chamber. The genre, as practiced by the Latin poets, characteristically includes the invocation to the Muses (sources of artistic inspiration), the bringing home of the bride, the singing and dancing at the wedding party, and the preparations for the wedding night. The first English example was written by Sir Philip Sidney (1554–1586; see pp. 188–99) in about

1580, and Edmund Spenser (ca. 1552–1599; see pp. 147–85) published perhaps the most well-known instance of the form in 1595.
8. A short form of the name Richard; a generic name for a man. The names used below (in lines 22–24) are all conventional or type names for men. "Bridget" and "Nell" are conventional peasant names for women (line 132).
9. A busy center in London located near the Haymarket; originally the site of a stone cross erected by King Edward I (1239–1307) in memory of his queen, Eleanor.

There is a house with stairs;
10 And there did I see coming down
Such folk as are not in our town,
      Forty, at least, in pairs.

Amongst the rest, one pest'lent[1] fine
(His beard no bigger, though, than thine)
15   Walked on before the rest.
Our landlord looks like nothing to him;
The king (God bless him!), 'twould undo him
      Should he go still° so dressed.   *always*

At course-a-park,[2] without all doubt,
20 He should have first been taken out
      By all the maids i' th' town,
Though lusty Roger there had been,
Or little George upon the Green,
      Or Vincent of the Crown.

25 But wot° you what? the youth was going   *know*
To make an end of all his wooing;
      The parson for him stayed.
Yet by his leave, for all his haste,
He did not so much wish all past,
30   Perchance, as did the maid.

The maid (and thereby hangs a tale),
For such a maid no Whitsun-ale[3]
      Could ever yet produce;
No grape, that's kindly[4] ripe, could be
35 So round, so plump, so soft as she,
      Nor half so full of juice.

Her finger was so small the ring
Would not stay on, which they did bring;
      It was too wide a peck:[5]
40 And to say truth (for out it must),
It looked like the great collar (just)
      About our young colt's neck.

Her feet beneath her petticoat,
Like little mice, stole in and out,
45   As if they feared the light;
But oh, she dances such a way,
No sun upon an Easter day
      Is half so fine a sight!

He would have kissed her once or twice,
50 But she would not, she was so nice,°   *delicate*

1. Exceptionally (deadly) fine.
2. A rural game in which a girl chooses a boy to chase her.
3. A church festival, or "ale," at which much ale was drunk; held at Whitsuntide.
4. Naturally; i.e., vine-ripened.
5. A measure of capacity.

She would not do 't in sight;
And then she looked as who should say,
   "I will do what I list° today;   *desire*
And you shall do 't at night."

55 Her cheeks so rare a white was on,
No daisy makes comparison
   (Who sees them is undone),
For streaks of red were mingled there,
Such as are on a Catherine pear[6]
60   (The side that's next the sun).

Her lips were red, and one was thin
Compared to that was next her chin
   (Some bee had stung it newly);
But, Dick, her eyes so guard her face
65 I durst no more upon them gaze
   Than on the sun in July.

Her mouth so small, when she does speak,
Thou 'dst swear her teeth her words did break,
   That they might passage get;
70 But she so handled still the matter,
They came as good as ours, or better,
   And are not spent a whit.[7]

If wishing should be any sin,
The parson himself had guilty been
75   (She looked that day so purely);
And did the youth so oft the feat
At night, as some did in conceit,°   *imagination*
   It would have spoiled him, surely.

Passion o' me, how I run on![8]
80 There's that that would be thought upon,
   I trow,° besides the bride.   *suppose*
The business of the kitchen's great,
For it is fit that man should eat,
   Nor was it there denied.

85 Just in the nick the cook knocked thrice,
And all the waiters in a trice
   His summons did obey;
Each serving-man, with dish in hand,
Marched boldly up, like our trained band,°   *militia*
90   Presented, and away.

When all the meat was on the table,
What man of knife or teeth was able

---

6. A small variety of pear.
7. To a very small extent.
8. In the 1646 edition this stanza, with the first three lines following the last three, appears after line 96. The order preferred here is that of the 1648 and subsequent editions.

To stay to be entreated?[9]
And this the very reason was,
95 Before the parson could say grace,
The company was seated.

Now hats fly off, and youths carouse;
Healths° first go round, and then the house;   *toasts*
The bride's came thick and thick:
100 And when 'twas named another's health,
Perhaps he made it hers by stealth;
And who could help it, Dick?

O' th' sudden up they rise and dance;
Then sit again and sigh and glance;
105   Then dance again and kiss.
Thus several ways the time did pass,
Till every woman wished her place,
And every man wished his!

By this time all were stolen aside
110 To counsel and undress the bride,
But that he must not know;
But yet 'twas thought he guessed her mind,
And did not mean to stay behind
Above an hour or so.

115 When in he came, Dick, there she lay
Like new-fallen snow melting away
('Twas time, I trow,° to part);   *believe*
Kisses were now the only stay,
Which soon she gave, as who would say,
120   "God b' w' ye,[1] with all my heart."

But just as heaven would have, to cross it,
In came the bridesmaids with the posset.[2]
The bridegroom ate in spite,
For had he left the women to 't,
125 It would have cost two hours to do 't,
Which were too much that night.

At length the candle's out, and now
All that they had not done, they do.
What that is, who can tell?
130 But I believe it was no more
Than thou and I have done before
With Bridget and with Nell.

ca. 1641   1646

---

9. I.e., what man able to eat could wait to be asked to sit down?
1. A contraction for "God be with ye," pro-
nounced in two syllables.
2. A hot drink of spiced milk curdled with ale or wine.

Out upon It!

Out upon it! I have loved
　Three whole days together;
And am like to love three more,
　If it prove fair weather.

5　Time shall molt away his wings,
　Ere he shall discover
In the whole wide world again
　Such a constant lover.

But the spite on 't is, no praise
10　Is due at all to me;
Love with me had made no stays[3]
　Had it any been but she.

Had it any been but she,
　And that very face,
15　There had been at least ere this
　A dozen dozen in her place.

1659

ANNE BRADSTREET

ca. 1612–1672

In Honor of that High and Mighty Princess, Queen Elizabeth, of Most Happy Memory[1]

The Proem

Although, great Queen, thou now in silence lie,
Yet thy loud herald fame doth to the sky
Thy wondrous worth proclaim in every clime,°　　　*climate, region*
And so has vowed, whilst there is world, or time;
5　So great's thy glory, and thine excellence,
The sound thereof raps° every humane sense;　　　*enraptures*
That men account it no impiety,
To say, thou wert a fleshly deity.
Thousands bring off'rings, (though out of date)
10　Thy world of honors to accumulate,
'Mongst hundred hecatombs of roaring[2] verse,
Mine bleating[3] stands before thy royal herse:°　　　*grave*
Thou never didst, nor canst thou now disdain,
T' accept the tribute of a loyal brain;
15　Thy clemency did yerst° esteem as much　　　*formerly*
The acclamations of the poor, as rich;

3. I.e., found no support.
1. Queen Elizabeth I (1533–1603), who ruled England for forty-four years, died in 1603, before Bradstreet was born.
2. Loud; "hecatombs": a great number of things presented as an offering (originally from the Greek, the sacrifice of one hundred oxen).
3. Crying of a sheep, goat, or calf, used contemptuously for a human utterance.

Which makes me deem,° my rudeness is no wrong,   *think*
Though I resound thy greatness 'mongst the throng.

The Poem

No phoenix pen, nor Spenser's poetry,
20   No Speed's, nor Camden's learned history,[4]
Eliza's° works, wars, praise, can e're compact,°   *Elizabeth's / compose*
The world's the theater where she did act;
No memories, nor volumes can contain,
The nine Olimp'ades[5] of her happy reign,
25   Who was so good, so just, so learned, so wise,
From all the kings on earth she won the prize;
Nor say I more than duly is her due,
Millions will testify that this is true;
She hath wiped off th' aspersion of her sex,
30   That women wisdom lack to play the Rex;°   *King*
Spain's monarch says not so; nor yet his host,°   *followers*
She taught them better manners to their cost.[6]
The Salique law[7] had not in force now been,
If France had ever hoped for such a Queen;
35   But can you Doctors[8] now this point dispute,
She's argument enough to make you mute;
Since first the sun did run, his ne'er runned° race,   *never finished*
And earth had twice a year, a new-old face;[9]
Since time was time, and man unmanly man,[1]
40   Come show me such a phoenix[2] if you can;
Was ever people better ruled than hers?
Was ever land more happy, freed from stirs?°   *public disturbances*
Did ever wealth in England so abound?
Her victories in foreign coasts resound?
45   Ships more invincible then Spain's, her foe
She racked, she sacked, she sunk his Armadoe;°   *Armada*
Her stately troops advanced to Lisbon's wall,
Don Anthony in's right for to install;[3]

4. William Camden (1551–1623) wrote *Annales or The History of the Most Renowned and Victorious Princess Elizabeth* (translated from the Latin by R. Norton, 1630). The "Phoenix" here refers to Sir Philip Sidney (1554–1586); Edmund Spenser (ca. 1552–1599) wrote *The Faerie Queene* (1590, 1596), the title of which refers to Queen Elizabeth. John Speed (1552–1629) wrote *Historie of Great Britaine under the Conquests of the Romans, Saxons, Danes and Normans from Julius Caesar to our most gracious Soveraign King James* (1611).
5. Olympiads: periods of four years reckoned from one celebration of the Olympics to the next, by which the ancient Greeks computed time. The version of this poem published in 1678 has "'leven" in place of "nine"; eleven corresponds to Elizabeth's forty-four-year reign, while the meaning of nine is unclear.
6. Spain's monarch was Philip II (1527–1598); his great naval fleet, the Spanish Armada, was defeated by the British naval forces in 1588.
7. A much-debated law excluding females from succession to the French crown.
8. Learned men, or more specifically, men proficient in the knowledge of law.

9. A reference to the seasonal changes of spring and fall, at which times the earth dons a "new" face, though "old" because recurring annually.
1. Time became measurable with the creation of day and night, and distinct from eternity when God made humans mortal as punishment for the sin of Adam and Eve; as a result of the Fall, Adam lost his true manly nature, thus becoming "unmanly man."
2. A legendary bird, the only one of its kind. It is represented as living five hundred years in the Arabian desert before setting itself on fire, then rising anew from its own ashes; the Phoenix was an emblem used to represent Queen Elizabeth (who was often called the "Virgin Queen") because of its associations with the Virgin Mary (the bird is both virginal and fertile).
3. Don Antonio of Crato (1531–1595), a claimant to the throne of Portugal, was used by Elizabeth to cause trouble for King Philip II of Spain. In 1589 he went on an expedition to coastal Portugal and Spain with Sir Francis Drake (1546–1596) and Sir John Norris (1547–1597), their intention being to provoke rebellion in Portugal against the rule of Philip. The expedition was a failure.

She frankly helpe'd Frank's (brave) distressèd King,[4]
50 The states united now her fame do sing;[5]
She their protectrix was, they well do know,
Unto our dread virago,[6] what they owe;
Her nobles sacrificed their noble blood,
Nor men, nor coin she spared, to do them good;
55 The rude untamed Irish she did quell,
And Tiron[7] bound, before her picture fell.
Had ever Prince such counsellors as she?
Her self Minerva,[8] caused them so to be;
Such soldiers, and such captains never seen,
60 As were the subjects of our (Pallas) Queen;
Her sea-men through all straights[9] the world did round,
Terra incognitae[1] might know her sound;
Her Drake came laded home with Spanish gold,[2]
Her Essex took Cades, their Herculean hold.[3]
65 But time would fail me, so my wit would too,
To tell of half she did, or she could do;
Semiramis[4] to her is but obscure,
More infamy than fame she did procure;
She placed her glory but on Babel's walls,
70 World's wonder for a time, but yet it falls;
Fierce Tomris[5] (Cyrus' heads-man, Sythians' Queen)
Had put her harness off, had she but seen
Our Amazon i'th' camp at Tilberry:[6]
(Judging all valor, and all majesty)
75 Within that Princess to have residence,
And prostrate yielded to her excellence:
Dido[7] first foundress of proud Carthage walls,
(Who living consummates her funerals)
A great Eliza, but compared with ours,
80 How vanisheth her glory, wealth, and powers;

4. From 1589 to 1590 Elizabeth sent troops and £300,000 to Henry IV, the Huguenot king of France, first against the Catholic League, which raised a puppet king against him, and later against Spain.
5. A reference to the provinces of the Low Countries (the representative assembly of the Netherlands was called the States General). Elizabeth aided the Protestant Netherlands in their wars against Spain.
6. A vigorous, heroic woman; a female warrior.
7. Hugh O'Neill, second earl of Tyrone (ca. 1540–1616) and an Irish chieftain, intrigued with both the Spanish and the Scots against England. He was defeated by Lord Mountjoy and the English forces in 1601.
8. The Roman goddess of war, wisdom, chastity, the arts, and justice; also called Pallas Athena (Greek).
9. Narrow waterways connecting two large bodies of water; may also mean difficulties.
1. "Unknown lands" (Latin).
2. In his expedition of 1577–80, Drake plundered Spanish settlements along the coast of Chile and Peru, and returned with spoils of immense value.
3. Robert Devereux (1566–1601), second earl of Essex, captured Cádiz, a Spanish port, in 1596;

Hercules was a mythological hero with superhuman strength; thus "Herculean" suggests that the port was very strong or well fortified.
4. Late-ninth-century queen of Assyria famed for her beauty, her military prowess, and her promiscuity; she ruled after the death of her husband Ninus (in whose murder she may have had a hand); she reputedly built Babylon.
5. First-century queen of the Massagetae, a Scythian tribe, defeated Cyrus the Great of Persia; she had his head cut off and thrown into a pot of blood, because, she said, he thirsted for it.
6. A fortification on the north bank of the Thames River, near London. In August 1588 the English army was assembled there, in readiness to repulse an expected Spanish invasion. Queen Elizabeth reviewed the troops and gave a celebrated address. She reportedly wore a silver breastplate over her white dress and carried a truncheon; the Amazons were a legendary tribe of women warriors.
7. Legendary queen of Carthage, who burned herself on a funeral pyre, either to escape marriage to Iarbas, a local king, or, according to Virgil, because she had been abandoned by Aeneas, who left her to pursue his own destiny, the founding of Rome.

Proud profuse Cleopatra,[8] whose wrong name,
Instead of glory proved her country's shame:
Of her what worth in story's to be seen,
But that she was a rich Egyptian Queen;
85   Zenobia,[9] potent empress of the East,
And of all these without compare the best;
(Whom none but great Aurelius could quell)
Yet for our Queen is no fit parallel:
She was a phoenix Queen, so shall she be,
90   Her ashes not revived more phoenix she;
Her personal perfections, who would tell,
Must dip his pen i'th' Heliconian well;[1]
Which I may not, my pride doth but aspire,
To read what others write, and then admire.
95   Now say, have women worth, or have they none?
Or had they some, but with our Queen is't gone?
Nay Masculines, you have thus taxed us long,
But she though dead, will vindicate our wrong.
Let such, as say our sex is void of reason,
100   Know 'tis a slander now, but once was treason.
But happy England, which had such a Queen,
O happy, happy, had those days still been,
But happiness lies in a higher sphere;
Then wonder not, Eliza moves not here.
105   Full fraught with honor, riches, and with days,
She set, she set, like Titan° in his rays.   *the sun*
No more shall rise or set such glorious sun
Until the heavens' great revolution:[2]
If then new things, their old form must retain,
110   Eliza shall rule Albion° once again.   *England*

Her Epitaph

Here sleeps the Queen, this is the royal bed.
O'th' damask Rose, sprung from the white and red,[3]
Whose sweet perfume fills the all-filling air,
This Rose is withered, once so lovely fair,
115   *On neither tree did grow such Rose before,*
The greater was our gain, our loss the more.

---

8. First-century Egyptian queen and mistress of Julius Caesar, she married Marc Antony and the two were defeated by Octavius at the battle of Actium; she killed herself rather than be paraded in triumph by Octavius. Her story is told in Shakespeare's play *Antony and Cleopatra*. "Cleopatra" means "glory to the father" in Greek; Bradstreet evidently takes Cleopatra's name as referring by metaphorical extension to her "fatherland."
9. (d. after A.D. 274); queen of Palmyra, a city-state in Syria. After the death of her husband, Odaenathus, whom she may have murdered, she embarked on wars of expansion and called herself "Augusta" and the "Empress of the East"; she distinguished herself in warfare but was finally defeated by the Roman Emperor Aurelian in 273.
1. The Hippocrene Spring on Mount Helicon was the haunt of the Muses, the nine Greek goddesses who were believed to be the sources of inspiration for the arts.
2. A reference to the Apocalypse, after which a "new heaven and a new earth" (Revelation 21.1), eternal and idyllic, will be established.
3. Queen Elizabeth I was the daughter of Henry VIII, whose father was Henry VII, of the House of Lancaster, and whose mother was Elizabeth, daughter of Edward IV, of the house of York. These two houses, whose symbols were the red rose and the white rose respectively, warred upon each other for many years. The "Damask Rose," a pink or variegated red-and-white rose, is here used to represent the merging of the two houses in the person of Elizabeth.

Another

> Here lies the pride of Queens, pattern of Kings,
> So blaze it fame, here's feathers for thy wings,
> Here lies the envied, yet unparralelled Prince
> 120 Whose living virtues speak (though dead long since)
> If many worlds, as that fantastic framed,
> In every one, be her great glory famed.

1643

The Prologue[4]

1

To sing of wars, of captains, and of kings,
Of cities founded, common-wealths begun,
For my mean° pen, are too superior things,   *inferior*
And how they all, or each, their dates have run
5 Let poets, and historians set these forth,
My obscure verse shall not so dim their worth.

2

But when my wond'ring eyes, and envious heart,
Great Bartas'[5] sugared lines do but read o'er,
Fool, I do grudge the Muses[6] did not part°   *divide*
10 'Twixt him and me that over-fluent store;
A Bartas can do what a Bartas will,
But simple I, according to my skill.

3

From school-boys tongue, no rhetoric[7] we expect,
Nor yet a sweet consort,° from broken strings,   *concert, harmony*
15 Nor perfect beauty, where's a main defect;
My foolish, broken, blemished Muse so sings;
And this to mend, alas, no art is able,
'Cause nature made it so irreparable.

4

Nor can I, like that fluent sweet-tongued Greek[8]
20 Who lisped at first, speak afterwards more plain.
By art, he gladly found what he did seek,
A full requital of his striving pain:
Art can do much, but this maxim's most sure.
A weak or wounded brain admits no cure.

---

4. This poem appeared at the beginning of Bradstreet's first volume of poetry, *The Tenth Muse Lately Sprung Up in America* (1650); this volume was evidently published without Bradstreet's knowledge.
5. Guillaume du Bartas (1544–1590), a French poet and author of *La Semaine* (1578), an epic poem on Christian history; his works greatly influenced Bradstreet.
6. The nine Greek goddesses believed to be a source of inspiration for the arts.
7. Skill in using eloquent and persuasive language.
8. Demosthenes (384–322 B.C.), Greek orator, who was said to have overcome a speech defect.

5

25 I am obnoxious° to each carping tongue,   *vulnerable*
    Who says my hand a needle better fits;
    A poet's pen all scorn I should thus wrong;
    For such despite° they cast on female wits: *scorn*
    If what I do prove well, it won't advance,
30 They'll say it's stolen, or else it was by chance.

6

    But sure the antick[9] Greeks were far more mild,
    Else of our sex, why feigned° they those nine,[1]   *invented*
    And poesy made Calliope's owne child?[2]
    So 'mongst the rest, they placed the arts divine:
35 But this weak knot[3] they will full soon untie,
    The Greeks did nought, but play the fool and lie.

7

    Let Greeks be Greeks, and women what they are,
    Men have precedency,[4] and still excel;
    It is but vain, unjustly to wage war;
40 Men can do best, and women know it well;
    Preeminence in each and all is yours,
    Yet grant some small acknowledgement of ours.

8

    And oh, ye high flown quills[5] that soar the skies,
    And ever with your prey, still catch your praise,
45 If e'er you deign° these lowly lines your eyes,   *think fit for*
    Give wholesome parsley wreath, I ask no bays:[6]
    This mean and unrefinèd stuff of mine,
    Will make your glistering gold but more to shine.

                                                              1650

Before the Birth of One of Her Children

    All things within this fading world hath end,
    Adversity doth still our joys attend;
    No ties so strong, no friends so dear and sweet,
    But with death's parting blow is sure to meet.
5   The sentence past is most irrevocable,[7]
    A common thing, yet oh inevitable;
    How soon, my dear,[8] death may my steps attend,

---

9. Ancient, but also absurd, bizarre.
1. I.e., the nine Muses.
2. Calliope was the Muse of heroic poetry.
3. I.e., this argument for women's right to compose poetry; "they" refers to those who disapprove of women writing poetry; the last line of the stanza is what "they" might say to refute the argument made by the speaker in the first four lines of the stanza.
4. Superiority in rank or estimation; also, priority

in time or succession.
5. Feathers, poetic for wings; also, pens.
6. Leaves of the bay tree, woven into a wreath to reward a poet; hence, the fame or repute gained by poetic achievement.
7. The sin of Adam and Eve brought the "sentence" of death to humans.
8. The poet addresses her husband; death due to complications in childbirth was common at this time.

How soon't may be thy lot to lose thy friend;
We both are ignorant, yet love bids me
10 These farewell lines to recommend to thee,
That when that knot's untied[9] that made us one,
I may seem thine, who in effect am none.
And if I see not half my days that's due,[1]
What nature would, God grant to yours and you;
15 The many faults that well you know I have,
Let be interr'd in my oblivion's[2] grave;
If any worth or virtue were in me,
Let that live freshly in thy memory,
And when thou feel'st no grief, as I no harms,
20 Yet love thy dead, who long lay in thine arms:
And when thy loss shall be repaid with gains,
Look to my little babes, my dear remains.
And if thou love thy self, or loved'st me,
These O protect from step-dame's injury.
25 And if chance to thine eyes shall bring this verse,
With some sad sighs honor my absent Hearse;°   *corpse*
And kiss this paper for thy love's dear sake,
Who with salt tears this last farewell did take.

1678

To My Dear and Loving Husband

If ever two were one, then surely we.
If ever man were loved by wife, then thee;
If ever wife was happy in a man,
Compare with me ye women if you can.
5 I prize thy love more than whole mines of gold,
Or all the riches that the East doth hold.
My love is such that rivers cannot quench,
Nor ought but love from thee give recompense.
Thy love is such I can no way repay;
10 The heavens reward thee manifold, I pray.
Then while we live, in love let's so persever,
That when we live no more we may live ever.

1678

The Author to Her Book[3]

Thou ill-formed offspring of my feeble brain,
Who after birth didst by my side remain,
Till snatched from thence by friends, less wise than true,
Who thee abroad, exposed to public view,
5 Made thee in rags, halting to th' press to trudge,
Where errors were not lessened (all may judge).
At thy return my blushing was not small,

---

9. I.e., the "knot" of marriage, "untied" by death.
1. I.e., she fears that she may die before she reaches the age of thirty-five, half of the seventy years traditionally seen as humankind's allotment.
2. Some editors emend to "oblivious."
3. Bradstreet is thought to have written this poem in 1666, when a second edition was contemplated.

My rambling brat (in print) should mother call,
I cast thee by as one unfit for light,
10 The visage was so irksome in my sight;
Yet being mine own, at length affection would
Thy blemishes amend, if so I could.
I washed thy face, but more defects I saw,
And rubbing off a spot still made a flaw.
15 I stretched thy joints to make thee even feet,[4]
Yet still thou run'st more hobbling than is meet;
In better dress to trim thee was my mind,
But nought save homespun cloth i' th' house I find.
In this array 'mongst vulgars[5] may'st thou roam.
20 In critic's hands beware thou dost not come,
And take thy way where yet thou art not known;
If for thy father asked, say thou hadst none;
And for thy mother, she alas is poor,
Which caused her thus to send thee out of door.

1678

A Letter to Her Husband, Absent upon Public Employment[6]

My head, my heart, mine eyes, my life, nay, more,
My joy, my magazine° of earthly store,   *storehouse*
If two be one, as surely thou and I,
How stayest thou there, whilst I at Ipswich[7] lie?
5 So many steps, head[8] from the heart to sever,
If but a neck, soon should we be together.
I, like the Earth this season, mourn in black,
My Sun is gone so far in's zodiac,
Whom whilst I 'joyed, nor storms, nor frost I felt,
10 His warmth such frigid colds did cause to melt.
My chillèd limbs now numbèd lie forlorn;
Return; return, sweet Sol, from Capricorn;[9]
In this dead time, alas, what can I more
Than view those fruits[1] which through thy heat I bore?
15 Which sweet contentment yield me for a space,
True living pictures of their father's face.
O strange effect! now thou art southward[2] gone,
I weary grow the tedious day so long;
But when thou northward to me shalt return,
20 I wish my Sun may never set, but burn
Within the Cancer[3] of my glowing breast,
The welcome house of him my dearest guest.
Where ever, ever stay, and go not thence,
Till nature's sad decree shall call thee hence;

---

4. I.e., metrical feet; to smooth out the lines.
5. Common people.
6. Simon Bradstreet was in Boston as a member of the General Court, which was working to combine several individual colonies into the United Colonies of New England.
7. Ipswich, Massachusetts, is north of Boston.
8. Perhaps including an allusion to the Biblical idea that "the head of the woman is the man" (1 Corinthians 11.3).
9. Capricorn, the tenth sign of the zodiac, represents winter; "Sol": sun.
1. Their children.
2. Toward Boston.
3. Cancer, the fourth sign of the zodiac, represents summer.

25 Flesh of thy flesh, bone of thy bone,[4]
    I here, thou there, yet both but one.

1678

Here Follows Some Verses upon the Burning of Our House July 10th, 1666

Copied Out of a Loose Paper

    In silent night when rest I took
    For sorrow near I did not look
    I wakened was with thund'ring noise
    And piteous shrieks of dreadful voice.
5 That fearful sound of "Fire!" and "Fire!"
    Let no man know is my desire.[5]
    I, starting up, the light did spy,
    And to my God my heart did cry
    To strengthen me in my distress
10 And not to leave me succorless.°   *without aid*
    Then, coming out, beheld a space[6]
    The flame consume my dwelling place.
    And when I could no longer look,
    I blest His name that gave and took,[7]
15 That laid my goods now in the dust.
    Yea, so it was, and so 'twas just.
    It was His own, it was not mine,
    Far be it that I should repine;°   *complain*
    He might of all justly bereft
20 But yet sufficient for us left.
    When by the ruins oft I past
    My sorrowing eyes aside did cast,
    And here and there the places spy
    Where oft I sat and long did lie:
25 Here stood that trunk, and there that chest,
    There lay that store I counted best.
    My pleasant things in ashes lie,
    And them behold no more shall I.
    Under thy roof no guest shall sit,
30 Nor at thy table eat a bit.
    No pleasant tale shall e'er be told,
    Nor things recounted done of old.
    No candle e'er shall shine in thee,
    Nor bridegroom's voice e'er heard shall be.
35 In silence ever shall thou lie,
    Adieu, Adieu, all's vanity.
    Then straight I 'gin my heart to chide,
    And did thy wealth on earth abide?
    Didst fix thy hope on mold'ring dust?
40 The arm of flesh didst make thy trust?

---

4. After God created Eve from Adam's rib, Adam said, "This is now bone of my bones, and flesh of my flesh" (Genesis 2.23).
5. I.e., I desire that no man know that "fearful sound."
6. I.e., for a time.
7. "The Lord gave, and the Lord hath taken away; blessed be the name of the Lord" (Job 1.21).

Raise up thy thoughts above the sky
That dunghill mists away may fly.
Thou hast an house on high erect,
Framed by that mighty Architect,
45 With glory richly furnished,
Stands permanent though this be fled.
It's purchasèd and paid for too
By Him[8] who hath enough to do.
A price so vast as is unknown
50 Yet by His gift is made thine own;
There's wealth enough, I need no more,
Farewell, my pelf,[9] farewell my store.
The world no longer let me love,
My hope and treasure lies above.

1867

RICHARD CRASHAW
1613–1649

On the Baptized Ethiopian[1]

Let it no longer be a forlorn hope
    To wash[2] an Ethiope;
He's washed, his gloomy skin a peaceful shade
    For his white soul is made,
5 And now, I doubt not, the Eternal Dove[3]
    A black-faced house will love.

1646

To the Infant Martyrs[4]

Go, smiling souls, your new-built cages[5] break,
In heaven you'll learn to sing, ere here to speak,
Nor let the milky fonts[6] that bathe your thirst
    Be your delay;

8. I.e., Christ, whose death is said to pay for the sins of Adam and Eve.
9. Possessions, usually in the sense of being falsely gained.
1. Acts 8.26–39 tells how an Ethiopian eunuch of great authority under Queen Candace was converted and baptized by Philip the Evangelist.
    A follower of George Herbert, Crashaw entitled his second volume of poetry *Steps to the Temple* as a tribute to Herbert (who published *The Temple* in 1633). These religious poems were paired with secular poems (entitled *The Delights of the Muses*) in a combined volume, published in 1646. Thirty-two of Crashaw's already published religious poems also appeared in the posthumous volume *Carmen Deo Nostro* of 1652.

2. I.e., baptize. Perhaps an allusion to the phrase "washing an Ethiope white," used as an expression for an impossible task.
3. I.e., the Holy Spirit; the spirit of God descends "like a dove" on Christ during his baptism (Matthew 3.16).
4. The Holy Innocents, all the children of Bethlehem of two years and under, who were slain by Herod in an effort to destroy the one who, according to prophecy, would become the ruler of Israel, i.e., Jesus (Matthew 2.16).
5. I.e., the bodies that confined them to an earthly existence.
6. "Fonts": receptacles used in the sacrament of baptism; i.e., a reference both to baptism and to mother's milk.

5   The place that calls you hence is, at the worst,
                Milk all the way.[7]

                                      1646

Upon the Infant Martyrs

To see both blended in one flood,
The mothers' milk, the children's blood,
Make me doubt° if heaven will gather   *wonder*
Roses hence, or lilies rather.

                                        1646

A Hymn to the Name and Honor of the Admirable Saint Teresa,[8]

Foundress of the reformation of the discalced[9] Carmelites,
both men and women.
A woman for angelical height of speculation,
for masculine courage of performance,
more than a woman; who yet a child outran maturity,
and durst plot a martyrdom.

Love, thou art absolute sole lord
Of life and death. To prove the word,
We'll now appeal to none of all
Those thy old soldiers, great and tall,
5   Ripe men of martyrdom, that could reach down
With strong arms their triumphant crown;
Such as could with lusty breath
Speak loud into the face of death
Their great Lord's glorious name; to none
10 Of those whose spacious bosoms spread a throne
For Love at large to fill. Spare blood and sweat,[1]
And see Him take a private seat;
Making His mansion in the mild
And milky soul of a soft child.
15 Scarce has she learnt to lisp the name
Of Martyr, yet she thinks it shame
Life should so long play with that breath
Which spent can buy so brave a death.
She never undertook to know
20 What death with love should have to do;
Nor has she e'er yet understood
Why to show love she should shed blood;
Yet though she cannot tell you why,
She can love and she can die.

---

7. I.e., at worst, the Milky Way will replace their mothers' milk; at best, they will be even higher in the heavens.
8. (1515–1582); Spanish mystic, canonized in 1622. Her autobiography records how, at the age of six, she ran away from home to convert the Moors; an English translation of this work was pub-lished in 1642, and Crashaw showed his devotion to Teresa by publishing three poems about her including this one.
9. Barefoot.
1. I.e., refrain from using "old soldiers" (those martyrs of "blood and sweat").

25   Scarce has she blood enough to make
      A guilty sword blush for her sake;
      Yet has she a heart dares hope to prove
      How much less strong is death than love.
          Be love but there, let poor six years
30   Be posed with° the maturest fears   *placed against*
      Man trembles at, you straight shall find
      Love knows no nonage,[2] nor the mind.
      'Tis love, not years or limbs, that can
      Make the martyr or the man.
35   Love touched her heart, and lo it beats
      High, and burns with such brave heats,
      Such thirsts to die, as dares drink up
      A thousand cold deaths in one cup.
      Good reason, for she breathes all fire;
40   Her weak breast heaves with strong desire
      Of what she may with fruitless wishes
      Seek for amongst her mother's kisses.
          Since 'tis not to be had at home,
      She'll traval° to a martyrdom.   *labor, journey*
45   No home for hers confesses she
      But where she may a martyr be.
          She'll to the Moors and trade with them
      For this unvalued° diadem.°   *invaluable / crown*
      She'll offer them her dearest breath,
50   With Christ's name in 't, in change for death.
      She'll bargain with them, and will give
      Them God, teach them how to live
      In Him; or, if they this deny,
      For Him she'll teach them how to die.
55   So shall she leave amongst them sown
      Her Lord's blood, or at least her own.
          Farewell then, all the world, adieu!
      Teresa is no more for you.
      Farewell, all pleasures, sports, and joys,
60   Never till now esteeméd toys;
      Farewell, whatever dear may be,
      Mother's arms, or father's knee;
      Farewell house and farewell home,
      She's for the Moors and martyrdom!
65   Sweet, not so fast! lo, thy fair Spouse[3]
      Whom thou seek'st with so swift vows
      Calls thee back, and bids thee come
      T' embrace a milder martyrdom.
          Blest powers forbid thy tender life
70   Should bleed upon a barbarous knife;
      Or some base hand have power to rase°   *cut*
      Thy breast's chaste cabinet, and uncase
      A soul kept there so sweet; oh no,
      Wise Heav'n will never have it so.
75   Thou art Love's victim, and must die

---

2. Period of being underage.   3. I.e., Christ.

A death more mystical and high;[4]
Into Love's arms thou shalt let fall
A still surviving funeral.[5]
His is the dart must make the death

80   Whose stroke shall taste thy hallowed breath;
A dart thrice dipped in that rich flame
Which writes thy Spouse's radiant name
Upon the roof of heaven, where aye°   *always*
It shines, and with a sovereign ray

85   Beats bright upon the burning faces
Of souls which in that name's sweet graces
Find everlasting smiles. So rare,
So spiritual, pure, and fair
Must be th' immortal instrument

90   Upon whose choice point shall be sent
A life so loved; and that there be
Fit executioners for thee,
The fair'st and first-born sons of fire,
Blest seraphim,[6] shall leave their choir

95   And turn Love's soldiers, upon thee
To exercise their archery.
     Oh, how oft shalt thou complain
Of a sweet and subtle pain,
Of intolerable joys,

100 Of a death, in which who dies
Loves his death and dies again,
And would for ever so be slain,
And lives and dies, and knows not why
To live, but that he thus may never leave to die!

105   How kindly will thy gentle heart
Kiss the sweetly killing dart!
And close in his embraces keep
Those delicious wounds, that weep
Balsam[7] to heal themselves with. Thus

110 When these thy deaths, so numerous,
Shall all at last die into one,
And melt thy soul's sweet mansion;
Like a soft lump of incense, hasted
By too hot a fire, and wasted

115 Into perfuming clouds, so fast
Shalt thou exhale to heaven at last
In a resolving sigh; and then,
Oh, what? Ask not the tongues of men;
Angels cannot tell; suffice,

120 Thyself shall feel thine own full joys
And hold them fast for ever. There,
So soon as thou shalt first appear,

---

4. According to Teresa's autobiography, in later visions she saw a seraph (angel of the highest order) who pierced her heart repeatedly with a fire-tipped golden dart, simultaneously causing intense pain and joy. These "wounds of love" constitute the "death more mystical and high"; the erotic image draws upon "death" as a popular metaphor for sexual climax, as well as the arrows (or darts) of Cupid, the mythological god of erotic love.
5. I.e., a continuing or repeated death.
6. Angels of the highest order, distinguished by dwelling continuously in the fire of divine love.
7. A resin, often used for healing wounds or easing pain.

The moon of maiden stars, thy white
Mistress, attended by such bright
125 Souls as thy shining self, shall come
And in her first ranks make thee room;
Where 'mongst her snowy family
Immortal welcomes wait for thee.
Oh, what delight when revealed life shall stand
130 And teach thy lips heaven with his hand,
On which thou now mayst to thy wishes
Heap up thy consecrated kisses.
What joys shall seize thy soul when she,
Bending her blessed eyes on thee,
135 Those second smiles of heaven, shall dart
Her mild rays through thy melting heart!
   Angels, thy old friends, there shall greet thee,
Glad at their own home now to meet thee.
   All thy good works which went before
140 And waited for thee at the door
Shall own° thee there, and all in one   *claim*
Weave a constellatiön
Of crowns, with which the King, thy Spouse,
Shall build up thy triumphant brows.
145   All thy old woes shall now smile on thee,
And thy pains sit bright upon thee;
All thy sorrows here shall shine,
All thy sufferings be divine;
Tears shall take comfort and turn gems,
150 And wrongs repent to diadems.
Even thy deaths shall live, and new
Dress the soul that erst they slew;
Thy wounds shall blush to such bright scars
As keep account of the Lamb's[8] wars.
155   Those rare works where thou shalt leave writ
Love's noble history, with wit
Taught thee by none but Him, while here
They feed our souls, shall clothe thine there.
Each heavenly word by whose hid flame
160 Our hard hearts shall strike fire, the same
Shall flourish on thy brows, and be
Both fire to us and flame to thee,
Whose light shall live bright in thy face
By glory, in our hearts by grace.
165   Thou shalt look round about and see
Thousands of crowned souls throng to be
Themselves thy crown; sons of thy vows,[9]
The virgin-births with which thy sovereign Spouse
Made fruitful thy fair soul, go now
170 And with them all about thee, bow
To Him. "Put on," He'll say, "put on,
My rosy love, that, thy rich zone
Sparkling with the sacred flames

---

8. I.e., Christ's.   9. I.e., those whom she converted.

Of thousand souls whose happy names
175 Heav'n keeps upon thy score. Thy bright
Life brought them first to kiss the light
That kindled them to stars." And so
Thou with the Lamb, thy Lord, shalt go,
And whereso'er He sets His white
180 Steps, walk with Him those ways of light
Which who in death would live to see
Must learn in life to die like thee.

1646, 1652

ABRAHAM COWLEY

1618–1667

The Wish

Well then; I now do plainly see,
This busy world and I shall ne'er agree;
The very honey of all earthly joy
    Does of all meats the soonest cloy;[1]
5   And they, methinks, deserve my pity
Who for it can endure the stings,
The crowd, and buzz, and murmurings
    Of this great hive, the city.

    Ah, yet, ere I descend to the grave
10 May I a small house and large garden have!
And a few friends, and many books, both true,
    Both wise, and both delightful too!
    And since love ne'er will from me flee,
A mistress moderately fair,
15 And good as guardian angels are,
    Only beloved, and loving me!

    O fountains, when in you shall I
Myself, eased of unpeaceful thoughts, espy?
O fields! O woods! when, when shall I be made
20   The happy tenant of your shade?
    Here's the spring-head of pleasure's flood,
Here's wealthy Nature's treasury,
Where all the riches lie that she
    Has coined and stamped for good.

25   Pride and ambition here
Only in farfetched metaphors appear;
Here naught but winds can hurtful murmurs scatter,
    And naught but Echo flatter.
    The gods, when they descended, hither
30 From heaven did always choose their way;

---

1. Overfeed to the point of loathing.

And therefore we may boldly say
That 'tis the way, too, thither.[2]

How happy here should I
And one dear she live and, embracing, die!
35 She who is all the world, and can exclude
In deserts, solitude.
I should have then this only fear,
Lest men, when they my pleasures see,
Should hither throng to live like me,
40 And so make a city here.

1647

Platonic Love[3]

1

Indeed I must confess,
When souls mix 'tis an happiness,
But not complete till bodies too do join,
And both our wholes into one whole combine;
5 But half of heaven the souls in glory taste
Till by love in heaven at last
Their bodies too are placed.

2

In thy immortal part
Man, as well as I, thou art.[4]
10 But something 'tis that differs° thee and me,   *distinguishes*
And we must one even in that difference be.
I thee both as a man and woman prize,[5]
For a perfect love implies
Love in all capacities.

3

15 Can that for true love pass
When a fair woman courts her glass?°   *mirror*
Something unlike must in love's likeness be:
His[6] wonder is one and variety.
For he whose soul nought but a soul can move
20 Does a new Narcissus[7] prove,
And his own image love.

4

That souls do beauty know
'Tis to the body's help they owe;
If when they know't they straight abuse that trust

---

2. I.e., since the gods always come here when they descend from heaven, we can say that the way to heaven ("thither") is from here.
3. Based on the ideas of Plato (ca. 428–347 B.C.), the Greek philosopher, the concept of Platonic love (as it was expressed by many Renaissance writers) held that physical beauty is the outer sign of a moral and spiritual beauty of the soul; the proper Platonic lover adores the beloved's physical beauty

only as a manifestation of spirit.
4. I.e., in your soul, you are equal to man.
5. I.e., I value you both as my equal (as a "man") and as a lover (as a "woman").
6. I.e., love's.
7. I.e., prove to be a new Narcissus: in Greek mythology, a youth who fell in love with his own reflection in a pool of water, and drowned in an attempt to embrace the reflection.

25 And shut the body from't, 'tis as unjust
As if I brought my dearest friend to see
My mistress and at th' instant he
Should steal her quite from me.

1656

RICHARD LOVELACE
1618–1658

To Althea, from Prison[1]

When Love with unconfinèd wings[2]
Hovers within my gates,
And my divine Althea brings
To whisper at the grates;
5 When I lie tangled in her hair
And fettered to her eye,
The gods[3] that wanton in the air
Know no such liberty.

When flowing cups run swiftly round,
10 With no allaying Thames,[4]
Our careless heads with roses bound,
Our hearts with loyal flames;
When thirsty grief in wine we steep,
When healths° and draughts go free,   *toasts*
15 Fishes, that tipple° in the deep,   *drink*
Know no such liberty.

When, like committed° linnets,° I   *caged / finches*
With shriller throat shall sing
The sweetness, mercy, majesty,
20 And glories of my King;
When I shall voice aloud how good
He is, how great should be,
Enlargèd winds, that curl the flood,
Know no such liberty.

25 Stone walls do not a prison make,
Nor iron bars a cage;
Minds innocent and quiet take
That for an hermitage.
If I have freedom in my love,
30 And in my soul am free,
Angels alone, that soar above,
Enjoy such liberty.

1. Lovelace published a volume called *Lucasta* in 1649; all the poems here are from that volume, and several (e.g., "To Amarantha") were set to music.
2. I.e., Cupid, the winged god of erotic love in classical mythology.
3. Some seventeenth-century versions read "birds" for "gods."
4. I.e., with no mixture of water in the wine (the Thames River flows through London).

To Lucasta, Going to the Wars

Tell me not, sweet, I am unkind,
    That from the nunnery
Of thy chaste breast and quiet mind,
    To war and arms I fly.

5   True, a new mistress now I chase,
    The first foe in the field;
And with a stronger faith embrace
    A sword, a horse, a shield.

Yet this inconstancy is such
10   As you too shall adore;
I could not love thee, dear, so much,
    Loved I not honor more.

To Amarantha, That She Would Dishevel Her Hair

Amarantha sweet and fair,
Ah, braid no more that shining hair!
    As my curious hand or eye,
Hovering round thee, let it fly.

5   Let it fly as unconfined
As its calm ravisher, the wind,
    Who hath left his darling, th' East,
To wanton o'er that spicy nest.

Every tress must be confessed[5]
10   But neatly tangled at the best,
    Like a clue° of golden thread,   *ball*
Most excellently ravelèd.

Do not then wind up that light
In ribands,° and o'ercloud in night;   *ribbons*
15   Like the sun in's early ray,
But shake your head and scatter day.

See, 'tis broke![6] Within this grove,
The bower and the walks of love,
    Weary lie we down and rest
20   And fan each other's panting breast.

Here we'll strip and cool our fire
In cream below, in milk-baths higher;
    And when all wells are drawn dry,
I'll drink a tear out of thine eye.

5. I.e., said to be.
6. I.e., the morning has broken, or started (a continuation of the previous stanza, in which the speaker compares Amarantha's hair to the sun, and encourages her to shake it free, as the sun scatters its light and begins day).

25   Which our very joys shall leave,
            That sorrows thus we can deceive;
                Or our very sorrows weep,
            That joys so ripe so little keep.

The Grasshopper[7]

To My Noble Friend, Mr. Charles Cotton[8]

O thou that swing'st upon the waving hair
    Of some well-fillèd oaten beard,[9]
Drunk every night with a delicious tear°   dew, water
    Dropped thee from heaven, where now th' art reared;[1]

5   The joys of earth and air are thine entire,
        That with thy feet and wings dost hop and fly;
    And, when thy poppy° works, thou dost retire   sleeping potion
        To thy carved acorn-bed to lie.

    Up with the day, the sun thou welcom'st then,
10   Sport'st in the gilt-plats° of his beams,   hair braids
    And all these merry days mak'st merry men,
        Thyself, and melancholy streams.[2]

    But ah, the sickle! Golden ears are cropped;
        Ceres and Bacchus[3] bid good night;
15 Sharp, frosty fingers all your flowers have topped,
        And what scythes spared, winds shave off quite.

    Poor verdant° fool, and now green ice! thy joys,   green
        Large and as lasting as thy perch of grass,
    Bid us lay in[4] 'gainst winter rain, and poise°   balance
20   Their floods with an o'erflowing glass.

    Thou best of men and friends! we will create
        A genuine summer in each other's breast,
    And spite of this cold time and frozen fate,
        Thaw us a warm seat to our rest.

25 Our sacred hearths shall burn eternally,
        As vestal flames;[5] the North Wind, he
    Shall strike his frost-stretched wings, dissolve, and fly
        This Etna in epitome.[6]

---

7. This poem embellishes the traditional ant and grasshopper fable, in which the ant dutifully prepares for the coming winter, while the grasshopper plays instead of working. The circumstances are evidently those of the Interregnum, a winter of Puritanism for Royalists such as Lovelace.
8. A scholar and friend of Lovelace.
9. I.e., grain.
1. I.e., where you are growing up.
2. "Men," "thyself" and "melancholy streams" are all possible objects of "mak'st merry."
3. The grain and the grape, from Ceres, goddess of the harvest, and Bacchus, god of wine.
4. Prepare for by storing food and drink ("o'erflowing glass"). "Now green ice": i.e., the grasshopper has frozen.
5. The vestal virgins, consecrated to the Roman goddess Vesta, kept a sacred fire burning perpetually on her altar.
6. I.e., the North wind strikes (or folds up) his wings and flees from the underground warmth of Etna, a Sicilian volcano, whose flame serves as an emblem (or "epitome") of the flame of friendship.

Dropping December shall come weeping in,
30   Bewail th' usurping of his reign:
But when in showers of old Greek we begin,
    Shall cry he hath his crown again![7]

Night, as clear Hesper, shall our tapers whip
    From the light casements where we play,
35 And the dark hag[8] from her black mantle strip,
    And stick there everlasting day.

Thus richer than untempted kings[9] are we,
    That, asking nothing, nothing need:
Though lord of all what seas embrace,[1] yet he
40   That wants himself is poor indeed.

1649

ANDREW MARVELL

1621–1678

The Coronet[1]

When for the thorns with which I long, too long,
    With many a piercing wound,
    My Savior's head have crowned,
I seek with garlands[2] to redress that wrong;
5   Through every garden, every mead,°   *meadow*
I gather flowers (my fruits are only flowers)
    Dismantling all the fragrant towers°   *high headdresses*
That once adorned my shepherdess's head.
And now when I have summed up all my store,
10   Thinking (so I myself deceive)
    So rich a chaplet° thence to weave   *garland*
As never yet the king of glory[3] wore;
    Alas I find the serpent old[4]
    That, twining in his speckled breast,
15   About the flowers disguised does fold,
    With wreaths° of fame and interest.[5]   *coils*
Ah, foolish man, that wouldst debase with them,
    And mortal glory, heaven's diadem!°   *crown*
    But Thou who only couldst the serpent tame,[6]
20 Either his slippery knots at once untie,

7. Greek wine was favored in the classical world, and drinkers often wore festive crowns; also, December "crowns" or terminates the year.
8. Hecate, sometimes described as the daughter of Night; by keeping their lights ("tapers") burning all night, they will strip her black garment ("mantle") from her. "Hesper": Hesperus, the morning star.
9. I.e., kings who have everything.
1. I.e., even one who is lord of all and can embrace the seas is poor, if he "wants" himself (does not have self-knowledge).
1. Marvell's poems (including all the selections

here) were first published in 1681, three years after his death. "Coronet": a wreath of flowers; also, a small crown. This poem is a lyric in the religious pastoral mode.
2. Wreaths; also, garlands were a symbol of poetic achievement. I.e., poems of praise.
3. I.e., Christ.
4. A reference to the serpent who tempted Eve with an apple from the Tree of Knowledge, leading to the Fall from Paradise (Genesis 3).
5. I.e., self-glorification and self-advancement.
6. I.e., Christ.

And disentangle all his winding snare;
Or shatter too with him my curious° frame,°   *elaborate / structure*
And let these wither, so that he may die,
Though set with skill and chosen out with care,
25   That they, while Thou on both their spoils dost tread,
May crown Thy feet, that could not crown Thy head.

Bermudas

Where the remote Bermudas ride,°   *float*
In th' ocean's bosom unespied,
From a small boat that rowed along,
The listening winds received this song:
5   "What should we do but sing His praise,
That led us through the watery maze
Unto an isle so long unknown,
And yet far kinder than our own?
Where He the huge sea monsters wracks,°   *casts ashore*
10   That lift the deep upon their backs;
He lands us on a grassy stage,
Safe from the storms, and prelate's rage.[7]
He gave us this eternal spring
Which here enamels everything,
15   And sends the fowls to us in care,
On daily visits through the air;
He hangs in shades the orange bright,
Like golden lamps in a green night,
And does in the pomegranates close
20   Jewels more rich than Ormus[8] shows;
He makes the figs our mouths to meet,
And throws the melons at our feet;
But apples° plants of such a price,   *pineapples*
No tree could ever bear them twice;
25   With cedars, chosen by His hand,
From Lebanon,[9] He stores the land;
And makes the hollow seas, that roar,
Proclaim the ambergris[1] on shore;
He cast (of which we rather[2] boast)
30   The Gospel's pearl upon our coast,
And in these rocks for us did frame
A temple, where to sound His name.
O! let our voice His praise exalt,
Till it arrive at heaven's vault,
35   Which, thence (perhaps) rebounding, may
Echo beyond the Mexique Bay."[3]
Thus sung they in the English boat,
An holy and a cheerful note;

---

7. Storms at sea are here associated with bishops (thus indicating a Puritan stance by Marvell).
8. An island off Persia whence gems were exported.
9. The tree called the cedar of Lebanon from its most famous early locality.

1. The roaring seas announce ("proclaim") their bounty. "Ambergris": a soapy secretion of the sperm whale, gathered on beaches and used in perfumes.
2. More properly.
3. I.e., the Gulf of Mexico.

And all the way, to guide their chime,
40   With falling oars they kept the time.

A Dialogue Between the Soul and Body[4]

Soul

Oh, who shall from this dungeon raise
A soul enslaved so many ways?[5]
With bolts of bones that fettered stands
In feet, and manacled in hands;
5   Here blinded with an eye, and there
Deaf with the drumming of an ear;
A soul hung up, as 'twere, in chains
Of nerves and arteries and veins;
Tortured, besides each other part,
10   In a vain head and double° heart.   *deceitful*

Body

Oh, who shall me deliver whole
From bonds of this tyrannic soul?
Which stretched upright, impales me so
That mine own precipice[6] I go,
15   And warms and moves this needless frame[7] —
A fever could but do the same —
And, wanting where[8] its spite to try,
Has made me live to let me die:
A body that could never rest,
20   Since this ill spirit it possessed.

Soul

What magic could me thus confine
Within another's grief to pine?
Where whatsoever it complain,
I feel, that cannot feel,[9] the pain,
25   And all my care itself employs,
That to preserve which me destroys,
Constrained not only to endure
Diseases, but, what's worse, the cure;
And ready oft the port[1] to gain,
30   And shipwrecked into health again.

---

4. Deriving from the medieval "débat," a literary form wherein two speakers dispute a topic.
5. Compare St. Paul's Epistle to the Romans (7.24): "O wretched man that I am! who shall deliver me from the body of this death?"
6. Humans walk "upright" instead of prowling like animals because they possess souls; however, possession of a soul is also the reason why they can fall and be damned, so the soul is an internal "precipice."
7. I.e., this frame, which does not need it.
8. I.e., lacking an object.
9. I.e., the soul can sympathize even though it has no power of physical sensation.
1. I.e., death.

Body

But physic° yet could never reach   *medicine*
The maladies thou me dost teach:
Whom first the cramp of hope does tear,
And then the palsy shakes of fear;
35   The pestilence of love does heat,
Or hatred's hidden ulcer eat;
Joy's cheerful madness does perplex,
Or sorrow's other madness vex;
Which knowledge forces me to know,
40   And memory will not forgo.
What but a soul could have the wit
To build me up for sin so fit?
So architects do square and hew
Green trees that in the forest grew.

To His Coy² Mistress

Had we but world enough, and time,
This coyness, lady, were no crime.
We would sit down, and think which way
To walk, and pass our long love's day.
5   Thou by the Indian Ganges' side
Shoudst rubies³ find; I by the tide
Of Humber would complain.⁴ I would
Love you ten years before the flood,
And you should, if you please, refuse
10   Till the conversion of the Jews.⁵
My vegetable⁶ love should grow
Vaster than empires and more slow;
An hundred years should go to praise
Thine eyes, and on thy forehead gaze;
15   Two hundred to adore each breast,
But thirty thousand to the rest;
An age at least to every part,
And the last age should show your heart.
For, lady, you deserve this state,°   *dignity*
20   Nor would I love at lower rate.⁷
    But at my back I always hear
Time's wingèd chariot hurrying near;
And yonder all before us lie
Deserts of vast eternity.
25   Thy beauty shall no more be found;
Nor, in thy marble vault, shall sound
My echoing song; then worms shall try

---

2. In the seventeenth century, "coy" could mean "shy" or quiet as well as "coquettish," the common modern meaning.
3. Rubies were thought to help preserve virginity. "Ganges": the Ganges River.
4. The Humber River flows through Marvell's native town of Hull; "complain" implies plaintive lyrics of unavailing love.
5. To occur, as Christian tradition had it, at the end of recorded history.
6. I.e., characterized by growth; in context, increasing without conscious nurturing.
7. I.e., at any smaller amounts of time ("lower rate") than what I've just mentioned.

That long-preserved virginity,
And your quaint[8] honor turn to dust,
30 And into ashes all my lust:
The grave's a fine and private place,
But none, I think, do there embrace.
    Now therefore, while the youthful hue
Sits on thy skin like morning dew,[9]
35 And while thy willing soul transpires°   *breathes out*
At every pore with instant fires,
Now let us sport us while we may,
And now, like amorous birds of prey,
Rather at once our time devour
40 Than languish in his slow-chapped° power.   *slow-jawed*
Let us roll all our strength and all
Our sweetness up into one ball,
And tear our pleasures with rough strife
Thorough the iron gates[1] of life:
45 Thus, though we cannot make our sun
Stand still,[2] yet we will make him run.

The Gallery

Clora, come view my soul, and tell
Whether I have contrived° it well.   *designed*
Now all its several lodgings lie
Composed into one gallery;
5 And the great arras-hangings, made
Of[3] various faces, by are laid;
That, for all furniture,° you'll find   *furnishings*
Only your picture in my mind.

Here thou art painted in the dress
10 Of an inhuman murderess;
Examining° upon our hearts   *testing*
Thy fertile shop of cruel arts:
Engines° more keen than ever yet   *instruments*
Adornèd tyrant's cabinet;[4]
15 Of which the most tormenting are
Black eyes, red lips, and curlèd hair.

But, on the other side, thou'rt drawn
Like to Aurora[5] in the dawn;

8. Has several meanings, including: fine, elegant, fastidious, and oversubtle; also with a pun on the Middle English noun "queynte," or pudendum.
9. In the 1681 text, line 34 ends with the word "glew," rhyming with "hew." Some modern editors emend to "glow" rather than "dew." One recent scholar argues for retaining "glew" on the grounds that the term had a specific meaning in alchemical processes of distillation and that Marvell, like Donne, was deeply interested in alchemy.
1. The obscure "iron gates" suggests that the "ball"

of line 42 has become a missile from a siege gun, battering its way into a citadel.
2. An allusion to the power of Zeus, who, to prolong his night with the mortal Alcamena, ordered the sun not to shine; also, see Joshua 10.12–13.
3. I.e., depicting various faces. "Arras-hangings": tapestries, so called for Arras, the French town noted for their production.
4. A room devoted to the display of works of art.
5. Goddess of the dawn in Greek mythology.

When in the east she slumb'ring lies,
20 And stretches out her milky thighs;
While all the morning choir does sing,
And manna[6] falls, and roses spring;
And, at thy feet, the wooing doves[7]
Sit perfecting their harmless loves.

25 Like an enchantress here thou show'st,
Vexing thy restless lover's ghost;
And, by a light obscure, dost rave
Over his entrails,[8] in the cave;
Divining thence, with horrid care,
30 How long thou shalt continue fair;
And (when informed) them throw'st away,
To be the greedy vulture's prey.

But, against° that, thou sit'st afloat   *opposite*
Like Venus in her pearly boat.[9]
35 The halcyons,[1] calming all that's nigh,
Betwixt the air and water fly:
Or, if some rolling wave appears,
A mass of ambergris[2] it bears:
Nor blows more wind than what may well
40 Convoy the perfume to the smell.

These pictures and a thousand more,
Of thee, my gallery do store;
In all the forms thou canst invent
Either to please me, or torment:
45 For thou alone to people me,
Art grown a num'rous colony;
And a collection choicer far
Than or° Whitehall's, or Mantua's were.[3]   *either*

But, of these pictures and the rest,
50 That at the entrance likes me best;
Where the same posture, and the look
Remains, with which I first was took:
A tender shepherdess, whose hair
Hangs loosely playing in the air,
55 Transplanting flowers from the green hill,
To crown her head, and bosom fill.

6. Food divinely supplied, or spiritual nourish-
ment. Manna was the substance miraculously sup-
plied as food to the Children of Israel during the
time in the wilderness described in Exodus 16.
7. Turtledoves, emblems of steadfastness in love.
8. An allusion to the Roman practice of divining
the future through examination of the entrails of
sacrificial victims.
9. Venus (often identified with Aphrodite) was
commonly depicted as rising from the sea.

1. Birds believed to nest on the surface of the sea;
hence representative of calm weather.
2. A soapy secretion of the sperm whale, gathered
on beaches and used in perfumes.
3. References to well-known collections of paint-
ings, the first assembled by Charles I of England
(1600–1649; owner of Whitehall Palace) and the
second by Vincenzo Gonzaga (1562–1612), duke
of Mantua.

The Fair Singer[4]

To make a final conquest of all me,
Love did compose so sweet an enemy,
In whom both beauties to my death agree,
Joining themselves in fatal harmony;
5   That while she with her eyes my heart does bind,
She with her voice might captivate my mind.

I could have fled from one but singly fair:
My disentangled soul itself might save,
Breaking the curlèd trammels[5] of her hair.
10   But how should I avoid to be her slave,
Whose subtle art invisibly can wreathe
My fetters of the very air I breathe?

It had been easy fighting in some plain,
Where victory might hang in equal choice,
15   But all resistance against her is vain,
Who has th' advantage both of eyes and voice,
And all my forces needs must be undone,
She having gainèd both the wind and sun.[6]

The Definition of Love[7]

My Love is of a birth as rare
As 'tis, for object, strange and high;[8]
It was begotten by Despair
Upon Impossibility.

5   Magnanimous Despair alone
Could show me so divine a thing,
Where feeble Hope could ne'er have flown
But vainly flapped its tinsel[9] wing.

And yet I quickly might arrive
10   Where my extended soul is fixed;[1]
But Fate does iron wedges drive,
And always crowds itself betwixt.

For Fate with jealous eye does see
Two perfect loves, nor lets them close;°   unite
15   Their union would her ruin be,
And her tyrannic power depose.[2]

4. A poem in the genre of the courtly compliment paid to a lady to commend her skill in music or dancing.
5. Tresses; also, fetters.
6. In earlier warfare (especially at sea) the force with the wind and sun behind it had distinct advantages.
7. The poem plays upon a Platonic definition of love as an unfulfilled longing.
8. I.e., my love's lineage is as rare as my love itself is strange and high.
9. Glittering; also, flashy, with little or no intrinsic worth.
1. The speaker describes his soul as having gone out of his body ("extended") and attached ("fixed") itself to his mistress.
2. A reference to the idea that an even mixture of pure elements formed an altogether stable compound, able to withstand any sudden change, and hence, in context, defying fate.

And therefore her decrees of steel
Us as the distant poles have placed
(Though Love's whole world on us doth wheel),[3]
20   Not by themselves to be embraced,

Unless the giddy heaven fall,
And earth some new convulsion tear,
And, us to join, the world should all
Be cramped into a planisphere.[4]

25   As lines, so loves oblique may well
Themselves in every angle greet;[5]
But ours, so truly parallel,
Though infinite, can never meet.

Therefore the love which us doth bind,
30   But Fate so enviously debars,
Is the conjunction of the mind,
And opposition of the stars.[6]

The Picture of Little T. C. in a Prospect[7] of Flowers

See with what simplicity
This nymph[8] begins her golden days!
In the green grass she loves to lie,
And there with her fair aspect tames
5   The wilder flowers, and gives them names;
But only with the roses plays,
     And them does tell
What color best becomes them, and what smell.

Who can foretell for what high cause
10   This darling of the gods was born?
Yet this is she whose chaster laws
The wanton Love[9] shall one day fear,
And, under her command severe,
See his bow broke and ensigns torn.
15   Happy who can
Appease this virtuous enemy of man!

---

3. Though by decree of Fate the lovers are as far apart as the two poles of the Earth, the relationship (literally, the line) between them forms the axis on which Love's world turns.
4. A chart formed by the projection of a sphere on a plane; the two poles could come together only if the charted world were collapsed.
5. I.e., the lines may converge at any angle.
6. In this astronomical image, the minds of the lovers are in accord (literally in *conjunction*, or occupying the same celestial longitude), but the stars determining their destinies are entirely hostile (literally in *opposition*, or 180 degrees apart).
7. A background scene, or representation of a view. "T. C.": an unknown little girl; possibly Theophila Cornewall, who was baptized on Sep-

tember 26, 1644, the second daughter of that name in the family. The first Theophila had died two days after birth.
8. A young beautiful female; also, nymphs were beautiful female spirits in mythology, who inhabited a particular place, object, or natural phenomenon.
9. I.e., Cupid. The speaker predicts that "T. C." will follow "chaster laws," with a likely allusion to those laws followed by Diana, the mythological goddess of chastity and hunting. By doing battle with Cupid, breaking his bow and tearing his flags ("ensigns"), she ("T. C.") will be a "virtuous enemy" to man (i.e., one whose chaste virtue causes her to be the foe of love).

O then let me in time compound°   *bargain*
And parley[1] with those conquering eyes,
Ere they have tried their force to wound;
20   Ere with their glancing wheels they drive
In triumph over hearts that strive,[2]
And them that yield but more despise:
        Let me be laid
Where I may see thy glories from some shade.

25   Meantime, whilst every verdant° thing   *green*
Itself does at thy beauty charm,[3]
Reform the errors of the spring;
Make that the tulips may have share
Of sweetness, seeing they are fair;
30   And roses of their thorns disarm;
        But most procure
That violets may a longer age endure.

But, O young beauty of the woods,
Whom nature courts with fruits and flowers,
35   Gather the flowers, but spare the buds,
Lest Flora, angry at thy crime
To kill her infants[4] in their prime,
Do quickly make the example yours;
        And ere we see,
40   Nip in the blossom all our hopes and thee.

The Mower Against Gardens[5]

Luxurious man, to bring his vice in use,[6]
    Did after him the world seduce,
And from the fields the flowers and plants allure,
    Where Nature was most plain and pure.
5   He first enclosed within the gardens square
    A dead and standing pool of air,
And a more luscious earth for them did knead,
    Which stupefied them while it fed.
The pink grew then as double as his mind;[7]
10   The nutriment did change the kind.
With strange perfumes he did the roses taint;
    And flowers themselves were taught to paint.
The tulip white did for complexion seek,
    And learned to interline its cheek;
15   Its onion root they then so high did hold,
    That one was for a meadow sold:[8]
Another world was searched through oceans new,

---

1. Speak; also, hold a conference with the enemy.
2. Her eyes are compared to a war chariot driving over her foes.
3. Enchants itself at thy beauty.
4. I.e., the buds. "Flora": Roman goddess of flowers.
5. One of four "mower" poems that examine different aspects of rural life; "mower": one who cuts grass with a scythe.
6. I.e., to establish his vice as custom; "luxurious": lustful, and voluptuous.
7. The double pink carnation is produced by a hypocritical ("double") mind, i.e., one who counterfeits the natural color.
8. A tulip fad in the 1630s brought extremely high prices for rare varieties. "Onion root": bulb.

To find the Marvel of Peru;[9]
And yet these rarities might be allowed
20   To man, that sovereign thing and proud,
Had he not dealt between the bark and tree,[1]
    Forbidden mixtures there to see.
No plant now knew the stock from which it came;
    He grafts upon the wild the tame,
25   That the uncertain and adulterate° fruit   *counterfeit*
    Might put the palate in dispute.[2]
His green seraglio[3] has its eunuchs too,
    Lest any tyrant him outdo;
And in the cherry he does Nature vex,
30   To procreate without a sex.[4]
'Tis all enforced, the fountain and the grot,[5]
    While the sweet fields do lie forgot,
Where willing Nature does to all dispense
    A wild and fragrant innocence;
35   And fauns[6] and fairies do the meadows till
    More by their presence than their skill.
Their statues[7] polished by some ancient hand,
    May to adorn the gardens stand;
But, howsoe'er the figures do excel,
40   The Gods themselves with us do dwell.

The Mower[8] to the Glowworms

Ye living lamps, by whose dear light
The nightingale does sit so late,
And studying all the summer night,
    Her matchless songs[9] does meditate;

5   Ye country comets, that portend
No war nor prince's funeral,[1]
Shining unto no higher end
    Than to presage° the grass's fall;   *foretell*

Ye glowworms, whose officious° flame   *serviceable*
10   To wandering mowers shows the way,

9. A tuliplike flower (*mirabilis jalapa*) that
expands at night.
1. I.e., by grafting; proverbial for audacity.
2. I.e., the result of which grafting confuses the
palate as to what it tastes.
3. The part of a Muhammadan house where the
women dwell, hence a place of confinement;
"eunuchs": castrated male slaves. I.e., his garden
("green seraglio") has its castrated slaves (the
grafted plants, some of which could not repro-
duce) just like any tyrant.
4. Cherries are often propagated by budding on
the stocks of sturdier but less productive varieties.
5. Grotto, a picturesque structure made to imitate
a cave, serving as a cool retreat.
6. In classical mythology, half-goat, half-man
woodland gods associated with lust and drinking
(although the fauns were often described as less
wild than the satyrs).

7. I.e., statues of the fauns and fairies are placed
in the gardens for decoration.
8. See n. 5 (p. 440). "Glowworms": insects, the
females of which emit a shining green light from
the abdomen.
9. The nightingale is known for its sweet and sad
song, which has perhaps given rise to one tradition
that the bird's song laments the tragic result of
wrongful love. Another tale of the nightingale, as
told by Ovid, has the mournful song refer to the
violence committed on Philomela, who was raped
by her brother-in-law, Tereus, who then tore out
her tongue so that she could not speak. She wove
the story in a tapestry and sent it to her sister, who
rescued her. She was later changed into a nightin-
gale while in flight from Tereus, after seeking
revenge on him.
1. Comets were sometimes believed to be portents
of approaching disasters.

That in the night have lost their aim,
And after foolish fires[2] do stray;

Your courteous lights in vain you waste,
Since Juliana here is come,
15   For she my mind hath so displaced
That I shall never find my home.

The Garden

How vainly men themselves amaze°   *perplex*
To win the palm, the oak, or bays,[3]
And their incessant° labors see   *unceasing*
Crowned from some single herb, or tree,
5   Whose short and narrow-vergèd[4] shade
Does prudently their toils upbraid;
While all flowers and all trees do close°   *join*
To weave the garlands of repose!

Fair Quiet, have I found thee here,
10   And Innocence, thy sister dear?
Mistaken long, I sought you then
In busy companies of men.
Your sacred plants,° if here below,   *cuttings*
Only among the plants will grow;
15   Society is all but rude[5]
To° this delicious solitude.   *compared to*

No white nor red[6] was ever seen
So amorous as this lovely green.
Fond° lovers, cruel as their flame,   *foolish*
20   Cut in these trees their mistress' name:[7]
Little, alas, they know or heed
How far these beauties hers exceed!
Fair trees, wheresoe'er your barks I wound,
No name shall but your own be found.

25   When we have run our passion's heat,°   *course*
Love hither makes his best retreat.
The gods, that mortal beauty chase,
Still in a tree did end their race:[8]

---

2. *Ignis fatuus* (Latin), also known as the will-o'-the-wisp; said to draw travelers astray by holding a false light before them; the phenomenon of nocturnal light is caused by the combustion of marsh gas.
3. The wreaths awarded, respectively, for athletic, civic, and poetic accomplishments.
4. Confined, not spreading luxuriantly like the living branch.
5. I.e., all merely barbarous.
6. The colors conventionally used to depict female beauty in love poetry (in the Petrarchan tradition).

7. According to a poetic tradition, a lover carved his beloved's name in a tree (as Petrarch did with Laura's).
8. I.e., even the gods who chase after their desired nymphs (described in the following lines) succeed only in achieving a garden prize (the laurel and the reed) for their endeavors. According to Ovid's versions of these two myths, the nymphs (Daphne and Syrinx) both elude the unwanted sexual advances of their pursuers (Apollo and Pan, respectively) only after being metamorphosed into a laurel tree (Daphne) and reeds (Syrinx) through the intervention of sympathetic deities.

Apollo hunted Daphne so,
30 Only that she might laurel grow;
And Pan did after Syrinx speed,
Not as a nymph, but for a reed.

What wondrous life is this I lead!
Ripe apples drop about my head;
35 The luscious clusters of the vine
Upon my mouth do crush their wine;
The nectarine and curious° peach   *exquisite*
Into my hands themselves do reach;
Stumbling on melons,[9] as I pass,
40 Insnared with flowers, I fall on grass.

Meanwhile the mind, from pleasure less,[1]
Withdraws into its happiness;
The mind, that ocean where each kind
Does straight its own resemblance find;[2]
45 Yet it creates, transcending these,
Far other worlds and other seas,
Annihilating all that's made
To a green thought in a green shade.

Here at the fountain's sliding foot,
50 Or at some fruit tree's mossy root,
Casting the body's vest[3] aside,
My soul into the boughs does glide:
There, like a bird, it sits and sings,
Then whets° and combs its silver wings,   *preens*
55 And, till prepared for longer flight,
Waves in its plumes the various° light.   *iridescent*

Such was that happy garden-state,
While man there walked without a mate:
After a place so pure and sweet,
60 What other help could yet be meet![4]
But 'twas beyond a mortal's share
To wander solitary there:
Two paradises 'twere in one
To live in paradise alone.[5]

65 How well the skillful gardener drew
Of flowers and herbs this dial[6] new,
Where, from above, the milder sun
Does through a fragrant zodiac run;

9. "Melon" has an etymological root in the Greek word for apple; perhaps an allusion to the apple that led to the Fall (or "stumbling") of humankind.
1. "Less" may modify either "pleasure" or "mind."
2. As every land creature was thought to have its counterpart sea creature, so also in the ocean of the mind.
3. Garment; i.e., the body itself.
4. Fit, suitable; also, God created Eve because "for

Adam there was not found an help meet for him" (Genesis 2.20).
5. I.e., it would be twice as wonderful to be alone in Paradise (i.e., before Eve).
6. Flowers planted to form a dial face, through which the sun follows its course; it is "milder" because its intense rays are tempered by the flowers through which they filter.

And as it works, th' industrious bee
70   Computes its time as well as we!
How could such sweet and wholesome hours
Be reckoned but with herbs and flowers?

An Horatian Ode[7]

Upon Cromwell's Return from Ireland[8]

The forward youth that would appear
Must now forsake his Muses[9] dear,
      Nor in the shadows sing
      His numbers° languishing: *poems*

5   'Tis time to leave the books in dust,
And oil the unusèd armor's rust,
      Removing from the wall
      The corslet of the hall.[1]

So restless Cromwell could not cease
10   In the inglorious arts of peace,
      But through adventurous war
      Urgèd his active star;

And like the three-forked lightning, first
Breaking the clouds where it was nursed,
15   Did thorough° his own side   *through*
      His fiery way divide.[2]

For 'tis all one to courage high,
The emulous[3] or enemy;
      And with such to inclose
20   Is more than to oppose.[4]

Then burning through the air he went,
And palaces and temples rent;°   *tore*

7. Originally a classical form, an ode is a serious lyric poem, dignified by its theme, occasion, or subject. In contrast to the odes of the Greek poet Pindar (ca. 522–ca. 438 B.C.), which typically praised or glorified someone, a Horatian ode, derived from the work of the Roman poet Horace (65–8 B.C.), promises a poem of cool and balanced judgement. Balanced judgments of Oliver Cromwell (see note 1, below) were not politic in the Restoration: the poem was canceled from all but two known copies of the 1681 edition of *Miscellaneous Poems*.
8. Oliver Cromwell (1599–1658), English general and statesman, lord protector of England, returned from conquering Ireland in May 1650, about eighteen months after the execution of Charles I. His victory over the Irish was sometimes taken as a sign that God did not disapprove of the beheading of Charles I.

9. The nine Greek goddesses believed to be sources of inspiration for the arts.
1. The suit of armor belonging to the household.
2. Cromwell had begun as a Presbyterian, but became the leader of the more radical group known as the "Independents," or the "Rump." The comparison to the "three-forked lightning" links him to Zeus, the king of the classical gods, whose daughter Athena sprang fully formed from Zeus' head.
3. One who is greedy for praise or power; also, one who imitates or rivals.
4. Possible paraphrase of stanza: It challenges high courage as much to deal with competitors as to deal with the enemy; and to make common cause with men like the sectarians of the Parliamentary party is more of an accomplishment than effectually to oppose them. (Marvell's obscurities may be deliberate and politic.)

And Caesar's head at last
Did through his laurels blast.[5]

25 'Tis madness to resist or blame
The force of angry heaven's flame;[6]
And if we would speak true,
Much to the man is due,

Who, from his private gardens, where
30 He lived reservèd and austere
(As if his highest plot
To plant the bergamot[7]),

Could by industrious valor climb
To ruin the great work of time,
35 And cast the kingdom old
Into another mold;[8]

Though Justice against Fate complain,
And plead the ancient rights in vain;
But those do hold or break,
40 As men are strong or weak.

Nature, that hateth emptiness,
Allows of penetration less,[9]
And therefore must make room
Where greater spirits come.

45 What field of all the civil wars,
Where his were not the deepest scars?
And Hampton shows what part
He had of wiser art;[1]

Where, twining subtle fears with hope,
50 He wove a net of such a scope
That Charles himself might chase
To Carisbrooke's narrow case,[2]

That thence the royal actor borne
The tragic scaffold might adorn;
55 While round the armèd bands
Did clap their bloody hands.

5. I.e., like lightning, Cromwell beheaded
Charles I ("Caesar"). Laurels were used for classi-
cal crowns because they were supposed to protect
from lightning, which represented the gods' jeal-
ousy.
6. The lightning hurled by Zeus represents divine
judgment.
7. A variety of pear; its etymology (from the Turk-
ish, "prince's pear") may hold the insinuation that
Cromwell had been plotting for power even in his
early days of private life.

8. I.e., a reference to the change from monarchy
to republic.
9. I.e., Nature, which abhors a vacuum, is even
less willing to let two bodies occupy the same
space.
1. Cromwell purportedly let Charles escape from
Hampton Court to Carisbrooke Castle on the Isle
of Wight, in order to convince the Parliament that
the king could not be trusted and must be exe-
cuted.
2. "Case" may mean either "plight" or "prison."

He[3] nothing common did or mean
Upon that memorable scene,
   But with his keener eye
60   The axe's edge did try;[4]

Nor called the gods with vulgar spite
To vindicate his helpless right;
   But bowed his comely head
   Down, as upon a bed.

65 This was that memorable hour
Which first assured the forcèd power:
   So, when they did design
   The Capitol's first line,

A bleeding head, where they begun,
70 Did fright the architects to run;
   And yet in that the state
   Foresaw its happy fate.[5]

And now the Irish are ashamed
To see themselves in one year tamed;
75   So such one man can do
   That does both act and know.

They can affirm his praises best,
And have, though overcome, confessed
   How good he is, how just,
80   And fit for highest trust.

Nor yet grown stiffer with command,
But still in the republic's hand—
   How fit he is to sway
   That can so well obey!

85 He to the Commons' feet presents
A kingdom for his first year's rents;
   And, what he may, forbears
   His fame to make it theirs;

And has his sword and spoils ungirt,
90 To lay them at the public's skirt:[6]
   So when the falcon high
   Falls heavy from the sky,

---

3. I.e., Charles.
4. The Latin word *acies* means "the front of a battle line," "the edge of a sword or ax blade," and the "beam of an eye."
5. When foundations were being dug for Jupiter's temple in Rome (according to Pliny), a bloody head was uncovered. The workers at first thought it was an ill omen, but then were persuaded to believe it to mean that Rome would be "head" of an empire. The temple and the hill on which it stood were thereafter called Capitoline or the Capitol (from the Latin *caput*, "head").
6. I.e., at the feet of the Republic, conceived as a Roman senator wearing a toga.

She, having killed, no more does search
But on the next green bough to perch;
95   Where, when he first does lure,[7]
        The falconer has her sure.

What may not, then, our isle presume,
While victory his crest[8] does plume?
        What may not others fear,
100   If thus he crown each year?

A Caesar he, ere long, to Gaul
To Italy an Hannibal,[9]
        And to all states not free
        Shall climactèric[1] be.

105   The Pict no shelter now shall find
Within his parti-colored mind,[2]
        But from this valor sad°   *serious*
        Shrink underneath the plaid;°   *tartan kilts*

Happy if in the tufted brake°   *bushes*
110   The English hunter him mistake,
        Nor lay his hounds in near
        The Caledonian° deer.[3]   *Scottish*

But thou, the war's and fortune's son,
March indefatigably on!
115   And for the last effect,
        Still keep thy sword erect;

Besides the force it has to fright
The spirits of the shady night,[4]
        The same arts that did gain
120   A power must it maintain.

1681

---

7. I.e., when the falconer casts out his lure—a bunch of feathers attached to a cord and baited with meat.
8. Of the falcon; also the plumed helmet of the warrior.
9. The Roman general Gaius Julius Caesar (100–44 B.C.) conquered Gaul; the Carthaginian general Hannibal (247?–183 B.C.) conquered Italy.
1. I.e., ushering in a new epoch.
2. The Scots, called *Picti* ("painted men") by the Romans because they painted their bodies for battle, are stigmatized as factious (with a pun on "party" and "parti-colored"). They were in fact torn between their Calvinism and their loyalty to the Catholic or Anglo-Catholic Stuart kings.
3. I.e., the "Pict" shall be happy if the English hunter mistakenly misses him and fails to send his hounds in after him.
4. The underworld spirits of classical mythology were said to fear cold iron.

HENRY VAUGHAN

1622–1695

Regeneration[1]

A ward, and still in bonds,[2] one day
    I stole abroad;
It was high spring, and all the way
    Primrosed and hung with shade;
5   Yet was it frost within,
      And surly winds
Blasted my infant buds, and sin
    Like clouds eclipsed my mind.

Stormed thus, I straight perceived my spring
10   Mere stage and show,
My walk a monstrous,° mountained thing,   *strange, unnatural*
    Roughcast with rocks and snow;
    And as a pilgrim's eye,
      Far from relief,
15   Measures the melancholy sky,
    Then drops and rains for grief,

So sighed I upwards still;[3] at last
    'Twixt steps and falls
I reached the pinnacle,° where placed   *summit*
20   I found a pair of scales;
    I took them up and laid
    In th' one, late pains;
The other smoke and pleasures weighed,
    But proved the heavier grains.[4]

25   With that some cried, "Away!" Straight I
    Obeyed, and led
Full east, a fair, fresh field could spy;[5]
    Some called it Jacob's bed,[6]
    A virgin soil which no
30   Rude feet ere trod,
Where, since he stepped there, only go
    Prophets and friends of God.

1. This poem, like the others by Vaughan printed here, is from Vaughan's book *Silex Scintillans* ("sparkling, or fiery, flint" [Latin]). First published in 1650 and reissued with additional poems in 1655, the volume dramatizes Vaughan's experience of religious conversion. The book's title alludes to the poet's "stony" heart, from which God strikes divine, purifying sparks. In the 1650 edition, the subtitle on the engraved title page acknowledges Vaughan's indebtedness to George Herbert, who had used the same subtitle for *The Temple* (1633): "Sacred Poems and Private Ejaculations."
2. I.e., constrained—by the legal limits set on words or, metaphorically, by the bondage of sin; "a ward": one who is under the protection or control of another.
3. I.e., as a pilgrim still far from relief looks up at the dark sky—but also, albeit perhaps unknowingly, up toward God—then cries, so did I keep sighing as I climbed.
4. I.e., his sins ("smoke and pleasures"), being compared to grains of corn or other seed, weigh more than his recent penance ("late pains").
5. I.e., being led to the east, toward the place of rebirth, I could spy a field.
6. Sleeping in a field, Jacob saw a ladder reaching from earth to heaven, with angels ascending and descending on it (Genesis 28.10–12).

Here I reposed; but scarce well set,
    A grove descried[7]
35 Of stately height, whose branches met
    And mixed on every side;
    I entered, and once in,
      Amazed to see 't,
Found all was changed, and a new spring
40   Did all my senses greet.

The unthrift sun shot vital gold,
    A thousand pieces,[8]
And heaven its azure did unfold,
    Checkered with snowy fleeces;
45   The air was all in spice,
      And every bush
A garland wore; thus fed my eyes,
    But all the ear lay hush.°   *quiet*

Only a little fountain[9] lent
50   Some use for ears,
And on the dumb shades language spent°   *expended*
    The music of her tears;
    I drew her near, and found
      The cistern full
55 Of divers stones, some bright and round,
    Others ill-shaped and dull.[1]

The first, pray mark, as quick as light
    Danced through the flood,[2]
But the last, more heavy than the night,
60   Nailed to the center stood;[3]
    I wondered much, but tired
      At last with thought,
My restless eye that still desired
    As strange an object brought.[4]

65 It was a bank of flowers, where I descried
    Though 'twas midday,
Some fast asleep, others broad-eyed
    And taking in the ray;[5]
    Here, musing long, I heard
70   A rushing wind
Which still increased, but whence it stirred
    No where I could not find.

---

7. I.e., he was scarcely settled for rest when he saw a grove of trees.
8. I.e., the sun like a spendthrift tosses away pieces of gold (its rays).
9. Perhaps alluding to a baptismal font.
1. Critics have proposed various interpretations of the stones, e.g., ideas, images, and souls.
2. The water. "Pray mark": i.e., take note.
3. Probably the "heaviest stone" is the idea of Christ's crucifixion, with the cross as the "center" of Christian theology. Other interpretations of "center" include earth and hell.
4. I.e., his eye, still desiring to see something, brought to his sight an object as strange as the one just described.
5. God and Christ were often symbolized by the sun. "Fast asleep": i.e., spiritually sluggish.

I turned me round, and to each shade
    Dispatched an eye
75 To see if any leaf had made
    Least motion or reply,
    But while I listening sought
        My mind to ease
    By knowing where 'twas, or where not,
80   It whispered, "Where I please."[6]

"Lord," then said I, "on me one breath,[7]
And let me die before my death!"

Cant. chap. 5. ver. 17[8]

*Arise O North, and come thou South-wind and blow upon my garden,
that the spices thereof may flow out.*

1650

The Retreat

Happy those early days! when I
Shined in my angel infancy.
Before I understood this place
Appointed for my second race,[9]
5 Or taught my soul to fancy aught
But a white, celestial thought;
When yet I had not walked above
A mile or two from my first love,[1]
And looking back, at that short space,
10 Could see a glimpse of His bright face;
When on some gilded cloud or flower
My gazing soul would dwell an hour,
And in those weaker glories spy
Some shadows of eternity;
15 Before I taught my tongue to wound
My conscience with a sinful sound,
Or had the black art to dispense
A several° sin to every sense,   separate
But felt through all this fleshly dress[2]
20 Bright shoots of everlastingness.
    O, how I long to travel back,
And tread again that ancient track!
That I might once more reach that plain
Where first I left my glorious train,[3]

6. "The wind bloweth where it listeth, and thou hearest the sound thereof, but canst not tell whence it cometh, and whither it goeth: so is every one that is born of the Spirit" (John 3.8).
7. I.e., blow one of your life-giving (and perhaps also poetry-inspiring) breaths upon me.
8. The poem ends by merging its voice, imaged as breath, with that of the Biblical "Song of Solomon"; the quoted verse actually comes from chapter 4.16.
9. "Race" is a traditional Christian metaphor for

"life"; by "second" race Vaughan evidently alludes to a belief in the soul's heavenly existence prior to its human life. Such a belief was held by some Christian Neoplatonists and Hermetic authors; it reappears in Wordsworth's "Ode: Intimations of Immortality" (see pp. 728–32).
1. I.e., Christ.
2. I.e., the mortal body.
3. I.e., my previous mode of existence, or, possibly, my place in God's angelic entourage.

25   From whence th' enlightened spirit sees
      That shady city of palm trees.[4]
      But, ah! my soul with too much stay°   *delay*
      Is drunk, and staggers in the way.
      Some men a forward motion love;
30   But I by backward steps would move,
      And when this dust falls to the urn,[5]
      In that state I came, return.

                      1650

They Are All Gone into the World of Light!

They are all gone into the world of light!
    And I alone sit lingering here;
Their very memory is fair and bright,
    And my sad thoughts doth clear.

5   It° glows and glitters in my cloudy breast   *the memory*
      Like stars upon some gloomy grove,
      Or those faint beams in which this hill is dressed
      After the sun's remove.

I see them walking in an air of glory,
10   Whose light doth trample on my days;
      My days, which are at best but dull and hoary,°   *gray, ancient*
      Mere glimmering and decays.

O holy hope! and high humility,
      High as the heavens above!
15   These are your walks, and you have showed them me
      To kindle my cold love.

Dear, beauteous death! the jewel of the just,
      Shining nowhere but in the dark;
      What mysteries do lie beyond thy dust,
20   Could man outlook that mark!°   *boundary*

He that hath found some fledged bird's nest may know[6]
      At first sight if the bird be flown;
      But what fair well° or grove he sings in now,   *spring*
      That is to him° unknown.   *the seeker*

25   And yet, as angels in some brighter dreams
      Call to the soul when man doth sleep,
      So some strange thoughts transcend our wonted themes,[7]
      And into glory peep.

If a star were confined into a tomb,[8]
30   Her captive flames must needs burn there;

---

4. Heaven or the Promised Land, as shown to Moses (Deuteronomy 34.1–4); for its identification with Jericho, see Deuteronomy 34.3.
5. Tomb; "this dust": my body.
6. The bird often symbolizes the human soul; cf. Herbert, "Easter Wings" (pp. 330–31); "Fledged": fit to fly.
7. I.e., accustomed ideas.
8. Probably a metaphor for the body, with the "star" as the soul.

But when the hand that locked her up gives room,
    She'll shine through all the sphere.

O Father of eternal life, and all
    Created glories under Thee!
35 Resume° Thy spirit from this world of thrall°   *take back / slavery*
    Into true liberty!

Either disperse these mists, which blot and fill
    My perspective[9] still as they pass;
Or else remove me hence unto that hill
40   Where I shall need no glass.[1]

                                             1655

The Waterfall

With what deep murmurs through time's silent stealth
Doth thy transparent, cool, and watery wealth
    Here flowing fall,
    And chide, and call,
5 As if his liquid, loose retinue[2] stayed
Lingering, and were of this steep place afraid,
    The common pass
    Where, clear as glass,
    All must descend—
10   Not to an end,
But quickened by this deep and rocky grave,
Rise to a longer course more bright and brave.[3]

    Dear stream! dear bank, where often I
    Have sat and pleased my pensive eye,
15   Why, since each drop of thy quick° store   *living*
    Runs thither whence it flowed before,[4]
    Should poor souls fear a shade or night,
    Who came, sure, from a sea of light?[5]
    Or since those drops are all sent back
20   So sure to thee, that none doth lack,
    Why should frail flesh doubt any more
    That what God takes He'll not restore?

    O useful element and clear!
    My sacred wash and cleanser here,

9. Literally, telescope; more generally, ability to see into the distance.
1. Vaughan superimposes the modern image of the magnifying telescope onto the traditional Christian and Platonic image of life as an experience of distorted vision or darkness; "for now we see through a glass, darkly; but then face to face" (1 Corinthians 13.12). "Hill": Sion hill, figuratively, heaven.
2. Those in service; i.e., the water that has not yet flowed over the edge is likened to Time's ("his") followers or "retainers," with a probable bilingual pun on *retenu:* "held back" (French).

3. I.e., elaborating on the central Christian paradox of resurrection, Vaughan imagines death as a "quickening" in the grave (a movement like that of a child in the womb) followed by a rising that defies the waterfall's apparently natural downward "course." "Brave": splendid. Cf. Herbert's "Virtue," line 5 (p. 337).
4. A reference to the cyclical movement of water (from river to sea to clouds to rain or snow to rivers again); often held to be a sign of the ordering of God's universe.
5. A Hermetic concept (see "The Retreat," n. 9, p. 450).

25 My first consignor[6] unto those
Fountains of life where the Lamb goes!
What sublime truths and wholesome themes
Lodge in thy mystical deep streams!
Such as dull man can never find
30 Unless that Spirit lead his mind
Which first upon thy face did move,[7]
And hatched all with His quickening love.
As this loud brook's incessant fall
In streaming rings restagnates° all,   *becomes stagnant*
35 Which reach by course the bank, and then
Are no more seen, just so pass men.
O my invisible estate,°   *condition*
My glorious liberty, still late![8]
Thou art the channel my soul seeks,
40 Not this with cataracts° and creeks.   *waterfalls*

                   1655

The Night

John 2.3[9]

Through that pure virgin shrine,[1]
That sacred veil drawn o'er Thy glorious noon,[2]
That men might look and live, as glowworms[3] shine,
   And face the moon,
5 Wise Nicodemus saw such light
 As made him know his God by night.[4]

  Most blest believer he!
Who in that land of darkness and blind eyes
Thy long-expected healing wings[5] could see,
10   When Thou didst rise!
 And, what can never more be done,
 Did at midnight speak with the Sun![6]

6. One who dispatches goods to another, i.e., the baptismal water ("cleanser here") delivers the speaker to eternal life ("where the Lamb goes"); compare Revelation 7.17: "For the Lamb which is in the midst of the throne shall feed them, and shall lead them unto living fountains of waters: and God shall wipe away all tears from their eyes."
7. A description of the beginning of creation (thus, "hatched all"): "And the Spirit of God moved upon the face of the waters" (Genesis 1.2).
8. I.e., not yet arrived (that is, the liberty of eternal life after death); compare Romans 8.21: "Because the creature itself also shall be delivered from the bondage of corruption into the glorious liberty of the children of God."
9. As at the end of "Regeneration," Vaughan or the typesetter mistook the exact biblical reference; the citation should be to the verse in John (3.2) describing how Nicodemus, a Pharisee, came to Jesus by night and was able, even in literal and spiritual darkness, to recognize Christ as a "teacher come from God."
1. Refers both to Christ's mortal body and to the night sky; the "virgin shrine" condenses allusions not only to Christ but also to his mother, Mary, and probably to Diana, virgin and goddess of the moon (according to pagan myth).
2. Christ was often figured as the sun; "sacred veil": Paul writes of "a new and living way which he [Christ] hath consecrated for us, through the veil, that is to say, his flesh" (Hebrews 10.20).
3. An insect, (the female of) which emits a shining green light from the abdomen; i.e. (perhaps), as the glowworms shine by reflecting the moon's light, so humans spiritually shine by reflecting Christ's light.
4. Nicodemus, coming to Christ at night, addressed him as "come from God"; in the same account Christ speaks of his coming as "the light" (John 3.1–21).
5. A prophecy of Christ's coming: "But unto you that fear my Name shall the Sun of righteousness arise with healing in his wings" (Malachi 4.2).
6. A reference back to Nicodemus, who spoke with Christ at midnight in a miracle the speaker thinks (perhaps erroneously) can never recur.

O who will tell me where
He found Thee at that dead and silent hour?
15 What hallowed solitary ground did bear
So rare a flower,
Within whose sacred leaves did lie
The fulness of the Deity?

No mercy-seat of gold,
20 No dead and dusty cherub, nor carved stone,
But His own living works did my Lord hold
And lodge alone;[7]
Where trees and herbs did watch and peep
And wonder, while the Jews did sleep.[8]

25 Dear night! this world's defeat;
The stop to busy fools; care's check and curb;
The day of spirits; my soul's calm retreat
Which none disturb!
Christ's progress, and His prayer time;[9]
30 The hours to which high heaven doth chime;

God's silent, searching flight;
When my Lord's head is filled with dew, and all
His locks are wet with the clear drops of night;
His still, soft call;
35 His knocking time;[1] the soul's dumb watch,
When spirits their fair kindred catch.

Were all my loud, evil days
Calm and unhaunted as is thy dark tent,
Whose peace but by some angel's wing or voice
40 Is seldom rent,°   torn
Then I in heaven all the long year
Would keep, and never wander here.

But living where the sun
Doth all things wake, and where all mix and tire
45 Themselves and others, I consent and run
To every mire,
And by this world's ill-guiding light,[2]
Err more than I can do by night.

---

7. God instructed Moses on how to make the ark of the Covenant: "And thou shalt make a mercy seat of pure gold . . . And thou shalt make two cherubims of gold, of beaten work shalt thou make them, in the two ends of the mercy seat" (Exodus 25.17–18). Vaughan contrasts the physical temples of the Old Testament with the "living works" in which Christ lodges.
8. Vaughan imputes to plants an eagerness for Christ's coming lacking in the Jews. Their spiritual lethargy ("sleep") prevents them from recognizing Christ's divinity.
9. "*Mark, chap.* i.35. *Luke, chap.* xxi.37" [Vaughan's note]. The cited passages mention

Christ's praying at night.
1. "I sleep, but my heart waketh: it is the voice of my beloved that knocketh, saying, Open to me, my sister, my love, my dove, my undefiled: for my head is filled with dew, and my locks with the drops of the night" (Song of Solomon 5.2).
2. The speaker's own "consent" to error, along with the "ill-guiding light" of the world, cause him to run into a spiritual swamp ("mire"). The "ill-guiding light" may allude to the will-o'-the-wisp, which was said to draw travelers astray into bogs by holding a false light before them; the phenomenon of nocturnal light is caused by the combustion of marsh gas.

There is in God, some say,
50 A deep but dazzling darkness, as men here
Say it is late and dusky, because they
    See not all clear.
 O for that night! where I in Him
 Might live invisible and dim!

                                1655

MARGARET CAVENDISH
1623–1673

An Apology for Writing So Much upon This Book[1]

Condemn me not, I make so much ado
About this book; it is my child, you know.
Just like a bird, when her young are in nest,
Goes in, and out, and hops, and takes no rest:
5 But when their young are fledg'd, their heads out-peep,
Lord! What a chirping does the old one keep!
So I, for fear my strengthless child should fall
Against a door, or stool, aloud I call;
Bid have a care of such a dangerous place:
10 Thus write I much, to hinder all disgrace.

The Sea Similized[2] to Meadows and Pastures: the Mariners, to Shepherds: the Mast, to a May-Pole: the Fish, to Beasts

The waves, like ridges of plow'd land, are high;
Whereat the ship oft stumbling, down doth lie.
But, in a calm, the sea's like meadows seen
Level; its saltness makes it look as green.
5 When ships thereon a slow soft pace do walk;
Then mariners, as shepherds, sing and talk:
Some whistle, and some on their pipes do play;
And thus, with mirth, they pass their time away.
And every mast is like a May-pole[3] high,
10 Round which they dance, though not so merrily
As shepherds do, when they their lasses bring
Garlands, to May-poles tied with a silk string.
Instead of garlands, they hang on their mast
Huge sails and ropes, to tie these garlands fast.
15 Instead of lasses, they do dance with Death;
And for their music, they have Boreas'[4] breath.
Instead of wine and wassails,[5] drink salt tears;

1. This poem appeared in slightly different versions at the beginning of all three editions of Margaret Cavendish's poems published during her lifetime (in 1653, 1664, and 1668, respectively; we reprint the 1668 text). For the metaphor of the book or poem as child, see Sir Philip Sidney, *Astrophil and Stella*, Sonnet 1 (p. 192) and Anne Bradstreet, "The Author to Her Book" (pp. 419–20).
2. Compared.
3. A high pole, painted with spiral stripes of different colors, decked with flowers, set up on a green for revelers to dance around at a May Day festival.
4. That of the north wind.
5. The liquor with which healths were drunk.

And for their meat, they feed on nought but fears.
For flocks of sheep, great schools of herrings swim;
20   The whales, as ravenous wolves, do feed on them.
As sportful kids skip over hillocks green,
So dancing dolphins, on the waves are seen.
The porpoise, like their watchful dog espies,
And gives them warning when great winds will rise.
25   Instead of barking, he his head doth show
Above the waters, when they roughly flow:
And, like as men, in time of show'ring rain
And wind, do not in open fields remain;
But quickly run for shelter to a tree:
30   So ships at anchor lie upon the sea.

Of Many Worlds in This World

Just like as in a nest of boxes[6] round,
degrees of sizes in each box are found:
So, in this world, may many others be
Thinner and less, and less still by degree:
5   Although they are not subject to our sense,
A world may be no bigger than two-pence.[7]
Nature is curious,° and such works may shape,   *ingenious, skillful*
Which our dull senses easily escape:
For creatures, small as atoms,[8] may be there,
10   If every one a creature's figure bear.
If atoms four, a world can make,[9] then see
What several worlds might in an ear-ring be:
For, millions of those atoms may be in
The head of one small, little, single pin.
15   And if thus small, then ladies may well wear
A world of worlds, as pendents in each ear.

1668

JOHN DRYDEN

1631–1700

Song from *The Indian Emperor*[1]

Ah, fading joy, how quickly art thou past!
Yet we thy ruin haste.

---

6. A set of boxes of graduated sizes packed inside one another.
7. An English silver coin having the value of two pennies; a very small amount.
8. A very minute or microscopic object.
9. In another poem Cavendish declares that the four elements—earth, water, air, and fire—are made out of four different kinds of atoms: "square flat atoms," "atoms round," "long straight atoms,"

and "sharpest atoms" respectively.
1. This play, first performed by the King's Company in the spring of 1665, focuses on the conquest of Mexico by Hernán Cortés (1485–1547), the Spanish conquistador. The song is sung by an Indian woman to a group of Spaniards reclining by a fountain (4.3); immediately after the song's end, they are captured by Indian forces.

As if the cares of human life were few,
    We seek out new:
5 And follow fate, which would too fast pursue.[2]

See how on every bough the birds express
    In their sweet notes their happiness.
    They all enjoy and nothing spare;
    But on their mother nature lay their care.
10 Why then should man, the lord of all below,
    Such troubles choose to know
    As none of all his subjects undergo?

Hark, hark, the waters fall, fall, fall,
    And with a murmuring sound
15   Dash, dash upon the ground,
    To gentle slumbers call.

                          1667

Song from *Troilus and Cressida*[3]

1

Can life be a blessing,
    Or worth the possessing,
Can life be a blessing, if love were away?
    Ah, no! though our love all night keep us waking,
5 And though he[4] torment us with cares all the day,
    Yet he sweetens, he sweetens our pains in the taking;
There's an hour at the last, there's an hour to repay.

2

In every possessing
    The ravishing blessing,
10 In every possessing the fruit of our pain,
    Poor lovers forget long ages of anguish,
Whate'er they have suffered and done to obtain;
    'Tis a pleasure, a pleasure to sigh and to languish,
When we hope, when we hope to be happy again.

                          1679

2. I.e., which, even if we did not conspire with it, would hurry us too quickly to our end. Dryden, in response to criticism of this metaphor, explained that it was borrowed from a line in the *Aeneid* (11.695).
3. *Troilus and Cressida, or Truth Found Too Late* is Dryden's third and last adaptation of a Shakespeare play; the Homeric story of two lovers, Troilus and Cressida, separated during the siege of Troy, had also been told by Chaucer (see p. 52). Dryden alters Shakespeare's play considerably; unlike Shakespeare, Dryden has both title charac-

ters die, for instance. In both versions Cressida's uncle, Pandarus, is a voyeuristic, lewd character who schemes to bring about the physical consummation of the lovers' desires, but only in Dryden's text does Pandarus use a song to serenade the lovers. In this scene (3.2), Pandarus listens outside the lovers' door the morning after they have consummated their love, and then instructs a group of musicians to sing this song.
4. Love is commonly personified as the young boy, Cupid.

From Absalom and Achitophel: A Poem[5]

In pious times, ere priestcraft did begin,
Before polygamy was made a sin;
When man on many multiplied his kind,
Ere one to one was cursedly confined;
5   When nature prompted and no law denied
Promiscuous use of concubine and bride;
Then Israel's monarch after Heaven's own heart,[6]
His vigorous warmth did variously impart
To wives and slaves; and, wide as his command,
10   Scattered his Maker's image through the land.
Michal,[7] of royal blood, the crown did wear,
A soil ungrateful to the tiller's care:
Not so the rest; for several mothers bore
To godlike David several sons before.
15   But since like slaves his bed they did ascend,
No true succession could their seed attend.
Of all this numerous progeny was none
So beautiful, so brave, as Absalom:
Whether, inspired by some diviner lust,
20   His father got° him with a greater gust,°   begot / enjoyment
Or that° his conscious destiny made way,   whether
By manly beauty, to imperial sway.[8]
Early in foreign fields he won renown,
With kings and states allied to Israel's crown:
25   In peace the thoughts of war he could remove,
And seemed as he were only born for love.
Whate'er he did, was done with so much ease,
In him alone 'twas natural to please;
His motions all accompanied with grace;
30   And paradise was opened in his face.
With secret joy indulgent David viewed

5. The title names refer the reader to 2 Samuel 13–18. Absalom there rebels against his father, King David; Achitophel advises Absalom to destroy David at once. Like many other texts from this period, Dryden's poem uses this biblical story as an analogue for the religious and political crisis of 1678 that came to be known as the "Popish Plot," and its aftermath of bitter political struggle between Charles II and the earl of Shaftesbury: David stands for Charles II and Absalom for the duke of Monmouth, Charles' illegitimate son. Achitophel represents the earl of Shaftesbury; he urged Monmouth to seek the succession in an attempt to displace Charles' brother James, the duke of York, an openly practicing Catholic. In 1678, Titus Oates offered sworn testimony of the existence of a Jesuit plot to assassinate the king, burn London, massacre Protestants, and restore the Catholic Church; this testimony, combined with the discovery of the murder of a London justice of the peace, Sir Edmund Berry Godfrey, who had received a copy of the oath for safekeeping, prompted fear of a Catholic uprising; Protestant leaders took advantage of the panic to try to exclude James from the succession. To what extent (if any) such a plot really existed is a matter of historical debate. Charles managed to retain his brother's position as heir, and charged Shaftesbury with high treason. Dryden anonymously published the first part of "Absalom and Achitophel" in 1681 while the earl was under arrest, apparently as an attempt to stir public opinion against him; however, the grand jury soon set the earl free (he died two years later). A second part appeared in 1682, although much of this work is attributed to Nahum Tate. After Charles II died in 1685 and James II succeeded to the throne, Dryden (and his two sons) converted to Catholicism in 1686; he remained a Catholic for the rest of his life.
6. God calls David "a man after mine own heart" in Acts 13.22.
7. David's childless wife. She stands for Charles' childless queen, Catherine of Portugal.
8. Although the lines are ambiguous, Dryden seems to be asking whether Absalom gained imperial power (sway) by heredity or by deliberate use of his "manly beauty." Dryden alludes here to Monmouth's personal attractiveness and, in the following lines, to his prowess in wars against the Dutch and later the French, and to his marriage (arranged by the king) to the Scottish heiress Anne Scott.

His youthful image in his son renewed:
To all his wishes nothing he denied;
And made the charming Annabel his bride.
35 What faults he had (for who from faults is free?)
His father could not, or he would not see.
Some warm excesses which the law forbore,
Were cònstrued youth that purged by boiling o'er:
And Amnon's murder,[9] by a specious name,
40 Was called a just revenge for injured fame.
Thus praised and loved the noble youth remained,
While David, undisturbed, in Sion[1] reigned.
But life can never be sincerely° blest;   *wholly*
Heaven punishes the bad, and proves° the best.   *tries*
45 The Jews,[2] a headstrong, moody, murmuring race,
As ever tried the extent and stretch of grace;
God's pampered people, whom, debauched with ease,
No king could govern, nor no God could please
(Gods they had tried of every shape and size
50 That god-smiths could produce, or priests devise);[3]
These Adam-wits,[4] too fortunately free,
Began to dream they wanted° liberty;   *lacked*
And when no rule, no precedent was found,
Of men by laws less circumscribed and bound,
55 They led their wild desires to woods and caves,[5]
And thought that all but savages were slaves.
They who, when Saul was dead, without a blow,
Made foolish Ishbosheth the crown forego;[6]
Who banished David did from Hebron[7] bring,
60 And with a general shout proclaimed him king:
Those very Jews, who, at their very best,
Their humor° more than loyalty expressed,   *caprice*
Now wondered why so long they had obeyed
An idol monarch,[8] which their hands had made;
65 Thought they might ruin him they could create,
Or melt him to that golden calf, a state.[9]
But these were random bolts;° no formed design   *shots*

9. Absalom had killed his half-brother Amnon to avenge his rape of Absalom's half-sister, Tamar (2 Samuel 13.28–29). The parallel with Monmouth is vague, although he had a reputation for violence in his youth, and his troopers had recently attacked an abusive Parliamentarian, Sir John Coventry. "Cònstrued": interpreted as the result of.
1. I.e., London.
2. I.e., the English.
3. Perhaps a reference to the novelties in church doctrine and practice that had issued in the disestablishment of the Anglican Church under the Commonwealth; more generally, the recent political and religious controversies that had divided England. The Israelites (God's chosen people) were frequently converted to the worship of the pagan gods of the tribes and peoples with whom they fought and traded.
4. The word calls attention to the supposedly untutored quality of the dissenters from the Anglican communion, and also the biblical Adam's rebellion against the single restraint imposed on

him: eating the fruit of the Tree of the Knowledge of Good and Evil (Genesis 2.16–17).
5. Dissenters from the Church of England were sometimes forced to worship in hiding.
6. Saul stands for Oliver Cromwell (1599–1658), English general and statesman, lord protector of England; Ishbosheth, Saul's son who briefly ruled Israel, here represents Richard Cromwell (1626–1712), who had succeeded his father as lord protector before being forced to abdicate in 1659.
7. David was first crowned king of the tribe of Judah, in Hebron, before becoming king of Israel (2 Samuel 1–5); Charles II was first crowned king in Scotland, before being restored to the throne in England in 1660.
8. I.e., Oliver Cromwell. Jews were not allowed to worship idols (Exodus 20.4).
9. I.e., that idol, a republic or commonwealth. The biblical reference is to the image of a calf, made of melted golden earrings, which the Israelites worshiped while Moses was on Mount Sinai (Exodus 32.1–4).

Nor interest made the factious crowd to join:
The sober part of Israel, free from stain,
70 Well knew the value of a peaceful reign;
And, looking backward with a wise affright,°   *fear*
Saw seams of wounds, dishonest° to the sight: *dishonorable*
In contemplation of whose ugly scars
They cursed the memory of civil wars.[1]
75 The moderate sort of men, thus qualified,°   *mollified*
Inclined the balance to the better side;
And David's mildness managed it so well,
The bad found no occasion to rebel.
But when to sin our biased nature leans,[2]
80 The careful° Devil is still at hand with means;   *watchful*
And providently pimps for ill desires:[3]
The Good Old Cause[4] revived, a plot requires.
Plots, true or false, are necessary things,
To raise up commonwealths and ruin kings.
85   The inhabitants of old Jerusalem
Were Jebusites;[5] the town so called from them;
And theirs the native right.
But when the chosen people[6] grew more strong,
The rightful cause at length became the wrong;
90 And every loss the men of Jebus bore,
They still were thought God's enemies the more.
Thus worn and weakened, well or ill content,
Submit they must to David's government:
Impoverished and deprived of all command,
95 Their taxes doubled as they lost their land;
And, what was harder yet to flesh and blood,
Their gods disgraced, and burnt like common wood.
This set the heathen priesthood[7] in a flame;
For priests of all religions are the same:
100 Of whatsoe'er descent their godhead be,
Stock,[8] stone, or other homely pedigree,
In his defense his servants are as bold,
As if he had been born of beaten gold.
The Jewish rabbins, though their enemies,
105 In this conclude them honest men and wise:[9]
For 'twas their duty, all the learned think,
To espouse his cause, by whom they eat and drink.[1]

---

1. I.e., such as the religious and political turmoil that had led to the beheading of Charles II's father, Charles I, in 1649.
2. "Biased": prejudiced, or inclined in some direction (the OED cites Dryden's line); i.e., when our human inclination to sin takes over.
3. I.e., the devil prudently provides the means ("pimps") for sinful desires.
4. A popular phrase referring to the Commonwealth.
5. The Jebusites (Judges 1.21) represent Roman Catholics; Jerusalem stands for London.
6. The Protestants, some of whom claimed for England a divinely appointed destiny like that of the Hebrews.
7. The Catholic clergy, suffering from the recent flare-up of prejudice as well as from the long his-

tory of restrictions to which Dryden has just alluded; in particular, many oppressive laws against Catholics were established under the reign (1558–1603) of Queen Elizabeth I (see pp. 130–32).
8. Block of wood, i.e., of humble descent.
9. I.e., even though the Anglican divines ("Jewish rabbins") are "enemies" to Catholics, they consider Catholics wise in their "bold" defense of their God.
1. I.e., Christ, whose body Catholics "eat and drink" in Communion; according to the Catholic doctrine of transubstantiation, the bread and wine actually become the body of Christ during Communion (whereas Protestant doctrine holds that the bread and wine symbolize or represent his body).

From hence began that Plot,[2] the nation's curse,
Bad in itself, but represented worse;
110   Raised in extremes, and in extremes decried;
With oaths affirmed, with dying vows denied;
Not weighed or winnowed[3] by the multitude;
But swallowed in the mass, unchewed and crude.
Some truth there was, but dashed° and brewed with lies,   *mixed*
115   To please the fools, and puzzle all the wise.
Succeeding times did equal folly call,
Believing nothing, or believing all.
The Egyptian[4] rites the Jebusites embraced,
Where gods were recommended by their taste.
120   Such savory deities must needs be good,
As served at once for worship and for food.
By force they could not introduce these gods,
For ten to one in former days was odds;[5]
So fraud was used (the sacrificer's trade):[6]
125   Fools are more hard to conquer than persuade.
Their busy teachers mingled with the Jews,
And raked for converts even the court and stews:°   *brothels*
Which Hebrew priests the more unkindly took,
Because the fleece accompanies the flock.[7]
130   Some thought they God's anointed[8] meant to slay
By guns, invented since full many a day:
Our author swears it not; but who can know
How far the Devil and Jebusites may go?
This Plot, which failed for want of common sense,
135   Had yet a deep and dangerous consequence:
For, as when raging fevers boil the blood,
The standing lake soon floats into a flood,
And every hostile humor, which before
Slept quiet in its channels, bubbles o'er;
140   So several factions from this first ferment
Work up to foam, and threat the government.
Some by their friends, more by themselves thought wise,
Opposed the power to which they could not rise.
Some had in courts been great, and thrown from thence,
145   Like fiends were hardened in impenitence;°   *unrepentance*
Some, by their monarch's fatal mercy, grown
From pardoned rebels kinsmen to the throne,
Were raised in power and public office high;
Strong bands, if bands ungrateful men could tie.
150   Of these the false Achitophel[9] was first;

---

2. I.e., the Catholic plot described in note 5 (p. 458).
3. According to this simile, in which the reports of a plot are compared to grain, the populace has not carefully "weighed" and "winnowed" (separated the good from the bad) the grain, but has swallowed it whole.
4. I.e., the French; hence, Roman Catholics. The allusion is to the Mass, incorporating the doctrine of transubstantiation.
5. I.e., because Protestants outnumbered Catholics (although the difference in numbers was prob-

ably much smaller than Dryden indicates).
6. I.e., those who use fraud sacrifice innocent people.
7. Dryden implies that the Anglican clergy ("Hebrew priests") resented any loss of tithes ("fleece") paid to the established church; such loss was caused by Catholic conversions.
8. The king.
9. Shaftesbury had been a member of Cromwell's council of state; later, he had helped to bring back Charles II, and was made a member of the Cabal, a powerful committee of the Privy Council.

A name to all succeeding ages cursed:
For close° designs, and crooked counsels fit;   secret
Sagacious, bold, and turbulent of wit;°   imagination
Restless, unfixed in principles and place;
155 In power unpleased, impatient of disgrace:
A fiery soul, which, working out its way, ⎤
Fretted the pygmy° body to decay, ⎬   overly small
And o'er-informed the tenement of clay.[1] ⎦
A daring pilot in extremity;
160 Pleased with the danger, when the waves went high,
He sought the storms; but, for a calm unfit,
Would steer too nigh the sands, to boast his wit.
Great wits° are sure to madness near allied,   geniuses
And thin partitions do their bounds divide;
165 Else why should he, with wealth and honor blest,
Refuse his age the needful hours of rest?
Punish a body which he could not please,
Bankrupt of life, yet prodigal of ease?
And all to leave what with his toil he won,
170 To that unfeathered two-legged thing,[2] a son;
Got,° while his soul did huddled° notions try;   begotten / confused
And born a shapeless lump, like anarchy.
In friendship false, implacable in hate,
Resolved to ruin or to rule the state.
175 To compass° this the triple bond he broke,[3] ⎤   accomplish
The pillars of the public safety shook, ⎬
And fitted Israel for a foreign yoke; ⎦
Then seized with fear, yet still affecting fame,
Usurped a patriot's all-atoning name.[4]
180 So easy still it proves in factious times,
With public zeal to cancel private crimes.
How safe is treason, and how sacred ill,
Where none can sin against the people's will!
Where crowds can wink, and no offense be known,
185 Since in another's guilt they find their own!
Yet fame deserved, no enemy can grudge;
The statesman we abhor, but praise the judge.
In Israel's courts ne'er sat an Abbethdin[5]
With more discerning eyes, or hands more clean;
190 Unbrided,[6] unsought, the wretched to redress;
Swift of dispatch, and easy of access.
Oh, had he been content to serve the crown,
With virtues only proper to the gown;°   judiciary
Or had the rankness of the soil been freed
195 From cockle,° that oppressed the noble seed;   weedlike plant

1. I.e., overanimated his body.
2. The ancient Greek philosopher Plato's defini-
tion of cloddish man.
3. Shaftesbury helped to bring about the war
against Holland, with France as an ally, in 1672;
"triple bond": an alliance between England, Swe-
den, and the Dutch Republic against France,
which was thought to pose the threat of an inva-

sion (line 177).
4. The name of "patriot" was affected, then and
thereafter, by the party out of power.
5. A rabbinical term for a justice. Shaftesbury pre-
sided over the Court of Chancery from 1672 to
1673.
6. I.e., not "married" or united with anyone seek-
ing to influence his actions in the court.

David for him his tuneful harp had strung,
And Heaven had wanted one immortal song.[7]
But wild Ambition loves to slide, not stand,
And Fortune's ice prefers to Virtue's land.
200 Achitophel, grown weary to possess
A lawful fame, and lazy happiness,
Disdained the golden fruit to gather free,
And lent the crowd his arm to shake the tree.
Now, manifest of° crimes contrived long since,   *detected in*
205 He stood at bold defiance with his prince;
Held up the buckler° of the people's cause   *protector*
Against the crown, and skulked behind the laws.
The wished occasion of the Plot he takes;
Some circumstances finds, but more he makes.
210 By buzzing emissaries fills the ears
Of listening crowds with jealousies° and fears   *suspicions*
Of arbitrary counsels brought to light,
And proves the king himself a Jebusite.
Weak arguments! which yet he knew full well
215 Were strong with people easy to rebel.
For, governed by the moon, the giddy Jews
Tread the same track when she the prime renews;[8]
And once in twenty years, their scribes record,
By natural instinct they change their lord.
220 Achitophel still wants a chief, and none
Was found so fit as warlike Absalom:
Not that he wished his greatness to create
(For politicians neither love nor hate),
But, for he knew his title not allowed,
225 Would keep him still depending on the crowd,
That kingly power, thus ebbing out, might be
Drawn to the dregs of a democracy.[9]
Him he attempts with studied arts to please,
And sheds his venom in such words as these:
230   "Auspicious prince, at whose nativity
Some royal planet[1] ruled the southern sky;
Thy longing country's darling and desire;
Their cloudy pillar and their guardian fire:
Their second Moses,[2] whose extended wand
235 Divides the seas, and shows the promised land;
Whose dawning day in every distant age
Has exercised the sacred prophet's rage:

---

7. I.e., heaven would have lacked one Psalm of David. Many interpretations exist for this difficult couplet: perhaps it is a reference to Psalm 3, written, as tradition would have it, when David fled from Absalom; other suggestions include Psalm 4 and Psalm 109. The application to Charles II is unclear; some have suggested that it refers to Dryden's poem.
8. The phases of the moon fall on the same day of the calendar year at roughly twenty-year intervals. Crises in English politics occurred in 1640 (the rebellion against Charles I), 1660 (the restoration of Charles II), and the time of the poem.
9. I.e., mob rule.

1. A planet whose influence determines that he (Absalom) should be king.
2. I.e., their guide; after their exodus from Egypt under the leadership of Moses, who separated the waters of the Red Sea long enough to allow them to escape, the Israelites were led in their forty-year wandering by a pillar of clouds by day and a pillar of fire by night (Exodus 13–14). In reference to Christ, Moses said, "A Prophet shall the Lord your God raise up unto you of your brethren, like unto me": Christ is sometimes referred to as "the second Moses" (see Acts 7.37). Here, Achitophel tells Absalom that he is meant to be a second Moses.

The people's prayer, the glad diviners' theme,
The young men's vision, and the old men's dream![3]
240 Thee, savior, thee, the nation's vows confess,
And, never satisfied with seeing, bless:
Swift unbespoken° pomps° thy steps proclaim,   voluntary / celebrations
And stammering babes are taught to lisp thy name.
How long wilt thou the general joy detain,
245 Starve and defraud the people of thy reign?
Content ingloriously to pass thy days
Like one of Virtue's fools that feeds on praise;
Till thy fresh glories, which now shine so bright,
Grow stale and tarnish with our daily sight.
250 Believe me, royal youth, thy fruit must be
Or° gathered ripe, or rot upon the tree.   either
Heaven has to all allotted, soon or late,
Some lucky revolution of their fate;
Whose motions if we watch and guide with skill
255 (For human good depends on human will),
Our Fortune rolls as from a smooth descent,[4]
And from the first impression takes the bent;
But, if unseized, she glides away like wind,
And leaves repenting Folly far behind.
260 Now, now she meets you with a glorious prize,
And spreads her locks before her as she flies.
Had thus Old David, from whose loins you spring,
Not dared, when Fortune called him, to be king,
At Gath[5] an exile he might still remain,
265 And heaven's anointing oil[6] had been in vain.
Let his successful youth your hopes engage;
But shun the example of declining age;
Behold him setting in his western skies,
The shadows lengthening as the vapors rise.[7]
270 He is not now, as when on Jordan's sand[8]
The joyful people thronged to see him land,
Covering the beach, and blackening all the strand;°   shore
But, like the Prince of Angels,[9] from his height
Comes tumbling downward with diminished light,
275 Betrayed by one poor plot to public scorn
(Our only blessing since his cursed return),[1]
Those heaps of people which one sheaf did bind,
Blown off and scattered by a puff of wind.[2]
What strength can he to your designs oppose,

---

3. Cf. the prophecy delivered to Joel: "And it shall come to pass afterward, that I will pour out my spirit upon all flesh; and your sons and your daughters shall prophesy, your old men shall dream dreams, your young men shall see visions" (Joel 2.28).
4. Achitophel stresses the workings of Fortune, or what emblem books called "Occasion," rather than divine Providence. He uses traditional images of Fortune standing on a ball and having to be seized by a forelock as she approaches, the back of her head being bald.
5. David escaped Saul by fleeing to Gath (1 Samuel 27.1–4); here, a reference to Brussels, where

Charles spent much of his exile.
6. God sent Samuel to anoint David as a token that he would finally come to the throne (1 Samuel 16.1–13).
7. The vapors or humors associated with night.
8. I.e., at Dover, where Charles II landed at the time of the Restoration.
9. I.e., Lucifer; compare Luke 10.18: "I beheld Satan as lightning fall from heaven."
1. I.e., the crisis of 1678 was the only favorable opportunity for the conspirators since the Restoration.
2. I.e., the unity and loyalty of the people who had supported the king are easily dispersed.

280 Naked of friends, and round beset with foes?
If Pharaoh's[3] doubtful succor he should use,
A foreign aid would more incense the Jews:
Proud Egypt would dissembled friendship bring;
Foment° the war, but not support the king: *heat, rouse*
285 Nor would the royal party e'er unite
With Pharaoh's arms to assist the Jebusite;
Or if they should, their interest soon would break,
And with such odious aid make David weak.
All sorts of men by my successful arts,
290 Abhorring kings, estrange their altered hearts
From David's rule: and 'tis the general cry,
'Religion, commonwealth, and liberty.'
If you, as champion of the public good,
Add to their arms a chief of royal blood,
295 What may not Israel hope, and what applause
Might such a general gain by such a cause?
Not barren praise alone, that gaudy flower
Fair only to the sight, but solid power;
And nobler is a limited command,
300 Given by the love of all your native land,
Than a successive title, long and dark,
Drawn from the moldy rolls of Noah's ark."[4]
    What cannot praise effect in mighty minds,
When flattery soothes, and when ambition blinds!
305 Desire of power, on earth a vicious weed,
Yet, sprung from high, is of celestial seed:
In God 'tis glory; and when men aspire,
'Tis but a spark too much of heavenly fire.[5]
The ambitious youth, too covetous of fame,
310 Too full of angel's metal[6] in his frame,
Unwarily was led from virtue's ways,
Made drunk with honor, and debauched with praise.
Half loath, and half consenting to the ill
(For loyal blood within him struggled still),
315 He thus replied: "And what pretense have I
To take up arms for public liberty?
My father governs with unquestioned right;
The faith's defender, and mankind's delight,
Good, gracious, just, observant of the laws:
320 And heaven by wonders has espoused his cause.
Whom has he wronged in all his peaceful reign?
Who sues for justice to his throne in vain?
What millions has he pardoned of his foes,
Whom just revenge did to his wrath expose?
325 Mild, easy, humble, studious of our good,
Inclined to mercy, and averse from blood;
If mildness ill with stubborn Israel suit,

---

3. I.e., King Louis XIV of France.
4. Achitophel (Shaftesbury) espouses constitutional monarchy ("a limited command") and parliamentary as opposed to hereditary determination of the succession.
5. Perhaps including a reference to Prometheus, who angered the gods by stealing fire for the benefit of mortals.
6. A double pun: the gold of which the coin "angel" is made, and the spirit ("mettle") of the rebellious angels led by Satan.

His crime is God's belovèd attribute.
What could he gain, his people to betray,
330 Or change his right for arbitrary sway?
Let haughty Pharaoh curse with such a reign
His fruitful Nile, and yoke a servile train.[7]
If David's rule Jerusalem displease,
The Dog Star[8] heats their brains to this disease.
335 Why then should I, encouraging the bad,
Turn rebel and run popularly mad?
Were he a tyrant, who, by lawless might
Oppressed the Jews, and raised the Jebusite,
Well might I mourn; but nature's holy bands
340 Would curb my spirits and restrain my hands:
The people might assert their liberty,
But what was right in them were crime in me.
His favor leaves me nothing to require,
Prevents my wishes, and outruns desire.
345 What more can I expect while David lives?
All but his kingly diadem he gives:
And that"—But there he paused; then sighing, said—
"Is justly destined for a worthier head.
For when my father from his toils shall rest
350 And late augment the number of the blest,[9]
His lawful issue shall the throne ascend,
Or the collateral° line, where that shall end.   brother's
His brother,[1] though oppressed with vulgar spite,
Yet dauntless, and secure of native right,
355 Of every royal virtue stands possessed;
Still dear to all the bravest and the best.
His courage foes,[2] his friends his truth proclaim;
His loyalty the king, the world his fame.
His mercy even the offending crowd will find,
360 For sure he comes of a forgiving kind.°   family
Why should I then repine° at heaven's decree,   complain
Which gives me no pretense to royalty?
Yet O that fate, propitiously° inclined,   favorably
Had raised my birth, or had debased my mind;
365 To my large soul not all her treasure lent,
And then betrayed it to a mean° descent!   low
I find, I find my mounting spirits bold,
And David's part disdains my mother's mold.
Why am I scanted by a niggard[3] birth?
370 My soul disclaims the kindred of her earth;[4]
And, made for empire, whispers me within,
'Desire of greatness is a godlike sin.' "

7. I.e., if King Louis XIV of France were to help
Charles II remain in power, he would only be curs-
ing his own country. In Exodus, the Pharaoh's
refusal to release the enslaved Israelites caused
God to visit a series of plagues on the Egyptian
people.
8. Sirius, the morning and evening star of late
summer, associated with crazing heat.
9. I.e., increase the number of souls in heaven.

1. Although Monmouth and the duke of York
were able to get along for many years, by 1679 they
were opposed to each other, and so it is unlikely
that Monmouth would have felt the emotions for
his uncle that Dryden here has him express.
2. I.e., his foes proclaim his courage.
3. Ungenerous; the birth of a king's son should
confer succession to the throne.
4. I.e., her body.

    Him staggering so when hell's dire agent[5] found,
    While fainting Virtue scarce maintained her ground,
375 He pours fresh forces in, and thus replies:
      "The eternal God, supremely good and wise,
    Imparts not these prodigious gifts in vain:
    What wonders are reserved to bless your reign!
    Against your will, your arguments have shown,
380 Such virtue's only given to guide a throne.
    Not that your father's mildness I contemn,
    But manly force becomes the diadem.
    'Tis true he grants the people all they crave;
    And more, perhaps, than subjects ought to have:
385 For lavish grants suppose a monarch tame,
    And more his goodness than his wit° proclaim.   *intelligence*
    But when should people strive their bonds to break,
    If not when kings are negligent or weak?
    Let him give on till he can give no more,
390 The thrifty Sanhedrin[6] shall keep him poor;
    And every shekel which he can receive,
    Shall cost a limb of his prerogative.[7]
    To ply him with new plots shall be my care;
    Or plunge him deep in some expensive war;
395 Which when his treasure can no more supply,
    He must, with the remains of kingship, buy.
    His faithful friends our jealousies and fears
    Call Jebusites, and Pharaoh's pensioners;
    Whom when our fury from his aid has torn,
400 He shall be naked left to public scorn.
    The next successor, whom I fear and hate,
    My arts have made obnoxious to the state;
    Turned all his virtues to his overthrow,
    And gained our elders[8] to pronounce a foe.
405 His right, for sums of necessary gold,
    Shall first be pawned, and afterward be sold;
    Till time shall ever-wanting David draw,
    To pass your doubtful title into law:
    If not, the people have a right supreme
410 To make their kings; for kings are made for them.
    All empire is no more than power in trust,
    Which, when resumed, can be no longer just.
    Succession, for the general good designed,
    In its own wrong a nation cannot bind;
415 If altering that the people can relieve,
    Better one suffer than a nation grieve.
    The Jews well know their power: ere Saul they chose,

---

5. I.e., as Absalom (Monmouth) wavers, tempted by the sin of pride to attempt the throne despite his own arguments against it, Achitophel (Shaftesbury), acting as "hell's agent," again tries to persuade him to rebel.
6. The high council of the Jews; here the Parliament, which provided the crown with its monies. The Whigs hoped to limit the powers of the crown by refusing to vote money to Charles, but he lived on French subsidies and refused to summon Parliament for the duration of the crisis.
7. A term used with particular reference to a sovereign's rights (in theory, subject to no restrictions).
8. In the Bible, the Jewish magistrates; in the poem, the Parliamentarians who voted to exclude James from the succession.

God was their king, and God they durst depose.[9]
Urge now your piety,° your filial name,   *dutifulness*
420   A father's right, and fear of future fame;
The public good, that universal call,
To which even heaven submitted, answers all.
Nor let his love enchant your generous mind;
'Tis Nature's trick to propagate her kind.
425   Our fond begetters, who would never die,
Love but themselves in their posterity.
Or let his kindness by the effects be tried,
Or let him lay his vain pretense aside.
God said he loved your father; could he bring
430   A better proof than to anoint him king?
It surely showed he loved the shepherd[1] well,
Who gave so fair a flock as Israel.
Would David have you thought his darling son?
What means he then, to alienate[2] the crown?
435   The name of godly he may blush to bear:
'Tis after God's own heart to cheat his heir.[3]
He to his brother gives supreme command;
To you a legacy of barren land,[4]
Perhaps the old harp, on which he thrums his lays,°   *songs*
440   Or some dull Hebrew ballad in your praise.
Then the next heir, a prince severe and wise,
Already looks on you with jealous eyes;
Sees through the thin disguises of your arts,
And marks your progress in the people's hearts.
445   Though now his mighty soul its grief contains,
He meditates revenge who least complains;
And, like a lion, slumbering in the way,
Or sleep dissembling, while he waits his prey,
His fearless foes within his distance draws,
450   Constrains his roaring, and contracts his paws;
Till at the last, his time for fury found,
He shoots with sudden vengeance from the ground;
The prostrate vulgar° passes o'er and spares,   *populace*
But with a lordly rage his hunters tears.
455   Your case no tame expedients will afford:
Resolve on death, or conquest by the sword,
Which for no less a stake than life you draw;
And self-defense is nature's eldest law.
Leave the warm people[5] no considering time;
460   For then rebellion may be thought a crime.

---

9. The Israelites' demand that a secular king (Saul, as it happened) replace the theocratic Judges was condemned as impious: "And the Lord said . . . , they have rejected me, that I should not reign over them" (1 Samuel 8.7). As Saul replaced the Judges, so, in the poem, Oliver Cromwell took over authority from the theocrats of the Commonwealth.
1. As a youth David tended sheep for his father.
2. I.e., transfer title to another (a legal term).
3. A reference to the story of Jacob and Esau (Genesis 27–28). Esau, the older twin, was entitled to the birthright and blessing of his father, but God chose Jacob to continue the covenant he had made with Abraham. Jacob tricked Esau out of his birthright and blessing, apparently with God's approval; see also line 981. Conflicting interpretations exist for how these lines apply to Charles II.
4. James had been titled generalissimo (the supreme commander of combined forces) in 1678; Monmouth had been exiled in the following year.
5. I.e., recently heated or roused in anger.

Prevail° yourself of what occasion gives,   *avail*
But try your title while your father lives;
And that your arms may have a fair pretense,°   *pretext*
Proclaim you take them in the king's defense;
465 Whose sacred life each minute would expose
To plots, from seeming friends, and secret foes.
And who can sound the depth of David's soul?
Perhaps his fear his kindness may control.[6]
He fears his brother, though he loves his son,
470 For plighted vows too late to be undone.
If so, by force he wishes to be gained,
Like women's lechery, to seem constrained.°   *forced*
Doubt not; but when he most affects the frown,
Commit a pleasing rape° upon the crown.   *seizure*
475 Secure his person to secure your cause:
They who possess the prince, possess the laws."
   He said, and this advice above the rest
With Absalom's mild nature suited best:
Unblamed of life (ambition set aside),[7]
480 Not stained with cruelty, nor puffed with pride,
How happy had he been, if destiny
Had higher placed his birth, or not so high!
His kingly virtues might have claimed a throne,
And blest all other countries but his own.
485 But charming greatness since so few refuse,
'Tis juster to lament him than accuse.
Strong were his hopes a rival to remove,
With blandishments to gain the public love;
To head the faction while their zeal was hot,
490 And popularly prosecute the Plot.
To further this, Achitophel unites
The malcontents of all the Israelites;[8]
Whose differing parties he could wisely join,
For several ends, to serve the same design:
495 The best (and of the princes some were such),
Who thought the power of monarchy too much;
Mistaken men, and patriots in their hearts;
Not wicked, but seduced by impious arts.
By these the springs of property were bent,
500 And wound so high, they cracked the government.
The next[9] for interest sought to embroil the state,
To sell their duty at a dearer rate;
And make their Jewish markets of the throne,
Pretending public good, to serve their own.
505 Others thought kings an useless heavy load,
Who cost too much, and did too little good.
These were for laying honest David by,
On principles of pure good husbandry.°   *economy*
With them joined all the haranguers of the throng,

---

6. I.e., perhaps his fear of James keeps Charles II
from being kind to you.
7. I.e., not guilty except perhaps for ambition.
8. Lines 492–543 describe the various groups that

Shaftesbury sought to unite against Charles II.
9. I.e., those primarily concerned with economic
gain, namely London merchants.

510 That thought to get preferment by the tongue.
Who follow next, a double danger bring,
Not only hating David, but the king:
The Solymaean rout,[1] well-versed of old
In godly faction, and in treason bold;
515 Cowering and quaking at a conqueror's sword,
But lofty to a lawful prince restored;
Saw with disdain an ethnic[2] plot begun,
And scorned by Jebusites to be outdone.
Hot Levites[3] headed these; who, pulled before
520 From the ark, which in the Judges' days they bore,
Resumed their cant, and with a zealous cry
Pursued their old beloved theocracy:
Where Sanhedrin and priest enslaved the nation,
And justified their spoils by inspiration:
525 For who so fit for reign as Aaron's race,[4]
If once dominion they could found in grace?
These led the pack; though not of surest scent,
Yet deepest-mouthed° against the government.   *baying loudest*
A numerous host of dreaming saints° succeed,   *sectarians*
530 Of the true old enthusiastic° breed: *fanatic*
'Gainst form and order they their power employ,
Nothing to build, and all things to destroy.
But far more numerous was the herd of such,
Who think too little, and who talk too much.
535 These out of mere instinct, they knew not why,
Adored their fathers' God and property;
And, by the same blind benefit of fate,
The Devil and the Jebusite did hate:
Born to be saved, even in their own despite,
540 Because they could not help believing right.[5]
Such were the tools; but a whole Hydra[6] more
Remains, of sprouting heads too long to score.°   *record*
Some of their chiefs were princes of the land:
In the first rank of these did Zimri[7] stand;
545 A man so various, that he seemed to be
Not one, but all mankind's epitome:
Stiff in opinions, always in the wrong;
Was everything by starts, and nothing long;
But, in the course of one revolving moon,
550 Was chemist, fiddler, statesman, and buffoon:
Then all for women, painting, rhyming, drinking,
Besides ten thousand freaks° that died in thinking.   *whims*
Blest madman, who could every hour employ,

1. The London populace. Solyma was a name for Jerusalem.
2. In the biblical context, gentile; in the historical, Catholic.
3. Men of the tribe of Levi conveyed the Ark of the Covenant when Israel moved camp (Numbers 4.15); the Presbyterian clergy administered the state religion under the Commonwealth ("in the Judges' days").
4. The priestly family; (derisively) the theocratically disposed dissenters.

5. Dryden calls attention to the Calvinist doctrines of predestination and election, and (in line 536) to the commercial origins of many dissenters.
6. Mythical beast with nine heads, each of which was replaced by two heads when it was cut off.
7. An Israelite executed for whoredom (Numbers 25); a second Zimri was a traitor and regicide (1 Kings 26.8–20). Dryden gives the name to George Villiers, duke of Buckingham, a latecomer to Monmouth's cause (described in lines 492–543).

With something new to wish, or to enjoy!
555 Railing and praising were his usual themes;
And both (to show his judgment) in extremes:
So over-violent, or over-civil,
That every man, with him, was God or Devil.
In squandering wealth with his peculiar art:
560 Nothing went unrewarded but desert.°   *worth*
Beggared by fools, whom still° he found too late,   *always*
He had his jest, and they had his estate.
He laughed himself from court; then sought relief
By forming parties, but could ne'er be chief;
565 For, spite of him, the weight of business fell
On Absalom and wise Achitophel:
Thus, wicked but in will, of means bereft,
He left not faction, but of that was left.[8]

      *   *   *

With all these loads of injuries oppressed,
And long revolving in his careful breast
935 The event° of things, at last, his patience tired,   *outcome*
Thus from his royal throne, by Heaven inspired,
The godlike David spoke: with awful fear
His train their Maker in their master hear.
    "Thus long have I, by native mercy swayed,
940 My wrongs dissembled, my revenge delayed:
So willing to forgive the offending age,
So much the father did the king assuage.
But now so far my clemency they slight,
The offenders question my forgiving right.[9]
945 That one was made for many, they contend;
But 'tis to rule; for that's a monarch's end.
They call my tenderness of blood my fear;
Though manly tempers can the longest bear.
Yet, since they will divert my native course,
950 'Tis time to show I am not good by force.
Those heaped affronts that haughty subjects bring,
Are burdens for a camel, not a king:
Kings are the public pillars of the State,
Born to sustain and prop the nation's weight:

8. The passage here omitted has five parts. (1) Lines 569–681: A further roll of the rebels or dissenters, including briefly "The well-hung Balaam and cold Caleb," "canting Nadab" and "bull-faced Jonas," and, extensively, Shimei (Slingsby Bethel, a sheriff of London), "whose youth did early promise bring / Of zeal to God and hatred to his king," and Corah (Titus Oates), whose "zeal to heaven made him his prince despise." (2) Lines 682–752: Absalom's courting of the people and the development of the plot against David. (3) Lines 753–810: Dryden's analysis of the issues involved in conflicts between the people (divinely obligated to obedience) and their monarchs (divinely obligated to just stewardship), culminating thus: "Yet, grant our lords the people kings can make, / What prudent men a settled throne would shake? / For whatsoe'er their sufferings were before, / That change they covet makes them suffer more.... If ancient fabrics nod, and threat to fall, / To patch the flaws, and buttress up the wall, / Thus far 'tis duty; but here fix the mark; / For all beyond it is to touch the ark" (lines 795–804; to touch the ark of the covenant, which contained the Ten Commandments, is to commit sacrilege). (4) Lines 811–913: A short roll of David's supporters, including at length Barzillai (the duke of Ormond)—"The court he practiced, not the courtier's art: / Large was his wealth, but larger was his heart"—and, briefly, Zadoc, Adriel, Jotham, Hushai, and Amiel. (5) Lines 914–932: A brief reprise of number 2, Absalom's courting of the people, and an indication of the mounting danger of open revolt.
9. The right of the king to pardon, questioned by some members of the opposition.

955 If my young Samson will pretend a call
To shake the column, let him share the fall:[1]
But, oh, that yet he would repent and live!
How easy 'tis for parents to forgive!
With how few tears a pardon might be won
960 From nature, pleading for a darling son!
Poor pitied youth, by my paternal care
Raised up to all the height his frame could bear:
Had God ordained his fate for empire born,
He would have given his soul another turn:
965 Gulled° with a patriot's name, whose modern sense   *deceived*
Is one that would by law supplant his prince:
The people's brave,[2] the politician's tool;
Never was patriot yet, but was a fool.
Whence comes it that religion and the laws
970 Should more be Absalom's than David's cause?
His old instructor, ere he lost his place,[3]
Was never thought indued° with so much grace.   *endowed*
Good heavens, how faction can a patriot paint!
My rebel ever proves my people's saint:
975 Would *they* impose an heir upon the throne?
Let Sanhedrins be taught to give their own.
A king's at least a part of government,
And mine as requisite as their consent;
Without my leave a future king to choose,
980 Infers a right the present to depose:
True, they petition me to approve their choice;
But Esau's hands suit ill with Jacob's voice.[4]
My pious subjects for my safety pray,
Which to secure, they take my power away.
985 From plots and treasons Heaven preserve my years,
But save me most from my petitioners.[5]
Unsatiate as the barren womb or grave;
God cannot grant so much as they can crave.
What then is left but with a jealous eye
990 To guard the small remains of royalty?
The law shall still direct my peaceful sway,
And the same law teach rebels to obey:
Votes shall no more established power control—
Such votes as make a part exceed the whole:
995 No groundless clamors shall my friends remove,
Nor crowds have power to punish ere they prove:
For gods and godlike kings their care express,
Still to defend their servants in distress.
O that my power to saving were confined: ⎫
1000 Why am I forced, like Heaven, against my mind, ⎬
To make examples of another kind?   ⎭

1. Samson, pulling down the supporting columns of a Philistine temple, was destroyed in the ruin (Judges 16.29–30).
2. I.e., hero (derisive); show-off.
3. Shaftesbury had been dismissed as chancellor in 1673 and as lord president of the Council in 1679.
4. Jacob deceived his old blind father by making his hands hairy (like Esau's) with animal fur; but he could not mask his voice (Genesis 27).
5. Shaftesbury (and others) made use of petitions in attempts to force the king to meet the demands of the Parliament in 1681.

Must I at length the sword of justice draw?
O curst effects of necessary law!
How ill my fear they by my mercy scan![6]
1005 Beware the fury of a patient man.
Law they require, let Law then show her face;
They could not be content to look on Grace,
Her hinder parts, but with a daring eye
To tempt the terror of her front and die.[7]
1010 By their own arts, 'tis righteously decreed,
Those dire artificers of death shall bleed.
Against themselves their witnesses will swear,
Till viper-like their mother Plot they tear:
And suck for nutriment that bloody gore,[8]
1015 Which was their principle of life before.
Their Belial with their Belzebub[9] will fight;
Thus on my foes, my foes shall do me right:
Nor doubt the event,° for factious crowds engage,   outcome
In their first onset, all their brutal rage.
1020 Then let 'em take an unresisted course,
Retire and traverse, and delude their force:
But when they stand all breathless, urge the fight,
And rise upon 'em with redoubled might:
For lawful power is still superior found,
1025 When long driven back, at length it stands the ground."
    He said. The Almighty, nodding, gave consent;
And peals of thunder shook the firmament.°   heavens
Henceforth a series of new time began,
The mighty years in long procession ran:
1030 Once more the godlike David was restored,
And willing nations knew their lawful lord.

1681

Mac Flecknoe[1]

All human things are subject to decay,
And when fate summons, monarchs must obey.

6. I.e., how wrong they are to estimate my fear (determine that I am afraid) by the fact that I am merciful.
7. Moses, on Mount Sinai, was forbidden upon pain of death to look upon the face of God, but he glimpsed Him from behind after He had passed by (Exodus 33.20–23).
8. The simile is based on a common idea that vipers eat their own mothers.
9. I.e., their principal leaders; in Milton's *Paradise Lost*, Belial and Beelzebub, leaders of Satan's host, disagree about their course of action (Book 2).
1. Or Thomas Shadwell (1640–1692), a comic playwright who considered himself the dramatic heir of Ben Jonson and the champion of the type of comedy that Jonson had written, the "comedy of humors." Such plays allude to the medical theory that said a healthy human body was composed of four humors, kept in careful balance. Characters without such a balance have a predominant humor portrayed as a comic eccentricity. Dryden and Shadwell conducted a public argument for years on the merits of Jonson's plays. Dryden names Shadwell "Mac" (Gaelic for "son of") Flecknoe, making him heir not of Jonson but of the recently dead Irish priest Richard Flecknoe, a poet Dryden considered not only prolific but tiresome.
    "Mac Flecknoe" was probably circulated in manuscript for a few years before being printed in a pirated edition in 1682 by an obscure publisher. A subtitle, "Or a Satire Upon the True-Blue Protestant Poet, T. S.," evoked contemporary political controversies by referring to Shadwell's membership in the Whig party, the political haven of dissenting Protestants. This subtitle, presumably added when the poem was published to stimulate sales, was removed in the 1684 edition and all others that Dryden oversaw.

This Flecknoe found, who, like Augustus,[2] young
Was called to empire, and had governed long;
5   In prose and verse, was owned, without dispute,
Through all the realms of Nonsense, absolute.
This agèd prince, now flourishing in peace,
And blest with issue of a large increase,[3]
Worn out with business, did at length debate
10   To settle the succession of the state;[4]
And, pondering which of all his sons was fit
To reign, and wage immortal war with wit,[5]
Cried: " 'Tis resolved; for Nature pleads that he
Should only rule, who most resembles me.
15   Sh——[6] alone my perfect image bears,
Mature in dullness from his tender years:
Sh—— alone, of all my sons, is he
Who stands confirmed in full stupidity.
The rest to some faint meaning make pretense,
20   But Sh—— never deviates into sense.
Some beams of wit on other souls may fall,
Strike through, and make a lucid interval;[7]
But Sh——'s genuine night admits no ray,
His rising fogs prevail upon the day.
25   Besides, his goodly fabric[8] fills the eye,
And seems designed for thoughtless majesty:
Thoughtless as monarch oaks that shade the plain,
And, spread in solemn state, supinely reign.
Heywood and Shirley[9] were but types of thee,
30   Thou last great prophet of tautology.[1]
Even I, a dunce of more renown than they,
Was sent before but to prepare thy way;
And, coarsely clad in Norwich drugget,[2] came
To teach the nations in thy greater name.
35   My warbling lute, the lute I whilom° strung,   *formerly*
When to King John of Portugal I sung,[3]
Was but the prelude to that glorious day,
When thou on silver Thames didst cut thy way,[4]
With well-timed oars before the royal barge,
40   Swelled with the pride of thy celestial charge;

---

2. Augustus (Octavian) became the first Roman emperor at thirty-three and reigned from 30 B.C. to A.D. 14.
3. Figuratively, children; perhaps also a more specific reference to Flecknoe's practice of collecting pieces from his earlier publications and publishing them again with a new title. "Increase" was stressed on the second syllable.
4. Comic allusion to the serious question of who would succeed Charles II. "Business": with a play on sexual intercourse.
5. "Wit," here as in other poems of the time, variously denotes the intellect, the poetic imagination, and a general sprightliness of mind.
6. A transparent pretense of anonymity for Shadwell. The use of dashes is a common device of the period's satire. Also, a scatological suggestion. The name is spelled out in some manuscripts.

7. A bright period; also, a medical term referring to periods of sanity between attacks of lunacy.
8. His body; Shadwell was corpulent.
9. Thomas Heywood (1574?–1641) and James Shirley (1596–1666), prolific playwrights of the time of Charles I, now out of fashion. Dryden suggests that they prefigure Shadwell as the Old Testament prophets and (in lines 31–34) John the Baptist prefigured Christ.
1. A repetition of the same point in different words.
2. A coarse cloth.
3. Flecknoe visited the king of Portugal and claimed him as a patron.
4. Dryden alludes here to the royal pageants performed on the river Thames, which flows through London.

And big with hymn, commander of a host,
The like was ne'er in Epsom blankets tossed.[5]
Methinks I see the new Arion[6] sail,
The lute still trembling underneath thy nail.°   *fingernail*
45 At thy well-sharpened thumb from shore to shore
The treble squeaks for fear, the basses roar;
Echoes from Pissing Alley Sh—— call,
And Sh—— they resound from A—— Hall.[7]
About thy boat the little fishes throng,
50 As at the morning toast[8] that floats along.
Sometimes, as prince of thy harmonious band,
Thou wield'st thy papers in thy threshing hand.[9]
St. André's feet[1] ne'er kept more equal time,
Not ev'n the feet of thy own *Psyche's* rhyme,
55 Though they in number° as in sense excel: *meter*
So just, so like tautology, they° fell,   *the papers*
That, pale with envy, Singleton forswore ⎤
The lute and sword, which he in triumph bore, ⎬
And vowed he ne'er would act Villerius[2] more." ⎦
60 Here stopped the good old sire, and wept for joy
In silent raptures of the hopeful boy.[3]
All arguments, but most his plays, persuade,
That for anointed dullness[4] he was made.
  Close to the walls which fair Augusta[5] bind
65 (The fair Augusta much to fears inclined),
An ancient fabric° raised to inform the sight   *building*
There stood of yore, and Barbican it hight:°   *was called*
A watchtower once; but now, so fate ordains,
Of all the pile an empty name remains.
70 From its old ruins brothel houses rise,
Scenes of lewd loves, and of polluted joys,
Where their vast courts the mother-strumpets keep,
And, undisturbed by watch, in silence sleep.
Near these a Nursery[6] erects its head,
75 Where queens are formed, and future heroes bred;

---

5. A simultaneous reference to two of Shadwell's plays: *The Virtuoso* (1676), in which a character who thinks himself a "wit" is tossed in a blanket in a farcical scene, and *Epsom Wells* (1673).
6. When the semilegendary Greek poet Arion was cast into the sea, a dolphin, charmed by his singing, bore him ashore. Shadwell was proud of his own musical accomplishments.
7. This scatologically named hall, written out as "Aston" in the 1682 edition, has not been located. Pissing Alley ran between the Strand and the Thames.
8. A comic metaphor for sewage.
9. I.e., his hand beats or strikes as with a flail, with a pun on the violence of his "beating," or writing, and the accents or beats in measured verse. In the following lines, Dryden continues to make fun of the mechanical metrics of the songs in Shadwell's opera *Psyche* (1675). Shadwell had apologized for his use of rhyme in the preface to the printed text.
1. With a pun on dancing and metrical feet. "St. André": a French dancing-master, choreographer

of Shadwell's *Psyche*.
2. A role in Sir William Davenant's *The Siege of Rhodes* (1656), the first English opera. "Singleton": John Singleton (d. 1686), a musician of the Theatre Royal. Dryden seems to be suggesting (sarcastically) that Shadwell's art is so skilled that it evokes the admiration of an undistinguished performer.
3. I.e., Mac Flecknoe, or Shadwell (who was in his mid-thirties). "Good old sire": i.e., Flecknoe.
4. The expected phrase is "anointed majesty," since English kings are anointed with oil at their coronations; i.e., all arguments favor Mac Flecknoe's ascent to the throne of dullness, but most of all his plays.
5. I.e., London; an allusion to contemporary fears of a Catholic plot to burn down the city (see "*From Absalom and Achitophel: A Poem*," n. 5, p. 458).
6. The name of a training school for young actors built in the Barbican in 1671, against the wishes of many residents.

Where unfledged actors learn to laugh and cry,
Where infant punks° their tender voices try,   *prostitutes*
And little Maximins[7] the gods defy.
Great Fletcher never treads in buskins here,
80 Nor greater Jonson dares in socks[8] appear;
But gentle Simkin[9] just reception finds
Amidst this monument of vanished minds:
Pure clinches° the suburbian Muse[1] affords,   *puns*
And Panton° waging harmless war with words.   *a punster*
85 Here Flecknoe, as a place to fame well known,
Ambitiously designed his Sh——'s throne;
For ancient Dekker[2] prophesied long since,
That in this pile would reign a mighty prince,
Born for a scourge of wit, and flail of sense;[3]
90 To whom true dullness should some *Psyches* owe,
But worlds of *Misers* from his pen should flow;[4]
Humorists and *Hypocrites* it should produce,
Whole Raymond families, and tribes of Bruce.
     Now Empress Fame had published the renown
95 Of Sh——'s coronation through the town.
Roused by report of Fame, the nations meet,
From near Bunhill, and distant Watling Street.[5]
No Persian carpets spread the imperial way,
But scattered limbs of mangled poets lay;
100 From dusty shops neglected authors come,
Martyrs of pies, and relics of the bum.[6]
Much Heywood, Shirley, Ogilby[7] there lay,
But loads of Sh—— almost choked the way.
Bilked stationers[8] for yeomen stood prepared,
105 And H—— was captain of the guard.
The hoary° prince in majesty appeared,   *gray, aged*
High on a throne of his own labors reared.
At his right hand our young Ascanius[9] sate,
Rome's other hope, and pillar of the state.
110 His brows thick fogs, instead of glories, grace,

7. The bombastic Roman emperor in Dryden's own *Tyrannic Love* (1669).
8. "Buskins," the high-soled boots worn in Athenian tragedy, are opposed to "socks," the low shoes worn in comedy (thus the reference to Ben Jonson). "Fletcher": John Fletcher (1579–1625), a playwright.
9. A clown; a popular character in farces.
1. The nine Muses were Greek goddesses believed to be sources of inspiration for the arts; this Muse, unlike the classical ones, is associated with the licentious suburbs of London, where brothels and theaters were located.
2. Thomas Dekker (ca. 1572–1632), a playwright satirized by Ben Jonson in *The Poetaster* (1602). He probably figures in the line of poets leading up to Shadwell because he was a city poet and a proponent of a dramatic realism that Dryden deplored.
3. I.e., born to be one who punishes wit and whips sense.
4. In these lines Dryden names plays of (and characters in plays by) Shadwell.
5. Victims of the plague (1665–66) were buried in Bunhill. Because these locations are both within half-mile of the scene of the supposed coronation ("the Nursery"), Mac Flecknoe's fame is narrowly circumscribed; furthermore, his subjects live in the unfashionable commercial center of the city, regarded as a place of bad taste and vulgarity.
6. I.e., unsold books, the paper of which was used in bakers' shops and in privies (toilets).
7. John Ogilby (1600–1676), a translator of Virgil and Homer and a dramatic entrepreneur derided by Dryden (and later by Pope); Thomas Heywood and James Shirley (see n. 9, p. 474).
8. Booksellers, impoverished because they had stocked the works of Shadwell and others, stood guard to protect what remained of their interests. Their "captain," Henry Herringman, however, referred to in line 105, had been Dryden's publisher as well as Shadwell's.
9. Aeneas' son; hence, like Shadwell, the destined heir. Virgil referred to him as "*spes altera Romae*" ("Rome's other hope") (*Aeneid* 12.168); as Troy fell, his favor with the gods was marked by a flickering ("lambent") flame that played around his head (*Aeneid* 2.680–84).

And lambent dullness played around his face.
As Hannibal did to the altars come,
Sworn by his sire a mortal foe to Rome,[1]
So Sh—— swore, nor should his vow be vain,
115 That he till death true dullness would maintain;
And, in his father's right, and realm's defense,
Ne'er to have peace with wit, nor truce with sense.
The king himself the sacred unction° made,   *ointment*
As king by office, and as priest by trade.
120 In his sinister[2] hand, instead of ball,
He placed a mighty mug of potent ale;
Love's Kingdom[3] to his right he did convey,
At once his scepter, and his rule of sway;
Whose righteous lore the prince had practiced young,
125 And from whose loins recorded *Psyche* sprung.
His temples, last, with poppies[4] were o'erspread,
That nodding seemed to consecrate his head.
Just at that point of time, if fame not lie,
On his left hand twelve reverend owls[5] did fly.
130 So Romulus, 'tis sung, by Tiber's brook,
Presage of sway from twice six vultures took.[6]
The admiring throng loud acclamations make,
And omens of his future empire take.
The sire then shook the honors[7] of his head,
135 And from his brows damps° of oblivion shed   *vapors*
Full on the filial dullness: long he stood, ⎫
Repelling from his breast the raging god; ⎬
At length burst out in this prophetic mood: ⎭
        "Heavens bless my son, from Ireland let him reign
140 To far Barbadoes on the western main;[8]
Of his dominion may no end be known,
And greater than his father's be his throne;
Beyond *Love's Kingdom* let him stretch his pen!"
He paused, and all the people cried, "Amen."
145 Then thus continued he: "My son, advance
Still in new imprudence, new ignorance.
Success let others teach, learn thou from me
Pangs without birth, and fruitless industry.
Let *Virtuosos* in five years be writ;
150 Yet not one thought accuse thy toil of wit.[9]

---

1. Hannibal (247–183 B.C.), the Carthaginian general who invaded Italy, swore enmity to Rome.
2. In British coronations the monarch holds in his or her left ("sinister") hand a globe surmounted by a cross.
3. A pastoral tragicomedy by Flecknoe, apparently visualized by Dryden as a rolled-up manuscript held like a scepter. Shadwell's *Psyche*, a pastoral opera, could be described as the child ("from whose loins") of *Love's Kingdom* (1644).
4. Connoting both intellectual heaviness and Shadwell's addiction to opiates; a parody of the laurel wreath with which a poet was traditionally crowned as a sign of poetic achievement.
5. Symbols of dullness.

6. When the site ("Tiber's brook") that Romulus had chosen for Rome was visited by twelve vultures, or twice as many as had visited the site picked by his brother Remus, the kingship ("sway") of Romulus was presaged.
7. Locks; in Virgil's *Aeneid* it is Zeus, ruler of the gods, who shakes his locks. Here and in the following lines, Dryden parodies two epic motifs: the father influencing his son and the Sybil receiving the "rasing God" who speaks through her (see *Aeneid* 6.46–51).
8. I.e., a realm of empty ocean.
9. I.e., even if Shadwell spent five years writing a comedy, it would still lack wit.

Let gentle George[1] in triumph tread the stage,
Make Dorimant betray, and Loveit rage;
Let Cully, Cockwood, Fopling, charm the pit,
And in their folly show the writer's wit.
155 Yet still thy fools shall stand in thy defense,
And justify their author's want of sense.
Let 'em be all by thy own model made
Of dullness, and desire no foreign aid;
That they to future ages may be known,
160 Not copies drawn, but issue of thy own.
Nay, let thy men of wit too be the same,
All full of thee, and differing but in name.
But let no alien S—dl—y[2] interpose,
To lard with wit[3] thy hungry *Epsom* prose.
165 And when false flowers of rhetoric thou wouldst cull,
Trust nature, do not labor to be dull;
But write thy best, and top; and, in each line,
Sir Formal's[4] oratory will be thine:
Sir Formal, though unsought, attends thy quill,
170 And does thy northern dedications[5] fill.
Nor let false friends seduce thy mind to fame,
By arrogating Jonson's hostile name.
Let father Flecknoe fire thy mind with praise,
And uncle Ogilby thy envy raise.
175 Thou art my blood, where Jonson has no part:
What share have we in nature, or in art?
Where did his wit on learning fix a brand,
And rail at arts he did not understand?[6]
Where made he love in Prince Nicander's vein,
180 Or swept the dust in *Psyche's* humble strain?[7]
Where sold he bargains,[8] 'whip-stitch, kiss my arse,'
Promised a play and dwindled to a farce?
When did his Muse from Fletcher scenes purloin,°   steal
As thou whole Eth'rege dost transfuse to thine?
185 But so transfused, as oil on water's flow,
His always floats above, thine sinks below.
This is thy province, this thy wondrous way,
New humors[9] to invent for each new play:
This is that boasted bias of thy mind,
190 By which one way, to dullness, 'tis inclined;
Which makes thy writings lean on one side still,
And, in all changes, that way bends thy will.
Nor let thy mountain-belly make pretense

1. Sir George Etherege (ca. 1635–1691), playwright who set the tone for stylish Restoration comedy; Dryden proceeds to name five of his characters.
2. Sir Charles Sedley (ca. 1639–1701), Restoration wit who had contributed a prologue and (Dryden suggests in line 184) a part of the text to Shadwell's *Epsom Wells* (1673).
3. The phrase recalls a sentence in *Anatomy of Melancholy* (1621) by the English clergyman and scholar Robert Burton (1577–1640): "They lard their lean books with the fat of others' works."
4. Sir Formal Trifle was an inflated orator in *The Virtuoso*.
5. I.e., to Shadwell's patron the duke of Newcastle, whose seat was in northern England.
6. Perhaps an allusion to the satire on experimental science in *The Virtuoso*.
7. Nicander pays court to the title character Psyche in Shadwell's opera.
8. A "bargain" is a gross rejoinder to an innocent question. The rest of the line, itself a kind of bargain, echoes a farcical character in *The Virtuoso*.
9. Parodying Shadwell's Dedication to *The Virtuoso*, in which he claims that "four of the humours are entirely new."

Of likeness; thine's a tympany[1] of sense.
195   A tun of man in thy large bulk is writ,
But sure thou'rt but a kilderkin[2] of wit.
Like mine, thy gentle numbers° feebly creep;   *verses*
Thy tragic Muse gives smiles, thy comic sleep.
With whate'er gall thou sett'st thyself to write,
200   Thy inoffensive satires never bite.
In thy felonious heart though venom lies,
It does but touch thy Irish pen, and dies.
Thy genius[3] calls thee not to purchase fame
In keen iambics,[4] but mild anagram.[5]
205   Leave writing plays, and choose for thy command
Some peaceful province in acrostic land.
There thou may'st wings display and altars raise,
And torture one poor word ten thousand ways.
Or, if thou wouldst thy different talent suit,
210   Set thy own songs, and sing them to thy lute."
     He said: but his last words were scarcely heard ⎤
For Bruce and Longville had a trap prepared,   ⎬
And down they sent the yet declaiming bard.[6]   ⎦
Sinking he left his drugget° robe behind,   *coarse*
215   Borne upwards by a subterranean wind.
The mantle fell to the young prophet's part,[7]
With double portion of his father's art.

ca. 1676   1682, 1684

To the Memory of Mr. Oldham[8]

Farewell, too little, and too lately known,
Whom I began to think and call my own:
For sure our souls were near allied, and thine
Cast in the same poetic mold with mine.[9]
5   One common note on either lyre did strike,
And knaves and fools we both abhorred alike.
To the same goal did both our studies° drive;   *endeavors*
The last set out the soonest did arrive.
Thus Nisus[1] fell upon the slippery place,
10   While his young friend performed° and won the race.   *completed*

---

1. A swelling caused by air.
2. A little cask. "Tun": a big cask.
3. The tutelary spirit allotted to every person at birth to govern his or her fortunes and determine the individual's character. Dryden terms Shadwell Irish as an insult.
4. The meter of (Greek) satire; hence satire itself.
5. The transposition of letters in a word so as to make a new word; "mild": tame, feeble. Dryden scorns this form of ingenuity, and the others that follow, as trivial. "Acrostic": a poem in which the first letter of each line, read downward, makes up the name of the person or thing that is the subject of the poem. "Wings" and "altars": references to poems in the shape of their subjects, such as George Herbert's "Easter Wings" (pp. 330–31) and "The Altar" (p. 329).
6. These characters in *The Virtuoso* so trap Sir

Formal Trifle.
7. When the prophet Elijah was carried to heaven in a chariot of fire borne on a whirlwind, his mantle fell on Elisha, his successor (2 Kings 2.8–14). Flecknoe's "subterranean wind" is a fart, and an allusion to the moment in *Paradise Lost* where Satan lands on ground seemingly destroyed by "the force / Of subterranean wind" (1.231).
8. John Oldham (1653–1683), author of *Satires Upon the Jesuits* (1681), was a promising young poet, harsh (partly by calculation) in metrics and manner, but earnest and vigorous. He died of smallpox.
9. Dryden cast horoscopes and had the same birthday as Oldham.
1. A footracer in Virgil's *Aeneid*; his young friend Euryalus came from behind to reach the goal before him (5.315 ff.).

O early ripe! to thy abundant store
What could advancing age have added more?
It might (what nature never gives the young)
Have taught the numbers° of thy native tongue.   *metrics*
15   But satire needs not those, and wit will shine
Through the harsh cadence of a rugged line:
A noble error, and but seldom made,
When poets are by too much force betrayed.
Thy generous fruits, though gathered ere their prime, ⎫
20   Still showed a quickness,° and maturing time   ⎬   *sharpness*
But mellows what we write to the dull sweets of rhyme. ⎭
Once more, hail and farewell; farewell, thou young,
But ah too short, Marcellus² of our tongue;
Thy brows with ivy, and with laurels bound;
25   But fate and gloomy night encompass thee around.³

1684

A Song for St. Cecilia's Day⁴

1

From harmony, from heavenly harmony
This universal frame⁵ began:
When Nature⁶ underneath a heap
Of jarring atoms lay,
5   And could not heave her head,
The tuneful voice was heard from high:
"Arise, ye more than dead."
Then cold, and hot, and moist, and dry,⁷
In order to their stations leap,
10   And Music's power obey.
From harmony, from heavenly harmony
This universal frame began:
From harmony to harmony
Through all the compass° of the notes it ran,   *full range*
15   The diapason⁸ closing full in man.

2

What passion cannot Music raise and quell!
When Jubal⁹ struck the corded shell,
His listening brethren stood around,
And, wondering, on their faces fell

2. Roman Emperor Augustus Caesar's nephew, who died at twenty after a meteoric military career.
3. The Roman elegiac phrase "Hail and farewell!" in line 22; the mention of Marcellus (line 23) and of the classical poet's wreath, a symbol of poetic achievement (line 24); and the echo of Virgil's lament for Marcellus (see *Aeneid* 6.566) conspire to Romanize Oldham.
4. St. Cecilia, a Roman martyr of the second or third century, was patron saint of music, customarily represented at the organ (cf. line 52). Celebrations of her festival day (November 22) in England were usually devoted to music, and from about 1683 to 1703 the "Musical Society" in London annually commemorated it with a religious service and a public concert. Dryden's ode was set to music (by Giovanni Battista Draghi) for this occasion in 1687.
5. The physical universe.
6. Created nature as distinguished from chaos.
7. The four elements: earth, fire, water, and air.
8. The entire range or scale of tones; representing the perfection of God's harmony in his final creation, humankind. The just gradation of notes in a scale is analogous to the equally just gradation in the ascending scale of created beings according to the idea of the Chain of Being (in which the creation is ordered from inanimate nature up to humans, God's best and final work).
9. "Father of all such as handle the harp and organ" (Genesis 4.21). The "corded" or stringed tortoise "shell" is a harp or lyre.

20   To worship that celestial sound.
  Less than a god they thought there could not dwell
    Within the hollow of that shell
    That spoke so sweetly and so well.
  What passion cannot Music raise and quell!

3

25   The trumpet's loud clangor
    Excites us to arms,
   With shrill notes of anger,
    And mortal alarms.
   The double double double beat
30   Of the thundering drum
  Cries: "Hark! the foes come;
  Charge, charge, 'tis too late to retreat."

4

  The soft complaining flute
  In dying notes discovers
35   The woes of hopeless lovers,
  Whose dirge is whispered by the warbling lute.

5

  Sharp violins[1] proclaim
  Their jealous pangs, and desperation,
  Fury, frantic indignation,
40 Depth of pains, and height of passion,
   For the fair, disdainful dame.

6

  But O! what art can teach,
  What human voice can reach,
  The sacred organ's praise?
45   Notes inspiring holy love,
  Notes that wing their heavenly ways
   To mend the choirs above.[2]

7

  Orpheus could lead the savage race;
  And trees unrooted left their place,
50   Sequacious of[3] the lyre;
  But bright Cecilia raised the wonder higher:
  When to her organ vocal breath[4] was given,
  An angel heard, and straight appeared,
   Mistaking earth for heaven.

Grand Chorus

55 *As from the power of sacred lays°*   songs
  The spheres began to move,[5]

1. A reference to the bright tone of the violin, recently introduced into England. The tone of the old-fashioned viol is much duller.
2. I.e., to improve the music of the angels.
3. Following. "Orpheus": son of the Muse Calliope, he played so wonderfully on the lyre that wild beasts ("the savage race") grew tame and followed him, as did even rocks and trees.
4. I.e., its ability to sustain notes as the human voice does.
5. As it was harmony that ordered the universe, so it was angelic song ("sacred lays") that put the celestial bodies ("spheres") in motion. The harmonious chord that results from the traditional "music of the spheres" is a hymn of "praise" sung by created nature to its "Creator."

And sung the great Creator's praise
To all the blest above;
So, when the last and dreadful hour
60 *This crumbling pageant⁶ shall devour,*
The trumpet⁷ shall be heard on high,
The dead shall live, the living die,
And Music shall untune the sky.⁸

1687

KATHERINE PHILIPS

1632–1664

Epitaph

On her Son H. P. at St. Syth's Church where her body
also lies Interred.

What on Earth deserves our trust?
Youth and beauty both are dust.
Long we gathering are with pain,
What one moment calls again.
5 Seven years childless marriage past,
A son, a son is born at last;
So exactly limbed¹ and fair,
Full of good spirits, mien, and air,²
As a long life promised,
10 Yet, in less than six weeks dead.
Too promising, too great a mind
In so small room to be confined:
Therefore, fit in Heaven to dwell,
He quickly broke the prison shell.
15 So the subtle alchimist,³
Can't with Hermes' seal⁴ resist
The powerful spirit's subtler flight,
But t'will bid him long good night.
So the Sun if it arise
20 Half so glorious as his eyes,
Like this infant, takes a shroud,
Buried in a morning cloud.

1655   1667

6. The universe, the stage on which the drama of human salvation has been acted out. "The last and dreadful hour": Judgment Day.
7. The sounding of the last trumpet announces the Resurrection (in which the "dead shall live") and the Last Judgement (1 Corinthians 15.52).
8. I.e., the sounding of the last trumpet will end the harmony of the spheres, concentric transparent shells containing the heavenly bodies in Ptolemaic astronomy; they were thought to produce angelic music as they turned.
1. I.e., having perfect limbs.
2. Apparent character or disposition; "mien": appearance or expression.
3. Alchemy was the science aiming to achieve the transmutation of baser metals into gold and also to find a panacea or universal remedy.
4. Hermetic seal, the air-tight closure of a container.

To Mr. Henry Lawes[5]

Nature, which is the vast creation's soul,
That steady curious agent[6] in the whole,
The art of Heaven, the order of this frame,
Is only number[7] in another name.
5 For as some king conqu'ring what was his own,
Hath choice of several titles to his crown;
So harmony on this score now, that then,
Yet still is all that takes and governs men.[8]
Beauty is but composure, and we find
10 Content° is but the concord of the mind,   *contentment*
Friendship the unison of well-tuned hearts,
Honor the chorus of the noblest parts,[9]
And all the world on which we can reflect
Music to th'ear, or to the intellect.
15 If then each man a little world must be,[1]
How many worlds are copied out in thee,
Who art so richly formed, so complete
T'epitomize all that is good and great;
Whose stars[2] this brave advantage did impart,
20 Thy nature's as harmonious as thy art?
Thou dost above the poets' praises live,
Who fetch from thee th'eternity they give.
And as true reason triumphs over sense,
Yet is subjected to intelligence:[3]
25 So poets on the lower world look down,
But Lawes on them; his height is all his own.
For, like Divinity it self, his lyre
Rewards the wit it did at first inspire.[4]
And thus by double right poets allow

---

5. A friend of Philips', and a well-known musician and composer, he set to music the words of some of the most prominent poets of his day, including Ben Jonson, Davenant, Waller, Herrick, Carew, Lovelace, Cartwright, and Milton (see "To Mr. H. Lawes, On His Airs," pp. 375–76).
6. The material cause whereby effects are produced. In the *Timaeus*, Plato gives an account of the generation of the soul of the world in terms of the Pythagorean generation of the consonant intervals in music; in the *Somnium Scipionis*, Cicero describes the musical creation of the universe in terms of proportional intervals and tones. Many early Christian writers also explained the creation of the world in Pythagorean terms.
7. Music; drawing on Pythagorean ideas, many classical and Neoplatonic writers believed that to understand God, the universe, or humankind, one had to understand numbers and their relationships. Music, based on numerical relationships, spatial measurements of intervals, and metrical measurements of time, afforded one access to the measurements of those things that were intangible or invisible.
8. I.e., just as a king, who has conquered lands that are by rights his, may be called by the title of any of those lands, so harmony, by natural right, may be credited with being both the force that ini-

tiates and preserves the order of the natural world ("that then" refers to this topic, mentioned in the first four lines) and that which "takes and governs" the world of human society (as the poet goes on to demonstrate in the next four lines, thus "on this score now").
9. In these lines Philips plays on the musical meanings of words; "composure": collectedness, but also referring to a musical composition; "concord": agreement, but also referring to a combination of notes that is pleasing to the ear; "unison": a sound or note of the same pitch as another; "chorus": both a choir and the song sung by the choir.
1. Perhaps a reference to the Platonic idea that the soul of humankind and the soul of the universe are similarly harmonious, and therefore music may reveal to the human being ("a little world") the divine harmony of the universe, or larger world, in which his or her soul shares.
2. Destiny as determined by astrology.
3. According to Aristotle, reason governs the lesser faculties of the soul—the physical senses and the appetites that they generate; both reason and sense are subject to intelligence, which Aristotle believed to be the divine element in humans.
4. I.e., his songs "reward" (by setting to music) the poetry originally inspired by his art.

30 His and their laurel should adorn his brow.[5]
Live then, great soul of nature, to assuage
The savage dulness of this sullen age.
Charm us to sense; for though experience fail
And reason too,[6] thy numbers° may prevail.   *songs*
35 Then, like those ancients, strike, and so command
All nature to obey thy gen'rous hand.[7]
None will resist but such who needs will be
More stupid° than a stone, a fish, a tree.   *senseless*
Be it thy care our age to new-create:
40 What built a world may sure repair a state.[8]

1667

On the Welch Language[9]

If honor to an ancient name be due,
Or riches challenge it for one that's new,
The British language[1] claims in either sense
Both for its age, and for its opulence.°   *wealth*
5 But all great things must be from us removed,
To be with higher reverence beloved.
So landskips° which in prospects distant lie,   *landscapes*
With greater wonder draw the pleasèd eye.
Is not great Troy to one dark ruin hurled?
10 Once the fam'd scene of all the fighting world.[2]
Where's Athens now, to whom Rome learning owes,
And the safe laurels that adorned her brows?[3]
A strange reverse of fate she did endure,
Never once greater, than she's now obscure.

---

5. The laurel was a symbol of poetic achievement.
6. According to Aristotle, sense experience gives knowledge of the concrete, while reason acts on that knowledge to arrive at an understanding of universal or first principles.
7. Perhaps a reference to Orpheus, famed for his singing and playing upon the lyre, who was said to be able to charm birds, animals, rocks, and trees with his music; other "ancients" that the poet may have had in mind: Amphion, who with his music caused stones to build the walls of Thebes, and Arion, whose singing won him the love of dolphins; "strike": here, to play upon a stringed instrument.
8. Philips is thought to have had Royalist sympathies; therefore this line, along with the reference to "this sullen age" in line 32, may refer to her dissatisfaction with the British government during the Interregnum (1649–60).
9. The Welsh language appears here to mean that language spoken by the earliest settlers of Britain, namely the Britons, or Celts. That language was thought to have survived in Wales, which was a stronghold of resistance against the Romans in the first century A.D. and against the Anglo-Saxons in the fourth and fifth centuries. After the defeat of

Wales by Edward I, in the thirteenth century, Welsh cultural identity began to erode, and in 1636, when Wales was officially incorporated into England, Welshmen holding positions in Henry VIII's regime were required to speak English. In the seventeenth century, however, some interest developed among the Welsh in preserving their language. Philips moved with her husband to Cardigan, Wales, when she was seventeen years old and lived there for twelve years.
1. The language spoken by the ancient Britons.
2. Troy was the site of the legendary Trojan War, in which the Greeks fought with the Trojans to possess Helen. Helen, married to Menelaus, a Greek king, was carried off by Paris, a son of the king of Troy. At the end of the ten-year war, the Greeks defeated the Trojans and destroyed the city.
3. Athens was the Greek city that became the cultural, military, and economic center of an extensive empire (during the sixth and fifth centuries B.C.). The city was taken over by the Romans in 86 B.C.; the Romans adopted and imitated Greek culture and learning; laurel wreaths, sometimes worn on the head, were symbols of both poetic and military achievement.

15 Even Rome her self can but some footsteps show
Of Scipio's times, or those of Cicero.[4]
And as the Roman and the Grecian state,
The British fell,[5] the spoil of time and fate.
But though the language hath the beauty lost,
20 Yet she has still some great remains to boast.
For 'twas in that,[6] the sacred bards of old,
In deathless numbers° did their thoughts unfold.   *poetry*
In groves, by rivers, and on fertile plains,
They civilized and taught the listening swains;°   *rustics*
25 Whilst with high raptures, and as great success,
Virtue they clothed in music's charming dress.
This Merlin spoke, who in his gloomy cave,
Even Destiny her self seemed to enslave.
For to his sight the future time was known,
30 Much better than to others is their own;
And with such state, predictions from him fell,
As if he did decree, and not foretell.
This spoke King Arthur,[7] who, if fame be true,
Could have compelled mankind to speak it too.
35 In this once Boadicca[8] valor taught,
And spoke more nobly than her soldiers fought:
Tell me what hero could be more than she,
Who fell at once for fame and liberty?
Nor could a greater sacrifice belong,
40 Or° to her children's, or her country's wrong.   *either*
This spoke Caractacus,[9] who was so brave,
That to the Roman fortune check he gave:
And when their yoke he could decline no more,
He it so decently and nobly wore,
45 That Rome her self with blushes did believe,
A Britain° would the law of honor[1] give;   *a Briton, British person*
And hastily his chains away she threw,
Lest her own captive else should her subdue.

1667

4. Marcus Tullius Cicero (106–43 B.C.), a Roman statesman and orator who was executed on the order of Marc Antony after the assassination of Julius Caesar. There were two "Scipios": Scipio the Great, or Publius Cornelius Scipio (236–184 B.C.), a Roman general and statesman who distinguished himself in the Punic Wars; and Aemilianus Numantinus, who was represented by Cicero as the ideal of wise statesmanship.
5. A reference to the Roman conquest of the British Isles. By 78 A.D. Wales had been brought under Roman control, but its language survived.
6. I.e., the Welsh language, also the referent of "this" in lines 27, 33, 35, and 41.
7. A legendary king of Britain, who, according to Geoffrey of Monmouth's *Historia Regum Britanniae*, defeated a Roman army but was mortally wounded in battle during a rebellion at home by

his nephew, Mordred. Chrétien de Troyes added to the legend of King Arthur in the late twelfth century, as did Thomas Malory in his *Le Morte Darthur*, written in the fifteenth century; Merlin, a magician who could foresee the future, served both Arthur and his father, Uther Pendragon.
8. A British queen who led a revolt against the Romans but was finally defeated in A.D. 61.
9. A king of Silures in the west of Britain during the reign of Claudius, Caractacus, or Caraduc, was defeated by the Romans and taken as a prisoner to Rome in A.D. 51. The Roman emperor was so impressed by his noble spirit that he pardoned and released him.
1. Perhaps a reference to the agreement between the Roman emperor and Caractacus that Caractacus, if pardoned, would not engage in armed resistance against the Romans.

To My Excellent Lucasia, on Our Friendship[2]

I did not live until this time
   Crowned my felicity,
When I could say without a crime,
   I am not thine, but thee.

5 This carcass breathed, and walked, and slept,
   So that the world believed
There was a soul the motions kept;[3]
   But they were all deceived.

For as a watch by art[4] is wound
10   To motion, such was mine:
But never had Orinda[5] found
   A soul till she found thine;

Which now inspires, cures and supplies,
   And guides my darkened breast:
15 For thou art all that I can prize,
   My joy, my life, my rest.

No bridegroom's nor crown-conqueror's mirth
   To mine compared can be:
They have but pieces of the earth,
20   I've all the world in thee.

Then let our flames still light and shine,
   And no false fear control,
As innocent as our design,
   Immortal as our soul.

1667

THOMAS TRAHERNE*

1637–1674

The Salutation

These little limbs,
These eyes and hands which here I find,
These rosy cheeks wherewith my life begins,
   Where have ye been? behind

2. In her poems on the theme of friendship, Philips frequently employs the terminology and imagery of love poems. The addressee of this poem is Mrs. Anne Owens, whom she calls "Lucasia," a name taken from William Cartwright's play *The Lady Errant* (1636).
3. I.e., that guided the body's movements.
4. I.e., by artificial means.
5. Philips' name for herself.

*Traherne's poems were discovered in 1903 by a scholar (Bertram Dobell) who found a poetic manuscript and attributed it to Traherne after comparing it with the one work that Traherne published in his lifetime, an anti-Catholic prose tract called *Roman Forgeries* (1673). Traherne's poems do not appear to have circulated widely (if at all) during his lifetime.

5   What curtain were ye from me hid so long?
Where was, in what abyss, my speaking tongue?

When silent I
So many thousand, thousand years
Beneath the dust did in a chaos lie,
10   How could I smiles or tears,
Or lips or hands or eyes or ears perceive?
Welcome ye treasures which I now receive.

I that so long
Was nothing from eternity,
15   Did little think such joys as ear or tongue
To celebrate or see:
Such sounds to hear, such hands to feel, such feet,
Beneath the skies on such a ground to meet.

New burnished joys,
20   Which yellow gold and pearls excel!
Such sacred treasures are the limbs in boys,
In which a soul doth dwell;
Their organizèd joints and azure veins
More wealth include than all the world contains.

25   From dust I rise,
And out of nothing now awake;
These brighter regions which salute mine eyes,
A gift from God I take.
The earth, the seas, the light, the day, the skies,
30   The sun and stars are mine if those I prize.

Long time before
I in my mother's womb was born,
A God, preparing, did this glorious store,°   *storehouse*
The world, for me adorn.
35   Into this Eden so divine and fair,
So wide and bright, I come His son and heir.

A stranger here
Strange things doth meet, strange glories see;
Strange treasures lodged in this fair world appear,
40   Strange all and new to me;
But that they mine should be, who nothing was,
That strangest is of all, yet brought to pass.

ca. 1665   1903

Wonder

How like an angel came I down!
How bright are all things here!
When first among his works I did appear
Oh, how their glory me did crown!
5   The world resembled his eternity,

In which my soul did walk;
And everything that I did see
      Did with me talk.

The skies in their magnificence,
10   The lively, lovely air,
Oh, how divine, how soft, how sweet, how fair!
      The stars did entertain my sense,
And all the works of God, so bright and pure,
      So rich and great did seem,
15   As if they ever must endure
            In my esteem.

A native health and innocence
      Within my bones did grow;
And while my God did all his glories show,
20   I felt a vigor in my sense
That was all Spirit. I within did flow
      With seas of life, like wine;
I nothing in the world did know
      But° 'twas divine.   *except that*

25   Harsh ragged objects were concealed;
      Oppressions, tears, and cries,
Sins, griefs, complaints, dissensions, weeping eyes
      Were hid, and only things revealed
Which heavenly spirits and the angels prize.
30   The state of innocence
And bliss, not trades° and poverties,   *goods*
      Did fill my sense.

The streets were paved with golden stones,
      The boys and girls were mine,
35   Oh, how did all their lovely faces shine!
      The sons of men were holy ones,
In joy and beauty they appeared to me,
      And everything I found,
      While like an angel I did see,
40   Adorned the ground.

Rich diamond and pearl and gold
      In every place was seen;
Rare splendors, yellow, blue, red, white, and green,
      Mine eyes did everywhere behold.
45   Great wonders clothed with glory did appear,
      Amazement was my bliss,
That and my wealth met everywhere;
      No joy to° this!   *compared to*

Cursed and devised proprieties,[1]
50   With envy, avarice,

---

1. Properties, including both private property and the self.

And fraud, those fiends that spoil even paradise,
  Flew from the splendor of mine eyes;
And so did hedges, ditches, limits, bounds:
    I dreamed not aught of those,
55   But wandered over all men's grounds,
        And found repose.

Proprieties themselves were mine,
    And hedges ornaments;
Walls, boxes, coffers, and their rich contents
60   To make me rich combine.
Clothes, ribbons, jewels, laces, I esteemed
    My joys by others worn:
For me they all to wear them seemed
        When I was born.

ca. 1665   1903

To the Same Purpose

To the same purpose: he, not long before
  Brought home from nurse, going to the door
    To do some little thing
    He must not do within,
5   With wonder cries,
        As in the skies
He saw the moon, "O yonder is the moon,
  Newly come after me to town,
That shined at Lugwardin² but yesternight,
10   Where I enjoyed the self-same sight."

As if it had ev'n twenty thousand faces,
  It shines at once in many places;
    To all the earth so wide
    God doth the stars divide,
15   With so much art
        The moon impart,
They serve us all; serve wholly every one
  As if they servèd him alone.
While every single person hath such store,
20   'Tis want of sense that makes us poor.

ca. 1665   1910

Shadows in the Water

In unexperienced° infancy   *inexperienced*
Many a sweet mistake doth lie:
Mistake though false, intending° true;   *directing to*
A seeming somewhat more than view;³
5   That doth instruct the mind
    In things that lie behind,

2. A town in south central England on the Lugg   3. I.e., an outward appearance ("seeming") that
River.   suggests more than what is visible to the eye.

And many secrets to us show
Which afterwards we come to know.

Thus did I by the water's brink
10 Another world beneath me think;
And while the lofty spacious skies
Reversèd there, abused mine eyes,
    I fancied other feet
    Came mine to touch or meet;
15 As by some puddle I did play
Another world within it lay.

Beneath the water people drowned,
Yet with another heaven crowned,
In spacious regions seemed to go
20 As freely moving to and fro:
    In bright and open space
    I saw their very face;
Eyes, hands, and feet they had like mine;
Another sun did with them shine.

25 'Twas strange that people there should walk,
And yet I could not hear them talk:
That through a little watery chink,
Which one dry ox or horse might drink,
    We other worlds should see,
30   Yet not admitted be;
And other confines there behold
Of light and darkness, heat and cold.

I called them oft, but called in vain;
No speeches we could entertain:
35 Yet did I there expect to find
Some other world, to please my mind.
    I plainly saw by these
    A new antipodes,[4]
Whom, though they were so plainly seen,
40 A film kept off that stood between.

By walking men's reversèd feet
I chanced another world to meet;
Though it did not to view exceed
A phantom, 'tis a world indeed,
45   Where skies beneath us shine,
    And earth by art divine
Another face presents below,
Where people's feet against ours go.

Within the regions of the air,
50 Compassed about with heavens fair,
Great tracts of land there may be found

---

4. People living at a diametrically opposite point on the globe (literally, "with the feet opposite").

Enriched with fields and fertile ground;
    Where many numerous hosts
    In those far distant coasts,
55 For other great and glorious ends
    Inhabit, my yet unknown friends.

    O ye that stand upon the brink,
    Whom I so near me through the chink
    With wonder see: what faces there,
60 Whose feet, whose bodies, do ye wear?
        I my companions see
        In you, another me.
    They seemèd others, but are we;
    Our second selves these shadows be.

65 Look how far off those lower skies
    Extend themselves! scarce with mine eyes
    I can them reach. O ye my friends,
    What secret borders on those ends?
        Are lofty heavens hurled
70   'Bout your inferior world?
    Are yet the representatives
    Of other peoples' distant lives?

    Of all the playmates which I knew
    That here I do the image view
75 In other selves, what can it mean?
    But that below the purling° stream   *swirling, murmuring*
        Some unknown joys there be
        Laid up in store for me;
    To which I shall, when that thin skin
80 Is broken, be admitted in.

ca. 1665   1910

THE MASSACHUSETTS BAY PSALM BOOK

Psalm 58[1]

1
Do ye, o congregation,
    indeed speak righteousness?
and o ye sons of earthly men,
    do ye judge unrightness?

1. Cf. other translations of this psalm by Mary Sidney (pp. 199–200), Isaac Watts (pp. 536–37), and Christopher Smart (pp. 623–25). This version, from the first book published in the new colony of Massachusetts, was compiled by twelve Puritan clergymen who sought (as John Cotton explained in his preface) a plainer, more literal rendering of the Hebrew than occurs in other Protestant translations of the Psalms. Often reprinted, in England and Scotland as well as in North America, this Psalter was one of the two most commonly owned books in New England (the other being *The New England Primer*).

2

5   Yea you in heart will working be
     injurious-wickedness;
   and in the land you will weigh out
     your hands' violence.

3

   The wicked are estranged from
10   the womb, they go astray
   as soon as ever they are borne;
     uttering lies are they.

4

   Their poison's like serpent's poison;
     they like deaf asp,° her ear   *small poisonous snake*
15 that stops. Though charmer wisely charm,
     his voice she will not hear.

5

   Within their mouth do thou their teeth
     break out, O God most strong,
   do thou Jehovah, the great teeth
20   break of the lion's young.

6

   As waters let them melt away,
     that run continually:
   and when he bends his shafts, let them
     as cut asunder be.

7

25 Like to a snail that melts, so let
     each of them pass away;
   like to a woman's untimely birth
     see sun that never they may.

8

   Before your pots can feel the thorns,
30   take them away shall he,
   as with a whirlwind both living,
     and in his jealousy.

9

   The righteous will rejoice when as
     the vengeance he doth see;
35 his feet wash shall he in the blood
     of them that wicked be.

10

   So that a man shall say, surely
     for righteous, there is fruit:
   sure there's a God that in the earth
40   judgement doth execute.

1640

EDWARD TAYLOR

ca. 1642–1729

Meditation 8[1]

I kenning° through astronomy divine[2]   *discerning, knowing*
 The world's bright battlement,° wherein I spy   *heavens*
A golden path my pencil cannot line,
 From that bright throne unto my threshold lie.
5 And while my puzzled thoughts about it pore
 I find the bread of life in it at my door.

When that this bird of paradise[3] put in
 This wicker cage (my corpse)[4] to tweedle° praise   *sing*
Had pecked the fruit forbad,[5] and so did fling
10 Away its food, and lost its golden days,
 It fell into celestial famine sore,
 And never could attain a morsel more.

Alas! alas! Poor bird, what wilt thou do?
 The creatures' field no food for souls e'er gave.
15 And if thou knock at angels' doors they show
 An empty barrel; they no soul bread have.
 Alas! Poor bird, the world's white loaf is done,
 And cannot yield thee here the smallest crumb.

In this sad state, God's tender bowels[6] run
20 Out streams of grace; and he to end all strife
The purest wheat in heaven, his dear, dear son
 Grinds, and kneads up into this bread of life.
 Which bread of life from heaven down came and stands
 Dished on my table up by angels' hands.

25 Did God mould up this bread in heaven, and bake,
 Which from his table came, and to thine goeth?
Doth he bespeak thee thus: This soul bread take;
 Come eat thy fill of this thy God's white loaf?
 It's food too fine for angels, yet come, take
30 And eat thy fill: it's heaven's sugar cake.

What grace is this knead° in this loaf? This thing   *kneaded*
 Souls are but petty things it to admire.
Ye angels, help. This fill would to the brim

---

1. Based on the words of Christ in John 6.51: "I am the living bread that came down from heaven; if any man eat of this bread, he shall live forever; and the bread that I will give is my flesh, which I will give for the life of the world."
2. To discover or make out by supernatural or magical insight.
3. I.e., the soul.
4. In this context, the living body, with an emphasis on its mortality.
5. A reference to the sin of Adam and Eve, who ate the fruit of the Tree of Knowledge of Good and Evil, which God had forbidden them (Genesis 3).
6. I.e., God's powers of mercy and compassion.

Heaven's whelmed-down[7] crystal meal bowl, yea and higher,
35   This bread of life dropped in thy mouth, doth cry:
        Eat, eat me, soul, and thou shalt never die.

1684   1937

Upon Wedlock, and Death of Children[8]

A curious knot[9] God made in paradise,
        And drew it out enameled° neatly fresh.   *variously colored*
It was the truelove knot, more sweet than spice
        And set with all the flowers of grace's dress.
5   Its wedding knot, that ne'er can be untied;
        No Alexander's sword can it divide.[1]

The slips° here planted, gay and glorious grow,   *sprigs*
        Unless an hellish breath do singe their plumes.
Here primrose, cowslips, roses, lilies blow°   *bloom*
10   With violets and pinks that void° perfumes: *give off, exude*
        Whose beauteous leaves o'er laid with honey-dew,
        And chanting birds chirp out sweet music true.

When in this knot I planted was, my stock[2]
        Soon knotted, and a manly flower out brake.
15   And after it my branch again did knot;
        Brought out another flower its sweet breathed mate.
        One knot gave one t'other the t'other's place;
        Whence chuckling smiles fought in each other's face.

But oh! a glorious hand from glory came
20   Guarded with angels, soon did crop this flower
        Which almost tore the root up of the same
        At that unlooked for, dolesome, darksome hour.
        In prayer to Christ perfumed it did ascend,
        And angels bright did it to heaven tend.

25   But pausing on't, this sweet[3] perfumed my thought,
        Christ would in glory have a flower, choice, prime,
        And having choice, chose this my branch forth brought.
        Lord take't. I thank thee, thou takest aught° of mine, *nothing*
        It is my pledge in glory; part of me
30   Is now in it, Lord, glorified with thee.

        But praying o'er my branch, my branch did sprout
        And bore another manly flower, and gay;

7. Turned over upon something so as to cover it.
8. Taylor had fourteen children; this poem appears to allude to his first four children: two daughters who died in childhood and two sons who lived to maturity.
9. In this poem, Taylor plays on several meanings of the word "knot," including the marriage bond; an intricately laid out flower bed; the base of a woody branch enclosed in the stem from which it arises; figuratively, something intricate, involved, or difficult to trace out or explain; as a verb, of

plants: to bud, to begin to develop fruit.
1. In Greek mythology, Gordius, king of Phrygia, devised a complicated knot to be undone only by the person who was to rule Asia. Alexander the Great cut the knot with a blow of his sword; Jesus said, concerning marriage, "what, therefore, God hath joined together, let not man put asunder" (Matthew 19.6).
2. Stem, but also genealogical tree.
3. I.e., this sweet thought or idea.

And after that another, sweet, brake out,
  The which the former hand soon got° away.   *took*
35   But oh! the tortures, vomit, screechings, groans,
  And six weeks fever would pierce hearts like stones.

Grief o'er doth flow, and nature fault would find
  Were not thy will, my spell charm, joy, and gem;
That as I said, I say, take, Lord, they're thine.
40   I piecemeal pass to glory bright in them.
  I joy, may I sweet flowers for glory breed,
    Whether thou getst them green, or let them seed.

ca. 1682   1937

Upon a Spider Catching a Fly

Thou sorrow, venom elf:
  Is this thy ploy,
To spin a web out of thyself
  To catch a fly?
5   For why?

I saw a pettish° wasp   *peevish, petulant*
  Fall foul therein,
Whom yet thy whorl-pins[4] did not clasp
  Lest he should fling
10   His sting.

But as afraid, remote
  Didst stand hereat
And with thy little fingers stroke
  And gently tap
15   His back.

Thus gently him didst treat
  Lest he should pet,°   *take offense*
And in a froppish,° waspish heat   *fretful*
  Should greatly fret
20   Thy net.

Whereas the silly fly,
  Caught by its leg
Thou by the throat tookst hastily
  And hind° the head   *behind*
25   Bite dead.

This goes to pot, that not[;][5]
  Nature doth call.

4. Technically, the pin that attaches the spindle of a spinning wheel to the whorl, the flywheel on the spindle that regulates speed. Here, the spider's legs.
5. An enigmatic statement, especially because the manuscript supplies no punctuation between "not" and "Nature." If punctuation is supplied editorially, one can paraphrase, "This (i.e., the fly) deteriorates, that (i.e., the spider) does not, according to the law ('call') of nature." Another possible meaning: "this goes to show ('pot' as an old form of 'put,' as in put forward for consideration) that what is 'not nature' (i.e., the hellish spider) compels or calls."

Strive not above what strength hath got
   Lest in the brawl
30   Thou fall.

This fray seems thus to us.
   Hell's spider gets
His entrails spun to whip-cords[6] thus,
   And wove to nets
35   And sets.

To tangle Adam's race
   In's° strategems   *in his*
To their destructions, spoiled, made base
   By venom things,
40   Damned sins.

But mighty, gracious Lord
   Communicate
Thy grace to break the cord, afford
   Us glory's gate
45   And state.

We'll nightingale sing like
   When perched on high
In glory's cage, thy glory, bright,
   And thankfully,
50   For joy.

ca. 1680–82   1939

Housewifery

Make me, O Lord, thy spinning wheel complete.[7]
   Thy holy word my distaff make for me.
Make mine affections thy swift flyers neat,
   And make my soul thy holy spool to be.
5   My conversation make to be thy reel,
   And reel the yarn thereon spun on thy wheel.

Make me thy loom then, knit therein this twine;
   And make thy holy spirit, Lord, wind quills.[8]
Then weave the web thyself. The yarn is fine.
10   Thine ordinances make my fulling mills.[9]
   Then dye the same in heavenly colors choice,
   All pinked° with varnished° flowers of paradise.   *ornamented / luminous*

Then clothe therewith mine understanding, will,
   Affections, judgment, conscience, memory,

---

6. Strong cord or binding, like that made of hemp or catgut.

7. In the first stanza, parts of the spinning wheel specified are: the "distaff," which holds the material to be spun; "flyers," which twist the thread as it conducts it to and winds it upon the bobbin;

"spool," on which the thread is wound as it is spun; "reel," which receives the finished thread.

8. "Quills" are the spools of a looming machine.

9. In the "fulling mills," the cloth is "fulled" or milled by being pressed between rollers and cleansed with soap or fuller's earth.

15 My words, and actions, that their shine may fill
   My ways with glory and thee glorify.
   Then mine apparel shall display before ye
   That I am clothed in holy robes for glory.
1682–83   1939

APHRA BEHN
1640?–1689

Song
Love Armed[1]

Love in fantastic triumph[2] sat,
Whilst bleeding hearts a round him flowed,
For whom fresh pains he did create,
And strange tyrannic power he showed;
5 From thy bright eyes he took his fire,
Which round about, in sport he hurled;
But 'twas from mine he took desire,
Enough to undo the amorous world.

From me he took his sighs and tears,
10 From thee his pride and cruelty;
From me his languishments and fears,
And every killing dart from thee;
Thus thou and I, the God have armed,
And set him up a deity;
15 But my poor heart alone is harmed,
Whilst thine the victor is, and free.

                                                          1677

The Disappointment[3]
I

One day the amorous *Lysander*,[4]
By an impatient passion swayed,

1. This lyric, one of Behn's most popular, was first published at the beginning of her play *Abdelazar, or the Moor's Revenge*. The song arouses the heroic villain Abdelazar to action and seems initially to describe the emotional condition of the queen who illicitly loves him—and whom he secretly scorns. The song ironically foreshadows the Moor's own fate of suffering from unrequited love.
2. A formal celebration of conquest in which the defeated party in a war was, according to Roman tradition, paraded through the streets as a trophy of victory; a popular Renaissance masque (a court entertainment that included dancing, song, drama, and spectacle) was the Triumph of Cupid, in which Cupid displays his spoils; the scene in this poem is reminiscent of the masque of Cupid depicted in Edmund Spenser's *The Faerie Queene* in which Amoret appears carrying her own heart, steeped in blood, "in silver basin layd, / Quite through transfixèd with a deadly dart" (3.12.21.2–3).
3. Several of Behn's male contemporaries wrote poems on impotence, including the earl of Rochester and George Etherege. Both called their poems "The Imperfect Enjoyment." Ovid has a poem on the subject in *Amores* 3.7. Janet Todd, one modern editor of Behn, has identified a French poem, "Sur une Impuissance," as the immediate source of "The Disappointment."
4. A conventional name for a male lover in pastoral poetry.

Surprised fair *Cloris*,[5] that loved maid,
Who could defend her self no longer.
5 All things did with his love conspire;
The gilded planet of the day,[6]
In his gay chariot drawn by fire,
Was now descending to the sea,
And left no light to guide the world,
10 But what from *Cloris'* brighter eyes was hurled.

II

In a lone thicket made for love,
Silent as yielding maids' consent,
She with a charming languishment,
Permits his force, yet gently strove;°   struggled
15 Her hands his bosom softly meet,
But not to put him back designed,
Rather to draw 'em on inclined;
Whilst he lay trembling at her feet,
Resistance 'tis in vain to show;
20 She wants° the power to say—*Ah! What d'ye do?*[7]   lacks

III

Her bright eyes sweet, and yet severe,
Where love and shame confusedly strive,
Fresh vigor to *Lysander* give;
And breathing faintly in his ear,
25 She cried—*Cease, cease—your vain desire,*
Or I'll call out—What would you do?
My dearer honor ev'n to you
I cannot, must not give—retire,
Or take this life, whose chiefest part
30 *I gave you with the conquest of my heart.*

IV

But he as much unused to fear,
As he was capable of love,
The blessed minutes to improve,°   employ to advantage
Kisses her mouth, her neck, her hair;
35 Each touch her new desire alarms,
His burning trembling hand he prest
Upon her swelling snowy brest,
While she lay panting in his arms.
All her unguarded beauties lie
40 The spoils and trophies of the enemy.

V

And now without respect or fear,
He seeks the object of his vows,

5. A conventional name for a young woman in pastoral poetry.
6. I.e., the sun; according to myth, Apollo drove his chariot, the sun, across the sky daily.

7. The question of whether an alleged victim of rape had "shown resistance" by crying out was important in English trials for rape.

(His love no modesty allows)
By swift degrees advancing—where
45 His daring hand that altar seized,
Where gods of love do sacrifice:
That awful[8] throne, that paradise
Where rage is calmed, and anger pleased;
That fountain where delight still flows,
50 And gives the universal world repose.

VI

Her balmy lips incountring° his,   *encountering*
Their bodies, as their souls, are joyned;
Where both in transports unconfined
Extend themselves upon the moss.
55 *Cloris* half dead and breathless lay;
Her soft eyes cast a humid light,
Such as divides the day and night;
Or falling stars, whose fires decay:
And now no signs of life she shows,
60 But what in short-breathed sighs returns and goes.

VII

He saw how at her length she lay;
He saw her rising bosom bare;
Her loose thin robes, through which appear
A shape designed for love and play;
65 Abandoned by her pride and shame,
She does her softest joys dispense,
Off'ring her virgin-innocence
A victim to loves sacred flame;
While the o'er-ravished shepherd lies
70 Unable to perform the sacrifice.

VIII

Ready to taste a thousand joys,
The too transported hapless swain°   *rustic fellow*
Found the vast pleasure turned to pain;
Pleasure which too much love destroys:
75 The willing garments by he laid,
And heaven all opened to his view,
Mad to possess, himself he threw
On the defenseless lovely maid.
But Oh what envying gods conspire
80 To snatch his power, yet leave him the desire!

IX

Nature's support, (without whose aid
She can no human being give)[9]

8. Awe-inspiring; the word has the sense both of "causing dread" and of "commanding profound respect or reverential fear."

9. I.e., the aid of "Nature's support," without which Nature ("she") cannot give life ("being") to any human.

It self now wants the art to live;
Faintness its slackened nerves invade:
85   In vain th' enragèd youth essayed°   tried
To call its fleeting vigor back,
No motion 'twill from motion take;
Excess of love his love betrayed;
In vain he toils, in vain commands;
90   The insensible fell weeping in his hand.

X

In this so amorous cruel strife,
Where love and fate were too severe,
The poor *Lysander* in despair
Renounced his reason with his life:
95   Now all the brisk and active fire
That should the nobler part inflame,
Served to increase his rage and shame,
And left no spark for new desire:
Not all her naked charms could move
100   Or calm that rage that had debauched his love.

XI

Cloris returning from the trance
Which love and soft desire had bred,
Her timorous hand she gently laid
(Or° guided by design or chance)   whether
105   Upon that Fabulous *Priapus*,[1]
That potent god, as poets feign;
But never did young shepherdess,
Gath'ring of fern upon the plain,
More nimbly draw her fingers back,
110   Finding beneath the verdant leaves a snake;

XII

Than *Cloris* her fair hand withdrew,
Finding that god of her desires
Disarmed of all his awful fires,
And cold as flowers bathed in the morning dew.
115   Who can the Nymph's confusion guess?
The blood forsook the hinder place,
And strewed with blushes all her face,
Which both disdain and shame exprest:
And from *Lysander's* arms she fled,
120   Leaving him fainting on the gloomy bed.

XIII

Like lightning through the grove she hies,
Or *Daphne* from the *Delphick God*,[2]

1. A god of fertility often represented with grotesquely enlarged genitals; here the word is used as a euphemism for penis.
2. The nymph Daphne spurned the advances of the god Apollo ("the Delphick God"). Fleeing from him, she begged assistance from her father, a river god, and was turned into a laurel.

No print upon the grassy road
She leaves, t' instruct pursuing eyes.
125 The wind that wantoned in her hair,
And with her ruffled garments played,
Discovered in the flying maid
All that the gods e'er made, if fair.
So *Venus*, when her love was slain,
130 With fear and haste flew o'er the fatal plain.[3]

XIV

The Nymph's resentments none but I
Can well imagine or condole:
But none can guess *Lysander's* soul,
But° those who swayed his destiny.   *except*
135 His silent griefs swell up to storms,
And not one god his fury spares;
He cursed his birth, his fate, his stars;
But more the shepherdess's charms,
Whose soft bewitching influence
140 Had damn'd him to the hell of impotence.

1680

On the Death of the Late Earl of Rochester[4]

Mourn, mourn, ye Muses,[5] all your loss deplore,
The young, the noble *Strephon*[6] is no more.
Yes, yes, he fled quick as departing light,
And ne'er shall rise from Death's eternal night,
5 So rich a prize the *Stygian*[7] gods ne'er bore,
Such wit, such beauty, never graced their shore.
He was but lent this duller world t' improve
In all the charms of poetry, and love;
Both were his gift, which freely he bestowed,
10 And like a god, dealt to the wond'ring crowd.
Scorning the little vanity of fame,
Spight° of himself attained a glorious name.   *in spite*
But oh! in vain was all his peevish[8] pride,
The sun as soon might his vast luster hide,
15 As piercing, pointed, and more lasting bright,
As suffering no vicissitudes[9] of night.
    Mourn, mourn, ye Muses, all your loss deplore,
    The young, the noble *Strephon* is no more.

---

3. Adonis, the beloved of Venus, was killed by a wild boar during a hunt. She rushed to his side but was unable to save him.
4. This poem eulogizes John Wilmot, the second earl of Rochester (see pp. 505–11), a lyric poet, satirist, and leading member of the "court wits" at the court of Charles II. Rochester lived a fashionable life in London, reputedly had several mistresses, and, according to Samuel Johnson, "blazed out his youth and health in lavish voluptuousness."
5. The nine Greek goddesses believed to be the sources of inspiration for the arts.
6. A name for a pastoral lover.
7. Infernal; Styx was one of the rivers of the underworld, over which Charon ferried the shades of the dead.
8. Obstinate; "peevish" can also be an epithet of disparagement expressing the speaker's feeling toward, rather than a quality of, the object referred to.
9. Changes, mutations; particularly an alternation of opposite or contrasting things or conditions.

Now uninspired upon your banks[1] we lie,
20   Unless when we would mourn his elegy;[2]
His name's a genius[3] that would wit dispense,
And give the theme a soul, the words a sense.
But all fine thought that ravisht° when it spoke,   *enraptured*
With the soft youth eternal leave has took;
25   Uncommon wit that did the soul o'ercome,
Is buried all in *Strephon's* worshiped tomb;
Satire has lost its art, its sting is gone,
The Fop and Cully[4] now may be undone;
That dear instructing rage is now allayed,°   *laid down*
30   And no sharp pen dares tell 'em how they've strayed;
Bold as a god was ev'ry lash he took,
But kind and gentle the chastizing stroke.
    Mourn, mourn, ye youths, whom fortune has betrayed,
    The last reproacher of your vice is dead.

35   Mourn, all ye beauties, put your *Cyprus*[5] on,
The truest swain[6] that e're adored you's gone;
Think how he loved, and writ, and sighed, and spoke,
Recall his mien,° his fashion, and his look.   *bearing, manner*
By what dear arts the soul he did surprise,
40   Soft as his voice, and charming as his eyes.
Bring garlands all of never-dying flowers,
Bedewed with everlasting falling showers;
Fix your fair eyes upon your victimed slave,
Sent gay and young to his untimely grave.
45   See where the noble swain extended lies,
Too sad a triumph of your victories;[7]
Adorned with all the graces Heaven e'er lent, ⎫
All that was great, soft, lovely, excellent   ⎬
You've laid into his early monument. ⎭
50   Mourn, mourn, ye beauties, your sad loss deplore,
    The young, the charming *Strephon* is no more.

Mourn, all ye little gods of love,[8] whose darts
Have lost their wonted° power of piercing hearts;   *usual*
Lay by the gilded quiver and the bow,
55   The useless toys can do no mischief now,
Those eyes that all your arrows' points inspired,
Those lights[9] that gave ye fire are now retired,
Cold as his tomb, pale as your mother's doves;[1]
Bewail him then oh all ye little loves,

1. According to mythology, the Muses sang on the banks of the Hippocrene spring on Mt. Helicon.
2. A funeral song or lament; here, to utter in a sorrowful manner.
3. A spirit with the capacity to influence or inspire the character, conduct, or fortunes of a person.
4. A dupe, one easily taken in; "Fop": a fool; these types were frequent objects of satire in Restoration literature.
5. A light, transparent material like lawn or crepe, much used for mourning, but also perhaps with reference to a branch of the cypress tree, regarded as a symbol of mourning.

6. Lover, but also shepherd, in keeping with the pastoral references in the poem.
7. Triumph here refers to the defeated party in a war, who was, according to Roman tradition, paraded through the streets as a trophy of victory.
8. Figures of Eros, or Cupid, the god of love, who was often portrayed as a winged child or boy armed with a quiver and bow. His gold-tipped arrows incited his victims to love.
9. I.e., eyes.
1. Venus, the mother of Cupid, was often depicted attended by doves.

60 For you the humblest votary° have lost   *devoted worshiper*
    That ever your divinities could boast;
    Upon your hands your weeping heads decline,
    And let your wings encompass round his shrine;
    In stead of flowers your broken arrows strow,°   *scatter about*
65 And at his feet lay the neglected bow.
      Mourn, all ye little gods, your loss deplore,
      The soft, the charming *Strephon* is no more.

    Large was his fame, but short his glorious race,
    Like young *Lucretius*[2] lived and died apace.°   *quickly*
70 So early roses fade, so over all
    They cast their fragrant scents, then softly fall,
    While all the scattered perfumed leaves declare,
    How lovely 'twas when whole, how sweet, how fair.
    Had he been to the Roman Empire known,
75 When great *Augustus*[3] filled the peaceful throne;
    Had he the noble wond'rous poet[4] seen,
    And known his genius, and surveyed his mien,
    (When wits, and heroes graced divine abodes),
    He had increased the number of their gods;
80 The royal judge[5] had temples rear'd to's° name,   *to his*
    And made him as immortal as his fame;
    In love and verse his *Ovid* he'ad[6] out-done,
    And all his laurels, and his *Julia*[7] won.
      Mourn, mourn, unhappy world, his loss deplore,
85 The great, the charming *Strephon* is no more.

                  1685

To the Fair Clarinda, Who Made Love[8] to Me, Imagined More Than Woman

By Mrs. B.

    Fair lovely maid, or if that title be
    Too weak, too feminine for nobler thee,
    Permit a name that more approaches truth:
    And let me call thee, lovely charming youth.[9]
5 This last will justify my soft complaint,[1]

2. A Roman poet of the early first century B.C., author of *De Rerum Natura* ("On the Nature of Things"), the themes of which included the mortality of the soul and the pointlessness of the fear of death; he was said to have committed suicide.
3. The first Roman emperor, Augustus ruled from 27 B.C. until his death in A.D. 14, a period of time marked by relative peace, cultural achievement, and civil improvements. Virgil, Horace, and Ovid were among the writers of this period.
4. I.e., if "he," Augustus, had seen Rochester, "the noble wond'rous poet"; this line begins an "if . . . then" construction: if Augustus had known Rochester, then he (Augustus) would have added the English poet to the ranks of the Roman gods, built temples in his honor, and made him immortal.
5. I.e., Augustus.
6. He had, i.e., he would have. Ovid is famous for,

among other things, his love poems, including the *Amores*, purportedly based on his own experiences. Ovid was popular during the Restoration for his wit and sensuality.
7. The daughter of Augustus, thought to have been Ovid's mistress and one cause of his being banished from Rome by Augustus; "his laurels" refers to Ovid's poetic achievement.
8. Paid amorous attention to; Clarinda is a typical pastoral name, under which Behn refers, probably, to one of her contemporaries.
9. Young man; although "youth" can denote simply a young person, it is used here in opposition to the title of "maid," i.e., young woman, in line 1.
1. A lyric poem in which the speaker bewails the misery caused by his or her absent or unresponsive beloved.

While they may serve to lessen my constraint;
And without blushes I the youth pursue,
When so much beauteous woman is in view.
Against thy charms we struggle but in vain
10 With thy deluding form thou giv'st us pain,
While the bright nymph betrays us to the swain.[2]
In pity to our sex sure thou wer't sent,
That we might love, and yet be innocent:
For sure no crime with thee we can commit;
15 Or if we should—thy form excuses it.
For who, that gathers fairest flowers believes
A snake lies hid beneath the fragrant leaves.

Thou beauteous wonder of a different kind,
Soft *Cloris* with the dear *Alexis*[3] joined;
20 When e'r the manly part of thee, would plead
Thou tempts us with the image of the maid,
While we the noblest passions do extend
The love to *Hermes*, *Aphrodite*[4] the friend.

1688

A Thousand Martyrs[5]

A thousand martyrs I have made,
    All sacrificed to my desire;
A thousand beauties have betrayed,
    That languish in resistless fire.
5 The untamed heart to hand I brought,
And fixed the wild and wandering thought.

I never vowed nor sighed in vain
    But both, though false, were well received.
The fair are pleased to give us pain,
10   And what they wish is soon believed.
And though I talked of wounds and smart,
Love's pleasures only touched my heart.

Alone the glory and the spoil
    I always laughing bore away;
15 The triumphs, without pain or toil,
    Without the hell, the heav'n of joy.
And while I thus at random rove
Despise the fools that whine for love.

1688

---

2. The nymph and the swain are conventional
characters of pastoral poetry. The nymph is a
young, beautiful woman; the swain is a young
male shepherd or rustic.
3. I.e., she combines features of stock male and
female pastoral figures.
4. Hermaphroditus was the son of Hermes (Mer-
cury) and Aphrodite (Venus), the goddess of love
and beauty. Bathing in the fountain of the nymph
Salmacis, whose love he spurned, he merged with
her and became male and female in one body.

Behn herself was described by a contemporary,
Daniel Kendricks, as belonging to a "third" sex:
"ah, more than woman, more than man she is," he
wrote in 1688.
5. This lyric is from Behn's *Lycidus: Or the Lover
in Fashion*, a prose work with verse interspersed
that translates *Le Second Voyage de l'Isle d'Amour*
(1664) by the Abbé Paul Tallemant. This song is
introduced by the narrator with the line "Take
then the history of my heart, which I assure, boasts
itself of the conquests it has made."

JOHN WILMOT, EARL OF ROCHESTER
1647–1680

A Satire against Reason and Mankind

Were I (who to my cost already am
One of those strange, prodigious creatures, man)
A spirit free to choose, for my own share,
What case of flesh and blood I pleased to wear,
5   I'd be a dog, a monkey, or a bear,
Or anything but that vain animal
Who is so proud of being rational.
   The senses are too gross,[1] and he'll contrive
A sixth, to contradict the other five,
10 And before certain instinct, will prefer
Reason, which fifty times for one does err;
Reason, an *ignis fatuus*[2] in the mind,
Which, leaving light of nature, sense, behind,
Pathless and dangerous wandering ways it takes
15 Through error's fenny° bogs and thorny brakes;°   *swampy / thickets*
Whilst the misguided follower climbs with pain
Mountains of whimseys, heaped in his own brain;
Stumbling from thought to thought, falls headlong down
Into doubt's boundless sea, where, like to drown,
20 Books bear him up awhile, and make him try
To swim with bladders[3] of philosophy;
In hopes still to o'ertake th' escaping light,
The vapor dances in his dazzling° sight   *dazzled*
Till, spent, it leaves him to eternal night.
25 Then old age and experience, hand in hand,
Lead him to death, and make him understand,
After a search so painful and so long,
That all his life he has been in the wrong.
Huddled in dirt the reasoning engine lies,
30 Who was so proud, so witty, and so wise.
   Pride drew him in, as cheats their bubbles° catch,   *dupes*
And made him venture to be made a wretch.
His wisdom did his happiness destroy,
Aiming to know that world he should enjoy.
35 And wit was his vain, frivolous pretense
Of pleasing others at his own expense,
For wits are treated just like common whores:
First they're enjoyed, and then kicked out of doors.
The pleasure past, a threatening doubt remains
40 That frights th' enjoyer with succeeding pains.
Women and men of wit are dangerous tools,
And ever fatal to admiring° fools: *wondering*

1. Lacking in delicacy of perception; coarse, or inferior; "gross" may also mean dealing with the material or that which is perceptible to the senses as opposed to that which is spiritual or impalpable.
2. "Foolish fire" (Latin), also known as the will-o'-the-wisp; said to draw travelers astray by holding a false light before them. The phenomenon of nocturnal light is caused by the combustion of marsh gas.
3. Bladders of animals inflated and used as a float but also an inflated, pretentious man, a windbag.

Pleasure allures, and when the fops° escape,   *fools*
'Tis not that they're belov'd, but fortunate,
45 And therefore what they fear at heart, they hate.
    But now, methinks, some formal band and beard[4]
Takes me to task. Come on, sir; I'm prepared.
    "Then, by your favor, anything that's writ
Against this gibing, jingling[5] knack called wit
50 Likes° me abundantly; but you take care   *pleases*
Upon this point, not to be too severe.
Perhaps my muse[6] were fitter for this part,
For I profess I can be very smart
On wit, which I abhor with all my heart.
55 I long to lash it in some sharp essay,
But your grand indiscretion bids me stay
And turns my tide of ink another way.
    "What rage ferments in your degenerate mind
To make you rail at reason and mankind?
60 Blest, glorious man! to whom alone kind heaven
An everlasting soul has freely given,
Whom his great Maker took such care to make
That from himself he did the image take[7]
And this fair frame in shining reason dressed
65 To dignify his nature above beast;
Reason, by whose aspiring influence
We take a flight beyond material sense,
Dive into mysteries, then soaring pierce
The flaming limits of the universe,
70 Search heaven and hell, find out what's acted there,
And give the world true grounds of hope and fear."
    Hold, mighty man, I cry, all this we know
From the pathetic pen of Ingelo,
From Patrick's *Pilgrim*, Sibbes' soliloquies,[8]
75 And 'tis this very reason I despise:
This supernatural gift, that makes a mite°   *minute insect*
Think he's the image of the infinite,
Comparing his short life, void of all rest,
To the eternal and the ever blest;
80 This busy, puzzling stirrer-up of doubt
That frames deep mysteries, then finds 'em out,
Filling with frantic crowds of thinking fools
Those reverend bedlams,° colleges and schools;   *madhouses*
Borne on whose wings, each heavy sot° can pierce   *fool*
85 The limits of the boundless universe;
So charming° ointments make an old witch fly   *magic*
And bear a crippled carcass through the sky.
'Tis this exalted power, whose business lies

---

4. A Geneva band is worn by the clergy. A "band and beard" is hence a venerable parson.
5. The affected repetition of a series of similar sounds without regard to sense; "gibing": mocking, taunting.
6. One of the nine Greek goddesses believed to be sources of inspiration for the arts.
7. According to Genesis 1.26, humankind was made in the image of God.
8. Simon Patrick's *The Parable of the Pilgrim* (another allegory), and Richard Sibbes' discourses (none actually called *Soliloquies*) were current instructional works. Nathaniel Ingello, whose pen is derisively called "pathetic" (heart-rending), wrote an allegorical romance, *Bentivolio and Urania*.

In nonsense and impossibilities,
90 This made a whimsical philosopher[9]
Before the spacious world, his tub prefer,
And we have modern cloistered coxcombs° who   *foolish, conceited persons*
Retire to think, 'cause they have nought to do.
    But thoughts are given for action's government;
95 Where action ceases, thought's impertinent.°   *irrelevant*
Our sphere of action is life's happiness,
And he who thinks beyond, thinks like an ass.
Thus, whilst against false reasoning I inveigh,
I own° right reason, which I would obey: *acknowledge*
100 That reason which distinguishes by sense
And gives us rules of good and ill from thence,
That bounds desires with a reforming will
To keep 'em more in vigor, not to kill.
Your reason hinders, mine helps to enjoy,
105 Renewing appetites yours would destroy.
My reason is my friend, yours is a cheat;
Hunger calls out, my reason bids me eat;
Perversely, yours your appetite does mock:
This asks for food, that answers, "What's o'clock?"
110 This plain distinction, sir, your doubt° secures:°   *suspicion / confirms*
'Tis not true reason I despise, but yours.
    Thus I think reason righted, but for man,
I'll ne'er recant; defend him if you can.
For all his pride and his philosophy,
115 'Tis evident beasts are, in their degree,
As wise at least, and better far than he.
Those creatures are the wisest who attain,
By surest means, the ends at which they aim.
If therefore Jowler[1] finds and kills his hares
120 Better than Meres[2] supplies committee chairs,
Though one's a statesman, th' other but a hound,
Jowler, in justice, would be wiser found.
    You see how far man's wisdom here extends;
Look next if human nature makes amends:
125 Whose principles most generous are, and just,
And to whose morals you would sooner trust.
Be judge yourself, I'll bring it to the test:
Which is the basest creature, man or beast?
Birds feed on birds, beasts on each other prey,
130 But savage man alone does man betray.
Pressed by necessity, they kill for food;
Man undoes man to do himself no good.
With teeth and claws by nature armed, they hunt
Nature's allowance, to supply their want.°   *needs*
135 But man, with smiles, embraces, friendship, praise,
Inhumanly his fellow's life betrays;
With voluntary pains works his distress,
Not through necessity, but wantonness.

---

9. Diogenes the Cynic, of ancient Greece, who (in legend) inhabited a tub.
1. A hunting dog.
2. Sir Thomas Meres, a Whig member of Parliament.

For hunger or for love they fight and tear,
140 Whilst wretched man is still in arms for fear.
For fear he arms, and is of arms afraid,
By fear to fear successively betrayed;
Base fear, the source whence his best passions came:
His boasted honor, and his dear-bought fame;
145 That lust of power, to which he's such a slave,
And for the which alone he dares be brave;
To which his various projects are designed;
Which makes him generous, affable, and kind;
For which he takes such pains to be thought wise,
150 And screws° his actions in a forced disguise,   distorts
Leading a tedious life in misery
Under laborious, mean hypocrisy.
Look to the bottom of his vast design,
Wherein man's wisdom, power, and glory join:
155 The good he acts, the ill he does endure,
'Tis all from fear, to make himself secure.
Merely for safety, after fame we thirst,
For all men would be cowards if they durst.
And honesty's against all common sense:
160 Men must be knaves,° 'tis in their own defence.   unprincipled men
Mankind's dishonest; if you think it fair
Amongst known cheats to play upon the square,[3]
You'll be undone.
Nor can weak truth your reputation save:
165 The knaves will all agree to call you knave.
Wronged shall he live, insulted o'er, oppressed,
Who dares be less a villain than the rest.
Thus, sir, you see what human nature craves:
Most men are cowards, all men should be knaves.
170 The difference lies, as far as I can see,
Not in the thing itself, but the degree,
And all the subject matter of debate
Is only: Who's a knave of the first rate?

All this with indignation have I hurled
175 At the pretending part of the proud world,
Who, swollen with selfish vanity, devise
False freedoms, holy cheats, and formal lies
Over their fellow slaves to tyrannize.
But if in Court so just a man there be
180 (In Court a just man, yet unknown to me)
Who does his needful flattery direct,
Not to oppress and ruin, but protect
(Since flattery, which way soever laid,
Is still a tax on that unhappy trade);
185 If so upright a statesman you can find,
Whose passions bend to his unbiased mind,
Who does his arts and policies apply
To raise his country, not his family,
Nor, whilst his pride owned avarice withstands,

3. I.e., play in a fair, honest, and straightforward manner.

190 Receives close° bribes through friends' corrupted hands—   *secret*
    Is there a churchman who on God relies;
Whose life, his faith and doctrine justifies?
Not one blown up with vain prelatic pride,[4]
Who, for reproof of sins, does man deride;
195 Whose envious heart makes preaching a pretense,
With his obstreperous, saucy eloquence,
To chide at kings, and rail at men of sense;
None of that sensual tribe whose talents lie
In avarice, pride, sloth, and gluttony;
200 Who hunt good livings, but abhor good lives;
Whose lust exalted to that height arrives
They act adultery with their own wives,
And ere a score of years completed be,
Can from the lofty pulpit proudly see
205 Half a large parish their own progeny;
Nor doting bishop who would be adored
For domineering at the council board,
A greater fop in business at fourscore,°   *eighty*
Fonder of serious toys, affected more,
210 Than the gay, glittering fool at twenty proves
With all his noise, his tawdry clothes, and loves;
    But a meek, humble man of honest sense,
Who, preaching peace, does practice continence;
Whose pious life's a proof he does believe
215 Mysterious truths, which no man can conceive.
If upon earth there dwell such God-like men,
I'll here recant my paradox[5] to them,
Adore those shrines of virtue, homage pay,
And, with the rabble world, their laws obey.
220   If such there be, yet grant me this at least:
Man differs more from man, than man from beast.

                             1675

Love and Life

All my past life is mine no more;
    The flying hours are gone,
Like transitory dreams given o'er
Whose images are kept in store
5   By memory alone.

Whatever is to come is not:
    How can it then be mine?
The present moment's all my lot,
And that, as fast as it is got,
10   Phyllis,[6] is wholly thine.

Then talk not of inconstancy,
    False hearts, and broken vows;

---

4. I.e., pride in being a prelate, an ecclesiastical dignitary of high rank.

5. A tenet contrary to received opinion or belief.

6. A conventional poetic name for a woman.

If I, by miracle, can be
This livelong minute true to thee,
15   'Tis all that heaven allows.

1677

The Disabled Debauchee

As some brave admiral, in former war
    Deprived of force, but pressed with courage still,
Two rival fleets appearing from afar,
    Crawls to the top of an adjacent hill;

5   From whence, with thoughts full of concern, he views
    The wise and daring conduct of the fight,
Whilst each bold action to his mind renews
    His present glory and his past delight;

From his fierce eyes flashes of fire he throws,
10   As from black clouds when lightning breaks away;
Transported, thinks himself amidst the foes,
    And absent, yet enjoys the bloody day;

So, when my days of impotence approach,
    And I'm by pox[7] and wine's unlucky chance
15 Forced from the pleasing billows of debauch
    On the dull shore of lazy temperance,

My pains at least some respite shall afford
    While I behold the battles you maintain
When fleets of glasses sail about the board,°   table
20   From whose broadsides volleys of wit shall rain.

Nor let the sight of honorable scars,
    Which my too forward valor did procure,
Frighten new-listed° soldiers from the wars: newly enlisted
    Past joys have more than paid what I endure.

25 Should any youth (worth being drunk) prove nice,°   reluctant, fastidious
    And from his fair inviter meanly shrink,
'Twill please the ghost of my departed vice
    If, at my counsel, he repent and drink.

Or should some cold-complexioned sot° forbid,   fool
30   With his dull morals, our bold night-alarms,
I'll fire his blood by telling what I did
    When I was strong and able to bear arms.

I'll tell of whores attacked, their lords at home;
    Bawds' quarters beaten up,[8] and fortress won;

---

7. Venereal disease often left extensive scarring.
8. Aroused, disturbed; "bawds' quarters": ("bawds" are madams).

35 Windows demolished, watches° overcome;   *watchmen*
  And handsome ills by my contrivance done.

  Nor shall our love-fits, Chloris,[9] be forgot,
    When each the well-looked linkboy[1] strove t' enjoy,
  And the best kiss was the deciding lot
40   Whether the boy fucked you, or I the boy.

  With tales like these I will such thoughts inspire
    As to important mischief shall incline:
  I'll make him long some ancient church to fire,
    And fear no lewdness he's called to by wine.

45 Thus, statesmanlike, I'll saucily impose,
    And safe from action, valiantly advise;
  Sheltered in impotence, urge you to blows,
    And being good for nothing else, be wise.

                                                              1680

A Song of a Young Lady to Her Ancient Lover

          Ancient person, for whom I
          All the flattering youth defy,
          Long be it ere thou grow old,
          Aching, shaking, crazy, cold;
5   But still continue as thou art,
          Ancient person of my heart.

          On thy withered lips and dry,
          Which like barren furrows lie,
          Brooding kisses I will pour
10   Shall thy youthful [heat] restore
          (Such kind showers in autumn fall,
          And a second spring recall);
            Nor from thee will ever part,
            Ancient person of my heart.

15   Thy nobler part, which but to name
          In our sex would be counted shame,
          By age's frozen grasp possessed,
          From [his] ice shall be released,
          And soothed by my reviving hand,
20   In former warmth and vigor stand.
          All a lover's wish can reach
          For thy joy my love shall teach,
          And for they pleasure shall improve
          All that art can add to love.
25   Yet still I love thee without art,
            Ancient person of my heart.

                                                              1691

9. A conventional poetic name for a woman.
1. A boy employed to carry a torch to light the way for people in the streets.

ANNE KILLIGREW
1660–1685

Alexandreis[1]

I sing the man that never equal knew,
Whose mighty arms all *Asia* did subdue,[2]
Whose conquests through the spacious world do ring,
That city-raser,[3] king-destroying king,
5   Who o'er the warlike *Macedons* did reign,
And worthily the name of *Great* did gain.
This is the prince (if fame you will believe,
To ancient story any credit give.)
Who when the globe of Earth he had subdued,
10   With tears the easy victory pursued;
Because that no more worlds there were to win,
No further scene to act his glories in.

    Ah that some pitying *Muse*[4] would now inspire
My frozen style with a poetic fire,
15   And raptures worthy of his matchless fame,
Whose deeds I sing, whose never fading name
Long as the world shall fresh and deathless last,
No less to future ages, then° the past.   *than*
Great my presumption is, I must confess,
20   But if I thrive, my glory's ne'er the less;
Nor will it from his conquests derogate°   *detract*
A female pen his acts did celebrate.
If thou O *Muse* wilt thy assistance give,
Such as made *Naso* and great *Maro*[5] live,
25   With him whom *Melas*[6] fertile banks did bear,
Live, though their bodies dust and ashes are;
Whose laurels[7] were not fresher, than their fame
Is now, and will for ever be the same.
If the like favor thou wilt grant to me,
30   O Queen of Verse,[8] I'll not ungrateful be,
My choicest hours to thee I'll dedicate,
'Tis thou shalt rule, 'tis thou shalt be my fate.
But if coy goddess thou shalt this deny,

1. This unfinished poem was an early work of the young poet, who apparently (according to the note, reprinted here, at the end of the poem in the volume of collected works published after her death in 1686) felt herself unequal to the task of completing an epic poem about Alexander the Great. Alexander (356–323 B.C.), considered one of the greatest military leaders of all time, became king of Macedon in 336 B.C. and succeeded during his short life in conquering Egypt and most of Southeast Asia.
2. The opening lines of the poem echo the beginning of Virgil's great epic, the *Aeneid*, which begins: "Of arms and the man I sing. . . ."
3. One who razes, or obliterates, cities. In 335 B.C., Thebes, a Greek state, revolted. Alexander put down the revolt and destroyed the city. In the course of his conquests (of Phoenicia, Egypt, Tyre, Asia Minor, Persia, and the Punjab), Alexander destroyed many kings.
4. The Muses were nine Greek goddesses believed to be the sources of inspiration for the arts. The invocation of the Muse, requesting divine aid in the writing of the poem, is an epic convention.
5. Publius Vergilius Maro (70–19 B.C.) is the full name of the Roman poet Virgil; Publius Ovidius Naso is the full name of the Roman poet Ovid (43 B.C.–A.D. 17), author of the *Metamorphoses*.
6. The Greek poet Homer, author of the *Iliad* and the *Odyssey*, was said to have been born and lived by the Melas River.
7. The laurel was a symbol of poetic achievement.
8. I.e., the Muse of epic poetry, Calliope.

And from my humble suit disdaining fly,
35 I'll stoop and beg no more, since I know this,
Writing of him, I cannot write amiss:
His lofty deeds will raise each feeble line,
And god-like acts will make my verse divine.
'Twas at the time the golden sun doth rise,
40 And with his beams enlights the azure skies,
When lo a troop in silver arms drew near,
The glorious sun did nere° so bright appear;   *never*
Dire[9] scarlet plumes adorned their haughty crests,°   *helmets*
And crescent shields did shade their shining breasts;
45 Down from their shoulders hung a panthers hide,
A bow and quiver rattled by their side;
Their hands a knotty well tried spear did bear,
Jocund° they seemed, and quite devoid of fear.   *merry*
These warlike virgins were, that do reside
50 Near *Thermodons'* smooth banks[1] and verdant° side,   *green*
The plains of *Themiscyre*[2] their birth do boast,
Thalestris[3] now did head the beauteous host;
She emulating that illustrious dame,
Who to the aid of *Troy* and *Priam* came,[4]
55 And her who the *Retulian* prince did aid,[5]
Though dearly both for their assistance paid.
But fear she scorned, nor the like fate did dread,
Her host she often to the field had led,
As oft in triumph had returned again,
60 Glory she only fought for all her pain.
    This martial queen had heard how loudly fame,
Echoed our conqueror's redoubted° name,   *respected, dreaded*
Her soul his conduct and his courage fired,
To see the hero she so much admired;
65 And to *Hyrcania* for this cause she went,
Where *Alexander* (wholly then intent
On triumphs[6] and such military sport)
At truce with war held both his camp and court.
And while before the town she did attend°   *await*
70 Her messengers return, she saw ascend
A cloud of dust, that covered all the sky,
And still at every pause there stroke° her eye.   *struck*
The interrupted beams of burnisht gold,
As dust the splendor hid, or did unfold;

9. Terrible, in the sense of inspiring terror or fear in an onlooker.
1. The Amazons were a tribe of warrior women believed to live on the plain of the Thermodon River, which sprang from the Amazonian Mountains and emptied into the Black Sea.
2. The capital city of the Amazons.
3. Thalestris was a queen of the Amazons who desired to have a daughter sired by Alexander. Legend has it that she consorted with him for thirteen days at Hyrcania, but died shortly after returning to her own country.
4. Penthesilea, an earlier queen of the Amazons, fought in the Trojan War against the Greeks. In most versions of her story, she arrives in Troy after the death of the Trojan hero Hector, with the Trojans all but defeated. She and a small band of Amazons fight valiantly against the Greeks, killing many Greek heroes, before she is killed by Achilles, who is so impressed by her beauty and valor that he laments her death and prevents the Greeks from desecrating her body. Priam was the king of Troy.
5. In the *Aeneid*, Virgil records the bravery of the warrior-queen, Camilla, who fought with Turnus, prince of the Rutulians, against Aeneas and the Trojans. She is killed in the battle.
6. Formal celebrations of conquests.

75 Loud neighings of the steeds, and trumpets sound
    Filled all the air, and echoed from the ground:
    The gallant *Greeks* with a brisk march drew near,
    And their great chief did at their head appear.
    And now come up to th'*Amazonian* band,
80 They made a halt and a respectful stand:
    And both the troops (with like amazement strook°)   struck
    Did each on other with deep silence look.
    Th'heroic queen (whose high pretence to war
    Cancelled the bashful laws and nicer bar[7]
85 Of modesty, which did her sex restrain)
    First boldly did advance before her train,
    And thus she spake. All but a god in name,
    And that a debt time owes unto thy fame.

    This was the first essay° of this young lady in   attempt
    poetry, but finding the task she had undertaken
    hard, she laid it by till practice and more time
    should make her equal to so great a work.

                                                              1686

ANNE FINCH, COUNTESS OF WINCHILSEA
1661–1720

Friendship Between Ephelia and Ardelia[1]

Eph.   What Friendship is, Ardelia show.
Ard.   'Tis to love, as I love you.
Eph.   This account, so short (tho' kind)
         Suits not my inquiring mind.
5   Therefore farther now repeat:
         What is Friendship when complete?
Ard.   'Tis to share all joy and grief;
         'Tis to lend all due relief
         From the tongue, the heart, the hand;
10   'Tis to mortgage house and land;
         For a friend be sold a slave;
         'Tis to die upon a grave,
         If a friend therein do lie.
Eph.   This indeed, tho' carried high,[2]
15   This, tho' more than e'er was done
         Underneath the rolling sun,
         This has all been said before.

7. Stricter obstacle; "bashful": characterized by extreme modesty.
1. Ardelia is a poetic name that Finch sometimes used to refer to herself.
2. I.e., expressed loudly or in high style; or, perhaps, highly esteemed.

Can Ardelia say no more?
Ard.   Words indeed no more can show:
20   *But 'tis to love, as I love you.*

1713

Adam Posed[3]

Could our first father, at his toilsome plow,
Thorns in his path, and labor on his brow,
Clothed only in a rude, unpolished skin,
Could he a vain fantastic nymph[4] have seen,
5 In all her airs, in all her antic° graces,   *bizarre*
Her various fashions, and more various faces;
How had it posed that skill, which late assigned
Just appellations to each several kind![5]
A right idea of the sight to frame;
10 T'have guessed from what new element[6] she came;
T'have hit the wav'ring form,[7] or giv'n this thing a name.

1713

To Death

O King of terrors, whose unbounded sway
All that have life must certainly obey;
The King, the Priest, the Prophet, all are thine,
Nor would ev'n God (in flesh) thy stroke decline.[8]
5 My name is on thy roll, and sure I must
Increase thy gloomy kingdom in the dust.
My soul at this no apprehension feels,
But trembles at thy swords, thy racks, thy wheels;[9]
Thy scorching fevers, which distract the sense,
10 And snatch us raving, unprepared, from hence;
At thy contagious darts, that wound the heads
Of weeping friends, who wait at dying beds.
Spare these, and let thy time be when it will;
My bus'ness is to die, and thine to kill.
15 Gently thy fatal scepter on me lay,
And take to thy cold arms, insensibly, thy prey.

1713

3. Perplexed.
4. "Fantastic" may mean "capricious" or "foppish in attire," but may also have the sense of "imaginary" or "unreal." "Nymph" is a conventional pastoral word for a young woman. The character is a coquette, or flirtatious young woman, a type much commented on and satirized during the Restoration. Attacks on artificiality and the use of cosmetics were common during the Renaissance and still popular during the Restoration.
5. According to Genesis 2.19, Adam named ("assign'd / just appellations to") all the animals.
6. I.e., she is not created from one of the four elements—earth, air, water, and fire—out of which all things were believed to be composed.
7. I.e., to have accurately identified the nature of her changing form.
8. I.e., Christ (God in his human incarnation) suffered death on the Cross.
9. "Racks" and "wheels" are instruments of torture.

The Spleen[1]

A *Pindarik Poem*[2]

What art thou, Spleen, which ev'ry thing dost ape?
    Thou Proteus[3] to abused mankind,
    Who never yet thy real cause could find,
Or fix thee to remain in one continued shape.
5   Still varying thy perplexing form,
    Now a Dead Sea[4] thou'lt represent,
    A calm of stupid° discontent,   *unfeeling, unreasoning*
Then, dashing on the rocks wilt rage into a storm.
    Trembling sometimes thou dost appear,
10   Dissolved into a panic fear;
    On sleep intruding dost thy shadows spread,
    Thy gloomy terrors round the silent bed,
And crowd with boding° dreams the melancholy head;   *forboding*
    Or, when the midnight hour is told,
15   And drooping lids thou still dost waking hold,
    Thy fond delusions cheat° the eyes,   *deceive*
    Before them antick° spectres dance,   *bizarre*
Unusual fires their pointed heads advance,
    And airy phantoms rise.
20   Such was the monstrous vision seen,
When Brutus[5] (now beneath his cares opprest,
And all Rome's fortunes rolling in his breast,
    Before Philippi's latest field,
Before his fate did to Octavius lead)
25   Was vanquished by the Spleen.

    Falsely, the mortal part we blame
    Of our depressed, and pond'rous° frame,°   *unwieldy / body*
    Which, till the first degrading sin
    Let thee, its dull attendant, in,
30   Still with the other did comply,[6]
Nor clogged the active soul, disposed to fly,
And range the mansions of its native sky.
    Nor, whilst in his own heaven he dwelt,
    Whilst Man his paradise possesed,
35   His fertile Garden in the fragrant East,
    And all united odors smelled,

---

1. A mysterious illness, believed to be connected with the organ of the same name, the effects of which were believed to be depression, hypochondria, ill-temper, melancholy, and a variety of other nervous disorders. Although considered largely a disease of women, it sometimes afflicted men. It was often affected by, for instance, lovers and poets. In this poem, Finch makes a distinction between those who pretend to be affected by the disorder and those who really do suffer from it. Finch suffered from "spleen" and was praised by at least one contemporary physician for this accurate portrayal of the symptoms of the disease.
2. Pindar (ca. 522–ca. 438 B.C.), a Greek poet, was an early practitioner of the ode form. An ode is a lyric poem, usually with a serious subject and a dignified style.
3. A shape-changing sea god.
4. The Dead Sea, located on the border between Israel and Jordan, is a salt lake, called "dead" because it contains no visible plant or animal life.
5. Before the Battle of Philippi (42 B.C.), Brutus saw the ghost of Caesar, whom he had assassinated. Brutus was defeated at Philippi by Marc Antony and Octavius, Caesar's nephew and eventual successor.
6. "Other": i.e., the soul; "Mortal Part": i.e., the body; thus, before the sin of Adam and Eve, or original sin ("the First degrading Sin"), the body "did comply," i.e., acted in accordance with, or yielded to, the soul.

No armèd sweets,[7] until thy reign,
   Could shock the sense, or in the face
   A flushed, unhandsome color place.
40 Now the jonquil° o'ercomes the feeble brain;   *daffodil*
   We faint beneath the aromatic pain,
   Till some offensive scent thy pow'rs appease,
   And pleasure we resign° for short, and nauseous ease.   *give up*

   In ev'ry one thou dost possess,
45 New are thy motions,° and thy dress: *effects*
   Now in some grove a list'ning friend
   Thy false suggestions must attend,
   Thy whispered griefs, thy fancied sorrows hear,
   Breathed in a sigh, and witnessed° by a tear;   *confirmed*
50 Whilst in the light and vulgar crowd,[8]
   Thy slaves, more clamorous and loud,
   By laughters unprovoked, thy influence too confess.
   In the imperious wife thou vapors[9] art,
   Which from o'erheated passions rise
55 In clouds to the attractive[1] brain,
   Until descending thence again,
   Through the o'er-cast and show'ring eyes,
   Upon her husband's softened heart,
   He the disputed point must yield,
60 Something resign of the contested field;
   Till lordly Man, born to imperial sway,
   Compounds° for peace, to make that right away,   *bargains*
   And Woman, arm'd with Spleen, does servilely obey.

   The fool, to imitate the wits,
65 Complains of thy pretended fits,
   And dullness, born with him, would lay
   Upon[2] thy accidental sway;
   Because, sometimes, thou dost presume
   Into the ablest heads to come:
70 That, often, men of thoughts refined,
   Impatient of unequal sense,
   Such slow returns, where they so much dispense,
   Retiring from the crowd, are to thy shades inclined.[3]
   O'er me alas! thou dost too much prevail:
75 I feel thy force, whilst I against thee rail;
   I feel my verse decay, and my cramped numbers° fail.   *verses, poetry*
   Through thy black jaundice I all objects see,
   As dark, and terrible as thee,
   My lines decried, and my employment thought

7. Finch seems to imply that sweet odors bring on the disorder and that foul odors can "appease" or lessen the symptoms.
8. "Light": frivolous, "vulgar": pretentious or lacking in cultivation; therefore a description of those who counterfeit the symptoms of "spleen," such as the two examples that follow: the "imperious wife" of line 53 and the "fool" of line 64.
9. A disorder associated with "spleen" and supposed to be caused by exhalations within the organs of the body and characterized by depression, hypochondria, hysteria, and other nervous disorders.
1. In the medical sense of having the property of drawing something (the "passions," in this case) to itself.
2. I.e., would blame.
3. According to Burton's *Anatomy of Melancholy* (1621), love of learning could be a cause of "spleen."

80   An useless folly, or presumptuous fault:
       Whilst in the Muses'[4] paths I stray,
    Whilst in their groves, and by their secret springs
    My hand delights to trace° unusual things,   *write*
    And deviates from the known and common way;
85   Nor will in fading silks compose
        Faintly th' inimitable rose,
    Fill up an ill-drawn bird, or paint on glass[5]
    The sov'reign's blurred and undistinguished face,
    The threat'ning angel, and the speaking ass.[6]

90   Patron thou art to ev'ry gross° abuse,   *flagrant*
        The sullen husband's feigned excuse,
    When the ill humor with his wife he spends,°   *exhausts*
    And bears recruited° wit, and spirits° to his   *strengthened / cheerfulness*
        friends.
        The son of Bacchus pleads thy pow'r,
95   As to the glass he still repairs,
        Pretends but to remove thy cares,[7]
    Snatch from thy shades one gay and smiling hour,
    And drown thy kingdom in a purple show'r.[8]
    When the Coquette,[9] whom ev'ry fool admires,
100   Would in variety be fair,
        And, changing hastily the scene,
        From light, impertinent, and vain,
        Assumes a soft, a melancholy air,
        And of her eyes rebates° the wand'ring fires,   *diminishes*
105   The careless posture, and the head reclined,
        The thoughtful, and composèd face,
    Proclaiming the withdrawn, the absent mind,
    Allows the Fop[1] more liberty to gaze,
    Who gently for the tender cause inquires;
110   The cause, indeed, is a defect in sense,
    Yet is the Spleen alledged,° and still the dull pretence.   *blamed*
        But these are thy fantastic° harms,   *imaginary*
        The tricks of thy pernicious stage,
        Which do the weaker sort engage;
115   Worse are the dire effects of thy more pow'rful charms.
        By thee Religion, all we know,
        That should enlighten here below,
        Is veiled in darkness, and perplexed
    With anxious doubts, with endless scruples° vexed,   *uncertainties*

---

4. The nine Greek goddesses believed to be sources of inspiration for the arts. Originally they were nymphs of wells or springs, which inspired those who drank from them and near which they were worshiped.
5. Acceptable artistic pursuits for women were embroidery, painting, and tapestry making. "Inimitable": surpassing or defying imitation.
6. The subjects of such art (see previous note): the "sov'reign" at this time would have been William of Orange (1650–1702); line 89 refers to the biblical story of the prophet Balaam and his ass. Intent on cursing the Israelites, Balaam ignores the commands of God until he is rebuked by his ass and

threatened by an angel of the Lord (Numbers 22).
7. Continually returns to. Bacchus, the Roman god of wine, sometimes called the "drunken god"; thus "Son of Bacchus" is one who indulges or overindulges in drink.
8. I.e., in wine or drink.
9. A flirtatious woman who uses arts to gain the admiration and affection of men for the gratification of vanity or desire for conquest. A type much commented on and satirized during the Restoration.
1. A fool or dandy; one who is foolishly attentive to his attentions and manners; another type satirized during the Restoration.

120   And some restraint implied from each perverted text.[2]
         Whilst touch not, taste not, what is freely giv'n,
      Is but thy niggard° voice, disgracing bounteous heav'n.[3]   *miserly*
         From speech restrained, by thy deceits abused,
         To deserts banished, or in cells reclused,
125   Mistaken vot'ries° to the pow'rs divine,   *devout worshipers*
         Whilst they a purer sacrifice design,
      Do but the Spleen obey, and worship at thy shrine.
         In vain to chase thee ev'ry art we try,
         In vain all remedies apply,
130   In vain the Indian leaf° infuse,   *tea*
         Or the parched Eastern berry° bruise;   *coffee*
      Some pass, in vain, those bounds, and nobler liquors use.
         Now harmony, in vain, we bring,
         Inspire the flute, and touch the string.
135   From harmony no help is had;
      Music but soothes thee, if too sweetly sad,
      And if too light, but turns thee gaily mad.
         Though the physicians greatest gains,
         Although his growing wealth he sees
140   Daily increased by ladies' fees,
      Yet dost thou baffle all his studious pains.
         Not skillful Lower[4] thy source could find,
         Or through the well-dissected body trace
         The secret, the mysterious ways,
145   By which thou dost surprise, and prey upon the mind.
         Though in the search, too deep for humane thought,
         With unsuccessful toil he wrought,°   *worked*
      'Till thinking thee to've catched, himself by thee was caught,
         Retained thy pris'ner, thy acknowledged slave,
150   And sunk beneath thy chain to a lamented grave.

                                                        1713

A Nocturnal Reverie

      In such a night, when every louder wind
      Is to its distant cavern safe confined;
      And only gentle Zephyr[5] fans his wings,
      And lonely Philomel, still waking,[6] sings;
5   Or from some tree, famed for the owl's delight,
      She, hollowing clear, directs the wand'rer right:
      In such a night, when passing clouds give place,
      Or thinly veil the heav'ns' mysterious face;
      When in some river, overhung with green,

2. I.e., some prohibition ("restraint") inferred from misreadings of biblical texts.
3. Puritan zeal was considered another manifestation of "spleen." The Puritans were seen as harshly repressive.
4. Richard Lower (1631–1691), an English physician noted for his research in anatomy and physiology; author of *Treatise on the Heart* (1669).
5. According to myth, Zephyr, the west wind, is warm and mild. The four winds resided in caves.
6. I.e., ever wakeful; according to myth, Philomela was raped by her brother-in-law, Tereus, who then tore out her tongue so that she could not speak. She wove the story into a tapestry and sent it to her sister, who rescued her. She was later changed into a nightingale while in flight from Tereus.

10   The waving moon and trembling leaves are seen;
When freshened grass now bears itself upright,
And makes cool banks to pleasing rest invite,
Whence springs the woodbind,° and the bramble-rose,   *honeysuckle*
And where the sleepy cowslip sheltered grows;
15   Whilst now a paler hue the foxglove takes,
Yet checkers still with red the dusky brakes[7]
When scatter'd glow-worms,[8] but in twilight fine,
Shew trivial beauties watch their hour to shine;[9]
Whilst Salisb'ry stands the test of every light,
20   In perfect charms, and perfect virtue bright:
When odors, which declined repelling day,[1]
Through temp'rate air uninterrupted stray;
When darkened groves their softest shadows wear,
And falling waters we distinctly hear;
25   When through the gloom more venerable[2] shows
Some ancient fabric, awful[3] in repose,
While sunburnt hills their swarthy looks conceal,
And swelling haycocks[4] thicken up the vale:
When the loosed horse now, as his pasture leads,
30   Comes slowly grazing through th' adjoining meads,°   *meadows*
Whose stealing pace, and lengthened shade we fear,
Till torn-up forage in his teeth we hear:
When nibbling sheep at large pursue their food,
And unmolested kine° rechew the cud;   *cattle*
35   When curlews[5] cry beneath the village walls,
And to her straggling brood the partridge calls;
Their shortlived jubilee the creatures keep,
Which but endures, whilst tyrant man does sleep;
When a sedate content the spirit feels,
40   And no fierce light disturb, whilst it reveals;
But silent musings urge the mind to seek
Something, too high for syllables to speak;
Till the free soul to a composedness charmed,
Finding the elements of rage disarmed,
45   O'er all below a solemn quiet grown,
Joys in th' inferior world, and thinks it like her own:
In such a night let me abroad remain,
Till morning breaks, and all's confused again;
Our cares, our toils, our clamors are renewed,
50   Or pleasures, seldom reached, again pursued.

1713

7. Thickets; tall ferns or bracken.
8. Insects, the females of which emit a shining green light from the abdomen.
9. I.e., show lesser beauties that, unlike the countess of Salisbury, Anne Tufton, of the following line, they must make the most of their limited opportunities to shine.
1. I.e., when the aromas ("odors") of field and wood, which refused to come forth ("declined") under the hot, "repelling" rays of the sun ("day").
2. Impressive or worthy of religious reverence.
3. May mean both awe-inspiring and causing fear or dread; "fabric": structure, i.e., building.
4. Conical piles of hay.
5. A kind of shore bird not unlike a sandpiper.

The Answer[6]

(To Pope's Impromptu)

Disarmed with so genteel an air,
    The contest I give o'er;
Yet, Alexander, have a care,
    And shock the sex no more.
5 We rule the world our life's whole race,
    Men but assume that right;
First slaves to ev'ry tempting face,
    Then martyrs to our spite.
You of one Orpheus[7] sure have read,
10   Who would like you have writ
Had he in London town been bred,
    And polished to[o] his wit;
But he poor soul thought all was well,
    And great should be his fame,
15 When he had left his wife in hell,
    And birds and beasts could tame.
Yet venturing then with scoffing rhymes
    The women to incense,
Resenting heroines of those times
20   Soon punished his offense.
And as the Hebrus rolled his skull,
    And harp besmeared with blood,
They clashing as the waves grew full,
    Still harmonized the flood.
25 But you our follies gently treat,
    And spin so fine the thread,
You need not fear his awkward fate,
    The lock[8] won't cost the head.
Our admiration you command
30   For all that's gone before;
What next we look for at your hand
    Can only raise it more.
Yet sooth° the Ladies I advise   *truly*
    (As me too pride has wrought)
35 We're born to wit, but to be wise
    By admonitions taught.

1734

---

6. Finch and Alexander Pope engaged in a dispute over some lines in his *The Rape of the Lock* that deprecated female wits (see Canto IV, lines 59–62 [p. 558]). He responded to her complaint in a short poem, "Impromptu," subtitled "To Lady Winchilsea" (see p. 576), in which he complimented her poetic talent while slighting the talent of earlier women poets. This poem is her response.
7. Orpheus, famed for his singing and playing upon the lyre, was said to be able to charm birds and animals with his music. According to myth, when his wife, Eurydice, died, he traveled to the underworld and charmed the infernal gods with his singing. He was granted permission to lead her out of hell on condition that he not look back to see her following. When they were nearly out of hell, he glimpsed over his shoulder and she returned to the ranks of the dead. Inconsolable, Orpheus never again took pleasure in women, but continued to sing, enchanting even the stones and trees. The Maenads, frenzied devotees of the god Dionysus, hated Orpheus (perhaps because of his lack of interest in them), and one day they tore him to pieces, casting his head and lyre into the river Hebros. The severed head continued to sing as it floated down the river.
8. A reference to *The Rape of the Lock*; see note 6, above.

The Introduction

Did I, my lines intend for public view,
How many censures, would their faults pursue,
Some would, because such words they do affect,
Cry they're insipid, empty, uncorrect.
5   And many have attained, dull and untaught,
The name of wit only by finding fault.
True judges might condemn their want of wit,
And all might say, they're by a woman writ.
Alas! a woman that attempts the pen,
10   Such an intruder on the rights of men,
Such a presumptuous creature, is esteemed,
The fault can by no virtue be redeemed.
They tell us we mistake our sex and way;
Good breeding, fashion, dancing, dressing, play
15   Are the accomplishments we should desire;
To write, or read, or think, or to inquire
Would cloud our beauty, and exhaust our time,
And interrupt the conquests of our prime;
Whilst the dull manage of a servile house
20   Is held by some our outmost° art, and use.   *utmost*
    Sure 'twas not ever thus, nor are we told
Fables, of women that excelled of old;
To whom, by the diffusive hand of Heaven
Some share of wit, and poetry was given.
25   On that glad day, on which the Ark returned,[9]
The holy pledge, for which the land had mourned,
The joyful tribes, attend it on the way,
The Levites do the sacred charge convey,
Whilst various instruments, before it play;
30   Here, holy virgins in the concert join
The louder notes, to soften, and refine,
And with alternate verse complete the hymn divine.
Lo! the young Poet,[1] after God's own heart,
By Him inspired, and taught the Muses'[2] art,
35   Returned from conquest, a bright chorus meets,
That sing his slain ten thousand in the streets.
In such loud numbers they his acts declare,
Proclaim the wonders of his early war,
That Saul upon the vast applause does frown,

---

9. The Ark of the Covenant was captured by the Philistines, but God forced them to return it by smiting them with pestilence. However, God did not allow the Ark to be returned to Jerusalem, because of the transgressions of the Israelites, and during its absence "all the house of Israel lamented after the Lord" (1 Samuel 7.2). The Ark was returned to Jerusalem twenty years later, during the reign of David. The Levites (the tribe of priests) were assigned to convey it to the city, and it was accompanied by a procession with much singing and music (1 Chronicles 15.25–28).
1. I.e., David, second king of Israel, who wrote many of the Psalms. Before he became king, during the reign of Saul, David won a great battle over the Philistines. Upon returning to Jerusalem, the women of the city sang and said, "Saul hath slain his thousands, and David his ten thousands" (1 Samuel 18.7). The prophet Samuel had earlier predicted Saul's downfall and replacement by "a neighbor of thine, who is better than thou" (1 Samuel 15.28), and the women's praise initiated Saul's jealous rage against David.
2. The nine Greek goddesses believed to be sources of inspiration for the arts.

40 And feels its mighty thunder shake the crown.
What, can the threatened judgment now prolong?
Half of the kingdom is already gone;
The fairest half, whose influence guides the rest,
Have David's empire o'er their hearts confessed.
45   A woman[3] here, leads fainting Israel on,
She fights, she wins, she triumphs with a song,
Devout, majestic, for the subject fit,
And far above her arms,[4] exalts her wit;
Then, to the peaceful, shady palm withdraws,
50 And rules the rescued nation, with her laws.
How are we fall'n, fall'n by mistaken rules?
And education's, more than nature's fools,
Debarred from all improvements of the mind,
And to be dull, expected and designed;°   *appointed, intended*
55 And if some one would soar above the rest,
With warmer fancy, and ambition pressed,
So strong th' opposing faction still appears,
The hopes to thrive can ne'er outweigh the fears,
Be cautioned then my Muse, and still[5] retired;
60 Nor be despised, aiming to be admired;
Conscious of wants, still with contracted wing,
To some few friends, and to thy sorrows sing;
For groves of laurel[6] thou wert never meant;
Be dark enough thy shades, and be thou there content.

1689   1902

On Myself

Good Heav'n, I thank thee, since it was designed
I should be framed, but of the weaker kind,
That yet, my Soul, is rescued from the love
Of all those trifles which their passions move.
5 Pleasures and praise and plenty have with me
But° their just value. If allowed they be,   *only*
Freely, and thankfully as much I taste,
As will not reason or religion waste.
If they're denied, I on my self can live,
10 And slight° those aids unequal chance does give.   *disdain*
When in the sun, my wings can be displayed,
And, in retirement, I can bless the shade.

                                                                          1902

---

3. Deborah, the fourth judge of Israel (before Israel had kings, judges administered the laws given by God; see Judges 4.5). When the Israelites were enslaved by the Canaanites, Deborah urged her fellow judge, Barak, to wage war against the enslavers and accompanied him to the site of the battle. After their victory Deborah and Barak wrote a song of praise (Judges 5).
4. I.e., her military feats.
5. Here and in line 61 may mean both "always" and "motionless."
6. The laurel was a symbol of poetic achievement.

MATTHEW PRIOR
1664–1721

A Fable

In Æsop's tales an honest wretch we find,
Whose years and comforts equally declined;
He in two wives had two domestic ills,
For different age they had, and different wills;
One plucked his black hairs out, and one his gray,   5
The man for quietness did both obey,
Till all his parish saw his head quite bare,
And thought he wanted brains as well as hair.

The Moral.

The parties, henpecked William,[1] are thy wives,
The hairs they pluck are thy prerogatives;[2]   10
Tories thy person hate, the Whigs thy power,[3]
Though much thou yieldest, still they tug for more,
Till this poor man and thou alike are shown,
He without hair, and thou without a crown.

1703

To a Lady: She Refusing to Continue a Dispute with Me, and Leaving Me in the Argument

1

Spare, gen'rous victor, spare the slave,
   Who did unequal war pursue;
That more than triumph he might have,
   In being overcome by you.

2

In the dispute whate'er I said,   5
   My heart was by my tongue belied;
And in my looks you might have read,
   How much I argued on your side.

3

You, far from danger as from fear,
   Might have sustained an open fight: 10
For seldom your opinions err;
   Your eyes are always in the right.

4

Why, fair one, would you not rely
   On reason's force with beauty's joined?
Could I their prevalence deny;   15
   I must at once be deaf and blind.

1. King William III (1650–1702), who ruled
England from 1689 until his death.
2. The rights of the king, previously not subject to
parliamentary restriction.
3. The Whigs and Tories were the two main polit-
ical parties in seventeenth- and eighteenth-century
England.

5

Alas! not hoping to subdue,
   I only to the fight aspired:
To keep the beauteous foe in view
20   Was all the glory I desired.

6

But she, howe'er of vict'ry sure,
   Contemns the wreath[4] too long delayed;
And, armed with more immediate pow'r,
   Calls cruel silence to her aid.

7

25 Deeper to wound, she shuns the fight:
   She drops her arms, to gain the field:
Secures her conquest by her flight;
   And triumphs, when she seems to yield.

8

So when the Parthian[5] turned his steed,
30   And from the hostile camp withdrew;
With cruel skill the backward reed°   *arrow*
   He sent; and as he fled, he slew.

1718

An Ode

The merchant, to secure his treasure,
   Conveys it in a borrowed name;
Euphelia serves to grace my measure,[6]
   But Cloe is my real flame.

5 My softest verse, my darling lyre,[7]
   Upon Euphelia's toilet° lay;   *dressing table*
When Cloe noted her desire
   That I should sing, that I should play.

My lyre I tune, my voice I raise,
10   But with my numbers° mix my sighs;   *songs*
And whilst I sing Euphelia's praise,
   I fix my soul on Cloe's eyes.

Fair Cloe blushed; Euphelia frowned;
   I sung and gazed; I played and trembled;
15 And Venus to the Loves around[8]
   Remarked how ill we all dissembled.

1718

---

4. A wreath of laurel or other leaves was a symbol of victory.
5. A people of western Asia, whose cavalry fought in the manner Prior describes.
6. I.e., Euphelia adorns or adds grace to my poetry, or is the name used in my poetry.

7. A stringed instrument similar to a harp.
8. Venus is the goddess of love; her attendant "Loves" are, in mythology, the goddesses of beauty; in the social context, they are attractive young ladies.

JONATHAN SWIFT

1667–1745

A Description of the Morning

Now hardly here and there a hackney-coach[1]
Appearing, showed the ruddy morn's approach.
Now Betty from her master's bed had flown,
And softly stole to discompose her own;
5   The slip-shod 'prentice from his master's door
Had pared the dirt and sprinkled round the floor.
Now Moll[2] had whirled her mop with dext'rous airs,
Prepared to scrub the entry and the stairs.
The youth with broomy stumps began to trace
10   The kennel-edge,[3] where wheels had worn the place.
The small-coal man[4] was heard with cadence deep,
Till drowned in shriller notes of chimney-sweep:
Duns° at his lordship's gate began to meet;   *bill collectors*
And brickdust Moll[5] had screamed through half the street.
15   The turnkey° now his flock returning sees,   *jailer*
Duly let out a-nights to steal for fees:[6]
The watchful bailiffs[7] take their silent stands,
And schoolboys lag with satchels in their hands.

1709

A Description of a City Shower

Careful observers may foretell the hour
(By sure prognostics) when to dread a shower:
While rain depends,° the pensive cat gives o'er   *impends*
Her frolics, and pursues her tail no more.
5   Returning home at night, you'll find the sink°   *sewer*
Strike your offended sense with double stink.
If you be wise, then go not far to dine;
You'll spend in coach hire more than save in wine.
A coming shower your shooting corns presage,
10   Old aches throb, your hollow tooth will rage.
Sauntering in coffeehouse is Dulman° seen;   *dull man*
He damns the climate and complains of spleen.°   *melancholy*
   Meanwhile the South,° rising with dabbled° wings,   *a wind / spattered*
A sable cloud athwart the welkin° flings,   *sky*
15   That swilled more liquor than it could contain,
And, like a drunkard, gives it up again.
Brisk Susan whips her linen from the rope,
While the first drizzling shower is borne aslope:°   *slanting*
Such is that sprinkling which some careless quean°   *wench*

1. A horse-drawn carriage, for hire.
2. A diminuitive form of Mary; a common name for a woman.
3. Curb of the road.
4. Seller of charcoal.
5. A woman selling powdered brick (used for cleaning knives).
6. Prisoners were allowed out to get money to pay their jailers, who could charge fees for allowing certain privileges, such as better accommodations.
7. I.e., sheriff's deputies.

20 Flirts° on you from her mop, but not so clean: *flicks*
 You fly, invoke the gods; then turning, stop
 To rail; she singing, still whirls on her mop.
 Not yet the dust had shunned the unequal strife,
 But, aided by the wind, fought still for life,
25 And wafted with its foe by violent gust,
 'Twas doubtful which was rain and which was dust.
 Ah! where must needy poet seek for aid,
 When dust and rain at once his coat invade?
 Sole coat, where dust cemented by the rain
30 Erects the nap,[8] and leaves a mingled stain.
  Now in contiguous drops the flood comes down,
 Threatening with deluge this devoted° town.   *doomed*
 To shops in crowds the daggled° females fly,   *spattered*
 Pretend to cheapen° goods, but nothing buy.   *price*
35 The Templar spruce,[9] while every spout's abroach,° *running*
 Stays till 'tis fair, yet seems to call a coach.
 The tucked-up sempstress° walks with hasty strides, *seamstress*
 While streams run down her oiled umbrella's sides.
 Here various kinds, by various fortunes led,
40 Commence acquaintance underneath a shed.
 Triumphant Tories and desponding Whigs[1]
 Forget their feuds, and join to save their wigs.
 Boxed in a chair° the beau impatient sits,   *sedan chair*
 While spouts run clattering o'er the roof by fits,
45 And ever and anon with frightful din
 The leather[2] sounds; he trembles from within.
 So when Troy chairmen bore the wooden steed,
 Pregnant with Greeks impatient to be freed
 (Those bully Greeks, who, as the moderns do,
50 Instead of paying chairmen, run them through),
 Laocoön struck the outside with his spear,
 And each imprisoned hero quaked for fear.[3]
  Now from all parts the swelling kennels° flow,   *gutters*
 And bear their trophies with them as they go:
55 Filth of all hues and odors seem to tell
 What street they sailed from, by their sight and smell.
 They, as each torrent drives with rapid force,
 From Smithfield or St. Pulchre's shape their course,
 And in huge confluence joined at Snow Hill ridge,
60 Fall from the conduit prone° to Holborn Bridge.[4] *downward*
 Sweepings from butchers' stalls, dung, guts, and blood, ⎤
 Drowned puppies, stinking sprats,° all drenched in mud, ⎬ *herring*
 Dead cats, and turnip tops, come tumbling down the flood. ⎦

                   1710

8. I.e., makes the fibers on the surface of the fabric stand up stiffly.
9. The dapper law student.
1. The Whigs and Tories were the two main political parties in seventeenth- and eighteenth-century England; the Tories (Swift's party) had recently assumed power.
2. Leather roof of the sedan chair.

3. In *Aeneid* 2, Laocoön so struck the side of the Trojan horse, frightening the Greeks within.
4. The offal from the Smithfield cattle market would be swept toward the Fleet Ditch, spanned by Holborn Bridge, where it would merge with garbage floating down the Snow Hill stream. "St. Pulchre's": St. Sepulchre's Church in Holborn.

A Satirical Elegy on the Death of a Late Famous General[5]

His Grace! impossible! what dead!
Of old age too, and in his bed!
And could that mighty warrior fall?
And so inglorious, after all!
5 Well, since he's gone, no matter how,
The last loud trump[6] must wake him now:
And, trust me, as the noise grows stronger,
He'd wish to sleep a little longer.
And could he be indeed so old
10 As by the newspapers we're told?
Threescore,° I think, is pretty high;   *sixty*
'Twas time in conscience he should die.
This world he cumbered° long enough;   *encumbered*
He burnt his candle to the snuff;°   *end*
15 And that's the reason, some folks think,
He left behind so great a s---k.
Behold his funeral appears,
Nor widow's sighs, nor orphan's tears,
Wont° at such times each heart to pierce,   *accustomed*
20 Attend the progress of his hearse.
But what of that, his friends may say,
He had those honors in his day.
True to his profit and his pride,
He made them weep before he died.
25   Come hither, all ye empty things,
Ye bubbles raised by breath of kings;
Who float upon the tide of state,
Come hither, and behold your fate.
Let pride be taught by this rebuke,
30 How very mean[7] a thing's a Duke;
From all his ill-got honors flung,
Turned to that dirt from whence he sprung.

1722, 1764

Stella's Birthday

March 13, 1727[8]

This day, whate'er the fates decree,
Shall still° be kept with joy by me: *always*
This day then, let us not be told
That you are sick, and I grown old,
5 Nor think on our approaching ills,
And talk of spectacles and pills;
Tomorrow will be time enough
To hear such mortifying° stuff.   *depressing*

5. The duke of Marlborough, who died on June 16, 1722, at the age of seventy-two.
6. Trumpet, calling the souls of the dead to judgment (1 Corinthians 15.52).
7. This word has a range of meanings, including poor, inferior, ignoble, destitute of moral dignity, undistinguished.
8. The forty-sixth birthday of Swift's devoted companion and protégée Esther Johnson.

Yet since from reason may be brought
10   A better and more pleasing thought,
Which can in spite of all decays
Support a few remaining days:
From not the gravest of divines,
Accept for once some serious lines.
15   Although we now can form no more
Long schemes of life, as heretofore;
Yet you, while time is running fast,
Can look with joy on what is past.
     Were future happiness and pain
20   A mere contrivance of the brain,
As atheists argue, to entice
And fit their proselytes° for vice   *converts*
(The only comfort they propose,
To have companions in their woes),
25   Grant this the case, yet sure 'tis hard
That virtue, styled its own reward,
And by all sages understood
To be the chief of human good,
Should acting, die, nor leave behind
30   Some lasting pleasure in the mind,
Which, by remembrance, will assuage
Grief, sickness, poverty, and age;
And strongly shoot a radiant dart,
To shine through life's declining part.
35   Say, Stella, feel you no content,
Reflecting on a life well spent?
Your skillful hand employed to save
Despairing wretches from the grave;
And then supporting from your store
40   Those whom you dragged from death before
(So Providence on mortals waits,
Preserving what it first creates);
Your generous boldness to defend
An innocent and absent friend;
45   That courage which can make you just,
To merit humbled in the dust:
The detestation you express
For vice in all its glittering dress:
That patience under torturing pain,
50   Where stubborn stoics[9] would complain.
     Must these like empty shadows pass,
Or forms reflected from a glass?
Or mere chimeras° in the mind,   *wild fancies*
That fly and leave no marks behind?
55   Does not the body thrive and grow
By food of twenty years ago?
And, had it not been still supplied,
It must a thousand times have died.
Then who with reason can maintain

---

9. Those who practice repression of emotion, indifference to pleasure and pain, and patient endurance.

60 That no effects of food remain?
And is not virtue in mankind
The nutriment that feeds the mind?
Upheld by each good action past,
And still continued by the last:
65 Then who with reason can pretend
That all effects of virtue end?
　　Believe me, Stella, when you show
That true contempt for things below,
Nor prize your life for other ends
70 Than merely to oblige your friends,
Your former actions claim their part,
And join to fortify your heart.
For virtue in her daily race,
Like Janus,[1] bears a double face,
75 Looks back with joy where she has gone,
And therefore goes with courage on.
She at your sickly couch will wait,
And guide you to some better state.
　　O then, whatever Heaven intends,
80 Take pity on your pitying friends;
Nor let your ills affect your mind,
To fancy they can be unkind.
Me, surely me, you ought to spare,
Who gladly would your sufferings share;
85 Or give my scrap of life to you,
And think it far beneath your due;
You, to whose care so oft I owe
That I'm alive to tell you so.

1727

The Lady's Dressing Room

Five hours, (and who can do it less in?)
By haughty Celia[2] spent in dressing;
The goddess from her chamber issues,
Arrayed in lace, brocades and tissues.[3]
5 　　Strephon, who found the room was void,
And Betty otherwise employed,
Stole in, and took a strict survey,
Of all the litter as it lay;
Whereof, to make the matter clear,
10 An inventory follows here.
　　And first a dirty smock appeared,
Beneath the armpits well besmeared.
Strephon, the rogue, displayed it wide,
And turned it round on every side.
15 On such a point few words are best,
And Strephon bids us guess the rest,
But swears how damnably the men lie,

1. The Roman god of doors, with opposed faces, one looking forward, the other back.
2. Celia and Strephon are conventional poetic names often used in pastoral poetry.
3. Fine, lightweight fabric; "brocades": a rich silk fabric with raised patterns in gold and silver.

In calling Celia sweet and cleanly.
Now listen while he next produces
20 The various combs for various uses,
Filled up with dirt so closely fixt,
No brush could force a way betwixt.
A paste of composition rare,
Sweat, dandruff, powder, lead[4] and hair;
25 A forehead cloth with oil upon't
To smooth the wrinkles on her front;°   brow
Here alum flower to stop the steams,[5]
Exhaled from sour unsavory streams,
There night-gloves made of Tripsy's hide,
30 Bequeathed by Tripsy when she died,
With puppy water,[6] beauty's help
Distilled from Tripsy's darling whelp;
Here gallypots[7] and vials placed,
Some filled with washes, some with paste,
35 Some with pomatum, paints and slops,
And ointments good for scabby chops.[8]
Hard by a filthy basin stands,
Fouled with the scouring of her hands;
The basin takes whatever comes
40 The scrapings of her teeth and gums,
A nasty compound of all hues,
For here she spits, and here she spews.
But oh! it turned poor Strephon's bowels,
When he beheld and smelled the towels,
45 Begummed, bemattered, and beslimed
With dirt, and sweat, and earwax grimed.
No object Strephon's eye escapes,
Here petticoats in frowzy° heaps;   ill-smelling, unkempt
Nor be the handkerchiefs forgot
50 All varnished o'er with snuff[9] and snot.
The stockings why should I expose,
Stained with the marks of stinking toes;
Or greasy coifs and pinners[1] reeking,
Which Celia slept at least a week in?
55 A pair of tweezers next he found
To pluck her brows in arches round,
Or hairs that sink the forehead low,
Or on her chin like bristles grow.
    The virtues we must not let pass,
60 Of Celia's magnifying glass.
When frighted Strephon cast his eye on't
It showed visage° of a giant.   face
A glass that can to sight disclose,

---

4. Then used to make hair glossy.
5. Vapors or exhalations produced as an excretion of the body, e.g., hot breath, perspiration, or the infectious effluvium of a disease; "alum flower": powdered mineral salt used in medicine.
6. The urine of a puppy, used as a cosmetic.
7. Small ceramic pots, often containers for medicine.

8. Painful fissures or cracks in the skin; "washes": liquid cosmetic for the complexion; "paste": either medicinal or cosmetic compound: "pomatum": scented ointment for application to the skin; "paints": rouges; "slops": refuse liquid.
9. Powdered tobacco inhaled through the nostrils.
1. Types of headwear.

The smallest worm in Celia's nose,
65 And faithfully direct her nail
To squeeze it out from head to tail;
For catch it nicely by the head,
It must come out alive or dead.
        Why Strephon will you tell the rest?
70 And must you needs describe the chest?[2]
That careless wench! no creature warn her
To move it out from yonder corner;
But leave it standing full in sight
For you to exercise your spite.
75 In vain the workman showed his wit
With rings and hinges counterfeit
To make it seem in this disguise
A cabinet to vulgar eyes;
For Strephon ventured to look in,
80 Resolved to go through thick and thin;
He lifts the lid, there needs no more,
He smelled it all the time before.
As from within Pandora's box,
When Epimetheus[3] op'd the locks,
85 A sudden universal crew
Of human evils upwards flew;
He still was comforted to find
That Hope at last remained behind;
So Strephon lifting up the lid,
90 To view what in the chest was hid.
The vapors flew from out the vent,
But Strephon cautious never meant
The bottom of the pan° to grope,   *vessel*
And foul his hands in search of Hope.
95 O never may such vile machine
Be once in Celia's chamber seen!
O may she better learn to keep
Those "secrets of the hoary deep!"[4]
        As mutton cutlets, prime of meat,
100 Which though with art you salt and beat
As laws of cookery require,
And toast them at the clearest fire;
If from adown the hopeful chops
The fat upon a cinder drops,
105 To stinking smoke it turns the flame
Pois'ning the flesh from whence it came,
And up exhales a greasy stench,
For which you curse the careless wench;
So things, which must not be expressed,
110 When plumped° into the reeking chest,   *dropped*
Send up an excremental smell

2. Celia's champber pot.
3. In Greek mythology, brother of Prometheus and husband of Pandora. Created by the gods as the first human woman, Pandora brought with her to Earth a box containing all human ills, which, when it was opened, were released into the world,
leaving only Hope behind.
4. From Milton's *Paradise Lost* (2.891), a poetic reference to the ocean; Swift puns on "hoary," which means ancient but may also mean corrupt, and perhaps also on the homonym, "hory," meaning filthy.

To taint the parts from whence they fell.
The petticoats and gown perfume,
Which waft a stink round every room.
115 Thus finishing his grand survey,
Disgusted Strephon stole away
Repeating in his amorous fits,
Oh! Celia, Celia, Celia shits!
    But Vengeance, goddess never sleeping
120 Soon punished Strephon for his peeping;
His foul imagination links
Each Dame he sees with all her stinks:
And, if unsavory odors fly,
Conceives a lady standing by:
125 All women his description fits,
And both ideas jump like wits:[5]
By vicious fancy coupled fast,
And still appearing in contrast.
I pity wretched Strephon blind
130 To all the charms of female kind;
Should I the queen of love[6] refuse,
Because she rose from stinking ooze?
To him that looks behind the scene,
Satira's but some pocky quean.[7]
135 When Celia in her glory shows,
If Strephon would but stop his nose
(Who now so impiously blasphemes
Her ointments, daubs, and paints and creams,
Her washes, slops, and every clout,°   *rag*
140 With which he makes so foul a rout°)   *fuss*
He soon would learn to think like me,
And bless his ravished sight to see
Such order from confusion sprung,
Such gaudy tulips raised from dung.

1730

ISAAC WATTS

1674–1748

The Day of Judgment

An Ode Attempted in English Sapphic[1]

When the fierce north wind with his airy forces
Rears up the Baltic to a foaming fury,
And the red lightning with a storm of hail comes
                    Rushing amain° down,   *violently*

5. "Jump": match; from the proverbial phrase, "good wits jump," i.e., great minds think alike.
6. Aphrodite or Venus, the classical goddess often depicted as rising out of the sea.
7. Whore; "Satira": probably Statira, one of the wives of Alexander the Great in Nathaniel Lee's

tragedy *Rival Queens* (1677); "pocky": infected with pox (usually syphilis), or marked with pocks or pustules.
1. A poetic form consisting of quatrains utilizing a meter derived from the Greek poet Sappho.

5   How the poor sailors stand amazed and tremble,
    While the hoarse thunder, like a bloody trumpet,
    Roars a loud onset° to the gaping waters,   assault
                    Quick to devour them!

    Such shall the noise be and the wild disorder,
10 (If things eternal may be like these earthly)
    Such the dire terror, when the great Archangel
                    Shakes the creation,

    Tears the strong pillars of the vault of heaven,
    Breaks up old marble, the repose of princes;
15 See the graves open, and the bones arising,
                    Flames all around 'em!

    Hark, the shrill outcries of the guilty wretches!
    Lively bright horror and amazing anguish
    Stare through their eyelids, while the living worm[2] lies
20   Gnawing within them.

    Thoughts like old vultures prey upon their heart-strings,
    And the smart twinges,[3] when the eye beholds the
    Lofty Judge frowning, and a flood of vengeance
                    Rolling afore him.

25 Hopeless immortals! how they scream and shiver,
    While devils push them to the pit wide-yawning
    Hideous and gloomy, to receive them headlong
                    Down to the center.[4]

    Stop here, my fancy: (all away ye horrid
30 Doleful° ideas); come, arise to Jesus;   gloomy
    How He sits God-like! and the saints around him
                    Throned, yet adoring!

    Oh may I sit there when he comes triumphant
    Dooming the nations! then ascend to glory
35 While our hosannas all along the passage
                    Shout the Redeemer.

                                                                1706

A Prospect of Heaven Makes Death Easy

            There is a land of pure delight
                Where saints immortal reign;
            Infinite day excludes the night,
                And pleasures banish pain.

2. Christ describes hell in Mark 9.44 as a place "where their worm dieth not."
3. Sharp pains.
4. At the Last Judgment, Christ will judge "all the nations," separating the believers from the unbelievers, casting the unbelievers into hell ("the pit"), and inviting believers to inherit the kingdom of heaven (Matthew 25.31–41).

5 There everlasting spring abides,
  And never-withering flowers;
 Death like a narrow sea divides
  This heavenly land from ours.

 Sweet fields beyond the swelling flood
10 Stand dressed in living green:
 So to the Jews old Canaan stood,
  While Jordan rolled between.[5]

 But timorous° mortals start° and shrink   *fearful / recoil*
  To cross this narrow sea,
15 And linger shivering on the brink,
  And fear to launch away.

 Oh could we make our doubts remove,
  These gloomy doubts that rise,
 And see the Canaan that we love,
20 With unbeclouded eyes;

 Could we but climb where Moses stood
  And view the landscape o'er,[6]
 Not Jordan's stream, nor death's cold flood,
  Should fright us from the shore.

             1707

Our God, Our Help[7]

Our God, our help in ages past,
 Our hope for years to come,
Our shelter from the stormy blast,
 And our eternal home:

5 Under the shadow of thy throne
  Thy saints have dwelt secure;
 Sufficient is thine arm alone,
  And our defense is sure.

 Before the hills in order stood
10 Or earth received her frame,[8]
 From everlasting thou art God,
  To endless years the same.

 Thy word commands our flesh to dust,
  "Return, ye sons of men";[9]

5. Canaan was the land "flowing with milk and honey" (Joshua 5.6) promised to the Israelites after their forty years of wandering in the wilderness. In order to reach it they had to cross the Jordan River.
6. Moses was allowed to ascend Mount Nebo to see the promised land, but was not allowed to enter Canaan because of his sins (Deuteronomy 34.1–4).

7. Originally entitled "Man Frail and God Eternal," the hymn derives from Psalm 90.
8. Structure, constitution.
9. From Psalm 90.3; God's curse after the sin of Adam and Eve: "In the sweat of thy face shalt thou eat bread, till thou return unto the ground; for out of it was thou taken: for dust thou art, and unto dust shalt thou return" (Genesis 3.19).

15   All nations rose from earth at first,
      And turn to earth again.

  A thousand ages in thy sight
      Are like an evening gone;
  Short as the watch[1] that ends the night
20   Before the rising sun.

  The busy tribes of flesh and blood,
      With all their lives and cares,
  Are carried downwards by thy flood,
      And lost in following years.

25   Time, like an ever-rolling stream,
      Bears all its sons away;
  They fly forgotten, as a dream
      Dies at the opening day.

  Like flowery fields the nations stand,
30   Pleased with the morning light;
  The flowers beneath the mower's hand
      Lie withering e'er 'tis night.

  Our God, our help in ages past,
      Our hope for years to come,
35   Be thou our guard while troubles last,
      And our eternal home.

                            1719

Psalm 58

Judges, who rule the world by laws,
Will ye despise the righteous cause,
  When th'injur'd poor before you stands?
Dare ye condemn the righteous poor,
5 And let rich sinners 'scape secure,
  While gold and greatness bribe your hands?

Have ye forgot or never knew
That God will judge the judges too?
  High in the Heavens his justice reigns;
10 Yet you invade the rights of God,
And send your bold decrees abroad
  To bind the conscience in your chains.

A poison'd arrow is your tongue,
The arrow sharp, the poison strong,
15   And death attends where e'er it wounds:
You hear no counsels, cries or tears;
So the deaf adder stops her ears
  Against the power of charming sounds.

---

1. One of the three, four, or five periods into which the night was divided.

Break out their teeth, eternal God,
20 Those teeth of lions dyed in blood;
     And crush the serpents in the dust:
     As empty chaff,[2] when whirlwinds rise,
     Before the sweeping tempest flies,
          So let their hopes and names be lost.

25 Th'Almighty thunders from the sky,
     Their grandeur melts, their titles die,
          As hills of snow dissolve and run,
     Or snails that perish in their slime,
     Or births that come before their time,
30   Vain births, that never see the sun.

     Thus shall the vengeance of the Lord
     Safety and joy to saints afford;
          And all that hear shall join and say,
     "Sure there's a God that rules on high,
35 "A God that hears his children cry,
          "And will their sufferings well repay."

1719

JOHN GAY

1685–1732

Songs from *The Beggar's Opera*[1]

Act I, Scene viii, Air X—"Thomas, I Cannot,"[2] *etc.*

Polly.   I like a ship in storms was tossed,
                   Yet afraid to put into land,
              For seized in the port the vessel's lost
                   Whose treasure is contraband.°   smuggled goods
5   The waves are laid,
                     My duty's° paid;   tax on imports
                 O joy beyond expression!
                 Thus safe ashore
                 I ask no more;
10   My all is in my possession.

2. The husks of the grain separated by threshing or winnowing.

1. *The Beggar's Opera* (1728) was the first ballad opera, a type of play in which the action, usually comic, is conveyed in prose interspersed with songs set to traditional or contemporary melodies. This opera is a satire of corrupt government, and its comic but realistic characters are the underclass of London. Polly, the daughter of Peacham (an informer and receiver of stolen goods), marries the handsome highwayman, Macheath. Peacham informs against Macheath (both to collect the reward and to rid himself of an unwanted son-in-law). Lucy Lockit, the prison warder's daughter, whom Macheath had previously seduced and promised to marry, effects his escape. Macheath is recaptured and sentenced to hang, but through an absurd twist the play ends happily.

Because all of the songs from *The Beggar's Opera* were published in 1728, we do not print the date for each.

2. A popular song, the tune to which these words are sung (each set of lyrics here is sung to a preexisting tune); Polly, having secretly married Macheath, has been first violently chided, then forgiven by her parents.

Act I, Scene ix, Air XI—"A Soldier and a Sailor"[3]

A fox may steal your hens, sir,
A whore your health and pence,° sir, money
Your daughter rob your chest, sir,
Your wife may steal your rest, sir,
5   A thief your goods and plate.
But this is all for picking,° pilfering, petty thievery
With rest, pence, chest and chicken;
It ever was decreed, sir,
If lawyer's hand is fee'd, sir,
10   He steals your whole estate.

Act I, Scene xiii, Air XVI—"Over the Hills, and Far Away"[4]

Mac.   Were I laid on Greenland's coast,
    And in my arms embraced my lass,
Warm amidst eternal frost,
    Too soon the half-year's night would pass.
5 Polly. Were I sold on Indian soil,
    Soon as the burning day was closed,
I could mock the sultry toil
    When on my charmer's breast reposed.
Mac.   And I would love you all the day,
10 Polly. Every night would kiss and play,
Mac.   If with me you'd fondly stray
Polly. Over the hills, and far away.

Act II, Scene iv, Air IV—Cotillion[5]

Youth's the season made for joys,
    Love is then our duty:
She alone who that employs,
    Well deserves her beauty.
5   Let's be gay
    While we may,
Beauty's a flower despised in decay.

Chorus.   Youth's the season, etc.

Let us drink and sport to-day,
10   Ours is not to-morrow:
Love with youth flies swift away,
    Age is naught but sorrow.
    Dance and sing,
    Time's on the wing,
15   Life never knows the return of spring.

Chorus.   Let us drink, etc.

---

3. Sung by Polly's father, Peacham; Polly's parents worry that Macheath may have several wives, so that if he were to die, her inheritance of his property would come into dispute.
4. Polly fears that Macheath will be deported to a penal settlement; here they sing about their desire not to be separated.
5. A dance of French origin; Macheath dances and sports with a group of women in a tavern.

Act II, Scene xv, Air XXII—"The Lass of Patie's Mill"[6]

Lucy.   I like the fox shall grieve,
             Whose mate hath left her side;
             Whom hounds, from morn to eve,
             Chase o'er the country wide.

5   Where can my lover hide?
             Where cheat the wary pack?
             If love be not his guide,
             He never will come back.

Act III, Scene xiii, Air XXVII—"Green Sleeves"[7]

Since laws were made, for every degree,
To curb vice in others, as well as me,
I wonder we han't better company
    Upon Tyburn tree.[8]
5 But gold from law can take out the sting;
And if rich men, like us, were to swing,
'Twould thin the land, such numbers to string
    Upon Tyburn tree.

1728

ALEXANDER POPE

1688–1744

From An Essay on Criticism

Part II

Of all the causes which conspire to blind
Man's erring judgment, and misguide the mind,
What the weak head with strongest bias rules,
Is pride, the never-failing vice of fools.
205 Whatever Nature has in worth denied,
She gives in large recruits° of needful pride;   *supplies*
For as in bodies, thus in souls, we find
What wants in blood and spirits swelled with wind:
Pride, where wit fails, steps in to our defense,
210 And fills up all the mighty void of sense.
If once right reason drives that cloud away,
Truth breaks upon us with resistless day.
Trust not yourself: but your defects to know,
Make use of every friend—and every foe.
215 A little learning is a dangerous thing;
Drink deep, or taste not the Pierian spring.[1]

6. Lucy has agreed to help Macheath escape, and he has promised to send for her when it is safe.
7. Macheath, recaptured and condemned to hang, sits in his jail cell, drinking and singing.

8. The gallows; Tyburn was a place of public execution in Middlesex until 1783.
1. The spring in Pieria on Mount Olympus, sacred to the Muses.

There shallow draughts intoxicate the brain,
And drinking largely sobers us again.
Fired at first sight with what the Muse imparts,
220 In fearless youth we tempt° the heights of arts,   *attempt*
While from the bounded level of our mind
Short views we take, nor see the lengths behind;
But more advanced, behold with strange surprise
New distant scenes of endless science rise!
225 So pleased at first the towering Alps we try,
Mount o'er the vales, and seem to tread the sky,
The eternal snows appear already past,
And the first clouds and mountains seem the last;
But, those attained, we tremble to survey
230 The growing labors of the lengthened way,
The increasing prospect tires our wandering eyes,
Hills peep o'er hills, and Alps on Alps arise!
     A perfect judge will read each work of wit
With the same spirit that its author writ:
235 Survey the whole, nor seek slight faults to find
Where Nature moves, and rapture warms the mind;
Nor lose, for that malignant dull delight,
The generous pleasure to be charmed with wit.
But in such lays as neither ebb nor flow,
240 Correctly cold, and regularly low,
That, shunning faults, one quiet tenor keep,
We cannot blame indeed—but we may sleep.
In wit, as nature, what affects our hearts
Is not the exactness of peculiar° parts;   *particular*
245 'Tis not a lip, or eye, we beauty call,
But the joint force and full result of all.
Thus when we view some well-proportioned dome
(The world's just wonder, and even thine, O Rome![2]),
No single parts unequally surprise,
250 All comes united to the admiring eyes:
No monstrous height, or breadth, or length appear;
The whole at once is bold and regular.
     Whoever thinks a faultless piece to see,
Thinks what ne'er was, nor is, nor e'er shall be.
255 In every work regard the writer's end,
Since none can compass more than they intend;
And if the means be just, the conduct true,
Applause, in spite of trivial faults, is due.
As men of breeding, sometimes men of wit,
260 To avoid great errors must the less commit,
Neglect the rules each verbal critic lays,
For not to know some trifles is a praise.
Most critics, fond of some subservient art,
Still make the whole depend upon a part:
265 They talk of principles, but notions prize,
And all to one loved folly sacrifice.

---

2. Refers either to the dome of St. Peter's, i.e., the wonder *in* (Catholic) Rome; or to the dome of St. Paul's, in London, i.e., a wonder *to* Rome.

Once on a time La Mancha's knight,[3] they say,
A certain bard encountering on the way,
Discoursed in terms as just, with looks as sage,
270 As e'er could Dennis,[4] of the Grecian stage;
Concluding all were desperate sots and fools
Who durst depart from Aristotle's rules.[5]
Our author, happy in a judge so nice,°   *overrefined*
Produced his play, and begged the knight's advice;
275 Made him observe the subject and the plot,
The manners, passions, unities; what not?
All which exact to rule were brought about,
Were but a combat in the lists° left out.   *arena*
"What! leave the combat out?" exclaims the knight.
280 "Yes, or we must renounce the Stagirite."[6]
"Not so, by Heaven!" he answers in a rage,
"Knights, squires, and steeds must enter on the stage."
"So vast a throng the stage can ne'er contain."
"Then build a new, or act it in a plain."
285   Thus critics of less judgment than caprice,
Curious,° not knowing, not exact, but nice,   *laboriously careful*
Form short ideas, and offend in arts
(As most in manners), by a love to parts.
    Some to conceit[7] alone their taste confine,
290 And glittering thoughts struck out at every line;
Pleased with a work where nothing's just or fit,
One glaring chaos and wild heap of wit.
Poets, like painters, thus unskilled to trace
The naked nature and the living grace,
295 With gold and jewels cover every part,
And hide with ornaments their want of art.
    True wit is Nature to advantage dressed,
What oft was thought, but ne'er so well expressed;
Something whose truth convinced at sight we find,
300 That gives us back the image of our mind.
As shades more sweetly recommend the light,
So modest plainness sets off sprightly wit;
For works may have more wit than does them good,
As bodies perish through excess of blood.
305   Others for language all their care express,
And value books, as women men, for dress.
Their praise is still—the style is excellent;
The sense they humbly take upon contènt.°   *mere acquiescence*
Words are like leaves; and where they most abound,
310 Much fruit of sense beneath is rarely found.
False eloquence, like the prismatic glass,
Its gaudy colors spreads on every place;
The face of Nature we no more survey,

3. Don Quixote, hero of Cervantes' novel; but this
story comes from a sequel to it by Don Alonzo Fer-
nandez de Avellaneda.
4. John Dennis (1657–1734), an English critic.
5. Refers to the description of the purpose and
forms of tragic drama contained in Aristotle's
Poetics.

6. I.e., Aristotle, who was a native of Stagira. One
of his principles was that tragic drama should
maintain unity of time and place.
7. Pointed wit, ingenuity and extravagance, or
affectation in the use of figures, especially similes
and metaphors.

All glares alike, without distinction gay.
315 But true expression, like the unchanging sun,⎱
Clears and improves whate'er it shines upon; ⎰
It gilds all objects, but it alters none.
Expression is the dress of thought, and still
Appears more decent as more suitable.
320 A vile conceit in pompous words expressed
Is like a clown° in regal purple dressed: *peasant*
For different styles with different subjects sort,
As several garbs with country, town, and court.
Some by old words to fame have made pretense,
325 Ancients in phrase, mere moderns in their sense.
Such labored nothings, in so strange a style,
Amaze the unlearned, and make the learned smile;
Unlucky as Fungoso[8] in the play,   ⎫
These sparks with awkward vanity display ⎬
330 What the fine gentleman wore yesterday; ⎭
And but so mimic ancient wits at best,
As apes our grandsires in their doublets[9] dressed.
In words as fashions the same rule will hold,
Alike fantastic if too new or old:
335 Be not the first by whom the new are tried,
Nor yet the last to lay the old aside.
      But most by numbers° judge a poet's song,   *versification*
And smooth or rough with them is right or wrong.
In the bright Muse though thousand charms conspire,
340 Her voice is all these tuneful fools admire,
Who haunt Parnassus[1] but to please their ear,   ⎫
Not mend their minds; as some to church repair, ⎬
Not for the doctrine, but the music there.   ⎭
These equal syllables alone require,
345 Though oft the ear the open vowels tire,
While expletives[2] their feeble aid do join,
And ten low words oft creep in one dull line:
While they ring round the same unvaried chimes,
With sure returns of still expected rhymes;
350 Where'er you find "the cooling western breeze,"
In the next line, it "whispers through the trees";
If crystal streams "with pleasing murmurs creep,"
The reader's threatened (not in vain) with "sleep";
Then, at the last and only couplet fraught
355 With some unmeaning thing they call a thought,
A needless Alexandrine[3] ends the song
That, like a wounded snake, drags its slow length along.
Leave such to tune their own dull rhymes, and know
What's roundly smooth or languishingly slow;
360 And praise the easy vigor of a line

---

8. A character in Ben Jonson's comedy *Every Man out of His Humor.*
9. Jackets in a style popular in the sixteenth and seventeenth centuries.
1. The mountain in Greece sacred to the Muses.

2. A word added to fill out a line—for example, "do" in this line.
3. A line in iambic hexameter—for example, the next line.

Where Denham's strength and Waller's sweetness join.[4]
True ease in writing comes from art, not chance,
As those move easiest who have learned to dance.
'Tis not enough no harshness gives offense,
365 The sound must seem an echo to the sense.
Soft is the strain when Zephyr[5] gently blows,
And the smooth stream in smoother numbers flows;
But when loud surges lash the sounding shore,
The hoarse, rough verse should like the torrent roar.
370 When Ajax[6] strives some rock's vast weight to throw,
The line too labors, and the words move slow;
Not so when swift Camilla scours the plain,
Flies o'er the unbending corn, and skims along the main.
Hear how Timotheus'[7] varied lays surprise,
375 And bid alternate passions fall and rise!
While at each change the son of Libyan Jove[8]
Now burns with glory, and then melts with love;
Now his fierce eyes with sparkling fury glow,
Now sighs steal out, and tears begin to flow:
380 Persians and Greeks like turns of nature[9] found
And the world's victor stood subdued by sound!
The power of music all our hearts allow,
And what Timotheus was is Dryden now.
    Avoid extremes; and shun the fault of such
385 Who still are pleased too little or too much.
At every trifle scorn to take offense:
That always shows great pride, or little sense.
Those heads, as stomachs, are not sure the best,
Which nauseate° all, and nothing can digest.   *vomit*
390 Yet let not each gay turn thy rapture move;
For fools admire,° but men of sense approve:[1]   *wonder*
As things seem large which we through mists descry,
Dullness is ever apt to magnify.
    Some foreign writers, some our own despise;
395 The ancients only, or the moderns prize.
Thus wit, like faith, by each man is applied
To one small sect, and all are damned beside.
Meanly they seek the blessing to confine,
And force that sun but on a part to shine,
400 Which not alone the southern wit sublimes,
But ripens spirits in cold northern climes;
Which from the first has shone on ages past,
Enlights the present, and shall warm the last;
Though each may feel increases and decays,
405 And see now clearer and now darker days.
Regard not then if wit be old or new,
But blame the false and value still the true.

4. Dryden, whom Pope echoes here, considered Sir John Denham (1615–1669) and Edmund Waller (1606–1687) to have been the principal shapers of the closed pentameter couplet.
5. The west wind.
6. The strongest, though not the most intelligent, of the Greek warriors in the war with Troy. He is contrasted with Camilla, a swift-footed messenger of the moon goddess, Diana.
7. The musician in Dryden's *Alexander's Feast*.
8. Alexander the Great.
9. Comparable alternations of feelings.
1. I.e., only after due deliberation.

Some ne'er advance a judgment of their own,
But catch the spreading notion of the town;
410   They reason and conclude by precedent,
And own[2] stale nonsense which they ne'er invent.
Some judge of authors' names, not works, and then
Nor praise nor blame the writings, but the men.
Of all this servile herd the worst is he
415   That in proud dullness joins with quality,
A constant critic at the great man's board,
To fetch and carry nonsense for my lord.
What woeful stuff this madrigal would be
In some starved hackney[3] sonneteer or me!
420   But let a lord once own[4] the happy lines,
How the wit brightens! how the style refines!
Before his sacred name flies every fault,
And each exalted stanza teems with thought!
    The vulgar thus through imitation err;
425   As oft the learn'd by being singular;°   *peculiar*
So much they scorn the crowd, that if the throng
By chance go right, they purposely go wrong.
So schìsmatics[5] the plain believers quit,
And are but damned for having too much wit.
430   Some praise at morning what they blame at night,
But always think the last opinion right.
A Muse by these is like a mistress used,
This hour she's idolized, the next abused;
While their weak heads like towns unfortified,
435   'Twixt sense and nonsense daily change their side.
Ask them the cause; they're wiser still, they say;
And still tomorrow's wiser than today.
We think our fathers fools, so wise we grow;
Our wiser sons, no doubt, will think us so.
440   Once school divines[6] this zealous isle o'erspread;
Who knew most sentences[7] was deepest read.
Faith, Gospel, all seemed made to be disputed,
And none had sense enough to be confuted.
Scotists and Thomists now in peace remain
445   Amidst their kindred cobwebs in Duck Lane.[8]
If faith itself has different dresses worn,
What wonder modes in wit should take their turn?
Oft, leaving what is natural and fit,
The current folly proves the ready wit;
450   And authors think their reputation safe,
Which lives as long as fools are pleased to laugh.
    Some valuing those of their own side or mind,
Still make themselves the measure of mankind:
Fondly° we think we honor merit then,   *foolishly*

---

2. Claim as their own.
3. For hire.
4. Acknowledge as his.
5. Those who divide the church on points of theology.
6. Scholastic philosophers such as the Scotists and Thomists (followers of the medieval theologians

Duns Scotus and St. Thomas Aquinas) mentioned below.
7. Alludes to Peter Lombard's *Book of Sentences*, a theological work.
8. Where secondhand and remaindered books were sold.

455   When we but praise ourselves in other men.
       Parties in wit attend on those of state,
       And public faction doubles private hate.
       Pride, Malice, Folly against Dryden rose,
       In various shapes of parsons, critics, beaux;
460   But sense survived, when merry jests were past;
       For rising merit will buoy up at last.
       Might he return and bless once more our eyes,
       New Blackmores and new Milbourns must arise.[9]
       Nay, should great Homer lift his awful head,
465   Zoilus[1] again would start up from the dead.
       Envy will merit, as its shade, pursue,
       But like a shadow, proves the substance true;
       For envied wit, like Sol° eclipsed, makes known   *the sun*
       The opposing body's grossness, not its own.
470   When first that sun too powerful beams displays,
       It draws up vapors which obscure its rays;
       But even those clouds at last adorn its way,
       Reflect new glories, and augment the day.
         Be thou the first true merit to befriend;
475   His praise is lost who stays till all commend.
       Short is the date, alas! of modern rhymes,
       And 'tis but just to let them live betimes.°   *early*
       No longer now that golden age appears,
       When patriarch wits survived a thousand years:
480   Now length of fame (our second life) is lost,
       And bare threescore is all even that can boast;
       Our sons their fathers' failing language see,
       And such as Chaucer is shall Dryden be.
       So when the faithful pencil has designed
485   Some bright idea of the master's mind,
       Where a new world leaps out at his command,
       And ready Nature waits upon his hand;
       When the ripe colors soften and unite,
       And sweetly melt into just shade and light;
490   When mellowing years their full perfection give,
       And each bold figure just begins to live,
       The treacherous colors the fair art betray,
       And all the bright creation fades away!
         Unhappy wit, like most mistaken° things,   *misunderstood*
495   Atones not for that envy which it brings.
       In youth alone its empty praise we boast,
       But soon the short-lived vanity is lost;
       Like some fair flower the early spring supplies,
       That gaily blooms, but even in blooming dies,
500   What is this wit, which must our cares employ?
       The owner's wife, that other men enjoy;
       Then most our trouble still when most admired,
       And still the more we give, the more required;
       Whose fame with pains we guard, but lose with ease,

9. Sir Richard Blackmore, physician and poet, had attacked Dryden for the immorality of his plays; the Rev. Luke Milbourn had attacked his translation of Virgil.
1. A Greek critic of the fourth century B.C. who wrote a book of carping criticism of Homer.

505   Sure some to vex, but never all to please;
'Tis what the vicious fear, the virtuous shun,
By fools 'tis hated, and by knaves undone!
    If wit so much from ignorance undergo,
Ah, let not learning too commence its foe!
510   Of old those met rewards who could excel,
And such were praised who but endeavored well;
Though triumphs were to generals only due,
Crowns were reserved to grace the soldiers too.
Now they who reach Parnassus' lofty crown
515   Employ their pains to spurn some others down;
And while self-love each jealous writer rules,
Contending wits become the sport of fools;
But still the worst with most regret commend,
For each ill author is as bad a friend.
520   To what base ends, and by what abject ways,
Are morals urged through sacred° lust of praise!   *accursed*
Ah, ne'er so dire a thirst of glory boast,
Nor in the critic let the man be lost!
Good nature and good sense must ever join;
525   To err is human, to forgive divine.
    But if in the noble minds some dregs remain
Nor yet purged off, spleen and sour disdain,
Discharge that rage on more provoking crimes,
Nor fear a dearth in these flagitious° times.   *shameful, wicked*
530   No pardon vile obscenity should find,
Though wit and art conspire to move your mind;
But dullness with obscenity must prove
As shameful sure as impotence in love.
In the fat age of pleasure, wealth, and ease
535   Sprung the rank weed, and thrived with large increase:
When love was all an easy monarch's[2] care,
Seldom at council, never in a war;
Jilts ruled the state, and statesmen farces writ;
Nay, wits had pensions, and young lords had wit;
540   The fair sat panting at a courtier's play,
And not a mask[3] went unimproved away;
The modest fan was lifted up no more,
And virgins smiled at what they blushed before.
The following license of a foreign reign[4]
545   Did all the dregs of bold Socinus[5] drain;
Then unbelieving priests reformed the nation,
And taught more pleasant methods of salvation;
Where Heaven's free subjects might their rights dispute,
Lest God himself should seem too absolute;
550   Pulpits their sacred satire learned to spare,
And Vice admired to find a flatterer there!
Encouraged thus, wit's Titans[6] braved the skies,

---

2. Charles II, king of England from 1660 to 1685.
The following lines describe the corruption of
morals and letters under this recently dead mon-
arch.
3. A woman in a mask, as at a masquerade.
4. That of William III, king of England from 1689

to 1702. He was born in Holland.
5. The name of two Italian theologians of the six-
teenth century who denied the divinity of Jesus.
6. Primordial giants, whose rule over the Earth
was broken by the Greek gods.

And the press groaned with licensed blasphemies.
These monsters, critics! with your darts engage,
555 Here point your thunder, and exhaust your rage!
Yet shun their fault, who, scandalously nice,
Will needs mistake[7] an author into vice;
All seems infected that the infected spy,
As all looks yellow to the jaundiced eye.

1709   1711

The Rape of the Lock

An Heroi-Comical Poem[8]

Nolueram, Belinda, tuos violare capillos;
sed juvat hoc precibus me tribuisse tuis.[9]
— MARTIAL

Canto I

What dire offense from amorous causes springs,
What mighty contests rise from trivial things,
I sing—This verse to Caryll, Muse! is due:
This, even Belinda may vouchsafe to view:
5 Slight is the subject, but not so the praise,
If she inspire, and he approve my lays.
Say what strange motive, Goddess! could compel
A well-bred lord to assault a gentle belle?
Oh, say what stranger cause, yet unexplored,
10 Could make a gentle belle reject a lord?
In tasks so bold can little men engage,
And in soft bosoms dwells such mighty rage?
Sol through white curtains shot a timorous ray,
And oped those eyes that must eclipse the day.[1]
15 Now lapdogs give themselves the rousing shake,
And sleepless lovers just at twelve awake:
Thrice rung the bell, the slipper knocked the ground,[2]
And the pressed watch returned a silver sound.[3]
Belinda still her downy pillow pressed,
20 Her guardian Sylph[4] prolonged the balmy rest:
'Twas he had summoned to her silent bed
The morning dream that hovered o'er her head.

---

7. I.e., give a wrong meaning to (an author's writings).
8. Based on an actual incident. A young man, Lord Petre, had sportively cut off a lock of a Miss Arabella Fermor's hair. She and her family were angered by the prank, and Pope's friend John Caryll (line 3), a relative of Lord Petre's, asked the poet to turn the incident into jest, so that good relations (and possibly negotiations toward a marriage between the principals) might be resumed. Pope responded by treating the incident in a mock epic or "heroi-comical poem." The epic conventions first encountered are the immediate statement of the topic, which the poet says he will "sing" as if

in oral recitation, and the request to the Muse (line 7) to grant him the necessary insight.
9. "I did not want, Belinda, to violate your locks, but it pleases me to have paid this tribute to your prayers" (Latin). Miss Fermor did not in fact request the poem.
1. The eyes of lovely young women—though Belinda herself is still asleep.
2. These are two ways of summoning servants.
3. In a darkened bed, one discovered the approximate time by a watch that chimed the hour and quarter-hour when the stem was pressed.
4. Air spirit. He accounts for himself in the lines below.

A youth more glittering than a birthnight beau[5]
(That even in slumber caused her cheek to glow)
25 Seemed to her ear his winning lips to lay,
And thus in whispers said, or seemed to say:
"Fairest of mortals, thou distinguished care[6]
Of thousand bright inhabitants of air!
If e'er one vision touched thy infant thought,
30 Of all the nurse and all the priest have taught,
Of airy elves by moonlight shadows seen,
The silver token, and the circled green,[7]
Or virgins visited by angel powers,
With golden crowns and wreaths of heavenly flowers,
35 Hear and believe! thy own importance know,
Nor bound thy narrow views to things below.
Some secret truths, from learned pride concealed,
To maids alone and children are revealed:
What though no credit doubting wits may give?
40 The fair and innocent shall still believe.
Know, then, unnumbered spirits round thee fly,
The light militia of the lower sky:
These, though unseen, are ever on the wing,
Hang o'er the box, and hover round the Ring.[8]
45 Think what an equipage thou hast in air,
And view with scorn two pages and a chair.°   *sedan chair*
As now your own, our beings were of old,
And once enclosed in woman's beauteous mold;
Thence, by a soft transition, we repair
50 From earthly vehicles[9] to these of air.
Think not, when woman's transient breath is fled,
That all her vanities at once are dead:
Succeeding vanities she still regards,
And though she plays no more, o'erlooks the cards.
55 Her joy in gilded chariots,° when alive,   *carriages*
And love of ombre,[1] after death survive.
For when the Fair in all their pride expire,
To their first elements their souls retire:[2]
The sprites of fiery termagants in flame
60 Mount up, and take a Salamander's name.
Soft yielding minds to water glide away,
And sip, with Nymphs, their elemental tea.[3]
The graver prude sinks downward to a Gnome,

---

5. Courtier dressed for a royal birthnight celebration.
6. I.e., object of care.
7. The silver token is the coin left by a fairy or elf, and the circled green is a ring of bright green grass, supposed dancing circle of fairies.
8. The box is a theater box; the Ring, the circular carriage course in Hyde Park.
9. Mediums of existence, with a side glance at the fondness of young women for riding in carriages.
1. A popular card game, pronounced *omber*. See n. 4, p. 554.
2. Namely, to fire, water, earth, and air, the four elements of the old cosmology and the several habitats (in the Rosicrucian myths upon which Pope

embroiders) of four different kinds of "spirit." Envisaging these spirits as the transmigrated souls of different kinds of women, Pope causes termagants (scolds) to become fire spirits or Salamanders (line 60); irresolute women to become water spirits or Nymphs (line 62); prudes, or women who delight in rejection and negation, to become earth spirits or Gnomes (line 63); and coquettes to become air spirits or Sylphs (line 65). Since "nymph" could designate either a water spirit or (in literary usage) a young lady, Pope permits his water spirits to claim tea as their native element (line 62) and to keep their former company at tea parties.
3. Pronounced *tay*.

In search of mischief still on earth to roam.
65 The light coquettes in Sylphs aloft repair,
    And sport and flutter in the fields of air.
        "Know further yet; whoever fair and chaste
    Rejects mankind, is by some Sylph embraced:
    For spirits, freed from mortal laws, with ease
70 Assume what sexes and what shapes they please.[4]
    What guards the purity of melting maids,
    In courtly balls, and midnight masquerades,
    Safe from the treacherous friend, the daring spark,
    The glance by day, the whisper in the dark,
75 When kind occasion prompts their warm desires,
    When music softens, and when dancing fires?
    'Tis but their Sylph, the wise Celestials know,
    Though Honor is the word with men below.
        "Some nymphs there are, too conscious of their face,
80 For life predestined to the Gnomes' embrace.
    These swell their prospects and exalt their pride,
    When offers are disdained, and love denied:
    Then gay ideas° crowd the vacant brain,   *imaginings*
    While peers, and dukes, and all their sweeping train,
85 And garters, stars, and coronets[5] appear,
    And in soft sounds, 'your Grace' salutes their ear.
    'Tis these that early taint the female soul,
    Instruct the eyes of young coquettes to roll,
    Teach infant cheeks a bidden blush to know,
90 And little hearts to flutter at a beau.
        "Oft, when the world° imagine women stray,   *fashionable people*
    The Sylphs through mystic mazes guide their way,
    Through all the giddy circle they pursue,
    And old impertinence expel by new.
95 What tender maid but must a victim fall
    To one man's treat, but for another's ball?
    When Florio speaks what virgin could withstand,
    If gentle Damon did not squeeze her hand?
    With varying vanities, from every part,
100 They shift the moving toyshop of their heart;
    Where wigs with wigs, with sword-knots sword-knots strive,[6]
    Beaux banish beaux, and coaches coaches drive.
    This erring mortals levity may call;
    Oh, blind to truth! the Sylphs contrive it all.
105   "Of these am I, who thy protection claim,
    A watchful sprite, and Ariel is my name.
    Late, as I ranged the crystal wilds of air,
    In the clear mirror of thy ruling star
    I saw, alas! some dread event impend,
110 Ere to the main[7] this morning sun descend,
    But Heaven reveals not what, or how, or where:
    Warned by the Sylph, O pious maid, beware!

4. Like Milton's angels (*Paradise Lost* 1.423 ff.).
5. Insignia of rank and court status.
6. Sword knots are ribbons tied to hilts. The verbal repetition and the tangled syntax recall descrip-
tions of the throng and press of battle appearing in English translations of classical epic.
7. Broad expanse of land or sea (figuratively, the horizon). Cf. Canto II, lines 2 and 85.

This to disclose is all thy guardian can:
Beware of all, but most beware of Man!"
115   He said; when Shock,[8] who thought she slept too long,
Leaped up, and waked his mistress with his tongue.
'Twas then, Belinda, if report say true,
Thy eyes first opened on a billet-doux;[9]
Wounds, charms, and ardors were no sooner read,
120   But all the vision vanished from thy head.
    And now, unveiled, the toilet stands displayed,
Each silver vase in mystic order laid.
First, robed in white, the nymph intent adores,
With head uncovered, the cosmetic powers.
125   A heavenly image in the glass[1] appears;
To that she bends, to that her eyes she rears.
The inferior priestess, at her altar's side,
Trembling begins the sacred rites of pride.
Unnumbered treasures ope at once, and here
130   The various offerings of the world appear;
From each she nicely culls with curious toil,
And decks the goddess with the glittering spoil.
This casket India's glowing gems unlocks,
And all Arabia[2] breathes from yonder box.
135   The tortoise here and elephant unite,
Transformed to combs, the speckled and the white.
Here files of pins extend their shining rows,
Puffs, powders, patches, Bibles, billet-doux.
Now awful Beauty put on all its arms;
140   The fair each moment rises in her charms,
Repairs her smiles, awakens every grace,
And calls forth all the wonders of her face;
Sees by degrees a purer blush arise,
And keener lightnings quicken in her eyes.
145   The busy Sylphs surround their darling care,
These set the head, and those divide the hair,
Some fold the sleeve, whilst others plait the gown;
And Betty's praised for labors not her own.

Canto II

Not with more glories, in the ethereal plain,
The sun first rises o'er the purpled main,
Than, issuing forth, the rival of his beams[3]
Launched on the bosom of the silver Thames.
5   Fair nymphs and well-dressed youths around her shone,
But every eye was fixed on her alone.
On her white breast a sparkling cross she wore,
Which Jews might kiss, and infidels adore.
Her lively looks a sprightly mind disclose,

8. A name for lapdogs (like "Poll" for parrots); they looked like little "shocks" of hair.
9. A love letter. The affected language of the fashionable love letter is exhibited in the next line.
1. The mirror. Her image is the object of veneration, the "goddess" named later. Belinda presides over the appropriate rites. Betty, her maid, is the "inferior priestess."
2. Source of perfumes.
3. I.e., Belinda. She is en route to Hampton Court, a royal palace some twelve miles up the river Thames from London.

10 Quick as her eyes, and as unfixed as those:
  Favors to none, to all she smiles extends;
  Oft she rejects, but never once offends.
  Bright as the sun, her eyes the gazers strike,
  And, like the sun, they shine on all alike.
15 Yet graceful ease, and sweetness void of pride,
  Might hide her faults, if belles had faults to hide:
  If to her share some female errors fall,
  Look on her face, and you'll forget 'em all.
    This nymph, to the destruction of mankind,
20 Nourished two locks which graceful hung behind
  In equal curls, and well conspired to deck
  With shining ringlets the smooth ivory neck.
  Love in these labyrinths his slaves detains,
  And mighty hearts are held in slender chains.
25 With hairy springes° we the birds betray,   *snares*
  Slight lines of hair surprise the finny prey,
  Fair tresses man's imperial race ensnare,
  And beauty draws us with a single hair.
    The adventurous Baron the bright locks admired,
30 He saw, he wished, and to the prize aspired.
  Resolved to win, he meditates the way,
  By force to ravish, or by fraud betray;
  For when success a lover's toil attends,
  Few ask if fraud or force attained his ends.
35   For this, ere Phoebus⁴ rose, he had implored
  Propitious Heaven, and every power adored,
  But chiefly Love—to Love an altar built,
  Of twelve vast French romances, neatly gilt.
  There lay three garters, half a pair of gloves,
40 And all the trophies of his former loves.
  With tender billet-doux he lights the pyre,
  And breathes three amorous sighs to raise the fire.
  Then prostrate falls, and begs with ardent eyes
  Soon to obtain, and long possess the prize:
45 The powers gave ear, and granted half his prayer,
  The rest the winds dispersed in empty air.
    But now secure the painted vessel glides,
  The sunbeams trembling on the floating tides,
  While melting music steals upon the sky,
50 And softened sounds along the waters die.
  Smooth flow the waves, the zephyrs⁵ gently play,
  Belinda smiled, and all the world was gay.
  All but the Sylph—with careful thoughts oppressed,
  The impending woe sat heavy on his breast.
55 He summons straight his denizens° of air;   *inhabitants*
  The lucid squadrons round the sails repair:°   *assemble*
  Soft o'er the shrouds aërial whispers breathe
  That seemed but zephyrs to the train beneath.
  Some to the sun their insect-wings unfold,
60 Waft on the breeze, or sink in clouds of gold.
  Transparent forms too fine for mortal sight,

---

4. Apollo, god of the sun.   5. West winds.

Their fluid bodies half dissolved in light,
Loose to the wind their airy garments flew,
Thin glittering textures of the filmy dew,[6]
65   Dipped in the richest tincture of the skies,
Where light disports in ever-mingling dyes,
While every beam new transient colors flings,
Colors that change whene'er they wave their wings.
Amid the circle, on the gilded mast,
70   Superior by the head was Ariel placed;
His purple° pinions opening to the sun,   *brilliant*
He raised his azure wand, and thus begun:
    "Ye Sylphs and Sylphids, to your chief give ear!
Fays, Fairies, Genii, Elves, and Daemons, hear!
75   Ye know the spheres and various tasks assigned
By laws eternal to the aërial kind.
Some in the fields of purest ether play,
And bask and whiten in the blaze of day.
Some guide the course of wandering orbs on high,
80   Or roll the planets through the boundless sky.
Some less refined, beneath the moon's pale light
Pursue the stars that shoot athwart the night,
Or suck the mists in grosser air below,
Or dip their pinions in the painted bow,°   *rainbow*
85   Or brew fierce tempests on the wintry main,
Or o'er the glebe° distill the kindly rain.   *farmland*
Others on earth o'er human race preside,
Watch all their ways, and all their actions guide:
Of these the chief the care of nations own,
90   And guard with arms divine the British Throne.
    "Our humbler province is to tend the Fair,
Not a less pleasing, though less glorious care:
To save the powder from too rude a gale,
Nor let the imprisoned essences exhale;
95   To draw fresh colors from the vernal flowers;
To steal from rainbows e'er they drop in showers
A brighter wash;° to curl their waving hairs,   *(cosmetic) wash*
Assist their blushes, and inspire their airs;
Nay oft, in dreams invention we bestow,
100 To change a flounce, or add a furbelow.°   *ornamental pleat*
    "This day black omens threat the brightest fair,
That e'er deserved a watchful spirit's care;
Some dire disaster, or° by force or slight,   *whether*
But what, or where, the Fates have wrapped in night:
105 Whether the nymph shall break Diana's law,[7]
Or some frail china jar receive a flaw,
Or stain her honor or her new brocade,
Forget her prayers, or miss a masquerade,
Or lose her heart, or necklace, at a ball;
110 Or whether Heaven has doomed that Shock[8] must fall.
Haste, then, ye spirits! to your charge repair:
The fluttering fan be Zephyretta's care;

6. The supposed material of spider webs.   8. See Canto I, line 115.
7. Of chastity.

The drops° to thee, Brillante, we consign;   *earrings*
And, Momentilla, let the watch be thine;
115   Do thou, Crispissa,⁹ tend her favorite Lock;
Ariel himself shall be the guard of Shock.
    "To fifty chosen Sylphs, of special note,
We trust the important charge, the petticoat;
Oft have we known that sevenfold fence to fail,
120   Though stiff with hoops, and armed with ribs of whale.
Form a strong line about the silver bound,
And guard the wide circumference around.
    "Whatever spirit, careless of his charge,
His post neglects, or leaves the fair at large,
125   Shall feel sharp vengeance soon o'ertake his sins,
Be stopped in vials, or transfixed with pins,
Or plunged in lakes of bitter washes lie,
Or wedged whole ages in a bodkin's° eye;   *large needle's*
Gums and pomatums shall his flight restrain,
130   While clogged he beats his silken wings in vain,
Or alum styptics with contracting power
Shrink his thin essence like a riveled° flower: *shriveled*
Or, as Ixion¹ fixed, the wretch shall feel
The giddy motion of the whirling mill,°   *cocoa mill*
135   In fumes of burning chocolate shall glow,
And tremble at the sea that froths below!"
    He spoke; the spirits from the sails descend;
Some, orb in orb, around the nymph extend;
Some thread the mazy ringlets of her hair;
140   Some hang upon the pendants of her ear:
With beating hearts the dire event they wait,
Anxious, and trembling for the birth of Fate.

Canto III

    Close by those meads,° forever crowned with flowers,   *meadows*
Where Thames with pride surveys his rising towers,
There stands a structure of majestic frame,²
Which from the neighboring Hampton takes its name.
5   Here Britain's statesmen oft the fall foredoom
Of foreign tyrants and of nymphs at home;
Here thou, great Anna!³ whom three realms obey,
Dost sometimes counsel take—and sometimes tea.
    Hither the heroes and the nymphs resort,
10   To taste awhile the pleasures of a court;
In various talk the instructive hours they passed,
Who gave the ball, or paid the visit last;
One speaks the glory of the British Queen,
And one describes a charming Indian screen;
15   A third interprets motions, looks, and eyes;
At every word a reputation dies.
    Snuff, or the fan, supply each pause of chat,

---

9. To "crisp" is to curl (hair).   2. Hampton Court.
1. For an affront to Juno, Ixion was bound eter- 3. Anne, queen of England.
nally to a turning wheel.

With singing, laughing, ogling, and all that.
   Meanwhile, declining from the noon of day,
20 The sun obliquely shoots his burning ray;
The hungry judges soon the sentence sign,
And wretches hang that jurymen may dine;
The merchant from the Exchange° returns in peace,   *stock market*
And the long labors of the toilet cease.
25 Belinda now, whom thirst of fame invites,
Burns to encounter two adventurous knights,
At ombre⁴ singly to decide their doom,
And swells her breast with conquests yet to come.
Straight the three bands prepare in arms° to join,   *combat*
30 Each band the number of the sacred nine.
Soon as she spreads her hand, the aërial guard
Descend, and sit on each important card:
First Ariel perched upon a Matadore,
Then each according to the rank they bore;
35 For Sylphs, yet mindful of their ancient race,
Are, as when women, wondrous fond of place.
   Behold, four Kings in majesty revered,
With hoary whiskers and a forky beard;
And four fair Queens whose hands sustain a flower,
40 The expressive emblem of their softer power;
Four Knaves in garbs succinct,⁵ a trusty band,
Caps on their heads, and halberts⁶ in their hand;
And parti°-colored troops, a shining train,   *variously*
Draw forth to combat on the velvet plain.
45   The skillful nymph reviews her force with care;
"Let Spades be trumps!" she said, and trumps they were
   Now move to war her sable Matadores,
In show like leaders of the swarthy Moors.
Spadillio first, unconquerable lord!
50 Led off two captive trumps, and swept the board.
As many more Manillio forced to yield,
And marched a victor from the verdant field.
Him Basto followed, but his fate more hard
Gained but one trump and one plebeian card.
55 With his broad saber next, a chief in years,
The hoary Majesty of Spades appears,
Puts forth one manly leg, to sight revealed,

---

4. This game is like three-handed bridge with some features of poker added. From a deck lacking 8s, 9s, and 10s, nine cards are dealt to each player (line 30) and the rest put in a central pool. A declarer called the *Ombre* (Spanish *hombre:* "man") commits himself to taking more tricks than either of his opponents individually; hence Belinda would "encounter two knights *singly.*" Declarer, followed by the other players, then selects discards and replenishes his hand with cards drawn sight unseen from the pool (line 45). He proceeds to name his trumps (line 46). The three principal trumps, called *Matadors* (line 47), always include the black aces. When spades are declared, the Matadors are, in order of value, the ace of spades (called *Spadille*, line 49), the deuce

of spades (called *Manille*, line 51), and the ace of clubs (called *Basto*, line 53). The remaining spades fill out the trump suit. In the game here described, Belinda leads out her high trumps (lines 49–56), but the suit breaks badly (line 54); the Baron retains the queen (line 67), with which he presently trumps her king of clubs (line 69). He then leads high diamonds until she is on the verge of a set (called *Codille*, line 92). But she makes her bid at the last trick (line 94), taking his ace of hearts with her king (line 95), this being, in ombre, the highest card in the heart suit. The game is played on a green velvet cloth (line 44).
5. Hemmed up short, not flowing.
6. Weapons combining pike and ax on a single shaft.

The rest his many-colored robe concealed.
The rebel Knave,° who dares his prince engage,   *jack*
60 Proves the just victim of his royal rage.
Even mighty Pam,[7] that kings and queens o'erthrew
And mowed down armies in the fights of loo,
Sad chance of war! now destitute of aid,
Falls undistinguished by the victor Spade.
65   Thus far both armies to Belinda yield;
Now to the Baron fate inclines the field.
His warlike amazon her host invades,
The imperial consort of the crown of Spades.
The Club's black tyrant first her victim died,
70 Spite of his haughty mien and barbarous pride.
What boots the regal circle on his head,
His giant limbs, in state unwieldy spread?
That long behind he trails his pompous robe.
And of all monarchs only grasps the globe?
75   The Baron now his Diamonds pours apace;
The embroidered King who shows but half his face,
And his refulgent Queen, with powers combined
Of broken troops an easy conquest find.
Clubs, Diamonds, Hearts, in wild disorder seen,
80 With throngs promiscuous strew the level green.
Thus when dispersed a routed army runs,
Of Asia's troops, and Afric's sable sons,
With like confusion different nations fly,
Of various habit,° and of various dye,°   *dress / color*
85 The pierced battalions disunited fall
In heaps on heaps; one fate o'erwhelms them all.
     The Knave of Diamonds tries his wily arts,
And wins (oh, shameful chance!) the Queen of Hearts.
At this, the blood the virgin's cheek forsook,
90 A livid paleness spreads o'er all her look;
She sees, and trembles at the approaching ill,
Just in the jaws of ruin, and Codille,
And now (as oft in some distempered state)
On one nice trick depends the general fate.
95   An Ace of Hearts steps forth: the King unseen
Lurked in her hand, and mourned his captive Queen.
He springs to vengeance with an eager pace,
And falls like thunder on the prostrate Ace.
The nymph exulting fills with shouts the sky,
100 The walls, the woods, and long canals[8] reply.
     O thoughtless mortals! ever blind to fate,
Too soon dejected, and too soon elate:
Sudden these honors shall be snatched away,
And cursed forever this victorious day.
105   For lo! the board with cups and spoons is crowned,
The berries crackle, and the mill turns round;[9]
     On shining altars of Japan[1] they raise

---

7. The jack of clubs, paramount trump in the game of loo.
8. Passages between avenues of trees.
9. As coffee beans are roasted and ground.
1. Lacquered tables.

The silver lamp; the fiery spirits blaze:
From silver spouts the grateful liquors glide,
110 While China's earth[2] receives the smoking tide.
At once they gratify their scent and taste,
And frequent cups prolong the rich repast.
Straight hover round the fair her airy band;
Some, as she sipped, the fuming liquor fanned,
115 Some o'er her lap their careful plumes displayed,
Trembling, and conscious of the rich brocade.
Coffee (which makes the politician wise,
And see through all things with his half-shut eyes)
Sent up in vapors to the Baron's brain
120 New stratagems, the radiant Lock to gain.
Ah, cease, rash youth! desist ere 'tis too late,
Fear the just Gods, and think of Scylla's fate![3]
Changed to a bird, and sent to flit in air,
She dearly pays for Nisus' injured hair!
125   But when to mischief mortals bend their will,
How soon they find fit instruments of ill!
Just then, Clarissa drew with tempting grace
A two-edged weapon from her shining case:
So ladies in romance assist their knight,
130 Present the spear, and arm him for the fight.
He takes the gift with reverence, and extends
The little engine on his fingers' ends;
This just behind Belinda's neck he spread,
As o'er the fragrant steams she bends her head.
135 Swift to the Lock a thousand sprites repair,
A thousand wings, by turns, blow back the hair,
And thrice they twitched the diamond in her ear,
Thrice she looked back, and thrice the foe drew near.
Just in that instant, anxious Ariel sought
140 The close recesses of the virgin's thought;
As on the nosegay° in her breast reclined,   *posy*
He watched the ideas rising in her mind,
Sudden he viewed, in spite of all her art,
An earthly lover lurking at her heart.
145 Amazed, confused, he found his power expired,[4]
Resigned to fate, and with a sigh retired.
     The Peer now spreads the glittering forfex° wide,   *scissors*
To enclose the Lock; now joins it, to divide.
Even then, before the fatal engine closed,
150 A wretched Sylph too fondly interposed;
Fate urged the shears, and cut the Sylph in twain
(But airy substance soon unites again):[5]
The meeting points the sacred hair dissever
From the fair head, forever, and forever!

2. Ceramic cups.
3. Scylla cut from the head of her father, Nisus, the lock of hair on which his life depended and gave it to her lover Minos of Crete, who was besieging Nisus' city. For this she was turned into a sea bird relentlessly pursued by an eagle.

4. Belinda, being strongly attracted to the Baron (line 144), can no longer merely coquette. She hence passes beyond Ariel's control.
5. Again as with Milton's angels (*Paradise Lost* 6.329–31).

155 Then flashed the living lightning from her eyes,
And screams of horror rend the affrighted skies.
Not louder shrieks to pitying heaven are cast,
When husbands, or when lapdogs breathe their last;
Or when rich china vessels fallen from high,
160 In glittering dust and painted fragments lie!
"Let wreaths of triumph now my temples twine,"
The victor cried, "the glorious prize is mine!
While fish in streams, or birds delight in air,
Or in a coach and six the British Fair,
165 As long as *Atalantis*[6] shall be read,
Or the small pillow grace a lady's bed,
While visits shall be paid on solemn days,
When numerous wax-lights in bright order blaze,[7]
While nymphs take treats, or assignations give,
170 So long my honor, name, and praise shall live!
What Time would spare, from Steel receives its date,°   termination
And monuments, like men, submit to fate!
Steel could the labor of the Gods destroy,[8]
And strike to dust the imperial towers of Troy;
175 Steel could the works of mortal pride confound,
And hew triumphal arches to the ground.
What wonder then, fair nymph! thy hairs should feel,
The conquering force of unresisted Steel?"

Canto IV

But anxious cares the pensive nymph oppressed,
And secret passions labored in her breast.
Not youthful kings in battle seized alive,
Not scornful virgins who their charms survive,
5 Not ardent lovers robbed of all their bliss,
Not ancient ladies when refused a kiss,
Not tyrants fierce that unrepenting die,
Not Cynthia when her manteau's[9] pinned awry,
E'er felt such rage, resentment, and despair,
10 As thou, sad virgin! for thy ravished hair.
For, that sad moment, when the Sylphs withdrew
And Ariel weeping from Belinda flew,
Umbriel,[1] a dusky, melancholy sprite
As ever sullied the fair face of light,
15 Down to the central earth, his proper scene,
Repaired to search the gloomy Cave of Spleen.[2]
Swift on his sooty pinions flits the Gnome,
And in a vapor reached the dismal dome.

6. A set of memoirs that, under thin disguise, recounted actual scandals.
7. Attending the formal evening visits of the previous line.
8. Troy (named in the next line) was built by Apollo and Poseidon.
9. I.e., robe is.
1. Suggesting *umbra*, shadow; and *umber*, brown. The final *el* of this name is a further reminiscence of Milton's angels: Gabriel, Abdiel, Zophiel.

2. This journey is formally equivalent to Odysseus' and Aeneas' visits to the underworld. "Spleen" refers to the human organ, the supposed seat of melancholy; hence to melancholy itself. Believed to be induced by misty weather such as the east wind brings (lines 18–20), the condition was also called the "vapors." In its severer manifestations it tends toward madness; in its milder forms, it issues in peevishness and suspicion.

No cheerful breeze this sullen region knows,
20   The dreaded east is all the wind that blows.
Here in a grotto, sheltered close from air,
And screened in shades from day's detested glare,
She sighs forever on her pensive bed,
Pain at her side, and Megrim° at her head.   *migraine*
25   Two handmaids wait° the throne: alike in place,   *attend*
But differing far in figure and in face.
Here stood Ill-Nature like an ancient maid,
Her wrinkled form in black and white arrayed;
With store of prayers for mornings, nights, and noons,
30   Her hand is filled; her bosom with lampoons.°   *slanders*
    There Affectation, with a sickly mien,
Shows in her cheek the roses of eighteen,
Practiced to lisp, and hang the head aside,
Faints into airs, and languishes with pride,
35   On the rich quilt sinks with becoming woe,
Wrapped in a gown, for sickness and for show.
The fair ones feel such maladies as these,
When each new nightdress gives a new disease.
    A constant vapor o'er the palace flies.
40   Strange phantoms rising as the mists arise;
Dreadful as hermit's dreams in haunted shades,
Or bright as visions of expiring maids.
Now glaring fiends, and snakes on rolling spires,°   *coils*
Pale specters, gaping tombs, and purple fires;
45   Now lakes of liquid gold, Elysian scenes,
And crystal domes, and angels in machines.[3]
    Unnumbered throngs on every side are seen
Of bodies changed to various forms by Spleen.
Here living teapots stand, one arm held out,
50   One bent; the handle this, and that the spout:
A pipkin[4] there, like Homer's tripod, walks;
Here sighs a jar, and there a goose pie talks;
Men prove with child, as powerful fancy works,
And maids, turned bottles, call aloud for corks.
55   Safe passed the Gnome through this fantastic band,
A branch of healing spleenwort[5] in his hand.
Then thus addressed the Power: "Hail, wayward Queen!
Who rule the sex to fifty from fifteen:
Parent of vapors and of female wit,
60   Who give the hysteric or poetic fit,
On various tempers act by various ways,
Make some take physic,° others scribble plays;   *medicine*
Who cause the proud their visits to delay,
And send the godly in a pet° to pray.   *fit of anger*
65   A nymph there is that all thy power disdains,
And thousands more in equal mirth maintains.
But oh! if e'er thy Gnome could spoil a grace,

---

3. These images are both 1) the hallucinations of insane melancholy and 2) parodies of stage properties and effects.
4. An earthen pot; it walks like the three-legged stools that Vulcan made for the gods in *Iliad* 18.
5. A kind of fern, purgative of spleen; suggesting the golden bough that Aeneas bore as a passport to Hades in *Aeneid* 6.

Or raise a pimple on a beauteous face,
Like citron-waters° matrons' cheeks inflame,   *orange brandy*
70 Or change complexions at a losing game;
If e'er with airy horns I planted heads,[6]
Or rumpled petticoats, or tumbled beds,
Or caused suspicion when no soul was rude,
Or discomposed the headdress of a prude,
75 Or e'er to costive° lapdog gave disease,   *constipated*
Which not the tears of brightest eyes could ease,
Hear me, and touch Belinda with chagrin:°   *annoyance*
That single act gives half the world the spleen."
    The Goddess with a discontented air
80 Seems to reject him though she grants his prayer.
A wondrous bag with both her hands she binds,
Like that where once Ulysses held the winds;[7]
There she collects the force of female lungs,
Sighs, sobs, and passions, and the war of tongues.
85 A vial next she fills with fainting fears,
Soft sorrows, melting griefs, and flowing tears.
The Gnome rejoicing bears her gifts away,
Spreads his black wings, and slowly mounts to day.
    Sunk in Thalestris'[8] arms the nymph he found,
90 Her eyes dejected and her hair unbound.
Full o'er their heads the swelling bag he rent,
And all the Furies issued at the vent.
Belinda burns with more than mortal ire,
And fierce Thalestris fans the rising fire.
95 "O wretched maid!" she spreads her hands, and cried
(While Hampton's echoes, "Wretched maid!" replied),
"Was it for this you took such constant care
The bodkin,° comb, and essence° to prepare?   *hairpin / perfume*
For this your locks in paper durance bound,
100 For this with torturing irons wreathed around?
For this with fillets° strained your tender head,   *bands*
And bravely bore the double loads of lead?[9]
Gods! shall the ravisher display your hair,
While the fops envy, and the ladies stare!
105 Honor forbid! at whose unrivaled shrine
Ease, pleasure, virtue, all, our sex resign.
Methinks already I your tears survey,
Already hear the horrid things they say,
Already see you a degraded toast,
110 And all your honor in a whisper lost!
How shall I, then, your helpless fame defend?
'Twill then be infamy to seem your friend!
And shall this prize, the inestimable prize,
Exposed through crystal to the gazing eyes,
115 And heightened by the diamond's circling rays,
On that rapacious hand forever blaze?

---

6. I.e., made men imagine they were being cuck-
olded.
7. Aeolus, the wind god, enabled Odysseus (Ulys-
ses) so to contain all adverse winds in *Odyssey* 10.

8. The name of an Amazon.
9. The means by which Belinda's locks were fash-
ioned into a ringlet: lead strips held her curl papers
in place.

Sooner shall grass in Hyde Park Circus[1] grow,
And wits take lodgings in the sound of Bow;[2]
Sooner let earth, air, sea, to chaos fall,
120 Men, monkeys, lapdogs, parrots, perish all!"
    She said; then raging to Sir Plume repairs,
And bids her beau demand the precious hairs
(Sir Plume of amber snuffbox justly vain,
And the nice° conduct° of a clouded cane).   *precise / handling*
125 With earnest eyes, and round unthinking face,
He first the snuffbox opened, then the case,
And thus broke out—"My Lord, why, what the devil!
Zounds! damn the lock! 'fore Gad, you must be civil!
Plague on't! 'tis past a jest—nay prithee, pox!
130 Give her the hair"—he spoke, and rapped his box.
    "It grieves me much," replied the Peer again,
"Who speaks so well should ever speak in vain.
But by this Lock, this sacred Lock I swear
(Which never more shall join its parted hair;
135 Which never more its honors shall renew,
Clipped from the lovely head where late it grew),
That while my nostrils draw the vital air,
This hand, which won it, shall forever wear."
He spoke, and speaking, in proud triumph spread
140 The long-contended honors° of her head.   *ornaments*
    But Umbriel, hateful Gnome, forbears not so;
He breaks the vial whence the sorrows flow.
Then see! the nymph in beauteous grief appears,
Her eyes half languishing, half drowned in tears;
145 On her heaved bosom hung her drooping head,
Which with a sigh she raised, and thus she said:
    "Forever cursed be this detested day,
Which snatched my best, my favorite curl away!
Happy! ah, ten times happy had I been,
150 If Hampton Court these eyes had never seen!
Yet am not I the first mistaken maid,
By love of courts to numerous ills betrayed.
Oh, had I rather unadmired remained
In some lone isle, or distant northern land;
155 Where the gilt chariot never marks the way,
Where none learn ombre, none e'er taste bohea!°   *fine tea*
There kept my charms concealed from mortal eye,
Like roses that in deserts bloom and die.
What moved my mind with youthful lords to roam?
160 Oh, had I stayed, and said my prayers at home!
'Twas this the morning omens seemed to tell,
Thrice from my trembling hand the patch box[3] fell;
The tottering china shook without a wind,
Nay, Poll sat mute, and Shock was most unkind!
165 A Sylph too warned me of the threats of fate,

---

1. The fashionable carriage course (the "Ring" of 1.44).
2. I.e., the sound of the church bells of St. Mary Le Bow in the unfashionable commercial section of London.
3. A box for ornamental patches to accent the face.

In mystic visions, now believed too late!
See the poor remnants of these slighted hairs!
My hands shall rend what e'en thy rapine spares.
These in two sable ringlets taught to break,
170 Once gave new beauties to the snowy neck;
The sister lock now sits uncouth, alone,
And in its fellow's fate foresees its own;
Uncurled it hands, the fatal shears demands,
And tempts once more thy sacrilegious hands.
175 Oh, hadst thou, cruel! been content to seize
Hairs less in sight, or any hairs but these!"

Canto V

She said: the pitying audience melt in tears.
But Fate and Jove had stopped the Baron's ears.
In vain Thalestris with reproach assails,
For who can move when fair Belinda fails?
5 Not half so fixed the Trojan could remain,
While Anna begged and Dido raged in vain.[4]
Then grave Clarissa graceful waved her fan;
Silence ensued, and thus the nymph began:
"Say why are beauties praised and honored most,
10 The wise man's passion, and the vain man's toast?
Why decked with all that land and sea afford,
Why angels called, and angel-like adored?
Why round our coaches crowd the white-gloved beaux,
Why bows the side box[5] from its inmost rows?
15 How vain are all these glories, all our pains,
Unless good sense preserve what beauty gains;
That men may say when we the front box grace,
'Behold the first in virtue as in face!'
Oh! if to dance all night, and dress all day,
20 Charmed the smallpox, or chased old age away,
Who would not scorn what housewife's cares produce,
Or who would learn one earthly thing of use?
To patch, nay ogle, might become a saint,
Nor could it sure be such a sin to paint.°   apply cosmetics
25 But since, alas! frail beauty must decay,
Curled or uncurled, since locks will turn to gray;
Since painted, or not painted, all shall fade,
And she who scorns a man must die a maid;
What then remains but well our power to use,
30 And keep good humor still whate'er we lose?
And trust me, dear, good humor can prevail
When airs, and flights, and screams, and scolding fail.
Beauties in vain their pretty eyes may roll;
Charms strike the sight, but merit wins the soul."[6]
35 So spoke the dame, but no applause ensued;

4. Aeneas was determined to leave Carthage for Italy, though the enamored queen Dido raved and her sister Anna pleaded with him to stay.
5. I.e., at the theater.

6. Clarissa's address parallels a speech in *Iliad* 12, wherein Sarpedon tells Glaucus that, as leaders of the army, they must justify their privilege by extraordinary prowess.

Belinda frowned, Thalestris called her prude.
"To arms, to arms!" the fierce virago cries,
And swift as lightning to the combat flies.
All side in parties, and begin the attack;
40   Fans clap, silks rustle, and tough whalebones crack;
Heroes' and heroines' shouts confusedly rise,
And bass and treble voices strike the skies.
No common weapons in their hands are found,
Like Gods they fight, nor dread a mortal wound.
45   So when bold Homer makes the Gods engage,
And heavenly breasts with human passions rage;
'Gainst Pallas, Mars; Latona, Hermes arms;[7]
And all Olympus rings with loud alarms:
Jove's thunder roars, heaven trembles all around,
50   Blue Neptune[8] storms, the bellowing deeps resound:
Earth shakes her nodding towers, the ground gives way,
And the pale ghosts start at the flash of day!
    Triumphant Umbriel on a sconce's° height   *mounted candlestick*
Clapped his glad wings, and sat to view the fight:
55   Propped on the bodkin spears, the sprites survey
The growing combat, or assist the fray.
    While through the press enraged Thalestris flies,
And scatters death around from both her eyes,
A beau and witling perished in the throng,
60   One died in metaphor, and one in song.
"O cruel nymph! a living death I bear,"
Cried Dapperwit, and sunk beside his chair.
A mournful glance Sir Fopling upwards cast,
"Those eyes are made so killing"—was his last.
65   Thus on Maeander's[9] flowery margin lies
The expiring swan, and as he sings he dies.
    When bold Sir Plume had drawn Clarissa down,
Chloe stepped in, and killed him with a frown;
She smiled to see the doughty hero slain,
70   But, at her smile, the beau revived again.
    Now Jove suspends his golden scales in air,[1]
Weighs the men's wits against the lady's hair;
The doubtful beam long nods from side to side;
At length the wits mount up, the hairs subside.
75   See, fierce Belinda on the Baron flies,
With more than usual lightning in her eyes;
Nor feared the chief the unequal fight to try,
Who sought no more than on his foe to die.[2]
    But this bold lord with manly strength endued,
80   She with one finger and a thumb subdued:
Just where the breath of life his nostrils drew,
A charge of snuff the wily virgin threw;
The Gnomes direct, to every atom just,
The pungent grains of titillating dust.

7. Mars arms against Pallas, and Hermes against
Latona in *Iliad* 20. The tangled syntax is supposed
to mirror the press of battle.
8. Neptune is god of the sea.
9. A river in Asia Minor noted for its wandering

course.
1. He so weighs the fortunes of war in classical
epic.
2. I.e., to experience sexual bliss.

85 Sudden, with starting tears each eye o'erflows,
And the high dome re-echoes to his nose.
    "Now meet thy fate," incensed Belinda cried,
And drew a deadly bodkin[3] from her side.
(The same, his ancient personage to deck,
90 Her great-great-grandsire wore about his neck,
In three seal rings; which after, melted down,
Formed a vast buckle for his widow's gown:
Her infant grandame's whistle next it grew,
The bells she jingled, and the whistle blew;
95 Then in a bodkin graced her mother's hairs,
Which long she wore, and now Belinda wears.)
    "Boast not my fall," he cried, "insulting foe!
Thou by some other shalt be laid as low.
Nor think to die dejects my lofty mind:
100 All that I dread is leaving you behind!
Rather than so, ah, let me still survive,
And burn in Cupid's flames—but burn alive."
    "Restore the Lock!" she cries; and all around
"Restore the Lock!" the vaulted roofs rebound.
105 Not fierce Othello in so loud a strain
Roared for the handkerchief that caused his pain.[4]
But see how oft ambitious aims are crossed,
And chiefs contend till all the prize is lost!
The lock, obtained with guilt, and kept with pain,
110 In every place is sought, but sought in vain:
With such a prize no mortal must be blessed,
So Heaven decrees! with Heaven who can contest?
    Some thought it mounted to the lunar sphere,
Since all things lost on earth are treasured there.
115 There heroes' wits are kept in ponderous vases,
And beaux' in snuffboxes and tweezer cases.
There broken vows and deathbed alms are found,
And lovers' hearts with ends of riband bound,
The courtier's promises, and sick man's prayers,
120 The smiles of harlots, and the tears of heirs,
Cages for gnats, and chains to yoke a flea,
Dried butterflies, and tomes of casuistry.
    But trust the Muse—she saw it upward rise,
Though marked by none but quick, poetic eyes
125 (So Rome's great founder to the heavens withdrew,[5]
To Proculus alone confessed in view);
A sudden star, it shot through liquid° air,   clear
And drew behind a radiant trail of hair.
Not Berenice's locks first rose so bright,[6]
130 The heavens bespangling with disheveled light.
The Sylphs behold it kindling as it flies,
And pleased pursue its progress through the skies.

---

3. Here an ornamental hairpin. Its history suggests that of Agamemnon's scepter in *Iliad* 2. "Seal rings" (line 91) are for impressing seals on letters and legal documents.
4. In *Othello* 3.4.

5. Romulus was borne heavenward in a storm cloud and later deified.
6. The locks that the Egyptian queen Berenice dedicated to her husband's safe return were turned into a constellation.

This the beau monde shall from the Mall[7] survey,
And hail with music its propitious ray.
135 This the blest lover shall for Venus take,
And send up vows from Rosamonda's Lake.
This Partridge soon shall view in cloudless skies,
When next he looks through Galileo's eyes;[8]
And hence the egregious wizard shall foredoom
140 The fate of Louis, and the fall of Rome.
    Then cease, bright nymph! to mourn thy ravished hair,
Which adds new glory to the shining sphere!
Not all the tresses that fair head can boast,
Shall draw such envy as the Lock you lost.
145 For, after all the murders of your eye,
When, after millions slain, yourself shall die:
When those fair suns shall set, as set they must,
And all those tresses shall be laid in dust,
This Lock the Muse shall consecrate to fame,
150 And 'midst the stars inscribe Belinda's name.

1712   1714

Epistle to Miss Blount[9]

On Her Leaving the Town, After the Coronation

As some fond virgin, whom her mother's care
Drags from the town to wholesome country air,
Just when she learns to roll a melting eye,
And hear a spark,[1] yet think no danger nigh;
5 From the dear man unwilling she must sever,
Yet takes one kiss before she parts forever:
Thus from the world fair Zephalinda[2] flew,
Saw others happy, and with sighs withdrew;
Not that their pleasures caused her discontent;
10 She sighed not that they stayed, but that she went.
    She went to plain-work,° and to purling[3] brooks,   needlework
Old-fashioned halls, dull aunts, and croaking rooks:[4]
She went from opera, park, assembly, play,
To morning walks, and prayers three hours a day;
15 To part her time 'twixt reading and bohea,[5]
To muse, and spill her solitary tea,
Or o'er cold coffee trifle with the spoon,
Count the slow clock, and dine exact at noon;
Divert her eyes with pictures in the fire,
20 Hum half a tune, tell stories to the squire;
Up to her godly garret after seven,
There starve and pray, for that's the way to heaven.
    Some squire, perhaps, you take delight to rack,°   torture

---

7. A fashionable walk that (like Rosamonda's Lake [line 136]) was in St. James's Park.
8. "Galileo's eyes": the telescope. "Partridge": A London astrologer who predicted calamities for the enemies of England and Protestantism.
9. Teresa Blount, sister of Pope's lifelong friend Martha Blount. The "coronation" was that of

George I (1714).
1. Beau, gallant.
2. A fanciful name for Miss Blount.
3. Gently rippling.
4. Crowlike birds.
5. A high-grade Chinese tea.

Whose game is whist, whose treat a toast in sack;°   *wine, sherry*
25 Who visits with a gun, presents you birds,
Then gives a smacking buss, and cries—"No words!"
Or with his hounds comes hollowing from the stable,
Makes love with nods and knees beneath a table;
Whose laughs are hearty, though his jests are coarse,
30 And loves you best of all things—but his horse.
     In some fair evening, on your elbow laid,
You dream of triumphs in the rural shade;
In pensive thought recall the fancied scene,
See coronations rise on every green:
35 Before you pass the imaginary sights
Of lords and earls and dukes and gartered knights,
While the spread fan o'ershades your closing eyes;
Then gives one flirt, and all the vision flies.
Thus vanish scepters, coronets, and balls,
40 And leave you in lone woods, or empty walls!
     So when your slave,[6] at some dear idle time
(Not plagued with headaches or the want of rhyme)
Stands in the streets, abstracted from the crew,
And while he seems to study, thinks of you;
45 Just when his fancy points[7] your sprightly eyes,
Or sees the blush of soft Parthenia[8] rise,
Gay[9] pats my shoulder, and you vanish quite;
Streets, chairs,° and coxcombs[1] rush upon my sight;   *sedan chairs*
Vexed to be still in town, I knit my brow,
50 Look sour, and hum a tune—as you may now.

                            1717

Epistle to Dr. Arbuthnot[2]

P. Shut, shut the door, good John![3] (fatigued, I said),
Tie up the knocker, say I'm sick, I'm dead.
The Dog Star[4] rages! nay 'tis past a doubt
All Bedlam, or Parnassus,[5] is let out:
5 Fire in each eye, and papers in each hand,
They rave, recite, and madden round the land.
     What walls can guard me, or what shades can hide?
They pierce my thickets, through my grot[6] they glide,
By land, by water, they renew the charge,
10 They stop the chariot, and they board the barge.[7]
No place is sacred, not the church is free;
Even Sunday shines no Sabbath day to me:

6. I.e., the speaker, Pope.
7. Focuses or zeroes in on.
8. Like Zephalinda (line 7), a fanciful name for Miss Blount.
9. John Gay, the poet, Pope's friend.
1. Dandies, fops.
2. John Arbuthnot, former physician to Queen Anne, was Pope's physician, and friend and literary collaborator of Pope, Swift, and Gay. He had asked Pope to moderate his attacks on his personal and literary enemies and was hence a logical person to whom to address an apology for writing satire.
3. Pope's servant, John Serle.
4. The summer star Sirius, attendant upon crazing heat. In ancient Rome, late summer was a season for public recitations of poetry.
5. Bedlam is a hospital for the insane; Mt. Parnassus, the haunt of the Muses.
6. Pope's "grotto," one entrance to the grounds of his villa at Twickenham.
7. Pope often traveled from Twickenham to London by water.

Then from the Mint[8] walks forth the man of rhyme,
Happy to catch me just at dinner time.
15   Is there a parson, much bemused in beer,
A maudlin poetess, a rhyming peer,
A clerk foredoomed his father's soul to cross,
Who pens a stanza when he should engross?[9]
Is there who,[1] locked from ink and paper, scrawls
20   With desperate charcoal round his darkened walls?
All fly to Twit'nam,° and in humble strain   Twickenham
Apply to me to keep them mad or vain.
Arthur,[2] whose giddy son neglects the laws,
Imputes to me and my damned works the cause:
25   Poor Cornus[3] sees his frantic wife elope,
And curses wit, and poetry, and Pope.
Friend to my life (which did not you prolong,
The world had wanted many an idle song)
What drop or nostrum° can this plague remove?   drug
30   Or which must end me, a fool's wrath or love?
A dire dilemma! either way I'm sped,°   ruined
If foes, they write, if friends, they read me dead.
Seized and tied down to judge, how wretched I!
Who can't be silent, and who will not lie.
35   To laugh were want of goodness and of grace,
And to be grave exceeds all power of face.
I sit with sad° civility, I read   sober
With honest anguish and an aching head,
And drop at last, but in unwilling ears,
40   This saving counsel, "Keep your piece nine years."[4]
"Nine years!" cries he, who high in Drury Lane,[5]
Lulled by soft zephyrs through the broken pane,
Rhymes ere he wakes, and prints before term°   the publishing season
      ends,
Obliged by hunger and request of friends:
45   "The piece, you think, is incorrect? why, take it,
I'm all submission, what you'd have it, make it."
Three things another's modest wishes bound,
My friendship, and a prologue, and ten pound.
Pitholeon[6] sends to me: "You know his Grace,
50   I want a patron; ask him for a place."
Pitholeon libeled me—"but here's a letter
Informs you, sir, 'twas when he knew no better.
Dare you refuse him? Curll[7] invites to dine,
He'll write a *Journal*, or he'll turn divine."[8]
55   Bless me! a packet.—" 'Tis a stranger sues,

8. A sanctuary for debtors. They emerged on Sunday, being everywhere immune from arrest on that day.
9. Prepare legal documents.
1. I.e., one who.
2. Arthur Moore, father of James Moore Smythe, a playwright who had plagiarized some lines from Pope.
3. From Latin *cornu*: "horn"; hence a cuckold.
4. Horace's advice (*Ars Poetica*, 386–89).
5. The theater district, where the speaker occupies a garret.
6. "A foolish poet of Rhodes, who pretended much to Greek" [Pope's note]. He stands for Leonard Welsted, translator of Longinus and an enemy of Pope's.
7. Edmund Curll, an unscrupulous publisher; the bookseller principally derided in the *Dunciad*.
8. Referring to attacks on Pope in *The London Journal* and (perhaps) to Welsted's theological writing.

A virgin tragedy, an orphan Muse."
If I dislike it, "Furies, death, and rage!"
If I approve, "Commend it to the stage."
There (thank my stars) my whole commission ends,
60 The players and I are, luckily, no friends.
Fired that the house° reject him, " 'Sdeath, I'll print it,   *playhouse*
And shame the fools—Your interest, sir, with Lintot!"[9]
Lintot, dull rogue, will think your price too much.
"Not, sir, if you revise it, and retouch."
65 All my demurs but double his attacks;
At last he whispers, "Do; and we go snacks."°   *shares*
Glad of a quarrel, straight I clap the door,
"Sir, let me see your works and you no more."
'Tis sung, when Midas' ears began to spring
70 (Midas, a sacred person and a king),
His very minister who spied them first
(Some say his queen) was forced to speak, or burst.[1]
And is not mine, my friend, a sorer case,
When every coxcomb perks them in my face?
75 A. Good friend, forbear! you deal in dangerous things.
I'd never name queens, ministers, or kings;
Keep close to ears, and those let asses prick;
'Tis nothing— P. Nothing? if they bite and kick?
Out with it, *Dunciad!* let the secret pass,
80 That secret to each fool, that he's an ass:
The truth once told (and wherefore should we lie?)
The queen of Midas slept, and so may I.
You think this cruel? take it for a rule,
No creature smarts so little as a fool.
85 Let peals of laughter, Codrus![2] round thee break,
Thou unconcerned canst hear the mighty crack.
Pit, box, and gallery in convulsions hurled,
Thou stand'st unshook amidst a bursting world.
Who shames a scribbler? break one cobweb through,
90 He spins the slight, self-pleasing thread anew:
Destroy his fib or sophistry, in vain;
The creature's at his dirty work again,
Throned in the center of his thin designs,
Proud of a vast extent of flimsy lines.
95 Whom have I hurt? has poet yet or peer
Lost the arched eyebrow or Parnassian[3] sneer?
And has not Colley[4] still his lord and whore?
His butchers Henley? his freemasons Moore?[5]
Does not one table Bavius still admit?
100 Still to one bishop Philips seem a wit?

9. Bernard Lintot, an early publisher of Pope's.
1. King Midas, preferring Pan's music to Apollo's, was given ass's ears by the affronted god. His barber (in Chaucer's version of the tale, his wife) discovered the ears and, fairly bursting with the secret, whispered it into a hole in the ground. It is suggested that the prime minister (Walpole) and Queen Caroline know that George II is an ass.
2. A poet ridiculed by Virgil and Juvenal.
3. Pertaining to poetry and the Muses.

4. Colley Cibber, poet laureate.
5. John Henley ("Orator Henley") was an independent preacher with a mass following. James Moore Smythe was a member of the Masonic order. Bavius (line 99) is a bad poet referred to by Virgil. The bishop of Armagh employed Ambrose Philips (line 100 [called "Namby-Pamby" by the wits]) as his secretary. "Sappho" (line 101) is the poet Lady Mary Wortley Montagu.

Still Sappho—— A. Hold! for God's sake—you'll offend.
No names—be calm—learn prudence of a friend.
I too could write, and I am twice as tall;
But foes like these!—— P. One flatterer's worse than all.
105 Of all mad creatures, if the learn'd are right,
It is the slaver° kills, and not the bite.   spittle
A fool quite angry is quite innocent:
Alas! 'tis ten times worse when they repent.
    One dedicates in high heroic prose,
110 And ridicules beyond a hundred foes;
One from all Grub Street[6] will my fame defend,
And, more abusive, calls himself my friend.
This prints my letters,[7] that expects a bribe,
And others roar aloud, "Subscribe, subscribe!"[8]
115   There are, who to my person pay their court:
I cough like Horace, and, though lean, am short;
Ammon's great son° one shoulder had too high,   Alexander the Great
Such Ovid's nose, and "Sir! you have an eye—"
Go on, obliging creatures, make me see
120 All that disgraced my betters met in me.
Say for my comfort, languishing in bed,
"Just so immortal Maro° held his head":   Virgil
And when I die, be sure you let me know
Great Homer died three thousand years ago.
125   Why did I write? what sin to me unknown
Dipped me in ink, my parents', or my own?
As yet a child, nor yet a fool to fame,
I lisped in numbers, for the numbers came.
I left no calling for this idle trade,
130 No duty broke, no father disobeyed.
The Muse but served to ease some friend, not wife,
To help me through this long disease, my life,
To second, Arbuthnot! thy art and care,
And teach the being° you preserved, to bear.   life
135   A. But why then publish? P. Granville the polite,[9]
And knowing Walsh, would tell me I could write;
Well-natured Garth inflamed with early praise,
And Congreve loved, and Swift endured my lays;
The courtly Talbot, Somers, Sheffield, read;
140 Even mitered Rochester[1] would nod the head,
And St. John's[2] self (great Dryden's friends before)
With open arms received one poet more.
Happy my studies, when by these approved!
Happier their author, when by these beloved!
145 From these the world will judge of men and books,
Not from the Burnets, Oldmixons, and Cookes.[3]
    Soft were my numbers; who could take offense
While pure description held the place of sense?

---

6. The traditional haunt of hack writers.
7. As Curll had done without permission.
8. Pay for copies in advance of publication.
9. There follow the names of poets and men of letters, Pope's early friends. They were literary elder statesmen, chiefly, who had befriended Dry-
den in the preceding century.
1. The bishop of Rochester.
2. Pronounced *sinjin*.
3. Thomas Burnet, John Oldmixon, and Arthur Cooke had all attacked Pope or his works.

Like gentle Fanny's[4] was my flowery theme,
150 A painted mistress, or a purling stream.
Yet then did Gildon[5] draw his venal quill;
I wished the man a dinner, and sat still.
Yet then did Dennis[6] rave in furious fret;
I never answered, I was not in debt.
155 If want provoked, or madness made them print,
I waged no war with Bedlam or the Mint.[7]
     Did some more sober critic come abroad?
If wrong, I smiled; if right, I kissed the rod.
Pains, reading, study are their just pretense,
160 And all they want is spirit, taste, and sense.
Commas and points they set exactly right,
And 'twere a sin to rob them of their mite.
Yet ne'er one sprig of laurel graced these ribalds,°   *rascals*
From slashing Bentley down to piddling Tibbalds.[8]
165 Each wight° who reads not, and but scans and spells,   *man*
Each word-catcher that lives on syllables,
Even such small critics some regard may claim,
Preserved in Milton's or in Shakespeare's name.
Pretty! in amber to observe the forms
170 Of hairs, or straws, or dirt, or grubs, or worms!
The things, we know, are neither rich nor rare,
But wonder how the devil they got there.
     Were others angry? I excused them too;
Well might they rage; I gave them but their due.
175 A man's true merit 'tis not hard to find;
But each man's secret standard in his mind,
That casting weight[9] pride adds to emptiness,
This, who can gratify? for who can guess?
The bard whom pilfered pastorals renown,
180 Who turns a Persian tale for half a crown,[1]
Just writes to make his barrenness appear,
And strains from hard-bound brains eight lines a year:
He, who still wanting, though he lives on theft,
Steals much, spends little, yet has nothing left;
185 And he who now to sense, now nonsense leaning,
Means not, but blunders round about a meaning:
And he whose fustian's° so sublimely bad,   *pretentious writing's*
It is not poetry, but prose run mad:
All these, my modest satire bade translate,
190 And owned that nine such poets made a Tate.[2]
How did they fume, and stamp, and roar, and chafe!
And swear, not Addison[3] himself was safe.

---

4. Lord Hervey, satirized as Sporus in lines 305 ff.
5. Charles Gildon, a critic who had, as Pope believed, written against him "venally," to curry favor with Addison.
6. John Dennis, who wrote a furious condemnation of Pope's *Essay on Criticism.*
7. See note 8 to line 13, above.
8. Richard Bentley, a classical scholar, had edited *Paradise Lost* with undue license on the grounds that Milton was blind and never saw his text. Lewis Theobald, no wit but a closer scholar than Pope, had exposed the faults of Pope's edition of Shakespeare in a subsequent edition of his own.
9. Weight tipping the scales.
1. Ambrose Philips (named in line 100), who had competed with the youthful Pope as a pastoral poet; author of *Persian Tales.*
2. Nahum Tate, successor to Dryden as poet laureate.
3. Joseph Addison, coauthor of *The Tatler* and *The Spectator*, and arbiter of polite taste.

Peace to all such! but were there one whose fires
True Genius kindles, and fair Fame inspires;
195　Blessed with each talent and each art to please,
And born to write, converse, and live with ease:
Should such a man, too fond to rule alone,
Bear, like the Turk, no brother near the throne;[4]
View him with scornful, yet with jealous eyes,
200　And hate for arts that caused himself to rise;
Damn with faint praise, assent with civil leer,
And without sneering, teach the rest to sneer;
Willing to wound, and yet afraid to strike,
Just hint a fault, and hesitate dislike;
205　Alike reserved to blame or to commend,
A timorous foe, and a suspicious friend;
Dreading even fools; by flatterers besieged,
And so obliging that he ne'er obliged;
Like Cato, give his little senate laws,[5]
210　And sit attentive to his own applause;
While wits and Templars° every sentence raise, 　　　　*law students*
And wonder with a foolish face of praise —
Who but must laugh, if such a man there be?
Who would not weep, if Atticus[6] were he?
215　　What though my name stood rubric° on the walls? 　　*in red letters*
Or plastered posts, with claps,° in capitals? 　　　　　　　*posters*
Or smoking forth, a hundred hawkers' load,
On wings of winds came flying all abroad?
I sought no homage from the race that write;
220　I kept, like Asian monarchs, from their sight:
Poems I heeded (now berhymed so long)
No more than thou, great George![7] a birthday song.
I ne'er with wits or witlings passed my days
To spread about the itch of verse and praise;
225　Nor like a puppy daggled° through the town 　　　　*dragged about*
To fetch and carry sing-song up and down;
Nor at rehearsals sweat, and mouthed, and cried,
With handkerchief and orange at my side;
But sick of fops, and poetry, and prate,
230　To Bufo left the whole Castalian state.[8]
　　Proud as Apollo on his forkèd hill,[9]
Sat full-blown Bufo, puffed by every quill;
Fed with soft dedication all day long,
Horace and he went hand in hand in song.
235　His library (where busts of poets dead
And a true Pindar stood without a head)
Received of wits an undistinguished race,
Who first his judgment asked, and then a place:

4. The Ottoman emperors, Europeans believed, regularly killed their principal kinsmen upon ascending the throne.
5. Addison (author of the immensely popular tragedy *Cato*) presided over an admiring company of political and literary partisans at Button's Coffee House.
6. A friend of Cicero's; here a pseudonym for Addison.
7. George II.
8. Pope leaves Bufo the whole republic of letters, named from the spring Castalia, which was sacred to Apollo and the Muses. Bufo is perhaps a composite of Lord Halifax and "Bubo," Bubb Dodington.
9. The twin peaks of Parnassus.

Much they extolled his pictures, much his seat,°   estate
240 And flattered every day, and some days eat:°   ate
Till grown more frugal in his riper days,
He paid some bards with port, and some with praise;
To some a dry° rehearsal was assigned,   *without performance*
And others (harder still) he paid in kind.[1]
245 Dryden alone (what wonder?) came not nigh;
Dryden alone escaped this judging eye:
But still the great have kindness in reserve;
He helped to bury whom he helped to starve.
      May some choice patron bless each gray goose quill!°   *quill pen*
250 May every Bavius have his Bufo still!
So when a statesman wants a day's defense,
Or Envy holds a whole week's war with Sense,
Or simple Pride for flattery makes demands,
May dunce by dunce be whistled off my hands!
255 Blessed be the great! for those they take away,
And those they left me—for they left me Gay;[2]
Left me to see neglected genius bloom,
Neglected die, and tell it on his tomb;
Of all thy blameless life the sole return
260 My verse, and Queensberry weeping o'er thy urn!
Oh, let me live my own, and die so too!
("To live and die is all I have to do")[3]
Maintain a poet's dignity and ease,
And see what friends, and read what books I please;
265 Above a patron, though I condescend
Some times to call a minister my friend.
I was not born for courts or great affairs;
I pay my debts, believe, and say my prayers,
Can sleep without a poem in my head,
270 Nor know if Dennis be alive or dead.
      Why am I asked what next shall see the light?
Heavens! was I born for nothing but to write?
Has life no joys for me? or (to be grave)
Have I no friend to serve, no soul to save?
275 "I found him close with Swift"—"Indeed? no doubt,"
Cries prating Balbus, "something will come out."
'Tis all in vain, deny it as I will.
"No, such a genius never can lie still,"
And then for mine obligingly mistakes
280 The first lampoon Sir Will or Bubo[4] makes.
Poor guiltless I! and can I choose but smile,
When every coxcomb knows me by my style?
      Cursed be the verse, how well soe'er it flow,
That tends to make one worthy man my foe,
285 Give Virtue scandal, Innocence a fear,
Or from the soft-eyed virgin steal a tear!
But he who hurts a harmless neighbor's peace,

1. I.e., he read them his poetry in turn.   3. Pope quotes Denham's "Of Prudence."
2. John Gay, author of *The Beggar's Opera*, associ-   4. Sir William Yonge or Bubb Dodington. Both
ate of Pope and Swift; befriended (line 260) by the   were Pope's political adversaries as well as, in some
duke and duchess of Queensberry.   degree, silly men.

Insults fallen worth, or Beauty in distress,
Who loves a lie, lame Slander helps about,
290 Who writes a libel, or who copies out:
That fop whose pride affects a patron's name,
Yet absent, wounds an author's honest fame;
Who can your merit selfishly approve,
And show the sense of it without the love;
295 Who has the vanity to call you friend,
Yet wants the honor, injured, to defend;
Who tells whate'er you think, whate'er you say,
And, if he lie not, must at least betray:
Who to the dean and silver bell can swear,
300 And sees at Cannons what was never there:[5]
Who reads but with a lust to misapply,
Make satire a lampoon, and fiction, lie:
A lash like mine no honest man shall dread,
But all such babbling blockheads in his stead.
305   Let Sporus[6] tremble —— A. What? that thing of silk,
Sporus, that mere white curd of ass's milk?
Satire or sense, alas! can Sporus feel?
Who breaks a butterfly upon a wheel?
        P. Yet let me flap this bug with gilded wings,
310 This painted child of dirt, that stinks and stings;
Whose buzz the witty and the fair annoys,
Yet wit ne'er tastes, and beauty ne'er enjoys;
So well-bred spaniels civilly delight
In mumbling of the game they dare not bite.
315 Eternal smiles his emptiness betray,
As shallow streams run dimpling all the way.
Whether in florid impotence he speaks,
And, as the prompter breathes, the puppet squeaks;
Or at the ear of Eve,[7] familiar toad,
320 Half froth, half venom, spits himself abroad,
In puns, or politics, or tales, or lies,
Or spite, or smut, or rhymes, or blasphemies.
His wit all seesaw between *that* and *this*, ⎫
Now high, now low, now master up, now miss, ⎬
325 And he himself one vile antithesis.   ⎭
Amphibious thing! that acting either part,
The trifling head or the corrupted heart,
Fop at the toilet, flatterer at the board,
Now trips° a lady, and now struts a lord.   *walks like*
330 Eve's tempter thus the rabbins° have expressed,   *Hebrew scholars*
A cherub's face, a reptile all the rest;
Beauty that shocks you, parts° that none will trust,   *talents*
Wit that can creep, and pride that licks the dust.
        Not Fortune's worshiper, nor Fashion's fool,

---

5. In his *Epistle to Burlington*, Pope satirized "Timon's Villa," an estate where a silver bell and an obsequious dean invite worshipers to an overstuffed chapel. Mischief-makers had identified this estate with Cannons, the ostentatious home of Pope's well-wisher the duke of Chandos.
6. Roman eunuch, victim of the Emperor Nero's perversions; in the poem, Lord Hervey, a foppish and effeminate courtier who was Pope's personal, political, and literary enemy. He attested his frailty by drinking ass's milk as a tonic.
7. Like Satan in Eden (*Paradise Lost* 4.790 ff.). Hervey was Queen Caroline's confidant; the word "familiar" suggests a demonic ministrant.

335   Not Lucre's° madman, nor Ambition's tool,   *Money's*
      Not proud, nor servile, be one poet's praise,
      That if he pleased, he pleased by manly ways:
      That flattery, even to kings, he held a shame,
      And thought a lie in verse or prose the same:
340   That not in fancy's maze he wandered long,
      But stooped[8] to truth, and moralized his song:
      That not for fame, but Virtue's better end,
      He stood the furious foe, the timid friend,
      The damning critic, half approving wit,
345   The coxcomb hit, or fearing to be hit;
      Laughed at the loss of friends he never had,
      The dull, the proud, the wicked, and the mad;
      The distant threats of vengeance on his head,
      The blow unfelt, the tear he never shed;
350   The tale revived, the lie so oft o'erthrown,
      The imputed trash, and dullness not his own;
      The morals blackened when the writings 'scape,
      The libeled person, and the pictured shape;[9]
      Abuse on all he loved, or loved him, spread,
355   A friend in exile, or a father dead;
      The whisper,[1] that to greatness still too near,
      Perhaps yet vibrates on his sovereign's ear—
      Welcome for thee, fair Virtue! all the past!
      For thee, fair Virtue! welcome even the last!
360   A. But why insult the poor, affront the great?
      P. A knave's a knave to me in every state:
      Alike my scorn, if he succeed or fail,
      Sporus at court, or Japhet[2] in a jail,
      A hireling scribbler, or a hireling peer,
365   Knight of the post[3] corrupt, or of the shire,
      If on a pillory, or near a throne,
      He gain his prince's ear, or lose his own.
          Yet soft by nature, more a dupe than wit,
      Sappho can tell you how this man was bit:°   *deceived*
370   This dreaded satirist Dennis will confess
      Foe to his pride, but friend to his distress:[4]
      So humble, he has knocked at Tibbald's door,
      Has drunk with Cibber, nay, has rhymed for Moore.
      Full ten years slandered, did he once reply?
375   Three thousand suns went down on Welsted's lie.[5]
      To please a mistress one[6] aspersed° his life;   *maligned*
      He lashed him not, but let her be his wife.
      Let Budgell charge low Grub Street on his quill,
      And write whate'er he pleased, except his will;[7]
380   Let the two Curlls, of town and court,[8] abuse

8. Swooped down, perceiving prey (a term from falconry).
9. Cartoons were drawn of Pope's hunched posture.
1. Hervey's whisper to Queen Caroline.
2. Japhet Crook, a forger; his ears were cropped for his crime (line 367).
3. "Knight of the post": professional witness.
4. Pope contributed to a benefit performance for the aging Dennis.
5. Welsted had accused Pope of causing the death of a lady.
6. William Windham.
7. Budgell (perhaps falsely) attributed to Pope a squib in the *Grub-Street Journal* charging that Budgell had forged a will.
8. Edmund Curll, the publisher; and Lord Hervey.

His father, mother, body, soul, and muse.
Yet why? that father held it for a rule,
It was a sin to call our neighbor fool;
That harmless mother thought no wife a whore:
385   Hear this, and spare his family, James Moore![9]
Unspotted names, and memorable long,
If there be force in virtue, or in song.
     Of gentle blood (part shed in honor's cause,
While yet in Britain honor had applause)
390   Each parent sprung—— A. What fortune, pray?—— P. Their own,
And better got than Bestia's[1] from the throne.
Born to no pride, inheriting no strife,
Nor marrying discord in a noble wife,
Stranger to civil and religious rage,
395   The good man walked innoxious° through his age.   *harmless*
No courts he saw, no suits would ever try,
Nor dared an oath, nor hazarded a lie.[2]
Unlearned, he knew no schoolman's subtle art,
No language but the language of the heart.
400   By nature honest, by experience wise,
Healthy by temperance, and by exercise;
His life, though long, to sickness passed unknown,
His death was instant, and without a groan.
Oh, grant me thus to live, and thus to die!
405   Who sprung from kings shall know less joy than I.
     O friend! may each domestic bliss be thine!
Be no unpleasing melancholy mine:
Me, let the tender office long engage,
To rock the cradle of reposing Age,
410   With lenient arts extend a mother's breath,[3]
Make Languor smile, and smooth the bed of Death,
Explore the thought, explain the asking eye,
And keep a while one parent from the sky!
On cares like these if length of days attend,
415   May Heaven, to bless those days, preserve my friend,
Preserve him social, cheerful, and serene,
And just as rich as when he served a Queen![4]
   A. Whether that blessing be denied or given,
Thus far was right—the rest belongs to Heaven.

1735

The Universal Prayer

Father of all! in every age,
   In every clime adored,
By saint, by savage, and by sage,
   Jehovah, Jove, or Lord!

9. See lines 23 and 373.
1. A Roman consul who was bribed to arrange a dishonorable peace; in the poem, probably the duke of Marlborough.
2. He did not take the special oath required of Catholics wanting to enter public life or the professions, nor did he evade by falsehood the restric-

tions on Catholics.
3. Pope was nursing his sick mother when he first wrote these lines.
4. Arbuthnot, who had sought no professional profit as physician to Queen Anne, continued to earn the same income after her death.

5   Thou Great First Cause,[5] least understood:
     Who all my sense confined
   To know but this—that thou art good,
     And that myself am blind:

   Yet gave me, in this dark estate,
10   To see the good from ill;
   And binding Nature fast in fate,
     Left free the human will.

   What conscience dictates to be done,
     Or warns me not to do,
15   This, teach me more than Hell to shun,
     That, more than Heaven pursue.[6]

   What blessings thy free bounty gives,
     Let me not cast away;
   For God is paid when man receives,
20   To enjoy is to obey.

   Yet not to earth's contracted span,
     Thy goodness let me bound,
   Or think thee Lord alone of man,
     When thousand worlds are round:

25   Let not this weak, unknowing hand
     Presume thy bolts to throw,[7]
   And deal damnation round the land,
     On each I judge thy foe.

   If I am right, thy grace impart,
30   Still in the right to stay;
   If I am wrong, oh teach my heart
     To find that better way.

   Save me alike from foolish pride,
     Or impious discontent,
35   At aught thy wisdom has denied,
     Or aught thy goodness lent.

   Teach me to feel another's woe,
     To hide the fault I see;
   That mercy I to others show,
40   That mercy show to me.

   Mean though I am, not wholly so
     Since quickened by thy breath;
   Oh lead me wheresoe'er I go,
     Through this day's life or death.

---

5. God considered as the first principle, creator of all creatures, cause of all truth and goodness.
6. I.e., teach me to refine my conscience here on Earth instead of concerning myself overmuch with the afterlife.
7. Zeus's weapons, thunderbolts.

45   This day, be bread and peace[8] my lot:
     All else beneath the sun,
     Thou know'st if best bestowed or not,
     And let thy will be done.

     To thee, whose temple is all space,
50   Whose altar, earth, sea, skies!
     One chorus let all being raise!
     All Nature's incense rise!

ca. 1715   1738

Impromptu

To Lady Winchelsea,
Occasioned by four Satirical Verses on Women Wits,
In The Rape of the Lock[9]

In vain you boast poetic names of yore,
And cite those Sapphos we admire no more:[1]
Fate doomed the fall of every female wit;
But doomed it then, when first Ardelia[2] writ.
5 Of all examples by the world confessed,
I knew Ardelia could not quote the best;
Who, like her mistress on Britannia's throne,
Fights and subdues in quarrels not her own.[3]
To write their praise you but in vain essay;
10 Even while you write, you take that praise away.
Light to the stars the sun does thus restore,
but shines himself till they are seen no more.

ca. 1715   1741

From The Dunciad

[The Triumph of Dulness][4]

In vain, in vain,—the all-composing hour
Resistless° falls: the Muse obeys the power.   *irresistibly*

---

8. Perhaps an allusion to the Lord's Prayer.
9. Ostensibly written casually, without premeditation ("impromptu"), this poem to Anne Finch, countess of Winchilsea, replies to some verses she had sent Pope in response to Canto IV, lines 59–62, of *The Rape of the Lock* (see p. 558). Since these lines, from the "Cave of Spleen" episode, are directed specifically against female poets, and Anne Finch was herself the author of a poem entitled "The Spleen" (pp. 516–19), it seems likely that she correctly read Pope's verses as containing a comic slur directed at her. Her initial response to Pope has not survived, but her witty "Answer" to this "Impromptu" was printed in 1717 (p. 521). In a letter to a male friend written in 1713, Pope complained that the experience of hearing Lady Win-

chilsea read her poetry at a dinner party gave him a headache—an ailment that in the *Rape* he associates only with women. For another view of spleen—an ailment similar to depression—see the selection from Matthew Green's poem on that subject (p. 582).
1. Applies to all female poets the name of a Greek poet born in 612 B.C.
2. The name under which Anne Finch sometimes wrote.
3. An allusion to Queen Anne (reigned 1702–14), who involved England in wars (of the Spanish Succession) that Pope viewed as irrelevant to the national interest.
4. *Dunciad* (B) 4.627–56.

She comes! she comes![5] the sable throne behold
630 Of *Night* primeval, and of *Chaos* old![6]
Before her, *Fancy*'s gilded clouds decay,
And all its varying rainbows die away.
Wit shoots in vain its momentary fires,
The meteor drops, and in a flash expires.
635 As one by one, at dread Medea's strain,
The sickening stars fade off the ethereal plain;[7]
As Argus' eyes by Hermes' wand oppressed,
Closed one by one to everlasting rest;[8]
Thus at her felt approach, and secret might,
640 *Art* after *Art* goes out, and all is night.
See skulking *Truth* to her old cavern fled,[9]
Mountains of casuistry heaped o'er her head!
Philosophy, that leaned on Heaven before,
Shrinks to her second cause,[1] and is no more.
645 *Physic*° of *Metaphysic* begs defense,   natural science
And *Metaphysic* calls for aid on *Sense*!
See *Mystery*° to *Mathematics* fly!   mystical knowledge
In vain! they gaze, turn giddy, rave, and die.
Religion blushing veils her sacred fires,
650 And unawares *Mortality* expires.
Nor public flame, nor private, dares to shine;
Nor human spark is left, nor glimpse divine!
Lo! thy dread empire, Chaos is restored;
Light dies before thy uncreating word:[2]
655 Thy hand, great Anarch! lets the curtain fall;
And universal darkness buries all.

1743

LADY MARY WORTLEY MONTAGU

1689–1762

The Lover: A Ballad

At length, by so much importunity pressed,
Take, C,——[1] at once, the inside of my breast;
This stupid indifference so often you blame
Is not owing to nature, to fear, or to shame;

---

5. Dulness, the center of a mock-apocalyptic vision in which the light of the arts and sciences is extinguished.
6. Milton, in *Paradise Lost* 1.543, describes the elements separating heaven and hell as "Chaos and old Night," or disorder and darkness, the first materials of the cosmos.
7. In Seneca's *Medea*, the stars obey the curse of Medea, a magician and avenger.
8. Hermes, the Greek gods' messenger, charmed the hundred-eyed watchman, Argus, to sleep and then killed him.

9. "Alluding to the saying of Democritus, that Truth lay at the bottom of a deep well" [Pope's note].
1. In classical philosophy, God is defined as the first cause of all things. Under the sway of Dulness, a materialistic explanation (or "second cause") is substituted.
2. As opposed to God's first creating words in Genesis, "Let there be light."
1. Probably Richard Chandler, a friend of Lady Mary. The ideal "lover" of the title, however, is not to be identified with any particular person.

5   I am not as cold as a Virgin in lead,[2]
Nor is Sunday's sermon so strong in my head;
I know but too well how time flies along,
That we live but few years and yet fewer are young.

But I hate to be cheated, and never will buy
10 Long years of repentance for moments of joy.
Oh was there a man (but where shall I find
Good sense and good nature so equally joined?)
Would value his pleasure, contribute to mine,
Not meanly would boast, nor would lewdly design,°   *plot*
15 Not over severe, yet not stupidly vain,
For I would have the power though not give the pain;

No pedant yet learnèd, not rakehelly° gay   *like a libertine*
Or laughing because he has nothing to say,
To all my whole sex obliging and free,
20 Yet never be fond of any but me;
In public preserve the decorum that's just,
And show in his eyes he is true to his trust,
Then rarely approach, and respectfully bow,
Yet not fulsomely pert, nor yet foppishly low.

25 But when the long hours of public are past
And we meet with champagne and a chicken at last,
May every fond pleasure that hour endear,
Be banished afar both discretion and fear,
Forgetting or scorning the airs of the crowd
30 He may cease to be formal, and I to be proud,
Till lost in the joy we confess that we live,
And he may be rude, and yet I may forgive.

And that my delight may be solidly fixed,
Let the friend and the lover be handsomely mixed,
35 In whose tender bosom my soul might confide,
Whose kindness can sooth me, whose counsel could guide.
From such a dear lover as here I describe
No danger should fright me, no millions should bribe;
But till this astonishing creature I know,
40 As I long have lived chaste, I will keep myself so.

I never will share with the wanton coquette,
Or be caught by a vain affectation of wit.
The toasters and songsters may try all their art
But never shall enter the pass of my heart.
45 I loathe the lewd rake, the dressed fopling despise;
Before such pursuers the nice° virgin flies;   *fastidious*

---

2. I.e., an image of the Virgin Mary, either as a leaden statue or as a stained-glass window framed in lead.

And as Ovid has sweetly in parables told
We harden like trees, and like rivers are cold.[3]

1747

A Receipt to Cure the Vapors[4]

I

Why will Delia thus retire,
    And idly languish life away?
While the sighing crowd admire,
    'Tis too soon for hartshorn tea:[5]

II

5   All those dismal looks and fretting
    Cannot Damon's life restore;
Long ago the worms have eat him,
    You can never see him more.

III

Once again consult your toilette,[6]
10   In the glass your face review:
So much weeping soon will spoil it,
    And no spring your charms renew.

IV

I, like you, was born a woman,
    Well I know what vapors mean:
15   The disease, alas! is common;
    Single, we have all the spleen.[7]

V

All the morals that they tell us,
    Never cured the sorrow yet:
Chuse, among the pretty fellows,
20   One of honor, youth, and wit.

VI

Prithee hear him every morning
    At the least an hour or two;
Once again at night returning—
    I believe the dose will do.

ca. 1730 1748

---

3. In Ovid's *Metamorphoses* Daphne, to escape Apollo, was turned into a laurel; and Arethusa, escaping Alpheus, became a fountain.
4. This poem was apparently written to Lady Anne Irwin, widowed eight or nine years previously and addressed here under the stereotypical name Delia. "Receipt": formula of a remedy for a disease; "vapors": a disorder supposed to be caused by exhalations within the organs of the body and characterized by depression, hypochondria, hyste-ria, and other nervous disorders. Synonymous with the malaise of "spleen" analyzed by Anne Finch (see pp. 516–19).
5. A medicinal tea made from ammonia.
6. I.e., consider your manner of dressing.
7. I.e., we alone (i.e., women only) are affected by vapors; or, alternatively, women are affected by vapors when they are "single" (i.e., without the company of a man).

Epistle from Mrs. Yonge to Her Husband[8]

Think not this paper comes with vain pretense
To move your pity, or to mourn th' offense.
Too well I know that hard obdurate heart;
No softening mercy there will take my part,
5   Nor can a woman's arguments prevail,
When even your patron's wise example fails.[9]
But this last privilege I still retain;
Th' oppressed and injured always may complain.
   Too, too severely laws of honor bind
10 The weak submissive sex of womankind.
If sighs have gained or force compelled our hand,
Deceived by art, or urged by stern command,
Whatever motive binds the fatal tie,
The judging world expects our constancy.
15   Just heaven! (for sure in heaven does justice reign,
Though tricks below that sacred name profane)
To you appealing I submit my cause,
Nor fear a judgment from impartial laws.
All bargains but conditional[1] are made;
20 The purchase void, the creditor unpaid;
Defrauded servants are from service free;
A wounded slave regains his liberty.
For wives ill used no remedy remains,
To daily racks condemned, and to eternal chains.
25   From whence is this unjust distinction grown?
Are we not formed with passions like your own?
Nature with equal fire our souls endued,
Our minds as haughty, and as warm our blood;
O'er the wide world your pleasures you pursue, ⎤
30 The change is justified by something new; ⎬
But we must sigh in silence—and be true. ⎦
Our sex's weakness you expose and blame
(Of every prattling fop the common theme),
Yet from this weakness you suppose is due
35 Sublimer virtue than your Cato[2] knew.
Had heaven designed us trials so severe,
It would have formed our tempers then to bear.
And I have borne (oh what have I not borne!)

---

8. In 1724 the notorious libertine William Yonge, separated from his wife, Mary, discovered that she (like him) had committed adultery. He sued her lover, Colonel Norton, for damages and collected £1,500. Later that year, according to the law of the time, he petitioned the Houses of Parliament for a divorce. The case was tried in public, Mrs. Yonge's love letters were read aloud, and two men testified that they had found her and Norton "together in naked bed." Yonge was granted the divorce, his wife's dowry, and the greater part of her fortune.
   Though the *Epistle* is obviously based on this sensational affair, it is also a work of imagination. Like Pope's *Eloisa to Abelard*—addressed to Lady Mary herself—it takes the form of a heroic epistle, the passionate outcry of an abandoned woman. The poet, entering into the feelings of Mrs. Yonge,

justifies her conduct with reasons both of the heart and head. The objects of her attack include the institution of marriage, which binds wives in "eternal chains"; the double standard of morality, which requires chastity from women but not men; the hypocrisy of society, which condemns the very behavior it secretly lusts after; and the craven greed and cruelty of the husband himself. But eighteenth-century women seldom dared to speak like this in public, and the *Epistle* was not published until the 1970s.

9. Sir Robert Walpole, Yonge's friend at court, was rumored to tolerate his own wife's infidelities.

1. Only conditionally.

2. The asceticism and self-discipline of the Roman statesman Cato had been emphasized in Addison's famous tragedy *Cato* (1713).

The pang of jealousy, the insults of scorn.
40 Wearied at length, I from your sight remove,
And place my future hopes in secret love.
In the gay bloom of glowing youth retired,
I quit the woman's joy to be admired,
With that small pension your hard heart allows,
45 Renounce your fortune, and release your vows.
To custom (though unjust) so much is due;
I hide my frailty from the public view.
My conscience clear, yet sensible of shame,
My life I hazard, to preserve my fame.
50 And I prefer this low inglorious state   ⎫
To vile dependence on the thing I hate— ⎬
But you pursue me to this last retreat.   ⎭
Dragged into light, my tender crime is shown
And every circumstance of fondness known.
55 Beneath the shelter of the law you stand,
And urge my ruin with a cruel hand,
While to my fault thus rigidly severe,
Tamely submissive to the man you fear.[3]
    This wretched outcast, this abandoned wife,
60 Has yet this joy to sweeten shameful life:
By your mean conduct, infamously loose,
You are at once my accuser and excuse.
Let me be damned by the censorious prude
(Stupidly dull, or spiritually lewd),
65 My hapless case will surely pity find
From every just and reasonable mind.
When to the final sentence I submit,
The lips condemn me, but their souls acquit.
    No more my husband, to your pleasures go,
70 The sweets of your recovered freedom know.
Go: court the brittle friendship of the great,
Smile at his board, or at his levee[4] wait;
And when dismissed, to madam's toilet fly,[5]
More than her chambermaids, or glasses,° lie,   mirrors
75 Tell her how young she looks, how heavenly fair,
Admire the lilies and the roses there.
Your high ambition may be gratified,
Some cousin of her own be made your bride,
And you the father of a glorious race
80 Endowed with Ch——l's strength and Low——r's face.[6]

1724   1972

3. I.e., Walpole. Lady Mary suggests that the whole political establishment of England takes sides against Mrs. Yonge.
4. Morning reception of visitors; "board": dining table.
5. It was fashionable for women like Lady Walpole to receive visitors during the last stages of dressing (their "toilet").

6. General Churchill was rumored to have had an affair with Lady Walpole; Anthony Lowther was a notorious gallant. The author implies that Yonge's next wife may be as untrue as his first. Mrs. Yonge remarried immediately after her divorce; five years later Yonge himself (whose divorce had made him rich) married the daughter of a baron.

MATTHEW GREEN
1696–1737

From The Spleen[1]

AN EPISTLE TO MR. CUTHBERT JACKSON

This motley piece to you I send,
Who always were a faithful friend;
Who, if disputes should happen hence,
Can best explain the author's sense;
5   And, anxious for the public weal,
Do, what I sing, so often feel.[2]

The want of method pray excuse,
Allowing for a vapored Muse;[3]
Nor to a narrow path confined,
10   Hedge in by rules a roving mind.

The child is genuine, you may trace
Throughout the sire's transmitted[4] face.
Nothing is stolen: my Muse, though mean,°   *lowly, poor*
Draws from the spring she finds within;
15   Nor vainly° buys what Gildon[5] sells,   *in vain*
Poetic buckets for dry wells.

School-helps I want,[6] to climb on high,
Where all the ancient treasures lie,
And there unseen commit a theft
20   On wealth in Greek exchequers° left.   *treasuries*
Then where? from whom? what can I steal,
Who only with the moderns deal?
This were attempting to put on
Raiment from naked bodies won:[7]
25   They safely sing before a thief,
They cannot give who want relief;
Some few excepted, names well known,
And justly laureled[8] with renown,
Whose stamp of genius marks their ware,
30   And theft detects: of theft beware;

---

1. The effects of "the spleen" were believed to be depression, hypochondria, ill-temper, melancholy, and a variety of other nervous disorders. Green wrote this poem supposedly in reply to a friend who asked him how he coped with this malady. Although he does cite causes and treatments for the disorder, Green uses the subject to write a satire on religion, politics, and contemporary social practices. See Anne Finch, "The Spleen" (pp. 516–19).
2. Green claims to suffer from "what I sing," i.e., "spleen" as a result of his concern for the "public weal," i.e., the public welfare, a reference to his job as a clerk in a Custom House (the office responsible for levying taxes on imported and exported goods) in London.
3. The Muses were the nine Greek goddesses sup-posed to be the sources of inspiration for the arts; "vapored": i.e., afflicted with the vapors, a disorder supposed to be caused by exhalations within the organs of the body and characterized by depression, hypochondria, hysteria, and other nervous disorders.
4. Passed on by heredity.
5. Charles Gildon (1665–1724) wrote *The Complete Art of English Poetry*.
6. Lack; Green claims to not have a classical education, a claim somewhat belied by the many learned allusions in the poem.
7. Perhaps a reference to a line from Edward Howard's epic poem *British Princes* (1669): "A painted vest Prince Vortiger had on, / Which from a naked Pict his grandsire won."
8. The laurel was a symbol of poetic achievement.

From More so lashed,[9] example fit,
Shun petty larceny in wit.

    First know, my friend, I do not mean
To write a treatise on the spleen;
35 Nor to prescribe when nerves convulse;
Nor mend th' alarum watch, your pulse.
If I am right, your question lay,
What course I take to drive away
The day-mare[1] Spleen, by whose false pleas
40 Men prove mere suicides in ease;[2]
And how I do myself demean°   *manage*
In stormy world to live serene.

    When by its magic lantern[3] Spleen
With frightful figures spreads life's scene,
45 And threat'ning prospects° urged my fears,   *expectations*
A stranger to the luck of heirs;[4]
Reason, some quiet to restore,
Showed part was substance, shadow more;
With Spleen's dead weight though heavy grown,
50 In life's rough tide I sunk not down,
But swam, 'till Fortune threw a rope,
Buoyant on bladders[5] fill'd with hope.

    I always choose the plainest food
To mend viscidity° of blood.   *glutinousness*
55 Hail! water-gruel,° healing power,   *thin porridge*
Of easy access to the poor;
Thy help love's confessors implore,
And doctors secretly adore;
To thee, I fly, by thee dilute—[6]
60 Through veins my blood doth quicker shoot,
And by swift current throws off clean
Prolific particles of Spleen.

    I never sick by drinking grow,
Nor keep myself a cup too low,[7]
65 And seldom Cloe's lodgings haunt,
Thrifty of spirits, which I want.[8]

    Hunting I reckon very good
To brace the nerves, and stir the blood:
But after no field-honors[9] itch,

---

9. James More Smith (1702–1734), a playwright, wrote a comedy, "The Rival Modes" (1727); in *The Dunciad* 2.50, Alexander Pope "lashed," i.e., castigated, him for plagiarism.
1. Similar to a nightmare, but occurring during wakefulness; a term coined by Green.
2. Without hesitation; or, at leisure; "mere": unassisted (legal).
3. An optical instrument by means of which a magnified image of a picture on glass is thrown upon a white screen or wall in a darkened room.
4. I.e., he has no hope of an inheritance.

5. Bladders of animals, inflated and used as flotation devices.
6. "Blood" in the next line is the noun acted on by the past participle, "dilute": i.e., "blood," diluted by the gruel, "doth quicker shoot" through the veins.
7. I.e., sad, gloomy.
8. I.e., economical of liveliness or energy, which I lack; "C[h]loe": a conventional poetic name for a young woman.
9. I.e., honors won in the hunt.

70　Achieved by leaping hedge and ditch,
　　While Spleen lies soft relaxed in bed,
　　Or o'er coal fires inclines the head,
　　Hygeia's sons[1] with hound and horn,
　　And jovial cry awake the morn.

*　　*　　*

　　To cure the mind's wrong bias, Spleen,
90　Some recommend the bowling-green;[2]
　　Some, hilly walks; all, exercise;
　　Fling but a stone, the giant dies;[3]
　　Laugh and be well. Monkeys have been
　　Extreme good doctors for the Spleen;
95　And kitten, if the humor hit,
　　Has harlequinned away the fit.[4]

*　　*　　*

125　If spleen-fogs rise at close of day,
　　I clear my evening with a play,
　　Or to some concert take my way.
　　The company, the shine of lights,
　　The scenes of humor, music's flights,
130　Adjust and set the soul to rights.

　　Life's moving pictures, well-wrought plays,
　　To others' grief attention raise:
　　Here, while the tragic fictions glow,
　　We borrow joy by pitying woe;
135　There gaily comic scenes delight,
　　And hold true mirrors to our sight.
　　Virtue, in charming dress arrayed,
　　Calling the passions to her aid,
　　When moral scenes just actions join,
140　Takes shape, and shows her face divine.

*　　*　　*

　　Sometimes I dress, with women sit,
　　And chat away the gloomy fit;
　　Quit the stiff garb of serious sense,
185　And wear a gay impertinence,°　　　　　　　　　　*indifference*
　　Nor think nor speak with any pains,
　　But lay on fancy's neck the reins;
　　Talk of unusual swell of waist
　　In maid of honor[5] loosely laced,
190　And beauty borr'wing Spanish red,[6]
　　And loving pair with sep'rate bed,
　　And jewels pawned for loss of game,

1. Hygeia is the goddess of health; thus, her "sons" are healthy men.
2. The lawn on which bowls, a popular English game, is played.
3. The metaphor alludes to the story from 1 Samuel 17, in which a young David kills the Philistine giant, Goliath, with a stone from his sling.
4. "Harlequin": to conjure away; "if the humor hit": i.e., if it affects the disposition.
5. An unmarried woman, usually of noble birth, who attends upon a queen or princess.
6. A cosmetic that added reddish color to the cheeks.

And then redeemed by loss of fame;
Of Kitty (aunt left in the lurch
195 By grave pretence to go to church)
Perceived in hack° with lover fine,   rented carriage
Like Will and Mary on the coin:[7]
And thus in modish° manner we,   fashionable
In aid of sugar, sweeten tea.

200   Permit, ye fair,° your idol form,   beautiful woman
Which e'en the coldest heart can warm,
May with its beauties grace my line,
While I bow down before its shrine,
And your thronged altars with my lays°   songs
205 Perfume, and get by giving praise.
With speech so sweet, so sweet a mien,°   appearance
You excommunicate the Spleen.

*   *   *

1737

JAMES THOMSON

1700–1748

From The Seasons

From *Winter*

The keener tempests come: and, fuming dun
From all the livid east or piercing north,
225 Thick clouds ascend, in whose capacious womb
A vapory deluge lies, to snow congealed.
Heavy they roll their fleecy world along,
And the sky saddens with the gathered storm.
Through the hushed air the whitening shower descends,
230 At first thin-wavering; till at last the flakes
Fall broad and wide and fast, dimming the day
With a continual flow. The cherished fields
Put on their winter robe of purest white.
'Tis brightness all; save where the new snow melts
235 Along the mazy current. Low the woods
Bow their hoar head; and, ere the languid sun
Faint from the west emits his evening ray,
Earth's universal face, deep-hid and chill,
Is one wild dazzling waste that buries wide
240 The works of man. Drooping, the laborer-ox
Stands covered o'er with snow, and then demands
The fruit of all his toil. The fowls of heaven,

---

7. William and Mary were joint rulers of England from 1689 until her death in 1694. During their reign, coins were minted that bore the likenesses of their two heads in profile.

Tamed by the cruel season, crowd around
The winnowing store, and claim the little boon
245   Which Providence assigns them. One alone,
The redbreast, sacred to the household gods,
Wisely regardful of the embroiling sky,
In joyless fields and thorny thickets leaves
His shivering mates, and pays to trusted man
250   His annual visit. Half afraid, he first
Against the window beats; then brisk alights
On the warm hearth; then, hopping o'er the floor,
Eyes all the smiling family askance,
And pecks, and starts, and wonders where he is—
255   Till, more familiar grown, the table crumbs
Attract his slender feet. The foodless wilds
Pour forth their brown inhabitants. The hare,
Though timorous of heart, and hard beset
By death in various forms, dark snares, and dogs,
260   And more unpitying men, the garden seeks,
Urged on by fearless want. The bleating kind[1]
Eye the bleak heaven, and next the glistening earth,
With looks of dumb despair; then, sad-dispersed,
Dig for the withered herb through heaps of snow.
265   Now, shepherds, to your helpless charge be kind;
Baffle the raging year, and fill their pens
With food at will; lodge them below the storm,
And watch them strict, for, from the bellowing east,
In this dire season, oft the whirlwind's wing
270   Sweeps up the burden of whole wintry plains
In one wide weft,° and o'er the hapless flocks,   *web*
Hid in the hollow of two neighboring hills,
The billowy tempest whelms,° till, upward urged,   *engulfs*
The valley to a shining mountain swells,
275   Tipped with a wreath high-curling in the sky.
     As thus the snows arise, and, foul and fierce,
All Winter drives along the darkened air,
In his own loose-revolving° fields the swain   *giddily turning*
Disastered stands; sees other hills ascend,
280   Of unknown joyless brow, and other scenes,
Of horrid prospect, shag° the trackless plain;   *make shaggy*
Nor finds the river nor the forest, hid
Beneath the formless wild, but wanders on
From hill to dale, still more and more astray,
285   Impatient flouncing through the drifted heaps,
Stung with the thoughts of home—the thoughts of home
Rush on his nerves and call their vigor forth
In many a vain attempt. How sinks his soul!
What black despair, what horror fills his heart,
290   When, for the dusky spot which fancy feigned
His tufted cottage rising through the snow,
He meets the roughness of the middle waste,
Far from the track and blest abode of man,
While round him night resistless closes fast,

1. Sheep.

295 And every tempest, howling o'er his head,
Renders the savage wilderness more wild.
Then throng the busy shapes into his mind
Of covered pits, unfathomably deep,
A dire descent! beyond the power of frost;
300 Of faithless bogs; of precipices huge,
Smoothed up with snow; and (what is land unknown,
What water) of the still unfrozen spring,
In the loose marsh or solitary lake,
Where the fresh fountain from the bottom boils.
305 These check his fearful steps; and down he sinks
Beneath the shelter of the shapeless drift,
Thinking o'er all the bitterness of death,
Mixed with the tender anguish nature shoots
Through the wrung bosom of the dying man—
310 His wife, his children, and his friends unseen.
In vain for him the officious° wife prepares   *dutiful*
The fire fair-blazing and the vestment warm;
In vain his little children, peeping out
Into the mingling storm, demand their sire
315 With tears of artless innocence. Alas!
Nor wife nor children more shall he behold,
Nor friends, nor sacred home. On every nerve
The deadly winter seizes, shuts up sense,
And, o'er his inmost vitals creeping cold,
320 Lays him along the snows a stiffened corse,°   *corpse*
Stretched out and bleaching in the northern blast.
     Ah! little think the gay licentious proud,
Whom pleasure, power, and affluence surround—
They who their thoughtless hours in giddy mirth,
325 And wanton, often cruel, riot° waste—   *revelry*
Ah! little think they, while they dance along,
How many feel, this very moment, death
And all the sad variety of pain;
How many sink in the devouring flood,
330 Or more devouring flame; how many bleed,
By shameful variance° betwixt man and man;   *quarreling*
How many pine in want, and dungeon glooms,
Shut from the common air and common use
Of their own limbs; how many drink the cup
335 Of baleful grief, or eat the bitter bread
Of misery; sore pierced by wintry winds,
How many shrink into the sordid hut
Of cheerless poverty; how many shake
With all the fiercer tortures of the mind,
340 Unbounded passion, madness, guilt, remorse—
Whence, tumbled headlong from the height of life,
They furnish matter for the Tragic Muse;
Even in the vale, where wisdom loves to dwell,
With friendship, peace, and contemplation joined,
345 How many, racked with honest passions, droop
In deep retired distress; how many stand
Around the death-bed of their dearest friends,

And point° the parting anguish! Thought fond man　　*accentuate*
Of these, and all the thousand nameless ills
350　That one incessant struggle render life,[2]
One scene of toil, of suffering, and of fate,
Vice in his high career would stand appalled,
And heedless rambling Impulse learn to think;
The conscious° heart of Charity would warm,　　*sympathetic*
355　And her wide wish Benevolence dilate;°　　*diffuse*
The social tear would rise, the social sigh;
And into clear perfection, gradual° bliss,　　*progressive*
Refining still, the social passions work.

1726

CHARLES WESLEY

1707–1788

Hymns[1]

[My God! I know, I feel thee mine]

1

My God! I know, I feel thee mine,[2]
　And will not quit my claim
Till all I have is lost in thine,
　And all renewed I am.

2

5　I hold thee with a trembling hand,
　But will not let thee go
Till steadfastly by faith I stand,
　And all thy goodness know.

3

When shall I see the welcome hour
10　That plants my God in me!
Spirit of health, and life, and power,
　And perfect liberty!

2. I.e., if foolish man thought of these, and of all the thousand nameless ills that render life one incessant struggle.

1. The tenets of the Methodist movement, founded by John Wesley (1703–1791), are often expressed in the hymns of his brother, Charles. Some Methodists believed in the assurance of salvation (rejecting the Calvinist doctrine of predestination) and acquired their name by advocating methodical study and devotion as a means of attaining Christian perfection. Charles Wesley wrote more than six thousand hymns and helped to popularize the tradition of hymn singing in the English language at worship services. The hymns selected below were first printed in different editions of the Wesleys' *Hymns and Sacred Prayers;* we follow the text of the 1780 *Hymnbook.*

2. The subtext for this hymn is Romans 4.13: "For the promise that he should be the heir of the world was not to Abraham, or to his seed, through the law, but through the righteousness of faith."

4

Jesu, thine all-victorious love
    Shed in my heart abroad!
15 Then shall my feet no longer rove,
    Rooted and fixed in God.

5

Love only can the conquest win,
    The strength of sin subdue
(Mine own unconquerable sin),
20   And form my soul anew.

6

Love can bow down the stubborn neck,
    The stone to flesh convert;
Soften, and melt, and pierce, and break
    An adamantine° heart.   *unyielding, hard*

7

25 Oh, that in me the sacred fire
    Might now begin to glow,
Burn up the dross of base desire,
    And make the mountains flow!

8

Oh, that it now from heaven might fall,
30   And all my sins consume!
Come, Holy Ghost, for thee I call,
    Spirit of burning, come!

9

Refining fire, go through my heart,
    Illuminate my soul;
35 Scatter thy life through every part,
    And sanctify the whole.

10

Sorrow and sin shall then expire,
    While, entered into rest,
I only live my God t'admire—
40   My God forever blest.

11

No longer then my heart shall mourn,
    While purified by grace
I only for his glory burn,
    And always see his face.

12

45 My steadfast soul, from falling free,
    Shall then no longer move;
But Christ be all the world to me,
    And all my heart be love.

1740

[*None is like Jeshuron's God*]³

1

None is like Jeshuron's God!
    So great, so strong, so high!
Lo! he spreads his wings abroad,
    He rides upon the sky!
5 Israel is his firstborn son;
    God, th' almighty God, is thine,
See him in thy help come down,
    The excellence divine.

2

To thee the great Jehovah deigns
10   To succor and defend;
Thee th' eternal God sustains,
    Thy maker and thy friend;
Sinner, what hast thou to dread?
    Safe from all impending harms,
15 Round thee and beneath are spread
    The everlasting arms.

3

God is thine; disdain to fear
    The enemy within;
God shall in thy flesh appear,
20   And make an end of sin;
God the man of sin shall slay,
    Fill thee with triumphant joy;
God shall thrust him out, and say,
    Destroy them all, destroy!

4

25 All the struggle then is o'er
    And wars and fightings cease;
Israel then shall sin no more,
    But dwell in perfect peace.
All his enemies are gone;
30   Sin shall have in him no part;
Israel now shall dwell alone,
    With Jesus in his heart.

5

In a land of corn and wine
    His lot shall be below;
35 Comforts there and blessings join,
    And milk and honey flow.
Jacob's well is in his soul;⁴

---

3. This hymn is based on Deuteronomy 33.26–29: "There is none like unto the God of Jeshurun, who rideth upon the heaven in thy help, and in his excellency on the sky. The eternal God is thy refuge, and underneath are the everlasting arms; and he shall thrust out the enemy from before thee, and shall say, Destroy them. Israel then shall dwell in safety alone; the fountain of Jacob shall be upon a land of corn and wine; also his heavens shall drop down dew. Happy art thou, O Israel! Who is like unto thee, O people saved by the Lord, the shield of thy help, and who is the sword of thy excellency? And thine enemies shall be found liars unto thee, and thou shalt tread upon their high places." Jeshuron (Jeshurun in the Bible) is a designation for Israel.
4. In John 4, Jesus offers the Samaritan woman "living water" from Jacob's well.

Gracious dew his heavens distil,
Fill his soul, already full,
40   And shall forever fill.

6

Blest, O Israel, art thou!
    What people is like thee?
Saved from sin by Jesus now
    Thou art, and still shalt be.
45 Jesus is thy sevenfold[5] shield,
    Jesus is thy flaming sword;
Earth, and hell, and sin shall yield
    To God's almighty word.

1742

[*Come on, my partners in distress*]

1

Come on, my partners in distress,
My comrades through the wilderness,
    Who still your bodies feel;
Awhile forget your griefs and fears,
5   And look beyond this vale of tears
    To that celestial hill.[6]

2

Beyond the bounds of time and space
Look forward to that heavenly place,
    The saints' secure abode;
10 On faith's strong eagle pinions rise,
And force your passage to the skies,
    And scale the mount of God.

3

Who suffer with our Master[7] here,
We shall before his face appear,
15   And by his side sit down;
To patient faith the prize is sure,
And all that to the end endure
    The cross, shall wear the crown.[8]

4

Thrice blessed bliss-inspiring hope!
20 It lifts the fainting spirits up,
    It brings to life the dead;
Our conflicts here shall soon be past,
And you and I ascend at last
    Triumphant with our head.[9]

---

5. Seven is traditionally seen as a number of perfection.
6. The heavenly Jerusalem is located on a hill, specifically Mt. Sion. "Wilderness": where the Israelites wandered for forty years; also the place where Christ was tempted, thus a place of suffering, testing, wandering, used here as a metaphor for earthly life. "Vale of tears": this world, regarded as a place of trouble, sorrow, misery, or weeping.
7. I.e., Christ.
8. The New Testament promises a "crown of life" to the faithful Christian (James 1.12).
9. I.e., Christ; "the head of every man is Christ" (1 Corinthians 11.3).

5

25 That great mysterious Deity
We soon with open face shall see;
    The beatific sight[1]
Shall fill heaven's sounding courts with praise,
And wide diffuse the golden blaze
30 Of everlasting light.

6

The Father shining on his throne,
The glorious, co-eternal Son,
    The Spirit, one and seven,[2]
Conspire our rapture to complete,
35 And lo! we fall before his feet,
    And silence heightens heaven.

7

In hope of that ecstatic pause,
Jesu, we now sustain the cross,
    And at thy footstool fall,
40 Till thou our hidden life reveal,
Till thou our ravished spirits fill,
    And God is all in all.

1749

JOHN DYER

1700–1758

Grongar Hill[1]

Silent nymph,[2] with curious eye!
Who, the purple evening, lie[3]
On the mountain's lonely van,°   brow, summit
Beyond the noise of busy man,
5 Painting fair the form of things,
While the yellow linnet[4] sings;
Or the tuneful nightingale
Charms the forest with her tale;
Come with all thy various hues,
10 Come, and aid thy sister Muse;
Now while Phoebus riding high[5]
Gives luster to the land and sky!
Grongar Hill invites my song,
Draw the landscape bright and strong;
15 Grongar, in whose mossy cells

1. A sight of the glories of heaven, especially that first granted to a disembodied spirit.
2. The "seven spirits of God" are referred to in Revelations 1.4, 3.1, 4.5, 5.6.
1. An eminence rising off the river Towy (line 23) in Dyer's native South Wales.
2. I.e., the Muse of painting. Her "sister" (line 10) is the Muse of poetry.
3. An apparent agrammaticism common to early editions. The writer and critic Samuel Johnson said of this poem, "It is not, indeed, very accurately written."
4. Probably the yellowhammer, a species of bunting.
5. Apollo, (Greek and Roman god of) the sun and leader of the Muses.

Sweetly musing Quiet dwells;
Grongar, in whose silent shade,
For the modest Muses made,
So oft I have, the evening still,
20   At the fountain of a rill,
Sate upon a flowery bed,
With my hand beneath my head;
While strayed my eyes o'er Towy's flood,
Over mead and over wood,
25   From house to house, from hill to hill,
Till Contemplation had her fill.
    About his checkered sides I wind,
And leave his brooks and meads behind,
And groves, and grottoes where I lay,
30   And vistas shooting beams of day;
Wide and wider spreads the vale,
As circles on a smooth canal;
The mountains round—unhappy fate,
Sooner or later, of all height—
35   Withdraw their summits from the skies,
And lessen as the others rise;[6]
Still the prospect wider spreads,
Adds a thousand woods and meads,
Still it widens, widens still,
40   And sinks the newly-risen hill.
    Now I gain the mountain's brow,
What a landscape lies below!
No clouds, no vapors intervene,
But the gay, the open scene
45   Does the face of Nature show
In all the hues of heaven's bow,
And, swelling to embrace the light,
Spreads around beneath the sight.
    Old castles on the cliffs arise,
50   Proudly towering in the skies!
Rushing from the woods, the spires
Seem from hence ascending fires!
Half his beams Apollo sheds
On the yellow mountain-heads,
55   Gilds the fleeces of the flocks,
And glitters on the broken rocks!
    Below me trees unnumbered rise,
Beautiful in various dyes:
The gloomy pine, the poplar blue,
60   The yellow beech, the sable yew,
The slender fir that taper grows,
The sturdy oak with broad-spread boughs.
And beyond the purple grove,
Haunt of Phyllis,[7] queen of love!
65   Gaudy as the opening dawn,
Lies a long and level lawn,
On which a dark hill, steep and high,

---

6. I.e., the nearby peaks seem smaller as I ascend.   7. Conventional name for a pastoral beauty.

Holds and charms the wandering eye!
Deep are his feet in Towy's flood,
His sides are clothed with waving wood,
And ancient towers crown his brow,
That cast an awful look below;
Whose ragged walls the ivy creeps,
And with her arms from falling keeps;
So both a safety from the wind
On mutual dependence find.
  'Tis now the raven's bleak abode;
'Tis now the apartment of the toad;
And there the fox securely feeds;
And there the poisonous adder breeds,
Concealed in ruins, moss, and weeds,
While, even and anon, there falls
Huge heaps of hoary moldered walls.
Yet Time has seen, that lifts the low,
And level lays the lofty brow,
Has seen this broken pile complete,
Big with the vanity of state;
But transient is the smile of Fate!
A little rule, a little sway,
A sunbeam in a winter's day,
Is all the proud and mighty have
Between the cradle and the grave.
  And see the rivers, how they run
Through woods and meads, in shade and sun;
Sometimes swift, sometimes slow,
Wave succeeding wave, they go
A various journey to the deep,
Like human life to endless sleep!
Thus is Nature's vesture wrought,
To instruct our wandering thought;
Thus she dresses green and gay,
To disperse our cares away.
  Ever charming, ever new,
When will the landscape tire the view!
The fountain's fall, the river's flow,
The woody valleys warm and low;
The windy summit, wild and high,
Roughly rushing on the sky;
The pleasant seat, the ruined tower,
The naked rock, the shady bower,
The town and village, dome and farm,
Each give each a double charm,
As pearls upon an Ethiop's arm.
  See on the mountain's southern side,
Where the prospect opens wide,
Where the evening gilds the tide,
How close and small the hedges lie!
What streaks of meadows cross the eye!
A step methinks may pass the stream,
So little distant dangers seem;

So we mistake the future's face,
Eyed through Hope's deluding glass;
As yon summits soft and fair,
Clad in colors of the air,
125 Which to those who journey near,
Barren, brown, and rough appear;
Still we tread the same coarse way,
The present's still a cloudy day.
    Oh, may I with myself agree,°   *be pleased*
130 And never covet what I see,
Content me with an humble shade,
My passions tamed, my wishes laid;
For while our wishes wildly roll,
We banish quiet from the soul;
135 'Tis thus the busy beat the air,
And misers gather wealth and care.
    Now, even now, my joys run high,
As on the mountain turf I lie;
While the wanton Zephyr[8] sings,
140 And in the vale perfumes his wings;
While the waters murmur deep,
While the shepherd charms his sheep,
While the birds unbounded fly,
And with music fill the sky;
145 Now, even now, my joys run high.
    Be full, ye courts, be great who will;
Search for Peace with all your skill;
Open wide the lofty door;
Seek her on the marble floor;
150 In vain you search, she is not there;
In vain ye search the domes of Care!
Grass and flowers Quiet treads,
On the meads and mountain-heads,
Along with Pleasure, close allied,
155 Ever by each other's side:
And often, by the murmuring rill,
Hears the thrush, while all is still,
Within the groves of Grongar Hill.

1726

SAMUEL JOHNSON

1709–1784

Prologue Spoken by Mr. Garrick[1]

At the Opening of the Theater Royal, Drury Lane, 1747

When Learning's triumph o'er her barbarous foes
First reared the stage, immortal Shakespeare rose;

---

8. The west wind, personified.
1. David Garrick (1717–1779), English actor and theater-manager.

Each change of many-colored life he drew,
Exhausted worlds, and then imagined new:
5   Existence saw him spurn her bounded reign,
And panting Time toiled after him in vain.
His powerful strokes presiding Truth impressed,
And unresisted Passion stormed the breast.
    Then Jonson came, instructed from the school
10   To please in method and invent by rule;
His studious patience and laborious art
By regular approach essayed the heart;
Cold Approbation gave the lingering bays,
For those who durst not censure, scarce could praise.
15   A mortal born, he met the general doom,
But left, like Egypt's kings, a lasting tomb.
    The wits of Charles[2] found easier ways to fame,
Nor wished for Jonson's art, or Shakespeare's flame;
Themselves they studied; as they felt, they writ;
20   Intrigue was plot, obscenity was wit.
Vice always found a sympathetic friend;
They pleased their age, and did not aim to mend.°   *amend it*
Yet bards like these aspired to lasting praise,
And proudly hoped to pimp in future days.
25   Their cause was general, their supports were strong,
Their slaves were willing, and their reign was long:
Till Shame regained the post that Sense betrayed,
And Virtue called Oblivion to her aid.
    Then, crushed by rules, and weakened as refined,
30   For years the power of Tragedy declined;
From bard to bard the frigid caution crept,
Till Declamation roared while Passion slept;
Yet still did Virtue deign the stage to tread;
Philosophy remained though Nature fled;
35   But forced at length her ancient reign to quit,
She saw great Faustus[3] lay the ghost of Wit;
Exulting Folly hailed the joyous day,
And Pantomime and Song confirmed her sway.
    But who the coming changes can presage,
40   And mark the future periods of the stage?
Perhaps if skill could distant times explore,
New Behns, new Durfeys,[4] yet remain in store;
Perhaps where Lear has raved, and Hamlet died,
On flying cars new sorcerers may ride;
45   Perhaps (for who can guess the effects of chance?)
Here Hunt may box, or Mahomet may dance.[5]
    Hard is his lot that, here by fortune placed,
Must watch the wild vicissitudes of taste;
With every meteor of caprice must play,
50   And chase the new-blown bubbles of the day.
    Ah! let not censure term our fate our choice,

2. The comic playwrights of the Restoration.
3. As treated in current farce and pantomime.
4. Aphra Behn (1640?–1689; see pp. 497–504), Restoration author admired by Dryden but attacked by some for her racy plays; and Thomas

D'Urfey (1653–1723), playwright and poetaster who was a standing joke among the wits.
5. A pugilist and a tightrope dancer currently popular.

The stage but echoes back the public voice;
The drama's laws, the drama's patrons give,
For we that live to please, must please to live.
55   Then prompt no more the follies you decry,
As tyrants doom their tools of guilt to die;
'Tis yours this night to bid the reign commence
Of rescued Nature and reviving Sense;
To chase the charms of Sound, the pomp of Show,
60 For useful Mirth and salutary Woe;
Bid scenic Virtue form the rising age,
And Truth diffuse her radiance from the stage.

                                                    1747

The Vanity of Human Wishes

In Imitation of the Tenth Satire of Juvenal

Let Observation, with extensive view,
Survey mankind, from China to Peru;
Remark each anxious toil, each eager strife,
And watch the busy scenes of crowded life;
5   Then say how hope and fear, desire and hate
O'erspread with snares the clouded maze of fate,
Where wavering man, betrayed by venturous pride
To tread the dreary paths without a guide,
As treacherous phantoms in the mist delude,
10 Shuns fancied ills, or chases airy good;
How rarely Reason guides the stubborn choice,
Rules the bold hand, or prompts the suppliant voice;
How nations sink, by darling schemes oppressed,
When Vengeance listens to the fool's request.[6]
15 Fate wings with every wish the afflictive dart,
Each gift of nature, and each grace of art;[7]
With fatal heat impetuous courage glows,
With fatal sweetness elocution flows,
Impeachment stops the speaker's powerful breath,
20 And restless fire precipitates on death.[8]
      But scarce observed, the knowing and the bold
Fall in the general massacre of gold;
Wide-wasting pest! that rages unconfined,
And crowds with crimes the records of mankind;
25 For gold his sword the hireling ruffian draws,
For gold the hireling judge distorts the laws;
Wealth heaped on wealth, nor truth nor safety buys,
The dangers gather as the treasures rise.
      Let History tell where rival kings command,
30 And dubious title shakes the madded land,
When statutes glean the refuse of the sword,

---

6. I.e., when vengeance hangs over a nation, ready to descend on it if the proposals of political fools prevail.
7. The sense of this couplet is that men can be hurried toward misery by their desires and even by their talents and accomplishments.
8. Perhaps, that is, impetuous energy hastens men to their death.

How much more safe the vassal than the lord,
Low skulks the hind beneath the rage of power,
And leaves the wealthy traitor in the Tower,[9]
35 Untouched his cottage, and his slumbers sound,
Though Confiscation's vultures hover round.
    The needy traveler, serene and gay,
Walks the wild heath, and sings his toil away.
Does envy seize thee? crush the upbraiding joy,
40 Increase his riches and his peace destroy;
New fears in dire vicissitude invade,
The rustling brake° alarms, and quivering shade,   thicket
Nor light nor darkness bring his pain relief,
One shows the plunder, and one hides the thief.
45   Yet still one general cry the skies assails,
And gain and grandeur load the tainted gales;
Few know the toiling statesman's fear or care,
The insidious rival and the gaping heir.
    Once more, Democritus,[1] arise on earth,
50 With cheerful wisdom and instructive mirth,
See motley life in modern trappings dressed,
And feed with varied fools the eternal jest:
Thou who couldst laugh where Want enchained Caprice,
Toil crushed Conceit, and man was of a piece;
55 Where Wealth unloved without a mourner died;
And scarce a sycophant was fed by Pride;
Where ne'er was known the form of mock debate,
Or seen a new-made mayor's unwieldy state;°   pomp
Where change of favorites made no change of laws,
60 And senates heard before they judged a cause;
How wouldst thou shake at Britain's modish tribe,
Dart the quick taunt, and edge the piercing gibe?
Attentive truth and nature to descry,
And pierce each scene with philosophic eye,
65 To thee were solemn toys or empty show
The robes of pleasures and the veils of woe:
All aid the farce, and all thy mirth maintain,
Whose joys are causeless, or whose griefs are vain.
    Such was the scorn that filled the sage's mind,
70 Renewed at every glance on human kind;
How just that scorn ere yet thy voice declare,
Search every state, and canvass every prayer.
    Unnumbered suppliants crowd Preferment's gate,
Athirst for wealth, and burning to be great;
75 Delusive Fortune hears the incessant call,
They mount, they shine, evaporate, and fall.
On every stage the foes of peace attend,
Hate dogs their flight, and Insult mocks their end.
Love ends with hope, the sinking statesman's door
80 Pours in the morning worshiper no more;[2]
For growing names the weekly scribbler lies,

---

9. Tower of London (a prison).
1. Greek philosopher of the late fifth century B.C.,
a fatalist who exalted cheerfulness and derided all
immoderate pretensions.
2. Important personages received petitions and
official calls in the morning.

To growing wealth the dedicator flies;
From every room descends the painted face,
That hung the bright palladium[3] of the place;
85 And smoked in kitchens, or in auctions sold,
To better features yields the frame of gold;
For now no more we trace in every line
Heroic worth, benevolence divine:
The form distorted justifies the fall,
90 And Detestation rids the indignant wall.
　　But will not Britain hear the last appeal,
Sign her foes' doom, or guard her favorites' zeal?
Through Freedom's sons no more remonstrance rings,
Degrading nobles and controlling kings;
95 Our supple tribes repress their patriot throats,
And ask no questions but the price of votes,
With weekly libels and septennial ale.[4]
Their wish is full° to riot and to rail.　　　　　　　　　*satisfied*
　　In full-blown dignity, see Wolsey[5] stand,
100 Law in his voice, and fortune in his hand:
To him the church, the realm, their powers consign,
Through him the rays of regal bounty shine;
Turned by his nod the stream of honor flows,
His smile alone security bestows:
105 Still to new heights his restless wishes tower,
Claim leads to claim, and power advances power;
Till conquest unresisted ceased to please,
And rights submitted, left him none to seize.
At length his sovereign frowns—the train of state[6]
110 Mark the keen glance, and watch the sign to hate.
Where'er he turns, he meets a stranger's eye,
His suppliants scorn him, and his followers fly;
At once is lost the pride of awful state,
The golden canopy, the glittering plate,
115 The regal palace, the luxurious board,
The liveried army, and the menial lord.
With age, with cares, with maladies oppressed,
He seeks the refuge of monastic rest.
Grief aids disease, remembered folly stings,
120 And his last sighs reproach the faith of kings.
　　Speak thou, whose thoughts at humble
　　　　peace repine,°　　　　　　　　　　　　　　　*complain*
Shall Wolsey's wealth, with Wolsey's end be thine?
Or liv'st thou now, with safer pride content,
The wisest justice on the banks of Trent?[7]
125 For why did Wolsey, near the steeps of fate,
On weak foundations raise the enormous weight?
Why but to sink beneath misfortune's blow,
With louder ruin to the gulfs below?

3. An image of Pallas that supposedly preserved Troy from capture as long as it remained in the city; hence, a safeguard.
4. I.e., public attacks in the weekly press and ale distributed at the parliamentary elections held every seventh year.
5. Thomas Cardinal Wolsey (ca. 1475–1530), lord chancellor under Henry VIII.
6. I.e., followers of the king.
7. A river flowing through the English Midlands.

What gave great Villiers[8] to the assassin's knife,
130   And fixed disease on Harley's closing life?
What murdered Wentworth, and what exiled Hyde,
By kings protected and to kings allied?
What but their wish indulged in courts to shine,
And power too great to keep or to resign?
135   When first the college rolls receive his name,
The young enthusiast quits his ease for fame;
Resistless burns the fever of renown
Caught from the strong contagion of the gown:[9]
O'er Bodley's dome his future labors spread,
140   And Bacon's mansion trembles o'er his head.[1]
Are these thy views? proceed, illustrious youth,
And Virtue guard thee to the throne of Truth!
Yet should thy soul indulge the generous heat,
Till captive Science yields her last retreat;
145   Should Reason guide thee with her brightest ray,
And pour on misty Doubt resistless day;
Should no false kindness lure to loose delight,
Nor praise relax, nor difficulty fright;
Should tempting Novelty thy cell refrain,°   *pass by, avoid*
150   And Sloth effuse her opiate fumes in vain;
Should Beauty blunt on fops her fatal dart,
Nor claim the triumph of a lettered heart;
Should no disease thy torpid veins invade,
Nor Melancholy's phantoms haunt thy shade;
155   Yet hope not life from grief or danger free,
Nor think the doom of man reversed for thee:
Deign on the passing world to turn thine eyes,
And pause a while from letters, to be wise;
There mark what ills the scholar's life assail,
160   Toil, envy, want, the patron, and the jail.
See nations slowly wise, and meanly just,
To buried merit raise the tardy bust.
If dreams yet flatter, once again attend,
Hear Lydiat's life, and Galileo's end.[2]
165   Nor deem, when Learning her last prize bestows,
The glittering eminence exempt from foes;
See when the vulgar 'scapes, despised or awed,
Rebellion's vengeful talons seize on Laud.[3]
From meaner minds though smaller fines content,

---

8. George Villiers, duke of Buckingham, court favorite of James I and Charles I; assassinated in 1628. Robert Harley (line 130), earl of Oxford, a member of the Tory ministry under Queen Anne, was subsequently imprisoned and suffered a decline. Thomas Wentworth, earl of Strafford, advisor to Charles I, was executed under the Long Parliament. Edward Hyde, earl of Clarendon, who was Charles II's lord chancellor and whose daughter married into the royal family, was impeached and exiled in 1667.
9. Academic gown, put on upon entering the university, with allusion to the shirt of Nessus, the flaming robe that clung to Hercules and drove him to his death.

1. "There is a tradition, that the study of friar Bacon, built on an arch over the bridge, will fall, when a man greater than Bacon shall pass under it" [Johnson's note]. "Bodley's dome": the Bodleian Library at Oxford; "dome": *domus*, "house" (Latin).
2. Galileo (1564–1642), the Italian astronomer, was imprisoned for heresy by the Inquisition; he died blind. Thomas Lydiat (1572–1646), the Oxford mathematician and don, endured lifelong poverty.
3. William Laud (1573–1645), archbishop of Canterbury under Charles I; executed in 1645 for his devotion to episcopacy.

170   The plundered palace, or sequestered° rent;   *confiscated*
      Marked out by dangerous parts he meets the shock,
      And fatal Learning leads him to the block:
      Around his tomb let Art and Genius weep,
      But hear his death, ye blockheads, hear and sleep.[4]
175   The festal blazes, the triumphal show,
      The ravished standard, and the captive foe,
      The senate's thanks, the gàzette's pompous tale,
      With force resistless o'er the brave prevail.
      Such bribes the rapid Greek[5] o'er Asia whirled,
180   For such the steady Romans shook the world;
      For such in distant lands the Britons shine,
      And stain with blood the Danube or the Rhine;
      This power has praise that virtue scarce can warm,[6]
      Till fame supplies the universal charm.
185   Yet Reason frowns on War's unequal game,
      Where wasted nations raise a single name,
      And mortgaged states their grandsires' wreaths regret
      From age to age in everlasting debt;
      Wreaths which at last the dear-bought right convey
190   To rust on medals, or on stones decay.
          On what foundation stands the warrior's pride,
      How just his hopes, let Swedish Charles[7] decide;
      A frame of adamant, a soul of fire,
      No dangers fright him, and no labors tire;
195   O'er love, o'er fear, extends his wide domain,
      Unconquered lord of pleasure and of pain;
      No joys to him pacific scepters yield,
      War sounds the trump, he rushes to the field;
      Behold surrounding kings their powers combine,
200   And one capitulate, and one resign;[8]
      Peace courts his hand, but spreads her charms in vain;
      "Think nothing gained," he cries, "till naught remain,
      On Moscow's walls till Gothic° standards fly,   *Teutonic*
      And all be mine beneath the polar sky."
205   The march begins in military state,
      And nations on his eye suspended wait;
      Stern Famine guards the solitary coast,
      And Winter barricades the realms of Frost;
      He comes, nor want nor cold his course delay—
210   Hide, blushing Glory, hide Pultowa's day:
      The vanquished hero leaves his broken bands,
      And shows his miseries in distant lands;
      Condemned a needy supplicant to wait,
      While ladies interpose, and slaves debate.
215   But did not Chance at length her error mend?

4. Rest secure, that is, since you lack Laud's learning and gifts.
5. I.e., Alexander the Great (356–323 B.C.).
6. I.e., praise has a power (to activate the brave) that an abstract love of virtue can scarcely begin to kindle.
7. King Charles XII (1682–1718). Peter the Great (1672–1725), czar of Russia, defeated him at Pul-towa in 1709. Escaping, "a needy supplicant," he sought an alliance with the Turkish Sultan. He was killed in an attack on "a petty fortress," Fredriks-hald in Norway.
8. Frederick IV of Denmark capitulated in 1700, and Augustus II of Poland resigned his throne in 1704.

Did no subverted empire mark his end?
Did rival monarchs give the fatal wound?
Or hostile millions press him to the ground?
His fall was destined to a barren strand,
220 A petty fortress, and a dubious hand;
He left the name at which the world grew pale,
To point a moral, or adorn a tale.
    All times their scenes of pompous woes afford,
From Persia's tyrant to Bavaria's lord.⁹
225 In gay hostility, and barbarous pride,
With half mankind embattled at his side,
Great Xerxes comes to seize the certain prey,
And starves exhausted regions in his way;
Attendant Flattery counts his myriads o'er,
230 Till counted myriads soothe his pride no more;
Fresh praise is tried till madness fires his mind,
The waves he lashes, and enchains the wind;
New powers are claimed, new powers are still bestowed,
Till rude resistance lops the spreading god;
235 The daring Greeks deride the martial show,
And heap their valleys with the gaudy foe;
The insulted sea with humbler thought he gains,
A single skiff to speed his flight remains;
The encumbered oar scarce leaves the dreaded coast
240 Through purple° billows and a floating host.   blood-stained
    The bold Bavarian, in a luckless hour,
Tries the dread summits of Caesarean° power,   imperial
With unexpected legions bursts away,
And sees defenseless realms receive his sway;
245 Short sway! fair Austria spreads her mournful charms,
The queen, the beauty, sets the world in arms;
From hill to hill the beacon's rousing blaze
Spreads wide the hope of plunder and of praise;
The fierce Croatian, and the wild Hussar,¹
250 With all the sons of ravage crowd the war;
The baffled prince, in honor's flattering bloom,
Of hasty greatness finds the fatal doom;
His foes' derision, and his subjects' blame,
And steals to death from anguish and from shame.
255   Enlarge my life with multitude of days!
In health, in sickness, thus the suppliant prays;
Hides from himself his state, and shuns to know,
That life protracted is protracted woe.
Time hovers o'er, impatient to destroy,
260 And shuts up all the passages of joy;
In vain their gifts the bounteous seasons pour,
The fruit autumnal, and the vernal flower;
With listless eyes the dotard views the store,
He views, and wonders that they please no more;

---

9. Charles Albert, elector of Bavaria, who success-
fully aspired to the crown of the Holy Roman
Empire but was deposed in a few years through the
political skill of Maria Theresa ("fair Austria," line

245). "Persia's tyrant": Xerxes, emperor whose
forces the Greeks defeated by sea at Salamis in 480
B.C. and later, on land, at Plataea.
1. Hungarian cavalryman.

265 Now pall the tasteless meats, and joyless wines,
And Luxury with sighs her slave resigns.
Approach, ye minstrels, try the soothing strain,
Diffuse the tuneful lenitives° of pain: *softeners*
No sounds, alas! would touch the impervious ear,
270 Though dancing mountains witnessed Orpheus near;[2]
Nor lute nor lyre his feeble powers attend,
Nor sweeter music of a virtuous friend,
But everlasting dictates crowd his tongue,
Perversely grave, or positively wrong.
275 The still returning tale, and lingering jest,
Perplex the fawning niece and pampered guest,
While growing hopes scarce awe the gathering sneer,
And scarce a legacy can bribe to hear;
The watchful guests still hint the last offense;
280 The daughter's petulance, the son's expense,
Improve° his heady rage with treacherous skill,   *play upon*
And mold his passions till they make his will.
    Unnumbered maladies his joints invade,
Lay siege to life and press the dire blockade;
285 But unextinguished avarice still remains,
And dreaded losses aggravate his pains;
He turns, with anxious heart and crippled hands,
His bonds of debt, and mortgages of lands;
Or views his coffers with suspicious eyes,
290 Unlocks his gold, and counts it till he dies.
    But grant, the virtues of a temperate prime
Bless with an age exempt from scorn or crime;
An age that melts with unperceived decay,
And glides in modest innocence away;
295 Whose peaceful day Benevolence endears,
Whose night congratulating Conscience cheers;
The general favorite as the general friend:
Such age there is, and who shall wish its end?
    Yet even on this her load Misfortune flings,
300 To press the weary minutes' flagging wings;
New sorrow rises as the day returns,
A sister sickens, or a daughter mourns.
Now kindred Merit fills the sable bier,
Now lacerated Friendship claims a tear;
305 Year chases year, decay pursues decay,
Still drops some joy from withering life away;
New forms arise, and different views engage,
Superfluous lags the veteran[3] on the stage,
Till pitying Nature signs the last release,
310 And bids afflicted Worth retire to peace.
    But few there are whom hours like these await,
Who set unclouded in the gulfs of Fate.
From Lydia's monarch[4] should the search descend,
By Solon cautioned to regard his end,

---

2. The legendary Thracian bard whose playing could move even trees and hills.
3. I.e., an aged person.

4. Croesus (d. ca. 547 B.C.), whom Solon advised to regard no living man as securely happy, was later deposed by the Persian Cyrus (d. 529 B.C.).

315 In life's last scene what prodigies surprise,
Fears of the brave, and follies of the wise!
From Marlborough's eyes the streams of dotage flow,
And Swift expires a driveler and a show.[5]
The teeming mother, anxious for her race,
320 Begs for each birth the fortune of a face:
Yet Vane could tell what ills from beauty spring;[6]
And Sedley cursed the form that pleased a king.
Ye nymphs of rosy lips and radiant eyes,
Whom Pleasure keeps too busy to be wise,
325 Whom Joys with soft varieties invite,
By day the frolic, and the dance by night;
Who frown with vanity, who smile with art,
And ask the latest fashion of the heart;
What care, what rules your heedless charms shall save,
330 Each nymph your rival, and each youth your slave?
Against your fame with Fondness Hate combines,
The rival batters, and the lover mines.°   undermines
With distant voice neglected Virtue calls,
Less heard and less, the faint remonstrance falls;
335 Tired with contempt, she quits the slippery reign,
And Pride and Prudence take her seat in vain.
In crowd at once, where none the pass defend,
The harmless freedom, and the private friend.
The guardians yield, by force superior plied:
340 To Interest, Prudence; and to Flattery, Pride.
Now Beauty falls betrayed, despised, distressed,
And hissing Infamy proclaims the rest.
    Where then shall Hope and Fear their objects find?
Must dull Suspense corrupt the stagnant mind?
345 Must helpless man, in ignorance sedate,
Roll darkling down the torrent of his fate?
Must no dislike alarm, no wishes rise,
No cries invoke the mercies of the skies?
Inquirer, cease; petitions yet remain,
350 Which Heaven may hear, nor deem religion vain.
Still raise for good the supplicating voice,
But leave to Heaven the measure and the choice.
Safe in His power, whose eyes discern afar
The secret ambush of a specious prayer.
355 Implore His aid, in His decisions rest,
Secure, whate'er He gives, He gives the best.
Yet when the sense of sacred presence fires,
And strong devotion to the skies aspires,
Pour forth thy fervors for a healthful mind,
360 Obedient passions, and a will resigned;
For love, which scarce collective man can fill;
For patience sovereign o'er transmuted ill;[7]
For faith, that panting for a happier seat,

5. Both John Churchill, duke of Marlborough (the military hero), and the English writer Jonathan Swift (1667–1745) declined into senility.
6. Anne Vane, the mistress of Frederick, prince of Wales, died in 1736 at the age of thirty-one. Catherine Sedley was mistress to James II.
7. I.e., a capacity for love such that all mankind together can hardly engage it fully; and for patience, which, by asserting sovereignty over ills, changes their nature.

Counts death kind Nature's signal of retreat:
365 These goods for man the laws of Heaven ordain,
These goods He grants, who grants the power to gain;
With these celestial Wisdom calms the mind,
And makes the happiness she does not find.

1749

On the Death of Dr. Robert Levet[8]

Condemned to Hope's delusive mine,
   As on we toil from day to day,
By sudden blasts, or slow decline,
   Our social comforts drop away.

5 Well tried through many a varying year,
   See Levet to the grave descend;
Officious,° innocent, sincere,   *dutiful*
   Of every friendless name the friend.

Yet still he fills Affection's eye,
10   Obscurely wise, and coarsely kind;
Nor, lettered Arrogance, deny
   Thy praise to merit unrefined.

When fainting Nature called for aid,
   And hovering Death prepared the blow,
15 His vigorous remedy displayed
   The power of art without the show.

In Misery's darkest cavern known,
   His useful care was ever nigh,
Where hopeless Anguish poured his groan,
20   And lonely Want retired to die.

No summons mocked by chill delay,
   No petty gain disdained by pride,
The modest wants of every day
   The toil of every day supplied.

25 His virtues walked their narrow round,
   Nor made a pause, nor left a void;
And sure the Eternal Master found
   The single talent[9] well employed.

The busy day, the peaceful night,
30   Unfelt, uncounted, glided by;
His frame was firm, his powers were bright,
   Though now his eightieth year was nigh.

8. An unlicensed physician, practicing among the poor, who had long lived in Johnson's house. He was uncouth in appearance and stiff in manner.

9. An allusion to the portion of wealth given in trust in the parable of the talents (Matthew 25.14–30).

Then with no throbbing fiery pain,
    No cold gradations of decay,
35 Death broke at once the vital chain,
    And freed his soul the nearest way.

1783

THOMAS GRAY

1716–1771

Ode on a Distant Prospect of Eton College

Ἄνθρωπος· ἱκανὴ πρόφασις εἰς τὸ δυστυχεῖν.[1]
—MENANDER

Ye distant spires, ye antique towers,
    That crown the watery glade,
Where grateful Science° still adores   learning
    Her Henry's holy shade;[2]
5 And ye, that from the stately brow
Of Windsor's heights the expanse below
    Of grove, of lawn, of mead survey,
Whose turf, whose shade, whose flowers among
Wanders the hoary Thames along
10   His silver-winding way.

Ah happy hills, ah pleasing shade,
    Ah fields beloved in vain,
Where once my careless childhood strayed,
    A stranger yet to pain!
15 I feel the gales, that from ye blow,
A momentary bliss bestow,
    As waving fresh their gladsome wing,
My weary soul they seem to soothe,
And, redolent of joy and youth,
20   To breathe a second spring.

Say, Father Thames, for thou hast seen
    Full many a sprightly race
Disporting on thy margent green
    The paths of pleasure trace,
25 Who foremost now delight to cleave
With pliant arm thy glassy wave?
    The captive linnet which enthrall?°   imprison
What idle progeny succeed[3]
To chase the rolling circle's[4] speed,
30   Or urge the flying ball?

1. "I am a man, and that is reason enough for being miserable" (Greek).
2. Henry VI, founder of Eton.
3. Follow the example of the preceding generation.
4. "The rolling circle": the hoop.

While some on earnest business bent
  Their murmuring labors ply
'Gainst graver hours, that bring constraint
  To sweeten liberty:
35 Some bold adventurers disdain
The limits of their little reign,
  And unknown regions dare descry:°   *discover*
Still as they run they look behind,
They hear a voice in every wind,
40 And snatch a fearful joy.

Gay hope is theirs by fancy fed,
  Less pleasing when possessed;
The tear forgot as soon as shed,
  The sunshine of the breast:
45 Theirs buxom° health of rosy hue,   *vigorous*
Wild wit, invention ever new,
  And lively cheer of vigor born;
The thoughtless day, the easy night,
The spirits pure, the slumbers light,
50 That fly the approach of morn.

Alas, regardless of their doom,
  The little victims play!
No sense have they of ills to come,
  Nor care beyond today.
55 Yet see how all around 'em wait
The ministers of human fate,
  And black Misfortune's baleful train!
Ah, show them where in ambush stand
To seize their prey the murderous band!
60 Ah, tell them they are men!

These shall the fury Passions tear,
  The vultures of the mind,
Disdainful Anger, pallid Fear,
  And Shame that skulks behind;
65 Or pining Love shall waste their youth,
Or Jealousy with rankling tooth,
  That inly gnaws the secret heart,
And Envy wan, and faded Care,
Grim-visaged comfortless Despair,
70 And Sorrow's piercing dart.

Ambition this[5] shall tempt to rise,
  Then whirl the wretch from high,
To bitter Scorn a sacrifice,
  And grinning Infamy.
75 The stings of Falsehood those[6] shall try,
And hard Unkindness' altered eye,
  That mocks the tear it forced to flow;

---

5. I.e., one of them.   6. I.e., others.

And keen Remorse with blood defiled,
And moody Madness laughing wild
80   Amid severest woe.

Lo, in the vale of years beneath
    A grisly troop are seen,
The painful family of Death,
    More hideous than their queen:
85 This racks the joints, this fires the veins,
    That every laboring sinew strains,
        Those in the deeper vitals rage:
Lo, Poverty, to fill the band,
That numbs the soul with icy hand,
90   And slow-consuming Age.

To each his sufferings: all are men,
    Condemned alike to groan;
The tender for another's pain,
    The unfeeling for his own.
95 Yet ah! why should they know their fate?
Since sorrow never comes too late,
    And happiness too swiftly flies.
Thought would destroy their paradise.
No more; where ignorance is bliss,
100   'Tis folly to be wise.

1742

1747

Ode

On the Death of a Favorite Cat, Drowned in a Tub of Goldfishes

'Twas on a lofty vase's side,
Where China's gayest art had dyed
    The azure flowers that blow;°   bloom
Demurest of the tabby kind,
5   The pensive Selima, reclined,
    Gazed on the lake below.

Her conscious tail her joy declared;
The fair round face, the snowy beard,
    The velvet of her paws,
10 Her coat, that with the tortoise vies,
Her ears of jet, and emerald eyes,
    She saw; and purred applause.

Still had she gazed; but 'midst the tide
Two angel forms were seen to glide,
15   The genii° of the stream: guardian spirits
Their scaly armor's Tyrian hue
Through richest purple to the view
    Betrayed a golden gleam.[7]

7. "Tyrian" and (in classical reference) "purple" cover a considerable spectrum, including crimson. The fish are seen, through red highlights, as golden.

The hapless nymph with wonder saw:
20   A whisker first and then a claw,
    With many an ardent wish,
She stretched in vain to reach the prize.
What female heart can gold despise?
    What cat's averse to fish?

25   Presumptuous maid! with looks intent
Again she stretched, again she bent,
    Nor knew the gulf between.
(Malignant Fate sat by and smiled)
The slippery verge her feet beguilded,
30   She tumbled headlong in.

Eight times emerging from the flood
She mewed to every watery god,
    Some speedy aid to send.
No dolphin came, no Nereid stirred;[8]
35   Nor cruel Tom, nor Susan heard;
    A favorite has no friend!

From hence, ye beauties, undeceived,
Know, one false step is ne'er retrieved,
    And be with caution bold.
40   Not all that tempts your wandering eyes
And heedless hearts, is lawful prize;
    Nor all that glisters, gold.

1747   1748

Elegy Written in a Country Churchyard

The curfew° tolls the knell of parting day,   *evening bell*
  The lowing herd wind slowly o'er the lea,
The plowman homeward plods his weary way,
  And leaves the world to darkness and to me.

5 Now fades the glimmering landscape on the sight,
  And all the air a solemn stillness holds,
Save where the beetle wheels his droning flight,
  And drowsy tinklings lull the distant folds;

Save that from yonder ivy-mantled tower
10   The moping owl does to the moon complain
Of such, as wandering near her secret bower,
  Molest her ancient solitary reign.

Beneath those rugged elms, that yew tree's shade,
  Where heaves the turf in many a moldering heap,
15 Each in his narrow cell forever laid,
  The rude° forefathers of the hamlet sleep.   *rustic*

8. A dolphin appeared to save the singer Arion when he was cast overboard. Nereids are sea nymphs.

The breezy call of incense-breathing morn,
  The swallow twittering from the straw-built shed,
  The cock's shrill clarion, or the echoing horn,°   *hunting horn*
20 No more shall rouse them from their lowly bed.

For them no more the blazing hearth shall burn,
  Or busy housewife ply her evening care;
No children run to lisp their sire's return,
  Or climb his knees the envied kiss to share.

25 Oft did the harvest to their sickle yield,
  Their furrow oft the stubborn glebe° has broke;   *soil*
How jocund did they drive their team afield!
  How bowed the woods beneath their sturdy stroke!

Let not Ambition mock their useful toil,
30 Their homely joys, and destiny obscure;
Nor Grandeur hear with a disdainful smile
  The short and simple annals of the poor.

The boast of heraldry,[9] the pomp of power,
  And all that beauty, all that wealth e'er gave,
35 Awaits alike the inevitable hour.
  The paths of glory lead but to the grave.

Nor you, ye proud, impute to these the fault,
  If Memory o'er their tomb no trophies[1] raise,
Where through the long-drawn aisle and fretted° vault   *ornamented*
40 The pealing anthem swells the note of praise.

Can storied urn[2] or animated° bust   *lifelike*
  Back to its mansion call the fleeting breath?
Can Honor's voice provoke° the silent dust,   *call forth*
  Or Flattery soothe the dull cold ear of Death?

45 Perhaps in this neglected spot is laid
  Some heart once pregnant with celestial fire;
Hands that the rod of empire might have swayed,
  Or waked to ecstasy the living lyre.

But Knowledge to their eyes her ample page
50 Rich with the spoils of time did ne'er unroll;
Chill Penury repressed their noble rage,
  And froze the genial current of the soul.

Full many a gem of purest ray serene,
  The dark unfathomed caves of ocean bear:
55 Full many a flower is born to blush unseen,
  And waste its sweetness on the desert air.

---

9. I.e., noble family.
1. Memorials to military heroes; typically, statuary representations of arms captured in battle.
2. Funeral urn with descriptive epitaph.

Some village Hampden,[3] that with dauntless breast
    The little tyrant of his fields withstood;
Some mute inglorious Milton here may rest,
60   Some Cromwell guiltless of his country's blood.

The applause of listening senates to command,
    The threats of pain and ruin to despise,
To scatter plenty o'er a smiling land,
    And read their history in a nation's eyes,

65   Their lot forbade: nor circumscribed alone
    Their growing virtues, but their crimes confined;
Forbade to wade through slaughter to a throne,
    And shut the gates of mercy on mankind,

The struggling pangs of conscious truth to hide,
70   To quench the blushes of ingenuous shame,
Or heap the shrine of Luxury and Pride
    With incense kindled at the Muse's flame.

Far from the madding[4] crowd's ignoble strife,
    Their sober wishes never learned to stray;
75   Along the cool sequestered vale of life
    They kept the noiseless tenor of their way.

Yet even these bones from insult to protect
    Some frail memorial still erected nigh,
With uncouth rhymes and shapeless sculpture decked,
80   Implores the passing tribute of a sigh.

Their name, their years, spelt by the unlettered Muse,
    The place of fame and elegy supply:
And many a holy text around she strews,
    That teach the rustic moralist to die.

85   For who to dumb Forgetfulness a prey,
    This pleasing anxious being e'er resigned,
Left the warm precincts of the cheerful day,
    Nor cast one longing lingering look behind?

On some fond breast the parting soul relies,
90   Some pious drops the closing eye requires;
Even from the tomb the voice of Nature cries,
    Even in our ashes live their wonted fires.

For thee, who mindful of the unhonored dead
    Dost in these lines their artless tale relate;
95   If chance, by lonely contemplation led,
    Some kindred spirit shall inquire thy fate,

3. Leader of the opposition to Charles I in the   civil wars.
controversy over ship money; killed in battle in the   4. I.e., either maddening or acting madly.

Haply some hoary-headed swain may say,
  "Oft have we seen him at the peep of dawn
Brushing with hasty steps the dews away
100   To meet the sun upon the upland lawn.

"There at the foot of yonder nodding beech
  That wreathes its old fantastic roots so high,
His listless length at noontide would he stretch,
  And pore upon the brook that babbles by.

105 "Hard by yon wood, now smiling as in scorn,
  Muttering his wayward fancies he would rove,
Now drooping, woeful wan, like one forlorn,
  Or crazed with care, or crossed in hopeless love.

"One morn I missed him on the customed hill,
110   Along the heath and near his favorite tree;
Another came; nor yet beside the rill,
  Nor up the lawn, nor at the wood was he;

"The next with dirges due in sad array
  Slow through the churchway path we saw him borne.
115 Approach and read (for thou canst read) the lay,
  Graved on the stone beneath yon aged thorn."

The Epitaph

Here rests his head upon the lap of Earth
  A youth to Fortune and to Fame unknown.
Fair Science° frowned not on his humble birth,   Learning
120   And Melancholy marked him for her own.

Large was his bounty, and his soul sincere,
  Heaven did a recompense as largely send:
He gave to Misery all he had, a tear,
  He gained from Heaven ('twas all he wished) a friend.

125 No farther seek his merits to disclose,
  Or draw his frailties from their dread abode
(There they alike in trembling hope repose),
  The bosom of his Father and his God.

ca. 1742–50   1751

Sonnet

On the Death of Mr. Richard West[5]

In vain to me the smiling mornings shine,
  And reddening Phoebus° lifts his golden fire;   the sun god
The birds in vain their amorous descant join,°   harmonize
  Or cheerful fields resume their green attire;
5   These ears, alas! for other notes repine,

5. West, a friend of Gray's since preparatory school, had died at the age of twenty-six.

A different object do these eyes require;°   *ask for*
My lonely anguish melts no heart but mine,
   And in my breast the imperfect joys expire.
Yet morning smiles the busy race to cheer,
10   And newborn pleasure brings to happier men;
The fields to all their wonted tribute bear;
   To warm their little loves the birds complain:[6]
I fruitless mourn to him that cannot hear,
   And weep the more, because I weep in vain.

1742   1775

WILLIAM COLLINS

1721–1759

Ode Written in the Beginning of the Year 1746[1]

How sleep the brave who sink to rest
By all their country's wishes blest!
When Spring, with dewy fingers cold,
Returns to deck their hallowed mold,
5 She there shall dress a sweeter sod
Than Fancy's feet have ever trod.

By fairy hands their knell is rung,
By forms unseen their dirge is sung;
There Honor comes, a pilgrim gray,
10 To bless the turf that wraps their clay,
And Freedom shall awhile repair,
To dwell a weeping hermit there!

                                            1746

Ode on the Poetical Character

Strophe[2]

As once, if not with light regard,
I read aright that gifted bard
(Him whose school above the rest
His loveliest Elfin Queen has blest).[3]
5 One, only one, unrivaled fair,
Might hope the magic girdle[4] wear,
At solemn tourney hung on high,
The wish of each love-darting eye;
Lo! to each other nymph in turn applied,

6. I.e., sing of their unfulfilled desire.
1. The poem celebrates Englishmen who fell resisting the pretender to the throne ("Bonnie Prince Charlie," the grandson of James II) in the previous year.
2. Initial segment of the Greek choral ode, delivered with the chorus in motion; normally followed by the antistrophe, with the chorus in reverse motion, and then by the epode, with the chorus standing still.
3. Edmund Spenser, whose followers ("school") have exalted his *Faerie Queene* above his other poems.
4. A belt, "band" (line 12), "zone" (line 16), or "cest" (line 19) described in *Faerie Queene* 4.5: it "gave the virtue of chaste love and wifehood to all that did it bear." "Peerless was she thought" that wore it.

10   As if, in air unseen, some hovering hand,
      Some chaste and angel-friend to virgin-fame,
            With whispered spell had burst the starting band,
      It left unblest her loathed dishonored side;
            Happier, hopeless fair, if never
15   Her baffled hand with vain endeavor
      Had touched that fatal zone to her denied!
      Young Fancy thus, to me divinest name,
            To whom, prepared and bathed in Heaven
            The cest[5] of amplest power is given;
20   To few the godlike gift assigns,
            To gird their blest, prophetic loins,
      And gaze her visions wild, and feel unmixed her flame!

Epode

      The band, as fairy legends say,
      Was wove on that creating day,
25   When He, who called with thought to birth
      Yon tented sky, this laughing earth,
      And dressed with springs, and forests tall,
      And poured the main engirting all,
      Long by the loved Enthusiast[6] wooed,
30   Himself in some diviner mood,
      Retiring, sate with her alone,
      And placed her on his sapphire throne;
      The whiles, the vaulted shrine around,
      Seraphic wires were heard to sound,
35   Now sublimest triumph swelling,
      Now on love and mercy dwelling;
      And she, from out the veiling cloud,
      Breathed her magic notes aloud:
      And thou, thou rich-haired Youth of Morn,[7]
40   And all thy subject life was born!
      The dangerous Passions kept aloof,
      Far from the sainted growing woof;[8]
      But near it sate ecstatic Wonder,
      Listening the deep applauding thunder;
45   And Truth, in sunny vest arrayed,
      By whose the tarsel's° eyes were made;   *male falcon's*
      All the shadowy tribes of Mind,
      In braided dance their murmurs joined,
      And all the bright uncounted Powers
50   Who feed on Heaven's ambrosial flowers.
      Where is the bard, whose soul can now
      Its high presuming hopes avow?
      Where he who thinks, with rapture blind,
      This hallow'd work for him designed?

---

5. From *cestus* (Latin): "girdle" or "belt."   7. Apollo, the sun, god of poetry.
6. Literally, one inspired by God; i.e., Fancy.   8. The fabric of the girdle (line 6).

Antistrophe

55 High on some cliff, to Heaven up-piled,
Of rude access, of prospect wild,
Where, tangled round the jealous steep,
Strange shades o'erbrow the valleys deep,
And holy Genii guard the rock,
60 Its glooms embrown, its springs unlock,
While on its rich ambitious head,
An Eden, like his[9] own, lies spread;
I view that oak, the fancied glades among,
By which as Milton lay, his evening ear,
65 From many a cloud that dropped ethereal dew,
Nigh sphered in Heaven its native strains could hear;
On which that ancient trump[1] he reached was hung;
Thither oft, his glory greeting,
From Waller's[2] myrtle shades retreating,
70 With many a vow from Hope's aspiring tongue,
My trembling feet his guiding steps pursue;
In vain—such bliss to one alone,
Of all the sons of soul was known,
And Heaven, and Fancy, kindred powers,
75 Have now o'erturned the inspiring bowers,
Or curtained close such scene from every future view.

1746

Ode to Evening

If aught of oaten stop,[3] or pastoral song,
May hope, chaste Eve, to soothe thy modest ear,
Like thy own solemn springs,
Thy springs and dying gales,
5 O nymph reserved, while now the bright-haired sun
Sits in yon western tent, whose cloudy skirts,
With brede° ethereal wove,   *braid*
O'erhang his wavy bed:
Now air is hushed, save where the weak-eyed bat,
10 With short shrill shriek flits by on leathern wing,
Or where the beetle winds
His small but sullen horn,
As oft he rises 'midst the twilight path,
Against the pilgrim° borne in heedless hum: *wayfarer*
15 Now teach me, maid composed,
To breathe some softened strain,
Whose numbers, stealing through thy darkening vale,
May not unseemly with its stillness suit,
As, musing slow, I hail
20 Thy genial loved return!

---

9. Milton's.
1. Milton's epic or sublime trumpet. The line echoes "Il Penseroso," lines 59–60 ("While Cynthia checks her Dragon yoke, / Gently o'er th'accustomed Oke"), and "Nativity Ode," line 156 ("The wakefull trump").
2. Edmund Waller. The "myrtle," sacred to Venus, is an emblem of love.
3. I.e., if any modulation of a (shepherd's) reed.

For when thy folding-star[4] arising shows
His paly° circlet, at his warning lamp   *pale*
   The fragrant Hours, and elves
   Who slept in flowers the day,
25 And many a nymph who wreaths her brows with sedge,
And sheds the freshening dew, and, lovelier still,
   The pensive Pleasures sweet,
   Prepare thy shadowy car.
Then lead, calm votaress, where some sheety lake
30 Cheers the lone heath, or some time-hallowed pile
   Or upland fallows[5] gray
   Reflect its last cool gleam.
But when chill blustering winds, or driving rain,
Forbid my willing feet, be mine the hut
35   That from the mountain's side
   Views wilds, and swelling floods,
And hamlets° brown, and dim-discovered spires,   *villages*
And hears their simple bell, and marks o'er all
   Thy dewy fingers draw
40   The gradual dusky veil.
While Spring shall pour his showers, as oft he wont,
And bathe thy breathing tresses, meekest Eve;
   While Summer loves to sport
   Beneath thy lingering light;
45 While sallow Autumn fills thy lap with leaves;
Or Winter, yelling through the troublous air,
   Affrights thy shrinking train,
   And rudely rends thy robes;
So long, sure-found beneath the sylvan shed,[6]
50 Shall Fancy, Friendship, Science, rose-lipped Health,
   Thy gentlest influence own,
   And hymn thy favorite name!

                                          1746, 1748

MARY LEAPOR

1722–1746

Mira's Will

Imprimis[1]—my departed shade I trust
To Heaven—my body to the silent dust;
My name to public censure I submit,
To be disposed of as the world thinks fit;
5 My vice and folly let oblivion close,°   *end*
The world already is o'erstocked with those;
My wit I give, as misers give their store,

---

4. The evening star, which, when it becomes visible, tells the shepherd to drive his flock to the sheepfold.
5. I.e., ploughed land. Cf. Milton, "L'Allegro," line 71 (p. 367).

6. I.e., secure beneath the shelter of the forest.
1. "In the first place" (Latin); this word is used to introduce the first of a number of items in a formal will.

To those who think they had enough before.
Bestow my patience to compose the lives
10 Of slighted virgins and neglected wives;
To modish[2] lovers I resign my truth,
My cool reflection to unthinking youth;
And some good-nature give ('tis my desire)
To surly husbands, as their needs require;
15 And first discharge my funeral—and then
To the small poets I bequeath my pen.

Let a small sprig (true emblem of my rhyme)
Of blasted laurel[3] on my hearse recline;
Let some grave wight,° that struggles for renown,   *person*
20 By chanting dirges° through a market-town,   *funeral songs*
With gentle step precede the solemn train;
A broken flute[4] upon his arm shall lean.
Six comic poets may the corpse surround,
And all free-holders,[5] if they can be found:
25 Then follow next the melancholy throng,
As shrewd instructors, who themselves
        are wrong.
The virtuoso,° rich in sun-dried weeds,°   *learned person, scholar / clothes*
The politician, whom no mortal heeds,
The silent lawyer, chambered all the day,
30 And the stern soldier that receives no pay.
But stay—the mourners should be first our care,
Let the freed prentice lead the miser's heir;
Let the young relict° wipe her mournful eye,   *widow*
And widowed husbands o'er their garlic cry.

35   All this let my executors fulfil,
And rest assured that this is Mira's will,
Who was, when she these legacies designed,
In body healthy, and composed in mind.

                                                    1748

The Epistle of Deborah Dough

Dearly beloved Cousin, these
Are sent to thank you for your cheese;
The price of oats is greatly fell:
I hope your children all are well
5 (Likewise the calf you take delight in),
As I am at this present writing.
But I've no news to send you now;
Only I've lost my brindled° cow,   *streaked, spotted*
And that has greatly sunk my dairy.
10 But I forgot our neighbor Mary;

2. Following the prevailing fashion; usually used disparagingly.
3. The laurel is a symbol of poetic achievement.
4. According to pastoral convention, the poet often plays a flute or pipe, symbolizing his poetry writing.

5. Those who possessed a free-hold estate, i.e., tenure in real property held fee-simple (inheritable without limitation to any particular class of heirs), fee-tail (inheritable but limited to a particular class of heirs), or for term of life.

Our neighbor Mary—who, they say,
Sits scribble-scribble all the day,
And making—what—I can't remember;
But sure 'tis something like December;
15   A frosty morning—let me see—
O! now I have it to a T:
She throws away her precious time
In scrawling nothing else but rhyme;
Of which, they say, she's mighty proud,
20   And lifts her nose above the crowd;
Though my young daughter Cicely
Is taller by a foot than she,
And better learned (as people say);
Can knit a stocking in a day;
25   Can make a pudding, plump and rare;°   excellent
And boil her bacon to an hair;[6]
Will coddle° apples nice and green,   stew
And fry her pancakes—like a queen.

But there's a man, that keeps a dairy,
30   Will clip the wings of neighbor Mary:
Things wonderful they talk of him,
But I've a notion 'tis a whim.
Howe'er, 'tis certain he can make
Your rhymes as thick as plums in cake;
35   Nay more, they say that from the pot
He'll take his porridge, scalding hot,
And drink 'em down;—and yet they tell ye
Those porridge shall not burn his belly;
A cheesecake o'er his head he'll throw,
40   And when 'tis on the stones below,
It shan't be found so much as quaking,
Provided 'tis of his wife's making.
From this some people would infer
That this good man's a conjuror:°   magician
45   But I believe it is a lie;
I never thought him so, not I,
Though Win'fred Hobble who, you know,
Is plagued with corns on every toe,
Sticks on his verse with fastening spittle,
50   And says it helps her feet a little.
Old Frances too his paper tears,
And tucks it close behind his ears;
And (as she told me t'other day)
It charmed her toothache quite away.[7]

55   Now as thou'rt better learned than me,
Dear Cos', I leave it all to thee

6. With the utmost exactness.
7. Charms were verbal formulas believed to have healing powers when written down and applied directly to the ailing body part. Evidence seems to suggest a fairly widespread use of such charms before the Reformation, which brought a gradual decline as official Protestant theology rejected charms as a superstitious, Catholic practice. By the time this poem was written, such charms would probably have been considered an outmoded folk remedy.

To judge about this puzzling man,
And ponder wisely—for you can.

Now Cousin, I must let you know
60   That, while my name is Deborah Dough,
I shall be always glad to see ye,
And what I have, I'll freely gi' ye.

'Tis one o'clock, as I'm a sinner;
The boys are all come home to dinner,
65   And I must bid you now farewell.
I pray remember me to Nell;
And for your friend I'd have you know
Your loving Cousin,
                    DEBORAH DOUGH

ca. 1746   1751

JEAN ELLIOT
1727–1805

The Flowers of the Forest[1]

I've heard the lilting[2] at our yowe°-milking,	*ewe*
Lasses a-lilting before the dawn o' day;	
But now they are moaning on ilka° green loaning:[3]	*each*
"The Flowers of the Forest are a' wede away."[4]	

5   At buchts,° in the morning, nae° blythe lads are scorning;°   *sheepfolds / no*
                                                                                                           teasing
      The lasses are lonely, and dowie,° and wae;°   *sad / wretched*
      Nae daffin',° nae gabbin', but sighing and sabbing:°   *foolish playing*
                                                                                                           sobbing
      Ilk ane° lifts her leglen,° and hies her away.   *each one / milk pail*

      In hairst,° at the shearing, nae youths now are jeering,   *harvest*
10   The bandsters[5] are lyart, and runkled and gray;
      At fair or at preaching, nae wooing, nae fleeching:°   *flattering*
      The Flowers of the Forest are a' wede away.

      At e'en, in the gloaming,° nae swankies[6] are roaming   *twilight*
      'Bout stacks[7] wi' the lasses at bogle° to play,   *hide-and-seek*

1. This poem is a ballad on the battle of Flodden, an English victory over the Scots in 1513. James IV of Scotland, in alliance with France, had invaded the north of England. At Flodden in Northumberland, James' army occupied a strong position and outnumbered the English troops, but James proved an incompetent, though brave, general. More than ten thousand Scots were killed at Flodden, including James himself. Elliot set the words of the ballad to an old Scottish air, from which she takes her first and fourth lines; cf. Pete Seeger, "Where Have All the Flowers Gone?" (p. 1746).
2. Sweet and cheerful singing.
3. Uncultivated ground used for milking.
4. Carried off, especially by death.
5. Those who bind sheaves behind the reaper.
6. Strapping young men.
7. Large piles of dried peat erected outdoors as a fuel store.

15   But ilk ane sits drearie, lamenting her dearie:
        The Flowers of the Forest are a' wede away.

    Dule° and wae° for the order sent our lads to the Border;   *grief / woe*
        The English, for ance,° by guile wan° the day;   *once / won*
    The Flowers of the Forest, that foucht aye the foremost,
20   The prime o' our land, are cauld° in the clay.   *cold*

    We'll hear nae mair° lilting at our yowe-milking,   *more*
        Women and bairns° are heartless and wae;   *children*
    Sighing and moaning on ilka green loaning:
        "The Flowers of the Forest are a' wede away."

1769

CHRISTOPHER SMART

1722–1771

From A Song to David[1]

David the son of Jesse said, and the man who was raised up on high, the anointed of the God of Jacob, and the sweet psalmist of Israel, said, "The Spirit of the Lord spake by me, and His Word was in my tongue."

—2 Samuel 23.1, 2

1

    O Thou, that sit'st upon a throne,   *[Invocation]*[2]
    With harp of high majestic tone,
        To praise the King of kings;
    And voice of heav'n-ascending swell,
5   Which, while its deeper notes excel,
        Clear, as a clarion,° rings: *trumpet*

2

    To bless each valley, grove and coast,
    And charm the cherubs[3] to the post
        Of gratitude in throngs;
10   To keep the days on Zion's[4] mount,
    And send the year to his account,
        With dances and with songs:[5]

1. David was the second king of Israel. In an advertisement for the first edition (printed in *Poems on Several Occasions* 1763]), Smart called this work "A Poem composed in a Spirit of affection and thankfulness to the great Author of the Book of Gratitude, which is the Psalms of David the King." Smart's main sources for the poem were the Bible and Patrick Delaney's *An Historical Account of the Life and Reign of David King of Israel* (1740).
2. In the first edition, Smart prefaced the poem with a summary, which is here reprinted as a series of marginal glosses. The invocation is a poetic convention in which the poet requests divine inspiration and assistance to write his poem. Smart here calls upon David.

3. One of the nine orders of angels.
4. Zion is the name of one of the hills of Jerusalem and may be used figuratively to connote the Israelites, the Christian Church, the heavenly Jerusalem, or a place of worship.
5. David's task, to "keep the days," is both to observe the religious rites and festivals and to maintain a record of the history of the Israelites in order to "send the year to his [God's] account," i.e., to his reckoning, for his sake, or to his credit. (One of Smart's own projects was to compose a complete cycle of hymns for the major occasions in the calendar of the Anglican Church.)

3

O Servant of God's holiest charge,
The minister of praise at large,
15   Which thou may'st now receive;[6]
From thy blessed mansion hail and hear,
From topmost eminence appear
      To this the wreath I weave.[7]

4

Great, valiant, pious, good, and clean,   [*The excellence and luster*
20   Sublime, contemplative, serene,   *of David's character in*
      Strong, constant, pleasant, wise![8]   *twelve points of view;*]
Bright effluence° of exceeding grace;   *outflowing*
Best man!—the swiftness and the race,
      The peril, and the prize!

5

25   Great—from the luster of his crown,   [*proved from the*
From Samuel's horn[9] and God's renown,   *history of his life*]
      Which is the people's voice;
From all the host° from rear to van,°   *Israelites / front*
Applauded and embraced the man—
30   The man of God's own choice.

6

Valiant—the word, and up he rose—
The fight—he triumphed o'er the foes,
      Whom God's just laws abhor;°   *hate*
And armed in gallant faith he took
35   Against the boaster,[1] from the brook
      The weapons of the war,

7

Pious—magnificent and grand;
'Twas he the famous temple planned:
      (The seraph in his soul)[2]
40   Foremost to give the Lord his dues,
Foremost to bless the welcome news,
      And foremost to condole.

8

Good—from Jehudah's genuine vein,
From God's best nature good in grain,[3]
45   His aspect and his heart;

---

6. I.e., David, whose responsibility is praise of God, will now receive the praise of the poet.
7. Smart compares his poem to a wreath; the laurel wreath was a symbol of poetic achievement.
8. The next twelve stanzas will give an example from David's life of each of these twelve virtues. (In "Jubilate Agno," Smart associates these twelve virtues with the twelve tribes of Israel.)
9. God sent Samuel to Bethlehem to choose David, a then unknown shepherd-boy, to be the next king of Israel: "Then Samuel took the horn of oil, and anointed him in the midst of his brethren: and the spirit of the Lord came upon David from that day forward" (1 Samuel 16.13).
1. The Philistine giant, Goliath, whom David

killed using his sling and a stone from a brook.
2. David received the "pattern" or plan for the temple "by the Spirit" (1 Chronicles 28.12); the "seraph" seems to be an invention of Delaney's. Although David wanted to build the temple himself, he was told by the prophet Nathan that God would not allow him to do so. He was promised that his son, Solomon, would build the temple; "welcome news" is the Davidic Covenant, God's promise that David's line would be established kings of Israel.
3. In background and substance; David came from the tribe of Judah (Jehudah is a variation of Judah).

To pity, to forgive, to save,
Witness En-gedi's conscious cave,[4]
And Shimei's blunted dart.[5]

9

Clean—if perpetual prayer be pure,
50   And love, which could itself inure°   *accustom*
    To fasting and to fear—
Clean in his gestures, hands, and feet,
To smite the lyre,° the dance complete,   *stringed instrument*
    To play the sword and spear.

10

55 Sublime—invention ever young,
Of vast conception, towering tongue,
    To God the external theme;
Notes from yon exaltations caught,
Unrivaled royalty of thought,
60   O'er meaner strains supreme.

11

Contemplative—on God to fix
His musings, and above the six
    The sabbath-day he blessed;
'Twas then his thoughts self-conquest pruned,
65 And heavenly melancholy tuned,
    To bless and bear the rest.

12

Serene—to sow the seeds of peace,
Remembering, when he watched the fleece,
    How sweetly Kidron[6] purled°—   *murmured*
70 To further knowledge, silence vice,
And plant perpetual paradise
    When God had calmed the world.

13

Strong—in the Lord, who could defy
Satan, and all his powers that lie
75   In sempiternal° night;   *everlasting*
And hell, and horror, and despair
Were as the lion and the bear[7]
    To his undaunted might.

14

Constant—in love to God The Truth,
80 Age, manhood, infancy, and youth—
    To Jonathan his friend
Constant, beyond the verge of death;

---

4. Before David became king of Israel, Saul, the reigning king, pursued him with an army in an attempt to kill him. One day, in the wilderness of Engedi, Saul wandered alone into a cave where David and his men were hiding. Although his men urged him to take advantage of this easy opportunity to kill Saul, David refused.
5. Shimei, a relative of Saul, cursed and threw stones at King David, but David refused to kill him.
6. A brook that borders the district of Jerusalem. As a youth, David tended his father's flocks near this brook.
7. In 1 Samuel 17, David credits God with helping him kill a lion and a bear that were ravaging his flock.

And Ziba, and Mephibosheth
His endless fame attend.[8]

15

85 Pleasant—and various as the year;
Man, soul, and angel, without peer,
Priest, champion, sage and boy;
In armor, or in ephod° clad,   *priestly vestment*
His pomp, his piety was glad;
90 Majestic was his joy.

16

Wise—in recovery from his fall,[9]
Whence rose his eminence o'er all,
Of all the most reviled;
The light of Israel in his ways,
95 Wise are his precepts, prayer and praise,
And counsel to his child.[1]

17

His muse, bright angel of his verse,   *[He consecrates his*
Gives balm for all the thorns that pierce,   *genius for consolation*
For all the pangs that rage   *and edification]*
100 Blessed light, still gaining on the gloom,
The more than Michal of his bloom,
The Abishag of his age.[2]

18

He sung of god—the mighty source   *[The subjects he*
Of all things—the stupendous force   *made choice of—the*
105 Of which all strength depends;   *Supreme Being;]*
From whose right arm, beneath whose eyes,
All period,[3] power, and enterprise
Commences, reigns, and ends.

1763   1763

Psalm 58[4]

Ye congregation of the tribes,[5]
On justice do you set your mind;

8. During the time that Saul was trying to kill him, David became fast friends with Saul's son Jonathan. David made a covenant with Jonathan, promising to extend his kindness to Jonathan's house, even after Jonathan's death (1 Samuel 20.15). David honored this covenant many years later when he restored Saul's land to Jonathan's son, Mephibosheth, and invited him to eat at David's own table (2 Samuel 9). The stewardship of the land was awarded to Ziba (a servant of Saul) and his family.
9. David's "fall" was the result of his lust for Bathsheba and his arranging to have her husband, Uriah, killed in battle. David repented of his sin and asked God's forgiveness (Psalm 51). It is Delaney who emphasizes David's repentance and insists that his greatness rose out of his recovery from sin.
1. According to 1 Kings 2 and 1 Chronicles 22,

just before his death David gave advice to Solomon, his son and successor. David counseled Solomon to keep the commandments of God and to build the temple. Delaney notes that David left precepts for his son in the Psalms and Proverbs.
2. Michal was David's first wife; Abishag, a young woman who nursed him in his old age.
3. Possibly meaning accomplishments, achievements; or, set amount of time (during which one has power).
4. Cf. the versions of this Psalm by Mary Sidney (pp. 199–200), by Isaac Watts (pp. 536–37), and from *The Massachusetts Bay Psalm Book* (pp. 491–92).
5. "Congregation," a common Protestant term for members of a church, here refers to the collective body of the Israelites; there were twelve tribes of Israel.

And are ye free from guile and bribes
   Ye judges of mankind?

5   Nay, ye of frail and mortal mould
     Imagine mischief in your heart;
   Your suffrages[6] and selves are sold
     Unto the general mart.

Men of unrighteous seed betray
10   Perverseness from their mother's womb;[7]
   As soon as they can run astray,
     Against the truth presume.

They are with foul infection stained,
     Ev'n with the serpent's taint impure;
15   Their ears to blest persuasion chained,
     And locked against her lure.[8]

Though Christ himself the pipe should tune,
     They will not to the measure tread,[9]
   Nor will they with his grief commune°   *sympathize*
20   Though tears of blood he shed.

Lord, humanize their scoff and scorn,
     And their malevolence defeat;
   Of water and the spirit born[1]
     Let grace their change complete.

25   Let them with pious ardor burn,
     And make thy holy church their choice;
   To thee with all their passions turn,
     And in thy light rejoice.

As quick as lightning to its mark,
30   So let thy gracious angel speed;
   And take their spirits in thine ark[2]
     To their eternal mead.°   *reward*

The righteous shall exult the more
   As he such powerful mercy sees,

---

6. Intercessory prayers; petitions to god; supplications; also, in the Church of England, various versicles and their responses in morning and evening prayer and in the Litany.

7. The doctrine of original sin holds that children are born sinful, but Smart seems here to allude to the Calvinist idea that some people are predestined to damnation.

8. Cf. the King James Bible's image (in Psalm 58) of an adder that "stoppeth up her ear" so that the charmer cannot charm her.

9. "To tread a measure" is to dance in a rhythmic or stately manner.

1. Jesus uses these terms in the New Testament: "Except a man be born of water and of the Spirit, he cannot enter the kingdom of God" (John 3.5); but in the Old Testament, God, in forming a new covenant with the people of Israel, says, "Then will I sprinkle clean water upon you, and ye shall be clean; from all your filthiness, and from all your idols, will I cleanse you. A new heart also will I give you, and a new spirit will I put within you" (Ezekiel 36.25–26).

2. The Ark of the covenant contained "the two tables of stone, which Moses put there at Horeb, when the Lord made a covenant with the children of Israel, when they came out of the land of Egypt" (1 Kings 8.9); thus it is a symbol of God's promise to guide and protect the Israelites.

35   Such wrecks and ruins safe on shore,
      Such tortured souls at ease.

    So that a man shall say, no doubt,
      The penitent has his reward;
    There is a God to bear him out,
40   And he is Christ our Lord.

1763   1765

From Jubilate Agno[3]

For I will consider my Cat Jeoffry.
For he is the servant of the Living God, duly and daily serving
    him.
For at the first glance of the glory of God in the East he worships
    in his way.
700 For is this done by wreathing his body seven times round with
    elegant quickness.
For then he leaps up to catch the musk,[4] which is the blessing of
    God upon his prayer.
For he rolls upon prank[5] to work it in.
For having done duty and received blessing he begins to consider
    himself.
For this he performs in ten degrees.
705 For first he looks upon his forepaws to see if they are clean.
For secondly he kicks up behind to clear away there.
For thirdly he works it upon stretch with the forepaws extended.
For fourthly he sharpens his paws by wood.
For fifthly he washes himself.
710 For sixthly he rolls upon wash.
For seventhly he fleas himself, that he may not be interrupted
    upon the beat.[6]
For eighthly he rubs himself against a post.
For ninthly he looks up for his instructions.
For tenthly he goes in quest of food.
715 For having considered God and himself he will consider his
    neighbor.
For if he meets another cat he will kiss her in kindness.
For when he takes his prey he plays with it to give it a chance.
For one mouse in seven escapes by his dallying.
For when his day's work is done his business more properly
    begins.
720 For he keeps the Lord's watch in the night against the adversary.
For he counteracts the powers of darkness by his electrical skin
    and glaring eyes.
For he counteracts the Devil, who is death, by brisking about the
    life.

---

3. "Rejoice in the Lamb" (Latin); i.e., in Jesus, the Lamb of God; written while Smart was confined for insanity. The form of the poem derives from the biblical Psalms.

4. His own or another animal's scent, or perhaps a plant odor.
5. I.e., in display or jest.
6. Upon his daily round, possibly of hunting.

For in his morning orisons he loves the sun and the sun loves
    him.
For he is of the tribe of Tiger.
725 For the Cherub Cat is a term of the Angel Tiger.[7]
For he has the subtlety and hissing of a serpent, which in good-
    ness he suppresses.
For he will not do destruction if he is well-fed, neither will he
    spit without provocation.
For he purrs in thankfulness when God tells him he's a good Cat.
For he is an instrument for the children to learn benevolence
    upon.
730 For every house is incomplete without him, and a blessing is
    lacking in the spirit.
For the Lord commanded Moses concerning the cats at the
    departure of the Children of Israel from Egypt.
For every family had one cat at least in the bag.[8]
For the English Cats are the best in Europe.
For he is the cleanest in the use of his forepaws of any quadruped.
735 For the dexterity of his defense is an instance of the love of God
    to him exceedingly.
For he is the quickest to his mark of any creature.
For he is tenacious of his point.
For he is a mixture of gravity and waggery.
For he knows that God is his Saviour.
740 For there is nothing sweeter than his peace when at rest.
For there is nothing brisker than his life when in motion.
For he is of the Lord's poor, and so indeed is he called by benevo-
    lence perpetually—Poor Jeoffry! poor Jeoffry! the rat has bit
    thy throat.
For I bless the name of the Lord Jesus that Jeoffry is better.
For the divine spirit comes about his body to sustain it in com-
    plete cat.
745 For his tongue is exceeding pure so that it has in purity what it
    wants in music.
For he is docile and can learn certain things.
For he can sit up with gravity, which is patience upon approba-
    tion.
For he can fetch and carry, which is patience in employment.
For he can jump over a stick, which is patience upon proof posi-
    tive.
750 For he can spraggle upon waggle at the word of command.
For he can jump from an eminence into his master's bosom.
For he can catch the cork and toss it again.
For he is hated by the hypocrite and miser.
For the former is afraid of detection.
755 For the latter refuses the charge.
For he camels his back to bear the first notion of business.
For he is good to think on, if a man would express himself neatly.
For he made a great figure in Egypt for his signal services.

---

7. Smart apparently thinks of Jeoffry as an imma-
ture or diminutive phase of a larger creature—
cherubs being by artistic convention small and
childlike.

8. The Israelites took with them silver and gold
ornaments and raiment, as well as flocks and herds
(Exodus 11.2 and 12.32, 35). Smart adds the cats.

For he killed the Icneumon rat, very pernicious by land.[9]
760 For his ears are so acute that they sting again.
For from this proceeds the passing quickness of his attention.
For by stroking of him I have found out electricity.
For I perceived God's light about him both wax and fire.
For the electrical fire is the spiritual substance which God sends
    from heaven to sustain the bodies both of man and beast.
765 For God has blessed him in the variety of his movements.
For, though he cannot fly, he is an excellent clamberer.
For his motions upon the face of the earth are more than any
    other quadruped.
For he can tread to all the measures upon the music.
For he can swim for life.
770 For he can creep.

ca. 1760   1939

OLIVER GOLDSMITH

1730–1774

When Lovely Woman Stoops to Folly

When lovely woman stoops to folly,
    And finds too late that men betray,
What charm can soothe her melancholy,
    What art can wash her guilt away?

5   The only art her guilt to cover,
    To hide her shame from every eye,
To give repentance to her love,
    And wring his bosom — is to die.

1766

The Deserted Village

Sweet Auburn![1] loveliest village of the plain,
Where health and plenty cheered the laboring swain,
Where smiling spring its earliest visit paid,
And parting summer's lingering blooms delayed:
5 Dear lovely bowers of innocence and ease,
Seats of my youth, when every sport could please,
How often have I loitered o'er thy green,
Where humble happiness endeared each scene;
How often have I paused on every charm,
10 The sheltered cot, the cultivated farm,
The never-failing brook, the busy mill,
The decent church that topped the neighboring hill,

---

9. The rats encountered by Jeoffry may have impressed Smart as resembling mongooses (one sense of *ichneumon*); or there may be some reference to the ichneumon fly, a wasplike insect parasitic upon caterpillars.
1. Apparently a fictional, ideal village; there is much debate about its exact prototype.

The hawthorn bush, with seats beneath the shade,
For talking age and whispering lovers made;
15   How often have I blessed the coming day,°   *holiday*
When toil remitting lent its turn to play,
And all the village train, from labor free,
Led up their sports beneath the spreading tree,
While many a pastime circled in the shade,
20   The young contending as the old surveyed;
And many a gambol frolicked o'er the ground,
And sleights of art and feats of strength went round;
And still as each repeated pleasure tired,
Succeeding sports the mirthful band inspired;
25   The dancing pair that simply sought renown,
By holding out to tire each other down;
The swain mistrustless of his smutted face,
While secret laughter tittered round the place;
The bashful virgin's sidelong looks of love,
30   The matron's glance that would those looks reprove:
These were thy charms, sweet village! sports like these,
With sweet succession, taught even toil to please;
These round thy bowers their cheerful influence shed,
These were thy charms—But all these charms are fled.
35   Sweet smiling village, loveliest of the lawn,
Thy sports are fled, and all thy charms withdrawn;
Amidst thy bowers the tyrant's hand is seen,
And desolation saddens all thy green:
One only master grasps the whole domain,
40   And half a tillage² stints thy smiling plain;
No more thy glassy brook reflects the day,
But choked with sedges, works its weedy way;
Along thy glades, a solitary guest,
The hollow-sounding bittern guards its nest;
45   Amidst thy desert walks the lapwing flies,
And tires their echoes with unvaried cries.
Sunk are thy bowers, in shapeless ruin all,
And the long grass o'ertops the moldering wall,
And, trembling, shrinking from the spoiler's hand,
50   Far, far away thy children leave the land.
    Ill fares the land, to hastening ills a prey,
Where wealth accumulates, and men decay;³
Princes and lords may flourish, or may fade;
A breath can make them, as a breath has made;
55   But a bold peasantry, their country's pride,
When once destroyed, can never be supplied.
    A time there was, ere England's griefs began,
When every rood⁴ of ground maintained its man;
For him light labor spread her wholesome store,
60   Just gave what life required, but gave no more:

---

2. I.e., only half the land is cultivated under the new monopoly; or, the land was being plowed and was left unfinished when ownership changed. The significant landowners were displacing less prosperous freeholders and at the same time appropriating land formerly held in common.

3. In the opening dedication to Sir Joshua Reynolds, Goldsmith writes, "I . . . continue to think those luxuries prejudicial to states, by which so many vices are introduced, and so many kingdoms have been undone."
4. A measure of land, varying by locality.

His best companions, innocence and health;
And his best riches, ignorance of wealth.
    But times are altered; Trade's unfeeling train
Usurp the land and dispossess the swain;
65 Along the lawn, where scattered hamlets rose,
Unwieldy wealth, and cumbrous pomp repose;
And every want to opulence allied,
And every pang that folly pays to pride.
These gentle hours that plenty bade to bloom,
70 Those calm desires that asked but little room,
Those healthful sports that graced the peaceful scene,
Lived in each look, and brightened all the green;
These far departing seek a kinder shore,
And rural mirth and manners are no more.
75   Sweet Auburn! parent of the blissful hour,
Thy glades forlorn confess the tyrant's power.
Here, as I take my solitary rounds,
Amidst thy tangling walks, and ruined grounds,
And, many a year elapsed, return to view
80 Where once the cottage stood, the hawthorn grew,
Remembrance wakes with all her busy train,
Swells at my breast, and turns the past to pain.
    In all my wanderings round this world of care,
In all my griefs—and God has given my share—
85 I still had hopes my latest hours to crown,
Amidst these humble bowers to lay me down;
To husband out life's taper at the close,
And keep the flame from wasting by repose.
I still had hopes, for pride attends us still,
90 Amidst the swains to show my book-learned skill,
Around my fire an evening group to draw,
And tell of all I felt, and all I saw;
And, as an hare whom hounds and horns pursue,
Pants to the place from whence at first she flew,
95 I still had hopes, my long vexations past,
Here to return—and die at home at last.
    O blest retirement, friend to life's decline,
Retreats from care that never must be mine,
How happy he who crowns in shades like these
100 A youth of labor with an age of ease;
Who quits a world where strong temptations try,
And, since 'tis hard to combat, learns to fly!
For him no wretches, born to work and weep,
Explore the mine, or tempt the dangerous deep;
105 No surly porter stands in guilty state
To spurn imploring famine from the gate;
But on he moves to meet his latter end,
Angels around befriending virtue's friend;
Bends to the grave with unperceived decay,
110 While Resignation gently slopes the way;
And, all his prospects brightening to the last,
His Heaven commences ere the world be passed!
    Sweet was the sound when oft at evening's close,

Up yonder hill the village murmur rose;
115   There, as I passed with careless steps and slow,
The mingling notes came softened from below;
The swain responsive as the milkmaid sung,
The sober herd that lowed to meet their young,
The noisy geese that gabbled o'er the pool,
120   The playful children just let loose from school;
The watchdog's voice that bayed the whispering wind,
And the loud laugh that spoke the vacant° mind;   *carefree*
These all in sweet confusion sought the shade,
And filled each pause the nightingale had made.
125   But now the sounds of population fail,
No cheerful murmurs fluctuate in the gale,
No busy steps the grass-grown footway tread,
For all the bloomy flush of life is fled.
All but yon widowed, solitary thing
130   That feebly bends beside the plashy° spring;   *marshy*
She, wretched matron, forced, in age, for bread,
To strip the brook with mantling cresses spread,
To pick her wintry faggot° from the thorn,   *firewood*
To seek her nightly shed, and weep till morn;
135   She only left of all the harmless train,
The sad historian of the pensive plain.
      Near yonder copse,° where once the garden smiled,   *grove*
And still where many a garden flower grows wild,
There, where a few torn shrubs the place disclose,
140   The village preacher's modest mansion[5] rose.
A man he was, to all the country dear,
And passing rich with forty pounds a year;
Remote from towns he ran his godly race,
Nor e'er had changed, nor wished to change his place;
145   Unpracticed he to fawn, or seek for power,
By doctrines fashioned to the varying hour;
Far other aims his heart had learned to prize,
More skilled to raise the wretched than to rise.
His house was known to all the vagrant train,
150   He chid their wanderings, but relieved their pain;
The long-remembered beggar was his guest,
Whose beard descending swept his aged breast;
The ruined spendthrift, now no longer proud,
Claimed kindred there, and had his claims allowed;
155   The broken soldier, kindly bade to stay,
Sate by his fire, and talked the night away;
Wept o'er his wounds, or tales of sorrow done,
Shouldered his crutch, and showed how fields were won.
Pleased with his guests, the good man learned to glow,
160   And quite forgot their vices in their woe;
Careless their merits, or their faults to scan,
His pity gave ere charity began.
      Thus to relieve the wretched was his pride,
And even his failings leaned to Virtue's side;

---

5. There seem to have been no conventional mansions in Goldsmith's village; see lines 195 and 238, and Crabbe, "The Parish Register," line 19 (p. 663).

165　But in his duty prompt at every call,
　　He watched and wept, he prayed and felt, for all.
　　And, as a bird each fond endearment tries,
　　To tempt its new-fledged offspring to the skies,
　　He tried each art, reproved each dull delay,
170　Allured to brighter worlds, and led the way.
　　　　Beside the bed where parting life was laid,
　　And sorrow, guilt, and pain, by turns dismayed,
　　The reverend champion stood. At his control,
　　Despair and anguish fled the struggling soul;
175　Comfort came down the trembling wretch to raise,
　　And his last faltering accents whispered praise.
　　　　At church, with meek and unaffected grace,
　　His looks adorned the venerable place;
　　Truth from his lips prevailed with double sway,
180　And fools, who came to scoff, remained to pray.
　　The service past, around the pious man,
　　With steady zeal each honest rustic ran;
　　Even children followed with endearing wile,
　　And plucked his gown, to share the good man's smile.
185　His ready smile a parent's warmth expressed,
　　Their welfare pleased him, and their cares distressed;
　　To them his heart, his love, his griefs were given,
　　But all his serious thoughts had rest in Heaven.
　　As some tall cliff that lifts its awful form,
190　Swells from the vale, and midway leaves the storm,
　　Though round its breast the rolling clouds are spread,
　　Eternal sunshine settles on its head.
　　　　Beside yon straggling fence that skirts the way,
　　With blossomed furze unprofitably gay,
195　There, in his noisy mansion, skilled to rule,
　　The village master taught his little school;
　　A man severe he was, and stern to view,
　　I knew him well, and every truant knew;
　　Well had the boding° tremblers learned to trace　　　*anxious*
200　The day's disasters in his morning face;
　　Full well they laughed with counterfeited glee,
　　At all his jokes, for many a joke had he;
　　Full well the busy whisper circling round,
　　Conveyed the dismal tidings when he frowned;
205　Yet he was kind, or if severe in aught,
　　The love he bore to learning was in fault;[6]
　　The village all declared how much he knew;
　　'Twas certain he could write, and cipher too;
　　Lands he could measure, terms and tides presage,[7]
210　And even the story ran that he could gauge.
　　In arguing too, the parson owned his skill,[8]
　　For even though vanquished, he could argue still;
　　While words of learned length, and thundering sound,
　　Amazed the gazing rustics ranged around;

---

6. Pronounced like *fought*.
7. He could calculate (for example) when rents were due and the date of the next Easter. "Tides"
here means "times." To "gauge" (line 210) is to calculate the fluid content of vessels.
8. I.e., admitted his (the schoolmaster's) skill.

215 And still they gazed, and still the wonder grew,
That one small head could carry all he knew.
  But past is all his fame. The very spot
Where many a time he triumphed, is forgot.
Near yonder thorn, that lifts its head on high,
220 Where once the signpost caught the passing eye,
Low lies that house where nut-brown draughts inspired,[9]
Where graybeard Mirth and smiling Toil retired,
Where village statesmen talked with looks profound,
And news much older than their ale went round.
225 Imagination fondly stoops to trace
The parlor splendors of that festive place:
The whitewashed wall, the nicely sanded floor,
The varnished clock that clicked behind the door;
The chest contrived a double debt to pay,
230 A bed by night, a chest of drawers by day;
The pictures placed for ornament and use,
The twelve good rules, the royal game of goose;[1]
The hearth, except when winter chilled the day,
With aspen boughs, and flowers, and fennel gay,
235 While broken teacups, wisely kept for show,
Ranged o'er the chimney, glistened in a row.
  Vain transitory splendors! Could not all
Reprieve the tottering mansion from its fall!
Obscure it sinks, nor shall it more impart
240 An hour's importance to the poor man's heart;
Thither no more the peasant shall repair
To sweet oblivion of his daily care;
No more the farmer's news, the barber's tale,
No more the woodman's ballad shall prevail;
245 No more the smith his dusky brow shall clear,
Relax his ponderous strength, and lean to hear;
The host himself no longer shall be found
Careful to see the mantling bliss[2] go round;
Nor the coy maid, half willing to be pressed,
250 Shall kiss the cup to pass it to the rest.
  Yes! let the rich deride, the proud disdain,
These simple blessings of the lowly train,
To me more dear, congenial to my heart,
One native charm, than all the gloss of art;
255 Spontaneous joys, where nature has its play,
The soul adopts, and owns their first-born sway;
Lightly they frolic o'er the vacant mind,
Unenvied, unmolested, unconfined.
But the long pomp, the midnight masquerade,
260 With all the freaks of wanton wealth arrayed,
In these, ere° triflers half their wish obtain,   *before*
The toiling pleasure sickens into pain;
And, even while fashion's brightest arts decoy,

9. I.e., the public house where ale inspired the customers. Contrast with Crabbe's "The Parish Register," which transfers Goldsmith's "twelve good rules" (line 232) to the cottage of the "industrious swain" and describes the pub as a place of crime and corruption.
1. The "twelve good rules" are rules of conduct often posted in taverns; "goose" is a board game.
2. The ale covering itself with foam.

The heart distrusting asks if this be joy.
265   Ye friends to truth, ye statesmen, who survey
The rich man's joys increase, the poor's decay,
'Tis yours to judge how wide the limits stand
Between a splendid and an happy land.
Proud swells the tide with loads of freighted ore,
270   And shouting Folly hails them from her shore;
Hoards, even beyond the miser's wish abound,
And rich men flock from all the world around.
Yet count our gains. This wealth is but a name
That leaves our useful products still the same.
275   Not so the loss. The man of wealth and pride,
Takes up a space that many poor supplied;
Space for his lake, his park's extended bounds,
Space for his horses, equipage, and hounds;
The robe that wraps his limbs in silken sloth
280   Has robbed the neighboring fields of half their growth;
His seat, where solitary sports are seen,
Indignant spurns the cottage from the green;
Around the world each needful product flies,
For all the luxuries the world supplies:
285   While thus the land adorned for pleasure, all
In barren splendor feebly waits the fall.
      As some fair female unadorned and plain,
Secure to please while youth confirms her reign,
Slights every borrowed charm that dress supplies,
290   Nor shares with art the triumph of her eyes;
But when those charms are past, for charms are frail,
When time advances, and when lovers fail,
She then shines forth, solicitous to bless,
In all the glaring impotence of dress:
295   Thus fares the land, by luxury betrayed;
In nature's simplest charms at first arrayed;
But verging to decline, its splendors rise,
Its vistas strike, its palaces surprise;
While scourged by famine from the smiling land,
300   The mournful peasant leads his humble band;
And while he sinks without one arm to save,
The country blooms—a garden, and a grave.
      Where then, ah where, shall Poverty reside,
To 'scape the pressure of contiguous Pride?
305   If to some common's fenceless limits strayed,
He drives his flock to pick the scanty blade,
Those fenceless fields the sons of wealth divide,
And even the bare-worn common is denied.[3]
      If to the city sped—What waits him there?
310   To see profusion that he must not share;
To see ten thousand baneful arts combined
To pamper luxury, and thin mankind;
To see those joys the sons of pleasure know,
Extorted from his fellow creature's woe.
315   Here, while the courtier glitters in brocade,

---

3. Refers to the enclosure and appropriation of common land.

There the pale artist° plies the sickly trade;   *artisan*
Here, while the proud their long-drawn pomps display,
There the black gibbet glooms beside the way.
The dome where Pleasure holds her midnight reign,
320   Here, richly decked, admits the gorgeous train;
Tumultuous grandeur crowds the blazing square,
The rattling chariots clash, the torches glare.
Sure scenes like these no troubles e'er annoy!
Sure these denote one universal joy!
325   Are these thy serious thoughts?—Ah, turn thine eyes
Where the poor houseless shivering female lies.
She once, perhaps, in village plenty blest,
Has wept at tales of innocence distressed;
Her modest looks the cottage might adorn,
330   Sweet as the primrose peeps beneath the thorn;
Now lost to all; her friends, her virtue fled,
Near her betrayer's door she lays her head,
And pinched with cold, and shrinking from the shower,
With heavy heart deplores that luckless hour,
335   When idly first, ambitious of the town,
She left her wheel and robes of country brown.
     Do thine, sweet Auburn, thine, the loveliest train,
Do thy fair tribes participate her pain?
Even now, perhaps, by cold and hunger led,
340   At proud men's doors they ask a little bread!
     Ah, no. To distant climes, a dreary scene,
Where half the convex world intrudes between,
Through torrid tracts with fainting steps they go,
Where wild Altama[4] murmurs to their woe.
345   Far different there from all that charmed before,
The various terrors of that horrid shore;
Those blazing suns that dart a downward ray,
And fiercely shed intolerable day;
Those matted woods where birds forget to sing,
350   But silent bats in drowsy clusters cling,
Those poisonous fields with rank luxuriance crowned,
Where the dark scorpion gathers death around;
Where at each step the stranger fears to wake
The rattling terrors of the vengeful snake;
355   Where crouching tigers° wait their hapless prey,   *pumas*
And savage men, more murderous still than they;
While oft in whirls the mad tornado flies,
Mingling the ravaged landscape with the skies.
Far different these from every former scene,
360   The cooling brook, the grassy-vested green,
The breezy covert of the warbling grove,
That only sheltered thefts of harmless love.
     Good Heaven! what sorrows gloomed that parting day,
That called them from their native walks away;
365   When the poor exiles, every pleasure past,
Hung round their bowers, and fondly looked their last,
And took a long farewell, and wished in vain

---

4. Altahama, a river in Georgia.

For seats like these beyond the western main;
And shuddering still to face the distant deep,
370   Returned and wept, and still returned to weep.
The good old sire the first prepared to go
To new-found worlds, and wept for other's woe;
But for himself, in conscious virtue brave,
He only wished for worlds beyond the grave.
375   His lovely daughter, lovelier in her tears,
The fond companion of his helpless years,
Silent went next, neglectful of her charms,
And left a lover's for a father's arms.
With louder plaints the mother spoke her woes,
380   And blessed the cot where every pleasure rose;
And kissed her thoughtless babes with many a tear,
And clasped them close in sorrow doubly dear;
Whilst her fond husband strove to lend relief
In all the silent manliness of grief.
385   O luxury! Thou cursed by Heaven's decree,
How ill exchanged are things like these for thee!
How do thy potions, with insidious joy,
Diffuse their pleasures only to destroy!
Kingdoms, by thee, to sickly greatness grown,
390   Boast of a florid vigor not their own.
At every draught more large and large they grow,
A bloated mass of rank unwieldy woe;
Till sapped their strength, and every part unsound,
Down, down they sink, and spread a ruin round.
395   Even now the devastation is begun,
And half the business of destruction done;
Even now, methinks, as pondering here I stand,
I see the rural Virtues leave the land.
Down where yon anchoring vessel spreads the sail,
400   That idly waiting flaps with every gale,
Downward they move, a melancholy band,
Pass from the shore, and darken all the strand.
Contented Toil, and hospitable Care,
And kind connubial Tenderness are there;
405   And Piety, with wishes placed above,
And steady Loyalty, and faithful Love:
And thou, sweet Poetry, thou loveliest maid,
Still first to fly where sensual joys invade;
Unfit in these degenerate times of shame,
410   To catch the heart, or strike for honest fame;
Dear charming Nymph, neglected and decried,
My shame in crowds, my solitary pride;
Thou source of all my bliss, and all my woe,
That found'st me poor at first, and keep'st me so;
415   Thou guide by which the nobler arts excel,
Thou nurse of every virtue, fare thee well.
Farewell, and O! where'er thy voice be tried,
On Torno's cliffs, or Pambamarca's side,[5]
Whether where equinoctial fervors glow,

5. I.e., on the cliffs overlooking the river Torne in Sweden or the side of Mount Pambamarca in Ecuador.

420 Or winter wraps the polar world in snow,
Still let thy voice, prevailing over time,
Redress the rigors of the inclement clime;
Aid slighted truth, with thy persuasive strain
Teach erring man to spurn the rage of gain;
425 Teach him that states of native strength possessed,
Though very poor, may still be very blest;
That Trade's proud empire hastes to swift decay,
As ocean sweeps the labored mole° away;   *breakwater*
While self-dependent power can time defy,
430 As rocks resist the billows and the sky.[6]

1770

WILLIAM COWPER

1731–1800

From Olney Hymns[1]

Light Shining out of Darkness

God moves in a mysterious way,
    His wonders to perform;
He plants his footsteps in the sea,
    And rides upon the storm.

5   Deep in unfathomable mines
        Of never failing skill,
    He treasures up his bright designs,
        And works his sovereign will.

    Ye fearful saints, fresh courage take,
10   The clouds ye so much dread
    Are big with mercy, and shall break
        In blessings on your head.

    Judge not the Lord by feeble sense,
        But trust him for his grace;
15 Behind a frowning providence,
        He hides a smiling face.

    His purposes will ripen fast,
        Unfolding every hour;
    The bud may have a bitter taste,
20   But sweet will be the flower.

    Blind unbelief is sure to err,
        And scan his work in vain;

6. The last four lines are by Samuel Johnson.
1. Cowper moved to Olney, in Buckinghamshire,

in 1767, and lived there until 1786.

God is his own interpreter,
    And he will make it plain.

1779

Epitaph on a Hare

Here lies, whom hound did ne'er pursue,
    Nor swifter greyhound follow,
Whose foot ne'er tainted° morning dew,   *left a scent on*
    Nor ear heard huntsman's hallo',

5 Old Tiney, surliest of his kind,
    Who, nursed with tender care,
And to domestic bounds confined,
    Was still a wild jack-hare.

Though duly from my hand he took
10   His pittance every night,
He did it with a jealous look,
    And, when he could, would bite.

His diet was of wheaten bread,
    And milk, and oats, and straw,
15 Thistles, or lettuces instead,
    With sand to scour his maw.

On twigs of hawthorn he regaled,°   *feasted*
    On pippins'° russet peel;   *apples'*
And, when his juicy salads failed,
20   Sliced carrot pleased him well.

A Turkey carpet was his lawn,[2]
    Whereon he loved to bound,
To skip and gambol like a fawn,
    And swing his rump around.

25 His frisking was at evening hours,
    For then he lost his fear;
But most before approaching showers,
    Or when a storm drew near.

Eight years and five round-rolling moons
30   He thus saw steal away,
Dozing out all his idle noons,
    And every night at play.

I kept him for his humor's sake,
    For he would oft beguile
35 My heart of thoughts that made it ache,
    And force me to a smile.

---

2. Cowper exercised his hares on his parlor carpet of Turkey red.

But now, beneath this walnut-shade
He finds his long, last home,
And waits in snug concealment laid,
40   Till gentler Puss shall come.

He,[3] still more agèd, feels the shocks
From which no care can save,
And, partner once of Tiney's box,
Must soon partake his grave.

1783   1784

From The Task[4]

From *Book IV: The Winter Evening*

Just when our drawing-rooms begin to blaze
With lights, by clear reflection multiplied
From many a mirror, in which he of Gath,
Goliath, might have seen his giant bulk
5   Whole without stooping, towering crest and all,
My pleasures too begin. But me perhaps
The glowing hearth may satisfy awhile
With faint illumination, that uplifts
The shadow to the ceiling, there by fits
10   Dancing uncouthly to the quivering flame.
Not undelightful is an hour to me
So spent in parlour twilight; such a gloom
Suits well the thoughtful or unthinking mind,
The mind contemplative, with some new theme
15   Pregnant, or indisposed alike to all.
Laugh ye, who boast your more mercurial powers
That never feel a stupor, know no pause,
Nor need one; I am conscious, and confess,
Fearless, a soul that does not always think.
20   Me oft has fancy ludicrous and wild
Soothed with a waking dream of houses, towers,
Trees, churches, and stranger visages expressed
In the red cinders, while with poring eye
I gazed, myself creating what I saw.[5]
25   Nor less amused have I quiescent watched
The sooty films that play upon the bars
Pendulous, and foreboding in the view
Of superstition, prophesying still,
Though still deceived, some stranger's near approach
30   'Tis thus the understanding takes repose
In indolent vacuity of thought,
And sleeps and is refreshed. Meanwhile the face
Conceals the mood lethargic with a mask
Of deep deliberation, as° the man   *as if*
35   Were tasked to his full strength, absorbed and lost.

3. Puss, the longest-lived of Cowper's three hares.
4. So called because, when he complained of the want of a poetic topic, a friend, Lady Austen (the "fair" of line 7), set him the task of writing about the parlor sofa. The completed work ran to six books and ranged over a diversity of subjects.
5. Compare the following passage with Coleridge's "Frost at Midnight" (pp. 742–44).

Thus oft reclined at ease, I lose an hour
At evening, till at length the freezing blast
That sweeps the bolted shutter, summons home
The recollected powers, and, snapping short
40 The glassy threads with which the fancy weaves
Her brittle toys, restores me to myself.
How calm is my recess! and how the frost
Raging abroad, and the rough wind, endear
The silence and the warmth enjoyed within!
45 I saw the woods and fields at close of day
A variegated show; the meadows green
Though faded, and the lands, where lately waved
The golden harvest, of a mellow brown,
Upturned so lately by the forceful share;°   *plough*
50 I saw far off the weedy fallows° smile   *dormant land*
With verdure not unprofitable, grazed
By flocks fast feeding, and selecting each
His favorite herb; while all the leafless groves
That skirt th' horizon wore a sable hue,
55 Scarce noticed in the kindred dusk of eve.
Tomorrow brings a change, a total change,
Which even now, though silently perform'd
And slowly, and by most unfelt, the face
Of universal nature undergoes.
60 Fast falls a fleecy shower; the downy flakes,
Descending and with never-ceasing lapse
Softly alighting upon all below,
Assimilate all objects. Earth receives
Gladly the thickening mantle, and the green
65 And tender blade that feared the chilling blast,
Escapes unhurt beneath so warm a veil.

From *Book VI: The Winter Walk at Noon*

The groans of nature in this nether world,
730 Which Heaven has heard for ages, have an end.
Foretold by prophets, and by poets sung,
Whose fire was kindled at the prophets' lamp,
The time of rest, the promised Sabbath, comes.[6]
Six thousand years[7] of sorrow have well-nigh
735 Fulfilled their tardy and disastrous course
Over a sinful world; and what remains
Of this tempestuous state of human things
Is merely as the working of a sea
Before a calm, that rocks itself to rest:
740 For He, whose car° the winds are, and the clouds   *chariot*
The dust that waits upon his sultry march,
When sin hath moved him, and his wrath is hot,
Shall visit earth in mercy; shall descend,
Propitious, in his chariot paved with love;

6. An allusion to the end of the world and the second coming of Christ, when God will make "a new heaven and a new earth" (Revelation 21.1). Lines 759–817 are Cowper's visionary description of this "promised Sabbath."

7. The creation of the world was traditionally believed to have taken place four thousand years before the birth of Christ.

745 And what his storms have blasted and defaced
For man's revolt shall with a smile repair.
     Sweet is the harp of prophecy; too sweet
Not to be wronged by a mere mortal touch:
Nor can the wonders it records be sung
750 To meaner music, and not suffer loss.
But, when a poet, or when one like me,
Happy to rove among poetic flowers,
Though poor in skill to rear them, lights at last
On some fair theme, some theme divinely fair,
755 Such is the impulse and the spur he feels
To give it praise proportioned to its worth,
That not t' attempt it, arduous as he deems
The labor, were a task more arduous still.
     Oh scenes surpassing fable, and yet true,
760 Scenes of accomplished bliss! which who can see,
Though but in distant prospect, and not feel
His soul refreshed with foretaste of the joy?
Rivers of gladness water all the earth,
And clothe all climes with beauty; the reproach
765 Of barrenness is past. The fruitful field
Laughs with abundance; and the land, once lean,
Or fertile only in its own disgrace,
Exults to see its thistly curse repealed.
The various seasons woven into one,
770 And that one season an eternal spring,
The garden fears no blight, and needs no fence,
For there is none to covet, all are full.
The lion, and the libbard,° and the bear   leopard
Graze with the fearless flocks; all bask at noon
775 Together, or all gambol in the shade
Of the same grove, and drink one common stream.
Antipathies are none. No foe to man
Lurks in the serpent now: the mother sees,
And smiles to see, her infant's playful hand
780 Stretched forth to dally with the crested worm,°   serpent
To stroke his azure neck, or to receive
The lambent homage of his arrowy tongue.
All creatures worship man, and all mankind
One Lord, one Father. Error has no place:
785 That creeping pestilence is driven away;
The breath of heaven has chased it. In the heart
No passion touches a discordant string,
But all is harmony and love. Disease
Is not: the pure and uncontaminate blood
790 Holds its due course, nor fears the frost of age.
One song employs all nations; and all cry,
"Worthy the Lamb, for he was slain for us!"
The dwellers in the vales and on the rocks
Shout to each other, and the mountain tops
795 From distant mountains catch the flying joy;
Till, nation after nation taught the strain,
Earth rolls the rapturous hosanna round.

Behold the measure of the promise filled;
See Salem[8] built, the labor of a God!
800 Bright as a sun the sacred city shines;
All kingdoms and all princes of the earth
Flock to that light; the glory of all lands
Flows into her; unbounded is her joy,
And endless her increase. Thy rams are there,
805 Nebaioth, and the flocks of Kedar there;[9]
The looms of Ormus, and the mines of Ind,
And Saba's spicy groves, pay tribute there.[1]
Praise is in all her gates: upon her walls,
And in her streets, and in her spacious courts,
810 Is heard salvation. Eastern Java there
Kneels with the native of the farthest west;
And Ethiopia spreads abroad the hand,
And worships. Her report has traveled forth
Into all lands. From every clime they come
815 To see thy beauty and to share thy joy,
O Sion![2] an assembly such as earth
Saw never, such as heaven stoops down to see.
    Thus heaven-ward all things tend. For all were once
Perfect, and all must be at length restored.
820 So God has greatly purposed; who would else
In his dishonored works himself endure
Dishonor, and be wronged without redress.
Haste, then, and wheel away a shattered world,
Ye slow-revolving seasons! we would see
825 (A sight to which our eyes are strangers yet)
A world that does not dread and hate his laws,
And suffer for its crime; would learn how fair
The creature is that God pronounces good,
How pleasant in itself what pleases him.
830 Here every drop of honey hides a sting,
Worms wind themselves into our sweetest flowers;
And even the joy that haply° some poor heart   *luckily*
Derives from heaven, pure as the fountain is,
Is sullied in the stream, taking a taint
835 From touch of human lips, at best impure.
Oh for a world in principle as chaste
As this is gross and selfish! over which
Custom and prejudice shall bear no sway,
That govern all things here, shouldering aside
840 The meek and modest truth, and forcing her
To seek a refuge from the tongue of strife
In nooks obscure, far from the ways of men;

8. Jerusalem; not only the terrestrial city but the New Jerusalem or Holy City, God's perfect and eternal order of the future. See Revelation 31.2: "And I John saw the holy city, new Jerusalem, coming down from God out of heaven."
9. "Nebaioth and Kedar, the sons of Ishmael and progenitors of the Arabs, in the prophetic Scripture here alluded to may be reasonably considered as representatives of the Gentiles at large" [Cowper's note]. By "the prophetic Scripture here alluded to"

Cowper means Isaiah 60.3–7, in which God promises a blessed future to Jerusalem: "And the Gentiles shall come to thy light. . . . All the flocks of Kedar shall be gathered together unto thee, the rams of Nebaioth shall minister unto thee."
1. Ormus (an island in the Persian Gulf), India, and Saba (Sheba, a country in Arabia) were renowned for their wealth.
2. Often, as here, equivalent to Jerusalem.

Where violence shall never lift the sword,
Nor cunning justify the proud man's wrong,
845 Leaving the poor no remedy but tears;
Where he that fills an office shall esteem
Th' occasion it presents of doing good
More than the perquisite;° where law shall speak   *profits*
Seldom, and never but as wisdom prompts
850 And equity; not jealous more to guard
A worthless form, than to decide aright;
Where fashion shall not sanctify abuse,
Nor smooth good breeding (supplemental grace)
With lean performance ape the work of love!
855   Come then, and, added to thy many crowns,
Receive yet one, the crown of all the earth,
Thou who alone art worthy! It was thine
By ancient covenant, ere nature's birth;
And thou hast made it thine by purchase since,
860 And overpaid its value with thy blood.
Thy saints proclaim thee king; and in their hearts
Thy title is engraven with a pen
Dipped in the fountain of eternal love.
Thy saints proclaim thee king; and thy delay
865 Gives courage to their foes, who, could they see
The dawn of thy last advent, long desired,
Would creep into the bowels of the hills,
And flee for safety to the falling rocks.
The very spirit of the world is tired
870 Of its own taunting question, asked so long,
"Where is the promise of your Lord's approach?"
The infidel has shot his bolts° away,   *arrows*
Till, his exhausted quiver yielding none,
He gleans the blunted shafts that have recoiled,
875 And aims them at the shield of truth again.
The veil is rent, rent too by priestly hands,
That hides divinity from mortal eyes;[3]
And all the mysteries to faith proposed,
Insulted and traduced, are cast aside,
880 As useless, to the moles and to the bats.
They now are deemed the faithful, and are praised,
Who, constant only in rejecting thee,
Deny thy Godhead with a martyr's zeal,
And quit their office for their error's sake.
885 Blind, and in love with darkness! yet even these
Worthy, compared with sycophants, who knee
Thy name adoring, and then preach thee man!
So fares thy church. But how thy church may fare
The world takes little thought. Who will may preach,
890 And what they will. All pastors are alike
To wandering sheep, resolved to follow none.

---

3. The veil of the Temple in Jerusalem divided the inner sanctuary from the rest of the Temple. For Christians, rending of the veil represented gaining direct access to God, notably through Christ's death. "And Jesus cried with a loud voice, and gave up the ghost. And the veil of the temple was rent in twain from the top to the bottom" (Mark 15.37–8).

Two gods divide them all—Pleasure and Gain:
For these they live, they sacrifice to these,
And in their service wage perpetual war
895 With conscience and with thee. Lust in their hearts,
And mischief in their hands, they roam the earth
To prey upon each other: stubborn, fierce,
High-minded, foaming out their own disgrace.
Thy prophets speak of such; and, noting down
900 The features of the last degenerate times,
Exhibit every lineament of these.
Come then, and, added to thy many crowns,
Receive yet one, as radiant as the rest,
Due to thy last and most effectual work,
905 Thy word fulfilled, the conquest of a world!

1785

The Castaway

Obscurest night involved the sky,
   The Atlantic billows roared,
When such a destined wretch as I,
   Washed headlong from on board,
5 Of friends, of hope, of all bereft,
His floating home forever left.

No braver chief could Albion boast
   Than he with whom he went,[4]
Nor ever ship left Albion's coast,
10   With warmer wishes sent.
He loved them both, but both in vain,
Nor him beheld, nor her again.

Not long beneath the whelming brine,
   Expert to swim, he lay;
15 Nor soon he felt his strength decline,
   Or courage die away;
But waged with death a lasting strife,
Supported by despair of life.

He shouted; nor his friends had failed
20   To check the vessel's course,
But so the furious blast prevailed,
   That, pitiless perforce,
They left their outcast mate behind,
And scudded still before the wind.

25 Some succor yet they could afford;
   And, such as storms allow,
The cask, the coop, the floated cord,
   Delayed not to bestow.

4. Namely, George, Lord Anson, who told the castaway's story in his memoir, *Voyage Round the World* (1748).

But he (they knew) nor ship, nor shore,
30 Whate'er they gave, should visit more.

Nor, cruel as it seemed, could he
    Their haste himself condemn,
Aware that flight, in such a sea,
    Alone could rescue them;
35 Yet bitter felt it still to die
Deserted, and his friends so nigh.

He long survives, who lives an hour
    In ocean, self-upheld;
And so long he, with unspent power,
40   His destiny repelled;
And ever, as the minutes flew,
Entreated help, or cried, "Adieu!"

At length, his transient respite past,
    His comrades, who before
45 Had heard his voice in every blast,
    Could catch the sound no more.
For then, by toil subdued, he drank
The stifling wave, and then he sank.

No poet wept him; but the page
50   Of narrative sincere,
That tells his name, his worth, his age,
    Is wet with Anson's tear.
And tears by bards or heroes shed
Alike immortalize the dead.

55 I therefore purpose not, or dream,
    Descanting on his fate,
To give the melancholy theme
    A more enduring date:
But misery still delights to trace
60 Its semblance in another's case.

No voice divine the storm allayed,
    No light propitious shone,
When, snatched from all effectual aid,
    We perished, each alone;
65 But I beneath a rougher sea,
And whelmed in deeper gulfs than he.

1799   1803

Lines Written During a Period of Insanity

Hatred and vengeance, my eternal portion,
Scarce can endure delay of execution,
Wait, with impatient readiness, to seize my
                    Soul in a moment.

5   Damned below Judas:[5] more abhorred than he was,
    Who for a few pence sold his holy Master.
    Twice betrayed Jesus me, the last delinquent,
                Deems the profanest.[6]

    Man disavows, and Deity disowns me:
10 Hell might afford my miseries a shelter;
    Therefore hell keeps her ever hungry mouths all
                Bolted against me.

    Hard lot! encompassed with a thousand dangers;
    Weary, faint, trembling with a thousand terrors;
15 I'm called, if vanquished, to receive a sentence
                Worse than Abiram's.[7]

    Him the vindictive rod of angry justice
    Sent quick and howling to the center headlong;
    I, fed with judgment, in a fleshly tomb, am
20   Buried above ground.

ca. 1774   1816

ANNA LAETITIA BARBAULD

1743–1825

To Mr. S. T. Coleridge

Midway the hill of science, after steep
And rugged paths that tire the' unpractised feet,
A grove extends; in tangled mazes wrought,
And filled with strange enchantment:—dubious shapes
5   Flit through dim glades, and lure the eager foot
Of youthful ardor to eternal chase.
Dreams hang on every leaf: unearthly forms
Glide through the gloom; and mystic visions swim
Before the cheated sense. Athwart the mists,
10 Far into vacant space, huge shadows stretch,
And seem realities; while things of life,
Obvious to sight and touch, all glowing round,
Fade to the hue of shadows—Scruples° here,   *doubts*
With filmy net, most like the autumnal webs
15 Of floating gossamer,° arrest the foot   *cobwebs*
Of generous enterprise; and palsy° hope   *render powerless*

---

5. Judas betrayed Jesus to the chief priests for money (Matthew 26.14–16).
6. I.e., Jesus, betrayed by me as well as by Judas, deems me the most profane.
7. Abirim, rebelling against the authority of Moses and Aaron, was swallowed up with his fellow dissidents in a cleft of the earth. They "went down alive into the pit, and the earth closed upon them" (Numbers 16.33).

And fair ambition with the chilling touch
Of sickly hesitation and blank fear.
Nor seldom[1] Indolence these lawns among
20 Fixes her turf-built seat; and wears the garb
Of deep philosophy, and museful sits,
In dreamy twilight of the vacant mind,
Soothed by the whispering shade; for soothing soft
The shades; and vistas lengthening into air,
25 With moonbeam rainbows tinted.—Here each mind
Of finer mould, acute and delicate,
In its high progress to eternal truth
Rests for a space, in fairy bowers[2] entranced;
And loves the softened light and tender gloom;
30 And, pampered with most unsubstantial food,
Looks down indignant on the grosser° world,   coaser, inferior
And matter's cumbrous° shapings. Youth beloved   cumbersome
Of Science—of the Muse[3] beloved,—not here,
Not in the maze of metaphysic[4] lore,
35 Build thou thy place of resting! lightly tread
The dangerous ground, on noble aims intent;
And be this Circe[5] of the studious cell
Enjoyed, but still subservient. Active scenes
Shall soon with healthful spirit brace thy mind;
40 And fair exertion, for bright fame sustained,
For friends, for country, chase each spleen-fed[6] fog
That blots the wide creation.—
Now Heaven conduct thee with a parent's love!

1797   1799

The Rights of Woman[7]

Yes, injured Woman! rise, assert thy right!
Woman! too long degraded, scorned, opprest;
O born to rule in partial° Law's despite,°   biased / contempt
Resume thy native empire o'er the breast!

5 Go forth arrayed in panoply[8] divine;
That angel pureness which admits no stain;
Go, bid proud Man his boasted rule resign,
And kiss the golden scepter of thy reign.

---

1. I.e., and not infrequently, i.e., often.
2. Leafy coverts or arbors; "bower" is also a poetic word for an idealized abode.
3. One of the nine Greek goddesses believed to be sources of inspiration for the arts.
4. Metaphysics is the branch of speculative inquiry that deals with the first principles of things, including such concepts as being, essence, time, space, cause, etc.
5. An enchantress in Homer's *Odyssey*. When Odysseus stopped at Circe's island on his return home from the Trojan War, she fell in love with him and transformed his men into swine. He dallied on the island for a year before Circe restored

his men to their human forms and he continued on his way.
6. The spleen was the organ deemed responsible for a variety of neurotic disorders including ill-temper, moroseness, and depression. See Anne Finch, "The Spleen" (pp. 516–19); and Matthew Green, "The Spleen" (pp. 582–85).
7. Until the last two stanzas, a seemingly positive response to Mary Wollstonecraft's *A Vindication of the Rights of Woman* (1792), a radical look at the place of women in society.
8. Ephesians 6.11: "Put on the whole armor of God, that ye may be able to stand against the wiles of the devil."

Go, gird thyself with grace; collect thy store
10 Of bright artillery glancing° from afar;   *gleaming*
Soft melting tones thy thundering cannon's roar,
Blushes and fears thy magazine⁹ of war.

Thy rights are empire: urge no meaner° claim,—   *humbler*
Felt, not defined, and if debated, lost;
15 Like sacred mysteries, which withheld from fame,
Shunning discussion, are revered the most.

Try all that wit and art suggest to bend
Of thy imperial foe the stubborn knee;
Make treacherous Man thy subject, not thy friend;
20 Thou mayst command, but never canst be free.

Awe the licentious, and restrain the rude;
Soften the sullen, clear the cloudy brow:
Be, more than princes' gifts, thy favors sued;°—   *sought*
She hazards all, who will the least allow.

25 But hope not, courted idol of mankind,
On this proud eminence secure to stay;
Subduing and subdued, thou soon shalt find
Thy coldness soften, and thy pride give way.

Then, then, abandon each ambitious thought,
30 Conquest or rule thy heart shall feebly move,
In Nature's school, by her soft maxims taught,
That separate rights are lost in mutual love.

ca. 1795   1825

To the Poor

Child of distress, who meet'st the bitter scorn
Of fellow-men to happier prospects born,
Doomed Art and Nature's various stores to see
Flow in full cups of joy—and not for thee;
5 Who seest the rich, to heaven and fate resigned,
Bear *thy* afflictions with a patient mind;
Whose bursting heart disdains unjust control,
Who feel'st oppression's iron in thy soul,
Who dragg'st the load of faint and feeble years,
10 Whose bread is anguish, and whose water tears;
Bear, bear thy wrongs—fulfill thy destined hour,
Bend thy meek neck beneath the foot of Power;
But when thou feel'st the great deliverer nigh,
And thy freed spirit mounting seeks the sky,
15 Let no vain fears thy parting hour molest,
No whispered terrors shake thy quiet breast:
Think not their threats can work thy future woe,

---

9. Storage place for weapons or ammunition.

Nor deem the Lord above like lords below; —
Safe in the bosom of that love repose
20   By whom the sun gives light, the ocean flows;
Prepare to meet a Father undismayed,
Nor fear the God whom priests and kings have made.

1795   1825

Life

Animula, vagula, blandula.[1]

Life! I know not what thou art,
But know that thou and I must part;
And when, or how, or where we met,
I own° to me's a secret yet.   *acknowledge*
5   But this I know, when thou art fled,
Where'er they lay these limbs, this head,
No clod so valueless shall be,
As all that then remains of me.
O whither, whither dost thou fly,
10   Where bend unseen thy trackless course,
      And in this strange divorce,
Ah tell where I must seek this compound I?

To the vast ocean of empyreal flame,
    From whence thy essence came,
15   Dost thou thy flight pursue, when freed
    From matter's base encumbering weed?
      Or dost thou, hid from sight,
      Wait, like some spell-bound knight,
Through blank oblivious years th' appointed hour,
20   To break thy trance and reassume thy power?
Yet canst thou without thought or feeling be?
O say what art thou, when no more thou 'rt thee?

    Life! we've been long together,
    Through pleasant and through cloudy weather;
25   'Tis hard to part when friends are dear;
      Perhaps 't will cost a sigh, a tear;
      Then steal away, give little warning,
        Choose thine own time;
    Say not Good night, but in some brighter clime
30   Bid me Good morning.

                                                  1825

---

1. "Charming little soul, hastening away" (Latin); the first line of a poem supposedly composed by the Roman Emperor Hadrian (A.D. 76–138) on his deathbed, quoted from Aelius Spartianus, *Life of Hadrian* 25.

HANNAH MORE

1745–1833

Inscription in a Beautiful Retreat Called Fairy Bower[1]

Airy spirits, you who love
Cooling bower, or shady grove;
Streams that murmur as they flow,
Zephyrs[2] bland that softly blow;

5   Babbling echo,[3] or the tale
Of the lovelorn Nightingale;[4]
Hither, airy spirits, come,
This is your peculiar° home.   *own*

If you love a verdant° glade,   *green*
10   If you love a noon-tide shade,
Hither, Sylphs[5] and Fairies, fly,
Unobserved of earthly eye.

Come, and wander every night,
By the moonbeam's glimmering light;
15   And again at early day
Brush the silver dews away.

Mark where first the daisies blow,°   *bloom*
Where the bluest violets grow;
Where the sweetest linnet[6] sings,
20   Where the earliest cowslip springs;

Where the largest acorn lies,
Precious in a Fairy's eyes:
Sylphs, though unconfined to place,
Love to fill an acorn's space.

25   Come, and mark within what bush
Builds the blackbird or the thrush;
Great his joy who first espies,
Greater his who spares the prize.

Come, and watch the hallowed bower,
30   Chase the insect from the flower;

---

1. A leafy covert or arbor, but also a poetic word for an idealized abode.
2. Zephyr, the west wind, is a mild wind.
3. Echo was a nymph whose chatter distracted Hera, the queen of the gods, while Zeus, Hera's husband, consorted with other nymphs and mortal women. Hera punished her by depriving her of speech, save to repeat the words of others. Later, Echo pined for the youth Narcissus, who spurned her love, until nothing was left of her but her voice.
4. The nightingale is known for its sweet noctur-

nal song; there are several classical myths about nightingales. Ovid tells the story of Philomela: she was raped by her brother-in-law, Tereus, who then tore out her tongue so that she could not speak. She wove the story into a tapestry and sent it to her sister, who rescued her. She was later changed into a nightingale while in flight from Tereus; Philomela was "lovelorn" only in the ironic sense of being victimized by another's passion.
5. Spirits supposed to inhabit the air.
6. A songbird.

Little offices like these,
Gentle souls and Fairies please.

Mortals! formed of grosser clay,
From our haunts keep far away;
35   Or, if you should dare appear,
See that you from vice are clear.

Folly's minion,° Fashion's fool,   *darling*
Mad ambition's restless tool!
Slave of passion, slave of power,
40   Fly, ah fly! this tranquil bower!

Son of avarice,° soul of frost,   *greed*
Wretch! of Heaven abhorred the most,
Learn to pity others' wants,   *needs*
Or avoid these hallowed haunts.

45   Eye, unconscious of a tear,
When affliction's train appear;
Heart that never heaved a sigh,
For another, come not nigh.

But, ye darling sons of Heaven,
50   Giving freely what was given,
You, whose liberal hands dispense
The blessings of benevolence:

You, who wipe the tearful eye,
You, who stop the rising sigh;
55   You, whose souls have understood
The luxury of doing good,

Come, ye happy virtuous few,
Open is my bower to you;
You, these mossy banks may press;
60   You, each guardian Fay° shall bless.   *fairy*

1774

From The Slave Trade

Strange power of song![7] the strain that warms the heart
Seems the same inspiration to impart;
Touched by the extrinsic° energy alone,   *external*
We think the flame which melts us is our own;
5   Deceived, for genius we mistake delight,

---

7. The "song" refers to Thomas Southerne's "Tragedy of Oroonoko" (1695), a stage adaptation of Aphra Behn's *Oroonoko or the History of the Royal Slave*. Both the novel and the play critiqued some aspects of the slave trade. The title character is an African prince, sold into slavery in Surinam, who leads a slave revolt and is eventually executed. Southerne is the "sweet Bard" referred to in line 7, below.

Charmed as we read, we fancy we can write.[8]
   Though not to me, sweet Bard, thy powers belong,
The cause I plead shall sanctify my song.
The Muse[9] awakes no artificial fire,
10   For Truth rejects what Fancy would inspire:
Here Art would weave her gayest flowers in vain,
The bright invention Nature would disdain.
For no fictitious ills these numbers° flow,   *verses*
But living anguish, and substantial woe;
15   No individual griefs my bosom melt,
For millions feel what Oronoko felt:
Fired by no single wrongs, the countless host
I mourn, by rapine° dragged from Afric's coast.   *seizure*
   Perish the illiberal[1] thought which would debase
20   The native genius of the sable° race!   *dark-complexioned*
Perish the proud philosophy, which sought
To rob them of the powers of equal thought![2]
Does then the immortal principle within
Change with the casual color of a skin?
25   Does matter° govern spirit? or is mind   *body*
Degraded by the form to which 'tis joined?
   No; they have heads to think, and hearts to feel,
And souls to act, with firm, though erring zeal;[3]
For they have keen affections, kind desires,
30   Love strong as death, and active patriot fires;
All the rude energy, the fervid flame,
Of high-souled passion, and ingenuous[4] shame:
Strong, but luxuriant virtues boldly shoot
From the wild vigor of a savage root.
35   Nor weak their sense of honor's proud control,
For pride is virtue in a Pagan soul;
A sense of worth, a conscience° of desert,°   *consciousness / worth*
A high, unbroken haughtiness of heart;
That self-same stuff which erst° proud empires swayed,   *formerly*
40   Of which the conquerors of the world were made.
Capricious fate of men! that very pride
In Afric scourged, in Rome was deified.
   No Muse, O Qua-shi![5] shall thy deeds relate,
No statue snatch thee from oblivious fate!
45   For thou wast born where never gentle Muse
On Valor's grave the flowers of Genius strews;
And thou wast born where no recording page
Plucks the fair deed from Time's devouring rage.
Had Fortune placed thee on some happier coast,

---

8. I.e., we mistake the pleasure we receive from reading for genius of our own, leading us to think we can write.
9. One of the nine Greek goddesses believed to be the source of inspiration for the arts.
1. Not generous in respect of the rights or liberties of others, narrow-minded or bigoted.
2. Perhaps an allusion to Aristotle's theory (in the *Politics* 1.5) that some are "naturally" born as slaves or inferior persons.
3. Erring because not Christian.
4. Noble, freeborn; the slaves feel shame because they are "ingenuous."
5. A slave who killed himself rather than undergo punishment by the master with whom he had been brought up as a playfellow.

50 Where *polished*[6] Pagans souls heroic boast,
To thee, who soughtest a voluntary grave,
The uninjured honors of thy name to save,
Whose generous arm thy barbarous Master spared,[7]
Altars had smoked, and temples had been reared.
55   Whenever to Afric's shores I turn my eyes,
Horrors of deepest, deadliest guilt arise;
I see, by more than Fancy's mirror[8] shewn,
The burning village, and the blazing town:
See the dire victim torn from social life,
60 The shrieking babe, the agonizing wife!
She, wretch forlorn! is dragged by hostile hands,
To distant tyrants sold, in distant lands!
Transmitted[9] miseries, and successive chains,
The sole sad heritage her child obtains!
65 Even this last wretched boon° their foes deny,   request
To weep together, or together die.
By felon hands, by one relentless stroke,
See the fond links of feeling Nature broke!
The fibres twisting round a parent's heart,
70 Torn from their grasp, and bleeding as they part.

1788

CHARLOTTE SMITH
1749–1806

Written in the church yard at Middleton in Sussex

Pressed by the moon, mute arbitress of tides,
   While the loud equinox its power combines,
   The sea no more its swelling surge confines,
But o'er the shrinking land sublimely rides.
5 The wild blast, rising from the western cave,
   Drives the huge billows from their heaving bed,
   Tears from their grassy tombs the village dead,
And breaks the silent sabbath of the grave!
With shells and sea-weed mingled, on the shore
10   Lo! their bones whiten in the frequent wave;
   But vain to them the winds and waters rave;
They hear the warring elements no more:
While I am doomed—by life's long storm oppressed,
To gaze with envy on their gloomy rest.

1789

---

6. Made more refined or elegant by the stories told about them.
7. When his master tries to punish him, Quashi resists. In the struggle that ensues, Quashi gains the upper hand and draws a knife, but uses it to kill himself rather than the master.
8. Fictions generated by imagination; perhaps referring to Southerne's play or other theatrical or literary works.
9. Passed by inheritance.

To the shade of Burns[1]

Mute is thy wild harp, now, O Bard sublime!
  Who, amid Scotia's° mountain solitude,   *Scotland's*
Great Nature taught to "build the lofty rhyme,"[2]
  And even beneath the daily pressure, rude,°   *harsh*
5   Of laboring Poverty,[3] thy generous blood,
Fired with the love of freedom—Not subdued
  Wert thou by thy low fortune: But a time
  Like this we live in, when the abject chime
Of echoing Parasite is best approved,[4]
10   Was not for thee—Indignantly is fled
Thy noble Spirit; and no longer moved
  By all the ills o'er which thine heart has bled,
  Associate worthy of the illustrious dead,
Enjoys with them "the Liberty it loved."[5]

1796   1797

Written near a port on a dark evening

Huge vapors brood above the clifted shore,
  Night on the Ocean settles, dark and mute,
Save where is heard the repercussive roar
  Of drowsy billows,° on the rugged foot   *waves*
5   Of rocks remote; or still more distant tone
  Of seamen in the anchored bark° that tell   *ship*
The watch relieved; or one deep voice alone
  Singing the hour, and bidding "Strike the bell."
All is black shadow, but the lucid line
10   Marked by the light surf on the level sand,
Or where afar the ship-lights faintly shine
  Like wandering fairy fires,[6] that oft on land
Mislead the Pilgrim—Such the dubious ray
That wavering Reason lends, in life's long darkling way.

                                                  1797

Written in October

The blasts of Autumn as they scatter round
  The faded foliage of another year,
And muttering many a sad and solemn sound,
  Drive the pale fragments o'er the stubble sere,°   *dry, withered*
5   Are well attuned to my dejected mood;
    (Ah! better far than airs that breathe of Spring!)

1. This sonnet was written upon the death of the Scottish poet Robert Burns (1759–1796; see pp. 684–95).
2. Cf. Milton, *Lycidas*, line 11 (p. 354).
3. Burns was the son of an unsuccessful farmer; his own health was broken by efforts to earn a living at farming.
4. I.e., in our time (unlike Burns'), public taste favors "low," unoriginal (parasitical) poetry.

5. Cf. Alexander Pope, "Epitaph on Sir William Trumbull," lines 11–12: "Such this man was, who now, from earth remov'd, / At length enjoys that Liberty he lov'd."
6. The will-o'-the-wisp was said to draw travelers astray by holding a false light before them; the phenomenon of nocturnal light is caused by the combustion of marsh gas.

While the high rooks, that hoarsely clamoring
Seek in black phalanx[7] the half-leafless wood,
I rather hear, than that enraptured lay°   song
10 Harmonious, and of Love and Pleasure born,
Which from the golden furze,[8] or flowering thorn
Awakes the Shepherd in the ides° of May;   fifteenth
Nature delights *me* most when most she mourns,
For never more to me the Spring of Hope returns!

1797

Nepenthe[9]

Oh! for imperial Polydamna's art,
Which to bright Helen was in Egypt taught,
To mix with magic power the oblivious draught[1]
Of force to staunch the bleeding of the heart,
5   And to Care's wan and hollow cheek impart
The smile of happy youth, uncursed with thought.
Potent indeed the charm that could appease
Affection's ceaseless anguish, doomed to weep
O'er the cold grave; or yield even transient ease
10 By soothing busy Memory to sleep!
—Around me those who surely must have tried
Some charm of equal power, I daily see,
But still to *me* Oblivion is denied,
There's no Nepenthe, now, on earth for me.

1797

Stanzas

Ah! think'st thou, Laura,[2] then, that wealth
Should make me thus my youth, and health,
And freedom and repose resign?—
Ah, no!—I toil to gain by stealth
5   One look, one tender glance of thine.

Born where huge hills on hills are piled,
In Caledonia's[3] distant wild,
Unbounded Liberty was mine:
But thou upon my hopes hast smiled,
10   And bade me be a slave of thine!

Amid these gloomy haunts of gain,
Of weary hours I not complain,

7. A flock of rooks (a species of crow that nests in
a colony and hence looks like a phalanx).
8. A spiny evergreen shrub with yellow flowers.
9. A drink or drug supposed to bring forgetfulness
of trouble or grief, used by Helen (in Homer,
Odyssey 4.219–32) to quell the lament over the
apparently lost Odysseus. In a note to this poem,
Smith cites lines from Alexander Pope's "Odys-
sey," which describes Helen mixing the potion and
her acquisition of the drug from "Thone's imperial

wife," i.e., Polydamna, the Egyptian woman from
whom she learned the art of herbs.
1. A potion or drink producing forgetfulness.
2. This poem originally appeared in Smith's *The
Young Philosopher: A Novel* (1798), in which it is
written by the character Glenmorris to Laura, his
future wife.
3. Caledonia is the Roman name for the northern
part of Britain; hence, used poetically for Scotland.

While Hope forbids me to repine,°   *complain*
And whispering tells me I obtain
15   Pity from that soft heart of thine.

Tho' far capricious Fortune flies,
Yet Love will bless the sacrifice,
    And all his purer joys combine;
While I my little world comprise
20   In that fair form, and fairer soul of thine.

                                       1798

Ode to death

Friend of the wretched! wherefore° should the eye   *why*
    Of blank Despair, whence tears have ceased to flow,
Be turned from thee?—Ah! wherefore fears to die
    He, who compelled each poignant grief to know,
5   Drains to its lowest dregs the cup of woe?

Would Cowardice postpone thy calm embrace,
    To linger out long years in torturing pain?
Or not prefer thee to the ills that chase
    Him, who too much impoverished to obtain
10   From British Themis[4] *right*, implores her aid in vain!

Sharp goading Indigence° who would not fly,   *poverty*
    That urges toil the exhausted strength above?
Or shun the *once* fond friend's averted eye?
    Or who to *thy* asylum not remove,
15   To lose the wasting pain of unrequited love?

Can then the wounded wretch who must deplore
    What most she loved, to thy cold arms consigned,
Who hears the voice that soothed her soul no more,[5]
    Fear *thee*, O Death!—Or hug the chains that bind
20   To joyless, cheerless life, her sick, reluctant mind?

Oh! Misery's Cure; who e'er in pale dismay
    Has watched the angel form they could not save,
And seen their dearest blessing tore away,
    May well the terrors of *thy* triumph brave,
25   Nor pause in fearful dread before the opening grave!

                                1797, 1800

From Beachy Head[6]

On thy stupendous summit, rock sublime!
That o'er the channel reared, half way at sea

---

4. The British judicial system; Smith spent many years embroiled in the legal system, trying to settle her father-in-law's will in order to allow her children to claim their shares in his estate.
5. Smith refers to the death of her daughter, Anna Augusta de Foville, who died while giving birth in 1795.
6. This long poem (732 lines) appeared in Smith's last volume of poetry, *Beachy Head and Other Poems*, published after her death in 1807. The notes below are Smith's own, printed originally as endnotes in the 1807 edition.

The mariner at early morning hails,[7]
I would recline; while Fancy should go forth,
5 And represent the strange and awful hour
Of vast concussion;[8] when the Omnipotent
Stretched forth his arm, and rent the solid hills,
Bidding the impetuous main flood rush between
The rifted shores, and from the continent
10 Eternally divided this green isle.
Imperial lord of the high southern coast!
From thy projecting head-land I would mark
Far in the east the shades of night disperse,
Melting and thinned, as from the dark blue wave
15 Emerging, brilliant rays of arrowy light
Dart from the horizon; when the glorious sun
Just lifts above it his resplendent orb.
Advances now, with feathery silver touched,
The rippling tide of flood; glisten the sands,
20 While, inmates of the chalky clefts that scar
Thy sides precipitous, with shrill harsh cry,
Their white wings glancing in the level beam,
The terns, and gulls, and tarrocks, seek their food,[9]
And thy rough hollows echo to the voice
25 Of the gray choughs,[1] and ever restless daws,
With clamor, not unlike the chiding hounds,
While the lone shepherd, and his baying dog,
Drive to thy turfy crest his bleating flock.

The high meridian of the day is past,
30 And Ocean now, reflecting the calm Heaven,
Is of cerulean hue; and murmurs low
The tide of ebb, upon the level sands.
The sloop, her angular canvas shifting still,
Catches the light and variable airs
35 That but a little crisp the summer sea,
Dimpling its tranquil surface.

1807

PHILIP FRENEAU

1752–1832

The Indian Burying Ground

In spite of all the learned have said,
I still my opinion keep;

7. "In crossing the Channel from the coast of France, Beachy-Head is the first land made."
8. "Alluding to an idea that this Island was once joined to the continent of Europe, and torn from it by some convulsion of Nature. I confess I never could trace the resemblance between the two countries. Yet the cliffs about Dieppe, resemble the chalk cliffs on the southern coast. But Nor- mandy has no likeness whatever to the part of England opposite to it."
9. "Terns. *Sterna hirundo,* or Sea Swallow. Gulls. *Larus canus.* Tarrocks. *Larus tridactylus.*"
1. "Gray choughs. *Corvus Graculus,* Cornish Choughs, or, as these birds are called by the Sussex people, Saddle-backed Crows, build in great num- bers on this coast."

The posture, that we give the dead,
    Points out the soul's eternal sleep.

5 Not so the ancients of these lands—
    The Indian, when from life released,
Again is seated with his friends,[1]
    And shares again the joyous feast.

His imaged birds, and painted bowl,
10   And venison, for a journey dressed,[2]
Bespeak the nature of the soul,
    Activity, that knows no rest.

His bow, for action ready bent,
    And arrows, with a head of stone,
15 Can only mean that life is spent,
    And not the old ideas gone.

Thou, stranger, that shalt come this way,
    No fraud upon the dead commit—
Observe the swelling turf, and say
20   They do not lie, but here they sit.

Here still a lofty rock remains,
    On which the curious eye may trace
(Now wasted, half, by wearing rains)
    The fancies of a ruder race.

25 Here still an aged elm aspires,
    Beneath whose far-projecting shade
(And which the shepherd still admires)
    The children of the forest played!

There oft a restless Indian queen
30   (Pale Shebah,[3] with her braided hair)
And many a barbarous form is seen
    To chide the man that lingers there.

By midnight moons, o'er moistening dews;
    In habit for the chase arrayed,
35 The hunter still the deer pursues,
    The hunter and the deer, a shade!

And long shall timorous fancy see
    The painted chief, and pointed spear,
And Reason's self shall bow the knee
40   To shadows and delusions here.

1787   1788

1. Referring to the ancient Indian custom of bury-
ing the dead in a sitting position.
2. Pun on "dress": to prepare for cooking as well
as to clothe.
3. The name evokes Sheba, the queen who visited
Solomon (1 Kings 10.1–13).

To Sir Toby[4]

A *Sugar Planter in the Interior Parts of Jamaica, Near the City of
San Jago De La Vega, (Spanish Town) 1784*

"The motions of his spirit are black as night,
And his affections dark as Erebus."
—SHAKESPEARE[5]

If there exists a hell—the case is clear—
Sir Toby's slaves enjoy that portion here:
Here are no blazing brimstone lakes—'tis true;
But kindled rum too often burns as blue;
5   In which some fiend, whom nature must detest,
Steeps Toby's brand, and marks poor Cudjoe's breast.[6]
Here whips on whips excite perpetual fears,
And mingled howlings vibrate on my ears:
Here nature's plagues abound, to fret and tease,
10   Snakes, scorpions, despots, lizards, centipedes—
No art, no care escapes the busy lash;
All have their dues—and all are paid in cash—
The eternal driver keeps a steady eye
On a black herd, who would his vengeance fly,
15   But chained, imprisoned, on a burning soil,
For the mean avarice of a tyrant toil![7]
The lengthy cart-whip guards this monster's reign—
And cracks, like pistols, from the fields of cane.
    Ye powers! who formed these wretched tribes, relate,
20   What had they done, to merit such a fate!
Why were they brought from Eboe's[8] sultry waste,
To see that plenty which they must not taste—
Food, which they cannot buy, and dare not steal;
Yams and potatoes—many a scanty meal!—
25   One, with a gibbet° wakes his negro's fears,   *gallows*
One to the windmill nails him by the ears;
One keeps his slave in darkened dens, unfed,
One puts the wretch in pickle[9] ere he's dead:
This, from a tree suspends him by the thumbs,
30   That, from his table grudges even the crumbs!
    O'er yond' rough hills a tribe of females go,
Each with her gourd,° her infant, and her hoe;   *water cup*
Scorched by a sun that has no mercy here,
Driven by a devil, whom men call overseer—
35   In chains, twelve wretches to their labors haste;
Twice twelve I saw, with iron collars graced!—
    Are such the fruits that spring from vast domains?
Is wealth, thus got, Sir Toby, worth your pains!—

4. First published in the *National Gazette*, July 21, 1792, and entitled "The Island Field Hand."
5. *The Merchant of Venice* 5.1.79. Freneau has substituted the word "black" for "dull." "Erebus": darkness; the name given to part of the underworld.
6. Cudge or Cudjoe was a common name for a slave. "This passage has a reference to the West Indian custom (sanctioned by law) of branding a newly imported slave on the breast, with a red hot iron, as evidence of the purchaser's property" [Freneau's note].
7. Lines 13–16 were added in 1809.
8. "A small Negro kingdom near the river Senegal" [Freneau's note].
9. I.e., rubs salt or salt and vinegar on the slave's back after a flogging.

Who would your wealth on terms, like these, possess,
40   Where all we see is pregnant with distress—
Angola's[1] natives scourged by ruffian hands,
And toil's hard product shipped to foreign lands.
    Talk not of blossoms, and your endless spring;
What joy, what smile, can scenes of misery bring?—
45   Though Nature, here, has every blessing spread,
Poor is the laborer—and how meanly fed!—
    Here Stygian[2] paintings light and shade renew,
Pictures of hell, that Virgil's[3] pencil drew:
Here, surly Charons make their annual trip,
50   And ghosts arrive in every Guinea ship,[4]
To find what beasts these western isles afford,
Plutonian[5] scourges, and despotic lords:—
    Here, they, of stuff determined to be free,
Must climb the rude cliffs of the Liguanee;[6]
55   Beyond the clouds, in sculking haste repair,
And hardly safe from brother traitors[7] there.—

1784   1792

PHILLIS WHEATLEY

1753–1784

A Farewell to America. To Mrs. S. W.[1]

I

Adieu, New-England's smiling meads,°   *meadows*
    Adieu, the flow'ry plain:
I leave thine op'ning charms, O spring,
And tempt the roaring main.°   *sea*

II

5   In vain for me the flow'rets rise,
    And boast their gaudy pride,
While here beneath the northern skies
    I mourn for health denied.[2]

1. West African Portuguese colony's.
2. Hellish; alluding to the river Styx, which, in Greek mythology, souls must cross to enter Hades. They were ferried across to the underworld by Charon.
3. "See *Aeneid*, Book 6th.—and Fenelon's Telemachus, Book 18" [Freneau's note]. Aeneas descends to the underworld in the sixth book of the epic by the Latin poet Virgil (70–19 B.C.); François de Salignac de La Mothe-Fénelon (1651–1715) wrote *Télémaque* (1699), a didactic romance concerning the son of Ulysses as he searches for his father.
4. Slave ships from West Africa.
5. Hellish; Pluto was the Roman name for the god of the underworld.
6. "The mountains northward of the kingdom" [Freneau's note].
7. "Alluding to the *Independent* negroes in the blue mountains, who, for a stipulated reward, deliver up every fugitive that falls into their hands, to the English Government" [Freneau's note].
1. Phillis Wheatley departed Boston for London in May 1773. "Mrs. S. W.": Susanna Wheatley (1709–1774), Phillis's owner and mistress, who had afforded her an excellent education and had encouraged her writing.
2. Wheatley was frail and sickly for much of her life, and part of her reason for going to England was to improve her health.

III

Celestial maid of rosy hue,[3]
    O let me feel thy reign!°   *influence, dominion*
I languish till thy face I view,
    Thy vanished joys regain.

IV

Susannah mourns, nor can I bear
    To see the crystal show'r,
Or mark the tender falling tear
    At sad departure's hour;

V

Not unregarding can I see
    Her soul with grief opprest;
But let no sighs, no groans for me,
    Steal from her pensive breast.

VI

In vain the feathered warblers sing,
    In vain the garden blooms,
And on the bosom of the spring
    Breathes out her sweet perfumes,

VII

While for Britannia's distant shore
    We sweep the liquid plain,
And with astonished eyes explore
    The wide-extended main.

VIII

Lo! Health appears! celestial dame!
    Complacent and serene,
With Hebe's[4] mantle o'er her frame,
    With soul-delighting mien.°   *appearance, expression*

IX

To mark the vale° where London lies   *valley*
    With misty vapors crowned,
Which cloud Aurora's[5] thousand dyes,
    And veil her charms around,

X

Why, Phoebus,[6] moves thy car so slow?
    So slow thy rising ray?
Give us the famous town to view,
    Thou glorious king of day!

XI

For thee, Britannia, I resign
    New England's smiling fields;
To view again her charms divine,
    What joy the prospect yields!

3. I.e., New England (or America?).
4. Hebe, the goddess of youth, performed small services for the gods, including cup-bearing (until replaced by Ganymede); she was considered the personification of youthful beauty. "Health" in this stanza may refer to Hygieia, goddess of health.
5. The goddess of the dawn.
6. The god of the sun, who daily drove his chariot ("car"), the sun, across the sky.

XII

45 But thou! Temptation hence away,
    With all thy fatal train
Nor once seduce my soul away,
    By thine enchanting strain.

XIII

Thrice happy they, whose heav'nly shield
50   Secures their souls from harms,
And fell° Temptation on the field   *destructive*
    Of all its pow'r disarms!

Boston, May 7, 1773

On Being Brought from Africa to America[7]

'Twas mercy brought me from my pagan land,
Taught my benighted[8] soul to understand
That there's a God, that there's a Savior too:
Once I redemption neither sought nor knew.
5 Some view our sable race with scornful eye,
"Their color is a diabolic die."   *dye*
Remember, Christians, Negros, black as Cain,[9]
May be refined, and join th' angelic train.

To S. M.,[1] a Young African Painter, on Seeing His Works

To show the lab'ring bosom's deep intent,
And thought in living characters to paint,
When first thy pencil did those beauties give,
And breathing figures learnt from thee to live,
5 How did those prospects give my soul delight,
A new creation rushing on my sight?
Still,° wond'rous youth! each noble path pursue,   *always*
On deathless glories fix thine ardent view:
Still may the painter's and the poet's fire
10 To aid thy pencil, and thy verse conspire!
And may the charms of each seraphic[2] theme
Conduct thy footsteps to immortal fame!
High to the blissful wonders of the skies
Elate thy soul, and raise thy wishful eyes.
15 Thrice happy, when exalted to survey
That splendid city, crowned with endless day,
Whose twice six gates on radiant hinges ring:
Celestial Salem[3] blooms in endless spring.

7. Wheatley was brought from West Africa to Boston in July 1761, as a child of eight.
8. Overtaken by darkness; also, figuratively, involved in intellectual or moral darkness, involved in obscurity.
9. The son of Adam and Eve, Cain killed his brother Abel, and God punished him with this curse: "When thou tillest the ground, it shall not henceforth yield unto thee its strength; a fugitive and a vagabond shalt thou be in the earth" (Genesis 4.12).
1. Scipio Moorhead, the slave of a Boston clergyman, John Moorhead.
2. Resembling a seraph (a member of one of the nine orders of angels) either in beauty or in fervor of exalted devotion.
3. The heavenly Jerusalem.

Calm and serene thy moments glide along,
20   And may the muse inspire each future song!
Still, with the sweets of contemplation blessed,
May peace with balmy wings your soul invest!
But when these shades of time are chased away,
And darkness ends in everlasting day,
25   On what seraphic pinions° shall we move,   *wings*
And view the landscapes in the realms above?
There shall thy tongue in heav'nly murmurs flow,
And there my muse[4] with heav'nly transport glow:
No more to tell of Damon's[5] tender sighs,
30   Or rising radiance of Aurora's[6] eyes,
For nobler themes demand a nobler strain,
And purer language on th' ethereal plain.
Cease, gentle muse! the solemn gloom of night
Now seals the fair creation from my sight.

1773

GEORGE CRABBE

1754–1832

From The Parish Register[1]

Part I

BAPTISMS

Tum porro puer (ut sævis projectus ab undis,
Navita) nudus humi jacet infans indigus omni
Vitali auxilio, . . .
Vagituque locum lugubri complet, ut æquum est,
Cui tantum in vitå restat transire malorum.[2]

The year revolves, and I again explore
The simple Annals of my Parish poor;
What Infant-members in my flock appear,
What Pairs I blessed in the departed year;
5   And who, of Old or Young, or Nymphs or Swains,
Are lost to Life, its pleasures and its pains.
    No Muse I ask, before my view to bring
The humble actions of the swains I sing. —
How passed the youthful, how the old their days;
10   Who sank in sloth, and who aspired to praise;

---

4. The Muses were nine Greek goddesses believed to be the sources of inspiration for the arts.
5. According to one version of the Greek legend, Damon was a friend of Pythias, who had been condemned to death by the tyrant Dionysius. Damon stood pledge for Pythias as the latter left to settle his affairs. When Pythias returned, Dionysius was so impressed by the actions of both men that he pardoned Pythias.
6. The goddess of the dawn's.
1. Crabbe's poem is modeled on the parish regis-

ters in which baptisms, marriages, and deaths were recorded. The following section, although titled "Baptisms," serves as an introduction to the whole poem.
2. From Lucretius, *De Rerum Natura* (Latin, "On the Nature of Things") 5.222–24, 225–27: "Then the child, like a sailor thrown forth by the cruel waves, lies naked on the ground, speechless, needing all kinds of vital support . . . and he fills the surrounding air with sad cries—as is appropriate, given that so much trouble awaits in life."

Their tempers, manners, morals, customs, arts,
What parts they had, and how they employed their parts;
By what elated, soothed, seduced, depressed,
Full well I know—these Records give the rest.
15   Is there a place, save one the poet sees,
A land of love, of liberty and ease;
Where labor wearies not, nor cares suppress
Th' eternal flow of rustic happiness;
Where no proud mansion frowns in awful state,
20   Or keeps the sunshine from the cottage-gate;
Where young and old, intent on pleasure, throng,
And half man's life is holiday and song?
Vain search for scenes like these! no view appears;
By sighs unruffled or unstained by tears;
25   Since vice the world subdued and waters drowned,
Auburn[3] and Eden can no more be found.
       Hence good and evil mixed, but man has skill
And power to part them, when he feels the will!
Toil, care, and patience bless th' abstemious few,
30   Fear, shame, and want the thoughtless herd pursue.
       Behold the Cot!° where thrives th' industrious swain,   cottage
Source of his pride, his pleasure, and his gain;
Screened from the winter's wind, the sun's last ray
Smiles on the window and prolongs the day;
35   Projecting thatch the woodbine's branches stop,
And turn their blossoms to the casement's top:
All need requires is in that cot contained,
And much that taste untaught and unrestrained
Surveys delighted; there she loves to trace,
40   In one gay picture, all the royal race;
Around the walls are heroes, lovers, kings;
The print that shows them and the verse that sings.
       Here the last Lewis on his throne is seen,
And there he stands imprisoned, and his Queen;[4]
45   To these the mother takes her child, and shows
What grateful duty to his God he owes;
Who gives to him a happy home, where he
Lives and enjoys his freedom with the free;
When kings and queens, dethroned, insulted, tried,
50   Are all these blessings of the poor denied.
       There is King Charles, and all his Golden Rules,[5]
Who proved Misfortune's was the best of schools:
And there his Son, who, tried by years of pain,
Proved that misfortunes may be sent in vain.
55   The Magic-mill that grinds the gran'nams young,[6]
Close at the side of kind Godiva hung;[7]

3. The fictive village invoked by Goldsmith in "The Deserted Village" (pp. 627–36). The opening section of Crabbe's poem argues explicitly against Goldsmith's views of village life.
4. Louis XVI and Marie Antoinette of France, who were guillotined in 1793.
5. Charles I was thought to have authored twelve popular maxims shortly before he died.

6. A popular contemporary print depicting the Guildford Mill, comically imagined to grind old women into young ones.
7. An eleventh-century noblewoman reputed to have ridden naked through the streets of Coventry to dissuade her husband from imposing heavy taxes on the citizens.

She, of her favorite place the pride and joy,
Of charms at once most lavish and most coy,
By wanton act the purest fame could raise,
60 And give the boldest deed the chastest praise.
There stands the stoutest Ox in England fed;[8]
There fights the boldest Jew, Whitechapel bred;[9]
And here Saint Monday's worthy votaries live,
In all the joys that ale and skittles[1] give.
65 Now lo! on Egypt's coast that hostile fleet,
By nations dreaded and by NELSON beat;[2]
And here shall soon another triumph come,
A deed of glory in a day of gloom;
Distressing glory! grievous boon of fate!
70 The proudest conquest, at the dearest rate.[3]
On shelf of deal beside the cuckoo-clock,
Of cottage-reading rests the chosen stock;
Learning we lack, not books, but have a kind
For all our wants, a meat for every mind:
75 The tale for wonder and the joke for whim,
The half-sung sermon and the half-groaned hymn.
No need of classing; each within its place,
The feeling finger in the dark can trace;
"First from the corner, farthest from the wall,"
80 Such all the rules, and they suffice for all.
There pious works for Sunday's use are found;
Companions for that Bible newly bound;
That Bible, bought by sixpence weekly saved,
Has choicest prints by famous hands engraved;
85 Has choicest notes by many a famous head,
Such as to doubt, have rustic readers led;
Have made them stop to reason *why?* and *how?*
And, where they once agreed, to cavil now.
Oh! rather give me commentators plain,
90 Who with no deep researches vex the brain;
Who from the dark and doubtful love to run,
And hold their glimmering tapers to the sun;
Who simple truth with nine-fold reasons back,
And guard the point no enemies attack.
95 Bunyan's famed Pilgrim rests that shelf upon,
A genius rare but rude was honest John;[4]
Not one who, early by the Muse beguiled,
Drank from her well the waters undefiled;[5]
Not one who slowly gained the hill sublime,[6]
100 Then often sipped and little at a time;
But one who dabbled in the sacred springs,
And drank them muddy, mixed with baser things.

8. A Lancashire ox famous for its size.
9. The boxer Daniel Mendoza.
1. An English bowling game. "Saint Monday's . . . votaries" are working people devoted to taking Monday (as well as Sunday) as "holy days."
2. At the Battle of the Nile in 1798.
3. I.e., the Battle of Trafalgar in 1805, in which Admiral Horatio Nelson died.
4. John Bunyan (1628–1688), English preacher

and author of *Pilgrim's Progress* (1678).
5. A phrase applied by Spenser (*Faerie Queene* 5.2.32) to Chaucer, and by Samuel Johnson (in the preface to his *Dictionary*) to Spenser and others.
6. Perhaps Milton (pp. 354–407), who contrasted his "slow-endeavoring art" to Shakespeare's "easy numbers" ("On Shakespeare") and who stressed the idea of temperance throughout *Paradise Lost.*

Here to interpret dreams we read the rules,
Science our own! and never taught in schools;
105 In moles and specks we Fortune's gifts discern,
And Fate's fixed will from Nature's wanderings learn.
Of Hermit Quarll we read, in island rare,[7]
Far from mankind and seeming far from care;
Safe from all want, and sound in every limb;
110 Yes! there was he, and there was care with him.
Unbound and heaped, these valued tomes beside,
Lay humbler works, the pedlar's pack supplied;
Yet these, long since, have all acquired a name;
The Wandering Jew has found his way to fame;[8]
115 And fame, denied to many a labored song,
Crowns Thumb the Great, and Hickathrift the strong.
There too is he, by wizard-power upheld,
Jack[9], by whose arm the giant-brood were quelled:
His shoes of swiftness on his feet he placed;
120 His coat of darkness on his loins he braced;
His sword of sharpness in his hand he took,
And off the heads of doughty giants stroke:
Their glaring eyes beheld no mortal near;
No sound of feet alarmed the drowsy ear;
125 No English blood their pagan sense could smell,
But heads dropt headlong, wondering why they fell.
These are the peasant's joy, when placed at ease,
Half his delighted offspring mount his knees.
To every cot° the lord's indulgent mind   *cottage*
130 Has a small space for garden-ground assigned;
Here—till return of morn dismissed the farm—
The careful peasant plies the sinewy arm,
Warmed as he works, and casts his look around
On every foot of that improving ground:
135 It is his own he sees; his master's eye
Peers not about, some secret fault to spy;
Nor voice severe is there, nor censure known;—
Hope, profit, pleasure,—they are all his own.
Here grow the humble cives,° and, hard by them,   *chives*
140 The leek with crown globose and reedy stem;
High climb his pulse° in many an even row,   *peas, beans*
Deep strike the ponderous roots in soil below;
And herbs of potent smell and pungent taste,
Give a warm relish to the night's repast.
145 Apples and cherries grafted by his hand,
And clustered nuts for neighboring market stand.
Nor thus concludes his labor; near the cot,
The reed-fence rises round some favorite spot;
Where rich carnations, pinks with purple eyes,
150 Proud hyacinths, the least some florist's prize,
Tulips tall-stemmed and pounced auriculas rise.

7. Attributed to Edward Dorrington, *The Hermit, or Unparalleled Sufferings and Surprising Adventures of Philip Quarll* tells the story of a Robinson Crusoe–like hero. First published in 1727, it was often adapted for children.

8. A proverbial figure condemned to a life of eternal wandering as punishment for his cruelty to Christ.

9. Jack the Giant Killer, like Tom Thumb and Tom Hickathrift, was a popular folk-hero.

Here on a Sunday-eve, when service ends,
Meet and rejoice a family of friends;
All speak aloud, are happy and are free,
155 And glad they seem, and gaily they agree.
    What, though fastidious ears may shun the speech,
Where all are talkers, and where none can teach;
Where still the welcome and the words are old,
And the same stories are for ever told;
160 Yet theirs is joy that, bursting from the heart,
Prompts the glad tongue these nothings to impart;
That forms these tones of gladness we despise,
That lifts their steps, that sparkles in their eyes;
That talks or laughs or runs or shouts or plays,
165 And speaks in all their looks and all their ways.
    Fair scenes of peace! ye might detain us long,
But vice and misery now demand the song;
And turn our view from dwellings simply neat,
To this infected row, we term our Street.
170   Here, in cabal,° a disputatious crew   *illegal assembly*
Each evening meet; the sot, the cheat, the shrew:
Riots are nightly heard:—the curse, the cries
Of beaten wife, perverse in her replies;
While shrieking children hold each threatening hand,
175 And sometimes life, and sometimes food demand:
Boys, in their first-stolen rags, to swear begin,
And girls, who heed not dress, are skilled in gin:
Snarers° and smugglers here their gains divide;   *poachers*
Ensnaring females here their victims hide;
180 And here is one, the Sibyl[1] of the Row,
Who knows all secrets, or affects to know.
Seeking their fate, to her the simple run,
To her the guilty, theirs awhile to shun;
Mistress of worthless arts, depraved in will,
185 Her care unblest and unrepaid her skill,
Slave to the tribe, to whose command she stoops,
And poorer than the poorest maid she dupes.
    Between the road-way and the walls, offence
Invades all eyes and strikes on every sense:
190 There lie, obscene, at every open door,
Heaps from the hearth and sweepings from the floor,
And day by day the mingled masses grow,
As sinks are disembogued° and kennels flow.   *drained*
    There hungry dogs from hungry children steal;
195 There pigs and chickens quarrel for a meal;
There dropsied infants wail without redress,
And all is want and wo and wretchedness:
Yet should these boys, with bodies bronzed and bare,
High-swollen and hard, outlive that lack of care—
200 Forced on some farm, the unexerted strength,
Though loth to action, is compelled at length,
When warmed by health, as serpents in the spring,

1. Name given by the Greeks and Romans to certain women who prophesied and claimed divine inspiration.

Aside their slough of indolence they fling.
　　Yet, ere they go, a greater evil comes—
205　See! crowded beds in those contiguous rooms;
Beds but ill parted, by a paltry screen
Of papered lath or curtain dropt between;
Daughters and sons to yon compartments creep,
And parents here beside their children sleep:
210　Ye who have power, these thoughtless people part,
Nor let the ear be first to taint the heart.
　　Come! search within, nor sight nor smell regard;
The true physician walks the foulest ward.
See! on the floor, what frousy patches rest!
215　What nauseous fragments on yon fractured chest!
What downy dust beneath yon window-seat!
And round these posts that serve this bed for feet;
This bed where all those tattered garments lie,
Worn by each sex, and now perforce thrown by!
220　See! as we gaze, an infant lifts its head,
Left by neglect and burrowed in that bed;
The Mother-gossip has the love suppressed
An infant's cry once wakened in her breast;
And daily prattles, as her round she takes,
225　(With strong resentment) of the want she makes.
　　Whence all these woes?—From want of virtuous will,
Of honest shame, of time-improving skill;
From want of care t' employ the vacant hour,
And want of ev'ry kind but want of power.
230　Here are no wheels for either wool or flax,
But packs of cards—made up of sundry packs;
Here is no clock, nor will they turn the glass,
And see how swift th' important moments pass;
Here are no books, but ballads on the wall,
235　Are some abusive, and indecent all;
Pistols are here, unpaired; with nets and hooks,
Of every kind, for rivers, ponds, and brooks;
An ample flask, that nightly rovers fill
With recent poison from the Dutchman's still;[2]
240　A box of tools, with wires of various size,
Frocks, wigs, and hats, for night or day disguise,
And bludgeons stout to gain or guard a prize.
　　To every house belongs a space of ground,
Of equal size, once fenced with paling round;
245　That paling now by slothful waste destroyed,
Dead gorse and stumps of elder fill the void;
Save in the center-spot, whose walls of clay
Hide sots and striplings at their drink or play:
Within, a board,[3] beneath a tiled retreat,
250　Allures the bubble° and maintains the cheat;　　　　　　*dupe*
Where heavy ale in spots like varnish shows,
Where chalky tallies yet remain in rows;
Black pipes and broken jugs the seats defile,

---

2. Illegally imported alcohol.　　　　　3. Probably a gambling table.

The walls and windows, rhymes and reck'nings vile;
255   Prints of the meanest kind disgrace the door,
And cards, in curses torn, lie fragments on the floor.
    Here his poor bird th' inhuman Cocker[4] brings,
Arms his hard heel and clips his golden wings;
With spicy food th' impatient spirit feeds,
260   And shouts and curses as the battle bleeds.
Struck through the brain, deprived of both his eyes,
The vanquished bird must combat till he dies;
Must faintly peck at his victorious foe,
And reel and stagger at each feeble blow:
265   When fallen, the savage grasps his dabbled plumes,
His blood-stained arms, for other deaths assumes;
And damns the craven-fowl, that lost his stake,
And only bled and perished for his sake.
    Such are our Peasants, those to whom we yield
270   Praise with relief,° the fathers of the field;   *welfare*
And these who take from our reluctant hands,
What Burn advises[5] or the Bench commands.
    Our Farmers round, well pleased with constant gain,
Like other farmers, flourish and complain. —
275   These are our groups; our Portraits next appear,
And close our Exhibition for the year.

                                    1807

From The Borough

From *Letter XXII, The Poor of The Borough: Peter Grimes*

165   Alas! for Peter, not a helping hand,
So was he hated, could he now command.[6]
Alone he rowed his boat, alone he cast
His nets beside, or made his anchor fast;
To hold a rope or hear a curse was none —
170   He toiled and railed, he groaned and swore alone.
    Thus by himself compelled to live each day,
To wait for certain hours the tide's delay;
At the same times the same dull views to see,
The bounding marsh-bank and the blighted tree;
175   The water only, when the tides were high,
When low, the mud half-covered and half-dry;
The sun-burnt tar that blisters on the planks,
And bank-side stakes in their uneven ranks;
Heaps of entangled weeds that slowly float,
180   As the tide rolls by the impeded boat.
    When tides were neap° and, in the sultry day,   *low*
Through the tall bounding mud-banks made their way,
Which on each side rose swelling, and below
The dark warm flood ran silently and slow;

---

4. The owner of fighting cocks.
5. Richard Burn (1709–1795), English legal scholar who wrote *Justice of the Peace* and *Ecclesiastical Law.*

6. Grimes has fatally exploited three boys provided by the workhouses as child laborers and has been forbidden to employ any more.

185   There anchoring, Peter chose from man to hide, ⎫
      There hang his head, and view the lazy tide   ⎬
      In its hot slimy channel slowly glide;   ⎭
      Where the small eels that left the deeper way
      For the warm shore within the shallows play;
190   Where gaping mussels, left upon the mud,
      Slope their slow passage to the fallen flood.
      Here dull and hopeless he'd lie down and trace
      How sidelong crabs had scrawled their crooked race,
      Or sadly listen to the tuneless cry
195   Of fishing gull or clanging golden-eye;°   *species of wild duck*
      What time the sea-birds to the marsh would come, ⎫
      And the loud bittern, from the bulrush° home,   ⎬   *cattail*
      Gave from the salt-ditch side the bellowing boom. ⎭
      He nursed the feelings these dull scenes produce,
200   And loved to stop beside the opening sluice;
      Where the small stream, confined in narrow bound,
      Ran with a dull, unvaried, saddening sound;
      Where all, presented to the eye or ear,
      Oppressed the soul with misery, grief, and fear.
205   Besides these objects, there were places three,
      Which Peter seemed with certain dread to see;
      When he drew near them he would turn from each,
      And loudly whistle till he passed the reach.[7]
        A change of scene to him brought no relief;
210   In town, 'twas plain, men took him for a thief.
      The sailors' wives would stop him in the street,
      And say, "Now, Peter, thou'st no boy to beat!"
      Infants at play, when they perceived him, ran,
      Warning each other—"That's the wicked man!"
215   He growled an oath, and in an angry tone
      Cursed the whole place and wished to be alone.
        Alone he was, the same dull scenes in view,
      And still more gloomy in his sight they grew;
      Though man he hated, yet employed alone
220   At bootless labor, he would swear and groan,
      Cursing the shoals° that glided by the spot,   *schools of fish*
      And gulls that caught them when his arts could not.
        Cold nervous tremblings shook his sturdy frame,
      And strange disease—he couldn't say the name;
225   Wild were his dreams, and oft he rose in fright,
      Waked by his view of horrors in the night—
      Horrors that would the sternest minds amaze,
      Horrors that demons might be proud to raise;
      And though he felt forsaken, grieved at heart   ⎫
230   To think he lived from all mankind apart,   ⎬
      Yet, if a man approached, in terrors he would start. ⎭
        A winter passed since Peter saw the town,
      And summer lodgers were again come down.
      These, idly curious, with their glasses° spied   *telescopes*
235   The ships in bay as anchored for the tide—

---

7. A "reach" is the distance between two points on a river, or along its banks. The places correspond to the three dead boys.

The river's craft—the bustle of the quay—
And sea-port views, which landmen love to see.
   One, up the river, had a man and boat
Seen day by day, now anchored, now afloat;
₂₄₀ Fisher he seemed, yet used no net nor hook, ⎫
Of sea-fowl swimming by no heed he took, ⎬
But on the gliding waves still fixed his lazy look. ⎭
At certain stations he would view the stream,
As if he stood bewildered in a dream,
₂₄₅ Or that[8] some power had chained him for a time,
To feel a curse or meditate on crime.
   This known, some curious, some in pity went,
And others questioned—"Wretch, dost thou repent?"
He heard, he trembled, and in fear resigned
₂₅₀ His boat; new terror filled his restless mind;
Furious he grew, and up on the country ran,
And there they seized him—a distempered man.
Him we received, and to a parish-bed,[9]
Followed and cursed, the groaning man was led.

1810

WILLIAM BLAKE

1757–1827

FROM POETICAL SKETCHES

To the Muses[1]

Whether on Ida's[2] shady brow,
   Or in the chambers of the East,
The chambers of the sun, that now
   From antient melody have ceas'd;

₅ Whether in Heav'n ye wander fair,
   Or the green corners of the earth,
Or the blue regions of the air,
   Where the melodious winds have birth;

Whether on chrystal rocks ye rove,
₁₀   Beneath the bosom of the sea
Wand'ring in many a coral grove,
   Fair Nine, forsaking Poetry!

How have you left the antient love
   That bards of old enjoy'd in you!
₁₅ The languid strings do scarcely move!
   The sound is forc'd, the notes are few!

1783

8. I.e., or as if.
9. A bed in the charity hospital.
1. Nine goddesses who, in Greek myth, preside over the arts and sciences, especially poetry.

2. Mountain in Asia Minor, distant from the mountains sacred to the Muses (Helicon and Parnassus) in Greece.

Song

How sweet I roam'd from field to field,
    And tasted all the summer's pride,
'Till I the prince of love beheld,
    Who in the sunny beams did glide!

5   He shew'd me lilies for my hair,
    And blushing roses for my brow;
He led me through his gardens fair,
    Where all his golden pleasures grow.

With sweet May dews my wings were wet,
10   And Phoebus fir'd my vocal rage;[3]
He caught me in his silken net,
    And shut me in his golden cage.

He loves to sit and hear me sing,
    Then, laughing, sports and plays with me;
15   Then stretches out my golden wing,
    And mocks my loss of liberty.

1783

To the Evening Star

Thou fair-hair'd angel of the evening,
Now, while the sun rests on the mountains, light
Thy bright torch of love; thy radiant crown
Put on, and smile upon our evening bed!
5   Smile on our loves; and, while thou drawest the
Blue curtains of the sky, scatter thy silver dew
On every flower that shuts its sweet eyes
In timely sleep. Let thy west wind sleep on
The lake; speak silence with thy glimmering eyes,
10   And wash the dusk with silver. Soon, full soon,
Dost thou withdraw; then the wolf rages wide,
And the lion glares thro' the dun forest:
The fleeces of our flocks are cover'd with
Thy sacred dew: protect them with thine influence.[4]

1783

FROM SONGS OF INNOCENCE

Introduction

Piping down the valleys wild
Piping songs of pleasant glee
On a cloud I saw a child,
    And he laughing said to me,

3. Impassioned song. Phoebus is Apollo, god of
poetic inspiration.

4. In astrology, the effect that heavenly bodies
exert on earthly things and creatures.

5   "Pipe a song about a Lamb";
So I piped with merry chear.
"Piper pipe that song again"—
So I piped, he wept to hear.

"Drop thy pipe thy happy pipe
10   Sing thy songs of happy chear";
So I sung the same again
While he wept with joy to hear.

"Piper sit thee down and write
In a book that all may read"—
15   So he vanish'd from my sight.
And I pluck'd a hollow reed,

And I made a rural pen,
And I stain'd the water clear,
And I wrote my happy songs
20   Every child may joy to hear.

1789

The Lamb

Little Lamb, who made thee?
Dost thou know who made thee?
Gave thee life & bid thee feed,
By the stream & o'er the mead;
5   Gave thee clothing of delight,
Softest clothing wooly bright;
Gave thee such a tender voice,
Making all the vales rejoice!
Little Lamb who made thee?
10   Dost thou know who made thee?

Little Lamb I'll tell thee,
Little Lamb I'll tell thee!
He° is callèd by thy name,   *Christ*
For he calls himself a Lamb:
15   He is meek & he is mild,
He became a little child:
I a child & thou a lamb,
We are callèd by his name.
Little Lamb God bless thee.
20   Little Lamb God bless thee.

1789

Holy Thursday [I.]

'Twas on a Holy Thursday,[5] their innocent faces clean,
The children[6] walking two & two, in red & blue & green,

5. Probably Ascension Day (forty days after Easter).

6. Here the children of charity schools are depicted in St. Paul's Cathedral, London.

Gray headed beadles[7] walkd before with wands as white as snow,
Till into the high dome of Paul's they like Thames' waters flow.

5 O what a multitude they seemd, these flowers of London town!
Seated in companies they sit with radiance all their own.
The hum of multitudes was there, but multitudes of lambs,
Thousands of little boys & girls raising their innocent hands.

Now like a mighty wind they raise to heaven the voice of song,
10 Or like harmonious thunderings the seats of heaven among.
Beneath them sit the aged men, wise guardians of the poor;
Then cherish pity, lest you drive an angel from your door.

1789

The Divine Image

To Mercy, Pity, Peace, and Love,
All pray in their distress:
And to these virtues of delight
Return their thankfulness.

5 For Mercy, Pity, Peace, and Love,
Is God, our father dear:
And Mercy, Pity, Peace, and Love,
Is Man, his child and care.

For Mercy has a human heart,
10 Pity, a human face:
And Love, the human form divine,
And Peace, the human dress.

Then every man of every clime,
That prays in his distress,
15 Prays to the human form divine,
Love, Mercy, Pity, Peace.

And all must love the human form,
In heathen, Turk, or Jew.
Where Mercy, Love, & Pity dwell,
20 There God is dwelling too.

1789

The Little Black Boy

My mother bore me in the southern wild,
And I am black, but O! my soul is white;
White as an angel is the English child:
But I am black as if bereav'd of light.

5 My mother taught me underneath a tree,
And sitting down before the heat of day,

7. Ushers charged with keeping order.

She took me on her lap and kisséd me,
And pointing to the east, began to say:

"Look on the rising sun: there God does live,
10   And gives his light, and gives his heat away;
And flowers and trees and beasts and men receive
Comfort in morning, joy in the noon day.

"And we are put on earth a little space,
That we may learn to bear the beams of love,
15   And these black bodies and this sun-burnt face
Is but a cloud, and like a shady grove.

"For when our souls have learn'd the heat to bear,
The cloud will vanish; we shall hear his voice,
Saying: 'Come out from the grove, my love & care,
20   And round my golden tent like lambs rejoice.' "

Thus did my mother say, and kisséd me;
And thus I say to little English boy:
When I from black and he from white cloud free,
And round the tent of God like lambs we joy,

25   I'll shade him from the heat till he can bear
To lean in joy upon our father's knee;
And then I'll stand and stroke his silver hair,
And be like him, and he will then love me.

1789

The Little Boy Lost

"Father, father, where are you going?
O do not walk so fast.
Speak father, speak to your little boy
Or else I shall be lost."

5   The night was dark, no father was there,
The child was wet with dew.
The mire was deep, & the child did weep,
And away the vapor flew.

1789

The Little Boy Found

The little boy lost in the lonely fen,
Led by the wand'ring light,[8]
Began to cry, but God ever nigh
Appeard like his father in white.

5   He kissed the child & by the hand led
And to his mother brought,

8. A will-o'-the-wisp.

Who in sorrow pale, thro' the lonely dale,
Her little boy weeping sought.

1789

The Book of Thel[9]

Thel's Motto

Does the Eagle know what is in the pit?
Or wilt thou go ask the Mole?
Can Wisdom be put in a silver rod?
Or Love in a golden bowl?

1

5 The daughters of Mne[1] Seraphim led round their sunny flocks,
All but the youngest; she in paleness sought the secret air,
To fade away like morning beauty from her mortal day;
Down by the river of Adona[2] her soft voice is heard,
And thus her gentle lamentation falls like morning dew:

10 "O life of this our spring! why fades the lotus of the water?
Why fade these children of the spring? born but to smile & fall.
Ah! Thel is like a watry bow, and like a parting cloud,
Like a reflection in a glass, like shadows in the water,
Like dreams of infants, like a smile upon an infant's face,
15 Like the dove's voice, like transient day, like music in the air.
Ah! gentle may I lay me down, and gentle rest my head,
And gentle sleep the sleep of death and gentle hear the voice
Of him that walketh in the garden in the evening time."

The Lilly of the valley, breathing in the humble grass,
20 Answer'd the lovely maid and said: "I am a watry weed,
And I am very small, and love to dwell in lowly vales;
So weak, the gilded butterfly scarce perches on my head;
Yet I am visited from heaven, and he that smiles on all
Walks in the valley and each morn over me spreads his hand,
25 Saying: 'Rejoice, thou humble grass, thou new-born lilly flower,
Thou gentle maid of silent valleys and of modest brooks;
For thou shalt be clothed in light, and fed with morning manna,
Till summer's heat melts thee beside the fountains and the springs
To flourish in eternal vales.' Then why should Thel complain?

30 Why should the mistress of the vales of Har utter a sigh?"

She ceasd & smild in tears, then sat down in her silver shrine.

Thel answerd: "O thou little virgin of the peaceful valley,
Giving to those that cannot crave, the voiceless, the o'ertired;
Thy breath doth nourish the innocent lamb, he smells thy milky
  garments,

---

9. "Thel," like the other proper names in the poem, is Blake's invention, and its meaning can only be inferred.
1. Possibly a misprint for "the." Seraphim are angels who guard Jehovah's throne.
2. Probably the river Adonis in Milton's *Paradise Lost* 1.540–42, associated with rituals of fertility and of death and rebirth.

35 He crops thy flowers, while thou sittest smiling in his face,
Wiping his mild and meekin[3] mouth from all contagious taints.
Thy wine doth purify the golden honey; thy perfume,
Which thou dost scatter on every little blade of grass that springs,
Revives the milkéd cow, & tames the fire-breathing steed.
40 But Thel is like a faint cloud kindled at the rising sun:
I vanish from my pearly throne, and who shall find my place?"
"Queen of the vales," the Lilly answered, "ask the tender cloud,
And it shall tell thee why it glitters in the morning sky,
And why it scatters its bright beauty thro' the humid air.
45 Descend, O little cloud, & hover before the eyes of Thel."

The Cloud descended, and the Lilly bowd her modest head,
And went to mind her numerous charge among the verdant grass.

2

"Oh little Cloud," the virgin said, "I charge thee tell to me,
Why thou complainest not when in one hour thou fade away:
50 Then we shall seek thee but not find; ah, Thel is like to Thee.
I pass away, yet I complain, and no one hears my voice."

The Cloud then shew'd his golden head & his bright form emerg'd,
Hovering and glittering on the air before the face of Thel.

"O virgin, know'st thou not our steeds drink of the golden springs
55 Where Luvah[4] doth renew his horses? Look'st thou on my youth,
And fearest thou, because I vanish and am seen no more,
Nothing remains? O maid, I tell thee, when I pass away,
It is to tenfold life, to love, to peace, and raptures holy:
Unseen descending, weigh my light wings upon balmy flowers,
60 And court the fair eyed dew, to take me to her shining tent;
The weeping virgin trembling kneels before the risen sun,
Till we arise link'd in a golden band, and never part,
But walk united, bearing food to all our tender flowers."

"Dost thou O little Cloud? I fear that I am not like thee;
65 For I walk through the vales of Har and smell the sweetest flowers,
But I feed not the little flowers; I hear the warbling birds,
But I feed not the warbling birds; they fly and seek their food;
But Thel delights in these no more, because I fade away,
And all shall say, 'Without a use this shining woman liv'd,
70 Or did she only live to be at death the food of worms?' "

The Cloud reclind upon his airy throne and answer'd thus:

"Then if thou are the food of worms, O virgin of the skies,
How great thy use, how great thy blessing! Every thing that lives
Lives not alone, nor for self; fear not, and I will call
75 The weak worm from its lowly bed, and thou shalt hear its voice.
Come forth, worm of the silent valley, to thy pensive queen."

---

3. Perhaps describing a lamb's delicately wrinkling mouth.

4. In Blake's mythology, a sun god of Love (Love, Lover, Luvah).

The helpless worm arose, and sat upon the Lilly's leaf,
And the bright Cloud saild on, to find his partner in the vale.

3

Then Thel astonish'd view'd the Worm upon its dewy bed.

80 "Art thou a Worm? Image of weakness, art thou but a Worm?
I see thee like an infant wrapped in the Lilly's leaf;
Ah, weep not, little voice, thou can'st not speak, but thou can'st weep.
Is this a Worm? I see thee lay helpless & naked, weeping,
And none to answer, none to cherish thee with mother's smiles."

85 The Clod of Clay heard the Worm's voice, & raisd her pitying head;
She bow'd over the weeping infant, and her life exhal'd
In milky fondness; then on Thel she fix'd her humble eyes.

"O beauty of the vales of Har! we live not for ourselves;
Thou seest me the meanest thing, and so I am indeed.
90 My bosom of itself is cold, and of itself is dark;

But he that loves the lowly, pours his oil upon my head,
And kisses me, and binds his nuptial bands around my breast,
And says: 'Thou mother of my children, I have lovéd thee,
And I have given thee a crown that none can take away.'
95 But how this is, sweet maid, I know not, and I cannot know;
I ponder, and I cannot ponder; yet I live and love."

The daughter of beauty wip'd her pitying tears with her white veil,
And said: "Alas! I knew not this, and therefore did I weep.
That God would love a Worm, I knew, and punish the evil foot
100 That, wilful, bruis'd its helpless form; but that he cherish'd it
With milk and oil I never knew; and therefore did I weep,
And I complaind in the mild air, because I fade away,
And lay me down in thy cold bed, and leave my shining lot."

"Queen of the vales," the matron Clay answerd, "I heard thy sighs,
105 And all thy moans flew o'er my roof, but I have call'd them down.
Wilt thou, O Queen, enter my house? 'Tis given thee to enter
And to return; fear nothing, enter thy virgin feet."

4

The eternal gates' terrific porter lifted the northern bar:[5]
Thel enter'd in & saw the secrets of the land unknown.
110 She saw the couches of the dead, & where the fibrous roots
Of every heart on earth infixes deep its restless twists:
A land of sorrows & of tears where never smile was seen.

She wanderd in the land of clouds thro' valleys dark, listning
Dolours & lamentations; waiting oft beside a dewy grave,
115 She stood in silence, listning to the voices of the ground,

---

5. Possibly, the gate through which a soul or spirit enters the world of earthly life and death.

Till to her own grave plot she came, & there she sat down,
And heard this voice of sorrow breathéd from the hollow pit:

"Why cannot the Ear be closed to its own destruction?
Or the glistning Eye to the poison of a smile?
120 Why are Eyelids stord with arrows ready drawn,
Where a thousand fighting men in ambush lie?
Or an Eye of gifts & graces, show'ring fruits & coinéd gold?
Why a Tongue impress'd with honey from every wind?
Why an Ear, a whirlpool fierce to draw creations in?
125 Why a Nostril wide inhaling terror, trembling, & affright?
Why a tender curb upon the youthful burning boy?
Why a little curtain of flesh on the bed of our desire?"

The Virgin started from her seat, & with a shriek
Fled back unhinderd till she came into the vales of Har.
THE END

1789–91

FROM SONGS OF EXPERIENCE

Introduction

Hear the voice of the Bard!
Who Present, Past, & Future sees,
Whose ears have heard
The Holy Word
5 That walk'd among the ancient trees;[6]

Calling the lapséd Soul
And weeping in the evening dew;
That might controll
The starry pole,
10 And fallen fallen light renew!

"O Earth O Earth return!
Arise from out the dewy grass;
Night is worn,
And the morn
15 Rises from the slumberous mass.

"Turn away no more:
Why wilt thou turn away?
The starry floor
The watry shore
20 Is giv'n thee till the break of day."

1794

6. "And Adam and Eve heard the voice of the Lord God walking in the garden in the cool of the day"
(Genesis 3.8).

A Divine Image

Cruelty has a Human heart
And Jealousy a Human Face,
Terror, the Human Form Divine,
And Secrecy, the Human Dress.

5   The Human Dress is forgéd Iron,
The Human Form, a fiery Forge,
The Human Face, a Furnace seal'd,
The Human Heart, its hungry Gorge.°   *throat*

1790–91   1921

Holy Thursday [II.]

Is this a holy thing to see,
In a rich and fruitful land,
Babes reducd to misery,
Fed with cold and usurous hand?

5   Is that trembling cry a song?
Can it be a song of joy?
And so many children poor?
It is a land of poverty!

And their sun does never shine,
10   And their fields and bleak & bare,
And their ways are fill'd with thorns;
It is eternal winter there.

For where-e'er the sun does shine,
And where-e'er the rain does fall,
15   Babe can never hunger there,
Nor poverty the mind appall.

1794

The Clod & the Pebble

"Love seeketh not Itself to please,
Nor for itself hath any care;
But for another gives its ease,
And builds a Heaven in Hells despair."

5   So sang a little Clod of Clay,
Trodden with the cattle's feet;
But a Pebble of the brook,
Warbled out these meters meet:°   *appropriate*

"Love seeketh only Self to please,
10   To bind another to its delight,
Joys in another's loss of ease,
And builds a Hell in Heaven's despite."

1794

The Sick Rose

O Rose, thou art sick.
The invisible worm
That flies in the night
In the howling storm

5   Has found out thy bed
Of crimson joy,
And his dark secret love
Does thy life destroy.

1794

A Poison Tree

I was angry with my friend:
I told my wrath, my wrath did end.
I was angry with my foe:
I told it not, my wrath did grow.

5   And I waterd it in fears,
Night & morning with my tears;
And I sunnéd it with smiles,
And with soft deceitful wiles.

And it grew both day and night,
10 Till it bore an apple bright.
And my foe beheld it shine,
And he knew that it was mine,

And into my garden stole,
When the night had veild the pole;
15 In the morning glad I see
My foe outstretchd beneath the tree.

1794

The Tyger

Tyger! Tyger! burning bright
In the forests of the night,
What immortal hand or eye
Could frame thy fearful symmetry?

5   In what distant deeps or skies
Burnt the fire of thine eyes?
On what wings dare he aspire?
What the hand, dare seize the fire?

And what shoulder, & what art,
10 Could twist the sinews of thy heart?
And when thy heart began to beat,
What dread hand? & what dread feet?

What the hammer? what the chain?
In what furnace was thy brain?
15 What the anvil? what dread grasp
Dare its deadly terrors clasp?

When the stars threw down their spears,
And water'd heaven with their tears,
Did he smile his work to see?
20 Did he who made the Lamb make thee?

Tyger! Tyger! burning bright
In the forests of the night,
What immortal hand or eye
Dare frame thy fearful symmetry?

1794

Ah Sun-flower

Ah Sun-flower! weary of time,
Who countest the steps of the Sun,
Seeking after that sweet golden clime
Where the traveller's journey is done;

5 Where the Youth pined away with desire,
And the pale Virgin shrouded in snow,
Arise from their graves and aspire,
Where my Sun-flower wishes to go.

1794

The Garden of Love

I went to the Garden of Love,
And saw what I never had seen:
A Chapel was built in the midst,
Where I used to play on the green.

5 And the gates of this Chapel were shut,
And "Thou shalt not" writ over the door;
So I turn'd to the Garden of Love,
That so many sweet flowers bore,

And I saw it was filled with graves,
10 And tomb-stones where flowers should be:
And Priests in black gowns were walking their rounds,
And binding with briars my joys & desires.

1794

London

I wander thro' each charter'd[7] street,
Near where the charter'd Thames does flow,

7. Mapped out, legally defined, constricted.

And mark in every face I meet
Marks of weakness, marks of woe.

5   In every cry of every man,
In every Infant's cry of fear,
In every voice, in every ban,[8]
The mind-forg'd manacles I hear.

How the Chimney-sweeper's cry
10 Every blackning Church appalls;°   horrifies, casts a pall over
And the hapless Soldier's sigh
Runs in blood down Palace walls.

But most thro' midnight streets I hear
How the youthful Harlot's curse
15 Blasts the new-born Infant's tear,
And blights with plagues the Marriage hearse.

1794

FROM SONGS AND BALLADS

I Askéd a Thief

I askéd a thief to steal me a peach,
He turned up his eyes;
I ask'd a lithe lady to lie her down,
Holy & meek she cries.

5   As soon as I went
An angel came.
He wink'd at the thief
And smild at the dame—

And without one word said
10 Had a peach from the tree
And still as a maid
Enjoy'd the lady.

1796   1863

Mock on, Mock on, Voltaire, Rousseau

Mock on, Mock on, Voltaire, Rousseau;[9]
Mock on, Mock on, 'tis all in vain.
You throw the sand against the wind,
And the wind blows it back again.

5   And every sand becomes a Gem
Reflected in the beams divine;
Blown back, they blind the mocking Eye,
But still in Israel's paths they shine.

8. A law or notice commanding or forbidding; a
published penalty.
9. Leaders of the pre-Revolutionary French

"Enlightenment"; critics of the established order,
here representing thinkers who destroy without
creating.

The Atoms of Democritus
10 And Newton's Particles of light[1]
Are sands upon the Red sea shore,[2]
Where Israel's tents do shine so bright.

1800–08   1863

Eternity

He who binds to himself a joy
Does the wingéd life destroy
But he who kisses the joy as it flies
Lives in eternity's sun rise.

1800–08   1863

A Question Answered

What is it men in women do require?
The lineaments of Gratified Desire.
What is it women do in men require?
The lineaments of Gratified Desire.

1800–08   1863

FROM MILTON

And Did Those Feet

And did those feet in ancient time
Walk upon England's mountains green?
And was the holy Lamb of God
On England's pleasant pastures seen?

5   And did the Countenance Divine
Shine forth upon our clouded hills?
And was Jerusalem builded here,
Among these dark Satanic Mills?[3]

Bring me my Bow of burning gold:
10 Bring me my Arrows of desire:
Bring me my Spear: O clouds unfold!
Bring me my Chariot of fire!

I will not cease from Mental Fight,
Nor shall my Sword sleep in my hand,
15 Till we have built Jerusalem
In England's green & pleasant Land.

1804–10

---

1. Democritus (Greek philosopher, fifth century B.C.) and Sir Isaac Newton (1642–1727), both represented as nonsensically reducing nature to inanimate matter.
2. Where God delivered the Israelites from the Egyptians (Exodus 14).
3. The primary meaning is "millstone"—two heavy cylindrical stones that grind grain into meal between them; "factory" is an extended meaning.

FROM JERUSALEM

England! Awake! Awake! Awake!

England! awake! awake! awake!
Jerusalem thy Sister calls!
Why wilt thou sleep the sleep of death?
And close her from thy ancient walls.

5   Thy hills & valleys felt her feet,
                               Gently upon their bosoms move:
                               Thy gates beheld sweet Zions ways;
                               Then was a time of joy and love.

                      And now the time returns again:
10   Our souls exult & Londons towers,
                      Receive the Lamb of God to dwell
                      In Englands green & pleasant bowers.

1804–09   1818

ROBERT BURNS

1759–1796

To a Mouse

On Turning Her up in Her Nest with the Plough, November, 1785

Wee, sleekit,° cow'rin, tim'rous beastie,   *sleek*
O, what a panic's in thy breastie!
Thou need na start awa sae hasty,
                       Wi' bickering° brattle!°   *hurried / scamper*
5   I wad be laith to rin an' chase thee,
                       Wi' murd'ring pattle!°   *plowstaff ("paddle")*

I'm truly sorry man's dominion
Has broken Nature's social union,
An' justifies that ill opinion
10   Which makes thee startle
At me, thy poor earth-born companion,
                       An' fellow-mortal!

I doubt na, whiles,° but thou may thieve;   *sometimes*
What then? poor beastie, thou maun° live!   *must*
15   A daimen° icker° in a thrave°   *random / corn-ear / shock*
                       'S a sma' request:
I'll get a blessin wi' the lave,°   *rest*
                       And never miss't!

Thy wee bit housie, too, in ruin!
20   Its silly° wa's the win's are strewin!   *frail*

An' naething, now, to big° a new ane,   *build*
      O' foggage° green!   *mosses*
An' bleak December's winds ensuin,
      Baith snell° an' keen!   *bitter*

25 Thou saw the fields laid bare and waste,
An' weary winter comin fast,
An' cozie here, beneath the blast,
      Thou thought to dwell,
Till crash! the cruel coulter° past   *plowshare*
30   Out thro' thy cell.

That wee bit heap o' leaves an' stibble°   *stubble*
Has cost thee mony a weary nibble!
Now thou's turned out, for a' thy trouble,
      But° house or hald,°   *without / home ("hold")*
35 To thole° the winter's sleety dribble,   *endure*
      An' cranreuch° cauld!   *hoarfrost*

But, Mousie, thou art no thy lane,[1]
In proving foresight may be vain:
The best laid schemes o' mice an' men
40   Gang° aft a-gley.°   *go / astray*
An' lea'e us nought but grief an' pain
      For promised joy.

Still thou art blest, compared wi' me!
The present only toucheth thee:
45 But och! I backward cast my e'e
      On prospects drear!
An' forward, tho' I canna see,
      I guess an' fear!

                                     1785, 1786

Holy Willie's[2] Prayer

O Thou, wha in the heavens dost dwell,
Wha, as it pleases best thysel',
Sends ane to heaven and ten to hell,
      A' for thy glory,
5 And no for ony guid or ill
      They've done afore thee!

I bless and praise thy matchless might,
Whan thousands thou hast left in night,
That I am here afore thy sight,
10   For gifts an' grace
A burnin' an' a shinin' light,
      To a' this place.

1. "No thy lane": not alone.
2. William Fisher, an elder in the church at Mauchline, the seat of Burns' farm. He habitually censured other men's behavior and doctrine, but was himself rebuked for drunkenness and was suspected of stealing church funds.

What was I, or my generation,
That I should get sic exaltation?
15 I, wha deserve most just damnation,
      For broken laws,
Sax thousand years 'fore my creation,
      Thro' Adam's cause.

When frae my mither's womb I fell,
20 Thou might hae plungéd me in hell,
To gnash my gums, to weep and wail,
      In burnin lakes,
Where damnéd devils roar and yell,
      Chained to their stakes;

25 Yet I am here a chosen sample,
To show thy grace is great and ample;
I'm here a pillar in thy temple,
      Strong as a rock,
A guide, a buckler,° an example   *protector*
30   To a' thy flock.

O Lord, thou kens what zeal I bear,
When drinkers drink, and swearers swear.
And singin' there and dancin' here,
      Wi' great an' sma':
35 For I am keepit by thy fear
      Free frae them a'.

But yet, O Lord! confess I must
At times I'm fashed° wi' fleshy lust;   *troubled*
An' sometimes too, wi' warldly trust,
40   Vile self gets in;
But thou remembers we are dust,
      Defiled in sin.

O Lord! yestreen,° thou kens, wi' Meg—   *last night*
Thy pardon I sincerely beg;
45 O! may't ne'er be a livin' plague
      To my dishonor,
An' I'll ne'er lift a lawless leg
      Again upon her.

Besides I farther maun allow,
50 Wi' Lizzie's lass, three times I trow—
But, Lord, that Friday I was fou,°   *full (of liquor)*
      When I cam near her,
Or else thou kens thy servant true
      Wad never steer° her.   *touch ("stir")*

55 May be thou lets this fleshly thorn
Beset thy servant e'en and morn
Lest he owre high and proud should turn,
      That he's sae gifted;

If sae, thy hand maun e'en be borne,
60   Until thou lift it.

Lord, bless thy chosen in this place,
For here thou hast a chosen race;
But God confound their stubborn face,
    And blast their name,
65 Wha bring thy elders to disgrace
    An' public shame.

Lord, mind Gawn Hamilton's[3] deserts,
He drinks, an' swears, an' plays at cartes,
Yet has sae mony takin arts
70   Wi' great an' sma',
Frae God's ain priest the people's hearts
    He steals awa'.

An' when we chastened him therefor,
Thou kens how he bred sic a splore°   *row*
75 As set the warld in a roar
    O' laughin' at us;
Curse thou his basket and his store,
    Kail° and potatoes.   *cabbage*

Lord, hear my earnest cry an' pray'r,
80 Against that presbytery o' Ayr;
Thy strong right hand, Lord, make it bare
    Upo' their heads;
Lord, weigh it down, and dinna spare,
    For their misdeeds.

85 O Lord my God, that glib-tongued Aiken,
My very heart and soul are quakin',
To think how we stood sweatin, shakin,
    An' pissed wi' dread,
While he, wi' hingin° lips and snakin,° *hanging / sneering*
90   Held up his head.

Lord in the day of vengeance try him;
Lord, visit them wha did employ him,
And pass not in thy mercy by them,
    Nor hear their pray'r:
95 But, for thy people's sake, destroy them,
    And dinna spare.

But, Lord, remember me and mine
Wi' mercies temp'ral and divine,
That I for gear° and grace may shine   *wealth*
100   Excelled by nane,

3. Gavin Hamilton, a convivial lawyer friend of Burns'. Accused of Sabbath-breaking and other offenses by the elders of Mauchline church, he was cleared by the Presbytery of Ayr (line 80) with the help of his counsel, Robert Aiken (line 85).

And a' the glory shall be thine,
            Amen, Amen!
1785   1808

Green Grow the Rashes

Green grow the rashes,° O;   *tall grasses or rushes*
    Green grow the rashes, O;
The sweetest hours that e'er I spend,
    Are spent amang the lasses, O!

5   There's nought but care on ev'ry han',
        In ev'ry hour that passes, O:
    What signifies the life o' man,
        An'° 'twere na for the lasses, O.   *if*

    Green grow the rashes, O; . . .

10   The warly° race may riches chase,   *worldly*
        An' riches still may fly them, O;
    An' though at last they catch them fast,
        Their hearts can ne'er enjoy them, O.

    Green grow the rashes, O; . . .

15   But gie me a canny° hour at e'en,   *pleasant*
        My arms about my dearie, O;
    An' warly cares, an' warly men,
        May a' gae tapsalteerie,° O!   *topsy turvy*

    Green grow the rashes, O; . . .

20   For you sae douce,° ye sneer at this,   *prudent*
        Ye're nought but senseless asses, O:
    The wisest man[4] the warl' saw,
        He dearly loved the lasses, O.

    Green grow the rashes, O; . . .

25   Auld nature swears, the lovely dears
        Her noblest work she classes, O:
    Her prentice han' she tried on man,
        An' then she made the lasses, O.

    Green grow the rashes, O; . . .
1784   1787

4. King Solomon, who had many wives.

Of A' the Airts[5]

Of a' the airts° the wind can blaw,   *quarters*
   I dearly like the west,
For there the bonie lassie lives,
   The lassie I lo'e best:
5 There's wild woods grow, and rivers row,°   *flow*
   And mony a hill between;
But day and night my fancy's flight
   Is ever wi' my Jean.

I see her in the dewy flowers,
10 I see her sweet and fair;
I hear her in the tunefu' birds,
   I hear her charm the air:
There's not a bonie flower that springs
   By fountain, shaw,° or green,   *wood*
15 There's not a bonie bird that sings,
   But minds me o' my Jean.

1788   1790

John Anderson, My Jo

John Anderson my jo,° John,   *joy*
   When we were first acquent,
Your locks were like the raven,
   Your bonie brow was brent;[6]
5 But now your brow is beld, John,
   Your locks are like the snow;
But blessings on your frosty pow,°   *head*
   John Anderson, my jo.

John Anderson my jo, John,
10 We clamb° the hill thegither;   *climbed*
And mony a canty° day, John,   *merry*
   We've had wi' ane anither:
Now we maun totter down, John,
   And hand in hand we'll go,
15 And sleep thegither at the foot,
   John Anderson, my jo.

1789   1790

Tam O'Shanter

Of Brownyis and of Bogillis full is this Buke.[7]
         —GAWIN DOUGLAS

When chapman° billies° leave the street,   *peddler / fellows*
And drouthy° neebors neebors meet,   *thirsty*

---

5. Written from Dumfriesshire to Burns' wife, Jean Armour, in Ayrshire, the county to the west. 6. Straight, steep; not rounding off into a bald pate.

7. From the prologue to the sixth book of the *Aeneid*, translated into Scots dialect by Gavin Douglas (1474–1522). Brownies are friendly goblins and bogles unfriendly.

As market-days are wearing late,
An' folk begin to tak the gate;°   road
5   While we sit bousing at the nappy,°   ale
An' getting fou° and unco happy,   full
We think na on the lang Scots miles,
The mosses,° waters, slaps,° and styles,   bogs / gaps in walls
That lie between us and our hame,
10 Where sits our sulky sullen dame,
Gathering her brows like gathering storm,
Nursing her wrath to keep it warm.
    This truth fand° honest Tam o' Shanter,   found
As he frae Ayr ae night did canter,
15 (Auld Ayr, wham ne'er a town surpasses
For honest men and bonnie lasses).
    O Tam! hadst thou but been sae wise,
As ta'en thy ain wife Kate's advice!
She tauld thee weel thou was a skellum,°   good-for-nothing
20 A bletherin',° blusterin', drunken blellum,°   babbling / windbag
That frae November till October,
Ae market-day thou was na sober;
That ilka° melder,° wi' the miller   every / meal-grinding
Thou sat as lang as thou had siller;°   silver
25 That every naig° was ca'd° a shoe on,   horse / driven
The smith and thee gat roarin' fou on;
That at the Lord's house, even on Sunday,
Thou drank wi' Kirkton Jean[8] till Monday.
She prophesied that, late or soon,
30 Thou would be found deep drowned in Doon;
Or catched wi' warlocks° in the mirk,°   wizards / dark
By Alloway's auld haunted kirk.[9]
    Ah, gentle dames! it gars° me greet°   makes / weep
To think how mony counsels sweet,
35 How mony lengthened sage advices,
The husband frae the wife despises!
    But to our tale: Ae market night,
Tam had got planted unco° right;   uncommonly
Fast by an ingle,° bleezing° finely,   fireplace / blazing
40 Wi' reaming° swats,° that drank divinely;   foaming / ale
And at his elbow, Souter° Johnny,   cobbler
His ancient, trusty, drouthy crony;
Tam lo'ed him like a vera brither;
They had been fou for weeks thegither.
45 The night drave on wi' sangs and clatter;°   talk
And aye the ale was growing better:
The landlady and Tam grew gracious,
Wi' favors secret, sweet, and precious:
The souter tauld his queerest stories;
50 The landlord's laugh was ready chorus:
The storm without might rair° and rustle,   roar
Tam did na mind the storm a whistle.
    Care, mad to see a man sae happy,

8. Mistress of a tavern.   object of much superstitious dread.
9. The ruins of a church near Burns' home, the

E'en drowned himsel amang the nappy;
55 As bees flee hame wi' lades° o' treasure,   *loads*
The minutes winged their way wi' pleasure;
Kings may be blest, but Tam was glorious,
O'er a' the ills o' life victorious!
    But pleasures are like poppies spread,
60 You seize the flow'r, its bloom is shed;
Or like the snow falls in the river,
A moment white—then melts for ever;
Or like the borealis race,
That flit ere you can point their place;
65 Or like the rainbow's lovely form
Evanishing amid the storm—
Nae man can tether time nor tide;
The hour approaches Tam maun ride;
That hour, o' night's black arch the key-stane,
70 That dreary hour, he mounts his beast in;
And sic a night he taks the road in,
As ne'er poor sinner was abroad in.
    The wind blew as 'twad° blawn its last;   *it would have*
The rattling show'rs rose on the blast;
75 The speedy gleams the darkness swallowed;
Loud, deep, and lang, the thunder bellowed:
That night, a child might understand,
The Deil° had business on his hand.   *Devil*
    Weel mounted on his gray mare, Meg,
80 A better never lifted leg,
Tam skelpit° on thro' dub° and mire,   *hurried / puddle*
Despising wind, and rain, and fire;
Whiles° holding fast his guid blue bonnet;   *sometimes*
Whiles crooning° o'er some auld Scots sonnet;°   *humming / song*
85 Whiles glow'ring° round wi' prudent cares,   *staring*
Lest bogles° catch him unawares.   *bogies*
Kirk-Alloway was drawing nigh,
Whare ghaists and houlets° nightly cry.   *owls*
    By this time he was cross the ford,
90 Where in the snaw the chapman smoored;°   *smothered*
And past the birks° and meikle° stane,°   *birches / great / stone*
Where drunken Charlie brak's neck-bane;
And thro' the whins,° and by the cairn,   *furze*
Where hunters fand the murdered bairn;
95 And near the thorn, aboon° the well,   *above*
Where Mungo's mither hanged hersel.
Before him Doon pours all his floods;
The doubling storm roars thro' the woods;
The lightnings flash from pole to pole;
100 Near and more near the thunders roll:
When, glimmering thro' the groaning trees,
Kirk-Alloway seemed in a bleeze;°   *blaze*
Thro' ilka° bore° the beams were glancing;   *every / chink*
And loud resounded mirth and dancing.
105   Inspiring bold John Barleycorn!
What dangers thou canst make us scorn!

Wi' tippenny,° we fear nae evil;   *twopenny ale*
Wi' usquebae° we'll face the devil!   *whisky*
The swats° sae reamed° in Tammie's noddle,   *ale / foamed*
110 Fair play, he cared na deils a boddle.°   *farthing*
But Maggie stood right sair° astonished,   *sorely*
Till, by the heel and hand admonished,
She ventured forward on the light;
And, vow! Tam saw an unco sight!
115 Warlocks and witches in a dance;
Nae cotillon° brent° new frae France,   *dance / brand*
But hornpipes, jigs, strathspeys,° and reels,   *Highland dances*
Put life and mettle in their heels.
A winnock-bunker° in the east,   *window-seat*
120 There sat auld Nick, in shape o' beast;
A touzie° tyke,° black, grim, and large!   *tousled / dog*
To gie them music was his charge:
He screwed the pipes and gart° them skirl,°   *made / shrill*
Till roof and rafters a' did dirl.°   *ring*
125 Coffins stood round like open presses,°   *closets*
That shawed the dead in their last dresses;
And by some devilish cantraip° slight°   *weird / trick*
Each in its cauld hand held a light,
By which heroic Tam was able
130 To note upon the haly table
A murderer's banes in gibbet-airns;°   *-irons*
Twa span-lang, wee, unchristened bairns;°   *children*
A thief new-cutted frae a rape,
Wi' his last gasp his gab° did gape;   *mouth*
135 Five tomahawks, wi' blude red-rusted;
Five scymitars, wi' murder crusted;
A garter, which a babe had strangled;
A knife, a father's throat had mangled,
Whom his ain son o' life bereft,
140 The gray hairs yet stack to the heft;
Wi' mair of horrible and awfu',
Which even to name wad be unlawfu'.
    As Tammie glowred,° amazed, and curious,   *stared*
The mirth and fun grew fast and furious:
145 The piper loud and louder blew;
The dancers quick and quicker flew;
They reeled, they set, they crossed, they cleekit,°   *joined hands*
Till ilka carlin° swat° and reekit,°   *witch / sweated / steamed*
And coost° her duddies° to the wark,   *cast off / dress*
150 And linkit° at it in her sark!°   *tripped nimbly / shift*
    Now Tam, O Tam! had thae been queans,°   *girls*
A' plump and strapping in their teens;
Their sarks, instead o' creeshie° flannen,°   *greasy / flannel*
Been snaw-white seventeen hunder linen![1]
155 Thir° breeks o' mine, my only pair,   *these*
That ance were plush, o' gude blue hair,
I wad hae gi'en them off my hurdies,°   *buttocks*

---

1. Fine linen, with seventeen hundred threads to a width.

For ae blink o' the bonie burdies!°   *maidens*
    But wither'd beldams,° auld and droll,   *old women*
160 Rigwoodie° hags wad spean° a foal,   *scrawny / wean*
    Louping° and flinging on a crummock,°   *leaping / staff*
    I wonder didna turn thy stomach.
        But Tam kend what was what fu' brawlie,°   *well*
    There was ae winsome wench and wawlie°   *buxom*
165 That night enlisted in the core,°   *company*
    Lang after kent° on Carrick shore   *known*
    (For mony a beast to dead she shot,
    And perished mony a bonie boat,
    And shook baith meikle° corn and bear,°   *much / barley*
170 And kept the country-side in fear).
    Her cutty° sark, o' Paisley harn,°   *short / coarse cloth*
    That while a lassie she had worn,
    In longitude tho' sorely scanty,
    It was her best, and she was vauntie.
175 Ah! little kend thy reverend grannie
    That sark she coft° for her wee Nannie   *bought*
    Wi' twa pund Scots ('twas a' her riches)
    Wad ever graced a dance of witches!
        But here my Muse her wing maun cour;°   *stoop*
180 Sic flights are far beyond her pow'r—
    To sing how Nannie lap° and flang,   *leaped*
    (A souple jade she was, and strang),
    And how Tam stood, like ane bewitched,
    And thought his very een enriched;
185 Even Satan glow'd, and fidged° fu' fain,°   *wriggled / happy*
    And hotched° and blew wi' might and main: *hitched (himself)*
    Till first ae caper, syne° anither,   *then*
    Tam tint° his reason a' thegither,   *lost*
    And roars out, "Weel done, Cutty-sark!"
190 And in an instant all was dark!
    And scarcely had he Maggie rallied,
    When out the hellish, legion sallied.
        As bees bizz out wi' angry fyke,°   *fuss*
    When plundering herds° assail their byke;°   *shepherds / hive*
195 As open° pussie's° mortal foes,   *bay / the hare's*
    When pop! she starts before their nose;
    As eager runs the market-crowd,
    When "Catch the thief!" resounds aloud;
    So Maggie runs; the witches follow,
200 Wi' mony an eldritch° skriech and hollow.   *unearthly*
        Ah, Tam! ah, Tam! thou'll get thy fairin!°   *punishment*
    In hell they'll roast thee like a herrin!
    In vain thy Kate awaits thy comin!
    Kate soon will be a woefu' woman!
205 Now do thy speedy utmost, Meg,
    And win the key-stane° o' the brig;°   *central stone / bridge*
    There at them thou thy tail may toss,
    A running stream they darena cross.
    But ere the key-stane she could make,
210 The fient a° tail she had to shake!   *devil-a*

For Nannie, far before the rest,
Hard upon noble Maggie prest,
And flew at Tam wi' furious ettle;°   purpose
But little wist she Maggie's mettle.
215 Ae spring brought off her master hale,°   whole
But left behind her ain gray tail:
The carlin° claught her by the rump,   old woman
And left poor Maggie scarce a stump.
    Now, wha this tale o' truth shall read,
220 Each man and mother's son, take heed:
Whene'er to drink you are inclined,
Or cutty-sarks rin in your mind,
Think! ye may buy the joys o'er dear;
Remember Tam o' Shanter's mare.

1790   1791

Bonie Doon

Ye flowery banks o' bonie Doon,
    How can ye blume sae fair?
How can ye chant, ye little birds,
    And I sae fu' o' care?

5 Thou'll break my heart, thou bonie bird,
    That sings upon the bough;
Thou minds me o' the happy days,
    When my fause° luve was true.   false

Thou'll break my heart, thou bonie bird,
10   That sings beside thy mate;
For sae I sat, and sae I sang,
    And wist° na o' my fate.   knew

Aft hae I roved by bonie Doon
    To see the wood-bine twine,
15 And ilka° bird sang o' its luve,   every
    And sae did I o' mine.

Wi' lightsome heart I pu'd a rose
    Frae aff its thorny tree;
And my fause luver staw° my rose   stole
20   But left the thorn wi' me.

1791   1792

A Red, Red Rose

O my luve's like a red, red rose,
    That's newly sprung in June;
O my luve's like the melodie
    That's sweetly played in tune.

5 As fair art thou, my bonnie lass,
    So deep in luve am I;

And I will luve thee still, my dear,
    Till a' the seas gang dry.

     Till a' the seas gang dry, my dear,
10   And the rocks melt wi' the sun:
O I will love thee still, my dear,
    While the sands o' life shall run.

And fare thee weel, my only luve,
    And fare thee weel awhile!
15   And I will come again, my luve,
    Though it were ten thousand mile.

                          1796

O, Wert Thou in the Cauld Blast

O, wert thou in the cauld blast
    On yonder lea, on yonder lea,
My plaidie to the angry airt,°   *quarter (of the wind)*
    I'd shelter thee, I'd shelter thee.
5   Or did misfortune's bitter storms
    Around thee blaw, around thee blaw,
Thy bield° should be my bosom,   *shelter*
    To share it a', to share it a'.

Or were I in the wildest waste,
10   Sae black and bare, sae black and bare,
The desert were a paradise,
    If thou wert there, if thou wert there.
Or were I monarch o' the globe,
    Wi' thee to reign, wi' thee to reign,
15   The brightest jewel in my crown
    Wad be my queen, wad be my queen.

1796   1800

HELEN MARIA WILLIAMS

1761–1827

To the Moon

The glittering colors of the day are fled—
    Come, melancholy orb! that dwell'st with night,
Come, and o'er earth thy wandering luster shed,
    Thy deepest shadow, and thy softest light.
5   To me congenial is the gloomy grove,
    When with faint rays the sloping uplands shine;
That gloom, those pensive rays,[1] alike I love,

---

1. Compare this phrase and the entire poem to Milton's "Il Penseroso" (pp. 369–73), especially the address to the "pensive nun" and the description of the moon (lines 31 ff. and 67 ff. respectively).

Whose sadness seems in sympathy with mine.
But most for this, pale orb! thy light is dear,
10   For this, benignant orb! I hail thee most,
That while I pour the unavailing tear,
    And mourn that hope to me in youth is lost—
Thy light can visionary thoughts impart,
And lead the Muse to soothe a suffering heart.

To the Torrid Zone[2]

Pathway of light! o'er thy empurpled zone,
With lavish charms perennial summer strays;
Soft 'midst thy spicy groves the zephyr° plays,   *west wind*
While far around the rich perfumes are thrown:
5   The amadavid-bird[3] for thee alone,
Spreads his gay plumes that catch thy vivid rays;
For thee the gems with liquid luster blaze,
And nature's various wealth is all thy own.
But, ah! not thine is twilight's doubtful gloom,
10   Those mild gradations, mingling day with night;
Here, instant darkness shrouds thy genial bloom,
Nor leaves my pensive soul that ling'ring light,
When musing mem'ry would each trace resume
Of fading pleasures in successive flight.

1801

JOANNA BAILLIE
1762–1851

A Mother to her Waking Infant

Now in thy dazzling° half-oped eye,   *dazed*
Thy curlèd nose and lip awry,
Thy up-hoist arms and noddling° head,   *nodding*
And little chin with crystal spread,
5   Poor helpless thing! what do I see,
    That I should sing of thee?

From thy poor tongue no accents come,
Which can but rub thy toothless gum;
Small understanding boasts thy face,
10   Thy shapeless limbs nor step nor grace;
A few short words thy feats may tell,
    And yet I love thee well.

When sudden wakes the bitter shriek,
And redder swells thy little cheek;

2. This sonnet is number six in a series entitled "Sonnets from Paul and Virginia." The title alludes to the French writer Bernardin de Saint-Pierre's (1737–1814) sentimental novel *Paul et* *Virginie* (1783), much read by the Romantics.
3. A brown songbird with white spots found in India and called "amadavat" or "avadavat" in various Indian languages.

15   When rattled keys thy woes beguile,
    And through the wet eye gleams the smile,
    Still for thy weakly self is spent
      Thy little silly plaint.

    But when thy friends are in distress,
20   Thou'lt laugh and chuckle ne'er the less;
    Nor e'en with sympathy be smitten,
    Though all are sad but thee and kitten;
    Yet little varlet° that thou art,   *rascal*
      Thou twitchest at the heart.

25   Thy rosy cheek so soft and warm;
    Thy pinky hand and dimpled arm;
    Thy silken locks that scantly peep,
    With gold-tipped ends, where circles deep
    Around thy neck in harmless grace
30   So soft and sleekly hold their place,
    Might harder hearts with kindness fill,
      And gain our right good will.

    Each passing clown bestows his blessing,
    Thy mouth is worn with old wives' kissing:
35   E'en lighter looks the gloomy eye
    Of surly sense, when thou art by;
    And yet I think whoe'er they be,
      They love thee not like me.

    Perhaps when time shall add a few
40   Short years to thee, thou'lt love me too.
    Then wilt thou through life's weary way
    Become my sure and cheering stay:
    Wilt care for me, and be my hold,
      When I am weak and old.

45   Thou'lt listen to my lengthened tale,
    And pity me when I am frail—
    But see, the sweepy spinning fly
    Upon the window takes thine eye.
    Go to thy little senseless play—
50   Thou dost not heed my lay.°   *song*
                            1790

Up! quit thy bower[1]

Up! quit thy bower, late wears the hour;
Long have the rooks caw'd round thy tower;
On flower and tree, loud hums the bee;
The wilding kid[2] sports merrily:
5   A day so bright, so fresh, so clear,
    Shineth when good fortune's near.

1. The opening song from Act 1 of Baillie's *The*   (1812).
Beacon: A Serious Musical Drama in Two Acts   2. Wild young goat.

Up! lady fair, and braid thy hair,
And rouse thee in the breezy air;
The lulling stream, that sooth'd thy dream,
10   Is dancing in the sunny beam:
And hours so sweet, so bright, so gay,
Will waft good fortune on its way.

Up! time will tell; the friar's bell
Its service sound hath chimed well;
15   The aged crone keeps house alone,
And reapers to the fields are gone:
The active day, so boon and bright,
May bring good fortune ere the night.

1812

Song: Woo'd and married and a'

The bride she is winsome and bonny,
    Her hair it is snooded° sae sleek,   *bound up with a ribbon*
And faithfu' and kind is her Johnny,
    Yet fast fa' the tears on her cheek.
5   New pearlins° are cause of her sorrow,   *lace trimmings*
    New pearlins and plenishing° too,   *furnishings*
The bride that has a' to borrow,
    Has e'en right mickle ado,
        Woo'd and married and a'!
10   Woo'd and married and a'!
    Is na' she very weel aff
        To be woo'd and married at a'?

Her mither then hastily spak,
    "The lassie is glaikit° wi' pride;   *foolish*
15   In my pouch I had never a plack°   *farthing*
    On the day when I was a bride.
E'en tak' to your wheel, and be clever,
    And draw out your thread in the sun;
The gear° that is gifted,° it never   *goods, wealth / given*
20   Will last like the gear that is won.°   *earned*
        Woo'd and married and a'!
        Wi' havins° and toucher° sae sma',   *possessions / dowry*
    I think ye are very weel aff,
        To be woo'd and married at a'!"

25   "Toot, toot!" quo' her gray-headed faither,
    "She's less o' a bride than a bairn;°   *child*
She's ta'en like a cout° frae the heather,   *colt*
    Wi' sense and discretion to learn.
Half husband, I trow, and half daddy,
30   As humor inconstantly leans,
The chiel° maun° be patient and steady,   *man / must*

That yokes wi' a mate in her teens.
  A kerchief sae douce° and sae neat,   *sedate, respectable*
  O'er her locks that the winds used to blaw!
35 I'm baith like to laugh and to greet,°   *weep*
  When I think o' her married at a'!"

Then out spak' the wily bridegroom;
  Weel waled° were his wordies, I ween—   *chosen*
  "I'm rich, though my coffer be toom,°   *empty*
40 Wi' the blinks o' your bonny blue een.°   *eyes*
I'm prouder o' thee by my side,
  Though thy ruffles or ribbons be few,
Than if Kate o' the Croft were my bride,
  Wi' purfles° and pearlins enow.   *embroidered trimmings*
45 Dear and dearest of ony!
  Ye're woo'd and buikit³ and a'!"
And do ye think scorn o' your Johnny,
  And grieve to be married at a'?"

She turn'd, and she blush'd, and she smiled,
50 And she looket sae bashfully down;
The pride o' her heart was beguiled,
  And she played wi' the sleeves o' her gown;
She twirled the tag o' her lace,
  And she nippet her boddice sae blue,
55 Syne° blinket sae sweet in his face,   *then*
  And aff like a maukin° she flew.   *hare*
  Woo'd and married and a'!
  Wi' Johnny to roose° her and a'!   *praise*
She thinks hersel very weel aff,
60 To be woo'd and married at a'!

               1822

WILLIAM WORDSWORTH
1770–1850

Lines

Composed a Few Miles Above Tintern Abbey on Revisiting the Banks of the Wye During a Tour. July 13, 1798[1]

Five years have passed; five summers, with the length
Of five long winters! and again I hear
These waters, rolling from their mountain-springs
With a soft inland murmur. Once again
5 Do I behold these steep and lofty cliffs,
That on a wild secluded scene impress
Thoughts of more deep seclusion; and connect

---

3. "Booked," i.e., officially registered as engaged
in the book of the session clerk.
1. Ruins of a medieval abbey situated in the valley
of the river Wye, in Monmouthshire, noted for its
scenery.

The landscape with the quiet of the sky.
The day is come when I again repose
10   Here, under this dark sycamore, and view
These plots of cottage ground, these orchard tufts,
Which at this season, with their unripe fruits,
Are clad in one green hue, and lose themselves
'Mid groves and copses. Once again I see
15   These hedgerows, hardly hedgerows, little lines
Of sportive wood run wild; these pastoral farms,
Green to the very door; and wreaths of smoke
Sent up, in silence, from among the trees!
With some uncertain notice, as might seem
20   Of vagrant dwellers in the houseless woods,
Or of some Hermit's cave, where by his fire
The Hermit sits alone.

                              These beauteous forms,
Through a long absence, have not been to me
As is a landscape to a blind man's eye;
25   But oft, in lonely rooms, and 'mid the din
Of towns and cities, I have owed to them,
In hours of weariness, sensations sweet,
Felt in the blood, and felt along the heart;
And passing even into my purer mind,
30   With tranquil restoration—feelings too
Of unremembered pleasure; such, perhaps,
As have no slight or trivial influence
On that best portion of a good man's life,
His little, nameless, unremembered, acts
35   Of kindness and of love. Nor less, I trust,
To them I may have owed another gift,
Of aspect more sublime; that blessed mood,
In which the burthen of the mystery,
In which the heavy and the weary weight
40   Of all this unintelligible world,
Is lightened—that serene and blessed mood,
In which the affections gently lead us on—
Until, the breath of this corporeal frame
And even the motion of our human blood
45   Almost suspended, we are laid asleep
In body, and become a living soul;
While with an eye made quiet by the power
Of harmony, and the deep power of joy,
We see into the life of things.

                                        If this
50   Be but a vain belief, yet, oh! how oft—
In darkness and amid the many shapes
Of joyless daylight; when the fretful stir
Unprofitable, and the fever of the world,
Have hung upon the beatings of my heart—
55   How oft, in spirit, have I turned to thee,

O sylvan Wye! thou wanderer through the woods,
How often has my spirit turned to thee!

And now, with gleams of half-extinguished thought,
With many recognitions dim and faint,
60 And somewhat of a sad perplexity,
The picture of the mind revives again;
While here I stand, not only with the sense
Of present pleasure, but with pleasing thoughts
That in this moment there is life and food
65 For future years. And so I dare to hope,
Though changed, no doubt, from what I was when first
I came among these hills; when like a roe
I bounded o'er the mountains, by the sides
Of the deep rivers, and the lonely streams,
70 Wherever nature led—more like a man
Flying from something that he dreads than one
Who sought the thing he loved. For nature then
(The coarser[2] pleasures of my boyish days,
And their glad animal movements all gone by)
75 To me was all in all.—I cannot paint
What then I was. The sounding cataract
Haunted me like a passion; the tall rock,
The mountain, and the deep and gloomy wood,
Their colors and their forms, were then to me
80 An appetite; a feeling and a love,
That had no need of a remoter charm,
By thought supplied, nor any interest
Unborrowed from the eye.—That time is past,
And all its aching joys are now no more,
85 And all its dizzy raptures. Not for this
Faint° I, nor mourn nor murmur; other gifts   *become discouraged*
Have followed; for such loss, I would believe,
Abundant recompense. For I have learned
To look on nature, not as in the hour
90 Of thoughtless youth; but hearing oftentimes
The still, sad music of humanity,
Nor harsh nor grating, though of ample power
To chasten and subdue. And I have felt
A presence that disturbs me with the joy
95 Of elevated thoughts; a sense sublime
Of something far more deeply interfused,
Whose dwelling is the light of setting suns,
And the round ocean and the living air,
And the blue sky, and in the mind of man:
100 A motion and a spirit, that impels
All thinking things, all objects of all thought,
And rolls through all things. Therefore am I still
A lover of the meadows and the woods,
And mountains; and of all that we behold
105 From this green earth; of all the mighty world

2. I.e., primarily physical.

Of eye, and ear—both what they half create,
And what perceive; well pleased to recognize
In nature and the language of the sense
The anchor of my purest thoughts, the nurse,
110 The guide, the guardian of my heart, and soul
Of all my moral being.

                          Nor perchance,
If I were not thus taught, should I the more
Suffer my genial spirits° to decay: *vital energies*
For thou art with me here upon the banks
115 Of this fair river; thou my dearest Friend,[3]
My dear, dear Friend; and in thy voice I catch
The language of my former heart, and read
My former pleasures in the shooting lights
Of thy wild eyes. Oh! yet a little while
120 May I behold in thee what I was once,
My dear, dear Sister! and this prayer I make,
Knowing that Nature never did betray
The heart that loved her; 'tis her privilege,
Through all the years of this our life, to lead
125 From joy to joy: for she can so inform
The mind that is within us, so impress
With quietness and beauty, and so feed
With lofty thoughts, that neither evil tongues,
Rash judgments, nor the sneers of selfish men,
130 Nor greetings where no kindness is, nor all
The dreary intercourse of daily life,
Shall e'er prevail against us, or disturb
Our cheerful faith, that all which we behold
Is full of blessings. Therefore let the moon
135 Shine on thee in thy solitary walk;
And let the misty mountain winds be free
To blow against thee: and, in after years,
When these wild ecstasies shall be matured
Into a sober pleasure; when thy mind
140 Shall be a mansion for all lovely forms,
Thy memory be as a dwelling place
For all sweet sounds and harmonies; oh! then,
If solitude, or fear, or pain, or grief
Should be thy portion, with what healing thoughts
145 Of tender joy wilt thou remember me,
And these my exhortations! Nor, perchance—
If I should be where I no more can hear
Thy voice, nor catch from thy wild eyes these gleams
Of past existence—wilt thou then forget
150 That on the banks of this delightful stream
We stood together; and that I, so long
A worshiper of Nature, hither came
Unwearied in that service; rather say
With warmer love—oh! with far deeper zeal
155 Of holier love. Nor wilt thou then forget,

3. Wordsworth's sister Dorothy, who accompanied him on the walking trip here commemorated.

That after many wanderings, many years
Of absence, these steep woods and lofty cliffs,
And this green pastoral landscape, were to me
More dear, both for themselves and for thy sake!

1798

The Ruined Cottage[4]

First Part

'Twas Summer and the sun was mounted high.
Along the south the uplands feebly glared
Through a pale steam, and all the northern downs,
In clearer air ascending, showed far off
5 Their surfaces with shadows dappled o'er
Of deep embattled clouds. Far as the sight
Could reach those many shadows lay in spots
Determined° and unmoved, with steady beams   *exactly fixed*
Of clear and pleasant sunshine interposed—
10 Pleasant to him who on the soft cool grass
Extends his careless limbs beside the root
Of some huge oak whose agèd branches make
A twilight of their own, a dewy shade
Where the wren warbles while the dreaming man,
15 Half conscious of that soothing melody,
With sidelong eye looks out upon the scene,
By those impending branches made more soft,
More soft and distant.

                Other lot was mine.
Across a bare wide Common I had toiled
20 With languid feet which by the slippery ground
Were baffled still, and when I stretched myself
On the brown earth my limbs from very heat
Could find no rest, nor my weak arm disperse
The insect host which gathered round my face
25 And joined their murmurs to the tedious noise
Of seeds of bursting gorse that crackled round.
I rose and turned towards a group of trees
Which midway in that level stood alone;
And thither come at length, beneath a shade
30 Of clustering elms that sprang from the same root
I found a ruined house, four naked walls
That stared upon each other. I looked round
And near the door I saw an agèd Man,
Alone and stretched upon the cottage bench,
35 An iron-pointed staff lay at his side.
With instantaneous joy I recognized
That pride of nature and of lowly life,
The venerable Armytage,° a friend   *hermitage*
As dear to me as is the setting sun.

4. A shorter version of a narrative that comprised the first book of *The Excursion* (1814). First published
by Jonathan Wordsworth in *The Music of Humanity* (1969).

                                        Two days before
40   We had been fellow travelers. I knew
     That he was in this neighborhood, and now
     Delighted found him here in the cool shade.
     He lay, his pack of rustic merchandise
     Pillowing his head. I guess he had no thought
45   Of his way-wandering life. His eyes were shut,
     The shadows of the breezy elms above
     Dappled his face. With thirsty heat oppressed
     At length I hailed him, glad to see his hat
     Bedewed with waterdrops, as if the brim
50   Had newly scooped a running stream. He rose
     And pointing to a sunflower, bade me climb
     The [   ] wall where that same gaudy flower
     Looked out upon the road.

                                     It was a plot
     Of garden ground now wild, its matted weeds
55   Marked with the steps of those whom as they passed,
     The gooseberry trees that shot in long lank slips,
     Or currants hanging from their leafless stems
     In scanty strings, had tempted to o'erleap
     The broken wall. Within that cheerless spot,
60   Where two tall hedgerows of thick alder boughs
     Joined in a damp cold nook, I found a well
     Half covered up with willow flowers and grass.
     I slaked my thirst and to the shady bench
     Returned, and while I stood unbonneted
65   To catch the motion of the cooler air,
     The old Man said, "I see around me here
     Things which you cannot see. We die, my Friend,
     Nor we alone, but that which each man loved
     And prized in his peculiar nook of earth
70   Dies with him, or is changed, and very soon
     Even of the good is no memorial left.
     The Poets, in their elegies and songs
     Lamenting the departed, call the groves,
     They call upon the hills and streams to mourn,
75   And senseless rocks—nor idly, for they speak
     In these their invocations with a voice
     Obedient to the strong creative power
     Of human passion. Sympathies there are
     More tranquil, yet perhaps of kindred birth,
80   That steal upon the meditative mind
     And grow with thought. Beside yon spring I stood,
     And eyed its waters till we seemed to feel
     One sadness, they and I. For them a bond
     Of brotherhood is broken; time has been
85   When every day the touch of human hand
     Disturbed their stillness, and they ministered
     To human comfort. When I stopped to drink
     A spider's web hung to the water's edge,
     And on the wet and slimy footstone lay

90   The useless fragment of a wooden bowl.
      It moved my very heart.

                    "The day has been
      When I could never pass this road but she
      Who lived within these walls, when I appeared,
      A daughter's welcome gave me, and I loved her
95   As my own child. Oh Sir, the good die first,
      And they whose hearts are dry as summer dust
      Burn to the socket. Many a passenger
      Has blessed poor Margaret for her gentle looks
      When she upheld the cool refreshment drawn
100   From that forsaken spring, and no one came
      But he was welcome, no one went away
      But that it seemed she loved him. She is dead,
      The worm is on her cheek, and this poor hut,
      Stripped of its outward garb of household flowers,
105   Of rose and sweetbriar, offers to the wind
      A cold bare wall whose earthy top is tricked
      With weeds and the rank spear grass. She is dead,
      And nettles rot and adders sun themselves
      Where we have sate together while she nursed
110   Her infant at her breast. The unshod colt,
      The wandring heifer and the Potter's ass,
      Find shelter now within the chimney wall
      Where I have seen her evening hearthstone blaze
      And through the window spread upon the road
115   Its cheerful light. You will forgive me, sir,
      But often on this cottage do I muse
      As on a picture, till my wiser mind
      Sinks, yielding to the foolishness of grief.

      "She had a husband, an industrious man,
120   Sober and steady. I have heard her say
      That he was up and busy at his loom
      In summer ere the mower's scythe had swept
      The dewy grass, and in the early spring
      Ere the last star had vanished. They who passed
125   At evening, from behind the garden fence
      Might hear his busy spade, which he would ply
      After his daily work till the daylight
      Was gone, and every leaf and flower were lost
      In the dark hedges. So they passed their days
130   In peace and comfort, and two pretty babes
      Were their best hope next to the God in Heaven.

      "You may remember, now some ten years gone,
      Two blighting seasons when the fields were left
      With half a harvest. It pleased heaven to add
135   A worse affliction in the plague of war,
      A happy land was stricken to the heart,
      'Twas a sad time of sorrow and distress.
      A wanderer among the cottages,

I with my pack of winter raiment saw
140 The hardships of that season. Many rich
Sunk down as in a dream among the poor,
And of the poor did many cease to be,
And their place knew them not. Meanwhile, abridged
Of daily comforts, gladly reconciled
145 To numerous self-denials, Margaret
Went struggling on through those calamitous years
With cheerful hope. But ere the second autumn
A fever seized her husband. In disease
He lingered long, and when his strength returned
150 He found the little he had stored to meet
The hour of accident, or crippling age,
Was all consumed. As I have said, 'twas now
A time of trouble: shoals of artisans
Were from their daily labor turned away
155 To hang for bread on parish charity,
They and their wives and children, happier far
Could they have lived as do the little birds
That peck along the hedges, or the kite
That makes her dwelling in the mountain rocks.

160 "Ill fared it now with Robert, he who dwelt
In this poor cottage. At his door he stood
And whistled many a snatch of merry tunes
That had no mirth in them, or with his knife
Carved uncouth figures on the heads of sticks.
165 Then idly sought about through every nook
Of house or garden any casual task
Of use or ornament, and with a strange
Amusing but uneasy novelty
He blended where he might the various tasks
170 Of summer, autumn, winter, and of spring.
But this endured not, his good humor soon
Became a weight in which no pleasure was,
And poverty brought on a petted° mood   *irritable*
And a sore temper. Day by day he drooped.
175 And he would leave his home, and to the town
Without an errand would he turn his steps,
Or wander here and there among the fields.
One while he would speak lightly of his babes
And with a cruel tongue, at other times
180 He played with them wild freaks of merriment.
And 'twas a piteous thing to see the looks
Of the poor innocent children. 'Every smile,'
Said Margaret to me here beneath these trees,
'Made my heart bleed.' "

                              At this the old Man paused
185 And looking up to those enormous elms
He said, " 'Tis now the hour of deepest noon.
At this still season of repose and peace,
This hour when all things which are not at rest

Are cheerful, while this multitude of flies
190 Fills all the air with happy melody,
Why should a tear be in an old man's eye?
Why should we thus with an untoward mind,
And in the weakness of humanity,
From natural wisdom turn our hearts away.
195 To natural comfort shut our eyes and ears.
And, feeding on disquiet, thus disturb
The calm of Nature with our restless thoughts?"

END OF THE FIRST PART

Second Part

He spake with somewhat of a solemn tone,
But when he ended there was in his face
200 Such easy cheerfulness, a look so mild,
That for a little time it stole away
All recollection, and that simple tale
Passed from my mind like a forgotten sound.
A while on trivial things we held discourse
205 To me soon tasteless. In my own despite
I thought of that poor woman as of one
Whom I had known and loved. He had rehearsed
Her homely tale with such familiar power,
With such an active countenance, an eye
210 So busy, that the things of which he spake
Seemed present, and, attention now relaxed,
There was a heartfelt chillness in my veins.
I rose, and turning from that breezy shade
Went out into the open air, and stood
215 To drink the comfort of the warmer sun.
Long time I had not stayed ere, looking round
Upon that tranquil ruin, I returned
And begged of the old man that for my sake
He would resume his story.

                              He replied,
220 "It were a wantonness, and would demand
Severe reproof, if we were men whose hearts
Could hold vain dalliance with the misery
Even of the dead, contented thence to draw
A momentary pleasure, never marked
225 By reason, barren of all future good.
But we have known that there is often found
In mournful thoughts, and always might be found,
A power to virtue friendly; were't not so
I am a dreamer among men, indeed
230 An idle dreamer. 'Tis a common tale
By moving accidents[5] uncharactered,
A tale of silent suffering, hardly clothed

5. High adventures; the phrase is Shakespeare's: *Othello* 1.3.135.

In bodily form, and to the grosser sense
But ill adapted, scarcely palpable
235 To him who does not think. But at your bidding
I will proceed.

                    "While thus it fared with them
To whom this cottage till that hapless year
Had been a blessed home, it was my chance
To travel in a country far remote;
240 And glad I was when, halting by yon gate
That leads from the green lane, again I saw
These lofty elm trees. Long I did not rest:
With many pleasant thoughts I cheered my way
O'er the flat common. At the door arrived,
245 I knocked, and when I entered, with the hope
Of usual greeting, Margaret looked at me
A little while, then turned her head away
Speechless, and sitting down upon a chair
Wept bitterly. I wist not what to do,
250 Or how to speak to her. Poor wretch, at last
She rose from off her seat, and then, oh Sir,
I cannot tell how she pronounced my name.
With fervent love, and with a face of grief
Unutterably helpless, and a look
255 That seemed to cling upon me, she enquired
If I had seen her husband. As she spake
A strange surprise and fear came to my heart,
Nor had I power to answer ere she told
That he had disappeared—just two months gone.
260 He left his house: two wretched days had passed,
And on the third by the first break of light,
Within her casement full in view she saw
A purse of gold.[6] 'I trembled at the sight,'
Said Margaret, 'for I knew it was his hand
265 That placed it there. And on that very day
By one, a stranger, from my husband sent,
The tidings came that he had joined a troop
Of soldiers going to a distant land.
He left me thus. Poor Man, he had not heart
270 To take farewell of me, and he feared
That I should follow with my babes, and sink
Beneath the misery of a soldier's life.'

"This tale did Margaret tell with many tears,
And when she ended I had little power
275 To give her comfort, and was glad to take
Such words of hope from her own mouth as served
To cheer us both. But long we had not talked
Ere we built up a pile of better thoughts,
And with a brighter eye she looked around,
280 As if she had been shedding tears of joy.

6. The payment her husband had received for enlisting.

We parted. It was then the early spring:
I left her busy with her garden tools,
And well remember, o'er that fence she looked,
And, while I paced along the footway path,
285 Called out and sent a blessing after me,
With tender cheerfulness, and with a voice
That seemed the very sound of happy thoughts.

"I roved o'er many a hill and many a dale
With this my weary load, in heat and cold,
290 Through many a wood and many an open ground,
In sunshine or in shade, in wet or fair,
Now blithe, now drooping, as it might befall;
My best companions now the driving winds
And now the 'trotting brooks'[7] and whispering trees,
295 And now the music of my own sad steps,
With many a short-lived thought that passed between
And disappeared.

             "I came this way again
Towards the wane of summer, when the wheat
Was yellow, and the soft and bladed grass
300 Sprang up afresh and o'er the hay field spread
Its tender green. When I had reached the door
I found that she was absent. In the shade,
Where we now sit, I waited her return.
Her cottage in its outward look appeared
305 As cheerful as before, in any show
Of neatness little changed, but that I thought
The honeysuckle crowded round the door,
And from the wall hung down in heavier tufts,
And knots of worthless stonecrop started out
310 Along the window's edge, and grew like weeds
Against the lower panes. I turned aside
And strolled into her garden. It was changed.
The unprofitable bindweed spread his bells
From side to side, and with unwieldy wreaths
315 Had dragged the rose from its sustaining wall
And bent it down to earth. The border tufts,
Daisy, and thrift, and lowly camomile,
And thyme, had straggled out into the paths
Which they were used to deck.

                  "Ere this an hour
320 Was wasted. Back I turned my restless steps,
And as I walked before the door it chanced
A stranger passed, and guessing whom I sought,
He said that she was used to ramble far.
The sun was sinking in the west, and now
325 I sate with sad impatience. From within
Her solitary infant cried aloud.

---

7. "Trotting brooks": slightly misquoted ("trotting burns") from Robert Burns' "Epistle to William Simpson," a poem in praise of natural feelings.

The spot though fair seemed very desolate,
The longer I remained more desolate;
And looking round I saw the cornerstones,
330   Till then unmarked, on either side the door
With dull red stains discolored, and stuck o'er
With tufts and hairs of wool, as if the sheep
That feed upon the commons thither came
Familiarly, and found a couching place
Even at her threshold.

335   "The house clock struck eight:
I turned and saw her distant a few steps.
Her face was pale and thin, her figure too
Was changed. As she unlocked the door she said,
'It grieves me you have waited here so long,
340   But in good truth I've wandered much of late,
And sometimes, to my shame I speak, have need
Of my best prayers to bring me back again.'
While on the board she spread our evening meal,
She told me she had lost her elder child,
345   That he for months had been a serving boy,
Apprenticed by the parish. 'I perceive
You look at me, and you have cause. Today
I have been travelling far, and many days
About the fields I wander, knowing this
350   Only, that what I seek I cannot find.
And so I waste my time: for I am changed,
And to myself,' she said, 'have done much wrong,
And to this helpless infant. I have slept
Weeping, and weeping I have waked. My tears
355   Have flowed as if my body were not such
As others are, and I could never die.
But I am now in mind and in my heart
More easy, and I hope,' she said, 'that heaven
Will give me patience to endure the things
Which I behold at home.'

360   "It would have grieved
Your very soul to see her. Sir, I feel
The story linger in my heart. I fear
'Tis long and tedious, but my spirit clings
To that poor woman. So familiarly
365   Do I perceive her manner and her look
And presence, and so deeply do I feel
Her goodness, that not seldom in my walks
A momentary trance comes over me,
And to myself I seem to muse on one
370   By sorrow laid asleep or borne away,
A human being destined to awake
To human life, or something very near
To human life, when he shall come again
For whom she suffered. Sir, it would have grieved

375 Your very soul to see her: evermore
     Her eyelids drooped, her eyes were downward cast,
     And when she at her table gave me food
     She did not look at me. Her voice was low,
     Her body was subdued. In every act
380 Pertaining to her house affairs appeared
     The careless stillness which a thinking mind
     Gives to an idle matter. Still she sighed,
     But yet no motion of the breast was seen,
     No heaving of the heart. While by the fire
385 We sate together, sighs came on my ear,
     I knew not how, and hardly whence they came.
     I took my staff, and when I kissed her babe
     The tears stood in her eyes. I left her then
     With the best hope and comfort I could give:
390 She thanked me for my will, but for my hope
     It seemed she did not thank me.

                              "I returned
     And took my rounds along this road again
     Ere on its sunny bank the primrose flower
     Had chronicled the earliest day of spring.
395 I found her sad and drooping. She had learned
     No tidings of her husband; if he lived,
     She knew not that he lived; if he were dead,
     She knew not he was dead. She seemed the same
     In person or appearance, but her house
400 Bespoke a sleepy hand of negligence.
     The floor was neither dry nor neat, the hearth
     Was comfortless,
     The windows too were dim, and her few books,
     Which one upon the other heretofore
405 Had been piled up against the corner panes
     In seemly order, now with straggling leaves
     Lay scattered here and there, open or shut,
     As they had chanced to fall. Her infant babe
     Had from its mother caught the trick of grief,
410 And sighed among its playthings. Once again
     I turned towards the garden gate, and saw
     More plainly still that poverty and grief
     Were now come nearer to her. The earth was hard,
     With weeds defaced and knots of withered grass;
415 No ridges there appeared of clear black mold,
     No winter greenness. Of her herbs and flowers
     It seemed the better part were gnawed away
     Or trampled on the earth. A chain of straw,
     Which had been twisted round the tender stem
420 Of a young apple tree, lay at its root;
     The bark was nibbled round by truant sheep.
     Margaret stood near, her infant in her arms,
     And, seeing that my eye was on the tree,
     She said, 'I fear it will be dead and gone
     Ere Robert come again.'

425   "Towards the house
Together we returned, and she enquired
If I had any hope. But for her Babe,
And for her little friendless Boy, she said,
She had no wish to live—that she must die

430 Of sorrow. Yet I saw the idle loom
Still in its place. His Sunday garments hung
Upon the selfsame nail, his very staff
Stood undisturbed behind the door. And when
I passed this way beaten by Autumn winds,

435 She told me that her little babe was dead,
And she was left alone. That very time,
I yet remember, through the miry lane
She walked with me a mile, when the bare trees
Trickled with foggy damps, and in such sort

440 That any heart had ached to hear her, begged
That wheresoe'r I went I still would ask
For him whom she had lost. We parted then,
Our final parting; for from that time forth
Did many seasons pass ere I returned
Into this tract again.

445   "Five tedious years
She lingered in unquiet widowhood,
A wife and widow. Needs must it have been
A sore heart-wasting. I have heard, my friend,
That in that broken arbor she would sit

450 The idle length of half a sabbath day;
There, where you see the toadstool's lazy head;
And when a dog passed by she still would quit
The shade and look abroad. On this old Bench
For hours she sate, and evermore her eye

455 Was busy in the distance, shaping things
Which made her heart beat quick. Seest thou that path?
The green sward now has broken its gray line—
There to and fro she paced through many a day
Of the warm summer, from a belt of flax

460 That girt her waist, spinning the long-drawn thread
With backward steps. Yet ever as there passed
A man whose garments showed the Soldier's red,
Or crippled Mendicant in Sailor's garb,
The little child who sate to turn the wheel

465 Ceased from his toil, and she, with faltering voice,
Expecting still to hear her husband's fate,
Made many a fond enquiry; and when they
Whose presence gave no comfort, were gone by,
Her heart was still more sad. And by yon gate,

470 Which bars the traveler's road, she often stood,
And when a stranger horseman came, the latch
Would lift, and in his face look wistfully,
Most happy if from aught discovered there
Of tender feeling she might dare repeat
The same sad question.

475   "Meanwhile her poor hut
Sunk to decay; for he was gone, whose hand
At the first nippings of October frost
Closed up each chink, and with fresh bands of straw
Chequered the green-grown thatch. And so she lived
480 Through the long winter, reckless° and alone,   *not caring for herself*
Till this reft° house, by frost, and thaw, and rain,   *emptied*
Was sapped; and when she slept, the nightly damps
Did chill her breast, and in the stormy day
Her tattered clothes were ruffled by the wind
485 Even at the side of her own fire. Yet still
She loved this wretched spot, nor would for worlds
Have parted hence; and still that length of road,
And this rude bench, one torturing hope endeared,
Fast rooted at her heart. And here, my friend,
490 In sickness she remained; and here she died,
Last human tenant of these ruined walls."

The old Man ceased: he saw that I was moved.
From that low bench rising instinctively,
I turned aside in weakness, nor had power
495 To thank him for the tale which he had told.
I stood, and leaning o'er the garden gate
Reviewed that Woman's sufferings; and it seemed
To comfort me while with a brother's love
I blessed her in the impotence of grief.
500 At length towards the cottage I returned
Fondly, and traced with milder interest,
That secret spirit of humanity
Which, 'mid the calm oblivious tendencies
Of nature, 'mid her plants, her weeds and flowers,
505 And silent overgrowings, still survived.
The old man seeing this resumed, and said,
"My friend, enough to sorrow have you given,
The purposes of Wisdom ask no more:
Be wise and cheerful, and no longer read
510 The forms of things with an unworthy eye.
She sleeps in the calm earth, and peace is here.
I well remember that those very plumes,
Those weeds, and the high spear grass on that wall,
By mist and silent raindrops silvered o'er,
515 As once I passed, did to my mind convey
So still an image of tranquility,
So calm and still, and looked so beautiful
Amid the uneasy thoughts which filled my mind,
That what we feel of sorrow and despair
520 From ruin and from change, and all the grief
The passing shows of being leave behind,
Appeared an idle dream that could not live
Where meditation was. I turned away,
And walked along my road in happiness."

525   He ceased. By this the sun declining shot
A slant and mellow radiance, which began

To fall upon us where beneath the trees
We sate on that low bench. And now we felt,
Admonished thus, the sweet hour coming on:
530 A linnet warbled from those lofty elms,
A thrush sang loud, and other melodies
At distance heard, peopled the milder air.
The old man rose and hoisted up his load.
Together casting then a farewell look
535 Upon those silent walls, we left the shade;
And, ere the stars were visible, attained
A rustic inn, our evening resting place.

THE END

1797–99   1968

From The Prelude

From *Book I*

Fair seedtime had my soul, and I grew up
Fostered alike by beauty and by fear:
Much favored in my birthplace,[8] and no less
In that belovèd Vale[9] to which erelong
305 We were transplanted—there were we let loose
For sports of wider range. Ere I had told
Ten birthdays, when among the mountain slopes
Frost, and the breath of frosty wind, had snapped
The last autumnal crocus, 'twas my joy
310 With store of springes° o'er my shoulder hung   snares
To range the open heights where woodcocks run
Along the smooth green turf. Through half the night,
Scudding away from snare to snare, I plied
That anxious visitation—moon and stars
315 Were shining o'er my head. I was alone,
And seemed to be a trouble to the peace
That dwelt among them. Sometimes it befell
In these night wanderings, that a strong desire
O'erpowered my better reason, and the bird
320 Which was the captive of another's toil
Became my prey; and when the deed was done
I heard among the solitary hills
Low breathings coming after me, and sounds
Of undistinguishable motion, steps
325 Almost as silent as the turf they trod.

Nor less, when spring had warmed the cultured° Vale,   *cultivated*
Moved we as plunderers where the mother bird
Had in high places built her lodge; though mean
Our object and inglorious, yet the end
330 Was not ignoble. Oh! when I have hung
Above the raven's nest, by knots of grass

8. Cockermouth, in the northern part of the Eng-   9. Esthwaite, also in the Lakes.
lish Lake District.

And half-inch fissures in the slippery rock
But ill sustained, and almost (so it seemed)
Suspended by the blast that blew amain,
335   Shouldering the naked crag, oh, at that time
While on the perilous ridge I hung alone,
With what strange utterance did the loud dry wind
Blow through my ear! the sky seemed not a sky
Of earth—and with what motion moved the clouds!

340   Dust as we are, the immortal spirit grows
Like harmony in music; there is a dark
Inscrutable workmanship that reconciles
Discordant elements, makes them cling together
In one society. How strange that all
345   The terrors, pains, and early miseries,
Regrets, vexations, lassitudes interfused
Within my mind, should e'er have borne a part,
And that a needful part, in making up
The calm existence that is mine when I
350   Am worthy of myself! Praise to the end!
Thanks to the means which Nature deigned to employ;
Whether her fearless visitings, or those
That came with soft alarm, like hurtless light
Opening the peaceful clouds; or she may use
355   Severer interventions, ministry
More palpable, as best might suit her aim.

     One summer evening (led by her) I found
A little boat tied to a willow tree
Within a rocky cave, its usual home.
360   Straight I unloosed her chain, and stepping in
Pushed from the shore. It was an act of stealth
And troubled pleasure, nor without the voice
Of mountain echoes did my boat move on;
Leaving behind her still, on either side,
365   Small circles glittering idly in the moon,
Until they melted all into one track
Of sparkling light. But now, like one who rows,
Proud of his skill, to reach a chosen point
With an unswerving line, I fixed my view
370   Upon the summit of a craggy ridge,
The horizon's utmost boundary; for above
Was nothing but the stars and the gray sky.
She was an elfin pinnace; lustily
I dipped my oars into the silent lake,
375   And, as I rose upon the stroke, my boat
Went heaving through the water like a swan;
When, from behind that craggy steep till then
The horizon's bound, a huge peak, black and huge,
As if with voluntary power instinct,
380   Upreared its head. I struck and struck again,
And growing still in stature the grim shape
Towered up between me and the stars, and still,

For so it seemed, with purpose of its own
And measured motion like a living thing,
385 Strode after me. With trembling oars I turned,
And through the silent water stole my way
Back to the covert of the willow tree;
There in her mooring place I left my bark,
And through the meadows homeward went, in grave
390 And serious mood; but after I had seen
That spectacle, for many days, my brain
Worked with a dim and undetermined sense
Of unknown modes of being; o'er my thoughts
There hung a darkness, call it solitude
395 Or blank desertion. No familiar shapes
Remained, no pleasant images of trees,
Of sea or sky, no colors of green fields;
But huge and mighty forms, that do not live
Like living men, moved slowly through the mind
400 By day, and were a trouble to my dreams.

    Wisdom and Spirit of the universe!
Thou Soul that art the eternity of thought,
That givest to forms and images a breath
And everlasting motion, not in vain
405 By day or starlight thus from my first dawn
Of childhood didst thou intertwine for me
The passions that build up our human soul;
Not with the mean and vulgar works of man,
But with high objects, with enduring things—
410 With life and nature—purifying thus
The elements of feeling and of thought,
And sanctifying, by such discipline,
Both pain and fear, until we recognize
A grandeur in the beating of the heart.
415 Nor was this fellowship vouchsafed to me
With stinted kindness. In November days,
When vapors rolling down the valley made
A lonely scene more lonesome, among woods,
At noon and 'mid the calm of summer nights,
420 When, by the margin of the trembling lake,
Beneath the gloomy hills homeward I went
In solitude, such intercourse was mine;
Mine was it in the fields both day and night,
And by the waters, all the summer long.

425   And in the frosty season, when the sun
Was set, and visible for many a mile
The cottage windows blazed through twilight gloom,
I heeded not their summons: happy time
It was indeed for all of us—for me
430 It was a time of rapture! Clear and loud
The village clock tolled six—I wheeled about,
Proud and exulting like an untired horse
That cares not for his home. All shod with steel,

We hissed along the polished ice in games
435 Confederate, imitative of the chase
And woodland pleasures—the resounding horn,
The pack loud chiming, and the hunted hare.
So through the darkness and the cold we flew,
And not a voice was idle; with the din
440 Smitten, the precipices rang aloud;
The leafless trees and every icy crag
Tinkled like iron; while far distant hills
Into the tumult sent an alien sound
Of melancholy not unnoticed, while the stars
445 Eastward were sparkling clear, and in the west
The orange sky of evening died away.
Not seldom from the uproar I retired
Into a silent bay, or sportively
Glanced sideway, leaving the tumultuous throng,
450 To cut across the reflex° of a star   *reflection*
That fled, and, flying still before me, gleamed
Upon the glassy plain; and oftentimes,
When we had given our bodies to the wind,
And all the shadowy banks on either side
455 Came sweeping through the darkness, spinning still
The rapid line of motion, then at once
Have I, reclining back upon my heels,
Stopped short; yet still the solitary cliffs
Wheeled by me—even as if the earth had rolled
460 With visible motion her diurnal round!
Behind me did they stretch in solemn train,
Feebler and feebler, and I stood and watched
Till all was tranquil as a dreamless sleep.

Ye Presences of Nature in the sky
465 And on the earth! Ye Visions of the hills!
And Souls of lonely places! can I think
A vulgar° hope was yours when ye employed   *lowly*
Such ministry, when ye, through many a year
Haunting me thus among my boyish sports,
470 On caves and trees, upon the woods and hills,
Impressed upon all forms the characters
Of danger or desire; and thus did make
The surface of the universal earth
With triumph and delight, with hope and fear,
Work like a sea?
475   Not uselessly employed,
Might I pursue this theme through every change
Of exercise and play, to which the year
Did summon us in his delightful round.

We were a noisy crew; the sun in heaven
480 Beheld not vales more beautiful than ours;
Nor saw a band in happiness and joy
Richer, or worthier of the ground they trod.
I could record with no reluctant voice

The woods of autumn, and their hazel bowers
485   With milk-white clusters hung; the rod and line,
True symbol of hope's foolishness, whose strong
And unreproved enchantment led us on
By rocks and pools shut out from every star,
All the green summer, to forlorn cascades
490   Among the windings hid of mountain brooks.
—Unfading recollections! at this hour
The heart is almost mine with which I felt,
From some hill-top on sunny afternoons,
The paper kite high among fleecy clouds
495   Pull at her rein like an impetuous courser;
Or, from the meadows sent on gusty days,
Beheld her breast the wind, then suddenly
Dashed headlong, and rejected by the storm.

        Ye lowly cottages wherein we dwelt,
500   A ministration of your own was yours;
Can I forget you, being as you were
So beautiful among the pleasant fields
In which ye stood? or can I here forget
The plain and seemly countenance with which
505   Ye dealt out your plain comforts? Yet had ye
Delights and exultations of your own.
Eager and never weary we pursued
Our home-amusements by the warm peat-fire
At evening, when with pencil, and smooth slate
510   In square divisions parceled out and all
With crosses and with cyphers scribbled o'er,
We schemed and puzzled, head opposed to head
In strife too humble to be named in verse:
Or round the naked table, snow-white deal,°   pine board
515   Cherry or maple, sate in close array,
And to the combat, Loo or Whist,[1] led on
A thick-ribbed army; not, as in the world,
Neglected and ungratefully thrown by
Even for the very service they had wrought,
520   But husbanded through many a long campaign.
Uncouth assemblage was it, where no few
Had changed their functions; some, plebeian cards
Which Fate, beyond the promise of their birth,
Had dignified, and called to represent
525   The persons of departed potentates.
Oh, with what echoes on the board they fell!
Ironic diamonds,—clubs, hearts, diamonds, spades,
A congregation piteously akin!
Cheap matter offered they to boyish wit,
530   Those sooty knaves, precipitated down
With scoffs and taunts, like Vulcan[2] out of heaven:

---

1. Card games resembling poker and bridge; the pack of cards described in lines 516–35 through long use has been damaged and repaired, with low (line 522, "plebeian") cards made into high (line 525, "potentates") and others partially defaced.
2. In Roman mythology, the god of fire, or the smith of the gods (hence "sooty," line 530); his father, Jove, once hurled him out of heaven.

The paramount ace, a moon in her eclipse,
Queens gleaming through their splendor's last decay,
And monarchs surly at the wrongs sustained
535   By royal visages. Meanwhile abroad
Incessant rain was falling, or the frost
Raged bitterly, with keen and silent tooth;
And, interrupting oft that eager game,
From under Esthwaite's splitting fields of ice
540   The pent-up air, struggling to free itself,
Gave out to meadow grounds and hills a loud
Protracted yelling, like the noise of wolves
Howling in troops along the Bothnic main.[3]

     Nor, sedulous as I have been to trace
545   How Nature by extrinsic passion first
Peopled the mind with forms sublime or fair,
And made me love them, may I here omit
How other pleasures have been mine, and joys
Of subtler origin; how I have felt,
550   Not seldom even in that tempestuous time,
Those hallowed and pure motions of the sense
Which seem, in their simplicity, to own
An intellectual charm; that calm delight
Which, if I err not, surely must belong
555   To those first-born affinities that fit
Our new existence to existing things,
And, in our dawn of being, constitute
The bond of union between life and joy.

     Yes, I remember when the changeful earth,
560   And twice five summers on my mind had stamped
The faces of the moving year, even then
I held unconscious intercourse with beauty
Old as creation, drinking in a pure
Organic pleasure from the silver wreaths
565   Of curling mist, or from the level plain
Of waters colored by impending clouds.

     The sands of Westmoreland, the creeks and bays
Of Cumbria's rocky limits,[4] they can tell
How, when the Sea threw off his evening shade,
570   And to the shepherd's hut on distant hills
Sent welcome notice of the rising moon,
How I have stood, to fancies such as these
A stranger, linking with the spectacle
No conscious memory of a kindred sight,
575   And bringing with me no peculiar sense
Of quietness or peace; yet have I stood,
Even while mine eye hath moved o'er many a league
Of shining water, gathering as it seemed,
Through every hairbreadth in that field of light,
580   New pleasure like a bee among the flowers.

3. Baltic Sea.   4. Coastline areas of the Lake District.

Thus oft amid those fits of vulgar° joy   *ordinary, unreflective*
Which, through all seasons, on a child's pursuits
Are prompt attendants, 'mid that giddy bliss
Which, like a tempest, works along the blood
585   And is forgotten; even then I felt
Gleams like the flashing of a shield—the earth
And common face of Nature spake to me
Rememberable things; sometimes, 'tis true,
By chance collisions and quaint accidents
590   (Like those ill-sorted unions, work supposed
Of evil-minded fairies), yet not vain
Nor profitless, if haply they impressed
Collateral objects and appearances,
Albeit lifeless then, and doomed to sleep
595   Until maturer seasons called them forth
To impregnate and to elevate the mind.
—And if the vulgar joy by its own weight
Wearied itself out of the memory,
The scenes which were a witness of that joy
600   Remained in their substantial lineaments
Depicted on the brain, and to the eye
Were visible, a daily sight; and thus
By the impressive discipline of fear,
By pleasure and repeated happiness,
605   So frequently repeated, and by force
Of obscure feelings representative
Of things forgotten, these same scenes so bright,
So beautiful, so majestic in themselves,
Though yet the day was distant, did become
610   Habitually dear, and all their forms
And changeful colors by invisible links
Were fastened to the affections
                        I began
My story early—not misled, I trust,
By an infirmity of love for days
615   Disowned by memory—fancying flowers where none
Not even the sweetest do or can survive
For him at least whose dawning day they cheered.
Nor will it seem to thee, O Friend![5] so prompt
In sympathy, that I have lengthened out
620   With fond and feeble tongue a tedious tale.
Meanwhile, my hope has been, that I might fetch
Invigorating thoughts from former years;
Might fix the wavering balance of my mind,
And haply meet reproaches too, whose power
625   May spur me on, in manhood now mature,
To honorable toil. Yet should these hopes
Prove vain, and thus should neither I be taught
To understand myself, nor thou to know
With better knowledge how the heart was framed
630   Of him thou lovest; need I dread from thee

---

5. Samuel Taylor Coleridge, the poet and philosopher to whom *The Prelude* was addressed; Wordsworth's particular friend and collaborator.

Harsh judgments, if the song be loth to quit
Those recollected hours that have the charm
Of visionary things, those lovely forms
And sweet sensations that throw back our life,
635 And almost make remotest infancy
A visible scene, on which the sun is shining?

One end at least hath been attained; my mind
Hath been revived, and if this genial mood
Desert me not, forthwith shall be brought down
640 Through later years the story of my life.
The road lies plain before me—'tis a theme
Single and of determined bounds; and hence
I choose it rather at this time, than work
Of ampler or more varied argument,
645 Where I might be discomfited and lost:
And certain hopes are with me, that to thee
This labor will be welcome, honored Friend!
1798–1800   1850

She Dwelt Among the Untrodden Ways

She dwelt among the untrodden ways
        Beside the springs of Dove.[6]
A Maid whom there were none to praise
        And very few to love;

5   A violet by a mossy stone
        Half hidden from the eye!
—Fair as a star, when only one
        Is shining in the sky.

She lived unknown, and few could know
10   When Lucy ceased to be;
But she is in her grave, and, oh,
        The difference to me!
                                                1800

Three Years She Grew

Three years she grew in sun and shower,
Then Nature said, "A lovelier flower
On earth was never sown;
This Child I to myself will take;
5   She shall be mine, and I will make
A Lady of my own.

"Myself will to my darling be
Both law and impulse: and with me
The Girl, in rock and plain,

6. Several rivers in England are named Dove.

10 In earth and heaven, in glade and bower,
    Shall feel an overseeing power
    To kindle or restrain.

    "She shall be sportive as the fawn
    That wild with glee across the lawn
15 Or up the mountain springs;
    And hers shall be the breathing balm,
    And hers the silence and the calm
    Of mute insensate things.

    "The floating clouds their state shall lend
20 To her; for her the willow bend;
    Nor shall she fail to see
    Even in the motions of the Storm
    Grace that shall mold the Maiden's form
    By silent sympathy.

25 "The stars of midnight shall be dear
    To her; and she shall lean her ear
    In many a secret place
    Where rivulets dance their wayward round,
    And beauty born of murmuring sound
30 Shall pass into her face.

    "And vital feelings of delight
    Shall rear her form to stately height,
    Her virgin bosom swell;
    Such thoughts to Lucy I will give
35 While she and I together live
    Here in this happy dell."

    Thus Nature spake—the work was done—
    How soon my Lucy's race was run!
    She died, and left to me
40 This health, this calm, and quiet scene;
    The memory of what has been,
    And never more will be.

                                                    1800

A Slumber Did My Spirit Seal

    A slumber did my spirit seal;
        I had no human fears:
    She seemed a thing that could not feel
        The touch of earthly years.

5   No motion has she now, no force;
        She neither hears nor sees;
    Rolled round in earth's diurnal course,
        With rocks, and stones, and trees.

                                                    1800

Resolution and Independence

1

There was a roaring in the wind all night;
The rain came heavily and fell in floods;
But now the sun is rising calm and bright;
The birds are singing in the distant woods;
5   Over his own sweet voice the Stock-dove broods;
The Jay makes answer as the Magpie chatters;
And all the air is filled with pleasant noise of waters.

2

All things that love the sun are out of doors;
The sky rejoices in the morning's birth;
10   The grass is bright with rain-drops;—on the moors
The hare is running races in her mirth;
And with her feet she from the plashy earth
Raises a mist; that, glittering in the sun,
Runs with her all the way, wherever she doth run.

3

15   I was a Traveler then upon the moor;
I saw the hare that raced about with joy;
I heard the woods and distant waters roar;
Or heard them not, as happy as a boy:
The pleasant season did my heart employ:
20   My old remembrances went from me wholly;
And all the ways of men, so vain and melancholy.

4

But, as it sometimes chanceth, from the might
Of joy in minds that can no further go,
As high as we have mounted in delight
25   In our dejection do we sink as low;
To me that morning did it happen so;
And fears and fancies thick upon me came;
Dim sadness—and blind thoughts, I knew not, nor could name.

5

I heard the sky-lark warbling in the sky;
30   And I bethought me of the playful hare:
Even such a happy Child of earth am I;
Even as these blissful creatures do I fare;
Far from the world I walk, and from all care;
But there may come another day to me—
35   Solitude, pain of heart, distress, and poverty.

6

My whole life I have lived in pleasant thought,
As if life's business were a summer mood;
As if all needful things would come unsought
To genial faith, still rich in genial good;
40   But how can He expect that others should
Build for him, sow for him, and at his call
Love him, who for himself will take no heed at all?

7

I thought of Chatterton,[7] the marvelous Boy,
The sleepless Soul that perished in his pride;
45 Of Him[8] who walked in glory and in joy
Following his plow, along the mountain-side:
By our own spirits are we deified:
We Poets in our youth begin in gladness;
But thereof come in the end despondency and madness.

8

50 Now, whether it were by peculiar grace,
A leading from above, a something given,
Yet it befell, that, in this lonely place,
When I with these untoward thoughts had striven,
Beside a pool bare to the eye of heaven
55 I saw a Man before me unawares:
The oldest man he seemed that ever wore gray hairs.

9

As a huge stone is sometimes seen to lie
Couched on the bald top of an eminence;
Wonder to all who do the same espy,
60 By what means it could thither come, and whence;
So that it seems a thing endued with sense:
Like a sea-beast crawled forth, that on a shelf
Of rock or sand reposeth, there to sun itself;

10

Such seemed this Man, not all alive nor dead,
65 Nor all asleep—in his extreme old age:
His body was bent double, feet and head
Coming together in life's pilgrimage;
As if some dire constraint of pain, or rage
Of sickness felt by him in times long past,
70 A more than human weight upon his frame had cast.

11

Himself he propped, limbs, body, and pale face,
Upon a long gray staff of shaven wood:
And, still as I drew near with gentle pace,
Upon the margin of that moorish flood
75 Motionless as a cloud the old Man stood,
That heareth not the loud winds when they call;
And moveth all together, if it move at all.

12

At length, himself unsettling, he the pond
Stirred with his staff, and fixedly did look
80 Upon the muddy water, which he conned,°   studied
As if he had been reading in a book:
And now a stranger's privilege I took;
And, drawing to his side, to him did say,
"This morning gives us promise of a glorious day."

---

7. Thomas Chatterton (1752–1770), a gifted young English poet who committed suicide.

8. Robert Burns (1759–1796), who died before achieving his later great renown.

13

85   A gentle answer did the old Man make,
    In courteous speech which forth he slowly drew:
    And him with further words I thus bespake,
    "What occupation do you there pursue?
    This is a lonesome place for one like you."
90   Ere he replied, a flash of mild surprise
    Broke from the sable orbs of his yet-vivid eyes.

14

    His words came feebly, from a feeble chest,
    But each in solemn order followed each,
    With something of a lofty utterance drest—
95   Choice word and measured phrase, above the reach
    Of ordinary men; a stately speech;
    Such as grave Livers[9] do in Scotland use,
    Religious men, who give to God and man their dues.

15

    He told, that to these waters he had come
100   To gather leeches,[1] being old and poor:
    Employment hazardous and wearisome!
    And he had many hardships to endure:
    From pond to pond he roamed, from moor to moor;
    Housing, with God's good help, by choice or chance;
105   And in this way he gained an honest maintenance.

16

    The old Man still stood talking by my side;
    But now his voice to me was like a stream
    Scarce heard; nor word from word could I divide;
    And the whole body of the Man did seem
110   Like one whom I had met with in a dream;
    Or like a man from some far region sent,
    To give me human strength, by apt admonishment.

17

    My former thoughts returned: the fear that kills;
    And hope that is unwilling to be fed;
115   Cold, pain, and labor, and all fleshly ills;
    And mighty Poets in their misery dead.
    —Perplexed, and longing to be comforted,
    My question eagerly did I renew,
    "How is it that you live, and what is it you do?"

18

120   He with a smile did then his words repeat;
    And said, that, gathering leeches, far and wide
    He traveled; stirring thus about his feet
    The waters of the pools where they abide.

9. Those who live austerely and gravely. See Wordsworth's "The Excursion," Book I, lines 113–17; the reference is to a Scottish family:

> Pure livers were they all, austere and grave,
> And fearing God; the very children taught
> Stern self-respect, a reverence for God's word,
> And an habitual piety, maintained
> With strictness scarcely known on English ground.

1. Aquatic bloodsuckers, once widely used for medicinal bloodletting.

"Once I could meet with them on every side;
125 But they have dwindled long by slow decay;
Yet still I persevere, and find them where I may."

19

While he was talking thus, the lonely place,
The old Man's shape, and speech—all troubled me:
In my mind's eye I seemed to see him pace
130 About the weary moors continually,
Wandering about alone and silently.
While I these thoughts within myself pursued,
He, having made a pause, the same discourse renewed.

20

And soon with this he other matter blended,
135 Cheerfully uttered, with demeanor kind,
But stately in the main; and when he ended,
I could have laughed myself to scorn to find
In that decrepit Man so firm a mind.
"God," said I, "be my help and stay secure;
140 I'll think of the Leech-gatherer on the lonely moor!"
1802   1807

It Is a Beauteous Evening[2]

It is a beauteous evening, calm and free,
The holy time is quiet as a Nun
Breathless with adoration; the broad sun
Is sinking down in its tranquility;
5 The gentleness of heaven broods o'er the Sea:
Listen! the mighty Being is awake,
And doth with his eternal motion make
A sound like thunder—everlastingly.
Dear Child! dear Girl! that walkest with me here,
10 If thou appear untouched by solemn thought,
Thy nature is not therefore less divine:
Thou liest in Abraham's bosom[3] all the year,
And worship'st at the Temple's inner shrine,[4]
God being with thee when we know it not.

1807

London, 1802

Milton! thou shouldst be living at this hour:
England hath need of thee: she is a fen
Of stagnant waters: altar, sword, and pen,
Fireside, the heroic wealth of hall and bower,

---

2. Wordsworth told Isabella Fenwick in 1843:
"This was composed on the beach near Calais in
the autumn of 1802." The "Dear Child" was Caro-
line (then ten years old), his daughter by Annette

Vallon.
3. Where souls in heaven rest (as in Luke 16.22).
4. The holy of holies (as in the ancient temple in
Jerusalem); where God is present.

5   Have forfeited their ancient English dower
Of inward happiness. We are selfish men;
Oh! raise us up, return to us again;
And give us manners, virtue, freedom, power.
Thy soul was like a Star, and dwelt apart;
10   Thou hadst a voice whose sound was like the sea:
Pure as the naked heavens, majestic, free,
So didst thou travel on life's common way,
In cheerful godliness; and yet thy heart
The lowliest duties on herself did lay.

1807

Composed upon Westminster Bridge, September 3, 1802

Earth has not anything to show more fair:
Dull would he be of soul who could pass by
A sight so touching in its majesty;
This City now doth, like a garment, wear
5   The beauty of the morning; silent, bare,
Ships, towers, domes, theaters, and temples lie
Open unto the fields, and to the sky;
All bright and glittering in the smokeless air.
Never did sun more beautifully steep
10   In his first splendor, valley, rock, or hill;
Ne'er saw I, never felt, a calm so deep!
The river glideth at his own sweet will:
Dear God! the very houses seem asleep;
And all that mighty heart is lying still!

1807

Nuns Fret Not at Their Convent's Narrow Room

Nuns fret not at their convent's narrow room;
And hermits are contented with their cells;
And students with their pensive citadels;
Maids at the wheel, the weaver at his loom,
5   Sit blithe and happy; bees that soar for bloom,
High as the highest Peak of Furness-fells,[5]
Will murmur by the hour in foxglove bells:
In truth the prison, into which we doom
Ourselves, no prison is: and hence for me,
10   In sundry moods, 'twas pastime to be bound
Within the Sonnet's scanty plot of ground;
Pleased if some Souls (for such there needs must be)
Who have felt the weight of too much liberty,
Should find brief solace there, as I have found.

1807

---

5. Mountains in the English Lake District.

My Heart Leaps Up

My heart leaps up when I behold
   A rainbow in the sky:
So was it when my life began;
So is it now I am a man;
5   So be it when I shall grow old,
   Or let me die!
The Child is father of the Man;
And I could wish my days to be
Bound each to each by natural piety.

1807

Ode

Intimations of Immortality from Recollections of Early Childhood

> The Child is father of the Man;
> And I could wish my days to be
> Bound each to each by natural piety.[6]

1

There was a time when meadow, grove, and stream,
The earth, and every common sight,
    To me did seem
   Appareled in celestial light,
5 The glory and the freshness of a dream.
It is not now as it hath been of yore—
    Turn whereso'er I may,
    By night or day,
The things which I have seen I now can see no more.

2

10   The Rainbow comes and goes,
    And lovely is the Rose,
    The Moon doth with delight
Look round her when the heavens are bare,
    Waters on a starry night
15   Are beautiful and fair;
  The sunshine is a glorious birth;
  But yet I know, where'er I go,
That there hath passed away a glory from the earth.

3

Now, while the birds thus sing a joyous song,
20   And while the young lambs bound
    As to the tabor's sound,[7]
To me alone there came a thought of grief:
A timely utterance gave that thought relief,
    And I again am strong:
25 The cataracts blow their trumpets from the steep;
No more shall grief of mine the season wrong;
I hear the Echoes through the mountains throng,

6. Final lines of Wordsworth's "My Heart Leaps Up."   7. "Tabor": a small drum.

The Winds come to me from the fields of sleep,
    And all the earth is gay;
30   Land and sea
    Give themselves up to jollity,
        And with the heart of May
    Doth every Beast keep holiday—
        Thou Child of Joy,
35 Shout round me, let me hear thy shouts, thou happy Shepherd-boy!

4

Ye blessèd Creatures, I have heard the call
    Ye to each other make; I see
The heavens laugh with you in your jubilee;
    My heart is at your festival,
40   My head hath its coronal,
The fullness of your bliss, I feel—I feel it all.
      Oh, evil day! if I were sullen
      While Earth herself is adorning,
        This sweet May morning,
45   And the Children are culling
        On every side,
    In a thousand valleys far and wide,
    Fresh flowers; while the sun shines warm,
And the Babe leaps up on his Mother's arm—
50   I hear, I hear, with joy I hear!
    —But there's a Tree, of many, one,
A single Field which I have looked upon,
Both of them speak of something that is gone:
      The Pansy at my feet
55   Doth the same tale repeat:
Whither is fled the visionary gleam?
Where is it now, the glory and the dream?

5

Our birth is but a sleep and a forgetting:
The Soul that rises with us, our life's Star,
60   Hath had elsewhere its setting,
       And cometh from afar:
    Not in entire forgetfulness,
    And not in utter nakedness,
But trailing clouds of glory do we come
65   From God, who is our home:
Heaven lies about us in our infancy!
Shades of the prison-house begin to close
      Upon the growing Boy
        But he
70 Beholds the light, and whence it flows,
      He sees it in his joy;
The Youth, who daily farther from the east
      Must travel, still is Nature's Priest,
      And by the vision splendid
75   Is on his way attended;
At length the Man perceives it die away,
And fade into the light of common day.

6

Earth fills her lap with pleasures of her own;
Yearnings she hath in her own natural kind,
80 And, even with something of a Mother's mind,
            And no unworthy aim,
      The homely° Nurse doth all she can   *simple, kindly*
To make her foster child, her Inmate Man,
      Forget the glories he hath known,
85 And that imperial palace whence he came.

7

Behold the Child among his newborn blisses,
A six-years' Darling of a pygmy size!
See, where 'mid work of his own hand he lies,
Fretted° by sallies of his mother's kisses,   *vexed*
90 With light upon him from his father's eyes!
See, at his feet, some little plan or chart,
Some fragment from his dream of human life,
Shaped by himself with newly-learnèd art;
            A wedding or a festival,
95   A mourning or a funeral;
            And this hath now his heart,
            And unto this he frames his song;
                  Then will he fit his tongue
To dialogues of business, love, or strife;
100   But it will not be long
               Ere this be thrown aside,
               And with new joy and pride
The little Actor cons° another part;   *commits to memory*
Filling from time to time his "humorous stage"[8]
105 With all the Persons,° down to palsied Age,   *dramatis personae*
That Life brings with her in her equipage;°   *group of servants*
               As if his whole vocation
               Were endless imitation.

8

Thou, whose exterior semblance doth belie
110   Thy Soul's immensity;
Thou best Philosopher, who yet dost keep
Thy heritage, thou Eye among the blind,
That, deaf and silent, read'st the eternal deep,
Haunted forever by the eternal mind—
115   Mighty Prophet! Seer blest!
            On whom those truths do rest,
Which we are toiling all our lives to find,
In darkness lost, the darkness of the grave;
Thou, over whom thy Immortality
120 Broods like the Day, a Master o'er a Slave,
A Presence which is not to be put by;
Thou little Child, yet glorious in the might
Of heaven-born freedom on thy being's height,

---

8. I.e., playing the parts of characters with various temperaments, called "humors" by Elizabethan poets and playwrights: "humorous stage" is a quo- tation from line 1 of Samuel Daniel's dedicatory sonnet to Fulke Greville in *Musophilus*.

Why with such earnest pains dost thou provoke
125 The years to bring the inevitable yoke,
Thus blindly with thy blessedness at strife?
Full soon thy Soul shall have her earthly freight,
And custom lie upon thee with a weight,
Heavy as frost, and deep almost as life!

9

130   O joy! that in our embers
      Is something that doth live,
     That nature yet remembers
      What was so fugitive!
The thought of our past years in me doth breed
135 Perpetual benediction: not indeed
For that which is most worthy to be blest;
Delight and liberty, the simple creed
Of Childhood, whether busy or at rest,
With new-fledged hope still fluttering in his breast—
140   Not for these I raise
      The song of thanks and praise;
    But for those obstinate questionings
     Of sense and outward things,
     Fallings from us, vanishings;
145   Blank misgivings of a Creature
Moving about in worlds not realized,
High instincts before which our mortal Nature
Did tremble like a guilty Thing surprised;
     But for those first affections,
150   Those shadowy recollections,
    Which, be they what they may,
Are yet the fountain light of all our day,
Are yet a master light of all our seeing;
    Uphold us, cherish, and have power to make
155 Our noisy years seem moments in the being
Of the eternal Silence: truths that wake,
      To perish never;
Which neither listlessness, nor mad endeavor,
      Nor Man nor Boy,
160 Nor all that is at enmity with joy,
Can utterly abolish or destroy!
     Hence in a season of calm weather
      Though inland far we be,
Our Souls have sight of that immortal sea
165   Which brought us hither,
     Can in a moment travel thither,
And see the Children sport upon the shore,
And hear the mighty waters rolling evermore.

10

Then sing, ye Birds, sing, sing a joyous song!
170   And let the young Lambs bound
      As to the tabor's sound!
We in thought will join your throng,
     Ye that pipe and ye that play,

Ye that through your hearts today
175   Feel the gladness of the May!
What though the radiance which was once so bright
Be now forever taken from my sight,
    Though nothing can bring back the hour
Of splendor in the grass, of glory in the flower;
180   We will grieve not, rather find
    Strength in what remains behind;
    In the primal sympathy
    Which having been must ever be;
    In the soothing thoughts that spring
185   Out of human suffering;
    In the faith that looks through death,
In years that bring the philosophic mind.

11

And O, ye Fountains, Meadows, Hills, and Groves,
Forebode not any severing of our loves!
190 Yet in my heart of hearts I feel your might;
I only have relinquished one delight
To live beneath your more habitual sway.
I love the Brooks which down their channels fret,
Even more than when I tripped lightly as they;
195 The innocent brightness of a newborn Day
    Is lovely yet;
The clouds that gather round the setting sun
Do take a sober coloring from an eye
That hath kept watch o'er man's mortality;
200 Another race hath been, and other palms° are won.   *symbols of victory*
Thanks to the human heart by which we live,
Thanks to its tenderness, its joys, and fears,
To me the meanest° flower that blows° can give   *most ordinary / blooms*
Thoughts that do often lie too deep for tears.

1802–04   1807

I Wandered Lonely As a Cloud

I wandered lonely as a cloud
That floats on high o'er vales and hills,
When all at once I saw a crowd,
A host, of golden daffodils;
5   Beside the lake, beneath the trees,
Fluttering and dancing in the breeze.

Continuous as the stars that shine
And twinkle on the milky way,
They stretched in never-ending line
10   Along the margin of a bay:
Ten thousand saw I at a glance,
Tossing their heads in sprightly dance.

The waves beside them danced; but they
Outdid the sparkling waves in glee;
15   A poet could not but be gay,
In such a jocund° company;   *cheerful*
I gazed—and gazed—but little thought
What wealth the show to me had brought:

For oft, when on my couch I lie
20   In vacant or in pensive mood,
They flash upon that inward eye
Which is the bliss of solitude;
And then my heart with pleasure fills,
And dances with the daffodils.

1807

She Was a Phantom of Delight

She was a Phantom° of delight   *vivid image*
When first she gleamed upon my sight;
A lovely Apparition, sent
To be a moment's ornament;
5   Her eyes as stars of Twilight fair;
Like Twilight's, too, her dusky hair;
But all things else about her drawn
From May-time and the cheerful Dawn;
A dancing Shape, an Image gay,
10   To haunt, to startle, and way-lay.

I saw her upon nearer view,
A Spirit, yet a Woman too!
Her household motions light and free,
And steps of virgin-liberty;
15   A countenance in which did meet
Sweet records, promises as sweet;
A Creature not too bright or good
For human nature's daily food;
For transient sorrows, simple wiles,
20   Praise, blame, love, kisses, tears, and smiles.

And now I see with eye serene
The very pulse of the machine;[9]
A Being breathing thoughtful breath,
A Traveler between life and death;
25   The reason firm, the temperate will,
Endurance, foresight, strength, and skill;
A perfect Woman, nobly planned,
To warn, to comfort, and command;
And yet a Spirit still, and bright
30   With something of angelic light.

1807

9. Complete organism.

Elegiac Stanzas[1]

Suggested by a Picture of Peele Castle, in a Storm, Painted by Sir George Beaumont

I was thy neighbor once, thou rugged Pile!
Four summer weeks I dwelt in sight of thee:
I saw thee every day; and all the while
Thy Form was sleeping on a glassy sea.

5   So pure the sky, so quiet was the air!
So like, so very like, was day to day!
Whene'er I looked, thy Image still was there;
It trembled, but it never passed away.

How perfect was the calm! it seemed no sleep;
10   No mood, which season takes away, or brings:
I could have fancied that the mighty Deep
Was even the gentlest of all gentle Things.

Ah! THEN, if mine had been the Painter's hand,
To express what then I saw; and add the gleam,
15   The light that never was, on sea or land,
The consecration, and the Poet's dream;

I would have planted thee, thou hoary Pile
Amid a world how different from this!
Beside a sea that could not cease to smile;
20   On tranquil land, beneath a sky of bliss.

Thou shouldst have seemed a treasure house divine
O peaceful years; a chronicle of heaven—
Of all the sunbeams that did ever shine
The very sweetest had to thee been given.

25   A Picture had it been of lasting ease,
Elysian[2] quiet, without toil or strife;
No motion but the moving tide, a breeze,
Or merely silent Nature's breathing life.

Such, in the fond illusion of my heart,
30   Such Picture would I at that time have made,
And seen the soul of truth in every part,
A steadfast peace that might not be betrayed.

So once it would have been—'tis so no more;
I have submitted to a new control:
35   A power is gone, which nothing can restore;
A deep distress hath humanized my Soul.

---

1. In memory of the poet's brother, John, lost at sea in February 1805 (see lines 36–39).

2. In Greek myth the souls of the blest dwelt in the Elysian Fields.

Not for a moment could I now behold
A smiling sea, and be what I have been:
The feeling of my loss will ne'er be old;
40 This, which I know, I speak with mind serene.

Then, Beaumont, Friend! who would have been the Friend,
If he had lived, of him whom I deplore,°   *lament*
This work of thine I blame not, but commend;
This sea in anger, and that dismal shore.

45 O 'tis a passionate Work!—yet wise and well,
Well chosen is the spirit that is here;
That Hulk which labors in the deadly swell,
This rueful sky, this pageantry of fear!

And this huge Castle, standing here sublime,
50 I love to see the look with which it braves,
Cased in the unfeeling armor of old time,
The lightning, the fierce wind, and trampling waves.

Farewell, farewell the heart that lives alone,
Housed in a dream, at distance from the Kind!°   *mankind*
55 Such happiness, wherever it be known,
Is to be pitied; for 'tis surely blind.

But welcome fortitude, and patient cheer,
And frequent sights of what is to be borne!
Such sights, or worse, as are before me here.
60 Not without hope we suffer and we mourn.

                                         1807

The World Is Too Much with Us

The world is too much with us; late and soon,
Getting and spending, we lay waste our powers;
Little we see in Nature that is ours;
We have given our hearts away, a sordid boon!°   *gift*
5 This Sea that bares her bosom to the moon,
The winds that will be howling at all hours,
And are up-gathered now like sleeping flowers,
For this, for everything, we are out of tune;
It moves us not.—Great God! I'd rather be
10 A Pagan suckled in a creed outworn;
So might I, standing on this pleasant lea,°   *open meadow*
Have glimpses that would make me less forlorn;
Have sight of Proteus rising from the sea;
Or hear old Triton blow his wreathèd horn.[3]

                                         1807

3. In Greek myth Proteus, the "Old Man of the Sea," rises from the sea at midday and can be forced to read the future by anyone who holds him while he takes many frightening shapes. Triton is the son of the sea god, Neptune; the sound of his conch-shell horn calms the waves.

The Solitary Reaper

Behold her, single in the field,
Yon solitary Highland Lass!
Reaping and singing by herself;
Stop here, or gently pass!
5 Alone she cuts and binds the grain,
And sings a melancholy strain;
O listen! for the Vale profound
Is overflowing with the sound.

No Nightingale did ever chaunt
10 More welcome notes to weary bands
Of travelers in some shady haunt,
Among Arabian sands;
A voice so thrilling ne'er was heard
In springtime from the Cuckoo bird,
15 Breaking the silence of the seas
Among the farthest Hebrides.

Will no one tell me what she sings?—
Perhaps the plaintive numbers flow
For old, unhappy, far-off things,
20 And battles long ago;
Or is it some more humble lay,
Familiar matter of today?
Some natural sorrow, loss, or pain,
That has been, and may be again?

25 Whate'er the theme, the Maiden sang
As if her song could have no ending;
I saw her singing at her work,
And o'er the sickle bending—
I listened, motionless and still;
30 And, as I mounted up the hill,
The music in my heart I bore,
Long after it was heard no more.

1807

Surprised by Joy

Surprised by joy—impatient as the Wind
I turned to share the transport—Oh! with whom
But thee,[4] deep buried in the silent tomb,
That spot which no vicissitude can find?
5 Love, faithful love, recalled thee to my mind—
But how could I forget thee? Through what power,
Even for the least division of an hour,
Have I been so beguiled as to be blind
To my most grievous loss!—That thought's return

4. The poet's daughter Catharine, who died at the age of four, in 1812.

10   Was the worst pang that sorrow ever bore,
     Save one, one only, when I stood forlorn,
     Knowing my heart's best treasure was no more;
     That neither present time, nor years unborn
     Could to my sight that heavenly face restore.

1815

Mutability

     From low to high doth dissolution climb,
     And sink from high to low, along a scale
     Of awful notes, whose concord shall not fail;
     A musical but melancholy chime,
5   Which they can hear who meddle not with crime,
     Nor avarice, nor over-anxious care.
     Truth fails not; but her outward forms that bear
     The longest date do melt like frosty rime,°   *thin coating*
     That in the morning whitened hill and plain
10 And is no more; drop like the tower sublime
     Of yesterday, which royally did wear
     His crown of weeds, but could not even sustain
     Some casual shout that broke the silent air,
     Or the unimaginable touch of Time.

1822

Scorn Not the Sonnet

     Scorn not the sonnet; critic, you have frowned,
     Mindless of its just honors; with this key
     Shakespeare unlocked his heart; the melody
     Of this small lute gave ease to Petrarch's[5] wound;
5   A thousand times this pipe did Tasso[6] sound;
     With it Camöens soothed an exile's grief;[7]
     The sonnet glittered a gay myrtle leaf
     Amid the cypress with which Dante crowned
     His visionary brow; a glow-worm lamp,
10 It cheered mild Spenser, called from Faeryland
     To struggle through dark ways; and, when a damp°   *dark mist*
     Fell round the path of Milton, in his hand
     The thing became a trumpet; whence he blew
     Soul-animating strains—alas, too few!

1827

5. (1304–1374); Italian poet, whose "wound" was his unconsummated love for "Laura."
6. (1544–1595); Italian poet.
7. Camoëns (1524?–1580), a Portuguese poet, was banished from the royal court.

MARY TIGHE

1772–1810

Sonnet Addressed to My Mother

Oh, thou! whose tender smile most partially°   *with partiality*
    Hath ever blessed thy child: to thee belong
    The graces which adorn my first wild song,
If aught° of grace it knows: nor thou deny   *anything*
5 Thine ever prompt attention to supply.
    But let me lead thy willing ear along,
    Where virtuous love still bids the strain° prolong   *offspring*
His innocent applause; since from thine eye
    The beams of love first charmed my infant breast,
10 And from thy lip Affection's soothing voice
    That eloquence of tenderness expressed,
Which still my grateful heart confessed divine:
Oh! ever may its accents sweet rejoice
The soul which loves to own° whate'er it has is thine!   *acknowledge*

From Psyche[1]

1

Let not the rugged brow[2] the rhymes accuse,
    Which speak of gentle knights and ladies fair,
    Nor scorn the lighter labors of the muse,[3]
    Who yet, for cruel battles would not dare
5 The low-strung chords of her weak lyre[4] prepare;
    But loves to court repose in slumbery° lay,°   *sleepy / song*
    To tell of goodly bowers[5] and gardens rare,
    Of gentle blandishments[6] and amorous play,
And all the lore of love, in courtly verse essay.°   *attempt*

2

10 And ye whose gentle hearts in thraldom° held   *servitude*
    The power of mighty Love already own,°   *acknowledge*
    When you the pains and dangers have beheld,
    Which erst your lord[7] hath for his Psyche known,

1. This is the proem to a long poem that tells the story of Psyche, a mortal woman so beautiful that she inspires Venus' jealousy. Venus sends her son, Cupid, the god of love, to make Psyche fall in love with a man of low rank. Instead Cupid falls in love with Psyche and becomes her lover, but he visits her only at night and forbids her to see his face or seek his identity. Persuaded by her sisters that she is sleeping with a monster, Psyche takes a lamp and looks at Cupid one night while he sleeps. When a drop of hot oil from the lamp spills on him, he wakens and flees, angry at her disobedience, and Psyche searches for him throughout the Earth. Venus then sets her a series of impossible tasks. Although Psyche dies while accomplishing the last of these tasks, Cupid revives her, gets Jupi- ter's permission to marry her, and brings her to heaven to live. Psyche means "soul" in Greek, and the story is often interpreted as the journey of the soul through life on Earth, with its suffering and death, to its final union with the divine. Tighe's poem is believed to have influenced Keats' "Ode to Psyche" (pp. 843–45).
2. Furrowed or frowning forehead or countenance.
3. One of the nine Greek goddesses believed to be the sources of inspiration for the arts.
4. A harplike stringed instrument.
5. Leafy coverts or arbors.
6. Allurements, or gently flattering speech or actions.
7. I.e., Cupid.

For all your sorrows this may well atone,
15 That he you serve the same hath suffered;
And sure, your fond applause the tale will crown
In which your own distress is pictured,
And all that weary way which you yourselves must tread.

3

Most sweet would to my soul the hope appear,
20 That sorrow in my verse a charm might find,
To smooth the brow long bent with bitter cheer,
Some short distraction to the joyless mind
Which grief, with heavy chain, hath fast confined
To sad remembrance of its happier state;
25 For to myself I ask no boon° more kind   *favor*
Than power another's woes to mitigate,
And that soft soothing art which anguish can abate.

4

And thou, sweet sprite,[8] whose sway doth far extend,
Smile on the mean° historian of thy fame!   *humble, lowly*
30 My heart in each distress and fear befriend,
Nor ever let it feel a fiercer flame
Than innocence may cherish free from blame,
And hope may nurse, and sympathy may own;
For, as thy rights I never would disclaim,
35 But true allegiance offered to thy throne,
So may I love but one, by one beloved alone.

5

That anxious torture may I never feel,
Which, doubtful, watches o'er a wandering heart.
Oh! who that bitter torment can reveal,
40 Or tell the pining anguish of that smart!
In those affections may I ne'er have part,
Which easily transferred can learn to rove:
No, dearest Cupid! when I feel thy dart,[9]
For thy sweet Psyche's sake may no false love
45 The tenderness I prize lightly from me remove!

1811

SAMUEL TAYLOR COLERIDGE

1772–1834

The Aeolian Harp[1]

Composed at Clevedon, Somersetshire

My pensive Sara![2] thy soft cheek reclined
Thus on mine arm, most soothing sweet it is

---

8. I.e., Psyche.
9. The victims of Cupid's gold-tipped arrows fell
hopelessly in love.
1. The wind-harp (named after Aeolus, classical
god of winds) has a sounding board equipped with

a set of strings that vibrate in response to air cur-
rents; it was much in favor with German and
English Romantic writers.
2. Coleridge's bride; the poem was composed dur-
ing their honeymoon.

To sit beside our Cot,° our Cot o'ergrown   *cottage*
With white-flowered Jasmin, and the broad-leaved Myrtle,
5   (Meet° emblems they of Innocence and Love!)   *appropriate*
And watch the clouds, that late were rich with light,
Slow saddening round, and mark the star of eve
Serenely brilliant (such should Wisdom be)
Shine opposite! How exquisite the scents
10 Snatched from yon bean-field! and the world *so* hushed!
The stilly murmur of the distant Sea
Tells us of silence.

               And that simplest Lute,
Placed length-ways in the clasping casement, hark!
How by the desultory breeze caressed,
15 Like some coy maid half yielding to her lover,
It pours such sweet upbraiding, as must needs
Tempt to repeat the wrong! And now, its strings
Boldlier swept, the long sequacious° notes   *uninterruptedly flowing*
Over delicious surges sink and rise,
20 Such a soft floating witchery of sound
As twilight Elfins make, when they at eve
Voyage on gentle gales from Fairy-Land,
Where Melodies round honey-dropping flowers,
Footless and wild, like birds of Paradise,[3]
25 Nor pause, nor perch, hovering on untamed wing!
O! the one Life within us and abroad,
Which meets all motion and becomes its soul,
A light in sound, a sound-like power in light,
Rhythm in all thought, and joyance everywhere—
30 Methinks, it should have been impossible
Not to love all things in a world so filled;
Where the breeze warbles, and the mute still air
Is Music slumbering on her instrument.

        And thus, my Love! as on the midway slope
35 Of yonder hill I stretch my limbs at noon,
Whilst through my half-closed eyelids I behold
The sunbeams dance, like diamonds, on the main,
And tranquil muse upon tranquility:
Full many a thought uncalled and undetained,
40 And many idle flitting phantasies,
Traverse my indolent and passive brain,
As wild and various as the random gales
That swell and flutter on this subject Lute!

        And what if all of animated nature
45 Be but organic Harps diversely framed,
That tremble into thought, as o'er them sweeps
Plastic and vast, one intellectual breeze,
At once the Soul of each, and God of all?

---

3. Bright-plumaged birds of New Guinea and nearby islands; mistakenly supposed to have no feet and to spend their lives on the wing.

But thy more serious eye a mild reproof
50 Darts, O belovéd Woman! nor such thoughts
Dim and unhallowed dost thou not reject,
And biddest me walk humbly with my God.
Meek Daughter in the family of Christ!
Well hast thou said and holily dispraised
55 These shapings of the unregenerate mind;
Bubbles that glitter as they rise and break
On vain Philosophy's aye-babbling spring.
For never guiltless may I speak of him,
The Incomprehensible! save when with awe
60 I praise him, and with Faith that inly *feels*;
Who with his saving mercies healéd me,
A sinful and most miserable man,
Wildered and dark, and gave me to possess
Peace, and this Cot, and thee, heart-honored Maid!

1796, 1817

Kubla Khan[4]

Or a Vision in a Dream. A Fragment

In Xanadu did Kubla Khan
A stately pleasure dome decree:
Where Alph, the sacred river, ran
Through caverns measureless to man
5   Down to a sunless sea.
So twice five miles of fertile ground
With walls and towers were girdled round:
And there were gardens bright with sinuous rills,
Where blossomed many an incense-bearing tree;
10 And here were forests ancient as the hills,
Enfolding sunny spots of greenery.

But oh! that deep romantic chasm which slanted
Down the green hill athwart a cedarn cover!
A savage place! as holy and enchanted
15 As e'er beneath a waning moon was haunted

4. The first *khan*, or ruler, of the Mongol dynasty in thirteenth-century China. The topography and place-names are fictitious. In a prefatory note to the poem, Coleridge gave the following background: "In the summer of the year 1797, the author, then in ill health, had retired to a lonely farmhouse between Porlock and Linton, on the Exmoor confines of Somerset and Devonshire. In consequence of a slight indisposition, an anodyne had been prescribed, from the effects of which he fell asleep in his chair at the moment that he was reading the following sentence, or words of the same substance, in *Purchas's Pilgrimage:* 'Here the Khan Kubla commanded a palace to be built, and a stately garden thereunto. And thus ten miles of fertile ground were inclosed with a wall.' The author continued for about three hours in a profound sleep, at least of the external sense, during which time he has the most vivid confidence that he could not have composed less than from two to three hundred lines; if that indeed can be called composition in which all the images rose up before him as *things*, with a parallel production of the correspondent expressions, without any sensation or consciousness of effort. On awaking he appeared to himself to have a distinct recollection of the whole, and taking his pen, ink, and paper, instantly and eagerly wrote down the lines that are here preserved. At this moment he was unfortunately called out by a person on business from Porlock, and detained by him above an hour, and on his return to his room, found, to his no small surprise and mortification, that though he still retained some vague and dim recollection of the general purport of the vision, yet, with the exception of some eight or ten scattered lines and images, all the rest had passed away like the images on the surface of a stream into which a stone has been cast, but, alas! without the after restoration of the latter!"

By woman wailing for her demon lover!
And from this chasm, with ceaseless turmoil seething,
As if this earth in fast thick pants were breathing,
A mighty fountain momently was forced:
20 Amid whose swift half-intermitted burst
Huge fragments vaulted like rebounding hail,
Or chaffy grain beneath the thresher's flail:
And 'mid these dancing rocks at once and ever
It flung up momently the sacred river.
25 Five miles meandering with a mazy motion
Through wood and dale the sacred river ran,
Then reached the caverns measureless to man,
And sank in tumult to a lifeless ocean:
And 'mid this tumult Kubla heard from far
30 Ancestral voices prophesying war!

    The shadow of the dome of pleasure
    Floated midway on the waves;
    Where was heard the mingled measure
    From the fountain and the caves.
35 It was a miracle of rare device,
    A sunny pleasure dome with caves of ice!

    A damsel with a dulcimer[5]
    In a vision once I saw:
    It was an Abyssinian maid,
40 And on her dulcimer she played,
    Singing of Mount Abora.
    Could I revive within me
    Her symphony and song,
    To such a deep delight 'twould win me,
45 That with music loud and long,
    I would build that dome in air,
    That sunny dome! those caves of ice!
    And all who heard should see them there,
    And all should cry, Beware! Beware!
50 His flashing eyes, his floating hair!
    Weave a circle round him thrice,
    And close your eyes with holy dread,
    For he on honey-dew hath fed,
    And drunk the milk of Paradise.

1797–98   1816

Frost at Midnight

    The Frost performs its secret ministry,
    Unhelped by any wind. The owlet's cry
    Came loud—and hark, again! loud as before.
    The inmates of my cottage, all at rest,
5   Have left me to that solitude, which suits
    Abstruser musings: save that at my side

___

5. A harplike instrument.

My cradled infant[6] slumbers peacefully.
'Tis calm indeed! so calm, that it disturbs
And vexes meditation with its strange
10   And extreme silentness. Sea, hill, and wood,
This populous village! Sea, and hill, and wood,
With all the numberless goings-on of life,
Inaudible as dreams! the thin blue flame
Lies on my low-burnt fire, and quivers not;
15   Only that film,[7] which fluttered on the grate,
Still flutters there, the sole unquiet thing.
Methinks its motion in this hush of nature
Gives it dim sympathies with me who live,
Making it a companionable form,
20   Whose puny flaps and freaks the idling Spirit
By its own moods interprets, everywhere
Echo or mirror seeking of itself,
And makes a toy of Thought.

But O! how oft,
How oft, at school, with most believing mind,
25   Presageful,° have I gazed upon the bars,   *foretelling*
To watch that fluttering *stranger!* and as oft
With unclosed lids, already had I dreamt
Of my sweet birthplace, and the old church tower,
Whose bells, the poor man's only music, rang
30   From morn to evening, all the hot Fair-day,[8]
So sweetly, that they stirred and haunted me
With a wild pleasure, falling on mine ear
Most like articulate sounds of things to come!
So gazed I, till the soothing things, I dreamt,
35   Lulled me to sleep, and sleep prolonged my dreams!
And so I brooded all the following morn,
Awed by the stern preceptor's° face, mine eye   *schoolmaster's*
Fixed with mock study on my swimming book:[9]
Save if the door half opened, and I snatched
40   A hasty glance, and still my heart leaped up,
For still I hoped to see the *stranger's* face,
Townsman, or aunt, or sister more beloved,
My playmate when we both were clothed alike![1]

Dear Babe, that sleepest cradled by my side,
45   Whose gentle breathings, heard in this deep calm,
Fill up the interspersèd vacancies
And momentary pauses of the thought!
My babe so beautiful! it thrills my heart
With tender gladness, thus to look at thee,
50   And think that thou shalt learn far other lore,
And in far other scenes! For I was reared
In the great city, pent 'mid cloisters dim,

6. Coleridge's eldest son, Hartley.
7. Bits of soot fluttering in a fireplace; in folklore, said to foretell the arrival of an unexpected guest, and hence called "strangers" (lines 26, 41).
8. Market-day, often a time of festivities.
9. I.e., seen unclearly because of emotion.
1. In early childhood, when boys and girls wore the same kind of infants' clothing.

And saw nought lovely but the sky and stars.
But *thou,* my babe! shalt wander like a breeze
55   By lakes and sandy shores, beneath the crags
Of ancient mountain, and beneath the clouds,
Which image in their bulk both lakes and shores
And mountain crags: so shalt thou see and hear
The lovely shapes and sounds intelligible
60   Of that eternal language, which thy God
Utters, who from eternity doth teach
Himself in all, and all things in himself.
Great universal Teacher! he shall mold
Thy spirit, and by giving make it ask.

65   Therefore all seasons shall be sweet to thee,
Whether the summer clothe the general° earth   generative, vernal
With greenness, or the redbreast sit and sing
Betwixt the tufts of snow on the bare branch
Of mossy apple tree, while the nigh thatch
70   Smokes in the sun-thaw; whether the eave-drops fall
Heard only in the trances of the blast,
Or if the secret ministry of frost
Shall hang them up in silent icicles,
Quietly shining to the quiet Moon.

1798

The Rime of the Ancient Mariner

IN SEVEN PARTS

*Facile credo, plures esse Naturas invisibiles quam visibiles in rerum universitate.
Sed horum [sic] omnium familiam quis nobis enarrabit? et gradus et cognationes et discrimina et singulorum munera? Quid agunt? quae loca habitant?
Harum rerum notitiam semper ambivit ingenium humanum, nunquam attigit.
Juvat, interea, non diffiteor, quandoque in animo, in tabulâ, majoris et melioris
mundi imaginem contemplari: ne mens assuefacta hodiernae vitae minutiis se
contrahat nimis, et tota subsidat in pusillas cogitationes. Sed veritati interea
invigilandum est, modusque servandus, ut certa ab incertis, diem a nocte, distinguamus.*

—T. BURNET[2]

Part I

*An ancient Mariner
meeteth three Gal-
lants bidden to a
wedding feast, and
detaineth one.*

It is an ancient Mariner
And he stoppeth one of three.
— "By thy long gray beard and glittering eye,
Now wherefore stopp'st thou me?

2. From *Archaeologiae Philosophiae*, p. 68. "I can easily believe that there are more invisible than visible beings in the universe. But of their families, degrees, connections, distinctions, and functions, who shall tell us? How do they act? Where are they found? About such matters the human mind has always circled without attaining knowledge. Yet I do not doubt that sometimes it is well for the soul to contemplate as in a picture the image of a larger and better world, lest the mind, habituated to the small concerns of daily life, limit itself too much and sink entirely into trivial thinking. But meanwhile we must be on watch for the truth, avoiding extremes, so that we may distinguish certain from uncertain, day from night." Burnet was a seventeenth-century English theologian.

The Bridegroom's doors are opened wide,   5
And I am next of kin;
The guests are met, the feast is set:
May'st hear the merry din."

He holds him with his skinny hand,
"There was a ship," quoth he.   10
"Hold off! unhand me, graybeard loon!"
Eftsoons° his hand dropped he.   *straightway*

*The Wedding Guest
is spellbound by the
eye of the old seafar-
ing man, and con-
strained to hear his
tale.*

He holds him with his glittering eye—
The Wedding Guest stood still,
And listens like a three years' child: 15
The Mariner hath his will.

The Wedding Guest sat on a stone:
He cannot choose but hear;
And thus spake on that ancient man,
The bright-eyed Mariner.   20

"The ship was cheered, the harbor cleared,
Merrily did we drop
Below the kirk,° below the hill,   *church*

*The Mariner tells
how the ship sailed
southward with a
good wind and fair
weather, till it
reached the line.*

Below the lighthouse top.

The Sun came up upon the left,   25
Out of the sea came he!
And he shone bright, and on the right
Went down into the sea.

Higher and higher every day,
Till over the mast at noon—"   30
The Wedding Guest here beat his breast,
For he heard the loud bassoon.

*The Wedding Guest
heareth the bridal
music; but the Mari-
ner continueth his
tale.*

The bride hath paced into the hall,
Red as a rose is she;
Nodding their heads before her goes   35
The merry minstrelsy.

The Wedding Guest he beat his breast,
Yet he cannot choose but hear;
And thus spake on that ancient man,
The bright-eyed Mariner.   40

*The ship driven by a
storm toward the
South Pole.*

"And now the STORM-BLAST came, and he
Was tyrannous and strong;
He struck with his o'ertaking wings,
And chased us south along.

With sloping masts and dipping prow,   45
As who pursued with yell and blow
Still treads the shadow of his foe,
And forward bends his head,

The ship drove fast, loud roared the blast,
And southward aye we fled.   50

And now there came both mist and snow,
And it grew wondrous cold:
And ice, mast-high, came floating by,
As green as emerald.

The land of ice, and
of fearful sounds
where no living
thing was to be seen.
And through the drifts the snowy clifts°   *cliffs* 55
Did send a dismal sheen:
Nor shapes of men nor beasts we ken—
The ice was all between.

The ice was here, the ice was there,
The ice was all around: 60
It cracked and growled, and roared and howled,
Like noises in a swound!°   *swoon*

Till a great sea bird,
called the Albatross,
came through the
snow-fog, and was
received with great
joy and hospitality.
At length did cross an Albatross,
Thorough the fog it came;
As if it had been a Christian soul,   65
We hailed it in God's name.

It ate the food it ne'er had eat,
And round and round it flew.
The ice did split with a thunder-fit;
The helmsman steered us through!   70

And lo! the Alba-
tross proveth a bird
of good omen, and
followeth the ship as
it returned north-
ward through fog
and floating ice.
And a good south wind sprung up behind;
The Albatross did follow,
And every day, for food or play,
Came to the mariners' hollo!

In mist or cloud, on mast or shroud,   75
It perched for vespers° nine;   *evenings*
Whiles all the night, through fog-smoke white,
Glimmered the white Moon-shine."

The ancient Mari-
ner inhospitably kil-
leth the pious bird of
good omen.
"God save thee, ancient Mariner!
From the fiends, that plague thee thus!—   80
Why look'st thou so?"—With my crossbow
I shot the ALBATROSS.

Part II

The Sun now rose upon the right:
Out of the sea came he,
Still hid in mist, and on the left   85
Went down into the sea.

And the good south wind still blew behind,
But no sweet bird did follow,

Nor any day for food or play
Came to the mariners' hollo!   90

*His shipmates cry
out against the
ancient Mariner, for
killing the bird of
good luck.*
And I had done a hellish thing,
And it would work 'em woe:
For all averred, I had killed the bird
That made the breeze to blow.
Ah wretch! said they, the bird to slay,   95
That made the breeze to blow!

*But when the fog
cleared off, they jus-
tify the same, and
thus make them-
selves accomplices in
the crime.*
Nor dim nor red, like God's own head,
The glorious Sun uprist:°   *arose*
Then all averred, I had killed the bird
That brought the fog and mist.   100
'Twas right, said they, such birds to slay,
That bring the fog and mist.

*The fair breeze con-
tinues; the ship
enters the Pacific
Ocean, and sails
northward, even till
it reaches the Line.*
The fair breeze blew, the white foam flew,
The furrow followed free;
We were the first that ever burst   105
Into that silent sea.

*The ship hath been
suddenly becalmed.*
Down dropped the breeze, the sails dropped down,
'Twas sad as sad could be;
And we did speak only to break
The silence of the sea!   110

All in a hot and copper sky,
The bloody Sun, at noon,
Right up above the mast did stand,
No bigger than the Moon.

Day after day, day after day,   115
We stuck, nor breath nor motion;
As idle as a painted ship
Upon a painted ocean.

*And the Albatross
begins to be
avenged.*
Water, water, everywhere,
And all the boards did shrink;   120
Water, water, everywhere,
Nor any drop to drink.

The very deep did rot: O Christ!
That ever this should be!
Yea, slimy things did crawl with legs   125
Upon the slimy sea.

About, about, in reel and rout
The death-fires danced at night;
The water, like a witch's oils,
Burnt green, and blue and white.   130

And some in dreams assuréd were
Of the Spirit that plagued us so;
Nine fathom deep he had followed us
From the land of mist and snow.

*A Spirit had fol-
lowed them; one
of the invisible
inhabitants of this
planet, neither
departed souls nor angels; concerning whom the learned Jew, Josephus, and the Platonic Constantinopoli-
tan, Michael Psellus, may be consulted. They are very numerous, and there is no climate or element with-
out one or more.*

And every tongue, through utter drought,   135
Was withered at the root;
We could not speak, no more than if
We had been choked with soot.

*The shipmates, in
their sore distress,
would fain throw the
whole guilt on the
ancient Mariner: in
sign whereof they
hang the dead sea
bird round his neck.*

Ah! well-a-day! what evil looks
Had I from old and young!   140
Instead of the cross, the Albatross
About my neck was hung.

Part III

There passed a weary time. Each throat
Was parched, and glazed each eye.
A weary time! a weary time!   145
How glazed each weary eye,

*The ancient Mari-
ner beholdeth a sign
in the element afar
off.*

When looking westward, I beheld
A something in the sky.

At first it seemed a little speck,
And then it seemed a mist;   150
It moved and moved, and took at last
A certain shape, I wist.°   knew

A speck, a mist, a shape, I wist!
And still it neared and neared:
As if it dodged a water sprite,   155
It plunged and tacked and veered.

*As its nearer
approach, it seemeth
him to be a ship;
and at a dear ran-
som he freeth his
speech from the
bonds of thirst.*

With throats unslaked, with black lips baked,
We could nor laugh nor wail;
Through utter drought all dumb we stood!
I bit my arm, I sucked the blood,   160
And cried, A sail! a sail!

With throats unslaked, with black lips baked,
Agape they heard me call:

A flash of joy;

Gramercy!° they for joy did grin,   *thank heavens!*
And all at once their breath drew in,   165
As they were drinking all.

*And horror follows.
For can it be a ship
that comes onward
without wind or
tide?*

See! see! (I cried) she tacks no more!
Hither to work us weal;°   *benefit*
Without a breeze, without a tide,
She steadies with upright keel!   170

The western wave was all aflame.
The day was well nigh done!
Almost upon the western wave
Rested the broad bright Sun;
When that strange shape drove suddenly   175
Betwixt us and the Sun.

It seemeth him but the skeleton of a ship.

And straight the Sun was flecked with bars,
(Heaven's Mother send us grace!)
As if through a dungeon grate he peered
With broad and burning face.   180

And its ribs are seen as bars on the face of the setting Sun.

Alas! (thought I, and my heart beat loud)
How fast she nears and nears!
Are those *her* sails that glance in the Sun,
Like restless gossameres?°   cobwebs

The Specter-Woman and her Deathmate, and no other on board the skeleton ship.

Are those *her* ribs through which the Sun   185
Did peer, as through a grate?
And is that Woman all her crew?
Is that a DEATH? and are there two?
Is DEATH that woman's mate?

Like vessel, like crew!

Her lips were red, *her* looks were free,   190
Her locks were yellow as gold:
Her skin was as white as leprosy,
The Nightmare LIFE-IN-DEATH was she,
Who thicks man's blood with cold.

Death and Life-in-Death have diced for the ship's crew and she (the latter) winneth the ancient Mariner.

The naked hulk alongside came,   195
And the twain were casting dice;
"The game is done! I've won! I've won!"
Quoth she, and whistles thrice.

No twilight within the courts of the Sun.

The Sun's rim dips; the stars rush out:
At one stride comes the dark;   200
With far-heard whisper, o'er the sea,
Off shot the specter-bark.

At the rising of the Moon,

We listened and looked sideways up!
Fear at my heart, as at a cup,
My lifeblood seemed to sip!   205
The stars were dim, and thick the night,
The steersman's face by his lamp gleamed white;
From the sails the dew did drip—
Till clomb° above the eastern bar   climbed
The hornéd Moon, with one bright star   210
Within the nether tip.

One after another,

One after one, by the star-dogged Moon,
Too quick for groan or sigh,
Each turned his face with ghastly pang,
And cursed me with his eye.   215

His shipmates drop down dead.

Four times fifty living men,
(And I heard nor sigh nor groan)
With heavy thump, a lifeless lump,
They dropped down one by one.

But Life-in-Death begins her work on the ancient Mariner.

The souls did from their bodies fly—   220
They fled to bliss or woe!
And every soul, it passed me by,
Like the whizz of my cross-bow!

Part IV

The Wedding Guest feareth that a Spirit is talking to him;

"I fear thee, ancient Mariner!
I fear thy skinny hand!   225
And thou art long, and lank, and brown,
As is the ribbed sea-sand.

I fear thee and thy glittering eye,
And thy skinny hand, so brown."—

But the ancient Mariner assureth him of his bodily life, and proceedeth to relate his horrible penance.

Fear not, fear not, thou Wedding Guest!   230
This body dropped not down.

Alone, alone, all, all alone,
Alone on a wide wide sea!
And never a saint took pity on
My soul in agony.   235

He despiseth the creatures of the calm,

The many men, so beautiful!
And they all dead did lie:
And a thousand thousand slimy things
Lived on; and so did I.

And envieth that they should live, and so many lie dead.

I looked upon the rotting sea,   240
And drew my eyes away;
I looked upon the rotting deck,
And there the dead men lay.

I looked to heaven, and tried to pray;
But or ever a prayer had gushed,   245
A wicked whisper came, and made
My heart as dry as dust.

I closed my lids, and kept them close,
And the balls like pulses beat,
For the sky and the sea, and the sea and the sky   250
Lay like a load on my weary eye,
And the dead were at my feet.

But the curse liveth for him in the eye of the dead men.

The cold sweat melted from their limbs,
Nor rot nor reek did they:
The look with which they looked on me   255
Had never passed away.

An orphan's curse would drag to hell
A spirit from on high;
But oh! more horrible than that
Is the curse in a dead man's eye!   260
Seven days, seven nights, I saw that curse,
And yet I could not die.

The moving Moon went up the sky,
And nowhere did abide:
In his loneliness and Softly she was going up,   265
fixedness he year- And a star or two beside—
neth towards the
journeying Moon,
and the stars that Her beams bemocked the sultry main,
still sojourn, yet still Like April hoar-frost spread;
move onward; and But where the ship's huge shadow lay,
everywhere the blue The charméd water burnt alway   270
sky belongs to them, A still and awful red.
and is their
appointed rest, and
their native coun-
try and their own natural homes, which they enter unannounced, as lords that are certainly expected and
yet there is a silent joy at their arrival.

By the light of the Beyond the shadow of the ship,
Moon he beholdeth I watched the water snakes:
God's creatures of They moved in tracks of shining white,
the great calm. And when they reared, the elfish light   275
Fell off in hoary° flakes.   gray or white

Within the shadow of the ship
I watched their rich attire:
Blue, glossy green, and velvet black,
They coiled and swam; and every track   280
Was a flash of golden fire.

Their beauty and O happy living things! no tongue
their happiness. Their beauty might declare:
A spring of love gushed from my heart,
He blesseth them in And I blessed them unaware: 285
his heart. Sure my kind saint took pity on me,
And I blessed them unaware.

The spell begins to The self-same moment I could pray;
break. And from my neck so free
The Albatross fell off, and sank   290
Like lead into the sea.

Part V

Oh sleep! it is a gentle thing,
Beloved from pole to pole!
To Mary Queen the praise be given!
She sent the gentle sleep from Heaven,   295
That slid into my soul.

By grace of the holy
Mother, the ancient
Mariner is refreshed
with rain.

The silly° buckets on the deck,   *lowly, harmless*
That had so long remained,
I dreamt that they were filled with dew;
And when I awoke, it rained.   300

My lips were wet, my throat was cold,
My garments all were dank;
Sure I had drunken in my dreams,
And still my body drank.

I moved, and could not feel my limbs: 305
I was so light—almost
I thought that I had died in sleep,
And was a blessèd ghost.

He heareth sounds
and seeth strange
sights and commo-
tions in the sky and
the element.

And soon I heard a roaring wind:
It did not come anear;   310
But with its sound it shook the sails,
That were so thin and sere.°   *dry, withered*

The upper air burst into life!
And a hundred fire-flags sheen,°   *shone*
To and fro they were hurried about!   315
And to and fro, and in and out,
The wan stars danced between.

And the coming wind did roar more loud,
And the sails did sigh like sedge;[3]
And the rain poured down from one black cloud;
The Moon was at its edge.   320

The thick black cloud was cleft, and still
The Moon was at its side:
Like waters shot from some high crag,
The lightning fell with never a jag,
A river steep and wide.   325

The bodies of the
ship's crew are
inspirited, and the
ship moves on;

The loud wind never reached the ship,
Yet now the ship moved on!
Beneath the lightning and the Moon
The dead men gave a groan.   330

They groaned, they stirred, they all uprose,
Nor spake, nor moved their eyes;
It had been strange, even in a dream,
To have seen those dead men rise.

The helmsman steered, the ship moved on;   335
Yet never a breeze up-blew;
The mariners all 'gan work the ropes,
Where they were wont to do;

3. Rushlike plants bordering streams and lakes.

They raised their limbs like lifeless tools—
We were a ghastly crew.   340

The body of my brother's son
Stood by me, knee to knee:
The body and I pulled at one rope,
But he said nought to me.

But not by the souls of the men, nor by demons of earth or middle air, but by a blesséd troop of angelic spirits, sent down by the invocation of the guardian saint.

"I fear thee, ancient Mariner!"   345
Be calm, thou Wedding Guest!
'Twas not those souls that fled in pain,
Which to their corses° came again,   *corpses*
But a troop of spirits blest:

For when it dawned—they dropped their arms,   350
And clustered round the mast;
Sweet sounds rose slowly through their mouths,
And from their bodies passed.

Around, around, flew each sweet sound,
Then darted to the Sun;   355
Slowly the sounds came back again,
Now mixed, now one by one.

Sometimes a-dropping from the sky
I heard the sky-lark sing;
Sometimes all little birds that are,   360
How they seemed to fill the sea and air
With their sweet jargoning!°   *warbling*

And now 'twas like all instruments,
Now like a lonely flute;
And now it is an angel's song,   365
That makes the heavens be mute.

It ceased; yet still the sails made on
A pleasant noise till noon,
A noise like of a hidden brook
In the leafy month of June,   370
That to the sleeping woods all night
Singeth a quiet tune.

Till noon we quietly sailed on,
Yet never a breeze did breathe:
Slowly and smoothly went the ship,   375
Moved onward from beneath.

The lonesome Spirit from the South Pole carries on the ship as far as the Line, in obedience to the angelic troop, but still requireth vengeance.

Under the keel nine fathom deep,
From the land of mist and snow,
The spirit slid: and it was he
That made the ship to go.   380
The sails at noon left off their tune,
And the ship stood still also.

The Sun, right up above the mast,
Had fixed her to the ocean:
But in a minute she 'gan stir,   385
With a short uneasy motion—
Backwards and forwards half her length
With a short uneasy motion.

Then like a pawing horse let go,
She made a sudden bound: 390
It flung the blood into my head,
And I fell down in a swound.

How long in that same fit I lay,
I have not° to declare;   cannot
But ere my living life returned,   395
I heard and in my soul discerned
Two voices in the air.

The Polar Spirit's fellow demons, the invisible inhabitants of the element, take part in his wrong; and two of them relate, one to the other, that penance long and heavy for the ancient Mariner hath been accorded to the Polar Spirit, who returneth southward.

"Is it he?" quoth one, "Is this the man?
By him who died on cross,
With his cruel bow he laid full low   400
The harmless Albatross.

The spirit who bideth by himself
In the land of mist and snow,
He loved the bird that loved the man
Who shot him with his bow."   405

The other was a softer voice,
As soft as honey-dew:
Quoth he, "The man hath penance done,
And penance more will do."

Part VI

FIRST VOICE

"But tell me, tell me! speak again,   410
Thy soft response renewing—
What makes that ship drive on so fast?
What is the ocean doing?"

SECOND VOICE

"Still as a slave before his lord,
The ocean hath no blast;   415
His great bright eye most silently
Up to the Moon is cast—

If he may know which way to go;
For she guides him smooth or grim.
See, brother, see! how graciously   420
She looketh down on him."

FIRST VOICE

The Mariner hath
been cast into a
trance; for the
angelic power
causeth the vessel to
drive northward
faster than human
life could endure.

"But why drives on that ship so fast,
Without or wave or wind?"

SECOND VOICE

"The air is cut away before,
And closes from behind.   425

Fly, brother, fly! more high, more high!
Or we shall be belated:
For slow and slow that ship will go,
When the Mariner's trance is abated."

The supernatural
motion is retarded;
the Mariner awakes,
and his penance
begins anew.

I woke, and we were sailing on   430
As in a gentle weather:
'Twas night, calm night, the moon was high;
The dead men stood together.

All stood together on the deck,
For a charnel-dungeon fitter: 435
All fixed on me their stony eyes,
That in the Moon did glitter.

The pang, the curse, with which they died,
Had never passed away:
I could not draw my eyes from theirs,   440
Nor turn them up to pray.

The curse is finally
expiated.

And now this spell was snapped: once more
I viewed the ocean green,
And looked far forth, yet little saw
Of what had else been seen—   445

Like one, that on a lonesome road
Doth walk in fear and dread,
And having once turned round walks on,
And turns no more his head;
Because he knows, a frightful fiend   450
Doth close behind him tread.

But soon there breathed a wind on me,
Nor sound nor motion made:
Its path was not upon the sea,
In ripple or in shade.   455

It raised my hair, it fanned my cheek
Like a meadow-gale of spring—
It mingled strangely with my fears,
Yet it felt like a welcoming.

Swiftly, swiftly flew the ship,   460
Yet she sailed softly too:

Sweetly, sweetly blew the breeze—
On me alone it blew.

*And the ancient
Mariner beholdeth
his native country.*
Oh! dream of joy! is this indeed
The lighthouse top I see? 465
Is this the hill? is this the kirk?
Is this mine own countree?

We drifted o'er the harbor-bar,
And I with sobs did pray—
O let me be awake, my God 470
Or let me sleep alway.

The harbor-bay was clear as glass,
So smoothly it was strewn!
And on the bay the moonlight lay,
And the shadow of the Moon. 475

The rock shone bright, the kirk no less,
That stands above the rock:
The moonlight steeped in silentness
The steady weathercock.

And the bay was white with silent light, 480
Till rising from the same,
*The angelic spirits
leave the dead
bodies,*
Full many shapes, that shadows were,
In crimson colors came.

A little distance from the prow
Those crimson shadows were: 485
*And appear in their
own forms of light.*
I turned my eyes upon the deck—
Oh, Christ! what saw I there!

Each corse lay flat, lifeless and flat,
And, by the holy rood!° *cross of Christ*
A man all light, a seraph°-man, *angel-like* 490
On every corse there stood.

This seraph-band, each waved his hand:
It was a heavenly sight!
They stood as signals to the land,
Each one a lovely light; 495

This seraph-band, each waved his hand,
No voice did they impart—
No voice; but oh! the silence sank
Like music on my heart.

But soon I heard the dash of oars, 500
I heard the Pilot's cheer;
My head was turned perforce away
And I saw a boat appear.

The Pilot and the Pilot's boy,
I heard them coming fast: 505
Dear Lord in Heaven! it was a joy
The dead men could not blast.

I saw a third—I heard his voice:
It is the Hermit good!
He singeth loud his godly hymns   510
That he makes in the wood.
He'll shrieve[4] my soul, he'll wash away
The Albatross's blood.

Part VII

The Hermit of the
Wood

This Hermit good lives in that wood
Which slopes down to the sea.   515
How loudly his sweet voice he rears!
He loves to talk with marineres
That come from a far countree.

He kneels at morn, and noon, and eve—
He hath a cushion plump: 520
It is the moss that wholly hides
The rotted old oak stump.

The skiff-boat neared: I heard them talk,
"Why, this is strange, I trow!
Where are those lights so many and fair,   525
That signal made but now?"

Approacheth the
ship with wonder.

"Strange, by my faith!" the Hermit said—
"And they answered not our cheer!
The planks looked warped! and see those sails,
How thin they are and sere!   530
I never saw aught like to them,
Unless perchance it were

Brown skeletons of leaves that lag
My forest-brook along;
When the ivy tod° is heavy with snow,   *bushy clump* 535
And the owlet whoops to the wolf below,
That eats the she-wolf's young."

"Dear Lord! it hath a fiendish look,"
The Pilot made reply,
"I am a-feared"—"Push on, push on!"   540
Said the Hermit cheerily.

The boat came closer to the ship,
But I nor spake nor stirred;

---

4. Set free from sin.

The boat came close beneath the ship,
And straight a sound was heard.   545

The ship suddenly sinketh.

Under the water it rumbled on,
Still louder and more dread:
It reached the ship, it split the bay;
The ship went down like lead.

The ancient Mariner is saved in the Pilot's boat.

Stunned by that loud and dreadful sound,   550
Which sky and ocean smote,
Like one that hath been seven days drowned
My body lay afloat;
But swift as dreams, myself I found
Within the Pilot's boat.   555

Upon the whirl, where sank the ship,
The boat spun round and round;
And all was still, save that the hill
Was telling of the sound.

I moved my lips—the Pilot shrieked   560
And fell down in a fit;
The holy Hermit raised his eyes,
And prayed where he did sit.

I took the oars: the Pilot's boy,
Who now doth crazy go,   565
Laughed loud and long, and all the while
His eyes went to and fro.
"Ha! ha!" quoth he, "full plain I see,
The Devil knows how to row."

And now, all in my own countree,   570
I stood on the firm land!
The Hermit stepped forth from the boat,
And scarcely he could stand.

The ancient Mariner earnestly entreateth the Hermit to shrieve him; and the penance of life falls on him.

"O shrieve me, shrieve me, holy man!"
The Hermit crossed⁵ his brow.   575
"Say quick," quoth he, "I bid thee say—
What manner of man art thou?"

Forthwith this frame of mine was wrenched
With a woeful agony,
Which forced me to begin my tale;   580
And then it left me free.

And ever and anon throughout his future life an agony constraineth him to travel from land to land;

Since then, at an uncertain hour,
That agony returns:
And till my ghastly tale is told,
This heart within me burns.   585

5. Made the sign of the cross upon.

I pass, like night, from land to land;
I have strange power of speech;
That moment that his face I see,
I know the man that must hear me:
To him my tale I teach.   590

What loud uproar bursts from that door!
The wedding guests are there:
But in the garden-bower the bride
And bridemaids singing are:
And hark the little vesper bell,   595
Which biddeth me to prayer!

O Wedding Guest! this soul hath been
Alone on a wide wide sea:
So lonely 'twas, that God himself
Scarce seeméd there to be.   600

O sweeter than the marriage feast,
'Tis sweeter far to me,
To walk together to the kirk
With a goodly company!

To walk together to the kirk,   605
And all together pray,
While each to his great Father bends,
Old men, and babes, and loving friends
And youths and maidens gay!

And to teach, by his
own example, love   Farewell, farewell! but this I tell   610
and reverence to all To thee, thou Wedding Guest!
things that God   He prayeth well, who loveth well
made and loveth.   Both man and bird and beast.

He prayeth best, who loveth best
All things both great and small;   615
For the dear God who loveth us,
He made and loveth all.

The Mariner, whose eye is bright,
Whose beard with age is hoar,
Is gone: and now the Wedding Guest   620
Turned from the bridegroom's door.

He went like one that hath been stunned,
And is of sense forlorn:°   *deprived*
A sadder and a wiser man,
He rose the morrow morn.   625
1798   1817

Dejection: An Ode

Late, late yestreen I saw the new Moon,
With the old Moon in her arms;
And I fear, I fear, my master dear!
We shall have a deadly storm.
Ballad of Sir Patrick Spence

1

Well! If the bard was weather-wise, who made
  The grand old ballad of Sir Patrick Spence,
    This night, so tranquil now, will not go hence
Unroused by winds, that ply a busier trade
5 Than those which mold yon cloud in lazy flakes,
Or the dull sobbing draft, that moans and rakes
Upon the strings of this Aeolian lute,[6]
    Which better far were mute.
    For lo! the New-moon winter-bright!
10   And overspread with phantom light,
    (With swimming phantom light o'erspread
    But rimmed and circled by a silver thread)
I see the old Moon in her lap, foretelling
  The coming-on of rain and squally blast.
15 And oh! that even now the gust were swelling,
  And the slant night shower driving loud and fast!
Those sounds which oft have raised me, whilst they awed,
    And sent my soul abroad,
Might now perhaps their wonted° impulse give,   *usual*
20 Might startle this dull pain, and make it move and live!

2

A grief without a pang, void, dark, and drear,
  A stifled, drowsy, unimpassioned grief,
  Which finds no natural outlet, no relief,
    In word, or sigh, or tear —
25 O Lady! in this wan and heartless mood,
To other thoughts by yonder throstle° wooed,   *song thrush*
  All this long eve, so balmy and serene,
Have I been gazing on the western sky,
  And its peculiar tint of yellow green:
30 And still I gaze — and with how blank an eye!
And those thin clouds above, in flakes and bars,
That give away their motion to the stars;
Those stars, that glide behind them or between,
Now sparkling, now bedimmed, but always seen:
35 Yon crescent Moon, as fixed as if it grew
In its own cloudless, starless lake of blue;
I see them all so excellently fair,
I see, not feel, how beautiful they are!

3

    My genial spirits° fail;   *vital energies*
40   And what can these avail

6. The wind-harp (named after Aeolus, classical god of winds) has a sounding board equipped with a set of strings that vibrate in response to air currents.

To lift the smothering weight from off my breast?
    It were a vain endeavor,
      Though I should gaze forever
On that green light that lingers in the west:
45 I may not hope from outward forms to win
The passion and the life, whose fountains are within.

4

O Lady! we receive but what we give,
And in our life alone does Nature live:
Ours is her wedding garment, ours her shroud!
50   And would we aught behold, of higher worth,
Than that inanimate cold world allowed
To the poor loveless ever-anxious crowd,
    Ah! from the soul itself must issue forth
A light, a glory, a fair luminous cloud
55   Enveloping the Earth—
And from the soul itself must there be sent
    A sweet and potent voice, of its own birth,
Of all sweet sounds the life and element!

5

O pure of heart! thou need'st not ask of me
60 What this strong music in the soul may be!
What, and wherein it doth exist,
This light, this glory, this fair luminous mist,
This beautiful and beauty-making power.
    Joy, virtuous Lady! Joy that ne'er was given,
65 Save to the pure, and in their purest hour,
Life, and Life's effluence, cloud at once and shower,
Joy, Lady! is the spirit and the power,
Which wedding Nature to us gives in dower
    A new Earth and new Heaven,
70 Undreamt of by the sensual and the proud—
Joy is the sweet voice, Joy the luminous cloud—
    We in ourselves rejoice!
And thence flows all that charms or ear or sight,
    All melodies the echoes of that voice,
75 All colors a suffusion from that light.

6

There was a time when, though my path was rough,
    This joy within me dallied with distress,
And all misfortunes were but as the stuff
    Whence Fancy made me dreams of happiness:
80 For hope grew round me, like the twining vine,
And fruits, and foliage, not my own, seemed mine.
But now afflictions bow me down to earth:
Nor care I that they rob me of my mirth;
    But oh! each visitation
85 Suspends what nature gave me at my birth,
    My shaping spirit of Imagination.

For not to think of what I needs must feel,
    But to be still and patient, all I can;

And happly by abstruse research to steal
90   From my own nature all the natural man—
This was my sole resource, my only plan:
Till that which suits a part infects the whole,
And now is almost grown the habit of my soul.

7

Hence, viper thoughts, that coil around my mind,
95   Reality's dark dream!
I turn from you, and listen to the wind,
   Which long has raved unnoticed. What a scream
Of agony by torture lengthened out
That lute sent forth! Thou Wind, that rav'st without,
100   Bare crag, or mountain tairn,° or blasted tree,   *pool*
Or pine grove whither woodman never clomb,
Or lonely house, long held—the witches' home,
   Methinks were fitter instruments for thee,
Mad lutanist! who in this month of showers,
105 Of dark-brown gardens, and of peeping flowers,
Mak'st devils' yule,[7] with worse than wintry song,
The blossoms, buds, and timorous leaves among.
   Thou actor, perfect in all tragic sounds!
Thou mighty poet, e'en to frenzy bold!
110   What tell'st thou now about?
   'Tis of the rushing of an host in rout,
With groans, of trampled men, with smarting wounds—
At once they groan with pain, and shudder with the cold!
But hush! there is a pause of deepest silence!
115   And all that noise, as of a rushing crowd,
With groans, and tremulous shudderings—all is over—
   It tells another tale, with sounds less deep and loud!
    A tale of less affright,
    And tempered with delight,
120 As Otway's[8] self had framed the tender lay—
    'Tis of a little child
    Upon a lonesome wild,
Not far from home, but she hath lost her way:
And now moans low in bitter grief and fear,
125 And now screams loud, and hopes to make her mother hear.

8

'Tis midnight, but small thoughts have I of sleep:
Full seldom may my friend such vigils keep!
Visit her, gentle Sleep! with wings of healing,
   And may this storm be but a mountain birth,
130 May all the stars hang bright above her dwelling,
   Silent as though they watched the sleeping Earth!
    With light heart may she rise,
    Gay fancy, cheerful eyes,
Joy lift her spirit, joy attune her voice;
135 To her may all things live, from pole to pole,

---

7. A winter storm in spring; hence, an unnatural or "devils'" Christmas.
8. Thomas Otway (1652–1685), poet and drama- tist, author of "The Poet's Complaint of His Muse" (1680), a work thought to have influenced Cole- ridge.

Their life the eddying of her living soul!
  O simple spirit, guided from above,
Dear Lady! friend devoutest of my choice,
Thus mayest thou ever, evermore rejoice.

1802   1817

WALTER SAVAGE LANDOR
1775–1864

Rose Aylmer[1]

Ah what avails the sceptered race,
  Ah what the form divine!
What every virtue, every grace!
  Rose Aylmer, all were thine.
5 Rose Aylmer, whom these wakeful eyes
    May weep, but never see,
A night of memories and of sighs
  I consecrate to thee.

1806, 1831, 1846

Past Ruined Ilion Helen[2] Lives

Past ruined Ilion Helen lives,
  Alcestis[3] rises from the shades;
Verse calls them forth; 'tis verse that gives
  Immortal youth to mortal maids.

5 Soon shall Oblivion's deepening veil
    Hide all the peopled hills you see,
The gay, the proud, while lovers hail
  In distant ages you and me.

The tear for fading beauty check,
10   For passing glory cease to sigh;
One form shall rise above the wreck,
  One name, Ianthe,[4] shall not die.

1831

Dirce

Stand close around, ye Stygian set,[5]
  With Dirce in one boat conveyed!

---

1. The Honorable Rose Whitworth Aylmer (1779–1800), whom Landor had known in Wales, died suddenly in Calcutta on March 2, 1800.
2. Helen of Troy ("Ilion").
3. Alcestis sacrificed her life for her husband, who was stricken with a mortal illness. She acted in accordance with Apollo's promise that he might thus be saved; she was then brought back from the underworld by Hercules.
4. The name given by Landor to Sophia Jane Swift, an Irishwoman who eventually became Countess de Morlandé.
5. The shades of the dead who were ferried by Charon over the river Styx to Hades.

Or Charon, seeing may forget
That he is old and she a shade.

1831, 1846

To Robert Browning

There is delight in singing, though none hear
Beside the singer; and there is delight
In praising, though the praiser sit alone
And see the praised far off him, far above.
5   Shakspeare is not *our* poet, but the world's,
Therefore on him no speech; and short for thee,
Browning! Since Chaucer was alive and hale,
No man hath walked along our roads with step
So active, so inquiring eye, or tongue
10   So varied in discourse. But warmer climes
Give brighter plumage, stronger wing; the breeze
Of Alpine heights thou playest with, borne on
Beyond Sorrento and Amalfi,[6] where
The Siren waits thee, singing song for song.

1845

Dying Speech of an Old Philosopher

I strove with none, for none was worth my strife:
   Nature I loved, and, next to Nature, Art:
I warmed both hands before the fire of Life;
   It sinks; and I am ready to depart.

1849

Death Stands Above Me, Whispering Low

Death stands above me, whispering low
   I know not what into my ear:
Of his strange language all I know
   Is, there is not a word of fear.

1853

Death of the Day

My pictures blacken in their frames
   As night comes on,
And youthful maids and wrinkled dames
   Are now all one.

5   Death of the day! a sterner Death
   Did worse before;
The fairest form, the sweetest breath,
   Away he bore.

1858

6. Towns near Naples that Browning had visited on his second trip to Italy in 1844, and that figure in some of his early poems. According to legend, the Sirens had drowned themselves in despair when Odysseus escaped the lure of their song; one of them, Parthenope, cast up on the shore of the bay of Naples, gave that city its ancient name.

FRANCIS SCOTT KEY

1779–1843

Defence of Fort McHenry[1]

O! say can you see, by the dawn's early light,
  What so proudly we hail'd at the twilight's last gleaming,
Whose broad stripes and bright stars through the perilous fight,
  O'er the ramparts we watch'd, were so gallantly streaming?
5   And the rockets' red glare, the bombs bursting in air,
    Gave proof through the night that our flag was still there—
      O! say, does that star-spangled banner yet wave
      O'er the land of the free, and the home of the brave?

On the shore, dimly seen through the mists of the deep,
10   Where the foe's haughty host in dread silence reposes,
What is that which the breeze o'er the towering steep,
  As it fitfully blows, half conceals, half discloses?
    Now it catches the gleam of the morning's first beam,
    In full glory reflected now shines on the stream—
15   'Tis the star-spangled banner, O! long may it wave
      O'er the land of the free, and the home of the brave.

And where is that band who so vauntingly swore
  That the havock of war and the battle's confusion
A home and a country should leave us no more?
20   Their blood has wash'd out their foul foot-steps' pollution.
    No refuge could save the hireling and slave,
    From the terror of flight or the gloom of the grave;
      And the star-spangled banner in triumph doth wave
      O'er the land of the free, and the home of the brave.

25 O! thus be it ever when freemen shall stand
  Between their lov'd home, and the war's desolation,
Blest with vict'ry and peace, may the heav'n-rescued land
  Praise the power that hath made and preserv'd us a nation!
    Then conquer we must, when our cause it is just,
30   And this be our motto—"In God is our trust!"
      And the star-spangled banner in triumph shall wave
      O'er the land of the free, and the home of the brave.

1814   1814, 1857

1. A version of what is called "The Star-Spangled Banner," now the national anthem of the United States. Key witnessed the British bombardment of Baltimore in 1814. On the dawn of September 14, he was moved to see the American flag still flying over Fort McHenry.

GEORGE GORDON, LORD BYRON
1788–1824

Written After Swimming from Sestos to Abydos[1]

1

If, in the month of dark December,
    Leander, who was nightly wont
(What maid will not the tale remember?)
    To cross thy stream, broad Hellespont!

2

5 If, when the wintry tempest roared,
    He sped to Hero, nothing loath,
And thus of old thy current poured,
    Fair Venus! how I pity both!

3

For *me*, degenerate modern wretch,
10   Though in the genial month of May,
My dripping limbs I faintly stretch,
    And think I've done a feat today.

4

But since he crossed the rapid tide,
    According to the doubtful story,
15 To woo—and—Lord knows what beside,
    And swam for Love, as I for Glory;

5

'Twere hard to say who fared the best:
    Sad mortals! thus the gods still plague you!
He lost his labor, I my jest;
20   For he was drowned, and I've the ague.°   *chills and fever*

                                                1812

The Destruction of Sennacherib[2]

1

The Assyrian came down like the wolf on the fold,
And his cohorts were gleaming in purple and gold;
And the sheen of their spears was like stars on the sea,
When the blue wave rolls nightly on deep Galilee.

2

5 Like the leaves of the forest when summer is green,
That host with their banners at sunset were seen:
Like the leaves of the forest when autumn hath blown,
That host on the morrow lay withered and strown.

---

1. The Hellespont, or Dardanelles, is the strait separating Europe from Asia Minor, between Abydos on the Greek shore and Sestos on the Asian. In Greek legend, Leander used to swim from Abydos to visit his sweetheart, Hero, at Sestos. 2. Assyrian king, whose armies, while besieging Jerusalem (701 B.C.), were attacked by a violent plague (2 Kings 19.35).

3

For the Angel of Death spread his wings on the blast,
10 And breathed in the face of the foe as he passed;
And the eyes of the sleepers waxed deadly and chill,
And their hearts but once heaved, and forever grew still!

4

And there lay the steed with his nostril all wide,
But through it there rolled not the breath of his pride;
15 And the foam of his gasping lay white on the turf,
And cold as the spray of the rock-beating surf.

5

And there lay the rider distorted and pale,
With the dew on his brow, and the rust on his mail:
And the tents were all silent, the banners alone,
20 The lances unlifted, the trumpet unblown.

6

And the widows of Ashur[3] are loud in their wail,
And the idols are broke in the temple of Baal;[4]
And the might of the Gentile,[5] unsmote by the sword,
Hath melted like snow in the glance of the Lord!

1815

She Walks in Beauty

1

She walks in beauty, like the night
    Of cloudless climes and starry skies;
And all that's best of dark and bright
    Meet in her aspect and her eyes:
5 Thus mellowed to that tender light
    Which heaven to gaudy day denies.

2

One shade the more, one ray the less,
    Had half impaired the nameless grace
Which waves in every raven tress,
10   Or softly lightens o'er her face;
Where thoughts serenely sweet express
    How pure, how dear their dwelling place.

3

And on that cheek, and o'er that brow,
    So soft, so calm, yet eloquent,
15 The smiles that win, the tints that glow,
    But tell of days in goodness spent,
A mind at peace with all below,
    A heart whose love is innocent!

1815

3. Assyria.
4. Deity of the Assyrians.

5. Here, Sennacherib; anyone not a Hebrew.

When We Two Parted

When we two parted
   In silence and tears,
Half broken-hearted
   To sever for years,
5 Pale grew thy cheek and cold,
   Colder thy kiss;
Truly that hour foretold
   Sorrow to this.

The dew of the morning
10   Sunk chill on my brow—
It felt like the warning
   Of what I feel now.
Thy vows are all broken,
   And light is thy fame;
15 I hear thy name spoken,
   And share in its shame.

They name thee before me,
   A knell to mine ear;
A shudder comes o'er me—
20   Why wert thou so dear?
They know not I knew thee,
   Who knew thee too well—
Long, long shall I rue thee,
   Too deeply to tell.

25 In secret we met—
   In silence I grieve,
That thy heart could forget,
   Thy spirit deceive.
If I should meet thee
30   After long years,
How should I greet thee?—
   With silence and tears.

1813   1816

So We'll Go No More A-Roving

1

So we'll go no more a-roving
   So late into the night,
Though the heart be still as loving,
   And the moon be still as bright.

2

5 For the sword outwears its sheath,
   And the soul wears out the breast,
And the heart must pause to breathe,
   And Love itself have rest.

3

Though the night was made for loving,
10   And the day returns too soon,
Yet we'll go no more a-roving
    By the light of the moon.

1817   1836

From Don Juan[6]

Fragment
On the Back of the Ms. of Canto I

I would to Heaven that I were so much clay,
    As I am blood, bone, marrow, passion, feeling—
Because at least the past were passed away,
    And for the future—(but I write this reeling,
5 Having got drunk exceedingly to-day,
    So that I seem to stand upon the ceiling)
I say—the future is a serious matter—
And so—for God's sake—hock and soda-water![7]

From *Canto the First*

1

I want° a hero: an uncommon want,   *lack*
    When every year and month sends forth a new one,
Till, after cloying the gazettes[8] with cant,
    The age discovers he is not the true one;
5 Of such as these I should not care to vaunt,
    I'll therefore take our ancient friend Don Juan—
We all have seen him, in the pantomime,[9]
Sent to the Devil somewhat ere his time.

2

Vernon, the butcher Cumberland, Wolfe, Hawke,
10 Prince Ferdinand, Granby, Burgoyne, Keppel, Howe,[1]
Evil and good, have had their tithe of talk,
    And filled their sign-posts then, like Wellesley now;
Each in their turn like Banquo's monarchs stalk,
    Followers of Fame, "nine farrow" of that sow:
15 France, too, had Buonaparté and Dumourier
Recorded in the *Moniteur* an *Courier*.[2]

---

6. The hero is a legendary Spanish nobleman, a notorious seducer of women; in most versions, but not Byron's satire, finally carried off to hell. Canto I comprises 222 stanzas; stanzas 1–119, given here, conclude with the end of the romance between Don Juan and Donna Julia.
7. Hock is Rhine wine, a supposed remedy for the hangover.
8. Official notices or newspapers.
9. I.e., on the stage, in one or another of many adaptations.
1. British military leaders of the eighteenth century, their fame extinguished by more recent "heroes," such as Wellesley (line 12), the duke of Wellington, who defeated Napoleon at Waterloo.
2. "Banquo's monarchs" (line 13), in *Macbeth* 4.1.112–13. The sow, "Fame" (line 14), eats her own offspring ("farrow")—i.e., the "heroes" just listed. "Buonaparté" (line 15) is Napoleon, and Dumourier a French general, whose victories and defeats were chronicled in the French newspapers *Gazette Nationale; ou le Moniteur Universel* and *le Courier Republicain*.

3

Barnave, Brissot, Condorcet, Mirabeau,
　　Petion, Clootz, Danton, Marat, La Fayette[3]
Were French, and famous people, as we know;
20　　And there were others, scarce forgotten yet,
Joubert, Hoche, Marceau, Lannes, Desaix, Moreau,[4]
　　With many of the military set,
Exceedingly remarkable at times,
But not at all adapted to my rhymes.

4

25　Nelson[5] was once Britannia's god of War,
　　And still should be so, but the tide is turned;
There's no more to be said of Trafalgar,
　　'Tis with our hero quietly inurned;
Because the army's grown more popular,
30　　At which the naval people are concerned;
Besides, the Prince is all for the land-service,
Forgetting Duncan, Nelson, Howe, and Jervis.[6]

5

Brave men were living before Agamemnon[7]
　　And since, exceeding valorous and sage,
35　A good deal like him too, though quite the same none;
　　But then they shone not on the poet's page,
And so have been forgotten:—I condemn none,
　　But can't find any in the present age
Fit for my poem (that is, for my new one);
40　So, as I said, I'll take my friend Don Juan.

6

Most epic poets plunge *"in medias res"*[8]
　　(Horace makes this the heroic turnpike road),
And then your hero tells, when'er you please,
　　What went before—by way of episode,
45　While seated after dinner at his ease,
　　Beside his mistress in some soft abode,
Palace, or garden, paradise, or cavern,
Which serves the happy couple for a tavern.

7

That is the usual method, but not mine—
50　My way is to begin with the beginning;
The regularity of my design
　　Forbids all wandering as the worst of sinning,
And therefore I shall open with a line
　　(Although it cost me half an hour in spinning),
55　Narrating somewhat of Don Juan's father,
And also of his mother, if you'd rather.

---

3. French generals and politicians connected with the French Revolution, many of them guillotined.
4. Other French military men; most of these died in battle.
5. British naval hero, fatally wounded at the Battle of Trafalgar, 1805.
6. British naval commanders. "The Prince" (line 31): the Prince of Wales.
7. Commander of the Greeks at the siege of Troy.
8. Horace (65–68 B.C.; Roman poet and satirist) asserted, in *Ars Poetica* 148–49, that the writer of an epic should rush his readers "into the middle of the story."

8

In Seville was he born, a pleasant city,
  Famous for oranges and women—he
Who has not seen it will be much to pity,
60   So says the proverb—and I quite agree;
Of all the Spanish towns is none more pretty,
  Cadiz perhaps—but that you soon may see;
Don Juan's parents lived beside the river,
A noble stream, and called the Guadalquivir.

9

65 His father's name was José—*Don*, of course,—
  A true Hidalgo,[9] free from every stain
Of Moor or Hebrew blood, he traced his source
  Through the most Gothic gentlemen of Spain;[1]
A better cavalier ne'er mounted horse,
70   Or, being mounted, e'er got down again,
Than José, who begot our hero, who
Begot—but that's to come—Well, to renew:

10

His mother was a learnéd lady, famed
  For every branch of every science known—
75 In every Christian language ever named,
  With virtues equaled by her wit alone:
She made the cleverest people quite ashamed,
  And even the good with inward envy groan,
Finding themselves so very much exceeded,
80 In their own way, by all the things that she did.

11

Her memory was a mine: she knew by heart
  All Calderon and greater part of Lopé,[2]
So, that if any actor missed his part,
  She could have served him for the prompter's copy;
85 For her Feinagle's[3] were an useless art,
  And he himself obliged to shut up shop—he
Could never make a memory so fine as
That which adorned the brain of Donna Inez.

12

Her favorite science was the mathematical,
90   Her noblest virtue was her magnanimity,
Her wit (she sometimes tried at wit) was Attic[4] all,
  Her serious sayings darkened to sublimity;
In short, in all things she was fairly what I call
  A prodigy—her morning dress was dimity,
95 Her evening silk, or, in the summer, muslin,
And other stuffs, with which I won't stay puzzling.

---

9. Spanish noble of minor degree.
1. Descended from the Visigoths, who conquered Spain in the fifth century A.D.
2. Calderón (1600–1681) and Lopé de Vega (1562–1635), preeminent Spanish dramatists.
3. Gregor von Feinagle (1765–1819) was the originator of mnemonics, a method of memorization. He lectured in England in 1811.
4. Athenian: i.e., refined, learned.

13

She knew the Latin—that is, "the Lord's prayer,"
    And Greek—the alphabet—I'm nearly sure;
She read some French romances here and there,
100   Although her mode of speaking was not pure;
For native Spanish she had no great care,
    At least her conversation was obscure;
Her thoughts were theorems, her words a problem,
As if she deemed that mystery would ennoble 'em.

14

105 She liked the English and the Hebrew tongue,
    And said there was analogy between 'em;
She proved it somehow out of sacred song,
    But I must leave the proofs of those who've seen 'em;
But this I heard her say, and can't be wrong,
110   And all may think which way their judgments lean 'em,
" 'Tis strange—the Hebrew noun which means 'I am,'[5]
The English always use to govern d——n."

15

Some women use their tongues—she *looked* a lecture,
    Each eye a sermon, and her brow a homily,
115 An all-in-all sufficient self-director,
    Like the lamented late Sir Samuel Romilly,[6]
The Law's expounder, and the State's corrector,
    Whose suicide was almost an anomaly—
One sad example more, that "All is vanity"—
120 (The jury brought their verdict in "Insanity!")

16

In short, she was a walking calculation,
    Miss Edgeworth's novels stepping from their covers,
Or Mrs. Trimmer's books on education,
    Or "Coelebs' Wife"[7] set out in quest of lovers,
125 Morality's prim personifation,
    In which not Envy's self a flaw discovers;
To others' share let "female errors fall,"[8]
For she had not even one—the worst of all.

17

Oh! she was perfect past all parallel—
130   Of any modern female saint's comparison;
So far above the cunning powers of Hell,
    Her Guardian Angel had given up his garrison;
Even her minutest motions went as well
    As those of the best time-piece made by Harrison;[9]
135 In virtues nothing earthly could surpass her,
    Save thine "incomparable oil," Macassar![1]

5. The name of God, "I am that I am" (see Exodus 3.14); English gentlemen traveling on the European continent were sometimes known as "Goddams," from their habitual profanity.
6. Lawyer for Byron's wife in a suit for separation.
7. A novel by Hannah More, who like Maria Edgeworth (line 122) and Sarah Trimmer (line 123) was a writer whom Byron could not take seriously.
8. Quoted from Pope, *The Rape of the Lock* 2.17; frailties or foibles.
9. John Harrison (1693–1776) improved the accuracy of watches and chronometers.
1. A much-advertised hairdressing.

18

Perfect she was, but as perfection is
    Insipid in this naughty world of ours,
Where our first parents² never learned to kiss
140   Till they were exiled from their earlier bowers,
Where all was peace, and innocence, and bliss,
    (I wonder how they got through the twelve hours),
Don José, like a lineal son of Eve,
Went plucking various fruit without her leave.

19

145 He was a mortal of the careless kind,
    With no great love for learning, or the learned,
Who chose to go where'er he had a mind,
    And never dreamed his lady was concerned;
The world, as usual, wickedly inclined
150   To see a kingdom or a house o'erturned,
Whispered he had a mistress, some said *two*.
But for domestic quarrels *one* will do.

20

Now Donna Inez had, with all her merit,
    A great opinion of her own good qualities;
155 Neglect, indeed, requires a saint to bear it,
    And such, indeed, she was in her moralities;°   *moralizing*
But then she had a devil of a spirit,
    And sometimes mixed up fancies with realities,
And let few opportunities escape
160 Of getting her liege lord into a scrape.

21

This was an easy matter with a man
    Oft in the wrong, and never on his guard;
And even the wisest, do the best they can,
    Have moments, hours, and days, so unprepared,
165 That you might "brain them with their lady's fan";³
    And sometimes ladies hit exceeding hard,
And fans turn into falchions° in fair hands,   *swords*
And why and wherefore no one understands.

22

'Tis pity learnéd virgins ever wed
170   With persons of no sort of education,
Or gentlemen, who, though well born and bred,
    Grow tired of scientific conversation:
I don't choose to say much upon this head,
    I'm a plain man, and in a single station,
175 But—Oh! ye lords of ladies intellectual,
Inform us truly, have they not hen-pecked you all?

23

Don José and his lady quarrelled—*why*,
    Not any of the many could divine,

---

2. I.e., Adam and Eve.
3. Modified quotation from Shakespeare, *1 Henry IV* 2.3.

Though several thousand people chose to try,
180   'Twas surely no concern of theirs nor mine;
I loath that low vice—curiosity;
    But if there's anything in which I shine,
'Tis in arranging all my friends' affairs,
Not having, of my own, domestic cares.

24

185 And so I interfered, and with the best
    Intentions, but their treatment was not kind;
I think the foolish people were possessed,
    For neither of them could I ever find,
Although their porter afterwards confessed—
190   But that's no matter, and the worst's behind,
For little Juan o'er me threw, down stairs,
A pail of housemaid's water unawares.

25

A little curly-headed, good-for-nothing,
    And mischief-making monkey from his birth;
195 His parents ne'er agreed except in doting
    Upon the most unquiet imp on earth;
Instead of quarrelling, had they been but both in
    Their senses, they'd have sent young master forth
To school, or had him soundly whipped at home,
200 To teach him manners for the time to come.

26

Don José and the Donna Inez led
    For some time an unhappy sort of life,
Wishing each other, not divorced, but dead;
    They lived respectably as man and wife,
205 Their conduct was exceedingly well-bred,
    And gave no outward signs of inward strife,
Until at length the smothered fire broke out,
And put the business past all kind of doubt.

27

For Inez called some druggists and physicians,
210   And tried to prove her loving lord was *mad*,
But as he had some lucid intermissions,
    She next decided he was only *bad*;
Yet when they asked her for her depositions,
    No sort of explanation could be had,
215 Save that her duty both to man and God
Required this conduct—which seemed very odd.

28

She kept a journal, where his faults were noted,
    And opened certain trunks of books and letters,
All which might, if occasion served, be quoted;
220   And then she had all Seville for abettors,
Besides her good old grandmother (who doted);
    The hearers of her case became repeaters,
Then advocates, inquisitors, and judges,
Some for amusement, others for old grudges.

29

225 And then this best and meekest woman bore
    With such serenity her husband's woes,
Just as the Spartan ladies did of yore,
    Who saw their spouses killed, and nobly chose
Never to say a word about them more—
230   Calmly she heard each calumny that rose,
And saw *his* agonies with such sublimity,
That all the world exclaimed, "What magnanimity!"

30

No doubt this patience, when the world is damning us,
    Is philosophic in our former friends;
235 'Tis also pleasant to be deemed magnanimous,
    The more so in obtaining our own ends;
And what the lawyers call a *"malus animus"*[4]
    Conduct like this by no means comprehends:
Revenge in person's certainly no virtue,
240 But then 'tis no *my* fault, if *others* hurt you.

31

And if our quarrels should rip up old stories,
    And help them with a lie or two additional,
I'm not to blame, as you well know—no more is
    Any one else—they were become traditional;
245 Besides, their resurrection aids our glories
    By contrast, which is what we just were wishing all:
And Science profits by this resurrection—
Dead scandals form good subjects for dissection.

32

Their friends had tried at reconciliation,
250   Then their relations, who made matters worse.
('Twere hard to tell upon a like occasion
    To whom it may be best to have recourse—
I can't say much for friend or yet relation):
    The lawyers did their utmost for divorce,
255 But scarce a fee was paid on either side
Before, unluckily, Don José died.

33

He died: and most unluckily, because,
    According to all hints I could collect
From Counsel learnéd in those kinds of laws,
260   (Although their talk's obscure and circumspect)
His death contrived to spoil a charming cause;°   legal case
    A thousand pities also with respect
To public feeling, which on this occasion
Was manifested in a great sensation.

34

265 But ah! he died; and buried with him lay
    The public feeling and the lawyers' fees:
His house was sold, his servants sent away,

---

4. "Malicious intent" (Latin).

A Jew took one of his two mistresses,
A priest the other—at least so they say:
270   I asked the doctors after his disease—
He died of the slow fever called the tertian,[5]
And left his widow to her own aversion.

35

Yet José was an honorable man,
    That I must say, who knew him very well;
275   Therefore his frailties I'll no further scan,
    Indeed there were not many more to tell:
And if his passions now and then outran
    Discretion, and were not so peaceable
As Numa's (who was also named Pompilius),[6]
280   He had been ill brought up, and was born bilious.

36

Whate'er might be his worthlessness or worth,
    Poor fellow! he had many things to wound him.
Let's own—since it can do no good on earth—
    It was a trying moment that which found him
285   Standing alone beside his desolate hearth,
    Where all his household gods lay shivered° round him: *broken*
No choice was left his feelings or his pride,
Save Death or Doctor's Commons° so he died.   *divorce courts*

37

Dying intestate,° Juan was sole heir   *leaving no will*
290   To a chancery suit,[7] and messuages,° and lands,   *household lands*
Which, with a long minority[8] and care,
    Promised to turn out well in proper hands:
Inez became sole guardian, which was fair,
    And answered but to Nature's just demands;
295   An only son left with an only mother
Is brought up much more wisely than another.

38

Sagest of women, even of widows, she
    Resolved that Juan should be quite a paragon,
And worthy of the noblest pedigree,
300   (His Sire was of Castile, his Dam from Aragon):
Then, for accomplishments of chivalry,
    In case our Lord the King should go to war again,
He learned the arts of riding, fencing, gunnery,
And how to scale a fortress—or a nunnery.

39

305   But that which Donna Inez most desired,
    And saw into herself each day before all
The learnéd tutors whom for him she hired,
    Was, that his breeding should be strictly moral:
Much into all his studies she inquired,
310   And so they were submitted first to her, all,

---

5. A form of malaria.
6. Ancient Roman king, famed for the compara-
tive peace of his forty-three-year reign.

7. Drawn-out legal proceedings over inheritance
of property.
8. Before he should come of age.

Arts, sciences—no branch was made a mystery
To Juan's eyes, excepting natural history.

40

The languages, especially the dead,
  The sciences, and most of all the abstruse,
315 The arts, at least all such as could be said
    To be the most remote from common use,
In all these he was much and deeply read:
    But not a page of anything that's loose,
Or hints continuation of the species,
320 Was ever suffered, lest he should grow vicious.

41

His classic studies made a little puzzle,
    Because of filthy loves of gods and goddesses,
Who in the earlier ages raised a bustle,
    But never put on pantaloons or bodices;
325 His reverend tutors had at times a tussle,
    And for their Aeneids, Iliads, and Odysseys,
Were forced to make an odd sort of apology,
For Donna Inez dreaded the Mythology.

42

Ovid's a rake, as half his verses show him,
330   Anacreon's morals are a still worse sample,
Catullus scarcely has a decent poem,
    I don't think Sappho's Ode a good example,[9]
Although Longinus[1] tells us there is no hymn
    Where the Sublime soars forth on wings more ample;
335 But Virgil's songs are pure, except that horrid one
Beginning with *"Formosum Pastor Corydon."*[2]

43

Lucretius' irreligion is too strong
    For early stomachs, to prove wholesome food;
I can't help thinking Juvenal was wrong,
340   Although no doubt his real intent was good,
For speaking out so plainly in his song,
    So much indeed as to be downright rude;
And then what proper person can be partial
To all those nauseous epigrams of Martial?[3]

44

345 Juan was taught from out the best edition,
    Expurgated by learnéd men, who place,
Judiciously, from out the schoolboy's vision,
    The grosser parts; but, fearful to deface
Too much their modest bard by this omission,
350   And pitying sore his mutilated case,

9. These lines name Greek and Roman classic and erotic poets.
1. The presumed author (first century A.D.) of a treatise on "the sublime" in literature.
2. "Handsome Shepherd Corydon": opening words of Virgil's Second Eclogue (a pastoral poem), concerned with love between young men.
3. Like Lucretius (line 337) and Juvenal (line 339), a Roman poet. Lucretius was a philosophic atheist; Juvenal and Martial were severe and sometimes obscene satirists.

They only add them all in an appendix,[4]
Which saves, in fact, the trouble of an index;

45

For there we have them all "at one fell swoop,"[5]
    Instead of being scattered through the pages;
355 They stand forth marshaled in a handsome troop,
    To meet the ingenuous youth of future ages,
Till some less rigid editor shall stoop
    To call them back into their separate cages,
Instead of standing staring all together,
360 Like garden gods[6]—and not so decent either.

46

The Missal too (it was the family Missal)
    Was ornamented in a sort of way
Which ancient mass-books often are, and this all
    Kinds of grotesques illumined; and how they,
365 Who saw those figures on the margin kiss all,
    Could turn their optics to the text and pray,
Is more than I know—But Don Juan's mother
Kept this herself, and gave her son another.

47

Sermons he read, and lectures he endured,
370   And homilies, and lives of all the saints;
To Jerome and to Chrysostom[7] inured,
    He did not take such studies for restraints;
But how Faith is acquired, and then insured,
    So well not one of the aforesaid paints
375 As Saint Augustine[8] in his fine Confessions,
Which make the reader envy his transgressions.

48

This, too, was a sealed book to little Juan—
    I can't but say that his mamma was right,
If such an education was the true one.
380   She scarcely trusted him from out her sight;
Her maids were old, and if she took a new one,
    You might be sure she was a perfect fright;
She did this during even her husband's life—
I recommend as much to every wife.

49

385 Young Juan waxed in goodliness and grace;
    At six a charming child, and at eleven
With all the promise of as fine a face
    As e'er to man's maturer growth was given:
He studied steadily, and grew apace,

---

4. "Fact! There is, or was, such an edition, with all the obnoxious epigrams of Martial placed by themselves at the end" [Byron's note].
5. Allusion to Macduff's reaction, upon learning of the death of his family: "What! All my pretty chickens and their dam / At one fell swoop?" (Shakespeare, *Macbeth* 4.3.219).
6. Statues of fertility deities, often phallic.
7. Saints and teachers of the early Church.
8. Another early father of the Church; his autobiography candidly describes his worldy life before conversion.

390   And seemed, at least, in the right road to Heaven,
       For half his days were passed at church, the other
       Between his tutors, confessor,° and mother.   *private chaplain*

50

       At six, I said, he was a charming child,
          At twelve he was a fine, but quiet boy;
395   Although in infancy a little wild,
          They tamed him down amongst them: to destroy
       His natural spirit not in vain they toiled,
          At least it seemed so; and his mother's joy
       Was to declare how sage, and still, and steady,
400   Her young philosopher was grown already.

51

       I had my doubts, perhaps I have them still,
          But what I say is neither here nor there:
       I knew his father well, and have some skill
          In character—but it would not be fair
405   From sire to son to augur good or ill:
          He and his wife were an ill-sorted pair—
       But scandal's my aversion—I protest
       Against all evil speaking, even in jest.

52

       For my part I say nothing—nothing—but
410   *This* I will say—my reasons are my own—
       That if I had an only son to put
          To school (as God be praised that I have none),
       'Tis not with Donna Inez I would shut
          Him up to learn his catechism[9] alone,
415   No—no—I'd send him out betimes to college,
       For there it was I picked up my own knowledge.

53

       For there one learns—'tis not for me to boast,
          Though I acquired—but I pass over *that,*
       As well as all the Greek I since have lost:
420   I say that there's the place—but *"Verbum sat,"*[1]
       I think I picked up too, as well as most,
          Knowledge of matters—but no matter *what*—
       I never married—but, I think, I know
       That sons should not be educated so.

54

425   Young Juan now was sixteen years of age,
          Tall, handsome, slender, but well knit: he seemed
       Active, though not so sprightly, as a page;
          And everybody but his mother deemed
       Him almost man; but she flew in a rage
430   And bit her lips (for else she might have screamed)
       If any said so—for to be precocious
       Was in her eyes a thing the most atrocious.

---

9. A brief summary of Christian teaching.   1. "A word to the wise suffices" (Latin).

55

Amongst her numerous acquaintance, all
    Selected for discretion and devotion,
435 There was the Donna Julia, whom to call
    Pretty were but to give a feeble notion
Of many charms in her as natural
    As sweetness to the flower, or salt to Ocean,
Her zone° to Venus,[2] or his bow to Cupid,   *girdle*
440 (But this last simile is trite and stupid.)

56

The darkness of her Oriental eye
    Accorded with her Moorish origin;
(Her blood was not all Spanish; by the by,
    In Spain, you know, this is a sort of sin;)
445 When proud Granada fell, and, forced to fly,
    Boabdil[3] wept: of Donna Julia's kin
Some went to Africa, some stayed in Spain—
Her great great grandmamma chose to remain.

57

She married (I forget the pedigree)
450   With an Hidalgo, who transmitted down
His blood less noble than such blood should be;
    At such alliances his sires would frown,
In that point so precise in each degree
    That they bred *in and in*, as might be shown,
455 Marrying their cousins—nay, their aunts, and nieces,
Which always spoils the breed, if it increases.

58

This heathenish cross restored the breed again,
    Ruined its blood,[4] but much improved its flesh;
For from a root the ugliest in Old Spain
460   Sprung up a branch as beautiful as fresh;
The sons no more were short, the daughters plain:
    But there's a rumor which I fain would hush,
'Tis said that Donna Julia's grandmamma
Produced her Don more heirs at love than law.

59

465 However this might be, the race went on
    Improving still through every generation,
Until it centered in an only son,
    Who left an only daughter; my narration
May have suggested that this single one
470   Could be but Julia (whom on this occasion
I shall have much to speak about), and she
Was married, charming, chaste, and twenty-three.

60

Her eye (I'm very fond of handsome eyes)
    Was large and dark, suppressing half its fire

---

2. The magical girdle of Venus (Aphrodite) made its wearer sexually attractive.
3. The last Mohammedan ruler of Granada, a province of Spain.
4. Bloodline, i.e., pure lineage.

475 Until she spoke, then through its soft disguise
    Flashed an expression more of pride than ire,
And love than either; and there would arise
    A something in them which was not desire,
But would have been, perhaps, but for the soul
480 Which struggled through and chastened down the whole.

61

Her glossy hair was clustered o'er a brow
    Bright with intelligence, and fair, and smooth;
Her eyebrow's shape was like the aërial bow,°   *rainbow*
    Her cheek all purple° with the beam of youth,   *rosy*
485 Mounting, at times, to a transparent glow,
    As if her veins ran lightning; she, in sooth,
Possessed an air and grace by no means common:
Her stature tall—I hate a dumpy woman.

62

Wedded she was some years, and to a man
490   Of fifty, and such husbands are in plenty;
And yet, I think, instead of such a ONE
    'Twere better to have TWO of five-and-twenty,
Especially in countries near the sun:
    And now I think on't, "*mi vien in mente,*"[5]
495 Ladies even of the most uneasy virtue
Prefer a spouse whose age is short of thirty.

63

'Tis a sad thing, I cannot choose but say,
    And all the fault of that indecent sun,
Who cannot leave alone our helpless clay,
500   But will keep baking, broiling, burning on,
That howsoever people fast and pray,
    The flesh is frail, and so the soul undone:
What men call gallantry, and gods adultery,
Is much more common where the climate's sultry.

64

505 Happy the nations of the moral North!
    Where all is virtue, and the winter season
Sends sin, without a rag on, shivering forth
    ('Twas snow that brought St. Anthony to reason);[6]
Where juries cast up what a wife is worth,
510   By laying whate'er sum, in mulct,° they please on   *as a fine*
The lover, who must pay a handsome price,
Because it is a marketable vice.

65

Alfonso was the name of Julia's lord,
    A man well looking for his years, and who
515 Was neither much beloved nor yet abhorred:
    They lived together as most people do,
Suffering each other's foibles by accord,

---

5. "It comes to my mind" (Italian).   snow as a remedy for lust.
6. St. Anthony recommended the application of

And not exactly either *one* or *two*;
　　Yet he was jealous, though he did not show it,
520　For Jealousy dislikes the world to know it.

66

Julia was—yet I never could see why—
　　With Donna Inez quite a favorite friend;
Between their tastes there was small sympathy,
　　For not a line had Julia ever penned:
525　Some people whisper (but, no doubt, they lie,
　　For Malice still imputes some private end)
That Inez had, ere Don Alfonso's marriage,
Forgot with him her very prudent carriage;°　　　　　　behavior

67

And that still keeping up the old connection,
530　　Which Time had lately rendered much more chaste,
She took his lady also in affection,
　　And certainly this course was much the best:
She flattered Julia with her sage protection,
　　And complimented Don Alfonso's taste;
535　And if she could not (who can?) silence scandal,
At least she left it a more slender handle.

68

I can't tell whether Julia saw the affair
　　With other people's eyes, or if her own
Discoveries made, but none could be aware
540　　Of this, at least no symptom e'er was shown;
Perhaps she did not know, or did not care,
　　Indifferent from the first, or callous grown:
I'm really puzzled what to think or say,
She kept her counsel in so close a way.

69

545　Juan she saw, and, as a pretty child,
　　Caressed him often—such a thing might be
Quite innocently done, and harmless styled,
　　When she had twenty years, and thirteen he;
But I am not so sure I should have smiled
550　　When he was sixteen, Julia twenty-three;
These few short years make wondrous alterations,
Particularly amongst sun-burnt nations.

70

Whate'er the cause might be, they had become
　　Changed; for the dame grew distant, the youth shy,
555　Their looks cast down, their greetings almost dumb,
　　And much embarrassment in either eye;
There surely will be little doubt with some
　　That Donna Julia knew the reason why,
But as for Juan, he had no more notion
560　Than he who never saw the sea of Ocean.

71

Yet Julia's very coldness still was kind,
　　And tremulously gentle her small hand

Withdrew itself from his, but left behind
　　A little pressure, thrilling, and so bland
565 And slight, so very slight, that to the mind
　　　'Twas but a doubt; but ne'er magician's wand
　　Wrought change with all Armida's[7] fairy art
　　Like what this light touch left on Juan's heart.

72

And if she met him, though she smiled no more,
570 　　She looked a sadness sweeter than her smile,
　　As if her heart had deeper thoughts in store
　　　She must not own, but cherished more the while
　　For that compression in its burning core;
　　　Even Innocence itself has many a wile,
575 And will not dare to trust itself with truth,
　　And Love is taught hypocrisy from youth.

73

But Passion most dissembles, yet betrays
　　　Even by its darkness; as the blackest sky
Foretells the heaviest tempest, it displays
580 　　Its workings through the vainly guarded eye,
　　And in whatever aspect it arrays
　　　Itself, 'tis still the same hypocrisy;
　　Coldness or Anger, even Disdain or Hate,
　　Are masks it often wears, and still too late.

74

585 Then there were sighs, the deeper for suppression,
　　　And stolen glances, sweeter for the theft,
　　And burning blushes, though for no transgression,
　　　Tremblings when met, and restlessness when left;
　　All these are little preludes to possession,
590 　　Of which young Passion cannot be bereft,
　　And merely tend to show how greatly Love is
　　Embarrassed at first starting with a novice.

75

Poor Julia's heart was in an awkward state;
　　　She felt it going, and resolved to make
595 The noblest efforts for herself and mate,
　　　For Honor's, Pride's, Religion's, Virtue's sake:
　　Her resolutions were most truly great,
　　　And almost might have made a Tarquin[8] quake:
　　She prayed the Virgin Mary for her grace,
600 As being the best judge of a lady's case.

76

She vowed she never would see Juan more,
　　　And next day paid a visit to his mother,
　　And looked extremely at the opening door,
　　　Which, by the Virgin's grace, let in another;
605 Grateful she was, and yet a little sore —

---

7. An enchantress who seduces Christian knights
in Tasso's *Jerusalem Delivered.*
8. The ravisher of a Roman noblewoman

renowned for her chastity, in Shakespeare's *Rape
of Lucrece.*

Again it opens, it can be no other,
'Tis surely Juan now—No! I'm afraid
That night the Virgin was no further prayed.

77

She now determined that a virtuous woman
610   Should rather face and overcome temptation,
That flight was base and dastardly, and no man
    Should ever give her heart the least sensation,
That is to say, a thought beyond the common
    Preference, that we must feel, upon occasion,
615   For people who are pleasanter than others,
But then they only seem so many brothers.

78

And even if by chance—and who can tell?
    The Devil's so very sly—she should discover
That all within was not so very well,
620   And, if still free,[9] that such or such a lover
Might please perhaps, a virtuous wife can quell
    Such thoughts, and be the better when they're over;
And if the man should ask, 'tis but denial:
I recommend young ladies to make trial.

79

625   And, then, there are such things as Love divine,
    Bright and immaculate, unmixed and pure,
Such as the angels think so very fine,
    And matrons, who would be no less secure,
Platonic, perfect, "just such love as mine;"
630   Thus Julia said—and thought so, to be sure;
And so I'd have her think, were I the man
On whom her reveries celestial ran.

80

Such love is innocent, and may exist
    Between young persons without any danger.
635   A hand may first, and then a lip be kissed;
    For my part, to such doings I'm a stranger,
But hear these freedoms form the utmost list
    Of all o'er which such love may be a ranger:
If people go beyond, 'tis quite a crime,
640   But not my fault—I tell them all in time.

81

Love, then, but Love within its proper limits,
    Was Julia's innocent determination
In young Don Juan's favor, and to him its
    Exertion might be useful on occasion;
645   And, lighted at too pure a shrine to dim its
    Ethereal luster, with what sweet persuasion
He might be taught, by Love and her together—
I really don't know what, nor Julia either.

9. I.e., if she were not already married.

82

Fraught with this fine intention, and well fenced
650   In mail of proof—her purity of soul—
She, for the future, of her strength convinced,
    And that her honor was a rock, or mole,°   *breakwater*
Exceeding sagely from that hour dispensed
    With any kind of troublesome control;
655   But whether Julia to the task was equal
Is that which must be mentioned in the sequel.

83

Her plan she deemed both innocent and feasible,
    And, surely, with a stripling of sixteen
Not Scandal's fangs could fix on much that's seizable,
660   Or if they did so, satisfied to mean
Nothing but what was good, her breast was peaceable—
    A quiet conscience makes one so serene!
Christians have burnt each other, quite persuaded
That all the Apostles would have done as they did.

84

665   And if in the mean time her husband died,
    But Heaven forbid that such a thought should cross
Her brain, though in a dream! (and then she sighed)
    Never could she survive that common loss;
But just suppose that moment should betide,
670   I only say suppose it—*inter nos:*[1]
(This should be *entre nous*, for Julia thought
In French, but then the rhyme would go for nought.)

85

I only say, suppose this supposition:
    Juan being then grown up to man's estate
675   Would fully suit a widow of condition,
    Even seven years hence it would not be too late;
And in the interim (to pursue this vision)
    The mischief, after all, could not be great,
For he would learn the rudiments of Love,
680   I mean the *seraph*° way of those above.   *angelic, pure*

86

So much for Julia! Now we'll turn to Juan.
    Poor little fellow! he had no idea
Of his own case, and never hit the true one;
    In feelings quick as Ovid's Miss Medea,[2]
685   He puzzled over what he found a new one,
    But not as yet imagined it could be a
Thing quite in course, and not at all alarming,
Which, with a little patience, might grow charming.

87

Silent and pensive, idle, restless, slow,
690   His home deserted for the lonely wood,

---

1. "Just between ourselves" (Latin).
2. In Ovid's *Metamorphoses*, the young Medea finds herself irresistibly infatuated with the hero Jason.

Tormented with a wound he could not know,
 His, like all deep grief, plunged in solitude:
I'm fond myself of solitude or so,
 But then, I beg it may be understood,
695 By solitude I mean a Sultan's (not
 A Hermit's), with a harem for a grot.

88

"Oh Love! in such a wilderness as this,
 Where Transport and Security entwine,
Here is the Empire of thy perfect bliss,
700 And here thou art a God indeed divine."
The bard[3] I quote from does not sing amiss,
 With the exception of the second line,
For that same twining "Transport and Security"
Are twisted to a phrase of some obscurity.

89

705 The Poet meant, no doubt, and thus appeals
 To the good sense and senses of mankind,
The very thing which everybody feels,
 As all have found on trial, or may find,
That no one likes to be disturbed at meals
710 Or love—I won't say more about "entwined"
Or "Transport," as we knew all that before,
But beg "Security" will bolt the door.

90

Young Juan wandered by the glassy brooks,
 Thinking unutterable things; he threw
715 Himself at length within the leafy nooks
 Where the wild branch of the cork forest grew;
There poets find materials for their books,
 And every now and then we read them through,
So that their plan and prosody are eligible,
720 Unless, like Wordsworth, they prove unintelligible.

91

He, Juan (and not Wordsworth), so pursued
 His self-communion with his own high soul,
Until his mighty heart, in its great mood,
 Had mitigated part, though not the whole
725 Of its disease; he did the best he could
 With things not very subject to control,
And turned, without perceiving his condition,
Like Coleridge, into a metaphysician.

92

He thought about himself, and the whole earth,
730 Of man the wonderful, and of the stars,
And how the deuce they ever could have birth;
 And then he thought of earthquakes, and of wars,
How many miles the moon might have in girth,
 Of air-balloons, and of the many bars

---

3. Byron's contemporary, Thomas Campbell, whose *Gertrude of Wyoming* is here paraphrased.

735 To perfect knowledge of the boundless skies;—
And then he thought of Donna Julia's eyes.

93

In thoughts like these true Wisdom may discern
    Longings sublime, and aspirations high,
Which some are born with, but the most part learn
740   To plague themselves withal, they know not why:
'Twas strange that one so young should thus concern
    His brain about the action of the sky;
If you think 'twas Philosophy that this did,
I can't help thinking puberty assisted.

94

745 He pored upon the leaves, and on the flowers,
    And heard a voice in all the winds; and then
He thought of wood-nymphs and immortal bowers,
    And how the goddesses came down to men:
He missed the pathway, he forgot the hours,
750   And when he looked upon his watch again,
He found how much old Time had been a winner—
He also found that he had lost his dinner.

95

Sometimes he turned to gaze upon his book,
    Boscan, or Garcilasso;[4]—by the wind
755 Even as the page is rustled while we look,
    So by the poesy of his own mind
Over the mystic leaf his soul was shook,
    As if 'twere one whereon magicians bind
Their spells, and give them to the passing gale,
760 According to some good old woman's tale.

96

Thus would he while his lonely hours away
    Dissatisfied, not knowing what he wanted;
Nor glowing reverie, nor poet's lay,
    Could yield his spirit that for which it panted,
765 A bosom whereon he his head might lay,
    And hear the heart beat with the love it granted,
With—several other things, which I forget,
Or which, at least, I need not mention yet.

97

Those lonely walks, and lengthening reveries,
770   Could not escape the gentle Julia's eyes;
She saw that Juan was not at his ease;
    But that which chiefly may, and must surprise,
Is, that the Donna Inez did not tease
    Her only son with question or surmise;
775 Whether it was she did not see, or would not,
Or, like all very clever people, could not.

---

4. Spanish poets of the early sixteenth century.

98

This may seem strange, but yet 'tis very common;
   For instance—gentlemen, whose ladies take
Leave to o'erstep the written rights of Woman,
780   And break the——Which commandment is't they break?
(I have forgot the number, and think no man
   Should rashly quote, for fear of a mistake;)
I say, when these same gentlemen are jealous,
They make some blunder, which their ladies tell us.

99

785 A real husband always is suspicious,
   But still no less suspects in the wrong place,
Jealous of some one who had no such wishes,
   Or pandering blindly to his own disgrace,
By harboring some dear friend extremely vicious;
790   The last indeed's infallibly the case:
And when the spouse and friend are gone off wholly,
He wonders at their vice, and not his folly.

100

Thus parents also are at times short-sighted:
   Though watchful as the lynx, they ne'er discover,
795 The while the wicked world beholds delighted,
   Young Hopeful's mistress, or Miss Fanny's lover,
Till some confounded escapade has blighted
   The plan of twenty years, and all is over;
And then the mother cries, the father swears,
800 And wonders why the devil he got heirs.

101

But Inez was so anxious, and so clear
   Of sight, that I must think, on this occasion,
She had some other motive much more near
   For leaving Juan to this new temptation,
805 But what that motive was, I shan't say here;
   Perhaps to finish Juan's education,
Perhaps to open Don Alfonso's eyes,
In case he thought his wife too great a prize.

102

It was upon a day, a summer's day—
810   Summer's indeed a very dangerous season,
And so is spring about the end of May;
   The sun, no doubt, is the prevailing reason;
But whatsoe'er the cause is, one may say,
   And stand convicted of more truth than treason,
815 That there are months which nature grows more merry in,—
March has its hares, and May must have its heroine.

103

'Twas on a summer's day—the sixth of June:
   I like to be particular in dates,
Not only of the age, and year, but moon;
820   They are a sort of post-house, where the Fates
Change horses, making History change its tune,

Then spur away o'er empires and o'er states,
Leaving at last not much besides chronology,
Excepting the post-obits[5] of theology.

104

825 'Twas on the sixth of June, about the hour
Of half-past six—perhaps still nearer seven—
When Julia sate within as pretty a bower
As e'er held houri[6] in that heathenish heaven
Described by Mahomet, and Anacreon Moore,[7]
830 To whom the lyre and laurels have been given,
With all the trophies of triumphant song—
He won them well, and may he wear them long!

105

She sate, but not alone; I know not well
How this same interview had taken place,
835 And even if I knew, I should not tell—
People should hold their tongues in any case;
No matter how or why the thing befell,
But there were she and Juan, face to face—
When two such faces are so, 'twould be wise,
840 But very difficult, to shut their eyes.

106

How beautiful she looked! her conscious heart[8]
Glowed in her cheek, and yet she felt no wrong:
Oh Love! how perfect is thy mystic art,
Strengthening the weak, and trampling on the strong!
845 How self-deceitful is the sagest part
Of mortals whom thy lure hath led along!
The precipice she stood on was immense,
So was her creed° in her own innocence.   *trust*

107

She thought of her own strength, and Juan's youth,
850 And of the folly of all prudish fears,
Victorious Virtue, and domestic Truth,
And then of Don Alfonso's fifty years:
I wish these last had not occurred, in sooth,
Because that number rarely much endears,
855 And through all climes, the snowy and the sunny,
Sounds ill in love, whate'er it may in money.

108

When people say, "I've told you *fifty* times,"
They mean to scold, and very often do;
When poets say, "I've written *fifty* rhymes,"
860 They make you dread that they'll recite them too;
In gangs of *fifty*, thieves commit their crimes;
At *fifty* love for love is rare, 'tis true,

5. Loans repaid from the estate of a person after his or her death; probably referring to rewards or punishments in the afterlife.
6. A beautiful maiden said to entertain faithful Muslims in paradise.
7. Byron's friend, Thomas Moore, author of oriental tales in his long poem *Lalla Rookh*, and translator of love poems by the ancient Greek poet Anacreon.
8. Deep emotion.

But then, no doubt, it equally as true is,
A good deal may be bought for *fifty* Louis[9]

109

865 Julia had honor, virtue, truth, and love
For Don Alfonso; and she inly swore,
By all the vows below to Powers above,
She never would disgrace the ring she wore,
Nor leave a wish which wisdom might reprove;
870 And while she pondered this, besides much more,
One hand on Juan's carelessly was thrown,
Quite by mistake—she thought it was her own;

110

Unconsciously she leaned upon the other,
Which played within the tangles of her hair;
875 And to contend with thoughts she could not smother
She seemed by the distraction of her air.
'Twas surely very wrong in Juan's mother
To leave together this imprudent pair,
She who for many years had watched her son so—
880 I'm very certain *mine* would not have done so.

111

The hand which still held Juan's, by degrees
Gently, but palpably confirmed its grasp,
As if it said, "Detain me, if you please";
Yet there's no doubt she only meant to clasp
885 His fingers with a pure Platonic squeeze;
She would have shrunk as from a toad, or asp,
Had she imagined such a thing could rouse
A feeling dangerous to a prudent spouse.

112

I cannot know what Juan thought of this,
890 But what he did, is much what you would do;
His young lip thanked it with a grateful kiss,
And then, abashed at its own joy, withdrew
In deep despair, lest he had done amiss—
Love is so very timid when 'tis new:
895 She blushed, and frowned not, but she strove to speak,
And held her tongue, her voice was grown so weak.

113

The sun set, and up rose the yellow moon:
The Devil's in the moon for mischief; they
Who called her CHASTE, methinks, began too soon
900 Their nomenclature; there is not a day,
The longest, not the twenty-first of June,
Sees half the business in a wicked way,
On which three single hours of moonshine smile—
And then she looks so modest all the while!

9. French gold coins.

114

905 There is a dangerous silence in that hour,
  A stillness, which leaves room for the full soul
To open all itself, without the power
  Of calling wholly back its self-control;
The silver light which, hallowing tree and tower,
910 Sheds beauty and deep softness o'er the whole,
Breathes also to the heart, and o'er it throws
A loving languor, which is not repose.

115

And Julia sate with Juan, half embraced
  And half retiring from the glowing arm,
915 Which trembled like the bosom where 'twas placed;
  Yet still she must have thought there was no harm,
Or else 'twere easy to withdraw her waist;
  But then the situation had its charm,
And then——God knows what next—I can't go on;
920 I'm almost sorry that I e'er begun.

116

Oh Plato! Plato! you have paved the way,
  With your confounded fantasies, to more
Immoral conduct by the fancied sway
  Your system feigns o'er the controlless core
925 Of human hearts, than all the long array
  Of poets and romancers:—You're a bore,
A charlatan, a coxcomb—and have been,
At best, no better than a go-between.

117

And Julia's voice was lost, except in sighs,
930 Until too late for useful conversation;
The tears were gushing from her gentle eyes,
  I wish, indeed, they had not had occasion;
But who, alas! can love, and then be wise?
  Not that Remorse did not oppose Temptation;
935 A little still she strove, and much repented,
And whispering "I will ne'er consent"—consented.

118

'Tis said that Xerxes[1] offered a reward
  To those who could invent him a new pleasure:
Methinks the requisition's rather hard,
940 And must have cost his Majesty a treasure:
For my part, I'm a moderate-minded bard,
  Fond of a little love (which I call leisure);
I care not for new pleasures, as the old
Are quite enough for me, so they but hold.

119

945 Oh Pleasure! you're indeed a pleasant thing,
  Although one must be damned for you, no doubt:

---

1. King of Persia, fifth century B.C.

I make a resolution every spring
 Of reformation, ere the year run out,
But somehow, this my vestal vow takes wing,
950 Yet still, I trust, it may be kept throughout:
I'm very sorry, very much ashamed,
And mean, next winter, to be quite reclaimed.

1819

Stanzas

When a Man Hath No Freedom to Fight for at Home

When a man hath no freedom to fight for at home,
 Let him combat for that of his neighbors;
Let him think of the glories of Greece and of Rome,
 And get knocked on his head for his labors.

5 To do good to mankind is the chivalrous plan,
  And is always as nobly requited;
Then battle for freedom wherever you can,
 And, if not shot or hanged, you'll get knighted.

1824

On This Day I Complete My Thirty-sixth Year

Missolonghi,[2] January 22, 1824

'Tis time this heart should be unmoved,
 Since others it hath ceased to move:
Yet, though I cannot be beloved,
  Still let me love!

5 My days are in the yellow leaf;
 The flowers and fruits of love are gone;
The worm, the canker,° and the grief   *deep infection*
  Are mine alone!

The fire that on my bosom preys
10 Is lone as some volcanic isle;
No torch is kindled at its blaze—
  A funeral pile.

The hope, the fear, the jealous care,
 The exalted portion of the pain
15 And power of love, I cannot share,
  But wear the chain.

But 'tis not *thus*—and 'tis not *here*—
 Such thoughts should shake my soul, nor *now*,
Where glory decks the hero's bier,
20   Or binds his brow.

---

2. A town in Greece, where Byron had gone to support the Greek war for independence from Turkey, and where he died, April 19, 1824.

The sword, the banner, and the field,
    Glory and Greece, around me see!
The Spartan, borne upon his shield,
        Was not more free.

25 Awake! (not Greece—she *is* awake!)
    Awake, my spirit! Think through *whom*
Thy life-blood tracks its parent lake,
        And then strike home!

    Tread those reviving passions down,
30   Unworthy manhood!—unto thee
Indifferent should the smile or frown
        Of beauty be.

    If thou regrett'st thy youth, *why live?*
    The land of honorable death
35 Is here:—up to the field, and give
        Away thy breath!

    Seek out—less often sought than found—
    A soldier's grave, for thee the best;
Then look around, and choose thy ground,
40   And take thy rest.

                  1824

PERCY BYSSHE SHELLEY

1792–1822

To Wordsworth

Poet of Nature, thou hast wept to know
    That things depart which never may return;
    Childhood and youth, friendship and love's first glow,
    Have fled like sweet dreams, leaving thee to mourn.
5 These common woes I feel. One loss is mine,
    Which thou too feel'st, yet I alone deplore;
    Thou wert as a lone star whose light did shine
    On some frail bark in winter's midnight roar;
Thou hast like to a rock-built refuge stood
10   Above the blind and battling multitude;
    In honored poverty thy voice did weave
Songs consecrate to truth and liberty;—
    Deserting these, thou leavest me to grieve,
    Thus having been, that thou shouldst cease to be.[1]

                  1816

---

1. I.e., Wordsworth had ceased to champion the liberal and revolutionary ideas of his youth and, in Shelley's view, had compromised himself.

Hymn to Intellectual Beauty[2]

1

The awful shadow of some unseen Power
   Floats though unseen among us—visiting
   This various world with as inconstant wing
As summer winds that creep from flower to flower—
5   Like moonbeams that behind some piny mountain shower,
      It visits with inconstant glance
      Each human heart and countenance;
   Like hues and harmonies of evening—
      Like clouds in starlight widely spread—
10   Like memory of music fled—
      Like aught that for its grace may be
Dear, and yet dearer for its mystery.

2

Spirit of BEAUTY, that dost consecrate
   With thine own hues all thou dost shine upon
15   Of human thought or form—where art thou gone?
Why dost thou pass away and leave our state,
This dim vast vale of tears, vacant and desolate?
      Ask why the sunlight not forever
      Weaves rainbows o'er yon mountain river,
20   Why aught should fail and fade that once is shown,
      Why fear and dream and death and birth
      Cast on the daylight of this earth
      Such gloom—why man has such a scope
For love and hate, despondency and hope?

3

25   No voice from some sublimer world hath ever
      To sage or poet these responses given—
   Therefore the names of Daemon, Ghost, and Heaven,
Remain the records of their vain endeavor,
Frail spells—whose uttered charm might not avail to sever,
30   From all we hear and all we see,
      Doubt, chance, and mutability.
Thy light alone—like mist o'er mountains driven,
      Or music by the night wind sent
      Through strings of some still instrument,
35   Or moonlight on a midnight stream,
Gives grace and truth to life's unquiet dream.

4

Love, Hope, and Self-esteem, like clouds depart
   And come, for some uncertain moments lent.
   Man were immortal, and omnipotent,
40   Didst thou, unknown and awful as thou art,
Keep with thy glorious train° firm state within his heart.   *company*
      Thou messenger of sympathies,
      That wax and wane in lovers' eyes—

---

2. Beauty perceived not by the senses but by spiritual illumination.

Thou—that to human thought art nourishment,
45   Like darkness to a dying flame!
      Depart not as thy shadow came,
      Depart not—lest the grave should be,
Like life and fear, a dark reality.

5

While yet a boy I sought for ghosts, and sped
50   Through many a listening chamber, cave and ruin,
      And starlight wood, with fearful steps pursuing
Hopes of high talk with the departed dead.
I called on poisonous names[3] with which our youth is fed;
      I was not heard—I saw them not—
55   When musing deeply on the lot
Of life, at that sweet time when winds are wooing
      All vital things that wake to bring
      News of birds and blossoming—
      Sudden, thy shadow fell on me;
60 I shrieked, and clasped my hands in ecstasy!

6

I vowed that I would dedicate my powers
      To thee and thine—have I not kept the vow?
      With beating heart and streaming eyes, even now
I call the phantoms of a thousand hours
65 Each from his voiceless grave: they have in visioned bowers
      Of studious zeal or love's delight
      Outwatched with me the envious night—
They know that never joy illumed my brow
      Unlinked with hope that thou wouldst free
70   This world from its dark slavery,
      That thou—O awful LOVELINESS,
Wouldst give whate'er these words cannot express.

7

The day becomes more solemn and serene
      When noon is past—there is a harmony
75   In autumn, and a luster in its sky,
Which through the summer is not heard or seen,
As if it could not be, as if it had not been!
      Thus let thy power, which like the truth
      Of nature on my passive youth
80 Descended, to my onward life supply
      Its calm—to one who worships thee,
      And every form containing thee,
      Whom, SPIRIT fair, thy spells did bind
To fear himself, and love all human kind.

1817

---

3. Possibly alluding to attempts to summon spirits of the dead by means of magic rites.

Mont Blanc[4]

Lines Written in the Vale of Chamouni[5]

1

The everlasting universe of things
Flows through the mind, and rolls its rapid waves,
Now dark—now glittering—now reflecting gloom—
Now lending splendor, where from secret springs
5   The source of human thought its tribute brings
Of waters,—with a sound but half its own,
Such as a feeble brook will oft assume
In the wild woods, among the mountains lone,
Where waterfalls around it leap for ever,
10   Where woods and winds contend, and a vast river
Over its rocks ceaselessly bursts and raves.

2

Thus thou, Ravine of Arve—dark, deep Ravine—
Thou many-colored, many voicèd vale,
Over whose pines, and crags, and caverns sail
15   Fast cloud-shadows and sunbeams: awful° scene,   *awesome*
Where Power in likeness of the Arve comes down
From the ice-gulfs that gird his secret throne,
Bursting through these dark mountains like the flame
Of lightning through the tempest;—thou dost lie,
20   Thy giant brood of pines around thee clinging,
Children of elder time, in whose devotion
The chainless winds still come and ever came
To drink their odors, and their mighty swinging
To hear—an old and solemn harmony;
25   Thine earthly rainbows stretched across the sweep
Of the ethereal waterfall, whose veil
Robes some unsculptured image; the strange sleep
Which when the voices of the desert fail
Wraps all in its own deep eternity;—
30   Thy caverns echoing to the Arve's commotion,
A loud, lone sound no other sound can tame;
Thou art pervaded with that ceaseless motion,
Thou art the path of that unresting sound—
Dizzy Ravine! and when I gaze on thee
35   I seem as in a trance sublime and strange
To muse on my own separate fantasy,
My own, my human mind, which passively
Now renders and receives fast influencings,
Holding an unremitting interchange
40   With the clear universe of things around;
One legion of wild thoughts, whose wandering wings
Now float above thy darkness, and now rest
Where that or thou art no unbidden guest,
In the still cave of the witch Poesy,[6]

---

4. The highest of the Alps.
5. Through the Chamouni valley flows the river Arve, which originates in a glacier on the moun- tain and empties into Lake Geneva, whence flows the Rhone, which reaches the Mediterranean.
6. The power of the imagination.

45 Seeking among the shadows that pass by
Ghosts of all things that are, some shade of thee,
Some phantom, some faint image; till the breast
From which they fled recalls them, thou art there!

3

Some say that gleams of a remoter world
50 Visit the soul in sleep,—that death is slumber,
And that its shapes the busy thoughts outnumber
Of those who wake and live.—I look on high;
Has some unknown omnipotence unfurled
The veil of life and death? or do I lie
55 In dream, and does the mightier world of sleep
Spread far around and inaccessibly
Its circles? For the very spirit fails,
Driven like a homeless cloud from steep to steep
That vanishes among the viewless gales!
60 Far, far above, piercing the infinite sky,
Mont Blanc appears,—still, snowy, and serene—
Its subject mountains their unearthly forms
Pile around it, ice and rock; broad vales between
Of frozen floods, unfathomable deeps,
65 Blue as the overhanging heaven, that spread
And wind among the accumulated steeps;
A desert peopled by the storms alone,
Save when the eagle brings some hunter's bone,
And the wolf tracks her there—how hideously
70 Its shapes are heaped around! rude, bare, and high,
Ghastly, and scarred, and riven.—Is this the scene
Where the old Earthquake-demon⁷ taught her young
Ruin? Were these their toys? or did a sea
Of fire envelop once this silent snow?
75 None can reply—all seems eternal now.
The wilderness has a mysterious tongue
Which teaches awful° doubt, or faith so mild,   *profoundly disturbing*
So solemn, so serene, that man may be,
But for such faith, with nature reconciled;⁸
80 Thou hast a voice, great Mountain, to repeal
Large codes of fraud and woe; not understood
By all, but which the wise, and great, and good
Interpret, or make felt, or deeply feel.

4

The fields, the lakes, the forests, and the streams,
85 Ocean, and all the living things that dwell
Within the daedal⁹ earth; lightning, and rain,
Earthquake, and fiery flood, and hurricane,
The torpor of the year when feeble dreams
Visit the hidden buds, or dreamless sleep
90 Holds every future leaf and flower;—the bound

7. Personification of geologic forces.
8. A debated passage; perhaps to be paraphrased
as, the "tongue" may teach either that the cosmos
and the human mind are deeply at odds, or that
we may have "faith" that they are in harmony.
9. Intricately made, as by Daedalus, the legendary
Greek craftsman.

With which from that detested trance they leap;
The works and ways of man, their death and birth,
And that of him and all that his may be;
All things that move and breathe with toil and sound
95   Are born and die; revolve, subside, and swell.
Power dwells apart in its tranquility,
Remote, serene, and inaccessible:
And *this*, the naked countenance of earth,
On which I gaze, even these primeval mountains
100   Teach the adverting mind. The glaciers creep
Like snakes that watch their prey, from their far fountains,
Slow rolling on; there, many a precipice,
Frost and the Sun in scorn of mortal power
Have piled: dome, pyramid, and pinnacle,
105   A city of death, distinct with many a tower
And wall impregnable of beaming ice.
Yet not a city, but a flood of ruin
Is there, that from the boundaries of the sky
Rolls its perpetual stream; vast pines are strewing
110   Its destined path, or in the mangled soil
Branchless and shattered stand; the rocks, drawn down
From yon remotest waste, have overthrown
The limits of the dead and living world,
Never to be reclaimed. The dwelling-place
115   Of insects, beasts, and birds, becomes its spoil
Their food and their retreat for ever gone,
So much of life and joy is lost. The race
Of man flies far in dread; his work and dwelling
Vanish, like smoke before the tempest's stream,
120   And their place is not known. Below, vast caves
Shine in the rushing torrents' restless gleam,
Which from those secret chasms in tumult welling
Meet in the vale, and one majestic River,
The breath and blood of distant lands, for ever
125   Rolls its loud waters to the ocean-waves,
Breathes its swift vapors to the circling air.[1]

5

Mont Blanc yet gleams on high:—the power is there,
The still and solemn power of many sights,
And many sounds, and much of life and death.
130   In the calm darkness of the moonless nights,
In the lone glare of day, the snows descend
Upon that Mountain; none beholds them there,
Nor when the flakes burn in the sinking sun,
Or the star-beams dart through them:—Winds contend
135   Silently there, and heap the snow with breath
Rapid and strong, but silently! Its home
The voiceless lightning in these solitudes
Keeps innocently, and like vapor broods
Over the snow. The secret Strength of things

---

1. Compare Coleridge, "Kubla Khan," lines 12–24 (pp. 741–42).

140   Which governs thought, and to the infinite dome
      Of Heaven is as a law, inhabits thee![2]
      And what were thou, and earth, and stars, and sea,
      If to the human mind's imaginings
      Silence and solitude were vacancy?

July 23, 1816   1817

Ozymandias[3]

      I met a traveler from an antique land
      Who said: Two vast and trunkless legs of stone
      Stand in the desert . . . Near them, on the sand,
      Half sunk, a shattered visage lies, whose frown,
5   And wrinkled lip, and sneer of cold command,
      Tell that its sculptor well those passions read
      Which yet survive, stamped on these lifeless things,
      The hand that mocked them, and the heart that fed:
      And on the pedestal these words appear:
10   "My name is Ozymandias, king of kings:
      Look on my works, ye Mighty, and despair!"
      Nothing beside remains. Round the decay
      Of that colossal wreck, boundless and bare
      The lone and level sands stretch far away.

                                                              1818

Stanzas Written in Dejection, Near Naples

                            1
      The sun is warm, the sky is clear,
          The waves are dancing fast and bright,
      Blue isles and snowy mountains wear
          The purple noon's transparent might,
5   The breath of the moist earth is light,
      Around its unexpanded buds;
          Like many a voice of one delight,
      The winds, the birds, the ocean floods,
      The City's voice itself is soft like Solitude's.

                            2
10   I see the Deep's untrampled floor
          With green and purple seaweeds strown;
      I see the waves upon the shore,
          Like light dissolved in star-showers, thrown:
          I sit upon the sands alone—
15   The lightning of the noontide ocean
          Is flashing round me, and a tone
      Arises from its measured motion;
      How sweet! did any heart now share in my emotion.

---

2. I.e., Mont Blanc.
3. Greek name for the Egyptian monarch Ramses

II (thirteenth century B.C.), who is said to have
erected a huge statue of himself.

3

Alas! I have nor hope nor health,
20   Nor peace within nor calm around,
Nor that content surpassing wealth
        The sage in meditation found,
        And walked with inward glory crowned—
Nor fame, nor power, nor love, nor leisure.
25   Others I see whom these surround—
Smiling they live, and call life pleasure;
To me that cup has been dealt in another measure.

4

Yet now despair itself is mild,
        Even as the winds and waters are;
30 I could lie down like a tired child,
        And weep away the life of care
        Which I have borne and yet must bear,
Till death like sleep might steal on me,
        And I might feel in the warm air
35 My cheek grow cold, and hear the sea
Breathe o'er my dying brain its last monotony.

5

Some might lament that I were cold,
        As I, when this sweet day is gone,
Which my lost heart, too soon grown old,
40   Insults with this untimely moan;
        They might lament—for I am one
Whom men love not—and yet regret,
        Unlike this day, which, when the sun
        Shall on its stainless glory set,
45 Will linger, though enjoyed, like joy in memory yet.

1818   1824

England in 1819

An old, mad, blind, despised, and dying king[4]—
Princes, the dregs of their dull race,[5] who flow
Through public scorn—mud from a muddy spring;
Rulers who neither see, nor feel, nor know,
5   But leechlike to their fainting country cling,
Till they drop, blind in blood, without a blow;
A people starved and stabbed in the untilled field—
An army, which liberticide[6] and prey
Makes as a two-edged sword to all who wield;
10 Golden and sanguine[7] laws which tempt and slay;
Religion Christless, Godless—a book sealed;
A Senate—Time's worst statute[8] unrepealed—

---

4. George III (1738–1820), who lived for years in a state of advanced senility. The "Princes" of line 2 are George III's sons, including the Prince-Regent, later George IV, whom Shelley detested.
5. The "Hanoverian" line of English monarchs, beginning in 1714 with George I.

6. Destruction of liberty.
7. Sanguinary; causing bloodshed.
8. I.e., probably the Act of Union (1801), uniting Ireland to England and excluding Roman Catholics from exercising full citizenship.

Are graves, from which a glorious Phantom[9] may
Burst, to illumine our tempestuous day.

1819   1839

Ode to the West Wind[1]

1

O wild West Wind, thou breath of Autumn's being,
Thou, from whose unseen presence the leaves dead
Are driven, like ghosts from an enchanter fleeing,

Yellow, and black, and pale, and hectic red,
5   Pestilence-stricken multitudes: O thou,
Who chariotest to their dark wintry bed

The wingéd seeds, where they lie cold and low,
Each like a corpse within its grave, until
Thine azure sister of the Spring shall blow

10   Her clarion[2] o'er the dreaming earth, and fill
(Driving sweet buds like flocks to feed in air)
With living hues and odors plain and hill:

Wild Spirit, which art moving everywhere;
Destroyer and preserver; hear, oh, hear!

2

15   Thou on whose stream, mid the steep sky's commotion,
Loose clouds like earth's decaying leaves are shed,
Shook from the tangled boughs of Heaven and Ocean,

Angels[3] of rain and lightning: there are spread
On the blue surface of thine aëry surge,
20   Like the bright hair uplifted from the head

Of some fierce Maenad,[4] even from the dim verge
Of the horizon to the zenith's height,
The locks of the approaching storm. Thou dirge

Of the dying year, to which this closing night
25   Will be the dome of a vast sepulcher,
Vaulted with all thy congregated might

Of vapors, from whose solid atmosphere
Black rain, and fire, and hail will burst: oh, hear!

---

9. I.e., the spirit of liberty.
1. "This poem was conceived and chiefly written in a wood that skirts the Arno, near Florence, and on a day when that tempestuous wind, whose temperature is at once mild and animating, was collecting the vapours which pour down the autumnal rains" [Shelley's note]. Florence was the home of Dante Alighieri (1265–1321), who originated the verse form of Shelley's Ode (see *terza rima*, p. lxxii) for his masterpiece, *The Divine Comedy* (*La divina commedia*).
2. Melodious trumpet-call.
3. In Greek derivation, messengers or divine messengers.
4. Frenzied dancer, worshiper of Dionysus (Greek god of wine and fertility).

3

Thou who didst waken from his summer dreams
30   The blue Mediterranean, where he lay,
Lulled by the coil of his crystálline streams,

Beside a pumice isle in Baiae's bay,[5]
And saw in sleep old palaces and towers
Quivering within the wave's intenser day,

35   All overgrown with azure moss and flowers
So sweet, the sense faints picturing them! Thou
For whose path the Atlantic's level powers

Cleave themselves into chasms, while far below
The sea-blooms and the oozy woods which wear
40   The sapless foliage of the ocean, know

Thy voice, and suddenly grow gray with fear,
And tremble and despoil themselves: oh, hear!

4

If I were a dead leaf thou mightest bear;
If I were a swift cloud to fly with thee;
45   A wave to pant beneath thy power, and share

The impulse of thy strength, only less free
Than thou, O uncontrollable! If even
I were as in my boyhood, and could be

The comrade of thy wanderings over Heaven,
50   As then, when to outstrip thy skyey speed
Scarce seemed a vision; I would ne'er have striven

As thus with thee in prayer in my sore need.
Oh, lift me as a wave, a leaf, a cloud!
I fall upon the thorns of life! I bleed!

55   A heavy weight of hours has chained and bowed
One too like thee: tameless, and swift, and proud.

5

Make me thy lyre,[6] even as the forest is:
What if my leaves are falling like its own!
The tumult of thy mighty harmonies

60   Will take from both a deep, autumnal tone,
Sweet though in sadness. Be thou, Spirit fierce,
My spirit! Be thou me, impetuous one!

Drive my dead thoughts over the universe
Like withered leaves to quicken a new birth!
65   And, by the incantation of this verse,

---

5. Near Naples, Italy.   songs and recited poems.
6. Small harp traditionally used to accompany

Scatter, as from an unextinguished hearth
Ashes and sparks, my words among mankind!
Be through my lips to unawakened earth

The trumpet of a prophecy! O Wind,
70   If Winter comes, can Spring be far behind?

1820

The Cloud

I bring fresh showers for the thirsting flowers,
    From the seas and the streams;
I bear light shade for the leaves when laid
    In their noonday dreams.
5 From my wings are shaken the dews that waken
    The sweet buds every one,
When rocked to rest on their mother's breast,
    As she dances about the sun.
I wield the flail of the lashing hail,
10   And whiten the green plains under,
And then again I dissolve it in rain,
    And laugh as I pass in thunder.

I sift the snow on the mountains below,
    And their great pines groan aghast;
15 And all the night 'tis my pillow white,
    While I sleep in the arms of the blast.
Sublime on the towers of my skyey bowers,
    Lightning my pilot[7] sits;
In a cavern under is fettered the thunder,
20   It struggles and howls at fits;°   intermittently
Over earth and ocean, with gentle motion,
    This pilot is guiding me,
Lured by the love of the genii that move
    In the depths of the purple sea;
25 Over the rills, and the crags, and the hills,
    Over the lakes and the plains,
Wherever he dream, under mountain or stream,
    The Spirit he loves remains;
And I all the while bask in Heaven's blue smile,
30   Whilst he is dissolving in rains.

The sanguine Sunrise, with his meteor eyes,
    And his burning plumes outspread,
Leaps on the back of my sailing rack,[8]
    When the morning star shines dead;
35 As on the jag of a mountain crag,
    Which an earthquake rocks and swings,
An eagle alit one moment may sit

---

7. Electrical energy, here represented as directing   charges ("genii," line 23) under the sea.
the cloud in response to the attraction of opposite   8. Wind-driven clouds.

In the light of its golden wings.
And when Sunset may breathe, from the lit sea beneath,
40   Its ardors of rest and of love,
And the crimson pall of eve may fall
      From the depth of Heaven above,
With wings folded I rest, on mine aëry nest,
      As still as a brooding dove.

45 That orbéd maiden with white fire laden,
      Whom mortals call the Moon,
Glides glimmering o'er my fleecelike floor,
      By the midnight breezes strewn;
And wherever the beat of her unseen feet,
50   Which only the angels hear,
May have broken the woof° of my tent's thin roof,   *fabric*
      The stars peep behind her and peer;
And I laugh to see them whirl and flee,
      Like a swarm of golden bees,
55 When I widen the rent in my wind-built tent,
      Till the calm rivers, lakes, and seas,
Like strips of the sky fallen through me on high,
      Are each paved with the moon and these.

I bind the Sun's throne with a burning zone,°   *belt*
60   And the Moon's with a girdle of pearl;
The volcanoes are dim, and the stars reel and swim,
      When the whirlwinds my banner unfurl.
From cape to cape, with a bridgelike shape,
      Over a torrent sea,
65 Sunbeam-proof, I hang like a roof—
      The mountains its columns be.
The triumphal arch through which I march
      With hurricane, fire, and snow,
When the Powers of the air are chained to my chair,
70   Is the million-colored bow;
The sphere-fire above its soft colors wove,
      While the moist Earth was laughing below.

I am the daughter of Earth and Water,
      And the nursling of the Sky;
75 I pass through the pores of the ocean and shores;
      I change, but I cannot die.
For after the rain when with never a stain
      The pavilion of Heaven is bare,
And the winds and sunbeams with their convex° gleams   *upward-arching*
80   Build up the blue dome of air,
I silently laugh at my own cenotaph,[9]
      And out of the caverns of rain,
Like a child from the womb, like a ghost from the tomb,
      I arise and unbuild it again.

1820

9. Monument honoring a person who is buried elsewhere.

To a Skylark

Hail to thee, blithe Spirit!
  Bird thou never wert,
That from Heaven, or near it,
  Pourest thy full heart
5 In profuse strains of unpremeditated art.

    Higher still and higher
  From the earth thou springest
Like a cloud of fire;
  The blue deep thou wingest,
10 And singing still dost soar, and soaring ever singest.

    In the golden lightning
  Of the sunken sun,
O'er which clouds are bright'ning,
  Thou dost float and run;
15 Like an unbodied joy whose race is just begun.

    The pale purple even
  Melts around thy flight;
Like a star of Heaven,
  In the broad daylight
20 Thou art unseen, but yet I hear thy shrill delight,

    Keen as are the arrows
  Of that silver sphere,°   *star*
Whose intense lamp narrows
  In the white dawn clear
25 Until we hardly see—we feel that it is there.

    All the earth and air
  With thy voice is loud,
As, when night is bare,
  From one lonely cloud
30 The moon rains out her beams, and Heaven is overflowed.

    What thou art we know not;
  What is most like thee?
From rainbow clouds there flow not
  Drops so bright to see
35 As from thy presence showers a rain of melody.

    Like a Poet hidden
  In the light of thought,
Singing hymns unbidden,
  Till the world is wrought
40 To sympathy with hopes and fears it heeded not:

    Like a high-born maiden
  In a palace tower,
Soothing her love-laden

Soul in secret hour
45 With music sweet as love, which overflows her bower:

Like a glowworm golden
In a dell of dew,
Scattering unbeholden
Its aërial hue
50 Among the flowers and grass, which screen it from the view!

Like a rose embowered
In its own green leaves,
By warm winds deflowered,
Till the scent it gives
55 Makes faint with too much sweet those heavy-wingéd thieves:

Sound of vernal showers
On the twinkling grass,
Rain-awakened flowers,
All that ever was
60 Joyous, and clear, and fresh, thy music doth surpass:

Teach us, Sprite° or Bird,   *spirit*
What sweet thoughts are thine:
I have never heard
Praise of love or wine
65 That panted forth a flood of rapture so divine.

Chorus Hymeneal,[1]
Or triumphal chant,
Matched with thine would be all
But an empty vaunt,
70 A thing wherein we feel there is some hidden want.

What objects are the fountains
Of thy happy strain?
What fields, or waves, or mountains?
What shapes of sky or plain?
75 What love of thine own kind? what ignorance of pain?

With thy clear keen joyance
Languor cannot be:
Shadow of annoyance
Never came near thee:
80 Thou lovest—but ne'er knew love's sad satiety.

Waking or asleep,
Thou of death must deem
Things more true and deep
Than we mortals dream,
85 Or how could thy notes flow in such a crystal stream?

1. As for a wedding.

We look before and after,
  And pine for what is not:
Our sincerest laughter
  With some pain is fraught;
90 Our sweetest songs are those that tell of saddest thought.

Yet if we could scorn
  Hate, and pride, and fear;
If we were things born
  Not to shed a tear,
95 I know not how thy joy we ever should come near.

Better than all measures
  Of delightful sound,
Better than all treasures
  That in books are found,
100 Thy skill to poet were, thou scorner of the ground!

Teach me half the gladness
  That thy brain must know,
Such harmonious madness
  From my lips would flow
105 The world should listen then—as I am listening now.

1820

Adonais[1]

An Elegy on the Death of John Keats, Author of Endymion, Hyperion, etc.

ἀστὴρ πρὶν μὲν ἔλαμπες ἐνὶ ζωοῖσιν ἑῷος,
νῦν δὲ θανὼν λάμπεις ἕσπερος ἐν φθιμένοις.[2]
—PLATO

1

I weep for Adonais—he is dead!
Oh, weep for Adonais! though our tears
Thaw not the frost which binds so dear a head!
And thou, sad Hour, selected from all years
5 To mourn our loss, rouse thy obscure compeers,°   equals
And teach them thine own sorrow, say: with me
Died Adonais; till the Future dares
Forget the Past, his fate and fame shall be
An echo and a light unto eternity!

---

1. A name derived from Adonis, in Greek legend a young hunter beloved of Aphrodite (Venus) and killed by a wild boar. The root meaning of his name, Adon, is "the lord," and in the form Adonai appears in Hebrew scriptures as a synonym for God.

2. "Thou wert the morning star among the living, / Ere thy fair light had fled— / Now, having died, thou art as Hesperus, giving / New splendor to the dead" [Shelley's translation]; Venus is both Hesperus, the evening star, and the morning star.

2

10 Where wert thou mighty Mother,[3] when he lay,
    When thy Son lay, pierced by the shaft which flies
    In darkness? where was lorn Urania
    When Adonais died? With veiléd eyes,
    'Mid listening Echoes, in her Paradise
15 She sate, while one, with soft enamored breath,
    Rekindled all the fading melodies,
    With which, like flowers that mock the corse° beneath,   corpse
    He had adorned and hid the coming bulk of death.

3

    Oh, weep for Adonais—he is dead!
20 Wake, melancholy Mother, wake and weep!
    Yet wherefore? Quench within their burning bed
    Thy fiery tears, and let thy loud heart keep
    Like his, a mute and uncomplaining sleep;
    For he is gone, where all things wise and fair
25 Descend:—oh, dream not that the amorous Deep
    Will yet restore him to the vital air;
    Death feeds on his mute voice, and laughs at our despair.

4

    Most musical of mourners, weep again!
    Lament anew, Urania!—He[4] died,
30 Who was the Sire of an immortal strain,
    Blind, old, and lonely, when his country's pride,
    The priest, the slave, and the liberticide,
    Trampled and mocked with many a loathéd rite
    Of lust and blood; he went, unterrified,
35 Into the gulf of death; but his clear Sprite°   spirit
    Yet reigns o'er earth; the third among the sons of light.[5]

5

    Most musical of mourners, weep anew!
    Not all to that bright station dared to climb;
    And happier they their happiness who knew,
40 Whose tapers yet burn through that night of time
    In which suns perished; others more sublime,
    Struck by the envious wrath of man or God,
    Have sunk, extinct in their refulgent° prime;   shining
    And some yet live, treading the thorny road,
45 Which leads, through toil and hate, to Fame's serene abode.

6

    But now, thy youngest, dearest one, has perished,
    The nursling of thy widowhood, who grew,
    Like a pale flower by some sad maiden cherished,
    And fed with true-love tears, instead of dew;
50 Most musical of mourners, weep anew!
    Thy extreme° hope, the loveliest and the last,   highest, latest

---

3. Urania, "heavenly one," Venus invoked as the Muse of noble poetry. Adonais is represented as her son.
4. Milton, who also invoked the aid of Urania (see *Paradise Lost* 1.6–16).
5. Rivaled as a poet by only two predecessors, Homer and Dante.

The bloom, whose petals nipped before they blew
Died on the promise of the fruit, is waste;
The broken lily lies—the storm is overpast.

7

55 To that high Capital,[6] where kingly Death
Keeps his pale court in beauty and decay,
He came; and bought, with price of purest breath,
A grave among the eternal.—Come away!
Haste, while the vault of blue Italian day
60 Is yet his fitting charnel-roof! while still
He lies, as if in dewy sleep he lay;
Awake him not! surely he takes his fill
Of deep and liquid rest, forgetful of all ill.

8

He will awake no more, oh, never more!—
65 Within the twilight chamber spreads apace
The shadow of white Death, and at the door
Invisible Corruption waits to trace
His extreme way to her dim dwelling-place;
The eternal Hunger sits, but pity and awe
70 Soothe her pale rage, nor dares she to deface
So fair a prey, till darkness and the law
Of change, shall o'er his sleep the mortal curtain draw.

9

Oh, weep for Adonais!—The quick Dreams,
The passion-wingéd Ministers of thought,
75 Who were his flocks, whom near the living streams
Of his young spirit he fed, and whom he taught
The love which was its music, wander not—
Wander no more, from kindling brain to brain,
But droop there, whence they sprung; and mourn their lot
80 Round the cold heart, where, after their sweet pain,
They ne'er will gather strength, or find a home again.

10

And one with trembling hand clasps his cold head,
And fans him with her moonlight wings, and cries,
"Our love, our hope, our sorrow, is not dead;
85 See, on the silken fringe of his faint eyes,
Like dew upon a sleeping flower, there lies
A tear some Dream has loosened from his brain."
Lost Angel of a ruined Paradise!
She knew not 'twas her own; as with no stain
90 She faded, like a cloud which had outwept its rain.

11

One from a lucid urn of starry dew
Washed his light limbs as if embalming them;
Another clipped her profuse locks, and threw
The wreath upon him, like an anadem,°   garland
95 Which frozen tears instead of pearls begem;

---

6. Rome, where Keats died.

Another in her willful grief would break
Her bow and wingéd reeds, as if to stem
A greater loss with one which was more weak;
And dull the barbéd fire against his frozen cheek.

12

100 Another Splendor on his mouth alit,
That mouth, whence it was wont to draw the breath
Which gave it strength to pierce the guarded wit,[7]
And pass into the panting heart beneath
With lightning and with music: the damp death
105 Quenched its caress upon its icy lips;
And, as a dying meteor stains a wreath
Of moonlight vapor, which the cold night clips,°   *envelops*
It flushed through his pale limbs, and passed to its eclipse.

13

And others came . . . Desires and Adorations,
110 Wingéd Persuasions and veiled Destinies,
Splendors, and Glooms, and glimmering Incarnations
Of hopes and fears, and twilight Phantasies;
And Sorrow, with her family of Sighs,
And Pleasure, blind with tears, led by the gleam
115 Of her own dying smile instead of eyes,
Came in slow pomp;—the moving pomp might seem
Like pageantry of mist on an autumnal stream.

14

All he had loved, and molded into thought
From shape, and hue, and odor, and sweet sound,
120 Lamented Adonais. Morning sought
Her eastern watch-tower, and her hair unbound,
Wet with the tears which should adorn the ground,
Dimmed the aërial eyes that kindle day;
Afar the melancholy thunder moaned,
125 Pale Ocean in unquiet slumber lay,
And the wild Winds flew round, sobbing in their dismay.

15

Lost Echo[8] sits amid the voiceless mountains,
And feeds her grief with his remembered lay,
And will no more reply to winds or fountains,
130 Or amorous birds perched on the young green spray,
Or herdsman's horn, or bell at closing day;
Since she can mimic not his lips, more dear
Than those for whose disdain she pined away
Into a shadow of all sounds:—a drear
135 Murmur, between their songs, is all the woodmen hear.

16

Grief made the young Spring wild, and she threw down
Her kindling buds, as if she Autumn were,

---

7. The defensive analytical mind.
8. A nymph who loved Narcissus and who pined away into a mere voice when that youth fell in love with his own reflection in a pool.

Or they dead leaves; since her delight is flown
For whom should she have waked the sullen year?
140   To Phoebus was not Hyacinth[9] so dear,
Nor to himself Narcissus, as to both
Thou, Adonais; wan they stand and sere
Amid the faint companions of their youth,
With dew all turned to tears; odor, to sighing ruth.°   *pity*

17

145   Thy spirit's sister, the lorn° nightingale,   *lost, abandoned*
Mourns not her mate with such melodious pain;
Not so the eagle, who like thee could scale
Heaven, and could nourish in the sun's domain
Her mighty youth,[1] with morning, doth complain,
150   Soaring and screaming round her empty nest,
As Albion° wails for thee: the curse of Cain[2]   *England*
Light on his head who[3] pierced thy innocent breast,
And scared the angel soul that was its earthly guest!

18

Ah, woe is me! Winter is come and gone,
155   But grief returns with the revolving year;
The airs and streams renew their joyous tone;
The ants, the bees, the swallows reappear;
Fresh leaves and flowers deck the dead Seasons' bier;
The amorous birds now pair in every brake,°   *thicket*
160   And build their mossy homes in field and brere;°   *briar*
And the green lizard, and the golden snake,
Like unimprisoned flames, out of their trance awake.

19

Through wood and stream and field and hill and Ocean,
A quickening life from the Earth's heart has burst
165   As it has ever done, with change and motion,
From the great morning of the world when first
God dawned on Chaos; in its stream immersed
The lamps of Heaven flash with a softer light;
All baser things pant with life's sacred thirst;
170   Diffuse themselves; and spend in love's delight,
The beauty and the joy of their renewéd might.

20

The leprous corpse touched by this spirit tender
Exhales itself in flowers of gentle breath;
Like incarnations of the stars, when splendor
175   Is changed to fragrance, they illumine death
And mock the merry worm that wakes beneath;
Nought we know, dies. Shall that alone which knows
Be as a sword consumed before the sheath

9. Youth loved by Apollo ("Phoebus"), who killed him by accident.
1. In folklore an eagle could recapture its youth by soaring close to the sun.
2. God's curse upon Cain for having slain his brother Abel was that nothing should grow for him and that he should be homeless (Genesis 3.11–12).
3. The anonymous critic whose venomous review of Keats' *Endymion* had hastened, Shelley believed, Keats' death.

By sightless⁴ lightning?—the intense atom⁵ glows
180 A moment, then is quenched in a most cold repose.

21

Alas! that all we loved of him should be,
But for our grief, as if it had not been.
And grief itself be mortal! Woe is me!
Whence are we, and why are we? of what scene
185 The actors or spectators? Great and mean
Meet massed in death, who lends what life must borrow.
As long as skies are blue, and fields are green,
Evening must usher night, night urge the morrow,
Month follow month with woe, and year wake year to sorrow.

22

190 *He* will awake no more, oh, never more!
"Wake thou," cried Misery, "childless Mother, rise
Out of thy sleep, and slake, in thy heart's core,
A wound more fierce than his with tears and sighs."
And all the Dreams that watched Urania's eyes,
195 And all the Echoes whom their sister's song
Had held in holy silence, cried, "Arise!"
Swift as a Thought by the snake Memory stung,
From her ambrosial° rest the fading Splendor sprung.   *immortal*

23

She rose like an autumnal Night, that springs
200 Out of the East, and follows wild and drear
The golden Day, which, on eternal wings,
Even as a ghost abandoning a bier,
Has left the Earth a corpse. Sorrow and fear
So struck, so roused, so rapt Urania;
205 So saddened round her like an atmosphere
Of stormy mist; so swept her on her way
Even to the mournful place where Adonais lay.

24

Out of her secret Paradise she sped,
Through camps and cities rough with stone, and steel,
210 And human hearts, which to her aery tread
Yielding not, wounded the invisible
Palms of her tender feet where'er they fell:
And barbéd tongues, and thoughts more sharp than they,
Rent the soft Form they never could repel,
215 Whose sacred blood, like the young tears of May,
Paved with eternal flowers that undeserving way.

25

In the death-chamber for a moment Death,
Shamed by the presence of that living Might,
Blushed to annihilation, and the breath
220 Revisited those lips, and life's pale light

---

4. Unseeing and unseen.   that exists.
5. Indivisible and indestructible unit of anything

Flashed through those limbs, so late her dear delight.
"Leave me not wild and drear and comfortless,
As silent lightning leaves the starless night!
Leave me not!" cried Urania: her distress
225 Roused Death: Death rose and smiled, and met her vain caress.

26

"Stay yet awhile! speak to me once again;
Kiss me, so long but as a kiss may live;
And in my heartless breast and burning brain
That word, that kiss, shall all thoughts else survive,
230 With food of saddest memory kept alive,
Now thou art dead, as if it were a part
Of thee, my Adonais! I would give
All that I am to be as thou now art,
But I am chained to Time, and cannot thence depart!

27

235 "O gentle child, beautiful as thou wert,
Why didst thou leave the trodden paths of men
Too soon, and with weak hands though mighty heart
Dare the unpastured dragon in his den?
Defenseless as thou wert, oh! where was then
240 Wisdom the mirrored shield, or scorn the spear?[6]
Or hadst thou waited the full cycle, when
Thy spirit should have filled its crescent sphere,
The monsters of life's waste had fled from thee like deer.

28

"The herded wolves, bold only to pursue;
245 The obscene ravens, clamorous o'er the dead;
The vultures, to the conqueror's banner true,
Who feed where Desolation first has fed,
And whose wings rain contagion;—how they[7] fled,
When like Apollo, from his golden bow,
250 The Pythian of the age[8] one arrow sped
And smiled!—The spoilers tempt no second blow,
They fawn on the proud feet that spurn them lying low.

29

"The sun comes forth, and many reptiles spawn;
He sets, and each ephemeral insect then
255 Is gathered into death without a dawn,
And the immortal stars awake again;
So is it in the world of living men:
A godlike mind soars forth, in its delight
Making earth bare and veiling heaven, and when
260 It sinks, the swarms that dimmed or shared its light
Leave to its kindred lamps the spirit's awful night."

6. An allusion to Perseus, who killed the monster
Medusa, evading her gaze, which could turn him
into stone, by using his shield as a mirror.
7. Critics, here characterized as beasts and birds
of prey.

8. Byron, Shelley's friend, who attacked the critics
in *English Bards and Scotch Reviewers*; here com-
pared to Apollo the Pythian, who slew the monster
Python near Delphi.

30

Thus ceased she: and the mountain shepherds came
Their garlands sere, their magic mantles rent;
The Pilgrim of Eternity,[9] whose fame
265   Over his living head like Heaven is bent,
An early but enduring monument,
Came, veiling all the lightnings of his song
In sorrow; from her wilds Ierne° sent   *Ireland*
The sweetest lyrist of her saddest wrong,[1]
270   And love taught grief to fall like music from his tongue.

31

Midst others of less note, came one frail Form,[2]
A phantom among men; companionless
As the last cloud of an expiring storm,
Whose thunder is its knell; he, as I guess,
275   Had gazed on Nature's naked loveliness,
Actaeon-like,[3] and now he fled astray
With feeble steps o'er the world's wilderness,
And his own thoughts, along that rugged way,
Pursued, like raging hounds, their father and their prey.

32

280   A pardlike[4] Spirit beautiful and swift—
A Love in desolation masked;—a Power
Girt round with weakness;—it can scarce uplift
The weight of the superincumbent hour;
It is a dying lamp, a falling shower,
285   A breaking billow;—even whilst we speak
Is it not broken? On the withering flower
The killing sun smiles brightly: on a cheek
The life can burn in blood, even while the heart may break.

33

His head was bound with pansies overblown,
290   And faded violets, white, and pied,° and blue;   *multicolored*
And a light spear topped with a cypress cone,
Round whose rude shaft dark ivy-tresses grew
Yet dripping with the forest's noonday dew,
Vibrated, as the ever-beating heart
295   Shook the weak hand that grasped it; of that crew
He came the last, neglected and apart;
A herd-abandoned deer, struck by the hunter's dart.

34

All stood aloof, and at his partial moan[5]
Smiled through their tears; well knew that gentle band
300   Who in another's fate now wept his own;
As in the accents of an unknown land,

9. Byron, as author of *Childe Harold's Pilgrimage.*
1. Thomas Moore (1779–1852), poet, author of *Irish Melodies.*
2. Shelley, as poet-mourner, here wearing emblems of the god Dionysus.
3. Actaeon, a young hunter, offended the goddess Diana by discovering her while she was bathing.

She transformed him into a stag, and he was torn to pieces by his hounds.
4. Leopardlike; the leopard was sacred to Dionysus.
5. Expressing a bond of sympathy (partiality) toward Adonais.

He sung new sorrow; sad Urania scanned
The Stranger's mien,° and murmured: "Who art thou?"   *expressions*
He answered not, but with a sudden hand
305   Made bare his branded and ensanguined brow,
Which was like Cain's or Christ's—oh! that it should be so!

35

What softer voice is hushed over the dead?
Athwart what brow is that dark mantle thrown?
What form leans sadly o'er the white death-bed,
310   In mockery° of monumental stone,   *imitation*
The heavy heart heaving without a moan?
If it be He,[6] who, gentlest of the wise,
Taught, soothed, loved, honored the departed one;
Let me not vex, with inharmonious sighs,
315 The silence of that heart's accepted sacrifice.

36

Our Adonais has drunk poison—oh!
What deaf and viperous murderer could crown
Life's early cup with such a draught of woe?
The nameless worm[7] would now itself disown:
320   It felt, yet could escape the magic tone
Whose prelude held° all envy, hate and wrong,   *held off*
But what was howling in one breast alone,
Silent with expectation of the song,
Whose master's hand is cold, whose silver lyre unstrung.

37

325 Live thou, whose infamy is not thy fame!
Live! fear no heavier chastisement from me,
Thou noteless blot on a remembered name!
But be thyself, and know thyself to be!
And ever at thy season be thou free
330   To spill the venom when thy fangs o'erflow:
Remorse and Self-contempt shall cling to thee;
Hot Shame shall burn upon thy secret brow,
And like a beaten hound tremble thou shalt—as now.

38

Nor let us weep that our delight is fled
335   Far from these carrion kites° that scream below;   *scavenger hawks*
He wakes or sleeps with the enduring dead;
Thou canst not soar where he is sitting now.
Dust to the dust! but the pure spirit shall flow
Back to the burning fountain whence it came,
340   A portion of the Eternal, which must glow
Through time and change, unquenchably the same,
Whilst thy[8] cold embers choke the sordid hearth of shame.

39

Peace, peace! he is not dead, he doth not sleep—
He hath awakened from the dream of life—

6. Leigh Hunt (1784–1859), poet and critic, friend   152).
of Keats and Shelley.   8. The reviewer's.
7. Serpent; the anonymous reviewer (see line

345   'Tis we, who lost in stormy visions, keep
    With phantoms an unprofitable strife,
    And in mad trance strike with our spirit's knife
    Invulnerable nothings.—We decay
    Like corpses in a charnel; fear and grief
350   Convulse us and consume us day by day,
And cold hopes swarm like worms within our living clay.

40

He has outsoared the shadow of our night;
Envy and calumny and hate and pain,
And that unrest which men miscall delight,
355   Can touch him not and torture not again;
From the contagion of the world's slow stain
He is secure, and now can never mourn
A heart grown cold, a head grown gray in vain;
Nor, when the spirit's self has ceased to burn,
360   With sparkless ashes load an unlamented urn.

41

He lives, he wakes—'tis Death is dead, not he;
Mourn not for Adonais.—Thou young Dawn,
Turn all thy dew to splendor, for from thee
The spirit thou lamentest is not gone;
365   Ye caverns and ye forests, cease to moan!
Cease ye faint flowers and fountains, and thou Air,
Which like a morning veil thy scarf hadst thrown
O'er the abandoned Earth, now leave it bare
Even to the joyous stars which smile on its despair!

42

370   He is made one with Nature: there is heard
His voice in all her music, from the moan
Of thunder, to the song of night's sweet bird;
He is a presence to be felt and known
In darkness and in light, from herb and stone,
375   Spreading itself where'er that Power may move
Which has withdrawn his being to its own;
Which wields the world with never wearied love,
Sustains it from beneath, and kindles it above.

43

He is a portion of the loveliness
380   Which once he made more lovely: he doth bear
His part, while the one Spirit's plastic° stress   *formative*
Sweeps through the dull dense world, compelling there
All new successions to the forms they wear;
Torturing the unwilling dross° that checks its flight   *coarse matter*
385   To its own likeness, as each mass may bear;
And bursting in its beauty and its might
From trees and beasts and men into the Heaven's light.

44

The splendors of the firmament of time
May be eclipsed, but are extinguished not;
390   Like stars to their appointed height they climb,

And death is a low mist which cannot blot
The brightness it may veil. When lofty thought
Lifts a young heart above its mortal lair,
And love and life contend in it, for what
395   Shall be its earthly doom, the dead live there
And move like winds of light on dark and stormy air.

45

The inheritors of unfulfilled renown
Rose from their thrones, built beyond mortal thought,
Far in the Unapparent. Chatterton[9]
400   Rose pale, his solemn agony had not
Yet faded from him; Sidney,[1] as he fought
And as he fell and as he lived and loved
Sublimely mild, a Spirit without spot,
Arose; and Lucan,[2] by his death approved:°   *vindicated*
405   Oblivion as they rose shrank like a thing reproved.

46

And many more, whose names on Earth are dark
But whose transmitted effluence cannot die
So long as fire outlives the parent spark,
Rose, robed in dazzling immortality.
410   "Thou art become as one of us," they cry,
"It was for thee yon kingless sphere has long
Swung blind in unascended majesty,
Silent alone amid an Heaven of Song.
Assume thy wingéd throne, thou Vesper of our throng!"

47

415   Who mourns for Adonais? Oh, come forth,
Fond wretch! and know thyself and him aright.
Clasp with thy panting soul the pendulous[3] Earth;
As from a center, dart thy spirit's light
Beyond all worlds, until its spacious might
420   Satiate the void circumference: then shrink
Even to a point within our day and night;
And keep thy heart light lest it make thee sink
When hope has kindled hope, and lured thee to the brink.

48

Or go to Rome, which is the sepulcher,
425   Oh, not of him, but of our joy: 'tis nought
That ages, empires, and religions there
Lie buried in the ravage they have wrought;
For such as he can lend—they borrow not
Glory from those who made the world their prey;
430   And he is gathered to the kings of thought
Who waged contention with their time's decay,
And of the past are all that cannot pass away.

---

9. Thomas Chatterton (1752–1770), a gifted young
poet who committed suicide.
1. Sir Philip Sidney (1554–1586), a poet, critic,
courtier, and soldier, fatally wounded in battle. See
pp. 188–99.

2. Lucan, a young Roman poet, took his own life
rather than die under sentence of the notorious
emperor Nero, against whom he had conspired.
3. Floating poised in space.

49

Go thou to Rome,—at once the Paradise,
The grave, the city, and the wilderness;
435 And where its wrecks like shattered mountains rise,
And flowering weeds, and fragrant copses dress
The bones of Desolation's nakedness
Pass, till the Spirit of the spot shall lead
Thy footsteps to a slope of green access
440 Where, like an infant's smile, over the dead
A light of laughing flowers along the grass is spread,

50

And gray walls moulder round, on which dull Time
Feeds, like slow fire upon a hoary brand;
And one keen pyramid[4] with wedge sublime,
445 Pavilioning the dust of him who planned
This refuge for his memory, doth stand
Like flame transformed to marble; and beneath,
A field is spread, on which a newer band
Have pitched in Heaven's smile their camp of death,
450 Welcoming him we lose with scarce extinguished breath.

51

Here pause: these graves are all too young as yet
To have outgrown the sorrow which consigned
Its charge to each; and if the seal is set,
Here, on one fountain of a mourning mind,
455 Break it not thou! too surely shalt thou find
Thine own well full, if thou returnest home,
Of tears and gall. From the world's bitter wind
Seek shelter in the shadow of the tomb.
What Adonais is, why fear we to become?

52

460 The One remains, the many change and pass;
Heaven's light forever shines, Earth's shadows fly;
Life, like a dome of many-colored glass,
Stains the white radiance of Eternity,
Until Death tramples it to fragments.—Die,
465 If thou wouldst be with that which thou dost seek!
Follow where all is fled!—Rome's azure sky,
Flowers, ruins, statues, music, words, are weak
The glory they transfuse with fitting truth to speak.

53

Why linger, why turn back, why shrink, my Heart?
470 Thy hopes are gone before: from all things here
They have departed; thou shouldst now depart!
A light is past from the revolving year,
And man, and woman; and what still is dear
Attracts to crush, repels to make thee wither.
475 The soft sky smiles,—the low wind whispers near:

4. Tomb of Gaius Cestius, an officer of ancient Rome, beside the Protestant cemetery where Keats and
Shelley are buried.

'Tis Adonais calls! oh, hasten thither,
No more let life divide what Death can join together.

54

That Light whose smile kindles the Universe,
That Beauty in which all things work and move,
480   That Benediction which the eclipsing Curse
Of birth can quench not, that sustaining Love
Which through the web of being blindly wove
By man and beast and earth and air and sea,
Burns bright or dim, as each are mirrors of
485   The fire for which all thirst; now beams on me,
Consuming the last clouds of cold mortality.

55

The breath whose might I have invoked in song
Descends on me; my spirit's bark° is driven,   *small ship*
Far from the shore, far from the trembling throng
490   Whose sails were never to the tempest given;
The massy earth and spheréd skies are riven!
I am borne darkly, fearfully, afar;
Whilst burning through the inmost veil of Heaven,
The soul of Adonais, like a star,
495 Beacons from the abode where the Eternal are.

                                  1821

Mutability

1

The flower that smiles today
    Tomorrow dies;
All that we wish to stay,
    Tempts and then flies.
5 What is this world's delight?
Lightning that mocks the night,
  Brief even as bright.

2

Virtue, how frail it is!
    Friendship how rare!
10 Love, how it sells poor bliss
    For proud despair!
But we, though soon they fall,
Survive their joy and all
  Which ours we call.

3

15 Whilst skies are blue and bright,
    Whilst flowers are gay,
Whilst eyes that change ere night
    Make glad the day,
Whilst yet the calm hours creep,
20 Dream thou—and from thy sleep
  Then wake to weep.

                                  1824

From Hellas:[5] *Two Choruses*

Worlds on Worlds

Worlds on worlds are rolling ever
From creation to decay,
Like the bubbles on a river
　　Sparkling, bursting, borne away.
5　　But they[6] are still immortal
　　Who, through birth's orient portal
And death's dark chasm hurrying to and fro,
　　Clothe their unceasing flight
　　In the brief dust and light
10　Gathered around their chariots as they go;
　　New shapes they still may weave,
　　New gods, new laws receive,
Bright or dim are they as the robes they last
　　On Death's bare ribs had cast.

15　　A power from the unknown God,[7]
　　A Promethean conqueror,[8] came;
Like a triumphal path he trod
　　The thorns of death and shame.
　　A mortal shape to him
20　　Was like the vapor dim
Which the orient planet animates with light;
　　Hell, Sin, and Slavery came,
　　Like bloodhounds mild and tame,
Nor preyed, until their Lord had taken flight;
25　　The moon of Mahomet[9]
　　Arose, and it shall set:
While blazoned as on Heaven's immortal noon
　　The cross leads generations on.

　　Swift as the radiant shapes of sleep
30　　From one whose dreams are Paradise
Fly, when the fond wretch wakes to weep,
　　And Day peers forth with her blank eyes;
　　So fleet, so fain, so fair,
　　The Powers of earth and air
35　Fled from the folding-star[1] of Bethlehem:
　　Apollo, Pan, and Love,
　　And even Olympian Jove[2]
Grew weak, for killing Truth had glared on them;
　　Our hills and seas and streams,

---

5. *Hellas,* an ancient name for Greece, is the title
of a drama in which Shelley celebrates the con-
temporary Greek struggle for independence,
which he saw as heralding the return of the legend-
ary "Age of Saturn" or "Age of Gold," the first, best
period of human history.
6. "The first stanza contrasts the immortality of
the living and thinking beings which inhabit the
planets, and to use a common and inadequate
phrase, *clothe themselves in matter,* with the tran-
sience of the noblest manifestations of the external

world" [Shelley's note].
7. At Athens St. Paul proclaimed the "unknown
god," i.e., the One God of the Hebraic and Chris-
tian faiths (Acts 17.22–28).
8. Christ; likened to the Greek Titan Prometheus,
who befriended and suffered for mankind.
9. Crescent moon, symbol of Mohammedanism.
1. Star that rises at the hour when sheep are
brought to the fold at evening.
2. Gods worshiped in Greece until Christianity
displaced them.

40   Dispeopled of their dreams,
   Their waters turned to blood, their dew to tears,
      Wailed for the golden years.

1822

The World's Great Age

The world's great age begins anew,
   The golden years return,
The earth doth like a snake[3] renew
   Her winter weeds[4] outworn:
5 Heaven smiles, and faiths and empires gleam,
Like wrecks of a dissolving dream.

A brighter Hellas rears its mountains
   From waves serener far;
A new Peneus[5] rolls his fountains
10   Against the morning star.
Where fairer Tempes[6] bloom, there sleep
Young Cyclads[7] on a sunnier deep.

A loftier Argo[8] cleaves the main,
   Fraught with a later prize;
15 Another Orpheus[9] sings again,
   And loves, and weeps, and dies.
A new Ulysses leaves once more
Calypso[1] for his native shore.

Oh, write no more the tale of Troy,
20   If earth Death's scroll must be!
Nor mix with Laian rage[2] the joy
   Which dawns upon the free:
Although a subtler Sphinx renew
Riddles of death Thebes never knew.

25 Another Athens shall arise,
   And to remoter time
Bequeath, like sunset to the skies,
   The splendor of its prime;
And leave, if nought so bright may live,
30 All earth can take or Heaven can give.

Saturn and Love their long repose
   Shall burst, more bright and good

---

3. Shedding its skin after hibernation, a symbol of regeneration.
4. Clothes, especially mourning garments.
5. Greek river of legendary beauty.
6. Valley of the Peneus.
7. Or Cyclades, islands in the Aegean Sea.
8. In Greek legend, the first of seagoing vessels, on which Jason sailed to gain the "prize" (line 14) of the Golden Fleece.
9. Legendary Greek poet and musician of magical genius whose playing on the lyre caused his wife, Eurydice, to be released from the realm of the dead on condition that he would not look at her until they had reached the upper world. Breaking his pledge at the last moment, he lost her forever.
1. Island-nymph with whom Ulysses (Odysseus) lived for seven years during his return to Ithaca from the Trojan War.
2. Ignorant of his own identity, Oedipus in a rage killed King Laius of Thebes (in fact his father). Oedipus then delivered Thebes from the power of a sphinx by answering her riddles and won Jocasta (in fact his mother) as his wife and queen.

Than all who fell, than One who rose,
   Than many unsubdued:[3]
35 Not gold, not blood, their altar dowers,
But votive tears and symbol flowers.

Oh, cease! must hate and death return?
   Cease! must men kill and die?
Cease! drain not to its dregs the urn
40   Of bitter prophecy.
The world is weary of the past,
Oh, might it die or rest at last!

                            1822

JOHN CLARE

1793–1864

Badger

When midnight comes a host of dogs and men
Go out and track the badger to his den,
And put a sack within the hole, and lie
Till the old grunting badger passes by.
5 He comes and hears—they let the strongest loose.
The old fox hears the noise and drops the goose.
The poacher shoots and hurries from the cry,
And the old hare half wounded buzzes by.
They get a forkéd stick to bear him down
10 And clap the dogs and take him to the town,
And bait him all the day with many dogs,
And laugh and shout and fright the scampering hogs.
He runs along and bites at all he meets:
They shout and hollo down the noisy streets.

15 He turns about to face the loud uproar
And drives the rebels to their very door.
The frequent stone is hurled where'er they go;
When badgers fight, then everyone's a foe.
The dogs are clapped and urged to join the fray;
20 The badger turns and drives them all away.
Though scarcely half as big, demure and small,
He fights with dogs for hours and beats them all.
The heavy mastiff, savage in the fray,
Lies down and licks his feet and turns away.
25 The bulldog knows his match and waxes cold,
The badger grins and never leaves his hold.

---

3. Saturn and Love are the restored deities of the "world's great age"; "all who fell" are the deities who "fell" when Christ arose from the dead; the "many unsubdued" are idols still worshiped throughout the world.

He drives the crowd and follows at their heels
And bites them through—the drunkard swears and reels.

30 The frighted women take the boys away,
The blackguard laughs and hurries on the fray.
He tries to reach the woods, an awkward race,
But sticks and cudgels quickly stop the chase.
He turns again and drives the noisy crowd
And beats the many dogs in noises loud.
35 He drives away and beats them every one,
And then they loose them all and set them on.
He falls as dead and kicked by boys and men,
Then starts and grins and drives the crowd again;
Till kicked and torn and beaten out he lies
40 And leaves his hold and crackles, groans, and dies.

1835–37   1920

Gypsies

The snow falls deep; the forest lies alone;
The boy goes hasty for his load of brakes,°   brushwood
Then thinks upon the fire and hurries back;
The gypsy knocks his hands and tucks them up,
5 And seeks his squalid camp, half hid in snow,
Beneath the oak which breaks away the wind,
And bushes close in snow like hovel warm;
There tainted mutton wastes upon the coals,
And the half-wasted dog squats close and rubs,
10 Then feels the heat too strong, and goes aloof;
He watches well, but none a bit can spare,
And vainly waits the morsel thrown away.
'Tis thus they live—a picture to the place,
A quiet, pilfering, unprotected race.

1837–41   1920

Song: Love Lives Beyond the Tomb

Love lives beyond
The tomb, the earth, which fades like dew—
I love the fond,
The faithful, and the true.

5   Love lives in sleep,
'Tis happiness of healthy dreams,
Eve's dews may weep,
But love delightful seems.

'Tis seen in flowers,
10 And in the even's pearly dew
On earth's green hours,
And in the heaven's eternal blue.

'Tis heard in spring
When light and sunbeams, warm and kind,
On angel's wing
Brings love and music to the wind.

And where's the voice
So young, so beautiful, and sweet
As nature's choice,
Where spring and lovers meet?

Love lives beyond
The tomb, the earth, the flowers, and dew.
I love the fond,
The faithful, young, and true.

1842–64   1873

First Love

I ne'er was struck before that hour
With love so sudden and so sweet,
Her face it bloomed like a sweet flower
And stole my heart away complete.
My face turned pale as deadly pale.
My legs refused to walk away,
And when she looked, what could I ail?
My life and all seemed turned to clay.

And then my blood rushed to my face
And took my eyesight quite away,
The trees and bushes round the place
Seemed midnight at noonday.
I could not see a single thing,
Words from my eyes did start—
They spoke as chords do from the string,
And blood burnt round my heart.

Are flowers the winter's choice?
Is love's bed always snow?
She seemed to hear my silent voice,
Not love's appeals to know.
I never saw so sweet a face
As that I stood before.
My heart has left its dwelling-place
And can return no more.

1842–64   1920

Farewell

Farewell to the bushy clump close to the river
And the flags[1] where the butter-bump° hides in forever;   *bittern*

1. Irises (tall plants).

Farewell to the weedy nook, hemmed in by waters;
Farewell to the miller's brook and his three bonny daughters;
5   Farewell to them all while in prison I lie—
In the prison a thrall sees naught but the sky.

Shut out are the green fields and birds in the bushes;
In the prison yard nothing builds, blackbirds or thrushes.
Farewell to the old mill and dash of the waters,
10   To the miller and, dearer still, to his three bonny daughters.

In the nook, the larger burdock grows near the green willow;
In the flood, round the moor-cock dashes under the billow;
To the old mill farewell, to the lock, pens, and waters,
To the miller himsel', and his three bonny daughters.

1842–64   1920

I Am

I am: yet what I am none cares or knows
    My friends forsake me like a memory lost,
I am the self-consumer of my woes—
    They rise and vanish in oblivious host,
5   Like shadows in love's frenzied, stifled throes—
And yet I am, and live—like vapors tossed

Into the nothingness of scorn and noise,
    Into the living sea of waking dreams,
Where there is neither sense of life or joys,
10   But the vast shipwreck of my life's esteems;
Even the dearest, that I love the best,
Are strange—nay, rather stranger than the rest.

I long for scenes, where man hath never trod,
    A place where woman never smiled or wept—
15   There to abide with my Creator, God,
    And sleep as I in childhood sweetly slept,
Untroubling, and untroubled where I lie,
The grass below—above the vaulted sky.

1842–64   1865

FELICIA DOROTHEA HEMANS

1793–1835

England's Dead

Son of the ocean isle!
Where sleep your mighty dead?
Show me what high and stately pile
Is reared o'er Glory's bed.

5   Go, stranger! track the deep,
    Free, free the white sail spread!
   Wave may not foam, nor wild wind sweep,
    Where rest not England's dead.

   On Egypt's burning plains,
10   By the pyramid o'erswayed,
   With fearful power the noonday reigns,
    And the palm trees yield no shade.[1]

   But let the angry sun
    From heaven look fiercely red,
15 Unfelt by those whose task is done! —
    There slumber England's dead.

   The hurricane hath might
    Along the Indian shore,
  And far by Ganges' banks at night,
20   Is heard the tiger's roar.

   But let the sound roll on!
    It hath no tone of dread,
  For those that from their toils are gone; —
    There slumber England's dead.

25 Loud rush the torrent floods
    The western wilds among,
  And free, in green Columbia's woods,
    The hunter's bow is strung.

   But let the floods rush on!
30   Let the arrow's flight be sped!
  Why should *they* reck° whose task is done? —   *care*
    There slumber England's dead!

   The mountain storms rise high
    In the snowy Pyrenees,
35 And toss the pine boughs through the sky,
    Like rose leaves on the breeze.

   But let the storm rage on!
    Let the fresh wreaths be shed!
  For the Roncesvalles' field[2] is won, —
40   *There* slumber England's dead.

   On the frozen deep's repose
    'Tis a dark and dreadful hour,

---

1. This specific reference—to the defeat of French forces by the British at Alexandria in the spring of 1801—is followed by more general military references: to eighteenth- and early-nineteenth-century battles in India (lines 17–24), America (lines 25–32), Spain (lines 33–40), and on the sea (lines 41–48).
2. During the Peninsular War (1808–14) between France and Great Britain, fighting occurred in Roncesvalles, a pass in the Pyrenees (mountains separating France and Spain).

When round the ship the ice-fields close,
    And the northern night clouds lower.°   *look threatening*

45   But let the ice drift on!
    Let the cold-blue desert spread!
Their course with mast and flag is done,—
    Even there sleep England's dead.

    The warlike of the isles,
50   The men of field and wave!
Are not the rocks their funeral piles,
    The seas and shores their grave?

    Go, stranger! track the deep,
    Free, free the white sail spread!
55   Wave may not foam, nor wild wind sweep,
    Where rest not England's dead.

                              1822

The Landing of the Pilgrim Fathers in New England

> Look now abroad—another race has fill'd
>   Those populous borders—wide the wood recedes,
> And towns shoot up, and fertile realms are till'd;
>   The land is full of harvests and green meads.
>   —BRYANT[3]

The breaking waves dashed high
    On a stern and rock-bound coast,
And the woods against a stormy sky
    Their giant branches tossed;

5   And the heavy night hung dark,
    The hills and waters o'er,
When a band of exiles moored their bark°   *ship*
    On the wild New England shore.

Not as the conqueror comes,
10   They, the true-hearted, came;
Not with the roll of the stirring drums,
    And the trumpet that sings of fame;

Not as the flying come,
    In silence and in fear;—
15   They shook the depths of the desert gloom
    With their hymns of lofty cheer.

Amidst the storm they sang,
    And the stars heard and the sea;
And the sounding aisles of the dim woods rang
20   To the anthem of the free!

---

3. William Cullen Bryant, *The Ages* (1821), lines 280–83.

The ocean eagle soared
     From his nest by the white wave's foam;
And the rocking pines of the forest roared—
     This was their welcome home!

25   There were men with hoary hair
          Amidst that pilgrim band;—
     Why had *they* come to wither there,
          Away from their childhood's land?

     There was woman's fearless eye,
30   Lit by her deep love's truth;
     There was manhood's brow serenely high,
          And the fiery heart of youth.

     What sought they thus afar?
          Bright jewels of the mine?
35   The wealth of seas, the spoils of war?—
          They sought a faith's pure shrine!

     Aye, call it holy ground,
          The soil where first they trod.
     They have left unstained what there they found—
40   Freedom to worship God.

                                                      1826

Indian Woman's Death-Song[4]

[An Indian woman, driven to despair by her husband's desertion of her for another wife, entered a canoe with her children, and rowed it down the Mississippi towards a cataract. Her voice was heard from the shore singing a mournful death-song, until overpowered by the sound of the waters in which she perished. The tale is related in Long's "Expedition to the Source of St. Peter's River."]

"*Non, je ne puis vivre avec un coeur brisé. Il faut que je retrouve la joie, et que je m'unisse aux esprits libres de l'air.*"[5]
                              —*Bride of Messina*—Translated by MADAME DE STAEL

"Let not my child be a girl, for very sad is the life of a woman."
                                                      The Prairie[6]

     Down a broad river of the western wilds,
     Piercing thick forest-glooms, a light canoe
     Swept with the current: fearful was the speed
     Of the frail bark, as by a tempest's wing
5   Borne leaf-like on to where the mist of spray
     Rose with the cataract's thunder. Yet within,
     Proudly, and dauntlessly, and all alone,

---

4. From Hemans' *Records of Women* (1828).
5. "No, I can't live with a broken heart. I must retrieve my happiness, and be reunited with the spirits of the air" (French). *The Bride of Messina* (1803) is a play by Friedrich von Schiller (1759–

1805), German poet and dramatist. Madame Anne-Louise-Germaine de Staël (1766–1817), French writer and hostess of literary salon.
6. An 1827 novel by the American writer James Fenimore Cooper (1789–1851).

Save that a babe lay sleeping at her breast,
A woman stood! Upon her Indian brow
10 Sat a strange gladness, and her dark hair waved
As if triumphantly. She pressed her child,
In its bright slumber, to her beating heart,
And lifted her sweet voice, that rose awhile
Above the sound of waters, high and clear,
15 Wafting a wild proud strain—a song of death.

"Roll swiftly to the spirit's land, thou mighty stream and free!
Father of ancient waters, roll! and bear our lives with thee!
The weary bird that storms have tossed would seek the sunshine's calm,
And the deer that hath the arrow's hurt flies to the woods of balm.

20 "Roll on!—my warrior's eye hath looked upon another's face,
And mine hath faded from his soul, as fades a moonbeam's trace:
My shadow comes not o'er his path, my whisper to his dream,
He flings away the broken reed. Roll swifter yet, thou stream!

"The voice that spoke of other days is hushed within *his* breast,
25 But *mine* its lonely music haunts, and will not let me rest;
It sings a low and mournful song of gladness that is gone—
I cannot live without that light. Father of waves! roll on!

"Will he not miss the bounding step that met him from the chase?
The heart of love that made his home an ever-sunny place?
30 The hand that spread the hunter's board, and decked his couch of yore?
He will not! Roll, dark foaming stream, on to the better shore!

"Some blessèd fount amidst the woods of that bright land must flow,
Whose waters from my soul may lave the memory of this woe;
Some gentle wind must whisper there, whose breath may waft away
35 The burden of the heavy night, the sadness of the day.

"And thou, my babe! though born, like me, for woman's weary lot,
Smile!—to that wasting of the heart, my own! I leave thee not;
Too bright a thing art *thou* to pine in aching love away—
Thy mother bears thee far, young fawn! from sorrow and decay.

40 "She bears thee to the glorious bowers where none are heard to weep,
And where the unkind one hath no power again to trouble sleep;
And where the soul shall find its youth, as wakening from a dream:
One moment, and that realm is ours. On, on, dark rolling stream!"

1828

WILLIAM CULLEN BRYANT
1794–1878

To a Waterfowl

Whither, 'midst falling dew,
While glow the heavens with the last steps of day,
Far, through their rosy depths, dost thou pursue
    Thy solitary way?

5   Vainly the fowler's° eye   *bird hunter's*
Might mark thy distant flight, to do thee wrong,
As, darkly seen against the crimson sky,
    Thy figure floats along.

Seek'st thou the plashy brink
10 Of weedy lake, or marge of river wide,
Or where the rocking billows rise and sink
    On the chaféd ocean side?

There is a Power, whose care
Teaches thy way along that pathless coast,—
15 The desert and illimitable air,
    Lone wandering, but not lost,

All day thy wings have fanned,
At that far height, the cold thin atmosphere;
Yet stoop not, weary, to the welcome land,
20   Though the dark night is near.

And soon that toil shall end,
Soon shalt thou find a summer home, and rest,
And scream among thy fellows; reeds shall bend,
    Soon, o'er thy sheltered nest.

25   Thou'rt gone, the abyss of heaven
Hath swallowed up thy form, yet, on my heart
Deeply hath sunk the lesson thou hast given,
    And shall not soon depart.

He, who, from zone to zone,
30 Guides through the boundless sky thy certain flight,
In the long way that I must trace alone,
    Will lead my steps aright.

1815   1818, 1821

JOHN KEATS

1795–1821

On First Looking into Chapman's Homer[1]

Much have I traveled in the realms of gold,
   And many goodly states and kingdoms seen;
   Round many western islands have I been
Which bards in fealty° to Apollo[2] hold.   *allegiance*
5 Oft of one wide expanse had I been told
   That deep-browed Homer ruled as his demesne;°   *domain*
   Yet did I never breathe its pure serene°   *atmosphere*
Till I heard Chapman speak out loud and bold:
Then felt I like some watcher of the skies
10   When a new planet swims into his ken;
Or like stout Cortez[3] when with eagle eyes
   He stared at the Pacific—and all his men
Looked at each other with a wild surmise—
   Silent, upon a peak in Darien.

1816

On the Sea

It keeps eternal whisperings around
   Desolate shores, and with its mighty swell
   Gluts twice ten thousand Caverns, till the spell
Of Hecate[4] leaves them their old shadowy sound.
5 Often 'tis in such gentle temper found,
   That scarcely will the very smallest shell
   Be moved for days from where it sometime fell,
When last the winds of Heaven were unbound.
Oh ye! who have your eyeballs vexed and tired,
10   Feast them upon the wideness of the Sea;
   Oh ye! whose ears are dinned with uproar rude,
Or fed too much with cloying melody—
   Sit ye near some old Cavern's Mouth and brood,
Until ye start, as if the sea nymphs quired!°   *choired*

1817

On Sitting Down to Read *King Lear* Once Again

O golden-tongued Romance with serene lute!
   Fair pluméd Siren!° Queen of far away!   *enchantress*
   Leave melodizing on this wintry day,
Shut up thine olden pages, and be mute:
5 Adieu! for once again the fierce dispute

---

1. Translations from Homer, in particular *Odyssey*, Book 5, by George Chapman, a contemporary of Shakespeare's.
2. God of poetic inspiration.
3. Spanish conqueror of Mexico; in fact, Balboa, not Cortez, was the first European to see the Pacific, from Darien, in Panama.
4. Greek goddess associated with witchcraft and the underworld.

Betwixt damnation and impassioned clay
Must I burn through; once more humbly assay°   test
The bitter-sweet of this Shakespearean fruit.
Chief Poet! and ye clouds of Albion,[5]
10   Begetters of our deep eternal theme,
When through the old oak forest I am gone,
Let me not wander in a barren dream,
But when I am consuméd in the fire,
Give me new Phoenix[6] wings to fly at my desire.

1818   1838

When I Have Fears

When I have fears that I may cease to be
Before my pen has gleaned my teeming brain,
Before high-piléd books, in charact'ry,°   written symbols
Hold like rich garners the full-ripened grain;
5   When I behold, upon the night's starred face,
Huge cloudy symbols of a high romance,
And think that I may never live to trace
Their shadows, with the magic hand of chance;
And when I feel, fair creature of an hour,
10   That I shall never look upon thee more,
Never have relish in the faery° power   magical
Of unreflecting love!—then on the shore
Of the wide world I stand alone, and think
Till Love and Fame to nothingness do sink.

1818   1848

To Homer[7]

Standing aloof in giant ignorance,[8]
Of thee I hear and of the Cyclades,[9]
As one who sits ashore and longs perchance
To visit dolphin-coral in deep seas.
5   So thou wast blind!—but then the veil was rent;
For Jove[1] uncurtain'd Heaven to let thee live,
And Neptune made for thee a spumy tent,
And Pan made sing for thee his forest-hive;
Aye, on the shores of darkness there is light,
10   And precipices show untrodden green;
There is a budding morrow in midnight;
There is a triple sight in blindness keen;
Such seeing hadst thou, as it once befel
To Dian,[2] Queen of Earth, and Heaven, and Hell.

1818?   1848

5. Ancient name for England, especially referring to pre-Roman Britain, the era of King Lear.
6. Fabled Arabian bird that, after living for centuries, consumes itself in fire and is reborn.
7. By tradition, blind; here a symbol of poetic illumination.
8. Keats could not read Homer's Greek.
9. Islands near the Greek coast.
1. Jove, Neptune, and Pan: Homer's gods of heaven, sea, and land.
2. The "three-formed" goddess presiding in the moon, in forests, and in the underworld.

The Eve of St. Agnes[3]

1

St. Agnes' Eve—Ah, bitter chill it was!
The owl, for all his feathers, was a-cold;
The hare limped trembling through the frozen grass,
And silent was the flock in woolly fold:
5   Numb were the Beadsman's[4] fingers, while he told
His rosary, and while his frosted breath,
Like pious incense from a censer old,
Seemed taking flight for heaven, without a death,
Past the sweet Virgin's picture, while his prayer he saith.

2

10   His prayer he saith, this patient, holy man;
Then takes his lamp, and riseth from his knees,
And back returneth, meager, barefoot, wan,
Along the chapel aisle by slow degrees:
The sculptured dead, on each side, seem to freeze,
15   Imprisoned in black, purgatorial rails:
Knights, ladies, praying in dumb orat'ries,[5]
He passeth by; and his weak spirit fails
To think how they may ache in icy hoods and mails.

3

Northward he turneth through a little door,
20   And scarce three steps, ere Music's golden tongue
Flattered to tears this aged man and poor;
But no—already had his deathbell rung:
The joys of all his life were said and sung:
His was harsh penance on St. Agnes' Eve:
25   Another way he went, and soon among
Rough ashes sat he for his soul's reprieve,
And all night kept awake, for sinner's sake to grieve.

4

That ancient Beadsman heard the prelude soft;
And so it chanced, for many a door was wide,
30   From hurry to and fro. Soon, up aloft,
The silver, snarling trumpets 'gan to chide:
The level chambers, ready with their pride,
Were glowing to receive a thousand guests:
The carvéd angels, ever eager-eyed,
35   Stared, where upon their heads the cornice rests,
With hair blown back, and wings put crosswise on their breasts.

5

At length burst in the argent revelry,[6]
With plume, tiara, and all rich array,
Numerous as shadows haunting faerily

---

3. January 20, proverbially the coldest winter night. St. Agnes, martyred in the fourth century A.D., is patroness of virgins. Traditionally, a maiden who observes the ritual of St. Agnes' Eve will see a vision of her husband-to-be.
4. From Middle English *bede*, meaning "prayer."

A needy dependent, paid a small stipend to pray regularly for his benefactor. "Rosary" (line 6): a string of beads on which a series of short prayers are counted ("told," line 5).
5. Small chapels in a larger one.
6. Brightly dressed revelers.

40 The brain, new stuffed, in youth, with triumphs gay
Of old romance. These let us wish away,
And turn, sole-thoughted, to one Lady there,
Whose heart had brooded, all that wintry day,
On love, and winged St. Agnes' saintly care,
45 As she had heard old dames full many times declare.

6

They told her how, upon St. Agnes' Eve,
Young virgins might have visions of delight,
And soft adorings from their loves receive
Upon the honeyed middle of the night,
50 If ceremonies due they did aright;
As, supperless to bed they must retire,
And couch supine their beauties, lily white;
Nor look behind, nor sideways, but require
Of Heaven with upward eyes for all that they desire.

7

55 Full of this whim was thoughtful Madeline:
The music, yearning like a God in pain,
She scarcely heard: her maiden eyes divine,
Fixed on the floor, saw many a sweeping train
Pass by—she heeded not at all: in vain
60 Came many a tiptoe, amorous cavalier,
And back retired; not cooled by high disdain;
But she saw not: her heart was otherwhere:
She sighed for Agnes' dreams, the sweetest of the year.

8

She danced along with vague, regardless eyes,
65 Anxious her lips, her breathing quick and short:
The hallowed hour was near at hand: she sighs
Amid the timbrels,° and the thronged resort   hand drums
Of whisperers in anger, or in sport;
'Mid looks of love, defiance, hate, and scorn,
70 Hoodwinked with faery fancy; all amort,[7]
Save to St. Agnes and her lambs unshorn,[8]
And all the bliss to be before tomorrow morn.

9

So, purposing each moment to retire,
She lingered still. Meantime, across the moors,
75 Had come young Porphyro, with heart on fire
For Madeline. Beside the portal doors,
Buttressed from moonlight,[9] stands he, and implores
All saints to give him sight of Madeline,
But for one moment in the tedious hours,
80 That he might gaze and worship all unseen;
Perchance speak, kneel, touch, kiss—in sooth such things have been.

---

7. Dead; i.e., oblivious.
8. Symbolically associated with St. Agnes; new wool offered at the Mass commemorating the saint
was later spun and woven by the nuns (lines 115–17).
9. I.e., concealed in dark shadows.

10

He ventures in: let no buzzed whisper tell:
All eyes be muffled, or a hundred swords
Will storm his heart, Love's fev'rous citadel:
85   For him, those chambers held barbarian hordes,
Hyena foemen, and hot-blooded lords,
Whose very dogs would execrations howl
Against his lineage: not one breast affords
Him any mercy, in that mansion foul,
90   Save one old beldame,° weak in body and in soul.   *old woman*

11

Ah, happy chance! the aged creature came,
Shuffling along with ivory-headed wand,
To where he stood, hid from the torch's flame,
Behind a broad hall-pillar, far beyond
95   The sound of merriment and chorus bland:°   *harmonizing*
He startled her; but soon she knew his face,
And grasped his fingers in her palsied hand,
Saying, "Mercy, Porphyro! hie thee from this place;
They are all here tonight, the whole bloodthirsty race!

12

100   "Get hence! get hence! there's dwarfish Hildebrand;
He had a fever late, and in the fit
He curséd thee and thine, both house and land:
Then there's that old Lord Maurice, not a whit
More tame for his gray hairs—Alas me! flit!
105   Flit like a ghost away."—"Ah, Gossip[1] dear,
We're safe enough; here in this armchair sit,
And tell me how"—"Good Saints! not here, not here;
Follow me, child, or else these stones will be thy bier."

13

He followed through a lowly archéd way,
110   Brushing the cobwebs with his lofty plume,
And as she muttered "Well-a—well-a-day!"
He found him in a little moonlight room,
Pale, latticed, chill, and silent as a tomb.
"Now tell me where is Madeline," said he,
115   "O tell me, Angela, by the holy loom
Which none but secret sisterhood may see,
When they St. Agnes' wool are weaving piously."

14

"St Agnes! Ah! it is St. Agnes' Eve—
Yet men will murder upon holy days:
120   Thou must hold water in a witch's sieve,
And be liege lord of all the Elves and Fays,[2]
To venture so: it fills me with amaze
To see thee, Porphyro!—St. Agnes' Eve!

---

1. Old kinswoman or household retainer.
2. I.e., to hold water in a sieve and to command elves and fairies ("Fays"), Porphyro would have to be a magician.

God's help! my lady fair the conjuror plays[3]
125   This very night: good angels her deceive!
But let me laugh awhile, I've mickle° time to grieve."   much

15

Feebly she laugheth in the languid moon,
While Porphyro upon her face doth look,
Like puzzled urchin on an aged crone
130   Who keepeth closed a wondrous riddle-book,
As spectacled she sits in chimney nook.
But soon his eyes grew brilliant, when she told
His lady's purpose; and he scarce could brook°   check
Tears, at the thought of those enchantments cold,
135   And Madeline asleep in lap of legends old.

16

Sudden a thought came like a full-blown rose,
Flushing his brow, and in his painéd heart
Made purple riot: then doth he propose
A stratagem, that makes the beldame start:
140   "A cruel man and impious thou art:
Sweet lady, let her pray, and sleep, and dream
Alone with her good angels, far apart
From wicked men like thee. Go, go!—I deem
Thou canst not surely be the same that thou didst seem."

17

145   "I will not harm her, by all saints I swear,"
Quoth Porphyro: "O may I ne'er find grace
When my weak voice shall whisper its last prayer,
If one of her soft ringlets I displace,
Or look with ruffian passion in her face:
150   Good Angela, believe me by these tears;
Or I will, even in a moment's space,
Awake, with horrid shout, my foemen's ears,
And beard° them, though they be more fanged than wolves   confront
    and bears."

18

"Ah! why wilt thou affright a feeble soul?
155   A poor, weak, palsy-stricken, churchyard thing,[4]
Whose passing bell[5] may ere the midnight toll;
Whose prayers for thee, each morn and evening,
Were never missed."—Thus plaining,° doth she bring   complaining
A gentler speech from burning Porphyro;
160   So woeful and of such deep sorrowing,
That Angela gives promise she will do
Whatever he shall wish, betide her weal or woe.

19

Which was, to lead him, in close secrecy,
Even to Madeline's chamber, and there hide

---

3. I.e., is trying magic spells.   5. Tolled when a person died ("passed away").
4. I.e., soon to die.

165 Him in a closet, of such privacy
That he might see her beauty unespied,
And win perhaps that night a peerless bride,
While legioned faeries paced the coverlet,
And pale enchantment held her sleepy-eyed.
170 Never on such a night have lovers met,
Since Merlin paid his Demon all the monstrous debt.[6]

20

"It shall be as thou wishest," said the Dame:
"All cates° and dainties shall be storéd there   *delicacies*
Quickly on this feast[7] night: by the tambour frame[8]
175 Her own lute thou wilt see: no time to spare,
For I am slow and feeble, and scarce dare
On such a catering trust my dizzy head.
Wait here, my child, with patience; kneel in prayer
The while: Ah! thou must needs the lady wed,
180 Or may I never leave my grave among the dead."

21

So saying, she hobbled off with busy fear.
The lover's endless minutes slowly passed:
The dame returned, and whispered in his ear
To follow her; with aged eyes aghast
185 From fright of dim espial. Safe at last,
Through many a dusky gallery, they gain
The maiden's chamber, silken, hushed, and chaste;
Where Porphyro took covert, pleased amain.°   *greatly*
His poor guide hurried back with agues in her brain.

22

190 Her falt'ring hand upon the balustrade,
Old Angela was feeling for the stair,
When Madeline, St. Agnes' charméd maid,
Rose, like a missioned spirit, unaware:
With silver taper's light, and pious care,
195 She turned, and down the aged gossip led
To a safe level matting. Now prepare,
Young Porphyro, for gazing on that bed;
She comes, she comes again, like ringdove frayed° and fled.   *affrighted*

23

Out went the taper as she hurried in;
200 Its little smoke, in pallid moonshine, died:
She closed the door, she panted, all akin
To spirits of the air, and visions wide:
No uttered syllable, or, woe betide!
But to her heart, her heart was voluble,
205 Paining with eloquence her balmy side;
As though a tongueless nightingale should swell
Her throat in vain, and die, heart-stifled, in her dell.

6. Possibly alluding to the tale that Merlin, in Arthurian legend a great wizard, lies bound for ages by a spell that he gave to an evil woman to buy her love.
7. The festival, or Mass, honoring St. Agnes.
8. A circular embroidery frame.

24

A casement high and triple-arched there was,
All garlanded with carven imag'ries
210   Of fruits, and flowers, and bunches of knot-grass,
And diamonded with panes of quaint device,
Innumerable of stains and splendid dyes,
As are the tiger-moth's deep-damasked wings;
And in the midst, 'mong thousand heraldries,
215   And twilight saints, and dim emblazonings,
A shielded scutcheon blushed with blood of queens and kings.[9]

25

Full on this casement shone the wintry moon,
And threw warm gules[1] on Madeline's fair breast,
As down she knelt for heaven's grace and boon;°   *gift*
220   Rose-bloom fell on her hands, together pressed,
And on her silver cross soft amethyst,
And on her hair a glory,° like a saint: *halo*
She seemed a splendid angel, newly dressed,
Save wings, for heaven—Porphyro grew faint:
225 She knelt, so pure a thing, so free from mortal taint.

26

Anon his heart revives: her vespers done,
Of all its wreathéd pearls her hair she frees;
Unclasps her warméd jewels one by one;
Loosens her fragrant bodice; by degrees
230   Her rich attire creeps rustling to her knees:
Half-hidden, like a mermaid in sea-weed,
Pensive awhile she dreams awake, and sees,
In fancy, fair St. Agnes in her bed,
But dares not look behind, or all the charm is fled.

27

235   Soon, trembling in her soft and chilly nest,
In sort of wakeful swoon, perplexed she lay,
Until the poppied warmth of sleep oppressed
Her soothéd limbs, and soul fatigued away;
Flown, like a thought, until the morrow-day;
240   Blissfully havened both from joy and pain;
Clasped like a missal where swart Paynims[2] pray;
Blinded alike from sunshine and from rain,
As though a rose should shut, and be a bud again.

28

Stol'n to this paradise, and so entranced,
245   Porphyro gazed upon her empty dress,
And listened to her breathing, if it chanced
To wake into a slumberous tenderness;
Which when he heard, that minute did he bless,
And breathed himself: then from the closet crept,
250   Noiseless as fear in a wide wilderness,

---

9. A shield representing a coat of arms ("scutch-
eon") showed the red pigments ("blushed") indi-
cating royal ancestry.

1. Heraldic red; here, in stained glass.
2. Dark pagans.

And over the hushed carpet, silent, stepped,
And 'tween the curtains peeped, where, lo!—how fast she slept.

29

Then by the bedside, where the faded moon
Made a dim, silver twilight, soft he set
255   A table, and, half anguished, threw thereon
A cloth of woven crimson, gold, and jet—
O for some drowsy Morphean amulet![3]
The boisterous, midnight, festive clarion,
The kettledrum, and far-heard clarinet,
260   Affray his ears, though but in dying tone—
The hall door shuts again, and all the noise is gone.

30

And still she slept an azure-lidded sleep,
In blanchéd linen, smooth, and lavendered,
While he from forth the closet brought a heap
265   Of candied apple, quince, and plum, and gourd;
With jellies soother than the creamy curd,
And lucent syrups, tinct° with cinnamon;   *tinctured*
Manna and dates, in argosy transferred
From Fez;[4] and spicéd dainties, every one,
270   From silken Samarcand to cedared Lebanon.[5]

31

These delicates he heaped with glowing hand
On golden dishes and in baskets bright
Of wreathéd silver: sumptuous they stand
In the retiréd quiet of the night,
275   Filling the chilly room with perfume light.—
"And now, my love, my seraph° fair, awake!   *angel*
Thou art my heaven, and I thine eremite:[6]
Open thine eyes, for meek St. Agnes' sake,
Or I shall drowse beside thee, so my soul doth ache."

32

280   Thus whispering, his warm, unnervéd arm
Sank in her pillow. Shaded was her dream
By the dusk curtains: 'twas a midnight charm
Impossible to melt as icéd stream:
The lustrous salvers° in the moonlight gleam;   *serving dishes*
285   Broad golden fringe upon the carpet lies:
It seemed he never, never could redeem
From such a steadfast spell his lady's eyes;
So mused awhile, entoiled in wooféd° fantasies.   *enwoven*

33

Awakening up, he took her hollow lute—
290   Tumultuous—and, in chords that tenderest be,
He played an ancient ditty, long since mute,
In Provence called *"La belle dame sans merci"*[7]

3. An object, such as an engraved stone, exerting the power of Morpheus, god of sleep.
4. Morocco.
5. Places associated with ancient luxury and wealth.
6. Hermit, religious devotee.
7. "The lady beautiful but without mercy" (French).

Close to her ear touching the melody;
Wherewith disturbed, she uttered a soft moan:
295 He ceased—she panted quick—and suddenly
Her blue affrayéd eyes wide open shone:
Upon his knees he sank, pale as smooth-sculptured stone.

34

Her eyes were open, but she still beheld,
Now wide awake, the vision of her sleep:
300 There was a painful change, that nigh expelled
The blisses of her dream so pure and deep,
At which fair Madeline began to weep,
And moan forth witless words with many a sigh;
While still her gaze on Porphyro would keep,
305 Who knelt, with joinéd hands and piteous eye,
Fearing to move or speak, she looked so dreamingly.

35

"Ah, Porphyro!" said she, "but even now
Thy voice was at sweet tremble in mine ear,
Made tunable with every sweetest vow;
310 And those sad eyes were spiritual and clear:
How changed thou art! how pallid, chill, and drear!
Give me that voice again, my Porphyro,
Those looks immortal, those complainings dear!
Oh leave me not in this eternal woe,
315 For if thou diest, my Love, I know not where to go."

36

Beyond a mortal man impassioned far
At these voluptuous accents, he arose,
Ethereal, flushed, and like a throbbing star
Seen mid the sapphire heaven's deep repose;
320 Into her dream he melted, as the rose
Blendeth its odor with the violet—
Solution sweet: meantime the frost-wind blows
Like Love's alarum° pattering the sharp sleet   *signal, call to arms*
Against the windowpanes; St. Agnes' moon hath set.

37

325 'Tis dark: quick pattereth the flaw-blown° sleet: *gust-blown*
"This is no dream, my bride, my Madeline!"
'Tis dark: the icéd gusts still rave and beat:
"No dream, alas! alas! and woe is mine!
Porphyro will leave me here to fade and pine.—
330 Cruel! what traitor could thee hither bring?
I curse not, for my heart is lost in thine,
Though thou forsakest a deceivéd thing—
A dove forlorn and lost with sick unprunéd[8] wing."

38

"My Madeline! sweet dreamer! lovely bride!
335 Say, may I be for aye thy vassal blest?

8. Unpreened; i.e., disarranged, rumpled.

Thy beauty's shield, heart-shaped and vermeil° dyed?   *vermilion*
Ah, silver shrine, here will I take my rest
After so many hours of toil and quest,
A famished pilgrim—saved by miracle.
340   Though I have found, I will not rob thy nest
Saving of thy sweet self; if thou think'st well
To trust, fair Madeline, to no rude infidel.

39

"Hark! 'tis an elfin-storm from faery land,
Of haggard° seeming, but a boon indeed: *wild, ugly*
345   Arise—arise! the morning is at hand—
The bloated wassaillers° will never heed—   *drunken revelers*
Let us away, my love, with happy speed;
There are no ears to hear, or eyes to see—
Drowned all in Rhenish and the sleepy mead:[9]
350   Awake! arise! my love, and fearless be,
For o'er the southern moors I have a home for thee."

40

She hurried at his words, beset with fears,
For there were sleeping dragons all around,
At glaring watch, perhaps, with ready spears—
355   Down the wide stairs a darkling way they found.—
In all the house was heard no human sound.
A chain-dropped lamp was flickering by each door;
The arras, rich with horseman, hawk, and hound,
Fluttered in the besieging wind's uproar;
360   And the long carpets rose along the gusty floor.

41

They glide, like phantoms, into the wide hall;
Like phantoms, to the iron porch, they glide;
Where lay the Porter, in uneasy sprawl,
With a huge empty flagon by his side:
365   The wakeful bloodhound rose, and shook his hide,
But his sagacious eye an inmate owns:°   *recognizes*
By one, and one, the bolts full easy slide:
The chains lie silent on the footworn stones;
The key turns, and the door upon its hinges groans.

42

370   And they are gone: aye, ages long ago
These lovers fled away into the storm.
That night the Baron dreamt of many a woe,
And all his warrior-guests, with shade and form
Of witch, and demon, and large coffin-worm,
375   Were long be-nightmared. Angela the old
Died palsy-twitched, with meager face deform;
The Beadsman, after thousand aves[1] told,
For aye unsought for slept among his ashes cold.

1819   1820

9. Rhine wine, and fermented honey and water.   the Virgin.
1. As in *Ave Maria* ("Hail Mary"), a salutation to

On the Sonnet

If by dull rhymes our English must be chained,
    And, like Andromeda,² the Sonnet sweet
Fettered, in spite of painéd loveliness;
    Let us find out, if we must be constrained,
5   Sandals more interwoven and complete
To fit the naked foot of poesy;
    Let us inspect the lyre, and weigh the stress
Of every chord, and see what may be gained
    By ear industrious, and attention meet;
10   Misers of sound and syllable, no less
Than Midas³ of his coinage, let us be
    Jealous° of dead leaves in the bay-wreath crown;⁴   *intolerant*
So, if we may not let the Muse be free,
    She will be bound with garlands of her own.

1819   1848

La Belle Dame sans Merci⁵

O what can ail thee, Knight at arms,
    Alone and palely loitering?
The sedge has withered from the Lake
    And no birds sing!

5 O what can ail thee, Knight at arms,
    So haggard, and so woebegone?
The squirrel's granary is full
    And the harvest's done.

I see a lily on thy brow
10   With anguish moist and fever dew,
And on thy cheeks a fading rose
    Fast withereth too.

"I met a Lady in the Meads,°   *meadows*
    Full beautiful, a faery's child,
15 Her hair was long, her foot was light
    And her eyes were wild.

"I made a Garland for her head,
    And bracelets too, and fragrant Zone;°   *girdle*
She looked at me as she did love
20   And made sweet moan.

"I set her on my pacing steed
    And nothing else saw all day long,

---

2. A beautiful princess chained naked to a rock as a sacrifice to a sea monster; rescued by the hero Perseus.
3. A fabulously wealthy king who wished to turn all that he touched into gold; granted his wish by the gods, he quickly repented it.
4. Awarded as prize to a true poet.
5. "The lady beautiful but without mercy" (French). This is an earlier (and widely preferred) version of a poem first published in 1820.

For sidelong would she bend and sing
    A faery's song.

25   "She found me roots of relish sweet,
    And honey wild, and manna dew,
And sure in language strange she said
    'I love thee true.'

"She took me to her elfin grot
30   And there she wept and sighed full sore,
And there I shut her wild wild eyes
    With kisses four.

"And there she lulléd me asleep,
    And there I dreamed, Ah Woe betide!
35 The latest° dream I ever dreamt   *last*
    On the cold hill side.

"I saw pale Kings, and Princes too,
    Pale warriors, death-pale were they all;
They cried, 'La belle dame sans merci
40   Hath thee in thrall!'

"I saw their starved lips in the gloam
    With horrid warning gapéd wide,
And I awoke, and found me here
    On the cold hill's side.

45 "And this is why I sojourn here,
    Alone and palely loitering;
Though the sedge is withered from the Lake
    And no birds sing."

April 1819   1888

Ode to Psyche[6]

O Goddess! hear these tuneless numbers,° wrung   *verses*
    By sweet enforcement and remembrance dear,
And pardon that thy secrets should be sung
    Even into thine own soft-conchéd° ear;   *shell-like*
5 Surely I dreamt today, or did I see
    The wingéd Psyche with awakened eyes?
I wandered in a forest thoughtlessly,
    And, on the sudden, fainting with surprise,
Saw two fair creatures, couchéd side by side
10   In deepest grass, beneath the whisp'ring roof
Of leaves and trembled blossoms, where there ran
    A brooklet, scarce espied:

6. In Greek legend, Psyche (meaning "soul") was loved in secret and in darkness by Cupid, the "wingéd" son of the goddess Venus. After many trials Psyche was united with Cupid in immortality.

'Mid hushed, cool-rooted flowers, fragrant-eyed,
   Blue, silver-white, and budded Tyrian,[7]
15 They lay calm-breathing on the bedded grass;
   Their arms embracéd, and their pinions° too;   *wings*
   Their lips touched not, but had not bade adieu,
As if disjoinéd by soft-handed slumber,
And ready still past kisses to outnumber
20 At tender eye-dawn of aurorean° love: *dawning*
    The wingéd boy I knew;
   But who wast thou, O happy, happy dove?
   His Psyche true!

O latest born and loveliest vision far
25   Of all Olympus' faded hierarchy![8]
Fairer than Phoebe's° sapphire-regioned star,   *the moon's*
  Or Vesper;° amorous glowworm of the sky;   *the evening star*
Fairer than these, though temple thou hast none,
  Nor altar heaped with flowers;
30 Nor virgin choir to make delicious moan
    Upon the midnight hours;
No voice, no lute, no pipe, no incense sweet
  From chain-swung censer teeming;
No shrine, no grove, no oracle, no heat
35   Of pale-mouthed prophet dreaming.

O brightest! though too late for antique vows,
  Too, too late for the fond believing lyre,
When holy were the haunted forest boughs,
  Holy the air, the water, and the fire;
40 Yet even in these days so far retired
  From happy pieties, thy lucent fans,°   *wings*
  Fluttering among the faint Olympians,
I see, and sing, by my own eyes inspired.
So let me be thy choir, and make a moan
45   Upon the midnight hours;
Thy voice, thy lute, thy pipe, thy incense sweet
  From swingéd censer teeming;
Thy shrine, thy grove, thy oracle, thy heat
  Of pale-mouthed prophet dreaming.

50 Yes, I will be thy priest, and build a fane°   *temple*
  In some untrodden region of my mind,
Where branchéd thoughts, new grown with pleasant pain,
  Instead of pines shall murmur in the wind:
Far, far around shall those dark-clustered trees
55   Fledge the wild-ridgéd mountains steep by steep;
And there by zephyrs,° streams, and birds, and bees,   *breezes*
  The moss-lain Dryads° shall be lulled to sleep; *tree nymphs*
And in the midst of this wide quietness
A rosy sanctuary will I dress

---

7. Purple or red, as in the "royal" dye made in ancient Tyre.

8. Lines 24–25: last of the deities to be added to the company of the Greek Olympian gods.

60 With the wreathed trellis of a working brain,
        With buds, and bells, and stars without a name,
    With all the gardener Fancy e'er could feign,
        Who breeding flowers, will never breed the same:
    And there shall be for thee all soft delight
65   That shadowy thought can win,
    A bright torch, and a casement ope at night,
        To let the warm Love⁹ in!

1819   1820

Ode to a Nightingale

1

My heart aches, and a drowsy numbness pains
    My sense, as though of hemlock¹ I had drunk,
Or emptied some dull opiate to the drains
    One minute past, and Lethe-wards² had sunk:
5 'Tis not through envy of thy happy lot,
    But being too happy in thine happiness—
        That thou, light-wingéd Dryad of the trees,
            In some melodious plot
    Of beechen green, and shadows numberless,
10   Singest of summer in full-throated ease.

2

O, for a draught of vintage! that hath been
    Cooled a long age in the deep-delvéd earth,
Tasting of Flora³ and the country green,
    Dance, and Provençal song,⁴ and sunburnt mirth!
15 O for a beaker full of the warm South,
    Full of the true, the blushful Hippocrene,⁵
        With beaded bubbles winking at the brim,
            And purple-stainéd mouth;
    That I might drink, and leave the world unseen,
20   And with thee fade away into the forest dim:

3

Fade far away, dissolve, and quite forget
    What thou among the leaves hast never known,
The weariness, the fever, and the fret
    Here, where men sit and hear each other groan;
25 Where palsy shakes a few, sad, last gray hairs,
    Where youth grows pale, and specter-thin, and dies,
        Where but to think is to be full of sorrow
            And leaden-eyed despairs,
    Where Beauty cannot keep her lustrous eyes,
30   Or new Love pine at them beyond tomorrow.

---

9. I.e., Cupid.
1. Opiate made from a poisonous herb.
2. Towards the river Lethe, whose waters in Hades
bring the dead forgetfulness.
3. Roman goddess of springtime and flowers.

4. Of the late-medieval troubadours of Provence,
in southern France.
5. The fountain of the Muses (goddesses of poetry
and the arts) on Mt. Helicon in Greece; its waters
induce poetic inspiration.

4

Away! away! for I will fly to thee,
  Not charioted by Bacchus and his pards,[6]
But on the viewless° wings of Poesy,   *invisible*
  Though the dull brain perplexes and retards:
35 Already with thee! tender is the night,
  And haply the Queen-Moon is on her throne,
    Clustered around by all her starry Fays;°   *fairies*
      But here there is no light,
  Save what from heaven is with the breezes blown
40   Through verdurous glooms and winding mossy ways.

5

I cannot see what flowers are at my feet,
  Nor what soft incense hangs upon the boughs,
But, in embalméd° darkness, guess each sweet   *perfumed*
  Wherewith the seasonable month endows
45 The grass, the thicket, and the fruit tree wild;
  White hawthorn, and the pastoral eglantine;[7]
    Fast fading violets covered up in leaves;
      And mid-May's eldest child,
  The coming musk-rose, full of dewy wine,
50   The murmurous haunt of flies on summer eves.

6

Darkling° I listen; and for many a time   *in darkness*
  I have been half in love with easeful Death,
Called him soft names in many a muséd rhyme,
  To take into the air my quiet breath;
55 Now more than ever seems it rich to die,
  To cease upon the midnight with no pain,
    While thou art pouring forth thy soul abroad
      In such an ecstasy!
  Still wouldst thou sing, and I have ears in vain—
60   To thy high requiem become a sod.

7

Thou wast not born for death, immortal Bird!
  No hungry generations tread thee down;
The voice I hear this passing night was heard
  In ancient days by emperor and clown:
65 Perhaps the selfsame song that found a path
  Through the sad heart of Ruth,[8] when, sick for home,
    She stood in tears amid the alien corn;
      The same that ofttimes hath
  Charmed magic casements, opening on the foam
70   Of perilous seas, in faery lands forlorn.

8

Forlorn! the very word is like a bell
  To toll me back from thee to my sole self!
Adieu! the fancy cannot cheat so well

---

6. "Bacchus": god of wine, often depicted in a chariot drawn by leopards ("pards").
7. Sweetbrier; wood roses.
8. In the Old Testament, a woman of great loyalty and modesty who, as a stranger in Judah, won a husband while gleaning in the barley fields ("the alien corn," line 67).

As she is famed to do, deceiving elf.
75 Adieu! adieu! thy plaintive anthem fades
Past the near meadows, over the still stream,
Up the hill side; and now 'tis buried deep
In the next valley-glades:
Was it a vision, or a waking dream?
80 Fled is that music:—Do I wake or sleep?

May 1819   1820

Ode on Melancholy

1

No, no, go not to Lethe,[9] neither twist
Wolfsbane, tight-rooted, for its poisonous wine;
Nor suffer thy pale forehead to be kissed
By nightshade,[1] ruby grape of Proserpine;[2]
5   Make not your rosary of yew-berries,[3]
Nor let the beetle, nor the death-moth be
Your mournful Psyche, nor the downy owl[4]
A partner in your sorrow's mysteries;
For shade to shade will come too drowsily,
10   And drown the wakeful anguish of the soul.

2

But when the melancholy fit shall fall
Sudden from heaven like a weeping cloud,
That fosters the droop-headed flowers all,
And hides the green hill in an April shroud;
15   Then glut thy sorrow on a morning rose,
Or on the rainbow of the salt sand-wave,
Or on the wealth of globéd peonies;
Or if thy mistress some rich anger shows,
Imprison her soft hand, and let her rave,
20   And feed deep, deep upon her peerless eyes.

3

She[5] dwells with Beauty—Beauty that must die;
And Joy, whose hand is ever at his lips
Bidding adieu; and aching Pleasure nigh,
Turning to Poison while the bee-mouth sips:
25   Aye, in the very temple of Delight
Veiled Melancholy has her sov'reign shrine,
Though seen of none save him whose strenuous tongue
Can burst Joy's grape against his palate fine;°   sensitive
His soul shall taste the sadness of her might,
30   And be among her cloudy trophies[6] hung.

May 1819   1820

9. River in Hades, the waters of which bring for-
getfulness to the dead.
1. "Nightshade" and "wolfsbane" are poisonous
herbs from which sedatives and opiates were
extracted.
2. Queen of Hades.
3. Symbols of mourning; often growing in ceme-
teries.

4. Beetles, moths, and owls have been tradition-
ally associated with darkness, death, and burial;
Psyche (meaning "soul") has sometimes been sym-
bolized by a moth that escapes the mouth in sleep
or at death.
5. The goddess Melancholy.
6. Symbols of victory, such as banners, hung in
religious shrines.

Ode on a Grecian Urn

1

Thou still unravished bride of quietness,
   Thou foster child of silence and slow time,
Sylvan historian, who canst thus express
   A flowery tale more sweetly than our rhyme:
5   What leaf-fringed legend haunts about thy shape
     Of deities or mortals, or of both,
       In Tempe or the dales of Arcady?[7]
     What men or gods are these? What maidens loath?
   What mad pursuit? What struggle to escape?
10   What pipes and timbrels? What wild ecstasy?

2

Heard melodies are sweet, but those unheard
   Are sweeter; therefore, ye soft pipes, play on;
Not to the sensual ear, but, more endeared,
   Pipe to the spirit ditties of no tone:
15   Fair youth, beneath the trees, thou canst not leave
     Thy song, nor ever can those trees be bare;
       Bold Lover, never, never canst thou kiss,
   Though winning near the goal—yet, do not grieve;
     She cannot fade, though thou hast not thy bliss,
20   Forever wilt thou love, and she be fair!

3

Ah, happy, happy boughs! that cannot shed
   Your leaves, nor ever bid the Spring adieu;
And, happy melodist, unwearièd,
   Forever piping songs forever new;
25   More happy love! more happy, happy love!
     Forever warm and still to be enjoyed,
       Forever panting, and forever young;
All breathing human passion far above,
     That leaves a heart high-sorrowful and cloyed,
30   A burning forehead, and a parching tongue.

4

Who are these coming to the sacrifice?
   To what green altar, O mysterious priest,
Lead'st thou that heifer lowing at the skies,
   And all her silken flanks with garlands dressed?
35   What little town by river or sea shore,
     Or mountain-built with peaceful citadel,
       Is emptied of this folk, this pious morn?
And, little town, thy streets forevermore
     Will silent be; and not a soul to tell
40   Why thou art desolate, can e'er return.

5

O Attic[8] shape! Fair attitude! with brede°   *woven pattern*
   Of marble men and maidens overwrought,

---

7. Tempe and Arcady (or Arcadia), in Greece, are   8. Greek, especially Athenian.
traditional symbols of perfect pastoral landscapes.

With forest branches and the trodden weed;
    Thou, silent form, dost tease us out of thought
45 As doth eternity: Cold Pastoral!
    When old age shall this generation waste,
      Thou shalt remain, in midst of other woe
    Than ours, a friend to man, to whom thou say'st,
  "Beauty is truth, truth beauty,"[9]—that is all
50   Ye know on earth, and all ye need to know.

May 1819   1820

To Autumn

1

Season of mists and mellow fruitfulness,
    Close bosom-friend of the maturing sun;
Conspiring with him how to load and bless
    With fruit the vines that round the thatch-eaves run;
5 To bend with apples the mossed cottage-trees,
    And fill all fruit with ripeness to the core;
      To swell the gourd, and plump the hazel shells
    With a sweet kernel; to set budding more,
And still more, later flowers for the bees,
10 Until they think warm days will never cease,
      For Summer has o'er-brimmed their clammy cells.

2

Who hath not seen thee oft amid thy store?
    Sometimes whoever seeks abroad may find
Thee sitting careless on a granary floor,
15   Thy hair soft-lifted by the winnowing wind;[1]
Or on a half-reaped furrow sound asleep,
    Drowsed with the fume of poppies, while thy hook[2]
      Spares the next swath and all its twinéd flowers:
And sometimes like a gleaner[3] thou dost keep
20   Steady thy laden head across a brook;
    Or by a cider-press, with patient look,
      Thou watchest the last oozings hours by hours.

3

Where are the songs of Spring? Aye, where are they?
    Think not of them, thou hast thy music too—
25 While barréd clouds bloom the soft-dying day,
    And touch the stubble-plains with rosy hue;
Then in a wailful choir the small gnats mourn
    Among the river sallows,° borne aloft   *low-growing willows*
      Or sinking as the light wind lives or dies;
30 And full-grown lambs loud bleat from hilly bourn;°   *field*
    Hedge crickets sing; and now with treble soft

---

9. The quotation marks around this phrase are absent from some other versions also having good authority. This discrepancy has led some readers to ascribe only this phrase to the voice of the Urn; others ascribe to the Urn the whole of the two concluding lines.

1. "Winnowing": blowing the grain clear of the lighter chaff.
2. Small curved blade for cutting grain; sickle.
3. Someone who gathers up ears of corn after reapers have passed.

The redbreast whistles from a garden-croft;[4]
And gathering swallows twitter in the skies.
September 19, 1819   1820

Bright Star

Bright star, would I were steadfast as thou art—
  Not in lone splendor hung aloft the night
And watching, with eternal lids apart,
  Like nature's patient, sleepless Eremite,°   *hermit, devotee*
5 The moving waters at their priestlike task
  Of pure ablution round earth's human shores,
Or gazing on the new soft fallen mask
  Of snow upon the mountains and the moors—
No—yet still steadfast, still unchangeable,
10 Pillowed upon my fair love's ripening breast,
To feel forever its soft fall and swell,
  Awake forever in a sweet unrest,
Still, still to hear her tender-taken breath,
And so live ever—or else swoon to death.
1819   1838

This Living Hand[5]

This living hand, now warm and capable
Of earnest grasping, would, if it were cold
And in the icy silence of the tomb,
So haunt thy days and chill thy dreaming nights
5 That thou wouldst wish thine own heart dry of blood
So in my veins red life might stream again,
And thou be conscience-calmed—see here it is—
I hold it towards you.
1819?   1898

RALPH WALDO EMERSON
1803–1882

Concord Hymn

Sung at the Completion of the Battle Monument,[1] July 4, 1837

By the rude bridge that arched the flood,
  Their flag to April's breeze unfurled,
Here once the embattled farmers stood
  And fired the shot heard round the world.

---

4. Small field, as for a vegetable garden, near a house.
5. Written on a manuscript page of Keats' unfin-

ished poem, *The Cap and Bells.*
1. Commemorating the battles of Lexington and Concord, April 19, 1775.

5 The foe long since in silence slept;
  Alike the conqueror silent sleeps;
 And Time the ruined bridge has swept
  Down the dark stream which seaward creeps.

 On this green bank, by this soft stream,
10 We set to-day a votive° stone;   *offered in gratitude*
 That memory may their deed redeem,
  When, like our sires, our sons are gone.

 Spirit, that made those heroes dare
  To die, and leave their children free,
15 Bid Time and Nature gently spare
  The shaft we raise to them and thee.

              1837, 1876

The Rhodora[2]

On Being Asked, Whence Is the Flower?

In May, when sea-winds pierced our solitudes,
I found the fresh Rhodora in the woods,
Spreading its leafless blooms in a damp nook,
To please the desert and the sluggish brook.
5 The purple petals, fallen in the pool,
Made the black water with their beauty gay;
Here might the red-bird come his plumes to cool,
And court the flower that cheapens his array.
Rhodora! if the sages ask thee why
10 This charm is wasted on the earth and sky,
Tell them, dear, that if eyes were made for seeing,
Then Beauty is its own excuse for being:
Why thou wert there, O rival of the rose!
I never thought to ask, I never knew;
15 But, in my simple ignorance, suppose
The self-same Power that brought me there brought you.

1834   1839, 1847

The Snow-Storm

Announced by all the trumpets of the sky,
Arrives the snow, and, driving o'er the fields,
Seems nowhere to alight: the whited air
Hides hills and woods, the river, and the heaven,
5 And veils the farmhouse at the garden's end.
The sled and traveler stopped, the courier's feet
Delayed, all friends shut out, the housemates sit
Around the radiant fireplace, enclosed
In a tumultuous privacy of storm.

10 Come see the north wind's masonry.
Out of an unseen quarry evermore

2. An azalea native to the northeastern United States.

Furnished with tile, the fierce artificer
Curves his white bastions with projected roof
Round every windward stake, or tree, or door.
15 Speeding, the myriad-handed, his wild work
So fanciful, so savage, nought cares he
For number or proportion. Mockingly,
On coop or kennel he hangs Parian³ wreaths;
A swan-like form invests the hidden thorn;
20 Fills up the farmer's lane from wall to wall,
Maugre° the farmer's sighs; and, at the gate,   *in spite of*
A tapering turret overtops the work.
And when his hours are numbered, and the world
Is all his own, retiring, as he were not,
25 Leaves, when the sun appears, astonished Art
To mimic in slow structures, stone by stone,
Built in an age, the mad wind's night-work,
The frolic architecture of the snow.

1841, 1847

Ode

*Inscribed to W. H. Channing*⁴

Though loath to grieve
The evil time's sole patriot,
I cannot leave
My honied thought
5 For the priest's cant,
Or statesman's rant.

If I refuse
My study for their politique,
Which at the best is trick,
10 The angry Muse
Puts confusion in my brain.

But who is he that prates
Of the culture of mankind,
Of better arts and life?
15 Go, blindworm, go,
Behold the famous States
Harrying Mexico
With rifle and with knife!⁵

Or who, with accent bolder,
20 Dare praise the freedom-loving mountaineer?
I found by thee, O rushing Contoocook!⁶

---

3. I.e., like the fine white marble from the Greek island of Paros.
4. William Henry Channing (1810–1884), a clergyman and abolitionist who urged Emerson to involve himself more actively in the antislavery movement.
5. A reference to the war between the United States and Mexico (1846–48) chiefly over the question of the boundaries of Texas. Emerson was among those Americans who believed that the United States' position was an immoral, imperialist enterprise that would result in extending slaveholding territory.
6. Part of the Merrimack River in New Hampshire.

And in thy valleys, Agiochook![7]
The jackals of the negro-holder.

The God who made New Hampshire
25   Taunted the lofty land
With little men;—
Small bat and wren
House in the oak:—
If earth-fire cleave
30   The upheaved land, and bury the folk,
The southern crocodile would grieve.
Virtue palters;° Right is hence;   *hesitates, equivocates*
Freedom praised, but hid;
Funeral eloquence
35   Rattles the coffin-lid.

What boots° thy zeal,   *profits*
O glowing friend,
That would indignant rend
The northland from the south?
40   Wherefore? to what good end?
Boston Bay and Bunker Hill[8]
Would serve things still;—
Things are of the snake.

The horseman serves the horse,
45   The neatherd serves the neat,[9]
The merchant serves the purse,
The eater serves his meat;
'Tis the day of the chattel,
Web to weave, and corn to grind;
50   Things are in the saddle,
And ride mankind.

There are two laws discrete,
Not reconciled,—
Law for man, and law for things;
55   The last builds town and fleet,
But it runs wild,
And doth the man unking.

'Tis fit the forest fall,
The steep be graded,
60   The mountain tunnelled,
The sand shaded,
The orchard planted,
The glebe tilled,
The prairie granted,
65   The steamer built.

7. The White Mountains of New Hampshire.
8. Hill in Charlestown, Massachusetts, site of the first major battle of the American Revolutionary War, on June 17, 1775; "Boston Bay": site of the Boston Tea Party, on December 16, 1773, an incident that helped provoke the Revolutionary War.
9. Archaic terms for "cowherd" and "cow."

Let man serve law for man;
Live for friendship, live for love,
For truth's and harmony's behoof;°   benefit
The state may follow how it can,
70   As Olympus follows Jove.[1]

          Yet do not I implore
The wrinkled shopman to my surrounding woods,
Nor bid the unwilling senator
Ask votes of thrushes in the solitudes.
75   Every one to his chosen work;—
Foolish hands may mix and mar;
Wise and sure the issues are.
Round they roll till dark is light,
Sex to sex, and even to odd;—
80   The over-god
Who marries Right to Might,
Who peoples, unpeoples,—
He who exterminates
Races by stronger races,
85   Black by white faces,—
Knows to bring honey
Out of the lion;[2]
Grafts gentlest scion
On pirate and Turk.

90   The Cossack eats Poland,[3]
Like stolen fruit;
Her last noble is ruined,
Her last poet mute:
Straight, into double band
95   The victors divide;
Half for freedom strike and stand;—
The astonished Muse finds thousands at her side.

                                                    1847

Intellect[4]

Rule which by obeying grows
Knowledge not its fountain knows
Wave removing whom it bears
From the shores which he compares
5   Adding wings thro° things to range   through
Makes him to his own blood strange

1851   1903

---

1. Jove (Jupiter or Zeus) was the chief of the Greek and Roman gods, who lived on Mount Olympus.
2. The allusion in lines 83–87 is to Samson, who killed a lion and returned later to find the carcass filled with honey (Judges 14.5–10).
3. Russian military despotism, established in Poland after the popular insurrections of 1830–31, was challenged by a new Polish uprising (lines 94–96) in 1846.
4. An untitled notebook entry of Emerson's; the title was added posthumously in 1903.

Brahma[5]

If the red slayer think he slays,
  Or if the slain think he is slain,
They know not well the subtle ways
  I keep, and pass, and turn again.

5 Far or forgot to me is near;
  Shadow and sunlight are the same;
The vanished gods to me appear;
  And one to me are shame and fame.

They reckon ill who leave me out;
10 When me they fly, I am the wings;
I am the doubter and the doubt,
  And I the hymn the Brahmin sings.

The strong gods pine for my abode,
  And pine in vain the sacred Seven,[6]
15 But thou, meek lover of the good!
  Find me, and turn thy back on heaven.

1856   1857, 1867

Days

Daughters of Time, the hypocritic Days,
Muffled and dumb like barefoot dervishes,°   *whirling dancers*
And marching single in an endless file,
Bring diadems and fagots[7] in their hands.
5 To each they offer gifts after his will,
Bread, kingdom, stars, and sky that holds them all.
I, in my pleachéd garden,[8] watched the pomp,
Forgot my morning wishes, hastily
Took a few herbs and apples, and the Day
10 Turned and departed silent. I, too late,
Under her solemn fillet° saw the scorn.   *hair band*
                                     1857, 1867

Fate

Her planted eye to-day controls,
Is in the morrow most at home,
And sternly calls to being souls
That curse her when they come.

                                            1867

---

5. The supreme God of Hindu mythology and, in later theological developments, the divine reality itself, once thought to comprehend the entire universe.
6. Perhaps the seven saints high in the Brahman hierarchy, but lesser than Brahma.
7. Bundles of sticks; "diadems": crowns.
8. To pleach is to entwine, plait, or arrange foliage artificially.

ELIZABETH BARRETT BROWNING

1806–1861

Sonnets from the Portuguese[1]

1

I thought once how Theocritus had sung[2]
  Of the sweet years, the dear and wished-for years,
  Who each one in a gracious hand appears
To bear a gift for mortals, old or young:
5   And, as I mused it in his antique tongue,
  I saw, in gradual vision through my tears,
  The sweet, sad years, the melancholy years,
Those of my own life, who by turns had flung
A shadow across me. Straightway I was 'ware,
10   So weeping, how a mystic Shape did move
Behind me, and drew me backward by the hair;[3]
  And a voice said in mastery, while I strove,—
"Guess now who holds thee?"—"Death," I said. But, there,
  The silver answer rang,—"Not Death, but Love."

43

How do I love thee? Let me count the ways.
I love thee to the depth and breadth and height
My soul can reach, when feeling out of sight
For the ends of Being and ideal Grace.
5   I love thee to the level of everyday's
Most quiet need, by sun and candle-light.
I love thee freely, as men strive for Right;
I love thee purely, as they turn from Praise.
I love thee with the passion put to use
10   In my old griefs, and with my childhood's faith.
I love thee with a love I seemed to lose
With my lost saints—I love thee with the breath,
Smiles, tears, of all my life!—and, if God choose,
I shall but love thee better after death.

1845–46   1850

---

1. The "Sonnets from the Portuguese" were written between 1845, when Elizabeth Barrett met Robert Browning, and 1846, when they were married. An earlier poem, "Catrina to Camoëns," in which Barrett had assumed the persona of the girl who was loved by the sixteenth-century Portuguese poet Camoëns, suggested the lightly disguising title when the sonnets were published in 1850.
2. In Idyll 15 of Theocritus, the Greek pastoral poet of the third century B.C., a singer describes (lines 100–5) the Hours, who have brought Adonis back from the underworld, as "the dear soft-footed Hours, slowest of all the Blessed Ones; but their coming is always longed for, and they bring something for all men."
3. In the *Iliad* 1, just as Achilles is drawing his sword to raise it against his leader, Agamemnon, Pallas Athene, standing behind him and hence invisible to the others, catches him by his hair to warn him.

From Aurora Leigh

From *Book 5*

[POETS AND THE PRESENT AGE]

The critics say that epics have died out
140   With Agamemnon and the goat-nursed gods;[4]
I'll not believe it. I could never deem,
As Payne Knight[5] did (the mythic mountaineer
Who travelled higher than he was born to live,
And showed sometimes the goitre[6] in his throat
145   Discoursing of an image seen through fog),
That Homer's heroes measured twelve feet high.
They were but men:—his Helen's hair turned gray
Like any plain Miss Smith's who wears a front;[7]
And Hector's infant whimpered at a plume[8]
150   As yours last Friday at a turkey-cock.
All actual heroes are essential men,
And all men possible heroes: every age,
Heroic in proportions, double-faced,
Looks backward and before, expects a morn
And claims an epos.[9]
155   Ay, but every age
Appears to souls who live in 't (ask Carlyle)[1]
Most unheroic. Ours, for instance, ours:
The thinkers scout it, and the poets abound
Who scorn to touch it with a finger-tip:
160   A pewter age,[2]—mixed metal, silver-washed;
An age of scum, spooned off the richer past,
An age of patches for old gaberdines,[3]
An age of mere transition,[4] meaning nought
Except that what succeeds must shame it quite
165   If God please. That's wrong thinking, to my mind,
And wrong thoughts make poor poems.
                  Every age,
Through being beheld too close, is ill-discerned
By those who have not lived past it. We'll suppose
Mount Athos carved, as Alexander schemed,

---

4. References to Greek mythological figures: Zeus, king of the gods, had been nursed by a goat; Agamemnon, a chieftain, returned from the Trojan War and was murdered by his wife, Clytemnestra.

5. Richard Payne Knight (1750–1824), a classical philologist, argued that not all of the Elgin Marbles—sculptures and architectural details brought to England from the Parthenon by Lord Elgin—were Greek.

6. An enlargement of the thyroid gland, symptomatic of a disease often caught in mountainous regions and due to a lack of iodine in the water supply.

7. A hairpiece worn by women over the forehead.

8. In the *Iliad* 6, when the warrior Hector attempts to hold his infant son, the boy is so frightened by the crest on his father's helmet that he clings to his nurse and cries.

9. An epic poem.

1. In *On Heroes, Hero-Worship, and the Heroic in History* (1841), Thomas Carlyle (1795–1881), a British historian and essayist, called for a renewed interest in heroism.

2. I.e., a debased time; refers to the practice, initiated by the Greek poet Hesiod (first century B.C.), of assigning the names of increasingly less valuable metals to increasingly less elevated periods in history, such as the Golden Age, the Silver Age, and the Bronze Age.

3. Coats or other garments made of gabardine; also, the smocks of English laborers.

4. "An age of transition" is a quotation from *The Spirit of the Age* (1831) by John Stuart Mill (1806–1873), English philosopher and economist.

170　　To some colossal statute of a man.[5]
　　　　The peasants, gathering brushwood in his ear,
　　　　Had guessed as little as the browsing goats
　　　　Of form or feature of humanity
　　　　Up there,—in fact, had travelled five miles off
175　　Or ere the giant image broke on them,
　　　　Full human profile, nose and chin distinct,
　　　　Mouth, muttering rhythms of silence up the sky
　　　　And fed at evening with the blood of suns;
　　　　Grand torso,—hand, that flung perpetually
180　　The largesse° of a silver river down　　　　　　　　　　　　*bounty*
　　　　To all the country pastures. 'Tis even thus
　　　　With times we live in,—evermore too great
　　　　To be apprehended near.
　　　　　　　　　　　　　　　But poets should
　　　　Exert a double vision; should have eyes
185　　To see near things as comprehensively
　　　　As if afar they took their point of sight,
　　　　And distant things as intimately deep
　　　　As if they touched them. Let us strive for this.
　　　　I do distrust the poet who discerns.
190　　No character or glory in his times,
　　　　And trundles back his soul five hundred years,
　　　　Past moat and drawbridge, into a castle-court,
　　　　To sing—oh, not of lizard or of toad
　　　　Alive i' the ditch there,—'twere excusable,
195　　But of some black chief, half knight, half sheep-lifter,
　　　　Some beauteous dame, half chattel and half queen,
　　　　As dead as must be, for the greater part,
　　　　The poems made on their chivalric bones;
　　　　And that's no wonder: death inherits death.

200　　Nay, if there's room for poets in this world
　　　　A little overgrown (I think there is),
　　　　Their sole work is to represent the age,
　　　　Their age, not Charlemagne's,[6] —this live, throbbing age,
　　　　That brawls, cheats, maddens, calculates, aspires,
205　　And spends more passion, more heroic heat,
　　　　Betwixt the mirrors of its drawing-rooms,
　　　　Than Roland[7] with his knights at Roncesvalles.
　　　　To flinch from modern varnish, coat or flounce,
　　　　Cry out for togas and the picturesque,
210　　Is fatal,—foolish too. King Arthur's self
　　　　Was commonplace to Lady Guenever;
　　　　And Camelot to minstrels seemed as flat
　　　　As Fleet Street[8] to our poets.

5. According to legend, Alexander the Great (356–323 B.C.), king of Macedon, considered a proposal by the sculptor Dionocrates to carve Mount Athos into the statue of a conqueror. In his left hand this massive figure would have held a city, while in his right hand he would have held a basin to catch the waters of the region and to irrigate the pastures below.
6. Charles the Great, or Charles I (A.D. 742–814), a Frankish king and the ruler of a European empire.
7. Hero of the medieval epic *Chanson de Roland*.
8. Street in London, center of the London newspaper and book-publishing district.

Never flinch,
But still, unscrupulously epic, catch
215   Upon the burning lava of a song
The full-veined, heaving, double-breasted Age:
That, when the next shall come, the men of that
May touch the impress with reverent hand, and say
"Behold,—behold the paps° we all have sucked!   *breasts*
220   This bosom seems to beat still, or at least
It sets ours beating: this is living art,
Which thus presents and thus records true life."

1853–56   1857

A Musical Instrument

What was he doing, the great god Pan,[9]
    Down in the reeds by the river?
Spreading ruin and scattering ban,°   *baleful influence*
Splashing and paddling with hoofs of a goat,
5   And breaking the golden lilies afloat
    With the dragonfly on the river.

He tore out a reed, the great god Pan,
    From the deep cool bed of the river;
The limpid water turbidly ran,
10   And the broken lilies a-dying lay,
And the dragonfly had fled away,
    Ere he brought it out of the river.

High on the shore sat the great god Pan
    While turbidly flowed the river;
15   And hacked and hewed as a great god can,
With his hard bleak steel at the patient reed,
Till there was not a sign of the leaf indeed
    To prove it fresh from the river.

He cut it short, did the great god Pan
20   (How tall it stood in the river!),
Then drew the pith, like the heart of a man,
Steadily from the outside ring,
And notched the poor dry empty thing
    In holes, as he sat by the river.

25   "This is the way," laughed the great god Pan
        (Laughed while he sat by the river),
"The only way, since gods began
To make sweet music, they could succeed."
Then, dropping his mouth to a hole in the reed,
30   He blew in power by the river.

9. In Greek mythology, an Arcadian god, in shape half goat, half human, son of Hermes; his function was to make the flocks fertile. He is also musical, his instrument the reed flute, and later pastoral poets made him the patron of their art. One of his loves was the nymph Syrinx; trying to escape him, she sought help from the river nymphs, who turned her into a reed bed: and from a reed Pan made his flute.

Sweet, sweet, sweet, O Pan!
  Piercing sweet by the river!
Blinding sweet, O great god Pan!
The sun on the hill forgot to die,
35 And the lilies revived, and the dragonfly
  Came back to dream on the river.

Yet half a beast is the great god Pan,
  To laugh as he sits by the river,
Making a poet out of a man;
40 The true gods sigh for the cost and pain—
For the reed which grows nevermore again
  As a reed with the reeds in the river.

1860   1862

HENRY WADSWORTH LONGFELLOW
1807–1882

From Evangeline[1]

This is the forest primeval. The murmuring pines and the hemlocks,
Bearded with moss, and in garments green, indistinct in the twilight,
Stand like Druids of eld,[2] with voices sad and prophetic,
Stand like harpers hoar,[3] with beards that rest on their bosoms.
5 Loud from its rocky caverns, the deep-voiced neighbouring ocean
Speaks, and in accents disconsolate answers the wail of the forest.

This is the forest primeval; but where are the hearts that beneath it
Leaped like the roe, when he hears in the woodland the voice of the
    huntsman?
Where is the thatch-roofed village, the home of Acadian farmers,—
10 Men whose lives glided on like rivers that water the woodlands,
Darkened by shadows of earth, but reflecting an image of heaven?
Waste are those pleasant farms, and the farmers forever departed!
Scattered like dust and leaves, when the mighty blasts of October
Seize them, and whirl them aloft, and sprinkle them far o'er the ocean.
15 Naught but tradition remains of the beautiful village of Grand-Pré.

1847

The Jewish Cemetery at Newport[4]

How strange it seems! These Hebrews in their graves,
  Close by the street of this fair seaport town,

1. Some introductory verses to a long poem, a tale of divided lovers, based on a true story told to Nathaniel Hawthorne, and by him to Longfellow. The poem opens in Nova Scotia, Canada (where Longfellow never visited), a region often called Acadia or Acadie, which France ceded to Great Britain in 1713. When the French and Indian War broke out, the French inhabitants who refused to take an oath of allegiance were shipped off; about three thousand were deported in 1755, like those of the village of Grand Pré. The poem is credited with having provoked a wider interest in English hexameter.
2. "Druids of eld (old)": members of a prophetic priesthood in ancient Gaul, Britain, and Ireland.
3. Ancient harpists.
4. The oldest synagogue in the United States is in Newport, R.I.

Silent beside the never-silent waves,
    At rest in all this moving up and down!

5   The trees are white with dust, that o'er their sleep
    Wave their broad curtains in the southwind's breath,
While underneath these leafy tents they keep
    The long, mysterious Exodus[5] of Death.

And these sepulchral stones, so old and brown,
10   That pave with level flags their burial-place,
Seem like the tablets of the Law, thrown down
    And broken by Moses at the mountain's base.[6]

The very names recorded here are strange,
    Of foreign accent, and of different climes;
15   Alvares and Rivera[7] interchange
    With Abraham and Jacob of old times.

"Blessed be God! for he created Death!"
    The mourners said, "and Death is rest and peace;"
Then added, in the certainty of faith,
20   "And giveth Life that nevermore shall cease."

Closed are the portals of their Synagogue,
    No Psalms of David now the silence break,
No Rabbi reads the ancient Decalogue°   *Ten Commandments*
    In the grand dialect the Prophets spake.

25   Gone are the living, but the dead remain,
    And not neglected; for a hand unseen,
Scattering its bounty, like a summer rain,
    Still keeps their graves and their remembrance green.

How came they here? What burst of Christian hate,
30   What persecution, merciless and blind,
Drove o'er the sea—that desert desolate—
    These Ishmaels and Hagars of mankind?[8]

They lived in narrow streets and lanes obscure,
    Ghetto and Judenstrass,[9] in mirk and mire;
35   Taught in the school of patience to endure
    The life of anguish and the death of fire.

All their lives long, with the unleavened bread
    And bitter herbs of exile and its fears,

---

5. The flight of Moses and the Israelites from Egypt.
6. Moses, angered by the disobedience of the Israelites, broke the tablets of the law that God had given them (see Exodus 32.19).
7. Many of the early Jewish families in New England were from Spain and Portugal.
8. Hagar, concubine of Abraham, wandered in the desert with Ishmael, her son by Abraham, after she was sent away by Abraham and Sarah (see Genesis 21.9–21). In many countries, Jews faced legal restrictions as well as prejudice.
9. "Street of Jews" (German); "ghetto": originally, the section of a city in which Jews were forced to live.

The wasting famine of the heart they fed,
40   And slaked its thirst with marah[1] of their tears.

Anathema maranatha![2] was the cry
    That rang from town to town, from street to street;
At every gate the accursed Mordecai[3]
    Was mocked and jeered, and spurned by Christian feet.

45 Pride and humiliation hand in hand
    Walked with them through the world where'er they went;
Trampled and beaten were they as the sand,
    And yet unshaken as the continent.

For in the background figures vague and vast
50   Of patriarchs and of prophets rose sublime,
And all the great traditions of the Past
    They saw reflected in the coming time.

And thus forever with reverted look
    The mystic volume of the world they read,
55 Spelling it backward, like a Hebrew book,[4]
    Till life became a Legend of the Dead.

But ah! what once has been shall be no more!
    The groaning earth in travail and in pain
Brings forth its races, but does not restore,
60   And the dead nations never rise again.

1852   1854, 1858

Snow-Flakes

Out of the bosom of the Air,
    Out of the cloud-folds of her garments shaken,
Over the woodlands brown and bare,
    Over the harvest-fields forsaken,
5   Silent, and soft, and slow
        Descends the snow.

Even as our cloudy fancies take
    Suddenly shape in some divine expression,
Even as the troubled heart doth make
10   In the white countenance confession,
        The troubled sky reveals
        The grief it feels.

---

1. The Hebrew word for "bitter" or "bitterness," and the name of a bitter spring the fleeing Israelites found (Exodus 15.23). Salt water (symbolizing tears), unleavened bread, and bitter herbs are all part of the Passover meal, which commemorates the Exodus.
2. A Greek-Aramaic phrase signifying a terrible curse, applied to those who "love not the Lord Jesus Christ" (1 Corinthians 16.22), and later specifically to the Jews.
3. When Haman, the favored advisor of Ahasuerus (Xerxes), king of Persia, sought to destroy Mordecai and the rest of the Jews, Mordecai stood at the king's gate crying out against the persecution. See Esther 3–4.
4. Hebrew is read from right to left.

This is the poem of the air,
   Slowly in silent syllables recorded;
15 This is the secret of despair,
   Long in its cloudy bosom hoarded,
     Now whispered and revealed
     To wood and field.

                                           1863

The Cross of Snow[5]

In the long, sleepless watches of the night,
   A gentle face—the face of one long dead—
   Looks at me from the wall, where round its head
   The night-lamp casts a halo of pale light.
5 Here in this room she died; and soul more white
   Never through martyrdom of fire was led
   To its repose; nor can in books be read
   The legend of a life more benedight.°   *blessed*
There is a mountain in the distant West
10   That, sun-defying, in its deep ravines
   Displays a cross of snow upon its side.
Such is the cross I wear upon my breast
   These eighteen years, through all the changing scenes
   And seasons, changeless since the day she died.

1879   1886

JOHN GREENLEAF WHITTIER

1807–1892

Telling the Bees[1]

Here is the place; right over the hill
   Runs the path I took;
You can see the gap in the old wall still,
   And the stepping-stones in the shallow brook.

5 There is the house, with the gate red-barred,
   And the poplars tall;
And the barn's brown length, and the cattle-yard,
   And the white horns tossing above the wall.

There are the beehives ranged in the sun;
10   And down by the brink
Of the brook are her poor flowers, weed-o'errun,
   Pansy and daffodil, rose and pink.

---

5. Longfellow's second wife, Fanny, died in 1861 when her dress caught fire; he too was burned trying to save her. The poem was found in his portfolio after his death.
1. Whittier's note explains the former custom in rural New England of informing the bees of the death of a family member and dressing their hives in mourning to prevent them from leaving the hives for a new home.

A year has gone, as the tortoise goes,
   Heavy and slow;
15 And the same rose blows, and the same sun glows,
   And the same brook sings of a year ago.

There's the same sweet clover-smell in the breeze;
   And the June sun warm
Tangles his wings of fire in the trees,
20   Setting, as then, over Fernside farm.

I mind me how with a lover's care
   From my Sunday coat
I brushed off the burrs, and smoothed my hair,
   And cooked at the brookside my brow and throat.

25 Since we parted, a month had passed,—
   To love, a year;
Down through the beeches I looked at last
   On the little red gate and the well-sweep near.

I can see it all now,—the slantwise rain
30   Of light through the leaves,
The sundown's blaze on her window-pane,
   The bloom of her roses under the eaves.

Just the same as a month before,—
   The house and the trees,
35 The barn's brown gable, the vine by the door,—
   Nothing changed but the hives of bees.

Before them, under the garden wall,
   Forward and back,
Went drearily singing the chore-girl small,
40   Draping each hive with a shred of black.

Trembling, I listened: the summer sun
   Had the chill of snow;
For I knew she was telling the bees of one
   Gone on the journey we all must go!

45 Then I said to myself, "My Mary weeps
   For the dead to-day:
Haply her blind old grandsire sleeps
   The fret and the pain of his age away."

But her dog whined low; on the doorway sill,
50   With his cane to his chin,
The old man sat; and the chore-girl still
   Sang to the bees stealing out and in.

And the song she was singing ever since
   In my ear sounds on:—

55   "Stay at home, pretty bees, fly not hence!
    Mistress Mary is dead and gone!"

1858

Abraham Davenport[2]

In the old days (a custom laid aside
With breeches and cocked hats) the people sent
Their wisest men to make the public laws.
And so, from a brown homestead, where the Sound[3]
5 Drinks the small tribute of the Mianus,
Waved over by the woods of Rippowams,
And hallowed by pure lives and tranquil deaths,
Stamford[4] sent up to the councils of the State
Wisdom and grace in Abraham Davenport.

10   'Twas on a May-day of the far old year
Seventeen hundred eighty, that there fell
Over the bloom and sweet life of the Spring,
Over the fresh earth and the heaven of noon,
A horror of great darkness, like the night
15 In day of which the Norland sagas tell,
The Twilight of the Gods.[5] The low-hung sky
Was black with ominous clouds, save where its rim
Was fringed with a dull glow, like that which climbs
The crater's sides from the red hell below.
20 Birds ceased to sing, and all the barnyard fowls
Roosted; the cattle at the pasture bars
Lowed, and looked homeward; bats on leathern wings
Flitted abroad; the sounds of labor died;
Men prayed, and women wept, all ears grew sharp
25 To hear the doom-blast of the trumpet[6] shatter
The black sky, that the dreadful face of Christ
Might look from the rent clouds, not as He looked
A loving guest at Bethany,[7] but stern
As Justice and inexorable Law.

30   Meanwhile in the old State House, dim as ghosts,
Sat the lawgivers of Connecticut,
Trembling beneath their legislative robes.
"It is the Lord's Great Day! Let us adjourn,"
Some said; and then, as if with one accord,
35 All eyes were turned to Abraham Davenport.
He rose, slow cleaving with his steady voice
The intolerable hush. "This well may be

2. "The famous Dark Day of New England, May 19, 1780, was a physical puzzle for many years to our ancestors. . . . The incident of Colonel Abraham Davenport's sturdy protest is a matter of history" [Whittier's note].
3. Long Island Sound, into which the Mianus and Rippowams Rivers flow from western Connecticut.
4. Town in southwestern Connecticut.
5. *Ragnarok* in Scandinavian, and *Götterdämmerung* in German mythology: the total destruction of the universe, as the sun dims, in a final battle between the gods and the giants. Afterward, creation begins again.
6. The trumpet of the Last Judgment. See 1 Corinthians 15.51–53.
7. Where Christ was compassionate and mild when his disciples criticized the woman who poured precious ointment on his head (Matthew 26.6–13).

The Day of Judgment which the world awaits;
But be it so or not, I only know
40   My present duty, and my Lord's command
To occupy till He come. So at the post
Where He hath set me in His providence,
I choose, for one, to meet Him face to face,
No faithless servant frightened from my task,
45   But ready when the Lord of the harvest[8] calls;
And therefore, with all reverence, I would say,
Let God do His work, we will see to ours.
Bring in the candles." And they brought them in.

Then by the flaring lights the Speaker read,
50   Albeit with husky voice and shaking hands,
An act to amend an act to regulate
The shad and alewive[9] fisheries. Whereupon
Wisely and well spake Abraham Davenport,
Straight to the question, with no figures of speech
55   Save the ten Arab signs,[1] yet not without
The shrewd dry humor natural to the man:
His awe-struck colleagues listening all the while,
Between the pauses of his argument,
To hear the thunder of the wrath of God
60   Break from the hollow trumpet of the cloud.

And there he stands in memory to this day,
Erect, self-poised, a rugged face, half seen
Against the background of unnatural dark,
A witness to the ages as they pass,
65   That simple duty hath no place for fear.

                                        1866, 1867

EDWARD FITZGERALD
1809–1883

The Rubáiyát of Omar Khayyám of Naishápúr[1]

1

Wake! For the Sun, who scattered into flight
The Stars before him from the Field of Night,
    Drives Night along with them from Heav'n, and strikes
The Sultán's Turret with a Shaft of Light.

2

5   Before the phantom of False morning died,
Methought a Voice within the Tavern cried,

---

8. See Luke 10.2.
9. A fish in the herring family, like the shad.
1. Arabic numerals.
1. Omar Khayyám (ca. 1050–1132?), Persian poet, mathematician, and astronomer, lived at Nisha-pur, in the province of Khurasan. FitzGerald trans-

lated his epigrammatic quatrains (Rubáiyát, plural of ruba'i, "quatrain"), which he first published in 1859; in three subsequent editions (the fourth edition is printed here) FitzGerald made many alterations of detail, arrangement, and number of stanzas.

"When all the Temple is prepared within,
"Why nods the drowsy Worshipper outside?"

3

And, as the Cock crew, those who stood before
10   The Tavern shouted—"Open then the Door!
    "You know how little while we have to stay,
  "And, once departed, may return no more."

4

Now the New Year[2] reviving old Desires,
The thoughtful Soul to Solitude retires,
15   Where the WHITE HAND OF MOSES on the Bough
Puts out, and Jesus from the Ground suspires.[3]

5

Irám[4] indeed is gone with all his Rose,
And Jamshýd's Sev'n-ringed Cup[5] where no one knows;
  But still a Ruby kindles in the Vine,
20 And many a Garden by the Water blows.

6

And David's lips are lockt; but in divine
High-piping Pehleví,[6] with "Wine! Wine! Wine!
  "Red Wine!"—the Nightingale cries to the Rose
That sallow cheek of hers to incarnadine.°   *redden*

7

25 Come, fill the Cup, and in the fire of Spring
Your Winter-garment of Repentance fling:
  The Bird of Time has but a little way
To flutter—and the Bird is on the Wing.

8

Whether at Naishápúr or Babylon,
30 Whether the Cup with sweet or bitter run,
  The Wine of Life keeps oozing drop by drop,
The Leaves of Life keep falling one by one.

9

Each Morn a thousand Roses brings, you say;
Yes, but where leaves the Rose of Yesterday?
35   And this first Summer month that brings the Rose
Shall take Jamshýd and Kaikobád away.

10

Well, let it take them! What have we to do
With Kaikobád the Great, or Kaikhosrú?

2. "Beginning with the Vernal Equinox, it must be remembered" [FitzGerald's note].
3. The blossoming of trees is compared to the whiteness of Moses' hand as it is described in Exodus 4.6, and the sweetness of flowers to the sweetness of the breath of Jesus.
4. "A royal Garden now sunk somewhere in the Sands of Arabia" [FitzGerald's note].
5. In Persian mythology, Jamshýd was a king of the peris (celestial beings), who, because he had boasted of his immortality, was compelled to live on Earth in human form for seven hundred years, becoming one of the kings of Persia. His cup, the invention of Kai-Kosru (line 38), another Persian king, great-grandson of Kai-Kobad (line 36), was decorated with signs enabling its possessor to foretell the future.
6. The ancient literary language of Persia.

Let Zál and Rustum[7] bluster as they will,
40   Or Hátim[8] call to Supper—heed not you.

                    11

With me along the strip of Herbage strown
That just divides the desert from the sown,
        Where name of Slave and Sultán is forgot—
And Peace to Mahmúd[9] on his golden Throne!

                    12

45   A Book of Verses underneath the Bough,
A Jug of Wine, a Loaf of Bread—and Thou
        Beside me singing in the Wilderness—
Oh, Wilderness were Paradise enow!

                    13

Some for the Glories of This World; and some
50   Sigh for the Prophet's[1] Paradise to come;
        Ah, take the Cash, and let the Credit go,
Nor heed the rumble of a distant Drum!

                    14

Look to the blowing Rose about us—"Lo,
"Laughing," she says, "into the world I blow,
55   "At once the silken tassel of my Purse
"Tear, and its Treasure on the Garden throw."

                    15

And those who husbanded the Golden grain,
And those who flung it to the winds like Rain,
        Alike to no such aureate Earth are turned
60   As, buried once, Men want dug up again.

                    16

The Worldly Hope men set their Hearts upon
Turns Ashes—or it prospers; and anon,
        Like Snow upon the Desert's dusty Face,
Lighting a little hour or two—is gone.

                    17

65   Think, in this battered Caravanserai°   inn
Whose Portals are alternate Night and Day,
        How Sultán after Sultán with his Pomp
Abode his destined Hour, and went his way.

                    18

They say the Lion and the Lizard keep
70   The Courts where Jamshýd gloried and drank deep:
        And Bahrám,[2] that great Hunter—the Wild Ass
Stamps o'er his Head, but cannot break his Sleep.

                    19

I sometimes think that never blows so red
The Rose as where some buried Caesar bled;

---

7. "The 'Hercules' of Persia, and Zál his Father"
[FitzGerald's note].
8. Hátim Tai: a Persian chieftain, an archetype of
Eastern hospitality.
9. Sultan Máhmúd (A.D. 971–1031) of Ghazni, in

Afghanistan, renowned both as ruler and as the
conqueror of India.
1. I.e., Mohammed's.
2. A Sassanian king who, according to legend, met
his death while hunting the wild ass.

75   That every Hyacinth the Garden wears
       Dropt in her Lap from some once lovely Head.

20

And this reviving Herb whose tender Green
Fledges the river-lip on which we lean—
    Ah, lean upon it lightly! for who knows
80   From what once lovely Lip it springs unseen!

21

Ah, my Belovéd, fill the Cup that clears
TODAY of past Regrets and future Fears:
    Tomorrow!—Why, Tomorrow I may be
Myself with Yesterday's Sev'n thousand Years.

22

85 For some we loved, the loveliest and the best
That from his Vintage rolling Time hath prest,
    Have drunk their Cup a Round or two before,
And one by one crept silently to rest.

23

And we, that make merry in the Room
90 They left, and Summer dresses in new bloom,
    Ourselves must we beneath the Couch of Earth
Descend—ourselves to make a Couch—for whom?

24

Ah, make the most of what we yet may spend,
Before we too into the Dust descend;
95   Dust into Dust, and under Dust to lie,
Sans Wine, sans Song, sans Singer, and sans End!

25

Alike for those who for TODAY prepare,
And those that after some TOMORROW stare,
    A Muezzín[3] from the Tower of Darkness cries,
100 "Fools! your Reward is neither Here nor There."

26

Why, all the Saints and Sages who discussed
Of the Two Worlds so wisely—they are thrust
    Like foolish Prophets forth; their Words to Scorn
Are scattered, and their Mouths are stopt with Dust.

27

105 Myself when young did eagerly frequent
Doctor and Saint, and heard great argument
    About it and about: but evermore
Came out by the same door where in I went.

28

With them the seed of Wisdom did I sow,
110 And with mine own hand wrought to make it grow;
    And this was all the Harvest that I reaped—
"I came like Water, and like Wind I go."

---

3. The crier who calls the hours of prayer from tower or minaret.

29

Into this Universe, and *Why* not knowing
Nor *Whence*, like Water willy-nilly flowing;
115   And out of it, as Wind along the Waste,
I know not *Whither*, willy-nilly blowing.

30

What, without asking, hither hurried *Whence?*
And, without asking, *Whither* hurried hence!
    Oh, many a Cup of this forbidden Wine[4]
120   Must drown the memory of that insolence!

31

Up from Earth's Center through the Seventh Gate
I rose, and on the Throne of Saturn[5] sate,
    And many a Knot unraveled by the Road;
But not the Master-knot of Human Fate.

32

125   There was the Door to which I found no Key;
There was the Veil through which I might not see:
    Some little talk awhile of ME and THEE
There was—and then no more of THEE and ME.

33

Earth could not answer; nor the Seas that mourn
130   In flowing Purple, of their Lord forlorn;
    Nor rolling Heaven, with all his Signs revealed
And hidden by the sleeve of Night and Morn.

34

Then of the THEE IN ME who works behind
The Veil, I lifted up my hands to find
135   A lamp amid the Darkness; and I heard,
As from Without—"THE ME WITHIN THEE BLIND!"

35

Then to the Lip of this poor earthen Urn
I leaned, the Secret of my Life to learn:
    And Lip to Lip it murmured—"While you live,
140   "Drink! for, once dead, you never shall return."

36

I think the Vessel, that with fugitive
Articulation answered, once did live,
    And drink; and Ah! the passive Lip I kissed,
How many Kisses might it take—and give!

37

145   For I remember stopping by the way
To watch a Potter thumping his wet Clay:
    And with its all-obliterated Tongue
It murmured—"Gently, Brother, gently, pray!"

---

4. Alcohol is forbidden to Mohammedans.
5. "Lord of the Seventh Heaven" [FitzGerald's note]. In ancient astronomy, Saturn was the most remote of the seven known planets; hence, Omar had reached the bounds of astronomical knowledge.

38

And has not such a Story from of Old
150   Down Man's successive generations rolled
    Of such a clod of saturated Earth
  Cast by the Maker into Human mold?

39

And not a drop that from our Cups we throw
For Earth to drink of, but may steal below
155   To quench the fire of Anguish in some Eye
There hidden—far beneath, and long ago.

40

As then the Tulip for her morning sup
Of Heav'nly Vintage from the soil looks up,
    Do you devoutly do the like, till Heav'n
160   To Earth invert you—like an empty Cup.

41

Perplext no more with Human or Divine,
Tomorrow's tangle to the winds resign,
    And lose your fingers in the tresses of
The Cypress-slender Minister of Wine.[6]

42

165   And if the Wine you drink, the Lip you press,
End in what All begins and ends in—Yes;
    Think then you are TODAY what YESTERDAY
You were—TOMORROW you shall not be less.

43

So when that Angel of the darker Drink
170   At last shall find you by the river-brink,
    And, offering his Cup, invite your Soul
Forth to your Lips to quaff—you shall not shrink.

44

Why, if the Soul can fling the Dust aside,
And naked on the Air of Heaven ride,
175   Were't not a Shame—were't not a Shame for him
In this clay carcase crippled to abide?

45

'Tis but a Tent where takes his one day's rest
A Sultán to the realm of Death addrest;
    The Sultán rises, and the dark Ferrásh[7]
180   Strikes, and prepares it for another Guest.

46

And fear not lest Existence closing your
Account, and mine, should know the like no more;
    The Eternal Sákí ° from that Bowl has poured   *cup-bearer*
Millions of Bubbles like us, and will pour.

---

6. The maidservant who pours the wine.
7. The servant charged with setting up and striking the tent.

47

185 When You and I behind the Veil are past,
Oh, but the long, long while the World shall last,
   Which of our Coming and Departure heeds
As the Sea's self should heed a pebble-cast.

48

A Moment's Halt—a momentary taste
190 Of BEING from the Well amid the Waste—
   And Lo!—the phantom Caravan has reached
The NOTHING it set out from—Oh, make haste!

49

Would you that spangle of Existence spend
About THE SECRET—quick about it, Friend!
195   A Hair perhaps divides the False and True—
And upon what, prithee, may life depend?

50

A Hair perhaps divides the False and True;
Yes; and a single Alif[8] were the clue—
   Could you but find it—to the Treasure-house,
200 And peradventure to THE MASTER too;

51

Whose secret Presence, through Creation's veins
Running Quicksilver-like eludes your pains;
   Taking all shapes from Máh to Máhi;[9] and
They change and perish all—but He remains;

52

205 A moment guessed—then back behind the Fold
Immerst of Darkness round the Drama rolled
   Which, for the Pastime of Eternity,
He doth Himself contrive, enact, behold.

53

But if in vain, down on the stubborn floor
210 Of Earth, and up to Heav'n's unopening Door,
   You gaze TODAY, while You are You—how then
TOMORROW, You when shall be You no more?

54

Waste not your Hour, nor in the vain pursuit
Of This and That endeavor and dispute;
215   Better be jocund with the fruitful Grape
Than sadden after none, or bitter, Fruit.

55

You know, my Friends, with what a brave Carouse
I made a Second Marriage in my house;
   Divorced old barren Reason from my Bed,
220 And took the Daughter of the Vine to Spouse.

---

8. First letter of Arabic alphabet, consisting of a   9. From lowest to highest.
single vertical stroke.

56

For "Is" and "Is-not" though with Rule and Line
And "Up-and-down" by Logic I define,
   Of all that one should care to fathom, I
Was never deep in anything but—Wine.

57

225 Ah, but my Computations, People say,
Reduced the Year to better reckoning?[1]—Nay,
   'Twas only striking from the Calendar
Unborn Tomorrow, and dead Yesterday.

58

And lately, by the Tavern Door agape,
230 Came shining through the Dusk an Angel Shape
   Bearing a Vessel on his Shoulder; and
He bid me taste of it; and 'twas—the Grape!

59

The Grape that can with Logic absolute
The Two-and-Seventy jarring Sects[2] confute:
235   The sovereign Alchemist that in a trice
Life's leaden metal into Gold transmute:

60

The mighty Mahmúd, Allah-breathing Lord,[3]
That all the misbelieving and black Horde
   Of Fears and Sorrows that infest the Soul
240 Scatters before him with his whirlwind Sword.

61

Why, be this Juice the growth of God, who dare
Blaspheme the twisted tendril as a Snare?
   A Blessing, we should use it, should we not?
And if a Curse—why, then, Who set it there?

62

245 I must abjure the Balm of Life, I must,
Scared by some After-reckoning ta'en on trust,
   Or lured with Hope of some Diviner Drink,
To fill the Cup—when crumbled into Dust!

63

Oh threats of Hell and Hopes of Paradise!
250 One thing at least is certain—*This* Life flies;
   One thing is certain and the rest is Lies;
The Flower that once has blown for ever dies.

64

Strange, is it not? that of the myriads who
Before us passed the door of Darkness through,
255   Not one returns to tell us of the Road,
Which to discover we must travel too.

---

1. Omar was one of the learned men who had been charged with reforming the calendar.
2. "The 72 sects into which Islamism so soon split" [FitzGerald's note].
3. "This alludes to Máhmúd's Conquest of India and its swarthy Idolators" [FitzGerald's note].

65

The Revelations of Devout and Learned
Who rose before us, and as Prophets burned,
   Are all but Stories, which, awoke from Sleep
260 They told their comrades, and to Sleep returned.

66

I sent my Soul through the Invisible,
Some letter of that Afterlife to spell:
   And by and by my Soul returned to me,
And answered "I Myself am Heav'n and Hell:"

67

265 Heav'n but the Vision of fulfilled Desire,
And Hell the Shadow from a Soul on fire,
   Cast on the Darkness into which Ourselves,
So late emerged from, shall so soon expire.

68

We are no other than a moving row
270 Of Magic Shadow-shapes that come and go
   Round with the Sun-illumined Lantern held
In Midnight by the Master of the Show;

69

But helpless Pieces of the Game He plays
Upon his Checkerboard of Nights and Days;
275   Hither and thither moves, and checks, and slays,
And one by one back in the Closet lays.

70

The Ball no question makes of Ayes and Noes,
But Here or There as strikes the Player goes;
   And He that tossed you down into the Field,
280 *He* knows about it all—HE knows—HE knows!

71

The Moving Finger writes; and, having writ,
Moves on: nor all your Piety nor Wit
   Shall lure it back to cancel half a Line,
Nor all your Tears wash out a Word of it.

72

285 And that inverted Bowl they call the Sky,
Whereunder crawling cooped we live and die,
   Lift not your hands to *It* for help—for It
As impotently moves as you or I.

73

With Earth's first Clay They did the Last Man knead,
290 And there of the Last Harvest sowed the Seed:
   And the first Morning of Creation wrote
What the Last Dawn of Reckoning shall read.

74

YESTERDAY *This* Day's Madness did prepare;
TOMORROW's Silence, Triumph, or Despair:

295　　Drink! for you know not whence you came, nor why:
　　　Drink! for you know not why you go, nor where.

75

I tell you this—When, started from the Goal,
Over the flaming shoulders of the Foal[4]
　　Of Heav'n, Parwín and Mushtarí[5] they flung,
300　In my predestined Plot of Dust and Soul.

76

The Vine had struck a fiber: which about
If clings my Being—let the Dervish[6] flout;
　　Of my Base metal may be filed a Key,
That shall unlock the Door he howls without.

77

305　And this I know: whether the one True Light
　　　Kindle to Love, or Wrath consume me quite,
　　　　One Flash of It within the Tavern caught
　　　Better than in the Temple lost outright.

78

What! out of senseless Nothing to provoke
310　A conscious Something to resent the yoke
　　　　Of unpermitted Pleasure, under pain
　　　Of Everlasting Penalties, if broke!

79

What! from his helpless Creature be repaid
Pure Gold for what he lent him dross-allayed—
315　　Sue for a Debt he never did contract,
　　　And cannot answer—Oh the sorry trade!

80

Oh Thou, who didst with pitfall and with gin°　　　　　　　　　　trap
Beset the Road I was to wander in,
　　　Thou wilt not with Predestined Evil round
320　Enmesh, and then impute my Fall to Sin!

81

Oh Thou, who Man of baser Earth didst make,
And ev'n with Paradise devise the Snake:
　　　For all the Sin wherewith the Face of Man
Is blackened—Man's forgiveness give—and take!

82

325　As under cover of departing Day
　　　Slunk hunger-stricken Ramazán[7] away,
　　　　Once more within the Potter's house alone
　　　I stood, surrounded by the Shapes of Clay.

---

4. The constellation known as the Colt (*Equu-leus*) or Foal.
5. "The Pleiads and Jupiter" [FitzGerald's note]; Omar ascribes his fate to the position of the stars and planets at the time of his birth.

6. Member of any of several Muslim orders taking vows of austerity and poverty.
7. The Mohammedans' annual thirty-day fast, during which no food may be taken from dawn to sunset.

83

Shapes of all Sorts and Sizes, great and small,
330   That stood along the floor and by the wall;
    And some loquacious Vessels were; and some
  Listened perhaps, but never talked at all.

84

Said one among them—"Surely not in vain
"My substance of the common Earth was ta'en
335   "And to this Figure molded, to be broke,
"Or trampled back to shapeless Earth again."

85

Then said a Second—"Ne'er a peevish Boy
"Would break the Bowl from which he drank in joy;
    "And He that with his hand the Vessel made
340   "Will surely not in after Wrath destroy."

86

After a momentary silence spake
Some Vessel of a more ungainly Make;
    "They sneer at me for leaning all awry:
"What! did the Hand then of the Potter shake?"

87

345 Whereat some one of the loquacious Lot—
I think a Súfi° pipkin—waxing hot—   *mystic*
    "All this of Pot and Potter—Tell me then,
"Who is the Potter, pray, and who the Pot?"

88

"Why," said another, "Some there are who tell
350   "Of one who threatens he will toss to Hell
    "The luckless Pots he marred in making—Pish!
"He's a Good Fellow, and 'twill all be well."

89

"Well," murmured one, "Let whoso make or buy,
"My Clay with long Oblivion is gone dry:
355   "But fill me with the old familiar Juice,
"Methinks I might recover by and by."

90

So while the Vessels one by one were speaking,
The little Moon[8] looked in that all were seeking:
    And then they jogged each other, "Brother! Brother!
360   "Now for the Porter's shoulder-knot[9] a-creaking!"

———————

91

Ah, with the Grape my fading Life provide,
And wash the Body whence the Life has died,
    And lay men shrouded in the living Leaf,
By some not unfrequented Garden-side.

---

8. The new moon, which signaled the end of Ramazán.

9. The knot on the porter's shoulder strap from which the wine jars were hung.

92

365 That ev'n my buried Ashes such a snare
 Of Vintage shall fling up into the Air
  As not a True-believer passing by
 But shall be overtaken unaware.

93

 Indeed the Idols I have loved so long
370 Have done my credit in this World much wrong:
  Have drowned my Glory in a shallow Cup,
 And sold my Reputation for a Song.

94

 Indeed, indeed, Repentance oft before
 I swore—but was I sober when I swore?
375 And then and then came Spring, and Rose-in-hand
 My threadbare Penitence apieces tore.

95

 And much as Wine has played the Infidel,
 And robbed me of my Robe of Honor—Well,
  I wonder often what the Vintners buy
380 One half so precious as the stuff they sell.

96

 Yet Ah, that Spring should vanish with the Rose!
 That Youth's sweet-scented manuscript should close!
  The Nightingale that in the branches sang,
 Ah whence, and whither flown again, who knows!

97

385 Would but the Desert of the Fountain yield
 One glimpse—if dimly, yet indeed, revealed,
  To which the fainting Traveler might spring,
 As springs the trampled herbage of the field!

98

 Would but some wingéd Angel ere too late
390 Arrest the yet unfolded Roll of Fate,
  And make the stern Recorder otherwise
 Enregister, or quite obliterate!

99

 Ah Love! could you and I with Him conspire
 To grasp this sorry Scheme of Things entire,
395 Would not we shatter it to bits—and then
 Remold it nearer to the Heart's Desire!

100

 Yon rising Moon that looks for us again—
 How oft hereafter will she wax and wane;
  How oft hereafter rising look for us
400 Through this same Garden — and for *one* in vain!

101

 And when like her, oh Sákí, you shall pass
 Among the Guests Star-scattered on the Grass,

And in your joyous errand reach the spot
Where I made One—turn down an empty Glass!
                                              TAMÁM[1]

                                                              1859, 1879

OLIVER WENDELL HOLMES
1809–1894

The Chambered Nautilus[1]

This is the ship of pearl, which, poets feign,
    Sails the unshadowed main,°   *sea*
      The venturous bark that flings
On the sweet summer wind its purpled wings
5 In gulfs enchanted, where the Siren[2] sings,
      And coral reefs lie bare,
Where the cold sea-maids rise to sun their streaming hair.

Its webs of living gauze no more unfurl;
    Wrecked is the ship of pearl!
10   And every chambered cell,
Where its dim dreaming life was wont to dwell,
As the frail tenant shaped his growing shell,
      Before thee lies revealed,
Its irised° ceiling rent, its sunless crypt unsealed!   *iridescent*

15 Year after year beheld the silent toil
    That spread his lustrous coil;
      Still, as the spiral grew,
He left the past year's dwelling for the new,
Stole with soft step its shining archway through,
20   Built up its idle door,
Stretched in his last-found home, and knew the old no more.

Thanks for the heavenly message brought by thee,
    Child of the wandering sea,
      Cast from her lap, forlorn!
25 From thy dead lips a clearer note is born
Than ever Triton[3] blew from wreathéd horn!
      While on mine ear it rings,
Through the deep caves of thought I hear a voice that sings:

Build thee more stately mansions,[4] O my soul,
30   As the swift seasons roll!

---

1. "It is ended."

1. A small mollusk with an external spiral shell, pearly on the inside (lines 1, 9), that grows as chambers are added; the webbed membranes on its back were once thought to function as sails.
2. In classical mythology, a female creature whose magically sweet song drew sailors to their deaths

on the reef of her island.
3. Son of Poseidon, god of the ocean, who blows on a sea conch; cf. Wordsworth, "The World Is Too Much with Us," line 14 (p. 735).
4. Cf. John 14.2: "In my Father's house are many mansions."

Leave thy low-vaulted past!
Let each new temple, nobler than the last,
Shut thee from heaven with a dome more vast,
    Till thou at length art free,
35 Leaving thine outgrown shell by life's unresting sea!

1858

EDGAR ALLAN POE
1809–1849

Sonnet—To Science

Science! true daughter of Old Time thou art!
    Who alterest all things with thy peering eyes.
Why preyest thou thus upon the poet's heart,
    Vulture, whose wings are dull realities?
5   How should he love thee? or how deem thee wise?
    Who wouldst not leave him in his wandering
To seek for treasure in the jeweled skies,
    Albeit he soared with an undaunted wing?
Hast thou not dragged Diana[1] from her car?
10   And driven the Hamadryad[2] from the wood
To seek a shelter in some happier star?
    Hast thou not torn the Naiad° from her flood,   *freshwater nymph*
The Elfin from the green grass, and from me
The summer dream beneath the tamarind tree?[3]

1829   1829, 1845

To Helen

Helen, thy beauty is to me
    Like those Nicéan barks[4] of yore,
That gently, o'er a perfumed sea,
    The weary, way-worn wanderer bore
5   To his own native shore.

On desperate seas long wont to roam,
    Thy hyacinth hair,[5] thy classic face,
Thy Naiad airs have brought me home
    To the glory that was Greece
10 And the grandeur that was Rome.

Lo! in yon brilliant window-niche
    How statue-like I see thee stand,

1. Roman goddess of the hunt, revered for her chastity; her "car" is the moon.
2. Wood nymph said to live and die with the tree she inhabits.
3. An Asian tree the fruit of which is used for medicine and for food.
4. Boats, perhaps from some Mediterranean loca-

tion; variously interpreted by Poe scholars.
5. In his story "Ligeia" (1838), Poe calls "the raven-black, the glossy, the luxuriant and naturally curling tresses . . . 'hyacinthine.'" The blood of the slain youth Hyacinthus, whom Apollo loved, was changed into a purple flower.

The agate lamp within thy hand!
Ah! Psyche,[6] from the regions which
15   Are Holy Land!

1823   1831, 1845

The City in the Sea

Lo! Death has reared himself a throne
In a strange city lying alone
Far down within the dim West,[7]
Where the good and the bad and the worst and the best
5   Have gone to their eternal rest.
There shrines and palaces and towers
(Time-eaten towers that tremble not!)
Resemble nothing that is ours.
Around, by lifting winds forgot,
10   Resignedly beneath the sky
The melancholy waters lie.

No rays from the holy heaven come down
On the long night-time of that town;
But light from out the lurid sea
15   Streams up the turrets silently—
Gleams up the pinnacles far and free—
Up domes—up spires—up kingly halls—
Up fanes—up Babylon-like[8] walls—
Up shadowy long-forgotten bowers
20   Of sculptured ivy and stone flowers—
Up many and many a marvelous shrine
Whose wreathéd friezes intertwine
The viol, the violet, and the vine.

Resignedly beneath the sky
25   The melancholy waters lie.
So blend the turrets and shadows there
That all seem pendulous in air,
While from a proud tower in the town
Death looks gigantically down.

30   There open fanes° and gaping graves   *temples, churches*
Yawn level with the luminous waves;
But not the riches there that lie
In each idol's diamond eye—
Not the gaily-jeweled dead
35   Tempt the waters from their bed;
For no ripples curl, alas!
Along that wilderness of glass—
No swellings tell that winds may be

6. Having lost her lover, Cupid, because she dis-
obeyed his order not to look at him (he awakened
when a drop of hot oil from her lamp fell on him),
Psyche appealed for help to his mother, Venus.
One punitive task set by Venus was that Psyche
bring her a portion of the beauty of Proserpina,
queen of the underworld.
7. To "go west" is to die.
8. Babylon traditionally symbolizes the wicked
city doomed (see, for example, Isaiah 14.4–23 and
Revelation 16.18–19).

Upon some far-off happier sea—
40 No heavings hint that winds have been
On seas less hideously serene.

But lo, a stir is in the air!
The wave—there is a movement there!
As if the towers had thrust aside,
45 In slightly sinking, the dull tide—
As if their tops had feebly given
A void within the filmy Heaven.
The waves have now a redder glow—
The hours are breathing faint and low—
50 And when, amid no earthly moans,
Down, down that town shall settle hence,
Hell, rising from a thousand thrones,
Shall do it reverence.

1831, 1845

The Raven[9]

1 Once upon a midnight dreary, while I pondered, weak and weary,
Over many a quaint and curious volume of forgotten lore—
While I nodded, nearly napping, suddenly there came a tapping,
As of some one gently rapping, rapping at my chamber door.
5 " 'Tis some visiter," I muttered, "tapping at my chamber door—
Only this and nothing more."

Ah, distinctly I remember it was in the bleak December;
And each separate dying ember wrought its ghost upon the floor.
Eagerly I wished the morrow;—vainly I had sought to borrow
10 From my books surcease of sorrow—sorrow for the lost Lenore—
For the rare and radiant maiden whom the angels name Lenore—
Nameless *here* for evermore.

And the silken, sad, uncertain rustling of each purple curtain
Thrilled me—filled me with fantastic terrors never felt before;
15 So that now, to still the beating of my heart, I stood repeating
" 'Tis some visiter entreating entrance at my chamber door—
Some late visiter entreating entrance at my chamber door;—
This it is and nothing more."

Presently my soul grew stronger; hesitating then no longer,
20 "Sir," said I, "or Madam, truly your forgiveness I implore;
But the fact is I was napping, and so gently you came rapping,
And so faintly you came tapping, tapping at my chamber door,
That I scarce was sure I heard you"—here I opened wide the door;—
Darkness there and nothing more.

25 Deep into that darkness peering, long I stood there wondering, fearing,
Doubting, dreaming dreams no mortal ever dared to dream before;

---

9. Many slightly different texts of this poem exist; reprinted here is the version published in *The Raven and Other Poems*.

But the silence was unbroken, and the stillness gave no token,
And the only word there spoken was the whispered word, "Lenore?"
This I whispered, and an echo murmured back the word, "Lenore!"
30   Merely this and nothing more.

Back into the chamber turning, all my soul within me burning,
Soon again I heard a tapping somewhat louder than before.
"Surely," said I, "surely that is something at my window lattice;
Let me see, then, what thereat is, and this mystery explore—
35 Let my heart be still a moment and this mystery explore;—
                      'Tis the wind and nothing more!"

Open here I flung the shutter, when, with many a flirt and flutter,
In there stepped a stately Raven of the saintly days of yore;
Not the least obeisance made he; not a minute stopped or stayed he;
40 But, with mien of lord or lady, perched above my chamber door—
Perched upon a bust of Pallas[1] just above my chamber door—
                        Perched, and sat, and nothing more.

Then this ebony bird beguiling my sad fancy into smiling,
By the grave and stern decorum of the countenance it wore,
45 "Though thy crest be shorn and shaven, thou," I said, "art sure no craven,
Ghastly grim and ancient Raven wandering from the Nightly shore—
Tell me what thy lordly name is on the Night's Plutonian[2] shore!"
                        Quoth the Raven "Nevermore."

Much I marvelled this ungainly fowl to hear discourse so plainly,
50 Though its answer little meaning—little relevancy bore;
For we cannot help agreeing that no living human being
Ever yet was blessed with seeing bird above his chamber door—
Bird or beast upon the sculptured bust above his chamber door,
                        With such name as "Nevermore."

55 But the Raven, sitting lonely on the placid bust, spoke only
That one word, as if his soul in that one word he did outpour.
Nothing farther then he uttered—not a feather then he fluttered—
Till I scarcely more than muttered "Other friends have flown before—
On the morrow *he* will leave me, as my Hopes have flown before."
60   Then the bird said "Nevermore."

Startled at the stillness broken by reply so aptly spoken,
"Doubtless," said I, "what it utters is its only stock and store
Caught from some unhappy master whom unmerciful Disaster
Followed fast and followed faster till his songs one burden bore—
65 Till the dirges of his Hope that melancholy burden bore
                        Of 'Never—nevermore.' "

But the Raven still beguiling my sad fancy into smiling,
Straight I wheeled a cushioned seat in front of bird, and bust and door;
Then, upon the velvet sinking, I betook myself to linking
70 Fancy unto fancy, thinking what this ominous bird of yore—

---

1. Athena, Greek goddess of wisdom and the arts.
2. Black; Pluto was the Greek god of the underworld.

What this grim, ungainly, ghastly, gaunt, and ominous bird of yore
                                   Meant in croaking "Nevermore."

This I sat engaged in guessing, but no syllable expressing
To the fowl whose fiery eyes now burned into my bosom's core;
75 This and more I sat divining, with my head at ease reclining
On the cushion's velvet lining that the lamp-light gloated o'er,
But whose velvet-violet lining with the lamp-light gloating o'er,
                                   She shall press, ah, nevermore!

Then, methought, the air grew denser, perfumed from an unseen censer
80 Swung by seraphim[3] whose foot-falls tinkled on the tufted floor.
"Wretch," I cried, "thy God hath lent thee—by these angels he hath sent
        thee
Respite—respite and nepenthe[4] from thy memories of Lenore;
Quaff, oh quaff this kind nepenthe and forget this lost Lenore!"
                                   Quoth the Raven "Nevermore."

85 "Prophet!" said I, "thing of evil!—prophet still, if bird or devil!—
Whether Tempter° sent, or whether tempest tossed thee here   *devil*
        ashore,
Desolate yet all undaunted, on this desert land enchanted—
On this home by Horror haunted—tell me truly, I implore—
Is there—*is* there balm in Gilead?[5]—tell me—tell me, I implore!"
90   Quoth the Raven "Nevermore."

"Prophet!" said I, "thing of evil!—prophet still, if bird or devil!
By that Heaven that bends above us—by that God we both adore—
Tell this soul with sorrow laden if, within the distant Aidenn,[6]
It shall clasp a sainted maiden whom the angels name Lenore—
95 Clasp a rare and radiant maiden whom the angels name Lenore."
                                   Quoth the Raven "Nevermore."

"Be that word our sign of parting, bird or fiend!" I shrieked, upstarting—
"Get thee back into the tempest and the Night's Plutonian shore!
Leave no black plume as a token of that lie thy soul hath spoken!
100 Leave my loneliness unbroken!—quit the bust above my door!
Take thy beak from out my heart, and take thy form from off my door!"
                                   Quoth the Raven "Nevermore."

And the Raven, never flitting, still is sitting, *still* is sitting
On the pallid bust of Pallas just above my chamber door;
105 And his eyes have all the seeming of a demon's that is dreaming,
And the lamp-light o'er him streaming throws his shadow on the floor;
And my soul from out that shadow that lies floating on the floor
                                   Shall be lifted—nevermore!
                                                             1845

---

3. Angels of the highest order.
4. Oblivion-inducing drug.
5. As in Jeremiah 8.22: "Is there no balm in Gilead; is there no physician there?" Evergreens grow-
ing in Gilead, a mountainous area east of the Jordan River, were tapped for medicinal resins.
6. Invented place-name, suggestive of Eden.

Eldorado[7]

Gaily bedight,°   *equipped*
A gallant knight,
In sunshine and in shadow,
Had journeyed long,
Singing a song,
In search of Eldorado.

But he grew old—
This knight so bold—
And o'er his heart a shadow
Fell as he found
No spot of ground
That looked like Eldorado.

And, as his strength
Failed him at length,
He met a pilgrim shadow—
"Shadow," said he,
"Where can it be—
This land of Eldorado?"

"Over the Mountains
Of the Moon,
Down the Valley of the Shadow,
Ride, boldly ride,"
The shade replied,—
"If you seek for Eldorado!"

1849

Annabel Lee

It was many and many a year ago,
In a kingdom by the sea,
That a maiden there lived whom you may know
By the name of Annabel Lee;
And this maiden she lived with no other thought
Than to love and be loved by me.

She was a child and *I* was a child,
In this kingdom by the sea,
But we loved with a love that was more than love—
I and my Annabel Lee—
With a love that the wingéd seraphs[8] of Heaven
Coveted her and me.

And this was the reason that, long ago,
In this kingdom by the sea,
A wind blew out of a cloud by night

7. "The gilded one" (Spanish). The name of a mythical South American land of gold and vast wealth, sought by European explorers beginning in the sixteenth century; more generally, any such place.
8. Angels of the highest order.

Chilling my Annabel Lee;
So that her highborn kinsmen came
    And bore her away from me,
To shut her up in a sepulchre
20   In this kingdom by the sea.

The angels, not half so happy in Heaven,
    Went envying her and me:
Yes! that was the reason (as all men know,
    In this kingdom by the sea)
25 That the wind came out of the cloud, chilling
    And killing my Annabel Lee.

But our love it was stronger by far than the love
    Of those who were older than we—
    Of many far wiser than we—
30 And neither the angels in Heaven above
    Nor the demons down under the sea,
Can ever dissever my soul from the soul
    Of the beautiful Annabel Lee:

For the moon never beams without bringing me dreams
35   Of the beautiful Annabel Lee;
And the stars never rise but I see the bright eyes
    Of the beautiful Annabel Lee;
And so, all the night-tide, I lie down by the side
Of my darling, my darling, my life and my bride,
40   In her sepulchre there by the sea—
    In her tomb by the side of the sea.

                    1849, 1850

ALFRED, LORD TENNYSON

1809–1892

Mariana

"Mariana in the moated grange."
    —*Measure for Measure*[1]

With blackest moss the flower-plots
    Were thickly crusted, one and all;
The rusted nails fell from the knots
    That held the pear to the gable-wall.
5   The broken sheds looked sad and strange:
    Unlifted was the clinking latch;
    Weeded and worn the ancient thatch
Upon the lonely moated grange.
      She only said, "My life is dreary,
10   He cometh not," she said;

---

1. Cf. Shakespeare's *Measure for Measure* 3.1.277.

She said, "I am aweary, aweary,
    I would that I were dead!"

Her tears fell with the dews at even;
    Her tears fell ere the dews were dried;
15 She could not look on the sweet heaven,
    Either at morn or eventide.
After the flitting of the bats,
    When thickest dark did trance the sky,
She drew her casement-curtain by,
20 And glanced athwart the glooming flats.
    She only said, "The night is dreary,
        He cometh not," she said;
    She said, "I am aweary, aweary,
        I would that I were dead!"

25 Upon the middle of the night,
    Waking she heard the night-fowl crow;
The cock sung out an hour ere light;
    From the dark fen the oxen's low
Came to her: without hope of change,
30   In sleep she seemed to walk forlorn,
    Till cold winds woke the gray-eyed morn
About the lonely moated grange.
    She only said, "The day is dreary,
        He cometh not," she said;
35   She said, "I am aweary, aweary,
        I would that I were dead!"

About a stone-cast from the wall
    A sluice with blackened waters slept,
And o'er it many, round and small,
40   The clustered marish°-mosses crept.   *marsh-*
Hard by a poplar shook alway,
    All silver-green with gnarlèd bark:
For leagues no other tree did mark
    The level waste, the rounding gray.
45   She only said, "My life is dreary,
        He cometh not," she said;
    She said, "I am aweary, aweary,
        I would that I were dead!"

And ever when the moon was low,
50   And the shrill winds were up and away,
In the white curtain, to and fro,
    She saw the gusty shadow sway.
But when the moon was very low,
    And wild winds bound within their cell,
55   The shadow of the poplar fell
Upon her bed, across her brow.
    She only said, "The night is dreary,
        He cometh not," she said;

She said, "I am aweary, aweary,
60   I would that I were dead!"

All day within the dreamy house,
    The doors upon their hinges creaked;
The blue fly sung in the pane; the mouse
    Behind the moldering wainscot shrieked,
65 Or from the crevice peered about.
        Old faces glimmered through the doors,
        Old footsteps trod the upper floors,
    Old voices called her from without.
        She only said, "My life is dreary,
70   He cometh not," she said;
        She said, "I am aweary, aweary,
            I would that I were dead!"

The sparrow's chirrup on the roof,
    The slow clock ticking, and the sound
75 Which to the wooing wind aloof
    The poplar made, did all confound
Her sense; but most she loathed the hour
        When the thick-moted sunbeam lay
        Athwart the chambers, and the day
80 Was sloping toward his western bower.
        Then, said she, "I am very dreary,
            He will not come," she said;
        She wept, "I am aweary, aweary,
            Oh God, that I were dead!"

                                            1830

The Kraken[2]

Below the thunders of the upper deep;
Far, far beneath in the abysmal sea,
His ancient, dreamless, uninvaded sleep
The Kraken sleepeth: faintest sunlights flee
5   About his shadowy sides: above him swell
Huge sponges of millennial growth and height;
And far away into the sickly light,
From many a wondrous grot and secret cell
Unnumbered and enormous polypi[3]
10 Winnow with giant fins the slumbering green.
There hath he lain for ages and will lie
Battening upon huge seaworms in his sleep,
Until the latter fire shall heat the deep;[4]

2. A mythical sea monster, called in an eigh-
teenth-century *Natural History of Norway* "the
largest and most surprising of all the animal cre-
ation" (O.E.D.).
3. Octopuslike creatures.
4. At the end of the world, "the elements shall
melt with fervent heat, the earth also and the works
that are therein shall be burned up" (2 Peter 3.10).
See also Revelation 8.8–9: "And the second angel
sounded, and as it were a great mountain burning
with fire was cast into the sea: and the third part of
the sea became blood; and there died the third part
of the creatures which were in the sea."

Then once by men and angels to be seen,
15   In roaring he shall rise and on the surface die.

1830

The Lady of Shalott
Part I

On either side the river lie
Long fields of barley and of rye,
That clothe the wold° and meet the sky;   *rolling plain*
And through the field the road runs by
5   To many towered Camelot;[5]
And up and down the people go,
Gazing where the lilies blow°   *bloom*
Round an island there below,
          The island of Shalott.

10   Willows whiten, aspens quiver,
Little breezes dusk and shiver
Through the wave that runs for ever
By the island in the river
          Flowing down to Camelot.
15   Four gray walls, and four gray towers,
Overlook a space of flowers,
And the silent isle imbowers
          The Lady of Shalott.

By the margin, willow-veiled,
20   Slide the heavy barges trailed
By slow horses; and unhailed
The shallop° flitteth silken-sailed   *light open boat*
          Skimming down to Camelot:
But who hath seen her wave her hand?
25   Or at the casement seen her stand?
Or is she known in all the land,
          The Lady of Shalott?

Only reapers, reaping early
In among the bearded barley,
30   Hear a song that echoes cheerly
From the river winding clearly,
          Down to towered Camelot:
And by the moon the reaper weary,
Piling sheaves in uplands airy,
35   Listening, whispers " 'Tis the fairy
          Lady of Shalott."

Part II

There she weaves by night and day
A magic web with colors gay.

5. King Arthur's castle.

She has heard a whisper say,
40 A curse is on her if she stay
  To look down to Camelot.
She knows not what the curse may be,
And so she weaveth steadily,
And little other care hath she,
45   The Lady of Shalott.

And moving through a mirror clear[6]
That hangs before her all the year,
Shadows of the world appear.
There she sees the highway near
50   Winding down to Camelot:
There the river eddy whirls,
And there the surly village-churls,
And the red cloaks of market girls,
  Pass onward from Shalott.

55 Sometimes a troop of damsels glad,
An abbot on an ambling pad,[7]
Sometimes a curly shepherd-lad,
Or long-haired page in crimson clad,
  Goes by to towered Camelot;
60 And sometimes through the mirror blue
The knights come riding two and two:
She hath no loyal knight and true,
  The Lady of Shalott.

But in her web she still delights
65 To weave the mirror's magic sights,
For often through the silent nights
A funeral, with plumes and lights
  And music, went to Camelot:
Or when the moon was overhead.
70 Came two young lovers lately wed;
"I am half sick of shadows," said
  The Lady of Shalott

Part III

A bow-shot from her bower-eaves,
He rode between the barley-sheaves,
75 The sun came dazzling through the leaves,
And flamed upon the brazen greaves
  Of bold Sir Lancelot.
A red-cross knight for ever kneeled
To a lady in his shield,
80 That sparkled on the yellow field,
  Beside remote Shalott.

6. Weavers placed mirrors facing their looms in   7. Easy-paced horse.
order to see the progress of their work.

The gemmy bridle glittered free,
Like to some branch of stars we see
Hung in the golden Galaxy.
85   The bridle bells rang merrily
      As he rode down to Camelot:
And from his blazoned baldric slung
A mighty silver bugle hung,
And as he rode his armor rung,
90   Beside remote Shalott.

All in the blue unclouded weather
Thick-jewelled shone the saddle-leather,
The helmet and the helmet-feather
Burned like one burning flame together,
95   As he rode down to Camelot.
As often through the purple night,
Below the starry clusters bright,
Some bearded meteor, trailing light,
      Moves over still Shalott.

100 His broad clear brow in sunlight glowed;
On burnished hooves his war-horse trode;
From underneath his helmet flowed
His coal-black curls as on he rode,
      As he rode down to Camelot.
105 From the bank and from the river
He flashed into the crystal mirror,
"Tirra lirra," by the river
      Sang Sir lancelot.

She left the web, she left the loom,
110 She made three paces through the room,
She saw the water-lily bloom,
She saw the helmet and the plume,
      She looked down to Camelot.
Out flew the web and floated wide;
115 The mirror cracked from side to side;
"The curse is come upon me," cried
      The Lady of Shalott.

Part IV

In the stormy east-wind straining,
The pale yellow woods were waning,
120 The broad stream in his banks complaining.
Heavily the low sky raining
      Over towered Camelot;
Down she came and found a boat
Beneath a willow left afloat,
125 And round about the prow she wrote
      The Lady of Shalott.

And down the river's dim expanse
Like some bold seër in a trance,
Seeing all his own mischance—
130   With a glassy countenance
        Did she look to Camelot.
And at the closing of the day
She loosed the chain, and down she lay;
The broad stream bore her far away,
135   The Lady of Shalott.

Lying, robed in snowy white
That loosely flew to left and right—
The leaves upon her falling light—
Through the noises of the night
140   She floated down to Camelot:
And as the boat-head wound along
The willowy hills and fields among,
They heard her singing her last song,
        The Lady of Shalott.

145   Heard a carol, mournful, holy,
Chanted loudly, chanted lowly,
Till her blood was frozen slowly,
And her eyes were darkened wholly,
        Turned to towered Camelot.
150   For ere she reached upon the tide
The first house by the water-side,
Singing in her song she died,
        The Lady of Shalott.

Under tower and balcony,
155   By garden-wall and gallery,
A gleaming shape she floated by,
Dead-pale between the houses high,
        Silent into Camelot.
Out upon the wharfs they came,
160   Knight and burgher, lord and dame,
And round the prow they read her name,
        The Lady of Shalott.

Who is this? and what is here?
And in the lighted palace near
165   Died the sound of royal cheer;
And they crossed themselves for fear,
        All the knights at Camelot:
But Lancelot mused a little space;
He said, "She has a lovely face;
170   God in his mercy lend her grace,
        The Lady of Shalott."

1831–32   1832, 1842

The Lotos-Eaters[8]

"Courage!" he[9] said, and pointed toward the land,
"This mounting wave will roll us shoreward soon."
In the afternoon they came unto a land
In which it seemèd always afternoon.
All round the coast the languid air did swoon,
Breathing like one that hath a weary dream.
Full-faced above the valley stood the moon;
And, like a downward smoke, the slender stream
Along the cliff to fall and pause and fall did seem.

A land of streams! some, like a downward smoke,
Slow-dropping veils of thinnest lawn,[1] did go;
And some through wavering lights and shadows broke,
Rolling a slumbrous sheet of foam below.
They saw the gleaming river seaward flow
From the inner land: far off three mountain-tops,
Three silent pinnacles of agèd snow,
Stood sunset-flushed; and, dewed with showery drops,
Up-clomb the shadowy pine above the woven copse.

The charmèd sunset lingered low adown
In the red West; through mountain clefts the dale
Was seen far inland, and the yellow down
Bordered with palm, and many a winding vale
And meadow, set with slender galingale;[2]
A land where all things always seemed the same!
And round about the keel with faces pale,
Dark faces pale against that rosy flame,
The mild-eyed melancholy Lotos-eaters came.

Branches they bore of that enchanted stem,
Laden with flower and fruit, whereof they gave
To each, but whoso did receive of them
And taste, to him the gushing of the wave
Far far away did seem to mourn and rave
On alien shores; and if his fellow spake,
His voice was thin, as voices from the grave;
And deep-asleep he seemed, yet all awake,
And music in his ears his beating heart did make.

They sat them down upon the yellow sand,
Between the sun and moon upon the shore;
And sweet it was to dream of Fatherland,
Of child, and wife, and slave; but evermore
Most weary seemed the sea, weary the oar,
Weary the wandering fields of barren foam.
Then some one said, "We will return no more;"

---

8. In Greek legend, a people who ate the fruit of
the lotos, the effect of which was to induce drowsy
languor and forgetfulness. The visit of Odysseus
and his men to their island is described in the
Odyssey 9.82–97.
9. I.e., Odysseus.
1. Sheer cotton fabric.
2. A reedlike plant, a species of sedge.

And all at once they sang, "Our island home
45 Is far beyond the wave; we will no longer roam."

Choric Song

1

There is sweet music here that softer falls
Than petals from blown roses on the grass,
Or night-dews on still waters between walls
Of shadowy granite, in a gleaming pass;
50 Music that gentlier on the spirit lies,
Than tired eyelids upon tired eyes;
Music that brings sweet sleep down from the blissful skies.
Here are cool mosses deep,
And through the moss the ivies creep,
55 And in the stream the long-leaved flowers weep,
And from the craggy ledge the poppy hangs in sleep.

2

Why are we weighed upon with heaviness,
And utterly consumed with sharp distress,
While all things else have rest from weariness?
60 All things have rest: why should we toil alone,
We only toil, who are the first of things,
And make perpetual moan,
Still from one sorrow to another thrown;
Nor ever fold our wings,
65 And cease from wanderings,
Nor steep our brows in slumber's holy balm;
Nor harken what the inner spirit sings,
"There is no joy but calm!"
Why should we only toil, the roof and crown of things?

3

70 Lo! in the middle of the wood,
The folded leaf is wooed from out the bud
With winds upon the branch, and there
Grows green and broad, and takes no care,
Sun-steeped at noon, and in the moon
75 Nightly dew-fed; and turning yellow
Falls, and floats adown the air.
Lo! sweetened with the summer light,
The full-juiced apple, waxing over-mellow,
Drops in a silent autumn night.
80 All its allotted length of days,
The flower ripens in its place,
Ripens and fades, and falls, and hath no toil,
Fast-rooted in the fruitful soil.

4

Hateful is the dark-blue sky,
85 Vaulted o'er the dark-blue sea.
Death is the end of life; ah, why
Should life all labor be?
Let us alone. Time driveth onward fast

And in a little while our lips are dumb.
90 Let us alone. What is it that will last?
All things are taken from us, and become
Portions and parcels of the dreadful Past.
Let us alone. What pleasure can we have
To war with evil? Is there any peace
95 In ever climbing up the climbing wave?
All things have rest, and ripen toward the grave
In silence; ripen, fall, and cease:
Give us long rest or death, dark death, or dreamful ease.

5

How sweet it were, hearing the downward stream,
100 With half-shut eyes ever to seem
Falling asleep in a half-dream!
To dream and dream, like yonder amber light,
Which will not leave the myrrh-bush on the height;
To hear each other's whispered speech;
105 Eating the Lotos day by day,
To watch the crisping ripples on the beach,
And tender curving lines of creamy spray;
To lend our hearts and spirits wholly
To the influence of mild-minded melancholy;
110 To muse and brood and live again in memory,
With those old faces of our infancy
Heaped over with a mound of grass,
Two handfuls of white dust, shut in an urn of brass!

6

Dear is the memory of our wedded lives,
115 And dear the last embraces of our wives
And their warm tears: but all hath suffered change:
For surely now our household hearths are cold:
Our sons inherit us: our looks are strange:
And we should come like ghosts to trouble joy.
120 Or else the island princes³ over-bold
Have eat our substance, and the minstrel sings
Before them of the ten years' war in Troy,
And our great deeds, as half-forgotten things.
Is there confusion in the little isle?⁴
125 Let what is broken so remain.
The Gods are hard to reconcile:
'Tis hard to settle order once again.
There *is* confusion worse than death,
Trouble on trouble, pain on pain,
130 Long labor unto agèd breath,
Sore tasks to hearts worn out by many wars
And eyes grown dim with gazing on the pilot-stars.

7

But, propt on beds of amaranth⁵ and moly,
How sweet (while warm airs lull us, blowing lowly)

---

3. The princes who had remained behind in Ith-
aca while Odysseus was at Troy.
4. I.e., Ithaca.

5. A legendary flower, reputed not to fade; "moly":
an herb of magical properties.

135 With half-dropt eyelid still,
    Beneath a heaven dark and holy,
    To watch the long bright river drawing slowly
    His waters from the purple hill—
    To hear the dewy echoes calling
140 From cave to cave through the thick-twinèd vine—
    To watch the emerald-colored water falling
    Through many a woven acanthus-wreath divine!
    Only to hear and see the far-off sparkling brine,
    Only to hear were sweet, stretched out beneath the pine.

8

145 The Lotos blooms below the barren peak,
    The Lotos blows by every winding creek;
    All day the wind breathes low with mellower tone;
    Through every hollow cave and alley lone
    Round and round the spicy downs the yellow Lotos-dust is blown.
150 We have had enough of action, and of motion we,
    Rolled to starboard, rolled to larboard, when the surge was seething free,
    Where the wallowing monster spouted his foam-fountains in the sea.
    Let us swear an oath, and keep it with an equal mind,
    In the hollow Lotos-land to live and lie reclined
155 On the hills like Gods together, careless of mankind.
    For they lie beside their nectar, and the bolts are hurled
    Far below them in the valleys, and the clouds are lightly curled
    Round their golden houses, girdled with the gleaming world:
    Where they smile in secret, looking over wasted lands,
160 Blight and famine, plague and earthquake, roaring deeps and fiery sands,
    Clanging fights, and flaming towns, and sinking ships, and praying hands.
    But they smile, they find a music centered in a doleful song
    Steaming up, a lamentation and an ancient tale of wrong,
    Like a tale of little meaning though the words are strong;
165 Chanted from an ill-used race of men that cleave the soil,
    Sow the seed, and reap the harvest with enduring toil,
    Storing yearly little dues of wheat, and wine and oil;
    Till they perish and they suffer—some, 'tis whispered—down in hell
    Suffer endless anguish, others in Elysian valleys dwell,
170 Resting weary limbs at last on beds of asphodel.[6]
    Surely, surely, slumber is more sweet than toil, the shore
    Than labor in the deep mid-ocean, wind and wave and oar;
    O, rest ye, brother mariners, we will not wander more.

1832, 1842

Break, Break, Break

    Break, break, break,
      On thy cold gray stones, O Sea!
    And I would that my tongue could utter
      The thoughts that arise in me.

5   O well for the fisherman's boy,
      That he shouts with his sister at play!

6. Any one of a number of plants of the lily family.

O well for the sailor lad,
  That he sings in his boat on the bay!

And the stately ships go on
10   To their haven under the hill;
  But O for the touch of a vanished hand,
    And the sound of a voice that is still!

Break, break, break,
  At the foot of thy crags, O Sea!
15 But the tender grace of a day that is dead
    Will never come back to me.

1834   1842

Ulysses[7]

It little profits that an idle king,
By this still hearth, among these barren crags,
Matched with an aged wife, I mete and dole
Unequal laws unto a savage race,
5   That hoard, and sleep, and feed, and know not me.

I cannot rest from travel: I will drink
Life to the lees: all times I have enjoyed
Greatly, have suffered greatly, both with those
That loved me, and alone; on shore, and when
10 Through scudding drifts the rainy Hyades[8]
Vext the dim sea I am become a name;
For always roaming with a hungry heart
Much have I seen and known; cities of men
And manners, climates, councils, governments,
15 Myself not least, but honored of them all;
And drunk delight of battle with my peers,
Far on the ringing plains of windy Troy.
I am a part of all that I have met;
Yet all experience is an arch wherethrough
20 Gleams that untravelled world whose margin fades
For ever and for ever when I move.
How dull it is to pause, to make an end,
To rust unburnished, not to shine in use!
As though to breathe were life! Life piled on life
25 Were all too little, and of one to me
Little remains: but every hour is saved
From that eternal silence, something more,
A bringer of new things; and vile it were
For some three suns to store and hoard myself,
30 And this gray spirit yearning in desire

---

7. Tennyson's Ulysses (Greek *Odysseus*), restless
after his return to Ithaca, eager to renew the life of
great deeds he had known during the Trojan War
and the adventures of his ten-year journey home,
resembles the figure of Ulysses presented by
Dante, *Inferno* 26.
8. A group of stars in the constellation Taurus,
believed to foretell the coming of rain when they
rose with the sun.

To follow knowledge like a sinking star,
Beyond the utmost bound of human thought.

This is my son, mine own Telemachus,
To whom I leave the scepter and the isle—
35   Well-loved of me, discerning to fulfill
This labor, by slow prudence to make mild
A rugged people, and through soft degrees
Subdue them to the useful and the good.
Most blameless is he, centered in the sphere
40   Of common duties, decent not to fail
In offices of tenderness, and pay
Meet adoration to my household gods,
When I am gone. He works his work, I mine.

There lies the port; the vessel puffs her sail:
45   There gloom the dark, broad seas. My mariners,
Souls that have toiled, and wrought, and thought with me—
That ever with a frolic welcome took
The thunder and the sunshine, and opposed
Free hearts, free foreheads—you and I are old;
50   Old age hath yet his honor and his toil;
Death closes all: but something ere the end,
Some work of noble note, may yet be done,
Not unbecoming men that strove with Gods.
The lights begin to twinkle from the rocks:
55   The long day wanes: the slow moon climbs: the deep
Moans round with many voices. Come, my friends,
'Tis not too late to seek a newer world.
Push off, and sitting well in order smite
The sounding furrows; for my purpose holds
60   To sail beyond the sunset, and the baths
Of all the western stars, until I die.
It may be that the gulfs will wash us down:
It may be we shall touch the Happy Isles,[9]
And see the great Achilles, whom we knew.
65   Though much is taken, much abides; and though
We are not now that strength which in old days
Moved earth and heaven; that which we are, we are,
One equal temper of heroic hearts,
Made weak by time and fate, but strong in will
70   To strive, to seek, to find, and not to yield.

1833   1842

Songs from *The Princess*

The Splendor Falls

The splendor falls on castle walls
And snowy summits old in story:

---

9. The Islands of the Blessed, or Elysium, the abode after death of those favored by the gods, especially heroes and patriots: supposed, in earlier myth, to be located beyond the western limits of the known world.

The long light shakes across the lakes,
   And the wild cataract leaps in glory.
5 Blow, bugle, blow, set the wild echoes flying,
Blow, bugle; answer, echoes, dying, dying, dying.

O hark, O hear! how thin and clear,
   And thinner, clearer, farther going!
O sweet and far from cliff and scar[1]
10   The horns of Elfland faintly blowing!
Blow, let us hear the purple glens replying:
Blow, bugle; answer, echoes, dying, dying, dying.

O love, they die in yon rich sky,
   They faint on hill or field or river:
15 Our echoes roll from soul to soul,
   And grow for ever and for ever.
Blow, bugle, blow, set the wild echoes flying,
And answer, echoes, answer, dying, dying, dying.

                                          1850

Tears, Idle Tears

Tears, idle tears, I know not what they mean,
Tears from the depth of some divine despair
Rise in the heart, and gather to the eyes,
In looking on the happy Autumn-fields,
5 And thinking of the days that are no more.

Fresh as the first beam glittering on a sail,
That brings our friends up from the underworld,
Sad as the last which reddens over one
That sinks with all we love below the verge;
10 So sad, so fresh, the days that are no more.

Ah, sad and strange as in dark summer dawns
The earliest pipe of half-awakened birds
To dying ears, when unto dying eyes
The casement slowly grows a glimmering square;
15 So sad, so strange, the days that are no more.

Dear as remembered kisses after death,
And sweet as those by hopeless fancy feigned
On lips that are for others; deep as love,
Deep as first love, and wild with all regret;
20 O Death in Life, the days that are no more!

                                          1847

Now Sleeps the Crimson Petal

Now sleeps the crimson petal, now the white;
Nor waves the cypress in the palace walk;
Nor winks the gold fin in the porphyry font:
The firefly wakens: waken thou with me.

---

1. Isolated rock, or rocky height.

5 Now droops the milkwhite peacock like a ghost,
And like a ghost she glimmers on to me.

Now lies the Earth all Danaë² to the stars,
And all thy heart lies open unto me.

Now slides the silent meteor on, and leaves
10 A shining furrow, as thy thoughts in me.

Now folds the lily all her sweetness up,
And slips into the bosom of the lake:
So fold thyself, my dearest, thou, and slip
Into my bosom and be lost in me.

1847

From In Memoriam A. H. H.³

OBIIT. MDCCCXXXIII

1

I held it truth, with him who sings
    To one clear harp in divers tones,⁴
    That men may rise on stepping-stones
Of their dead selves to higher things.

5 But who shall so forecast the years
    And find in loss a gain to match?
    Or reach a hand through time to catch
The far-off interest of tears?

Let Love clasp Grief lest both be drowned,
10   Let darkness keep her raven gloss:
    Ah, sweeter to be drunk with loss,
To dance with death, to beat the ground,

Than that the victor Hours should scorn
    The long result of love, and boast,
15   "Behold the man that loved and lost,
But all he was is overworn."

2

Old Yew, which graspest at the stones
    That name the under-lying dead,
    Thy fibers net the dreamless head,
Thy roots are wrapt about the bones.

---

2. Daughter of a king of Argos in ancient Greece who, warned by an oracle that she would bear a son who would kill him, shut her up in a bronze chamber, where she was visited by Zeus in a shower of gold.
3. Arthur Henry Hallam (1811–1833) had been Tennyson's close friend at Cambridge, they had traveled together in France and Germany, and Hallam had been engaged to the poet's sister. To his associates at Cambridge, Hallam had seemed to give the most brilliant promise of greatness. In the summer of 1833, when he had been traveling on the Continent with his father, Hallam died of a stroke at Vienna.
4. I.e., Goethe.

5   The seasons bring the flowers again,
      And bring the firstling to the flock;
      And in the dusk of thee, the clock
   Beats out the little lives of men.

   O not for thee the glow, the bloom,
10   Who changest not in any gale,
      Nor branding summer suns avail
   To touch thy thousand years of gloom:

   And gazing on thee, sullen tree,
      Sick for thy stubborn hardihood,
15   I seem to fail from out my blood
   And grow incorporate into thee.

7

   Dark house, by which once more I stand
      Here in the long unlovely street,[5]
      Doors, where my heart was used to beat
   So quickly, waiting for a hand,

5   A hand that can be clasped no more—
      Behold me, for I cannot sleep,
      And like a guilty thing I creep
   At earliest morning to the door.

   He is not here; but far away
10   The noise of life begins again,
      And ghastly through the drizzling rain
   On the bald street breaks the blank day.

11

   Calm is the morn without a sound,
      Calm as to suit a calmer grief,
      And only through the faded leaf
   The chestnut pattering to the ground:

5   Calm and deep peace on this high wold,°   *upland plain*
      And on these dews that drench the furze,
      And all the silvery gossamers
   That twinkle into green and gold:

   Calm and still light on yon great plain
10   That sweeps with all its autumn bowers,
      And crowded farms and lessening towers,
   To mingle with the bounding main:

   Calm and deep peace in this wide air,
      These leaves that redden to the fall;

5. I.e., Wimpole St., where Hallam had been living after he left Cambridge.

15   And in my heart, if calm at all,
      If any calm, a calm despair:

      Calm on the seas, and silver sleep,
         And waves that sway themselves in rest,
         And dead calm in the noble breast
20   Which heaves but with the heaving deep.

19

      The Danube to the Severn gave
         The darkened heart that beat no more;[6]
         They laid him by the pleasant shore,
      And in the hearing of the wave.

5   There twice a day the Severn fills;
         The salt sea-water passes by,
         And hushes half the babbling Wye,[7]
      And makes a silence in the hills.

      The Wye is hushed nor moved along,
10   And hushed my deepest grief of all,
         When filled with tears that cannot fall,
      I brim with sorrow drowning song.

      The tide flows down, the wave again
         Is vocal in its wooded walls;
15   My deeper anguish also falls,
      And I can speak a little then.

50

      Be near me when my light is low,
         When the blood creeps, and the nerves prick
         And tingle; and the heart is sick,
      And all the wheels of Being slow.

5   Be near me when the sensuous frame
         Is racked with pangs that conquer trust;
         And Time, a maniac scattering dust,
      And Life, a Fury slinging flame.

      Be near me when my faith is dry,
10   And men the flies of latter spring,
         That lay their eggs, and sting and sing
      And weave their petty cells and die.

      Be near me when I fade away,
         To point the term of human strife,

6. Vienna, where Hallam died, is on the Danube; the Severn empties into the Bristol Channel near Clevedon, Somersetshire, Hallam's burial place.
7. The Wye, a tributary of the Severn, also runs into the Bristol Channel; the incoming tide deepens the river and makes it quiet, but as the tide ebbs the Wye once more becomes voluble.

15   And on the low dark verge of life
          The twilight of eternal day.

54

Oh yet we trust that somehow good
    Will be the final goal of ill,
    To pangs of nature, sins of will,
Defects of doubt, and taints of blood;

5   That nothing walks with aimless feet;
      That not one life shall be destroyed,
      Or cast as rubbish to the void,
When God hath made the pile complete;

That not a worm is cloven in vain;
10   That not a moth with vain desire
      Is shriveled in a fruitless fire,
Or but subserves another's gain.

Behold, we know not anything;
    I can but trust that good shall fall
15   At last—far off—at last, to all,
And every winter change to spring.

So runs my dream: but what am I?
    An infant crying in the night:
    An infant crying for the light:
20 And with no language but a cry.

55

The wish, that of the living whole
    No life may fail beyond the grave,
    Derives it not from what we have
The likest God within the soul?

5   Are God and Nature then at strife,
      That Nature lends such evil dreams?
      So careful of the type° she seems,   *species*
So careless of the single life;

That I, considering everywhere
10   Her secret meaning in her deeds,
      And finding that of fifty seeds
She often brings but one to bear,

I falter where I firmly trod,
    And falling with my weight of cares
15   Upon the great world's altar-stairs
That slope through darkness up to God,

I stretch lame hands of faith, and grope,
    And gather dust and chaff, and call

To what I feel is Lord of all,
20   And faintly trust the larger hope.

56

"So careful of the type?" but no.
    From scarpèd[8] cliff and quarried stone
    She[9] cries, "A thousand types are gone;
I care for nothing, all shall go.

5   "Thou makest thine appeal to me:
    I bring to life, I bring to death:
    The spirit does but mean the breath:
I know no more." And he, shall he,

Man, her last work, who seemed so fair,
10   Such splendid purpose in his eyes,
    Who rolled the psalm to wintry skies,
Who built him fanes° of fruitless prayer,   *temples, churches*

Who trusted God was love indeed
    And love Creation's final law—
15   Though Nature, red in tooth and claw
With ravine, shrieked against his creed—

Who loved, who suffered countless ills,
    Who battled for the True, the Just,
    Be blown about the desert dust,
20   Or sealed within the iron hills?

No more? A monster then, a dream,
    A discord. Dragons of the prime,
    That tare° each other in their slime,   *tore (archaic)*
Were mellow music matched with him.

25   O life as futile, then, as frail!
    O for thy voice to soothe and bless!
    What hope of answer, or redress?
Behind the veil, behind the veil.

67

When on my bed the moonlight falls,
    I know that in thy place of rest
    By that broad water of the west
There comes a glory on the walls;[1]

5   Thy marble bright in dark appears,
    As slowly steals a silver flame
    Along the letters of thy name,
And o'er the number of thy years.

---

8. Cut down vertically, thus displaying the strata
of geologic growth and the fossils they contain.
9. I.e., Nature.

1. Hallam's tomb is inside Clevedon Church, just
south of Clevedon, Somersetshire, on a hill over-
looking the Bristol Channel.

The mystic glory swims away;
10   From off my bed the moonlight dies;
And closing eaves of wearied eyes
I sleep till dusk is dipt in gray:

And then I know the mist is drawn
A lucid veil from coast to coast,
15   And in the dark church like a ghost
Thy tablet glimmers to the dawn.

88

Wild bird, whose warble, liquid sweet,
Rings Eden through the budded quicks,[2]
O tell me where the senses mix,
O tell me where the passions meet,

5   Whence radiate: fierce extremes employ
Thy spirits in the darkening leaf,
And in the midmost heart of grief
Thy passion clasps a secret joy:

And I—my harp would prelude woe—
10   I cannot all command the strings;
The glory of the sum of things
Will flash along the chords and go.

95

By night we lingered on the lawn,
For underfoot the herb was dry;
And genial warmth; and o'er the sky
The silvery haze of summer drawn;

5   And calm that let the tapers burn
Unwavering: not a cricket chirred;
The brook alone far-off was heard,
And on the board the fluttering urn:[3]

And bats went round in fragrant skies,
10   And wheeled or lit the filmy shapes
That haunt the dusk, with ermine capes
And woolly breasts and beaded eyes;

While now we sang old songs that pealed
From knoll to knoll, where, couched at ease,
15   The white kine° glimmered, and the trees   *cattle*
Laid their dark arms about the field.

But when those others, one by one,
Withdrew themselves from me and night,

2. Hawthorn hedgerow.   a fluttering flame beneath.
3. I.e., on the table a tea- or coffee-urn heated by

And in the house light after light
20 Went out, and I was all alone,

A hunger seized my heart; I read
Of that glad year which once had been,
In those fallen leaves which kept their green,
The noble letters of the dead:

25 And strangely on the silence broke
The silent-speaking words, and strange
Was love's dumb cry defying change
To test his worth; and strangely spoke

The faith, the vigor, bold to dwell
30 On doubts that drive the coward back,
And keen through wordy snares to track
Suggestion to her inmost cell.

So word by word, and line by line,
The dead man touched me from the past,
35 And all at once it seemed at last
The living soul was flashed on mine,

And mine in this was wound, and whirled
About empyreal heights of thought,
And came on that which is, and caught
40 The deep pulsations of the world,

Æonian music[4] measuring out
The steps of Time—the shocks of Chance—
The blows of Death. At length my trance
Was cancelled, stricken through with doubt.

45 Vague words! but ah, how hard to frame
In matter-molded forms of speech,
Or even for intellect to reach
Through memory that which I became:

Till now the doubtful dusk revealed
50 The knolls once more where, couched at ease,
The white kine glimmered, and the trees
Laid their dark arms about the field:

And sucked from out the distant gloom
A breeze began to tremble o'er
55 The large leaves of the sycamore,
And fluctuate all the still perfume,

And gathering freshlier overhead,
Rocked the full-foliaged elms, and swung

---

4. I.e., the rhythm of the universe; it has persisted for eons.

The heavy-folded rose, and flung
60   The lilies to and fro, and said

"The dawn, the dawn," and died away;
  And East and West, without a breath,
  Mixt their dim lights, like life and death,
To broaden into boundless day.

119

Doors, where my heart was used to beat
  So quickly, not as one that weeps
  I come once more; the city sleeps;
I smell the meadow in the street;

5   I hear a chirp of birds; I see
  Betwixt the black fronts long-withdrawn
  A light-blue lane of early dawn,
And think of early days and thee,

And bless thee, for thy lips are bland,
10   And bright the friendship of thine eye;
  And in my thoughts with scarce a sigh
I take the pressure of thine hand.

121

Sad Hesper o'er the buried sun
  And ready, thou, to die with him,
  Thou watchest all things ever dim
And dimmer, and a glory done:

5   The team is loosened from the wain,°   wagon
  The boat is drawn upon the shore;
  Thou listenest to the closing door,
And life is darkened in the brain.

Bright Phosphor, fresher for the night,
10   By thee the world's great work is heard
  Beginning, and the wakeful bird;
Behind thee comes the greater light:

The market boat is on the stream,
  And voices hail it from the brink;
15   Thou hear'st the village hammer clink,
And see'st the moving of the team.

Sweet Hesper-Phosphor, double name[5]
  For what is one, the first, the last,
  Thou, like my present and my past,
20   Thy place is changed; thou art the same.

---

5. Hesper, the evening star, and Phosphor, the morning star, are both the planet Venus.

130

Thy voice is on the rolling air;
  I hear thee where the waters run;
  Thou standest in the rising sun,
And in the setting thou art fair.

5 What are thou then? I cannot guess;
  But though I seem in star and flower
  To feel thee some diffusive power,
I do not therefore love thee less:

My love involves the love before;
10   My love is vaster passion now;
  Though mixed with God and Nature thou,
I seem to love thee more and more.

Far off thou art, but ever nigh;
  I have thee still, and I rejoice;
15   I prosper, circled with thy voice;
I shall not lose thee though I die.

1833–50   1850

The Eagle

Fragment

He clasps the crag with crooked hands;
Close to the sun in lonely lands,
Ringed with the azure world, he stands.

The wrinkled sea beneath him crawls;
5 He watches from his mountain walls,
And like a thunderbolt he falls.

                                           1851

The Charge of the Light Brigade[6]

1

Half a league, half a league,
  Half a league onward,
All in the valley of Death
  Rode the six hundred.
5 "Forward, the Light Brigade!
Charge for the guns!" he said:
Into the valley of Death
  Rode the six hundred.

---

6. A section of the British army's cavalry that carried few pieces of heavy equipment and could therefore move quickly.

2

"Forward, the Light Brigade!"
10   Was there a man dismayed?
Not though the soldier knew
      Some one had blundered:
Their's not to make reply,
Their's not to reason why,
15   Their's but to do and die:
Into the valley of Death
      Rode the six hundred.

3

Cannon to right of them,
Cannon to left of them,
20   Cannon in front of them
      Volleyed and thundered;
Stormed at with shot and shell,
Boldly they rode and well,
Into the jaws of Death,
25   Into the mouth of Hell
      Rode the six hundred.

4

Flashed all their sabers° bare,   curved swords
Flashed as they turned in air
Sabring the gunners there,
30   Charging an army, while
      All the world wondered:
Plunged in the battery-smoke
Right through the line they broke;
Cossack and Russian
35   Reeled from the saber-stroke
      Shattered and sundered.
Then they rode back, but not
      Not the six hundred.

5

Cannon to right of them,
40   Cannon to left of them,
Cannon behind them
      Volleyed and thundered;
Stormed at with shot and shell,
While horse and hero fell,
45   They that had fought so well
Came through the jaws of Death,
Back from the mouth of Hell,
All that was left of them,
      Left of six hundred.

6

50   When can their glory fade?
O the wild charge they made!
      All the world wondered.
Honor the charge they made!

Honor the Light Brigade,
55   Noble six hundred!

1854   1855

Tithonus[7]

The woods decay, the woods decay and fall,
The vapors weep their burthen to the ground,
Man comes and tills the field and lies beneath,
And after many a summer dies the swan.
5 Me only cruel immortality
Consumes: I wither slowly in thine arms,
Here at the quiet limit of the world,
A white-haired shadow roaming like a dream
The ever-silent spaces of the East,
10 Far-folded mists, and gleaming halls of morn.

Alas! for this gray shadow, once a man—
So glorious in his beauty and thy choice,
Who madest him thy chosen, that he seemed
To his great heart none other than a God!
15 I asked thee, "Give me immortality."
Then didst thou grant mine asking with a smile,
Like wealthy men who care not how they give.
But thy strong Hours indignant worked their wills,
And beat me down and marred and wasted me,
20 And though they could not end me, left me maimed
To dwell in presence of immortal youth.
Immortal age beside immortal youth,
And all I was, in ashes. Can thy love,
Thy beauty, make amends, though even now,
25 Close over us, the silver star,[8] thy guide,
Shines in those tremulous eyes that fill with tears
To hear me? Let me go: take back thy gift:
Why should a man desire in any way
To vary from the kindly race of men,
30 Or pass beyond the goal of ordinance
Where all should pause, as is most meet for all?

A soft air fans the cloud apart; there comes
A glimpse of that dark world where I was born.
Once more the old mysterious glimmer steals
35 From thy pure brows, and from thy shoulders pure,
And bosom beating with a heart renewed.
Thy cheek begins to redden through the gloom,
Thy sweet eyes brighten slowly close to mine,
Ere yet they blind the stars, and the wild team
40 Which love thee, yearning for thy yoke, arise,
And shake the darkness from their loosened manes,

7. A Trojan prince beloved by Aurora (Greek
Eos), goddess of the dawn, who took him as her
spouse. She begged Zeus to grant him eternal life,
but forgot to ask also for the gift of eternal youth.
8. I.e., the morning star.

And beat the twilight into flakes of fire.
Lo! ever thus thou growest beautiful
In silence, then before thine answer given
45 Departest, and thy tears are on my cheek.

Why wilt thou ever scare me with thy tears,
And make me tremble lest a saying learnt,
In days far-off, on that dark earth, be true?
"The Gods themselves cannot recall their gifts."
50 Ay me! ay me! with what another heart
In days far-off, and with what other eyes
I used to watch — if I be he that watched —
The lucid outline forming round thee; saw
The dim curls kindle into sunny rings;
55 Changed with thy mystic change, and felt my blood
Glow with the glow that slowly crimsoned all
Thy presence and thy portals, while I lay,
Mouth, forehead, eyelids, growing dewy-warm
With kisses balmier than half-opening buds
60 Of April, and could hear the lips that kissed
Whispering I knew not what of wild and sweet,
Like that strange song I heard Apollo sing,
While Ilion like a mist rose into towers.[9]

Yet hold me not for ever in thine East:
65 How can my nature longer mix with thine?
Coldly thy rosy shadows bathe me, cold
Are all thy lights, and cold my wrinkled feet
Upon thy glimmering thresholds, when the steam
Floats up from those dim fields about the homes
70 Of happy men that have the power to die,
And grassy barrows of the happier dead.
Release me, and restore me to the ground;
Thou seëst all things, thou wilt see my grave:
Thou wilt renew thy beauty morn by morn;
75 I earth in earth forget these empty courts,
And thee returning on thy silver wheels.

1833, 1859   1860

"Frater Ave atque Vale"[1]

Row us out from Desenzano, to your Sirmione row!
So they rowed, and there we landed — "O venusta Sirmio!"[2]
There to me through all the groves of olive in the summer glow,
There beneath the Roman ruin where the purple flowers grow,
5 Came that "Ave atque Vale" of the Poet's hopeless woe,
Tenderest of Roman poets nineteen-hundred years ago,

9. According to legend, the walls and towers of Ilion (Troy) were raised by the sound of Apollo's song, as related by Ovid, *Heroides* 16.179.
1. The title (Latin, "Brother, hail and farewell") repeats the concluding phrase of poem number 101, in which Catullus records the journey to visit his brother's tomb in Asia Minor. Tennyson's poem, written on a visit to the little peninsula of Sirmio, on Lake Garda in northern Italy, shortly after his own brother had died, echoes phrases from another poem (31) in which Catullus describes his pleasure in returning to Sirmio after a long absence.
2. "O lovely Sirmio" (Latin).

"Frater Ave atque Vale"—as we wandered to and fro
Gazing at the Lydian laughter of the Garda Lake below[3]
Sweet Catullus's all-but-island, olive-silvery Sirmio!

1880   1885

Crossing the Bar

Sunset and evening star,
    And one clear call for me!
And may there be no moaning of the bar,
    When I put out to sea,

5   But such a tide as moving seems asleep,
    Too full for sound and foam,
When that which drew from out the boundless deep
    Turns again home.

Twilight and evening bell,
10   And after that the dark!
And may there be no sadness of farewell,
    When I embark;

For though from out our bourne of Time and Place
    The flood may bear me far,
15   I hope to see my Pilot face to face
    When I have crost the bar.

1889

ROBERT BROWNING

1812–1889

My Last Duchess[1]

Ferrara

That's my last duchess painted on the wall,
Looking as if she were alive. I call
That piece a wonder, now: Frà Pandolf's hands
Worked busily a day, and there she stands.
5 Will't please you sit and look at her? I said
"Frà Pandolf" by design, for never read
Strangers like you that pictured countenance,
The depth and passion of its earnest glance,

3. Catullus's line, "And rejoice, O Lydian waves of the lake" (31.13) alludes to the old belief that the Etruscans of the Garda region had originated in Lydia, in Asia Minor.
1. The events of Browning's poem parallel historical events, but its emphasis is rather on truth to Renaissance attitudes than on historic specificity. Alfonso II d'Este, duke of Ferrara (born 1533), in Northern Italy, had married his first wife, daughter of Cosimo I de'Medici, duke of Florence, in 1558, when she was fourteen; she died on April 21, 1561, under suspicious circumstances, and soon afterwards he opened negotiations for the hand of the niece of the count of Tyrol, the seat of whose court was at Innsbruck, in Austria. "Fra Pandolf" and "Claus of Innsbruck" are types rather than specific artists.

But to myself they turned (since none puts by
10   The curtain I have drawn for you, but I)
And seemed as they would ask me, if they durst,
How such a glance came there; so, not the first
Are you to turn and ask thus. Sir, 'twas not
Her husband's presence only, called that spot
15   Of joy into the Duchess' cheek: perhaps
Frà Pandolf chanced to say "Her mantle laps
"Over my lady's wrist too much," or "Paint
"Must never hope to reproduce the faint
"Half-flush that dies along her throat": such stuff
20   Was courtesy, she thought, and cause enough
For calling up that spot of joy. She had
A heart—how shall I say?—too soon made glad,
Too easily impressed; she liked whate'er
She looked on, and her looks went everywhere.
25   Sir, 'twas all one! My favor at her breast,
The dropping of the daylight in the West,
The bough of cherries some officious fool
Broke in the orchard for her, the white mule
She rode with round the terrace—all and each
30   Would draw from her alike the approving speech,
Or blush, at least. She thanked men—good! but thanked
Somehow—I know not how—as if she ranked
My gift of a nine-hundred-years-old name
With anybody's gift. Who'd stoop to blame
35   This sort of trifling? Even had you skill
In speech—which I have not—to make your will
Quite clear to such an one, and say, "Just this
"Or that in you disgusts me; here you miss,
"Or there exceed the mark"—and if she let
40   Herself be lessoned so, nor plainly set
Her wits to yours, forsooth, and made excuse,
—E'en then would be some stooping; and I choose
Never to stoop. Oh sir, she smiled, no doubt,
Whene'er I passed her; but who passed without
45   Much the same smile? This grew; I gave commands;
Then all smiles stopped together. There she stands
As if alive. Will 't please you rise? We'll meet
The company below, then. I repeat,
The Count your master's known munificence
50   Is ample warrant that no just pretense
Of mine for dowry will be disallowed;
Though his fair daughter's self, as I avowed
At starting, is my object. Nay, we'll go
Together down, sir. Notice Neptune, though,
55   Taming a sea-horse, thought a rarity,
Which Claus of Innsbruck cast in bronze for me!

1842

Soliloquy of the Spanish Cloister

1

Gr-r-r—there go, my heart's abhorrence!
    Water your damned flower-pots, do!
If hate killed men, Brother Lawrence,
    God's blood, would not mine kill you!
5 What? your myrtle-bush wants trimming?
    Oh, that rose has prior claims—
Needs its leaden vase filled brimming?
    Hell dry you up with its flames!

2

At the meal we sit together:
10   *Salve tibi!*[2] I must hear
Wise talk of the kind of weather,
    Sort of season, time of year:
Not a plenteous cork-crop: scarcely
    Dare we hope oak-galls,[3] *I doubt:*
15 *What's the Latin name for "parsley"?*
    What's the Greek name for Swine's Snout?

3

Whew! We'll have our platter burnished,
    Laid with care on our own shelf!
With a fire-new spoon we're furnished,
20   And a goblet for ourself,
Rinsed like something sacrificial
    Ere 'tis fit to touch our chaps—
Marked with L for our initial!
    (He-he! There his lily snaps!)

4

25 *Saint,* forsooth! While brown Dolores
    Squats outside the Convent bank
With Sanchicha, telling stories,
    Steeping tresses in the tank,
Blue-black, lustrous, thick like horsehairs,
30   —Can't I see his dead eye glow,
Bright as 'twere a Barbary corsair's?[4]
    (That is, if he'd let it show!)

5

When he finishes refection,°   *dinner*
    Knife and fork he never lays
35 Cross-wise, to my recollection,
    As do I, in Jesu's praise.
I the Trinity illustrate,
    Drinking watered orange-pulp—
In three sips the Arian[5] frustrate;
40   While he drains his at one gulp.

---

2. "Hail to thee!" (Spanish).
3. Growths produced on oak leaves by gallflies.
4. "Barbary corsair": pirate from the Berber coun-
tries on the north coast of Africa.
5. Arius, a fourth-century Alexandrian heretic,
denied the doctrine of the Trinity.

6

Oh, those melons? If he's able
 We're to have a feast! so nice!
One goes to the Abbot's table,
 All of us get each a slice.
45 How go on your flowers? None double?
 Not one fruit-sort can you spy?
Strange! And I, too, at such trouble,
 Keep them close-nipped on the sly!

7

There's a great text in Galatians,[6]
50 Once you trip on it, entails
Twenty-nine distinct damnations,
 One sure, if another fails:
If I trip him just a-dying,
 Sure of heaven as sure can be,
55 Spin him around and send him flying
 Off to hell, a Manichee?[7]

8

Or, my scrofulous° French novel   *morally corrupt*
 On gray paper with blunt type!
Simply glance at it, you grovel
60 Hand and foot in Belial's[8] gripe:
If I double down its pages
 At the woeful sixteenth print,
When he gathers his greengages,
 Ope a sieve and slip it in't?

9

65 Or, there's Satan! one might venture
 Pledge one's soul to him, yet leave
Such a flaw in the indenture
 As he'd miss till, past retrieve,
Blasted lay that rose-acacia
70 We're so proud of![9] *Hy, Zy, Hine*[1] . . .
'St, there's vespers! *Plena gratiâ*
 Ave, Virgo![2] Gr-r-r—you swine!

1842

Home-Thoughts, From Abroad

1

Oh, to be in England
Now that April's there,

---

6. The line has sometimes been taken as referring to Galatians 3.10; but see Galatians 5.14–15, with its ironic applicability to the spirit of the monologue, and also 5.16–24.
7. The Manichean heresy, which the speaker hopes to lure Brother Lawrence into accepting, claimed that the world was divided between forces of good and forces of evil.
8. Hebrew personification of lawlessness, hence one of the names for the Devil.

9. The speaker seems to say that, if all else fails, he might secure Brother Lawrence's damnation by pledging his own soul to the Devil in return—but being careful to leave a flaw in the contract that would invalidate it.
1. Possibly an incantation used in calling up the Devil.
2. "*Plena gratiâ / Ave, Virgo*": the speaker reverses the opening words of the Ave Maria: "Hail Mary, full of grace."

And whoever wakes in England
Sees, some morning, unaware,
5 That the lowest boughs and the brushwood sheaf
Round the elm-tree bole are in tiny leaf,
While the chaffinch sings on the orchard bough
In England—now!

2

And after April, when May follows,
10 And the whitethroat builds, and all the swallows!
Hark, where my blossomed pear-tree in the hedge
Leans to the field and scatters on the clover
Blossoms and dewdrops—at the bent spray's edge—
That's the wise thrush; he sings each song twice over,
15 Lest you should think he never could recapture
The first fine careless rapture!
And though the fields look rough with hoary dew
All will be gay when noontide wakes anew
The buttercups, the little children's dower
20 —Far brighter than this gaudy melon-flower!

1845

The Bishop Orders His Tomb at Saint Praxed's Church[3]

Rome, 15—

Vanity, saith the preacher, vanity![4]
Draw round my bed: is Anselm keeping back?
Nephews—sons mine . . . ah God, I know not! Well—
She, men would have to be your mother once,
5 Old Gandolf envied me, so fair she was!
What's done is done, and she is dead beside,
Dead long ago, and I am Bishop since,
And as she died so must we die ourselves,
And thence ye may perceive the world's a dream.
10 Life, how and what is it? As here I lie
In this state-chamber, dying by degrees,
Hours and long hours in the dead night, I ask
"Do I live, am I dead?" Peace, peace seems all.
Saint Praxed's ever was the church for peace;
15 And so, about this tomb of mine. I fought
With tooth and nail to save my niche, ye know:
—Old Gandolf cozened° me, despite my care;   *cheated*
Shrewd was that snatch from out the corner south
He graced his carrion with, God curse the same!
20 Yet still my niche is not so cramped but thence
One sees the pulpit o' the epistle-side,[5]
And somewhat of the choir, those silent seats,

3. The church of Santa Prassede, in Rome, dedicated to a Roman virgin, dates from the fifth century but was rebuilt early in the ninth and restored at later times. The sixteenth-century bishop who speaks here is a fictional figure, as is his predecessor, Gandolf.

4. An echo of Ecclesiastes 1.2: "Vanity of vanities, saith the Preacher, vanity of vanities; all is vanity."
5. The right-hand side as one faces the altar, the side from which the Epistles of the New Testament were read.

And up into the aery dome where live
The angels, and a sunbeam's sure to lurk:
25 And I shall fill my slab of basalt there,
And 'neath my tabernacle[6] take my rest,
With those nine columns round me, two and two,
The odd one at my feet where Anselm stands:
Peach-blossom marble all, the rare, the ripe
30 As fresh-poured red wine of a mighty pulse.
—Old Gandolf with his paltry onion-stone,
Put me where I may look at him! True peach,
Rosy and flawless: how I earned the prize!
Draw close: that conflagration of my church
35 —What then? So much was saved if aught were missed!
My sons, ye would not be my death? Go dig
The white-grape vineyard where the oil-press stood,
Drop water gently till the surface sink,
And if ye find . . . Ah God, I know not, I! . . .
40 Bedded in store of rotten fig-leaves soft,
And corded up in a tight olive-frail,°   *olive basket*
Some lump, ah God, of *lapis lazuli*,[7]
Big as a Jew's head cut off at the nape,
Blue as a vein o'er the Madonna's breast . . .
45 Sons, all have I bequeathed you, villas, all,
That brave Frascati[8] villa with its bath,
So, let the blue lump poise between my knees,
Like God the Father's globe on both his hands
Ye worship in the Jesu Church[9] so gay,
50 For Gandolf shall not choose but see and burst!
Swift as a weaver's shuttle fleet our years:[1]
Man goeth to the grave, and where is he?
Did I say basalt for my slab, sons? Black—
'Twas ever antique-black I meant! How else
55 Shall ye contrast my frieze to come beneath?
The bas-relief in bronze ye promised me,
Those Pans and Nymphs ye wot of, and perchance
Some tripod, thyrsus,[2] with a vase or so,
The Saviour at his sermon on the mount,
60 Saint Praxed in a glory,[3] and one Pan
Ready to twitch the Nymph's last garment off,
And Moses with the tables . . . but I know
Ye mark me not! What do they whisper thee,
Child of my bowels, Anselm? Ah, ye hope
65 To revel down my villas while I gasp
Bricked o'er with beggar's moldy travertine[4]
Which Gandolf from his tomb-top chuckles at!
Nay, boys, ye love me—all of jasper,[5] then!

6. Canopy over his tomb.
7. A vivid blue stone, one of the so-called hard stones, used for ornament.
8. A resort town in the mountains.
9. The splendid baroque church Il Gesù. The sculptured group of the Trinity includes a terrestrial globe carved from the largest known block of lapis lazuli.
1. See Job 7.6 ("My days are swifter than a weaver's shuttle, and are spent without hope").
2. A staff ornamented with ivy or vine leaves, carried by followers of Bacchus, the Roman god of wine and revelry.
3. Rays of gold, signifying sanctity, around the head or body of the saint portrayed.
4. Ordinary limestone used in building.
5. A variety of quartz.

'T is jasper ye stand pledged to, lest I grieve
70 My bath must needs be left behind, alas!
One block, pure green as a pistachio-nut,
There's plenty jasper somewhere in the world—
And have I not Saint Praxed's ear to pray
Horses for ye, and brown Greek manuscripts,
75 And mistresses with great smooth marbly limbs?
—That's if ye carve my epitaph aright,
Choice Latin, picked phrase, Tully's[6] every word,
No gaudy ware like Gandolf's second line—
Tully, my masters? Ulpian[7] serves his need!
80 And then how I shall lie through centuries,
And hear the blessed mutter of the mass,
And see God made and eaten all day long,[8]
And feel the steady candle-flame, and taste
Good strong thick stupefying incense-smoke!
85 For as I lie here, hours of the dead night,
Dying in state and by such slow degrees,
I fold my arms as if they clasped a crook,[9]
And stretch my feet forth straight as stone can point,
And let the bedclothes, for a mortcloth,[1] drop
90 Into great laps and folds of sculptor's-work:
And as yon tapers dwindle, and strange thoughts
Grow, with a certain humming in my ears,
About the life before I lived this life,
And this life too, popes, cardinals and priests,
95 Saint Praxed at his sermon on the mount,[2]
Your tall pale mother with her talking eyes,
And new-found agate urns as fresh as day,
And marble's language, Latin pure, discreet,
—Aha, ELUCESCEBAT[3] quoth our friend?
100 No Tully, said I, Ulpian at the best!
Evil and brief hath been my pilgrimage.
All *lapis*, all, son! Else I give the Pope
My villas! Will ye ever eat my heart?
Ever your eyes were as a lizard's quick,
105 They glitter like your mother's for my soul,
Or ye would heighten my impoverished frieze,
Piece out its starved design, and fill my vase
With grapes, and add a vizor and a Term,[4]
And to the tripod ye would tie a lynx
110 That in his struggle throws the thyrsus down,
To comfort me on my entablature
Whereon I am to lie till I must ask
"Do I live, am I dead?" There, leave me, there!
For ye have stabbed me with ingratitude

6. Familiar name for Cicero (Marcus Tullius Cicero).
7. His Latin would be stylistically inferior to that of Cicero.
8. Refers to the doctrine of transubstantiation.
9. I.e., the bishop's crozier, with its emblematic resemblance to a shepherd's crook.
1. The pall with which a coffin is draped.
2. As the bishop's mind wanders, he attributes Christ's Sermon on the Mount to Santa Prassede.
3. A word from Gandolf's epitaph (a form of the Latin verb meaning "to shine forth"); the bishop claims that this form is inferior to *elucebat*, which Cicero would have used.
4. A pillar adorned with a bust; "visor": a mask. Both are motifs of classical sculpture imitated by the Renaissance.

115 To death—ye wish it—God, ye wish it! Stone—
Gritstone, a-crumble! Clammy squares which sweat
As if the corpse they keep were oozing through—
And no more *lapis* to delight the world!
Well, go! I bless ye. Fewer tapers there,
120 But in a row: and, going, turn your backs
—Ay, like departing altar-ministrants,
And leave me in my church, the church for peace,
That I may watch at leisure if he leers—
Old Gandolf, at me, from his onion-stone,
125 As still he envied me, so fair she was!

1845, 1849

Fra Lippo Lippi[5]

I am poor brother Lippo, by your leave!
You need not clap your torches to my face.
Zooks, what's to blame? you think you see a monk!
What, 'tis past midnight, and you go the rounds,
5 And here you catch me at an alley's end
Where sportive ladies leave their doors ajar?
The Carmine's my cloister:[6] hunt it up,
Do—harry out, if you must show your zeal,
Whatever rat, there, haps on his wrong hole,
10 And nip each softling of a wee white mouse,
Weke, weke, that's crept to keep him company!
Aha, you know your betters! Then, you'll take
Your hand away that's fiddling on my throat,
And please to know me likewise. Who am I?
15 Why, one, sir, who is lodging with a friend
Three streets off—he's a certain . . . how d'ye call?
Master—a . . . Cosimo of the Medici,[7]
I' the house that caps the corner. Boh! you were best!
Remember and tell me, the day you're hanged,
20 How you affected such a gullet's-gripe![8]
But you, sir, it concerns you that your knaves
Pick up a manner nor discredit you:
Zooks, are we pilchards,° that they sweep the streets   fish
And count fair prize what comes into their net?
25 He's Judas to a tittle, that man is![9]
Just such a face! Why, sir, you make amends.
Lord, I'm not angry! Bid your hangdogs go
Drink out this quarter-florin to the health
Of the munificent House that harbors me

5. (ca. 1406–1469); Florentine painter, whose life Browning knew from Vasari's *Lives of the Most Eminent Painters, Sculptors, and Architects,* and from other sources, and whose paintings he had learned to know at first hand during his years in Florence.
6. Fra Lippo had entered the Carmelite cloister while still a boy. He gave up monastic vows on June 6, 1421, but was clothed by the monastery until 1431 and was called "Fra Filippo" in documents until his death.
7. Cosimo de'Medici (1389–1464), Fra Lippo's wealthy patron and an important political power in Florence.
8. I.e., grip on my throat.
9. Of one of the watchmen who have arrested him, he says he looks exactly like Judas.

30 (And many more beside, lads! more beside!)
    And all's come square again. I'd like his face—
    His, elbowing on his comrade in the door
    With the pike and lantern—for the slave that holds
    John Baptist's head a-dangle by the hair
35 With one hand ("Look you, now," as who should say)
    And his weapon in the other, yet unwiped!
    It's not your chance to have a bit of chalk,
    A wood-coal or the like? or you should see!
    Yes, I'm the painter, since you style me so.
40 What, brother Lippo's doings, up and down,
    You know them and they take you? like enough!
    I saw the proper twinkle in your eye—
    'Tell you, I liked your looks at very first.
    Let's sit and set things straight now, hip to haunch.
45 Here's spring come, and the nights one makes up bands
    To roam the town and sing out carnival,
    And I've been three weeks shut within my mew,[1]
    A-painting for the great man, saints and saints
    And saints again. I could not paint all night—
50 Ouf! I leaned out of window for fresh air.
    There came a hurry of feet and little feet,
    A sweep of lute-strings, laughs, and whiffs of song—
    Flower o' the broom,
    Take away love, and our earth is a tomb!
55 *Flower o' the quince,*
    I let Lisa go, and what good in life since?
    Flower o' the thyme—and so on. Round they went.
    Scarce had they turned the corner when a titter
    Like the skipping of rabbits by moonlight—
        three slim shapes,
60 And a face that looked up . . . zooks, sir, flesh and blood,
    That's all I'm made of! Into shreds it went,
    Curtain and counterpane and coverlet,
    All the bed-furniture—a dozen knots,
    There was a ladder! Down I let myself,
65 Hands and feet, scrambling somehow, and so dropped,
    And after them. I came up with the fun
    Hard by Saint Laurence,[2] hail fellow, well met—
    Flower o' the rose,
    If I've been merry, what matter who knows?
70 And so as I was stealing back again
    To get to bed and have a bit of sleep
    Ere I rise up to-morrow and go work
    On Jerome knocking at his poor old breast[3]
    With his great round stone to subdue the flesh,
75 You snap me of the sudden. Ah, I see!
    Though your eye twinkles still, you shake your head—
    Mine's shaved—a monk, you say—the sting's in that!
    If Master Cosimo announced himself,

---

1. I.e., within the confines of my quarters (in the Medici palace).
2. The church of San Lorenzo, not far from the Medici palace.
3. I.e., on a painting of St. Jerome in the Desert.

Mum's the word naturally; but a monk!
80 Come, what am I a beast for? tell us, now!
I was a baby when my mother died
And father died and left me in the street.
I starved there, God knows how, a year or two
On fig-skins, melon-parings, rinds and shucks,
85 Refuse and rubbish. One fine frosty day,
My stomach being empty as your hat,
The wind doubled me up and down I went.
Old Aunt Lapaccia trussed me with one hand,
(Its fellow was a stinger as I knew)
90 And so along the wall, over the bridge,
By the straight cut to the convent. Six words there,
While I stood munching my first bread that month:
"So, boy, you're minded," quoth the good fat father
Wiping his own mouth, 't was refection-time—
95 "To quit this very miserable world?
"Will you renounce" . . . "the mouthful of bread?" thought I;
By no means! Brief, they made a monk of me;
I did renounce the world, its pride and greed,
Palace, farm, villa, shop and banking-house,
100 Trash, such as these poor devils of Medici
Have given their hearts to—all at eight years old.
Well, sir, I found in time, you may be sure,
'T was not for nothing—the good bellyful,
The warm serge and the rope that goes all round,
105 And day-long blessed idleness beside!
"Let's see what the urchin's fit for"—that came next.
Not overmuch their way, I must confess.
Such a to-do! They tried me with their books:
Lord, they'd have taught me Latin in pure waste!
110 *Flower o' the clove,*
All the Latin I construe is, "amo" I love!
But, mind you, when a boy starves in the streets
Eight years together, as my fortune was,
Watching folk's faces to know who will fling
115 The bit of half-stripped grape-bunch he desires,
And who will curse or kick him for his pains—
Which gentleman processional and fine,
Holding a candle to the Sacrament,
Will wink and let him lift a plate and catch
125 The droppings of the wax to sell again,
Or holla for the Eight[4] and have him whipped—
How say I? nay, which dog bites, which lets drop
His bone from the heap of offal in the street—
Why, soul and sense of him grow sharp alike,
125 He learns the look of things, and none the less
For admonition from the hunger-pinch.
I had a store of such remarks, be sure,
Which, after I found leisure, turned to use.
I drew men's faces on my copy-books,

---

4. The Florentine magistrates.

130 Scrawled them within the antiphonary's[5] marge,
Joined legs and arms to the long music-notes,
Found eyes and nose and chin for A's and B's,
And made a string of pictures of the world
Betwixt the ins and outs of verb and noun,
135 On the wall, the bench, the door. The monks looked black.
"Nay," quoth the Prior, "turn him out, d'ye say?
"In no wise. Lose a crow and catch a lark.
"What if at last we get our man of parts,
"We Carmelites, like those Camaldolese[6]
140 "And Preaching Friars,[7] to do our church up fine
"And put the front on it that ought to be!"
And hereupon he bade me daub away.
Thank you! my head being crammed, the walls a blank,
Never was such prompt disemburdening.
145 First, every sort of monk, the black and white,
I drew them, fat and lean: then, folk at church,
From good old gossips waiting to confess
Their cribs° of barrel-droppings, candle-ends —   minor thefts
To the breathless fellow at the altar-foot,
150 Fresh from his murder, safe and sitting there
With the little children round him in a row
Of admiration, half for his beard and half
For that white anger of his victim's son
Shaking a fist at him with one fierce arm,
155 Signing[8] himself with the other because of Christ
(Whose sad face on the cross sees only this
After the passion of a thousand years)
Till some poor girl, her apron o'er her head,
(Which the intense eyes looked through) came at eve
160 On tiptoe, said a word, dropped in a loaf,
Her pair of earrings and a bunch of flowers
(The brute took growling), prayed, and so was gone.
I painted all, then cried " 'Tis ask and have;
"Choose, for more's ready!" — laid the ladder flat,
165 And showed my covered bit of cloister-wall.
The monks closed in a circle and praised loud
Till checked, taught what to see and not to see,
Being simple bodies — "That's the very man!
"Look at the boy who stoops to pat the dog!
170 "That woman's like the Prior's niece who comes
"To care about his asthma: it's the life!"
But there my triumph's straw-fire flared and funked;[9]
Their betters took their turn to see and say:
The Prior and the learned pulled a face
175 And stopped all that in no time. "How? what's here?
"Quite from the mark of painting, bless us all!
"Faces, arms, legs and bodies like the true
"As much as pea and pea! it's devil's-game!

5. The book containing the antiphons, or responses chanted in the liturgy.
6. Members of a religious order at Camaldoli, in the Apennines.
7. I.e., Dominicans.
8. Making the sign of the cross with one hand, because of the image of Christ on the altar.
9. Expired in smoke.

"Your business is not to catch men with show,
180 "With homage to the perishable clay,
"But lift them over it, ignore it all,
"Make them forget there's such a thing as flesh.
"Your business is to paint the souls of men—
"Man's soul, and it's a fire, smoke . . . no, it's not . . .
185 "It's vapor done up like a new-born babe—
"(In that shape when you die it leaves your mouth)
"It's . . . well, what matters talking, it's the soul!
"Give us no more of body than shows soul!
"Here's Giotto,[1] with his Saint a-praising God,
190 "That sets us praising—why not stop with him?
"Why put all thoughts of praise out of our head
"With wonder at lines, colors, and what not?
"Paint the soul, never mind the legs and arms!
"Rub all out, try at it a second time.
195 "Oh, that white smallish female with the breasts,
"She's just my niece . . . Herodias,[2] I would say—
"Who went and danced and got men's heads cut off!
"Have it all out!" Now, is this sense, I ask?
A fine way to paint soul, by painting body
200 So ill, the eye can't stop there, must go further
And can't fare worse! Thus, yellow does for white
When what you put for yellow's simply black,
And any sort of meaning looks intense
When all beside itself means and looks nought.
205 Why can't a painter lift each foot in turn,
Left foot and right foot, go a double step,
Make his flesh liker and his soul more like,
Both in their order? Take the prettiest face,
The Prior's niece . . . patron-saint—is it so pretty
210 You can't discover if it means hope, fear,
Sorrow or joy? won't beauty go with these?
Suppose I've made her eyes all right and blue,
Can't I take breath and try to add life's flash,
And then add soul and heighten them threefold?
215 Or say there's beauty with no soul at all—
(I never saw it—put the case the same—)
If you get simple beauty and nought else,
You get about the best thing God invents:
That's somewhat: and you'll find the soul you have missed,
220 Within yourself, when you return him thanks.
"Rub all out!" Well, well, there's my life, in short,
And so the thing has gone on ever since.
I'm grown a man no doubt, I've broken bounds:
You should not take a fellow eight years old
225 And make him swear to never kiss the girls.
I'm my own master, paint now as I please—
Having a friend, you see, in the Corner-house![3]

1. The great Florentine painter Giotto di Bondone (1267–1337).
2. Sister-in-law of the tetrarch Herod. She had
demanded that John the Baptist be imprisoned:
when her daughter Salome so pleased the king

with her dancing that he promised her anything
she asked, Herodias instructed her to ask for the
head of John the Baptist on a platter (Matthew
14.1–12).
3. I.e., the Medici palace.

Lord, it's fast holding by the rings in front—
Those great rings serve more purposes than just
230 To plant a flag in, or tie up a horse!
And yet the old schooling sticks, the old grave eyes
Are peeping o'er my shoulder as I work,
The heads shake still—"It's art's decline, my son!
"You're not of the true painters, great and old;
235 "Brother Angelico's the man, you'll find;
"Brother Lorenzo⁴ stands his single peer:
"Fag on at flesh, you'll never make the third!"
Flower o' the pine,
You keep your mistr . . . manners, and I'll stick to mine!
240 I'm not the third, then: bless us, they must know!
Don't you think they're the likeliest to know,
They with their Latin? So, I swallow my rage,
Clench my teeth, suck my lips in tight, and paint
To please them—sometimes do and sometimes don't;
245 For, doing most, there's pretty sure to come
A turn, some warm eve finds me at my saints—
A laugh, a cry, the business of the world—
(Flower o' the peach,
Death for us all, and his own life for each!)
250 And my whole soul revolves, the cup runs over,
The world and life's too big to pass for a dream,
And I do these wild things in sheer despite,
And play the fooleries you catch me at,
In pure rage! The old mill-horse, out at grass
255 After hard years, throws up his stiff heels so,
Although the miller does not preach to him
The only good of grass is to make chaff.
What would men have? Do they like grass or no—
May they or mayn't they? all I want's the thing
260 Settled for ever one way. As it is,
You tell too many lies and hurt yourself:
You don't like what you only like too much,
You do like what, if given you at your word,
You find abundantly detestable.
265 For me, I think I speak as I was taught;
I always see the garden and God there
A-making man's wife: and, my lesson learned,
The value and significance of flesh,
I can't unlearn ten minutes afterwards.

270 You understand me: I'm a beast, I know.
But see, now—why, I see as certainly
As that the morning-star's about to shine,
What will hap some day. We've a youngster here
Comes to our convent, studies what do,
275 Slouches and stares and lets no atom drop:
His name is Guidi—he'll not mind the monks—

---

4. Fra Angelico (1387–1455), and Fra Lorenzo Monaco (1370–1425).

They call him Hulking Tom,[5] he lets them talk—
He picks my practice up—he'll paint apace,
I hope so—though I never live so long,
280 I know what's sure to follow. You be judge!
You speak no Latin more than I, belike;
However, you're my man, you've seen the world
—The beauty and the wonder and the power,
The shapes of things, their colors, lights and shades,
285 Changes, surprises—and God made it all!
—For what? Do you feel thankful, ay or no,
For this fair town's face, yonder river's line,
The mountain round it and the sky above,
Much more the figures of man, woman, child,
290 These are the frame to? What's it all about?
To be passed over, despised? or dwelt upon,
Wondered at? oh, this last of course!—you say.
But why not do as well as say, paint these
Just as they are, careless what comes of it?
295 God's works—paint anyone, and count it crime
To let a truth slip. Don't object, "His works
"Are here already; nature is complete:
"Suppose you reproduce her (which you can't)
"There's no advantage! you must beat her, then."
300 For, don't you mark? we're made so that we love
First when we see them painted, things we have passed
Perhaps a hundred times nor cared to see;
And so they are better, painted—better to us,
Which is the same thing. Art was given for that;
305 God uses us to help each other so,
Lending our minds out. Have you noticed, now,
Your cullion's° hanging face? A bit of chalk,   rascal's
And trust me but you should, though! How much more,
If I drew higher things with the same truth!
310 That were to take the Prior's pulpit-place,
Interpret God to all of you! Oh, oh,
It makes me mad to see what men shall do
And we in our graves! This world's no blot for us,
Nor blank; it means intensely, and means good:
315 To find its meaning is my meat and drink.
"Ay, but you don't so instigate to prayer!"
Strikes in the Prior: "when your meaning's plain
"It does not say to folk—remember matins,
"Or, mind you fast next Friday!" Why, for this
320 What need of art at all? A skull and bones,
Two bits of stick nailed crosswise, or, what's best,
A bell to chime the hour with, does as well.
I painted a Saint Laurence six months since
At Prato,[6] splashed the fresco in fine style:

5. The painter Tommaso Guidi (1401–1428), known as Masaccio (from *Tomasaccio*, meaning "Big Tom" or "Hulking Tom"). The series of frescoes that he painted in Santa Maria del Carmine, of key importance in the history of Florentine painting, was completed by Fra Lippo's son, Filippino Lippi, and it is in fact more likely that Fra Lippo learned from Masaccio than that he saw him as a promising newcomer.
6. Smaller town near Florence, where Fra Lippo painted some of his most important pictures.

325 "How looks my painting, now the scaffold's down?"
I ask a brother: "Hugely," he returns—
"Already not one phiz° of your three slaves   *face*
"Who turn the Deacon off his toasted side,[7]
"But's scratched and prodded to our heart's content,
330 "The pious people have so eased their own
"With coming to say prayers there in a rage:
"We get on fast to see the bricks beneath.
"Expect another job this time next year,
"For pity and religion grow i' the crowd—
355 "Your painting serves its purpose!" Hang the fools!

    —That is—you'll not mistake an idle word
Spoke in a huff by a poor monk, God wot,
Tasting the air this spicy night which turns
The unaccustomed head like Chianti wine!
340 Oh, the church knows! don't misreport me, now!
It's natural a poor monk out of bounds
Should have his apt word to excuse himself:
And hearken how I plot to make amends.
I have bethought me: I shall paint a piece
345 . . . There's for you! Give me six months, then go, see
Something in Sant' Ambrogio's![8] Bless the nuns!
They want a cast o' my office.[9] I shall paint
God in the midst, Madonna and her babe,
Ringed by a bowery flowery angel-brood,
350 Lilies and vestments and white faces, sweet
As puff on puff of grated orris-root
When ladies crowd to Church at midsummer.
And then i' the front, of course a saint or two—
Saint John, because he saves the Florentines,[1]
355 Saint Ambrose, who puts down in black and white
The convent's friends and gives them a long day,
And Job, I must have him there past mistake,
The man of Uz (and Us without the z,
Painters who need his patience). Well, all these
360 Secured at their devotion, up shall come
Out of a corner when you least expect,
As one by a dark stair into a great light,
Music and talking, who but Lippo! I!
Mazed, motionless and moonstruck—I'm the man!
365 Back I shrink—what is this I see and hear?
I, caught up with my monk's-things by mistake,
My old serge gown and rope that goes all round,
I, in this presence, this pure company!
Where's a hole, where's a corner for escape?
370 Then steps a sweet angelic slip of a thing
Forward, puts out a soft palm—"Not so fast!"

---

7. Saint Lawrence was martyred by being roasted on a gridiron; according to legend, he urged his executioners to turn him over, saying that he was done on one side.
8. Fra Lippo painted the *Coronation of the Virgin*, here described, for the high altar of Sant' Ambrogio in 1447.
9. A sample of my work.
1. San Giovanni is the patron saint of Florence.

—Addresses the celestial presence, "nay—
"He made you and devised you, after all,
"Though he's none of you! Could Saint John there draw—
375 "His camel-hair² make up a painting-brush?
"We come to brother Lippo for all that,
"*Iste perfecit opus!*"³ So, all smile—
I shuffle sideways with my blushing face
Under the cover of a hundred wings
380 Thrown like a spread of kirtles⁴ when you're gay
And play hot cockles,⁵ all the doors being shut,
Till, wholly unexpected, in there pops
The hothead husband! Thus I scuttle off
To some safe bench behind, not letting go
385 The palm of her, the little lily thing
That spoke the good word for me in the nick,
Like the Prior's niece . . . Saint Lucy, I would say.
And so all's saved for me, and for the church
A pretty picture gained. Go, six months hence!
390 Your hand, sir, and good-bye: no lights, no lights!
The street's hushed, and I know my own way back,
Don't fear me! there's the gray beginning. Zooks!

1855

A Toccata of Galuppi's⁶

1

Oh Galuppi, Baldassare, this is very sad to find!
I can hardly misconceive you; it would prove me deaf and blind;
But although I take your meaning, 'tis with such a heavy mind!

2

Here you come with your old music, and here's all the good it brings.
5 What, they lived once thus at Venice where the merchants were the kings,
Where Saint Mark's is, where the Doges used to wed the sea with rings?⁷

3

Ay, because the sea's the street there; and 'tis arched by . . . what you call
. . . Shylock's bridge⁸ with houses on it, where they kept the carnival:
I was never out of England—it's as if I saw it all.

---

2. John the Baptist is often portrayed wearing a rough robe of camel's hair, in accord with Mark 1.6.
3. The figure that Browning took to be that of the painter is more likely that of the patron, the Very Reverend Francesco Marenghi, who ordered the painting in 1441, and that the words on the scroll before him (*Is [te] perfecit opus*, Latin for "This man accomplished the work") refer to the commissioning of the project.
4. Women's gowns or skirts.
5. A game in which a blindfolded player must guess who has struck him.
6. The poem presents the reflections of a nineteenth-century Englishman, as he plays a toccata

by the eighteenth-century Venetian composer Baldassare Galuppi. (A toccata is a "touch-piece," the word derived from the Italian verb *toccare*, "to touch": "a composition intended to exhibit the touch and execution of the performer," and hence often having the character of "showy improvisation" [*Grove's Dictionary of Music and Musicians*]. In stanzas 7–9, the quoted words represent the thoughts, feelings, or casual remarks of the earlier Venetian audience, now dispersed by death.
7. Each year the Doge, chief magistrate of the Venetian republic, threw a ring into the sea with the ceremonial words, "We wed thee, O sea, in sign of true and everlasting dominion."
8. The Rialto Bridge over the Grand Canal.

4

10 Did young people take their pleasure when the sea was warm in May?
Balls and masks begun at midnight, burning ever to mid-day,
When they made up fresh adventures for the morrow, do you say?

5

Was a lady such a lady, cheeks so round and lips so red—
On her neck the small face buoyant, like a bellflower on its bed,
15 O'er the breast's superb abundance where a man might base his head?

6

Well, and it was graceful of them—they'd break talk off and afford
—She, to bite her mask's black velvet—he, to finger on his sword,
While you sat and played Toccatas, stately at the clavichord?[9]

7

What? Those lesser thirds so plaintive, sixths diminished, sigh on sigh,
20 Told them something? Those suspensions, those solutions—"Must we
die?"
Those commiserating sevenths[1]—"Life might last! we can but try!"

8

"Were you happy?" "Yes." "And are you still as happy?" "Yes. And you?"
"Then, more kisses!" "Did I stop them, when a million seemed so few?"
Hark, the dominant's persistence till it must be answered to!

9

25 So, an octave struck the answer. Oh, they praised you, I dare say!
"Brave Galuppi! that was music! good alike at grave and gay!
"I can always leave off talking when I hear a master play!"

10

Then they left you for their pleasure: till in due time, one by one,
Some with lives that came to nothing, some with deeds as well undone,
30 Death stepped tacitly and took them where they never see the sun.

11

But when I sit down to reason, think to take my stand nor swerve,
While I triumph o'er a secret wrung from nature's close reserve,
In you come with your cold music[2] till I creep through every nerve.

12

Yes, you, like a ghostly cricket, creaking where a house was burned:
35 "Dust and ashes, dead and done with, Venice spent what Venice earned.
"The soul, doubtless, is immortal—where a soul can be discerned.

13

"Yours for instance: you know physics, something of geology,
"Mathematics are your pastime; souls shall rise in their degree;
"Butterflies may dread extinction—you'll not die, it cannot be!

---

9. "A keyboard instrument, precursor of the piano" [Webster].
1. This term and others in these lines all refer to the technical devices used by Galuppi to produce alternating moods in his music, conflict in each case being resolved into harmony. Thus the "dominant" (the fifth note of the scale), after being persistently sounded, is answered by a resolving chort (lines 24–25).
2. In stanzas 12–15, the quoted words are the words he imagines the composer as speaking to him.

14

40 "As for Venice and her people, merely born to bloom and drop,
"Here on earth they bore their fruitage, mirth and folly were the crop:
"What of soul was left, I wonder, when the kissing had to stop?

15

"Dust and ashes!" So you creak it, and I want° the heart to scold.   lack
Dear dead women, with such hair, too—what's become of all the gold
45 Used to hang and brush their bosoms? I feel chilly and grown old.
ca. 1847   1855

"Childe Roland to the Dark Tower Came"

(See Edgar's Song in "Lear")[3]

1

My first thought was, he lied in every word,
    That hoary cripple, with malicious eye
    Askance to watch the working of his lie
On mine, and mouth scarce able to afford
5 Suppression of the glee, that pursed and scored
    Its edge, at one more victim gained thereby.

2

What else should he be set for, with his staff?
    What, save to waylay with his lies, ensnare
    All travelers who might find him posted there,
10 And ask the road? I guessed what skull-like laugh
    Would break, what crutch 'gin write my epitaph
    For pastime in the dusty thoroughfare,

3

If at his counsel I should turn aside
    Into that ominous tract which, all agree,
15   Hides the Dark Tower. Yet acquiescingly
I did turn as he pointed: neither pride
    Nor hope rekindling at the end descried,
    So much as gladness that some end might be.

4

For, what with my whole world-wide wandering,
20   What with my search drawn out through years, my hope
    Dwindled into a ghost not fit to cope
With that obstreperous joy success would bring,—
    I hardly tried now to rebuke the spring
    My heart made, finding failure in its scope.

5

25 As when a sick man very near to death
    Seems dead indeed, and feels begin and end
    The tears, and takes the farewell of each friend,
    And hears one bid the other go, draw breath

---

3. In Shakespeare's *King Lear* 2.4, Edgar, Gloucester's son, disguised as a madman, meets Lear in the midst of a storm; at the end of the scene, Edgar sings: "Child Rowland to the dark tower came; / His word was still, 'Fie, foh, and fum, / I smell the blood of a British man.'" ("Childe": medieval title applied to a youth awaiting knighthood.)

Freelier outside, ("since all is o'er," he saith,
30   "And the blow fallen no grieving can amend;")

6

While some discuss if near the other graves
    Be room enough for this, and when a day
    Suits best for carrying the corpse away,
With care about the banners, scarves and staves:
35 And still the man hears all, and only craves
    He may not shame such tender love and stay.

7

Thus, I had so long suffered in this quest,
    Heard failure prophesied so oft, been writ
    So many times among "The Band"—to wit,
40 The knights who to the Dark Tower's search addressed
    Their steps—that just to fail as they, seemed best,
    And all the doubt was now—should I be fit?

8

So, quiet as despair, I turned from him,
    That hateful cripple, out of his highway
45   Into the path he pointed. All the day
Had been a dreary one at best, and dim
Was settling to its close, yet shot one grim
    Red leer to see the plain catch its estray.[4]

9

For mark! no sooner was I fairly found
50   Pledged to the plain, after a pace or two,
    Than, pausing to throw backward a last view
O'er the safe road, 'twas gone; gray plain all round:
Nothing but plain to the horizon's bound.
    I might go on; naught else remained to do.

10

55 So, on I went. I think I never saw
    Such starved ignoble nature; nothing throve:
    For flowers—as well expect a cedar grove!
But cockle, spurge,[5] according to their law
Might propagate their kind, with none to awe,
60   You'd think: a burr had been a treasure trove.

11

No! penury, inertness and grimace,
    In some strange sort, were the land's portion. "See
    Or shut your eyes," said Nature peevishly,
"It nothing skills:[6] I cannot help my case:
65 'Tis the Last Judgment's fire must cure this place,
    Calcine° its clods and set my prisoners free."   *burn to powder*

12

If there pushed any ragged thistle-stalk
    Above its mates, the head was chopped; the bents°   *reeds, rushes*

---

4. A stray or unclaimed domestic animal.   spurge, a plant with minute flowers.
5. Cockle here is a weed that grows in wheatfields;   6. I.e., it is useless.

Were jealous else. What made those holes and rents
70 In the dock's⁷ harsh swarth° leaves, bruised as to balk   *dark*
All hope of greenness? 'tis a brute must walk
    Pashing° their life out, with a brute's intents.   *crushing*

13

As for the grass, it grew as scant as hair
    In leprosy; thin dry blades pricked the mud
75   Which underneath looked kneaded up with blood.
One stiff blind horse, his every bone a-stare,
    Stood stupefied, however he came there:
    Thrust out past service from the devil's stud!

14

Alive? he might be dead for aught I know,
80   With that red gaunt colloped° neck a-strain,   *chafed, ridged*
    And shut eyes underneath the rusty mane;
Seldom went such grotesqueness with such woe;
I never saw a brute I hated so;
    He must be wicked to deserve such pain.

15

85 I shut my eyes and turned them on my heart.
    As a man calls for wine before he fights,
    I asked one draught of earlier, happier sights,
Ere fitly I could hope to play my part.
Think first, fight afterwards—the soldier's art:
90   One taste of the old time sets all to rights.

16

Not it! I fancied Cuthbert's reddening face
    Beneath its garniture of curly gold,
    Dear fellow, till I almost felt him fold
An arm in mine to fix me to the place,
95   That way he used. Alas, one night's disgrace!
    Out went my heart's new fire and left it cold.

17

Giles then, the soul of honor—there he stands
    Frank as ten years ago when knighted first.
    What honest man should dare (he said) he durst.
100 Good—but the scene shifts—faugh! what hangman hands
    Pin to his breast a parchment? His own bands
    Read it. Poor traitor, spit upon and curst!

18

Better this present than a past like that;
    Back therefore to my darkening path again!
105   No sound, no sight as far as eye could strain.
Will the night send a howlet° or a bat?   *owl*
I asked: when something on the dismal flat
    Came to arrest my thoughts and change their train.

19

A sudden little river crossed my path
110   As unexpected as a serpent comes.

7. Coarse weedy plant's.

No sluggish tide congenial to the glooms;
  This, as it frothed by, might have been a bath
  For the fiend's glowing hoof—to see the wrath
Of its black eddy bespate° with flakes and spumes.   *spattered*

20

115 So petty yet so spiteful! All along,
  Low scrubby alders kneeled down over it;
  Drenched willows flung them headlong in a fit
Of mute despair, a suicidal throng:
  The river which had done them all the wrong,
120   Whate'er that was, rolled by, deterred no whit.

21

Which, while I forded,—good saints, how I feared
  To set my foot upon a dead man's cheek,
  Each step, or feel the spear I thrust to seek
For hollows, tangled in his hair or beard!
125   —It may have been a water-rat I speared,
  But, ugh! it sounded like a baby's shriek.

22

Glad was I when I reached the other bank.
  Now for a better country. Vain presage!
  Who were the strugglers, what war did they wage,
130 Whose savage trample thus could pad the dank
  Soil to a plash?° Toads in a poisoned tank,   *puddle*
  Or wild cats in a red-hot iron cage—

23

The fight must so have seemed in that fell cirque.[8]
  What penned them there, with all the plain to choose?
135   No footprint leading to that horrid mews,°   *stabling area*
None out of it. Mad brewage set to work
  Their brains, no doubt, like galley-slaves the Turk
  Pits for his pastime, Christians against Jews.

24

And more than that—a furlong on—why, there!
140   What bad use was that engine° for, that wheel,   *mechanical contrivance*
  Or brake,[9] not wheel—that harrow fit to reel
Men's bodies out like silk? with all the air
  Of Tophet's° tool, on earth left unaware,   *Hell's*
  Or brought to sharpen its rusty teeth of steel.

25

145 Then came a bit of stubbed ground, once a wood,
  Next a marsh, it would seem, and now mere earth
  Desperate and done with; (so a fool finds mirth,
Makes a thing and then mars it, till his mood
  Changes and off he goes!) within a rood[1]—
150   Bog, clay and rubble, sand and stark black dearth.

---

8. Rounded hollow encircled by heights.
9. Here in the sense of a tool for breaking up flax
or hemp, to separate the fiber.

1. Linear measure, varying locally from six to
eight yards.

26

Now blotches rankling,° colored gay and grim,   *festering*
  Now patches where some leanness of the soil's
  Broke into moss or substances like boils;
Then came some palsied oak, a cleft in him
155 Like a distorted mouth that splits its rim
  Gaping at death, and dies while it recoils.

27

And just as far as ever from the end!
  Nought in the distance but the evening, nought
  To point my footstep further! At the thought,
160 A great black bird, Apollyon's[2] bosom-friend,
Sailed past, nor beat his wide wing dragon-penned[3]
  That brushed my cap—perchance the guide I sought.

28

For, looking up, aware I somehow grew,
  'Spite of the dusk, the plain had given place
165   All round to mountains—with such name to grace
Mere ugly heights and heaps now stolen in view.
How thus they had surprised me,—solve it, you!
  How to get from them was no clearer case.

29

Yet half I seemed to recognize some trick
170   Of mischief happened to me, God knows when—
  In a bad dream perhaps. Here ended, then,
Progress this way. When, in the very nick
Of giving up, one time more, came a click
  As when a trap shuts—you're inside the den!

30

175 Burningly it came on me all at once,
  This was the place! those two hills on the right,
  Crouched like two bulls locked horn in horn in fight;
While to the left, a tall scalped mountain . . . Dunce,
Dotard, a-dozing at the very nonce,°   *moment*
180   After a life spent training for the sight!

31

What in the midst lay but the Tower itself?
  The round squat turret, blind as the fool's heart,
  Built of brown stone, without a counterpart
In the whole world. The tempest's mocking elf
185 Points to the shipman thus the unseen shelf
  He strikes on, only when the timbers start.

32

Not see? because of night perhaps?—why, day
  Came back again for that! before it left,
  The dying sunset kindled through a cleft:

---

2. ". . . The angel of the bottomless pit, whose name in the Hebrew tongue is Abaddon, but in the Greek tongue . . . Apollyon" (Revelation 9.11).
3. With pinions like a dragon's.

190   The hills, like giants at a hunting, lay,
      Chin upon hand, to see the game at bay,—
        "Now stab and end the creature—to the heft!"[4]

33

      Not hear? when noise was everywhere! it tolled
        Increasing like a bell. Names in my ears
195   Of all the lost adventurers my peers,—
      How such a one was strong, and such was bold,
        And such was fortunate, yet each of old
        Lost, lost! one moment knelled the woe of years.

34

      There they stood, ranged along the hillsides, met
200   To view the last of me, a living frame
        For one more picture! in a sheet of flame
      I saw them and I knew them all. And yet
      Dauntless the slug-horn[5] to my lips I set,
        And blew. *"Childe Roland to the Dark Tower came."*

1855

Memorabilia[6]

1

Ah, did you once see Shelley plain,
    And did he stop and speak to you
And did you speak to him again?
    How strange it seems and new!

2

5 But you were living before that,
    And also you are living after;
And the memory I started at—
    My starting moves your laughter.

3

I crossed a moor, with a name of its own
10   And a certain use in the world no doubt,
Yet a hand's-breadth of it shines alone
    'Mid the blank miles round about:

4

For there I picked up on the heather
    And there I put inside my breast
15 A moulted feather, an eagle-feather!
    Well, I forget the rest.

1855

---

4. Handle of a dagger or knife.   cow.
5. Rough trumpet made from the horn of an ox or   6. Memorable things.

Andrea del Sarto[7]

Called "The Faultless Painter"

But do not let us quarrel any more,
No, my Lucrezia; bear with me for once:
Sit down and all shall happen as you wish.
You turn your face, but does it bring your heart?
5   I'll work then for your friend's friend, never fear,
Treat his own subject after his own way,
Fix his own time, accept too his own price,
And shut the money into this small hand
When next it takes mine. Will it? tenderly?
10 Oh, I'll content him—but tomorrow, Love!
I often am much wearier than you think,
This evening more than usual, and it seems
As if—forgive now—should you let me sit
Here by the window with your hand in mine
15 And look a half-hour forth on Fiesole,[8]
Both of one mind, as married people use,
Quietly, quietly the evening through
I might get up tomorrow to my work
Cheerful and fresh as ever. Let us try.
20 Tomorrow, how you shall be glad for this!
Your soft hand is a woman of itself,
And mine the man's bared breast she curls inside.
Don't count the time lost, neither; you must serve
For each of the five pictures we require:
25 It saves a model. So! keep looking so—
My serpenting beauty, rounds on rounds!
—How could you ever prick those perfect ears,
Even to put the pearl there! oh, so sweet—
My face, my moon, my everybody's moon,
30 Which everybody looks on and calls his,
And, I suppose, is looked on by in turn,
While she looks—no one's: very dear, no less.
You smile? why, there's my picture ready made,
There's what we painters call our harmony!
35 A common grayness silvers everything,
All in a twilight, you and I alike
—You, at the point of your first pride in me
(That's gone you know)—but I, at every point;
My youth, my hope, my art, being all toned down
40 To yonder sober pleasant Fiesole.
There's the bell clinking from the chapel-top;
That length of convent-wall across the way

---

7. Andrea del Sarto (1486–1530), the Florentine painter, spent his entire life in Florence except for a year's sojourn at the court of the French king, Francis I, at Fontainebleau, 1518–19. He had been married since 1517 to Lucrezia del Fede, a widow, and in response to her pleading he left Fontainebleau, with the understanding that he would soon return to complete work for which he had been paid. But he did not return, and he spent money that the king had given him to purchase works of art in Italy on a house in Florence for him and Lucrezia. These and other facts Browning derived from Vasari's *Life* of Andrea (in his *Lives of the Most Eminent Painters, Sculptors, and Architects*). But the poem also depends inevitably on Browning's own response to Andrea's art.
8. A small town on the crown of a hill above Florence.

Holds the trees safer, huddled more inside;
The last monk leaves the garden; days decrease,
45 And autumn grows, autumn in everything.
Eh? the whole seems to fall into a shape
As if I saw alike my work and self
And all that I was born to be and do,
A twilight-piece. Love, we are in God's hand.
50 How strange now, looks the life he makes us lead;
So free we seem, so fettered fast we are!
I feel he laid the fetter: let it lie!
This chamber for example—turn your head—
All that's behind us! You don't understand
55 Nor care to understand about my art,
But you can hear at least when people speak:
And that cartoon,⁹ the second from the door
—It is the thing, Love! so such things should be—
Behold Madonna! I am bold to say.
60 I can do with my pencil what I know,
What I see, what at bottom of my heart
I wish for, if I ever wish so deep—
Do easily, too—when I say, perfectly,
I do not boast, perhaps: yourself are judge,
65 Who listened to the Legate's¹ talk last week,
And just as much they used to say in France.
At any rate 'tis easy, all of it!
No sketches first, no studies, that's long past:
I do what many dream of, all their lives,
70 —Dream? strive to do, and agonize to do,
And fail in doing. I could count twenty such
On twice your fingers, and not leave this town,
Who strive—you don't know how the others strive
To paint a little thing like that you smeared
75 Carelessly passing with your robes afloat—
Yet do much less, so much less, Someone says,
(I know his name, no matter)—so much less!
Well, less is more, Lucrezia: I am judged.
There burns a truer light of God in them,
80 In their vexed beating stuffed and stopped-up brain,
Heart, or whate'er else, than goes on to prompt
This low-pulsed forthright craftsman's hand of mine.
Their works drop groundward, but themselves, I know,
Reach many a time a heaven that's shut to me,
85 Enter and take their place there sure enough,
Though they come back and cannot tell the world.
My works are nearer heaven, but I sit here.
The sudden blood of these men! at a word—
Praise them, it boils, or blame them, it boils too.
90 I, painting from myself and to myself,
Know what I do, am unmoved by men's blame
Or their praise either. Somebody remarks

9. A preparatory drawing, on heavy paper, of the
same size as the painting to be executed from it in
oil or fresco.
1. The Pope's representative's.

Morello's[2] outline there is wrongly traced,
His hue mistaken; what of that? or else,
95   Rightly traced and well ordered; what of that?
Speak as they please, what does the mountain care?
Ah, but a man's reach should exceed his grasp,
Or what's a heaven for? All is silver-gray
Placid and perfect with my art: the worse!
100 I know both what I want and what might gain,
And yet how profitless to know, to sigh
"Had I been two, another and myself,
Our head would have o'erlooked the world!" No doubt.
Yonder's a work now, of that famous youth
105 The Urbinate[3] who died five years ago.
('Tis copied, George Vasari[4] sent it me.)
Well, I can fancy how he did it all,
Pouring his soul, with kings and popes to see,
Reaching, that heaven might so replenish him,
110 Above and through his art—for it gives way;
That arm is wrongly put—and there again—
A fault to pardon in the drawing's lines,
Its body, so to speak: its soul is right,
He means right—that, a child may understand.
115 Still, what an arm! and I could alter it:
But all the play, the insight and the stretch—
Out of me, out of me! And wherefore out?
Had you enjoined them on me, given me soul,
We might have risen to Rafael, I and you!
120 Nay, Love, you did give all I asked, I think—
More than I merit, yes, by many times.
But had you—oh, with the same perfect brow,
And perfect eyes, and more than perfect mouth,
And the low voice my soul hears, as a bird
125 The fowler's° pipe, and follows to the snare—   bird-catcher's
Had you, with these the same, but brought a mind!
Some women do so. Had the mouth there urged
"God and the glory! never care for gain.
The present by the future, what is that?
130 Live for fame, side by side with Agnolo![5]
"Rafael is waiting: up to God, all three!"
I might have done it for you. So it seems:
Perhaps not. All is as God over-rules.
Beside, incentives come from the soul's self;
135 The rest avail not. Why do I need you?
What wife had Rafael, or has Agnolo?
In this world, who can do a thing, will not;
And who would do it, cannot, I perceive:
Yet the will's somewhat—somewhat, too, the power—
140 And thus we half-men struggle. At the end,
God, I conclude, compensates, punishes.

---

2. Monte Morello is a mountain lying a little to the northwest of Florence in the Apennines.
3. The painter Raphael (1483–1520), so called because he was born at Urbino.
4. Giorgio Vasari, the biographer, himself a painter and an architect, had been Andrea's pupil.
5. I.e., Michelangelo (1475–1564).

'Tis safer for me, if the award be strict,
That I am something underrated here,
Poor this long while, despised, to speak the truth.
145 I dared not, do you know, leave home all day,
For fear of chancing on the Paris lords.
The best is when they pass and look aside;
But they speak sometimes; I must bear it all.
Well may they speak! That Francis, that first time,
150 And that long festal year at Fontainebleau![6]
I surely then could sometimes leave the ground,
Put on the glory, Rafael's daily wear,
In that humane great monarch's golden look—
One finger in his beard or twisted curl
155 Over his mouth's good mark that made the smile,
One arm about my shoulder, round my neck,
The jingle of his gold chain in my ear,
I painting proudly with his breath on me,
All his court round him, seeing with his eyes,
160 Such frank French eyes, and such a fire of souls
Profuse, my hand kept plying by those hearts—
And, best of all, this, this, this face beyond,
This in the background, waiting on my work,
To crown the issue with a last reward!
165 A good time, was it not, my kingly days?
And had you not grown restless . . . but I know—
'Tis done and past; 'twas right, my instinct said;
Too live the life grew, golden and not gray,
And I'm the weak-eyed bat no sun should tempt
170 Out of the grange° whose four walls make his world.   *country house*
How could it end in any other way?
You called me, and I came home to your heart.
The triumph was—to reach and stay there; since
I reached it ere the triumph, what is lost?
175 Let my hands frame your face in your hair's gold,
You beautiful Lucrezia that are mine!
"Rafael did this, Andrea painted that;
"The Roman's[7] is the better when you pray,
"But still the other's Virgin was his wife—"
180 Men will excuse me. I am glad to judge
Both pictures in your presence; clearer grows
My better fortune, I resolve to think.
For, do you know, Lucrezia, as God lives,
Said one day Agnolo, his very self,
185 To Rafael . . . I have known it all these years . . .
(When the young man was flaming out his thoughts
Upon a palace-wall for Rome to see,
Too lifted up in heart because of it)
"Friend, there's a certain sorry little scrub
190 Goes up and down our Florence, none cares how,
Who, were he set to plan and execute

---

6. The village southwest of Paris where Francis I built the royal palace.

7. Refers to Raphael, who worked in Rome for the last twelve years of his life.

As you are, pricked on by your popes and kings,
Would bring the sweat into that brow of yours!"
To Rafael's! And indeed the arm is wrong.
195 I hardly dare . . . yet, only you to see,
Give the chalk here—quick, thus the line should go!
Ay, but the soul! he's Rafael! rub it out!
Still, all I care for, if he spoke the truth,
(What he? why, who but Michel Agnolo?
200 Do you forget already words like those?)
If really there was such a chance, so lost,
Is, whether you're—not grateful—but more pleased.
Well, let me think so. And you smile indeed!
This hour has been an hour! Another smile?
205 If you would sit thus by me every night
I should work better, do you comprehend?
I mean that I should earn more, give you more.
See, it is settled dusk now; there's a star;
Morello's gone, the watch-lights show the wall,
210 The cue-owls[8] speak the name we call them by.
Come from the window, love—come in, at last,
Inside the melancholy little house
We built to be so gay with. God is just.
King Francis may forgive me: oft at nights
215 When I look up from painting, eyes tired out,
The walls become illumined, brick from brick
Distinct, instead of mortar, fierce bright gold,
That gold of his I did cement them with!
Let us but love each other. Must you go?
220 That Cousin here again? he waits outside?
Must see you—you, and not with me? Those loans?
More gaming debts to pay? you smiled for that?
Well, let smiles buy me! have you more to spend?
While hand and eye and something of a heart
225 Are left me, work's my ware, and what's it worth?
I'll pay my fancy. Only let me sit
The gray remainder of the evening out,
Idle, you call it, and muse perfectly
How I could paint, were I but back in France,
230 One picture, just one more—the Virgin's face,
Not yours this time! I want you at my side
To hear them—that is, Michel Agnolo—
Judge all I do and tell you of its worth.
Will you? Tomorrow, satisfy your friend.
235 I take the subjects for his corridor,
Finish the portrait out of hand—there, there,
And throw him in another thing or two
If he demurs; the whole should prove enough
To pay for this same Cousin's freak. Beside,
240 What's better and what's all I care about,
Get you the thirteen scudi[9] for the ruff!

---

8. A Mediterranean owl whose name derives from its cry, *ki-ou.*

9. A *scudo* ("shield," in Italian) was a silver coin bearing a shield.

Love, does that please you? Ah, but what does he,
The Cousin! what does he to please you more?

I am grown peaceful as old age tonight.
245 I regret little, I would change still less.
Since there my past life lies, why alter it?
The very wrong to Francis! it is true
I took his coin, was tempted and complied,
And built this house and sinned, and all is said.
250 My father and my mother died of want.
Well, had I riches of my own? you see
How one gets rich! Let each one bear his lot.
They were born poor, lived poor, and poor they died:
And I have labored somewhat in my time
255 And not been paid profusely. Some good son
Paint my two hundred pictures—let him try!
No doubt, there's something strikes a balance. Yes,
You loved me quite enough, it seems tonight.
This must suffice me here. What would one have?
260 In heaven, perhaps, new chances, one more chance—
Four great walls in the New Jerusalem,[1]
Meted on each side by the angel's reed,
For Leonard,[2] Rafael, Agnolo and me
To cover—the three first without a wife,
265 While I have mine! So—still they overcome
Because there's still Lucrezia—as I choose.

Again the Cousin's whistle! Go, my Love.

1855

Two in the Campagna[3]

1

I wonder do you feel today
    As I have felt since, hand in hand,
We sat down on the grass, to stray
    In spirit better through the land,
5   This morn of Rome and May?

2

For me, I touched a thought, I know,
    Has tantalized me many times,
(Like turns of thread the spiders throw
    Mocking across our path) for thymes
10   To catch at and let go.

3

Help me to hold it! First it left
    The yellowing fennel,[4] run to seed

1. Mentioned in Revelation 21.10–21.
2. I.e., Leonardo da Vinci (1452–1519).
3. The grassy, rolling countryside around Rome; it was malarial, and hence semideserted, until Mussolini reclaimed the Pontine marshes.
4. A yellow-flowered plant, whose aromatic seeds are used as a condiment.

There, branching from the brickwork's cleft,
   Some old tomb's ruin: yonder weed
15 Took up the floating weft,°   *spider-web*

4

Where one small orange cup amassed
   Five beetles—blind and green they grope
Among the honey-meal: and last,
   Everywhere on the grassy slope
20 I traced it. Hold it fast!

5

The champaign⁵ with its endless fleece
   Of feathery grasses everywhere!
Silence and passion, joy and peace,
   An everlasting wash of air—
25 Rome's ghost since her decease.

6

Such life here, through such lengths of hours,
   Such miracles performed in play,
Such primal naked forms of flowers,
   Such letting nature have her way
30 While heaven looks from its towers!

7

How say you? Let us, O my dove,
   Let us be unashamed of soul,
As earth lies bare to heaven above!
   How is it under our control
35 To love or not to love?

8

I would that you were all to me,
   You that are just so much, no more.
Nor yours nor mine, nor slave nor free!
   Where does the fault lie? What the core
40 O' the wound, since wound must be?

9

I would I could adopt your will,
   See with your eyes, and set my heart
Beating by yours, and drink my fill
   At your soul's springs—your part my part
45 In life, for good and ill.

10

No. I yearn upward, touch you close,
   Then stand away. I kiss your cheek,
Catch your soul's warmth—I pluck the rose
   And love it more than tongue can speak—
50 Then the good minute goes.

11

Already how am I so far
   Out of that minute? Must I go

5. I.e., grassland—here, the Campagna itself.

Still like the thistle-ball, no bar,
   Onward, whenever light winds blow,
55 Fixed by no friendly star?
12

Just when I seemed about to learn!
   Where is the thread now? Off again!
The old trick! Only I discern—
   Infinite passion, and the pain
60 Of finite hearts that yearn.

1855

JONES VERY

1813–1880

The Dead[1]

I see them crowd on crowd they walk the earth
Dry, leafless trees no Autumn wind laid bare;
And in their nakedness find cause for mirth,
And all unclad would winter's rudeness° dare;   *harshness*
5 No sap doth through their clattering branches flow,
Whence springing leaves and blossoms bright appear;
Their hearts the living God have ceased to know,
Who gives the spring time to th'expectant year;
They mimic life, as if from him to steal
10 His glow of health to paint the livid° cheek;   *pale*
They borrow words for thoughts they cannot feel,
That with a seeming heart their tongue may speak;
And in their show of life more dead they live
Than those that to the earth with many tears they give.

1838
1839

The Lost

The fairest day that ever yet has shone,
  Will be when thou the day within shalt see;
The fairest rose that ever yet has blown,
  When thou the flower thou lookest on shalt be.
5 But thou art far away among Time's toys;
  Thyself the day thou lookest for in them,
Thyself the flower that now thine eye enjoys,
  But wilted now thou hang'st upon thy stem.
The bird thou hearest on the budding tree,
10 Thou hast made sing with thy forgotten voice;
But when it swells again to melody,
  The song is thine in which thou wilt rejoice;

---

1. In September of 1838 Very, a tutor of Greek at Harvard, had a mystical experience; he told his students that the Holy Spirit was speaking through him, and that the end of the world was at hand. His employment at Harvard was terminated, and he was sent briefly to an asylum, though many considered him sane. Both of these poems date from his visionary period.

And thou new risen 'midst these wonders live,
That now to them dost all thy substance give.

1838–40   1883

EDWARD LEAR
1812–1888

There Was an Old Man with a Beard

There was an Old Man with a beard,
Who said, "It is just as I feared! —
Two Owls and a Hen, four Larks and a Wren,
Have all built their nests in my beard!"

1846

There Was an Old Man in a Tree

There was an Old Man in a tree,
Who was horribly bored by a Bee;
When they said, "Does it buzz?" he replied, "Yes, it does!"
"It's a regular brute of a Bee!"

1846

There Was an Old Man Who Supposed

There was an Old Man who supposed,
That the street door was partially closed;
But some very large rats, ate his coats and his hats,
While that futile old gentleman dozed.

1846

The Owl and the Pussy-Cat

1

The Owl and the Pussy-cat went to sea
    In a beautiful pea-green boat,
They took some honey, and plenty of money,
    Wrapped up in a five-pound note.
5   The Owl looked up to the stars above,
    And sang to a small guitar,
"O lovely Pussy! O Pussy, my love,
    What a beautiful Pussy you are,
            You are,
10   You are!
    What a beautiful Pussy you are!"

2

Pussy said to the Owl, "You elegant fowl!
    How charmingly sweet you sing!

O let us be married! too long we have tarried:
15   But what shall we do for a ring?"
They sailed away, for a year and a day,
    To the land where the Bong-tree grows
And there in a wood a Piggy-wig stood
    With a ring at the end of his nose,
20   His nose,
        His nose,
    With a ring at the end of his nose.

3

"Dear Pig, are you willing to sell for one shilling
    Your ring?" Said the Piggy, "I will."
25 So they took it away, and were married next day
    By the Turkey who lives on the hill.
They dined on mince, and slices of quince,
    Which they ate with a runcible spoon;[1]
And hand in hand, on the edge of the sand,
30   They danced by the light of the moon,
        The moon,
        The moon,
    They danced by the light of the moon.

1871

How Pleasant to Know Mr. Lear

How pleasant to know Mr. Lear!
    Who has written such volumes of stuff!
Some think him ill-tempered and queer,
    But a few think him pleasant enough.

5 His mind is concrete and fastidious,
    His nose is remarkably big;
His visage is more or less hideous,
    His beard it resembles a wig.

He has ears, and two eyes, and ten fingers,
10   Leastways if you reckon two thumbs;
Long ago he was one of the singers,
    But now he is one of the dumbs.

He sits in a beautiful parlor,
    With hundreds of books on the wall;
15 He drinks a great deal of Marsala,[2]
    But never gets tipsy at all.

He has many friends, laymen and clerical;
    Old Foss is the name of his cat;
His body is perfectly spherical,
20   He weareth a runcible hat.

1. Fork with three broad, curved prongs and sharpened edge. Lear coined the word "runcible" and used it often in his nonsense verse.
2. A dark, sweet Spanish wine.

When he walks in a waterproof° white,   *raincoat*
 The children run after him so!
Calling out, "He's come out in his night-
 Gown, that crazy old Englishman, oh!"

25 He weeps by the side of the ocean,
 He weeps on the top of the hill;
He purchases pancakes and lotion,
 And chocolate shrimps from the mill.

He reads but he cannot speak Spanish,
30 He cannot abide ginger-beer:
Ere the days of his pilgrimage vanish,
 How pleasant to know Mr. Lear!

              1871

HENRY DAVID THOREAU
1817–1862

I Am a Parcel of Vain Strivings Tied

I am a parcel of vain strivings tied
 By a chance bond together,
 Dangling this way and that, their links
  Were made so loose and wide,
5   Methinks,
   For milder weather.

A bunch of violets without their roots,
 And sorrel intermixed,
 Encircled by a wisp of straw
10 Once coiled about their shoots,
    The law
   By which I'm fixed.

A nosegay which Time clutched from out
 Those fair Elysian fields,[1]
15 With weeds and broken stems, in haste,
  Doth make the rabble rout
    That waste
   The day he yields.

And here I bloom for a short hour unseen,
20 Drinking my juices up,
 With no root in the land
  To keep my branches green,
    But stand
   In a bare cup.

              1841

---

1. In Greek and Roman mythology, the home of the blessed in the afterlife.

Smoke

Light-winged Smoke, Icarian bird,[2]
Melting thy pinions in thy upward flight;
Lark without song, and messenger of dawn,
Circling above the hamlets as thy nest;
5   Or else, departing dream, and shadowy form
Of midnight vision, gathering up thy skirts;
By night star-veiling, and by day
Darkening the light and blotting out the sun;
Go thou my incense upward from this hearth,
10 And ask the gods to pardon this clear flame.

1843, 1854

EMILY BRONTË
1818–1848

[Long Neglect Has Worn Away]

Long neglect has worn away
Half the sweet enchanting smile;
Time has turned the bloom to gray;
Mold and damp the face defile.

5   But that lock of silky hair,
Still beneath the picture twined,
Tells what once those features were,
Paints their image on the mind.

Fair the hand that traced that line,
10 "Dearest, ever deem me true";
Swiftly flew the fingers fine
When the pen that motto drew.

1837   1923

Hope

Hope was but a timid friend—
She sat without° my grated den   *outside*
Watching how my fate would tend
Even as selfish-hearted men.

5   She was cruel in her fear.
Through the bars, one dreary day,
I looked out to see her there
And she turned her face away!

2. Icarus and his father, Daedalus, escaped from Crete by flying with wings of wax and feathers. When Icarus flew too near the sun, his wings melted.

Like a false guard false watch keeping
10 Still in strife she whispered peace;
    She would sing while I was weeping,
    If I listened, she would cease.

    False she was, and unrelenting.
    When my last joys strewed the ground
15 Even Sorrow saw repenting
    Those sad relics scattered round;

    Hope—whose whisper would have given
    Balm to all that frenzied pain—
    Stretched her wings and soared to heaven;
20 Went—and ne'er returned again!

1843   1846

Remembrance[1]

Cold in the earth—and the deep snow piled above thee,
Far, far removed, cold in the dreary grave!
Have I forgot, my only Love, to love thee,
Severed at last by Time's all-severing wave?

5   Now, when alone, do my thoughts no longer hover
    Over the mountains, on that northern shore,
    Resting their wings where heath and fern leaves cover
    Thy noble heart forever, ever more?

    Cold in the earth—and fifteen wild Decembers,
10 From those brown hills, have melted into spring;
    Faithful, indeed, is the spirit that remembers
    After such years of change and suffering!

    Sweet Love of youth, forgive, if I forget thee,
    While the world's tide is bearing me along;
15 Other desires and other hopes beset me,
    Hopes which obscure, but cannot do thee wrong!

    No later light has lightened up my heaven,
    No second morn has ever shone for me;
    All my life's bliss from thy dear life was given,
20 All my life's bliss is in the grave with thee.

    But, when the days of golden dreams had perished,
    And even Despair was powerless to destroy,
    Then did I learn how existence could be cherished,
    Strengthened, and fed without the aid of joy.

25 Then did I check the tears of useless passion—
    Weaned my young soul from yearning after thine;

1. One of the Gondal poems. As children, Emily
and Anne Brontë had written poems and stories
about the inhabitants of Gondal, an imaginary
island in the North Pacific, and Emily, at least,
continued to write Gondal poems throughout her
life.

Sternly denied its burning wish to hasten
Down to that tomb already more than mine.

And, even yet, I dare not let it languish,
30   Dare not indulge in memory's rapturous pain;
Once drinking deep of that divinest anguish,
How could I seek the empty world again?

1845   1846

The Prisoner

"Still let my tyrants know, I am not doomed to wear
Year after year in gloom, and desolate despair;
A messenger of Hope comes every night to me,
And offers for short life, eternal liberty.

5   "He comes with western winds, with evening's wandering airs,
With that clear dusk of heaven that brings the thickest stars,
Winds take a pensive tone, and stars a tender fire,
And visions rise, and change, that kill me with desire.

"Desire for nothing known in my maturer years,
10   When Joy grew mad with awe, at counting future tears.
When, if my spirit's sky was full of flashes warm,
I knew not whence they came, from sun or thunderstorm.

"But, first, a hush of peace—a soundless calm descends;
The struggle of distress, and fierce impatience ends;
15   Mute music soothes my breast—unuttered harmony,
That I could never dream, till Earth was lost to me.

"Then dawns the Invisible; the Unseen its truth reveals;
My outward sense is gone, my inward essence feels:
Its wings are almost free—its home, its harbor found,
20   Measuring the gulf, it stoops and dares the final bound.

"O! dreadful is the check—intense the agony—
When the ear begins to hear, and the eye begins to see;
When the pulse begins to throb, the brain to think again;
The soul to feel the flesh, and the flesh to feel the chain.

25   "Yet I would lose no sting, would wish no torture less;
The more that anguish racks, the earlier it will bless;
And robed in fires of hell, or bright with heavenly shine,
If it but herald death, the vision is divine!"

1845   1846

No Coward Soul Is Mine

No coward soul is mine,
No trembler in the world's storm-troubled sphere!

I see Heaven's glories shine,
And Faith shines equal, arming me from Fear.

5   O God within my breast,
Almighty ever-present Deity!
Life, that in me hast rest
As I, undying Life, have power in thee!

Vain are the thousand creeds
10 That move men's hearts, unutterably vain;
Worthless as withered weeds,
Or idlest froth, amid the boundless main

To waken doubt in one
Holding so fast by thy infinity,
15 So surely anchored on
The steadfast rock of Immortality.

With wide-embracing love
Thy spirit animates eternal years,
Pervades and broods above,
20 Changes, sustains, dissolves, creates and rears.

Though earth and moon were gone,
And suns and universes ceased to be,
And thou were left alone,
Every Existence would exist in thee.

25 There is not room for Death,
Nor atom that his might could render void
Since thou art Being and Breath,
And what thou art may never be destroyed.

1850

ARTHUR HUGH CLOUGH
1819–1861

[Say not the struggle nought availeth]

Say not the struggle nought availeth,
　The labor and the wounds are vain,
The enemy faints not, nor faileth,
　And as things have been, things remain.

5   If hopes were dupes, fears may be liars;
　It may be, in yon smoke concealed,
Your comrades chase e'en now the fliers,
　And, but for you, possess the field.

For while the tired waves, vainly breaking,
10 　Seem here no painful inch to gain,

Far back through creeks and inlets making
  Came, silent, flooding in, the main,°   *sea*

And not by eastern windows only,
  When daylight comes, comes in the light,
15   In front the sun climbs slow, how slowly,
  But westward, look, the land is bright.

1849   1855

From Amours de Voyage

Canto I

Over the great windy waters, and over the clear crested summits,
  Unto the sun and the sky, and unto the perfecter earth,
Come, let us go,—to a land wherein gods of the old time wandered,
  Where every breath even now changes to ether[1] divine.
5 *Come, let us go; though withal a voice whisper, "The world that we*
    live in,
  Whithersoever we turn, still is the same narrow crib;
'Tis but to prove limitation, and measure a cord, that we travel;
  Let who would 'scape and be free go to his chamber and think;
'Tis but to change idle fancies for memories wilfully falser;
10 *'Tis but to go and have been."—Come, little bark!°*   *small boat*
    let us go.

I. CLAUDE TO EUSTACE

Dear Eustatio, I write that you may write me an answer,
Or at the least to put us again en rapport[2] with each other.
Rome disappoints me much,—St. Peter's, perhaps, in especial;
Only the Arch of Titus and view from the Lateran please me:
15 This, however, perhaps, is the weather, which truly is horrid.
Greece must be better, surely; and yet I am feeling so spiteful,
That I could travel to Athens, to Delphi, and Troy, and Mount Sinai,
Though but to see with my eyes that these are vanity also.
  Rome disappoints me much; I hardly as yet understand, but
20 *Rubbishy* seems the word that most exactly would suit it.
All the foolish destructions, and all the sillier savings,
All the incongruous things of past incompatible ages,
Seem to be treasured up here to make fools of present and future.
Would to Heaven the old Goths[3] had made a cleaner sweep of it!
25 Would to Heaven some new ones would come and destroy these
    churches!
However, one can live in Rome as also in London.
Rome is better than London, because it is other than London.
It is a blessing, no doubt, to be rid, at least for a time, of
All one's friends and relations,—yourself (forgive me!) included,—
30 All the *assujettissement*[4] of having been what one has been,
What one thinks one is, or thinks that others suppose one;
Yet, in despite of all, we turn like fools to the English.

---

1. The clear upper air, or a heavenly material not matter.
2. "In sympathy" (French).
3. One of the barbarian tribes that sacked ancient Rome.
4. "Constraint" (French).

Vernon has been my fate; who is here the same that you knew him,—
Making the tour, it seems, with friends of the name of Trevellyn.

II. CLAUDE TO EUSTACE

35   Rome disappoints me still; but I shrink and adapt myself to it.
Somehow a tyrannous sense of a superincumbent° oppression   *overlying*
Still, wherever I go, accompanies ever, and makes me
Feel like a tree (shall I say?) buried under a ruin of brickwork.
Rome, believe me, my friend, is like its own Monte Testaceo,
40   Merely a marvellous mass of broken and castaway wine-pots.
Ye gods! what do I want with this rubbish of ages departed,
Things that Nature abhors, the experiments that she has failed in?
What do I find in the Forum? An archway and two or three pillars.
Well, but St. Peter's? Alas, Bernini has filled it with sculpture!
45   No one can cavil, I grant, at the size of the great Coliseum.
Doubtless the notion of grand and capacious and massive amusement,
This the old Romans had; but tell me, is this an idea?
Yet of solidity much, but of splendor little is extant:
"Brickwork I found thee, and marble I left thee!" their Emperor
       vaunted;
50   "Marble I thought thee, and brickwork I find thee!" the Tourist may
       answer.

III. GEORGINA TREVELLYN TO LOUISA

At last, dearest Louisa, I take up my pen to address you.
Here we are, you see, with the seven-and-seventy boxes,
Courier, Papa and Mamma, the children, and Mary and Susan:
Here we all are at Rome, and delighted of course with St. Peter's,
55   And very pleasantly lodged in the famous Piazza di Spagna.
Rome is a wonderful place, but Mary shall tell you about it;
Not very gay, however; the English are mostly at Naples;
There are the A.s, we hear, and most of the W. party.
George, however, is come; did I tell you about his mustachios?
60   Dear, I must really stop, for the carriage, they tell me, is waiting.
Mary will finish; and Susan is writing, they say, to Sophia.
Adieu, dearest Louise,—evermore your faithful Georgina.
Who can a Mr. Claude be whom George has taken to be with?
Very stupid, I think, but George says so *very* clever.

                                                        1858

The Latest Decalogue⁵

Thou shalt have one God only; who
Would be at the expense of two?
No graven images may be
Worshipped, except the currency:
5   Swear not at all; for for thy curse
Thine enemy is none the worse:
At church on Sunday to attend
Will serve to keep the world thy friend:

---

5. "Decalogue": The Ten Commandments.

Honor thy parents; that is, all
10   From whom advancement may befall:
Thou shalt not kill; but needst not strive
Officiously to keep alive:
Do not adultery commit;
Advantage rarely comes of it:
15   Thou shalt not steal; an empty feat,
When it's so lucrative to cheat:
Bear not false witness; let the lie
Have time on its own wings to fly:
Thou shalt not covet; but tradition
20   Approves all forms of competition.

The sum of all is, thou shalt love,
If any body, God above:
At any rate shall never labor
More than thyself to love thy neighbor.

1862

From Dipsychus

Scene VI

"There is no God," the wicked saith,
    "And truly it's a blessing,
For what he might have done with us
    It's better only guessing."

5   "There is no God," a youngster thinks,
    "Or really, if there may be,
He surely didn't mean a man
    Always to be a baby."

"There is no God, or if there is,"
10   The tradesman thinks, " 'twere funny
If he should take it ill in me
    To make a little money."

"Whether there be," the rich man says,
    "It matters very little,
15   For I and mine, thank somebody,
    Are not in want of victual."°   food

Some others, also, to themselves
    Who scarce so much as doubt it,
Think there is none, when they are well,
20   And do not think about it.

But country folks who live beneath
    The shadow of the steeple;
The parson and the parson's wife,
    And mostly married people;

25   Youths green and happy in first love,
            So thankful for illusion;
        And men caught out in what the world
            Calls guilt, in first confusion;

        And almost every one when age,
30   Disease, or sorrows strike him,
        Inclines to think there is a God,
            Or something very like Him.

1865

JULIA WARD HOWE

1819–1910

Battle-Hymn of the Republic[1]

Mine eyes have seen the glory of the coming of the Lord:
He is trampling out the vintage where the grapes of wrath are stored;
He hath loosed the fateful lightning of his terrible swift sword:
        His truth is marching on.

5   I have seen Him in the watch-fires of a hundred circling camps;
    They have builded Him an altar in the evening dews and damps;
    I can read His righteous sentence by the dim and flaring lamps.
        His day is marching on.

    I have read a fiery gospel, writ in burnished rows of steel:
10 "As ye deal with my contemners,° so with you my grace shall   condemners
        deal;
    Let the Hero, born of woman, crush the serpent with his heel,
        Since God is marching on."

    He has sounded forth the trumpet that shall never call retreat;
    He is sifting out the hearts of men before his judgment-seat:
15 Oh! be swift, my soul, to answer Him! be jubilant, my feet!
        Our God is marching on.

    In the beauty of the lilies Christ was born across the sea,
    With a glory in his bosom that transfigures you and me:
    As he died to make men holy, let us die to make men free,
20   While God is marching on.
1861   1866

1. When Howe saw Union troops camped along the roadside in Washington, D.C., she joined friends in singing the popular Civil War song that begins "John Brown's body lies a-mouldering in the grave." That night, she responded to someone's suggestion that she write new verses to the same tune. Howe here compares the reckoning that will come at the end of the war with the Day of Jehovah; see especially Isaiah 63.

HERMAN MELVILLE

1819–1891

The Portent

Hanging from the beam,
   Slowly swaying (such the law),
Gaunt the shadow on your green,
   Shenandoah!¹
5 The cut is on the crown
   (Lo, John Brown),²
And the stabs shall heal no more.

Hidden in the cap
   Is the anguish none can draw;
10 So your future veils its face,
   Shenandoah!
But the streaming beard is shown
   (Weird John Brown),
The meteor of the war.

1859   1866

The March into Virginia

Ending in the First Manassas³ (July 1861)

Did all the lets° and bars appear   *obstructions*
   To every just or larger end,
Whence should come the trust and cheer?
   Youth must its ignorant impulse lend—
5 Age finds place in the rear.
   All wars are boyish, and are fought by boys,
   The champions and enthusiasts of the state:
     Turbid ardours and vain joys
     Not barrenly abate—
10   Stimulants to the power mature,
     Preparatives of fate.

Who here forecasteth the event?
What heart but spurns at precedent
And warnings of the wise,
15 Contemned foreclosures of surprise?
The banners play, the bugles call,
The air is blue and prodigal.
     No berrying party, pleasure-wooed,
     No picnic party in the May,
20   Ever went less loth than they
     Into that leafy neighborhood.

1. Valley in northern Virginia; the scene of famous Civil War battles between 1862 and 1864. 2. Abolitionist who was hanged in 1859 for leading a raid on the United States armory at Harpers Ferry, West Virginia, near the Shenandoah Valley. 3. The battle on July 21, 1861, at Bull Run, where the Union forces were routed; it was the first major engagement of the Civil War.

In Bacchic glee they file toward Fate,
Moloch's[4] uninitiate;
Expectancy, and glad surmise
25 Of battle's unknown mysteries.

All they feel is this: 'tis glory,
A rapture sharp, though transitory,
Yet lasting in belaureled story.
So they gaily go to fight,
30 Chatting left and laughing right.

But some who this blithe mood present,
 As on in lightsome files they fare,
Shall die experienced ere three days are spent—
 Perish, enlightened by the volleyed glare;
35 Or shame survive, and, like to adamant,[5]
 The throe of Second Manassas[6] share.

1861   1866

Shiloh[7]

A Requiem (April 1862)

Skimming lightly, wheeling still,
 The swallows fly low
Over the field in clouded days,
 The forest-field of Shiloh—
5 Over the field where April rain
Solaced the parched one stretched in pain
Through the pause of night
That followed the Sunday fight
 Around the church of Shiloh—
10 The church so lone, the log-built one,
That echoed to many a parting groan
  And natural prayer
 Of dying foemen mingled there—
Foemen at morn, but friends at eve—
15 Fame or country least their care:
(What like a bullet can undeceive!)
 But now they lie low,
While over them the swallows skim,
 And all is hushed at Shiloh.

                       1866

4. That of the Semitic god to whom children were sacrificed in Old Testament days (for example, see Leviticus 18.21, 20.2). "Bacchic": like reveling followers of Bacchus, Roman god of wine.
5. Hard, unbreakable substance.
6. The second defeat of the Union forces at Man-

assas was on August 30, 1862.
7. The battle at Shiloh Church in Tennessee on April 6 and 7, 1862, was one of the bloodiest of the Civil War; close to twenty-four thousand men died.

The Maldive Shark

About the Shark, phlegmatical one,
Pale sot° of the Maldive sea,[8]   *habitual drunkard*
The sleek little pilot-fish, azure and slim,
How alert in attendance be.
5   From his saw-pit of mouth, from his charnel of maw,
They have nothing of harm to dread,
But liquidly glide on his ghastly flank
Or before his Gorgonian[9] head;
Or lurk in the port of serrated teeth
10   In white triple tiers of glittering gates,
And there find a haven when peril's abroad,
An asylum in jaws of the Fates!

They are friends; and friendly they guide him to prey,
Yet never partake of the treat—
15   Eyes and brains to the dotard lethargic and dull,
Pale ravener of horrible meat.

                                                        1888

The Berg

A Dream

I saw a Ship of martial build
(Her standards set, her brave apparel on)
Directed as by madness mere
Against a stolid iceberg steer,
5   Nor budge it, though the infatuate° Ship went down.   *foolish, stupefied*
The impact made huge ice-cubes fall
Sullen, in tons that crashed the deck;
But that one avalanche was all—
No other movement save the foundering wreck.

10   Along the spurs of ridges pale,
Not any slenderest shaft and frail,
A prism over glass-green gorges lone,
Toppled; nor lace of traceries fine,
Nor pendant drops in grot or mine
15   Were jarred, when the stunned Ship went down.

Nor sole the gulls in cloud that wheeled
Circling one snow-flanked peak afar,
But nearer fowl the floes that skimmed
And crystal beaches, felt no jar.
20   No thrill transmitted stirred the lock
Of jack-straw needle-ice at base;
Towers undermined by waves—the block
Atilt impending—kept their place.

8. I.e., the area around the Maldives, a group of islands in the Indian Ocean.
9. In classical mythology, the Gorgons were three sisters (Medusa was one) with terrifying faces and serpent hair; whoever looked at them turned to stone.

Seals, dozing sleek on sliddery ledges
25 Slipt never, when by loftier edges,
Through very inertia overthrown,
The impetuous ship in bafflement went down.

Hard Berg (methought), so cold, so vast,
With mortal damps self-overcast;
30 Exhaling still thy dankish breath—
Adrift dissolving, bound for death;
Though lumpish thou, a lumbering one—
A lumbering lubbard loitering slow,
Impingers rue thee and go down,
35 Sounding thy precipice below,
Nor stir the slimy slug that sprawls
Along thy dead indifference of walls.[1]

1888

Monody[2]

To have known him, to have loved him
After loneness long;
And then to be estranged in life,
And neither in the wrong;
5 And now for death to set his seal—
Ease me, a little ease, my song!

By wintry hills his hermit-mound
The sheeted snow-drifts drape,
And houseless there the snow-bird flits
10 Beneath the fir-trees' crape:
Glazed now with ice the cloistral vine
That hid the shyest grape.

1891

The Bench of Boors

In bed I muse on Tenier's[3] boors,
Embrowned and beery losels° all: *ne'er-do-wells*
A wakeful brain
Elaborates pain:
5 Within low doors the slugs of boors
Laze and yawn and doze again.

In dreams they doze, the drowsy boors,
Their hazy hovel warm and small:
Thought's ampler bound
10 But chill is found:

1. Manuscript version of Melville's final line. In his first published edition of the poem, the final line reads "Along thy dense stolidity of walls."
2. Lament; originally, a Greek ode sung by a single voice, as in a tragedy. Some critics have surmised that Melville may have been writing about a cooled friendship with the American writer Nathaniel Hawthorne (1804–1864).
3. That of the Flemish painter David Teniers the Younger (1610–1690).

Within low doors the basking boors
Snugly hug the ember-mound.

Sleepless, I see the slumberous boors
Their blurred eyes blink, their eyelids fall:
15   Thought's eager sight
       Aches—overbright!
Within low doors the boozy boors
Cat-naps take in pipe-bowl light.

1891

Fragments of a Lost Gnostic[4] Poem of the Twelfth Century

   .   .   .   .   .

Found a family, build a state,
The pledged event is still the same:
Matter in end will never abate
His ancient brutal claim.

   .   .   .   .

5 Indolence is heaven's ally here,
And energy the child of hell:
The good man pouring from his pitcher clear
But brims the poisoned well.

1891

Greek Architecture

Not magnitude, not lavishness,
But form—the site;
Not innovating wilfulness,
But reverence for the archetype.

1891

SPIRITUALS

Go Down, Moses[1]

Go down, Moses,
Way down in Egyptland
Tell old Pharaoh
To let my people go.

5 When Israel was in Egyptland
Let my people go

---

4. Gnosticism, a philosophical and religious movement of the early Christian era, was condemned as heretical by orthodox Christians.
1. Hebrew lawgiver; according to the Old Testament, he led his people out of bondage in Egypt to the edge of Canaan. Cf. Exodus 5: "Afterward Moses . . . went to Pharaoh and said, 'Thus says the Lord, the God of Israel, "Let my people go, that they may hold a feast to me in the wilderness." ' "

Oppressed so hard they could not stand
Let my people go.

Go down, Moses,
10   Way down in Egyptland
Tell old Pharaoh
"Let my people go."

"Thus saith the Lord," bold Moses said,
"Let my people go;
15   If not I'll smite your first-born dead[2]
Let my people go.

"No more shall they in bondage toil,
Let my people go;
Let them come out with Egypt's spoil,
20   Let my people go."

The Lord told Moses what to do
Let my people go;
To lead the children of Israel through,
Let my people go.

25   Go down, Moses,
Way down in Egyptland,
Tell old Pharaoh,
"Let my people go!"

Steal Away to Jesus

Steal away, steal away, steal away to Jesus,
Steal away, steal away home,
I ain't got long to stay here.

My Lord, He calls me,
5   He calls me by the thunder,
The trumpet sounds within-a my soul,
I ain't got long to stay here.

Steal away, steal away, steal away to Jesus,
Steal away, steal away home,
10   I ain't got long to stay here.

Green trees a-bending,
Po' sinner stands a-trembling,
The trumpet sounds within-a my soul,
I ain't got long to stay here.

15   Steal away, steal away, steal away to Jesus,
Steal away, steal away home,
I ain't got long to stay here.

---

2. After Pharaoh refused to free the Israelites, God sent a series of miracles, plagues, and punishments. Cf. Exodus 11: "And Moses said, 'Thus says the Lord: About midnight I will go forth in the midst of Egypt; and all the first-born in the land of Egypt shall die.'"

Ezekiel Saw the Wheel[3]

Ezek'el saw the wheel
'Way up in the middle o' the air,
Ezek'el saw the wheel
'Way up in the middle o' the air.

5   The big wheel moved by Faith,
The little wheel moved by the Grace of God,
A wheel in a wheel,
'Way up in the middle o' the air.

Jes' let me tell you what a hypocrite'll do,
10   'Way up in the middle o' the air,
He'll talk about me an' he'll talk about you!
'Way up in the middle o' the air.

Ezek'el saw the wheel
'Way up in the middle o' the air,
15   Ezek'el saw the wheel
'Way up in the middle o' the air.

The big wheel moved by Faith,
The little wheel moved by the Grace of God,
A wheel in a wheel,
20   'Way up in the middle o' the air.

Watch out my sister how you walk on the cross,
'Way up in the middle o' the air,
Your foot might slip and your soul get lost!
'Way up in the middle o' the air.

25   Ezek'el saw the wheel
'Way up in the middle o' the air,
Ezek'el saw the wheel
'Way up in the middle o' the air.

The big wheel moved by Faith,
30   The little wheel moved by the Grace of God,
A wheel in a wheel,
'Way up in the middle o' the air.

You say the Lord has set you free,
'Way up in the middle o' the air,
35   Why don't you let your neighbors be!
'Way up in the middle o' the air.

3. Old Testament prophecy; cf. Ezekiel 15: "Now as I looked at the living creatures, I saw a wheel upon the earth beside the living creatures, one for each of the four of them . . . their construction being as it were a wheel within a wheel. . . . And when the living creatures went, the wheels went beside them; and when the living creatures rose from the earth, the wheels rose. Wherever the spirit would go, they went, and the wheels rose along with them; for the spirit of the living creatures was in the wheels."

Ezek'el saw the wheel
'Way up in the middle o' the air,
Ezek'el saw the wheel
40 'Way up in the middle o' the air.

The big wheel moved by Faith,
The little wheel moved by the Grace of God,
A wheel in a wheel,
'Way up in the middle o' the air.

My Lord, What a Mornin'

My Lord, what a mornin',
My Lord, what a mornin',
My Lord, what a mornin',
When de stars begin to fall.

5   My Lord, what a mornin',
My Lord, what a mornin',
My Lord, what a mornin',
When de stars begin to fall.

You'll hear de trumpet sound,
10 To wake de nations underground,
Lookin' to my God's right hand,
When de stars begin to fall.

My Lord, what a mornin',
My Lord, what a mornin',
15 My Lord, what a mornin',
When de stars begin to fall.

You'll hear de sinner moan,
To wake de nations underground,
Lookin' to my God's right hand,
20 When de stars begin to fall.

My Lord, what a mornin',
My Lord, what a mornin',
My Lord, what a mornin',
When de stars begin to fall.

25 You'll hear de Christians shout,
To wake de nations underground,
Lookin' to my God's right hand,
When de stars begin to fall.

My Lord, what a mornin',
30 My Lord, what a mornin',
My Lord, what a mornin',
When de stars begin to fall.

WALT WHITMAN

1819–1892

From Song of Myself[1]

1

I celebrate myself, and sing myself,
And what I assume you shall assume,
For every atom belonging to me as good belongs to you.

I loafe and invite my soul,
5 I lean and loafe at my ease observing a spear of summer grass.

My tongue, every atom of my blood, form'd from this soil, this air,
Born here of parents born here from parents the same, and their
        parents the same,
I, now thirty-seven years old in perfect health begin,
Hoping to cease not till death.

10 Creeds and schools in abeyance,
Retiring back a while sufficed at what they are, but never forgotten,
I harbor for good or bad, I permit to speak at every hazard,
Nature without check with original energy.

6

A child said *What is the grass?* fetching it to me with full hands;
100 How could I answer the child? I do not know what it is any more than
        he.

I guess it must be the flag of my disposition, out of hopeful green stuff
        woven.

Or I guess it is the handkerchief of the Lord,
A scented gift and remembrancer designedly dropt,
Bearing the owner's name someway in the corners, that we may see and
        remark, and say *Whose?*

105 Or I guess the grass is itself a child, the produced babe of the vegetation.

Or I guess it is a uniform hieroglyphic,
And it means, Sprouting alike in broad zones and narrow zones,
Growing among black folks as among white,
Kanuck, Tuckahoe, Congressman, Cuff,[2] I give them the same, I
        receive them the same.

---

1. The title Whitman gave in 1881 to the poem
that constituted more than half of *Leaves of Grass,*
originally published in 1855. The book, radical in
both form and content (particularly in its explicit
treatment of sexual themes), was years in the mak-
ing and underwent many, though often slight,
revisions.
   "Song of Myself" was both untitled and unsec-

tioned in its first appearance. This version is based
on the Blodgett and Bradley Norton Critical Edi-
tion of *Leaves of Grass* (1973), which was itself
based on Whitman's 1891–92 text.
2. Slang for an African-American; "Kanuck": a
French-Canadian; "Tuckahoe": an inhabitant of
the lowlands of Virginia.

110 And now it seems to me the beautiful uncut hair of graves.

Tenderly will I use you curling grass,
It may be you transpire from the breasts of young men,
It may be if I had known them I would have loved them,
It may be you are from old people, or from offspring taken soon out of
    their mothers' laps,
115 And here you are the mothers' laps.

This grass is very dark to be from the white heads of old mothers,
Darker than the colorless beards of old men,
Dark to come from under the faint red roofs of mouths.

O I perceive after all so many uttering tongues,
120 And I perceive they do not come from the roofs of mouths for nothing.

I wish I could translate the hints about the dead young men and
    women,
And the hints about old men and mothers, and the offspring taken soon
    out of their laps.

What do you think has become of the young and old men?
And what do you think has become of the women and children?

125 They are alive and well somewhere,
The smallest sprout shows there is really no death,
And if ever there was it led forward life, and does not wait at the end to
    arrest it,
And ceas'd the moment life appear'd.

All goes onward and outward, nothing collapses,
130 And to die is different from what any one supposed, and luckier.

11

Twenty-eight young men bathe by the shore,
200 Twenty-eight young men and all so friendly;
Twenty-eight years of womanly life and all so lonesome.

She owns the fine house by the rise of the bank,
She hides handsome and richly drest aft the blinds of the window.

Which of the young men does she like the best?
205 Ah the homeliest of them is beautiful to her.

Where are you off to, lady? for I see you,
You splash in the water there, yet stay stock still in your room.

Dancing and laughing along the beach came the twenty-ninth bather,
The rest did not see her, but she saw them and loved them.

210 The beards of the young men glisten'd with wet, it ran from their long
    hair,
Little streams, pass'd all over their bodies.

An unseen hand also pass'd over their bodies,
It descended tremblingly from their temples and ribs.

The young men float on their backs, their white bellies bulge to the
    sun, they do not ask who seizes fast to them,
215 They do not know who puffs and declines with pendant and bending
    arch,
They do not think whom they souse with spray.

24

Walt Whitman, a kosmos, of Manhattan the son,
Turbulent, fleshy, sensual, eating, drinking and breeding,
No sentimentalist, no stander above men and women or apart from
    them,
500 No more modest than immodest.

Unscrew the locks from the doors!
Unscrew the doors themselves from their jambs!

Whoever degrades another degrades me,
And whatever is done or said returns at last to me.

505 Through me the afflatus° surging and surging, through   *inspiration*
    me the current and index.

I speak the pass-word primeval, I give the sign of democracy,
By God! I will accept nothing which all cannot have their counterpart
    of on the same terms.

Through me many long dumb voices,
Voices of the interminable generations of prisoners and slaves,
510 Voices of the diseas'd and despairing and of thieves and dwarfs,
Voices of cycles of preparation and accretion,
And of the threads that connect the stars, and of wombs and of the
    father-stuff,
And of the rights of them the others are down upon,
Of the deform'd, trivial, flat, foolish, despised,
515 Fog in the air, beetles rolling balls of dung.

Through me forbidden voices,
Voices of sexes and lusts, voices veil'd and I remove the veil,
Voices indecent by me clarified and transfigur'd.

I do not press my fingers across my mouth,
520 I keep as delicate around the bowels as around the head and heart,
Copulation is no more rank to me than death is.

I believe in the flesh and the appetites,
Seeing, hearing, feeling, are miracles, and each part and tag of me is a
    miracle.

Divine am I inside and out, and I make holy whatever I touch or am
    touch'd from,

525 The scent of these arm-pits aroma finer than prayer,
This head more than churches, bibles, and all the creeds.

If I worship one thing more than another it shall be the spread of my
own body, or any part of it,
Translucent mould of me it shall be you!
Shaded ledges and rests it shall be you!
530 Firm masculine colter[3] it shall be you!
Whatever goes to the tilth[4] of me it shall be you!
You my rich blood! your milky stream pale strippings of my life!
Breast that presses against other breasts it shall be you!
My brain it shall be your occult convolutions!
535 Root of wash'd sweet-flag! timorous pond-snipe! nest of guarded
duplicate eggs! it shall be you!
Mix'd tussled hay of head, beard, brawn, it shall be you!
Trickling sap of maple, fibre of manly wheat, it shall be you!
Sun so generous it shall be you!
Vapors lighting and shading my face it shall be you!
540 You sweaty brooks and dews it shall be you!
Winds whose soft-tickling genitals rub against me it shall be you!
Broad muscular fields, branches of live oak, loving lounger in my
winding paths, it shall be you!
Hands I have taken, face I have kiss'd, mortal I have ever touch'd, it
shall be you.

I dote on myself, there is that lot of me and all so luscious,
545 Each moment and whatever happens thrills me with joy,
I cannot tell how my ankles bend, nor whence the cause of my faintest
wish,
Nor the cause of the friendship I emit, nor the cause of the friendship I
take again.

That I walk up my stoop, I pause to consider if it really be,
A morning-glory at my window satisfies me more than the metaphysics
of books.

550 To behold the day-break!
The little light fades the immense and diaphanous shadows,
The air tastes good to my palate.

Hefts of the moving world at innocent gambols silently rising, freshly
exuding,
Scooting obliquely high and low.

555 Something I cannot see puts upward libidinous prongs,
Seas of bright juice suffuse heaven.

The earth by the sky staid with, the daily close of their junction,
The heav'd challenge from the east that moment over my head,
The mocking taunt, See then whether you shall be master!

---

3. A cutting edge fastened to a plow ahead of the
plowshare.

4. Land under cultivation; also, the act of cultivat-
ing soil.

52

The spotted hawk swoops by and accuses me, he complains of my gab
　　and my loitering.

I too am not a bit tamed, I too am untranslatable,
I sound my barbaric yawp over the roofs of the world.

The last scud of day holds back for me,
1335　It flings my likeness after the rest and true as any on the shadow'd wilds,
It coaxes me to the vapor and the dusk.

I depart as air, I shake my white locks at the runaway sun,
I effuse my flesh in eddies, and drift it in lacy jags.

I bequeath myself to the dirt to grow from the grass I love,
1340　If you want me again look for me under your boot-soles.

You will hardly know who I am or what I mean,
But I shall be good health to you nevertheless,
And filter and fibre your blood.

Failing to fetch me at first keep encouraged,
1345　Missing me one place search another,
I stop somewhere waiting for you.

　　　　　　　　　　　　　　　　　　　　　　1855, 1881

Crossing Brooklyn Ferry

1

Flood-tide below me! I see you face to face!
Clouds of the west—sun there half an hour high—I see you also face to
　　face.

Crowds of men and women attired in the usual costumes, how curious
　　you are to me!
On the ferry-boats the hundreds and hundreds that cross, returning
　　home, are more curious to me than you suppose,
5　And you that shall cross from shore to shore years hence are more to me,
　　and more in my meditations, than you might suppose.

2

The impalpable sustenance of me from all things at all hours of the day,
The simple, compact, well-join'd scheme, myself disintegrated, every
　　one disintegrated yet part of the scheme,
The similitudes of the past and those of the future,
The glories strung like beads on my smallest sights and hearings, on the
　　walk in the street and the passage over the river,
10　The current rushing so swiftly and swimming with me far away,
The others that are to follow me, the ties between me and them,
The certainty of others, the life, love, sight, hearing of others.

Others will enter the gates of the ferry and cross from shore to shore,
Others will watch the run of the flood-tide,
15 Others will see the shipping of Manhattan north and west, and the
heights of Brooklyn to the south and east,
Others will see the islands large and small;
Fifty years hence, others will see them as they cross, the sun half an hour
high,
A hundred years hence, or ever so many hundred years hence, others
will see them,
Will enjoy the sunset, the pouring-in of the flood-tide, the falling-back
to the sea of the ebb-tide.

3

20 It avails not, time nor place—distance avails not,
I am with you, you men and women of a generation, or ever so many
generations hence,
Just as you feel when you look on the river and sky, so I felt,
Just as any of you is one of a living crowd, I was one of a crowd,
Just as you are refresh'd by the gladness of the river and the bright flow,
I was refresh'd,
25 Just as you stand and lean on the rail, yet hurry with the swift current, I
stood yet was hurried,
Just as you look on the numberless masts of ships and the thick-stemm'd
pipes of steamboats, I look'd.

I too many and many a time cross'd the river of old,
Watched the Twelfth-month° sea-gulls, saw them high in   *December*
the air floating with motionless wings, oscillating their bodies,
Saw how the glistening yellow lit up parts of their bodies and left the
rest in strong shadow,
30 Saw the slow-wheeling circles and the gradual edging toward the south,
Saw the reflection of the summer sky in the water,
Had my eyes dazzled by the shimmering track of beams,
Look'd at the fine centrifugal spokes of light round the shape of my head
in the sunlit water,
Look'd on the haze on the hills southward and south-westward,
35 Look'd on the vapor as it flew in fleeces tinged with violet,
Look'd toward the lower bay to notice the vessels arriving,
Saw their approach, saw aboard those that were near me,
Saw the white sails of schooners and sloops, saw the ships at anchor,
The sailors at work in the rigging or out astride the spars,
40 The round masts, the swinging motion of the hulls, the slender
serpentine pennants,
The large and small steamers in motion, the pilots in their pilot-houses,
The white wake left by the passage, the quick tremulous whirl of the
wheels,
The flags of all nations, the falling of them at sunset,
The scallop-edged waves in the twilight, the ladled cups, the frolicsome
crests and glistening,
45 The stretch afar growing dimmer and dimmer, the gray walls of the
granite storehouses by the docks,

On the river the shadowy group, the big steam-tug closely flank'd on
    each side by the barges, the hay-boat, the belated lighter,[5]
On the neighboring shore the fires from the foundry chimneys burning
    high and glaringly into the night,
Casting their flicker of black contrasted with wild red and yellow light
    over the tops of houses, and down into the clefts of streets.

4

These and all else were to me the same as they are to you,
50 I loved well those cities, loved well the stately and rapid river,
The men and women I saw were all near to me,
Others the same—others who look back on me because I look'd forward
    to them,
(The time will come, though I stop° here to-day and to-night.)   *stay*

5

What is it then between us?
55 What is the count of the scores or hundreds of years between us?

Whatever it is, it avails not—distance avails not, and place avails not,
I too lived, Brooklyn of ample hills was mine,
I too walk'd the streets of Manhattan island, and bathed in the waters
    around it,
I too felt the curious abrupt questionings stir within me,
60 In the day among crowds of people sometimes they came upon me,
In my walks home late at night or as I lay in my bed they came upon
    me,
I too had been struck from the float forever held in solution,
I too had receiv'd identity by my body,
That I was I knew was of my body, and what I should be I knew I should
    be of my body.

6

65 It is not upon you alone the dark patches fall,
The dark threw its patches down upon me also,
The best I had done seem'd to me blank and suspicious,
My great thoughts as I supposed them, were they not in reality meagre?
Nor is it you alone who know what it is to be evil,
70 I am he who knew what it was to be evil,
I too knitted the old knot of contrariety,
Blabb'd, blush'd, resented, lied, stole, grudg'd,
Had guile, anger, lust, hot wishes I dared not speak,
Was wayward, vain, greedy, shallow, sly, cowardly, malignant,
75 The wolf, the snake, the hog, not wanting in me,
The cheating look, the frivolous word, the adulterous wish, not wanting,
Refusals, hates, postponements, meanness, laziness, none of these
    wanting,
Was one with the rest, the days and haps of the rest,
Was call'd by my nighest name by clear loud voices of young men as
    they saw me approaching or passing,

---

5. Barge used for loading and unloading ships.

80 Felt their arms on my neck as I stood, or the negligent leaning of their
        flesh against me as I sat,
    Saw many I loved in the street or ferry-boat or public assembly, yet never
        told them a word,
    Lived the same life with the rest, the same old laughing, gnawing,
        sleeping,
    Play'd the part that still looks back on the actor or actress,
    The same old role, the role that is what we make it, as great as we like,
85 Or as small as we like, or both great and small.

7

    Closer yet I approach you,
    What thought you have of me now, I had as much of you—I laid in my
        stores in advance,
    I consider'd long and seriously of you before you were born.

    Who was to know what should come home to me?
90 Who knows but I am enjoying this?
    Who knows, for all the distance, but I am as good as looking at you now,
        for all you cannot see me?

8

    Ah, what can ever be more stately and admirable to me than mast-
        hemm'd Manhattan?
    River and sunset and scallop-edg'd waves of flood-tide?
    The sea-gulls oscillating their bodies, the hay-boat in the twilight, and
        the belated lighter?
95 What gods can exceed these that clasp me by the hand, and with voices I
        love call me promptly and loudly by my nighest name as I approach?
    What is more subtle than this which ties me to the woman or man that
        looks in my face?
    Which fuses me into you now, and pours my meaning into you?

    We understand then do we not?
    What I promis'd without mentioning it, have you not accepted?
100 What the study could not teach—what the preaching could not
        accomplish is accomplish'd, is it not?

9

    Flow on, river! flow with the flood-tide, and ebb with the ebb-tide!
    Frolic on, crested and scallop-edg'd waves!
    Gorgeous clouds of the sunset! drench with your splendor me, or the
        men and women generations after me!
    Cross from shore to shore, countless crowds of passengers!
105 Stand up, tall masts of Mannahatta![6] stand up, beautiful hills of
        Brooklyn!
    Throb, baffled and curious brain! throw out questions and answers!
    Suspend here and everywhere, eternal float of solution!
    Gaze, loving and thirsting eyes, in the house or street or public assembly!
    Sound out, voices of young men! loudly and musically call me by my
        nighest name!

6. Variant for the Indian word normally spelled Manhattan.

110   Live, old life! play the part that looks back on the actor or actress!
      Play the old role, the role that is great or small according as one makes
           it!
      Consider, you who peruse me, whether I may not in unknown ways be
           looking upon you;
      Be firm, rail over the river, to support those who lean idly, yet haste with
           the hasting current;
      Fly on, sea birds! fly sideways, or wheel in large circles high in the air;
115   Receive the summer sky, you water, and faithfully hold it till all downcast
           eyes have time to take it from you!
      Diverge, fine spokes of light, from the shape of my head, or any one's
           head, in the sunlit water!
      Come on, ships from the lower bay! pass up or down, white-sail'd
           schooners, sloops, lighters!
      Flaunt away, flags of all nations! be duly lower'd at sunset!
      Burn high your fires, foundry chimneys! cast black shadows at nightfall!
           cast red and yellow light over the tops of the houses!
120   Appearances, now or henceforth, indicate what you are,
      You necessary film, continue to envelop the soul,
      About my body for me, and your body for you, be hung our divinest
           aromas,
      Thrive, cities—bring your freight, bring your shows, ample and sufficient
           rivers,
      Expand, being than which none else is perhaps more spiritual,
125   Keep your places, objects than which none else is more lasting.

      You have waited, you always wait, you dumb, beautiful ministers,
      We receive you with free sense at last, and are insatiate[7] henceforward,
      Not you any more shall be able to foil us, or withhold yourselves from
           us,
      We use you, and do not cast you aside—we plant you permanently
           within us,
130   We fathom you not—we love you—there is perfection in you also,
      You furnish your parts toward eternity,
      Great or small, you furnish your parts toward the soul.
1856   1881

When I Heard the Learn'd Astronomer

      When I heard the learn'd astronomer,
      When the proofs, the figures, were ranged in columns before me,
      When I was shown the charts and diagrams, to add, divide, and measure
           them,
      When I sitting heard the astronomer where he lectured with much
           applause in the lecture-room,
5   How soon unaccountable I became tired and sick,
      Till rising and gliding out I wander'd off by myself,
      In the mystical moist night-air, and from time to time,
      Look'd up in perfect silence at the stars.
1865   1865

7. Insatiable.

I Saw in Louisiana a Live-Oak Growing

I saw in Louisiana a live-oak growing,
All alone stood it and the moss hung down from the branches,
Without any companion it grew there uttering joyous leaves of
    dark green,
And its look, rude, unbending, lusty, made me think of myself,
5 But I wonder'd how it could utter joyous leaves standing alone
    there without its friend near, for I knew I could not,
And I broke off a twig with a certain number of leaves upon it,
    and twined around it a little moss,
And brought it away, and I have placed it in sight in my room,
It is not needed to remind me as of my own dear friends,
(For I believe lately I think of little else than of them,)
10 Yet it remains to me a curious token, it makes me think of manly
    love;
For all that, and though the live-oak glistens there in Louisiana
    solitary in a wide flat space,
Uttering joyous leaves all its life without a friend a lover near,
I know very well I could not.

1860   1867

Vigil Strange I Kept on the Field One Night

Vigil strange I kept on the field one night;
When you my son and my comrade dropt at my side that day,
One look I but gave which your dear eyes return'd with a look I
    shall never forget,
One touch of your hand to mine O boy, reach'd up as you lay on
    the ground,
5 Then onward I sped in the battle, the even-contested battle,
Till late in the night reliev'd to the place at last again I made my way,
Found you in death so cold dear comrade, found your body son
    of responding kisses, (never again on earth responding,)
Bared your face in the starlight, curious the scene, cool blew the
    moderate night-wind,
Long there and then in vigil I stood, dimly around me the battle-
    field spreading,
10 Vigil wondrous and vigil sweet there in the fragrant silent night,
But not a tear fell, not even a long-drawn sigh, long I gazed,
Then on the earth partially reclining sat by your side leaning my
    chin in my hands,
Passing sweet hours, immortal and mystic hours with you dearest
    comrade — not a tear, not a word,
Vigil of silence, love and death, vigil for you my son and my soldier,
15 As onward silently stars aloft, eastward new ones upward stole,
Vigil final for you brave boy, (I could not save you, swift was your
    death,
I faithfully loved you and cared for you living, I think we shall
    surely meet again,)
Till at latest lingering of the night, indeed just as the dawn appear'd,
My comrade I wrapt in his blanket, envelop'd well his form,

20 Folded the blanket well, tucking it carefully over head and care-
    fully under feet,
And there and then and bathed by the rising sun, my son in his
    grave, in his rude-dug grave I deposited,
Ending my vigil strange with that, vigil of night and battle-field dim,
Vigil for boy of responding kisses, (never again on earth responding,)
Vigil for comrade swiftly slain, vigil I never forget, how as day
    brighten'd,
25 I rose from the chill ground and folded my soldier well in his blanket,
And buried him where he fell.

1865   1867

Beat! Beat! Drums!

Beat! beat! drums!—blow! bugles! blow!
Through the windows—through doors—burst like a ruthless force,
Into the solemn church, and scatter the congregation,
Into the school where the scholar is studying;
5 Leave not the bridegroom quiet—no happiness must he have now
    with his bride,
Nor the peaceful farmer any peace, ploughing his field or gathering
    his grain,
So fierce you whirr and pound you drums—so shrill you bugles blow.

Beat! beat! drums!—blow! bugles! blow!
Over the traffic of cities—over the rumble of wheels in the streets;
10 Are beds prepared for sleepers at night in the houses? no sleepers
    must sleep in those beds,
No bargainers' bargains by day—no brokers or speculators—
    would they continue?
Would the talkers be talking? would the singer attempt to sing?
Would the lawyer rise in the court to state his case before the judge?
Then rattle quicker, heavier drums—you bugles wilder blow.

15 Beat! beat! drums!—blow! bugles! blow!
Make no parley—stop for no expostulation,
Mind not the timid—mind not the weeper or prayer,
Mind not the old man beseeching the young man,
Let not the child's voice be heard, nor the mother's entreaties,
20 Make even the trestles to shake the dead where they lie awaiting the
    hearses,
So strong you thump O terrible drums—so loud you bugles blow.

1861   1867

By the Bivouac's Fitful Flame[8]

By the bivouac's fitful flame,
A procession winding around me, solemn and sweet and slow—but
    first I note,
The tents of the sleeping army, the fields' and woods' dim outline,

8. "Bivouac": an overnight encampment in the open air.

The darkness lit by spots of kindled fire, the silence,
5   Like a phantom far or near an occasional figure moving,
The shrubs and trees, (as I lift my eyes they seem to be stealthily
    watching me,)
While wind in procession thoughts, O tender and wondrous thoughts,
Of life and death, of home and the past and loved, and of those that
    are far away;
A solemn and slow procession there as I sit on the ground,
10   By the bivouac's fitful flame.
1865   1867

Cavalry Crossing a Ford

A line in long array where they wind betwixt green islands,
They take a serpentine course, their arms flash in the sun—hark to
    the musical clank,
Behold the silvery river, in it the splashing horses loitering stop to
    drink,
Behold the brown-faced men, each group, each person a picture, the
    negligent rest on the saddles,
5   Some emerge on the opposite bank, others are just entering the
    ford—while,
Scarlet and blue and snowy white,
The guidon[9] flags flutter gayly in the wind.
1865   1871

The World below the Brine

The world below the brine,
Forests at the bottom of the sea, the branches and leaves,
Sea-lettuce, vast lichens, strange flowers and seeds, the thick tangle,
    openings, and pink turf,
Different colors, pale gray and green, purple, white, and gold, the play
    of light through the water,
5   Dumb swimmers there among the rocks, coral, gluten, grass, rushes, and
    the aliment[1] of the swimmers,
Sluggish existences grazing there suspended, or slowly crawling close to
    the bottom,
The sperm-whale at the surface blowing air and spray, or disporting with
    his flukes,
The leaden-eyed shark, the walrus, the turtle, the hairy sea-leopard, and
    the sting-ray,
Passions there, wars, pursuits, tribes, sight in those ocean-depths,
    breathing that thick-breathing air, as so many do,
10   The change thence to the sight here, and to the subtle air breathed
    by beings like us who walk this sphere,
The change onward from ours to that of beings who walk other spheres.
1860   1871

---

9. Small flag or banner used by a military unit as a signal or guide.

1. Food. "Gluten": obsolete geological term for a tenacious mass (as of clay).

Out of the Cradle Endlessly Rocking

Out of the cradle endlessly rocking,
Out of the mocking-bird's throat, the musical shuttle,
Out of the Ninth-month[2] midnight,
Over the sterile sands and the fields beyond, where the child leaving his
    bed wander'd alone, bareheaded, barefoot,
5 Down from the shower'd halo,
Up from the mystic play of shadows twining and twisting as if they
    were alive,
Out from the patches of briers and blackberries,
From the memories of the bird that chanted to me,
From your memories sad brother, from the fitful risings and fallings I
    heard,
10 From under that yellow half-moon late-risen and swollen as if with tears,
From those beginning notes of yearning and love there in the mist,
From the thousand responses of my heart never to cease,
From the myriad thence-arous'd words,
From the word stronger and more delicious than any,
15 From such as now they start the scene revisiting,
As a flock, twittering, rising, or overhead passing,
Borne hither, ere all eludes me, hurriedly,
A man, yet by these tears a little boy again,
Throwing myself on the sand, confronting the waves,
20 I, chanter of pains and joys, uniter of here and hereafter,
Taking all hints to use them, but swiftly leaping beyond them,
A reminiscence sing.

Once Paumanok,[3]
When the lilac-scent was in the air and Fifth-month grass was growing,
25 Up this seashore in some briers,
Two feather'd guests from Alabama, two together,
And their nest, and four light-green eggs spotted with brown,
And every day the he-bird to and fro near at hand,
And every day the she-bird crouch'd on her nest, silent, with bright eyes,
30 And every day I, a curious boy, never too close, never disturbing them,
Cautiously peering, absorbing, translating.

Shine! shine! shine!
Pour down your warmth, great sun!
While we bask, we two together.

35 *Two together!*
Winds blow south, or winds blow north,
Day come white, or night come black,
Home, or rivers and mountains from home,
Singing all time, minding no time,
40 *While we two keep together.*

Till of a sudden,
May-be kill'd, unknown to her mate,

2. The Quaker designation for September may
here also suggest the human cycle of fertility and
birth, in contrast with "sterile sands" in the next
line.
3. The Indian name for Long Island.

One forenoon the she-bird crouch'd not on the nest,
Nor return'd that afternoon, nor the next,
45 Nor ever appear'd again.

And thenceforward all summer in the sound of the sea,
And at night under the full of the moon in calmer weather,
Over the hoarse surging of the sea,
Or flitting from brier to brier by day,
50 I saw, I heard at intervals the remaining one, the he-bird,
The solitary guest from Alabama.

Blow! blow! blow!
Blow up sea-winds along Paumanok's shore;
I wait and I wait till you blow my mate to me.

55 Yes, when the stars glisten'd,
All night long on the prong of a moss-scallop'd stake,
Down almost amid the slapping waves,
Sat the lone singer wonderful causing tears.

He call'd on his mate,
60 He pour'd forth the meanings which I of all men know.

Yes my brother I know,
The rest might not, but I have treasur'd every note,
For more than once dimly down to the beach gliding,
Silent, avoiding the moonbeams, blending myself with the shadows,
65 Recalling now the obscure shapes, the echoes, the sounds and sights
      after their sorts,
The white arms out in the breakers tirelessly tossing,
I, with bare feet, a child, the wind wafting my hair,
Listen'd long and long.

Listen'd to keep, to sing, now translating the notes,
70 Following you my brother.

Soothe! soothe! soothe!
Close on its wave soothes the wave behind,
And again another behind embracing and lapping, every one close,
But my love soothes not me, not me.

75 *Low hangs the moon, it rose late,*
It is lagging—O I think it is heavy with love, with love.

O madly the sea pushes upon the land,
With love, with love.

O night! do I not see my love fluttering out among the breakers?
80 *What is that little black thing I see there in the white?*

Loud! loud! loud!
Loud I call to you, my love!

High and clear I shoot my voice over the waves,
Surely you must know who is here, is here,
85 *You must know who I am, my love.*

Low-hanging moon!
What is that dusky spot in your brown yellow?
O it is the shape, the shape of my mate!
O moon do not keep her from me any longer.

90 *Land! land! O land!*
Whichever way I turn, O I think you could give me my mate back again if
*   you only would,*
For I am almost sure I see her dimly whichever way I look.

O rising stars!
Perhaps the one I want so much will rise, will rise with some of you.

95 *O throat! O trembling throat!*
Sound clearer through the atmosphere!
Pierce the woods, the earth,
Somewhere listening to catch you must be the one I want.

Shake out carols!
100 *Solitary here, the night's carols!*
Carols of lonesome love! death's carols!
Carols under that lagging, yellow, waning moon!
O under that moon where she droops almost down into the sea!
O reckless despairing carols.

105 *But soft! sink low!*
Soft! let me just murmur,
And do you wait a moment you husky-nois'd sea,
For somewhere I believe I heard my mate responding to me,
So faint, I must be still, be still to listen,
110 *But not altogether still, for then she might not come immediately to me.*

Hither my love!
Here I am! here!
With this just-sustain'd note I announce myself to you,
This gentle call is for you my love, for you.

115 *Do not be decoy'd elsewhere,*
That is the whistle of the wind, it is not my voice,
That is the fluttering, the fluttering of the spray,
Those are the shadows of leaves.

O darkness! O in vain!
120 *O I am very sick and sorrowful.*

O brown halo in the sky near the moon, drooping upon the sea!
O troubled reflection in the sea!
O throat! O throbbing heart!
And I singing uselessly, uselessly all the night.

125 *O past! O happy life! O songs of joy!*
In the air, in the woods, over fields,
Loved! loved! loved! loved! loved!
But my mate no more, no more with me!
We two together no more.

130 The aria sinking,
All else continuing, the stars shining,
The winds blowing, the notes of the bird continuous echoing,
With angry moans the fierce old mother incessantly moaning,
On the sands of Paumanok's shore gray and rustling,
135 The yellow half-moon enlarged, sagging down, drooping, the face of the
sea almost touching,
The boy ecstatic, with his bare feet the waves, with his hair the
atmosphere dallying,
The love in the heart long pent, now loose, now at last tumultuously
bursting,
The aria's meaning, the ears, the soul, swiftly depositing,
The strange tears down the cheeks coursing,
140 The colloquy there, the trio, each uttering,
The undertone, the savage old mother incessantly crying,
To the boy's soul's questions sullenly timing, some drown'd secret
hissing,
To the outsetting bard.

Demon or bird! (said the boy's soul,)
145 Is it indeed toward your mate you sing? or is it really to me?
For I, that was a child, my tongue's use sleeping, now I have heard you,
Now in a moment I know what I am for, I awake,
And already a thousand singers, a thousand songs, clearer, louder and
more sorrowful than yours,
A thousand warbling echoes have started to life within me, never to die.

150 O you singer solitary, singing by yourself, projecting me,
O solitary me listening, never more shall I cease perpetuating you,
Never more shall I escape, never more the reverberations,
Never more the cries of unsatisfied love be absent from me,
Never again leave me to be the peaceful child I was before what there
in the night,
155 By the sea under the yellow and sagging moon,
The messenger there arous'd, the fire, the sweet hell within,
The unknown want, the destiny of me.

O give me the clew! (it lurks in the night here somewhere,)
O if I am to have so much, let me have more!

160 A word then, (for I will conquer it,)
The word final, superior to all,
Subtle, sent up—what is it?—I listen;
Are you whispering it, and have been all the time, you sea-waves?
Is that it from your liquid rims and wet sands?

165 Whereto answering, the sea,
Delaying not, hurrying not,

Whisper'd me through the night, and very plainly before daybreak,
Lisp'd to me the low and delicious word death,
And again death, death, death, death,
170 Hissing melodious, neither like the bird nor like my arous'd child's heart,
But edging near as privately for me rustling at my feet,
Creeping thence steadily up to my ears and laving me softly all over,
Death, death, death, death, death.

Which I do not forget,
175 But fuse the song of my dusky demon and brother,
That he sang to me in the moonlight on Paumanok's gray beach,
With the thousand responsive songs at random,
My own songs awaked from that hour,
And with them the key, the word up from the waves,
180 The word of the sweetest song and all songs,
That strong and delicious word which, creeping to my feet,
(Or like some old crone rocking the cradle, swathed in sweet garments,
    bending aside,)
The sea whisper'd me.

1859   1881

On the Beach at Night

On the beach at night,
Stands a child with her father,
Watching the east, the autumn sky.

Up through the darkness,
5 While ravening clouds, the burial clouds, in black masses spreading,
Lower sullen and fast athwart and down the sky,
Amid a transparent clear belt of ether yet left in the east,
Ascends large and calm the lord-star Jupiter,
And nigh at hand, only a very little above,
10 Swim the delicate sisters the Pleiades.[4]

From the beach the child holding the hand of her father,
Those burial-clouds that lower victorious soon to devour all,
Watching, silently weeps.

Weep not, child,
15 Weep not, my darling,
With these kisses let me remove your tears,
The ravening clouds shall not long be victorious,
They shall not long possess the sky, they devour the stars only in
    apparition,
Jupiter shall emerge, be patient, watch again another night, the Pleiades
    shall emerge,
20 They are immortal, all those stars both silvery and golden shall shine out
    again,

---

4. "Lord" because the largest of the planets, and because Jupiter was the greatest of the Roman gods. According to Greek mythology, the seven sisters became the constellation known as the Pleiades.

The great stars and the little ones shall shine out again, they endure,
The vast immortal suns and the long-enduring pensive moons shall again
    shine.

Then dearest child mournest thou only for Jupiter?
Considerest thou alone the burial of the stars?

25 Something there is,
    (With my lips soothing thee, adding I whisper,
    I give thee the first suggestion, the problem and indirection,)
    Something there is more immortal even than the stars,
    (Many the burials, many the days and nights, passing away,)
30 Something that shall endure longer even than lustrous Jupiter,
    Longer than sun or any revolving satellite,
    Or the radiant sisters the Pleiades.
1871   1881

The Dalliance of the Eagles

Skirting the river road, (my forenoon walk, my rest,)
Skyward in air a sudden muffled sound, the dalliance of the eagles,
The rushing amorous contact high in space together,
The clinching interlocking claws, a living, fierce, gyrating wheel,
5 Four beating wings, two beaks, a swirling mass tight grappling,
    In tumbling turning clustering loops, straight downward falling,
    Till o'er the river pois'd, the twain yet one, a moment's lull,
    A motionless still balance in the air, then parting, talons loosing,
    Upward again on slow-firm pinions slanting, their separate diverse flight,
10 She hers, he his, pursuing.
1880   1881

Reconciliation

Word over all, beautiful as the sky,
Beautiful that war and all its deeds of carnage must in time be utterly
    lost,
That the hands of the sisters Death and Night incessantly softly wash
    again, and ever again, this soil'd world;
For my enemy is dead, a man divine as myself is dead,
5 I look where he lies white-faced and still in the coffin—I draw near,
    Bend down and touch lightly with my lips the white face in the coffin.
1865–66   1881

When Lilacs Last in the Dooryard Bloom'd[5]

1

When lilacs last in the dooryard bloom'd,
And the great star early droop'd in the western sky in the night,
I mourn'd, and yet shall mourn with ever-returning spring.

---

5. Composed immediately after the assassination of President Abraham Lincoln, April 14, 1865.

Ever-returning spring, trinity sure to me you bring,
5   Lilac blooming perennial and drooping star in the west,
And thought of him I love.

2

O powerful western fallen star!
O shades of night—O moody, tearful night!
O great star disappear'd—O the black murk that hides the star!
10   O cruel hands that hold me powerless—O helpless soul of me!
O harsh surrounding cloud that will not free my soul.

3

In the dooryard fronting an old farm-house near the white-wash'd
    palings,
Stands the lilac-bush tall-growing with heart-shaped leaves of rich green,
With many a pointed blossom rising delicate, with the perfume strong I
    love,
15   With every leaf a miracle—and from this bush in the dooryard,
With delicate-color'd blossoms and heart-shaped leaves of rich green,
A sprig with its flower I break.

4

In the swamp in secluded recesses,
A shy and hidden bird is warbling a song.

20   Solitary the thrush,
The hermit withdrawn to himself, avoiding the settlements,
Sings by himself a song.

Song of the bleeding throat,
Death's outlet song of life, (for well dear brother I know,
25   If thou wast not granted to sing thou would'st surely die.)

5

Over the breast of the spring, the land, amid cities,
Amid lanes and through old woods, where lately the violets peep'd from
    the ground, spotting the gray debris,
Amid the grass in the fields each side of the lanes, passing the endless
    grass,
Passing the yellow-spear'd wheat, every grain from its shroud in the dark-
    brown fields uprisen,
30   Passing the apple-tree blows of white and pink in the orchards,
Carrying a corpse to where it shall rest in the grave,
Night and day journeys a coffin.

6

Coffin that passes through lanes and streets,[6]
Through day and night with the great cloud darkening the land,
35   With the pomp of the inloop'd flags with the cities draped in black,

6. The funeral procession of Lincoln traveled from Washington to Springfield, Illinois, stopping at cities
and towns all along the way for the people to honor the murdered president.

With the show of the States themselves as of crape-veil'd women
    standing,
With processions long and winding and the flambeaus[7] of the night,
With the countless torches lit, with the silent sea of faces and the
    unbared heads,
With the waiting depot, the arriving coffin, and the sombre faces,
40   With dirges through the night, with the thousand voices rising strong
    and solemn,
With all the mournful voices of the dirges pour'd around the coffin,
The dim-lit churches and the shuddering organs—where amid these you
    journey,
With the tolling tolling bells' perpetual clang,
Here, coffin that slowly passes,
45   I give you my sprig of lilac.

7

(Nor for you, for one alone,
Blossoms and branches green to coffins all I bring,
For fresh as the morning, thus would I chant a song for you O sane and
    sacred death.

All over bouquets of roses,
50   O death, I cover you over with roses and early lilies,
But mostly and now the lilac that blooms the first,
Copious I break, I break the sprigs from the bushes,
With loaded arms I come, pouring for you,
For you and the coffins all of you O death.)

8

55   O western orb sailing the heaven,
Now I know what you must have meant as a month since I walk'd,
As I walk'd in silence the transparent shadowy night,
As I saw you had something to tell as you bent to me night after night,
As you droop'd from the sky low down as if to my side, (while the other
    stars all look'd on,)
60   As we wander'd together the solemn night, (for something I know not
    what kept me from sleep,)
As the night advanced, and I saw on the rim of the west how full you
    were of woe,
As I stood on the rising ground in the breeze in the cool transparent
    night,
As I watch'd where you pass'd and was lost in the netherward black of
    the night,
As my soul in its trouble dissatisfied sank, as where you sad orb,
65   Concluded, dropt in the night, and was gone.

9

Sing on there in the swamp,
O singer bashful and tender, I hear your notes, I hear your call,
I hear, I come presently, I understand you,

---

7. Flaming torches.

But a moment I linger, for the lustrous star has detain'd me,
70   The star my departing comrade holds and detains me.

10

O how shall I warble myself for the dead one there I loved?
And how shall I deck my song for the large sweet soul that has gone?
And what shall my perfume be for the grave of him I love?

Sea-winds blown from east and west,
75   Blown from the Eastern sea and blown from the Western sea, till there
          on the prairies meeting,
These and with these and the breath of my chant,
I'll perfume the grave of him I love.

11

O what shall I hang on the chamber walls?
And what shall the pictures be that I hang on the walls,
80   To adorn the burial-house of him I love?

Pictures of growing spring and farms and homes,
With the Fourth-month° eve at sundown, and the gray smoke   *April*
          lucid and bright,
With floods of the yellow gold of the gorgeous, indolent, sinking sun,
          burning, expanding the air,
With the fresh sweet herbage under foot, and the pale green leaves of
          the trees prolific,
85   In the distance the flowing glaze, the breast of the river, with a wind-
          dapple here and there,
With ranging hills on the banks, with many a line against the sky, and
          shadows,
And the city at hand with dwellings so dense, and stacks of chimneys,
And all the scenes of life and the workshops, and the workmen
          homeward returning.

12

Lo, body and soul—this land,
90   My own Manhattan with spires, and the sparkling and hurrying tides,
          and the ships,
The varied and ample land, the South and the North in the light, Ohio's
          shores and flashing Missouri,
And ever the far-spreading prairies cover'd with grass and corn.

Lo, the most excellent sun so calm and haughty,
The violet and purple morn with just-felt breezes,
95   The gentle soft-born measureless light,
The miracle spreading bathing all, the fulfill'd noon,
The coming eve delicious, the welcome night and the stars,
Over my cities shining all, enveloping man and land.

13

Sing on, sing on you gray-brown bird,
100   Sing from the swamps, the recesses, pour your chant from the bushes,
Limitless out of the dusk, out of the cedars and pines.

Sing on dearest brother, warble your reedy song,
Loud human song, with voice of uttermost woe.

O liquid and free and tender!
105   O wild and loose to my soul—O wondrous singer!
You only I hear—yet the star holds me, (but will soon depart,)
Yet the lilac with mastering odor holds me.

14

Now while I sat in the day and look'd forth,
In the close of the day with its light and the fields of spring, and the
    farmers preparing their crops,
110   In the large unconscious scenery of my land with its lakes and forests,
In the heavenly aerial beauty, (after the perturb'd winds and the storms,)
Under the arching heavens of the afternoon swift passing, and the voices
    of children and women,
The many-moving sea-tides, and I saw the ships how they sail'd,
And the summer approaching with richness, and the fields all busy with
    labor,
115   And the infinite separate houses, how they all went on, each with its
    meals and minutia of daily usages,
And the streets how their throbbings throbb'd, and the cities pent—lo,
    then and there,
Falling upon them all and among them all, enveloping me with the rest,
Appear'd the cloud, appear'd the long black trail,
And I knew death, its thought, and the sacred knowledge of death.

120   Then with the knowledge of death as walking one side of me,
And the thought of death close-walking the other side of me,
And I in the middle as with companions, and as holding the hands of
    companions,
I fled forth to the hiding receiving night that talks not,
Down to the shores of the water, the path by the swamp in the dimness,
125   To the solemn shadowy cedars and ghostly pines so still.

And the singer so shy to the rest receiv'd me,
The gray-brown bird I know receiv'd us comrades three,
And he sang the carol of death, and a verse for him I love.

From deep secluded recesses,
130   From the fragrant cedars and the ghostly pines so still,
Came the carol of the bird.

And the charm of the carol rapt me,
As I held as if by their hands my comrades in the night,
And the voice of my spirit tallied the song of the bird.

135   *Come lovely and soothing death,*
Undulate round the world, serenely arriving, arriving,
In the day, in the night, to all, to each,
Sooner or later delicate death.

Prais'd be the fathomless universe,
140 *For life and joy, and for objects and knowledge curious,*
And for love, sweet love—but praise! praise! praise!
For the sure-enwinding arms of cool-enfolding death.

Dark mother always gliding near with soft feet,
Have none chanted for thee a chant of fullest welcome?
145 *Then I chant it for thee, I glorify thee above all,*
I bring thee a song that when thou must indeed come, come unfalteringly.

Approach strong deliveress,
When it is so, when thou hast taken them I joyously sing the dead,
Lost in the loving floating ocean of thee,
150 *Laved in the flood of thy bliss O death.*

From me to thee glad serenades,
Dances for thee I propose saluting thee, adornments and feastings for thee,
And the sights of the open landscape and the high-spread sky are fitting,
And life and the fields, and the huge and thoughtful night.

155 *The night in silence under many a star,*
The ocean shore and the husky whispering wave whose voice I know,
And the soul turning to thee O vast and well-veil'd death,
And the body gratefully nestling close to thee.

Over the tree-tops I float thee a song,
160 *Over the rising and sinking waves, over the myriad fields and the prairies*
wide,
Over the dense-pack'd cities all and the teeming wharves and ways,
I float this carol with joy, with joy to thee O death.

15

To the tally of my soul,
Loud and strong kept up the gray-brown bird,
165 With pure deliberate notes spreading filling the night.

Loud in the pines and cedars dim,
Clear in the freshness moist and the swamp-perfume,
And I with my comrades there in the night.

While my sight that was bound in my eyes unclosed,
170 As to long panoramas of visions.

And I saw askant the armies,
I saw as in noiseless dreams hundreds of battle-flags,
Borne through the smoke of the battles and pierc'd with missiles I saw
them,
And carried hither and yon through the smoke, and torn and bloody,
175 And at last but a few shreds left on the staffs, (and all in silence,)
And the staffs all splinter'd and broken.

I saw battle-corpses, myriads of them,
And the white skeletons of young men, I saw them,
I saw the debris and debris of all the slain soldiers of the war,
180 But I saw they were not as was thought,
They themselves were fully at rest, they suffer'd not,
The living remain'd and suffer'd, the mother suffer'd,
And the wife and the child and the musing comrade suffer'd,
And the armies that remain'd suffer'd.

16

185 Passing the visions, passing the night,
Passing, unloosing the hold of my comrades' hands,
Passing the song of the hermit bird and the tallying song of my soul,
Victorious song, death's outlet song, yet varying ever-altering song,
As low and wailing, yet clear the notes, rising and falling, flooding the
night,
190 Sadly sinking and fainting, as warning and warning, and yet again
bursting with joy,
Covering the earth and filling the spread of the heaven,
As that powerful psalm in the night I heard from recesses,
Passing, I leave thee lilac with heart-shaped leaves,
I leave thee there in the door-yard, blooming, returning with spring.

195 I cease from my song for thee,
From my gaze on thee in the west, fronting the west, communing with
thee,
O comrade lustrous with silver face in the night.

Yet each to keep and all, retrievements out of the night,
The song, the wondrous chant of the gray-brown bird,
200 And the tallying chant, the echo arous'd in my soul,
With the lustrous and drooping star with the countenance full of woe,
With the holders holding my hand nearing the call of the bird,
Comrades mine and I in the midst, and their memory ever to keep, for
the dead I loved so well,
For the sweetest, wisest soul of all my days and lands—and this for his
dear sake,
205 Lilac and star and bird twined with the chant of my soul,
There in the fragrant pines and the cedars dusk and dim.
1865–66   1881

A Noiseless Patient Spider

A noiseless patient spider,
I mark'd where on a little promontory it stood isolated,
Mark'd how to explore the vacant vast surrounding,
It launch'd forth filament, filament, filament, out of itself,
5 Ever unreeling them, ever tirelessly speeding them.

And you O my soul where you stand,
Surrounded, detached, in measureless oceans of space,
Ceaselessly musing, venturing, throwing, seeking the spheres to connect
them,

Till the bridge you will need be form'd, till the ductile anchor hold,
10 Till the gossamer thread you fling catch somewhere, O my soul.
1868   1881

To a Locomotive in Winter

Thee for my recitative,
Thee in the driving storm even as now, the snow, the winter-day
    declining,
Thee in thy panoply, thy measur'd dual throbbing and thy beat
    convulsive,
Thy black cylindric body, golden brass and silvery steel,
5   Thy ponderous side-bars, parallel and connecting rods, gyrating, shuttling
    at thy sides,
Thy metrical, now swelling pant and roar, now tapering in the distance,
Thy great protruding head-light fix'd in front,
Thy long, pale, floating vapor-pennants, tinged with delicate purple,
The dense and murky clouds out-belching from thy smoke-stack,
10 Thy knitted frame, thy springs and valves, the tremulous twinkle of thy
    wheels,
Thy train of cars behind, obedient, merrily following,
Through gale or calm, now swift, now slack, yet steadily careering;
Type of the modern—emblem of motion and power—pulse of the
    continent,
For once come serve the Muse and merge in verse, even as here I see
    thee,
15 With storm and buffeting gusts of wind and falling snow,
By day thy warning ringing bell to sound its notes,
By night thy silent signal lamps to swing.

Fierce-throated beauty!
Roll through my chant with all thy lawless music, thy swinging lamps at
    night,
20 Thy madly-whistled laughter, echoing, rumbling like an earthquake,
    rousing all,
Law of thyself complete, thine own track firmly holding,
(No sweetness debonair of tearful harp or glib piano thine,)
Thy trills of shrieks by rocks and hills return'd,
Launch'd o'er the prairies wide, across the lakes,
25 To the free skies unpent and glad and strong.
1876   1881

FREDERICK GODDARD TUCKERMAN

1821–1873

From Sonnets, First Series

10

An upper chamber in a darkened house,
Where, ere his footsteps reached ripe manhood's brink,

Terror and anguish were his lot to drink;
I cannot rid the thought nor hold it close
5   But dimly dream upon that man alone:
Now though the autumn clouds most softly pass,
The cricket chides beneath the doorstep stone
And greener than the season grows the grass.
Nor can I drop my lids nor shade my brows,
10   But there he stands beside the lifted sash;
And with a swooning of the heart, I think
Where the black shingles slope to meet the boughs
And, shattered on the roof like smallest snows,
The tiny petals of the mountain ash.

28

Not the round natural world, not the deep mind,
The reconcilement holds: the blue abyss
Collects it not; our arrows sink amiss
And but in Him may we our import° find.   *meaning*
5   The agony to know, the grief, the bliss
Of toil, is vain and vain: clots of the sod
Gathered in heat and haste and flung behind
To blind ourselves and others, what but this
Still grasping dust and sowing toward the wind?
10   No more thy meaning seek, thine anguish plead,
But leaving straining thought and stammering word,
Across the barren azure pass to God;
Shooting the void in silence like a bird,
A bird that shuts his wings for better speed.

                              1860

From Sonnets, Second Series

7

His heart was in his garden; but his brain
Wandered at will among the fiery stars:
Bards, heroes, prophets, Homers, Hamilcars,[1]
With many angels, stood, his eye to gain;
5   The devils, too, were his familiars.
And yet the cunning florist held his eyes
Close to the ground, —a tulip-bulb his prize, —
And talked of tan and bone-dust, cutworms, grubs,
As though all Nature held no higher strain;
10   Or, if he spoke of Art, he made the theme
Flow through box-borders, turf, and flower-tubs;
Or, like a garden-engine's, steered the stream, —
Now spouted rainbows to the silent skies;
Now kept it flat, and raked the walks and shrubs.

---

1. Hamilcar Barca (d. 229 / 228 B.C.), general and conqueror, who assumed command of Carthaginian forces in Sicily during the last years of the First Punic War with Rome; father of Hannibal. "Homer": Greek epic poet of the eighth century B.C., author of the *Iliad* and the *Odyssey*.

29

How oft in schoolboy-days, from the school's sway
Have I run forth to Nature as to a friend,—
With some pretext of o'erwrought sight, to spend
My school-time in green meadows far away!
5 Careless of summoning bell, or clocks that strike,
I marked with flowers the minutes of my day:
For still the eye that shrank from hated hours,
Dazzled with decimal and dividend,
Knew each bleached alder-root that plashed° across   *splashed*
10 The bubbling brook, and every mass of moss;
Could tell the month, too, by the vervain-spike,[2]—
How far the ring of purple tiny flowers
Had climbed; just starting, may-be, with the May,
Half-high, or tapering off at Summer's end.

1860

MATTHEW ARNOLD

1822–1888

Shakespeare

Others abide our question. Thou art free.
We ask and ask—thou smilest and art still,
Out-topping knowledge. For the loftiest hill,
Who to the stars uncrowns his majesty,

5 Planting his stedfast footsteps in the sea,
Making the heaven of heavens his dwelling-place,
Spares but the cloudy border of his base
To the foiled searching of mortality;

And thou, who didst the stars and sunbeams know,
10 Self-schooled, self-scanned, self-honored, self-secure,
Didst tread on earth unguessed at—better so!

All pains the immortal spirit must endure,
All weakness which impairs, all griefs which bow,
Find their sole speech in that victorious brow.

1849

To Marguerite

Yes! in the sea of life enisled,
With echoing straits between us thrown,
Dotting the shoreless watery wild,
We mortal millions live *alone*.
5 The islands feel the enclasping flow,
And then their endless bounds they know.

---

2. "Vervain": a spiky-flowered plant of the genus Verbena.

But when the moon their hollows lights,
And they are swept by balms of spring,
And in their glens, on starry nights,
10 The nightingales divinely sing;
And lovely notes, from shore to shore,
Across the sounds and channels pour—

Oh! then a longing like despair
Is to their farthest caverns sent;
15 For surely once, they feel, we were
Parts of a single continent!
Now round us spreads the watery plain—
Oh might our marges° meet again!   *margins*

Who ordered, that their longing's fire
20 Should be, as soon as kindled, cooled?
Who renders vain their deep desire?—
A God, a God their severance ruled!
And bade betwixt their shores to be
The unplumbed, salt, estranging sea.

1852

The Scholar-Gypsy[1]

Go, for they call you, shepherd, from the hill;
 Go, shepherd, and untie the wattled cotes![2]
  No longer leave thy wistful flock unfed,
  Nor let thy bawling fellows rack their throats,
5   Nor the cropped herbage shoot another head.
    But when the fields are still,
 And the tired men and dogs all gone to rest,
  And only the white sheep are sometimes seen
  Cross and recross the strips of moon-blanched green,
10 Come, shepherd, and again begin the quest!

Here, where the reaper was at work of late—
 In this high field's dark corner, where he leaves
  His coat, his basket, and his earthen cruse,°   *vessel*
  And in the sun all morning binds the sheaves,
15   Then here, at noon, comes back his stores to use—
    Here will I sit and wait,

1. " 'There was very lately a lad in the University of Oxford, who was by his poverty forced to leave his studies there; and at last to join himself to a company of vagabond gypsies. Among these extravagant people, by the insinuating subtlety of his carriage, he quickly got so much of their love and esteem as that they discovered to him their mystery. After he had been a pretty while well exercised in the trade, there chanced to ride by a couple of scholars, who had formerly been of his acquaintance. They quickly spied out their old friend among the gypsies; and he gave them an account of the necessity which drove him to that kind of life, and told them that the people he went with were not such impostors as they were taken for, but that they had a traditional kind of learning among them, and could do wonders by the power of imagination, their fancy binding that of others: that himself had learned much of their art, and when he had compassed the whole secret, he intended, he said, to leave their company, and give the world an account of what he had learned.'— Glanvil's *Vanity of Dogmatizing*, 1661" [Arnold's note].
2. Sheepfolds made of woven boughs (wattles).

While to my ear from uplands far away
  The bleating of the folded flocks is borne,
    With distant cries of reapers in the corn°—   *grain*
20   All the live murmur of a summer's day.

Screened is this nook o'er the high, half-reaped field,
  And here till sundown, shepherd! will I be.
    Through the thick corn the scarlet poppies peep,
  And round green roots and yellowing stalks I see
25   Pale pink convolvulus in tendrils creep;
      And air-swept lindens yield
  Their scent, and rustle down their perfumed showers
  Of bloom on the bent grass where I am laid,
  And bower me from the August sun with shade;
30   And the eye travels down to Oxford's towers.

And near me on the grass lies Glanvil's book—
  Come, let me read the oft-read tale again!
    The story of the Oxford scholar poor,
  Of pregnant parts[3] and quick inventive brain,
35   Who, tired of knocking at preferment's door,
      One summer-morn forsook
  His friends, and went to learn the gypsy-lore,
  And roamed the world with that wild brotherhood,
  And came, as most men deemed, to little good,
40   But came to Oxford and his friends no more.

But once, years after, in the country-lanes,
  Two scholars, whom at college erst he knew,
    Met him, and of his way of life enquired;
  Whereat he answered, that the gypsy-crew,
45   His mates, had arts to rule as they desired
      The workings of men's brains,
  And they can bind them to what thoughts they will.
  "And I," he said, "the secret of their art,
  When fully learned, will to the world impart;
50   But it needs heaven-sent moments for this skill."

This said, he left them, and returned no more.—
  But rumors hung about the country-side,
    That the lost Scholar long was seen to stray,
  Seen by rare glimpses, pensive and tongue-tied,
55   In hat of antique shape, and cloak of gray.
      The same the gypsies wore.
  Shepherds had met him on the Hurst[4] in spring;
  At some lone alehouse in the Berkshire moors,
  On the warm ingle-bench, the smock-frocked boors°   *rustics*
60   Had found him seated at their entering,

---

3. I.e., of quick intellectual abilities.
4. A hill near Oxford. (All place-names in the poem, with the obvious exception of the Mediter-ranean localities of the last two stanzas, refer to the countryside around Oxford.)

But, 'mid their drink and clatter, he would fly.
  And I myself seem half to know thy looks,
    And put the shepherds, wanderer! on thy trace;
    And boys who in lone wheatfields scare the rooks
65   I ask if thou hast passed their quiet place;
        Or in my boat I lie
    Moored to the cool bank in the summer-heats,
      'Mid wide grass meadows which the sunshine fills,
      And watch the warm, green-muffled Cumner hills,
70   And wonder if thou haunt'st their shy retreats.

For most, I know, thou lov'st retired ground!
  Thee at the ferry Oxford riders blithe,
    Returning home on summer-nights, have met
  Crossing the stripling Thames at Bab-lock-hithe,
75   Trailing in the cool stream thy fingers wet,
        As the punt's rope chops round;[5]
  And leaning backward in a pensive dream,
    And fostering in thy lap a heap of flowers
    Plucked in shy fields and distant Wychwood bowers,
80   And thine eyes resting on the moonlit stream.

And then they land, and thou art seen no more!
  Maidens, who from the distant hamlets come
    To dance around the Fyfield elm in May,
  Oft through the darkening fields have seen thee roam,
85   Or cross a stile into the public way.
        Oft thou hast given them store
  Of flowers—the frail-leafed, white anemone,
    Dark bluebells drenched with dews of summer eves,
    And purple orchises with spotted leaves—
90   But none hath words she can report of thee.

And, above Godstow Bridge, when hay-time's here
  In June, and many a scythe in sunshine flames,
    Men who through those wide fields of breezy grass
  Where black-winged swallows haunt the glittering Thames,
95   To bathe in the abandoned lasher[6] pass,
        Have often passed thee near
  Sitting upon the river bank o'ergrown;
    Marked thine outlandish garb, thy figure spare,
    Thy dark vague eyes, and soft abstracted air—
100   But, when they came from bathing, thou wast gone!

At some lone homestead in the Cumner hills,
  Where at her open door the housewife darns,
    Thou hast been seen, or hanging on a gate
  To watch the threshers in the mossy barns.
105   Children, who early range these slopes and late
        For cresses from the rills,
  Have known thee eying, all an April-day,

---

5. I.e., as the rope tying the small boat to the bank shifts around.

6. Slack water above a weir or dam, or the weir itself.

The springing pastures and the feeding kine;
And marked thee, when the stars come out and shine,
110   Through the long dewy grass move slow away.

In autumn, on the skirts of Bagley Wood—
Where most the gypsies by the turf-edged way
        Pitch their smoked tents, and every bush you see
With scarlet patches tagged and shreds of gray,
115   Above the forest-ground called Thessaly—
            The blackbird, picking food,
Sees thee, nor stops his meal, nor fears at all;
        So often has he known thee past him stray,
        Rapt, twirling in thy hand a withered spray,
120   And waiting for the spark from heaven to fall.

And once, in winter, on the causeway chill
Where home through flooded fields foot-travelers go,
        Have I not passed thee on the wooden bridge,
Wrapt in thy cloak and battling with the snow,
125   Thy face tow'rd Hinksey and its wintry ridge?
            And thou hast climbed the hill,
And gained the white brow of the Cumner range;
        Turned once to watch, while thick the snowflakes fall,
        The line of festal light in Christ Church hall—
130   Then sought thy straw in some sequestered grange.

But what—I dream! Two hundred years are flown
Since first thy story ran through Oxford halls,
        And the grave Glanvil did the tale inscribe
That thou wert wandered from the studious walls
135   To learn strange arts, and join a gypsy-tribe;
            And thou from earth art gone
Long since, and in some quiet churchyard laid—
        Some country-nook, where o'er thy unknown grave
        Tall grasses and white flowering nettles wave,
140   Under a dark, red-fruited yew-tree's shade.

—No, no, thou hast not felt the lapse of hours!
For what wears out the life of mortal men?
        'Tis that from change to change their being rolls;
        'Tis that repeated shocks, again, again,
145   Exhaust the energy of strongest souls
            And numb the elastic powers.
Till having used our nerves with bliss and teen,°   *vexation*
        And tired upon a thousand schemes our wit,
        To the just-pausing Genius[7] we remit
150   Our worn-out life, and are—what we have been.

Thou hast not lived, why should'st thou perish, so?
Thou hadst *one* aim, *one* business, *one* desire;
        Else wert thou long since numbered with the dead!

7. In classical mythology, the protecting spirit assigned to each being to see it through the world and
finally to usher it out.

Else hadst thou spent, like other men, thy fire!
155   The generations of thy peers are fled.
    And we ourselves shall go;
  But thou possessest an immortal lot,
  And we imagine thee exempt from age
  And living as thou liv'st on Glanvil's page,
160   Because thou hadst—what we, alas! have not.

For early didst thou leave the world, with powers
  Fresh, undiverted to the world without,
    Firm to their mark, not spent on other things;
  Free from the sick fatigue, the languid doubt,
165   Which much to have tried, in much been baffled, brings.
    O life unlike to ours!
Who fluctuate idly without term or scope,
  Of whom each strives, nor knows for what he strives,
  And each half lives a hundred different lives;[8]
170   Who wait like thee, but not, like thee, in hope.

Thou waitest for the spark from heaven! and we,
  Light half-believers of our casual creeds,
    Who never deeply felt, nor clearly willed,
  Whose insight never has borne fruit in deeds,
175   Whose vague resolves never have been fulfilled;
    For whom each year we see
Breeds new beginnings, disappointments new;
  Who hesitate and falter life away,
  And lose tomorrow the ground won today—
180   Ah! do not we, wanderer! await it too?

Yes, we await it! but it still delays,
  And then we suffer! and amongst us one,[9]
    Who most has suffered, takes dejectedly
  His seat upon the intellectual throne;
185   And all his store of sad experience he
    Lays bare of wretched days;
Tells us his misery's birth and growth and signs,
  And how the dying spark of hope was fed,
  And how the breast was soothed, and how the head,
190   And all his hourly varied anodynes.

This for our wisest! and we others pine,
  And wish the long unhappy dream would end,
    And waive all claim to bliss, and try to bear;
  With close-lipped patience for our only friend,
195   Sad patience, too near neighbor to despair—
    But none has hope like thine!
Thou through the fields and through the woods dost stray,
  Roaming the countryside, a truant boy,
  Nursing thy project in unclouded joy,
200   And every doubt long blown by time away.

---

8. I.e., half-heartedly lives a hundred different lives.

9. Both Goethe and Tennyson have been suggested as being meant here.

O born in days when wits were fresh and clear,
   And life ran gaily as the sparkling Thames;
      Before this strange disease of modern life,
   With its sick hurry, its divided aims,
205   Its head o'ertaxed, its palsied hearts, was rife—
        Fly hence, our contact fear!
   Still fly, plunge deeper in the bowering wood!
      Averse, as Dido did with gesture stern
      From her false friend's approach in Hades turn,[1]
210   Wave us away, and keep thy solitude!

Still nursing the unconquerable hope,
   Still clutching the inviolable shade,
      With a free, onward impulse brushing through,
   By night, the silvered branches of the glade—
215   Far on the forest-skirts, where none pursue,
        On some mild pastoral slope
   Emerge, and resting on the moonlit pales°   *fences*
      Freshen thy flowers as in former years
      With dew, or listen with enchanted ears,
220   From the dark dingles,° to the nightingales!   *valleys*

But fly our paths, our feverish contact fly!
   For strong the infection of our mental strife,
      Which, though it gives no bliss, yet spoils for rest;
   And we should win thee from thy own fair life,
225   Like us distracted, and like us unblest.
        Soon, soon thy cheer would die,
   Thy hopes grow timorous, and unfixed thy powers,
      And thy clear aims be cross and shifting made;
      And then thy glad perennial youth would fade,
230   Fade, and grow old at last, and die like ours.

Then fly our greetings, fly our speech and smiles!
   —As some grave Tyrian[2] trader, from the sea,
      Descried at sunrise an emerging prow
   Lifting the cool-haired creepers stealthily,
235   The fringes of a southward-facing brow
        Among the Aegean isles;
   And saw the merry Grecian coaster come,
      Freighted with amber grapes, and Chian[3] wine,
      Green, bursting figs, and tunnies steeped in brine—
240   And knew the intruders on his ancient home,

The young light-hearted masters of the waves—
   And snatched his rudder, he shook out more sail;
      And day and night held on indignantly
   O'er the blue Midland waters with the gale,
245   Betwixt the Syrtes[4] and soft Sicily,

1. Dido, queen of Carthage, had been deserted by Aeneas after giving her love to him. Aeneas later encountered her in the underworld, among the shades of those who had died of unhappy love, but when he greeted her she turned her back on him.
2. A native of the ancient Phoenician city of Tyre, in the eastern Mediterranean.
3. From the island of Chios, famous for its wine.
4. Two gulfs on the North African coast, one off Cyrenaica, the other off Tunisia.

To where the Atlantic raves
Outside the western straits;[5] and unbent sails
There, where down cloudy cliffs, through sheets of foam,
Shy traffickers, the dark Iberians[6] come;
250   And on the beach undid his corded bales.

1853

Thyrsis

A Monody,[7] to Commemorate the Author's Friend, Arthur Hugh Clough, Who Died at Florence, 1861[8]

How changed is here each spot man makes or fills!
In the two Hinkseys[9] nothing keeps the same;
The village street its haunted mansion lacks,
And from the sign is gone Sibylla's name,[1]
5   And from the roofs the twisted chimney-stacks—
Are ye too changed, ye hills?
See, 'tis no foot of unfamiliar men
Tonight from Oxford up your pathway strays!
Here came I often, often, in old days—
10   Thyrsis and I; we still had Thyrsis then.

Runs it not here, the track by Childsworth Farm,
Past the high wood, to where the elm-tree crowns
The hill behind whose ridge the sunset flames?
The signal-elm, that looks on Ilsley Downs,
15   The Vale, the three lone weirs,° the youthful Thames?   *river-dams*
This winter-eve is warm,
Humid the air! leafless, yet soft as spring,
The tender purple spray on copse and briers!
And that sweet city with her dreaming spires,
20   She needs not June for beauty's heightening,

Lovely all times she lies, lovely tonight!
Only, methinks, some loss of habit's power
Befalls me wandering through this upland dim.
Once passed I blindfold here, at any hour;
25   Now seldom come I, since I came with him.
That single elm-tree bright
Against the west—I miss it! is it gone?
We prized it dearly; while it stood, we said,
Our friend, the Gypsy-Scholar, was not dead;
30   While the tree lived, he in these fields lived on.

---

5. I.e., the Straits of Gibraltar.
6. Ancient name for the inhabitants of Spain.
7. Species of poem in which a single mourner laments.
8. The friendship between Arnold and Clough (1819–1861), himself a distinguished poet, had been at its closest while they were at Oxford, and Arnold chooses as the framework for his poem a visit to Oxford—at least in reminiscence—and more specifically to a hill above the town crowned by the signal-elm. The tree had had a particular significance for them, since they connected it with the continuing symbolic presence in the country-side of the Scholar-Gypsy and his lonely faithful-ness to an ideal of truth-seeking. (See Arnold's poem "The Scholar-Gypsy" and his note to it, above.) As the name Thyrsis (and later, Corydon) indicates, Arnold is adopting the conventions of the Greek and Latin pastoral elegy for his poem.
9. Two villages (North and South Hinksey) near Oxford.
1. Sibylla Kerr, a tavern-keeper when Arnold and Clough were students.

Too rare, too rare, grow now my visits here,
But once I knew each field, each flower, each stick;
And with the country-folk acquaintance made
By barn in threshing-time, by new-built rick.
35   Here, too, our shepherd-pipes we first assayed.
Ah me! this many a year
My pipe is lost, my shepherd's holiday!
Needs must I lose them, needs with heavy heart
Into the world and wave of men depart;
40   But Thyrsis of his own will went away.[2]

It irked him to be here, he could not rest.
He loved each simple joy the country yields,
He loved his mates; but yet he could not keep,
For that a shadow loured on the fields,
45   Here with the shepherds and the silly° sheep.   *innocent*
Some life of men unblest
He knew, which made him droop; and filled his head.
He went; his piping took a troubled sound
Of storms that rage outside our happy ground;
50   He could not wait their passing, he is dead.

So, some tempestuous morn in early June,
When the year's primal burst of bloom is o'er,
Before the roses and the longest day—
When garden-walks and all the grassy floor
55   With blossoms red and white of fallen May
And chestnut-flowers are strewn—
So have I heard the cuckoo's parting cry,
From the wet field, through the vext garden-trees,
Come with the volleying rain and tossing breeze:
60   *The bloom is gone, and with the bloom go I!*

Too quick despairer, wherefore wilt thou go?
Soon will the high Midsummer pomps come on,
Soon will the musk carnations break and swell,
Soon shall we have gold-dusted snapdragon,
65   Sweet-William with his homely cottage-smell,
And stocks in fragrant blow;
Roses that down the alleys shine afar,
And open, jasmine-muffled lattices,
And groups under the dreaming garden-trees,
70   And the full moon, and the white evening-star.

He hearkens not! light comer, he is flown!
What matters it? next year he will return,
And we shall have him in the sweet spring-days,
With whitening hedges, and uncrumpling fern,
75   And bluebells trembling by the forest-ways,
And scent of hay new-mown.
But Thyrsis never more we swains shall see;

2. Clough resigned his fellowship at Oxford in 1848, rather than subscribe to the Thirty-nine Articles of
the Anglican Church.

See him come back, and cut a smoother reed,
  And blow a strain the world at last shall heed—
80 For Time, not Corydon, hath conquered thee!

Alack, for Corydon no rival now!
  But when Sicilian shepherds lost a mate,
    Some good survivor with his flute would go,
  Piping a ditty sad for Bion's fate;[3]
85   And cross the unpermitted ferry's flow,[4]
      And relax Pluto's brow,
  And make leap up with joy the beauteous head
Of Proserpine, among whose crownéd hair
Are flowers first opened on Sicilian air,
90 And flute his friend, like Orpheus,[5] from the dead.

O easy access to the hearer's grace
  When Dorian[6] shepherds sang to Proserpine!
    For she herself had trod Sicilian fields,
  She knew the Dorian water's gush divine,
95   She knew each lily white which Enna yields,
      Each rose with blushing face;
  She loved the Dorian pipe, the Dorian strain.
But ah, of our poor Thames she never heard!
Her foot the Cumner cowslips never stirred;
100 And we should tease her with our plaint in vain!

Well! wind-dispersed and vain the words will be,
  Yet, Thyrsis, let me give my grief its hour
    In the old haunt, and find our tree-topped hill!
  Who, if not I, for questing here hath power?
105   I know the wood which hides the daffodil,
      I know the Fyfield tree,
  I know what white, what purple fritillaries°   *flowers*
    The grassy harvest of the river-fields,
    Above by Ensham, down by Sandford, yields,
110 And what sedged brooks are Thames's tributaries;

I know these slopes; who knows them if not I?
  But many a dingle° on the loved hillside,   *valley*
    With thorns once studded, old, white-blossomed trees,
  Where thick the cowslips grew, and far descried
115   High towered the spikes of purple orchises,
      Hath since our day put by
  The coronals of that forgotten time;[7]
    Down each green bank hath gone the ploughboy's team,

---

3. Refers to a Greek pastoral poet of the first century B.C. who lived in Sicily and who was mourned in "Lament for Bion," sometimes ascribed to his pupil Moschus.
4. The ferry across the river Styx to Hades, ruled over by Pluto and his queen, Proserpine, whom he had abducted while she was gathering flowers in the fields near Enna, in Sicily. She spent half of

each year in the underworld and half on Earth.
5. Orpheus, because of the power and charm of his music, had been permitted to attempt to lead his wife, Eurydice, back from the dead.
6. One of the ancient Greek lyrical modes, characterized by simplicity and nobility.
7. I.e., the flowers that once crowned them.

And only in the hidden brookside gleam
120   Primroses, orphans of the flowery prime.

Where is the girl, who by the boatman's door,
    Above the locks, above the boating throng,
        Unmoored our skiff when through the Wytham flats,
    Red loosestrife and blond meadow-sweet among
125   And darting swallows and light water-gnats,
            We tracked the shy Thames shore?
    Where are the mowers, who, as the tiny swell
        Of our boat passing heaved the river-grass,
        Stood with suspended scythe to see us pass?
130   They all are gone, and thou art gone as well!

Yes, thou art gone! and round me too the night
    In ever-nearing circle weaves her shade.
        I see her veil draw soft across the day,
    I feel her slowly chilling breath invade
135   The cheek grown thin, the brown hair sprent° with gray;   *sprinkled*
            I feel her finger light
    Laid pausefully upon life's headlong train;
        The foot less prompt to meet the morning dew,
        The heart less bounding at emotion new,
140   And hope, once crushed, less quick to spring again.

And long the way appears, which seemed so short
    To the less practiced eye of sanguine youth;
        And high the mountain-tops, in cloudy air,
    The mountain-tops where is the throne of Truth,
145   Tops in life's morning-sun so bright and bare!
            Unbreachable the fort
    Of the long-battered world uplifts its wall;
        And strange and vain the earthly turmoil grows,
        And near and real the charm of thy repose,
150   And night as welcome as a friend would fall.

But hush! the upland hath a sudden loss
    Of quiet!—Look, adown the dusk hillside,
        A troop of Oxford hunters going home,
    As in old days, jovial and talking, ride!
155   From hunting with the Berkshire hounds they come.
            Quick! let me fly, and cross
    Into yon farther field!—'Tis done; and see,
        Backed by the sunset, which doth glorify
        The orange and pale violet evening-sky,
160   Bare on its lonely ridge, the Tree! the Tree!

I take the omen! Eve lets down her veil,
    The white fog creeps from bush to bush about,
        The west unflushes, the high stars grow bright,
    And in the scattered farms the lights come out.
165   I cannot reach the signal-tree to-night,

Yet, happy omen, hail!
Hear it from thy broad lucent Arno-vale[8]
(For there thine earth-forgetting eyelids keep
The morningless and unawakening sleep
170   Under the flowery oleanders pale),

Hear it, O Thyrsis, still our tree is there!
Ah, vain! These English fields, this upland dim,
These brambles pale with mist engarlanded,
That lone, sky-pointing tree, are not for him;
175   To a boon southern country he is fled,
And now in happier air,
Wandering with the great Mother's train divine[9]
(And purer or more subtle soul than thee,
I trow, the mighty Mother doth not see)
180   Within a folding of the Apennine,[1]

Thou hearest the immortal chants of old!
Putting his sickle to the perilous grain
In the hot cornfield of the Phrygian king,
For thee the Lityerses-song again
185   Young Daphnis with his silver voice doth sing;[2]
Sings his Sicilian fold,
His sheep, his hapless love, his blinded eyes—
And how a call celestial round him rang,
And heavenward from the fountain-brink he sprang,
190   And all the marvel of the golden skies.

There thou art gone, and me thou leavest here
Sole in these fields! yet will I not despair.
Despair I will not, while I yet descry
Neath the mild canopy of English air
195   That lonely tree against the western sky.
Still, still these slopes, 'tis clear,
Our Gypsy-Scholar haunts, outliving thee!
Fields where soft sheep from cages pull the hay,
Woods with anemonies in flower till May,
200   Know him a wanderer still; then why not me?

A fugitive and gracious light he seeks,
Shy to illumine; and I seek it too.
This does not come with houses or with gold,

8. Clough is buried in the Protestant cemetery in Florence, through which city the Arno flows.
9. The devotees of Cubele (Rhea), "the Great Mother," mother of the gods.
1. The Apennines are a mountain range in Italy.
2. "Daphnis, the ideal Sicilian shepherd of Greek pastoral poetry, was said to have followed into Phrygia his mistress Piplea, who had been carried off by robbers, and to have found her in the power of the king of Phrygia, Lityerses. Lityerses used to make strangers try a contest with him in reaping corn, and to put them to death if he overcame them. Hercules arrived in time to save Daphnis, took upon himself the reaping-contest with Lity-erses, overcame him, and slew him. The Lityerses-song connected with this tradition was, like the Linus-song, one of the early plaintive strains of Greek popular poetry, and used to be sung by corn-reapers. Other traditions represented Daphnis as beloved by a nymph who exacted from him an oath to love no one else. He fell in love with a princess, and was struck blind by the jealous nymph. Mercury, who was his father, raised him to heaven, and made a fountain spring up in the place from which he ascended. At this fountain the Sicilians offered yearly sacrifices.—See Servius, *Comment. in Virgil. Bucol.*, v.20 and viii.68" [Arnold's note].

With place, with honor, and a flattering crew;
205   'Tis not in the world's market bought and sold—
          But the smooth-slipping weeks
Drop by, and leave its seeker still untired;
      Out of the heed of mortals he is gone,
      He wends unfollowed, he must house alone;
210 Yet on he fares, by his own heart inspired.

Thou too, O Thyrsis, on like quest wast bound;
      Thou wanderest with me for a little hour!
          Men gave thee nothing; but this happy quest,
      If men esteemed thee feeble, gave thee power,
215   If men procured thee trouble, gave thee rest.
          And this rude Cumner ground,
      Its fir-topped Hurst, its farms, its quiet fields,
      Here cam'st thou in thy jocund youthful time,
      Here was thine height of strength, thy golden prime!
220 And still the haunt beloved a virtue yields.

What though the music of thy rustic flute
      Kept not for long its happy, country tone;
          Lost it too soon, and learnt a stormy note
      Of men contention-tost, of men who groan,
225   Which tasked thy pipe too sore, and tired thy throat—
          It failed, and thou wast mute!
      Yet hadst thou alway visions of our light,
      And long with men of care thou couldst not stay,
      And soon thy foot resumed its wandering way,
230 Left human haunt, and on alone till night.

Too rare, too rare, grow now my visits here!
      'Mid city-noise, not, as with thee of yore,
          Thyrsis! in reach of sheep-bells is my home.
      —Then through the great town's harsh, heart-wearying roar,
235   Let in thy voice a whisper often come,
          To chase fatigue and fear:
      Why faintest thou? I wandered till I died.
      Roam on! The light we sought is shining still.
      Dost thou ask proof? Our tree yet crowns the hill,
240 *Our Scholar travels yet the loved hillside.*

                                                    1866

Dover Beach

      The sea is calm tonight.
      The tide is full, the moon lies fair
      Upon the straits; on the French coast the light
      Gleams and is gone; the cliffs of England stand,
5   Glimmering and vast, out in the tranquil bay.
      Come to the window, sweet is the night-air!
      Only, from the long line of spray
      Where the sea meets the moon-blanched land,
      Listen! you hear the grating roar

10 Of pebbles which the waves draw back, and fling,
At their return, up the high strand,
Begin, and cease, and then again begin,
With tremulous cadence slow, and bring
The eternal note of sadness in.

15 Sophocles long ago
Heard it on the Aegean, and it brought
Into his mind the turbid ebb and flow
Of human misery;[3] we
Find also in the sound a thought,
20 Hearing it by this distant northern sea.

The Sea of Faith
Was once, too, at the full, and round earth's shore
Lay like the folds of a bright girdle furled.
But now I only hear
25 Its melancholy, long withdrawing roar,
Retreating, to the breath
Of the night-wind, down the vast edges drear
And naked shingles[4] of the world.

Ah, love, let us be true
30 To one another! for the world, which seems
To lie before us like a land of dreams,
So various, so beautiful, so new,
Hath really neither joy, nor love, nor light,
Nor certitude, nor peace, nor help for pain;
35 And we are here as on a darkling plain
Swept with confused alarms of struggle and flight,
Where ignorant armies clash by night.

1867

DANTE GABRIEL ROSSETTI
1828–1882

The Blessed Damozel[1]

The blessed damozel leaned out
From the gold bar of Heaven;
Her eyes were deeper than the depth
Of waters stilled at even;
5 She had three lilies in her hand,
And the stars in her hair were seven.

Her robe, ungirt from clasp to hem,
No wrought flowers did adorn,

3. Compare Sophocles' *Antigone*, lines 583–91.
4. Beaches covered with water-worn small stones and pebbles.
1. Older form of *damsel*, meaning "young unmar-ried lady," preferred by Romantic and later writers because it avoids the simpler, homelier associations of *damsel*.

But a white rose of Mary's gift,
10   For service meetly worn;
Her hair that lay along her back
    Was yellow like ripe corn.°   *wheat, grain*

Herseemed she scarce had been a day
    One of God's choristers;
15 The wonder was not yet quite gone
    From that still look of hers;
Albeit, to them she left, her day
    Had counted as ten years.

(To one, it is ten years of years.
20   . . . Yet now, and in this place,
Surely she leaned o'er me — her hair
    Fell all about my face. . . .
Nothing: the autumn fall of leaves.
    The whole year sets apace.)

25 It was the rampart of God's house
    That she was standing on;
By God built over the sheer depth
    The which is Space begun;
So high, that looking downward thence
30   She scarce could see the sun.

It lies in Heaven, across the flood
    Of ether, as a bridge.
Beneath, the tides of day and night
    With flame and darkness ridge
35 The void, as low as where this earth
    Spins like a fretful midge.

Around her, lovers, newly met
    In joy no sorrow claims,
Spoke evermore among themselves
40   Their rapturous new names;
And the souls mounting up to God
    Went by her like thin flames.

And still she bowed herself and stooped
    Out of the circling charm;
45 Until her bosom must have made
    The bar she leaned on warm,
And the lilies lay as if asleep
    Along her bended arm.

From the fixed place of Heaven she saw
50   Time like a pulse shake fierce
Through all the worlds. Her gaze still strove
    Within the gulf to pierce
Its path; and now she spoke as when
    The stars sang in their spheres.

55 The sun was gone now; the curled moon
   Was like a little feather
 Fluttering far down the gulf; and now
   She spoke through the still weather.
 Her voice was like the voice the stars
60   Had when they sang together.

   (Ah sweet! Even now, in that bird's song,
     Strove not her accents there,
   Fain to be hearkened? When those bells
     Possessed the midday air,
65   Strove not her steps to reach my side
     Down all the echoing stair?)

   "I wish that he were come to me,
     For he will come," she said.
   "Have I not prayed in Heaven?—on earth,
70   Lord, Lord, has he not prayed?
   Are not two prayers a perfect strength?
     And shall I feel afraid?

   "When round his head the aureole clings,
     And he is clothed in white,
75   I'll take his hand and go with him
     To the deep wells of light;
   We will step down as to a stream,
     And bathe there in God's sight.

   "We two will stand beside that shrine,
80   Occult, withheld, untrod,
   Whose lamps are stirred continually
     With prayer sent up to God;
   And see our old prayers, granted, melt
     Each like a little cloud.

85   "We two will lie i' the shadow of
     That living mystic tree
   Within whose secret growth the Dove
     Is sometimes felt to be,
   While every leaf that His plumes touch
90   Saith His Name audibly.

   "And I myself will teach to him,
     I myself, lying so,
   The songs I sing here; which his voice
     Shall pause in, hushed and slow,
95   And find some knowledge at each pause,
     Of some new thing to know."

   (Alas! We two, we two, thou say'st!
     Yea, one wast thou with me
   That once of old. But shall God lift
100   To endless unity

The soul whose likeness with thy soul
    Was but its love for thee?)

"We two," she said, "will seek the groves
    Where the lady Mary is,
105 With her five handmaidens, whose names
    Are five sweet symphonies,
Cecily, Gertrude, Magdalen,
    Margaret and Rosalys.

"Circlewise sit they, with bound locks
110   And foreheads garlanded;
Into the fine cloth white like flame
    Weaving the golden thread,
To fashion the birth-robes for them
    Who are just born, being dead.

115 "He shall fear, haply, and be dumb:
    Then will I lay my cheek
To his, and tell about our love,
    Not once abashed or weak:
And the dear Mother will approve
120   My pride, and let me speak.

"Herself shall bring us, hand in hand,
    To Him round whom all souls
Kneel, the clear-ranged unnumbered heads
    Bowed with their aureoles:
125 And angels meeting us shall sing
    To their citherns and citoles.[2]

"There will I ask of Christ the Lord
    Thus much for him and me: —
Only to live as once on earth
130   With Love — only to be,
As then awhile, forever now
    Together, I and he."

She gazed and listened and then said,
    Less sad of speech than mild,
135 "All this is when he comes." She ceased.
    The light thrilled towards her, filled
With angels in strong level flight.
    Her eyes prayed, and she smiled.

(I saw her smile.) But soon their path
140   Was vague in distant spheres:
And then she cast her arms along
    The golden barriers,

---

2. Antique musical instruments: the cithern (seventeenth century), a guitarlike instrument with wire strings; the citole, a stringed instrument dating from the thirteenth to the fifteenth century.

And laid her face between her hands,
And wept. (I heard her tears.)

1846   1850

Sudden Light

I have been here before,
  But when or how I cannot tell:
I know the grass beyond the door,
  The sweet keen smell,
5   The sighing sound, the lights around the shore.

You have been mine before,
  How long ago I may not know:
But just when at that swallow's soar
  Your neck turned so,
10   Some veil did fall—I knew it all of yore.

Has this been thus before?
  And shall not thus time's eddying flight
Still with our lives our love restore
  In death's despite,
15   And day and night yield one delight once more?

1854   1863

The Woodspurge

The wind flapped loose, the wind was still,
Shaken out dead from tree and hill:
I had walked on at the wind's will—
I sat now, for the wind was still.

5   Between my knees my forehead was—
My lips, drawn in, said not Alas!
My hair was over in the grass,
My naked ears heard the day pass.

My eyes, wide open, had the run
10   Of some ten weeds to fix upon;
Among those few, out of the sun,
The woodspurge flowered, three cups in one.

From perfect grief there need not be
Wisdom or even memory:
15   One thing then learnt remains to me—
The woodspurge has a cup of three.

1856   1870

From The House of Life

A Sonnet

A Sonnet is a moment's monument,—
   Memorial from the Soul's eternity
   To one dead deathless hour. Look that it be,
Whether for lustral° rite or dire portent,   *purificatory*
5 Of its own arduous fullness reverent:
   Carve it in ivory or in ebony,
   As Day or Night may rule; and let Time see
Its flowering crest impearled and orient.

A Sonnet is a coin: its face reveals
10 The soul—its converse, to what Power 'tis due:
Whether for tribute to the august appeals
   Of Life, or dower in Love's high retinue,
It serve; or, 'mid the dark wharf's cavernous breath,
In Charon's³ palm it pay the toll to Death.

19. *Silent Noon*

Your hands lie open in the long fresh grass—
   The finger-points look through like rosy blooms:
   Your eyes smile peace. The pasture gleams and glooms
'Neath billowing skies that scatter and amass.
5 All round our nest, far as the eye can pass,
   Are golden kingcup-fields with silver edge
   Where the cow-parsley skirts the hawthorn-hedge.
'Tis visible silence, still as the hour-glass.

Deep in the sun-searched growths the dragonfly
10 Hangs like a blue thread loosened from the sky:
   So this winged hour is dropt to us from above.
Oh! clasp we to our hearts, for deathless dower,
This close-companioned inarticulate hour
   When twofold silence was the song of love.

70. *The Hill Summit*

This feast-day of the sun, his altar there
   In the broad west has blazed for vesper-song;
   And I have loitered in the vale too long
And gaze now a belated worshipper.
5 Yet may I not forget that I was 'ware,
   So journeying, of his face at intervals
   Transfigured where the fringed horizon falls,
A fiery bush with coruscating° hair.   *glittering*

And now that I have climbed and won this height,
10 I must tread downward through the sloping shade
   And travel the bewildered tracks till night.

---

3. Charon received a coin, an *obolus,* for ferrying the shades of the newly dead across the river Styx to Hades.

Yet for this hour I still may here be stayed
And see the gold air and the silver fade
And the last bird fly into the last light.

83. Barren Spring

Once more the changed year's turning wheel returns:
    And as a girl sails balanced in the wind,
    And now before and now again behind
Stoops as it swoops, with cheek that laughs and burns—
5   So Spring comes merry towards me here, but earns
    No answering smile from me, whose life is twined
    With the dead boughs that winter still must bind,
And whom to-day the Spring no more concerns.

Behold, this crocus is a withering flame;
10 This snowdrop, snow; this apple-blossom's part
    To breed the fruit that breeds the serpent's art.
Nay, for these Spring-flowers, turn thy face from them,
    Nor gaze till on the year's last lily-stem
    The white cup shrivels round the golden heart.

91. Lost on Both Sides

As when two men have loved a woman well,
    Each hating each, through Love's and Death's deceit;
    Since not for either this stark marriage-sheet
And the long pauses of this wedding-bell;
5   Yet o'er her grave the night and day dispel
    At last their feud forlorn, with cold and heat;
    Nor other than dear friends to death may fleet
The two lives left that most of her can tell:

So separate hopes, which in a soul had wooed
10 The one same Peace, strove with each other long,
    And Peace before their faces perished since:
So through that soul, in restless brotherhood,
    They roam together now, and wind among
    Its bye-streets, knocking at the dusty inns.

97. A Superscription

Look in my face; my name is Might-have-been;
    I am also called No-more, Too-late, Farewell;
    Unto thine ear I hold the dead-sea shell
Cast up thy Life's foam-fretted feet between;
5   Unto thine eyes the glass where that is seen
    Which had Life's form and Love's, but by my spell
    Is now a shaken shadow intolerable,
Of ultimate things unuttered the frail screen.

Mark me, how still I am! But should there dart
10 One moment through thy soul the soft surprise
    Of that winged Peace which lulls the breath of sighs,
Then shalt thou see me smile, and turn apart

Thy visage to mine ambush at thy heart
Sleepless with cold commemorative eyes.

1847–80   1870, 1881

GEORGE MEREDITH

1828–1909

Modern Love[1]

1

By this he knew she wept with waking eyes:
That, at his hand's light quiver by her head,
The strange low sobs that shook their common bed
Were called into her with a sharp surprise,
5 And strangled mute, like little gaping snakes,
Dreadfully venomous to him. She lay
Stone-still, and the long darkness flowed away
With muffled pulses. Then, as midnight makes
Her giant heart of Memory and Tears
10 Drink the pale drug of silence, and so beat
Sleep's heavy measure, they from head to feet
Were moveless, looking through their dead black years,
By vain regret scrawled over the blank wall.
Like sculptured effigies they might be seen
15 Upon their marriage-tomb,[2] the sword between;
Each wishing for the sword that severs all.

17

At dinner, she is hostess, I am host.
Went the feast ever cheerfuller? She keeps
The Topic over intellectual deeps
In buoyancy afloat. They see no ghost.
5 With sparkling surface-eyes we ply the ball:
It is in truth a most contagious game:
HIDING THE SKELETON, shall be its name.
Such play as this the devils might appall!
But here's the greater wonder; in that we,
10 Enamored of an acting naught can tire,
Each other, like true hypocrites, admire;
Warm-lighted looks, Love's ephemerioe,[3]
Shoot gaily o'er the dishes and the wine.
We waken envy of our happy lot.
15 Fast, sweet, and golden, shows the marriage-knot.
Dear guests, you now have seen Love's corpse-light shine.

---

1. *Modern Love* is a sequence of fifty sixteen-line sonnets, a kind of novel in verse about the breakup of a marriage. For most of the sequence the husband is the speaker, but the opening and closing sections are told in the third person.

2. I.e., as motionless as sculptured stone statues on a tomb. In medieval legend, a naked sword between lovers symbolized chastity.

3. Short-lived creatures.

30

What are we first? First, animals; and next
Intelligences at a leap; on whom
Pale lies the distant shadow of the tomb,
And all that draweth on the tomb for text.
5 Into which state comes Love, the crowning sun:
Beneath whose light the shadow loses form.
We are the lords of life, and life is warm.
Intelligence and instinct now are one.
But nature says: "My children most they seem
10 When they least know me: therefore I decree
That they shall suffer." Swift doth young Love flee,
And we stand wakened, shivering from our dream.
Then if we study Nature we are wise.
Thus do the few who live but with the day:
15 The scientific animals are they—
Lady, this is my sonnet to your eyes.[4]

48

Their sense is with their senses all mixed in,
Destroyed by subtleties these women are![5]
More brain, O Lord, more brain! or we shall mar
Utterly this fair garden we might win.
5 Behold! I looked for peace, and thought it near.
Our inmost hearts had opened, each to each.
We drank the pure daylight of honest speech.
Alas! that was the fatal draught, I fear.
For when of my lost Lady came the word,
10 This woman, O this agony of flesh!
Jealous devotion bade her break the mesh,
That I might seek that other like a bird.
I do adore the nobleness! despise
The act! She has gone forth, I know not where.
15 Will the hard world my sentience of her share?
I feel the truth; so let the world surmise.

49

He found her by the ocean's moaning verge,
Nor any wicked change in her discerned;
And she believed his old love had returned,
Which was her exultation, and her scourge.
5 She took his hand, and walked with him, and seemed
The wife he sought, though shadow-like and dry.
She had one terror, lest her heart should sigh,
And tell her loudly she no longer dreamed.
She dared not say, "This is my breast: look in."

4. A poetic convention of love sonnets was the praise of one of the lady's features, such as her eyes. Meredith uses it as an ironic close to a statement of his theory of evolution.
5. Earlier, the couple had at last talked together about the wife's affair with another man, and had become reconciled. But when the husband tells her of his own recent passing affair with his "lost Lady" (line 9), she resolves to give him up to his mistress. Her resolve is a noble one but, in his view, without "sense" or "brain."

10   But there's a strength to help the desperate weak.
      That night he learned how silence best can speak
      The awful things when Pity pleads for Sin.
      About the middle of the night her call
      Was heard, and he came wondering to the bed.
15   "Now kiss me, dear! it may be, now!" she said.
      Lethe[6] had passed those lips, and he knew all.

50

      Thus piteously Love closed what he begat:
      The union of this ever-diverse pair!
      These two were rapid falcons in a snare,
      Condemned to do the flitting of the bat.
5   Lovers beneath the singing sky of May,
      They wandered once; clear as the dew on flowers:
      But they fed not on the advancing hours:
      Their hearts held cravings for the buried day.
      Then each applied to each that fatal knife,
10   Deep questioning, which probes to endless dole.°   *sorrow*
      Ah, what a dusty answer gets the soul
      When hot for certainties in this our life!—
      In tragic hints here see what evermore
      Moves dark as yonder midnight ocean's force,
15   Thundering like ramping° hosts of warrior horse,   *rearing*
      To throw that faint thin line upon the shore!

1862

Lucifer in Starlight

      On a starred night Prince Lucifer uprose.
      Tired of his dark dominion, swung the fiend
      Above the rolling ball, in cloud part screened,
      Where sinners hugged their specter of repose.
5   Poor prey to his hot fit of pride were those.
      And now upon his western wing he leaned,
      Now his huge bulk o'er Afric's sands careened,
      Now the black planet shadowed Arctic snows.
      Soaring through wider zones that pricked his scars
10   With memory of the old revolt from Awe,[7]
      He reached a middle height, and at the stars,
      Which are the brain of heaven, he looked, and sank.
      Around the ancient track marched, rank on rank,
      The army of unalterable law.

1883

---

6. River of forgetfulness in Hades, the mythological Greek underworld.
7. I.e., God. Satan is reminded of the wounds he suffered when his revolt against God was crushed and he was hurled from heaven into hell.

EMILY DICKINSON*
1830–1886

49

I never lost as much but twice,
And that was in the sod.
Twice have I stood a beggar
Before the door of God!

5   Angels—twice descending
Reimbursed my store—
Burglar! Banker—Father!
I am poor once more!

1890

59

A little East of Jordan,
Evangelists record,[1]
A Gymnast and an Angel
Did wrestle long and hard—

5   Till morning touching mountain—
And Jacob, waxing strong,
The Angel begged permission
To Breakfast—to return—

Not so, said cunning Jacob!
10   "I will not let thee go
Except thou bless me"—Stranger!
The which acceded to—

Light swung the silver fleeces[2]
"Peniel" Hills beyond,
15   And the bewildered Gymnast
Found he had worsted God!

ca. 1859

1914

67

Success is counted sweetest
By those who ne'er succeed.
To comprehend a nectar
Requires sorest need.

---

* The order and numbering of the poems are those established by Thomas H. Johnson in his *Poems of Emily Dickinson* (1955).
1. The story actually occurs in Genesis 32.24–30. Jacob wrestled with the angel for a blessing; having succeeded, "Jacob called the place Peniel: for I have seen God face to face, and my life is preserved."
2. Clouds; also, a possible allusion to the Golden Fleece, of Greek myth, that Jason long traveled to find.

5 Not one of all the purple Host°   *army*
  Who took the Flag today
  Can tell the definition
  So clear of Victory

  As he defeated—dying—
10 On whose forbidden ear
  The distant strains of triumph
  Burst agonized and clear!

ca. 1859   1878

185

"Faith" is a fine invention
When Gentlemen can *see*—
But *Microscopes* are prudent
In an Emergency.

ca. 1860   1891

216

Safe in their Alabaster[3] Chambers—
Untouched by Morning
And untouched by Noon—
Sleep the meek members of the Resurrection—
5 Rafter of satin,
  And Roof of stone.

Light laughs the breeze
In her Castle above them—
Babbles the Bee in a stolid Ear,
10 Pipe the Sweet Birds in ignorant cadence—
  Ah, what sagacity perished here!

version of 1859   1862

216[4]

Safe in their Alabaster Chambers—
Untouched by Morning—
And untouched by Noon—
Lie the meek members of the Resurrection—
5 Rafter of Satin—and Roof of Stone!

3. Translucent white mineral.
4. The composition of this poem illustrates Dickinson's characteristic trying and retrying of various articulations of her poetic idea. The 1859 version was sent to Sue Dickinson, her sister-in-law, for advice, and Sue evidently did not like it much. The notes between the two women (they lived in adjoining houses) show Dickinson's labors over the poem, and her 1861 version was an attempt to meet her own and Sue's exactions. It was printed once during her lifetime (1862) in the 1859 version, but when she began her famous correspondence with Thomas W. Higginson, the literary critic and editor, she sent a modified version of the 1861 poem. When Higginson edited Emily Dickinson's poetry for posthumous publication (1890), he combined the two versions, and it is this three-stanza poem that readers had known as Dickinson's until Thomas H. Johnson's definitive edition of the poems in 1955.

Grand go the Years—in the Crescent—above them—
Worlds scoop their Arcs—
And Firmaments—row—
Diadems°—drop—and Doges⁵—surrender—   *crowns*
10   Soundless as dots—on a Disc of Snow—
version of 1861   1890

241

I like a look of Agony,
Because I know it's true—
Men do not sham Convulsion,
Nor simulate, a Throe—

5   The Eyes glaze once—and that is Death—
Impossible to feign
The Beads upon the Forehead
By homely Anguish strung.

ca. 1861   1890

249

Wild Nights—Wild Nights!
Were I with thee
Wild Nights should be
Our luxury!

5   Futile—the Winds—
To a Heart in port—
Done with the Compass—
Done with the Chart!

Rowing in Eden—
10   Ah, the Sea!
Might I but moor—Tonight—
In Thee!

ca. 1861   1891

254

"Hope" is the thing with feathers—
That perches in the soul—
And sings the tune without the words—
And never stops—at all—

5   And sweetest—in the Gale—is heard—
And sore must be the storm—
That could abash the little Bird
That kept so many warm—

5. Chief magistrates in the republics of Venice and Genoa from the eleventh through the sixteenth centuries.

I've heard it in the chillest land—
10 And on the strangest Sea—
Yet, never, in Extremity,
It asked a crumb—of Me.

ca. 1861   1891

258

There's a certain Slant of light,
Winter Afternoons—
That oppresses, like the Heft
Of Cathedral Tunes—

5 Heavenly Hurt, it gives us—
We can find no scar,
But internal difference,
Where the Meanings, are—

None may teach it—Any—
10 'Tis the Seal Despair—
An imperial affliction
Sent us of the Air—

When it comes, the Landscape listens—
Shadows—hold their breath—
15 When it goes, 'tis like the Distance
On the look of Death—

ca. 1861   1890

280

I felt a Funeral, in my Brain,
And Mourners to and fro
Kept treading—treading—till it seemed
That Sense was breaking through—

5 And when they all were seated,
A Service, like a Drum—
Kept beating—beating—till I thought
My Mind was going numb—

And then I heard them lift a Box
10 And creak across my Soul
With those same Boots of Lead, again,
Then Space—began to toll,

As all the Heavens were a Bell,
And Being, but an Ear,
15 And I, and Silence, some strange Race
Wrecked, solitary, here—

And then a Plank in Reason, broke,
And I dropped down, and down—

And hit a World, at every plunge,
20 And Finished knowing—then—

ca. 1861   1896

287

A Clock stopped—
Not the Mantel's—
Geneva's farthest skill[6]
Can't put the puppet bowing—
5   That just now dangled still—

An awe came on the Trinket!
The Figures hunched, with pain—
Then quivered out of Decimals—
Into Degreeless Noon—

10   It will not stir for Doctors—
This Pendulum of snow—
This Shopman importunes it—
While cool—concernless No—

Nods from the Gilded pointers—
15   Nods from the Seconds slim—
Decades of Arrogance between
The Dial life—
And Him—

ca. 1861   1896

303

The Soul selects her own Society—
Then—shuts the Door—
To her divine Majority—
Present no more—

5   Unmoved—she notes the Chariots—pausing—
At her low Gate—
Unmoved—an Emperor be kneeling
Upon her Mat—

I've known her—from an ample nation—
10   Choose One—
Then—close the Valves of her attention—
Like Stone—

ca. 1862   1890

328

A Bird came down the Walk—
He did not know I saw—

6. Geneva, Switzerland, is traditionally famous for watchmaking.

He bit an Angleworm in halves
And ate the fellow, raw,

5   And then he drank a Dew
From a convenient Grass—
And then hopped sidewise to the Wall
To let a Beetle pass—

He glanced with rapid eyes
10   That hurried all around—
They looked like frightened Beads, I thought—
He stirred his Velvet Head

Like one in danger, Cautious,
I offered him a Crumb
15   And he unrolled his feathers
And rowed him softer home—

Than Oars divide the Ocean,
Too silver for a seam—
Or Butterflies, off Banks of Noon
20   Leap, plashless° as they swim.   *splashless*

ca. 1862   1891

341

After great pain, a formal feeling comes—
The Nerves sit ceremonious, like Tombs—
The stiff Heart questions was it He, that bore,
And Yesterday, or Centuries before?

5   The Feet, mechanical, go round—
Of Ground, or Air, or Ought[7]—
A Wooden way
Regardless grown,
A Quartz contentment, like a stone—

10   This is the Hour of Lead—
Remembered, if outlived,
As Freezing persons, recollect the Snow—
First—Chill—then Stupor—then the letting go—

ca. 1862   1929

435

Much Madness is divinest Sense—
To a discerning Eye—
Much Sense—the starkest Madness—
'Tis the Majority
5   In this, as All, prevail—
Assent—and you are sane—

7. Nothing, or anything.

Demur—you're straightway dangerous—
And handled with a Chain—

ca. 1862   1890

465

I heard a Fly buzz—when I died—
The Stillness in the Room
Was like the Stillness in the Air—
Between the Heaves of Storm—

5   The Eyes around—had wrung them dry—
And Breaths were gathering firm
For that last Onset—when the King
Be witnessed—in the Room—

I willed my Keepsakes—Signed away
10 What portion of me be
Assignable—and then it was
There interposed a Fly—

With Blue—uncertain stumbling Buzz—
Between the light—and me—
15 And then the Windows failed—and then
I could not see to see—

ca. 1862   1896

505

I would not paint—a picture—
I'd rather be the One
Its bright impossibility
To dwell—delicious—on—
5   And wonder how the fingers feel
Whose rare—celestial—stir—
Evokes so sweet a Torment—
Such sumptuous—Despair—

I would not talk, like Cornets—
10 I'd rather be the One
Raised softly to the Ceilings—
And out, and easy on—
Through Villages of Ether—
Myself endued° Balloon   endowed
15 By but a lip of Metal—
The pier to my Pontoon°—   boat

Nor would I be a Poet—
It's finer—own the Ear—
Enamored—impotent—content—
20 The License to revere,
A privilege so awful°   awesome
What would the Dower° be,   dowry, gift

Had I the Art to stun myself
With Bolts of Melody!

ca. 1862   1945

528

Mine—by the Right of the White Election!
Mine—by the Royal Seal!
Mine—by the Sign in the Scarlet prison—
Bars—cannot conceal!

5   Mine—here—in Vision—and in Veto!
Mine—by the Grave's Repeal—
Titled—Confirmed—
Delirious Charter!
Mine—long as Ages steal!

ca. 1862   1890

536

The Heart asks Pleasure—first—
And then—Excuse from Pain—
And then—those little Anodynes°   *painkillers*
That deaden suffering—

5   And then—to go to sleep—
And then—if it should be
The will of its Inquisitor
The privilege to die—

ca. 1862   1890

569

I reckon—when I count at all—
First—Poets—Then the Sun—
Then Summer—Then the Heaven of God—
And then—the List is done—

5   But, looking back—the First so seems
To Comprehend the Whole—
The Others look a needless Show—
So I write—Poets—All—

Their Summer—lasts a Solid Year—
10   They can afford a Sun
The East—would deem extravagant—
And if the Further Heaven—

Be Beautiful as they prepare
For Those who worship Them—
15   It is too difficult a Grace—
To justify the Dream—

ca. 1862   1929

585

I like to see it lap the Miles—
And lick the Valleys up—
And stop to feed itself at Tanks—
And then—prodigious step

5   Around a Pile of Mountains—
And supercilious peer
In Shanties—by the sides of Roads—
And then a Quarry pare

To fit its Ribs
10 And crawl between
Complaining all the while
In horrid—hooting stanza—
Then chase itself down Hill—

And neigh like Boanerges[8]—
15 Then—punctual as a Star
Stop—docile and omnipotent
At its own stable door—

ca. 1862   1891

613

They shut me up in Prose—
As when a little Girl
They put me in the Closet—
Because they liked me "still"—

5   Still! Could themself have peeped—
And seen my Brain—go round—
They might as wise have lodged a Bird
For Treason—in the Pound—

Himself has but to will
10 And easy as a Star
Abolish his Captivity—
And laugh—No more have I—

ca. 1862   1935

640

I cannot live with You—
It would be Life—
And Life is over there—
Behind the Shelf

5   The Sexton keeps the Key to—
Putting up

8. Like thunder. Cf. Mark 3.17: "And James the son of Zebedee, and John the brother of James; and he surnamed them Boanerges, which is, The sons of thunder."

Our Life—His Porcelain—
Like a Cup—

Discarded of the Housewife—
10   Quaint—or Broke—
A newer Sevres⁹ pleases—
Old Ones crack—

I could not die—with You—
For One must wait
15   To shut the Other's Gaze down—
You—could not—

And I—could I stand by
And see You—freeze—
Without my Right of Frost—
20   Death's privilege?

Nor could I rise—with You—
Because Your Face
Would put out Jesus'—
That New Grace

25   Glow plain—and foreign
On my homesick Eye—
Except that You than He
Shone closer by—

They'd judge Us—How—
30   For You—served Heaven—You know,
Or sought to—
I could not—

Because You saturated Sight—
And I had no more Eyes
35   For sordid excellence
As Paradise

And were You lost, I would be—
Though My Name
Rang loudest
40   On the Heavenly fame—

And were You—saved—
And I—condemned to be
Where You were not—
That self—were Hell to Me—

45   So We must meet apart—
You there—I—here—
With just the Door ajar
That Oceans are—and Prayer—

9. A fine and expensive French porcelain.

And that White Sustenance—
50 Despair—

ca. 1862   1890

709

Publication—is the Auction
Of the Mind of Man—
Poverty—be justifying
For so foul a thing

5   Possibly—but We—would rather
From Our Garret go
White—Unto the White Creator—
Than invest—Our Snow—

Thought belong to Him who gave it—
10   Then—to Him Who bear
Its Corporeal illustration—Sell
The Royal Air—

In the Parcel—Be the Merchant
Of the Heavenly Grace—
15   But reduce no Human Spirit
To Disgrace of Price—

ca. 1863   1929

712

Because I could not stop for Death—
He kindly stopped for me—
The Carriage held but just Ourselves—
And Immortality.

5   We slowly drove—He knew no haste
And I had put away
My labor and my leisure too,
For His Civility—

We passed the School, where Children strove
10   At Recess—in the Ring—
We passed the Fields of Gazing Grain—
We passed the Setting Sun—

Or rather—He passed Us—
The Dews drew quivering and chill—
15   For only Gossamer, my Gown—
My Tippet—only Tulle[1]—

We paused before a House that seemed
A Swelling of the Ground—

1. A sheer silk net; "Tippet": a shoulder cape.

The Roof was scarcely visible—
20   The Cornice°—in the Ground—   *crowning point*

Since then—'tis Centuries—and yet
Feels shorter than the Day
I first surmised the Horses' Heads
Were toward Eternity—

ca. 1863   1890

744

Remorse—is Memory—awake—
Her Parties all astir—
A Presence of Departed Acts—
At window—and at Door—

5   Its Past—set down before the Soul
And lighted with a Match—
Perusal—to facilitate—
And help Belief to stretch—

Remorse is cureless—the Disease
10   Not even God—can heal—
For 'tis His institution—and
The Adequate of Hell—

ca. 1863   1891

745

Renunciation—is a piercing Virtue—
The letting go
A Presence—for an Expectation—
Not now—
5   The putting out of Eyes—
Just Sunrise—
Lest Day—
Day's Great Progenitor—
Outvie
10   Renunciation—is the Choosing
Against itself—
Itself to justify
Unto itself—
When larger function—
15   Make that appear—
Smaller—that Covered Vision—Here—

ca. 1863   1929

754

My Life had stood—a Loaded Gun—
In Corners—till a Day
The Owner passed—identified—
And carried Me away—

5 And now We roam in Sovereign Woods—
And now We hunt the Doe—
And every time I speak for Him—
The Mountains straight reply—

And do I smile, such cordial light
10 Upon the Valley glow—
It is as a Vesuvian face[2]
Had let its pleasure through—

And when at Night—Our good Day done—
I guard My Master's Head—
15 'Tis better than the Eider-Duck's
Deep Pillow[3]—to have shared—

To foe of His—I'm deadly foe—
None stir the second time—
On whom I lay a Yellow Eye—
20 Or an emphatic Thumb—

Though I than He—may longer live
He longer must—then I—
For I have but the power to kill,
Without—the power to die—

ca. 1863   1929

789

On a Columnar Self—
How ample to rely
In Tumult—or Extremity—
How good the Certainty

5 That Lever cannot pry—
And Wedge cannot divide
Conviction—That Granitic Base—
Though None be on our Side—

Suffice Us—for a Crowd—
10 Ourself—and Rectitude—
And that Assembly—not far off
From furthest Spirit—God—

1863   1929

861

Split the Lark—and you'll find the Music—
Bulb after Bulb, in Silver rolled—
Scantily dealt to the Summer Morning
Saved for your Ear when Lutes be old.

2. I.e., a face capable of erupting like Mount Ve-   3. I.e., pillow stuffed with feathers or down.
suvius, the volcano near Naples.

5   Loose the Flood—you shall find it patent—
Gush after Gush, reserved for you—
Scarlet Experiment! Sceptic Thomas![4]
Now, do you doubt that your Bird was true?

ca. 1864   1896

986

A narrow Fellow in the Grass
Occasionally rides—
You may have met Him—did you not
His notice sudden is—

5   The Grass divides as with a Comb—
A spotted shaft is seen—
And then it closes at your feet
And opens further on—

He likes a Boggy Acre
10 A Floor too cool for Corn—
Yet when a Boy, and Barefoot—
I more than once at Noon
Have passed, I thought, a Whip lash
Unbraiding in the Sun
15 When stooping to secure it
It wrinkled, and was gone—

Several of Nature's People
I know, and they know me—
I feel for them a transport
20 Of cordiality—

But never met this Fellow
Attended, or alone
Without a tighter breathing
And Zero at the Bone—

ca. 1865   1866

1068

Further in Summer than the Birds
Pathetic from the Grass
A minor Nation[5] celebrates
Its unobtrusive Mass.

5 No Ordinance° be seen   *prescribed usage*
So gradual the Grace
A pensive Custom it becomes
Enlarging Loneliness.

4. Doubting Thomas, who would not believe he had seen the Lord until he had seen the print of the nails in Jesus' hands and thrust a hand into His side (John 20.25).
5. I.e., insects.

Antiquest felt at Noon
10   When August burning low
Arise this spectral Canticle°   *liturgical song*
Repose to typify

Remit as yet no Grace
No Furrow on the Glow
15   Yet a Druidic[6] Difference
Enhances Nature now

ca. 1866   1891

1078

The Bustle in a House
The Morning after Death
Is solemnest of industries
Enacted upon Earth—

5   The Sweeping up the Heart
And putting Love away
We shall not want to use again
Until Eternity.

ca. 1866   1890

1129

Tell all the Truth but tell it slant—
Success in Circuit lies
Too bright for our infirm Delight
The Truth's superb surprise

5   As Lightning to the Children eased
With explanation kind
The Truth must dazzle gradually
Or every man be blind—

ca. 1868   1945

1463

A Route of Evanescence
With a revolving Wheel—
A Resonance of Emerald—
A Rush of Cochineal°—   *red dye*
5   And every Blossom on the Bush
Adjusts its tumbled Head—
The mail from Tunis,[7] probably,
An easy Morning's Ride—

ca. 1879   1891

---

6. Pertaining to the ancient sacred lore of the   7. City on the north coast of Africa.
Celtic priest-magicians.

1540

As imperceptibly as Grief
The Summer lapsed away—
Too imperceptible at last
To seem like Perfidy—
5   A Quietness distilled
As Twilight long begun,
Or Nature spending with herself
Sequestered Afternoon—
The Dusk drew earlier in—
10   The Morning foreign shone—
A courteous, yet harrowing Grace,
As Guest, that would be gone—
And thus, without a Wing
Or service of a Keel
15   Our Summer made her light escape
Into the Beautiful.

ca. 1865   1891

1545

The Bible is an antique Volume—
Written by faded Men
At the suggestion of Holy Specters—
Subjects—Bethlehem—
5   Eden—the ancient Homestead—
Satan—the Brigadier—
Judas—the Great Defaulter—
David—the Troubadour—
Sin—a distinguished Precipice
10   Others must resist—
Boys that "believe" are very lonesome—
Other Boys are "lost"—
Had but the Tale a warbling Teller—
All the Boys would come—
15   Orpheus' Sermon[8] captivated—
It did not condemn—

ca. 1882   1924

1763

Fame is a bee.
It has a song—
It has a sting—
Ah, too, it has a wing.

?   1898

8. The music of the legendary Greek musician Orpheus attracted and controlled beasts, rocks, and trees.

CHRISTINA ROSSETTI
1830–1894

Song

When I am dead, my dearest,
  Sing no sad songs for me;
Plant thou no roses at my head,
  Nor shady cypress tree:
5 Be the green grass above me
  With showers and dewdrops wet;
And if thou wilt, remember,
  And if thou wilt, forget.

I shall not see the shadows,
10 I shall not feel the rain;
I shall not hear the nightingale
  Sing on, as if in pain:
And dreaming through the twilight
  That doth not rise nor set,
15 Haply I may remember,
  And haply may forget.

1848   1862

Remember

Remember me when I am gone away,
  Gone far away into the silent land;
  When you can no more hold me by the hand,
Nor I half turn to go yet turning stay.
5 Remember me when no more day by day
  You tell me of our future that you planned:
  Only remember me; you understand
It will be late to counsel then or pray.
Yet if you should forget me for a while
10 And afterwards remember, do not grieve:
  For if the darkness and corruption leave
  A vestige of the thoughts that once I had,
Better by far you should forget and smile
  Than that you should remember and be sad.

1858   1862

Echo

Come to me in the silence of the night;
  Come in the speaking silence of a dream;
Come with soft rounded cheeks and eyes as bright
  As sunlight on a stream;
5   Come back in tears,
O memory, hope, love of finished years.

Oh dream how sweet, too sweet, too bitter sweet,
  Whose wakening should have been in Paradise,
Where souls brimful of love abide and meet;
10   Where thirsting longing eyes
      Watch the slow door
That opening, letting in, lets out no more.

Yet come to me in dreams, that I may live
  My very life again tho' cold in death:
15 Come back to me in dreams, that I may give
  Pulse for pulse, breath for breath:
    Speak low, lean low,
As long ago, my love, how long ago.

1854   1862

In an Artist's Studio

One face looks out from all his canvases,
  One selfsame figure sits or walks or leans:
  We found her hidden just behind those screens,
That mirror gave back all her loveliness.
5 A queen in opal or in ruby dress,
  A nameless girl in freshest summer-greens,
  A saint, an angel—every canvas means
The same one meaning, neither more nor less.
He feeds upon her face by day and night,
10 And she with true kind eyes looks back on him,
Fair as the moon and joyful as the light:
  Not wan with waiting, not with sorrow dim;
Not as she is, but was when hope shone bright;
  Not as she is, but as she fills his dream.

1856   1896

Up-Hill

Does the road wind up-hill all the way?
  Yes, to the very end.
Will the day's journey take the whole long day?
  From morn to night, my friend.

5 But is there for the night a resting-place?
  A roof for when the slow dark hours begin.
May not the darkness hide it from my face?
  You cannot miss that inn.

Shall I meet other wayfarers at night?
10 Those who have gone before.
Then must I knock, or call when just in sight?
  They will not keep you standing at that door.

Shall I find comfort, travel-sore and weak?
  Of labor you shall find the sum.

15   Will there be beds for me and all who seek?
      Yea, beds for all who come.

1858   1862

The Convent Threshold

There's blood between us, love, my love,
There's father's blood, there's brother's blood;
And blood's a bar I cannot pass:
I choose the stairs that mount above,
5   Stair after golden skyward stair,
To city and to sea of glass.
My lily feet are soiled with mud,
With scarlet mud which tells a tale
Of hope that was, of guilt that was,
10 Of love that shall not yet avail;
Alas, my heart, if I could bare
My heart, this selfsame stain is there:
I seek the sea of glass and fire
To wash the spot, to burn the snare;
15 Lo, stairs are meant to lift us higher:
Mount with me, mount the kindled stair.

Your eyes look earthward, mine look up.
I see the far-off city grand,
Beyond the hills a watered land,
20 Beyond the gulf a gleaming strand
Of mansions where the righteous sup;
Who sleep at ease among their trees,
Or wake to sing a cadenced hymn
With Cherubim and Seraphim;[1]
25 They bore the Cross, they drained the cup,
Racked, roasted, crushed, wrenched limb from limb,
They the offscouring[2] of the world:
The heaven of starry heavens unfurled,
The sun before their face is dim.

30 You looking earthward, what see you?
Milk-white, wine-flushed among the vines,
Up and down leaping, to and fro,
Most glad, most full, made strong with wines,
Blooming as peaches pearled with dew,
35 Their golden windy hair afloat,
Love-music warbling in their throat,
Young men and women come and go.

You linger, yet the time is short:
Flee for your life, gird up your strength
40 To flee; the shadows stretched at length
Show that day wanes, that night draws nigh;

---

1. Plurals (Hebrew, Biblical) of, respectively, "cherub" and "seraph"; seraphim are the highest order of angels, just above the cherubim.

2. What is "scoured off," hence refuse, that which is rejected.

Flee to the mountain, tarry not.
Is this a time for smile and sigh,
For songs among the secret trees
45   Where sudden blue birds nest and sport?
The time is short and yet you stay:
Today while it is called today
Kneel, wrestle, knock, do violence, pray;
Today is short, tomorrow nigh:
50   Why will you die? why will you die?

You sinned with me a pleasant sin:
Repent with me, for I repent.
Woe's me the lore I must unlearn!
Woe's me that easy way we went,
55   So rugged when I would return!
How long until my sleep begin,
How long shall stretch these nights and days?
Surely, clean Angels cry, she prays;
She laves her soul with tedious tears:
60   How long must stretch these years and years?

I turn from you my cheeks and eyes,
My hair which you shall see no more—
Alas for joy that went before,
For joy that dies, for love that dies.
65   Only my lips still turn to you,
My livid lips that cry, Repent.
Oh weary life, Oh weary Lent,
Oh weary time whose stars are few.

How should I rest in Paradise,
70   Or sit on steps of heaven alone?
If Saints and Angels spoke of love
Should I not answer from my throne:
Have pity upon me, ye my friends,
For I have heard the sound thereof:
75   Should I not turn with yearning eyes,
Turn earthwards with a pitiful pang?
Oh save me from a pang in heaven.
By all the gifts we took and gave,
Repent, repent, and be forgiven:
80   This life is long, but yet it ends;
Repent and purge your soul and save:
No gladder song the morning stars
Upon their birthday morning sang
Than Angels sing when one repents.

85   I tell you what I dreamed last night:
A spirit with transfigured face
Fire-footed clomb an infinite space.
I heard his hundred pinions° clang,   *feathered wings*
Heaven-bells rejoicing rang and rang,
90   Heaven-air was thrilled with subtle scents,

Worlds spun upon their rushing cars:
He mounted shrieking: "Give me light."
Still light was poured on him, more light;
Angels, Archangels he outstripped
95 Exultant in exceeding might,
And trod the skirts of Cherubim.
Still "Give me light," he shrieked; and dipped
His thirsty face, and drank a sea,
Athirst with thirst it could not slake.
100 I saw him, drunk with knowledge, take
From aching brows the aureole crown[3] —
His locks writhed like a cloven snake —
He left his throne to grovel down
And lick the dust of Seraphs' feet:
105 For what is knowledge duly weighed?
Knowledge is strong, but love is sweet;
Yea all the progress he had made
Was but to learn that all is small
Save love, for love is all in all.

110 I tell you what I dreamed last night:
It was not dark, it was not light,
Cold dews had drenched my plenteous hair
Thro' clay; you came to seek me there.
And "Do you dream of me?" you said.
115 My heart was dust that used to leap
To you; I answered half asleep:
"My pillow is damp, my sheets are red,
There's a leaden tester[4] to my bed:
Find you a warmer playfellow,
120 A warmer pillow for your head,
A kinder love to love than mine."
You wrung your hands; while I like lead
Crushed downwards thro' the sodden earth:
You smote your hands but not in mirth,
125 And reeled but were not drunk with wine.

For all night long I dreamed of you:
I woke and prayed against my will,
Then slept to dream of you again.
At length I rose and knelt and prayed:
130 I cannot write the words I said,
My words were slow, my tears were few;
But thro' the dark my silence spoke
Like thunder. When this morning broke,
My face was pinched, my hair was gray,
135 And frozen blood was on the sill
Where stifling in my struggle I lay.

If now you saw me you would say:
Where is the face I used to love?

---

3. Golden crown or halo.   4. Canopy over a bed.

And I would answer: Gone before;
140   It tarries veiled in paradise.
When once the morning star shall rise,
When earth with shadow flees away
And we stand safe within the door,
Then you shall lift the veil thereof.
145   Look up, rise up: for far above
Our palms are grown, our place is set;
There we shall meet as once we met
And love with old familiar love.

1858   1862

Passing Away, Saith the World, Passing Away

Passing away, saith the World, passing away:
Chances, beauty and youth sapped day by day:
Thy life never continueth in one stay.
Is the eye waxen dim, is the dark hair changing to gray
5   That hath won neither laurel nor bay?[5]
I shall clothe myself in Spring and bud in May:
Thou, root-stricken, shalt not rebuild thy decay
On my bosom for aye.
Then I answered: Yea.

10   Passing away, saith my Soul, passing away:
With its burden of fear and hope, of labor and play;
Hearken what the past doth witness and say:
Rust in thy gold, a moth is in thine array,
A canker is in thy bud, thy leaf must decay.
15   At midnight, at cockcrow, at morning, one certain day
Lo the bridegroom shall come and shall not delay:
Watch thou and pray.
Then I answered: Yea.

Passing away, saith my God, passing away:
20   Winter passeth after the long delay:
New grapes on the vine, new figs on the tender spray,
Turtle calleth turtle in Heaven's May.
Tho' I tarry, wait for Me, trust Me, watch and pray.
Arise, come away, night is past and lo it is day,
25   My love, My sister, My spouse, thou shalt hear Me say.
Then I answered: Yea.

1860   1862

Amor Mundi[6]

"Oh where are you going with your love-locks flowing
On the west wind blowing along this valley track?"

---

5. In ancient Greece, victors in the Pythian games were crowned with a wreath made from the leaves of the laurel, and later such wreaths were bestowed on the winners of academic or poetic honors. "Bay" is synonymous with laurel.
6. "Love of the world" (Latin).

"The downhill path is easy, come with me an it please ye,
 We shall escape the uphill by never turning back."

5   So they two went together in glowing August weather,
     The honey-breathing heather lay to their left and right;
 And dear she was to dote on, her swift feet seemed to float on
     The air like soft twin pigeons too sportive to alight.

 "Oh what is that in heaven where gray cloud-flakes are seven,
10   Where blackest clouds hang riven just at the rainy skirt?"
 Oh that's a meteor sent us, a message dumb, portentous,
     An undeciphered solemn signal of help or hurt."

 "Oh what is that glides quickly where velvet flowers grow thickly,
     Their scent comes rich and sickly?"—"A scaled and hooded worm."
15   "Oh what's that in the hollow, so pale I quake to follow?"
     "Oh that's a thin dead body which waits the eternal term."

 "Turn again, O my sweetest,—turn again, false and fleetest:
     This beaten way thou beatest I fear is hell's own track."
 "Nay, too steep for hill-mounting; nay, too late for cost-counting:
20   This downhill path is easy, but there's no turning back."
1865   1875

LEWIS CARROLL
(CHARLES LUTWIDGE DODGSON)
1832–1898

Jabberwocky[1]

There was a book lying near Alice on the table, and while she sat watching the White King (for she was still a little anxious about him, and had the ink all ready to throw over him, in case he fainted again), she turned over the leaves, to find some part that she could read, "—for it's all in some language I don't know," she said to herself. It was like this:

Jabberwocky

"Twas brillig, and the slithy toves
 Did gyre and gimble in the wabe:
All mimsy were the borogoves,
And the mome raths outgrabe.

She puzzled over this for some time, but at last a bright thought struck her. "Why, it's a Looking-glass book, of course! And, if I hold it up to a glass, the words will all go the right way again."

This was the poem that Alice read:

---

1. From *Through the Looking-Glass*, Chapter I.

Jabberwocky

'Twas brillig, and the slithy toves
    Did gyre and gimble in the wabe:
All mimsy were the borogoves,
    And the mome raths outgrabe.

5   "Beware the Jabberwock, my son!
    The jaws that bite, the claws that catch!
Beware the Jubjub bird, and shun
    The frumious Bandersnatch!"

He took his vorpal sword in hand:
10   Long time the manxome foe he sought—
So rested he by the Tumtum tree,
    And stood awhile in thought.

And, as in uffish thought he stood,
    The Jabberwock, with eyes of flame,
15   Came whiffling through the tulgey wood,
    And burbled as it came!

One, two! One, two! And through and through
    The vorpal blade went snicker-snack!
He left it dead, and with its head
20   He went galumphing back.

"And hast thou slain the Jabberwock?
    Come to my arms, my beamish boy!
O frabjous day! Callooh! Callay!"
    He chortled in his joy.

25   'Twas brillig, and the slithy toves
    Did gyre and gimble in the wabe:
All mimsy were the borogoves,
    And the mome raths outgrabe.

[*Humpty Dumpty's Explication of* Jabberwocky][2]

"You seem very clever at explaining words, Sir," said Alice. "Would you kindly tell me the meaning of the poem *Jabberwocky?*"

"Let's hear it," said Humpty Dumpty. "I can explain all the poems that ever were invented—and a good many that haven't been invented just yet."

This sounded very hopeful, so Alice repeated the first verse:

    " 'Twas brillig, and the slithy toves
        Did gyre and gimble in the wabe;
    All mimsy were the borogoves,
        And the mome raths outgrabe."

"That's enough to begin with," Humpty Dumpty interrupted: "there are plenty of hard words there. 'Brillig' means four o'clock in the afternoon—the time when you begin *broiling* things for dinner."

---

2. From *Through the Looking-Glass*, Chapter VI.

"That'll do very well," said Alice: "and 'slithy'?"[3]

"Well, 'slithy' means 'lithe and slimy.' 'Lithe' is the same as 'active.' You see it's like a portmanteau—there are two meanings packed up into one word."

"I see it now," Alice remarked thoughtfully: "and what are 'toves'?"

"Well, 'toves' are something like badgers—they're something like lizards—and they're something like corkscrews."

"They must be very curious creatures."

"They are that," said Humpty Dumpty: "also they make their nests under sundials—also they live on cheese."

"And what's to 'gyre' and to 'gimble'?"

"To 'gyre' is to go round and round like a gyroscope. To 'gimble' is to make holes like a gimlet."

"And the 'wabe' is the grass plot round a sundial, I suppose?" said Alice, surprised at her own ingenuity.

"Of course it is. It's called 'wabe,' you know, because it goes a long way before it, and a long way behind it—"

"And a long way beyond it on each side," Alice added.

"Exactly so. Well then, 'mimsy' is 'flimsy and miserable' (there's another portmanteau for you). And a 'borogove' is a thin shabby-looking bird with its feathers sticking out all round—something like a live mop."

"And then 'mome raths'?" said Alice. "If I'm not giving you too much trouble." '

"Well, a 'rath' is a sort of green pig: but 'mome' I'm not certain about. I think it's short for 'from home'—meaning that they'd lost their way, you know."

"And what does 'outgrabe' mean?"

"Well, 'outgribing' is something between bellowing and whistling, with a kind of sneeze in the middle: however, you'll hear it done, maybe—down in the wood yonder—and when you've once heard it you'll be *quite* content. Who's been repeating all that hard stuff to you?"

"I read it in a book," said Alice.

1871

The White Knight's Song[4]

Haddock's Eyes or *The Aged Aged Man* or
Ways and Means or *A-Sitting On A Gate*

I'll tell thee everything I can;
   There's little to relate.
I saw an aged, aged man,
   A-sitting on a gate.
5   "Who are you, aged man?" I said.
   "And how is it you live?"
And his answer trickled through my head
   Like water through a sieve.

---

3. Concerning the pronunciation of these words, Carroll later said: "The 'i' in 'slithy' is long, as in 'writhe'; and 'toves' is pronounced so as to rhyme with 'groves.' Again, the first 'o' in 'borogoves' is pronounced like the 'o' in 'borrow.' I have heard people try to give it the sound of the 'o' in 'worry.' Such is Human Perversity."

4. The Knight is a character in *Through the Looking-Glass*; the song is in part a parody of Wordsworth's "Resolution and Independence."

He said "I look for butterflies
10   That sleep among the wheat;
I make them into mutton-pies,
    And sell them in the street.
I sell them unto men," he said,
    "Who sail on stormy seas;
15 And that's the way I get my bread—
    A trifle, if you please."

But I was thinking of a plan
    To dye one's whiskers green,
And always use so large a fan
20   That it could not be seen.
So, having no reply to give
    To what the old man said,
I cried, "Come, tell me how you live!"
    And thumped him on the head.

25 His accents mild took up the tale;
    He said, "I go my ways,
And when I find a mountain-rill,
    I set it in a blaze;
And thence they make a stuff they call
30   Rowland's Macassar Oil—[5]
Yet twopence-halfpenny is all
    They give me for my toil."

But I was thinking of a way
    To feed oneself on batter,
35 And so go on from day to day
    Getting a little fatter.
I shook him well from side to side,
    Until his face was blue;
"Come, tell me how you live," I cried
40   "And what it is you do!"

He said, "I hunt for haddocks' eyes
    Among the heather bright,
And work them into waistcoat-buttons
    In the silent night.
45 And these I do not sell for gold
    Or coin of silvery shine,
But for a copper halfpenny,
    And that will purchase nine.

"I sometimes dig for buttered rolls,
50   Or set limed twigs for crabs;
I sometimes search the grassy knolls
    For wheels of hansom-cabs.
And that's the way" (he gave a wink)
    "By which I get my wealth—

5. A patented hairdressing.

55   And very gladly will I drink
        Your Honor's noble health."

        I heard him then, for I had just
        Completed my design
        To keep the Menai bridge[6] from rust
60   By boiling it in wine.
        I thanked him much for telling me
        The way he got his wealth,
        But chiefly for his wish that he
        Might drink my noble health.

65   And now, if e'er by chance I put
        My fingers into glue,
        Or madly squeeze a right-hand foot
        Into a left-hand shoe,
        Or if I drop upon my toe
70   A very heavy weight,
        I weep, for it reminds me so
        Of that old man I used to know—
        Whose look was mild, whose speech was slow,
        Whose hair was whiter than the snow,
75   Whose face was very like a crow,
        With eyes, like cinders, all aglow,
        Who seemed distracted with his woe,
        Who rocked his body to and fro,
        And muttered mumblingly and low,
80   As if his mouth were full of dough,
        Who snorted like a buffalo—
        That summer evening long ago
        A-sitting on a gate.

                                                    1871

WILLIAM MORRIS

1834–1896

The Haystack in the Floods[1]

        Had she come all the way for this,
        To part at last without a kiss?
        Yea, had she borne the dirt and rain
        That her own eyes might see him slain
5   Beside the haystack in the floods?

        Along the dripping leafless woods,
        The stirrup touching either shoe,

---

6. A large bridge in Wales.
1. The events of the poem take place immediately after the battle of Poitiers (1356), in which the English defeated the French. An English knight, Sir Robert de Marny, and his mistress, Jehane, are attempting to escape the French by reaching Gascony, held by the English.

She rode astride as troopers do;
With kirtle kilted to her knee,
10 To which the mud splashed wretchedly;
And the wet dripped from every tree
Upon her head and heavy hair,
And on her eyelids broad and fair;
The tears and rain ran down her face.
15 By fits and starts they rode apace,
And very often was his place
Far off from her; he had to ride
Ahead, to see what might betide
When the roads crossed; and sometimes, when
20 There rose a murmuring from his men,
Had to turn back with promises;
Ah me! she had but little ease;
And often for pure doubt and dread
She sobbed, made giddy in the head
25 By the swift riding; while, for cold,
Her slender fingers scarce could hold
The wet reins; yea, and scarcely, too,
She felt the foot within her shoe
Against the stirrup: all for this,
30 To part at last without a kiss
Beside the haystack in the floods.

For when they neared that old soaked hay,
They saw across the only way
That Judas, Godmar, and the three
35 Red running lions dismally
Grinned from his pennon,° under which,   *banner*
In one straight line along the ditch,
They counted thirty heads.

                                So then,
40 While Robert turned round to his men,
She saw at once the wretched end,
And, stooping down, tried hard to rend
Her coif the wrong way from her head,
And hid her eyes; while Robert said:
45 "Nay, love, 'tis scarcely two to one,
At Poitiers where we made them run
So fast—why, sweet my love, good cheer.
The Gascon frontier is so near,
Nought after this."

50   But, "O," she said,
"My God! my God! I have to tread
The long way back without you; then
The court at Paris; those six men;[2]
The gratings of the Chatelet;[3]
55 The swift Seine on some rainy day

---

2. I.e., the judges.   3. A prison in Paris.

Like this, and people standing by,
And laughing, while my weak hands try
To recollect how strong men swim,[4]
All this, or else a life with him,
60   For which I should be damned at last,
Would God that this next hour were past!"

He answered not, but cried his cry,
"St. George for Marny!" cheerily;
And laid his hand upon her rein.
65   Alas! no man of all his train
Gave back that cheery cry again;
And, while for rage his thumb beat fast
Upon his sword-hilts, someone cast
About his neck a kerchief long,
70   And bound him.
                    Then they went along
To Godmar; who said: "Now, Jehane,
Your lover's life is on the wane
So fast, that, if this very hour
75   You yield not as my paramour,
He will not see the rain leave off—
Nay, keep your tongue from gibe and scoff,
Sir Robert, or I slay you now."

She laid her hand upon her brow,
80   Then gazed upon the palm, as though
She thought her forehead bled, and—"No,"
She said, and turned her head away,
As there were nothing else to say,
And everything were settled: red
85   Grew Godmar's face from chin to head:
"Jehane, on yonder hill there stands
My castle, guarding well my lands:
What hinders me from taking you,
And doing that I list to do
90   To your fair willful body, while
Your knight lies dead?"
                         A wicked smile
Wrinkled her face, her lips grew thin,
A long way out she thrust her chin:
95   "You know that I should strangle you
While you were sleeping; or bite through
Your throat, by God's help—ah!" she said,
"Lord Jesus, pity your poor maid!
For in such wise they hem me in,
100   I cannot choose but sin and sin,
Whatever happens: yet I think
They could not make me eat or drink,

4. When captured, she will have to undergo trial by water to determine whether or not she is a witch: if she drowns, she is innocent; but if she swims, it will be by virtue of her powers as a witch, and she will be burned at the stake.

And so should I just reach my rest."
"Nay, if you do not my behest,
105 O Jehane! though I love you well,"
Said Godmar, "would I fail to tell
All that I know." "Foul lies," she said.
"Eh? lies my Jehane? by God's head,
At Paris folks would deem them true!
110 Do you know, Jehane, they cry for you,
'Jehane the brown! Jehane the brown!
Give us Jehane to burn or drown!' —
Eh — gag me Robert! — sweet my friend,
This were indeed a piteous end
115 For those long fingers, and long feet,
And long neck, and smooth shoulders sweet;
An end that few men would forget
That saw it — so, an hour yet:
Consider, Jehane, which to take
120 Of life or death!"

                So, scarce awake,
Dismounting, did she leave that place,
And totter some yards: with her face
Turned upward to the sky she lay,
125 Her head on a wet heap of hay,
And fell asleep: and while she slept,
And did not dream, the minutes crept
Round to the twelve again; but she,
Being waked at last, sighed quietly,
130 And strangely childlike came, and said:
"I will not." Straightway Godmar's head,
As though it hung on strong wires, turned
Most sharply round, and his face burned.

For Robert — both his eyes were dry,
135 He could not weep, but gloomily
He seemed to watch the rain; yea, too,
His lips were firm; he tried once more
To touch her lips; she reached out, sore
And vain desire so tortured them,
140 The poor gray lips, and now the hem
Of his sleeve brushed them.
                    With a start
Up Godmar rose, thrust them apart;
From Robert's throat he loosed the bands
Of silk and mail; with empty hands
145 Held out, she stood and gazed, and saw,
The long bright blade without a flaw
Glide out from Godmar's sheath, his hand
In Robert's hair; she saw him bend
Back Robert's head; she saw him send
150 The thin steel down; the blow told well,
Right backward the knight Robert fell,
And moaned as dogs do, being half dead,

Unwitting, as I deem: so then
Godmar turned grinning to his men,
155 Who ran, some five or six, and beat
His head to pieces at their feet.

Then Godmar turned again, and said:
"So, Jehane, the first fitte⁵ is read!
Take note, my lady, that your way
160 Lies backward to the Chatelet!"
She shook her head and gazed awhile
At her cold hands with a rueful smile,
As though this thing had made her mad.

This was the parting that they had
165 Beside the haystack in the floods.

1858

The Earthly Paradise⁶

Of heaven or hell I have no power to sing,
I cannot ease the burden of your fears,
Or make quick-coming death a little thing,
Or bring again the pleasure of past years,
5 Nor for my words shall ye forget your tears,
Or hope again for aught that I can say,
The idle singer of an empty day.

But rather, when, aweary of your mirth,
From full hearts still unsatisfied ye sigh,
10 And, feeling kindly unto all the earth,
Grudge every minute as it passes by,
Made the more mindful that the sweet days die—
Remember me a little then I pray,
The idle singer of an empty day.

15 The heavy trouble, the bewildering care
That weighs us down who live and earn our bread,
These idle verses have no power to bear;
So let me sing of names rememberéd,
Because they, living not, can ne'er be dead,
20 Or long time take their memory quite away
From us poor singers of an empty day.

Dreamer of dreams, born out of my due time,
Why should I strive to set the crooked straight?
Let it suffice me that my murmuring rhyme
25 Beats with light wing against the ivory gate,⁷

5. Division of a song, poem, or tale.
6. The dedicatory stanzas to Morris' poem *The Earthly Paradise* (1868–70), consisting of a prologue and twenty-four tales on classical and medieval—especially Norse—subjects.

7. In Homer, dreams came through one or the other of two gates: through the gates of ivory, those that were untrue; through the gates of horn, those that were true.

Telling a tale not too importunate
To those who in the sleepy region stay,
Lulled by the singer of an empty day.

Folk say, a wizard to a northern king
30 At Christmas-tide such wondrous things did show,
That through one window men beheld the spring,
And through another saw the summer glow,
And through a third the fruited vines a-row,
While still, unheard, but in its wonted way,
35 Piped the drear wind of that December day.

So with this Earthly Paradise it is,
If ye will read aright, and pardon me,
Who strive to build a shadowy isle of bliss
Midmost the beating of the steely sea,
40 Where tossed about all hearts of men must be;
Whose ravening monsters mighty men shall slay,
Not the poor singer of an empty day.

1868–70

W. S. GILBERT

1836–1911

I Am the Very Model of a Modern Major-General[1]

I am the very model of a modern Major-General,
I've information vegetable, animal, and mineral,
I know the kings of England, and I quote the fights historical,
From Marathon to Waterloo, in order categorical;[2]
5   I'm very well acquainted too with matters mathematical,
I understand equations, both the simple and quadratical,
About binomial theorem I'm teeming with a lot o' news—
With many cheerful facts about the square of the hypotenuse.[3]

ALL   With many cheerful facts, etc.

10 GEN. I'm very good at integral and differential calculus,
I know the scientific names of beings animalculous;[4]
In short, in matters vegetable, animal, and mineral,
I am the very model of a modern Major-General.

ALL   In short, in matters vegetable, animal, and mineral,
15   He is the very model of a modern Major-General.

GEN. I know our mythic history, King Arthur's and Sir Caradoc's,
I answer hard acrostics, I've a pretty taste for paradox,

---

1. Sung by the Major-General on his entrance in Act I of *The Pirates of Penzance*.
2. The Greeks defeated the Persians in a famous battle at Marathon in 490 B.C.; the duke of Wel-lington won his decisive victory over Napoleon at Waterloo in 1815.
3. All these are mathematical terms.
4. Microscopic organisms.

I quote in elegiacs all the crimes of Heliogabalus,
In conics I can floor peculiarities parabolous.[5]

20 I can tell undoubted Raphaels from Gerard Dows and Zoffanies,
I know the croaking chorus from the *Frogs* of Aristophanes,
Then I can hum a fugue of which I've heard the music's dinafore,
And whistle all the airs from that infernal nonsense *Pinafore*.[6]

ALL   And whistle all the airs, etc.

25 GEN.   Then I can write a washing bill in Babylonic cuneiform,
And tell you every detail of Caractacus's uniform;[7]
In short, in matters vegetable, animal, and mineral,
I am the very model of a modern Major-General.

ALL   In short, in matters vegetable, animal, and mineral,
30   He is the very model of a modern Major-General.

GEN.   In fact, when I know what is meant by "mamelon" and "ravelin,"
When I can tell at sight a chassepôt rifle from a javelin,
When such affairs as sorties and surprises I'm more wary at,
And when I know precisely what is meant by "commissariat",
35   When I have learnt what progress has been made in modern
      gunnery,
When I know more of tactics than a novice in a nunnery:[8]
In short, when I've a smattering of elemental strategy,
You'll say a better Major-Gene*ral* has never *sat* a gee —[9]

ALL   You'll say a better, etc.

40 GEN.   For my military knowledge, though I'm plucky and adventury,
Has only been brought down to the beginning of the century;
But still in matters vegetable, animal, and mineral,
I am the very model of a modern Major-General.

ALL   But still in matters vegetable, animal, and mineral,
45   He is the very model of a modern Major-General.

1879

---

5. More examples of the Major-General's abstruse bits of knowledge: Sir Caradoc was a legendary figure in British history, supposedly one of King Arthur's knights; "acrostics" are word puzzles (fore-runners of crossword puzzles); "elegiacs" were a classical verse form of praise, quite unsuitable to describe the life of the most depraved of the Roman emperors; "conics" are the study of three-dimensional figures, of which the parabola is one.
6. Raphael was one of the great painters of the early Italian Renaissance, as opposed to Gerhard Dou and Johann Zoffany, undistinguished seven-teenth- and eighteenth-century painters; in *The Frogs*, by Aristophanes, the great classical comic playwright, a chorus of frogs chants "Brekke-ko-ax, ko-ax, ko-ax"; a "fugue" is a learned (and, inciden-tally, multivoiced) musical composition; the last line of the verse is Gilbert's sly dig at the immense popularity of the previous Gilbert and Sullivan operetta, *H.M.S. Pinafore* (1878).
7. Cuneiform was a form of writing (made by pressing a stick into clay) practiced in ancient Bab-ylonia; Caractacus is an alternate form of "Car-adoc."
8. The Major-General has just listed his "smatter-ing" of military terms: a "mamelon" is a fortified mound, while a "ravelin" is a detached outwork also used in fortification; the "chassepôt rifle" was a bolt-action, breech-loading rifle, very recently invented in Gilbert's time, while a "javelin" is a light spear that has been used in warfare for centu-ries; "sorties" and "surprises" both refer to sudden military attacks; a "commissariat" is the system for supplying an army with food.
9. Horse (usually a work horse).

Titwillow[1]

On a tree by a river a little tom-tit
    Sang "Willow, titwillow, titwillow!"
And I said to him, "Dicky-bird, why do you sit
    Singing 'Willow, titwillow, titwillow'?"
5   "Is it weakness of intellect, birdie?" I cried,
    "Or a rather tough worm in your little inside?"
With a shake of his poor little head, he replied,
    "Oh, willow, titwillow, titwillow!"

He slapped at his chest, as he sat on that bough,
10   Singing "Willow, titwillow, titwillow!"
And a cold perspiration bespangled his brow,
    Oh, willow, titwillow, titwillow!
He sobbed and he sighed, and a gurgle he gave,
Then he plunged himself into the billowy wave,
15 And an echo arose from the suicide's grave—
    "Oh, willow, titwillow, titwillow!"

Now I feel just as sure as I'm sure that my name
    Isn't Willow, titwillow, titwillow,
That 'twas blighted affection that made him exclaim
20   "Oh, willow, titwillow, titwillow!"
And if you remain callous and obdurate, I
Shall perish as he did, and you will know why,
Though I probably shall not exclaim as I die,
    "Oh, willow, titwillow, titwillow!"

1885

ALGERNON CHARLES SWINBURNE
1837–1909

Chorus from *Atalanta in Calydon*
When the Hounds of Spring Are on Winter's Traces

When the hounds of spring are on winter's traces,
    The mother of months[1] in meadow or plain
Fills the shadows and windy places
    With lisp of leaves and ripple of rain;
5   And the brown bright nightingale amorous
    Is half assuaged for Itylus,[2]

---

1. Sung by Ko-Ko in Act II of *The Mikado*.
1. Artemis (in Roman mythology, Diana), called "mother of months" because of her role as moon goddess.
2. Procne and Philomela were the daughters of Pandion, legendary king of Athens. Procne was the wife of Tereus, king of Thrace, who fell in love with Philomela, ravished her, and cut out her tongue to ensure her silence. But Philomela wove the story of his deed into a tapestry, and in revenge Procne served up to her husband the cooked flesh of their child Itys (or Itylus) at a banquet. The sisters, fleeing from Tereus, were changed into birds before he could overtake them, Procne into a swallow, Philomela into a nightingale.

For the Thracian ships and the foreign faces,
　　The tongueless vigil, and all the pain.

Come with bows bent and with emptying of quivers,
10　　Maiden most perfect, lady of light,
With a noise of winds and many rivers,
　　With a clamor of waters, and with might;
Bind on thy sandals, O thou most fleet,
Over the splendor and speed of thy feet;
15　For the faint east quickens, the wan west shivers,
　　Round the feet of the day and the feet of the night.

Where shall we find her, how shall we sing to her,
　　Fold our hands round her knees, and cling?
O that man's heart were as fire and could spring to her,
20　　Fire, or the strength of the streams that spring!
For the stars and the winds are unto her
As raiment, as songs of the harp-player;
For the risen stars and the fallen cling to her,
　　And the southwest wind and the west wind sing.

25　For winter's rains and ruins are over,
　　And all the season of snows and sins;
The days dividing lover and lover,
　　The light that loses, the night that wins;
And time remembered is grief forgotten,
30　And frosts are slain and flowers begotten,
And in green underwood and cover
　　Blossom by blossom the spring begins.

The full streams feed on flower of rushes,
　　Ripe grasses trammel a traveling foot,
35　The faint fresh flame of the young year flushes
　　From leaf to flower and flower to fruit;
And fruit and leaf are as gold and fire,
And the oat° is heard above the lyre,　　　　　　　*musical pipe*
And the hooféd heel of a satyr[3] crushes
40　　The chestnut-husk at the chestnut-root.

And Pan by noon and Bacchus by night,[4]
　　Fleeter of foot than the fleet-foot kid,
Follows with dancing and fills with delight
　　The Maenad and the Bassarid;
45　And soft as lips that laugh and hide
The laughing leaves of the trees divide,
And screen from seeing and leave in sight
　　The god pursuing, the maiden hid.

The ivy falls with the Bacchanal's hair
50　　Over her eyebrows hiding her eyes;

3. A woodland god, half man, half beast.
4. Pan, in Greek mythology, was the god of flocks and shepherds; Bacchus, or Dionysus, was god of wine and was accompanied in his revels by a train of devotees that included Maenads and Bassarids (line 44).

The wild vine slipping down leaves bare
   Her bright breast shortening into sighs;
The wild vine slips with the weight of its leaves,
But the berried ivy catches and cleaves
55 To the limbs that glitter, the feet that scare
   The wolf that follows, the fawn that flies.

                                     1865

The Garden of Proserpine[5]

Here, where the world is quiet;
   Here, where all trouble seems
Dead winds' and spent waves' riot
   In doubtful dreams of dreams;
5 I watch the green field growing
For reaping folk and sowing,
For harvest-time and mowing,
   A sleepy world of streams.

I am tired of tears and laughter,
10   And men that laugh and weep;
Of what may come hereafter
   For men that sow to reap:
I am weary of days and hours,
Blown buds of barren flowers,
15 Desires and dreams and powers
   And everything but sleep.

Here life has death for neighbor,
   And far from eye or ear
Wan waves and wet winds labor,
20   Weak ships and spirits steer;
They drive adrift, and whither
They wot not who make thither;
But no such winds blow hither,
   And no such things grow here.

25 No growth of moor or coppice,
    No heather-flower or vine,
But bloomless buds of poppies,
   Green grapes of Proserpine,
Pale beds of blowing rushes
30 Where no leaf blooms or blushes
Save this whereout she crushes
   For dead men deadly wine.

Pale, without name or number,
   In fruitless fields of corn,°   *wheat*
35 They bow themselves and slumber
   All night till light is born;

5. Persephone, in Roman mythology Proserpine, the daughter of Zeus and Demeter, had been abducted by Hades (the Roman Pluto), god of the underworld (over which she ruled with him thereafter as his queen).

And like a soul belated,
In hell and heaven unmated,
By cloud and mist abated
40   Comes out of darkness morn.

Though one were strong as seven,
   He too with death shall dwell,
Nor wake with wings in heaven,
   Nor weep for pains in hell;
45 Though one were fair as roses,
   His beauty clouds and closes;
And well though love reposes,
   In the end it is not well.

Pale, beyond porch and portal,
50   Crowned with calm leaves, she stands
Who gathers all things mortal
   With cold immortal hands;
Her languid lips are sweeter
Than love's who fears to greet her
55 To men that mix and meet her
   From many times and lands.

She waits for each and other,
   She waits for all men born;
Forgets the earth her mother,
60   The life of fruits and corn;
And spring and seed and swallow
Take wing for her and follow
Where summer song rings hollow
   And flowers are put to scorn.

65 There go the loves that wither,
   The old loves with wearier wings;
And all dead years draw thither,
   And all disastrous things;
Dead dreams of days forsaken,
70 Blind buds that snows have shaken,
Wild leaves that winds have taken,
   Red strays of ruined springs.

We are not sure of sorrow,
   And joy was never sure;
75 Today will die tomorrow;
   Time stoops to no man's lure;[6]
And love, grown faint and fretful,
With lips but half regretful
Sighs, and with eyes forgetful
80   Weeps that no love endure.

From too much love of living,
   From hope and fear set free,

6. In falconry, the lure is a device used to recall the hawk to the falconer's wrist.

We thank with brief thanksgiving
    Whatever gods may be
85 That no life lives for ever;
    That dead men rise up never;
    That even the weariest river
        Winds somewhere safe to sea.

    Then star nor sun shall waken,
90   Nor any change of light:
    Nor sound of waters shaken,
        Nor any sound or sight:
    Nor wintry leaves nor vernal,
    Nor days nor things diurnal;
95 Only the sleep eternal
        In an eternal night.

                                        1866

A Forsaken Garden

In a coign of the cliff between lowland and highland,
    At the sea-down's edge between windward and lee,
Walled round with rocks as an inland island,
    The ghost of a garden fronts the sea.
5 A girdle of brushwood and thorn encloses
    The steep square slope of the blossomless bed
Where the weeds that grew green from the graves of its roses
        Now lie dead.

The fields fall southward, abrupt and broken,
10   To the low last edge of the long lone land.
If a step should sound or a word be spoken,
    Would a ghost not rise at the strange guest's hand?
So long have the grey bare walks lain guestless,
    Through branches and briars if a man make way,
15 He shall find no life but the sea-wind's, restless
        Night and day.

The dense hard passage is blind and stifled
    That crawls by a track none turn to climb
To the strait waste place that the years have rifled
20   Of all but the thorns that are touched not of time.
The thorns he spares when the rose is taken;
    The rocks are left when he wastes the plain.
The wind that wanders, the weeds wind-shaken,
        These remain.

25 Not a flower to be pressed of the foot that falls not;
    As the heart of a dead man the seed-plots are dry;
From the thicket of thorns whence the nightingale calls not,
    Could she call, there were never a rose to reply.
Over the meadows that blossom and wither
30   Rings but the note of a sea-bird's song;

Only the sun and the rain come hither
    All year long.

The sun burns sere° and the rain dishevels   *dry*
    One gaunt bleak blossom of scentless breath.
35 Only the wind here hovers and revels
    In a round where life seems barren as death.
Here there was laughing of old, there was weeping,
    Haply, of lovers none ever will know,
Whose eyes went seaward a hundred sleeping
40   Years ago.

Heart handfast in heart as they stood, "Look thither,"
    Did he whisper? "look forth from the flowers to the sea,
For the foam-flowers endure when the rose-blossoms wither,
    And men that love lightly may die—but we?"
45 And the same wind sang and the same waves whitened,
    And or ever the garden's last petals were shed,
In the lips that had whispered, the eyes that had lightened,
        Love was dead.

Or they loved their life through, and then went whither?
50   And were one to the end—but what end who knows?
Love deep as the sea as a rose must wither,
    As the rose-red seaweed that mocks the rose.
Shall the dead take thought for the dead to love them?
    What love was ever as deep as a grave?
55 They are loveless now as the grass above them
        Or the wave.

All are at one now, roses and lovers,
    Not known of the cliffs and the fields and the sea.
Not a breath of the time that has been hovers
60   In the air now soft with a summer to be.
Not a breath shall there sweeten the seasons hereafter
    Of the flowers or the lovers that laugh now or weep,
When as they that are free now of weeping and laughter
        We shall sleep.

65 Here death may deal not again for ever;
    Here change may come not till all change end.
From the graves they have made they shall rise up never,
    Who have left nought living to ravage and rend.
Earth, stones, and thorns of the wild ground growing,
70   While the sun and the rain live, these shall be;
Till a last wind's breath upon all these blowing
        Roll the sea.

Till the slow sea rise and the sheer cliff crumble,
    Till terrace and meadow the deep gulfs drink,
75 Till the strength of the waves of the high tides humble
    The fields that lessen, the rocks that shrink,
Here now in his triumph where all things falter,

Stretched out on the spoils that his own hand spread,
As a god self-slain on his own strange altar,
80   Death lies dead.
1876   1878

THOMAS HARDY
1840–1928

Hap

If but some vengeful god would call to me
From up the sky, and laugh: "Thou suffering thing,
Know that thy sorrow is my ecstasy,
That thy love's loss is my hate's profiting!"

5   Then would I bear it, clench myself, and die,
Steeled by the sense of ire unmerited;
Half-eased in that a Powerfuller than I
Had willed and meted me the tears I shed.

But not so. How arrives it joy lies slain,
10 And why unblooms the best hope ever sown?
—Crass Casualty obstructs the sun and rain,
And dicing Time for gladness casts a moan. . . .
These purblind Doomsters had as readily strown
Blisses about my pilgrimage as pain.
1866   1898

Neutral Tones

We stood by a pond that winter day,
And the sun was white, as though chidden of° God,   *rebuked by*
And a few leaves lay on the starving sod;°   *turf*
    —They had fallen from an ash, and were grey.

5   Your eyes on me were as eyes that rove
Over tedious riddles of years ago;
And some words played between us to and fro
    On which lost the more by our love.

The smile on your mouth was the deadest thing
10 Alive enough to have strength to die;
And a grin of bitterness swept thereby
    Like an ominous bird a-wing. . .

Since then, keen lessons that love deceives,
And wrings with wrong, have shaped to me
15 Your face, and the God-curst sun, and a tree,
    And a pond edged with greyish leaves
1867   1898

Thoughts of Phena[1]

At News of Her Death

Not a line of her writing have I,
    Not a thread of her hair,
No mark of her late time as dame in her dwelling, whereby
    I may picture her there;
5   And in vain do I urge my unsight
      To conceive my lost prize
At her close, whom I knew when her dreams were upbrimming with light,
    And with laughter her eyes.

What scenes spread around her last days,
10   Sad, shining, or dim?
Did her gifts and compassions enray and enarch her sweet ways
    With an aureate nimb?°   *nimbus*
Or did life-light decline from her years,
    And mischances control
15 Her full day-star; unease, or regret, or forebodings, or fears
    Disennoble her soul?

Thus I do but the phantom retain
    Of the maiden of yore
As my relic; yet haply the best of her—fined° in my brain   *refined*
20   It may be the more
That no line of her writing have I,
    Nor a thread of her hair,
No mark of her late time as dame in her dwelling, whereby
    I may picture her there.

March 1890   1898

I Look into My Glass

I look into my glass,
    And view my wasting skin,
And say, "Would God it came to pass
    My heart had shrunk as thin!"

5   For then, I, undistrest
    By hearts grown cold to me,
Could lonely wait my endless rest
    With equanimity.

But Time, to make me grieve,
10   Part steals, lets part abide;
And shakes this fragile frame at eve
    With throbbings of noontide.

                                                1898

---

1. The name under which, at various places in his writings, Hardy lightly concealed the identity of Tryphena Sparks, a young woman with whom he had a liaison in the late 1860s and early 1870s; she terminated their engagement in 1873. (See J. O. Bailey, *The Poetry of Thomas Hardy*, 1970, pp. 35–37.)

Drummer Hodge[2]

1

They throw in Drummer Hodge, to rest
    Uncoffined—just as found:
His landmark is a kopje-crest[3]
    That breaks the veldt around;
5   And foreign constellations west
    Each night above his mound.

2

Young Hodge the Drummer never knew—
    Fresh from his Wessex home—
The meaning of the broad Karoo,
10   The Bush, the dusty loam,
And why uprose to nightly view
    Strange stars amid the gloam.

3

Yet portion of that unknown plain
    Will Hodge forever be;
15 His homely Northern breast and brain
    Grow to some Southern tree,
And strange-eyed constellations reign
    His stars eternally.

1902

A Broken Appointment

    You did not come,
And marching Time drew on, and wore me numb.
Yet less for loss of your dear presence there
Than that I thus found lacking in your make
5   That high compassion which can overbear
Reluctance for pure lovingkindness' sake
Grieved I, when, as the hope-hour stroked its sum,
    You did not come.

    You love not me,
10 And love alone can lend you loyalty;
    —I know and knew it. But, unto the store
Of human deeds divine in all but name,
Was it not worth a little hour or more
To add yet this: Once you, a woman, came
15 To soothe a time-torn man; even though it be
    You love not me?

1902

2. The poem presents an incident from the Boer War (1899–1902) and when first published bore this note: "One of the Drummers killed was a native of a village near Casterbridge," i.e., Dorchester, the principal city of the region of southern England to which, in his novels and poems, Hardy gave its medieval name of Wessex.
3. In Afrikaans, the language of the Dutch settlers in South Africa, the crest of a small hill. The veldt (line 4) is open country, unenclosed pasture land; the Karoo (line 9), barren tracts of plateau-land.

The Darkling Thrush

I leant upon a coppice[4] gate
    When Frost was spectre-grey,
And Winter's dregs made desolate
    The weakening eye of day.
5 The tangled bine-stems[5] scored the sky
    Like strings of broken lyres,
And all mankind that haunted nigh
    Had sought their household fires.

The land's sharp features seemed to be
10   The Century's corpse outleant,
His crypt the cloudy canopy,
    The wind his death-lament.
The ancient pulse of germ and birth
    Was shrunken hard and dry,
15 And every spirit upon earth
    Seemed fervourless as I.

At once a voice arose among
    The bleak twigs overhead
In a full-hearted evensong
20   Of joy illimited;
An aged thrush, frail, gaunt, and small,
    In blast-beruffled plume,
Had chosen thus to fling his soul
    Upon the growing gloom.

25 So little cause for carolings
    Of such ecstatic sound
Was written on terrestrial things
    Afar or nigh around,
That I could think there trembled through
30   His happy good-night air
Some blessed Hope, whereof he knew
    And I was unaware.

December 31, 1900   1902

The Ruined Maid

"O'Melia, my dear, this does everything crown!
Who could have supposed I should meet you in Town?
And whence such fair garments, such prosperi-ty?"
"O didn't you know I'd been ruined?" said she.

5 "You left us in tatters, without shoes or socks,
Tired of digging potatoes, and spudding up docks;[6]
And now you've gay bracelets and bright feathers three!"
"Yes: that's how we dress when we're ruined," said she.

---

4. Thicket or wood consisting of small trees.   6. Digging up weedy herbs.
5. Shoots or stems of a climbing plant.

"At home in the barton° you said 'thee' and 'thou,'   *farm*
10   And 'thik oon,' and 'theäs oon,' and 't'other'; but now
Your talking quite fits 'ee for high compa-ny!"
"Some polish is gained with one's ruin," said she.

"Your hands were like paws then, your face blue and bleak
But now I'm bewitched by your delicate cheek,
15   And your little gloves fit as on any la-dy!"
"We never do work when we're ruined," said she.

"You used to call home-life a hag-ridden dream,
And you'd sigh, and you'd sock; but at present you seem
To know not of megrims° or melancho-ly!"   *low spirits*
20   "True. One's pretty lively when ruined," said she.

"I wish I had feathers, a fine sweeping gown,
And a delicate face, and could strut about Town!"
"My dear—a raw country girl, such as you be,
Cannot quite expect that. You ain't ruined," said she.

1866   1902

The Convergence of the Twain

Lines on the Loss of the Titanic[7]

1

In a solitude of the sea
Deep from human vanity,
And the Pride of Life that planned her, stilly couches she.

2

Steel chambers, late the pyres
5   Of her salamandrine fires,[8]
Cold currents thrid,° and turn to rhythmic tidal lyres.   *thread*

3

Over the mirrors meant
To glass the opulent
The sea-worm crawls—grotesque, slimed, dumb, indifferent.

4

10   Jewels in joy designed
To ravish the sensuous mind
Lie lightless, all their sparkles bleared and black and blind.

5

Dim moon-eyed fishes near
Gaze at the gilded gear
15   And query: "What does this vaingloriousness down here?"

7. The White Star liner R.M.S. *Titanic* was sunk, with great loss of life, as the result of collision with an iceberg on its maiden voyage from Southampton to New York on April 15, 1912.

8. The ship's fires, which burn though immersed in water, are compared to the salamander, a lizardlike creature that according to fable could live in the midst of fire.

6

Well: while was fashioning
This creature of cleaving wing,
The Immanent Will that stirs and urges everything

7

Prepared a sinister mate
20   For her—so gaily great—
A Shape of Ice, for the time far and dissociate.

8

And as the smart ship grew
In stature, grace, and hue,
In shadowy silent distance grew the Iceberg too.

9

25   Alien they seemed to be:
No mortal eye could see
The intimate welding of their later history,

10

Or sign that they were bent
By paths coincident
30 On being anon twin halves of one august event,

11

Till the Spinner of the Years
Said "Now!" And each one hears,
And consummation comes, and jars two hemispheres.

1912

Channel Firing

That night your great guns, unawares,
Shook all our coffins as we lay,
And broke the chancel window-squares,
We thought it was the Judgment-day

5 And sat upright. While drearisome
Arose the howl of wakened hounds:
The mouse let fall the altar-crumb,
The worms drew back into the mounds,

The glebe cow[9] drooled. Till God called, "No;
10 It's gunnery practice out at sea
Just as before you went below;
The world is as it used to be:

"All nations striving strong to make
Red war yet redder. Mad as hatters
15 They do no more for Christés sake
Than you who are helpless in such matters.

"That this is not the judgment-hour
For some of them's a blessed thing,

9. Cow pastured on the glebe, a piece of land attached to a vicarage or rectory.

For if it were they'd have to scour
20   Hell's floor for so much threatening. . . .

"Ha, ha. It will be warmer when
I blow the trumpet (if indeed
I ever do; for you are men,
And rest eternal sorely need)."

25   So down we lay again. "I wonder,
Will the world ever saner be,"
Said one, "than when He sent us under
In our indifferent century!"

And many a skeleton shook his head.
30   "Instead of preaching forty year,"
My neighbour Parson Thirdly said,
"I wish I had stuck to pipes and beer."

Again the guns disturbed the hour,
Roaring their readiness to avenge,
35   As far inland as Stourton Tower,
And Camelot, and starlit Stonehenge.[1]

April 1914   1914

Under the Waterfall

"Whenever I plunge my arm, like this,
In a basin of water, I never miss
The sweet sharp sense of a fugitive day
Fetched back from its thickening shroud of grey.
5   Hence the only prime
               And real love-rhyme
               That I know by heart,
               And that leaves no smart,
Is the purl[2] of a little valley fall
10   About three spans wide and two spans tall
Over a table of solid rock
And into a scoop of the self-same block;
The purl of a runlet that never ceases
In stir of kingdoms, in wars, in peaces;
15   With a hollow boiling voice it speaks
And has spoken since hills were turfless peaks."

"And why gives this the only prime
Idea to you of a real love-rhyme?
And why does plunging your arm in a bowl
20   Full of spring water, bring throbs to your soul?"

1. Stourton Tower, built in 1772, and locally known as "Alfred's Tower," stands on the highest point of the estate of Stourhead, in Wiltshire, close to the Somersetshire border. Camelot, the seat of King Arthur's court, has been variously associated with Winchester and with certain places in Somer- setshire. Stonehenge is a circular grouping of megalithic monuments on Salisbury Plain, Wilt- shire, dating back to the late Neolithic or early Bronze Age.
2. Flow with a murmuring sound.

"Well, under the fall, in a crease of the stone,
Though where precisely none ever has known,
Jammed darkly, nothing to show how prized,
And by now with its smoothness opalized,
25   Is a drinking-glass:
           For, down that pass
           My lover and I
           Walked under a sky
Of blue with a leaf-wove awning of green,
30 In the burn of August, to paint the scene,
And we placed our basket of fruit and wine
By the runlet's rim, where we sat to dine;
And when we had drunk from the glass together,
Arched by the oak-copse from the weather,
35 I held the vessel to rinse in the fall,
Where it slipped, and sank, and was past recall,
Though we stooped and plumbed the little abyss
With long bared arms. There the glass still is.
And, as said, if I thrust my arm below
40 Cold water in basin or bowl, a throe[3]
From the past awakens a sense of that time,
And the glass we used, and the cascade's rhyme.
The basin seems the pool, and its edge
The hard smooth face of the brook-side ledge,
45 And the leafy pattern of china-ware
The hanging plants that were bathing there.

"By night, by day, when it shines or lours,°   *darkens*
There lies intact that chalice of ours,
And its presence adds to the rhyme of love
50 Persistently sung by the fall above.
No lip has touched it since his and mine
In turns therefrom sipped lovers' wine."

                                              1914

The Voice

Woman much missed, how you call to me, call to me,
Saying that now you are not as you were
When you had changed from the one who was all to me,
But as at first, when our day was fair.

5 Can it be you that I hear? Let me view you, then,
Standing as when I drew near to the town
Where you would wait for me: yes, as I knew you then,
Even to the original air-blue gown!

Or is it only the breeze, in its listlessness
10 Travelling across the wet mead to me here,
You being ever dissolved to wan wistlessness,°   *heedlessness*
Heard no more again far or near?

3. Violent pang.

Thus I; faltering forward,
Leaves around me falling,
15 Wind oozing thin through the thorn from norward,
And the woman calling.

December 1912   1914

During Wind and Rain

They sing their dearest songs—
He, she, all of them—yea,
Treble and tenor and bass,
    And one to play;
5 With the candles mooning each face. . . .
    Ah, no; the years O!
How the sick leaves reel down in throngs!

They clear the creeping moss—
Elders and juniors—aye,
10 Making the pathways neat
    And the garden gay;
And they build a shady seat. . . .
    Ah, no; the years, the years;
See, the white storm-birds wing across.

15 They are blithely° breakfasting all—   *cheerfully*
Men and maidens—yea,
Under the summer tree,
    With a glimpse of the bay,
While pet fowl come to the knee. . . .
20   Ah, no; the years O!
And the rotten rose is ript from the wall.

They change to a high new house,
He, she, all of them—aye,
Clocks and carpets and chairs
25   On the lawn all day,
And brightest things that are theirs. . . .
    Ah, no; the years, the years
Down their carved names the rain-drop ploughs.

                                                                            1917

In Time of "The Breaking of Nations"[4]

1

Only a man harrowing clods
    In a slow silent walk
With an old horse that stumbles and nods
    Half asleep as they stalk.

---

4. See Jeremiah 51.20: "Thou art my battle ax and weapons of war: for with thee will I break in pieces the nations, and with thee will I destroy kingdoms."

2

5   Only thin smoke without flame
     From the heaps of couch-grass;
   Yet this will go onward the same
     Though Dynasties pass.

3

   Yonder a maid and her wight°   *man*
10   Come whispering by:
   War's annals will cloud into night
     Ere their story die.

1915   1916

Afterwards

When the Present has latched its postern° behind my   *back gate*
   tremulous stay
And the May month flaps its glad green leaves like wings,
Delicate-filmed as new-spun silk, will the neighbours say,
   "He was a man who used to notice such things"?

5   If it be in the dusk when, like an eyelid's soundless blink,
     The dewfall-hawk comes crossing the shades to alight
   Upon the wind-warped upland thorn, a gazer may think,
     "To him this must have been a familiar sight."

   If I pass during some nocturnal blackness, mothy and warm,
10   When the hedgehog travels furtively over the lawn,
   One may say, "He strove that such innocent creatures should come to
     no harm,
     But he could do little for them; and now he is gone."

   If, when hearing that I have been stilled at last, they stand at the door,
     Watching the full-starred heavens that winter sees,
15   Will this thought rise on those who will meet my face no more,
     "He was one who had an eye for such mysteries"?

   And will any say when my bell of quittance is heard in the gloom,
     And a crossing breeze cuts a pause in its outrollings,
   Till they rise again, as they were a new bell's boom,
20   "He hears it not now, but used to notice such things"?

                                                          1917

SIDNEY LANIER

1842–1881

From the Flats[1]

What heartache—ne'er a hill!
Inexorable, vapid, vague, and chill

---

1. Written in Tampa, Florida; Lanier was from Georgia.

The drear sand-levels drain my spirit low.
With one poor word they tell me all they know;
5   Whereat their stupid tongues, to tease my pain,
Do drawl it o'er again and o'er again.
They hurt my heart with griefs I cannot name:
     Always the same, the same.

     Nature hath no surprise,
10 No ambuscade of beauty 'gainst mine eyes
From brake or lurking dell or deep defile;°   *narrow pass*
No humors, frolic forms—this mile, that mile;
No rich reserves or happy-valley hopes
Beyond the bends of roads, the distant slopes.
15 Her fancy fails, her wild is all run tame:
     Ever the same, the same.

     Oh, might I through these tears
But glimpse some hill my Georgia high uprears,
Where white the quartz and pink the pebble shine,
20 The hickory heavenward strives, the muscadine°   *grapevine*
Swings o'er the slope, the oak's far-falling shade
Darkens the dogwood in the bottom glade,
    And down the hollow from a ferny nook
     Bright leaps a living brook!

                                 1877

The Marshes of Glynn[2]

Glooms of the live-oaks,[3] beautiful-braided and woven
With intricate shades of the vines that myriad-cloven
   Clamber the forks of the multiform boughs,—
      Emerald twilights,—
5   Virginal shy lights,
Wrought of the leaves to allure to the whisper of vows,
When lovers pace timidly down through the green colonnades
   Of the dim sweet woods, of the dear dark woods,
      Of the heavenly woods and glades,
10 That run to the radiant marginal sand-beach within
     The wide sea-marshes of Glynn;—

Beautiful glooms, soft dusks in the noon-day fire,—
Wildwood privacies, closets of lone desire,
Chamber from chamber parted with wavering arras° of   *tapestry*
   leaves,—
15 Cells for the passionate pleasure of prayer to the soul that grieves,
   Pure with a sense of the passing of saints through the wood,
   Cool for the dutiful weighing of ill with good;—

O braided dusks of the oak and woven shades of the vine,
While the riotous noon-day sun of the June-day long did shine,

2. Glynn County, Georgia.
3. Evergreen oak, indigenous to the American South.

20 Ye held me fast in your heart and I held you fast in mine;
But now when the noon is no more, and riot is rest,
And the sun is a-wait at the ponderous gate of the West,
And the slant yellow beam down the wood-aisle doth seem
Like a lane into heaven that leads from a dream,—
25 Ay, now, when my soul all day hath drunken the soul of the oak,
And my heart is at ease from men, and the wearisome sound of the stroke
Of the scythe of time and the trowel of trade is low,
And belief overmasters doubt, and I know that I know,
And my spirit is grown to a lordly great compass within,
30 That the length and the breadth and the sweep of the marshes of
Glynn
Will work me no fear like the fear they have wrought me of yore
When length was fatigue, and when breadth was but bitterness sore,
And when terror and shrinking and dreary unnamable pain
Drew over me out of the merciless miles of the plain,—
35 Oh, now, unafraid, I am fain° to face   *would like*
The vast sweet visage of space.
To the edge of the wood I am drawn, I am drawn,
Where the gray beach glimmering runs, as a belt of the dawn,
For a mete° and a mark   *measure*
40 To the forest-dark:—
So:
Affable live-oak, leaning low,—
Thus—with your favor—soft, with a reverent hand,
(Not lightly touching your person, Lord of the land!)
45 Bending your beauty aside, with a step I stand
On the firm-packed sand,
Free
By a world of marsh that borders a world of sea.
Sinuous southward and sinuous northward the shimmering band
50 Of the sand-beach fastens the fringe of the marsh to the folds of the land.
Inward and outward to northward and southward the beachlines linger
and curl
As a silver-wrought garment that clings to and follows the firm sweet
limbs of a girl.
Vanishing, swerving, evermore curving again into sight,
Softly the sand-beach wavers away to a dim gray looping of light.
55 And what if behind me to westward the wall of the woods stands high?
The world lies east: how ample, the marsh and the sea and the sky!
A league[4] and a league of marsh-grass, waist-high, broad in the blade,
Green, and all of a height, and unflecked with a light or a shade,
Stretch leisurely off, in a pleasant plain,
60 To the terminal blue of the main.°   *sea*

Oh, what is abroad in the marsh and the terminal sea?
Somehow my soul seems suddenly free
From the weighing of fate and the sad discussion of sin,
By the length and the breadth and the sweep of the marshes of
Glynn.
65 Ye marshes, how candid and simple and nothing-withholding and free

---

4. An English unit of about three miles.

Ye publish yourselves to the sky and offer yourselves to the sea!
Tolerant plains, that suffer the sea and the rains and the sun,
Ye spread and span like the catholic man who hath mightily won
 God out of knowledge and good out of infinite pain
70 And sight out of blindness and purity out of a stain.

 As the marsh-hen secretly builds on the watery sod,
 Behold I will build me a nest on the greatness of God:
 I will fly in the greatness of God as the marsh-hen flies
 In the freedom that fills all the space 'twixt the marsh and the skies:
75 By so many roots as the marsh-grass sends in the sod
 I will heartily lay me a-hold on the greatness of God:
 Oh, like to the greatness of God is the greatness within
 The range of the marshes, the liberal marshes of Glynn.

 And the sea lends large, as the marsh: lo, out of his plenty the sea
80 Pours fast: full soon the time of the flood-tide must be:
  Look how the grace of the sea doth go
 About and about through the intricate channels that flow
   Here and there,
   Everywhere,
85 Till his waters have flooded the uttermost creeks and the low-lying lanes,
  And the marsh is meshed with a million veins,
 That like as with rosy and silvery essences flow
  In the rose-and-silver evening glow.
   Farewell, my lord Sun!
90 The creeks overflow: a thousand rivulets run
 'Twixt the roots of the sod; the blades of the marsh-grass stir;
Passeth a hurrying sound of wings that westward whirr;
Passeth, and all is still; and the currents cease to run;
  And the sea and the marsh are one.

95 How still the plains of the waters be!
  The tide is in his ecstasy.
  The tide is at his highest height:
   And it is night.

 And now from the Vast of the Lord will the waters of sleep
100 Roll in on the souls of men,
 But who will reveal to our waking ken°   *range of vision*
 The forms that swim and the shapes that creep
  Under the waters of sleep?
And I would I could know what swimmeth below when the tide comes in
105 On the length and the breadth of the marvellous marshes of Glynn.
                              1878

GERARD MANLEY HOPKINS

1844–1889

God's Grandeur

The world is charged with the grandeur of God.
  It will flame out, like shining from shook foil;[1]
  It gathers to a greatness, like the ooze of oil
Crushed.[2] Why do men then now not reck his rod?
5　Generations have trod, have trod, have trod;
  And all is seared with trade; bleared, smeared with toil;
  And wears man's smudge and shares man's smell: the soil
Is bare now, nor can foot feel, being shod.

And for all this, nature is never spent;
10　There lives the dearest freshness deep down things;
And though the last lights off the black West went
  Oh, morning, at the brown brink eastward, springs—
Because the Holy Ghost over the bent
  World broods with warm breast and with ah! bright wings.

1877　　　　　　　　　　　　　　　　　　　　　　　　　　　1895

The Windhover[3]

To Christ Our Lord

I caught this morning morning's minion,° king-　　　　*darling, favorite*
  dom of daylight's dauphin,[4] dapple-dawn-drawn Falcon,
    in his riding
Of the rolling level underneath him steady air, and striding
High there, how he rung upon the rein of a wimpling° wing　　*rippling*
5　In his ecstasy! then off, off forth on swing,
  As a skate's heel sweeps smooth on a bow-bend: the hurl and gliding
  Rebuffed the big wind. My heart in hiding
Stirred for a bird,—the achieve of, the mastery of the thing!

Brute beauty and valour and act, oh, air, pride, plume, here
10　Buckle![5] AND the fire that breaks from thee then, a billion
Times told lovelier, more dangerous, O my chevalier![6]

---

1. In a letter to Robert Bridges (January 4, 1883), Hopkins says: "I mean foil in its sense of leaf or tinsel, and no other word whatever will give the effect I want. Shaken goldfoil gives off broad glares like sheet lightning and also, and this is true of nothing else, owing to its zigzag dints and crossings and network of small many cornered facets, a sort of fork lightning too."
2. I.e., as when olives are crushed for their oil.
3. "A name for the kestrel [a species of small hawk], from its habit of hovering or hanging with its head to the wind" [O.E.D.].
4. The eldest son of the king of France was called the *dauphin:* hence, the word here means heir to a splendid, kingly condition.
5. The word "buckle" brings to a single focus the several elements of line 9, both in their literal sense, as descriptive of a single, sudden movement of the airborne bird, and in their symbolic sense as descriptive of Christ and with further reference to the poet himself and the lesson he draws from his observation. It may be read either as indicative or imperative, and in one or another of its possible meanings: "to fasten," "to join closely," "to equip for battle," "to grapple with, engage," but also "to cause to bend, give way, crumple."
6. Knight, nobleman, champion.

No wonder of it: shéer plód makes plough down sillion°   *furrow*
  Shine, and blue-bleak embers, ah my dear,
    Fall, gall themselves, and gash gold-vermilion.

1877   1918

Pied Beauty[7]

Glory be to God for dappled things—
  For skies of couple-colour as a brinded° cow;   *streaked, brindled*
    For rose-moles all in stipple upon trout that swim;
  Fresh-firecoal chestnut-falls;[8] finches' wings;
5   Landscape plotted and pieced—fold, fallow, and plough;[9]
    And áll trádes, their gear and tackle and trim.
  All things counter, original, spare, strange;
    Whatever is fickle, freckled (who knows how?)
    With swift, slow; sweet, sour; adazzle, dim;
10 He fathers-forth whose beauty is past change:
                  Praise him.

1877   1918

Felix Randal

Felix Randal the farrier,° O is he dead then? my duty   *blacksmith*
  all ended,
Who have watched his mould of man, big-boned and hardy-
  handsome
Pining, pining, till time when reason rambled in it and some
Fatal four disorders, fleshed there, all contended?

5 Sickness broke him. Impatient, he cursed at first, but mended
Being anointed and all; though a heavenlier heart began some
Months earlier, since I had our sweet reprieve and ransom
Tendered to him.[1] Ah well, God rest him all road ever he offended![2]

This seeing the sick endears them to us, us too it endears.
10 My tongue had taught thee comfort, touch had quenched thy tears,
Thy tears that touched my heart, child, Felix, poor Felix Randal;

How far from then forethought of, all thy more boisterous years,
When thou at the random[3] grim forge, powerful amidst peers,
Didst fettle[4] for the great grey drayhorse his bright and battering sandal!

1880   1918

---

7. "Pied": having two or more colors, in patches or blotches.
8. In his *Journals* Hopkins writes of "chestnuts as bright as coals or spots of vermilion."
9. The land makes a pattern of varicolored patches by reason of its several uses, as for pasture, or being left fallow for a season, or being plowed and sown.
1. I.e., since I had a priest visit him to hear his confession and give absolution.

2. I.e., for any way in which he may have offended.
3. Ramshackle, as applied to the forge itself; but also meaning that the man's life as a blacksmith was merely one casual earthly life as opposed to the sure way of Christian salvation.
4. To line or cover with a refractory material; hence, to shoe.

Spring and Fall

To a Young Child

Márgarét, áre you gríeving
Over Goldengrove unleaving?
Leáves, líke the things of man, you
With your fresh thoughts care for, can you?
5 Áh! ás the heart grows older
It will come to such sights colder
By and by, nor spare a sigh
Though worlds of wanwood leafmeal lie;[5]
And yet you *will* weep and know why.
10 Now no matter, child, the name:
Sórrow's spríngs áre the same.
Nor mouth had, no nor mind, expressed
What heart heard of, ghost° guessed: *spirit, soul*
It ís the blight man was born for,
15 It is Margaret you mourn for.

1880   1893

[As Kingfishers Catch Fire, Dragonflies Draw Flame]

As kingfishers catch fire, dragonflies draw flame;[6]
   As tumbled over rim in roundy wells
Stones ring; like each tucked° string tells, each   *touched, plucked*
      hung bell's
Bow swung finds tongue to fling out broad its name;
5 Each mortal thing does one thing and the same:
   Deals out that being indoors each one dwells;[7]
   Selves[8]—goes itself; *myself* it speaks and spells,
Crying *What I do is me: for that I came.*

I say more: the just man justices;
10   Keeps gráce: thát keeps all his goings graces;
Acts in God's eye what in God's eye he is—
   Chríst. For Christ plays in ten thousand places,
Lovely in limbs, and lovely in eyes not his
   To the Father through the features of men's faces.

1882?   1918

[Carrion Comfort]

Not, I'll not, carrion[9] comfort, Despair, not feast on thee;
Not untwist—slack they may be—these last strands of man
In me ór, most weary, cry *I can no more.* I can;
Can something, hope, wish day come, not choose not to be.

---

5. "Wanwood": *pale* or *dim*—the groves are pale because of their light-colored autumn foliage, or dim because of the filtered light. "Leafmeal" (a word coined by Hopkins by analogy with "piecemeal"): *leaf by leaf* or *leaf mold*—in the first sense, the foliage lies about the grove, having fallen leaf by leaf; in the second, foliage gradually decays to leaf mold.
6. I.e., as their bright colors flash in the light.
7. I.e., gives utterance to the essential nature that dwells within ("indoors") each individual being.
8. I.e., gives being to its own individuality.
9. Dead and putrefying flesh.

5 But ah, but O thou terrible, why wouldst thou rude° on me   *roughly*
     Thy wring-world right foot[1] rock? lay a lionlimb against me? scan
     With darksome devouring eyes my bruisèd bones? and fan,
     O in turns of tempest, me heaped there; me frantic to avoid thee
       and flee?

     Why? That my chaff might fly; my grain lie, sheer and clear.
10 Nay in all that toil, that coil, since (seems) I kissed the rod,
     Hand[2] rather, my heart lo! lapped strength, stole joy, would laugh, chéer.
     Cheer whom though? The hero whose heaven-handling flung me,
       fóot tród
     Me? or me that fought him? O which one? is it each one? That night,
       that year
     Of now done darkness I wretch lay wrestling with (my God!) my God.
1885   1918

[No Worst, There Is None. Pitched Past Pitch of Grief]

     No worst, there is none. Pitched past pitch of grief,
     More pangs will, schooled at forepangs, wilder wring.
     Comforter, where, where is your comforting?
     Mary, mother of us, where is your relief?

5 My cries heave, herds-long; huddle in a main, a chief-
     woe, world-sorrow; on an age-old anvil wince and sing—
     Then lull, then leave off. Fury had shrieked "No ling-
     ering! Let me be fell:° force° I must be brief".   *fierce / perforce*

     O the mind, mind has mountains; cliffs of fall
10 Frightful, sheer, no-man-fathomed. Hold them cheap
     May who ne'er hung there. Nor does long our small
     Durance° deal with that steep or deep. Here! creep,   *endurance*
     Wretch, under a comfort serves in a whirlwind: all
     Life death does end and each day dies with sleep.
1885   1918

[I Wake and Feel the Fell of Dark, Not Day]

     I wake and feel the fell[3] of dark, not day.
     What hours, O what black hoürs we have spent
     This night! what sights you, heart, saw; ways you went!
     And more must, in yet longer light's delay.

5 With witness I speak this. But where I say
     Hours I mean years, mean life. And my lament
     Is cries countless, cries like dead° letters sent   *undelivered*
     To dearest him that lives alas! away.

---

1. I.e., the foot capable of causing the world to writhe or twist.
2. I.e., the hand that wields the rod.
3. "Fell" is capable of being read in a number of senses: as "the hide or hairy skin of a beast," or, in an obsolete or rare sense, as "gall, bitterness; hence, animosity, rancor" [O.E.D.], or possibly as the adjective "fell"—fierce, savage, cruel—used as a noun.

I am gall, I am heartburn. God's most deep decree
10   Bitter would have me taste: my taste was me;
Bones built in me, flesh filled, blood brimmed the curse.

Selfyeast of spirit a dull dough sours. I see
The lost are like this, and their scourge to be
As I am mine, their sweating selves, but worse.

1885   1918

[My Own Heart Let Me More Have Pity On]

My own heart let me more have pity on; let
Me live to my sad self hereafter kind,
Charitable; not live this tormented mind
With this tormented mind tormenting yet.

5   I cast for comfort I can no more get
By groping round my comfortless, than blind
Eyes in their dark can day or thirst can find
Thirst's all-in-all in all a world of wet.[4]

Soul, self; come, poor Jackself,[5] I do advise
10   You, jaded, let be; call off thoughts awhile
Elsewhere; leave comfort root-room;[6] let joy size°   grow

At God knows when to God knows what;[7] whose smile
's not wrung,[8] see you; unforeseen times rather—as skies
Betweenpie mountains[9]—lights a lovely mile.

1885   1918

That Nature is a Heraclitean[1] Fire and of the comfort of the Resurrection

Cloud-puffball, torn tufts, tossed pillows | flaunt forth, then
        chevy° on an air-   race, scamper
built thoroughfare: heaven-roysterers, in gay-gangs | they throng;
        they glitter in marches.

4. I.e., as shipwrecked persons adrift without drinking water cannot quench their thirst, even though they are surrounded by "wet." The noun "world" is common to all three instances: the speaker's "comfortless" world, the blind man's "dark" world, the "world of wet" in which the shipwrecked are adrift.
5. The humble self—"Jack" used in a pitying, deprecating sense (as in "jack-of-all-trades").
6. Room for its roots to grow.
7. "At God knows when": at unpredictable times; "to God knows what": until it reaches an unpredictable condition.
8. Cannot be forced, but must come as it will.
9. "Betweenpie" (a verb of Hopkins' invention [see "Pied Beauty"]): the brightness of skies seen between mountains—which makes a variegated patterning of light and dark.
1. Heraclitus of Ephesus (flourished 500 B.C.) was the founder of an important school of pre-Socratic

philosophy who taught that the world had its origin in fire and would end in fire. "He is best known for his doctrine of perpetual change and impermanence in nature." For him the principle of the universe was "a law of opposites, whose conflicts were controlled by eternal justice and whose contrary tensions produced the apparent stability of being. Fire, the underlying primary substance, is the prototype of the world, which is an 'ever-living fire with measures of it kindling and measures of it going out.' Fire passes by combustion through the fiery waterspout . . . into water and earth; and the reverse process occurs simultaneously, when part of the earth liquefies and passes by evaporation and 'exhalation' as fuel into fire. Thus are constituted a 'way up' and a 'way down,' a two-way process of interchange between the elements, with approximate balance of 'measures.' 'All is perpetual flux and nothing abides.' " [A. J. D. Porteous, in *Chambers's Encyclopedia*]

Down roughcast,[2] down dazzling whitewash, | wherever an elm arches,
Shivelights[3] and shadowtackle[4] in long | lashes lace, lance, and pair.
5   Delightfully the bright wind boisterous | ropes, wrestles, beats earth bare
Of yestertempest's creases; | in pool and rutpeel parches
Squandering ooze to squeezed | dough, crust, dust; stanches, starches
Squadroned masks and manmarks | treadmire toil there
Footfretted in it. Million-fuelèd, | nature's bonfire burns on.
10 But quench her bonniest, dearest | to her, her clearest-selvèd spark
Man, how fast his firedint,[5] | his mark on mind, is gone!
Both are in an unfathomable, all is in an enormous dark
Drowned. O pity and indig | nation! Manshape, that shone
Sheer off, disseveral,[6] a star, | death blots black out; nor mark
15   Is any of him at all so stark
But vastness blurs and time | beats level. Enough! the Resurrection,
A heart's-clarion! Away grief's gasping, | joyless days, dejection.
          Across my foundering deck shone
A beacon, an eternal beam. | Flesh fade, and mortal trash
20 Fall to the residuary worm; | world's wildfire, leave but ash:
          In a flash, at a trumpet crash,
I am at once what Christ is, | since he was what I am, and
This Jack,[7] joke, poor potsherd, | patch, matchwood, immortal diamond,
          Is immortal diamond.

1888   1918

[Thou Art Indeed Just, Lord . . .]

*Justus quidem tu es, Domine, si disputem tecum: verumtamen
justa loquar ad te: Quare via impiorum prosperatur? & c.*[8]

Thou art indeed just, Lord, if I contend
With thee; but, sir, so what I plead is just.
Why do sinners' ways prosper? and why must
Disappointment all I endeavour end?
5   Wert thou my enemy, O thou my friend,
How wouldst thou worse, I wonder, than thou dost
Defeat, thwart me? Oh, the sots and thralls of lust
Do in spare hours more thrive than I that spend,
Sir, life upon thy cause. See, banks and brakes
10 Now, leavèd how thick! lacèd they are again
With fretty chervil,[9] look, and fresh wind shakes
Them; birds build—but not I build; no, but strain,
Time's eunuch, and not breed one work that wakes.
Mine, O thou lord of life, send my roots rain.

1889   1893

---

2. A mixture of lime and gravel used to coat walls.
3. Light in splinters, fragments.
4. Shadows in complicated shapes, as of ship's ropes, tackle, gear.
5. Hopkins' compound, meaning the mark made by the flame of man's spirit, the spirit's power to make its mark.
6. Separate.
7. Common mortal, like "poor Jackself" in "[My Own Heart Let Me More Have Pity On]."
8. The Latin epigraph is from the Vulgate version of Jeremiah 12.1; the first three lines of Hopkins' poem translate it. The "&c" indicates that the whole of Jeremiah 12 is relevant to the poem, which, while it does not continue to translate it directly, parallels it frequently.
9. An herb of the carrot or parsley family, with curled leaves.

EMMA LAZARUS

1849–1887

The New Colossus[1]

Not like the brazen giant of Greek fame,
With conquering limbs astride from land to land;
Here at our sea-washed, sunset gates shall stand
A mighty woman with a torch, whose flame
5   Is the imprisoned lightning, and her name
Mother of Exiles. From her beacon-hand
Glows world-wide welcome; her mild eyes command
The air-bridged harbor that twin cities frame.
"Keep, ancient lands, your storied pomp!"[2] cries she
10   With silent lips. "Give me your tired, your poor,
Your huddled masses yearning to breathe free,
The wretched refuse of your teeming shore.
Send these, the homeless, tempest-tost° to me,   *tossed*
I lift my lamp beside the golden door!"

1883   1888

A. E. HOUSMAN

1859–1936

Loveliest of Trees, the Cherry Now

Loveliest of trees, the cherry now
Is hung with bloom along the bough,
And stands about the woodland ride
Wearing white for Eastertide.

5   Now, of my threescore years and ten,
Twenty will not come again,
And take from seventy springs a score,
It only leaves me fifty more.

And since to look at things in bloom
10   Fifty springs are little room,
About the woodlands I will go
To see the cherry hung with snow.

1896

1. Written as part of a fundraising campaign for the Statue of Liberty, in New York harbor. The poem was recited in 1866 at the statue's dedication; later its final lines were engraved on the pedestal. Lazarus compares the Statue of Liberty to the Colossus of Rhodes, one of the Seven Wonders of the World, a statue to the sun god Helios that stood in the harbor at Rhodes, Greece. Contrary to legend that dates from the Middle Ages (see line 2), the statue could not have straddled the harbor entrance.
2. The splendors of your history.

Reveille

Wake: the silver dusk returning
　　Up the beach of darkness brims,
And the ship of sunrise burning
　　Strands upon the eastern rims.

5　Wake: the vaulted shadow shatters,
　　Trampled to the floor it spanned,
And the tent of night in tatters
　　Straws° the sky-pavilioned land.　　　　　　　*strews*

Up, lad, up, 'tis late for lying:
10　　Hear the drums of morning play;
Hark, the empty highways crying
　　"Who'll beyond the hills away?"

Towns and countries woo together,
　　Forelands beacon, belfries call;
15　Never lad that trod on leather
　　Lived to feast his heart with all.

Up, lad; thews° that lie and cumber　　　　　　*limbs*
　　Sunlit pallets never thrive;
Morns abed and daylight slumber
20　　Were not meant for man alive.

Clay lies still, but blood's a rover;
　　Breath's a ware that will not keep.
Up, lad: when the journey's over
　　There'll be time enough to sleep.

　　　　　　　　　　　　　　　　　　1896

When I Watch the Living Meet

When I watch the living meet,
　　And the moving pageant file
Warm and breathing through the street
　　Where I lodge a little while,

5　If the heats of hate and lust
　　In the house of flesh are strong,
Let me mind the house of dust
　　Where my sojourn shall be long.

In the nation that is not
10　　Nothing stands that stood before;
There revenges are forgot,
　　And the hater hates no more;

Lovers lying two and two
　　Ask not whom they sleep beside,

15   And the bridegroom all night through
      Never turns him to the bride.

1896

To an Athlete Dying Young

The time you won your town the race
We chaired you through the market-place;
Man and boy stood cheering by,
And home we brought you shoulder-high.

5   Today, the road all runners come,
    Shoulder-high we bring you home,
    And set you at your threshold down,
    Townsman of a stiller town.

    Smart lad, to slip betimes away
10   From fields where glory does not stay
    And early though the laurel grows
    It withers quicker than the rose.

    Eyes the shady night has shut
    Cannot see the record cut,
15   And silence sounds no worse than cheers
    After earth has stopped the ears:

    Now you will not swell the rout
    Of lads that wore their honours out,
    Runners whom renown outran
20   And the name died before the man.

    So set, before its echoes fade,
    The fleet foot on the sill of shade,
    And hold to the low lintel up
    The still-defended challenge-cup.

25   And round that early-laurelled head
    Will flock to gaze the strengthless dead,
    And find unwithered on its curls
    The garland briefer than a girl's.

1896

Is My Team Ploughing

"Is my team ploughing,
    That I was used to drive
And hear the harness jingle
    When I was man alive?"

5   Ay, the horses trample,
    The harness jingles now;
No change though you lie under
    The land you used to plough.

"Is football playing
10   Along the river shore,
With lads to chase the leather,
        Now I stand up no more?"

Ay, the ball is flying,
        The lads play heart and soul;
15 The goal stands up, the keeper
        Stands up to keep the goal.

"Is my girl happy,
        That I thought hard to leave,
And has she tired of weeping
20   As she lies down at eve?"

Ay, she lies down lightly,
        She lies not down to weep:
Your girl is well contented.
        Be still, my lad, and sleep.

25 "Is my friend hearty,
        Now I am thin and pine,
And has he found to sleep in
        A better bed than mine?"

Yes, lad, I lie easy,
30   I lie as lads would choose;
I cheer a dead man's sweetheart,
        Never ask me whose.

                                        1896

On Wenlock Edge the Wood's in Trouble

On Wenlock Edge[1] the wood's in trouble;
        His forest fleece the Wrekin[2] heaves;
The gale, it plies the saplings double,
        And thick on Severn[3] snow the leaves.

5 'Twould blow like this through holt and hanger[4]
        When Uricon[5] the city stood:
'Tis the old wind in the old anger,
        But then it threshed another wood.

Then, 'twas before my time, the Roman
10   At yonder heaving hill would stare:
The blood that warms an English yeoman,
        The thoughts that hurt him, they were there.

There, like the wind through woods in riot,
        Through him the gale of life blew high;

---

1. A range of hills in Shropshire.
2. A prominent, isolated hill in Shropshire.
3. The river Severn.
4. A holt is a wood or wooded hill; a hanger is a steep wooded slope.
5. The Roman town Uriconium, on the site of the modern town of Wroxeter, Shropshire.

15   The tree of man was never quiet:
         Then 'twas the Roman, now 'tis I.

      The gale, it plies the saplings double,
         It blows so hard, 'twill soon be gone:
      To-day the Roman and his trouble
20   Are ashes under Uricon.

                                                    1896

From Far, from Eve and Morning

      From far, from eve and morning
         And yon twelve-winded sky,[6]
      The stuff of life to knit me
         Blew hither: here am I.

5   Now—for a breath I tarry
         Nor yet disperse apart—
      Take my hand quick and tell me,
         What have you in your heart.

      Speak now, and I will answer;
10   How shall I help you, say;
      Ere to the wind's twelve quarters
         I take my endless way.

                                                    1896

With Rue My Heart Is Laden

      With rue my heart is laden
         For golden friends I had,
      For many a rose-lipt maiden
         And many a lightfoot lad.

5   By brooks too broad for leaping
         The lightfoot boys are laid;
      The rose-lipt girls are sleeping
         In fields where roses fade.

                                                    1896

"Terence,[7] This Is Stupid Stuff . . ."

      "Terence, this is stupid stuff:
      You eat your victuals fast enough;
      There can't be much amiss, 'tis clear,
      To see the rate you drink your beer.
5   But oh, good Lord, the verse you make,
      It gives a chap the belly-ache.
      The cow, the old cow, she is dead;

6. I.e., winds blowing from the twelve compass points.
7. Housman had at first planned to call the vol-ume in which this poem appeared *The Poems of Terence Hearsay.*

It sleeps well, the hornéd head:
We poor lads, 'tis our turn now
10 To hear such tunes as killed the cow.
Pretty friendship 'tis to rhyme
Your friends to death before their time
Moping melancholy mad:
Come, pipe a tune to dance to, lad."

15   Why, if 'tis dancing you would be,
There's brisker pipes than poetry.
Say, for what were hop-yards meant,
Or why was Burton built on Trent?[8]
Oh many a peer of England brews
20 Livelier liquor than the Muse,
And malt does more than Milton can
To justify God's ways to man.
Ale, man, ale's the stuff to drink
For fellows whom it hurts to think:
25 Look into the pewter pot
To see the world as the world's not.
And faith, 'tis pleasant till 'tis past:
The mischief is that 'twill not last.
Oh I have been to Ludlow[9] fair
30 And left my necktie God knows where,
And carried halfway home, or near,
Pints and quarts of Ludlow beer:
Then the world seemed none so bad,
And I myself a sterling lad;
35 And down in lovely muck I've lain,
Happy till I woke again.
Then I saw the morning sky:
Heigho, the tale was all a lie;
The world, it was the old world yet,
40 I was I, my things were wet,
And nothing now remained to do
But begin the game anew.

        Therefore, since the world has still
Much good, but much less good than ill,
45 And while the sun and moon endure
Luck's a chance, but trouble's sure,
I'd face it as a wise man would,
And train for ill and not for good.
'Tis true, the stuff I bring for sale
50 Is not so brisk a brew as ale:
Out of a stem that scored the hand
I wrung it in a weary land.
But take it: if the smack is sour,
The better for the embittered hour;
55 It should do good to heart and head
When your soul is in my soul's stead;

8. Burton-on-Trent, a town in Staffordshire, the   9. A town in Shropshire.
principal industry of which is the brewing of ale.

And I will friend you, if I may,
In the dark and cloudy day.

There was a king reigned in the East:
60   There, when kings will sit to feast,
They get their fill before they think
With poisoned meat and poisoned drink.
He gathered all that springs to birth
From the many-venomed earth;
65   First a little, thence to more,
He sampled all her killing store;
And easy, smiling, seasoned sound,
Sate the king when healths went round.
They put arsenic in his meat
70   And stared aghast to watch him eat;
They poured strychnine in his cup
And shook to see him drink it up:
They shook, they stared as white's their shirt:
Them it was their poison hurt.
75   —I tell the tale that I heard told.
Mithridates, he died old.[1]

1896

Astronomy

The Wain[2] upon the northern steep
Descends and lifts away.
Oh I will sit me down and weep
For bones in Africa.[3]

5   For pay and medals, name and rank,
Things that he has not found,
He hove the Cross[4] to heaven and sank
The pole-star underground.

And now he does not even see
10   Signs of the nadir° roll   *lowest point*
At night over the ground where he
Is buried with the pole.

1922

Epitaph on an Army of Mercenaries[5]

These, in the day when heaven was falling,
The hour when earth's foundations fled,
Followed their mercenary calling
And took their wages and are dead.

1. Mithridates VI, king of Pontus in Asia Minor in the first century B.C., produced in himself an immunity to certain poisons by administering them to himself in small, gradual doses.
2. The constellation of Ursa Minor.
3. Housman's brother Herbert died fighting in the Anglo-Boer War in 1901.
4. The Southern Cross, a constellation visible from the southern hemisphere.
5. Professional soldiers of the British regular army killed in the first year of World War I. For a response to this poem, see p. 1268.

5   Their shoulders held the sky suspended;
       They stood, and earth's foundations stay;
    What God abandoned, these defended,
       And saved the sum of things for pay.

1915   1922

Crossing Alone the Nighted Ferry

Crossing alone the nighted ferry
    With the one coin for fee,[6]
Whom, on the wharf of Lethe waiting,
    Count you to find? Not me.

5   The brisk fond lackey to fetch and carry,
       The true, sick-hearted slave,
    Expect him not in the just city
       And free land of the grave.

                                               1936

Here Dead Lie We Because We Did Not Choose

Here dead lie we because we did not choose
    To live and shame the land from which we sprung.
Life, to be sure, is nothing much to lose;
    But young men think it is, and we were young.

                                               1936

CHARLES G. D. ROBERTS

1860–1943

Marsyas[1]

A little grey hill-glade, close-turfed, withdrawn
Beyond resort or heed of trafficking feet,
Ringed round with slim trunks of the mountain ash.
Through the slim trunks and scarlet bunches flash—
5   Beneath the clear chill glitterings of the dawn—
Far off, the crests, where down the rosy shore
The Pontic[2] surges beat.
The plains lie dim below. The thin airs wash
The circuit of the autumn-coloured hills,
10   And this high glade, whereon
The satyr pipes, who soon shall pipe no more.

6. The shades of the dead were ferried over the river Styx to Hades by Charon, paying him an obolus (a Greek coin) as fee. Lethe, in Greek mythology, was another of the rivers of the underworld: its water, drunk by souls about to be reincarnated, would cause them to forget their previous existences.

1. In Greek myth, a satyr who played the flute so well that he challenged the god Apollo, who played the lyre, to a musical contest. The victor could do what he wished to the loser; when Apollo won, he tied Marsyas to a tree and flayed him alive.
2. As in Pontus, the Black Sea, in Asia Minor.

He sits against the beech-tree's mighty bole,—
He leans, and with persuasive breathing fills
The happy shadows of the slant-set lawn.
15 The goat-feet fold beneath a gnarlèd root;
And sweet, and sweet the note that steals and thrills
From slender stops of that shy flute.
Then to the goat-feet comes the wide-eyed fawn
Hearkening; the rabbits fringe the glade, and lay
20 Their long ears to the sound;
In the pale boughs the partridge gather round,
And quaint hern° from the sea-green river reeds;   *heron*
The wild ram halts upon a rocky horn
O'erhanging; and, unmindful of his prey,
25 The leopard steals with narrowed lids to lay
His spotted length along the ground.
The thin airs wash, the thin clouds wander by,
And those hushed listeners move not. All the morn
He pipes, soft-swaying, and with half-shut eye,
30 In rapt content of utterance,—
          nor heeds
The young God standing in his branchy place,
The languor on his lips, and in his face,
Divinely inaccessible, the scorn.

1893

RUDYARD KIPLING

1865–1936

Tommy[1]

I went into a public-'ouse to get a pint o'beer,
The publican° 'e up an' sez, "We serve no red-coats here." *bar-keeper*
The girls be'ind the bar they laughed an' giggled fit to die,
I outs into the street again an' to myself sez I:
5 O it's Tommy this, an' Tommy that, an' "Tommy, go away";
  But it's "Thank you, Mister Atkins," when the band begins to
    play—
  The band begins to play, my boys, the band begins to play,
  O it's "Thank you, Mister Atkins," when the band begins to play.

I went into a theatre as sober as could be,
10 They gave a drunk civilian room, but 'adn't none for me;
They sent me to the gallery or round the music-'alls,[2]
But when it comes to fightin', Lord! they'll shove me in the stalls!
  For it's Tommy this, an' Tommy that, an' "Tommy, wait outside";
  But its "Special train for Atkins" when the trooper's on the tide—
15 The troopship's on the tide, my boys, the troopship's on the tide,
  O it's "Special train for Atkins" when the trooper's on the tide.

1. Derived from "Thomas Atkins," as the typical name for a soldier in the British army.

2. Cheaper seats in a theater, in the balcony; the best seats, in the orchestra, are the stalls.

Yes, makin' mock o' uniforms that guard you while you sleep
Is cheaper than them uniforms, an' they're starvation cheap;
An' hustlin' drunken soldiers when they're goin' large a bit
20 Is five times better business than paradin' in full kit.
     Then it's Tommy this, an' Tommy that, an' "Tommy, 'ow's yer
        soul?"
     But it's "Thin red line of 'eroes"[3] when the drums begin to roll—
     The drums begin to roll, my boys, the drums begin to roll,
     O it's "Thin red line of 'eroes" when the drums begin to roll.

25 We aren't no thin red 'eroes, nor we aren't no blackguards too,
But single men in barricks, most remarkable like you;
An' if sometimes our conduck isn't all your fancy paints,
Why, single men in barricks don't grow into plaster saints;
     While it's Tommy this, an' Tommy that, an' "Tommy, fall
        be'ind,"
30   But it's "Please to walk in front, sir," when there's trouble in the
        wind—
     There's trouble in the wind, my boys, there's trouble in the wind,
     O it's "Please to walk in front, sir," when there's trouble in the
        wind.

You talk o' better food for us, an' schools, an' fires, an' all:
We'll wait for extry rations if you treat us rational.
35 Don't mess about the cook-room slops, but prove it to our face
The Widow's Uniform[4] is not the soldier-man's disgrace.
     For it's Tommy this, an' Tommy that, an' "Chuck him out, the
        brute!"
     But it's "Saviour of 'is country" when the guns begin to shoot;
     An' it's Tommy this, an' Tommy that, an' anything you please;
40   An' Tommy ain't a bloomin' fool—you bet that Tommy sees!

                          1890

Recessional[5]

1897[6]

God of our fathers, known of old,
   Lord of our far-flung battle-line,
Beneath whose awful Hand we hold
   Dominion over palm and pine—
5 Lord God of Hosts, be with us yet,
   Lest we forget—lest we forget!

The tumult and the shouting dies;
   The Captains and the Kings depart:

---

3. W. H. Russell, a London *Times* correspondent, had used the phrase "thin red line tipped with steel" to describe the 93rd Highlanders infantry regiment as they stood to meet the advancing Russian cavalry at Balaclava (1854), in the Crimean War.
4. I.e., the queen's uniform. In his poems and stories Kipling occasionally referred to Queen Victoria as "The Widow at Windsor."
5. A piece of music or a hymn to be played or sung at the close of a religious service.
6. The year of Queen Victoria's Diamond Jubilee, celebrating the sixtieth year of her reign, the occasion serving also to celebrate the current great extent, power, and prosperity of the British Empire.

Still stands Thine ancient sacrifice,
10   An humble and a contrite heart.[7]
Lord God of Hosts, be with us yet,
Lest we forget—lest we forget!

Far-called, our navies melt away;
    On dune and headland sinks the fire:[8]
15 Lo, all our pomp of yesterday
    Is one with Nineveh and Tyre![9]
Judge of the Nations, spare us yet,
Lest we forget—lest we forget!

If, drunk with sight of power, we loose
20   Wild tongues that have not Thee in awe,
Such boastings as the Gentiles use,
    Or lesser breeds without the Law—[1]
Lord God of Hosts, be with us yet,
Lest we forget—lest we forget!

25 For heathen heart that puts her trust
    In reeking tube and iron shard,
All valiant dust that builds on dust,
    And guarding, calls not Thee to guard,
For frantic boast and foolish word—
30 Thy mercy on Thy People, Lord!

1897   1899

Epitaphs of the War

1914–18

"Equality of Sacrifice"

A. "I was a Have." B. "I was a 'have-not.' "
    (Together.) "What hast thou given which I gave not?"

A Servant

We were together since the war began.
He was my servant—and the better man.

A Son

My son was killed while laughing at some jest. I would I knew
What it was, and it might serve me in a time when jests are few.

An Only Son

I have slain none except my mother. She
(Blessing her slayer) died of grief for me.

---

7. Cf. Psalms 51.17.
8. On the night of the anniversary of Victoria's accession to the throne, bonfires were lit on high points throughout Great Britain.
9. Nineveh, ancient capital of Assyria, and Tyre, capital of Phoenicia, were once great cities that later dwindled to insignificance.
1. Cf. Romans 2.14.

Ex-clerk

Pity not! The army gave
Freedom to a timid slave:
In which freedom did he find
Strength of body, will, and mind:
By which strength he came to prove
Mirth, companionship, and love:
For which love to death he went:
In which death he lies content.

The Wonder

Body and spirit I surrendered whole
To harsh instructors—and received a soul . . .
If mortal man could change me through and through
From all I was—what may the God not do?

Hindu Sepoy[2] in France

This man in his own country prayed we know not to what powers.
We pray them to reward him for his bravery in ours.

The Coward

I could not look on death, which being known,
Men led me to him, blindfold and alone.

Shock

My name, my speech, my self I had forgot.
My wife and children came—I knew them not.
I died. My mother followed. At her call
And on her bosom I remembered all.

A Grave Near Cairo

Gods of the Nile, should this stout fellow here
Get out—get out! He knows not shame nor fear.

Pelicans in the Wilderness

(A GRAVE NEAR HALFA)[3]

The blown sand heaps on me, that none may learn
Where I am laid for whom my children grieve. . . .
O wings that beat at dawning, ye return
Out of the desert to your young at eve!

Two Canadian Memorials

1

We giving all gained all.
Neither lament us nor praise.

---

2. Native of India employed as soldier under   3. In the Sudan.
European (especially British) discipline.

    Only in all things recall,
      It is fear, not death that slays.

2

    From little towns in a far land we came,
      To save our honour and a world aflame.
    By little towns in a far land we sleep;
      And trust that world we won for you to keep.

The Favour

Death favoured me from the first, well knowing I could not endure
    To wait on him day by day. He quitted my betters and came
Whistling over the fields, and, when he had made all sure,
    "Thy line is at end," he said, "but at least I have saved its name."

The Beginner

    On the first hour of my first day
      In the front trench I fell.
    (Children in boxes at a play
      Stand up to watch it well.)

R.A.F. (Aged Eighteen)

    Laughing through clouds, his milk-teeth still unshed,
    Cities and men he smote from overhead.
    His deaths delivered, he returned to play
    Childlike, with childish things now put away.

The Refined Man

I was of delicate mind. I stepped aside for my needs,
    Disdaining the common office. I was seen from afar and killed. . . .
How is this matter for mirth? Let each man be judged by his deeds.
    I have paid my price to live with myself on the terms that I willed.

Native Water-Carrier (M.E.F.)[4]

    Prometheus brought down fire to men.
      This brought up water.
    The Gods are jealous—now, as then,
      Giving no quarter.

Bombed in London

    On land and sea I strove with anxious care
    To escape conscription. It was in the air!

The Sleepy Sentinel

    Faithless the watch that I kept: now I have none to keep.
    I was slain because I slept: now I am slain I sleep.
    Let no man reproach me again, whatever watch is unkept—
    I sleep because I am slain. They slew me because I slept.

---

4. Mediterranean Expeditionary Force.

Batteries Out of Ammunition

If any mourn us in the workshop, say
We died because the shift kept holiday.

Common Form

If any question why we died,
Tell them, because our fathers lied.

A Dead Statesman

I could not dig: I dared not rob:
Therefore I lied to please the mob.
Now all my lies are proved untrue
And I must face the men I slew.
What tale shall serve me here among
Mine angry and defrauded young?

The Rebel

If I had clamoured at Thy gate
   For gift of life on earth,
And, thrusting through the souls that wait,
   Flung headlong into birth—
Even then, even then, for gin and snare
   About my pathway spread,
Lord, I had mocked Thy thoughtful care
   Before I joined the dead!
But now? . . . I was beneath Thy hand
   Ere yet the planets came.
And now—though planets pass, I stand
   The witness to Thy shame!

The Obedient

Daily, though no ears attended,
   Did my prayers arise.
Daily, though no fire descended,
   Did I sacrifice.
Though my darkness did not lift,
   Though I faced no lighter odds,
Though the Gods bestowed no gift,
     Nonetheless,
   Nonetheless, I served the Gods!

A Drifter Off Tarentum[5]

He from the wind-bitten North with ship and companions descended,
   Searching for eggs of death spawned by invisible hulls.
Many he found and drew forth. Of a sudden the fishery ended
   In flame and a clamorous breath known to the eye-pecking gulls.

---

5. Roman name for Taranto, just under the heel of the Italian peninsula.

Destroyers in Collision

For fog and fate no charm is found
  To lighten or amend.
I, hurrying to my bride, was drowned—
  Cut down by my best friend.

Convoy Escort

I was a shepherd to fools
  Causelessly bold or afraid.
They would not abide by my rules.
  Yet they escaped. For I stayed.

Unknown Female Corpse

Headless, lacking foot and hand,
Horrible I come to land.
I beseech all women's sons
Know I was a mother once.

Raped and Revenged

One used and butchered me: another spied
Me broken—for which thing an hundred died.
So it was learned among the heathen hosts
How much a freeborn woman's favour costs.

Salonikan[6] Grave

I have watched a thousand days
  Push out and crawl into night
Slowly as tortoises.
  Now I, too, follow these.
It is fever, and not the fight—
  Time, not battle,—that slays.

The Bridegroom

Call me not false, beloved,
  If, from thy scarce-known breast
So little time removed,
  In other arms I rest.

For this more ancient bride,
  Whom coldly I embrace,
Was constant at my side
  Before I saw thy face.

Our marriage, often set—
  By miracle delayed—
At last is consummate,
  And cannot be unmade.

---

6. Thessalonia, the second largest city in Greece, was destroyed by fire in 1917.

Live, then, whom life shall cure,
  Almost, of memory,
And leave us to endure
  Its immortality.

V.A.D.[7] *(Mediterranean)*

Ah, would swift ships had never been, for then we ne'er had found,
These harsh Aegean rocks between, this little virgin drowned,
Whom neither spouse nor child shall mourn, but men she nursed through
  pain
And—certain keels for whose return the heathen look in vain.

Actors

ON A MEMORIAL TABLET IN HOLY TRINITY CHURCH,
STRATFORD-ON-AVON

We counterfeited once for your disport
  Men's joy and sorrow: but our day has passed.
We pray you pardon all where we fell short—
  Seeing we were your servants to this last.

Journalists

ON A PANEL IN THE HALL OF THE INSTITUTE OF JOURNALISTS

We have served our day.

1919, 1940

WILLIAM BUTLER YEATS*

1865–1939

The Stolen Child

Where dips the rocky highland
Of Sleuth Wood[1] in the lake,
There lies a leafy island
Where flapping herons wake
5   The drowsy water-rats;
There we've hid our faery vats,
Full of berries
And of reddest stolen cherries.
Come away, O human child!
10 *To the waters and the wild*
With a faery, hand in hand,
For the world's more full of weeping than you can understand.

---

7. Voluntary Aid Detachment.
*Yeats' poems are arranged here in the order in which they appear in *The Collected Poems of William Butler Yeats* (1940).

1. Place names throughout the poem refer to the area near Sligo, in the west of Ireland: Rosses Point on Sligo Bay, and Glen-Car, a small lake near Sligo.

Where the wave of moonlight glosses
The dim grey sands with light,
15 Far off by furthest Rosses
We foot it all the night,
Weaving olden dances,
Mingling hands and mingling glances
Till the moon has taken flight;
20 To and fro we leap
And chase the frothy bubbles,
While the world is full of troubles
And is anxious in its sleep.
Come away, O human child!
25 *To the waters and the wild*
With a faery, hand in hand,
For the world's more full of weeping than you can understand.

Where the wandering water gushes
From the hills above Glen-Car,
30 In pools among the rushes
That scarce could bathe a star,
We seek for slumbering trout
And whispering in their ears
Give them unquiet dreams;
35 Leaning softly out
From ferns that drop their tears
Over the young streams.
Come away, O human child!
To the waters and the wild
40 *With a faery, hand in hand,*
For the world's more full of weeping than you can understand.

Away with us he's going,
The solemn-eyed:
He'll hear no more the lowing
45 Of the calves on the warm hillside
Or the kettle on the hob
Sing peace into his breast,
Or see the brown mice bob
Round and round the oatmeal-chest.
50 *For he comes, the human child!*
To the waters and the wild
With a faery, hand in hand,
From a world more full of weeping than he can understand.

1889

The Lake Isle of Innisfree

I will arise and go now, and go to Innisfree,
And a small cabin build there, of clay and wattles[2] made:
Nine bean-rows will I have there, a hive for the honey-bee,
And live alone in the bee-loud glade.

2. Rods interwoven with twigs or branches to form a framework for walls or roof.

5 And I shall have some peace there, for peace comes dropping slow,
   Dropping from the veils of the morning to where the cricket sings;
   There midnight's all a glimmer, and noon a purple glow,
   And evening full of the linnet's wings.

   I will arise and go now, for always night and day
10 I hear lake water lapping with low sounds by the shore;
   While I stand on the roadway, or on the pavements grey,
   I hear it in the deep heart's core.

                                                        1892

When You Are Old[3]

When you are old and grey and full of sleep,
And nodding by the fire, take down this book,
And slowly read, and dream of the soft look
Your eyes had once, and of their shadows deep;

5 How many loved your moments of glad grace,
And loved your beauty with love false or true,
But one man loved the pilgrim soul in you,
And loved the sorrows of your changing face;

And bending down beside the glowing bars,
10 Murmur, a little sadly, how Love fled
And paced upon the mountains overhead
And hid his face amid a crowd of stars.

                                                        1893

The Man Who Dreamed of Faeryland

He stood among a crowd at Drumahair;[4]
His heart hung all upon a silken dress,
And he had known at last some tenderness,
Before earth took him to her stony care;
5 But when a man poured fish into a pile,
It seemed they raised their little silver heads,
And sang what gold morning or evening sheds
Upon a woven world-forgotten isle
Where people love beside the ravelled seas;
10 That Time can never mar a lover's vows
Under that woven changeless roof of boughs:
The singing shook him out of his new ease.

He wandered by the sands of Lissadell;
His mind ran all on money cares and fears,
15 And he had known at last some prudent years

---

3. The poem's point of departure is a sonnet by
the French poet Pierre de Ronsard (1524–1585)
that begins "Quand vous serez bien vieille, au soir
à la chandelle" ("When you are very old, in the
evening, by candlelight"), but is a free adaptation
rather than a translation.

4. Localities named in the poem, all in the west
of Ireland: Drumahair, or Dromahair, a town in
County Leitrim; Lissadell, the estate of the Gore-
Booth family in County Sligo; Scanavin, a town in
County Sligo; Lugnagall, a hill near Ben Bulben,
in County Sligo.

Before they heaped his grave under the hill;
But while he passed before a plashy place,
A lug-worm with its grey and muddy mouth
Sang that somewhere to north or west or south
20   There dwelt a gay, exulting, gentle race
Under the golden or the silver skies;
That if a dancer stayed his hungry foot
It seemed the sun and moon were in the fruit:
And at that singing he was no more wise.

25   He mused beside the well of Scanavin,
He mused upon his mockers: without fail
His sudden vengeance were a country tale,
When earthy night had drunk his body in;
But one small knot-grass growing by the pool
30   Sang where—unnecessary cruel voice—
Old silence bids its chosen race rejoice,
Whatever ravelled waters rise and fall
Or stormy silver fret the gold of day,
And midnight there enfold them like a fleece
35   And lover there by lover be at peace.
The tale drove his fine angry mood away.

He slept under the hill of Lugnagall;
And might have known at last unhaunted sleep
Under that cold and vapour-turbaned steep,
40   Now that the earth had taken man and all:
Did not the worms that spired about his bones
Proclaim with that unwearied, reedy cry
That God has laid His fingers on the sky,
That from those fingers glittering summer runs
45   Upon the dancer by the dreamless wave.
Why should those lovers that no lovers miss
Dream, until God burn Nature with a kiss?
The man has found no comfort in the grave.

1893

Adam's Curse[5]

We sat together at one summer's end,
That beautiful mild woman, your close friend,[6]
And you and I, and talked of poetry.
I said, "A line will take us hours maybe;
5   Yet if it does not seem a moment's thought,
Our stitching and unstitching has been naught.
Better go down upon your marrow-bones
And scrub a kitchen pavement, or break stones
Like an old pauper, in all kinds of weather;
10   For to articulate sweet sounds together
Is to work harder than all these, and yet

5. Genesis 3.17–19.
6. The two women who figure in the poem are
Maud Gonne and, rather than a friend, her sister
Kathleen Pilcher.

Be thought an idler by the noisy set
Of bankers, schoolmasters, and clergymen
The martyrs call the world."

                                        And thereupon
15   That beautiful mild woman for whose sake
There's many a one shall find out all heartache
On finding that her voice is sweet and low
Replied, "To be born woman is to know—
Although they do not talk of it at school—
20   That we must labour to be beautiful."

I said, "It's certain there is no fine thing
Since Adam's fall but needs much labouring.
There have been lovers who thought love should be
So much compounded of high courtesy
25   That they would sigh and quote with learned looks
Precedents out of beautiful old books;
Yet now it seems an idle trade enough."

We sat grown quiet at the name of love;
We saw the last embers of daylight die,
30   And in the trembling blue-green of the sky
A moon, worn as if it had been a shell
Washed by time's waters as they rose and fell
About the stars and broke in days and years.

I had a thought for no one's but your ears:
35   That you were beautiful, and that I strove
To love you in the old high way of love;
That it had all seemed happy, and yet we'd grown
As weary-hearted as that hollow moon.

                                        1904

The Wild Swans at Coole[7]

The trees are in their autumn beauty,
The woodland paths are dry,
Under the October twilight the water
Mirrors a still sky;
5   Upon the brimming water among the stones
Are nine-and-fifty swans.

The nineteenth autumn has come upon me
Since I first made my count;[8]
I saw, before I had well finished,
10   All suddenly mount
And scatter wheeling in great broken rings
Upon their clamorous wings.

7. Coole Park, the estate in western Ireland of Lady Augusta Gregory, Yeats' patroness and friend.

8. Yeats had first visited Coole Park in 1897; the poem was written in October 1916.

I have looked upon those brilliant creatures,
And now my heart is sore.
15 All's changed since I, hearing at twilight,
The first time on this shore,
The bell-beat of their wings above my head,
Trod with a lighter tread.

Unwearied still, lover by lover,
20 They paddle in the cold
Companionable streams or climb the air;
Their hearts have not grown old;
Passion or conquest, wander where they will,
Attend upon them still.

25 But now they drift on the still water,
Mysterious, beautiful;
Among what rushes will they build,
By what lake's edge or pool
Delight men's eyes when I awake some day
30 To find they have flown away?

1917

An Irish Airman Foresees His Death[9]

I know that I shall meet my fate
Somewhere among the clouds above;
Those that I fight I do not hate,
Those that I guard I do not love;
5 My country is Kiltartan Cross,[1]
My countrymen Kiltartan's poor,
No likely end could bring them loss
Or leave them happier than before.
Nor law, nor duty bade me fight,
10 Nor public men, nor cheering crowds,
A lonely impulse of delight
Drove to this tumult in the clouds;
I balanced all, brought all to mind,
The years to come seemed waste of breath,
15 A waste of breath the years behind
In balance with this life, this death.

1919

The Scholars

Bald heads forgetful of their sins,
Old, learned, respectable bald heads
Edit and annotate the lines
That young men, tossing on their beds,

9. The airman, who was killed in action in Italy in
January 1918, is Major Robert Gregory, son of
Yeats' friend and patron Lady Augusta Gregory.

1. A village near the Gregory estate, Coole Park,
in County Galway, western Ireland.

5   Rhymed out in love's despair
     To flatter beauty's ignorant ear.

     All shuffle there; all cough in ink;
     All wear the carpet with their shoes;
     All think what other people think;
10   All know the man their neighbour knows.
     Lord, what would they say
     Did their Catullus[2] walk that way?

1917

Easter 1916[3]

     I have met them at close of day
     Coming with vivid faces
     From counter or desk among grey
     Eighteenth-century houses.
5   I have passed with a nod of the head
     Or polite meaningless words,
     Or have lingered awhile and said
     Polite meaningless words,
     And thought before I had done
10   Of a mocking tale or a gibe
     To please a companion
     Around the fire at the club,
     Being certain that they and I
     But lived where motley is worn:
15   All changed, changed utterly:
     A terrible beauty is born.

     That woman's days were spent
     In ignorant good will,
     Her nights in argument
20   Until her voice grew shrill.
     What voice more sweet than hers
     When, young and beautiful,
     She rode to harriers?[4]
     This man had kept a school
25   And rode our wingéd horse;[5]
     This other his helper and friend
     Was coming into his force;

---

2. Gaius Valerius Catullus (ca. 84–ca. 54 B.C.), Roman poet famous for his erotic verse.

3. An Irish Nationalist uprising had been planned for Easter Sunday 1916, and although the German ship that was bringing munitions had been intercepted by the British, attempts to postpone the uprising failed; it began in Dublin on Easter Monday. "Fifteen hundred men seized key points and an Irish republic was proclaimed from the General Post Office. After the initial surprise prompt British military action was taken, and when over 300 lives had been lost the insurgents were forced to surrender on 29 April. . . . The seven signatories of the republican proclamation, including [Pádraic] Pearse and [James] Connolly, and nine others were shot after court martial between 3 and 12 May; 75 were reprieved and over 2000 held prisoners" [From "Ireland: History," by D. B. Quinn, in *Chambers's Encyclopedia*].

4. Countess Constance Georgina Markiewicz, *née* Gore-Booth, about whom Yeats wrote "On a Political Prisoner" and a later poem, "In Memory of Eva Gore-Booth and Con Markiewicz."

5. Pádraic Pearse, headmaster of St. Enda's School, and a prolific writer of poems, plays, and stories as well as of essays on Irish politics and Gaelic literature. The winged mythological horse, Pegasus, is here used as a symbol of poetic inspiration. "This other" was Thomas MacDonough, also a schoolteacher.

He might have won fame in the end,
So sensitive his nature seemed,
30   So daring and sweet his thought.
This other man I had dreamed
A drunken, vainglorious lout.[6]
He had done most bitter wrong
To some who are near my heart,
35   Yet I number him in the song;
He, too, has resigned his part
In the casual comedy;
He, too, has been changed in his turn,
Transformed utterly:
40   A terrible beauty is born.

Hearts with one purpose alone
Through summer and winter seem
Enchanted to a stone
To trouble the living stream.
45   The horse that comes from the road,
The rider, the birds that range
From cloud to tumbling cloud,
Minute by minute they change;
A shadow of cloud on the stream
50   Changes minute by minute;
A horse-hoof slides on the brim,
And a horse plashes within it;
The long-legged moor-hens dive,
And hens to moor-cocks call;
55   Minute by minute they live:
The stone's in the midst of all.

Too long a sacrifice
Can make a stone of the heart.
O when may it suffice?
60   That is Heaven's part, our part
To murmur name upon name,
As a mother names her child
When sleep at last has come
On limbs that had run wild.
65   What is it but nightfall?
No, no, not night but death;
Was it needless death after all?
For England may keep faith
For all that is done and said.
70   We know their dream; enough
To know they dreamed and are dead;
And what if excess of love
Bewildered them till they died?
I write it out in a verse—
75   MacDonagh and MacBride
And Connolly and Pearse

6. Major John MacBride, who had married Maud Gonne (the woman with whom Yeats had for years been hopelessly in love) in 1903 and separated from her in 1905.

Now and in time to be,
Wherever green is worn,
Are changed, changed utterly.
80   A terrible beauty is born.

September 25, 1916   1916

The Second Coming

Turning and turning in the widening gyre[7]
The falcon cannot hear the falconer;
Things fall apart; the centre cannot hold;
Mere anarchy is loosed upon the world,
5   The blood-dimmed tide is loosed, and everywhere
The ceremony of innocence is drowned;
The best lack all conviction, while the worst
Are full of passionate intensity.

Surely some revelation is at hand;
10   Surely the Second Coming is at hand:
The Second Coming! Hardly are those words out
When a vast image out of *Spiritus Mundi*[8]
Troubles my sight: somewhere in sands of the desert
A shape with lion body and the head of a man,[9]
15   A gaze blank and pitiless as the sun,
Is moving its slow thighs, while all about it
Reel shadows of the indignant desert birds.
The darkness drops again; but now I know
That twenty centuries of stony sleep
20   Were vexed to nightmare by a rocking cradle,
And what rough beast, its hour come round at last,
Slouches towards Bethlehem to be born?

1921

7. The gyre—the conical shape is traced in the falcon's sweep upward and out in widening circles from the falconer who should control its flight—involves a reference to the geometrical figure of the interpenetrating cones, the "fundamental symbol" Yeats used to diagram his cyclical view of history. (See the opening pages of "The Great Wheel," in *A Vision* [1937]). He saw the cycle of Greco-Roman civilization as having been brought to a close by the advent of Christianity, and in the violence of his own times—"the growing murderousness of the world"—he saw signs that the two-thousand-year cycle of Christianity was itself about to end and to be replaced by a system antithetical to it.
8. Or *Anima Mundi*, "the Great Memory" (Latin). "Before the mind's eye, whether in sleep or waking, came images that one was to discover presently in some book one had never read, and after looking in vain for explanation to the current theory of forgotten personal memory, I came to believe in a great memory passing on from generation to generation.... Our daily thought was certainly but the line of foam at the shallow edge of a vast luminous sea" [*Per Amica Silentia Lunae,* "Anima Mundi," § ii].
9. In the introduction to his play *The Resurrection* (in *Wheels and Butterflies,* 1935), Yeats describes the way in which the sphinx image had first manifested itself to him: "Our civilisation was about to reverse itself, or some new civilisation about to be born from all that our age had rejected...; because we had worshipped a single god it would worship many.... Had I begun "On Baile's Strand" or not when I began to imagine, as always at my left side just out of the range of the sight, a brazen winged beast (afterwards described in my poem "The Second Coming") that I associated with laughing, ecstatic destruction?"

A Prayer for My Daughter[1]

Once more the storm is howling, and half hid
Under this cradle-hood and coverlid
My child sleeps on. There is no obstacle
But Gregory's wood and one bare hill
5 Whereby the haystack- and roof-levelling wind,
Bred on the Atlantic, can be stayed;
And for an hour I have walked and prayed
Because of the great gloom that is in my mind.

I have walked and prayed for this young child an hour
10 And heard the sea-wind scream upon the tower,[2]
And under the arches of the bridge, and scream
In the elms above the flooded stream;
Imagining in excited reverie
That the future years had come,
15 Dancing to a frenzied drum,
Out of the murderous innocence of the sea.

May she be granted beauty and yet not
Beauty to make a stranger's eye distraught,
Or hers before a looking glass, for such,
20 Being made beautiful overmuch,
Consider beauty a sufficient end,
Lose natural kindness and maybe
The heart-revealing intimacy
That chooses right, and never find a friend.

25 Helen[3] being chosen found life flat and dull
And later had much trouble from a fool,
While that great Queen,[4] that rose out of the spray,
Being fatherless could have her way
Yet chose a bandy-leggèd smith for man.
30 It's certain that fine women eat
A crazy salad with their meat,
Whereby the Horn of Plenty is undone.

In courtesy I'd have her chiefly learned;
Hearts are not had as a gift but hearts are earned
35 By those that are not entirely beautiful;
Yet many, that have played the fool
For beauty's very self, has charm made wise,
And many a poor man that has roved,

---

1. Yeats' daughter, Anne Butler Yeats, was born on February 26, 1919.
2. For Yeats' tower, which he called Thoor Bal-lylee, see note to the next poem.
3. Helen of Troy, whose beauty was legendary. The daughter of Zeus and Leda, she married Menelaus, brother of the Greek leader, Agamemnon. She was abducted by Paris, son of the king of Troy; the Greeks undertook an expedition to Troy to bring her back, besieged the city for ten years,
and finally took it. Helen was reunited with Menelaus.
4. Aphrodite, Greek goddess of love. "Fatherless" in the sense that, in Hesiod's version of the myth, "she sprang from the foam (aphros) of the sea that gathered about the severed member of Uranus when Cronos . . . mutilated him" (Oxford Companion to Classical Literature). She was married to Hephaestus, the smith, lame from birth, who forged thunderbolts for the gods.

Loved and thought himself beloved,
40   From a glad kindness cannot take his eyes.

May she become a flourishing hidden tree
That all her thoughts may like the linnet[5] be,
And have no business but dispensing round
Their magnanimities of sound,
45   Nor but in merriment begin a chase,
Nor but in merriment a quarrel.
Oh, may she live like some green laurel
Rooted in one dear perpetual place.

My mind, because the minds that I have loved,
50   The sort of beauty that I have approved,
Prosper but little, has dried up of late,
Yet knows that to be choked with hate
May well be of all evil chances chief.
If there's no hatred in a mind
55   Assault and battery of the wind
Can never tear the linnet from the leaf.

An intellectual hatred is the worst,
So let her think opinions are accursed.
Have I not seen the loveliest woman born[6]
60   Out of the mouth of Plenty's horn,
Because of her opinionated mind
Barter that horn and every good
By quiet natures understood
For an old bellows full of angry wind?

65   Considering that, all hatred driven hence,
The soul recovers radical innocence
And learns at last that it is self-delighting,
Self-appeasing, self-affrighting,
And that its own sweet will is Heaven's will;
70   She can, though every face should scowl
And every windy quarter howl
Or every bellows burst, be happy still.

And may her bridegroom bring her to a house
Where all's accustomed, ceremonious;
75   For arrogance and hatred are the wares
Peddled in the thoroughfares.
How but in custom and in ceremony
Are innocence and beauty born?
Ceremony's a name for the rich horn,
80   And custom for the spreading laurel tree.

1919   1921

5. Small European bird of the finch family.
6. Doubtless Maud Gonne, whom Yeats had
loved hopelessly since meeting her in 1889, and
who had married Major John MacBride in 1903;
often to Yeats' dismay, she was a very daring activist
in the cause of Irish liberation.

To Be Carved on a Stone at Thoor Ballylee[7]

I, the poet William Yeats,
With old mill boards and sea-green slates,
And smithy work from the Gort forge,
Restored this tower for my wife George;
5   And may these characters remain
When all is ruin once again.

1918   1921

Sailing to Byzantium[8]

1

That is no country for old men. The young
In one another's arms, birds in the trees
—Those dying generations—at their song,
The salmon-falls, the mackerel-crowded seas,
5   Fish, flesh, or fowl, commend all summer long
Whatever is begotten, born, and dies.
Caught in that sensual music all neglect
Monuments of unaging intellect.

2

An aged man is but a paltry thing,
10   A tattered coat upon a stick, unless
Soul clap its hands and sing, and louder sing
For every tatter in its mortal dress,
Nor is there singing school but studying
Monuments of its own magnificence;
15   And therefore I have sailed the seas and come
To the holy city of Byzantium.

---

7. In June 1917, Yeats had purchased a small plot of land and the buildings on it, including a ruined Norman tower, Thoor Ballylee (Thoor: Gaelic for "tower"), part of the Gregory estate, Coole Park, in Kiltartan, near the village of Gort, County Galway. After marrying Miss George Hyde-Lees in October 1917, he made the tower and two cottages suitable for habitation. An earlier version of this poem was "to be inscribed on a great stone beside the front door."

8. Of the ancient city of Byzantium—on the site of modern Istanbul, capital of the Eastern Roman Empire, and the center, especially in the fifth and sixth centuries, of highly developed and characteristic forms of art and architecture—Yeats made a many-faceted symbol, which, since it is a symbol, should not be brought within the limits of too narrowly specific interpretation. Byzantine painting and the mosaics that decorated its churches (Yeats had seen later derivatives of these mosaics in Italy, at Ravenna and elsewhere) were stylized and formal, making no attempt at the full naturalistic rendering of human forms, so that the city and its art can appropriately symbolize a way of life in which art is frankly accepted and proclaimed as artifice. As artifice, as a work of the intellect, this art is not subject to the decay and death that overtake the life of "natural things." But while such an opposi-

tion of artifice and nature is central to the poem, there are references to Byzantium in Yeats' prose that suggest the wider range of meaning that the city held for him. In A Vision, particularly, he makes of it an exemplar of a civilization that had achieved "Unity of Being": "I think if I could be given a month of Antiquity and leave to spend it where I chose, I would spend it in Byzantium a little before Justinian [who ruled at Byzantium from 527 to 565] opened St. Sophia and closed the Academy of Plato. I think I could find in some little wineshop some philosophical worker in mosaic who could answer all my questions, the supernatural descending nearer to him than to Plotinus even, for the pride of his delicate skill would make what was an instrument of power to princes and clerics, a murderous madness in the mob, show as a lovely flexible presence like that of a perfect human body. . . . I think that in early Byzantium, maybe never before or since in recorded history, religious, aesthetic and practical life were one, that architect and artificers . . . spoke to the multitude and the few alike. The painter, the mosaic worker, the worker in gold and silver, the illuminator of sacred books, were almost impersonal, almost perhaps without the consciousness of individual design, absorbed in their subject-matter and that the vision of a whole people."

3

O sages standing in God's holy fire
As in the gold mosaic of a wall,
Come from the holy fire, perne in a gyre,[9]
20   And be the singing-masters of my soul.
Consume my heart away; sick with desire
And fastened to a dying animal
It knows not what it is; and gather me
Into the artifice of eternity.

4

25   Once out of nature I shall never take
My bodily form from any natural thing,
But such a form as Grecian goldsmiths make
Of hammered gold and gold enamelling
To keep a drowsy Emperor awake;
30   Or set upon a golden bough to sing
To lords and ladies of Byzantium
Of what is past, or passing, or to come.

1927

Leda and the Swan[1]

A sudden blow: the great wings beating still
Above the staggering girl, her thighs caressed
By the dark webs, her nape caught in his bill,
He holds her helpless breast upon his breast.

5   How can those terrified vague fingers push
The feathered glory from her loosening thighs?
And how can body, laid in that white rush,
But feel the strange heart beating where it lies?

A shudder in the loins engenders there
10   The broken wall, the burning roof and tower
And Agamemnon dead.
                  Being so caught up,
So mastered by the brute blood of the air,
Did she put on his knowledge with his power
Before the indifferent beak could let her drop?

1923   1924

9. Out of the noun "pern" (usually "pirn"), a weaver's bobbin, spool, or reel, Yeats makes a verb meaning to move in the spiral pattern taken by thread being unwound from a bobbin or being wound upon it. Here the speaker entreats the sages to descend to him in this manner, to come down into the gyres of history, the cycles of created life, out of their eternity in "the simplicity of fire" where is "all music and all rest." (For "the two realities, the terrestrial and the condition of fire," see *Per Amica Silentia Lunae*, "Anima Mundi," § x.)

1. Leda, possessed by Zeus in the guise of a swan, gave birth to Helen of Troy and the twins Castor and Pollux. (Leda was also the mother of Clytemnestra, Agamemnon's wife, who murdered him on his return from the war at Troy.) Helen's abduction by Paris from her husband, Menelaus, brother of Agamemnon, was the cause of the Trojan War. Yeats saw Leda as the recipient of an annunciation that would found Greek civilization, as the Annunciation to Mary would found Christianity.

Among School Children

1

I walk through the long schoolroom questioning;
A kind old nun in a white hood replies;
The children learn to cipher and to sing,
To study reading-books and histories,
5   To cut and sew, be neat in everything
In the best modern way—the children's eyes
In momentary wonder stare upon
A sixty-year-old smiling public man.

2

I dream of a Ledaean body,[2] bent
10 Above a sinking fire, a tale that she
Told of a harsh reproof, or trivial event
That changed some childish day to tragedy—
Told, and it seemed that our two natures blent
Into a sphere from youthful sympathy,
15 Or else, to alter Plato's parable,
Into the yolk and white of the one shell.[3]

3

And thinking of that fit of grief or rage
I look upon one child or t'other there
And wonder if she stood so at that age—
20 For even daughters of the swan can share
Something of every paddler's heritage—
And had that colour upon cheek or hair,
And thereupon my heart is driven wild:
She stands before me as a living child.

4

25 Her present image floats into the mind—
Did Quattrocento finger[4] fashion it
Hollow of cheek as though it drank the wind
And took a mess of shadows for its meat?
And I though never of Ledaean kind
30 Had pretty plumage once—enough of that,
Better to smile on all that smile, and show
There is a comfortable kind of old scarecrow.

5

What youthful mother, a shape upon her lap
Honey of generation had betrayed,[5]

2. I.e., the body of a woman the poet has known and loved and who has seemed to him as beautiful as Leda or her daughter, Helen of Troy.
3. In Plato's *Symposium*, one of the speakers, to explain the origin of human love, recounts the legend according to which human beings were originally double their present form until Zeus, fearful of their power, decided to cut them in two, which he did "as men cut sorbapples in two when they are preparing them for pickling, or as they cut eggs in two with a hair." Since then, "each of us is . . . but the half of a human being, . . . each is forever seeking his missing half."

4. I.e., the hand of an Italian artist of the fifteenth century.
5. In a note to the poem, Yeats says: "I have taken the 'honey of generation' from Porphyry's essay on 'The Cave of the Nymphs' but find no warrant in Porphyry for considering it the 'drug' that destroys the 'recollection' of pre-natal freedom." In the essay explaining the symbolism of a passage from the *Odyssey*, Book 13, Porphyry (ca. A.D. 232–305) makes such statements as that "the sweetness of honey signifies . . . the same thing as the pleasure arising from copulation," the pleasure "which draws souls downward to generation."

35 And that must sleep, shriek, struggle to escape
As recollection or the drug decide,
Would think her son, did she but see that shape
With sixty or more winters on its head,
A compensation for the pang of his birth,
40 Or the uncertainty of his setting forth?

6

Plato thought nature but a spume that plays
Upon a ghostly paradigm of things;[6]
Solider Aristotle played the taws
Upon the bottom of a king of kings;[7]
45 World-famous golden-thighed Pythagoras[8]
Fingered upon a fiddle-stick or strings
What a star sang and careless Muses heard:
Old clothes upon old sticks to scare a bird.

7

Both nuns and mothers worship images,
50 But those the candles light are not as those
That animate a mother's reveries,
But keep a marble or a bronze repose.
And yet they too break hearts—O Presences
That passion, piety or affection knows,
55 And that all heavenly glory symbolize—
O self-born mockers of man's enterprise;

8

Labour is blossoming or dancing where
The body is not bruised to pleasure soul,
Nor beauty born out of its own despair,
60 Nor blear-eyed wisdom out of midnight oil.
O chestnut-tree, great-rooted blossomer,
Are you the leaf, the blossom or the bole?°   *trunk*
O body swayed to music, O brightening glance,
How can we know the dancer from the dance?

1927

Byzantium[9]

The unpurged images of day recede;
The Emperor's drunken soldiery are abed;

6. In Plato's idealistic philosophy the world of nature, of appearances, that we know is but the copy of a world of ideal, permanently enduring prototypes.
7. The philosophy of Aristotle differed most markedly from that of Plato in that it emphasized the systematic investigation of verifiable phenomena. Aristotle was tutor to the son of King Philip of Macedonia, later Alexander the Great. "Played the taws": whipped.
8. A Greek philosopher (sixth century B.C.), about whom clustered many legends even in his own lifetime, as that he was the incarnation of Apollo, that he had a golden hipbone or thighbone, and so on. Central to the Pythagorean school of philosophy

(along with the doctrine of the transmigration of souls) was the premise that the universe is mathematically regular, which premise had as one of its starting points the Pythagoreans' observations of the exact mathematical relationships underlying musical harmony.
9.Under the heading "Subject for a Poem, April 30th," Yeats wrote in his *1930 Diary:* "Describe Byzantium as it is in the system [that is, his system in *A Vision*] towards the end of the first Christian millennium. A walking mummy. Flames at the street corners where the soul is purified, birds of hammered gold singing in the golden trees, in the harbor [dolphins], offering their backs to the wailing dead that they may carry them to Paradise."

Night resonance recedes, night-walkers' song
After great cathedral gong;
5   A starlit or a moonlit dome disdains[1]
All that man is,
All mere complexities,
The fury and the mire of human veins.

Before me floats an image, man or shade,
10   Shade more than man, more image than a shade;
For Hades' bobbin bound in mummy-cloth
May unwind the winding path;[2]
A mouth that has no moisture and no breath
Breathless mouths may summon;[3]
15   I hail the superhuman;
I call it death-in-life and life-in-death.

Miracle, bird or golden handiwork,
More miracle than bird or handiwork,
Planted on the starlit golden bough,
20   Can like the cocks of Hades crow,[4]
Or, by the moon embittered, scorn aloud
In glory of changeless metal
Common bird or petal
And all complexities of mire or blood.

25   At midnight on the Emperor's pavement flit
Flames that no faggot feeds, nor steel has lit,
Nor storm disturbs, flames begotten of flame,
Where blood-begotten spirits come
And all complexities of fury leave,
30   Dying into a dance,
An agony of trance,
An agony of flame that cannot singe a sleeve.

Astraddle on the dolphin's mire and blood,
Spirit after spirit! The smithies break the flood.

1. If the dome is seen as "starlit" at the dark of the moon and as "moonlit" at the full, then these terms may be seen as referring to Phase 1 and Phase 15, respectively, of the twenty-eight phases of the moon in the system of *A Vision*. As Michael Robartes says in *The Phases of the Moon*, "There's no human life at the full or the dark," these being "the superhuman phases," opposite to one another on the Wheel of Being. Phase 1 is the phase of complete objectivity, the soul being "completely absorbed by its supernatural environment," waiting to be formed, in a state of "complete plasticity." Phase 15 is the state of complete subjectivity, when the soul is completely absorbed in an achieved state, "a phase of complete beauty." Thus, the world of "mere complexities," the world in which man is in a state of becoming, is banished from the poem at the beginning, as the "unpurged images of day" have been banished.
2. The soul and/or body of the dead. The comparison to the bobbin or spindle is at first visual, to describe the figure of the dead, wrapped in a winding-sheet or mummy-cloth, but it also emphasizes the idea that the soul may unwind the thread of its fate by retracing its path, returning to the world to serve as guide, instructor, inspiration.
3. The two lines have been read in two different ways, depending on which of the two phrases ("a mouth" or "breathless mouths") is seen as subject and which as object of "may summon." Taking "breathless mouths" as subject: mouths of the living, breathless with the intensity of the act of invocation, may call up the mouths of the dead to instruct them.
4. A symbol of rebirth and resurrection. In a book on Roman sculpture that Yeats is believed to have known, *Apotheosis and After Life* (1915), Mrs. Arthur Strong says: "The great vogue of the cock on later Roman tombstones is due . . . to the fact that as herald of the sun he becomes by an easy transition the herald of rebirth and resurrection." In the next sentence she mentions another visual symbol, which figures in the poem's last stanza: "The dolphins and marine monsters, another frequent decoration, form a mystic escort of the dead to the Islands of the Blest."

35 The golden smithies of the Emperor!
    Marbles of the dancing floor
    Break bitter furies of complexity,
    Those images that yet
    Fresh images beget,
40 That dolphin-torn, that gong-tormented sea.

1930   1932

Crazy Jane Talks with the Bishop

    I met the Bishop on the road
    And much said he and I.
    "Those breasts are flat and fallen now,
    Those veins must soon be dry;
5   Live in a heavenly mansion,
    Not in some foul sty."

    "Fair and foul are near of kin,
    And fair needs foul," I cried.
    "My friends are gone, but that's a truth
10 Nor grave nor bed denied,
    Learned in bodily lowliness
    And in the heart's pride.

    "A woman can be proud and stiff
    When on love intent;
15 But Love has pitched his mansion in
    The place of excrement;
    For nothing can be sole or whole
    That has not been rent."

                                                                       1933

Lapis Lazuli[5]

(For Harry Clifton)

    I have heard that hysterical women say
    They are sick of the palette and fiddle-bow,
    Of poets that are always gay,
    For everybody knows or else should know
5   That if nothing drastic is done
    Aeroplane and Zeppelin will come out,
    Pitch like King Billy[6] bomb-balls in
    Until the town lie beaten flat.

    All perform their tragic play,
10 There struts Hamlet, there is Lear,

5. A deep-blue semiprecious stone. In a letter dated July 6, 1935, Yeats wrote, "Someone has sent me a present of a great piece [of lapis lazuli] carved by some Chinese sculptor into the semblance of a mountain with temple, trees, paths and an ascetic and pupil about to climb the mountain. Ascetic, pupil, hard stone, eternal theme of the sensual east. The heroic cry in the midst of despair. But no, I am wrong, the east has its solutions always and therefore knows nothing of tragedy. It is we, not the east, that must raise the heroic cry."
6. At the Battle of the Boyne on July 1, 1690, William III, king of England since 1689, had defeated the forces of the deposed king, James II.

That's Ophelia, that Cordelia;
Yet they, should the last scene be there,
The great stage curtain about to drop,
If worthy their prominent part in the play,
15 Do not break up their lines to weep.
They know that Hamlet and Lear are gay;
Gaiety transfiguring all that dread.
All men have aimed at, found and lost;
Black out; Heaven blazing into the head:
20 Tragedy wrought to its uttermost.
Though Hamlet rambles and Lear rages,
And all the drop-scenes drop at once
Upon a hundred thousand stages,
It cannot grow by an inch or an ounce.

25 On their own feet they came, or on shipboard,
Camelback, horseback, ass-back, mule-back,
Old civilizations put to the sword.
Then they and their wisdom went to rack:
No handiwork of Callimachus,[7]
30 Who handled marble as if it were bronze,
Made draperies that seemed to rise
When sea-wind swept the corner, stands;
His long lamp-chimney shaped like the stem
Of a slender palm, stood but a day;
35 All things fall and are built again,
And those that build them again are gay.

Two Chinamen, behind them a third,
Are carved in lapis lazuli,
Over them flies a long-legged bird,
40 A symbol of longevity;
The third, doubtless a serving-man,
Carries a musical instrument.

Every discolouration of the stone,
Every accidental crack or dent,
45 Seems a water-course or an avalanche,
Or lofty slope where it still snows
Though doubtless plum or cherry-branch
Sweetens the little half-way house
Those Chinamen climb towards, and I
50 Delight to imagine them seated there;
There, on the mountain and the sky,
On all the tragic scene they stare.
One asks for mournful melodies;
Accomplished fingers begin to play.

---

7. Greek sculptor of the fifth century B.C., of whom Yeats says in *A Vision* that only one example of his work remains, a marble chair, and goes on to mention "that bronze lamp [in the Erechtheum, a temple of the guardian deities of Athens] shaped like a palm, known to us by a description in Pausanias."

55 Their eyes mid many wrinkles, their eyes,
Their ancient, glittering eyes, are gay.

1938

Long-Legged Fly

That civilisation may not sink,
Its great battle lost,
Quiet the dog, tether the pony
To a distant post;
5 Our master Caesar is in the tent
Where the maps are spread,
His eyes fixed upon nothing,
A hand under his head.
Like a long-legged fly upon the stream
10 *His mind moves upon silence.*

That the topless towers be burnt
And men recall that face,[8]
Move most gently if move you must
In this lonely place.
15 She thinks, part woman, three parts a child,
That nobody looks; her feet
Practice a tinker shuffle
Picked up on a street.
Like a long-legged fly upon the stream
20 *Her mind moves upon silence.*

That girls at puberty may find
The first Adam in their thought,
Shut the door of the Pope's chapel,[9]
Keep those children out.
25 There on that scaffolding reclines
Michael Angelo.
With no more sound than the mice make
His hand moves to and fro.
Like a long-legged fly upon the stream
30 *His mind moves upon silence.*

1939

The Circus Animals' Desertion

1

I sought a theme and sought for it in vain,
I sought it daily for six weeks or so.

8. An echo of Marlowe's lines on Helen of Troy in Dr. *Faustus:* "Was this the face that launched a thousand ships, / And burnt the topless towers of Ilium?"

9. On the ceiling of the Sistine Chapel, so called because it was built under Pope Sixtus IV, Michelangelo painted a series of biblical scenes, including the creation of Adam.

Maybe at last, being but a broken man,
I must be satisfied with my heart, although
5   Winter and summer till old age began
My circus animals were all on show,
Those stilted boys, that burnished chariot,[1]
Lion and woman and the Lord knows what.

2

What can I but enumerate old themes?
10 First that sea-rider Oisin[2] led by the nose
Through three enchanted islands, allegorical dreams,
Vain gaiety, vain battle, vain repose,
Themes of the embittered heart, or so it seems,
That might adorn old songs or courtly shows;
15 But what cared I that set him on to ride,
I, starved for the bosom of his faery bride?

And then a counter-truth filled out its play,
The Countess Cathleen[3] was the name I gave it;
She, pity-crazed, had given her soul away,
20 But masterful Heaven had intervened to save it.
I thought my dear[4] must her own soul destroy,
So did fanaticism and hate enslave it,
And this brought forth a dream and soon enough
This dream itself had all my thought and love.

25 And when the Fool and Blind Man stole the bread
Cuchulain fought the ungovernable sea;[5]
Heart-mysteries there, and yet when all is said
It was the dream itself enchanted me:
Character isolated by a deed
30 To engross the present and dominate memory.
Players and painted stage took all my love,
And not those things that they were emblems of.

3

Those masterful images because complete
Grew in pure mind, but out of what began?

---

1. The images of lines 7–8 may refer to motifs from specific earlier works by Yeats (in his play *The Unicorn from the Stars*, for instance, a gilded state coach, adorned with lion and unicorn, is being built on stage), but it is at least as likely that they are merely generalized images, in line with the title and argument of the poem, of the people and things to be encountered in the heightened, unreal world of a circus.
2. The hero of Yeats' long allegorical (and symbolic) poem, *The Wanderings of Oisin* (pronounced *Usheen*), 1889, is led by the fairy Niamh (pronounced *Nee-ave*) in succession to the three Islands of, respectively, Dancing (changeless joy), Victories (also called "Of Many Fears"), and Forgetfulness.

3. Yeats' first play, 1892. In it the people, in a time of famine, are selling their souls to emissaries of the devil. To save their souls, the Countess Cathleen sells hers "for a great price." She dies, but an angel announces that she is "passing to the floor of peace."
4. Maud Gonne, whom Yeats had loved since first meeting her in 1889, and who had married John MacBride in 1903; she was a daring, even violent, activist in the cause of Irish liberation.
5. In another early play, *On Baile's Strand* (1904), Cuchulain (pronounced *Cuhoolin*) unwittingly kills his own son; maddened, he rushes out to fight the waves. As the people run to the shore to watch, the fool and the blind man hurry off to steal the bread from their ovens.

35 A mound of refuse or the sweeping of a street,
    Old kettles, old bottles, and a broken can,
    Old iron, old bones, old rags, that raving slut
    Who keeps the till. Now that my ladder's gone,
    I must lie down where all the ladders start,
40 In the foul rag-and-bone shop of the heart.

1939

Under Ben Bulben[6]

1

Swear by what the sages spoke
Round the Mareotic Lake[7]
That the Witch of Atlas knew,
Spoke and set the cocks a-crow.[8]

5   Swear by those horsemen, by those women
    Complexion and form prove superhuman,
    That pale, long-visaged company
    That air in immortality
    Completeness of their passions won;
10 Now they ride the wintry dawn
    Where Ben Bulben sets the scene.[9]

Here's the gist of what they mean.

2

Many times man lives and dies
Between his two eternities,
15 That of race and that of soul,
    And ancient Ireland knew it all.
    Whether man die in his bed
    Or the rifle knocks him dead,
    A brief parting from those dear
20 Is the worst man has to fear.
    Though gravediggers' toil is long,
    Sharp their spades, their muscles strong,
    They but thrust their buried men
    Back in the human mind again.

6. A mountain in County Sligo, in the west of Ireland, that overlooks Drumcliff Churchyard, where Yeats is buried. The last three lines of the poem are carved on his tombstone.
7. Lake Mareotis, a salt lake in northern Egypt, near which the members of the Thebaid, among them St. Anthony (A.D. 251–356) had withdrawn to contemplation. About the Thebaid, in his 1930 *Diary*, Yeats wrote that "men went on pilgrimage to Saint Anthony that they might learn about their spiritual states, what was about to happen and why it happened, and Saint Anthony would reply neither out of traditional casuistry nor common sense but from spiritual powers."
8. In Shelley's poem "The Witch of Atlas," the

protagonist, a spirit of love, beauty, and freedom, visits Egypt and the Mareotic Lake in the course of her magic journeyings. The knowledge and belief that Yeats describes as common to her and to the sages "set the cocks a-crow" in the sense that, like "the cocks of Hades" and the golden bird in "Byzantium," they summon to a spiritual rebirth.
9. In another late poem, "Alternative Song for the Severed Head in 'The King of the Great Clock Tower,'" Yeats reintroduces some of the Irish mythological or legendary heroes and heroines who figure in his early poems—Cuchulain, Niam, and others—with whom the supernatural riders of these lines may be identified.

3

25   You that Mitchel's prayer have heard,
"Send war in our time, O Lord!"[1]
Know that when all words are said
And a man is fighting mad,
Something drops from eyes long blind,
30   He completes his partial mind,
For an instant stands at ease,
Laughs aloud, his heart at peace.
Even the wisest man grows tense
With some sort of violence
35   Before he can accomplish fate,
Know his work or choose his mate.

4

Poet and sculptor, do the work,
Nor let the modish painter shirk
What his great forefathers did,
40   Bring the soul of man to God,
Make him fill the cradles right.

Measurement began our might:[2]
Forms a stark Egyptian thought,
Forms that gentler Phidias wrought.
45   Michael Angelo left a proof
On the Sistine Chapel roof,
Where but half-awakened Adam
Can disturb globe-trotting Madam
Till her bowels are in heat,
50   Proof that there's a purpose set
Before the secret working mind:
Profane perfection of mankind.
Quattrocento[3] put in paint
On backgrounds for a God or Saint
55   Gardens where a soul's at ease;
Where everything that meets the eye,
Flowers and grass and cloudless sky,
Resemble forms that are or seem
When sleepers wake and yet still dream,
60   And when it's vanished still declare,
With only bed and bedstead there,
That heavens had opened.
                    Gyres[4] run on;
When that greater dream had gone
Calvert and Wilson, Blake and Claude,

1. John Mitchel (1815–1875), the Irish patriot, wrote in his *Jail Journal, or Five Years in British Prisons* (published in New York, 1854): "Czar, I bless thee, I kiss the hem of thy garment. I drink to thy health and longevity. Give us war in our time, O Lord" [quoted by T. R. Henn, *The Lonely Tower*].
2. The achievements of Western civilization— now, according to the poem, being challenged or destroyed—began with the exact mathematical rules that the Egyptians followed in working out the proportions of their sculptured figures—rules that Phidias (line 44), the great Greek sculptor of the fifth century B.C., used, and that have been implicit in the greatest Western art up to the present, when "confusion [falls] upon our thought."
3. The Italian fifteenth century.
4. I.e., the cycles of history.

65   Prepared a rest for the people of God,
      Palmer's phrase, but after that[5]
      Confusion fell upon our thought.

                        5

      Irish poets, learn your trade,
      Sing whatever is well made,
70   Scorn the sort now growing up
      All out of shape from toe to top,
      Their unremembering hearts and heads
      Base-born products of base beds.
      Sing the peasantry, and then
75   Hard-riding country gentlemen,
      The holiness of monks, and after
      Porter-drinkers' randy laughter;
      Sing the lords and ladies gay
      That were beaten into the clay
80   Through seven heroic centuries;
      Cast your mind on other days
      That we in coming days may be
      Still the indomitable Irishry.

                        6

      Under bare Ben Bulben's head
85   In Drumcliff churchyard Yeats is laid.
      An ancestor was rector there
      Long years ago, a church stands near,
      By the road an ancient cross.
      No marble, no conventional phrase;
90   On limestone quarried near the spot
      By his command these words are cut:

                 Cast a cold eye
                 On life, on death.
                 Horseman, pass by!

September 4, 1938   1939

ERNEST DOWSON

1867–1900

Vitae summa brevis spem nos vetat incohare longam[1]

They are not long, the weeping and the laughter,
      Love and desire and hate:

---

5. The verse paragraph assembles five artists who had provided Yeats with images and with ideals of what art should be. Claude Lorrain (1600–1682), the great French landscape painter, was a central standard for landscape painters up to the early nineteenth century, including those mentioned here, especially Richard Wilson (1714–1782).

Edward Calvert (1799–1883) and Samuel Palmer (1805–1881), visionaries, landscape painters, and engravers, had found inspiration in many aspects of Blake's life and work.
1. "The brevity of life forbids us to entertain hopes of long duration" (Latin): Horace, *Odes* 1.4.15.

I think they have no portion in us after
    We pass the gate.

5 They are not long, the days of wine and roses:
      Out of a misty dream
    Our path emerges for a while, then closes
      Within a dream.

Non sum qualis eram bonae sub regno Cynarae[2]

Last night, ah, yesternight, betwixt her lips and mine
There fell thy shadow, Cynara! thy breath was shed
Upon my soul between the kisses and the wine;
And I was desolate and sick of an old passion,
5   Yea, I was desolate and bowed my head:
I have been faithful to thee, Cynara! in my fashion.

All night upon mine heart I felt her warm heart beat,
Night-long within mine arms in love and sleep she lay;
Surely the kisses of her bought red mouth were sweet;
10 But I was desolate and sick of an old passion,
      When I awoke and found the dawn was grey:
I have been faithful to thee, Cynara! in my fashion.

I have forgot much, Cynara! gone with the wind,
Flung roses, roses riotously with the throng,
15 Dancing, to put thy pale, lost lilies out of mind;
But I was desolate and sick of an old passion,
      Yea, all the time, because the dance was long:
I have been faithful to thee, Cynara! in my fashion.

I cried for madder music and for stronger wine,
20 But when the feast is finished and the lamps expire,
Then falls thy shadow, Cynara! the night is thine;
And I am desolate and sick of an old passion,
      Yea hungry for the lips of my desire:
I have been faithful to thee, Cynara! in my fashion.

1891   1896

EDWIN ARLINGTON ROBINSON
1869–1935

Richard Cory

Whenever Richard Cory went down town,
We people on the pavement looked at him:
He was a gentleman from sole to crown,
Clean favored, and imperially slim.

---

2. Horace, *Odes* 4.1.3–4: the poet urges Venus to spare him new efforts in her service: "I am not as I was under the reign of the good Cynara" (Latin).

5   And he was always quietly arrayed,
    And he was always human when he talked;
    But still he fluttered pulses when he said,
    "Good-morning," and he glittered when he walked.

    And he was rich—yes, richer than a king—
10   And admirably schooled in every grace:
    In fine, we thought that he was everything
    To make us wish that we were in his place.

    So on we worked, and waited for the light,
    And went without the meat, and cursed the bread;
15   And Richard Cory, one calm summer night,
    Went home and put a bullet through his head.

1869

George Crabbe[1]

    Give him the darkest inch your shelf allows,
    Hide him in lonely garrets, if you will,
    But his hard, human pulse is throbbing still
    With the sure strength that fearless truth endows.
5   In spite of all fine science disavows,
    Of his plain excellence and stubborn skill
    There yet remains what fashion cannot kill,
    Though years have thinned the laurel[2] from his brows.

    Whether or not we read him, we can feel
10   From time to time the vigor of his name
    Against us like a finger for the shame
    And emptiness of what our souls reveal
    In books that are as altars where we kneel
    To consecrate the flicker, not the flame.

1897

Reuben Bright

    Because he was a butcher and thereby
    Did earn an honest living (and did right),
    I would not have you think that Reuben Bright
    Was any more a brute than you or I;

5   For when they told him that his wife must die,
    He stared at them, and shook with grief and fright,
    And cried like a great baby half that night,
    And made the women cry to see him cry.

    And after she was dead, and he had paid
10   The singers and the sexton and the rest,

---

1. (1754–1832); English poet, physician, and curate, known for his realistic narrative poems (see pp. 662–70).

2. In classical Greece, laurel was associated with prophecy and poetry; laurel wreaths crowned poets as well as the victors in athletic contests.

He packed a lot of things that she had made
Most mournfully away in an old chest
Of hers, and put some chopped-up cedar boughs
In with them, and tore down the slaughter-house.

1897

Miniver Cheevy

Miniver Cheevy, child of scorn,
  Grew lean while he assailed the seasons;
He wept that he was ever born,
  And he had reasons.

5 Miniver loved the days of old
  When swords were bright and steeds were prancing;
The vision of a warrior bold
  Would set him dancing.

Miniver sighed for what was not,
10 And dreamed, and rested from his labors;
He dreamed of Thebes and Camelot,
  And Priam's neighbors.[3]

Miniver mourned the ripe renown
  That made so many a name so fragrant;
15 He mourned Romance, now on the town,
  And Art, a vagrant.

Miniver loved the Medici,[4]
  Albeit he had never seen one;
He would have sinned incessantly
20 Could he have been one.

Miniver cursed the commonplace
  And eyed a khaki suit with loathing;
He missed the medieval grace
  Of iron clothing.

25 Miniver scorned the gold he sought,
  But sore annoyed was he without it;
Miniver thought, and thought, and thought,
  And thought about it.

Miniver Cheevy, born too late,
30 Scratched his head and kept on thinking;
Miniver coughed, and called it fate,
  And kept on drinking.

1910

---

3. "Priam": king of Troy during the Trojan War, immortalized in Homer's *Iliad*. "Thebes": ancient Greek city, famous in history and legend; "Camelot": legendary site of King Arthur's court.

4. Merchant-princes of Renaissance Florence, known both for cruelty and for their support of learning and art.

Eros Turannos[5]

She fears him, and will always ask
    What fated her to choose him;
She meets in his engaging mask
    All reasons to refuse him;
5   But what she meets and what she fears
Are less than are the downward years,
Drawn slowly to the foamless weirs[6]
    Of age, were she to lose him.

Between a blurred sagacity
10   That once had power to sound him,
And Love, that will not let him be
    The Judas[7] that she found him,
Her pride assuages her almost,
As if it were alone the cost.
15   He sees that he will not be lost,
    And waits and looks around him.

A sense of ocean and old trees
    Envelopes and allures him;
Tradition, touching all he sees,
20   Beguiles and reassures him;
And all her doubts of what he says
Are dimmed with what she knows of days—
Till even prejudice delays
    And fades, and she secures him.

25   The falling leaf inaugurates
    The reign of her confusion;
The pounding wave reverberates
    The dirge of her illusion;
And home, where passion lived and died,
30   Becomes a place where she can hide,
While all the town and harbor side
    Vibrate with her seclusion.

We tell you, tapping on our brows,
    The story as it should be,
35   As if the story of a house
    Were told, or ever could be;
We'll have no kindly veil between
Her visions and those we have seen,
As if we guessed what hers have been,
40   Or what they are or would be.

Meanwhile we do no harm; for they
    That with a god have striven,
Not hearing much of what we say,
    Take what the god has given;

---

5. "Love, the King" (Greek); the title alludes both to Sophocles' tragedy (*Oidipous Turannos,* or *Oedipus Tyrannos*) and to the English word "tyrant."
6. Dams; also, the water dammed (especially a millpond).
7. The disciple who betrayed Jesus.

45   Though like waves breaking it may be,
      Or like a changed familiar tree,
      Or like a stairway to the sea
        Where down the blind are driven.

                                       1916

The Mill

    The miller's wife had waited long,
      The tea was cold, the fire was dead;
    And there might yet be nothing wrong
      In how he went and what he said:
5   "There are no millers any more,"
      Was all that she had heard him say;
    And he had lingered at the door
      So long that it seemed yesterday.

    Sick with a fear that had no form
10   She knew that she was there at last;
    And in the mill there was a warm
      And mealy fragrance of the past.
    What else there was would only seem
      To say again what he had meant;
15   And what was hanging from a beam
      Would not have heeded where she went.

    And if she thought it followed her,
      She may have reasoned in the dark
    That one way of the few there were
20   Would hide her and would leave no mark:
    Black water, smooth above the weir°   *milldam*
      Like starry velvet in the night,
    Though ruffled once, would soon appear
      The same as ever to the sight.

                                         1920

Mr. Flood's Party

    Old Eben Flood, climbing alone one night
    Over the hill between the town below
    And the forsaken upland hermitage
    That held as much as he should ever know
5   On earth again of home, paused warily.
    The road was his with not a native near;
    And Eben, having leisure, said aloud,
    For no man else in Tilbury Town to hear:

    "Well, Mr. Flood, we have the harvest moon
10   Again, and we may not have many more;
    The bird is on the wing, the poet says,[8]
    And you and I have said it here before.

8. A paraphrase of the seventh stanza of *The Rubáiyát of Omar Khayyám* as translated in 1859 by the English poet Edward FitzGerald (1809–1883; see pp. 866–78).

Drink to the bird." He raised up to the light
The jug that he had gone so far to fill,
15   And answered huskily: "Well, Mr. Flood,
Since you propose it, I believe I will."

Alone, as if enduring to the end
A valiant armor of scarred hopes outworn,
He stood there in the middle of the road
20   Like Roland's ghost winding a silent horn.[9]
Below him, in the town among the trees,
Where friends of other days had honored him,
A phantom salutation of the dead
Rang thinly till old Eben's eyes were dim.

25   Then, as a mother lays her sleeping child
Down tenderly, fearing it may awake,
He set the jug down slowly at his feet
With trembling care, knowing that most things break;
And only when assured that on firm earth
30   It stood, as the uncertain lives of men
Assuredly did not, he paced away,
And with his hand extended paused again:

"Well, Mr. Flood, we have not met like this
In a long time; and many a change has come
35   To both of us, I fear, since last it was
We had a drop together. Welcome home!"
Convivially returning with himself,
Again he raised the jug up to the light;
And with an acquiescent quaver said:
40   "Well, Mr. Flood, if you insist, I might.

"Only a very little, Mr. Flood—
For auld lang syne.[1] No more, sir; that will do."
So, for the time, apparently it did,
And Eben evidently thought so too;
45   For soon amid the silver loneliness
Of night he lifted up his voice and sang,
Secure, with only two moons listening,
Until the whole harmonious landscape rang—

"For auld lang syne." The weary throat gave out,
50   The last word wavered; and the song being done,
He raised again the jug regretfully
And shook his head, and was again alone.
There was not much that was ahead of him,
And there was nothing in the town below—
55   Where strangers would have shut the many doors
That many friends had opened long ago.

1920

9. The hero of the French medieval poem *The Song of Roland* (ca. 1000) had an enchanted horn; at Roncevalles (A.D. 778), he sounded his horn for help just before dying.

1. Literally, "old long since" (Scottish), the days of long ago: the title and refrain of a famous song by the Scottish poet Robert Burns (1759–1796; see pp. 684–95).

CHARLOTTE MEW
1869–1928

The Farmer's Bride

Three Summers since I chose a maid,
Too young maybe—but more's to do
At harvest-time than bide and woo.
　　When us was wed she turned afraid
5　　Of love and me and all things human;
Like the shut of a winter's day.
Her smile went out, and 'twasn't a woman—
　　More like a little frightened fay.°   *fairy*
　　　One night, in the Fall, she runned away.

10　"Out 'mong the sheep, her be," they said,
'Should properly have been abed;
But sure enough she wasn't there
Lying awake with her wide brown stare.
So over seven-acre field and up-along across the down°   *upland pasture*
15　We chased her, flying like a hare
Before our lanterns. To Church-Town
　　All in a shiver and a scare
We caught her, fetched her home at last
And turned the key upon her, fast.

20　She does the work about the house
As well as most, but like a mouse:
　　Happy enough to chat and play
　　With birds and rabbits and such as they,
　　So long as men-folk keep away.
25　"Not near, not near!" her eyes beseech
When one of us comes within reach.
　　The women say that beasts in stall
　　Look round like children at her call.
　　I've hardly heard her speak at all.

30　Shy as a leveret,° swift as he,   *young hare*
Straight and slight as a young larch tree,
Sweet as the first wild violets, she,
To her wild self. But what to me?

The short days shorten and the oaks are brown,
35　　The blue smoke rises to the low grey sky,
One leaf in the still air falls slowly down,
　　A magpie's spotted feathers lie
On the black earth spread white with rime,°   *frozen dew*
The berries redden up to Christmas-time.
40　　What's Christmas-time without there be
　　Some other in the house than we!

She sleeps up in the attic there
Alone, poor maid. 'Tis but a stair
Betwixt us. Oh! my God! the down,°   *light, soft body hair*
45   The soft young down of her, the brown,
The brown of her—her eyes, her hair, her hair!

1912   1916

In Nunhead Cemetery

It is the clay that makes the earth stick to his spade;
    He fills in holes like this year after year;
The others have gone; they were tired, and half afraid
    But I would rather be standing here;

5   There is nowhere else to go. I have seen this place
    From the windows of the train that's going past
Against the sky. This is rain on my face—
    It was raining here when I saw it last.

There is something horrible about a flower;
10   This, broken in my hand, is one of those
He threw in just now: it will not live another hour;
    There are thousands more: you do not miss a rose.

One of the children hanging about
    Pointed at the whole dreadful heap and smiled
15   This morning, after THAT was carried out;
    There is something terrible about a child.

We were like children, last week, in the Strand;[1]
    That was the day you laughed at me
Because I tried to make you understand
20   The cheap, stale chap I used to be
Before I saw the things you made me see.

This is not a real place; perhaps by-and-by
    I shall wake—I am getting drenched with all this rain:
To-morrow I will tell you about the eyes of the Crystal Palace[2] train
25   Looking down on us, and you will laugh and I shall see what you
         see again.

    Not here, not now. We said "Not yet
    Across our low stone parapet
Will the quick shadows of the sparrows fall."

    But still it was a lovely thing
30   Through the grey months to wait for Spring
    With the birds that go a-gypsying
In the parks till the blue seas call.
    And next to these, you used to care

1. Street in central London.   in London's Great Exhibition of 1851.
2. Large building, made of glass and iron, erected

For the lions in Trafalgar Square,
35 Who'll stand and speak for London when her bell of Judgment
tolls—
And the gulls at Westminster that were
The old sea-captains' souls.
To-day again the brown tide splashes, step by step, the river stair,
And the gulls are there!

40 By a month we have missed our Day:
The children would have hung about
Round the carriage and over the way
As you and I came out.

We should have stood on the gulls' black cliffs and heard the sea
45 And seen the moon's white track,
I would have called, you would have come to me
And kissed me back.

You have never done that: I do not know
Why I stood staring at your bed
50 And heard you, though you spoke so low,
But could not reach your hands, your little head.
There was nothing we could not do, you said,
And you went, and I let you go!

Now I will burn you back, I will burn you through,
55 Though I am damned for it we two will lie
And burn, here where the starlings fly
To these white stones from the wet sky—;
Dear, you will say this is not I—
It would not be you, it would not be you!

60 If for only a little while
You will think of it you will understand,
If you will touch my sleeve and smile
As you did that morning in the Strand
I can wait quietly with you
65 Or go away if you want me to—
God! What is God? but your face has gone and your hand!
Let me stay here too.

When I was quite a little lad
At Christmas-time we went half mad
70 For joy of all the toys we had,
And then we used to sing about the sheep
The shepherds watched by night;
We used to pray to Christ to keep
Our small souls safe till morning light—;
75 I am scared, I am staying with you to-night—
Put me to sleep.

I shall stay here: here you can see the sky;
The houses in the streets are much too high;

There is no one left to speak to there;
80   Here they are everywhere,
And just above them fields and fields of roses lie—
If he would dig it all up again they would not die.

                                                                    1916

STEPHEN CRANE

1871–1900

From The Black Riders and Other Lines[1]

I

BLACK RIDERS CAME FROM THE SEA.
THERE WAS CLANG AND CLANG OF SPEAR AND SHIELD,
AND CLASH AND CLASH OF HOOF AND HEEL,
WILD SHOUTS AND THE WAVE OF HAIR
5   IN THE RUSH UPON THE WIND:
THUS THE RIDE OF SIN.

III

IN THE DESERT
I SAW A CREATURE, NAKED, BESTIAL,
WHO, SQUATTING UPON THE GROUND,
HELD HIS HEART IN HIS HANDS,
5   AND ATE OF IT.
I SAID, "IS IT GOOD, FRIEND?"
"IT IS BITTER—BITTER," HE ANSWERED;
"BUT I LIKE IT
"BECAUSE IT IS BITTER,
10   "AND BECAUSE IT IS MY HEART."

XXIV

I SAW A MAN PURSUING THE HORIZON;
ROUND AND ROUND THEY SPED.
I WAS DISTURBED AT THIS;
I ACCOSTED THE MAN.
5   "IT IS FUTILE," I SAID,
"YOU CAN NEVER——"

"YOU LIE," HE CRIED,
AND RAN ON.

XXV

BEHOLD, THE GRAVE OF A WICKED MAN,
AND NEAR IT, A STERN SPIRIT.

1. The stylish Boston publishers of Crane's first poetry collection, *The Black Riders and Other Lines*, proposed what they called a "severely classic" design, printing the poems in capitals only— which greatly pleased Crane. Modern editors have reproduced the poems in standard typography; here the original look of the "lines" ("I never call them poems," Crane said) is more closely approximated.

THERE CAME A DROOPING MAID WITH VIOLETS,
BUT THE SPIRIT GRASPED HER ARM.
5   "NO FLOWERS FOR HIM," HE SAID.
THE MAID WEPT:
"AH, I LOVED HIM."
BUT THE SPIRIT, GRIM AND FROWNING:
"NO FLOWERS FOR HIM."

10   NOW, THIS IS IT——
IF THE SPIRIT WAS JUST,
WHY DID THE MAID WEEP?

LVI

A MAN FEARED THAT HE MIGHT FIND AN ASSASSIN;
ANOTHER THAT HE MIGHT FIND A VICTIM.
ONE WAS MORE WISE THAN THE OTHER.

1895

From War is Kind[2]

Do not weep, maiden, for war is kind.
Because your lover threw wild hands toward the sky
And the affrighted steed ran on alone,
Do not weep.
5   War is kind.

Hoarse, booming drums of the regiment
Little souls who thirst for fight,
These men were born to drill and die
The unexplained glory flies above them
10   Great is the battle-god, great, and his kingdom——
A field where a thousand corpses lie.

Do not weep, babe, for war is kind.
Because your father tumbled in the yellow trenches,
Raged at his breast, gulped and died,
15   Do not weep.
War is kind.

Swift, blazing flag of the regiment
Eagle with crest of red and gold,
These men were born to drill and die
20   Point for them the virtue of slaughter
Make plain to them the excellence of killing
And a field where a thousand corpses lie.

Mother whose heart hung humble as a button
On the bright splendid shroud of your son,
25   Do not weep.
War is kind.

1899

2. The poems in Crane's second and final collection of verse were printed conventionally, with upper-
and lowercase letters.

[A man adrift on a slim spar]

A man adrift on a slim spar
A horizon smaller than the rim of a bottle
Tented waves rearing lashy dark points
The near whine of froth in circles.
5   God is cold.

The incessant raise and swing of the sea
And growl after growl of crest
The sinkings, green, seething, endless
The upheaval half-completed.
10   God is cold.

The seas are in the hollow of The Hand;
Oceans may be turned to a spray
Raining down through the stars
Because of a gesture of pity toward a babe.
15 Oceans may become grey ashes,
Die with a long moan and a roar
Amid the tumult of the fishes
And the cries of the ships,
Because The Hand beckons the mice.

20 A horizon smaller than a doomed assassin's cap,
Inky, surging tumults
A reeling, drunken sky and no sky
A pale hand sliding from a polished spar.
                     God is cold.

25 The puff of a coat imprisoning air.
A face kissing the water-death
A weary slow sway of a lost hand
And the sea, the moving sea, the sea.
                     God is cold.

ca. 1897   1929

PAUL LAURENCE DUNBAR

1872–1906

A Summer's Night

The night is dewy as a maiden's mouth,
  The skies are bright as are a maiden's eyes,
  Soft as a maiden's breath, the wind that flies
Up from the perfumed bosom of the South.
5 Like sentinels, the pines stand in the park;
  And hither hastening like rakes that roam,
  With lamps to light their wayward footsteps home,
The fire-flies come stagg'ring down the dark.

                                               1895

We Wear the Mask

We wear the mask that grins and lies,
It hides our cheeks and shades our eyes —
This debt we pay to human guile;
With torn and bleeding hearts we smile,
5   And mouth with myriad subtleties.

Why should the world be over-wise,
In counting all our tears and sighs?
Nay, let them only see us, while
        We wear the mask.

10   We smile, but, O great Christ, our cries
To thee from tortured souls arise.
We sing, but oh the clay is vile
Beneath our feet, and long the mile;
But let the world dream otherwise,
15   We wear the mask!

1896

Little Brown Baby

Little brown baby wif spa'klin' eyes,
    Come to yo' pappy an' set on his knee.
What you been doin', suh—makin' san' pies?
    Look at dat bib—you's ez du'ty ez me.
5   Look at dat mouf—dat's merlasses, I bet;
    Come hyeah, Maria, an' wipe off his han's.
Bees gwine to ketch you an' eat you up yit,
    Bein' so sticky an sweet—goodness lan's!

Little brown baby wif spa'klin' eyes,
10   Who's pappy's darlin' an' who's pappy's chile?
Who is it all de day nevah once tries
    Fu' to be cross, er once loses dat smile?
Whah did you git dem teef? My, you's a scamp!
    Whah did dat dimple come f'om in yo' chin?
15   Pappy do' know you—I b'lieves you's a tramp;
    Mammy, dis hyeah's some ol' straggler got in!

Let's th'ow him outen de do' in de san',
    We do' want stragglers a-layin' 'roun' hyeah;
Let's gin him 'way to de big buggah-man;
20   I know he's hidin' erroun' hyeah right neah.
Buggah-man, buggah-man, come in de do',
Hyeah's a bad boy you kin have fu' to eat,
Mammy an' pappy do' want him no mo',
    Swaller him down f'om his haid to his feet!

25   Dah, now, I t'ought dat you'd hug me up close.
    Go back, ol' buggah, you sha'n't have dis boy.
He ain't no tramp, ner no straggler, of co'se;

He's pappy's pa'dner an' playmate an' joy.
Come to you' pallet now—go to yo' res';
30   Wisht you could allus know ease an' cleah skies;
Wisht you could stay jes' a chile on my breas'—
Little brown baby wif spa'klin' eyes!

1899?

Sympathy

I know what the caged bird feels, alas!
    When the sun is bright on the upland slopes;
When the wind stirs soft through the springing grass,
And the river flows like a stream of glass;
5   When the first bird sings and the first bud opes,°   opens
And the faint perfume from its chalice steals—
I know what the caged bird feels!

I know why the caged bird beats his wing
    Till its blood is red on the cruel bars;
10   For he must fly back to his perch and cling
When he fain would be° on the bough a-swing;   would like to be
    And a pain still throbs in the old, old scars
And they pulse again with a keener sting—
I know why he beats his wing!

15   I know why the caged bird sings, ah me,
    When his wing is bruised and his bosom sore,—
When he beats his bars and he would be free;
It is not a carol of joy or glee,
    But a prayer that he sends from his heart's deep core,
20   But a plea, that upward to Heaven he flings—
I know why the caged bird sings!

1899

JOHN McCRAE
1872–1918

In Flanders Fields[1]

In Flanders fields the poppies blow
Between the crosses, row on row,
    That mark our place; and in the sky

1. Written in April 1915 during the second battle of Ypres, France, in the region (once the country) called Flanders, which encompasses parts of modern France, Belgium, and the Netherlands. McRae, a Canadian soldier and physician, survived massive German shelling in one of the bloodiest chapters in World War I. Major-General E. W. B. Morrison, who commanded McRae's brigade, wrote: "During periods in the battle men who were shot actually rolled down the bank [of the Ypres Canal] into his dressing station. . . . [H]e and I watched [men] burying their dead whenever there was a lull. Thus the crosses, row on row, grew into a good-sized cemetery." The poem, first published in *Punch* in December 1915, achieved instant international fame, and was memorized by soldiers.

The larks, still bravely singing, fly
5   Scarce heard amid the guns below.

We are the Dead. Short days ago
We lived, felt dawn, saw sunset glow,
    Loved and were loved, and now we lie,
        In Flanders fields.

10   Take up our quarrel with the foe:
To you from failing hands we throw
    The torch; be yours to hold it high.
    If ye break faith with us who die
We shall not sleep, though poppies grow
15   In Flanders fields.

1915   1919

WALTER DE LA MARE

1873–1956

The Listeners

"Is there anybody there?" said the Traveller,
    Knocking on the moonlit door;
And his horse in the silence champed the grasses
    Of the forest's ferny floor:
5   And a bird flew up out of the turret,
    Above the Traveller's head:
And he smote upon the door again a second time;
    "Is there anybody there?" he said.
But no one descended to the Traveller;
10   No head from the leaf-fringed sill
Leaned over and looked into his grey eyes,
    Where he stood perplexed and still.
But only a host of phantom listeners
    That dwelt in the lone house then
15 Stood listening in the quiet of the moonlight
    To that voice from the world of men:
Stood thronging the faint moonbeams on the dark stair,
    That goes down to the empty hall,
Hearkening in an air stirred and shaken
20   By the lonely Traveller's call.
And he felt in his heart their strangeness,
    Their stillness answering his cry,
While his horse moved, cropping the dark turf,
    'Neath the starred and leafy sky;
25 For he suddenly smote on the door, even
    Louder, and lifted his head:—
"Tell them I came, and no one answered,
    That I kept my word," he said.
Never the least stir made the listeners,

30   Though every word he spake
Fell echoing through the shadowiness of the still house
      From the one man left awake:
Ay, they heard his foot upon the stirrup,
      And the sound of iron on stone,
35   And how the silence surged softly backward,
      When the plunging hoofs were gone.

1912

Fare Well

When I lie where shades of darkness
Shall no more assail mine eyes,
Nor the rain make lamentation
      When the wind sighs;
5   How will fare the world whose wonder
Was the very proof of me?
Memory fades, must the remembered
      Perishing be?

Oh, when this my dust surrenders
10   Hand, foot, lip, to dust again,
May these loved and loving faces
      Please other men!
May the rusting harvest hedgerow
Still the Traveller's Joy[1] entwine,
15   And as happy children gather
      Posies once mine.

Look thy last on all things lovely,
Every hour. Let no night
Seal thy sense in deathly slumber
20   Till to delight
Thou have paid thy utmost blessing;
Since that all things thou wouldst praise
Beauty took from those who loved them
      In other days.

1918

ROBERT FROST

1874–1963

Mending Wall

Something there is that doesn't love a wall,
That sends the frozen-ground-swell under it,
And spills the upper boulders in the sun;
And makes gaps even two can pass abreast.

---

1. Wild climbing plant also known as Virgin's Bower or Old Man's Beard.

5   The work of hunters is another thing:
I have come after them and made repair
Where they have left not one stone on a stone,
But they would have the rabbit out of hiding,
To please the yelping dogs. The gaps I mean,
10   No one has seen them made or heard them made,
But at spring mending-time we find them there.
I let my neighbor know beyond the hill;
And on a day we meet to walk the line
And set the wall between us once again.
15   We keep the wall between us as we go.
To each the boulders that have fallen to each.
And some are loaves and some so nearly balls
We have to use a spell to make them balance:
'Stay where you are until our backs are turned!'
20   We wear our fingers rough with handling them.
Oh, just another kind of outdoor game,
One on a side. It comes to little more:
There where it is we do not need the wall:
He is all pine and I am apple orchard.
25   My apple trees will never get across
And eat the cones under his pines, I tell him.
He only says, 'Good fences make good neighbors.'
Spring is the mischief in me, and I wonder
If I could put a notion in his head:
30   '*Why* do they make good neighbors? Isn't it
Where there are cows? But here there are no cows.
Before I built a wall I'd ask to know
What I was walling in or walling out,
And to whom I was like to give offense.
35   Something there is that doesn't love a wall,
That wants it down.' I could say 'Elves' to him,
But it's not elves exactly, and I'd rather
He said it for himself. I see him there
Bringing a stone grasped firmly by the top
40   In each hand, like an old-stone savage armed.
He moves in darkness as it seems to me,
Not of woods only and the shade of trees.
He will not go behind his father's saying,
And he likes having thought of it so well
45   He says again, 'Good fences make good neighbors.'

1914

The Death of the Hired Man

Mary sat musing on the lamp-flame at the table
Waiting for Warren. When she heard his step,
She ran on tip-toe down the darkened passage
To meet him in the doorway with the news
5   And put him on his guard. 'Silas is back.'
She pushed him outward with her through the door
And shut it after her. 'Be kind,' she said.
She took the market things from Warren's arms

And set them on the porch, then drew him down
10 To sit beside her on the wooden steps.

'When was I ever anything but kind to him?
But I'll not have the fellow back,' he said.
'I told him so last haying, didn't I?
If he left then, I said, that ended it.
15 What good is he? Who else will harbor him
At his age for the little he can do?
What help he is there's no depending on.
Off he goes always when I need him most.
He thinks he ought to earn a little pay,
20 Enough at least to buy tobacco with,
So he won't have to beg and be beholden.
"All right," I say, "I can't afford to pay
Any fixed wages, though I wish I could."
"Someone else can." "Then someone else will have to."
25 I shouldn't mind his bettering himself
If that was what it was. You can be certain,
When he begins like that, there's someone at him
Trying to coax him off with pocket-money,—
In haying time, when any help is scarce.
30 In winter he comes back to us. I'm done.'

'Sh! Not so loud: he'll hear you,' Mary said.

'I want him to: he'll have to soon or late.'

'He's worn out. He's asleep beside the stove.
When I came up from Rowe's I found him here,
35 Huddled against the barn-door fast asleep,
A miserable sight, and frightening, too—
You needn't smile—I didn't recognize him—
I wasn't looking for him—and he's changed.
Wait till you see.'

40   'Where did you say he'd been?'

'He didn't say. I dragged him to the house,
And gave him tea and tried to make him smoke.
I tried to make him talk about his travels.
Nothing would do: he just kept nodding off.'

45 'What did he say? Did he say anything?'

'But little.'

                    'Anything? Mary, confess
He said he'd come to ditch the meadow for me.'

'Warren!'

50   'But did he? I just want to know.'

'Of course he did. What would you have him say?
Surely you wouldn't grudge the poor old man
Some humble way to save his self-respect.
He added, if you really care to know,
55 He meant to clear the upper pasture, too.
That sounds like something you have heard before?
Warren, I wish you could have heard the way
He jumbled everything. I stopped to look
Two or three times—he made me feel so queer—
60 To see if he was talking in his sleep.
He ran on Harold Wilson—you remember—
The boy you had in haying four years since.
He's finished school, and teaching in his college.
Silas declares you'll have to get him back.
65 He says they two will make a team for work:
Between them they will lay this farm as smooth!
The way he mixed that in with other things.
He thinks young Wilson a likely lad, though daft
On education—you know how they fought
70 All through July under the blazing sun,
Silas up on the cart to build the load,
Harold along beside to pitch it on.'

'Yes, I took care to keep well out of earshot.'

'Well, those days trouble Silas like a dream.
75 You wouldn't think they would. How some things linger!
Harold's young college boy's assurance piqued him.
After so many years he still keeps finding
Good arguments he sees he might have used.
I sympathize. I know just how it feels
80 To think of the right thing to say too late.
Harold's associated in his mind with Latin.
He asked me what I thought of Harold's saying
He studied Latin like the violin
Because he liked it—that an argument!
85 He said he couldn't make the boy believe
He could find water with a hazel prong—
Which showed how much good school had ever done him.
He wanted to go over that. But most of all
He thinks if he could have another chance
90 To teach him how to build a load of hay—'

'I know, that's Silas' one accomplishment.
He bundles every forkful in its place,
And tags and numbers it for future reference,
So he can find and easily dislodge it
95 In the unloading. Silas does that well.
He takes it out in bunches like big birds' nests.
You never see him standing on the hay
He's trying to lift, straining to lift himself.'

'He thinks if he could teach him that, he'd be
100 Some good perhaps to someone in the world.

He hates to see a boy the fool of books.
Poor Silas, so concerned for other folk,
And nothing to look backward to with pride,
And nothing to look forward to with hope,
105 So now and never any different.'

Part of a moon was falling down the west,
Dragging the whole sky with it to the hills.
Its light poured softly in her lap. She saw it
And spread her apron to it. She put out her hand
110 Among the harp-like morning-glory strings,
Taut with the dew from garden bed to eaves,
As if she played unheard some tenderness
That wrought on him beside her in the night.
'Warren,' she said, 'he has come home to die:
115 You needn't be afraid he'll leave you this time.'

'Home,' he mocked gently.

                              'Yes, what else but home?
It all depends on what you mean by home.
Of course he's nothing to us, any more
120 Than was the hound that came a stranger to us
Out of the woods, worn out upon the trail.'

'Home is the place where, when you have to go there,
They have to take you in.'

                              'I should have called it
125 Something you somehow haven't to deserve.'

Warren leaned out and took a step or two,
Picked up a little stick, and brought it back
And broke it in his hand and tossed it by.
'Silas has better claim on us you think
130 Than on his brother? Thirteen little miles
As the road winds would bring him to his door.
Silas has walked that far no doubt today.
Why doesn't he go there? His brother's rich,
A somebody—director in the bank.'

135 'He never told us that.'

                              'We know it though.'

'I think his brother ought to help, of course.
I'll see to that if there is need. He ought of right
To take him in, and might be willing to—
140 He may be better than appearances.
But have some pity on Silas. Do you think
If he had any pride in claiming kin
Or anything he looked for from his brother,
He'd keep so still about him all this time?'

145 'I wonder what's between them.'

                                      'I can tell you.
Silas is what he is—we wouldn't mind him—
But just the kind that kinsfolk can't abide.
He never did a thing so very bad.
150 He don't know why he isn't quite as good
As anybody. Worthless though he is,
He won't be made ashamed to please his brother.'

'I can't think Si ever hurt anyone.'

'No, but he hurt my heart the way he lay
155 And rolled his old head on that sharp-edged chair-back.
He wouldn't let me put him on the lounge.
You must go in and see what you can do.
I made the bed up for him there tonight.
You'll be surprised at him—how much he's broken.
160 His working days are done; I'm sure of it.'

'I'd not be in a hurry to say that.'

'I haven't been. Go, look, see for yourself.
But, Warren, please remember how it is:
He's come to help you ditch the meadow.
165 He has a plan. You mustn't laugh at him.
He may not speak of it, and then he may.
I'll sit and see if that small sailing cloud
Will hit or miss the moon.'

                                It hit the moon.
170 Then there were three there, making a dim row,
The moon, the little silver cloud, and she.

Warren returned—too soon, it seemed to her,
Slipped to her side, caught up her hand and waited.

'Warren?' she questioned.

175   'Dead,' was all he answered.

                                                  1914

The Wood-Pile

Out walking in the frozen swamp one gray day,
I paused and said, 'I will turn back from here.
No, I will go on farther—and we shall see.'
The hard snow held me, save where now and then
5 One foot went through. The view was all in lines
Straight up and down of tall slim trees
Too much alike to mark or name a place by
So as to say for certain I was here
Or somewhere else: I was just far from home.

10   A small bird flew before me. He was careful
      To put a tree between us when he lighted,
      And say no word to tell me who he was
      Who was so foolish as to think what *he* thought.
      He thought that I was after him for a feather—
15   The white one in his tail; like one who takes
      Everything said as personal to himself.
      One flight out sideways would have undeceived him.
      And then there was a pile of wood for which
      I forgot him and let his little fear
20   Carry him off the way I might have gone,
      Without so much as wishing him good-night.
      He went behind it to make his last stand.
      It was a cord of maple, cut and split
      And piled—and measured, four by four by eight.
25   And not another like it could I see.
      No runner tracks in this year's snow looped near it.
      And it was older sure than this year's cutting,
      Or even last year's or the year's before.
      The wood was gray and the bark warping off it
30   And the pile somewhat sunken. Clematis
      Had wound strings round and round it like a bundle.
      What held it though on one side was a tree
      Still growing, and on one a stake and prop,
      These latter about to fall. I thought that only
35   Someone who lived in turning to fresh tasks
      Could so forget his handiwork on which
      He spent himself, the labor of his ax,
      And leave it there far from a useful fireplace
      To warm the frozen swamp as best it could
40   With the slow smokeless burning of decay.

                                      1914

The Road Not Taken

      Two roads diverged in a yellow wood,
      And sorry I could not travel both
      And be one traveler, long I stood
      And looked down one as far as I could
5   To where it bent in the undergrowth;

      Then took the other, as just as fair,
      And having perhaps the better claim,
      Because it was grassy and wanted wear;
      Though as for that the passing there
10   Had worn them really about the same,

      And both that morning equally lay
      In leaves no step had trodden black.
      Oh, I kept the first for another day!
      Yet knowing how way leads on to way,
15   I doubted if I should ever come back.

I shall be telling this with a sigh
Somewhere ages and ages hence:
Two roads diverged in a wood, and I—
I took the one less traveled by,
20   And that has made all the difference.

1916

The Oven Bird

There is a singer everyone has heard,
Loud, a mid-summer and a mid-wood bird,
Who makes the solid tree trunks sound again.
He says that leaves are old and that for flowers
5   Mid-summer is to spring as one to ten.
He says the early petal-fall is past
When pear and cherry bloom went down in showers
On sunny days a moment overcast;
And comes that other fall we name the fall.
10   He says the highway dust is over all.
The bird would cease and be as other birds
But that he knows in singing not to sing.
The question that he frames in all but words
Is what to make of a diminished thing.

1916

Birches

When I see birches bend to left and right
Across the lines of straighter darker trees,
I like to think some boy's been swinging them.
But swinging doesn't bend them down to stay
5   As ice-storms do. Often you must have seen them
Loaded with ice a sunny winter morning
After a rain. They click upon themselves
As the breeze rises, and turn many-colored
As the stir cracks and crazes their enamel.
10   Soon the sun's warmth makes them shed crystal shells
Shattering and avalanching on the snow-crust—
Such heaps of broken glass to sweep away
You'd think the inner dome of heaven had fallen.
They are dragged to the withered bracken° by the load,   *ferns*
15   And they seem not to break; though once they are bowed
So low for long, they never right themselves:
You may see their trunks arching in the woods
Years afterwards, trailing their leaves on the ground
Like girls on hands and knees that throw their hair
20   Before them over their heads to dry in the sun.
But I was going to say when Truth broke in
With all her matter-of-fact about the ice-storm
I should prefer to have some boy bend them
As he went out and in to fetch the cows—
25   Some boy too far from town to learn baseball,
Whose only play was what he found himself,

Summer or winter, and could play alone.
One by one he subdued his father's trees
By riding them down over and over again
30   Until he took the stiffness out of them,
And not one but hung limp, not one was left
For him to conquer. He learned all there was
To learn about not launching out too soon
And so not carrying the tree away
35   Clear to the ground. He always kept his poise
To the top branches, climbing carefully
With the same pains you use to fill a cup
Up to the brim, and even above the brim.
Then he flung outward, feet first, with a swish,
40   Kicking his way down through the air to the ground.
So was I once myself a swinger of birches.
And so I dream of going back to be.
It's when I'm weary of considerations,
And life is too much like a pathless wood
45   Where your face burns and tickles with the cobwebs
Broken across it, and one eye is weeping
From a twig's having lashed across it open.
I'd like to get away from earth awhile
And then come back to it and begin over.
50   May no fate willfully misunderstand me
And half grant what I wish and snatch me away
Not to return. Earth's the right place for love:
I don't know where it's likely to go better.
I'd like to go by climbing a birch tree,
55   And climb black branches up a snow-white trunk
Toward heaven, till the tree could bear no more,
But dipped its top and set me down again.
That would be good both going and coming back.
One could do worse than be a swinger of birches.

1916

The Hill Wife

Loneliness

HER WORD

One ought not to have to care
     So much as you and I
Care when the birds come round the house
     To seem to say good-by;

5   Or care so much when they come back
     With whatever it is they sing;
The truth being we are as much
     Too glad for the one thing

As we are too sad for the other here—
10   With birds that fill their breasts

But with each other and themselves
And their built or driven nests.

House Fear

Always—I tell you this they learned—
Always at night when they returned
To the lonely house from far away
To lamps unlighted and fire gone gray,
5 They learned to rattle the lock and key
To give whatever might chance to be
Warning and time to be off in flight:
And preferring the out- to the in-door night,
They learned to leave the house-door wide
10 Until they had lit the lamp inside.

The Smile

HER WORD

I didn't like the way he went away.
That smile! It never came of being gay.
Still he smiled—did you see him?—I was sure!
Perhaps because we gave him only bread
5 And the wretch knew from that that we were poor.
Perhaps because he let us give instead
Of seizing from us as he might have seized.
Perhaps he mocked at us for being wed,
Or being very young (and he was pleased
10 To have a vision of us old and dead).
I wonder how far down the road he's got.
He's watching from the woods as like as not.

The Oft-Repeated Dream

She had no saying dark enough
  For the dark pine that kept
Forever trying the window-latch
  Of the room where they slept.

5 The tireless but ineffectual hands
  That with every futile pass
Made the great tree seem as a little bird
  Before the mystery of glass!

It never had been inside the room,
10   And only one of the two
Was afraid in an oft-repeated dream
  Of what the tree might do.

The Impulse

It was too lonely for her there,
  And too wild,
And since there were but two of them,
  And no child,

5 And work was little in the house,
  She was free,
 And followed where he furrowed field,
  Or felled tree.

 She rested on a log and tossed
10 The fresh chips,
 With a song only to herself
  On her lips.

 And once she went to break a bough
  Of black alder.
15 She strayed so far she scarcely heard
  When he called her—

 And didn't answer—didn't speak—
  Or return.
 She stood, and then she ran and hid
20 In the fern.

 He never found her, though he looked
  Everywhere,
 And he asked at her mother's house
  Was she there.

25 Sudden and swift and light as that
  The ties gave,
 And he learned of finalities
  Besides the grave.

1916

Stopping by Woods on a Snowy Evening

 Whose woods these are I think I know.
 His house is in the village though;
 He will not see me stopping here
 To watch his woods fill up with snow.

5 My little horse must think it queer
 To stop without a farmhouse near
 Between the woods and frozen lake
 The darkest evening of the year.

 He gives his harness bells a shake
10 To ask if there is some mistake.
 The only other sound's the sweep
 Of easy wind and downy flake.

 The woods are lovely, dark and deep,
 But I have promises to keep,
15 And miles to go before I sleep,
 And miles to go before I sleep.

1923

To Earthward

Love at the lips was touch
As sweet as I could bear;
And once that seemed too much;
I lived on air

5   That crossed me from sweet things,
The flow of—was it musk
From hidden grapevine springs
Down hill at dusk?

I had the swirl and ache
10   From sprays of honeysuckle
That when they're gathered shake
Dew on the knuckle.

I craved strong sweets, but those
Seemed strong when I was young;
15   The petal of the rose
It was that stung.

Now no joy but lacks salt
That is not dashed with pain
And weariness and fault;
20   I crave the stain

Of tears, the aftermark
Of almost too much love,
The sweet of bitter bark
And burning clove.

25   When stiff and sore and scarred
I take away my hand
From leaning on it hard
In grass and sand,

The hurt is not enough:
30   I long for weight and strength
To feel the earth as rough
To all my length.

1923

Acquainted with the Night

I have been one acquainted with the night.
I have walked out in rain—and back in rain.
I have outwalked the furthest city light.

I have looked down the saddest city lane.
5 I have passed by the watchman on his beat
And dropped my eyes, unwilling to explain.

I have stood still and stopped the sound of feet
When far away an interrupted cry
Came over houses from another street,

10 But not to call me back or say good-by;
And further still at an unearthly height,
One luminary clock against the sky

Proclaimed the time was neither wrong nor right.
I have been one acquainted with the night.

1928

West-Running Brook

'Fred, where is north?'

'North? North is there, my love.
The brook runs west.'

'West-running Brook then call it.'
5 (West-running Brook men call it to this day.)
'What does it think it's doing running west
When all the other country brooks flow east
To reach the ocean? It must be the brook
Can trust itself to go by contraries
10 The way I can with you—and you with me—
Because we're—we're—I don't know what we are.
What are we?'

'Young or new?'

'We must be something.
15 We've said we two. Let's change that to we three.
As you and I are married to each other,
We'll both be married to the brook. We'll build
Our bridge across it, and the bridge shall be
Our arm thrown over it asleep beside it.
20 Look, look, it's waving to us with a wave
To let us know it hears me.'

'Why, my dear,
That wave's been standing off this jut of shore—'
(The black stream, catching on a sunken rock,
25 Flung backward on itself in one white wave,
And the white water rode the black forever,
Not gaining but not losing, like a bird
White feathers from the struggle of whose breast

Flecked the dark stream and flecked the darker pool
30 Below the point, and were at last driven wrinkled
In a white scarf against the far shore alders.)
'That wave's been standing off this jut of shore
Ever since rivers, I was going to say,
Were made in heaven. It wasn't waved to us.'

35 'It wasn't, yet it was. If not to you
It was to me—in an annunciation.'

'Oh, if you take it off to lady-land,
As't were the country of the Amazons[1]
We men must see you to the confines of
40 And leave you there, ourselves forbid to enter,—
It is your brook! I have no more to say.'

'Yes, you have, too. Go on. You thought of something.'

'Speaking of contraries, see how the brook
In that white wave runs counter to itself.
45 It is from that in water we were from
Long, long before we were from any creature.
Here we, in our impatience of the steps,
Get back to the beginning of beginnings,
The stream of everything that runs away.
50 Some say existence like a Pirouot
And Pirouette, forever in one place,
Stands still and dances, but it runs away,
It seriously, sadly, runs away
To fill the abyss' void with emptiness.
55 It flows beside us in this water brook,
But it flows over us. It flows between us
To separate us for a panic moment.
It flows between us, over us, and *with* us.
And it is time, strength, tone, light, life, and love—
60 And even substance lapsing unsubstantial;
The universal cataract of death
That spends to nothingness—and unresisted,
Save by some strange resistance in itself,
Not just a swerving, but a throwing back,
65 As if regret were in it and were sacred.
It has this throwing backward on itself
So that the fall of most of it is always
Raising a little, sending up a little.
Our life runs down in sending up the clock.
70 The brook runs down in sending up our life.
The sun runs down in sending up the brook.
And there is something sending up the sun.
It is this backward motion toward the source,
Against the stream, that most we see ourselves in,
75 The tribute of the current to the source.

1. Legendary female warriors who inhabited a country without men.

It is from this in nature we are from.
It is most us.'

           'Today will be the day
You said so.'

80   'No, today will be the day
You said the brook was called West-running Brook.'

'Today will be the day of what we both said.'

                             1928

Neither Out Far Nor In Deep

    The people along the sand
    All turn and look one way.
    They turn their back on the land.
    They look at the sea all day.

5   As long as it takes to pass
    A ship keeps raising its hull;
    The wetter ground like glass
    Reflects a standing gull.

    The land may vary more;
10 But wherever the truth may be—
    The water comes ashore,
    And the people look at the sea.

    They cannot look out far.
    They cannot look in deep.
15 But when was that ever a bar
    To any watch they keep?

                            1936

Design

    I found a dimpled spider, fat and white,
    On a white heal-all,[2] holding up a moth
    Like a white piece of rigid satin cloth—
    Assorted characters of death and blight
5 Mixed ready to begin the morning right,
    Like the ingredients of a witches' broth—
    A snow-drop spider, a flower like a froth,
    And dead wings carried like a paper kite.

    What had that flower to do with being white,
10 The wayside blue and innocent heal-all?
    What brought the kindred spider to that height,
    Then steered the white moth thither in the night?

2. One of a variety of plants in the mint family; the flowers are usually violet-blue.

What but design of darkness to appall?—
If design govern in a thing so small.

1936

Provide, Provide

The witch that came (the withered hag)
To wash the steps with pail and rag,
Was once the beauty Abishag,[3]

The picture pride of Hollywood.
5   Too many fall from great and good
For you to doubt the likelihood.

Die early and avoid the fate.
Or if predestined to die late,
Make up your mind to die in state.

10   Make the whole stock exchange your own!
If need be occupy a throne,
Where nobody can call *you* crone.

Some have relied on what they knew;
Others on being simply true.
15   What worked for them might work for you.

No memory of having starred
Atones for later disregard,
Or keeps the end from being hard.

Better to go down dignified
20   With boughten friendship at your side
Than none at all. Provide, provide!

1934

1936

The Silken Tent

She is as in a field a silken tent
At midday when a sunny summer breeze
Has dried the dew and all its ropes relent,
So that in guys[4] it gently sways at ease,
5   And its supporting central cedar pole,
That is its pinnacle to heavenward
And signifies the sureness of the soul,
Seems to owe naught to any single cord,
But strictly held by none, is loosely bound
10   By countless silken ties of love and thought
To everything on earth the compass round,
And only by one's going slightly taut

---

3. A beautiful maiden brought to warm King
David in his old age (1 Kings 1.2–4).   4. Ropes or cables used to steady an object.

In the capriciousness of summer air
Is of the slightest bondage made aware.

                                                              1942

Come In

As I came to the edge of the woods,
Thrush music—hark!
Now if it was dusk outside,
Inside it was dark.

5   Too dark in the woods for a bird
By sleight of wing
To better its perch for the night,
Though it still could sing.

The last of the light of the sun
10 That had died in the west
Still lived for one song more
In a thrush's breast.

Far in the pillared dark
Thrush music went—
15 Almost like a call to come in
To the dark and lament.

But no, I was out for stars:
I would not come in.
I meant not even if asked,
20 And I hadn't been.

                                                              1942

Never Again Would Birds' Song Be the Same

He would declare and could himself believe
That the birds there in all the garden round
From having heard the daylong voice of Eve
Had added to their own an oversound,
5   Her tone of meaning but without the words.
Admittedly an eloquence so soft
Could only have had an influence on birds
When call or laughter carried it aloft.
Be that as may be, she was in their song.
10 Moreover her voice upon their voices crossed
Had now persisted in the woods so long
That probably it never would be lost.
Never again would birds' song be the same.
And to do that to birds was why she came.

                                                              1942

The Most of It

He thought he kept the universe alone;
For all the voice in answer he could wake
Was but the mocking echo of his own
From some tree-hidden cliff across the lake.
5   Some morning from the boulder-broken beach
He would cry out on life, that what it wants
Is not its own love back in copy speech,
But counter-love, original response.
And nothing ever came of what he cried
10 Unless it was the embodiment that crashed
In the cliff's talus⁵ on the other side,
And then in the far distant water splashed,
But after a time allowed for it to swim,
Instead of proving human when it neared
15 And someone else additional to him,
As a great buck it powerfully appeared,
Pushing the crumpled water up ahead,
And landed pouring like a waterfall,
And stumbled through the rocks with horny tread,
20 And forced the underbrush—and that was all.

1942

The Gift Outright

The land was ours before we were the land's.
She was our land more than a hundred years
Before we were her people. She was ours
In Massachusetts, in Virginia,
5   But we were England's, still colonials,
Possessing what we still were unpossessed by,
Possessed by what we now no more possessed.
Something we were withholding made us weak
Until we found it was ourselves
10 We were withholding from our land of living,
And forthwith found salvation in surrender.
Such as we were we gave ourselves outright
(The deed of gift was many deeds of war)
To the land vaguely realizing westward,
15 But still unstoried, artless, unenhanced,
Such as she was, such as she would become.

1942

Directive

Back out of all this now too much for us,
Back in a time made simple by the loss
Of detail, burned, dissolved, and broken off
Like graveyard marble sculpture in the weather,
5   There is a house that is no more a house

---

5. Slope rock debris at the foot of a cliff.

Upon a farm that is no more a farm
And in a town that is no more a town.
The road there, if you'll let a guide direct you
Who only has at heart your getting lost,
10   May seem as if it should have been a quarry—
Great monolithic knees the former town
Long since gave up pretense of keeping covered.
And there's a story in a book about it:
Besides the wear of iron wagon wheels
15   The ledges show lines ruled southeast northwest,
The chisel work of an enormous Glacier
That braced his feet against the Arctic Pole.
You must not mind a certain coolness from him
Still said to haunt this side of Panther Mountain.
20   Nor need you mind the serial ordeal
Of being watched from forty cellar holes
As if by eye pairs out of forty firkins.°   *small wooden tubs*
As for the woods' excitement over you
That sends light rustle rushes to their leaves,
25   Charge that to upstart inexperience.
Where were they all not twenty years ago?
They think too much of having shaded out
A few old pecker-fretted[6] apple trees.
Make yourself up a cheering song of how
30   Someone's road home from work this once was,
Who may be just ahead of you on foot
Or creaking with a buggy load of grain.
The height of the adventure is the height
Of country where two village cultures faded
35   Into each other. Both of them are lost.
And if you're lost enough to find yourself
By now, pull in your ladder road behind you
And put a sign up CLOSED to all but me.
Then make yourself at home. The only field
40   Now left's no bigger than a harness gall.[7]
First there's the children's house of make believe,
Some shattered dishes underneath a pine,
The playthings in the playhouse of the children.
Weep for what little things could make them glad.
45   Then for the house that is no more a house,
But only a belilaced cellar hole,
Now slowly closing like a dent in dough.
This was no playhouse but a house in earnest.
Your destination and your destiny's
50   A brook that was the water of the house,
Cold as a spring as yet so near its source,
Too lofty and original to rage.
(We know the valley streams that when aroused
Will leave their tatters hung on barb and thorn.)
55   I have kept hidden in the instep arch
Of an old cedar at the waterside

6. I.e., marked by woodpeckers.   7. A sore caused by chafing against a harness.

A broken drinking goblet like the Grail
Under a spell so the wrong ones can't find it,
So can't get saved, as Saint Mark says they mustn't.[8]
60 (I stole the goblet from the children's playhouse.)
Here are your waters and your watering place.
Drink and be whole again beyond confusion.

1947

AMY LOWELL
1874–1925

Patterns

I walk down the garden paths,
And all the daffodils
Are blowing, and the bright blue squills.[1]
I walk down the patterned garden-paths
5   In my stiff, brocaded gown.
With my powdered hair and jewelled fan,
I too am a rare
Pattern. As I wander down
The garden paths.

10 My dress is richly figured,
And the train
Makes a pink and silver stain
On the gravel, and the thrift
Of the borders.
15 Just a plate of current fashion,
Tripping by in high-heeled, ribboned shoes.
Not a softness anywhere about me,
Only whalebone and brocade.
And I sink on a seat in the shade
20 Of a lime tree. For my passion
Wars against the stiff brocade.
The daffodils and squills
Flutter in the breeze
As they please.
25 And I weep;
For the lime-tree is in blossom
And one small flower has dropped upon my bosom.

And the plashing of waterdrops
In the marble fountain
30 Comes down the garden-paths.
The dripping never stops.

8. Cf. Mark 16.16: "He that believeth and is bap-
tized shall be saved; but he that believeth not shall
be damned." "The Grail": the cup used by Jesus
at the Last Supper, the object of many quests in
medieval and Arthurian romance.
1. Plants of the lily family.

Underneath my stiffened gown
Is the softness of a woman bathing in a marble basin,
A basin in the midst of hedges grown
35   So thick, she cannot see her lover hiding,
But she guesses he is near,
And the sliding of the water
Seems the stroking of a dear
Hand upon her.
40   What is Summer in a fine brocaded gown!
I should like to see it lying in a heap upon the ground.
All the pink and silver crumpled up on the ground.

I would be the pink and silver as I ran along the paths,
And he would stumble after,
45   Bewildered by my laughter.
I should see the sun flashing from his sword-hilt and the buckles on his
        shoes.
I would choose
To lead him in a maze along the patterned paths,
A bright and laughing maze for my heavy-booted lover.
50   Till he caught me in the shade,
And the buttons of his waistcoat bruised my body as he clasped me,
Aching, melting, unafraid.
With the shadows of the leaves and the sundrops,
And the plopping of the waterdrops,
55   All about us in the open afternoon—
I am very like to swoon
With the weight of this brocade,
For the sun sifts through the shade.

Underneath the fallen blossom
60   In my bosom,
Is a letter I have hid.
It was brought to me this morning by a rider from the Duke.
"Madam, we regret to inform you that Lord Hartwell
Died in action Thursday se'nnight."°   *a week ago*
65   As I read it in the white, morning sunlight,
The letters squirmed like snakes.
"Any answer, Madam," said my footman.
"No," I told him.
"See that the messenger takes some refreshment.
70   No, no answer."
And I walked into the garden,
Up and down the patterned paths,
In my stiff, correct brocade.
The blue and yellow flowers stood up proudly in the sun,
75   Each one.
I stood upright too,
Held rigid to the pattern
By the stiffness of my gown.
Up and down I walked,
80   Up and down.

In a month he would have been my husband.
In a month, here, underneath this lime,
We would have broke the pattern;
He for me, and I for him,
85   He as Colonel, I as Lady,
On this shady seat.
He had a whim
That sunlight carried blessing.
And I answered, "It shall be as you have said."
90   Now he is dead.

In Summer and in Winter I shall walk
Up and down
The patterned garden-paths
In my stiff, brocaded gown.
95   The squills and daffodils
Will give place to pillared roses, and to asters, and to snow.
I shall go
Up and down,
In my gown.
100   Gorgeously arrayed,
Boned and stayed.
And the softness of my body will be guarded from embrace
By each button, hook, and lace.
For the man who should loose me is dead,
105   Fighting with the Duke in Flanders,[2]
In a pattern called a war.
Christ! What are patterns for?

                                                        1916

The Weather-Cock Points South

I put your leaves aside,
One by one:
The stiff, broad outer leaves;
The smaller ones,
5   Pleasant to touch, veined with purple;
The glazed inner leaves.
One by one
I parted you from your leaves,
Until you stood up like a white flower
10   Swaying slightly in the evening wind.

White flower,
Flower of wax, of jade, of unstreaked agate;
Flower with surfaces of ice,
With shadows faintly crimson.
15   Where in all the garden is there such a flower?
The stars crowd through the lilac leaves

---

2. A medieval country; later the term for a region comprised of parts of France, Belgium, and the Netherlands. The poem was written during World War I, when Flanders was also a famous site of battle.

To look at you.
The low moon brightens you with silver.

The bud is more than the calyx.[3]
20   There is nothing to equal a white bud,
Of no colour, and of all,
Burnished by moonlight,
Thrust upon by a softly-swinging wind.

1919

GERTRUDE STEIN

1874–1946

From Stanzas in Meditation[1]

Part I

STANZA XIII

She may count three little daisies very well
By multiplying to either six nine or fourteen
Or she can be well mentioned as twelve
Which they may like which they can like soon
5   Or more than ever which they wish as a button
Just as much as they arrange which they wish
Or they can attire where they need as which say
Can they call a hat or a hat a day
Made merry because it is so.

Part III

STANZA II

I think very well of Susan but I do not know her name
I think very well of Ellen but which is not the same
I think very well of Paul I tell him not to do so
I think very well of Francis Charles but do I do so
5   I think very well of Thomas but I do not not do so
I think very well of not very well of William
I think very well of any very well of him
I think very well of him.
It is remarkable how quickly they learn
10   But if they learn and it is very remarkable how quickly they learn
It makes not only but by and by
And they can not only be not here
But not there

---

3. Outermost group of the parts of a flower.
1. Written in the same year as Stein's hugely popular *Autobiography of Alice B. Toklas, Stanzas in Meditation* is a long-neglected five-part poem with autobiographical elements, but which resists straightforward interpretation. "These austere 'stanzas' are made up almost entirely of colorless connecting words such as 'where,' 'which,' 'there,' 'of,' 'not,' 'have,' 'about,' and so on, though now and then Miss Stein throws in an orange, a lilac, or an Albert to remind us that it really is the world, our world, that she has been talking about" [John Ashbery]. In the *Autobiography*, Stein writes that she considers the *Stanzas* "her real achievement of the commonplace."

Which after all makes no difference
15 After all this does not make any does not make any difference
I add added it to it.
I could rather be rather be here.

STANZA V

It is not a range of a mountain
Of average of a range of a average mountain
Nor can they of which of which of arrange
To have been not which they which
5   Can add a mountain to this.
Upper an add it then maintain
That if they were busy so to speak
Add it to and
It not only why they could not add ask
10 Or when just when more each other
There is no each other as they like
They add why then emerge an add in
It is of absolutely no importance how often they add it.

Part V

STANZA XXXVIII

Which I wish to say is this
There is no beginning to an end
But there is a beginning and an end
To beginning.
5   Why yes of course.
Any one can learn that north of course
Is not only north but north as north
Why were they worried.
What I wish to say is this.
10 Yes of course

STANZA LXIII

I wish that I had spoken only of it all.

1932   1956

TRUMBULL STICKNEY

1874–1904

[And, the last day being come, Man stood alone]

And, the last day being come,[1] Man stood alone
Ere sunrise on the world's dismantled verge,°   *edge*
Awaiting how from everywhere should urge
The Coming of the Lord. And, behold, none

---

1. Stickney's apocalyptic vision of the Lord's coming partakes of imagery in Revelation and other books of the Bible, but is essentially original.

5 Did come,—but indistinct from every realm
Of earth and air and water, growing more
And louder, shriller, heavier, a roar
Up the dun° atmosphere did overwhelm   *dark*

His ears; and as he looked affrighted round
10 Every manner of beast innumerable
All thro' the shadows crying grew, until
The wailing was like grass upon the ground.

Asudden then within his human side
Their anguish, since the goad[2] he wielded first,
15 And, since he gave them not to drink, their thirst,
Darted compressed and vital.—As he died,

Low in the East now lighting gorgeously
He saw the last sea-serpent iris-mailed[3]
Which, with a spear transfixèd, yet availed
20 To pluck the sun down into the dead sea.

1905

An Athenian Garden

The burned and dusty garden said:
"My leaves are echoes, and thy earth
Is packed with footsteps of the dead.

"The strength of spring-time brought to birth
5 Some needles on the crooked fir,—
A rose, a laurel[4]—little worth.

"Come here, ye dreaming souls that err
Among the immortals of the grave:[5]
My summer is your sepulchre.

10 "On earth what darker voices rave
Than now this sea-breeze, driving dust
And whirling radiance wave on wave,

"With lulls so fearful thro' the gust
That on the shapeless flower-bed
15 Like timber splits the yellow crust.

"O thirsty, thirsty are the dead,[6]
Still thirsty, ever unallayed.
Where is no water, bring no bread."

2. A pointed stick for driving cattle and other animals.
3. In rainbow-colored armor.
4. The laurel is a symbol of glory; the fir, of time; the rose, of love.
5. Stickney, a devotee of the Greek philosopher Plato (ca. 428–347 B.C.), may be referring to Plato's Myth of Er, according to which immortal souls are given lots that allow them to choose, wisely or unwisely, from an assortment of next lives (*Republic* 10).
6. In Greek mythology, the dead are often represented as thirsty.

      I then had almost answer made,
20   When round the path in pleasure drew
      Three golden children to the shade.

      They stirred the dust with pail and hoe.
      Then did the littlest from his fears
      Come up and with his eyes of blue

25   Give me some berries seriously.
      And as he turned to his brother, I
      Looked after him thro' happy tears.

1903   1905

From Fragments

IX[7]

I hear a river thro' the valley wander
Whose water runs, the song alone remaining.
A rainbow stands and summer passes under.

                                              1905

CARL SANDBURG
1878–1967

Chicago

Hog Butcher for the World,
Tool Maker, Stacker of Wheat,
Player with Railroads and the Nation's Freight Handler;
Stormy, husky, brawling,
5 City of the Big Shoulders:

They tell me you are wicked and I believe them, for I have seen your
    painted women under the gas lamps luring the farm boys.
And they tell me you are crooked and I answer: Yes, it is true I have seen
    the gunman kill and go free to kill again.
And they tell me you are brutal and my reply is: On the faces of women
    and children I have seen the marks of wanton hunger.
And having answered so I turn once more to those who sneer at this my
    city, and I give them back the sneer and say to them:
10 Come and show me another city with lifted head singing so proud to be
    alive and coarse and strong and cunning.
Flinging magnetic curses amid the toil of piling job on job, here is a tall
    bold slugger set vivid against the little soft cities;
Fierce as a dog with tongue lapping for action, cunning as a savage pitted
    against the wilderness,
        Bareheaded,

---

7. Cf. John Hollander's homage to this poem, "Variations on a Fragment by Trumbull Stickney"
(p. 1665).

Shoveling,
15   Wrecking,
Planning,
Building, breaking, rebuilding,
Under the smoke, dust all over his mouth, laughing with white teeth,
Under the terrible burden of destiny laughing as a young man laughs,
20 Laughing even as an ignorant fighter laughs who has never lost a battle,
Bragging and laughing that under his wrist is the pulse, and under his
    ribs the heart of the people,
          Laughing!
Laughing the stormy, husky, brawling laughter of Youth, half-naked,
    sweating, proud to be Hog Butcher, Tool Maker, Stacker of Wheat,
Player with Railroads and Freight Handler to the Nation.

1916

Grass

Pile the bodies high at Austerlitz[1] and Waterloo.
Shovel them under and let me work—
         I am the grass; I cover all.

And pile them high at Gettysburg
5 And pile them high at Ypres and Verdun.
Shovel them under and let me work.
Two years, ten years, and passengers ask the conductor:
         What place is this?
         Where are we now?

10   I am the grass.
         Let me work.

1918

EDWARD THOMAS

1878–1917

Adlestrop

Yes, I remember Adlestrop—
The name, because one afternoon
Of heat the express-train drew up there
Unwontedly. It was late June.

5   The steam hissed. Someone cleared his throat.
No one left and no one came
On the bare platform. What I saw
Was Adlestrop—only the name

And willows, willow-herb, and grass,
10   And meadowsweet, and haycocks dry,

---

1. The places listed here are sites of major, bloody battles in the Napoleonic Wars, the Civil War, and World War I.

No whit less still and lonely fair
Than the high cloudlets in the sky.

And for that minute a blackbird sang
Close by, and round him, mistier,
15   Farther and farther, all the birds
Of Oxfordshire and Gloucestershire.

1915   1917

The Owl

Downhill I came, hungry, and yet not starved;
Cold, yet had heat within me that was proof
Against the North wind; tired, yet so that rest
Had seemed the sweetest thing under a roof.

5   Then at the inn I had food, fire, and rest,
Knowing how hungry, cold, and tired was I.
All of the night was quite barred out except
An owl's cry, a most melancholy cry

Shaken out long and clear upon the hill,
10   No merry note, nor cause of merriment,
But one telling me plain what I escaped
And others could not, that night, as in I went.

And salted was my food, and my repose,
Salted and sobered, too, by the bird's voice
15   Speaking for all who lay under the stars,
Soldiers and poor, unable to rejoice.

1917

In Memoriam [Easter 1915]

The flowers left thick at nightfall in the wood
This Eastertide call into mind the men,
Now far from home, who, with their sweethearts, should
Have gathered them and will do never again.

1915   1917

Rain

Rain, midnight rain, nothing but the wild rain
On this bleak hut, and solitude, and me
Remembering again that I shall die
And neither hear the rain nor give it thanks
5   For washing me cleaner than I have been
Since I was born into this solitude.
Blessed are the dead that the rain rains upon:
But here I pray that none whom once I loved
Is dying tonight or lying still awake
10   Solitary, listening to the rain,

Either in pain or thus in sympathy
Helpless among the living and the dead,
Like a cold water among broken reeds,
Myriads of broken reeds all still and stiff,
15   Like me who have no love which this wild rain
Has not dissolved except the love of death,
If love it be towards what is perfect and
Cannot, the tempest tells me, disappoint.

1916   1917

As the team's head brass[1]

As the team's head brass flashed out on the turn
The lovers disappeared into the wood.
I sat among the boughs of the fallen elm
That strewed an angle of the fallow, and
5   Watched the plough narrowing a yellow square
Of charlock.[2] Every time the horses turned
Instead of treading me down, the ploughman leaned
Upon the handles to say or ask a word,
About the weather, next about the war.
10 Scraping the share he faced towards the wood,
And screwed along the furrow till the brass flashed
Once more.
             The blizzard felled the elm whose crest
I sat in, by a woodpecker's round hole,
The ploughman said. "When will they take it away?"
15 "When the war's over." So the talk began—
One minute and an interval of ten,
A minute more and the same interval.
"Have you been out?" "No." "And don't want to, perhaps?"
"If I could only come back again, I should.
20 I could spare an arm. I shouldn't want to lose
A leg. If I should lose my head, why, so,
I should want nothing more. . . . Have many gone
From here?" "Yes." "Many lost?" "Yes, a good few.
Only two teams work on the farm this year.
25 One of my mates is dead. The second day
In France they killed him. It was back in March,
The very night of the blizzard, too. Now if
He had stayed here we should have moved the tree."
"And I should not have sat here. Everything
30 Would have been different. For it would have been
Another world." "Ay, and a better, though
If we could see all all might seem good." Then
The lovers came out of the wood again:
The horses started and for the last time
35 I watched the clods crumble and topple over
After the ploughshare and the stumbling team.

1916   1917

1. A team of horses pulling a plow; a head brass is an ornamental plaque of brass attached to a horse's bridle.
2. Wild mustard, a common yellow field-weed.

The Gypsy

A fortnight before Christmas Gypsies were everywhere:
Vans were drawn up on wastes, women trailed to the fair.
"My gentleman," said one, "you've got a lucky face."
"And you've a luckier," I thought, "if such a grace
5   And impudence in rags are lucky." "Give a penny
For the poor baby's sake." "Indeed I have not any
Unless you can give change for a sovereign,³ my dear."
"Then just half a pipeful of tobacco can you spare?"
I gave it. With that much victory she laughed content.
10 I should have given more, but off and away she went
With her baby and her pink sham flowers to rejoin
The rest before I could translate to its proper coin
Gratitude for her grace. And I paid nothing then,
As I pay nothing now with the dipping of my pen
15 For her brother's music when he drummed the tambourine
And stamped his feet, which made the workmen passing grin,
While his mouth-organ changed to a rascally Bacchanal⁴ dance
"Over the hills and far away." This and his glance
Outlasted all the fair, farmer, and auctioneer,
20 Cheap-jack,° balloon-man, drover with crooked stick, and steer,   *peddler*
Pig, turkey, goose, and duck, Christmas corpses to be.
Not even the kneeling ox had eyes like the Romany.°   *gypsy*
That night he peopled for me the hollow wooded land,
More dark and wild than stormiest heavens, that I searched and scanned
25 Like a ghost new-arrived. The gradations of the dark
Were like an underworld of death, but for the spark
In the Gypsy boy's black eyes as he played and stamped his tune,
"Over the hills and far away," and a crescent moon.

1918

WALLACE STEVENS
1879–1955

The Snow Man

One must have a mind of winter
To regard the frost and the boughs
Of the pine-trees crusted with snow;

And have been cold a long time
5   To behold the junipers shagged with ice,
The spruces rough in the distant glitter

Of the January sun; and not to think
Of any misery in the sound of the wind,
In the sound of a few leaves,

---

3. Formerly, a British gold coin, value one pound,
so called because it bore the effigy of the ruler on
one face.

4. Like Bacchus (Greek and Roman god of wine)
or his drunken, riotous rites.

10 Which is the sound of the land
    Full of the same wind
    That is blowing in the same bare place

    For the listener, who listens in the snow,
    And, nothing himself, beholds
15 Nothing that is not there and the nothing that is.

                                                    1923

The Emperor of Ice-Cream

    Call the roller of big cigars,
    The muscular one, and bid him whip
    In kitchen cups concupiscent curds.
    Let the wenches dawdle in such dress
5   As they are used to wear, and let the boys
    Bring flowers in last month's newspapers.
    Let be be finale of seem.
    The only emperor is the emperor of ice-cream.

    Take from the dresser of deal.°   *pine or firwood*
10 Lacking the three glass knobs, that sheet
    On which she embroidered fantails[1] once
    And spread it so as to cover her face.
    If her horny feet protrude, they come
    To show how cold she is, and dumb.
15 Let the lamp affix its beam.
    The only emperor is the emperor of ice-cream.

                                                    1923

Sunday Morning

                            1
    Complacencies of the peignoir, and late
    Coffee and oranges in a sunny chair,
    And the green freedom of a cockatoo
    Upon a rug mingle to dissipate
5   The holy hush of ancient sacrifice.
    She dreams a little, and she feels the dark
    Encroachment of that old catastrophe,
    As a calm darkens among water-lights.
    The pungent oranges and bright, green wings
10 Seem things in some procession of the dead,
    Winding across wide water, without sound.
    The day is like wide water, without sound,
    Stilled for the passing of her dreaming feet
    Over the seas, to silent Palestine,
15 Dominion of the blood and sepulchre.[2]

                            2
    Why should she give her bounty to the dead?
    What is divinity if it can come

---

1. Fantail pigeons.
2. I.e., the holy sepulcher, the cave in Jerusalem where Jesus was entombed; much blood was shed during the Crusades (eleventh–thirteenth centuries) as Christians attempted to gain control of Palestine.

Only in silent shadows and in dreams?
Shall she not find in comforts of the sun,
20　In pungent fruit and bright, green wings, or else
In any balm or beauty of the earth,
Things to be cherished like the thought of heaven?
Divinity must live within herself:
Passions of rain, or moods in falling snow;
25　Grievings in loneliness, or unsubdued
Elations when the forest blooms; gusty
Emotions on wet roads on autumn nights;
All pleasures and all pains, remembering
The bough of summer and the winter branch.
30　These are the measures destined for her soul.

3

Jove[3] in the clouds had his inhuman birth.
No mother suckled him, no sweet land gave
Large-mannered motions to his mythy mind
He moved among us, as a muttering king,
35　Magnificent, would move among his hinds,°　　*farmhands, rustics*
Until our blood, commingling, virginal,
With heaven, brought such requital to desire
The very hinds discerned it, in a star.
Shall our blood fail? Or shall it come to be
40　The blood of paradise? And shall the earth
Seem all of paradise that we shall know?
The sky will be much friendlier then than now,
A part of labor and a part of pain,
And next in glory to enduring love,
45　Not this dividing and indifferent blue.

4

She says, "I am content when wakened birds,
Before they fly, test the reality
Of misty fields, by their sweet questionings;
But when the birds are gone, and their warm fields
50　Return no more, where, then, is paradise?"
There is not any haunt of prophecy,
Nor any old chimera[4] of the grave,
Neither the golden underground, nor isle
Melodious, where spirits gat them home,
55　Nor visionary south, nor cloudy palm
Remote on heaven's hill, that has endured
As April's green endures; or will endure
Like her remembrance of awakened birds,
Or her desire for June and evening, tipped
60　By the consummation of the swallow's wings.

5

She says, "But in contentment I still feel
The need of some imperishable bliss."

3. Jove, or Jupiter, was the greatest of the Roman gods; "Jupiter" etymologically means "sky father."
4. In Greek mythology, a monster with a lion's head, goat's body, and serpent's tail. Also, an illusion or fabrication of the mind.

Death is the mother of beauty; hence from her,
Alone, shall come fulfilment to our dreams
65 And our desires. Although she strews the leaves
Of sure obliteration on our paths,
The path sick sorrow took, the many paths
Where triumph rang its brassy phrase, or love
Whispered a little out of tenderness,
70 She makes the willow shiver in the sun
For maidens who were wont to sit and gaze
Upon the grass, relinquished to their feet.
She causes boys to pile new plums and pears
On disregarded plate.[5] The maidens taste
75 And stray impassioned in the littering leaves.

6

Is there no change of death in paradise?
Does ripe fruit never fall? Or do the boughs
Hang always heavy in that perfect sky,
Unchanging, yet so like our perishing earth,
80 With rivers like our own that seek for seas
They never find, the same receding shores
That never touch with inarticulate pang?
Why set the pear upon those river-banks
Or spice the shores with odors of the plum?
85 Alas, that they should wear our colors there,
The silken weavings of our afternoons,
And pick the strings of our insipid lutes!
Death is the mother of beauty, mystical,
Within whose burning bosom we devise
90 Our earthly mothers waiting, sleeplessly.

7

Supple and turbulent, a ring of men
Shall chant in orgy on a summer morn
Their boisterous devotion to the sun,
Not as a god, but as a god might be,
95 Naked among them, like a savage source.
Their chant shall be a chant of paradise,
Out of their blood, returning to the sky;
And in their chant shall enter, voice by voice,
The windy lake wherein their lord delights,
100 The trees, like serafin,[6] and echoing hills,
That choir among themselves long afterward.
They shall know well the heavenly fellowship
Of men that perish and of summer morn.
And whence they came and whither they shall go
105 The dew upon their feet shall manifest.

8

She hears, upon that water without sound,
A voice that cries, "The tomb in Palestine

5. "Plate is used in the sense of so-called family
plate. Disregarded refers to the disuse into which
things fall that have been possessed for a long time.
I mean, therefore, that death releases and renews"

[*Letters of Wallace Stevens*, New York, 1966, pp.
183–84].
6. I.e., seraphim, the highest order of angels.

Is not the porch of spirits lingering.
It is the grave of Jesus, where he lay."
110 We live in an old chaos of the sun,
Or old dependency of day and night,
Or island solitude, unsponsored, free,
Of that wide water, inescapable.
Deer walk upon our mountains, and the quail
115 Whistle about us their spontaneous cries;
Sweet berries ripen in the wilderness;
And, in the isolation of the sky,
At evening, casual flocks of pigeons make
Ambiguous undulations as they sink,
120 Downward to darkness, on extended wings.

1915   1923

Anecdote of the Jar

I placed a jar in Tennessee,
And round it was, upon a hill.
It made the slovenly wilderness
Surround that hill.

5 The wilderness rose up to it,
And sprawled around, no longer wild.
The jar was round upon the ground
And tall and of a port in air.

It took dominion everywhere.
10 The jar was gray and bare.
It did not give of bird or bush,
Like nothing else in Tennessee.

1923

To the One of Fictive Music

Sister and mother and diviner love,
And of the sisterhood of the living dead
Most near, most clear, and of the clearest bloom,
And of the fragrant mothers the most dear
5 And queen, and of diviner love the day
And flame and summer and sweet fire, no thread
Of cloudy silver sprinkles in your gown
Its venom of renown, and on your head
No crown is simpler than the simple hair.

10 Now, of the music summoned by the birth
That separates us from the wind and sea,
Yet leaves us in them, until earth becomes,
By being so much of the things we are,
Gross effigy and simulacrum, none
15 Gives motion to perfection more serene
Than yours, out of our imperfections wrought,

Most rare, or ever of more kindred air
In the laborious weaving that you wear.

For so retentive of themselves are men
20   That music is intensest which proclaims
The near, the clear, and vaunts the clearest bloom,
And of all vigils musing the obscure,
That apprehends the most which sees and names,
As in your name, an image that is sure,
25   Among the arrant spices of the sun,
O bough and bush and scented vine, in whom
We give ourselves our likest issuance.

Yet not too like, yet not so like to be
Too near, too clear, saving a little to endow
30   Our feigning with the strange unlike, whence springs
The difference that heavenly pity brings.
For this, musician, in your girdle fixed
Bear other perfumes. On your pale head wear
A band entwining, set with fatal stones.
35   Unreal, give back to us what once you gave:
The imagination that we spurned and crave.

1923

Thirteen Ways of Looking at a Blackbird

1

Among twenty snowy mountains,
The only moving thing
Was the eye of the blackbird.

2

I was of three minds,
5   Like a tree
In which there are three blackbirds.

3

The blackbird whirled in the autumn winds.
It was a small part of the pantomime.

4

A man and a woman
10   Are one.
A man and a woman and a blackbird
Are one.

5

I do not know which to prefer,
The beauty of inflections
15   Or the beauty of innuendoes,
The blackbird whistling
Or just after.

6

Icicles filled the long window
With barbaric glass.
20   The shadow of the blackbird
Crossed it to and fro.
The mood
Traced in the shadow
An indecipherable cause.

7

25   O thin men of Haddam,[7]
Why do you imagine golden birds?
Do you not see how the blackbird
Walks around the feet
Of the women about you?

8

30   I know noble accents
And lucid, inescapable rhythms;
But I know, too,
That the blackbird is involved
In what I know.

9

35   When the blackbird flew out of sight,
It marked the edge
Of one of many circles.

10

At the sight of blackbirds
Flying in a green light,
40   Even the bawds of euphony
Would cry out sharply.

11

He rode over Connecticut
In a glass coach.
Once, a fear pierced him
45   In that he mistook
The shadow of his equipage
For blackbirds.

12

The river is moving.
The blackbird must be flying.

13

50   It was evening all afternoon.
It was snowing
And it was going to snow.
The blackbird sat
In the cedar-limbs.

1923

---

7. A town in Connecticut. Stevens explains: "The thin men of Haddam are entirely fictitious. . . . I just like the name. . . . It has a completely Yankee sound" [*Letters*, p. 340].

Peter Quince at the Clavier[8]

I

Just as my fingers on these keys
Make music, so the selfsame sounds
On my spirit make a music, too.

5 Music is feeling, then, not sound;
And thus it is that what I feel,
Here in this room, desiring you,

Thinking of your blue-shadowed silk,
Is music. It is like the strain
Waked in the elders by Susanna.[9]

10 Of a green evening, clear and warm,
She bathed in her still garden, while
The red-eyed elders watching, felt

The basses of their beings throb
In witching chords, and their thin blood
15 Pulse pizzicati of Hosanna.[1]

II

In the green water, clear and warm,
Susanna lay.
She searched
The touch of springs,
20 And found
Concealed imaginings.
She sighed,
For so much melody.

Upon the bank, she stood
25 In the cool
Of spent emotions.
She felt, among the leaves,
The dew
Of old devotions.

30 She walked upon the grass,
Still quavering.
The winds were like her maids,
On timid feet,
Fetching her woven scarves,
35 Yet wavering.

---

8. Early keyboard instrument. Peter Quince is one of the rustic actors who clumsily perform a "tragedy" within Shakespeare's comedy A *Midsummer Night's Dream*.
9. In Daniel 13, the Apocrypha, Susanna refused seduction by two Hebrew elders, who then falsely accused her of a liaison with a young man. Daniel protected her from being punished.
1. Great praise. "Pizzicata": musical passages in which strings are plucked.

A breath upon her hand
Muted the night.
She turned—
A cymbal crashed,
40 And roaring horns.

III

Soon, with a noise like tambourines,
Came her attendant Byzantines.[2]

They wondered why Susanna cried
Against the elders by her side;

45 And as they whispered, the refrain
Was like a willow swept by rain.

Anon, their lamps' uplifted flame
Revealed Susanna and her shame.

And then, the simpering Byzantines
50 Fled, with a noise like tambourines.

IV

Beauty is momentary in the mind—
The fitful tracing of a portal;
But in the flesh it is immortal.
The body dies; the body's beauty lives.
55 So evenings die, in their green going,
A wave, interminably flowing.
So gardens die, their meek breath scenting
The cowl of winter, done repenting.
So maidens die, to the auroral
60 Celebration of a maiden's choral.
Susanna's music touched the bawdy strings
Of those white elders; but, escaping,
Left only Death's ironic scraping.
Now, in its immortality, it plays
65 On the clear viol of her memory,
And makes a constant sacrament of praise.

1923   1931

The Idea of Order at Key West

She sang beyond the genius of the sea.
The water never formed to mind or voice,
Like a body wholly body, fluttering
Its empty sleeves; and yet its mimic motion
5 Made constant cry, caused constantly a cry,
That was not ours although we understood,
Inhuman, of the veritable ocean.

2. People of the Byzantine Empire of the fourth through the fifteenth centuries A.D.; an anachronism, as they postdated Susanna.

The sea was not a mask. No more was she.
The song and water were not medleyed sound
10 Even if what she sang was what she heard,
Since what she sang was uttered word by word.
It may be that in all her phrases stirred
The grinding water and the gasping wind;
But it was she and not the sea we heard.
15 For she was the maker of the song she sang.
The ever-hooded, tragic-gestured sea
Was merely a place by which she walked to sing.
Whose spirit is this? we said, because we knew
It was the spirit that we sought and knew
20 That we should ask this often as she sang.

If it was only the dark voice of the sea
That rose, or even colored by many waves;
If it was only the outer voice of sky
And cloud, of the sunken coral water-walled,
25 However clear, it would have been deep air,
The heaving speech of air, a summer sound
Repeated in a summer without end
And sound alone. But it was more than that,
More even than her voice, and ours, among
30 The meaningless plungings of water and the wind,
Theatrical distances, bronze shadows heaped
On high horizons, mountainous atmospheres
Of sky and sea.
                     It was her voice that made
35 The sky acutest at its vanishing.
She measured to the hour its solitude.
She was the single artificer of the world
In which she sang. And when she sang, the sea,
Whatever self it had, became the self
40 That was her song, for she was the maker. Then we,
As we beheld her striding there alone,
Knew that there never was a world for her
Except the one she sang and, singing, made.

Ramon Fernandez,[3] tell me, if you know,
45 Why, when the singing ended and we turned
Toward the town, tell why the glassy lights,
The lights in the fishing boats at anchor there,
As the night descended, tilting in the air,
Mastered the night and portioned out the sea,
50 Fixing emblazoned zones and fiery poles,
Arranging, deepening, enchanting night.

Oh! Blessed rage for order, pale Ramon,
The maker's rage to order words of the sea,
Words of the fragrant portals, dimly-starred,

---

3. Stevens claimed that he had simply combined two common Spanish names at random, without conscious reference to the French literary critic and essayist Ramon Fernandez (1894–1944).

55   And of ourselves and of our origins,
    In ghostlier demarcations, keener sounds.

1935

Waving Adieu, Adieu, Adieu[4]

That would be waving and that would be crying,
Crying and shouting and meaning farewell,
Farewell in the eyes and farewell at the centre,
Just to stand still without moving a hand.

5   In a world without heaven to follow, the stops
    Would be endings, more poignant than partings, profounder,
    And that would be saying farewell, repeating farewell,
    Just to be there and just to behold.

To be one's singular self, to despise
10   The being that yielded so little, acquired
    So little, too little to care, to turn
    To the ever-jubilant weather, to sip

One's cup and never to say a word,
Or to sleep or just to lie there still,
15   Just to be there, just to be beheld,
    That would be bidding farewell, be bidding farewell.

One likes to practice the thing. They practice,
Enough, for heaven. Ever-jubilant,
What is there here but weather, what spirit
20   Have I except it comes from the sun?

1935

The Poems of Our Climate

1

Clear water in a brilliant bowl,
Pink and white carnations. The light
In the room more like a snowy air,
Reflecting snow. A newly-fallen snow
5   At the end of winter when afternoons return.
    Pink and white carnations—one desires
    So much more than that. The day itself
    Is simplified: a bowl of white,
    Cold, a cold porcelain, low and round,
10 With nothing more than the carnations there.

2

Say even that this complete simplicity
Stripped one of all one's torments, concealed

4. Cf. Mark Strand's homage to this poem in *Dark Harbor*, XVI (p. 1759).

The evilly compounded, vital I
And made it fresh in a world of white,
15   A world of clear water, brilliant-edged,
Still one would want more, one would need more,
More than a world of white and snowy scents.

3

There would still remain the never-resting mind,
So that one would want to escape, come back
20   To what had been so long composed.
The imperfect is our paradise.
Note that, in this bitterness, delight,
Since the imperfect is so hot in us,
Lies in flawed words and stubborn sounds.

1942

The House Was Quiet and the World Was Calm

The house was quiet and the world was calm.
The reader became the book; and summer night

Was like the conscious being of the book.
The house was quiet and the world was calm.

5   The words were spoken as if there was no book,
Except that the reader leaned above the page,

Wanted to lean, wanted much most to be
The scholar to whom his book is true, to whom

The summer night is like a perfection of thought.
10   The house was quiet because it had to be.

The quiet was part of the meaning, part of the mind:
The access of perfection to the page.

And the world was calm. The truth in a calm world,
In which there is no other meaning, itself

15   Is calm, itself is summer and night, itself
Is the reader leaning late and reading there.

1947

Table Talk

Granted, we die for good.
Life, then, is largely a thing
Of happens to like, not should.

And that, too, granted, why
5   Do I happen to like red bush,
Gray grass and green-gray sky?

What else remains? But red,
Gray, green, why those of all?
That is not what I said:

10 Not those of all. But those.
One likes what one happens to like.
One likes the way red grows.

It cannot matter at all.
Happens to like is one
15 Of the ways things happen to fall.

ca. 1935   1957

A Room on a Garden

O stagnant east-wind, palsied mare,
Giddap! The ruby roses' hair
Must blow.

Behold how order is the end
5 Of everything. The roses bend
As one.

Order, the law of hoes and rakes,
May be perceived in windy quakes
And squalls.

10 The gardener searches earth and sky
The truth in nature to espy
In vain.

He well might find that eager balm
In lilies' stately-statued calm;
15 But then

He well might find it in this fret
Of lilies rusted, rotting, wet
With rain.

ca. 1935   1957

Of Mere Being

The palm at the end of the mind,
Beyond the last thought, rises
In the bronze decor,[5]

A gold-feathered bird
5 Sings in the palm, without human meaning,
Without human feeling, a foreign song.

5. In the first published version of this poem, the 1957 *Opus Posthumous* incorrectly gave "decor" as "distance." The 1989 edition provided a correction.

You know then that it is not the reason
That makes us happy or unhappy.
The bird sings. Its feathers shine.

10   The palm stands on the edge of space.
The wind moves slowly in the branches.
The bird's fire-fangled feathers dangle down.

1955?   1957, 1989

WITTER BYNNER
1881–1968

Haskell[1]

Here in Kansas is a school
Made of square stones and windows,
Where Indian boys are taught to use a tool,
A printing-press, a book,
5   And Indian girls
To read, to dress, to cook.
And as I watch today
The orderly industrious classes,
Only their color and silence and the way
10   The hair lies flat and black on their heads proclaims them Sioux,
Comanche, Choctaw, Cherokee,
Creek, Chippewa, Paiute[2]—and the red and blue
Of the girls' long sweaters and the purple and yellow,
And the tawny slant of the machine-made shirts . . .

15   Noon—and out they come. And one tall fellow,
Breaking from the others with a glittering yell and crouching slim,
Gives a leap like the leap of Mordkin,[3]
And the sun carves under him
A canyon of glory . . .
20   And then it shadows, and he darts,
With head hung, to the dormitory.

1920

From Chinese Drawings

A Philosopher

What though they conquer us?
The tea has come.
In at most nine hundred years,
Someone will conquer them.

1920

1. Town in Kansas.   3. Mikhail Mordkin (1881–1944), Russian ballet
2. Names of Native American tribes.   dancer.

The Wintry Mind

Winter uncovers distances, I find;
And so the cold and so the wintry mind
Takes leaves away, till there is left behind
A wide cold world. And so the heart grows blind
5 To the earth's green motions lying warm below
Field upon field, field upon field, of snow.

1940

More Lovely than Antiquity

There comes a moment in her veins
Not of the earth, not of the rains,
Something not of stalks and stems
But of dim crowns and diadems,°   *royal headbands*
5 Something commanding her to be
More ancient than antiquity
And to soothe her head on a pike above
The vacant circumstance of love.

1947

E. J. PRATT

1883–1964

Come Not the Seasons Here

Comes not the springtime here,
    Though the snowdrop came,
And the time of the cowslip is near,
    For a yellow flame
5 Was found in a tuft of green;
    And the joyous shout
    Of a child rang out
That a cuckoo's eggs were seen.

Comes not the summer here,
10   Though the cowslip be gone,
Though the wild rose blow as the year
    Draws faithfully on;
Though the face of the poppy be red
    In the morning light,
15   And the ground be white
With the bloom of the locust shed.

Comes not the autumn here,
    Though someone said
He found a leaf in the sere°   *withered state*
20   By an aster dead;

And knew that the summer was done,
    For a herdsman cried
That his pastures were brown in the sun,
    And his wells were dried.

25   Nor shall the winter come,
      Though the elm be bare,
    And every voice be dumb
      On the frozen air;
    But the flap of a waterfowl
30   In the marsh alone,
    Or the hoot of a horned owl
      On a glacial stone.

1923

From Stone to Steel

From stone to bronze, from bronze to steel
Along the road-dust of the sun
Two revolutions of the wheel
From Java to Geneva run.[1]

5   The snarl Neanderthal is worn
Close to the smiling Aryan[2] lips,
The civil polish of the horn
Gleams from our praying finger tips.

The evolution of desire
10   Has but matured a toxic wine,
Drunk long before its heady fire
Reddened Euphrates or the Rhine.[3]

Between the temple and the cave
The boundary lies tissue-thin:
15   The yearlings still the altars crave
As satisfaction for a sin.

The road goes up, the road goes down—
Let Java or Geneva be—
But whether to the cross or crown,
20   The path lies through Gethsemane.[4]

1932

---

1. Java, now part of Indonesia, was the site of fossil excavations, where the bones of an early type of prehistoric man ("Neanderthal," line 5) were found. Geneva, in Switzerland, was the headquarters of the League of Nations from 1919 until the outbreak of World War II.
2. According to Nazi racial theory, the Aryan "race" was superior to all others.

3. The Euphrates was one of the two great river valleys of ancient Mesopotamian civilization; the Rhine flows through western Germany and the Netherlands.
4. The garden where Christ prayed while his disciples slept, and where Judas betrayed him (Matthew 26.36–56).

WILLIAM CARLOS WILLIAMS
1883–1963

Danse Russe

If when my wife is sleeping
and the baby and Kathleen
are sleeping
and the sun is a flame-white disc
5   in silken mists
above shining trees,—
if I in my north room
dance naked, grotesquely
before my mirror
10 waving my shirt round my head
and singing softly to myself:
"I am lonely, lonely.
I was born to be lonely,
I am best so!"
15 If I admire my arms, my face,
my shoulders, flanks, buttocks
against the yellow drawn shades,—

Who shall say I am not
the happy genius[1] of my household?

1917

The Red Wheelbarrow

so much depends
upon

a red wheel
barrow

5 glazed with rain
water

beside the white
chickens.

1923

Queen-Ann's-Lace[2]

Her body is not so white as
anemone petals nor so smooth—nor
so remote a thing. It is a field
of the wild carrot taking
5 the field by force; the grass
does not raise above it.

1. The pervading and guardian spirit of a place.   2. A common field-flower.

Here is no question of whiteness,
white as can be, with a purple mole
at the center of each flower.
10 Each flower is a hand's span
of her whiteness. Wherever
his hand has lain there is
a tiny purple blemish. Each part
is a blossom under his touch
15 to which the fibres of her being
stem one by one, each to its end,
until the whole field is a
white desire, empty, a single stem,
a cluster, flower by flower,
20 a pious wish to whiteness gone over—
or nothing.

                                      1925

This Is Just to Say[3]

I have eaten
the plums
that were in
the icebox

5 and which
you were probably
saving
for breakfast

Forgive me
10 they were delicious
so sweet
and so cold   1934

Poem

As the cat
climbed over
the top of

the jamcloset
5 first the right
forefoot

carefully
then the hind
stepped down

10 into the pit of
the empty
flowerpot   1934

3. Cf. Kenneth Koch, "Variations on a Theme by William Carlos Williams" (1962; pp. 1584–85).

The Yachts

contend in a sea which the land partly encloses
shielding them from the too-heavy blows
of an ungoverned ocean which when it chooses

tortures the biggest hulls, the best man knows
5 to pit against its beatings, and sinks them pitilessly.
Mothlike in mists, scintillant in the minute

brilliance of cloudless days, with broad bellying sails
they glide to the wind tossing green water
from their sharp prows while over them the crew crawls

10 ant-like, solicitously grooming them, releasing,
making fast as they turn, lean far over and having
caught the wind again, side by side, head for the mark.

In a well guarded arena of open water surrounded by
lesser and greater craft which, sycophant, lumbering
15 and flittering follow them, they appear youthful, rare

as the light of a happy eye, live with the grace
of all that in the mind is fleckless, free and
naturally to be desired. Now the sea which holds them

is moody, lapping their glossy sides, as if feeling
20 for some slightest flaw but fails completely.
Today no race. Then the wind comes again. The yachts

move, jockeying for a start, the signal is set and they
are off. Now the waves strike at them but they are too
well made, they slip through, though they take in canvas.

25 Arms with hands grasping seek to clutch at the prows.
Bodies thrown recklessly in the way are cut aside.
It is a sea of faces about them in agony, in despair

until the horror of the race dawns staggering the mind,
the whole sea become an entanglement of watery bodies
30 lost to the world bearing what they cannot hold. Broken,

beaten, desolate, reaching from the dead to be taken up
they cry out, failing, failing! their cries rising
in waves still as the skillful yachts pass over.

1935

A Sort of a Song

Let the snake wait under
his weed
and the writing
be of words, slow and quick, sharp

5 to strike, quiet to wait,
  sleepless.

  —through metaphor to reconcile
  the people and the stones.
  Compose. (No ideas
10 but in things) Invent!
  Saxifrage[4] is my flower that splits
  the rocks.

           1944

The Dance

 In Breughel's[5] great picture, The Kermess,
 the dancers go round, they go round and
 around, the squeal and the blare and the
 tweedle of bagpipes, a bugle and fiddles
5 tipping their bellies (round as the thick-
 sided glasses whose wash they impound)
 their hips and their bellies off balance
 to turn them. Kicking and rolling about
 the Fair Grounds, swinging their butts, those
10 shanks must be sound to bear up under such
 rollicking measures, prance as they dance
 in Breughel's great picture, The Kermess.

           1944

From Asphodel, That Greeny Flower[6]

Book I

 Of asphodel, that greeny flower,
   like a buttercup
      upon its branching stem—
save that it's green and wooden—
5   I come, my sweet,
       to sing to you.
We lived long together
   a life filled,
      if you will,
10 with flowers. So that
    I was cheered
      when I came first to know

4. Literally, "breaking rocks" (Latin); a perennial herb.
5. Pieter Brueghel (d. 1569), Flemish painter of peasant life; "kermess": a fair or dance.
6. A tripartite love poem, with coda, for the poet's wife. The green asphodel first impressed Williams as a child in Switzerland, and appears in his early work *Kora in Hell: Improvisations* (1920). (Kora— or *Kore*, Greek for girl or young woman—is another name for the mythological figure Per-

sephone. The daughter of Demeter, she was carried to the underworld by its ruler, Hades. In the underworld of Homer's *Odyssey*, a grove of poplars sacred to Persephone stood at the entrance of *asphodel limona*, fields of asphodel inhabited by the souls of the dead.) The opening lines were originally published in *Poetry*, October 1952, as "Paterson, Book V: The River of Heaven," but were later removed from *Paterson*.

that there were flowers also
in hell.
15   Today
I'm filled with the fading memory of those flowers
that we both loved,
even to this poor
colorless thing—
20   I saw it
when I was a child—
little prized among the living
but the dead see,
asking among themselves:
25 What do I remember
that was shaped
as this thing is shaped?
while our eyes fill
with tears.
30   Of love, abiding love
it will be telling
though too weak a wash of crimson
colors it
to make it wholly credible.
35   There is something
something urgent
I have to say to you
and you alone
but it must wait
40 while I drink in
the joy of your approach,
perhaps for the last time.
And so
with fear in my heart
45   I drag it out
and keep on talking
for I dare not stop.
Listen while I talk on
against time.
50   It will not be
for long.
I have forgot
and yet I see clearly enough
something
55 central to the sky
which ranges round it.
An odor
springs from it!
A sweetest odor!
60   Honeysuckle! And now
there comes the buzzing of a bee!
and a whole flood
of sister memories!
Only give me time,
65   time to recall them
before I shall speak out.

Give me time,
   time.
When I was a boy
70   I kept a book
      to which, from time
to time,
     I added pressed flowers
      until, after a time,
75 I had a good collection.
     The asphodel,
      forebodingly,
among them.
     I bring you,
80   reawakened,
a memory of those flowers.
     They were sweet
      when I pressed them
and retained
85   something of their sweetness
      a long time.
It is a curious odor,
     a moral odor,
      that brings me
90 near to you.
     The color
      was the first to go.
There had come to me
     a challenge,
95   your dear self,
mortal as I was,
     the lily's throat
      to the hummingbird!
Endless wealth,
100   I thought,
      held out its arms to me.
A thousand tropics
     in an apple blossom.
      The generous earth itself
105 gave us lief.[7]
     The whole world
      became my garden!
But the sea
     which no one tends
110   is also a garden
when the sun strikes it
     and the waves
      are wakened.
I have seen it
115   and so have you
      when it puts all flowers
to shame.

---

7. Leave, or permission. Possibly a double meaning; "lief" also connotes gladness.

                  Too, there are the starfish
                      stiffened by the sun
120   and other sea wrack
                  and weeds. We knew that
                      along with the rest of it
        for we were born by the sea,
                knew its rose hedges
125   to the very water's brink.
        There the pink mallow grows
                and in their season
                      strawberries
        and there, later,
130   we went to gather
                    the wild plum.
        I cannot say
                that I have gone to hell
                    for your love
135   but often
                found myself there
                    in your pursuit.
        I do not like it
                and wanted to be
140   Do not turn away.
                    in heaven. Hear me out.
        I have learned much in my life
                from books
                    and out of them
145   about love.
               Death
                    is not the end of it.
        There is a hierarchy
                which can be attained,
150   I think,
        in its service.
               Its guerdon°   *reward*
                    is a fairy flower;
        a cat of twenty lives.
155   If no one came to try it
                    the world
        would be the loser.
                It has been
                    for you and me
160   as one who watches a storm
                come in over the water.
                    We have stood
        from year to year
                before the spectacle of our lives
165   with joined hands.
        The storm unfolds.
               Lightning
                    plays about the edges of the clouds.
        The sky to the north
170   is placid,

blue in the afterglow
as the storm piles up.
        It is a flower
            that will soon reach
175 the apex of its bloom.
        We danced,
           in our minds,
and read a book together.
        You remember?
180   It was a serious book.
And so books
        entered our lives.
The sea! The sea!
        Always
185   when I think of the sea
there comes to mind
        the *Iliad*
           and Helen's public fault
that bred it.[8]
190   Were it not for that
           there would have been
no poem but the world
        if we had remembered,
           those crimson petals
195 spilled among the stones,
        would have called it simply
           murder.
The sexual orchid that bloomed then
        sending so many
200   disinterested
men to their graves
        has left its memory
           to a race of fools
or heroes
205   if silence is a virtue.
           The sea alone
with its multiplicity
        holds any hope.
           The storm
210 has proven abortive
        but we remain
           after the thoughts it roused
to
        re-cement our lives.
215   It is the mind
the mind
        that must be cured
           short of death's
intervention,
220   and the will becomes again
        a garden. The poem

---

8. In Greek myth, the beautiful Helen (daughter of Zeus and Leda; wife of Menelaus) was abducted by Paris (son of the Trojan king, Priam). The dispute that followed was a cause of the Trojan War.

       is complex and the place made
            in our lives
                for the poem.
225   Silence can be complex too,
            but you do not get far
                with silence.
       Begin again.
           It is like Homer's
230   catalogue of ships:[9]
       it fills up the time.
           I speak in figures,
               well enough, the dresses
     you wear are figures also,
235   we could not meet
               otherwise. When I speak
   of flowers
          it is to recall
             that at one time
240   we were young.
          All women are not Helen,
             I know that,
    but have Helen in their hearts.
         My sweet,
245   you have it also, therefore
 I love you
        and could not love you otherwise.
          Imagine you saw
    a field made up of women
250   all silver-white.
            What should you do
   but love them?
         The storm bursts
          or fades! it is not
255   the end of the world.
         Love is something else,
            or so I thought it,
    a garden which expands,
         though I knew you as a woman
260   and never thought otherwise,
   until the whole sea
        has been taken up
           and all its gardens.
   It was the love of love,
265   the love that swallows up all else,
           a grateful love,
   a love of nature, of people,
        animals,
          a love engendering
270 gentleness and goodness
        that moved me

9. Cf. *Iliad* 2.484–785, where the Greek ships that sailed to Troy are listed.

and *that* I saw in you.
I should have known,
though I did not,
275   that the lily-of-the-valley
is a flower makes many ill
who whiff it.
We had our children,
rivals in the general onslaught.
280   I put them aside
though I cared for them
as well as any man
could care for his children
according to my lights.
285 You understand
I had to meet you
after the event
and have still to meet you.
Love
290   to which you too shall bow
along with me—
a flower
a weakest flower
shall be our trust
295   and not because
we are too feeble
to do otherwise
but because
at the height of my power
300 I risked what I had to do,
therefore to prove
that we love each other
while my very bones sweated
that I could not cry to you
305   in the act.
Of asphodel, that greeny flower,
I come, my sweet,
to sing to you!
My heart rouses
310   thinking to bring you news
of something
that concerns you
and concerns many men. Look at
what passes for the new.
315 You will not find it there but in
despised poems.
It is difficult
to get the news from poems
yet men die miserably every day
320   for lack
of what is found there.
Hear me out
for I too am concerned

and every man
325   who wants to die at peace in his bed
                    besides.

                                                              1955

D. H. LAWRENCE
1885–1930

Love on the Farm[1]

What large, dark hands are those at the window
Grasping in the golden light
Which weaves its way through the evening wind
        At my heart's delight?

5   Ah, only the leaves! But in the west
I see a redness suddenly come
Into the evening's anxious breast—
        'Tis the wound of love goes home!

The woodbine° creeps abroad   *honeysuckle*
10 Calling low to her lover:
        The sun-lit flirt who all the day
        Has poised above her lips in play
        And stolen kisses, shallow and gay
        Of pollen, now has gone away—
15   She woos the moth with her sweet, low word:
And when above her his moth-wings hover
Then her bright breast she will uncover
And yield her honey-drop to her lover.

Into the yellow, evening glow
20 Saunters a man from the farm below;
Leans, and looks in at the low-built shed
Where the swallow has hung her marriage bed.
        The bird lies warm against the wall.
        She glances quick her startled eyes
25   Towards him, then she turns away
        Her small head, making warm display
        Of red upon the throat. Her terrors sway
        Her out of the nest's warm, busy ball,
        Whose plaintive cry is heard as she flies
30   In one blue stoop from out the sties°   *pens for animals*
        Into the twilight's empty hall.
Oh, water-hen, beside the rushes
Hide your quaintly scarlet blushes,
Still your quick tail, lie still as dead,
35 Till the distance folds over his ominous tread!

1. Originally published as "Cruelty and Love," but retitled for the *Collected Poems* (1928).

The rabbit presses back her ears,
Turns back her liquid, anguished eyes
And crouches low; then with wild spring
Spurts from the terror of *his* oncoming;
40 To be choked back, the wire ring
Her frantic effort throttling:
      Piteous brown ball of quivering fears!
Ah, soon in his large, hard hands she dies,
And swings all loose from the swing of his walk!
45 Yet calm and kindly are his eyes
And ready to open in brown surprise
Should I not answer to his talk
Or should he my tears surmise.

I hear his hand on the latch, and rise from my chair
50 Watching the door open; he flashes bare
His strong teeth in a smile, and flashes his eyes
In a smile like triumph upon me; then careless-wise
He flings the rabbit soft on the table board
And comes towards me: ah! the uplifted sword
55 Of his hand against my bosom! and oh, the broad
Blade of his glance that asks me to applaud
His coming! With his hand he turns my face to him
And caresses me with his fingers that still smell grim
Of the rabbit's fur! God, I am caught in a snare!°   *wire trap*
60 I know not what fine wire is round my throat;
I only know I let him finger there
My pulse of life, and let him nose like a stoat[2]
Who sniffs with joy before he drinks the blood.

And down his mouth comes to my mouth! and down
65 His bright dark eyes come over me, like a hood
Upon my mind! his lips meet mine, and a flood
Of sweet fire sweeps across me, so I drown
Against him, die, and find death good.

1913

Piano

Softly, in the dusk, a woman is singing to me;
Taking me back down the vista of years, till I see
A child sitting under the piano, in the boom of the tingling strings
And pressing the small, poised feet of a mother who smiles as she sings.

5 In spite of myself, the insidious mastery of song
Betrays me back, till the heart of me weeps to belong
To the old Sunday evenings at home, with winter outside
And hymns in the cosy parlour, the tinkling piano our guide.

So now it is vain for the singer to burst into clamour
10 With the great black piano appassionato. The glamour

---

2. Small carnivorous animal of the weasel family.

Of childish days is upon me, my manhood is cast
Down in the flood of remembrance, I weep like a child for the past.

1918

Snake

A snake came to my water-trough
On a hot, hot day, and I in pyjamas for the heat,
To drink there.

In the deep, strange-scented shade of the great dark carob-tree
5 I came down the steps with my pitcher
And must wait, must stand and wait, for there he was at the trough before
me.

He reached down from a fissure in the earth-wall in the gloom
And trailed his yellow-brown slackness soft-bellied down, over the edge of
the stone trough
And rested his throat upon the stone bottom,
10 And where the water had dripped from the tap, in a small clearness,
He sipped with his straight mouth,
Softly drank through his straight gums, into his slack long body,
Silently.

Someone was before me at my water-trough,
15 And I, like a second comer, waiting.

He lifted his head from his drinking, as cattle do,
And looked at me vaguely, as drinking cattle do,
And flickered his two-forked tongue from his lips, and mused a moment,
And stooped and drank a little more,
20 Being earth-brown, earth-golden from the burning bowels of the earth
On the day of Sicilian July, with Etna smoking.
The voice of my education said to me
He must be killed,
For in Sicily the black, black snakes are innocent, the gold are venomous.

25 And voices in me said, If you were a man
You would take a stick and break him now, and finish him off.

But must I confess how I liked him,
How glad I was he had come like a guest in quiet, to drink at my water-
trough

And depart peaceful, pacified, and thankless,
30 Into the burning bowels of this earth?

Was it cowardice, that I dared not kill him?
Was it perversity, that I longed to talk to him?
Was it humility, to feel so honoured?
I felt so honoured.

35 And yet those voices:
    If you were not afraid, you would kill him!

    And truly I was afraid, I was most afraid,
    But even so, honoured still more
    That he should seek my hospitality
40 From out the dark door of the secret earth.

    He drank enough
    And lifted his head, dreamily, as one who has drunken,
    And flickered his tongue like a forked night on the air, so black,
    Seeming to lick his lips,
45 And looked around like a god, unseeing, into the air,
    And slowly turned his head,
    And slowly, very slowly, as if thrice adream,
    Proceeded to draw his slow length curving round
    And climb again the broken bank of my wall-face.

50 And as he put his head into that dreadful hole,
    And as he slowly drew up, snake-easing his shoulders, and entered farther,
    A sort of horror, a sort of protest against his withdrawing into that horrid
        black hole,
    Deliberately going into the blackness, and slowly drawing himself after,
    Overcame me now his back was turned.

55 I looked round, I put down my pitcher,
    I picked up a clumsy log
    And threw it at the water-trough with a clatter.

    I think it did not hit him,
    But suddenly that part of him that was left behind convulsed in undigni-
        fied haste.
60 Writhed like lightning, and was gone
    Into the black hole, the earth-lipped fissure in the wall-front,
    At which, in the intense still noon, I stared with fascination.

    And immediately I regretted it.
    I thought how paltry, how vulgar, what a mean act!
65 I despised myself and the voices of my accursed human education.

    And I thought of the albatross[3]
    And I wished he would come back, my snake.

    For he seemed to me again like a king,
    Like a king in exile, uncrowned in the underworld,
70 Now due to be crowned again.

    And so, I missed my chance with one of the lords
    Of life.[4]

---

3. In Coleridge's "Rime of the Ancient Mariner"   4. Cf. Meredith, "Modern Love," 30, line 7 (p.
(p. 744).   1008).

And I have something to expiate;
A pettiness.

Taormina.
1923

Elemental

Why don't people leave off being lovable
Or thinking they are lovable, or wanting to be lovable,
And be a bit elemental instead?

Since man is made up of the elements
5 Fire, and rain, and air, and live loam
And none of these is lovable
But elemental,
Man is lop-sided on the side of the angels.

I wish men would get back their balance among the elements
10 And be a bit more fiery, as incapable of telling lies
As fire is.
I wish they'd be true to their own variation, as water is,
Which goes through all the stages of steam and stream and ice
Without losing its head.

15 I am sick of lovable people,
Somehow they are a lie.

1929

Self-Protection

When science starts to be interpretive
It is more unscientific even than mysticism.

To make self-preservation and self-protection the first law of existence
Is about as scientific as making suicide the first law of existence,
5 And amounts to very much the same thing.

A nightingale singing at the top of his voice
Is neither hiding himself nor preserving himself nor propagating his
    species;
He is giving himself away in every sense of the word;
And obviously, it is the culminating point of his existence.

10 A tiger is striped and golden for his own glory.
He would certainly be much more invisible if he were grey-green.
And I don't suppose the ichthyosaurus sparkled like the humming-bird,
No doubt he was khaki-colored with muddy protective colouration,
So why didn't he survive?

15 As a matter of fact, the only creatures that seem to survive
Are those that give themselves away in flash and sparkle
And gay flicker of joyful life;

Those that go glittering abroad
With a bit of splendour.

20 Even mice play quite beautifully at shadows,
And some of them are brilliantly piebald.

I expect the dodo looked like a clod,
A drab and dingy bird.

1929

Trees in the Garden

Ah in the thunder air
How still the trees are!

And the lime-tree, lovely and tall, every leaf silent
Hardly looses even a last breath of perfume.

5 And the ghostly, creamy coloured little tree of leaves
White, ivory white among the rambling greens
How evanescent, variegated elder, she hesitates on the green grass
As if, in another moment, she would disappear
With all her grace of foam!

10 And the larch that is only a column, it goes up too tall to see:
And the balsam-pines that are blue with the grey-blue blueness of things
    from the sea,
And the young copper beech, its leaves red-rosy at the ends
How still they are together, they stand so still
In the thunder air, all strangers to one another
15 As the green grass glows upwards, strangers in the garden.

Lichtental.⁵
1932

The English Are So Nice!

The English are so nice
So awfully nice
They are the nicest people in the world.

And what's more, they're very nice about being nice
5 About your being nice as well!
If you're not nice they soon make you feel it.

Americans and French and Germans and so on
They're all very well
But they're not *really* nice, you know.
10 They're not nice in *our* sense of the word, are they now?

That's why one doesn't have to take them seriously.
We must be nice to them, of course,

5. A village near Baden-Baden, in south Germany, where Lawrence wrote the poem.

Of course, naturally.
But it doesn't really matter what you say to them,
15   They don't really understand
You can just say anything to them:
Be nice, you know, just nice
But you must never take them seriously, they wouldn't understand,
Just be nice, you know! oh, fairly nice,
20   Not too nice of course, they take advantage
But nice enough, just nice enough
To let them feel they're not quite as nice as they might be.

1932

Andraitx[6] — Pomegranate Flowers

It is June, it is June
The pomegranates are in flower,
The peasants are bending cutting the bearded wheat.

The pomegranates are in flower
5   Beside the high road, past the deathly dust,
And even the sea is silent in the sun.

Short gasps of flame in the green of night, way off
The pomegranates are in flower,
Small sharp red fires in the night of leaves.

10   And noon is suddenly dark, is lustrous, is silent and dark
Men are unseen, beneath the shading hats;
Only, from out the foliage of the secret loins
Red flamelets here and there reveal
A man, a woman there.

1932

Bavarian Gentians

Not every man has gentians in his house
in Soft September, at slow, sad Michaelmas.

Bavarian gentians, big and dark, only dark
darkening the daytime, torch-like with the smoking blueness of Pluto's
    gloom,
5   ribbed and torch-like, with their blaze of darkness spread blue
down flattening into points, flattened under the sweep of white day
torch-flower of the blue-smoking darkness, Pluto's dark-blue daze,
black lamps from the halls of Dis,[7] burning dark blue,
giving off darkness, blue darkness, as Demeter's pale lamps give off light,
10   lead me then, lead the way.

---

6. A town on the island of Majorca, Spain.
7. Another Roman name for Pluto (Greek Hades), ruler of the underworld. He had abducted Perse-
phone (Roman Proserpine) the daughter of Demeter (Roman Ceres), goddess of growing vege-
tation and living nature; Persephone ruled with him as queen of the underworld, but returned to spend six months of each year with her mother in the world above.

Reach me a gentian, give me a torch!
let me guide myself with the blue, forked torch of this flower
down the darker and darker stairs, where blue is darkened on blueness
even where Persephone goes, just now, from the frosted September
to the sightless realm where darkness is awake upon the dark
and Persephone herself is but a voice
or a darkness invisible enfolded in the deeper dark
of the arms Plutonic, and pierced with the passion of dense gloom,
among the splendour of torches of darkness, shedding darkness on the
    lost bride and her groom.

1932

The Ship of Death[8]

1

Now it is autumn and the falling fruit
and the long journey towards oblivion.

The apples falling like great drops of dew
to bruise themselves an exit from themselves.

And it is time to go, to bid farewell
to one's own self, and find an exit
from the fallen self.

2

Have you built your ship of death, O have you?
O build your ship of death, for you will need it.

The grim frost is at hand, when the apples will fall
thick, almost thundrous, on the hardened earth.

And death is on the air like a smell of ashes!
Ah! can't you smell it?

And in the bruised body, the frightened soul
finds itself shrinking, wincing from the cold
that blows upon it through the orifices.

3

And can a man his own quietus make
with a bare bodkin?[9]

With daggers, bodkins, bullets, man can make
a bruise or break of exit for his life;
but is that a quietus, O tell me, is it quietus?

---

8. In *Etruscan Places* (1932), the book that describes his visit to the Etruscan painted tombs in central Italy in the spring of 1927, Lawrence mentions that originally, before the tombs were pillaged, there would be found in the last chamber among "the sacred treasures of the dead, the little bronze ship that should bear [the soul of the dead] over to the other world."
9. From *Hamlet* 3.1.75–6.

Surely not so! for how could murder, even self-murder
ever a quietus make?

4

O let us talk of quiet that we know,
25   that we can know, the deep and lovely quiet
 of a strong heart at peace!

How can we this, our own quietus, make?

5

Build then the ship of death, for you must take
the longest journey, to oblivion.

30   And die the death, the long and painful death
that lies between the old self and the new.

Already our bodies are fallen, bruised, badly bruised,
already our souls are oozing through the exit
of the cruel bruise.

35   Already the dark and endless ocean of the end
is washing in through the breaches of our wounds,
already the flood is upon us.

Oh build your ship of death, your little ark
and furnish it with food, with little cakes, and wine
40   for the dark flight down oblivion.

6

Piecemeal the body dies, and the timid soul
has her footing washed away, as the dark flood rises.

We are dying, we are dying, we are all of us dying
and nothing will stay the death-flood rising within us
45   and soon it will rise on the world, on the outside world.

We are dying, we are dying, piecemeal our bodies are dying
and our strength leaves us,
and our soul cowers naked in the dark rain over the flood,
cowering in the last branches of the tree of our life.

7

50   We are dying, we are dying, so all we can do
is now to be willing to die, and to build the ship
of death to carry the soul on the longest journey.

A little ship, with oars and food
and little dishes, and all accoutrements
55   fitting and ready for the departing soul.

Now launch the small ship, now as the body dies
and life departs, launch out, the fragile soul
in the fragile ship of courage, the ark of faith
with its store of food and little cooking pans
60   and change of clothes,
upon the flood's black waste
upon the waters of the end
upon the sea of death, where still we sail
darkly, for we cannot steer, and have no port.

65   There is no port, there is nowhere to go
only the deepening blackness darkening still
blacker upon the soundless, ungurgling flood
darkness at one with darkness, up and down
and sideways utterly dark, so there is no direction any more.
70   and the little ship is there; yet she is gone.
She is not seen, for there is nothing to see her by.
She is gone! gone! and yet
somewhere she is there.
Nowhere!

8

75   And everything is gone, the body is gone
completely under, gone, entirely gone.
The upper darkness is heavy as the lower,
between them the little ship
is gone
80   she is gone.

It is the end, it is oblivion.

9

And yet out of eternity, a thread
separates itself on the blackness,
a horizontal thread
85   that fumes a little with pallor upon the dark.

Is it illusion? or does the pallor fume
A little higher?
Ah wait, wait, for there's the dawn,
the cruel dawn of coming back to life
90   out of oblivion.

Wait, wait, the little ship
drifting, beneath the deathly ashy grey
of a flood-dawn.

Wait, wait! even so, a flush of yellow
95   and strangely, O chilled wan soul, a flush of rose.

A flush of rose, and the whole thing starts again.

10

The flood subsides, and the body, like a worn sea-shell
emerges strange and lovely.
And the little ship wings home, faltering and lapsing
100   on the pink flood,
and the frail soul steps out, into her house again
filling the heart with peace.

Swings the heart renewed with peace
even of oblivion.

105   Oh build your ship of death, oh build it!
for you will need it.
For the voyage of oblivion awaits you.

1932

EZRA POUND

1885–1972

Portrait d'une Femme[1]

Your mind and you are our Sargasso Sea,[2]
London has swept about you this score years
And bright ships left you this or that in fee:
Ideas, old gossip, oddments of all things,
5   Strange spars of knowledge and dimmed wares of price.
Great minds have sought you—lacking someone else.
You have been second always. Tragical?
No. You preferred it to the usual thing:
One dull man, dulling and uxorious,
10   One average mind—with one thought less, each year.
Oh, you are patient, I have seen you sit
Hours, where something might have floated up.
And now you pay one. Yes, you richly pay.
You are a person of some interest, one comes to you
15   And takes strange gain away:
Trophies fished up; some curious suggestion;
Fact that leads nowhere; and a tale or two,
Pregnant with mandrakes,[3] or with something else
That might prove useful and yet never proves,
20   That never fits a corner or shows use,
Or finds its hour upon the loom of days:
The tarnished, gaudy, wonderful old work;
Idols and ambergris[4] and rare inlays,
These are your riches, your great store; and yet
25   For all this sea-hoard of deciduous things,
Strange woods half sodden, and new brighter stuff:

1. "Portrait of a Lady" (French).
2. A relatively calm part of the North Atlantic, named for an abundance of floating gulfweed.
3. Plants, the root of which, roughly shaped like a human body, traditionally was believed to promote female fertility.
4. Waxlike substance produced by sperm whales, used in making perfume.

In the slow float of differing light and deep,
No! there is nothing! In the whole and all,
Nothing that's quite your own.
30   Yet this is you.

                                                    1912

The Seafarer[5]

From the Anglo-Saxon

May I for my own self song's truth reckon,
Journey's jargon, how I in harsh days
Hardship endured oft.
Bitter breast-cares have I abided,
5   Known on my keel many a care's hold,
And dire sea-surge, and there I oft spent
Narrow nightwatch nigh the ship's head
While she tossed close to cliffs. Coldly afflicted,
My feet were by frost benumbed.
10   Chill its chains are; chafing sighs
Hew my heart round and hunger begot
Mere-weary° mood. Lest man know not   *sea-weary*
That he on dry land loveliest liveth,
List how I, care-wretched, on ice-cold sea,
15   Weathered the winter, wretched outcast
Deprived of my kinsmen;
Hung with hard ice-flakes, where hail-scur° flew,   *hail-storms*
There I heard naught save the harsh sea
And ice-cold wave, at whiles the swan cries,
20   Did for my games the gannet's° clamor,   *large seabird's*
Sea-fowls' loudness was for me laughter,
The mews'° singing all my mead-drink.   *seagulls'*
Storms, on the stone-cliffs beaten, fell on the stern
In icy feathers;[6] full oft the eagle screamed
With spray on his pinion.
25   Not any protector
May make merry man faring needy.
This he little believes, who aye in winsome life
Abides 'mid burghers some heavy business,
Wealthy and wine-flushed, how I weary oft
30   Must bide above brine.
Neareth nightshade, snoweth from north,
Frost froze the land, hail fell on earth then,
Corn of the coldest. Nathless° there knocketh now   *nevertheless*
The heart's thought that I on high streams
35   The salt-wavy tumult traverse alone.
Moaneth alway my mind's lust
That I fare forth, that I afar hence
Seek out a foreign fastness.°   *remote place*
For this there's no mood-lofty man over earth's midst,

---

5. Pound's poem translates, sometimes loosely, the first 99 lines of an Old English poem, 124 lines long, by an unknown author and of unknown date (see pp. 10–12).
6. An alcoholic drink made from fermented honey.

40 Not though he be given his good, but will have in his youth
        greed;
    Nor his deed to the daring, nor his king to the faithful
    But shall have his sorrow for sea-fare
    Whatever his lord will.
    He hath not heart for harping, nor in ring-having
45 Nor winsomeness to wife, nor world's delight
    Nor any whit else save the wave's slash,
    Yet longing comes upon him to fare forth on the water.
    Bosque° taketh blossom, cometh beauty of berries,   *grove*
    Fields to fairness, land fares brisker,
50 All this admonisheth man eager of mood,
    The heart turns to travel so that he then thinks
    On flood-ways to be far departing.
    Cuckoo calleth with gloomy crying,
    He singeth summerward, bodeth sorrow,
55 The bitter heart's blood. Burgher knows not—
    He the prosperous man—what some perform
    Where wandering them widest draweth.
    So that but now my heart burst from my breastlock,
    My mood 'mid the mere-flood,°   *sea-flood*
60 Over the whale's acre, would wander wide.
    On earth's shelter cometh oft to me,
    Eager and ready, the crying lone-flyer,
    Whets for the whale-path the heart irresistibly,
    O'er tracks of ocean; seeing that anyhow
65 My lord deems to me this dead life
    On loan and on land,[7] I believe not
    That any earth-weal eternal standeth
    Save there be somewhat calamitous
    That, ere a man's tide go, turn it to twain.
70 Disease or oldness or sword-hate
    Beats out the breath from doom-gripped body.
    And for this, every earl whatever, for those speaking
        after—
    Laud of the living, boasteth some last word,
    That he will work ere he pass onward,
75 Frame on the fair earth 'gainst foes his malice,
    Daring ado,° . . .   *brave deeds*
    So that all men shall honor him after
    And his laud beyond them remain 'mid the English,[8]
    Aye, for ever, a lasting life's-blast,
    Delight 'mid the doughty.°   *valiant*
80   Days little durable,
    And all arrogance of earthen riches,
    There come now no kings nor Cæsars°   *emperors*
    Nor gold-giving lords like those gone.
    Howe'er in mirth most magnified,

---

7. Behind Pound's phrase "on loan and on land" is the O. E. *læne on lond,* "briefly on earth." ("Because the Lord's joys are warmer to me than this dead life, brief on the earth.") But Pound has chosen to play down the Christian elements in the poem, perhaps believing that they are inconsistent with its essential spirit.

8. In the original, the sense is "with the angels," not "mid the English."

85   Whoe'er lived in life most lordliest,
     Drear all this excellence, delights undurable!
     Waneth the watch, but the world holdeth.
     Tomb hideth trouble. The blade is layed low.
     Earthly glory ageth and seareth.
90   No man at all going the earth's gait,
     But age fares against him, his face paleth,
     Gray-haired he groaneth, knows gone companions,
     Lordly men, are to earth o'ergiven,
     Nor may he then the flesh-cover, whose life ceaseth,
95   Nor eat the sweet nor feel the sorry,
     Nor stir hand nor think in mid heart,
     And though he strew the grave with gold,
     His born brothers, their buried bodies
     Be an unlikely treasure hoard.

1913, 1912

The Garden

En robe de parade.[9]
—SAMAIN

Like a skein of loose silk blown against a wall
She walks by the railing of a path in Kensington Gardens,[1]
And she is dying piecemeal
     of a sort of emotional anemia.

5   And round about there is a rabble
     Of the filthy, sturdy, unkillable infants of the very poor.
     They shall inherit the earth.

In her is the end of breeding.
Her boredom is exquisite and excessive.
10 She would like some one to speak to her,
     And is almost afraid that I
         will commit that indiscretion.

1913, 1916

Ts'ai Chi'h[2]

The petals fall in the fountain,
     the orange-colored rose-leaves,
Their ochre clings to the stone.

1913, 1916

---

9. "Dressed as for a state occasion." The phrase is from "The Infanta," a poem by the French poet Albert Samain (1858–1900).
1. Extensive public gardens in a residential district of London.
2. Ts'ai Chi'h, or more usually Ts'ao Chih, a Chinese poet (A.D. 192–232) who wrote "five-character poems."

In a Station of the Metro[3]

The apparition of these faces in the crowd;
Petals on a wet, black bough.

1913, 1916

The River-Merchant's Wife: a Letter[4]

While my hair was still cut straight across my forehead
I played about the front gate, pulling flowers.
You came by on bamboo stilts, playing horse,
You walked about my seat, playing with blue plums.
5 And we went on living in the village of Chokan:
Two small people, without dislike or suspicion.
At fourteen I married My Lord you.
I never laughed, being bashful.
Lowering my head, I looked at the wall.
10 Called to, a thousand times, I never looked back.

At fifteen I stopped scowling,
I desired my dust to be mingled with yours
Forever and forever and forever.
Why should I climb the look out?

15 At sixteen you departed,
You went into far Ku-to-yen, by the river of swirling eddies,
And you have been gone five months.
The monkeys make sorrowful noise overhead.

You dragged your feet when you went out.
20 By the gate now, the moss is grown, the different mosses,
Too deep to clear them away!
The leaves fall early this autumn, in wind.
The paired butterflies are already yellow with August
Over the grass in the West garden;
25 They hurt me. I grow older.
If you are coming down through the narrows of the river Kiang,
Please let me know beforehand,
And I will come out to meet you
              As far as Cho-fu-Sa.

By Rihaku
1915

---

3. Pound writes in *Gaudier-Brzeska: A Memoir* (1916) of having suddenly seen a succession of beautiful faces one day on the Paris Metro (subway), after which he tried all day to find words "as worthy, or as lovely as that sudden emotion. And that evening . . . I was still trying and I found, suddenly, the expression. I do not mean that I found words, but there came an equation . . . not in speech, but in little splotches of color. . . . The 'one-image poem' is a form of super-position, that is to say, it is one idea set on top of another. I found it useful in getting out of the impasse in which I had been left by my metro emotion. I wrote a thirty-line poem, and destroyed it. . . . Six months later I made the following *hokku*-like sentence."
4. Adaptation from the Chinese of Li Po (A.D. 701–762), named Rihaku in Japanese.

Hugh Selwyn Mauberley

LIFE AND CONTACTS[5]

E. P. Ode pour l'election de Son Sépulchre[6]

For three years, out of key with his time,
He strove to resuscitate the dead art
Of poetry; to maintain "the sublime"
In the old sense. Wrong from the start—

5   No, hardly, but seeing he had been born
In a half savage country, out of date;
Bent resolutely on wringing lilies from the acorn;
Capaneus;[7] trout for factitious° bait;   *false; artificial*

     Ἴδμεν γάρ τοι πάνθ' ὅσ' ἐνὶ Τροίῃ[8]
10   Caught in the unstopped ear;
Giving the rocks small lee-way
The chopped seas held him, therefore, that year.

His true Penelope[9] was Flaubert,[1]
He fished by obstinate isles;
15   Observed the elegance of Circe's[2] hair
Rather than the mottoes on sundials.

Unaffected by "the march of events,"
He passed from men's memory in *l'an trentiesme
De son eage;*[3] the case presents
20   No adjunct to the Muses' diadem.

II

The age demanded an image
Of its accelerated grimace,
Something for the modern stage,
Not, at any rate, an Attic[4] grace;

5   Not, not certainly, the obscure reveries
Of the inward gaze;

---

5. *Hugh Selwyn Mauberley* comprises two sets of poems: the thirteen poems reprinted here ("Life and Contacts," or "Contacts and Life," as Pound subtitled a 1957 edition) and five poems that follow, headed "Mauberley (1920)." The entire volume bore an epigraph from the fourth Eclogue of the third-century Carthaginian poet Nemesianus: *Vocat aestus in umbram* (Latin, "The heat calls us into the shade").
6. Cf. Pierre de Ronsard (1524–1585), *Odes* 4.5, "*De l'élection de son sépulchre*" [French, "Concerning the choice of his tomb"], in which the poet describes the kind of burial place and the kind of fame he would like to have.
7. In Aeschylus' tragedy *The Seven against Thebes* (467 B.C.), Capaneus swore he would sack that city despite Zeus and was struck dead with a thunderbolt.
8. "For we know all the things that [were suffered]

in Troy" (Greek); Homer, *Odyssey* 12.189. From the song of the Sirens, meant to lure Odysseus' ship onto the rocks. Odysseus plugged his companions' ears with wax, and he alone, bound to the mast, heard the song with "unstopped ear."
9. The paradigmatic faithful wife, she fended off suitors who besieged her husband during the ten years at the siege of Troy and another ten years returning home.
1. Gustave Flaubert (1821–1880), French realist novelist and meticulous craftsman.
2. Circe was a beautiful enchantress who seduced Odysseus; he stayed on her island for over a year.
3. "In the thirty-first year of his age" (Pound's age when his book *Lustra* was published); adapted from the beginning of *Le Grand Testament* by the fifteenth-century French poet François Villon: "In the thirtieth year of my age."
4. Athenian; i.e., simple, pure, classical.

Better mendacities
Than the classics in paraphrase!

The "age demanded" chiefly a mold in plaster,
10 Made with no loss of time,
A prose kinema,[5] not, not assuredly, alabaster
Or the "sculpture" of rhyme.

III

The tea-rose tea-gown, etc.
Supplants the mousseline of Cos,[6]
The pianola° "replaces"   *player piano*
Sappho's barbitos.[7]

5 Christ follows Dionysus,[8]
Phallic and ambrosial
Made way for macerations;°   *fastings*
Caliban casts out Ariel.[9]

All things are a flowing,
10 Sage Heracleitus[1] says;
But a tawdry cheapness
Shall outlast our days.

Even the Christian beauty
Defects—after Samothrace;[2]
15 We see τὸ καλόν[3]
Decreed in the market place.

Faun's flesh is not to us,
Nor the saint's vision.
We have the press for wafer;
20 Franchise for circumcision.

All men, in law, are equals.
Free of Pisistratus,[4]
We choose a knave or an eunuch
To rule over us.

25 O bright Apollo,
τίν' ἄνδρα, τίν' ἥρωα, τίνα θεόν,[5]

5. "Motion" (Greek), and an early spelling of "cinema" (motion pictures).
6. Greek island; "mousseline": fine cloth (muslin).
7. Lyre; Sappho (ca. 600 B.C.), a Greek lyric poet, sang her poems.
8. Greek god of fertility and wine, whose worship included ecstatic frenzies, sexual rites, and dramatic festivals.
9. In Shakespeare's *Tempest*, Caliban is earthbound and coarse, Ariel a beautiful spirit.
1. (fl. 500 B.C.); Greek philosopher whose teaching emphasized flux ("all things flow").

2. Greek island where a mystery cult was centered and where the famous statue *Winged Victory* was found.
3. Tò Kalón: "the beautiful" (Greek).
4. (d. 527 B.C.); three times the absolute ruler of Athens, he made the city the foremost power in Ionia and supported the arts.
5. Tín ándra, tín héroa, tín a theòn [keladésimon]: "what man, what hero, what god" (Greek); cf. the Greek poet Pindar's "Olympian Ode" 2.2: "What god, what hero, what man shall we loudly praise?"

What god, man, or hero
Shall I place a tin wreath upon!

IV

These fought in any case,
and some believing,

      pro domo,[6] in any case . . .

Some quick to arm,
5   some for adventure,
some from fear of weakness,
some from fear of censure,
some for love of slaughter, in imagination,
learning later . . .
10 some in fear, learning love of slaughter;

Died some, pro patria,

      non "dulce" non "et decor" . . .[7]
walked eye-deep in hell
believing in old men's lies, then unbelieving
15 came home, home to a lie,
home to many deceits,
home to old lies and new infamy;
usury age-old and age-thick
and liars in public places.

20 Daring as never before, wastage as never before.
Young blood and high blood,
fair cheeks, and fine bodies;
fortitude as never before

frankness as never before,
25 disillusions as never told in the old days,
hysterias, trench confessions,
laughter out of dead bellies.

V

There died a myriad,
And of the best, among them,
For an old bitch gone in the teeth,
For a botched civilization,

5   Charm, smiling at the good mouth,
Quick eyes gone under earth's lid,

For two gross of broken statues,
For a few thousand battered books.

---

6. "For home" (Latin).
7. The famous line from one of Horace's *Odes*
(3.2.13): *Dulce et decorum est pro patria mori*
(Latin, "Sweet and fitting it is to die for one's
country").

Yeux Glauques[8]

Gladstone[9] was still respected,
When John Ruskin produced
"King's Treasuries";[1] Swinburne
And Rossetti still abused.[2]

5 Fetid Buchanan lifted up his voice
When that faun's head of hers
Became a pastime for
Painters and adulterers.

The Burne-Jones cartons[3]
10 Have preserved her eyes;
Still, at the Tate, they teach
Cophetua to rhapsodize;

Thin like brook water,
With a vacant gaze.
15 The English Rubaiyat was stillborn[4]
In those days.

The thin, clear gaze, the same
Still darts out faunlike from the half-ruined face,
Questing and passive. . . .
20 "Ah, poor Jenny's case" . . .[5]

Bewildered that a world
Shows no surprise
At her last maquero's[6]
Adulteries.

"Siena Mi Fe'; Disfecemi Maremma"[7]

Among the pickled fetuses and bottled bones,
Engaged in perfecting the catalogue,

---

8. "Sea-green eyes" (French). Pound's poem focuses on the eyes of Elizabeth Siddal, wife of poet and painter Dante Gabriel Rossetti (1828–1882) and the model used for many of his paintings as well as for those of other Pre-Raphaelite painters, including Edward Burne-Jones (1833–1898), in whose painting *King Cophetua and the Beggar Maid* (1884; now in the Tate Gallery, London; see the third stanza, below) she appears as the beggar maid.
9. William Ewart Gladstone (1809–1898), active in British politics for over sixty years, was four times prime minister.
1. The English critic John Ruskin's sentimental *Sesame and Lilies* (1865) contained a chapter titled "Of Kings' Treasuries."
2. Rossetti and the poet Algernon Swinburne (1837–1909) were abused by Robert W. Buchanan (1841–1901) in "The Fleshly School of Poetry"

(1871).
3. I.e., cartoons: preliminary sketches.
4. Edward FitzGerald's translation of *The Rubáiyát of Omar Khayyám* (see pp. 866–78), first published in 1859, became popular only when the Pre-Raphaelites "discovered" it.
5. Buchanan had particularly attacked Rossetti's "Jenny," a sympathetic portrayal of a prostitute.
6. Perhaps a pun, suggesting both one who lacquers pictures (from the Spanish verb, *maquear*) and a pimp (from the French noun, *maquereau*).
7. "Siena made me; the Maremma undid me" (*Purgatorio* 5.134). Words spoken to Dante by the spirit of Pia de' Tolomei, encountered in Purgatory among those who died by violence and without absolution. She was murdered by her husband. The line carries with it the idea of exile from one's native place; the subject of Pound's poem had been born in Alsace.

I found the last scion of the
Senatorial families of Strasbourg, Monsieur Verog.[8]

5   For two hours he talked of Gallifet;[9]
Of Dowson; of the Rhymers' Club;[1]
Told me how Johnson (Lionel) died[2]
By falling from a high stool in a pub . . .

But showed no trace of alcohol
10   At the autopsy, privately performed—
Tissue preserved—the pure mind
Arose toward Newman[3] as the whiskey warmed.

Dowson found harlots cheaper than hotels;
Headlam for uplift; Image[4] impartially imbued
15   With raptures for Bacchus, Terpsichore[5] and the Church.
So spoke the author of "The Dorian Mood,"[6]

M. Verog, out of step with the decade,
Detached from his contemporaries,
Neglected by the young,
20   Because of these reveries.

Brennbaum[7]

The skylike limpid eyes,
The circular infant's face,
The stiffness from spats to collar
Never relaxing into grace;

5   The heavy memories of Horeb, Sinai and the forty years[8]
Showed only when the daylight fell
Level across the face
Of Brennbaum "The Impeccable."

8. Pound's model for Verog was the poet and librarian of the Royal College of Surgeons Victor Gustav Plarr (1863–1929), whose friends included the poets Ernest Dowson (1867–1900) and Lionel Johnson (1867–1902). He, like them, was a member of the Rhymers' Club (see line 6, note 1); he published a memoir of Dowson. Pound edited Johnson's *Poetical Works* (1915).
9. Marquis de Galliffet (1830–1909), a French general who led a cavalry charge at the battle of Sedan (1870) in the Franco-Prussian War.
1. London literary club founded in 1891 by the Irish poet William Butler Yeats (1865–1939) and his friends.
2. Johnson died from a fall in the street.
3. John Henry Newman (1801–1890), the most famous Victorian convert to Roman Catholicism (and eventually a cardinal). Johnson was also an ardent convert.
4. Selwyn Image (1849–1930), artist, poet, and clergyman; the Reverend Stewart Headlam (1847–1924), liberal clergyman who was for many years a vicar in the East End of London, writer on social and religious questions. Both were members of the Rhymers' Club.
5. Greek muse of the dance. "Bacchus": Roman god of wine.
6. Parr, "In the Dorian Mood" (poem, published in 1896). See note 2, above.
7. Often identified as Max Beerbohm (1872–1956), English critic and caricaturist, who was known as "the Incomparable Max." Pound mistakenly thought he was Jewish.
8. After the Exodus from Egypt, the Israelites, led by Moses, spent forty years in the wilderness. At Horeb, the Lord spoke to Moses from a burning bush (Exodus 3.1–4); on Mt. Sinai, Moses received the Ten Commandments (Exodus 19–20).

Mr. Nixon[9]

In the cream gilded cabin of his steam yacht
Mr. Nixon advised me kindly, to advance with fewer
Dangers of delay. "Consider
                Carefully the reviewer.

5   "I was as poor as you are;
"When I began I got, of course,
"Advance on royalties, fifty at first," said Mr. Nixon,
"Follow me, and take a column,
"Even if you have to work free.

10 "Butter reviewers. From fifty to three hundred
"I rose in eighteen months;
"The hardest nut I had to crack
"Was Dr. Dundas.

"I never mentioned a man but with the view
15 "Of selling my own works.
"The tip's a good one, as for literature
"It gives no man a sinecure.

"And no one knows, at sight, a masterpiece.
"And give up verse, my boy,
20 "There's nothing in it."

   . . . .

Likewise a friend of Bloughram's[1] once advised me:
Don't kick against the pricks,[2]
Accept opinion. The "Nineties" tried your game
And died, there's nothing in it.

X

Beneath the sagging roof
The stylist has taken shelter,
Unpaid, uncelebrated,
At last from the world's welter

5 Nature receives him;
With a placid and uneducated mistress
He exercises his talents
And the soil meets his distress.

The haven from sophistications and contentions
10 Leaks through its thatch;
He offers succulent cooking;
The door has a creaking latch.

9. Pound wrote that Nixon "is a fictitious name for a real person"—perhaps the English novelist Arnold Bennett (1867–1931), who did own a yacht.
1. A reference to the bishop in Browning's "Bishop Blougram's Apology" (1855), a man more practical than devotional in his beliefs.
2. Cf. Jesus' words to Saul: "It is hard for thee to kick against the pricks" (Acts 9.5).

XI

"Conservatrix of Milésien"[3]
Habits of mind and feeling,
Possibly. But in Ealing[4]
With the most bank-clerkly of Englishmen?

5   No, "Milésian" is an exaggeration.
No instinct has survived in her
Older than those her grandmother
Told her would fit her station.

XII

"Daphne with her thighs in bark
Stretches toward me her leafy hands,"[5] —
Subjectively. In the stuffed-satin drawing room
I await The Lady Valentine's commands,

5   Knowing my coat has never been
Of precisely the fashion
To stimulate, in her,
A durable passion;

   Doubtful, somewhat, of the value
10 Of well-gowned approbation
Of literary effort,
But never of The Lady Valentine's vocation:

   Poetry, her border of ideas,
The edge, uncertain, but a means of blending
15 With other strata
Where the lower and higher have ending;

   A hook to catch the Lady Jane's attention,
A modulation toward the theatre,
Also, in the case of revolution,
20 A possible friend and comforter.

   . . . .

   Conduct, on the other hand, the soul
"Which the highest cultures have nourished"[6]
To Fleet St. where
Dr. Johnson[7] flourished;

25 Beside this thoroughfare
The sale of half-hose has

---

3. I.e., preserver of Milesian tradition; the Greek city Miletus, a center of literature and philosophy, was also associated with the erotic stories of Aristides' *Milesian Tales* (second century B.C.).
4. Staid middle-class London suburb.
5. The first two lines translate two lines from "Le Château de Souvenir" by the French poet Théophile Gautier (1811–1872). Daphne, pursued by Apollo, was turned into a laurel to enable her to escape.
6. A translation of two lines from "Complainte de Pianos" by the French poet Jules Laforgue (1860–1887).
7. Samuel Johnson (1709–1784), poet, journalist, critic, essayist, lexicographer, and the dominant English man of letters of the mid-eighteenth century; "Fleet Street": the center of London newspaper publishing.

Long since superseded the cultivation
Of Pierian[8] roses.

Envoi (1919)

Go, dumb-born book,[9]
Tell her that sang me once that song of Lawes:
Hadst thou but song
As thou hast subjects known,
5 Then were there cause in thee that should condone
Even my faults that heavy upon me lie,
And build her glories their longevity

Tell her that sheds
Such treasure in the air,
10 Recking naught else but that her graces give
Life to the moment,
I would bid them live
As roses might, in magic amber laid,
Red overwrought with orange and all made
15 One substance and one color
Braving time.

Tell her that goes
With song upon her lips
But sings not out the song, nor knows
20 The maker of it, some other mouth,
May be as fair as hers,
Might, in new ages, gain her worshipers,
When our two dusts with Waller's shall be laid,
Siftings on siftings in oblivion,
25 Till change hath broken down
All things save Beauty alone.

1920

Medallion

Luini[1] in porcelain!
The grand piano
Utters a profane
Protest with her clear soprano.

5 The sleek head emerges
From the gold-yellow frock
As Anadyomene[2] in the opening
Pages of Reinach.

---

8. Pieria is a region of northern Greece associated with the Muses.
9. Here and throughout this poem Pound echoes "Go, Lovely Rose" by Edmund Waller (1607–1687; see pp. 352–53), which was set to music by Henry Lawes (1596–1662).
1. Bernardino Luini (ca. 1480–1532), Italian painter.
2. "Rising [from the sea]" (Greek); Aphroditē anaduomenē was a famous painting by Apelles (fourth century B.C.), and similar depictions of the goddess in sculpture are illustrated in Salomon Reinach's Apollo: An Illustrated History of Art throughout the Ages (1904).

Honey-red, closing the face-oval,
10   A basket-work of braids which seem as if they were
Spun in King Minos'[3] hall
From metal, or intractable amber;

The face-oval beneath the glaze,
Bright in its suave bounding-line, as,
15   Beneath half-watt rays,
The eyes turn topaz.

1920

FROM THE CANTOS

I[4]

And then went down to the ship,
Set keel to breakers, forth on the godly sea, and
We set up mast and sail on that swart ship,
Bore sheep aboard her, and our bodies also
5   Heavy with weeping, and winds from sternward
Bore us out onward with bellying canvas,
Circe's this craft, the trim-coifed goddess.[5]
Then sat we amidships, wind jamming the tiller,
Thus with stretched sail, we went over sea till day's end.
10   Sun to his slumber, shadows o'er all the ocean,
Came we then to the bounds of deepest water,
To the Kimmerian lands,[6] and peopled cities
Covered with close-webbed mist, unpierced ever
With glitter of sun-rays
15   Nor with stars stretched, nor looking back from heaven
Swartest night stretched over wretched men there.
The ocean flowing backward, came we then to the place
Aforesaid by Circe.
Here did they rites, Perimedes and Eurylochus,[7]
20   And drawing sword from my hip
I dug the ell-square pitkin;°   *small trench*
Poured we libations unto each the dead,
First mead[8] and then sweet wine, water mixed with white flour.
Then prayed I many a prayer to the sickly death's-heads;
25   As set in Ithaca, sterile bulls of the best
For sacrifice, heaping the pyre with goods,
A sheep to Tiresias only, black and a bell-sheep.[9]
Dark blood flowed in the fosse,°   *trench, ditch*

3. In Greek mythology, king of Crete.
4. The opening of Pound's *Cantos*, the complex poem of epic proportions on which he worked for over fifty years, is taken up, through line 67, with Pound's translation of the beginning of book 11 of Homer's *Odyssey*, not directly from the Greek but from the sixteenth-century Latin translation of Andreas Divus (see line 68). Book 11 describes Odysseus' trip to the underworld to consult the spirit of Tiresias, the blind Theban prophet, who will give him instructions for the final stages of his return to his home island, Ithaca.
5. Circe was the enchantress with whom Odysseus lived for over a year and who told him to seek Tiresias' advice.
6. The Cimmerians were a mythical people living in darkness and mist on the farthest borders of the known world.
7. Two of Odysseus' men.
8. Alcoholic drink made from fermented honey.
9. The sheep that leads the herd.

Souls out of Erebus,[1] cadaverous dead, of brides
30 Of youths and of the old who had borne much;
Souls stained with recent tears, girls tender,
Men many, mauled with bronze lance heads,
Battle spoil, bearing yet dreory[2] arms,
These many crowded about me; with shouting,
35 Pallor upon me, cried to my men for more beasts;
Slaughtered the herds, sheep slain of bronze;
Poured ointment, cried to the gods,
To Pluto[3] the strong, and praised Proserpine;
Unsheathed the narrow sword,
40 I sat to keep off the impetuous impotent dead,
Till I should hear Tiresias.
But first Elpenor[4] came, our friend Elpenor,
Unburied, cast on the wide earth,
Limbs that we left in the house of Circe,
45 Unwept, unwrapped in sepulchre, since toils urged other.
Pitiful spirit. And I cried in hurried speech:
"Elpenor, how art thou come to this dark coast?
"Cam'st thou afoot, outstripping seamen?"
      And he in heavy speech:
50 "Ill fate and abundant wine. I slept in Circe's ingle.°   *nook, corner*
"Going down the long ladder unguarded,
"I fell against the buttress,
"Shattered the nape-nerve, the soul sought Avernus.[5]
"But thou, O King, I bid remember me, unwept, unburied,
55 "Heap up mine arms, be tomb by sea-bord, and inscribed:
"*A man of no fortune, and with a name to come.*
"And set my oar up, that I swung mid fellows."

And Anticlea[6] came, whom I beat off, and then Tiresias Theban,
Holding his golden wand, knew me, and spoke first:
60 "A second time?[7] why? man of ill star,
"Facing the sunless dead and this joyless region?
"Stand from the fosse,[8] leave me my bloody bever°   *drink*
"For soothsay."
      And I stepped back,
65 And he strong with the blood, said then: "Odysseus
"Shalt return through spiteful Neptune, over dark seas,
"Lose all companions." And then Anticlea came.
Lie quiet Divus. I mean, that is Andreas Divus,[9]
In officina Wecheli, 1538, out of Homer.
70 And he sailed, by Sirens and thence outward and away

---

1. A dark place in the underworld, on the way to Hades.
2. "Bloody" (from Old English *dreorig*).
3. Latin name for the lord of the underworld (Hades); Proserpine, known by the Greeks as Persephone, is his queen.
4. The youngest of Odysseus' men, he had drunkenly fallen asleep on a loft on the eve of their departure from her island and fell to his death when he tried to climb down a ladder.
5. A lake near Cumae believed by the ancients to be the entrance to the underworld.
6. Odysseus' mother; according to the *Odyssey*,

Odysseus wept at seeing her, but obeyed Circe's instruction to speak to no one until he had heard Tiresias.
7. "A second time" correctly translates Divus' adverb *iterum*, but Homer's adverb does not have here the sense of "again."
8. The trench that Odysseus and his men have dug and in which the blood from the sacrifice has collected.
9. The sixteenth-century Italian whose translation of the *Odyssey* had been published "in officina Wecheli," at the printing shop of Chrétien Wechel, Paris, in 1538.

And unto Circe.[1]
    Venerandam,[2]
In the Cretan's phrase, with the golden crown, Aphrodite,
Cypri munimenta sortita est, mirthful, oricalchi,[3] with golden
75 Girdles and breast bands, thou with dark eyelids
Bearing the golden bough of Argicida.[4] So that:[5]

1921   1930

ELINOR WYLIE

1885–1928

Full Moon

My bands of silk and miniver°   *white fur*
Momently grew heavier;
The black gauze was beggarly thin;
The ermine muffled mouth and chin;
5 I could not suck the moonlight in.

Harlequin in lozenges[1]
Of love and hate, I walked in these
Striped and ragged rigmaroles;[2]
Along the pavement my footsoles
10 Trod warily on living coals.

Shouldering the thoughts I loathed,
In their corrupt disguises clothed,
Mortality I could not tear
From my ribs, to leave them bare
15 Ivory in silver air.

There I walked, and there I raged;
The spiritual savage caged
Within my skeleton, raged afresh

---

1. After this visit to the underworld, Odysseus returned to Circe and then, forewarned by her, successfully sailed past the Sirens.
2. "Worthy of worship," applied to Aphrodite. This, like the Latin words and phrases in the next lines, derives from a Latin translation of two Hymns to Aphrodite (among the so-called Homeric Hymns, dating from the eighth to the sixth century B.C.). This translation by Georgius Dartona Cretensis was contained in the volume in which Pound had found Divus' translation of the *Odyssey*. One hymn begins with the words that figure, in Latin or in English, in the closing lines of the Canto: "Reverend golden-crowned beautiful Aphrodite / I shall sing, who has received as her lot the citadels of all sea-girt Cyprus. . . ."
3. Brass. The Hours have adorned Aphrodite with earrings, flower-shaped, of brass and precious gold.
4. An epithet for Hermes, "slayer of Argos" (the many-eyed herdsman set to watch Io); from the other hymn, which recounts the union of Aphrodite and Anchises, a union that led to the birth of the Trojan leader Aeneas. Aphrodite, deceiving Anchises at first, says that she is a mortal maiden, that the "slayer of Argos, with wand of gold" has brought her to be his wife.
5. The Canto ends on the colon, going immediately into Canto II, which begins with the words "Hang it all, Robert Browning, / There can be but one 'Sordello.' "
1. Diamond shapes; "harlequin": a buffoon, a character in the Italian *commedia dell'arte*, or one dressed in fabric of certain variegated patterns.
2. Literally, confused or meaningless statements.

To feel, behind a carnal mesh,
20   The clean bones crying in the flesh.

1923

Doomsday

The end of everything approaches;
I hear it coming
Loud as the wheels of painted coaches
On turnpikes drumming;
5   Loud as the pomp of plumy hearses,
Or pennoned charges;[3]
Loud as when every oar reverses
Venetian barges;
Loud as the caves of covered bridges
10   Fulfilled with rumble
Of hooves; and loud as cloudy ridges
When glaciers tumble;
Like creeping thunder this continues
Diffused and distant,
15   Loud in our ears and in our sinews,
Insane, insistent;
Loud as a lion scorning carrion
Further and further;
Loud as the ultimate loud clarion
20   Or the first murther.°   murder

1932

H. D. (HILDA DOOLITTLE)

1886–1961

Sea Rose

Rose, harsh rose,
marred and with stint of petals,
meager flower, thin,
sparse of leaf,

5   more precious
than a wet rose
single on a stem—
you are caught in the drift.

Stunted, with small leaf,
10   you are flung on the sand,
you are lifted
in the crisp sand
that drives in the wind.

3. Military charges with streaming banners.

Can the spice-rose
15 drip such acrid fragrance
hardened in a leaf?

1916

Sea Violet

The white violet
is scented on its stalk,
the sea-violet
fragile as agate,
5 lies fronting all the wind
among the torn shells
on the sand-bank.

The greater blue violets
flutter on the hill,
10 but who would change for these
who would change for these
one root of the white sort?

Violet
your grasp is frail
15 on the edge of the sand-hill,
but you catch the light—
frost, a star edges with its fire.

1916

Helen[1]

All Greece hates
the still eyes in the white face,
the luster as of olives
where she stands,
5 And the white hands.

All Greece reviles
the wan face when she smiles,
hating it deeper still
when it grows wan and white,
10 remembering past enchantments
and past ills.

Greece sees unmoved,
God's daughter,[2] born of love,
the beauty of cool feet
15 and slenderest knees,
could love indeed the maid,

---

1. The beautiful wife of the Greek leader
Menelaus; given to the Trojan prince Paris by
Aphrodite, she was blamed for the Trojan War,
waged to regain her.
2. Helen was said to be the daughter of Zeus, ruler
of the gods, and Leda, a mortal woman.

only if she were laid,
white ash amid funereal cypresses.

1924

Wine Bowl

I will rise
from my troth
with the dead,
I will sweeten my cup
5 and my bread
with a gift;
I will chisel a bowl for the wine,
for the white wine
and red;
10 I will summon a Satyr[3] to dance,
a Centaur,
a Nymph
and a Faun;
I will picture
15 a warrior King,
a Giant,
a Naiad,
a Monster;
I will cut round the rim of the crater,[4]
20 some simple
familiar thing,
vine leaves
or the sea-swallow's wing;
I will work at each separate part
25 till my mind is worn out
and my heart:
in my skull,
where the vision had birth,
will come wine,
30 would pour song
of the hot earth,
of the flower and the sweet
of the hill,
thyme,
35 meadow-plant,
grass-blade and sorrel;
in my skull,
from which vision took flight,
will come wine
40 will pour song
of the cool night,

3. Here, and in the lines following, figures from classical mythology are evoked. "Nymphs" were minor nature goddesses; those who lived in springs, fountains, rivers, and lakes were called "naiads." In Greek mythology, "satyrs" were woodland spirits in the form of men with the legs of goats and with pointed ears or horns. The Romans identified satyrs with their own woodland spirits, the "fauns." "Centaurs" had the faces and chests of men and the bodies of horses. Satyrs are usually associated with lechery; centaurs, with savagery.
4. I.e., a *kratēr*, the usual Greek term for a drinking bowl.

of the silver and blade of the moon,
of the star,
of the sun's kiss at midnoon;
45   I will challenge the reed-pipe[5]
and stringed lyre,
to sing sweeter,
pipe wilder,
praise louder
50   the fragrance and sweet
of the wine jar,
till each lover
must summon another,
to proffer a rose
55   where all flowers are,
in the depths of the exquisite crater;
flower will fall upon flower
till the red shower
inflame all
60   with intimate fervor;
till:
men who travel afar
will look up,
sensing grape
65   and hill-slope
in the cup;
men who sleep by the wood
will arise,
hearing ripple and fall
70   of the tide,
being drawn by the spell of the sea;
the bowl will ensnare and enchant
men who crouch by the hearth
till they want
75   but the riot of stars in the night;
those who dwell far inland
will seek ships;
the deep-sea fisher,
plying his nets,
80   will forsake them
for wheat-sheaves and loam;
men who wander
will yearn for their home,
men at home
85   will depart.

I will rise
from my troth with the dead,
I will sweeten my cup
and my bread
90   *with a gift;*

5. The pipe was the instrument of Pan, god of forests, pastures, flocks, and herds; the lyre was the instrument of Apollo, Olympian god of the sun and patron of music and poetry.

I will chisel a bowl for the wine,
for the white wine
and red.

1931

From The Walls Do Not Fall[6]

[1]

An incident here and there,
and rails gone (for guns)
from your (and my) old town square:

mist and mist-grey, no colour,
5   still the Luxor[7] bee, chick and hare
pursue unalterable purpose

in green, rose-red, lapis;
they continue to prophesy
from the stone papyrus:

10   there, as here, ruin opens
the tomb, the temple; enter,
there as here, there are no doors:

the shrine lies open to the sky,
the rain falls, here, there
15   sand drifts; eternity endures:

ruin everywhere, yet as the fallen roof
leaves the sealed room
open to the air,

so, through our desolation,
20   thoughts stir, inspiration stalks us
through gloom:

unaware, Spirit announces the Presence;
shivering overtakes us,
as of old, Samuel:[8]

25   trembling at a known street-corner,
we know not nor are known;
the Pythian[9] pronounces—we pass on

6. The first of three book-length poems, including
Tribute to the Angels and *The Flowering of the Rod,*
that would be known as H. D.'s war trilogy. "The
parallel between ancient Egypt and 'ancient' Lon-
don is obvious. In I *(The Walls Do Not Fall)* the
'fallen roof leaves the sealed room open to the air'
is of course true of our own house of life—outer
violence touching the deepest hidden subcon-
scious terrors, etc. and we see so much of our past
'on show,' as it were 'another sliced wall where
poor utensils show like rare objects in a museum' "
(H. D., in a letter to Norman Holmes Pearson).
7. An Egyptian town on the Nile, near the ruins
of ancient Thebes. Representations of the bee,
chick, and hare appear on the Temple of Karnak
in Thebes.
8. Cf. 1 Samuel 28.15, where the prophet Samuel
is disturbed at being brought up from the dead,
and 1 Samuel 28.3: "When Saul saw the army of
the Philistines, he was afraid, and his heart trem-
bled greatly."
9. Pertaining to the oracle at Delphi.

to another cellar, to another sliced wall
where poor utensils show
30   like rare objects in a museum;

Pompeii[1] has nothing to teach us,
we know crack of volcanic fissure,
slow flow of terrible lava,

pressure on heart, lungs, the brain
35   about to burst its brittle case
(what the skull can endure!):

over us, Apocryphal[2] fire,
under us, the earth sway, dip of a floor,
slope of a pavement

40   where men roll, drunk
with a new bewilderment,
sorcery, bedevilment:

the bone-frame was made for
no such shock knit within terror,
45   yet the skeleton stood up to it:

the flesh? it was melted away,
the heart burnt out, dead ember,
tendons, muscles shattered, outer husk dismembered,

yet the frame held:
50   we passed the flame: we wonder
what saved us? what for?

1944

SIEGFRIED SASSOON

1886–1967

"They"

The Bishop tells us: "When the boys come back
They will not be the same; for they'll have fought
In a just cause: they lead the last attack
On Anti-Christ; their comrades' blood has bought
5   New right to breed an honourable race,
They have challenged Death and dared him face to face."

---

1. Ancient city on the bay of Naples, buried by an eruption of Mount Vesuvius in A.D. 79.
2. Or perhaps "apocalyptic," meaning the fiery judgments of the Apocalypse prophesied in the New Testament. Cf. 1 Corinthians 3.15: "If any man's work shall be burned, he shall suffer loss: but he himself shall be saved; yet so as by fire."

"We're none of us the same!" the boys reply.
"For George lost both his legs; and Bill's stone blind;
Poor Jim's shot through the lungs and like to die;
10   And Bert's gone syphilitic: you'll not find
A chap who's served that hasn't found *some* change."
And the Bishop said: "The ways of God are strange!"

1916   1917

The General

"Good-morning, good-morning!" the General said
When we met him last week on our way to the line.
Now the soldiers he smiled at are most of 'em dead,
And we're cursing his staff for incompetent swine.
5   "He's a cheery old card," grunted Harry to Jack
As they slogged up to Arras[1] with rifle and pack.

·   ·   ·

But he did for them both by his plan of attack.

1917   1918

Glory of Women

You love us when we're heroes, home on leave,
Or wounded in a mentionable place.
You worship decorations; you believe
That chivalry redeems the war's disgrace.
5   You make us shells. You listen with delight,
By tales of dirt and danger fondly thrilled.
You crown our distant ardours while we fight,
And mourn our laurelled memories when we're killed.
You can't believe that British troops "retire"
10   When hell's last horror breaks them, and they run,
Trampling the terrible corpses—blind with blood.
    O German mother dreaming by the fire,
While you are knitting socks to send your son
His face is trodden deeper in the mud.

1917   1918

Everyone Sang

Everyone suddenly burst out singing;
And I was filled with such delight
As prisoned birds must find in freedom,
Winging wildly across the white
5   Orchards and dark-green fields; on—on—and out of sight.

Everyone's voice was suddenly lifted;
And beauty came like the setting sun:

1. A city in northern France, in the front line throughout much of World War I. The British assault on the Western Front that began on April 9, 1917, was known as the Battle of Arras. The British suffered casualties of eighty-four thousand troops, inflicted casualties of seventy-five thousand on the Germans, and took thirteen thousand prisoners.

My heart was shaken with tears; and horror
Drifted away . . . O, but Everyone
10 Was a bird; and the song was wordless; the singing will never be done.
1919   1919

On Passing the New Menin Gate

Who will remember, passing through this Gate,[2]
The unheroic Dead who fed the guns?
Who shall absolve the foulness of their fate,—
Those doomed, conscripted, unvictorious ones?
5   Crudely renewed, the Salient holds its own.
Paid are its dim defenders by this pomp;
Paid, with a pile of peace-complacent stone,
The armies who endured that sullen swamp.

Here was the world's worst wound. And here with pride
10 "Their name liveth for ever," the Gateway claims.
Was ever an immolation so belied
As these intolerably nameless names?
Well might the Dead who struggled in the slime
Rise and deride this sepulchre of crime.
1927–28   1928

Christ and the Soldier

I

The straggled soldier halted—stared at Him—
Then clumsily dumped down upon his knees,
Gasping, "O blessed crucifix, I'm beat!"
And Christ, still sentried by the seraphim,[3]
5   Near the front-line, between two splintered trees,
Spoke him: "My son, behold these hands and feet."

The soldier eyed Him upward, limb by limb,
Paused at the Face; then muttered, "Wounds like these
Would shift a bloke to Blighty[4] just a treat!"
10 Christ, gazing downward, grieving and ungrim,
Whispered, "I made for you the mysteries,
Beyond all battles moves the Paraclete."[5]

II

The soldier chucked his rifle in the dust,
And slipped his pack, and wiped his neck, and said—
15 "O Christ Almighty, stop this bleeding fight!"
Above that hill the sky was stained like rust
With smoke. In sullen daybreak flaring red
The guns were thundering bombardment's blight.

---

2. 54,889 names of men killed in World War I are engraved on the gate.
3. Angels of the highest of nine orders. In the Bible (Isaiah 6), six-winged celestial beings.
4. Slang for Britain.
5. Advocate or counselor; sometimes, as here, applied to the Holy Ghost.

The soldier cried, "I was born full of lust,
20 With hunger, thirst, and wishfulness to wed.
Who cares today if I done wrong or right?"
Christ asked all pitying, "Can you put no trust
In my known word that shrives each faithful head?
Am I not resurrection, life and light?"

III

25 Machine-guns rattled from below the hill;
High bullets flicked and whistled through the leaves;
And smoke came drifting from exploding shells.
Christ said, "Believe; and I can cleanse your ill.
I have not died in vain between two thieves;
30 Nor made a fruitless gift of miracles."

The soldier answered, "Heal me if you will,
Maybe there's comfort when a soul believes
In mercy, and we need it in these hells.
But be you for both sides? I'm paid to kill
35 And if I shoot a man his mother grieves.
Does that come into what your teaching tells?"

A bird lit on the Christ and twittered gay;
Then a breeze passed and shook the ripening corn.
A Red Cross waggon bumped along the track.
40 Forsaken Jesus dreamed in the desolate day—
Uplifted Jesus, Prince of Peace forsworn—
An observation post for the attack.

"Lord Jesus, ain't you got no more to say?"
Bowed hung that head below the crown of thorns.
45 The soldier shifted, and picked up his pack,
And slung his gun, and stumbled on his way.
"O God," he groaned, "why ever was I born?" . . .
The battle boomed, and no reply came back.

1916   1973

ROBINSON JEFFERS

1887–1962

Shine, Perishing Republic

While this America settles in the mold of its vulgarity, heavily thick-
ening to empire,
And protest, only a bubble in the molten mass, pops and sighs out, and
the mass hardens,
I sadly smiling remember that the flower fades to make fruit, the fruit
rots to make earth.
out of the mother; and through the spring exultances, ripeness and
decadence; and home to the mother.

5   You making haste haste on decay: not blameworthy; life is good, bc it
        stubbornly long or suddenly
    A mortal splendor: meteors are not needed less than mountains: shine,
        perishing republic.

    But for my children, I would have them keep their distance from the
        thickening center; corruption
    Never has been compulsory, when the cities lie at the monster's feet there
        are left the mountains.

    And boys, be in nothing so moderate as in love of man, a clever servant,
        insufferable master.
10   There is the trap that catches noblest spirits, that caught—they say—
        God, when he walked on earth.[1]

                                               1924

Boats in a Fog

    Sports and gallantries, the stage, the arts, the antics of dancers,
    The exuberant voices of music,
    Have charm for children but lack nobility; it is bitter earnestness
    That makes beauty; the mind
5   Knows, grown adult.
               A sudden fog-drift muffled the ocean,
    A throbbing of engines moved in it,
    At length, a stone's throw out, between the rocks and the vapor,
    One by one moved shadows
10   Out of the mystery, shadows, fishing-boats, trailing each other,
    Following the cliff for guidance,
    Holding a difficult path between the peril of the sea-fog
    And the foam on the shore granite.
    One by one, trailing their leader, six crept by me,
15   Out of the vapor and into it,
    The throb of their engines subdued by the fog, patient and cautious,
    Coasting all round the peninsula
    Back to the buoys in Monterey harbor. A flight of pelicans
    Is nothing lovelier to look at;
20   The flight of the planets is nothing nobler; all the arts lose virtue
    Against the essential reality
    Of creatures going about their business among the equally
    Earnest elements of nature.

                                             1924

To the Stone-Cutters

    Stone-cutters fighting time with marble, you foredefeated
    Challengers of oblivion
    Eat cynical earnings, knowing rock splits, records fall down,
    The square-limbed Roman letters
5   Scale° in the thaws, wear in the rain. The poet as well   *flake off*
    Builds his monument mockingly;

---

1. I.e., Christ.

For man will be blotted out, the blithe earth die, the brave sun
Die blind, his heart blackening:
Yet stones have stood for a thousand years, and pained thoughts found
10   The honey peace in old poems.

1925

Hurt Hawks

1

The broken pillar of the wing jags from the clotted shoulder,
The wing trails like a banner in defeat,
No more to use the sky forever but live with famine
And pain a few days: cat nor coyote
5   Will shorten the week of waiting for death, there is game without talons.
He stands under the oak-bush and waits
The lame feet of salvation; at night he remembers freedom
And flies in a dream, the dawns ruin it.
He is strong and pain is worse to the strong, incapacity is worse.
10   The curs of the day come and torment him
At distance, no one but death the redeemer will humble that head,
The intrepid readiness, the terrible eyes.
The wild God of the world is sometimes merciful to those
That ask mercy, not often to the arrogant.
15   You do not know him, you communal people, or you have forgotten him;
Intemperate and savage, the hawk remembers him;
Beautiful and wild, the hawks, and men that are dying, remember him.

2

I'd sooner, except the penalties, kill a man than a hawk;
    but the great redtail°   *red-tailed hawk*
Had nothing left but unable misery
20   From the bone too shattered for mending, the wing that trailed under his
    talons when he moved.
We had fed him six weeks, I gave him freedom,
He wandered over the foreland hill and returned in the evening,
    asking for death,
Not like a beggar, still eyed with the old
Implacable arrogance. I gave him the lead gift in the twilight. What fell
    was relaxed,
25   Owl-downy, soft feminine feathers; but what
Soared: the fierce rush: the night-herons by the flooded river cried fear at
    its rising
Before it was quite unsheathed from reality.

1928

The Purse-Seine

Our sardine fishermen work at night in the dark of the moon;
    daylight or moonlight
They could not tell where to spread the net, unable to see the
    phosphorescence of the shoals° of fish.   *schools*

They work northward from Monterey, coasting Santa Cruz; off
   New Year's Point or off Pigeon Point[2]
The look-out man will see some lakes of milk-color light on the sea's
   night-purple; he points, and the helmsman
5 Turns the dark prow, the motorboat circles the gleaming shoal and drifts
   out her seine-net. They close the circle
And purse the bottom of the net, then with great labor haul it in.

                                       I cannot tell you
How beautiful the scene is, and a little terrible, then, when the crowded
   fish
Know they are caught, and wildly beat from one wall to the other of their
   closing destiny the phosphorescent
10 Water to a pool of flame, each beautiful slender body sheeted with flame,
   like a live rocket
A comet's tail wake of clear yellow flame; while outside the narrowing
Floats and cordage of the net great sea-lions come up to watch, sighing
   in the dark; the vast walls of night
Stand erect to the stars.

                       Lately I was looking from a night mountain-top
15 On a wide city, the colored splendor, galaxies of light: how could I help
   but recall the seine-net
Gathering the luminous fish? I cannot tell you how beautiful the city
   appeared, and a little terrible.
I thought, We have geared the machines and locked all together into
   interdependence; we have built the great cities; now
There is no escape. We have gathered vast populations incapable of free
   survival, insulated
From the strong earth, each person in himself helpless, on all dependent.
   The circle is closed, and the net
20 Is being hauled in. They hardly feel the cords drawing, yet they shine
   already. The inevitable mass-disasters
Will not come in our time nor in our children's, but we and our children
Must watch the net draw narrower, government take all powers—or revo-
   lution, and the new government
Take more than all, add to kept bodies kept souls—or anarchy, the mass-
   disasters.

             These things are Progress;
25 Do you marvel our verse is troubled or frowning, while it keeps its reason?
   Or it lets go, lets the mood flow
In the manner of the recent young men into mere hysteria, splintered
   gleams, crackled laughter. But they are quite wrong.
There is no reason for amazement: surely one always knew that cultures
   decay, and life's end is death.

                                   1937

---

2. Monterey, Santa Cruz, New Year's Point, and Pigeon Point are all places in the Monterey Bay area of
California.

Carmel Point[3]

The extraordinary patience of things!
This beautiful place defaced with a crop of suburban houses—
How beautiful when we first beheld it,
Unbroken field of poppy and lupin walled with clean cliffs;
5   No intrusion but two or three horses pasturing,
Or a few milch cows rubbing their flanks on the outcrop rock-heads—
Now the spoiler has come: does it care?
Not faintly. It has all time. It knows the people are a tide
That swells and in time will ebb, and all
10 Their works dissolve. Meanwhile the image of the pristine beauty
Lives in the very grain of the granite,
Safe as the endless ocean that climbs our cliff.—As for us:
We must uncenter our minds from ourselves;
We must unhumanize our views a little, and become confident
15 As the rock and ocean that we were made from.

1954

Birds and Fishes

Every October millions of little fish come along the shore,
Coasting this granite edge of the continent
On their lawful occasions: but what a festival for the sea-fowl.
What a witches' sabbath[4] of wings
5 Hides the dark water. The heavy pelicans shout "Haw!" like Job's friend's
     warhorse[5]
And dive from the high air, the cormorants[6]
Slip their long black bodies under the water and hunt like wolves
Through the green half-light. Screaming, the gulls watch,
Wild with envy and malice, cursing and snatching. What hysterical
     greed!
10 What a filling of pouches! the mob
Hysteria is nearly human—these decent birds!—as if they were finding
Gold in the street. It is better than gold,
It can be eaten: and which one in all this fury of wild-fowl pities the
     fish?
No one certainly. Justice and mercy
15 Are human dreams, they do not concern the birds nor the fish nor
     eternal God.
However—look again before you go.
The wings and wild hungers, the wave-worn skerries, the bright quick
     minnows
Living in terror to die in torment—
Man's fate and theirs—and the island rocks and immense ocean
     beyond, and Lobos[7]

3. On the California coast, below San Francisco.
4. Midnight meeting of witches and wizards, believed to be devil worshipers, to celebrate the witchcraft cult.
5. In Job 39.19–25, God describes the strength of the horse, who "saith among the trumpets Ha, ha; and he smelleth the battle afar off, the thunder of the captains and the shouting."
6. Aquatic birds with dark plumage.
7. Point Lobos, just below Carmel.

20   Darkening above the bay: they are beautiful?
That is their quality: not mercy, not mind, not goodness, but the beauty
    of God.

1963

RUPERT BROOKE
1887–1915

Sonnet

Oh! Death will find me, long before I tire
    Of watching you; and swing me suddenly
Into the shade and loneliness and mire°   *mud*
    Of the last land! There, waiting patiently,

5   One day, I think, I'll feel a cool wind blowing,
    See a slow light across the Stygian[1] tide,
And hear the Dead about me stir, unknowing,
    And tremble. And *I* shall know that you have died,

And watch you, a broad-browed and smiling dream,
10   Pass, light as ever, through the lightless host,
Quietly ponder, start, and sway, and gleam—
    Most individual and bewildering ghost!—

And turn, and toss your brown delightful head
Amusedly, among the ancient Dead.

April 1909   1911

From The Old Vicarage, Grantchester
(*Café des Westens, Berlin, May 1912*)

Just now the lilac is in bloom,
All before my little room;
And in my flower-beds, I think,
Smile the carnation and the pink;
5   And down the borders, well I know,
The poppy and the pansy blow . . .
Oh! there the chestnuts, summer through,
Beside the river make for you
A tunnel of green gloom, and sleep
10   Deeply above; and green and deep
The stream mysterious glides beneath,
Green as a dream and deep as death.
—Oh, damn! I know it! and I know
How the May fields all golden show,
15   And when the day is young and sweet,
Gild gloriously the bare feet

1. Of Styx, one of the mythological rivers of Hades, across which the ferryman Charon rowed the dead.

That run to bathe . . .
        Du lieber Gott![2]

Here am I, sweating, sick, and hot,
20 And there the shadowed waters fresh
    Lean up to embrace the naked flesh.
    Temperamentvoll[3] German Jews
    Drink beer around;—and *there* the dews
    Are soft beneath a morn of gold.
25 Here tulips bloom as they are told;
    Unkempt about those hedges blows
    An English unofficial rose;
    And there the unregulated sun
    Slopes down to rest when day is done,
30 And wakes a vague unpunctual star,
    A slippered Hesper; and there are
    Meads towards Haslingfield and Coton
    Where *das Betreten's* not *verboten.*[4]

    εἴθε γενοίμην[5] . . . would I were
35 In Grantchester, in Grantchester!—
    Some, it may be, can get in touch
    With Nature there, or Earth, or such.
    And clever modern men have seen
    A Faun a-peeping through the green,
40 And felt the Classics were not dead,
    To glimpse a Naiad's reedy head,
    Or hear the Goat-foot piping low: . . .
    But these are things I do not know.
    I only know that you may lie
45 Day-long and watch the Cambridge sky,
    And, flower-lulled in sleepy grass,
    Hear the cool lapse of hours pass,
    Until the centuries blend and blur
    In Grantchester, in Grantchester. . . .
50 Still in the dawnlit waters cool
    His ghostly Lordship swims his pool,[6]
    And tries the strokes, essays the tricks,
    Long learnt on Hellespont, or Styx.[7]
    Dan Chaucer hears his river still
55 Chatter beneath a phantom mill.
    Tennyson notes, with studious eye,
    How Cambridge waters hurry by . . .
    And in that garden, black and white,
    Creep whispers through the grass all night;
60 And spectral dance, before the dawn,
    A hundred Vicars down the lawn;

2. "[You] dear God!" (German).
3. "Temperamental" (German).
4. "Forbidden" (German); *das Betreten*: "walking on the grass" (German).
5. "Would I were" (Greek).
6. "Byron's Pool," a favorite bathing place in the river Cam.
7. One of the mythological rivers of Hades, over which Charon ferried the dead. "Hellespont": the "Sea of Helle"—now known as the Dardanelles—between Bulgaria and Turkey; straits across which Byron once swam.

Curates,[8] long dust, will come and go
On lissom,° clerical, printless toe;   *lithe, nimble*
And oft between the boughs is seen
65   The sly shade of a Rural Dean[9] . . .
Till, at a shiver in the skies,
Vanishing with Satanic cries,
The prim ecclesiastic rout
Leaves but a startled sleeper-out,
70   Grey heavens, the first bird's drowsy calls,
The falling house that never falls.[1]
. . . .
     Ah God! to see the branches stir
Across the moon at Grantchester!
To smell the thrilling-sweet and rotten
75   Unforgettable, unforgotten
River-smell, and hear the breeze
Sobbing in the little trees.
Say, do the elm-clumps greatly stand
Still guardians of that holy land?
80   The chestnuts shade, in reverend dream,
The yet unacademic stream?
Is dawn a secret shy and cold
Anadyomene,[2] silver-gold?
And sunset still a golden sea
85   From Haslingfield to Madingley?
And after, ere the night is born,
Do hares come out about the corn?
Oh, is the water sweet and cool,
Gentle and brown, above the pool?
90   And laughs the immortal river still
Under the mill, under the mill?
Say, is there Beauty yet to find?
And Certainty? and Quiet kind?
Deep meadows yet, for to forget
95   The lies, and truths, and pain? . . . Oh! yet
Stands the Church clock at ten to three?
And is there honey still for tea?

1912   1914

The Soldier

If I should die, think only this of me:
     That there's some corner of a foreign field
That is for ever England. There shall be
     In that rich earth a richer dust concealed;
5   A dust whom England bore, shaped, made aware,
     Gave, once, her flowers to love, her ways to roam,
A body of England's, breathing English air,
     Washed by the rivers, blest by suns of home.

---

8. Junior clergyman in the Church of England.   1. Forty-four lines omitted.
9. Clergyman in the Church of England with   2. "Rising" (Greek): name given to the goddess
responsibility for certain country parishes.   Aphrodite, who rose (at her birth) from the sea.

And think, this heart, all evil shed away,
10   A pulse in the eternal mind, no less
            Gives somewhere back the thoughts by England given;
        Her sights and sounds; dreams happy as her day;
        And laughter, learnt of friends; and gentleness,
            In hearts at peace, under an English heaven.

November–December 1914   1914

MARIANNE MOORE
1887–1972

Poetry[1]

I, too, dislike it: there are things that are important beyond all this
        fiddle.
    Reading it, however, with a perfect contempt for it, one discovers in
        it after all, a place for the genuine.
            Hands that can grasp, eyes
5   that can dilate, hair that can rise
                if it must, these things are important not because a

high-sounding interpretation can be put upon them but because they are
        useful. When they become so derivative as to become unintelligible,
        the same thing may be said for all of us, that we
10   do not admire what
            we cannot understand: the bat
                holding on upside down or in quest of something to

eat, elephants pushing, a wild horse taking a roll, a tireless wolf under
        a tree, the immovable critic twitching his skin like a horse that feels
        a flea, the base-
15   ball fan, the statistician—
            nor is it valid
                to discriminate against 'business documents and

school-books';[2] all these phenomena are important. One must make a
        distinction
    however: when dragged into prominence by half poets, the result is not
        poetry,
20   nor till the poets among us can be
            'literalists of
                the imagination'[3]—above
                    insolence and triviality and can present

1. Moore later cut this poem to include the first
three lines only.
2. "Diary of Tolstoy (Dutton), p. 84. 'Where the
boundary between prose and poetry lies, I shall
never be able to understand. The question is raised
in manuals of style, yet the answer to it lies beyond
me. Poetry is verse: prose is not verse. Or else
poetry is everything with the exception of business
documents and school books' " [Moore's note].
Leo Tolstoy (1828–1910), Russian novelist, philos-
opher, and mystic.

3. "Yeats: Ideas of Good and Evil (A. H. Bullen),
p. 182. 'The limitation of [Blake's] view was from
the very intensity of his vision; he was a too literal
realist of imagination, as others are of nature; and
because he believed that the figures seen by the
mind's eye, when exalted by inspiration, were
"eternal existences," symbols of divine essences, he
hated every grace of style that might obscure their
lineaments' " [Moore's note]. William Butler Yeats
(1865–1939), Irish poet and dramatist.

for inspection, 'imaginary gardens with real toads in them', shall we have
25   it. In the meantime, if you demand on the one hand,
       the raw material of poetry in
         all its rawness and
         that which is on the other hand
           genuine, you are interested in poetry.

                                         1921

The Steeple-Jack

Revised, 1961

Dürer[4] would have seen a reason for living
     in a town like this, with eight stranded whales
to look at; with the sweet sea air coming into your house
on a fine day, from water etched
5   with waves as formal as the scales
on a fish.

One by one in two's and three's, the seagulls keep
     flying back and forth over the town clock,
or sailing around the lighthouse without moving their wings—
10   rising steadily with a slight
       quiver of the body—or flock
mewing where

a sea the purple of the peacock's neck is
     paled to greenish azure as Dürer changed
15   the pine green of the Tyrol[5] to peacock blue and guinea
gray.[6] You can see a twenty-five-
       pound lobster; and fishnets arranged
to dry. The

whirlwind fife-and-drum of the storm bends the salt
20   marsh grass, disturbs stars in the sky and the
star on the steeple; it is a privilege to see so
much confusion. Disguised by what
       might seem the opposite, the sea-
side flowers and

25   trees are favored by the fog so that you have
       the tropics at first hand: the trumpet-vine,
fox-glove, giant snap-dragon, a salpiglossis[7] that has
spots and stripes; morning-glories, gourds,
       or moon-vines trained on fishing-twine
30   at the back

door; cat-tails, flags, blueberries and spiderwort,
     striped grass, lichens, sunflowers, asters, daisies—

4. Albrecht Dürer (1471–1528), great German Renaissance painter and engraver particularly gifted in rendering closely and meticulously observed detail.
5. The mountainous western area of Austria.
6. The slate gray, speckled with white, of the guinea fowl.
7. An herb with large, varicolored flowers that often have striking markings.

yellow and crab-claw ragged sailors with green bracts[8]—toad-plant,
    petunias, ferns; pink lilies, blue
35   ones, tigers; poppies; black sweet-peas.
The climate

is not right for the banyan, frangipani, or
    jack-fruit trees;[9] or an exotic serpent
life. Ring lizard and snake-skin for the foot, if you see fit;
40   but here they've cats, not cobras, to
        keep down the rats. The diffident
little newt

with white pin-dots on black horizontal spaced
    out bands lives here; yet there is nothing that
45   ambition can buy or take away. The college student
named Ambrose sits on the hillside
        with his not-native books and hat
and sees boats

at sea progress white and rigid as if in
50   a groove. Liking an elegance of which
the source is not bravado, he knows by heart the antique
sugar-bowl shaped summer-house of
        interlacing slats, and the pitch
of the church

55   spire, not true, from which a man in scarlet lets
        down a rope as a spider spins a thread;
he might be part of a novel, but on the sidewalk a
sign says C. J. Poole, Steeple Jack,
        in black and white; and one in red
60   and white says

Danger. The church portico has four fluted
    columns, each a single piece of stone, made
modester by white-wash. This would be a fit haven for
waifs, children, animals, prisoners,
65   and presidents who have repaid
sin-driven

senators by not thinking about them. The
    place has a school-house, a post-office in a
store, fish-houses, hen-houses, a three-masted
70   schooner on
the stocks. The hero, the student,
        the steeple-jack, each in his way,
is at home.

It could not be dangerous to be living
75   in a town like this, of simple people,

---

8. Flowerlike leaves on some plants (for instance, flowering dogwood).
9. The banyan is an East Indian tree some of whose branches send out trunks that grow downward; frangipani is a tropical American shrub (red jasmine is a species); the jack-fruit is a large East Indian tree with large edible fruit.

who have a steeple-jack placing danger-signs by the church
while he is gilding the solid-
    pointed star, which on a steeple
stands for hope.

                    1935

No Swan So Fine

'No water so still as the
    dead fountains of Versailles.'[1] No swan,
with swart blind look askance
and gondoliering legs,[2] so fine
5   as the chintz china one with fawn-
brown eyes and toothed gold
collar on to show whose bird it was.

Lodged in the Louis Fifteenth
    candelabrum-tree[3] of cockscomb-
10   tinted buttons, dahlias,
sea-urchins, and everlastings,[4]
    it perches on the branching foam
of polished sculptured
flowers—at ease and tall. The king is dead.

              1932, 1951

The Fish

wade
through black jade.
    Of the crow-blue mussel-shells, one keeps
    adjusting the ash-heaps;
5   opening and shutting itself like

an
injured fan.
    The barnacles which encrust the side
    of the wave, cannot hide
10   there for the submerged shafts of the

sun,
split like spun
    glass, move themselves with spotlight swiftness
    into the crevices—
15   in and out, illuminating

the
turquoise sea

---

1. "Percy Phillip, *New York Times Magazine*, May 10, 1931" [Moore's note]. Famed palace of French kings, including Louis XV, in the late seventeenth and early eighteenth centuries; now a museum.
2. Italian gondoliers paddle from the stern to propel their gondolas.
3. "A pair of Louis XV candelabra with Dresden figures of swans belonging to Lord Balfour" [Moore's note].
4. Plants with flowers that may be dried without losing their form or color; also, the flowers from such plants.

of bodies. The water drives a wedge
of iron through the iron edge
20   of the cliff; whereupon the stars,

pink
rice-grains, ink-
    bespattered jelly-fish, crabs like green
    lilies, and submarine
25   toadstools, slide each on the other.

All
external
    marks of abuse are present on this
    defiant edifice—
30   all the physical features of

ac-
cident—lack
    of cornice, dynamite grooves, burns, and
    hatchet strokes, these things stand
35   out on it; the chasm-side is

dead.
Repeated
    evidence has proved that it can live
    on what can not revive
40   its youth. The sea grows old in it.

                                      1921, 1935

Peter

    Strong and slippery,
built for the midnight grass-party
confronted by four cats, he sleeps his time away—
the detached first claw on the foreleg corresponding
5 to the thumb, retracted to its tip; the small tuft of fronds
or katydid-legs above each eye numbering all units
in each group; the shadbones[5] regularly set about the mouth
to droop or rise in unison like porcupine-quills.
He lets himself be flattened out by gravity,
10 as seaweed is tamed and weakened by the sun,
compelled when extended, to lie stationary.
Sleep is the result of his delusion that one must
do as well as one can for oneself,
sleep—epitome of what is to him the end of life.
15 Demonstrate on him how the lady placed a forked stick
on the innocuous neck-sides of the dangerous southern snake.
One need not try to stir him up; his prune-shaped head
and alligator-eyes are not party to the joke.
Lifted and handled, he may be dangled like an eel
20 or set up on the forearm like a mouse;

5. Long, very fine bones of the shad fish.

his eyes bisected by pupils of a pin's width,
are flickeringly exhibited, then covered up.
May be? I should have said might have been;
when he has been got the better of in a dream—
25   as in a fight with nature or with cats, we all know it.
Profound sleep is not with him a fixed illusion.
Springing about with froglike accuracy, with jerky cries
when taken in hand, he is himself again;
to sit caged by the rungs of a domestic chair
30   would be unprofitable—human. What is the good of hypocrisy?
it is permissible to choose one's employment,
to abandon the nail, or roly-poly,
when it shows signs of being no longer a pleasure,
to score the nearby magazine with a double line of strokes.
35   He can talk but insolently says nothing. What of it?
When one is frank, one's very presence is a compliment.
It is clear that he can see the virtue of naturalness,
that he does not regard the published fact as a surrender.
As for the disposition invariably to affront,
40   an animal with claws should have an opportunity to use them.
The eel-like extension of trunk into tail is not an accident.
To leap, to lengthen out, divide the air, to purloin, to pursue.
To tell the hen: fly over the fence, go in the wrong way
in your perturbation—this is life;
45   to do less would be nothing but dishonesty.

1935

A Grave

Man looking into the sea,
taking the view from those who have as much right to it as you have to it
    yourself,
it is human nature to stand in the middle of a thing,
but you cannot stand in the middle of this;
5   the sea has nothing to give but a well excavated grave.
The firs stand in a procession, each with an emerald turkey-foot at the
    top,
reserved as their contours, saying nothing;
repression, however, is not the most obvious characteristic of the sea;
the sea is a collector, quick to return a rapacious look.
10   There are others besides you who have worn that look—
whose expression is no longer a protest; the fish no longer investigate
    them
for their bones have not lasted:
men lower nets, unconscious of the fact that they are desecrating a grave,
and row quickly away—the blades of the oars
15   moving together like the feet of water-spiders as if there were no such
    thing as death.
The wrinkles progress among themselves in a phalanx[6]—beautiful under
    networks of foam,
and fade breathlessly while the sea rustles in and out of the seaweed;

6. Compact body of troops.

the birds swim through the air at top speed, emitting cat-calls as hereto-
   fore—
the tortoise-shell scourges about the feet of the cliffs, in motion beneath
   them;
20   and the ocean, under the pulsation of lighthouses and noise of bell-buoys,
advances as usual, looking as if it were not that ocean in which dropped
   things are bound to sink—
in which if they turn and twist, it is neither with volition nor
   consciousness.

1924, 1935

What Are Years?

What is our innocence,
what is our guilt? All are
   naked, none is safe. And whence
is courage: the unanswered question,
5   the resolute doubt,—
dumbly calling, deafly listening—that
in misfortune, even death,
      encourages others
      and in its defeat, stirs

10   the soul to be strong? He
sees deep and is glad, who
      accedes to mortality
and in his imprisonment rises
upon himself as
15   the sea in a chasm, struggling to be
free and unable to be,
      in its surrendering
      finds its continuing.

So he who strongly feels,
20   behaves. The very bird,
      grown taller as he sings, steels
his form straight up. Though he is captive,
his mighty singing
says, satisfaction is a lowly
25   thing, how pure a thing is joy.
      This is mortality,
      this is eternity.

1931–9   1941

Nevertheless

you've seen a strawberry
      that's had a struggle; yet
      was, where the fragments met,

a hedgehog or a star-
5   fish for the multitude
      of seeds. What better food

than apple-seeds—the fruit
within the fruit—locked in
like counter-curved twin

10 hazel-nuts? Frost that kills
the little rubber-plant-
leaves of *kok-saghyz*-stalks, can't

harm the roots; they still grow
in frozen ground. Once where
15 there was a prickly-pear-

leaf clinging to barbed wire,
a root shot down to grow
in earth two feet below;

as carrots form mandrakes
20 or a ram's-horn root some-
times. Victory won't come

to me unless I go
to it; a grape-tendril
ties a knot in knots till

25 knotted thirty times,—so
the bound twig that's under-
gone and over-gone, can't stir.

The weak overcomes its
menace, the strong over-
30 comes itself. What is there

like fortitude! What sap
went through that little thread
to make the cherry red!

1944

The Mind Is an Enchanting Thing

is an enchanted thing
like the glaze on a
katydid-wing
subdivided by sun
5 till the nettings are legion.
Like Gieseking playing Scarlatti;[7]

like the apteryx-awl[8]
as a beak, or the
kiwi's rain-shawl

---

7. Walter Wilhelm Gieseking (1895–1956), German pianist, was famous for his renditions of the music of the Italian composer Domenico Scarlatti

(1685–1757).
8. New Zealand bird, related to the kiwi, with an awl-shaped beak.

10   of haired feathers, the mind
                feeling its way as though blind,
         walks along with its eyes on the ground.

         It has memory's ear
                that can hear without
15   having to hear.
                Like the gyroscope's fall,
                truly unequivocal
         because trued° by regnant° certainty,   *balanced / authoritative*

         it is a power of
20   strong enchantment. It
         is like the dove-
                neck animated by
                sun; it is memory's eye;
         it's conscientious inconsistency.

25   It tears off the veil; tears
                the temptation, the
         mist the heart wears,
                from its eyes—if the heart
                has a face; it takes apart
30   dejection. It's fire in the dove-neck's

         iridescence; in the
                inconsistencies
         of Scarlatti.
                Unconfusion submits
35   its confusion to proof; it's
         not a Herod's oath[9] that cannot change.

                                                    1944

EDWIN MUIR

1887–1959

Childhood

Long time he lay upon the sunny hill,
    To his father's house below securely bound.
Far off the silent, changing sound was still,
    With the black islands lying thick around.

5   He saw each separate height, each vaguer hue,
        Where the massed islands rolled in mist away,
    And though all ran together in his view
        He knew that unseen straits between them lay.

---

9. Cf. Mark 6.22–27. Herod, ruler of Judea under the Romans, fulfilled an oath to Salome by having John the Baptist beheaded.

Often he wondered what new shores were there.
10   In thought he saw the still light on the sand,
The shallow water clear in tranquil air,
    And walked through it in joy from strand to strand.

Over the sound a ship so slow would pass
    That in the black hill's gloom it seemed to lie.
15 The evening sound was smooth like sunken glass,
    And time seemed finished ere the ship passed by.

Grey tiny rocks slept round him where he lay,
    Moveless as they, more still as evening came,
The grasses threw straight shadows far away,
20   And from the house his mother called his name.

1925

The Return of the Greeks

The veteran Greeks came home
Sleepwandering from the war.
We saw the galleys come
Blundering over the bar.
5   Each soldier with his scar
In rags and tatters came home.

Reading the wall of Troy[1]
Ten years without a change
Was such intense employ
10 (Just out of the arrows' range),
All the world was strange
After ten years of Troy.

Their eyes knew every stone
In the huge heartbreaking wall
15 Year after year grown
Till there was nothing at all
But an alley steep and small,
Tramped earth and towering stone.

Now even the hills seemed low
20 In the boundless sea and land,
Weakened by distance so.
How could they understand
Space empty on every hand
And the hillocks squat and low?

25 And when they arrived at last
They found a childish scene
Embosomed in the past,
And the war lying between—

---

1. The ancient city on the Asiatic shore of the Hellespont, besieged by the Greeks for ten years, as described in the *Iliad* of Homer.

A child's preoccupied scene
30　When they came home at last.

But everything trite and strange,
The peace, the parcelled ground,
The vinerows—never a change!
The past and the present bound
35　In one oblivious round
Past thinking trite and strange.

But for their grey-haired wives
And their sons grown shy and tall
They would have given their lives
40　To raise the battered wall
Again, if this was all
In spite of their sons and wives.

Penelope in her tower
Looked down upon the show
45　And saw within an hour
Each man to his wife go,
Hesitant, sure and slow:
She, alone in her tower.[2]

1946

Adam's Dream

They say the first dream Adam our father had
After his agelong daydream in the Garden[3]
When heaven and sun woke in his wakening mind,
The earth with all its hills and woods and waters,
5　The friendly tribes of trees and animals,
And earth's last wonder Eve (the first great dream
Which is the ground of every dream since then)—
They say he dreamt lying on the naked ground,
The gates shut fast behind him as he lay
10　Fallen in Eve's fallen arms, his terror drowned
In her engulfing terror, in the abyss
Whence there's no further fall, and comfort is—
That he was standing on a rocky ledge
High on the mountainside, bare crag behind,
15　In front a plain as far as eye could reach,
And on the plain a few small figures running
That were like men and women, yet were so far away
He could not see their faces. On they ran,
And fell, and rose again, and ran, and fell,
20　And rising were the same yet not the same,

---

2. Odysseus, Penelope's husband and one of the Greek leaders in the ten-year Trojan War, took another ten years to return home (as described in the *Odyssey*).
3. I.e., after the Fall. According to Genesis 3, Adam and Eve were expelled from the Garden of Eden because they ate the fruit of the one tree forbidden to them by God ("the tree of knowledge of good and evil").

Identical or interchangeable,
Different in indifference. As he looked
Still there were more of them, the plain was filling
As by an alien arithmetical magic
25 Unknown in Eden, a mechanical
Addition without meaning, joining only
Number to number in no mode or order,
Weaving no pattern. For these creatures moved
Towards no fixed mark even when in growing bands
30 They clashed against each other and clashing fell
In mounds of bodies. For they rose again,
Identical or interchangeable,
And went their way that was not like a way;
Some back and forward, back and forward, some
35 In a closed circle, wide or narrow, others
In zigzags on the sand. Yet all were busy,
And tense with purpose as they cut the air
Which seemed to press them back. Sometimes they paused
While one stopped one—fortuitous assignations
40 In the disorder, whereafter two by two
They ran awhile,
Then parted and again were single. Some
Ran straight against the frontier of the plain
Till the horizon drove them back. A few
45 Stood still and never moved. Then Adam cried
Out of his dream, "What are you doing there?"
And the crag answered "Are you doing there?"
"What are you doing there?"—"you doing there?"
The animals had withdrawn and from the caves
50 And woods stared out in fear or condemnation,
Like outlaws or like judges. All at once
Dreaming or half-remembering, "This is time,"
Thought Adam in his dream, and time was strange
To one lately in Eden. "I must see,"
55 He cried, "the faces. Where are the faces? Who
Are you all out there?" Then in his changing dream
He was a little nearer, and he saw
They were about some business strange to him
That had a form and sequence past their knowledge;
60 And that was why they ran so frenziedly.
Yet all, it seemed, made up a story, illustrated
By these the living, the unknowing, cast
Each singly for his part. But Adam longed
For more, not this mere moving pattern, not
65 This illustrated storybook of mankind
Always a-making, improvised on nothing.
At that he was among them, and saw each face
Was like his face, so that he would have hailed them
As sons of God but that something restrained him.
70 And he remembered all, Eden, the Fall,
The Promise, and his place, and took their hands
That were his hands, his and his children's hands,

Cried out and was at peace, and turned again
In love and grief in Eve's encircling arms.

1950, 1952

T. S. ELIOT
1888–1965

The Love Song of J. Alfred Prufrock

S'io credesse che mia risposta fosse
A persona che mai tornasse al mondo,
Questa fiamma staria senza piu scosse.
Ma perciocche giammai di questo fondo
Non torno vivo alcun, s'i'odo il vero,
Senza tema d'infamia ti rispondo.[1]

Let us go then, you and I,
When the evening is spread out against the sky
Like a patient etherised upon a table;
Let us go, through certain half-deserted streets,
5   The muttering retreats
Of restless nights in one-night cheap hotels
And sawdust restaurants with oyster-shells:
Streets that follow like a tedious argument
Of insidious intent
10   To lead you to an overwhelming question . . .
Oh, do not ask, "What is it?"
Let us go and make our visit.

In the room the women come and go
Talking of Michelangelo.

15   The yellow fog that rubs its back upon the window-panes,
The yellow smoke that rubs its muzzle on the window-panes
Licked its tongue into the corners of the evening,
Lingered upon the pools that stand in drains,
Let fall upon its back the soot that falls from chimneys,
20   Slipped by the terrace, made a sudden leap,
And seeing that it was a soft October night,
Curled once about the house, and fell asleep.

And indeed there will be time
For the yellow smoke that slides along the street,
25   Rubbing its back upon the window-panes;
There will be time, there will be time
To prepare a face to meet the faces that you meet;
There will be time to murder and create,

---

1. Dante, *Inferno* 27.61–66. These words are spoken by Guido da Montefeltro, whom Dante and Virgil have encountered among the false counselors (each spirit is concealed within a flame): "If I thought my answer were given / to anyone who would ever return to the world, / this flame would stand still without moving any further. / But since never from this abyss / has anyone ever returned alive, if what I hear is true, / without fear of infamy I answer you."

And time for all the works and days[2] of hands
30 That lift and drop a question on your plate;
Time for you and time for me,
And time yet for a hundred indecisions,
And for a hundred visions and revisions,
Before the taking of a toast and tea.

35   In the room the women come and go
Talking of Michelangelo.

And indeed there will be time
To wonder, "Do I dare?" and, "Do I dare?"
Time to turn back and descend the stair,
40 With a bald spot in the middle of my hair—
[They will say: "How his hair is growing thin!"]
My morning coat, my collar mounting firmly to the chin,
My necktie rich and modest, but asserted by a simple pin—
[They will say: "But how his arms and legs are thin!"]
45 Do I dare
Disturb the universe?
In a minute there is time
For decisions and revisions which a minute will reverse.

For I have known them all already, known them all—
50 Have known the evenings, mornings, afternoons,
I have measured out my life with coffee spoons;
I know the voices dying with a dying fall[3]
Beneath the music from a farther room.
So how should I presume?

55   And I have known the eyes already, known them all—
The eyes that fix you in a formulated phrase,
And when I am formulated, sprawling on a pin,
When I am pinned and wriggling on the wall,
Then how should I begin
60 To spit out all the butt-ends of my days and ways?
And how should I presume?

And I have known the arms already, known them all—
Arms that are braceleted and white and bare
[But in the lamplight, downed with light brown hair!]
65 Is it perfume from a dress
That makes me so digress?
Arms that lie along a table, or wrap about a shawl.
And should I then presume?
And how should I begin?

          .   .   .   .   .

70 Shall I say, I have gone at dusk through narrow streets
And watched the smoke that rises from the pipes
Of lonely men in shirt-sleeves, leaning out of windows? . . .

2. *Works and Days*, by the Greek poet Hesiod (eighth century B.C.), is a didactic poem about farming and family life.

3. An echo of Shakespeare's *Twelfth Night* (1.1.1–4): "If music be the food of love, play on. . . . That strain again, it had a dying fall."

I should have been a pair of ragged claws
Scuttling across the floors of silent seas.

. . . . .

75   And the afternoon, the evening, sleeps so peacefully!
Smoothed by long fingers,
Asleep . . . tired . . . or it malingers,
Stretched on the floor, here beside you and me.
Should I, after tea and cakes and ices,
80   Have the strength to force the moment to its crisis?
But though I have wept and fasted, wept and prayed,
Though I have seen my head [grown slightly bald] brought in
     upon a platter,[4]
I am no prophet—and here's no great matter;
I have seen the moment of my greatness flicker,
85   And I have seen the eternal Footman hold my coat, and snicker,
And in short, I was afraid.

And would it have been worth it, after all,
After the cups, the marmalade, the tea,
Among the porcelain, among some talk of you and me,
90   Would it have been worth while,
To have bitten off the matter with a smile,
To have squeezed the universe into a ball
To roll it toward some overwhelming question,
To say: "I am Lazarus,[5] come from the dead,
95   Come back to tell you all, I shall tell you all"—
If one, settling a pillow by her head,
     Should say: "That is not what I meant at all.
     That is not it, at all."

And would it have been worth it, after all,
100   Would it have been worth while,
After the sunsets and the dooryards and the sprinkled streets,
After the novels, after the teacups, after the skirts that trail along the
     floor—
And this, and so much more?—
It is impossible to say just what I mean!
105   But as if a magic lantern threw the nerves in patterns on a screen:
Would it have been worth while
If one, settling a pillow or throwing off a shawl,
And turning toward the window, should say:
     "That is not it at all,
110   That is not what I meant, at all."

. . . . .

No! I am not Prince Hamlet, nor was meant to be;
Am an attendant lord, one that will do
To swell a progress,[6] start a scene or two,
Advise the prince; no doubt, an easy tool,

---

4. The head of John the Baptist was presented to Salome on a plate at her request (Matthew 14.1–12).
5. On the resurrection of Lazarus, see John 11.

6. Journey made by a royal court, often depicted in the Elizabethan drama, in which the Fool was also a fixture.

115 Deferential, glad to be of use,
Politic, cautious, and meticulous;
Full of high sentence,° but a bit obtuse;   *sententiousness*
At times, indeed, almost ridiculous—
Almost, at times, the Fool.

120 I grow old . . . I grow old . . .
I shall wear the bottoms of my trousers rolled.

Shall I part my hair behind? Do I dare to eat a peach?
I shall wear white flannel trousers, and walk upon the beach.
I have heard the mermaids singing, each to each.

125 I do not think that they will sing to me.

I have seen them riding seaward on the waves
Combing the white hair of the waves blown back
When the wind blows the water white and black.

We have lingered in the chambers of the sea
130 By sea-girls wreathed with seaweed red and brown
Till human voices wake us, and we drown.

                                                    1917

Preludes

1

The winter evening settles down
With smell of steaks in passageways.
Six o'clock.
The burnt-out ends of smoky days.
5 And now a gusty shower wraps
The grimy scraps
Of withered leaves about your feet
And newspapers from vacant lots;
The showers beat
10 On broken blinds and chimney-pots
And at the corner of the street
A lonely cab-horse steams and stamps.
And then the lighting of the lamps.[7]

2

The morning comes to consciousness
15 Of faint stale smells of beer
From the sawdust-trampled street
With all its muddy feet that press
To early coffee-stands.
With the other masquerades
20 That time resumes,
One thinks of all the hands

---

7. Gas lamps, which were lit each night by a lamplighter.

That are raising dingy shades
In a thousand furnished rooms.

3

You tossed a blanket from the bed,
25   You lay upon your back, and waited;
You dozed, and watched the night revealing
The thousand sordid images
Of which your soul was constituted;
They flickered against the ceiling.
30   And when all the world came back
And the light crept up between the shutters
And you heard the sparrows in the gutters,
You had such a vision of the street
As the street hardly understands;
35   Sitting along the bed's edge, where
You curled the papers[8] from your hair,
Or clasped the yellow soles of feet
In the palms of both soiled hands.

4

His soul stretched tight across the skies
40   That fade behind a city block,
Or trampled by insistent feet
At four and five and six o'clock;
And short square fingers stuffing pipes,
And evening newspapers, and eyes
45   Assured of certain certainties,
The conscience of a blackened street
Impatient to assume the world.

I am moved by fancies[9] that are curled
Around these images, and cling;
50   The notion of some infinitely gentle
Infinitely suffering thing.

Wipe your hand across your mouth, and laugh;
The worlds revolve like ancient women
Gathering fuel in vacant lots.

1917

Sweeney Among the Nightingales

ὤμοι, πέπληγμαι καιρίαν πληγὴν ἔσω.[1]

Apeneck Sweeney spreads his knees
Letting his arms hang down to laugh,
The zebra stripes along his jaw
Swelling to maculate° giraffe.   *spotted*

---

8. Curling papers, used to create ringlets.
9. Imaginary associations.
1. Aeschylus, *Agamemnon*, line 1343. Agamem-

non's cry, heard from inside the palace, as he is
murdered by his wife: "Oh, I have been struck a
deadly blow, within!" (Greek).

5   The circles of the stormy moon
Slide westward toward the River Plate,[2]
Death and the Raven[3] drift above
And Sweeney guards the hornéd gate.[4]

Gloomy Orion[5] and the Dog
10   Are veiled; and hushed the shrunken seas;
The person in the Spanish cape
Tries to sit on Sweeney's knees

Slips and pulls the table cloth
Overturns a coffee-cup,
15   Reorganized upon the floor
She yawns and draws a stocking up;

The silent man in mocha brown
Sprawls at the window-sill and gapes;
The waiter brings in oranges
20   Bananas figs and hothouse grapes;

The silent vertebrate in brown
Contracts and concentrates, withdraws;
Rachel *née* Rabinovitch
Tears at the grapes with murderous paws;

25   She and the lady in the cape
Are suspect, thought to be in league;
Therefore the man with heavy eyes
Declines the gambit, shows fatigue,

Leaves the room and reappears
30   Outside the window, leaning in,
Branches of wistaria
Circumscribe a golden grin;

The host with someone indistinct
Converses at the door apart,
35   The nightingales[6] are singing near
The Convent of the Sacred Heart,

And sang within the bloody wood
When Agamemnon[7] cried aloud,
And let their liquid siftings fall
40   To stain the stiff dishonoured shroud.

1919

2. Rio de la Plata, an estuary of the Paraná and Uruguay rivers, between Uruguay and Argentina.
3. The southern constellation Corvus.
4. In Greek legend, dreams came to mortals from the underworld through two sets of gates: true dreams through the gates of horn, false through the gates of ivory.
5. A constellation in which is seen the figure of a hunter, with belt and sword; near it, the Dog Star,
Sirius, represents the hunter's dog.
6. The Greeks explained the mournful song of the nightingale by the story that she had been a woman who killed her son and fed him to her husband, who had raped and mutilated her sister.
7. Greek leader, who on his victorious return from the Trojan War was murdered by his wife, Clytemnestra.

The Waste Land[8]

"Nam Sibyllam quidem Cumis ego ipse oculis meis vidi in ampulla pendere, et cum illi pueri dicerent: Σίβυλλα τί θέλεις; respondebat illa: ἀποθανεῖν θέλω."[9]

FOR EZRA POUND

il miglior fabbro.[1]

I. The Burial of the Dead[2]

April is the cruellest month, breeding
Lilacs out of the dead land, mixing
Memory and desire, stirring
Dull roots with spring rain.
5   Winter kept us warm, covering
Earth in forgetful snow, feeding
A little life with dried tubers.
Summer surprised us, coming over the Starnbergersee[3]
With a shower of rain; we stopped in the colonnade,
10   And went on in sunlight, into the Hofgarten,
And drank coffee, and talked for an hour.
Bin gar keine Russin, stamm' aus Litauen, echt deutsch.[4]
And when we were children, staying at the arch-duke's,
My cousin's, he took me out on a sled,
15   And I was frightened. He said, Marie,
Marie, hold on tight. And down we went.
In the mountains, there you feel free.
I read, much of the night, and go south in the winter.

What are the roots that clutch, what branches grow
20   Out of this stony rubbish? Son of man,[5]
You cannot say, or guess, for you know only
A heap of broken images, where the sun beats,
And the dead tree gives no shelter, the cricket no relief,[6]

8. On its publication in book form, T. S. Eliot provided *The Waste Land* with many (and perhaps sometimes parodic) notes. They begin: "Not only the title, but the plan and a good deal of the incidental symbolism of the poem were suggested by Miss Jessie L. Weston's book on the Grail legend: *From Ritual to Romance* (Cambridge). Indeed, so deeply am I indebted, Miss Weston's book will elucidate the difficulties of the poem much better than my notes can do; and I recommend it (apart from the great interest of the book itself) to any who think such elucidation of the poem worth the trouble. To another work of anthropology I am indebted in general, one which has influenced our generation profoundly; I mean *The Golden Bough* [by Sir James Frazer; 12 volumes, 1890–1915]; I have used especially the two volumes *Adonis, Attis, Osiris.* Anyone who is acquainted with these works will immediately recognize in the poem certain references to vegetation ceremonies [i.e., fertility rites]."
9. "For indeed I myself have seen, with my own eyes, the Sibyl hanging in a bottle at Cumae, and when those boys would say to her: 'Sibyl, what do you want?' she replied, 'I want to die.' " From the *Satyricon* of Petronius (d. A.D. 66), chapter 48. The Sibyl of Cumae, a prophetess of Apollo, was immortal without eternal youth.
1. "The better craftsman" (Italian). So the poet Guido Guinizelli characterizes the Provençal poet Arnaut Daniel in Dante's *Purgatorio* 26.117.
2. The burial service of the Anglican Church.
3. Lake a few miles south of Munich. The Hofgarten (line 10) is a public garden in Munich, partly surrounded by a colonnaded walk.
4. "I am certainly no Russian, I come from Lithuania, a true German" (German).
5. "Cf. Ezekiel II, i" [Eliot's note], where God addressed Ezekiel, "Son of man, stand upon thy feet, and I will speak unto thee."
6. "Cf. Ecclesiastes XII, v" [Eliot's note], a description of times of fear and death, when "the grasshopper shall be a burden, and desire shall fail." The passage continues, "Then shall the dust return to the earth as it was" (12.7); cf. line 30 below.

And the dry stone no sound of water. Only
25 There is shadow under this red rock,
(Come in under the shadow of this red rock),[7]
And I will show you something different from either
Your shadow at morning striding behind you
Or your shadow at evening rising to meet you;
30 I will show you fear in a handful of dust.
    Frisch weht der Wind
    Der Heimat zu
    Mein Irisch Kind,
    Wo weilest du?[8]
35 "You gave me hyacinths first a year ago;
"They called me the hyacinth girl."
—Yet when we came back, late, from the Hyacinth garden,
Your arms full, and your hair wet, I could not
Speak, and my eyes failed, I was neither
40 Living nor dead, and I knew nothing,
Looking into the heart of light, the silence.
Oed' und leer das Meer.[9]

  Madame Sosostris,[1] famous clairvoyante,
Had a bad cold, nevertheless
45 Is known to be the wisest woman in Europe,
With a wicked pack of cards.[2] Here, said she,
Is your card, the drowned Phoenician Sailor,
(Those are pearls that were his eyes.[3] Look!)
Here is Belladonna, the Lady of the Rocks,
50 The lady of situations.
Here is the man with three staves, and here the Wheel,
And here is the one-eyed merchant, and this card,
Which is blank, is something he carries on his back,
Which I am forbidden to see. I do not find
55 The Hanged Man. Fear death by water.
I see crowds of people, walking round in a ring.
Thank you. If you see dear Mrs. Equitone,
Tell her I bring the horoscope myself:
One must be so careful these days.

---

7. Cf. Isaiah's prophecy of a Messiah who will be "as rivers of water in a dry place, as the shadow of a great rock in a weary land" (Isaiah 32.2).
8. "V. *Tristan und Isolde*, I, verses 5–8" [Eliot's note]. The sailor's song from Wagner's opera: "Fresh blows the wind / Toward home. / My Irish child, / Where are you waiting?"
9. "Id. III, verse 24" [Eliot's note]. "Empty and waste the sea" (German): that is, the ship bringing Isolde back to the dying Tristan is nowhere in sight.
1. A pseudo-Egyptian name assumed by a fortune-teller in Aldous Huxley's novel *Chrome Yellow* (1921).
2. "I am not familiar with the exact constitution of the Tarot pack of cards, from which I have obviously departed to suit my own convenience. The

Hanged Man, a member of the traditional pack, fits my purpose in two ways: because he is associated in my mind with the Hanged God of Frazer, and because I associate him with the hooded figure in the passage of the disciples to Emmaus in Part V. The Phoenician Sailor and the Merchant appear later; also the 'crowds of people' and Death by Water is executed in Part IV. The Man with Three Staves (an authentic member of the Tarot pack) I associate, quite arbitrarily, with the Fisher King himself" [Eliot's note]. The tarot cards are used in fortune-telling.
3. From Ariel's song in Shakespeare's *Tempest* 1.2: "Full fathom five thy father lies." "Phoenician sailor": the Phoenicians were seagoing merchants (cf. "Mr. Eugenides," line 209, and "Phlebas the Phoenician," line 312).

60   Unreal City,[4]
    Under the brown fog of a winter dawn,
    A crowd flowed over London Bridge, so many,
    I had not thought death had undone so many.[5]
    Sighs, short and infrequent, were exhaled,[6]
65   And each man fixed his eyes before his feet.
    Flowed up the hill and down King William Street,
    To where Saint Mary Woolnoth kept the hours
    With a dead sound on the final stroke of nine.[7]
    There I saw one I knew, and stopped him, crying: "Stetson!
70   "You who were with me in the ships at Mylae![8]
    "That corpse you planted last year in your garden,
    "Has it begun to sprout? Will it bloom this year?
    "Or has the sudden frost disturbed its bed?
    "Oh keep the Dog far hence, that's friend to men,
75   "Or with his nails he'll dig it up again![9]
    "You! hypocrite lecteur!—mon semblable,—mon frère!"[1]

II. A Game of Chess[2]

    The Chair she sat in, like a burnished throne,[3]
    Glowed on the marble, where the glass
    Held up by standards wrought with fruited vines
80   From which a golden Cupidon peeped out
    (Another hid his eyes behind his wing)
    Doubled the flames of sevenbranched candelabra[4]
    Reflecting light upon the table as
    The glitter of her jewels rose to meet it,
85   From satin cases poured in rich profusion;
    In vials of ivory and coloured glass
    Unstoppered, lurked her strange synthetic perfumes,

---

4. "Cf. Baudelaire: 'Fourmillante cité, cité pleine de rêves, / Où le spectre en plein jour raccroche le passant' " [Eliot's note]. The lines are from *Les Sept viellards (The Seven Old Men)*, one of the poems in *Les Fleurs du mal* (1857): "Swarming city, city filled with dreams, / Where the specter in broad daylight accosts the passerby" (French).
5. "Cf. Inferno III, 55–57: 'si lunga tratta / di gente, ch' io non avrei mai creduto / che morte tanta n'avesse disfatta' " [Eliot's note]. On his arrival in the Inferno, Dante sees the vast crowd, "such a long procession of people, that I would never have believed that death had undone so many" (Italian).
6. "Cf. Inferno IV, 25–27: 'Quivi, secondo che per ascoltare, / non avea pianto, ma' che di sospiri, / che l'aura eterna facevan tremare' " [Eliot's note]. Dante descends into the first circle of Hell, filled with virtuous pagans condemned to Limbo because they had lived before Christianity: "Here, if one trusted to hearing, there was no weeping but so many sighs as caused the everlasting air to tremble" (Italian).
7. "A phenomenon which I have often noticed" [Eliot's note]. The church and the other London sites are in the City, London's financial and business center.

8. Sicilian seaport; at the battle of Mylae (260 B.C.), the Romans defeated the Carthaginians.
9. "Cf. the Dirge in Webster's *White Devil* [1612]" [Eliot's note]. The song is sung by a crazed mother, who has witnessed one son murder another, and ends, "But keep the wolf far thence, that's foe to men; / For with his nails he'll dig them up again" (5.4.97–98).
1. "V. Baudelaire, Preface to *Fleurs du mal*" [Eliot's note]. Baudelaire's prefatory poem is entitled *To the Reader*, and Eliot quotes the last line: "Hypocrite reader!—my likeness,—my brother!" (French).
2. The title alludes to two plays by Thomas Middleton (1570–1627), *A Game at Chesse* (1627) and *Women Beware Women* (1657), both of which involve sexual intrigue. In the second, a game of chess is used to mark a seduction, the moves in the game paralleling its steps.
3. "Cf. *Antony and Cleopatra*, II, ii, 1. 190" [Eliot's note]. The long description of Cleopatra's first meeting with Antony on the River Cydnus begins: "The barge she sat in, like a burnished throne / Burned on the water." Eliot's language recalls the passage in Shakespeare.
4. The Menorah, used in Jewish worship.

Unguent,° powdered, or liquid—troubled, confused   *ointment*
And drowned the sense in odours; stirred by the air
90 That freshened from the window, these ascended
In fattening the prolonged candle-flames,
Flung their smoke into the laquearia,[5]
Stirring the pattern on the coffered[6] ceiling.
Huge sea-wood fed with copper
95 Burned green and orange, framed by the coloured stone,
In which sad light a carvéd dolphin swam.
Above the antique mantel was displayed
As though a window gave upon the sylvan scene[7]
The change of Philomel, by the barbarous king[8]
100 So rudely forced; yet there the nightingale[9]
Filled all the desert with inviolable voice
And still she cried, and still the world pursues,
"Jug Jug" to dirty ears.
And other withered stumps of time
105 Were told upon the walls; staring forms
Leaned out, leaning, hushing the room enclosed.
Footsteps shuffled on the stair.
Under the firelight, under the brush, her hair
Spread out in fiery points
110 Glowed into words, then would be savagely still.

"My nerves are bad to-night. Yes, bad. Stay with me.
"Speak to me. Why do you never speak. Speak.
"What are you thinking of? What thinking? What?
"I never know what you are thinking. Think."

115 I think we are in rats' alley[1]
Where the dead men lost their bones.

"What is that noise?"
                The wind under the door.[2]
"What is that noise now? What is the wind doing?"
120   Nothing again nothing.
                            "Do
"You know nothing? Do you see nothing? Do you remember
"Nothing?"

---

5. "Laquearia. V. *Aeneid*, I, 726: dependent lychni laquearibus aureis / Incensi, et noctem flammis funalia vincunt" [Eliot's note]. "Lighted lamps hang from the golden paneled ceiling [*laquearia*], and the torches conquer the night with their flames" (Latin). The lines describe the banquet hall where Dido welcomes Aeneas to Carthage (her passion for the visitor, like Cleopatra's, ended in suicide.
6. With recessed panels.
7. "Sylvan scene. V. Milton, *Paradise Lost*, IV, 140" [Eliot's note]. The phrase occurs in the description of Eden as first seen by Satan.
8. "V. Ovid, *Metamorphoses*, VI, Philomela"

[Eliot's note]. Ovid describes how Tereus raped his sister-in-law, Philomela, and cut out her tongue. To avenge her, his wife, Procne, murdered her son and fed him to Tereus. All three are changed into birds: the sisters into the nightingale and swallow, Tereus into the hoopoe pursuing them.
9. "Cf. Part III, l. 204" [Eliot's note]. "Jug Jug": the conventional rendering of the nightingale's song in Elizabethan poetry.
1. "Cf. Part III, l. 195" [Eliot's note].
2. "Cf. Webster: 'Is the wind in that door still?'" [Eliot's note], referring to John Webster's play *The Devil's Law Case* 3.2.162 (1623). In context, the speaker is asking if someone is still alive.

I remember
125 Those are pearls that were his eyes.[3]
"Are you alive, or not? Is there nothing in your head?"

But
O O O O that Shakespeherian Rag—
It's so elegant
130 So intelligent
"What shall I do now? What shall I do?"
"I shall rush out as I am, and walk the street
"With my hair down, so. What shall we do tomorrow?
"What shall we ever do?"
135   The hot water at ten.
And if it rains, a closed car at four.
And we shall play a game of chess,
Pressing lidless eyes and waiting for a knock upon the door.[4]

When Lil's husband got demobbed,[5] I said—
140 I didn't mince my words, I said to her myself,
HURRY UP PLEASE ITS TIME[6]
Now Albert's coming back, make yourself a bit smart.
He'll want to know what you done with that money he gave you
To get yourself some teeth. He did, I was there.
145 You have them all out, Lil, and get a nice set,
He said, I swear, I can't bear to look at you.
And no more can't I, I said, and think of poor Albert,
He's been in the army four years, he wants a good time,
And if you don't give it him, there's others will, I said.
150 Oh is there, she said. Something o' that, I said.
Then I'll know who to thank, she said, and give me a straight look.
HURRY UP PLEASE ITS TIME
If you don't like it you can get on with it, I said.
Others can pick and choose if you can't.
155 But if Albert makes off, it won't be for lack of telling.
You ought to be ashamed, I said, to look so antique.
(And her only thirty-one.)
I can't help it, she said, pulling a long face,
It's them pills I took, to bring it off, she said.
160 (She's had five already, and nearly died of young George.)
The chemist° said it would be all right, but I've never been   druggist
       the same.
You *are* a proper fool, I said.
Well, if Albert won't leave you alone, there it is, I said,
What you get married for if you don't want children?
165 HURRY UP PLEASE ITS TIME
Well, that Sunday Albert was home, they had a hot
       gammon,°   smoked ham
And they asked me in to dinner, to get the beauty of it hot—
HURRY UP PLEASE ITS TIME

---

3. "Cf. Part I, ll. 37, 48" [Eliot's note]. See n. 3, p. 1237.
4. "Cf. the game of chess in Middleton's *Women Beware Women*" [Eliot's note].
5. Demobilized (discharged from military service) after World War I.
6. Typical call of a British bartender to clear the bar at closing time.

Hurry up please its time

170 Goonight Bill. Goonight Lou. Goonight May. Goonight.
Ta ta. Goonight. Goonight.
Good night, ladies, good night, sweet ladies, good night, good
night.[7]

III. The Fire Sermon[8]

The river's tent is broken: the last fingers of leaf
Clutch and sink into the wet bank. The wind
175 Crosses the brown land, unheard. The nymphs are departed
Sweet Thames, run softly, till I end my song.[9]
The river bears no empty bottles, sandwich papers,
Silk handkerchiefs, cardboard boxes, cigarette ends
Or other testimony of summer nights. The nymphs are departed.
180 And their friends, the loitering heirs of city directors;
Departed, have left no addresses.
By the waters of Leman I sat down and wept[1] . . .
Sweet Thames, run softly till I end my song,
Sweet Thames, run softly, for I speak not loud or long.
185 But at my back in a cold blast I hear[2]
The rattle of the bones, and chuckle spread from ear to ear.
A rat crept softly through the vegetation
Dragging its slimy belly on the bank
While I was fishing in the dull canal
190 On a winter evening round behind the gashouse
Musing upon the king my brother's wreck[3]
And on the king my father's death before him.
White bodies naked on the low damp ground
And bones cast in a little low dry garret,
195 Rattled by the rat's foot only, year to year.
But at my back from time to time I hear[4]
The sound of horns and motors, which shall bring[5]
Sweeney to Mrs. Porter in the spring.
O the moon shone bright on Mrs. Porter[6]
200 And on her daughter

---

7. Quoting Ophelia's farewell before drowning; see *Hamlet* 4.5.71–72.
8. The title is that of the Buddha's Fire Sermon; see Eliot's notes to lines 308 and 309, below.
9. "V. Spenser, *Prothalamion*" [Eliot's note]. The line is the refrain from Spenser's marriage song (1596), which celebrates a wedding near the Thames, the river that flows through London.
1. An echo of the exiled Jews in Psalm 137: "By the rivers of Babylon, there we sat down, yea, we wept, when we remembered Zion." Lac Léman is the Lake of Geneva, and much of *The Waste Land* was written at Lausanne, on its shore. *Leman* is also an archaic word for lover or mistress.
2. Echoes Marvell's "To His Coy Mistress" (1681); see pp. 435–36: "But at my back I always hear / Time's winged chariot hurrying near."
3. "Cf. *The Tempest*, I, ii" [Eliot's note]. Just before Ariel sings "Full fathom five thy father lies" (see line 48), Ferdinand describes himself as "sitting on a bank, / Weeping again the King my father's wreck. / This music crept by me upon the waters."
4. "Cf. Marvell, *To His Coy Mistress*" [Eliot's note]. See line 185.
5. "Cf. Day, *Parliament of Bees*: "When of the sudden, listening, you shall hear, / A noise of horns and hunting, which shall bring / Actaeon to Diana in the spring'" [Eliot's note]. Actaeon saw Diana, chaste goddess of the hunt, naked as she bathed; the goddess changed him into a stag, which his own hounds killed. John Day (1574–ca. 1640), English poet.
6. "I do not know the origin of the ballad from which these lines are taken: it was reported to me from Sydney, Australia" [Eliot's note]. The bawdy song was popular with Australian soldiers in World War I. Sweeney (line 198) is the figure of vulgar, thoughtless sexual enterprise who figures in Eliot's "Sweeney Among the Nightingales" and "Sweeney Agonistes."

They wash their feet in soda water
Et O ces voix d'enfants, chantant dans la coupole![7]

Twit twit twit
Jug jug jug jug jug jug
205 So rudely forc'd.
Tereu[8]

Unreal City[9]
Under the brown fog of a winter noon
Mr. Eugenides, the Smyrna merchant
210 Unshaven, with a pocket full of currants
C.i.f. London: documents at sight,[1]
Asked me in demotic[2] French
To luncheon at the Cannon Street Hotel
Followed by a weekend at the Metropole.[3]

215 At the violet hour, when the eyes and back
Turn upward from the desk, when the human engine waits
Like a taxi throbbing waiting,
I Tiresias, though blind, throbbing between two lives,[4]
Old man with wrinkled female breasts, can see
220 At the violet hour, the evening hour that strives
Homeward, and brings the sailor home from sea,[5]
The typist home at teatime, clears her breakfast, lights
Her stove, and lays out food in tins.
Out of the window perilously spread
225 Her drying combinations° touched by the sun's last rays,   *underwear*

---

7. "V. Verlaine, *Parsifal*" [Eliot's note]. Quoted is the concluding line of Verlaine's sonnet (1886), which treats ironically Parsifal's conquering of some forms of fleshly temptation, only to be haunted—even in his purity—by others: "And, O those children's voices singing in the dome!" (French). In Wagner's opera *Parsifal* (1882), the feet of the questing knight are washed before he enters the sanctuary of the Grail.
8. Another conventional Elizabethan rendering of the song of the nightingale, as well as a form of the name "Tereus" (see note to Part I, line 99, p. 1239.
9. See note to Part I, line 60, p. 1238.
1. "The currants were quoted at a price 'carriage and insurance free to London'; and the Bill of Lading etc. were to be handled to the buyer upon payment of the sight draft" [Eliot's note]. "C.i.f." should be "cost, insurance, and freight." "Smyrna": port in west Turkey.
2. I.e., vulgar or simplified.
3. A large hotel at Brighton, a seaside town on the south coast. "Cannon Street Hotel": a very large hotel in London's commercial district.
4. "Tiresias, although a mere spectator and not indeed a 'character,' is yet the most important personage in the poem, uniting all the rest. Just as the one-eyed merchant, seller of currants, melts into the Phoenician sailor, and the latter is not wholly distinct from Ferdinand Prince of Naples, so all the women are one woman, and the two sexes meet in Tiresias. What Tiresias *sees*, in fact, is the substance of the poem. The whole passage from Ovid is of great anthropological interest" [Eliot's note]. Eliot's note then cites in Latin Ovid's version of why Tiresias was blinded by a goddess and then granted a seer's power by Zeus (*Metamorphoses* 3.320–38): "Jove [very drunk] said jokingly to Juno: 'You women have greater pleasure in love than that enjoyed by men.' She denied it. So they decided to refer the question to wise Tiresias who knew love from both points of view. For once, with a blow of his staff, he had separated two huge snakes who were copulating in the forest, and miraculously was changed instantly from a man into a woman and remained so for seven years. In the eighth year he saw the snakes again and said: 'If a blow against you is so powerful that it changes the sex of the author of it, now I shall strike you again.' With these words he struck them, and his former shape and masculinity were restored. As referee in the sportive quarrel, he supported Jove's claim. Juno, overly upset by the decision, condemned the arbitrator to eternal blindness. But the all-powerful father (inasmuch as no god can undo what has been done by another god) gave him the power of prophecy, with this honor compensating him for the loss of sight."
5. "This may not appear as exact as Sappho's lines, but I had in mind the 'longshore' or 'dory' fisherman, who returns at nightfall" [Eliot's note]. Fragment 104a (L-P) of Sappho (Greek poet ca. 600 B.C.): "Evening, bringing all that light-giving dawn has scattered, you bring the sheep, you bring the goat, you bring the child to its mother." But cf. Robert Louis Stevenson's *Requiem* (1887): "Home is the sailor, home from the sea."

On the divan are piled (at night her bed)
Stockings, slippers, camisoles, and stays.
I Tiresias, old man with wrinkled dugs°   breasts
Perceived the scene, and foretold the rest—
230 I too awaited the expected guest.
He, the young man carbuncular,° arrives,   with pimples
A small house agent's clerk, with one bold stare,
One of the low on whom assurance sits
As a silk hat on a Bradford[6] millionaire.
235 The time is now propitious, as he guesses,
The meal is ended, she is bored and tired,
Endeavours to engage her in caresses
Which still are unreproved, if undesired.
Flushed and decided, he assaults at once;
240 Exploring hands encounter no defence;
His vanity requires no response,
And makes a welcome of indifference.
(And I Tiresias have foresuffered all
Enacted on this same divan or bed;
245 I who have sat by Thebes below the wall[7]
And walked among the lowest of the dead.)
Bestows one final patronizing kiss,
And gropes his way, finding the stairs unlit . . .

She turns and looks a moment in the glass,
250 Hardly aware of her departed lover;
Her brain allows one half-formed thought to pass:
"Well now that's done: and I'm glad it's over."
When lovely woman stoops to folly and[8]
Paces about her room again, alone,
255 She smoothes her hair with automatic hand,
And puts a record on the gramophone.

"This music crept by me upon the waters"[9]
And along the Strand, up Queen Victoria Street.
O City city, I can sometimes hear
260 Beside a public bar in Lower Thames Street,
The pleasant whining of a mandolin
And a clatter and a chatter from within
Where fishmen lounge at noon: where the walls
Of Magnus Martyr[1] hold
265 Inexplicable splendour of Ionian white and gold.

The river sweats[2]
Oil and tar

6. A manufacturing town in Yorkshire, England, that enjoyed an industrial boom during World War I.
7. Tiresias was a Theban seer (see note to line 218, p. 1242) whose prophecies played a part in the tragedies of Oedipus and Creon; he continued to prophesy in the underworld.
8. "V. Goldsmith, the song in The Vicar of Wakefield" [Eliot's note] (1766; see p. 627).
9. "V. The Tempest, as above" [Eliot's note]. See note to line 191, p. 1241.

1. "The interior of St. Magnus Martyr is to my mind one of the finest among [Christopher] Wren's interiors" [Eliot's note].
2. "The song of the (three) Thames-daughters begins here. From line 292 to 306 inclusive they speak in turn. V. Götterdämmerung, III, i: the Rhine-daughters" [Eliot's note]. Lines 277–78 and 290–91 repeat the refrain of the Rhine maidens lamenting the lost beauty of their river in Richard Wagner's 1876 opera.

The barges drift
With the turning tide
270   Red sails
Wide
To leeward, swing on the heavy spar.
The barges wash
Drifting logs
275   Down Greenwich reach
Past the Isle of Dogs.[3]
              Weialala leia
              Wallala leialala

Elizabeth and Leicester[4]
280   Beating oars
The stern was formed
A gilded shell
Red and gold
The brisk swell
285   Rippled both shores
Southwest wind
Carried down stream
The peal of bells
White towers
290   Weialala leia
              Wallala leialala

'Trams and dusty trees.
Highbury bore me.[5] Richmond and Kew
Undid me. By Richmond I raised my knees
295   Supine on the floor of a narrow canoe.'

"My feet are at Moorgate,[6] and my heart
Under my feet. After the event
He wept. He promised 'a new start.'
I made no comment. What should I resent?"

300   "On Margate Sands.[7]
I can connect
Nothing with nothing.
The broken fingernails of dirty hands.
My people humble people who expect
305   Nothing."
             la la

---

3. A tongue of land extending into the Thames opposite Greenwich, a borough of London.

4. "V. Froude, [*Reign of*] Elizabeth, Vol. I, ch. iv, letter of De Quadra to Philip of Spain: 'In the afternoon we were in a barge, watching the games on the river. (The queen) was alone with the Lord Robert and myself on the poop, when they began to talk nonsense, and went so far that Lord Robert at last said, as I was on the spot there was no reason why they should not be married if the queen pleased' " [Eliot's note]. Sir Robert Dudley (1532?–1588), earl of Leicester, was a favorite of the queen.

5. "Cf. Purgatorio, V, 133" [Eliot's note]. "Remember me, who am la Pia; Sien made me, the Maremma unmade me"; also quoted by Ezra Pound in *Hugh Selwyn Mauberley: Life and Contacts* (1920; see n. 7, p. 1194). Highbury is a residential suburb in North London; Richmond is the object of a pleasant excursion up the river from London; Kew is another excursion point, chiefly because of its botanical gardens.

6. A slum in East London.

7. A beach resort in Kent, popular with London residents, where the Thames broadens into the Channel.

To Carthage then I came[8]
Burning burning burning burning[9]
O Lord Thou pluckest me out[1]
310   O Lord Thou pluckest

burning

IV. Death by Water

Phlebas the Phoenician, a fortnight dead,
Forgot the cry of gulls, and the deep sea swell
And the profit and loss.
315   A current under sea
Picked his bones in whispers. As he rose and fell
He passed the stages of his age and youth
Entering the whirlpool.
                    Gentile or Jew
320   O you who turn the wheel and look to windward,
Consider Phlebas, who was once handsome and tall as you.

V. What the Thunder Said[2]

After the torchlight red on sweaty faces
After the frosty silence in the gardens
After the agony in stony places
325   The shouting and the crying
Prison and palace and reverberation
Of thunder of spring over distant mountains
He who was living is now dead
We who were living are now dying
330   With a little patience

Here is no water but only rock
Rock and no water and the sandy road
The road winding above among the mountains
Which are mountains of rock without water
335   If there were water we should stop and drink
Amongst the rock one cannot stop or think
Sweat is dry and feet are in the sand
If there were only water amongst the rock
Dead mountain mouth of carious° teeth that cannot spit   *decayed*
340   Here one can neither stand nor lie nor sit
There is not even silence in the mountains
But dry sterile thunder without rain
There is not even solitude in the mountains

8. "V. St. Augustine's *Confessions*: 'to Carthage then I came, where a cauldron of unholy loves sang all about mine ears' " [Eliot's note]. Augustine is recounting his licentious youth.
9. "Taken from the complete text of the Buddha's Fire Sermon (which corresponds in importance to the Sermon on the Mount)" [Eliot's note].
1. "From St. Augustine's *Confessions* again. The collocation of these two representatives of eastern and western asceticism, as the culmination of this part of the poem, is not an accident" [Eliot's note]. Cf. Zechariah 3.2, where the Lord calls Joshua "a

brand plucked out of the fire."
2. "In the first part of Part V three themes are employed: the journey to Emmaus, the approach to the Chapel Perilous (see Miss Weston's book) and the present decay of eastern Europe" [Eliot's note]. On the third day after his crucifixion, Jesus appeared to two of his disciples as they walked to Emmaus, a village, but they knew him only when he vanished (Luke 24.13–34). The Chapel Perilous is connected with the quest for the Holy Grail, in which only those of perfect purity can succeed.

But red sullen faces sneer and snarl
345 From doors of mudcracked houses
                    If there were water
        And no rock
        If there were rock
        And also water
350   And water
        A spring
        A pool among the rock
        If there were the sound of water only
        Not the cicada[3]
355   And dry grass singing
        But sound of water over a rock
        Where the hermit-thrush sings in the pine trees[4]
        Drip drop drip drop drop drop drop
        But there is no water

360   Who is the third who walks always beside you?
        When I count, there are only you and I together[5]
        But when I look ahead up the white road
        There is always another one walking beside you
        Gliding wrapt in a brown mantle, hooded
365   I do not know whether a man or a woman
        —But who is that on the other side of you?

        What is that sound high in the air[6]
        Murmur of maternal lamentation
        Who are those hooded hordes swarming
370   Over endless plains, stumbling in cracked earth
        Ringed by the flat horizon only
        What is the city over the mountains
        Cracks and reforms and bursts in the violet air
        Falling towers
375   Jerusalem Athens Alexandria
        Vienna London
        Unreal

        A woman drew her long black hair out tight
        And fiddled whisper music on those strings
380   And bats with baby faces in the violet light
        Whistled, and beat their wings
        And crawled head downward down a blackened wall
        And upside down in air were towers

---

3. Cf. Part I, line 23, and note there (p. 1236).
4. "This is . . . the hermit-thrush which I have heard in Quebec Province. . . . Its 'water-dripping song' is justly celebrated" [Eliot's note].
5. "The following lines were stimulated by the account of one of the Antarctic expeditions (I forget which, but I think one of Shackleton's): it was related that the party of explorers, at the extremity of their strength, had the constant delusion that there was *one more member* than could actually be counted" [Eliot's note]. These lines also recall the journey to Emmaus; see note 2, above.

6. Eliot's note to lines 366–76 quotes a passage from Hermann Hesse's *Blick ins Chaos* (1920; A Glimpse into Chaos) that may be translated as follows: "Already half Europe, already at least half of Eastern Europe, is on the road to Chaos, drives drunken in holy madness along the abyss and sings the while, sings drunk and hymnlike as Dmitri Karamazov sang [in *The Brother's Karamazov* (1882), by Feodor Dostoevsky]. The bourgeois laughs, offended, at these songs, the saint and the prophet hear them with tears."

Tolling reminiscent bells, that kept the hours
385 And voices singing out of empty cisterns and exhausted wells.

In this decayed hole among the mountains
In the faint moonlight, the grass is singing
Over the tumbled graves, about the chapel
There is the empty chapel, only the wind's home.
390 It has no windows, and the door swings,
Dry bones can harm no one.
Only a cock stood on the rooftree
Co co rico co co rico[7]
In a flash of lightning. Then a damp gust
395 Bringing rain

Ganga[8] was sunken, and the limp leaves
Waited for rain, while the black clouds
Gathered far distant, over Himavant.
The jungle crouched, humped in silence.
400 Then spoke the thunder
Da
Datta:[9] what have we given?
My friend, blood shaking my heart
The awful daring of a moment's surrender
405 Which an age of prudence can never retract
By this, and this only, we have existed
Which is not to be found in our obituaries
Or in memories draped by the beneficent spider[1]
Or under seals broken by the lean solicitor
410 In our empty rooms
Da
Dayadhvam: I have heard the key[2]
Turn in the door once and turn once only
We think of the key, each in his prison
415 Thinking of the key, each confirms a prison
Only at nightfall, ethereal rumours
Revive for a moment a broken Coriolanus[3]
Da

---

7. When Peter denied Jesus, "immediately the cock crew," as Jesus had predicted (Matthew 26.34, 74–75). Also, ghosts traditionally vanish at a cock's crow.
8. The Sanskrit name of the River Ganges. Himavant is a peak in the Himalayas.
9. " 'Datta, dayadhvam, damyata' (Give, sympathize, control). The fable of the meaning of the Thunder is found in the *Brihadaranyaka—Upanishad*, 5, [ii]" [Eliot's note]. In the legend, the offspring of Prajapati ask him to tell them their duty. To each he says *Da*, which each interprets differently: the gods understand it as "be restrained" *(damyata)*, humans as "give alms" *(datta)*, and demons as "have compassion" *(dayadhvam)*. All are correct, and *da* is repeated by a divine voice with the force of thunder.
1. "Cf. Webster, *The White Devil*, V. vi: '. . . they'll remarry / Ere the worm pierce your winding-sheet, ere the spider / Make a thin curtain for your epitaphs' " [Eliot's note].
2. "Cf. *Inferno*, XXXIII, 46" [Eliot's note], where Ugolino recalls his imprisonment with his sons in the tower where they starved to death: "And I heard below the door of the horrible tower being locked up." Eliot also cited F. H. Bradley, *Appearance and Reality* (1893), p. 346: "My external sensations are no less private to myself than are my thoughts or my feelings. In either case my experience falls within my own circle, a circle closed on the outside; and, with all its elements alike, every sphere is opaque to the others which surround it. . . . In brief, regarded as an existence which appears in a soul, the whole world for each is peculiar and private to that soul."
3. Legendary Roman patrician, and hero of Shakespeare's tragedy *Coriolanus*, who joins forces with the enemy he had once defeated when the leaders of the Roman populace opposed him.

Damyata: The boat responded
420 Gaily, to the hand expert with sail and oar
The sea was calm, your heart would have responded
Gaily, when invited, beating obedient
To controlling hands

                             I sat upon the shore
425 Fishing, with the arid plain behind me[4]
Shall I at least set my lands in order?[5]
London Bridge is falling down falling down falling down[6]
Poi s'ascose nel foco che gli affina[7]
Quando fiam uti chelidon[8]—O swallow swallow
430 *Le Prince d'Aquitaine à la tour abolie*[9]
These fragments I have shored against my ruins
Why then Ile fit you. Hieronymo's mad againe.[1]
Datta. Dayadhvam. Damyata.
           Shantih   shantih   shantih[2]

                                        1922

Journey of the Magi[3]

    "A cold coming we had of it,[4]
Just the worst time of the year
For a journey, and such a long journey:
The ways deep and the weather sharp,
5 The very dead of winter."
And the camels galled, sore-footed, refractory,
Lying down in the melting snow.
There were times we regretted
The summer palaces on slopes, the terraces,
10 And the silken girls bringing sherbet.
Then the camel men cursing and grumbling
And running away, and wanting their liquor and women,
And the night-fires going out, and the lack of shelters,

4. "V. Weston: *From Ritual to Romance*; chapter on the Fisher King" [Eliot's note].
5. Cf. Isaiah 38.1: "Thus saith the Lord, Set thine house in order: for thou shalt die, and not live."
6. One of the later lines of this nursery rhyme is "Take the key and lock her up, my fair lady."
7. "V. *Purgatorio*, XXVI, 148" [Eliot's note]. Eliot here quotes the final lines of Dante's encounter with Arnaut Daniel, the late-twelfth-century poet, encountered among the lustful in Purgatory: " 'And so I pray you, by that Virtue which guides you to the top of the stair, be reminded in time of my pain.' Then he hid himself in the fire that purifies them" (Italian). This last line appears above in Eliot's text.
8. "V. *Pervigilium Veneris*. Cf. Philomela in Parts I and II" [Eliot's note]. *The Vigil of Venus*, an anonymous Latin poem (ca. second century A.D.) celebrating the spring festival of Venus, ends with an allusion to the Procne-Philomela-Tereus myth. The quoted line means "When shall I become like the swallow"; the Latin continues, "that I may cease to be silent." "O swallow swallow": Cf. Swinburne's *Itylus*, which begins: "Swallow, my sister, O sister swallow, / How can thine heart be full of spring?"; cf. also Tennyson's lyric in *The Princess*: "O Swallow, Swallow, flying, flying south."
9. "V. Gérard de Nerval, Sonnet *El Desdichado*" [Eliot's note]. The line reads: "The prince of Aquitania in the ruined tower" (French).
1. "V. Kyd's *Spanish Tragedy*" [Eliot's note]. The subtitle of Kyd's *Spanish Tragedy* (1594) is *Hieronymo's Mad Againe*. Hieronymo, driven mad by his son's death, "fits" the parts in a court masque so that in the course of it he kills his son's murderers before himself committing suicide.
2. "Shantih. Repeated as here, a formal ending to an Upanishad. 'The Peace which passeth understanding' is our nearest equivalent to this word" [Eliot's note]. The Upanishads are philosophical treatises, part of the ancient Hindu sacred literature.
3. The poem re-creates the recollections of one of the three Wise Men, or Magi, who followed the star to Bethlehem bearing gifts for the newly born Jesus (see Matthew 2.1–2).
4. The first five lines are adapted from the sermon preached at Christmas, 1622, by Bishop Lancelot Andrewes.

And the cities hostile and the towns unfriendly
15 And the villages dirty and charging high prices:
A hard time we had of it.
At the end we preferred to travel all night,
Sleeping in snatches,
With the voices singing in our ears, saying
20 That this was all folly.

Then at dawn we came down to a temperate valley,
Wet, below the snow line, smelling of vegetation;
With a running stream and a water-mill beating the darkness,
And three trees on the low sky,[5]
25 And an old white horse galloped away in the meadow.
Then we came to a tavern with vine-leaves over the lintel,
Six hands at an open door dicing for pieces of silver,
And feet kicking the empty wine-skins.
But there was no information, and so we continued
30 And arrived at evening, not a moment too soon
Finding the place; it was (you may say) satisfactory.

All this was a long time ago, I remember,
And I would do it again, but set down
This set down
35 This: were we led all that way for
Birth or Death? There was a Birth, certainly,
We had evidence and no doubt. I had seen birth and death,
But had thought they were different; this Birth was
Hard and bitter agony for us, like Death, our death.
40 We returned to our places, these Kingdoms,
But no longer at ease here, in the old dispensation,
With an alien people clutching their gods.
I should be glad of another death.

1927

FROM FOUR QUARTETS

The Dry Salvages[6]

I

I do not know much about gods; but I think that the river[7]
Is a strong brown god—sullen, untamed and intractable,
Patient to some degree, at first recognized as a frontier;
Useful, untrustworthy, as a conveyor of commerce;
5 Then only a problem confronting the builder of bridges.
The problem once solved, the brown god is almost forgotten
By the dwellers in cities—ever, however, implacable,

5. The image prefigures the three crosses of the
Crucifixion, as line 27 suggests the Roman soldiers
dicing for Jesus' robe, as well as the pieces of silver
paid to Judas for betraying him.
6. Eliot's prefatory note to the poem is as follows:
"(The Dry Salvages—presumably *les trois sau-
vages*—is a small group of rocks, with a beacon, off

the N.E. coast of Cape Ann, Massachusetts. *Sal-
vages* is pronounced to rhyme with *assuages*.
Groaner: a whistling buoy)." The poem was pub-
lished as a separate pamphlet in 1941 and took its
place as the third of the *Four Quartets* in 1943.
7. Mississippi. Eliot was born and grew up in St.
Louis, Missouri.

Keeping his seasons and rages, destroyer, reminder
Of what men choose to forget. Unhonoured, unpropitiated
10 By worshippers of the machine, but waiting, watching and waiting.
His rhythm was present in the nursery bedroom,
In the rank ailanthus[8] of the April dooryard,
In the smell of grapes on the autumn table,
And the evening circle in the winter gaslight.

15   The river is within us, the sea is all about us;
The sea is the land's edge also, the granite
Into which it reaches, the beaches where it tosses
Its hints of earlier and other creation:
The starfish, the hermit crab, the whale's backbone;
20 The pools where it offers to our curiosity
The more delicate algae and the sea anemone.
It tosses up our losses, the torn seine,°   *fishing-net*
The shattered lobsterpot, the broken oar
And the gear of foreign dead men. The sea has many voices,
Many gods and many voices.
25   The salt is on the briar rose,
The fog is in the fir trees.
                              The sea howl
And the sea yelp, are different voices
Often together heard; the whine in the rigging,
The menace and caress of wave that breaks on water,
30 The distant rote° in the granite teeth,   *roar*
And the wailing warning from the approaching headland
Are all sea voices, and the heaving groaner
Rounded homewards,[9] and the seagull:
And under the oppression of the silent fog
35 The tolling bell
Measures time not our time, rung by the unhurried
Ground swell,[1] a time
Older than the time of chronometers, older
Than time counted by anxious worried women
40 Lying awake, calculating the future,[2]
Trying to unweave, unwind, unravel
And piece together the past and the future,
Between midnight and dawn, when the past is all deception,
The future futureless, before the morning watch
45 When time stops and time is never ending;
And the ground swell, that is and was from the beginning,
Clangs
The bell.

II

    Where is there an end of it, the soundless wailing,
50 The silent withering of autumn flowers

---

8. A large tree native to southeastern Asia, culti-
vated in Europe and America for shade: "rank"
both because of its vigorous growth and because of
the unpleasant smell of its flowers.
9. I.e., the buoy is rounded by a ship on its way

homewards.
1. Broad, deep swell of the ocean, caused by a dis-
tant storm.
2. In Greek and Roman mythology, weaving is
associated with the Fates.

Dropping their petals and remaining motionless;
Where is there an end to the drifting wreckage,
The prayer of the bone on the beach, the unprayable
Prayer at the calamitous annunciation?

55   There is no end, but addition: the trailing
Consequence of further days and hours,
While emotion takes to itself the emotionless
Years of living among the breakage
Of what was believed in as the most reliable—
60   And therefore the fittest for renunciation.

There is the final addition, the failing
Pride or resentment at failing powers,
The unattached devotion which might pass for devotionless,
In a drifting boat with a slow leakage,
65   The silent listening to the undeniable
Clamour of the bell of the last annunciation.

Where is the end of them, the fishermen sailing
Into the wind's tail, where the fog cowers?
We cannot think of a time that is oceanless
70   Or of an ocean not littered with wastage
Or of a future that is not liable
Like the past, to have no destination.

We have to think of them as forever baling,
Setting and hauling, while the North East lowers°   *looks threatening*
75   Over shallow banks unchanging and erosionless
Or drawing their money, drying sails at dockage;
Not as making a trip that will be unpayable
For a haul that will not bear examination.

There is no end of it, the voiceless wailing,
80   No end to the withering of withered flowers,
To the movement of pain that is painless and motionless,
To the drift of the sea and the drifting wreckage,
The bone's prayer to Death its God. Only the hardly, barely prayable
Prayer of the one Annunciation.[3]

85   It seems, as one becomes older,
That the past has another pattern, and ceases to be a mere
     sequence—
Or even development: the latter a partial fallacy,
Encouraged by superficial notions of evolution,
Which becomes, in the popular mind, a means of disowning the
     past.
90   The moments of happiness—not the sense of well-being,
Fruition, fulfilment, security or affection,
Or even a very good dinner, but the sudden illumination—
We had the experience but missed the meaning,

---

3. The submissive prayer made by Mary at the Annunciation by the angel that she is to become the
mother of Jesus: "Behold the handmaid of the Lord; be it unto me according to thy word" (Luke 1.38).

And approach to the meaning restores the experience
95   In a different form, beyond any meaning
We can assign to happiness. I have said before
That the past experience revived in the meaning
Is not the experience of one life only
But of many generations—not forgetting
100 Something that is probably quite ineffable:
The backward look behind the assurance
Of recorded history, the backward half-look
Over the shoulder, towards the primitive terror.
Now, we come to discover that the moments of agony
105 (Whether, or not, due to misunderstanding,
Having hoped for the wrong things or dreaded the wrong things,
Is not in question) are likewise permanent
With such permanence as time has. We appreciate this better
In the agony of others, nearly experienced,
110 Involving ourselves, than in our own.
For our own past is covered by the currents of action,
But the torment of others remains an experience
Unqualified, unworn by subsequent attrition.
People change, and smile: but the agony abides.
115 Time the destroyer is time the preserver,
Like the river with its cargo of dead Negroes, cows and chicken
         coops,
The bitter apple and the bite in the apple.
And the ragged rock in the restless waters,
Waves wash over it, fogs conceal it;
120 On a halcyon° day it is merely a monument,   calm
In navigable weather it is always a seamark
To lay a course by: but in the sombre season
Or the sudden fury, is what it always was.

III

I sometimes wonder if that is what Krishna[4] meant—
125 Among other things—or one way of putting the same thing:
That the future is a faded song, a Royal Rose or a lavender spray
Of wistful regret for those who are not yet here to regret,
Pressed between yellow leaves of a book that has never been opened.
And the way up is the way down,[5] the way forward is the way back.
130 You cannot face it steadily, but this thing is sure,
That time is no healer: the patient is no longer here.
When the train starts, and the passengers are settled
To fruit, periodicals and business letters
(And those who saw them off have left the platform)
135 Their faces relax from grief into relief,
To the sleepy rhythm of a hundred hours.
Fare forward, travellers! not escaping from the past
Into different lives, or into any future;

---

4. An incarnation of the Hindu god Vishnu, the Preserver; his teachings are preserved in the *Bhagavad-Gītā* ("Song of the Lord"), which forms a part of the Hindu epic of the *Mahābhārata*. Eliot considered the *Bhagavad-Gītā* "the next greatest philosophical poem" to Dante's *Divine Comedy*.
5. "Burnt Norton," the first of the *Four Quartets*, bears two epigraphs from the Greek philosopher Heraclitus (ca. 540–475 B.C.): one of them is "The way up and the way down are one and the same."

You are not the same people who left that station
140 Or who will arrive at any terminus,
While the narrowing rails slide together behind you;
And on the deck of the drumming liner
Watching the furrow that widens behind you,
You shall not think "the past is finished"
145 Or "the future is before us".
At nightfall, in the rigging and the aerial,
Is a voice descanting[6] (though not to the ear,
The murmuring shell of time, and not in any language)
"Fare forward, you who think that you are voyaging;
150 You are not those who saw the harbour
Receding, or those who will disembark.
Here between the hither and the farther shore
While time is withdrawn, consider the future
And the past with an equal mind.
155 At the moment which is not of action or inaction
You can receive this: 'on whatever sphere of being
The mind of a man may be intent
At the time of death'[7]—that is the one action
(And the time of death is every moment)
160 Which shall fructify° in the lives of others: bear fruit
And do not think of the fruit of action.
Fare forward.
                         O voyagers, O seamen,
You who come to port, and you whose bodies
Will suffer the trial and judgment of the sea,
165 Or whatever event, this is your real destination".
So Krishna, as when he admonished Arjuna
On the field of battle.
                         Not fare well,
But fare forward, voyagers.

IV

Lady,[8] whose shrine stands on the promontory,
170 Pray for all those who are in ships, those
Whose business has to do with fish, and
Those concerned with every lawful traffic
And those who conduct them.

Repeat a prayer also on behalf of
175 Women who have seen their sons or husbands
Setting forth, and not returning:
Figlia del tuo figlio,[9]
Queen of Heaven.

Also pray for those who were in ships, and
180 Ended their voyage on the sand, in the sea's lips

6. Holding forth on a subject.
7. The quoted passage comes from the *Bhagavad-Gītā*. Arjuna, the hero of the poem, has hesitated to fight, and Krishna says: "On whatever sphere of being the mind of a man may be intent at the time of death, thither will he go. / Therefore meditate always on Me, and fight; if thy mind and thy reason be fixed on Me, to Me shalt thou surely come" [tr. by Shri Purohit Swāmi].
8. The Virgin Mary.
9. "The daughter of Thy Son." From St. Bernard's prayer to Mary in Dante, *Paradiso* 33.1.

Or in the dark throat which will not reject them
Or wherever cannot reach them the sound of the sea bell's
Perpetual angelus.[1]

V

To communicate with Mars, converse with spirits,
185 To report the behaviour of the sea monster,
Describe the horoscope, haruspicate or scry,[2]
Observe disease in signatures, evoke
Biography from the wrinkles of the palm
And tragedy from fingers; release omens
190 By sortilege,[3] or tea leaves, riddle the inevitable
With playing cards, fiddle with pentagrams[4]
Or barbituric acids, or dissect
The recurrent image into pre-conscious terrors—
To explore the womb, or tomb, or dreams; all these are usual
195 Pastimes and drugs, and features of the press:
And always will be, some of them especially
When there is distress of nations and perplexity
Whether on the shores of Asia, or in the Edgware Road.[5]
Men's curiosity searches past and future
200 And clings to that dimension. But to apprehend
The point of intersection of the timeless
With time, is an occupation for the saint—
No occupation either, but something given
And taken, in a lifetime's death in love,
205 Ardour and selflessness and self-surrender.
For most of us, there is only the unattended
Moment, the moment in and out of time,
The distraction fit, lost in a shaft of sunlight,
The wild thyme unseen, or the winter lightning
210 Or the waterfall, or music heard so deeply
That it is not heard at all, but you are the music
While the music lasts. These are only hints and guesses,
Hints followed by guesses; and the rest
Is prayer, observance, discipline, thought and action.
215 The hint half guessed, the gift half understood, is Incarnation.[6]
Here the impossible union
Of spheres of existence is actual,
Here the past and future
Are conquered, and reconciled,
220 Where action were otherwise movement
Of that which is only moved
And has in it no source of movement—

---

1. A Roman Catholic devotion commemorating the Incarnation, so called from its first word (*Angelus domini nuntiavit Mariae:* "The angel of the lord announced to Mary" [Latin]); it is repeated at morning, noon, and sunset, at the sound of a bell (also called *angelus*).
2. See visions in a crystal; "horoscope": i.e., foretell the future from the positions of the planets at a given time; "haruspicate": interpret the will of the gods by examining the entrails of sacrificed birds or animals.
3. Divination by drawing lots.
4. Five-pointed diagrams containing figures and symbols used in divination and sorcery.
5. A busy but unremarkable street in London.
6. I.e., the union of divinity with humanity in Jesus Christ.

Driven by daemonic, chthonic[7]
Powers. And right action is freedom
225 From past and future also.
For most of us, this is the aim
Never here to be realized;
Who are only undefeated
Because we have gone on trying;
230 We, content at the last
If our temporal reversion nourish
(Not too far from the yew-tree)[8]
The life of significant soil.

1941

JOHN CROWE RANSOM

1888–1974

Bells for John Whiteside's Daughter

There was such speed in her little body,
And such lightness in her footfall,
It is no wonder her brown study
Astonishes us all.

5 Her wars were bruited° in our high window.   *loudly voiced*
We looked among orchard trees and beyond
Where she took arms against her shadow,
Or harried unto the pond

The lazy geese, like a snow cloud
10 Dripping their snow on the green grass,
Tricking and stopping, sleepy and proud,
Who cried in goose, Alas,

For the tireless heart within the little
Lady with rod that made them rise
15 From their noon apple-dreams and scuttle
Goose-fashion under the skies!

But now go the bells, and we are ready,
In one house we are sternly stopped
To say we are vexed at her brown study,
20 Lying so primly propped.

1924

7. From the underworld (literally, "from the earth").
8. Throughout the *Four Quartets*, the yew-tree is a recurrent symbol for death, variously counterpointed or combined with the rose, a symbol of life.

Piazza¹ Piece

   —I am a gentleman in a dustcoat trying
   To make you hear. Your ears are soft and small
   And listen to an old man not at all,
   They want the young men's whispering and sighing.
5 But see the roses on your trellis dying
   And hear the spectral singing of the moon;
   For I must have my lovely lady soon,
   I am a gentleman in a dustcoat trying.

   —I am a lady young in beauty waiting
10 Until my truelove comes, and then we kiss.
   But what gray man among the vines is this
   Whose words are dry and faint as in a dream?
   Back from my trellis, Sir, before I scream!
   I am a lady young in beauty waiting.

1925   1927

Blue Girls

   Twirling your blue skirts, travelling the sward°   *grass, turf*
   Under the towers of your seminary,
   Go listen to your teachers old and contrary
   Without believing a word.

5 Tie the white fillets° then about your hair   *ribbons*
   And think no more of what will come to pass
   Than bluebirds that go walking on the grass
   And chattering on the air.

   Practise your beauty, blue girls, before it fail;
10 And I will cry with my loud lips and publish
   Beauty which all our power shall never establish,
   It is so frail.

   For I could tell you a story which is true;
   I know a woman with a terrible tongue,
15 Blear° eyes fallen from blue,   *bleary*
   All her perfections tarnished—yet it is not long
   Since she was lovelier than any of you.

                                          1927

Parting, without a Sequel

   She has finished and sealed the letter
   At last, which he so richly has deserved,
   With characters venomous and hatefully curved,
   And nothing could be better.

1. Porch.

5   But even as she gave it
Saying to the blue-capped functioner of doom,
"Into his hands," she hoped the leering groom
Might somewhere lose and leave it.

Then all the blood
10   Forsook the face. She was too pale for tears,
Observing the ruin of her younger years.
She went and stood

Under her father's vaunting oak
Who kept his peace in wind and sun, and glistened
15   Stoical in the rain; to whom she listened
If he spoke.

And now the agitation of the rain
Rasped his sere leaves, and he talked low and gentle
Reproaching the wan daughter by the lintel;
20   Ceasing and beginning again.

Away went the messenger's bicycle,
His serpent's track went up the hill forever,
And all the time she stood there hot as fever
And cold as any icicle.

1927

Lady Lost

This morning, flew up the lane
A timid lady bird to our birdbath
And eyed her image dolefully as death;
This afternoon, knocked on our windowpane
5   To be let in from the rain.

And when I caught her eye
She looked aside, but at the clapping thunder
And sight of the whole world blazing up like tinder
Looked in on us again so miserably
10   It was as if she would cry.

So I will go out into the park and say,
"Who has lost a delicate brown-eyed lady
In the West End section? Or has anybody
Injured some fine woman in some dark way
15   Last night, or yesterday?

"Let the owner come and claim possession,
No questions will be asked. But stroke her gently
With loving words, and she will evidently
Return to her full soft-haired white-breasted fashion
20   And her right home and her right passion."

1927

Dead Boy

The little cousin is dead, by foul subtraction,
A green bough from Virginia's aged tree,
And none of the county kin like the transaction,
Nor some of the world of outer dark, like me.

5 A boy not beautiful, nor good, nor clever,
A black cloud full of storms too hot for keeping,
A sword beneath his mother's heart—yet never
Woman bewept her babe as this is weeping.

A pig with a pasty face, so I had said,
10 Squealing for cookies, kinned by poor pretense
With a noble house. But the little man quite dead,
I see the forbears' antique lineaments.

The elder men have strode by the box of death
To the wide flag porch, and muttering low send round
15 The bruit° of the day. O friendly waste of breath!   news, report
Their hearts are hurt with a deep dynastic wound.

He was pale and little, the foolish neighbors say;
The first-fruits, saith the Preacher, the Lord hath taken;[2]
But this was the old tree's late branch wrenched away,
20 Grieving the sapless limbs, the shorn and shaken.

1927

CONRAD AIKEN

1889–1973

From Senlin:[1] A Biography

II. *His Futile Preoccupations,* 2[2]

It is morning, Senlin says, and in the morning
When the light drips through the shutters like the dew,
I arise, I face the sunrise,
And do the things my fathers learned to do.
5 Stars in the purple dusk above the rooftops
Pale in a saffron mist and seem to die,
And I myself on a swiftly tilting planet
Stand before a glass and tie my tie.

---

2. Cf. the commandment of God in Exodus 22.29: "Thou shalt not delay to offer the first of thy ripe fruits, and of thy liquors. The firstborn of thy sons shalt thou give unto me."
1. An invented name that, according to Aiken's preface to *The Divine Pilgrim* (1949), "means literally the 'little old man' that each of us must become . . . "; the poem poses "the basic and possibly unanswerable question, *who and what am I,* how is it that I am I, Senlin, and not someone else?"
2. This section has also been published separately under the title "Morning Song."

Vine leaves tap my window,
10 Dew-drops sing to the garden stones,
    The robin chirps in the chinaberry tree
    Repeating three clear tones.

    It is morning. I stand by the mirror
    And tie my tie once more.
15 While waves far off in a pale rose twilight
    Crash on a coral shore.
    I stand by a mirror and comb my hair:
    How small and white my face! —
    The green earth tilts through a sphere of air
20 And bathes in a flame of space.

    There are houses hanging above the stars
    And stars hung under a sea.
    And a sun far off in a shell of silence
    Dapples my walls for me.

25 It is morning, Senlin says, and in the morning
    Should I not pause in the light to remember god?
    Upright and firm I stand on a star unstable,
    He is immense and lonely as a cloud.[3]
    I will dedicate this moment before my mirror
30 To him alone, for him I will comb my hair.
    Accept these humble offerings, cloud of silence!
    I will think of you as I descend the stair.

    Vine leaves tap my window,
    The snail-track shines on the stones,
35 Dew-drops flash from the chinaberry tree
    Repeating two clear tones.

    It is morning, I awake from a bed of silence,
    Shining I rise from the starless waters of sleep.
    The walls are about me still as in the evening,
40 I am the same, and the same name still I keep.
    The earth revolves with me, yet makes no motion,
    The stars pale silently in a coral sky.
    In a whistling void I stand before my mirror,
    Unconcerned, and tie my tie.

45 There are horses neighing on far-off hills
    Tossing their long white manes,
    And mountains flash in the rose-white dusk,
    Their shoulders black with rains.
    It is morning. I stand by the mirror
50 And surprise my soul once more;
    The blue air rushes above my ceiling,
    There are suns beneath my floor.

---

3. An allusion to "I Wandered Lonely As a Cloud" (pp. 732–33) by the English poet William Wordsworth (1770–1850).

. . . It is morning, Senlin says, I ascend from darkness
And depart on the winds of space for I know not where,
My watch is wound, a key is in my pocket,
And the sky is darkened as I descend the stair.
There are shadows across the windows, clouds in heaven,
And a god among the stars; and I will go
Thinking of him as I might think of daybreak
And humming a tune I know.

Vine leaves tap at the window,
Dewdrops sing to the garden stones,
The robin chirps in the chinaberry tree
Repeating three clear tones.

1918

IVOR GURNEY

1890–1937

To His Love

He's gone, and all our plans
    Are useless indeed.
We'll walk no more on Cotswold[1]
    Where the sheep feed
    Quietly and take no heed.

His body that was so quick
    Is not as you
Knew it, on Severn river
    Under the blue
    Driving our small boat through.

You would not know him now . . .
    But still he died
Nobly, so cover him over
    With violets of pride
    Purple from Severn side.

Cover him, cover him soon!
    And with thick-set
Masses of memoried flowers—
    Hide that red wet
    Thing I must somehow forget.

1919

---

1. Range of hills in Gloucestershire, in western England.

Towards Lillers[2]

In October marching, taking the sweet air,
Packs riding lightly, and homethoughts soft coming,
"This is right marching, we are even glad to be here,
Or very glad?" But looking upward to dark smoke foaming,
5   Chimneys on the clear crest, no more shades for roaming,
Smoke covering sooty what man's heart holds dear,
Lillers we approached, a quench for thirsty frames,
And looked once more between houses and at queer names
Of estaminets,° longed for cool wine or cold beer.   *cafés*
10   This was war; we understood; moving and shifting about;
To stand or be withstood in the mixèd rout
Of fight to come after this. But that was a good dream
Of justice or strength-test with steel tool a gleam
Made to the hand. But barb-wire lay to the front,
15   Tiny aeroplanes circled as ever their wont
High over the two ditches of heart-sick men;
The times scientific, as evil as ever again.
October lovely bathing with sweet air the plain.

Gone outward to the east and the new skies
20   Are aeroplanes, and flat there as tiny as bright
As insects wonderful coloured after the night
Emerging lovely as ever into the new day's
First coolness and lucent gratefulness
Of the absorbing wide prayer of middle sight.
25   Men clean their rifles insentient at that delight;
Wonder increases as fast as the night dies.

Now up to the high above aeroplanes go
Swift bitter smoke puffs and spiteful flames,
None knows the pilots, none guesses at their names,
30   They fly unthought courses of common danger,
Honour rides on the frame with them through that anger,
As the heroes of Marathon[3] their renown we know.

1933

The Silent One

Who died on the wires,[4] and hung there, one of two—
Who for his hours of life had chattered through
Infinite lovely chatter of Bucks[5] accent:
Yet faced unbroken wires; stepped over, and went
5   A noble fool, faithful to his stripes—and ended.
But I weak, hungry, and willing only for the chance
Of line—to fight in the line, lay down under unbroken
Wires, and saw the flashes and kept unshaken,
Till the politest voice—a finicking accent, said:

2. In northwestern France, close to the front line.
3. The battle in which the Athenians defeated the invading Persians in 490 B.C., thus ending the first Persian War.
4. The barbed wire protecting the front from infantry attack.
5. Buckinghamshire, in southern England.

10   "Do you think you might crawl through there: there's a hole."
     Darkness, shot at: I smiled, as politely replied—
     "I'm afraid not, Sir." There was no hole no way to be seen
     Nothing but chance of death, after tearing of clothes.
     Kept flat, and watched the darkness, hearing bullets whizzing—
15   And thought of music—and swore deep heart's deep oaths
     (Polite to God) and retreated and came on again,
     Again retreated—and a second time faced the screen.

1954

First Time In

     After the dread tales and red yarns of the Line
     Anything might have come to us; but the divine
     Afterglow brought us up to a Welsh colony
     Hiding in sandbag ditches, whispering consolatory
5   Soft foreign things. Then we were taken in
     To low huts candle-lit, shaded close by slitten°   *slit*
     Oilsheets, and there the boys gave us kind welcome,
     So that we looked out as from the edge of home,
     Sang us Welsh things, and changed all former notions
10   To human hopeful things. And the next day's guns
     Nor any line-pangs ever quite could blot out
     That strangely beautiful entry to war's rout;
     Candles they gave us, precious and shared over-rations—
     Ulysses[6] found little more in his wanderings without doubt.
15   "David of the White Rock", the "Slumber Song" so soft, and that
     Beautiful tune to which roguish words by Welsh pit boys
     Are sung—but never more beautiful than there under the guns' noise.

1919–20   1982

ISAAC ROSENBERG

1890–1918

Break of Day in the Trenches

     The darkness crumbles away.
     It is the same old druid[1] Time as ever,
     Only a live thing leaps my hand,
     A queer sardonic rat,
5   As I pull the parapet's[2] poppy
     To stick behind my ear.
     Droll rat, they would shoot you if they knew
     Your cosmopolitan sympathies.
     Now you have touched this English hand
10   You will do the same to a German

6. The hero of Homer's *Odyssey*, who spent ten years wandering on his way home to Ithaca after the Trojan War.

1. Member of an ancient Celtic order of priest-magicians.
2. Wall protecting a trench in World War I.

Soon, no doubt, if it be your pleasure
To cross the sleeping green between.
It seems you inwardly grin as you pass
Strong eyes, fine limbs, haughty athletes,
15   Less chanced than you for life,
Bonds to the whims of murder,
Sprawled in the bowels of the earth,
The torn fields of France.
What do you see in our eyes
20   At the shrieking iron and flame
Hurled through still heavens?
What quaver—what heart aghast?
Poppies whose roots are in man's veins
Drop, and are ever dropping;
25   But mine in my ear is safe—
Just a little white with the dust.

Louse Hunting

Nudes—stark and glistening,
Yelling in lurid glee. Grinning faces
And raging limbs
Whirl over the floor one fire.
5   For a shirt verminously busy
Yon soldier tore from his throat, with oaths
Godhead might shrink at, but not the lice.
And soon the shirt was aflare
Over the candle he'd lit while we lay.

10   Then we all sprang up and stript
To hunt the verminous brood.
Soon like a demons' pantomime
The place was raging.
See the silhouettes agape,
15   See the gibbering shadows
Mixed with the battled arms on the wall.
See gargantuan hooked fingers
Pluck in supreme flesh
To smutch supreme littleness.
20   See the merry limbs in hot Highland fling[3]
Because some wizard vermin
Charmed from the quiet this revel
When our ears were half lulled
By the dark music
25   Blown from Sleep's trumpet.

Dead Man's Dump

The plunging limbers[4] over the shattered track
Racketed with their rusty freight,

3. Scottish dance.
4. Two-wheeled vehicles for pulling guns or caissons.

Struck out like many crowns of thorns,
And the rusty stakes like sceptres old
5   To stay the flood of brutish men
Upon our brothers dear.

The wheels lurched over sprawled dead
But pained them not, though their bones crunched,
Their shut mouths made no moan.
10   They lie there huddled, friend and foeman,
Man born of man, and born of woman,
And shells go crying over them
From night till night and now.

Earth has waited for them
15   All the time of their growth
Fretting for their decay:
Now she has them at last!
In the strength of their strength
Suspended—stopped and held.

20   What fierce imaginings their dark souls lit
Earth! have they gone into you?
Somewhere they must have gone,
And flung on your hard back
Is their souls' sack,
25   Emptied of God-ancestralled essences.
Who hurled them out? Who hurled?

None saw their spirits' shadow shake the grass,
Or stood aside for the half used life to pass
Out of those doomed nostrils and the doomed mouth,
30   When the swift iron burning bee
Drained the wild honey of their youth.

What of us, who flung on the shrieking pyre,
Walk, our usual thoughts untouched,
Our lucky limbs as on ichor[5] fed,
35   Immortal seeming ever?
Perhaps when the flames beat loud on us,
A fear may choke in our veins
And the startled blood may stop.

The air is loud with death,
40   The dark air spurts with fire
The explosions ceaseless are.
Timelessly now, some minutes past,
These dead strode time with vigorous life,
Till the shrapnel called "an end!"
45   But not to all. In bleeding pangs
Some borne on stretchers dreamed of home,
Dear things, war-blotted from their hearts.

5. In Greek mythology, the ethereal fluid flowing through the veins of the gods.

A man's brains splattered on
A stretcher-bearer's face;
50 His shook shoulders slipped their load,
But when they bent to look again
The drowning soul was sunk too deep
For human tenderness.

They left this dead with the older dead,
55 Stretched at the cross roads.

Burnt black by strange decay,
Their sinister faces lie
The lid over each eye,
The grass and coloured clay
60 More motion have than they,
Joined to the great sunk silences.

Here is one not long dead;
His dark hearing caught our far wheels,
And the choked soul stretched weak hands
65 To reach the living word the far wheels said,
The blood-dazed intelligence beating for light,
Crying through the suspense of the far torturing wheels
Swift for the end to break,
Or the wheels to break,
70 Cried as the tide of the world broke over his sight.

Will they come? Will they ever come?
Even as the mixed hoofs of the mules,
The quivering-bellied mules,
And the rushing wheels all mixed
75 With his tortured upturned sight,
So we crashed round the bend,
We heard his weak scream,
We heard his very last sound,
And our wheels grazed his dead face.

1922

HUGH MacDIARMID
(CHRISTOPHER MURRAY GRIEVE)
1892–1978

From Lament for the Great Music

Yet there is no great problem in the world to-day
Except disease and death men cannot end
If no man tries to dominate another.
The struggle for material existence is over. It has been won.
5 The need for repressions and disciplines has passed.
The struggle for truth and that indescribable necessity,

Beauty, begins now, hampered by none of the lower needs.
No one now needs live less or be less than his utmost.
And in the slow and devious development that has brought men to
    this stage
10 Scottish genius has played a foremost role. Yet I turn to you,
For unselfish intellect rises like a perfume
Above the faults and follies of the world of will.
But for the excellence of the typical swift life no nation
Deserves to be remembered more than the sands of the sea.

15 I am only that Job[1] in feathers, a heron myself,
Gaunt and unsubstantial—yet immune to the vicissitudes
Other birds accept as a matter of course; impervious to the effects
Of even the wildest weather, no mean consideration in a country
    like this;
And my appetite is not restricted to any particular fare.
20 Hence I am encountered in places far removed from one another
And widely different in an intimately topographical sense
—Spearing a rat at the mouth of a culvert at midnight
And bolting an eel on the seashore in the halflight of dawn—
Communal dweller yet lone hunter, lumbering yet swift and
    sustained flier,
25 The usual steely expression of my eyes does not flatter me;
Few birds perhaps have so successfully solved
The problem of existence as my grey lanky self
That in light or darkness, wet or shine, subsists
By a combination of alertness, patience, and passivity.
30 A kind of Caolite mac Ronain[2] too; but it takes
    All my wits in Scotland to-day.

This is the darkness where you have been; and have left
I think forever. It is the darkness from which nothing is cast out,
No loss, no wanton pain, no disease, no insanity,
35 None of the unripe intelligence of so-called dead nature,
Abortive attempts of nature to reflect itself.
All the unintelligible burden that alone leads to the height
Where it seems that extremes meet and I could reach you
i bh-fogus do dhul ar neamh-nidh,[3] with a *leim eanamhail.*
40 In this depth that I dare not leave
I who am no dilettante of chaos and find
No bitter gratification in the contemplation of ultimate Incoherence
Know that the world is at any given moment anything it may be
    called
And even more difficult to group round any central character,
45 Yet it is out of this aimless dispersion, all these zig-zagging efforts,
All this disorderly growth, that the ideal of an epoch ends
By disentangling itself. Myriads of human activities

1. Biblical character who has come to represent patience in adversity.
2. "The grey spare swift runner, he who saved Fionn once by that wonderful feat of gathering couples of all the wild beasts and birds of Ireland (a ram and a crimson sheep from Inis, two water-birds from the Erne, two cormorants from the Cliannth, two foxes from Slieve Gullion, and the rest)" [MacDiarmid's note].
3. "On the confines of vanishing" (Gaelic); *leim eanamhail:* "birdlike leap" (Gaelic).

Are scattered in all directions by the indifferent forces
Of self-interest, passion, crime, madness—but out of their number
50 Some few of these activities are endowed with a little constancy
By the pure in heart, for reasons which seem to respond
To the most elementary designs of the spirit.
Civilisation, culture, all the good in the world
Depends ultimately on the existence of a few men of good will.
55 The perspective will converge upon them yet.
I dare not leave this dark and distracted scene.
I believe in the necessary and unavoidable responsibility of man
And in the ineluctable certainty of the resurrection
And know that the mind of man creates no ideas
60 Though it is ideas alone that create.
Mind is the organ through which the Universe reaches
Such consciousness of itself as is possible now, and I must not brood
On the intermittence of genius, the way consciousness varies
Or declines, as in Scotland here, till it seems
65 Heaven itself may be only the best that is feasible
For most people, but a sad declension from music like yours.
Yes, I am prepared to see the Heavens open
And find the celestial music poor by comparison.
Yet my duty is here. It is now the duty of the Scottish genius
70 Which has provided the economic freedom for it
To lead in the abandonment of creeds and moral compromises
Of every sort and to commence to express the unity of life
By confounding the curse of short-circuited thought
Circumscribing consciousness, for that is the thought
75 Of compromise, the medium of the time-server.
This must be done to lead men to cosmic consciousness
And as it cannot be quick, except on occasion
And *that* the creative instant, the moment of divine realisation,
When the self is lit up by its own inner light
80 Caused in the self by its intensity of thought
Possibly over a long period, it must be thought of as a craft
In which the consummation of the idea, not in analysis but in
      synthesis,
Must be the subject of the object—life.
Wherefore I cannot take the bird-like leap to you
85 Though well I know that: "He that can endure
To follow with allegiance a fallen lord
Does conquer him that did his master conquer."

I dare not leap to you now. But after all since I cannot believe
You will ever be really for everyone or even for many
90 And are likely to pursue in the hereafter
A separate destiny from theirs—or simply because
I long to hear the great pipers play their great music themselves.
And they all dead (save one) centuries before I was born,
And have one glimpse of my beloved Scotland yet
95 As the land I have dreamt of where the supreme values
Which the people recognise are states of mind
Their ruling passion the attainment of higher consciousness,
And their actual rulers those in whom they find,

Or think they do, the requisite knowledge for such attainments
100 And where one is not required to believe anything
But even warned of the dangers of doing so
Except with infinite qualifications and care,
My duty done, I will try to follow you on the last day of the world,
And pray I may see you all standing shoulder to shoulder
105 With Patrick Mor MacCrimmon and Duncan Ban MacCrimmon
in the centre
In the hollow[4] at Boreraig or in front of Dunvegan Castle
Or on the lip of the broken graves in Kilmuir Kirkyard[5]
While, the living stricken ghastly in the eternal light
And the rest of the dead all risen blue-faced from their graves
110 (Though, the pipes to your hand, you will be once more
Perfectly at ease, and as you were in your prime)
All ever born crowd the islands and the West Coast of Scotland
Which has standing room for them all, and the air curdled with
angels,
And everywhere that feeling seldom felt on the earth before
115 Save in the hearts of parents or in youth untouched by tragedy
That in its very search for personal experience often found
A like impersonality and self-forgetfulness,
And you playing: "Farewell to Scotland, and the rest of the Earth,"
The only fit music there can be for that day
120 —And I will leap then and hide behind one of you,
Us Caismeachd phiob-mora bras shroiceadh am puirt.[6]

Look! Is that only the setting sun again?
Or a piper coming from far away?

1934

Another Epitaph on an Army of Mercenaries[7]

It is a God-damned lie to say that these
Saved, or knew, anything worth any man's pride.
They were professional murderers and they took
Their blood money and impious risks and died.
5 In spite of all their kind some elements of worth
With difficulty persist here and there on earth.

1935

4. I.e., the pipers' hollow where the students at the college of the MacCrimmons (1500–1800) practiced. Ten generations of MacCrimmons were the hereditary pipers of MacLeod of MacLeod, whose seat is at Dunvegan Castle in the Isle of Skye. Boreraig was where the MacCrimmons lived.
5. Near Dunvegan.

6. "While the notes of the great pipes shrilly sounded out their cries" (Gaelic; from Alasdair MacMhaighstir Alasdair).
7. "In reply to A. E. Housman's" [MacDiarmid's note]. See A. E. Housman's poem "Epitaph on an Army of Mercenaries" (pp. 1074–75).

Perfect[8]

ON THE WESTERN SEABOARD OF SOUTH UIST

Los muertos abren los ojos a los que viven[9]

I found a pigeon's skull on the machair,[1]
All the bones pure white and dry, and chalky,
But perfect,
Without a crack or a flaw anywhere.

5   At the back, rising out of the beak,
Were domes like bubbles of thin bone,
Almost transparent, where the brain had been
That fixed the tilt of the wings.

1939

From In Memoriam James Joyce

We Must Look at the Harebell[2]

We must look at the harebell as if
We had never seen it before.
Remembrance gives an accumulation of satisfaction
Yet the desire for change is very strong in us
5   And change is in itself a recreation.
To those who take any pleasure
In flowers, plants, birds, and the rest
An ecological change is recreative.
(Come. Climb with me. Even the sheep are different
10   And of new importance.
The coarse-fleeced, hardy Herdwick,
The Hampshire Down, artificially fed almost from birth,
And butcher-fat from the day it is weaned,
The Lincoln-Longwool, the biggest breed in England,
15   With the longest fleece, and the Southdown
Almost the smallest—and between them thirty other breeds,
Some whitefaced, some black,
Some with horns and some without,
Some long-wooled, some short-wooled,
20   In England where the men, and women too,
Are almost as interesting as the sheep.)
Everything is different, everything changes,
Except for the white bedstraw which climbs all the way
Up from the valleys to the tops of the high passes
25   The flowers are all different and more precious
Demanding more search and particularity of vision.
Look! Here and there a pinguicula[3] eloquent of the Alps
Still keeps a purple-blue flower

---

8. With the exception of the first line, the words of "Perfect" were taken from "Port-y-Rhyd," a short story in a collection by Glyn Jones entitled *The Blue Bed*, published by Jonathan Cape in 1937.
9. "The dead have things to tell the living" (Spanish).

1. A low-lying coastal strip of arable or grassland.
2. A blue flower, with bell-shaped head, that grows wild in Scotland.
3. The butterwort, a small herb that secretes a sticky liquid to catch insects.

On the top of its straight and slender stem.
30 Bog-asphodel, deep-gold, and comely in form,
The queer, almost diabolical, sundew,
And when you leave the bog for the stag moors and the rocks
The parsley fern—a lovelier plant
Than even the proud Osmunda Regalis[4]—
35 Flourishes in abundance
Showing off oddly contrasted fronds
From the cracks of the lichened stones.
It is pleasant to find the books
Describing it as "very local."
40 Here is a change indeed!
The universal *is* the particular.

1955

ARCHIBALD MacLEISH

1892–1982

Ars Poetica[1]

A poem should be palpable and mute
As a globed fruit,

Dumb
As old medallions to the thumb,

5   Silent as the sleeve-worn stone
Of casement ledges where the moss has grown—

A poem should be wordless
As the flight of birds.

*

A poem should be motionless in time
10 As the moon climbs,

Leaving, as the moon releases
Twig by twig the night-entangled trees,

Leaving, as the moon behind the winter leaves,
Memory by memory the mind—

15 A poem should be motionless in time
As the moon climbs.

*

A poem should be equal to:
Not true.

4. The flowering or "royal" fern.   by the Roman poet Horace (65–68 B.C.).
1. "The Art of Poetry," title of a poetical treatise

For all the history of grief
20   An empty doorway and a maple leaf.

For love
The leaning grasses and two lights above the sea—

A poem should not mean
But be.

1926

You, Andrew Marvell[2]

And here face down beneath the sun
And here upon earth's noonward height
To feel the always coming on
The always rising of the night

5   To feel creep up the curving east
The earthy chill of dusk and slow
Upon those under lands the vast
And ever climbing shadow grow

And strange at Ecbatan[3] the trees
10   Take leaf by leaf the evening strange
The flooding dark about their knees
The mountains over Persia change

And now at Kermanshah the gate
Dark empty and the withered grass
15   And through the twilight now the late
Few travelers in the westward pass

And Baghdad darken and the bridge
Across the silent river gone
And through Arabia the edge
20   Of evening widen and steal on

And deepen on Palmyra's street
The wheel rut in the ruined stone
And Lebanon fade out and Crete
High through the clouds and overblown

25   And over Sicily the air
Still flashing with the landward gulls
And loom and slowly disappear
The sails above the shadowy hulls

And Spain go under and the shore
30   Of Africa the gilded sand

2. Andrew Marvell (1621–1678) wrote "To His Coy Mistress" (see pp. 435–36), the poem to which MacLeish specifically alludes.
3. The poet's thoughts, following the daily path of the sun, move westward, from Ecbatana, once the capital of Media Magna (part of Persia), on to Kermanshah, Baghdad, Palmyra, Sicily, and so on.

And evening vanish and no more
The low pale light across that land

Nor now the long light on the sea
And here face downward in the sun
35   To feel how swift how secretly
The shadow of the night comes on. . . .

1930

The Snowflake Which Is Now and Hence Forever

Will it last? he says.
Is it a masterpiece?
Will generation after generation
Turn with reverence to the page?

5   Birdseye scholar of the frozen fish,
What would he make of the sole, clean, clear
Leap of the salmon that has disappeared?

To *be*, yes!—whether they like it or not!
But not to last when leap and water are forgotten,
10   A plank of standard pinkness in the dish.

They also live
Who swerve and vanish in the river.[4]

1952

EDNA ST. VINCENT MILLAY
1892–1950

First Fig[1]

My candle burns at both ends;
It will not last the night;
But ah, my foes, and oh, my friends—
It gives a lovely light!

1920

Second Fig[2]

Safe upon the solid rock the ugly houses stand:
Come and see my shining palace built upon the sand!

1920

---

4. An allusion to Milton, "When I Consider How My Light Is Spent" (p. 378), a sonnet that concludes, "They also serve who only stand and wait."
1. From *A Few Figs from Thistles*, a title derived from Matthew 7.16: "Do men gather grapes of thorns, or figs of thistles?"
2. See the preceding note and Matthew 7.26–27, referring to "a foolish man, which built his house upon the sand."

Euclid Alone Has Looked on Beauty Bare

Euclid[3] alone has looked on Beauty bare.
Let all who prate of Beauty hold their peace,
And lay them prone upon the earth and cease
To ponder on themselves, the while they stare
5   At nothing, intricately drawn nowhere
In shapes of shifting lineage; let geese
Gabble and hiss, but heroes seek release
From dusty bondage into luminous air.
O blinding hour, O holy, terrible day,
10 When first the shaft into his vision shone
Of light anatomized! Euclid alone
Has looked on Beauty bare. Fortunate they
Who, though once only and then but far away,
Have heard her massive sandal set on stone.

1920

Spring

To what purpose, April, do you return again?
Beauty is not enough.
You can no longer quiet me with the redness
Of little leaves opening stickily.
5   I know what I know.
The sun is hot on my neck as I observe
The spikes of the crocus.
The smell of the earth is good.
It is apparent that there is no death.
10 But what does that signify?
Not only under ground are the brains of men
Eaten by maggots.
Life in itself
Is nothing,
15 An empty cup, a flight of uncarpeted stairs.
It is not enough that yearly, down this hill,
April
Comes like an idiot, babbling and strewing flowers.

1920

I, Being Born a Woman and Distressed

I, being born a woman and distressed
By all the needs and notions of my kind,
Am urged by your propinquity to find
Your person fair, and feel a certain zest
5   To bear your body's weight upon my breast:
So subtly is the fume of life designed,
To clarify the pulse and cloud the mind,
And leave me once again undone, possessed.
Think not for this, however, the poor treason

---

3. The Greek formulator of the science of geometry, ca. 300 B.C.

10 Of my stout blood against my staggering brain,
I shall remember you with love, or season
My scorn with pity,—let me make it plain:
I find this frenzy insufficient reason
For conversation when we meet again.

1923

The Buck in the Snow

White sky, over the hemlocks bowed with snow,
Saw you not at the beginning of evening the antlered buck and his doe
Standing in the apple-orchard? I saw them. I saw them suddenly go,
Tails up, with long leaps lovely and slow,
5 Over the stone-wall into the wood of hemlocks bowed with snow.

Now lies he here, his wild blood scalding the snow.

How strange a thing is death, bringing to his knees, bringing to his antlers
The buck in the snow.
How strange a thing,—a mile away by now, it may be,
10 Under the heavy hemlocks that as the moments pass
Shift their loads a little, letting fall a feather of snow—
Life, looking out attentive from the eyes of the doe.

1928

I Dreamed I Moved among the Elysian Fields

I dreamed I moved among the Elysian fields,[4]
In converse with sweet women long since dead;
And out of blossoms which that meadow yields
I wove a garland for your living head.
5 Danae,[5] that was the vessel for a day
Of golden Jove, I saw, and at her side,
Whom Jove the Bull desired and bore away,
Europa[6] stood, and the Swan's featherless bride.[7]
All these were mortal women, yet all these
10 Above the ground had had a god for guest;
Freely I walked beside them and at ease,
Addressing them, by them again addressed,
And marveled nothing, for remembering you,
Wherefore I was among them well I knew.

1930

Ragged Island

There, there where those black spruces crowd
To the edge of the precipitous cliff,
Above your boat, under the eastern wall of the island;

4. In the Greek underworld, the abode of the
happy dead.
5. Whom Jove (Zeus) seduced by descending
upon her as a shower of gold.

6. A maiden carried away by Jove in the form of a
bull.
7. Leda, seduced by Jove in the form of a swan.

And no wave breaks; as if
5   All had been done, and long ago, that needed
Doing; and the cold tide, unimpeded
By shoal or shelving ledge, moves up and down,
Instead of in and out;
And there is no driftwood there, because there is no beach;
10 Clean cliff going down as deep as clear water can reach;

No driftwood, such as abounds on the roaring shingle,[8]
To be hefted home, for fires in the kitchen stove;
Barrels, banged ashore about the boiling outer harbor;
Lobster-buoys, on the eel-grass of the sheltered cove:

15 There, thought unbraids itself, and the mind becomes
      single.
There you row with tranquil oars, and the ocean
Shows no scar from the cutting of your placid keel;
Care becomes senseless there; pride and promotion
Remote; you only look; you scarcely feel.

20 Even adventure, with its vital uses,
Is aimless ardour now; and thrift is waste.

Oh, to be there, under the silent spruces,
Where the wide, quiet evening darkens without haste
Over a sea with death acquainted, yet forever chaste.

1954

Armenonville[9]

By the lake at Armenonville in the Bois de Boulogne
Small begonias had been set in the embankment, both pink and red;
With polished leaf and brittle, juicy stem;
They covered the embankment; there were wagon-loads of them,
5 Charming and neat, gay colours in the warm shade.

We had preferred a table near the lake, half out of view,
Well out of hearing, for a voice not raised above
A low, impassioned question and its low reply.
We both leaned forward with our elbows on the table, and you
10 Watched my mouth while I answered, and it made me shy.
I looked about, but the waiters knew we were in love,
And matter-of-factly left us blissfully alone.

There swam across the lake, as I looked aside, avoiding
Your eyes for a moment, there swam from under the pink and red
      begonias
15 A small creature; I thought it was a water-rat; it swam very well,
In complete silence, and making no ripples at all
Hardly; and when suddenly I turned again to you,

8. Stones on a seashore.
9. Pavilion in the park of the Bois de Boulogne in Paris.

Aware that you were speaking, and perhaps had been speaking for
  some time,
I was aghast at my absence, for truly I did not know
20 Whether you had been asking or telling.

1954

WILFRED OWEN
1893–1918

Anthem for Doomed Youth

What passing-bells for these who die as cattle?[1]
  —Only the monstrous anger of the guns.
  Only the stuttering rifles' rapid rattle
Can patter out their hasty orisons.
5   No mockeries now for them; no prayers nor bells;
    Nor any voice of mourning save the choirs,—
  The shrill, demented choirs of wailing shells;
  And bugles calling for them from sad shires.°   counties

What candles may be held to speed them all?
10   Not in the hands of boys but in their eyes
  Shall shine the holy glimmers of goodbyes.
    The pallor of girls' brows shall be their pall;
  Their flowers the tenderness of patient minds,
  And each slow dusk a drawing-down of blinds.

1917   1920

Dulce Et Decorum Est[2]

Bent double, like old beggars under sacks,
Knock-kneed, coughing like hags, we cursed through sludge,
Till on the haunting flares we turned our backs
And towards our distant rest began to trudge.
5   Men marched asleep. Many had lost their boots
But limped on, blood-shod. All went lame; all blind;
Drunk with fatigue; deaf even to the hoots
Of tired, outstripped Five-Nines[3] that dropped behind.

  Gas! GAS! Quick, boys!—An ecstasy of fumbling,
10 Fitting the clumsy helmets just in time;

1. Owen was probably responding to the anonymous Prefatory Note to *Poems of Today* (1916), of which he possessed a copy: "This book has been compiled in order that boys and girls, already perhaps familiar with the great classics of the English speech, may also know something of the newer poetry of their own day. Most of the writers are living, and the rest are still vivid memories among us, while one of the youngest, almost as these words are written, has gone singing to lay down his life for his country's cause.... There is no arbitrary isolation of one theme from another; they mingle and interpenetrate throughout, to the music of Pan's flute, and of Love's viol, and the bugle-call of Endeavour, and the passing-bells of Death."
2. "The famous Latin tag [from Horace, *Odes* 3.2.13] means, of course, *It is sweet and meet to die for one's country. Sweet! And decorous!*" [October 16, 1917, letter of Owen to his mother].
3. I.e., 5.9-inch caliber shells.

But someone still was yelling out and stumbling,
And flound'ring like a man in fire or lime . . .
Dim, through the misty panes[4] and thick green light,
As under a green sea, I saw him drowning.

15 In all my dreams, before my helpless sight,
He plunges at me, guttering, choking, drowning.

If in smothering dreams you too could pace
Behind the wagon that we flung him in,
And watch the white eyes writhing in his face,
20 His hanging face, like a devil's sick of sin;
If you could hear, at every jolt, the blood
Come gargling from the froth-corrupted lungs,
Obscene as cancer, bitter as the cud
Of vile, incurable sores on innocent tongues,—
25 My friend,[5] you would not tell with such high zest
To children ardent for some desperate glory,
The old Lie: Dulce et decorum est
Pro patria mori.

1917–18   1920

Insensibility

1

Happy are men who yet before they are killed
Can let their veins run cold.
Whom no compassion fleers°   *mocks*
Or makes their feet
5 Sore on the alleys cobbled[6] with their brothers.
The front line withers.
But they are troops who fade, not flowers,
For poets' tearful fooling:
Men, gaps for filling:
10 Losses, who might have fought
Longer; but no one bothers.

2

And some cease feeling
Even themselves or for themselves.
Dullness best solves
15 The tease and doubt of shelling,
And Chance's strange arithmetic
Comes simpler than the reckoning of their shilling.[7]
They keep no check on armies' decimation.

---

4. Of the gas mask's celluloid window.
5. Jessie Pope, to whom the poem was originally to have been dedicated, was the author of numerous prewar children's books as well as *Jessie Pope's War Poems* (1915).

6. "They are dying again at Beaumont Hamel, which already in 1916 was cobbled with skulls" [March 1918, letter of Owen to his sister].
7. A "King's shilling" was traditionally given to the newly established soldier by the recruiting officer.

3

Happy are these who lose imagination:
20   They have enough to carry with ammunition.
Their spirit drags no pack.
Their old wounds, save with cold, can not more ache.
Having seen all things red,
Their eyes are rid
25   Of the hurt of the colour of blood for ever.
And terror's first constriction over,
Their hearts remain small-drawn.
Their senses in some scorching cautery of battle
Now long since ironed,
30   Can laugh among the dying, unconcerned.

4

Happy the soldier home, with not a notion
How somewhere, every dawn, some men attack,
And many sighs are drained.
Happy the lad whose mind was never trained:
35   His days are worth forgetting more than not.
He sings along the march
Which we march taciturn, because of dusk,
The long, forlorn, relentless trend
From larger day to huger night.

5

40   We wise,[8] who with a thought besmirch
Blood over all our soul,
How should we see our task
But through his blunt and lashless eyes?
Alive, he is not vital overmuch;
45   Dying, not mortal overmuch;
Nor sad, nor proud,
Nor curious at all.
He cannot tell
Old men's placidity from his.

6

50   But cursed are dullards whom no cannon stuns,
That they should be as stones.
Wretched are they, and mean
With paucity that never was simplicity.
By choice they made themselves immune.
55   To pity and whatever moans in man
Before the last sea and the hapless stars;
Whatever mourns when many leave these shores;
Whatever shares
The eternal reciprocity of tears.

1917–18   1920

8. I.e., poets.

Strange Meeting[9]

It seemed that out of battle I escaped
Down some profound dull tunnel, long since scooped
Through granites which titanic wars had groined.

Yet also there encumbered sleepers groaned,
5   Too fast in thought or death to be bestirred.
Then, as I probed them, one sprang up, and stared
With piteous recognition in fixed eyes,
Lifting distressful hands, as if to bless.
And by his smile, I knew that sullen hall,—
10   By his dead smile I knew we stood in Hell.

With a thousand pains that vision's face was grained;
Yet no blood reached there from the upper ground,
And no guns thumped, or down the flues made moan.
"Strange friend," I said, "here is no cause to mourn."
15   "None," said that other, "save the undone years,
The hopelessness. Whatever hope is yours,
Was my life also; I went hunting wild
After the wildest beauty in the world,
Which lies not calm in eyes, or braided hair,
20   But mocks the steady running of the hour,
And if it grieves, grieves richlier than here.
For by my glee might many men have laughed.
And of my weeping something had been left,
Which must die now. I mean the truth untold,
25   The pity of war, the pity war distilled.[1]
Now men will go content with what we spoiled,
Or, discontent, boil bloody, and be spilled.
They will be swift with swiftness of the tigress.
None will break ranks, though nations trek from progress.
30   Courage was mine, and I had mystery,
Wisdom was mine, and I had mastery:
To miss the march of this retreating world
Into vain citadels that are not walled.
Then, when much blood had clogged their chariot-wheels,
35   I would go up and wash them from sweet wells,
Even with truths that lie too deep for taint.
I would have poured my spirit without stint
But not through wounds; not on the cess[2] of war.
Foreheads of men have bled where no wounds were.

40   "I am the enemy you killed, my friend.
I knew you in this dark: for so you frowned

---

9. Cf. Shelley, *The Revolt of Islam* 1828–32:

> And one whose spear had pierced me, leaned
>   beside,
> With quivering lips and humid eyes;—and all
> Seemed like some brothers on a journey wide
>   Gone forth, whom now strange meeting did
>   befall
> In a strange land.

The speaker of Owen's poem imagines his victim a poet like himself.
1. "My subject is War, and the pity of War. The Poetry is in the pity" [Owen's draft preface to his poems].
2. Luck, as in the phrase "bad cess to you" (may evil befall you); also muck or excrement, as in the word "cesspit."

Yesterday through me as you jabbed and killed.
I parried; but my hands were loath and cold.
Let us sleep now...."

1918   1920

Futility

Move him into the sun—
Gently its touch awoke him once,
At home, whispering of fields half-sown.
Always it woke him, even in France,
5   Until this morning and this snow.
If anything might rouse him now
The kind old sun will know.

Think how it wakes the seeds—
Woke once the clays of a cold star.
10   Are limbs, so dear achieved, are sides
Full-nerved, still warm, too hard to stir?
Was it for this the clay grew tall?
—O what made fatuous sunbeams toil
To break earth's sleep at all?

1918   1920

DOROTHY PARKER
1893–1967

Unfortunate Coincidence

By the time you swear you're his,
    Shivering and sighing,
And he vows his passion is
    Infinite, undying—
5   Lady, make a note of this:
    One of you is lying.

Résumé

Razors pain you;
Rivers are damp;
Acids stain you;
And drugs cause cramp.
5   Guns aren't lawful;
Nooses give;
Gas smells awful;
You might as well live.

One Perfect Rose

A single flow'r he sent me, since we met.
All tenderly his messenger he chose;

Deep-hearted, pure, with scented dew still wet—
One perfect rose.

5 I knew the language of the floweret;
"My fragile leaves," it said, "his heart enclose."
Love long has taken for his amulet
One perfect rose.

Why is it no one ever sent me yet
10 One perfect limousine, do you suppose?
Ah no, it's always just my luck to get
One perfect rose.

1926

E. E. CUMMINGS
1894–1962

All in green went my love riding

All in green went my love riding
on a great horse of gold
into the silver dawn.

four lean hounds crouched low and smiling
5 the merry deer ran before.

Fleeter be they than dappled dreams
the swift sweet deer
the red rare deer.

Four red roebuck at a white water
10 the cruel bugle sang before.

Horn at hip went my love riding
riding the echo down
into the silver dawn.

four lean hounds crouched low and smiling
15 the level meadows ran before.

Softer be they than slippered sleep
the lean lithe deer
the fleet flown deer.

Four fleet does at a gold valley
20 the famished arrow sang before.

Bow at belt went my love riding
riding the mountain down
into the silver dawn.

four lean hounds crouched low and smiling
25   the sheer peaks ran before.

Paler be they than daunting death
the sleek slim deer
the tall tense deer.

Four tall stags at a green mountain
30   the lucky hunter sang before.

All in green went my love riding
on a great horse of gold
into the silver dawn.

four lean hounds crouched low and smiling
35   my heart fell dead before.

1923

in Just-

in Just-
spring   when the world is mud-
luscious the little
lame balloonman

5   whistles   far   and wee

and eddieandbill come
running from marbles and
piracies and it's
spring

10   when the world is puddle-wonderful

the queer
old balloonman whistles
far   and   wee
and bettyandisbel come dancing

15   from hop-scotch and jump-rope and

it's
spring
and
    the

20   goat-footed[1]

---

1. A reference to the goat-footed, lecherous forest gods of classical mythology, the satyrs.

balloonMan   whistles
far
and
wee

1923

the Cambridge ladies who live in furnished souls

the Cambridge ladies who live in furnished souls
are unbeautiful and have comfortable minds
(also,with the church's protestant blessings
daughters,unscented shapeless spirited)
5   they believe in Christ and Longfellow,[2]both dead,
are invariably interested in so many things—
at the present writing one still finds
delighted fingers knitting for the is it Poles?
perhaps. While permanent faces coyly bandy
10   scandal of Mrs. N and Professor D
. . . . the Cambridge ladies do not care,above
Cambridge if sometimes in its box of
sky lavender and cornerless,the
moon rattles like a fragment of angry candy

1923

Spring is like a perhaps hand

Spring is like a perhaps hand
(which comes carefully
out of Nowhere)arranging
a window,into which people look(while
5   people stare
arranging and changing placing
carefully there a strange
thing and a known thing here)and

changing everything carefully

10   spring is like a perhaps
Hand in a window
(carefully to
and fro moving New and
Old things,while
15   people stare carefully
moving a perhaps
fraction of flower here placing
an inch of air there)and

without breaking anything.

1925

2. For most of his life, the American poet Henry Wadsworth Longfellow (1807–1882; see pp. 860–63) lived in Cambridge, Massachusetts.

"next to of course god america i

"next to of course god america i
love you land of the pilgrims' and so forth oh
say can you see by the dawn's early my
country 'tis of centuries come and go
5   and are no more what of it we should worry
in every language even deafanddumb
thy sons acclaim your glorious name by gorry
by jingo[3] by gee by gosh by gum
why talk of beauty what could be more beaut-
10   iful than these heroic happy dead
who rushed like lions to the roaring slaughter
they did not stop to think they died instead
then shall the voice of liberty be mute?"

He spoke. And drank rapidly a glass of water

1926

since feeling is first

since feeling is first
who pays any attention
to the syntax of things
will never wholly kiss you;

5   wholly to be a fool
while Spring is in the world

my blood approves,
and kisses are a better fate
than wisdom
10   lady i swear by all flowers. Don't cry
—the best gesture of my brain is less than
your eyelids' flutter which says

we are for each other:then
laugh,leaning back in my arms
15   for life's not a paragraph

And death i think is no parenthesis

1926

i sing of Olaf glad and big

i sing of Olaf glad and big
whose warmest heart recoiled at war:
a conscientious object-or[4]

---

3. "Jingo" is both part of a mild oath and a refer-
ence to jingoism: extreme nationalism, especially
as demonstrated in a belligerent foreign policy.
4. One who on moral or religious grounds refuses
to bear arms; this status was rarely granted in
World War I except to members of recognized
pacifist religious sects.

his wellbelovéd colonel(trig°   *primly neat*
5   westpointer most succinctly bred)
took erring Olaf soon in hand;
but—though an host of overjoyed
noncoms°(first knocking on the head *noncommissioned officers*
him)do through icy waters roll
10 that helplessness which others stroke
with brushes recently employed
anent° this muddy toiletbowl,   *concerning*
while kindred intellects evoke
allegiance per blunt instruments—
15 Olaf(being to all intents
a corpse and wanting any rag
upon what God unto him gave)
responds,without getting annoyed
"I will not kiss your fucking flag"

20 straightway the silver bird[5] looked grave
(departing hurriedly to shave)

but—though all kinds of officers
(a yearning nation's blueeyed pride)
their passive prey did kick and curse
25 until for wear their clarion
voices and boots were much the worse,
and egged the firstclassprivates on
his rectum wickedly to tease
by means of skillfully applied
30 bayonets roasted hot with heat—
Olaf(upon what were once knees)
does almost ceaselessly repeat
"there is some shit I will not eat"

our president,being of which
35 assertions duly notified
threw the yellowsonofabitch
into a dungeon,where he died

Christ(of His mercy infinite)
i pray to see;and Olaf,too

40 preponderatingly because
unless statistics lie he was
more brave than me:more blond than you.

                                          1931

somewhere i have never travelled,gladly beyond

somewhere i have never travelled,gladly beyond
any experience,your eyes have their silence:

---

5. The colonel; strictly speaking, his insignia of rank.

in your most frail gesture are things which enclose me,
or which i cannot touch because they are too near

5   your slightest look easily will unclose me
though i have closed myself as fingers,
you open always petal by petal myself as Spring opens
(touching skilfully,mysteriously)her first rose

or if your wish be to close me,i and
10 my life will shut very beautifully,suddenly,
as when the heart of this flower imagines
the snow carefully everywhere descending;

nothing which we are to perceive in this world equals
the power of your intense fragility:whose texture
15 compels me with the colour of its countries,
rendering death and forever with each breathing

(i do not know what it is about you that closes
and opens;only something in me understands
the voice of your eyes is deeper than all roses)
20 nobody,not even the rain,has such small hands

1931

anyone lived in a pretty how town

anyone lived in a pretty how town
(with up so floating many bells down)
spring summer autumn winter
he sang his didn't he danced his did.

5   Women and men(both little and small)
cared for anyone not at all
they sowed their isn't they reaped their same
sun moon stars rain

children guessed(but only a few
10 and down they forgot as up they grew
autumn winter spring summer)
that noone loved him more by more

when by now and tree by leaf
she laughed his joy she cried his grief
15 bird by snow and stir by still
anyone's any was all to her

someones married their everyones
laughed their cryings and did their dance
(sleep wake hope and then)they
20 said their nevers they slept their dream

stars rain sun moon
(and only the snow can begin to explain

how children are apt to forget to remember
with up so floating many bells down)

25 one day anyone died i guess
(and noone stooped to kiss his face)
busy folk buried them side by side
little by little and was by was

all by all and deep by deep
30 and more by more they dream their sleep
noone and anyone earth by april
wish by spirit and if by yes.

Women and men(both dong and ding)
summer autumn winter spring
35 reaped their sowing and went their came
sun moon stars rain

1940

my father moved through dooms of love

my father moved through dooms of love
through sames of am through haves of give,
singing each morning out of each night
my father moved through depths of height

5 this motionless forgetful where
turned at his glance to shining here;
that if(so timid air is firm)
under his eyes would stir and squirm

newly as from unburied which
10 floats the first who,his april touch
drove sleeping selves to swarm their fates
woke dreamers to their ghostly roots

and should some why completely weep
my father's fingers brought her sleep:
15 vainly no smallest voice might cry
for he could feel the mountains grow.

Lifting the valleys of the sea
my father moved through griefs of joy;
praising a forehead called the moon
20 singing desire into begin

joy was his song and joy so pure
a heart of star by him could steer
and pure so now and now so yes
the wrists of twilight would rejoice

25 keen as midsummer's keen beyond
conceiving mind of sun will stand,

so strictly(over utmost him
so hugely(stood my father's dream

his flesh was flesh his blood was blood:
30 no hungry man but wished him food;
no cripple wouldn't creep one mile
uphill to only see him smile.

Scorning the pomp of must and shall
my father moved through dooms of feel;
35 his anger was as right as rain
his pity was as green as grain

septembering arms of year extend
less humbly wealth to foe and friend
than he to foolish and to wise
40 offered immeasurable is

proudly and(by octobering flame
beckoned)as earth will downward climb,
so naked for immortal work
his shoulders marched against the dark

45 his sorrow was as true as bread:
no liar looked him in the head;
if every friend became his foe
he'd laugh and build a world with snow.

My father moved through theys of we,
50 singing each new leaf out of each tree
(and every child was sure that spring
danced when she heard my father sing)

then let men kill which cannot share,
let blood and flesh be mud and mire,
55 scheming imagine,passion willed,
freedom a drug that's bought and sold

giving to steal and cruel kind,
a heart to fear,to doubt a mind,
to differ a disease of same,
60 conform the pinnacle of am

though dull were all we taste as bright,
bitter all utterly things sweet,
maggoty minus and dumb death
all we inherit,all bequeath

65 and nothing quite so least as truth
—i say though hate were why men breathe—
because my father lived his soul
love is the whole and more than all

1940

JEAN TOOMER
1894–1967

FROM CANE[1]

Reapers

Black reapers with the sound of steel on stones
Are sharpening scythes. I see them place the hones
In their hip-pockets as a thing that's done,
And start their silent swinging, one by one.
5 Black horses drive a mower through the weeds,
And there, a field rat, startled, squealing bleeds,
His belly close to ground. I see the blade,
Blood-stained, continue cutting weeds and shade.

Face

Hair—
silver-gray,
like streams of stars,
Brows—
5 recurved canoes
quivered by the ripples blown by pain,
Her eyes—
mist of tears
condensing on the flesh below
10 And her channeled muscles
are cluster grapes of sorrow
purple in the evening sun
nearly ripe for worms.

Georgia Dusk

The sky, lazily disdaining to pursue
    The setting sun, too indolent to hold
    A lengthened tournament for flashing gold,
Passively darkens for night's barbecue,

5 A feast of moon and men and barking hounds,
    An orgy for some genius of the South
    With blood-hot eyes and cane-lipped scented mouth,
Surprised in making folksongs from soul sounds.

    The sawmill blows its whistle, buzz-saws stop,
10   And silence breaks the bud of knoll and hill,

1. A collection of fiction, drama, and poetry, published in 1923, that Toomer saw as a unified book that ought not be excerpted. Set in Georgia and in Washington, D.C., it was partly inspired by the period in which the urban Toomer, of black and white ancestry, worked in a school in Sparta, Georgia.

Soft settling pollen where plowed lands fulfill
Their early promise of a bumper crop.

Smoke from the pyramidal sawdust pile
Curls up, blue ghosts of trees, tarrying low
15   Where only chips and stumps are left to show
The solid proof of former domicile.

Meanwhile, the men, with vestiges of pomp,
Race memories of king and caravan,
High-priests, an ostrich, and a juju-man,[2]
20   Go singing through the footpaths of the swamp.

Their voices rise . . the pine trees are guitars,
Strumming, pine-needles fall like sheets of rain . .
Their voices rise . . the chorus of the cane
Is caroling a vesper to the stars. .

25   O singers, resinous and soft your songs
Above the sacred whisper of the pines,
Give virgin lips to cornfield concubines,
Bring dreams of Christ to dusky cane-lipped throngs.

Portrait in Georgia

Hair—braided chestnut,
    coiled like a lyncher's rope,
Eyes—fagots,°   *bundles of sticks*
Lips—old scars, or the first red blisters,
5   Breath—the last sweet scent of cane,
And her slim body, white as the ash
    of black flesh after flame.

Harvest Song

I am a reaper whose muscles set at sundown. All my oats are cradled.
But I am too chilled, and too fatigued to bind them. And I hunger.

I crack a grain between my teeth. I do not taste it.
I have been in the fields all day. My throat is dry. I hunger.

5   My eyes are caked with dust of oatfields at harvest-time.
I am a blind man who stares across the hills, seeking stacked fields of
    other harvesters.

It would be good to see them . . crook'd, split, and iron-ringed handles of
    the scythes. It would be good to see them, dust-caked and blind. I
    hunger.

2. One who controls the magic associated with jujus, the fetishes or charms of West African peoples.

(Dusk is a strange feared sheath their blades are dulled in.)
My throat is dry. And should I call, a cracked grain like the oats . . .
   eoho—

10 I fear to call. What should they hear me, and offer me their grain, oats,
    or wheat, or corn? I have been in the fields all day. I fear I could not
    taste it. I fear knowledge of my hunger.

My ears are caked with dust of oatfields at harvest-time.
I am a deaf man who strains to hear the calls of other harvesters whose
    throats are also dry.

It would be good to hear their songs . . reapers of the sweet-stalked cane,
    cutters of the corn . . even though their throats cracked and the
    strangeness of their voices deafened me.

I hunger. My throat is dry. Now that the sun has set and I am chilled, I
    fear to call. (Eoho, my brothers!)

15 I am a reaper. (Eoho!) All my oats are cradled. But I am too fatigued to
    bind them. And I hunger. I crack a grain. It has no taste to it. My
    throat is dry . . .

O my brothers, I beat my palms, still soft, against the stubble of my
    harvesting. (You beat your soft palms, too.) My pain is sweet. Sweeter
    than the oats or wheat or corn. It will not bring me knowledge of my
    hunger.

1923

ROBERT GRAVES

1895–1985

Love Without Hope

Love without hope, as when the young bird-catcher
Swept off his tall hat to the Squire's own daughter,
So let the imprisoned larks escape and fly
Singing about her head, as she rode by.

1925

In Broken Images

He is quick, thinking in clear images;
I am slow, thinking in broken images.

He becomes dull, trusting to his clear images;
I become sharp, mistrusting my broken images.

5 Trusting his images, he assumes their relevance;
Mistrusting my images, I question their relevance.

Assuming their relevance, he assumes the fact;
Questioning their relevance, I question the fact.

10 When the fact fails him, he questions his senses;
When the fact fails me, I approve my senses.

He continues quick and dull in his clear images;
I continue slow and sharp in my broken images.

He in a new confusion of his understanding;
I in a new understanding of my confusion.

1929

Warning to Children

Children, if you dare to think
Of the greatness, rareness, muchness,
Fewness of this precious only
Endless world in which you say
5 You live, you think of things like this:
Blocks of slate enclosing dappled
Red and green, enclosing tawny
Yellow nets, enclosing white
And black acres of dominoes,
10 Where a neat brown paper parcel
Tempts you to untie the string.
In the parcel a small island,
On the island a large tree,
On the tree a husky fruit.
15 Strip the husk and pare the rind off:
In the kernel you will see
Blocks of slate enclosed by dappled
Red and green, enclosed by tawny
Yellow nets, enclosed by white
20 And black acres of dominoes,
Where the same brown paper parcel—
Children, leave the string alone!
For who dares undo the parcel
Finds himself at once inside it,
25 On the island, in the fruit,
Blocks of slate about his head,
Finds himself enclosed by dappled
Green and red, enclosed by yellow
Tawny nets, enclosed by black
30 And white acres of dominoes,
With the same brown paper parcel
Still unopened on his knee.
And, if he then should dare to think
Of the fewness, muchness, rareness,
35 Greatness of this endless only
Precious world in which he says
He lives—he then unties the string.

1929

The Persian Version

Truth-loving Persians do not dwell upon
The trivial skirmish fought near Marathon.[1]
As for the Greek theatrical tradition
Which represents that summer's expedition
5   Not as a mere reconnaissance in force
By three brigades of foot and one of horse
(Their left flank covered by some obsolete
Light craft detached from the main Persian fleet)
But as a grandiose, ill-starred attempt
10   To conquer Greece—they treat it with contempt;
And only incidentally refute
Major Greek claims, by stressing what repute
The Persian monarch and the Persian nation
Won by this salutary demonstration:
15   Despite a strong defence and adverse weather
All arms combined magnificently together.

1945

To Juan at the Winter Solstice[2]

There is one story and one story only
That will prove worth your telling,
Whether as learned bard or gifted child;[3]
To it all lines or lesser gauds[4] belong
5   That startle with their shining
Such common stories as they stray into.

Is it of trees you tell, their months and virtues,[5]
Or strange beasts that beset you,
Of birds that croak at you the Triple will?[6]
10   Or of the Zodiac and how slow it turns
Below the Boreal Crown,[7]
Prison of all true kings that ever reigned?

Water to water, ark again to ark,
From woman back to woman:
15   So each new victim treads unfalteringly

---

1. The Battle of Marathon in 490 B.C. was a decisive Greek victory over the Persians.
2. Graves' "grammar of poetic myth," *The White Goddess* (1948), finds the only theme for true poetry in the story of the life cycle of the Sun God or Sun Hero, his marriage with the Goddess, and inevitable death at her hands or by her command. The poet's son Juan was born on December 21, 1945, one day before the winter solstice, which (being the time when the sun gives least heat and light to the north) is in many religions the birthday of the Sun Hero.
3. Graves has solved the riddle of the poem *The Battle of the Trees* by the Celtic bard Taliesin, who, as a "gifted child," outmatched twenty-four experienced court poets.
4. The larger beads placed between the decades

of "aves" in a Roman Catholic rosary (i.e., every eleventh bead).
5. Graves cites, in addition to Taliesin's *The Battle of the Trees*, an ancient Druidic "tree-calendar" that describes the natural and magic properties of different trees and associates each with a different month or season.
6. The Goddess sometimes speaks through such "prophetic" birds as the owl and eagle and has been called the Triple Goddess because of her threefold aspect as Goddess of the Underworld, Earth, and Sky.
7. "*Corona Borealis,* . . . which in Thracian-Libyan mythology carried to Bronze Age Britain, was the purgatory where Solar Heroes went after death" [Graves' note]. The twelve signs of the turning zodiac correspond to the twelve months.

The never altered circuit of his fate,
Bringing twelve peers[8] as witness
Both to his starry rise and starry fall.[9]

20 Or is it of the Virgin's silver beauty,
All fish below the thighs?
She in her left hand bears a leafy quince;[1]
When with her right she crooks a finger, smiling,
How may the King hold back?
Royally then he barters life for love.

25 Or of the undying snake from chaos hatched,
Whose coils contain the ocean,
Into whose chops with naked sword he springs,
Then in black water, tangled by the reeds,
Battles three days and nights,
30 To be spewed up beside her scalloped shore?[2]

Much snow is falling, winds roar hollowly,
The owl hoots from the elder,
Fear in your heart cries to the loving-cup:
Sorrow to sorrow as the sparks fly upward.
35 The log groans and confesses:[3]
There is one story and one story only.

Dwell on her graciousness, dwell on her smiling,
Do not forget what flowers
The great boar trampled down in ivy time.[4]
40 Her brow was creamy as the crested wave,
Her sea-grey eyes were wild[5]
But nothing promised that is not performed.

                                              1945

The White Goddess[6]

All saints revile her, and all sober men
Ruled by the God Apollo's golden mean[7] —
In scorn of which we sailed to find her
In distant regions likeliest to hold her
5 Whom we desired above all things to know,
Sister of the mirage and echo.

---

8. Perhaps the twelve knights of King Arthur's round table, Christ's twelve apostles, or the twelve signs of the zodiac.
9. The king (or Solar Hero), reincarnated, reappears at the winter solstice floating in an ark on the water.
1. Two forms of the Goddess are Aphrodite, Greek goddess of love, whose emblem is the quince, and Rahab, the Hebraic sea goddess, who was depicted with a fish's tail.
2. The snake, Ophion, was created by the Goddess and mated with her. From their egg, the world was hatched by the sun's rays. The king (or Solar

Hero) must kill the snake to win the Goddess, but in October the snake (perhaps reincarnated as the boar of line 39) must kill the king.
3. Cf. Job 5.7: "Man is born unto trouble, as the sparks fly upward." "The log is the Yule [or Christmas] log, burned at the year's end" [Graves' note].
4. Aphrodite's lover, Adonis, was killed by a boar.
5. Cf. Keats, "La Belle Dame sans Merci," line 16: "And her eyes were wild" (p. 842).
6. See n. 2, p. 1293.
7. The middle way, moderation. Apollo's motto was "Nothing in Excess."

It was a virtue not to stay,
To go our headstrong and heroic way
Seeking her out at the volcano's head,
10 Among pack ice, or where the track had faded
Beyond the cavern of the seven sleepers:[8]
Whose broad high brow was white as any leper's,
Whose eyes were blue, with rowan-berry lips,
With hair curled honey-coloured to white hips.

15 Green sap of Spring in the young wood a-stir
Will celebrate the Mountain Mother,
And every song-bird shout awhile for her;
But we are gifted, even in November
Rawest of seasons, with so huge a sense
20 Of her nakedly worn magnificence
We forget cruelty and past betrayal,
Heedless of where the next bright bolt may fall.

1948

The Song of Blodeuwedd

[Reassembled from the deliberately confused mediaeval poem medley,
Câd Goddeu, *in the* Red Book of Hergest, *hitherto regarded as*
nonsensical.]

Not of father nor of mother
Was my blood, was my body.
I was spellbound by Gwydion,
Prime enchanter of the Britons,
5   When he formed me from nine blossoms,
  Nine buds of various kind:
From primrose of the mountain,
Broom, meadow-sweet and cockle,
  Together intertwined,
10   From the bean in its shade bearing
A white spectral army
  Of earth, of earthy kind,
From blossoms of the nettle,
Oak, thorn and bashful chestnut—
15   Nine powers of nine flowers,
  Nine powers in me combined,
   Nine buds of plant and tree.
Long and white are my fingers
  As the ninth wave of the sea.

1948

---

8. Cf. Donne, "The Good Morrow," line 4: "Or snorted we in the Seven Sleepers' den?" (p. 263).

EDMUND BLUNDEN
1896–1974

Forefathers

Here they went with smock and crook,
   Toiled in the sun, lolled in the shade,
Here they mudded out the brook
   And here their hatchet cleared the glade:
5 Harvest-supper woke their wit,
Huntsman's moon their wooings lit.

From this church they led their brides,
   From this church themselves were led
Shoulder-high; on these waysides
10   Sat to take their beer and bread.
Names are gone—what men they were
These their cottages declare.

Names are vanished, save the few
   In the old brown Bible scrawled;
15 These were men of pith[1] and thew,°   *strong muscle*
   Whom the city never called;
Scarce could read or hold a quill,
Built the barn, the forge, the mill.

On the green they watched their sons
20   Playing till too dark to see,
As their fathers watched them once,
   As my father once watched me;
While the bat and beetle flew
On the warm air webbed with dew.

25 Unrecorded, unrenowned,
   Men from whom my ways begin,
Here I know you by your ground
   But I know you not within—
There is silence, there survives
30   Not a moment of your lives.

Like the bee that now is blown
   Honey-heavy on my hand,
From his toppling tansy[2]-throne
   In the green tempestuous land—
35 I'm in clover now, nor know
Who made honey long ago.

1922

---

1. I.e., forcible and sententious.   2. Tall yellow-flowered plant.

Vlamertinghe:[3] Passing the Chateau, July 1917

"And all her silken flanks with garlands drest"—[4]
But we are coming to the sacrifice.
Must those have flowers who are not yet gone West?[5]
May those have flowers who live with death and lice?
5   This must be the floweriest place
That earth allows; the queenly face
Of the proud mansion borrows grace for grace
Spite of those brute guns lowing at the skies.

Bold great daisies, golden lights,
10 Bubbling roses' pinks and whites—
Such a gay carpet! poppies by the million;
Such damask! such vermilion!
But if you ask me, mate, the choice of colour
Is scarcely right; this red should have been much duller.

                           1928

1916 seen from 1921

Tired with dull grief, grown old before my day,
I sit in solitude and only hear
Long silent laughters, murmurings of dismay,
The lost intensities of hope and fear;
5 In those old marshes yet the rifles lie,
On the thin breastwork flutter the grey rags,
The very books I read are there—and I
Dead as the men I loved, wait while life drags

Its wounded length from those sad streets of war
10 Into green places here, that were my own;
But now what once was mine is mine no more,
I seek such neighbours here and I find none.
With such strong gentleness and tireless will
Those ruined houses seared themselves in me,
15 Passionate I look for their dumb story still,
And the charred stub outspeaks the living tree.

I rise up at the singing of a bird
And scarcely knowing slink along the lane,
I dare not give a soul a look or word
20 Where all have homes and none's at home in vain:
Deep red the rose burned in the grim redoubt,[6]
The self-sown wheat around was like a flood,
In the hot path the lizard lolled time out,
The saints in broken shrines were bright as blood.

3. Village in Belgium, near Passchendaele, where
from July to November 1917 some of the heaviest
fighting of World War I took place.
4. Keats, "Ode on a Grecian Urn," line 34 (pp.
848–49).
5. Soldiers' slang for "died."
6. Earthwork defensive position enclosed on all
sides.

25 Sweet Mary's shrine between the sycamores!
There we would go, my friend of friends and I,
And snatch long moments from the grudging wars,
Whose dark made light intense to see them by.
Shrewd bit the morning fog, the whining shots
30 Spun from the wrangling wire;[7] then in warm swoon
The sun hushed all but the cool orchard plots,
We crept in the tall grass and slept till noon.

1922   1930

The Midnight Skaters

The hop-poles[8] stand in cones,
    The icy pond lurks under,
The pole-tops steeple to the thrones
    Of stars, sound gulfs of wonder;
5 But not the tallest there, 'tis said,
Could fathom to this pond's black bed.

Then is not death at watch
    Within those secret waters?
What wants he but to catch
10   Earth's heedless sons and daughters?
With but a crystal parapet
Between, he has his engines set.

Then on, blood shouts, on, on,
    Twirl, wheel and whip above him,
15 Dance on this ball-floor thin and wan,
    Use him as though you love him;
Court him, elude him, reel and pass,
And let him hate you through the glass.

1925   1926

LOUISE BOGAN
1897–1970

Medusa[1]

I had come to the house, in a cave of trees,
Facing a sheer sky.
Everything moved,—a bell hung ready to strike,
Sun and reflection wheeled by.

5 When the bare eyes were before me
And the hissing hair,

---

7. Barbed wire.
8. Poles supporting a climbing plant from the fruit of which beer is made.
1. One of the Gorgons, Greek mythological women of terrifying ugliness, with snakes for hair, the sight of whom turned people to stone. She was killed by Perseus, who cut off her head.

Held up at a window, seen through a door.
The stiff bald eyes, the serpents on the forehead
Formed in the air.

10 This is a dead scene forever now.
Nothing will ever stir.
The end will never brighten it more than this,
Nor the rain blur.

The water will always fall, and will not fall,
15 And the tipped bell make no sound.
The grass will always be growing for hay
Deep on the ground.

And I shall stand here like a shadow
Under the great balanced day,
20 My eyes on the yellow dust, that was lifting in the wind,
And does not drift away.

1923

Juan's Song

When beauty breaks and falls asunder
I feel no grief for it, but wonder.
When love, like a frail shell, lies broken,
I keep no chip of it for token.
5 I never had a man for friend
Who did not know that love must end.
I never had a girl for lover
Who could discern when love was over.
What the wise doubt, the fool believes—
10 Who is it, then, that love deceives?

1923

Man Alone

It is yourself you seek
In a long rage,
Scanning through light and darkness
Mirrors, the page,

5 Where should reflected be
Those eyes and that thick hair,
That passionate look, that laughter.
You should appear

Within the book, or doubled,
10 Freed, in the silvered glass;
Into all other bodies
Yourself should pass.

The glass does not dissolve;
Like walls the mirrors stand;

15 The printed page gives back
Words by another hand.

And your infatuate eye
Meets not itself below:
Strangers lie in your arms
20 As I lie now.

1937

Roman Fountain

Up from the bronze, I saw
Water without a flaw
Rush to its rest in air,
Reach to its rest, and fall.

5 Bronze of the blackest shade,
An element man-made,
Shaping upright the bare
Clear gouts of water in air.

O, as with arm and hammer,
10 Still it is good to strive
To beat out the image whole,
To echo the shout and stammer
When full-gushed waters, alive,
Strike on the fountain's bowl
15 After the air of summer.

1937

Song for the Last Act

Now that I have your face by heart, I look
Less at its features than its darkening frame
Where quince and melon, yellow as young flame,
Lie with quilled dahlias and the shepherd's crook.
5 Beyond, a garden. There, in insolent ease
The lead and marble figures watch the show
Of yet another summer loath to go
Although the scythes hang in the apple trees.

Now that I have your face by heart, I look.

10 Now that I have your voice by heart, I read
In the black chords upon a dulling page
Music that is not meant for music's cage,
Whose emblems mix with words that shake and bleed.
The staves[2] are shuttled over with a stark
15 Unprinted silence. In a double dream
I must spell out the storm, the running stream.
The beat's too swift. The notes shift in the dark.

2. Horizontal lines on which music is written.

Now that I have your voice by heart, I read.

Now that I have your heart by heart, I see
20 The wharves with their great ships and architraves;[3]
The rigging and the cargo and the slaves
On a strange beach under a broken sky.
O not departure, but a voyage done!
The bales stand on the stone; the anchor weeps
25 Its red rust downward, and the long vine creeps
Beside the salt herb, in the lengthening sun.

Now that I have your heart by heart, I see.

1954

Night

The cold remote islands
And the blue estuaries
Where what breathes, breathes
The restless wind of the inlets,
5   And what drinks, drinks
The incoming tide;

Where shell and weed
Wait upon the salt wash of the sea,
And the clear nights of stars
10 Swing their lights westward
To set behind the land;

Where the pulse clinging to the rocks
Renews itself forever;
Where, again on cloudless nights,
15 The water reflects
The firmament's partial setting;

—O remember
In your narrowing dark hours
That more things move
20 Than blood in the heart.

1968

HART CRANE
1899–1932

My Grandmother's Love Letters

There are no stars to-night
But those of memory.

3. Beams on columns.

Yet how much room for memory there is
In the loose girdle of soft rain.

5   There is even room enough
For the letters of my mother's mother,
Elizabeth,
That have been pressed so long
Into a corner of the roof
10   That they are brown and soft,
And liable to melt as snow.

Over the greatness of such space
Steps must be gentle.
It is all hung by an invisible white hair.
15   It trembles as birch limbs webbing the air.

And I ask myself:

"Are your fingers long enough to play
Old keys that are but echoes:
Is the silence strong enough
20   To carry back the music to its source
And back to you again
As though to her?"
Yet I would lead my grandmother by the hand
Through much of what she would not understand;
25   And so I stumble. And the rain continues on the roof
With such a sound of gently pitying laughter.

1926

At Melville's Tomb[1]

Often beneath the wave, wide from this ledge
The dice[2] of drowned men's bones he saw bequeath
An embassy. Their numbers as he watched,
Beat on the dusty shore and were obscured.

5   And wrecks passed without sound of bells,
The calyx[3] of death's bounty giving back
A scattered chapter, livid hieroglyph,
The portent wound in corridors of shells.

Then in the circuit calm of one vast coil,
10   Its lashings charmed and malice reconciled,
Frosted eyes there were that lifted altars;
And silent answers crept across the stars.

1. The American poet and novelist Herman Mel-
ville (1819–1891; see pp. 953–57), best known for
his works dealing with the sea.
2. Small, broken pieces; "Dice as a symbol of
chance and circumstance is also implied" [Crane's
note].

3. "This calyx refers in a double ironic sense both
to a cornucopia (cone-shaped receptacle) and the
vortex made by a sinking vessel" [Crane's note]. A
calyx is literally the outer whorl of a flower, formed
by modified leaves.

Compass, quadrant and sextant[4] contrive
No farther tides . . . High in the azure steeps
15 Monody[5] shall not wake the mariner.
This fabulous shadow only the sea keeps.

1926

Voyages

1

Above the fresh ruffles of the surf
Bright striped urchins flay each other with sand.
They have contrived a conquest for shell shucks,
And their fingers crumble fragments of baked weed
5   Gaily digging and scattering.

And in answer to their treble interjections
The sun beats lightning on the waves,
The waves fold thunder on the sand;
And could they hear me I would tell them:

10 O brilliant kids, frisk with your dog,
Fondle your shells and sticks, bleached
By time and the elements; but there is a line
You must not cross nor ever trust beyond it
Spry cordage° of your bodies to caresses   *ropes in ship's rigging*
15 Too lichen-faithful from too wide a breast.
The bottom of the sea is cruel.

2

—And yet this great wink of eternity,
Of rimless floods, unfettered leewardings,
Samite[6] sheeted and processioned where
Her undinal[7] vast belly moonward bends,
5   Laughing the wrapt inflections of our love;

Take this Sea, whose diapason° knells   *burst of sound*
On scrolls of silver snowy sentences,
The sceptered terror of whose sessions rends
As her demeanors motion well or ill.
10 All but the pieties of lovers' hands.

And onward, as bells off San Salvador[8]
Salute the crocus lusters of the stars,
In these poinsettia[9] meadows of her tides—

---

4. Instruments used in navigation: the compass determines geographic directions, the quadrant and sextant measure angles and reckon altitudes. Crane's note suggests that they "have inadvertently so extended the concepts of the entity they were invented to measure . . . that they may metaphorically be said to have extended the original boundaries of the entity measured."

5. Elegy or dirge sung by one person.
6. A rich, silky fabric interwoven with gold or silver.
7. The adjective suggests both waves and undines, or water spirits.
8. An island of the Bahamas group, Columbus' first landfall on the first voyage.
9. Showy plant native to Central America.

Adagios[1] of islands, O my Prodigal,
15   Complete the dark confessions her veins spell.

Mark how her turning shoulders wind the hours,
And hasten while her penniless rich palms
Pass superscription of bent foam and wave—
Hasten, while they are true—sleep, death, desire,
20   Close round one instant in one floating flower.

Bind us in time, O Seasons clear, and awe.
O minstrel galleons of Carib[2] fire,
Bequeath us to no earthly shore until
Is answered in the vortex of our grave
25   The seal's wide spindrift gaze toward paradise.

3

Infinite consanguinity° it bears—   *blood relationship*
This tendered theme of you that light
Retrieves from sea plains where the sky
Resigns a breast that every wave enthrones;
5   While ribboned water lanes I wind
Are laved and scattered with no stroke
Wide from your side, whereto this hour
The sea lifts, also, reliquary hands.[3]

And so, admitted through black swollen gates
10   That must arrest all distance otherwise,
Past whirling pillars and lithe pediments,
Light wrestling there incessantly with light,
Star kissing star through wave on wave unto
Your body rocking!
15   and where death, if shed,
Presumes no carnage, but this single change,
Upon the steep floor flung from dawn to dawn
The silken skilled transmemberment[4] of song;

Permit me voyage, love, into your hands . . .

4

Whose counted smile of hours and days, suppose
I know as spectrum of the sea and pledge
Vastly now parting gulf on gulf of wings
Whose circles bridge, I know, (from palms to the severe
5   Chilled albatross's[5] white immutability)
No stream of greater love advancing now
Than, singing, this mortality alone
Through clay aflow immortally to you.

---

1. The divisions of a composition that are musi-
cally slow and graceful.
2. Some of the West Indian islands, or the sea sur-
rounding them.
3. I.e., hands holding sacred relics.

4. Exchange or transformation of parts.
5. That of a large seabird capable of long, sus-
tained flights away from land, believed to sleep in
the air without moving its wings.

All fragrance irrefragibly,[6] and claim
10   Madly meeting logically in this hour
And region that is ours to wreathe again,
Portending eyes and lips and making told
The chancel[7] port and portion of our June—

Shall they not stem and close in our own steps
15   Bright staves of flowers and quills to-day as I
Must first be lost in fatal tides to tell?

In signature of the incarnate word
The harbor shoulders to resign in mingling
Mutual blood, transpiring as foreknown
20   And widening noon within your breast for gathering
All bright insinuations that my years have caught
For islands where must lead inviolably
Blue latitudes and levels of your eyes—

In this expectant, still exclaim receive
25   The secret oar and petals of all love.

5

Meticulous, past midnight in clear rime,°   *frost*
Infrangible and lonely, smooth as though cast
Together in one merciless white blade—
The bay estuaries fleck the hard sky limits.

5   —As if too brittle or too clear to touch!
The cables of our sleep so swiftly filed,
Already hang, shred ends from remembered stars.
One frozen trackless smile . . . What words
Can strangle this deaf moonlight? For we

10   Are overtaken. Now no cry, no sword
Can fasten or deflect this tidal wedge,
Slow tyranny of moonlight, moonlight loved
And changed . . . "There's

Nothing like this in the world," you say,
15   Knowing I cannot touch your hand and look
Too, into that godless cleft of sky
Where nothing turns but dead sands flashing.

"—And never to quite understand!" No,
In all the argosy[8] of your bright hair I dreamed
20   Nothing so flagless as this piracy.

But now
Draw in your head, alone and too tall here.

---

6. Undeniably; unalterably.
7. The part of a church that contains the altar and seats for the clergy and choir.

8. A rich supply; also, a large ship or a fleet of ships.

Your eyes already in the slant of drifting foam;
Your breath sealed by the ghosts I do not know:
25 Draw in your head and sleep the long way home.

6

Where icy and bright dungeons lift
Of swimmers their lost morning eyes,
And ocean rivers, churning, shift
Green borders under stranger skies,

5   Steadily as a shell secretes
Its beating leagues of monotone,
Or as many waters trough the sun's
Red kelson[9] past the cape's wet stone;

O rivers mingling toward the sky
10 And harbor of the phoenix'[1] breast—
My eyes pressed black against the prow,
—Thy derelict and blinded guest

Waiting, afire, what name, unspoke,
I cannot claim: let thy waves rear
15 More savage than the death of kings,
Some splintered garland for the seer.

Beyond siroccos[2] harvesting
The solstice thunders, crept away,
Like a cliff swinging or a sail
20 Flung into April's inmost day—

Creation's blithe and petaled word
To the lounged goddess when she rose
Conceding dialogue with eyes
That smile unsearchable repose—

25 Still fervid covenant, Belle Isle,[3]
—Unfolded floating dais before
Which rainbows twine continual hair—
Belle Isle, white echo of the oar!

The imaged Word, it is, that holds
30 Hushed willows anchored in its glow.
It is the unbetrayable reply
Whose accent no farewell can know.

1926

---

9. A beam laid parallel to the keel of a ship in order to hold together the flooring and the keel.
1. A mythological bird said to end its very long life by burning itself; from its ashes arises a new phoenix. The phoenix is also a symbol of the Resurrection.

2. Hot, moist winds, usually those from North African deserts.
3. Tiny island near Newfoundland that is the first land seen by boats coming from Europe.

From The Bridge

Proem: To Brooklyn Bridge

How many dawns, chill from his rippling rest
The seagull's wings shall dip and pivot him,
Shedding white rings of tumult, building high
Over the chained bay waters Liberty—

5   Then, with inviolate curve, forsake our eyes
As apparitional as sails that cross
Some page of figures to be filed away;
—Till elevators drop us from our day . . .

I think of cinemas, panoramic sleights
10 With multitudes bent toward some flashing scene
Never disclosed, but hastened to again,
Foretold to other eyes on the same screen;

And Thee,[4] across the harbor, silver-paced
As though the sun took step of thee, yet left
15 Some motion ever unspent in thy stride—
Implicitly thy freedom staying thee!

Out of some subway scuttle, cell or loft
A bedlamite° speeds to thy parapets,   *madman*
Tilting there momently, shrill shirt ballooning,
20 A jest falls from the speechless caravan.

Down Wall,[5] from girder into street noon leaks,
A rip-tooth of the sky's acetylene,
All afternoon the cloud-flown derricks turn . . .
Thy cables breathe the North Atlantic still.

25 And obscure as that heaven of the Jews,
Thy guerdon° . . . Accolade thou dost bestow   *reward*
Of anonymity time cannot raise:
Vibrant reprieve and pardon thou dost show.

O harp and altar, of the fury fused,
30 (How could mere toil align thy choiring strings!)[6]
Terrific threshold of the prophet's pledge,
Prayer of pariah, and the lover's cry—

Again the traffic lights that skim thy swift
Unfractioned idiom, immaculate sigh of stars,
35 Beading thy path—condense eternity:
And we have seen night lifted in thine arms.

Under thy shadow by the piers I waited;
Only in darkness is thy shadow clear.

---

4. I.e., Brooklyn Bridge.
5. Wall Street is less than half a mile south of the bridge's Manhattan end.

6. The suspension bridge has cables formed from parallel steel wires that were spun in place.

The City's fiery parcels all undone,
40   Already snow submerges an iron year . . .

O Sleepless as the river under thee,
Vaulting the sea, the prairies' dreaming sod,
Unto us lowliest sometime sweep, descend
And of the curveship lend a myth to God.

1930

The Broken Tower

The bell-rope that gathers God at dawn
Dispatches me as though I dropped down the knell
Of a spent day—to wander the cathedral lawn
From pit to crucifix, feet chill on steps from hell.

5   Have you not heard, have you not seen that corps
Of shadows in the tower, whose shoulders sway
Antiphonal carillons[7] launched before
The stars are caught and hived in the sun's ray?

The bells, I say, the bells break down their tower;
10   And swing I know not where. Their tongues engrave
Membrane through marrow, my long-scattered score
Of broken intervals . . . And I, their sexton slave!

Oval encyclicals in canyons heaping
The impasse high with choir. Banked voices slain!
15   Pagodas, campaniles° with reveilles[8] outleaping—   bell towers
O terraced echoes prostrate on the plain! . . .

And so it was I entered the broken world
To trace the visionary company of love, its voice
An instant in the wind (I know not whither hurled)
20   But not for long to hold each desperate choice.

My word I poured. But was it cognate, scored
Of that tribunal monarch of the air
Whose thigh embronzes earth, strikes crystal Word[9]
In wounds pledged once to hope—cleft to despair?

25   The steep encroachments of my blood left me
No answer (could blood hold such a lofty tower
As flings the question true?)—or is it she
Whose sweet mortality stirs latent power?

And through whose pulse I hear, counting the strokes
30   My veins recall and add, revived and sure

7. Bells, the playing of which is controlled by a   9. Cf. John 1.14: "And the Word was made flesh,
keyboard.   and dwelt among us."
8. Signals to awaken in the morning.

The angelus[1] of wars my chest evokes:
What I hold healed, original now, and pure . . .

And builds, within, a tower that is not stone
(Not stone can jacket heaven)—but slip
35   Of pebbles—visible wings of silence sown
In azure circles, widening as they dip

The matrix of the heart, lift down the eye
That shrines the quiet lake and swells a tower . . .
The commodious, tall decorum of that sky
40   Unseals her earth, and lifts love in its shower.

1933

To Emily Dickinson[2]

You who desired so much—in vain to ask—
Yet fed your hunger like an endless task,
Dared dignify the labor, bless the quest—
Achieved that stillness ultimately best,

5   Being, of all, least sought for: Emily, hear!
O sweet, dead Silencer, most suddenly clear
When singing that Eternity possessed
And plundered momently in every breast;

—Truly no flower yet withers in your hand,
10   The harvest you descried and understand
Needs more than wit to gather, love to bind.
Some reconcilement of remotest mind—

Leaves Ormus rubyless, and Ophir chill.[3]
Else tears heap all within one clay-cold hill.

1933

ALLEN TATE

1899–1979

Ode to the Confederate Dead

Row after row with strict impunity
The headstones yield their names to the element,
The wind whirrs without recollection;
In the riven troughs the splayed leaves
5   Pile up, of nature the casual sacrament
To the seasonal eternity of death;

---

1. The bell that announces the time for a devotion said in the morning, at noon, and in the evening (as well as the name of the prayer itself).
2. (1830–1886); American poet (see pp. 1010–25).

3. Ormus (or Ormuz), ancient city on the Persian Gulf; in the Old Testament (1 Kings 10.11), Solomon receives rich gifts, including gold and precious stones, from a region called Ophir.

Then driven by the fierce scrutiny
Of heaven to their election in the vast breath,
They sough° the rumor of mortality.   *moan*

10 Autumn is desolation in the plot
Of a thousand acres where these memories grow
From the inexhaustible bodies that are not
Dead, but feed the grass row after rich row.
Think of the autumns that have come and gone!
15 Ambitious November with the humors of the year,
With a particular zeal for every slab,
Staining the uncomfortable angels that rot
On the slabs, a wing chipped here, an arm there:
The brute curiosity of an angel's stare
20 Turns you, like them, to stone,
Transforms the heaving air
Till plunged to a heavier world below
You shift your sea-space blindly
Heaving, turning like the blind crab.

25   Dazed by the wind, only the wind
          The leaves flying, plunge

You know who have waited by the wall
The twilight certainty of an animal,
Those midnight restitutions of the blood
30 You know—the immitigable[1] pines, the smoky frieze
Of the sky, the sudden call: you know the rage,
The cold pool left by the mounting flood,
Of muted Zeno and Parmenides.[2]
You who have waited for the angry resolution
35 Of those desires that should be yours tomorrow,
You know the unimportant shrift of death
And praise the vision
And praise the arrogant circumstance
Of those who fall
40 Rank upon rank, hurried beyond decision—
Here by the sagging gate, stopped by the wall.

          Seeing, seeing only the leaves
          Flying, plunge and expire

Turn your eyes to the immoderate past,
45 Turn to the inscrutable infantry rising
Demons out of the earth—they will not last.
Stonewall, Stonewall, and the sunken fields of hemp,
Shiloh, Antietam, Malvern Hill, Bull Run.[3]
Lost in that orient of the thick and fast
50 You will curse the setting sun.

1. Unable to become less harsh.
2. Zeno and Parmenides were Greek philosophers
(fifth century B.C.) of the Eleatic school. They held
that what is various and changeable, all "develop-
ment," is illusory, for reality is one and changeless.

3. Names of important Civil War battles; "Stone-
wall": Thomas "Stonewall" Jackson (1824–1863),
Confederate general fatally wounded by his men
at Chancellorsville.

Cursing only the leaves crying
Like an old man in a storm

You hear the shout, the crazy hemlocks point
With troubled fingers to the silence which
55 Smothers you, a mummy, in time.

The hound bitch
Toothless and dying, in a musty cellar
Hears the wind only.

Now that the salt of their blood
60 Stiffens the saltier oblivion of the sea,
Seals the malignant purity of the flood,
What shall we who count our days and bow
Our heads with a commemorial woe
In the ribboned coats of grim felicity,
65 What shall we say of the bones, unclean,
Whose verdurous[4] anonymity will grow?

The ragged arms, the ragged heads and eyes
Lost in these acres of the insane green?
The gray lean spiders come, they come and go;
70 In a tangle of willows without light
The singular screech-owl's tight
Invisible lyric seeds the mind
With the furious murmur of their chivalry.

We shall say only the leaves
75 Flying, plunge and expire

We shall say only the leaves whispering
In the improbable mist of nightfall
That flies on multiple wing:
Night is the beginning and the end
80 And in between the ends of distraction
Waits mute speculation, the patient curse
That stones the eyes, or like the jaguar leaps
For his own image in a jungle pool, his victim.

What shall we say who have knowledge
85 Carried to the heart? Shall we take the act
To the grave? Shall we, more hopeful, set up the grave
In the house? The ravenous grave?

Leave now
The shut gate and the decomposing wall:
90 The gentle serpent, green in the mulberry bush,
Riots with his tongue through the hush—
Sentinel of the grave who counts us all!

1928

4. Green (i.e., vigorous) as growing vegetation.

BASIL BUNTING

1900–1985

What the Chairman Told Tom[1]

Poetry? It's a hobby.
I run model trains.
Mr Shaw there breeds pigeons.

It's not work. You dont sweat.
5   Nobody pays for it.
You *could* advertise soap.

Art, that's opera; or repertory—
The Desert Song.[2]
Nancy was in the chorus.

10   But to ask for twelve pounds a week—
married, aren't you?—
you've got a nerve.

How could I look a bus conductor
in the face
15   if I paid you twelve pounds?

Who says it's poetry, anyhow?
My ten year old
can do it *and* rhyme.

I get three thousand and expenses,
20   a car, vouchers,
but I'm an accountant.

They do what I tell them,
my company.
What do *you* do?

25   Nasty little words, nasty long words,
it's unhealthy.
I want to wash when I meet a poet.

They're Reds, addicts,
all delinquents.
30   What you write is rot.

Mr Hines says so, and he's a schoolteacher,
he ought to know.
Go and find *work*.

1965

1. T. S. Eliot; see pp. 1230–55.   2. A popular musical of the 1930s.

From Briggflats[3]

From *I*

Brag, sweet tenor bull,
descant on Rawthey's madrigal,[4]
each pebble its part
for the fells'[5] late spring.
5 Dance tiptoe, bull,
black against may.[6]
Ridiculous and lovely
chase hurdling shadows
morning into noon.
10 May on the bull's hide
and through the dale
furrows fill with may,
paving the slowworm's[7] way.

A mason times his mallet
15 to a lark's twitter,
listening while the marble rests,
lays his rule
at a letter's edge,
fingertips checking,
20 till the stone spells a name
naming none,
a man abolished.
Painful lark, labouring to rise!
the solemn mallet says:
25 In the grave's slot
he lies. We rot.

Decay thrusts the blade,
Wheat stands in excrement
trembling. Rawthey trembles.
30 Tongue stumbles, ears err
for fear of spring.
Rub the stone with sand,
wet sandstone rending
roughness away. Fingers
35 ache on the rubbing stone.
The mason says: Rocks
happen by chance.
No one here bolts the door,
love is so sore.

40 Stone smooth as skin,
cold as the dead they load

3. In the north of England, "flats" are low-lying fields along a waterway. In an interview, Bunting once remarked, "My autobiography is Briggflats." We reprint the opening lines of Part I.
4. Part-song for three or more voices; "descant": sing the upper part of a part-song. "Rawthey" is presumably the name of the itinerant mason, or stone-carver, of these lines.
5. In Britain, a "fell" is a hill or stretch of high moorland.
6. Flowers, pink or white, of the hawthorn tree.
7. Or "blind worm," a small, burrowing, limbless lizard.

on a low lorry[8] by night.
The moon sits on the fell
but it will rain.
45 Under sacks on the stone
two children lie,
hear the horse stale,°   *urinate*
the mason whistle,
harness mutter to shaft,
50 felloe[9] to axle squeak,
rut thud the rim,
crushed grit.

Stocking to stocking, jersey to jersey,[1]
head to a hard arm,
55 they kiss under the rain,
bruised by their marble bed.
In Garsdale, dawn;
at Hawes, tea from the can.[2]
Rain stops, sacks
60 steam in the sun, they sit up.
Copper-wire moustache,
sea-reflecting eyes
and Baltic plainsong speech
declare: By such rocks
65 men killed Bloodaxe.[3]

Fierce blood throbs in his tongue,
lean words.
Skulls cropped for steel caps
huddle round Stainmore.[4]
70 Their becks ring on limestone,
whisper to peat.[5]
The clogged cart pushes the horse downhill.
In such soft air
they trudge and sing,
75 laying the tune frankly on the air.
All sounds fall still,
fellside bleat,
hide-and-seek peewit.[6]

Her pulse their pace,
80 palm countering palm,
till a trench is filled,
stone white as cheese
jeers at the dale.

---

8. Britishism for "truck."
9. Or "felly," the exterior rim of a wheel.
1. "Sweater to sweater" (jerseys were worn by the working classes).
2. Metal container with handle and cover (not, that is, a modern sealed can). Garsdale and Hawes are small country towns in northern England.
3. Eric Bloodaxe, a Norse hero of the pirates (with "sea-reflecting eyes") from European countries around the Baltic Sea who began invading England in A.D. 450. Their "Baltic plainsong" refers to their rough yet rhythmic speech.
4. Desolate forest in the north of England; the "steel caps" are helmets.
5. "Beck" is a dialect word for a mattock, an agricultural instrument; it would "ring" on hard limestone, but "whisper" cutting into soft "peat," or decayed vegetable tissue in the earth.
6. Or "pewit," a bird noted for its shrill wailing cry.

Knotty wood, hard to rive,°   *split*
85 smoulders to ash;
    smell of October apples.
    The road again,
    at a trot.
    Wetter, warmed, they watch
90 the mason meditate
    on name and date.

    Rain rinses the road,
    the bull streams and laments.
    Sour rye porridge from the hob[7]
95 with cream and black tea,
    meat, crust and crumb.
    Her parents in bed
    the children dry their clothes.
    he has untied the tape
100 of her striped flannel drawers
    before the range. Naked
    on the pricked rag mat[8]
    his fingers comb
    thatch of his manhood's home.

105 Gentle generous voices weave
    over bare night
    words to confirm and delight
    till bird dawn.
    Rainwater from the butt
110 she fetches and flannel
    to wash him inch by inch,
    kissing the pebbles.
    Shining slowworm part of the marvel.
    The mason stirs:
115 Words!
    Pens are too light.
    Take a chisel to write.

    Every birth a crime,
    every sentence life.
120 Wiped of mould and mites
    would the ball run true?
    No hope of going back.
    Hounds falter and stray,
    Shame deflects the pen.
125 Love murdered neither bleeds nor stifles
    but jogs the draftsman's elbow.
    what can he, changed, tell
    her, changed, perhaps dead?
    Delight dwindles. Blame
130 stays the same.

---

7. Level projection in a fireplace, where a kettle   8. Rug made from strips of rag hooked through a
can be kept warm.   sacking base.

Brief words are hard to find,
shapes to carve and discard:
Bloodaxe, king of York,
king of Dublin, king of Orkney.[9]
135 Take no notice of tears;
letter the stone to stand
over love laid aside lest
insufferable happiness impede
flight to Stainmore,
140 to trace
lark, mallet,
becks, flocks
and axe knocks.

Dung will not soil the slowworm's
145 mosaic. Breathless lark
drops to nest in sodden trash;
Rawthey truculent, dingy.
Drudge at the mallet, the may is down,
fog on fells. Guilty of spring
150 and spring's ending
amputated years ache after
the bull is beef, love a convenience.
It is easier to die than to remember.
Name and date
155 split in soft slate
a few months obliterate.

1966

LAURA (RIDING) JACKSON

1901–1991

The Wind Suffers

The wind suffers of blowing,
The sea suffers of water,
And fire suffers of burning,
And I of a living name.

5 As stone suffers of stoniness,
As light of its shiningness,
As birds of their wingedness,
So I of my whoness.

And what the cure of all this?
10 What the not and not suffering?
What the better and later of this?
What the more me of me?

9. Islands off the northeast coast of Scotland; "king" here is in the sense of an early tribal chieftain.

How for the pain-world to be
More world and no pain?
15 How for the old rain to fall
More wet and more dry?

How for the wilful blood to run
More salt-red and sweet-white?
And how for me in my actualness
20 To more shriek and more smile?

By no other miracles,
By the same knowing poison,
By an improved anguish,
By my further dying.

Ding-Donging

With old hours all belfry heads
Are filled, as with thoughts.
With old hours ring the new hours
Between their bells.
5 And this hour-long ding-donging
So much employs the hour-long silences
That bells hang thinking when not striking,
When striking think of nothing.

Chimes of forgotten hours
10 More and more are played
While bells stare into space,
And more and more space wears
A look of having heard
But hearing not:
15 Forgotten hours chime louder
In the meantime, as if always,
And spread ding-donging back
More and more to yesterdays.

1938

STERLING A. BROWN

1901–1989

Slim in Atlanta[1]

Down in Atlanta,
    De whitefolks got laws
For to keep all de niggers
    From laughin' outdoors.

---

1. One of a series of poems about the character Slim Greer.

5   Hope to Gawd I may die
     If I ain't speakin' truth
     Make de niggers do deir laughin'
     In a telefoam booth.

     Slim Greer hit de town
10   An' de rebs² got him told,—
     "Dontcha laugh on de street,
     If you want to die old."

     Den dey showed him de booth,
     An' a hundred shines°   *black people*
15   In front of it, waitin'
     In double lines.

     Slim thought his sides
     Would bust in two,
     Yelled, "Lookout, everybody,
20   I'm coming through!"

     Pulled de other man out,
     An' bust in de box,
     An' laughed four hours
     By de Georgia clocks.

25   Den he peeked through de door,
     An' what did he see?
     Three hundred niggers there
     In misery.—

     Some holdin' deir sides,
30   Some holdin' deir jaws,
     To keep from breakin'
     De Georgia laws.

     An' Slim gave a holler,
     An' started again;
35   An' from three hundred throats
     Come a moan of pain.

     An' everytime Slim
     Saw what was outside,
     Got to whoopin' again
40   Till he nearly died.

     An' while de poor critters
     Was waitin' deir chance,
     Slim laughed till dey sent
     Fo' de ambulance.

---

2. Abbreviation for rebels, or members of the Confederacy in the Civil War; here, a general term for Southerners.

45   De state paid de railroad
            To take him away;
        Den, things was as usural
            In Atlanta, Gee A.[3]

1932

Chillen Get Shoes

Hush little Lily,
    Don't you cry;
You'll get your silver slippers
    Bye and bye.

5   Moll wears silver slippers
        With red heels,
    And men come to see her
        In automobiles.

    Lily walks wretched,
10   Dragging her doll,
    Worshipping stealthily
        Good-time Moll;

    Envying bitterly
        Moll's fine clothes,
15 And her plump legs clad
        In openwork hose.

    Don't worry, Lily,
        Don't you cry;
    You'll be like Moll, too,
20   Bye and bye.

1932

Bitter Fruit of the Tree

They said to my grandmother: "Please do not be bitter,"
When they sold her first-born and let the second die,
When they drove her husband till he took to the swamplands,
And brought him home bloody and beaten at last.
5 They told her, "It is better you should not be bitter,
Some must work and suffer so that we, who must, can live,
Forgiving is noble, you must not be heathen bitter;
These are your orders: you *are* not to be bitter."
And they left her shack for their porticoed house.

10 They said to my father: "Please do not be bitter,"
When he ploughed and planted a crop not his,
When he weatherstripped a house that he could not enter,
And stored away a harvest he could not enjoy.
They answered his questions: "It does not concern you,

---

3. Ga.; abbreviation for the state of Georgia.

15 It is not for you to know, it is past your understanding,
    All you need know is: you must not be bitter."

1939   1980

Conjured

"She done put huh little hands
On the back uh my head;
I cain't git away from her
Twill I'm dead.

5   "She done laid her little body
    Beneaf my breast,
    And I won't never
    Git no rest.

    "She done been in my arms
10 Twill the break of day
    Won't never
    Git away. . . .

    "She done put her little shoes
    Underneaf my bed
15 Never git away from her
    Twill I'm dead.

    "Won't want to leave her
    Then," he said.
    "Oh, baby, gotta lay
20 So long
    Alone. . . ."

1930s   1980

LANGSTON HUGHES

1902–1967

The Weary Blues

Droning a drowsy syncopated tune,
Rocking back and forth to a mellow croon,
    I heard a Negro play.
Down on Lenox Avenue[1] the other night
5   By the pale dull pallor of an old gas light
        He did a lazy sway. . . .
        He did a lazy sway. . . .
To the tune o' those Weary Blues.
With his ebony hands on each ivory key
10 He made that poor piano moan with melody.

---

1. A main thoroughfare in New York, in the heart of Harlem.

O Blues!
Swaying to and fro on his rickety stool
He played that sad raggy tune like a musical fool.
    Sweet Blues!
15 Coming from a black man's soul.
    O Blues!
In a deep song voice with a melancholy tone
I heard that Negro sing, that old piano moan—
    "Ain't got nobody in all this world,
20   Ain't got nobody but ma self.
    I's gwine to quit ma frownin'
    And put ma troubles on the shelf."
Thump, thump, thump, went his foot on the floor.
He played a few chords then he sang some more—
25   "I got the Weary Blues
        And I can't be satisfied.
        Got the Weary Blues
        And can't be satisfied—
        I ain't happy no mo'
30   And I wish that I had died."
And far into the night he crooned that tune.
The stars went out and so did the moon.
The singer stopped playing and went to bed
While the Weary Blues echoed through his head.
35 He slept like a rock or a man that's dead.

                                        1926

The Negro Speaks of Rivers

(To W. E. B. Du Bois)[2]

I've known rivers:
I've known rivers ancient as the world and older than the
    flow of human blood in human veins.
My soul has grown deep like the rivers.

5   I bathed in the Euphrates when dawns were young.
I built my hut near the Congo and it lulled me to sleep.
I looked upon the Nile and raised the pyramids above it.
I heard the singing of the Mississippi when Abe Lincoln
        went down to New Orleans, and I've seen its muddy
10   bosom turn all golden in the sunset.

I've known rivers:
Ancient, dusky rivers.

My soul has grown deep like the rivers.

                                        1926

---

2. (1868–1963); American historian, educator, and activist, he was one of the founders of the NAACP,
and in later life became increasingly interested in Pan-Africanism.

Dream Variations

To fling my arms wide
In some place of the sun,
To whirl and to dance
Till the white day is done.
5   Then rest at cool evening
Beneath a tall tree
While night comes on gently,
    Dark like me—
That is my dream!

10   To fling my arms wide
In the face of the sun,
Dance! Whirl! Whirl!
Till the quick day is done.
Rest at pale evening . . .
15   A tall, slim tree . . .
Night coming tenderly
Black like me.

1926

Cross

My old man's a white old man
And my old mother's black.
If ever I cursed my white old man
I take my curses back.

5   If ever I cursed my black old mother
And wished she were in hell,
I'm sorry for that evil wish
And now I wish her well.

My old man died in a fine big house.
10   My ma died in a shack.
I wonder where I'm gonna die,
Being neither white nor black?

1926

Bad Luck Card

Cause you don't love me
Is awful, awful hard.
Gypsy done showed me
My bad luck card.

5   There ain't no good left
In this world for me.
Gypsy done tole me—
Unlucky as can be.

I don't know what
10   Po' weary me can do.
Gypsy says I'd kill my self
If I was you.

1927

Song for a Dark Girl

Way Down South in Dixie
   (Break the heart of me)
They hung my black young lover
   To a cross roads tree.

5   Way Down South in Dixie
   (Bruised body high in air)
I asked the white Lord Jesus
   What was the use of prayer.

Way Down South in Dixie
10   (Break the heart of me)
Love is a naked shadow
   On a gnarled and naked tree.

1927

Harlem Sweeties

Have you dug the spill
Of Sugar Hill?[3]
Cast your gims
On this sepia° thrill: *brown*
5   Brown sugar lassie,
Caramel treat,
Honey-gold baby
Sweet enough to eat.
Peach-skinned girlie,
10 Coffee and cream,
Chocolate darling
Out of a dream.
Walnut tinted
Or cocoa brown,
15 Pomegranate-lipped
Pride of the town.
Rich cream-colored
To plum-tinted black,
Feminine sweetness
20 In Harlem's no lack.
Glow of the quince
To blush of the rose.

---

3. In the early part of the twentieth century, the most fashionable residential area of Harlem.

Persimmon bronze
To cinnamon toes.
25 Blackberry cordial,
Virginia Dare⁴ wine —
All those sweet colors
Flavor Harlem of mine!
Walnut or cocoa,
30 Let me repeat:
Caramel, brown sugar,
A chocolate treat.
Molasses taffy,
Coffee and cream,
35 Licorice, clove, cinnamon
To a honey-brown dream.
Ginger, wine-gold,
Persimmon, blackberry,
All through the spectrum
40 Harlem girls vary —
So if you want to know beauty's
Rainbow-sweet thrill,
Stroll down luscious,
Delicious, *fine* Sugar Hill.

1942

Harlem

What happens to a dream deferred?

Does it dry up
like a raisin in the sun?
Or fester like a sore —
5 And then run?
Does it stink like rotten meat?
Or crust and sugar over —
like a syrupy sweet?

Maybe it just sags
10 like a heavy load.

Or does it explode?

1951

Theme for English B

The instructor said,

*Go home and write
a page tonight.
And let that page come out of you —
5 Then, it will be true.*

4. A brand of wine.

I wonder if it's that simple?
I am twenty-two, colored, born in Winston-Salem.
I went to school there, then Durham, then here
to this college on the hill above Harlem.
10   I am the only colored student in my class.
The steps from the hill lead down into Harlem,
through a park, then I cross St. Nicholas,
Eighth Avenue, Seventh, and I come to the Y,
the Harlem Branch Y, where I take the elevator
15   up to my room, sit down, and write this page:

It's not easy to know what is true for you or me
at twenty-two, my age. But I guess I'm what
I feel and see and hear, Harlem, I hear you:
hear you, hear me—we two—you, me, talk on this page.
20   (I hear New York, too.) Me—who?
Well, I like to eat, sleep, drink, and be in love.
I like to work, read, learn, and understand life.
I like a pipe for a Christmas present,
or records—Bessie,[5] bop, or Bach.
25   I guess being colored doesn't make me *not* like
the same things other folks like who are other races.
So will my page be colored that I write?
Being me, it will not be white.
But it will be
30   a part of you, instructor.
You are white—
yet a part of me, as I am a part of you.
That's American.
Sometimes perhaps you don't want to be a part of me.
35   Nor do I often want to be a part of you.
But we are, that's true!
I guess you learn from me—
although you're older—and white—
and somewhat more free.

40   This is my page for English B.

1951

ROY CAMPBELL

1902–1957

The Zulu Girl

To F. C. Slater

When in the sun the hot red acres smoulder,
Down where the sweating gang its labour plies,

5. Bessie Smith (1894?–1937), American blues singer.

A girl flings down her hoe, and from her shoulder
Unslings her child tormented by the flies.

5 She takes him to a ring of shadow pooled
By thorn-trees: purpled with the blood of ticks,
While her sharp nails, in slow caresses ruled,
Prowl through his hair with sharp electric clicks,

His sleepy mouth, plugged by the heavy nipple,
10 Tugs like a puppy, grunting as he feeds:
Through his frail nerves her own deep languors ripple
Like a broad river sighing through its reeds.

Yet in that drowsy stream his flesh imbibes
An old unquenched unsmotherable heat—
15 The curbed ferocity of beaten tribes,
The sullen dignity of their defeat.

Her body looms above him like a hill
Within whose shade a village lies at rest,
Or the first cloud so terrible and still
20 That bears the coming harvest in its breast.

1926   1930

The Sisters

After hot loveless nights, when cold winds stream
Sprinkling the frost and dew, before the light,
Bored with the foolish things that girls must dream
Because their beds are empty of delight,

5 Two sisters rise and strip. Out from the night
Their horses run to their low-whistled pleas—
Vast phantom shapes with eyeballs rolling white
That sneeze a fiery steam about their knees:

Through the crisp manes their stealthy prowling hands,
10 Stronger than curbs, in slow caresses rove,
They gallop down across the milk-white sands
And wade far out into the sleeping cove:

The frost stings sweetly with a burning kiss
As intimate as love, as cold as death:
15 Their lips, whereon delicious tremors hiss,
Fume with the ghostly pollen of their breath.

Far out on the grey silence of the flood
They watch the dawn in smouldering gyres° expand *spiral turnings*
Beyond them: and the day burns through their blood
20 Like a white candle through a shuttered hand.

1926   1930

Choosing a Mast

This mast, new-shaved, through whom I rive° the ropes,   *pull*
Says she was once an oread[1] of the slopes,
Graceful and tall upon the rocky highlands,
A slender tree as vertical as noon,
5   And her low voice was lovely as the silence
Through which a fountain whistles to the moon,
Who now of the white spray must take the veil
And, for her songs, the thunder of the sail.

I chose her for her fragrance, when the spring
10   With sweetest resins swelled her fourteenth ring
And with live amber welded her young thews:°   *sinews*
I chose her for the glory of the Muse,[2]
Smoother of forms, that her hard-knotted grain,
Grazed by the chisel, shaven by the plane,
15   Might from the steel as cool a burnish take
As from the bladed moon a windless lake.

I chose her for her eagerness of flight
Where she stood tiptoe on the rocky height
Lifted by her own perfume to the sun,
20   While through her rustling plumes with eager sound
Her eagle spirit, with the gale at one,
Spreading wide pinions,° would have spurned the ground   *wings*
And her own sleeping shadow, had they not
With thymy fragrance charmed her to the spot.

25   Lover of song, I chose this mountain pine
Not only for the straightness of her spine
But for her songs: for there she loved to sing
Through a long noon's repose of wave and wing,
The fluvial° swirling of her scented hair   *riverlike*
30   Sole rill° of song in all that windless air,   *stream*
And her slim form the naiad of the stream
Afloat upon the languor of its theme;

And for the soldier's fare on which she fed:
Her wine the azure, and the snow her bread;
35   And for her stormy watches on the height,
For only out of solitude or strife
Are born the sons of valour and delight;
And lastly for her rich, exulting life,
That with the wind stopped not its singing breath
40   But carolled on, the louder for its death.

Under a pine, when summer days were deep,
We loved the most to lie in love or sleep:
And when in long hexameters[3] the west

---

1. Mountain nymph.   She was the inspiring goddess of poetry.
2. Calliope: in Greek and Roman mythology, one   3. Verse line of six metrical feet.
of the nine daughters of Zeus and Mnemosyne.

Rolled his grey surge, the forest for his lyre,
45 It was the pines that sang us to our rest,
Loud in the wind and fragrant in the fire,
With legioned voices swelling all night long,
From Pelion to Provence, their storm of song.

It was the pines that fanned us in the heat,
50 The pines, that cheered us in the time of sleet,
For which sweet gifts I set one dryad[4] free;
No longer to the wind a rooted foe,
This nymph shall wander where she longs to be
And with the blue north wind arise and go,
55 A silver huntress with the moon to run
And fly through rainbows with the rising sun;

And when to pasture in the glittering shoals
The guardian mistral[5] drives his thundering foals,
And when like Tartar[6] horsemen racing free
60 We ride the snorting fillies of the sea,
My pine shall be the archer of the gale
While on the bending willow curves the sail
From whose great bow the long keel shooting home
Shall fly, the feathered arrow of the foam.

1931   1939

OGDEN NASH

1902–1971

The Cow

The cow is of the bovine ilk;
One end is moo, the other, milk.

1931

Reflections on Ice-breaking

Candy
Is dandy
But liquor
Is quicker.

1931

Requiem

There was a young belle of old Natchez
Whose garments were always in patchez.

4. Tree nymph.
5. A violent northeast wind in southern France.
6. Originally "Tatar": member of a tribe in Chi-
nese Tartary. Name later extended to Mongol,
Turkish, and other fierce tribes.

When comment arose
On the state of her clothes,
5   She drawled, When Ah itchez, Ah scratchez!

1935

Columbus

Once upon a time there was an Italian,
And some people thought he was a rapscallion,
But he wasn't offended,
Because other people thought he was splendid,
5   And he said the world was round,
And everybody made an uncomplimentary sound,
But he went and tried to borrow some money from Ferdinand
But Ferdinand said America was a bird in the bush and he'd
        rather have a berdinand,
But Columbus' brain was fertile, it wasn't arid,
10 And he remembered that Ferdinand was married,
And he thought, there is no wife like a misunderstood one,
Because if her husband thinks something is a terrible idea she is
        bound to think it a good one,
So he perfumed his handkerchief with bay rum and citronella,
And he went to see Isabella,
15 And he looked wonderful but he had never felt sillier,
And she said, I can't place the face but the aroma is familiar,
And Columbus didn't say a word,
All he said was, I am Columbus, the fifteenth-century Admiral
        Byrd,[1]
And, just as he thought, her disposition was very malleable,
20 And she said, Here are my jewels, and she wasn't penurious like
        Cornelia the mother of the Gracchi,[2] she wasn't referring to
        her children, no, she was referring to her jewels, which were
        very very valuable,
So Columbus said, Somebody show me the sunset and somebody
        did and he set sail for it,
And he discovered America and they put him in jail for it,
And the fetters gave him welts,
And they named America after somebody else,[3]
25 So the sad fate of Columbus ought to be pointed out to every
        child and every voter,
Because it has a very important moral, which is, Don't be a
        discoverer, be a promoter.

1935

The Turtle

The turtle lives 'twixt plated decks
Which practically conceal its sex.

1. Richard Evelyn Byrd (1888–1957), American explorer of the North and South Poles.
2. Cornelia (second century B.C.) was the Roman model of matronly virtue. Though hardly penurious, she famously responded to a request to show her jewels by producing her two sons (famous men in their own right).
3. Amerigo Vespucci (1454–1512), Italian navigator and explorer who first sailed across the Atlantic in 1497.

I think it clever of the turtle
In such a fix to be so fertile.

1940

Arthur

There was an old man of Calcutta,
Who coated his tonsils with butta,
Thus converting his snore
From a thunderous roar
5   To a soft, oleaginous° mutta.   *oily*

1940

STEVIE SMITH

1902–1971

No Categories!

I cry I cry
To God who created me
Not to you Angels who frustrated me
Let me fly, let me die,
5   Let me come to Him.

Not to you Angels on the wing,
With your severe faces,
And your scholarly grimaces,
And your do this and that,
10   And your exasperating pit-pat
Of appropriate admonishment.

That is not what the Creator meant.
In the day of his gusty creation
He made this and that
15   And laughed to see them grow fat.

Plod on, you Angels say, do better aspire higher
And one day you may be like us, or those next below us, ˙
Or nearer the lowest,
Or lowest,
20   Doing their best.

Oh no no, you Angels, I say,
No hierarchies I pray.

Oh God, laugh not too much aside
Say not, it is a small matter.
25   See what your Angels do; scatter
Their pride; laugh them away.

Oh no categories I pray.

1950

Mr. Over

Mr. Over is dead
He died fighting and true
And on his tombstone they wrote
Over to You.

5 And who pray is this You
To whom Mr. Over is gone?
Oh if we only knew that
We should not do wrong.

But who is this beautiful You
10 We all of us long for so much
Is he not our friend and our brother
Our father and such?

Yes he is this and much more
This is but a portion
15 A sea-drop in a bucket
Taken from the ocean

So the voices spake
Softly above my head
And a voice in my heart cried: Follow
20 Where he has led

And a devil's voice cried: Happy
Happy the dead.

1950

The Death Sentence

Cold as No Plea,
Yet wild with all negation,
Weeping I come
To my heart's destination,
5 To my last bed
Between th' unhallowed boards—
The Law allows it
And the Court awards.

1950

Not Waving but Drowning

Nobody heard him, the dead man,
But still he lay moaning:
I was much further out than you thought
And not waving but drowning.

5 Poor chap, he always loved larking
And now he's dead

It must have been too cold for him his heart gave way,
They said.

Oh, no no no, it was too cold always
10 (Still the dead one lay moaning)
I was much too far out all my life
And not waving but drowning.

1957

The Celts

I think of the Celts[1] as rather a whining lady
Who was beautiful once but is not so much so now
She is not very loving, but there is one thing she loves
It is her grievance which she hugs and takes out walking.
5 The Celtic lady likes fighting very much for freedom
But when she has got it she is a proper tyrant
Nobody likes her much when she is governing.

The Celtic lady is not very widely popular
But the English love her oh they love her very much
10 Especially when the Celtic lady is Irish they love her
Which is odd as she hates them then more than anyone else,
When she's Welsh the English stupidly associate her chiefly
With national hats, eisteddfods[2] and Old Age Pensions.
(They don't think of her at all when she is Scotch, it is rather a problem.)

15 Oh the Celtic lady when she's Irish is the one for me
Oh she is so witty and wild, my word witty,
And flashing and spiteful this Celtic lady we love
All the same she is not so beautiful as she was.

1957

Thoughts about the Person from Porlock[3]

Coleridge received the Person from Porlock
And ever after called him a curse,
Then why did he hurry to let him in?
He could have hid in the house.

5 It was not right of Coleridge in fact it was wrong
(But often we all do wrong)
As the truth is I think he was already stuck
With Kubla Khan.

---

1. Peoples speaking languages related to those of
the ancient Gauls, including Bretons, Cornish,
Welsh, Irish, etc.
2. Traditional Welsh congresses of bards, min-
strels and poets, at which contests of minstrelsy,
singing, or oratory are conducted.
3. Coleridge attributed the fact that his poem

"Kubla Khan" was left unfinished to his having
been interrupted, while writing it, by "a person on
business from Porlock," to having been "detained
by him for above an hour," and then having been
unable to recapture the vision that was the sub-
stance of the poem. (See n. 4, p. 741.)

He was weeping and wailing: I am finished, finished,
10   I shall never write another word of it,
When along comes the Person from Porlock
And takes the blame for it.

It was not right, it was wrong,
But often we all do wrong.

15   May we enquire the name of the Person from Porlock?
Why, Porson, didn't you know?
He lived at the bottom of Porlock Hill
So had a long way to go,

He wasn't much in the social sense
20   Though his grandmother was a Warlock,
One of the Rutlandshire ones I fancy
And nothing to do with Porlock,

And he lived at the bottom of the hill as I said
And had a cat named Flo,
25   And had a cat named Flo.

I long for the Person from Porlock
To bring my thoughts to an end,
I am becoming impatient to see him
I think of him as a friend,

30   Often I look out the window
Often I run to the gate
I think, He will come this evening,
I think it is rather late.

I am hungry to be interrupted
35   For ever and ever amen
O Person from Porlock come quickly
And bring my thoughts to an end.

I felicitate the people who have a Person from Porlock
To break up everything and throw it away
40   Because then there will be nothing to keep them
And they need not stay.

Why do they grumble so much?
He comes like a benison°   *blessing*
They should be glad he has not forgotten them
45   They might have had to go on.

These thoughts are depressing I know. They are depressing,
I wish I was more cheerful, it is more pleasant,
Also it is a duty, we should smile as well as submitting
To the purpose of One Above who is experimenting
50   With various mixtures of human character which goes best,

All is interesting for him it is exciting, but not for us.
There I go again. Smile, smile, and get some work to do
Then you will be practically unconscious without positively having
    to go.

1962

Pretty

Why is the word pretty so underrated?
In November the leaf is pretty when it falls
The stream grows deep in the woods after rain
And in the pretty pool the pike stalks

5   He stalks his prey, and this is pretty too,
The prey escapes with an underwater flash
But not for long, the great fish has him now
The pike is a fish who always has his prey

And this is pretty. The water rat is pretty
10 His paws are not webbed, he cannot shut his nostrils
As the otter can and the beaver, he is torn between
The land and water. Not "torn," he does not mind.

The owl hunts in the evening and it is pretty
The lake water below him rustles with ice
15 There is frost coming from the ground, in the air mist
All this is pretty, it could not be prettier.

Yes, it could always be prettier, the eye abashes
It is becoming an eye that cannot see enough,
Out of the wood the eye climbs. This is prettier
20 A field in the evening, tilting up.

The field tilts to the sky. Though it is late
The sky is lighter than the hill field
All this looks easy but really it is extraordinary
Well, it is extraordinary to be so pretty.

25 And it is careless, and that is always pretty
This field, this owl, this pike, this pool are careless,
As Nature is always careless and indifferent
Who sees, who steps, means nothing, and this is pretty.

So a person can come along like a thief—pretty!—
30 Stealing a look, pinching the sound and feel,
Lick the icicle broken from the bank
And still say nothing at all, only cry pretty.

Cry pretty, pretty, pretty and you'll be able
Very soon not even to cry pretty
35 And so be delivered entirely from humanity
This is prettiest of all, it is very pretty.

1969

COUNTEE CULLEN

1903–1946

Heritage

For Harold Jackman

What is Africa to me:
Copper sun or scarlet sea,
Jungle star or jungle track,
Strong bronzed men, or regal black
5 Women from whose loins I sprang
When the birds of Eden sang?
One three centuries removed
From the scenes his fathers loved,
Spicy grove, cinnamon tree,
10 *What is Africa to me?*

So I lie, who all day long
Want no sound except the song
Sung by wild barbaric birds
Goading massive jungle herds,
15 Juggernauts[1] of flesh that pass
Trampling tall defiant grass
Where young forest lovers lie,
Plighting troth beneath the sky.
So I lie, who always hear,
20 Though I cram against my ear
Both my thumbs, and keep them there,
Great drums throbbing through the air.
So I lie, whose fount of pride,
Dear distress, and joy allied,
25 Is my somber flesh and skin,
With the dark blood dammed within
Like great pulsing tides of wine
That, I fear, must burst the fine
Channels of the chafing net
30 Where they surge and foam and fret.

Africa? A book one thumbs
Listlessly, till slumber comes.
Unremembered are her bats
Circling through the night, her cats
35 Crouching in the river reeds,
Stalking gentle flesh that feeds
By the river brink; no more
Does the bugle-throated roar
Cry that monarch claws have leapt
40 From the scabbards where they slept.
Silver snakes that once a year

---

1. Great forces or massive objects that crush everything in their path.

Doff the lovely coats you wear,
Seek no covert in your fear
Lest a mortal eye should see;
45　What's your nakedness to me?
Here no leprous flowers rear
Fierce corollas° in the air;　　　　　　　　　　　　　　*petals*
Here no bodies sleek and wet,
Dripping mingled rain and sweat,
50　Tread the savage measures of
Jungle boys and girls in love.
What is last year's snow to me,
Last year's anything? The tree
Budding yearly must forget
55　How its past arose or set—
Bough and blossom, flower, fruit,
Even what shy bird with mute
Wonder at her travail there,
Meekly labored in its hair.
60　*One three centuries removed*
From the scenes his fathers loved,
Spicy grove, cinnamon tree,
What is Africa to me?

So I lie, who find no peace
65　Night or day, no slight release
From the unremittent beat
Made by cruel padded feet
Walking through my body's street.
Up and down they go, and back,
70　Treading out a jungle track.
So I lie, who never quite
Safely sleep from rain at night—
I can never rest at all
When the rain begins to fall;
75　Like a soul gone mad with pain
I must match its weird refrain;
Ever must I twist and squirm,
Writhing like a baited worm,
While its primal measures drip
80　Through my body, crying, "Strip!
Doff this new exuberance.
Come and dance the Lover's Dance!"
In an old remembered way
Rain works on me night and day.

85　Quaint, outlandish heathen gods
Black men fashion out of rods,
Clay, and brittle bits of stone,
In a likeness like their own,
My conversion came high-priced;
90　I belong to Jesus Christ,
Preacher of Humility;
Heathen gods are naught to me.

Father, Son, and Holy Ghost,
So I make an idle boast;
95　Jesus of the twice-turned cheek,[2]
Lamb of God, although I speak
With my mouth thus, in my heart
Do I play a double part.
Ever at Thy glowing altar
100　Must my heart grow sick and falter,
Wishing He I served were black,
Thinking then it would not lack
Precedent of pain to guide it,
Let who would or might deride it;
105　Surely then this flesh would know
Yours had borne a kindred woe.
Lord, I fashion dark gods, too,
Daring even to give You
Dark despairing features where,
110　Crowned with dark rebellious hair,
Patience wavers just so much as
Mortal grief compels, while touches　•
Quick and hot, of anger, rise
To smitten cheek and weary eyes.
115　Lord, forgive me if my need
Sometimes shapes a human creed.
All day long and all night through,
One thing only must I do:
Quench my pride and cool my blood,
120　*Lest I perish in the flood,*
Lest a hidden ember set
Timber that I thought was wet
Burning like the dryest flax,
Melting like the merest wax,
125　*Lest the grave restore its dead.*
Not yet has my heart or head
In the least way realized
They and I are civilized.

Incident

Once riding in old Baltimore,
Heart-filled, head-filled with glee,
I saw a Baltimorean
Keep looking straight at me.

5　Now I was eight and very small,
And he was no whit bigger,
And so I smiled, but he poked out
His tongue, and called me, "Nigger."

I saw the whole of Baltimore
10　From May until December;

---

2. See Matthew 5.39: "I say unto you, that ye resist not evil: but whosoever shall smite thee on the right cheek, turn to him the other also."

Of all the things that happened there
That's all that I remember.

1925

EARLE BIRNEY
1904–1991

Slug in Woods

For eyes he waves greentipped
taut horns of slime   They dipped
hours back   across a reef
a salmonberry leaf
5   Then strained to grope past fin
of spruce   Now eyes suck in
as through the hemlock butts
of his day's ledge there cuts
a vixen chipmunk   Stilled
10   is he—green mucus chilled
or blotched and soapy stone
pinguid° in moss   alone   *fat*
Hours on   he will resume
his silver scrawl   illume
15   his palimpsest[1]   emboss
his diver's line across
that waving green illim-
itable seafloor   Slim
young jay his sudden shark
20   the wrecks he skirts are dark
and fungussed firlogs[2]   whom
spirea sprays emplume
encoral[3]   Dew his shell
while mounting boles foretell
25   of isles in dappled air
fathoms above his care
Azygous° muted life   *single*
himself his viscid wife
foodward he noses cold beneath his sea
30   So spends a summer's jasper° century   *stonelike*

1928

Bushed

He invented a rainbow but lightning struck it
shattered it into the lake-lap of a mountain
so big his mind slowed when he looked at it

---

1. A page from which writing has been erased to
make room for another text.
2. A neologism for logs of a fir tree.

3. "Emplume / encoral": to make appear like
plumes or coral.

Yet he built a shack on the shore
5 learned to roast porcupine belly and
wore the quills on his hatband

At first he was out with the dawn
whether it yellowed bright as wood-columbine
or was only a fuzzed moth in a flannel of storm
10 But he found the mountain was clearly alive
sent messages whizzing down every hot morning
boomed proclamations at noon and spread out
a white guard of goat
before falling asleep on its feet at sundown

15 When he tried his eyes on the lake   ospreys[4]
would fall like valkyries[5]
choosing the cut-throat
He took then to waiting
till the night smoke rose from the boil of the sunset

20 But the moon carved unknown totems
out of the lakeshore
owls in the beardusky woods derided him
moosehorned cedars circled his swamps and tossed
their antlers up to the stars
25 Then he knew   though the mountain slept   the winds
were shaping its peak to an arrowhead
poised

And now he could only
bar himself in and wait
30 for the great flint to come singing into his heart

1952

The Bear on the Delhi Road[6]

Unreal   tall as a myth
by the road the Himalayan bear
is beating the brilliant air
with his crooked arms
5 About him two men   bare
spindly as locusts   leap
One pulls on a ring
in the great soft nose   His mate
flicks   flicks with a stick
10 up at the rolling eyes

They have not led him here
down from the fabulous hills
to this bald alien plain

---

4. Large, fish-eating hawks.
5. In Norse mythology, the warrior-maidens of Odin; they selected the heroes who were to die in battle and afterwards carried them to Valhalla, the hall of the heroic slain.
6. In India.

and the clamorous world   to kill
15 but simply to teach him to dance

They are peaceful both   these spare
men of Kashmir[7]   and the bear
alive is their living   too
If   far on the Delhi way
20 around him galvanic[8] they dance
it is merely to wear   wear
from his shaggy body the tranced
wish forever to stay
only an ambling bear
25 four-footed in berries

It is no more joyous for them
in this hot dust to prance
out of reach of the praying claws
sharpened to paw for ants
30 in the shadows of deodars[9]
It is not easy to free
myth from reality
or rear this fellow up
to lurch   lurch with them
35 in the tranced dancing of men

1962   1975

C. DAY LEWIS

1904–1972

The Conflict

I sang as one
Who on a tilting deck sings
To keep men's courage up, though the wave hangs
That shall cut off their sun.

5   As storm-cocks sing,
Flinging their natural answer in the wind's teeth,
And care not if it is waste of breath
Or birth-carol of spring.

As ocean-flyer clings
10 To height, to the last drop of spirit driving on
While yet ahead is land to be won
And work for wings.

Singing I was at peace,
Above the clouds, outside the ring:

---

7. Mountainous region of northern India.   9. East Indian cedars.
8. I.e., exciting him as if with electric shock.

15   For sorrow finds a swift release in song
     And pride its poise.

     Yet living here,
     As one between two massing powers I live
     Whom neutrality cannot save
20   Nor occupation cheer.

     None such shall be left alive:
     The innocent wing is soon shot down,
     And private stars fade in the blood-red dawn
     Where two worlds strive.

25   The red advance of life
     Contracts pride, calls out the common blood,
     Beats song into a single blade,
     Makes a depth-charge of grief.

     Move then with new desires,
30   For where we used to build and love
     Is no man's land, and only ghosts can live
     Between two fires.

1935

Two Songs

I've heard them lilting at loom and belting,[1]
Lasses lilting before dawn of day:
But now they are silent, not gamesome and gallant—
The flowers of the town are rotting away.

5   There was laughter and loving in the lanes at evening;
Handsome were the boys then, and girls were gay.
But lost in Flanders[2] by medalled commanders
The lads of the village are vanished away.

     Cursed be the promise that takes our men from us—
10   All will be champion if you choose to obey:
They fight against hunger but still it is stronger—
The prime of our land grows cold as the clay.

     The women are weary, once lilted so merry,
Waiting to marry for a year and a day:
15   From wooing and winning, from owning or earning
The flowers of the town are all turned away.

     Come, live with me and be my love,[3]
     And we will all the pleasures prove

1. Cf. Elliot, "The Flowers of the Forest" (pp. 619–20).
2. Site of many of the most murderous battles of World War I.
3. Cf. Marlowe, "The Passionate Shepherd to His Love" (p. 233) and Ralegh, "The Nymph's Reply to the Shepherd" (pp. 140–41).

20　　Of peace and plenty, bed and board,
　　　That chance employment may afford.

　　　I'll handle dainties on the docks
　　　And thou shalt read of summer frocks:
　　　At evening by the sour canals
　　　We'll hope to hear some madrigals.

25　　Care on thy maiden brow shall put
　　　A wreath of wrinkles, and thy foot
　　　Be shod with pain: not silken dress
　　　But toil shall tire thy loveliness.

　　　Hunger shall make thy modest zone°　　　　　　　*belt*
30　　And cheat fond death of all but bone—
　　　If these delights thy mind may move,
　　　Then live with me and be my love.

　　　　　　　　　　　　　　　　　　　　　　　　　1935

The Stand-To[4]

Autumn met me today as I walked over Castle Hill.
The wind that had set our corn by the ears was blowing still:
Autumn, who takes the leaves and the long days, crisped the air
With a tang of action, a taste of death; and the wind blew fair

5　From the east for men and barges massed on the other side—[5]
　Men maddened by numbers or stolid by nature, they have their pride
　As we in work and children, but now a contracting will
　Crumples their meek petitions and holds them poised to kill.

　Last night a Stand-To was ordered. Thirty men of us here
10　Came out to guard the star-lit village—my men who wear
　Unwitting the season's beauty, the received truth of the spade—
　Roadmen, farm labourers, masons, turned to another trade.

　A dog barked over the fields, the candle stars put a sheen
　On the rifles ready, the sandbags fronded with evergreen:
15　The dawn wind blew, the stars winked out on the posts where we lay,
　The order came, Stand Down, and thirty went away.

　Since a cold wind from Europe blows back the words in my teeth,
　Since autumn shortens the days and the odds against our death,
　And the harvest moon is waxing and high tides threaten harm,
20　Since last night may be the last night all thirty men go home,

　I write this verse to record the men who have watched with me—
　Spot who is good at darts, Squibby at repartee,

---

4. "Stand-To" (a shortened form of "Stand to Arms!") is a British military command given when an enemy attack is thought to be imminent. In September 1940, volunteer soldiers of the British Home Guard were mobilized in anticipation of a German invasion.
5. Of the English Channel.

Mark and Cyril, the dead shots, Ralph with a ploughman's gait,
Gibson, Harris and Long, old hands for the barricade,

25 Whiller the lorry°-driver, Francis and Rattlesnake,   *truck*
Fred and Charl and Stan—these nights I have lain awake
And thought of my thirty men and the autumn wind that blows
The apples down too early and shatters the autumn rose.

Destiny, History, Duty, Fortitude, Honour—all
30 The words of the politicians seem too big or too small
For the ragtag fighters of lane and shadow, the love that has grown
Familiar as working-clothes, faithful as bone to bone.

Blow, autumn wind, upon orchard and rose! Blow leaves along
Our lanes, but sing through me for the lives that are worth a song!
35 Narrowing days have darkened the vistas that hurt my eyes,
But pinned to the heart of darkness a tattered fire-flag flies.
                                                            September 1940

Where are the War Poets?

They who in folly or mere greed
Enslaved religion, markets, laws,
Borrow our language now and bid
Us to speak up in freedom's cause.

5   It is the logic of our times,
No subject for immortal verse—
That we who lived by honest dreams
Defend the bad against the worse.
                                                            1943

RICHARD EBERHART

1904–

The Fury of Aerial Bombardment

You would think the fury of aerial bombardment
Would rouse God to relent; the infinite spaces
Are still silent. He looks on shock-pried faces.
History, even, does not know what is meant.

5   You would feel that after so many centuries
God would give man to repent; yet he can kill
As Cain[1] could, but with multitudinous will,
No farther advanced than in his ancient furies.

Was man made stupid to see his own stupidity?
10   Is God by definition indifferent, beyond us all?

_____
1. The firstborn son of Adam and Eve, he murdered his brother Abel (Genesis 4.8).

Is the eternal truth man's fighting soul
Wherein the Beast ravens in its own avidity?

Of Van Wettering I speak, and Averill,
Names on a list, whose faces I do not recall
15 But they are gone to early death, who late° in school   *recently*
Distinguished the belt feed lever from the belt holding pawl.[2]

1947

PATRICK KAVANAGH
1905–1967

Sanctity

To be a poet and not know the trade,
To be a lover and repel all women;
Twin ironies by which great saints are made,
The agonising pincer-jaws of Heaven.

1936

From The Great Hunger[1]

I

Clay is the word and clay is the flesh
Where the potato-gatherers like mechanised scarecrows move
Along the side-fall of the hill—Maguire and his men.
If we watch them an hour is there anything we can prove
5 Of life as it is broken-backed over the Book
Of Death? Here crows gabble over worms and frogs
And the gulls like old newspapers are blown clear of the hedges, luckily.
Is there some light of imagination in these wet clods?
Or why do we stand here shivering?
10   Which of these men
Loved the light and the queen
Too long virgin? Yesterday was summer. Who was it promised marriage
     to himself

---

2. Parts of the .50-caliber Browning machine gun, mounted in American aircraft during World War II. Eberhart was an aerial gunnery instructor during the summer of 1944.

1. Kavanagh's most famous work is his long poem in fourteen sections, *The Great Hunger* (1942), named for a severe famine that decimated the Irish population during the 1840s, but which concerns itself with the spiritual and sexual hunger of the Irish peasantry among whom Kavanagh grew up. The central figure is a potato farmer named Patrick Maguire, who is bound to the soil by the need not to leave his aged mother, and whose church-induced sense of sin is so strong that he dies a bachelor and perhaps a virgin. In the remarks with

which he prefaced a 1960 radio broadcast of the poem, Kavanagh says: "It was in 1942 in darkest Dublin . . . that I wrote *The Great Hunger* . . . and if I say now that I do not like it, this will not mean as some of you might think, a sensational repudiation of my own works. . . . I'm afraid I'm too involved in *The Great Hunger*; the poem remains a tragedy because it is not completely born. Tragedy is underdeveloped comedy: tragedy fully explored becomes comedy. . . . But I am not debunking the unfortunate poem entirely; I will grant that there are some remarkable things in it, but free it hardly is, for there's no laughter in it" (*November Haggard*, p. 15).

Before apples were hung from the ceilings for Hallowe'en?
We will wait and watch the tragedy to the last curtain,
15 Till the last soul passively like a bag of wet clay
Rolls down the side of the hill, diverted by the angles
Where the plough missed or a spade stands, straitening the way.

A dog lying on a torn jacket under a heeled-up cart,
A horse nosing along the posied headland, trailing
20 A rusty plough. Three heads hanging between wide-apart
Legs. October playing a symphony on a slack wire paling.
Maguire watches the drills flattened out
And the flints that lit a candle for him on a June altar
Flameless. The drills slipped by and the days slipped by
25 And he trembled his head away and ran free from the world's halter,
And thought himself wiser than any man in the townland[2]
When he laughed over pints of porter°   *strong dark ale*
Of how he came free from every net spread
In the gaps of experience. He shook a knowing head
30 And pretended to his soul
That children are tedious in hurrying fields of April
Where men are spanging° across wide furrows.   *leaping*
Lost in the passion that never needs a wife—
The pricks that pricked were the pointed pins of harrows.
35 Children scream so loud that the crows could bring
The seed of an acre away with crow-rude jeers.
Patrick Maguire, he called his dog and he flung a stone in the air
And hallooed the birds away that were the birds of the years.

Turn over the weedy clods and tease out the tangled skeins.
40 What is he looking for there?
He thinks it is a potato, but we know better
Than his mud-gloved fingers probe in this insensitive hair.

"Move forward the basket and balance it steady
In this hollow. Pull down the shafts of that cart, Joe,
45 And straddle the horse," Maguire calls.
"The wind's over Brannagan's, now that means rain.
Graip° up some withered stalks and see that no potato falls   *fork*
Over the tail-board going down the ruckety pass—
And *that's* a job we'll have to do in December,
50 Gravel it and build a kerb on the bog-side. Is that Cassidy's ass
Out in my clover? Curse o' God—
Where is that dog?
Never where he's wanted." Maguire grunts and spits
Through a clay-wattled moustache and stares about him from the height.
55 His dream changes again like the cloud-swung wind
And he is not so sure now if his mother was right
When she praised the man who made a field his bride.

Watch him, watch him, that man on a hill whose spirit
Is a wet sack flapping about the knees of time.

---

2. In Ireland, an area of land comparable to a township.

60 He lives that his little fields may stay fertile when his own body
   Is spread in the bottom of a ditch under two coulters crossed in
      Christ's Name.

   He was suspicious in his youth as a rat near strange bread,
   When girls laughed; when they screamed he knew that meant
   The cry of fillies in season. He could not walk
65 The easy road to his destiny. He dreamt
   The innocense of young brambles to hooked treachery.
   O the grip, O the grip of irregular fields! No man escapes.
   It could not be that back of the hills love was free
   And ditches straight.
70 No monster hand lifted up children and put down apes
   As here
                           "O God if I had been wiser!"
   That was his sigh like the brown breeze in the thistles.
   He looks towards his house and haggard.° "O God if I had   yard
      been wiser!"
75 But now a crumpled leaf from the whitethorn bushes
   Darts like a frightened robin, and the fence
   Shows the green of after-grass through a little window,
   And he knows that his own heart is calling his mother a liar.
   God's truth is life—even the grotesque shapes of its foulest fire.

80 The horse lifts its head and cranes
   Through the whins and stones
   To lip late passion in the crawling clover.
   In the gap there's a bush weighted with boulders like morality,
   The fools of life bleed if they climb over.

85 The wind leans from Brady's, and the coltsfoot leaves are holed
      with rust,
   Rain fills the cart-tracks and the sole-plate grooves;
   A yellow sun reflects in Donaghmoyne[3]
   The poignant light in puddles shaped by hooves.

   Come with me, Imagination, into this iron house
90 And we will watch from the doorway the years run back,
   And we will know what a peasant's left hand wrote on the page.
   Be easy, October. No cackle hen, horse neigh, tree sough, duck quack.

                                                              1942

Epic

   I have lived in important places, times
   When great events were decided, who owned
   That half a rood[4] of rock, a no-man's land
   Surrounded by our pitchfork-armed claims.
5   I heard the Duffys shouting "Damn your soul"
   And old McCabe stripped to the waist, seen
   Step the plot defying blue cast-steel—

3. A stream in County Monaghan.   4. A quarter of an acre.

"Here is the march along these iron stones"
That was the year of the Munich bother.[5] Which
10   Was more important? I inclined
To lose my faith in Ballyrush and Gortin
Till Homer's ghost came whispering to my mind
He said: I made the Iliad[6] from such
A local row. Gods make their own importance.

1951

Canal Bank Walk[7]

Leafy-with-love banks and the green waters of the canal
Pouring redemption for me, that I do
The will of God, wallow in the habitual, the banal,
Grow with nature again as before I grew.
5   The bright stick trapped, the breeze adding a third
Party to the couple kissing on an old seat,
And a bird gathering materials for the nest for the Word
Eloquently new and abandoned to its delirious beat.
O unworn world enrapture me, encapture me in a web
10   Of fabulous grass and eternal voices by a beech,
Feed the gaping need of my senses, give me ad lib
To pray unselfconsciously with overflowing speech
For this soul needs to be honoured with a new dress woven
From green and blue things and arguments that cannot be proven.

1960

STANLEY KUNITZ

1905–

He[1]

He runs before the wise men: he
Is moving on the hills like snow.
No gifts, no tears, no company
He brings, but wind-rise and water-flow.

5   In meadows of descended day
His motion leans, dividing air:
He takes the unforgiving way
Beneath the apostolic star.[2]

---

5. Diplomatic crisis of September 1939 (involving Britain, Czechoslovakia, France, and Germany) that precipitated World War II.
6. Homer's epic tale of the war between the Greeks and the Trojans.
7. "It was while recovering from a serious illness in the hot summer of nineteen fifty-five as I lay on the bank of the Grand Canal [in Dublin] that I learned the pleasures of being passive" (*November Haggard*, p. 85). Kavanagh saw this as a turning point in his poetical career, and claimed that his "birth as a poet" occurred at that time, when he was satisfied to "let the water lap idly on the shores of my mind. My purpose in life was to have no purpose" (*Collected Poems*, p. xiv).
1. Kunitz's preferred version of a poem he wrote at twenty-three, inspired by Luke's account, in the New Testament, of the Annunciation and Incarnation.
2. The star of Bethlehem.

She who has known him calls him stranger.
10　Parting the night's long hair, he steals
Within the heart, that humble manger
Where the white, astonished spirit kneels.

His vertical inflicting pride,
Whose shadow cuts the nib of space,
15　Bends to this virtue fructified.
But though he kiss the little face

Like rapture breaking on the mind,
The necessary fierce details
Implacably he has designed.
20　Redemption hangs upon the nails.

1928, 1958

1930, 1958

Robin Redbreast

It was the dingiest bird
you ever saw, all the color
washed from him, as if
he had been standing in the rain,
5　friendless and stiff and cold,
since Eden went wrong.
In the house marked For Sale,
where nobody made a sound,
in the room where I lived
10　with an empty page, I had heard
the squawking of the jays
under the wild persimmons
tormenting him.
So I scooped him up
15　after they knocked him down,
in league with that ounce of heart
pounding in my palm,
that dumb beak gaping.
Poor thing! Poor foolish life!
20　without sense enough to stop
running in desperate circles,
needing my lucky help
to toss him back into his element.
But when I held him high,
25　fear clutched my hand,
for through the hole in his head,
cut whistle-clean . . .
through the old dried wound
between his eyes
30　where the hunter's brand
had tunneled out his wits . . .
I caught the cold flash of the blue
unappeasable sky.

1971

Touch Me

Summer is late, my heart.
Words plucked out of the air
some forty years ago
when I was wild with love
5   and torn almost in two
scatter like leaves this night
of whistling wind and rain.
It is my heart that's late,
it is my song that's flown.
10   Outdoors all afternoon
under a gun-metal sky
staking my garden down,
I kneeled to the crickets trilling
underfoot as if about
15   to burst from their crusty shells;
and like a child again
marveled to hear so clear
and brave a music pour
from such a small machine.
20   What makes the engine go?
Desire, desire, desire.
The longing for the dance
stirs in the buried life.
One season only,
25   and it's done.
So let the battered old willow
thrash against the windowpanes
and the house timbers creak.
Darling, do you remember
30   the man you married? Touch me,
remind me who I am.

1995

ROBERT PENN WARREN

1905–1989

Bearded Oaks

The oaks, how subtle and marine,
Bearded, and all the layered light
Above them swims; and thus the scene,
Recessed, awaits the positive night.

5   So, waiting, we in the grass now lie
Beneath the languorous tread of light:
The grasses, kelp-like, satisfy
The nameless motions of the air.

Upon the floor of light, and time,
10 Unmurmuring, of polyp made,
We rest; we are, as light withdraws,
Twin atolls on a shelf of shade.

Ages to our construction went,
Dim architecture, hour by hour:
15 And violence, forgot now, lent
The present stillness all its power.

The storm of noon above us rolled,
Of light the fury, furious gold,
The long drag troubling us, the depth:
20 Dark is unrocking, unrippling, still.

Passion and slaughter, ruth, decay
Descend, minutely whispering down,
Silted down swaying streams, to lay
Foundation for our voicelessness.

25 All our debate is voiceless here,
As all our rage, the rage of stone;
If hope is hopeless, then fearless is fear,
And history is thus undone.

Our feet once wrought the hollow street
30 With echo when the lamps were dead
At windows, once our headlight glare
Disturbed the doe that, leaping, fled.

I do not love you less that now
The caged heart makes iron stroke,
35 Or less that all that light once gave
The graduate° dark should now revoke.   *increasing*

We live in time so little time
And we learn all so painfully,
That we may spare this hour's term
40 To practice for eternity.

1944

Masts at Dawn

Past second cock-crow yacht masts in the harbor go slowly white.

No light in the east yet, but the stars show a certain fatigue.
They withdraw into a new distance, have discovered our unworthiness.
    It is long since

The owl, in the dark eucalyptus, dire and melodious, last called, and

5   Long since the moon sank and the English
Finished fornicating in their ketches.[1] In the evening there was a strong
    swell.

Red died the sun, but at dark wind rose easterly, white sea nagged the
    black harbor headland.

When there is a strong swell, you may, if you surrender to it, experience
A sense, in the act, of mystic unity with that rhythm. Your peace is the
    sea's will.

10   But now no motion, the bay-face is glossy in darkness, like

An old window pane flat on black ground by the wall, near the ash heap.
    It neither
Receives nor gives light. Now is the hour when the sea

Sinks into meditation. It doubts its own mission. The drowned cat
That on the evening swell had kept nudging the piles of the pier and had
    seemed

15   To want to climb out and lick itself dry, now floats free. On that surface
    a slight convexity only, it is like

An eyelid, in darkness, closed. You must learn to accept the kiss of fate,
    for

The masts go white slow, as light, like dew, from darkness
Condensed on them, on oiled wood, on metal. Dew whitens in darkness.

I lie in my bed and think how, in darkness, the masts go white.

20   The sound of the engine of the first fishing dory dies seaward. Soon
In the inland glen wakes the dawn-dove. We must try

To love so well the world that we may believe, in the end, in God.

1968

There's a Grandfather's Clock in the Hall

There's a grandfather's clock in the hall, watch it closely. The
    minute hand stands still, then it jumps, and in between
    jumps there is no-Time,
And you are a child again watching the reflection of early
5   morning sunlight on the ceiling above your bed,

Or perhaps you are fifteen feet under water and holding your
    breath as you struggle with a rock-snagged anchor, or hold-
    ing your breath just long enough for one more long, slow
    thrust to make the orgasm really intolerable,

---

1. Sailing vessels.

10   Or you are wondering why you really do not give a damn, as they
       trundle you off to the operating room,

  Or your mother is standing up to get married and is very pretty,
       and excited and is a virgin, and your heart overflows, and
       you watch her with tears in your eyes, or
15   She is the one in the hospital room and she is really dying.

  They have taken out her false teeth, which are now in a tumbler
       on the bedside table, and you know that only the undertaker
       will ever put them back in.
  You stand there and wonder if you will ever have to wear false
20   teeth.

  She is lying on her back, and God, is she ugly, and
  With gum-flabby lips and each word a special problem, she is
       asking if it is a new suit that you are wearing.

  You say yes, and hate her uremic[2] guts, for she has no right to
25   make you hurt the way that question hurts.
  You do not know why that question makes your heart hurt like a
       kick in the scrotum,

  For you do not yet know that the question, in its murderous trivi-
       ality, is the last thing she will ever say to you,
30   Nor know what baptism is occurring in a sod-roofed hut or hole
       on the night-swept steppes of Asia, and a million mouths,
       like ruined stars in darkness, make a rejoicing that howls like
       wind, or wolves,

  Nor do you know the truth, which is: *Seize the nettle of innocence*
35   *in both your hands, for this is the only way, and every*
  Ulcer in love's lazaret[3] may, like a dawn-stung gem, sing—or even
       burst into whoops of, perhaps, holiness.

  But, in any case, watch the clock closely. Hold your breath
       and wait.
40   Nothing happens, nothing happens, then suddenly, quick as a
       wink, and slick as a mink's prick, Time thrusts through
       the time of no-Time.

              1974

Evening Hawk

  From plane of light to plane, wings dipping through
  Geometries and orchids that the sunset builds,
  Out of the peak's black angularity of shadow, riding
  The last tumultuous avalanche of
5   Light above pines and the guttural gorge,
  The hawk comes.

2. Characterized by a toxic condition associated with kidney disease.

3. Storeroom; also ("lazaretto") quarters for quarantine or contagious hospital.

His wing
Scythes down another day, his motion
Is that of the honed steel-edge, we hear
10   The crashless fall of stalks of Time.

The head of each stalk is heavy with the gold of our error.

Look! Look! he is climbing the last light
Who knows neither Time nor error, and under
Whose eye, unforgiving, the world, unforgiven, swings
15   Into shadow.

Long now,
The last thrush is still, the last bat
Now cruises in his sharp hieroglyphics. His wisdom
Is ancient, too, and immense. The star
20   Is steady, like Plato,[4] over the mountain.

If there were no wind we might, we think, hear
The earth grind on its axis, or history
Drip in darkness like a leaking pipe in the cellar.

1975

Sila

Sila, for the Eskimo, "is the air, not the sky; movement, not wind; the very
breath of life, but not physical life; he is clear-sighted energy, activating intelli-
gence; the powerful fluid circulating 'all around' and also within each indi-
vidual . . ."

—*Larousse World Mythology*

Upgrade, past snow-tangled bramble, past
Deadfall snow-buried, there—
The ruin of old stonework, where man-heart
Long ago had once lifted
5   In joy, and back muscles strained. "Stay, Sila!" the boy
Commanded the tawny great husky, broad-chested,
That in harness yet stood, forward-leaning. The boy
Stamped his cross-countries. Stared
At the ruin. Thought:
10   *Two hundred years back—and it might
Have been me.*

And wondered what name the man
Might have had. Thought:
*Well, summer, I'll come
15   And hunt for the gravestones.* Then thought
How letters that crude must be weathered away—how deeper
A skull must be pulping to earth, and now grinless.
But thought: *At least, I can touch it, whatever
It is, stone or skull.*

4. (427–347 B.C.); Greek philosopher; here, a symbol of the "steady" because he characterized physical
objects as impermanent representations of unchanging ideas.

20   *Was young,* then he thought, *young as me, maybe.*

Then felt muscles tighten and clinch
At a sudden impulse of surprise
To find here the old mark of life that for life
Once had sung, while the axe-edge glittered in sunlight.
25   *Oh, what are the years!* his heart cried, and he felt
His own muscles pulsing in joy, just as when
Hands clasp for the lift of the beauty of butt-swell.

Land benched here, great beeches,
Gray, leafless, arising parklike and artful
30   From snow artificial as Christmas.
"Stay, Sila!" he called, and on level ground now
Slick glided to where the blue gleam of ice-eyes
Looked up in his own, with a knowledge deeper than words.
He snapped harness loose, wrapped cords at his waist, and—
35   The dog exploded.

From behind a beech deadfall, the doe, it had leaped,
Cow-awkward on earth, but magically airy in flight,
And weightless as wind, forelegs airward prowing
To seem as frail as a spider's, but hooves aglitter like glass
40   To cleave sunlight. Then,
Suddenly knifing the ice-crust as deep
As a trap, while the husky's wide paw-spread
Had opened like snowshoes behind.
Five leaps—and first blood, at a haunch,
45   Flesh laid back like a hunter's thin knife-slice.

Again, two more leaps, and white slash at belly—
Red line drawn clean on the curve. The boy's order
No use now: "Stay! Damn it, stay!" Until
Hand on harness, at last and too late, for
50   Red blood dripped now from white fang
To whiteness of snow, and eyes blue as steel drove into
The boy's eyes brain-deep, while, that instant,
All eons of friendship fled.
Then dog-eyes went earthward. The guts
55   Of the doe slip forth blue on the ice-crust.

The husky, stiff as in bronze cast, waits.

Only one thing to do. Who'd leave the doe there,
Dying slow into sunset, while all the small teeth—
Fox, field mouse, and wildcat—emerge
60   For their nocturnal feast? So the boy's knees bend.
Break the snow-crust like prayer,
And he cuddles the doe's head, and widening brown eyes
Seem ready, almost, to forgive.

Throat fur is cream color, eyes flecked with gold glintings.
65   He longs for connection, to give explanation. Sudden,
The head, now helpless, drops back on his shoulder. Twin eyes

Hold his own entrapped in their depth,
But his free hand, as though unaware,
Slides slow back
70 To grope for the knife-sheath.

The boy could not shut his eyes to the task,
As some fool girl might, but set
Eyes deeper in eyes, as he cradled the head, and gently
Held up the soft chin
75 To tauten the fullness of throat, and then,
As scrupulous as a well-trained tailor, set
The knife's needle point where acuteness
Would enter without prick of pain, and
Slashed in a single, deep motion.

80 He was sure that the doe
Never twitched.

On snow unconsciously heaped, he let down the head,
Aware even yet of the last embracement of gaze.
He watched, bewitched by the beauty, how blood flowed,
85 Red petal by petal, a great rose that bloomed where he stood.
How petal on petal, curve swelling past curve,
Gleamed forth at his feet on the snow,
And each petal sparkled with flicker of ice through the crimson,
As rays of last sun found a special glory in smallness.

90 He lifted his head, knife yet in hand, and westward
Fixed eyes beyond beech-bench to the snow-hatched
Stone thrust of the mountain, above which sky, too,
More majestically bloomed, but petals paler as higher—
The rose of the blood of the day. Still as stone,
95 So he stood. Then slowly—so slowly—
He raised the blade of the knife he loved honing, and wiped
The sweet warmness and wetness across his own mouth,
And set tongue to the edge of the silk-whetted steel.

He knew he knew something at last
100 That he'd never before known.
No name for it—no!

He snow-cleaned the knife. Sheathed it. Called: "Come!"
The dog, now docile, obeyed. With bare hands full of snow,
The boy washed him of blood and, comblike,
105 With fingers ennobled the ruff.

Then suddenly clasping the creature, he,
Over raw fur, past beeches, the mountain's snow-snag,
And the sky's slow paling of petals,
Cried out into vastness
110 Of silence: "Oh, world!"

He felt like a fool when tears came.

Some sixty years later, propped on death's pillow,
Again will he see that same scene, and try,
Heart straining, to utter that cry?—But
115 Cannot, breath short.

1980

JOHN BETJEMAN

1906–1984

Death in Leamington[1]

She died in the upstairs bedroom
　By the light of the evening star
That shone through the plate glass window
　From over Leamington Spa.

5 Beside her the lonely crochet
　Lay patiently and unstirred,
But the fingers that would have worked it
　Were dead as the spoken word.

And Nurse came in with the tea-things
10 　Breast high 'mid the stands and chairs—
But Nurse was alone with her own little soul,
　And the things were alone with theirs.

She bolted the big round window,
　She let the blinds unroll,
15 She set a match to the mantle,[2]
　She covered the fire with coal.

And "Tea!" she said in a tiny voice
　"Wake up! It's nearly *five*."
Oh! Chintzy,[3] chintzy cheeriness,
20 　Half dead and half alive!

Do you know that the stucco is peeling?
　Do you know that the heart will stop?
From those yellow Italianate arches
　Do you hear the plaster drop?

25 Nurse looked at the silent bedstead,
　At the grey, decaying face,
As the calm of a Leamington evening
　Drifted into the place.

She moved the table of bottles
30 　Away from the bed to the wall;

1. Leamington Spa is a health resort in Warwick-
shire, with medicinal springs and baths.
2. The mantle of the gaslight jet.
3. Not in the current (American) slang sense, but
meaning that the room's hangings and furniture
coverings are of the flower-patterned glazed-cotton
fabric called chintz.

And tiptoeing gently over the stairs
Turned down the gas in the hall.

1932

The Arrest of Oscar Wilde at the Cadogan Hotel[4]

He sipped at a weak hock[5] and seltzer
As he gazed at the London skies
Through the Nottingham lace of the curtains
Or was it his bees-winged[6] eyes?

5   To the right and before him Pont Street
Did tower in her new built red,
As hard as the morning gaslight
That shone on his unmade bed,

"I want some more hock in my seltzer,
10   And Robbie,[7] please give me your hand—
Is this the end or beginning?
How can I understand?

"So you've brought me the latest *Yellow Book*:[8]
And Buchan[9] has got in it now:
15   Approval of what is approved of
Is as false as a well-kept vow.

"More hock, Robbie—where is the seltzer?
Dear boy, pull again at the bell!
They are all little better than *cretins*,
20   Though this *is* the Cadogan Hotel.

"One astrakhan coat is at Willis's—
Another one's at the Savoy:
Do fetch my morocco portmanteau,
And bring them on later, dear boy."

25   A thump, and a murmur of voices—
("Oh why must they make such a din?")
As the door of the bedroom swung open
And TWO PLAIN CLOTHES POLICEMEN came in:

"Mr. Woilde, we've come for tew take yew
30   Where felons and criminals dwell:
We must ask yew tew leave with us quoietly
For this *is* the Cadogan Hotel."

4. On May 27, 1895, Wilde was found guilty of offenses against Section 11 of the Criminal Law Amendment Act (1885), which punished "indecencies between grown men, in public or private," and was sentenced to two years hard labor.
5. Generic term for German white wine.
6. Filmed over, from "bees-wing": "a film of tartar scales formed in port and some other wines after long keeping" *(Webster's)*.
7. Robert Ross, a friend who remained loyal to Wilde after the latter's downfall.
8. *The Yellow Book* was an elaborately illustrated hardcover periodical, which appeared quarterly from 1894 to 1897, and in which many writers associated with the aesthetic movement were represented.
9. John Buchan, later Lord Tweedsmuir (1875–1940), author of several popular novels, including *Thirty-nine Steps* (1915).

He rose, and he put down *The Yellow Book.*
He staggered—and, terrible-eyed,
35 He brushed past the palms on the staircase
And was helped to a hansom outside.

1937

East Anglian Bathe[1]

Oh when the early morning at the seaside
Took us with hurrying steps from Horsey Mere
To see the whistling bent-grass on the leeside
And then the tumbled breaker-line appear,
5   On high, the clouds with mighty adumbration
Sailed over us to seaward fast and clear
And jellyfish in quivering isolation
Lay silted in the dry sand of the breeze
And we, along the tableland of beach blown
10 Went gooseflesh from our shoulders to our knees
And ran to catch the football, each to each thrown,
In the soft and swirling music of the seas.

There splashed about our ankles as we waded
Those intersecting wavelets morning-cold,
15 And sudden dark a patch of sea was shaded,
And sudden light, another patch would hold
The warmth of whirling atoms in a sun-shot
And underwater sandstorm green and gold.
So in we dived and louder than a gunshot
20 Sea water broke in fountains down the ear.
How cold the bathe, how chattering cold the drying,
How welcoming the inland reeds appear,
The wood smoke and the breakfast and the frying,
And your warm freshwater ripples, Horsey Mere.

1945

False Security

I remember the dread with which I at a quarter past four
Let go with a bang behind me our house front door
And, clutching a present for my dear little hostess tight,
Sailed out for the children's party into the night
5   Or rather the gathering night. For still some boys
In the near municipal acres were making a noise
Shuffling in fallen leaves and shouting and whistling
And running past hedges of hawthorn, spikey and bristling.
And black in the oncoming darkness stood out the trees
10 And pink shone the ponds in the sunset ready to freeze
And all was still and ominous waiting for dark
And the keeper was ringing his closing bell in the park
And the arc lights started to fizzle and burst into mauve

---

1. East Anglia comprises the English counties of Norfolk and Suffolk; Horsey Mere ("Mere," deriving from Latin *mare*, the sea, indicating the resort area of the town of Horsey) is on the coast of Norfolk, north of Great Yarmouth.

As I climbed West Hill to the great big house in The Grove,
15   Where the children's party was and the dear little hostess.
But halfway up stood the empty house where the ghost is
I crossed to the other side and under the arc
Made a rush for the next kind lamppost out of the dark
And so to the next and the next till I reached the top
20   Where the Grove branched off to the left. Then ready to drop
I ran to the ironwork gateway of number seven
Secure at last on the lamplit fringe of Heaven.
Oh who can say how subtle and safe one feels
Shod in one's children's sandals from Daniel Neal's,
25   Clad in one's party clothes made of stuff from Heal's?
And who can still one's thrill at the candle shine
On cakes and ices and jelly and blackcurrant wine,
And the warm little feel of my hostess's hand in mine?
Can I forget my delight at the conjuring show?
30   And wasn't I proud that I was the last to go?
Too overexcited and pleased with myself to know
That the words I heard my hostess's mother employ
To a guest departing, would ever diminish my joy,
I WONDER WHERE JULIA FOUND THAT STRANGE, RATHER COMMON
   LITTLE BOY?

1958

WILLIAM EMPSON

1906–1984

Legal Fiction[1]

Law makes long spokes of the short stakes of men.
Your well fenced out real estate of mind
No high flat of the nomad citizen
Looks over, or train leaves behind.

5   Your rights extend under and above your claim
Without bound; you own land in heaven and hell;
Your part of earth's surface and mass the same,
Of all cosmos' volume, and all stars as well.

Your rights reach down where all owners meet, in hell's
10   Pointed exclusive conclave, at earth's centre
(Your spun farm's root still on that axis dwells);
And up, through galaxies, a growing sector.

You are nomad yet; the lighthouse beam you own
Flashes, like Lucifer,[2] through the firmament.
15   Earth's axis varies; your dark central cone
Wavers a candle's shadow, at the end.

1935

1. Something assumed to be true for the purpose of legal argument, whether or not it is true.
2. The morning star (Venus); also, a name of Satan ("light-bearer") before he was cast out of heaven.

Missing Dates

Slowly the poison the whole blood stream fills.
It is not the effort nor the failure tires.
The waste remains, the waste remains and kills.

It is not your system or clear sight that mills
5 Down small to the consequence a life requires;
Slowly the poison the whole blood stream fills.

They bled an old dog dry yet the exchange rills°   *streams*
Of young dog blood gave but a month's desires;
The waste remains, the waste remains and kills.

10 It is the Chinese tombs and the slag hills
Usurp the soil, and not the soil retires.[3]
Slowly the poison the whole blood stream fills.

Not to have fire is to be a skin that shrills.
The complete fire is death. From partial fires
15 The waste remains, the waste remains and kills.

It is the poems you have lost, the ills
From missing dates, at which the heart expires.
Slowly the poison the whole blood stream fills.
The waste remains, the waste remains and kills.

1940

W. H. AUDEN
1907–1973

As I Walked Out One Evening

As I walked out one evening,
    Walking down Bristol Street,
The crowds upon the pavement
    Were fields of harvest wheat.

5 And down by the brimming river
    I heard a lover sing
Under an arch of the railway:
    "Love has no ending.

"I'll love you, dear, I'll love you
10   Till China and Africa meet,
And the river jumps over the mountain
    And the salmon sing in the street,

---

3. "It is true about the old dog, at least I saw it reported somewhere, but the legend that a fifth or some such part of the soil of China is given up to ancestral tombs is (by the way) not true" [Empson's note].

"I'll love till the ocean
 Is folded and hung up to dry
15 And the seven stars go squawking
 Like geese about the sky.

"The years shall run like rabbits,
 For in my arms I hold
The Flower of the Ages,
20 And the first love of the world."

But all the clocks in the city
 Began to whirr and chime:
"O let not Time deceive you,
 You cannot conquer Time.

25 "In the burrows of the Nightmare
 Where Justice naked is,
Time watches from the shadow
 And coughs when you would kiss.

"In headaches and in worry
30 Vaguely life leaks away,
And Time will have his fancy
 Tomorrow or today.

"Into many a green valley
 Drifts the appalling snow;
35 Time breaks the threaded dances
 And the diver's brilliant bow.

"O plunge your hands in water,
 Plunge them in up to the wrist;
Stare, stare in the basin
40 And wonder what you've missed.

"The glacier knocks in the cupboard,
 The desert sighs in the bed,
And the crack in the teacup opens
 A lane to the land of the dead.

45 "Where the beggars raffle the banknotes
 And the Giant is enchanting to Jack,
And the Lily-white Boy is a Roarer,
 And Jill goes down on her back.

"O look, look in the mirror,
50 O look in your distress;
Life remains a blessing
 Although you cannot bless.

"O stand, stand at the window
 As the tears scald and start;

55 You shall love your crooked neighbour
With your crooked heart."

It was late, late in the evening,
The lovers they were gone;
The clocks had ceased their chiming,
60 And the deep river ran on.

1940

From Twelve Songs

IX. [*Funeral Blues*]

Stop all the clocks, cut off the telephone,
Prevent the dog from barking with a juicy bone,
Silence the pianos and with muffled drum
Bring out the coffin, let the mourners come.

5 Let aeroplanes circle moaning overhead
Scribbling on the sky the message He Is Dead,
Put crêpe bows round the white necks of the public doves,
Let the traffic policemen wear black cotton gloves.

He was my North, my South, my East and West,
10 My working week and my Sunday rest,
My noon, my midnight, my talk, my song;
I thought that love would last for ever: I was wrong.

The stars are not wanted now: put out every one;
Pack up the moon and dismantle the sun;
15 Pour away the ocean and sweep up the wood;
For nothing now can ever come to any good.

1936?   1940

XII. [*Tell Me the Truth About Love*]

Some say that love's a little boy,
    And some say it's a bird,
Some say it makes the world go round,
    And some say that's absurd,
5 And when I asked the man next-door,
    Who looked as if he knew,
His wife got very cross indeed,
    And said it wouldn't do.

        Does it look like a pair of pyjamas,
10   Or the ham in a temperance hotel?
    Does its odour remind one of llamas,[1]
        Or has it a comforting smell?
    Is it prickly to touch as a hedge is,
        Or soft as eiderdown fluff?

1. South American camel-like animals.

15   Is it sharp or quite smooth at the edges?
          O tell me the truth about love.

Our history books refer to it
     In cryptic little notes,
It's quite a common topic on
20   The Transatlantic boats;
I've found the subject mentioned in
     Accounts of suicides,
And even seen it scribbled on
     The backs of railway-guides.

25   Does it howl like a hungry Alsatian,
          Or boom like a military band?
     Could one give a first-rate imitation
          On a saw or a Steinway Grand?[2]
     Is its singing at parties a riot?
30   Does it only like Classical stuff?
     Will it stop when one wants to be quiet?
          O tell me the truth about love.

I looked inside the summer-house;
     It wasn't ever there:
35 I tried the Thames at Maidenhead,
     And Brighton's bracing air.
I don't know what the blackbird sang,
     Or what the tulip said;
But it wasn't in the chicken-run,
40   Or underneath the bed.

     Can it pull extraordinary faces?
          Is it usually sick on a swing?
     Does it spend all its time at the races,
          Or fiddling with pieces of string?
45   Has it views of its own about money?
          Does it think Patriotism enough?
     Are its stories vulgar but funny?
          O tell me the truth about love.

     When it comes, will it come without warning
50   Just as I'm picking my nose?
     Will it knock on my door in the morning,
          Or tread in the bus on my toes?
     Will it come like a change in the weather?
          Will its greeting be courteous or rough?
55   Will it alter my life altogether?
          O tell me the truth about love.

January 1938   1940

---

2. Brand of grand piano.

Lullaby

Lay your sleeping head, my love,
Human on my faithless arm;
Time and fevers burn away
Individual beauty from
5   Thoughtful children, and the grave
Proves the child ephemeral:
But in my arms till break of day
Let the living creature lie,
Mortal, guilty, but to me
10   The entirely beautiful.

Soul and body have no bounds:
To lovers as they lie upon
Her tolerant enchanted slope
In their ordinary swoon,
15   Grave the vision Venus[3] sends
Of supernatural sympathy,
Universal love and hope;
While an abstract insight wakes
Among the glaciers and the rocks
20   The hermit's carnal ecstasy.

Certainty, fidelity
On the stroke of midnight pass
Like vibrations of a bell
And fashionable madmen raise
25   Their pedantic boring cry:
Every farthing[4] of the cost,
All the dreaded cards foretell,
Shall be paid, but from this night
Not a whisper, not a thought,
30   Not a kiss nor look be lost.

Beauty, midnight, vision dies:
Let the winds of dawn that blow
Softly round your dreaming head
Such a day of welcome show
35   Eye and knocking heart may bless,
Find our mortal world enough;
Noons of dryness find you fed
By the involuntary powers,
Nights of insult let you pass
40   Watched by every human love.

January 1937   1940

---

3. Roman goddess of love.   4. Old British coin worth one fourth of a penny.

Spain 1937[5]

Yesterday all the past. The language of size
Spreading to China along the trade-routes; the diffusion
        Of the counting-frame and the cromlech;
Yesterday the shadow-reckoning in the sunny climates.

5   Yesterday the assessment of insurance by cards,
The divination of water; yesterday the invention
        Of cart-wheels and clocks, the taming of
Horses; yesterday the bustling world of the navigators.

Yesterday the abolition of fairies and giants;
10   The fortress like a motionless eagle eyeing the valley,
        The chapel built in the forest;
Yesterday the carving of angels and of frightening gargoyles;

The trial of heretics among the columns of stone;
Yesterday the theological feuds in the taverns
15   And the miraculous cure at the fountain;
Yesterday the Sabbath of Witches. But to-day the struggle.

Yesterday the installation of dynamos and turbines;
The construction of railways in the colonial desert;
        Yesterday the classic lecture
20   On the origin of Mankind. But to-day the struggle.

Yesterday the belief in the absolute value of Greek;
The fall of the curtain upon the death of a hero;
        Yesterday the prayer to the sunset,
And the adoration of madmen. But to-day the struggle.

25   As the poet whispers, startled among the pines
Or, where the loose waterfall sings, compact, or upright
        On the crag by the leaning tower:
"O my vision. O send me the luck of the sailor."

And the investigator peers through his instruments
30   At the inhuman provinces, the virile bacillus
        Or enormous Jupiter finished:
"But the lives of my friends. I inquire, I inquire."

And the poor in their fireless lodgings dropping the sheets
Of the evening paper: "Our day is our loss. O show us
35   History the operator, the
Organiser, Time the refreshing river."

And the nations combine each cry, invoking the life
That shapes the individual belly and orders

---

5. Auden traveled to Spain in January 1936, saying he was going to drive an ambulance for the left-wing Republican forces then engaged in a civil war with the Fascist Nationalists, but returned shortly, without having done so, horrified by what he had seen.

The private nocturnal terror:
40 "Did you not found once the city state of the sponge,

"Raise the vast military empires of the shark
And the tiger, establish the robin's plucky canton?
        Intervene. O descend as a dove[6] or
A furious papa or a mild engineer:[7] but descend."

45 And the life, if it answers at all, replies from the heart
And the eyes and the lungs, from the shops and squares of the city:
        "O no, I am not the Mover,
Not to-day, not to you. To you I'm the

"Yes-man, the bar-companion, the easily-duped:
50 I am whatever you do; I am your vow to be
        Good, your humorous story;
I am your business voice; I am your marriage.

"What's your proposal? To build the Just City? I will.
I agree. Or is it the suicide pact, the romantic
55   Death? Very well, I accept, for
I am your choice, your decision: yes, I am Spain."

Many have heard it on remote peninsulas,
On sleepy plains, in the aberrant fishermen's islands,
        In the corrupt heart of the city;
60 Have heard and migrated like gulls or the seeds of a flower.

They clung like burrs to the long expresses that lurch
Through the unjust lands, through the night, through the alpine
        tunnel;
        They floated over the oceans;
They walked the passes: they came to present their lives.

65 On that arid square, that fragment nipped off from hot
Africa, soldered so crudely to inventive Europe,
        On that tableland scored by rivers,
Our fever's menacing shapes are precise and alive.

To-morrow, perhaps, the future: the research on fatigue
70 And the movements of packers; the gradual exploring of all the
        Octaves of radiation;
To-morrow the enlarging of consciousness by diet and breathing.

To-morrow the rediscovery of romantic love;
The photographing of ravens; all the fun under
75   Liberty's masterful shadow;
To-morrow the hour of the pageant-master and the musician.

---

6. In the Bible and Christian iconography, the Holy Ghost often takes the form of a dove descending to the Earth.
7. *Deus ex machina:* Latin translation of the Greek for "god from the machinery"; i.e., the device by which in Greek theater the gods were shown in the air.

To-morrow for the young the poets exploding like bombs,
The walks by the lake, the winter of perfect communion;
      To-morrow the bicycle races
80   Through the suburbs on summer evenings: but to-day the struggle.

To-day the inevitable increase in the chances of death;
The conscious acceptance of guilt in the fact of murder;[8]
      To-day the expending of powers
On the flat ephemeral pamphlet and the boring meeting.

85   To-day the makeshift consolations; the shared cigarette;
The cards in the candle-lit barn and the scraping concert,
      The masculine jokes; to-day the
Fumbled and unsatisfactory embrace before hurting.

The stars are dead; the animals will not look:
90   We are left alone with our day, and the time is short and
      History to the defeated
May say Alas but cannot help or pardon.
April 1937   1937, 1940

Musée des Beaux Arts[9]

About suffering they were never wrong,
The Old Masters: how well they understood
Its human position; how it takes place
While someone else is eating or opening a window or just walking dully
    along;
5   How, when the aged are reverently, passionately waiting
For the miraculous birth, there always must be
Children who did not specially want it to happen, skating
On a pond at the edge of the wood:
They never forgot
10 That even the dreadful martyrdom must run its course
Anyhow in a corner, some untidy spot
Where the dogs go on with their doggy life and the torturer's horse
Scratches its innocent behind on a tree.

In Brueghel's *Icarus*,[1] for instance: how everything turns away
15 Quite leisurely from the disaster; the ploughman may
Have heard the splash, the forsaken cry,
But for him it was not an important failure; the sun shone
As it had to on the white legs disappearing into the green
Water; and the expensive delicate ship that must have seen

8. At its first printing, this line read: "The conscious acceptance of guilt in the necessary murder." Auden later suppressed the poem, largely because of its seeming support for murder.
9. Museum of Fine Arts (French).
1. *The Fall of Icarus*, by Pieter Brueghel (ca. 1525–1569), the painting described here, is in the Musée d'Art Ancien, a section of the Musées Royaux des Beaux Arts, in Brussels. Daedalus, the greatly skilled Athenian craftsman, constructed for Minos, king of Crete, a labyrinth in which the Minotaur was kept, but was then imprisoned in it himself with his son, Icarus. He made wings of feathers and wax, with which they flew away, but Icarus flew too near the sun, the wax melted, and he fell into the sea.

20 Something amazing, a boy falling out of the sky,
    Had somewhere to get to and sailed calmly on.

1940

In Memory of W. B. Yeats[2]

(d. Jan. 1939)

I

He disappeared in the dead of winter:
The brooks were frozen, the airports almost deserted,
And snow disfigured the public statues;
The mercury sank in the mouth of the dying day.
5 What instruments we have agree
The day of his death was a dark cold day.

Far from his illness
The wolves ran on through the evergreen forests,
The peasant river was untempted by the fashionable quays;
10 By mourning tongues
The death of the poet was kept from his poems.

But for him it was his last afternoon as himself,
An afternoon of nurses and rumours;
The provinces of his body revolted,
15 The squares of his mind were empty,
Silence invaded the suburbs,
The current of his feeling failed; he became his admirers.

Now he is scattered among a hundred cities
And wholly given over to unfamiliar affections.
20 To find his happiness in another kind of wood[3]
And be punished under a foreign code of conscience.[4]
The words of a dead man
Are modified in the guts of the living.

But in the importance and noise of to-morrow
25 When the brokers are roaring like beasts on the floor of the Bourse,[5]
And the poor have the sufferings to which they are fairly accustomed,
And each in the cell of himself is almost convinced of his freedom,
A few thousand will think of this day
As one thinks of a day when one did something slightly unusual.

30 What instruments we have agree
The day of his death was a dark cold day.

---

2. Willian Butler Yeats (b. 1865), Irish poet and
dramatist, died in Roquebrune (southern France)
on January 29, 1939.
3. At the beginning of the *Inferno* (1.1–3), middle-
aged Dante finds himself in a metaphorical "dark

wood."
4. Yeats, as represented by his work, must endure
the judgment of the living; a veiled reference to
his Irish nationalism.
5. The French stock exchange.

II

You were silly like us;[6] your gift survived it all:
The parish of rich women,[7] physical decay,
Yourself. Mad Ireland hurt you into poetry.
35   Now Ireland has her madness and her weather still,
For poetry makes nothing happen: it survives
In the valley of its making where executives
Would never want to tamper, flows on south
From ranches of isolation and the busy griefs,
40   Raw towns that we believe and die in; it survives,
A way of happening, a mouth.

III

Earth, receive an honoured guest:
William Yeats is laid to rest.
Let the Irish vessel lie
45   Emptied of its poetry.[8]

In the nightmare of the dark
All the dogs of Europe bark.[9]
And the living nations wait,
Each sequestered in its hate;

50   Intellectual disgrace
Stares from every human face,
And the seas of pity lie
Locked and frozen in each eye.

Follow, poet, follow right
55   To the bottom of the night,
With your unconstraining voice
Still persuade us to rejoice;

With the farming of a verse
Make a vineyard of the curse,
60   Sing of human unsuccess
In a rapture of distress;

In the deserts of the heart.
Let the healing fountain start,
In the prison of his days
65   Teach the free man how to praise.

February 1939   1940

6. See Auden's prose pieces for his objections to
Yeats' thought, particularly to his interest in the
supernatural.
7. Lady Augusta Gregory (1852–1932), Irish dra-
matist, was one of several wealthy women who pro-
vided financial help for Yeats.
8. Three stanzas that originally followed this were
omitted in the 1966 edition of Auden's *Collected
Shorter Poems* and thereafter: "Time that is
intolerant / Of the brave and innocent, / And indif-
ferent in a week / To a beautiful physique, / / Wor-
ships language and forgives / Everyone by whom it

lives; / Pardons cowardice, conceit / Lays its hon-
ours at their feet, / / Time that with this strange
excuse / Pardoned Kipling and his views, / And
will pardon Paul Claudel, / Pardons him for writ-
ing well." Kipling's views were imperialistic and
jingoistic; Paul Claudel (1868–1955), French
poet, dramatist, and diplomat, was an extreme
right-winger in his political ideas. Yeats' own poli-
tics were at times antidemocratic and appeared to
favor dictatorship.
9. A reference to World War II, which began in
September 1939.

In Praise of Limestone

If it form the one landscape that we, the inconstant ones,
  Are consistently homesick for, this is chiefly
Because it dissolves in water. Mark these rounded slopes
  With their surface fragrance of thyme and, beneath,
5 A secret system of caves and conduits; hear the springs
  That spurt out everywhere with a chuckle,
Each filling a private pool for its fish and carving
  Its own little ravine whose cliffs entertain
The butterfly and the lizard; examine this region
10   Of short distances and definite places:
What could be more like Mother or a fitter background
  For her son, the flirtatious male who lounges
Against a rock in the sunlight, never doubting
  That for all his faults he is loved; whose works are but
15 Extensions of his power to charm? From weathered outcrop
  To hilltop temple, from appearing waters to
Conspicuous fountains, from a wild to a formal vineyard,
  Are ingenious but short steps that a child's wish
To receive more attention than his brothers, whether
20   By pleasing or teasing, can easily take.

Watch, then, the band of rivals as they climb up and down
  Their steep stone gennels° in twos and threes,   channels, passages
    at times
Arm in arm, but never, thank God, in step; or engaged
  On the shady side of a square at midday in
25 Voluble discourse, knowing each other too well to think
  There are any important secrets, unable
To conceive a god whose temper tantrums are moral
  And not to be pacified by a clever line
Or a good lay: for, accustomed to a stone that responds,
30   They have never had to veil their faces in awe
Of a crater whose blazing fury could not be fixed;
  Adjusted to the local needs of valleys
Where everything can be touched or reached by walking,
  Their eyes have never looked into infinite space
35 Through the latticework of a nomad's comb; born lucky,
  Their legs have never encountered the fungi
And insects of the jungle, the monstrous forms and lives
  With which we have nothing, we like to hope, in common.
So, when one of them goes to the bad, the way his mind works
40   Remains comprehensible: to become a pimp
Or deal in fake jewelry or ruin a fine tenor voice
  For effects that bring down the house, could happen to all
But the best and the worst of us . . .
                                That is why, I suppose,
  The best and worst never stayed here long but sought
45 Immoderate soils where the beauty was not so external,
  The light less public and the meaning of life

Something more than a mad camp. "Come!" cried the granite
    wastes,
  "How evasive is your humour, how accidental
Your kindest kiss, how permanent is death." (Saints-to-be
50   Slipped away sighing.) "Come!" purred the clays and gravels.
"On our plains there is room for armies to drill; rivers
  Wait to be tamed and slaves to construct you a tomb
In the grand manner: soft as the earth is mankind and both
  Need to be altered." (Intendant Caesars rose and
55 Left, slamming the door.) But the really reckless were fetched
  By an older colder voice, the oceanic whisper:
"I am the solitude that asks and promises nothing;
  That is how I shall set you free. There is no love;
There are only the various envies, all of them sad."
60   They were right, my dear, all those voices were right
And still are; this land is not the sweet home that it looks,
  Nor its peace the historical calm of a site
Where something was settled once and for all: A backward
  And dilapidated province, connected
65 To the big busy world by a tunnel, with a certain
  Seedy appeal, is that all it is now? Not quite:
It has a worldly duty which in spite of itself
  It does not neglect, but calls into question
All the Great Powers assume; it disturbs our rights. The poet,
70   Admired for his earnest habit of calling
The sun the sun, his mind Puzzle, is made uneasy
  By these marble statues which so obviously doubt
His antimythological myth; and these gamins,°   *street urchins*
  Pursuing the scientist down the tiled colonnade
75 With such lively offers, rebuke his concern for Nature's
  Remotest aspects: I, too, am reproached, for what
And how much you know. Not to lose time, not to get caught,
  Not to be left behind, not, please! to resemble
The beasts who repeat themselves, or a thing like water
80   Or stone whose conduct can be predicted, these
Are our Common Prayer, whose greatest comfort is music
  Which can be made anywhere, is invisible,
And does not smell. In so far as we have to look forward
  To death as a fact, no doubt we are right: But if
85 Sins can be forgiven, if bodies rise from the dead,
  These modifications of matter into
Innocent athletes and gesticulating fountains,
  Made solely for pleasure, make a further point:
The blessed will not care what angle they are regarded from,
90   Having nothing to hide. Dear, I know nothing of
Either, but when I try to imagine a faultless love
  Or the life to come, what I hear is the murmur
Of underground streams, what I see is a limestone landscape.

1951

The Shield of Achilles[1]

She looked over his shoulder
For vines and olive trees,
Marble well-governed cities
And ships upon untamed seas,
But there on the shining metal
His hands had put instead
An artificial wilderness
And a sky like lead.

A plain without a feature, bare and brown,
No blade of grass, no sign of neighbourhood,
Nothing to eat and nowhere to sit down,
Yet, congregated on its blankness, stood
An unintelligible multitude,
A million eyes, a million boots in line,
Without expression, waiting for a sign.

Out of the air a voice without a face
Proved by statistics that some cause was just
In tones as dry and level as the place:
No one was cheered and nothing was discussed;
Column by column in a cloud of dust
They marched away enduring a belief
Whose logic brought them, somewhere else, to grief.

She looked over his shoulder
For ritual pieties,
White flower-garlanded heifers,
Libation and sacrifice,
But there on the shining metal
Where the altar should have been,
She saw by his flickering forge-light
Quite another scene.

Barbed wire enclosed an arbitrary spot
Where bored officials lounged (one cracked a joke)
And sentries sweated for the day was hot:
A crowd of ordinary decent folk
Watched from without and neither moved nor spoke
As three pale figures were led forth and bound
To three posts driven upright in the ground.

Line numbers: 5, 10, 15, 20, 25, 30, 35.

---

1. Achilles, the chief Greek hero in the war with Troy, loses his armor when his great friend Patroclus, wearing it, is slain by Hector. While Achilles is mourning the death of his friend, his mother, the goddess Thetis, goes to Olympus to entreat Hephaestos to make new armor for him: both she and Hephaestos pity Achilles because he is fated to die soon and because his life has not been happy. The splendid shield, incorporating gold and silver as well as less precious metals, is described at length in *Iliad* 18.478–608, the scenes depicted on it constituting an epitome of the universe and the lives of men. Hephaestos portrays on it the Earth, the heavens, the sea, and the planets; a city in peace (with a wedding and a trial-at-law) and a city at war; scenes from country life, including a harvest feast and a grape-gathering; scenes from animal life, and the joyful life of young men and maidens. Around all these scenes, closing them in as the outer border, flows the ocean.

The mass and majesty of this world, all
    That carries weight and always weighs the same
40 Lay in the hands of others; they were small
    And could not hope for help and no help came:
    What their foes liked to do was done, their shame
Was all the worst could wish; they lost their pride
And died as men before their bodies died.

45   She looked over his shoulder
             For athletes at their games,
          Men and women in a dance
             Moving their sweet limbs
          Quick, quick, to music,
50   But there on the shining shield
          His hands had set no dancing-floor
          But a weed-choked field.

A ragged urchin, aimless and alone,
    Loitered about that vacancy, a bird
55 Flew up to safety from his well-aimed stone:
    That girls are raped, that two boys knife a third,
    Were axioms to him, who'd never heard
Of any world where promises were kept,
Or one could weep because another wept.

60   The thin-lipped armourer,
             Hephaestos hobbled away,
          Thetis of the shining breasts
             Cried out in dismay
          At what the god had wrought
65   To please her son, the strong
          Iron-hearted man-slaying Achilles
          Who would not live long.

1955

A. D. HOPE

1907–

Australia

A Nation of trees, drab green and desolate grey
In the field uniform of modern wars,
Darkens her hills, those endless, outstretched paws
Of Sphinx[1] demolished or stone lion worn away.

5 They call her a young country, but they lie:
    She is the last of lands, the emptiest,

---

1. A reference to the monumental stone sphinx of Egypt.

A woman beyond her change of life,[2] a breast
Still tender but within the womb is dry.

Without songs, architecture, history:
10   The emotions and superstitions of younger lands,
Her rivers of water drown among inland sands,
The river of her immense stupidity

Floods her monotonous tribes from Cairns to Perth.[3]
In them at last the ultimate men arrive
15   Whose boast is not: "we live" but "we survive."
A type who will inhabit the dying earth.

And her five cities, like five teeming sores,
Each drains her: a vast parasite robber-state
Where second-hand Europeans pullulate°   breed
20   Timidly on the edge of alien shores.

Yet there are some like me turn gladly home
From the lush jungle of modern thought, to find
The Arabian desert of the human mind,
Hoping, if still from the deserts the prophets come,

25   Such savage and scarlet as no green hills dare
Springs in that waste, some spirit which escapes
The learned doubt, the chatter of cultured apes
Which is called civilization over there.

1939

Imperial[4] Adam

Imperial Adam, naked in the dew,
Felt his brown flanks and found the rib was gone.
Puzzled he turned and saw where, two and two,
The mighty spoor of Jahweh° marked the lawn.   Jehovah

5   Then he remembered through mysterious sleep
The surgeon fingers probing at the bone,
The voice so far away, so rich and deep:
"It is not good for him to live alone."[5]

Turning once more he found Man's counterpart
10   In tender parody breathing at his side.
He knew her at first sight, he knew by heart
Her allegory of sense unsatisfied.

The pawpaw drooped its golden breasts above
Less generous than the honey of her flesh;

---

2. Menopause; i.e., she is past the years of child-bearing.
3. I.e., from one end of the continent to the other. Cairns is at the far northeast of Australia, Perth at the southwest.

4. I.e., emperor.
5. Genesis 2.18: "And the Lord said, It is not good that the man should be alone." Eve was created from one of Adam's ribs (cf. line 6).

15   The innocent sunlight showed the place of love;
    The dew on its dark hairs winked crisp and fresh.

    This plump gourd severed from his virile root,
    She promised on the turf of Paradise
    Delicious pulp of the forbidden fruit;
20   Sly as the snake she loosed her sinuous thighs,

    And waking, smiled up at him from the grass;
    Her breasts rose softly and he heard her sigh—
    From all the beasts whose pleasant task it was
    In Eden to increase and multiply

25   Adam had learned the jolly deed of kind:
    He took her in his arms and there and then,
    Like the clean beasts, embracing from behind,
    Began in joy to found the breed of men.

    Then from the spurt of seed within her broke
30   Her terrible and triumphant female cry,
    Split upward by the sexual lightning stroke.
    It was the beasts now who stood watching by:

    The gravid elephant, the calving hind,
    The breeding bitch, the she-ape big with young
35   Were the first gentle midwives of mankind;
    The teeming lioness rasped her with her tongue;

    The proud vicuña[6] nuzzled her as she slept
    Lax on the grass; and Adam watching too
    Saw how her dumb breasts at their ripening wept,
40   The great pod of her belly swelled and grew,

    And saw its water break, and saw, in fear,
    Its quaking muscles in the act of birth,
    Between her legs a pigmy face appear,
    And the first murderer[7] lay upon the earth.

1955

Advice to Young Ladies

A.U.C. 334:[8] about this date
For a sexual misdemeanour, which she denied,
The vestal virgin[9] Postumia was tried.
Livy records it among affairs of state.

---

6. Species of wild llama.
7. See Genesis 4: "And Adam knew Eve his wife; and she conceived, and bare Cain . . . and it came to pass . . . that Cain rose up against Abel his brother, and slew him."
8. *Ab urbe Condita*, "from the founding of the city" (Rome), traditionally in 753 B.C. In his *His-*

tory of Rome from its Foundation, Livy (59 B.C.– A.D. 17) records the incident narrated in the first three stanzas.
9. Vestal virgins were the young priestesses who tended the shrine of Vesta, goddess of the hearth. They were governed by the Pontifex Maximus (line 9), chief priest of the Roman religion.

5 They let her off: it seems she was perfectly pure;
  The charge arose because some thought her talk
  Too witty for a young girl, her eyes, her walk
  Too lively, her clothes too smart to be demure.

  The Pontifex Maximus, summing up the case,
10 Warned her in future to abstain from jokes,
  To wear less modish and more pious frocks.
  She left the court reprieved, but in disgrace.

  What then? With her the annalist is less
  Concerned than what the men achieved that year:
15 Plots, quarrels, crimes, with oratory to spare!
  I see Postumia with her dowdy dress,

  Stiff mouth and listless step; I see her strive
  To give dull answers. She had to knuckle down.
  A vestal virgin who scandalized that town
20 Had fair trial, then they buried her alive.[1]

  Alive, bricked up in suffocating dark,
  A ration of bread, a pitcher if she was dry,
  Preserved the body they did not wish to die
  Until her mind was quenched to the last spark.

25 How many the black maw has swallowed in its time!
  Spirited girls who would not know their place;
  Talented girls who found that the disgrace
  Of being a woman made genius a crime;

  How many others, who would not kiss the rod[2]
30 Domestic bullying broke or public shame?
  Pagan or Christian, it was much the same:
  Husbands, St. Paul declared,[3] rank next to God.

  Livy and Paul, it may be, never knew
  That Rome was doomed; each spoke of her with pride.
35 Tacitus,[4] writing after both had died,
  Showed that whole fabric rotten through and through.

  Historians spend their lives and lavish ink
  Explaining how great commonwealths collapse
  From great defects of policy—perhaps
40 The cause is sometimes simpler than they think.

  It may not seem so grave an act to break
  Postumia's spirit as Galileo's,[5] to gag

---

1. For breaking her vows of chastity a vestal virgin could be sentenced to be buried alive.
2. As the symbol of obedience and chastisement.
3. In Ephesians 5.22: "Wives, submit yourselves unto your own husbands, as unto the Lord."
4. (ca. A.D. 77–117); Roman historian, whose His-

tories of three Roman emperors who ruled and were successively deposed in A.D. 68–69 criticize the degeneracy of the times.
5. In 1633 the great Italian astronomer was forced by the Church to condemn his own scientific conclusions and was for a time imprisoned.

Hypatia as crush Socrates,[6] or drag
Joan as Giordano Bruno [7] to the stake.

45   Can we be sure? Have more states perished, then,
For having shackled the inquiring mind,
Than who, in their folly not less blind,
Trusted the servile womb to breed free men?

1966

Inscription for a War

> Stranger, go tell the Spartans
> we died here obedient to their commands.
> —Inscription at Thermopylae[8]

Linger not, stranger; shed no tear;
Go back to those who sent us here.

We are the young they drafted out
To wars their folly brought about.

5   Go tell those old men, safe in bed,
We took their orders and are dead.

1981

LOUIS MacNEICE

1907–1963

The Sunlight on the Garden[1]

The sunlight on the garden
Hardens and grows cold,
We cannot cage the minute
Within its nets of gold,
5   When all is told
We cannot beg for pardon.

Our freedom as free lances
Advances towards its end;
The earth compels, upon it
10   Sonnets and birds descend;

6. In 399 B.C. Socrates was sentenced to die by poion account of his supposedly subversive teachings. Hypatia was a lady of Alexandria, Egypt, noted for her learning and her beauty; she was murdered in A.D. 415, allegedly at the behest of an archbishop.
7. Both were burned at the stake, Joan of Arc in 1431 for heresy and sorcery, Bruno in 1600 for theological and scientific heresies.
8. Thermopylae takes its name from hot baths near the pass, twenty-five feet wide at its narrowest, between Thessaly and Locris in Greece. This place was defended by Leonides and three hundred Spartans (with seven hundred Thespians) against a huge Persian army led by Xerxes. The Persians infiltrated the Greek line by treachery, and the Spartans were wiped out.
1. MacNeice's farewell to his first wife, once the best dancer in Oxford (see line 12).

And soon, my friend,
We shall have no time for dances.

The sky was good for flying
Defying the church bells
15 And every evil iron
Siren and what it tells:
The earth compels,
We are dying, Egypt, dying[2]

And not expecting pardon,
20 Hardened in heart anew,
But glad to have sat under
Thunder and rain with you,
And grateful too
For sunlight on the garden.

1938

Bagpipe Music[3]

It's no go the merrygoround, it's no go the rickshaw,
All we want is a limousine and a ticket for the peepshow.
Their knickers[4] are made of crêpe-de-chine, their shoes are made
    of python,
Their halls are lined with tiger rugs and their walls with heads of bison.

5 John MacDonald found a corpse, put it under the sofa,
Waited till it came to life and hit it with a poker,
Sold its eyes for souvenirs, sold its blood for whiskey,
Kept its bones for dumbbells to use when he was fifty.

It's no go the Yogi-man, it's no go Blavatsky[5]
10 All we want is a bank balance and a bit of skirt in a taxi.

Annie MacDougall went to milk, caught her foot in the heather,
Woke to hear a dance record playing of Old Vienna.
It's no go your maidenheads, it's no go your culture,
All we want is a Dunlop tyre and the devil mend the puncture.

15 The Laird o' Phelps spent Hogmanay[6] declaring he was sober,
Counted his feet to prove the fact and found he had one foot over.
Mrs. Carmichael had her fifth, looked at the job with repulsion,
Said to the midwife "Take it away; I'm through with overproduction."

It's no go the gossip column, it's no go the Ceilidh,[7]
20 All we want is a mother's help and a sugar-stick for the baby.

2. From *Antony and Cleopatra* 4.15.41, Antony's speech to Cleopatra: "I am dying, Egypt, dying."
3. The poem is set in Scotland in the 1930s, the years of the Depression, years that led up to the Munich crisis of 1938 and to the outbreak of World War II in 1939.
4. Women's panties.
5. Madame Helena P. Blavatsky (1831–1891), Russian occultist, one of the founders of the Theo-sophical Society (to which W. B. Yeats had once belonged), which had flourished in London around the turn of the century and in whose writings there was renewed interest in the 1930s.
6. Scottish name given to the last day of the year.
7. Pronounced *kaley*; Gaelic term for a friendly social call or a session of traditional music, story-telling, or dancing.

Willie Murray cut his thumb, couldn't count the damage,
Took the hide of an Ayrshire cow and used it for a bandage.
His brother caught three hundred cran[8] when the seas were lavish,
Threw the bleeders back in the sea and went upon the parish.[9]

25 It's no go the Herring Board, it's no go the Bible,
All we want is a packet of fags° when our hands are idle.   *cigarettes*

It's no go the picture palace, it's no go the stadium,
It's no go the country cot with a pot of pink geraniums,
It's no go the Government grants, it's no go the elections,
30 Sit on your arse for fifty years and hang your hat on a pension.

It's no go my honey love, it's no go my poppet;
Work your hands from day to day, the winds will blow the profit.
The glass° is falling hour by hour, the glass with fall forever,   *barometer*
But if you break the bloody glass you won't hold up the weather.

                                                         1938

From Autumn Journal[1]

September has come and I wake
    And I think with joy how whatever, now or in future, the system
Nothing whatever can take
    The people away, there will always be people
5 For friends or for lovers though perhaps
    The conditions of love will be changed and its vices diminished
And affection not lapse
    To narrow possessiveness, jealousy founded on vanity.
September has come, it is *hers*
10   Whose vitality leaps in the autumn,
Whose nature prefers
    Trees without leaves and a fire in the fire-place;
So I give her this month and the next
    Though the whole of my year should be hers who has rendered
        already
15 So many of its days intolerable or perplexed
    But so many more so happy;
Who has left a scent on my life and left my walls
    Dancing over and over with her shadow,
Whose hair is twined in all my waterfalls
20   And all of London littered with remembered kisses.
So I am glad
    That life contains her with her moods and moments
More shifting and more transient than I had
    Yet thought of as being integral to beauty;
25 Whose mind is like the wind on a sea of wheat,
    Whose eyes are candour,
And assurance in her feet

8. A measure for the quantity of just-caught herrings.
9. I.e., went on relief.

1. A book-length "documentary" poem covering events (public and, as here, private) in autumn 1938.

Like a homing pigeon never by doubt diverted.
To whom I send my thanks
30   That the air has become shot silk, the streets are music,
And that the ranks
Of men are ranks of men, no more of cyphers.°   zeros
So that if now alone
I must pursue this life, it will not be only
35   A drag from numbered stone to numbered stone
But a ladder of angels, river turning tidal.
Off-hand, at times hysterical, abrupt,
You are one I always shall remember,
Whom cant can never corrupt
40   Nor argument disinherit.
Frivolous, always in a hurry, forgetting the address,
Frowning too often, taking enormous notice
Of hats and backchat—how could I assess
The thing that makes you different?
45   You whom I remember glad or tired,
Smiling in drink or scintillating anger,
Inopportunely desired
On boats, on trains, on roads when walking.
Sometimes untidy, often elegant,
50   So easily hurt, so readily responsive,
To whom a trifle could be an irritant
Or could be balm and manna.[2]
Whose words would tumble over each other and pelt
From pure excitement,
55   Whose fingers curl and melt
When you were friendly.
I shall remember you in bed with bright
Eyes or in a café stirring coffee
Abstractedly and on your plate the white
60   Smoking stub your lips had touched with crimson.
And I shall remember how your words could hurt
Because they were so honest
And even your lies were able to assert
Integrity of purpose.
65   And it is on the strength of knowing you
I reckon generous feeling more important
Than the mere deliberating what to do
When neither the pros nor cons affect the pulses.
And though I have suffered from your special strength
70   Who never flatter for points nor fake responses
I should be proud if I could evolve at length
An equal thrust and pattern.

1938

London Rain

The rain of London pimples
The ebony street with white

---

2. The food miraculously provided for the Israelites in the wilderness.

And the neon-lamps of London
Stain the canals of night
5   And the park becomes a jungle
In the alchemy of night.

My wishes turn to violent
Horses black as coal—
The randy mares of fancy,
10   The stallions of the soul—
Eager to take the fences
That fence about my soul.

Across the countless chimneys
The horses ride and across
15   The country to the channel
Where warning beacons toss,
To a place where God and No-God
Play at pitch and toss.

Whichever wins I am happy
20   For God will give me bliss
But No-God will absolve me
From all I do amiss
And I need not suffer conscience
If the world was made amiss.

25   Under God we can reckon
On pardon when we fall
But if we are under No-God
Nothing will matter at all,
Adultery and murder
30   Will count for nothing at all.

So reinforced by logic
As having nothing to lose
My lust goes riding horseback
To ravish where I choose,
35   To burgle all the turrets
Of beauty as I choose.

But now the rain gives over
Its dance upon the town,
Logic and lust together
40   Come dimly tumbling down,
And neither God nor No-God
Is either up or down.

The argument was wilful,
The alternatives untrue,
45   We need no metaphysics
To sanction what we do
Or to muffle us in comfort
From what we did not do.

Whether the living river
50   Began in bog or lake,
    The world is what was given,
The world is what we make.
And we only can discover
Life in the life we make.

55   So let the water sizzle
Upon the gleaming slates,
There will be sunshine after
When the rain abates
And rain returning duly
60   When the sun abates.

My wishes now come homeward,
Their gallopings in vain,
Logic and lust are quiet
And again it starts to rain;
65   Falling asleep I listen
To the falling London rain.

1941

Star-gazer

Forty-two years ago (to me if to no one else
The number is of some interest) it was a brilliant starry night
And the westward train was empty and had no corridors
So darting from side to side I could catch the unwonted sight
5   Of those almost intolerably bright
Holes, punched in the sky, which excited me partly because
Of their Latin names and partly because I had read in the textbooks
How very far off they were, it seemed their light
Had left them (some at least) long years before I was.

10   And this remembering now I mark that what
Light was leaving some of them at least then,
Forty-two years ago, will never arrive
In time for me to catch it, which light when
It does get here may find that there is not
15   Anyone left alive
To run from side to side in a late night train
Admiring it and adding noughts in vain.

1967

JOSEPHINE JACOBSEN
1908–

The Primer

I said in my youth
"they lie to children"
but it is not so.
Mother my goose[1] I know
5   told me the truth.

I remember that treetop minute.
That was a baby is a woman now;
in a rough wind, it was a broken bough
brought down the cradle with the baby in it.

10 I had a dumpy friend (you would not know his name,
though he indeed had several), after his fall
lay in live pieces by my garden wall
in a vain tide of epaulets and manes.

I had another friend (and you would know her name),
15 took up her candle on her way to bed.
She had a steady hand and a yellow head
up the tall stairwell, but the chopper came.

So small they meant to run away, from sightless eyes
three mice ran toward my mind instead;
20 I seized the shapely knife. They fled
in scarlet haste, the blind and tailless mice.

Cock robin was three birds of a single feather.
Three times cock robin fell when a breeze blew;
eye of fly watched; arrow of sparrow flew:
25 three times cock robin died in the same weather.

Sheep, cows, meander in the corn and meadow;
soundless the horn, fine, fine my seam;
nothing I feed, but rosy grows my cream.
My blue boy sleeps under the stack's huge shadow.

1974

Bush

It is the sound of lions lapping.
They drink themselves
from the gold shapes that waver
and grow shallower.

---

1. As in the Mother Goose nursery rhymes. Each stanza of the poem rewrites one of these rhymes.

5 Blue peels itself in the water-
hole; it is the sun coming.
Crouched, the lions meet
their matches at the surface.

The foxy jackals are far off
10 but the vultures cloud the flat treetop;
the drum of the zebra's body
is lined with red sunrise.

The jackals and vultures are waiting
for what happened under the moon.
15 The lions are through with it; they
lift their dripping chins and look ahead.

It is six o'clock on Christmas morning.
Now the lions have stopped lapping
the bush makes no sound
20 the vultures shift, but without sound.

The day is perfectly seamless.
Slowly the lions move like pistons past the dry grasses;
the jackals do not move yet;
the vultures show patience.

25 The lions pass a thornbush and melt.
Though the whole day is unbroken
the passage of the sun will represent heaven;
the bones will represent time.

1974

Hourglass

"Flawless" is the word, no doubt, for this third of May
that has landed on the grounds of Mayfair,
the Retirement Community par excellence.

Right behind the wheels of the mower, grass
5 explodes again, the bare trees most tenderly
push out their chartreuse tips.

Bottle bees are back. Feckless, reckless,
stingless, they probably have a function.
Above the cardinal, scarlet on the rim

10 of the birdbath, twinning himself,
they hover, cruise the flowers, mate.
The tiny water catches the sky.

On the circular inner road, the lady
untangles the poodle's leash from her cane.
15 He is wild to chase the splendid smells.

The small man with the small smile,
rapidly steering his Amigo,[2]
bowls past. She would wave, but can't.

All around, birds and sexual flowers
20 are intent on color, flight, fragrance.
The gardener sweeps his sweaty face

with a khaki sleeve. His tulips are shined
black at their centers. They have come along nicely.
He is young and will be gone before dark.

25 The man in the Amigo has in mind a May
a mirror of this, but unobtainable
as the touch of the woman in that glass.

The sun's force chills him. But the lady
with the curly poodle could melt her cane
30 in the very heat of her precious pleasure.

She perfectly understands the calendar
and the sun's passage. But she grips the leash
and leans on the air that is hers and here.

1995

THEODORE ROETHKE

1908–1963

Root Cellar

Nothing would sleep in that cellar, dank as a ditch,
Bulbs broke out of boxes hunting for chinks in the dark,
Shoots dangled and drooped,
Lolling obscenely from mildewed crates,
5 Hung down long yellow evil necks, like tropical snakes.
And what a congress of stinks!
Roots ripe as old bait,
Pulpy stems, rank, silo-rich,
Leaf-mold, manure, lime, piled against slippery planks.
10 Nothing would give up life:
Even the dirt kept breathing a small breath.

1948

Child on Top of a Greenhouse[1]

The wind billowing out the seat of my britches,
My feet crackling splinters of glass and dried putty,

2. Unidentified.
1. Roethke, author of a series of "greenhouse poems," called the greenhouse "my symbol for the whole of life, a womb, a heaven-on-earth." His father, a florist, owned a greenhouse in Saginaw, Michigan.

The half-grown chrysanthemums staring up like accusers,
Up through the streaked glass, flashing with sunlight,
5 A few white clouds all rushing eastward,
A line of elms plunging and tossing like horses,
And everyone, everyone pointing up and shouting!

1948

My Papa's Waltz

The whiskey on your breath
Could make a small boy dizzy;
But I hung on like death:
Such waltzing was not easy.

5 We romped until the pans
Slid from the kitchen shelf;
My mother's countenance
Could not unfrown itself.

The hand that held my wrist
10 Was battered on one knuckle;
At every step you missed
My right ear scraped a buckle.

You beat time on my head
With a palm caked hard by dirt,
15 Then waltzed me off to bed
Still clinging to your shirt.

1948

The Lost Son

1. The Flight

At Woodlawn[2] I heard the dead cry:
I was lulled by the slamming of iron,
A slow drip over stones,
Toads brooding wells.
5 All the leaves stuck out their tongues;
I shook the softening chalk of my bones,
Saying,
Snail, snail, glister me forward,
Bird, soft-sigh me home,
10 Worm, be with me.
This is my hard time.

Fished in an old wound,
The soft pond of repose;
Nothing nibbled my line,
15 Not even the minnows came.

2. The cemetery where Roethke's father was buried.

Sat in an empty house
Watching shadows crawl,
Scratching.
There was one fly.

20   Voice, come out of the silence.
Say something.
Appear in the form of a spider
Or a moth beating the curtain.

Tell me:
25   Which is the way I take;
Out of what door do I go,
Where and to whom?

Dark hollows said, lee° to the wind,   shelter
The moon said, back of an eel,
30   The salt said, look by the sea,
Your tears are not enough praise,
You will find no comfort here,
In the kingdom of bang and blab.

Running lightly over spongy ground,
35   Past the pasture of flat stones,
The three elms,
The sheep strewn on a field,
Over a rickety bridge
Toward the quick-water, wrinkling and rippling.

40   Hunting along the river,
Down among the rubbish, the bug-riddled foliage,
By the muddy pond-edge, by the bog-holes,
By the shrunken lake, hunting, in the heat of summer.

The shape of a rat?
45   It's bigger than that.
It's less than a leg
And more than a nose,
Just under the water
It usually goes.

50   Is it soft like a mouse?
Can it wrinkle its nose?
Could it come in the house
On the tips of its toes?

Take the skin of a cat
55   And the back of an eel,
Then roll them in grease,—
That's the way it would feel.

It's sleek as an otter
With wide webby toes

60   Just under the water
        It usually goes.

2. *The Pit*

        Where do the roots go?
            Look down under the leaves.
        Who put the moss there?
65   These stones have been here too long.
        Who stunned the dirt into noise?
            Ask the mole, he knows.[3]
        I feel the slime of a wet nest.
            Beware Mother Mildew.
70   Nibble again, fish nerves.

3. *The Gibber*[4]

        At the wood's mouth,
        By the cave's door,
        I listened to something
        I had heard before.

75   Dogs of the groin
        Barked and howled,
        The sun was against me,
        The moon would not have me.

        The weeds whined,
80   The snakes cried,
        The cows and briars
        Said to me: Die.

        What a small song. What slow clouds. What dark water.
        Hath the rain a father?[5] All the caves are ice. Only the snow's here.
85   I'm cold. I'm cold all over. Rub me in father and mother.
        Fear was my father, Father Fear.
        His look drained the stones.

            What gliding shape
            Beckoning through halls,
90   Stood poised on the stair,
            Fell dreamily down?

            From the mouths of jugs
            Perched on many shelves,
            I saw substance flowing
95   That cold morning.

            Like a slither of eels
            That watery cheek

---

3. Possible reference to *The Book of Thel* (1789–91) by the English poet William Blake: "Does the Eagle know what is in the pit? / Or wilt thou go ask the Mole."

4. A possible triple pun: meaningless utterance, the pouch at the base of the calyx of a flower, and working-class slang for a key.
5. Cf. Job 38.28.

As my own tongue kissed
My lips awake.

100 Is this the storm's heart? The ground is unstilling itself.
My veins are running nowhere. Do the bones cast out their fire?
Is the seed leaving the old bed? These buds are live as birds.
Where, where are the tears of the world?
Let the kisses resound, flat like a butcher's palm;
105 Let the gestures freeze; our doom is already decided.
All the windows are burning! What's left of my life?
I want the old rage, the lash of primordial milk!
Goodbye, goodbye, old stones, the time-order is going,
I have married my hands to perpetual agitation,
110 I run, I run to the whistle of money.

      Money money money
      Water water water

      How cool the grass is.
      Has the bird left?
115   The stalk still sways.
      Has the worm a shadow?
      What do the clouds say?

      These sweeps of light undo me.
      Look, look, the ditch is running white!
120   I've more veins than a tree!
      Kiss me, ashes, I'm falling through a dark swirl.

4. The Return

      The way to the boiler was dark,
      Dark all the way,
      Over slippery cinders
125   Through the long greenhouse.

      The roses kept breathing in the dark.
      They had many mouths to breathe with.
      My knees made little winds underneath
      Where the weeds slept.

130   There was always a single light
      Swinging by the fire-pit,
      Where the fireman pulled out roses,
      The big roses, the big bloody clinkers.[6]

      Once I stayed all night.
135   The light in the morning came slowly over the white
      Snow.
      There were many kinds of cool
      Air.
      Then came steam.

6. Literally, a mass of vitrified material ejected from a volcano.

140   Pipe-knock.

Scurry of warm over small plants.
Ordnung! ordnung!⁷
Papa is coming!

A fine haze moved off the leaves;
145   Frost melted on far panes;
The rose, the chrysanthemum turned toward the light.
Even the hushed forms, the bent yellowy weeds
Moved in a slow up-sway.

5. *"It was beginning winter"*

It was beginning winter,
150   An in-between time,
The landscape still partly brown:
The bones of weeds kept swinging in the wind,
Above the blue snow.

It was beginning winter,
155   The light moved slowly over the frozen field,
Over the dry seed-crowns,
The beautiful surviving bones
Swinging in the wind.

Light traveled over the wide field;
160   Stayed.
The weeds stopped swinging.
The mind moved, not alone,
Through the clear air, in the silence.

Was it light?
165   Was it light within?
Was it light within light?
Stillness becoming alive,
Yet still?

A lively understandable spirit
170   Once entertained you.
It will come again.
Be still.
Wait.

1948

Elegy for Jane

My Student, Thrown by a Horse

I remember the neckcurls, limp and damp as tendrils;
And her quick look, a sidelong pickerel smile;

---

7. "Order" (German). An expression meaning that all is in its proper place.

And how, once startled into talk, the light syllables leaped for her,
And she balanced in the delight of her thought,
5 A wren, happy, tail into the wind,
Her song trembling the twigs and small branches.
The shade sang with her;
The leaves, their whispers turned to kissing;
And the mold sang in the bleached valleys under the rose.

10 Oh, when she was sad, she cast herself down into such a pure depth,
Even a father could not find her:
Scraping her cheek against straw;
Stirring the clearest water.
My sparrow, you are not here,
15 Waiting like a fern, making a spiny shadow.
The sides of wet stones cannot console me,
Nor the moss, wound with the last light.

If only I could nudge you from this sleep,
My maimed darling, my skittery pigeon.
20 Over this damp grave I speak the words of my love:
I, with no rights in this matter,
Neither father nor lover.

1953

The Waking

I wake to sleep, and take my waking slow.
I feel my fate in what I cannot fear.
I learn by going where I have to go.

We think by feeling. What is there to know?
5 I hear my being dance from ear to ear.
I wake to sleep, and take my waking slow.

Of those so close beside me, which are you?
God bless the Ground! I shall walk softly there,
And learn by going where I have to go.

10 Light takes the Tree; but who can tell us how?
The lowly worm climbs up a winding stair;
I wake to sleep, and take my waking slow.

Great Nature has another thing to do
To you and me; so take the lively air,
15 And, lovely, learn by going where to go.

This shaking keeps me steady. I should know.
What falls away is always. And is near.
I wake to sleep, and take my waking slow.
I learn by going where I have to go.

1953

I Knew a Woman

I knew a woman, lovely in her bones,
When small birds sighed, she would sigh back at them;
Ah, when she moved, she moved more ways than one:
The shapes a bright container can contain!
5   Of her choice virtues only gods should speak,
Or English poets who grew up on Greek
(I'd have them sing in chorus, cheek to cheek).

How well her wishes went! She stroked my chin,
She taught me Turn, and Counter-turn, and Stand;[8]
10   She taught me Touch, that undulant white skin;
I nibbled meekly from her proffered hand;
She was the sickle; I, poor I, the rake,
Coming behind her for her pretty sake
(But what prodigious mowing we did make).

15   Love likes a gander, and adores a goose:
Her full lips pursed, the errant note to seize;
She played it quick, she played it light and loose,
My eyes, they dazzled at her flowing knees;
Her several parts could keep a pure repose,
20   Or one hip quiver with a mobile nose
(She moved in circles, and those circles moved).

Let seed be grass, and grass turn into hay:
I'm martyr to a motion not my own;
What's freedom for? To know eternity.
25   I swear she cast a shadow white as stone.
But who would count eternity in days?
These old bones live to learn her wanton ways:
(I measure time by how a body sways).

1958

Wish for a Young Wife

My lizard, my lively writher,
May your limbs never wither,
May the eyes in your face
Survive the green ice
5   Of envy's mean gaze;
May you live out your life
Without hate, without grief,
And your hair ever blaze,
In the sun, in the sun,
10   When I am undone,
When I am no one.

1964

---

8. Translations of the Greek literary terms *strophe, antistrophe,* and *epode* (more properly, "the song that follows"), which are the three parts of the Pindaric ode.

In a Dark Time

In a dark time, the eye begins to see,
I meet my shadow in the deepening shade;
I hear my echo in the echoing wood—
A lord of nature weeping to a tree.
5   I live between the heron and the wren,[9]
Beasts of the hill and serpents of the den.

What's madness but nobility of soul
At odds with circumstance? The day's on fire!
I know the purity of pure despair,
10 My shadow pinned against a sweating wall.
That place among the rocks—is it a cave,
Or winding path? The edge is what I have.

A steady storm of correspondences!
A night flowing with birds, a ragged moon,
15 And in broad day the midnight come again!
A man goes far to find out what he is—
Death of the self in a long, tearless night,
All natural shapes blazing unnatural light.

Dark, dark my light, and darker my desire.
20 My soul, like some heat-maddened summer fly,
Keeps buzzing at the sill. Which I is I?
A fallen man, I climb out of my fear.
The mind enters itself, and God the mind,
And one is One, free in the tearing[1] wind.

1964

RALPH GUSTAFSON

1909–

In the Yukon[1]

In Europe, you can't move without going down into history.
Here, all is a beginning. I saw a salmon jump,
Again and again, against the current,
The timbered hills a background, wooded green
5 Unpushed through; the salmon jumped, silver.
This was news, was commerce, at the end of the summer
The leap for dying. Moose came down to the water edge
To drink and the salmon turned silver arcs.
At night, the northern lights played, great over country
10 Without tapestry and coronations, kings crowned

---

9. The heron is a large, solitary wading bird, the wren a small, sociable songbird.
1. With a pun on "tearless" (line 17), according to a note of Roethke's.
1. Territory of Canada.

With weights of gold. They were green,
Green hangings and great grandeur, over the north
Going to what no man can hold hard in mind,
The dredge of that gravity, being without experience.

1960, 1979

Of Green Steps and Laundry

The man will put a large-headed nail,
Shiny as silver, into the green step,
Straightening winter's bias and spring
Thaw and his hammer will knock it crooked,
5 The bird come obtrusively to the bough above,
And it will have to be done again, and that
Will be important; and she will hang
Blue and white shirts and a patched quilt
On the laundry line that runs from the kitchen
10 Step to the yard telephone pole and sheets
That smell of winter's cold, and the pulley
Each time the line is launched will squeak,
And that will be important; and neither
She nor the man pounding the clear air
15 Fixing the green step with another nail,
Will be aware of the importance, twenty
Years later thought of by him
Who drove nails and saw laundry,
Who thought little of cardinals and clothespins
20 And now loves life, loves life.

1977

A. M. KLEIN
1909–1972

Indian Reservation: Caughnawaga[1]

Where are the braves, the faces like autumn fruit,
who stared at the child from the colored frontispiece?
And the monosyllabic chief who spoke with his throat?
Where are the tribes, the feathered bestiaries?[2] —
5 Rank Aesop's animals erect and red,
with fur on their names to make all live things kin' —
Chief Running Deer, Black Bear, Old Buffalo Head?

Childhood, that wished me Indian, hoped that
one afterschool I'd leave the classroom chalk,

1. Small Indian reservation in southern Quebec, across the St. Lawrence River from Montreal.
2. Old books describing, often with allegorical overtones, the habits of real and mythical animals; "Aesop" was the ancient Greek author of fables, many of which involved animal protagonists.

10   the varnish smell, the watered dust of the street,
to join the clean outdoors and the Iroquois track.
Childhood; but always,—as on a calendar,—
there stood that chief, with arms akimbo, waiting
the runaway mascot paddling to his shore.

15   With what strange moccasin stealth that scene is changed!
With French names, without paint, in overalls,
their bronze, like their nobility expunged,—
the men. Beneath their alimentary° shawls   *providing sustenance*
sit like black tents their squaws; while for the tourist's
20   brown pennies scattered at the old church door,
the ragged papooses° jump, and bite the dust.   *young children*

    Their past is sold in a shop: the beaded shoes,
the sweetgrass basket, the curio Indian,
burnt wood and gaudy cloth and inch-canoes—
25   trophies and scalpings for a traveler's den.
Sometimes, it's true, they dance, but for a bribe;
after a deal don the bedraggled feather
and welcome a white mayor to the tribe.

    This is a grassy ghetto, and no home.
30   And these are fauna in a museum kept.
The better hunters have prevailed. The game,
losing its blood, now makes these grounds its crypt.
The animals pale, the shine of the fur is lost,
bleached are their living bones. About them watch
35   as through a mist, the pious prosperous ghosts.

The Rocking Chair

    It seconds the crickets of the province. Heard
in the clean lamplit farmhouses of Quebec,—
wooden,—it is no less a national bird;
and rivals, in its cage, the mere stuttering clock.
5   To its time, the evenings are rolled away;
and in its peace the pensive mother knits
contentment to be worn by her family,
grown-up, but still cradled by the chair in which she sits.

    It is also the old man's pet, pair to his pipe,
10   the two aids of his arithmetic and plans,
plans rocking and puffing into market-shape;
and it is the toddler's game and dangerous dance.
Moved to the verandah, on summer Sundays, it is,
among the hanging plants, the girls, the boy-friends,
15   sabbatical and clumsy, like the white haloes
dangling above the blue serge suits of the young men.

    It has a personality of its own;
is a character (like that old drunk Lacoste,

exhaling amber, and toppling on his pins);
20   it is alive; individual; and no less
an identity than those about it. And
it is tradition. Centuries have been flicked
from its arcs, alternately flicked and pinned.
It rolls with the gait of St. Malo.[3] It is act

25   and symbol, symbol of this static folk
which moves in segments, and returns to base,—
a sunken pendulum: *invoke, revoke;*
loosed yon, leashed hither, motion on no space.
O, like some Anjou[4] ballad, all refrain,
30   which turns about its longing, and seems to move
to make a pleasure out of repeated pain,
its music moves, as if always back to a first love.

For the Sisters of the Hotel Dieu[5]

In pairs,
as if to illustrate their sisterhood,
the sisters pace the hospital garden walks.
In their robes black and white immaculate hoods
5   they are like birds,
the safe domestic fowl of the House of God.

O biblic birds,
who fluttered to me in my childhood illnesses
—me little, afraid, ill, not of your race,—
10   the cool wing for my fever, the hovering solace,
the sense of angels—
be thanked, O plumage of paradise, be praised.

1948

DOROTHY LIVESAY

1909–

Green Rain

I remember long veils of green rain
Feathered like the shawl of my grandmother—
Green from the half-green of the spring trees
Waving in the valley.

5   I remember the road
Like the one which leads to my grandmother's house,

<hr>

3. Breton town in France, from which many French Canadians came.
4. Both a town in southern Quebec and an ancient province in western France.
5. "Hotel" is used here in the broader French sense, which includes "hospital"; "Dieu": God. "Sisters" connotes both nuns and nurses.

A warm house, with green carpets,
Geraniums, a trilling canary
And shining horse-hair chairs;
10   And the silence, full of the rain's falling
Was like my grandmother's parlour
Alive with herself and her voice, rising and falling—
Rain and wind intermingled.

I remember on that day
15   I was thinking only of my love
And of my love's house.
But now I remember the day
As I remember my grandmother.
I remember the rain as the feathery fringe of her shawl.

1930   1932

The Uninvited

Always a third one's there
where any two are walking out
along a river-bank   so mirror-still
sheathed in sheets
5   of sky   pillows of cloud—
their footprints crunch the hardening earth
their eyes delight in trees   stripped clean
winter-prepared
with only the rose-hips red
10   and the plump fingers of sumach

And always between the two
(scuffling the leaves, laughing
and fingers locked)
goes a third lover   his or hers
15   who walked this way with one or other   once
flung back the head   snapped branches of dark
     pine
in armfuls   before snowfall

          I walk beside you
          trace
20   a shadow's shade
          skating on silver
          hear
          another voice
          singing under ice

1969   1971

MALCOLM LOWRY

1909–1957

Delirium in Vera Cruz[1]

Where has tenderness gone, he asked the mirror
Of the Biltmore Hotel, cuarto° 216. Alas,   *room*
Can its reflection lean against the glass
Too, wondering where I have gone, into what horror?
5   Is that it staring at me now with terror
Behind your frail tilted barrier? Tenderness
Was here, in this very bedroom, in this
Place, its form seen, cries heard, by you. What error
Is here? Am I that rashed image?
10 Is this the ghost of the love you reflected?
Now with a background of tequila, stubs, dirty collars,
Sodium perborate,[2] and a scrawled page
To the dead, telephone off the hook? In rage
He smashed all the glass in the room. (Bill: $50.)

1936   1962

The Wild Cherry[3]

We put a prop beneath the sagging bough
That yearned over the beach, setting four stones
Cairn-like against it, but we thought our groans
Were the wild cherry's, for it was as though
5   Utterly set with broken seams on doom
It listed wilfully down like a mast,
Stubborn as some smashed recalcitrant boom
That will neither be cut loose nor made fast.
Going—going—it was yet no bidder
10 For life, whether for such sober healing
We left its dead branches to consider
Until its sunward pulse renewed, feeling
The passionate hatred of that tree
Whose longing was to wash away to sea.

1940–47   1962, 1992

Eye-Opener[4]

How like a man, is Man, who rises late
And gazes on his unwashed dinner plate
And gazes on the bottles, empty too,

---

1. The chief seaport of Mexico; now Veracruz. Canadian-born Lowry spent nineteen months in Mexico, where his most celebrated work, the novel *Under the Volcano* (1947), was set. The state of Lowry's poem texts is extraordinarily complicated, and the versions here are chosen from among several, offered either by his first editor, Earle Birney (whose 1962 selected edition included some ques-
tionable changes), or the editor of the 1992 *Collected Poetry of Malcolm Lowry*, Kathleen Sherf. This poem is a Birney version.
2. A water-soluble solid used as a bleach and as an antiseptic.
3. Sherf version.
4. Sherf version.

All gulphed in last night's loud long how-do-you-do,
5   —Although one glass yet holds a gruesome bait—
How like to Man is this man and his fate—
Still drunk and stumbling through the rusty trees
To breakfast on stale rum sardines and peas.

1953   1962, 1992

Strange Type[5]

I wrote: in the dark cavern of our birth.
The printer had it tavern, which seems better:
But herein lies the subject of our mirth,
Since on the next page death appears as dearth.
5   So it may be that God's word was distraction,
Which to our strange type appears destruction,
Which is bitter.

1946–54   1962

STEPHEN SPENDER

1909–1995

I Think Continually of Those Who Were Truly Great

I think continually of those who were truly great.
Who, from the womb, remembered the soul's history
Through corridors of light where the hours are suns
Endless and singing. Whose lovely ambition
5   Was that their lips, still touched with fire,
Should tell of the Spirit clothed from head to foot in song.
And who hoarded from the Spring branches
The desires falling across their bodies like blossoms.

What is precious is never to forget
10   The essential delight of the blood drawn from ageless springs
Breaking through rocks in worlds before our earth.
Never to deny its pleasure in the morning simple light
Nor its grave evening demand for love.
Never to allow gradually the traffic to smother
15   With noise and fog the flowering of the spirit.

Near the snow, near the sun, in the highest fields
See how these names are fêted by the waving grass
And by the streamers of white cloud
And whispers of wind in the listening sky.
20   The names of those who in their lives fought for life
Who wore at their hearts the fire's centre.

5. The title is Birney's; Lowry left the poem unti-
tled. Though Sherf's punctuation is probably more
accurate, Birney's version is given here for its read-
ing of the last word, "bitter," which seems more
likely than Sherf's "better."

Born of the sun they travelled a short while towards the sun,
And left the vivid air signed with their honour.

1933

Ultima Ratio Regum[1]

The guns spell money's ultimate reason
In letters of lead on the Spring hillside.
But the boy lying dead under the olive trees
Was too young and too silly
5 To have been notable to their important eye.
He was a better target for a kiss.

When he lived, tall factory hooters never summoned him
Nor did restaurant plate-glass doors revolve to wave him in
His name never appeared in the papers.
10 The world maintained its traditional wall
Round the dead with their gold sunk deep as a well,
Whilst his life, intangible as a Stock Exchange rumour, drifted outside.

O too lightly he threw down his cap
One day when the breeze threw petals from the trees.
15 The unflowering wall sprouted with guns,
Machine-gun anger quickly scythed the grasses;
Flags and leaves fell from hands and branches;
The tweed cap rotted in the nettles.

Consider his life which was valueless
20 In terms of employment, hotel ledgers, news files.
Consider. One bullet in ten thousand kills a man.
Ask. Was so much expenditure justified
On the death of one so young, and so silly
Lying under the olive trees, O world, O death?

1939

Seascape

(In Memoriam, M.A.S.)

There are some days the happy ocean lies
Like an unfingered harp, below the land.
Afternoon gilds all the silent wires
Into a burning music for the eyes.
5 On mirrors flashing between fine-strung fires
The shore, heaped up with roses, horses, spires,
Wanders on water, walking above ribbed sand.

The motionlessness of the hot sky tires
And a sigh, like a woman's, from inland
10 Brushes the instrument with shadowing hand
Drawing across its wires some gull's sharp cries

---

1. Latin for "kings' ultimate reason" (for taking action).

Or bell, or shout, from distant, hedged-in shires;
These, deep as anchors, the hushing wave buries.

Then from the shore, two zig-zag butterflies,
15   Like errant dog-roses, cross the bright strand
Spiraling over sea in foolish gyres°   *spirals*
Until they fall into reflected skies.
They drown. Fishermen understand
Such wings sunk in such ritual sacrifice,

20   Recalling legends of undersea, drowned cities.
What voyagers, oh what heroes, flamed like pyres
With helmets plumed, have set forth from some island
And them the sea engulfed. Their eyes,
Contorted by the cruel waves' desires
25   Glitter with coins through the tide scarcely scanned,
While, above them, that harp assumes their sighs.

1947

ROBERT FITZGERALD
1910–1985

Figlio Maggiore[1]
Benedict Robert Campion Fitzgerald

Twitched in her belly, or he raised a fist,
and came and cried. O red and meager baby,
umbilical, priapic,° knobby,   *phallic*
mashed and wrinkled as an old pugilist.

5   A lyric name he got and a saint's name,
a third stout name from Pa, *cioè Roberto.*[2]
Think of this Christian if you care to
filling his giant napkin° without shame.   *diaper*

And soon for happy trilled at goldy leaves
10   by a summer air. What hours our boy would warble.
You find my doting lines intolerable?
Never was infant such under such eaves.

Behave. "I'm being hayve." With Harpo's[3] grin.
At three he shook his cap and bells, our jester,
15   or tented him in a souwester°   *rain hat*
and fragrant slicker to stay in the rain in.

---

1. "Eldest Son" (Italian).
2. "That is, Robert (Fitzgerald)" (Italian). "Lyric name": from Thomas Campion (1567–1620), English poet and composer; "saint's name": Bene-
dict.
3. Harpo Marx (1893–1964), one member of the Marx Brothrs comedy team.

Never (ah!) to inherit that dripping grove,
in a DC–6 he peered at cumulo-cirrus
"trees" on ocean. (Graciously hear us,
20 lord of that aircraft gaily named I LOVE)

Ligurian fry[4] inquired, "Why is your old man
home all day? What *mestiere*[5] has he?"
"*Da notte va fuori a rubare case.*"[6]
A penman's alibi. Tie it if you can.

25 Off iodine-scented rock pure undersea,
fronded, astir, awaited our explorer.
Noon. With a tentacled small horror
draped on his tines[7] he swam ashore in glee.

Daemonic lightning, ire of rebellious powers
30 could rend this patient hunter of the polyp.[8]
Bone-ache from one corrective wallop
disabled the parental hand for hours.

Child of my own rage, rippling in Tuscan speech
through five hard winters' *compiti*, my Benny,
35 *temi, storie, disegni!*[9]
What will the next years teach?

1971

NORMAN MacCAIG

1910–1996

Fetching cows

The black one, last as usual, swings her head
And coils a black tongue round a grass-tuft. I
Watch her soft weight come down, her split feet spread.

In front, the others swing and slouch; they roll
5 Their great Greek eyes and breathe out milky gusts
From muzzles black and shiny as wet coal.

The collie trots, bored, at my heels, then plops
Into the ditch. The sea makes a tired sound
That's always stopping though it never stops.

10 A haycart squats prickeared against the sky.
Hay breath and milk breath. Far out in the West
The wrecked sun founders though its colours fly.

---

4. Children in Liguria, Italy.
5. "Job, profession" (Italian).
6. " 'At night he goes out to burgle houses' "
(Italian).
7. Meant to suggest the tines of the triton of Nep-

tune, Roman god of the sea.
8. Tentacled sea creature.
9. "Themes, stories, drawings!" (Italian). *Compiti*:
"homework" (Italian).

The collie's bored. There's nothing to control . . .
The black cow is two native carriers
15   Bringing its belly home, slung from a pole.

1965

Solitary crow

Why solitary crow? He in his feathers
Is a whole world of crow—of a dry-stick nest,
Of windy distances where to be crow is best,
Of tough-guy clowning and of black things done
5   To a sprawled lamb whose blood beads in the sun.

Sardonic anarchist. Where he goes he carries,
Since there's no centre, what a centre is,
And that is crow, the ragged self that's his.
Smudged on a cloud, he jeers at the world then halts
10   To jeer at himself and turns two somersaults.

He ambles through the air, flops down and seesaws
On a blunt fencepost, hiccups and says *Caw*.
The sun glints greasy on his working craw
And adds a silver spot to that round eye
15   Whose black light bends and cocks the world awry.

1968

Ringed plover by a water's edge

They sprint eight feet and—
stop. Like that. They
sprintayard (like that) and
stop.

5   They have no acceleration
and no brakes.
Top speed's their only one.

They're alive—put life
through a burning-glass, they're
10   its focus—but they share
the world of delicate clockwork.

In spasmodic
Indian file
they parallel the parallel ripples.

15   When they stop
they, suddenly,
are gravel.

1974

Kingfisher

That kingfisher jewelling upstream
seems to leave a streak of itself behind it
in the bright air. The trees
are all the better for its passing.

5   It's not a mineral eater, though it looks it:
It doesn't nip nicks out of the edges
of rainbows. — It dives
into the burly water, then, perched
on a Japanese bough, gulps
10 into its own incandescence
a wisp of minnow, a warrior stickleback.
— Or it vanishes into its burrow, resplendent
Samurai, returning home
to his stinking slum.

1977

CHARLES OLSON

1910–1970

Merce[1] of Egypt

1

I sing the tree is a heron
I praise long grass
I wear the lion skin
over the long skirt
5 to the ankle. The ankle
is a heron
I look straightly backward. Or I bend to the side straightly
to raise the sheaf
up the stick of the leg
10 as the bittern's leg, raised
as slow as
his neck grows
as the wheat. The presentation,
the representation,
15 is flat,

I am followed by women and a small boy in white carrying a duck,
all have flat feet and, foot before foot, the women with black wigs
And I intent
upon idlers,
20 and flowers

---

1. Merce Cunningham (b. 1919?), the dancer and choreographer. While head of Black Mountain College, an experimental school in North Caro- lina, Olson brought him there to teach, and even participated in some of his dance classes.

2

  the sedge
as tall as I am, the rushes
as I am
  as far as I am animal, antelope
with such's attendant carnivores
      and rows of beaters
drive the game to the hunter, or into nets,
where it is thick-wooded or there are open spaces
with low shrubs

3

I speak downfall, the ball of my foot
on the neck of the earth, the hardsong
of the rise of all trees, the jay
who uses the air. I am the recovered sickle
with the grass-stains still on the flint of its teeth.
I am the six-rowed barley
they cut down.

I am tree. The boy of the back of my legs
is roots. I am water fowl
when motion is the season of my river, and the wild boar
casts me. But my time
is hawkweed,

4

I hold what the wind blows, and silt.
I hide in the swamps of the valley to escape civil war,
and marauding soldiers. In the new procession
I am first, and carry wine
made of dandelions. The new rites
are my bones

I built my first settlement
in groves

5

  as they would flail crops
when the spring comes, and flood, the tassels
rise, as my head

         1953

Variations Done for Gerald Van De Wiele[2]

I. Le Bonheur[3]

dogwood flakes
what is green

the petals
from the apple
5 blow on the road

mourning doves
mark the sway
of the afternoon, bees
dig the plum blossoms

10 the morning
stands up straight, the night
is blue from the full of the April moon

iris and lilac, birds
birds, yellow flowers
15 white flowers, the Diesel
does not let up dragging
the plow
      as the whippoorwill,
the night's tractor, grinds
20 his song

      and no other birds but us
are as busy (O saisons, o châteaux!

Délires![4]

      What soul
25 is without fault?

Nobody studies
happiness

Every time the cock crows
I salute him

30 I have no longer any excuse
for envy. My life

2. Van De Wiele was a student at Black Mountain College during Olson's time as head there.
3. The "Variations" allude repeatedly, and in complex, subtle ways, to a poem by Arthur Rimbaud (1854–1891), "Le Bonheur" ("Happiness"), the last of the poems that occur throughout Rimbaud's poem-prose complex *Une Saison en enfer* (*A Season in Hell*, 1873). Sometimes Olson cites a word or a phrase from the poem in French, some-times he translates a word by the English word it resembles (*"trépas"* as "trespass"), then later by the word that translates it correctly ("death").
4. Two sections of *Une Saison en enfer* are entitled "Délires" ("Deliriums," "Frenzies"), and "Le Bonheur" occurs in "Délires II." "O saisons, o châteaux!": the first line and refrain of "Le Bonheur" ("O seasons! o castles!").

has been given its orders: the seasons
seize

the soul and the body, and make mock
35   of any dispersed effort. The hour of death

is the only trespass

II. The Charge

dogwood flakes
the green

the petals from the apple-trees
40   fall for the feet to walk on

the birds are so many they are
loud, in the afternoon

they distract, as so many bees do
suddenly all over the place

45   With spring one knows today to see
that in the morning each thing

is separate but by noon
they have melted into each other

and by night only crazy things
50   like the full moon and the whippoorwill

and us, are busy. We are busy
if we can get by that whiskered bird,

that nightjar,° and get across, the moon   *nocturnal bird*
is our conversation, she will say

55   what soul
isn't in default?

can you afford not to make
the magical study

which happiness is? do you hear
60   the cock when he crows? do you know the charge,

that you shall have no envy, that your life
has its orders, that the seasons

seize you too, that no body and soul are one
if they are not wrought

65   in this retort? that otherwise efforts
are efforts? And that the hour of your flight

will be the hour of your death?

III. Spring

The dogwood
lights up the day.

70   The April moon
flakes the night.

Birds, suddenly,
are a multitude

The flowers are ravined°   *hollowed out*
75   by bees, the fruit blossoms

are thrown to the ground, the wind
the rain forces everything. Noise—

even the night is drummed
by whippoorwills, and we get

80   as busy, we plow, we move,
we break out, we love. The secret

which got lost neither hides
nor reveals itself, it shows forth

tokens. And we rush
85   to catch up. The body

whips the soul. In its great desire
it demands the elixir

In the roar of spring,
transmutations. Envy

90   drags herself off. The fault of the body and the soul
—that they are not one—

the matutinal° cock clangs   *morning*
and singleness: we salute you

season of no bungling

1960

ELIZABETH BISHOP

1911–1979

The Fish

I caught a tremendous fish
and held him beside the boat
half out of water, with my hook
fast in a corner of his mouth.
5   He didn't fight.
He hadn't fought at all.
He hung a grunting weight,
battered and venerable
and homely. Here and there
10   his brown skin hung in strips
like ancient wallpaper,
and its pattern of darker brown
was like wallpaper:
shapes like full-blown roses
15   stained and lost through age.
He was speckled with barnacles,
fine rosettes of lime,
and infested
with tiny white sea-lice,
20   and underneath two or three
rags of green weed hung down.
While his gills were breathing in
the terrible oxygen
—the frightening gills,
25   fresh and crisp with blood,
that can cut so badly—
I thought of the coarse white flesh
packed in like feathers,
the big bones and the little bones,
30   the dramatic reds and blacks
of his shiny entrails,
and the pink swim-bladder
like a big peony.
I looked into his eyes
35   which were far larger than mine
but shallower, and yellowed,
the irises backed and packed
with tarnished tinfoil
seen through the lenses
40   of old scratched isinglass.[1]
They shifted a little, but not
to return my stare.
—It was more like the tipping
of an object toward the light.

---

1. Here, mica in thin, transparent sheets; "isinglass" is also a gelatin prepared from the air bladder of certain fishes.

45 I admired his sullen face,
the mechanism of his jaw,
and then I saw
that from his lower lip
—if you could call it a lip—
50 grim, wet, and weaponlike,
hung five old pieces of fish-line,
or four and a wire leader
with the swivel still attached,
with all their five big hooks
55 grown firmly in his mouth.
A green line, frayed at the end
where he broke it, two heavier lines,
and a fine black thread
still crimped from the strain and snap
60 when it broke and he got away.
Like medals with their ribbons
frayed and wavering,
a five-haired beard of wisdom
trailing from his aching jaw.
65 I stared and stared
and victory filled up
the little rented boat,
from the pool of bilge
where oil had spread a rainbow
70 around the rusted engine
to the bailer rusted orange,
the sun-cracked thwarts,
the oarlocks on their strings,
the gunnels—until everything
75 was rainbow, rainbow, rainbow!
And I let the fish go.

1946

Filling Station

Oh, but it is dirty!
—this little filling station,
oil-soaked, oil-permeated
to a disturbing, over-all
5 black translucency.
Be careful with that match!

Father wears a dirty,
oil-soaked monkey suit
that cuts him under the arms,
10 and several quick and saucy
and greasy sons assist him
(it's a family filling station),
all quite thoroughly dirty.

Do they live in the station?
15 It has a cement porch

behind the pumps, and on it
a set of crushed and grease-
impregnated wickerwork;
on the wicker sofa
20   a dirty dog, quite comfy.

Some comic books provide
the only note of color—
of certain color. They lie
upon a big dim doily
25   draping a taboret°   *drum-shaped table*
(part of the set), beside
a big hirsute begonia.

Why the extraneous plant?
Why the taboret?
30   Why, oh why, the doily?
(Embroidered in daisy stitch
with marguerites,° I think,   *small daisies*
and heavy with gray crochet.)

Somebody embroidered the doily.
35   Somebody waters the plant,
or oils it, maybe. Somebody
arranges the rows of cans
so that they softly say:
ESSO—SO—SO—SO^2
40   to high-strung automobiles.
Somebody loves us all.

1965

The Armadillo[3]

For Robert Lowell

This is the time of year
when almost every night
the frail, illegal fire balloons appear.
Climbing the mountain height,

5   rising toward a saint
still honored in these parts,
the paper chambers flush and fill with light
that comes and goes, like hearts.

Once up against the sky it's hard
10   to tell them from the stars—
planets, that is—the tinted ones:
Venus going down, or Mars,

2. The company name "Esso" was subsumed by "Exxon."

3. Cf. Robert Lowell, "Skunk Hour" (pp. 1493–95), which is modeled on Bishop's poem.

or the pale green one. With a wind,
they flare and falter, wobble and toss;
15   but if it's still they steer between
the kite sticks of the Southern Cross,[4]

receding, dwindling, solemnly
and steadily forsaking us,
or, in the downdraft from a peak,
20   suddenly turning dangerous.

Last night another big one fell.
It splattered like an egg of fire
against the cliff behind the house.
The flame ran down. We saw the pair

25   of owls who nest there flying up
and up, their whirling black-and-white
stained bright pink underneath, until
they shrieked up out of sight.

The ancient owls' nest must have burned.
30   Hastily, all alone,
a glistening armadillo left the scene,
rose-flecked, head down, tail down,

and then a baby rabbit jumped out,
short-eared, to our surprise.
35   So soft!—a handful of intangible ash
with fixed, ignited eyes.

Too pretty, dreamlike mimicry!
O falling fire and piercing cry
and panic, and a weak mailed fist
40   *clenched ignorant against the sky!*

1965

Sestina

September rain falls on the house.
In the failing light, the old grandmother
sits in the kitchen with the child
beside the Little Marvel Stove,[5]
5   reading the jokes from the almanac,
laughing and talking to hide her tears.

She thinks that her equinoctial tears
and the rain that beats on the roof of the house
were both foretold by the almanac,
10   but only known to a grandmother.
The iron kettle sings on the stove.
She cuts some bread and says to the child,

4. Bright constellation.   5. Brand name of a wood- or coal-burning stove.

It's time for tea now; but the child
is watching the teakettle's small hard tears
15 dance like mad on the hot black stove,
the way the rain must dance on the house.
Tidying up, the old grandmother
hangs up the clever almanac

on its string. Birdlike, the almanac
20 hovers half open above the child,
hovers above the old grandmother
and her teacup full of dark brown tears.
She shivers and says she thinks the house
feels chilly, and puts more wood in the stove.

25 *It was to be,* says the Marvel Stove.
I know what I know, says the almanac.
With crayons the child draws a rigid house
and a winding pathway. Then the child
puts in a man with buttons like tears
30 and shows it proudly to the grandmother.

But secretly, while the grandmother
busies herself about the stove,
the little moons fall down like tears
from between the pages of the almanac
35 into the flower bed the child
has carefully placed in the front of the house.

Time to plant tears, says the almanac.
The grandmother sings to the marvelous stove
and the child draws another inscrutable house.

1965

In the Waiting Room

In Worcester, Massachusetts,
I went with Aunt Consuelo
to keep her dentist's appointment
and sat and waited for her
5 in the dentist's waiting room.
It was winter. It got dark
early. The waiting room
was full of grown-up people,
arctics and overcoats,
10 lamps and magazines.
My aunt was inside
what seemed like a long time
and while I waited I read
the *National Geographic*
15 (I could read) and carefully
studied the photographs:
the inside of a volcano,
black, and full of ashes;

then it was spilling over
20   in rivulets of fire.
Osa and Martin Johnson
dressed in riding breeches,
laced boots, and pith helmets.
A dead man slung on a pole
25   —"Long Pig,"[6] the caption said.
Babies with pointed heads
wound round and round with string;
black, naked women with necks
wound round and round with wire
30   like the necks of light bulbs.
Their breasts were horrifying.
I read it right straight through.
I was too shy to stop.
And then I looked at the cover:
35   the yellow margins, the date.

Suddenly, from inside,
came an *oh!* of pain
—Aunt Consuelo's voice—
not very loud or long.
40   I wasn't at all surprised;
even then I knew she was
a foolish, timid woman.
I might have been embarrassed,
but wasn't. What took me
45   completely by surprise
was that it was *me:*
my voice, in my mouth.
Without thinking at all
I was my foolish aunt,
50   I—we—were falling, falling,
our eyes glued to the cover
of the *National Geographic,*
February, 1918.

I said to myself: three days
55   and you'll be seven years old.
I was saying it to stop
the sensation of falling off
the round, turning world
into cold, blue-black space.
60   But I felt: you are an *I,*
you are an *Elizabeth,*
you are one of *them.*
Why should you be one, too?
I scarcely dared to look
65   to see what it was I was.
I gave a sidelong glance
—I couldn't look any higher—

6. Human flesh, food for cannibals.

at shadowy gray knees,
trousers and skirts and boots
70   and different pairs of hands
lying under the lamps.
I knew that nothing stranger
had ever happened, that nothing
stranger could ever happen.
75   Why should I be my aunt,
or me, or anyone?
What similarities—
boots, hands, the family voice
I felt in my throat, or even
80   the *National Geographic*
and those awful hanging breasts—
held us all together
or made us all just one?
How—I didn't know any
85   word for it—how "unlikely" . . .
How had I come to be here,
like them, and overhear
a cry of pain that could have
got loud and worse but hadn't?

90   The waiting room was bright
and too hot. It was sliding
beneath a big black wave,
another, and another.

Then I was back in it.
95   The War[7] was on. Outside,
in Worcester, Massachusetts,
were night and slush and cold,
and it was still the fifth
of February, 1918.

1976

The Moose

For Grace Bulmer Bowers

From narrow provinces[8]
of fish and bread and tea,
home of the long tides
where the bay leaves the sea
5   twice a day and takes
the herrings long rides,

where if the river
enters or retreats
in a wall of brown foam
10   depends on if it meets

---

7. World War I.
8. The maritime provinces of Canada, including   Nova Scotia, where Bishop was born, and New
Brunswick.

the bay coming in,
the bay not at home;

where, silted red,
sometimes the sun sets
15   facing a red sea,
and others, veins the flats'
lavender, rich mud
in burning rivulets;

on red, gravelly roads,
20   down rows of sugar maples,
past clapboard farmhouses
and neat, clapboard churches,
bleached, ridged as clamshells,
past twin silver birches,

25   through late afternoon
a bus journeys west,
the windshield flashing pink,
pink glancing off of metal,
brushing the dented flank
30   of blue, beat-up enamel;

down hollows, up rises,
and waits, patient, while
a lone traveller gives
kisses and embraces
35   to seven relatives
and a collie supervises.

Goodbye to the elms,
to the farm, to the dog.
The bus starts. The light
40   grows richer; the fog,
shifting, salty, thin,
comes closing in.

Its cold, round crystals
form and slide and settle
45   in the white hens' feathers,
in gray glazed cabbages,
on the cabbage roses
and lupins like apostles;

the sweet peas cling
50   to their wet white string
on the whitewashed fences;
bumblebees creep
inside the foxgloves,
and evening commences.

55   One stop at Bass River.
Then the Economies—

Lower, Middle, Upper;
Five Islands, Five Houses,[9]
where a woman shakes a tablecloth
60 out after supper.

A pale flickering. Gone.
The Tantramar marshes[1]
and the smell of salt hay.
An iron bridge trembles
65 and a loose plank rattles
but doesn't give way.

On the left, a red light
swims through the dark:
a ship's port lantern.
70 Two rubber boots show,
illuminated, solemn.
A dog gives one bark.

A woman climbs in
with two market bags,
75 brisk, freckled, elderly.
"A grand night. Yes, sir,
all the way to Boston."
She regards us amicably.

Moonlight as we enter
80 the New Brunswick woods,
hairy, scratchy, splintery;
moonlight and mist
caught in them like lamb's wool
on bushes in a pasture.

85 The passengers lie back.
Snores. Some long sighs.
A dreamy divagation
begins in the night,
a gentle, auditory,
90 slow hallucination. . . .

In the creakings and noises,
an old conversation
—not concerning us,
but recognizable, somewhere,
95 back in the bus:
Grandparents' voices

uninterruptedly
talking, in Eternity:
names being mentioned,
100 things cleared up finally;

9. Towns in Nova Scotia.   into the Bay of Fundy.
1. Marshes of the Tantramar River, which empties

what he said, what she said,
who got pensioned;

deaths, deaths and sicknesses;
the year he remarried;
105   the year (something) happened.
She died in childbirth.
That was the son lost
when the schooner foundered.

He took to drink. Yes.
110   She went to the bad.
When Amos began to pray
even in the store and
finally the family had
to put him away.

115   "Yes . . ." that peculiar
affirmative. "Yes . . ."
A sharp, indrawn breath,
half groan, half acceptance,
that means "Life's like that.
120   We know *it* (also death)."

Talking the way they talked
in the old featherbed,
peacefully, on and on,
dim lamplight in the hall,
125   down in the kitchen, the dog
tucked in her shawl.

Now, it's all right now
even to fall asleep
just as on all those nights.
130   —Suddenly the bus driver
stops with a jolt,
turns off his lights.

A moose has come out of
the impenetrable wood
135   and stands there, looms, rather,
in the middle of the road.
It approaches; it sniffs at
the bus's hot hood.

Towering, anterless,
140   high as a church,
homely as a house
(or, safe as houses).
A man's voice assures us
"Perfectly harmless. . . ."

145   Some of the passengers
exclaim in whispers,

childishly, softly,
"Sure are big creatures."
"It's awful plain."
150 "Look! It's a she!"

Taking her time,
she looks the bus over,
grand, otherworldly.
Why, why do we feel
155 (we all feel) this sweet
sensation of joy?

"Curious creatures,"
says our quiet driver,
rolling his r's.
160 "Look at that, would you."
Then he shifts gears.
For a moment longer,

by craning backward,
the moose can be seen
165 on the moonlit macadam;
then there's a dim
smell of moose, an acrid
smell of gasoline.   1976

One Art

The art of losing isn't hard to master;
so many things seem filled with the intent
to be lost that their loss is no disaster.

Lose something every day. Accept the fluster
5   of lost door keys, the hour badly spent.
The art of losing isn't hard to master.

Then practice losing farther, losing faster:
places, and names, and where it was you meant
to travel. None of these will bring disaster.

10 I lost my mother's watch. And look! my last, or
next-to-last, of three loved houses went.
The art of losing isn't hard to master.

I lost two cities, lovely ones. And, vaster,
some realms I owned, two rivers, a continent.
15 I miss them, but it wasn't a disaster.

—Even losing you (the joking voice, a gesture
I love) I shan't have lied. It's evident
the art of losing's not too hard to master
though it may look like (*Write* it!) like disaster.   1976

ALLEN CURNOW

1911–

Landfall in Unknown Seas[1]

The 300th Anniversary of the Discovery of New Zealand by Abel Tasman,
13 December 1642

I

Simply by sailing in a new direction
You could enlarge the world
                You picked your captain,
Keen on discoveries, tough enough to make them,
5   Whatever vessels could be spared from other
More urgent service for a year's adventure;
Took stock of the more probable conjectures
About the Unknown to be traversed, all
Guesses at golden coasts and tales of monsters
10 To be digested into plain instructions
For likely and unlikely situations.

All this resolved and done, you launched the whole
On a fine morning, the best time of year,
Skies widening and the oceanic furies
15 Subdued by summer illumination; time
To go and to be gazed at going
On a fine morning, in the Name of God
Into the nameless waters of the world.

O you had estimated all the chances
20 Of business in those waters, the world's waters
Yet unexploited.
             But more than the sea-empire's
Cannon, the dogs of bronze and iron barking
From Timor to the Straits, backed up the challenge.
25 Between you and the South an older enmity
Lodged in the searching mind, that would not tolerate
So huge a hegemony of ignorance.
There, where your Indies had already sprinkled
Their tribes like ocean rains, you aimed your voyage;
30 Like them invoked your God, gave seas to history
And islands to new hazardous tomorrows.

II

Suddenly exhilaration
Went off like a gun, the whole
Horizon, the long chase done,
35 Hove to. There was the seascape

---

1. Written as part of the tercentenary celebrations.

Crammed with coast, surprising
As new lands will, the sailor
Moving on the face of the waters,
Watching the earth take shape
40   Round the unearthly summits, brighter
Than its emerging colour.

Yet this, no far fool's errand,
Was less than the heart desired,
In its old Indian dream
45   The glittering gulfs ascending
Past palaces and mountains
Making one architecture.
Here the uplifted structure,
Peak and pillar of cloud—
50   O splendour of desolation—reared
Tall from the pit of the swell,
With a shadow, a finger of wind, forbade
Hopes of a lucky landing.

Always to islanders danger
55   Is what comes over the sea;
Over the yellow sands and the clear
Shallows, the dull filament
Flickers, the blood of strangers:
Death discovered the Sailor
60   O in a flash, in a flat calm,
A clash of boats in the bay
And the day marred with murder.
The dead required no further
Warning to keep their distance;
65   The rest, noting the failure,
Pushed on with a reconnaissance
To the north; and sailed away.

III

Well, home is the Sailor,[2] and that is a chapter
In a schoolbook, a relevant yesterday
70   We thought we knew all about, being much apter
    To profit, sure of our ground,
No murderers mooring in our Golden Bay.

But now there are no more islands to be found
And the eye scans risky horizons of its own
75   In unsettled weather, and murmurs of the drowned
    Haunt their familiar beaches—
Who navigates us towards what unknown

---

2. Cf. R. L. Stevenson, *Requiem*: "Home is the sailor, home from sea."

But not improbable provinces? Who reaches
A future down for us from the high shelf
80   Of spiritual daring? Not those speeches
          Pinning on the Past like a decoration
      For merit that congratulates itself,

O not the self-important celebration
Or most painstaking history, can release
85   The current of a discoverer's elation
          And silence the voices saying,
      "Here is the world's end where wonders cease."

Only by a more faithful memory, laying
On him the half-light of a diffident glory,
90   The Sailor lives, and stands beside us, paying
          Out into our time's wave
      The stain of blood that writes an island story.

1942   1943

You Will Know When You Get There

Nobody comes up from the sea as late as this
in the day and the season, and nobody else goes down

the last steep kilometre, wet-metalled where
a shower passed shredding the light which keeps

5   pouring out of its tank in the sky, through summits,
trees, vapours thickening and thinning. Too

credibly by half celestial, the dammed
reservoir up there keeps emptying while the light lasts

over the sea, where it "gathers the gold against
10   it". The light is bits of crushed rock randomly

glinting underfoot, wetted by the short
shower, and down you go and so in its way does

the sun which gets there first. Boys, two of them,
turn campfirelit faces, a hesitancy to speak

15   is a hesitancy of the earth rolling back and away
behind this man going down to the sea with a bag

to pick mussels, having an arrangement with the tide,
the ocean to be shallowed three point seven metres,

one hour's light to be left and there's the excrescent
20   moon sponging off the last of it. A door

slams, a heavy wave, a door, the sea-floor shudders.
Down you go alone, so late, into the surge-black fissure.

1982

IRVING LAYTON

1912–

The Birth of Tragedy[1]

And me happiest when I compose poems.
   Love, power, the huzza of battle
   are something, are much;
yet a poem includes them like a pool
5   water and reflection.
In me, nature's divided things—
   tree, mold on tree—
   have their fruition;
I am their core. Let them swap,
10 bandy, like a flame swerve
I am their mouth; as a mouth I serve.

And I observe how the sensual moths
   big with odor and sunshine
   dart into the perilous shrubbery;
15 or drop their visiting shadows
    upon the garden I one year made
of flowering stone to be a footstool
   for the perfect gods:
   who, friends to the ascending orders,
20 sustain all passionate meditations
and call down pardons
for the insurgent blood.

A quiet madman, never far from tears,
   I lie like a slain thing
25   under the green air the trees
inhabit, or rest upon a chair
   towards which the inflammable air
tumbles on many robins' wings;
   noting how seasonably
30   leaf and blossom uncurl
and living things arrange their death,
while someone from afar off
blows birthday candles for the world.

              1954

---

1. The title of the first book (1872) of the German philosopher Friedrich Nietzsche (1844–1900). The book defended the importance of Dionysian emotionalism as well as Apollonian rationalism in the creation of tragedy.

The Cold Green Element

At the end of the garden walk
the wind and its satellite wait for me;
their meaning I will not know
    until I go there,
5 but the black-hatted undertaker

who, passing, saw my heart beating in the grass,
is also going there. Hi, I tell him,
a great squall in the Pacific blew a dead poet
    out of the water,
10 Who now hangs from the city's gates.

Crowds depart daily to see it, and return
with grimaces and incomprehension;
if its limbs twitched in the air
    they would sit at its feet
15 peeling their oranges.

And turning over I embrace like a lover
the trunk of a tree, one of those
for whom the lightning was too much
    and grew a brilliant
20 hunchback with a crown of leaves.

The ailments escaped from the labels
of medicine bottles are all fled to the wind;
I've seen myself lately in the eyes
    of old women,
25 spent streams mourning my manhood,

in whose old pupils the sun became
a bloodsmear on broad catalpa leaves
and hanging from ancient twigs,
    my murdered selves
30 sparked the air like the muted collisions

of fruit. A black dog howls down my blood,
a black dog with yellow eyes;
he too by someone's inadvertence
    saw the bloodsmear
35 on the broad catalpa leaves.

But the furies[2] clear a path for me to the worm
who sang for an hour in the throat of a robin,
and misled by the cries of young boys
    I am again
40 a breathless swimmer in that cold green element.

1955

---

2. In classical mythology, female spirits who punished the doers of unavenged wrongs.

Berry Picking

Silently my wife walks on the still wet furze
Now darkgreen the leaves are full of metaphors
Now lit up is each tiny lamp of blueberry.
The white nails of rain have dropped and the sun is free.

5   And whether she bends or straightens to each bush
To find the children's laughter among the leaves
Her quiet hands seem to make the quiet summer hush—
Berries or children, patient she is with these.

I only vex and perplex her; madness, rage
10 Are endearing perhaps put down upon the page;
Even silence daylong and sullen can then
Enamor as restraint or classic discipline.

So I envy the berries she puts in her mouth,
The red and succulent juice that stains her lips;
15 I shall never taste that good to her, nor will they
Displease her with a thousand barbarous jests.

How they lie easily for her hand to take,
Part of the unoffending world that is hers;
Here beyond complexity she stands and stares
20 And leans her marvelous head as if for answers.

No more the easy soul my childish craft deceives
Nor the simpler one for whom yes is always yes;
No, now her voice comes to me from a far way off
Though her lips are redder than the raspberries.

1958

ROBERT HAYDEN

1913–1980

Those Winter Sundays

Sundays too my father got up early
and put his clothes on in the blueblack cold,
then with cracked hands that ached
from labor in the weekday weather made
5 banked fires blaze. No one ever thanked him.

I'd wake and hear the cold splintering, breaking.
When the rooms were warm, he'd call,
and slowly I would rise and dress,
fearing the chronic angers of that house,

10 Speaking indifferently to him,
who had driven out the cold

and polished my good shoes as well.
What did I know, what did I know
of love's austere and lonely offices?

1962

Mourning Poem for the Queen of Sunday

Lord's lost Him His mockingbird,
His fancy warbler;
Satan sweet-talked her,
four bullets hushed her.
5   Who would have thought
she'd end that way?

Four bullets hushed her. And the world a-clang with evil.
Who's going to make old hardened sinner men tremble now
and the righteous rock?
10   Oh who and oh who will sing Jesus down
to help with struggling and doing without and being colored
all through blue Monday?
Till way next Sunday?

All those angels
15   in their cretonne clouds and finery
the true believer saw
when she rared back her head and sang,
all those angels are surely weeping.
Who would have thought
20   she'd end that way?

Four holes in her heart. The gold works wrecked.
But she looks so natural in her big bronze coffin
among the Broken Hearts and Gates-Ajar,
it's as if any moment she'd lift her head
25   from its pillow of chill gardenias
and turn this quiet into shouting Sunday
and make folks forget what she did on Monday.

Oh, Satan sweet-talked her,
and four bullets hushed her.
30   Lord's lost Him His diva,
His fancy warbler's gone.
Who would have thought,
who would have thought she'd end that way?

1966

Night, Death, Mississippi

I

A quavering cry. Screech-owl?
Or one of them?

The old man in his reek
and gauntness laughs—

5   One of them, I bet—
and turns out the kitchen lamp,
limping to the porch to listen
in the windowless night.

Be there with Boy and the rest
10   if I was well again.
Time was. Time was.
White robes like moonlight

In the sweetgum[1] dark.
Unbucked that one then
15   and him squealing bloody Jesus
as we cut it off.

Time was. A cry?
A cry all right.
He hawks and spits,
20   fevered as by groinfire.

Have us a bottle,
Boy and me—
he's earned him a bottle—
when he gets home.

II

25   Then we beat them, he said,
beat them till our arms was tired
and the big old chains
messy and red.

O Jesus burning on the lily cross

30   Christ, it was better
than hunting bear
which don't know why
you want him dead.

O night, rawhead and bloodybones night

35   You kids fetch Paw
some water now so's he
can wash that blood
off him, she said.

O night betrayed by darkness not its own

1966

---

1. The dark woods of the sweet gum, a North American tree of a deep reddish brown grain.

The Night-Blooming Cereus[2]

And so for nights
we waited, hoping to see
the heavy bud
    break into flower.

5   On its neck-like tube
hooking down from the edge
of the leaf-branch
    nearly to the floor,

    the bud packed
10 tight with its miracle swayed
stiffly on breaths
    of air, moved

    as though impelled
by stirrings within itself.
15 It repelled as much
    as it fascinated me

    sometimes—snake,
eyeless bird head,
beak that would gape
20   with grotesque life-squawk.

    But you, my dear,
conceded less to the bizarre
than to the imminence
    of bloom. Yet we agreed

25 we ought
to celebrate the blossom,
paint ourselves, dance
    in honor of

    archaic mysteries
30 when it appeared. Meanwhile
we waited, aware
    of rigorous design.

    Backster's
polygraph,[3] I thought
35 would have shown
    (as clearly as it had

    a philodendron's
fear) tribal sentience

---

2. A species of cactus.
3. Lie detector, which, Cleve Backster argued in the late 1960s, could be used to demonstrate that plants responded to the feelings around them.

in the cactus, focused
40   energy of will.

That belling of
tropic perfume—that
signaling
   not meant for us;

45   the darkness
cloyed with summoning
fragrance. We dropped
   trivial tasks

and marveling
50   beheld at last the achieved
flower. Its moonlight
   petals were

still unfold-
ing, the spike fringe of the outer
55   perianth[4] recessing
   as we watched.

Luna presence,
foredoomed, already dying,
it charged the room
60   with plangency

older than human
cries, ancient as prayers
invoking Osiris, Krishna,
   Tezcátlipóca.[5]

65   We spoke
in whispers when
we spoke
   at all . . .

1972

" 'Mystery Boy' Looks for Kin in Nashville"

Puzzle faces in the dying elms
promise him treats if he will stay.
Sometimes they hiss and spit at him
like varmints caught
5   in a thicket of butterflies.

A black doll,
one disremembered time,
came floating down to him

---

4. The outer covering of a flower.   5. Major Egyptian, Indian, and Aztec gods.

through mimosa's fancywork leaves and blooms
10   to be his hidden bride.

From the road beyond the creepered walls
they call to him now and then,
and he'll take off in spite of the angry trees,
hearing like the loudening of his heart
15   the name he never can he never can repeat.

And when he gets to where the voices were—
Don't cry, his dollbaby wife implores;
I know where they are, don't cry.
We'll go and find them, we'll go
20   and ask them for your name again.

                                                              1977

Paul Laurence Dunbar⁶

For Herbert Martin

We lay red roses on his grave,
speak sorrowfully of him
as if he were but newly dead

          And so it seems to us
5   this raw spring day, though years
before we two were born he was
          a young poet dead.

          Poet of our youth—
his "cri du coeur"⁷ our own,
10   his verses "in a broken tongue"

          beguiling as an elder
brother's antic lore.
Their sad blackface lilt and croon
          survive him like

15   The happy look (subliminal
of victim, dying man)
          a summer's tintypes⁸ hold.

          The roses flutter in the wind;
we weight their stems
20   with stones, then drive away.

                                                              1978

6. (1872–1906); African-American poet (see pp. 1117–19).
7. Passionate appeal or protest (French: literally, "cry from the heart"). The next line is probably a reference to Dunbar's poems in dialect (blackface).
8. I.e., old photographs.

MURIEL RUKEYSER

1913–1980

Sand-Quarry with Moving Figures

Father and I drove to the sand-quarry across the ruined marshlands,
miles of black grass, burned for next summer's green.
I reached my hand to his beneath the lap-robe,
we looked at the stripe of fire, the blasted scene.

5   "It's all right," he said, "they can control the flames,
on one side men are standing, and on the other the sea;"
but I was terrified of stubble and waste of black
and his ugly villages he built and was showing me.

The countryside turned right and left about the car,
10 straight through October we drove to the pit's heart;
sand, and its yellow canyon and standing pools
and the wealth of the split country set us farther apart.
"Look," he said, "this quarry means rows of little houses,
stucco and a new bracelet for you are buried there;"
15 but I remembered the ruined patches, and I saw the land ruined,
exploded, burned away, and the fiery marshes bare.

"We'll own the countryside, you'll see how soon I will,
you'll have acres to play in" : I saw the written name
painted on stone in the face of the steep hill:
20 "That's your name, Father!   "And yours!" he shouted, laughing.
"No, Father, no!"   He caught my hand as I cried,
and smiling, entered the pit, ran laughing down its side.

                                                   1935

Night Feeding

Deeper than sleep but not so deep as death
I lay there sleeping and my magic head
remembered and forgot.   On first cry I
remembered and forgot and did believe.
5 I knew love and I knew evil:
woke to the burning song and the tree burning blind,
despair of our days and the calm milk-giver who
knows sleep, knows growth, the sex of fire and grass,
and the black snake with gold bones.

10 Black sleeps, gold burns;   on second cry I woke
fully and gave to feed and fed on feeding.
Gold seed, green pain, my wizards in the earth
walked through the house, black in the morning dark.
Shadows grew in my veins, my bright belief,
15 my head of dreams deeper than night and sleep.
Voices of all black animals crying to drink,

cries of all birth arise, simple as we,
found in the leaves, in clouds and dark, in dream,
deep as this hour, ready again to sleep.

1951

Rondel[1]

Now that I am fifty-six
Come and celebrate with me—

What happens to song and sex
Now that I am fifty-six?

5   They dance, but differently,
Death and distance in the mix;
Now that I'm fifty-six
Come and celebrate with me.

1973

Ballad of Orange and Grape

After you finish your work
after you do your day
after you've read your reading
after you've written your say—
5   you go down the street to the hot dog stand,
one block down and across the way.
On a blistering afternoon in East Harlem in the twentieth century.

Most of the windows are boarded up,
the rats run out of a sack—
10   sticking out of the crummy garage
one shiny long Cadillac;
at the glass door of the drug-addiction center,
a man who'd like to break your back.
But here's a brown woman with a little girl dressed in rose and pink, too.

15   Frankfurters frankfurters sizzle on the steel
where the hot-dog-man leans—
nothing else on the counter
but the usual two machines,
the grape one, empty, and the orange one, empty,
20   I face him in between.
A black boy comes along, looks at the hot dogs, goes on walking.

I watch the man as he stands and pours
in the familiar shape
bright purple in the one marked ORANGE
25   orange in the one marked GRAPE,
the grape drink in the machine marked ORANGE

---

1. Based only loosely on the French syllabic verse form, a thirteen-line poem that turns on two rhymes, with a refrain.

and orange drink in the GRAPE.
Just the one word large and clear, unmistakable, on each machine.

I ask him   :   How can we go on reading
30 and make sense out of what we read?—
How can they write and believe what they're writing,
the young ones across the street,
while you go on pouring grape into ORANGE
and orange into the one marked GRAPE—?
35 (How are we going to believe what we read and we write and we
  hear and we say and we do?)

He looks at the two machines and he smiles
and he shrugs and smiles and pours again.
It could be violence and nonviolence
it could be white and black women and men
40 it could be war and peace or any
binary system, love and hate, enemy, friend.
Yes and no, be and not-be, what we do and what we don't do.

On a corner in East Harlem
garbage, reading, a deep smile, rape,
45 forgetfulness, a hot street of murder,
misery, withered hope,
a man keeps pouring grape into ORANGE
and orange into the one marked GRAPE,
pouring orange into GRAPE and grape into ORANGE forever.

          1973

MAY SWENSON

1913–1989

Motherhood

She sat on a shelf,
her breasts two bellies
on her poked-out belly,
on which the navel looked
5 like a sucked-in mouth—
her knees bent and apart,
her long left arm raised,
with the large hand knuckled
to a bar in the ceiling—
10 her right hand clamping
the skinny infant to her chest—
its round, pale, new,
soft muzzle hunting
in the brown hair for a nipple,
15 its splayed, tiny hand picking
at her naked, dirty ear.
Twisting its little neck,

with tortured, ecstatic eyes
the size of lentils, it looked
20 into her severe, close-set,
solemn eyes, that beneath bald
eyelids glared—dull lights
in sockets of leather.

She twitched some chin-hairs,
25 with pain or pleasure,
as the baby-mouth found and
yanked at her nipple;
its pink-nailed, jointless
fingers, wandering her face,
30 tangled in the tufts
of her cliffy brows.
She brought her big
hand down from the bar—
with pretended exasperation
35 unfastened the little hand,
and locked it within her palm—
while her right hand,
with snag-nailed forefinger
and short, sharp thumb, raked
40 the new orange hair
of the infant's skinny flank—
and found a louse,
which she lipped, and
thoughtfully crisped
45 between broad teeth.
She wrinkled appreciative
nostrils which, without a nose,
stood open—damp holes
above the poke of her mouth.

50 She licked her lips, flicked
her leather eyelids—
then, suddenly flung
up both arms and grabbed
the bars overhead.
55 The baby's scrabbly fingers
instantly caught the hair—
as if there were metal rings there—
in her long, stretched armpits.
And, as she stately swung,
60 and then proudly, more swiftly
slung herself from corner
to corner of her cell—
arms longer than her round
body, short knees bent—
65 her little wild-haired,
poke-mouthed infant hung,
like some sort of trophy,
or decoration, or shaggy medal—

shaped like herself—but new,
70 clean, soft and shining
on her chest.

1967

Cardinal Ideograms[1]

0   A mouth. Can blow or breathe,
    be funnel, or Hello.

1   A grass blade or a cut.

2   A question seated. And a proud
    bird's neck.

3   Shallow mitten for two-fingered hand.

4   Three-cornered hut
    on one stilt. Sometimes built
    so the roof gapes.

5   A policeman. Polite.
    Wearing visored cap.

6   O unrolling,
    tape of ambiguous length
    on which is written the mystery
    of everything curly.

7   A step,
    detached from its stair.

8   The universe in diagram:
    A cosmic hourglass.
    (Note enigmatic shape,
    absence of any valve of origin,
    how end overlaps beginning.)
    Unknotted like a shoelace
    and whipped back and forth,
    can serve as a model of time.

1. Counting-numbers interpreted as if they were pictures.

9
Lorgnette for the right eye.
In England or if you are Alice[2]
the stem is on the left.

10
A grass blade or a cut
companioned by a mouth.
Open? Open. Shut? Shut.

1967

Waterbird

Part otter, part snake, part bird the bird Anhinga,[3]
jalousie wings, draped open, dry. When slack-
hinged, the wind flips them shut. Her cry,
a slatted clatter, inflates her chin-
5   pouch; it's like a fish's swim-
bladder. Anhinga's body, otter-
furry, floats, under water-
mosses, neck a snake with white-
rimmed blue round roving eyes. Those long feet stilt-
10   paddle the only bird of the marsh that flies
submerged. Otter-
quick over bream that hover in water-
shade, she feeds, finds fillets among the water-
weeds. Her beak, ferrule of a folded black
15   umbrella, with neat thrust impales her prey.
She flaps up to dry on the crooked, look-
dead-limb of the Gumbo Limbo,[4] her tan-
tipped wing fans spread, tail a shut fan dangled.

1987

Goodbye, Goldeneye[5]

Rag of black plastic, shred of a kite
caught on the telephone cable above the bay
has twisted in the wind all winter, summer, fall.

Leaves of birch and maple, brown paws of the oak
5   have all let go but this. Shiny black Mylar[6]
on stem strong as fishline, the busted kite string

whipped around the wire and knotted—how long
will it cling there? Through another spring?
Long barge nudged up channel by a snorting tug,

---

2. Alice, who sees the mirror images of things in
Through the Looking Glass by the English mathe-
matician and writer Lewis Carroll (1832–1898; see
pp. 1032–36).
3. Also known as snake-bird or water-turkey. With
a long fantail and thin neck, it swims submerged
up to the neck, thus resembling a snake.

4. Tropical American tree with a smooth, coppery
bark.
5. The goldeneye, like the grebe, scaup, and loon
mentioned in line 20, is a freshwater diving duck.
6. Brand of strong, thin polyester film, here used
in string.

10 its blunt front aproned with rot-black tires —
what is being hauled in slime-green drums?
The herring gulls that used to feed their young

on the shore — puffy, wide-beaked babies standing
spraddle-legged and crying — are not here this year.
15 Instead, steam shovel, bulldozer, cement mixer

rumble over sand, beginning the big new beach house.
There'll be a hotdog stand, flush toilets, trash —
plastic and glass, greasy cartons, crushed beercans,

barrels of garbage for water rats to pick through.
20 So, goodbye, goldeneye, and grebe and scaup and loon.
Goodbye, morning walks beside the tide tinkling

among clean pebbles, blue mussel shells and snail
shells that look like staring eyeballs. Goodbye,
kingfisher, little green, black crowned heron,

25 snowy egret. And, goodbye, oh faithful pair of
swans that used to glide — god and goddess
shapes of purity — over the wide water.

1987

R. S. THOMAS

1913–

Welsh Landscape

To live in Wales is to be conscious
At dusk of the spilled blood
That went to the making of the wild sky,
Dyeing the immaculate rivers
5 In all their courses.
It is to be aware,
Above the noisy tractor
And hum of the machine
Of strife in the strung woods,
10 Vibrant with sped arrows.
You cannot live in the present,
At least not in Wales.
There is the language for instance,
The soft consonants
15 Strange to the ear.
There are cries in the dark at night
As owls answer the moon,
And thick ambush of shadows,
Hushed at the fields' corners
20 There is no present in Wales,

And no future;
There is only the past,
Brittle with relics,
Wind-bitten towers and castles
25   With sham ghosts;
Mouldering quarries and mines;
And an impotent people,
Sick with inbreeding,
Worrying the carcase of an old song.

1955

The Lonely Farmer

Poor hill farmer astray in the grass:
There came a movement and he looked up, but
All that he saw was the wind pass.
There was a sound of voices on the air,
5   But where, where? It was only the glib stream talking
Softly to itself. And once when he was walking
Along a lane in spring he was deceived
By a shrill whistle coming through the leaves:
Wait a minute, wait a minute—four swift notes;
10   He turned, and it was nothing, only a thrush
In the thorn bushes easing its throat.
He swore at himself for paying heed,
The poor hill farmer, so often again
Stopping, staring, listening, in vain,
15   His ear betrayed by the heart's need.

1955

The View from the Window

Like a painting it is set before one,
But less brittle, ageless; these colours
Are renewed daily with variations
Of light and distance that no painter
5   Achieves or suggests. Then there is movement,
Change, as slowly the cloud bruises
Are healed by sunlight, or snow caps
A black mood; but gold at evening
To cheer the heart. All through history
10   The great brush has not rested,
Nor the paint dried; yet what eye,
Looking coolly, or, as we now,
Through the tears' lenses, ever saw
This work and it was not finished?

1958

On the Farm

There was Dai Puw. He was no good.
They put him in the fields to dock swedes,

And took the knife from him, when he came home
At late evening with a grin
5 Like the slash of a knife on his face.

There was Llew Puw, and he was no good.
Every evening after the ploughing
With the big tractor he would sit in his chair,
And stare into the tangled fire garden,
10 Opening his slow lips like a snail.

There was Huw Puw, too. What shall I say?
I have heard him whistling in the hedges
On and on, as though winter
Would never again leave those fields,
15 And all the trees were deformed.

And lastly there was the girl:
Beauty under some spell of the beast.
Her pale face was the lantern
By which they read in life's dark book
20 The shrill sentence: God is love.

1963

Lore

Job Davies, eighty-five
Winters old, and still alive
After the slow poison
And treachery of the seasons.

5 Miserable? Kick my arse!
It needs more than the rain's hearse,
Wind-drawn, to pull me off
The great perch of my laugh.

What's living but courage?
10 Paunch full of hot porridge,
Nerves strengthened with tea,
Peat-black, dawn found me

Mowing where the grass grew,
Bearded with golden dew.
15 Rhythm of the long scythe
Kept this tall frame lithe.

What to do? Stay green.
Never mind the machine,
Whose fuel is human souls.
20 Live large, man, and dream small.

1964

JOHN BERRYMAN

1914–1972

From Homage to Mistress Bradstreet[1]

[17]

The winters close, Springs open, no child stirs
130 under my withering heart, O seasoned heart
God grudged his aid.
All things else soil like a shirt.
Simon is much away. My executive[2] stales.
The town came through for the cartway by the pales,[3]
135 but my patience is short.
I revolt from, I am like, these savage foresters

[18]

whose passionless dicker in the shade, whose glance
impassive & scant, belie their murderous cries
when quarry seems to show.
140 Again I must have been wrong, twice.[4]
Unwell in a new way. Can that begin?
God brandishes. O love, O I love. Kin,
gather. My world is strange
and merciful, ingrown months, blessing a swelling trance.

[19]

145 So squeezed, wince you I scream? I love you & hate
off with you. Ages! *Useless.* Below my waist
he has me in Hell's vise.
Stalling. He let go. Come back: brace
me somewhere. No. No. Yes! everything down
150 hardens I press with horrible joy down
my back cracks like a wrist
shame I am voiding oh behind it is too late

[20]

hide me forever I work thrust I must free
now I all muscles & bones concentrate
155 what is living from dying?
Simon I must leave you so untidy
Monster you are killing me Be sure
I'll have you later Women do endure
I can *can* no longer
160 and it passes the wretched trap whelming and I am me

1. Berryman's book-length poem about, and mostly in the voice of, the early American poet Anne Bradstreet (ca. 1612–1672; see pp. 413–22). Bradstreet speaks here of her struggle in childbirth. For a discussion of the complex stanza form Berryman invented for this poem (modeled partly on W. B. Yeats' "In Memory of Major Gregory"), as well as the form of the "dream song," see the introduction to Berryman's *Collected Poems 1937–1971* (New York, 1989) by Charles Thornbury, pp. xl–xliii.
2. Power to act; "Simon": her husband.
3. Stockade fence.
4. That is, she failed to conceive.

[21]

drencht & powerful, I did it with my body!
One proud tug greens Heaven. Marvellous,
unforbidding Majesty.
Swell, imperious bells. I fly.
165 Mountainous, woman not breaks and will bend:
sways God nearby: anguish comes to an end.
Blossomed Sarah,[5] and I
blossom. Is that thing alive? I hear a famisht howl.

1948–53   1956

A Sympathy, A Welcome

Feel for your bad fall how could I fail,
poor Paul, who had it so good.
I can offer you only: this world like a knife.
Yet you'll get to know your mother
5 and humourless as you do look you will laugh
and all the others
will NOT be fierce to you, and loverhood
will swing your soul like a broken bell
deep in a forsaken wood, poor Paul,
10 whose wild bad father loves you well.

1958

From The Dream Songs[6]

1

Huffy Henry hid   the day,
unappeasable Henry sulked.
I see his point,—a trying to put things over.
It was the thought that they thought
5 they could *do* it made Henry wicked & away.
But he should have come out and talked.

All the world like a woolen lover
once did seem on Henry's side.
Then came a departure.
10 Thereafter nothing fell out as it might or ought.
I don't see how Henry, pried
open for all the world to see, survived.

What he has now to say is a long
wonder the world can bear & be.
15 Once in a sycamore I was glad

5. Wife of Abraham, who after long barrenness gave birth to Isaac (Genesis 17.19).
6. "[The Dream Songs are] essentially about an imaginary character (not the poet, not me) named Henry, a white American in early middle age sometimes in blackface, who has suffered an irreversible loss and talks about himself sometimes in the first person, sometimes in the third, sometimes even in the second; he has a friend, never named, who addresses him as Mr. Bones and variants thereof" [Berryman's note]. These poems were written over a period of thirteen years.

all at the top, and I sang.
Hard on the land wears the strong sea
and empty grows every bed.

1964

4

Filling her compact & delicious body
with chicken páprika, she glanced at me
twice.
Fainting with interest, I hungered back
5 and only the fact of her husband & four other people
kept me from springing on her

or falling at her little feet and crying
'You are the hottest one for years of night
Henry's dazed eyes
10 have enjoyed, Brilliance.' I advanced upon
(despairing) my spumoni.—Sir Bones: is stuffed,
de world, wif feeding girls.

—Black hair, complexion Latin, jeweled eyes
downcast . . . The slob beside her   feasts . . . What wonders is
15 she sitting on, over there?
The restaurant buzzes. She might as well be on Mars.
Where did it all go wrong? There ought to be a law against Henry.
—Mr. Bones: there is.

1964

14

Life, friends, is boring. We must not say so.
After all, the sky flashes, the great sea yearns,
we ourselves flash and yearn,
and moreover my mother told me as a boy
5 (repeatingly) 'Ever to confess you're bored
means you have no

Inner Resources.' I conclude now I have no
inner resources, because I am heavy bored.
Peoples bore me,
10 literature bores me, especially great literature,
Henry bores me, with his plights & gripes
as bad as achilles,[7]

who loves people and valiant art, which bores me.
And the tranquil hills, & gin, look like a drag
15 and somehow a dog
has taken itself & its tail considerably away

---

7. The Greek hero of Homer's *Iliad*, who with-drew from battle because of a slight from Agamem-non. Berryman claimed that some of the structure of *The Dream Songs* could be traced to parallel scenes in the *Iliad*. "The chief enemy, in Achilles' case, was Hector, whom Berryman explicitly equated with Henry's father" [John Haffenden, *John Berryman: A Critical Commentary*, New York, 1980, p. 55].

into mountains or sea or sky, leaving
behind: me, wag.

1964

29

There sat down, once, a thing on Henry's heart
só heavy, if he had a hundred years
& more, & weeping, sleepless, in all them time
Henry could not make good.
5   Starts again always in Henry's ears
the little cough somewhere, an odor, a chime.

And there is another thing he has in mind
like a grave Sienese face[8] a thousand years
would fail to blur the still profiled reproach of. Ghastly,
10 with open eyes, he attends, blind.
All the bells say: too late. This is not for tears;
thinking.

But never did Henry, as he thought he did,
end anyone and hacks her body up
15 and hide the pieces, where they may be found.
He knows: he went over everyone, & nobody's missing.
Often he reckons, in the dawn, them up.
Nobody is ever missing.

1964

40

I'm scared a lonely. Never see my son,
easy be not to see anyone,
combers out to sea
know they're goin somewhere but not me.
5   Got a little poison, got a little gun,
I'm scared a lonely.

I'm scared a only one thing, which is me,
from othering I don't take nothin, see,
for any hound dog's sake.
10 But this is where I livin, where I rake
my leaves and cop my promise,[9] this' where we
cry oursel's awake.

Wishin was dyin but I gotta make
it all this way to that bed on these feet
15 where peoples said to meet.
Maybe but even if I see my son
forever never, get back on the take,
free, black & forty-one.[1]

1964

8. The painters of thirteenth- and fourteenth-cen-
tury Siena, Italy, were known for their austere reli-
gious portraits.

9. Build my potential.
1. A play on the phrase "free, white and twenty-
one," connoting independence.

145

Also I love him: me he's done no wrong
for going on forty years—forgiveness time—
I touch now his despair,
he felt as bad as Whitman[2] on his tower
5 but he did not swim out with me or my brother
as he threatened—

a powerful swimmer, to   take one of us along
as company in the defeat sublime,
freezing my helpless mother:
10 he only, very early in the morning,
rose with his gun and went outdoors by my window
and did what was needed.

I cannot read that wretched mind, so strong
& so undone. I've always tried. I—I'm
15 trying to forgive
whose frantic passage, when he could not live
an instant longer, in the summer dawn
left Henry to live on.

                            1968

155[3]

I can't get him out of my mind, out of my mind,
Hé was out of his own mind for years,
in police stations & Bellevue.[4]
He drove up to my house in Providence[5]
5 ho ho at 8 a.m. in a Cambridge taxi
and told it to wait.

He walked my living-room, & did not want breakfast
or even coffee, or even a drink.
He paced, I'd say Sit down,
10 it makes me nervous, for a moment he'd sit down,
then pace. After an hour or so I had a drink.
He took it back to Cambridge,

we never learnt why he came, or what he wanted.
His mission was obscure. His mission was real,
15 but obscure.
I remember his electrical insight as the young man,
his wit & passion, gift, the whole young man
alive with surplus love.

                            1968

---

2. Charles Whitman, a sniper who, from a tower at the University of Texas at Austin, sprayed the campus with bullets for eighty minutes on August 1, 1966. Whitman wrote of fear and violent impulses before his mass killing. "He" here refers to Berryman's father, John Smith, who committed suicide when the poet was twelve years old.

3. The poem refers to Delmore Schwartz (1913–1966), a gifted but troubled writer and Berryman's friend.
4. Public hospital in New York City, to which mentally disturbed patients are taken.
5. City in Rhode Island, about fifty miles from Cambridge, Massachusetts.

324. An Elegy for W.C.W.,[6] The Lovely Man

Henry in Ireland to Bill underground:
Rest well, who worked so hard, who made a good sound
constantly, for so many years:
your high-jinks delighted the continents & our ears:
5   you had so many girls your life was a triumph
and you loved your one wife.

At dawn you rose & wrote—the books poured forth—
you delivered infinite babies,[7] in one great birth—
and your generosity
10   to juniors made you deeply loved, deeply:
if envy was a Henry trademark, he would envy you,
especially the being through.

Too many journeys lie for him ahead,
too many galleys & page-proofs to be read,
15   he would like to lie down
in your sweet silence, to whom was not denied
the mysterious late excellence which is the crown
of our trials & our last bride.

                                 1968

382

At Henry's bier let some thing fall out well:
enter there none who somewhat has to sell,
the music ancient & gradual,
the voices solemn but the grief subdued,
5   no hairy jokes but everybody's mood
subdued, subdued,

until the Dancer comes, in a short short dress
hair black & long & loose, dark dark glasses,
uptilted face,
10   pallor & strangeness, the music changes
to 'Give!' & 'Ow!' and how! the music changes,
she kicks a backward limb

on tiptoe, pirouettes, & she is free
to the knocking music, sails, dips, & suddenly
15   returns to the terrible gay
occasion hopeless & mad, she weaves, it's hell,
she flings to her head a leg, bobs, all is well,
she dances Henry away.

                                 1968

---

6. William Carlos Williams (1883–1963), American poet (see pp. 1166–76).

7. Williams was a physician whose specialty was pediatrics.

RANDALL JARRELL
1914–1965

The Death of the Ball Turret Gunner[1]

From my mother's sleep I fell into the State,
And I hunched in its belly till my wet fur froze.
Six miles from earth, loosed from its dream of life,
I woke to black flak and the nightmare fighters.
5   When I died they washed me out of the turret with a hose.

1945

Eighth Air Force[2]

If, in an odd angle of the hutment,°   *encampment*
A puppy laps the water from a can
Of flowers, and the drunk sergeant shaving
Whistles O Paradiso![3] —shall I say that man
5   Is not as men have said: a wolf to man?

The other murderers troop in yawning;
Three of them play Pitch,° one sleeps, and one   *card game*
Lies counting missions, lies there sweating
Till even his heart beats: One; One; One.
10   O murderers! . . . Still, this is how it's done:

This is a war. . . . But since these play, before they die,
Like puppies with their puppy; since, a man,
I did as these have done, but did not die—
I will content the people as I can
15   And give up these to them: Behold the man![4]

I have suffered, in a dream, because of him,
Many things;[5] for this last saviour, man,
I have lied as I lie now. But what is lying?
Men wash their hands, in blood, as best they can:
20   I find no fault in this just man.[6]

1945

1. "A ball turret was a plexiglass sphere set into the belly of a B-17 or B-24, and inhabited by two .50 caliber machine-guns and one man, a short small man. When this gunner tracked with his machine-guns a fighter attacking his bomber from below, he revolved with the turret; hunched upside-down in his little sphere, he looked like the foetus in the womb. The fighters which attacked him were armed with cannon firing explosive shells. The hose was a steam hose" [Jarrell's note].
2. "A poem about the air force which bombed the Continent from England. The man who lies counting missions has one to go before being sent home. The phrases from the Gospels compare such criminals and scapegoats as these with that earlier criminal and scapegoat about whom the Gospels were written" [Jarrell's note].
3. A popular operatic aria.
4. Quoting John 19.5: these are Pilate's words as he presents Jesus, scourged and wearing a crown of thorns, to the crowd.
5. Pilate's wife wrote to him about Jesus: "Have nothing to do with that just man: for I have suffered many things this day in a dream because of him" (Matthew 27.19).
6. After the crowd had called on him to free the robber Barabbas and execute Jesus, Pilate had Jesus brought forth, "that you may know that I find no fault in him" (John 19.4–5). Pilate washed his hands to symbolize his freedom from responsibility for Christ's death.

A Front[7]

Fog over the base: the beams ranging
From the five towers pull home from the night
The crews cold in fur, the bombers banging
Like lost trucks down the levels of the ice.
5   A glow drifts in like mist (how many tons of it?),
Bounces to a roll, turns suddenly to steel
And tires and turrets, huge in the trembling light.
The next is high, and pulls up with a wail,
Comes round again—no use. And no use for the rest
10 In drifting circles out along the range;
Holding no longer, changed to a kinder course,
The flights drone southward through the steady rain.
The base is closed. . . . But one voice keeps on calling,
The lowering pattern of the engines grows;
15 The roar gropes downward in its shaky orbit
For the lives the season quenches. Here below
They beg, order, are not heard; and hear the darker
Voice rising: *Can't you hear me? Over. Over*—
All the air quivers, and the east sky glows.

1945

A Field Hospital

He stirs, beginning to awake.
A kind of ache
Of knowing troubles his blind warmth; he moans,
And the high hammering drone
5 Of the first crossing fighters shakes
His sleep to pieces, rakes
The darkness with its skidding bursts, is done.
All that he has known

Floods in upon him; but he dreads
10 The crooked thread
Of fire upon the darkness: "The great drake
Flutters to the icy lake—
The shotguns stammer in my head.
I lie in my own bed,"
15 He whispers, "dreaming"; and he thinks to wake.
The old mistake.

A cot creaks; and he hears the groan
He thinks his own—
And groans, and turns his stitched, blind, bandaged head
20 Up to the tent-flap, red
With dawn. A voice says, "Yes, this one";
His arm stings; then, alone,

---

7. "A front is closing in over a bomber base; the bombers, guided in by signals from the five towers of the radio range, are landing. Only one lands before the base is closed; the rest fly south to fields that are still open. One plane's radio has gone bad—it still transmits, but doesn't receive—and this plane tries to land and crashes" [Jarrell's note].

He neither knows, remembers—but instead
Sleeps, comforted.

1948

A Sick Child

The postman comes when I am still in bed.
"Postman, what do you have for me today?"
I say to him. (But really I'm in bed.)
Then he says—what shall I have him say?

5   "This letter says that you are president
Of—this word here; it's a republic."
Tell them I can't answer right away.
"It's your duty." No, I'd rather just be sick.

Then he tells me there are letters saying everything
10 That I can think of that I want for them to say.
I say, "Well, thank you very much. Good-bye."
He is ashamed, and turns and walks away.

If I can think of it, it isn't what I want.
I want . . . I want a ship from some near star
15 To land in the yard, and beings to come out
And think to me: "So this is where you are!

Come." Except that they won't do,
I thought of them. . . . And yet somewhere there must be
Something that's different from everything.
20 All that I've never thought of—think of me!

1951

Next Day

Moving from Cheer to Joy, from Joy to All,
I take a box
And add it to my wild rice, my Cornish game hens.
The slacked or shorted, basketed, identical
5   Food-gathering flocks
Are selves I overlook. Wisdom, said William James,

Is learning what to overlook.[8] And I am wise
If that is wisdom.
Yet somehow, as I buy All from these shelves
10 And the boy takes it to my station wagon,
What I've become
Troubles me even if I shut my eyes.

When I was young and miserable and pretty
And poor, I'd wish
15 What all girls wish: to have a husband,

8. From *Principles of Psychology*, by the American philosopher William James (1842–1910).

A house and children. Now that I'm old, my wish
Is womanish:
That the boy putting groceries in my car

See me. It bewilders me he doesn't see me.
20 For so many years
I was good enough to eat: the world looked at me
And its mouth watered. How often they have undressed me,
The eyes of strangers!
And, holding their flesh within my flesh, their vile

25 Imaginings within my imagining,
I too have taken
The chance of life. Now the boy pats my dog
And we start home. Now I am good.
The last mistaken,
30 Ecstatic, accidental bliss, the blind

Happiness that, bursting, leaves upon the palm
Some soap and water—
It was so long ago, back in some Gay
Twenties, Nineties, I don't know . . . Today I miss
35 My lovely daughter
Away at school, my sons away at school,

My husband away at work—I wish for them.
The dog, the maid,
And I go through the sure unvarying days
40 At home in them. As I look at my life,
I am afraid
Only that it will change, as I am changing:

I am afraid, this morning, of my face.
It looks at me
45 From the rear-view mirror, with the eyes I hate,
The smile I hate. Its plain, lined look
Of gray discovery
Repeats to me: "You're old." That's all, I'm old.

And yet I'm afraid, as I was at the funeral
50 I went to yesterday.
My friend's cold made-up face, granite among its flowers,
Her undressed, operated-on, dressed body
Were my face and body.
As I think of her I hear her telling me

55 How young I seem; I *am* exceptional;
I think of all I have.
But really no one is exceptional,
No one has anything, I'm anybody,
I stand beside my grave
60 Confused with my life, that is commonplace and solitary.

1965

A Man Meets a Woman in the Street

Under the separated leaves of shade
Of the gingko, that old tree
That has existed essentially unchanged
Longer than any other living tree,
5   I walk behind a woman. Her hair's coarse gold
Is spun from the sunlight that it rides upon.
Women were paid to knit from sweet champagne
Her second skin: it winds and unwinds, winds
Up her long legs, delectable haunches,
10   As she sways, in sunlight, up the gazing aisle.
The shade of the tree that is called maidenhair,
That is not positively known
To exist in a wild state, spots her fair or almost fair
Hair twisted in a French twist; tall or almost tall,
15   She walks through the air the rain has washed, a clear thing
Moving easily on its high heels, seeming to men
Miraculous . . . Since I can call her, as Swann[9] couldn't,
A woman who is my type, I follow with the warmth
Of familiarity, of novelty, this new
20   Example of the type,
Reminded of how Lorenz's[1] just-hatched goslings
Shook off the last remnants of the egg
And, looking at Lorenz, realized that Lorenz
Was their mother. Quacking, his little family
25   Followed him everywhere; and when they met a goose,
Their mother, they ran to him afraid.

Imprinted upon me
Is the shape I run to, the sweet strange
Breath-taking contours that breathe to me: "I am yours,
30   Be mine!"
            Following this new
Body, somehow familiar, this young shape, somehow old,
For a moment I'm younger, the century is younger.
The living Strauss,[2] his moustache just getting gray,
35   Is shouting to the players: "Louder!
Louder! I can still hear Madame Schumann-Heink—"[3]
Or else, white, bald, the old man's joyfully
Telling conductors they must play *Elektra*
Like *A Midsummer Night's Dream*[4]—like fairy music;
40   Proust, dying, is swallowing his iced beer
And changing in proof the death of Bergotte[5]

---

9. Charles Swann, a protagonist of the first book in the seven-volume novel *À la recherche du temps perdu* ("In Search of Lost Time") by the French writer Marcel Proust (1871–1922). After Swann's infatuation with his lover Odette ceases, he remarks that she was never his type.
1. Konrad Lorenz (1903–1989), Austrian ethologist who, in a 1935 study, described the process of "imprinting." Just-hatched goslings preferred Lorenz to their natural mother after having received certain stimuli.
2. Richard Strauss (1864–1949), German composer, wrote the opera *Electra*.
3. Ernestine Schumann-Heink (1861–1936), American (Bohemian-born) contralto.
4. Incidental music, based on Shakespeare's play, by Felix Mendelssohn (1809–1847), German composer.
5. Character in Proust's novel, a distinguished writer.

According to his own experience; Garbo,[6]
A commissar in Paris, is listening attentively
To the voice telling how McGillicuddy met McGillivray,
45 And McGillivray said to McGillicuddy—no, McGillicuddy
Said to McGillivray—that is, McGillivray . . . Garbo
Says seriously: "I vish dey'd never met."

As I walk behind this woman I remember
That before I flew here—waked in the forest
50 At dawn, by the piece called *Birds Beginning Day*
That, each day, birds play to begin the day—
I wished as men wish: "May this day be different!"
The birds were wishing, as birds wish—over and over,
With a last firmness, intensity, reality—
55 "May this day be the same!"
                Ah, turn to me
And look into my eyes, say: "I am yours,
Be mine!"
            My wish will have come true. And yet
60 When your eyes meet my eyes, they'll bring into
The weightlessness of my pure wish the weight
Of a human being: someone to help or hurt,
Someone to be good to me, to be good to,
Someone to cry when I am angry
65 That she doesn't like *Elektra*, someone to start out on Proust with.
A wish, come true, is life. I have my life.
When you turn just slide your eyes across my eyes
And show in a look flickering across your face
As lightly as a leaf's shade, a bird's wing,
70 That there is no one in the world quite like me,
That if only . . . If only . . .
               That will be enough.

But I've pretended long enough: I walk faster
And come close, touch with the tip of my finger
75 The nape of her neck, just where the gold
Hair stops, and the champagne-colored dress begins.
My finger touches her as the gingko's shadow
Touches her.
          Because, after all, it *is* my wife
80 In a new dress from Bergdorf's, walking toward the park.
She cries out, we kiss each other, and walk arm in arm
Through the sunlight that's much too good for New York,
The sunlight of our own house in the forest.
Still, though, the poor things need it . . . We've no need
85 To start out on Proust, to ask each other about Strauss.
We first helped each other, hurt each other, years ago.
After so many changes made and joys repeated,
Our first bewildered, transcending recognition
Is pure acceptance. We can't tell our life
90 From our wish. Really I began the day

---

6. Greta Garbo (1905–1990), American (Swedish-born) film actress, famous for her unsmiling demeanor.
Here quoted in the film *Ninotchka* (1939), before she finally laughs for the first time on screen.

Not with a man's wish: "May this day be different,"
But with the birds' wish: "May this day
Be the same day, the day of my life."

1967

DOUGLAS LE PAN

1914–

An Incident

Arrange the scene with only a shade of difference
And he would be a boy in his own native
And fern-fronded providence,
With a map in his hand, searching for a portage overgrown
5 With brush. Slim he is as a moccasin-flower
With his throat open
To the winds, to the four winds, quivering,
Who alone by the worm-holed flower of the rose-pink house
Bears the weight of this many-ringed, foreign noon,
10 Shadowless, vast and pitiless.
Notched by the wedge of his frown, it takes no notice.
Light that, alive, would be pungent with resin,
Sapless, now weighs and ponders like limestone.

What is he waiting for
15 As he studies a map the colour of his youth?
Time stops and whirs in his ear like a humming-bird
As he gazes this way and that
For someone to relieve him
For someone to break through the thicket of his isolation.

20 In the silence
The grasshoppers crackle and crumble the summer
Between their thin wings
And their singing thighs.
And his head has begun to sing,
25 To sing with the heat.
Stampeding, his blood butts him like a bull-calf.
How should one so young have learned how to wait?

Ah! there is the relief.
A stray round has caught him at the nape of the neck
30 And splayed him flat on the earth,
His blood flung wide as a sunburst.

And the pink house, that eavesdropped
Through smoke-blackened holes to each palpitation,
Recovering its reserve,
35 Sucks in unblemished stillness;
While the wise light with petrified foliage

Having disposed of this awkward animal tremor
Again stands superb as a temple.

1953

NORMAN NICHOLSON
1914–1987

To the River Duddon

I wonder, Duddon, if you still remember
An oldish man with a nose like a pony's nose,
Broad bones, legs long and lean but strong enough
To carry him over Hardknott at seventy years of age.[1]
5 He came to you first as a boy with a fishing-rod
And a hunk of Ann Tyson's bread and cheese in his pocket,
Walking from Hawkshead across Walna Scar;
Then as a middle-aged Rydal landlord,
With a doting sister and a pension on the civil list,
10 Who left his verses gummed to your rocks like lichen,
The dry and yellow edges of a once-green spring.
He made a guide-book for you, from your source
There where you bubble through the moss on Wrynose
(Among the ribs of bald and bony fells°   *upland tracts*
15 With screes[2] scratched in the turf like grey scabs),
And twist and slither under humpbacked bridges—
Built like a child's house from odds and ends
Of stones that lie about the mountain side—
Past Cockley Beck Farm and on to Birk's Bridge,
20 Where the rocks stride about like legs in armour,
And the steel birches buckle and bounce in the wind
With a crinkle of silver foil in the crisp of the leaves;
On then to Seathwaite, where like a steam-navvy[3]
You shovel and slash your way through the gorge
25 By Wallabarrow Crag, broader now
From becks that flow out of black upland tarns
Or ooze through golden saxifrage and the roots of rowans;
Next Ulpha, where a stone dropped from the bridge
Swims like a tadpole down thirty feet of water
30 Between steep skirting-boards of rock; and thence
You dribble into lower Dunnerdale
Through wet woods and wood-soil and woodland flowers,
Tutson, the St. John's-wort with a single yellow bead,
Marsh marigold, creeping jenny and daffodils;
35 Here from hazel islands in the late spring
The catkins fall and ride along the stream
Like little yellow weasels, and the soil is loosed
From bulbs of the white lily that smells of garlic,
And dippers rock up and down on rubber legs,

---

1. William Wordsworth (1770–1850; see pp. 699–737).
2. Masses of debris at the foot of a cliff.
3. A navvy is a laborer; a steam-navvy is a steam-powered excavator.

40 And long-tailed tits are flung through the air like darts;
By Foxfield now you taste the salt in your mouth,
And thrift mingles with the turf, and the heron stands
Watching the wagtails. Wordsworth wrote:
"Remote from every taint of sordid industry".
45 But you and I know better, Duddon lass.
For I, who've lived for nearly thirty years
Upon your shore, have seen the slagbanks slant
Like screes sheer into the sand, and seen the tide
Purple with ore back up the muddy gullies
50 And wiped the sinter[4] dust from the farmyard damsons.
A hundred years of floods and rain and wind
Have washed your rocks clear of his words again,
Many of them half-forgotten, brimming the Irish Sea,
But that which Wordsworth knew, even the old man
55 When poetry had failed like desire, was something
I have yet to learn, and you, Duddon,
Have learned and re-learned to forget and forget again.
Not the radical, the poet and heretic,
To whom the water-forces shouted and the fells
60 Were like a blackboard for the scrawls of God,
But the old man, inarticulate and humble,
Knew that eternity flows in a mountain beck—
The long cord of the water, the shepherd's numerals
That run upstream, through the singing decades of dialect.
65 He knew, beneath mutation of year and season,
Flood and drought, frost and fire and thunder,
The frothy blossom on the rowan and the reddening of the berries,
The silt, the sand, the slagbanks and the shingle,
And the wild catastrophes of the breaking mountains,
70 There stands the base and root of the living rock,
Thirty thousand feet of solid Cumberland.

1944

For Hokey and Henrietta

Now it is midsummer and the long sun shines
At my bedtime as it does at yours,
And, however early you wake, the yellow lines

Of the sun are lying like straw on the bedroom chairs,
5 And there are bees and creatures without names,
And, if you remember to look, there are always flowers.

Winter is a name for strange forgotten times,
Times as distant as bananas, when
The frost in the wind was a boxer, and goodnight games

10 Stalked round the fire like gypsies in caravan.
But winter will be real when laburnum turns to fibre
And the windows are black and the stories bright again.

4. Siliceous or calcareous rock.

Hokey, of course, will be polite to October,
Introduce it to his mother and show no surprise,
15 And Henrietta will hug it like a new neighbour.

In a world where worms are friends, and visiting eyes
Look for camels in the kitchen or under the stairs,
Winter will fall as gently as the snow on the trees.

What more can you learn to ask for in your prayers,
20 Than years unpredicted as weather, and days
Adventurous as a lobby full of bears?

1944

Halley's Comet

My father saw it back in 1910,
The year King Edward died.
Above dark telegraph poles, above the high
Spiked steeple of the Liberal Club, the white
5 Gas-lit dials of the Market Clock,
Beyond the wide
Sunset-glow cirrus of blast-furnace smoke,
My father saw it fly
Its thirty-seven-million-mile-long kite
10 Across Black Combe's[5] black sky.

And what of me,
Born four years too late?
Will I have breath to wait
Till the long-circuiting commercial traveller
15 Turns up at his due?
In 1986, aged seventy-two,
Watery in the eyes and phlegmy in the flue
And a bit bad tempered at so delayed a date,
Will I look out above whatever is left of the town—
20 The Liberal Club long closed and the clock stopped,
And the chimneys smokeless above damped-down
Furnace fires? And then will I
At last have chance to see it
With my own as well as my father's eyes,
25 And share his long-ago Edwardian surprise
At that high, silent jet, laying its bright trail
Across Black Combe's black sky?

1981

5. Place-name meaning dark, armchair-shaped rock formation.

HENRY REED

1914–1986

Chard Whitlow

(Mr Eliot's Sunday Evening Postscript)[1]

As we get older we do not get any younger.
Seasons return, and today I am fifty-five,
And this time last year I was fifty-four,
And this time next year I shall be sixty-two.
5   And I cannot say I should care (to speak for myself)
To see my time over again—if you can call it time,
Fidgeting uneasily under a draughty stair,
Or counting sleepless nights in the crowded Tube.[2]

There are certain precautions—though none of them very reliable—
10   Against the blast from bombs, or the flying splinter,
But not against the blast from Heaven, *vento dei venti*,[3]
The wind within a wind, unable to speak for wind;
And the frigid burnings of purgatory will not be touched
By any emollient.
15   I think you will find this put,
Far better than I could ever hope to express it,
In the words of Kharma:[4] "It is, we believe,
Idle to hope that the simple stirrup-pump[5]
Can extinguish hell."

20   Oh, listeners,
And you especially who have switched off the wireless,
And sit in Stoke or Basingstoke, listening appreciatively to the silence
(Which is also the silence of hell), pray not for yourselves but your souls.

And pray for me also under the draughty stair.
25   As we get older we do not get any younger.

And pray for Kharma under the holy mountain.

1941   1946

---

1. Reed's title and subtitle evoke three of T. S. Eliot's titles: *Burnt Norton*, "Mr. Eliot's Sunday Morning Service," and "The *Boston Evening Transcript*." A whitlow is an inflammatory sore on the finger.
2. Colloquial term for the London subway, in which thousands of Londoners were sheltering during the fire-bombing of London (known as the Blitz) of World War II, when this poem was written.
3. "Wind of winds" (Italian).
4. A concept common to Hinduism, Buddhism, and Jainism, the doctrine of Karma asserts that one's state in this life is a result of actions in past incarnations, and that action in this life can determine one's destiny in future incarnations. Reed deliberately misspells Karma and confuses it with Buddha.
5. A portable foot-pump used to combat fires during the London Blitz.

Lessons of the War

TO ALAN MICHELL

Vixi duellis nuper idoneus
Et militavi non sine gloria[6]

1. Naming of Parts

Today we have naming of parts. Yesterday,
We had daily cleaning. And tomorrow morning,
We shall have what to do after firing. But today,
Today we have naming of parts. Japonica[7]
5   Glistens like coral in all of the neighbouring gardens,
     And today we have naming of parts.

This is the lower sling swivel. And this
Is the upper sling swivel, whose use you will see,
When you are given your slings. And this is the piling swivel,
10 Which in your case you have not got. The branches
Hold in the gardens their silent, eloquent gestures,
     Which in our case we have not got.

This is the safety-catch, which is always released
With an easy flick of the thumb. And please do not let me
15 See anyone using his finger. You can do it quite easy
If you have any strength in your thumb. The blossoms
Are fragile and motionless, never letting anyone see
     Any of them using their finger.

And this you can see is the bolt. The purpose of this
20 Is to open the breech, as you see. We can slide it
Rapidly backwards and forwards: we call this
Easing the spring.[8] And rapidly backwards and forwards
The early bees are assaulting and fumbling the flowers:
     They call it easing the Spring.

25 They call it easing the Spring: it is perfectly easy
If you have any strength in your thumb: like the bolt,
And the breech, and the cocking-piece, and the point of balance,
Which in our case we have not got; and the almond-blossom
Silent in all of the gardens and the bees going backwards and forwards,
30   For today we have naming of parts.

1942   1946

2. Judging Distances

Not only how far away, but the way that you say it
Is very important. Perhaps you may never get

6. The opening lines of a Latin poem by Horace (3.26), but with Horace's word *puellis* ("girls") changed to *duellis* ("war," "battles"): "Lately I have lived in the midst of battles, creditably enough, / And have soldiered, not without glory."
7. The flowering quince *(Cydonia japonica)*, a shrub with brilliant scarlet flowers.
8. "Ease springs!": a military command requiring British infantrymen to move the bolts of their rifles "rapidly backwards and forwards," thereby ejecting any bullets remaining in the magazine and taking pressure off the spring.

The knack of judging a distance, but at least you know
How to report on a landscape: the central sector,
5   The right of arc and that, which we had last Tuesday,
    And at least you know

That maps are of time, not place, so far as the army
Happens to be concerned—the reason being,
Is one which need not delay us. Again, you know
10 There are three kinds of tree, three only, the fir and the poplar,
    And those which have bushy tops to; and lastly
        That things only seem to be things.

A barn is not called a barn, to put it more plainly,
Or a field in the distance, where sheep may be safely grazing.
15 You must never be over-sure. You must say, when reporting:
    At five o'clock in the central sector is a dozen
    Of what appear to be animals; whatever you do,
        Don't call the bleeders *sheep.*

I am sure that's quite clear; and suppose, for the sake of example,
20 The one at the end, asleep, endeavours to tell us
    What he sees over there to the west, and how far away,
    After first having come to attention. There to the west,
    On the fields of summer the sun and the shadows bestow
        Vestments of purple and gold.

25 The still white dwellings are like a mirage in the heat,
    And under the swaying elms a man and a woman
    Lie gently together. Which is, perhaps, only to say
    That there is a row of houses to the left of arc,
    And that under some poplars a pair of what appear to be humans
30   Appear to be loving.

Well that, for an answer, is what we might rightly call
Moderately satisfactory only, the reason being,
Is that two things have been omitted, and those are important.
The human beings, now: in what direction are they,
35 And how far away, would you say? And do not forget
        There may be dead ground[9] in between.

There may be dead ground in between; and I may not have got
The knack of judging a distance; I will only venture
A guess that perhaps between me and the apparent lovers
40 (Who, incidentally, appear by now to have finished)
    At seven o'clock from the houses, is roughly a distance
        Of about one year and a half.

1943   1946

---

9. Military: "Space that cannot be reached by fire from a given weapon or a given point" (*Webster's Third New International Dictionary*).

The Château[1]

Yet will I fear no evil:[2] not even here.
Nor even now.
    Now, at the ending of the autumn afternoon,
And here, on the wide stone terrace confronting the great château,
5 The enormous flagstones with the small, scattered tables,
Where a few of us sit, apart from each other, indifferent.
(Yet I am not indifferent, I am most dearly concerned)

There are not many of us. We face the great grey mansion
Whose doors and windows glare back at the sunless light,
10 And from the high flagpoles the long pennants, unenflamed,
Droop into the colourless day.
        Is some great Someone here,
For whom these pennants hang? There is no one to ask.
And one might be too frightened to ask.
15   Yet will I fear no evil,
Not even here or now.

For surely beyond that great façade my life is being lived?
Lived, loved and filled with gaiety and ardour,
As though my life were endowed with a perpetual splendour
20 And radiance fell on it. It is surely only that I
Am not now with it, not with my life, but here,
Restlessly rigid, counting the flagstones while there within, it dances
Nightly the length of the lighted hall to the starry feast,
Stoops in the dawn to the kindly fountain, rests and, rested,
25 Breathes on a single breath its anthem of love and praise.

Surely there will be a signal? Inconspicuously,
One of the giant roses in the gardens around us
Will perhaps explode on to the autumn grass:
Something like that, perhaps. I know I shall know the moment.

30 And surely (and almost now) it will happen, and tell me
That now I must rise and with firm footsteps tread
Across the enormous flagstones, reach, find and know
My own and veritable door;
I shall open it, enter, and learn
35 That in all this hungry time I have never wanted,
But have, elsewhere, on honey and milk been fed,
Have in green pastures somewhere lain, and in the mornings,
Somewhere beside still waters have
Mysteriously, ecstatically, been led.

                     1991

1. "Castle" (French).   Psalm of the Bible.
2. This sentence and lines 37–8 echo the 23d

DYLAN THOMAS
1914–1953

The Force That
Through the Green Fuse
Drives the Flower

The force that through the green fuse drives the flower
Drives my green age; that blasts the roots of trees
Is my destroyer.
And I am dumb to tell the crooked rose
5   My youth is bent by the same wintry fever.

The force that drives the water through the rocks
Drives my red blood; that dries the mouthing streams
Turns mine to wax.
And I am dumb to mouth unto my veins
10   How at the mountain spring the same mouth sucks.

The hand that whirls the water in the pool
Stirs the quicksand; that ropes the blowing wind
Hauls my shroud sail.
And I am dumb to tell the hanging man
15   How of my clay is made the hangman's lime.

The lips of time leech to the fountain head;
Love drips and gathers, but the fallen blood
Shall calm her sores.
And I am dumb to tell a weather's wind
20   How time has ticked a heaven round the stars.

And I am dumb to tell the lover's tomb
How at my sheet goes the same crooked worm.

1934

The Hand That Signed the Paper

The hand that signed the paper felled a city;
Five sovereign fingers taxed the breath,
Doubled the globe of dead and halved a country;
These five kings did a king to death.

5   The mighty hand leads to a sloping shoulder,
The finger joints are cramped with chalk;
A goose's quill has put an end to murder
That put an end to talk.

The hand that signed the treaty bred a fever,
10   And famine grew, and locusts came;
Great is the hand that holds dominion over
Man by a scribbled name.

The five kings count the dead but do not soften
The crusted wound nor stroke the brow;
15   A hand rules pity as a hand rules heaven;
Hands have no tears to flow.

1936

After the Funeral

(In Memory of Ann Jones)[1]

After the funeral, mule praises, brays,
Windshake of sailshaped ears, muffle-toed tap
Tap happily of one peg in the thick
Grave's foot, blinds down the lids, the teeth in black,
5   The spittled eyes, the salt ponds in the sleeves,
Morning smack of the spade that wakes up sleep,
Shakes a desolate boy who slits his throat
In the dark of the coffin and sheds dry leaves,
That breaks one bone to light with a judgment clout,
10   After the feast of tear-stuffed time and thistles
In a room with a stuffed fox and a stale fern,
I stand, for this memorial's sake, alone
In the snivelling hours with dead, humped Ann
Whose hooded, fountain heart once fell in puddles
15   Round the parched worlds of Wales and drowned each sun
(Though this for her is a monstrous image blindly
Magnified out of praise; her death was a still drop;
She would not have me sinking in the holy
Flood of her heart's fame; she would lie dumb and deep
20   And need no druid[2] of her broken body).
But I, Ann's bard on a raised hearth, call all
The seas to service that her wood-tongued virtue
Babble like a bellbuoy over the hymning heads,
Bow down the walls of the ferned and foxy woods
25   That her love sing and swing through a brown chapel,
Bless her bent spirit with four, crossing birds.
Her flesh was meek as milk, but this skyward statue
With the wild breast and blessed and giant skull
Is carved from her in a room with a wet window
30   In a fiercely mourning house in a crooked year.
I know her scrubbed and sour humble hands
Lie with religion in their cramp, her threadbare
Whisper in a damp word, her wits drilled hollow,
Her fist of a face died clenched on a round pain;
35   And sculptured Ann is seventy years of stone.
These cloud-sopped, marble hands, this monumental
Argument of the hewn voice, gesture and psalm,
Storm me forever over her grave until
The stuffed lung of the fox twitch and cry Love
40   And the strutting fern lay seeds on the black sill.

1939

---

1. Ann [Williams] Jones was Dylan Thomas' aunt, his mother's sister, who had married a tenant farmer; their rented farm was Fern Hill. She died in 1933.

2. Priest, among ancient Celts of Gaul or Britain; also magician or soothsayer.

The Hunchback in the Park

The hunchback in the park
A solitary mister
Propped between trees and water
From the opening of the garden lock
5   That lets the trees and water enter
Until the Sunday sombre bell at dark[3]

Eating bread from a newspaper
Drinking water from the chained cup
That the children filled with gravel
10   In the fountain basin where I sailed my ship
Slept at night in a dog kennel
But nobody chained him up.

Like the park birds he came early
Like the water he sat down
15   And Mister they called Hey mister
The truant boys from the town
Running when he had heard them clearly
On out of sound

Past lake and rockery
20   Laughing when he shook his paper
Hunchbacked in mockery
Through the loud zoo of the willow groves
Dodging the park keeper
With his stick that picked up leaves.

25   And the old dog sleeper
Alone between nurses and swans
While the boys among willows
Made the tigers jump out of their eyes
To roar on the rockery stones
30   And the groves were blue with sailors

Made all day until bell time
A woman figure without fault
Straight as a young elm
Straight and tall from his crooked bones
35   That she might stand in the night
After the locks and chains

All night in the unmade park
After the railings and shrubberies
The birds the grass the trees the lake
40   And the wild boys innocent as strawberries
Had followed the hunchback
To his kennel in the dark.

1942

---

3. The bell that warns visitors that the park gates are about to be closed for the night.

A Refusal to Mourn the Death, by Fire,[4] of a Child in London

Never until the mankind making
Bird beast and flower
Fathering and all humbling darkness
Tells with silence the last light breaking
5   And the still hour
Is come of the sea tumbling in harness

And I must enter again the round
Zion of the water bead
And the synagogue of the ear of corn
10 Shall I let pray the shadow of a sound
Or sow my salt seed
In the least valley of sackcloth to mourn

The majesty and burning of the child's death.
I shall not murder
15 The mankind of her going with a grave truth
Nor blaspheme down the stations of the breath
With any further
Elegy of innocence and youth.

Deep with the first dead lies London's daughter,
20 Robed in the long friends,
The grains beyond age, the dark veins of her mother,
Secret by the unmourning water
Of the riding Thames.
After the first death, there is no other.

1946

The Conversation of Prayer

The conversation of prayers about to be said
By the child going to bed and the man on the stairs
Who climbs to his dying love in her high room,
The one not caring to whom in his sleep he will move
5 And the other full of tears that she will be dead,

Turns in the dark on the sound they know will arise
Into the answering skies from the green ground,
From the man on the stairs and the child by his bed.
The sound about to be said in the two prayers
10 For the sleep in a safe land and the love who dies

Will be the same grief flying. Whom shall they calm?
Shall the child sleep unharmed or the man be crying?
The conversation of prayers about to be said
Turns on the quick and the dead, and the man on the stairs
15 Tonight shall find no dying but alive and warm

---

4. During the firebombing of London, known as the Blitz, in World War II.

In the fire of his care his love in the high room.
And the child not caring to whom he climbs his prayer
Shall drown in a grief as deep as his true grave,
And mark the dark eyed wave, through the eyes of sleep,
20   Dragging him up the stairs to one who lies dead.

1946

Fern Hill[5]

Now as I was young and easy under the apple boughs
About the lilting house and happy as the grass was green,
        The night above the dingle[6] starry,
            Time let me hail and climb
5   Golden in the heydays of his eyes,
And honoured among wagons I was prince of the apple towns
And once below a time I lordly had the trees and leaves
            Trail with daisies and barley
        Down the rivers of the windfall light.

10   And as I was green and carefree, famous among the barns
About the happy yard and singing as the farm was home,
        In the sun that is young once only,
            Time let me play and be
            Golden in the mercy of his means,
15   And green and golden I was huntsman and herdsman, the calves
Sang to my horn, the foxes on the hills barked clear and cold,
            And the sabbath rang slowly
        In the pebbles of the holy streams.

All the sun long it was running, it was lovely, the hay
20   Fields high as the house, the tunes from the chimneys, it was air
        And playing, lovely and watery
            And fire green as grass.
        And nightly under the simple stars
As I rode to sleep the owls were bearing the farm away,
25   All the moon long I heard, blessed among stables, the night-jars[7]
        Flying with the ricks,[8] and the horses
            Flashing into the dark.

And then to awake, and the farm, like a wanderer white
With the dew, come back, the cock on his shoulder: it was all
30   Shining, it was Adam and maiden,
            The sky gathered again
        And the sun grew round that very day.
So it must have been after the birth of the simple light
In the first, spinning place, the spellbound horses walking warm
35   Out of the whinnying green stable
            On to the fields of praise.

---

5. Farm, rented by Thomas' uncle and aunt, in   7. Nocturnal birds.
which he spent summer holidays as a boy.   8. Haystacks.
6. Small wooded valley.

And honoured among foxes and pheasants by the gay house
Under the new made clouds and happy as the heart was long,
   In the sun born over and over,
40   I ran my heedless ways,
   My wishes raced through the house high hay
And nothing I cared, at my sky blue trades, that time allows
In all his tuneful turning so few and such morning songs
   Before the children green and golden
45   Follow him out of grace,

Nothing I cared, in the lamb white days, that time would take me
Up to the swallow thronged loft by the shadow of my hand,
   In the moon that is always rising,
     Nor that riding to sleep
50   I should hear him fly with the high fields
And wake to the farm forever fled from the childless land.
Oh as I was young and easy in the mercy of his means,
   Time held me green and dying
   Though I sang in my chains like the sea.

             1946

In My Craft or Sullen Art

   In my craft or sullen art
   Exercised in the still night
   When only the moon rages
   And the lovers lie abed
5 With all their griefs in their arms,
   I labour by singing light
   Not for ambition or bread
   Or the strut and trade of charms
   On the ivory stages
10 But for the common wages
   Of their most secret heart.

   Not for the proud man apart
   From the raging moon I write
   On these spindrift pages
15 Nor for the towering dead
   With their nightingales and psalms
   But for the lovers, their arms
   Round the griefs of the ages,
   Who pay no praise or wages
20 Nor heed my craft or art.

             1946

Do Not Go Gentle into That Good Night[9]

Do not go gentle into that good night,
Old age should burn and rave at close of day;
Rage, rage against the dying of the light.

9. This villanelle was written in May 1951, during the final illness of Dylan Thomas' father.

Though wise men at their end know dark is right,
5 Because their words had forked no lightning they
Do not go gentle into that good night.

Good men, the last wave by, crying how bright
Their frail deeds might have danced in a green bay,
Rage, rage against the dying of the light.

10 Wild men who caught and sang the sun in flight,
And learn, too late, they grieved it on its way,
Do not go gentle into that good night.

Grave men, near death, who see with blinding sight
Blind eyes could blaze like meteors and be gay,
15 Rage, rage against the dying of the light.

And you, my father, there on the sad height,
Curse, bless, me now with your fierce tears, I pray.
Do not go gentle into that good night.
Rage, rage against the dying of the light.

1952

ALUN LEWIS

1915–1944

All Day It Has Rained

All day it has rained, and we on the edge of the moors
Have sprawled in our bell-tents,[1] moody and dull as boors,
Groundsheets and blankets spread on the muddy ground
And from the first grey wakening we have found
5 No refuge from the skirmishing fine rain
And the wind that made the canvas heave and flap
And the taut wet guy-ropes ravel out and snap.
All day the rain has glided, wave and mist and dream,
Drenching the gorse and heather, a gossamer stream
10 Too light to stir the acorns that suddenly
Snatched from their cups by the wild south-westerly
Pattered against the tent and our upturned dreaming faces.
And we stretched out, unbuttoning our braces,
Smoking a Woodbine,[2] darning dirty socks,
15 Reading the Sunday papers—I saw a fox
And mentioned it in the note I scribbled home;—
And we talked of girls, and dropping bombs on Rome,
And thought of the quiet dead and the loud celebrities
Exhorting us to slaughter, and the herded refugees;
20 —Yet thought softly, morosely of them, and as indifferently
As of ourselves or those whom we
For years have loved, and will again

---

1. Conical tents with a central pole.   2. Brand of cheap cigarette.

Tomorrow maybe love; but now it is the rain
Possesses us entirely, the twilight and the rain.

25 And I can remember nothing dearer or more to my heart
Than the children I watched in the woods on Saturday
Shaking down burning chestnuts for the schoolyard's merry play,
Or the shaggy patient dog who followed me
By Sheet and Steep and up the wooded scree[3]
30 To the Shoulder o' Mutton where Edward Thomas brooded long
On death and beauty—till a bullet stopped his song.[4]

1940   1941, 1942

Song

(On seeing dead bodies floating off the Cape[5])

The first month of his absence
I was numb and sick
And where he'd left his promise
Life did not turn or kick.
5 The seed, the seed of love was sick.

The second month my eyes were sunk
In the darkness of despair,
And my bed was like a grave
And his ghost was lying there.
10 And my heart was sick with care.

The third month of his going
I thought I heard him say
"Our course deflected slightly
On the thirty-second day—"
15 The tempest blew his words away.

And he was lost among the waves,
His ship rolled helpless in the sea,
The fourth month of his voyage
He shouted grievously
20 "Beloved, do not think of me."

The flying fish like kingfishers
Skim the sea's bewildered crests,
The whales blow steaming fountains,
The seagulls have no nests
25 Where my lover sways and rests.

We never thought to buy and sell
This life that blooms or withers in the leaf,

---

3. Mass of debris at the foot of a cliff.
4. In the issue of the magazine *Horizon* in which this poem first appeared, Lewis also had a book review, of Edward Thomas' *The Trumpet and Other Poems*, in which he wrote: "I have been garrisoned for six months in Edward Thomas country and walked his walks. I have sheltered from the rain in the beautiful house he built but did not inhabit." "Sheet" and "Steep" are villages. The "Shoulder o' Mutton" is a hill in Hampshire.
5. The Cape of Good Hope, South Africa.

And I'll not stir, so he sleeps well,
Though cell by cell the coral reef
30   Builds an eternity of grief.

But oh! the drag and dullness of my Self;
The turning seasons wither in my head;
All this slowness, all this hardness,
The nearness that is waiting in my bed,
35   The gradual self-effacement of the dead.

1944

Goodbye

So we must say Goodbye, my darling,
And go, as lovers go, for ever;
Tonight remains, to pack and fix on labels
And make an end of lying down together.

5   I put a final shilling in the gas,[6]
And watch you slip your dress below your knees
And lie so still I hear your rustling comb
Modulate the autumn in the trees.

And all the countless things I shall remember
10   Lay mummy-cloths[7] of silence round my head;
I fill the carafe with a drink of water;
You say "We paid a guinea[8] for this bed,"

And then, "We'll leave some gas, a little warmth
For the next resident, and these dry flowers,"
15   And turn your face away, afraid to speak
The big word, that Eternity is ours.

Your kisses close my eyes and yet you stare
As though God struck a child with nameless fears;
Perhaps the water glitters and discloses
20   Time's chalice and its limpid useless tears.

Everything we renounce except our selves;
Selfishness is the last of all to go;
Our sighs are exhalations of the earth,
Our footprints leave a track across the snow.

25   We made the universe to be our home,
Our nostrils took the wind to be our breath,
Our hearts are massive towers of delight,
We stride across the seven seas of death.

---

6. Gas fire, the fuel supply of which is controlled by a meter that must be fed with shilling coins.
7. Bandages that wrap an Egyptian mummy.
8. Old British currency: one pound and one shilling (105p.).

Yet when all's done you'll keep the emerald
30   I placed upon your finger in the street;
And I will keep the patches[9] that you sewed
On my old battledress tonight, my sweet.

1945

MARGARET WALKER

1915–

Since 1619[1]

How many years since 1619 have I been singing Spirituals?
How long have I been praising God and shouting hallelujahs?
How long have I been hated and hating?
How long have I been living in hell for heaven?

5   When will I see my brother's face wearing another color?
When will I be ready to die in a honest fight?
When will I be conscious of the struggle—now to do or die?
When will these scales fall away from my eyes?[2]

What will I say when days of wrath descend:
10   When the money-gods take all my life away;
When the death knell sounds
And peace is a flag of far-flung blood and filth?

When will I understand the cheated and the cheaters;
Their paltry pittances and cold concessions to my pride?
15   When will I burst from my kennel an angry mongrel,
Lean and hungry and tired of my dry bones and years?

Childhood

When I was a child I knew red miners
dressed raggedly and wearing carbide lamps.
I saw them come down red hills to their camps
dyed with red dust from old Ishkooda mines.[3]
5   Night after night I met them on the roads,
or on the streets in town I caught their glance;
the swing of dinner buckets in their hands,
and grumbling undermining all their words.

I also lived in low cotton country
10   where moonlight hovered over ripe haystacks,
or stumps of trees, and croppers' rotting shacks

9. Cloth badges of rank attached to a soldier's uniform.
1. The year that the first African slaves arrived in Jamestown, Virginia, aboard a Dutch frigate.
2. Cf. the account of Saul's conversion in Acts 9.18: "And immediately there fell from his eyes as it had been scales: and he received sight forthwith, and arose, and was baptized."
3. South of Birmingham, Alabama, where Walker's family lived until she was five. The sestet of the sonnet shifts to her second childhood home, near New Orleans.

with famine, terror, flood, and plague near by;
where sentiment and hatred still held sway
and only bitter land was washed away.

1942

JUDITH WRIGHT

1915–

Woman to Man

The eyeless labourer in the night,
the selfless, shapeless seed I hold,
builds for its resurrection day—
silent and swift and deep from sight
5   foresees the unimagined light.

This is no child with a child's face;
this has no name to name it by:
yet you and I have known it well.
This is our hunter and our chase,
10   the third who lay in our embrace.

This is the strength that your arm knows,
the arc of flesh that is my breast,
the precise crystals of our eyes.
This is the blood's wild tree that grows
15   the intricate and folded rose.

This is the maker and the made;
this is the question and reply;
the blind head butting at the dark,
the blaze of light along the blade.
20   Oh hold me, for I am afraid.

1949

Train Journey

Glassed with cold sleep and dazzled by the moon,
out of the confused hammering dark of the train
I looked and saw under the moon's cold sheet
your delicate dry breasts, country that built my heart;

5   and the small trees on their uncoloured slope
like poetry moved, articulate and sharp
and purposeful under the great dry flight of air,
under the crosswise currents of wind and star.

Clench down your strength, box-tree and ironbark.
10   Break with your violent root the virgin rock.

Draw from the flying dark its breath of dew
till the unliving come to life in you.

Be over the blind rock a skin of sense,
under the barren height a slender dance . . .

15 I woke and saw the dark small trees that burn
suddenly into flowers more lovely than the white moon.

1953

Birds

Whatever the bird is, is perfect in the bird.
Weapon kestrel[1] hard as a blade's curve,
thrush round as a mother or a full drop of water
fruit-green parrot wise in his shrieking swerve —
5 all are what bird is and do not reach beyond bird.

Whatever the bird does is right for the bird to do —
cruel kestrel dividing in his hunger the sky,
thrush in the trembling dew beginning to sing,
parrot clinging and quarrelling and veiling his queer eye —
10 all these are as birds are and good for birds to do.

But I am torn and beleaguered by my own people.
The blood that feeds my heart is the blood they gave me,
and my heart is the house where they gather and fight for dominion —
all different, all with a wish and a will to save me,
15 to turn me into the ways of other people.

If I could leave their battleground for the forest of a bird
I could melt the past, the present and the future in one
and find the words that lie behind all these languages.
Then I could fuse my passions into one clear stone
20 and be simple to myself as the bird is to the bird.

1953

Request to a Year

If the year is meditating a suitable gift,
I should like it to be the attitude
of my great-great-grandmother,
legendary devotee of the arts,

5 who, having had eight children
and little opportunity for painting pictures,
sat one day on a high rock
beside a river in Switzerland

and from a difficult distance viewed
10 her second son, balanced on a small ice-floe,

1. Species of small falcon.

drift down the current towards a waterfall
that struck rock-bottom eighty feet below,

while her second daughter, impeded,
no doubt, by the petticoats of the day,
15 stretched out a last-hope alpenstock
(which luckily later caught him on his way).

Nothing, it was evident, could be done;
and with the artist's isolating eye
my great-great-grandmother hastily sketched the scene.
20 The sketch survives to prove the story by.

Year, if you have no Mother's day present planned;
reach back and bring me the firmness of her hand.

1953

Eve to Her Daughters

It was not I who began it.
Turned out into draughty caves,
hungry so often, having to work for our bread,
hearing the children whining,
5 I was nevertheless not unhappy.
Where Adam went I was fairly contented to go.
I adapted myself to the punishment: it was my life.

But Adam, you know . . . !
He kept on brooding over the insult,
10 over the trick They had played on us, over the scolding.
He had discovered a flaw in himself
and he had to make up for it.

Outside Eden the earth was imperfect,
the seasons changed, the game was fleet-footed,
15 he had to work for our living, and he didn't like it.
He even complained of my cooking
(it was hard to compete with Heaven).

So he set to work.
The earth must be made a new Eden
20 with central heating, domesticated animals,
mechanical harvesters, combustion engines,
escalators, refrigerators,
and modern means of communication
and multiplied opportunities for safe investment
25 and higher education for Abel and Cain
and the rest of the family.
You can see how his pride had been hurt.

In the process he had to unravel everything,
because he believed that mechanism
30 was the whole secret—he was always mechanical-minded.

He got to the very inside of the whole machine
exclaiming as he went, So this is how it works!
And now that I know how it works, why, I must have invented it.
As for God and the Other, they cannot be demonstrated,
35   and what cannot be demonstrated
doesn't exist.
You see, he had always been jealous.

Yes, he got to the centre
where nothing at all can be demonstrated.
40   And clearly he doesn't exist; but he refuses
to accept the conclusion.
You see, he was always an egotist.

It was warmer than this in the cave;
there was none of this fall-out.
45   I would suggest, for the sake of the children,
that it's time you took over.

But you are my daughters, you inherit my own faults of character;
you are submissive, following Adam
even beyond existence.
50   Faults of character have their own logic
and it always works out.
I observed this with Abel and Cain.

Perhaps the whole elaborate fable
right from the beginning
55   is meant to demonstrate this; perhaps it's the whole secret.
Perhaps nothing exists but our faults?
At least they can be demonstrated.

But it's useless to make
such a suggestion to Adam.
60   He has turned himself into God,
who is faultless, and doesn't exist.

1966

DAVID GASCOYNE

1916–

Yves Tanguy[1]

The worlds are breaking in my head
Blown by the brainless wind
That comes from afar
Swollen with dusk and dust
5   And hysterical rain

---

1. (1900–1955); American (French-born) Surrealist painter.

The fading cries of the light
Awaken the endless desert
Engrossed in its tropical slumber
Enclosed by the dead grey oceans
10   Enclasped by the arms of the night

The worlds are breaking in my head
Their fragments are crumbs of despair
The food of the solitary damned
Who await the gross tumult of turbulent
15   Days bringing change without end.

The worlds are breaking in my head
The fuming future sleeps no more
For their seeds are beginning to grow
To creep and to cry midst the
20   Rocks of the deserts to come

Planetary seed
Sown by the grotesque wind
Whose head is so swollen with rumours
Whose hands are so urgent with tumours
25   Whose feet are so deep in the sand.

                                                        1936

Ecce Homo[2]

Whose is this horrifying face,
This putrid flesh, discoloured, flayed,
Fed on by flies, scorched by the sun?
Whose are these hollow red-filmed eyes
5   And thorn-spiked head and spear-stuck side?
Behold the Man: He is Man's Son.

Forget the legend, tear the decent veil
That cowardice or interest devised
To make their mortal enemy a friend,
10   To hide the bitter truth all His wounds tell,
Lest the great scandal be no more disguised:
He is in agony till the world's end,

And we must never sleep during that time!
He is suspended on the cross-tree now
15   And we are onlookers at the crime,
Callous contemporaries of the slow
Torture of God. Here is the hill
Made ghastly by His spattered blood

Whereon He hangs and suffers still:
20   See, the centurions wear riding-boots,
Black shirts and badges and peaked caps,

---

2. "Behold the Man!" (Latin); Pilate's words when presenting Christ, with thorns, to the people.

Greet one another with raised-arm salutes;
They have cold eyes, unsmiling lips;
Yet these His brothers know not what they do.

25 And on his either side hang dead
A labourer and a factory hand,
Or one is maybe a lynched Jew
And one a Negro or a Red,
Coolie or Ethiopian, Irishman,
30 Spaniard or German democrat.

Behind His lolling head the sky
Glares like a fiery cataract
Red with the murders of two thousand years
Committed in His name and by
35 Crusaders, Christian warriors
Defending faith and property.

Amid the plain beneath His transfixed hands,
Exuding darkness as indelible
As guilty stains, fanned by funereal
40 And lurid airs, besieged by drifting sands
And clefted° landslides our about-to-be   cloven, split
Bombed and abandoned cities stand.

He who wept for Jerusalem
Now sees His prophecy extend
45 Across the greatest cities of the world,
A guilty panic reason cannot stem
Rising to raze° them all as He foretold;   knock down
And He must watch this drama to the end.

Though often named, He is unknown
50 To the dark kingdoms at His feet
Where everything disparages His words,
And each man bears the common guilt alone
And goes blindfolded to his fate,
And fear and greed are sovereign lords.

55 The turning point of history
Must come. Yet the complacent and the proud
And who exploit and kill, may be denied—
Christ of Revolution and of Poetry—
The resurrection and the life
60 Wrought by your spirit's blood.

Involved in their own sophistry
The black priest and the upright man
Faced by subversive truth shall be struck dumb,
Christ of Revolution and of Poetry,
65 While the rejected and condemned become
Agents of the divine.

Not from a monstrance[3] silver-wrought
But from the tree of human pain
Redeem our sterile misery,
70 Christ of Revolution and of Poetry,
That man's long journey through the night
May not have been in vain.

1943

Rex Mundi[4]

I heard a herald's note announce the coming of a king.

He who came sounding his approach was a small boy;
The household trumpet that he flourished a tin toy.

Then from a bench beneath the boughs that lately Spring
5 Had hung again with green across the avenue, I rose
To render to the king who came the homage subjects owe.

And as I waited, wondered why it was that such a few
Were standing there with me to see him pass; but understood
As soon as he came into sight, this was a monarch no
10 Crowds of this world can recognize, to hail him as they should.

He drove past in a carriage that was drawn by a white goat;
King of the world to come where all that shall be now is new,
Calmly he gazed on our pretentious present that is not.

Of morals, classes, business, war, this child
15 Knew nothing. We were pardoned when he smiled.

If you hear it in the distance, do not scorn the herald's note.

1950

P. K. PAGE
1916–

Stories of Snow

Those in the vegetable rain retain
an area behind their sprouting eyes
held soft and rounded with the dream of snow
precious and reminiscent as those globes—
5 souvenir of some never-nether land—
which hold their snow-storms circular, complete,
high in a tall and teakwood cabinet.

---

3. Open or transparent box in which the Host
(sanctified bread or wafer) is carried in the Roman
Catholic service known as "the Mass."
4. "King of the World" (Latin).

In countries where the leaves are large as hands
where flowers protrude their fleshy chins
10 and call their colors,
an imaginary snow-storm sometimes falls
among the lilies.
And in the early morning one will waken
to think the glowing linen of his pillow
15 a northern drift, will find himself mistaken
and lie back weeping.
And there the story shifts from head to head,
of how in Holland, from their feather beds
hunters arise and part the flakes and go
20 forth to the frozen lakes in search of swans—
the snow-light falling white along their guns,
their breath in plumes.
While tethered in the wind like sleeping gulls
ice-boats wait the raising of their wings
25 to skim the electric ice at such a speed
they leap jet strips of naked water,
and how these flying, sailing hunters feel
air in their mouths as terrible as ether.
And on the story runs that even drinks
30 in that white landscape dare to be no color;
how flasked and water clear, the liquor slips
silver against the hunters' moving hips.
And of the swan in death these dreamers tell
of its last flight and how it falls, a plummet,
35 pierced by the freezing bullet
and how three feathers, loosened by the shot,
descend like snow upon it.
While hunters plunge their fingers in its down
deep as a drift, and dive their hands
40 up to the neck of the wrist
in that warm metamorphosis of snow
as gentle as the sort that woodsmen know
who, lost in the white circle, fall at last
and dream their way to death.

45 And stories of this kind are often told
in countries where great flowers bar the roads
with reds and blues which seal the route to snow—
as if, in telling, raconteurs unlock
the color with its complement and go
50 through to the area behind the eyes
where silent, unrefractive whiteness lies.

1946

Deaf-Mute in the Pear Tree

His clumsy body is a golden fruit
pendulous in the pear tree

Blunt fingers among the multitudinous buds

Adriatic[1] blue the sky above and through
5 the forking twigs

Sun ruddying tree's trunk, his trunk
his massive head thick-nobbed with burnished curls
tight-clenched in bud

(Painting by Generalić.[2] Primitive.)

10 I watch him prune with silent secateurs°   *pruning shears*

Boots in the crotch of branches shift their weight
heavily as oxen in a stall

Hear small inarticulate mews from his locked mouth
a kitten in a box

15 Pear clippings fall
                soundlessly on the ground
  Spring finches sing
             soundlessly in the leaves

A stone. A stone in ears and on his tongue

20 Through palm and fingertip he knows the tree's
quick springtime pulse

Smells in its sap the sweet incipient pears

Pale sunlight's choppy water glistens on
his mutely snipping blades

25 and flags and scraps of blue
above him make regatta° of the day   *boat race*

But when he sees his wife's foreshortened shape
sudden and silent in the grass below
uptilt its face to him

30 then air is kisses, kisses

stone dissolves

his locked throat finds a little door

and through it feathered joy
flies screaming like a jay

                                          1985

---

1. Adriatic Sea, part of the Mediterranean.   the former Yugoslavia.
2. Ivan Generalić (b. 1914), a "peasant painter" of

GWENDOLYN BROOKS

1917–

kitchenette building

We are things of dry hours and the involuntary plan,
Grayed in, and gray. "Dream" makes a giddy sound, not strong
Like "rent," "feeding a wife," "satisfying a man."

But could a dream send up through onion fumes
5   Its white and violet, fight with fried potatoes
And yesterday's garbage ripening in the hall,
Flutter, or sing an aria down these rooms

Even if we were willing to let it in,
Had time to warm it, keep it very clean,
10   Anticipate a message, let it begin?

We wonder. But not well! not for a minute!
Since Number Five is out of the bathroom now,
We think of lukewarm water, hope to get in it.

1945

my dreams, my works, must wait till after hell

I hold my honey and I store my bread
In little jars and cabinets of my will.
I label clearly, and each latch and lid
I bid, Be firm till I return from hell.
5   I am very hungry. I am incomplete.
And none can tell when I may dine again.
No man can give me any word but Wait,
The puny light. I keep eyes pointed in;
Hoping that, when the devil days of my hurt
10   Drag out to their last dregs and I resume
On such legs as are left me, in such heart
As I can manage, remember to go home,
My taste will not have turned insensitive
To honey and bread old purity could love.

1945

the birth in a narrow room

Weeps out of western country something new.
Blurred and stupendous. Wanted and unplanned.
  Winks. Twines, and weakly winks
Upon the milk-glass fruit bowl, iron pot,
5   The bashful china child tipping forever
Yellow apron and spilling pretty cherries.

Now, weeks and years will go before she thinks
"How pinchy is my room! how can I breathe!
I am not anything and I have got
10 Not anything, or anything to do!"—
But prances nevertheless with gods and fairies
Blithely about the pump and then beneath
The elms and grapevines, then in darling endeavor
By privy foyer, where the screenings stand
15 And where the bugs buzz by in private cars
Across old peach cans and old jelly jars.

                                                                    1949

the rites for Cousin Vit

Carried her unprotesting out the door.
Kicked back the casket-stand. But it can't hold her,
That stuff and satin aiming to enfold her,
The lid's contrition nor the bolts before.
5 Oh oh. Too much. Too much. Even now, surmise,
She rises in the sunshine. There she goes,
Back to the bars she knew and the repose
In love-rooms and the things in people's eyes.
Too vital and too squeaking. Must emerge.
10 Even now she does the snake-hips with a hiss,
Slops the bad wine across her shantung,[1] talks
Of pregnancy, guitars and bridgework, walks
In parks or alleys, comes haply on the verge
Of happiness, haply hysterics. Is.

                                                                    1949

The Bean Eaters

They eat beans mostly, this old yellow pair.
Dinner is a casual affair.
Plain chipware on a plain and creaking wood,
Tin flatware.

5 Two who are Mostly Good.
Two who have lived their day,
But keep on putting on their clothes
And putting things away.

And remembering . . .
10 Remembering, with twinklings and twinges,
As they lean over the beans in their rented back room that is full of beads
    and receipts and dolls and clothes, tobacco crumbs, vases and
    fringes.

                                                                    1960

_____

1. A garment of an uneven texture.

We Real Cool

THE POOL PLAYERS.
SEVEN AT THE GOLDEN SHOVEL.

We real cool. We
Left school. We

Lurk late. We
Strike straight. We

5   Sing sin. We
Thin gin. We

Jazz June. We
Die soon.

1960

Medgar Evers[2]

For Charles Evers

The man whose height his fear improved he
arranged to fear no further. The raw
intoxicated time was time for better birth or
a final death.

5   Old styles, old tempos, all the engagement of
the day—the sedate, the regulated fray—
the antique light, the Moral rose, old gusts,
tight whistlings from the past, the mothballs
in the Love at last our man forswore.

10 Medgar Evers annoyed confetti and assorted
brands of businessmen's eyes.

The shows came down: to maxims and surprise.
And palsy.

Roaring no rapt arise-ye to the dead, he
15 leaned across tomorrow. People said that
he was holding clean globes in his hands.

1968

Boy Breaking Glass

To Marc Crawford From Whom the Commission

Whose broken window is a cry of art
(success, that winks aware

2. (1925–1963); a prominent black civil-rights activist, and the first field secretary of the NAACP in Mississippi, he was murdered by a white supremacist.

as elegance, as a treasonable faith)
is raw: is sonic: is old-eyed première.
5 Our beautiful flaw and terrible ornament.
Our barbarous and metal little man.

"I shall create! If not a note, a hole.
If not an overture, a desecration."

Full of pepper and light
10 and Salt and night and cargoes.

"Don't go down the plank
if you see there's no extension.
Each to his grief, each to
his loneliness and fidgety revenge.

15 Nobody knew where I was and now I am no longer there."

The only sanity is a cup of tea.
The music is in minors.

Each one other
is having different weather.

20 "It was you, it was you who threw away my name!
And this is everything I have for me."

Who has not Congress, lobster, love, luau,
the Regency Room, the Statue of Liberty,
runs. A sloppy amalgamation.
25 A mistake.
A cliff.
A hymn, a snare, and an exceeding sun.

1968

The Coora Flower

Today I learned the *coora* flower
grows high in the mountains of Itty-go-luba Bésa.
Province Meechee.
Pop. 39.

5 Now I am coming home.
This, at least, is Real, and what I know.

It was restful, learning nothing necessary.
School is tiny vacation. At least you can sleep.
At least you can think of love or feeling your boy friend against you
10 (which is not free from grief).

But now it's Real Business.
I am Coming Home.

My mother will be screaming in an almost dirty dress.
The crack³ is gone. So a Man will be in the house.

15   I must watch myself.
I must not dare to sleep.

1991

CHARLES CAUSLEY

1917–

Armistice Day¹

I stood with three comrades in Parliament Square
November her freights of grey fire unloading,
No sound from the city upon the pale air,
Above us the sea-bell eleven exploding.

5   Down by the bands and the burning memorial
Beats all the brass in a royal array,
But at our end we are not so sartorial:
Out of (as usual) the rig of the day.

Starry is wearing a split pusser's flannel²
10   Rubbed, as he is, by the regular tide;
Oxo the ducks³ that he ditched in the Channel
In June, 1940 (when he was inside).

Kitty recalls his abandon-ship station,
Running below at the Old Man's salute
15   And (with a deck-watch) going down for duration
Wearing his oppo's⁴ pneumonia-suit.

Comrades, for you the black captain of carracks⁵
Writes in Whitehall his appalling decisions,
But as was often the case in the Barracks
20   Several ratings are not at Divisions.⁶

Into my eyes the stiff sea-horses stare,
Over my head sweeps the sun like a swan.
As I stand alone in Parliament Square
A cold bugle calls, and the city moves on.

1957

---

3. A form of cocaine.
1. November 11, when, at the eleventh hour (of the eleventh day of the eleventh month), church services throughout Britain commemorate the dead of the two world wars.
2. Naval-issue shirt.
3. Suit made of white duck (a canvaslike mate-rial).
4. From "opposite number": friend, comrade; "pneumonia-suit": tropical rig, or canvas suit worn while painting a ship, etc.
5. Large merchant ships equipped for warfare.
6. The parade of a ship's company.

At the British War Cemetery, Bayeux[7]

I walked where in their talking graves
And shirts of earth five thousand lay,
When history with ten feasts of fire
Had eaten the red air away.

5   "I am Christ's boy," I cried. "I bear
In iron hands the bread, the fishes.[8]
I hang with honey and with rose
This tidy wreck of all your wishes.

"On your geometry of sleep
10   The chestnut and the fir-tree fly,
And lavender and marguerite
Forge with their flowers an English sky.

"Turn now towards the belling town
Your jigsaws of impossible bone,
15   And rising read your rank of snow
Accurate as death upon the stone."

About your easy heads my prayers
I said with syllables of clay.
"What gift," I asked, "shall I bring now
20   Before I weep and walk away?"

Take, they replied, *the oak and laurel.*
Take our fortune of tears and live
Like a spendthrift lover. All we ask
Is the one gift you cannot give.

                                            1957

Eden Rock

They are waiting for me somewhere beyond Eden Rock:
My father, twenty-five, in the same suit
Of Genuine Irish Tweed, his terrier Jack
Still two years old and trembling at his feet.

5   My mother, twenty-three, in a sprigged dress
Drawn at the waist, ribbon in her straw hat,
Has spread the stiff white cloth over the grass.
Her hair, the colour of wheat, takes on the light.

She pours tea from a Thermos, the milk straight
10   From an old H.P. sauce[9] bottle, a screw
Of paper for a cork; slowly sets out
The same three plates, the tin cups painted blue.

---

7. Town in northern France where many British soldiers killed in Normandy and Flanders during World War II are buried.

8. Allusion to Christ's feeding of the five thousand (St. John 6).

9. A brand of steak sauce.

The sky whitens as if lit by three suns.
My mother shades her eyes and looks my way
15 Over the drifted stream. My father spins
A stone along the water. Leisurely,

They beckon to me from the other bank.
I hear them call, "See where the stream-path is!
Crossing is not as hard as you might think."

20 I had not thought that it would be like this.

1988

ROBERT LOWELL

1917–1977

The Quaker Graveyard in Nantucket

(FOR WARREN WINSLOW, DEAD AT SEA)

Let man have dominion over the fishes of the sea and the fowls of the air and
the beasts and the whole earth, and every creeping creature that moveth upon
the earth.[1]

1

A brackish reach of shoal off Madaket[2]
The sea was still breaking violently and night
Had steamed into our North Atlantic Fleet,
When the drowned sailor clutched the drag-net. Light
5 Flashed from his matted head and marble feet,
He grappled at the net
With the coiled, hurdling muscles of his thighs:
The corpse was bloodless, a botch of reds and whites,
Its open, staring eyes
10 Were lusterless dead-lights°   *porthole covers*
Or cabin-windows on a stranded hulk
Heavy with sand.[3] We weight the body, close
Its eyes and heave it seaward whence it came,
Where the heel-headed dogfish barks its nose
15 On Ahab's[4] void and forehead; and the name
Is blocked in yellow chalk.
Sailors, who pitch this portent at the sea
Where dreadnaughts° shall confess   *battleships*
Its hell-bent deity,
20 When you are powerless
To sand-bag this Atlantic bulwark, faced

1. Genesis 1.26.
2. Small settlement on Nantucket Island, Massa-
chusetts. Nantucket was a center of the American
whaling industry.
3. Lines 1–12 are based on the opening chapter of
Cape Cod (1864) by Henry David Thoreau (1817–

1862; see pp. 944–45).
4. Captain Ahab, protagonist of Herman
Melville's *Moby-Dick* (1851) and a recurring pres-
ence in this sequence of poems, sailed from Nan-
tucket on the *Pequod* in obsessive pursuit of the
white whale.

By the earth-shaker, green, unwearied, chaste
In his steel scales: ask for no Orphean lute
To pluck life back.[5] The guns of the steeled fleet
25 Recoil and then repeat
The hoarse salute.

2

Whenever winds are moving and their breath
Heaves at the roped-in bulwarks of this pier,
The terns and sea-gulls tremble at your death
30 In these home waters. Sailor, can you hear
The Pequod's sea wings, beating landward, fall
Headlong and break on our Atlantic wall
Off 'Sconset,[6] where the yawing S-boats° splash   *racing sailboats*
The bellbuoy, with ballooning spinnakers,
35 As the entangled, screeching mainsheet clears
The blocks: off Madaket, where lubbers lash
The heavy surf and throw their long lead squids
For blue-fish? Sea-gulls blink their heavy lids
Seaward. The winds' wings beat upon the stones,
40 Cousin, and scream for you and the claws rush
At the sea's throat and wring it in the slush
Of this old Quaker graveyard where the bones
Cry out in the long night for the hurt beast
Bobbing by Ahab's whaleboats in the East.

3

45 All you recovered from Poseidon died
With you, my cousin, and the harrowed brine
Is fruitless on the blue beard of the god,
Stretching beyond us to the castles in Spain,
Nantucket's westward haven. To Cape Cod
50 Guns, cradled on the tide,
Blast the eelgrass about a waterclock
Of bilge and backwash, roil the salt and sand
Lashing earth's scaffold, rock
Our warships in the hand
55 Of the great God, where time's contrition blues
Whatever it was these Quaker sailors lost
In the mad scramble of their lives. They died
When time was open-eyed,
Wooden and childish; only bones abide
60 There, in the nowhere, where their boats were tossed
Sky-high, where mariners had fabled news
Of IS,[7] the whited monster. What it cost
Them is their secret. In the sperm-whale's slick
I see the Quakers drown and hear their cry:
65 "If God himself had not been on our side,
If God himself had not been on our side,

5. The legendary Greek musician succeeded in
using song to win his wife, Eurydice, back from
the underworld (though he lost her again before
he reached the surface). 'The earth-shaker': Posei-

don, Greek god of the sea.
6. Siasconset, a town on Nantucket.
7. Cf. God's naming of himself to Moses as "I
AM" (Exodus 3.14).

When the Atlantic rose against us, why,
Then it had swallowed us up quick."

4

This is the end of the whaleroad[8] and the whale
70 Who spewed Nantucket bones on the thrashed swell
And stirred the troubled waters to whirlpools
To send the Pequod packing off to hell:
This is the end of them, three-quarters fools,
Snatching at straws to sail
75 Seaward and seaward on the turntail whale,
Spouting out blood and water as it rolls,
Sick as a dog to these Atlantic shoals:
Clamavimus, O depths.[9] Let the sea-gulls wail

For water, for the deep where the high tide
80 Mutters to its hurt self, mutters and ebbs.
Waves wallow in their wash, go out and out,
Leave only the death-rattle of the crabs,
The beach increasing, its enormous snout
Sucking the ocean's side.
85 This is the end of running on the waves;
We are poured out like water. Who will dance
The mast-lashed master of Leviathans
Up from this field of Quakers in their unstoned graves?

5

When the whale's viscera go and the roll
90 Of its corruption overruns this world
Beyond tree-swept Nantucket and Wood's Hole[1]
And Martha's Vineyard, Sailor, will your sword
Whistle and fall and sink into the fat?
In the great ash-pit of Jehoshaphat[2]
95 The bones cry for the blood of the white whale,
The fat flukes arch and whack about its ears,
The death-lance churns into the sanctuary, tears
The gun-blue swingle,[3] heaving like a flail,
And hacks the coiling life out: it works and drags
100 And rips the sperm-whale's midriff into rags,
Gobbets of blubber spill to wind and weather,
Sailor, and gulls go round the stoven timbers
Where the morning stars sing out together
And thunder shakes the white surf and dismembers
105 The red flag hammered in the mast-head.[4] Hide,
Our steel, Jonas Messias,[5] in Thy side.

---

8. An Anglo-Saxon epithet for the sea.
9. Adaptation of the Vulgate opening of Psalm 130: "Out of the depths have I cried unto thee, O Lord" (here, "we have cried").
1. On the coast of Massachusetts, near the island of Martha's Vineyard, which lies to the west of Nantucket.
2. "The day of judgment" [Lowell's note]. Joel 3 places the Last Judgment in the valley of Jehosha-phat.
3. Rod for beating flax.
4. As was the flag in the concluding chapter of *Moby-Dick*.
5. The prophet Jonah, who emerged alive from the whale, is often linked with the messiah as a figure of salvation. Here he is identified with Jesus struck by the Roman soldier (cf. Matthew 12.39–41).

6. Our Lady of Walsingham[6]

There once the penitents took off their shoes
And then walked barefoot the remaining mile;
And the small trees, a stream and hedgerows file
₁₁₀ Slowly along the munching English lane,
Like cows to the old shrine, until you lose
Track of your dragging pain.
The stream flows down under the druid tree,
Shiloah's[7] whirlpools gurgle and make glad
₁₁₅ The castle of God. Sailor, you were glad
And whistled Sion by that stream. But see:

Our Lady, too small for her canopy,
Sits near the altar. There's no comeliness
At all or charm in that expressionless
₁₂₀ Face with its heavy eyelids. As before,
This face, for centuries a memory,
Non est species, neque decor,[8]
Expressionless, expresses God: it goes
Past castled Sion. She knows what God knows,
₁₂₅ Not Calvary's Cross nor crib at Bethlehem
Now, and the world shall come to Walsingham.

7

The empty winds are creaking and the oak
Splatters and splatters on the cenotaph,[9]
The boughs are trembling and a gaff°   spar
₁₃₀ Bobs on the untimely stroke
Of the greased wash exploding on a shoal-bell
In the old mouth of the Atlantic. It's well;
Atlantic, you are fouled with the blue sailors,
Sea-monsters, upward angel, downward fish:[1]
₁₃₅ Unmarried and corroding, spare of flesh
Mart once of supercilious, wing'd clippers,
Atlantic, where your bell-trap guts its spoil
You could cut the brackish winds with a knife
Here in Nantucket, and cast up the time
₁₄₀ When the Lord God formed man from the sea's slime
And breathed into his face the breath of life,
And blue-lung'd combers lumbered to the kill.
The Lord survives the rainbow of His will.[2]

1946

6. Walsingham is a small town in Norfolk, England; a shrine to the Virgin Mary, built in the eleventh century, was an object of pilgrimage until it was destroyed in the Reformation. Lowell points out that this section is adapted from the description in E. I. Watkin's *Catholic Art and Culture*.
7. Pool or stream in Jerusalem; according to John Milton's *Paradise Lost* 1.11 (see p. 381), it flowed by the Temple on Mount Sion. In Isaiah 51.11, the redeemed come "singing into Zion," the heavenly city.

8. "There is no beauty or charm" (Latin; quoted from Watkin).
9. An empty tomb or monument erected to the dead but not containing their remains.
1. Cf. Milton, *Paradise Lost* 1.462–63: "Dagon his name, sea monster, upward man / And downward fish."
2. The rainbow symbolizes God's covenant with Noah never again to destroy the earth by flood (see Genesis 9.11–17).

Mr. Edwards[3] and the Spider

I saw the spiders marching through the air,
Swimming from tree to tree that mildewed day
   In latter August when the hay
   Came creaking to the barn. But where
5   The wind is westerly,
Where gnarled November makes the spiders fly
Into the apparitions of the sky,
They purpose nothing but their ease and die
Urgently beating east to sunrise and the sea;

10   What are we in the hands of the great God?
   It was in vain you set up thorn and briar
    In battle array against the fire
    And treason crackling in your blood;
     For the wild thorns grow tame
15   And will do nothing to oppose the flame;
   Your lacerations tell the losing game
   You play against a sickness past your cure.
How will the hands be strong? How will the heart endure?[4]

   A very little thing, a little worm,
20   Or hourglass-blazoned spider,[5] it is said,
    Can kill a tiger. Will the dead
    Hold up his mirror and affirm
     To the four winds the smell
And flash of his authority? It's well
25   If God who holds you to the pit of hell,
   Much as one holds a spider, will destroy,
Baffle and dissipate your soul. As a small boy

On Windsor Marsh,[6] I saw the spider die
When thrown into the bowels of fierce fire:
30   There's no long struggle, no desire
    To get up on its feet and fly—
     It stretches out its feet
And dies. This is the sinner's last retreat;
Yes, and no strength exerted on the heat
35   Then sinews the abolished will, when sick
And full of burning, it will whistle on a brick.

---

3. Jonathan Edwards (1703–1758), Puritan theologian and preacher whose works are alluded to throughout. The first stanza draws upon a paper, "On Insects," probably written ca. 1719–20, in which Edwards records his observations of the behavior of spiders. The poem is also heavily indebted to Edwards' most famous sermon, "Sinners in the Hands of an Angry God," which compares humans to spiders: "The God that holds you over the pit of Hell, much as one holds a spider or some loathsome insect, over the fire, abhors you, and is dreadfully provoked; his wrath towards you burns like fire."
4. Cf. Ezekiel 22.14 (the point of departure of "Sinners in the Hands of an Angry God"): "Can thine heart endure, or can thine hands be strong, in the days that I shall be strong, in the days that I shall deal with thee?"
5. The black widow spider (*Latrodectus mactans*), common in North America, is marked with a red hourglass pattern on its abdomen.
6. Near East Windsor, Connecticut, Edwards' birthplace.

But who can plumb the sinking of that soul?
Josiah Hawley,[7] picture yourself cast
   Into a brick-kiln where the blast
40   Fans your quick vitals to a coal—
      If measured by a glass,
How long would it seem burning! Let there pass
A minute, ten, ten trillion; but the blaze
Is infinite, eternal: this is death,
45 To die and know it. This is the Black Widow, death.

                              1946

My Last Afternoon with Uncle Devereux Winslow

1922: THE STONE PORCH OF MY GRANDFATHER'S SUMMER HOUSE

1

"I won't go with you. I want to stay with Grandpa!"
That's how I threw cold water
on my Mother and Father's
watery martini pipe dreams at Sunday dinner.
5   . . . Fontainebleau,[8] Mattapoisett, Puget Sound. . . .
Nowhere was anywhere after a summer
at my Grandfather's farm.
Diamond-pointed, athirst and Norman,[9]
its alley of poplars
10 paraded from Grandmother's rose garden
to a scary stand of virgin pine,
scrub, and paths forever pioneering.

One afternoon in 1922,
I sat on the stone porch, looking through
15 screens as black-grained as drifting coal.
Tockytock, tockytock
clumped our Alpine, Edwardian cuckoo clock,
slung with strangled, wooden game.
Our farmer was cementing a root-house[1] under the hill.
20 One of my hands was cool on a pile
of black earth, the other warm
on a pile of lime. All about me
were the works of my Grandfather's hands:
snapshots of his *Liberty Bell* silver mine;
25 his high school at *Stuttgart am Neckar;*
stogie-brown beams; fools'-gold nuggets;
octagonal red tiles,
sweaty with a secret dank, crummy with ant-stale;
a Rocky Mountain chaise longue,
30 its legs, shellacked saplings.

---

7. Edwards' uncle, Joseph Hawley, who killed himself in 1735.
8. All desirable places to visit.
9. A version of Romanesque architecture devel-oped in Normandy (France) in the tenth century A.D.
1. Small building, partly underground, used for storing root vegetables, bulbs, etc.

A pastel-pale Huckleberry Finn
fished with a broom straw in a basin
hollowed out of a millstone.
Like my Grandfather, the décor
35 was manly, comfortable,
overbearing, disproportioned.

What were those sunflowers? Pumpkins floating shoulder-high?
It was sunset, Sadie and Nellie
bearing pitchers of ice-tea,
40 oranges, lemons, mint, and peppermints,
and the jug of shandygaff,
which Grandpa made by blending half and half
yeasty, wheezing homemade sarsaparilla with beer.
The farm, entitled *Char-de-sa*
45 in the Social Register,
was named for my Grandfather's children:
Charlotte, Devereux, and Sarah.
No one had died there in my lifetime . . .
Only Cinder, our Scottie puppy
50 paralyzed from gobbling toads.
I sat mixing black earth and lime.

2

I was five and a half.
My formal pearl gray shorts
had been worn for three minutes.
55 My perfection was the Olympian
poise of my models in the imperishable autumn
display windows
of Rogers Peet's boys' store below the State House
in Boston. Distorting drops of water
60 pinpricked my face in the basin's mirror.
I was a stuffed toucan
with a bibulous, multicolored beak.

3

Up in the air
by the lakeview window in the billiards-room,
65 lurid in the doldrums of the sunset hour,
my Great Aunt Sarah
was learning *Samson and Delilah*.[2]
She thundered on the keyboard of her dummy piano,
with gauze curtains like a boudoir table,
70 accordionlike yet soundless.
It had been bought to spare the nerves
of my Grandmother,
tone-deaf, quick as a cricket,
now needing a fourth for "Auction,"°   *auction bridge*
75 and casting a thirsty eye

2. An opera by Camille Saint-Saëns (1835–1921), here in a piano arrangement.

on Aunt Sarah, risen like the phoenix[3]
from her bed of troublesome snacks and Tauchnitz[4] classics.

Forty years earlier,
twenty, auburn headed,
80   grasshopper notes of genius!
Family gossip says Aunt Sarah
tilted her archaic Athenian nose
and jilted an Astor.[5]
Each morning she practiced
85   on the grand piano at Symphony Hall,
deathlike in the off-season summer—
its naked Greek statues draped with purple
like the saints in Holy Week. . . .
On the recital day, she failed to appear.

4

90   I picked with a clean finger nail at the blue anchor
on my sailor blouse washed white as a spinnaker.
What in the world was I wishing?
. . . A sail-colored horse browsing in the bullrushes . . .
A fluff of the west wind puffing
95   my blouse, kiting me over our seven chimneys,
troubling the waters. . . .
As small as sapphires were the ponds: *Quittacus, Snippituit,*
and *Assawompset,* halved by "the Island,"
where my Uncle's duck blind
100   floated in a barrage of smoke-clouds.
Double-barreled shotguns
stuck out like bundles of baby crow-bars.
A single sculler° in a camouflaged kayak   *rower*
was quacking to the decoys. . . .

105   At the cabin between the waters,
the nearest windows were already boarded.
Uncle Devereux was closing camp for the winter.
As if posed for "the engagement photograph,"
he was wearing his severe
110   war-uniform of a volunteer Canadian officer.
Daylight from the doorway riddled his student posters,
tacked helter-skelter on walls as raw as a boardwalk.
Mr. Punch,[6] a water melon in hockey tights,
was tossing off a decanter of Scotch.
115   *La Belle France* in a red, white and blue toga
was accepting the arm of her "protector,"

---

3. A long-lived mythological bird that consumed itself in flames and was then reborn from its ashes; "Aunt Sarah": Sarah Stark Winslow, Robert Lowell's mother's aunt.
4. German publisher of an extensive range of inexpensive paper-covered books, including many works by English and American authors in English.
5. In the nineteenth century, three generations of Astors in New York accumulated one of the largest fortunes in the world.
6. A cartoon figure used as emblem for the English humor magazine *Punch*.

the ingenu and porcine Edward VII.[7]
The pre-war music hall belles
had goose necks, glorious signatures, beauty-moles,
120   and coils of hair like rooster tails.
The finest poster was two or three young men in khaki kilts
being bushwhacked on the veldt[8] —
They were almost life-size. . . .

My Uncle was dying at twenty-nine.
125   "You are behaving like children,"
said my Grandfather,
when my Uncle and Aunt left their three baby daughters,
and sailed for Europe on a last honeymoon . . .
I cowered in terror.
130   I wasn't a child at all —
unseen and all-seeing, I was Agrippina[9]
in the Golden House of Nero. . . .
Near me was the white measuring-door
my Grandfather had penciled with my Uncle's heights.
135   In 1911, he had stopped growing at just six feet.
While I sat on the tiles,
and dug at the anchor on my sailor blouse,
Uncle Devereux stood behind me.
He was as brushed as Bayard, our riding horse.
140   His face was putty.
His blue coat and white trousers
grew sharper and straighter.
His coat was a blue jay's tail,
his trousers were solid cream from the top of the bottle.
145   He was animated, hierarchical,
like a ginger snap man in a clothes-press.
He was dying of the incurable Hodgkin's disease. . . .
My hands were warm, then cool, on the piles
of earth and lime,
150   a black pile and a white pile. . . .
Come winter,
Uncle Devereux would blend to the one color.

1959

Skunk Hour

(For Elizabeth Bishop)[1]

Nautilus Island's hermit
heiress still lives through winter in her Spartan cottage;
her sheep still graze above the sea.
Her son's a bishop. Her farmer

7. Edward VII, king of England from 1901 to 1910, helped initiate the era of good feeling between England and France known as "L'Entente Cordiale." He is pictured with an arm around the waist of Marianne, "La Belle France," the traditional emblem for France.
8. Open country in South Africa. The poster pictures soldiers in the Boer War (1899–1902), fought by the British against the descendants of Dutch settlers in South Africa.
9. Mother of Nero; her scheming helped make him Roman emperor. He later had her murdered.
1. Lowell said that his poem was modeled on Elizabeth Bishop's "The Armadillo" (see pp. 1411–12).

5   is first selectman[2] in our village;
    she's in her dotage.

Thirsting for
the hierarchic privacy
of Queen Victoria's century,
10 she buys up all
the eyesores facing her shore,
and lets them fall.

The season's ill—
we've lost our summer millionaire,
15 who seemed to leap from an L. L. Bean[3]
catalogue. His nine-knot yawl
was auctioned off to lobstermen.
A red fox stain covers Blue Hill.

And now our fairy
20 decorator brightens his shop for fall;
his fishnet's filled with orange cork,
orange, his cobbler's bench and awl;
there is no money in his work,
he'd rather marry.

25 One dark night,
my Tudor Ford climbed the hill's skull;
I watched for love-cars. Lights turned down,
they lay together, hull to hull,
where the graveyard shelves on the town. . . .
30 My mind's not right.

A car radio bleats,
"Love, O careless Love. . . ." I hear
my ill-spirit sob in each blood cell,
as if my hand were at its throat. . . .
35 I myself am hell;[4]
nobody's here—

only skunks, that search
in the moonlight for a bite to eat.
They march on their soles up Main Street:
40 white stripes, moonstruck eyes' red fire
under the chalk-dry and spar spire
of the Trinitarian Church.

I stand on top
of our back steps and breathe the rich air—
45 a mother skunk with her column of kittens swills the garbage pail.
She jabs her wedge-head in a cup

2. Many New England towns are administered by an elected Board of Selectmen.
3. A mail-order company in Maine, originally specializing in hunting, fishing, and camping gear.
4. See Satan in Milton's *Paradise Lost* 4.75: "Which way I fly is Hell; myself am Hell."

of sour cream, drops her ostrich tail,
and will not scare.

1957   1959

Water

It was a Maine lobster town—
each morning boatloads of hands
pushed off for granite
quarries on the islands,

5   and left dozens of bleak
white frame houses stuck
like oyster shells
on a hill of rock,

and below us, the sea lapped
10   the raw little match-stick
mazes of a weir,
where the fish for bait were trapped.

Remember? We sat on a slab of rock.
From this dance in time,
15   it seems the color
of iris, rotting and turning purpler,

but it was only
the usual gray rock
turning the usual green
20   when drenched by the sea.

The sea drenched the rock
at our feet all day,
and kept tearing away
flake after flake.

25   One night you dreamed
you were a mermaid clinging to a wharf-pile,
and trying to pull
off the barnacles with your hands.

We wished our two souls
30   might return like gulls
to the rock. In the end,
the water was too cold for us.

1964

For the Union Dead[5]

"Relinquunt Omnia Servare Rem Publicam."

The old South Boston Aquarium stands
in a Sahara of snow now. Its broken windows are boarded.
The bronze weathervane cod has lost half its scales.
The airy tanks are dry.

5 Once my nose crawled like a snail on the glass;
my hand tingled
to burst the bubbles
drifting from the noses of the cowed, compliant fish.

My hand draws back. I often sigh still
10 for the dark downward and vegetating kingdom
of the fish and reptile. One morning last March,
I pressed against the new barbed and galvanized

fence on the Boston Common. Behind their cage,
yellow dinosaur steamshovels were grunting
15 as they cropped up tons of mush and grass
to gouge their underworld garage.

Parking spaces luxuriate like civic
sandpiles in the heart of Boston.
A girdle of orange, Puritan-pumpkin colored girders
20 braces the tingling Statehouse,

shaking over the excavations, as it faces Colonel Shaw
and his bell-cheeked Negro infantry
on St. Gaudens' shaking Civil War relief,
propped by a plank splint against the garage's earthquake.

25 Two months after marching through Boston,
half the regiment was dead;
at the dedication,
William James[6] could almost hear the bronze Negroes breathe.

Their monument sticks like a fishbone
30 in the city's throat.
Its Colonel is as lean
as a compass-needle.

He has an angry wrenlike vigilance,
a greyhound's gentle tautness;

---

5. At the edge of Boston Common, across from the Massachusetts State House, stands a monument to Colonel Robert Gould Shaw (1837–1863) and the first all-black Civil War regiment, the 54th Massachusetts; Shaw and many of his troops were killed in the assault on Fort Wagner, South Carolina. The bronze relief by Augustus St. Gaudens (1848–1897) was dedicated in 1897. In the upper right it bears the Latin motto of the Society of the Cincinnati, *Omnia relinquit servare rem publicam* ("He gives up everything to serve the republic"). Lowell's epigraph changes "he gives" to "they give."
6. (1842–1910); philosopher and psychologist who taught at Harvard.

35 he seems to wince at pleasure,
    and suffocate for privacy.

    He is out of bounds now. He rejoices in man's lovely,
    peculiar power to choose life and die—
    when he leads his black soldiers to death,
40 he cannot bend his back.

    On a thousand small town New England greens,
    the old white churches hold their air
    of sparse, sincere rebellion; frayed flags
    quilt the graveyards of the Grand Army of the Republic

45 The stone statues of the abstract Union Soldier
    grow slimmer and younger each year—
    wasp-waisted, they doze over muskets
    and muse through their sideburns . . .

    Shaw's father wanted no monument
50 except the ditch,
    where his son's body was thrown
    and lost with his "niggers."

    The ditch is nearer.
    There are no statues for the last war here;
55 on Boylston Street,[7] a commercial photograph
    shows Hiroshima boiling

    over a Mosler Safe, the "Rock of Ages"
    that survived the blast. Space is nearer.
    When I crouch to my television set,
60 the drained faces of Negro school-children rise like balloons.[8]

    Colonel Shaw
    is riding on his bubble,
    he waits
    for the blesséd break.

65 The Aquarium is gone. Everywhere,
    giant finned cars nose forward like fish;
    a savage servility
    slides by on grease.

                                                1964

Harriet[9]

A repeating fly, blueback, thumbthick—so gross,
it seems apocalyptic[1] in our house—
whams back and forth across the nursery bed

7. Major street in Boston.
8. The struggles to integrate public schools (first in the South, and later in the North) were fre-
quently featured in television newscasts.
9. The poet's daughter, born January 4, 1945.
1. Foreboding doom.

manned by a madhouse of stuffed animals,
5   not one a fighter. It is like a plane
dusting apple orchards or Arabs on the screen—
one of the mighty . . . one of the helpless. It
bumbles and bumps its brow on this and that,
making a short, unhealthy life the shorter.
10   I kill it, and another instant's added
to the horrifying mortmain[2] of
ephemera: keys, drift, sea-urchin shells,
you packrat off with joy . . . a dead fly swept
under the carpet, wrinkling to fulfillment.

1970   1973

Epilogue

Those blessèd structures, plot and rhyme—
why are they no help to me now
I want to make
something imagined, not recalled?
5   I hear the noise of my own voice:
The painter's vision is not a lens,
it trembles to caress the light.
But sometimes everything I write
with the threadbare art of my eye
10   seems a snapshot,
lurid, rapid, garish, grouped,
heightened from life,
yet paralyzed by fact.
All's misalliance.
15   Yet why not say what happened?
Pray for the grace of accuracy
Vermeer[3] gave to the sun's illumination
stealing like the tide across a map
to his girl solid with yearning.
20   We are poor passing facts,
warned by that to give
each figure in the photograph
his living name.

                                                                           1977

AL PURDY

1918–

Wilderness Gothic

Across Roblin Lake,[1] two shores away,
they are sheathing the church spire
with new metal. Someone hangs in the sky

2. A legal term ("dead hand") referring to perpet-
ual ownership; more generally, the influence of
the past on the present.

3. Jan Vermeer (1632–1675), Dutch painter
known for his treatment of light.
1. Small lake in southeastern Ontario.

over there from a piece of rope,
5   hammering and fitting God's belly-scratcher,
working his way up along the spire
until there's nothing left to nail on—
Perhaps the workman's faith reaches beyond:
touches intangibles, wrestles with Jacob,[2]
10   replacing rotten timber with pine thews,
pounds hard in the blue cave of the sky,
contends heroically with difficult problems of
gravity, sky navigation and mythopeia,°   *mythmaking*
his volunteer time and labor donated to God,
15   minus sick benefits of course on a non-union job—

Fields around are yellowing into harvest,
nestling and fingerling are sky and water borne,
death is yodeling quiet in green woodlots,
and bodies of three young birds have disappeared
20   in the sub-surface of the new county highway—

That picture is incomplete, part left out
that might alter the whole Dürer[3] landscape:
gothic ancestors peer from medieval sky,
dour faces trapped in photograph albums escaping
25   to clop down iron roads with matched grays:
work-sodden wives groping inside their flesh
for what keeps moving and changing and flashing
beyond and past the long frozen Victorian day.
A sign of fire and brimstone? A two-headed calf
30   born in the barn last night? A sharp female agony?
An age and a faith moving into transition,
the dinner cold and new-baked bread a failure,
deep woods shiver and water drops hang pendant,
double yolked eggs and the house creaks a little—
35   Something is about to happen. Leaves are still.
Two shores away, a man hammering in the sky.
Perhaps he will fall.

                                   1968

The Blue City

Of such an intense azure
that it seeps into your bones
providing dull earth
with an upsidedown sky
5   My wife is still sleeping
tired from the long journey
I have awakened very early
and must let her sleep longer
Her face is turned to one wall

2. Jacob, the grandson of Abraham, wrestled an entire night with an angel who then blessed him and gave him the name "Israel" (Genesis 32.24–30).

3. Albrecht Dürer (1471–1528), German painter and engraver, noted for the rich and realistic detail of his work.

10 of the strange hotel room
not feeling my own excitement
at being here with blood thrumming
and pulse beating a little faster
from the sheer romance of Asia
15 She turns over and sighs
while I'm standing at the window
trying to glimpse a camel
outside on awakening streets:
a woman is sweeping cobblestones
20 with some kind of twig broom
charcoal burning in a brazier
much blue ceramic but no camels
It occurs to me that I will remember
this time for its inbetweenness
25 removed from the continuity of things
and it's as if I'm a long way off
somewhere else and watching myself
watching a woman in bed sleeping
seeing what I see for the second time
30 the wished-for camel and burning charcoal
a blue city slowly coming awake
the little pulse in my wife's throat
I will be seeing it a second time
or has that second time arrived?
35 —My wife awakening not exactly
here nor there and aware of oddness
disoriented she keeps looking at me
brown eyes puzzled for a long moment

Samarkand & Ameliasburg[4]

1984

LAWRENCE FERLINGHETTI

1919–

Sometime During Eternity . . .

Sometime during eternity
                    some guys show up
and one of them
            who shows up real late
5   is a kind of carpenter[1]
      from some square-type place
                  like Galilee[2]
      and he starts wailing

---

4. Samarkand: city in Uzbekistan, in the former
Soviet Union; Ameliasburg: city on Roblin Lake in
Ontario, Canada.

1. Jesus, like his father Joseph, was a carpenter.
2. Region in northern Israel, home of Jesus.

and claiming he is hip
10   to who made heaven
          and earth
             and that the cat
      who really laid it on us
          is his Dad

15   And moreover
      he adds
        It's all writ down
            on some scroll-type parchments
    which some henchmen
20   leave lying around the Dead Sea[3] somewheres
      a long time ago
          and which you won't even find
  for a coupla thousand years or so
          or at least for
25 nineteen hundred and fortyseven
          of them
      to be exact
        and even then
  nobody really believes them
30   or me
          for that matter

  You're hot
      they tell him

  And they cool him

35 They stretch him on the Tree to cool

    And everybody after that
          is always making models
      of this Tree
        with Him hung up
40 and always crooning His name
        and calling Him to come down
      and sit in
        on their combo
    as if he is *the* king cat[4]
45   who's got to blow
  or they can't quite make it

  Only he don't come down
      from His Tree

  Him just hang there
50   on His Tree

---

3. Sea between the West Bank and Jordan, where the Dead Sea Scrolls, fragments of the Jewish Essene order's library dating back to 130 B.C., were found in 1947.

4. Slang; "king cat": leader (Jesus was also called King of the Jews). "Combo": group of musicians, particularly jazz.

looking real Petered out[5]
and real cool
and also
according to a roundup
55   of late world news
from the usual unreliable sources
real dead

1958

WILLIAM MEREDITH

1919–

The Illiterate

Touching your goodness, I am like a man
Who turns a letter over in his hand
And you might think this was because the hand
Was unfamiliar but, truth is, the man
5 Has never had a letter from anyone;
And now he is both afraid of what it means
And ashamed because he has no other means
To find out what it says than to ask someone.

His uncle could have left the farm to him,
10 Or his parents died before he sent them word,
Or the dark girl changed and want him for beloved.
Afraid and letter-proud, he keeps it with him.
What would you call his feeling for the words
That keep him rich and orphaned and beloved?

1958

Rhode Island

Here at the seashore they use the clouds over & over
again, like the rented animals in Aïda.[1]
In the late morning the land breeze
turns and now the extras are driving
5 all the white elephants the other way.
What language are the children shouting in?
He[2] is lying on the beach listening.

The sand knocks like glass, struck by bare heels.
He tries to remember snow noise.
10 Would powder snow ping like that?

5. Pun referring both to a sense of defeat or exhaustion and to St. Peter, who denied being a disciple three times after Jesus' arrest (John 18.17–27).
1. In the triumphal procession in Act II of Verdi's 1871 opera, the victorious Egyptian forces return to Memphis with their captives; major companies often hire horses and elephants to augment the spectacle.
2. Hazard, the Painter (title character of the volume from which this poem comes); cf. line 25.

But you don't lie with your ear to powder snow.
Why doesn't the girl who takes care
of the children, a Yale girl without flaw,
know the difference between *lay* and *lie?*

15   He tries to remember snow, his season.
The mind is in charge of things then.
Summer is for animals, the ocean is erotic,
all that openness and swaying.
No matter how often you make love
20   in August you're always aware of genitalia,
your own and the half-naked others'.
Even with the gracefulest bathers
you're aware of their kinship with porpoises,
mammals disporting themselves in a blue element,
25   smelling slightly of fish. Porpoise Hazard
watches himself awhile, like a blue movie.

In the other hemisphere now people
are standing up, at work at their easels.
There they think about love at night
30   when they take off their serious clothes
and go to bed sandlessly, under blankets.

Today the children, his own among them,
are apparently shouting fluently in Portuguese,
using the colonial dialect of Brazil.
35   It is just as well, they have all been changed
into small shrill marginal animals,
he would not want to understand them again
until after Labor Day. He just lays there.

1975

AMY CLAMPITT

1920–1994

Beach Glass

While you walk the water's edge,
turning over concepts
I can't envision, the honking buoy
serves notice that at any time
5   the wind may change,
the reef-bell clatters
its treble monotone, deaf as Cassandra[1]
to any note but warning. The ocean,
cumbered by no business more urgent
10   than keeping open old accounts

---

1. In Greek mythology, the daughter of Priam (last king of Troy), and a prophetess who predicted the fall of Troy. Her gift of prophecy was marred by the curse of never being believed.

that never balanced,
goes on shuffling its millenniums
of quartz, granite, and basalt.
                              It behaves
15   toward the permutations of novelty—
driftwood and shipwreck, last night's
beer cans, spilt oil, the coughed-up
residue of plastic—with random
impartiality, playing catch or tag
20   or touch-last like a terrier,
turning the same thing over and over,
over and over. For the ocean, nothing
is beneath consideration.
                              The houses
25   of so many mussels and periwinkles
have been abandoned here, it's hopeless
to know which to salvage. Instead
I keep a lookout for beach glass—
amber of Budweiser, chrysoprase[2]
30   of Almadén and Gallo, lapis[3]
by way of (no getting around it,
I'm afraid) Phillips'
Milk of Magnesia, with now and then a rare
translucent turquoise or blurred amethyst
35   of no known origin.
                              The process
goes on forever: they came from sand,
they go back to gravel,
along with the treasuries
40   of Murano,[4] the buttressed
astonishments of Chartres,[5]
which even now are readying
for being turned over and over as gravely
and gradually as an intellect
45   engaged in the hazardous
redefinition of structures
no one has yet looked at.

                                             1983

Beethoven, Opus 111[6]

for Norman Carey

There are epochs . . . when mankind, not content with the present, longing
for time's deeper layers, like the plowman, thirsts for the virgin soil of time.
                                             —OSIP MANDELSTAM[7]

---

2. Green variety of chalcedony quartz.
3. Lapis lazuli, a deep-blue mineral.
4. An island suburb of Venice, famous for its man-
ufacture of fine glass.
5. The cathedral of Notre Dame de Chartres in
France, celebrated for its stained glass windows.
6. Beethoven's *Piano Sonata No. 32*, Opus 111,

the last work in the form, as Clampitt's note
remarks, by Ludwig van Beethoven (1770–1827).
The German composer, an exemplar of Romanti-
cism and revolution, became deaf progressively.
7. (1891–1938); Russian poet and critic, who was
arrested for a poem on Joseph Stalin and later died
in a transit camp.

—Or, conversely, hungers
for the levitations of the concert hall:
the hands like rafts of *putti*[8]
out of a region where the dolorous stars
5   are fixed in glassy cerements of Art;
the *ancien régime's*[9] diaphanous plash
athwart the mounting throb of hobnails—
shod squadrons of vibration
mining the air, its struck ores hardening
10   into a plowshare, a downward wandering
disrupting every formal symmetry:
from the supine harp-case, the strung-foot
tendons under the mahogany, the bulldozer
in the bass unearths a Piranesian[1]
15   catacomb: Beethoven ventilating,
with a sound he cannot hear, the cave-in
of recurring rage.
             In the tornado country
of mid-America, my father
20   might have been his twin—a farmer
hacking at sourdock, at the strangle-
roots of thistles and wild morning glories,
setting out rashly, one October,
to rid the fencerows of poison ivy:
25   livid seed-globs turreted
in trinities of glitter, ripe
with the malefic glee no farmer doubts
lives deep down things.[2] My father
was naïve enough—by nature
30   revolutionary, though he'd have
disowned the label—to suppose he might
in some way, minor but radical, disrupt
the givens of existence: set
his neighbors' thinking straight, undo
35   the stranglehold of reasons nations
send their boys off to war. That fall,
after the oily fireworks had cooled down
to trellises of hairy wicks,
he dug them up, rootstocks and all,
40   and burned them. Do-gooder!
The well-meant holocaust became
a mist of venom, sowing itself along
the sculptured hollows of his overalls,
braceleting wrists and collarbone—
45   a mesh of blisters spreading to a shirt
worn like a curse. For weeks
he writhed inside it. Awful.

---

8. "The stylized infant cherubs that appear to soar, plunge or hover in some Italian and Spanish paintings on Christian themes" [Clampitt's note].
9. French term for France's political and social system before the revolution in 1789.
1. As in the work of Giambattista Piranesi (1720–

1778), Italian architect, painter, and engraver.
2. An allusion to "God's Grandeur" by the English poet Gerard Manley Hopkins (1844–1889), in which "There lives the dearest freshness deep down things" (p. 1062).

High art
with a stiff neck: an upright Steinway[3]
50 bought in Chicago; a chromo of a Hobbema
tree-avenue, or of Millet's imagined peasant,[4]
the lark she listens to invisible, perhaps
irrelevant: harpstrings and fripperies of air
congealed into an object nailed against the wall,
55 its sole ironic function (if it has any)
to demonstrate that one, though he may
grunt and sweat at work, is not a clod.
Beethoven might declare the air
his domicile, the winds kin,[5] the tornado
60 a kind of second cousin; here,
his labor merely shimmers—a deracinated
album leaf, a bagatelle, the "Moonlight"[6]
rendered with a dying fall (the chords
subside, disintegrate, regroup
65 in climbing sequences *con brio*);[7] there's
no dwelling on the sweet past here,
there being no past to speak of
other than the setbacks: typhoid
in the wells, half the first settlers
70 dead of it before a year was out;
diphtheria and scarlet fever
every winter; drought, the Depression,
a mortgage on the mortgage. High art
as a susurrus,° the silk and perfume   *whisper*
75 of unsullied hands. Those hands!—
driving the impressionable wild with anguish
for another life entirely: the Lyceum[8] circuit,
the doomed diving bell of Art.
                                    Beethoven
80 in his workroom: ear trumpet,
conversation book and pencil, candlestick,
broken crockery, the Graf piano
wrecked by repeated efforts to hear himself—
out of a humdrum squalor the levitations,
85 the shakes and triplets, the *Adagio
molto semplice e cantabile*,[9] the Arietta°   *little air*
a disintegrating surf of blossom
opening along the keyboard, along the fencerows
the astonishment of sweetness. My father,
90 driving somewhere in Kansas or Colorado,
in dustbowl country, stopped the car
to dig up by the roots a flower
he'd never seen before—a kind

---

3. A Steinway piano.
4. Jean François Millet (1814–1875), French painter. Meindert Hobbema (1638–1709), Dutch painter.
5. "In a letter to Count Brunswick dated February 13, 1814, Beethoven wrote: 'As regards me, great heavens! my dominion is in the air; the tones whirl like the wind, and often there is a whirl in my soul' " [Clampitt's note].

6. Beethoven's *Piano Sonata in C Sharp Minor* (*Moonlight*), Opus 27, No. 2.
7. Musical direction meaning "with vigor" (Italian).
8. A building used for cultural activities, such as concerts.
9. "A slow movement, played very simply and in a songlike manner" (Italian).

of prickly poppy most likely, its luminousness
95   wounding the blank plains like desire.
He mentioned in a letter the disappointment
of his having hoped it might transplant—
an episode that brings me near tears,
still, as even his dying does not—
100   that awful dying, months-long, hunkered,
irascible. From a clod no plowshare
could deliver, a groan for someone
(because he didn't want to look
at anything) to take away the flowers,
105   a bawling as of slaughterhouses, slogans
of a general uprising: *Freiheit!*[1]
Beethoven, shut up with the four walls
of his deafness, rehearsing the unhearable
semplice e cantabile, somehow reconstituting
110   the blister shirt of the intolerable
into these shakes and triplets, a hurrying
into flowering along the fencerows: dying,
for my father, came to be like that
finally—in its messages the levitation
115   of serenity, as though the spirit might
aspire, in its last act,
                      to walk on air.

                                               1983

The Sun Underfoot Among the Sundews[2]

An ingenuity too astonishing
to be quite fortuitous is
this bog full of sundews, sphagnum-
lined and shaped like a teacup.
5   A step
down and you're into it; a
wilderness swallows you up:
ankle-, then knee-, then midriff-
to-shoulder-deep in wetfooted
10   understory, an overhead
spruce-tamarack horizon hinting
you'll never get out of here.
                        But the sun
among the sundews, down there,
15   is so bright, an underfoot
webwork of carnivorous rubies,
a star-swarm thick as the gnats
they're set to catch, delectable
double-faced cockleburs, each
20   hair-tip a sticky mirror
afire with sunlight, a million
of them and again a million,
each mirror a trap set to
unhand unbelieving,

---

1. "Freedom" (German).   2. Carnivorous bog plants.

25   that either
a First Cause° said once, "Let there   *God*
be sundews,"[3] and there were, or they've
made their way here unaided
other than by that backhand, round-
30 about refusal to assume responsibility
known as Natural Selection.[4]
                 But the sun
underfoot is so dazzling
down there among the sundews,
35 there is so much light
in the cup that, looking,
you start to fall upward.

                                  1983

The Cormorant in Its Element

That bony potbellied arrow, wing-pumping along
implacably, with a ramrod's rigid adherence,
airborne, to the horizontal, discloses talents
one would never have guessed at. Plummeting

5 waterward, big black feet splayed for a landing
gear, slim head turning and turning, vermilion-
strapped, this way and that, with a lightning glance
over the shoulder, the cormorant astounding-

ly, in one sleek involuted arabesque, a vertical
10 turn on a dime, goes into that inimitable
vanishing-and-emerging-from-under-the-briny-

deep act which, unlike the works of Homo Houdini,[5]
is performed for reasons having nothing at all
to do with ego, guilt, ambition, or even money.

                                  1983

Syrinx[6]

Like the foghorn that's all lung,
the wind chime that's all percussion,
like the wind itself, that's merely air
in a terrible fret,[7] without so much
5 as a finger to articulate
what ails it, the aeolian
syrinx, that reed
in the throat of a bird,

3. An allusion to Genesis 1.14: "And God said, Let there be lights in the firmament of the heaven."
4. The theory of evolution as formulated by the English naturalist Charles Darwin (1809–1882).
5. An invented term conflating the Latin *Homo sapiens*, or humankind, with the American magician Harry Houdini (1874–1926).
6. The vocal organ of birds, named after the Arcadian mountain nymph in Greek mythology who,

to protect her chastity from Pan, was transformed into a reed. From that reed Pan made the panpipe, also called the syrinx. Pastoral poets considered Pan a patron of their art.
7. In the double sense of 1) worried agitation and 2) a ridge set across the fingerboard of a stringed instrument to help the fingers stop the strings correctly.

when it comes to the shaping of
10   what we call consonants, is
too imprecise for consensus
about what it even seems to
be saying: is it *o-ka-lee*
or *con-ka-ree,* is it really *jug jug,*
15   is it *cuckoo* for that matter? —
much less whether a bird's call
means anything in
particular, or at all.

Syntax comes last, there can be
20   no doubt of it: came last,
can be thought of (is
thought of by some) as a
higher form of expression:
is, in extremity, first to
25   be jettisoned: as the diva
onstage, all soaring
pectoral breathwork,
takes off, pure vowel
breaking free of the dry,
30   the merely fricative
husk of the particular, rises
past saying anything, any
more than the wind in
the trees, waves breaking,
35   or Homer's gibbering
Thespesiae iachē:[8]

those last-chance vestiges
above the threshold, the all-
but dispossessed of breath.

1994

BARBARA GUEST

1920–

Roses

"painting has no air . . ."
—GERTRUDE STEIN[1]

That there should never be air
in a picture surprises me.

8. Clampitt's oblique commentary, in a note, is a quotation from Homer's *Odyssey* 10.34–43, as translated by A. T. Murray: "Then there gathered from out of Erebus the spirits of those that are dead, brides, and unwedded youths, and toil-worn old men, and tender maidens with hearts yet new to sorrow, and many, too, that had been wounded with bronze-tipped spears, men slain in fight, wearing their blood-stained armour. These came thronging in crowds about the pit from every side, with a wondrous cry . . ."
1. (1874–1946); American avant-garde writer (see pp. 1143–44), whose Paris home was a salon for leading artists and writers between the two world wars.

It would seem to be only a picture
of a certain kind, a portrait in paper
5   or glued, somewhere a stickiness
as opposed to a stick-to-it-ness
of another genre. It might be
quite new to do without
that air, or to find oxygen
10 on the landscape line
like a boat which is an object
or a shoe which never floats
and is stationary.

                 Still there
15 are certain illnesses that require
air, lots of it. And there are nervous
people who cannot manufacture
enough air and must seek
for it when they don't have plants,
20 in pictures. There is the mysterious
traveling that one does outside
the cube and this takes place
in air.

             It is why one develops
25 an attitude toward roses picked
in the morning air, even roses
without sun shining on them.
The roses of Juan Gris[2] from which
we learn the selflessness of roses
30 existing perpetually without air,
the lid being down, so to speak,
a 1912 fragrance sifting
to the left corner where we read
"The Marvelous" and escape.

                         1973

Twilight Polka Dots

The lake was filled with distinguished fish purchased
at much expense in their prime. It was a curious lake, half salt,
wishing to set a tone of solitude edged with poetry.
This was a conscious body aware of shelves and wandering
5 rootlings, duty suggested it provide a scenic atmosphere
of content, a solicitude for the brooding emotions.

It despised the fish who enriched the waters. Fish with
their lithesome bodies, and their disagreeable concern
with feeding. They disturbed the water which preferred
10 the cultivated echoes of a hunting horn. Inside a
mercantile heart the lake dwelt on boning and deboning,
skin and sharpened eyes, a ritual search through

2. (1887–1927); Spanish cubist painter.

dependable deposits for slimier luxuries. The surface
presented an appeal to meditation and surcease.

15 Situated below the mountain, surrounded by aged trees,
the lake offered a picture appealing both to young and
mature romance. At last it was the visual choice of two
figures who in the fixity of their shared glance were
admired by the lake. Tactfully they ignored the lacustrine[3]
20 fish, their gaze faltered lightly on the lapping
margins, their thoughts flew elsewhere, even beyond the
loop of her twisted hair and the accent of his poised tie-pin.

The scene supplied them with theatre, it was an evening
performance and the water understood and strained its
25 source for bugling echoes and silvered laments. The
couple referred to the lake without speech, by the turn
of a head, a hand waved, they placed a dignity upon the lake
brow causing an undercurrent of physical pleasure to
shake the water.

30 Until the letter fell. Torn into fragments the man tossed
it on the water, and the wind spilled the paper forward,
the cypress bent, the mountain sent a glacial flake.
Fish leapt. Polka dots now stippled the
twilight water and a superannuated gleam like a browned
35 autumnal stalk followed the couple where they shied in
the lake marsh grass like two eels who were caught.

                                                    1989

EDWIN MORGAN
1920–

Strawberries

There were never strawberries
like the ones we had
that sultry afternoon
sitting on the step
5   of the open french window
facing each other
your knees held in mine
the blue plates in our laps
the strawberries glistening
10 in the hot sunlight
we dipped them in sugar
looking at each other
not hurrying the feast
for one to come
15 the empty plates

3. Of or pertaining to a lake.

laid on the stone together
with the two forks crossed
and I bent towards you
sweet in that air
20 in my arms
abandoned like a child
from your eager mouth
the taste of strawberries
in my memory
25 lean back again
let me love you

let the sun beat
on our forgetfulness
one hour of all
30 the heat intense
and summer lightning
on the Kilpatrick hills

let the storm wash the plates

1965

King Billy

Grey over Riddrie[1] the clouds piled up,
dragged their rain through the cemetery trees.
The gates shone cold. Wind rose
flaring the hissing leaves, the branches
5 swung, heavy, across the lamps.
Gravestones huddled in drizzling shadow,
flickering streetlight scanned the requiescats,[2]
a name and an urn, a date, a dove
picked out, lost, half regained.
10 What is this dripping wreath, blown from its grave
red, white, blue, and gold
"To Our Leader of Thirty years Ago" —

Bareheaded, in dark suits, with flutes
and drums, they brought him here, in procession
15 seriously, King Billy of Brigton, dead,
from Bridgeton Cross: a memory of violence,
brooding days of empty bellies,
billiard smoke and a sour pint,
boots or fists, famous sherrickings,[3]
20 the word, the scuffle, the flash, the shout,
bloody crumpling in the close,
bricks for papish windows, get
the Conks next time, the Conks ambush
the Billy Boys, the Billy Boys the Conks till
25 Sillitoe scuffs the razors down the stank° —   drain

1. A district of Glasgow.
2. *Requiescat in pace* is Latin for "Rest in Peace"
(often shortened to R.I.P. on gravestones).
3. Scottish slang for "fuss over nothing."

No, but it isn't the violence they remember
but the legend of a violent man
born poor, gang-leader in the bad times
of idleness and boredom, lost in better days,
30   a bouncer in a betting club,
quiet man at last, dying
alone in Bridgeton in a box bed.
So a thousand people stopped the traffic
for the hearse of a folk hero and the flutes
35   threw 'Onward Christian Soldiers' to the winds
from unironic lips, the mourners kept
in step, and there were some who wept.

Go from the grave. The shrill flutes
are silent, the march dispersed.
40   Deplore what is to be deplored,
and then find out the rest.

                          1968

The Dowser[4]

With my forked branch of Lebanese cedar
I quarter the dunes like downs and guide
an invisible plough far over the sand.
But how to quarter such shifting acres
5   when the wind melts their shapes, and shadows
mass where all was bright before,
and landmarks walk like wraiths at noon?
All I know is that underneath,
how many miles no one can say,
10   an unbroken water-table waits
like a lake; it has seen no bird or sail
in its long darkness, and no man;
not even pharaohs dug so far
for all their thirst, or thirst of glory,
15   or thrust-power of ten thousand slaves.
I tell you I can smell it though,
that water. I am old and black
and I know the manners of the sun
which makes me bend, not break. I lose
20   my ghostly footprints without complaint.
I put every mirage in its place.
I watch the lizard make its lace.
Like one not quite blind I go
feeling for the sunken face.
25   So hot the days, the nights so cold,
I gather my white rags and sigh
but sighing step so steadily
that any vibrance in so deep
a lake would never fail to rise

---

4. Someone who searches for underground streams by holding a forked branch of cedar or hazel, which
twitches when it is above water.

30 towards the snowy cedar's bait.
Great desert, let your sweetness wake.

1986   1988

KEITH DOUGLAS
1920–1944

Vergissmeinnicht[1]

Three weeks gone and the combatants gone
returning over the nightmare ground
we found the place again, and found
the soldier sprawling in the sun.

5 The frowning barrel of his gun
overshadowing. As we came on
that day, he hit my tank with one
like the entry of a demon.

Look. Here in the gunpit spoil
10 the dishonoured picture of his girl
who has put: *Steffi. Vergissmeinnicht*
in a copybook gothic script.

We see him almost with content,
abased, and seeming to have paid
15 and mocked at by his own equipment
that's hard and good when he's decayed.

But she would weep to see today
how on his skin the swart flies move;
the dust upon the paper eye
20 and the burst stomach like a cave.

For here the lover and killer are mingled
who had one body and one heart.
And death who had the soldier singled
has done the lover mortal hurt.

1943   1944

Aristocrats[2]

"I think I am becoming a God"[3]

The noble horse with courage in his eye
clean in the bone, looks up at a shellburst:

---

1. "Forget me not" (German).
2. Dr. Desmond Graham, editor of *The Complete Poems of Keith Douglas* (1978), prefers and prints another, perhaps later but inferior, version of this

poem, titled "Sportsmen."
3. The dying words of Roman Emperor Vespasian were reportedly "Alas! I suppose I am turning into a god."

away fly the images of the shires[4]
but he puts the pipe back in his mouth.

5 Peter was unfortunately killed by an 88:[5]
it took his leg away, he died in the ambulance.
I saw him crawling on the sand; he said
It's most unfair, they've shot my foot off.

How can I live among this gentle
10 obsolescent breed of heroes, and not weep?
Unicorns, almost,
for they are falling into two legends
in which their stupidity and chivalry
are celebrated. Each, fool and hero, will be an immortal.

15 The plains were their cricket pitch[6]
and in the mountains the tremendous drop fences[7]
brought down some of the runners. Here then
under the stones and earth they dispose themselves,
I think with their famous unconcern.
20 It is not gunfire I hear but a hunting horn.[8]

Enfidaville, Tunisia, 1943   1946

Gallantry

The Colonel[9] in a casual voice
spoke into the microphone a joke
Which through a hundred earphones broke
into the ears of a doomed race.[1]

5 Into the ears of the doomed boy, the fool
whose perfectly mannered flesh fell
in opening the door for a shell
as he had learnt to do at school.

Conrad luckily survived the winter:
10 he wrote a letter to welcome
the auspicious spring: only his silken
intentions severed with a single splinter.

Was George fond of little boys?
We always suspected it,
15 but who will say: since George was hit
we never mention our surmise.

---

4. Counties. Cf. Wilfred Owen, "Anthem for Doomed Youth," line 8 (p. 1276).
5. A German tank fitted with an eighty-eight-millimeter gun.
6. Field on which the game of cricket is played.
7. Fences in the course of a steeplechase horse race.
8. See n. 9, below.
9. "Lt. Col. J. D. Player, killed in Tunisia, Enfidaville, February 1943, left £3,000 to the Beaufort Hunt, and directed that the incumbent of the living in his gift [i.e., the church whose vicar he was entitled to appoint] should be a 'man who approves of hunting, shooting, and all manly sports, which are the backbone of the nation.'" [Douglas' note on one of the manuscripts of "Aristocrats." Player was in fact killed in April.]
1. Cf. Wilfred Owen, "Anthem for Doomed Youth" (p. 1276).

It was a brave thing the Colonel said,
but the whole sky turned too hot
and the three heroes never heard what
20   it was, gone deaf with steel and lead.

But the bullets cried with laughter,
the shells were overcome with mirth,
plunging their heads in steel and earth —
(the air commented in a whisper).

April 1943   1949

On a Return from Egypt

To stand here in the wings of Europe
disheartened, I have come away
from the sick land where in the sun lay
the gentle sloe-eyed[2] murderers
5   of themselves, exquisites under a curse;
here to exercise my depleted fury.

For the heart is a coal, growing colder
when jewelled cerulean[3] seas change
into grey rocks, grey water-fringe,
10   sea and sky altering like a cloth
till colour and sheen are gone both:
cold is an opiate of the soldier.

And all my endeavours are unlucky explorers
come back, abandoning the expedition;
15   the specimens, the lilies of ambition
still spring in their climate, still unpicked:
but time, time is all I lacked
to find them, as the great collectors before me.

The next month, then, is a window
20   and with a crash I'll split the glass.
Behind it stands one I must kiss,
person of love or death
a person or a wraith,
I fear what I shall find.

March–April 1944?

HOWARD NEMEROV

1920–1991

The Goose Fish

On the long shore, lit by the moon
To show them properly alone,

---

2. Dark-eyed: a sloe is the dark fruit of the black-   3. Dark blue or green.
thorn.

Two lovers suddenly embraced
So that their shadows were as one.
5   The ordinary night was graced
For them by the swift tide of blood
That silently they took at flood,
And for a little time they prized
 Themselves emparadised.

10   Then, as if shaken by stage-fright
Beneath the hard moon's bony light,
They stood together on the sand
Embarrassed in each other's sight
But still conspiring hand in hand,
15   Until they saw, there underfoot,
As though the world had found them out,
The goose fish turning up, though dead,
 His hugely grinning head.

There in the china light he lay,
20   Most ancient and corrupt and gray
They hesitated at his smile,
Wondering what it seemed to say
To lovers who a little while
Before had thought to understand,
25   By violence upon the sand,
The only way that could be known
 To make a world their own.

It was a wide and moony grin
Together peaceful and obscene;
30   They knew not what he would express,
So finished a comedian
He might mean failure or success,
But took it for an emblem of
Their sudden, new and guilty love
35   To be observed by, when they kissed,
 That rigid optimist.

So he became their patriarch,
Dreadfully mild in the half-dark.
His throat that the sand seemed to choke,
40   His picket teeth, these left their mark
But never did explain the joke
That so amused him, lying there
While the moon went down to disappear
Along the still and tilted track
45   That bears the zodiac.

1955

A Primer of the Daily Round

A peels an apple, while B kneels to God,
C telephones to D, who has a hand

On E's knee, F coughs, G turns up the sod
For H's grave, I do not understand
5 But J is bringing one clay pigeon down
While K brings down a nightstick on L's head,
And M takes mustard, N drives into town,
O goes to bed with P, and Q drops dead,
R lies to S, but happens to be heard
10 By T, who tells U not to fire V
For having to give W the word
That X is now deceiving Y with Z,
Who happens just now to remember A
Peeling an apple somewhere far away.

                                                    1958

The Blue Swallows

Across the millstream below the bridge
Seven blue swallows divide the air
In shapes invisible and evanescent,
Kaleidoscopic beyond the mind's
5 Or memory's power to keep them there.

"History is where tensions were,"
"Form is the diagram of forces."
Thus, helplessly, there on the bridge,
While gazing down upon those birds—
10 How strange, to be above the birds!—
Thus helplessly the mind in its brain
Weaves up relation's spindrift web,
Seeing the swallows' tails as nibs
Dipped in invisible ink, writing . . .

15 Poor mind, what would you have them write?
Some cabalistic° history   occult
Whose authorship you might ascribe
To God? to Nature? Ah, poor ghost,
You've capitalized your Self enough.
20 That villainous William of Occam[1]
Cut out the feet from under that dream
Some seven centuries ago.
It's taken that long for the mind
To waken, yawn and stretch, to see
25 With opened eyes emptied of speech
The real world where the spelling mind
Imposes with its grammar book
Unreal relations on the blue
Swallows. Perhaps when you will have
30 Fully awakened, I shall show you
A new thing: even the water

1. Fourteenth-century scholastic philosopher; his central principle ("Occam's razor") was that the simplest, most economical explanation is always to be preferred to one that introduces unnecessary complications.

Flowing away beneath those birds
Will fail to reflect their flying forms,
And the eyes that see become as stones
35   Whence never tears shall fall again.

O swallows, swallows,[2] poems are not
The point. Finding again the world,
That is the point, where loveliness
Adorns intelligible things
40   Because the mind's eye lit the sun.

1967

Boy with Book of Knowledge[3]

He holds a volume open in his hands:
Sepia portraits of the hairy great,
The presidents and poets in their beards
Alike, simplified histories of the wars,
5   Conundrums, quizzes, riddles, games and poems,

"Immortal Poems"; at least he can't forget them,
Barbara Fritchie and the Battle Hymn,
And best of all America the Beautiful,[4]
Whose platitudinous splendors ended with
10   "From sea to shining sea," and made him cry

And wish to be a poet, only to say such things,
From sea to shining sea. Could that have been
Where it began? the vast pudding of knowledge,
With poetry rare as raisins in the midst
15   Of those gold-lettered volumes black and green?

Mere piety to think so. But being now
As near his deathday as his birthday then,
He would acknowledge all he will not know,
The silent library brooding through the night
20   With all its lights continuing to burn

Insomniac, a luxury liner on what sea
Unfathomable of ignorance who could say?
And poetry, as steady, still, and rare
As the lighthouses now unmanned and obsolete
25   That used to mark America's dangerous shores.

1975

---

2. Cf. T. S. Eliot, *The Waste Land* (1922), line 429 (p. 1248).
3. A type of reference book once used in schools.
4. "America the Beautiful" was often, and sometimes still is, sung in classrooms. "Barbara Friet- chie" (Nemerov misspelled it) by John Greenleaf Whittier (1807–1892) and the "Battle-Hymn of the Republic" (p. 952) by Julia Ward Howe (1819– 1910) were popular patriotic poems of the Civil War.

Easter

Even this suburb has overcome Death.
Overnight, by a slow explosion, or
A rapid burning, it begins again
Bravely disturbing the brown ground
5 With grass and even more elaborate
Unnecessaries such as daffodils
And tulips, till the whole sordid block
Of houses turned so inward on themselves,
So keeping of a winter's secret sleep,
10 Looks like a lady's hat, improbably
Nodding with life, with bluejays hooting
And pigeons caracoling[5] up among
The serious chimney pots, and pairs
Of small birds speeding behind the hedges
15 Readying to conceal them soon. Here,
Even here, Death has been vanquished again,
What was a bramble of green barbed wire
Becomes forsythia, as the long war
Begins again, not by our doing or desiring.

1980

The Historical Judas[6]

He too has an eternal part to play,
What did he understand? that good has scope
Only from evil, flowering in filth?
Did he go smiling, kissing, to betray
5 Out of a fine conviction of his truth,
Or some original wreckage of our hope?

If merely mistaken, at any rate,
He had a talent for the grand mistake,
The necessary one, without which not,
10 And managed to incur eternal hate
For triggering what destiny had got
Arranged from the beginning, for our sake.

Let us consider, then, if not forgive
This most distinguished of our fellow sinners,
15 Who sponsored our redemption with his sin,
And whose name, more than ours, shall surely live
To make our meanness look like justice in
All histories commissioned by the winners.

1980

---

5. Half turning to either side (a move performed by a horse and rider).
6. Judas Iscariot, the disciple who betrayed Jesus, identifying him with a kiss (see Matthew 26.14–50).

GEORGE MACKAY BROWN
1921–1996

The Old Women

Go sad or sweet or riotous with beer
Past the old women gossiping by the hour,
They'll fix on you from every close and pier
An acid look to make your veins run sour.

5 "No help," they say, "his grandfather that's dead
Was troubled with the same dry-throated curse,
And many a night he made the ditch his bed.
This blood comes welling from the same cracked source."

On every kind of merriment they frown.
10 But I have known a gray-eyed sober boy
Sail to the lobsters in a storm, and drown.
Over his body dripping on the stones
Those same old hags would weave into their moans
An undersong of terrible holy joy.

1959

Haddock Fishermen

Midnight. The wind yawing nor-east.
A low blunt moon.
Unquiet beside quiet wives we rest.

A spit of rain and a gull
5 In the open door.
The lit fire. A quick mouthful of ale.

We push the *Merle* at a sea of cold flame.
The oars drip honey.
Hook by hook uncoils under The Kame.

10 Our line breaks the trek of sudden thousands.
Twelve nobbled jaws,
Gray cowls, gape in our hands.

Twelve cold mouths scream without sound.
The sea is empty again.
15 Like tinkers° the bright ones endlessly shift their ground. *gypsies*

We probe emptiness all the afternoon,
Then pause and fill our teeth
With dependable food, beef and barley scone.

Sunset drags its butcher blade
20 From the day's throat.
We turn through an ebb salt and sticky as blood.

More stars than fish. Women, cats, a gull
Mewl at the rock.
The valley divides the meagre miracle.

1959

The Hawk

On Sunday the hawk fell on Bigging
  And a chicken screamed
  Lost in its own little snowstorm.
And on Monday he fell on the moor
5   And the Field Club
  Raised a hundred silent prisms.[1]
And on Tuesday he fell on the hill
  And the happy lamb
  Never knew why the loud collie straddled him.
10 And on Wednesday he fell on a bush
  And the blackbird
  Laid by his little flute for the last time.
And on Thursday he fell on Cleat
  And peerie Tom's rabbit
15 Swung in a single arc from shore to hill.
And on Friday he fell on a ditch
  But the rampant rat,
  That eye and that tooth, quenched his flame.
And on Saturday he fell on Bigging
20 And Jock lowered his gun
  And nailed a small wing over the corn.

1965

Shroud

Seven threads make the shroud,
  The white thread,
  A green corn thread,
  A blue fish thread,
5 A red stitch, rut and rieving and wrath,
  A gray thread
  (All winter failing hand falleth on wheel)
  The black thread,
  And a thread too bright for the eye.

1971

1. Lenses of binoculars.

MONA VAN DUYN

1921–

Letters from a Father

I

Ulcerated tooth keeps me awake, there is
such pain, would have to go to the hospital to have
it pulled or would bleed to death from the blood thinners,
but can't leave Mother, she falls and forgets her salve
5 and her tranquilizers, her ankles swell so and her bowels
are so bad, she almost had a stoppage and sometimes
what she passes is green as grass. There are big holes
in my thigh where my leg brace buckles the size of dimes.
My head pounds from the high pressure. It is awful
10 not to be able to get out, and I fell in the bathroom
and the girl could hardly get me up at all.
Sure thought my back was broken, it will be next time.
Prostate is bad and heart has given out,
feel bloated after supper. Have made my peace
15 because am just plain done for and have no doubt
that the Lord will come any day with my release.
You say you enjoy your feeder, I don't see why
you want to spend good money on grain for birds
and you say you have a hundred sparrows, I'd buy
20 poison and get rid of their diseases and turds.

II

We enjoyed your visit, it was nice of you to bring
the feeder but a terrible waste of your money
for that big bag of feed since we won't be living
more than a few weeks longer. We can see
25 them good from where we sit, big ones and little ones
but you know when I farmed I used to like to hunt
and we had many a good meal from pigeons
and quail and pheasant but these birds won't
be good for nothing and are dirty to have so near
30 the house. Mother likes the redbirds though.
My bad knee is so sore and I can't hardly hear
and Mother says she is hoarse from yelling but I know
it's too late for a hearing aid. I belch up all the time
and have a sour mouth and of course with my heart
35 it's no use to go to a doctor. Mother is the same.
Has a scab she thinks is going to turn to a wart.

III

The birds are eating and fighting, Ha! Ha! All shapes
and colors and sizes coming out of our woods
but we don't know what they are. Your Mother hopes
40 you can send us a kind of book that tells about birds.

There is one the folks called snowbirds, they eat on the ground,
we had the girl sprinkle extra there, but say,
they eat something awful. I sent the girl to town
to buy some more feed, she had to go anyway.

IV

45 Almost called you on the telephone
but it costs so much to call thought better write.
Say, the funniest thing is happening, one
day we had so many birds and they fight
and get excited at their feed you know
50 and it's really something to watch and two or three
flew right at us and crashed into our window
and bang, poor little things knocked themselves silly.
They come to after awhile on the ground and flew away.
And they been doing that. We felt awful
55 and didn't know what to do but the other day
a lady from our Church drove out to call
and a little bird knocked itself out while she sat
and she brought it in her hands right into the house,
it looked like dead. It had a kind of hat
60 of feathers sticking up on its head, kind of rose
or pinky color, don't know what it was,
and I petted it and it come to life right there
in her hands and she took it out and it flew. She says
they think the window is the sky on a fair
65 day, she feeds birds too but hasn't got
so many. She says to hang strips of aluminum foil
in the window so we'll do that. She raved about
our birds. P.S. The book just come in the mail.

V

Say, that book is sure good, I study
70 in it every day and enjoy our birds.
Some of them I can't identify
for sure, I guess they're females, the Latin words
I just skip over. Bet you'd never guess
the sparrows I've got here, House Sparrows you wrote,
75 but I have Fox Sparrows, Song Sparrows, Vesper Sparrows,
Pine Woods and Tree and Chipping and White Throat
and White Crowned Sparrows. I have six Cardinals,
three pairs, they come at early morning and night,
the males at the feeder and on the ground the females.
80 Juncos, maybe 25, they fight
for the ground, that's what they used to call snowbirds. I miss
the Bluebirds since the weather warmed. Their breast
is the color of a good ripe muskmelon. Tufted Titmouse
is sort of blue with a little tiny crest.
85 And I have Flicker and Red-Bellied and Red-
Headed Woodpeckers, you would die laughing
to see Red-Bellied, he hangs on with his head
flat on the board, his tail braced up under,

wing out. And Dickcissel and Ruby Crowned Ringlet
90 and Nuthatch stands on his head and Veery on top
the color of a bird dog and Hermit Thrush with spot
on breast, Blue Jay so funny, he will hop
right on the backs of the other birds to get the grain.
We bought some sunflower seeds just for him.
95 And Purple Finch I bet you never seen,
color of a watermelon, sits on the rim
of the feeder with his streaky wife, and the squirrels,
you know, they are cute too, they sit tall
and eat with their little hands, they eat bucketfuls.
100 I pulled my own tooth, it didn't bleed at all.

VI

It's sure a surprise how well Mother is doing,
she forgets her laxative but bowels move fine.
Now that windows are open she says our birds sing
all day. The girl took a Book of Knowledge[1] on loan
105 from the library and I am reading up
on the habits of birds, did you know some males have three
wives, some migrate some don't. I am going to keep
feeding all spring, maybe summer, you can see
they expect it. Will need thistle seed for Goldfinch and Pine
110 Siskin next winter. Some folks are going to come see us
from Church, some bird watchers, pretty soon.
They have birds in town but nothing to equal this.

So the world woos its children back for an evening kiss.

1982

Falling in Love at Sixty-Five

It is like the first and last time I tried a Coleman°   *lamp*
for reading in bed in Maine. Too early the camp
went dark for fossil habits, no longer could candleflame
convince my eyes, and I lit that scary lamp.
5 Instant outcry came from the savage white light
of the mantles, as if a star had been brought down
out of space and trapped by the unchinked logs of the bedroom,
roaring its threat to explode the walls and be gone,
or as if the lamp could tell time and knew that one tongue
10 was no longer enough to speak with, it must double its blare,
overwhelm two senses at once, that the jaded heart
might burst into ravished applause for its *son et lumière*.[2]

Perched on a pile of books on the seat of a chair
drawn to the head of the bed, the lamp called out
15 the guilty years and shamed them for cracks and shrivels
that bent the patient, scabbed logs of the walls and ceiling.

---

1. A general reference book.   2. "Sound and light show" (French).

Then I opened a book whose every radiant page
was illuminated in colors of lightning and thunder
by the quick-witted lamp in its artistry of rage.
20   The book and the lamp fused to one voice, whose sense
became mine, strokes of a slow, rhythmic broom
swept a dusty pith that seemed to lie still until
some other sense told me that there were wings in the room.

In one much earlier year I had fallen asleep
25   in the meadow, head near bright heights of fireweed, fireweed
strewn on my chest from a hand that let go its bouquet,
and had wakened at eyelash touches, the delicate need
of five blue butterflies that found me in bloom.
Now, striking my neck and cheeks, came the first
30   wave of this late invasion, three flying bugs
that hit me, lit, flew again, hit, an outburst
the lamp had called for through log-gaps and screenholes, then
more entered the air, winged in gray, brown, dun,
and more, as I tried to read on, in the muted shades
35   brushed on by sundown's dimming imagination.

Beetle-bodied or light as moths they came
and, big and small, bombed the lit skin of face,
arms, shoulders, rested, crawled, unfurled, and sent
the blind wanting that stuffed full each one's carapace
40   in a clicking crash at the lampglass, then crazily flew
back to me, the bared part of me becoming a plan
for plates of an insect book whose specimens
rearranged themselves fiercely over and over again.
For as long as the lantern lasted they would have kept coming,
45   as if the grave darkness had smiled at that tiny dawn
and had hurled them in fistfuls straight at the speaking light
in answer to what was being insisted upon.

1990

RICHARD WILBUR

1921–

First Snow in Alsace[1]

The snow came down last night like moths
Burned on the moon; it fell till dawn,
Covered the town with simple cloths.

Absolute snow lies rumpled on
5   What shellbursts scattered and deranged,
Entangled railings, crevassed lawn.

---

1. Region of northern France.

As if it did not know they'd changed,
Snow smoothly clasps the roofs of homes
Fear-gutted, trustless and estranged.

10   The ration stacks are milky domes;
Across the ammunition pile
The snow has climbed in sparkling combs.

You think: beyond the town a mile
Or two, this snowfall fills the eyes
15   Of soldiers dead a little while.

Persons and persons in disguise,
Walking the new air white and fine,
Trade glances quick with shared surprise.

At children's windows, heaped, benign,
20   As always, winter shines the most,
And frost makes marvelous designs.

The night guard coming from his post,
Ten first-snows back in thought, walks slow
And warms him with a boyish boast:

25   He was the first to see the snow.

1947

Praise in Summer

Obscurely yet most surely called to praise,
As sometimes summer calls us all, I said
The hills are heavens full of branching ways
Where star-nosed moles fly overhead the dead;
5   I said the trees are mines in air, I said
See how the sparrow burrows in the sky!
And then I wondered why this mad *instead*
Perverts our praise to uncreation, why
Such savor's in this wrenching things awry.
10   Does sense so stale that it must needs derange
The world to know it? To a praiseful eye
Should it not be enough of fresh and strange
That trees grow green, and moles can course in clay,
And sparrows sweep the ceiling of our day?

1947

Love Calls Us to the Things of This World[2]

The eyes open to a cry of pulleys,
And spirited from sleep, the astounded soul
Hangs for a moment bodiless and simple
As false dawn.

---

2. A quotation from St. Augustine (A.D. 354–430).

Outside the open window
5   The morning air is all awash with angels.

Some are in bed-sheets, some are in blouses,
Some are in smocks: but truly there they are.
Now they are rising together in calm swells
Of halcyon feeling, filling whatever they wear
10   With the deep joy of their impersonal breathing;

Now they are flying in place, conveying
The terrible speed of their omnipresence, moving
And staying like white water; and now of a sudden
They swoon down into so rapt a quiet
That nobody seems to be there.
15   The soul shrinks

From all that it is about to remember,
From the punctual rape of every blessèd day,
And cries,
        "Oh, let there be nothing on earth but laundry,
Nothing but rosy hands in the rising steam
20   And clear dances done in the sight of heaven."

Yet, as the sun acknowledges
With a warm look the world's hunks and colors,
The soul descends once more in bitter love
To accept the waking body, saying now
25   In a changed voice as the man yawns and rises,

"Bring them down from their ruddy gallows;
Let there be clean linen for the backs of thieves;
Let lovers go fresh and sweet to be undone,
And the heaviest nuns walk in a pure floating
Of dark habits,
30   keeping their difficult balance."

1956

Piazza di Spagna,[3] Early Morning

I can't forget
How she stood at the top of that long marble stair
Amazed, and then with a sleepy pirouette
Went dancing slowly down to the fountain-quieted square;

5   Nothing upon her face
But some impersonal loneliness, — not then a girl,
But as it were a reverie of the place,
A called-for falling glide and whirl;

As when a leaf, petal, or thin chip
10   Is drawn to the falls of a pool and, circling a moment above it,

3. Plaza in Rome, famous for its long, curved stairway.

Rides on over the lip—
Perfectly beautiful, perfectly ignorant of it.

1956

A Plain Song for Comadre[4]

Though the unseen may vanish, though insight fails
And doubter and downcast saint
Join in the same complaint,
What holy things were ever frightened off
5 By a fly's buzz, or itches, or a cough?
Harder than nails

They are, more warmly constant than the sun,
At whose continual sign
The dimly prompted vine
10 Upbraids itself to a green excellence.
What evening, when the slow and forced expense
Of sweat is done,

Does not the dark come flooding the straight furrow
Or filling the well-made bowl?
15 What night will not the whole
Sky with its clear studs and steady spheres
Turn on a sound chimney? It is seventeen years
Come tomorrow

That Bruna Sandoval has kept the church
20 Of San Ysidro,[5] sweeping
And scrubbing the aisles, keeping
The candlesticks and the plaster faces bright,
And seen no visions but the thing done right
From the clay porch

25 To the white altar. For love and in all weathers
This is what she has done.
Sometimes the early sun
Shines as she flings the scrubwater out, with a crash
Of grimy rainbows, and the stained suds flash
30 Like angel-feathers.

1956

A Baroque Wall-Fountain in the Villa Sciarra[6]

For Dore and Adja

Under the bronze crown
Too big for the head of the stone cherub whose feet
A serpent has begun to eat,
Sweet water brims a cockle[7] and braids down

---

4. Here, "peasant woman" (Spanish); can mean "midwife," "godmother," "neighbor." "Plain song" (or plainsong): the unisonous vocal music of the early Christian Church; also, any simple melody.

5. Village in San Diego County, near the Mexican border.
6. A large public park in Rome.
7. Shell-shaped basin, part of the fountain.

5   Past spattered mosses, breaks
On the tipped edge of a second shell, and fills
The massive third below. It spills
In threads then from the scalloped rim, and makes

     A scrim or summery tent
10   For a faun-ménage[8] and their familiar goose.
Happy in all that ragged, loose
Collapse of water, its effortless descent

     And flatteries of spray,
The stocky god upholds the shell with ease,
15   Watching, about his shaggy knees,
The goatish innocence of his babes at play;

     His fauness all the while
Leans forward, slightly, into a clambering mesh
Of water-lights, her sparkling flesh
20   In a saecular[9] ecstasy, her blinded smile

     Bent on the sand floor
Of the trefoil° pool, where ripple-shadows come   *three-leaved*
And go in swift reticulum,[1]
More addling to the eye than wine, and more

25   Interminable to thought
Than pleasure's calculus. Yet since this all
Is pleasure, flash, and waterfall,
Must it not be too simple? Are we not

     More intricately expressed
30   In the plain fountains that Maderna[2] set
Before St. Peter's—the main jet
Struggling aloft until it seems at rest

     In the act of rising, until
The very wish of water is reversed,
35   That heaviness borne up to burst
In a clear, high, cavorting head, to fill

     With blaze, and then in gauze
Delays, in a gnatlike shimmering, in a fine
Illumined version of itself, decline,
40   And patter on the stones its own applause?

     If that is what men are
Or should be, if those water-saints display

---

8. Group surrounding the faun, a lusty rural god usually pictured with a goat's legs and tail.
9. Lasting for ages (punning on *secular,* "worldly").
1. A netlike formation.

2. Carlo Maderno (1556–1629), architect and designer responsible for giving St. Peter's Basilica in Rome the shape of a cross, and for completing the facade.

The pattern of our areté,[3]
What of these showered fauns in their bizarre,

45   Spangled, and plunging house?
They are at rest in fulness of desire
    For what is given, they do not tire
Of the smart of the sun, the pleasant water-douse

        And riddled pool below,
50 Reproving our disgust and our ennui
    With humble insatiety.
Francis,[4] perhaps, who lay in sister snow

        Before the wealthy gate
Freezing and praising, might have seen in this
55   No trifle, but a shade of bliss—
That land of tolerable flowers, that state

        As near and far as grass
Where eyes become the sunlight, and the hand
    Is worthy of water: the dreamt land
60 Toward which all hungers leap, all pleasures pass.

1956

Advice to a Prophet

When you come, as you soon must, to the streets of our city,
    Mad-eyed from stating the obvious,
Not proclaiming our fall but begging us
    In God's name to have self-pity,

5 Spare us all word of the weapons, their force and range,
    The long numbers that rocket the mind;
Our slow, unreckoning hearts will be left behind,
    Unable to fear what is too strange.

Nor shall you scare us with talk of the death of the race.
10   How should we dream of this place without us?—
The sun mere fire, the leaves untroubled about us,
    A stone look on the stone's face?

Speak of the world's own change. Though we cannot conceive
    Of an undreamt thing, we know to our cost
15 How the dreamt cloud crumbles, the vines are blackened by frost,
    How the view alters. We could believe,

If you told us so, that the white-tailed deer will slip
    Into perfect shade, grown perfectly shy,
The lark avoid the reaches of our eye,
20 The jack-pine lose its knuckled grip

---

3. "A Greek word meaning roughly 'virtue'" [Wilbur's note].   4. I.e., St. Francis of Assisi (1182–1226), known for his vow of poverty and love of nature.

On the cold ledge, and every torrent burn
As Xanthus[5] once, its gliding trout
Stunned in a twinkling. What should we be without
The dolphin's arc, the dove's return,

25 These things in which we have seen ourselves and spoken?
Ask us, prophet, how we shall call
Our natures forth when that live tongue is all
Dispelled, that glass obscured or broken

In which we have said the rose of our love and the clean
30 Horse of our courage, in which beheld
The singing locust of the soul unshelled,
And all we mean or wish to mean.

Ask us, ask us whether with the worldless rose
Our hearts shall fail us; come demanding
35 Whether there shall be lofty or long standing
When the bronze annals of the oak-tree close.

1961

Junk

Huru Welandes
                    worc ne geswiceð
monna ænigum
                    ðara ðe Mimming can
heardne gehealdan.
                    —Waldere[6]

An axe angles
                    from my neighbor's ashcan;
It is hell's handiwork,
                    the wood not hickory,
5 The flow of the grain
                    not faithfully followed.
The shivered shaft
                    rises from a shellheap
Of plastic playthings,
10   paper plates,
And the sheer shards
                    of shattered tumblers
That were not annealed
                    for the time needful.
15 At the same curbside,
                    a cast-off cabinet
Of wavily-warped
                    unseasoned wood
Waits to be trundled

5. "Haphaestus, invoked by Achilles, scalded the river Xanthus (Scamander) in *Iliad, xxi*" [Wilbur's note].
6. *Waldere* (or *Waldhere*) is the name of an Old English heroic poem. "The epigraph, taken from a fragmentary Anglo-Saxon poem, concerns the leg- endary smith Wayland, and may roughly be translated: 'Truly, Wayland's handiwork—the sword Mimming which he made—will never fail any man who knows how to use it bravely' " [Wilbur's note].

20   in the trash-man's truck.
Haul them off! Hide them!
                           The heart winces
For junk and gimcrack,
                    for jerrybuilt things
25 And the men who make them
                         for a little money,
Bartering pride
              like the bought boxer
Who pulls his punches,
30   or the paid-off jockey
Who in the home stretch
                holds in his horse.
Yet the things themselves
              in thoughtless honor
35 Have kept composure,
              like captives who would not
Talk under torture.
           Tossed from a tailgate
Where the dump displays
40   its random dolmens,[7]
Its black barrows
            and blazing valleys,
They shall waste in the weather
              toward what they were.
45 The sun shall glory
            in the glitter of glass-chips,
Foreseeing the salvage
             of the prisoned sand,
And the blistering paint
50   peel off in patches,
That the good grain
            be discovered again.
Then burnt, bulldozed,
            they shall all be buried
55 To the depth of diamonds,
             in the making dark
Where halt Hephaestus[8]
           keeps his hammer
And Wayland's work
60   is worn away.

                                1961

Seed Leaves

Homage to R. F.[9]

Here something stubborn comes,
Dislodging the earth crumbs
And making crusty rubble.

---

7. Prehistoric monuments of horizontal stone slabs supported by upright stones, believed to be tombs.

8. Greek god of fire and the forge.

9. Robert Frost (1874–1963), American poet; see pp. 1121–40.

It comes up bending double,
5   And looks like a green staple.
It could be seedling maple,
Or artichoke, or bean.
That remains to be seen.

Forced to make choice of ends,
10 The stalk in time unbends,
Shakes off the seed-case, heaves
Aloft, and spreads two leaves
Which still display no sure
And special signature.
15 Toothless and fat, they keep
The oval form of sleep.

This plant would like to grow
And yet be embryo;
Increase, and yet escape
20 The doom of taking shape;
Be vaguely vast, and climb
To the tip end of time
With all of space to fill,
Like boundless Igdrasil[1]
25 That has the stars for fruit.

But something at the root
More urgent than that urge
Bids two true leaves emerge,
And now the plant, resigned
30 To being self-defined
Before it can commerce
With the great universe,
Takes aim at all the sky
And starts to ramify.

1969

DONALD DAVIE

1922–1995

Remembering the 'Thirties

I

Hearing one saga, we enact the next.
We please our elders when we sit enthralled;
But then they're puzzled; and at last they're vexed
To have their youth so avidly recalled.

---

1. Also Yggdrasil, in Scandinavian myth an enormous ash tree that grew in the middle of the world and united three realms: the underworld, the Earth, and the Aesir gods' home above.

5   It dawns upon the veterans after all
That what for them were agonies, for us
Are high-brow thrillers, though historical;
And all their feats quite strictly fabulous.

This novel written fifteen years ago,
10 Set in my boyhood and my boyhood home,
These poems about "abandoned workings", show
Worlds more remote than Ithaca or Rome.

The Anschluss,[1] Guernica—all the names
At which those poets thrilled or were afraid
15 For me mean schools and schoolmasters and games;
And in the process some-one is betrayed.

Ourselves perhaps. The Devil for a joke
Might carve his own initials on our desk,
And yet we'd miss the point because he spoke
20 An idiom too dated, Audenesque.

Ralegh's Guiana also killed his son.[2]
A pretty pickle if we came to see
The tallest story really packed a gun,
The Telemachiad an Odyssey.[3]

II

25 Even to them the tales were not so true
As not to be ridiculous as well;
The ironmaster met his Waterloo,[4]
But Rider Haggard[5] rode along the fell.

"Leave for Cape Wrath tonight!" They lounged away
30 On Fleming's trek or Isherwood's ascent.[6]
England expected every man that day
To show his motives were ambivalent.

They played the fool, not to appear as fools
In time's long glass. A deprecating air
35 Disarmed, they thought, the jeers of later schools;
Yet irony itself is doctrinaire,

And curiously, nothing now betrays
Their type to time's derision like this coy

---

1. "Union" (German): name given to the German seizure of Austria in March 1938; "Guernica": Spanish town bombed by German aircraft in the Spanish Civil War, an event commemorated by Picasso's famous painting called "Guernica" (1937).
2. In search of gold, Sir Walter Ralegh (ca. 1552–1618), courtier-poet (see pp. 139–46), led a military expedition to Guyana, in West Africa, on which his son was killed in 1617.

3. Telemachus was the son of Odysseus, the story of whose wandering and eventual return to his wife and son is told in Homer's Odyssey.
4. Battle of 1815 in which Napolean was finally defeated.
5. Writer of boys' adventure stories.
6. Reference to a play, The Ascent of F6 (1936), by Christopher Isherwood and W. H. Auden; Peter Fleming (1907–1971), British explorer and travel writer.

Insistence on the quizzical, their craze
40 For showing Hector[7] was a mother's boy.

A neutral tone is nowadays preferred.
And yet it may be better, if we must,
To praise a stance impressive and absurd
Than not to see the hero for the dust.

45 For courage is the vegetable king,
The sprig of all ontologies, the weed
That beards the slag-heap with his hectoring,
Whose green adventure is to run to seed.

1955

The Fountain

Feathers up fast, and steeples; then in clods
Thuds into its first basin; thence as surf
Smokes up and hangs; irregularly slops
Into its second, tattered like a shawl;
5 There, chill as rain, stipples a danker green,
Where urgent tritons lob their heavy jets.

For Berkeley[8] this was human thought, that mounts
From bland assumptions to inquiring skies,
There glints with wit, fumes into fancies, plays
10 With its negations, and at last descends,
As by a law of nature, to its bowl
Of thus enlightened but still common sense.

We who have no such confidence must gaze
With all the more affection on these forms,
15 These spires, these plumes, these calm reflections, these
Similitudes of surf and turf and shawl,
Graceful returns upon acceptances.
We ask of fountains only that they play,

Though that was not what Berkeley meant at all.

1957

Rejoinder to a Critic

You may be right: "How can I dare to feel?"
May be the only question I can pose,
"And haply by abstruse research to steal
From my own nature all the natural man"
5 My sole resource. And I do not suppose
That others may not have a better plan.

---

7. Leader of the Trojans at the siege of Troy.
8. George Berkeley (1685–1753), Irish bishop and philosopher, who maintained that the world is not an independent entity of which our minds may be an effect, but, rather, depends on our sensory perception for its existence.

And yet I'll quote again, and gloss it too
(You know by now my liking for collage):
Donne could be daring, but he never knew,
10   When he inquired, "Who's injured by my love?"[9]
Love's radio-active fall-out on a large
Expanse around the point it bursts above.

"Alas, alas, who's injured by my love?"
And recent history answers: Half Japan!
15   Not love, but hate? Well, both are versions of
The "feeling" that you dare me to . . . Be dumb!
Appear concerned only to make it scan!
How dare we now be anything but numb?

1957

Time Passing, Beloved

Time passing, and the memories of love
Coming back to me, carissima,[1] no more mockingly
Than ever before; time passing, unslackening,
Unhastening, steadily; and no more
5   Bitterly, beloved, the memories of love
Coming into the shore.

How will it end? Time passing and our passages of love
As ever, beloved, blind
As ever before; time binding, unbinding
10   About us; and yet to remember
Never less chastening, nor the flame of love
Less like an ember.

What will become of us? Time
Passing, beloved, and we in a sealed
15   Assurance unassailed
By memory. How can it end,
This siege of a shore that no misgivings have steeled,
No doubts defend?

1957

SIDNEY KEYES
1922–1943

From The Foreign Gate

The moon is a poor woman.
The moon returns to weep with us. The crosses
Burn raw and white upon the night's stiff banners.
The wooden crosses and the marble trees

9. Cf. John Donne, "The Canonization" (pp.   1. "Darling" (Italian).
266–67).

5   Shrink from the foreign moon.
     The iron gate glitters. Here the soldiers lie.
     Fold up the flags, muffle the soldier's drum;
     Silence the calling fife. O drape
     The soldier's drum with heavy crêpe;
10   With mourning weeds muffle the soldier's girl.
     It's a long way and a long march
     To the returning moon and to the soil
     No time at all.
             O call
15   The soldier's glory by another name:
     Shroud up the soldier's common shame
     And drape the soldier's drum, but spare
     The steel-caged brain, the feet that walk to war.

     Once striding under a horsehair plume
20   Once beating the taut drums for war
     The sunlight rang from brass and iron;
     History was an angry play—
     The boy grew tall and rode away;
     The door hung slack; the pale girl wept
25   And cursed the company he kept.
     And dumb men spoke
     Through the glib mouths of smoke;
     The servile learned to strike
     The proud to shriek;
30   And strangled in their lovers' lips
     The young fell short of glory in the sand
     Raking for graves among the scattered sand;
     The tattered flags strained at the wind
     Scaring the thrifty kite, mocking the dead.
35   But muffle the soldier's drum, hide his pale head,
     His face a spider's web of blood. O fold
     The hands that grip a splintered gun.
           The glittering gate
     Baffles him still, his starvecrow soul. O drape
40   The soldier's drum and cry, who never dare
     Defy the ironbound brain, the feet that walk to war.

     The cold hand clenches. The stupid mouth
     Writhes like a ripple. Now the field is full
     Of noises and dead voices . . .
45   "My rags flap
     Though the great flags are trampled . . ."
                     "My mouth speaks
     Terror and truth, instead of hard command."
     "Remember the torn lace, the fine coats slashed
50   With steel instead of velvet. Künersdorf
     Fought in the shallow sand was my relief."
     "I rode to Naseby" . . . "And the barren land
     Of Tannenberg drank me.[1] Remember now

1. Famous battles from different periods of history.

The grey and jointed corpses in the snow,
55   The struggle in the drift, the numb hands freezing
Into the bitter iron . . ."
                  "At Dunkirk I
Rolled in the shallows, and the living trod
Across me for a bridge . . ."
60   "Let me speak out
Against this sham of policy, for pain
Alone is true. I was a general
Who fought the cunning Africans, returned
Crowned with harsh laurel, frantically cheered
65   Through Roman streets. I spoke of fame and glory.
Women grabbed at my robe. Great poets praised me.
I died of cancer, screaming, in a year."
"I fell on a black Spanish hillside
Under the thorn-hedge, fighting for a dream
70   That troubled me in Paris; vomited
My faith and courage out among the stones . . ."
"I was a barb of light, a burning cross
Of wood and canvas, falling through the night."
"I was shot down at morning, in a yard."

75   The moon regards them without shame. The wind
Rises and twitters through the wreck of bone . . .
              "It is so hard to be alone
Continually, watching the great stars march
Their circular unending route; sharp sand
80   Straying about the eyes, blinding the quick-eyed spirit."
A soldier's death is hard;
There's no prescribed or easy word
For dissolution in the Army books.
The uniform of pain with pain put on is straiter
85   Than any lover's garment; yet the death
Of these is different, and their glory greater.
Once men, then moving figures on a map,
Patiently giving time and strength and vision
Even identity
90   Into the future's keeping;
Nourished on wounds and weeping
Faces and laughing flags and pointed laurels,
Their pain cries down the noise of poetry.

So muffle the soldier's drum, forget the battles;
95   Remember only fame's a way of living:
The writing may be greater than the speaking
And every death for something different
From time's compulsion, is a written word.
Whatever gift, it is the giving
100   Remains significant: whatever death
It is the dying matters.
                     Emblematic
Bronze eagle or bright banner or carved name
Of fighting ancestor; these never pardon

105 The pain and sorrow. It is the dying pardons,
For something different from man or emblem.
Then drape the soldier's drum
And carry him down
Beyond the moon's inspection, and the noise
110 Of bands and banners and the striking sun.
Scatter the soldier's emblems and his fame:
Shroud up the shattered face, the empty name;
Speak out the word and drape the drum and spare
The captive brain, the feet that walk to war
115 The ironbound brain, the hand unskilled in war
The shrinking brain, sick of an inner war.

1942   1942

War Poet

I am the man who looked for peace and found
My own eyes barbed.
I am the man who groped for words and found
An arrow in my hand.
5 I am the builder whose firm walls surround
A slipping land.
When I grow sick or mad
Mock me not nor chain me:
When I reach for the wind
10 Cast me not down:
Though my face is a burnt book
And a wasted town.

1942   1943

Elegy

(In memoriam S. K. K.)[2]

April again, and it is a year again
Since you walked out and slammed the door
Leaving us tangled in your words. Your brain
Lives in the bank-book, and your eyes look up
5 Laughing from the carpet on the floor:
And we still drink from your silver cup.

It is a year again since they poured
The dumb ground into your mouth:
And yet we know, by some recurring word
10 Or look caught unawares, that you still drive
Our thoughts like the smart cobs of your youth—
When you and the world were alive.

A year again, and we have fallen on bad times
Since they gave you to the worms.
15 I am ashamed to take delight in these rhymes

2. Keyes was sixteen when he wrote this elegy for his grandfather.

Without grief; but you need no tears.
We shall never forget nor escape you, nor make terms
With your enemies, the swift departing years.

1938   1945

PHILIP LARKIN ✦

1922–1985

Church Going

Once I am sure there's nothing going on
I step inside, letting the door thud shut.
Another church: matting, seats, and stone,
And little books; sprawlings of flowers, cut
5   For Sunday, brownish now; some brass and stuff
Up at the holy end; the small neat organ;
And a tense, musty unignorable silence,
Brewed God knows how long. Hatless, I take off
My cycle-clips in awkward reverence,

10   Move forward, run my hand around the font.
From where I stand, the roof looks almost new—
Cleaned, or restored? Someone would know: I don't.
Mounting the lectern, I peruse a few
Hectoring large-scale verses, and pronounce
15   "Here endeth" much more loudly than I'd meant.
The echoes snigger briefly. Back at the door
I sign the book, donate an Irish sixpence,[1]
Reflect the place was not worth stopping for.

Yet stop I did: in fact I often do,
20   And always end much at a loss like this,
Wondering what to look for; wondering, too,
When churches fall completely out of use
What we shall turn them into, if we shall keep
A few cathedrals chronically on show,
25   Their parchment, plate and pyx[2] in locked cases,
And let the rest rent-free to rain and sheep.
Shall we avoid them as unlucky places?

Or, after dark, will dubious women come
To make their children touch a particular stone;
30   Pick simples[3] for a cancer; or on some
Advised night see walking a dead one?
Power of some sort or other will go on
In games, in riddles, seemingly at random;
But superstition, like belief, must die,

---

1. An Irish sixpence has no value in England.   3. Medicinal herbs.
2. Box in which communion wafers are kept.

35 And what remains when disbelief has gone?
Grass, weedy pavement, brambles, buttress, sky,

A shape less recognisable each week,
A purpose more obscure. I wonder who
Will be the last, the very last, to seek
40 This place for what it was; one of the crew
That tap and jot and know what rood-lofts[4] were?
Some ruin-bibber, randy for antique,
Or Christmas-addict, counting on a whiff
Of gown-and-bands and organ-pipes and myrrh?[5]
45 Or will he be my representative,

Bored, uninformed, knowing the ghostly silt
Dispersed, yet tending to this cross of ground
Through suburb scrub because it held unspilt
So long and equably what since is found
50 Only in separation—marriage, and birth,
And death, and thoughts of these—for which was built
This special shell? For, though I've no idea
What this accoutred frowsty barn is worth,
It pleases me to stand in silence here;

55 A serious house on serious earth it is,
In whose blent air all our compulsions meet,
Are recognized, and robed as destinies.
And that much never can be obsolete,
Since someone will forever be surprising
60 A hunger in himself to be more serious,
And gravitating with it to this ground,
Which, he once heard, was proper to grow wise in,
If only that so many dead lie round.

1954   1955

For Sidney Bechet[6]

That note you hold, narrowing and rising, shakes
Like New Orleans reflected on the water,
And in all ears appropriate falsehood wakes,

Building for some a legendary Quarter
5 Of balconies, flower-baskets and quadrilles,[7]
Everyone making love and going shares—

Oh, play that thing! Mute glorious Storyvilles[8]
Others may license, grouping round their chairs
Sporting-house girls like circus tigers (priced

4. Galleries on top of carved screens separating the nave of a church from the choir.
5. Gum resin, from trees of genus *Commiphora*, used in the making of incense; one of three presents given by the Three Wise Men to the infant Jesus. "Gown-and-bands": gown and decorative collar worn by clergymen.
6. (1897–1959); American jazz clarinetist and saxophonist.
7. Square dance for couples.
8. Cf. Thomas Gray, "Elegy Written in a Country Churchyard" (p. 609): "Some mute inglorious Milton here may rest."

10 Far above rubies) to pretend their fads,
While scholars *manqués*[9] nod around unnoticed
Wrapped up in personnels like old plaids.

On me your voice falls as they say love should,
Like an enormous yes. My Crescent City
15 Is where your speech alone is understood,

And greeted as the natural noise of good,
Scattering long-haired grief and scored pity.

1954   1964

An Arundel[1] Tomb

Side by side, their faces blurred,
The earl and countess lie in stone,
Their proper habits° vaguely shown   costumes
As jointed armour, stiffened pleat,
5   And that faint hint of the absurd—
The little dogs under their feet.

Such plainness of the pre-baroque
Hardly involves the eye, until
It meets his left-hand gauntlet, still
10   Clasped empty in the other; and
One sees, with a sharp tender shock
His hand withdrawn, holding her hand.

They would not think to lie so long.
Such faithfulness in effigy
15   Was just a detail friends would see:
A sculptor's sweet commissioned grace
Thrown off in helping to prolong
The Latin names around the base.

They would not guess how early in
20   Their supine stationary voyage
The air would change to soundless damage,
Turn the old tenantry away;
How soon succeeding eyes begin
To look, not read. Rigidly they

25   Persisted, linked, through lengths and breadths
Of time. Snow fell, undated. Light
Each summer thronged the glass. A bright
Litter of birdcalls strewed the same
Bone-riddled ground. And up the paths
30   The endless altered people came,

Washing at their identity.
Now, helpless in the hollow of

9. Would-be scholars.   1. English aristocratic family.

An unarmorial age, a trough
Of smoke in slow suspended skeins
35   Above their scrap of history,
Only an attitude remains:

Time has transfigured them into
Untruth. The stone fidelity
They hardly meant has come to be
40   Their final blazon,° and to prove   record of virtue
Our almost-instinct almost true:
What will survive of us is love.

1956   1964

The Whitsun² Weddings

That Whitsun, I was late getting away:
        Not till about
One-twenty on the sunlit Saturday
Did my three-quarters-empty train pull out,
5   All windows down, all cushions hot, all sense
Of being in a hurry gone. We ran
Behind the backs of houses, crossed a street
Of blinding windscreens, smelt the fish-dock; thence
The river's level drifting breadth began,
10   Where sky and Lincolnshire and water meet.

All afternoon, through the tall heat that slept
        For miles inland,
A slow and stopping curve southwards we kept.
Wide farms went by, short-shadowed cattle, and
15   Canals with floatings of industrial froth;
A hothouse flashed uniquely: hedges dipped
And rose: and now and then a smell of grass
Displaced the reek of buttoned carriage-cloth
Until the next town, new and nondescript,
20   Approached with acres of dismantled cars.

At first, I didn't notice what a noise
        The weddings made
Each station that we stopped at: sun destroys
The interest of what's happening in the shade,
25   And down the long cool platforms whoops and skirls°   shrill cries
I took for porters larking with the mails,
And went on reading. Once we started, though,
We passed them, grinning and pomaded, girls
In parodies of fashion, heels and veils,
30   All posed irresolutely, watching us go,

As if out on the end of an event
        Waving goodbye

2. The seventh Sunday after Easter, commemorat-
ing the day of Pentecost, when converts to the
early Christian Church wore white robes. In the

1950s, British tax law made the Whitsun weekend
a financially advantageous time to be married.

To something that survived it. Struck, I leant
More promptly out next time, more curiously,
35   And saw it all again in different terms:
The fathers with broad belts under their suits
And seamy foreheads; mothers loud and fat;
An uncle shouting smut; and then the perms,
The nylon gloves and jewellery-substitutes,
40   The lemons, mauves, and olive-ochres that

Marked off the girls unreally from the rest.
   Yes, from cafés
And banquet-halls up yards, and bunting-dressed
Coach-party annexes, the wedding-days
45   Were coming to an end. All down the line
Fresh couples climbed aboard: the rest stood round;
The last confetti and advice were thrown,
And, as we moved, each face seemed to define
Just what it saw departing: children frowned
50   At something dull; fathers had never known

Success so huge and wholly farcical;
   The women shared
The secret like a happy funeral;
While girls, gripping their handbags tighter, stared
55   At a religious wounding. Free at last,
And loaded with the sum of all they saw,
We hurried towards London, shuffling gouts of steam.
Now fields were building-plots, and poplars cast
Long shadows over major roads, and for
60   Some fifty minutes, that in time would seem

Just long enough to settle hats and say
   I nearly died,
A dozen marriages got under way.
They watched the landscape, sitting side by side
65   —An Odeon° went past, a cooling tower,[3]   *cinema*
And someone running up to bowl[4]—and none
Thought of the others they would never meet
Or how their lives would all contain this hour.
I thought of London spread out in the sun,
70   Its postal districts packed like squares of wheat:

There we were aimed. And as we raced across
   Bright knots of rail
Past standing Pullmans,[5] walls of blackened moss
Came close, and it was nearly done, this frail
75   Travelling coincidence; and what it held
Stood ready to be loosed with all the power
That being changed can give. We slowed again,
And as the tightened brakes took hold, there swelled

3. Industrial structure for cooling hot water before reuse.
4. Throw a cricket ball at a batsman.

5. Railway saloons or sleeping cars first made in the United States by George M. Pullman.

A sense of falling, like an arrow-shower
80   Sent out of sight, somewhere becoming rain.

1958   1964

MCMXIV[6]

Those long uneven lines
Standing as patiently
As if they were stretched outside
The Oval or Villa Park,[7]
5   The crowns of hats, the sun
On moustached archaic faces
Grinning as if it were all
An August bank Holiday lark;

And the shut shops, the bleached,
10   Established names on the sunblinds,
The farthings and sovereigns,[8]
And dark-clothed children at play
Called after kings and queens,
The tin advertisements
15   For cocoa and twist,° and the pubs   tobacco
Wide open all day;

And the countryside not caring:
The place-names all hazed over
With flowering grasses, and fields
20   Shadowing Domesday lines[9]
Under wheat's restless silence;
The differently-dressed servants
With tiny rooms in huge houses,
The dust behind limousines;

25   Never such innocence,
Never before or since,
As changed itself to past
Without a word—the men
Leaving the gardens tidy,
30   The thousands of marriages
Lasting a little while longer:
Never such innocence again.

1960   1964

Talking in Bed

Talking in bed ought to be easiest,
Lying together there goes back so far,
An emblem of two people being honest.

6. 1914, in roman numerals, as incised on stone memorials to the dead of World War I.
7. London cricket ground and Birmingham football ground.
8. At that time, the least valuable and the most valuable British coins, respectively.
9. The still-visible boundaries of medieval farmers' long and narrow plots, ownership of which is recorded in William the Conqueror's *Domesday Book* (1085–86).

Yet more and more time passes silently.
5 Outside, the wind's incomplete unrest
Builds and disperses clouds about the sky,

And dark towns heap up on the horizon.
None of this cares for us. Nothing shows why
At this unique distance from isolation

10 It becomes still more difficult to find
Words at once true and kind,
Or not untrue and not unkind.

1960   1964

Ambulances

Closed like confessionals,[1] they thread
Loud noons of cities, giving back
None of the glances they absorb.
Light glossy grey, arms on a plaque,
5 They come to rest at any kerb:
All streets in time are visited.

Then children strewn on steps or road,
Or women coming from the shops
Past smells of different dinners, see
10 A wild white face that overtops
Red stretcher-blankets momently
As it is carried in and stowed,

And sense the solving emptiness
That lies just under all we do,
15 And for a second get it whole,
So permanent and blank and true.
The fastened doors recede. *Poor soul,*
They whisper at their own distress;

For borne away in deadened air
20 May go the sudden shut of loss
Round something nearly at an end,
And what cohered in it across
The years, the unique random blend
Of families and fashions, there

25 At last begin to loosen. Far
From the exchange of love to lie
Unreachable inside a room
The traffic parts to let go by
Brings closer what is left to come,
30 And dulls to distance all we are.

1961   1964

1. Enclosed stalls in Roman Catholic churches, in which priests hear confession.

The Trees

The trees are coming into leaf
Like something almost being said;
The recent buds relax and spread,
Their greenness is a kind of grief.

5 Is it that they are born again
And we grow old? No, they die too.
Their yearly trick of looking new
Is written down in rings of grain.

Yet still the unresting castles thresh
10 In fullgrown thickness every May.
Last year is dead, they seem to say,
Begin afresh, afresh, afresh.

1967   1974

Sad Steps[2]

Groping back to bed after a piss
I part thick curtains, and am startled by
The rapid clouds, the moon's cleanliness.

Four o'clock: wedge-shadowed gardens lie
5 Under a cavernous, a wind-picked sky.
There's something laughable about this,

The way the moon dashes through clouds that blow
Loosely as cannon-smoke to stand apart
(Stone-coloured light sharpening the roofs below)

10 High and preposterous and separate—
Lozenge of love! Medallion of art!
O wolves of memory! Immensements! No,

One shivers slightly, looking up there.
The hardness and the brightness and the plain
15 Far-reaching singleness of that wide stare

Is a reminder of the strength and pain
Of being young; that it can't come again,
But is for others undiminished somewhere.

1968   1974

The Explosion

On the day of the explosion
Shadows pointed towards the pithead.[3]
In the sun the slagheap slept.

---

2. Cf. Sir Philip Sidney, *Astrophil and Stella* 31: "With how sad steps, O Moon, thou climb'st the skies" (p. 194).

3. Entrance to a mine.

Down the lane came men in pitboots
5   Coughing oath-edged talk and pipe-smoke,
Shouldering off the freshened silence.

One chased after rabbits; lost them;
Came back with a nest of lark's eggs;
Showed them; lodged them in the grasses.

10   So they passed in beards and moleskins,
Fathers, brothers, nicknames, laughter,
Through the tall gates standing open.

At noon, there came a tremor; cows
Stopped chewing for a second; sun,
15   Scarfed as in a heat-haze, dimmed.

The dead go on before us, they
Are sitting in God's house in comfort,
We shall see them face to face—

Plain as lettering in the chapels
20   It was said, and for a second
Wives saw men of the explosion

Larger than in life they managed—
Gold as on a coin, or walking
Somehow from the sun towards them,

25   One showing the eggs unbroken.

1970   1974

Aubade[4]

I work all day, and get half-drunk at night.
Waking at four to soundless dark, I stare.
In time the curtain-edges will grow light.
Till then I see what's really always there:
5   Unresting death, a whole day nearer now,
Making all thought impossible but how
And where and when I shall myself die.
Arid interrogation: yet the dread
Of dying, and being dead,
10   Flashes afresh to hold and horrify.

The mind blanks at the glare. Not in remorse
—The good not done, the love not given, time
Torn off unused—nor wretchedly because
An only life can take so long to climb
15   Clear of its wrong beginnings, and may never;
But at the total emptiness for ever,
The sure extinction that we travel to

4. Music or poem announcing dawn.

And shall be lost in always. Not to be here,
Not to be anywhere,
20 And soon; nothing more terrible, nothing more true.

This is a special way of being afraid
No trick dispels. Religion used to try,
That vast moth-eaten musical brocade
Created to pretend we never die,
25 And specious stuff that says *No rational being*
Can fear a thing it will not feel, not seeing
That this is what we fear—no sight, no sound,
No touch or taste or smell, nothing to think with,
Nothing to love or link with,
30 The anaesthetic from which none come round.

And so it stays just on the edge of vision,
A small unfocused blur, a standing chill
That slows each impulse down to indecision.
Most things may never happen: this one will,
35 And realisation of it rages out
In furnace-fear when we are caught without
People or drink. Courage is no good:
It means not scaring others. Being brave
Lets no one off the grave.
40 Death is no different whined at than withstood.

Slowly light strengthens, and the room takes shape.
It stands plain as a wardrobe, what we know,
Have always known, know that we can't escape,
Yet can't accept. One side will have to go.
45 Meanwhile telephones crouch, getting ready to ring
In locked-up offices, and all the uncaring
Intricate rented world begins to rouse.
The sky is white as clay, with no sun.
Work has to be done.
50 Postmen like doctors go from house to house.

1977

HOWARD MOSS

1922–1987

Water Island[1]

To the memory of a friend,
drowned off Water Island, April, 1960

Finally, from your house, there is no view;
The bay's blind mirror shattered over you
And Patchogue took your body like a log

---

1. Island in New York State, between Long Island and Fire Island, near the town of Patchogue.

The wind rolled up to shore. The senseless drowned
5 Have faces nobody would care to see,
But water loves those gradual erasures
Of flesh and shoreline, greenery and glass,
And you belonged to water, it to you,
Having built, on a hillock, above the bay,
10 Your house, the bay giving you reason to,
Where now, if seasons still are running straight,
The horseshoe crabs clank armor night and day,
Their couplings far more ancient than the eyes
That watched them from your porch. I saw one once
15 Whose back was a history of how we live;
Grown onto every inch of plate, except
Where the hinges let it move, were living things,
Barnacles, mussels, water weeds—and one
Blue bit of polished glass, glued there by time:
20 The origins of art. It carried them
With pride, it seemed, as if endurance only
Matters in the end. Or so I thought.

Skimming traffic lights, starboard and port,
Steer through planted poles that mark the way,
25 And other lights, across the bay, faint stars
Lining the border of Long Island's shore,
Come on at night, they still come on at night,
Though who can see them now I do not know.
Wild roses, at your back porch, break their blood,
30 And bud to test surprises of sea air,
And the birds fly over, gliding down to feed
At the two feeding stations you set out with seed,
Or splash themselves in a big bowl of rain
You used to fill with water. Going across
35 That night, too fast, too dark, no one will know,
Maybe you heard, the last you'll ever hear,
The cry of the savage and endemic gull
Which shakes the blood and always brings to mind
The thought that death, the scavenger, is blind,
40 Blunders and is stupid, and the end
Comes with ironies so fine the seed
Falters in the marsh and the heron stops
Hunting in the weeds below your landing stairs,
Standing in a stillness that now is yours.

1965

The Persistence of Song

Although it is not yet evening,
The secretaries have changed their frocks
As if it were time for dancing,
And locked up in the scholars' books
5 There is a kind of rejoicing,
There is a kind of singing
That even the dark stone canyon makes

As though all fountains were going
At once, and the color flowed from bricks
10 In one wild, lit upsurging.

What is the weather doing?
And who arrived on a scallop shell
With the smell of the sea this morning?[2]
—Creating a small upheaval
15 High above the scaffolding
By saying, "All will be well.
There is a kind of rejoicing."

Is there a kind of rejoicing
In saying, "All will be well"?
20 High above the scaffolding,
Creating a small upheaval,
The smell of the sea this morning
Arrived on a scallop shell.
What was the weather doing

25 In one wild, lit upsurging?
At once, the color flowed from bricks
As though all fountains were going,
And even the dark stone canyon makes
Here a kind of singing,
30 And there a kind of rejoicing,
And locked up in the scholars' books
There is a time for dancing
When the secretaries have changed their frocks,
And though it is not yet evening,

35 There is the persistence of song.

1968

Tourists

Cramped like sardines on the Queens,[3] and sedated,
The sittings all first, the roommates mismated,

Three nuns at the table, the waiter a barber,
Then dumped with their luggage at some frumpish harbor,

5 Veering through rapids in a vapid *rapido*
To view the new moon from a ruin on the Lido,[4]

Or a sundown in London from a rundown Mercedes,
Then high-borne to Glyndebourne for Orfeo in Hades,[5]

---

2. Reference to Venus, goddess of love and beauty, who was said to have been born from a shell in the sea.
3. Ocean liner.
4. A chain of islands between the Lagoon of Venice and the Adriatic Sea. *Rapido*: Italian term for an express passenger boat in Venice.
5. Reference to the 1858 opera *Orphée aux Enfers* by the French composer Jacques Offenbach (1819–1880).

Embarrassed in Paris in Harris tweed, dying to
10   Get to the next museum piece that they're flying to,

Finding, in Frankfurt, that one indigestible
Comestible makes them too ill for the Festival,

Footloose in Lucerne, or taking a pub in in
Stratford or Glasgow, or maudlin in Dublin, in-

15   sensitive, garrulous, querulous, audible,
Drunk in the Dolomites, tuning a portable,

Homesick in Stockholm, or dressed to toboggan
At the wrong time of year in too dear° Copenhagen,   *expensive*

Generally being too genial or hostile—
20   Too grand at the Grand, too old at the Hostel—

Humdrum conundrums, what's to become of them?
Most will come home, but there will be some of them

Subsiding like Lawrence in Florence,[6] or crazily
Ending up tending shop up in Fiesole.[7]

                                    1976

JAMES DICKEY

1923–1997

The Lifeguard

In a stable of boats I lie still,
From all sleeping children hidden.
The leap of a fish from its shadow
Makes the whole lake instantly tremble.
5   With my foot on the water, I feel
The moon outside

Take on the utmost of its power.
I rise and go out through the boats.
I set my broad sole upon silver,
10   On the skin of the sky, on the moonlight,
Stepping outward from earth onto water
In quest of the miracle

This village of children believed
That I could perform as I dived
15   For one who had sunk from my sight.
I saw his cropped haircut go under.

6. D. H. Lawrence, English writer (1885–1930),   7. Town in Italy, near Florence.
lived in Italy several times.

I leapt, and my steep body flashed
Once, in the sun.

Dark drew all the light from my eyes.
20 Like a man who explores his death
By the pull of his slow-moving shoulders,
I hung head down in the cold,
Wide-eyed, contained, and alone
Among the weeds,

25 And my fingertips turned into stone
From clutching immovable blackness.
Time after time I leapt upward
Exploding in breath, and fell back
From the change in the children's faces
30 At my defeat.

Beneath them I swam to the boathouse
With only my life in my arms
To wait for the lake to shine back
At the risen moon with such power
35 That my steps on the light of the ripples
Might be sustained.

Beneath me is nothing but brightness
Like the ghost of a snowfield in summer.
As I move toward the center of the lake,
40 Which is also the center of the moon,
I am thinking of how I may be
The savior of one

Who has already died in my care.
The dark trees fade from around me.
45 The moon's dust hovers together.
I call softly out, and the child's
Voice answers through blinding water.
Patiently, slowly,

He rises, dilating to break
50 The surface of stone with his forehead.
He is one I do not remember
Having ever seen in his life.
The ground I stand on is trembling
Upon his smile.

55 I wash the black mud from my hands.
On a light given off by the grave
I kneel in the quick of the moon
At the heart of a distant forest
And hold in my arms a child
60 Of water, water, water.

1962

In the Marble Quarry

Beginning to dangle beneath
The wind that blows from the undermined wood,
   I feel the great pulley grind,

   The thread I cling to lengthen
5 And let me soaring and spinning down into marble,
   Hooked and weightlessly happy

   Where the squared sun shines
Back equally from all four sides, out of stone
   And years of dazzling labor,

10   To land at last among men
Who cut with power saws a Parian whiteness[1]
   And, chewing slow tobacco,

   Their eyebrows like frost,
Shunt house-sized blocks and lash them to cables
15   And send them heavenward

   Into small-town banks,
Into the columns and statues of government buildings,
   But mostly graves.

   I mount my monument and rise
20 Slowly and spinningly from the white-gloved men
   Toward the hewn sky

   Out of the basement of light,
Sadly, lifted through time's blinding layers
   On perhaps my tombstone

25   In which the original shape
Michelangelo believed was in every rock upon earth
   Is heavily stirring,

   Surprised to be an angel,
To be waked in North Georgia by the ponderous play
30   Of men with ten-ton blocks

   But no more surprised than I
To feel sadness fall off as though I myself
   Were rising from stone

   Held by a thread in midair,
35 Badly cut, local-looking, and totally uninspired,
   Not a masterwork

---

1. The whiteness of marble from the Greek island Paros.

Or even worth seeing at all
But the spirit of this place just the same,
Felt here as joy.

1964

Buckdancer's Choice

So I would hear out those lungs,
The air split into nine levels,
Some gift of tongues of the whistler

In the invalid's bed: my mother,
5 Warbling all day to herself
The thousand variations of one song;

It is called Buckdancer's Choice.
For years, they have all been dying
Out, the classic buck-and-wing[2] men

10 Of traveling minstrel shows;
With them also an old woman
Was dying of breathless angina,[3]

Yet still found breath enough
To whistle up in my head
15 A sight like a one-man band,

Freed black, with cymbals at heel,
An ex-slave who thrivingly danced
To the ring of his own clashing light

Through the thousand variations of one song
20 All day to my mother's prone music,
The invalid's warbler's note,

While I crept close to the wall
Sock-footed, to hear the sounds alter,
Her tongue like a mockingbird's break

25 Through stratum after stratum of a tone
Proclaiming what choices there are
For the last dancers of their kind,

For ill women and for all slaves
Of death, and children enchanted at walls
30 With a brass-beating glow underfoot,

Not dancing but nearly risen
Through barnlike, theaterlike houses
On the wings of the buck and wing.

1965

---

2. Tap-dance step invented by black entertainers.   pain, caused by heart disease.
3. A disease marked by spasmodic attacks of chest

Sled Burial, Dream Ceremony

While the south rains, the north
Is snowing, and the dead southerner
Is taken there. He lies with the top of his casket
Open, his hair combed, the particles in the air
5   Changing to other things. The train stops

In a small furry village, and men in flap-eared caps
And others with women's scarves tied around their heads
And business hats over those, unload him,
And one of them reaches inside the coffin and places
10   The southerner's hand at the center

Of his dead breast. They load him onto a sled,
An old-fashioned sled with high-curled runners,
Drawn by horses with bells, and begin
To walk out of town, past dull red barns
15   Inching closer to the road as it snows

Harder, past an army of gunny-sacked bushes,
Past horses with flakes in the hollows of their sway-backs,
Past round faces drawn by children
On kitchen windows, all shedding basic-shaped tears.
20   The coffin top still is wide open;

His dead eyes stare through his lids,
Not fooled that the snow is cotton. The woods fall
Slowly off all of them, until they are walking
Between rigid little houses of ice-fishers
25   On a plain which is a great plain of water

Until the last rabbit track fails, and they are
At the center. They take axes, shovels, mattocks,
Dig the snow away, and saw the ice in the form
Of his coffin, lifting the slab like a door
30   Without hinges. The snow creaks under the sled

As they unload him like hay, holding his weight by ropes.
Sensing an unwanted freedom, a fish
Slides by, under the hole leading up through the snow
To nothing, and is gone. The coffin's shadow
35   Is white, and they stand there, gunny-sacked bushes,

Summoned from village sleep into someone else's dream
Of death, and let him down, still seeing the flakes in the air
At the place they are born of pure shadow
Like his dead eyelids, rocking for a moment like a boat
40   On utter foreignness, before he fills and sails down.

1965

PETER KANE DUFAULT

1923–

A Letter for All-Hallows[1] (1949)

I am still hurt, Plin,
by your desertion. Now and again,
between rains, or among
sagged syllables on a page,
5   I am stopped suddenly by your grinning
lantern-jawed, monkey-eared beautiful face —
and I am hurt because you went to war
and died right in the middle of your letters
and never said goodbye.

10   And then your father followed you,
at a respectful distance,
and the high house on the hill went
for a Trappist monkery[2]. . . . I hope those monks
have veneration for the juniper
15   and the blackberries and the frogpond
and the dust of toy-soldiers in the attic
where we warred long November afternoons. —
Above all, for the black road that,
if I listen on All-Souls' Eve,[3] will clatter
20   to the gait of you riding home
from the white woods on Diamond, your horse.

The glue is long since dry
they made of him. Yet we mark well:
He was the last of the historic horses.
25   Revere rode him, and Sheridan,
and Sitting Bull[4]. . . .

I hope those monks treat you gently, shades
galloping alongside the emptying meadows,
from Concord and Lexington,
30   from the fords of the Shenandoah,
the forks of the Little Bighorn.[5]

Surely they would not be unmerciful
and frighten away with signs and bells and torches
so young an old-soldier and his friend

1. Or All Saints Day, a church festival celebrated November 1 in honor of all saints. Dufault writes in the aftermath of World War II.
2. The Trappist monks are members of a branch of the austere Cistercian order.
3. Evening of November 1, before All Souls Day (a day of prayer for all the dead).
4. Native American warrior, victor at the Battle of the Little Big Horn (1876). Paul Revere (1735–1818), American patriot famous for a horseback ride on the evening of April 18, 1775, in which he warned Massachusetts colonists of the arrival of British troops; Philip Henry Sheridan (1831–1888), Union general in the American Civil War.
5. Scenes of the battles associated with Revere, Sheridan, and Sitting Bull.

35 who, one way or another, were made ghosts
in all their country's wars.

1949   1978

The Mud Dauber Wasp

I take heart, breaking in
to the drab little pueblo[6]
of a dauber wasp: Inside,
wrinkled as a raisin
5   and rigid as Pharoah[7]
embalmed and mummified,

the dauber's pupa-doll[8]
sits in its shroud or pod—
a mere seed of a thing,
10   a bean, cold as the wall
it crooked against, and god-
forsaken now, though Spring

comes in a week . . . And god-
forsaken anyway,
15   for all entomologies—
or maths, or rockets—could
coerce its crumb of clay
to a metamorphosis.

And yet—the first warm days
20   suffice. A shudder in
the faint magnetic field?—
and undifferentiate clay's
quick, visual, wearing thin
wings—and at last unsealed

25   it flies away. No wonder
Pharoah lay spiralled in
a caul of similar kind
when he went under ground. Or
that I take heart—who've been
30   bowed-down, and barren of mind.

1961   1978

A First Night

It's the first night, I suppose,
in more than eighty year
Hattie has slept alone. . . .
And outdoors, in the falling
5   snow, without bedclothes

6. As in the adobe or stone dwellings of certain
Native Americans in the Southwest.
7. An ancient Egyptian king.

8. "Pupa": an insect in the nonfeeding, immobile
stage between the larva and the imago; sometimes
used to mean doll or puppet.

or night light and none near
but the deaf sunken stone
were one to awake calling.

What could old Hattie have done
10   wrong, anyway?—Made raw-
milk cheese, rubbed eggs, admired
her rose-red Christmas cactus, and
rocked, looking out at one
more mid-February thaw,
15   drifts melting and dungwagon mired—
that now like a reprimand

she might have heard sixty-eight
or seventy years ago,
(such as 'Hattie thinks she is clever,
20   but will go to bed with boxed ears
and no supper') she is told: 'Tonight
you'll sleep with shoes on in the snow
in the cemetery and never
never wake up in a million years.'

1978

Burden

I called you because I could not stand alone
looking north to that skyline-
tree globed with its yellow apples
balancing like a fountain of planets
5   in the bright light and the blue air.

And because on the way there
I looked at a smooth cirque°   *circle*
the brook had worn in a stone;
and nothing as soft as water
10   could, by taking care,
have so pestled° and polished   *pounded*
that granite mortar; only
by a thousand years of indifference,
of aiming elsewhere.

15   I wish we might do—or no,
look back and find we had done—
some un-advertized thing,
overwhelming and un-self-aware
as water streamlining a stone, or a tree's
20   kindling in an empty meadow
its casual Hesperides.[9]

1976   1978

9. The garden where the golden apples were grown in the Greek myth; the apple tree was a wedding gift of Gaea to Hera.

ANTHONY HECHT

1923–

A Hill

In Italy, where this sort of thing can occur,
I had a vision once—though you understand
It was nothing at all like Dante's,[1] or the visions of saints,
And perhaps not a vision at all. I was with some friends,
5   Picking my way through a warm sunlit piazza
In the early morning. A clear fretwork of shadows
From huge umbrellas littered the pavement and made
A sort of lucent shallows in which was moored
A small navy of carts. Books, coins, old maps,
10 Cheap landscapes and ugly religious prints
Were all on sale. The colors and noise
Like the flying hands were gestures of exultation,
So that even the bargaining
Rose to the ear like a voluble godliness.
15 And then, when it happened, the noises suddenly stopped,
And it got darker; pushcarts and people dissolved
And even the great Farnese Palace[2] itself
Was gone, for all its marble; in its place
Was a hill, mole-colored and bare. It was very cold,
20 Close to freezing, with a promise of snow.
The trees were like old ironwork gathered for scrap
Outside a factory wall. There was no wind,
And the only sound for a while was the little click
Of ice as it broke in the mud under my feet.
25 I saw a piece of ribbon snagged on a hedge,
But no other sign of life. And then I heard
What seemed the crack of a rifle. A hunter, I guessed;
At least I was not alone. But just after that
Came the soft and papery crash
30 Of a great branch somewhere unseen falling to earth.

And that was all, except for the cold and silence
That promised to last forever, like the hill.

Then prices came through, and fingers, and I was restored
To the sunlight and my friends. But for more than a week
35 I was scared by the plain bitterness of what I had seen.
All this happened about ten years ago,
And it hasn't troubled me since, but at last, today,
I remembered that hill; it lies just to the left
Of the road north of Poughkeepsie;[3] and as a boy
40 I stood before it for hours in wintertime.

1967

---

1. The Italian poet Dante Alighieri (1265–1321),
author of the visionary *Divine Comedy*.
2. Palace in Rome.
3. Town in upstate New York.

"More Light! More Light!"

For Heinrich Blücher and Hannah Arendt[4]

Composed in the Tower[5] before his execution
These moving verses, and being brought at that time
Painfully to the stake, submitted, declaring thus:
"I implore my God to witness that I have made no crime."

5   Nor was he forsaken of courage, but the death was horrible,
The sack of gunpowder failing to ignite.
His legs were blistered sticks on which the black sap
Bubbled and burst as he howled for the Kindly Light.[6]

And that was but one, and by no means one of the worst;
10 Permitted at least his pitiful dignity;
And such as were by made prayers in the name of Christ,
That shall judge all men, for his soul's tranquillity.

We move now to outside a German wood.[7]
Three men are there commanded to dig a hole
15 In which the two Jews are ordered to lie down
And be buried alive by the third, who is a Pole.

Not light from the shrine at Weimar beyond the hill
Nor light from heaven appeared. But he did refuse.
A Lüger[8] settled back deeply in its glove.
20 He was ordered to change places with the Jews.

Much casual death had drained away their souls.
The thick dirt mounted toward the quivering chin.
When only the head was exposed the order came
To dig him out again and to get back in.

25 No light, no light in the blue Polish eye.
When he finished a riding boot packed down the earth.
The Lüger hovered lightly in its glove.
He was shot in the belly and in three hours bled to death.

No prayers or incense rose up in those hours
30 Which grew to be years, and every day came mute
Ghosts from the ovens, sifting through crisp air,
And settled upon his eyes in a black soot.

1967

4. (1906–1975); political philosopher who wrote and lectured extensively on totalitarianism, coining the phrase "the banality of evil." She and her husband, Blücher, a philosophy professor, were refugees from Nazi Germany. "More light...": reportedly the dying words of German author Johann Wolfgang von Goethe (1749–1832).
5. The Tower of London, a fortress and sometimes a prison. Hecht explains that no specific execution is described; but such events took place during the Catholic and Protestant persecutions in England in the sixteenth century.
6. An allusion to the nineteenth-century hymn "Lead, Kindly Light," a petition for God's mercy in time of trouble.
7. Such as Buchenwald, on the outskirts of Weimar, site of the notorious Nazi death camp.
8. A German military pistol.

The Ghost in the Martini[9]

Over the rim of the glass
Containing a good martini with a twist
I eye her bosom and consider a pass,
    Certain we'd not be missed

5   In the general hubbub.
Her lips, which I forgot to say, are superb,
Never stop babbling once (Aye, there's the rub)[1]
    But who would want to curb

Such delicious, artful flattery?
10 It seems she adores my work, the distinguished grey
Of my hair. I muse on the salt and battery[2]
    Of the sexual clinch, and say

Something terse and gruff
About the marked disparity in our ages.
15 She looks like twenty-three, though eager enough.
    As for the famous wages

Of sin,[3] she can't have attained
Even to union scale, though you never can tell.
Her waist is slender and suggestively chained,
20   And things are going well.

The martini does its job,
God bless it, seeping down to the dark old id.
("Is there no cradle, Sir, you would not rob?"
    Says ego, but the lid

25 Is off. The word is Strike
While the iron's hot.) And now, ingenuous and gay,
She is asking me about what I was like
    At twenty. (Twenty, eh?)

You wouldn't have liked me then,
30 I answer, looking carefully into her eyes.
I was shy, withdrawn, awkward, one of those men
    That girls seemed to despise,

Moody and self-obsessed,
Unhappy, defiant, with guilty dreams galore,
35 Full of ill-natured pride, an unconfessed
    Snob and a thorough bore.

Her smile is meant to convey
How changed or modest I am, I can't tell which,

---

9. Alludes to the expression "the ghost in the machine," a way of describing the mind/body opposition.
1. Cf. *Hamlet* 3.1.64.

2. An ironic play on "assault and battery."
3. Cf. Romans 6.23: "For the wages of sin is death."

When I suddenly hear someone close to me say,
40   "You lousy son-of-a-bitch!"

A young man's voice, by the sound,
Coming, it seems, from the twist in the martini.
"You arrogant, elderly letch, you broken-down
Brother of Apeneck Sweeney![4]

45   Thought I was buried for good
Under six thick feet of mindless self-regard?
Dance on my grave, would you, you galliard° stud,   *lively*
Silenus[5] in leotard?

Well, summon me you did,
50   And I come unwillingly, like Samuel's ghost.[6]
'All things shall be revealed that have been hid.'[7]
There's something for you to toast!

You only got where you are
By standing upon my ectoplasmic° shoulders,   *ghostly*
55   And wherever that is may not be so high or far
In the eyes of some beholders.

Take, for example, me.
I have sat alone in the dark, accomplishing little,
And worth no more to myself, in pride and fee,
60   Than a cup of luke-warm spittle.

But honest about it, withal . . ."
("Withal," forsooth!) "Please not to interrupt.
And the lovelies went by, 'the long and the short and the tall,'[8]
Hankered for, but untupped.

65   Bloody monastic it was.
A neurotic mixture of self-denial and fear;
The verse halting, the cataleptic pause,
No sensible pain, no tear,

But an interior drip
70   As from an ulcer, where, in the humid deep
Center of myself, I would scratch and grip
The wet walls of the keep,

Or lie on my back and smell
From the corners the sharp, ammoniac, urine stink.

4. Cf. T. S. Eliot, "Sweeney Among the Nightingales" (pp. 1234–35).
5. In Greek myth, foster father and companion of the wine god Dionysus; of human form, with a horse's ears and tail. Generally old, bald, and bearded. A famous legend relates that Midas made Silenus drunk in order to learn his secrets.
6. Saul, fearful of the army of the Philistines, found his prayers for guidance unanswered, and so consulted a medium to bring the unwilling Samuel up from the dead (1 Samuel 28).
7. A rewriting of a recurrent theme in the Gospels, as in Luke 12.2 or Matthew 10.26.
8. As in the 1940 popular song by Jimmy Hughes and Frank Lake, "Bless 'Em All."

75 'No light, but rather darkness visible.'[9]
And plenty of time to think.

In that thick, fetid air
I talked to myself in giddy recitative:
'I have been studying how I may compare
80 This prison where I live

Unto the world . . .'[1] I learned
Little, and was awarded no degrees.
Yet all that sunken hideousness earned
Your negligence and ease.

85 Nor was it wholly sick,
Having procured you a certain modest fame;
A devotion, rather, a grim device to stick
To something I could not name."

Meanwhile, she babbles on
90 About men, or whatever, and the juniper juice
Shuts up at last, having sung, I trust, like a swan.[2]
Still given to self-abuse!

Better get out of here;
If he opens his trap again it could get much worse.
95 I touch her elbow, and, leaning toward her ear,
Tell her to find her purse.

1977

Still Life

Sleep-walking vapor, like a visitant ghost,
Hovers above a lake
Of Tennysonian[3] calm just before dawn.
Inverted trees and boulders waver and coast
5 In polished darkness. Glints of silver break
Among the liquid leafage, and then are gone.

Everything's doused and diamonded with wet.
A cobweg, woven taut
On bending stanchion° frames of tentpole grass,   upright prop
10 Sags like a trampoline or firemen's net
With all the glitter and riches it has caught,
Each drop a paperweight of Steuben glass.[4]

No birdsong yet, no cricket, nor does the trout
Explode in water-scrolls

---

9. Cf. Milton, *Paradise Lost* 1.61–63, where Satan views Hell: "A Dungeon horrible, on all sides round / As one great Furnace flam'd, yet from those flames / No light, but rather darkness visible."
1. Cf. the poetic, self-absorbed King Richard's soliloquy in prison (*Richard II* 5.5.1ff).
2. A swan is said to sing before it dies. Juniper juice is an ingredient used in flavoring gin.
3. As in the poetry of Alfred, Lord Tennyson (1809–1892; see pp. 885–911).
4. Brand of handmade, heavy lead crystal.

15 For a skimming fly. All that is yet to come.
Things are as still and motionless throughout
The universe as ancient Chinese bowls,
And nature is magnificently dumb.

Why does this so much stir me, like a code
20   Or muffled intimation
Of purposes and preordained events?
It knows me, and I recognize its mode
Of cautionary, spring-tight hesitation,
This silence so impacted and intense.

25 As in a water-surface I behold
    The first, soft, peach decree
Of light, its pale, inaudible commands.
I stand beneath a pine-tree in the cold,
Just before dawn, somewhere in Germany,
30 A cold, wet, Garand rifle in my hands.

1979

The Book of Yolek

Wir haben ein Gesetz,
Und nach dem Gesetz soll er sterben.[5]

The dowsed coals fume and hiss after your meal
Of grilled brook trout, and you saunter off for a walk
Down the fern trail, it doesn't matter where to,
Just so you're weeks and worlds away from home,
5 And among midsummer hills have set up camp
In the deep bronze glories of declining day.

You remember, peacefully, an earlier day
In childhood, remember a quite specific meal:
A corn roast and bonfire in summer camp.
10 That summer you got lost on a Nature Walk;
More than you dared admit, you thought of home;
No one else knows where the mind wanders to.

The fifth of August, 1942.
It was morning and very hot. It was the day
15 They came at dawn with rifles to The Home
For Jewish Children, cutting short the meal
Of bread and soup, lining them up to walk
In close formation off to a special camp.

How often you have thought about that camp,
20 As though in some strange way you were driven to,
And about the children, and how they were made to walk,

5. From the German translation of John 19.7 ("We have a law, and by that law he ought to die") by the theologian Martin Luther (1483–1546), leader in Germany of the Protestant Reformation. Hecht's poem is inspired by "Yanosz Korczak's Last Walk" by Hannah Mortkowicz-Olczakowa, in Jacob Glatstein and Israel Knox, eds., *Anthology of Holocaust Literature* (Atheneum, 1973), pp. 134–37, which recounts a historical event in Germany.

Yolek who had bad lungs, who wasn't a day
Over five years old, commanded to leave his meal
And shamble between armed guards to his long home.

25   We're approaching August again. It will drive home
The regulation torments of that camp
Yolek was sent to, his small, unfinished meal,
The electric fences, the numeral tattoo,
The quite extraordinary heat of the day
30   They all were forced to take that terrible walk.

Whether on a silent, solitary walk
Or among crowds, far off or safe at home,
You will remember, helplessly, that day,
And the smell of smoke, and the loudspeakers of the camp.
35   Wherever you are, Yolek will be there, too.
His unuttered name will interrupt your meal.

Prepare to receive him in your home some day.
Though they killed him in the camp they sent him to,
He will walk in as you're sitting down to a meal.

1990

Death the Painter[6]

Snub-nosed, bone-fingered, deft with engraving tools,
    I have alone been given
The powers of Joshua, who stayed the sun
    In its traverse of heaven.[7]
5   Here in this Gotham[8] of unnumbered fools
I have sought out and arrested everyone.

Under my watchful eye all human creatures
    Convert to a *still life,*
As with unique precision I apply
10   White lead and palette knife.
A model student of remodelled features,
The final barber, the last beautician, I.

You lordlings, what is Man, his blood and vitals,[9]
    When all is said and done?
15   A poor forked animal,[1] a nest of flies.
    Tell us, what is this one
Once shorn of all his dignities and titles,
Divested of his testicles and eyes?

1995

6. From *The Presumptions of Death*, a series of twenty-two poems written from the perspective of Death, to accompany woodcuts by the American artist Leonard Baskin (b. 1922).
7. Cf. Joshua 10.12–3; when Joshua asked the sun and the moon to stand still, "the sun stood still, and the moon stayed, until the people had avenged themselves upon their enemies."
8. Proverbial town (in England) known for its fool-ish inhabitants.
9. Cf. Psalm 8.4: "What is man, that thou art mindful of him?"
1. Cf. *King Lear* 3.4.101ff, where Lear encounters Edgar, disguised in rags as a madman, and laments, "Is man no more than this?" and "unac-commodated man is no more but such a poor, bare, fork'd animal as thou art."

The Mysteries of Caesar[2]

Known to the boys in his Latin class as "Sir,"
Balding, cologned, mild-mannered Mr. Sypher
Defied his sentence as a highschool lifer
With a fresh, carefully chosen boutonniere

5   As daily he heard the Helvetians[3] plead their cause
In chains while captives were brought face to face
With the impositions of the ablative case,
The torts and tortures of grammatic laws.

Gracelessly stalled by vast impediments
10 Of words and baggage as by a conqueror's shackles,
O'Rourke, his face a celestial sphere of freckles
(One Gaul brought down by the pluperfect tense),

Submitted to all the galls° and agonies   *irritations*
Of pained sight-readings from the *Gallic Wars.*
15 They all bore dark, dishonorable scars
From what their textbook called an "exercise"

At least as draining as the quarter-mile.
But Mr. Sypher listened with superb
Imperial hauteur, with imperturb-
20 able patience, and a somewhat cryptic smile.

"Thompson," he'd murmur, "please instruct our class."
And Thompson would venture timidly, much rattled,
"Caesar did withhold his men from battle,
And he did have enough in presentness

25 To prohibit the enemy from further wastings,
From foragings and rapines." And through a long
Winter campaign of floundering, grief, and wrong,
That little army force-marched without resting.

"Please aid us, Jones," Mr. Sypher would beseech;
30 And Jones would tremulously undertake
To decipher the old Caesarian mystique
In the mixed medium of cracked parts of speech.

"Which things being known, when surest things accede,
He did deem enough of cause . . . ," Jones volunteered.
35 Invariably it came out sounding weird,
The garbled utterance of some lesser breed

Without the law of common intercourse.
Long weeks of rain, followed by early frost

---

2. The poem concerns a Latin class in which the *Gallic Wars*, first book of the *Commentaries* by the Roman Emperor Julius Caesar, is translated. Caesar recounted his campaigns of 58 to 52 B.C. in Gaul (modern-day France).

3. Celtic tribe that tried to move from its territory northeast of Lake Geneva to settle in Gaul in the first century B.C. They were halted and driven back by the Romans.

Had not improved morale, and yet the worst
40   Is not when there can always still be worse.

They rather liked Mr. Sypher, who was kind,
An easy grader. Was he a widower?
It was thought he had lost a child some years before.
Often they wondered what passed through his mind

45   As he calmly attended to their halt and crude
Efforts, not guessing one or another boy
Served as Antinous[4] to that inward eye
Which is the pitiless bliss of solitude.[5]

1995

RICHARD HUGO

1923–1982

The Way a Ghost Dissolves

Where she lived the close remained the best.
The nearest music and the static cloud,
sun and dirt were all she understood.
She planted corn and left the rest
5   to elements, convinced that God
with giant faucets regulates the rain
and saves the crops from frost or foreign wind.

Fate assisted her with special cures.
Rub a half potato on your wart
10 and wrap it in a damp cloth. Close
your eyes and whirl three times and throw.
Then bury rag and spud exactly where
they fall. The only warts that I have now
are memories or comic on my nose.

15 Up at dawn. The earth provided food
if worked and watered, planted green
with rye grass every fall. Or driven wild
by snakes that kept the carrots clean,
she butchered snakes and carrots with a hoe.
20 Her screams were sea birds in the wind,
her chopping—nothing like it now.

I will garden on the double run,
my rhythm obvious in ringing rakes,
and trust in fate to keep me poor and kind

---

4. Bithynian youth, a great favorite of the Emperor Hadrian, who was drowned in the Nile in A.D. 130. Gossip and romantic legends surrounded his death. Hadrian founded the Egyptian city of Antinoöpolis and built temples in memory of Antinoüs.

5. Ironic allusion to Wordsworth's "I Wandered Lonely As a Cloud" (p. 732), which concludes, "They flash upon that inward eye / Which is the bliss of solitude; / And then my heart with pleasure fills, / And dances with the daffodils."

25   and work until my heart is short,
then go out slowly with a feeble grin,
my fingers flexing but my eyes gone gray
from cramps and the lack of oxygen.

Forget the tone. Call the neighbor's trumpet
30   golden as it grates. Exalt the weeds.
Say the local animals have class
or help me say that ghost has gone to seed.
And why attempt to see the cloud again—
the screaming face it was before it cracked
35   in wind from Asia and a wanton rain.

1961

The Lady in Kicking Horse Reservoir[1]

Not my hands but green across you now.
Green tons hold you down, and ten bass curve
teasing in your hair. Summer slime
will pile deep on your breast. Four months of ice
5   will keep you firm. I hope each spring
to find you tangled in those pads
pulled not quite loose by the spillway pour,
stars in dead reflection off your teeth.

Lie there lily still. The spillway's closed.
10   Two feet down most lakes are common gray.
This lake is dark from the black blue Mission range
climbing sky like music dying Indians once wailed.
On ocean beaches, mystery fish
are offered to the moon. Your jaws go blue.
15   Your hands start waving every wind.
Wave to the ocean where we crushed a mile of foam.

We still love there in thundering foam
and love. Whales fall in love with gulls
and tide reclaims the Dolly skeletons[2]
20   gone with a blast of aching horns to China.
Landlocked in Montana here
the end is limited by light, the final note
will trail off at the farthest point we see,
already faded, lover, where you bloat.

25   All girls should be nicer. Arrows rain
above us in the Indian wind. My future
should be full of windy gems, my past
will stop this roaring in my dreams.
Sorry. Sorry. Sorry. But the arrows sing:
30   no way to float her up. The dead sink

---

1. Both Kicking Horse Reservoir and the Mission mountain range (line 11) are on the Flathead Indian reservation in Montana.

2. Specifically, here, skeletons of the Dolly Varden trout (but see also line 54).

from dead weight. The Mission range
turns this water black late afternoons.

One boy slapped the other. Hard.
The slapped boy talked until his dignity
35   dissolved, screamed a single "stop"
and went down sobbing in the company pond.
I swam for him all night. My only suit
got wet and factory hands went home.
No one cared the coward disappeared.
40   Morning then: cold music I had never heard.

Loners like work best on second shift.
No one liked our product and the factory closed.
Off south, the bison multiply so fast
a slaughter's mandatory every spring
45   and every spring the creeks get fat
and Kicking Horse fills up. My hope is vague.
The far blur of your bones in May
may be nourished by the snow.

The spillway's open and you spill out
50   into weather, lover down the bright canal
and mother, irrigating crops
dead Indians forgot to plant.
I'm sailing west with arrows to dissolving foam
where waves strand naked Dollys.
55   Their eyes are white as oriental mountains
and their tongues are teasing oil from whales.

1973

DENISE LEVERTOV

1923–

Scenes from the Life of the Peppertrees

1

The peppertrees, the peppertrees!

Cats are stretching in the doorways,
sure of everything. It is morning.
      But the peppertrees
5   stand aside in diffidence, with berries
of modest red.
           Branch above branch, an air
of lightness; of shadows
scattered lightly.
10   A cat
closes upon its shadow.
Up and up goes the sun,

sure of everything.
     The peppertrees
15   shiver a little.
Robust
and soot-black, the cat
leaps to a low branch. Leaves
close about him.

2

20   The yellow moon dreamily
tipping buttons of light
down among the leaves. Marimba,
marimba—from beyond the
black street.
25   Somebody dancing,
somebody
          getting the hell
outta here. Shadows of cats
weave round the tree trunks,
30   the exposed knotty roots.

3

The man on the bed sleeping
defenseless. Look—
his bare long feet together
sideways, keeping each other
35   warm. And the foreshortened shoulders,
the head
barely visible.   He is good.
let him sleep.
           But the third peppertree
40   is restless, twitching
thin leaves in the light
of afternoon. After a while
it walks over and taps
on the upstairs window with a bunch
45   of red berries.   Will he wake?

1958

The Dead Butterfly

1

Now I see its whiteness
is not white but green, traced with green,
and resembles the stones
of which the city is built,
5   quarried high in the mountains.

2

Everywhere among the marigolds
the rainblown roses and the hedges
of tamarisk are white

butterflies this morning, in constant
10   tremulous movement, only those
that lie dead revealing
their rockgreen color and the bold
cut of the wings.

1959

Triple Feature

Innocent decision: to enjoy.
And the pathos
of hopefulness, of his solicitude:

—he in mended serape,
5   she having plaited carefully
magenta ribbons into her hair,
the baby a round half-hidden shape
slung in her rebozo,° and the young son steadfastly   *shawl*
gripping a fold of her skirt,
10   pale and severe under a
handed-down sombrero—

all regarding
the stills with full attention, preparing
to pay and go in—

15   to worlds of shadow-violence, half-
familiar, warm with popcorn, icy
with strange motives, barbarous splendors!

1959

O Taste and See

The world is
not with us enough.[1]
O taste and see

the subway Bible poster said,
5   meaning The Lord,[2] meaning
if anything all that lives
to the imagination's tongue,

grief, mercy, language,
tangerine, weather, to
10   breathe them, bite,
savor, chew, swallow, transform

into our flesh our
deaths, crossing the street, plum, quince,
living in the orchard and being

1. Cf. Wordsworth's sonnet "The World Is Too   2. "O taste and see that the Lord is good" (Psalms
Much with Us" (1807; p. 735).   34.8).

15   hungry, and plucking
     the fruit.

1964

The Closed World

"If the Perceptive Organs close, their
Objects seem to close also."
—BLAKE: *Jerusalem*

The house-snake dwells here still
under the threshold
but for months I have not seen it
nor its young, the inheritors.

5   Light and the wind enact
   passion and resurrection
   day in, day out
   but the blinds are down over my windows,
   my doors are shut.

10   When after the long drought at last
   silver and darkness swept over the hills
   the dry indifferent glare in my mind's eye
   wavered but burned on.

1967

Tenebrae[3]

(Fall of 1967)[4]

Heavy, heavy, heavy, hand and heart.
We are at war,
bitterly, bitterly at war.

And the buying and selling
5   buzzes at our heads, a swarm
of busy flies, a kind of innocence.

Gowns of gold sequins are fitted,
sharp-glinting. What harsh rustlings
of silver moiré° there are,   *watered silk*
10   to remind me of shrapnel splinters.

And weddings are held in full solemnity
not of desire but of etiquette,
the nuptial pomp of starched lace;
a grim innocence.

15   And picnic parties return from the beaches
   burning with stored sun in the dusk;

3. Literally, "darkness" (Latin): church service observed during the final part of Holy Week to commemorate the sufferings and death of Christ.

4. Time of a march on the Pentagon, to protest the continuing presence of American troops in Vietnam.

children promised a TV show when they get home
fall asleep in the backs of a million station wagons,
sand in their hair, the sound of waves
20 quietly persistent at their ears.
They are not listening.

Their parents at night
dream and forget their dreams.
They wake in the dark
25 and make plans. Their sequin plans
glitter into tomorrow.
They buy, they sell.

They fill freezers with food.
Neon signs flash their intentions
30 into the years ahead.

And at their ears the sound
of the war. They are
not listening, not listening.

1972

Caedmon[5]

All others talked as if
talk were a dance.
Clodhopper I, with clumsy feet
would break the gliding ring.
5 Early I learned to
hunch myself
close by the door:
then when the talk began
I'd wipe my
10 mouth and wend
unnoticed back to the barn
to be with the warm beasts,
dumb among body sounds
of the simple ones.
15 I'd see by a twist
of lit rush[6] the motes
of gold moving
from shadow to shadow
slow in the wake
20 of deep untroubled sighs.
The cows
munched or stirred or were still. I
was at home and lonely,
both in good measure. Until
25 the sudden angel affrighted me—light effacing

5. The earliest known English Christian poet, an unlettered cowherd who, the legend goes, received a divine call to praise the Lord in verse. (Cf. Cædmon's "Hymn," p. 1.) "The story comes, of course, from the Venerable Bede's *History of the* *English Church and People,* but I first read it as a child in John Richard Green's *History of the English People,* 1855" [Levertov's note].
6. Rush plants were lit to serve as candlewicks.

my feeble beam,
a forest of torches, feathers of flame, sparks upflying:
but the cows as before
were calm, and nothing was burning,
30   nothing but I, as that hand of fire
touched my lips and scorched my tongue
and pulled my voice
                    into the ring of the dance.

1987

JOHN ORMOND

1923–1990

To a Nun

after the 15th Century Welsh

Please God, forsake your water and dry bread
And fling the bitter cress you eat aside.
Put by your rosary. In Mary's name
Leave chanting creeds to mildewing monks in Rome.
5   Spring is at work in woodlands bright with sun;
Springtime's not made for living like a nun.
Your faith, my fairest lady, your religion
Show but a single face of love's medallion.
Slip on this ring and this green gown, these laces;
10   The wood is furnitured with resting-places.
Hide in the birch-tree's shade—upon your knees
Murmur the mass of cuckoos, litanies
Of spring's green foliage. There's no sacrilege
If we find heaven here against the hedge.
15   Remember Ovid's book and Ovid's truth:[1]
There's such a thing as having too much faith.
Let us discover the shapes, the earthly signs
Of our true selves, our souls, among the vines.
For surely God and all his saints above,
20   High in their other heaven, pardon love.

1969

Cathedral Builders

They climbed on sketchy ladders towards God,
With winch and pulley hoisted hewn rock into heaven,
Inhabited sky with hammers, defied gravity,
Deified stone, took up God's house to meet Him,

5   And came down to their suppers and small beer;
Every night slept, lay with their smelly wives,

---

1. Publius Ovidius Naso (43 B.C.–A.D. 18), Roman poet, author of the *Ars Amatoria* ("The Arts of Love").

Quarrelled and cuffed the children, lied,
Spat, sang, were happy or unhappy,

And every day took to the ladders again;
10   Impeded the rights of way of another summer's
Swallows, grew greyer, shakier, became less inclined
To fix a neighbour's roof of a fine evening,

Saw naves sprout arches, clerestories[2] soar,
Cursed the loud fancy glaziers for their luck,
15   Somehow escaped the plague, got rheumatism,
Decided it was time to give it up,

To leave the spire to others; stood in the crowd
Well back from the vestments at the consecration,
Envied the fat bishop his warm boots,
20   Cocked up a squint eye and said, "I bloody did that."

1969

Lament for a Leg

*Near the yew tree under which the body of Dafydd ap Gwilym[3] is buried
in Strata Florida, Cardiganshire, there stands a stone with the following
inscription: "The left leg and part of the thigh of Henry Hughes, Cooper,
was cut off and interr'd here, June 18, 1756". Later the rest of Henry
Hughes set off across the Atlantic in search of better fortune.*

A short service, to be sure,
With scarcely half a hymn they held,
Over my lost limb, suitable curtailment.
Out-of-tune notes a crow cawed
5   By the yew tree, and me,
My stump still tourniqued,
Awkward on my new crutch,
Being snatched towards the snack
Of a funeral feast they made.
10   With seldom a dry eye, for laughter,
They jostled me over the ale
I'd cut the casks for, and the mead.
"Catch me falling under a coach",
Every voice jested, save mine,
15   Henry Hughes, cooper. A tasteless caper!
Soon with my only, my best, foot forward
I fled, quiet, to far America:

Where, with my two tried hands, I plied
My trade and, true, in time made good
20   Though grieving for Pontrhydfendigaid.[4]
Sometimes, all at once, in my tall cups,

2. Upper stories with their own windows; "nave":   3. Fourteenth-century Welsh poet.
main section of a church.   4. Welsh place-name, as is Ystrad Fflur (line 23).

I'd cry in *hiraeth*[5] for my remembered thigh
Left by the grand yew in Ystrad Fflur's
Bare ground, near the good bard.
25 Strangers, astonished at my high
Beer-flush, would stare, not guessing,
Above the bar-board, that I, of the starry eye,
Had one foot in the grave; thinking me,
No doubt, a drunken dolt in whom a whim
30 Warmed to madness, not knowing a tease
Of a Welsh worm was tickling my distant toes.

"So I bequeath my leg", I'd say and sigh,
Baffling them, "my unexiled part, to Dafydd
The pure poet who, whole, lies near and far
35 From me, still pining for Morfudd's heart",[6]
Giving him, generous to a fault
With what was no more mine to give,
Out of that curt plot, my quarter grave,
Good help, I hope. What will the great God say
40 At Dafydd's wild-kicking-climbing extra leg,
Jammed hard in heaven's white doorway
(I'll limp unnimble round the narrow back)
Come the quick trumpet of the Judgement Day?

1973

JAMES SCHUYLER

1923–

Freely Espousing

a commingling sky

a semi-tropic night
that cast the blackest shadow
of the easily torn, untrembling banana leaf

5 or Quebec! what a horrible city
so Steubenville is better?
the sinking sensation
when someone drowns thinking, "This can't be happening to me!"
the profit of excavating the battlefield where Hannibal whomped the
Romans[1]
10 the sinuous beauty of words like allergy
the tonic resonance of
pill when used as in
"she is a pill"
on the other hand I am not going to espouse any short stories in which
lawn mowers clack.

---

5. "Longing, nostalgia" (Welsh).
6. The love of Morfudd.
1. The Carthaginian general Hannibal in 217–16

B.C. crossed the Alps and defeated Roman armies,
using brilliant military tactics.

15   No, it is absolutely forbidden
for words to echo the act described; or try to. Except very directly
as in
bong. And tickle. Oh it is inescapable kiss.
Marriages of the atmosphere
20   are worth celebrating
          where Tudor City[2]
catches the sky or the glass side
of a building lit up at night in fog
"What is that gold green tetrahedron down the river?"
25   "You are experiencing a new sensation."

        if the touch-me-nots
        are not in bloom
        neither are the chrysanthemums

the bales of pink cotton candy
30   in the slanting light
        are ornamental cherry trees.
        The greens around them, and
        the browns, the grays, are the park.
It's. Hmm. No.
35   Their scallop shell of quiet
      is the S.S. *United States.*
      It is not so quiet and they
      are a medium-size couple who
      when they fold each other up
40   well, thrill. That's their story.

                              1979

PATRICIA BEER

1924–

Grave Doubts

Peace to Lord Hamlet,[1] I have never heard
Gravediggers talking. Before the funeral
You see them from a distance, usually
In mist, moving eloquently
5   But without speech in a pas de deux.[2]

On that day when the clergyman's voice
Had had its say and gone back into its box,
In the silence of people turning to go home
And the receding mutter of an empty
10   Hearse, the gravediggers closed in.

---

2. Large apartment complex on the east side of New York City.
1. Shakespeare, *Hamlet* 5.1.

2. Ballet term: sequence of steps for two dancers, usually a ballerina and her partner.

Taciturn caterers, they stared down at the coffin
Spread out on its base of earth. Mutely
They sandwiched it in soil. And then they went
Away to wash their hands of it. I thought
15   That they would never cross my path again.

Many years later, the only relation left,
I came in search of the plot and could not find it.
The manager, in her steamy little hut,
Explained to me that the grave was "unpurchased".
20   "A *pauper's*° grave?" "That's what they used to say."   *penniless person's*

I asked her what might happen now. She said
The gravediggers could come back without a word
To me or anybody else, remove
The contents, add to it, or anything.
25   She liked telling me that. I purchased it.

A crested document arrived this morning
And I became, as in the childhood chapters
Of some second-rate autobiography,
The proud possessor of. Not of a bicycle
30   Not of a pony or a doll's house. Of a grave.

He was a distant cousin, but I am glad
To have bought one respectable old man
From the gravediggers. They deafened him once.
Now he will hold his peace in the deadpan dark
35   And will not hear spade voices ever again.

Footbinding

My grandmother had a small shelf of books
Hanging in a shadow. One of them
Was Foxe's Book of Martyrs.[3] All the rest
Were works by missionaries who had served
5   In China. They were handsome volumes, hard
With gold and angry colours, heavy with Empire.
I never saw her read them but she handed
Them out to me like medicine. As well
As every other heathen practice, they
10   Described footbinding. In their godly fashion
The missionaries revelled in the cracking
Of the maiden's bones, the consternation
Of her bloodstream, the whining of her sinews
And the two years of agony ahead.
15   It was far worse than Foxe's Book of Martyrs.

My mother's and her mother's feet were tiny.
Mine were thin but long and getting longer.

3. John Foxe (1516–1587), author of *Actes and Monuments* (1563), popularly known as the *Book of Martyrs*, an account of the lives of Christian martyrs.

Would those two organise a ceremony
Where women gathered and the screaming started?
20 Probably not. They planned on twisting me
Into a little lady if it killed them
But definitely would not want to be
Anything but the smallest feet in town.

Nowadays I think of those girls in China
25 Who ran and pounced and almost flew until
The day they never pounced or ran again.
Their fledgling feet did not grow into birds.
Some of them died of gangrene. Some went mad.
But those who lived, nubile, felt like orchids.
30 Their family's approval smelled of jasmine
As, fluttering in silk, they married Emperors.

An aim the missionaries did not mention.

1993

DONALD JUSTICE

1925–

Counting the Mad[1]

This one was put in a jacket,
This one was sent home,
This one was given bread and meat
But would eat none,
5 And this one cried No No No No
All day long.

This one looked at the window
As though it were a wall,
This one saw things that were not there,
10 This one things that were,
And this one cried No No No No
All day long.

This one thought himself a bird,
This one a dog,
15 And this one thought himself a man,
An ordinary man,
And cried and cried No No No No
All day long.

1960

1. The poem is inspired by the nursery rhyme that begins "this little pig went to market."

But That Is Another Story

I do not think the ending can be right.
How can they marry and live happily
Forever, these who were so passionate
At chapter's end? Once they are settled in
5   The quiet country house, what will they do,
So many miles from anywhere?
Those blond ancestral ghosts crowding the stair,
Surely they disapprove? Ah me,
I fear love will catch cold and die
10   From pacing naked through those drafty halls
Night after night. Poor Frank! Poor Imogene!
Before them now their lives
Stretch empty as great Empire beds
After the lovers rise and the damp sheets
15   Are stripped by envious chambermaids.

And if the first night passes brightly enough,
What with the bonfires lit with old love letters,
That is no inexhaustible fuel, perhaps?
God knows how it must end, not I.
20   Will Frank walk out one day
Alone through the ruined orchard with his stick,
Strewing the path with lissome heads
Of buttercups? Will Imogene
Conceal in the crotches of old trees
25   Love notes for beardless gardeners and such?
Meanwhile they quarrel and make it up
Only to quarrel again. A sudden storm
Pulls the last fences down. Now moonstruck sheep
Stray through the garden all night peering in
30   At the exhausted lovers where they sleep.

1967

Men at Forty

Men at forty
Learn to close softly
The doors to rooms they will not be
Coming back to.

5   At rest on a stair landing,
They feel it moving
Beneath them now like the deck of a ship,
Though the swell is gentle.

And deep in mirrors
10   They rediscover
The face of the boy as he practices tying
His father's tie there in secret,

And the face of that father,
Still warm with the mystery of lather.
15   They are more fathers than sons themselves now.
Something is filling them, something

That is like the twilight sound
Of the crickets, immense,
Filling the woods at the foot of the slope
20   Behind their mortgaged houses.

1967

Mrs. Snow

Busts of the great composers glimmered in niches,
Pale stars. Poor Mrs. Snow, who could forget her,
Calling the time out in that hushed falsetto?
(How early we begin to grasp what kitsch[2] is!)
5   But when she loomed above us like an alp,
We little towns below would feel her shadow.
Somehow her nods of approval seemed to matter
More than the stray flakes drifting from her scalp.
Her etchings of ruins, her mass-production Mings[3]
10   Were our first culture: she put us in awe of things.
And once, with her help, I composed a waltz,
Too innocent to be completely false
Perhaps, but full of marvellous clichés.
She beamed and softened then.
                              Ah, those were the days.

1987

KENNETH KOCH
1925–

Permanently

One day the Nouns were clustered in the street.
An Adjective walked by, with her dark beauty.
The Nouns were struck, moved, changed.
The next day a Verb drove up, and created the Sentence.

5   Each Sentence says one thing—for example. "Although it was a dark
          rainy day when the Adjective walked by, I shall remember the pure
          and sweet expression on her face until the day I perish from the
          green, effective earth."
Or, "Will you please close the window, Andrew?"

---

2. Something that appeals to an undiscriminating taste.
3. Cheap reproductions of the Ming porcelain
fashioned during the Ming Dynasty of China (1368–1644).

Or, for example, "Thank you, the pink pot of flowers on the window sill
has changed color recently to a light yellow, due to the heat from
the boiler factory which exists nearby."

In the springtime the Sentences and the Nouns lay silently on the grass.
A lonely Conjunction here and there would call, "And! But!"
10 But the Adjective did not emerge.

As the adjective is lost in the sentence,
So I am lost in your eyes, ears, nose, and throat—
You have enchanted me with a single kiss
Which can never be undone
15 Until the destruction of language.

                                                                    1962

You Were Wearing

You were wearing your Edgar Allan Poe printed cotton blouse.
In each divided up square of the blouse was a picture of Edgar Allan
    Poe.
Your hair was blonde and you were cute. You asked me, "Do most boys
    think that most girls are bad?"
I smelled the mould of your seaside resort hotel bedroom on your hair
    held in place by a John Greenleaf Whittier clip.
5   "No," I said, "it's girls who think that boys are bad." Then we read *Snow-
    bound* together.
And ran around in an attic, so that a little of the blue enamel was
    scraped off my George Washington, Father of His Country, shoes.

Mother was walking in the living room, her Strauss Waltzes comb in her
    hair.
We waited for a time and then joined her, only to be served tea in cups
    painted with pictures of Herman Melville
As well as with illustrations from his book *Moby Dick* and from his
    novella, *Benito Cereno*.
10 Father came in wearing his Dick Tracy necktie: "How about a drink,
    everyone?"
I said, "Let's go outside a while." Then we went onto the porch and sat
    on the Abraham Lincoln swing.
You sat on the eyes, mouth, and beard part, and I sat on the knees.
In the yard across the street we saw a snowman holding a garbage can
    lid smashed into a likeness of the mad English king, George the
    Third.

                                                                    1962

Variations on a Theme by William Carlos Williams[1]

1

I chopped down the house that you had been saving to live in next
    summer.
I am sorry, but it was morning, and I had nothing to do
and its wooden beams were so inviting.

---

1. See Williams' "This Is Just to Say" (1934; p. 1167). Williams was a physician (see line 12).

2

We laughed at the hollyhocks together
and then I sprayed them with lye.
Forgive me. I simply do not know what I am doing.

3

I gave away the money that you had been saving to live on for the next
    ten years.
The man who asked for it was shabby
and the firm March wind on the porch was so juicy and cold.

4

Last evening we went dancing and I broke your leg.
Forgive me. I was clumsy, and
I wanted you here in the wards, where I am the doctor!

1962

Girl and Baby Florist Sidewalk Pram
Nineteen Seventy Something

Sweeping past the florist's came the baby and the girl
I am the girl! I am the baby!
I am the florist who is filled with mood!
I am the mood. I am the girl who is inside the baby
For it is a baby girl. I am old style of life. I am the new
Everything as well. I am the evening in which you docked your first kiss.
And it came to the baby. And I am the boyhood of the girl
Which she never has. I am the florist's unknown baby
He hasn't had one yet. The florist is in a whirl
So much excitement, section, outside his shop
Or hers. Who is he? Where goes the baby? She
Is immensely going to grow up. How much
Does this rent for? It's more than a penny. It's more
Than a million cents. My dear, it is life itself. Roses?
Chrysanthemums? If you can't buy them I'll give
Them for nothing. Oh no, I can't.
Maybe my baby is allergic to their spores.
So then the girl and her baby go away. Florist stands whistling
Neither inside nor outside thinking about the mountains of Peru.

1982

Energy in Sweden

Those were the days
When there was so much energy in and around me
I could take it off and put it back on, like clothes
That one has bought only for a ski trip
But then finds that one is using every day
Because every day is like a ski trip—
I think that's how I was at twenty-three.

Seeing those six young women in a boat I was on a ski trip.
They said, We are all from Minneapolis. This was in Stockholm.

10   The melding of American and Swedish-American female looks was a ski
          trip
     Although I had no particular reason at that time to put all my energy on
     Yet there it was, I had it, the way a giant has the hegemony of his nerves
     In case he needs it, or the way a fisherman has all his poles and lines
          and lures, and a scholar all his books
     The way a water heater has all its gas
15   Whether it is being used or not, I had all that energy.
     Really, are you all from Minneapolis? I said, almost bursting with force.
     And yes, one of them, about the second prettiest, replied. We are here for
          several days.

     I thought about this moment from time to time
     For eight or ten years. It seemed to me I should have done something at
          the time,
20   To have used all that energy. Lovemaking is one way to use it and writ-
          ing is another.
     Both maybe are overestimated, because the relation is so clear.
     But that is probably human destiny and I'm not going to go against it
          here.
     Sometimes there are the persons and not the energy, sometimes the
          energy and not the persons.
     When the gods give both, a man shouldn't complain.

                                                                    1994

A. R. AMMONS
1926–

Silver

     I thought Silver must have snaked° logs   dragged
          when young:
     she couldn't stand to have the line brush her lower hind leg:
     in blinded halter she couldn't tell what had loosened behind her
5   and was coming
     as downhill
     to rush into her crippling her to the ground:

     and when she almost went to sleep, me dreaming at the slow plow,
     I would
10   at dream's end turning over the mind to a new chapter
               let the line drop and touch her leg
               and she would
     bring the plow out of the ground with speed but wisely
     fall soon again into the slow requirements of our dreams:
15   how we turned at the ends of rows without sense to new furrows
     and went back
               flicked by
               cornblades and hearing the circling in
     the cornblades of horseflies in pursuit:

I hitch up early, the raw spot on Silver's shoulder
sore to the collar,
get a wrench and change the plow's bull-tongue for a sweep,[1]
and go out, wrench in my hip pocket for later adjustments,
    down the ditch-path
25 by the white-bloomed briars, wet crabgrass, cattails,
    and rusting ferns,
riding the plow handles down,
   keeping the sweep's point from the ground,
the smooth bar under the plow gliding,
30 the traces loose, the raw spot wearing its soreness out
in the gentle movement to the fields:

       when snake-bitten in the spring pasture grass
Silver came up to the gate and stood head-down enchanted
    in her fate
35 I found her sorrowful eyes by accident and knew:
nevertheless the doctor could not keep her from all
the consequences, rolls in the sand, the blank extension
    of limbs,
    head thrown back in the dust,
40 useless unfocusing eyes, belly swollen
wide as I was tall
and I went out in the night and saw her in the solitude
    of her wildness:

but she lived and one day half got up
45 and looking round at the sober world took me back
    into her eyes
and then got up and walked and plowed again;
mornings her swollen snake-bitten leg wept bright as dew
and dried to streaks of salt leaked white from the hair.

                                      1961

Corsons Inlet[2]

I went for a walk over the dunes again this morning
to the sea,
then turned right along
    the surf
5   rounded a naked headland
            and returned

    along the inlet shore:

it was muggy sunny, the wind from the sea steady and high,
crisp in the running sand,
10   some breakthroughs of sun
    but after a bit
continuous overcast:

---

1. Cultivator blade for a plow; "bull-tongue": 2. Located on the southern New Jersey shore.
shovel blade for stirring soil or marking furrows.

the walk liberating, I was released from forms,
from the perpendiculars,
15   straight lines, blocks, boxes, binds
of thought
into the hues, shadings, rises, flowing bends and blends
        of sight:

                I allow myself eddies of meaning:
20   yield to a direction of significance
running
like a stream through the geography of my work:
        you can find
in my sayings
25   swerves of action
                like the inlet's cutting edge:
        there are dunes of motion,
organizations of grass, white sandy paths of remembrance
in the overall wandering of mirroring mind:

30   but Overall is beyond me: is the sum of these events
I cannot draw, the ledger I cannot keep, the accounting
beyond the account:

in nature there are few sharp lines: there are areas of
primrose
35   more or less dispersed;
disorderly orders of bayberry; between the rows
of dunes,
irregular swamps of reeds,
though not reeds alone, but grass, bayberry, yarrow, all . . .
40   predominantly reeds:

I have reached no conclusions, have erected no boundaries,
shutting out and shutting in, separating inside
        from outside: I have
        drawn no lines:
45   as

manifold events of sand
change the dune's shape that will not be the same shape
tomorrow,

so I am willing to go along, to accept
50   the becoming
thought, to stake off no beginnings or ends, establish
        no walls:

by transitions the land falls from grassy dunes to creek
to undercreek: but there are no lines, though
55   change in that transition is clear
        as any sharpness: but "sharpness" spread out,
allowed to occur over a wider range
than mental lines can keep:

the moon was full last night: today, low tide was low:
60   black shoals of mussels exposed to the risk
of air
and, earlier, of sun,
waved in and out with the waterline, waterline inexact,
caught always in the event of change:
65   a young mottled gull stood free on the shoals
       and ate
to vomiting: another gull, squawking possession, cracked a crab,
picked out the entrails, swallowed the soft-shelled legs, a ruddy
turnstone° running in to snatch leftover bits: *a shorebird*

70   risk is full: every living thing in
siege: the demand is life, to keep life: the small
white blacklegged egret, how beautiful, quietly stalks and spears
       the shallows, darts to shore
           to stab—what? I couldn't
75   see against the black mudflats—a frightened
     fiddler crab?

       the news to my left over the dunes and
reeds and bayberry clumps was
       fall: thousands of tree swallows
80   gathering for flight:
       an order held
       in constant change: a congregation
rich with entropy: nevertheless, separable, noticeable
       as one event,
85   not chaos: preparations for
flight from winter,
cheet, cheet, cheet, cheet, wings rifling the green clumps,
beaks
at the bayberries
90   a perception full of wind, flight, curve,
       sound:
       the possibility of rule as the sum of rulelessness:
the "field" of action
with moving, incalculable center:

95   in the smaller view, order tight with shape:
blue tiny flowers on a leafless weed: carapace of crab:
snail shell:
       pulsations of order
       in the bellies of minnows: orders swallowed,
100   broken down, transferred through membranes
to strengthen larger orders: but in the large view, no
lines or changeless shapes: the working in and out, together
       and against, of millions of events: this,
       so that I make
105   no form
       formlessness:

orders as summaries, as outcomes of actions override
or in some way result, not predictably (seeing me gain

the top of a dune,
110   the swallows
could take flight—some other fields of bayberry
    could enter fall
    berryless) and there is serenity:

      no arranged terror: no forcing of image, plan,
115 or thought:
no propaganda, no humbling of reality to precept:

terror pervades but is not arranged, all possibilities
of escape open: no route shut, except in
    the sudden loss of all routes:

120   I see narrow orders, limited tightness, but will
not run to that easy victory:
    still around the looser, wider forces work:
    I will try
    to fasten into order enlarging grasps of disorder, widening
125 scope, but enjoying the freedom that
Scope eludes my grasp, that there is no finality of vision,
    that I have perceived nothing completely,
      that tomorrow a new walk is a new walk.

1965

The City Limits

When you consider the radiance, that it does not withhold
itself but pours its abundance without selection into every
nook and cranny not overhung or hidden; when you consider

that birds' bones make no awful noise against the light but
5 lie low in the light as in a high testimony; when you consider
the radiance, that it will look into the guiltiest

swervings of the weaving heart and bear itself upon them,
not flinching into disguise or darkening; when you consider
the abundance of such resource as illuminates the glow-blue

10 bodies and gold-skeined wings of flies swarming the dumped
guts of a natural slaughter or the coil of shit and in no
way winces from its storms of generosity; when you consider

that air or vacuum, snow or shale, squid or wolf, rose or lichen,
each is accepted into as much light as it will take, then
15 the heart moves roomier, the man stands and looks about, the

leaf does not increase itself above the grass, and the dark
work of the deepest cells is of a tune with May bushes
and fear lit by the breadth of such calmly turns to praise.

1971

The Arc Inside and Out

For Harold Bloom

If, whittler and dumper, gross carver
into the shadiest curvings, I took branch
and meat from the stalk of life, threw

away the monies of the treasured,
5   treasurable mind, cleaved memory free
of the instant, if I got right down

shucking off periphery after periphery
to the glassy vague gray parabolas
and swoops of unnailable perception,

10   would I begin to improve the purity,
would I essentialize out the distilled
form, the glitter-stone that whether

the world comes or goes clicks gleams
and chinks of truth self-making, never
15   to be shuttered, the face-brilliant core

stone: or if I, amasser, heap shoveler,
depth pumper, took in all springs and
oceans, paramoecia and moons, massive

buttes and summit slants, rooted trunks
20   and leafages, anthologies of wise words,
schemata, all grasses (including the

tidal *Spartinas*,[3] marginal, salty
broadsweeps) would I finally come on a
suasion, large, fully-informed, restful

25   scape, turning back in on itself, its
periphery enclosing our system with
its bright dot and allowing in nonparlant

quantities at the edge void, void, and
void, would I then feel plenitude
30   brought to center and extent, a sweet

easing away of all edge, evil, and surprise:
these two ways to dream! dreaming them's
the bumfuzzlement—the impoverished

diamond, the heterogeneous abundance
35   starved into oneness: ultimately, either
way, which is our peace, the little

---

3. Genus of various swamp grasses.

arc-line appears, inside which is nothing,
outside which is nothing—however big,
nothing beyond: however small, nothing

40 within: neither way to go's to stay, stay
here, the apple an apple with its own hue
or streak, the drink of water, the drink,

the falling into sleep, restfully ever the
falling into sleep, dream, dream, and
45 every morning the sun comes, the sun.

1972

Pet Panther

My attention is a wild
animal: it will if idle
make trouble where there
was no harm: it will

5 sniff and scratch at the
breath's sills:
it will wind itself tight
around the pulse

or, undistracted by
10 verbal toys, pommel the
heart frantic: it will
pounce on a stalled riddle

and wrestle the mind numb:
attention, fierce animal
15 I cry, as it coughs in my
face, dislodges boulders

in my belly, lie down, be
still, have mercy, here
is song, coils of song, play
20 it out, run with it.

1983

JAMES K. BAXTER

1926–1972

Wild Bees

Often in summer, on a tarred bridge plank standing,
Or downstream between willows, a safe Ophelia drifting[1]

1. The young heroine of Shakespeare's *Hamlet*, who went mad and then drowned while drifting down a river (*Hamlet* 4.7.167–85).

In a rented boat—I had seen them come and go,
Those wild bees swift as tigers, their gauze wings a-glitter
5 In passionless industry, clustering black at the crevice
Of a rotten cabbage tree, where their hive was hidden low.

But never strolled too near. Till one half-cloudy evening
Of ripe January, my friends and I
Came, gloved and masked to the eyes like plundering desperadoes,
10 To smoke them out. Quiet beside the stagnant river
We trod wet grasses down, hearing the crickets chitter
And waiting for light to drain from the wounded sky.

Before we reached the hive their sentries saw us
And sprang invisible through the darkening air,
15 Stabbed, and died in stinging. The hive woke. Poisonous fuming
Of sulphur filled the hollow trunk, and crawling
Blue flame sputtered—yet still their suicidal
Live raiders dived and clung to our hands and hair.

O it was Carthage under the Roman torches,
20 Or loud with flames and falling timber, Troy![2]
A job well botched. Half of the honey melted
And half the rest young grubs. Through earth-black smoldering ashes
And maimed bees groaning, we drew out our plunder.
Little enough their gold, and slight our joy.

25 Fallen then the city of instinctive wisdom.
Tragedy is written distinct and small:
A hive burned on a cool night in summer.
But loss is a precious stone to me, a nectar
Distilled in time, preaching the truth of winter
30 To the fallen heart that does not cease to fall.

1953

East Coast Journey

About twilight we came to the whitewashed pub
On a knuckle of land above the bay

Where a log was riding and the slow
Bird-winged breakers cast up spray.

5 One of the drinkers round packing cases had
The worn face of a kumara[3] god,

Or so it struck me. Later on
Lying awake in the veranda bedroom

In great dryness of mind I heard the voice of the sea
10 Reverberating, and thought: As a man

2. References to the destruction by fire of two great cities of classical times—Carthage by the Romans in 146 B.C. and Troy by the Greeks at the end of the Trojan War.

3. Maori word for "sweet potato," a staple food of the Maoris, who are the Polynesian natives of New Zealand.

Grows older he does not want beer, bread, or the prancing flesh,
But the arms of the eater of life, Hine-nui-te-po,[4]

With teeth of obsidian and hair like kelp
Flashing and glimmering at the edge of the horizon.

1966

New Zealand

(For Monte Holcroft)

These unshaped islands, on the sawyer's bench,
Wait for the chisel of the mind,
Green canyons to the south, immense and passive,
Penetrated rarely, seeded only
5   By the deer-culler's shot,[5] or else in the north
Tribes of the shark and the octopus,
Mangroves, black hair on a boxer's hand.

The founding fathers with their guns and bibles,
Botanist, whaler, added bones and names
10   To the land, to us a bridle
As if the id were a horse: the swampy towns
Like dreamers that struggle to wake,

Longing for the poet's truth
And the lover's pride. Something new and old
15   Explores its own pain, hearing
The rain's choir on curtains of gray moss
Or fingers of the Tasman[6] pressing
On breasts of hardening sand, as actors
Find their own solitude in mirrors,

20   As one who has buried his dead,
Able at last to give with an open hand.

1969

From Jerusalem[7] Sonnets

(POEMS FOR COLIN DURNING)

1

The small gray cloudy louse that nests in my beard
Is not, as some have called it, "a pearl of God" —

No, it is a fiery tormentor
Waking me at two a.m.

5   Or thereabouts, when the lights are still on
In the houses in the pa,[8] to go across thick grass

---

4. Maori goddess of death.
5. A "deer-culler" is a kind of game warden, an agent of the government who controls the herds of deer.

6. The Tasman Sea, to the west of New Zealand.
7. Isolated Maori settlement to which Baxter retreated during the last years of his life.
8. "Village" (Maori).

Wet with rain, feet cold, to kneel
For an hour or two in front of the red flickering

Tabernacle light—what He sees inside
10 My meandering mind I can only guess—

A madman, a nobody, a raconteur
Whom He can joke with—"Lord," I ask Him,

"Do You or don't You expect me to put up with lice?"
His silent laugh still shakes the hills at dawn.

1970

ROBERT BLY

1926–

Waking from Sleep

Inside the veins there are navies setting forth,
Tiny explosions at the water lines,
And seagulls weaving in the wind of the salty blood.

It is the morning. The country has slept the whole winter.
5 Window seats were covered with fur skins, the yard was full
Of stiff dogs, and hands that clumsily held heavy books.

Now we wake, and rise from bed, and eat breakfast!—
Shouts rise from the harbor of the blood,
Mist, and masts rising, the knock of wooden tackle in the sunlight.

10 Now we sing, and do tiny dances on the kitchen floor.
Our whole body is like a harbor at dawn;
We know that our master has left us for the day.

1962

ROBERT CREELEY

1926–

I Know a Man

As I sd to my
friend, because I am
always talking,—John, I

sd, which was not his
5 name, the darkness sur-
rounds us, what

can we do against
it, or else, shall we &
why not, buy a goddamn big car,

10   drive, he sd, for
christ's sake, look
out where yr going.

1957

Heroes

In all those stories the hero
is beyond himself into the next
thing, be it those labors
of Hercules,[1] or Aeneas going into death.

5   I thought the instant of the one humanness
in Virgil's plan of it
was that it was of course human enough to die,
yet to come back, as he said, *hoc opus, hic labor est.*[2]

That was the Cumaean Sibyl speaking.
10   This is Robert Creeley, and Virgil
is dead now two thousand years, yet Hercules
and the *Aeneid*, yet all that industrious wis-

dom lives in the way the mountains
and the desert are waiting
15   for the heroes, and death also
can still propose the old labors.

1959

The World

I wanted so ably
to reassure you, I wanted
the man you took to be me,

to comfort you, and got
5   up, and went to the window,
pushed back, as you asked me to,

the curtain, to see
the outline of the trees
in the night outside.

10   The light, love,
the light we felt then,
grayly, was it, that

1. Greek hero of superhuman strength, best
known for his legendary twelve labors. Aeneas was
a Trojan hero whose adventures and travails are
recorded in Virgil's epic poem, *The Aeneid* (19
B.C.).

2. *Aeneid* 6.129. When Aeneas asks the Sibyl, a
priestess and prophet of Apollo, how he might visit
his dead father in the underworld, she answers that
the descent is easy, but to return—"That is the
task, that is the labor."

came in, on us, not
merely my hands or yours,
15   or a wetness so comfortable,

but in the dark then
as you slept, the gray
figure came so close

and leaned over,
20   between us, as you
slept, restless, and

my own face had to
see it, and be seen by it,
the man it was, your

25   gray lost tired bewildered
brother, unused, untaken—
hated by love, and dead,

but not dead, for an
instant, saw me, myself
30   the intruder, as he was not.

I tried to say, it is
all right, she is
happy, you are no longer

needed. I said,
35   he is dead, and he
went as you shifted

and woke, at first afraid,
then knew by my own knowing
what had happened—

40   and the light then
of the sun coming
for another morning
in the world.

                                        1969

Bresson's Movies[3]

A movie of Robert
Bresson's[4] showed a yacht,
at evening on the Seine,
all its lights on, watched

5   by two young, seemingly
poor people, on a bridge adjacent,

---

3. Robert Bresson (1907–   ), French director and   4. *Quatre Nuits d'Un Rêveur* ("Four Nights of a
screenwriter, known for his austere style.   Dreamer"), 1971.

the classic boy and girl
of the story, any one

one cares to tell. So
10   years pass, of course, but
I identified with the young,
embittered Frenchman,

knew his almost complacent
anguish and the distance
15   he felt from his girl. Yet another film

of Bresson's has the
aging Lancelot[5] with his
awkward armor standing
20   in a woods, of small trees,

dazed, bleeding, both he
and his horse are,
trying to get back to
the castle, itself of

25   no great size. It
moved me, that
life was after all
like that. You are

in love. You stand
30   in the woods, with
a horse, bleeding.
The story is true.

1982

ALLEN GINSBERG
1926–

From Howl

FOR CARL SOLOMON[1]

1

I saw the best minds of my generation destroyed by madness, starving
    hysterical naked,
dragging themselves through the negro streets at dawn looking for an
    angry fix,

5. *Lancelot du Lac* ("Lancelot of the Lake"), 1974.
1. Ginsberg met Solomon (b. 1928) while both
were patients in the Columbia Psychiatric Institute
in 1949. Many details in *Howl* come from the
"apocryphal history" that Solomon then told him.

angelheaded hipsters burning for the ancient heavenly connection to the
starry dynamo in the machinery of night,

who poverty and tatters and hollow-eyed and high sat up smoking in the
supernatural darkness of cold-water flats floating across the tops of
cities contemplating jazz,

5 who bared their brains to Heaven under the El[2] and saw Mohammedan
angels staggering on tenement roofs illuminated

who passed through universities with radiant cool eyes hallucinating
Arkansas and Blake-light[3] tragedy among the scholars of war,

who were expelled from the academies for crazy & publishing obscene
odes on the windows of the skull,

who cowered in unshaven rooms in underwear, burning their money in
wastebaskets and listening to the Terror through the wall,

who got busted in their pubic beards returning through Laredo with a
belt of marijuana for New York,

10 who ate fire in paint hotels or drank turpentine in Paradise Alley,[4] death,
or purgatoried their torsos night after night

with dreams, with drugs, with waking nightmares, alcohol and cock and
endless balls,

incomparable blind streets of shuddering cloud and lightning in the mind
leaping toward poles of Canada & Paterson,[5] illuminating all the
motionless world of Time between,

Peyote solidities of halls, backyard green tree cemetery dawns, wine
drunkenness over the rooftops, storefront boroughs of teahead joy-
ride neon blinking traffic light, sun and moon and tree vibrations in
the roaring winter dusks of Brooklyn, ashcan rantings and kind king
light of mind,

who chained themselves to subways for the endless ride from Battery to
holy Bronx[6] on benzedrine until the noise of wheels and children
brought them down shuddering mouth-wracked and battered bleak
of brain all drained of brilliance in the drear light of Zoo,

15 who sank all night in submarine light of Bickford's floated out and sat
through the stale beer afternoon in desolate Fugazzi's,[7] listening to
the crack of doom on the hydrogen jukebox,

who talked continuously seventy hours from park to pad to bar to Belle-
vue[8] to museum to the Brooklyn Bridge,

a lost battalion of platonic conversationalists jumping down the stoops off
fire escapes off windowsills off Empire State out of the moon,

yacketayakking screaming vomiting whispering facts and memories and
anecdotes and eyeball kicks and shocks of hospitals and jails and
wars,

whole intellects disgorged in total recall for seven days and nights with
brilliant eyes, meat for the Synagogue cast on the pavement,

20 who vanished into nowhere Zen New Jersey leaving a trail of ambiguous
picture postcards of Atlantic City Hall,

suffering Eastern sweats and Tangerian bone-grindings and migraines of
China under junk-withdrawal in Newark's bleak furnished room,

2. Elevated railway.
3. A reference to the English visionary poet and artist William Blake (1757–1827).
4. A slum courtyard in New York's East Village, the setting of Jack Kerouac's novel *The Subterraneans* (1958).
5. City in New Jersey where Ginsberg was born.
6. The south-north extremes of one set of New York subway lines; the zoo is in the Bronx.
7. A bar near Greenwich Village, New York's bohemian center. "Bickford's": one of a chain of cafetarias open twenty-four hours a day.
8. A public hospital in New York that serves as a receiving center for mental patients.

who wandered around and around at midnight in the railroad yard won-
dering where to go, and went, leaving no broken hearts,
who lit cigarettes in boxcars boxcars boxcars racketing through snow
toward lonesome farms in grandfather night,
who studied Plotinus Poe St. John of the Cross[9] telepathy and bop
kaballa[1] because the cosmos instinctively vibrated at their feet in
Kansas,
25   who loned it through the streets of Idaho seeking visionary indian angels
who were visionary indian angels,
who thought they were only mad when Baltimore gleamed in supernatu-
ral ecstasy,
who jumped in limousines with the Chinaman of Oklahoma on the
impulse of winter midnight streetlight smalltown rain,
who lounged hungry and lonesome through Houston seeking jazz or sex
or soup, and followed the brilliant Spaniard to converse about
America and Eternity, a hopeless task, and so took ship to Africa,
who disappeared into the volcanoes of Mexico leaving behind nothing
but the shadow of dungarees and the lava and ash of poetry scattered
in fireplace Chicago,
30   who reappeared on the West Coast investigating the F.B.I. in beards and
shorts with big pacifist eyes sexy in their dark skin passing out incom-
prehensible leaflets,
who burned cigarette holes in their arms protesting the narcotic tobacco
haze of Capitalism,
who distributed Supercommunist pamphlets in Union Square weeping
and undressing while the sirens of Los Alamos[2] wailed them down,
and wailed down Wall,[3] and the Staten Island ferry also wailed,
who broke down crying in white gymnasiums naked and trembling before
the machinery of other skeletons,
who bit detectives in the neck and shrieked with delight in policecars
for committing no crime but their own wild cooking pederasty and
intoxication,
35   who howled on their knees in the subway and were dragged off the roof
waving genitals and manuscripts,
who let themselves be fucked in the ass by saintly motorcyclists, and
screamed with joy,
who blew and were blown by those human seraphim,[4] the sailors, caresses
of Atlantic and Caribbean love,
who balled in the morning in the evenings in rosegardens and the grass
of public parks and cemeteries scattering their semen freely to
whomever come who may,
who hiccupped endlessly trying to giggle but wound up with a sob behind
a partition in a Turkish Bath when the blonde & naked angel came
to pierce them with a sword,[5]

---

9. Spanish poet and mystic (1542–1591), who
wrote *The Dark Night of the Soul*. Plotinus (A.D.
205–270): mystic philosopher. Edgar Allen Poe
(1809–1894): American poet and author of super-
natural tales as well as the cosmological *Eureka*.
1. "Bop" is a jazz style of the 1940s. The Kaballa is
a tradition of mystical interpretation of the Hebrew
scriptures.
2. In New Mexico, where the development of the
atomic bomb was completed.
3. Wall Street, the center of New York's financial

district, but also the Wailing Wall in Jerusalem, a
place of prayer and lamentation.
4. The highest order of angels.
5. An allusion to *The Ecstasy of St. Teresa*, a sculp-
ture by Lorenzo Bernini (1598–1680) based on St.
Teresa's (1515–1582) distinctly erotic description
of a religious vision. "Three old shrews": a refer-
ence to the three fates of Greek mythology, who
spun, wove, and finally cut the thread of every
mortal life.

40   who lost their loveboys to the three old shrews of fate the one eyed shrew
of the heterosexual dollar the one eyed shrew that winks out of the
womb and the one eyed shrew that does nothing but sit on her ass
and snip the intellectual golden threads of the craftsman's loom,

who copulated ecstatic and insatiate with a bottle of beer a sweetheart a
package of cigarettes a candle and fell off the bed, and continued
along the floor and down the hall and ended fainting on the wall
with a vision of ultimate cunt and come eluding the last gyzym of
consciousness,

who sweetened the snatches of a million girls trembling in the sunset, and
were red eyed in the morning but prepared to sweeten the snatch of
the sunrise, flashing buttocks under barns and naked in the lake,

who went out whoring through Colorado in myriad stolen night-cars,
N.C.,[6] secret hero of these poems, cocksman and Adonis of Den-
ver—joy to the memory of his innumerable lays of girls in empty
lots & diner backyards, moviehouses' rickety rows, on mountaintops
in caves or with gaunt waitresses in familiar roadside lonely petticoat
upliftings & especially secret gas-station solipsisms of johns, &
hometown alleys too,

who faded out in vast sordid movies, were shifted in dreams, woke on
a sudden Manhattan, and picked themselves up out of basements
hungover with heartless Tokay[7] and horrors of Third Avenue iron
dreams & stumbled to unemployment offices,

45   who walked all night with their shoes full of blood on the snowbank docks
waiting for a door in the East River to open to a room full of steam-
heat and opium,

who created great suicidal dramas on the apartment cliff-banks of the
Hudson under the wartime blue floodlight of the moon & their
heads shall be crowned with laurel in oblivion,

who ate the lamb stew of the imagination or digested the crab at the
muddy bottom of the rivers of Bowery,[8]

who wept at the romance of the streets with their pushcarts full of onions
and bad music,

who sat in boxes breathing in the darkness under the bridge, and rose up
to build harpsichords in their lofts,

50   who coughed on the sixth floor of Harlem crowned with flame under the
tubercular sky surrounded by orange crates of theology,

who scribbled all night rocking and rolling over lofty incantations which
in the yellow morning were stanzas of gibberish,

who cooked rotten animals lung heart feet tail borsht & tortillas dreaming
of the pure vegetable kingdom,

who plunged themselves under meat trucks looking for an egg,

who threw their watches off the roof to cast their ballot for Eternity out-
side of Time, & alarm clocks fell on their heads every day for the
next decade,

55   who cut their wrists three times successively unsuccessfully, gave up and
were forced to open antique stores where they thought they were
growing old and cried,

who were burned alive in their innocent flannel suits on Madison Ave-

---

6. Neal Cassady, a friend and lover of Ginsberg.
Also a friend of Jack Kerouac, he is the hero of
Kerouac's novel *On the Road* (1957).

7. Hungarian wine.
8. Street in lower Manhattan, traditional haunt of
alcoholics and derelicts.

nue[9] amid blasts of leaden verse & the tanked-up clatter of the iron
 regiments of fashion & the nitroglycerine shrieks of the fairies of
 advertising & the mustard gas of sinister intelligent editors, or were
 run down by the drunken taxicabs of Absolute Reality,
who jumped off the Brooklyn Bridge this actually happened and walked
 away unknown and forgotten into the ghostly daze of Chinatown
 soup alleyways & firetrucks, not even one free beer,
who sang out of their windows in despair, fell out of the subway window,
 jumped in the filthy Passaic,[1] leaped on negroes, cried all over the
 street, danced on broken wineglasses barefoot smashed phonograph
 records of nostalgic European 1930's German jazz finished the whis-
 key and threw up groaning into the bloody toilet, moans in their ears
 and the blast of colossal steamwhistles,
who barreled down the highways of the past journeying to each other's
 hotrod-Golgotha[2] jail-solitude watch or Birmingham jazz incarna-
 tion,
who drove crosscountry seventytwo hours to find out if I had a vision or
 you had a vision or he had a vision to find out Eternity,
who journeyed to Denver, who died in Denver, who came back to Den-
 ver & waited in vain, who watched over Denver & brooded & loned
 in Denver and finally went away to find out the Time, & now Den-
 ver is lonesome for her heroes,
who fell on their knees in hopeless cathedrals praying for each other's
 salvation and light and breasts, until the soul illuminated its hair for
 a second,
who crashed through their minds in jail waiting for impossible criminals
 with golden heads and the charm of reality in their hearts who sang
 sweet blues to Alcatraz,
who retired to Mexico to cultivate a habit, or Rocky Mount to tender
 Buddha or Tangiers to boys or Southern Pacific to the black locomo-
 tive or Harvard to Narcissus to Woodlawn[3] to the daisychain or
 grave,
who demanded sanity trials accusing the radio of hypnotism & were left
 with their insanity & their hands & a hung jury,
who threw potato salad at CCNY lecturers on Dadaism[4] and subse-
 quently presented themselves on the granite steps of the madhouse
 with shaven heads and harlequin speech of suicide, demanding
 instantaneous lobotomy,
and who were given instead the concrete void of insulin metrasol electric-
 ity hydrotherapy psychotherapy occupational therapy pingpong &
 amnesia,
who in humorless protest overturned only one symbolic pingpong table,
 resting briefly in catatonia,
returning years later truly bald except for a wig of blood, and tears and
 fingers, to the visible madman doom of the wards of the madtowns
 of the East,
Pilgrim State's Rockland's and Greystone's[5] foetid halls, bickering with

60

65

70

9. The center of New York's advertising industry.
Cf. *The Man in the Gray Flannel Suit*, Sloan Wil-
son's 1955 best-selling novel.
1. The river that flows through Paterson.
2. Hill where Jesus was crucified.
3. Cemetery in the Bronx.
4. An artistic movement based on absurdity and

accident; it flourished during World War I.
"CCNY": City College of New York.
5. Three mental hospitals near New York. Carl
Solomon was an inmate at Pilgrim State and Rock-
land, and Ginsberg's mother was institutionalized
at Greystone.

the echoes of the soul, rocking and rolling in the midnight solitude-
bench dolmen-realms[6] of love, dream of life a nightmare, bodies
turned to stone as heavy as the moon,
with mother finally ******, and the last fantastic book flung out of the
tenement window, and the last door closed at 4 AM and the last
telephone slammed at the wall in reply and the last furnished room
emptied down to the last piece of mental furniture, a yellow paper
rose twisted on a wire hanger in the closet, and even that imaginary,
nothing but a hopeful little bit of hallucination—
ah, Carl, while you are not safe I am not safe, and now you're really in
the total animal soup of time—
and who therefore ran through the icy streets obsessed with a sudden
flash of the alchemy of the use of the ellipse the catalog the meter &
the vibrating plane,
who dreamt and made incarnate gaps in Time & Space through images
juxtaposed, and trapped the archangel of the soul between 2 visual
images and joined the elemental verbs and set the noun and dash of
consciousness together jumping with sensation of Pater Omnipotens
Aeterna Deus[7]
75   to recreate the syntax and measure of poor human prose and stand before
you speechless and intelligent and shaking with shame, rejected yet
confessing out the soul to conform to the rhythm of thought in his
naked and endless head,
the madman bum and angel beat in Time, unknown, yet putting down
here what might be left to say in time come after death,
and rose reincarnate in the ghostly clothes of jazz in the goldhorn shadow
of the band and blew the suffering of America's naked mind for love
into an eli eli lamma lamma sabacthani[8] saxophone cry that shivered
the cities down to the last radio
with the absolute heart of the poem of life butchered out of their own
bodies good to eat a thousand years.
San Francisco 1955   1956

To Aunt Rose

Aunt Rose—now—might I see you
with your thin face and buck tooth smile and pain
of rheumatism—and a long black heavy shoe
for your bony left leg
5   limping down the long hall in Newark on the running carpet
past the black grand piano
in the day room
where the parties were
and I sang Spanish loyalist songs
10   in a high squeaky voice
(hysterical) the committee listening
while you limped around the room

6. Dolmens are prehistoric monuments of hori-
zontal stone slabs supported by upright stones,
found in Britain and France and believed to be
tombs.
7. "All-powerful Father, Eternal God" (Latin;
"Aeterna" is feminine, the nouns are masculine).

Paul Cézanne (1839–1906), the French Impres-
sionist painter, used this phrase to describe the
effects of nature on him.
8. "My God, my God, why have you forsaken
me?" (Hebrew). These are Jesus' last words from
the cross (Matthew 27.46; quoting Psalm 22.1).

                    collected the money—
        Aunt Honey, Uncle Sam, a stranger with a cloth arm
15   in his pocket
                    and huge young bald head
                    of Abraham Lincoln Brigade[9]

        —your long sad face
                    your tears of sexual frustration
20   (what smothered sobs and bony hips
                        under the pillows of Osborne Terrace)
        —the time I stood on the toilet seat naked
            and you powdered my thighs with Calomine
                against the poison ivy—my tender
25   and shamed first black curled hairs
        what were you thinking in secret heart then
                    knowing me a man already—
        and I am ignorant girl of family silence on the thin pedestal
                    of my legs in the bathroom—Museum of Newark.
30   Aunt Rose
        Hitler is dead, Hitler is in Eternity; Hitler is with
                    Tamburlane and Emily Brontë[1]

        Though I see you walking still, a ghost on Osborne Terrace
                    down the long dark hall to the front door
35   limping a little with a pinched smile
                    in what must have been a silken
                        flower dress
            welcoming my father, the Poet, on his visit to Newark
                    —see you arriving in the living room
40   dancing on your crippled leg
                        and clapping hands his book
                        had been accepted by Liveright

        Hitler is dead and Liveright's gone out of business
        The Attic of the Past and *Everlasting Minute* are out of print
45   Uncle Harry sold his last silk stocking
            Claire quit interpretive dancing school
                Buba[2] sits a wrinkled monument in Old
                    Ladies Home blinking at new babies

        last time I saw you was the hospital
50   pale skull protruding under ashen skin
                blue veined unconscious girl
                    in an oxygen tent
                the war in Spain has ended long ago
                    Aunt Rose
Paris 1958   1961

9. A group of American volunteers in the Spanish
Civil War (1936–39); they and the Spanish loyal-
ists were fighting againt the Fascists, whose even-
tual triumph led to Francisco Franco (1892–1975)
becoming dictator of Spain.
1. (1818–1848); English poet and novelist, whose

novel *Wuthering Heights* is in part a ghost story.
"Tamburlane": renowned fourteenth-century Tartar
conqueror and bloodthirsty hero of Christopher
Marlowe's tragedy *Tambulaine the Great* (1587).
2. "Grandmother" (Yiddish).

JAMES MERRILL
1926–1995

The Country of a Thousand Years of Peace[1]
to Hans Lodeizen (1924–1950)

Here they all come to die,
Fluent therein as in a fourth tongue.[2]
But for a young man not yet of their race
It was a madness you should lie

5   Blind in one eye, and fed
By the blood of a scrubbed face;
It was a madness to look down
On the toy city where

The glittering neutrality
10 Of clock and chocolate and lake and cloud[3]
Made every morning somewhat
Less than you could bear;

And makes me cry aloud
At the old masters of disease
15 Who dangling high above you on a hair
The sword that, never falling, kills[4]

Would coax you still back from that starry land
Under the world, which no one sees
Without a death, its finish and sharp weight
20 Flashing in his own hand.

1959

The Broken Home[5]

Crossing the street,
I saw the parents and the child
At their window, gleaming like fruit
With evening's mild gold leaf.

5 In a room on the floor below,
Sunless, cooler—a brimming
Saucer of wax, marbly and dim—
I have lit what's left of my life.

---

1. Expression for Switzerland.
2. In addition to the three national languages of Switzerland: French, German, and Italian.
3. Switzerland has a policy of neutrality. Clocks and chocolate are the country's most celebrated products; it is also known for its lakes.
4. Reference to Damocles, a courtier to Dionysius I of Syracuse in the fourth century B.C. After

Damocles overpraised the happiness of tyrants, Dionysius demonstrated the precariousness of happiness by placing him at a banquet where a sword dangled by a single hair over his head.
5. The poem is composed of sonnets, some "broken" into unconventional proportions and rhyme schemes.

I have thrown out yesterday's milk
10   And opened a book of maxims.
The flame quickens. The word stirs.

Tell me, tongue of fire,
That you and I are as real
At least as the people upstairs.

15   My father, who had flown in World War I,
Might have continued to invest his life
In cloud banks well above Wall Street and wife.[6]
But the race was run below, and the point was to win.

Too late now, I make out in his blue gaze
20   (Through the smoked glass of being thirty-six)
The soul eclipsed by twin black pupils, sex
And business; time was money in those days.

Each thirteenth year he married. When he died
There were already several chilled wives
25   In sable orbit—rings, cars, permanent waves.
We'd felt him warming up for a green bride.

He could afford it. He was "in his prime"
At three score ten. But money was not time.

When my parents were younger this was a popular act:
30   A veiled woman would leap from an electric, wine-dark car
To the steps of no matter what—the Senate or the Ritz Bar—
And bodily, at newsreel speed, attack

No matter whom—Al Smith or José Maria Sert
Or Clemenceau[7]—veins standing out on her throat
35   As she yelled *War mongerer! Pig! Give us the vote!*,
And would have to be hauled away in her hobble skirt.

What had the man done? Oh, made history.
Her business (he had implied) was giving birth,
Tending the house, mending the socks.

40   Always that same old story—
Father Time and Mother Earth,
A marriage on the rocks.

One afternoon, red, satyr-thighed
Michael, the Irish setter, head

6. Charles Merrill, the poet's father, was a cofounder of the investment firm Merrill, Lynch. Wall Street is the hub of the financial industry in New York City.
7. Georges Clemenceau (1841–1929): premier of France in World War I, visitor to the United States in 1922. Alfred Smith (1873–1944): 1928 candidate for the United States presidency; José Maria Sert y Badia (1874–1945): Spanish painter and muralist who decorated the Waldorf-Astoria Hotel in New York in 1930.

45 Passionately lowered, led
    The child I was to a shut door. Inside,

    Blinds beat sun from the bed.
    The green-gold room throbbed like a bruise.
    Under a sheet, clad in taboos
50 Lay whom we sought, her hair undone, outspread,

    And of a blackness found, if ever now, in old
    Engravings where the acid bit.
    I must have needed to touch it
    Or the whiteness—was she dead?
55 Her eyes flew open, startled strange and cold.
    The dog slumped to the floor. She reached for me. I fled.

    Tonight they have stepped out onto the gravel.
    The party is over. It's the fall
    Of 1931. They love each other still.

60 She: Charlie, I can't stand the pace.
    He: Come on, honey—why, you'll bury us all!

    A lead soldier guards my windowsill:
    Khaki rifle, uniform, and face.
    Something in me grows heavy, silvery, pliable.

65 How intensely people used to feel!
    Like metal poured at the close of a proletarian novel,
    Refined and glowing from the crucible,
    I see those two hearts, I'm afraid,
    Still. Cool here in the graveyard of good and evil,
70 They are even so to be honored and obeyed.

    . . . Obeyed, at least, inversely. Thus
    I rarely buy a newspaper, or vote.
    To do so, I have learned, is to invite
    The tread of a stone guest[8] within my house.

75 Shooting this rusted bolt, though, against him,
    I trust I am no less time's child than some
    Who on the heath impersonate Poor Tom[9]
    Or on the barricades risk life and limb.

    Nor do I try to keep a garden, only
80 An avocado in a glass of water—
    Roots pallid, gemmed with air. And later,

---

8. As in Molière's play *The Stone Feast*, in which a stone statue of the commander of Seville drags his murderer, Don Juan, down to hell.
9. The nickname that Edgar, the disowned son of Gloucester in Shakespeare's *King Lear*, gives to himself when he wanders the heath in disguise as a disheveled madman.

When the small gilt leaves have grown
Fleshy and green, I let them die, yes, yes,
And start another. I am earth's no less.

85   A child, a red dog roam the corridors,
Still, of the broken home. No sound. The brilliant
Rag runners halt before wide-open doors.
My old room! Its wallpaper—cream, medallioned
With pink and brown—brings back the first nightmares,
90   Long summer colds, and Emma, sepia-faced,
Perspiring over broth carried upstairs
Aswim with golden fats I could not taste.

The real house became a boarding school.
Under the ballroom ceiling's allegory
95   Someone at last may actually be allowed
To learn something; or, from my window, cool
With the unstiflement of the entire story,
Watch a red setter stretch and sink in cloud.

1966

The Victor Dog[1]

For Elizabeth Bishop

Bix to Buxtehude to Boulez,
The little white dog on the Victor label
Listens long and hard as he is able.
It's all in a day's work, whatever plays.

5   From judgment, it would seem, he has refrained.
He even listens earnestly to Bloch,
Then builds a church upon our acid rock.
He's man's—no—he's the Leiermann's best friend,[2]

Or would be if hearing and listening were the same.
10   Does he hear? I fancy he rather smells
Those lemon-gold arpeggios in Ravel's
"Les jets d'eau du palais de ceux qui s'aiment."[3]

He ponders the Schumann Concerto's tall willow hit
By lightning, and stays put. When he surmises
15   Through one of Bach's eternal boxwood mazes[4]
The oboe pungent as a bitch in heat,

1. Long a trademark of RCA, the dog "Victor" was
on the label of RCA Victor records, listening
intently to a gramophone, with the caption "His
master's voice." In the poem, passing reference is
made to jazz trumpeter Bix Beiderbecke (1903–
1931), to classical composers Dietrich Buxtehude
(1637–1707), Johann Sebastian Bach (1685–
1750), George Frederick Handel (1685–1759),
and Robert Schumann (1810–1856), and to mod-
ernists Pierre Boulez (b. 1925), Ernest Bloch
(1880–1959), and Maurice Ravel (1875–1937).
2. In the song Der Leiermann ("The Organ-
Grinder") by Franz Schubert, an old man cranks
his barrel-organ in the winter cold to an audience
of snarling dogs.
3. "The fountains of the palace of those who are
in love with each other" (French).
4. A labyrinth executed in living boxwood plants,
popular in eighteenth-century formal gardens.

Or when the calypso decants its raw bay rum
Or the moon in *Wozzeck*[5] reddens ripe for murder,
He doesn't sneeze or howl; just listens harder.
20 Adamant° needles bear down on him from   *diamond*

Whirling of outer space, too black, too near—
But he was taught as a puppy not to flinch,
Much less to imitate his bête noire Blanche
Who barked, fat foolish creature, at King Lear.[6]

25 Still others fought in the road's filth over Jezebel,[7]
Slavered on hearths of horned and pelted barons.
His forebears lacked, to say the least, forbearance.
Can nature change in him? Nothing's impossible.

The last chord fades. The night is cold and fine.
30 His master's voice rasps through the grooves' bare groves.
Obediently, in silence like the grave's
He sleeps there on the still-warm gramophone

Only to dream he is at the première of a Handel
Opera long thought lost—*Il Cane Minore.*[8]
35 Its allegorical subject is his story!
A little dog revolving round a spindle

Gives rise to harmonies beyond belief,
A cast of stars. . . . Is there in Victor's heart
No honey for the vanquished? Art is art.
40 The life it asks of us is a dog's life.

1972

Lost in Translation

for Richard Howard

*Diese Tage, die leer dir scheinen
und wertlos für das All,
haben Wurzeln zwischen den Steinen
und trinken dort überall.*[9]

A card table in the library stands ready
To receive the puzzle which keeps never coming.
Daylight shines in or lamplight down
Upon the tense oasis of green felt.

5. An opera by Alban Berg (1885–1935), in which the protagonist murders his unfaithful wife beneath a rising moon.
6. In *King Lear*, the mad king says, "The little dogs and all. / Trey, Blanch, and Sweetheart, see, they bark at me" (3.6.62–63).
7. The proverbial wicked woman, she was killed in the street; when the body was recovered for burial, dogs had eaten most of it, as had been prophesied earlier by Elijah (see 1 Kings 21, 2 Kings 9.30–37).
8. "The Little Dog" (Italian).
9. "These days which seem empty and entirely fruitless to you have roots between the stones and drink from everywhere" (German). From the translation by the Austrian poet Rainer Maria Rilke (1875–1926) of "Palme" by the French poet Paul Valéry (1871–1945). Ironically, the epigraph provides the very translation Merrill claims, within the poem, to be "lost"—or difficult to find. Though the expression "lost in translation" is in common use, Merrill may have meant to refer also to Robert Frost's definition of poetry as that which is lost in translation.

5   Full of unfulfillment, life goes on,
Mirage arisen from time's trickling sands
Or fallen piecemeal into place:
German lesson, picnic, see-saw, walk
With the collie who "did everything but talk"—
10   Sour windfalls of the orchard back of us.
A summer without parents is the puzzle,
Or should be. But the boy, day after day,
Writes in his Line-a-Day° *No puzzle.*   *diary*

He's in love, at least. His French Mademoiselle,
15   In real life a widow since Verdun,[1]
Is stout, plain, carrot-haired, devout.
She prays for him, as does a curé in Alsace,[2]
Sews costumes for his marionettes,
Helps him to keep behind the scene
20   Whose sidelit goosegirl, speaking with his voice,
Plays Guinevere as well as Gunmoll Jean.[3]
Or else at bedtime in his tight embrace
Tells him her own French hopes, her German fears,
Her—but what more is there to tell?
25   Having known grief and hardship, Mademoiselle
Knows little more. Her languages. Her place.
Noon coffee. Mail. The watch that also waited
Pinned to her heart, poor gold, throws up its hands—
No puzzle! Steaming bitterness
30   Her sugars draw pops back into his mouth, translated:
"Patience, chéri. Geduld, mein Shatz."[4]
(Thus, reading Valéry the other evening
And seeming to recall a Rilke version of "Palme,"
That sunlit paradigm whereby the tree
35   Taps a sweet wellspring of authority,
The hour came back. Patience dans l'azur.
Geduld im . . . Himmelblau? Mademoiselle.)

Out of the blue, as promised, of a New York
Puzzle-rental shop the puzzle comes—
40   A superior one, containing a thousand hand-sawn,
Sandal-scented pieces. Many take
Shapes known already—the craftsman's repertoire
Nice in its limitation—from other puzzles:
Witch on broomstick, ostrich, hourglass,
45   Even (surely not just in retrospect)
An inchling, innocently branching palm.
These can be put aside, made stories of
While Mademoiselle spreads out the rest face-up,

---

1. French-speaking governess, called Mademoiselle, widowed since the battle of Verdun in World War I.
2. Region of France on the border of Germany; *curé:* "priest" (French).
3. Term for a gangster's female accomplice. "Goosegirl": as in the fairy tale "The Goosegirl"; i.e., an impersonating voice. "Guinevere": wife of the legendary King Arthur.
4. " 'Patience, my dear' " (French and German). Merrill is reminded, in the lines to follow, of Valéry's "Palme" and Rilke's translation, "Patience in the Blue," which refers to the palm tree's patience in growth. The "blue" of the German "Himmelblau" provides Merrill with his own "Out of the blue."

Herself excited as a child; or questioned
50   Like incoherent faces in a crowd,
Each with its scrap of highly colored
Evidence the Law must piece together.
Sky-blue ostrich? Likely story.
Mauve of the witch's cloak white, severed fingers
55   Pluck? Detain her. The plot thickens
As all at once two pieces interlock.

Mademoiselle does borders[5]—(Not so fast.
A London dusk, December last.
Chatter silenced in the library
60   This grown man reenters, wearing grey.
A medium. All except him have seen
Panel slid back, recess explored,
An object at once unique and common
Displayed, planted in a plain tole[6]
65   Casket the subject now considers
Through shut eyes, saying in effect:
"Even as voices reach me vaguely
A dry saw-shriek drowns them out,
Some loud machinery—a lumber mill?
70   Far uphill in the fir forest
Trees tower, tense with shock,
Groaning and cracking as they crash groundward.
But hidden here is a freak fragment
Of a pattern complex in appearance only.
75   What it seems to show is superficial
Next to that long-term lamination
Of hazard and craft, the karma that has
Made it matter in the first place.
Plywood, Piece of a puzzle." Applause
80   Acknowledged by an opening of lids
Upon the thing itself. A sudden dread—
But to go back. All this lay years ahead.)

Mademoiselle does borders. Straight-edge pieces
Align themselves with earth or sky
85   In twos and threes, naive cosmogonists
Whose views clash. Nomad inlanders meanwhile
Begin to cluster where the totem
Of a certain vibrant egg-yolk yellow
Or pelt of what emerging animal
90   Acts on the straggler like a trumpet call
To form a more sophisticated unit.
By suppertime two ragged wooden clouds
Have formed. In one, a Sheik with beard
And flashing sword hilt (he is all but finished)
95   Steps forward on a tiger skin. A piece
Snaps shut, and fangs gnash out at us!

5. She fits the pieces on the "borders" of the puzzle, with the additional meaning of frontiers between nations, languages, or (as the lines following suggest) this world and the next. 6. Enameled or lacquered metal.

In the second cloud—they gaze from cloud to cloud
With marked if undecipherable feeling—
Most of a dark-eyed woman veiled in mauve
100 Is being helped down from her camel (kneeling)
By a small backward-looking slave or page-boy
(Her son, thinks Mademoiselle mistakenly)
Whose feet have not been found. But lucky finds
In the last minutes before bed
105 Anchor both factions to the scene's limits
And, by so doing, orient
Them eye to eye across the green abyss.
The yellow promises, oh bliss,
To be in time a sumptuous tent.

110 *Puzzle begun* I write in the day's space,
Then, while she bathes, peek at Mademoiselle's
Page to the curé: ". . . cette innocente mère,
Ce pauvre enfant, que deviendront-ils?"[7]
Her azure script is curlicued like pieces
115 Of the puzzle she will be telling him about.
(Fearful incuriosity of childhood!
"Tu as l'accent allemand,"[8] said Dominique.
Indeed. Mademoiselle was only French by marriage.
Child of an English mother, a remote
120 Descendant of the great explorer Speke,[9]
And Prussian father. No one knew. I heard it
Long afterwards from her nephew, a UN
Interpreter. His matter-of-fact account
Touched old strings. My poor Mademoiselle,
125 With 1939[1] about to shake
This world where "each was the enemy, each the friend"
To its foundations, kept, though signed in blood,
Her peace a shameful secret to the end.)
"Schlaf wohl, chéri."[2] Her kiss. Her thumb
130 Crossing my brow against the dreams to come.

This World that shifts like sand, its unforeseen
Consolidations and elate routine,
Whose Potentate had lacked a retinue?
Lo! it assembles on the shrinking Green.

135 Gunmetal-skinned or pale, all plumes and scars,
Of Vassalage the noblest avatars—[3]
The very coffee-bearer in his vair°   fur-trimmed
Vest is a swart Highness, next to ours.

Kef[4] easing Boredom, and iced syrups, thirst,
140 In guessed-at glooms old wives who know the worst

---

7. " 'This innocent mother, this poor child, what
will become of them?' " (French).
8. " 'You have a German accent' " (French).
9. Possible pun on *speak*: John Hanning Speke
(1827–1864), English explorer.

1. When World War II began.
2. " 'Sleep well, darling' " (German, French).
3. The noblest incarnations of slavery.
4. Narcotic made from hemp.

Outsweat that virile fiction of the New:
"Insh'Allah,[5] he will tire—" "—or kill her first!"

(Hardly a proper subject for the Home,
Work of—dear Richard, I shall let *you* comb
145 Archives and learned journals for his name—
A minor lion attending on Gérôme.[6])

While, thick as Thebes[7] whose presently complete
Gates close behind them, Houri and Afreet[8]
Both claim the Page.[9] He wonders whom to serve,
150 And what his duties are, and where his feet,

And if we'll find, as some before us did,
That piece of Distance deep in which lies hid
Your tiny apex sugary with sun,
Eternal Triangle, Great Pyramid!

155 Then Sky alone is left, a hundred blue
Fragments in revolution, with no clue
To where a Niche will open. Quite a task,
Putting together Heaven, yet we do.

It's done. Here under the table all along
160 Were those missing feet. It's done.

The dog's tail thumping. Mademoiselle sketching
Costumes for a coming harem drama
To star the goosegirl. All too soon the swift
Dismantling. Lifted by two corners,
165 The puzzle hung together—and did not.
Irresistibly a populace
Unstitched of its attachments, rattled down.
Power went to pieces as the witch
Slithered easily from Virtue's gown.
170 The blue held out for time, but crumbled, too.
The city had long fallen, and the tent,
A separating sauce mousseline,[1]
Been swept away. Remained the green
On which the grown-ups gambled. A green dusk.
175 First lightning bugs. Last glow of west
Green in the false eyes of (coincidence)
Our mangy tiger safe on his bared hearth.

Before the puzzle was boxed and readdressed
To the puzzle shop in the mid-Sixties,[2]
180 Something tells me that one piece contrived

5. " 'As Allah [the God of Islam] wills' " (Arabic).
6. Jean Léon Gérôme (1824–1940), French painter; also an allusion to Saint Jerome, who, the legend goes, pulled a thorn from the paw of a lion, which then befriended him.
7. Capital of ancient Upper Egypt; pun on "thick as thieves."

8. Arabian mythological figures. "Houri": beautiful virgin; "Afreet": evil demon.
9. The servant, with a suggestion too of the printed page.
1. A French white sauce.
2. The streets numbered in the mid-Sixties in Manhattan.

To stay in the boy's pocket. How do I know?
I know because so many later puzzles
Had missing pieces—Maggie Teyte's[3] high notes
Gone at the war's end, end of the vogue for collies,
185 A house torn down; and hadn't Mademoiselle
Kept back her pitiful bit of truth as well?
I've spent the last days, furthermore,
Ransacking Athens for that translation of "Palme."
Neither the Goethehaus[4] nor the National Library
190 Seems able to unearth it. Yet I can't
Just be imagining. I've seen it. Know
How much of the sun-ripe original
Felicity Rilke made himself forego
(Who loved French words—verger, mûr, parfumer[5])
195 In order to render its underlying sense.
Know already in that tongue of his
What Pains, what monolithic Truths
Shadow stanza to stanza's symmetrical
Rhyme-rutted pavement. Know that ground plan left
200 Sublime and barren, where the warm Romance
Stone by stone faded, cooled; the fluted nouns
Made taller, lonelier than life
By leaf-carved capitals in the afterglow.
The owlet umlaut[6] peeps and hoots
205 Above the open vowel. And after rain
A deep reverberation fills with stars.

Lost, is it, buried? One more missing piece?

But nothing's lost. Or else: all is translation
And every bit of us is lost in it
210 (Or found—I wander through the ruin of S
Now and then, wondering at the peacefulness)
And in that loss a self-effacing tree,
Color of context, imperceptibly
Rustling with its angel,[7] turns the waste
215 To shade and fiber, milk and memory.

1976

3. (1888–1976); English soprano known for her repertoire in French.
4. A German library.
5. "Orchard, ripe, to scent" (French).
6. German accent mark (¨), the two high dots of which resemble an owl's eyes.
7. Pun on "wrestling with its angel." Jacob wrestled with an angel, saying, "I will not let thee go, except thou bless me" (Genesis 32.26).

From The Book of Ephraim[8]

Correct but cautious, that first night, we asked
Our visitor's name, era, habitat.
EPHRAIM came the answer. A Greek Jew
Born AD 8 at XANTHOS   Where was that?
5   In Greece WHEN WOLVES & RAVENS WERE IN ROME
(Next day the classical dictionary yielded
A Xanthos on the Asia Minor Coast.)
NOW WHO ARE U   We told him. ARE U XTIANS
We guessed so. WHAT A COZY CATACOMB
10   Christ had WROUGHT HAVOC in *his* family,
ENTICED MY FATHER FROM MY MOTHERS BED
(I too had issued from a broken home[9]—
The first of several facts to coincide.)
Later a favorite of TIBERIUS[1] Died
15   AD 36 on CAPRI throttled
By the imperial guard for having LOVED
THE MONSTERS NEPHEW (sic) CALIGULA[2]
Rapidly he went on—changing the subject?
A long incriminating manuscript
20   Boxed in bronze lay UNDER PORPHYRY
Beneath the deepest excavations. He
Would help us find it, but we must please make haste
Because Tiberius wanted it destroyed.
Oh? And where, we wondered of the void,
25   *Was* Tiberius these days? STAGE THREE

Why was he telling *us*? He'd overheard us
Talking to SIMPSON   Simpson? His LINK WITH EARTH
His REPRESENTATIVE   A feeble nature
All but bestial, given to violent
30   Short lives—one ending lately among flames
In an Army warehouse. Slated for rebirth
But not in time, said Ephraim, to prevent
The brat from wasting, just now at our cup,[3]
Precious long distance minutes—don't hang up!

35   So much facetiousness—well, we were young
And these were matters of life and death—dismayed us.
Was he a devil? His reply MY POOR
INNOCENTS left the issue hanging fire.

---

8. The first part of an epic trilogy, *The Changing Light at Sandover*, which also includes *Mirabell: Books of Number* and *Scripts for the Pageant. The Book of Ephraim* originally appeared in the volume *Divine Comedies*, which made Merrill's debt to the tripartite *Divine Comedy* of Dante Alighieri (1265–1321) explicit. Merrill ("JM") records encounters through the Ouija board that he and his companion, David Jackson ("DJ"), have with spirits from the other world, who illuminate a system of reincarnation and purification as well as suggest theories about the creation and future of the universe. Merrill models the structure of each part of the trilogy on the design of the Ouija board; thus *Ephraim* is in twenty-six parts, one for each letter of the alphabet. In "C" (identified by the large initial letter), the spirit guide Ephraim introduces himself; uppercase letters indicate the "speech" of the Ouija board.
9. Cf. Merrill's poem "The Broken Home" (pp. 1605–08).
1. (42 B.C.–A.D. 37); Roman emperor.
2. (A.D. 12–41); Roman emperor.
3. JM and DJ place hands on a teacup to "read" the Ouija board.

As it flowed on, his stream-of-consciousness
40   Deepened. There was a buried room, a BED
      WROUGHT IN SILVER   I CAN LEAD U THERE
      IF   If? U GIVE ME   What? HA HA YR SOULS
      (Another time he'll say that he misread
      Our innocence for insolence that night,
45   And meant to scare us.) Our eyes met. What if . . .
      The blood's least vessel hoisted jet-black sails.
      Five whole minutes we were frightened stiff
      —But after all, we weren't *that* innocent.
      The Rover Boys[4] at thirty, still red-blooded
50   Enough not to pass up an armchair revel
      And pure enough at heart to beat the devil,
      Entered into the spirit, so to speak,
      And said they'd leave for Capri that same week.

      Pause. Then, as though we'd passed a test,
55   Ephraim's whole manner changed. He brushed aside
      Tiberius and settled to the task
      Of answering, like an experienced guide,
      Those questions we had lacked the wit to ask.

      Here on Earth—huge tracts of information
60   Have gone into these capsules flavorless
      And rhymed for easy swallowing—on Earth
      We're each the REPRESENTATIVE of a PATRON
      —Are there that many patrons? YES O YES
      These secular guardian angels fume and fuss
65   For what must seem eternity over us.
      It is forbidden them to INTERVENE
      Save, as it were, in the entr'acte° between   *intermission*
      One incarnation and another. Back
      To school from the disastrously long vac°   *summer vacation*
70   Goes the soul its patron crams yet once
      Again with savoir vivre.[5] Will the dunce
      Never—by rote, the hundredth time round—learn
      What ropes make fast that point of no return,
      A footing on the lowest of NINE STAGES
75   Among the curates and the minor mages?
      Patrons at last ourselves, an upward notch
      Our old ones move   THEYVE BORNE IT ALL FOR THIS
      And take delivery from the Abyss
      Of brand-new little savage souls to watch.
80   One difference: with every rise in station
      Comes a degree of PEACE FROM REPRESENTATION
      —Odd phrase, more like a motto for abstract
      Art—or for Autocracy—In fact
      Our heads are spinning—From the East a light—
85   BUT U ARE TIRED MES CHERS[6]   SWEET DREAMS   TOMORROW NIGHT

                                                                      1976

---

4. Heroes of a popular series of children's books.   6. "My dears" (French).
5. "Knowledge of how to live" (French).

FRANK O'HARA

1926–1966

The Day Lady[1] Died

It is 12:20 in New York a Friday
three days after Bastille day,[2] yes
it is 1959 and I go get a shoeshine
because I will get off the 4:19 in Easthampton[3]
5   at 7:15 and then go straight to dinner
and I don't know the people who will feed me

I walk up the muggy street beginning to sun
and have a hamburger and a malted and buy
an ugly NEW WORLD WRITING to see what the poets
10   in Ghana are doing these days
                              I go on to the bank
and Miss Stillwagon (first name Linda I once heard)
doesn't even look up my balance for once in her life
and in the GOLDEN GRIFFIN[4] I get a little Verlaine
15   for Patsy with drawings by Bonnard although I do
think of Hesiod, trans. Richmond Lattimore or
Brendan Behan's new play or *Le Balcon* or *Les Nègres*
of Genet, but I don't, I stick with Verlaine
after practically going to sleep with quandariness

20   and for Mike I just stroll into the PARK LANE
Liquor Store and ask for a bottle of Strega and
then I go back where I came from to 6th Avenue
and the tobacconist in the Ziegfeld Theatre and
casually ask for a carton of Gauloises and a carton
25   of Picayunes, and a NEW YORK POST with her face on it

and I am sweating a lot by now and thinking of
leaning on the john door in the 5 SPOT
while she whispered a song along the keyboard
to Mal Waldron[5] and everyone and I stopped breathing

1959   1964

How to Get There

White the October air, no snow, easy to breathe
beneath the sky, lies, lies everywhere writhing and gasping
clutching and tangling, it is not easy to breathe
lies building their tendrils into dim figures

1. Billie Holiday (1915–1959), called Lady Day, African-American jazz and blues singer.
2. July 14, the French national holiday that celebrates the storming of the Bastille prison in 1789.
3. One of "the Hamptons," towns on eastern Long Island, popular, especially in the summer, with New York City artists and writers.
4. An avant-garde bookshop in New York, near the Museum of Modern Art where O'Hara was a curator. All the works mentioned are quite highbrow.
5. (B. 1926); Billie Holiday's accompanist.

5   who disappear down corridors in west-side[6] apartments
into childhood's proof of being wanted, not abandoned, kidnaped
betrayal staving off loneliness, I see the fog lunge in
and hide it
           where are you?
10   here I am on the sidewalk
under the moonlike lamplight thinking how precious moss is
so unique and greenly crushable if you can find it
on the north side of the tree where the fog binds you
and then, tearing apart into soft white lies, spreads its disease
15   through the primal night of an everlasting winter
which nevertheless has heat in tubes, west-side and east-side
and its intricate individual pathways of white accompanied
by the ringing of telephone bells beside which someone sits in
silence denying their own number, never given out! nameless
20   like the sound of troika[7] bells rushing past suffering
in the first storm, it is snowing now, it is already too late
the snow will go away, but nobody will be there

police cordons for lying political dignitaries ringing too
the world becomes a jangle
25   from the index finger
to the vast empty houses filled with people, their echoes
of lies and the tendrils of fog trailing softly around their throats
now the phone can be answered, nobody calling, only an echo
all can confess to be home and waiting, all is the same
30   and we drift into the clear sky enthralled by our disappointment
never to be alone again
                never to be loved
sailing through space: didn't I have you once for my self? West Side?
    for a couple of hours, but I am not that person
1960   1964

Ave Maria[8]

Mothers of America
           let your kids go to the movies!
get them out of the house so they won't know what you're up to
it's true that fresh air is good for the body
5   but what about the soul
that grows in darkness, embossed by silvery images
and when you grow old as grow old you must
                  they won't hate you
they won't criticize you they won't know
10   they'll be in some glamorous country
they first saw on a Saturday afternoon or playing hookey

they may even be grateful to you
               for their first sexual experience

---

6. "West-side" and "east-side" in the poem refer to areas in Manhattan (east or west of Fifth Avenue).
7. A Russian vehicle drawn by three horses abreast.
8. "Hail Mary" (Latin): the Catholic prayer addressed to the Virgin Mary, mother of Jesus.

which only cost you a quarter
15   and didn't upset the peaceful home
they will know where candy bars come from
                       and gratuitous bags of popcorn
as gratuitous as leaving the movie before it's over
with a pleasant stranger whose apartment is in the Heaven on Earth
20   Bldg
near the Williamsburg Bridge[9]
                   oh mothers you will have made the little tykes
so happy because if nobody does pick them up in the movies
they won't know the difference
25   and if somebody does it'll be sheer gravy
and they'll have been truly entertained either way
instead of hanging around the yard
                  or up in their room
                        hating you
30 prematurely since you won't have done anything horribly mean yet
except keeping them from the darker joys
                  it's unforgivable the latter
so don't blame me if you won't take this advice
                 and the family breaks up
35 and your children grow old and blind in front of a TV set
                      seeing
movies you wouldn't let them see when they were young
1960   1964

Why I Am Not a Painter

I am not a painter, I am a poet.
Why? I think I would rather be
a painter, but I am not. Well,

for instance, Mike Goldberg[1]
5 is starting a painting. I drop in.
"Sit down and have a drink" he
says. I drink; we drink. I look
up. "You have SARDINES in it."
"Yes, it needed something there."
10 "Oh." I go and the days go by
and I drop in again. The painting
is going on, and I go, and the days
go by. I drop in. The painting is
finished. "Where's SARDINES?"
15 All that's left is just
letters, "It was too much," Mike says.

But me? One day I am thinking of
a color: orange. I write a line
about orange. Pretty soon it is a
20 whole page of words, not lines.

---

9. Bridge connecting lower Manhattan with the   1. (B. 1924); New York painter, whose silk-screen
Williamsburg section of Brooklyn.   prints appear in O'Hara's Odes (1960).

Then another page. There should be
so much more, not of orange, of
words, of how terrible orange is
and life. Days go by. It is even in
25 prose, I am a real poet. My poem
is finished and I haven't mentioned
orange yet. It's twelve poems, I call
it ORANGES. And one day in a gallery
I see Mike's painting, called SARDINES.

1971

W. D. SNODGRASS

1926–

April Inventory

The green catalpa tree has turned
All white; the cherry blooms once more.
In one whole year I haven't learned
A blessed thing they pay you for.
5   The blossoms snow down in my hair;
The trees and I will soon be bare.

The trees have more than I to spare.
The sleek, expensive girls I teach,
Younger and pinker every year,
10 Bloom gradually out of reach.
The pear tree lets its petals drop
Like dandruff on a tabletop.

The girls have grown so young by now
I have to nudge myself to stare.
15 This year they smile and mind me how
My teeth are falling with my hair.
In thirty years I may not get
Younger, shrewder, or out of debt.

The tenth time, just a year ago,
20 I made myself a little list
Of all the things I'd ought to know,
Then told my parents, analyst,
And everyone who's trusted me
I'd be substantial, presently.

25 I haven't read one book about
A book or memorized one plot.
Or found a mind I did not doubt.
I learned one date. And then forgot.
And one by one the solid scholars
30 Get the degrees, the jobs, the dollars.

And smile above their starchy collars.
I taught my classes Whitehead's[1] notions;
One lovely girl, a song of Mahler's.[2]
Lacking a source-book or promotions,
35   I showed one child the colors of
A luna moth and how to love.

I taught myself to name my name,
To bark back, loosen love and crying;
To ease my woman so she came,
40   To ease an old man who was dying.
I have not learned how often I
Can win, can love, but choose to die.

I have not learned there is a lie
Love shall be blonder, slimmer, younger;
45   That my equivocating eye
Loves only by my body's hunger;
That I have forces, true to feel,
Or that the lovely world is real.

While scholars speak authority
50   And wear their ulcers on their sleeves,
My eyes in spectacles shall see
These trees procure and spend their leaves.
There is a value underneath
The gold and silver in my teeth.

55   Though trees turn bare and girls turn wives,
We shall afford our costly seasons;
There is a gentleness survives
That will outspeak and has its reasons.
There is a loveliness exists,
60   Preserves us, not for specialists.

1959

From Heart's Needle[3]

For Cynthia

" 'Your father is dead.' 'That grieves me,' said he. 'Your mother is dead,' said
the lad. 'Now all pity for me is at an end,' said he. 'Your brother is dead,' said
Loingsechan. 'I am sorely wounded by that,' said Suibne. 'Your daughter is
dead,' said Loingsechan. 'And an only daughter is the needle of the heart,'
said Suibne. 'Dear is your son who used to call you "Father," ' said Loing-
sechan. 'Indeed,' said he, 'that is the drop that brings a man to the ground.' "

FROM AN OLD IRISH STORY,
The Frenzy of Suibne,
AS TRANSLATED BY MYLES DILLON

---

1. Alfred North Whitehead (1861–1947), English
philosopher.
2. Gustav Mahler (1860–1911), Austrian com-
poser.
3. Snodgrass's long poem for his daughter, after a
divorce, is written in ten sections.

2

Late April and you are three; today
We dug your garden in the yard.
To curb the damage of your play,
Strange dogs at night and the moles tunneling,
5   Four slender sticks of lath stand guard
Uplifting their thin string.

So you were the first to tramp it down.
And after the earth was sifted close
You brought your watering can to drown
10 All earth *and* us. But these mixed seeds are pressed
With light loam in their steadfast rows.
Child, we've done our best.

Someone will have to weed and spread
The young sprouts. Sprinkle them in the hour
15   When shadow falls across their bed.
You should try to look at them every day
Because when they come to full flower
I will be away.

3

The child between them on the street
Comes to a puddle, lifts his feet
And hangs on their hands. They start
At the live weight and lurch together,
5   Recoil to swing him through the weather,
Stiffen and pull apart.

We read of cold war[4] soldiers that
Never gained ground, gave none, but sat
Tight in their chill trenches.
10 Pain seeps up from some cavity
Through the ranked teeth in sympathy;
The whole jaw grinds and clenches

Till something somewhere has to give.
It's better the poor soldiers live
15   In someone else's hands
Than drop where helpless powers fall
On crops and barns, on towns where all
Will burn. And no man stands.

7

Here in the scuffled dust
is our ground of play.
I lift you on your swing and must
shove you away,

---

4. The post–World War II rivalry between the Soviet Union and the United States.

5   see you return again,
        drive you off again, then

        stand quiet till you come.
          You, though you climb
        higher, farther from me, longer,
10   will fall back to me stronger.
        Bad penny, pendulum,
          you keep my constant time

        to bob in blue July
          where fat goldfinches fly
15   over the glittering, fecund
          reach of our growing lands.
        Once more now, this second,
          I hold you in my hands.

10

The vicious winter finally yields
    the green winter wheat;
the farmer, tired in the tired fields
    he dare not leave will eat.

5   Once more the runs come fresh; prevailing
        piglets, stout as jugs,
    harry their old sow to the railing
        to ease her swollen dugs

    and game colts trail the herded mares
10   that circle the pasture courses;
    our seasons bring us back once more
        like merry-go-round horses.

    With crocus mouths, perennial hungers,
        into the park Spring comes;
15   we roast hot dogs on old coat hangers
        and feed the swan bread crumbs,

    pay our respects to the peacocks, rabbits,
        and leathery Canada goose
    who took, last Fall, our tame white habits
20   and now will not turn loose.

    In full regalia, the pheasant cocks
        march past their dubious hens;
    the porcupine and the lean, red fox
        trot around bachelor pens

25   and the miniature painted train
        wails on its oval track:
    you said, I'm going to Pennsylvania!
        and waved. And you've come back.

If I loved you, they said, I'd leave
30   and find my own affairs.
Well, once again this April, we've
    come around to the bears;

punished and cared for, behind bars,
  the coons on bread and water
35 stretch thin black fingers after ours.
    And you are still my daughter.

                      1959

Mementos, 1

Sorting out letters and piles of my old
  Canceled checks, old clippings, and yellow note cards
That meant something once, I happened to find
  Your picture. *That* picture. I stopped there cold,
5 Like a man raking piles of dead leaves in his yard
    Who has turned up a severed hand.

Still, that first second, I was glad: you stand
  Just as you stood—shy, delicate, slender,
In that long gown of green lace netting and daisies
10 That you wore to our first dance. The sight of you stunned
Us all. Well, our needs were different, then,
    And our ideals came easy.

Then through the war° and those two long years   *World War II*
  Overseas, the Japanese dead in their shacks
15 Among dishes, dolls, and lost shoes; I carried
  This glimpse of you, there, to choke down my fear,
Prove it had been, that it might come back.
    That was before we got married.

—Before we drained out one another's force
20 With lies, self-denial, unspoken regret
And the sick eyes that blame; before the divorce
  And the treachery. Say it: before we met. Still,
I put back your picture. Someday, in due course,
    I will find that it's still there.

                      1968

ELIZABETH JENNINGS
1926–

My Grandmother

She kept an antique shop—or it kept her.
Among Apostle spoons and Bristol glass,[1]
The faded silks, the heavy furniture,
She watched her own reflection in the brass
5 Salvers[2] and silver bowls, as if to prove
Polish was all, there was no need of love.

And I remember how I once refused
To go out with her, since I was afraid.
It was perhaps a wish not to be used
10 Like antique objects. Though she never said
That she was hurt, I still could feel the guilt
Of that refusal, guessing how she felt.

Later, too frail to keep a shop, she put
All her best things in one long narrow room.
15 The place smelt old, of things too long kept shut,
The smell of absences where shadows come
That can't be polished. There was nothing then
To give her own reflection back again.

And when she died I felt no grief at all,
20 Only the guilt of what I once refused.
I walked into her room among the tall
Sideboards and cupboards—things she never used
But needed: and no finger-marks were there,
Only the new dust falling through the air.

1961

One Flesh

Lying apart now, each in a separate bed,
He with a book, keeping the light on late,
She like a girl dreaming of childhood,
All men elsewhere—it is as if they wait
5 Some new event: the book he holds unread,
Her eyes fixed on the shadows overhead.

Tossed up like flotsam from a former passion,
How cool they lie. They hardly ever touch,
Or if they do it is like a confession
10 Of having little feeling—or too much.

---

1. Prized glassware of a deep blue color. "Apostle": set of teaspoons, the handles of which are in the form of male figures, supposedly the Apostles.
2. Round trays.

Chastity faces them, a destination
For which their whole lives were a preparation.

Strangely apart, yet strangely close together,
Silence between them like a thread to hold
15 And not wind in. And time itself's a feather
Touching them gently. Do they know they're old,
These two who are my father and my mother
Whose fire from which I came, has now grown cold?

1966

JOHN ASHBERY

1927–

The Painter

Sitting between the sea and the buildings
He enjoyed painting the sea's portrait.
But just as children imagine a prayer
Is merely silence, he expected his subject
5 To rush up the sand, and, seizing a brush,
Plaster its own portrait on the canvas.

So there was never any paint on his canvas
Until the people who lived in the buildings
Put him to work: "Try using the brush
10 As a means to an end. Select, for a portrait,
Something less angry and large, and more subject
To a painter's moods, or, perhaps, to a prayer."

How could he explain to them his prayer
That nature, not art, might usurp the canvas?
15 He chose his wife for a new subject,
Making her vast, like ruined buildings,
As if, forgetting itself, the portrait
Had expressed itself without a brush.

Slightly encouraged, he dipped his brush
20 In the sea, murmuring a heartfelt prayer:
"My soul, when I paint this next portrait
Let it be you who wrecks the canvas."
The news spread like wildfire through the buildings:
He had gone back to the sea for his subject.

25 Imagine a painter crucified by his subject!
Too exhausted even to lift his brush,
He provoked some artists leaning from the buildings
To malicious mirth: "We haven't a prayer
Now, of putting ourselves on canvas,
30 Or getting the sea to sit for a portrait!"

Others declared it a self-portrait.
Finally all indications of a subject
Began to fade, leaving the canvas
Perfectly white. He put down the brush.
35 At once a howl, that was also a prayer,
Arose from the overcrowded buildings.

They tossed him, the portrait, from the tallest of the buildings;
And the sea devoured the canvas and the brush
As though his subject had decided to remain a prayer.

1956

Rivers and Mountains

On the secret map the assassins
Cloistered, the Moon River was marked
Near the eighteen peaks and the city
Of humiliation and defeat—wan ending
5 Of the trail among dry, papery leaves
Gray-brown quills like thoughts
In the melodious but vast mass of today's
Writing through fields and swamps
Marked, on the map, with little bunches of weeds.
10 Certainly squirrels lived in the woods
But devastation and dull sleep still
Hung over the land, quelled
The rioters turned out of sleep in the peace of prisons
Singing on marble factory walls
15 Deaf consolation of minor tunes that pack
The air with heavy invisible rods
Pent in some sand valley from
Which only quiet walking ever instructs.
The bird flew over and
20 Sat—there was nothing else to do.
Do not mistake its silence for pride or strength
Or the waterfall for a harbor
Full of light boats that is there
Performing for thousands of people
25 In clothes some with places to go
Or games. Sometimes over the pillar
Of square stones its impact
Makes a light print.

So going around cities
30 To get to other places you found
It all on paper but the land
Was made of paper processed
To look like ferns, mud or other
Whose sea unrolled its magic
35 Distances and then rolled them up
Its secret was only a pocket
After all but some corners are darker
Than these moonless nights spent as on a raft

In the seclusion of a melody heard
40 As though through trees
And you can never ignite their touch
Long but there were homes
Flung far out near the asperities
Of a sharp, rocky pinnacle
45 And other collective places
Shadows of vineyards whose wine
Tasted of the forest floor
Fisheries and oyster beds
Tides under the pole
50 Seminaries of instruction, public
Places for electric light
And the major tax assessment area
Wrinkled on the plan
Of election to public office
55 Sixty-two years old bath and breakfast
The formal traffic, shadows
To make it not worth joining
After the ox had pulled away the cart.

Your plan was to separate the enemy into two groups
60 With the razor-edged mountains between.
It worked well on paper
But their camp had grown
To be the mountains and the map
Carefully peeled away and not torn
65 Was the light, a tender but tough bark
On everything. Fortunately the war was solved
In another way by isolating the two sections
Of the enemy's navy so that the mainland
Warded away the big floating ships.
70 Light bounced off the ends
Of the small gray waves to tell
Them in the observatory
About the great drama that was being won
To turn off the machinery
75 And quietly move among the rustic landscape
Scooping snow off the mountains rinsing
The coarser ones that love had
Slowly risen in the night to overflow
Wetting pillow and petal
80 Determined to place the letter
On the unassassinated president's desk
So that a stamp could reproduce all this
In detail, down to the last autumn leaf
And the affliction of June ride
85 Slowly out into the sun-blackened landscape.

1966

Melodic Trains

A little girl with scarlet enameled fingernails
Asks me what time it is—evidently that's a toy wristwatch
She's wearing, for fun. And it is fun to wear other
Odd things, like this briar pipe and tweed coat

5 Like date-colored sierras with the lines of seams
Sketched in and plunging now and then into unfathomable
Valleys that can't be deduced by the shape of the person
Sitting inside it—me, and just as our way is flat across
Dales and gulches, as though our train were a pencil

10 Guided by a ruler held against a photomural of the Alps
We both come to see distance as something unofficial
And impersonal yet not without its curious justification
Like the time of a stopped watch—right twice a day.

Only the wait in stations is vague and
15 Dimensionless, like oneself. How do they decide how much
Time to spend in each? One begins to suspect there's no
Rule or that it's applied haphazardly.

Sadness of the faces of children on the platform,
Concern of the grownups for connections, for the chances
20 Of getting a taxi, since these have no timetable.
You get one if you can find one though in principle

You can always find one, but the segment of chance
In the circle of certainty is what gives these leaning
Tower of Pisa figures their aspect of dogged
25 Impatience, banking forward into the wind.

In short any stop before the final one creates
Clouds of anxiety, of sad, regretful impatience
With ourselves, our lives, the way we have been dealing
With other people up until now. Why couldn't
30 We have been more considerate? These figures leaving

The platform or waiting to board the train are my brothers
In a way that really wants to tell me why there is so little
Panic and disorder in the world, and so much unhappiness.
If I were to get down now to stretch, take a few steps

35 In the wearying and world-weary clouds of steam like great
White apples, might I just through proximity and aping
Of postures and attitudes communicate this concern of mine
To them? That their jagged attitudes correspond to mine,

That their beefing strikes answering silver bells within
40 My own chest, and that I know, as they do, how the last
Stop is the most anxious one of all, though it means
Getting home at last, to the pleasures and dissatisfactions of home?

It's as though a visible chorus called up the different
Stages of the journey, singing about them and being them:
45　Not the people in the station, not the child opposite me
With currant fingernails, but the windows, seen through,

Reflecting imperfectly, ruthlessly splitting open the bluish
Vague landscape like a zipper. Each voice has its own
Descending scale to put one in one's place at every stage;
50　One need never not know where one is

Unless one give up listening, sleeping, approaching a small
Western town that is nothing but a windmill. Then
The great fury of the end can drop as the solo
Voices tell about it, wreathing it somehow with an aura

55　Of good fortune and colossal welcomes from the mayor and
Citizens' committees tossing their hats into the air.
To hear them singing you'd think it had already happened
And we had focused back on the furniture of the air.

1977

Rain Moving In

The blackboard is erased in the attic
And the wind turns up the light of the stars,
Sinewy now. Someone will find out, someone will know.
And if somewhere on this great planet
5　The truth is discovered, a patch of it, dried, glazed by the sun,
It will just hang on, in its own infamy, humility. No one
Will be better for it, but things can't get any worse.
Just keep playing, mastering as you do the step
Into disorder this one meant. Don't you see
10　It's all we can do? Meanwhile, great fires
Arise, as of haystacks aflame. The dial has been set
And that's ominous, but all your graciousness in living
Conspires with it, now that this is our home:
A place to be from, and have people ask about.

1984

Brute Image

It's a question of altitude, or latitude,
Probably. I see them leaving their offices.
By seven they are turning smartly into the drive
To spend the evening with small patterns and odd,
5　Oblique fixtures. Authentic what? Did I say,
Or more likely did you ask is there any
Deliverance from any of this? Why yes,
One boy says, one can step for a moment
Out into the hall. Spells bring some relief
10　And antique shrieking into the night
That was not here before, not like this.

This is only a stand-in for the more formal,
More serious side of it. There is partial symmetry here.
Later one protests: How did we get here
15   This way, unable to stop communicating?
And is it all right for the children to listen,
For the weeds slanting inward, for the cold mice
Until dawn? Now every yard has its tree,
Every heart its valentine, and only we
20   Don't know how to occupy the tent of night
So that what must come to pass shall pass.

1992

GALWAY KINNELL

1927–

First Song

Then it was dusk in Illinois, the small boy
After an afternoon of carting dung
Hung on the rail fence, a sapped thing
Weary to crying. Dark was growing tall
5   And he began to hear the pond frogs all
Calling on his ear with what seemed their joy.

Soon their sound was pleasant for a boy
Listening in the smoky dusk and the nightfall
Of Illinois, and from the fields two small
10   Boys came bearing cornstalk violins
And they rubbed the cornstalk bows with resins
And the three sat there scraping of their joy.

It was now fine music the frogs and the boys
Did in the towering Illinois twilight make
15   And into dark in spite of a shoulder's ache
A boy's hunched body loved out of a stalk
The first song of his happiness, and the song woke
His heart to the darkness and into the sadness of joy.

1960

The Correspondence School Instructor Says Goodbye to His Poetry Students

Goodbye, lady in Bangor, who sent me
snapshots of yourself, after definitely hinting
you were beautiful; goodbye,
Miami Beach urologist, who enclosed plain
5   brown envelopes for the return of your *very*
"Clinical Sonnets"; goodbye, manufacturer
of brassieres on the Coast, whose eclogues
give the fullest treatment in literature yet

to the sagging breast motif; goodbye, you in San Quentin,[1]
10 who wrote, "Being German my hero is Hitler,"
instead of "Sincerely yours," at the end of long,
neat-scripted letters demolishing
the pre-Raphaelites:[2]

I swear to you, it was just my way
15 of cheering myself up, as I licked
the stamped, self-addressed envelopes,
the game I had
of trying to guess which one of you, this time,
had poisoned his glue. I did care.
20 I did read each poem entire.
I did say what I thought was the truth
in the mildest words I knew. And now,
in this poem, or chopped prose, not any better,
I realize, than those troubled lines
25 I kept sending back to you,
I have to say I am relieved it is over:
at the end I could feel only pity
for that urge toward more life
your poems kept smothering in words, the smell
30 of which, days later, would tingle
in your nostrils as new, God-given impulses
to write.

Goodbye,
you who are, for me, the postmarks again
35 of shattered towns—Xenia, Burnt Cabins, Hornell—
their loneliness
given away in poems, only their solitude kept.

1968

After Making Love We Hear Footsteps

For I can snore like a bullhorn
or play loud music
or sit up talking with any reasonably sober Irishman
and Fergus will only sink deeper
5 into his dreamless sleep, which goes by all in one flash,
but let there be that heavy breathing
or a stifled come-cry anywhere in the house
and he will wrench himself awake
and make for it on the run—as now, we lie together,
10 after making love, quiet, touching along the length of our bodies,
familiar touch of the long-married,
and he appears—in his baseball pajamas, it happens,
the neck opening so small he has to screw them on—
and flops down between us and hugs us and snuggles himself to sleep,
15 his face gleaming with satisfaction at being this very child.

1. Prison in California.
2. A group of nineteenth-century English painters and poets, who advocated a close study of nature and wished to restore to art the methods and spirit of the arts before the Italian painter Raphael (1483–1520).

In the half darkness we look at each other
and smile
and touch arms across this little, startlingly muscled body—
this one whom habit of memory propels to the ground of his making,
20   sleeper only the mortal sounds can sing awake,
this blessing love gives again into our arms.

1980, 1993

W. S. MERWIN

1927–

The Drunk in the Furnace

    For a good decade
The furnace stood in the naked gully, fireless
And vacant as any hat. Then when it was
No more to them than a hulking black fossil
5 To erode unnoticed with the rest of the junk-hill
By the poisonous creek, and rapidly to be added
    To their ignorance.

    They were afterwards astonished
To confirm, one morning, a twist of smoke like a pale
10 Resurrection, staggering out of its chewed hole,
And to remark then other tokens that someone,
Cozily bolted behind the eye-holed iron
Door of the drafty burner, had there established
    His bad castle.

15   Where he gets his spirits
It's a mystery. But the stuff keeps him musical:
Hammer-and-anviling with poker and bottle
To his jugged bellowings, till the last groaning clang
As he collapses onto the rioting
20 Springs of a litter of car-seats ranged on the grates,
    To sleep like an iron pig.[1]

    In their tar-paper church
On a text about stoke-holes that are sated never
Their Reverend lingers. They nod and hate trespassers.
25 When the furnace wakes, though, all afternoon
Their witless offspring flock like piped rats to its siren
Crescendo, and agape on the crumbling ridge
    Stand in a row and learn.

1960

---

1. A crude block poured from a smelting furnace.

Odysseus[2]

For George Kirstein

Always the setting forth was the same,
Same sea, same dangers waiting for him
As though he had got nowhere but older.
Behind him on the receding shore
5   The identical reproaches, and somewhere
Out before him, the unraveling patience
He was wedded to. There were the islands
Each with its woman and twining welcome
To be navigated, and one to call "home."[3]
10   The knowledge of all that he betrayed
Grew till it was the same whether he stayed
Or went. Therefore he went. And what wonder
If sometimes he could not remember
Which was the one who wished on his departure
15   Perils that he could never sail through,
And which, improbable, remote, and true,
Was the one he kept sailing home to?

1960

Separation

Your absence has gone through me
Like thread through a needle.
Everything I do is stitched with its color.

1973

Strawberries

When my father died I saw   a narrow valley

it looked as though it began   across the river
from the landing where he was born   but there was no river

I was hoeing the sand   of a small vegetable plot
5   for my mother   in deepening twilight
and looked up in time   to see a farm wagon
dry and gray   horse already hidden
and no driver   going into the valley
carrying a casket

10   and another wagon
coming out of the valley   behind a gray horse
with a boy driving   and a high load
of two kinds of berries   one of them strawberries

that night when I slept   I dreamed of things
15   wrong in the house   all of them signs

2. Hero of Homer's *Odyssey*, who spent ten years of wandering after the Trojan War attempting to return home.

3. Alluding to Odysseus' encounters with the sorceress Circe and the nymph Calypso, and to his wife, Penelope, waiting for him on Ithaca.

the water of the shower   running brackish
and an insect of a kind   I had seen him kill
climbing around   the walls of his bathroom
     up in the morning   I stopped on the stairs
20 my mother was awake   already and asked me
if I wanted a shower   before breakfast
and for breakfast she said   we have strawberries

1983

Losing a Language

A breath leaves the sentences and does not come back
yet the old still remember something that they could say

but they know now that such things are no longer believed
and the young have fewer words

5   many of the things the words were about
no longer exist

the noun for standing in mist by a haunted tree
the verb for I

the children will not repeat
10 the phrases their parents speak

somebody has persuaded them
that it is better to say everything differently

so that they can be admired somewhere
farther and farther away

15 where nothing that is here is known
we have little to say to each other

we are wrong and dark
in the eyes of the new owners

the radio is incomprehensible
20 the day is glass

when there is a voice at the door it is foreign
everywhere instead of a name there is a lie

nobody has seen it happening
nobody remembers

25 this is what the words were made
to prophesy

here are the extinct feathers
here is the rain we saw

1988

CHARLES TOMLINSON

1927–

Farewell to Van Gogh[1]

The quiet deepens. You will not persuade
  One leaf of the accomplished, steady, darkening
Chestnut-tower to displace itself
  With more of violence than the air supplies
5 When, gathering dusk, the pond brims evenly
  And we must be content with stillness.

Unhastening, daylight withdraws from us its shapes
  Into their central calm. Stone by stone
Your rhetoric is dispersed until the earth
10 Becomes once more the earth, the leaves
  A sharp partition against cooling blue.

Farewell, and for your instructive frenzy
  Gratitude. The world does not end tonight
And the fruit that we shall pick tomorrow
15 Await us, weighing the unstripped bough.

1960

The Picture of J.T. in a Prospect of Stone[2]

    What should one
      wish a child
        and that, one's own
    emerging
5   from between
        the stone lips
    of a sheep-stile
      that divides
        village graves
10 and village green?
      —Wish her
        the constancy of stone.
    —But stone
      is hard.
15   —Say, rather
    it resists
      the slow corrosives
        and the flight
    of time
20   and yet it takes
      the play, the fluency
    from light.

1. (1853–1890); Dutch post-impressionist painter, who suffered bouts of insanity and finally killed himself.

2. Cf. Andrew Marvell's poem "The Picture of Little T. C. in a Prospect of Flowers" (pp. 439–40).

—How would you know.
the gift you'd give
25 was the gift
she'd wish to have?
—Gift is giving,
gift is meaning:
first
30   I'd give
then let her
live with it
to prove
its quality the better and
35   thus learn
to love
what (to begin with)
she might spurn.
—You'd
40 moralize a gift?
—I'd have her
understand
the gift I gave her.
—And so she shall
45   but let her play
her innocence away
emerging
as she does
between
50   her doom (unknown),
her unmown green.

1963

Mr. Brodsky

I had heard
before, of an
American who would have preferred
to be an Indian;
5 but not
until Mr. Brodsky, of one
whose professed and long
pondered-on passion
was to become a Scot,
10 who even sent for haggis[3] and oatcakes
across continent.
Having read him
in Cambridge English
a verse or two
15 from MacDiarmid,[4]
I was invited
to repeat the reading

3. Traditional Scottish dish, consisting of minced heart, lungs, and liver of sheep and calves, boiled in an artificial bag with oatmeal, etc.

4. Pen name of Christopher Murray Grieve (1892–1978), Scottish poet (see pp. 1265–70).

before a Burns Night Gathering[5]
where the Balmoral Pipers
20   of Albuquerque would
play in the haggis
out of its New York tin.
Of course, I said
No. No. I could *not* go
25   and then
half-regretted I had not been.
But to console
and cure the wish, came
Mr. Brodsky, bringing
30   his pipes and played
until the immense, distended
bladder of leather seemed
it could barely contain its water—
tears (idle
35   tears) for the bridal of Annie Laurie[6]
and Morton J. Brodsky.
A bagpipe in a dwelling is
a resonant instrument
and there he stood
40   lost in the gorse
the heather or whatever
six thousand
miles and more
from the infection's source,
45   in our neo–New Mexican parlour
where I had heard
before of an
American who would have preferred
to be merely an Indian.

1966

Ararat[7]

We shall sleep-out together through the dark
The earth's slow voyage across centuries
Towards whatever Ararat its ark
Is steering for. Our atoms then will feel
5   The jarring and arrival of that keel
In timelessness, and rise through galaxies,
Motes starred by the first and final light to show
Whether those shores are habitable or no.

1987

5. Evening of January 25, birthday of Robert
Burns (1759–1796), Scottish poet (see pp. 684–
95).

6. Subject of anonymous Scottish folk song.
7. The mountain on which Noah's ark came to
rest (Genesis 6–10).

JAMES WRIGHT

1927–1980

A Note Left in Jimmy Leonard's Shack

Near the dry river's water-mark we found
　　Your brother Minnegan,
Flopped like a fish against the muddy ground.
Beany, the kid whose yellow hair turns green,
5　Told me to find you, even in the rain,
　　And tell you he was drowned.

I hid behind the chassis on the bank,
　　The wreck of someone's Ford:
I was afraid to come and wake you drunk:
10　You told me once the waking up was hard,
The daylight beating at you like a board.
　　Blood in my stomach sank.

Besides, you told him never to go out
　　Along the river-side
15　Drinking and singing, clattering about.
You might have thrown a rock at me and cried
I was to blame, I let him fall in the road
　　And pitch down on his side.

Well, I'll get hell enough when I get home
20　　For coming up this far,
Leaving the note, and running as I came.
I'll go and tell my father where you are.
You'd better go find Minnegan before
　　Policemen hear and come.

25　Beany went home, and I got sick and ran,
　　You old son of a bitch.
You better hurry down to Minnegan;
He's drunk or dying now, I don't know which,
Rolled in the roots and garbage like a fish.
30　　The poor old man.

1959

A Blessing

Just off the highway to Rochester, Minnesota,
Twilight bounds softly forth on the grass.
And the eyes of those two Indian ponies
Darken with kindness.
5　They have come gladly out of the willows
To welcome my friend and me.
We step over the barbed wire into the pasture
Where they have been grazing all day, alone.

They ripple tensely, they can hardly contain their happiness
10 That we have come.
They bow shyly as wet swans. They love each other.
There is no loneliness like theirs.
At home once more,
They begin munching the young tufts of spring in the darkness.
15 I would like to hold the slenderer one in my arms,
For she has walked over to me
And nuzzled my left hand.
She is black and white,
Her mane falls wild on her forehead,
20 And the light breeze moves me to caress her long ear
That is delicate as the skin over a girl's wrist.
Suddenly I realize
That if I stepped out of my body I would break
Into blossom.

1963

Speak

To speak in a flat voice
Is all that I can do.
I have gone every place
Asking for you.
5 Wondering where to turn
And how the search would end
And the last streetlight spin
Above me blind.

Then I returned rebuffed
10 And saw under the sun
The race not to the swift
Nor the battle won.[1]
Liston[2] dives in the tank,
Lord, in Lewiston, Maine,
15 And Ernie Doty's drunk
In hell again.

And Jenny, oh my Jenny[3]
Whom I love, rhyme be damned,
Has broken her spare beauty
20 In a whorehouse old.
She left her new baby
In a bus-station can,
And sprightly danced away
Through Jacksontown.[4]

1. As in Ecclesiastes 9.11: "I returned, and saw under the sun, that the race is not to the swift, nor the battle to the strong . . ."
2. In a controversial bout for the heavyweight boxing title in 1965, Cassius Clay knocked out Sonny Liston in one minute.
3. Jenny, "a girl I was in love with who has been dead a long time" (Wright interview), appears in several poems in different guises, including the role of the Muse.
4. Town in central Ohio; Wright grew up in Martins Ferry, Ohio.

25   Which is a place I know,
One where I got picked up
A few shrunk years ago
By a good cop.
Believe it, Lord, or not.
30   Don't ask me who he was.
I speak of flat defeat
In a flat voice.

I have gone forward with
Some, few lonely some.
35   They have fallen to death.
I die with them.
Lord, I have loved Thy cursed,
The beauty of Thy house:
Come down. Come down. Why dost
40   Thou hide thy face?[5]

1968

PETER DAVISON

1928–

Equinox 1980

In the stillness after dawn we two
    paddled a noiseless boat
before wakefall across
    a bay smooth as a mirror,
5   changeless as its glass.
    Not a whisper of passage.
Hardly a single stir
    inside the horizon
except for the rippling
10   wrinkles pushed by our prow
and the faraway swoop and flurry
    of a squadron of terns.
The tide at its landward edge
    ignited a smudge of commotion,
15 skittering sandpipers
    along the farther shore.
In all the days of our marriage
    we had never seen
so unruffled a morning:
20   never had any event
shimmered with so costly a light
    as we ascended the meandering
creek in our sweet boat,
    surprising no one except
25 a bright-eyed otter.

5. As in Job 13.24: "Wherefore hidest thou thy face, and holdest me for thine enemy?"

> Pushed by mere hints
> from our paddles,
> 　　we rode up the thickening tide
> among heavy wands
> 30　　　of ripe marsh grass
> that wagged seed-bundles
> 　　high above our heads.
>
> Neither one speaking,
> 　　we rose to go ashore
> 35　and lugged away
> 　　our featherweight kayak
> to winter quarters,
> 　　　knowing as we stowed it
> that this would be the last time,
> 40　　that we would never set out to sea
> together again.

Peaches

> A mouthful of language to swallow:
> stretches of beach, sweet clinches,
> breaches in walls, pleached branches;
> britches hauled over haunches;
> 5　hunched leeches, wrenched teachers.
> What English can do: ransack
> the warmth that chuckles beneath
> fuzzed surfaces, smooth velvet
> richness, plashy juices.
> 10　I beseech you, peach,
> clench me into the sweetness
> of your reaches.

1989

DONALD HALL
1928–

Exile[1]

> A boy who played and talked and read with me
> Fell from a maple tree.
>
> I loved her, but I told her I did not,
> And wept, and then forgot.
>
> 5　I walked the streets where I was born and grew,
> And all the streets were new.

1951–55   1969

---

1. Many versions of this poem exist; cf. a much longer one, written earlier but published later (in Hall's 1990 *Old and New Poems*).

From The One Day[2]

Prophecy

I will strike down wooden houses; I will burn aluminum
clapboard skin; I will strike down garages
where crimson Toyotas sleep side by side; I will explode
palaces of gold, silver, and alabaster: — the summer
5 great house and its folly together. Where shopping malls
spread plywood and plaster out, and roadhouses
serve steak and potatoskins beside Alaska king crab;
where triangular flags proclaim tribes of identical campers;
where airplanes nose to tail exhale kerosene,
10 weeds and ashes will drowse in continual twilight.

I reject the old house and the new car; I reject
Tory and Whig[3] together; I reject the argument
that modesty of ambition is sensible because the bigger
they are the harder they fall; I reject Waterford;[4]
15 I reject the five and dime; I reject Romulus and Remus;[5]
I reject Martha's Vineyard and the slamdunk contest;
I reject leaded panes; I reject the appointment made
at the tennis net or on the seventeenth green; I reject
the Professional Bowlers Tour; I reject matchboxes;
20 I reject purple bathrooms with purple soap in them.

Men who lie awake worrying about taxes, vomiting
at dawn, whose hands shake as they administer Valium, —
skin will peel from the meat of their thighs.
Armies that march all day with elephants past pyramids
25 and roll pulling missiles past generals weary of saluting
and past president-emperors splendid in cloth-of-gold, —
soft rumps of armies will dissipate in rain. Where square
miles of corn waver in Minnesota, where tobacco ripens
in Carolina and apples in New Hampshire, where wheat
30 turns Kansas green, where pulpmills stink in Oregon, —

---

2. A three-part, book-length poem written over several decades. "Prophecy" is the first of the "Four Classic Texts" within the poem's central section, which is introduced with two epigraphs: "Of the opposites that which tends to birth or creation is called war or strife. That which tends to destruction by fire is called concord or peace" (Heraclitus) and "Poetry is preparation for death" (Nadezhda Mandelstam). The two principal voices of the poem, a female sculptor and the author, are set aside here for a "general consciousness that narrates. . . . There are many borrowings and allusions" [Hall's note]. The tone of "Prophecy" suggests particularly an indebtedness to Heraclitus

(ca. 540–ca. 480 B.C.), the Greek philosopher who argued that the essential stuff of the universe is pure fire, and to the first part of the book of Isaiah, who in a vision saw the vain and the wicked destroyed by fire. Nadezhda Mandelstam (d. 1980), memoirist, wife of the Russian poet Osip Mandelstam (1891–1938).
3. Historically, opposing parties in British politics.
4. Brand name of crystal made in Waterford, Ireland.
5. In Roman legend, twin sons of the god Mars and Rhea Silvia; descendants of Aeneas and the founders of the city of Rome.

dust will blow in the darkness and cactus die
before it flowers. Where skiers wait for chairlifts,
wearing money, low raspberries will part rib bones.
Where the drive-in church raises a chromium cross,
35 dandelions and milkweed will straggle through blacktop.
I will strike from the ocean with waves afire;
I will strike from the hill with rainclouds of lava;
I will strike from darkened air
with melanoma in the shape of decorative hexagonals.
40 I will strike down embezzlers and eaters of snails.

I reject Japanese smoked oysters, potted chrysanthemums
allowed to die, Tupperware parties, Ronald McDonald,
Kaposi's sarcoma, the Taj Mahal, Holsteins wearing
electronic necklaces, the Algonquin, Tunisian aqueducts,
45 Phi Beta Kappa keys, the Hyatt Embarcadero,[6] carpenters
jogging on the median, and betrayal that engorges
the corrupt heart longing for criminal surrender.
I reject shadows in the corner of the atrium
where Phyllis or Phoebe speaks with Billy or Marc
50 who says that afternoons are best although not reliable.

Your children will wander looting the shopping malls
for forty years, suffering for your idleness,
until the last dwarf body rots in a parking lot.
I will strike down lobbies and restaurants in motels
55 carpeted with shaggy petrochemicals
from Maine to Hilton Head, from the Skagit[7] to Tucson.
I will strike down hang gliders, wiry adventurous boys;
their thigh bones will snap, their brains
slide from their skulls. I will strike down
60 families cooking wildboar in New Mexico backyards.

Then landscape will clutter with incapable machinery,
acres of vacant airplanes and schoolbuses, ploughs
with seedlings sprouting and turning brown through colters.
Unlettered dwarves will burrow for warmth and shelter
65 in the caves of dynamos and Plymouths, dying
of old age at seventeen. Tribes wandering
in the wilderness of their ignorant desolation,
who suffer from your idleness, will burn your illuminated
missals to warm their rickety bodies.
70 Terrorists assemble plutonium because you are idle

6. A hotel. "Holsteins": cows. "Algonquin": a hotel. "Phi Beta Kappa keys": symbols of membership in a scholarly society.   7. A bay and county in the state of Washington; "Hilton Head": resort in South Carolina.

and industrious. The whip-poor-will shrivels
and the pickerel chokes under the government of self-love.
Vacancy burns air so that you strangle without oxygen
like rats in a biologist's bell jar. The living god sharpens
75 the scythe of my prophecy to strike down red poppies
and blue cornflowers. When priests and policemen
strike my body's match, Jehovah will flame out;
Jehovah will suck air from the vents of bombshelters.
Therefore let the Buick swell until it explodes;
80 therefore let anorexia starve and bulimia engorge.

When Elzira leaves the house wearing her tennis dress
and drives her black Porsche to meet Abraham,
quarrels, returns to husband and children, and sobs
asleep, drunk, unable to choose among them, —
85 lawns and carpets will turn into tar together
with lovers, husbands, and children.
Fat will boil in the sacs of children's clear skin.
I will strike down the nations, astronauts and judges;
I will strike down Babylon,[8] I will strike acrobats,
90 I will strike algae and the white birches.

Because professors of law teach ethics in dumbshow,
let the colonel become president; because chief executive
officers and commissars collect down for pillows,
let the injustice of cities burn city and suburb;
95 let the countryside burn; let the pineforests of Maine
explode like a kitchenmatch and the Book of Kells[9] turn
ash in a microsecond; let oxen and athletes
flash into grease: — I return to Appalachian rocks;
I shall eat bread; I shall prophesy through millennia
100 of Jehovah's day until the sky reddens over cities:

Then houses will burn, even houses of alabaster;
the sky will disappear like a scroll rolled up
and hidden in a cave from the industries of idleness.
Mountains will erupt and vanish, becoming deserts,
105 and the sea wash over the sea's lost islands
and the earth split open like a corpse's gassy
stomach and the sun turn as black as a widow's skirt
and the full moon grow red with blood swollen inside it

8. The city to which the Jews were carried in captivity (2 Kings 24–25); also, a great but fallen city, epitomizing sinfulness (Revelation 18).
9. An ornately illustrated manuscript of the Gospels of the New Testament, produced by Scottish and Irish monks and completed in Kells, Ireland, in the ninth century.

110 and stars fall from the sky like wind-blown apples, —
while Babylon's managers burn in the rage of the Lamb.[1]

1988

THOMAS KINSELLA
1928–

Another September

Dreams fled away, this country bedroom, raw
With the touch of the dawn, wrapped in a minor peace,
Hears through an open window the garden draw
Long pitch black breaths, lay bare its apple trees,
5 Ripe pear trees, brambles, windfall-sweetened soil,
Exhale rough sweetness against the starry slates.
Nearer the river sleeps St. John's,[1] all toil
Locked fast inside a dream with iron gates.

Domestic Autumn, like an animal
10 Long used to handling by those countrymen,
Rubs her kind hide against the bedroom wall
Sensing a fragrant child come back again
—Not this half-tolerated consciousness,
Its own cold season never done,
15 But that unspeaking daughter, growing less
Familiar where we fell asleep as one.

Wakeful moth-wings blunder near a chair,
Toss their light shell at the glass, and go
To inhabit the living starlight. Stranded hair
20 Stirs on the still linen. It is as though
The black breathing that billows her sleep, her name,
Drugged under judgment, waned and—bearing daggers
And balances—down the lampless darkness they came,
Moving like women: Justice, Truth, such figures.

1958

Ancestor

I was going up to say something,
and stopped. Her profile against the curtains
was old, and dark like a hunting bird's.

It was the way she perched on the high stool,
5 staring into herself, with one fist
gripping the side of the barrier around her desk
—or her head held by something, from inside.
And not caring for anything around her

1. The Lamb of God; i.e., Jesus. The stanza is a
freely reconceived paraphrase of Revelation 6.12–
16.
1. Church dedicated to St. John the Evangelist.

or anyone there by the shelves.
10   I caught a faint smell, musky and queer.

I may have made some sound—she stopped rocking
and pressed her fist in her lap; then she stood up
and shut down the lid of the desk, and turned the key.
She shoved a small bottle under her aprons
15   and came toward me, darkening the passageway.

Ancestor . . . among sweet- and fruit-boxes.
Her black heart . . .
                Was that a sigh?
—brushing by me in the shadows,
20   with her heaped aprons, through the red hangings
to the scullery, and down to the back room.

                                    1973

Tear

I was sent in to see her.
A fringe of jet drops
chattered at my ear
as I went in through the hangings.

5   I was swallowed in chambery dusk.
My heart shrank
at the smell of disused
organs and sour kidney.

The black aprons I used to
10   bury my face in
were folded at the foot of the bed
in the last watery light from the window

(Go in and say goodbye to her)
and I was carried off
15   to unfathomable depths.
I turned to look at her.

She stared at the ceiling
and puffed her cheek, distracted,
propped high in the bed
20   resting for the next attack.

The covers were gathered close
up to her mouth,
that the lines of ill-temper still
marked. Her grey hair

25   was loosened out like
a young woman's all over
the pillow, mixed with the shadows
criss-crossing her forehead

and at her mouth and eyes,
30   like a web of strands tying down her head
and tangling down toward the shadow
eating away the floor at my feet.

I couldn't stir at first, nor wished to,
for fear she might turn and tempt me
35   (my own father's mother)
with open mouth

—with some fierce wheedling whisper—
to hide myself one last time
against her, and bury my
40   self in her drying mud.

Was I to kiss her? As soon
kiss the damp that crept
in the flowered walls
of this pit.

45   Yet I had to kiss.
I knelt by the bulk of the death bed
and sank my face in the chill
and smell of her black aprons.

Snuff and musk, the folds against my eyelids,
50   carried me into a derelict place
smelling of ash: unseen walls and roofs
rustled like breathing.

I found myself disturbing
dead ashes for any trace
55   of warmth, when far off
in the vaults a single drop

splashed. And I found
what I was looking for
—not heat nor fire,
60   not any comfort,

but her voice, soft, talking to someone
about my father: "God help him, he cried
big tears over there by the machine
for the poor little thing." Bright

65   drops on the wooden lid for
my infant sister. My own
wail of child-animal grief
was soon done, with any early guess

at sad dullness and tedious pain
70   and lives bitter with hard bondage.
How I tasted it now—
her heart beating in my mouth!

She drew an uncertain breath
and pushed at the clothes
75 and shuddered tiredly.
I broke free

and left the room
promising myself
when she was really dead
80 I would really kiss.

My grandfather half looked up
from the fireplace as I came out,
and shrugged and turned back
with a deaf stare to the heat.

85 I fidgeted beside him for a minute
and went out to the shop.
It was still bright there
and I felt better able to breathe.

Old age can digest
90 anything: the commotion
at Heaven's gate—the struggle
in store for you all your life.

How long and hard it is
before you get to Heaven,
95 unless like little Agnes
you vanish with early tears.

1973

PHILIP LEVINE

1928–

They Feed They Lion

Out of burlap sacks, out of bearing butter,
Out of black bean and wet slate bread,
Out of the acids of rage, the candor of tar,
Out of creosote, gasoline, drive shafts, wooden dollies,
5   They Lion grow.
            Out of the gray hills
Of industrial barns, out of rain, out of bus ride,
West Virginia to Kiss My Ass, out of buried aunties,
Mothers hardening like pounded stumps, out of stumps,
10 Out of the bones' need to sharpen and the muscles' to stretch,
They Lion grow.
            Earth is eating trees, fence posts,
Gutted cars, earth is calling in her little ones,
"Come home, Come home!" From pig balls,

15 From the ferocity of pig driven to holiness,
From the furred ear and the full jowl come
The repose of the hung belly, from the purpose
They Lion grow.
                    From the sweet glues of the trotters
20 Come the sweet kinks of the fist, from the full flower
Of the hams the thorax of caves,
From "Bow Down" come "Rise Up,"
Come they Lion from the reeds of shovels,
The grained arm that pulls the hands,
25 They Lion grow.
                    From my five arms and all my hands,
From all my white sins forgiven, they feed,
From my car passing under the stars,
They Lion, from my children inherit,
30 From the oak turned to a wall, they Lion,
From they sack and they belly opened
And all that was hidden burning on the oil-stained earth
They feed they Lion and he comes.

                                                1972

You Can Have It

My brother comes home from work
and climbs the stairs to our room.
I can hear the bed groan and his shoes drop
one by one. You can have it, he says.

5   The moonlight streams in the window
and his unshaven face is whitened
like the face of the moon. He will sleep
long after noon and waken to find me gone.

Thirty years will pass before I remember
10 that moment when suddenly I knew each man
has one brother who dies when he sleeps
and sleeps when he rises to face this life,

and that together they are only one man
sharing a heart that always labors, hands
15 yellowed and cracked, a mouth that gasps
for breath and asks, Am I gonna make it?

All night at the ice plant he had fed
the chute its silvery blocks, and then I
stacked cases of orange soda for the children
20 of Kentucky, one gray boxcar at a time

with always two more waiting. We were twenty
for such a short time and always in
the wrong clothes, crusted with dirt
and sweat. I think now we were never twenty.

25 In 1948 in the city of Detroit, founded
by de la Mothe Cadillac for the distant purposes
of Henry Ford,[1] no one wakened or died,
no one walked the streets or stoked a furnace,

for there was no such year, and now
30 that year has fallen off all the old newspapers,
calendars, doctors' appointments, bonds,
wedding certificates, drivers licenses.

The city slept. The snow turned to ice.
The ice to standing pools or rivers
35 racing in the gutters. Then bright grass rose
between the thousands of cracked squares,

and that grass died. I give you back 1948.
I give you all the years from then
to the coming one. Give me back the moon
40 with its frail light falling across a face.

Give me back my young brother, hard
and furious, with wide shoulders and a curse
for God and burning eyes that look upon
all creation and say, You can have it.

1979

The Simple Truth

I bought a dollar and a half's worth of small red potatoes,
took them home, boiled them in their jackets
and ate them for dinner with a little butter and salt.
Then I walked through the dried fields
5 on the edge of town. In middle June the light
hung on in the dark furrows at my feet,
and in the mountain oaks overhead the birds
were gathering for the night, the jays and mockers
squawking back and forth, the finches still darting
10 into the dusty light. The woman who sold me
the potatoes was from Poland; she was someone
out of my childhood in a pink spangled sweater and sunglasses
praising the perfection of all her fruits and vegetables
at the road-side stand and urging me to taste
15 even the pale, raw sweet corn trucked all the way,
she swore, from New Jersey. "Eat, eat," she said,
"Even if you don't I'll say you did."
                        Some things
you know all your life. They are so simple and true
20 they must be said without elegance, meter and rhyme,
they must be laid on the table beside the salt shaker,

1. (1863–1947); American automobile manufac-
turer, associated with Detroit. Antoine Laumet de
la Mothe Cadillac (1658–1730), born in France,
established a fur-trade post, later the city of Detroit;
Cadillac cars are named for him.

the glass of water, the absence of light gathering
in the shadows of picture frames, they must be
naked and alone, they must stand for themselves.
25 My friend Henri and I arrived at this together in 1965
before I went away, before he began to kill himself,
and the two of us to betray our love. Can you taste
what I'm saying? It is onions or potatoes, a pinch
of simple salt, the wealth of melting butter, it is obvious,
30 it stays in the back of your throat like a truth
you never uttered because the time was always wrong,
it stays there for the rest of your life, unspoken,
made of that dirt we call earth, the metal we call salt,
in a form we have no words for, and you live on it.

1994

ANNE SEXTON

1928–1974

The Truth the Dead Know

For my mother, born March 1902, died March 1959,
and my father, born February 1900, died June 1959

Gone, I say and walk from church,
refusing the stiff procession to the grave,
letting the dead ride alone in the hearse.
It is June. I am tired of being brave.

5   We drive to the Cape. I cultivate
myself where the sun gutters from the sky,
where the sea swings in like an iron gate
and we touch. In another country people die.

My darling, the wind falls in like stones
10 from the whitehearted water and when we touch
we enter touch entirely. No one's alone.
Men kill for this, or for as much.

And what of the dead? They lie without shoes
in their stone boats. They are more like stone
15 than the sea would be if it stopped. They refuse
to be blessed, throat, eye and knucklebone.

1962

And One for My Dame

A born salesman,
my father made all his dough
by selling wool to Fieldcrest, Woolrich and Faribo.

A born talker,
5   he could sell one hundred wet-down bales
of that white stuff. He could clock the miles and sales

and make it pay.
At home each sentence he would utter
had first pleased the buyer who'd paid him off in butter.

10   Each word
had been tried over and over, at any rate,
on the man who was sold by the man who filled my plate.

My father hovered
over the Yorkshire pudding and the beef:
15   a peddler, a hawker, a merchant and an Indian chief.

Roosevelt! Willkie! and war![1]
How suddenly gauche I was
with my old-maid heart and my funny teenage applause.

Each night at home
20   my father was in love with maps
while the radio fought its battles with Nazis and Japs.

Except when he hid
in his bedroom on a three-day drunk,
he typed out complex itineraries, packed his trunk,

25   his matched luggage
and pocketed a confirmed reservation,
his heart already pushing over the red routes of the nation.

I sit at my desk
each night with no place to go,
30   opening the wrinkled maps of Milwaukee and Buffalo,

the whole U.S.,
its cemeteries, its arbitrary time zones,
through routes like small veins, capitals like small stones.

He died on the road,
35   his heart pushed from neck to back,
his white hanky signaling from the window of the Cadillac.

My husband,
as blue-eyed as a picture book, sells wool:
boxes of card waste, laps and rovings he can pull

40   to the thread
and say *Leicester, Rambouillet, Merino,*[2]
a half-blood, it's greasy and thick, yellow as old snow.

1. Franklin Delano Roosevelt (1882–1945), U.S.   Wendell Lewis Willkie (1892–1944).
President during World War II, was opposed by   2. Types of wool.

And when you drive off, my darling,
Yes, sir! Yes, sir! It's one for my dame,[3]
45 your sample cases branded with my father's name,

your itinerary open,
its tolls ticking and greedy,
its highways built up like new loves, raw and speedy.

1966

L. E. SISSMAN
1928–1976

From Dying: An Introduction[1]

IV. Path. Report

Bruisingly cradled in a Harvard chair
Whose orange arms cramp my pink ones, and whose black
Back stamps my back with splat marks, I receive
The brunt of the pathology report,
5 Bitingly couched in critical terms of my
Tissue of fabrications, which is bad.
That Tyrian° specimen on the limelit stage   *purplish*
Surveyed by Dr. Cyclops,[2] magnified
Countless diameters on its thick slide,
10 Turns out to end in -oma.[3] "But be glad
These things are treatable today," I'm told.
"Why, fifteen years ago—" a dark and grave-
Shaped pause. "But now, a course of radiation, and—"
Sun rays break through. "And if you want X-ray,
15 You've come to the right place." A history,
A half-life of the hospital. Marie
Curie must have endowed it. Cyclotrons,[4]
Like missile silos, lurk within its walls.
It's reassuring, anyway. But bland
20 And middle-classic as these environs are,
And sanguine as his measured words may be,
And soft his handshake, the webbed, inky hand
Locked on the sill, and the unshaven face
Biding outside the window still appall
25 Me as I leave the assignation place.

3. Allusion to the nursery rhyme "Baa Baa Black Sheep," which ends "One for the master / And one for the dame, / And one for the little boy / Who lives down the lane."
1. The final two parts of a long poem.
2. Named for the one-eyed giants of Greek myth.

3. I.e., a cancer.
4. Accelerators in which particles are propelled in spiral paths. "Half-life": time required for half the atoms of a radioactive substance to disintegrate. Marie Curie (1867–1934): Polish physicist in France, codiscoverer of radium.

V. *Outbound*

Outside, although November by the clock,
Has a thick smell of spring,
And everything—
The low clouds lit
5   Fluorescent green by city lights;
The molten, hissing stream
Of white car lights, cooling
To red and vanishing;
The leaves,
10 Still running from last summer, chattering
Across the pocked concrete;
The wind in trees;
The ones and twos,
The twos and threes
15 Of college girls,
Each shining in the dark,
Each carrying
A book or books,
Each laughing to her friend
20 At such a night in fall;
The two-and-twos
Of boys and girls who lean
Together in an A and softly walk
Slowly from lamp to lamp,
25 Alternatively lit
And nighted; Autumn Street,
Astonishingly named, a rivulet
Of asphalt twisting up and back
To some spring out of sight—and everything
30 Recalls one fall
Twenty-one years ago, when I,
A freshman, opening
A green door just across the river,
Found the source
35 Of spring in that warm night,
Surprised the force
That sent me on my way
And set me down
Today. Tonight. Through my
40 Invisible new veil
Of finity, I see
November's world—
Low scud, slick street, three giggling girls—
As, oddly, not as sombre
45 As December,
But as green
As anything:
As spring.

1968

A Deathplace

Very few people know where they will die,
But I do: in a brick-faced hospital,
Divided, not unlike Caesarean Gaul,[5]
Into three parts: the Dean Memorial
5 Wing, in the classic cast of 1910,
Green-grated in unglazed, Aeolian[6]
Embrasures; the Maud Wiggin Building, which
Commemorates a dog-jawed Boston bitch
Who fought the brass[7] down to their whipcord knees
10 In World War I, and won enlisted men
Some decent hospitals, and, being rich,
Donated her own granite monument;
The Mandeville Pavilion, pink-brick tent
With marble piping, flying snapping flags
15 Above the entry where our bloody rags
Are rolled in to be sponged and sewn again.
Today is fair; tomorrow, scourging rain
(If only my own tears) will see me in
Those jaundiced and distempered corridors
20 Off which the five-foot-wide doors slowly close.
White as my skimpy chiton°, I will cringe   gown
Before the pinpoint of the least syringe;
Before the buttered catheter goes in;
Before the I.V.'s lisp and drip begins
25 Inside my skin; before the rubber hand
Upon the lancet takes aim and descends
To lay me open, and upon its thumb
Retracts the trouble, a malignant plum;
And finally, I'll quail before the hour
30 When the authorities shut off the power
In that vast hospital, and in my bed
I'll feel my blood go thin, go white, the red,
The rose all leached away, and I'll go dead.
Then will the business of life resume:
35 The muffled trolley wheeled into my room,
The off-white blanket blanking off my face,
The stealing, secret, private, *largo°* race   slow
Down halls and elevators to the place
I'll be consigned to for transshipment, cased
40 In artificial air and light: the ward
That's underground; the terminal; the morgue.
Then one fine day when all the smart flags flap,
A booted man in black with a peaked cap
Will call for me and troll me down the hall
45 And slot me into his black car. That's all.

1969

5. Roman Emperor Julius Caesar (100–44 B.C.),   6. In the shape of an Aeolian harp.
in his conquest of Gaul, divided it into three parts.   7. High-ranking military officers.

Upon Finding *Dying: An Introduction*, by L. E. Sissman, Remaindered at 1s.[8]

I wandered lonely as a cloud in Foyles[9]
Of incandescent, tight-knit air, when I
Spied a remainder[1] counter, pied as a
Meadow in autumn with the relicts of
5 A foisonous summer: novels all the Réage[2]
Short weeks ago, now smutched with rusts and rots
Upon their colored calyces;[3] memoirs
Of august personages laid to rest
As early as October; ghosts of Mod
10 Nonce-figures,[4] once in, now as dead as God;
And there, a snip under a blackleg sign,[5]
"These books reduced to 1s.," there is mine,
Dying: An Introduction. Well, if you
Preach about dying, you must practice, too.

1969

U. A. FANTHORPE

1929–

The Person's Tale

"In consequence of a slight indisposition, an anodyne had been prescribed, from the effects of which [the author] fell asleep . . . On awaking . . . [he] eagerly wrote down the lines that are here preserved. At this moment he was unfortunately called out by a person on business from Porlock, and detained by him above an hour . . ."

S.T.C.[1]

That the Muses[2] have no more fervent
Devotee than myself may not be generally
Known outside Porlock. As a man of the cloth
I am, I trust, superior to mere vulgar
5 Appetite for fame. "Full many a gem
Of purest ray serene . . ."[3] I am, I hope, resigned
To being such a gem; an unseen blush.
But to allow myself to be presented
By Mr C — to posterity as a *person*
10 Goes beyond the limits of even clerical
Diffidence. It was, I may say, in pursuit
Of my pastoral duties that I made

---

8. One shilling.
9. Large London bookshop; a parody of "I Wandered Lonely As a Cloud" (pp. 732–33) by the English poet William Wordsworth (1770–1850).
1. A book whose price is reduced for quick sale.
2. Punning allusion to Pauline Réage, pseudonymous author of the notorious, sexually explicit French novel *Histoire d'O* ("Story of O"; 1954).
3. External parts of a flower; here, dust jackets.

4. "Nonce": for the moment; "Mod": modern, hip.
5. A bargain under a swindling sign.
1. Samuel Taylor Coleridge (1772–1834), English poet. See "Kubla Khan," n. 4 (p. 741).
2. The nine goddesses in Greek and Roman mythology who inspire artists, including poets.
3. Cf. Thomas Gray, "Elegy Written in a Country Churchyard," line 53 (p. 609).

The not inconsiderable journey from my parsonage
To the farmhouse, at Mr C——'s own
15 Most vehement behest. Prepared for any
Extreme office, I presented myself
Before Mr C——, *Sir*, said I, *I am here.*
The very man, quoth he, clasping me in
A distasteful embrace. *Most reverend sir*—
20 Then for two hours detained me at his door
With chronicles of colic, stomach, bowels,
Of nightly sweats, the nightmare, cramps, diarrhoea
(Your pardon, Delicacy! Merely the word appals),
All the while straining me to his bosom, like
25 His own deplorable Mariner,[4] neglected hygiene
Rendering contiguity less than welcome,
The more as I infallibly discerned
The less pleasing features of addiction
To the poppy,[5] prescribed, he affirmed,
30 As anodyne against the dysentery.
And now, it seems, I am the guilty *person*
Who cut off inspiration in its prime.
Quite otherwise. Myself had on the way
Entertained the notion of an Acrostick,[6] a form
35 Of harmless mirth whereby I have achieved
Some slender fame among the Porlock fair.°   ladies
Alas! the frail thing could not survive
Two hours of Mr C——'s internal ills.
I am the loser, first of my Acrostick,
40 Then of my character, for surely *person*
Denotes nonentity, a man of straw—
And the proud name of Porlock sullied too!

1984

Nativities

Godlings are born racily.

They are excavated
Into life by the strong licks
Of the world-cow, suckled
5   By goats, mares, wolves.[7]

Blossom of oak, blossom of broom,
Blossom of meadowsweet
Go to their making.[8]

They erupt through the paternal
10 Skull fully armed,[9] hatch from an egg,
Or appear, foam-born,

---

4. See Samuel Taylor Coleridge, "The Rime of the Ancient Mariner" (pp. 744–59).
5. From which opium is made.
6. A word game popular in the eighteenth century.
7. As were, for example, Romulus and Remus, sons of Mars.
8. As in the case of Blodeuwedd. See Robert Graves, "The Song of Blodeuwedd" (p. 1295).
9. Athene burst, fully armed, from the head of her father, Zeus. Helen of Troy hatched from an egg.

In Cyprus, in a shell,
Wearing a great deal of hair
And nothing else.[1]

15   This one[2] arrived
At the time of the early lambs
By means of the usual channels.

1987

THOM GUNN

1929–

On the Move

"Man, you gotta Go."

The blue jay scuffling in the bushes follows
Some hidden purpose, and the gust of birds
That spurts across the field, the wheeling swallows,
Have nested in the trees and undergrowth.
5   Seeking their instinct, or their poise, or both,
One moves with an uncertain violence
Under the dust thrown by a baffled sense
Or the dull thunder of approximate words.

On motorcycles, up the road, they come:
10   Small, black, as flies hanging in heat, the Boys,
Until the distance throws them forth, their hum
Bulges to thunder held by calf and thigh.
In goggles, donned impersonality,
In gleaming jackets trophied with the dust,
15   They strap in doubt—by hiding it, robust—
And almost hear a meaning in their noise.

Exact conclusion of their hardiness
Has no shape yet, but from known whereabouts
They ride, direction where the tyres press.
20   They scare a flight of birds across the field:
Much that is natural, to the will must yield.
Men manufacture both machine and soul,
And use what they imperfectly control
To dare a future from the taken routes.

25   It is a part solution, after all.
One is not necessarily discord
On earth; or damned because, half animal,

1. Aphrodite (Greek), or Venus (Roman), was
born from the foam and was depicted, in a famous
painting by the Italian artist Botticelli (1445–
1510), rising from a seashell.
2. Christ.

One lacks direct instinct, because one wakes
Afloat on movement that divides and breaks.
30 One joins the movement in a valueless world,
Choosing it, till, both hurler and the hurled,
One moves as well, always toward, toward.

A minute holds them, who have come to go:
The self-defined, astride the created will
35 They burst away; the towns they travel through
Are home for neither bird nor holiness,
For birds and saints complete their purposes.
At worst, one is in motion; and at best,
Reaching no absolute, in which to rest,
40 One is always nearer by not keeping still.

California   1957

A Map of the City

I stand upon a hill and see
A luminous country under me,
Through which at two the drunk must weave;
The transient's pause, the sailor's leave.

5 I notice, looking down the hill,
Arms braced upon a window sill;
And on the web of fire escapes
Move the potential, the grey shapes.

I hold the city here, complete:
10 And every shape defined by light
Is mine, or corresponds to mine,
Some flickering or some steady shine.

This map is ground of my delight.
Between the limits, night by night,
15 I watch a malady's advance,
I recognize my love of chance.

By the recurrent lights I see
Endless potentiality,
The crowded, broken, and unfinished!
20 I would not have the risk diminished.

1961

Black Jackets

In the silence that prolongs the span
Rawly of music when the record ends,
The red-haired boy who drove a van
In weekday overalls but, like his friends,

5 Wore cycle boots and jacket here
To suit the Sunday hangout he was in,

Heard, as he stretched back from his beer,
Leather creak softly round his neck and chin.

Before him, on a coal-black sleeve
10 Remote exertion had lined, scratched, and burned
Insignia that could not revive
The heroic fall or climb where they were earned.

On the other drinkers bent together,
Concocting selves for their impervious kit,
15 He saw it as no more than leather
Which, taut across the shoulders grown to it,

Sent through the dimness of a bar
As sudden and anonymous hints of light
As those that shipping give, that are
20 Now flickers in the Bay, now lost in night.

He stretched out like a cat, and rolled
The bitterish taste of beer upon his tongue,
And listened to a joke being told:
The present was the things he stayed among.

25 If it was only loss he wore,
He wore it to assert, with fierce devotion,
Complicity and nothing more.
He recollected his initiation,

And one especially of the rites.
30 For on his shoulders they had put tattoos:
The group's name on the left, The Knights,
And on the right the slogan Born To Lose.

1961

My Sad Captains

One by one they appear in
the darkness: a few friends, and
a few with historical
names. How late they start to shine!
5 but before they fade they stand
perfectly embodied, all

the past lapping them like a
cloak of chaos. They were men
who, I thought, lived only to
10 renew the wasteful force they
spent with each hot convulsion.
They remind me, distant now.

True, they are not at rest yet,
but now that they are indeed

15   apart, winnowed° from failures,   *separated*
they withdraw to an orbit
and turn with disinterested
hard energy, like the stars.

1961

From the Wave

It mounts at sea, a concave wall
Down-ribbed with shine,
And pushes forward, building tall
Its steep incline.

5   Then from their hiding rise to sight
Black shapes on boards
Bearing before the fringe of white
It mottles towards.

Their pale feet curl, they poise their weight
10   With a learn'd skill.
It is the wave they imitate
Keeps them so still.

The marbling bodies have become
Half wave, half men,
15   Grafted it seems by feet of foam
Some seconds, then,

Late as they can, they slice the face
In timed procession:
Balance is triumph in this place,
20   Triumph possession.

The mindless heave of which they rode
A fluid shelf
Breaks as they leave it, falls and, slowed,
Loses itself.

25   Clear, the sheathed bodies slick as seals
Loosen and tingle;
And by the board the bare foot feels
The suck of shingle.

They paddle in the shallows still;
30   Two splash each other;
Then all swim out to wait until
The right waves gather.

1971

The Missing

Now as I watch the progress of the plague,[1]
The friends surrounding me fall sick, grow thin,
And drop away. Bared, is my shape less vague
—Sharply exposed and with a sculpted skin?

5 I do not like the statue's chill contour,
Not nowadays. The warmth investing me
Let outward through mind, limb, feeling, and more
In an involved increasing family.

Contact of friend led to another friend,
10 Supple entwinement through the living mass
Which for all that I knew might have no end,
Image of an unlimited embrace.

I did not just feel ease, though comfortable:
Aggressive as in some ideal of sport,
15 With ceaseless movement thrilling through the whole,
Their push kept me as firm as their support.

But death—Their deaths have left me less defined:
It was their pulsing presence made me clear.
I borrowed from it, I was unconfined,
20 Who tonight balance unsupported here,

Eyes glaring from raw marble, in a pose
Languorously part-buried in the block,
Shins perfect and no calves, as if I froze
Between potential and a finished work.

25 —Abandoned incomplete, shape of a shape,
In which exact detail shows the more strange,
Trapped in unwholeness, I find no escape
Back to the play of constant give and change.

1987   1992

1. AIDS.

JOHN HOLLANDER

1929–

Swan and Shadow

```
                     Dusk
                  Above the
         water   hang    the
                     loud
                     flies
                     Here
                     O so
                     gray
                     then
                  What                    A pale signal will appear
                  When               Soon before its shadow fades
                  Where          Here in this pool of opened eye
                  In us      No Upon us As at the very edges
                of where we take shape in the dark air
                   this object bares its image awakening
                      ripples of recognition that will
                         brush darkness up into light
    even after this bird this hour both drift by atop the perfect sad instant now
                         already passing out of sight
                      toward yet-untroubled reflection
                   this image bears its object darkening
                 into memorial shades Scattered bits of
                  light          No of water Or something across
                  water             Breaking up No Being regathered
                  soon                 Yet by then a swan will have
                  gone                   Yes out of mind into what
                     vast
                     pale
                     hush
                     of a
                     place
                     past
         sudden   dark   as
            if   a   swan
                  sang                                                    1969
```

Adam's Task

"And Adam gave names to all cattle, and to the fowl of the air, and to every beast of the field . . ."

—Gen. 2:20

Thou, paw-paw-paw; thou, glurd; thou, spotted
Glurd; thou, whitestap, lurching through
The high-grown brush; thou, pliant-footed,
Implex; thou, awagabu.

5 Every burrower, each flier
Came for the name he had to give:
Gay, first work, ever to be prior,
Not yet sunk to primitive.

Thou, verdle; thou, McFleery's pomma;
10   Thou; thou; thou—three types of grawl;
Thou, flisket; thou, kabasch; thou, comma-
Eared mashawk; thou, all; thou, all.

Were, in a fire of becoming,
    Laboring to be burned away,
15   Then work, half-measuring, half-humming,
    Would be as serious as play.

Thou, pambler; thou, rivarn; thou, greater
    Wherret, and thou, lesser one;
Thou, sproal; thou, zant; thou, lily-eater.
20   Naming's over. Day is done.   1971

An Old-Fashioned Song

(Nous n'irons plus au bois)[1]

No more walks in the wood:
The trees have all been cut
Down, and where once they stood
Not even a wagon rut
5   Appears along the path
Low brush is taking over.

No more walks in the wood;
This is the aftermath
Of afternoons in the clover
10   Fields where we once made love
Then wandered home together
Where the trees arched above,
Where we made our own weather
When branches were the sky.
15   Now they are gone for good,
And you, for ill, and I
Am only a passer-by.

We and the trees and the way
Back from the fields of play
20   Lasted as long as we could.
No more walks in the wood.   1993

Variations on a Fragment by Trumbull Stickney[2]

I hear a river thro' the valley wander
Whose water runs, the song alone remaining.
A rainbow stands and summer passes under,

Flowing like silence in the light of wonder.
5   In the near distances it is still raining
Where now the valley fills again with thunder,

1. "*Nous n'irons plus au bois/ Les lauriers sont coupés*" (We'll go no more to the woods/ The laurels have been cut down)—from a French children's round dance" [Hollander's note].

2. Cf. "Fragments: IX" (p. 1146) by the American poet Trumbull Stickney (1874–1904). The three-line poem provides Hollander's first stanza.

Where now the river in her wide meander,
Losing at each loop what she had been gaining,
Moves into what one might as well call yonder.

10 The way of the dark water is to ponder
The way the light sings as of something waning.
The far-off waterfall can sound asunder

Stillness of distances, as if in blunder,
Tumbling over the rim of all explaining.
15 Water proves nothing, but can only maunder.

Shadows show nothing, but can only launder
The lovely land that sunset had been staining,
Long fields of which the falling light grows fonder.

Here summer stands while all its songs pass under,
20 A riverbank still time runs by, remaining.
I will remember rainbows as I wander.   1993

RICHARD HOWARD
1929–

Nikolaus Mardruz to his Master Ferdinand, Count of Tyrol, 1565[1]

A tribute to Robert Browning and in celebration of the 65th birthday of Harold Bloom, who made such tribute only natural.

My Lord recalls Ferrara?[2] How walls
rise out of water yet appear to recede
identically
into it, as if
5 built in both directions: soaring and sinking . . .
Such mirroring was my first dismay—
my next, having crossed
the moat, was making
out that, for all its grandeur, the great
10 pile, observed close to, is close to a ruin!
(Even My Lord's most
unstinting dowry
may not restore these wasted precincts to what
their deteriorating state demands.)
15 Queasy it made me,
glancing first down there
at swans in the moat apparently
feeding on their own doubled image, then up
at the citadel,

1. The poem is in the voice of the envoy of the Count of Tyrol, upon returning home to Austria from a visit to the Duke of Ferrara in "My Last Duchess" by the English poet Robert Browning (1812–1899). Browning's poem implies that the Duke ordered his first wife's death; the possibility of marriage between himself and the Count's niece closes the poem and provides the occasion for Howard's poem. Cf. footnote 1 to "My Last Duchess" (p. 911) for Browning's blending of fact and fiction.
2. City in northern Italy.

20 so high—or so deep,
and *everywhere* those carved effigies of
men and women, monsters among them
                        crowding the ramparts
                        and seeming at home
25   in the dingy water that somehow
held them up as if for our surveillance—ours?
anyone's who looked!
All that pretension
of marble display, the whole improbable
30   menagerie with but one purpose:
                having to be seen.
                        Such was the matter
of Ferrara, and such the manner,
when at last we met, of the Duke in greeting
35   My Lordship's Envoy:
        life in fallen stone!

Several hours were to elapse, in the keeping
        of his lackeys, before the Envoy
                of My Lord the Count
40   of Tyrol might see
        or even be seen to by His Grace
the Duke of Ferrara, though from such neglect
no *deliberate*
slight need be inferred:
45 now that I have had an opportunity
        —have had, indeed, the obligation—
                to fix on His Grace
                        that perlustration°   *thorough inspection*
or power of scrutiny for which
50   (I believe) My Lord holds his Envoy's service
in some favor still,
I see that the Duke,
by his own lights or, perhaps, more properly
        said, by his own *tenebrosity,*°   *obscurity*
55   could offer some excuse
                        for such cunctation . . .°   *tardiness*
        Appraising a set of cameos
just brought from Cairo by a Jew in his trust,
His Grace had been rapt
60   in connoisseurship,
that study which alone can distract him
        from his wonted courtesy; he was
                affability
                itself, once his mind
65   could be deflected from mere *objects.*

At last I presented (with those documents
        which in some detail
        describe and define
the duties of both signators) the portrait
70   of your daughter the Countess,

observing the while
his countenance. No
fault was found with our contract, of which
each article had been so correctly framed
75   (if I may say so)
as to ascertain
a pre-nuptial alliance which must persuade
and please the most punctilious (and
impecunious)
80   of future husbands.
Principally, or (if I may be
allowed the amendment) perhaps Ducally,
His Grace acknowledged
himself *beguiled* by
85   Cranach's[3] portrait of our young Countess, praising
the design, the hues, the glaze—the frame!
and appeared averse,
for a while, even
to letting the panel leave his hands!
90   Examining those same hands, I was convinced
that no matter what
the result of our
(at this point, promising) negotiations,
your daughter's likeness must now remain
95   "for good," as we say,
among Ferrara's
treasures, already one more trophy
in His Grace's multifarious *holdings,*
like those marble busts
100   lining the drawbridge,
like those weed-stained statues grinning up at us
from the still moat, and—inside as well
as out—those grotesque
figures and faces
105   fastened to the walls. So be it!

                    Real
bother (after all, one painting, for Cranach
—*and* My Lord—need be
no great forfeiture)
110   commenced only when the Duke himself led me
out of the audience-chamber and
laboriously
(he is no longer
a young man) to a secret penthouse
115   high on the battlements where he can indulge
those despotic tastes
he denominates,
half smiling over the heartless words,
"the relative consolations of semblance."
120   "Sir, suppose you draw

---

3. Lucas Cranach the Younger (1515–1586), German painter and graphic artist.

that curtain," smiling
in earnest now, and so I sought—
but what appeared a piece of drapery proved
a painted deceit!
125   My embarrassment
afforded a cue for audible laughter,
    and only then His Grace, visibly
        relishing his trick,
        turned the thing around,
130   whereupon appeared, on the reverse,
the late Duchess of Ferrara to the life!
Instanter the Duke
praised the portrait
so readily provided by one Pandolf[4]—
135   a monk by some profane article
           attached to the court,
           hence answerable
for taking likenesses *as required*
in but a day's diligence, so it was claimed . . .
140   Myself I find it
but a mountebank's
proficiency—another chicane, like that
    illusive curtain, a waxwork sort
        of nature called forth:
145   cold legerdemain!
Though *extranea* such as the hares
(copulating!), the doves, and a full-blown rose
were showily limned,
I could not discern
150 aught to be loved in that countenance itself,
    likely to rival, much less to excel
        the life illumined
        in Cranach's image
of *our* Countess, which His Grace had set
155 beside the dead woman's presentment . . . And took,
so evident was
the supremacy,
no further pains to assert Fra Pandolf's skill.
One last hard look, whereupon the Duke
160   resumed his discourse
        in an altered tone,
now some unintelligible rant
of *stooping*—His Grace chooses "never to stoop"
when he makes reproof . . .
165   My Lord will take this
as but a figure: not only is the Duke
    no longer young, his body is so
        queerly misshapen
        that even to *speak*
170   of "not stooping" seems absurdity:
the creature *is* stooped, whether by cruel or

---

4. Fra Pandolph, or Brother Pandolph, an artist invented by Browning.

impartial cause—say
Time or the Tempter°—   *the devil*
I shall not venture to hypothecate. Cause
175   or no cause, it would appear he marked
some motive for his
"reproof," a mortal
chastisement in fact inflicted on
his poor Duchess, *put away* (I take it so)
180   for smiling—at whom?
Brother Pandolf? or
some visitor to court during the sitting?
—too generally, if I construe
the Duke's clue rightly,
185   to survive the terms
of his . . . severe protocol. My Lord,
at the time it was delivered to me thus,
the admonition
if indeed it was
190   any such thing, seemed no more of a menace
than the rest of his rodomontade;°   *boasting*
item, he pointed,
as we toiled downstairs,
to that bronze *Neptune* by our old Claus
195   (there must be at least six of them cluttering
the Summer Palace
at Innsbruck), claiming
it was "cast in bronze for me."[5] Nonsense, of course.

But upon reflection, I suppose
200   we had better take
the old reprobate
at his unspeakable word . . . Why, even
assuming his boasts should be as plausible
as his avarice,
205   no "cause" for dismay:
once ensconced here as the Duchess, your daughter
need no more apprehend the Duke's
murderous temper
than his matchless taste.
210   For I have devised a means whereby
the dowry so flagrantly pursued by our
insolvent Duke ("no
just pretense of mine
be disallowed"[6] indeed!), instead of being
215   paid as he pleads in one globose sum,
should drip into his
coffers by degrees—
say, one fifth each year—then after five
such years, the dowry itself to be doubled,
220   always assuming
that Her Grace enjoys

5. Cf. "My Last Duchess," lines 54–56. Claus of   6. Cf. "My Last Duchess," lines 50–51.
Innsbruck is also fictional.

her usual smiling health. The years are her
  ally in such an arbitrament,
      and with confidence
225   My Lord can assure
  the new Duchess (assuming her Duke
abides by these stipulations and his own
  propensity for
  accumulating
230 "semblances") the long devotion (so long as
  he lasts) of her last Duke . . . Or more likely,
      if I guess aright
      your daughter's intent,
  of that young lordling I might make so
235 bold as to designate her next Duke, as well . . .

           Ever determined in
  My Lordship's service,
  I remain his Envoy
to Ferrara as to the world.
240   Nikolaus Mardruz.

                    1995

JOHN MONTAGUE

1929–

Like Dolmens[1] Round My Childhood, the Old People

Like dolmens round my childhood, the old people.

Jamie MacCrystal sang to himself,
A broken song without tune, without words;
He tipped me a penny every pension day.
5 Fed kindly crusts to winter birds.
When he died, his cottage was robbed,
Mattress and money box torn and searched.
Only the corpse they didn't disturb.

Maggie Owens was surrounded by animals,
10 A mongrel bitch and shivering pups,
Even in her bedroom a she-goat cried.
She was a well of gossip defiled,
Fanged chronicler of a whole countryside;
Reputed a witch, all I could find
15 Was her lonely need to deride.

The Nialls lived along a mountain lane
Where heather bells bloomed, clumps of foxglove.
All were blind, with Blind Pension[2] and Wireless,°   *radio*

---

1. Ancient standing stones.   2. State-provided income for sightless people.

Dead eyes serpent-flicked as one entered
20 To shelter from a downpour of mountain rain.
Crickets chirped under the rocking hearthstone
Until the muddy sun shone out again.

Mary Moore lived in a crumbling gatehouse,
Famous as Pisa[3] for its leaning gable.
25 Bag-apron and boots, she tramped the fields
Driving lean cattle from a miry stable.
A by-word for fierceness, she fell asleep
Over love stories, Red Star and Red Circle,[4]
Dreamed of gypsy love rites, by firelight sealed.

30 Wild Billy Eagleson married a Catholic servant girl
When all his Loyal[5] family passed on:
We danced round him shouting "To Hell with King Billy",[6]
And dodged from the arc of his flailing blackthorn.
Forsaken by both creeds, he showed little concern
35 Until the Orange° drums banged past in the summer   Protestant
And bowler and sash aggressively shone.

Curate and doctor trudged to attend them,
Through knee-deep snow, through summer heat,
From main road to lane to broken path,
40 Gulping the mountain air with painful breath.
Sometimes they were found by neighbours,
Silent keepers of a smokeless hearth,
Suddenly cast in the mould of death.

Ancient Ireland, indeed! I was reared by her bedside,
45 The rune and the chant, evil eye and averted head,
Fomorian[7] fierceness of family and local feud.
Gaunt figures of fear and of friendliness,
For years they trespassed on my dreams,
Until once, in a standing circle of stones,
50 I felt their shadows pass

Into that dark permanence of ancient forms.

1959

Old Mythologies

And now, at last, all proud deeds done,
Mouths dust-stopped, dark they embrace
Suitably disposed, as urns, underground.
Cattle munching soft spring grass
5 —Epicures of shamrock and the four-leaved clover—
Hear a whimper of ancient weapons,

---

3. The Leaning Tower of Pisa.
4. Cheap romance series.
5. Loyalist, Protestant.
6. A Roman Catholic taunt to Protestant coreligionists of King William III of England, who at the

Battle of the Boyne in 1690 defeated his predecessor, the Roman Catholic King James II, thereby establishing the Protestant domination of Ireland.
7. The Fomorians were demons or evil gods in Irish pagan mythology.

As a whole dormitory of heroes turn over,
Regretting their butchers' days.
This valley cradles their archaic madness
10 As once, on an impossibly epic morning,
It upheld their savage stride:
To bagpiped battle marching,
Wolfhounds, lean as models,
At their urgent heels.

1961

The Trout

Flat on the bank I parted
Rushes to ease my hands
In the water without a ripple
And tilt them slowly downstream
5 To where he lay, light as a leaf,
In his fluid sensual dream.

Bodiless lord of creation
I hung briefly above him
Savouring my own absence
10 Senses expanding in the slow
Motion, the photographic calm
That grows before action.

As the curve of my hands
Swung under his body
15 He surged, with visible pleasure.
I was so preternaturally close
I could count every stipple
But still cast no shadow, until

The two palms crossed in a cage
20 Under the lightly pulsing gills.
Then (entering my own enlarged
Shape, which rode on the water)
I gripped. To this day I can
Taste his terror on my hands.

1966

All Legendary Obstacles

All legendary obstacles lay between
Us, the long imaginary plain,
The monstrous ruck of mountains
And, swinging across the night,
5 Flooding the Sacramento, San Joaquin,
The hissing drift of winter rain.

All day I waited, shifting
Nervously from station to bar

As I saw another train sail
10   By, the San Francisco Chief or
Golden Gate, water dripping
From great flanged wheels.

At midnight you came, pale
Above the negro porter's lamp.
15   I was too blind with rain
And doubt to speak, but
Reached from the platform
Until our chilled hands met.

You had been travelling for days
20   With an old lady, who marked
A neat circle on the glass
With her glove, to watch us
Move into the wet darkness
Kissing, still unable to speak.

1966

PETER PORTER

1929–

A Consumer's Report

The name of the product I tested is *Life,*
I have completed the form you sent me
and understand that my answers are confidential.

I had it as a gift,
5   I didn't feel much while using it,
in fact I think I'd have liked to be more excited.
It seemed gentle on the hands
but left an embarrassing deposit behind.
It was not economical
10   and I have used much more than I thought
(I suppose I have about half left
but it's difficult to tell)—
although the instructions are fairly large
there are so many of them
15   I don't know which to follow, especially
as they seem to contradict each other.
I'm not sure such a thing
should be put in the way of children—
It's difficult to think of a purpose
20   for it. One of my friends says
it's just to keep its maker in a job.
Also the price is much too high.
Things are piling up so fast,
after all, the world got by

25   for a thousand million years
without this, do we need it now?
(Incidentally, please ask your man
to stop calling me "the respondent",
I don't like the sound of it.)
30   There seems to be a lot of different labels,
sizes and colours should be uniform,
the shape is awkward, it's waterproof
but not heat resistant, it doesn't keep
yet it's very difficult to get rid of:
35   whenever they make it cheaper they seem
to put less in—if you say you don't
want it, then it's delivered anyway.
I'd agree it's a popular product,
it's got into the language; people
40   even say they're on the side of it.
Personally I think it's overdone,
a small thing people are ready
to behave badly about. I think
we should take it for granted. If its
45   experts are called philosophers or market
researchers or historians, we shouldn't
care. We are the consumers and the last
law makers. So finally, I'd buy it.
But the question of a "best buy"
50   I'd like to leave until I get
the competitive product you said you'd send.

1970

An Angel in Blythburgh Church

Shot down from its enskied formation,
This stern-faced plummet rests against the wall;
Cromwell's soldiers peppered it[1] and now the death-
    watch beetle has it in thrall.[2]

5   If you make fortunes from wool, along
The weeping winter foreshores of the tide,
You build big churches with clerestories[3]
    And place angels high inside.

Their painted faces guard and guide. Now or
10   Tomorrow or whenever is the promise—
The resurrection comes: fix your eyes halfway
    Between Heaven and Diss.[4]

The face is crudely carved, simplified by wind;
It looks straight at God and waits for orders,

---

1. Cromwell led the anti-Royalist "Roundheads," who defeated the "Cavaliers" loyal to King Charles I in the English civil war. Largely Puritan, they defaced many church decorations that they considered idolatrous.
2. A bug that eats wood. See Keats, "La Belle Dame sans Merci," line 40 (p. 843).
3. Upper stories with their own windows.
4. A town in Norfolk, near Blythburgh; also, as Dis, the Roman god of the underworld.

15 Buffeted by the organ militant, and blasted
    By choristers and recorders.

    Faith would have our eyes as wooden and as certain.
    It might be worth it, to start the New Year's hymn
    Allowing for death as a mere calculation,
20   A depreciation, entered in.

    Or so I fancy looking at the roof beams
    Where the dangerous beetle sails. What is it
    Turns an atheist's mind to prayer in almost
        Any church on a country visit?

25 Greed for love or certainty or forgiveness?
    High security rising with the sea birds?
    A theology of self looking for precedents?
        A chance to speak old words?

    Rather, I think of a woman lying on her bed[5]
30 Staring for hours up to the ceiling where
    Nothing is projected—death the only angel
        To shield her from despair.

                                    1978

An Exequy[6]

    In wet May, in the months of change,
    In a country you wouldn't visit, strange
    Dreams pursue me in my sleep,
    Black creatures of the upper deep—
5   Though you are five months dead, I see
    You in guilt's iconography,
    Dear Wife, lost beast, beleaguered child,
    The stranded monster with the mild
    Appearance, whom small waves tease,
10 (Andromeda[7] upon her knees
    In orthodox deliverance)
    And you alone of pure substance,
    The unformed form of life, the earth
    Which Piero's brushes[8] brought to birth
15 For all to greet as myth, a thing
    Out of the box of imagining.
    This introduction serves to sing
    Your mortal death as Bishop King[9]
    Once hymned in tetrametric rhyme
20 His young wife, lost before her time;
    Though he lived on for many years

---

5. The poet's wife, who committed suicide in
1974.
6. Funeral rite.
7. Daughter of Cepheus and Cassiope. Her moth-
er's boasting of her beauty enraged the Nereids,
who persuaded Neptune to send a sea monster to
her homeland. An oracle demanded that Androm-
eda be sacrificed to the monster in expiation, but
she was saved by Perseus. After her death she was
placed among the stars.
8. Piero della Francesca (ca. 1410/20–1492), Ital-
ian Renaissance painter.
9. Bishop Henry King, author of "An Exequy" (see
p. 326).

His poem each day fed new tears
To that unreaching spot, her grave,
His lines a baroque architrave[1]
25   The Sunday poor with bottled flowers
Would by-pass in their mourning hours,
Esteeming ragged natural life
("Most dearly loved, most gentle wife"),
Yet, looking back when at the gate
30   And seeing grief in formal state
Upon a sculpted angel group,
Were glad that men of god could stoop
To give the dead a public stance
And freeze them in their mortal dance.

35   The words and faces proper to
My misery are private—you
Would never share your heart with those
Whose only talent's to suppose,
Nor from your final childish bed
40   Raise a remote confessing head—
The channels of our lives are blocked,
The hand is stopped upon the clock,
No one can say why hearts will break
And marriages are all opaque:
45   A map of loss, some posted cards,
The living house reduced to shards,
The abstract hell of memory,
The pointlessness of poetry—
These are the instances which tell
50   Of something which I know full well,
I owe a death to you—one day
The time will come for me to pay
When your slim shape from photographs
Stands at my door and gently asks
55   If I have any work to do
Or will I come to bed with you.
O scala enigmatica,[2]
I'll climb up to that attic where
The curtain of your life was drawn
60   Some time between despair and dawn—
I'll never know with what halt steps
You mounted to this plain eclipse
But each stair now will station me
A black responsibility
65   And point me to that shut-down room,
"This be your due appointed tomb."

I think of us in Italy:
Gin-and-chianti-fuelled, we
Move in a trance through Paradise,
70   Feeding at last our starving eyes,

---

1. Lintel or other molding around a door.
2. "O enigmatic stairs" (Latin); an allusion to the stairs leading to the attic in which the poet's wife committed suicide in 1974.

Two people of the English blindness
Doing each masterpiece the kindness
Of discovering it—from Baldovinetti
To Venice's most obscure jetty.
75 A true unfortunate traveller, I
Depend upon your nurse's eye
To pick the altars where no Grinner°   grotesque fiend
Puts us off our tourists' dinner
And in hotels to bandy words
80 With Genevan girls and talking birds,
To wear your feet out following me
To night's end and true amity,
And call my rational fear of flying
A paradigm of Holy Dying—
85 And, oh my love, I wish you were
Once more with me, at night somewhere
In narrow streets applauding wines,
The moon above the Apennines
As large as logic and the stars,
90 Most middle-aged of avatars,
As bright as when they shone for truth
Upon untried and avid youth.

The rooms and days we wandered through
Shrink in my mind to one—there you
95 Lie quite absorbed by peace—the calm
Which life could not provide is balm
In death. Unseen by me, you look
Past bed and stairs and half-read book
Eternally upon your home,
100 The end of pain, the left alone.
I have no friend, or intercessor,
No psychopomp³ or true confessor
But only you who know my heart
In every cramped and devious part—
105 Then take my hand and lead me out,
The sky is overcast by doubt,
The time has come, I listen for
Your words of comfort at the door,
O guide me through the shoals of fear—
110 "Fürchte dich nicht, ich bin bei dir."⁴

1978

3. Someone who acts as a guide of the soul; also,   4. "Fear not, I am with you" (German). This is the
a conductor of souls to the place of the dead.   opening sentence of Bach's motet BMV 228.

ADRIENNE RICH

1929–

Aunt Jennifer's Tigers

Aunt Jennifer's tigers prance across a screen,
Bright topaz denizens of a world of green.
They do not fear the men beneath the tree;
They pace in sleek chivalric certainty.

5   Aunt Jennifer's fingers fluttering through her wool
Find even the ivory needle hard to pull.
The massive weight of Uncle's wedding band
Sits heavily upon Aunt Jennifer's hand.

When Aunt is dead, her terrified hands will lie
10   Still ringed with ordeals she was mastered by.
The tigers in the panel that she made
Will go on prancing, proud and unafraid.

                                                        1951

Living in Sin

She had thought the studio would keep itself;
no dust upon the furniture of love.
Half heresy, to wish the taps less vocal,
the panes relieved of grime. A plate of pears,
5   a piano with a Persian shawl, a cat
stalking the picturesque amusing mouse
had risen at his urging.
Not that at five each separate stair would writhe
under the milkman's tramp; that morning light
10   so coldly would delineate the scraps
of last night's cheese and three sepulchral bottles;
that on the kitchen shelf among the saucers
a pair of beetle-eyes would fix her own —
envoy from some village in the moldings . . .
15   Meanwhile, he, with a yawn,
sounded a dozen notes upon the keyboard,
declared it out of tune, shrugged at the mirror,
rubbed at his beard, went out for cigarettes;
while she, jeered by the minor demons,
20   pulled back the sheets and made the bed and found
a towel to dust the table-top,
and let the coffee-pot boil over on the stove.
By evening she was back in love again,
though not so wholly but throughout the night
25   she woke sometimes to feel the daylight coming
like a relentless milkman up the stairs.

                                                        1955, 1975

Snapshots of a Daughter-in-Law

1

You, once a belle in Shreveport,
with henna-colored hair, skin like a peachbud,
still have your dresses copied from that time,
and play a Chopin prelude
5   called by Cortot: *"Delicious recollections*
float like perfume through the memory."[1]

Your mind now, moldering like wedding-cake,
heavy with useless experience, rich
with suspicion, rumor, fantasy,
10   crumbling to pieces under the knife-edge
of mere fact. In the prime of your life.

Nervy, glowering, your daughter
wipes the teaspoons, grows another way.

2

Banging the coffee-pot into the sink
15   she hears the angels chiding, and looks out
past the raked gardens to the sloppy sky.
Only a week since They said: *Have no patience.*

The next time it was: *Be insatiable.*
Then: *Save yourself; others you cannot save.*
20   Sometimes she's let the tapstream scald her arm,
a match burn to her thumbnail,

or held her hand above the kettle's snout
right in the woolly steam. They are probably angels,
since nothing hurts her anymore, except
25   each morning's grit blowing into her eyes.

3

A thinking woman sleeps with monsters.
The beak that grips her, she becomes.[2] And Nature,
that sprung-lidded, still commodious
steamer-trunk of *tempora* and *mores*[3]
30   gets stuffed with it all: the mildewed orange-flowers,
the female pills,[4] the terrible breasts
of Boadicea[5] beneath flat foxes' heads and orchids.

---

1. A remark made by Alfred Cortot (1877–1962), French pianist, in his *Chopin: 24 Preludes* (1930); he is referring specifically to Chopin's Prelude No. 7, Andantino, A Major. Frederic François Chopin (1810–1849), Polish composer and piano virtuoso who settled in Paris in 1831.
2. A reference to W. B. Yeats' "Leda and the Swan" (1924), in which Zeus in the shape of a swan rapes a girl and then lets her drop from "the indifferent beak" (see p. 1095).
3. Literally, "times and customs"—the Roman orator Cicero's famous phrase, "O tempora! O mores!" (i.e., "Alas for the degeneracy of our times and the low standard of our morals!").
4. Remedies for menstrual pain.
5. British queen of the first century A.D.; she led her people in a large though ultimately unsuccessful revolt against Roman rule.

Two handsome women, gripped in argument,
each proud, acute, subtle, I hear scream
35 across the cut glass and majolica
like Furies[6] cornered from their prey:
The argument *ad feminam*,[7] all the old knives
that have rusted in my back, I drive in yours,
ma semblable, ma soeur![8]

4

40 Knowing themselves too well in one another:
their gifts no pure fruition, but a thorn,
the prick filed sharp against a hint of scorn . . .
Reading while waiting
for the iron to heat,
45 writing, *My Life had stood—a Loaded Gun—*[9]
in that Amherst pantry while the jellies boil and scum,
or, more often,
iron-eyed and beaked and purposed as a bird,
dusting everything on the whatnot every day of life.

5

50 *Dulce ridens, dulce loquens,*[1]
she shaves her legs until they gleam
like petrified mammoth-tusk.

6

When to her lute Corinna sings[2]
neither words nor music are her own;
55 only the long hair dipping
over her cheek, only the song
of silk against her knees
and these
adjusted in reflections of an eye.

60 Poised, trembling and unsatisfied, before
an unlocked door, that cage of cages,
tell us, you bird, you tragical machine—
is this *fertilisante douleur?*[3] Pinned down
by love, for you the only natural action,
65 are you edged more keen
to prise the secrets of the vault? has Nature shown
her household books to you, daughter-in-law,
that her sons never saw?

6. Greek female spirits of vengeance. "Majolica": a glazed earthenware.
7. Feminine version of the phrase *ad hominem* (Latin; literally, "against the man"), referring to an argument directed not to reason but to personal prejudices and emotions.
8. The last line of Charles Baudelaire's poem "Au Lecteur" addresses "*Hypocrite lecteur!—mon semblable—mon frère!*" (French; "Hypocrite reader!—my likeness!—my brother!"); Rich here instead

addresses "*ma soeur*" ("my sister").
9. "*Emily Dickinson, Complete Poems*, ed. T. H. Johnson, 1960, p. 369" [Rich's note]; see p. 1021. Amherst, referred to in the next line, is the town where Dickinson lived her entire life (1830–1886).
1. "Sweetly laughing, sweetly speaking" (Latin; from Horace *Odes* 22.23–24).
2. First line of a poem by Thomas Campion (1567–1620); see p. 251.
3. "Fertilizing (or life-giving) sorrow" (French).

7

"To have in this uncertain world some stay
70 *which cannot be undermined, is*
of the utmost consequence."[4]
                              Thus wrote
a woman, partly brave and partly good,
who fought with what she partly understood.
Few men about her would or could do more,
75 hence she was labeled harpy, shrew and whore.

8

"You all die at fifteen," said Diderot,[5]
and turn part legend, part convention.
Still, eyes inaccurately dream
behind closed windows blankening with steam.
80 Deliciously, all that we might have been,
all that we were—fire, tears,
wit, taste, martyred ambition—
stirs like the memory of refused adultery
the drained and flagging bosom of our middle years.

9

85 *Not that it is done well, but*
that it is done at all?[6] Yes, think
of the odds! or shrug them off forever.
This luxury of the precocious child,
Time's precious chronic invalid,—
90 would we, darlings, resign it if we could?
Our blight has been our sinecure:
mere talent was enough for us—
glitter in fragments and rough drafts.

Sigh no more, ladies.[7]
                    Time is male
95 and in his cups drinks to the fair.
Bemused by gallantry, we hear
our mediocrities over-praised,
indolence read as abnegation,
slattern thought styled intuition,
100 every lapse forgiven, our crime
only to cast too bold a shadow
or smash the mold straight off.

---

4. "From Mary Wollstonecraft, *Thoughts on the Education of Daughters*, London, 1787" [Rich's note]. Wollstonecraft (1759–1797), one of the first feminist thinkers, is best known for her *Vindication of the Rights of Woman* (1792).
5. Denis Diderot (1713–1784), French philosopher, encyclopedist, playwright, and critic. " 'You all die at fifteen': 'Vous mourez toutes a quinze ans,' from the *Lettres à Sophie Volland*, quoted by Simone de Beauvoir in *Le Deuxième Sexe*, Vol. II,

pp. 123–24" [Rich's note].
6. An allusion to Samuel Johnson's remark to James Boswell: "Sir, a woman's preaching is like a dog's walking on his hinder legs. It is not done well; but you are surprised to find it done at all" (July 31, 1763).
7. Shakespeare, *Much Ado about Nothing* 2.3.62–63: "Sigh no more, ladies, sigh no more, / Men were deceivers ever."

For that, solitary confinement,
tear gas, attrition shelling.
105 Few applicants for that honor.

10

Well,
she's long about her coming, who must be
more merciless to herself than history.
Her mind full to the wind, I see her plunge
110 breasted and glancing through the currents,
taking the light upon her
at least as beautiful as any boy
or helicopter,[8]
poised, still coming,
her fine blades making the air wince

115 but her cargo
no promise then:
delivered
palpable
ours.

1958–60   1963

Orion[9]

Far back when I went zig-zagging
through tamarack pastures
you were my genius,° you   *attendant spirit*
my cast-iron Viking, my helmed
5 lion-heart king in prison.[1]
Years later now you're young

my fierce half-brother, staring
down from that simplified west
your breast open, your belt dragged down
10 by an oldfashioned thing, a sword
the last bravado you won't give over
though it weighs you down as you stride

and the stars in it are dim
and maybe have stopped burning.
15 But you burn, and I know it;
as I throw back my head to take you in
an old transfusion happens again:
divine astronomy is nothing to it.

8. "She comes down from the remoteness of ages, from Thebes, from Crete, from Chichén-Itzá; and she is also the totem set deep in the African jungle; she is a helicopter and she is a bird; and there is this, the greatest wonder of all: under her tinted hair the forest murmur becomes a thought, and words issue from her breasts" (Simone de Beauvoir, *The Second Sex*, trans. H. M. Parshley [New York, 1953], p. 729). (A translation of the passage from *Le Deuxième Sexe*, Vol. II, p. 574, cited in French by Rich.)

9. Constellation of the winter sky (known as "the Hunter") that appears as a warrior with belt and sword.

1. Alluding to the English king Richard the Lion-Hearted (1157–1199), imprisoned in Austria on his return from the Crusades.

Indoors I bruise and blunder,
20 break faith, leave ill enough
alone, a dead child born in the dark.
Night cracks up over the chimney,
pieces of time, frozen geodes[2]
come showering down in the grate.

25 A man reaches behind my eyes
and finds them empty
a woman's head turns away
from my head in the mirror
children are dying my death
30 and eating crumbs of my life.

Pity is not your forte.
Calmly you ache up there
pinned aloft in your crow's nest,[3]
my speechless pirate!
35 You take it all for granted
and when I look you back

it's with a starlike eye
shooting its cold and egotistical[4] spear
where it can do least damage.
40 Breathe deep! No hurt, no pardon
out here in the cold with you
you with your back to the wall.

1965   1969

A Valediction Forbidding Mourning[5]

My swirling wants. Your frozen lips.
The grammar turned and attacked me.
Themes, written under duress.
Emptiness of the notations.

5 They gave me a drug that slowed the healing of wounds.

I want you to see this before I leave:
the experience of repetition as death
the failure of criticism to locate the pain
the poster in the bus that said:
10 *my bleeding is under control.*

A red plant in a cemetery of plastic wreaths.

---

2. Small, spheroid stones, with a cavity often lined with crystals.
3. Lookout post on the mast of old ships.
4. "One of two phrases suggested by Gottfried Benn's essay, *Artists and Old Age* in *Primal Vision*, edited by E. B. Ashton, New Directions" [Rich's note]. Benn's advice to the modern artist is: "Don't lose sight of the cold and egotistical element in your mission. . . . With your back to the wall, care-worn and weary, in the gray light of the void, read Job and Jeremiah and keep going" (pp. 206–07).
5. The title of a famous poem by John Donne (1572–1631), in which he forbids his wife to lament his departure on a trip to the Continent; see p. 275.

A last attempt: the language is a dialect called metaphor.
These images go unglossed: hair, glacier, flashlight.
When I think of a landscape I am thinking of a time.
15 When I talk of taking a trip I mean forever.
I could say: those mountains have a meaning
but further than that I could not say.

To do something very common, in my own way.

1970   1971

Diving into the Wreck

First having read the book of myths,
and loaded the camera,
and checked the edge of the knife-blade,
I put on
5 the body-armor of black rubber
the absurd flippers
the grave and awkward mask.
I am having to do this
not like Cousteau[6] with his
10 assiduous team
aboard the sun-flooded schooner
but here alone.

There is a ladder.
The ladder is always there
15 hanging innocently
close to the side of the schooner.
We know what it is for,
we who have used it.
Otherwise
20 it is a piece of maritime floss
some sundry equipment.

I go down.
Rung after rung and still
the oxygen immerses me
25 the blue light
the clear atoms
of our human air.
I go down.
My flippers cripple me,
30 I crawl like an insect down the ladder
and there is no one
to tell me when the ocean
will begin.

First the air is blue and then
35 it is bluer and then green and then
black I am blacking out and yet

---

6. Jacques Cousteau (b. 1910), French underwater explorer, photographer, and author.

my mask is powerful
it pumps my blood with power
the sea is another story
40 the sea is not a question of power
I have to learn alone
to turn my body without force
in the deep element.

And now: it is easy to forget
45 what I came for
among so many who have always
lived here
swaying their crenellated[7] fans
between the reefs
50 and besides
you breathe differently down here.

I came to explore the wreck.
The words are purposes.
The words are maps.
55 I came to see the damage that was done
and the treasures that prevail.
I stroke the beam of my lamp
slowly along the flank
of something more permanent
60 than fish or weed

the thing I came for:
the wreck and not the story of the wreck
the thing itself and not the myth
the drowned face always staring
65 toward the sun
the evidence of damage
worn by salt and sway into this threadbare beauty
the ribs of the disaster
curving their assertion
70 among the tentative haunters.

This is the place.
And I am here, the mermaid whose dark hair
streams black, the merman in his armored body
We circle silently
75 about the wreck
we dive into the hold.
I am she: I am he

whose drowned face sleeps with open eyes
whose breasts still bear the stress
80 whose silver, copper, vermeil[8] cargo lies
obscurely inside barrels
half-wedged and left to rot

---

7. Notched with rounded or scalloped projections.   8. Gilded silver or bronze.

we are the half-destroyed instruments
that once held to a course
85   the water-eaten log
the fouled compass

We are, I am, you are
by cowardice or courage
the one who find our way
90   back to this scene
carrying a knife, a camera
a book of myths
in which
our names do not appear.

1973

From Eastern War Time[9]

1

Memory lifts her smoky mirror: 1943,
single isinglass window   kerosene
stove in the streetcar barn   halfset moon
8:15 a.m. Eastern War Time dark
5   Number 29 clanging in and turning
looseleaf notebook   *Latin for Americans*
Breasted's *History of the Ancient World*
on the girl's lap
money for lunch and war-stamps in her pocket
10   darkblue wool wet acrid on her hands
three pools of light   weak ceiling bulbs
a schoolgirl's hope-spilt terrified
sensations wired to smells
of kerosene wool and snow
15   and the sound of the dead language
praised as key   torchlight of the great dead
Grey spreading   behind still-flying snow
the lean and sway of the streetcar she must ride
to become one   of a hundred girls
20   rising white-cuffed and collared in a study hall
to sing *For those in peril on the sea*
under plaster casts of the classic frescoes
chariots horses draperies certitudes.

8

A woman wired in memories
stands by a house   collapsed in dust
her son beaten in prison   grandson
shot in the stomach   daughter
5   organizing the camps   an aunt's unpublished poems

9. Rich's invented term conflating "Eastern Stan-
dard Time," the time zone in which she grew up
in Baltimore, with the time of World War II. The
poem, in ten parts, juxtaposes Rich's childhood
memories, as an American Jew, with facts of the
Holocaust in Europe.

grandparents' photographs   a bridal veil
phased into smoke   up the obliterate air
With whom shall she let down and tell her story
Who shall hear her to the end
10 standing if need be for hours   in wind
that swirls the levelled dust
in sun that beats through their scarfed hair
at the lost gate by the shattered prickly pear
Who must hear her to the end
15 but the woman   forbidden to forget
the blunt groats freezing in the wooden ladle
old winds   dusting the ovens with light snow?

1995

A. K. RAMANUJAN

1929–1993

Snakes

No, it does not happen
when I walk through the woods.
But, walking in museums of quartz
or the aisles of bookstacks,
5 looking at their geometry
without curves
and the layers of transparency
that make them opaque,
dwelling on the yellower vein
10 in the yellow amber
or touching a book that has gold
on its spine,
        I think of snakes.

The twirls of their hisses
15 rise like the tiny dust-cones on slow-noon roads
winding through the farmers' feet.
Black lorgnettes are etched on their hoods,
ridiculous, alien, like some terrible aunt,
a crest among tiles and scales
20 that moult with the darkening half
of every moon.

A basketful of ritual cobras
comes into the tame little house,
their brown-wheat glisten ringed with ripples.
25 They lick the room with their bodies, curves
uncurling, writing a sibilant alphabet of panic
on my floor. Mother gives them milk
in saucers. She watches them suck
and bare the black-line design
30 etched on the brass of the saucer.

The snakeman wreathes their writhing
round his neck
for father's smiling
money. But I scream.

35 Sister ties her braids
with a knot of tassel.
But the weave of her knee-long braid has scales,
their gleaming held by a score of clean new pins.
I look till I see her hair again.
40 My night full of ghosts from a sadness
in a play, my left foot listens to my right footfall,
a clockwork clicking in the silence
within my walking.
                        The clickshod heel suddenly strikes
45 and slushes on a snake: I see him turn,
the green white of his belly
measured by bluish nodes, a water-bleached lotus stalk
plucked by a landsman hand. Yet panic rushes
my body to my feet, my spasms wring
50 and drain his fear and mine. I leave him sealed,
a flat-head whiteness on a stain.
                        Now
frogs can hop upon this sausage rope,
flies in the sun will mob the look in his eyes,

55 and I can walk through the woods.

Breaded Fish

Specially for me, she had some breaded
fish; even thrust a blunt-headed
smelt into my mouth;

and looked hurt when I could
5 neither sit nor eat, as a hood
of memory like a coil on a heath

opened in my eyes: a dark half-naked
length of woman, dead
on the beach in a yard of cloth,

10 dry, rolled by the ebb, breaded
by the grained indifference of sand. I headed
for the shore, my heart beating in my mouth.

Self-Portrait

I resemble everyone
but myself, and sometimes see
in shop-windows,
        despite the well-known laws

5   of optics,
       the portrait of a stranger,
       date unknown,
       often signed in a corner
       by my father.

                                                           1966

EDWARD KAMAU BRATHWAITE

1930–

FROM THE ARRIVANTS: A NEW WORLD TRILOGY

New World A-Comin'

1

Helpless like this
leader-
less like this,
heroless,
5 we met you: lover,
warrior, hater,
coming through the files
of the forest
soft foot
10 to soft soil
of silence:
we met in the soiled
tunnel of leaves.

Click lock
15 your fire-
lock fore-
arm fire-
arm flashed
fire and our firm
20 fleshed, flame
warm, fly
bitten warriors
fell.

How long
25 how long
O Lord
O devil
O fire
O flame
30 have we walked
have we journeyed
to this place
to this meeting

35 this shock
    and shame
    in the soiled
    silence.

    How long have we
    travelled down
40 valleys down
    slopes, silica
    glinted, stones
    dry as water,
    to this flash
45 of flame in the forest.
    O who now will help
    us, help-
    less, horse-
    less, leader-
50 less, no
    hope, no
    Hawkins,[1] no
    Cortez[2] to come.
    Prempeh[3] imprisoned,
55 Tawiah[4] dead,
    Asantewa[5] bridled
    and hung.
    O who now can help
    us: Geronimo, Tackie,
60 Montezuma[6] to come.

    And the fire, our
    fire, fashioning locks,
    rocks darker than iron;
    fire betrayed us once
65 in our village; now
    in the forest, fire falls
    us like birds, hot pods
    in our belly. Fire
    falls walls, fashions
70 these fire-
    locks darker than iron,
    and we filed down the path
    linked in a new
    clinked silence of iron.

1. Sir John Hawkins (1532–1595), the first Englishman to traffic in slaves.
2. Hernando Cortez (1485–1547), the Spanish conqueror of Mexico.
3. Prempeh (1888–1931), the last king of Ashanti in West Africa. He reigned from 1894 until 1896, when he was deposed by the British and exiled to the Seychelles.
4. Unidentified.
5. Yaa Asentewaa, the queen mother who led Ashanti opposition against the British. Captured in 1901, she was exiled to the Seychelles and died there in 1924.
6. Montezuma II (1480?–1520), the last Mexican emperor, was killed in the resistance against Cortez's conquest of Mexico. Geronimo (ca. 1829–1909), a chief of the Chiricahwa group of Apache Indians; his forces terrorized New Mexico and Arizona from 1875 until 1885, but surrendered to General George Cook in 1886. "Tackie": Tacky, a Caribbean priest/leader; the 1760 Tacky Rebellion in Jamaica was fomented and in places led by obeah men (spiritual leaders).

2

75　It will be a long long time before we see
this land again, these trees
again, drifting inland with the sound
of surf, smoke rising

It will be a long long time before we see
80　these farms again, soft wet slow green
again: Aburi, Akwamu,[7]
mist rising

Watch now these hard men, cold
clear eye'd like the water we ride,
85　skilful with sail and the rope and the tackle

Watch now these cold men, bold
as the water banging the bow in a sudden wild tide,
indifferent, it seems, to the battle

of wind in the water;
90　for our blood, mixed
soon with their passion in sport,

in indifference, in anger,
will create new soils, new souls, new
ancestors; will flow like this tide fixed

95　to the star by which this ship floats
to new worlds, new waters, new
harbours, the pride of our ancestors mixed

with the wind and the water
the flesh and the flies, the whips and the fixed
100　fear of pain in this chained and welcoming port.

1967

Ancestors

1

Every Friday morning my grandfather
left his farm of canefields, chickens, cows,
and rattled in his trap down to the harbour town
to sell his meat. He was a butcher.
5　Six-foot-three and very neat: high collar,
winged, a grey cravat, a waistcoat, watch-
chain just above the belt, thin narrow-
bottomed trousers, and the shoes his wife
would polish every night. He drove the trap
10　himself: slap of the leather reins

7. Towns in the Akan-speaking area of Ghana.

along the horse's back and he'd be off
with a top-hearted homburg on his head:
black English country gentleman.

Now he is dead. The meat shop burned,
15 his property divided. A doctor bought
the horse. His mad alsatians killed it.
The wooden trap was chipped and chopped
by friends and neighbours and used to stop-
gap fences and for firewood. One yellow
20 wheel was rolled across the former cowpen gate.
Only his hat is left. I "borrowed" it.
I used to try it on and hear the night wind
man go battering through the canes, cocks waking up and thinking
it was dawn throughout the clinking country night.
25 Great caterpillar tractors clatter down
the broken highway now; a diesel engine grunts
where pigs once hunted garbage.
A thin asthmatic cow shares the untrashed garage.

2

All that I can remember of his wife,
30 my father's mother, is that she sang us songs
("Great Tom Is Cast"[8] was one), that frightened me.
And she would go chug chugging with a jar
of milk until its white pap turned to yellow
butter. And in the basket underneath the stairs
35 she kept the polish for grandfather's shoes.

All that I have of her is voices:
laughing me out of fear because a crappaud°   *toad*
jumped and splashed the dark where I was huddled
in the galvanized tin bath; telling us stories
40 round her fat white lamp. It was her Queen
Victoria lamp, she said; although the stamp
read Ever Ready. And in the night, I listened to her singing
in a Vicks and Vapour Rub-like voice what you would call the blues

3

Come-a look
45 come-a look
see wha' happen

come-a look
come-a look
see wha' happen

50 Sookey dead
Sookey dead
Sookey dead-o

---

8. Song about the making (or "casting") of a bell.

Sookey dead
Sookey dead
55 Sookey dead-o.

Him a-wuk
him a-wuk
till 'e bleed-o

him a-wuk
60 him a-wuk
till 'e bleed-o

Sookey dead
Sookey dead
Sookey dead-o

65 Sookey dead
Sookey dead
Sookey dead-o . . .

1969

GREGORY CORSO
1930–

Marriage

Should I get married? Should I be good?
Astound the girl next door with my velvet suit and faustus hood?[1]
Don't take her to movies but to cemeteries
tell all about werewolf bathtubs and forked clarinets
5   then desire her and kiss her and all the preliminaries
and she going just so far and I understanding why
not getting angry saying You must feel! It's beautiful to feel!
Instead take her in my arms lean against an old crooked tombstone
and woo her the entire night the constellations in the sky—

10   When she introduces me to her parents
back straightened, hair finally combed, strangled by a tie,
should I sit knees together on their 3rd degree sofa
and not ask Where's the bathroom?
How else to feel other than I am,
15   often thinking Flash Gordon[2] soap—
O how terrible it must be for a young man
seated before a family and the family thinking
We never saw him before! He wants our Mary Lou!
After tea and homemade cookies they ask What do you do for a living?

1. The legendary Faust, a medieval alchemist, sold his soul to the devil. He gained not only knowledge and power but renewed youth and attractiveness to young women.

2. A science fiction "space opera" that first appeared as a comic strip, then as popular radio and movie serials in the 1930s.

20 Should I tell them? Would they like me then?
Say All right get married, we're losing a daughter
but we're gaining a son—
And should I then ask Where's the bathroom?

O God, and the wedding! All her family and her friends
25 and only a handful of mine all scroungy and bearded
just wait to get at the drinks and food—
And the priest! he looking at me as if I masturbated
asking me Do you take this woman for your lawful wedded wife?
And I trembling what to say say Pie Glue!
30 I kiss the bride all those corny men slapping me on the back
She's all yours, boy! Ha-ha-ha!
And in their eyes you could see some obscene honeymoon going on—
Then all that absurd rice and clanky cans and shoes
Niagara Falls! Hordes of us! Husbands! Wives! Flowers! Chocolates!
35 All streaming into cozy hotels
All going to do the same thing tonight
The indifferent clerk he knowing what was going to happen
The lobby zombies they knowing what
The whistling elevator man he knowing
40 The winking bellboy knowing
Everybody knowing! I'd be almost inclined not to do anything!
Stay up all night! Stare that hotel clerk in the eye!
Screaming: I deny honeymoon! I deny honeymoon!
running rampant into those almost climactic suites
45 yelling Radio belly! Cat shovel!
O I'd live in Niagara forever! in a dark cave beneath the Falls
I'd sit there the Mad Honeymooner
devising ways to break marriages, a scourge of bigamy
a saint of divorce—

50 But I should get married I should be good
How nice it'd be to come home to her
and sit by the fireplace and she in the kitchen
aproned young and lovely wanting my baby
and so happy about me she burns the roast beef
55 and comes crying to me and I get up from my big papa chair
saying Christmas teeth! Radiant brains! Apple deaf!
God what a husband I'd make! Yes, I should get married!
So much to do! like sneaking into Mr Jones' house late at night
and cover his golf clubs with 1920 Norwegian books
60 Like hanging a picture of Rimbaud[3] on the lawnmower
like pasting Tannu Tuva[4] postage stamps all over the picket fence
like when Mrs Kindhead comes to collect for the Community Chest
grab her and tell her There are unfavorable omens in the sky!
And when the mayor comes to get my vote tell him
65 When are you going to stop people killing whales!
And when the milkman comes leave him a note in the bottle
Penguin dust, bring me penguin dust, I want penguin dust—

---

3. Arthur Rimbaud (1854–1891), French sym-
bolist poet.
4. A Siberian republic of the Russian Federation,
located on the border between Russia and Mon-
golia.

Yet if I should get married and it's Connecticut and snow
and she gives birth to a child and I am sleepless, worn,
70   up for nights, head bowed against a quiet window, the past behind me,
finding myself in the most common of situations a trembling man
knowledged with responsibility not twig-smear nor Roman coin soup—
O what would that be like!
Surely I'd give it for a nipple a rubber Tacitus[5]
75   For a rattle a bag of broken Bach records
Tack Della Francesca[6] all over its crib
Sew the Greek alphabet on its bib
And build for its playpen a roofless Parthenon

No, I doubt I'd be that kind of father
80   Not rural not snow no quiet window
but hot smelly tight New York City
seven flights up, roaches and rats in the walls
a fat Reichian[7] wife screeching over potatoes Get a job!
And five nose running brats in love with Batman
85   And the neighbors all toothless and dry haired
like those hag masses of the 18th century
all wanting to come in and watch TV
The landlord wants his rent
Grocery store Blue Cross Gas & Electric Knights of Columbus
90   Impossible to lie back and dream Telephone snow, ghost parking—
No! I should not get married I should never get married!
But—imagine If I were married to a beautiful sophisticated woman
tall and pale wearing an elegant black dress and long black gloves
holding a cigarette holder in one hand and a highball in the other
95   and we lived high up in a penthouse with a huge window
from which we could see all of New York and ever farther on clearer days
No, can't imagine myself married to that pleasant prison dream—

O but what about love? I forget love
not that I am incapable of love
100   it's just that I see love as odd as wearing shoes—
I never wanted to marry a girl who was like my mother
And Ingrid Bergman[8] was always impossible
And there's maybe a girl now but she's already married
And I don't like men and—
105   but there's got to be somebody!
Because what if I'm 60 years old and not married,
all alone in a furnished room with pee stains on my underwear
and everybody else is married! All the universe married but me!

Ah, yet well I know that were a woman possible as I am possible
110   then marriage would be possible—

5. (A.D. 55?–117?); Roman historian. Punning on *tacitus*, "silent" (Latin).
6. Piero della Francesca (1420?–1492), Italian Renaissance painter.
7. Wilhelm Reich (1897–1957) founded a contro-versial school of psychiatry that emphasized love and sexual pleasure as the basis of mental health.
8. (1915–1982); Swedish actress in American films, known for her beauty.

Like SHE[9] in her lonely alien gaud waiting her Egyptian lover
so I wait—bereft of 2,000 years and the bath of life.

1960

TED HUGHES

1930–

The Thought-Fox

I imagine this midnight moment's forest:
Something else is alive
Beside the clock's loneliness
And this blank page where my fingers move.

5 Through the window I see no star:
Something more near
Though deeper within darkness
Is entering the loneliness:

Cold, delicately as the dark snow,
10 A fox's nose touches twig, leaf;
Two eyes serve a movement, that now
And again now, and now, and now

Sets neat prints into the snow
Between trees, and warily a lame
15 Shadow lags by stump and in hollow
Of a body that is bold to come

Across clearings, an eye,
A widening deepening greenness,
Brilliantly, concentratedly,
20 Coming about its own business

Till, with a sudden sharp hot stink of fox
It enters the dark hole of the head.
The window is starless still; the clock ticks,
The page is printed.

1957

Wind

This house has been far out at sea all night,
The woods crashing through darkness, the booming hills,
Winds stampeding the fields under the window
Floundering black astride and blinding wet

5 Till day rose; then under an orange sky
The hills had new places, and wind wielded

9. In H. Rider Haggard's novel of this name (1887), "She" gains eternal youth by bathing in a pillar of flame and waits thousands of years for the return of her lover.

Blade-light, luminous and emerald,
Flexing like the lens of a mad eye.

10 At noon I scaled along the house-side as far as
The coal-house door. I dared once to look up—
Through the brunt wind that dented the balls of my eyes
The tent of the hills drummed and strained its guyrope,

The fields quivering, the skyline a grimace,
At any second to bang and vanish with a flap:
15 The wind flung a magpie away and a black-
Back gull bent like an iron bar slowly. The house

Rang like some fine green goblet in the note
That any second would shatter it. Now deep
In chairs, in front of the great fire, we grip
20 Our hearts and cannot entertain book, thought,

Or each other. We watch the fire blazing,
And feel the roots of the house move, but sit on,
Seeing the window tremble to come in,
Hearing the stones cry out under the horizons.

1957

Relic

I found this jawbone at the sea's edge:
There, crabs, dogfish, broken by the breakers or tossed
To flap for half an hour and turn to a crust
Continue the beginning. The deeps are cold:
5 In that darkness camaraderie does not hold:
Nothing touches but, clutching, devours. And the jaws,
Before they are satisfied or their stretched purpose
Slacken, go down jaws; go gnawn bare. Jaws
Eat and are finished and the jawbone comes to the beach:
10 This is the sea's achievement; with shells,
Vertebrae, claws, carapaces, skulls.

Time in the sea eats its tail, thrives, casts these
Indigestibles, the spars of purposes
That failed far from the surface. None grow rich
15 In the sea. This curved jawbone did not laugh
But gripped, gripped and is now a cenotaph.[1]

1960

Pike

Pike, three inches long, perfect
Pike in all parts, green tigering the gold.
Killers from the egg: the malevolent aged grin.
They dance on the surface among the flies.

---

1. Monument to the dead.

5   Or move, stunned by their own grandeur,
Over a bed of emerald, silhouette
Of submarine delicacy and horror.
A hundred feet long in their world.

In ponds, under the heat-struck lily pads—
10 Gloom of their stillness:
Logged on last year's black leaves, watching upwards.
Or hung in an amber cavern of weeds

The jaws' hooked clamp and fangs
Not to be changed at this date;
15 A life subdued to its instrument;
The gills kneading quietly, and the pectorals.

Three we kept behind glass,
Jungled in weed: three inches, four,
And four and a half: fed fry[2] to them—
20 Suddenly there were two. Finally one

With a sag belly and the grin it was born with.
And indeed they spare nobody.
Two, six pounds each, over two feet long,
High and dry and dead in the willow-herb—

25 One jammed past its gills down the other's gullet:
The outside eye stared: as a vice locks—
The same iron in this eye
Though its film shrank in death.

A pond I fished, fifty yards across,
30 Whose lilies and muscular tench[3]
Had outlasted every visible stone
Of the monastery that planted them—

Stilled legendary depth:
It was as deep as England. It held
35 Pike too immense to stir, so immense and old
That past nightfall I dared not cast

But silently cast and fished
With the hair frozen on my head
For what might move, for what eye might move.
40 The still splashes on the dark pond,

Owls hushing the floating woods
Frail on my ear against the dream
Darkness beneath night's darkness had freed,
That rose slowly towards me, watching.

1959, 1960

---

2. Young fishes.   3. Variety of freshwater fish.

Theology

No, the serpent did not
Seduce Eve to the apple.
All that's simply
Corruption of the facts.

5 Adam ate the apple.
Eve ate Adam.
The serpent ate Eve.
This is the dark intestine.

The serpent, meanwhile,
10 Sleeps his meal off in Paradise—
Smiling to hear
God's querulous calling.

1967

Examination at the Womb-Door[4]

Who owns these scrawny little feet? *Death.*
Who owns this bristly scorched-looking face? *Death.*
Who owns these still-working lungs? *Death.*
Who owns this utility coat of muscles? *Death.*
5 Who owns these unspeakable guts? *Death.*
Who owns these questionable brains? *Death.*
All this messy blood? *Death.*
These minimum-efficiency eyes? *Death.*
This wicked little tongue? *Death.*
10 This occasional wakefulness? *Death.*

Given, stolen, or held pending trial?
Held.

Who owns the whole rainy, stony earth? *Death.*
Who owns all of space? *Death.*

15 Who is stronger than hope? *Death.*
Who is stronger than the will? *Death.*
Stronger than love? *Death.*
Stronger than life? *Death.*

But who is stronger than death?
                              Me, evidently.
20 Pass, Crow.

1970

River

Fallen from heaven, lies across
The lap of his mother, broken by world.

---

4. The demonic hero of the "Crow" myth is interrogated by an unidentified questioner.

But water will go on
Issuing from heaven

5   In dumbness uttering spirit brightness
Through its broken mouth.

Scattered in a million pieces and buried
Its dry tombs will split, at a sign in the sky,

At a rending of veils.
10   It will rise, in a time after times,

After swallowing death and the pit
It will return stainless

For the delivery of this world.
So the river is a god

15   Knee-deep among reeds, watching men,
Or hung by the heels down the door of a dam

It is a god, and inviolable.
Immortal. And will wash itself of all deaths.

1983

Walt

I *Under High Wood*[5]

Going up for the assault that morning
They passed the enclosure of prisoners.
"A big German stood at the wire," he said,
"A big German, and he caught my eye.
5   And he cursed me. I felt his eye curse me."

Halfway up the field, the bullet
Hit him in the groin. He rolled
Into a shell-hole. The sun rose and burned.
A sniper clipped his forehead. He wormed
10   Deeper down. Bullet after bullet
Dug at the crater rim, searching for him.
Another clipped him. Then the sniper stopped.

All that day he lay. He went walks
Along the Heights Road, from Peckett to Midgley,
15   Down to Mytholmroyd (past Ewood
Of his ancestors, past the high-perched factory
Of his future life). Up the canal bank,
Up Redacre, along and down into Hebden,
Then up into Crimsworth Dene, to their old campground
20   In the happy valley,

5. Scene of fierce infantry battles in World War I.

And up over Shackleton Hill, to Widdop,
Back past Greenwood Lea, above Hardcastles,
To Heptonstall—all day
He walked about that valley,[6] as he lay
25   Under High Wood in the shell-hole.

I knew the knot of scar on his temple.

We stood in the young March corn
Of a perfect field. His fortune made.
His life's hope over. Me beside him
30   Just the age he'd been when that German
Took aim with his eye and hit him so hard
It brought him and his wife down together,
With all his children one after the other.

A misty rain prickled and hazed.
35   "Here," he hazarded. "Somewhere just about here.
This is where he stopped me. I got this far."

He frowned uphill towards the skyline tree-fringe
As through binoculars
Towards all that was left.

II *The Atlantic*

Night after night he'd sat there,
Eighty-four, still telling the tale.
With his huge thirst for anaesthetics.
"Time I were dead," I'd heard. "I want to die."

5   That's altered.
                    We lean to a cliff rail
Founded in tremblings.
Beneath us, two thousand five hundred
Miles of swung worldweight
10   Hit England's western wall
With a meaningless bump.

"Aye!" he sighs. Over and over. "Aye!"
And massages his temples.

Can he grasp what's happened? His frown
15   Won't connect. Familiar eagle frown—
Dark imperial eye. The ground flinches.
Mountains of dissolution
Boil cold geysers, bespatter us.
                                    Tranquillizers,
20   Steroids, and a whole crateful
Of escapist Madeira,[7] collided
Three evenings ago—

---

6. In Yorkshire, England.   7. A fortified wine.

They swamped and drowned
The synapses, the breath-born spinnaker[8] shells
25　Of consonants and vowels.
　　　　　　　　　　　　　I found him
Trying to get up out of a chair,
Fish-eyed, and choking, clawing at air,
Dumbness like a bone stuck in his throat
30　He's survived with a word—one last word.
A last mouthful. I listen.
And I almost hear a new baby's
Eyeless howl of outrage—sobered to "Aye!"
Sighed slow. Like blessed breath. He breathes it.

35　I dare hardly look at him. I watch.
He'd crept into my care.
A cursed hulk of marriage, a full-rigged fortune
Cast his body, crusted like Job's,[9]
Onto my threshold. Strange Dead Sea creature.
40　He crawled in his ruins, like Timon.[1]
The Times Index[2] was his morning torture.
Fairy gold of a family of dead leaves.
"Why?" he'd cried. "Why can't I just die?"
His memory was so sharp—a potsherd.
45　He raked at his skin, whispering "God! God!"
Nightly, a nurse eased his scales with ointment.

I've brought him out for air. And the cliffs. And there
The sea towards America—wide open.
Untrodden, glorious America!
50　Look, a Peregrine Falcon—they're rare!

Nothing will connect.
He peers down past his shoes
Into a tangle of horizons—

Black, tilted bedrock struggling up,
55　Mouthing disintegration.

Every weedy breath of the sea
Is another swell of overwhelming.
Meaningless. And a sigh. Meaningless.

Now he's closed his eyes. He caresses
60　His own skull, over and over, comforting.
The Millmaster, the Caesar whose frown
Tossed my boyhood the baffling coin "guilty".
His fingers are my mother's. They seem astray
In quaverings and loss
65　As he strokes and strokes at his dome.

---

8. Triangular sail opposite the mainsail of a ship
sailing before the wind; "synapses": connections of
nerve cells.
9. Biblical character who suffered from, among

other things, an outbreak of boils.
1. Misanthropic hero of Shakespeare's tragedy
Timon of Athens.
2. Stockmarket price list in British newspaper.

The sea thuds and sighs. Bowed at the rail
He seems to be touching at a wound he dare not touch.
He seems almost to find the exact spot.
His eyelids quiver, in the certainty of touch—

70 And "Aye!" he breathes. "Aye!"

We turn away. Then as he steadies himself,
Still gripping the rail, his reaching stare
Meets mine watching him. I can't escape it
Or hold it. Walt! Walt!
75   I bury it
Hugger-mugger anyhow
Inside my shirt.

                                            1989

HARRY MATHEWS

1930–

Histoire[1]

Tina and Seth met in the midst of an overcrowded militarism.
"Like a drink?" he asked her. "They make great Alexanders[2] over at the
    Marxism-Leninism."
She agreed. They shared cocktails. They behaved cautiously, as in a
    period of pre-fascism.
Afterwards he suggested dinner at a restaurant renowned for its Maoism.
5 "O.K.," she said, but first she had to phone a friend about her ailing
    Afghan, whose name was Racism.
Then she followed Seth across town past twilit alleys of sexism.

The waiter brought menus and announced the day's specials. He treated
    them with condescending sexism,
So they had another drink. Tina started her meal with a dish of milita-
    rism,
While Seth, who was hungrier, had a half portion of stuffed baked racism.
10 Their main dishes were roast duck for Seth, and for Tina broiled
    Marxism-Leninism.
Tina had pecan pie à la for dessert, Seth a compote of stewed Maoism.
They lingered. Seth proposed a liqueur. They rejected sambuca and
    agreed on fascism.

During the meal, Seth took the initiative. He inquired into Tina's fas-
    cism,
About which she was reserved, not out of reticence but because Seth's
    sexism
15 Had aroused in her a desire she felt she should hide—as though her
    Maoism

1. "Story" (French).   2. Iced cocktails.

Would willy-nilly betray her feelings for him. She was right. Even her
deliberate militarism
Couldn't keep Seth from realizing that his attraction was reciprocated.
His own Marxism-Leninism
Became manifest, in a compulsive way that piled the Ossa of confusion
on the Peleion[3] of racism.

Next, what? Food finished, drinks drunk, bills paid—what racism
20 Might not swamp their yearning in an even greater confusion of fascism?
But women are wiser than words. Tina rested her hand on his thigh and,
a-twinkle with Marxism-Leninism,
Asked him, "My place?" Clarity at once abounded under the flood-lights
of sexism,
They rose from the table, strode out, and he with the impetuousness of
young militarism
Hailed a cab to transport them to her lair, heaven-haven of Maoism.

25 In the taxi he soon kissed her. She let him unbutton her Maoism
And stroke her resilient skin, which was quivering with shudders of
racism.
When beneath her jeans he sensed the superior Lycra of her militarism,
His longing almost strangled him. Her little tongue was as potent as fas-
cism
In its elusive certainty. He felt like then and there tearing off her sexism,
30 But he reminded himself: "Pleasure lies in patience, not in the greedy
violence of Marxism-Leninism."

Once home, she took over. She created a hungering aura of Marxism-
Leninism
As she slowly undressed him where he sat on her overstuffed art-deco
Maoism,
Making him keep still, so that she could indulge in caresses, in sexism,
In the pursuit of knowing him. He groaned under the exactness of her
racism
35 —Fingertip sliding up his nape, nails incising his soles, teeth nibbling his
fascism.
At last she guided him to bed, and they lay down on a patchwork of Old
American militarism.

Biting his lips, he plunged his militarism into the popular context of her
Marxism-Leninism,
Easing one thumb into her fascism, with his free hand coddling the tip
of her Maoism,
Until, gasping with appreciative racism, both together sink into the
revealed glory of sexism.

1982

---

3. Mathews reverses the image from Greek
mythology, in which the giants called Aloadae
tried to pile the Pelion, a range of mountains in
southeastern Thessaly, onto Ossa, a mountain also
in Thessaly.

GARY SNYDER
1930–

Mid-August at Sourdough Mountain[1] Lookout

Down valley a smoke haze
Three days heat, after five days rain
Pitch glows on the fir-cones
Across rocks and meadows
5   Swarms of new flies.

I cannot remember things I once read
A few friends, but they are in cities.
Drinking cold snow-water from a tin cup
Looking down for miles
10   Through high still air.

1959

Above Pate Valley

We finished clearing the last
Section of trail by noon,
High on the ridge-side
Two thousand feet above the creek
5   Reached the pass, went on
Beyond the white pine groves,
Granite shoulders, to a small
Green meadow watered by the snow,
Edged with Aspen—sun
10   Straight high and blazing
But the air was cool.
Ate a cold fried trout in the
Trembling shadows. I spied
A glitter, and found a flake
15   Black volcanic glass-obsidian—
By a flower. Hands and knees
Pushing the Bear grass, thousands
Of arrowhead leavings over a
Hundred yards. Not one good
20   Head, just razor flakes
On a hill snowed all but summer,
A land of fat summer deer,
They came to camp. On their
Own trails. I followed my own
25   Trail here. Picked up the cold-drill,
Pick, singlejack,[2] and sack
Of dynamite.
Ten thousand years.

1959

1. Many of Snyder's poems are set in the Pacific Northwest.
2. A cold-drill and singlejack (a short-handled hammer) are used to cut holes in solid rock for dynamite.

Four Poems for Robin

Siwashing it out once in Siuslaw Forest[3]

I slept under   rhododendron
All night   blossoms fell
Shivering on   a sheet of cardboard
Feet stuck   in my pack
5   Hands deep   in my pockets
Barely   able   to   sleep.
I remembered   when we were in school
Sleeping together   in a big warm bed
We were   the youngest lovers
10   When we broke up   we were still nineteen.
Now our   friends are married
You teach   school back east
I dont mind   living this way
Green hills   the long blue beach
15   But sometimes   sleeping in the open
I think back   when I had you.

A spring night in Shokoku-ji[4]

Eight years ago this May
We walked under cherry blossoms
At night in an orchard in Oregon.
20   All that I wanted then
Is forgotten now, but you.
Here in the night
In a garden of the old capital
I feel the trembling ghost of Yugao[5]
25   I remember your cool body
Naked under a summer cotton dress.

An autumn morning in Shokoku-ji

Last night watching the Pleiades,[6]
Breath smoking in the moonlight,
Bitter memory like vomit
30   Choked my throat.
I unrolled a sleeping bag
On mats on the porch
Under thick autumn stars.
In dream you appeared
35   (Three times in nine years)
Wild, cold, and accusing.
I woke shamed and angry:

3. West of Eugene, Oregon; "siwashing": camping with light equipment, roughing it.
4. Fourteenth-century Zen monastery in Kyoto, once the capital of Japan.
5. In the medieval Japanese novel *Genji monogatori (The Tale of Genji)*, written between A.D. 1001 and 1006, Murasaki-no-Shikibu (Lady Murasaki) recounts the amorous exploits of the young Prince Genji. Genji has a brief liaison with a young woman, Yugao, who dies suddenly and mysteriously. After her death, coming upon a dress of hers, he writes a poem.
6. A cluster of stars (named after the seven daughters of Atlas, in Greek mythology) in the constellation Taurus.

The pointless wars of the heart.
Almost dawn. Venus and Jupiter.[7]
40 The first time I have
Ever seen them close.

December at Yase[8]

You said, that October,
In the tall dry grass by the orchard
When you chose to be free,
45 "Again someday, maybe ten years."
After college I saw you
One time. You were strange.
And I was obsessed with a plan.

Now ten years and more have
50 Gone by: I've always known
where you were—
I might have gone to you
Hoping to win your love back.
You still are single.

55 I didn't.
I thought I must make it alone. I
Have done that.

Only in dream, like this dawn,
Does the grave, awed intensity
60 Of our young love
Return to my mind, to my flesh.

We had what the others
All crave and seek for;
We left it behind at nineteen.

65 I feel ancient, as though I had
Lived many lives.

And may never now know
If I am a fool
Or have done what my
70   karma demands.

1968

7. Snyder both names the plants and alludes to the Roman gods (Venus, the god of love; Jupiter, the ruler of all the gods).
8. Near northeast Kyoto.

DEREK WALCOTT

1930–

A Far Cry from Africa

A wind is ruffling the tawny pelt
Of Africa. Kikuyu,[1] quick as flies,
Batten upon the bloodstreams of the veldt.[2]
Corpses are scattered through a paradise.
5 Only the worm, colonel of carrion, cries:
"Waste no compassion on these separate dead!"
Statistics justify and scholars seize
The salients of colonial policy.
What is that to the white child hacked in bed?
10 To savages, expendable as Jews?

Threshed out by beaters,[3] the long rushes break
In a white dust of ibises whose cries
Have wheeled since civilization's dawn
From the parched river or beast-teeming plain.
15 The violence of beast on beast is read
As natural law, but upright man
Seeks his divinity by inflicting pain.
Delirious as these worried beasts, his wars
Dance to the tightened carcass of a drum,
20 While he calls courage still that native dread
Of the white peace contracted by the dead.

Again brutish necessity wipes its hands
Upon the napkin of a dirty cause, again
A waste of our compassion, as with Spain,[4]
25 The gorilla wrestles with the superman.
I who am poisoned with the blood of both,
Where shall I turn, divided to the vein?
I who have cursed
The drunken officer of British rule, how choose
30 Between this Africa and the English tongue I love?
Betray them both, or give back what they give?
How can I face such slaughter and be cool?
How can I turn from Africa and live?

1962

Nights in the Gardens of Port of Spain[5]

Night, the black summer, simplifies her smells
into a village; she assumes the impenetrable

---

1. An east African tribe whose members, as Mau Mau fighters, conducted an eight-year terrorist campaign against British colonial settlers in Kenya.
2. Open country, neither cultivated nor forest (Afrikaans).
3. In big-game hunting, natives are hired to beat the brush, driving birds—such as ibises—and other animals into the open.
4. The Spanish Civil War (1936–39).
5. Capital of Trinidad, British West Indies.

musk of the negro, grows secret as sweat,
her alleys odorous with shucked oyster shells,

5 coals of gold oranges, braziers of melon.
Commerce and tambourines increase her heat.

Hellfire or the whorehouse: crossing Park Street,
a surf of sailors' faces crests, is gone

with the sea's phosphoresence; the boites-de-nuit[6]
10 tinkle like fireflies in her thick hair.

Blinded by headlamps, deaf to taxi klaxons,
she lifts her face from the cheap, pitch oil flare

towards white stars, like cities, flashing neon,
burning to be the bitch she must become.

15 As daylight breaks the coolie turns his tumbril[7]
of hacked, beheaded coconuts towards home.

1964

The Glory Trumpeter

Old Eddie's face, wrinkled with river lights,
Looked like a Mississippi man's. The eyes,
Derisive and avuncular at once,
Swivelling, fixed me. They'd seen
5 Too many wakes, too many cathouse nights.
The bony, idle fingers on the valves
Of his knee-cradled horn could tear
Through "Georgia on My Mind" or "Jesus Saves"
With the same fury of indifference,
10 If what propelled such frenzy was despair.

Now, as the eyes sealed in the ashen flesh,
And Eddie, like a deacon at his prayer,
Rose, tilting the bright horn, I saw a flash
Of gulls and pigeons from the dunes of coal
15 Near my grandmother's barracks on the wharves,
I saw the sallow faces of those men
Who sighed as if they spoke into their graves
About the Negro in America. That was when
The Sunday comics sprawled out on her floor,
20 Sent from the States, had a particular odour,
A smell of money mingled with man's sweat.

And yet, if Eddie's features held our fate,
Secure in childhood I did not know then
A jesus-ragtime or gut-bucket blues
25 To the bowed heads of lean, compliant men

6. "Nightclubs" (French).
7. Open cart used in the French Revolution to
carry victims to the guillotine.

Back from the States in their funereal serge,
Black, rusty Homburgs[8] and limp waiters' ties
With honey accents and lard-coloured eyes
Was Joshua's ram's horn wailing for the Jews
30 Of patient bitterness or bitter siege.[9]

Now it was that as Eddie turned his back
On our young crowd out fêteing, swilling liquor,
And blew, eyes closed, one foot up, out to sea,
His horn aimed at those cities of the Gulf,
35 Mobile and Galveston and sweetly meted
The horn of plenty through a bitter cup,
In lonely exaltation blaming me
For all whom race and exile have defeated,
For my own uncle in America,
40 That living there I never could look up.

1964

The Gulf

[FOR JACK AND BARBARA HARRISON]

I

The airport coffee tastes less of America.
Sour, unshaven, dreading the exertion
of tightening, racked nerves fuelled with liquor,

some smoky, resinous Bourbon,
5 the body, buckling at its casket hole,
a roar like last night's blast racing its engines,

watches the fumes of the exhausted soul
as the trans-Texas jet, screeching, begins
its flight and friends diminish. So, to be aware

10 of the divine union the soul detaches
itself from created things.[1] "We're in the air,"
the Texan near me grins. All things: these matches

from LBJ's[2] campaign hotel, this rose
given me at dawn in Austin by a child,
15 this book of fables by Borges,[3] its prose

a stalking, moonlit tiger. What was willed
on innocent, sun-streaked Dallas,[4] the beast's claw
curled round that hairspring rifle is revealed

8. Old-fashioned felt hats. "Funereal serge": cheap dark suits.
9. At the fall of the city of Jericho (Joshua 6.1–21).
1. With reference to the neoplatonic doctrine that earthly relationships and attachments contaminate the striving for spiritual union with God; in contrast to the teaching that divine love is manifested in the created world and in human relationships.
2. Lyndon Baines Johnson (1906–1973), thirty-sixth president of the United States.
3. Jorge Luis Borges (1899–1986), Argentinian man of letters, best known for his short stories.
4. With an allusion to the assassination there of John F. Kennedy, November 22, 1963.

on every page as lunacy or feral law;
20   circling that wound we leave Love Field.[5]
Fondled, these objects conjure hotels,

quarrels, new friendships, brown limbs
nakedly moulded as these autumn hills
memory penetrates as the jet climbs

25   the new clouds over Texas; their home means
an island suburb, forest, mountain water;
they are the simple properties for scenes

whose joy exhausts like grief, scenes where we learn,
exchanging the least gifts, this rose, this napkin,
30   that those we love are objects we return,

that this lens on the desert's wrinkled skin
has priced our flesh, all that we love in pawn
to that brass ball, that the gifts, multiplying

clutter and choke the heart, and that I shall
35   watch love reclaim its things as I lie dying.
My very flesh and blood! Each seems a petal

shrivelling from its core. I watch them burn,
by the nerves' flare I catch their skeletal
candour! Best never to be born

40   the great dead cry.[6] Their works shine on our shelves,
by twilight tour their gilded gravestone spines,
and read until the lamplit page revolves

to a white stasis° whose detachment shines   *stillness*
like a propeller's rainbowed radiance.
45   Circling like us; no comfort for their loves!

II

The cold glass darkens. Elizabeth wrote once
that we make glass the image of our pain;
I watch clouds boil past the cold, sweating pane

above the Gulf. All styles yearn to be plain
50   as life. The face of the loved object under glass
is plainer still. Yet, somehow, at this height,

above this cauldron boiling with its wars,
our old earth, breaking to familiar light,
that cloud-bound mummy with self-healing scars

5. The Dallas airport.
6. For example, Sophocles, in *Oedipus at Colo-nus*: "Not to be born surpasses thought and speech. / The second best is to have seen the light / And then to go back quickly whence we came."

55 peeled of her cerements° again looks new;   *grave clothes*
     some cratered valley heals itself with sage,
     through that grey, fading massacre a blue

     light-hearted creek flutes of some seige
     to the amnesia of drumming water.
60 Their cause is crystalline: the divine union

     of these detached, divided States, whose slaughter
     darkens each summer now, as one by one,
     the smoke of bursting ghettos clouds the glass

     down every coast where filling-station signs
65 proclaim the Gulf, an air, heavy with gas,
     sickens the state, from Newark to New Orleans.

III

     Yet the South felt like home. Wrought balconies,
     the sluggish river with its tidal drawl,
     the tropic air charged with the extremities

70 of patience, a heat heavy with oil,
     canebrakes, that legendary jazz. But fear
     thickened my voice, that strange, familiar soil

     prickled and barbed the texture of my hair,
     my status as a secondary soul.
75 The Gulf, your gulf, is daily widening,

     each blood-red rose warns of that coming night
     when there's no rock cleft to go hidin' in[7]
     and all the rocks catch fire, when that black might,

     their stalking, moonless panthers turn from Him
80 whose voice they can no more believe, when the black X's[8]
     mark their passover with slain seraphim.[9]

IV

     The Gulf shines, dull as lead. The coast of Texas
     glints like a metal rim. I have no home
     as long as summer bubbling to its head

85 boils for that day when in the Lord God's name
     the coals of fire are heaped upon the head
     of all whose gospel is the whip and flame,

     age after age, the uninstructing dead.

1969

7. A reference to the hymn that begins "Rock of Ages, cleft for me, / Let me hide myself in thee." The "rock" signifies Christ, "cleft" in his crucifixion.

8. Such as Malcolm X, the Black Muslim leader, assassinated February 21, 1965, and the Black Panthers, a militant black organization.
9. Angels of the highest order.

From The Schooner *Flight*

1   Adios,[1] Carenage

In idle August, while the sea soft,
and leaves of brown islands stick to the rim
of this Caribbean, I blow out the light
by the dreamless face of Maria Concepcion
5   to ship as a seaman on the schooner *Flight.*
Out in the yard turning grey in the dawn,
I stood like a stone and nothing else move
but the cold sea rippling like galvanize
and the nail holes of stars in the sky roof,
10   till a wind start to interfere with the trees.
I pass me dry neighbour sweeping she yard
as I went downhill, and I nearly said:
"Sweep soft, you witch, 'cause she don't sleep hard,"
but the bitch look through me like I was dead.
15   A route taxi pull up, park-lights still on.
The driver size up my bags with a grin:
"This time, Shabine, like you really gone!"
I ain't answer the ass, I simply pile in
the back seat and watch the sky burn
20   above Laventille pink as the gown
in which the woman I left was sleeping,
and I look in the rearview and see a man
exactly like me, and the man was weeping
for the houses, the streets, the whole fucking island.
25   Christ have mercy on all sleeping things!
From that dog rotting down Wrightson Road
to when I was a dog on these streets;
if loving these islands must be my load,
out of corruption my soul takes wings,
30   But they had started to poison my soul
with their big house, big car, big-time bohbohl,
coolie, nigger, Syrian, and French Creole,
so I leave it for them and their carnival —
I taking a sea-bath, I gone down the road.
35   I know these islands from Monos to Nassau,
a rusty head sailor with sea-green eyes
that they nickname Shabine, the patois for
any red nigger, and I, Shabine, saw
when these slums of empire was paradise.
40   I'm just a red nigger who love the sea,
I had a sound colonial education,
I have Dutch, nigger, and English in me,
and either I'm nobody, or I'm a nation.

But Maria Concepcion was all my thought
45   watching the sea heaving up and down
as the port side of dories, schooners, and yachts
was painted afresh by the strokes of the sun

---

1. "Goodbye" (Spanish).

signing her name with every reflection;
I knew when dark-haired evening put on
50 her bright silk at sunset, and, folding the sea,
sidled under the sheet with her starry laugh,
that there'd be no rest, there'd be no forgetting.
Is like telling mourners round the graveside
about resurrection, they want the dead back,
55 so I smile to myself as the bow rope untied
and the *Flight* swing seaward: "Is no use repeating
that the sea have more fish. I ain't want her
dressed in the sexless light of a seraph,
I want those round brown eyes like a marmoset, and
60 till the day when I can lean back and laugh,
those claws that tickled my back on sweating
Sunday afternoons, like a crab on wet sand."
As I worked, watching the rotting waves come
past the bow that scissor the sea like silk,
65 I swear to you all, by my mother's milk,
by the stars that shall fly from tonight's furnace,
that I loved them, my children, my wife, my home;
I loved them as poets love the poetry
that kills them, as drowned sailors the sea.

70 You ever look up from some lonely beach
and see a far schooner? Well, when I write
this poem, each phrase go be soaked in salt;
I go draw and knot every line as tight
as ropes in this rigging; in simple speech
75 my common language go be the wind,
my pages the sails of the schooner *Flight*.

1979

Midsummer

Certain things here[2] are quietly American—
that chain-link fence dividing the absent roars
of the beach from the empty ball park, its holes
muttering the word umpire instead of empire;
5 the gray, metal light where an early pelican
coasts, with its engine off, over the pink fire
of a sea whose surface is as cold as Maine's.
The light warms up the sides of white, eager Cessnas[3]
parked at the airstrip under the freckling hills
10 of St. Thomas. The sheds, the brown, functional hangar,
are like those of the Occupation in the last war.
The night left a rank smell under the casuarinas,[4]
the villas have fenced-off beaches where the natives walk,
illegal immigrants from unlucky islands
15 who envy the smallest polyp its right to work.
Here the wetback crab and the mollusc are citizens,

2. I.e., in Trinidad.
3. Make of small aircraft.
4. Trees with jointed branches.

and the leaves have green cards. Bulldozers jerk
and gouge out a hill, but we all know that the dust
is industrial and must be suffered. Soon —
20   the sea's corrugations are sheets of zinc
soldered by the sun's steady acetylene. This
drizzle that falls now is American rain,
stitching stars in the sand. My own corpuscles
are changing as fast. I fear what the migrant envies:
25   the starry pattern they make — the flag on the post office —
the quality of the dirt, the fealty changing under my foot.

1984

From Omeros

Chapter XXX

1

He yawned and watched the lilac horns of his island
lift the horizon.
           "I know you ain't like to talk,"
the mate said, "but this morning I could use a hand.

5 Where your mind was whole night?"
                      "Africa."
                            "Oh? You walk?"
The mate held up his T-shirt, mainly a red hole,
and wriggled it on. He tested the bamboo pole

10 that trawled the skipping lure from the fast-shearing hull
with the Trade behind them.
                  "Mackerel running," he said.
"Africa, right! You get sunstroke, chief. That is all

You best put that damn captain-cap back on your head."
15 All night he had worked the rods without any sleep,
watching Achille cradled in the bow; he had read

the stars and known how far out they were and how deep
the black troughs were and how long it took them to lift,
but he owed it to his captain, who took him on

20 when he was stale-drunk. He had not noticed the swift.
"You know what we ketch last night? One *mako* size 'ton,' "
using the patois for kingfish, blue albacore.

"Look by your foot."
              The kingfish, steel-blue and silver,
25 lay fresh at his feet, its eye like a globed window
ringing with cold, its rim the circular river

of the current that had carried him back, with the spoon
bait in its jaw, the ton was his deliverer,
now its cold eye in sunlight was blind as the moon.

30 A grey lens clouded the gaze of the albacore
    that the mate had gaffed and clubbed. It lay there, gaping,
    its blue flakes yielding the oceanic colour

    of the steel-cold depth from which it had shot, leaping,
    stronger than a stallion's neck tugging its stake,
35 sounding, then bursting its trough, yawning at the lure

    of a fishhook moon that was reeled in at daybreak
    round the horizon's wrist. Tired of slapping water,
    the tail's wedge had drifted into docility.

    Achille had slept through the fight. Cradled at the bow
40 like a foetus, like a sea-horse, his memory
    dimmed in the sun with the scales of the albacore.

    "Look, land!" the mate said. Achille altered the rudder
    to keep sideways in the deep troughs without riding
    the crests, then he looked up at an old man-o'-war

45 tracing the herring-gulls with that endless gliding
    that made it the sea-king.
                    "Them stupid gulls does fish
    for him every morning. He himself don't catch none,

    white slaves for a black king."
50   "When?" the mate said. "You wish."
    "Look him dropping." Achille pointed. "Look at that son-
    of-a-bitch stealing his fish for the whole fucking week!"

    A herring-gull climbed with silver bent in its beak
    and the black magnificent frigate met the gull
55 halfway with the tribute; the gull dropped the mackerel

    but the frigate-bird caught it before it could break
    the water and soared.
                    "The black bugger beautiful,
    though!" The mate nodded, and Achille felt the phrase lift

60 his heart as high as the bird whose wings wrote the word
    "Afolabe," in the letters of the sea-swift.
    "The king going home," he said as he and the mate

    watched the frigate steer into that immensity
    of seraphic space whose cumuli were a gate
65 dividing for a monarch entering his city.

                                    1990

JAY MacPHERSON

1931–

The Swan

White-habited, the mystic Swan
Walks her rank° cloister as the night draws down,   *overgrown*
In sweet communion with her sister shade,
Matchless and unassayed.

5   The tower of ivory sways,
Gaze bends to mirrored gaze:
This perfect arc embraces all her days.
And when she comes to die,
The treasures of her silence patent lie:
10   'I am all that is and was and shall be,
My garment may no man put by.'

1957

A Lost Soul

Some are plain lucky—we ourselves among them:
Houses with books, with gardens, all we wanted,
Work we enjoy, with colleagues we feel close to—
Love we have, even:

5   True love and candid, faithful, strong as gospel,
Patient, untiring, fond when we are fretful.
Having so much, how is it that we ache for
Those darker others?

Some days for them we could let slip the whole damn
10   Soft bed we've made ourselves, our friends in Heaven
Let slip away, buy back with blood our ancient
Vampires and demons.

First loves and oldest, what names shall I call you?
Older to me than language, old as breathing,
15   Born with me, in this flesh: by now I know you're
Greed, pride and envy.

Too long I've shut you out, denied acquaintance,
Favoured less barefaced vices, hoped to pass for
Reasonable, rate with those who more inclined to
20   Self-hurt than murder.

You were my soul: in arrogance I banned you.
Now I recant—return, possess me, take my
Hands, bind my eyes, infallibly restore my
Share in perdition.

1981

The Well

A winter hanging over the dark well,
My back turned to the sky,
To see if in that blackness something stirs,
Or glints, or winks an eye:

5 Or, from the bottom looking up, I see
Sky's white, my pupil head—
Lying with all that's lost, with all that shines
My winter with the dead:

A well of truth, of images, of words.
10 Low where Orion[1] lies
I watch the solstice pit become a stair,
The constellations rise.

1981

CARTER REVARD

1931–

October, Isle of Skye[1]

Wading up Brunigill's[2] rush
for a long time is a question
of where to place each boot
on a rock that will hold, advance;
5 of not slipping on moss-slime's
green blackness under the swashing
of water past boots—
then eyes raise to a pool
too golden-deep for boots,
10 and before climbing around it, pause
and stretch and look down through
amber lucence where
slow gold-lit ripplings touch
white crystals in rockbed,
15 till a rowan-berry comes bobbing,
red-round and lightly,
to ride through the pool—
then boots go up over sheep-paths
to the heathery ridge and
20 a bumblebee knee-brushed from
purple paper-firm bells
drops wet and stunned,
chill mist on her wings,
tumbles in browning blossoms

---

1. A constellation named after the hunter of
Greek myth; associated with stormy weather.
1. Island in the Inner Hebrides, off the west coast
of Scotland.
2. Stream on the northwest peninsula of the Isle
of Skye.

25 and on her back caught
in the jungle of heather her front legs
rise drowned and waking, hook
slowly a heather-twig, pull
the fur-body up as antennae wag
30 through green and amber sensing
late pollen, nectar
for bee-bread in burrows—
and light changes dazzling
in downstreaming mist,
35 blue brilliance,
cloudrush,
soft greyblue
sunfilled,
while newlit water
40 birdshrills and gurgles,
and down again climbing
bootplace by bootplace
to the stream and
its rowanberry raft
45 by moss-edge of pool—
that from scarlet seed
over amber movement
a green tree may sway.

Birch Canoe

Red men embraced   my body's whiteness,
cutting into me   carved it free,
sewed it tight   with sinews taken
from lightfoot deer   who leaped this stream—
5 now in my ghost-skin   they glide over clouds
at home in the fish's   fallen heaven.

1993

GEOFFREY HILL

1932–

The Distant Fury of Battle

Grass resurrects to mask, to strangle
Words glossed on stone, lopped stone-angel;
But the dead maintain their ground—
That there's no getting round—

5 Who in places vitally rest,
Named, anonymous; who test
Alike the endurance of yews
Laurels, moonshine, stone, all tissues;

With whom, under licence and duress,
10   There are pacts made, if not peace.
Union with the stone-wearing dead
Claims the born leader, the prepared

Leader, the devourers and all lean men.
Some, finally, learn to begin.
15   Some keep to the arrangement of love
(Or similar trust) under whose auspices move

Most subjects, toward the profits of this
Combine of doves and witnesses.
Some, dug out of hot-beds, are brought bare,
20   Not past conceiving but past care.

1955   1959

The Guardians

The young, having risen early, had gone,
Some with excursions beyond the bay-mouth,
Some toward lakes, a fragile reflected sun.
Thunder-heads drift, awkwardly, from the south;

5   The old watch them. They have watched the safe
Packed harbours topple under sudden gales,
Great tides irrupt, yachts burn at the wharf
That on clean seas pitched their effective sails.

There are silences. These, too, they endure:
10   Soft comings-on; soft aftershocks of calm.
Quietly they wade the disturbed shore;
Gather the dead as the first dead scrape home.

1956   1959

September Song

Born 19.6.32—Deported 24.9.42[1]

Undesirable you may have been, untouchable
you were not. Not forgotten
or passed over at the proper time.

As estimated, you died. Things marched,
5   sufficient, to that end.
Just so much Zyklon[2] and leather, patented
terror, so many routine cries.

(I have made
an elegy for myself it
10   is true)

---

1. Hill was born on June 18, 1932, one day before
the birthdate given in the subtitle.
2. Hydrocyanic acid, used in fumigation; also
(Zyklon-B) used in the gas chambers of the German concentration camps.

September fattens on vines. Roses
flake from the wall. The smoke
of harmless fires drifts to my eyes.

This is plenty. This is more than enough.

1968

From Mercian Hymns[3]

VI

The princes of Mercia were badger and raven. Thrall
to their freedom, I dug and hoarded. Orchards
fruited above clefts. I drank from honeycombs of
chill sandstone.

5   "A boy at odds in the house, lonely among brothers."
But I, who had none, fostered a strangeness; gave
myself to unattainable toys.

Candles of gnarled resin, apple-branches, the tacky
mistletoe. "Look" they said and again "look." But
10   I ran slowly; the landscape flowed away, back to
its source.

In the schoolyard, in the cloakrooms, the children
boasted their scars of dried snot; wrists and
knees garnished with impetigo.

VII

Gasholders, russet among fields. Milldams, marlpools[4]
that lay unstirring. Eel-swarms. Coagulations of
frogs; once, with branches and half-bricks, he
battered a ditchful; then sidled away from the
5   stillness and silence.

Ceolred[5] was his friend and remained so, even after
the day of the lost fighter: a biplane, already
obsolete and irreplaceable, two inches of heavy
snub silver. Ceolred let it spin through a hole
10   in the classroom-floorboards, softly, into the
rat droppings and coins.

After school he lured Ceolred, who was sniggering
with fright, down to the old quarries, and flayed

---

3. "The historical Offa reigned over Mercia (and
the greater part of England south of the Humber)
in the years A.D. 757–796. During early medieval
times he was already becoming a creature of leg-
end. The Offa who figures in this sequence might
perhaps most usefully be regarded as the presiding
genius of the West Midlands, his dominion endur-
ing from the middle of the eighth century until the
middle of the twentieth (and possibly beyond).

The indication of such a timespan will, I trust,
explain and to some extent justify a number of
anachronisms" [Hill's note].
4. Pools in deposits of crumbling clay and chalk;
"gasholders": or gasometers, large metal recepta-
cles for gas.
5. Ceolred was a ninth-century bishop of Leices-
ter, but the name is here used as a characteristic
Anglo-Saxon Mercian name.

15 him. Then, leaving Ceolred, he journeyed for hours,
        calm and alone, in his private derelict sandlorry[6]
        named *Albion*.

VIII

The mad are predators. Too often lately they harbour
    against us. A novel heresy exculpates all maimed
    souls. Abjure it! I am the King of Mercia, and
    I know.

5   Threatened by phone-calls at midnight, venomous let-
        ters, forewarned I have thwarted their imminent
        devices.

Today I name them; tomorrow I shall express the new
    law. I dedicate my awakening to this matter.

X

He adored the desk, its brown-oak inlaid with ebony,
    assorted prize pens, the seals of gold and base
    metal into which he had sunk his name.

5   It was there that he drew upon grievances from the
        people; attended to signatures and retributions;
        forgave the death-howls of his rival. And there
        he exchanged gifts with the Muse of History.

What should a man make of remorse, that it might
    profit his soul? Tell me. Tell everything to
10 Mother, darling, and God bless.

He swayed in sunlight, in mild dreams. He tested the
    little pears. He smeared catmint on his palm for
    his cat Smut to lick. He wept, attempting to mas-
    ter *ancilla* and *servus*.[7]

XVI

Clash of salutation. As keels thrust into shingle.
    Ambassadors, pilgrims. What is carried over? The
    Frankish[8] gift, two-edged, regaled with slaughter.

The sword is in the king's hands; the crux a crafts-
5   man's triumph. Metal effusing its own fragrance,
        a variety of balm. And other miracles, other
        exchanges.

6. Sand truck. Albion was an old Celtic name for England; it is also the name of a famous make of British truck.
7. Latin for "maidservant" and "manservant" (or slave).

8. The Franks were members of a confederation of German tribes who formed the Frankish Empire in the Dark Ages. In the ninth century they gave way to the medieval kingdoms that became known as France, Germany, and Italy.

Shafts from the winter sun homing upon earth's rim.
Christ's mass: in the thick of a snowy forest the
10   flickering evergreen fissured with light.

Attributes assumed, retribution entertained. What is
borne amongst them? Too much or too little. In-
dulgences of bartered acclaim; an expenditure, a
hissing. Wine, urine and ashes.

XXVIII

Processes of generation; deeds of settlement. The
urge to marry well; wit to invest in the proper-
ties of healing-springs. Our children and our
children's children, o my masters.

5   Tracks of ancient occupation. Frail ironworks rust-
ing in the thorn-thicket. Hearthstones; charred
lullabies. A solitary axe-blow that is the echo
of a lost sound.

Tumult recedes as though into the long rain. Groves
10   of legendary holly; silverdark the ridged gleam.

XXX

And it seemed, while we waited, he began to walk to-
wards us   he vanished

he left behind coins, for his lodging, and traces of
red mud.

1971

From Lachrimae[9]

OR

SEVEN TEARS FIGURED IN SEVEN PASSIONATE PAVANS

> Passions I allow, and loves I approve, onely
> I would wish that men would alter their
> object and better their intent.
>   —ST. ROBERT SOUTHWELL,[1] *Mary Magda-
> len's Funeral Tears*, 1591

1. *Lachrimae Verae*

Crucified Lord, you swim upon your cross
and never move. Sometimes in dreams of hell
the body moves but moves to no avail
and is at one with that eternal loss.

---

9. "Tears" (Latin). Hill takes his title from the six-
teenth-century composer John Dowland's compo-
sition for viols and lutes. Dowland's "Lachrimae"
is divided into seven parts: "Antiquae," "Novae,"
"Genentes," "Tristes," "Coactae," "Amantis," and
"Verae" ("true"). A pavan is a stately dance or the
music for this.
1. (1561–1595); English Jesuit priest and poet.

5 You are the castaway of drowned remorse,
 you are the world's atonement on the hill.
 This is your body twisted by our skill
 into a patience proper for redress.

 I cannot turn aside from what I do;
10 you cannot turn away from what I am.
 You do not dwell in me nor I in you
 however much I pander to your name
 or answer to your lords of revenue,
 surrendering the joys that they condemn.

1978

From An Apology for the Revival of Christian Architecture in England

the spiritual, Platonic old England . . .[2]
—STC, Anima Poetae

"Your situation," said Coningsby, looking up
the green and silent valley, "is absolutely
poetic."
"I try sometimes to fancy," said Mr. Millbank,
with a rather fierce smile, "that I am in the
New World."
—BENJAMIN DISRAELI,[3] Coningsby

9. *The Laurel Axe*

Autumn resumes the land, ruffles the woods
with smoky wings, entangles them. Trees shine
out from their leaves, rocks mildew to moss-green;
the avenues are spread with brittle floods.

5 Platonic England, house of solitudes,
 rests in its laurels and its injured stone,
 replete with complex fortunes that are gone,
 beset by dynasties of moods and clouds.

 It stands, as though at ease with its own world,
10 the mannerly extortions, languid praise,
 all that devotion long since bought and sold,

 the rooms of cedar and soft-thudding baize,[4]
 tremulous boudoirs where the crystals kissed
 in cabinets of amethyst and frost.

1978

---

2. I.e., an idealized orderly rural England. "STC": Samuel Taylor Coleridge (1772–1834). English poet and philosopher (see pp. 739–63).
3. British novelist and statesman (1804–1881); the "New World" referred to is that of an idealized rural America.

4. I.e., billiard rooms in great old British homes; the "soft-thudding baize" refers to the soft green cloth covering billiard tables as well as to the "green-baize door" traditionally dividing the family quarters in a grand house from the servants' quarters.

Veni Coronaberis[5]

A Garland for Helen Waddell

The crocus armies from the dead
rise up; the realm of love renews
the battle it was born to lose,
though for a time the snows have fled

5 and old stones blossom in the south
with sculpted vine and psaltery[6]
and half-effaced adultery
the bird-dung dribbling from its mouth;

and abstinence crowns all our care
10 with martyr-laurels for this day.
Towers and steeples rise away
into the towering gulfs of air.

1978

DOUGLAS LIVINGSTONE

1932–

Lake Morning in Autumn

Before sunrise the stork was there
resting the pillow of his body
on stick legs growing from the water.

A flickering gust of pencil-slanted rain
5 swept over the chill autumn morning;
and he, too tired to arrange

his wind-buffeted plumage,
perched swaying a little,
neck flattened, ruminative,

10 beak on chest, contemplative eye
filmy with star vistas and hollow
black migratory leagues, strangely,

ponderously alone and some weeks
early. The dawn struck and everything,
15 sky, water, bird, reeds

was blood and gold. He sighed.
Stretching his wings he clubbed
the air; slowly, regally, so very tired,

5. "Come and you will be crowned" (Latin).
Helen Waddell (1889–1965), a British scholar,
translated several volumes of Latin poems, most
notably *Medieval Latin Lyrics.*
6. Ancient and medieval stringed instrument.

aiming his beak he carefully climbed
20   inclining to his invisible tunnel of sky,
his feet trailing a long, long time.

One Time

It seems a certain time ago: a-maybe
seven years or less, he
first took a woman underwater. In aqualungs
and bathing suits, hanging
5   in the pale liquid air
of a blue cathedral
—the sleeping pool of the limestone caves
to be precise—
face mask to mask,
10   wide-eyed and glass to glass,
they triumphed over the first knotty cotton fumblings
in the allembracing wetness.

Her hair, like a damp Medusa's,[1]
flared upwards.

15   He remembers their delight at the silent
new experience,
their emulations of the passions
of dolphins
who are not after all
20   unhonourable
and very humorous
and humouring in their loveplay.

Then, he recalls his panic
when, with a mounting climax,
25   perhaps upside down, certainly weightless,
he had to cram her mouthpiece
back into her vacant lips, fishwide and cyanosed,[2]
her eyes lightly closed,
and it was a long swim away
30   to the surface. (Her hair hung down on the journey.)

She did, of course, recover adequately
after a few splutters and with him gently
squeezing her ribs regularly
while finning desperately
35   upwards.
        But it was some time
before they tried it again
—some time after
and in shallower water.

1964

1. In Greek mythology, chief of the Gorgons, who had snakes for hair and looked so terrible that the sight of them turned men to stone.
2. Skin turning blue.

SYLVIA PLATH
1932–1963

The Colossus[1]

I shall never get you put together entirely,
Pieced, glued, and properly jointed.
Mule-bray, pig-grunt and bawdy cackles
Proceed from your great lips.
5   It's worse than a barnyard.

Perhaps you consider yourself an oracle,
Mouthpiece of the dead, or of some god or other.
Thirty years now I have labored
To dredge the silt from your throat.
10   I am none the wiser.

Scaling little ladders with gluepots and pails of lysol
I crawl like an ant in mourning
Over the weedy acres of your brow
To mend the immense skull plates and clear
15   The bald, white tumuli[2] of your eyes.

A blue sky out of the Oresteia[3]
Arches above us. O father, all by yourself
You are pithy and historical as the Roman Forum.
I open my lunch on a hill of black cypress.
20   Your fluted bones and acanthine[4] hair are littered

In their old anarchy to the horizon-line.
It would take more than a lightning-stroke
To create such a ruin.
Nights, I squat in the cornucopia
25   Of your left ear, out of the wind,

Counting the red stars and those of plum-color.
The sun rises under the pillar of your tongue.
My hours are married to shadow.
No longer do I listen for the scrape of a keel
30   On the blank stones of the landing.

1959   1960

Morning Song

Love set you going like a fat gold watch.
The midwife slapped your footsoles, and your bald cry
Took its place among the elements.

---

1. Alluding to the gigantic statue of this name that stood at the entrance of the harbor to Rhodes, Greece, in the third century B.C.
2. I.e., grave mounds.
3. A trilogy of plays by Aeschylus, performed in 458 B.C., that recounts the story of Orestes' efforts to avenge the murder of his father, Agamemnon, by his mother, Clytemnestra.
4. I.e., curved (as the capitals of some Greek columns) like the acanthus plant.

Our voices echo, magnifying your arrival. New statue.
5   In a drafty museum, your nakedness
Shadows our safety. We stand round blankly as walls.

I'm no more your mother
Than the cloud that distills a mirror to reflect its own slow
Effacement at the wind's hand.

10   All night your moth-breath
Flickers among the flat pink roses. I wake to listen:
A far sea moves in my ear.

One cry, and I stumble from bed, cow-heavy and floral
In my Victorian nightgown.
15   Your mouth opens clean as a cat's. The window square

Whitens and swallows its dull stars. And now you try
Your handful of notes;
The clear vowels rise like balloons.

1961   1965

Tulips

The tulips are too excitable, it is winter here.
Look how white everything is, how quiet, how snowed-in.
I am learning peacefulness, lying by myself quietly
As the light lies on these white walls, this bed, these hands.
5   I am nobody; I have nothing to do with explosions.
I have given my name and my day-clothes up to the nurses
And my history to the anaesthetist and my body to surgeons.

They have propped my head between the pillow and the sheet-cuff
Like an eye between two white lids that will not shut.
10   Stupid pupil, it has to take everything in.
The nurses pass and pass, they are no trouble,
They pass the way gulls pass inland in their white caps,
Doing things with their hands, one just the same as another,
So it is impossible to tell how many there are.

15   My body is a pebble to them, they tend it as water
Tends to the pebbles it must run over, smoothing them gently.
They bring me numbness in their bright needles, they bring me sleep.
Now I have lost myself I am sick of baggage—
My patent leather overnight case like a black pillbox,
20   My husband and child smiling out of the family photo;
Their smiles catch onto my skin, little smiling hooks.

I have let things slip, a thirty-year-old cargo boat
Stubbornly hanging on to my name and address.
They have swabbed me clear of my loving associations.
25   Scared and bare on the green plastic-pillowed trolley
I watched my tea-set, my bureaus of linen, my books

Sink out of sight, and the water went over my head.
I am a nun now, I have never been so pure.

I didn't want any flowers, I only wanted
30 To lie with my hands turned up and be utterly empty.
How free it is, you have no idea how free—
The peacefulness is so big it dazes you,
And it asks nothing, a name tag, a few trinkets.
It is what the dead close on, finally; I imagine them
35 Shutting their mouths on it, like a Communion tablet.

The tulips are too red in the first place, they hurt me.
Even through the gift paper I could hear them breathe
Lightly, through their white swaddlings, like an awful baby.
Their redness talks to my wound, it corresponds.
40 They are subtle: they seem to float, though they weigh me down,
Upsetting me with their sudden tongues and their color,
A dozen red lead sinkers round my neck.

Nobody watched me before, now I am watched.
The tulips turn to me, and the window behind me
45 Where once a day the light slowly widens and slowly thins,
And I see myself, flat, ridiculous, a cut-paper shadow
Between the eye of the sun and the eyes of the tulips,
And I have no face, I have wanted to efface myself.
The vivid tulips eat my oxygen.

50 Before they came the air was calm enough,
Coming and going, breath by breath, without any fuss.
Then the tulips filled it up like a loud noise.
Now the air snags and eddies round them the way a river
Snags and eddies round a sunken rust-red engine.
55 They concentrate my attention, that was happy
Playing and resting without committing itself.

The walls, also, seem to be warming themselves.
The tulips should be behind bars like dangerous animals;
They are opening like the mouth of some great African cat,
60 And I am aware of my heart: it opens and closes
Its bowl of red blooms out of sheer love of me.
The water I taste is warm and salt, like the sea,
And comes from a country far away as health.

1961   1965

Elm

For Ruth Fainlight

I know the bottom, she says. I know it with my great tap root:
It is what you fear.
I do not fear it: I have been there.

Is it the sea you hear in me,
5　Its dissatisfactions?
Or the voice of nothing, that was your madness?

Love is a shadow.
How you lie and cry after it.
Listen: these are its hooves: it has gone off, like a horse.

10　All night I shall gallop thus, impetuously,
Till your head is a stone, your pillow a little turf,
Echoing, echoing.

Or shall I bring you the sound of poisons?
This is rain now, this big hush.
15　And this is the fruit of it: tin-white, like arsenic.

I have suffered the atrocity of sunsets.
Scorched to the root
My red filaments burn and stand, a hand of wires.

Now I break up in pieces that fly about like clubs.
20　A wind of such violence
Will tolerate no bystanding: I must shriek.

The moon, also, is merciless: she would drag me
Cruelly, being barren.
Her radiance scathes me. Or perhaps I have caught her.

25　I let her go. I let her go
Diminished and flat, as after radical surgery.
How your bad dreams possess and endow me.

I am inhabited by a cry.
Nightly it flaps out
30　Looking, with its hooks, for something to love.

I am terrified by this dark thing
That sleeps in me;
All day I feel its soft, feathery turnings, its malignity.

Clouds pass and disperse.
35　Are those the faces of love, those pale irretrievables?
Is it for such I agitate my heart?

I am incapable of more knowledge.
What is this, this face
So murderous in its strangle of branches? —

40　Its snaky acids kiss.
It petrifies the will. These are the isolate, slow faults
That kill, that kill, that kill.

1962   1965

Daddy

You do not do, you do not do
Any more, black shoe
In which I have lived like a foot
For thirty years, poor and white,
5   Barely daring to breathe or Achoo.

Daddy, I have had to kill you.
You died before I had time —
Marble-heavy, a bag full of God,
Ghastly statue with one gray toe[1]
10   Big as a Frisco seal

And a head in the freakish Atlantic
Where it pours bean green over blue
In the waters off beautiful Nauset.
I used to pray to recover you.
15   Ach, du.[2]

In the German tongue, in the Polish town[3]
Scraped flat by the roller
Of wars, wars, wars.
But the name of the town is common.
20   My Polack friend

Says there are a dozen or two.
So I never could tell where you
Put your foot, your root,
I never could talk to you.
25   The tongue stuck in my jaw.

It stuck in a barb wire snare.
Ich, ich, ich, ich,[4]
I could hardly speak.
I thought every German was you.
30   And the language obscene

An engine, an engine
Chuffing me off like a Jew.
A Jew to Dachau, Auschwitz, Belsen.[5]
I began to talk like a Jew.
35   I think I may well be a Jew.

The snows of the Tyrol,[6] the clear beer of Vienna
Are not very pure or true.
With my gypsy ancestress and my weird luck
And my Taroc pack and my Taroc pack[7]
40   I may be a bit of a Jew.

---

1. Plath's father's toe turned black from gangrene.
2. "Ah, you"; the first of a series of references to her father's German origins.
3. Grabów, in Poland, Otto Plath's birthplace.
4. "I, I, I, I" (German).

5. German concentration camps, where millions of Jews were murdered during World War II.
6. Austrian Alpine region.
7. Tarot cards, used for fortune-telling.

I have always been scared of *you*,
With your Luftwaffe,[8] your gobbledygoo.
And your neat moustache
And your Aryan eye, bright blue.
45 Panzer[9]-man, panzer-man, O You——

Not God but a swastika
So black no sky could squeak through.
Every woman adores a Fascist,
The boot in the face, the brute
50 Brute heart of a brute like you.

You stand at the blackboard, daddy,
In the picture I have of you,
A cleft in your chin instead of your foot
But no less a devil for that, no not
55 Any less the black man who

Bit my pretty red heart in two.
I was ten when they buried you.
At twenty I tried to die
And get back, back, back to you.
60 I thought even the bones would do.

But they pulled me out of the sack,
And they stuck me together with glue,[1]
And then I knew what to do.
I made a model of you,
65 A man in black with a Meinkampf[2] look

And a love of the rack and the screw.
And I said I do, I do.
So daddy, I'm finally through.
The black telephone's off at the root,
70 The voices just can't worm through.

If I've killed one man, I've killed two——
The vampire who said he was you
And drank my blood for a year,
Seven years, if you want to know.
75 Daddy, you can lie back now.

There's a stake in your fat black heart
And the villagers never liked you.
They are dancing and stamping on you.
They always *knew* it was you.
80 Daddy, daddy, you bastard, I'm through.

1962   1965

---

8. The German air force.
9. "Armor" (German), especially, during World War II, referring to the German armored tank corps.

1. An allusion to Plath's first suicide attempt.
2. *Mein Kampf* ("My Struggle") is the title of Hitler's political autobiography and Nazi polemic, written before his rise to power.

Ariel[3]

Stasis in darkness.
Then the substanceless blue
Pour of tor° and distances.   *craggy hill*

God's lioness,
5 How one we grow,
Pivot of heels and knees!—The furrow

Splits and passes, sister to
The brown arc
Of the neck I cannot catch,

10 Nigger-eye
Berries cast dark
Hooks—

Black sweet blood mouthfuls,
Shadows.
15 Something else

Hauls me through air—
Thighs, hair;
Flakes from my heels.

White
20 Godiva,[4] I unpeel—
Dead hands, dead stringencies.

And now I
Foam to wheat, a glitter of seas.
The child's cry

25 Melts in the wall.
And I
Am the arrow,

The dew that flies
Suicidal, at one with the drive
30 Into the red

Eye, the cauldron of morning.

1962   1965

---

3. The name of a horse Plath often rode; also, the airy spirit in Shakespeare's *Tempest*.
4. According to legend, Lady Godiva (ca. 1010– 1067) rode naked through the streets of Coventry in order to persuade her husband, the local lord, to lower taxes.

Lady Lazarus[5]

I have done it again.
One year in every ten
I manage it—

A sort of walking miracle, my skin
5   Bright as a Nazi lampshade,[6]
My right foot

A paperweight,
My face a featureless, fine
Jew linen.

10   Peel off the napkin
O my enemy.
Do I terrify?—

The nose, the eye pits, the full set of teeth?
The sour breath
15   Will vanish in a day.

Soon, soon the flesh
The grave cave ate will be
At home on me

And I a smiling woman.
20   I am only thirty.
And like the cat I have nine times to die.

This is Number Three.
What a trash
To annihilate each decade.

25   What a million filaments.
The peanut-crunching crowd
Shoves in to see

Them unwrap me hand and foot—
The big strip tease.
30   Gentleman, ladies,

These are my hands,
My knees.
I may be skin and bone,

Nevertheless, I am the same, identical woman.
35   The first time it happened I was ten.
It was an accident.

---

5. Lazarus was raised by Jesus from the dead (John 11.1–44).
6. In the Nazi death camps, the skins of victims were sometimes used to make lampshades and the bodies to make soap.

The second time I meant
To last it out and not come back at all.
I rocked shut

40 As a seashell.
They had to call and call
And pick the worms off me like sticky pearls.

Dying
Is an art, like everything else.
45 I do it exceptionally well.

I do it so it feels like hell.
I do it so it feels real.
I guess you could say I've a call.

It's easy enough to do it in a cell.
50 It's easy enough to do it and stay put.
It's the theatrical

Comeback in broad day
To the same place, the same face, the same brute
Amused shout:

55 "A miracle!"
That knocks me out.
There is a charge

For the eyeing of my scars, there is a charge
For the hearing of my heart—
60 It really goes.

And there is a charge, very large charge,
For a word or a touch
Or a bit of blood

Or a piece of my hair or my clothes.
65 So, so, Herr Doktor.
So, Herr Enemy.

I am your opus,
I am your valuable,
The pure gold baby

70 That melts to a shriek.
I turn and burn.
Do not think I underestimate your great concern.

Ash, ash—
You poke and stir.
75 Flesh, bone, there is nothing there—

A cake of soap,
A wedding ring,
A gold filling.

Herr God, Herr Lucifer,[7]
80   Beware
Beware.

Out of the ash[8]
I rise with my red hair
And I eat men like air.

1965

Black Rook in Rainy Weather

On the stiff twig up there
Hunches a wet black rook
Arranging and rearranging its feathers in the rain.
I do not expect miracle
5   Or an accident

To set the sight on fire
In my eye, nor seek
Any more in the desultory weather some design,
But let spotted leaves fall as they fall,
10   Without ceremony, or portent

Although, I admit, I desire,
Occasionally, some backtalk
From the mute sky, I can't honestly complain:
A certain minor light may still
15   Leap incandescent

Out of kitchen table or chair
As if a celestial burning took
Possession of the most obtuse objects now and then—
Thus hallowing an interval
20   Otherwise inconsequent

By bestowing largesse, honor,
One might say love. At any rate, I now walk
Wary (for it could happen
Even in this dull, ruinous landscape); skeptical,
25   Yet politic; ignorant

Of whatever angel may choose to flare
Suddenly at my elbow. I only know that a rook
Ordering its black feathers can so shine

---

7. The devil. "Beware / Beware": cf. the end of S. T. Coleridge's "Kubla Khan" (1816; pp. 741–42).

8. An allusion to the phoenix, the mythical bird that dies in flames and is reborn from its own ashes.

As to seize my senses, haul
30   My eyelids up, and grant

A brief respite from fear
Of total neutrality. With luck,
Trekking stubborn through this season
Of fatigue, I shall
35   Patch together a content

Of sorts. Miracles occur,
If you care to call those spasmodic
Tricks of radiance miracles. The wait's begun again,
The long wait for the angel,
40   For that rare, random descent.

1956   1971

JOHN UPDIKE

1932–

Snapshots

How good of Mrs. Metz! The blur
Must be your cousin Christopher.

A scenic shot Jim took near Lyme.
Those rocks seemed lovely at the time.

5   And here's a product of the days
When Jim went through his gnarled-tree phase.

The man behind the man in shorts—
His name is Shorer, Shaw, or Schwartz.

The kids at play. This must be Keith.
10   Can that be Wilma underneath?

I'd give my life to know why Josh
Sat next to Mrs. McIntosh.

Jim looked so well in formal clothes.
I was much slimmer than this shows.

15   Yes, Jim and I were so in love.
That hat: what *was* I thinking of?

This disappointed Mrs. Weicker.
I don't know why, it's very like her.

The dog is Skip. He loved to play.
20   We had to have him put away.

I guess these people are the Wrens.
An insect landed on the lens.

This place is where I was inspired
To—stop me, if your eyes are tired.

1954

V. B. Nimble, V. B. Quick

Science, Pure and Applied, by V. B. Wigglesworth, F.R.S.,[1] Quick Professor of
Biology in the University of Cambridge.
—a talk listed in the B.B.C.'s *Radio Times*

V. B. Wigglesworth wakes at noon,
Washes, shaves, and very soon
Is at the lab; he reads his mail,
Tweaks a tadpole by the tail,
5   Undoes his coat, removes his hat,
Dips a spider in a vat
Of alkaline, phones the press,
Tells them he is F.R.S.,
Subdivides six protocells,
10 Kills a rat by ringing bells,
Writes a treatise, edits two
Symposia on "Will Man Do?,"
Gives a lecture, audits three,
Has the Sperm Club in for tea,
15 Pensions off an aging spore,
Cracks a test tube, takes some pure
Science and applies it, finds
His hat, adjusts it, pulls the blinds,
Instructs the jellyfish to spawn,
20 And, by one o'clock, is gone.

1954

I Missed His Book, but I Read His Name

"The Silver Pilgrimage," by M. Anantanarayanan . . . 160 pages. Criterion.
$3.95.
—*The New York Times*

Though authors are a dreadful clan
To be avoided if you can,
I'd like to meet the Indian,
M. Anantanarayanan.

5   I picture him as short and tan.
We'd meet, perhaps, in Hindustan.[2]
I'd say, with admirable *élan*,°   zest
"Ah, Anantanarayanan—

---

1. Fellow of the Royal Society.   2. Predominantly Hindu area of India.

I've heard of you. The *Times* once ran
10   A notice on your novel, an
    Unusual tale of God and Man."
    And Anantanarayanan

    Would seat me on a lush divan
    And read his name—that sumptuous span
15   Of "a"s and "n"s more lovely than
    "In Xanadu did Kubla Khan"[3]—

    Aloud to me all day. I plan
    Henceforth to be an ardent fan
    Of Anantanarayanan—
20   M. Anantanarayanan.

1963

ANNE STEVENSON

1933–

Temporarily in Oxford

Where they will bury me
I don't know.
Many places might not be
sorry to store me.

5   The Midwest has right of origin.
Already it has welcomed my mother
to its flat sheets.

The English fens that bore me
have been close curiously often.
10   It seems I can't get away from
dampness and learning.

If I stay where I am
I could sleep in this educated earth.

But if they are kind
15   they'll burn me and
send me to Vermont.

I'd be an education for the trees
and would relish, really,
flaring into maple each October—
20   my scarlet letter to you.

Your stormy north is possible.
You will be there, engrossed in its peat.

3. First line of "Kubla Khan" (p. 741) by the English poet Samuel Taylor Coleridge (1772–1834).

*   It would be handy not to have to
                cross the whole Atlantic
25   each time I wanted to
                lift up the turf
                and slip in beside you.

Willow Song

For Frances Horowitz[1]

I went down to the railway
But the railway wasn't there.
A long scar lay across the waste
Bound up with vetch and maidenhair
5   And birdsfoot trefoils everywhere.
But the clover and the sweet hay,
The cranesbill and the yarrow
Were as nothing to the rose bay
        the rose bay, the rose bay,
10   As nothing to the rose bay willow.

I went down to the river
But the river wasn't there.
A hill of slag lay in its course
With pennycress and cocklebur
15   And thistles bristling with fur.
But ragweed, dock and bitter may
And hawkbit in the hollow
Were as nothing to the rose bay,
        the rose bay, the rose bay
20   As nothing to the rose bay willow.

I went down to find my love,
My sweet love wasn't there.
A shadow stole into her place
And spoiled the loosestrife of her hair
25   And counselled me to pick despair.
Old elder and young honesty
Turned ashen, but their sorrow
Was as nothing to the rose bay
        the rose bay, the rose bay,
30   As nothing to the rose bay willow.

O I remember summer
When the hemlock was in leaf.
The sudden poppies by the path
Were little pools of crimson grief,
35   Sick henbane cowered like a thief.
But self-heal sprang up in her way,
And mignonette's light yellow,
To flourish with the rose bay,

1. (1938–1983); British poet.

the rose bay, the rose bay,
40 To flourish with the rose bay willow.

Its flames took all the wasteland
And all the river's silt,
But as my dear grew thin and grey
They turned as white as salt or milk.
45 Great purples withered out of guilt,
And bright weeds blew away
In cloudy wreathes of summer snow,
And the first one was the rose bay,
the rose bay, the rose bay,
50 The first one was the rose bay willow.

1983   1985

FLEUR ADCOCK

1934–

The Ex-Queen Among the Astronomers

They serve revolving saucer eyes,
dishes of stars; they wait upon
huge lenses hung aloft to frame
the slow procession of the skies.

5   They calculate, adjust, record,
watch transits, measure distances.
They carry pocket telescopes
to spy through when they walk abroad.

Spectra[1] possess their eyes; they face
10 upwards, alert for meteorites,
cherishing little glassy worlds:
receptacles for outer space.

But she, exile, expelled, ex-queen,
swishes among the men of science
15 waiting for cloudy skies, for nights
when constellations can't be seen.

She wears the rings he let her keep;
she walks as she was taught to walk
for his approval, years ago.
20 His bitter features taunt her sleep.

And so when these have laid aside
their telescopes, when lids are closed

---

1. Images retained for a time on the retina of the eye when turned away after gazing fixedly at bright objects.

between machine and sky, she seeks
terrestrial bodies to bestride.

25 She plucks this one or that among
the astronomers, and is become
his canopy, his occultation;[2]
she sucks at earlobe, penis, tongue

mouthing the tubes of flesh; her hair
30 crackles, her eyes are comet-sparks.
She brings the distant briefly close
above his dreamy abstract stare.

Poem Ended by a Death

They will wash all my kisses and fingerprints off you
and my tearstains—I was more inclined to weep
in those wild-garlicky days—and our happier stains,
thin scales of papery silk . . . Fuck that for a cheap
5 opener; and false too—any such traces
you pumiced away yourself, those years ago
when you sent my letters back, in the week I married
that anecdotal ape. So start again. So:

They will remove the tubes and drips and dressings
10 which I censor from my dreams. They will, it is true,
wash you; and they will put you into a box.
After which whatever else they may do
won't matter. This is my laconic style.
You praised it, as I praised your intricate pearled
15 embroideries; these links laced us together,
plain and purl across the ribs of the world . . .

The Soho Hospital for Women

1

Strange room, from this angle:
white door open before me,
strange bed, mechanical hum, white lights.
There will be stranger rooms to come.

5 As I almost slept I saw the deep flower opening
and leaned over into it, gratefully.
It swimmingly closed in my face. I was not ready.
It was not death, it was acceptance.

*

Our thin patient cat died purring,
10 her small triangular head tilted back,

---

2. Concealment of a heavenly body behind the body of the Earth.

the nurse's fingers caressing her throat,
my hand on her shrunken spine; the quick needle.

That was the second death by cancer.
The first is not for me to speak of.
15   It was telephone calls and brave letters
and a friend's hand bleeding under the coffin.

*

Doctor, I am not afraid of a word.
But neither do I wish to embrace that visitor,
to engulf it as Hine-Nui-te-Po
20   engulfed Maui;[3] that would be the way of it.

And she was the winner there: her womb crushed him.
Goddesses can do these things.
But I have admitted the gloved hands and the speculum[4]
and must part my ordinary legs to the surgeon's knife.

2

25   Nellie has only one breast
ample enough to make several.
Her quilted dressing-gown softens
to semi-doubtful this imbalance
and there's no starched vanity
30   in our abundant ward-mother:
her silvery hair's in braids, her slippers
loll, her weathered smile holds true.
When she dresses up in her black
with her glittering marcasite brooch[5] on
35   to go for the weekly radium treatment
she's the bright star of the taxi-party—
whatever may be growing under her ribs.

*

Doris hardly smokes in the ward—
and hardly eats more than a dreamy spoonful—
40   but the corridors and bathrooms
reek of her Players Number 10,
and the drug-trolley pauses
for long minutes by her bed.
Each week for the taxi-outing
45   she puts on her skirt again
and has to pin the slack waistband
more tightly over her scarlet sweater.
Her face, a white shadow through smoked glass,
lets Soho display itself unregarded.

---

3. Supernatural hero in Polynesian mythology, Maui the sun-snarer, fire-stealer, monster-slayer, entered the womb of Hine, sleeping goddess of the underworld, in search of immortality. He intended to depart through her mouth, but when his bird companion laughed at the sight, Hine awoke and crushed Maui to death.
4. Surgical instrument for dilating orifices of the body to facilitate examination or operation.
5. Cheap brooch made of crystallized iron pyrites.

*

50   Third in the car is Mrs Golding
      who never smiles. And why should she?

                        3

      The senior consultant on his rounds
      murmurs in so subdued a voice
      to the students marshalled behind
55   that they gather in, forming a cell,
      a cluster, a rosette around him
      as he stands at the foot of my bed
      going through my notes with them,
      half-audibly instructive, grave.

60   The slight ache as I strain forward
      to listen still seems imagined.

      Then he turns his practised smile on me:
      "How are you this morning?" "Fine,
      very well, thank you." I smile too.
65   And possibly all that murmurs within me
      is the slow dissolving of stitches.

                        4

      I am out in the supermarket choosing—
      this very afternoon, this day—
      picking up tomatoes, cheese, bread,

70   things I want and shall be using
      to make myself a meal, while they
      eat their stodgy suppers in bed:

      Janet with her big freckled breasts,
      her prim Scots voice, her one friend,
75   and never in hospital before,

      who came in to have a few tests
      and now can't see where they'll end;
      and Coral in the bed by the door

      who whimpered and gasped behind a screen
80   with nurses to and fro all night
      and far too much of the day;

      pallid, bewildered, nineteen.
      And Mary, who will be all right
      but gradually. And Alice, who may.

85   Whereas I stand almost intact,
      giddy with freedom, not with pain.
      I lift my light basket, observing

how little I needed in fact;
and move to the checkout, to the rain,
90 to the lights and the long street curving.

1979

POPULAR BALLADS OF
THE TWENTIETH CENTURY

Pete Seeger (1919–) · Where Have All the Flowers Gone?[1]

Where have all the flowers gone?—long time passing
Where have all the flowers gone?—long time ago
Where have all the flowers gone?—girls have picked them every one
When will they ever learn? When will they ever learn?

5   Where have all the young girls gone?—long time passing
Where have all the young girls gone?—long time ago
Where have all the young girls gone?—they've taken husbands every one
When will they ever learn? When will they ever learn?

Where have all the young men gone?—long time passing
10 Where have all the young men gone?—long time ago
Where have all the young men gone?—gone for soldiers every one
When will they ever learn? When will they ever learn?

Where have all the soldiers gone?—long time passing
Where have all the soldiers gone?—long time ago
15 Where have all the soldiers gone?—gone to graveyards everyone
When will they ever learn? When will they ever learn?

Where have all the graveyards gone?—long time passing
Where have all the graveyards gone?—long time ago
Where have all the graveyards gone?—gone to flowers everyone
20 When will they ever learn? When will they ever learn?

1961

Bob Dylan (1941–) · Boots of Spanish Leather

Oh, I'm sailing away my own true love,
I'm sailin' away in the morning,
Is there something I can send you from across the sea,
From the place that I'll be landing.

5   No, there's nothing you can send me my own true love,
There's nothin' I wish to be ownin',
Just carry yourself back to me unspoiled,
From across that lonesome ocean.

1. With additional verse by Joe Hickerson. Cf. Jean Elliot, "The Flowers of the Forest" (pp. 619–20).

Oh, but I just thought you might long want something fine
10 Made of silver or of golden,
Either from the mountains of Madrid
Or from the coast of Barcelona.

Oh, but if I had the stars from the darkest night
And the diamonds from the deepest ocean,
15 I'd forsake them all for your sweet kiss
For that's all I'm wishin' to be ownin'.

That I might be gone a long ole time
And it's only that I'm askin',
Is there somethin' I can send you to remember me by
20 To make your time more easy passin'.

Oh, how can, how can you ask me again,
It only brings me sorrow,
The same thing I want from you today
I would want again tomorrow.

25 I got a letter on a lonesome day,
It was from her ship a-sailin'
Saying I don't know when I'll be comin' back again,
It depends on how I'm a-feelin'.

Well, if you my love must think that-a-way,
30 I'm sure your mind is roamin',
I'm sure your heart is not with me,
But with the country to where you're goin'.

So take heed, take heed of the western wind,
Take heed of the stormy weather,
35 And yes, there's something you can send back to me,
Spanish boots of Spanish leather.

1963

Dudley Randall (1914–) · Ballad of Birmingham

(On the bombing of a church in Birmingham, Alabama, 1963)[2]

"Mother dear, may I go downtown
Instead of out to play,
And march the streets of Birmingham
In a Freedom March today?"

5 "No, baby, no, you may not go,
For the dogs are fierce and wild,
And clubs and hoses, guns and jails
Aren't good for a little child."

---

2. Two weeks after Martin Luther King's August 23rd March on Washington; in Birmingham, King had led nonviolent civil-rights demonstrations that were met with attack dogs, tear gas, cattle prods, and firehoses.

"But, mother, I won't be alone.
10   Other children will go with me,
And march the streets of Birmingham
To make our country free."

"No, baby, no, you may not go,
For I fear those guns will fire.
15   But you may go to church instead
And sing in the children's choir."

She has combed and brushed her night-dark hair,
And bathed rose petal sweet,
And drawn white gloves on her small brown hands,
20   And white shoes on her feet.

The mother smiled to know her child
Was in the sacred place,
But that smile was the last smile
To come upon her face.

25   For when she heard the explosion,
Her eyes grew wet and wild.
She raced through the streets of Birmingham
Calling for her child.

She clawed through bits of glass and brick,
30   Then lifted out a shoe.
"O, here's the shoe my baby wore,
But, baby, where are you?"

1969

Gordon Lightfoot (1938–) · The Wreck of the Edmund Fitzgerald[3]

The legend lives on from the Chippewa on down
Of the big lake they called "Gitche Gumee".
The lake, it is said, never gives up her dead
When the skies of November turn gloomy.
5   With a load of iron ore twenty-six thousand tons more
Than the Edmund Fitzgerald weighed empty,
That good ship and true was a bone to be chewed
When the gales of November came early.

The ship was the pride of the American side
10   Coming back from some mill in Wisconsin.
As the big freighters go, it was bigger than most
With a crew and good captain well seasoned;
Concluding some terms with a couple of steel firms
When they left fully loaded for Cleveland.
15   And later that night when the ship's bell rang
Could it be the north wind they'd been feelin'?

3. The *Edmund Fitzgerald* sank in Lake Superior on November 10, 1975.

The wind in the wires made a tattle-tale sound
And a wave broke over the railing.
And every man knew, as the captain did too,
20 T'was the witch of November come stealin'.
The dawn came late and the breakfast had to wait
When the gales of November came slashin'.
When afternoon came it was freezin' rain
In the face of a hurricane west wind.

25 When suppertime came, the old cook came on deck sayin'
Fellas, it's too rough to feed ya.
At Seven P.M. a main hatchway caved in, he said
Fellas, it's been good t'know ya.
The captain wired in he had water comin' in
30 And the good ship and crew was in peril.
And later that night when his lights went outta sight
Came the wreck of the Edmund Fitzgerald.

Does any one know where the love of God goes
When the waves turn the minutes to hours?
35 The searches all say they'd have made Whitefish Bay
If they'd put fifteen more miles behind her.
They might have split up or they might have capsized;
May have broke deep and took water.
And all that remains is the faces and the names
40 Of the wives and the sons and the daughters.

Lake Huron rolls, Superior sings
In the rooms of her ice-water mansion.
Old Michigan steams like a young man's dreams;
The islands and bays are for sportsmen.
45 And farther below Lake Ontario
Takes in what Lake Erie can send her,
And the iron boats go as the mariners all know
With the gales of November remembered.

In a musty old hall in Detroit they prayed,
50 In the Maritime Sailors' Cathedral.
The church bell chimed till it rang twenty-nine times
For each man on the Edmund Fitzgerald.
The legend lives on from the Chippewa on down
Of the big lake they call "Gitche Gumee".
55 Superior, they said, never gives up her dead
When the gales of November come early!

1976

AMIRI BARAKA (LEROI JONES)

1934–

In Memory of Radio

Who has ever stopped to think of the divinity of Lamont Cranston?[1]
(Only Jack Kerouac, that I know of: & me.
The rest of you probably had on WCBS and Kate Smith,
Or something equally unattractive.)

5 What can I say?
It is better to have loved and lost
Than to put linoleum in your living rooms?

Am I a sage or something?
Mandrake's hypnotic gesture of the week?
10 (Remember, I do not have the healing powers of Oral Roberts . . .
I cannot, like F. J. Sheen, tell you how to get saved & rich!
I cannot even order you to gaschamber satori[2] like Hitler or Goody
    Knight

& Love is an evil word.
Turn it backwards / see, what I mean?
15 An evol word. & besides
Who understands it?
I certainly wouldn't like to go out on that kind of limb.

Saturday mornings we listened to *Red Lantern* & his undersea folk.
At 11, *Let's Pretend* / & we did / & I, the poet, still do, Thank God!

20 What was it he used to say (after the transformation, when he was safe
& invisible & the unbelievers couldn't throw stones?) "Heh, heh, heh,
Who knows what evil lurks in the hearts of men? The Shadow knows."

O, yes he does
O, yes he does.
25 An evil word it is,
This Love.

1961

An Agony. As Now.

I am inside someone
who hates me. I look

---

1. The alter ego of the hero of the radio serial "The Shadow." The poem refers to prominent characters (Mandrake) and personalities that Jones would have heard on the radio as a boy: Kate Smith (1907–1986), a popular American singer, best known for her frequent performances of "God Bless America"; Oral Roberts (b. 1918), evangelist; Fulton J. Sheen (1895–1979), Roman Catholic popularizer of religion; Goodwin Knight (1896–1970), one of the first politicians to exploit radio and television—as governor of California in the 1950s, he wanted University of California teachers to sign a loyalty oath as a condition of employment. Jack Kerouac (1922–1969), American writer, was the leading chronicler of the "Beat Generation" (an artistic and social movement of the 1950s).
2. Japanese; state of spiritual enlightenment sought in Zen Buddhism.

out from his eyes. Smell
what fouled tunes come in
5   to his breath. Love his
wretched women.

Slits in the metal, for sun. Where
my eyes sit turning, at the cool air
the glance of light, or hard flesh
10   rubbed against me, a woman, a man,
without shadow, or voice, or meaning.

This is the enclosure (flesh,
where innocence is a weapon. An
abstraction. Touch. (Not mine.
15   Or yours, if you are the soul I had
and abandoned when I was blind and had
my enemies carry me as a dead man
(if he is beautiful, or pitied.

It can be pain. (As now, as all his
20   flesh hurts me.) It can be that. Or
pain. As when she ran from me into
that forest.
           Or pain, the mind
silver spiraled whirled against the
25   sun, higher than even old men thought
God would be. Or pain. And the other. The
yes. (Inside his books, his fingers. They
are withered yellow flowers and were never
beautiful.) The yes. You will, lost soul, say
30   'beauty.' Beauty, practiced, as the tree. The
slow river. A white sun in its wet sentences.

Or, the cold men in their gale. Ecstasy. Flesh
or soul. The yes. (Their robes blown. Their bowls
empty. They chant at my heels, not at yours.) Flesh
35   or soul, as corrupt. Where the answer moves too quickly.
Where the God is a self, after all.)

Cold air blown through narrow blind eyes. Flesh,
white hot metal. Glows as the day with its sun.
It is a human love. I live inside. A bony skeleton
40   you recognize as words or simple feeling.

But it has no feeling. As the metal, is hot, it is not,
given to love.

It burns the thing
inside it. And that thing
45   screams.

1964

The New World

The sun is folding, cars stall and rise
beyond the window. The workmen leave
the street to the bums and painters' wives
pushing their babies home. Those who realize
5   how fitful and indecent consciousness is
stare solemnly out on the emptying street.
The mourners and soft singers. The liars,
and seekers after ridiculous righteousness. All
my doubles, and friends, whose mistakes cannot
10   be duplicated by machines, and this is all of our
arrogance. Being broke or broken, dribbling
at the eyes. Wasted lyricists, and men
who have seen their dreams come true, only seconds
after they knew those dreams to be horrible conceits
15   and plastic fantasies of gesture and extension,
shoulders, hair and tongues distributing misinformation
about the nature of the understanding. No one is that simple
or priggish, to be alone out of spite and grown strong
in its practice, mystics in two-pants suits. Our style,
20   and discipline, controlling the method of knowledge.
Beatniks,[3] like Bohemians, go calmly out of style. And boys
are dying in Mexico, who did not get the word.
The lateness of their fabrication: mark their holes
with filthy needles. The lust of the world. This will not
25   be news. The simple damning lust,

> float flat magic in low changing
> evenings. Shiver your hands
> in dance. Empty all of me for
> knowing, and will the danger
30   > of identification,

> Let me sit and go blind in my dreaming
> and be that dream in purpose and device.
> A fantasy of defeat, a strong strong man
> older, but no wiser than the defect of love.

1969

AUDRE LORDE

1934–1992

Coal

I
is the total black, being spoken
from the earth's inside.

---

3. The terms, not what they represent, go out of style; "Beatnik" in the 1950s and early 1960s replaced the earlier "Bohemian" to label one who chooses to live an unconventional life.

There are many kinds of open
5 how a diamond comes into a knot of flame
how sound comes into a word, colored
by who pays what for speaking.

Some words are open like a diamond
on glass windows
10 singing out within the passing crash of sun
Then there are words like stapled wagers
in a perforated book—buy and sign and tear apart—
and come whatever wills all chances
the stub remains
15 an ill-pulled tooth with a ragged edge.
Some words live in my throat
breeding like adders. Others know sun
seeking like gypsies over my tongue
to explode through my lips
20 like young sparrows bursting from shell.
Some words
bedevil me.

Love is a word, another kind of open.
As the diamond comes into a knot of flame
25 I am Black because I come from the earth's inside
now take my word for jewel in the open light.

                                        1976

From the House of Yemanjá[1]

My mother had two faces and a frying pot
where she cooked up her daughters
into girls
before she fixed our dinner.
5 My mother had two faces
and a broken pot
where she hid out a perfect daughter
who was not me
I am the sun and moon and forever hungry
10 for her eyes.

I bear two women upon my back
one dark and rich and hidden
in the ivory hungers of the other
mother
15 pale as a witch
yet steady and familiar

1. "Mother of the other *Orisha* [the goddesses and gods . . . of the Yoruba peoples of Western Nigeria], Yemanjá is also the goddess of oceans. Rivers are said to flow from her breasts. One legend has it that a son tried to rape her. She fled until she collapsed, and from her breasts, the rivers flowed. Another legend says that a husband insulted Yemanjá's long breasts, and when she fled with her pots he knocked her down. From her breasts flowed the rivers, and from her body then sprang forth all the other *Orisha*. River-smooth stones are Yemanjá's symbol, and the sea is sacred to her followers. Those who please her are blessed with many children" [Lorde's note].

brings me bread and terror
in my sleep
her breasts are huge exciting anchors
20 in the midnight storm.

All this has been
before
in my mother's bed
time has no sense
25 I have no brothers
and my sisters are cruel.

Mother I need
mother I need
mother I need your blackness now
30 as the august earth needs rain.

I am
the sun and moon and forever hungry
the sharpened edge
where day and night shall meet
35 and not be
one.

1978

Hanging Fire

I am fourteen
and my skin has betrayed me
the boy I cannot live without
still sucks his thumb
5 in secret
how come my knees are
always so ashy
what if I die
before morning
10 and momma's in the bedroom
with the door closed.

I have to learn how to dance
in time for the next party
my room is too small for me
15 suppose I die before graduation
they will sing sad melodies
but finally
tell the truth about me
There is nothing I want to do
20 and too much
that has to be done
and momma's in the bedroom
with the door closed.

Nobody even stops to think
25   about my side of it
I should have been on Math Team
my marks were better than his
why do I have to be
the one
30   wearing braces
I have nothing to wear tomorrow
will I live long enough
to grow up
and momma's in the bedroom
35   with the door closed

1978

Echoes

There is a timbre of voice
that comes from not being heard
and knowing   you are not being
heard   noticed only
5   by others   not heard
for the same reason.

The flavor of midnight fruit   tongue
calling your body through dark light
piercing the allure of safety
10   ripping the glitter of silence
around you
        dazzle me with color
        and perhaps I won't notice
till after you're gone
15   your hot grain smell tattooed
into each new poem   resonant
beyond escape   I am listening
in that fine space
between desire and always
20   the grave stillness
before choice.

As my tongue unravels
in what pitch
will the scream hang unsung
25   or shiver like lace on the borders
of never   recording
which dreams heal   which
dream can kill
stabbing a man and burning his body
30   for cover   being caught
making love to a woman
I do not know.

1993

N. SCOTT MOMADAY
1934–

Headwaters

Noon in the intermountain plain:
There is scant telling of the marsh—
A log, hollow and weather-stained,
An insect at the mouth, and moss—
5   Yet waters rise against the roots,
Stand brimming to the stalks. What moves?
What moves on this archaic force
Was wild and welling at the source.

The Eagle-Feather Fan

The eagle is my power,
And my fan is an eagle.
It is strong and beautiful
In my hand. And it is real.
5   My fingers hold upon it
As if the beaded handle
Were the twist of bristlecone.
The bones of my hand are fine
And hollow; the fan bears them.
10 My hand veers in the thin air
Of the summits. All morning
It scuds on the cold currents;
All afternoon it circles
To the singing, to the drums.

The Gift

For Bobby Jack Nelson

Older, more generous,
We give each other hope.
The gift is ominous:
Enough praise, enough rope.

Two Figures

These figures moving in my rhyme,
Who are they? Death and Death's dog, Time.

1976

WOLE SOYINKA

1934–

Telephone Conversation

The price seemed reasonable, location
Indifferent. The landlady swore she lived
Off premises. Nothing remained
But self-confession. "Madam," I warned,
5   "I hate a wasted journey—I am African."
Silence. Silenced transmission of
Pressurized good-breeding. Voice, when it came,
Lipstick coated, long gold-rolled
Cigarette-holder pipped. Caught I was, foully.
10 "HOW DARK?" . . . I had not misheard . . . "ARE YOU LIGHT
OR VERY DARK?" Button B. Button A.[1] Stench
Of rancid breath of public hide-and-speak.
Red booth. Red pillar-box. Red double-tiered
Omnibus squelching tar. It *was* real! Shamed
15 By ill-mannered silence, surrender
Pushed dumbfoundment to beg simplification.
Considerate she was, varying the emphasis—
"ARE YOU DARK? OR VERY LIGHT?" Revelation came.
"You mean—like plain or milk chocolate?"
20 Her assent was clinical, crushing in its light
Impersonality. Rapidly, wave-length adjusted,
I chose. "West African sepia"—and as afterthought,
"Down in my passport." Silence for spectroscopic
Flight of fancy, till truthfulness clanged her accent
25 Hard on the mouthpiece. "WHAT'S THAT?" conceding
"DON'T KNOW WHAT THAT IS." "Like brunette."
"THAT'S DARK, ISN'T IT?" "Not altogether.
Facially, I am brunette, but, madam, you should see
The rest of me. Palm of my hand, soles of my feet
30 Are a peroxide blond. Friction, caused—
Foolishly, madam—by sitting down, has turned
My bottom raven black—One moment, madam!"—sensing
Her receiver rearing on the thunderclap
About my ears—"Madam," I pleaded, "wouldn't you rather
35 See for yourself?"

1962

---

1. Buttons to be pressed by caller who has inserted a coin into an old type of British public pay phone.

MARK STRAND

1934–

The Prediction

That night the moon drifted over the pond,
turning the water to milk, and under
the boughs of the trees, the blue trees,
a young woman walked, and for an instant

5   the future came to her:
rain falling on her husband's grave, rain falling
on the lawns of her children, her own mouth
filling with cold air, strangers moving into her house,

a man in her room writing a poem, the moon drifting into it,
10 a woman strolling under its trees, thinking of death,
thinking of him thinking of her, and the wind rising
and taking the moon and leaving the paper dark.

1970

Always

for Charles Simic

Always so late in the day
In their rumpled clothes, sitting
Around a table lit by a single bulb,
The great forgetters were hard at work.
5   They tilted their heads to one side, closing their eyes.
Then a house disappeared, and a man in his yard
With all his flowers in a row.
The great forgetters wrinkled their brows.
Then Florida went and San Francisco
10 Where tugs and barges leave
Small gleaming scars across the Bay.
One of the great forgetters struck a match.
Gone were the harps of beaded lights
That vault the rivers of New York.
15 Another filled his glass
And that was it for crowds at evening
Under sulphur yellow streetlamps coming on.
And afterwards Bulgaria was gone, and then Japan.
"Where will it stop?" one of them said.
20 "Such difficult work, pursuing the fate
Of everything known," said another.
"Down to the last stone," said a third,
"And only the cold zero of perfection
Left for the imagination." And gone
25 Were North and South America,

And gone as well the moon.
Another yawned, another gazed at the window:
No grass, no trees . . .
The blaze of promise everywhere.

1990

FROM DARK HARBOR[1]

XVI

It is true, as someone has said, that in
A world without heaven all is farewell.[2]
Whether you wave your hand or not,

It is farewell, and if no tears come to your eyes
5   It is still farewell, and if you pretend not to notice,
Hating what passes, it is still farewell.

Farewell no matter what. And the palms as they lean
Over the green, bright lagoon, and the pelicans
Diving, and the glistening bodies of bathers resting,

10   Are stages in an ultimate stillness, and the movement
Of sand, and of wind, and the secret moves of the body
Are part of the same, a simplicity that turns being

Into an occasion for mourning, or into an occasion
Worth celebrating, for what else does one do,
15   Feeling the weight of the pelicans' wings,

The density of the palms' shadows, the cells that darken
The backs of bathers? These are beyond the distortions
Of chance, beyond the evasions of music. The end

Is enacted again and again. And we feel it
20   In the temptations of sleep, in the moon's ripening,
In the wine as it waits in the glass.

XX

Is it you standing among the olive trees
Beyond the courtyard? You in the sunlight
Waving me closer with one hand while the other

Shields your eyes from the brightness that turns
5   All that is not you dead white? Is it you
Around whom the leaves scatter like foam?

1. These poems are included in a forty-five sec-
tion, book-length poem in which Strand recounts
a spiritual quest while paying homage to several
guiding influences in poetry. Among the most
important are Dante (whose three-line stanzas he
borrows, though not Dante's *terza rima* rhyme

scheme) and Wordsworth.
2. Cf. "Waving Adieu, Adieu, Adieu" by the
American poet Wallace Stevens (1879–1955),
lines 5–8 (p. 1160). The final section of *Dark Har-
bor* also alludes to Stevens.

You in the murmuring night that is scented
With mint and lit by the distant wilderness
Of stars? Is it you? Is it really you

10   Rising from the script of waves, the length
Of your body casting a sudden shadow over my hand
So that I feel how cold it is as it moves

Over the page? You leaning down and putting
Your mouth against mine so I should know
15   That a kiss is only the beginning

Of what until now we could only imagine?
Is it you or the long compassionate wind
That whispers in my ear: alas, alas?

1993

DARYL HINE
1936–

Letting Go

I loved you first the time I saw you last,
I knew you best before I let you go.
All the misapprehensions of the past
Dissipated in an hour or so,
5   Naked to the human eye you lay
Candid as a cadaver on the couch
I could have slept on, but I went away
Ashamed to stay, afraid almost to touch.

Lost, you seemed the only vivid thing
10   In a world made moribund and flat
By worldliness. Renunciations bring
Their own reward, apparently, like that
Last look of yours, ironical or tender,
A valediction and a benediction,
15   Which endless reruns will not soon surrender,
The indispensable, improper fiction
Of your unforgettable perfection.

Côte de Liesse[1]

For David Tacium

My disaffected gaze falls on the city
Of my youth, what's left of it. It winks
Back with insomniac, hypnotic eyes
Which sunrise is beginning to surprise.

---

1. "Coast of Jubilance" (French); major road leading west of Montreal, Canada.

5   Distinct, but less distinguished than it thinks,
The sleepy urban university[2]

Where I matriculated twenty odd
Years ago, seen from this twenty-third
Floor has altered out of recognition,
10 As if a revolution had occurred
Without my knowledge in the intermission
Between the acts—perhaps an act of god?

A handful of pedestrians like pigeons
Flutters across the pavement, obsolescent
15 Not only because they hunt and peck on foot,
But as the scattered relics of religion's
Locally outmoded, adolescent
Habits as impeccable as soot.

Light filters into focus, fills my field
20 Of vision till I long to turn away,
Discomfited by dawn's proximity.
At last the night that napkined up the day
Unfolds, and Royal Mountain[3] is revealed
Ridiculous in its sublimity,

25 A pimple on the spotty, pock-marked plain
That stretches, interrupted by the river,
Cluttered by indifferent slum clearance
And building blocks, apparently forever . . .
The past is nothing but a disappearance
30 The present is unable to explain,

Little of either visible to my
Myopic, lackadaisical researches
Into the afterlife of Montreal,
At the rate that cities live and die,
35 Changed beyond recall. So are we all.
Bells keep tinkling in the empty churches.

Riddle

Invisible, chimerical
Revolution of the air,
Fickle, hyperactive, fair,
Impulsive, unpredictable
5 Flibbertigibbet capable
Of never settling anywhere;
Fortuitously musical
Condition of the atmosphere,
Zephyr, monsoon, hurricane,
10 Tempest, typhoon, gust or gale—

2. McGill University.
3. The city of Montreal is built around and upon Royal Mountain.

When will inspiration fail?—
Accomplice of the hail and rain,
Blind but palpable as braille

Wind animates the weathervane.

1990

C. K. WILLIAMS
1936–

Repression

More and more lately, as, not even minding the slippages yet, the aches
and sad softenings,
I settle into my other years, I notice how many of what I once thought
were evidences of repression,
sexual or otherwise, now seem, in other people anyway, to be varieties of
dignity, withholding, tact,
and sometimes even in myself, certain patiences I would have once called
lassitude, indifference,
5 now seem possibly to be if not the rewards then at least the unsuspected,
undreamed-of conclusions
to many of the even-then-preposterous self-evolved disciplines, rigors,
almost mortifications
I inflicted on myself in my starting-out days, improvement days, days
when the idea alone of psychic peace,
of intellectual, of emotional quiet, the merest hint, would have meant
inconceivable capitulation.

1987

Snow: II

It's very cold, Catherine is bundled in a coat, a poncho on top of that,
high boots, gloves,
a long scarf around her neck, and she's sauntering up the middle of the
snowed-in street,
eating, of all things, an apple, the blazing redness of which shocks against
the world of white.
No traffic yet, the *crisp crisp* of her footsteps keeps reaching me until she
turns the corner.
5 I write it down years later, and the picture still holds perfectly, precise,
unwanting,
and so too does the sense of being suddenly bereft as she passes abruptly
from my sight,
the quick wash of desolation, the release again into the memory of
affection, and then affection,
as the first trucks blundered past, chains pounding, the first delighted
children rushed out with sleds.

1987

The Question

The middle of the night, she's wide awake, carefully lying as far away as
    she can from him.
He turns in his sleep and she can sense him realizing she's not in the
    place she usually is,
then his sleep begins to change, he pulls himself closer, his arm comes
    comfortably around her.
"Are you awake?" she says, then, afraid that he might think she's asking
    him for sex,
5   she hurries on, "I want to know something; last summer, in Cleveland,
    did you have someone else?"
She'd almost said—she was going to say—"Did you have a *lover?*" but
    she'd caught herself;
she'd been frightened by the word, she realized; it was much too definite,
    at least for now.
Even so, it's only after pausing that he answers, "No," with what feeling
    she can't tell.
He moves his hand on her, then with a smile in his voice asks, "Did you
    have somebody in Cleveland?"
10   "That's not what I was asking you," she says crossly. "But that's what I
    asked *you*," he answers.
She's supposed to be content now, the old story, she knows that she's
    supposed to be relieved,
but she's not relieved, her tension hasn't eased the slightest bit, which
    doesn't surprise her.
She's so confused that she can't really even say now if she wants to believe
    him or not.
Anyway, what about that pause? Was it because in the middle of the night
    and six months later
15   he wouldn't have even known what she was talking about, or was it
    because he needed that moment
to frame an answer which would neutralize what might after all have
    been a shocking thrust
with a reasonable deflection, in this case, his humor: a laugh that's like a
    lie and is.
"When would I have found the time?" he might have said, or, "Who in
    Cleveland could I love?"
Or, in that so brief instant, might he have been finding a way to stay in
    the realm of truth,
20   as she knew he'd surely want to, given how self-righteously he esteemed
    his ethical integrities?
It comes to her with a start that what she most deeply and painfully
    suspects him of is a *renunciation.*
She knows that he has no one now; she thinks she knows there's been no
    contact from Cleveland,
but she still believes that there'd been something then, and if it was as
    important as she thinks,
it wouldn't be so easily forgotten, it would still be with him somewhere
    as a sad regret,
25   perhaps a precious memory, but with that word, renunciation, hooked to
    it like a price tag.

Maybe that was what so rankled her, that she might have been the object
    of his charity, his *goodness*.
That would be too much; that he would have wronged her, then
    sacrificed himself for her.
Yes, "Lover," she should have said it, "Lover, lover," should have made
    him try to disavow it.
She listens to his breathing; he's asleep again, or has he taught himself to
    feign that, too?
30   "No, last summer in Cleveland I didn't have a lover, I have never been
    to Cleveland, I love you.
There is no Cleveland, I adore you, and, as you'll remember, there was
    no last summer:
the world last summer didn't yet exist, last summer still was universal
    darkness, chaos, pain."

1992

TONY HARRISON

1937–

On Not Being Milton

for Sergio Vieira & Armando Guebuza (Frelimo)[1]

Read and committed to the flames, I call
these sixteen lines that go back to my roots
my *Cahier d'un retour au pays natal*,[2]
my growing black enough to fit my boots.

5   The stutter of the scold out of the branks[3]
of condescension, class and counter-class
thickens with glottals[4] to a lumpen mass
of Ludding[5] morphemes closing up their ranks.
Each swung cast-iron Enoch[6] of Leeds stress
10   clangs a forged music on the frames of Art,
the looms of owned language smashed apart!

Three cheers for mute ingloriousness![7]

1. Mozambique freedom-fighters.
2. "Notebook of a return to one's land of birth" (French). The title of a poem by the Martinican poet, historian, and politician Aimé Césaire. Published in 1939, *Cahier d'un retour au pays natal* is a seminal work in the literature of *négritude*, describing the condition of colonized black (in Césaire's case West Indian) people, and charting a literal and physical journey back from exile to the homeland.
3. "Bridles," or gagging devices put over the mouths of "scolds," people who habitually complain and nag. As the old northern word for poet is "scald," the line could refer to poets who speak out in defiance of the society that silences them, as well as to political agitators and revolutionaries.

4. Sounds made by opening and closing the larynx. The Leeds dialect uses glottal stops, the sound made when the word "butter" is pronounced as two syllables without an intervening "t."
5. The Luddites were reactionary groups opposed to the mechanization of mills and factories, a change that led to unemployment and starvation.
6. "An 'Enoch' is an iron sledge-hammer used by the Luddites to smash the frames which were also made by the same Enoch Taylor of Marsden. The cry was: 'Enoch made them, Enoch shall break them!' " [Tony Harrison's note].
7. A reference to Thomas Gray, "Elegy Written in a Country Churchyard," line 59: "Some mute inglorious Milton here may rest" (p. 611).

Articulation is the tongue-tied's fighting.
In the silence round all poetry we quote
15 Tidd the Cato Street conspirator[8] who wrote:

Sir, I Ham a very Bad Hand at Righting.

1978

Classics Society

(Leeds Grammar School 1552–1952)[9]

*The grace of Tullies eloquence doth excell
any Englishmans tongue . . . my barbarous stile . . .*[1]

The tongue our leaders use to cast their spell
was once denounced as "rude", "gross", "base" and "vile".

5 How fortunate we are who've come so far!

We boys can take old Hansards[2] and translate
the British Empire into SPQR[3]
but nothing demotic or too up-to-date,
and *not* the English that I speak at home,
10 not Hansard standards, and if Antoninus[4]
spoke like delinquent Latin back in Rome
he'd probably get gamma double minus.[5]

And so the lad who gets the alphas works
the hardest in his class at his translation
15 and finds good Ciceronian for Burke's:

a dreadful schism in the British nation.[6]

1978

8. An eighteenth-century plot to assassinate the British cabinet. The conspirators met in a loft on Cato Street, near London's Edgware Road.
9. Tony Harrison won a scholarship to Leeds Grammar School, a highly academic school for pupils aged eleven to eighteen, which was otherwise for fee-paying students.
1. A quotation from Robert Recorde's preface to his *The Grounde of Artes* (1543), a work that expresses the ethos of Leeds Grammar School in preferring the (now defunct) language of "Tully," Marcus Tullius Cicero, to contemporary English.
2. Printed reports of debates in the British Houses of Parliament.
3. *Senatus Populusque Romanus*: "the senate and people of Rome" (Latin).
4. A third-century Roman emperor. As Harrison's first name, Tony, has been wrongly taken to be a

diminutive of Anthony (see "Them & [uz]," p. 1766), this could be a humorous reference to an imaginary self in ancient Rome.
5. Marking in British schools and universities is often based on the Greek alphabet. Thus alpha would be A, beta B, and gamma double minus C − −, or fail.
6. Edmund Burke (1729–1797), an Irishman who became one of Britain's foremost political thinkers. His writings advocated a sound constitutional statesmanship in a time of misgovernment and corruption. Though he was against the concept of inalienable human rights, he supported the notion of the "social contract." He warned that the "dreadful schism" in British society could lead to revolution and regicide as in France, and called for the suppression of free opinions.

Them & [uz]

for Professors Richard Hoggart & Leon Cortez[7]

I

αἰαῖ, ay, ay! . . . stutterer Demosthenes[8]
gob full of pebbles outshouting seas—

4 words only of *mi 'art aches*[9] and . . . "Mine's broken,
you barbarian, T.W.!" [1] *He* was nicely spoken.
5   "Can't have our glorious heritage done to death!"

I played the Drunken Porter in *Macbeth.*

"Poetry's the speech of kings. You're one of those
Shakespeare gives the comic bits to: prose!
All poetry (even Cockney Keats?) you see
10   's been dubbed by [ʌs][2] into RP,
Received Pronunciation, please believe [ʌs]
your speech is in the hands of the Receivers."

"We say [ʌs] not [uz], T.W.!" That shut my trap.
I doffed my flat a's (as in "flat cap")
15   my mouth all stuffed with glottals,[3] great
lumps to hawk up and spit out . . . *E-nun-ci-ate!*

II

So right, yer buggers, then! We'll occupy
your lousy leasehold Poetry.

I chewed up Littererchewer and spat the bones
20   into the lap of dozing Daniel Jones,
dropped the initials I'd been harried as
and used my *name* and own voice: [uz] [uz] [uz],
ended sentences with by, with, from,
and spoke the language that I spoke at home.
25   RIP RP, RIP T.W.
I'm *Tony* Harrison no longer you!

You can tell the Receivers where to go
(and not aspirate it) once you know
Wordsworth's *matter / water* are full rhymes,
30   [uz] can be loving as well as funny.

---

7. Richard Hoggart is an academic and, like Tony
Harrison, from a working-class, north-of-England
background. "Professor" Leon Cortez was a music-
hall comedian, whose act included recitations of
Shakespeare's *Macbeth* in Cockney (working-class
London) English.
8. (385?–322 B.C.); an Athenian orator.
9. See John Keats, "Ode to a Nightingale," line 1
(p. 845). To the despair of his teacher, the young
Harrison, speaking the Leeds dialect, says "mi 'art"
instead of "my heart."

1. Harrison's first names are Tony William. His
first work was published under the name T. W.
Harrison.
2. Phonetic transcription representing the Re-
ceived pronunciation form of "us." The northern
dialect form is "uz."
3. Sounds made by opening and closing the lar-
ynx. The Leeds dialect uses glottal stops, the sound
made when the word "butter" is pronounced as
two syllables without an intervening "t."

My first mention in the *Times*[4]
automatically made Tony Anthony!

1978

A Kumquat for John Keats

Today I found the right fruit for my prime,
not orange, not tangelo, and not lime,
nor moon-like globes of grapefruit that now hang
outside our bedroom, nor tart lemon's tang
5   (though last year full of bile and self-defeat
I wanted to believe no life was sweet)
nor the tangible sunshine of the tangerine,
and no incongruous citrus ever seen
at greengrocers' in Newcastle or Leeds
10   mis-spelt by the spuds° and mud-caked swedes,°   potatoes / Swedish turnips
a fruit an older poet might substitute
for the grape John Keats thought fit to be Joy's fruit,
when, two years before he died, he tried to write
how Melancholy dwelled inside Delight,[5]
15   and if he'd known the citrus that I mean
that's not orange, lemon, lime or tangerine,
I'm pretty sure that Keats, though he had heard
"of candied apple, quince and plum and gourd"[6]
instead of "grape against the palate fine"[7]
20   would have, if he'd known it, plumped for mine,
this Eastern citrus scarcely cherry size
he'd bite just once and then apostrophize
and pen one stanza how the fruit had all
the qualities of fruit before the Fall,
25   but in the next few lines be forced to write
how Eve's apple tasted at the second bite,
and if John Keats had only lived to be,
because of extra years, in need like me,
at 42 he'd help me celebrate
30   that Micanopy[8] kumquat that I ate
whole, straight off the tree, sweet pulp and sour skin—
or was it sweet outside, and sour within?
For however many kumquats that I eat
I'm not sure if it's flesh or rind that's sweet,
35   and being a man of doubt at life's mid-way
I'd offer Keats some kumquats and I'd say:
You'll find that one part's sweet and one part's tart:
say where the sweetness or the sourness start.

I find I can't, as if one couldn't say
40   exactly where the night became the day,
which makes for me the kumquat taken whole

---

4. A London "quality" newspaper.
5. See John Keats, "Ode to a Nightingale," (pp. 845–47).
6. See John Keats, "The Eve of St. Agnes," line
265 (p. 839).
7. See John Keats, "Ode on Melancholy," line 28 (p. 847).
8. Place in southern Florida.

best fruit, and metaphor, to fit the soul
of one in Florida at 42 with Keats
crunching kumquats, thinking, as he eats
45   the flesh, the juice, the pith, the pips, the peel,
that this is how a full life ought to feel,
its perishable relish prick the tongue,
when the man who savours life 's no longer young,
the fruits that were his futures far behind.
50   Then it's the kumquat fruit expresses best
how days have darkness round them like a rind,
life has a skin of death that keeps its zest.

History, a life, the heart, the brain
flow to the taste buds and flow back again.
55   That decade or more past Keats's span
makes me an older not a wiser man,
who knows that it's too late for dying young,
but since youth leaves some sweetnesses unsung,
he's granted days and kumquats to express
60   Man's Being ripened by his Nothingness.
And it isn't just the gap of sixteen years,
a bigger crop of terrors, hopes and fears,
but a century of history on this earth
between John Keats's death and my own birth—
65   years like an open crater, gory, grim,
with bloody bubbles leering at the rim;[9]
a thing no bigger than an urn explodes
and ravishes all silence, and all odes,
Flora[1] asphyxiated by foul air
70   unknown to either Keats or Lemprière,[2]
dehydrated Naiads, Dryad[3] amputees
dragging themselves through slagscapes with no trees,
a shirt of Nessus fire that gnaws and eats[4]
children half the age of dying Keats . . .

75   Now were you twenty five or six years old
when that fevered brow at last grew cold?
I've got no books to hand to check the dates.
My grudging but glad spirit celebrates
that all I've got to hand 's the kumquats, John,
80   the fruit I'd love to have your verdict on,
but dead men don't eat kumquats, or drink wine,
they shiver in the arms of Proserpine,[5]
not warm in bed beside their Fanny Brawne,[6]
nor watch her pick ripe grapefruit in the dawn
85   as I did, waking, when I saw her twist,
with one deft movement of a sunburnt wrist,
the moon, that feebly lit our last night's walk

---

9. See Keats, "Ode to a Nightingale," line 17 (p. 845).
1. Roman goddess of flowers.
2. Eighteenth-century author of *The Classical Dictionary*—for many years a standard work.

3. Wood nymph; "Naiads": water nymphs.
4. A magical shirt that once donned cannot be removed and that consumes the wearer in flames.
5. Queen of the underworld.
6. A young woman loved by John Keats.

past alligator swampland, off its stalk.
I thought of moon-juice juleps[7] when I saw,
90   as if I'd never seen the moon before,
the planet glow among the fruit, and its pale light
make each citrus on the tree its satellite.

Each evening when I reach to draw the blind
stars seem the light zest squeezed through night's black rind;
95   the night's peeled fruit the sun, juiced of its rays,
first stains, then streaks, then floods the world with days,
days, when the very sunlight made me weep,
days, spent like the nights in deep, drugged sleep,
days in Newcastle by my daughter's bed,
100 wondering if she, or I, weren't better dead,
days in Leeds, grey days, my first dark suit,
my mother's wreaths stacked next to Christmas fruit,
and days, like this in Micanopy. Days!

As strong sun burns away the dawn's grey haze
105 I pick a kumquat and the branches spray
cold dew in my face to start the day.
The dawn's molasses make the citrus gleam
still in the orchards of the groves of dream.

The limes, like Galway after weeks of rain,
110 glow with a greenness that is close to pain,
the dew-cooled surfaces of fruit that spent
all last night flaming in the firmament.
The new day dawns. O days! My spirit greets
the kumquat with the spirit of John Keats.
115 O kumquat, comfort for not dying young,
both sweet and bitter, bless the poet's tongue!
I burst the whole fruit chilled by morning dew
against my palate. Fine, for 42!

I search for buzzards as the air grows clear
120 and see them ride fresh thermals overhead.
Their bleak cries were the first sound I could hear
when I stepped at the start of sunrise out of doors,
and a noise like last night's bedsprings on our bed
from Mr Fowler sharpening farmers' saws.

1981

The Heartless Art

in memoriam S.T., died 4 April 1985

Death is in your house, but I'm out here
sackclothing kumquats against the forecast freeze,
filling the hole you took two days to clear
of briars, beercans, and bleached, barkless trees,
5   with hackberry leaves, pine needles, stuff like that.

---

7. Drinks made from spirits, sugar, ice, and mint.

Next spring, when you're no longer here
we'll have the land grassed over and quite flat.

When the Southern sun starts setting it sets fast.
I've time to tip one more load if I run.
10 Because I know this light could be your last
I drain the day of every drop of sun.
The barrow wheel spins round with a clock's tick.
I hear, three fields away, a hunter's gun,
you, in the silence after, being sick.

15 I watched you, very weak, negotiate
the childproof pill jar, panting to draw breath,
and when you managed it you poured your hate
more on the poured-out contents than on death,
and, like Baptists uttering Beelzebub
20 syllable by syllable, spat *Meth-
a-done*, and there's also the poetic rub!

I've often heard my fellow poets (or those
who write in metres something like my own
with rhyme and rhythm, not in chopped-up prose
25 and brood on man's mortality) bemoan
the insufficiency of rhymes for death—
hence my syllabifying *Methadone*
instead of just saying that you fought for breath.

Maybe the main but not the only cause;
30 a piece of engineering I'll explain
Each syllable *was* followed by a pause
for breathlessness, and scorn of drugs for pain.
Another reason, though, was to delay
the use of one more rhyme stored in my brain
35 that, alas, I'll have a use for any day.

I'd stored away this rhyme when we first met.
Knowing you crawled on hands and knees to prime
our water pump, I'll expiate one debt
by finally revealing that stored rhyme
40 that has the same relentlessness as death
and comes to every one of us in time
and comes to you this April full moon, SETH!

In return for all those oily working parts
you took the time and trouble to explain,
45 the pump that coughs, the saw that never starts,
I'll show you to distract you from the pain
you feel, except when napping, all the time
because you won't take drugs that dull the brain,
a bit about my metre, line and rhyme.

50 In Arthur Symons' *St Teresa* Nazaréth
is stressed on the last against its spoken flow

to engineer the contrast Jesus/Death.
Do I endorse that contrast? I don't, no!
To have a life on Earth and then want Heaven
55 seems like that all-night bar sign down below
that says that *Happy Hour's* from 4 to 7.

Package lounges are like ambulances:
the Bourbon-bibber stares at us and glowers
at what he thinks are pained or pitying glances.
60 We don't see his face but he sees ours.
The non-dying don't see you but you see them
passing by to other rooms with flowers
as you fill the shining kidney with red phlegm.

I've left some spaces (   )[8]
65 benumbed by morphia and *Methadone*
until the (   )[9] of April, (   )[1]
When I began these lines could I have known
that the nurse's registration of the time
you let your spirit go with one last groan
70 would help complete the first and third line rhyme?

Those bits I added later. Them apart
I wrote this *in memoriam* for Seth,
meant to show him something of my art,
almost a whole week before his death.
75 The last thing the dying want to read,
I thought, 's a poem, and didn't show it,
and you, not dying yet, why should you need
to know the final failure of the poet?

1985

ELEANOR WILNER

1937–

Reading the Bible Backwards[1]

All around the altar, huge lianas
curled, unfurled the dark green
of their leaves to complement the red
of blood spilled there—a kind of Christmas
5 decoration, overhung with heavy vines
and over them, the stars.
When the angels came, messengers like birds
but with the oiled flesh of men, they hung
over the scene with smoldering swords,[2]

8. "how you stayed alive" [Harrison's note].
9. "4th" [Harrison's note].
1. "10.05" [Harrison's note].
1. Or from the Apocalypse in Revelation, the final book of the New Testament, to the Creation in

Genesis, the first book of the Old Testament. Wilner fuses details from both testaments throughout the poem.
2. Suggests the flaming sword of the cherubim stationed east of the Garden of Eden (Genesis 3.24).

10   splashing the world when they beat
       their rain-soaked wings against the turning sky.

       The child was bright in his basket[3]
       as a lemon, with a bitter smell from his wet
       swaddling clothes. His mother bent
15   above him, singing a lullaby
       in the liquid tongue invented
       for the very young—short syllables
       like dripping from an eave
       mixed with the first big drops of rain
20   that fell, like tiny silver pears, from
       the glistening fronds of palm. The three
       who gathered there—old kings uncrowned:
       the cockroach, condor and the leopard, lords
       of the cracks below the ground, the mountain
25   pass and the grass-grown plain, were not
       adorned, did not bear gifts, had not
       come to adore; they were simply drawn
       to gawk at this recurrent, awkward son
       whom the wind had said would spell
30   the end of earth as it had been.

       Somewhere north of this familiar scene
       the polar caps were melting, the water was
       advancing in its slow, relentless
       lines, swallowing the old
35   landmarks, swelling the seas that pulled
       the flowers and the great steel cities down.
       The dolphins sport in the rising sea,
       anemones wave their many arms like hair
       on a drowned gorgon's head,[4] her features
40   softened by the sea beyond all recognition.

       On the desert's edge where the oasis dies
       in a wash of sand, the sphinx[5] seems to shift
       on her haunches of stone, and the rain, as it runs down,
       completes the ruin of her face. The Nile
45   merges with the sea, the waters rise
       and drown the noise of earth. At the forest's
       edge, where the child sleeps, the waters gather—
       as if a hand were reaching for the curtain
       to drop across the glowing, lit tableau.

50   When the waves closed over, completing the green
       sweep of ocean, there was no time for mourning.
       No final trump,[6] no thunder to announce

---

3. Moses' mother hid him in a covered wicker basket, which she set in reeds by the Nile, to protect him from Pharoah's command to cast all sons into the river (Exodus 2.2–3). The lines following return to Christ's nativity and the gifts brought to him by the Three Wise Men (Matthew 2.1–12).
4. The water imagery suggests both the flood from which Noah escaped in the ark (Genesis 7) and the end of the Ice Age. The Gorgons of classical myth were three sisters who had snakes for hair.
5. Wilner's sphinx evokes not the Egyptian but the Greek model, a winged creature with a woman's head and lion's body.
6. The final trumpet; image of the last judgment.

the silent steal of waters; how soundlessly
it all went under: the little family
55   and the scene so easily mistaken
for an adoration. Above, more clouds poured in
and closed their ranks across the skies;
the angels, who had seemed so solid, turned
quicksilver in the rain.
60   Now, nothing but the wind
moves on the rain-pocked face
of the swollen waters, though far below
where giant squid lie hidden in shy tangles,
the whales, heavy-bodied as the angels,
65   their fins like vestiges of wings,
sing some mighty epic of their own—
a great day when the ships would all withdraw,
the harpoons fail of their aim, the land
dissolve into the waters, and they would swim
70   among the peaks of mountains, like eagles
of the deep, while far below them, the old
nightmares of earth would settle
into silt among the broken cities, the empty
basket of the child would float
75   abandoned in the seaweed until the work of water
unraveled it in filaments of straw,
till even that straw rotted
in the planetary thaw the whales prayed for,
sending their jets of water skyward
80   in the clear conviction they'd spill back
to ocean with their will accomplished
in the miracle of rain: *And the earth
was without form and void, and darkness
was upon the face of the deep. And*
85   *the Spirit moved upon the face of the waters.*[7]

High Noon at Los Alamos[8]

To turn a stone
with its white squirming
underneath, to pry the disc
from the sun's eclipse—white heat
5   coiling in the blinded eye: to these malign
necessities we come
from the dim time of dinosaurs
who crawled like breathing lava
from the earth's cracked crust, and swung
10   their tiny heads above the lumbering tons
of flesh, brains no bigger than a fist
clenched to resist the white flash
in the sky the day the sun-flares
pared them down to relics for museums,

---

7. Direct quotation from Genesis 1.2.
8. Los Alamos, New Mexico; a major site of the   Manhattan Project to develop an atomic bomb (1942–45).

15 turned glaciers back, seared Sinai's
    meadows[9] black—the ferns withered, the swamps
    were melted down to molten mud, the cells
    uncoupled, recombined, and madly
    multiplied, huge trees toppled to the ground,
20 the slow life there abandoned hope,
    a caterpillar stiffened in the grass.
    Two apes, caught in the act of coupling,
    made a mutant child
    who woke to sunlight wondering, his mother
25 torn by the huge new head
    that forced the narrow birth canal.[1]

    As if compelled to repetition
    and to unearth again
    white fire at the heart of matter—fire
30 we sought and fire we spoke,
    our thoughts, however elegant, were fire
    from first to last—like sentries set to watch
    at Argos for the signal fire
    passed peak to peak from Troy
35 to Nagasaki,[2] triumphant echo of the burning
    city walls and prologue to the murders
    yet to come—we scan the sky
    for that bright flash,
    our eyes stared white from watching
40 for the signal fire that ends
    the epic—a cursèd line
    with its caesura, a pause
    to signal peace, or a rehearsal
    for the silence.

1989

DOM MORAES

1938–

Kanheri Caves

Over these blunted, these tormented hills,
Hawks hail and wheel, glissading down the sky:
It seems this green ambiguous landscape tilts
And teeters the perspective of the eye.
5 Only two centuries after Christ, this cliff

9. In the Sinai Peninsula, a triangular region linking Africa with Asia.
1. The effects of extreme radiation can include gene mutation.
2. Japanese city, site of the second atomic bomb explosion in 1945. Lines 32–34 refer to the beginning of *Agamemnon*, the first play in the *Oresteia*

trilogy by Aeschylus (524?–456 B.C.). The play opens with a watchman in Argos—a city on the lower peninsula of Greece, and the home of Agamemnon—looking for "the light, the signal-fire / breaking out of Troy" (i.e., signalling Greek victory in the Trojan War).

Was colonized by a mild antique race,
Who left us, like a faded photograph,
Their memories that dry up in this place.

They left no ghosts. The rock alone endures.
10   Their drains and cisterns work: storms wrecked the stairs:
Blocks are fallen: sunlight cracks those floors
And fidgets in a courtyard where a pair
Of giant Buddhas smile and wait their crash;
Then temples, audience-halls, a lonely tomb.
15   I touch its side. The stone's worn smooth as flesh.
A stranger dangles peaceful in that womb.

Worm he will be, if born: blink in the sun.
I'll crawl into his dark: perhaps he'll climb
Beyond the trippers to the final stone
20   Flat of the hillock, there to grow in Time.
Dry pubic ferns prickle the bitter sand.
Hawks in a hot concentric ecstasy
Of flight and shriek will wake his vision. And,
When the clouds lift, he'll glimpse the miles-off sea.

1957

Snow on a Mountain

That dream, her eyes like rocks studded the high
Mountain of her body that I was to climb.
One moment past my hands had swum
The chanting streams of her thighs:
5   Then I was lost, breathless among the pines.

Alone, alone with the nervous noise of water,
Climbing, I hoped to emerge on a path, but I knew
When the spurred trees were past
I should go on no farther
10   But fall there, dazzled by the miles of snow.

My dream was broken by the knock of day.
Yet, within my mind, these pictures linger:
I touch her with my clumsy words of love
And sense snow in her eye,
15   Mists, and the winds that warn, Stranger, O stranger!

1957

From Two from Israel

Rendezvous

(FOR NATHAN ALTERMANN)

Altermann, sipping wine, reads with a look
Of infinite patience and slight suffering.
When I approach him, he puts down his book,

Waves to the chair beside him like a king,
5   Then claps his hands, and an awed waiter fetches
Bread, kosher sausage, cake, a chicken's wing,

More wine, some English cigarettes, and matches.
"Eat, eat," Altermann says, "this is good food."
Through the awning over us the sunlight catches

10   His aquiline sad head, till it seems hewed
From tombstone marble. I accept some bread.
I've lunched already, but would not seem rude.

When I refuse more, he feeds me instead,
Heaping my plate, clapping for wine, his eyes
15   —Expressionless inside the marble head—

Appearing not to notice how the flies
Form a black, sticky icing on the cake.
Thinking of my health now, I visualise

The Aryan snow floating, flake upon flake,
20   Over the ghetto wall where only fleas
Fed well, and they and hunger kept awake

Under sharp stars, those waiting for release.
Birds had their nests, but Jews nowhere to hide
When visited by vans and black police.

25   The shekinah° rose where a people died,   *divine presence*
A pillar of flame by night, of smoke by day.
From Europe then the starved and terrified

Flew. Now their mourner sits in this café,
Telling me how to scan a Hebrew line.
30   Though my attention has moved far away

His features stay marble and aquiline.
But the eternal gesture of his race
Flowing through the hands that offer bread and wine

Reveals the deep love sealed in the still face.

                                                                                  1965

LES MURRAY

1938–

Noonday Axeman

Axe-fall, echo and silence. Noonday silence.
Two miles from here, it is the twentieth century:

cars on the bitumen,[1] powerlines vaulting the farms.
Here, with my axe, I am chopping into the stillness.

5 Axe-fall, echo and silence. I pause, roll tobacco,
twist a cigarette, lick it. All is still.
I lean on my axe. A cloud of fragrant leaves
hangs over me moveless, pierced everywhere by sky.

Here, I remember all of a hundred years:
10 candleflame, still night, frost and cattle bells,
the draywheels'[2] silence final in our ears,
and the first red cattle spreading through the hills

and my great-great-grandfather here with his first sons,
who would grow old, still speaking with his Scots accent,
15 having never seen those highlands that they sang of.
A hundred years. I stand and smoke in the silence.

A hundred years of clearing, splitting, sawing,
a hundred years of timbermen, ringbarkers, fencers
and women in kitchens, stoking loud iron stoves
20 year in, year out, and singing old songs to their children

have made this silence human and familiar
no farther than where the farms rise into foothills,
and, in that time, how many have sought their graves
or fled to the cities, maddened by this stillness?

25 Things are so wordless. These two opposing scarves
I have cut in my red-gum squeeze out jewels of sap
and stare. And soon, with a few more axe-strokes,
the tree will grow troubled, tremble, shift its crown

and, leaning slowly, gather speed and colossally
30 crash down and lie between the standing trunks.
And then, I know, of the knowledge that led my forebears
to drink and black rage and wordlessness, there will be silence.

After the tree falls, there will reign the same silence
as stuns and spurs us, enraptures and defeats us,
35 as seems to some a challenge, and seems to others
to be waiting here for something beyond imagining.

Axe-fall, echo and silence. Unhuman silence.
A stone cracks in the heat. Through the still twigs, radiance
stings at my eyes. I rub a damp brow with a handkerchief
40 and chop on into the stillness. Axe-fall and echo.

The great mast murmurs now. The scarves in its trunk
crackle and squeak now, crack and increase as the hushing

---

1. Name given to various inflammable mineral   2. Wheels of a long, heavy cart.
substances, here probably asphalt.

weight of high branches heels outward, and commences
tearing and falling, and the collapse is tremendous.

45 Twigs fly, leaves puff and subside. The severed trunk
slips off its stump and drops along its shadow.
And then there is no more. The stillness is there
as ever. And I fall to lopping branches.

Axe-fall, echo and silence. It will be centuries
50 before many men are truly at home in this country,
and yet, there have always been some, in each generation,
there have always been some who could live in the presence of
silence.

And some, I have known them, men with gentle broad hands,
who would die if removed from these unpeopled places,
55 some again I have seen, bemused and shy in the cities,
you have built against silence, dumbly trudging through noise

past the railway stations, looking up through the traffic
at the smoky halls, dreaming of journeys, of stepping
down from the train at some upland stop to recover
60 the crush of dry grass underfoot, the silence of trees.

Axe-fall, echo and silence. Dreaming silence.
Though I myself run to the cities, I will forever
be coming back here to walk, knee-deep in ferns,
up and away from this metropolitan century,

65 to remember my ancestors, axemen, dairymen, horse-breakers,
now coffined in silence, down with their beards and dreams,
who, unwilling or rapt, despairing or very patient,
made what amounts to a human breach in the silence,

made of their lives the rough foundation of legends—
70 men must have legends, else they will die of strangeness—
then died in their turn, each, after his own fashion,
resigned or agonized, from silence into great silence.

Axe-fall, echo and axe-fall. Noonday silence.
Though I go to the cities, turning my back on these hills,
75 for the talk and dazzle of cities, for the sake of belonging
for months and years at a time to the twentieth century,

the city will never quite hold me. I will be always
coming back here on the up-train, peering, leaning
out of the window to see, on far-off ridges,
80 the sky between the trees, and over the racket
of the rails to hear the echo and the silence.

I shoulder my axe and set off home through the stillness.

1965

Once in a Lifetime, Snow

For Chris and Mary Sharah

Winters at home brought wind,
black frost and raw
grey rain in barbed-wire fields,
but never more

5　until the day my uncle
rose at dawn
and stepped outside—to find
his paddocks gone,

his cattle to their hocks
10　in ghostly ground
and unaccustomed light
for miles around.

And he stopped short, and gazed
lit from below,
15　and half his wrinkles vanished
murmuring *Snow.*

A man of farm and fact
he stared to see
the facts of weather raised
20　to a mystery

white on the world he knew
and all he owned.
Snow? Here? he mused. I see.
High time I learned.

25　Here, guessing what he meant
had much to do
with that black earth dread old men
are given to,

he stooped to break the sheer
30　crust with delight
at finding the cold unknown
so deeply bright,

at feeling it take his prints
so softly deep,
35　as if it thought he knew
enough to sleep,

or else so little he
might seek to shift
its weight of wintry light
40　by a single drift,

perceiving this much, he scuffed
his slippered feet
and scooped a handful up
to taste, and eat

45   in memory of the fact
that even he
might not have seen the end
of reality . . .

Then, turning, he tiptoed in
50   to a bedroom, smiled,
and wakened a murmuring child
and another child.

1969

The Quality of Sprawl

Sprawl is the quality
of the man who cut down his Rolls-Royce
into a farm utility truck, and sprawl
is what the company lacked when it made repeated efforts
5   to buy the vehicle back and repair its image.

Sprawl is doing your farming by aeroplane, roughly,
or driving a hitchhiker that extra hundred miles home.
It is the rococo[3] of being your own still centre.
It is never lighting cigars with ten-dollar notes:
10   that's idiot ostentation and murder of starving people.
Nor can it be bought with the ash of million-dollar deeds.

Sprawl lengthens the legs; it trains greyhounds on liver and beer.
Sprawl almost never says Why not? with palms comically raised
nor can it be dressed for, not even in running shoes worn
15   with mink and a nose ring. That is Society. That's Style.
Sprawl is more like the thirteenth banana in a dozen
or anyway the fourteenth.

Sprawl is Hank Stamper in *Never Give an Inch*
bisecting an obstructive official's desk with a chainsaw.
20   Not harming the official. Sprawl is never brutal
though it's often intransigent. Sprawl is never Simon de Montfort[4]
at a town-storming: Kill them all! God will know his own.
Knowing the man's name this was said to might be sprawl.

Sprawl occurs in art. The fifteenth to twenty-first
25   lines in a sonnet, for example. And in certain paintings;
I have sprawl enough to have forgotten which paintings.
Turner's glorious *Burning of the Houses of Parliament*[5]

3. Style of architecture, decoration, and furniture prevalent in Louis XV's France. Characteristically, asymmetrical, overornamented, and florid.
4. Thirteenth-century earl of Leicester. Leader of the barons in disaffection against Henry III. Arche-
typal "overmighty subject."
5. Famous landscape by the English artist Joseph Mallord William Turner (1775–1851), whose painting, in watercolor and, later, oil, foreshadowed impressionism.

comes to mind, a doubling bannered triumph of sprawl —
except, he didn't fire them.

30 Sprawl gets up the nose of many kinds of people
(every kind that comes in kinds) whose futures don't include it.
Some decry it as criminal presumption, silken-robed Pope Alexander[6]
dividing the new world between Spain and Portugal.
If he smiled *in petto*[7] afterwards, perhaps the thing did have sprawl.

35 Sprawl is really classless, though. It's John Christopher Frederick Murray
asleep in his neighbours' best bed in spurs and oilskins
but not having thrown up:
sprawl is never Calum who, drunk, along the hallways of our house,
reinvented the Festoon. Rather
40 it's Beatrice Miles going twelve hundred ditto in a taxi,
No Lewd Advances, No Hitting Animals, No Speeding,
on the proceeds of her two-bob-a-sonnet Shakespeare readings.
An image of my country. And would that it were more so.

No, sprawl is full-gloss murals on a council-house wall.
45 Sprawl leans on things. It is loose-limbed in its mind.
Reprimanded and dismissed
it listens with a grin and one boot up on the rail
of possibility. It may have to leave the Earth.
Being roughly Christian, it scratches the other cheek
50 and thinks it unlikely. Though people have been shot for sprawl.

                                                            1983

Morse

Tuckett. Bill Tuckett. Telegraph operator, Hall's Creek,
which is way out back of the Outback, but he stuck it,
quite likely liked it, despite heat, glare, dust and the lack
of diversion or doctors. Come disaster you trusted to luck,
5 ingenuity and pluck. This was back when nice people said pluck,
the sleevelink and green eyeshade epoch.
                        Faced, though, like Bill Tuckett
with a man needing surgery right on the spot, a lot
would have done their dashes. It looked hopeless (dot dot dot)
10 Lift him up on the table, said Tuckett, running the key hot
till Head Office turned up a doctor who coolly instructed
up a thousand miles of wire, as Tuckett advanced slit by slit
with a safety razor blade, pioneering on into the wet,
copper-wiring the rivers off, in the first operation conducted
15 along dotted lines, with rum drinkers gripping the patient:
d-d-dash it, take care, Tuck!
                        And the vital spark stayed unshorted.
Yallah! breathed the camelmen. Tuckett, you did it, you did it!
cried the spattered la-de-dah jodhpur-wearing Inspector of Stock.

---

6. Eight popes took the name Alexander. Possibly
Alexander VI, Rodrigo Borgia (1431–1503), father
of Caesar, Lucretia, and other children. He
secured the papal throne through blatant bribery.
7. "To himself" (Italian).

20 We imagine, some weeks later, a properly laconic
convalescent averring Without you, I'd have kicked the bucket . . .

From Chungking to Burrenjuck, morse keys have mostly gone silent
and only old men meet now to chit-chat in their electric
bygone dialect. The last letter many will forget
25 is dit-dit-dit-dah, V for Victory. The coders' hero had speed,
resource and a touch. So ditditdit daah for Bill Tuckett.

1983

CHARLES SIMIC
1938–

Watch Repair

A small wheel
Incandescent,
Shivering like
A pinned butterfly.

5 Hands
Pointing in all directions:
The crossroads
One enters
In a nightmare.

10 Higher than anyone
Number 12 presides
Like a beekeeper
Over the swarming honeycomb
Of the open watch.

15 —Other wheels
That could fit
Inside a raindrop,

Tools
That must be splinters
20 Of arctic starlight . . .

Tiny golden mills
Grinding invisible
Coffee beans.

When the coffee's boiling,
25 Cautiously,
So it doesn't burn us,

We raise it
To the lips
Of the nearest
30 Ear.

1974

A Book Full of Pictures

Father studied theology through the mail
And this was exam time.
Mother knitted. I sat quietly with a book
Full of pictures. Night fell.
5   My hands grew cold touching the faces
Of dead kings and queens.

There was a black raincoat
   in the upstairs bedroom
Swaying from the ceiling,
10   But what was it doing there?
Mother's long needles made quick crosses.
They were black
Like the inside of my head just then.

The pages I turned sounded like wings.
15   "The soul is a bird," he once said.
In my book full of pictures
A battle raged: lances and swords
Made a kind of wintry forest
With my heart spiked and bleeding in its branches.

1992

MARGARET ATWOOD

1939–

This Is a Photograph of Me

It was taken some time ago.
At first it seems to be
a smeared
print: blurred lines and gray flecks
5   blended with the paper;

then, as you scan
it, you see in the left-hand corner
a thing that is like a branch: part of a tree
(balsam or spruce) emerging
10   and, to the right, halfway up
what ought to be a gentle
slope, a small frame house.

In the background there is a lake,
and beyond that, some low hills.

15   (The photograph was taken
the day after I drowned.

I am in the lake, in the center
of the picture, just under the surface.

It is difficult to say where
20   precisely, or to say
how large or small I am:

the effect of water
on light is a distortion

but if you look long enough,
25   eventually
you will be able to see me.)

1966

At the Tourist Center in Boston

There is my country under glass,
a white relief-
map with red dots for the cities,
reduced to the size of a wall

5   and beside it 10 blownup snapshots
one for each province,
in purple-browns and odd reds,
the green of the trees dulled;
all blues however
10   of an assertive purity.

Mountains and lakes and more lakes
(though Quebec is a restaurant and Ontario the empty
interior of the parliament buildings),
with nobody climbing the trails and hauling out
15   the fish and splashing in the water

but arrangements of grinning tourists —
look here, Saskatchewan
is a flat lake, some convenient rocks
where two children pose with a father
20   and the mother is cooking something
in immaculate slacks by a smokeless fire,
her teeth white as detergent.

Whose dream is this, I would like to know:
is this a manufactured
25   hallucination, a cynical fiction, a lure
for export only?

I seem to remember people,
at least in the cities, also slush,
machines and assorted garbage. Perhaps
30   that was my private mirage

which will just evaporate
when I go back. Or the citizens will be gone,
run off to the peculiarly-
green forests
35   to wait among the brownish mountains
for the platoons of tourists
and plan their odd red massacres.

Unsuspecting
window lady, I ask you:

40   Do you see nothing
watching you from under the water?

Was the sky ever that blue?

Who really lives there?

                          1968

You Begin

You begin this way:
this is your hand,
this is your eye,
that is a fish, blue and flat
5   on the paper, almost
the shape of an eye.
This is your mouth, this is an O
or a moon, whichever
you like. This is yellow.

10   Outside the window
is the rain, green
because it is summer, and beyond that
the trees and then the world,
which is round and has only
15   the colors of these nine crayons.

This is the world, which is fuller
and more difficult to learn than I have said.
You are right to smudge it that way
with the red and then
20   the orange: the world burns.

Once you have learned these words
you will learn that there are more
words than you can ever learn.
The word *hand* floats above your hand
25   like a small cloud over a lake.
The word *hand* anchors
your hand to this table,
your hand is a warm stone
I hold between two words.

30 This is your hand, these are my hands, this is the world,
which is round but not flat and has more colors
than we can see.

It begins, it has an end,
this is what you will
35 come back to, this is your hand.

1978

Flowers

Right now I am the flower girl.
I bring fresh flowers,
dump out the old ones, the greenish water
that smells like dirty teeth
5 into the bathroom sink, snip off the stem ends
with surgical scissors I borrowed
from the nursing station,
put them into a jar
I brought from home, because they don't have vases
10 in this hotel for the ill,
place them on the table beside my father
where he can't see them
because he won't open his eyes.

He lies flattened under the white sheet.
15 He says he is on a ship,
and I can see it—
the functional white walls, the minimal windows,
the little bells, the rubbery footsteps of strangers,
the whispering all around
20 of the air-conditioner, or else the ocean,
and he is on a ship;
he's giving us up, giving up everything
but the breath going in
and out of his diminished body;
25 minute by minute he's sailing slowly away,
away from us and our waving hands
that do not wave.

The women come in, two of them, in blue;
it's no use being kind, in here,
30 if you don't have hands like theirs—
large and capable, the hands
of plump muscular angels,
the ones that blow trumpets and lift swords.
They shift him carefully, tuck in the corners.
35 It hurts, but as little as possible.
Pain is their lore. The rest of us
are helpless amateurs.

A suffering you can neither cure nor enter—
there are worse things, but not many.
40 After a while it makes us impatient.
Can't we do anything but feel sorry?

I sit there, watching the flowers
in their pickle jar. He is asleep, or not.
I think: He looks like a turtle.
45 Or: He looks erased.
But somewhere in there, at the far end of the tunnel
of pain and forgetting he's trapped in
is the same father I knew before,
the one who carried the green canoe
50 over the portage, the painter trailing,
myself with the fishing rods, slipping
on the wet boulders and slapping flies.
That was the last time we went there.

There will be a last time for this also,
55 bringing cut flowers to this white room.
Sooner or later I too
will have to give everything up,
even the sorrow that comes with these flowers,
even the anger,
60 even the memory of how I brought them
from a garden I will no longer have by then,
and put them beside my dying father,
hoping I could still save him.

1995

Up

You wake up filled with dread.
There seems no reason for it.
Morning light sifts through the window,
there is birdsong,
5 you can't get out of bed.

It's something about the crumpled sheets
hanging over the edge like jungle
foliage, the terry slippers gaping
their dark pink mouths for your feet,
10 the unseen breakfast—some of it
in the refrigerator you do not dare
to open—you will not dare to eat.

What prevents you? The future. The future tense,
immense as outer space.
15 You could get lost there.
No. Nothing so simple. The past, its density
and drowned events pressing you down,
like sea water, like gelatin
filling your lungs instead of air.

20   Forget all that and let's get up.
     Try moving your arm.
     Try moving your head.
     Pretend the house is on fire
     and you must run or burn.
25   No, that one's useless.
     It's never worked before.

     Where is it coming from, this echo,
     this huge No that surrounds you,
     silent as the folds of the yellow
30   curtains, mute as the cheerful

     Mexican bowl with its cargo
     of mummified flowers?
     (You chose the colours of the sun,
     not the dried neutrals of shadow.
35   God knows you've tried.)

     Now here's a good one:
     you're lying on your deathbed.
     You have one hour to live.
     Who is it, exactly, you have needed
40   all these years to forgive?

1995

SEAMUS HEANEY

1939–

Digging

Between my finger and my thumb
The squat pen rests; snug as a gun.

Under my window, a clean rasping sound
When the spade sinks into gravelly ground:
5   My father, digging. I look down

Till his straining rump among the flowerbeds
Bends low, comes up twenty years away
Stooping in rhythm through potato drills[1]
Where he was digging.

---

1. Small furrows in which seeds are sown.

10   The coarse boot nestled on the lug, the shaft
Against the inside knee was levered firmly.
He rooted out tall tops, buried the bright edge deep
To scatter new potatoes that we picked
Loving their cool hardness in our hands.

15   By god, the old man could handle a spade.
Just like his old man.

My grandfather cut more turf[2] in a day
Than any other man on Toner's bog.
Once I carried him milk in a bottle
20   Corked sloppily with paper. He straightened up
To drink it, then fell to right away
Nicking and slicing neatly, heaving sods
Over his shoulder, going down and down
For the good turf. Digging.

25   The cold smell of potato mould, the squelch and slap
Of soggy peat, the curt cuts of an edge
Through living roots awaken in my head.
But I've no spade to follow men like them.

Between my finger and my thumb
30   The squat pen rests.
I'll dig with it.

1966

The Forge

All I know is a door into the dark.
Outside, old axles and iron hoops rusting;
Inside, the hammered anvil's short-pitched ring,
The unpredictable fantail of sparks
5   Or hiss when a new shoe toughens in water.
The anvil must be somewhere in the centre,
Horned as a unicorn, at one end square,
Set there immoveable: an altar
Where he expends himself in shape and music.
10   Sometimes, leather-aproned, hairs in his nose,
He leans out on the jamb, recalls a clatter
Of hoofs where traffic is flashing in rows;
Then grunts and goes in, with a slam and flick
To beat real iron out, to work the bellows.

1969

---

2. Slabs of peat that, when dried, are a common domestic fuel in Ireland.

Punishment[3]

I can feel the tug
of the halter at the nape
of her neck, the wind
on her naked front.

5 It blows her nipples
to amber beads,
it shakes the frail rigging
of her ribs.

I can see her drowned
10 body in the bog,
the weighing stone,
the floating rods and boughs.

Under which at first
she was a barked sapling
15 that is dug up
oak-bone, brain-firkin:[4]

her shaved head
like a stubble of black corn,
her blindfold a soiled bandage,
20 her noose a ring

to store
the memories of love.
Little adulteress,
before they punished you

25 you were flaxen-haired,
undernourished, and your
tar-black face was beautiful.
My poor scapegoat,

I almost love you
30 but would have cast, I know,
the stones of silence.
I am the artful voyeur

---

3. In 1951 the peat-stained body of a young girl, who lived in the late first century A.D., was recovered from a bog in Windeby, Germany. As P. V. Glob describes her in *The Bog People*, she "lay naked in the hole in the peat, a bandage over the eyes and a collar round the neck. The band across the eyes was drawn tight and had cut into the neck and the base of the nose. We may feel sure that it had been used to close her eyes to this world. There was no mark of strangulation on the neck, so that it had not been used for that purpose." Her hair "had been shaved off with a razor on the left side of the head. . . . When the brain was removed the convolutions and folds of the surface could be clearly seen [Glob reproduces a photograph of her brain]. . . . This girl of only fourteen had had an inadequate winter diet. . . . To keep the young body under, some birch branches and a big stone were laid upon her." According to the Roman historian Tacitus, the Germanic peoples punished adulterous women by shaving off their hair and then scourging them out of the village or killing them. In recent years, her "betraying sisters" have sometimes been shaved, stripped, tarred, and handcuffed by the IRA to the railings of Belfast in punishment for keeping company with British soldiers.
4. A small wooden cask or vessel.

of your brain's exposed
and darkened combs,
35   your muscles' webbing
and all your numbered bones:

I who have stood dumb
when your betraying sisters,
cauled[5] in tar,
40   wept by the railings,

who would connive
in civilized outrage
yet understand the exact
and tribal, intimate revenge.

1975

The Skunk

Up, black, striped and damasked like the chasuble[6]
At a funeral mass, the skunk's tail
Paraded the skunk. Night after night
I expected her like a visitor.

5   The refrigerator whinnied into silence.
My desk light softened beyond the verandah.
Small oranges loomed in the orange tree.
I began to be tense as a voyeur.

After eleven years I was composing
10   Love-letters again, broaching the word "wife"
Like a stored cask, as if its slender vowel
Had mutated into the night earth and air

Of California. The beautiful, useless
Tang of eucalyptus spelt your absence.
15   The aftermath of a mouthful of wine
Was like inhaling you off a cold pillow.

And there she was, the intent and glamorous,
Ordinary, mysterious skunk,
Mythologized, demythologized,
20   Snuffing the boards five feet beyond me.

It all came back to me last night, stirred
By the sootfall of your things at bedtime,
Your head-down, tail-up hunt in a bottom drawer
For the black plunge-line nightdress.

1979

5. Wrapped or enclosed. A caul is the inner fetal membrane that at birth, when it is unruptured, sometimes covers the infant's head.

6. Sleeveless vestment worn by the priest celebrating mass, its color regulated by the feast of the day.

A Dream of Jealousy

Walking with you and another lady
In wooded parkland, the whispering grass
Ran its fingers through our guessing silence
And the trees opened into a shady
5 Unexpected clearing where we sat down.
I think the candour of the light dismayed us.
We talked about desire and being jealous,
Our conversation a loose single gown
Or a white picnic tablecloth spread out
10 Like a book of manners in the wilderness.
"Show me," I said to our companion, "what
I have much coveted, your breast's mauve star."
And she consented. O neither these verses
Nor my prudence, love, can heal your wounded stare.

1979

From Station Island[7]

12

Like a convalescent, I took the hand
stretched down from the jetty, sensed again
an alien comfort as I stepped on ground

to find the helping hand still gripping mine,
5 fish-cold and bony, but whether to guide
or to be guided I could not be certain

for the tall man in step at my side
seemed blind, though he walked straight as a rush
upon his ash plant,[8] his eyes fixed straight ahead.

10 Then I knew him in the flesh
out there on the tarmac among the cars,
wintered hard and sharp as a blackthorn bush.

His voice eddying with the vowels of all rivers[9]
came back to me, though he did not speak yet,
15 a voice like a prosecutor's or a singer's,

7. "*Station Island* is a sequence of dream encounters with familiar ghosts, set on Station Island on Lough Derg in Co. Donegal. The island is also known as St. Patrick's Purgatory because of a tradition that Patrick was the first to establish the penitential vigil of fasting and praying which still constitutes the basis of the three-day pilgrimage. Each unit of the contemporary pilgrim's exercises is called a 'station,' and a large part of each station involves walking barefoot and praying round the 'beds,' stone circles which are said to be the remains of early medieval monastic cells" [Heaney's note]. In this last section of the poem, the familiar ghost is that of Heaney's countryman James Joyce.
8. Walking stick made of ash. Joyce was almost blind.
9. The Anna Livia Plurabelle episode of Joyce's *Finnegans Wake* resounds with the names of many rivers.

cunning,[1] narcotic, mimic, definite
as a steel nib's downstroke, quick and clean,
and suddenly he hit a litter basket

20 with his stick, saying, "Your obligation
is not discharged by any common rite.
What you must do must be done on your own

so get back in harness. The main thing is to write
for the joy of it. Cultivate a work-lust
that imagines its haven like your hands at night

25 dreaming the sun in the sunspot of a breast.
You are fasted now, light-headed, dangerous.
Take off from here. And don't be so earnest,

let others wear the sackcloth and the ashes.[2]
Let go, let fly, forget.
30 You've listened long enough. Now strike your note."

It was as if I had stepped free into space
alone with nothing that I had not known
already. Raindrops blew in my face

as I came to. "Old father, mother's son,
35 there is a moment in Stephen's diary
for April the thirteenth, a revelation

set among my stars—that one entry
has been a sort of password in my ears,
the collect of a new epiphany,[3]

40 the Feast of the Holy Tundish."[4] "Who cares,"
he jeered, "any more? The English language
belongs to us. You are raking at dead fires,

a waste of time for somebody your age.
That subject people stuff is a cod's° game,   fool's
45 infantile, like your peasant pilgrimage.

You lose more of yourself than you redeem
doing the decent thing. Keep at a tangent.
When they make the circle wide, it's time to swim

---

1. "The only arms I allow myself to use—silence, exile, and cunning" (Joyce, *Portrait of the Artist as a Young Man*).
2. As worn by penitents in biblical times and later.
3. Manifestation of a superhuman being, as of the infant Jesus to the Magi (Matthew 2). In the Christian calendar, the Feast of the Epiphany is January 6. "Collect": short prayer assigned to a particular day.

4. "See the end of James Joyce's *Portrait of the Artist as a Young Man*" [Heaney's note]: "13 *April*: That tundish [funnel] has been on my mind for a long time. I looked it up and find it English and good old blunt English too. Damn the dean of studies and his funnel! What did he come here for to teach us his own language or to learn it from us? Damn him one way or the other!"

out on your own and fill the element
50   with signatures on your own frequency,
echo soundings, searches, probes, allurements,

elver-gleams[5] in the dark of the whole sea."
The shower broke in a cloudburst, the tarmac
fumed and sizzled. As he moved off quickly
55   the downpour loosed its screens round his straight walk.

1984

A Ship of Death[6]

Scyld was still a strong man when his time came
and he crossed over into Our Lord's keeping.
His warrior band did what he bade them
when he laid down the law among the Danes:
5   they shouldered him out to the sea's flood,
the chief they revered who had long ruled them.
A ring-necked prow rode in the harbour,
clad with ice, its cables tightening.
They stretched their beloved lord in the boat,
10   laid out amidships by the mast
the great ring-giver. Far-fetched treasures
were piled upon him, and precious gear.
I never heard before of a ship so well furbished
with battle-tackle, bladed weapons
15   and coats of mail. The treasure was massed
on top of him: it would travel far
on out into the sway of ocean.
They decked his body no less bountifully
with offerings than those first ones did
20   who cast him away when he was a child
and launched him out alone over the waves.
And they set a gold standard up
high above his head and let him drift
to wind and tide, bewailing him
25   and mourning their loss. No man can tell,
no wise man in the hall or weathered veteran
knows for certain who salvaged that load.

1987

Casting and Gathering
for Ted Hughes[7]

Years and years ago, these sounds took sides:

On the left bank, a green silk tapered cast
Went whispering through the air, saying *hush*

---

5. Gleams as of young eels.
6. See pp. 2–6 for a translation of *Beowulf*, lines
1–193.
7. British poet (b. 1930; see pp. 1697–1704).

And *lush*, entirely free, no matter whether
5   It swished above the hayfield or the river.

On the right bank, like a speeded-up corncrake,[8]
A sharp ratcheting went on and on
Cutting across the stillness as another
Fisherman gathered line-lengths off his reel.

10 I am still standing there, awake and dreamy,
I have grown older and can see them both
Moving their arms and rods, working away,
Each one absorbed, proofed by the sounds he's making.

One sound is saying. "You are not worth tuppence,
15 But neither is anybody. Watch it! Be severe."
The other says, "Go with it! Give and swerve.
You are everything you feel beside the river."

I love hushed air. I trust contrariness.
Years and years go past and I do not move
20 For I see that when one man casts, the other gathers
And then *vice versa*, without changing sides.

1991

MICHAEL LONGLEY

1939–

The Linen Industry

Pulling up flax after the blue flowers have fallen
And laying our handfuls in the peaty water
To rot those grasses to the bone, or building stooks[1]
That recall the skirts of an invisible dancer,

5 We become a part of the linen industry
And follow its processes to the grubby town
Where fields are compacted into window-boxes
And there is little room among the big machines.

But even in our attic under the skylight
10 We make love on a bleach green, the whole meadow
Draped with material turning white in the sun
As though snow reluctant to melt were our attire.

What's passion but a battering of stubborn stalks,
Then a gentle combing out of fibres like hair
15 And a weaving of these into christening robes,
Into garments for a marriage or funeral?

---

8. Bird with a distinctive cry.   1. Sheaves standing together

Since it's like a bereavement once the labour's done
To find ourselves last workers in a dying trade,
Let flax be our matchmaker, our undertaker,
20   The provider of sheets for whatever the bed—

And be shy of your breasts in the presence of death,
Say that you look more beautiful in linen
Wearing white petticoats, the bow on your bodice
A butterfly attending the embroidered flowers.

1979

Gorse Fires

Cattle out of their byres° are dungy still, lambs   *cowsheds*
Have stepped from last year as from an enclosure.
Five or six men stand gazing at a rusty tractor
Before carrying implements to separate fields.

5   I am travelling from one April to another.
It is the same train between the same embankments.
Gorse fires are smoking, but primroses burn
And celandines and white may and gorse flowers.

1991

Ghetto

I

Because you will suffer soon and die, your choices
Are neither right nor wrong: a spoon will feed you,
A flannel keep you clean, a toothbrush bring you back
To your bathroom's view of chimney-pots and gardens.
5   With so little time for inventory or leavetaking,
You are packing now for the rest of your life
Photographs, medicines, a change of underwear, a book,
A candlestick, a loaf, sardines, needle and thread.
These are your heirlooms, perishables, worldly goods.
10   What you bring is the same as what you leave behind,
Your last belonging a list of your belongings.

II

As though it were against the law to sleep on pillows
They have filled a cathedral with confiscated feathers:
Silence irrefrangible, no room for angels' wings,
15   Tons of feathers suffocating cherubim and seraphim.[2]

III

The little girl without a mother behaves like a mother
With her rag doll to whom she explains fear and anguish,
The meagreness of the bread ration, how to make it last,

2. Types of angels.

How to get back to the doll's house and lift up the roof
20 And, before the flame-throwers and dynamiters destroy it,
How to rescue from their separate rooms love and sorrow,
Masterpieces the size of a postage stamp, small fortunes.

IV

From among the hundreds of thousands I can imagine one
Behind the barbed-wire fences as my train crosses Poland.
25 I see him for long enough to catch the sprinkle of snowflakes
On his hair and schoolbag, and then I am transported
Away from that world of broken hobby-horses and silent toys.
He turns into a little snowman and refuses to melt.

V

For street-singers in the marketplace, weavers, warp-makers,
30 Those who suffer in sewing-machine repair shops, excrement-
Removal workers, there are not enough root vegetables,
Beetroots, turnips, swedes, nor for the leather-stitchers
Who are boiling leather so that their children may eat;
Who are turning like a thick slice of potato-bread
35 This page, which is everything I know about potatoes,
My delivery of Irish Peace, Beauty of Hebron, Home
Guard, Arran Banners, Kerr's Pinks,[3] resistant to eelworm,
Resignation, common scab, terror, frost, potato-blight.

VI

There will be performances in the waiting room, and time
40 To jump over a skipping rope, and time to adjust
As though for a dancing class the ribbons in your hair.[4]
This string quartet is the most natural thing in the world.

VII

Fingers leave shadows on a violin, harmonics,
A blackbird fluttering between electrified fences.

VIII

45 Lessons were forbidden in that terrible school.
Punishable by death were reading and writing
And arithmetic, so that even the junior infants
Grew old and wise in lofts studying these subjects.
There were drawing lessons, and drawings of kitchens
50 And farms, farm animals, butterflies, mothers, fathers
Who survived in crayon until in pen and ink
They turned into guards at executions and funerals
Torturing and hanging even these stick figures.
There were drawings of barracks and latrines as well
55 And the only windows were the windows they drew.

1991

3. Varieties of potatoes.   frock" (pp. 1230–33).
4. Cf. T. S. Eliot, "The Love Song of J. Alfred Pru-

ROBERT PINSKY
1940–

From Essay on Psychiatrists

IV. A Lakeside Identification

Yes, crazy to suppose one could describe them—
And yet, there was this incident: at the local beach
Clouds of professors and the husbands of professors

Swam, dabbled or stood to talk with arms folded
5   Gazing at the lake . . . and one of the few townsfolk there,
With no faculty status—a matter-of-fact, competent,

Catholic woman of twenty-seven with five children
And a first-rate body—pointed her finger
At the back of one certain man and asked me,

10 "Is that guy a psychiatrist?" and by god he was! "Yes,"
She said, "He *looks* like a psychiatrist."
Grown quiet, I looked at his pink back, and thought.

V. Physical Comparison With Professors And Others

Pink and a bit soft-bodied, with a somewhat jazzy
Middle-class bathing suit and sandy sideburns, to me
He looked from the back like one more professor.

And from the front, too—the boyish, unformed carriage
5   Which foreigners always note in American men, combined
As in a professor with that liberal, quizzical,

Articulate gaze so unlike the more focused, more
Tolerant expression worn by a man of action (surgeon,
Salesman, athlete). On closer inspection was there,

10 Perhaps, a self-satisfied or benign air, a studied
Gentleness toward the child whose hand he held loosely?
Absurd to speculate; but then—the woman saw *something*.

1975

A Long Branch[1] Song

Some days in May, little stars
Winked all over the ocean. The blue
Barely changed all morning and afternoon:

---

1. Long Branch, New Jersey, where Pinsky was born.

The chimes of the bank's bronze clock;
5   The hoarse voice of Cookie, hawking
     The Daily Record for thirty-five years.

1984

The Street

Streaked and fretted with effort, the thick
Vine of the world, red nervelets
Coiled at its tips.

All roads lead from it.[2] All night
5   Wainwrights and upholsterers work finishing
The wheeled coffin

Of the dead favorite of the Emperor,
The child's corpse propped seated
On brocade, with yellow

10   Oiled curls, kohl on the stiff lids.
Slaves throw petals on the roadway
For the cortege, white

Languid flowers shooting from dark
Blisters on the vine, ramifying
15   Into streets. On mine,

Rockwell Avenue, it was embarrassing:
Trouble—fights, the police, sickness—
Seemed never to come

For anyone when they were fully dressed.
20   It was always underwear or dirty pyjamas,
Unseemly stretches

Of skin showing through a torn housecoat.
Once a stranger drove off in a car
With somebody's wife,

25   And he ran after them in his undershirt
And threw his shoe at the car. It bounced
Into the street

Harmlessly, and we carried it back to him;
But the man had too much dignity
30   To put it back on,

So he held it and stood crying in the street:
"He's breaking up my home," he said,
"The son of a bitch

---

2. A twist on the expression "all roads lead to Rome."

Bastard is breaking up my home." The street
35 Rose undulant in pavement-breaking coils
And the man rode it,

Still holding his shoe and stiffly upright
Like a trick rider in the circus parade
That came down the street

40 Each August. As the powerful dragonlike
Hump swelled he rose cursing and ready
To throw his shoe—woven

Angular as a twig into the fabulous
Rug or brocade with crowns and camels,
45 Leopards and rosettes,

All riding the vegetable wave of the street
From the John Flock Mortuary Home
Down to the river.

It was a small place, and off the center,
50 But so much a place to itself, I felt
Like a young prince

Or aspirant squire. I knew that Ivanhoe[3]
Was about race. The Saxons[4] were Jews,
Or even Coloreds,

55 With their low-ceilinged, unbelievably
Sour-smelling houses down by the docks.
Everything was written

Or woven, ivory and pink and emerald—
Nothing was too ugly or petty or terrible
60 To be weighed in the immense

Silver scales of the dead: the looming
Balances set right onto the live, dangerous
Gray bark of the street.

1984

---

3. Historical novel by the Scottish writer Sir Walter Scott (1771–1832), considered the inventor of the form.
4. The Germanic peoples in ancient times, some of whom invaded Britain in the fifth and sixth centuries; here, used to mean an English person or Anglo-Saxon. In the first pages of Ivanhoe, Scott reflects on the social effects of the Norman Conquest of England in 1066: "Four generations had not sufficed to blend the hostile blood of the Normans and Anglo-Saxons, or to unite, by common language and mutual interests, two hostile races." The Saxons were dispossessed of both land and status.

ROBERT HASS

1941–

Meditation at Lagunitas[1]

All the new thinking is about loss.
In this it resembles all the old thinking.
The idea, for example, that each particular erases
the luminous clarity of a general idea. That the clown-
5   faced woodpecker probing the dead sculpted trunk
of that black birch is, by his presence,
some tragic falling off from a first world
of undivided light. Or the other notion that,
because there is in this world no one thing
10   to which the bramble of *blackberry* corresponds,
a word is elegy to what it signifies.
We talked about it late last night and in the voice
of my friend, there was a thin wire of grief, a tone
almost querulous. After a while I understood that,
15   talking this way, everything dissolves: *justice,*
pine, hair, woman, you and *I.* There was a woman
I made love to and I remembered how, holding
her small shoulders in my hands sometimes,
I felt a violent wonder at her presence
20   like a thirst for salt, for my childhood river
with its island willows, silly music from the pleasure boat,
muddy places where we caught the little orange-silver fish
called *pumpkinseed.* It hardly had to do with her.
Longing, we say, because desire is full
25   of endless distances. I must have been the same to her.
But I remember so much, the way her hands dismantled bread,
the thing her father said that hurt her, what
she dreamed. There are moments when the body is as numinous[2]
as words, days that are the good flesh continuing.
30   Such tenderness, those afternoons and evenings,
saying *blackberry, blackberry, blackberry.*

1979

Tahoe[3] in August

What summer proposes is simply happiness:
heat early in the morning, jays
raucous in the pines. Frank and Ellen have a tennis game
at nine, Bill and Cheryl sleep on the deck
5   to watch a shower of summer stars. Nick and Sharon

1. A small town in California, near San Francisco (literally, "little lake" [Spanish]).
2. Filled with a sense of divinity.
3. A lake in the Sierra Nevada Mountains, in both eastern California and western Nevada.

stayed in, sat and talked the dark on,
drinking tea, and Jeanne walked into the meadow
in a white smock to write in her journal
by a grazing horse who seemed to want the company.
10   Some of them will swim in the afternoon.
Someone will drive to the hardware store to fetch
new latches for the kitchen door. Four o'clock;
the joggers jogging—it is one of them who sees
down the flowering slope the woman with her notebook
15   in her hand beside the white horse, gesturing, her hair
from a distance the copper color of the hummingbirds
the slant light catches on the slope; the hikers
switchback down the canyon from the waterfall;
the readers are reading, Anna is about to meet Vronsky,[4]
20   that nice M. Swann is dining in Combray
with the aunts, and Carrie[5] has come to Chicago.
What they want is happiness: someone to love them,
children, a summer by the lake. The woman who sets aside
her book blinks against the fuzzy dark,
25   re-entering the house. Her daughter drifts downstairs;
out late the night before, she has been napping,
and she's cross. Her mother tells her David telephoned.
"He's such a dear," the mother says, "I think
I made him nervous." The girl tosses her head as the horse
30   had done in the meadow while Jeanne read it her dream.
"You can call him now, if you want," the mother says,
"I've got to get the chicken started,
I won't listen." "Did I say you would?"
the girl says quickly. The mother who has been slapped
35   this way before and done the same herself another summer
on a different lake says, "Ouch." The girl shrugs
sulkily. "I'm sorry." Looking down: "Something
about the way you said that pissed me off."
"Hannibal has wandered off," the mother says,
40   wryness in her voice, she is thinking it is August,
"why don't you see if he's at the Finleys' house
again." The girl says, "God." The mother: "He loves
small children. It's livelier for him there."
The daughter, awake now, flounces out the door,
45   which slams. It is for all of them the sound of summer.
The mother she looks like stands at the counter snapping beans.

1989

4. The lover of Anna Karenina, in the novel of the same name by the Russian novelist Leo Tolstoy (1828–1910).
5. The heroine of *Sister Carrie*, by the American novelist Theodore Dreiser (1871–1945). "M. Swann": Charles Swann, a protagonist of *Swann's Way*, the first book in the seven-volume *A la recherche du temps perdu* ("In Search of Lost Time") by the French novelist Marcel Proust (1871–1922). Swann visits the aunts of the narrator, Marcel, at Combray, a town based on Illiers, near Chartres.

DEREK MAHON

1941–

In Carrowdore Churchyard

(at the grave of Louis MacNeice)[1]

Your ashes will not stir, even on this high ground,
However the wind tugs, the headstones shake.
This plot is consecrated, for your sake,
To what lies in the future tense. You lie
5   Past tension now, and spring is coming round
Igniting flowers on the peninsula.

Your ashes will not fly, however the rough winds burst
Through the wild brambles and the reticent trees.
All we may ask of you we have; the rest
10 Is not for publication, will not be heard.
Maguire, I believe, suggested a blackbird
And over your grave a phrase from Euripides.[2]

Which suits you down to the ground, like this churchyard
With its play of shadow, its humane perspective.
15 Locked in the winter's fist, these hills are hard
As nails, yet soft and feminine in their turn
When fingers open and the hedges burn.
This, you implied, is how we ought to live—

The ironical, loving crush of roses against snow,
20 Each fragile, solving ambiguity. So
From the pneumonia of the ditch, from the ague°   *fever*
Of the blind poet and the bombed-out town you bring
The all-clear to the empty holes of spring,
Rinsing the choked mud, keeping the colours new.

1968

A Disused Shed in Co. Wexford

Let them not forget us, the weak souls among the asphodels.
—SEFERIS, *Mythistorema*, tr. Keeley and Sherrard

(for J. G. Farrell)

Even now there are places where a thought might grow—
Peruvian mines, worked out and abandoned
To a slow clock of condensation,
An echo trapped for ever, and a flutter
5 Of wild-flowers in the lift-shaft,
Indian compounds where the wind dances

---

1. (1907–1963); Irish poet (see pp. 1377–82), buried in Carrowdore Churchyard, County Down, Northern Ireland.

2. The suggested phrase from the Greek dramatist Euripides was not carved on MacNeice's gravestone.

And a door bangs with diminished confidence,
Lime crevices behind rippling rain-barrels,
Dog corners for bone burials;
10 And in a disused shed in Co. Wexford,

Deep in the grounds of a burnt-out hotel,
Among the bathtubs and the washbasins
A thousand mushrooms crowd to a keyhole.
This is the one star in their firmament
15 Or frames a star within a star.
What should they do there but desire?
So many days beyond the rhododendrons
With the world waltzing in its bowl of cloud,
They have learnt patience and silence
20 Listening to the rooks querulous in the high wood.

They have been waiting for us in a foetor°   *fetid aura*
Of vegetable sweat since civil war days,
Since the gravel-crunching, interminable departure
Of the expropriated mycologist.[3]
25 He never came back, and light since then
Is a keyhole rusting gently after rain.
Spiders have spun, flies dusted to mildew
And once a day, perhaps, they have heard something—
A trickle of masonry, a shout from the blue
30 Or a lorry changing gear at the end of the lane.

There have been deaths, the pale flesh flaking
Into the earth that nourished it;
And nightmares, born of these and the grim
Dominion of stale air and rank moisture.
35 Those nearest the door grow strong—
"Elbow room! Elbow room!"
The rest, dim in a twilight of crumbling
Utensils and broken pitchers, groaning
For their deliverance, have been so long
40 Expectant that there is left only the posture.

A half century, without visitors, in the dark—
Poor preparation for the cracking lock
And creak of hinges. Magi,° moonmen,   *wise men*
Powdery prisoners of the old regime,
45 Web-throated, stalked like triffids, racked by drought
And insomnia, only the ghost of a scream
At the flash-bulb firing-squad we wake them with
Shows there is life yet in their feverish forms.
Grown beyond nature now, soft food for worms,
50 They lift frail heads in gravity and good faith.

They are begging us, you see, in their wordless way,
To do something, to speak on their behalf

---

3. Someone who studies mushrooms.

Or at least not to close the door again.
Lost people of Treblinka and Pompeii![4]
55   "Save us, save us," they seem to say,
"Let the god not abandon us
Who have come so far in darkness and in pain.
We too had our lives to live.
You with your light meter and relaxed itinerary,
60   Let not our naive labours have been in vain!"

1975

Girls on the Bridge

—*Pykene na Brukken*, Munch, 1900[5]

Audible trout,
Notional midges. Beds,
Lamplight and crisp linen wait
In the house there for the sedate
5   Limbs and averted heads
Of the girls out

Late on the bridge.
The dusty road that slopes
Past is perhaps the high road south,
10   A symbol of world-wondering youth,
Of adolescent hopes
And privileges;

But stops to find
The girls content to gaze
15   At the unplumbed, reflective lake,
Their plangent conversational quack
Expressive of calm days
And peace of mind.

Grave daughters
20   Of time, you lightly toss
Your hair as the long shadows grow
And night begins to fall. Although
Your laughter calls across
The dark waters,

25   A ghastly sun
Watches in pale dismay.
Oh, you may laugh, being as you are
Fair sisters of the evening star,
But wait—if not today
30   A day will dawn

---

4. Roman city preserved under ash and lava after a volcanic eruption that killed most of its inhabitants. "Treblinka"; place in northern Poland; site of one of the principal German concentration camps in World War II.
5. "Girls on a Bridge," title of a famous painting in expressionist style by Edvard Munch (1863–1944), Norwegian artist.

When the bad dreams
You scarcely know will scatter
The punctual increment of your lives.
The road resumes, and where it curves,
35   A mile from where you chatter,
Somebody screams.

The girls are dead,
The house and pond have gone.
Steel bridge and concrete highway gleam
40   And sing in the arctic dark; the scream
We started at is grown
The serenade

Of an insane
And monstrous age. We live
45   These days as on a different planet,
One without trout or midges on it,
Under the arc-lights of
A mineral heaven;

And we have come,
50   Despite ourselves, to no
True notion of our proper work,
But wander in the dazzling dark
Amid the drifting snow
Dreaming of some

55   Lost evening when
Our grandmothers, if grand
Mothers we had, stood at the edge
Of womanhood on a country bridge
And gazed at a still pond
60   And knew no pain.

1982

ERIC ORMSBY

1941–

Starfish

The stellar sea crawler, maw
Concealed beneath, with offerings of
Prismed crimson now darkened, now like
The smile of slag, a thing made rosy
5 As poured ingots, or suddenly dimmed—

I appreciate the studious labour
Of your rednesses, the scholarly fragrance
Of your sex. To mirror tidal drifts

The light ripples across or to enhance darkness
10 With palpable tinctures, dense as salt.

You crumple like a puppet's fist
Or erect, bristling, your tender luring barbs.
Casual abandon, like a dropped fawn glove.
Tensile symmetries, like a hawk's claw.

15 You clutch the seafloor.

You taste what has fallen.

1990

Skunk Cabbage

The skunk cabbage with its smug and opulent smell
Opens in plump magnificence near the edge
Of garbage-strewn canals, or you see its shape
Arise near the wet roots of the marsh.
5 How vigilant it looks with its glossy leaves
Parted to disclose its bruised insides,
That troubled purple of its blossom!
It always seemed so squat, dumpy and rank,
A noxious efflorescence of the swamp,
10 Until I got down low and looked at it.
Now I search out its blunt totemic shape
And bow when I see its outer stalks
Drawn aside, like the frilly curtains of the ark,
For the foul magenta of its gorgeous heart.

1990

Origins

I wanted to go down to where the roots begin,
to find words nested in their almond-skin,
the seed-curls of their birth, their sprigs of origin.

At night the dead set words upon my tongue,
5 drew back their coverings, laid bare the long
sheaths of their roots where the earth still clung.

I wanted to draw their words from the mouths of the dead,
I wanted to strip the coins from their heavy eyes,
I wanted the rosy breath to gladden their skins.

10 At night the dead remembered their origins,
at night they nested in the curve of my eyes,
and I tasted the savour of their seed-bed.

1993

DOUGLAS DUNN

1942–

A Removal from Terry Street

On a squeaking cart, they push the usual stuff,
A mattress, bed ends, cups, carpets, chairs,
Four paperback westerns. Two whistling youths
In surplus U.S. Army battle-jackets
5   Remove their sister's goods. Her husband
Follows, carrying on his shoulders the son
Whose mischief we are glad to see removed,
And pushing, of all things, a lawnmower.
There is no grass in Terry Street. The worms
10   Come up cracks in concrete yards in moonlight.
That man, I wish him well. I wish him grass.

1969

In the Grounds

Yorkshire, 1975

Barbarians in a garden, softness does
Approve of who we are as it does those
Who when we speak proclaim us barbarous
And say we have no business with the rose.

5   Gently the grass waves, and its green applauds
The justice, not of progress, but of growth.
We walk as people on the paths of gods
And in our minds we harmonize them both.

Disclosures of these grounds—a river view,
10   Two Irish wolfhounds watching on a lawn;
A spinster with her sewing stares at you,
And begs you leave her pretty world alone.

More books than prejudice in our young minds . . .
We could not harm her, would not, would prefer
15   A noise less military and more kind
Than our boots make across her wide *parterre*.[1]

We are intransigent, at odds with them.
They see our rabble-dreams as new contempt
For England's art of house and leaf. Condemn
20   Our clumsiness—you do not know, how, unkempt

And coarse, we hurt a truth with truth, still true
To who we are: barbarians, whose chins

---

1. French landscaping term for an arrangement of flower beds.

Drool with ale-stinking hair, whose horses chew
Turf owned by watching, frightened mandarins,

25 Their surly nephews lounging at each gate,
Afraid we'll steal their family's treasured things,
Then hawk them—pictures, furniture and plate—
Round the encampments of our saddle-kings.

1979

From Elegies

Thirteen Steps and the Thirteenth of March

She sat up on her pillows, receiving guests.
I brought them tea or sherry like a butler,
Up and down the thirteen steps from my pantry.
I was running out of vases.

5 More than one visitor came down, and said,
"Her room's so cheerful. She isn't afraid."
Even the cyclamen and lilies were listening,
Their trusty tributes holding off the real.

Doorbells, shopping, laundry, post and callers,
10 And twenty-six steps up the stairs
From door to bed, two times thirteen's
Unlucky numeral in my high house.

And visitors, three, four, five times a day;
My wept exhaustions over plates and cups
15 Drained my self-pity in these days of grief
Before the grief. Flowers, and no vases left.

Tea, sherry, biscuits, cake, and whisky for the weak . . .
She fought death with an understated mischief—
"I suppose I'll have to make an effort"—
20 Turning down painkillers for lucidity.

Some sat downstairs with a hankie
Nursing a little cry before going up to her.
They came back with their fears of dying amended.
"Her room's so cheerful. She isn't afraid."

25 Each day was duty round the clock.
Our kissing conversations kept me going,
Those times together with the phone switched off,
Remembering our lives by candlelight.

John and Stuart brought their pictures round,
30 A travelling exhibition. Dying,
She thumbed down some, nodded at others,
An artist and curator to the last,

Honesty at all costs. She drew up lists,
Bequests, gave things away. It tore my heart out.
35 Her friends assisted at this tidying
In a conspiracy of women.

At night, I lay beside her in the unique hours.
There were mysteries in candle-shadows,
Birds, aeroplanes, the rabbits of our fingers,
40 The lovely, erotic flame of the candlelight.

Sad? Yes. But it was beautiful also.
There was a stillness in the world. Time was out
Walking his dog by the low walls and privet.
There was anonymity in words and music.

45 She wanted me to wear her wedding ring.
It wouldn't fit even my little finger.
It jammed on the knuckle. I knew why.
Her fingers dwindled and her rings slipped off.

After the funeral, I had them to tea and sherry
50 At the Newland Park. They said it was thoughtful.
I thought it was ironic—one last time—
A mad reprisal for their loyalty.

1985

ALFRED CORN

1943–

Navidad, St. Nicholas Ave.[1]

An infant quirk of a pine
with aerosol frosting, spangles,
and bulbs that blink red-blue-gold.
Manolito, three days home, they've put

5 in his picket-fence crib,
paper diaper cinched tight,
eyes squinted in a mask
that looks Chinese or in pain.

Asleep. Trailing sighs and smiles
10 they tiptoe out to where the Magnavox
screen extolls some *producto*[2]
whose logo's a crystal star.

1. Street in the Harlem section of Manhattan, in New York City; here, the name alludes to St. Nick, or Santa Claus. *Navidad*: "nativity" (Spanish).

2. "Product" (Spanish). "Magnavox": brand of television; literally, "great voice" (Latin).

> She glances up at the window
> brimming with sodium light.
> 15 And, *mira*, snow begins to fall
> like manna[3] in the warming air
>
> as from down the avenue a taxi
> beeps a brass triad. Then an offended
> wail summons mother, father,
> 20 *todo el mundo*[4] back to his side.

1988

Contemporary Culture and the Letter "K"

First inroads were made in our 19-aughts
(Foreshadowed during the last century by nothing
More central than "Kubla Khan," Kipling, Greek
Letter societies, including the grotesque KKK—
5 Plus the kiwi, koala, and kookaburra from Down Under)[5]
When certain women applied to their moist eyelids
A substance pronounced *coal* but spelled *kohl*,
Much of the effect captured on Kodak film
With results on and off camera now notorious.
10 They were followed and sometimes chased by a platoon
Of helmeted cutups styled the *Keystone Kops*,[6] who'd
Freeze in the balletic pose of the letter itself,
Left arm on hip, leg pointed back at an angle,
Waiting under klieg lights next a worried kiosk
15 To put the kibosh on Knickerbocker[7] misbehavior.
Long gone, they couldn't help when that hirsute royal
King Kong arrived to make a desperate last stand,
Clinging from the Empire State, swatting at biplanes,
Fay Wray fainting away in his leathern palm
20 As in the grip of African might. Next, marketing
Stepped up with menthol tobacco and the brand name
Kool, smoked presumably by models and archetypes
Superior in every way to Jukes and Kallikaks.[8]
By then the race was on, if only because
25 Of German *Kultur*'s° increasing newsworthiness   *culture's*
On the international front. The nation that had canned
Its Kaiser went on to sponsor debuts for the hero
Of *Mein Kampf*, Wotan of his day, launching thunderbolts

---

3. The food that miraculously fell to the Israelites in the wilderness (Exodus 16.14–36). *Mira*: "look" (Spanish).
4. "All the world" (Spanish).
5. Australia. "Kubla Kahn": a fragment, composed under the influence of laudanum and dream, by the English poet Samuel Taylor Coleridge (1772–1834; see pp. 739–63). Rudyard Kipling (1865–1936; see pp. 1076–83), English writer best known for his celebration of English imperialism. "Greek letter societies": fraternities. "KKK": Ku Klux Klan, a secret white-supremacist organization founded in

the 1860s, disbanded during Reconstruction, refounded in 1915. "Kookaburra": a kingfisher bird.
6. Comically bungling policemen in silent films produced by the Keystone Motion Picture Co.
7. New Yorker. "Klieg lights": carbon arc lamps used in making motion pictures. "Put the kibosh on": put a stop to.
8. Fictitious names of two troubled familes, the subjects of psychological studies exploring the role of heredity.

And Stukas,[9] along with a new social order astonishing
30   In its industrial efficiency. His annexing
Of Bohemia cannot have been spurred by reflecting
That after all Prague had sheltered the creator
And in some sense alter-ego of Josef K.,[1]
Whose trial remained a local fact until the fall
35   Of the Empire of a Thousand Years, unheard of in "Amerika"[2]
Of the Jazz Age. But musicians Bix Beiderbecke and Duke
Ellington[3] somehow always took care to include the token
Grapheme in their names, for which precaution fans
Of certain priceless '78s can only be grateful.
40   They skipped and rippled through a long post-war glow
Still luminous in the memory of whoever recalls
Krazy Kat, Kleenex, Deborah Kerr, Korea, Kool-Aid,
And Jack Kennedy.[4] Small wonder if New York had
A special feeling for the theme, considering radical
45   Innovations of De Kooning, Kline, and Rothko.[5] This last
Can remind us that bearers of the letter often suffered
Bereavement and despair (cf. Chester Kallman) and even,
As with Weldon Kees,[6] self-slaying. Impossible not to see
Symptoms of a malaise more widespread still in a culture
50   That collects kitsch° and Krugerrands,[7] with a just-kids   *tasteless objects*
     lifestyle
Whose central shrine is the shopping mall—K-Mart, hail to thee!
To "Kuntry Kitchen," "Kanine Kennels," and a host of other
Kreative misspellings kreeping through the korpus
Of kontemporary lingo like an illness someone someday
55   (The trespass of metaphor) is going to spell "kancer."

True, there have been recidivists in opposite
Direction (a falling away perhaps from the Platonic ideal
Of *tò kalón*) like "calisthenics" and Maria Callas,[8]
Who seem to have preferred the less marblelike romance
60   Of traditional English. This and related factors make all
Supporters of the letter "k" in legitimate forms
And avatars cherish it with fiery intensity—

9. First bombers employed in World War II, by Germany against Poland. "Kaiser": Kaiser Wilhelm, or Wilhelm II (1859–1941) of Germany, defeated in world War I. Seen as the "debut" for Adolph Hitler (1889–1945), who before becoming dictator of Germany wrote *Mein Kampf* ("My Struggle"), a political manifesto outlining his racist ideology. "Wotan": chief Germanic god, corresponding to the Scandinavian war god Ódin.
1. On March 15, 1939, Hitler annexed Bohemia, including the city of Prague, birthplace and sometime home of the writer Franz Kafka (1883–1924). In Kafka's 1925 novel *The Trial*, seen as an anticipation of modern totalitarianism, Josef K. is a bank official arrested and executed on charges never made clear.
2. America; also the title of a 1927 novel by Kafka. "Empire of a Thousand Years": Hitler intended his regime, the Third Reich, to last a thousand years.
3. (1899–1974); band leader, composer, and arranger. Bix Beiderbecke (1903–1931), cornet player. Both jazz musicians.

4. U.S. President John Fitzgerald Kennedy (1917–1963). "Krazy Kat": character in George Herriman's short animated films, first produced in 1916 and revived for television in the 1960s. Deborah Kerr (b. 1921), Socttish stage and film actress.
5. Mark Rothko (1903–1970), Willem de Kooning (b. 1904), and Franz Kline (1910–1962), all abstract expressionists associated with New York City.
6. (1914–1955); American poet, filmmaker, and painter, who disappeared, an apparent suicide. Chester Kallman (1921–1975), American poet and librettist, longtime companion of the American (English-born) poet W. H. Auden (1907–1973; see pp. 1360–73), whom he survived.
7. One-ounce gold coins of the Republic of South Africa.
8. (1923–1977); operatic soprano, born Maria Kalogeropoulos; like "calisthenics," her Greek (sur)name began with a "k." *Tò kalón*: "the beautiful" (Greek).

All the more when besieged by forces beyond
Anyone's control, at least, with social or medical
65   Remedies now available. Dr. Kaposi named it,
That sarcoma[9] earmarking a mortal syndrome thus far
Incurable and spreading overland like acid rain.
A sense of helplessness is not in the repertory
Of our national consciousness, we have no aptitude
70   For standing by as chill winds rise, the shadows gather,
And gray light glides into the room where a seated figure
Has taken up his post by the window, facing away from us,
No longer bothering to speak, his mind at one with whatever
Is beyond the ordinary spell of language, whatever dreams us
75   Into that placeless place, its nearest image a cloudless
Sky at dusk, just before the slow ascent of the moon.

                                                     1992

LOUISE GLÜCK

1943–

Gretel in Darkness

This is the world we wanted.
All who would have seen us dead
are dead. I hear the witch's cry
break in the moonlight through a sheet
5   of sugar: God rewards.
Her tongue shrivels into gas. . . .

        Now, far from women's arms
and memory of women, in our father's hut
we sleep, are never hungry.
10   Why do I not forget?
My father bars the door, bars harm
from this house, and it is years.

No one remembers. Even you, my brother,
summer afternoons you look at me as though
15   you meant to leave,
as though it never happened.
But I killed for you. I see armed firs,
the spires of that gleaming kiln—

Nights I turn to you to hold me
20   but you are not there.
Am I alone? Spies
hiss in the stillness, Hansel,
we are there still and it is real, real,
that black forest and the fire in earnest.

                                                     1975

---

9. "Kaposi's sarcoma": form of cancer first reported by Dr. Moritz Kaposi; formerly rare, now prevalent among AIDS patients.

The Garden

I couldn't do it again,
I can hardly bear to look at it—

in the garden, in light rain
the young couple planting
5   a row of peas, as though
no one has ever done this before,
the great difficulties have never as yet
been faced and solved—

They cannot see themselves,
10   in fresh dirt, starting up
without perspective,
the hills behind them pale green, clouded with flowers—

She wants to stop;
he wants to get to the end,
15   to stay with the thing—

Look at her, touching his cheek
to make a truce, her fingers
cool with spring rain;
in thin grass, bursts of purple crocus—

20   even here, even at the beginning of love,
her hand leaving his face makes
an image of departure

and they think
they are free to overlook
25   this sadness.

1992

MICHAEL ONDAATJE

1943–

Letters & Other Worlds

*'for there was no more darkness for him and, no doubt like Adam before the fall,
he could see in the dark'*

My father's body was a globe of fear
His body was a town we never knew
He hid that he had been where we were going
His letters were a room he seldom lived in
5   In them the logic of his love could grow

My father's body was a town of fear
He was the only witness to its fear dance

He hid where he had been that we might lose him
His letters were a room his body scared

10 He came to death with his mind drowning.
On the last day he enclosed himself
in a room with two bottles of gin, later
fell the length of his body
so that brain blood moved
15 to new compartments
that never knew the wash of fluid
and he died in minutes of a new equilibrium.

His early life was a terrifying comedy
and my mother divorced him again and again.
20 He would rush into tunnels magnetized
by the white eye of trains
and once, gaining instant fame,
managed to stop a Perahara[1] in Ceylon
—the whole procession of elephants dancers
25 local dignitaries—by falling
dead drunk onto the street.

As a semi-official, and semi-white at that,
the act was seen as a crucial
turning point in the Home Rule Movement
30 and led to Ceylon's independence in 1948.

(My mother had done her share too—
her driving so bad
she was stoned by villagers
whenever her car was recognized)

35 For 14 years of marriage
each of them claimed he or she
was the injured party.
Once on the Colombo docks
saying goodbye to a recently married couple
40 my father, jealous
at my mother's articulate emotion,
dove into the waters of the harbour
and swam after the ship waving farewell.
My mother pretending no affiliation
45 mingled with the crowd back to the hotel.

Once again he made the papers
though this time my mother
with a note to the editor
corrected the report—saying he was drunk
50 rather than broken hearted at the parting of friends.

1. Or Anuradhapura Perahera, an annual Cey-
lonese religious festival commemorating the birth
of Vishnu, one of the three primary Hindu gods.
On its fifth and final day the festival culminates in
nocturnal processions such as that described here,
the elephants bearing shrines and relics.

The married couple received both editions
of *The Ceylon Times* when their ship reached Aden.[2]

And then in his last years
he was the silent drinker,
55 the man who once a week
disappeared into his room with bottles
and stayed there until he was drunk
and until he was sober.

There speeches, head dreams, apologies,
60 the gentle letters, were composed.
With the clarity of architects
he would write of the row of blue flowers
his new wife had planted,
the plans for electricity in the house,
65 how my half-sister fell near a snake
and it had awakened and not touched her.
Letters in a clear hand of the most complete empathy
his heart widening and widening and widening
to all manner of change in his children and friends
70 while he himself edged
into the terrible acute hatred
of his own privacy
till he balanced and fell
the length of his body
75 the blood entering
the empty reservoir of bones
the blood searching in his head without metaphor.

1979

From Rock Bottom

(*Ends of the Earth*)

For you I have slept
like a pure arrow in the hall
pointing towards your wakefulness
. . . a few misdemeanors but otherwise
5 lost without your company, you
in intricate time zones

And wary
piece by piece
we put each other together
10   your past
that of one who has walked
through fifteen strange houses
in order to be here

the charm of Wichita
15 gunmen in your bones

2. A country southwest of Arabia, then a British colony.

the 19th century
strolling like a storm
through your long body

that history I read in comic books
20 and on the flickering screen
when I was thirteen

Now we are cats-cradled
in the Pacific
how does one avoid this?
25 Go to the ends of the earth?
The loose moon follows

                    Wet moonlight
                    recalls childhood

the long legged daughter
30 the stars   the lights
of Wichita in the distance

midnight and hugging
against her small chest
the favourite book,
35 *Goodnight Moon*[3]

under the covers she
reads its courtly order
its list of farewells
to everything

40   We grow less complex
We reduce ourselves   The way lovers
have their small cheap charms
silver lizard,
a stone

45 Ancient customs
that grow from dust
                    swirled out
from prairie into tropic

Strange how the odours meet

50 How, however briefly, bedraggled
history
        focusses

                                        1984

3. Classic book for very young children by the American writer Margaret Wise Brown (1910–1952).

MICHAEL PALMER

1943–

Of this cloth doll which

(Sarah's fourth)

Of this cloth doll which
says Oh yes
and then its face changes
to Once upon a time
5   to Wooden but alive
to Like the real
to Late into the night
to There lived an old
to Running across ice
10 (but shadows followed)
to Finally it sneezed
to The boat tipped over
to Flesh and blood
to Out of the whale's mouth[1]

1984

Fifth Prose

Because I'm writing about the snow not the sentence
Because there is a card—a visitor's card—and on that card there are
    words of ours arranged in a row

and on those words we have written house, we have written leave this
    house, we
have written be this house, the spiral of a house, channels through this
    house

5   and we have written The Provinces and The Reversal and something
    called the Human Poems
though we live in a valley on the Hill of Ghosts

Still for many days the rain will continue to fall
A voice will say Father I am burning

Father I've removed a stone from a wall, erased a picture from that wall,
10 a picture of ships—cloud ships—pressing toward the sea

words only
taken limb by limb apart

Because we are not alive not alone
but ordinary extracts from the tablets

---

1. The fractured sentence of the poem borrows phrases from fairy tales, and especially from the 1883 children's story *The Adventures of Pinocchio* by the Italian writer Carlo Collodi (1826–1890).

15   Hassan the Arab and his wife
   who did vaulting and balancing

   Coleman and Burgess, and Adele Newsome
   pitched among the spectators one night

   Lizzie Keys
20   and Fred who fell from the trapeze

   into the sawdust
   and wasn't hurt at all

   and Jacob Hall the rope-dancer
   Little Sandy and Sam Sault[2]

25   Because there is a literal shore, a letter that's blood-red
   Because in this dialect the eyes are crossed or quartz

   seeing swimmer and seeing rock
   statue then shadow

   and here in the lake
30   first a razor then a fact

1988

EAVAN BOLAND

1944–

That the Science of Cartography Is Limited[1]

   —and not simply by the fact that this shading of
   forest cannot show the fragrance of balsam,
   the gloom of cypresses
   is what I wish to prove.

5   When you and I were first in love we drove
   to the borders of Connacht[2]
   and entered a wood there.

   Look down you said: this was once a famine road.

   I looked down at ivy and the scutch grass
10   rough-cast stone had
   disappeared into as you told me
   in the second winter of their ordeal, in

---

2. Probably a pun on "somersault."   2. Western province of Ireland.
1. "Cartography": mapmaking.

1847, when the crop[3] had failed twice,
Relief Committees gave
15 the starving Irish such roads to build.

Where they died, there the road ended

and ends still and when I take down
the map of this island, it is never so
I can say here is
20 the masterful, the apt rendering of

the spherical as flat, nor
an ingenious design which persuades a curve
into a plane,
but to tell myself again that

25 the line which says woodland and cries hunger
and gives out among sweet pine and cypress,
and finds no horizon

will not be there.

The Dolls Museum in Dublin

The wounds are terrible. The paint is old.
The cracks along the lips and on the cheeks
cannot be fixed. The cotton lawn[4] is soiled.
The arms are ivory dissolved to wax.

5 Recall the Quadrille. Hum the waltz.
Promenade on the yacht-club terraces.
Put back the lamps in their copper holders,
the carriage wheels on the cobbled quays.

And recreate Easter in Dublin.[5]
10 Booted officers. Their mistresses.
Sunlight criss-crossing College Green.
Steam hissing from the flanks of horses.

Here they are. Cradled and cleaned,
held close in the arms of their owners.
15 Their cold hands clasped by warm hands,
their faces memorized like perfect manners.

The altars are mannerly with linen.
The lilies are whiter than surplices.[6]
The candles are burning and warning:
20 Rejoice, they whisper. After sacrifice.

3. Of potatoes, staple diet of Irish peasants in the nineteenth century.
4. Usually fine linen, but also, as here, fine cotton.
5. What became known as the "Easter Rising" began on Easter Monday, 1916, when fifteen hundred Irish Nationalists seized key points in Dublin and an Irish Republic was proclaimed from the General Post Office. See W. B. Yeats, "Easter 1916" (pp. 1089–91).
6. White linen vestments worn over cassocks.

Horse-chestnuts hold up their candles.
The Green is vivid with parasols.
Sunlight is pastel and windless.
The bar of the Shelbourne[7] is full.

25 Laughter and gossip on the terraces.
Rumour and alarm at the barracks.
The Empire is summoning its officers.
The carriages are turning: they are turning back.

Past children walking with governesses,
30 Looking down, cossetting their dolls,
then looking up as the carriage passes,
the shadow chilling them. Twilight falls.

It is twilight in the dolls' museum. Shadows
remain on the parchment-coloured waists,
35 are bruises on the stitched cotton clothes,
are hidden in the dimples on the wrists.

The eyes are wide. They cannot address
the helplessness which has lingered in
the airless peace of each glass case:
40 to have survived. To have been stronger than

a moment. To be the hostages ignorance
takes from time and ornament from destiny. Both.
To be the present of the past. To infer the difference
with a terrible stare. But not feel it. And not know it.

The Pomegranate

The only legend I have ever loved is
the story of a daughter lost in hell.
And found and rescued there.
Love and blackmail are the gist of it.
5 Ceres and Persephone the names.[8]
And the best thing about the legend is
I can enter it anywhere. And have.
As a child in exile in
a city of fogs and strange consonants,
10 I read it first and at first I was
an exiled child in the crackling dusk of
the underworld, the stars blighted. Later
I walked out in a summer twilight
searching for my daughter at bed-time.
15 When she came running I was ready

7. Large Dublin hotel.
8. In Roman myth, Ceres was the born goddess
(Greek, Demeter). Her daughter, Proserpine
(Greek, Persephone), was carried off to the under-
world by its king. Her mother searched for an even-
tually found her, but by then Proserpina/

Persephone had eaten six pomegranate seeds and
was condemned to spend six months of every year
in Hades (when the world mourns) and six above
ground (when the Earth rejoices and fertility
returns).

to make any bargain to keep her.
I carried her back past whitebeams
and wasps and honey-scented buddleias.
But I was Ceres then and I knew
20 winter was in store for every leaf
on every tree on that road.
Was inescapable for each one we passed.
And for me.
               It is winter
25 and the stars are hidden.
I climb the stairs and stand where I can see
my child asleep beside her teen magazines,
her can of Coke, her plate of uncut fruit.
The pomegranate! How did I forget it?
30 She could have come home and been safe
and ended the story and all
our heart-broken searching but she reached
out a hand and plucked a pomegranate.
She put out her hand and pulled down
35 the French sound for apple and
the noise of stone and the proof
that even in the place of death,
at the heart of legend, in the midst
of rocks full of unshed tears
40 ready to be diamonds by the time
the story was told, a child can be
hungry. I could warn her. There is still a chance.
The rain is cold. The road is flint-coloured.
The suburb has cars and cable television.
45 The veiled stars are above ground.
It is another world. But what else
can a mother give her daughter but such
beautiful rifts in time?
If I defer the grief I will diminish the gift.
50 The legend will be hers as well as mine.
She will enter it. As I have.
She will wake up. She will hold
the papery flushed skin in her hand.
And to her lips. I will say nothing.

1994

CRAIG RAINE

1944–

The Onion, Memory

Divorced, but friends again at last,
we walk old ground together
in bright blue uncomplicated weather.
We laugh and pause

5 to hack to bits these tiny dinosaurs,
prehistoric, crenellated, cast
between the tractor ruts in mud.

On the green, a junior Douglas Fairbanks,[1]
swinging on the chestnut's unlit chandelier,
10 defies the corporation spears[2] —
a single rank around the bole,°   *tree trunk*
rusty with blood.
Green, tacky phalluses curve up, romance.
A gust—the old flag blazes on its pole.

15 In the village bakery
the pasty babies pass
from milky slump to crusty cadaver,
from crib to coffin—without palaver.
All's over in a flash,
20 too silently . . .

Tonight the arum lilies fold
back napkins monogrammed in gold,
crisp and laundered fresh.
Those crustaceous gladioli, on the sly,
25 reveal the crimson flower-flesh
inside their emerald armour plate.
The uncooked herrings blink a tearful eye.
The candles palpitate.
The Oistrakhs bow and scrape
30 in evening dress, on Emi-tape.[3]

Outside the trees are bending over backwards
to please the wind : the shining sword
grass flattens on its belly.
The white-thorn's frillies offer no resistance.
35 In the fridge, a heart-shaped jelly
strives to keep a sense of balance.

I slice up the onions. You sew up a dress.
This is the quiet echo—flesh—
white muscle on white muscle,
40 intimately folded skin,
finished with a satin rustle.
One button only to undo, sewn up with shabby thread.
It is the onion, memory,
that makes me cry.

45 Because there's everything and nothing to be said,
the clock with hands held up before its face,
stammers softly on, trying to complete a phrase—

---

1. Film actor famous for his swashbuckling dare-
devil exploits in the 1920s and 1930.
2. I.e., spiked fence put up by the town corpora-
tion.
3. A popular British brand of audiotape; David
and Igor Oistrakh, celebrated Russian violinists.

while we, together and apart,
repeat unfinished gestures got by heart.

50 And afterwards, I blunder with the washing on the line—
headless torsos, faceless lovers, friends of mine.

1978

A Martian Sends a Postcard Home

Caxtons[4] are mechanical birds with many wings
and some are treasured for their markings—

they cause the eyes to melt
or the body to shriek without pain.

5 I have never seen one fly, but
sometimes they perch on the hand.

Mist is when the sky is tired of flight
and rests its soft machine on ground:

then the world is dim and bookish
10 like engravings under tissue paper.

Rain is when the earth is television.
It has the property of making colours darker.

Model T[5] is a room with the lock inside—
a key is turned to free the world

15 for movement, so quick there is a film
to watch for anything missed.

But time is tied to the wrist
or kept in a box, ticking with impatience.

In homes, a haunted apparatus sleeps,
20 that snores when you pick it up.

If the ghost cries, they carry it
to their lips and soothe it to sleep

with sounds. And yet, they wake it up
deliberately, by tickling with a finger.

25 Only the young are allowed to suffer
openly. Adults go to a punishment room

with water but nothing to eat.
They lock the door and suffer the noises

---

4. I.e., books, which William Caxton (ca. 1422–1491) was the first to print in English; in the next couplet the Martian observes the effects of books on their readers, but does not know the words for "cry" or "laugh."
5. I.e., automobiles; the "key" is the ignition key.

alone. No one is exempt
30   and everyone's pain has a different smell.

At night, when all the colours die,
they hide in pairs

and read about themselves—
in colour, with their eyelids shut.

1979

WENDY COPE

1945–

Bloody Men

Bloody men are like bloody buses—
You wait for about a year
And as soon as one approaches your stop
Two or three others appear.

5   You look at them flashing their indicators,
Offering you a ride.
You're trying to read the destinations,
You haven't much time to decide.

If you make a mistake, there is no turning back.
10   Jump off, and you'll stand there and gaze
While the cars and the taxis and lorries° go by   trucks
And the minutes, the hours, the days.

Flowers

Some men never think of it.
You did. You'd come along
And say you'd nearly brought me flowers
But something had gone wrong.

5   The shop was closed. Or you had doubts—
The sort that minds like ours
Dream up incessantly. You thought
I might not want your flowers.

It made me smile and hug you then.
10   Now I can only smile.
But, look, the flowers you nearly brought
Have lasted all this while.

Valentine

My heart has made its mind up
And I'm afraid it's you.
Whatever you've got lined up,
My heart has made its mind up
5   And if you can't be signed up
This year, next year will do.
My heart has made its mind up
And I'm afraid it's you.

Serious Concerns

"She is witty and unpretentious, which is both her strength and her limita-
tion." (ROBERT O'BRIEN in the *Spectator*, 25.10.86)

I'm going to try and overcome my limitation—
Away with sloth!
Now should I work at being less witty? Or more pretentious?
Or both?

"They (Roger McGough and Brian Patten)[1] have something in common with
her, in that they all write to amuse." (IBID.)

5   Write to amuse? What an appalling suggestion!
I write to make people anxious and miserable and to worsen their
indigestion.

1992

BERNARD O'DONOGHUE

1945–

The Weakness

It was the frosty early hours when finally
The cow's despairing groans rolled him from bed
And into his boots, hardly awake yet.
He called "Dan! come on, Dan!
5   She's calving", and stumbled without his coat
Down the icy path to the haggard.

Castor and Pollux[1] were fixed in line
Over his head but he didn't see them,
This night any more than another.
10   He crossed to the stall, past the corner
Of the fairy-fort[2] he'd levelled last May.
But this that stopped him, like the mind's step

---

1. Two of the so-called Liverpool poets, popular
in the late 1960s and early 1970s.
1. The constellation named after the twin sons of
Zeus and Leda.

2. Probably a round barrow, an ancient burial site
associated in Irish folklore with the fairy people
known as the *Sidhe*.

Backward: what was that, more insistent
Than the calf's birth-pangs? "Hold on, Dan.
15   I think I'm having a weakness.
I never had a weakness, Dan, before."
And down he slid, groping for the lapels
Of the shocked boy's twenty-year old jacket.

The Apparition

More surprising than a moving statue
Of the Blessed Virgin, that yellow plane
Stationary in an Irish farmer's field
In the 'fifties: a four-day shrine until
5   Its tilted take-off, a wing-heavy heron.

That wasn't the end of it: disputation
Ran for months about its origins: what age
It came from, or what place; in what hangar
It wintered, north or south; whether our climate
10   Was too hot or cold for it: too dry or wet.

Last night I dreamt I saw it once again,
Thirty years later, on an empty patch
Beside the jumbo runway at Heathrow
From the window of a transatlantic jet
15   Through the pre-departure gauze of heat.

I tried to call "what message have you brought
From Bill Casey's field?" But the Boeing's whine
Defeated me as it carefully conducted
Its slow, elephantine pirouette.
20   Accepting that I'd never hear the truth,

I settled back to study our flight-path;
But as we drifted past it, gathering speed,
I saw clearly the notice I'd forgotten
Chalked on cardboard in the pilot's seat:
25   "Out of fuel. Back when we've got some more".

1991

YUSEF KOMUNYAKAA

1947–

Banking Potatoes

Daddy would drop purple-veined vines
Along rows of dark loam
& I'd march behind him
Like a peg-legged soldier,

5   Pushing down the stick
       With a V cut into its tip.

       Three weeks before the first frost
       I'd follow his horse-drawn plow
       That opened up the soil & left
10   Sweet potatoes sticky with sap,
       Like flesh-colored stones along a riverbed
       Or diminished souls beside a mass grave.

       They lay all day under the sun's
       Invisible weight, & by twilight
15   We'd bury them under pine needles
       & then shovel in two feet of dirt.
       Nighthawks scalloped the sweaty air,
       Their wings spread wide

       As plowshares. But soon the wind
20   Knocked on doors & windows
       Like a frightened stranger,
       & by mid-winter we had tunneled
       Back into the tomb of straw,
       Unable to divide love from hunger.

The Smokehouse

       In the hickory scent
       Among slabs of pork
       Glistening with salt,
       I played Indian
5   In a headdress of redbird feathers
       & brass buttons
       Off my mother's winter coat.
       Smoke wove
       A thread of fire through meat, into December
10   & January. The dead weight
       Of the place hung around me,
       Strung up with sweetgrass.
       The hog had been sectioned,
       A map scored into skin;
15   Opened like love,
       From snout to tail,
       The goodness
       No longer true to each bone.
       I was a wizard
20   In that hazy world,
       & knew I could cut
       Slivers of meat till my heart
       Grew more human & flawed.

Sunday Afternoons

       They'd latch the screendoors
       & pull venetian blinds,

Telling us not to leave the yard.
But we always got lost
5   Among mayhaw & crabapple.

Juice spilled from our mouths,
& soon we were drunk & brave
As birds diving through saw vines.
Each nest held three or four
10   Speckled eggs, blue as rage.

Where did we learn to be unkind,
There in the power of holding each egg
While watching dogs in June
Dust & heat, or when we followed
15   The hawk's slow, deliberate arc?

In the yard, we heard cries
Fused with gospel on the radio,
Loud as shattered glass
In a Saturday-night argument
20   About trust & money.

We were born between Oh Yeah
& Goddammit. I knew life
Began where I stood in the dark,
Looking out into the light,
25   & that sometimes I could see

Everything through nothing.
The backyard trees breathed
Like a man running from himself
As my brothers backed away
30   From the screendoor. I knew

If I held my right hand above my eyes
Like a gambler's visor, I could see
How their bedroom door halved
The dresser mirror like a moon
35   Held prisoner in the house.

1992

JANE SHORE

1947–

High Holy Days[1]

It was hot. A size too large,
my wool winter suit scratched.

1. Also called "Days of Awe," combining Rosh Hashanah, the Jewish New Year, with Yom Kippur, the Day of Atonement, ten days later; generally in September and October.

Indian summer flaring up through fall.
The shul's[2] broken window
5 bled sunlight on the congregation; the Red Sea
of the scarlet carpet parted the women from the men.[3]
Mother next to daughter, father next to son
flipped through prayerbooks in unison
trying to keep the place. Across the aisle,
10 my father wore a borrowed prayershawl.
A black yarmulke[4] covered his bald spot.

The rabbi unlocked the ark[5]
and slid the curtain open. Propped inside,
two scrolls of the Torah[6] dressed like matching dolls,
15 each, a king and a queen. Ribbons hung down
from their alabaster satin jackets;
each one wore two silver crowns.
I wondered, could the ancient kings
have been so small? So small,
20 and still have vanquished our enemies?

The cantor's voice rose
like smoke over a sacrificial altar,
and lambs,[7] we rose to echo the refrain.
Each time we sat down
25 my mother rearranged her skirt.
Each time we stood up
my head hurt from the heat, dizzy
from tripping over the alphabet's
black spikes and lyres,
30 stick-figure batallions marching to defend
the Second Temple of Jerusalem.[8]

Rocking on their heels, boats
anchored in the harbor of devotion,
the temple elders davenned Kaddish,[9] mourning the dead.
35 Our neighbor who owned the laundry down the street
covered his left wrist out of habit—
numbers indelible as those
he inked on my father's shirt collars.[1]
Once, I saw that whole arm disappear
40 into a tub of soapy shirts,

---

2. "Synagogue" (Yiddish).
3. Men and women are seated separately in Orthodox Jewish congregations. Shore's "Red Sea" of carpet, acting as a divider, reverses the image in Exodus 14.21–22, where Moses parted the Red Sea, allowing the nation of Israel to escape pursuit by the Egyptians.
4. Skullcap worn, like the "prayershawl" (a garment), by Jewish men during services.
5. A large cabinet on the altar, in which the locked Torahs are kept; the Jewish equivalent of the Ark of the Covenant (Exodus 25.10–22).
6. The five books of Moses (Genesis, Exodus, Leviticus, Numbers, and Deuteronomy), written in Hebrew. The scrolls, on two wooden rollers, are decorated with sterling-silver crowns and wrapped in fabric; called the "king's possessions" because of their centrality to Jewish religious life.
7. Under a system instituted by Moses, sins were atoned for by the sacrificing of a lamb (or ox, goat, or bird) as a burnt offering to the Lord. "Cantor": religious official who sings or chants prayers.
8. Temple built after the Jews returned from captivity in Babylon in the sixth century B.C.; destroyed by the Romans in 70 A.D.
9. Recited prayers in memory of the dead.
1. Reference to the Nazi practice of tattooing registration numbers on the left arms of some prisoners before they were sent to concentration camps.

rainbowed, buoyant as the pastel clouds
in *The Illustrated Children's Bible,*
where God's enormous hand reached down
and stopped a heathen army in its tracks.[2]
45 But on the white-hot desert of the page
I was reading, it was noon,
the marching letters swam, the regiments
wavered in the heat,
a red rain falling on their ranks.
50 I watched it fall one drop at a time.
I felt faint. And breathed out sharply,
my nose spattering blood across the page.[3]

I watched it fall, and thought,
you are a Chosen One,[4]
55 *the child to lead your tribe.*
I looked around the swaying room.
Why would God choose me
to lead this congregation of mostly strangers,
defend them against the broken windows,
60 the spray-painted writing on the walls?[5]

Overhead, the red bulb of the everlasting light[6]
was burning. As if God held me in His fist,
I stumbled down the synagogue stairs
just in time to hear
65 a cyclone of breath twist through
the shofar,[7] a battle cry so powerful
it blasted city walls to rubble.
And I reeled home through the dazed traffic
of the business day—
70 past shoppers, past my school,
in session as usual,
spat like Jonah from the whale[8]
back into the Jew-hating world.

1987

---

2. God's hand is commonly said to bring Israel deliverance from its enemies (e.g., 1 Samuel 7.13).
3. One of the three readings required on the morning of Yom Kippur (Leviticus 16.1–34) details how the priest is to consecrate the Ark of the Covenant by sprinkling the blood of a sacrificed bull and goat on the cover.
4. Moses underscored the special role of the descendants of Abraham, Isaac, and Jacob as the Lord's chosen people.
5. Reference to *Kristallnacht* ("Night of the Broken Glass"), November 9 and 10, 1938, when, in a pogrom throughout Germany and Austria, the Nazis committed such violent acts as breaking the windows of Jewish stores.
6. A red electric light, symbolic of God's eternal presence, is kept burning continuously in the ceiling of an Orthodox synagogue.
7. Trumpet made of ram's horn; blown in synagogues on the High Holy Days. In Joshua 6.20, when the people heard the priests blow a shofar, they raised such a great shout that the walls of Jericho fell.
8. After Jonah had been swallowed by a great fish, the Lord spoke to it and it spew Jonah out (Jonah 2.10). The Book of Jonah is read in its entirety on Yom Kippur.

LESLIE MARMON SILKO
1948–

Prayer to the Pacific

I traveled to the ocean
    distant
        from my southwest land of sandrock
        to the moving blue water
5   Big as the myth of origin.

Pale
pale water in the yellow-white light of
        sun   floating west
            to China
10   where ocean herself was born.
Clouds that blow across the sand are wet.

Squat in the wet sand and speak to the Ocean:
        I return to you   turquoise   the red coral you sent us,
            sister spirit of Earth.
15 Four round stones in my pocket   I carry back the ocean
        to suck and to taste.

Thirty thousand years ago
        Indians came riding across the ocean
        carried by giant sea turtles.
20 Waves were high that day
        great sea turtles waded   slowly out
            from the gray sundown sea.
Grandfather Turtle rolled in the sand   four times
        and disappeared
25   swimming into the sun.

And so   from that time
        immemorial,
            as the old people say,
rain clouds drift from the west
30   gift from the ocean.

Green leaves in the wind
Wet earth on my feet
        swallowing raindrops
            clear from China.

1981

RICHARD KENNEY

1948–

Aubade

Cold snap. Five o'clock.
Outside, a heavy frost—dark
footprints in the brittle
grass; a cat's. Quick coffee,
5 jacket, watch-cap, keys.
Stars blaze across the black
gap between horizons;
pickup somehow strikes
its own dim spark—an arc—
10 starts. Inside, familiar
metal cab, an icebox
full of lightless air,
limns green with dash-light. Vinyl
seat cracks, cold and brittle;
15 horn ring gleams, and chrome
cuts hard across the wrist
where the sleeve falls off the glove,
as moon-track curves its cool tiara
somewhere underneath your sleep
20 this very moment, love—

Apples on Champlain[1]

Oil-slick, slack shocks, ancient engine
smoking like a burning tire,
Augustus' old truck yaws and slews,
its leaf-springs limp these centuries
5 suspending apples, somehow pulls
the last hill past the bridge at Isle
La Motte.[2] I hear the iron arches
groaning. Why not? Whole orchards
rattling, empty racks behind us,
10 emptied into grain sacks, piled
behind us—home ahead, we broach
the mile-long causeway cross from Grande Isle[3]
back.
     A blue heron's motionless
15 in marsh grass to my right, and pole
and icepack at my left—one line,
two lanes, a roostertail of blue
exhaust, we part the cooling waters
of Champlain.

1. Lake Champlain, which divides the states of New York and Vermont near the Canadian border.
2. Vermont town on one of the islands in Lake Champlain.
3. Group of four islands in Lake Champlain.

20 The moon's a pool
of mercury. It's zero. Ice soon.
Steaming like a teacup, losing
heat, the lake is tossing clouds up
all around the truck; and tucked
25 so in its fragile ribcage creel,
the cold heart *thump* accordions
to keep alive, and fills, as apples
interrupt this landscape's black-
on-grey like heartbeats full of blood,
30 strung beads, a life of little suns
gone rolling down the press and sump
of memory and changing form
as *thump*, horizon groans and ladles
light, and the real sun comes up,
35 sudden, weightless, warm.

Sawmill

Snap tempered tooth chips
sawyer shouts *steel in sawlog*
lock engine off slack
line carriage back echo
5 like a gunshot ricochets
off galvanized tin roof the great
blade ringing like a gong
and every man down low:
look, along the log's sheer face,
10 the bright metal shows itself:
a tap, a nail, a bit of buried
wire, some wrong coordinate
or undetected intercept
exactly *there* — count the rings —
15 just forty years ago.

Plume

In the orchard,
puffs, plumes,
odd gusts —
when suddenly
5 the trees toss up
their blooms at once:
white petals
chimney up
and braid together
10 in the sky
like sweet smoke
from the same flame —
so beautiful!
And still, a shame.

1985

AGHA SHAHID ALI

1949–

The Dacca[1] Gauzes

. . . for a whole year he sought to accumulate the most exquisite Dacca gauzes.

—OSCAR WILDE / *The Picture of Dorian Gray*

Those transparent Dacca gauzes
known as woven air, running
water, evening dew:

a dead art now, dead over
5   a hundred years. "No one
now knows," my grandmother says,

"what it was to wear
or touch that cloth." She wore
it once, an heirloom sari from

10   her mother's dowry, proved
genuine when it was pulled, all
six yards, through a ring.

Years later when it tore,
many handkerchiefs embroidered
15   with gold-thread paisleys

were distributed among
the nieces and daughters-in-law.
Those too now lost.

In history we learned: the hands
20   of weavers were amputated,
the looms of Bengal silenced,

and the cotton shipped raw
by the British to England.
History of little use to her,

25   my grandmother just says
how the muslins of today
seem so coarse and that only

in autumn, should one wake up
at dawn to pray, can one
30   feel that same texture again.

1. City in Bangladesh.

One morning, she says, the air
was dew-starched: she pulled
it absently through her ring.

1987

I See Chile in My Rearview Mirror

For Carol Houck Smith

By dark the world is once again intact,
Or so the mirrors, wiped clean, try to reason . . .
—JAMES MERRILL

This dream of water—what does it harbor?
I see Argentina and Paraguay
under a curfew of glass, their colors
breaking, like oil. The night in Uruguay

5   is black salt. I'm driving toward Utah,
keeping the entire hemisphere in view—
Colombia vermilion, Brazil blue tar,
some countries wiped clean of color: Peru

is titanium white. And always oceans
10 that hide in mirrors: when beveled edges
arrest tides or this world's destinations
forsake ships. There's Sedona, Nogales

far behind. Once I went through a mirror—
from there too the world, so intact, resembled
15 only itself. When I returned I tore
the skin off the glass. The sea was unsealed

by dark, and I saw ships sink off the coast
of a wounded republic. Now from a blur
of tanks in Santiago, a white horse
20 gallops, riderless, chased by drunk soldiers

in a jeep; they're firing into the moon.
And as I keep driving in the desert,
someone is running to catch the last bus, men
hanging on to its sides. And he's missed it.

25 He is running again; crescents of steel
fall from the sky. And here the rocks
are under fog, the cedars a temple,
Sedona carved by the wind into gods—

each shadow their worshiper. The siren
30 empties Santiago; he watches
—from a hush of windows—blindfolded men
blurred in gleaming vans. The horse vanishes

into a dream. I'm passing skeletal
figures carved in 700 B.C.
35 Whoever deciphers these canyon walls
remains forsaken, alone with history,

no harbor for his dream. And what else will
this mirror now reason, filled with water?
I see Peru without rain, Brazil
40 without forests—and here in Utah a dagger

of sunlight: it's splitting—it's the summer
solstice—the quartz center of a spiral.
Did the Anasazi[2] know the darker
answer also—given now in crystal

45 by the mirrored continent? The solstice,
but of winter? A beam stabs the window,
diamonds him, a funeral in his eyes.
In the lit stadium of Santiago,

this is the shortest day. He's taken there.
50 Those about to die are looking at him,
his eyes the ledger of the disappeared.
What will the mirror try now? I'm driving,

still north, always followed by that country,
its floors ice, its citizens so lovesick
55 that the ground—sheer glass—of every city
is torn up. They demand the republic

give back, jeweled, their every reflection.
They dig till dawn but find only corpses.
He has returned to this dream for his bones.
60 The waters darken. The continent vanishes.

1991

JAMES FENTON

1949–

Dead Soldiers

When His Excellency Prince Norodom Chantaraingsey
Invited me to lunch on the battlefield
I was glad of my white suit for the first time that day.
They lived well, the mad Norodoms, they had style.
5 The brandy and the soda arrived in crates.
Bricks of ice, tied around with raffia,
Dripped from the orderlies' handlebars.

2. Culturally advanced, cliff-dwelling Indians in the southwestern United States (A.D. 1000–1300) who
mysteriously abandoned their cities.

And I remember the dazzling tablecloth
As the APCs[1] fanned out along the road,
10 The dishes piled high with frogs' legs,
Pregnant turtles, their eggs boiled in the carapace,
Marsh irises in fish sauce
And inflorescence[2] of a banana salad.

On every bottle, Napoleon Bonaparte
15 Pleaded for the authenticity of the spirit.[3]
They called the empties Dead Soldiers
And rejoiced to see them pile up at our feet.

Each diner was attended by one of the other ranks[4]
Whirling a table-napkin to keep off the flies.
20 It was like eating between rows of morris dancers[5] —
Only they didn't kick.

In a diary, I refer to Pol Pot's[6] brother as the Jockey Cap.
A few weeks later, I find him "in good form
And very skeptical about Chantaraingsey."
25 "But one eats well there," I remark.
"So one should," says the Jockey Cap:
"The tiger always eats well,
It eats the raw flesh of the deer,
And Chantaraingsey was born in the year of the tiger.
30 So, did they show you the things they do
With the young refugee girls?"

And he tells me how he will one day give me the gen.°   *inside information*
He will tell me how the prince financed the casino
And how the casino brought Lon Nol to power.[7]
35 He will tell me this.
He will tell me all these things.
All I must do is drink and listen.

In those days, I thought that when the game was up
The prince would be far, far away—
40 In a limestone faubourg,° on the promenade at Nice,   *suburb*
Reduced in circumstances but well enough provided for.
In Paris, he would hardly require his private army.
The Jockey Cap might suffice for café warfare,
And matchboxes for APCs.

45 But we were always wrong in these predictions.
It was a family war. Whatever happened,
The principals were obliged to attend its issue.

---

1. Armed Personnel Carriers: armored trucks for transporting troops.
2. Arrangement of flowers on an axis; blossoming.
3. Napolean brandy (i.e., of high quality).
4. General infantrymen.
5. Performers of British folk dances, which include the waving of scarves, handkerchiefs, and sometimes wooden staves.

6. Pol Pot was a Kampuchean politician. Part of the anti-French resistance in the 1940s, he became leader of the pro-French Communist Party, and Prime Minister in 1976. His government was overthrown after the Vietnamese invasion of 1979.
7. General Lon Nol, a right-wing politician, became president of Cambodia in 1970 after his faction overthrew Sihanouk (see note 8, below).

A few were cajoled into leaving, a few were expelled,
And there were villains enough, but none of them
50 Slipped away with the swag.°   *loot*

For the prince was fighting Sihanouk,[8] his nephew,
And the Jockey Cap was ranged against his brother
Of whom I remember nothing more
Than an obscure reputation for virtue.
55 I have been told that the prince is still fighting
Somewhere in the Cardamoms or the Elephant Mountains.
But I doubt that the Jockey Cap would have survived his good
        connections.
I think the lunches would have done for him—
Either the lunches or the dead soldiers.

                                                            1981

A German Requiem

(To T. J. G.-A.)

For as at a great distance of place, that which wee look at, appears dimme,
and without distinction of the smaller parts; and as Voyces grow weak, and
inarticulate: so also after great distance of time, our imagination of the Past is
weak; and wee lose (for example) of Cities wee have seen, many particular
Streets; and of Actions, many particular circumstances. This *decaying sense*,
when wee would express the thing it self, (I mean *fancy* it selfe,) wee call
Imagination, as I said before: But when we would express the *decay*, and
signifie that the Sense is fading, old, and past, it is called Memory. So that
Imagination and *Memory* are but one thing . . .
                                        —HOBBES, *Leviathan*

It is not what they built. It is what they knocked down.
It is not the houses. It is the spaces between the houses.
It is not the streets that exist. It is the streets that no longer exist.
It is not your memories which haunt you.
5 It is not what you have written down.
It is what you have forgotten, what you must forget.
What you must go on forgetting all your life.
And with any luck oblivion should discover a ritual.
You will find out that you are not alone in the enterprise.
10 Yesterday the very furniture seemed to reproach you.
Today you take your place in the Widow's Shuttle.[9]

                                *

The bus is waiting at the southern gate
To take you to the city of your ancestors
Which stands on the hill opposite, with gleaming pediments,[1]
15 As vivid as this charming square, your home.
Are you shy? You should be. It is almost like a wedding,
The way you clasp your flowers and give a little tug at your veil. Oh,
The hideous bridesmaids, it is natural that you should resent them

8. Norodom Sihanouk Varmon was made king of
Cambodia by the French in 1941.
9. Popular name for bus going to the cemetery.

1. Triangular structures crowning the fronts of
buildings.

Just a little, on this first day.
20 But that will pass, and the cemetery is not far.
Here comes the driver, flicking a toothpick into the gutter,
His tongue still searching between his teeth.
See, he has not noticed you. No one has noticed you.
It will pass, young lady, it will pass.

*

25 How comforting it is, once or twice a year,
To get together and forget the old times.
As on those special days, ladies and gentlemen,
When the boiled shirts[2] gather at the graveside
And a leering waistcoat approaches the rostrum.
30 It is like a solemn pact between the survivors.
The mayor has signed it on behalf of the freemasonry.[3]
The priest has sealed it on behalf of all the rest.
Nothing more need be said, and it is better that way—

*

The better for the widow, that she should not live in fear of surprise,
35 The better for the young man, that he should move at liberty
            between the armchairs,
The better that these bent figures who flutter among the graves
Tending the nightlights and replacing the chrysanthemums
Are not ghosts,
That they shall go home.
40 The bus is waiting, and on the upper terraces
The workmen are dismantling the houses of the dead.

*

But when so many had died, so many and at such speed,
There were no cities waiting for the victims.
They unscrewed the name-plates from the shattered doorways
45 And carried them away with the coffins.
So the squares and parks were filled with the eloquence of young
            cemeteries:
The smell of fresh earth, the improvised crosses
And all the impossible directions in brass and enamel.

*

"Doctor Gliedschirm, skin specialist, surgeries 14–16 hours or by
            appointment."
50 Professor Sargnagel was buried with four degrees, two associate
            memberships
And instructions to tradesmen to use the back entrance.
Your uncle's grave informed you that he lived on the third floor, left.
You were asked please to ring, and he would come down in the lift[4]
To which one needed a key . . .

2. (Men wearing) dress shirts with starched fronts.   rituals.
3. Fraternity for mutual help, called "Free and   4. Elevator.
Accepted Masons" and having elaborate secret

*

55 Would come down, would ever come down
    With a smile like thin gruel, and never too much to say.
    How he shrank through the years.
    How you towered over him in the narrow cage.[5]
    How he shrinks now . . .

*

60 But come. Grief must have its term? Guilt too, then.
    And it seems there is no limit to the resourcefulness of recollection.
    So that a man might say and think:
    When the world was at its darkest,
    When the black wings passed over the rooftops[6]
65 (And who can divine His purposes?) even then
    There was always, always a fire in this hearth.
    You see this cupboard? A priest-hole!
    And in that lumber-room whole generations have been housed and fed.
    Oh, if I were to begin, if I were to begin to tell you
70 The half, the quarter, a mere smattering of what we went through!

*

His wife nods, and a secret smile,
Like a breeze with enough strength to carry one dry leaf
Over two pavingstones, passes from chair to chair.
Even the enquirer is charmed.
75 He forgets to pursue the point.
It is not what he wants to know.
It is what he wants not to know.
It is not what they say.
It is what they do not say.

1982

God, A Poem

A nasty surprise in a sandwich,
A drawing-pin caught in your sock,
The limpest of shakes from a hand which
You'd thought would be firm as a rock,

5 A serious mistake in a nightie,
A grave disappointment all round
Is all that you'll get from th'Almighty,
Is all that you'll get underground.

Oh he *said*: "If you lay off the crumpet°   *women*
10 I'll see you alright in the end.
Just hang on until the last trumpet.
Have faith in me, chum—I'm your friend."

---

5. Of the wire-screened elevator.
6. Cf. Exodus 12.27: "It is the sacrifice of the Lord's passover, who passed over the houses of the children of Israel in Egypt, when he smote the Egyptians, and delivered our houses."

But if you remind him, he'll tell you:
"I'm sorry, I must have been pissed—
15   Though your name rings a sort of a bell. You
Should have guessed that I do not exist.

"I didn't exist at Creation,
I didn't exist at the Flood,
And I won't be around for Salvation
20   To sort out the sheep from the cud—

"Or whatever the phrase is. The fact is
In soteriological° terms   *salvational*
I'm a crude existential malpractice
And you are a diet of worms.

25   "You're a nasty surprise in a sandwich.
You're a drawing-pin caught in my sock.
You're the limpest of shakes from a hand which
I'd have thought would be firm as a rock,

"You're a serious mistake in a nightie,
30   You're a grave disappointment all round—
That's all that you are," says th'Almighty,
"And that's all that you'll be underground."

                                                                1983

In Paris with You

Don't talk to me of love. I've had an earful
And I get tearful when I've downed a drink or two.
I'm one of your talking wounded.
I'm a hostage. I'm maroonded.
5   But I'm in Paris with you.

Yes I'm angry at the way I've been bamboozled
And resentful at the mess that I've been through.
I admit I'm on the rebound
And I don't care where are *we* bound.
10   I'm in Paris with you.

Do you mind if we do *not* go to the Louvre,
If we say sod off to sodding Notre Dame,
If we skip the Champs Elysées
And remain here in this sleazy
15   Old hotel room
Doing this and that
To what and whom
Learning who you are,
Learning what I am.

20   Don't talk to me of love. Let's talk of Paris,
The little bit of Paris in our view.
There's that crack across the ceiling

And the hotel walls are peeling
And I'm in Paris with you.

25 Don't talk to me of love. Let's talk of Paris.
I'm in Paris with the slightest thing you do.
I'm in Paris with your eyes, your mouth,
I'm in Paris with . . . all points south.
Am I embarrassing you?
30 I'm in Paris with you.

1993

DEBORA GREGER

1949–

From Lives of the Saints

The Hustler de Paris[1]

Notre Dame, Sainte Chapelle, Sacré Coeur[2] by foot—
deep in the Louvre the Mona Lisa[3] smirks
at the good tourist who grants her a minute
for each star in the Michelin,[4] then soldiers on.
5 So all of Paris could be mine?

Quel est le prix d'entrée?[5]
For the price of admission, I can sit in defeat
and view an *arrondissement*° from home: district of Paris
a small-town main street, a gas station
10 somewhere on a studio's back lot. A car

like a loaf of bread pulls up. Two men get out.
One's the young god, Paul Newman,
about to step into a pool hall's gloom
undubbed, only the picket fence
15 of French subtitles between him and us.

Like a sleepy sexton, the janitor performs
uncalled-for miracles, raising the blinds
to flood the hall with daylight
so dirty it must be divine.
20 "Like a church," Newman says,

"Church of the Good Hustler."[6]
Even in black and white his eyes are blue.

1. An amalgam of the title of the 1961 American film *The Hustler* (which stars Paul Newman as Fast Eddie Felson, a pool shark) and the French "of Paris."
2. The cathedral, a chapel, and a basilica, all tourist landmarks in Paris.
3. Popular name for the painting *La Gioconda* by the Italian artist Leonardo da Vinci (1452–1519); a principal attraction of the Louvre Museum.
4. Tourist guidebook that awards stars for each attraction.
5. "What is the price of admission?" (French).
6. An ironic play on The Good Shepherd, or Jesus.

The fair Savior of Western art,
devil too handsome for his own good.
25   The fat man[7] with a carnation in his lapel

opens his great, soft palms
to receive the ritual talcum,
his the hands of a priest, so dainty, so mechanical.
At midnight he intones the litany of his shots.
30   Gray bills rain down on the gray felt.

To the gargoyles who watch,[8] it's the old story,
boy hustles anything that moves, even pain.
La petite escourgette[9] to mortify the flesh,
the Crown of Thorns, the Holy Sponge,
35   *un morceau considérable* of the True Cross[1] —

that is the smell of money,
of nights just a few thousand old.
Now the saint of the broken thumbs:
"I came to play pool, Fats."
40   *Très bien, Eddie Vite. Combien?*[2]

How much the things of this world
have darkened while we were inside.
Even the late light hurts,
the old stone cleaned of the centuries
45   we sat through, until it glows.

Just ahead of a last sweep by *les flics*,[3]
street sellers roll up their rugs,
their little Winged Victories,[4]
and weave into the nearest throng,
50   saints without permit passing among us.

The Frog in the Swimming Pool

A wet green velvet scums the swimming pool,
furring the cracks. The deep end swims
in a hatful of rain, not enough to float

the bedspring barge, the tug of shopping cart.
5   Green-wet himself, the bullfrog holds his court,
sounding the summons to a life so low

7. Minnesota Fats, the pool champion, beating whom is Fast Eddie's major challenge.
8. Gargoyles are carved in the roof of Notre Dame Cathedral.
9. "The little scourge" (Old French).
1. The scourge, the crown of thorns, the Holy Sponge, and the cross are all instruments of the Crucifixion. *Un morceau considérable*: "a considerable piece" (French).
2. "All right, Fast Eddie. How much?" (French).

Eddie's thumbs had earlier been broken in retaliation for hustling at pool.
3. "The police" (French slang).
4. Models of the Winged Victory of Samothrace, the great early Hellenistic sculpture, headless and armless, on display at the Louvre; like the "Mona Lisa," a tourist's symbol of Paris. Street vendors in Paris are often illegal residents; hence the flight from police.

he's yet to lure a mate. Under the lip
of concrete slab he reigns, a rumble of rock,
a flickering of sticky tongue that's licked

10   at any morsel winging into view.
How would he love her? Let me count the waves[5]
that scrape the underside of night and then

let go, the depth of love unplumbed, the breadth,
the height of the pool all he needs to know.
15   How do I love him? Let me add the weight

of one hush to another, the mockingbird
at midnight echoing itself, not him,
one silence torn in two, sewn shut again.

Down to his level in time wings everything.
20   He calls the night down on his unlovely head,
on the slimy skin that breathes the slimy air—

the skin that's shed and still he is the same,
the first voice in the world, the last each night.
His call has failed to fill the empty house

25   across the street, the vacant swing that sways
halfheartedly, the slide slid into rust,
the old griefs waiting burial by the new.

1994

DANA GIOIA

1950–

Prayer

Echo of the clocktower, footstep
in the alleyway, sweep
of the wind sifting the leaves.

Jeweller of the spiderweb, connoisseur
5   of autumn's opulence, blade of lightning
harvesting the sky.

Keeper of the small gate, choreographer
of entrances and exits, midnight
whisper travelling the wires.

---

5. An allusion to the first line of *Sonnets from the Portuguese*, 43 (p. 856), by the English poet Elizabeth Barrett Browning (1806–1861). Greger alters Browning's opening again in line 15.

10   Seducer, healer, deity or thief,
     I will see you soon enough—
     in the shadow of the rainfall,

     in the brief violet darkening a sunset—
     but until then I pray watch over him
15   as a mountain guards its covert ore

     and the harsh falcon its flightless young.

The Next Poem

     How much better it seems now
     than when it is finally done—
     the unforgettable first line,
     the cunning way the stanzas run.

5   The rhymes soft-spoken and suggestive
     are barely audible at first,
     an appetite not yet acknowledged
     like the inkling of a thirst.

     While gradually the form appears
10   as each line is coaxed aloud—
     the architecture of a room
     seen from the middle of a crowd.

     The music that of common speech
     but slanted so that each detail
15   sounds unexpected as a sharp
     inserted in a simple scale.

     No jumble box of imagery
     dumped glumly in the reader's lap
     or elegantly packaged junk
20   the unsuspecting must unwrap.

     But words that could direct a friend
     precisely to an unknown place,
     those few unshakeable details
     that no confusion can erase.

25   And the real subject left unspoken
     but unmistakable to those
     who don't expect a jungle parrot
     in the black and white of prose.

     How much better it seems now
30   than when it is finally written.
     How hungrily one waits to feel
     the bright lure seized, the old hook bitten.

1991

NICHOLAS CHRISTOPHER

1951–

The Palm Reader

In her storefront living room—
overstuffed couch, oversized TV, a bowl of mints
on the Plexiglas coffee table—
she watches *Edge of Night*[1] and files her nails.
5 The paraphernalia pertaining to her trade
crowd a shelf beneath the large green hand
painted onto the window: a Tarot deck,
coins and obelisks, a chalky bust with numbered
phrenological divisions on the skull.
10 Through the beaded curtain in the rear
some clues emerge as to *her* life:
two children trading insults,
a man calling out, "Eggs!"
as a frying pan clatters into a sink,
15 a dog running by with a wig in his mouth.
She herself is plump, heavily made up,
wearing a red dress and a shawl imprinted
with the signs of the zodiac.
A gold pyramid hangs from her throat
20 and she has combed glittering
silver stars through her black hair.
From a plush rocker she beckons you,
at the window, to a straight-back chair
in which she will divine (according to the sign
25 on the door) "the roads into your future,
and helpful information from the Beyond."
Though the latter, especially, tempts
you powerfully, you decline,
and she shrugs with a rueful smile.
30 And because it is close to noon,
and the sidewalk is empty, as you cross
the street she closes up for lunch.
Her living room in which matters of life
and death—of human destiny laid bare—
35 suddenly reverts to its other function:
husband slumped on the couch clutching a beer,
children sopping bread across paper plates,
the dog sprawled under the table.
All of them watching *Edge of Night* now.
40 The fate of whose characters, which keeps
a faithful public tuning in day after day,
year after year, is presumably known

---

1. A soap opera.

to this woman, lighting a cigarette
and surveying that room, open to all passersby
45   yet utterly remote, as inescapable
as the future itself, that jumps out
at her from every stranger's hand.

Far from Home

A broken-down hotel on an inhospitable sea,
and behind it, a field of thorns in which
a man wearing white gloves is digging a hole
with the exact proportions of a grave.

5   Down the hall, the young chambermaid
is staring into a basin full of red water.
Her hair is white and her hands are wrinkled.
A shark tooth dangles from her ear.

In the evening she leaves a tray by my door:
10   a glass, a carafe of water, and a bottle
containing liquor that swirls like mist.
Mornings she brings bitter tea and a map.

Always the same map—not of the island
we're on, but of one I left long ago.
15   (If it were this island, I wouldn't know,
having never ventured from the hotel.)

There is a bowl of black seashells by my bed.
The maps—thirteen of them—are stacked
between the lamp that flickers like a star
20   and the quartz lions veined with light.

The clerk at the front desk could be a statue.
His dark glasses reflect the bare lobby,
its leafless plants and shuttered windows.
At his fingertips is a tumbler filled with dust.

25   The day I check out, the other guests line
the balcony, wrapped in sheets, speaking
a language I've never heard—sibilant as
the sea, but with no two words sounding alike.

The man in white gloves appears, to carry
30   my suitcase, and pauses before a mirror
in which I see, not his image, but towering
iron waves, rising to mesh with an iron sky.

1995

JORIE GRAHAM

1951–

What the End Is For

[GRAND FORKS, NORTH DAKOTA]¹

A boy just like you took me out to see them,
    the five hundred B-52's on alert on the runway,
fully loaded fully manned pointed in all the directions,
    running every minute
5 of every day.
    They sound like a sickness of the inner ear,

where the heard foams up into the noise of listening,
    where the listening arrives without being extinguished.
The huge hum soaks up into the dusk.
10   The minutes spring open. Six is too many.
From where we watch,
    from where even watching is an anachronism,

from the 23rd of March from an open meadow,
    the concertina wire in its double helix
15 designed to tighten round a body if it turns
    is the last path the sun can find to take out,
each barb flaring gold like a braille being read,
    then off with its knowledge and the sun
is gone. . . .

20 That's when the lights on all the extremities, like an outline like a dress,
    become loud in the story,
and a dark I have not seen before
    sinks in to hold them one
by one.
25   Strange plot made to hold so many inexhaustible
screams.
    Have you ever heard in a crowd mutterings of
blame

that will not modulate that will not rise?
30   He tells me, your stand-in, they *stair-step* up.
He touches me to have me look more deeply
    in
to where for just a moment longer
    color still lives:
35 the belly white so that it looks like sky, the top
    some kind of brown, some soil—How does it look

---

1. Site of Grand Forks Air Force Base, where B-52 aircraft remained until 1986. Graham uses poetic license in greatly exaggerating the number of planes; fewer than a squadron (fifteen planes) would actually run their engines at a time, for no more than about an hour.

from up there now
        this meadow we lie on our bellies in, this field Iconography
tells me stands for sadness
40   because the wind can move through it uninterrupted?
What is it the wind
        would have wanted to find and didn't

leafing down through this endless admiration unbroken
        because we're too low for it
45 to find us?
        Are you still there for me now in that dark
we stood in for hours
        letting it sweep as far as it could down over us
unwilling to move, irreconcilable? What *he*
50   wants to tell me,

his whisper more like a scream
        over this eternity of engines never not running,
is everything: how the crews assigned to each plane
        for a week at a time, the seven boys, must live
55 inseparable,
        how they stay together for life,
how the wings are given a life of
        seven feet of play,

how they drop practice bombs called *shapes* over Nevada,
60   how the measures for counterattack in air
have changed and we
        now forego firepower for jamming, for the throwing
of false signals. The meadow, the meadow hums, love, with the planes,
        as if every last blade of grass were wholly possessed

65 by this practice, wholly prepared. The last time I saw you,
        we stood facing each other as dusk came on.
I leaned against the refrigerator, you leaned against the door.
        The picture window behind you was slowly extinguished,
the tree went out, the two birdfeeders, the metal braces on them.
70   The light itself took a long time,

bits in puddles stuck like the useless
        splinters of memory, the chips
of history, hopes, laws handed down. *Here, hold these* he says, these
        grasses these
75 torn pods, he says, smiling over the noise another noise, *take these*
        he says, my hands wrong for

the purpose, here,
        not-visible-from-the-sky, prepare yourself with these, boy and
bouquet of
80   thistleweed and wort and william and
timothy. We stood there. Your face went out a long time
        before the rest of it. Can't see you anymore I said. *Nor I,*

you, whatever you still were
    replied.
85 When I asked you to hold me you refused.
    When I asked you to cross the six feet of room to hold me

you refused. Until I
    couldn't rise out of the patience either any longer
to make us
90   take possession.
Until we were what we must have wanted to be:
    shapes the shapelessness was taking back.
Why should I lean out?
    Why should I move?
95 When the Maenads tear Orpheus limb from limb,
    they throw his head

out into the river.[2]
    Unbodied it sings
all the way downstream, all the way to the single ocean,
100   head floating in current downriver singing,
until the sound of the cataracts grows,
    until the sound of the open ocean grows and the voice.

                                                    1987

Opulence

The self-brewing of the amaryllis rising before me.
Weeks of something's decomposing—like hearsay
growing—into this stringent self-analysis—
a tyranny of utter self-reflexiveness—
5   its nearness to the invisible a deep fissure
the days suck round as its frontiers trill, slur
—a settling-ever-upward and then,
                        now,
this utterly sound-free-though-tongued opening
10 where some immortal scale is screeched—
bits of *clench, jolt, fray* and *assuage*—
bits of *gnaw* and *pulse* and, even, *ruse*
—impregnable dribble—wingbeat at a speed
too slow to see—stepping out of the casing outstretched,
15   high-heeled—
something from underneath coaxing the packed buds up,
loosening their perfect fit—the smooth skin between them
                            striating then
beginning to wrinkle and fold
20 so as to loosen the tight dictation of the four inseparable polished
                            and bullioned
buds—color seeping up till the icy green releases the sensation of

2. The Maenads, also called Bacchae and Thyi- / pieces for not honoring their god. His severed
ads, were women inspired to frenzy by Dionysus, / head, said to continue speaking, floated down the
Greek god of wine and ecstasy. One legend holds / Thracian river Hebrus to the island of Lesbos,
that it was they who tore the poet Orpheus to / home of lyric poetry.

a set of reds

imprisoned in it, flushed, though not yet truly
25   visible—the green still starchy—clean—
till the four knots grow loose in their armor,
and the two dimensions of their perfect-fit fill out and a third,
shadow, seeps in

loosening and loosening,
30   and the envelope rips,
and the fringes slip off and begin to fray at their newly freed tips,
and the enameled, vaulting, perfectly braided
Immaculate

is jostled, unpacked—
35   the force, the phantom, now sending armloads up
into the exclamation,
and the skin marbles, and then, when I look again,
has already begun to speckle, then blush, then a solid un-
avoidable incarnadine,
40   the fourness of it now maneuvering, vitalized,
like antennae rearranging constantly,
the monologue reduced—or is it expanded—to
this chatter seeking all the bits of light,
the four of them craning this way then that according to
45   the time

of day, the drying wrinkled skirts of the casing
now folded-down beneath, formulaic,
the light wide-awake around it—or is it the eye—
yes yes yes yes says the mechanism of the underneath tick tock—
50   and no footprints to or from the place—
no footprints to or from—

1993

PAUL MULDOON

1951–

Why Brownlee Left

Why Brownlee left, and where he went,
Is a mystery even now.
For if a man should have been content
It was him; two acres of barley,
5   One of potatoes, four bullocks,
A milker, a slated farmhouse.
He was last seen going out to plough
On a March morning, bright and early.

By noon Brownlee was famous;
10   They had found all abandoned, with
The last rig[1] unbroken, his pair of black

---

1. Ridge between a pair of plow furrows.

Horses, like man and wife,
Shifting their weight from foot to
Foot, and gazing into the future.

1980

Gathering Mushrooms

The rain comes flapping through the yard
like a tablecloth that she hand-embroidered.
My mother has left it on the line.
It is sodden with rain.
5   The mushroom shed is windowless, wide,
its high-stacked wooden trays
hosed down with formaldehyde.[2]
And my father has opened the Gates of Troy[3]
to that first load of horse manure.
10 Barley straw. Gypsum.[4] Dried blood. Ammonia.
Wagon after wagon
blusters in, a self-renewing gold-black dragon
we push to the back of the mind.
We have taken our pitchforks to the wind.

15 All brought back to me that September evening
fifteen years on. The pair of us
tripping through Barnett's fair demesne°   *domain*
like girls in long dresses
after a hail-storm.
20 We might have been thinking of the fire-bomb
that sent Malone House sky-high
and its priceless collection of linen
sky-high.
We might have wept with Elizabeth McCrum.
25 We were thinking only of psilocybin.[5]
You sang of the maid you met on the dewy grass—
And she stooped so low gave me to know
it was mushrooms she was gathering O.

He'll be wearing that same old donkey-jacket[6]
30 and the sawn-off waders.
He carries a knife, two punnets,[7] a bucket.
He reaches far into his own shadow.
We'll have taken him unawares
and stand behind him, slightly to one side.
35 He is one of those ancient warriors
before the rising tide.
He'll glance back from under his peaked cap
without breaking rhythm:
his coaxing a mushroom—a flat or a cup—

2. Formic-acid antiseptic.
3. Troy was the city besieged by the Greeks in Homer's *Iliad*. Its walls could not be destroyed from without, and it was finally captured only by a trick.
4. Hydrated calcium sulfate, used for making plaster of Paris.
5. Hallucinogenic drug made from mushrooms.
6. Strong jacket with leather shoulder patches.
7. Small shallow baskets for fruit or vegetables.

40   the nick against his right thumb;
the bucket then, the punnet to left or right,
and so on and so forth till kingdom come.

We followed the overgrown tow-path by the Lagan.
The sunset would deepen through cinnamon
45   to aubergine,
the wood-pigeon's concerto for oboe and strings,
allegro, blowing your mind.
And you were suddenly out of my ken, hurtling
towards the ever-receding ground,
50   into the maw
of a shimmering green-gold dragon.
You discovered yourself in some outbuilding
with your long-lost companion, me,
though my head had grown into the head of a horse
55   that shook its dirty-fair mane
and spoke this verse:

*Come back to us. However cold and raw, your feet
were always meant
to negotiate terms with bare cement.*
60   *Beyond this concrete wall is a wall of concrete
and barbed wire. Your only hope
is to come back. If sing you must, let your song
tell of treading your own dung,
let straw and dung give a spring to your step.*
65   *If we never live to see the day we leap
into our true domain,
lie down with us now and wrap
yourself in the soiled grey blanket of Irish rain
that will, one day, bleach itself white.*
70   *Lie down with us and wait.*

1983

Meeting the British

We met the British in the dead of winter.
The sky was lavender

and the snow lavender-blue.
I could hear, far below,

5   the sound of two streams coming together
(both were frozen over)

and, no less strange,
myself calling out in French

across that forest-
10   clearing. Neither General Jeffrey Amherst

nor Colonel Henry Bouquet
could stomach our willow-tobacco.

As for the unusual
scent when the Colonel shook out his hand-

15   kerchief: *C'est la lavande,*
une fleur mauve comme le ciel.[8]

They gave us six fishhooks
and two blankets embroidered with smallpox.

1987

Brock[9]

Small wonder
he's not been sighted all winter;
this old brock's
been to Normandy and back

5   through the tunnels and trenches
of his subconscious.
His father fell victim
to mustard-gas at the Somme;[1]

one of his sons lost a paw
10   to a gin-trap at Lisbellaw:
another drills
on the Antrim hills'

still-molten lava
in a moth-eaten Balaclava.[2]
15   An elaborate
system of foxholes and duckboards

leads to the terminal moraine[3]
of an ex-linen baron's
croquet-lawn
20   where he's part-time groundsman.

I would find it somewhat *infra dig*[4]
to dismiss him simply as a pig
or heed Gerald of Wales'[5]
tall tales

25   of badgers keeping badger-slaves.
For when he shuffles

8. "It is lavender, a flower as mauve as the sky" (French).
9. Popular name for badger.
1. Area in northern France, scene of some of the fiercest fighting of World War I.
2. Knitted helmet covering head and neck, with an opening for the face.
3. Final deposits of a glacier.
4. *Infra dignitatem*: "beneath one's dignity" (Latin).
5. Medieval cleric who wrote a topographical study of Wales.

across the esker[6]
I glimpse my grandfather's whiskers

stained with tobacco-pollen.
30   When he piddles against a bullaun[7]
I know he carries bovine TB
but what I *see*

is my father in his Sunday suit's
bespoke lime and lignite,°   *wood*
35   patrolling his now-diminished estate
and taking stock of this and that.

1987

Milkweed and Monarch

As he knelt by the grave of his mother and father
the taste of dill, or tarragon—
he could barely tell one from the other—

filled his mouth. It seemed as if he might smother.
5   Why should he be stricken
with grief, not for his mother and father,

but a woman slinking from the fur of a sea-otter
in Portland, Maine, or, yes, Portland, Oregon—
he could barely tell one from the other—

10   and why should he now savour
the tang of her, her little pickled gherkin,
as he knelt by the grave of his mother and father?

*

He looked about. He remembered her palaver
on how both earth and sky would darken—
15   "You could barely tell one from the other"—

while the Monarch butterflies passed over
in their milkweed-hunger: "A wing-beat, some reckon,
may trigger off the mother and father

of all storms, striking your Irish Cliffs of Moher
20   with the force of a hurricane."
Then: "Milkweed and Monarch 'invented' each other."

*

He looked about. Cow's-parsley in a samovar.[8]
He'd mistaken his mother's name, "Regan", for "Anger":

---

6. A ridge of sand and gravel deposited by a sub-glacial stream or retreating glacier (*eiscir:* "ridge" [Irish]).

7. Ancient "standing stones" (Irish) or cairn of stones.

8. Russian tea urn.

as he knelt by the grave of his mother and father
25   he could barely tell one from the other.

1994

ROO BORSON

1952–

Rain

The bay the color of steel, of a warship
with scattered sun and cloud on its flanks,
the color of a battlefield
after it's all over,
5   of a soldier's mind when there's nothing left to kill,
in the immediate vicinity anyway,
and he can rest
but what is that kind of rest worth?
There's always going to be something left alive.

10   The water from a tin cup
tastes thin and substanceless,
you can never get enough.
It's not that the first time wakens
a bloodthirst, it's that you cross over
15   to a country where everything's different,
a country of men
who don't know what they're after.
Everything tastes thin.
You take it all in, trying to get satisfied.
20   Then you just shut off.

Rain zig-zags down between the hills.
It shatters on rooves, and there are people inside
just sitting around listening.

If you're an ex-soldier you're out walking in the rain,
25   you're used to it. Hands in pockets,
the sidewalk full of shoes scraping past,
trousers, the bunched hems of dresses under coats.
You look at people from the bottom up.
Sometimes a pair of women's eyes catches
30   at your throat, at the way it was when you were a kid,
always wanting to know what came next,
like a movie full of possible surprise endings,
which way would it turn out?

But you never expected this. Never thought
35   the whole thing could just go on and on,
no end in sight, not much happening, just the rain,
the grey sidewalk and the shoes, soggy shoes

filled with other people's lives. The warm women
hurrying beneath their dresses.
40 Out on the street
you see people in-between things, never
the place they've left or where they're going, only
their faces with that look of expectation.

Except of course for the ones who live out on the street,
45 who stay there rain or shine, slumped in doorways,
sunk in their own eyes.

Further off the hills are blurred with white mist.
It's coming down hard there too. But from here
it just looks like a white mist that slowly blows and changes.

1984

RITA DOVE

1952–

Parsley[1]

1. The Cane Fields

There is a parrot imitating spring
in the palace, its feathers parsley green.
Out of the swamp the cane appears

to haunt us, and we cut it down. El General
5   searches for a word; he is all the world
there is. Like a parrot imitating spring,

we lie down screaming as rain punches through
and we come up green. We cannot speak an R—
out of the swamp, the cane appears

10 and then the mountain we call in whispers *Katalina*.
The children gnaw their teeth to arrowheads.
There is a parrot imitating spring.

El General has found his word: *perejil*.
Who says it, lives. He laughs, teeth shining
15 out of the swamp. The cane appears

in our dreams, lashed by wind and streaming.
And we lie down. For every drop of blood
there is a parrot imitating spring.
Out of the swamp the cane appears.

1. "On October 2, 1957, Rafael Trujillo (1891–
1961), dictator of the Dominican Republic,
ordered 20,000 blacks killed because they could
not pronounce the letter r in *perejil*, the Spanish
word for parsley" [Dove's note].

2. *The Palace*

20 The word the general's chosen is parsley.
It is fall, when thoughts turn
to love and death; the general thinks
of his mother, how she died in the fall
and he planted her walking cane at the grave
25 and it flowered, each spring stolidly forming
four-star blossoms. The general

pulls on his boots, he stomps to
her room in the palace, the one without
curtains, the one with a parrot
30 in a brass ring. As he paces he wonders
Who can I kill today. And for a moment
the little knot of screams
is still. The parrot, who has traveled

all the way from Australia in an ivory
35 cage, is, coy as a widow, practising
spring. Ever since the morning
his mother collapsed in the kitchen
while baking skull-shaped candies
for the Day of the Dead,[2] the general
40 has hated sweets. He orders pastries
brought up for the bird; they arrive

dusted with sugar on a bed of lace.
The knot in his throat starts to twitch;
he sees his boots the first day in battle
45 splashed with mud and urine
as a soldier falls at his feet amazed—
how stupid he looked!—at the sound
of artillery. *I never thought it would sing*
the soldier said, and died. Now

50 the general sees the fields of sugar
cane, lashed by rain and streaming.
He sees his mother's smile, the teeth
gnawed to arrowheads. He hears
the Haitians sing without R's
55 as they swing the great machetes:
Katalina, they sing, *Katalina*,

mi madle, mi amol en muelte. God knows
his mother was no stupid woman; she
could roll an R like a queen. Even
60 a parrot can roll an R! In the bare room
the bright feathers arch in a parody

2. All Souls' Day, November 2. An Aztec festival
for the spirits of the dead that coincides with the
Catholic calendar. Friends and relatives of the
dead process into cemeteries, bearing candles, flowers, and food, all of which may be shaped to resemble symbols of death, such as skulls or coffins.

of greenery, as the last pale crumbs
disappear under the blackened tongue. Someone

calls out his name in a voice
65   so like his mother's, a startled tear
splashes the tip of his right boot.
My mother, my love in death.
The general remembers the tiny green sprigs
men of his village wore in their capes
70   to honor the birth of a son. He will
order many, this time, to be killed

for a single, beautiful word.

                               1983

Dusting[3]

Every day a wilderness—no
shade in sight. Beulah
patient among knicknacks,
the solarium a rage
5   of light, a grainstorm
as her gray cloth brings
dark wood to life.

Under her hand scrolls
and crests gleam
10   darker still. What
was his name, that
silly boy at the fair with
the rifle booth? And his kiss and
the clear bowl with one bright
15   fish, rippling
wound!

Not Michael—
something finer. Each dust
stroke a deep breath and
20   the canary in bloom.
Wavery memory: home
from a dance, the front door
blown open and the parlor
in snow, she rushed
25   the bowl to the stove, watched
as the locket of ice
dissolved and he
swam free.

That was years before
30   Father gave her up

3. The poem is part of a book-length narrative, *Thomas and Beulah*, about which Doves writes in introduction, "These poems tell two sides of a story and are meant to be read in sequence." The main characters are African Americans born at the beginning of the twentieth century.

with her name, years before
her name grew to mean
Promise, then
Desert-in-Peace.
35 Long before the shadow and
sun's accomplice, the tree.

Maurice.

1986

The Bistro Styx[4]

She was thinner, with a mannered gauntness
as she paused just inside the double
glass doors to survey the room, silvery cape
billowing dramatically behind her. *What's this,*

5   I thought, lifting a hand until
she nodded and started across the parquet;
that's when I saw she was dressed all in gray,
from a kittenish cashmere skirt and cowl

down to the graphite signature of her shoes.
10 "Sorry I'm late," she panted, though
she wasn't, sliding into the chair, her cape

tossed off in a shudder of brushed steel.
We kissed. Then I leaned back to peruse
my blighted child, this wary aristocratic mole.

15 "How's business?" I asked, and hazarded
a motherly smile to keep from crying out:
Are you content to conduct your life
as a cliché and, what's worse,

an anachronism, the brooding artist's demimonde?
20 Near the rue Princesse[5] they had opened
a gallery *cum*° souvenir shop which featured   *with*
fuzzy off-color Monets[6] next to his acrylics, no doubt,

plus bearded African drums and the occasional miniature
gargoyle from Notre Dame[7] the Great Artist had
25 carved at breakfast with a pocket knife.

4. The poem is part of a sonnet sequence in *Mother Love*, a book-length modernization of the Greek myth of Persephone, the girl who is abducted to the underworld by Hades, and whose mother, Demeter, goddess of agriculture, is so grief-stricken she allows the crops to wither. "Before returning to the surface, the girl eats a few pomegranate seeds, not realizing that anyone who partakes of the food of the dead cannot be wholly restored to the living" [Dove's note]. Persephone spends half of each year with Hades thereafter, and her return to Earth heralds spring. In Dove's version, she resurfaces in modern Paris, in a restaurant named for the Styx, the river in the underworld over which dead souls were ferried.
5. Street in Paris.
6. Reproductions of work by the French painter Claude Monet (1840–1926).
7. Notre Dame de Paris, the cathedral.

"Tourists love us. The Parisians, of course"—
she blushed—"are amused, though not without
a certain admiration . . ."
                    The Chateaubriand[8]

arrived on a bone-white plate, smug and absolute
30   in its fragrant crust, a black plug steaming
like the heart plucked from the chest of a worthy enemy;
one touch with her fork sent pink juices streaming.

"Admiration for what?" Wine, a bloody
Pinot Noir, brought color to her cheeks. "Why,
35   the aplomb with which we've managed
to support our Art"—meaning he'd convinced

her to pose nude for his appalling canvases,
faintly futuristic landscapes strewn
with carwrecks and bodies being chewed

40   by rabid cocker spaniels. "I'd like to come by
the studio," I ventured, "and see the new stuff."
"Yes, if you wish . . ." A delicate rebuff

before the warning: "He dresses all
in black now. Me, he drapes in blues and carmine—
45   and even though I think it's kinda cute,
in company I tend toward more muted shades."

She paused and had the grace
to drop her eyes. She did look ravishing,
spookily insubstantial, a lipstick ghost on tissue,
50   or as if one stood on a fifth-floor terrace

peering through a fringe of rain at Paris'
dreaming chimney pots, each sooty issue
wobbling skyward in an ecstatic oracular spiral.

"And he never thinks of food. I wish
55   I didn't have to plead with him to eat. . . ." Fruit
and cheese appeared, arrayed on leaf-green dishes.

I stuck with café crème. "This Camembert's[9]
so ripe," she joked, "it's practically grown hair,"
mucking a golden glob complete with parsley sprig
60   onto a heel of bread. Nothing seemed to fill

her up: She swallowed, sliced into a pear,
speared each tear-shaped lavaliere[1]

---

8. Elegant beef dish.
9. A French cheese; "café crème": coffee with
cream.

1. Jeweled pendant necklace; here, the jewel
itself.

and popped the dripping mess into her pretty mouth.
Nowhere the bright tufted fields, weighted

65 vines and sun poured down out of the south.
"But are you happy?" Fearing, I whispered it
quickly. "What? You know, Mother"—

she bit into the starry rose of a fig—
"one really should try the fruit here."
70 *I've lost her,* I thought, and called for the bill.

1995

DANIEL HALL

1952–

Love-Letter-Burning

The archivist in us shudders at such cold-
blooded destruction of the word, but since
we're only human, we commit our sins
to the flames. Sauve qui peut;[1] fear makes us bold.

5   Tanka[2] was bolder: when the weather turned
from fair to frigid, he saw his way clear
to build a sacrificial fire
in which a priceless temple Buddha burned.

(The pretext? Simple: what he sought
10 was legendary Essence in the ash.
But if it shows up only in the flesh—?
He grinned and said, Let's burn the lot!)

Believers in the afterlife perform
this purifying rite. At last
15 a match is struck: it's done. The past
will shed some light, but never keep us warm.

1990

Mangosteens

These are the absolute top of the line,
I was telling him, they even surpass
the Jiangsu peach and the McIntosh°   *apple*

1. "Save (yourself) if you can" (French); also, a
panic or stampede.
2. The Zen master Tan-hsai, or Tanka (A.D. 738–
824). "It was so cold at the temple . . . that he took
one of the three images from the altar and burned
it for firewood. When the horrified chief monk
asked him . . . how he dared profane the sacred
image of the Buddha, he replied that he was burn-
ing it to obtain its *sarira* (an indestructible sub-
stance believed to reside in the ashes of holy men)"
(M. Conrad Hyers, *Zen and the Comic Spirit*). Not
finding *sarira* in one wooden Buddha, Tanka pro-
posed burning the other two as well.

for lusciousness and subtlety. . . . (He frowned:
5 McIntosh. How spelling.) We were eating
our way through another kilogram
of mangosteens, for which we'd both fallen
hard. I'd read that Queen Victoria[3]
(no voluptuary) once offered a reward
10 for an edible mangosteen: I don't know
how much, or whether it was ever claimed.
(But not enough, I'd guess, and no, I hope.)
Each thick skin yields to a counter-twist,
splits like rotted leather. Inside, snug
15 as a brain in its cranium, half a dozen
plump white segments, all but dry, part
to the tip of the tongue like lips—they *taste*
like lips, before they're bitten, a saltiness
washed utterly away; crushed, they release
20 a flood of unfathomable sweetness,
gone in a trice. He lay
near sleep, sunk back against a slope
of heaped-up bedding, stroked slantwise by fingers
of afternoon sun. McIntosh, he said again,
25 still chewing. I'd also been reading *The Spoils
of Poynton,*[4] so slowly the plot seemed to unfold
in real-time. " 'Things' were of course
the sum of the world," James tosses out
in that mock-assertive, contradiction-baffling
30 way he has, quotation marks gripped like a tweezers
lest he soil his hands on *things,*
as if the only things that mattered
were that homage be paid to English widowhood,
or whether another of his young virgins
35 would ever marry. (She wouldn't, but she would,
before the novel closed, endure one shattering
embrace, a consummation.) I spent the day
sleepwalking the halls of museums, a vessel
trembling at the lip. Lunch was a packet
40 of rice cakes and an apple in a garden
famed for its beauty, and deemed beautiful
for what had been taken away. I can still hear it,
still *taste* it, his quick gasp of astonishment
caught in my own mouth. I can feel that house
45 going up with a shudder, a clockwise funnel
howling to the heavens, while the things of her world
explode or melt or shrivel to ash
in the ecstatic emptying. The old woman set the fire
herself, she must have, she had to. His letter,
50 tattooed with postmarks, was waiting for me
back at the ryokan,[5] had overtaken me

3. Queen of Great Britain from 1837 to 1901.
4. Novel by British (American-born) writer Henry James (1843–1916). Mrs. Gereth, a recently widowed collector of beautiful things, is faced with giving up her house, Poynton, to her son, who has inherited it. She attempts unsuccessfully to make a match between him and an intense young woman friend. When Poynton is destroyed by fire, the cause is not given; here, Hall suspects Mrs. Gereth.
5. "Inn" (Japanese).

at last, half in Chinese, half in hard-won
English, purer than I will ever write —

Please don't give up me in tomorrow

55 The skin was bitter. It stained the tongue.

I want with you more time

1993   1996

GARY SOTO

1952–

The Soup

The lights off, the clock glowing 2:10,
And Molina is at the table drawing what he thinks is soup
And its carrots rising through a gray broth.

He adds meat and peppers it with pencil markings.
5   The onion has gathered the peas in its smile.
The surface is blurred with the cold oils squeezed from a lime.

He adds hominy and potato that bob
In a current of pork fat, from one rim to the other,
Crashing into the celery that has canoed such a long way.

10   *Spoon handle that is a plank an ant climbs.*
Saucer that is the slipped disk of a longhorn.
Napkin that is shredded into a cupful of snow.

1978

Not Knowing

By then, by the time my brother
Was getting married, weeks before the old
Apartment was pulled down,
The evenings were warm and the sounds of
5   Freight trains absorbed by three oleanders,°   *evergreen shrubs*
Whipped by wind and iron clanging.
By then, by the time I was nineteen
And the crickets were hauling their armor
Into the weeds and dusty bushes,
10   I was thinking that I would have to read more.
I had to put together the meaning of our neighbors
Fighting in bed, then loving in bed from 3:30 to 4:00.
I would have to read more. My other neighbor
Had painted his porch light blue, and the first
15   Black family on our college-poor street
Were so friendly that they disturbed my views

About trust and mistrust. And I was stymied
When my brother and I tried
To remove the refrigerator
20 Down a narrow flight of steps.
Now it was stuck, lodged between
The walls, an absurd physics for the wrecking crew
To solve. The beast of machinery would start up
And the old apartment would come down
25 The weekend my brother would pin
A carnation to his lapel, the ruffle of petal
Perfuming the air as he walked down the aisle.
By then, by the time my brother was ready
And the refrigerator was leaking
30 Its gray liquids and gases,
I would sit my sorrow on a lawn,
Flattening the grass with the heel of my palm.
The grass springing back from this kind of pressure,
Another physics I couldn't figure on paper
35 Or a blackboard of low math. The spin
Of light and wind
And the residue
Of an exhausted star told me nothing.
After my brother was gone
40 I sat with a book on the lawn,
The evening blood-red in the west
And my palm pressing the balance of solitary grass,
The world of unknowable forces stirring
Every live and dead tree.

1995

BRAD LEITHAUSER

1953–

The Buried Graves

From the pier, at dusk, the dim
    Billowing arms of kelp
Seem the tops of trees, as though
        Not long ago
5   A summer wood stood here, before a dam
    Was built, a valley flooded.

    Such a forest would release
        Its color only slowly,
And the leafy branches sway, as they'd
10   More lightly swayed
    Under a less distant sun and far less
        Even weather. Now, deeper down,

    Those glimmers of coral might
        Be the lots of some hard-luck

15 Town, or—depositing on the dead
        A second bed—
    A submerged cemetery. . . . To this mute,
    Envisioned, birdless wood would

    Come a kind of autumn, a tame
20   Sea-season, with foliage tumbling
    Through a weighty, trancelike fall;
        And come, as well,
    Soon in the emptying fullness of time,
    A mild but an endless winter.

                                          1985

In Minako Wada's House

    In old Minako Wada's house
    Everything has its place,
    And mostly out of sight:
        Bedding folded away
5   All day, brought down
    From the shelf at night,

    Tea things underneath
    Low tea table and tablecloth—
    And sliding screen doors,
10   Landscape-painted, that hide
    Her clothes inside a wash
    Of mountains. Here, the floors

    Are a clean-fitting mosaic,
    Mats of a texture like
15 A broom's; and in a niche
        In the tearoom wall
    Is a shrine to all of her
    Ancestors, before which

    She sets each day
20 A doll-sized cup of tea,
    A doll-sized bowl of rice.
        She keeps a glass jar
    Of crickets that are fed fish
    Shavings, an eggplant slice,

25   And whose hushed chorus,
    Like the drowsy toss
    Of a baby's rattle, moves in
        On so tranquil a song
        It's soon no longer heard.
30 The walls are thin

    In Minako Wada's little house,
    Open to every lifting voice
    On the street—by day, the cries

Of the children, at night
35   Those excited, sweet,
Reiterated goodbyes

Of men full of beer who now
Must hurry home. Just to
Wake in the night inside this nest,
40   Late, the street asleep (day done,
Day not yet begun), is what
Perhaps she loves best.

1985

Old Bachelor Brother

Here from his prominent but thankfully
uncentral position at the head of the church—
a flanking member of the groom's large party—
he stands and waits to watch the women march

5   up the wide aisle, just the way they did
at last night's long and leaden-joked rehearsal.
Only this time, it's all changed. There's now a crowd,
of course, and walls of lit stained glass, and Purcell[1]

ringing from the rented organist,
10 and yet the major difference, the one
that hits his throat as a sort of smoky thirst,
is how, so far away, the church's main

doors are flung back, uncovering a square
of sun that streams into the narthex,° so that   *covered walkway*
15 the women who materialize there
do so in blinding silhouette,

and these are not the women he has helloed
and kissed, and who have bored, ignored, or teased him,
but girls—whose high, garlanded hair goes haloed
20 by the noon-light . . . The years have dropped from them.

One by one they're bodied forth, edged with flame,
as new as flame, destined to part the sea
of faces on each side, and approaching him
in all their passionate anonymity.

1990

1. Henry Purcell (1658?–1695), English composer.

GJERTRUD SCHNACKENBERG

1953–

Darwin in 1881[1]

Sleepless as Prospero back in his bedroom
In Milan, with all his miracles
Reduced to sailors' tales,[2]
He sits up in the dark. The islands loom.
5 His seasickness upwells,
Silence creeps by in memory as it crept
By him on water,[3] while the sailors slept,
From broken eggs and vacant tortoise shells.
His voyage around the cape of middle age
10 Comes, with a feat of insight, to a close,
The same way Prospero's
Ended before he left the stage
To be led home across the blue-white sea,
When he had spoken of the clouds and globe,
15 Breaking his wand, and taking off his robe:[4]
Knowledge increases unreality.

He quickly dresses.
Form wavers like his shadow on the stair
As he descends, in need of air
20 To cure his dizziness,
Down past the ship-sunk emptiness
Of grownup children's rooms and hallways where
The family portraits stare,
All haunted by each other's likenesses.

25 Outside, the orchard and a piece of moon
Are islands, he an island as he walks,
Brushing against weed stalks.
By hook and plume
The seeds gathering on his trouser legs
30 Are archipelagoes, like nests he sees
Shadowed in branching, ramifying trees,
Each with unique expressions in its eggs.
Different islands conjure
Different beings; different beings call
35 From different isles. And after all
His scrutiny of Nature
All he can see
Is how it will grow small, fade, disappear,

---

1. The English naturalist Charles Darwin (1809–
1882), who developed a theory of evolution.
2. Prospero, the usurped and exiled Duke of
Milan in Shakespeare's *The Tempest*, is a magician
who is restored to his dukedom.
3. Cf. *The Tempest* 1.2.392: "This music crept by
me upon the waters."

4. Allusion to Prospero's words: "the great globe
itself, / Yea, all which it inherit, shall dissolve, /
And like this insubstantial pageant faded / Leave
not a rack behind" (4.1.153–55) and "But this
rough magic / I here abjure. . . . I'll break my staff"
(5.1.50–54).

A coastline fading from a traveler
40 Aboard a survey ship. Slowly,
As coasts depart,
Nature had left behind a naturalist
Bound for a place where species don't exist,
Where no emergence has a counterpart.

45 He's heard from friends
About the other night, the banquet hall
Ringing with bravos—like a curtain call,
He thinks, when the performance ends,
Failing to summon from the wings
50 An actor who had lost his taste for verse,
Having beheld, in larger theaters,
Much greater banquet vanishings
Without the quaint device and thunderclap
Required in Act 3.[5]
55 He wrote, Let your indulgence set me free,[6]
To the Academy, and took a nap
Beneath a *London Daily* tent,
Then puttered on his hothouse walk
Watching his orchids beautifully stalk
60 Their unreturning paths, where each descendant
Is the last—
Their inner staircases
Haunted by vanished insect faces
So tiny, so intolerably vast.
65 And, while they gave his proxy the award,
He dined in Downe[7] and stayed up rather late
For backgammon with his beloved mate,
Who reads his books and is, quite frankly, bored.

Now, done with beetle jaws and beaks of gulls
70 And bivalve hinges, now, utterly done,
One miracle remains, and only one.
An ocean swell of sickness rushes, pulls,
He leans against the fence
And lights a cigarette and deeply draws,
75 Done with fixed laws,
Done with experiments
Within his greenhouse heaven where
His offspring, Frank, for half the afternoon
Played, like an awkward angel, his bassoon
80 Into the humid air
So he could tell
If sound would make a Venus's-flytrap close.
And, done for good with scientific prose,
That raging hell
85 Of tortured grammars writhing on their stakes,

---

5. Prospero conjures up a banquet and then makes it disappear with thunder and (as in the stage direction) "a quaint device" (3.3).
6. Prospero's final speech, the last line of the play (Epilogue 20). "Academy": The Royal Society for the Improving of Natural Knowledge.
7. Darwin's home.

He'd turned to his memoirs, chuckling to write
About his boyhood in an upright
Home: a boy preferring gartersnakes
To schoolwork, a lazy, strutting liar
90   Who quite provoked her aggravated look,
Shushed in the drawing room behind her book,
His bossy sister itching with desire
To tattletale—yes, that was good.
But even then, much like the conjurer
95   Grown cranky with impatience to abjure
All his gigantic works and livelihood
In order to immerse
Himself in tales where he could be the man
In Once upon a time there was a man,

100   He'd quite by chance beheld the universe:
A disregarded game of chess
Between two love-dazed heirs
Who fiddle with the tiny pairs
Of statues in their hands,[8] while numberless
105   Abstract unseen
Combinings on the silent board remain
Unplayed forever when they leave the game
To turn, themselves, into a king and queen.
Now, like the coming day,
110   Inhaled smoke illuminates his nerves.
He turns, taking the sandwalk as it curves
Back to the yard, the house, the entrance way
Where, not to waken her,

He softly shuts the door,
115   And leans against it for a spell before
He climbs the stairs, holding the banister,
Up to their room: there
Emma sleeps, moored
In illusion, blown past the storm he conjured
120   With his book,[9] into a harbor
Where it all comes clear,
Where island beings leap from shape to shape
As to escape
Their terrifying turns to disappear.
125   He lies down on the quilt,
He lies down like a fabulous-headed
Fossil in a vanished riverbed,
In ocean drifts, in canyon floors, in silt,
In lime, in deepening blue ice,
130   In cliffs obscured as clouds gather and float;
He lies down in his boots and overcoat,
And shuts his eyes.

1982

8. That is, playing chess, as in *The Tempest* 5.1.172 ff.
9. Prospero's book of magic helped him conjure a tempest. Darwin's book *On the Origin of Species by Means of Natural Selection* (1859) was equally powerful.

Supernatural Love

My father at the dictionary-stand
Touches the page to fully understand
The lamplit answer, tilting in his hand

His slowly scanning magnifying lens,
5   A blurry, glistening circle he suspends
Above the word "Carnation." Then he bends

So near his eyes are magnified and blurred,
One finger on the miniature word,
As if he touched a single key and heard

10   A distant, plucked, infinitesimal string,
"The obligation due to every thing
That's smaller than the universe." I bring

My sewing needle close enough that I
Can watch my father through the needle's eye,
15   As through a lens ground for a butterfly

Who peers down flower-hallways toward a room
Shadowed and fathomed as this study's gloom
Where, as a scholar bends above a tomb

To read what's buried there, he bends to pore
20   Over the Latin blossom. I am four,
I spill my pins and needles on the floor

Trying to stitch "Beloved" X by X.
My dangerous, bright needle's point connects
Myself illiterate to this perfect text

25   I cannot read. My father puzzles why
It is my habit to identify
Carnations as "Christ's flowers," knowing I

Can give no explanation but "Because."
Word-roots blossom in speechless messages
30   The way the thread behind my sampler does

Where following each X I awkward move
My needle through the word whose root is love.
He reads, "A pink variety of Clove,

Carnatio, the Latin, meaning flesh."
35   As if the bud's essential oils brush
Christ's fragrance through the room, the iron-fresh

Odor carnations have floats up to me,
A drifted, secret, bitter ecstasy,
The stems squeak in my scissors, Child, it's me,

40 He turns the page to "Clove" and reads aloud:
"The clove, a spice, dried from a flower-bud."
Then twice, as if he hasn't understood,

He reads, "From French, for *clou*, meaning a nail."
He gazes, motionless. "Meaning a nail."
45 The incarnation blossoms, flesh and nail,

I twist my threads like stems into a knot
And smooth "Beloved," but my needle caught
Within the threads, *Thy blood so dearly bought,*

The needle strikes my finger to the bone.
50 I lift my hand, it is myself I've sewn,
The flesh laid bare, the threads of blood my own,

I lift my hand in startled agony
And call upon his name, "Daddy daddy" —
My father's hand touches the injury

55 As lightly as he touched the page before,
Where incarnation bloomed from roots that bore
The flowers I called Christ's when I was four.

1985

LOUISE ERDRICH

1954–

The Butcher's Wife

1

Once, my braids swung heavy as ropes.
Men feared them like the gallows.
Night fell
When I combed them out.
5 No one could see me in the dark.

Then I stood still
Too long and the braids took root.
I wept, so helpless.
The braids tapped deep and flourished.

10 A man came by with an ox on his shoulders.
He yoked it to my apron
And pulled me from the ground.
From that time on I wound the braids around my head
So that my arms would be free to tend him.

2

15 He could lift a grown man by the belt with his teeth.
In a contest, he'd press a whole hog, a side of beef.
He loved his highballs, his herring, and the attentions of women.
He died pounding his chest with no last word for anyone.

The gin vessels in his face broke and darkened. I traced them
20 Far from that room into Bremen on the Sea.[1]
The narrow streets twisted down to the piers.
And far off, in the black, rocking water, the lights of trawlers
Beckoned, like the heart's uncertain signals,
Faint, and final.

1984

I Was Sleeping Where the Black Oaks Move

We watched from the house
as the river grew, helpless
and terrible in its unfamiliar body.
Wrestling everything into it,
5 the water wrapped around trees
until their life-hold was broken.
They went down, one by one,
and the river dragged off their covering.

Nests of the herons, roots washed to bones,
10 snags of soaked bark on the shoreline:
a whole forest pulled through the teeth
of the spillway. Trees surfacing
singly, where the river poured off
into arteries for fields below the reservation.

15 When at last it was over, the long removal,
they had all become the same dry wood.
We walked among them, the branches
whitening in the raw sun.
Above us drifted herons,
20 alone, hoarse-voiced, broken,
settling their beaks among the hollows.

Grandpa said, *These are the ghosts of the tree people,*
moving above us, unable to take their rest.

Sometimes now, we dream our way back to the heron dance.
25 Their long wings are bending the air
into circles through which they fall.
They rise again in shifting wheels.
How long must we live in the broken figures
their necks make, narrowing the sky.

1984

1. Germany's oldest seaport, today the second largest after Hamburg.

Birth

When they were wild
When they were not yet human
When they could have been anything,
I was on the other side ready with milk to lure them,
5 And their father, too, each name a net in his hands.

1989

CAROL ANN DUFFY

1955–

Warming Her Pearls

Next to my own skin, her pearls. My mistress
bids me wear them, warm them, until evening
when I'll brush her hair. At six, I place them
round her cool, white throat. All day I think of her,

5 resting in the Yellow Room, contemplating silk
or taffeta, which gown tonight? She fans herself
whilst I work willingly, my slow heat entering
each pearl. Slack on my neck, her rope.

She's beautiful. I dream about her
10 in my attic bed; picture her dancing
with tall men, puzzled by my faint, persistent scent
beneath her French perfume, her milky stones.

I dust her shoulders with a rabbit's foot,
watch the soft blush seep through her skin
15 like an indolent sigh. In her looking-glass
my red lips part as though I want to speak.

Full moon. Her carriage brings her home. I see
her every movement in my head. . . . Undressing,
taking off her jewels, her slim hand reaching
20 for the case, slipping naked into bed, the way

she always does. . . . And I lie here awake,
knowing the pearls are cooling even now
in the room where my mistress sleeps. All night
I feel their absence and I burn.

1993

Prayer

Some days, although we cannot pray, a prayer
utters itself. So, a woman will lift
her head from the sieve of her hands and stare
at the minims° sung by a tree, a sudden gift.   *short notes*

5 Some nights, although we are faithless, the truth
enters our hearts, that small familiar pain;
then a man will stand stock-still, hearing his youth
in the distant Latin chanting of a train.

Pray for us now. Grade I piano scales[1]
10 console the lodger looking out across
a Midlands town. Then dusk, and someone calls
a child's name as though they named their loss.

Darkness outside. Inside, the radio's prayer —
Rockall. Malin. Dogger. Finisterre.[2]

1993

CATHY SONG

1955–

Girl Powdering Her Neck

from a ukiyo-e print by Utamaro[1]

The light is the inside
sheen of an oyster shell,
sponged with talc and vapor,
moisture from a bath.

5 A pair of slippers
are placed outside
the rice-paper doors.
She kneels at a low table
in the room,
10 her legs folded beneath her
as she sits on a buckwheat pillow.

Her hair is black
with hints of red,
the color of seaweed
15 spread over rocks.

Morning begins the ritual
wheel of the body,
the application of translucent skins.
She practices pleasure:
20 the pressure of three fingertips
applying powder.
Fingerprints of pollen
some other hand will trace.

---

1. Musical exercises for beginners.
2. Coastal regions named in British weather forecasts.
1. Kitagawa Utamaro (1753–1806), Japanese artist; *Ukiyo-e:* Japanese wood-block prints, mostly of the seventeenth to nineteenth centuries, depicting everyday scenes and pleasures of the moment; literally, "pictures of the floating world."

The peach-dyed kimono
25 patterned with maple leaves
drifting across the silk,
falls from right to left
in a diagonal, revealing
the nape of her neck
30 and the curve of a shoulder
like the slope of a hill
set deep in snow in a country
of huge white solemn birds.
Her face appears in the mirror,
35 a reflection in a winter pond,
rising to meet itself.

She dips a corner of her sleeve
like a brush into water
to wipe the mirror;
40 she is about to paint herself.
The eyes narrow
in a moment of self-scrutiny.
The mouth parts
as if desiring to disturb
45 the placid plum face;
break the symmetry of silence.
But the berry-stained lips,
stenciled into the mask of beauty,
do not speak.

50 Two chrysanthemums
touch in the middle of the lake
and drift apart.

                                                    1983

DIONISIO D. MARTINEZ
1956–

In a Duplex Near the San Andreas Fault[1]

When she tells him about the lump in her breast,
he kisses her on the shoulder for the first time—a natural
reflex twenty-some years in the making. Suddenly,

their entire vocabulary revolves around *benign*
5 and *malignant*—words reserved
for these occasions—though they will say

very little now, then nothing for a long time. His hands
are just as pale and nearly as fragile as rice paper,
but she's not familiar with rice paper

---

1. An active strike-slip fault extending from San Francisco to southern California.

10   and what she wants most desperately now
is a point of reference. Calla lilies bloom
like some glorious, abandoned music out on the lawn.

She takes one of his hands and thinks
of the spathe, which has the responsibility
15   of being leaf and petal, content and shape: without it

there would be no calla lily to remember,
nothing to see when she closes
her eyes and places his hand on her breast.

From What the Men Talk About When the Women Leave the Room

Stieglitz[2]

The room itself. The women. The absence of women
in the room. What the absence of women does
to a room. The sound of all those women getting

up and leaving; all of them at once, like wild
5   birds or hunger. How the world can be conquered
if only . . . Just don't tell the women.

What the absence of women will do to men
eventually. Fears. Men talk about fears, bad
dreams, women leaving, the room swelling with

10   the absence of women. Bad dreams have a way
of walking in the room when the women leave.
Each dream is an afterimage of a woman leaving.

1995

LI-YOUNG LEE

1957–

Persimmons

In sixth grade Mrs. Walker
slapped the back of my head
and made me stand in the corner
for not knowing the difference
5   between *persimmon* and *precision*.
How to choose

persimmons. This is precision.
Ripe ones are soft and brown-spotted.

2. Alfred Stieglitz (1864–1946), American photographer; husband of the artist Georgia O'Keeffe.

Sniff the bottoms. The sweet one
10   will be fragrant. How to eat:
put the knife away, lay down newspaper.
Peel the skin tenderly, not to tear the meat.
Chew the skin, suck it,
and swallow. Now, eat
15   the meat of the fruit,
so sweet,
all of it, to the heart.

Donna undresses, her stomach is white.
In the yard, dewy and shivering
20   with crickets, we lie naked,
face-up, face-down.
I teach her Chinese.
Crickets: *chiu chiu*. Dew: I've forgotten.
Naked: I've forgotten.
25   *Ni, wo:* you and me.
I part her legs,
remember to tell her
she is beautiful as the moon.

Other words
30   that got me into trouble were
fight and *fright, wren* and *yarn.*
Fight was what I did when I was frightened,
fright was what I felt when I was fighting.
Wrens are small, plain birds,
35   yarn is what one knits with.
Wrens are soft as yarn.
My mother made birds out of yarn.
I loved to watch her tie the stuff;
a bird, a rabbit, a wee man.

40   Mrs. Walker brought a persimmon to class
and cut it up
so everyone could taste
a *Chinese apple.* Knowing
it wasn't ripe or sweet, I didn't eat
45   but watched the other faces.

My mother said every persimmon has a sun
inside, something golden, glowing,
warm as my face.

Once, in the cellar, I found two wrapped in newspaper,
50   forgotten and not yet ripe.
I took them and set both on my bedroom windowsill,
where each morning a cardinal
sang, *The sun, the sun.*

Finally understanding
55   he was going blind,

my father sat up all one night
waiting for a song, a ghost.
I gave him the persimmons,
swelled, heavy as sadness,
60   and sweet as love.

This year, in the muddy lighting
of my parents' cellar, I rummage, looking
for something I lost.
My father sits on the tired, wooden stairs,
65   black cane between his knees,
hand over hand, gripping the handle.
He's so happy that I've come home.
I ask how his eyes are, a stupid question.
All gone, he answers.

70   Under some blankets, I find a box.
Inside the box I find three scrolls.
I sit beside him and untie
three paintings by my father:
Hibiscus leaf and a white flower.
75   Two cats preening.
Two persimmons, so full they want to drop from the cloth.

He raises both hands to touch the cloth,
asks, *Which is this?*

This is persimmons, Father.

80   *Oh, the feel of the wolftail on the silk,*
the strength, the tense
precision in the wrist.
I painted them hundreds of times
eyes closed. These I painted blind.
85   *Some things never leave a person:*
scent of the hair of one you love,
the texture of persimmons,
in your palm, the ripe weight.

1986

CYNTHIA ZARIN

1959–

The Ant Hill

Sand pyramid, size of a child, each September
it was moved thirty feet back from the veranda's
longest shadow, which stopped in its daily

violet slope near the withering yew. Moved gently,
5   with a wide flat shovel. From the kitchen,
      the wrecked hill was a slag heap, its mussel

color germinating in rain to brown, to velvet, to mica,
    so that after a time a reflection shone from it
      and scattered, and each June, Mother said aloud

10 that it seemed the house moved closer to the hill,
    even though the hill was long moved back.
      For the little girls who watched, who heard,

each tremble-leg was a signal in their own patois,
    a wave good-bye, the whole a black bead curtain
15   like the one at Mrs. Hennessey's, where sometimes,

of an afternoon, they were left—her doorway with its
    there, not there, its speechless partings, the
      dark italic hedge too small to read. A decade

of exile: of school, of being sent to bed, of being
20   told to put the book down, as every year the ants
      were wrenched from their own tenacious fondness

for the veranda pilings, for the black blossoms of old tires
    that clung to them like clematis until—a moving
      picture of transit—the ants crossed over again

25 for their mysterious attendance on the flagstones,
    the hill again grown pointed, night-colored, earth
      turned to mirror-water, a satellite by

the fence post that was flattened, excavated, removed.
    And then the white house was a flipped coin,
30   by and by deserted, its face showing not

the sun but the moon, and the girls who drew with a stick
    under the yew and learned their letters now
      stood under its cracked limbs to bicker, to

divide the world between them to say what Mother
35   said, to speak too subtly, about the ant hill now
      taller than the pilings, the veranda

turned violet as its shadow.

                          1993

Song

My heart, my dove, my snail, my sail, my
 milktooth, shadow, sparrow, fingernail,
  flower-cat and blossom-hedge, mandrake

root now put to bed, moonshell, sea-swell,
5 manatee, emerald shining back at me,
  nutmeg, quince, tea leaf and bone, zither,

cymbal, xylophone; paper, scissors, then
 there's stone—Who doesn't come through the door
  to get home?

1993

Biographical Sketches

Fleur Adcock (1934–)
Fleur Adcock was born in Papakura, New Zealand, but lived in England until 1947. She was educated at Victoria University, New Zealand, and taught Classics there and at Otago University before becoming a librarian, working in Otago and in London, at the Foreign and Commonwealth Office. Since 1979 Adcock has been a freelance writer based in London, though she has spent time at universities in the north of England, as a Northern Arts Fellow. She has translated works from Romanian and medieval Latin, and edited the *Faber Book of Twentieth-Century Women's Poetry*. Much of her work employs jarring images that make us see the domestic, familiar, and mundane as if for the first time, juxtaposing the calm daytime world and the frightening nighttime world, where "something angry, or nightmarish, or discomforting leaps out." Whether written in syllabics and an exacting rhyme scheme or in free verse, her poems are remarkable for their clarity and thoughtfulness and for their startling formal innovations. They range from the tightly controlled to the relaxed and conversational, but have become increasingly narrative.

Conrad Aiken (1889–1973)
Conrad Aiken was born in Savannah, Georgia, and raised there until the age of eleven, when his father shot his mother and himself to death and Aiken was sent to live with relatives in Cambridge, Massachusetts. He was educated at Harvard University, where he and his classmate T. S. Eliot began a lifelong troubled friendship. After traveling extensively in Europe, he settled into a career as a writer. During the 1920s and 1930s he lived in New York, but spent much time abroad, mostly in England. In his later years, he lived in Savannah and on Cape Cod, Massachusetts. An exceptionally prolific writer, Aiken published some thirty volumes of poetry, five novels, dozens of short stories, a multitude of essays and reviews, and an autobiography. His *Senlin* (1918) employs what he called the "symphony" form, where each section of the poem functions like a musical movement, images and themes recur frequently but usually with variation, and development is circular rather than linear. The poem was clearly influenced thematically by Eliot's *Love Song of J. Alfred Prufrock* (1917). Aiken's mellifluous verse has often been compared to Swinburne's.

Agha Shahid Ali (1949–)
Agha Shahid Ali was born in New Delhi, India, and raised in Kashmir. He was educated at the University of Kashmir, Srinagar, the University of Delhi, Pennsylvania State University (where he received a Ph.D.), and the University of Arizona, Tucson (where he received an M.F.A.). He teaches at the University of Massachusetts, Amherst. In addition to his own poetry, Ali has written on T. S. Eliot and has translated the work of Faiz Ahmed Faiz from Urdu. One of the few Indians from an Islamic background to write poetry in English, Ali has identified a "triple heritage" of Hindu, Muslim, and Western culture that informs his poems. He considers himself an "Indo-English" writer, and his predominant themes are uprootedness and exile.

A. R. Ammons (1926–)
A. R. Ammons was born and raised in Whiteville, North Carolina. He started writing poetry while serving on a navy destroyer in the South Pacific during World War II. Ammons received a B.S. from Wake Forest University and later did graduate work in English at the University of California at Berkeley. For one year he was principal of an elementary school on Cape Hatteras. In 1964, after working for nearly a decade as an executive at a glassmaking firm, he began an academic career at Cornell University, where he is currently poet-in-residence. Ammons began his career writing short lyrics, but since then has experimented with form and length. Often called an American Romantic, he values the meditative function of poetry, and his work frequently explores the relationship between humanity and nature, between matter and spirit, and between the Many and the One. Although he works in a fluid style, he values "clarity, order, meaning, structure, [and] rationality," believing them "necessary to whatever provisional stability we have."

Matthew Arnold (1822–1888)
Matthew Arnold was born in Laleham-on-Thames, England, and educated at Balliol College, Oxford, where he became a close friend of the poet Arthur Clough, whom he later eulogized in "Thyrsis" (1866). In 1851 Arnold became an inspector of schools, a position he held for thirty-five years. His writing on education advocated the study of the Bible and the humanities as the remedy for what he saw as the philistinism and insularity of the times, and he worked indefatigably to improve standards and introduce rigor into the school curriculum. After writing most of his memorable poetry between 1845 and 1867, he turned away from poetry, believing himself unable to convey "Joy." "It is not enough that the Poet should add to the knowledge of men, it is required of him also that he should add to their happiness," he wrote in the preface to his 1853 edition of *Poems*. Although he was elected professor of poetry at Oxford University in 1858, other than *New Poems* (1867) he subsequently published only prose.

John Ashbery (1927–)
John Ashbery was born in Rochester, New York, and raised on a farm near Lake Ontario. He attended Harvard, Columbia, and New York Universities, then worked as a copywriter in New York City. Beginning in 1955, he worked for a decade as an art reviewer in Paris. He has since served as poetry editor of the *Partisan Review* and art critic for *New York* and *Newsweek* magazines. He joined the faculty of Brooklyn College in 1974. In addition to poetry, Ashbery has written three plays and (with James Schuyler) a collaborative novel. Loosely connected to what has been called the New York school—along with Schuyler and fellow poets Frank O'Hara and Kenneth Koch—he frequently adopts and adapts the techniques of musicians as well as abstract expressionist and surrealist painters. His poems are characterized by radical disjunctions. Like Gertrude Stein, about whom he has written, Ashbery is concerned not so much with events themselves as with the way events

happen. He aims "to record a kind of generalized transcript of what's really going on in our minds all day long."

Anne Askew (1521–1546)

Anne Askew (or Ascue) was born into an old Lincolnshire (England) family that educated her well. As a young woman she devoted herself to study of the Bible and engaged the local clergy in disputes about the interpretation of scripture. Forced into marriage and eventually turned out of doors by her husband, Askew went to London and became a friend of Joan Bocher, a Protestant of known heterodoxy. Examined for heretical views about the sacraments in 1545, she was not found guilty but, in June 1546, was condemned by a special commission that called no jury and no witnesses. The next day she was tortured and after four weeks was burned at the stake. The Protestant Bishop John Bale (1495–1563) published two accounts of her examination and death, first published in 1546 and 1547. John Foxe's *Acts and Monuments* (1563) contains a description of her sufferings as a Protestant martyr, and ballads about her were written in the seventeenth century.

Margaret Atwood (1939–)

Margaret Atwood was born in Ottawa, Canada, and raised there and in Toronto. As a child, she spent much time in the woods of northern Quebec, where her father conducted entomological research. Educated at the University of Toronto, Radcliffe College, and Harvard University, Atwood has taught at a number of Canadian universities and has worked as an editor for the Anansi publishing house. Though known primarily as a novelist, she has also published poetry, short stories, children's books, critical essays, and a study of Canadian literature, and she has edited several collections of verse. She is an active supporter of Amnesty International and other human rights organizations. The subjects of her work include the social roles of women, as mothers and as daughters, and the power dynamics between men and women, nation and nation, those in control and those who have been marginalized. Her poems, generally in free verse, are at times ironic and dark, as in her recent elegies for her father.

W. H. Auden (1907–1973)

W(ystan) H(ugh) Auden was born in York, England, and educated at Christ Church College, Oxford, where he became a friend of "Pylon" poets Stephen Spender and Cecil Day Lewis. In the 1930s, Auden embarked on a series of formative travels: to Germany, where he was introduced to the work of Sigmund Freud; Iceland, which he visited with the poet Louis MacNeice; Spain, as a Republican sympathizer, during the Spanish Civil War; China, and the United States, to which he emigrated in 1939, taking American citizenship in 1946. With the move to America, Auden threw off the conflict between his privileged background and youthful left-wing sympathies that characterized his early poetry, and gradually returned to the Anglican faith of his mother, a change that left a strong imprint on his later poetry. In addition to poetry, Auden published prose, drama, and (in collaboration with Chester Kallman) libretti. He taught at a number of institutions, including Oxford, where he was professor of poetry from 1956 until 1960. Although his early work carried an inchoate sense of gloominess and doom, by the 1930s he had developed a new style, rooted in the literary tradition, and demonstrating a mastery of form and meter, but thoroughly modern in its diction and concerns. Auden diagnosed his century's banalities and horrors with relentless honesty and incisive wit, but also with compassion. Though he cherished poetry's power to palliate his generation's pain, he assigned it a sobering mission: "by telling the truth to disenchant and disintoxicate."

Joanna Baillie (1762–1851)

Joanna Baillie was born in Lanarkshire, Scotland, the daughter of Dorothea Hunter and James Baillie, a Presbyterian clergyman. At age ten she was sent to a boarding school in Glasgow. In 1783, Baillie, her mother, and her sister moved to London to keep house for her brother, who had inherited a small medical college. Baillie was introduced to London literary circles by her aunt, a minor poet, and was friends with the poet Anna Laetitia Barbauld. After her mother's death in 1806, Baillie traveled extensively in England and on the Continent. Her *Poems* appeared in 1790, but during her lifetime she was best known for her verse dramas, which were published in three volumes (1798–1812) under the title *Series of Plays, in which it is attempted to delineate the stranger passions of the mind.* The preface to her first volume of plays, anticipating Wordsworth's preface to the 1800 edition of *Lyrical Ballads,* calls for "natural" diction, "realness" in subject matter, and a plain style "less embellished with poetical decorations" and "less constrained by that lofty seriousness which [had] so generally been considered as necessary" by her contemporaries. She wrote in a wide range of traditional forms, including folk songs, narratives, occasional poems, and hymns. Though her poetry usually follows a strict measure (often iambic) and rhyme scheme, it is also characteristically lively, and her Scottish dialect poems have been compared to those of Robert Burns.

Amiri Baraka (LeRoi Jones) (1934–)

Amiri Baraka was born LeRoi Jones in Newark, New Jersey. He earned a B.A. from Howard University and an M.A. from Columbia University. From 1954 until 1956 he served in the United States Air Force. Since then he has taught at, among other schools, the New School for Social Research and Columbia University and has devoted himself to various experimental artistic ventures and radical political causes. He was instrumental in the founding of several small magazines, the Black Arts Repertory Theatre in Harlem, and Spirit House in Newark. In the 1970s, when he became a Black Muslim and took the name Imamu Amiri Baraka (although he later dropped Imamu), he began to write polemic poetry espousing black militancy. He later joined the Communist Party. In addition to poetry, he has written a novel, a collection of short stories, an autobiography, several plays, and numerous tracts on social issues. Baraka cites Allen Ginsberg as a major influence on his work, the primary themes of which include the nature of identity and the despair inherent in the human condition. He satirizes bourgeois values, but at the same time attempts to salvage and praise whatever "is useful & can be saved out of all the garbage of our lives." His poetry manifests the fluidity and improvisational qualities associated with jazz and scat, and is particularly well suited to public performance.

Anna Laetitia Barbauld (1743–1825)

Anna Laetitia Barbauld (née Aikin) was born at Kibworth Harcourt, Leicestershire, England, and taught at home by her father, a schoolmaster who became a classical tutor at the new Warrington Academy for Dissenters, an intellectual center where Barbauld spent fifteen years. She married in 1774 and followed her husband to Palgrave, where they managed a school for which she taught and wrote textbooks, one of which, *Hymns in Prose to Children* (1781), went through thirty editions and was translated into five languages. The Barbaulds left Palgrave in 1785 and settled in London, where Anna devoted herself to writing tracts in support of causes such as dissenting politics, democratic government, public education, and the French Revolution; and to literary work, such as editing the poetry of William Collins, collecting six volumes of the correspondence of Samuel Richardson, and writing prefaces to the entries in all fifty volumes of *The British Novelists*. In 1773 she published a volume of poems containing works in a variety of genres: the ode, the hymn, the fable, and the satire. In 1808 her husband drowned, having become mentally ill and violent. Barbauld published an anthology for girls, *The Female Speaker*, in 1811, and a poem entitled *Eighteen Hundred and Eleven*, in 1812, that was so badly reviewed that she published very little during the final thirteen years of her life.

James K. Baxter (1926–1972)

James K. Baxter was born in Dunedin, New Zealand, and educated at Quaker schools in New Zealand and England, the University of Otago, and the University of Victoria at Wellington. He worked as a laborer, journalist, and teacher, and from 1954 until 1960 edited the Wellington magazine *Numbers*. Following a long battle against alcoholism, he became a Roman Catholic in 1958, and subsequently founded a religious commune and became active in social welfare programs. Baxter began writing poetry at the age of seven and published his first collection when he was eighteen. From the beginning his work earned the praise of poets such as Allen Curnow. An extraordinarily prolific writer, Baxter published more than thirty collections of poetry as well as plays and literary criticism. His work shows a deep understanding of complex political and social issues and often attacks exploitation and materialism. Later poems express his appreciation of indigenous Maori culture and disdain for those who threatened it. His early poems were lyrical and employed regular meter and rhyme, but during the 1960s he adopted a leaner style and increasingly worked in "carped, carved little two-line stanzas," a form derived from Lawrence Durrell. His final works, which are based on his experiences in a Maori village called Jerusalem, and which profess his fervent religious faith, are written as sonnets made up of seven of these spare stanzas.

Patricia Beer (1924–)

Patricia Beer was born in Exmouth, Devon, England, and was educated at Exeter University and St. Hugh's College, Oxford. From 1946 to 1953 Beer lived in Italy, where she lectured on English at a number of institutions. Upon her return to England, she worked at odd jobs and continued to write. From 1962 to 1968 she taught at Goldsmith's College in London. She currently lives in Devon. Her favored themes are mortality, good and evil, religious faith, love, nature, and the passing of time. Frequently, she locates herself in the domestic realm and draws her poems from her own experience, employing the narrative mode and focusing intensely on a given topic or single anecdote. A respected critic as well as poet, Beer published her pioneering study of nineteenth-century British women novelists, *Reader, I Married Him*, in 1974.

Aphra Behn (1640?–1689)

Different accounts and opinions exist about Aphra Behn's date of birth, parentage, religion, given name, and marital status. Most historians agree, however, that she visited Surinam with her family in her youth, returned to England when the colony was handed over to the Dutch, and was briefly married to a merchant of Dutch extraction. While spying for Charles II in Antwerp in 1666, she seems to have uncovered a Dutch plot to sail up the Thames and burn the British fleet; letters survive in which she complains of the king's failure to pay her for her work, and she may have been briefly imprisoned for debt in the late 1660s. Writing plays became her main means of support, and she was one of the most prolific playwrights of the Restoration era. Her first play, *The Forced Marriage*, was produced in 1670; she subsequently wrote seventeen plays, among them *The Rover* (1677), *The City Heiress* (1682), and other comedies that characteristically satirize the consequences of ill-suited marriages. Her one tragedy, *Abdelazar* (1676), draws on previous dramatic portraits, including Shakespeare's in *Othello* and *Titus Andronicus*, of black men who love white women. Her prose romance, *Oroonoko, or the Royal Slave* (1688), was based on her experiences in Surinam and criticized the enslavement and subsequent torture and execution of a princely black hero whom the white female narrator greatly admires. Behn also wrote occasional poems, elegies, prologues and epilogues for other dramatists, including John Dryden, and erotic pastoral poems such as "The Disappointment." Her tragicomedy set in colonial Virginia, *The Widow Ranter*, was performed and published the year after Behn died.

John Berryman (1914–1972)

John Berryman was born John Smith in McAlester, Oklahoma. When he was ten, his family moved to Tampa, Florida, where his father committed suicide, shooting himself outside his son's window. The family moved to Massachusetts, then resettled in New York, where Mrs. Smith married a banker named John Berryman, who adopted her sons. The younger John Berryman was educated at Columbia University and Clare College, Cambridge University, where he studied Shakespeare. An erudite scholar and celebrated teacher, whose students included the poets Donald Justice, Philip Levine, and W. D. Snodgrass, Berryman taught at, among other schools, Harvard University, Princeton University, and the University of Minnesota. He also wrote a biography of Stephen Crane. Dogged by alcoholism and a nervous temperament, he committed suicide in 1972. Although his work was often tortured, he intended it "to terrify and comfort," his concern being with what he called "the epistemology of loss." His most enduring works show the influence of his studies in drama: *Homage to Mistress Bradstreet* (1956) is a dialogue between himself and his own version of Anne Bradstreet, and *The Dream Songs* (1964–77) is a sequence in the voices of two imaginary characters. Extraordinarily inventive in form and syntax, Berryman created voices that could be sardonic, tragic, and feisty all at once.

John Betjeman (1906–1984)

John Betjeman was born in London and attended Madgalen College, Oxford, which he left without taking a degree. During World War II he held posts in several government agencies, including the Books Department of the British Council. He later served as United Kingdom press attaché in Dublin. Betjeman had a lifelong avidity for architecture and devoted considerable energies to the preservation of historic landmarks and scenic views. After 1945 he worked as a freelance writer and journalist and a television personality; in 1969 he was knighted. In his youth, despite his former association with Auden and MacNeice, Betjeman seemed untouched by modernism; traditional modes of thinking, living, and writing held a stronger appeal. His preference for the past is evident in his pantheon of literary influences: "In the eighteenth century Dr. Watts, Swift, . . . Thomson, . . . Cowper and Burns are easily among my favourites, not for their finer flights, but for their topographical atmosphere. In the nineteenth century Crabbe, Praed, Hood, Clare, . . . Tennyson, . . . Meredith, William Morris." His verse exhibits tenderness for the often eccentric characters who inhabit his vividly evoked landscapes and is often comic, though his later work sometimes strikes a melancholy note.

Earle Birney (1904–1991)

Earle Birney was born in Calgary, Alberta, and raised on a farm in Erickson, British Columbia. He worked as a bank clerk, a farm laborer, and a park ranger before attending the University of British Columbia, the University of Toronto, and the University of California at Berkeley, from which he earned a Ph.D. in Old and Middle English. He then taught at the Universities of Utah, Toronto, and British Columbia. During World War II, Birney served with the Canadian Army as a personnel-selection officer and as supervisor of the International Service of the Canadian Broadcasting Corporation. Comfortable working in diverse styles and modes, he typically wrote in free verse and employed colloquial diction. Over the years, his work became increasingly playful and included experiments with form, sound, punctuation, spacing, and typeface. In addition to poetry, he published novels, radio plays, and literary essays.

Elizabeth Bishop (1911–1979)

Elizabeth Bishop was born in Worcester, Massachusetts. After her father's death in 1911 and her mother's permanent hospitalization for mental illness in 1917, Bishop lived with relatives in Nova Scotia and Massachusetts. She was educated at Vassar College, and while there Bishop met the poet Marianne Moore, who recognized her promise and became her mentor. Bishop traveled extensively and often addressed questions of travel in her work. In 1952 she settled in Rio de Janeiro with Lota de Macedo Soares, a Brazilian architect and landscape designer; the relationship ended tragically with Lota's suicide in 1967. Bishop returned to the United States to teach, first at the University of Washington in Seattle, then at Harvard University. In addition to poetry, she wrote short stories and essays, and she also translated from the French, Spanish, and Portuguese. Although she frequently wrote of loss and displacement, Bishop deplored nihilism. A close observer (and a fine amateur painter), she took delight and found moments of epiphany in the smallest details. During her lifetime she won the respect of her peers, and since her death she has come to be regarded as among the major poets of the century. Indeed, her tact, precision, and gentle humor, as well as a seeming spontaneousness that masks painstaking craftsmanship, make her a model for many contemporary poets.

William Blake (1757–1827)

William Blake was born in London. He attended art schools, including the Royal Academy school, and at the age of fourteen was apprenticed to an engraver. In 1800 he secured a patron at Felpham, but found the arrangement stultifying. Determined to follow his "Divine Visions," he returned to London. He published numerous collections of poetry illustrated with his own fantastic etchings until the 1820s, when he devoted himself exclusively to pictorial art. His early work reveals his dissatisfaction with the prevailing literary styles of his day; he took as his models the Elizabethan and early-seventeenth-century poets, the Ossianic poems, and the work of Collins, Chatterton, and other eighteenth-century poets working outside the prevailing contemporary literary conventions. He discarded the heroic couplet for lines ending in near and partial rhyme, and employed novel rhythms and bold figures of speech that conveyed a multiplicity of meanings. Between 1795 and 1820, Blake developed a complex mythology to explain human history and suffering and came to see himself as a visionary, prophetic figure, or Bard. His writings in this vein center around the biblical stories of the Fall, the Redemption, and the reestablishment of Eden, but Blake gave these materials his own spin. In his mythos, the Fall is seen as a psychic disintegration that results from the "original sin" of Selfhood, and the Redemption and return to Eden as a restitution of psychic wholeness, a "Resurrection to Unity." His schema centers around a "Universal Man" who incorporates God rather than around a transcendent Being distinct from humanity.

Edmund Blunden (1896–1974)

Edmund Blunden was born in London and raised in Yalding, Kent. In 1915 he joined the army and was sent to the front in France. Upon his return to England, he briefly attended Queen's College, Oxford; then moved to London to work as an assistant to J. Middleton Murry at the *Athenaeum* magazine. In 1922 he traveled to South America to convalesce from lingering physical and emotional effects of the war. For the next thirty years Blunden led a peripatetic existence, but in 1964 he returned to England for good. He taught at Tokyo University, the University of Hong Kong, Oxford University, and Merton College, Oxford, and was a writer for the *Times Literary Supplement*. In addition to publishing his own work, Blunden edited collections of poetry by John Clare, Wilfred Owen, and Ivor Gurney that brought about revivals of their flagging reputations. Unlike many poets of World War I, Blunden did not engage in antiwar invective. He focused instead on the experience of the men in the trenches, recording the "agony" etched into "each grey face" but also acknowledging the moments of happiness amid the slaughter. He was one of the only poets to mourn the devastation of the European landscape, and his poems about the English countryside are considered among his finest.

Robert Bly (1926–)

Robert Bly was born in the town of Madison, in rural Minnesota, where he has lived nearly all his life. He studied as an undergraduate at St. Olaf's College and Harvard University and as a graduate student at the University of Iowa Writers' Workshop. From 1944 until 1946 he served in the navy. Bly founded and continues to edit an influential journal named for each decade—*The Fifties, The Sixties, The Seventies, The Eighties,* and *The Nineties.* He has translated into English the work of many important poets, including Rilke, Goethe, Neruda, and Vallejo. In recent years, he has figured prominently in the men's movement. His work is informed by his study of the seventeenth-century German mystic Jakob Boehme and twentieth-century Spanish surrealist poets. Following their example, he champions intuitive perception over rationalism and empiricism. Believing that modernist poets moved in "a destructive motion outward," he advocates a "plunge inward, trying for intensity." Consequently, he employs "deep images" drawn from the unconscious and understood through the emotions rather than through the rational mind.

Louise Bogan (1897–1970)

Louise Bogan was born in Livermore Falls, Maine. She attended Boston University for one year, then left school to marry. In 1919, newly single, Bogan moved to New York City to pursue writing. She became the poetry critic for *The New Yorker* in 1931 and held the post until she retired in 1969. Bogan taught at several universities, including the University of Washington, the University of Chicago, the University of Arkansas, and Brandeis University. She also translated Jünger, Goethe, and Jules Renard and wrote two influential critical works, *Achievement in American Poetry 1900–1950* and *Selected Criticism: Poetry and Prose* (1955). Despite her professional success, she was dogged by loneliness and depression, and her standards were so exacting that she published only 105 poems in her lifetime. The virtues of her poetry—spareness, restraint, objectivity, and intricately wrought form—reflect her love for classical literature. She believed form essential, but thought each generation ought to find formal patterns appropriate to its temper, materials, and speech patterns. Despite these strictures, or perhaps because of them, Bogan's work conveys great emotion, particularly grief.

Eavan Boland (1944–)

Eavan Boland, the daughter of the Irish diplomat F. H. Boland and the post-expressionist painter Frances Kelley, was born in Dublin, but educated in London, where her father was Irish ambassador, and New York, where he was a representative to the United Nations. After graduating from Trinity College, Dublin, she lectured in English there but found herself "completely unsuited to being an academic," and subsequently taught on a short-term basis at institutions in Ireland and the United States in order to devote her energies to writing. In addition to her own poems, she has written essays on contemporary Irish literature, translated Irish poetry and work by Horace, Mayakovsky, and Nelly Sachs, and is a well-regarded reviewer and broadcaster. Her work takes up a number of themes both public—including Irish history, politics, and legend, and the position of women in contemporary Irish life—and private, including domesticity, love, and motherhood. She is acutely aware of the past and explores its relationship to the present, recounting specific moments but setting them in relation to larger cycles of existence. She draws parallels between contemporary experience and classical and biblical myth, but never evades direct confrontation of her subject matter.

Roo Borson (1952–)

Roo (Ruth Elizabeth) Borson was born and raised in Berkeley, California. Educated at the University of California at Santa Barbara, Goddard College, and the University of British Columbia, Borson worked as a librarian, a laboratory technician, and an administrative assistant before taking up writing as a career in 1983. She has lived in Canada since the 1970s and has taught at several Canadian universities, including the University of Western Ontario. Her work is distinguished by its observation and contemplation of the physical world and by its attempts to portray emotional states of being and to communicate the inexorability of change.

Anne Bradstreet (ca. 1612–1672)

Anne Bradstreet (née Dudley) was born in Northampton, England, daughter of a gentlewoman named Dorothy Yorke and of Thomas Dudley, a nonconformist minister who managed the business interests of the earl of Lincoln. Educated by private tutors in the earl's households, she married Simon Bradstreet, a future governor of the Massachusetts Bay Colony, in 1628; in 1630, Bradstreet emigrated to America with her husband and parents. When she first came to the colonies, she "found a new world and new manners," as she later remembered. "But after I was convinced it was the way of God I submitted to it and joined to the church of Boston." While caring for her growing family (she had

eight children), she continued to write. A volume of poems was published in London in 1650. Entitled *The Tenth Muse Lately Sprung Up in America*, the book was published by Bradstreet's brother-in-law without her knowledge (or so he claimed). It sold very well; a second edition, containing numerous corrections and additions, appeared six years after her death. Her work shows the influence of, among others, Philip Sidney, Walter Ralegh, and Queen Elizabeth; Bradstreet sees the dead queen as an example of feminine achievement and an argument against "masculines" who think women are "void of reason." She compiled but did not publish a collection of prose meditations on life and death for her son Simon when he was about to become minister in 1664.

Edward Kamau Brathwaite (1930–)

Edward Kamau Brathwaite was born in Bridgetown, Barbados, and educated at Harrison College, Pembroke College, Cambridge University, and Sussex University, from which he received a Ph.D. After working for the Ministry of Education in Ghana (Africa) from 1955 until 1962, he returned to his homeland to become a professor of social and cultural history at the University of the West Indies. Since the 1970s, he has taught at a variety of institutions in the United States. He has published scholarly works on West Indian history and culture and on dialect. Brathwaite has described two of his primary themes as "what caused the death of the Amerindians" and "the holocaust of slavery." He is best known for his trilogy of narrative poems, *The Arrivants*, which through a mixture of real and imagined history, tells the story of the dispossession, exile, and homecoming of African peoples, and explores African, Caribbean, and West Indian identity and folk culture. The trilogy reveals Brathwaite's remarkable imaginative sympathy in convincingly entering into the minds of both conquered and conqueror.

Emily Brontë (1818–1848)

Emily Brontë, sister of novelists Charlotte and Anne, was raised in a parsonage at Haworth, on the North Yorkshire moors of England. She was educated largely at home, leaving to work as a governess in 1837. In 1842 she went to Brussels with Charlotte to study language and music, and on her return began to write feverishly. For her first published work, the joint collection *Poems by Currer, Ellis and Acton Bell* (1846), she assumed a pseudonym to avoid being stereotyped as a "lady poet." The book was largely ignored, and she is best remembered for the novel *Wuthering Heights* (1847). Many of her poems (including "The Prisoner" and "Remembrance") were originally written (with Anne) as part of the "Gondal" saga, a series of intricate and elaborate tales set in an imaginary kingdom. The meter and form of Emily Brontë's poems often derive from the Wesleyan hymns she sang as a child. Much of her imagery is Gothic, and her concern with the transience of human life and beauty, as well as her reliance on a personal inner vision, links her to the Romantics. Her uniqueness lies in her brooding mysticism and in the way that her characters yearn for a power or presence that will transport them beyond the bleak, inhospitable physical realm.

Rupert Brooke (1887–1915)

Rupert Brooke was born in Rugby, England, where his father was a housemaster of the famous public school, and educated there and at King's College, Cambridge. After graduation, he established himself in the house immortalized in "The Old Vicarage, Grantchester." Following an unhappy love affair, he traveled in Europe, the United States, Canada, and the South Seas. When war broke out he returned to England and was commissioned into the Royal Naval Division. He saw action in Belgium in 1914 and spent the following winter training in Dorset, where he composed his "war sonnets." The following year, while on a troopship bound for Gallipoli, he died after contracting dysentery and blood poisoning. Much of his early work was published in Edward Marsh's anthologies of Georgian verse and was praised for its conversational diction, vivid descriptions, and delight in the commonplace. His war sonnets celebrate patriotism, peace, friendship, and love, and the values that galvanized the British public in the early days of the conflict—values Brooke had once derided as "Nineteenth Century grandiose thoughts, about the Destiny of Man, the Irresistibility of Fate, the Doom of Nations, the fact that Death awaits us All." Brooke was a formalist, and his preferred forms were the sonnet and the octosyllabic couplet.

Gwendolyn Brooks (1917–)

Gwendolyn Brooks was born in Topeka, Kansas, and raised in Chicago, Illinois. A graduate of Wilson Junior College, she studied modern poetry with Inez Cunning Stark Boulton at Chicago's Southside Community Art Center. Since becoming a writer, she has run workshops for underprivileged youths and has taught her craft at various schools, including City College in New York. Brooks's primary subject is the African-American experience: her first book, A Street in Bronzeville (1945), takes its title from the name journalists applied to Chicago's black ghetto. Like Langston Hughes, Brooks depicts the lives of "ordinary" people; without succumbing to sentimentality, she celebrates their vitality in the face of hardship. Since 1967, when Brooks' "Blackness . . . [confronted her] with a shrill spelling of itself," her work has grown more militant and political. Her poetry relies on strong rhythms, and its textured diction derives in part from gospel preachers and from street talk. She has increasingly moved away from closed forms to open, improvisational ones.

George Mackay Brown (1921–1996)

George Mackay Brown was born in Stromness, a small fishing and shipbuilding seaport in the Orkney Islands of Scotland. Apart from the time he spent at Newbattle Abbey College and the University of Edinburgh, he remained in the Orkneys all his life. A sufferer from tuberculosis, he underwent several periods of extended treatment and convalescence in local sanatoriums. He became a Roman Catholic in 1961. Whether in poetry or in his lyrical short stories and plays, Brown wrote almost invariably on themes connected with his remote northern homeland. His work was inspired by Norse saga, Catholic liturgy and ceremony, elemental rituals, ballad, myth, legend, island folklore, and local history, recorded and imagined. Both narrative and lyric, his poems are tied to the cycles of nature and village life. In addition, they have strong cadences and use litanylike repetition, yet produce an effect of natural speech. Brown also attributed aspects of his style to his interest in the patterns of arithmetic, insisting that the disciplines of geometry and trigonometry "taught me to reverence form" and "the beauty and inevitability of numbers."

Sterling A. Brown (1901–1989)

Sterling A. Brown was born in Washington, D.C., and educated at Williams College and at Harvard University. Upon graduation from Harvard, he embarked on a long and distinguished academic career, during which he taught at Virginia Seminary College and Lincoln, Fisk, and (for nearly fifty years) Howard Universities. From 1936 until 1939, Brown worked with the Federal Writers' Project of the Works Progress Administration (WPA). For a time he edited Negro Affairs magazine, and he later worked at Opportunity. In addition to poetry, he published several seminal works on African-American literature: The Negro in American Fiction, Negro Poetry and Drama, and The Negro Caravan. Brown cited the regionalists and realists E. A. Robinson and Robert Frost as important influences. Like Jean Toomer he set his work primarily in rural surroundings, and like Langston Hughes, to whom Brown is often compared, he wrote dialect poetry and derived many of his forms from the ballad, the work song, jazz, and the blues.

William Browne (1591?–1643?)

William Browne was born in Tavistock, Devon (England), a region he idealized in the Arcadian setting of his pastoral poetry, describing "Tavy's voiceful stream to whom I owe more strains than from my pipe can ever flow." He was educated at Exeter College, Oxford, and in 1611 entered the Inner Temple in London to study law. Tutor to Robert Dormer (the future earl of Carnavon), he later was taken into the household of the noble Herbert family; dedicated book 2 of his major work, Britannia's Pastorals (1616), to William Herbert, the third earl; and wrote an eloquent epitaph for William's mother, Mary Sidney. A friend of Michael Drayton and Ben Jonson, he admired the works of Philip Sidney and Edmund Spenser. Browne's pastoral poetry, published in a multiauthored collection called The Shepheard's Pipe (1614) and in Britannia's Pastorals, influenced Milton's "Lycidas," "L'Allegro," and "Il Penseroso," as well as works by later poets such as John Keats.

Elizabeth Barrett Browning (1806–1861)

Elizabeth Barrett was raised in Herefordshire, England. She received no formal education, but studied the classics at home and was extremely well-educated for a woman of her day. In 1846 she secretly married the poet Robert Browning and eloped to Italy. In England, she had lived the life of an invalid, but in Italy her strength and spirits revived. She developed a passion for Italian politics, supporting unification and writing energetically on behalf of the cause. Her poetry was well-received in its day, and at the time of her death, her reputation outstripped her husband's. She is best known for Sonnets from the Portuguese (1850), a sequence of forty-four Petrarchan sonnets that document her burgeoning love for Browning, but she is most admired for Aurora Leigh (1857), a nine-book verse novel that documents the emerging artistic consciousness of a young orphan sent from Italy to live with her aunt, a British spinster who prides herself on her conventionality. The work shocked many of its readers, who took offense at Browning's criticism of the stultifying social forms imposed on women, but deeply impressed contemporary writers, including John Ruskin, who called it "the greatest poem written in English," and Virginia Woolf. Her late work is sometimes criticized for its didacticism, but it is also praised for its realism, which ran counter to the prevailing style of the day.

Robert Browning (1812–1889)

Robert Browning was born in a suburb of London. He attended London University, but received most of his education by reading voraciously in his father's eclectic library. In 1846 he eloped with the poet Elizabeth Barrett and lived with her in Italy until her death in 1861. His early work, which included drama and poetry, was poorly received by the public, but brought him the respect of such influential literary figures as John Forster, Thomas Carlyle, Charles Dickens, and Alfred, Lord Tennyson. With the publication of *Dramatis Personae* in 1861, followed by the popular *The Ring and the Book* in 1864, Browning's reputation grew prodigious. Writing drama schooled Browning in the art of the dramatic monologue, which he used masterfully in his middle period. At their best, his monologues hide their careful construction under the guise of conversational language, a poetic commonplace now, but a startling innovation in an age that prized poetic diction. He frequently selected subject matter from obscure historical scenes in which he found parallels to his own age and through them discussed such issues as the nature of good and evil, the right use of power, the purpose of art, and the role of faith in modern life, but without making overt moral pronouncements about them.

William Cullen Bryant (1794–1878)
William Cullen Bryant was born in Cummington, Massachusetts, a descendant of early Puritan immigrants. He spent a year at Williams College and, at his father's urging, three years reading law at Worthington and Bridgewater Colleges. Bryant's reputation was established in 1817 with the publication of the poem "Thanatopsis" (Greek for "a view of death"), which he wrote at the age of sixteen. In 1825 he abandoned law for literature. He served on the editorial board of several journals, including the *New York Review*, and in 1829 he assumed the editorship of New York's *Evening Post*, a position he held for nearly fifty years. In his later years, he devoted much energy to translating the *Iliad* (1870) and *Odyssey* (1871–72) into blank verse. He wrote essays and travel journals, and also published his speeches and orations, but his essential work is contained in *Poems* (1832 edition). Committed to establishing an indigenous American poetry, Bryant filled his poems with precise descriptions of local flora and fauna. Sometimes called "the American Wordsworth," Bryant considered nature a physical manifestation of God's omnipotence and caring presence.

Basil Bunting (1900–1985)
Basil Bunting was born in Newcastle, Northumberland. He attended the London School of Economics. After being imprisoned for six months as a conscientious objector during World War I, he lived a bohemian existence that took him to France (where he met the poet Ezra Pound), Greece, Italy, Germany, and the Canary Islands. He enlisted in the Royal Air Force on the outbreak of World War II, served in a number of posts across the globe, and after the war was appointed to the British Embassy in Tehran. He returned to Northumberland in 1953 and went to work for a small newspaper. After the publication of *Briggflatts* in 1966, he was much in demand on the university circuit and taught at several institutions in England and the United States. Like Pound, Bunting exploited the deep connection between poetry and music, and his major poems are written in forms he identified as the "ode" and the "sonata." His contemporary reputation rests largely on *Briggflats*, a work organized around the narrative of Bunting's life, the seasons, and the sonata form, with its repetitions, echoings, and variations on images and themes. Its unique music results from the use of diction drawn from Northumbrian dialects and Anglo-Saxon poetic devices such as heavy alliteration, monosyllabic feet, and marked caesuras.

Robert Burns (1759–1796)
Robert Burns was born into a farming family in Ayrshire, Scotland. He received a modest education at the "adventure" school established by his father and his neighbors, but was largely self-taught. He spent a year and a half in Edinburgh following the publication of his immensely popular first book, *Poems, Chiefly in the Scottish Dialect* (1786), but returned home the following year when he was awarded a sinecure in the Excise Office. Burns farmed and performed his official duties until 1791, when he gave up his land and moved to Dumfries. He devoted his last years to collecting Scottish folk songs as part of a project to preserve Scottish culture and the Scottish national identity. He most often wrote in Scots, a form of English spoken by the Scottish peasantry that incorporates many dialect words, and his subject matter was frequently drawn from Scottish folk tales and legends, Scottish landscapes, and local events. He has been compared to figures such as Robert Henryson, William Dunbar, and Gavin Douglas, who wrote in the fifteenth and sixteenth centuries, the golden age of Scottish literature, and spawned a revival of interest in Scottish culture. Burns was by no means parochial, however. He is a precursor of the Romantics in his sensitivity to nature, high regard for sentiment, homely subject matter, and conversational diction. His genres ranged from the satire to the mock-heroic and narrative; his stanza forms from the intricate Spenserian to blank verse; and his tone from satiric to sentimental.

Witter Bynner (1881–1968)
Witter Bynner was born in Brooklyn, New York, and raised in Norwalk, Connecticut, and Brookline, Massachusetts. He was educated at Harvard University, where the poet Wallace Stevens and future president Franklin Delano Roosevelt were among his classmates. Until 1906 he worked as an editor, then quit to devote himself to writing. Bynner traveled extensively in the United States and in China, and he eventually established homes in Santa Fe, New Mexico, and near Guadalajara, Mexico. In addition to poetry, he published several verse dramas and numerous essays. With the assistance of Kiang Kang-hu, he undertook this century's first significant translation of Chinese poetry into English. Bynner gained fame, or infamy, for perpetuating the "Spectricism" hoax, in which he and Arthur Davidson Ficke published a well-received volume of poems intended as a spoof on imagism. Although the poems were games, they also revealed hallmarks of Bynner's own style: spareness, directness, and clarity. Bynner's range ran wide, from witty social verse to deeply expressive lyrics. His verse shares the merits of the T'ang Dynasty poems he studied so closely, particularly—in his own words—their "intuitional sense of oneness in man, nature and eternity."

George Gordon, Lord Byron (1788–1824)
George Gordon Byron was born near Aberdeen, Scotland, to dissolute aristocratic parents who had fallen on hard times. Their difficulties were alleviated when Byron inherited his title at the age of ten. Upon graduation from Trinity College, Cambridge, he embarked on a two-year tour of Portugal, Spain, Malta, Greece, and Asia-Minor, during which he gathered much of the material for his most important poems. He became a celebrity overnight in 1812 with the publication of his first collection of poems, but notoriety supplanted fame when Byron's affair with his half-sister, whom he had met as an adult, became public knowledge. His marriage collapsed and he was forced to leave England in 1816. He followed the poet Percy Bysshe Shelley to Geneva and Italy, then went on to Greece where he organized a contingent of soldiers to fight for independence from the Turks. After he fell sick in the woods during a training exercise and died, he was mourned as a national hero throughout Greece. His work was widely known in Eu-

rope and was immensely influential on the major European writers of his day. Perhaps his most significant contribution to literature was the development of the Byronic hero, a doomed but impassioned wanderer, often driven by guilt and alienated from his society, but superior to it. Byron's work was deeply rooted in the literary tradition; he turned to the past for models, drawing heavily on the Cavalier tradition of paying elaborate compliments to ladies, the satiric tradition of launching witty criticisms of modern civilization, and the narrative tradition. In *Don Juan*, his masterpiece, he uses the narrator to attack such institutions as the government, the church, and marriage; criticize such vices as hypocrisy, greed, and lust; and subtly extol such virtues as courage, loyalty, and candor. Although many critics considered the poem a wanton celebration of the misadventures of a profligate, Byron himself called it "the most moral of poems." His formal achievement was great. He worked with apparent facility in established meters, such as blank verse, terza-rima, and ottava-rima, and elaborate forms such as the ode and the Spenserian stanza.

Roy Campbell (1902–1957)

Roy Campbell was born in Natal, South Africa. After living briefly in England in his early twenties, he returned to South Africa and worked on the literary magazine *Voorslag* ("Whiplash"), which satirized the values of the Afrikaners. Among the volumes of poetry he produced during the 1920s and 1930s were *The Georgiad*, an attack on the Bloomsbury group; *Flowering Reeds*, a return to his earlier lyricism; and *Flowering Rifle*, in which he eulogized the Spanish dictator Francisco Franco. In 1935 Campbell became a Roman Catholic, and during World War II he served in the English army. He died in a car crash in Portugal. In addition to poetry, he wrote two autobiographical works. His translations of Spanish and Portuguese fiction, and particularly of Federico García Lorca's poetry and Charles Baudelaire's *Les Fleurs du Mal*, are highly regarded.

Thomas Campion (1567–1620)

Thomas Campion was born in London and educated at Peterhouse, Cambridge, which he left without taking a degree but with a taste for classical literature, and at Gray's Inn, though he was never called to the bar. After receiving an M.D. from the University of Caen in 1605, he was practicing medicine in London by 1606. He considered himself to be first and foremost a classicist and a composer, however, his chief aim being to "couple my words and notes lovingly together." He fulfilled this ambition in a number of lyrics in four *Bookes of Ayres* for lute and voice, and in his composition of court masques including *The Lord Hay's Masque*, performed in 1607, and the *Somerset Masque* and the *Lord's Masque*, both performed in 1613. Five poems by Campion were published, anonymously, in 1591, and his *Poemata*, consisting of Latin panegyrics, elegies, and epigrams, appeared in 1595. In his treatise *Observations in the Art of English Poesie* (1602), he advocated the classical or "quantitative" system of meter, prompting Samuel Daniel's *Defence of Rhyme* (1602). Though Campion dismissed his own early, mainly rhymed, verse as "superfluous blossoms of my deeper studies," his unrhymed experimental poems have a musical quality no less impressive than that of his rhyming poems.

Thomas Carew (1598?–1639?)

Thomas Carew (pronounced "Carey") was born in West Wickham, Kent, England. Son of Sir Matthew Carew, who worked in the court of law known as the Chancery, Carew was educated at Merton College, Oxford, and the

law school of the Middle Temple. He was secretary to Sir Dudley Carleton, the ambassador to Venice and later to The Hague, from 1613 to 1616, when he returned to England. He was next employed by Sir Edward Herbert, the ambassador to France, during which time he established his reputation as a poet and found favor with Charles I, who made him a gentleman of the privy chamber in 1628. Carew is the earliest of those authors who, like his friends Sir John Suckling and Richard Lovelace, are today known as "Cavalier" poets. They were Royalist in politics, looked to the classical poets (through Ben Jonson) for their models, and composed graceful, witty, elegantly crafted verse. Carew saw his own work as "a mine of rich and pregnant fancy," and brought lucidity, directness, a frank sexuality, and urbane cynicism to amatory verse, but also wrote on other themes, most notably in his "An Elegy upon the Death of the Dean of Paul's, Dr. John Donne." He also composed several longer poems, including "A Rapture" and "To Saxham," the latter showing the influence of Jonson's "To Penshurst." Carew's masque, *Coelum Britannicum*, was performed before Charles I in 1634, and a collection, *Poems*, was published in 1640.

Lewis Carroll (Charles Lutwidge Dodgson) (1832–1898)

Charles Lutwidge Dodgson was born in Daresbury, Cheshire, England, and educated at Rugby and Christ Church, Oxford, on whose grounds he was to live for the rest of his life. In 1855 he became a lecturer in mathematics and thereafter published several books on the subject, including a defense of Euclid. Although he became a clergyman in 1861, his habitual shyness caused a bad stammer that kept him from preaching often. In addition to poems, puns, pastiche, conundrums, problems of logic, and some adventurous linguistics, he wrote children's books (under the pseudonym Lewis Carroll, a Latinized form of Lutwidge Charles). *Alice's Adventures Under Ground* (1865), now usually known as *Alice's Adventures in Wonderland*, like its sequel, *Through the Looking-glass and What Alice Found There* (1871), began in tales told during boating trips on the Thames to the three daughters (one of whom was Alice) of Henry Liddell, dean of Christ Church. The stories were an instant and enduring success, perhaps because of the absence of the "improving" matter found in most children's literature of the time.

Charles Causley (1917–   )

Charles Causley was born in Launceston, Cornwall, and has lived there all his life. His father, a private soldier, returned from France after World War I a hopeless invalid, and died seven years later from the residual effects of nerve gas. Causley was educated at a local grammar school, then worked in a builder's office and later for a small electrical supply company. His service in the Royal Navy from 1940 until 1946 proved decisive to his literary career, drawing him from prose to poetry and providing him with a subject. After the war, Causley became a teacher, retiring in 1965 to become a full-time writer, but subsequently accepting offers to teach in various colleges and universities in Australia, Canada, and the United States. He has published plays, short stories, poetry, and children's verse, and edited numerous collections of poetry. His poems are mostly drawn from his naval experience and from the Cornish landscape and people, and many are poignant elegies for the war dead. Like those of John Clare, his verse forms and narrative devices derive from the oral folk tradition, especially the ballad and other song forms, and he combines jaunty cadences with agile interweaving of ancient and modern diction.

Margaret Cavendish (1623–1673)

Margaret Cavendish was born in England to an aristocratic family and became a maid of honor to Queen Henrietta Maria. At twenty-two she married the Royalist William Cavendish, then marquis of Newcastle, later first duke. She met him in Paris, where they both lived in exile during the Commonwealth. In 1651, having returned to England to try to recover part of her husband's estate, she wrote *Fancies* (1st edition, 1653) and *Philosophical Fancies* (1653; revised as part of *Philosophical and Physical Opinions*, 1655). Her wide-ranging intellectual interests, among them chemistry and natural philosophy, inform these and subsequent writings in a variety of genres, including the deliberately hybrid *Worlds of Olio* of 1655 (the term "Olio" refers to a Portuguese stew with many ingredients). She explores the question of women's "secondary" status from many and sometimes contradictory perspectives in volumes of plays (1662 and 1668), in *Natures Pictures* (with autobiography) (1656), in her *Sociable Letters* (1664), and in her utopian narrative *The New Blazing World* (1668). She made a visit to the Royal Society, a newly instituted scientific institution, in 1667 and was viewed as an "eccentric" both in her own time and later. Both in her poetry and in her prose she demonstrates a fascination with "similizing," or comparing elements from apparently disparate realms. In the "life" of herself she appended to her biography of her husband, she compared her thoughts to "silk worms" that spin "out of their own bowels."

Geoffrey Chaucer (ca. 1343–1400)

Geoffrey Chaucer was born into a middle-class merchant family and at about fifteen years of age became a page to the countess of Ulster. While serving her husband, Lionel (the second son of King Edward III) during the Hundred Years War, Chaucer was captured at the siege of Reims and eventually ransomed. In 1365 he married Philippa Roet, sister-in-law of the powerful peer John of Gaunt, who was the uncle and advisor of King Richard II. In 1367, Chaucer was granted an annuity in the royal household and soon began to travel on diplomatic missions: to Spain (1366), to France (1368), and to Italy (1372 and 1378). During his travels he encountered works by French and Italian authors such as Jean Froissart, Guillaume Machaut, Dante, Petrarch, and Boccaccio. These authors influenced Chaucer in a variety of ways; his first important original work, *The Book of the Duchess*, shows the influence of French courtly poetry; and his later *House of Fame* parodies Dante's *Divine Comedy* by depicting a poet's journey—in the talons of an eagle—to the celestial palace of the goddess of Fame. And his *Troilus and Criseide* (1385) was deeply indebted to Boccaccio's *Filostrato*. Chaucer's work also shows the influence of two texts that he translated into English from French and Latin respectively: a thirteenth-century drama vision entitled *The Romance of the Rose* and a fourth-century philosophical dialogue by Boethius, *The Consolation of Philosophy*.

At a time when many of his contemporaries were writing in French and Latin, Chaucer's use of English helped to establish the vernacular as a viable medium for serious poetry. He was an innovator in both technique and language; a great number of words and phrases, many of French origin, appear for the first time in his writings. His *Canterbury Tales*, begun in 1386, is an unfinished group of tales told by members of a company of pilgrims. The tales reflect Chaucer's own experience of many different social roles and events. He lived through several plagues and the Peasant's Revolt of 1381; he served as controller of the export tax on wool, sheep-skins, and leather for the port of London; he was justice of the peace and a member of Parliament for the county of Kent, and he was also a deputy forester. In 1380, he was released from a legal charge of rape by a woman named Cecily Champaigne. He succeeded in surviving, as many of his friends did not, the transition from Richard II to Henry IV. Although he never completed his plan of writing one hundred and ten Canterbury Tales (four for each pilgrim to tell on the way to Canterbury, two for the way back), the twenty-two tales and two fragments that he did complete contain, as John Dryden said, "God's plenty."

Nicholas Christopher (1951–)

Nicholas Christopher was born and raised in New York City and has lived there most of his life. He was educated at Harvard University, where he studied with the poets Robert Lowell and Anthony Hecht. A freelance writer and an educator, he has taught at New York and Columbia Universities. He has published poetry and novels—as well as an amalgam of the two in his "novella in verse," *Desperate Characters* (1989)—and he has edited two collections of contemporary American poetry. Although he often works in regular stanza forms and regularly accented lines, Christopher is not a strict formalist. Many of his poems have surrealistic elements; some take on the clipped, brusque tone of a detective novel; and still others are purely lyrical.

Amy Clampitt (1920–1994)

Amy Clampitt was born and raised in New Providence, Iowa. She was educated at Grinnell College. After working as an editor at Oxford University Press and E. P. Dutton and as a reference librarian at the National Audubon Society, she became a freelance writer in 1982. Clampitt published her first collection of poetry at the age of sixty-three and subsequently served as visiting professor at several colleges and universities. In addition to poetry, she authored a play and a collection of essays. In her poems Clampitt typically ponders commonplace objects and scenes until they are transformed under her gaze. Her keen powers of observation, ornate stanza forms, precise diction, complex syntax, and concern with morality link her to Gerard Manley Hopkins and Marianne Moore. And like John Keats, about whom she wrote a series of poems, she revels in the sensuousness of the natural world—while remaining aware of the transience of life and of beauty.

John Clare (1793–1864)

John Clare was born in the small rural village of Helpstone, in Northamptonshire, England. After leaving school at twelve he worked on the land, as gardener, hedge-settler, lime-burner, and field hand, and published his first collection, *Poems Descriptive of Rural Life and Scenery*, in 1820. The book was a success, but as literary tastes changed, and the vogue for "ploughman poets" declined, subsequent volumes were not. Clare had a strong sense of place and was deeply attached to his native countryside. A move to a village four miles distant from his birthplace seems to have been the catalyst for chronic mental insecurity and, along with his parting from his first love, Mary Joyce, provided the theme of loss so prevalent in his writing. After manifesting signs of mental illness for many years, he was sent to an asylum in 1836 and, having been declared insane, transferred to Northampton General Asylum, where he remained until his death. His descriptions of rural landscape and elegies for a dying pastoral England are highly evocative. Though the images are powerful, they do not cross into the symbolic; when Keats advised him to link "Images from Nature" with "particular sentiments," Clare resisted, deeming the practice "wearisome." He also resisted the prevalent artificial poetic diction (though he admired the work of James Thomson), writing in his own combination of dialect and idiosyncratic grammar. Clare's poetry remained in semiobscurity until this century, when his evident authenticity of feeling and complex sensibility were made available through new editions of his poems, autobiographical prose, and letters.

Arthur Hugh Clough (1819–1861)

Arthur Hugh Clough (rhymes with "rough") was born in Liverpool to a cotton merchant and the daughter of a banker. His family moved to South Carolina in 1822, but Clough returned to England in 1828 to attend first Rugby School then Oxford. In 1842 he earned a fellowship at Oriel College, Oxford, where he became friends with the poet Matthew Arnold. Like Arnold, Clough struggled with his religious beliefs, and in 1848 he resigned from his fellowship because he would not take clerical orders without sincerely believing the doctrines of the Church of England. That same year he published his first work, *The Bothie of Tober-na-Vuolich*, a verse novel about the romance between a student and a Scottish peasant. After traveling to Rome and writing more poetry, including *Amours de Voyage*, he took an administrative position at the University of London; however, in 1851 uncertainties about his religious faith again led him to resign. During the next year Clough returned to America with the thought of emigrating; he settled in Boston, where he tutored, wrote for magazines, and established a lasting friendship with Ralph Waldo Emerson. However, he returned to England in 1853, took an appointment in the Education Office, and married a cousin of Florence Nightingale. He died in Florence, Italy, while touring the Continent in the hope of improving his health, and Matthew Arnold wrote "Thyrsis" in memory of his friend. Most of Clough's work was published posthumously; many readers of the Victorian era identified with his themes of religious uncertainty, but his works are also remembered for their ironic wit and moments of playfulness.

Samuel Taylor Coleridge (1772–1834)

Samuel Taylor Coleridge was born in Ottery St. Mary, a rural village in Devon, and raised in London. He was educated at Jesus College, Cambridge, but fell into a dissolute lifestyle. He fled to London and served in the Light Dragoons until his brothers secured his release some months later. In 1795 he met Wordsworth, with whom he published *Lyrical Ballads* (1798), one of the most revolutionary collections of poetry in the history of English literature. From the age of thirty, Coleridge largely gave up poetry for philosophy and criticism. He is credited with introducing the works of the philosophers Immanuel Kant, Friedrich von Schlegel, and Friedrich von Schelling to England. At the height of his powers, he became addicted to opium, which had been prescribed to relieve agonizing physical pains that Wordsworth said were so unbearable they drove Coleridge to "throw himself down and writhe like a worm upon the ground." He spent his last years in the care of a clergyman, writing and attempting to be reconciled with estranged family and friends. In an age dominated by skepticism and empiricism, Coleridge held fast to his belief in the powers of the imagination, which he believed capable of leading humanity to Truth—not through appeals to reason, but to the senses. Like Wordsworth, he strove to express "natural thoughts with natural diction" and to use simple syntax. His accessible style reached its culmination in his meditative, blank-verse "Conversational poems," which influenced writers as diverse as Matthew Arnold, T. S. Eliot, and Robert

Frost. Coleridge worked in both established forms, such as the ode, and fluid forms of his own making. He eschewed the use of conventional "mechanic" or "preordained" forms that did not arise "out of the properties of the material" but were imposed from without, as when "to a mass of wet clay we give whatever shape we wish it to retain when hardened," for "organic" form, which arises "out of the properties of the material" and "shapes as it develops itself from within." If Wordsworth determined the content of a century or more of English poetry, Coleridge determined its shape. His theories on "organic form" provided a basis for the development of a freer poetic, and may have been the progenitor of many twentieth-century experiments in free verse.

William Collins (1721–1759)

William Collins was born in Chichester, England, where his father was twice mayor. Educated at Winchester School and Magdalen College, Oxford, he published *Persian Eclogues* as an undergraduate. Allegedly "too indolent even for the army," he went to London to earn a living from writing. His finances were always insecure, and ruin was averted only by the action of friends such as Samuel Johnson. His *Odes on Several Descriptive and Allegoric Subjects* (1747) was not esteemed at the time of publication, but a small inheritance enabled Collins to return to Chichester, where he could study and write. In 1750 he gave the Scottish playwright John Home an unfinished draft of "Ode on the Superstitions of the Highlands," in which (as the poet Robert Lowell put it) "the whole Romantic School is foreshadowed." Soon after, Collins' melancholia worsened, and after unsuccessfully seeking a cure in France he was confined to a Chelsea asylum. Soon committed to the care of his sister, he remained with her, experiencing spells of lucidity, until his death. Though he left fewer than fifteen hundred lines of verse, he was one of the most influential poets of his time.

Wendy Cope (1945–)

Wendy Cope was born in Erith, Kent, and educated at St. Hilda's College, Oxford, and the Westminster School of Education, Oxford. She has been a primary school teacher, a music teacher, the arts and books editor of the Inner London Education Authority's *Contact* magazine, and television columnist for the *Spectator*. She began writing while undergoing psychoanalysis for severe depression following her father's death. In addition to her verse for adults and children, she has edited a collection of poetry by women. Cope's acerbic, witty, epigrammatic poems invite comparison with the work of Dorothy Parker and Stevie Smith. Like them, she has serious aims, and asserts that "a humorous poem can also be . . . deeply felt and saying something that matters." Much of her work is satirical or parodic, and she has invented a character, "Jason Strugnell," a second-rate poet from South London, to be the "author" of a number of sonnets and a sequence of song lyrics in a pretentious and portentous style. Cope typically works in elaborate forms such as the ballade, rondeau, villanelle, and triolet, all of which depend upon regular meter and rhymes, and on refrains, repetition, and variation.

Alfred Corn (1943–)

Alfred Corn was born in Bainbridge, Georgia, and raised in Valdosta, Georgia. He was educated at Emory and Columbia Universities. His graduate studies were in French literature, and he has spent extensive time abroad, notably in France. A reviewer and essayist, as well as an art critic, Corn has taught at, among other schools, Columbia, Connecticut College, Yale University, and the City University of New York. He also has published a book of literary essays and edited a collection of writings on the New Testament. Two of Corn's volumes of poetry, *Notes from a Child of Paradise* (1984) and *Autobiographies* (1992), unfold long narratives that use many of the techniques of fiction. Each gives a sweeping view of America in a particular moment (the 1960s and 1990s, respectively). Corn's work frequently employs rhyme and a loose iambic line and has been described as simultaneously innovative and traditional. Clarity and irony—as well as playfulness—are hallmarks of his style.

Abraham Cowley (1618–1667)

Abraham Cowley (pronounced "Cooley") was born after the death of his father, a wealthy London stationer, and was educated at Westminster School and Trinity College, Cambridge. At fifteen he published his first book of poems, containing among other works a verse romance he had written at ten. In 1638, he published a pastoral drama, *Loves Riddle*, and a Latin comedy, *Naufragium Joculare*. Given a fellowship at his college in 1640, he lost it when the Civil War began, for he was a Royalist and went to France as secretary of the queen. He was imprisoned when he returned to England ten years later, because he was working as a spy and partly because he had published a satire, *The Puritan and the Papist*, in 1643. A political epic, *The Civil War*, was not published until 1679, but he celebrated the king's return to power with an "Ode, Upon the Blessed Restoration" (1660). In his "Pindarique Odes," included in *Poems* (1656), he introduced the irregular ode form that would influence John Dryden, among others.

William Cowper (1731–1800)

William Cowper (pronounced "Cooper") was born in Great Berkhamstead, Herfordshire, England, and was educated at a private school and Westminster; his experience of bullying at the former leading to the attack on private schools in his "Tirocinium" (1785). He studied law at the Inner Temple and was called up to the bar, but never practiced. From his early years he suffered from depression, which was accelerated into mental instability both by his father's forbidding his marriage to his cousin, Theodora, and by an uncle's attempt to get him a sinecure in the House of Lords, the prospect of examination for which brought on a suicide attempt. Treated at St. Albans asylum, Cowper turned to the consolations of evangelical Christianity, and on his release became "a sort of adopted son" in the household of the Reverend Morley Unwin. After Unwin's death, Cowper, Mary Unwin, and her children set up house together in Olney, Buckinghamshire. Under the influence of John Newton, an evangelical with Calvinistic leanings, Cowper's mental health again declined and eventually collapsed, but nursed by Mary he began to write again. They lived together until her death in 1794, after which Cowper never fully recovered his physical and mental health.

George Crabbe (1754–1832)

George Crabbe was born to poverty in Aldeburgh, Suffolk, England, and was educated largely at home. He was parish doctor of Aldeburgh before leaving for London and a literary career in 1780. With the help of his friend and admirer Edmund Burke, he published *The Library* (1781), was introduced to contemporary literary circles, and was encouraged to join the clergy in order to relieve his financial distress. In 1781 he became curate of Aldeburgh, and from 1782 until 1785 was chaplain to the duke of Rutland. Burke and Samuel Johnson helped him revise *The Village* (1783), a grimly realist portrait of rural poverty. After a period when he published little,

in 1807 he produced a collection of earlier and new works including "The Parish Register," which established him as a narrative poet. He published several more collections during his lifetime and left a quantity of unpublished work on his death. Known for his use of the heroic couplet characteristic of the departing Augustan Age, he was, according to Lord Byron, "Nature's sternest painter yet the best."

Hart Crane (1899–1932)

Hart (Harold) Crane was born in Garrettsville, Ohio, and raised in Cleveland. He left high school in 1916 and moved to New York. From 1918 to 1923, he shuttled between New York and Cleveland and worked for advertising agencies (where he wrote copy), a munitions plant, a local newspaper, and his father's candy company. In 1923 Crane settled in New York, but in 1931 he sailed to Mexico, where he planned to write an epic about the Spanish Conquest. On a return trip to the United States he committed suicide by leaping into shark-infested waters. Although his mature poems show the influence of T. S. Eliot (and the French symbolists), his work differs from Eliot's in significant ways, particularly in his emphasis on the positive and even ecstatic. This stance culminated in *The Bridge*, Crane's "mythical synthesis of America," which followed in the tradition of Walt Whitman. Its fifteen sections of varying length move westward, from New York to California; feature historical figures, including Pocahontas and Rip Van Winkle; and celebrate natural and technological wonders, such as the Mississippi River, the clipper ship *Cutty Sark*, the New York City subway system, and the Brooklyn Bridge.

Stephen Crane (1871–1900)

Stephen Crane was born in Newark, New Jersey, and was raised in upstate New York. He attended Lafayette College and Syracuse University for a year apiece before moving to New York City, where he worked as a reporter and began to write fiction. His first novel, a naturalistic account of urban poverty called *Maggie: A Girl of the Streets* (1893), was poorly received, but his next book, *The Red Badge of Courage* (1894–95), earned him fame. Although Crane had written this Civil War narrative without seeing combat, he received commissions to report on conflicts across the globe, including the Cuban Insurrection, the Turkish War, and the Spanish-American War. He died in Germany, where he had gone in search of a cure for his tuberculosis. Although he became famous for his prose, Crane preferred his poems, which were innovative for their time and, like his first fiction, badly received. Now considered pioneering examples of "free verse," they are deliberately plain, unmetered and unrhymed, often brief and epigrammatic, and thematically unorthodox. It took the efforts of the poet John Berryman, his biographer, to revive Crane's flagging posthumous reputation.

Richard Crashaw (1613–1649)

Richard Crashaw's mother and stepmother both died before he was nine years old, and he spent most of his life rebelling against the austere religion of his father, a Puritan preacher. Crashaw was educated at Charterhouse and Pembroke Hall, Cambridge, where he was influenced by the Anglican Nicholas Ferrar (1592–1637), whose religious community at Little Gidding inspired one of T. S. Eliot's *Four Quartets* (1944). After losing his fellowship at Peterhouse with the Royalists' defeat, Crashaw spent two years in exile, converting to Catholicism in 1645 and fleeing to Paris, where another friend, the writer Abraham Cowley, persuaded Queen Henrietta Maria to get Crashaw a position as an attendant to an

Italian cardinal and, subsequently, as a subcanon at the Cathedral of Loretto. In 1634 Crashaw published a book of Latin poems, *Epigrammatum Sacrorum Liber*. His *Steps to the Temple, Sacred Poems with other Delights of the Muses* (1646, revised and enlarged 1648) contains both religious and secular poems and indicates its debt to George Herbert in its title. Crashaw differs from Herbert, however, in using striking, even violent, images shaped by Continental models of poetry, art, and Roman Catholic devotional practice. A passionate admirer of the Spanish mystic Saint Teresa, Crashaw sought to represent the experience of religious ecstasy in words and, perhaps, in visual media. The manuscript as well as the printed volumes of his poetry contain elaborate titles in different-sized letters; and the emblematic engravings in his final (posthumously published) volume, the *Carmen Deo Nostro* (1652), may be by his own hand.

Robert Creeley (1926–)

Robert Creeley was born in Arlington, Massachusetts, and educated at Harvard University. From 1944 to 1945 he interrupted his studies to drive an ambulance for the American Field Service in the India-Burma theater, then later left Harvard during his last semester to take up subsistence farming. He traveled to France and Mallorca, Spain (where he established the Divers Press), and returned to the United States in 1955. As a member of the faculty at the experimental Black Mountain College, Creeley founded its influential *Review*. After the college closed, he moved to Albuquerque, did graduate study at the University of New Mexico, and taught English in the local school system. In 1966 he began teaching at the State University of New York at Buffalo. Deeply influenced by Charles Olson, William Carlos Williams, and the Beats, all of whom composed their poems (as Allen Ginsberg put it) directly from feeling, he writes in organic forms that mimic the cadences of conversation and the rhythms of jazz. He has written that form "is never more than an extension of content," and his spare, compressed, minimalist verse often depicts a struggle between the interior self and the exterior world.

Countee Cullen (1903–1946)

Countee Cullen was born in Louisville, Kentucky; at the age of fifteen he was adopted by an Episcopal minister from New York City. Cullen was educated at New York University and Harvard University. He worked as an assistant editor at *Opportunity* magazine, a prominent periodical of the Harlem Renaissance, from 1926 until 1928, when a fellowship enabled him to spend a year in Paris. From 1934 onward he taught English and French in the New York City public schools. In addition to writing five collections of poetry, Cullen translated Euripides, published a novel about life in Harlem, edited an influential anthology of African-American poetry, and wrote two children's books. Wanting to be known foremost "as a poet and not as a Negro poet," he was called "the black Keats" for his lyricism, his facility with difficult meters and forms, and his subject matter, such as the transience of beauty. Themes of injustice and prejudice recur in his work.

E. E. Cummings (1894–1962)

E(dward) E(stlin) Cummings was born in Cambridge, Massachusetts, and educated at Harvard University. In the early 1920s he lived in both New York City (where he was affiliated with the *Dial* magazine group, which included the poet Marianne Moore) and Paris (where he met the poets Ezra Pound, Hart Crane, and Archibald MacLeish). In his later years he lived primarily in New York. Cummings has always had a mixed critical reception, but at the time of his death he was one of the best-

known and best-liked American poets. Like his paintings, Cummings' poems reflect his devotion to the avant-garde; he was influenced by the impressionist and cubist movements in the visual arts and by imagism, vorticism, and futurism in literature. Through his radical experiments with syntax, typography, and line, he defamiliarized common subjects and thus challenged conventional ways of perceiving the world. Yet he respected many poetic conventions: regular rhyme schemes and traditional forms are often discernible under the fractured surface of his poems; the sonnet was a particular favorite. His satires of "mostpeople" who blindly make their way through the "unworld" are often scathing, and his poems convey an anarchistic, rebellious stance toward politics and religion, but Cummings, who celebrated joy, beauty, and sexual love, shared the Transcendentalists' faith in humanity and their appreciation of the natural world.

Allen Curnow (1911–)

Allen Curnow was born in Timaru, New Zealand, the son of an Anglican clergyman and author of light verse and his wife. He worked as a journalist before attending the Universities of Canterbury and Auckland and beginning studies for the ministry (which he later abandoned) at St. John's College. He taught English at Auckland University from 1950 until 1976. In addition to serious poetry, Curnow has published satirical verse under the pseudonym "Whim-Wham," as well as plays and literary criticism. He is the editor of two landmark anthologies, *A Book of New Zealand Verse* and *The Penguin Book of New Zealand Verse*. In the 1930s, Curnow was involved with poets associated with the left-wing magazine *Phoenix*, and his early work reflects their shared belief in the importance of establishing a national literature for New Zealand. These poems characteristically make detailed observation of the natural world. In 1972, after a fifteen-year silence, Curnow began writing in a new mode, exploring the relationship between self and place, the mystery of nature, and death. Whether political, satiric, or meditative, Curnow's work is rooted in literary tradition and filled with arresting imagery.

Samuel Daniel (ca. 1562–1619)

Samuel Daniel was born near Taunton (England), studied at Oxford, and traveled widely throughout Europe, learning several languages. He enjoyed the patronage of Mary Sidney, countess of Pembroke, to whose son he was tutor; and his neoclassical tragedy *Cleopatra* (1594, revised 1607), was influenced by Mary Sidney's translation of a French play about Cleopatra and Antony (*Antonie*, 1592). Daniel wrote works in a variety of genres, from a history of the War of the Roses to tragic and pastoral dramas, to court masques. His *Defence of Rhyme* (1602?), a response to Thomas Campion's treatise alleging the superiority of classical prosody, occupies an important place in the debate on the status of the vernacular as a literary language. In 1592 Daniel published his sonnet cycle to "Delia," a romance, *The Complaint of Rosamond*, appeared in the same volume. Another collection, *Certain Small Poems* (1605) caused Daniel to lose the favor of King James because it contained a tragedy whose protagonist, Philotas, was identified with Queen Elizabeth's rebellious courtier, the earl of Essex. Daniel was nonetheless patronized by James's queen, Anne, and he continued to write masques for the court, including *Tethys' Festival* (1610) and *Hymen's Triumph* (1615). Ben Jonson, with whom Daniel was "at jealousies," criticized his poetry but others, including Samuel Taylor Coleridge, have praised his poetic language.

Donald Davie (1922–1995)

Donald Davie was born in Barnsley, Yorkshire, England, to Baptist parents, and brought up in "the industrially ravaged landscape" of the West Riding. He was educated at Barnsley Hogate Grammar School and at St. Catherine's College, Cambridge, where he was greatly influenced by the critic F. R. Leavis. His studies were interrupted by service in the Royal Navy, but he then returned to Cambridge and took his B.A., M.A., and Ph.D. He taught at Trinity College, Dublin, the University of California at Santa Barbara, and Gonville and Caius College, Cambridge. A founder of the University of Essex, he served on its faculty from 1964 until 1968, when he moved to Stanford University. In 1978 he moved to Vanderbilt University, from which he retired in 1987 to live in Devon. In addition to poetry, Davie published a number of influential studies of English poetry, diction, and syntax, as well as criticism of the work of Hardy, Pound, and Pasternak, translations of the work of Polish, Hungarian, and Russian writers, and a study of English hymnology. His editorial work included several collections of poetry, including the *New Oxford Book of Christian Verse*. Davie's *Purity of Diction in English Verse* was virtually a manifesto for The Movement, a group of writers who eschewed the symbolism and syntactical disjunctions of imagism and symbolism in favor of paraphrasable logic, plain diction, straightforward syntax, and traditional forms.

Peter Davison (1928–)

Peter Davison was born in New York City and raised in Colorado. He was educated at Harvard University and St. John's College, Cambridge, and spent two years in the United States Army. Davison has held editorial jobs at Harcourt, Brace; Harvard University Press; and the Atlantic Monthly Press. Currently a senior editor at Houghton Mifflin, he has been the poetry editor of *The Atlantic Monthly* since 1972 and lives in Boston and Gloucester, Massachusetts. His work is by turns narrative, discursive, meditative, and elegiac (particularly a series of poems in memory of his first wife). Influenced by Robert Frost and by his father, the English poet Edward Davison, he typically employs traditional meters and forms and depicts correspondences between interior experience and the exterior landscape. He also engages in serious verbal play and makes quiet allusions to the classics.

Walter de la Mare (1873–1956)

Walter de la Mare was born in Charlton, Kent, England. In 1890 he took a job as a bookkeeper at the London offices of the Standard Oil Company, a position he held for eighteen years, until a government pension allowed him to devote himself full-time to writing. In 1902 he published his first collection of poetry, *Songs of Childhood*, under the pseudonym Walter Ramal, and over the next four and a half decades he published voluminously, producing novels, short stories, critical studies, and poetry, as well as editing several influential anthologies of literature. Written in the original Romantic tradition, his poetry typically portrays the speaker as a solitary traveler making his way through a disquieted world, occasionally taking solace in the intense beauty of nature or in a dimly apprehended dreamlike vision, but constantly threatened by the cold, impersonal forces that loom over him.

James Dickey (1923–1997)

James Dickey was born in Atlanta, Georgia, and raised in one of its suburbs. In 1942 he attended Clemson College, in South Carolina, then left to join the air force. After serving as a fighter-bomber pilot during World War II, he attended Vanderbilt University, where he began writing poetry. He received B.A. and M.A. degrees from Vanderbilt and did further graduate work there and at Rice University, in Texas. Following another two years in the air force (this time as a training officer during the Korean War), he spent six years as a writer of advertising copy. In 1960 he published his first book of poetry, and in the following years he was a teacher, lecturer, and writer-in-residence at a number of colleges and universities. From 1966 to 1968 he served as poetry consultant to the Library of Congress. In addition to poetry, he published fiction, including the best-selling novel *Deliverance* (1970)—which he adapted into a major Hollywood film—and nonfiction, including autobiographical works and reviews of other poets. Much of his work explored the limits of the self as well as conflicts between and within human beings, between one human being and another, and between human beings and nature. His early work was characterized by objective descriptions and short lines, but he subsequently developed a style based on tension-filled phrases, spaces, and associative leaps.

Emily Dickinson (1830–1886)

Emily Dickinson was born in Amherst, Massachusetts, to a prominent family. For one year she attended Mount Holyoke Female Seminary (now College), in nearby South Hadley, then withdrew and returned to Amherst. Her adult life was as short on external incident as it was long on imagination. Dickinson lived at her family home in Amherst from 1848 on, she rarely received visitors, and in her mature years she never went out. Suffering from agoraphobia (the fear of public places) and perhaps from an eye disorder called exotropia, she became known as the "Myth" and "the *character* of Amherst." Fewer than a dozen of her poems were published in her lifetime. Such a solitary life hardly dulled her sensibilities, however, for Dickinson's collected works—nearly two thousand poems, plus voluminous correspondence—brim with intense feeling, from terror to joy. The poems also reveal her intimate knowledge of the Bible, classical myth, and the works of Shakespeare; in addition, she admired the work of Transcendentalists Thoreau and Emerson and read the Brontës, the Brownings, Keats, and George Eliot. In an era marked by its evangelical fervor, Dickinson adopted skepticism—though she did not arrive at it easily—and her poems are remarkable for their irony, ambiguity, paradox, and sardonic wit. She succinctly defined her aesthetic in the epigrammatic lines "Tell the Truth but tell it slant— / Success in Circuit lies," and she once told a friend: "If I read a book [and] it makes my whole body so cold no fire ever can warm me I know that is poetry. If I feel physically as if the top of my head were taken off, I know that is poetry." She wrote in the meters of hymns and made masterful use of the ballad stanza, often using slant rhyme. Although her innovations initially baffled critics, the public's fascination with her life soon extended to her verse. She is, along with Walt Whitman, the most revered and influential of nineteenth-century American poets.

John Donne (1572–1631)

John Donne's father was a London ironmonger and his mother, a devout Catholic, was the daughter of the dramatist John Heywood as well as a descendent of Sir Thomas More. Donne studied at Oxford without taking a degree, because to do so would have required him to swear an oath affirming that the English monarch was head of the Church. After travel in Europe, Donne entered the legal institution of Lincoln's Inn in 1592. The next year his brother Henry, convicted of harboring a Catholic priest, died in prison. In 1595, Donne participated in a naval expedition against Spain and in 1596 joined an expedition to the Azores. On his return he became private secretary to Sir Thomas Egerton, lord keeper of the Great Seal, but was dismissed when his secret marriage to Lady Egerton's seventeen-year-old niece, Ann More, was discovered. The marriage effectively blocked

Donne's career as a courtier; and after many years of seeking offices and patrons, he took orders in the Church of England in 1615—as King James had been urging him to do since 1607. Two years later his wife died. He became dean of St. Paul's Cathedral in 1621, and his sermons were very well-attended. His private devotions (in prose) were published in 1624, but very few of the poems he had been writing since the 1590s were printed during his lifetime; instead, they circulated widely in manuscript, creating many textual variants and many questions about dating for future editors and readers. His poems were divided into nine generic groups in the second edition of his poetry (1635), including the *Elegies*, modeled on Ovid's erotic verse; the *Songs and Sonnets*, containing a variety of secular love poems; and the *Holy Sonnets*.

H. D. (Hilda Doolittle) (1886–1961)

Hilda Doolittle was born in Bethlehem, Pennsylvania. In 1901 she met the poet Ezra Pound, who encouraged her writing. Doolittle attended Bryn Mawr College, then moved to Greenwich Village, where she established her reputation as a writer. She traveled to London in 1911 intending to visit Pound, but lived in Europe for the rest of her life. In 1912 Pound submitted three of Doolittle's poems to Harriet Monroe, editor of *Poetry* magazine, signing them "H. D. Imagiste." Although H. D. moved beyond imagism—and vorticism, its quick successor—fairly early, her reputation has remained closely tied to that short-lived but momentous movement. In 1933 H. D. entered psychoanalysis with Sigmund Freud, and as a result of their sessions she developed a deep interest in symbologies. She dedicated herself to studying Moravian symbols and ritual, numerology, the cabal, the tarot, and classical mythology. Much like T. S. Eliot, in *The Waste Land*, and Pound, in the *Cantos*, H. D. set her own experience against the great storehouses of literature, myth, history, religion, and the occult, selecting and assembling material in order to explore, and even reconstruct, her own identity. In addition to poetry, she published numerous volumes of prose. She also did work in translation and wrote verse dramas.

Charles d'Orléans (1391–1465)

Charles, duke of Orléans (brother of King Charles VI of France), married his cousin Isabella (widow of Richard II of England), in 1406. Commander of the French forces at the battle of Agincourt in 1415, he was captured after their defeat by the English army under Henry V. He spent the next twenty-five years in prison, and during this time composed his poems in English as well as French. He produced *chansons*, *complaintes*, and translations, as well as poems in intricate forms such as the ballade and rondel, usually on the theme of courtly love. After payment of a huge ransom, he was released from prison and returned to France in 1440. He spent his last years at Blois, where his court became a center of music and literature.

Keith Douglas (1920–1944)

Keith Douglas was born in Tunbridge Wells, Kent, England, and brought up near Cranleigh. His childhood was difficult, as his father became a drifter and his mother was stricken with "sleepy sickness." At Merton College, Oxford, his tutor was Edmund Blunden, the soldier-poet of World War I. In 1941 Douglas enlisted and was posted to Egypt; though ordered to remain in reserve, he commandeered a truck and joined his regiment at the front. He was badly injured when he stepped on a land mine, but after convalescence in Palestine was sent to the European front, and was killed during the invasion of Normandy. Before his death Douglas had prepared a collection for publication, but it did not reach print until 1966. He also wrote a memoir, *Alamein to Zem*

Zem, based on his experiences in the Middle East. After his first years in the war, Douglas exchanged the lyricism of his early work for what he termed "reportage" and "extrospective writing." His later poems testify to the dehumanizing effect of war, but display little overt pity for the fallen, instead exploring war's ambiguities and paradoxes. Douglas presents himself in dual roles, victim and killer, satirist and eulogist, and disinterested spectator and committed participant. He wrote in four- and six-line rhymed stanzas, and shaped his rhythms "to be *read* as significant speech," finding "no reason to be either musical or sonorous about things at present."

Rita Dove (1952–)

Rita Dove was born in Akron, Ohio. She was educated at Miami University (Ohio), the University of Tübingen (Germany), and the University of Iowa, and has taught at Arizona State University and the University of Virginia. Dove has traveled widely and has lived abroad, notably in Berlin and Jerusalem. She was the youngest person ever to become poet laureate of the United States. In addition to poetry, she has written fiction and drama. One of her primary concerns is history: in "Parsley," for instance, she not only documents the slaughter of tens of thousands of Haitians, but also attempts to understand the "arbitrary cruelty" of General Trujillo. In *Thomas and Beulah* (1986), she presents her family history, specifically that of her maternal grandparents, within a larger picture of the millions of African Americans who moved north in the early decades of this century. Dove also makes frequent use of myth: *Mother Love* (1995), for example, is a series of poems that cast in a modern context the story of Demeter and Persephone.

Ernest Dowson (1867–1900)

Ernest Dowson was born in Kent, England. He attended Queen's College, Oxford. Dowson studied Latin poetry, and through extended stays on the Continent became familiar with French literature. With the writers Lionel Johnson, Ernest Rhys, Arthur Symons, William Butler Yeats, and others, Dowson formed the Rhymers' Club, an informal writers' group based in London that published two collections of verse. In 1891 he met "Missie," for whom he harbored a lifelong but unrequited passion and who became a symbol of love and innocence in his poetry. From 1895 onward, Dowson lived an increasingly dissolute life, traveling between England, Ireland, and France, and supporting himself through translation. His last years were marred by poverty and ill health. He was affiliated with the Decadent movement, which flourished in France in the second half of the century and in England in the 1890s. The movement's credo, "art for art's sake," which removed art from the realms of politics and morality and privileged studied artificiality over naturalness, found its culmination in the work of Oscar Wilde, a longtime friend of Dowson. While Dowson shared the Decadents' obsession with aesthetics and fascination with death and decay, his work contained an atypical measure of sincerity and innocence, typically concerning nature, religion, and love.

Michael Drayton (1563–1631)

Michael Drayton was a year older than Shakespeare and born in the same county, Warwickshire (England). Drayton was brought up as a page in the house of Sir Henry Goodyere, whose daughter Anne (later Lady Rainsford) Drayton loved (perforce platonically) for many years. At the age of ten he dedicated himself to a poetic career, and without benefit of a university education he became a learned and accomplished practitioner of most of the Renaissance poetic genres. He settled in London in 1590 and the next year published his first work, *The Harmony of the Church*. This series of verse paraphrases of the Bible was suppressed by public order except for forty copies (of which only one has survived) retained by the bishop of Canterbury. The reason for the suppression is obscure, but perhaps the highly Puritan flavor of the prefatory address to the readers offended Anglican authorities, along with Drayton's reliance on the Geneva Bible (1560), which had never been sanctioned for use in the Church of England. In 1593, he published *Idea: The Shepherd's Garland* (1593), which shows the influence of Spenser's pastoral poetry. A collection of sonnets, *Idea's Mirror*, appeared the next year (it was frequently revised and expanded); in both works Drayton honored Anne Goodyere under the name "Idea." He considered his *Poly-Olbion* his greatest poem, but this thirty-thousand-line celebration of the topography of Britain (1612–22), describing all the counties of England and Wales, proved less popular than most of Drayton's other works, among them *England's Heroical Epistles* (1597), modeled on Ovid's *Heroides*. Although Drayton wrote a poem of fulsome praise when King James took the crown, he never found favor at the court after Elizabeth's death; and his vision of the English nation as well as his most popular poetry suggests that he belonged to the Elizabethan Age even though he long outlived it. In the lyrics of *Nimphidia* (included in the 1627 volume entitled *The Battaile of Againcourt*) he echoes Spenser's *Faerie Queen* and Shakespeare's *A Midsummer Night's Dream* in evoking a folk landscape populated by Puck, Oberon, and Queen Mab; and in his late pastoral drama *The Muses Elizium*, he nostalgically envisions a poet's "Elizabethan" paradise.

John Dryden (1631–1700)

John Dryden, the son of a country gentleman and his wife, was educated at Westminster School and Trinity College, Cambridge. Although he wrote his first poem—the *Heroic Stanzas* of 1659—to commemorate the death of Oliver Cromwell, he celebrated the return of Charles II in *Astraea Redux* (1660). A loyal Royalist for the rest of his life, he was made poet laureate in 1668. He wrote twenty-four plays for the newly reopened London theaters and numerous important songs, poems, and elegies. Many of these were written for specific occasions such as a coronation, a military victory, or a death. These poems, together with his long works of political and literary satire, such as *Absalom and Achitophel* (1681) and the mock-heroic *Mac Flecknoe* (published 1682), affirmed the public role of the poet and established the basic forms of verse, most notably the heroic couplet, that dominated the neoclassical period and persisted into the early nineteenth century. His introductions and essays, at once learned and commonsensical, earned him the title of "the father of English criticism" from his successor Samuel Johnson and helped shape English prose style for centuries. In his later years, after writing a poem defending the Anglican church, Dryden converted to Catholicism. This decision, which led his enemies to charge him with opportunism (James II, a Catholic, had recently succeeded to the throne), eventually resulted in Dryden's losing his public offices and stipends, when the Protestant rulers William and Mary replaced James in 1688. Nearing sixty, Dryden supported himself by writing plays and making translations of classical writers, as well as of Chaucer and Boccaccio. Samuel Johnson praised him for his ability to "think naturally and express forcibly."

Peter Kane Dufault (1923–)

Peter Kane Dufault was born in Newark, New Jersey, and attended Harvard University. During World War II,

he served in the United States Army Air Force. Since then he has worked as a news editor, a house painter, a tree surgeon, a folk singer, a fiddler, a country-dance caller, an actor, and a teacher of writing at Williams College and Berkshire Community College (Massachusetts). He lives in Hillsdale, New York. His work typically observes the natural world closely and carefully, sometimes imbuing its subjects with mystical qualities. Its descriptions of flora and fauna of the American Northeast have elicited comparisons between his work and that of Marianne Moore, Elizabeth Bishop, Richard Wilbur, May Swenson, and Amy Clampitt. By turns celebratory and elegiac, his poems skilfully blend formal and free prosodic techniques.

Carol Ann Duffy (1955–)

Carol Ann Duffy was born in Glasgow, Scotland, brought up in Staffordshire, England, and studied philosophy at the University of Liverpool. She has been poetry editor of *Ambit* magazine since 1983, and has been a visiting professor and a writer-in-residence at a number of institutions. The hallmarks of her poetry—her ability to invent plausible characters, to explore a range of points of view, and to pace her poetry so as to surprise readers—derive in large part from her experience of writing for the stage. Like Robert Browning, she favors the dramatic monologue, and like him she creates personae with complex emotions, questionable ethics, and rich fantasy lives. She also writes in satirical and lyrical modes, and on subjects and themes including history, persecution, death, domesticity, loss, and artistic creation. A sense of menace lurks beneath the surface of many of her poems, and many of her protagonists, often working-class and poorly educated, are both oppressed and dispossessed, but her work is infused with humor and eroticism. She employs poetic devices such as rhyme and pararhyme and combines the diction of everyday speech with arresting and original imagery.

Paul Laurence Dunbar (1872–1906)

Paul Laurence Dunbar was born in Dayton, Ohio, the son of former slaves. His father had escaped to Canada via the Underground Railroad, but returned to the United States to enlist in the second black regiment of the Union Army. Dunbar attended a white high school, where he showed an early talent for writing. He was unable to fund further education, however, and went to work as an elevator operator. When his reputation as a writer grew, the abolitionist Frederick Douglass secured a job for him at the Columbian Exposition in Chicago. From 1897 to 1898 he worked as an assistant in the reading room of the Library of Congress, and he later supported himself by writing and lecturing in the United States and England. In addition to poetry, Dunbar published four novels and four volumes of short stories. Although Booker T. Washington once called him "the poet laureate of the Negro race," Dunbar's reputation declined after his death from tuberculosis, partly because he had adopted forms and conventions associated with the white literary canon. Dunbar often worked like a blues musician, though, conveying sorrow and pain in mellifluous and honest poems, and in his dialect poems he paid tribute to the language and experience of rural blacks, whose voices had rarely been heard.

William Dunbar (ca. 1460–ca. 1525)

William Dunbar was born to a noble Scottish family and apparently took an M.A. from St. Andrews University (near Edinburgh) in 1479. He became a Franciscan friar and traveled in England and France before leaving the order. Employed in various civil and diplomatic capacities abroad by James IV of Scotland, he went to England with the ambassadorial mission to arrange the king's marriage to Margaret Tudor, for which occasion (in 1503) he wrote *The Thrissil and the Rois*, a political allegory in which James is the thistle, Margaret the rose. This was followed by poems allegorical, satirical, visionary, and narrative, on both religious and secular themes. Influenced by Chaucer and the French poet François Villon, Dunbar wrote in a Scottish form of English, describing, in *The Flyting [Quarrel] of Dunbar and Kennedie*, the antipathy between "Inglis"-speaking southern borderlanders and the Scots/Gaelic-speakers of the highlands and west. He received a royal pension in 1500 and some of his poems—"The Queenis Progress at Aberdeen," for instance, and perhaps his "In Prais of Wemen"—suggest that Queen Margaret was his real or desired patron.

Douglas Dunn (1942–)

Douglas Dunn was born in Inchinnan, Renfrewshire, Scotland, and was educated at the Scottish School of Librarianship and the University of Hull. He worked as a librarian in a number of places including Akron, Ohio, but left the United States after fourteen months to avoid the Vietnam War draft. At the University of Hull he worked under Philip Larkin, whose influence can be seen in Dunn's early poems. From 1981 until 1982 he was a creative writing fellow at the University of Dundee. In 1984 he settled in Tayport, Fife. Dunn has published poetry, short stories, and plays for radio and television, and has translated Racine's *Andromache*. He has edited a selection of Delmore Schwartz's poems, a collection of work by Hull poets, and *The Faber Book of Twentieth-Century Scottish Poetry*. His early poems graphically describe the squalid living conditions and impoverished cultural and intellectual life of the underprivileged of Hull. Later work explores class conflict, largely from the point of view of a resentful working class. Perhaps his most memorable poems are the moving *Elegies* for his wife, an artist and curator who died of cancer at the age of thirty-seven.

John Dyer (1700–1758)

John Dyer was born in Llanfynnydd, Carmarthenshire (Wales). He reluctantly prepared for a career in law, but upon the death of his father, a solicitor, abandoned the profession and moved to London to study with Jonathan Richardson, a well-known artist and critic. Unable to establish himself as a painter, Dyer took up farming, for which he was ill-suited. Ordained in 1741, he preached in Leicestershire, Coningsby, and Lincolnshire. He is best known for "Grongar Hill," published as an irregular "Pindaric Ode" in 1726, but rewritten for a 1727 printing as a more regular poem of 150 octosyllabic lines rhymed in couplets. His longest work, a didactic blank-verse epic called *The Fleece*, was published in 1757.

Richard Eberhart (1904–)

Richard Eberhart was born in Austin, Minnesota. He received his undergraduate education at the University of Minnesota and Dartmouth College. As a member of the crew on a tramp steamer he made his way to England, where he undertook studies in English at St. John's College, Cambridge. Upon his return to the United States, Eberhart did graduate study at Harvard University, then taught at St. Mark's School (near Boston), where the poet Robert Lowell was one of his pupils. During World War II Eberhart served as an aerial gunnery instructor. In the mid-1940s he joined his father-in-law's floor-wax company, but in the 1950s he began an academic career and taught at, among other schools, the University of Washington, Princeton University, and Dartmouth College. In addition, he helped to found the Poets' Theatre in Cambridge, Massachusetts. Simple

and direct, his poetry frequently takes up concrete images to find moral truths, exploring the tension between spirit and matter, order and chaos.

T. S. Eliot (1888–1965)

T(homas) S(tearns) Eliot was born to a distinguished New England family, raised in St. Louis, Missouri, and educated at Harvard University, the Sorbonne, and Oxford University, where he wrote his Ph.D. dissertation on the English logician and metaphysician F. H. Bradley. The critic Arthur Symons' work on the French symbolists was a seminal influence on Eliot, as was the poet Ezra Pound, who encouraged him to stay in Europe. From 1917 until 1925 he worked in the International Department at Lloyd's Bank, after which he joined the publishing house of Faber and Faber, where he published the work of W. H. Auden, Stephen Spender, Louis MacNeice, and other young poets. He also edited the *Egoist* magazine and founded the influential *Criterion*. In 1927 Eliot took British citizenship and joined the Church of England. In his later years, he wrote compelling critical studies on literature, culture, society, and religion, and he generally is considered the most influential critic of the century. In addition, he wrote several successful verse dramas. Eliot was awarded the Nobel Prize for Literature in 1948. Although he dismissed *The Waste Land*, which he wrote largely while hospitalized for a breakdown in 1921, as "the relief of a personal and wholly insignificant grouse against life," his generation considered it a definitive explication of its distress. Eliot intended to amalgamate the disparate "fragments" in the poem—taken from classical, English, and European literatures, Hindu texts, and popular culture, and spoken by multiple voices and characters—into a new whole offering a form of spiritual renewal. *The Waste Land* (which Pound helped edit), like "The Love Song of J. Alfred Prufrock" (which Pound helped publish) and other early poems of Eliot's, comments on the barrenness of modern civilization and displays a rich complexity of tone, which ranges from satiric to lyrical and elegiac. Eliot's later work documents his conversion to Christianity and culminates in *Four Quartets*, which he considered his masterpiece.

Queen Elizabeth I (1533–1603)

The daughter of Henry VIII and his second wife, Anne Boleyn, Elizabeth was declared a bastard by her father, who executed her mother on probably spurious grounds of adultery in 1534. Questions about the legitimacy of Elizabeth's birth (at a time when Henry's first wife, Katharine of Aragon, was still living) fueled many later attacks on her, especially those by Catholics who supported the claims to the throne of Mary Tudor, Elizabeth's elder half-sister, or later, those of Mary Queen of Scots, Elizabeth's cousin. Elizabeth replaced Mary Tudor on the throne of England in 1558, supported by many of the Protestants who had welcomed her half-brother Edward VI's brief reign (1547–53). Elizabeth was, however, more adroit at religious compromise than Edward or Mary had been; the years of Elizabeth's long reign were relatively peaceful, despite the plots on her life and the criticisms made by many of her male subjects—most notoriously, the Scottish preacher John Knox—of a woman's right to rule England.

Elizabeth maintained and augmented her power through various strategies, including her refusal to marry; her shaping of various positive images of the female ruler, including the image of the "virgin" queen, married her to her kingdom; and her manipulation of her courtiers and advisors through Petrarchan love conventions that prescribed adoration of a woman whose purity rendered her unattainable. Well-educated in languages and rhetoric, the youthful Elizabeth translated works by Boethius, Petrarch, and Marguerite of Navarre, among others; as a queen, Elizabeth wrote eloquent speeches and letters as well as a few (extant) lyric poems. In one lyric ("Ah silly pugg"), she responds playfully to a poem by her courtier Walter Ralegh; in another ("The doubt of future foes"), she replies with grim wit to a petitionary sonnet from Mary Queen of Scots. In her writings Elizabeth often sought to control, and sometimes to counter, the many images of her produced by her subjects. If some of the most famous Elizabethans portrayed her as a "fairy queen" (Spenser did so in his epic of that name, as did Shakespeare in his play A *Midsummer Night's Dream*), she preferred to portray herself as a woman who had the "heart and stomach of a king."

Jean Elliot (1727–1805)

Jean (or Jane) Elliot was born in Teviotdale, Scotland. Her father, Sir Gilbert Elliot, was a judge who supported the royal family of England against the claims of the "Jacobites," those who adhered to the Stuart cause after the last Stuart king, James II, had been exiled in 1688. When a party of Jacobites came for Jean Elliot's father in 1545, she distracted them while he successfully made his escape. On her father's death, she, her mother, and her sister moved to Edinburgh, where Elliot remained until returning to Teviotdale shortly before her death. She was the author of probably the most popular version of the old ballad "The Flowers of the Forest," a haunting lament for the dead of the Battle of Flodden (Field), fought in September 1513 and a crushing defeat for Scotland. Published anonymously in 1756, Elliot's poem was greatly admired by the poets Robert Burns and Walter Scott, among others. "The manner of the ancient minstrels is so happily imitated," wrote Scott, "that it required the most positive evidence to convince me that the song was of modern date." Indeed, many readers assumed the poem was a genuine relic of the sixteenth century.

Ralph Waldo Emerson (1803–1882)

Ralph Waldo Emerson was born and raised in Boston, the son of a Unitarian minister and his wife. He was educated at Harvard University and Harvard Divinity School. Ordained as junior pastor of Boston's Second Church, he left the church in 1832 because of deep doubts concerning organized religion. That same year he traveled to Europe, where he met the poets William Wordsworth and Samuel Taylor Coleridge and the essayist and historian Thomas Carlyle, who became a close friend and great influence. He also was introduced to German idealism, and this philosophy, along with the writings of Plato and Swedenborg and the sacred texts of Hinduism, largely determined Emerson's interpretation of Transcendentalism. Although he never developed his beliefs into a full-fledged system, Emerson preached self-reliance and optimism and promoted instinct over reason. The Transcendental circle that formed around him included the writers Henry David Thoreau, Jones Very, Margaret Fuller, and Nathaniel Hawthorne. Although he used conventional meters and forms for his early poems, Emerson came to believe that "a thought so passionate and alive . . . has an architecture of its own," and this "organic" theory of composition informed his later works.

William Empson (1906–1984)

William Empson was born at Yokefleet Hall, near Howden, Yorkshire, and educated at Magdalene College, Cambridge. He took degrees in mathematics and, under the tutelage of critic I. A. Richards, English. After spending the 1930s abroad, teaching at the Tokyo University of Literature and Science and for the Southwest Associated Universities in China, Empson returned to England when World War II broke out and worked for the BBC, where he edited scripts for foreign broadcast. In 1947 he returned to China to teach at the University of Peking, and there he witnessed the Chinese civil war and the subsequent rise of communism. Empson returned to England in 1952 and was appointed professor of literature at Sheffield University, a position he held until his retirement in 1971. In addition to poetry, he published several scholarly studies. Like John Donne and the Metaphysical poets, Empson constructed his poems around witty intellectual arguments and drew his imagery from the realms of science, mathematics, and commerce. Philip Larkin was among the poets who took Empson's work as a model, confronting the despair inherent in the modern condition with grace and stoicism.

Louise Erdrich (1954–)

Louise Erdrich was born in Little Falls, Minnesota, and raised in Wahpeton, North Dakota, a small town near the Turtle Mountain Reservation and the Minnesota border. She was educated at Dartmouth College—where she studied with Michael Dorris, now her husband and collaborator—and at Johns Hopkins University. She has worked at a variety of jobs, including teaching poetry in prisons and editing a newspaper dedicated to Native American affairs (her mother was of French-Chippewa descent). Known primarily as a novelist and short-story writer, Erdrich is a consummate storyteller in both prose and poetry. Many of her poems are dramatic monologues spoken by the inhabitants of a mythical small town in the early twentieth century. Her penchant for storytelling, her tendency to work in loose pentameters that approximate the rhythms of spoken language, and her skill in creating music through repetition place her work alongside the Native American tradition.

U. A. Fanthorpe (1929–)

U(rsula) A(skham) Fanthorpe was born at Lee Green, London, and educated at St. Anne's College, Oxford, the University of London Institute for Education, and University College at Swansea. She was an assistant English teacher and later head of English at Cheltenham Ladies' College, Gloucestershire, but abandoned teaching to work as a hospital clerk in Bristol. She subsequently served as a writing fellow at St. Martin's College, Launceton, and at the Universities of Newcastle-upon-Tyne and Durham. Fanthorpe published her first collection of poetry when she was nearly fifty years old. Many of her poems express "anger, at the hierarchical system" and give visibility and voice to those who are typically overlooked and silenced, such as psychiatric patients, day laborers, and women; in addition, her work takes up questions of masculinity and feminity.

James Fenton (1949–)

James Fenton was born in Lincoln, England, and educated at Magdalen College, Oxford, where he studied politics, philosophy, and psychology. He worked as a literary and political journalist, and as a foreign correspondent in Germany, Cambodia, and Vietnam. He has published collections of poetry, theater reviews, and accounts of his travels and his experiences as a war reporter. He has translated Verdi's *Rigoletto* for the English National Opera and collaborated on the musical version of Hugo's *Les Miserables*, which has been running in New York and London for over a decade. He is currently professor of poetry at Oxford University. Fenton's poems are politically astute but avoid partisanship. His style might be described as reporterly in that it is laconic, objective, factual, declamatory, and unflinching. His poems contain much sardonic wit, which he uses not to mitigate the brutal impact of his often gory materials but to heighten their poignancy. Comfortable in both highly formal and free verse, he has also written light verse, much of which modulates into the surreal, and his newer work is extremely musical and suited to stage performance.

Lawrence Ferlinghetti (1919–   )

Lawrence Ferlinghetti was born in Yonkers, New York. Upon graduation from the University of North Carolina at Chapel Hill, he joined the navy and served during World War II. He worked for *Time* magazine and later resumed his education at Columbia University and the Sorbonne. After moving to San Francisco, he started the City Lights Bookstore and the City Lights Press, which launched the careers of a generation of American poets. He was associated with the San Francisco Group, started by the poet Kenneth Rexroth, and with the Beats, whose prominent members included Allen Ginsberg, Jack Kerouac, William Burroughs, and Gregory Corso. Ferlinghetti's poems display Beat and abstract expressionist aesthetics; they take up topical subjects, use "hip" diction, and imitate the rhythms of jazz and the blues. His satires against "Terrible People" who "perpetuate the system," his praise for the human spirit and the natural world, and his punning and verbal play are also reminiscent of E. E. Cummings.

Anne Finch, Countess of Winchilsea (1661–1720)

Anne Finch was born in Sydmonton, Berkshire, England, the daughter of Sir William Kingsmill and his wife, Anne Haslewood. After her parents died, she was raised and educated by an uncle. In 1683, with the poet Anne Killigrew, Finch became a maid of honor to Mary Modena, the duchess of York and future wife of James II, and at court met Colonel Heneage Finch, future earl of Winchilsea, who became her husband. Colonel Finch was arrested while attempting to follow King James to France after the king was deposed in 1688; following his release, he and his wife retired to their estate in Eastwell, Kent. Encouraged by her husband, Anne Finch began to write in the 1680s, and her long poem "The Spleen" was published in an anthology in 1701. In 1709 Jonathan Swift addressed a poem called "Apollo Outwitted" to her, and she engaged in an exchange of poems with Alexander Pope about the representation of "female wits" in his *Rape of the Lock* (1714). In 1713 she published her *Miscellany Poems on Several Occasions*, which included a tragedy, *Aristomenes*, but many of her poems remained in manuscript at her death. William Wordsworth praised her nature poems, especially "A Nocturnal Reverie," and included seventeen of her poems in an anthology he compiled for Lady Mary Lowther in 1819. Only recently, however, have Finch's satiric poems and meditations on the problems of women writers achieved their due recognition.

Edward FitzGerald (1809–1883)

Edward FitzGerald was born in Bredfield, Suffolk, England, and educated at Trinity College, Cambridge, where he met the writers William Thackeray and Alfred, Lord Tennyson. He never adopted a trade, but lived a retired and abstemious life occupied with study and translation. In the 1850s he took up oriental studies, a prevalent interest of mid-nineteenth-century intellectuals, and in 1856 produced his first translation. The work for which he is best known is his free translation of *The Rubáiyát of Omar Khayyám of Naishápúr*, which he

published anonymously in 1859, expanded in 1868, and revised further in 1872 and 1879. FitzGerald maintained the structure of Omar Khayyám's epigrammatic *ruba'i*, or quatrains, including their *aaba* rhyme scheme and mounting tension, but deviated significantly from the twelfth-century Persian manuscript. Imposing unity on the work by introducing a time frame and dramatic situation, he stripped it down to its essential themes, including the evanescence of life, the consequent necessity to "seize the day" *(carpe diem)*, the vanity of human pride, and the paradoxical nature of the Deity, who created evil but punished humanity for acting in evil ways. Initially ignored, the work rapidly gained in popularity when it was discovered by the painter and poet Dante Gabriel Rossetti and his Victorian coterie, the Pre-Raphaelites, who found its themes and tone strikingly contemporary.

Robert Fitzgerald (1910–1985)

Robert Fitzgerald was born in Geneva, New York, and grew up in Springfield, Illinois. He was educated at Harvard University and also did informal studies at Trinity College, Cambridge. After working as a reporter for the *New York Herald Tribune* and later for *Time* magazine, he served in the navy during World War II. Beginning in 1949, Fitzgerald divided his time between the United States and Italy. He was poetry editor of *The New Republic* and taught at, among other schools, Sarah Lawrence College and Princeton, Harvard, and Yale Universities. Known primarily for his translations of Homer and Virgil, he (with Dudley Fitts) also translated Euripides and Sophocles. His own poetry—lyrical, often humorous, always carefully crafted—is informed by a strong sense of history, and his frequent juxtapositions of classical allusions with images from modern life have been compared to T. S. Eliot's and Ezra Pound's.

John Fletcher (1579–1625)

John Fletcher was born in Rye, Sussex, England, and was educated at Benet College, Cambridge. After the death of his father, bishop of London, Fletcher was left to make his own way. In London he befriended Francis Beaumont, with whom he cowrote a number of plays for the fashionable boys' companies. Along with Shakespeare, Fletcher and Beaumont became leading playwrights of the King's Men, the most prominent theatrical company of the day. Their joint works include *Philaster* (ca. 1609), *The Maid's Tragedy* (ca. 1610), and *A King and No King* (1611). Following Beaumont's early retirement and death, Fletcher collaborated with other playwrights, most notably Philip Massinger, with whom he wrote *Sir John van Olden Barnavelt* (ca. 1619) and *The Beggar's Bush* (ca. 1622), among other plays, and Shakespeare, with whom he probably wrote *Henry VIII* (1613) and *The Two Noble Kinsmen* (1613). Fletcher is credited with sole authorship of a number of plays, including *The Faithful Shepherdess* (ca. 1609), *The Chances* (ca. 1617), *The Wild-Goose Chase* (ca. 1621), and *Rule a Wife and Have a Wife* (1624). His success reflected his alertness to changing tastes as well as his deft handling of tragicomedy and the comedy of manners. Like many dramatists of his day, he included lyrics and songs in his plays. "Hence all you vain delights," from *The Nice Valour* (1647), influenced Milton's "Il Penseroso." The first stanza of "Take, Oh, Take Those Lips Away" appears in Shakespeare's *Measure for Measure* and may have originated in that play.

Philip Freneau (1752–1832)

Philip Freneau was born and raised in New York City. He was educated at the College of New Jersey (now Princeton University), where he was a classmate of

James Madison, future president of the United States. From 1776 until nearly 1779 he worked as a secretary to a plantation owner in the West Indies. Upon a second trip to the West Indies in 1780, he was captured by the British and held as a prisoner of war. Freneau later worked in a Philadelphia post office for three years and gained a reputation as a satirist, journalist, and poet before returning to the high seas. In 1790 he became a clerk of foreign languages for the State Department, and he later worked for a number of journals. He spent his last years on his family's plantation in New Jersey, fell into poverty and obscurity, and died of exposure when he lost his way home during a snowstorm. Best known for his satires (many of which were anti-British), his polemics, and his lyrics, Freneau was called "the poet of the American Revolution," and many consider him the first major American poet. Determined to establish an indigenous literature, he drew heavily in his work on local flora and fauna. His temperament anticipated that of the Romantics, as evidenced by his treatment of transience and death.

Robert Frost (1874–1963)

Robert Frost was born and raised (until the age of eleven) in San Francisco. He attended Dartmouth and Harvard Colleges. For a decade, around the turn of the century, he worked as a farmer in New Hampshire. From 1912 until 1915 he, his wife, and their four children lived in England, where he met the poets Ezra Pound and Edward Thomas, both of whose shrewd reviews helped establish his reputation. Upon his return to America, Frost held a number of teaching appointments, his most enduring association being with Amherst College. In the years following the publication of his second book, *North of Boston* (1914), Frost became one of the best-known and most celebrated of American poets, and in 1961 he read his poem "The Gift Outright" at President John F. Kennedy's inauguration. Rooted in the rugged New England landscape, his poems were phrased in plain speech, set to traditional meters made to sound more like sentences than song, and housed in modified classical forms. Some intellectuals dismissed him as provincial, and modernists who preferred conspicuous difficulty and radical innovation thought him conventional. Even Frost's adoring public was often hoodwinked by his pithiness into missing the menacing forces at work beneath the surface. Astute readers saw an altogether different sensibility, however, one possessed of a propensity toward darkness and terror, in which a poem is "a momentary stay against confusion."

George Gascoigne (ca. 1535–1577)

George Gascoigne was probably educated at Trinity College, Cambridge, and entered Gray's Inn in 1555. Seeking a career as a courtier, he sold his patrimony to cover his debts. In 1561, he wed the already married Elizabeth Boyes and was imprisoned for debt in 1570. Having served twice in Parliament in the late 1550s, he was refused his seat in 1572 on the grounds of his bad reputation. From 1572 until 1573, he served as a soldier in the Netherlands, during which time an unauthorized edition of his play and poems, *A Hundredth Sundrie Flowres bound up in one small Posie*, appeared, which he corrected and extended as *The Posies of George Gascoigne*. Acknowledging Chaucer as his poetic master, Gascoigne translated from the Italian Ariosto's *The Supposes* and wrote the first original poem in English, *The Steele Glass*, a satire. His *The Adventures of Master F. J.* is a pioneering work of novelistic prose. He divided his poems into three categories, "Floures, Hearbes, and Weedes," the flowers representing "pleasant" poems written on "light occasions," the herbs representing "profitable" poems on moral subjects, and the weeds

representing poems "neither delightful nor yet profitable" on his own follies. His *Certayne notes of Instruction concerning the making of verse or ryme in English*, the first important work on English prosody, is a pithy and practical handbook showing a wide knowledge of poetic forms.

David Gascoyne (1916–)

David Gascoyne was born in Harrow, Middlesex, England, and educated at Regent Street Polytechnic, London. He published his first collection of poems at the age of sixteen. In 1933 he traveled to Paris to investigate the surrealist movement (and wrote the first English study of it when he was nineteen) and lived in France from 1937 to 1939 and 1954 to 1965. He joined the Communist Party in 1936 and made a brief sojourn in Spain, but his support for the party proved ephemeral, though his interest in social and political issues endured. In the late years of World War II, he became an actor. Psychological problems following his war experiences culminated in several nervous breakdowns, and as a result he has written little poetry in the last forty years. In addition to poetry, he has published a semiautobiographical novel and has translated the work of several European poets, including Jean Jouve. His poems convey his sense that life is "a long and painful operation performed without an anaesthetic." Not content simply to document the "spiritual crisis" and "universal anguish" that surround him, he sees the artist as a prophet or visionary who must be prepared to risk madness, despair, and death for the sake of the world and the Word, and often expresses his vision in admonitory Christian imagery. Gascoyne characteristically works in an Eliotesque free verse of strongly cadenced lines and recurring but not regular metrical patterns.

John Gay (1685–1732)

John Gay was born in Barnstaple, Devon, England. Educated at a Devon school, he was apprenticed to a London silk mercer, but was released from service due to poor health and began to haunt London literary society. He soon gained the attention of Alexander Pope, Jonathan Swift, and John Arbuthnot, with whom he founded the "Scriblerus Club." With their help he obtained posts with influential figures, including the duchess of Monmouth, widow of the duke figured in Dryden's *Absalom and Achitophel*; Lord Clarendon, whom he followed to the court of Hanover; the earl of Bath; and the duke and duchess of Queensberry, who housed him at their estate and managed his financial affairs. He was eventually awarded a modest sinecure as lottery commissioner. Gay achieved fame with *The Beggar's Opera* (1728), a satire on Italian opera and English politics. This work's evocative lyrics and pleasing tunes established Gay's reputation as the premiere lyricist of his day.

W. S. Gilbert (1836–1911)

W(illiam) S(chwenck) Gilbert was born in London. Educated at King's College, University of London, he studied law at the Inner Temple, though his career as a barrister was unsatisfying and, therefore, brief. In 1857 he joined the militia, in which he served for twenty years. He began writing comic verse and operatic burlesques during the 1860s, and in 1869 met the eminent composer Arthur Sullivan, with whom he wrote a series of exceptionally popular operettas, including *Trial by Jury*, which satirizes the English legal system; *H.M.S. Pinafore*, which parodies the Royal Navy; *Patience*, a wry satire on aesthetes such as Oscar Wilde, Dante Gabriel Rossetti, and James McNeill Whistler; *The Pirates of Penzance*; and *The Mikado*. Gilbert and

Sullivan's collaboration ended in 1896 due to differences in temperament. The public adored Gilbert's poems and libretti, but he referred to himself disparagingly as "a doggerel bard." Satiric verse was his forte. His wit was so biting and incisive that some thought he exhibited bad taste and others that he bordered on the seditious. Queen Victoria, for instance, snubbed Gilbert at a public performance of his work by leaving his name off the program and knighting him in 1907, twenty-five years after Sullivan was knighted.

Allen Ginsberg (1926–   )
Allen Ginsberg was born in Newark, New Jersey. He was educated at Columbia University. After spending much time in Greenwich Village with William Burroughs, Jack Kerouac, and other Beat writers, he moved to San Francisco, where Lawrence Ferlinghetti's City Lights Press published *Howl and Other Poems* (1956)—its title poem functioning as a condemnation of bourgeois culture, an introduction to the emergent counterculture, a celebration of sexuality, and a manifesto for the Beat movement. Before dropping out of the workaday world, Ginsberg held a variety of jobs, and has since traveled across England, the Far East, and the United States; been active in radical politics; and taught at a variety of schools. He has closely studied Zen Buddhism and such Western mystics as William Blake. His work frequently has an elegiac quality, mourning not a world that has disappeared, but one that has failed to reach its inherent potential. Ginsberg's prosody derives from the extended *vers-libre* lines of Walt Whitman and Christopher Smart and the organic forms of William Carlos Williams (his most important mentor).

Dana Gioia (1950–   )
(Michael) Dana Gioia was born in Los Angeles, California, and raised in a nearby working-class suburb. He was educated at Stanford University, Harvard University (where he studied with the poets Robert Fitzgerald and Elizabeth Bishop), and the Stanford University Business School. From 1977 until 1992, he worked as an executive at General Foods in New York City and simultaneously published poems, reviews, and essays. He subsequently left the business world to devote himself to writing, and he now lives in Santa Rosa, California. Gioia has edited the stories of Weldon Kees, coedited two anthologies of Italian poetry, and translated poets Eugenio Montale and Nina Cassian. Author of such controversial essays as "Notes on the New Formalism" and "Can Poetry Matter?", he works in regular meters and frequently employs rhyme, striving to achieve "tension" in his poems "either by experimenting with new forms or by playing with the rules of traditional patterns to achieve something slightly unexpected."

Louise Glück (1943–   )
Louise Glück was born in New York City and raised on Long Island. She was educated at Sarah Lawrence College and Columbia University, where she studied with the poet Stanley Kunitz. Glück has taught at, among other schools, Columbia, the University of Iowa, and Williams College. She lives in Plainfield, Vermont. In addition to poetry, she has written one volume of criticism. The subjects of her work include childhood, family, life, love, and motherhood. Recently she has turned to metaphysical questions and to explorations of the modern connotations of classical myth.

Oliver Goldsmith (1730–1774)
Oliver Goldsmith was born at Pallas, County Longford, Ireland, the son of an Anglo-Irish clergyman and his wife. He was brought up in rural parishes including Lis-

soy, which may be one source for his poem "The Deserted Village" (1770). After graduation from Trinity College, Dublin, his worldly career began with a series of misstarts: rejected for the ministry, he considered reading law, decided on medicine and enrolled at the University of Edinburgh, withdrew to study in Leyden, wandered the continent, and on his return failed the surgeon's exam. He settled on hack writing—which, through a favorable review of Edmund Burke's *Philosophical Enquiry*, brought him the author's friendship. Through a series of essays, poems, plays, histories, and biographies, he also attracted the attention of Samuel Johnson and Sir Joshua Reynolds. The former saved him from prosecution for debt by arranging the sale (for £60) of *The Vicar of Wakefield* (1766), the novel for which Goldsmith is chiefly remembered. His great comedy, *She Stoops to Conquer* (1773), was an immediate success.

Jorie Graham (1951–   )
Jorie Graham was born in Italy to religious historian Curtis Graham and sculptor Beverly Pepper. She was raised in Italy and France and educated at the Sorbonne, Columbia University, and the University of Iowa. Graham has served on the faculties of Murray State, Humboldt State, Columbia, and, since 1983, Iowa. Her poems make sophisticated philosophical and metaphysical inquiries: they are concerned with moral questions, but are not dogmatic. Linked to the Romantics, as well as to Emily Dickinson and Wallace Stevens, Graham works in regular stanza forms as well as long, loose lines and irregular verse paragraphs.

Robert Graves (1895–1985)
Robert Graves was born in Wimbledon, England. In the early days of World War I he left school and took a commission with the Royal Welsh Fusiliers. Sent to the front in France, where he met the poet Siegfried Sassoon, he was gravely injured in 1916 at the battle of the Somme and sent home. Upon his return, Graves attended St. John's College, Oxford, and in 1926 he taught English at the University of Cairo, Egypt. That same year he began a relationship with the American poet Laura Riding, with whom he founded the Seizin Press (London) and wrote several books. He wrote prolifically in a number of genres, including poetry, fiction, biography, autobiography, criticism, and translation, and his career can be divided into several distinct phases. When a young man, he was published in Edward Marsh's anthologies of Georgian poetry. As a result of the pressures of war, however, which shattered his faith in the values with which he had been raised, he began writing bald transcriptions of life on the battlefield, though he later suppressed this work, believing it inferior to the war poetry of Sassoon and Wilfred Owen. Under Riding's influence he experimented with modernism. While doing research for a novel, Graves constructed the mythological system that lay behind his late work, centering around a figure he called the White Goddess, a proud, narcissistic muse. In this phase, poetry attained an especially high status for Graves, and he believed, like William Blake and W. B. Yeats, that it gave him access to worlds beyond those acknowledged by the rational mind and conventional society.

Thomas Gray (1716–1771)
Thomas Gray was born in Cornhill, London, the son of a scrivener and his wife, and the only child of twelve to survive infancy. Educated at Eton and Peterhouse College, Cambridge, he divided his time between London and Stoke Poges before settling into a fellowship at Cambridge, where he pursued his studies in Classics, early English poetry, and ancient Welsh and Norse lit-

eratures. Other than brief stays in London and tours of the Lake District and Scotland in search of the picturesque, Gray rarely left the university. He embarked on a tour of France and Italy with the writer Horace Walpole in 1739, but after a quarrel returned alone. He began to write English poetry in about 1741. Little of his work was published in his lifetime, but his poems circulated in manuscript among friends. In Gray's "Elegy Written in a Country Churchyard" Samuel Johnson found "sentiments to which every bosom returns an echo" and "images which find a mirror in every mind."

Matthew Green (1696–1737)

Little is known about Matthew Green's life, except that he was born into a Quaker family and employed at the London Customs House. He published nothing during his lifetime, but left his manuscripts to his friend Richard Glover, who brought some of the poems to press after Green's death. Green's reputation rests solely on "The Spleen"; indeed, its author came to be known as "Spleen-Green."

Debora Greger (1949–)

Debora Greger was born in Walsenburg, Colorado, and raised in Richland, Washington. Educated at Whitman College, the University of Washington, and the University of Iowa, she has served on the faculties of George Mason University, California State University at Chico, and, since 1985, the University of Florida at Gainesville. She is also a gifted artist. Greger has traveled extensively and, besides her home in Florida, has another home in England. Her poems typically play several interrelated narrative lines off each other as they interweave myth, literary and cultural sources, memory, and the present. Her work relies greatly on allusion, irony, and wit.

Fulke Greville, Lord Brooke (1554–1628)

Fulke Greville was born into a family of Warwickshire (England) landowners and was sent to Shrewsbury School in the same year as Sir Philip Sidney, who became his close friend. After attending Jesus College, Cambridge, Greville went to court, where he was introduced to the "Areopagus" club, an association of courtiers and poets named after the meeting place of the Athenian aristocratic council. Knighted in 1597, he served as treasurer to the navy from 1589 to 1604. Although he fell from favor in the early years of James I's reign, he served as chancellor of the exchequer from 1614 to 1622 and was made first baron Brooke in 1621. Warwick Castle, granted to him on his elevation to the peerage, was the scene of his murder by a servant, who stabbed first Greville and then himself. Greville is perhaps best known for *The Life of the Renowned Sir Philip Sidney* (1652), which expresses Greville's political disillusionment after Queen Elizabeth's death and which helped to establish Sidney's reputation as the greatest of the Renaissance chivalric courtier-poets. Greville was also the author of *Caelica*, a sequence of songs and sonnets; the neo-Stoic *Letter to an Honourable Lady*; a verse *Treatise of Monarchy*; and two Senecan tragedies, *Alaham* and *Mustapha*, which deal with political and religious themes.

Nicholas Grimald (1519?–1562?)

Nicholas Grimald was educated at Christ's College, Cambridge, and became a chaplain to the Protestant Bishop Nicholas Ridley. After Wyatt and Surrey, Grimald was the best-represented poet in the first edition of the important collection of English poems by Richard Tottel, *Songs and Sonnets* (1557), but was drastically cut in the next edition, possibly because his name

had been besmirched by political and religious controversy. Because of his association with Ridley, he had been arrested during the reign of the Catholic Queen Mary and apparently recanted his Protestant beliefs and betrayed his friends. He was an influential translator of Cicero and Virgil and the author of two original Latin dramas. In his lament on the death of his mother, and in other poems, Grimald, with Henry Howard, Earl of Surrey and George Gascoigne and later Christopher Marlowe, helped confirm the pentameter line's importance to the theory and practice of English verse.

Barbara Guest (1920–)

Barbara Guest was born in Wilmington, North Carolina, and raised in California and Florida. She was educated at the University of North Carolina, the University of California at Los Angeles, and the University of California at Berkeley. From 1951 to 1954 Guest served as an associate editor at *ARTnews*. In addition to poetry, she has written plays, fiction, and a biography of H. D. Often associated with the New York school poets and the Language poets who descended from them, Guest has identified her concerns as "what happens every day, . . . memory, . . . conscience, . . . the brevity of ideas, . . . time, disorder, flux, etc." Influenced by surrealism and abstract expressionism, Guest employs radical disjunctions that mirror the incongruities of daily life and, in some cases, the process of composition itself. She generally works in free verse, striving to create melodic effects.

Thom Gunn (1929–)

Thom Gunn was born in Gravesend, Kent, England, but moved frequently as a child in the wake of his father, a journalist. After school, Gunn served in the army for two years, then went to Paris, where he worked on the Métro by day and attempted to write a novel by night, and to Rome. He then went up to Trinity College, Cambridge, where he attended lectures by the critic F. R. Leavis. He did graduate work at Stanford University under the formalist poet Yvor Winters. Except for a year in San Antonio, Texas, Gunn has lived in San Francisco since 1958. He taught at Berkeley from 1958 until 1966, but gave up full-time teaching to devote himself to writing. In addition to his own poetry and essays, he has edited collections of verse by Ben Jonson and Fulke Greville. His early work was influenced by Shakespeare, Donne, and the existentialist philosopher Jean-Paul Sartre. It typically married abstract ideas with concrete images, seeking to make the metaphysical or inchoate vivid and comprehensible, and fused traditional meter, contemporary subject matter, and colloquial idiom. In the 1950s, Gunn moved from statement to exploration, often of personal themes, such as his emergent homosexuality and, more recently, the toll exacted by the HIV virus from him and from the gay community. His later poetry is freer and more accessible than his earlier work.

Ivor Gurney (1890–1937)

Ivor Gurney was born in Gloucester, England. He attended the Royal College of Music, London, until 1914, when he enlisted in the army. Sent to the front in France, he was gassed at Ypres in 1917 and sent home; he suffered a breakdown the following year. Gurney returned briefly to his studies at the Royal College, where the composer Ralph Vaughan Williams became his tutor. From 1919 to 1922 he lived restlessly, continuing to compose music and to write but also working at a number of odd jobs, ranging from organist to cinema pianist to tax clerk. In 1922, suffering from schizophrenia, he was committed to the City of London Mental Hospital, where he eventually died. Gurney shared many of the Georgian poets' preoccupations—a reverence for place, an aversion to change, and a celebration of seclusion—but also displayed a modern sensibility; a sense of regret runs through his work, and his tone has been described as "teasing" and even "mildly malicious." His war poems differ from his contemporaries' in that they do not take an overt stance against the war or describe its most gruesome horrors, but instead remark on gentler, yet strikingly evocative, particulars of the scene.

Ralph Gustafson (1909–)

Ralph Gustafson was born in Lime Ridge, Quebec, and was educated at Bishop's University and at Oxford University. After briefly teaching in Canada, he returned to England and worked as a tutor and freelance writer. In 1939 he moved to New York City, and during World War II he worked with the British Information Services, assessing and reporting on American attitudes toward the British. Gustafson returned to Canada in 1963. He has subsequently been writer-in-residence at Bishop's, music critic for the Canadian Broadcasting Corporation, and a freelance writer. In addition to poetry, Gustafson has published short stories and a verse play and has edited several anthologies of Canadian poetry. Unlike his dense early poems, Gustafson's late poems are direct, elemental, and meditative. Rendered in spare, chiseled lines, they pay homage to beauty and to the concrete particulars of daily life in the eastern townships of Quebec, where Gustafson currently lives.

Daniel Hall (1952–)

Daniel Hall was born in Pittsfield, Massachusetts. He has traveled extensively throughout the British Isles and Asia, particularly China. He currently lives in western Massachusetts and works as a freelance indexer. His poetry is concise and precise—each gesture conveying multiple meanings—and it displays a deep regard for both the ancient and the immediate. Hall writes in a number of modes, ranging from the meditative to the narrative, from the formal to the free.

Donald Hall (1928–)

Donald Hall was born in New Haven, Connecticut. Educated at Harvard and Oxford universities, he has served as poetry editor at the Paris Review, as a member of the editorial board for poetry at Wesleyan University Press, and as a poetry consultant for Harper & Row. After teaching at Stanford University, Harvard University, and the University of Michigan, he retired in 1975 and moved back to his family home in Danbury, New Hampshire, to work full-time as a writer. In addition to poetry, Hall has published literary criticism, personal reminiscences, textbooks, and children's books, and has edited a number of anthologies. Long concerned with morality and ethics, particularly in the realm of politics, he has sometimes adopted a vatic, or prophetic, voice. Although he began writing in traditional meters and forms, his recent "anecdotal" poems, as he calls them, display a looser style.

Thomas Hardy (1840–1928)

Thomas Hardy was born in Dorset, England. He left school at sixteen to work as an apprentice for an architect who specialized in church restoration. Though he seriously considered taking holy orders, he lost his faith, in part because of the writings of prominent agnostics of his day, such as Charles Darwin. In 1867, after spending several years in London, he returned to Dorset, where he lived for the rest of his life. Known primarily as a novelist, he published no poetry until 1897, after the publication of his last novel, The Well-Beloved.

Claiming to love poetry more than prose, he dedicated the last thirty years of his life to it. Like Geoffrey Chaucer, William Wordsworth, and Hardy's contemporary Robert Browning, he wrote in a colloquial diction, in rhythms that, while regular, mimic the sounds of speech. A versatile poet, he wrote lyrics, ballads, sonnets, dramatic monologues, and a series of exceptional love songs composed upon the death of his first wife, Emma. He took "the intense interests, passions, and strategy that throb through the commonest [sic] lives" as his primary subject and often depicted humankind as locked in a struggle against overwhelming impersonal forces

Tony Harrison (1937–)

Tony Harrison was born in Leeds, England, and was educated at Leeds University, where he read Classics and linguistics and published his first poems. He lectured in Nigeria from 1962 until 1966, and in Prague from 1966 until 1967. Upon his return to England he became the first Northern Arts Fellow at the Universities of Newcastle-upon-Tyne and Durham. In addition to a number of original verse plays, many of which he also directed, he has written films and adaptations of works by Molière, Racine, and others, including acclaimed versions of the Oresteia and the medieval Mystery plays. His poetry explores the relationship between so-called "correct" English and political power, giving voice to those excluded and silenced by the ruling classes, and is characterized by strict forms (such as the sonnet, rhyming couplets, and iambic tetrameter), its treatment of popular culture and aggressively oppositional politics, and its use of dialect, slang, and profanity.

Robert Hass (1941–)

Robert Hass was born in San Francisco, California. He was educated at St. Mary's College and at Stanford University, from which he received a Ph.D. (and where he studied under the formalist poet Yvor Winters). He has taught at the State University of New York at Buffalo, St. Mary's College, and the University of California at Berkeley. In addition to poetry, he has written essays and criticism and translated European poetry, including that of Czeslaw Milosz. His work tends toward the meditative and reveals an interest in the relationship between words and the objects they represent, in affirming the value of physical and sensual pleasures, and in probing intense states of consciousness. Although his poems are rarely rendered in strict meters and forms, they can recall traditional prosody; many are written in modified blank verse and contain loose rhymes.

Robert Hayden (1913–1980)

Robert Hayden was born Asa Bundy Sheffey in a poor neighborhood of Detroit, Michigan, and raised by foster parents. He was educated at Detroit City College (now Wayne State University) and the University of Michigan at Ann Arbor, where he studied with W. H. Auden. In 1936 Hayden joined the Writers' Project of the Works Progress Administration, and the research he did on local folklore and the history of Michigan's Underground Railroad later made its way into many of his poems. Hayden taught at Fisk University in Nashville, Tennessee, from 1946 until 1969, and at the University of Michigan from then until his retirement. He professed the Baha'i faith and beginning in 1967 served a long tenure as editor of its World Order journal. In addition, he wrote a play on Malcolm X, published a collection of prose, and edited several anthologies. His poems display his strong interest in narrative and in character, as well as in historical events. He also wrote a good deal in the meditative mode and once described his work as "a form of prayer—a prayer for illumination." Hayden was a formalist, but increasingly turned from established meters and forms to those of his own devising.

Seamus Heaney (1939–)

Seamus Heaney was born in Mossbawn, County Derry, Northern Ireland, to a Catholic farmer and his wife. He was educated at Queen's University, Belfast, where he later lectured in English. He has also taught at the University of California, Berkeley, and Harvard and Oxford Universities, where he was professor of poetry from 1989 until 1994. He now lives in Dublin. In addition to poetry, Heaney has written wide-ranging criticism and has published his lectures on poetry. In 1995 he was awarded the Nobel Prize for Literature. His early poems are closely tied to the elemental rhythms of rural life and show the influence of W. B. Yeats, Robert Frost, Ted Hughes, and Patrick Kavanagh. Memory and history are recurring themes, and he depicts the Irish peat bog as a "memory bank," a record of the country and its people from primordial times. The strict pentameters of his early work have given way to looser forms, but his more recent work continues to present his keen insights and vivid observations in straightforward language.

Anthony Hecht (1923–)

Anthony Hecht was born in New York City. After graduation from Bard College, he joined the army and was stationed in Europe and Japan. He later taught at Kenyon College, where he studied informally with fellow faculty member John Crowe Ransom, then returned to New York and did graduate work at Columbia University. Since then he has taught at, among other schools, the University of Rochester and Georgetown University. In addition to poetry, he has published three books of criticism—including a study of W. H. Auden (a key influence)—and has undertaken translation, most notably of Aeschylus and Joseph Brodsky. He also has collaborated with artist Leonard Baskin on several series of poems. A gifted writer of light verse, he is coinventor (with John Hollander) of the comic "double dactyl," and even his graver poems often register moments of humor and transcendent joy. He frequently works in traditional meters and subtly alludes to the Bible, classical myth, and the literary canon.

Felicia Dorothea Hemans (1793–1835)

Felicia Dorothea Hemans was born in Liverpool, England, and raised in Wales. She was educated at home by her mother, who recognized her writing talent. Hemans was exceptionally prolific, publishing her first two volumes of poetry at the age of fifteen, and publishing a volume almost every year during the last two decades of her life. She was immensely popular in her day and is thought to be England's first professional female poet. From 1827 until 1831 she lived in the Liverpool suburb of Wavertree, where she had gone to secure an education for her sons, and from 1831 until her death she lived in Dublin. She carried on an active correspondence with many eminent writers of her day, including Joanna Baillie, Sir Walter Scott, and William Wordsworth. The gravity of her subject matter—on the themes of domesticity, chivalry, courage, and patriotism—her elevated tone, and her concern for morality led to her being credited with restoring the public's opinion of Romanticism following the disapproval occasioned by Lord Byron, and with setting the stage for Victorian poetry. Hemans typically set her poems in vibrant and sublime settings that corresponded to the portentousness of her subjects and to her intensity of feel-

ing about them. Although she rarely deviated from well-established meters and stanza forms, she used these materials so masterfully that her dramatic effects have been compared to Longfellow's.

George Herbert (1593–1633)

George Herbert was the fifth son of Richard Herbert, who died when the poet was three, and the younger brother of Edward, Lord Herbert of Cherbury, also a writer. A student at Westminster School and King's Scholar of Trinity College, Cambridge, Herbert at sixteen sent his mother, Magdalen, two accomplished and devout sonnets with a letter announcing his dedication of his poetic powers to God, though this did not preclude his harboring worldly ambition. His fellowship at Trinity required him to join the clergy within seven years, but after being elected public orator (a springboard into higher positions at court), he left his university duties to proxies while he pursued a secular career. Two terms as a member of Parliament evidently disillusioned him. He was ordained deacon, installed as canon of Lincoln Cathedral, and in 1630, having been ordained priest, received a living as rector of Bemerton, near Salisbury. In 1629 he married his stepfather's cousin, Jane Danvers, and they adopted his two orphaned nieces. In addition to a prose treatise, A Priest to the Temple: Or the Country Parson, his Character and Rule of Life (1652), he wrote many poems in both English and Latin. Shortly before his death, he sent his English poems to his friend, the Anglican clergyman Nicholas Ferrar, asking him to publish them if he believed that they could "turn to the advantage of any dejected soul;" otherwise, Ferrar was to burn them. The poems collected in The Temple (1633) represented, Herbert wrote, "a picture of the many spiritual conflicts that have passed betwixt God and my soul, before I could subject mine to the will of Jesus my master." Like John Donne, Herbert uses colloquial language and ingenious conceits and dramatizes the meeting of a powerful intellect and intense faith.

Robert Herrick (1591–1674)

Robert Herrick was born into a family of wealthy London goldsmiths. Apprenticed to his uncle at sixteen, he did not go up to Cambridge until 1613. After taking his M.A. in 1620, Herrick returned to London, where he became an admirer and friend of Ben Jonson. He joined the clergy in 1623, acted as a chaplain on the duke of Buckingham's disastrous expedition to the Isle of Rhé, and as a reward was given the living of dean priory, in Devon, a position he took up in 1630. The rural tranquillity of the parish, though at first alien to the urbane and social Herrick, made possible his prolific writing career; he produced over twenty-five hundred compositions, many written to imaginary mistresses, others about his maid, his dog, his cat, and rural customs and pleasures. He also wrote on religious themes. Dispossessed of his living by the Puritans, he returned to London and published in 1648 a volume containing his secular poems, the Hesperides, and his religious poems, the Noble Numbers. Among the former were his imitations of the classical poets Catullus and Horace. After the restoration of the monarchy in 1660, Herrick returned to Devon and spent his last years quietly, apparently without composing further poems.

Geoffrey Hill (1932–)

Geoffrey Hill was born in Bromsgrove, Worcestershire, England. He was educated at Keble College, Oxford, and has taught at the University of Leeds, Emmanuel and Trinity Colleges, Cambridge, and, since 1988, Boston University, as well as being a visiting lecturer at several institutions in England, Nigeria, and the

United States. He has published a collection of critical essays and produced a verse translation of Ibsen's *Brand* for the London stage. Rather than renounce obscurity, as have many of his contemporaries, Hill appears to revel in it. He often works in a sternly formal style and uses baroque diction, making frequent allusions to arcane history and legend, classical myth, European and English literature, and tumultuous events such as the Holocaust. Interwoven with and sometimes inseparable from these are Hill's personal history and concerns; for example, in *Mercian Hymns* (1971), a sequence of thirty innovative prose poems, Hill conflates an account of the powerful eighth-century Mercian (West Midland) King Offa with a reconstruction of his own younger self.

Daryl Hine (1936–   )

Daryl Hine was born in Vancouver, British Columbia, and was educated at McGill University and the University of Chicago, where he earned a Ph.D. He taught at Chicago until 1968, when he became editor of *Poetry* magazine. After serving in this post for a decade, he returned to teaching, mostly in the Chicago area. In addition to poetry, he has published a novel, a travel book, and several plays. He also has coedited an anthology of verse and has translated Homer and Theocritus. Often dubbed a "poet's poet," Hine works in established forms, such as the sonnet and the villanelle, and in elaborate constructions and rhyme schemes of his own devising. Hine's poems are by turns emotional, meditative, and playful. They frequently take up personal subjects, such as his homosexuality, and modern themes such as the search for order amidst chaos.

John Hollander (1929–   )

John Hollander was born in New York City. He was educated at Columbia University and Indiana University at Bloomington, from which he received a Ph.D. Upon graduation, he embarked on an academic career, during which he has taught at Harvard University, Connecticut College, Hunter College, and Yale University. In addition to poetry, Hollander has written plays, children's verse, and several scholarly works on prosody. He has edited numerous anthologies of essays and poems, perhaps most importantly a comprehensive edition of nineteenth-century American poetry. He is also coinventor (with Anthony Hecht) of the "double dactyl" verse form. Like Wallace Stevens, Hollander considers such philosophical issues as the nature of meaning and the role of imagination in the construction of meaning, and he makes frequent literary and biblical allusions. He works in both traditional forms and elaborate constructions of his own making and is one of the few contemporary poets known for shaped picture-poems.

Oliver Wendell Holmes (1809–1894)

Oliver Wendell Holmes was born in Cambridge, Massachusetts. He studied law at Harvard University, underwent two years of medical training in Europe, and returned to Harvard to complete his M.D. A dedicated Unitarian, he served as professor of anatomy at Dartmouth College and at Harvard, and later as dean of Harvard Medical School. He established his reputation in medicine by discovering that puerperal fever, commonly associated with childbirth and often fatal, was contagious; his work helped to stem its spread. He began writing in earnest shortly after earning his medical degree, and he was a popular lecturer on the New England lyceum circuit. *The Autocrat of the Breakfast-Table* (1858), a series of witty essays first published in *The Atlantic Monthly*, is generally considered his best work. Although his best-known poem is perhaps "Old Ironsides"

(a stirring "vers d'occasion" that rescued the *U.S.S. Constitution* from the salvage yard), "The Chambered Nautilus" was his favorite.

A. D. Hope (1907–   )

A(lec) D(erwent) Hope was born in Cooma, New South Wales, Australia. He was educated at Sydney University and University College, Oxford. Upon graduation he taught English in the New South Wales school system, and in 1937 became a lecturer in education at Sydney Teachers' College. He taught English at the University of Melbourne from 1945 to 1965 and at Canberra University College from 1965 to 1968, when he retired to devote himself to writing. Although his work is rich in literary, biblical, and mythological allusions, he recrafts traditional myths to fit the times in which he lives. Despite his propensity for conventional poetic materials and his use of traditional forms, he links himself to Chaucer, Hardy, Browning, and other poets who employed such prosaic modes as narrative, argument, and exposition—he values general statement over local or particular detail and individual expression. In a voice ferociously witty and authoritative, often sardonic and satiric, he typically approaches modern life with disdain, although he has softened this stance in his late work.

Gerard Manley Hopkins (1844–1889)

Gerard Manley Hopkins was born in Stratford, Essex, England, and was educated at Balliol College, Oxford. Under the influence of Cardinal John Henry Newman, he converted to Catholicism in 1866, became a novitiate of the Society of Jesuits two years later, and was ordained in 1877. Hopkins served as a parish priest and teacher of Classics, his lengthiest appointment being with University College, Dublin. After a promising start, Hopkins stopped writing poetry in 1868, believing it interfered with his priestly vocation. Encouraged by Church authorities, he resumed writing in 1875, with "The Wreck of the Deutschland," a poem commemorating the death of several Franciscan nuns, exiled from Germany by the Falck Laws, in a shipwreck at the mouth of the Thames. In his subsequent poems, Hopkins explored his relationship to God. Central to his complex theories on prosody are the terms "inscape," "instress," and, most important to future poets, "sprung rhythm." Little of his poetry was published during his lifetime, but the poet Robert Bridges, Hopkins' friend since Oxford, brought out an edition in 1918.

A. E. Housman (1859–1936)

A. E. Housman was born in Fockbury, Worcestershire, England, and was educated at St. John's College, Oxford. For a decade he worked for the Patent Office in London, while continuing his studies and publishing scholarly essays in literary journals. He held appointments at University College, London, and Trinity College, Cambridge. While he published extensively on the classics (in particular Propertius, Juvenal, Lucan, and Manilius), he came to poetry relatively late and had to publish his first collection, *A Shropshire Lad* (1896), at his own expense. In a well-known lecture, *The Name and Nature of Poetry* (1933), Housman asserted that "the peculiar function of poetry" is "not to transmit thought" but "to transfuse emotion." He disparaged poets, such as John Milton and Alexander Pope, who overprivileged the intellect and praised those who, like Christopher Smart and William Blake, induced in readers a physical response to their work. The chiseled clarity and flawless execution of Housman's poems is reminiscent of the classical poets he knew well. Infusing the pastoral tradition with irony, a staple of the modern temperament, he displayed baleful sentiment and a preoccupation with death that connect him to Decadent poets such as Ernest Dowson, and his evocation of Shropshire, less a geographic locale than an emotional one, bears a resemblance to the Decadents' evocations of the natural world.

Henry Howard, Earl of Surrey (ca. 1517–1547)

Henry Howard, also known as "Surrey," was the eldest son of an old aristocratic family. His father, who became third duke of Norfolk, had royal ancestors and so did his mother. Two of his nieces, Anne Boleyn and Catherine Howard, were wives of Henry VIII, and the king's illegitimate son, Henry Fitzroy, was a childhood friend. Surrey fought ably in campaigns against the French and was imprisoned in 1537 on suspicion of sympathizing with the so-called "Pilgrimage of Grace" rebellion against the dissolution of the monasteries. During his brief life (at thirty he was executed with his father on a frivolous charge of treason), Surrey wrote courtly poems and circulated them in manuscript. He followed Wyatt in translating sonnets from Petrarch's Italian and wrote his first English poem in blank verse, a translation of books 2 and 4 of Virgil's *Aeneid*. His work in this "strange meter," as the publisher called it, appeared in print in 1554 (book 4) and 1557 (book 2). Many of his lyrics were included, along with Wyatt's, in Tottel's *Songs and Sonnets* (1557). His (probably fictional) love for "Geraldine" is dramatized in Thomas Nashe's *The Unfortunate Traveller*, where Surrey appears as the traveler's "master."

Richard Howard (1929–)

Richard Howard was born in Cleveland, Ohio, and educated at Columbia University and the Sorbonne. In Cleveland and New York City he worked as a lexicographer for the World Publishing Company, then turned to translation and has since brought into English more than 150 French texts, including works by Baudelaire, Barthes, de Beauvoir, Breton, Camus, and Gide. In addition, he has worked as a poetry editor for such journals as *The New Republic*, the *Paris Review*, and *Shenandoah*, and has taught at, among other schools, Johns Hopkins University and the universities of Houston and Cincinnati. He currently lives in New York City and Houston. Known for his mastery of the dramatic monologue, Howard writes about contemporary dilemmas and personal concerns while speaking in the voices of others. Among his signature themes is the relationship between art and society. He has a gift for evoking settings; for choosing quirky, penetrating details; and for presenting startling twists, irony, and paradox. He has written formal verse and is especially skilled in syllabics.

Julia Ward Howe (1819–1910)

Julia Ward was born in New York City to a prominent family and was educated at home. In 1843 she married Samuel Gridley Howe, the social activist and reformer who founded the Perkins Institute for the Blind. The couple settled in Boston, where the poet gave birth to six children in rapid succession. She devoted herself not only to motherhood and to her writing but to the abolition and women's suffrage movements. In addition to poetry, Howe published two plays and much prose, including a well-received biography of Margaret Fuller. She is best remembered for the apocalyptic "Battle-Hymn of the Republic," which was first published, to great acclaim, in *The Atlantic Monthly* of February 1862. Despite her support for the Union in this poem, Howe later wrote a poem called "Save the Old South!", which offers a "counter mandate" to the "cruel overthrow and waste" that Northern troops ("manhood in its zeal and haste") inflicted on the South.

Langston Hughes (1902–1967)

Langston Hughes was born in Joplin, Missouri, and raised in Missouri, Kansas, Illinois, and Ohio. He attended Columbia University from 1921 until 1922, then traveled extensively in South America and Europe before moving to Washington, D.C., in 1925. The next year Hughes published his first collection of poems, *The Weary Blues*, to great acclaim. In 1929 he received a B.A. from Lincoln University in Pennsylvania, but from 1928 until 1930 he lived in New York City and was a prominent figure in the Harlem Renaissance. In addition to poetry, he wrote fiction, drama, screenplays, essays, and autobiography. Because of his journalistic work in support of the Republican side during the Spanish Civil War and his sympathies for the American Communists, in 1953 he was called to testify before Senator Joseph McCarthy's committee on subversive activities, and for many years following he worked to restore his reputation. Always concerned "largely . . . with the depicting of Negro life in America," Hughes—like Whitman, Sandburg, and Dunbar—populated his poems with urban figures, such as busboys, elevator operators, cabaret singers, and streetwalkers. He documented their troubles in social-protest poems, drawing his meters and moods from street language, jazz, and the blues.

Ted Hughes (1930–)

Ted Hughes was born in Mytholmroyd, South Yorkshire, England, and was raised in Mexborough, a coal-mining town in South Yorkshire. He won a scholarship to Pembroke College, Cambridge, but served two years in the Royal Air Force before matriculating. He studied English, archaeology, and anthropology, specializing in mythological systems (an interest that continues to inform his poetry). He later worked as a gardener, night watchman, zookeeper, script writer, and teacher. In 1956 he married the American poet Sylvia Plath, and the couple spent a year in the United States before moving to England in 1959. Plath committed suicide in 1963. In 1970 Hughes settled on a farm in Devon. In addition to poetry, he has written plays, short stories, and books for children. He has also edited numerous collections of verse and prose, and was a founding editor of *Modern Poetry in Translation* magazine. He currently is poet laureate of England. In his poetry, Hughes vividly describes the beauty of the natural world, but celebrates its raw, elemental energies. He often embodies the primal forces of nature as mythic animals such as the pike, the hawk, and "Crow," a central character in a long cycle of poems. Hughes has gradually abandoned traditional forms, asserting that the "very sound of metre calls up the ghosts of the past and it is difficult to sing one's own tune against that choir."

Richard Hugo (1923–1982)

Richard Hugo was born in Seattle and educated at the University of Washington, where he studied with Theodore Roethke. A bombardier in the United States Army Air Corps during World War II, he subsequently worked for the Boeing Corporation, then began an academic career, during which he taught at the University of Washington, the University of Iowa Writers' Workshop, and (from 1964 until 1982) the University of Montana at Missoula. From 1977 until 1982 he served as editor of the Yale Younger Poets series. His poems typically project a variety of emotional states onto desolate landscapes in the American West. Although his early work was ornately wrought, he later turned to a freer and somewhat confessional mode.

Laura (Riding) Jackson (1901–1991)

Laura Riding was born in New York City. She attended Cornell University. For a short time she was affiliated with the Fugitives, a prominent group of Southern writers; the poets Allen Tate and John Crowe Ransom particularly admired her work. In the 1930s Riding was involved with the poet and critic Robert Graves, with whom she wrote *A Survey of Modernist Poetry* (1927), an influential study that advocated close textual reading. Riding and Graves also founded the Seizin Press (London). In 1938, convinced that poetry could not render truth because it appealed more to the senses than to the intellect, she stopped writing verse, returned to the United States, and with Schuyler Jackson, her second husband, embarked on a series of lexicographic and linguistic studies, eventually published as *Rational Meaning: A New Foundation for the Definition of Words* (1974). In her poems, Riding tried to depict "ultimate reality"—or "truth," to use her term—through bare essentials, letting each word convey its full and exact meaning. She also avoided using concrete details, which might circumscribe a work to a specific time and place and thus limit its claims to universality. She believed that form and meter should arise implicitly from the materials in the poem rather than be imposed from without. Subtle formal constructions often lurk beneath the seemingly casual surface of her poems.

Josephine Jacobsen (1908–   )

Josephine Jacobsen was born in Cobourg, Ontario, to American parents. She was raised in New York City and on Long Island until the age of five, when her father died and her family began moving from place to place. Educated by private tutors until the age of fourteen (when her family settled in Baltimore), she later attended school but did not pursue higher education. Jacobsen worked in the theater until she married, then devoted herself to writing and to raising her family. She has traveled extensively in South America, Europe, and Africa, and many of her poems are based on her experiences abroad. In addition to poetry, she has published well-received short stories (which she began writing at the age of sixty), literary criticism, and (in collaboration with William R. Mueller) dramatic criticism. Her poetry tends to explore the relationship between the physical and the spiritual. Although themes of disappointment, isolation, displacement, and mortality recur in her work, and her tone can be gritty and sardonic, she remains a poet of affirmation.

Randall Jarrell (1914–1965)

Randall Jarrell was born in Nashville, Tennessee, but spent some of his early years in California. He was educated at Vanderbilt University, where he studied psychology and English (with the poet John Crowe Ransom) and wrote his M.A. thesis on A. E. Housman. He taught at several schools, including Kenyon College, where he roomed with novelist Peter Taylor and poet Robert Lowell; the University of Texas at Austin; and Women's College, University of North Carolina at Greensboro. Jarrell enlisted in the army in 1942. He was stationed stateside, instructing aviators and working with B-29 crews, and, based largely on their reports from the front, wrote some of the most sensitive and authentic poems to come out of World War II. He also earned a reputation as an astute, acerbic, and influential critic of poetry, known for brief, sweeping dismissals and for lengthy appreciations. Williams, Frost, Bishop, and Lowell were among those he favored. In addition to poetry, he wrote a novel and children's stories, as well as translations of Goethe, Chekhov, and several of Grimm's fairy tales. Though some suspected suicide, his death when a car struck him was deemed accidental. His style is marked by a colloquial plainness, yet reveals a Rilkean longing for transformation. Indeed, some of his most famous and successful poems are narrated in the voices of women.

Robinson Jeffers (1887–1962)

(John) Robinson Jeffers was born in Pittsburgh, Pennsylvania. He was educated at Occidental College. Before turning to writing, he studied medicine and forestry at the graduate level. In 1914 he moved to Carmel, California, where he lived in relative isolation—in a home overlooking the dramatic Pacific coastline that figures prominently in his work. Jeffers' philosophical stance, which he dubbed "inhumanism" and defined as "a shifting emphasis and significance from man to not-man," led many critics to label him a misanthrope. However, his intent was to challenge humanity's overreliance on the flawed social structures of its own making and to urge its return to a more primal relation with the natural world. There is a dynamic tension in Jeffers' work between violent energy and quiet endurance, symbolized as hawk and rock. Often expansive and rhetorical, his poems employ a line adapted, in part, from Walt Whitman's lines, and distinguish themselves clearly from the compact symbolist and spare imagist poems prevalent early in the century.

Elizabeth Jennings (1926–   )

Elizabeth Jennings was born in Boston, Lincolnshire, England, and educated at St. Anne's College, Oxford. She worked at various professions—including advertising, librarianship, and publishing—before devoting herself exclusively to writing. In the 1960s she suffered recurrent mental breakdowns, which resulted in hospitalization. Her later work documents her illness and subsequent recovery. In addition to poetry, she has published critical essays, children's verse, and a translation of Michelangelo's sonnets. Jennings typically sets her work in the domestic sphere and takes up personal but not autobiographical subjects. While she excels at presenting the significance of a given moment or precisely describing an isolated feeling, her powers are not limited to small subjects. She usually works in regular verse forms and meters.

Samuel Johnson (1709–1784)

Samuel Johnson was born in Lichfield, England, to a bookseller and his wife. As a child he contracted scrofula (tuberculosis of the lymphatic system) and smallpox, a combination that left him badly scarred, with impaired sight and hearing, and prone to involuntary gesticulation. He went to Pembroke College, Oxford, but financial difficulties forced him to leave after fourteen months. After a period spent teaching in Birmingham, in 1737 he settled in London, where he worked on *The Gentleman's Magazine*, and the next year published "London," an imitation of Juvenal's satires that was an immediate success, as was his second satire, "The Vanity of Human Wishes" (1749). Johnson's contribution to literary scholarship, criticism, and lexicography is incalculable. In addition to his many reviews and essays, he published the ambitious *Lives of the Poets* (1779–81), founded and edited *The Rambler* magazine, collected the works of Shakespeare, and produced his monumental, if idiosyncratic, *A Dictionary of the English Language* (1755).

Ben Jonson (1572–1637)

Ben(jamin) Jonson was born in London after the death of his father, a clergyman. Educated at Westminster School, he was working for his stepfather as a bricklayer by the early 1590s. He volunteered for military service in the Low Countries and after returning to England began a career in the theater, first as an actor, then as a playwright. In 1598 he killed a fellow actor in a duel but escaped hanging by claiming "benefit of clergy," that is, by demonstrating his ability to read a verse from the

Bible. His conversion to Catholicism in that same year no doubt contributed to the charges of "popery" and treason leveled against him after he published his neo-classical tragedy *Sejanus* (1606), which dramatized conspiracy and assassination. Jonson had also incurred the wrath of authorities by coauthoring *The Isle of Dogs* (1597) and *Eastward Hoe* (1605); the former, considered a "lewd play, containing very seditious and slanderous matter," caused its authors to be briefly imprisoned and was so effectively censored that no copies now exist; the latter, which also led to Jonson's imprisonment, contained a passage about the Scots that offended the court and the Scottish king, James I. Jonson soon gained the king's favor, however, with the series of court masques he began to create—with the designer Inigo Jones—in 1605; in 1616, after he had published his *Works* and had returned (in 1610) to the Church of England, he received a substantial pension from the king and effectively occupied the position of poet laureate. Learned in the classics and skilled in a variety of poetic and dramatic forms, Jonson first acquired fame as the author of "comedies of humors" satirizing the eccentricities and "ruling passions" of his characters. In addition to his many successful plays—*Volpone* (1605), *The Alchemist* (1610), and *Bartholomew Fair* (1614), for instance—Jonson wrote poetry in a variety of forms, including witty epigrams, epitaphs, songs (both freestanding and designed for plays and masques), and "occasional" poems celebrating events and people; his "To Penshurst" is an early example of the "country house" poem. In contrast to his contemporary Shakespeare, whose plays were collected only posthumously, Jonson was concerned with constructing an imposing authorial persona. Modeling himself in part on such classical writers as Martial and Horace, he was the first English poet to inspire a "school": the "sons" and "tribes" of Ben that included such poets as Robert Herrick and Thomas Carew.

Donald Justice (1925–)

Donald Justice was born and raised in Miami, Florida. He earned a B.A. from the University of Miami, an M.A. from the University of North Carolina at Chapel Hill, and a Ph.D. from the University of Iowa, where his teachers included the poets John Berryman, Robert Lowell, and Karl Shapiro. He also studied with Yvor Winters at Stanford University. He has taught at, among other schools, the University of Iowa Writers' Workshop and the University of Florida at Gainesville. Often compared to Wallace Stevens in his purity of phrasing, Justice remains committed to the "well-wrought" poem. His diction is accessible and exact, his forms derived from literary tradition. His work frequently takes up dark themes, such as isolation, madness, and terror, but can also be humorous.

Patrick Kavanagh (1905–1967)

Patrick Kavanagh was born in Inniskeen, County Monaghan, Ireland. He left school at the age of twelve to go to work. During the 1930s he became active on the Dublin literary scene, writing reviews for local publications while supporting himself by farming. In 1949 he sold his land and devoted himself entirely to literature. He made a precarious living over the next two decades; despite the critical success of *The Great Hunger* (1942), sales were sluggish and he had difficulty finding a publisher for subsequent work. His difficulties brought him close to despair, but in 1955 he experienced a powerful spiritual rebirth and his work enjoyed a brief revival. Kavanagh has been credited with maintaining public interest in Irish peasant culture in the period following the Celtic Twilight. He was no conventional champion of Irish culture, for he eschewed sentimentality and stereo-type. Kavanagh's detractors labeled him a "provincial" based on his use of traditional forms and meters, his plain language, and his narrow range (virtually all of his poems are set in Monaghan). He rejected this label, arguing that the "provincial" has "no mind of his own" and "does not trust what his eyes see until he has heard what the metropolis . . . has to say on the subject." He called himself a "parochial," concerned with "fundamentals" and "universals" revealed through careful study of the local.

John Keats (1795–1821)

John Keats was born in London, the son of a livery stableman and his wife. At the age of fifteen he was apprenticed to an apothecary-surgeon, and on completion of his apprenticeship did further training at Guy's Hospital, London. Having qualified, Keats abandoned medicine for poetry. In 1818 he fell in love with Fanny Brawne, but was prevented from marrying her by financial difficulties. In 1819, his *annus mirabilis*, he produced all of his great odes, a number of fine sonnets, and several other masterpieces. The following year, he developed tuberculosis, the disease that had killed his mother and beloved younger brother, Tom. Hoping to prolong his life, he traveled to Italy, but died in Rome the following spring. At the time of his death he had published only fifty-four poems, and his reputation as a great poet was by no means secure. In his poetry he struggled to make sense of a world riddled with "misery, heartache and pain, sickness and oppression." Rather than take solace in religious or philosophical creeds, as did Wordsworth and Coleridge, he strove to develop "negative capability," the ability to exist in a condition of "uncertainties, Mysteries, doubts, without any reaching after fact and reason." He looked to sensation, passion, and imagination to guide him: "I am certain of nothing but of the holiness of the Heart's affections and the truth of Imagination—What the imagination seizes as Beauty must be truth," he wrote to a friend. Despite the brevity of his life and writing career, Keats mastered a number of difficult forms, producing complex variations of the ode and the Petrarchan and Shakespearian sonnets.

Richard Kenney (1948–)

Richard Kenney was born in Glens Falls, New York. He attended Dartmouth College and studied Celtic lore in Ireland and Scotland. Kenney has worked at various jobs, including schoolbus driving and house painting, and he currently teaches English at the University of Washington in Seattle. He is well versed in science, history, and philosophy, and his work reflects a study of Hopkins, Browning, Crane, and Frost. Frequently composed of brief phrases that accrete into large and complex structures, his poems are the products of his lively mind and breadth of learning.

Francis Scott Key (1779–1843)

Francis Scott Key was born at Terra Rubra, his family's county seat in Carroll County, Maryland. He graduated from St. John's College at Annapolis in 1796 and went into legal practice with his brother-in-law, Roger B. Taney, later a Supreme Court justice. Key served twice as United States Attorney for the District of Columbia. Although he wrote devotional and occasional poems all his life, his reputation as a poet rests almost exclusively on "Defense of Fort McHenry." Written to fit the tune of "To Anacreon in Heaven," a popular English drinking song, it later was renamed the "Star-Spangled Banner" and became the United States National Anthem.

Sidney Keyes (1922–1943)

Sidney Keyes was born in Dartford, England. He was educated at Tonbridge School, where he began to write poetry, and at Queen's College, Oxford, where he became friends with John Heath-Stubbs and Michael Meyer, coeditors of *Eight Oxford Poets*, which includes some of Keyes' work. In 1942 he was commissioned into his father's regiment, the Queen's Own Royal West Kent. After only two weeks of active service he was captured at Tunisia and died there under mysterious circumstances. In addition to poetry, he wrote plays and stories, which were first published in 1948. Keyes found inspiration in the works of visionaries and masters of the macabre, but also felt an affinity for the Romantics, especially Wordsworth, and nature poets John Clare, Thomas Hardy, A. E. Housman, and Edward Thomas. In the war poems he wrote before joining up, he portrays death as a real presence to which the good soldier must submit courageously and with a measure of detachment. Confronted with the reality of death, he changed his stance, advocating active resistance against the forces of extinction.

Anne Killigrew (1660–1685)

Anne Killigrew was born in London. Her father, an amateur dramatist and chaplain to the duke of York, encouraged Anne's literary talents and oversaw the posthumous publication (in 1685–86) of the poems she produced before dying, at twenty-five, of small pox. In the ode John Dryden composed for this memorial volume, he praises her accomplishments in the "sister arts" of poetry and painting (two of her poems describe her own paintings), but also presents her as an entirely "artless" poet whose gifts were from "nature." Killigrew herself, however, might have disputed that view, for she worked at her craft by writing in a variety of poetic genres including a heroic poem on Alexander. Recognizing that a female writer's desire to create "deathless numbers" might be viewed as overly ambitious by some readers, Killigrew drew inspiration from her near-contemporary Katherine Philips: "Nor did sex at all obstruct her fame," Killigrew wrote about Philips, in a poem addressed to those who impugned Killigrew's status as an author by saying that her verses "Were Made by Another."

Henry King (1592–1669)

Henry King was the son of a bishop of London and his wife. Educated at Westminster and Christ Church, Oxford, he entered the Church of England and rose steadily through its ranks, becoming the bishop of Chichester in 1642. A staunch opponent of Puritanism, he was ejected from his position by Parliamentarians in 1643. After seventeen years in retirement with friends, he was reinstated as bishop in 1660, following the return of the monarchy. He published a verse translation of the Psalms in 1651 and composed both sacred and secular poems—including elegies on his friend John Donne, Ben Jonson, and Sir Walter Ralegh—that were published anonymously in an unauthorized edition called *Poems, Elegies, Paradoxes and Sonnets* (1657). He was known as an impressive preacher, and a number of his sermons have been published. His best known work, however, is "An Exequy to His Matchless, Never-to-Be-Forgotten Friend," a moving lament for his wife, Anne Berkeley, who died in 1624 at the age of twenty-four.

Galway Kinnell (1927–)

Galway Kinnell was born in Providence, Rhode Island. He was educated at Princeton University and the University of Rochester. From 1945 until 1946 he served in the navy, and then did field work for the Congress on Racial Equality. He has traveled widely in the Middle East and Europe and has taught at, among other schools,

the University of California at Irvine, the University of Pittsburgh, Sarah Lawrence College, and New York University. He lives in Vermont and New York City. Kinnell's poems, often tender and humorous, strive to find joy and even transcendence in daily life. His recent work explores humanity's relationship to the forces of the natural world; transience is his great theme. Kinnell began writing in a highly formal style, but subsequently moved to a freer verse that corresponds to "the rhythm of what's being said."

Thomas Kinsella (1928–)

Thomas Kinsella was born in Dublin, Ireland. He studied science at University College, Dublin, but left to work for the Irish Civil Service. After retiring from the Department of Finance in 1965, he taught in the United States. In 1972, in Dublin, he founded the Peppercanister Press, which published much of his own work. He has translated Gaelic poetry and has edited the *New Oxford Book of Irish Verse*. Although Kinsella is an Irish poet, he has avoided traditional Irish subjects "as being limited in themselves" and has instead concentrated on such universal themes as love, death, the passage of time, and the creative act. Although he occasionally writes public poetry, he has increasingly turned "downward into the psyche toward origin and myth," and to images inspired by Jungian archetypes. Many of his early poems are elaborate constructions following strict rhyme schemes and metrical patterns, but he has since loosened his poetic, the better to explore the fluid worlds of the psyche and the dream.

Rudyard Kipling (1865–1936)

Rudyard Kipling was born in Bombay, India, to British parents. He was educated in England, but in 1882 returned to India to work as a journalist. When he moved back to England in 1889, he enjoyed celebrity status for the prose he had written abroad and republished at home. Although he was awarded the Nobel Prize for Literature in 1907, by the time of his death his reputation had slipped considerably, due largely to the jingoism that pervaded his writings during the Boer War and World War I. In addition to poetry, Kipling wrote prose and fiction, including the acclaimed *Jungle Book* (1894), *The Second Jungle Book* (1895), and *Kim* (1901). The rousing rhythms that propel many of his poems are derived from music-hall songs and Protestant hymns, leading T. S. Eliot to call his work "the poetry of oratory." Although as a child of Empire, Kipling held in high regard what he considered the glories of civilization, in a moving series of monologues from the mouths of common soldiers he explores and acknowledges the cost of attaining such values as justice, patriotism, and sacrifice of self to a larger ideal.

A. M. Klein (1909–1972)

A(braham) M(oses) Klein was born in Ratno, Ukraine. After his parents immigrated to Canada in 1910, he was raised in a ghetto in Montreal, where he was immersed in Jewish culture. Klein was educated at McGill University and the University of Montreal Law School. He practiced law until 1955 and was actively involved in a number of publications, including the *Canadian Jewish Chronicle*, which he edited from 1938 until 1955; his insightful editorials documented the rise of the Third Reich, the progress of the Holocaust, and the establishment of a homeland in Israel. He also taught poetry at McGill University for three years, retiring in 1956 after a debilitating nervous collapse. In his early collections Klein took up mainly Jewish concerns, but by the time of *The Rocking Chair and Other Poems* (1948) he had extended his range to other minority groups—including

French-Canadians and Canadian Indians—whose traditional ways of life were threatened. Throughout his career he was an impassioned defender of cultural heritage.

Kenneth Koch (1925–   )
Kenneth Koch was born in Cincinnati, Ohio. He served as a rifleman in the Pacific theater during World War II, then attended Harvard University and Columbia University, from which he received a Ph.D. Aside from four years spent in France and Italy, Koch has lived, since 1950, in New York City. With John Ashbery, Frank O'Hara, and James Schuyler he was part of what became known as the New York school of poetry. In addition to poems, Koch has written several books on teaching children to write poetry, a novel, and a book of short stories. His plays have frequently been performed, and there have been several exhibitions of his collaborations with painters. His work might be described as an elevated form of play involving radical disjunctions and seeming randomness that cohere on a larger scale.

Yusef Komunyakaa (1947–   )
Yusef Komunyakaa was born in Bogalusa, Louisiana. He served in Vietnam as a war correspondent and for a time edited the *Southern Cross*. Following his years in the military, Komunyakaa studied at the University of Colorado, Colorado State, and the University of California at Irvine. He lived briefly in New Orleans, where he taught English at the Lakefront Campus of the University of New Orleans and served as poet-in-the-schools, and he has also lived in Australia, Saint Thomas, Puerto Rico, and Japan. He currently teaches at Indiana University, but many of his poems harken back to his childhood in a poor, rural, and largely black Southern community. They grapple with hard realities, including race and social class, and difficult themes, such as isolation and vulnerability. Their rhythms and melodic effects are influenced by jazz and the blues.

Stanley Kunitz (1905–   )
Stanley Kunitz was born and raised in Worcester, Massachusetts. After graduation from Harvard University, he worked as an editor in New York City. During World War II he served in the army, and during the academic career that followed he taught at, among other schools, Columbia University. He has been an influential teacher to many poets, including Louise Glück and Robert Hass. In addition to writing poetry, he has assembled (in collaboration with Howard Haycraft) nine biographical dictionaries of literary figures, edited a collection of William Blake's work, and translated the work of Anna Akhmatova from the Russian. His early poems are witty, elaborately constructed, and learned. Subsequent poems adopt an intimate, even confessional style that has been compared to that of Randall Jarrell and Robert Lowell. Characterized by spareness, directness, accessibility, and the rhythms of speech, Kunitz's poems frequently explore loss and regret.

Walter Savage Landor (1775–1864)
Walter Savage Landor was born in Warwick, England, and was educated at Trinity College, Oxford. In 1811 he married "a girl without a sixpence and with very few accomplishments," as he put it. The marriage eventually collapsed, but its interludes of domestic tranquility provided the basis for several of his most interesting poems. He lived in Italy from 1815 until 1835 and from 1857 until his death. During that time he polished his fluency in French, Italian, and Greek and deepened his prodigious knowledge of history. Landor was steeped in classicism, and his most enduring works,

based on his studies, made him an important figure to poets such as Robert Browning and Ezra Pound. He often composed in Latin, only subsequently translating his poems into English. He once remarked, "I am sometimes at a loss for an English word, for a Latin never." Influenced by Milton, however, he eventually abandoned Latin for English, and the classical hexameter couplet for blank verse, which he considered the best meter for conveying weighty matter in his native tongue. His spare, serene, elegant lyrics articulate a variety of classical themes and subjects; celebrate bodily pleasure and physical beauty; eulogize noble ideals; pay extravagant compliments to ladies (in particular, "Ianthe," a woman whom Landor loved but could not marry); and, in elegies for venerable persons and lost friends, mourn the brevity of life and love. Conventional modes of address and carefully wrought formal structures hold personal sentiment in check in Landor's verse.

William Langland (fl. 1375)
A note found in the margins of an early manuscript of *Piers Plowman* in a fifteenth-century hand is the single piece of evidence that ascribes this poem to a man named William Langland. The note, which many scholars accept as reliable, states that William Langland was the son of Stacy de Rokayle, a man of gentle birth who lived in Shipton-under-Wychwood and was tenant of Lord Spenser in the county of Oxfordshire. The note concludes, "this aforesaid William made the book that is called Piers Plowman."

Texts of the poem itself both support and elaborate on the note's information. In line 52 of Passus 15 of the B-text, the narrator seems to offer a cryptogram of the name "Langland": " 'I have lyved in londe,' quod I, 'my name is Longe Wille.' " At the beginning of the poem the narrator depicts himself awakening from his dream in the "Malvern Hills" in the West Midland region of England; elsewhere he presents himself as a man who has moved from the country to the city and is at the time of the poem's composition living in Cornhill, in London, making a living as a cleric who chants prayers for the souls of the dead. The poem further presents the narrator as elderly, as learned in the Bible and in Latin, and as the husband of Kit and the father of Calotte; from these details we may infer that the author had received a clerical education, but had never been ordained a priest. Passus 5 of the C-text states that the narrator comes from "franklins," or free man, and from married parents. This latter detail may serve to counter suspicions about the legitimacy of the poet's birth.

Sidney Lanier (1842–1881)
Sidney Lanier was born in Macon, Georgia. He was educated at Oglethorpe College. In 1861 he enlisted in the Confederate Army and in 1864 was captured by Union forces and imprisoned for four months at Point Lookout, Maryland, where he probably contracted the tuberculosis from which he later died. After the war, Lanier played in the Peabody Symphony as a flutist and, in 1879, became lecturer in literature at Johns Hopkins University. In addition to poetry, he wrote novels—including *Tiger-Lilies* (1867), which documents his war experience—and critical studies—including *The Science of English Verse* (1880), in which he argues that the same laws govern music and poetry. This view led Lanier to develop an innovative, fluid line that has the evocative power of music. In his poetry and criticism, Lanier explored the degenerative effect of commercialism on the human spirit and championed, as correctives, love and chivalric ideals such as honor, kinship, and propriety. As he grew sicker, poorer, and less sanguine about

the power of love to surmount all human difficulties, Lanier increasingly explored spiritual issues, although he never embraced traditional Christianity.

Aemilia Lanyer (1569–1645)

Aemilia Lanyer was the daughter of Baptist Bassano, an Italian court musician, and his wife, Margaret Johnson. She was probably educated in the noble household of Susan Wingfield, countess of Kent. As the mistress of Henry Cary, Lord Hunsdun, a wealthy courtier forty-five years her senior, she enjoyed a luxurious and privileged life until she became pregnant; she then married Captain Alfonso Lanyer, another court musician, in 1592. In 1617 she set up a school in the fashionable St. Giles in the Fields for the children of the nobility and gentlemen, but it failed in 1619. Lanyer was the first Englishwoman to publish a substantial collection of original poems in her own name, as well as actively to seek patronage from a host of noble ladies addressed in the prefatory poems affixed to her collection, *Salve Deus Rex Judaeorum* (1611). Her "Description of Cooke-ham," is, like Ben Jonson's "To Penshurst," an early example of the English "country house" poem.

Philip Larkin (1922–1985)

Philip Larkin was born in Coventry and studied at King Henry VIII School and St. John's College, Oxford. He worked as a librarian for the rest of his life, starting in the small town of Wellington and moving through the university libraries of Leicester and Belfast before settling at Hull. Although he tried to achieve recognition as a novelist, with *Jill* in 1946 and *A Girl in Winter* in 1947, it was in poetry that he made his reputation. Along with Donald Davie, Thom Gunn, and his college friend Kingsley Amis, Larkin came to be known as a writer of "the Movement," a group of postwar poets anthologized in Robert Conquest's *New Lines* (1956). As Conquest put it, these poets' work "is free from both mystical and logical compulsions and—like modern philosophy—is empirical in its attitude to all that comes." Although Larkin produced only four volumes of poetry in his lifetime—*The North Ship* (1945), *The Less Deceived* (1955), *The Whitsun Weddings* (1965), and *High Windows* (1974)—he was a highly influential presence in the second half of the twentieth century.

D. H. Lawrence (1885–1930)

D(avid) H(erbert) Lawrence was born in Eastwood, Nottinghamshire, England, and attended University College, Nottingham. In 1912 he embarked on a tempestuous and nomadic existence that took him around the globe—Italy, Ceylon, Australia, Mexico, the United States, and other countries—and brought him into the company of some of the foremost writers of the day, including Aldous and Maria Huxley, Bertrand Russell, Richard Aldington, and H. D. In addition to poetry, Lawrence wrote many controversial but acclaimed novels. In his mature work, Lawrence saw "man as imprisoned within his body . . . a mechanism grown incapable of passion." Skeptical of bourgeois Victorian civility, which he believed to have a stultifying effect on the human spirit, he turned to the natural order, with its infinite potential for renewal, and sexuality, with its liberating and generative possibilities. He sought to capture "creative change, creative mutation," which he believed to be the impulse behind all life.

Irving Layton (1912–)

Irving Layton was born in Romania to Jewish parents who emigrated to Montreal, Canada, the year after his birth. He was educated at Macdonald College, served briefly in the Canadian Army, then attended McGill University. Layton taught English in secondary schools and colleges until 1970, when he joined the faculty of York University (Toronto). He retired from teaching in 1978. One of the most prolific poets of this century, he has published some fifty volumes of poetry. He also has written political essays and a memoir and has edited numerous collections of verse. His poetry has garnered attention for its Dionysian celebrations of the vital and the sensual as well as the intellectually provocative. He takes up subjects generally considered unpoetic and chastises those, such as academics, critics, and religious leaders, who would stifle the irrational and thereby impede the creative process. For all his defiance, Layton is also a tender and reflective poet who values order, subscribes to a strong moral code, and considers the artist akin to the prophet—striving to enlighten a misguided world.

Emma Lazarus (1849–1887)

Emma Lazarus was born in New York City to a prominent Sefardic (Spanish Jewish) family. She was educated at home. In 1868 she met the writer Ralph Waldo Emerson, who became her literary mentor. In the 1880s, Lazarus developed a passionate interest in Semitism. She translated medieval Hebrew poets (from the German) and wrote impassioned essays on behalf of the wave of Jewish immigrants seeking refuge from persecution in Europe after the assassination of Russian Czar Alexander II in 1881. Lazarus was appalled by the squalid conditions in which many of these refugees were forced to live and sympathetic to their difficulty in finding employment, yet she was grateful to her country for opening its doors to them. She wrote "The New Colossus," the poem for which she is best remembered, in 1865. Its last five lines were engraved on the pedestal of the Statue of Liberty, which was dedicated in 1886. Lazarus's words thus greeted the millions of immigrants who arrived at Ellis Island by boat around the turn of the century.

Mary Leapor (1722–1746)

Mary Leapor was born in Marston St. Lawrence, Northamptonshire, England, and was educated at home. She showed an early talent for writing, which her parents encouraged as long as it did not interfere with her work or lead her to feel dissatisfied with her station in life. In her mid-teens she was put to work as a scullery maid; upon her mother's death she was recalled home to assist her father in his nursery. Leapor died of measles at the age of twenty-four. Thanks to the efforts of her patronness Bridget Freemantle, two volumes of her work were published posthumously. Her work appealed to readers who believed her to be a "natural poet," her talents innate and untainted by excessive education or contact with mannered society. In reality, she had thoroughly schooled herself in the poetic conventions of her day. She wrote in rhymed iambic couplets and in popular eighteenth-century genres—including satires, pastorals, elegies, and country-house poems. She frequently imitated canonical English poets, especially Pope. Her verses contain allusions to classical myth and the Bible. Her achievement lay in her ability not only to use these inherited materials but also to turn them on their heads through the skillful use of irony, wit, and satire. She frequently mocked high society, lamented the social condition of women in her century, and provided an unsentimental portrait of the hidden world of housekeepers, cooks, gardeners, and laborers whose exertions kept the estates of the landed gentry running smoothly.

Edward Lear (1812–1888)

Edward Lear was born in Holloway, London, and in 1832 began to work as an illustrator. In 1846 he published *A Book of Nonsense*, complete with illustrations by his own hand, which he had written to amuse the grandchildren of his patron, the earl of Derby. In the 1830s Lear became a wanderer, supporting himself by painting landscapes across Europe—he became known for his watercolors—and writing travel journals. He popularized the limerick, a verse form of uncertain origin that rhymes *aabba* and follows a strict syllable count and quantitative meter (Lear collapsed the third and fourth lines into one). Following his example, poets as diverse as Dante Gabriel Rossetti, Algernon Swinburne, Rudyard Kipling, and Alfred, Lord Tennyson, in the nineteenth century, and Ogden Nash, in the twentieth, employed the form. Lear's nonsense verse, particularly admired for its ability to convey emotion, frequently presents eccentric individuals at odds with conventional society. These figures, with their long beards and bulbous noses, often resemble the poet himself, just as the illustrations that accompany the text are frequently self-parodic.

Li-Young Lee (1957–)

Li-Young Lee was born in Jakarta, Indonesia, to Chinese parents. In 1959 his father, a former personal physician to Mao Tse-tung, escaped from the work camp where he had been held as a political prisoner; the family fled Indonesia and lived in Hong Kong, Macau, and Japan before settling in the United States in 1964. Lee was educated at the University of Pittsburgh, the University of Arizona, and the State University of New York at Brockport. He has worked as an artist for a fashion-accessories company in Chicago and has taught at, among other schools, Northwestern University and the University of Iowa. Family history is an important element in his work, which is by turns narrative and quietly meditative. He organizes his material through repetition and parallelism, employs montage to establish relationships between images, and works in a spare, free-verse line.

Brad Leithauser (1953–)

Brad Leithauser was born and raised in Detroit, Michigan. He attended Harvard College and Harvard Law School. For three years he was a research fellow at the Kyoto Comparative Law Center in Japan, and has subsequently lived in Italy, England, Iceland, and France. In addition to three volumes of poetry, he has published three novels and a book of essays, and has edited *The Norton Book of Ghost Stories*. He is currently an Emily Dickinson Lecturer in the Humanities at Mount Holyoke College. His work is suffused with a passion for the scientific and the mathematical as well as an interest in animals and landscape. A fondness for prosodic experimentation is his hallmark.

Douglas Le Pan (1914–)

Douglas Le Pan was born in Toronto and educated at the University of Toronto and Oxford University. He taught at Harvard University from 1938 until 1941. During World War II he served with the Canadian Army as a gunner in Italy, and after the war he joined the diplomatic corps. He held several positions of high rank within the Canadian government and was dispatched to London and the United States. In 1959 Le Pan returned to the academic life and since then has taught at Queen's University and the University of Toronto. In addition to poetry, Le Pan has written a memoir and a novel. During the period in which he composed "An Incident," Le Pan's predominant theme was humanity's quest to establish order (and maintain such ideals as freedom and justice) in the midst of a morally confused and often brutal world. Le Pan works in an essentially formal mode.

Denise Levertov (1923–)

Denise Levertov was born in Ilford, Essex (England), and educated at home. After working as a nurse in London during World War II, she immigrated to the United States in 1948. From 1956 to 1959 she lived in Mexico. Since then she has taught at, among other schools, Stanford University. In addition to poetry, she has published two collections of prose. Her early work was written in a predominantly English Romantic vein, but as a result of her associations with imagists William Carlos Williams, Ezra Pound, and H. D., and Black Mountain poets Robert Creeley, Cid Corman, and Robert Duncan, she remade herself into a quintessentially American poet. Although she often writes in a visionary style that borders on "magical realism," her commitment to material reality has resulted in a willingness to take on difficult social issues. She retains concreteness, precision, and intensity while working in freer forms.

Philip Levine (1928–)

Philip Levine was born in Detroit, Michigan. After graduation from Wayne State University, he worked at, as he put it, "a succession of stupid jobs," then left Detroit "for good." In 1957 he earned an M.F.A. from the University of Iowa, where Robert Lowell and John Berryman were his teachers. From 1958 until his retirement he taught at California State University in Fresno. In addition to poetry, he has written criticism and autobiography, and he has translated the work of several Spanish poets. Like Walt Whitman and William Carlos Williams, Levine identifies strongly with the working class and its struggles. Setting many of his poems in the decimated industrial landscape of Detroit, he bears witness to his subjects' tenacity and dignity in the face of extreme difficulty. He also writes about family and relationships, exploring his own vulnerabilities and the durability of love. Able to work in a wide range of modes—from the visionary and surrealistic to the lyric and the narrative—he uses colloquial diction masterfully.

Alun Lewis (1915–1944)

Alun Lewis was born in Cwmaman, a depressed mining town near Aberdare, South Wales. His parents were both schoolteachers, and he excelled in his years at Aberystwyth College, coming first in history and writing for the college magazine. He earned his M.A. at Manchester University and returned to Aberystwyth for a teacher's training course. Although he wavered at the thought of participating in the war, he enlisted in the army in 1940. In 1941 he married Gweno Ellis. Both his collection of short stories, *The Last Inspection*, and his first collection of poetry, *Raider's Dawn*, were published in 1942 and focused on the experiences of English soldiers. Lewis traveled with his battalion to India and finally to Burma to face the Japanese, but under the influences of the war, a love affair, Eastern religions, and culture shock, he began to feel he was losing his grasp on his own fate. He shot himself in 1944. A collection of the poems he had written while overseas, *Ha! Ha! Among the Trumpets*, was published posthumously in 1945.

C. Day Lewis (1904–1972)

C(ecil) Day Lewis was born in Ballintubber, Ireland, and raised in England. He was educated at Wadham College, Oxford, where he associated with the poets W. H. Auden, Louis MacNeice, and Stephen Spender. In the 1930s Day Lewis became active in left-wing politics and was a member of the Communist Party for three years, but grew disillusioned when the movement fell short of its ideals. In addition to poetry, Day Lewis wrote a series of successful detective stories under the pseudonym "Nicholas Blake," and several novels under his own name. He also translated Virgil, whose influence can be detected in his later poems. Like his fellow "Pylon" poets, as the Oxford group was sometimes called, Day Lewis introduced modern diction into his poems and made broad reference to the issues of the day. Like Auden, he resisted writing propagandistic works on behalf of liberal causes, but conveyed the plight of modern human beings with tenderness and affection. He had an enduring fascination with the transience of things, particularly of human relationships and communities.

Dorothy Livesay (1909–)

Dorothy Livesay was born in Winnipeg, Manitoba, and educated at the University of Toronto, the Sorbonne, and the University of British Columbia. She has worked as a social worker, a newspaper correspondent, a documentary scriptwriter, and a college professor. During the 1960s she taught English in Zambia. In addition to poetry, Livesay has published a novel, short stories, plays, and autobiographical prose, and she has edited several collections of poetry by Canadian women. Her own poetry has undergone many transformations over the course of her six-decade career: Livesay began as an imagist, but in the 1930s, influenced by W. H. Auden, she began to write political and social verse, and in the 1950s she adopted a lyrical, intimate style. She has identified her primary concerns as "love and . . . relationships between lovers, parents, children" and "achieving the just society."

Douglas Livingstone (1932–)

Douglas Livingstone was born in Kuala Lumpur, Malaya, and raised in Africa after the age of ten. He was educated at schools in Malaya, Australia, and South Africa, and attended Kearney College in Natal, South Africa. He studied pathogenic bacteriology at the Pasteur Institute in Salisbury, Rhodesia, and worked at the Pathological Laboratory at the General Hospital in Zambia from 1959 until 1963, before becoming a marine biologist in Natal. Livingstone has published poetry, plays, several studies in marine biology, and translations of a wide variety of European poets. His work treats African themes and subjects drawn from nature, his powers of observation no doubt honed by his scientific study.

Thomas Lodge (1558–1625)

Thomas Lodge, the son of a lord mayor of London and his wife, was educated at Merchant Taylors' School and Trinity College, Oxford. He entered Lincoln's Inn to study law in 1578, but soon turned to writing; in 1580, he wrote a "Defence" of plays in response to Stephen Gosson's attack on the theater in *The School of Abuse* (1579). Gosson answered Lodge in another pamphlet, and in 1584 Lodge retorted with a lively attack on the usurers; in this work he depicted the dangers that money lenders presented for young spendthrifts. Himself short of funds, he joined several voyages to the New World. During one, he wrote *Rosalynde, Euphues Golden Legacy* (1590), a prose romance with verse interludes that is the source for Shakespeare's *As You Like It*. Lodge returned from a later voyage with another prose romance interspersed with many lyrics, *A Margarite of America*. He translated many French love lyrics (for instance, from Pierre Ronsard's *Amours*), and after his conversion to Catholicism in 1600 translated prose works by ancient authors such as Seneca and the Jewish historian Josephus. Having turned away from secular poetry after his conversion, Lodge became a noted physician in London.

Henry Wadsworth Longfellow (1807–1882)

Henry Wadsworth Longfellow was born in Portland, Maine (then part of Massachusetts). He was educated at Bowdoin College, where Nathaniel Hawthorne was a classmate, and where he delivered a speech at graduation calling for a national literature. He spent three years in Europe studying foreign languages and, upon his return, was appointed professor of modern languages at his alma mater. In 1835 he accepted a similar position at Harvard University, where he remained until 1854, when he devoted himself to writing. He already had attained fame before the publication of his first book in 1839, and later works such as *Evangeline* (1847) and *The Song of Hiawatha* (1855) were hugely popular. In 1843 he became partially blind, and in 1861 he was badly injured as he tried to extinguish the flames that, when her dress caught fire, burned his second wife to death. Longfellow translated Dante, as well as many poets he collected in his anthology *The Poets and Poetry of Europe* (1845). He also wrote fiction and verse drama. Greatly beloved in his day, though his reputation later declined, Longfellow has been credited with popularizing American themes abroad and bringing European themes home. His greatest strengths lay in his mastery of rhythm, his gift for narrative, and his ability to evoke the poetic qualities of everyday things.

Michael Longley (1939–)

Michael Longley was born in Belfast, Northern Ireland, and educated at Trinity College, Dublin, where he read Classics. He worked as a schoolteacher until 1970, when he joined the Arts Council of Northern Ireland. Under the council's auspices, Longley compiled an anthology of verse written by children. His preferred themes are landscape, love, grief, and family, and he focuses as much on the constricting aspects of home as on its tenderness. He writes precise descriptions of the everyday and commonplace, but his work sometimes enters the realm of the surreal. He writes taut, disciplined verse while consistently employing colloquial language.

Audre Lorde (1934–1992)

Audre Lorde was born in New York City to West Indian parents. She was educated at Hunter College and Columbia University, where she earned a master's degree in library science. In addition to working as a librarian, she taught at Tougaloo College and throughout the City University of New York system. She published numerous collections of poetry and two prose memoirs, one about her struggle with cancer and the other about her emergent lesbian identity. Although she once described herself as a "black lesbian feminist warrior poet," her contemporary Adrienne Rich added the appellations "mother," "daughter," and "visionary." In her poems, Lorde succeeded in conflating these several identities into a cohesive whole. Her work is informed by African mythology and history and by the "legends of . . . struggle and survival" embedded in the work of African-American writers such as Toni Morrison and Ralph Ellison. She employed loose, organic forms, organized by repetitions and propelled by the rhythms of natural speech.

Richard Lovelace (1618–1658)

Richard Lovelace was born in England to a wealthy Kentish family and was educated at the Charterhouse School and Gloucester Hall, Oxford. Handsome and witty, he lived the life of a cultured courtier before taking arms for the king in the Scottish expeditions of 1639–40. He was imprisoned by Parliament in 1642 for presenting a Royalist petition, and he was jailed again in 1648 after returning to England from battles where he had fought with the French against the Spanish. Although he was released from prison after the king's execution in 1649, Lovelace spent his final years in poverty. One of the group of Royalist writers now known as "Cavalier" poets, he was strongly influenced by Ben Jonson. Lovelace is best known for occasional poems and lyrics that were written mostly during his periods of imprisonment; his "To Althea, from Prison" regained popularity after its inclusion in Percy's *Reliques of Ancient English Poetry* (1765), as did his "To Lucasta, Going to the Wars." The name Lucasta (from *Lux casta* [Latin], "pure light") probably refers to Lucy Sacheverell, Lovelace's fiancée, who married another man after receiving a false report of Lovelace's death. She is honored in the title of Lovelace's one volume of poems published during his lifetime (*Lucasta*, 1649) and again in the posthumous collection published by Lovelace's brother (*Lucasta Poems Posthume*, 1659).

Amy Lowell (1874–1925)

Amy Lowell was born, in Brookline, Massachusetts, into one of Boston's most prominent families; the poet James Russell Lowell was a distant uncle, and the poet Robert Lowell a distant nephew. She was educated at home and mainly self-taught. From 1914 on she lived with the actress Ada Dwyer Russell, who inspired many of her poems. In addition to poetry, Lowell wrote a biography of John Keats and much influential criticism. Flamboyant and eccentric, she generously supported many struggling artists. In January 1913, after reading several poems by H. D. in the magazine *Poetry*, Lowell traveled to England to meet with the imagist circle. When the poet Ezra Pound left imagism for vorticism, she assumed leadership of the first group, which Pound later referred to derisively as "Amy-gism." Having sparked a revolution in her style, imagism changed under her direction, its poems becoming discursive and mystical and moving closer to free verse. Although Lowell is best remembered for her association with imagism—of which she edited three collections—she also popularized "polyphonic prose," which made use of such poetic methods as rhyme, alliteration, and assonance.

Robert Lowell (1917–1977)

Robert Lowell was born in Boston, Massachusetts, to a distinguished family; his ancestors include poets James Russell Lowell and Amy Lowell. Following his family's expectations, he attended Harvard University, but under the advice of the psychiatrist who treated him for the first of many breakdowns and manic episodes, transferred to Kenyon College. There he studied with poets John Crowe Ransom and Allen Tate, and met lifelong friends and literary mentors Peter Taylor and Randall Jarrell, in addition to his first wife, fiction writer Jean Stafford. After graduation from Kenyon, Lowell moved to Louisiana State University, where he worked with New Critics Robert Penn Warren and Cleanth Brooks. He was imprisoned as a conscientious objector during World War II, and his fiercely held Catholicism was central in his early, often oracular and opaque poetry. In the late 1950s he began writing in an autobiographical strain. The publication of *Life Studies* (1959) heralded his much freer prosody, as well as what would be called the confessional school of poetry. Later, partly influenced by John Berryman's *Dream Songs* (1964–77), Lowell wrote sonnet sequences in which he explored the events—failures and accomplishments—of his first fifty years. Lowell also was a controversially freehanded translator of poetry, a critical essayist, and the adaptor of several classic works for the stage. He held teaching appointments at a number of universities, including Harvard, Oxford, and Essex. At the time of his sudden death in a taxi, he was returning to his second wife, Elizabeth Hardwick, after breaking with his third, Lady Caroline Blackwood.

Malcolm Lowry (1909–1957)

Malcolm Lowry was born in Birkenhead, Cheshire, just outside of Liverpool (England). Before attending St. Catherine's College, Cambridge (from which he received a B.A.), he worked as a crew member on a freighter bound for China and on a ship sailing to Oslo. He lived in London and then Paris until 1935, when he moved to the United States, where he lived in Hollywood, and then to Cuernevaca, Mexico, which became the setting of his most famous novel, *Under the Volcano* (1947). From 1940 until 1954 he lived in a primitive cabin in Dollarton, British Columbia, and from 1954 until his death he lived in Italy and then England. Best known as a novelist, he wrote plays, film scripts, and hundreds of poems, only a handful of which were published during his lifetime. His poetry traces the course of his hopes and terrors, recording struggles with alcohol and drugs, probing painful themes such as desperation, isolation, and guilt.

John Lyly (1554–1606)

John Lyly, born in Kent (England), was the grandson of William Lyly, the humanist author of a famous Latin grammar book. Educated at Magdalen College, Oxford, and later at Cambridge, Lyly was employed for a while by Elizabeth's treasurer, Lord Burghley, and was appointed vice-master of the St. Paul's choristers. After supporting the Anglican bishops in the "Marprelate" controversy, he served several terms as a Member of Parliament and possibly hoped to obtain a place at court. He had gained fame as the author of a romance in two parts, *Euphues, or the Anatomie of Wit* (1578) and *Euphues and His England* (1580). Lyly also wrote several plays that combined classical and traditional English dramatic forms. The striking style of these works, which has given us the term "euphuism," entails an elaborate sentence structure marked by balance, antithesis, and alliteration, among other rhetorical effects, as well as fulsome use of imagery drawn mainly from the works of the ancient naturalist Pliny.

Norman MacCaig (1910–1996)

Norman MacCaig was born in Edinburgh, Scotland. He was educated at the University of Edinburgh, where he took a degree in Classics. During World War II he served time in prison as a conscientious objector. MacCaig was a primary school teacher until 1970, when he was appointed a lecturer (and later a reader) in poetry at the University of Stirling. His early work was heavily influenced by the New Apocalypse movement, in which he was a central figure, and which concerned itself with the relationship between art and the unconscious. He later repudiated his work in this mode and began what he called "the long haul back to lucidity." His later poems are generally succinct, tightly constructed, and "metaphysical" in the manner of John Donne's poetry, though most recently he had moved toward an even freer style, one less taken up with metaphor-making.

Hugh MacDiarmid (Christopher Murray Grieve) (1892–1978)

Hugh MacDiarmid was born in Langholm, Dumfriesshire, near the Scottish border. He worked on several local newspapers before joining the Royal Army Medical Corps in 1912. After serving in the Balkans and France, he was sent home with malaria in 1918, then resumed his career in journalism and became active in communist and Scottish nationalist politics, involvement in each movement bringing him difficulty with the other. Although he moved often and traveled frequently, he lived in Shetland and Lanarkshire for extended periods of time. MacDiarmid was a central figure of the Scottish Renaissance, a loose collection of artists, writers, and musicians dedicated to reinvigorating Scottish culture and countering the sentimentality and insipidness that had crept into the arts since the time of Robert Burns. He wrote many of his early poems in "Lallans," a synthesized language culled from the dialects of several regions of Scotland—"an inexhaustible quarry of subtle and significant sound," as he put it. His linguistic experiments influenced those of, among others, James Joyce. In the 1930s he wrote politically committed poetry; from the 1940s on, he increasingly drew on philosophy, linguistics, and science. MacDiarmid worked in a wide range of styles with remarkable facility. His shorter poems are typically written in traditional meters and forms and employ regular rhyme, and his longer poems are in a looser style organized around a strong meter and carefully orchestrated music.

Archibald MacLeish (1892–1982)

Archibald MacLeish was born and raised in Illinois. He was educated at Yale University and Harvard Law School. During World War I, he volunteered to serve at the front. In the early 1920s he lived in Paris, and throughout the 1930s he served on the editorial board of *Fortune* magazine. MacLeish was influential in the upper echelons of American government under Franklin Delano Roosevelt and held the posts of Librarian of Congress and Assistant Secretary of State, among others. After leaving government, he taught at Harvard University. In addition to poetry, he wrote prose; verse plays, most famously *J.B.* (1957); radio plays; and the Oscar-winning screenplay for *The Eleanor Roosevelt Story* (1965). Like fellow modernists and expatriates Ezra Pound and T. S. Eliot, MacLeish looked deep into the literary past, hoping to salvage something of meaning to the present generation. Classical poets, the Elizabethans, and the Symbolists were among his sources and influences. In his later work, MacLeish attempted to reconcile the deep conflict between his famous dictum "A poem should not mean / but be" and his political commitment.

Louis MacNeice (1907–1963)

(Frederick) Louis MacNeice was born in Belfast, Ireland, and raised in Carrickfergus, whose landscape figures prominently in his work. He was educated at Marlborough College and later Merton College, Oxford, where he became a friend of poets W. H. Auden, Cecil Day Lewis, and Stephen Spender. After teaching Greek for several years, he worked as a script writer and producer for the BBC. He died from pneumonia after a recording session in a damp mine. Like his friend the poet John Betjeman, MacNeice eschewed the opacity of such modernists as T. S. Eliot and Ezra Pound, his immediate predecessors, in favor of accessibility, directness, and openness. He believed the poet ought to engage himself in the world rather than live in a rarified atmosphere, but he located himself in the realms of both the physical and the metaphysical, his work delighting in the sensuous while acknowledging and even mourning how quickly the sensuous vanishes.

Jay MacPherson (1931–)

Jay (Jean) MacPherson was born in England. When she was nine, her family emigrated to Canada and settled in Newfoundland. MacPherson was educated at Carleton College, McGill University, University College (London), and the University of Toronto, where she studied with the literary critic Northrop Frye and earned a Ph.D. She has been a member of the faculty at Toronto since 1957. MacPherson's first collection of poems, issued when she was twenty-one, was published by Robert Graves' Seizen Press; her next collection bears the imprint of her own press, Emblem Books. MacPherson employs traditional stanza forms and strict metrics. Her poems contain echoes of classical and biblical myth, Elizabethan verse, ballads, nursery rhymes, and fairy tales. Although they often have a fantastic quality, they pose sophisticated philosophical and metaphysical questions, recognizing and exploring the dark impulses in the psyche.

Derek Mahon (1941–)

Derek Mahon was born in Belfast, Northern Ireland, and read French at Trinity College, Dublin. After graduation, he traveled in France, Canada, and the United States, supporting himself through teaching and odd jobs. Since 1970, he has lived for extended periods in London and New York before returning, in 1996, to Ireland. He has worked as a scriptwriter for the BBC and a freelance writer and reviewer for a number of newspapers, and has been drama critic of the *Listener*, features editor of *Vogue*, and poetry and fiction editor of the *New Statesman*. In addition to poetry, Mahon has published translations of French writers including Molière and Philippe Jaccottet. In Mahon's poetry the commonplace reveals its beauty and mystery and provokes meditations on power, oppression, estrangement, loss, and hopelessness. Although his poems are deeply serious and often take up social and political themes, his work is also conversational, humorous, and witty.

Christopher Marlowe (1564–1593)

Christopher Marlowe was born in Canterbury, England, to an artisan family (his father was a successful shoemaker) and attended Corpus Christi College, Cambridge, on a fellowship designated for students preparing to become ministers. Marlowe, however, spent his university years writing plays (his tragedy, *Dido Queen of Carthage*, perhaps written with Thomas Nashe, apparently dates from the 1580s) and working as a spy abroad; when university officials wanted to deny Marlowe his M.A. in 1587, the Privy Council intervened, citing his service to the queen in "matters touching the benefit of his country." His contacts at court also seem to have intervened on his behalf in 1589, when he was involved in a murderous brawl but only briefly imprisoned; in 1592, when he was arrested for counterfeiting coins in the Netherlands but spared imprisonment; and again in 1593, when he was arrested on suspicion of dangerous religious views, having been denounced by his onetime friend Thomas Kyd for atheism and treason. Despite his wild life, he found time for writing: in the same year that he received his Cambridge M.A., his enormously popular play *Tamburlaine* was produced on the London stage; a sequel soon followed, and in both plays Marlowe used a powerfully rhetorical blank-verse line to explore a character driven by passionate ambition to rule the world. In his other plays, too, including *The Jew of Malta* and *Doctor Faustus*, a Marlovian hero-villain (often played by the great actor Edward Allyn) strives to fulfill his desires gloriously, amorally, and against great odds—and fails in the end. In his chronicle history play *Edward II*, Marlowe depicted the king's homoerotic love for his favorite, Gaveston, with boldness and subtlety. In addition to writing his seven plays, Marlowe translated from the Latin Ovid's *Amores* and Lucan's *Pharsalia* (about the Roman civil wars) and wrote the erotic mythological poem *Hero and Leander*, which was entered in the Stationers' Register in September 1593, just a few months after the poet's mysterious death from a knife wound in a barroom brawl. His short lyric "The Passionate Shepherd to His Love" was immensely popular, and many later poets, including Sir Walter Ralegh, John Donne, and Robert Herrick, wrote replies to it.

Dionisio D. Martinez (1956–)

Dionisio D. Martinez was born in Cuba. Following his family's exile from their homeland in 1965, he lived in northern Spain and southern California. He settled in Tampa, Florida, in 1972 and currently works as a poet in the schools, an affiliate writer at the University of Tampa, and a collaborating artist with the YMCA National Writer's Voice Project. His work frequently explores feelings of exile and mourns loss, but takes solace in language and in the work of such artists as Alfred Stieglitz and Marcel Duchamp. Despite their painful themes, his poems convey a sense of wonder that recalls the work of Frank O'Hara. Martinez works in relaxed meters and fairly regular forms, which give shape and rigor to his colloquial diction.

Andrew Marvell (1621–1678)

Andrew Marvell was born in Yorkshire, England, son of a Calvinist minister and his wife; moved to Hull on his father's appointment as lecturer at Holy Trinity Church; and was educated at Hull Grammar School and Trinity College, Cambridge. He spent the Civil War years touring Europe, finding "the Cause too good to have been fought for," and on his return moved in London literary circles, befriending, among others, John Milton and Richard Lovelace. From 1650 until 1652 he tutored the daughter of the Parliamentarian General Fairfax; at Fairfax's house, Nun Appleton in Yorkshire, Marvell wrote a number of poems about gardens and rural life, including the famous "country house" poem "Upon Appleton." He became Oliver Cromwell's unofficial laureate, and in 1657 replaced Milton as secretary to the Council of State. In 1659 he became a member of Parliament for Hull and adroitly managed to retain that seat after the Restoration. He fought for toleration of religious dissenters in verse and prose satires, many published anonymously, and some attacking the king's corrupt ministers and even the king himself. Most of Marvell's poems were not published until after his death, the lyrics in 1681, the satires in 1689, after the "Glorious Revolution."

The Massachusetts Bay Psalm Book

The *Bay Psalm Book*, also known as *The Whole Booke of Psalmes Faithfully Translated into English Metre*, was the authoritative hymnal of the Massachusetts Bay Colony and the first book published in America (1640). Translated by Richard Mather, John Eliot, and Thomas Weld, this work replaced a version produced in England that the Bay Puritans felt to be corrupted by the translators' willingness to employ poetic license in their renderings. The Puritan translators, by contrast, took scrupulous pains to render the poems as they appeared in the original, devoid of added ornamentation. "God's Altar needs not our Polishings," John Cotton declared in his preface to the work. The book enjoyed a wide circulation for nearly a century and was reprinted numerous times.

Harry Mathews (1930–)

Harry Mathews was born in New York City. After serving in the United States Navy from 1948 to 1949, he studied at Princeton and Harvard universities. Matthews has taught at Bennington College and Columbia University, among other schools, but has lived primarily in France. Known for his experimental novels as well as his offbeat but ingenious verse, he is often associated with New York school poets such as John Ashbery, Kenneth Koch, and James Schuyler, and he belongs to the Oulipo, a writers' association in Paris whose members are engaged in inventing new compositional methods. Although his poems show a narrative impulse, their primary aim is to engage the reader in the pleasurable activity of reading. Often humorous, his work is characterized by a rare combination of technical virtuosity—usually found in more conventional poets—and radical disjunctions of surface and subject.

John McCrae (1872–1918)

John McCrae was born in Guelph, Ontario, and educated at the University of Toronto. An accomplished physician and researcher, he practiced medicine at several hospitals in the United States and Canada and frequently published in highly regarded medical journals. McCrae served as a medical officer in the Canadian Army during the Boer War and World War I. In the latter, he was initially stationed at the front in France, then transferred to a military hospital in Boulogne, where he contracted a fatal case of double pneumonia. He published only a handful of poems in his lifetime and is best remembered for "In Flanders Field," which he composed during the second battle of Ypres. The poem, a call to courage and duty, was frequently invoked by military recruiters in the United States; blood-smeared copies of it were found in the breast pockets of many fallen soldiers. The poem is sometimes still memorized by schoolchildren and read aloud during Remembrance Day ceremonies.

Herman Melville (1819–1891)

Herman Melvill (the *e* was added in the 1830s) was born and raised in New York City. He left school at age fifteen to help support his family. In 1839 he sailed to Liverpool as a cabin boy, and this voyage inculcated in him an enduring love for the sea. In 1841 he sailed on a whaler, but jumped ship in the Marquesas Islands. Captured by cannibalistic natives, he escaped and went to Tahiti, where he worked as a field laborer, and Honolulu, where he enlisted as a seaman. In 1843 he returned home and began writing romantic novels based on his exotic adventures. His early work sold well and won him a wide following, but Melville himself thought little of it. His masterpieces, including the novel *Moby-Dick* (1851), were critical and commercial failures, and his poems, which he began writing in the 1870s, were largely ignored. In 1866 Melville went to work as a customs inspector in New York City, and he died in near obscurity and dire poverty. The Civil War had made Melville a poet (as the poet and critic Robert Penn Warren put it), in that it gave him a subject of magnitude and complexity. In his war poems (*Battle Pieces*, 1866), Melville explores the equivocal nature of experience. Later poems record his frustrated meditations on the mysterious natures of time and fate.

George Meredith (1828–1909)

George Meredith was born in Portsmouth, England. He received little education except for two years at a Moravian academy at Neuweid. In 1845 he was apprenticed to a lawyer, but found the work uncongenial. Needing money, he turned to journalism, then to publishing; he was a reader for Chapman and Hall from 1860 until 1895. In 1864 Meredith settled in Flint Cottage at Box Hill, Surrey. Like his admirer Thomas Hardy, he was better known for his novels than for his poetry, but preferred the latter to the former. His most enduring work of verse is *Modern Love* (1862), a cycle of fifty sonnets about the breakup of a marriage. Its inception was autobiographical — Meredith's marriage to the widowed daughter of Thomas Love Peacock collapsed in 1857 — but Meredith significantly changed real events and drafted protagonists distinct from himself and his wife for the work. Written in a sixteen-line stanza form developed by Meredith that employs iambic pentameter and a strict rhyme scheme, it shares the merits of all Meredith's successful work: acute psychological insight, a skillful narrative line, and incisive dialogue. Including dramatic imagery, biblical diction, and poetic conventions from the pastoral and courtly love traditions, and making reference to sources as diverse as Darwinian theory (*The Origin of Species* was published just three years before) and medieval legend, *Modern Love* has influenced such works as Robert Lowell's *The Mills of the Kavanaughs* and W. D. Snodgrass's *Heart's Needle*.

William Meredith (1919–)

William Meredith was born in New York City and was educated at Princeton University. After working as a reporter for *The New York Times* in the early 1940s, he spent five years in the armed forces, mainly as a naval aviator in the Pacific theater of World War II. During the academic career that followed, he taught at, among other schools, Princeton, the University of Hawaii, and Connecticut College. He has been an opera critic for the *Hudson Review*, poetry consultant to the Library of Congress, and a chancellor of the Academy of American Poets. In addition to poetry, he has published criticism and a libretto; he has edited several collections of poetry; and he has translated the poetry of Guillaume Apollinaire.

James Merrill (1926–1995)

James Merrill was born and raised in New York City, a son of Charles Merrill, founding partner of the Merrill Lynch investment firm. He was educated at Amherst College. Near the end of World War II he interrupted his studies to serve a year with the United States Army. In 1954 he settled in Stonington, Connecticut, and eventually divided his time between Connecticut and Florida, although he spent long periods in Greece. In addition to poetry, he published novels, plays, a collection of criticism, and a memoir. Widely admired from the outset of his career, Merrill achieved a major breakthrough in the 1960s, developing a poetic that was autobiographical without being "confessional." Comfortable working in many modes and in a wide range of traditional forms and meters, he controlled his material through an elegant, witty, highly wrought style that reflected the influence of Marcel Proust and Henry James. Throughout his oeuvre, he skillfully employed irony and word play, masterfully combining literary allusions with material from his day-to-day existence. His epic *The Changing Light at Sandover* (1977–1982), a seventeen-thousand-line trilogy, is one of the major achievements of twentieth-century poetry.

W. S. Merwin (1927–)

W(illiam) S(tanley) Merwin was born in New York City and raised in Union City, New Jersey, and Scranton, Pennsylvania. He was educated at Princeton University, where he studied with the poets John Berryman and R. P. Blackmur. He later traveled through Europe, and in Mallorca, Spain, was a tutor to the poet Robert Graves' son. For several years he worked as a translator at the BBC in London, and from 1951 until 1953 he was poetry editor at *The Nation*. He has since lived in, among other places, Mexico and France, and currently resides in Hawaii. In addition to poetry, Merwin has

written several plays, and has translated Latin, Greek, French, Spanish, Chinese, and Japanese poetry into English. His early work relied heavily on legend and mythology, and it demonstrated his virtuosity with difficult meters and forms. He has since moved to an autobiographical mode and a freer style; these poems eschew punctuation and capitalization and divide lines into phrases that approximate breaths.

Charlotte Mew (1869–1928)

Charlotte Mew was born in London and educated at home. She worked as a teacher for a time after her father's death and lived briefly in Paris. In her thirties, Mew wrote short stories; in her forties, she turned to poetry. Her work was much admired by, for instance, the poets John Masefield, Walter de la Mare, and Thomas Hardy, who became a close friend and once called her "far and away the best living woman poet." Her adult years were punctuated by difficulty and sadness. She watched two siblings succumb to madness and was herself institutionalized in 1927. She committed suicide a short time later. Reminiscent of Robert Browning and the young Robert Frost, she often wrote narrative poems or dramatic monologues that, while formal in construction, imitate the rough, even awkward, rhythms of natural speech and amount to psychological studies of the lonely and eccentric figures who speak them. Her most common subjects were madness, isolation — both physical and spiritual — failed relationships, ephemerality, and death. Her tone typically ranged from melancholic to elegiac, yet was restrained; deep pain lurks beneath the objective, conversational surface of her poems.

Edna St. Vincent Millay (1892–1950)

Edna St. Vincent Millay was born in Rockland, Maine. In 1912 she gained national attention when her precocious poem "Renascence" was published in *The Lyric Year*, an anthology of contemporary poetry. After graduation from Vassar College in 1917, Millay moved to Greenwich Village, where her literary reputation quickly flourished, and where she associated with many of the prominent artists, writers, and political radicals of her day, including the poets Hart Crane and Wallace Stevens, the playwright Eugene O'Neill, the editor Max Eastman, and the critic Edmund Wilson. In 1925 she settled with her husband in Austerlitz, New York, where she lived for the rest of her life. Millay captured the fleeting passions of her war-torn generation in poems employing nineteenth-century diction and traditional forms, yet she also excelled at free verse. From fairly commonplace materials she forged a means of personal expression, placing considerable emotional intensity beneath the unperturbed surfaces of her verse and tempering that intensity with archness and wit.

John Milton (1608–1674)

John Milton was born in London, son of Sara and John Milton. The latter earned his living by composing music and working as a "scrivener," that is, drawing up contracts and performing other business tasks requiring writing. The young Milton was educated at St. Paul's School and Christ's College, Cambridge, where he received his B.A. in 1629 and his M.A. in 1632, and where his "niceness of nature" and "honest haughtiness" (and, perhaps, his flowing locks), earned him the nickname "the lady of Christ's." According to his own testimony in the volume of the early poems he published (and carefully arranged) in 1645, his earliest poetic endeavors were two paraphrases of Psalms done when he was fifteen. During his university years Milton wrote various poems in both English and Latin, and his 1645 book opens with "On the Morning of Christ's Nativity," written in 1629, while he was still at Cambridge. From 1632 until 1638 he lived at his parents' house, studying and writing, supported by his father. During this period he wrote his masque, *Comus*, in collaboration with the musician Henry Lawes; performed in 1634, it was not published under Milton's name until 1645. His first published poem was "On Shakespeare," an epitaph printed in the Second Folio (1632) of Shakespeare's plays. In November of 1637, the year his mother died, Milton published his pastoral elegy "Lycidas" in a volume memorializing Edward King, a Cambridge student who had drowned. In 1638 Milton traveled to France and then to Italy, where he met, among others, the astronomer and physicist Galileo. Upon returning to an England entering the era of political and religious conflict known as the Civil Wars, he began the career as political writer that led him to advocate freedom of divorce (in pamphlets published soon after Milton's own hasty marriage, to Mary Powell, had failed in 1642); freedom from censorship of the press (*Areopagitica*, 1644); and freedom from what he and others considered tyranny. An ardent supporter of Oliver Cromwell's republican regime, Milton supported the execution of King Charles in 1649 and became Cromwell's "Secretary for foreign tongues" that same year. As an official defender of the new regime, Milton wrote many prose tracts during the 1650s, despite having become completely blind by 1652, the same year that Mary (who had returned to him in 1645, and with whom he had three daughters) died. He remarried in 1655 to Katherine Woodstock, but she died in childbirth in 1658. With the restoration of the monarchy in 1660, Milton was in danger of execution; friends, including the writer Andrew Marvell, intervened, and Milton was able to return to writing poetry during his final years. In 1633 he married a third time, in 1667 he published *Paradise Lost*, and in 1671 he published a volume containing his "brief epic," *Paradise Regained*, and his closet drama *Samson Agonistes*.

N. Scott Momaday (1934–)

N. Scott Momaday was born in Lawton, Oklahoma, a member of the Kiowa Native American tribe. He was educated at the University of New Mexico and Stanford University, from which he received a Ph.D. Since then he has taught at Stanford, the University of California at Santa Barbara, the University of California at Berkeley, and the University of Arizona at Tucson. Known primarily as a novelist, he is also a landscape artist. Although his work is rooted in the Native American literary tradition, it reveals broader influences. He writes in a plain style, frequently in an epigrammatic mode, often in rhyme and syllabics. Believing that "words are powerful beyond our knowledge" and contain an element of magic, he acknowledges their musicality through rhyme, assonance, and consonance.

Lady Mary Wortley Montagu (1689–1762)

Lady Mary Wortley Montagu was born Lady Mary Pierrepont, daughter of a wealthy Whig peer who became duke of Kingston in 1715 and of Lady Mary Fielding, who died when her daughter was thirteen. Educated at home, Lady Mary taught herself Latin. In 1712, she eloped with Edward Wortley Montagu, whom she followed to Turkey when he was appointed ambassador to Constantinople in 1716. Her letters from her travels were witty and immensely popular. On her return to England in 1718 she popularized the practice of inoculation against smallpox. She left England again in 1739, largely to escape her by then loveless marriage, and lived in Europe, mostly Italy, for the rest of her life, returning home only to die. She was connected to most of contemporary literary London: the novelist Henry Fielding was her second cousin; the poet Alexander

Pope was initially a friend, but after she spurned a declaration of love, he bitterly mocked her in *The Dunciad* and "Epistle to a Lady." Joseph Addison and Sir Richard Steele, founders of the *Spectator*, were her first publishers, and the writers William Congreve and John Gay were acquaintances. In "Epistle from Mrs. Yonge to Her Husband," she critiques sexual inequality and advises women trapped in loveless marriages to take lovers, as she had in her later years.

John Montague (1929–)

John Montague was born in Brooklyn, New York, where his Irish parents had fled in 1920 to avoid prosecution for Republican activities (his father had reputedly burned the homes of absentee landlords), and was brought up by his aunts on a farm in Garvaghey, County Tyrone, Northern Ireland. He was educated at University College, Dublin, Yale University, and the Universities of Iowa and California at Berkeley. He worked as a journalist before becoming a lecturer in poetry at University College, Cork, and he has been a visiting lecturer at several institutions in the United States, Europe, and Britain. While literary director of Claddagh Records (from 1962 until 1975), he organized recordings of poets such as Robert Graves, Seamus Heaney, Thomas Kavanagh, Thomas Kinsella, and Hugh MacDiarmid. In addition to poetry, Montague has published short stories, a play, and a novella, and has translated Gaelic writing and edited collections of Irish verse. His skillful cadences and assonance convey a sense of the melodic speech patterns of Irish. Like his antecedents Yeats and Joyce, Montague depicts Ireland as maiden and hag, variously repellent and attractive; explores the encroachment of modern life on ancient culture; displays affection for country people and their traditions; and expresses nostalgia for Ireland's past greatness.

Marianne Moore (1887–1972)

Marianne Moore was born in Kirkwood, Missouri, and was raised in Carlisle, Pennsylvania. After receiving a degree in biology from Bryn Mawr College, she took business courses at Carlisle Commercial College, taught business skills and commercial law at the U.S. Industrial Indian School in Carlisle, and traveled to Europe with her mother. Moore lived all her adult life with her mother, first in New Jersey, then in New York City's Greenwich Village (where she met leaders of the avant-garde), then in Brooklyn. Her first collection of poetry, *Poems* (1921), was brought out by the writers H. D., whom she had befriended at Bryn Mawr, and Bryher (Winifred Ellerman). Although she devoted most of her energies to writing poetry and criticism, Moore worked variously as a teacher, a secretary, and a librarian, and she edited the influential modernist magazine *Dial* from 1925 until 1929, when it ceased publication. In her poetry, she united precise and even scientific observation with ornate diction and complex stanza forms, using elaborate patterns of internal and end rhyme and strict syllable counts. The poet William Carlos Williams likened the "edge-to-edge contact" between things in Moore's poems to Picasso's cubist portraits and the swift movement from image to image to Emily Dickinson's poetry. Her work is as innovative as Picasso's and as passionate as Dickinson's, yet this thoroughly modern verse is marked overall by a formality so carefully wrought that it constitutes a moral vision, a statement concerning the proper balance of feeling and form.

Dom Moraes (1938–)

Dom(inic) Moraes was born in Bombay, India. He moved to England in 1954 and matriculated at Jesus College, Oxford, then published his first collection of poetry at nineteen. He has been a journalist, scriptwriter, and editor; has worked for the United Nations Fund for Populations; and has served as an honorary colonel with the United States Army in Vietnam. He eventually returned to India, where he married the actress Leela Naidu. In addition to poetry, Moraes has published an acclaimed prose autobiography and collections of essays on writing and on life in India and Pakistan. In its direct manner of address and themes of exile, failed love, and wasted time, his early work resembles his mentor W. H. Auden's. He later took up public themes, including politics and human rights. From 1965 to 1982, he wrote virtually no poetry at all, but in the early 1980s began writing in a wholly new style characterized by disillusionment, world-weariness, and sagacity.

Hannah More (1745–1833)
Hannah More was born in Stapleton, Gloucestershire, England, the daughter of Jacob More, a master of a Free School, and his wife, Mary Grace, a farmer's child. Sent to the boarding school opened in Bristol by her three older sisters, she there learned French, Italian, Spanish, and Latin, and eventually joined the staff. A year after the publication of her first play, *The Search for Happiness* (1773), her tragedy *The Inflexible Captive* was printed with a postscript by the famous actor David Garrick. More had met Garrick during a visit to London in 1774; she later met Samuel Johnson, Johnson's biographer James Boswell, Sir Joshua Reynolds, and other important London men of letters. She was also introduced to the "Bluestockings," a circle of women centered on Elizabeth Montagu (1720–1800). Although More became a popular and respected dramatist, she gradually moved from secular to religious and didactic writing and became a popular advocate of social reform in education and the relief of poverty. In her poem "Slavery," she argued that the captives about to be sold into slavery are in no way inferior to their captors. At her death she left £30,000 to more than seventy charities.

Edwin Morgan (1920–)
Edwin Morgan was born in Glasgow, Scotland, and educated at the University of Glasgow, interrupting his studies to serve in the Royal Army Medical Corps, but returning in 1947 as a lecturer. He was a visiting professor at Strathclyde University from 1987 until 1990. Morgan has translated *Beowulf* as well as the work of numerous poets, including several Latin Americans whose magical-realist mode has influenced his own work. He has also published many essays and reviews and has edited several collections of poetry, prose, and drama. He writes in a variety of modes: comedic, dialogic, narrative, parodic, satiric, and surrealistic. He is best known for his ingenious experimental and "concrete" poems, but also works in traditional forms. His themes and subjects are equally diverse, springing from the real world and the present moment, and his settings range from his native city to surreal, even apocalyptic landscapes inspired by his study of science fiction and of the New Apocalypse writers.

William Morris (1834–1896)
William Morris was born in Walthamstow, England, and educated at Exeter College, Oxford, where he became lifelong friends with the painter and designer Edward Burne-Jones. Their circle was strongly influenced by the Pre-Raphaelite school, which they encountered in about 1854. After graduation from Oxford, Morris joined an architectural firm, but left to paint and to design the furnishings for which the company he founded, Morris, Marshall, Faulkner and Co. (later Morris and Co.) is still famous. Producing his own furniture out of

frustration at not being able to find anything suitable for the striking Red House designed for him by Philip Webb, Morris started a revival of the decorative arts and a revolution in Victorian taste. He founded the Society for the Preservation of Ancient Buildings, joined the Social Democratic Federation, on its dissolution assumed the leadership of the Socialist League, and wrote and lectured for the cause of socialism with unflagging enthusiasm. As a poet (and a translator) Morris drew on the traditions of Icelandic, Anglo-Saxon, and classical literature. He combined the two strands of his talent in 1891 when he founded the Kelmscott Press at Kelmscott Manor (which he shared with Dante Gabriel Rossetti), producing books designed for beauty rather than for economy.

Howard Moss (1922–1987)
Howard Moss was born in New York City. He received his undergraduate education at the University of Michigan and Wisconsin University and did postgraduate work at Harvard and Columbia Universities. During World War II he served in the War Information Office, and between 1945 and 1948 he was an editor at *Time* magazine and the *Junior Bazaar*. In 1948 he joined the staff of *The New Yorker*, where he served as poetry editor for nearly forty years and helped establish the reputations of a wide range of poets, including Theodore Roethke, Elizabeth Bishop, Amy Clampitt, Donald Justice, James Merrill, Galway Kinnell, John Ashbery, Anne Sexton, Sylvia Plath, and Mark Strand. Considered one of the preeminent figures in twentieth-century American letters, he published poetry, light verse, plays, and criticism and edited several anthologies of poetry. He also taught at, among other schools, Barnard College and Columbia University. Renowned for his technical ingenuity in established forms, he also wrote in freer styles. His poetry moved among the realist, surrealist, comic, and satiric modes.

Edwin Muir (1887–1959)
Edwin Muir was born in the Orkney Islands. In 1901, his family moved to Glasgow in search of work, but within five years both of his parents and two of his brothers had died due to the harsh conditions in the city's slums and sweatshops. Muir left school at the age of eleven and worked in a beer-bottling factory, several law offices, and a factory that burned bones to charcoal. In 1919 he moved to London and began a literary career. From 1921 until 1956 he moved around Europe, England, and Scotland, eventually settling in Cambridgeshire, England. Muir often wrote in a narrative mode, and many of his poems take the form of dream-journeys that move forward in or back through time. He derived much of his imagery from the vanished landscapes of his childhood and was particularly fascinated with the myth of Eden and humanity's expulsion from the Garden. Muir is also known for his vivid descriptions of a post-apocalyptic world.

Paul Muldoon (1951–)
Paul Muldoon was born in Portadown, County, Armagh, Northern Ireland, and was raised in The Moy, a small village featured prominently in many of his poems. He was educated at Queen's University, Belfast, where he met Seamus Heaney, Michael Longley, and other poets of the Belfast "Group." Muldoon worked for the BBC in Belfast until the mid-1980s, when he became a freelance writer and moved to the United States, where he has taught at a number of institutions. In addition to poetry, he has written a children's book and has translated Gaelic verse and collaborated on the opera *Shining Brow*. His poems are humorous, but

their themes tend to be grim: "The Troubles" (to which he refers obliquely), warfare, oppression, mortality, futile attempts to recapture the past, and the commerce between lovers. Among the sources of their literary, historical, and cultural allusions are both Irish legend and Native American mythology, in particular journey and quest myths. Like his poetic models Edward Thomas and Robert Frost, he creates landscapes that transcend the literal to reflect moral and psychological concerns.

Les Murray (1938–)

Les Murray was born in the Nabiac, New South Wales (Australia), and raised on a dairy farm in nearby Bunyah. After studying arts and modern languages at the University of Sydney, he worked as a translator of foreign scholarly and technical materials at the Australian National University before embarking on a career as a freelance writer. He has been writer-in-residence at various institutions. In 1975 he repurchased part of the family farm in Bunyah, and in 1985 he returned there to live. An exceptionally prolific writer, he has published, in addition to poetry, several collections of critical essays and an acclaimed verse novel. He has been coeditor of *Poetry Australia*; poetry editor of Angus & Robertson; and, since 1991, literary editor of *Quadrant*. He compiled *The New Oxford Book of Australian Verse* and *The Anthology of Australian Religious Verse*. His work is by turns meditative, narrative, and declamatory, but his concerns have remained consistent: family, folklore, landscape, and history. He simultaneously displays reverence for the Bushland, Aborigines, and Aboriginal culture; respect for pioneers like his own ancestors, who came to Australia in the 1840s; and admiration for what has become the characteristic Australian temperament—independent, egalitarian, easygoing, pragmatic, and laconic. Murray works in a style uniquely his own—vernacular, loquacious, accessible, freeflowing, at once public and intimate.

Ogden Nash (1902–1971)

Ogden Nash was born in Rye, New York. He attended Harvard University for one year, then taught French, sold bonds—he often joked that he sold just one, to his godmother—and wrote copy for streetcar advertisements before embarking on a literary career. Nash worked for Doubleday and Rinehart Presses, and in 1929 he joined the staff of the fledgling *New Yorker* magazine. In addition to writing poetry, Nash wrote children's books, collaborated on several musicals, the most successful of which was the Broadway hit *One Touch of Venus* (1943), and lectured across the country. Nash once defined "the vast Mississippi" of American humor as "a unique blend of three ingredients: one of these [is] a sort of illogical playfulness. . . . The second, more full-blooded, originated with the tall tales, the sly understatement and uproarious overstatement of the pioneers. . . . The third arrived with our Jewish immigrants, tired, sad, and gently cynical after generations of oppression." His work expertly combines all three strains and, in addition, is at times quite lyrical.

Thomas Nashe (1567–1601)

Thomas Nashe, the son of a poor curate and his wife, became a "sizar," or fellowship student, at John's College, Cambridge, and was graduated in 1586. After touring France and Italy, he joined the circle of London writers that included Robert Greene. His first published work, a preface to Greene's *Menaphon* (1589), was an indictment of contemporary drama and poetry; his second, *The Anatomy of Absurdity* (1589), attacked the artificiality of recent romances. He contributed pamphlets such as *An Almond for a Parrot* (1590) to the religious disputes known as the Martin Marprelate controversy and used his pen as a weapon on the side of, and probably in the pay of, Anglican bishops against Puritans. When Richard Harvey accused Nashe of presumption in writing the preface to *Menaphon*, Nashe replied with a tract called *Pierce Penniless his Supplication to the Devil* (1592). When Gabriel Harvey wrote a contentious description of the end of Robert Greene's life in *Four Letters* (1592), Nashe replied in *Four Letters Confuted* (1593). The exchange was finally ended, in 1599, by Episcopal decree and confiscation of the adversaries' publications. Nashe's other works include *The Unfortunate Traveler* (1594), which has been called the first "picaresque" novel in English, and the plays *Summer's Last Will* (1592) and (with Ben Jonson) *The Isle of Dogs* (1597), which was suppressed for its allegedly lewd and seditious content. Though his reputation was based on his stinging wit and his rhetorical skills (he coined many new words in his prose works), Nashe also wrote fine lyrics.

Howard Nemerov (1920–1991)

Howard Nemerov was born and raised in New York City. Upon graduation from Harvard University, he entered the Canadian Air Force to fight in World War II and later transferred to the United States Air Force. After the war he returned to New York and worked as an editor at *Furioso* magazine for one year. During the academic career that followed he taught at, among other schools, Hamilton College, Bennington College, Brandeis University, and (from 1969 on) Washington University. From 1963 until 1964 he served as consultant in poetry to the Library of Congress. Influenced by Yeats, Eliot, and Auden, Nemerov was known for his wit, his use of irony and paradox, and his mastery of form. Both his serious and his more humorous poems asked thorny questions, avoided facile answers, and thus addressed the limitations of human perception and intellect. In addition to poetry, he wrote fiction.

Norman Nicholson (1914–1987)

Norman Nicholson was born in Millom, Cumberland, in the Lake District of England. Except for the years 1930–32, which he spent in a sanitorium undergoing treatment for tuberculosis, he lived in Millom all his life, in a small apartment above the tailor shop where his father had worked. In addition to poetry, he wrote autobiography and several prose works about the Lake District. He also edited a selection of Wordworth's poetry. Nicholson identified his main theme as the "sense of community, of organic relationship between man and his environment"; continuity and change are also important themes in his work, the imagery of which is drawn predominantly from the Bible—at twenty-three he "reconverted" to Christianity—and the natural world. Though he wrote in traditional meters and forms, he often employed colloquial diction and conversational rhythms.

Bernard O'Donoghue (1945–)

Bernard O'Donoghue was born in Cullen, County Cork, Republic of Ireland, to a farmer and a teacher, and educated at Lincoln College, Oxford. He worked for a year as a systems analyst before becoming a lecturer in medieval English. He is now a fellow of Wadham College, Oxford. In addition to publishing collections of his own poetry and studies of medieval secular lyrics and the poetry of Seamus Heaney, he has edited the *Selected Poetry of Hoccleve* and compiled a collection of essays on the courtly love tradition. He has been an editor of the *English Review* since 1989. Although he spends most of the year in England, Ireland and Irish literature inform his work socially, linguistically, and historically. His poems, which usually employ regular meter, are unflinchingly honest and gently humorous, and are characterized by sharp observation, especially of the incongruous, sublime, or ridiculous in the midst of the mundane.

Frank O'Hara (1926–1966)

Frank O'Hara was born in Baltimore, Maryland, and raised in Grafton, Massachusetts. From 1944 until 1946 he served in the navy in the South Pacific. He was educated at Harvard and the University of Michigan, and in 1951 he settled in New York. A fringe member of the Beats and a central figure in the New York school of poets, whose practitioners included John Ashbery, Kenneth Koch, and James Schuyler, he enjoyed a long association with the Museum of Modern Art (where he served for a time as associate curator) and was friends with such abstract expressionist artists as Willem De Kooning, Jackson Pollock, and Franz Kline. He also edited Art News from 1953 until 1955. Like the painters he admired, O'Hara stressed the process of composition. His poems are filled with the bric-a-brac of contemporary life—hamburgers, malts, cigarettes, coffee, and the like—and pay tribute to popular figures such as Billie Holiday. His work also contains a strongly autobiographical element, and its tone is simultaneously exuberant, sophisticated, and campy.

Charles Olson (1910–1970)

Charles Olson was born in Worcester, Massachusetts, and educated at Wesleyan, Harvard, and Yale Universities. In 1948 he began his association with the experimental Black Mountain College, which he directed from 1951 until it closed in 1956. During Olson's tenure, the composer John Cage, the choreographer Merce Cunningham, and the artist Franz Kline taught at the school; poets Robert Creeley, Robert Duncan, and Denise Levertov studied there; and writers Allen Ginsberg, Jack Kerouac, and Louis Zukofsky published early work in its influential magazine, The Black Mountain Review. In 1957 Olson settled in Gloucester, Massachusetts, and began work on the "Maximus" poems, which occupied him for the rest of his life. In a 1950 essay, Olson dubbed his poetry "Projective Verse." Believing that art "does not seek to describe but to enact," he attempted to convey in his work a sense of immediacy, action, and energy. He matched his lines to the length of a breath and abandoned traditional syntax for one he thought would better approximate "the rhythms of thinking, breathing, and gesturing."

Michael Ondaatje (1943–)

Michael Ondaatje was born in Colombo, Ceylon (now Sri Lanka), to parents of Sinhalese, Tamil, and Dutch origin, and, following the dissolution of their marriage, was raised in England from the age of nine. In 1962 he moved to Canada, where he studied at Bishop's University, the University of Toronto, and Queen's University. Ondaatje has taught at the University of Western Ontario and York University, has worked as an editor at Coach House Press, and has directed several films. In addition to poetry, he has written memoirs, plays, literary criticism, and highly acclaimed fiction. He also has edited a collection of long poems and several volumes of short stories. Ondaatje's poems explore the erotic, the ironic, and the pathetic: they typically depict emotional domestic situations as well as individuals at odds with society and themselves. His subjects are lifted from the realm of the personal through Ondaatje's skillful conflations of autobiography, history, folktale, and myth.

Much of his recent work is rife with discontinuities and ambiguities; it challenges readers to perceive existence as surreal, inchoate, and dynamic.

John Ormond (1923–1990)

John Ormond (Thomas) was born at Dunvant near Swansea, Glamorgan, Wales. He was educated at the University College of Swansea and studied drawing at the Swansea School of Art. After graduation, he worked as a journalist from 1945 until 1955, then joined the BBC as a television news assistant. He worked as a documentary filmmaker from 1957 until his retirement, and is best remembered for the series of films he produced on Welsh poets and writers. Ormond was first published in 1943, but grew increasingly dissatisfied with his poems and largely stopped writing until the 1960s, when new work showed that he had found a new voice. Ormond subsequently established himself as one of the foremost Welsh poets of his generation. His poems are typically rooted in his native Swansea: he creates interesting personae and compelling narratives that seem to derive from local folklore, and inserts himself into the distant past, which he renders vividly and convincingly. His main concerns include humanity's relationship to the past, to the natural world, to other humans, and to God.

Eric Ormsby (1941–)

Eric Ormsby was raised in Florida and later moved to Canada. He currently lives in Montreal and is director of libraries at McGill University. Displaying his remarkable powers of observation, his highly concentrated poems address "the loveliness of the familiar" and are exceptionally musical. A formalist but not a traditionalist, Ormsby uses rhyme intermittently and works in loose accentual verse.

Wilfred Owen (1893–1918)

Wilfred Owen was born in Oswestry, Shropshire, England. He left school in 1911, served as an assistant to a vicar in Oxfordshire, and taught English in Bordeaux. In 1915 he returned to England to enlist in the army and was sent to the front in France. Two years later, having been evacuated to the Craiglockhart War Hospital with shellshock, he met the poets Siegfried Sassoon and Robert Graves. After returning to combat in 1918, he was killed in action one week before the signing of the armistice. His war poems expose the horror of life in the trenches and satirize the blind jingoism of those who cheered the war from the comfort and safety of their parlors, but primarily they elegize the generation of young men who died on the plains of Europe. Although he claimed not to be concerned with "Poetry," his work is celebrated for its technical excellence and its poignance. His depiction of the subterranean world of the trenches hearkens back to Virgil's Underworld and Dante's Inferno; his haunting dreamscapes and spectral figures share similarities with the work of the symbolists; and his unique combination of beauty and terror is reminiscent of Percy Bysshe Shelley's poetry.

P. K. Page (1916–)

P. K. Page was born in Swanage, Dorset (England). Her family emigrated to Canada when she was three years old and settled in Red Deer, Alberta. After high school, Page worked as a shop assistant, a radio actress, a filing clerk, a researcher, and a scriptwriter. She then taught poetry at the Writers' Workshop in Toronto and at the University of Victoria. From 1942 until 1945 she worked on the editorial board of Preview magazine. From 1953 until 1964 she accompanied her husband, an ambassador, to Australia, Brazil, and Mexico, and while living abroad she resumed her earlier studies in painting. In addition to poetry, Page has written essays, short stories, a romance, and a memoir of her days in Brazil. Her earliest poems, rendered in a richly textured and highly allusive style that lent itself to irony and paradox, bear the mark of Auden and other socially conscious poets of the 1930s and 1940s. They satirize technology and regimentation, but are compassionate toward the isolated and dispossessed. Page subsequently adopted a sparer style and shifted her attention inward, and she now often explores metaphysical questions. Her concern with perspective, light, shadow, color, and shape reveals the powerful effect of the visual arts on her poetry.

Michael Palmer (1943–)

Michael Palmer was born and raised in New York City and educated at Harvard University. He has taught intermittently at several schools, such as the New College of California. In addition to writing poetry, Palmer has translated French literature and literary theory and has collaborated on books with painters and dancers. Like the artists and theorists he admires—including Gertrude Stein, Louis Zukofsky, Robert Creeley, and the Surrealists—Palmer in his work frequently examines the way in which words signify meaning. Like the Language poets, with whom he is associated, he regards the reader as a cocreator of his text. His poems are characterized by disjunctions and non sequiturs; an obliteration of the personality of the speaker; a resistance to conventional narrative structures, coherence, and closure; and an insistence on verbal play as an end in itself—all of which frequently lend his poetry an unusual humor.

Dorothy Parker (1893–1967)

Dorothy Parker was born and raised in New York City. Early in her career she worked for a number of prominent magazines, including Vogue, Vanity Fair, where she developed her reputation as an acerbic wit with a talent for bons mots, and The New Yorker, for which she wrote the popular "Constant Reader" column. In the 1930s she and her second husband, Alan Campbell, moved to Hollywood and wrote screenplays; with Lillian Hellman and Dashiell Hammett, Parker helped found the Screen Writers' Guild. In the 1920s and 1930s she became active in leftist politics—declaring herself a Communist and taking an early stand against Fascism and Nazism—for which she was blacklisted during the McCarthy era. An emancipated woman, considered one of the foremost wits of her day, Parker was celebrated for her short stories as for her poetry, but she spent her later years in isolation in New York. Disappointment and even despair lurk beneath the polished surfaces of her concise poems, which most often take up frustrated love and the shallowness of modern life.

George Peele (1557–1596)

George Peele was the son of James Peele, a clerk of Christ's Hospital who wrote pageants as well as a book on accounting, and his wife. After taking a B.A. and an M.A. from Oxford, Peele moved to London and made a bare living from writing pageants, plays, and poems. He is portrayed as a dissolute man-about-town in the anonymous book Merrie conceited Jests of George Peele (1607), but the portrait seems to bear little relation to Peele's actual life. While still at university, he translated the Iphigenia of Euripides, and he later may have worked as an actor in London. His first play, The Araygnment of Paris (ca. 1584), was performed before Elizabeth I and combines pastoral and debate, with songs interspersed. In this and other plays (including a historical one on Edward II that may predate Christo-

pher Marlowe's play on the same tragic king), Peele uses blank-verse lines and lyric interludes in ways that anticipate Shakespeare. Peele also used blank verse effectively in nondramatic poems, many of them published in Polyhymnia (1590) and The Honour of the Garter (1593).

Katherine Philips (1632–1664)

Katherine Philips, daughter of a London merchant and his wife, first went to school in Hackney (England), then moved to Pembrokeshire when her widowed mother remarried in 1646. Katherine was married to James Philips, thirty-eight years her senior, when she was sixteen, and spent twelve quiet years in Wales—the culture of which she celebrated in her poems on the Welsh language—while her husband served as a member of Oliver Cromwell's Parliament. Philips claimed that she "never writ a line in my life with intention to have it printed," but her poetry was being circulated before 1651, when Henry Vaughan eulogized her in his Olor Iscanus ("Swan of Usk," 1651). In 1655, her son Hector was born; when he died two weeks later, she lamented his death in an epitaph. Known as "the matchless Orinda" in her circle of friends and in the wider literary world, she named her school friend Mary Aubrey "Rosania" in several poems and addressed her friend Anne Owen as "Lucasia" in others. Despite being born, and having married, a Puritan, Philips had Royalist sympathies and contributed panegyrics to the returning monarchy, although her husband's fortunes declined after the Restoration. On a visit to Ireland in 1662, Philips translated Pierre Corneille's La Morte de Pompée, which was staged and printed in Dublin the next year. Though only her initials appeared on the title page, Philips gained fame, eventually becaming the best-known female poet of her age. An unauthorized edition of her poems (By the Incomparable Mrs. K. P.) appeared in 1664; suppressed four days later, it closely resembles the authorized edition published in 1667.

Robert Pinsky (1940–)

Robert Pinsky was born in Long Branch, New Jersey. He was educated at Rutgers University and Stanford University, where he studied under the poet Yvor Winters and earned a Ph.D. He has taught at Wellesley College, the University of California at Berkeley, and Boston University, and has served as poetry editor of The New Republic. In addition to his own poetry, Pinsky has published two volumes of criticism, a translation of Dante's Inferno, and translations (with Robert Hass) of the writings of Polish poet Czeslaw Milosz. Pinsky's work aims for discursiveness, morality, rationality, and temperateness. He draws much of his subject matter from the quotidian, in particular from his childhood, and his tone can be tender. He also has a strongly spiritual bent, which has resulted in rather mystical meditations. Although he readily modifies established forms to meet the demands of his materials, he works primarily in regular stanzas and frequently employs off-rhyme.

Sylvia Plath (1932–1963)

Sylvia Plath was born in Boston, Massachusetts. She was educated at Smith College and Newnham College, Cambridge, where she met her husband, the poet Ted Hughes. In 1953, following a month in New York City working as one of a dozen "Guest Editors" on the fashion magazine Mademoiselle, Plath suffered a bout of depression, attempted suicide, and was hospitalized for six months; these events form the gist of her novel, The Bell Jar (1963). In 1958 she attended Robert Lowell's verse-writing seminar at Boston University, where the poet Anne Sexton was a fellow student. In 1963, following the dissolution of her marriage, she suffered another bout of depression and committed suicide. Like Lowell and Sexton, Plath is generally considered a "confessional" poet. As personal as her poems are, however, they succeed because Plath transmutes autobiography into a representative account of agony, setting her personal, even generational drama against the backdrops of classical myth, nature, and history, and turning family members into archetypes. As Robert Lowell writes in his preface to *Ariel*, the posthumously published swansong that established her reputation, in her poems "Sylvia Plath becomes . . . one of those super-real, hypnotic, great classical heroines."

Edgar Allan Poe (1809–1849)

Edgar Poe was born in Boston to itinerant actors, orphaned in 1811, and then raised by John Allan, a Richmond merchant. He attended the University of Virginia for one year. When he ran up gambling debts his adoptive father withdrew support, and Poe enlisted in the army. Although he received an appointment to West Point, he found himself ill suited to military life and intentionally failed. He then embarked on a literary career, which took him to Baltimore, Richmond, Philadelphia, and New York. He won numerous prizes and published in respected journals, but earned too little money to survive; he and his young wife nearly starved and she died of tuberculosis in 1845. Poe, who had struggled long with mental instability and alcoholism, tried in 1849 to stop drinking, but he failed and died, probably of alcohol poisoning. Poe was more concerned with conveying mood—especially the melancholic—than idea; he considered poems "written solely for the poem's sake" superior to those written to convey, for instance, "the precepts of Duty." Holding beauty in such high esteem, he carefully crafted the form and music of his poems, which were highly original and were greatly appreciated by the French symbolists and other adherents of "pure poetry," such as Dante Gabriel Rossetti, Algernon Swinburne, and Ernest Dowson.

Alexander Pope (1688–1744)

Alexander Pope was born in London to a Catholic linen-draper and his wife. Debarred from university by his religion, he learned Greek, Latin, Italian, and French with the help of a local priest. At twelve he contracted a form of tuberculosis, probably Pott's Disease, which left his spine weakened, his growth stunted, and his health permanently damaged. His family moved to Binfield, in Windsor Forest, where at sixteen Pope composed his "Pastorals" (published 1709). His friend the playwright William Wycherley introduced him to London literary society, and his *Essay on Criticism* (1711) attracted the attention of Joseph Addison, though Pope was to leave Addison's circle for the "Sciblerus Club," which included John Gay, Jonathan Swift, and other writers. *The Rape of the Lock* appeared in 1712, and the first volume of his translation of the *Iliad* into heroic couplets followed in 1715. This, together with his translation of the *Odyssey* (1725–26), brought him financial security, and he moved to Twickenham, the Jacobite rebellion having made Catholics no longer welcome in the city center. The famous villa with its extensive grounds enabled Pope to indulge in gardening and landscaping in the new "picturesque" style. From there he wrote *The Dunciad* (1728–42, revised 1743), a satire on the alleged dullness of contemporary culture; the wittily and wickedly satirical "Epistle to Dr. Arbuthnot" (1735); and the *Essay on Man*, the first volume of a projected work in four books, reflecting Pope's interest in philosophical and intellectual speculation.

Peter Porter (1929–   )

Peter Porter was born in Brisbane, Australia, and educated at local grammar schools. He worked as a journalist and in the clothing industry before moving to London in 1951, where he worked as a clerk, a bookseller, and an advertising copywriter, and later served as a visiting lecturer at several English and Australian universities. During the 1950s, he was associated with the Group, a circle of poets who critiqued one another's work with the aim of achieving accessible verse. Porter has published several volumes of poetry and a collection of translations. His early work displays his gifts as satirist and tragedian. Typically positioned as an outsider in order to reflect upon "belonging," he sets his sights on sex, pretentious artists, and social posers. His work has become increasingly meditative, allusive, and complex, its wide and erudite range of reference including Baroque music and opera, Renaissance painting, and the Italian landscape.

Ezra Pound (1885–1972)

Ezra Pound was born in Hailey, Idaho, and raised in a suburb of Philadelphia. He was educated at Hamilton College and at the University of Pennsylvania, where he studied languages and became lifelong friends with the poet William Carlos Williams. In 1908 Pound moved to London, where he met the most prominent artists and writers of his day, including W. B. Yeats, for whom he worked as secretary. He also championed the careers of such promising writers as Robert Frost, T. S. Eliot, and James Joyce. Pound moved to Paris in 1920, and to Rapallo, Italy, in 1924. In 1930 he met the Italian dictator Benito Mussolini and began to write on economics and politics. During World War II he made a series of pro-Fascist and anti-Semitic radio broadcasts that culminated in an indictment for treason. Flown to the United States to stand trial, he was adjudged mentally unfit and sentenced to St. Elizabeth's Hospital for the Criminally Insane in Washington, D.C., where he remained until 1958. Upon his release he returned to Italy. In 1912, Pound, H. D., and Richard Aldington had launched imagism, a literary movement whose manifesto promised: "1. Direct treatment of the 'thing' whether subjective or objective. 2. To use absolutely no word that does not contribute to the presentation. 3. As regarding rhythm: to compose in the sequence of a musical phrase, not in sequence of a metronome." Soon dissatisfied with a slackness he saw creeping into the imagist movement, and increasingly influenced by avant-garde visual artists such as Wyndham Lewis, Pound moved on to vorticism, whose practitioners strove to depict dynamic energies rather than represent static images. In 1920, Pound's attempts to modernize his work, to "make it new," while preserving the best history had to offer, resulted in *Hugh Selwyn Mauberley*, whose foreign phrases, literary fragments, and abrupt shifts of scene anticipated Eliot's *The Waste Land* (1922), which Pound edited masterfully. The crowning achievement of his career is the *Cantos*, which he began to write in earnest in 1924 but never finished to his satisfaction. Both turgid and brilliant, the *Cantos* are "a mosaic of images, ideas, phrases—politics, ethics, economics—anecdotes, insults, denunciations—English, Greek, Italian, Provençal, Chinese," and so on, which attack the corruption Pound thought endemic to modern civilization. The poems follow no easily discernible pattern or line of logic. According to Pound, however, "the *forma*, the immortal *concetto*," or underlying organizing concept, is a dynamic one that might be compared to "the rose-pattern driven into the dead iron filings by the magnet."

E. J. Pratt (1883–1964)

E(dwin) J(ohn) Pratt was born in Western Bay, Newfoundland, Canada. An ordained Methodist minister, he taught and preached in several remote communities. Pratt held degrees in philosophy and theology from Victoria College, University of Toronto. He was a staff psychologist at the college until 1919, when he joined the English department, where he taught until his retirement in 1953. In 1936 he helped found, and until 1942 was an editor of, the *Canadian Poetry Magazine*, which launched the careers of many important Canadian poets. Pratt worked in traditional forms, and the sensibility in his early work is Romantic, the tone largely elegiac. Beginning in the 1930s, he moved outward and adopted a socially conscious stance. Pratt is best known for his "story-poems," in which conflict, struggle, and heroism are frequent themes.

Matthew Prior (1664–1721)

Matthew Prior was born in Wimborne, Dorset, England, the son of a joiner and his wife. Through the patronage of Lord Dorset he was educated at Westminster School, and with a scholarship from the duchess of Somerset went to St. John's College, Cambridge. He was secretary to the ambassador at The Hague, but turned Tory in Queen Anne's reign, acted as a secret agent, and was instrumental in bringing about the Treaty of Utrecht (1713), for which he was imprisoned for two years after the queen's death. He never held public office again, but Tory friends prevented his ruin by subscribing to a deluxe folio edition of Prior's work (1719). A gift of £4,000 from Lord Harley enabled him to buy Down Hall in Essex. Prior wrote in a variety of forms, including "Public Panegyrics, Amorous Odes, Serious Reflections, [and] Idle Tales," and defended his enjoyment of a range of verse forms thus: "He that writes in Rhimes, dances in Fetters: And as his Chain is more extended, he may certainly take larger steps."

Al Purdy (1918–)

Al(fred Wellington) Purdy was raised in Trenton, Ontario. He attended Albert College and the Trenton Collegiate Institute, but left school during the Depression and took up a number of odd jobs in cities across Canada. He served in the Royal Canadian Air Force during World War II, and subsequently conducted writing workshops at community arts centers and served as poet-in-residence at a number of Canadian universities. He currently lives at Roblin Lake, outside Trenton, in a home he built with his own hands. A prolific writer, Purdy has published some thirty volumes of verse, a historical novel, and a collection of loosely autobiographical essays. He also edited several books of verse and a colloquy of statements by Canadian writers on their conception of the United States. Most of his poems are set either in exotic locales or at Roblin Lake. Rendered with immediacy, they also resonate with echoes from the past, mixing the familiar with the historical and mythic.

Craig Raine (1944–)

Craig Raine was born in Bishop Aukland, County Durham, England. He was educated at Exeter College, Oxford, where he became a lecturer. He has worked for a number of journals and for ten years was poetry editor at Faber and Faber. Currently a fellow of New College, Oxford, Raine has written the libretto for the opera *The Electrification of the Soviet Union*, which was adapted from Pasternak's novella *The Last Summer*, and has adapted Racine's *Andromaque* for the stage. He is married to Pasternak's niece. His work is characterized by arresting, inventive metaphors that defamiliarize the commonplace, and the poet James Fenton has dubbed Raine and his followers "The Martian School," because poems such as "A Martian Sends a Postcard Home" have "taught us to become strangers in our familiar world, to release the faculty of perception." Raine's ingenious metaphors invite comparisons with the Metaphysicals, and the poems' precision and dynamism invite comparison with the imagists.

Sir Walter Ralegh (ca. 1552–1618)

Sir Walter Ralegh was born in Devonshire to a "gentle" but not wealthy family and was educated at Oriel College, Oxford, and became a favorite of Queen Elizabeth, whom he praised in many poems. He was renowned for his courage as a sailor, soldier, and explorer as well as for his eloquence and courtly wit. He lost the queen's favor when he seduced and married one of her maids of honor in 1592. She nonetheless gave him a royal patent to pursue an ill-fated search for gold in Guiana in 1595. Earlier, he had directed the colonization of Virginia, which he had named after his queen; he introduced tobacco from the colony to England. After Elizabeth died, the new king, James, had Ralegh imprisoned in the Tower of London on a questionable charge of treason. There he began his history of the world—which was to have been dedicated to his supporter, Henry, the prince of Wales. But Henry died in 1612 and Ralegh never finished the *History*. Although he was briefly released to pursue a second (and equally unsuccessful) search for gold in Guiana, he spent most of his later years in prison until he was executed on the old charge of treason.

A. K. Ramanujan (1929–1993)

A(ttipat) K(rishnaswami) Ramanujan was born in Mysore, Karnataka, India, and educated at Mysore University, Deccan College, and Indiana University, where he took a Ph.D. From 1950 until 1958 he taught English at various colleges and universities in India, and from 1962 until his death he taught at the University of Chicago. Ramanujan was a respected scholar of Dravidian languages, linguistics, culture, and folklore; a gifted translator of works in classical Tamil and medieval and modern Kannada; and an engaging poet in both English and Kannada. In addition to poetry, he published plays, a novel, short stories, and an autobiography (the last in Kannada). His poems are haunted by a sense of irrevocable loss and of the transience and insubstantiality of life. Although they are strongly rooted in the local, they are also eerily rootless, conveying a sense of displacement and seeming to exist in an internalized dreamscape that frequently assumes nightmarish qualities. Their rhythms imitate the cadences of natural speech.

John Crowe Ransom (1888–1974)

John Crowe Ransom was born in Pulaski, Tennessee. He was educated at Vanderbilt University and Christ Church College, Oxford. After enlisting in the army during World War I, he served on the front in France. A member of the Vanderbilt faculty from 1914 until 1937, he spearheaded the Agrarian Movement, whose members included the poet and novelist Robert Penn Warren and the poets Allen Tate and Donald Davidson. The group championed a somewhat nostalgic vision of an agrarian economy based on old Southern values—which they saw as a corrective for an urban Northern economy based on progressive values—and a rigorous poetic style that promoted traditional, or ornate, form and concrete detail over the sentimental commonplaces found in much Southern literature of the day. Ransom later joined the faculty of Kenyon College, where he founded the influential *Kenyon Review* and helped spur New Criticism, a critical school that emphasized close textual scrutiny and would dominate the American literary scene for several decades. Although Ransom wanted his poetry to "carry the dearest possible values to which we have attached ourselves," he was aware that these values were not shared by the modern world. He championed the mystery inherent in Christianity, but later, like many of his fellow modernists, Ransom came to view art as a substitute, albeit an imperfect one, for religion.

Henry Reed (1914–1986)

Henry Reed was born in Birmingham, Warwickshire, and educated at Birmingham University. From 1937 to 1941 he worked as a teacher and as a journalist. During World War II he served one year in the Royal Army Ordnance Corps and three as a cryptographer in the department of Naval Intelligence. In 1945 he went to work as a broadcaster, journalist, and playwright for the BBC, where his coworkers included the poets W. H. Auden, Louis MacNeice, and Dylan Thomas. He later taught at the University of Washington in Seattle. His reputation rests almost exclusively on the five-part poem "Lessons of the War," which may be the most anthologized poem of World War II. In the poem, which arose from Reed's comic imitations of officious drill-sergeants in charge of training new recruits, he juxtaposes the sergeant's jargon-filled harangue with the enlisted man's thoughtful and moving interior monologues on the absurdity of his training and the splendor of nature.

Carter Revard (1931–)

Carter Revard was born in Pawhuska, Oklahoma, a member of the Osage Indian Nation. He was educated at the University of Tulsa, Oxford University, and Yale University, from which he received a Ph.D. In addition to having taught at Amherst College, Washington University, the University of Tulsa, and the University of Oklahoma, he has worked as a linguist and as a consultant in lexicography. Although his early work employed the alliteration and strong stresses of Anglo-Saxon, his later work has increasingly accommodated the sounds and rhythms of Native American speech. His poems draw simultaneously from Native American and Euro-American literary traditions as they celebrate the delicacy, mystery, and goodness of the natural world.

Adrienne Rich (1929–)

Adrienne Rich was born in Baltimore, Maryland, and educated at Radcliffe College. In 1953 she married Alfred Conrad, an economist at Harvard, with whom she had three sons. During the 1960s Rich and Conrad lived in New York City, where they were active in radical politics and the antiwar movement. The marriage ended in 1970; that same year Conrad committed suicide. In 1976 Rich entered into a relationship with Michelle Cliff, with whom she edited the lesbian-feminist journal *Sinister Wisdom*. She has taught at, among other schools, Douglass College and Stanford University; she now lives in California. In addition to numerous widely acclaimed collections of poetry, she has published influential prose works combining autobiography with history and anthropology. Rich's poetry has mirrored her biography in its shifts of content and style. The poems in her first book, *A Change of World* (1951), employed meter and emphasized formal qualities, but as Rich became politically active and began to write more directly about her experiences as a woman, a lesbian, and a Jew, such constructions gave way to a looser, freer style, and her "quiet" and "respectful" tone to a tenser, angrier one. She strove also to convey a sense of immediacy, even urgency. "Instead of poems *about* experiences I am getting poems that *are* experiences," Rich wrote in 1964. Although she has devoted much energy to discovering what might be described as a "feminist style," her per-vasive concern has been for all who are silenced and crippled by the "world masculinity made / unfit for women or men."

Charles G. D. Roberts (1860–1943)

Charles G. D. Roberts was born near Fredericton, New Brunswick, and educated at the University of New Brunswick. Upon graduation, he taught school in Fredericton and was later appointed professor of English literature at King's College. In 1897, Roberts moved to New York, where he worked as associate editor of the *Illustrated American* and as a freelance journalist. During World War I, he enlisted at the age of fifty-four. He subsequently traveled in Europe and Africa and spent nearly fifteen years in England before returning to Canada. In addition to poetry, Roberts published a popular series of animal stories and several novels, romances, and travel guides. He also translated the work of French-Canadian writers into English and edited two collections of poems by Canadians. Due to his prolific output and his proficiency in several genres, Roberts is frequently referred to as "the father of Canadian fiction." He was knighted in 1935. Roberts was among the first Canadian writers to mythologize, in poetry and prose, the rich heritage and natural beauty of the Maritime region.

Edwin Arlington Robinson (1869–1935)

Edwin Arlington Robinson was born in Head Tide, Maine, and raised in Gardiner, Maine, the model for "Tilbury Town," the setting of many of his poems. He attended Harvard University. In 1896 Robinson moved to New York City, where he worked as a subway-construction inspector and, with the aid of President Theodore Roosevelt, who admired his work, in the Customs House. In 1910, despite financial difficulties, he devoted himself full-time to writing poetry. Robinson's early work received little recognition; fame came to him late, with the publication of *The Town Down the River* (1910) and *The Man against the Sky* (1916). By the time of his death, he was one of the most acclaimed poets in America. Although he wrote lyric poems, dramatic monologues, and, later, long blank-verse narratives (such as his trilogy of verse novels based on Arthurian legend), he is most remembered for his pastiches on eccentric New England types. Often considered a philosophical poet, he advocated (in the poet Yvor Winters' words) "stoical endurance" in the face of adversity. He tempered the unhappiness in his work with wry humor and, like the American Transcendentalists Emerson and Thoreau, maintained an optimistic outlook.

Theodore Roethke (1908–1963)

Theodore Roethke was born and raised in Saginaw, Michigan, where his German grandfather, his uncle, and his father operated greenhouses, which would figure prominently in Roethke's work. Roethke was educated at the University of Michigan and, briefly, Harvard University. In 1935 he was hospitalized for the first of several mental breakdowns. From 1947 until his death he taught at the University of Washington, where his students included the poets Richard Hugo and James Wright. His early work was typically comprised of short, tightly structured, adept lyrics; a breakthrough occurred with *The Lost Son and Other Poems* (1948). According to Roethke, these poems trace the spiritual and personal history "of a protagonist (not 'I' personally but of all haunted and harried men)." The stylistically innovative title poem uses nursery rhymes, nonsense verse, puns, and other forms of wordplay to explore prerational states of being. Elsewhere, as in the greenhouse sequence, intense observation of the natural world yields insight about the violence, comedy, eroticism, and regenerative potentiality inherent in all life. Like W. B. Yeats and Richard Wilbur, Roethke found spiritual correspondences in physical things: an "awareness of one's own self, *and*, even more mysteriously, in some instances, a feeling of the oneness of the universe."

Isaac Rosenberg (1890–1918)

Isaac Rosenberg was born in Bristol and raised in the East End of London. He left school at the age of fifteen and began working at an engraving firm. He did further training at the London School of Photo-Engraving and Lithography and took art lessons at Birbeck College and the Slade School. His first ambition was to be a painter, and he earned a modest reputation in the art world. In 1914 he traveled to South Africa to seek treatment for a worsening pulmonary illness, but returned to England the next year and enlisted in the army. Sent to the front in France in 1916, he was killed in action. Unlike most poets of World War I—including Wilfred Owen and Siegfried Sassoon, with whom he is often linked—Rosenberg did not write about patriotism or the falsity of patriotism. Nor did he express nostalgia for the older way of life that rapidly disappeared in the wake of the war. Life in the trenches was his subject, and he treated it with stoicism, sardonic wit, and passionate feeling, never shying away from the physical realities of war. Indeed, his talent lay in transforming materials as mean as a louse, repugnant as a rat, and horrifying as a pile of corpses, into art.

Christina Rossetti (1830–1894)

Christina Rossetti, sister of the poet and Pre-Raphaelite painter Dante Gabriel Rossetti, was born in London. Except for two brief trips abroad, she lived with her mother (who educated her) all her life. A committed High Anglican, she was deeply influenced by the Tractarian, or Oxford, Movement. Her first poems were published pseudonymously in the first issue of *The Germ*, in 1850. Her first major collection, *Goblin Market and Other Poems*, was published in 1866; the last collection published during her lifetime was the devout *The Face of the Deep: A Devotional Commentary on the Apocalypse* (1892). Rossetti displayed a virtuosic mastery of difficult forms, such as the sonnet, the rondeau, and the ballad. Heavily influenced by the Bible, especially the apocalyptic books, and the writings of Augustine, Thomas à Kempis, Plato, and Dante, she also admired the work of the Romantic poets as well as that of devotional poets such as George Herbert and John Donne. Her chief themes were love, often unrequited and addressed to God, death, and religion, and her most successful poems betray a deep conflict between the asceticism she imposed on herself and the aestheticism in which she revels.

Dante Gabriel Rossetti (1828–1882)

Dante Gabriel Rossetti, brother of the poet Christina Rossetti, was born in London. As a promising painter he attended various art schools, including the Royal Academy Antique School. In 1848, along with several painters, poets, and critics, he formed the short-lived but influential Pre-Raphaelite Brotherhood, which set itself in opposition to the "flimsy, frivolous, and conventional" art of its day by reviving the simplicity, clarity, brilliant color, and attention to detail that marked the work of the Italian *quattrocento*, and by introducing a "temper of wonder, reverence, and awe" into its productions. During the 1850s Rossetti moved away from the naturalism of the Pre-Raphaelites toward aestheticism. He joined a coterie of unconventional thinkers—including the designer and poet William Morris, the painter and designer Edward Burne-Jones, and the poet

Algernon Swinburne—whose work set a new standard of taste and thinking and influenced the Aesthetes and Decadents of the next generation, including the writers Walter Pater and Oscar Wilde. *The House of Life*, a sequence of 102 sonnets written between 1847 and 1881 and organized loosely on the theme of love, is generally considered Rossetti's masterpiece. His work was deeply influenced by Plato, the Bible (although he used Christian iconography for its evocative power rather than its theological significance), Dante (whom he translated), the medieval troubadours, and the Romantic poets.

Muriel Rukeyser (1913–1980)

Muriel Rukeyser was born in New York City. She attended Vassar College—where she, the poet Elizabeth Bishop, and the novelist Mary McCarthy founded the left-wing *Student Review*—and Columbia University. She taught writing at the California Labor School in Berkeley, California, and later at Sarah Lawrence College. In addition to poetry, Rukeyser published biographies of mathematicians Willard Gibbs and Thomas Hariot and Republican presidential candidate Wendell Willkie, collections of literary criticism, and children's books. She also translated the work of Gunnar Ekelof, Bertold Brecht, and Octavio Paz. Although social and political issues were her primary concern, Rukeyser also took up personal subjects, including her experiences as a daughter, mother, lover, and lesbian. Rukeyser's phrase "no more masks!" became a rallying cry for feminists, including the poets Adrienne Rich and Anne Sexton. Influenced early in her career by W. H. Auden, she later loosened her technique, and by the 1960s her sweeping forms, eclectic subject matter, and copious use of detail demonstrated her affinities with Walt Whitman.

Carl Sandburg (1878–1967)

Carl Sandburg was born in Galesburg, Illinois. He left school after the eighth grade to help support his family, but later attended Lombard College. In 1897 he embarked on a series of travels across America. His first collection of poetry, *Chicago Poems*, was published in 1914 and was followed by several highly acclaimed and immensely popular volumes, including *Cornhuskers* (1918), which documents Sandburg's war experience, and *Smoke and Steel* (1920), in which his disillusionment with post–World War I America anticipates T. S. Eliot's. Sandburg was a leading figure in the Chicago Renaissance, along with architect Frank Lloyd Wright, novelist Theodore Dreiser, and poets Vachel Lindsay and Edgar Lee Masters. In the 1930s Sandburg became active in the Socialist movement. In addition to writing poetry, he devoted thirty years to the study of Abraham Lincoln and traveled the country in search of folk songs and ballads, which he collected as *The American Songbag* (1927). He also wrote novels and children's stories. Overall, he shared Walt Whitman's and the Futurists' appreciation for the rhythms of the American urban scene and admiration for the spirit of common laborers. Although his work eventually lost its once immense popularity, Sandburg's interest in and passion for ordinary life never waned.

Siegfried Sassoon (1886–1967)

Siegfried Sassoon was born in Kent, England, and attended Clare College, Cambridge. For several years he divided his time between London, where he moved in fashionable literary circles, and his family's country estate, where he lived as a leisured Edwardian gentleman. At the outbreak of World War I he enlisted and went to the front with the Royal Welsh Fusiliers. By 1917, disillusioned with the war, he publicly protested that it was being "deliberately prolonged by those who have the power to end it." His actions landed him in the Craiglockhart War Hospital (authorities claimed he was suffering from "shell shock"), where he befriended the poet Wilfred Owen. Although Edward Marsh included some of Sassoon's early work in his anthologies of Georgian poetry, these poems bear little resemblance to those for which Sassoon is best remembered. Under the pressures of combat, and the influence of fellow poet and soldier Robert Graves, Sassoon produced poetry with an immediacy unmatched by his contemporaries' work. He not only exposed the horrors of trench warfare, but also castigated those at home who blithely sent a generation of young men to die.

Gjertrud Schnackenberg (1953–)

Gjertrud Schnackenberg was born in Tacoma, Washington. She attended Mount Holyoke College and earned early and wide admiration for her writing. She has traveled extensively, has lived in Rome, and currently resides in Boston. A technically deft and highly allusive poet, Schnackenberg works in a variety of modes, including the elegiac, the narrative, the meditative, and the comic. Often writing about attempts to construct meaning through science, history, religious belief, and poetry itself, she probes such complex subjects with authority and grace. Like H. D., she also writes in a palimpsestic fashion, layering texts one over the other but ensuring that each remains legible. In her book A Gilded Lapse of Time (1992), for example, she fuses her personal history with Dante's journey in The Divine Comedy.

James Schuyler (1923–1991)

James Schuyler was born in Chicago and raised in Washington, D.C., and western New York State. He was educated at Bethany College. After living in Italy during the 1950s, he settled in New York City. Like the poet Frank O'Hara, Schuyler worked at the Museum of Modern Art and served on the editorial board of Art News. In addition to poetry, he wrote three novels, all of them comedies of manners. Deeply influenced by the practices of avant-garde artists, he employed surreal imagery and experimental narrative techniques in his poems, the tone of which is generally urbane, witty, and conversational.

Anne Sexton (1928–1974)

Anne Sexton was born in Newton, Massachusetts, and attended Garland Junior College. Following the birth of her older child in 1951, she suffered the first in a series of mental breakdowns, which culminated in her suicide in 1974. Sexton began writing poetry in earnest in 1957. She studied under Robert Lowell and W. D. Snodgrass, whose Heart's Needle (1959) influenced her profoundly, and developed important friendships with Sylvia Plath and Maxine Kumin. Along with teaching poetry in high schools, at mental institutions, and at colleges and universities (including Harvard, Radcliffe, Oberlin, and Boston), she coauthored three children's books with Kumin. Sexton wrote "confessional" poetry, in which the speaker is the poet herself, laying bare the intimate traumas of her life and her times; she viewed the act of writing as an affirmation of life or, at least, a rebellion against that threatened to overwhelm her. Although her later poems were often in free verse, she frequently employed syllabics as well as traditional meters and forms, and she showed particular facility with rhyme.

William Shakespeare (1564–1616)

We know less about Shakespeare's life than we know about that of almost any other major English writer. He was born the third of eight children in Stratford-on-Avon. His father, John, was a maker of gloves who became an alderman and a bailiff before suffering financial troubles. Shakespeare's mother, Mary Arden, was the daughter of a rich farmer and brought land to the marriage. Shakespeare probably attended the Stratford grammar school, but received no university education and was referred to as an "upstart crow" by one of the better-educated "university wits" when he arrived in London in the early 1590s. The first record of him after his christening dates from 1582, when he married Anne Hathaway; they had a daughter in 1583 and twins, Judith and Hamnet, in 1585. For most of his career he was an actor and shareholder in, and principal playwright of, the most successful theatrical company of his time. He quickly gained a reputation as "the most excellent" English dramatist in both comedy and tragedy and was well known for his history plays, narrative poems, and the "sugared Sonnets" that were circulated "among his private friends." After the turn of the century he composed in rapid succession his tragic masterpieces Hamlet, Othello, King Lear, Macbeth, and Antony and Cleopatra. He apparently retired to Stratford around 1610, and during his later years worked mainly in the genres of romance and tragicomedy. When he died, no collected edition of his works had been published; the First Folio, a collection of his plays (but not his narrative poems or sonnets) appeared only in 1623.

Percy Bysshe Shelley (1792–1822)

Percy Bysshe Shelley was born near Horsham, Sussex, to a well-to-do, conservative family. In 1810 he went to University College, Oxford, but was expelled in his first year for refusing to recant an atheistic pamphlet he had published with a classmate. He married a young schoolgirl the following year. In 1813 he moved to London, where he worked for a number of social causes and came under the influence of the radical social philosopher William Godwin. Shelley fell in love with Godwin's daughter, Mary Wollstonecraft Godwin (author of the novel Frankenstein), and eloped to Europe with her. Byron joined them in Switzerland in 1816 and followed them to Italy in 1818. Shelley was drowned when his small boat was caught in a squall on the Gulf of Spezia. Lord Byron eulogized him as "without exception, the best and least selfish man I ever knew." The superlative opinion of friends did not reflect public opinion at large, however. Due to his radical social, political, and philosophical ideas and his unorthodox lifestyle, Shelley had few admirers in his lifetime. An avid student of Hume and Plato, he was deeply influenced by skeptical empiricism and idealism; he distrusted all claims to certainty—he never confessed a religious or philosophical creed—but held fast to his faith in the redeeming powers of love and the imagination. It is the latter that especially informs his poetry. In the influential essay "A Defence of Poetry," he asserts: "A Poet is a nightingale who sits in darkness and sings to cheer its own solitude with sweet sounds." His formal achievement was great: he worked in elaborate, elegant stanza forms, many of his own invention, and displayed a complex tone of voice, which ranged from passionate to dignified and urbane.

James Shirley (1596–1666)

James Shirley was born in London and, like Edmund Spenser, was educated at Merchant Taylor's School. He went on to St. John's, Oxford, and St. Catherine's Hall, Cambridge. After joining the Anglican clergy he served in St. Alban's and taught at the town's grammar school from 1623 until 1625, but lost his position there when he converted to Catholicism in 1624–25. Returning to

London, he began a career as a dramatist with *The School of Compliment* (later, *Love Tricks*; 1625). This was the first of thirty-six plays he wrote, many for the Cockpit Theatre, until 1640, when he succeeded Phillip Massinger as principle dramatist for the King's Men. Shirley's plays were largely comedies and tragicomedies in the style of (Francis) Beaumont and (John) Fletcher, and dramatized patriotic debates such as *The Contention of Ajax and Ulysses for the Armour of Achilles* (1658), but Shirley also composed masques such as *The Triumph of Peace*, commissioned by the Inns of Court in 1634, and poetry. As a Royalist and Catholic, Shirley was fortunate in finding employment as a school teacher during Oliver Cromwell's Commonwealth, but his luck did not long outlast it; he died of exposure during the Great Fire of London. His most famous poem, "Dirge" ("The Glories of Our Blood and State") comes from *The Contention of Ajax and Ulysses for the Armour of Achilles*. Other examples of his verse survive in *Poems* (1646), which contains "Narcissus," a revision of what is probably his first composition, of 1618, then entitled "Echo."

Jane Shore (1947–   )

Jane Shore was born in Newark, New Jersey, and educated at Goddard College and the University of Iowa. She was fellow in poetry at the Radcliffe Institute from 1971 until 1973. During the mid-1970s she taught at Harvard University—where one of her colleagues was the poet Elizabeth Bishop, a clear influence on Shore—and subsequently has taught at a variety of schools. She now lives in Washington, D.C., and in Vermont. Her poems contain a strong narrative impulse: they tend to be both autobiographical (often about her childhood) and historical, exploring the ways in which the past informs the present. Her style is characterized by attention to visual detail and to metaphor, and her tone is richly nuanced, at times humorous.

Mary Sidney (1568–1621)

Mary Sidney was the third of eleven children born to Sir Henry Sidney and his wife, Mary. Well-educated at home, Mary became proficient in Latin as well as in French and Italian; between 1575 and 1577, she acquired a courtly education by serving, as her mother had before her, as a lady-in-waiting to Queen Elizabeth. In 1577, she married Henry Herbert, the second earl of Pembroke, and lived with him at the great house of Wilton. As a patron of letters and inspiration to poets ranging from Edmund Spenser to Isabella Whitney, Mary Sidney Herbert made Wilton into an intellectual center. In the early 1580s, when he had been banished from court for rashly criticizing the queen's plans to marry a Frenchman, Mary's eldest brother, Philip, spent time at Wilton and probably wrote his *Defense of Poesy* there along with portions of his *Arcadia*, the second version of which was left unfinished when Philip died in 1586. He had dedicated the first version to his sister, and in 1590 she published a composite version of the two texts, an enormously influential work known as *The Countesse of Pembroke's Arcadia*. Sharing with her brother a hope that England would become a defender of Protestantism in Europe, Mary worked after his death to complete a series of verse translations of the Psalms that he had begun; having revised the forty-three psalms that he had finished, she composed another hundred and seven in a wide variety of meters and forms. The poem she wrote to the queen to accompany a presentation copy of these Psalms displays a delicately ambivalent—and sometimes obliquely critical—attitude toward the monarch; Elizabeth had often frustrated Philip's ambitions and was regarded as insufficiently

zealous by many English Protestants. Mary Sidney articulated some of her own religious beliefs not only in her versions of the Psalms (which often differ in interesting ways from those of other Protestant writers) but also in her translation of Du Plessis Mornay's *Discourse of Life and Death* and in her rendering, in *terza rima*, of Petrarch's *Triumph of Death*. In 1591, she published her *Antonie*, a translation of a French play by Robert Garnier. She has only recently begun to be studied as a poet in her own right, one whose original verse often appears under the "handmaidenly" cloak of translation and even, perhaps, under others' names: some critics have recently argued for her authorship of the "Lay of Clorinda" long attributed to Spenser and published in *Astrophil*, the elegy for Philip Sidney that Spenser dedicated to Mary.

Sir Philip Sidney (1554–1586)

Philip Sidney was born at Penshurst in Kent (England) to an aristocratic family that included among its poets Sidney's brother Robert, his sister Mary, and his niece, Mary Wroth. Sidney's mother, also Mary, was the sister of Queen Elizabeth's sometime favorite, Robert Dudley, earl of Leicester, and Sidney's father, Sir Henry, had served the queen as lord deputy of Ireland; nonetheless, Philip Sidney's relations with the queen proved to be vexed. After attending Shrewesbury School with his friend (and later, biographer) Fulke Greville, Sidney spent time at Oxford and Cambridge. From 1572 until 1575 he traveled in Europe, during which time he established a firm friendship with Hubert Languet, a French Huguenot who encouraged Sidney's own zealous Protestantism. When in 1580 Queen Elizabeth dallied with the idea of marrying a French Catholic, the duke of Alençon, Sidney criticized the idea in a letter and was consequently banished from court (a lower-born critic of the same prospective royal marriage, Philip Stubbes, incurred a more severe punishment: having his hand cut off). Sidney spent his enforced "idleness" composing poetry; his famous work of literary criticism, the *Defense of Poesy*; and two versions of his pastoral romance, *The Arcadia*, which was dedicated to his sister Mary (it was probably composed at her country estate) and which she published after Sidney's death in a widely read version that conflates Sidney's first text, the *Old Arcadia*, with his unfinished revision, the *New Arcadia*. In the *Defense of Poesy*, he calls the writing of verse his "unelected vocation" and insists (with considerable historical irony, given the queen's distaste for expensive military campaigns) that poetry is a vehicle for educating monarchs as well as a fit "companion" of the soldiers camp. Knighted in 1583, Sidney was finally granted a chance to fight for Protestantism in the Low Countries after being made governor of Flushing (an English possession in the Low Countries) in 1586. Sidney fought bravely but—Spenser implies in his elegy, *Astrophil*—somewhat rashly; he died of gangrene from a wound in the leg at the age of thirty-two. Legendary in life and death as the quintessential Elizabethan gentleman, Sidney was in reality more marked by the "great expectation" he mentions in one of his sonnets than by political or romantic success. His sonnet sequence *Astrophil and Stella* uses (and revises) Petrarchan conventions to record various experiences of unfulfilled desire. These include, but are not exhausted by, the erotic frustration caused by Sidney's failure to win Penelope Devereux, the historical model for Stella, as his wife. Although she was briefly engaged to Sidney, in 1581 she married Lord Robert Rich, upon whose name Sidney frequently puns in the sonnets; Sidney himself was married to Frances, daughter of the powerful courtier Sir Francis Walsingham, in 1583. *Astrophil and Stella* is the first great sonnet sequence in

English; like Sidney's other poetic works, it was circulated in manuscript but not published until after his death.

Leslie Marmon Silko (1948–)

Leslie Marmon Silko was born in Albuquerque, New Mexico, and raised in Old Laguna, a village located on a grazing ground of Pueblo cattle-keepers. Educated at the University of New Mexico, she entered law school, but left to become a writer and teacher. She has taught at the Navajo Community College, the University of New Mexico, and the University of Arizona. Particularly drawn to storytelling—the traditional means through which Native Americans have preserved their culture—she roots her work in the landscape of the Southwest and in the spirituality with which it has become imbued for her. Silko eschews traditional prosody, working in fluid stanzas that approximate the dynamism of the natural world.

Charles Simic (1938–)

Charles Simic was born in the former Yugoslavia and raised there during the Nazi occupation. At the age of eleven, he emigrated to the United States with his family. Simic was educated at the University of Chicago and New York University. Besides serving in the United States Army, he has worked as a bookkeeper, an accountant, a house painter, and a salesman. Since then he has taught at California State College and the University of New Hampshire. In addition to poetry, Simic has published two collections of essays and has translated several European poets into English. His poems tend toward the sinister, their senses of mystery and danger deriving in large part from folklore and fairy tale. At once a realist and a surrealist, Simic employs a deadpan tone and simple diction. He works primarily in free verse.

L. E. Sissman (1928–1976)

L(ouis) E(dward) Sissman was raised in Detroit, Michigan. After graduation from Harvard University he held a series of odd jobs: shelving books in a library, editing copy in a New York publishing house, working on John F. Kennedy's first Senate campaign, and selling vacuum cleaners and Fuller brushes. In 1956 he began a successful career in advertising. In 1958, after a ten-year hiatus, he began to write poetry in earnest, and he published prolifically from that time until his death from Hodgkins' disease. In addition, he regularly wrote for The Atlantic Monthly. He lived in Boston nearly all his adult life. Although his illness was a primary subject (another was his days at Harvard), Sissman never succumbed to self-pity. Like W. H. Auden and Philip Larkin, he treated personal subject matter with irony, urbanity, wit, and grim cheer. Beneath the chatty, prosaic surfaces of his poems—with their clever word play, their learned conceits and allusions—lies not only a strong, regular meter but a sense of the preciousness of life.

John Skelton (1460–1529)

Skelton often referred to himself as "poet laureate," a title conferred on him by the universities of Oxford and Cambridge in 1490 and 1493 respectively. Trained in Latin and in rhetoric, he was ordained a priest and subsequently served as a tutor for the future king Henry VIII. After writing a satire on court life, The Bowge of Court, in 1498, he became rector of the parish church of Diss, a town in Norfolk. While at Diss (from approximately 1502 until 1511), Skelton apparently kept a mistress and fathered children; he also wrote his comic lament "Phillip Sparow" and "Ware the Hawk," which denounces the actions of a neighboring priest who pursued his quarry, a hawk, into the sanctified

space of Skelton's church. Both in its (highly original) form and in some of its content, this poem anticipates Skelton's later attacks on Henry VIII's chancellor, Cardinal Wolsey; Wolsey's desecration of monastic spaces are the object of Skelton's comic invective in long poems such as Speak Parrot, Why Come Ye Not to Court, and Colin Clout, all from the early 1520s, when Skelton was living at the Abbey of Westminster, protected by the laws of sanctuary from Wolsey's (and perhaps also the king's) anger. The latter poem, which influenced Spenser, is a complaint by a vagabond poet-figure. Skelton also wrote The Turning of Eleanor Rumming, a satiric portrait of an alewife; a morality play, Magnificence; and a number of short lyrics including the ironic song "Mannerly Margery Milk and Ale." The "Skeltonic" style that he invented typically blends high and low diction in short rhymed lines containing from two to five beats.

Christopher Smart (1722–1771)

Christopher Smart was born in Kent, England, and educated in Durham and at Pembroke College, Cambridge, where he became a fellow. He was a brilliant classical scholar, but began to exhibit symptoms of obsessive behavior, including a compulsion to public prayer. After moving to London in 1749 he won prizes for poetry, but his illness worsened, and he was several times committed to the lunatics' ward at St. Luke's Hospital, where he divided his time between writing, gardening, and his cat, Jeoffry. In 1758 he was transferred to a private institution at Bethnal Green. Released from poverty, and in 1770 was remanded to the King's Bench debtor's prison, where he died. William Butler Yeats regarded Smart's A Song to David as the inaugural poem of the Romantic period. Smart's other well-known work, Jubilate Agno, which he referred to as his "Magnificat," was, like A Song to David, composed during Smart's confinement, but was unpublished until 1939.

Charlotte Smith (1749–1806)

Charlotte Smith (née Turner) was born in London, brought up on her family's estate, Bignor Park, in Sussex, and educated at schools in Sussex and London. At fifteen she married a wealthy merchant in the West Indies trade. When he was imprisoned for debt and subsequently fled to France, she was left to bring up twelve children and turned to writing to earn money. Her first publication was a translation of Antoine-François Prévost's Manon Lescaut, but she became better known as a poet and a novelist. A prolific writer, she published three collections of poetry, six children's books, and ten novels. Her first collection, Elegiac Sonnets and Other Essays (1774), went through eleven editions and was translated into French and Italian.

Stevie Smith (1902–1971)

Stevie Smith was born Florence Margaret Smith in Hull, Yorkshire (England). She was raised by an aunt in the north London suburb of Palmers Green and lived there for the rest of her life. A secretary in the magazine publishing house of Newnes, Pearson, Ltd for thirty years, she retired in 1953 following a severe breakdown and devoted the rest of her life to writing. In addition to poetry, she published three novels. A master of tone, she frequently directed her acerbic wit at bourgeois conventionality and religious orthodoxy. Often writing in the ballad stanza, she employed meter even when deviating from traditional forms. The remarkable diction in her poems is an amalgamation of clichés, street talk, nursery rhymes, the Bible, and vocabulary derived from Latinate and Anglo-Saxon roots.

W. D. Snodgrass (1926–)

W(illiam) D(eWitt) Snodgrass was born in Wilkinsburg, Pennsylvania, and raised in Beaver Falls, Pennsylvania, where he began undergraduate studies at Geneva College before entering the navy. He served in the Pacific during the last months of World War II. After the war he studied at the University of Iowa, where he attended Robert Lowell's poetry workshops. Snodgrass has held teaching appointments at a number of universities, including Cornell, Rochester, Wayne State, Syracuse, Old Dominion, and Delaware. In 1959 he published *Heart's Needle*, a revolutionary work credited, along with Robert Lowell's *Life Studies* (published the same year), with spawning the so-called confessional school. However, Snodgrass's intricate, restrained, and gently self-mocking poems often differ significantly in tone from the work of his fellow members Lowell, Sylvia Plath, and Anne Sexton. Snodgrass often takes up complex moral issues—in *The Führer Bunker* (1977), he presents a series of dramatic monologues spoken by prominent figures in the Third Reich during the final days of the Nazi regime. He strives to write "not what is acceptable; not what my favorite intellect would think in this situation; not what I wish I felt. Only what I cannot help thinking."

Gary Snyder (1930–)

Gary Snyder was born in San Francisco and raised on a farm near Seattle. He was educated at Reed College. In the early 1950s he worked as a logger, forest-fire lookout, trail-crew worker, carpenter, proofreader, seaman, and teacher. He subsequently studied Asian languages at the University of California at Berkeley and spent a dozen years in Japan, where he studied Zen Buddhism. Upon his return to the United States, he settled in a remote community in the Sierra Nevadas. He currently teaches literature at the University of California at Davis. Influenced by "five-and-seven-character line Chinese poems . . . which work like sharp blows on the mind," he arranges "tough, simple, short words" into powerful abbreviated lines. Writing in the first person and in a plain style, working with organic meters and forms, he favors direct statement over metaphor and allusion.

Cathy Song (1955–)

Cathy Song, a descendant of Korean immigrants, was born in Honolulu, Hawaii, and raised in Wahiawa, a small village on the island of Oahu. She was educated at the University of Hawaii, Wellesley College, and Boston University, and her first book, *Picture Bride* (1982), was published in the Yale series of Younger Poets. Song has taught creative writing at various colleges and universities on the mainland, but lives permanently in Hawaii. Her poems seek meaning in daily activities, common objects, and familiar scenes, often establishing a mood of serenity in order to complicate it. Although Song eschews regular metrics, she renders her work with clarity and subtlety.

Gary Soto (1952–)

Gary Soto was born in Fresno, California. He has worked as a field hand and in a tire factory. Educated at California State University, Fresno (where he studied with Philip Levine), and the University of California at Irvine (from which he earned an M.F.A.), he has been a visiting instructor at San Diego State University and the University of Cincinnati, and he currently teaches Chicano studies and English at the University of California at Berkeley. In addition to poetry, he has published a memoir and a collection of essays on poetry, and he has edited a book of recollections and stories about California. His poetry often acknowledges the sufferings of the downtrodden and dispossessed and explores their bitterness and anger. His work has been praised for its spare diction and striking imagery.

Robert Southwell (1561–1595)

Robert Southwell was born into a Catholic family in Harsham, Norwich (England), and was educated at the Jesuit School in Douai, France, accepted for the Jesuit novitiate in Rome, and ordained in 1585. Despite the law of 1584 forbidding English-born subjects who had taken Catholic orders since the queen's accession to remain in England longer than forty days, on pain of death, Southwell returned to England to minister to Catholics in 1586. In 1589 he became chaplain to Ann Howard, countess of Arundel, whose husband had been imprisoned, and to whom Southwell addressed his *Epistle of Comfort*. In 1592 Southwell was arrested while saying mass, tortured, imprisoned in the Tower, and finally executed. He was beatified as a martyr in 1929 and canonized in 1970. He wrote religious prose and verse in both Latin and English. His narrative poem, "St. Peter's Complaint," and his best-known lyric, "The Burning Babe," were both published in 1595. The latter is an unusually fine example of a poem in "fourteeners," or fourteen-syllable lines, a form that Sir Philip Sidney had parodied in "What Length of Verse?" Southwell's work became popular soon after his death, and Ben Jonson told a friend that he would willingly have destroyed many of his own poems if he could have written "The Burning Babe."

Wole Soyinka (1934–)

Wole Soyinka was born in Ijebut Isara, Nigeria, and spent his early years in Abeokuta. Educated at University College, Ibadan, and Leeds University, he has taught at the Universities of Lagos, Ibadan, and Ife, and lectured all over the world. In the late 1950s he worked as a reporter for the BBC. From August 1967 to October 1969 he was imprisoned as a political prisoner by the Federal Military Government of Nigeria. An exceptionally prolific writer, Soyinka has published poetry, novels, autobiography, critical essays, an anthology of African poetry, and numerous plays for radio, television, and the stage. He was founding director of Masks Theatre, the Orison Theatre, and the Guerrilla Theatre Unit of the University of Ife. He was awarded the 1986 Nobel Prize for Literature. Although astringent political comment established Soyinka's reputation, his later work draws on traditional Yoruban folk materials and on European literary tradition and takes up increasingly somber themes. Soyinka often weaves musical and dramatic elements into his poems, making his work particularly well suited to live performance.

Stephen Spender (1909–1995)

Stephen Spender was born in London and attended University College, Oxford, where he became friends with the writers W. H. Auden, Christopher Isherwood, and Louis MacNeice, with whom he shared an interest in left-wing politics. In 1937 he joined the British Communist Party and traveled to Spain to write propaganda for the Spanish Republicans' fight against fascism, but soon grew to feel that Communism was intolerant of individual vision and freedom of expression. In the 1930s he, Auden, MacNeice, and fellow poet Cecil Day Lewis were dubbed by critics the "Pylon" school, after Spender's poem "The Pylons," for their conspicuous use of industrial imagery. In his early work, Spender presented the technological progress of his age in fairly upbeat terms. He depicted poverty, suffering, and degradation with candor and compassion, but despite his modernism he displayed a Romantic strain, evident in his love of nature. Increasingly Spender looked to the constructs of the imagination, rather than those of the external world, for solace and renewal. In addition to writing his own poetry, he translated from Spanish, German, and Greek. He was knighted in 1983.

Edmund Spenser (ca. 1552–1599)

Edmund Spenser was born in London and educated at the Merchant Taylor's School by Richard Mulcaster, a respected humanist and educational theorist. After studying as a "poor scholar" at Cambridge, Spenser served as secretary to several prominent men, including the powerful earl of Leicester, uncle of Spenser's friend Sir Philip Sidney. In 1580 he was appointed secretary to the lord governor of Ireland, whose job it was to defend the English settlement there against the Irish "rebels" who objected to English rule of their land. Spenser remained in Ireland, as civil servant, settler, and landholder, for the rest of his life, and in 1596 wrote A *viewe of the present state of Ireland*, a political treatise detailing his views on the "Irish problem." Though born to a family in modest circumstances, Spenser wanted nothing less than to be the national poet of England, and he consciously modeled his career on that of Virgil, the great poet of imperial Rome. Like Virgil, Spenser initially wrote in the mode of pastoral, publishing in 1591 his *Shepheardes Calender*, a series of twelve pastoral eclogues set in the English countryside and corresponding to the months of the year. Chaucer was another of Spenser's main sources of inspiration, as were Italian writers such as Ludovico Ariosto and Torquato Tasso. Ariosto's *Orlando Furioso* (1516) provided, in its blending of epic and romance narrative structures, a particularly important model for Spenser's *The Faerie Queene*. That poem's first three books, published in 1590, were well received, and in 1596 Spenser republished the poem with three additional completed books and a portion of a seventh. He thus completed only a little over half of the poem he described, in a prefatory letter to Walter Ralegh, as designed to fashion a gentleman by illustrating twelve moral virtues in twelve books. He received a modest royal pension after the first three books of *The Faerie Queene* were published, but he never received a post at court nor the royal recognition he had hoped for. His disappointed expectations and his belief that the queen was mismanaging affairs in Ireland may have contributed to the sometimes critical ways in which he represented her in *The Faerie Queene*. Elizabeth was the name not only of the queen whom he "shadowed," but also of his wife; she is figured in his sonnet sequence *Amoretti* and also in his two marriage poems, *Epithalamion* and *Prothalamion*.

Gertrude Stein (1874–1946)

Gertrude Stein was born in Allegheny, Pennsylvania, and raised in Oakland, California. She was educated at Radcliffe College, where she studied with the psychologist and philosopher William James (whose theories about consciousness existing as a continuous "stream," located in the continuous present, influenced her deeply) and at Johns Hopkins University, where she studied medicine. In 1902 Stein and her brother, Leo, moved to Paris and established a salon that attracted the most prominent avant-garde artists of the day, including Pablo Picasso, Georges Braque, and Henri Matisse. In 1907 she began a relationship with Alice B. Toklas, and (apart from Stein's very successful lecture tour of the United States in 1934) they resided permanently in France. Stein's work—in prose, poetry, drama, and autobiography—was experimental in the extreme and frequently incomprehensible (she was called "the Mama

of dada"). Stein's experimentation can be compared to the cubists', for like them she was concerned not with presenting an accurate pictorial representation of a thing, but with conveying its unique "essence." Her radical dislocations of meaning and syntax were intended to challenge the reader; to free words of stale associations; and, perhaps above all, to convey the living moment.

Wallace Stevens (1879–1955)

Wallace Stevens was born and raised in Reading, Pennsylvania. After attending Harvard University for three years, Stevens moved to New York City, where he went to law school, worked in a number of law firms, and associated with prominent avant-garde artists, including the poets William Carlos Williams and Marianne Moore. In 1916, he went to work for the Hartford Accident and Indemnity Company, and he stayed with the firm for the rest of his life, becoming a vice president in 1934. His quiet life in an upper-class neighborhood in Hartford, Connecticut, seemed in sharp contrast with the vitality and sensuousness of so many of his poems. In his early work—dandified, ornate, and musical—Stevens explored the dynamic interplay between reality and the imagination. He adopted a plainer but more abstract style in his later work, both praised and criticized as a "poetry of ideas." In place of conventional faiths, Stevens posited a Romantic's belief in poetry, or more precisely, in the regenerative and redemptive act of imagining and reimagining. The poet, Stevens believed, "creates the world to which we turn incessantly and without knowing it and . . . gives to life the supreme fictions without which we are unable to conceive of it."

Anne Stevenson (1933–   )

Anne Stevenson was born of American parents in Cambridge, England, and raised in the United States, primarily in Cambridge, Massachusetts, and New Haven, Connecticut. She was educated at the University of Michigan, where she studied with the poet Donald Hall. In the early 1950s, she worked as a schoolteacher, settling in England in 1956, where she taught at a number of institutions and held several fellowships. She was the founder of the Poetry Bookshop at Hay-on-Wye, Wales. Her publications include a study of Elizabeth Bishop, a biography of Sylvia Plath, and several radio plays. Her best-known collection, *Correspondences*, is a sequence of epistolary poems interspersed with journal entries recounting her family history. Elsewhere she takes up feminist themes. Whatever her subject, she cultivates close ties to the natural world and establishes correspondences between physical landscapes and the emotions. Typically working in a simple style, she strives, she has said, for the "true sightness of seeing."

Trumbull Stickney (1874–1904)

Trumbull Stickney was born in Geneva, Switzerland, and spent his early years abroad. He was educated by his father, a Classics scholar, until he entered Harvard University, and he later became the first American to earn a Ph.D. at the Sorbonne. He taught Greek at Harvard for one year, then died suddenly of a brain tumor. Although during his lifetime he published only one book, *Dramatic Verses* (1902), he left much work in manuscript, and the poet William Vaughn Moody, a friend of Stickney's from Harvard, helped assemble a posthumous collection. The tone of Stickney's poetry is often intensely melancholic; yet it also contains a strain of humor. He also has been called a late Romantic; the quick passage of time was a frequent subject of his spare but richly sensuous poems.

Mark Strand (1934–)

Mark Strand was born on Prince Edward Island, Canada, and raised in various cities across the United States. He was educated at Antioch College, Yale University, the University of Florence, and the University of Iowa, where he studied with the poet Donald Justice. Strand taught for many years at the University of Utah and is currently a professor of English at Johns Hopkins University and the poetry editor of *The New Republic.* A noted anthologist, a translator of several European and Latin American poets, he also has written short stories, books for children, and a study of Edward Hopper. Though his work is sometimes impersonal in tone, he has written affecting and intimate poems about family members, particularly an elegy for his father, and his book-length poem *Dark Harbor* (1993) obliquely recounts a journey of the mind through memory and into the afterlife.

Sir John Suckling (1609–1642)

John Suckling was born into an old Norfolk (England) family through which he inherited great estates. Educated at Trinity College, Cambridge, he traveled in Holland and was knighted on his return in 1630. He was part of the 1631 embassy to Germany, returning the next year to court and a life of dissipation—the biographer John Aubrey described him as "the greatest gallant of his time, and the greatest Gamester, both for Bowling and Cards." In 1639 Suckling fought on the (losing) Royalist side against the Scots, and in 1641 levied a force to free the imprisoned earl of Strafford. The conspiracy, named the "Army Plot," was uncovered, and Suckling fled to France where, Aubrey suggests, he committed suicide by drinking poison. Like other "Cavalier" poets who supported the cause of Charles Stuart, Suckling embodied the courtly quality of *sprezzatura*, in which the most highly refined and polished style is disguised as effortless effusion. His literary reputation was established by 1637, when his satirical mock-ballad *The Wits (or Sessions of the Poets)* was sung before Charles I. Following the success of his tragedy *Aglaura* in 1638, it was restaged with a new fifth act, circumventing the tragedy. The protagonist of another of his plays, *Brennoralt,* is said to be a self-portrait. Poems such as "Song" ("Why so pale and wan, fond lover?") and "A Ballad upon a Wedding," collected in *Fragmenta Aurea* (1646), demonstrate the graceful cynicism for which Suckling is chiefly remembered.

May Swenson (1913–1989)

May Swenson was born in Logan, Utah, to a Mormon family. After graduation from Utah State University, she moved to New York and worked with the Writer's Project of the Works Progress Administration. From 1956 until 1966 she was an editor at New Directions Press. In addition, she was a visiting professor at many colleges and universities. Her poetry, like that of her friend Elizabeth Bishop, is marked by keen visual perception (particularly of the natural world), a passion for the exotic, and a capacity for self-effacement. The language in her poems is marked by witty and playful use of repetition, alliteration, rhyme, and pararhyme. Swenson often invented forms to suit her subjects, and her innovations included daring experiments with shaped poems and with typography.

Jonathan Swift (1667–1745)

Jonathan Swift was born in Dublin, Ireland, to English parents, but after his mother's return to England he lived in the care of his uncle. He was educated at Trinity College, Dublin. From 1689 until 1699 he was secretary to his kinsman Sir William Temple and tutor to "Stella," Ester Johnson (daughter of the companion to Temple's sister), to whom "Stella's Birthday" is addressed, and for whom Swift developed a lasting passion. Swift frequented London, where he became active in Tory politics and met the leading literary figures of the day. In 1694 he returned to Ireland to join the clergy, and he later served in several parishes and was appointed dean of St. Patrick's Cathedral in 1713. Despite his staunch conservatism, he became an ardent champion of Irish resistance to English oppression. Best known for *Gulliver's Travels* (1726), the only piece of writing for which he was paid, he was a prolific author of poetry, prose, pamphlets, letters, dialogues, and satires.

Algernon Charles Swinburne (1837–1909)

Algernon Charles Swinburne was born in London and attended Balliol College, Oxford, where he became a friend of the poet and Pre-Raphaelite painter Dante Gabriel Rossetti, the painter and designer Edward Burne-Jones, and the designer and poet William Morris. Swinburne introduced the phrase "art for art's sake" into the English aesthetic lexicon in an 1862 review of the French poet Charles Baudelaire's *Les Fleurs du Mal.* He became an adherent of Baudelaire's aesthetic, until, in 1867, he met Giuseppe Mazzini, whose fervor for Italian independence from Austrian rule caused Swinburne to repudiate "art for art's sake" and turn to politically motivated poetry. Swinburne wrote prolifically, and his work, which characteristically explores the relationship between pleasure and pain, love and death, shows the influence of sources as diverse as the Marquis de Sade, the Bible, Greek drama, and the Border Ballads. The technical virtuosity of *Poems and Ballads* (1866), his first poetry collection, brought him praise, as well as rebuke from those who found its denunciation of formal Christianity morally reprehensible. *Songs Before Sunrise* (1871) celebrates liberty and expresses a Blakean distrust of authority. The elegiac, stoical *Poems and Ballads* (1878) marks the end of Swinburne's greatest period of writing and mourns the effects of time on humanity.

Allen Tate (1899–1979)

Allen Tate was born in Winchester, Kentucky. He was educated at Vanderbilt University, where he roomed with the poet Robert Penn Warren and was affiliated with the Fugitive movement. Along with Warren, and Vanderbilt professors John Crowe Ransom and Donald Davidson, Tate later joined the Agrarians, who called for an agriculturally based Southern economy and championed traditional Southern values. In 1924 he moved to New York to embark on a literary career; the poet Hart Crane lived in his household for a time. In 1928–29 Tate lived in England and France, and spent time with fiction writers Ford Madox Ford, Ernest Hemingway, and F. Scott Fitzgerald. He later taught at, among other schools, Princeton University, New York University, and the University of Minnesota. In addition to poetry, he published biographies, a novel, and several collections of erudite and insightful criticism. His poetry was often elegiac, bemoaning the dearth of ideals such as "chivalry" and "heroism" in the modern age, which he found mechanistic and solipsistic.

Edward Taylor (ca. 1642–1729)

Edward Taylor was born in Leicestershire, England, but migrated to Massachusetts in 1668. After graduation from Harvard University in 1671, he served as the minister of Westfield, Massachusetts, then a frontier town. His writing remained in manuscript on his instructions, but was discovered among the papers in the Yale University library in 1937 and published. Taylor was a conservative in religion, preaching the doctrine of salvation by grace and requiring members of his church to give a public account of their conversion before allowing them to take the sacraments. In addition to occasional pieces, he composed *Meditations*, whose starting points are images from biblical texts, and the series *God's Determinations Touching his Elect; and the Elect's Combat in Their Conversion, and Coming up to God in Christ: Together with the Comfortable Effects Thereof.*

Alfred, Lord Tennyson (1809–1892)

Alfred, Lord Tennyson was born in Somersby, Lincolnshire (England). He was educated at Trinity College, Cambridge, where he met Arthur Henry Hallam, whom he later immortalized in *In Memoriam* (1850). Tennyson began to write when a child, largely to escape the oppressiveness of his homelife, made miserable by his father's drinking and violence. He published some of his best-known poems, such as "Mariana" and "The Kraken," when he was only twenty; in "Mariana," he displays his early, and enduring, gift for using objects and landscapes to convey states of mind and particular emotions. Between 1833, the date of Hallam's death, and 1843, when Tennyson received an annual government pension to support his writing, he was especially hard-hit by the melancholia that would plague him all his life and so dominate his poetry. In the wake of Hallam's death, Tennyson's work assumed a decidedly darker note. He expressed his grief abstrusely in such poems as "Ulysses" and "Break, Break, Break" and directly in *In Memoriam*, a series of 131 quatrain stanzas written in iambic tetrameter, which Tennyson began within days of Hallam's death and continued to write over a period of seventeen years. With the publication of *In Memoriam*, he finally attained the public recognition long denied him and earned sufficient money to marry Emily Sellwood after a ten-year on-again off-again courtship. He remained immensely popular until his death. His last major work was *Idylls of the King*, a project that occupied him for nearly fifty years; the first four idylls were published in 1859, and the complete cycle of twelve in 1885. In the work, which popularized the then obscure Arthurian legend, Tennyson upholds medieval ideals, such as community, heroism, and courtly love, and compares the decay of the Round Table to the moral decline of his own society.

Dylan Thomas (1914–1953)

Dylan Thomas was born in the Welsh seaport of Swansea. Ignoring his father's advice to attend university, he left school in 1931 to embark on a literary career. After working at the local newspaper, he headed for London in 1934. He worked as a broadcaster, prose writer, poet, and lecturer, and this varied career necessitated his traveling through the United Kingdom, Europe, and the United States. He died in New York City during a reading tour, his excessive drinking and generally riotous lifestyle hastening his early death but also responsible, in part, for the burning intensity of his poems, whose exuberant rhetoric sometimes masks his careful crafting. He governed the unruly energies of his oratory with strict syllable counts, complicated rhyme schemes, and demanding formal constructions, such as the villanelle. "My poetry," he once said, "is the record of my individual struggle from darkness towards some measure of light." Greatly admired and imitated, his work was also greatly despised. The "New Apocalypse" writers took him as a model; "the Movement" writers, including Philip Larkin, were said to have formed in reaction to the excesses, personal and poetic, of Thomas and his admirers.

Edward Thomas (1878–1917)

Edward Thomas was born in the London suburb of Lambeth and educated at Lincoln College, Oxford. His arduous biographical, critical, and review work often left him drained and depressed, but he was forced to be prolific in order to support a growing family. He began to write poetry in 1914 with the encouragement of the poet Robert Frost, whom he greatly admired. After joining the army in 1915, he was killed in battle at Arris. Compared with the oblique, experimental writing of T. S. Eliot and Ezra Pound, for example, his work was relatively accessible and conventional. Its simple appearance is deceptive, however. The revolutionary character of his poetry consists of its ability to convey the mystery and significance of the everyday, its recognition of the tenuous nature of things, and its capturing of the rhythms of plain speech within the confines of regular metrics and commonplace images.

R. S. Thomas (1913–)

R(obert) S(tuart) Thomas was born in Cardiff, Wales, and raised in Holyhead. He studied Classics at the University College of North Wales and theology at St. Michael's College in Llandaff. Ordained in the Anglican Church, he served at Chirk, Denbighshire, and a number of rural parishes before retiring from the Church in 1978. Having learned to speak Welsh in college in order to communicate with his parishioners and to gain a deeper understanding of Welsh culture, he pays quiet homage to his homeland in his poetry, but seems torn between preserving its old ways and welcoming potentially invigorating change. His work is propelled by strong stresses, arranged not in regular patterns but to imitate the rhythms of Anglo-Saxon poetry. He eschews ornamentation in favor of spare directness and lately has moved from traditional aural rhyme to a rhyme based on image or concept.

James Thomson (1700–1748)

James Thomson was born in Ednam Manse, Kelso, Scotland, and educated at Jedburgh School and Edinburgh University, preparing for the ministry. After abandoning his studies, he tried to make a living as a writer in London, where he became friendly with the leading writers of the day, including John Arbuthnot, Thomas Gay, and Alexander Pope. "Winter," a short blank-verse poem, appeared in 1726, and "Summer" and "Spring" in 1727 and 1728 respectively. *The Seasons*, which collected all three with "Autumn," was published in 1730. In 1731 Thomson accompanied Charles Talbot, son of the solicitor-general, on the Grand Tour, which provided the inspiration for his patriotic poem *Liberty* (1735–36), dedicated to the prince of Wales, who awarded him a pension. Further patronage came through the poem *Britannia* (1729), together with sinecures such as the surveyor-generalship of the Leeward Islands. Thomson's *Alfred, a Masque* (1740) includes the famous song "Rule Britannia," also attributed to his friend, David Mallet. His *Seasons* was one of the most popular and influential poems of the century, heralding the shift of poetic attention from humanity (the center of the Augustan universe) to nature, and ushering in the period of topographical poetry and the "cult of the picturesque."

Henry David Thoreau (1817–1862)

Henry David Thoreau was born and lived nearly all his life in Concord, Massachusetts. He was educated at Harvard University, where the poet Jones Very was his tutor. After graduation, he worked briefly as a schoolteacher, but was ill suited for the position. He lived in the writer Ralph Waldo Emerson's household for a time and became active in Emerson's Transcendentalist club. From 1845 until 1947 Thoreau lived in a wooden hut at Walden Pond, an experience he documented in his prose work *Walden* (1854). A rugged individualist whose primary concern was sincerity, he regarded moral law more highly than civil law, as demonstrated in his refusal to pay poll and church taxes and in his early support for the as yet unpopular abolition movement. In his poetry, most of it written before 1840, he spurned the sentimentality and facile optimism found in most verse of his day. Most critics failed to notice his classical influence—Thoreau favored the ode form, popularized by Pindar—and underappreciated the vitality, originality, and sensuousness of his work.

Chidiock Tichborne (d. 1586)
The Tichbornes were an old, probably pre-Conquest family of Hampshire (England) and were pious Catholics. Chidiock Tichborne was interrogated on several occasions on suspicion of "Popish practices" (i.e., attending mass) and in 1586 was involved in a plot led by Anthony Babington against the life of Queen Elizabeth I. Tichborne was arrested and sentenced to be hanged and disemboweled. Imprisoned in the Tower of London, he is said to have written his "Elegy" on the eve of his execution. The poem is based on the *contemptus mundi* theme summed up in its line "I lookte for life, and sawe it was a shade." Its line structure follows a popular late-medieval device of paradoxical pairing, for example, "My cropp of corne, is but a field of tares." Tichborne's speech from the scaffold, his poem of farewell, became widely known in the Elizabethan and Jacobean periods.

Mary Tighe (1772–1810)
Mary Tighe (pronounced "Tie") (née Blanchford) was born in Dublin, Ireland, and lived in County Wicklow. Her father was a rector and librarian, and her mother a prominent supporter of the Methodist movement. Educated at home, she learned Latin, Greek, and modern languages and studied poetry. In 1793 she married her cousin, Henry Tighe, a member of the Irish Parliament, a historian, and a poet. A short time after her marriage, Mary Tighe developed consumption, which eventually proved fatal. Her *Psyche; or The Legend of Love* (1805) was very popular in the early nineteenth century and went through several editions in England and America.

Charles Tomlinson (1927–)
Charles Tomlinson was born in Stoke-on-Trent, England, and educated at Queens' College, Cambridge, where he studied with the poet Donald Davie, and the University of London. He taught at a London school for a number of years and worked as a private secretary in Italy before joining the faculty of the University of Bristol in 1957. He has also taught at various institutions in the United States. In addition to poetry, Tomlinson has published literary criticism, and has edited several collections of work by and about Marianne Moore and William Carlos Williams. He edited *The Oxford Book of Verse in English Translation*, for which he translated the work of several poets. In addition, he is an accomplished painter. Indebted to the English meditative tradition, he describes his work as "phenomenological poetry, with roots in Wordsworth and in Ruskin." Tomlinson rarely works in traditional prosodic forms but instead develops forms to suit his materials: his meters have been described as "syncopated"—that is, based on regular patterns with evocative variations.

Jean Toomer (1894–1967)
Jean Toomer was born in Washington, D.C. He was raised by his mother and maternal grandfather, P. B. S. Pinchback, who had served as acting governor of Louisiana during Reconstruction. He attended several colleges, but never received a degree. Toomer spent much of his early adulthood in New York City; his work was both influenced by and influential on the Harlem Renaissance. In 1921 he taught in Sparta, Georgia, where he gathered material for *Cane* (1923), a mosaic of poetry, prose, and drama on black themes, and the work on which his reputation stands. In his later years, Toomer wrote extensively on religion and philosophy—he had studied the work of the Russian mystic Gurdjieff and had become a Quaker—but was unable to find a publisher for his work. He once said that he was of "seven blood mixtures: French, Dutch, Welsh, Negro, German, Jewish, and Indian" and that in his work he "strived for a spiritual fusion analogous to the fact of racial intermingling." The subjects of his work include racial tension and exploitation, but diverse audiences have found resonant his explorations of the displacement of humans by machines and of the decay of culture and tradition.

Thomas Traherne (1637–1674)
Thomas Traherne was the son of a Hereford (England) shoemaker and his wife—who, it is thought, died when Thomas and his brother were young, leaving them to be brought up by Philip Traherne, a wealthy innkeeper who was twice mayor of the city. Thomas was educated at Brasenose College, Oxford, and became rector of Credenhill, Herefordshire, in 1657. He was ordained in 1660, the year before taking his M.A. In 1669 he was made B.D., probably in recognition of his *Roman Forgeries* (which exposed ecclesiastical forgery of documents), and appointed chaplain to Sir Orlando Bridgeman, lord keeper of the Great Seal, after which he lived in London. His *Christian Ethics* appeared a year after his death, but his poems and prose meditations remained unknown until the early twentieth century, when manuscript volumes began to be discovered and published; more may still come to light. His *Centuries of Meditation* was probably written during his time at Credenhill, when he was part of a religious circle led by Susanna Hopton (1627–1709), a High Anglican who converted for a time to Catholicism and to whom Traherne dedicated the *Centuries*.

Frederick Goddard Tuckerman (1821–1873)
Frederick Goddard Tuckerman was born in Boston, Massachusetts, to a distinguished New England family. He was educated at Harvard University (where the poet Jones Very was one of his tutors) and Harvard Law School. In the late 1840s Tuckerman gave up the law to study his first loves: astronomy, botany, and poetry. He lived a retired and scholarly life at his family home in Greenfield, Massachusetts. Tuckerman's one published volume of poems was well received by the best poets of his day, including Emerson, Longfellow, and Tennyson, yet his name fell into obscurity until the twentieth century, when his work was rediscovered by the poet Witter Bynner. Among the poems not published during Tuckerman's lifetime are three sonnet sequences, unique for their time in that, as Bynner said, Tuckerman wrote them "straightly to himself" rather than directing them to an external audience. They seem to be near-transcripts of a deeply personal and intensely spiritual exploration. In addition, Tuckerman took surprising liberties with the sonnet form, diverging from conventional Petrarchan and English rhyme schemes, anticipating Gerard Manley Hopkins' experiments with sprung rhythm, and intentionally obfuscating grammar and syntax to add mystery and complexity to his work.

John Updike (1932–)
John Updike was born in Reading, Pennsylvania, and raised in nearby Shillington. He was educated at Harvard

University and studied drawing at the Ruskin School of Drawing and Fine Arts, in Oxford, England. Upon his return to the United States, he joined the staff of *The New Yorker*. In 1957, he and his family moved from New York City to Ipswich, Massachusetts, where he concentrated wholly on writing. One of the most versatile and highly acclaimed contemporary American writers, Updike has published many novels, short stories, plays, poems, essays, and reviews. Although his poems are typically playful appreciations of the commonplace, they also explore the rather sober themes that recur in his novels, in particular the bittersweet appeal of memory, the threat of mutability, and the diminishment of life with the passage of time. Even when he explores these darker themes, Updike's tone is consistently witty and bemused. His light verse reveals his delight in language and an exceptional deftness with rhyme and form.

Mona Van Duyn (1921–)

Mona Van Duyn was born in Waterloo, Iowa. She was educated at the University of Northern Iowa and the University of Iowa at Iowa City. She has taught at, among other schools, the University of Iowa, the University of Louisville, and Washington University. From 1974 to 1978, Van Duyn and her husband, Jarvis Thurston, edited *Perspective: A Quarterly of Literature*. Generally writing about ordinary people and the realities of their lives, she also finds inspiration in current events, literature, and philosophy. A formalist poet, she most often works in long, loosely metered lines and complex patterns of rhyme and slant rhyme.

Henry Vaughan (1622–1695)

Henry Vaughan was born in Newton-upon-Usk, Breconshire, the son of a Welsh gentleman and his wife, and the twin of Thomas, who became a natural physician or alchemist. Henry attended Jesus College, Oxford, and went on to London to study law, but was deflected by the Civil War. He may have fought for the Royalists before returning to Breconshire, where he seems to have taken up medicine, or "physic," perhaps in the 1640s. A poem in his first collection of 1646, "Upon the Priory Grove," records his courtship of Catherine Wise, whom he was to marry and whose younger sister, Elizabeth, became his second wife. The collection is almost entirely secular, as was his second, *Olor Iscanus* ("Swan of Usk," 1651), but his third, *Silex Scintillans* (1655), and his subsequent work, is of religious and devotional nature. Vaughan often sought what he called "shadows of eternity" in clouds, flowers, and other natural objects; contemplation of nature led him to meditation on holy themes and moments of transcendent vision. An interest in Hermeticism appears in several poems, which allude to theories found in his brother's treatises on the subject. Vaughan acknowledged George Herbert as a significant influence, writing that his "holy life and verse gained many pious Converts (of whom I am the least)."

Jones Very (1813–1880)

Jones Very was born in Salem, Massachusetts. He was educated at Harvard College, then became a tutor in Greek while he pursued a degree at the Divinity School. In 1838, after a conversion experience, Very repudiated Unitarianism for a rigorous mysticism and felt compelled to surrender himself completely to the will of God. Remanded to an asylum for evaluation at the request of his colleagues, he was declared sane and released, after which he retired to his parental home in Salem, where he lived a scholarly and reclusive life. In the eighteen months following his release, Very wrote some three hundred poems, including a mystical sonnet sequence. During this period, he was more concerned with theological matters than aesthetic ones; believing the Holy Ghost was dictating to him, he took liberties with the sonnet form and did little editing. Although the results have a raw and gnomic quality, their immediacy and intensity are remarkable. His one published collection, *Essays and Poems* (1839), was edited by Ralph Waldo Emerson. Very's work fell into obscurity until the twentieth century, when it was rediscovered by the poet and critic Yvor Winters. As his genius came to light, critics compared him to English metaphysical and devotional poets, including George Herbert.

Derek Walcott (1930–)

Derek Walcott was born on the West Indian island of St. Lucia. He was educated at the University of the West Indies, Jamaica, after which he moved to Trinidad, where he worked as a reviewer, art critic, playwright, and artistic director of a theater workshop. He has been poet-in-residence at a number of American institutions and currently teaches at Boston University. In 1992 he was awarded the Nobel Prize for Literature. His poems display his simultaneous attraction to and exclusion from both the English literary tradition and native West Indian culture. Walcott's primary themes are isolation, estrangement, race, and identity, and he also explores his relationships to his God, country, community, and family. Perhaps his most enduring theme is evil, especially its manifestation as political tyranny and racism. Often working in declamatory lines that are by turns lyrical, lush, and spartan, and that owe as much to Creole dialect, dance, and oral tradition as to canonical English poetry, he works with equal facility in strict meter and rhyme and in open forms.

Margaret Walker (1915–)

Margaret Walker was born in Birmingham, Alabama. She received her B.A. from Northwestern University and M.A. and Ph.D. from the University of Iowa. From 1936 until 1939 she was employed by the Writer's Project of the Works Progress Administration in Iowa, where she struck up a mutually beneficial association with her coworker Richard Wright. She subsequently worked as a social worker, reporter, and magazine editor and taught at Livingston College, West Virginia State College, and Jackson State College (now University). She retired in 1979. In addition to poetry, she published a biography of Wright and a collection of autobiographical essays. Walker's parents encouraged her to immerse herself in African-American culture and to read a wide variety of literary classics, from the Bible to Shakespeare and the "wisdom literature of the East." In her early work, she was especially fond of the sonnet and the folk ballad, but she later moved toward a freer style. She also writes lyric poems set in a Southern landscape and often urges African Americans to take action against oppressive social conditions.

Edmund Waller (1607–1687)

Edmund Waller was the eldest son of a wealthy landowner in Hertfordshire (England) and his wife. Educated at Eton and King's College, Cambridge, he became a Member of Parliament at only sixteen and swiftly gained a reputation as a brilliant orator. In his thirties he courted Dorothy Sidney, granddaughter of Robert Sidney and grandniece of Philip and Mary Sidney; he addressed her under the poetic name of "Saccharissa" (Sweetness). After participating in the philosophical circle around Lucius Cary at Great Tew, Oxfordshire, he changed his political stance from Parliamentarian to Royalist. His part in a plot to secure London for the king was discovered in 1643, but he avoided execution by a confession and an eloquent plea for clemency. Exiled, he traveled in France, Italy, and Switzerland with his friend John Evelyn until 1651, when he was allowed to return to England; although he wrote in praise of Oliver Cromwell, he regained a place in Parliament after the Restoration and advocated religious toleration. Waller's first known poem, commemorating Prince Charles' escape from shipwreck (ca. 1625) is an early example of the use of heroic couplets in English. His *Instructions to a Painter* appeared in 1666. John Dryden was among his admirers, praising the "sweetness" of Waller's style.

Robert Penn Warren (1905–1989)

Robert Penn Warren was born in Guthrie, Kentucky. He was educated at Vanderbilt University, the University of California at Berkeley, Yale University, and Oxford University. At Vanderbilt, Warren associated with the Fugitives, a literary group whose members included professors John Crowe Ransom and Donald Davidson and fellow student Allen Tate. He later became a member of the Agrarian movement, which called for an agriculturally based Southern economy and promoted traditional Southern values. Warren taught at, among other schools, Vanderbilt; Louisiana State University, where with Cleanth Brooks he cofounded the influential *Southern Review*; the University of Minnesota; and Yale. In addition to poetry, he wrote fiction (his novel *All the King's Men* won the Pulitzer Prize in 1946), drama, and criticism (including the influential New Critical treatise "Pure and Impure Poetry"). Warren was named the nation's first poet laureate. His early work was ornate and often cosmic in scope, and his reputation as an important poet was solidified with the publication of *Brother to Dragons* (1953), a verse drama that explores the nature of evil. Warren's later work was more accessible; its masterful use of irony and "resistance," or tensions between elements, conveys the multiplicity of experience.

Isaac Watts (1674–1748)

Isaac Watts was born in Southampton, England, and educated in the city's grammar school and the Nonconformist academy at Stoke Newington. His father was a clothier who later became a Nonconformist school master. Watts became minister of Mark Lane Chapel, London, in 1702, and when overwork led to illness in 1712, he moved into the household of Sir Thomas and Lady Abney, where he remained the rest of his life. Although he wrote theological and educational works, Pindaric odes, blank verse, and experimental poems such as "The Day of Judgment," which is in English Sapphics, he is chiefly remembered for his *Divine Songs for Children* (1715) and four collections of hymns. The volume entitled *The Psalms of David imitated in the language of the New Testament* (1719) contains some of the most famous hymns in English. Watts wanted his poems to "elevate" readers "to the most delightful and divine Sensations" and to provide models of appropriate Christian responses to trial and difficulty.

Charles Wesley (1707–1788)

Charles Wesley was born at Epworth Rectory, Lincolnshire, England. Like his older brother John Wesley, the founder of Methodism, he was educated at Christ Church, Oxford. Ordained in the Anglican Church, he accompanied John to Georgia in 1735 to act as secretary to James Edward Oglethorpe, governor of the colony, but returned to England the following year. When the established Church charged him with "irregularity," he became an itinerant minister. For seventeen years he traveled the countryside, preaching and helping groups of believers to found churches. He retired in 1756 due to poor health and lived out his last years in Bath and London. An accomplished poet who wrote on a variety of subjects—including love, marriage, and family life—he is best known as an extraordinarily prolific hymn writer, publishing some sixty-five hundred hymns in his lifetime, many of which remain popular today.

Phillis Wheatley (1753–1784)

Phillis Wheatley was born in Africa, sold into slavery, and in 1761 shipped to the slave market in Boston. She was bought by John Wheatley, a prosperous tailor, for his wife, Susannah. The family gave Phillis a good education and encouraged her writing talent, and she published a poem in a Boston newspaper in 1767. In 1773 they sent Phillis to London with their son, in the hope of strengthening her frail constitution. She published a collection of poems during her stay, but returned after a few months when her mistress fell ill. Freed on her return, she married John Peters, a free black man, in 1778 and after bearing and burying three children, she died in poverty and obscurity. Influenced by John Milton and Alexander Pope, she characteristically wrote in rhymed iambic-pentameter couplets or the ballad form, often using highly artificial diction. Like other Puritan colonial writers, however, she employed an emotionally restrained, highly accessible "plain" style for poems on religious subjects. In a poem about the American Revolution, "To the Right Honourable William, Earl of Dartmouth," she draws a parallel between the colonists' rebellion against the king and the slave's desire for freedom; and in her elegies, many for children, she figures death as a release from bondage.

Walt Whitman (1819–1892)

Walt Whitman was born on Long Island, New York, and raised in Brooklyn. He left school at the age of eleven and worked as an office boy, a printer's apprentice, and a teacher before establishing himself as a journalist affiliated with several prominent New York newspapers. In 1862, deeply moved by the scenes he witnessed while staying with his brother (a wounded Union soldier) in Washington, D.C., he spent several months visiting and nursing Civil War veterans. After the war, Whitman worked briefly at the Department of the Interior—he was fired for being the author of the "scandalous" *Leaves of Grass* (1855)—and for several years at the office of the attorney general. After suffering a debilitating stroke in 1873, he moved to his brother's home in Camden, New Jersey, where he remained until his death. In *Leaves of Grass*, his masterpiece, Whitman assumed the mantle of the public poet; his preface to the 1855 edition calls "the United States themselves" his subject. Although his poetry offers a Transcendentalist view of the human being as wholly attuned with divine creation, individual poems that celebrated the body and sexuality opened him up to charges of obscenity. His prosody proved as controversial as his subject matter, and one critic stated that he was "as unacquainted with art as a hog is with mathematics." In fact, Whitman's refusal to follow the prevailing taste for regular meter, standard forms, and studied artifice was based on long and careful thought. His direct, realistic, intense, and exuberant poems have profoundly influenced modern poetry (for instance, William Carlos Williams' *Paterson* and the work of the Beats) as well as American culture.

Isabella Whitney (fl. 1567–1573)

Isabella Whitney was born into a middle-class, Reformist family and apparently had two brothers (one of whom published a collection of poetry) and several sisters. Almost nothing is known of her personal life, although it is thought that by 1600 she had married and begun raising two children. Of the three books of poetry published by English women during the sixteenth century, two are hers. *Copy of a Letter Lately Written in Meter, by a Young Gentlewoman: to her Unconstant Lover. With an Admonition to All Young Gentlewomen, and to All Other Maids in General to Beware of Men's Flattery* (1567) contains both the letter described and the gentleman's reply; *A Sweet Nosegay or Pleasant Posy, Containing a Hundred and Ten Philosophical Flowers* (1573) was the first book of poems ever published by an Englishwoman. The "flowers," which render folk and Christian wisdom in ballad-stanza form, have not yet been republished in their entirety.

John Greenleaf Whittier (1807–1892)

John Greenleaf Whittier was born on a farm near Haverhill, Massachusetts. Except for a year's study at Haverhill Academy, he received little formal education. With the help of literary-minded friends, Whittier found a number of jobs with small newspapers. In the 1830s, he became an early, ardent abolitionist and wrote poems supporting the cause; in the late 1860s, following the Civil War, he turned his full attention to writing, often on behalf of the causes he espoused. Fame came in 1866 with the publication of *Snow-Bound*, a recollective idyll on his childhood. Several of his religious poems were set to music and became popular hymns, but his reputation rests on the poems, composed later in life, filled with concrete details that capture the essence of preindustrial life in the agricultural villages of New England. His character sketches have been said to anticipate the work of Edward Arlington Robinson and Robert Frost, in that they convincingly portray the staunchness of the New England character.

Richard Wilbur (1921–)

Richard Wilbur was born in New York City and raised in New Jersey. He was educated at Amherst College and Harvard University. After enlisting in the army in 1942, he served as a cryptographer with the 36th Infantry in Africa, southern France, and Italy. He began to write while in the army, in an attempt to create a measure of order in the midst of war. Since then Wilbur has taught at, among other schools, Harvard, Wellesley College, Wesleyan University, and Smith College. In addition to poetry, he has written literary essays and children's books, and he has translated Molière, Voltaire, and Racine. His poems are ornately but elegantly wrought and often witty. Like Marianne Moore and William Carlos Williams, Wilbur has an avid affection for, in his words, "the things of this world." He meditates on common physical objects in order to gain access to the spiritual realm, and in this practice he has been compared to William Blake.

C. K. Williams (1936–)

C(harles) K(enneth) Williams was born in Newark, New Jersey. He was educated at Bucknell College and the University of Pennsylvania. He established a poetry-therapy program for emotionally disturbed adolescents, served as a contributing editor to *American Poetry Review*, and ghostwrote articles on psychiatry and architecture before beginning an academic career. Having taught at a number of colleges and universities, he now teaches at Princeton University and lives part of each year in Paris. In addition to poetry, he has published translations of Sophocles' *Women of Trachis* and Euripides' *The Bacchae*. Although typically concerned with the darker dimensions of existence, his work is not without tenderness, grace, or humor. Williams writes almost exclusively in long and discursive lines and has a particular facility for depicting dramatic situations.

Helen Maria Williams (1761–1827)

Helen Maria Williams was born to a Welsh army officer and his Scottish wife, brought up in Berwick-upon-Tweed, and like most women of her day, educated at home. In 1781 she moved to London, where she moved in literary circles. She became increasingly attracted to dissenting religious ideas and radical politics, and in 1790 journeyed to France to witness the French Revolution. Her home in Paris became a center for expatriates who sympathized with the French revolutionaries, including Thomas Paine and Mary Wollstonecraft. Williams was, however, imprisoned by Robespierre in 1793 and narrowly escaped the guillotine. Her first published work was *Edwin and Eltruda* (1782), a ballad. She subsequently translated works from French and German, and wrote poems, novels, prose, and a series of letters (1790–95) that illuminate French life during the Revolution. Wordsworth was an admirer, and his first printed poem (for which he adopted the pseudonym "Axiologus") was "On Seeing Miss Helen Maria Williams Weep at a Tale of Distress" (1787). Her unadorned style contrasted starkly with the contemporary vogue for heavy ornamentation and anticipated the kind of plain poetic diction Wordsworth advocated in the preface to the third edition of his and Coleridge's *Lyrical Ballads* (1802).

William Carlos Williams (1883–1963)

William Carlos Williams was born in Rutherford, New Jersey. In 1906 he earned an M.D. from the University of Pennsylvania, where he met the poets Ezra Pound and H. D. and the painter Charles Demuth. In 1910 he opened a pediatrics practice in Rutherford, where, except for a year's "sabbatical" in Europe, he lived and practiced medicine for the rest of his life. Although strongly established in Rutherford, Williams was hardly provincial. He moved in New York's avant-garde circles—along with the poets Marianne Moore and Wallace Stevens and the artist Marcel Duchamp—and was affiliated with several short-lived but influential journals. In addition to poetry, he wrote fiction, drama, and essays. Influenced by Pound, Williams was an early proponent of imagism, a movement he valued for its stripping away of conventions that obfuscated the true significance of things. Later he regretted that imagism had "dribbled off into so called 'free verse'" and declared himself an objectivist, valuing the rigor of form. Williams called on his contemporaries to create a distinctly American art, arising out of the materials of the place, responding to contemporary necessities, firmly rooted in particulars: "No ideas but in things," he insisted time and again. These edicts find their culmination in Williams' masterpiece *Paterson* (1946–58), a five-volume poem that recounts the history of Rutherford and nearby Paterson and transforms the locale into the embodiment of modern humanity.

John Wilmot, Earl of Rochester (1647–1680)

John Wilmot was born at Ditchley, Oxfordshire (England), to a Cavalier hero and a devout Puritanical mother. After attending Wadham College, Oxford, he toured Europe, returning in 1664. He quickly became a favorite of Charles II and a leading member of the court "wits." At eighteen he abducted the heiress Elizabeth Malet and was consequently imprisoned in the Tower of London. He married her eighteen months later, having regained his position by serving courageously in the second Dutch War (1665). His time was then divided between family life in the country and life in London with a number of mistresses, including Elizabeth Barry, a popular actress. According to Samuel Johnson, Rochester "blazed out his youth and health in lavish voluptuousness" (he claimed that he went five years without being sober); and by his early thirties, drink and venereal disease were exacting a price. He consulted a number of theologians, including the royal chaplain, Gilbert Burnet, who wrote a highly popular pamphlet describing Rochester's renunciation of skepticism and conversion to Christianity. A friend of many poets including John Dryden and Aphra Behn, Rochester was renowned both as a satirist and as the author of erotic, sometimes pornographic, poetry, much of which was meant to be circulated in manuscript. He also wrote dramatic prologues and epilogues, imitations and adaptations of classical authors, and dramatic poems of self-analysis both comic and grim.

Eleanor Wilner (1937–)

Eleanor Wilner was born in Cleveland, Ohio. She was educated at Goucher College and Johns Hopkins University, from which she received a Ph.D. She worked as a newspaper reporter, as a feature writer at a radio station, and as a consultant to the Maryland State Commission on the Aging before beginning an academic career. She has taught at Goucher and at Morgan State University. Her work is complex and richly ambiguous, offering original and provocative rereadings of myth and history. By referring to the foundations of the Western canon, her poems affirm their value; by rewriting those materials, her work questions their monolithic authority. Although Wilner does not often work in traditional forms, her poems are strongly measured and musical, often employing internal rhyme with special ingenuity.

William Wordsworth (1770–1850)

William Wordsworth was born in Cockermouth, Cumberland, in the north of England's Lake District, and was educated at St. John's College, Cambridge. A walking tour of Europe in his early twenties brought him into contact with the first throes of the French Revolution, whose ideals he supported until the onset of the Terror. Upon his return to England, he settled with his sister, Dorothy, in the Lake District, where, apart from some few brief travels, he remained for the rest of his life. In 1795 he met the poet Samuel Taylor Coleridge, with whom he published *Lyrical Ballads* (1798), one of the most important works in the history of English literature, both for its innovative poetry and for Wordsworth's preface to its second edition (1800). In his later years Wordsworth grew increasingly conservative, and many former devotees accused him of apostasy, but his poetry remained both popular and influential — so influential and so formative of modern ideas about poetry that the scope of his achievement is easily overlooked. In his preface to the *Lyrical Ballads*, Wordsworth attacks the poetic diction and elaborate figures of speech characteristic of eighteenth-century poetry, asserting that he had "taken as much pains to avoid it as others take to produce it," and advocating the "language really used by men." He rejected the notion of a poetic hierarchy ranking epic and tragedy over the subjective mode of lyric; declared "incidents and situations from common life" as fit subjects for art; and substituted sincerity for studied artifice. The accessibility of Wordsworth's poetry and his "democratizing" theory should not divert attention from his painstaking and complex technique. Many of his poems are written in strict and elaborate forms, or blank verse; their effect might be one of spontaneity, but it results from careful construction. Wordsworth ascribed to art the duty of cultivating emotional and moral response in an increasingly desensitized age, one more interested in titillation than meditation.

James Wright (1927–1980)

James Wright was born and raised in Martin's Ferry, Ohio. Upon graduation from high school, he joined the army and was stationed in occupied Japan. After his military service, he attended Kenyon College, where he studied with John Crowe Ransom, and the University of Washington, where he studied with Theodore Roethke. He later taught at the University of Minnesota and Hunter College. In the first phase of his career, Wright was often concerned with guilt and suffering. Influenced by the psychologist Carl Jung, the expressionist poet Georg Trakl, and South American surrealists Pablo Neruda and Caesar Vallejo, he then began writing in what he called an "entirely different" mode, juxtaposing disparate images and relying on the subconscious mind to intuit connections between them. He worked in both closed and open forms, the plain surfaces of his free-verse poems sometimes masking the craft underneath.

Judith Wright (1915–)

Judith Wright was born in Armidale, New South Wales, Australia. She was educated at the Universities of Sydney and Queensland. Wright was active in the antiwar movement of the 1960s and is now a conservationist. She ascribes her interest in the environment to working the land at her family's estate at Willamumbi during World War II. Wright made her home at Mount Tambourine, Queensland, for many years, but currently lives on an animal preserve near Braidwood, New South Wales. She has written prolifically in a number of genres, including poetry, criticism, fiction, and children's fiction. Her early work was deeply rooted in the soil of Australia, yet intensely personal and sensuous. She has since moved outward toward a poetry of ideas that increasingly addresses social wrongs, seeking out what is worthy of "praise" in the modern "urban technological" wasteland.

Mary Wroth (1587?–1651?)

Lady Mary Wroth was born into an aristocratic family. Her mother, Barbara Gamage, a first cousin of Sir Walter Ralegh, was praised by Ben Jonson for ensuring that her children were "well taught." Wroth's father, Robert Sidney, her uncle, Philip Sidney, and her aunt, Mary Sidney, were all poets. Her arranged marriage to Sir Robert Wroth was unhappy, and after his death in 1614, she had two children by her lover and cousin, William Herbert, third earl of Pembroke and Montgomery. In 1621 she boldly published *The Countesse of Montgomerie's Urania*, addressed to her lover's wife. Like Philip Sidney's *Arcadia*, on which it is modeled, this long prose romance is interspersed with poems in a variety of forms and meters. Appended to the romance is a sonnet sequence, *Pamphilia to Amphilanthus*, similarly modeled on Sidney's sonnet sequence, *Astrophil and Stella*, but with a male love-object and narrated from the perspective of a woman. The *Urania* caused a scandal because it contained thinly veiled satire of well-known court figures, and Wroth's continuation of the work, like her pastoral verse play, *Love's Victorie*, was not published. Ben Jonson dedicated *The Alchemist* to Wroth and, in a sonnet addressed to her, praised her own poems for making him a "better lover, and much better poet."

Thomas Wyatt (1503–1542)

Thomas Wyatt was born at Allingham Castle, Kent (England), and educated at Cambridge. He held various positions at court and served on diplomatic missions to France, Spain, and Italy. Although he was knighted in 1535, his position as a courtier was never secure. Imprisoned for brawling and perhaps for sexual misconduct in 1534 (he had separated from his wife), he was again imprisoned, after a quarrel with the duke of Suffolk, in 1536. Some have linked this imprisonment also with the fall of Henry VIII's second wife, Anne Boleyn. Said to have been Wyatt's mistress, Anne Boleyn is almost certainly an allegorical referent of Wyatt's poem "Whoso List to Hunt" and perhaps of other poems as well. Released soon after her execution—which he witnessed through a grate from his own cell in Bell Tower of the Tower of London, as he recorded in a poem with the refrain "Circa regnat tonat" ("it thunders through the realm")—Wyatt fell from royal favor again in 1541, when he was accused of treason; and in 1554, during the reign of Queen Mary, his son, Thomas Wyatt "the younger," was hanged for treason. It was probably to avoid any associations to Wyatt's son that Richard Tottel left Wyatt "the elder's" name off the title page of the famous anthology of "songs and sonnets" that he published in the last year of Mary's reign (1557). Although Tottel praises the "weightiness of the deepwitted Sir Thomas Wyatt the Elder's verse" in the preface and includes ninety-seven of Wyatt's poems in the first edition of the anthology, the title page mentions only Wyatt's younger poetic imitator, Henry Howard, "late earl of Surrey." Tottel regularized the meter of many of Wyatt's poems and added titles to them. Fortunately, most also survive in manuscript versions, some of which are written and corrected in Wyatt's own hand; they exhibit a great variety of tones, forms, and rhythms. As a translator of Petrarch, Wyatt introduced the sonnet form to English; he also enriched English literature with satiric verse epistles modeled on classical and Italian poems.

Elinor Wylie (1885–1928)

Elinor Wylie (née Hoyt) was born in Somerville, New Jersey, to a prominent family. Apart from a college preparatory course, she was educated at home, learning French and German and being taught to draw. A socialite, she lived at various times in England, New York City, and Washington, D.C., and counted the writers Dorothy Parker, Ernest Hemingway, Edmund Wilson, and Edna St. Vincent Millay among her friends. In addition, her work brought her the respect of such prominent writers as W. B. Yeats, who admired her poems, and William Faulkner, Max Beerbohm, and Aldous Huxley, who praised her fiction. Due to her several marriages and affairs, Wylie was as notorious as she was celebrated, and she sought to disengage from the world in order to immerse herself more thoroughly in art. Her formal skill and musicality are still much admired.

William Butler Yeats (1865–1939)

William Butler Yeats was born in Dublin, but spent over half his life outside Ireland. He studied painting at the Dublin Metropolitan School of Art before turning his full attention to literature. Central themes of his poetry are Irish history, folklore, and contemporary politics. His early work belonged to the "Celtic revival" school and, in long allegorical poems and verse dramas, showed the influence of the "immortal world" of the intellect and the revolutionary Maud Gonne, whose politics at first excited, then, as they led to violence and betrayal, repulsed him. Another abiding interest, in mysticism and the occult, provided a source of poetic symbols, as well as a philosophical "key" to his writing, A Vision (1925, 1937). Though he sought respite in his imagination and its artifices and venerated the "immortal world" of the intellect and the soul, Yeats never rejected the sensuous world of the mortal body. Exploring the tensions between mortal and immortal in his later years and grounded his poetry in "the foul rag-and-bone shop of the heart." Perhaps his greatest achievement lay in his ability to create poems of extraordinary lyricism or dramatic intensity from the idiom and syntax of ordinary speech. He said that his estranging vision of extraordinary experience evoked "monstrous familiar images" that "bewilder" and "perturb the mind." Far from frozen by these images, the mind continued to explore, to question, to explain.

Cynthia Zarin (1959–)

Cynthia Zarin was born in New York City and raised on Long Island. She was educated at Harvard College and Columbia University. A staff writer at The New Yorker from 1985 until 1994, she currently teaches at Princeton University and lives in New York City, where she is a writer-in-residence at the Cathedral of St. John the Divine. In addition to poetry, she has written children's books, essays, and reviews. Her work reflects the influences of Marianne Moore (in its tendency to view the natural world in moral terms) and Elizabeth Bishop (in its oblique approach to subjects); it grounds abstract, weighty reflections in familiar, concrete, and precise details. Zarin writes formal verse as well as freer modes, often employing complicated stanza forms and inventive rhymes.

PERMISSIONS ACKNOWLEDGMENTS

Fleur Adcock, "The Ex-Queen Among the Astronomers," "Poem Ended by a Death," and "The Soho Hospital for Women" from *Selected Poems*. Copyright © 1983 by Fleur Adcock. Reprinted with the permission of Oxford University Press, Ltd.

Conrad Aiken, from *Senlin: A Biography*: II. "His Futile Preoccupations, 2" from *The Divine Pilgrim*, republished in *Collected Poems, Second Edition*. Copyright 1918, 1953, © 1970 by Conrad Aiken. Reprinted with the permission of Oxford University Press.

Agha Shahid Ali, "The Dacca Gauzes" from *The Half-Inch Himalayas* (Wesleyan, Conn.: Wesleyan University Press, 1987). Copyright © 1987 by Agha Shahid Ali. Reprinted with the permission of University Press of New England. "I See Chile in My Rearview Mirror" from *A Nostalgist's Map of America*. Originally published in *Field*. Copyright © 1991 by Agha Shahid Ali. Reprinted with the permission of W. W. Norton & Company, Inc.

A. R. Ammons, "Corsons Inlet," "The City Limits," "The Arc Inside and Out," from *The Selected Poems: Expanded Edition*. Copyright © 1986 by A. R. Ammons. "Silver" from *Collected Poems 1951–1971*. Originally published in *The Hudson Review* 13 (Autumn 1960). Copyright © 1960 by A. R. Ammons. "Pet Panther" from *Lake Effect Country*. Copyright © 1983 by A. R. Ammons. All reprinted with the permission of W. W. Norton & Company, Inc.

John Ashbery, "The Painter" from *Some Trees* (New York: The Ecco Press, 1977). Copyright © 1956 by John Ashbery. "Melodic Trains" from *Houseboat Days* (New York: The Viking Press, 1977). Copyright © 1975, 1976, 1977 by John Ashbery. "Rivers and Mountains" from *Rivers and Mountains* (New York: The Ecco Press, 1977). Copyright © 1962, 1963, 1964, 1966 by John Ashbery. "Rain Moving In" from *A Wave* (New York: The Viking Press, 1984). Copyright © 1984 by John Ashbery. All reprinted with the permission of Georges Borchardt, Inc. and Carcanet Press, Ltd. "Brute Image" from *Hotel Lautreamont*. Copyright © 1992 by John Ashbery. Reprinted with the permission of Alfred A. Knopf, Inc. and Carcanet Press, Ltd.

Margaret Atwood, "This Is a Photograph of Me" from *The Circle Game*. Copyright © 1966 by Margaret Atwood. Reprinted with the permission of Stoddart Publishing Company. "At the Tourist Center in Boston" from *The Animals in That Country*. Copyright © 1968 by Margaret Atwood. Reprinted with the permission of Oxford University Press Canada. "You Begin" from *Selected Poems 1966–1984*. Copyright © 1990 by Margaret Atwood. Reprinted with the permission of the author, c/o Phoebe Larmore Literary Agency and Oxford University Press Canada. "Up" and "Flowers" from *Morning in the Burnt House*. Copyright © 1995 by Margaret Atwood. Reprinted with the permission of Houghton Mifflin Company and McClelland & Stewart.

W. H. Auden, "As I Walked Out One Evening," "Musée des Beaux Arts," "In Praise of Limestone," "The Shield of Achilles," from *Twelve Songs*: IX ("Funeral Blues") and XII ("Tell Me the Truth about Love"), "Lullaby" ("Lay your sleeping head"), and "In Memory of W. B. Yeats" from *W. B. Auden: Collected Poems*, edited by Edward Mendelson. Copyright © 1940, 1941, 1951, 1952 and renewed 1968, 1969 by W. H. Auden. Copyright © 1976 by Edward Mendelson, William Meredith, and Monroe K. Spears. "Spain 1937" from *The English Auden: Poems, Essays, and Dramatic Writings 1927–1939*, edited by Edward Mendelson. Copyright © 1940 and renewed 1968 by W. H. Auden. All reprinted with the permission of Random House, Inc. and Faber and Faber, Ltd.

Amiri Baraka (LeRoi Jones), "In Memory of Radio" from *The Music: Reflections on Jazz and Blues* (New York: William Morrow & Company, 1987). Copyright © 1987 by Amiri Baraka. "The New World" and "An Agony. As Now." from *The Dead Lec-*

Index